Reader's Guide to

AMERICAN

HISTORY

Reader's Guide to

AMERICAN HISTORY

Editor

PETER J. PARISH

FITZROY DEARBORN PUBLISHERS
LONDON AND CHICAGO

Copyright © 1997 by
FITZROY DEARBORN PUBLISHERS

All rights reserved including the right of reproduction in whole or
in part in any form. For information write to:

FITZROY DEARBORN PUBLISHERS
70 East Walton Street
Chicago, Illinois 60611
USA

or

11 Rathbone Place
London WIP IDE
England

British Library Cataloguing in Publication Data
Reader's guide to American history
    1. United States – History   2. United States – History Abstracts
    I. Parish, Peter J.
    973

ISBN 1–884964–22–2

Library of Congress Cataloging in Publication Data is available.

First published in the USA and UK 1997

Typeset by Florencetype Ltd, Stoodleigh, Devon
Printed by Braun-Brumfield, Inc., Ann Arbor, Michigan

CONTENTS

EDITOR'S NOTE

Aims, Scope, and Selection of Entries

Few subjects can match the sheer volume of published work which has been devoted to the history of the United States, and the torrent of new books continues unabated. Among them are many admirable examples of readable and authoritative treatments of large topics, addressed to a wide audience. However, a great deal of the recent work has reflected the intense specialization within the subject; increasingly professional historians have been producing monographs addressed to a relatively restricted audience of fellow-specialists and their graduate students. Frequently, they engage in debates among themselves on issues which, fascinating and important as they often are, can be confusing or even mystifying to a wider readership.

One positive feature of this activity is the widening range of American historiography. Political history remains important, and there is greater depth and breadth in modern work on the subject. However, the most conspicuous area of expansion has been in social history, with increasing concentration on issues of class, race, ethnicity and gender. For example, interest in women's history, African American history and Native American history has grown tremendously, and such areas as labor history, urban history and western history have dramatically expanded their scope or shifted their emphasis.

The array of reading that is available is hugely impressive, but can also be daunting. The aim of the *Reader's Guide to American History* is to offer some help to those who wish to explore the riches of American historical writing, in all its diversity. In the belief that a simple listing of books will not suffice for this purpose, the *Reader's Guide* takes the form of a series of essays which describe and assess books on some 600 different topics – some specialized and very specific, others much broader and more general. It aims to provide constructive and authoritative guidance to readers on the use of a range of books on each topic. This approach is designed to help readers of various kinds and at various levels: students (both undergraduate and graduate) looking for assistance with their next written assignment or research paper; teachers in schools, colleges and universities – and particularly those who are faced with the challenge of preparing courses or classes on topics in which they are not specialists; and, equally important, those readers who simply have an interest in a particular subject, and seek advice on what to read next.

Entries fall into three main categories, dealing respectively with events, individuals, and broader themes and issues. Events are the very stuff of history – particularly, but by no means exclusively, of political history – and must be accorded a prominent place.

However, in order to keep the number of entries in this category within bounds, groups or sequences of events have often been brought together under a broader heading (e.g., on the coming of the Revolution or the approach of the Civil War). The substantial number of entries on individuals is partly a tribute to the richness of the biographical literature, and partly an acknowledgment that many readers, particularly non-specialists, find it helpful to approach a subject through study of the contributions of prominent individuals (e.g., Frederick Douglass on 19th-century African American history, or Susan B. Anthony on women's suffrage, or Rachel Carson on the environment). The entries on general topics and broader themes can often be used in conjunction with more specific entries on particular events or individuals. For example, the entries on constitutional and legal history might lead a reader on to the entries on the Supreme Court and the judiciary, and then on to entries on John Marshall, Roger B. Taney, Felix Frankfurter, Earl Warren and other leading justices – and then perhaps on again to the entry on the approach to Civil War which includes the Dred Scott case, or to the New Deal entry which examines constitutional issues, or to the entry on the Civil Rights Acts. The hope is that this kind of "multi-layered" approach will enable the user to proceed from the general to the particular, or vice versa, as his or her needs and inclinations dictate.

Even a volume with the generous proportions of this *Reader's Guide* cannot hope to be comprehensive in its coverage or in its treatment of each topic. Lines had to be drawn to make the project manageable within the scope of a single volume. Given that the approach had to be selective, the reader is entitled to know something of the principles on which selection has been based. These are:

1. The *Reader's Guide* concentrates on political, social and economic history. It does not include literary history, or the history of art and architecture, or the history of science and medicine. It includes only a few general entries on the history of technology, and on the history of popular culture (which could well be the subject of a volume of its own). In this volume there are no entries on movie stars or sporting heroes or popular musicians, and literary figures are included only if they played some wider public role.

2. Within the fields of political, social and economic history, selection of topics was based on a combination of two main factors: the importance and interest of the subject, and the quality and quantity of the literature on the subject – although a few entries do highlight surprising gaps even in such a crowded field as American history. Some of the individuals were selected as representative figures to illuminate the history of the causes or movements or events with which they were associated.

3. For each entry, the contributor was free, within the editorial guidelines, to make his or her own choice of books to be discussed. In most cases, the emphasis is on more recently published work, but, where appropriate, contributors were encouraged to include earlier books which influenced subsequent writing on the subject. New work appears constantly, and there has been no single cut-off point for inclusion of books in the *Reader's Guide*: it may be assumed in the case of most entries that books published through 1995 could have been selected for inclusion. In a few cases, it has been possible to include books published in 1996, and even one or two published in 1997.

4. The emphasis is predominantly on books (and contributions to books), as opposed to articles in journals and magazines. Articles are normally included only when they are of seminal importance, or when there is no adequate treatment of a particular aspect of the subject in a book-length study.

5. The *Reader's Guide* is a guide to the secondary literature, and not to primary sources, or to collections of printed source material. There are two limited exceptions to this rule. An editorial introduction to a collection of source material (e.g., the collected works of a major figure) may be of sufficient importance to justify inclusion of the volume(s) concerned. Second, there are a few entries on individuals where the exclusion of an autobiographical work would throw the whole entry out of balance (e.g., William Allen White or Malcolm X).

Arrangement of the Entries

Entries appear in alphabetical order; a complete list of them can be found in the **Alphabetical List of Entries** (p. xv). Where there are several entries sharing the same general heading (e.g., African American History, American Revolution, Colonial History, Native American History, Slavery), the order does not normally proceed alphabetically. In entries on events or a series of events (e.g., Civil War, Approach to), the order is normally chronological. In the case of entries on broader topics (e.g., Colonial History, Women's History) the order proceeds as far as possible from the more general to the more particular, and otherwise proceeds in what seems the most logical and helpful manner. Where there is a "General" entry in such a group, it is always placed first. In cases where these criteria offer no guidance (e.g., in Foreign Policy since 1945: Special Aspects), alphabetical order is followed.

While the overall arrangement of entries is alphabetical, there are other aids to facilitate access to the contents of the *Reader's Guide*. These are:

1. **Thematic List** (pp. xxi). This should be consulted to see the full range of entries in the *Reader's Guide* on a particular period or a particular subject area, such as African American History, Ethnicity and Immigration, Military and Naval History, or Southern History.
2. **Booklist Index** (pp. 789). This lists in alphabetical order of author all books and articles discussed in any of the entries, and can be used to locate discussion of the work of particular historians.
3. **General Index** (pp. 839). This lists events, individuals and topics mentioned in any of the entries. This index may be particularly useful for locating references to events or individuals or other topics that have no entry of their own.
4. **Cross References.** At the end of many entries there are *See Also* notes, which refer the reader to entries on related topics.

Format within Entries

Each entry begins with a list of the books/articles to be discussed. Publication details are provided, including dates of first publication and, where appropriate, the most recent revised edition. Reprints and paperback editions are normally omitted. In the text of each essay, the first significant mention of each author appears in capital letters. In cases where more than one book by the same author is discussed in the same entry, each book is introduced by the author's name in capital letters, followed by date of publication in parentheses. Although the list of books in each entry proceeds in alphabetical order of author, books are not normally discussed in the text in that order. It was left to the judgment of contributors to decide whether to discuss books in order of publication, or, more often, according to the subject matter and emphasis of each book.

Acknowledgments

Although, in his darker moments, the editor sometimes felt that his word processor was his only companion in this project, he does realise, and wishes to acknowledge, his utter dependence on a large number of other people. First, I should like to thank all those who have written for this volume. I am deeply impressed by the generosity and willing co-operation of all concerned, notably some distinguished American historians, whom I did not know personally, but who offered not only to contribute entries themselves but to encourage others to do so. I am equally grateful to friends, former colleagues and former students in Britain who have worked long and hard to help in many different ways. Advisers on both sides of the Atlantic were extremely helpful, both in the selection of entries to be included in the *Reader's Guide* and in suggesting names of suitable contributors.

The resources of the British Library, the University of London Library, and the Cambridge University Library have been invaluable. Alison Cowden, of the University of London Library, has made an outstanding contribution to the *Reader's Guide*, both through her unrivalled bibliographical knowledge of American history, and by her superb proof-reading skills. Particular thanks go to a number of people at Fitzroy Dearborn – to Mark Hawkins-Dady and Carol Jones, and above all to Daniel Kirkpatrick, the inspiration behind the whole project, whose special combination of patience, persistence and hard work has seen it through to publication. I am also grateful to my wife, Norma, who has witnessed, with only occasional protest, the invasion of more and more of our modest home by *Reader's Guide* files and papers, and my daughter, Helen, who has been my technical adviser, problem solver and crisis manager on all matters relating to my word processor.

PETER J. PARISH

ADVISERS

Anthony J. Badger
M. Les Benedict
Colin Bonwick
Peter G. Boyle
R.A. Burchell
Richard J. Carwardine
Catherine Clinton
Michael F. Holt

Stuart McConnell
James T. Patterson
Jim Potter
Donald J. Ratcliffe
W.A. Speck
John A. Thompson
Robert Wiebe

CONTRIBUTORS

David Adams
Giles Alston
Bernard Aspinwall
Fred Arthur Bailey
Jean H. Baker
Gordon Morris Bakken
William L. Barney
John C. Barrow III
Nikola Baumgarten
M. Les Benedict
Jean V. Berlin
Stephen W. Berry
Roger Biles
Jeremy Black
Kenneth J. Blume
Frederick A. Bode
John B. Boles
Christine Bolt
Colin Bonwick
Jerome D. Bowers II
Peter G. Boyle
James C. Bradford
H.W. Brands
T.R. Brereton

Teri F. Brewer
John D. Buenker
Steven C. Bullock
R.A. Burchell
Orville Vernon Burton
William Carrigan
Francis M. Carroll
James Taylor Carson
Richard J. Carwardine
Kathryn Castle
Geoffrey Channon
Elizabeth J. Clapp
Christopher Clark
Sally H. Clarke
Peter A. Coates
Donald B. Cole
Bruce W. Collins
James L. Conrad, Jr.
George Conyne
Emily Walker Cook
Robert Cook
Richard Coopey
Martin Crawford
Maureen Cressey-Hackett

Philip Cullis
Neil Curtin
Roger Daniels
Gareth Davies
Michael G. Davis
Vanessa L. Davis
Joseph G. Dawson III
Richard de Zoysa
Robert L. Dietle
Brian Dirck
Saki Dockrill
John Dumbrell
Elizabeth E. Dunn
Douglas Eden
Richard E. Ellis
Sylvia Ellis
Clive Emsley
Adam Fairclough
Peter Fearon
Daniel Feller
William M. Ferraro
Paul Finkelman
Wayne Flynt
Richard J. Follett
Robert P. Forbes
Gaines M. Foster
Richard M. Fried
Craig Thompson Friend
Dan R. Frost
Robert Garson
Roger L. Geiger
Mary K. Geiter
Louis S. Gerteis
J. David Gillespie
Jon Gjerde
Philip K. Goff
John Steele Gordon
Lewis L. Gould
Hugh Davis Graham
S-M. Grant
Dewey W. Grantham
Elna C. Green
Daniel P. Greene
Sally Foreman Griffith
Anne-Marie Grimaud
Martin Halliwell
J. William Harris
Lowell H. Harrison
Robert Harrison
Richard A. Hawkins
Ellis W. Hawley
R.J. Heinig
Robin L.E. Hemenway
Candida N. Hepworth
Brian Holden Reid
Max Holland
Sean P. Holmes
Michael F. Hopkins
S.J.S. Ickringill
William Issel

Jonathan Jeffrey
Shawn Johansen
Daniel J. Johnson
Wayne J. Johnson
Peter d'A. Jones
Theresa Kaminski
John Kentleton
Andrew E. Kerston
Stuart Kidd
John R. Killick
John A. Kirk
S.J. Kleinberg
Ann Kordas
Kent M. Krause
Michael A. Krysko
Andrew D. Lambert
Harry S. Laver
Shawn Lay
Thomas C. Leonard
W. Bruce Leslie
David W. Levy
Lawrence S. Little
Andreas Loizou
Charles D. Lowery
Maxine N. Lurie
Ted V. McAllister
Peter McCaffery
Stuart McConnell
Ronald MacKinnon
John R. McKivigan
John Major
Anthony Mann
John F. Marszalek
Fran Mason
Keith Mason
James I. Matray
Richard Middleton
David J. Mikosz
Andrew Thompson Miller
Randall M. Miller
Vivien M.L. Miller
Tim Minchin
Deborah Dash Moore
Gwenda Morgan
Iwan W. Morgan
Malcolm F. Morrison
J. Thomas Murphy
Andrew Neather
Mark Newman
Julia L. Oatham
Christopher J. Olsen
Bruce A. Olson
Shari L. Osborn
Richard Ostrander
Ted Ownby
Niall Andrew Palmer
Peter K. Parides
Peter J. Parish
Craig S. Pascoe
Michael Perman

Lawrence A. Peskin
Craig Phelan
Matthew Pinsker
Emil Pocock
Joy Porter
Jim Potter
Linda C.A. Przybyszewski
Stephen G. Rabe
Howard N. Rabinowitz
George C. Rable
James Ralph
Donald J. Ratcliffe
Patrick Renshaw
David Reynolds
John Saillant
Steven J. Sarson
Christopher MacGregor Scribner
Gunja SenGupta
William G. Shade
David B. Sicilia
Joel H. Silbey
Brooks D. Simpson
David Curtis Skaggs
Dennis B. Smith
Joseph Smith
Mark M. Smith
S.G.F. Spackman
Alasdair Spark
W.A. Speck
Melvyn Stokes
Mark A. Stoler
Daniel W. Stowell
Timothy E. Sullivan

Richard Sylla
Michael Tadman
Jon C. Teaford
John A. Thompson
Geoffrey Till
Hugh Tulloch
David Turley
William M. Tuttle, Jr.
Geoffrey Tweedale
Alexander Urbiel
Rudolph J. Vecoli
Fiona Venn
Michael Vorenberg
Steve R. Waddell
Xi Wang
Matthew C. Ward
Graham Watson
Harry L. Watson
Trent A. Watts
Clive Webb
Michael Wesley
John White
Mark J. White
Drew Whitelegg
William M. Wiecek
Hugh Wilford
Robert Williams
Neil A. Wynn
Melvin Yazawa
Nancy Beck Young
Frank Zelko
Robert H. Zieger

ALPHABETICAL
LIST OF ENTRIES

THEMATIC LIST

Entries by Category

Categories are listed in the following order: 1) periods of American history in chronological order; 2) broad categories of political, economic, and social history, reflecting the main emphasis of the topics covered in the *Reader's Guide*; 3) specific topics listed in alphabetical order.

PERIODS OF AMERICAN HISTORY

Colonial Period, to 1763
1763–1800: Era of the American Revolution
1800–1848: Early National and Jacksonian Periods
1848–1877: Civil War and Reconstruction

1877–1917: Gilded Age and Progressive Era
1917–1945: World Wars, Great Depression, and New Deal
Recent History: the United States since 1945

POLITICAL, ECONOMIC, AND SOCIAL HISTORY

Political History
   1) Periods, Policies, Issues, and Events
   2) Parties, Political Movements, and Elections
   3) Presidents and Other Political Figures

Economic History
   1) General
   2) Business and Industry
   3) Finance, Trade, and Transport

Social History
   1) Social Structure: Class, Race, Ethnicity, Gender, Family
   2) Issues, Influences, Policies, Movements

Note: Many topics in political and, particularly, social history are covered in greater detail under the specific topics listed below

SPECIFIC TOPICS

African American History
Cities, States, and Regions of the United States
Constitutional and Legal History
Education
Environmental History
Ethnicity and Immigration
Foreign Relations and Foreign Policy
   1) 1775–1865
   2) 1865–1945
   3) Since 1945
   4) Relations with Other Nations or Regions
Government and Government Agencies

Ideas, Ideology, and Social Commentary
Labor History
Media and Communications
Military and Naval History
Native American History
Reform and Protest Movements
Religion
Slavery and Antislavery
Southern History
Sports, Entertainment, and Leisure
Urban History
Western History
Women's History

PERIODS OF AMERICAN HISTORY

1) Colonial Period, to 1763

African American History: Colonial
    Beginnings to 1860
Agriculture, to 1860
Britain and the American Colonies,
    1651–1763
British Americans
British-French Rivalry in North America
Colonial History: General
Colonial History: Colonies, settlement and
    growth
    1) Chesapeake Bay
    2) New England
    3) Middle Atlantic
    4) Carolinas and Georgia
Colonial History: Government and
    Politics

Colonial History: Economic Development
Colonial History: Society
Colonial History: Education
Colonial History: Religion
Colonial History: Slavery and Indentured
    Servitude
Colonial History: Non-English Settlements
    in North America
Colonial History: Relations with Native
    Americans
Colonial History: Westward Expansion
Early Exploration of North America
Edwards, Jonathan
Great Awakening
Hutchinson, Anne
Mather, Cotton and Increase Mather

Native Americans: General
Native Americans: White Encounter
    with
Native Americans: Indian Wars
Native Americans: Cultures
    1) Northeast
    2) Southeast
Penn, William
Pilgrim Fathers
Puritanism
Seven Years' War, 1754–1763
Slavery: Slave Trade, External
Smith, John
South: Colonial Period to Civil War
Williams, Roger
Winthrop, John

2) 1763–1800: Era of the American Revolution

Adams, Abigail
Adams, John
African American History: Colonial
    Beginnings to 1860
Agriculture, to 1860
Alien and Sedition Acts, and Virginia and
    Kentucky Resolutions, 1798–99
American Revolution: General
American Revolution: Causes
American Revolution: Development of a
    Crisis, 1763–1770
American Revolution: Development of a
    Crisis, 1770–1775
American Revolution: Character, Scope, and
    Significance
Articles of Confederation
Bill of Rights, 1789–1791
Boone, Daniel
Clark, George Rogers
Constitution: the Document
Constitution: Philadelphia Convention, 1787
Constitution: Ratification

Constitutional History: General
Constitutional History, 1789–1877
Continental Congress
Declaration of Independence, 1776
Early National Period, 1789–1815: General
Elections:
    1) 1789–1860
Federal Government: Establishment of,
    1789–1793
Federalist Papers
Federalist Party
Financial History, 1780s–1930s
France and America, 1760–1815
Franklin, Benjamin
Hamilton, Alexander
Hamilton, Alexander: Financial and
    Economic Program, 1789–1795
Hutchinson, Thomas
Jefferson, Thomas
Jeffersonian Republican Party
Jones, John Paul
Loyalists

Madison, James
Marshall, John
Monroe, James
Morris, Robert
Northwest Ordinances, 1784–1787
Paine, Thomas
Republicanism
Rush, Benjamin
Schools: from the Revolution to 1900
Slavery: Slave Trade, External
South: Colonial Period to Civil War
State Constitutions and State Politics,
    1776–1789
States Rights
Universities and Colleges: 1783–1900
War of Independence, 1775–1783: Military
    History
War of Independence, 1775–1783:
    Diplomacy
Washington, George
Webster, Noah
Whitney, Eli

3) 1800–1848: Early National and Jacksonian Periods

Abolitionism/Antislavery Movement
Adams, John Quincy
Adams Family
African American History: Colonial
    Beginnings to 1860
Agriculture, to 1860
Antimasonry
Astor, John Jacob
Beecher Family
Benton, Thomas Hart
Boone, Daniel
Burr, Aaron
Bushnell, Horace
Calhoun, John C.
Carson, Kit
Child, Lydia Maria

Clay, Henry
Constitutional History, 1789–1877
Crandall, Prudence
Dix, Dorothea Lynde
Douglas, Stephen A.
Douglass, Frederick
Early National Period, 1789–1815:
    General
Elections:
    1) 1789–1860
Era of Good Feelings, c.1815–1824
Erie Canal
Expansionism
France and America, 1760–1815
Frémont, John C. and Jessie Benton
    Frémont

Fulton, Robert
Gallatin, Albert
Garrison, William Lloyd
Greeley, Horace
Grimké, Angelina and Sarah Grimké
Internal Improvements
Jackson, Andrew
Jacksonian Era, 1824–1848: General
Jefferson, Thomas
Jeffersonian Republican Party
Lewis, Meriwether and William Clark
Louisiana Purchase, 1803
McGuffey, William H.
Madison, James
Manifest Destiny, 1840s–1850s
Mann, Horace

4) 1848–1877: Civil War and Reconstruction

5) 1877–1917: Gilded Age and Progressive Era

6) 1917–1945: World Wars, Great Depression, and New Deal

Versailles, Treaty of, and League of
　　Nations
War Debts and Reparations, 1920s–1930s
Washington Treaties, 1921–1922
White, William Allen
Wilson, Woodrow
World War I: American Neutrality,
　　1914–1917

World War I: the United States at War,
　　1917–1918
World War II, Approach to
　　1) European War and American
　　　　Neutrality
　　2) Japan and the United States,
　　　　1931–1941
World War II, United States and

　　1) Campaigns in Europe
　　2) War Against Japan
　　3) Naval War
　　4) Air Power
　　5) Atomic Bomb
　　6) Relations with Allies
　　7) Economic Impact
　　8) Home Front

7) Recent History: the United States since 1945

Acheson, Dean
African American History: 1870s–1954, the
　　North
African American History: 1870s–1954, the
　　South
African American History: since 1954
Agriculture, since 1860
American Federation of Labor
Anticommunism
Black Power
Carter, Jimmy
Central Intelligence Agency
Civil Rights Acts, 1950s–1960s
Civil Rights Movement, 1950s–1960s
Cold War, Origins of
Computers and Data Processing
Congress of Industrial Organizations
Constitutional History, since 1877
Counterculture, 1960s
Cuban Missile Crisis, 1962
Du Bois, W.E.B.
Dulles, John Foster
Eisenhower, Dwight
Elections:
　　3) Since 1932
Federal Bureau of Investigation
Financial History, since 1940s
Foreign Policy since 1945: General
Foreign Policy since 1945: Special Aspects:
　　1) Relations with Asia
　　2) Relations with China

　　3) Relations with Europe
　　4) Relations with Israel and the Middle
　　　　East
　　5) Relations with the Soviet Union
　　6) Relations with the Western Hemisphere
Frankfurter, Felix
Friedan, Betty
Gay and Lesbian Movements, since 1960s
Graham, Billy
Great Society
Hamer, Fannie Lou
Jackson, Jesse
Johnson, Lyndon Baines
Kennedy, John F.
Kennedy, John F.: Assassination of
Kennedy Family
King, Martin Luther, Jr.
Kissinger, Henry A.
Korean War, 1950–1953: Military and
　　Diplomatic History
Korean War, 1950–1953: Political and
　　Economic Impact
Lewis, John L.
Lippmann, Walter
MacArthur, Douglas
McCarthy, Joseph R.
McCarthyism
Malcolm X
Marshall, George C.
Marshall, Thurgood
Marshall Plan, 1947–1951

Mumford, Lewis
National Association for the Advancement
　　of Colored People
Native Americans: Recent History (since
　　1960s)
Niebuhr, Reinhold
Nixon, Richard M.
Radio and Television
Reagan, Ronald
Recent American History (since 1945):
　　General
Reuther, Walter
Roads and Road Transport, 20th century:
　　Automobiles, Buses, and Trucks
Roosevelt, Eleanor
Schools: 20th century
South: since 1865
Space Policy and Program
Stevenson, Adlai E.
Truman, Harry S.
United Nations, United States and
Universities and Colleges: 20th century
Vietnam War: Military and Diplomatic
　　History
Vietnam War: Political and Social
　　Consequences
Wallace, George C.
Warren, Earl
Watergate
Women's History: Women's Liberation
　　Movement

POLITICAL, ECONOMIC, AND SOCIAL HISTORY

Political History: 1) Periods, Policies, Issues, and Events

Agrarian Discontent, 1865–1896
Alien and Sedition Acts, and Virginia and
　　Kentucky Resolutions, 1798–99
American Revolution: Causes
American Revolution: Development of a
　　Crisis, 1763–1770
American Revolution: Development of a
　　Crisis, 1770–1775
Anti-Evolution Crusade (1920s)
Antitrust Legislation and Court Cases,
　　1880s–1920s
Articles of Confederation
Bill of Rights, 1789–1791
Britain and the American Colonies,
　　1651–1763
Church and State

Citizenship
Civil Rights Acts, 1950s–1960s
Civil War, Approach to
　　1) 1846–1854: Wilmot Proviso,
　　　　Compromise of 1850, and fugitive
　　　　slaves
　　2) 1854–1860: Kansas-Nebraska Act,
　　　　"Bleeding Kansas," and Dred Scott
　　3) 1854–1860: Political realignment,
　　　　North and South; rise of Republican
　　　　party
　　4) 1860–1861: Secession crisis and
　　　　outbreak of war
Civil War: Debate on Causes
Civil War: the North
　　1) Wartime government and politics

Colonial History: Government and Politics
Compromise of 1877
Confederate States of America: Constitution,
　　Government, and Politics
Congress
Constitution: Philadelphia Convention, 1787
Constitution: Ratification
Continental Congress
Declaration of Independence, 1776
Democracy
Early National Period, 1789–1815: General
Emancipation Proclamations, 1862–1863
Era of Good Feelings, c.1815–1824
Expansionism
Federal Government: Establishment of,
　　1789–1793

Political History: 2) Parties, Political Movements, and Elections

Political History: 3) Presidents and Other Political Figures

Economic History: 1) General

Agriculture, to 1860
Agriculture, since 1860
Class
Colonial History: Economic Development
Economic Growth
Economic History: General
Economic Thought
Energy
Environment
Foreign Policy: Financial and Economic
    Aspects
Government and the Economy: Promotion
    and Regulation
Great Crash and Great Depression,
    1929–1939
Hamilton, Alexander: Financial and
    Economic Program, 1789–1795
Industrialization
Korean War, 1950–1953: Political and
    Economic Impact
Legal History: Special Aspects
Market Revolution, 1815–1850s
Marshall Plan, 1947–1951
New Deal: Economic Impact
Population
Poverty
Scientific Management
Slavery: Economics of
Slavery: Slave Trade, External
Slavery: Slave Trade, Internal
Technology and Invention
Tennessee Valley Authority
Urban History: Economic and Social
    Aspects
Wealth
World War II, United States and
    7) Economic Impact

Economic History: 2) Business and Industry

Advertising
Antitrust Legislation and Court Cases,
    1880s–1920s
Astor, John Jacob
Aviation and Aerospace
Bell, Alexander Graham
Business Cycle
Business History: General
Business History: Big Business
Business History: Individual Corporations
Carnegie, Andrew
Cattle Kingdom
Communications and Media: General
Computers and Data Processing
Du Pont Family
Edison, Thomas A.
Energy
Ford, Henry
Foreign Policy: Financial and Economic
    Aspects
Great Crash and Great Depression,
    1929–1939
Industrialization
McCormick, Cyrus
Manufacturing Industry: General
Manufacturing Industry: Individual
    Industries
Marketing and Distribution
Mellon, Andrew
Morgan, J. Pierpont
Morris, Robert
New Deal: Legislation and Agencies
    1) Business, Industry, and
    Agriculture
Oil and Natural Gas
Radio and Television
Railroads: General
Railroads: Legislation and Court Cases,
    1880s–1920s
Rockefeller, John D.
Scientific Management
Slater, Samuel
Technology and Invention
Telegraph and Telephone
Whitney, Eli

Economic History: 3) Finance, Trade, and Transport

Advertising
Astor, John Jacob
Aviation and Aerospace
Business Cycle
Business History: General
Business History: Big Business
Business History: Individual Corporations
Colonial History: Economic Development
Erie Canal
Financial History, 1780s–1930s
Financial History, since 1940s
Ford, Henry
Foreign Policy: Financial and Economic
    Aspects
Foreign Trade
Fulton, Robert
Gold Rushes
Great Crash and Great Depression,
    1929–1939
Hamilton, Alexander: Financial and
    Economic Program, 1789–1795
Internal Improvements
Investment: Foreign Investment in the
    United States
Investment: United States Investment
    Abroad
Japan: Matthew Perry and the Reopening
    of, 1853–1854
Market Revolution, 1815–1850s
Marketing and Distribution
Marshall Plan, 1947–1951
"Money Question," 1865–1896
Morgan, J. Pierpont
Morris, Robert
Open Door Policy
Panama Canal
Railroads: General
Railroads: Legislation and Court Cases,
    1880s–1920s
Rivers and Canals

Roads and Road Transport, to 1900
Roads and Road Transport, 20th century:
    Automobiles, Buses, and Trucks
Second Bank of the United States
Shipping
Stock Market
Transport: General
War Debts and Reparations,
    1920s–1930s
Wright, Orville and Wilbur Wright

Social History: 1) Social Structure: Class, Race, Ethnicity, Gender, Family

African American History entries
Children and Youth
Citizenship
Class
Colonial History: Colonies, settlement and
    growth
1) Chesapeake Bay
2) New England
3) Middle Atlantic
4) Carolinas and Georgia
Colonial History: Society
Democracy
Equality
Family
Gender
Immigration and Ethnicity: General
Industrialization
Marriage and Divorce

Middle Classes
Native Americans entries
Population
Poverty
Professions

Race
Slavery entries
Small Towns
Social Mobility
Suburbs

Urban History: General
Urban History: Economic and Social Aspects
Wealth
Women's History entries
Working Classes

Social History: 2) Issues, Influences, Policies, Movements

Abolitionism/Antislavery Movement
American Revolution: Character, Scope, and
    Significance
Birth Control
Black Power
Civil Rights Movement, 1950s–1960s
Civil War: the Common Soldiers
Civil War: the North
    2) Home Front
Communications and Media: General
Confederate States of America: Home Front
Counterculture, 1960s
Crime and Punishment
Feminism
Food
Gay and Lesbian Movements, since 1960s
Great Crash and Great Depression,
    1929–1939
Great Society
Homosexuality
Immigration: Acculturation and
    Americanization

Jim Crow: Segregation and Disfranchisement
    in the South, 1870s–1917
Labor History: General
Legal History: Special Aspects
Marketing and Distribution
Nativism
Nature: Attitudes to
New Deal: Legislation and Agencies
    2) Public Works, Social Security, and
    Labor
New Deal: Social Impact
Newspapers and Magazines
Philanthropy
Police and Law Enforcement
Prisons and Asylums
Prohibition
Prostitution
Radio and Television
Reform Movements, 1820s–1850s
Riots
Roads and Road Transport, 20th century:
    Automobiles, Buses, and Trucks

Settlement House Movement
Social Darwinism
Social Gospel
Social Welfare/Social Security
Social Work/Social Reform
Strikes
Suburbs
Technology and Invention
Telegraph and Telephone
Temperance
Utopian and Communitarian Movements
Vietnam War: Political and Social
    Consequences
Violence
Westward Expansion
Women's History: Women's Liberation
    Movement
World War I: the United States at War,
    1917–1918
World War II, United States and
    8) Home Front

SPECIFIC TOPICS

African American History

Abolitionism/Antislavery Movement
African American History: General
African American History: Colonial
    Beginnings to 1860
African American History: Civil War,
    Emancipation, and Reconstruction
African American History: 1870s–1954, the
    North
African American History: 1870s–1954, the
    South
African American History: since 1954
African American History: Religion
Bethune, Mary McLeod
Black Power
Brown, John
Child, Lydia Maria
Civil Rights Acts, 1950s–1960s
Civil Rights Movement, 1950s–1960s
Civil War, Approach to
    1) 1846–1854: Wilmot Proviso,
        Compromise of 1850, and fugitive
        slaves
    2) 1854–1860: Kansas-Nebraska Act,
        "Bleeding Kansas," and Dred Scott

Colonial History: Slavery and Indentured
    Servitude
Compromise of 1877
Crandall, Prudence
Douglass, Frederick
Du Bois, W.E.B.
Emancipation Proclamations, 1862–1863
Equality
Garrison, William Lloyd
Garvey, Marcus
Grimké, Angelina and Sarah Grimké
Hamer, Fannie Lou
Harlan, John M.
Jackson, Jesse
Jim Crow: Segregation and Disfranchisement
    in the South, 1870s–1917
King, Martin Luther, Jr.
Ku Klux Klan
Malcolm X
Marshall, Thurgood
Missouri Compromise, 1819–1821
Mott, Lucretia
National Association for the Advancement
    of Colored People

Phillips, Wendell
Race
Reconstruction: General
Reconstruction: Policy and Politics
    1) 1861–1869
    2) 1869–1877
Reconstruction: in the Southern States
Reconstruction: Economic Aspects
Reform Movements, 1820s–1850s
Slavery: General
Slavery: Economics of
Slavery: Legal Aspects
Slavery: Slave Trade, External
Slavery: Slave Trade, Internal
Slavery: Slave Culture and Community
Slavery: Slave Resistance and Rebellion
Slavery: Proslavery Thought
Truth, Sojourner
Tubman, Harriet
Turner, Nat
Washington, Booker T.
Weld, Theodore Dwight
Wells-Barnett, Ida B.

Cities, States, and Regions of the United States

Appalachia
Boston
California
Chicago
Colonial History: Colonies, settlement and
    growth
  1) Chesapeake Bay
  2) New England
  3) Middle Atlantic
  4) Carolinas and Georgia

Colonial History: Westward Expansion
Great Plains
Los Angeles
Louisiana Purchase, 1803
Middle Atlantic States
Midwest
New England
New Orleans
New York City
Pacific Northwest

Philadelphia
Rocky Mountains
San Francisco
South: General
South: Colonial Period to Civil War
South: since 1865
Southwest
Texas, Annexation of
Washington DC
Westward Expansion

Constitutional and Legal History

Antitrust Legislation and Court Cases,
    1880s–1920s
Articles of Confederation
Bill of Rights, 1789–1791
Brandeis, Louis D.
Bryce, James
Calhoun, John C.
Chase, Salmon P.
Church and State
Citizenship
Civil Rights Acts, 1950s–1960s
Civil War, Approach to
  2) 1854–1860: Kansas-Nebraska Act,
     "Bleeding Kansas," and Dred Scott
  4) 1860–1861: Secession crisis and
     outbreak of war
Confederate States of America:
    Constitution, Government, and
    Politics
Congress
Constitution: the Document
Constitution: Philadelphia Convention,
    1787
Constitution: Ratification

Constitutional History: General
Constitutional History, 1789–1877
Constitutional History, since 1877
Continental Congress
Crime and Punishment
Darrow, Clarence
Declaration of Independence, 1776
Equality
Federal Government: Establishment of,
    1789–1793
Federalism
Federalist Papers
Frankfurter, Felix
Government and the Economy: Promotion
    and Regulation
Harlan, John M.
Holmes, Oliver Wendell, Jr.
Hughes, Charles Evans
Judiciary
Labor History: Legal and Political
    Framework
Legal History: General
Legal History: Special Aspects
Legal Thought/Jurisprudence

Madison, James
Marshall, John
Marshall, Thurgood
New Deal: Political and Constitutional
    Issues
Nullification Crisis, 1832–1833
Police and Law Enforcement
Presidency
Prisons and Asylums
Railroads: Legislation and Court Cases,
    1880s–1920s
Slavery: Legal Aspects
State Constitutions and State Politics,
    1776–1789
States Rights
Story, Joseph
Suffrage
Supreme Court
Taft, William Howard
Taney, Roger B.
Warren, Earl
Watergate
Webster, Daniel
Women's History: Suffrage

Education

Beecher Family
Bethune, Mary McLeod
Colonial History: Education
Crandall, Prudence
Dewey, John
Education: General
Eliot, Charles W.

Finney, Charles Grandison
Franklin, Benjamin
McGuffey, William H.
Mann, Horace
Rush, Benjamin
Schools: from the Revolution to 1900
Schools: 20th century

Universities and Colleges: 1783–1900
Universities and Colleges: 20th century
Washington, Booker T.
Webster, Noah
Women's History: Education

Environmental History

Carson, Rachel
Cattle Kingdom
Conservation
Environment
Great Plains
Muir, John
Mumford, Lewis

National Parks
Nature: Attitudes to
Olmsted, Frederick Law
Pacific Northwest
Pinchot, Gifford
Powell, John Wesley
Public Land Policy

Rocky Mountains
Small Towns
Southwest
Suburbs
Tennessee Valley Authority
Urban History: General
Westward Expansion

Ethnicity and Immigration

Alien and Sedition Acts, and Virginia and
    Kentucky Resolutions, 1798–99
Anticommunism
Asian Americans
British Americans
Citizenship
Colonial History: Non-English Settlements
    in North America
German Americans
Hispanic Americans
Immigration and Ethnicity: General
Immigration: Federal Policy towards
Immigration: Acculturation and
    Americanization
Irish Americans
Italian Americans
Jewish Americans
Know Nothings
Mexican Americans
Nativism
Red Scare, 1919–1920
Scandinavian Americans
Women's History: Women in Ethnic
    Minority Groups

Foreign Relations and Foreign Policy: 1) 1775–1865

Adams, John Quincy
Britain and the United States: General
Canada and the United States
Civil War: International Aspects
Expansionism
Foreign Policy: General
Foreign Policy: Financial and Economic
    Aspects
Foreign Trade
France and America, 1760–1815
Investment: Foreign Investment in the
    United States
Investment: United States Investment
    Abroad
Japan: Matthew Perry and the Reopening
    of, 1853–1854
Jefferson, Thomas
Latin America and the United States
Louisiana Purchase, 1803
Manifest Destiny, 1840s–1850s
Mexican War: 1846–1848, Politics and
    Diplomacy
Mexico and the United States
Monroe, James
Monroe Doctrine
Pacifism
Polk, James K.
Seward, William H.
Texas, Annexation of
Tyler, John
War of 1812: Causes
War of 1812: Course and
    Consequences
War of Independence, 1775–1783:
    Diplomacy
Webster, Daniel

Foreign Relations and Foreign Policy: 2) 1865–1945

Alabama Claims and Treaty of Washington,
    1869–1872
Britain and the United States: General
Bryan, William Jennings
Bryce, James
Canada and the United States
China and the United States
Cuba and the United States
Expansionism
Foreign Policy: General
Foreign Policy: Financial and Economic
    Aspects
Foreign Policy, 1865–1918
Foreign Policy, 1919–1941
Foreign Trade
Hoover, Herbert
Hughes, Charles Evans
Imperialism and Anti-Imperialism,
    1890–1914
Investment: Foreign Investment in the
    United States
Investment: United States Investment
    Abroad
Isolationism
Latin America and the United States
Lippmann, Walter
Lodge, Henry Cabot
McKinley, William
Mahan, Alfred Thayer
Mexico and the United States
Monroe Doctrine
Open Door Policy
Pacifism
Panama Canal
Pearl Harbor, 1941
Roosevelt, Franklin D.
Roosevelt, Theodore
Spanish-American War, 1898
Taft, William Howard
Versailles, Treaty of, and League of
    Nations
War Debts and Reparations,
    1920s–1930s
Washington Treaties, 1921–1922
Wilson, Woodrow
World War I: American Neutrality,
    1914–1917
World War I: the United States at War,
    1917–1918
World War II, Approach to
    1) European War and American
        Neutrality
    2) Japan and the United States,
        1931–1941
World War II, United States and
    5) Atomic Bomb
    6) Relations with Allies

Foreign Relations and Foreign Policy: 3) Since 1945

Acheson, Dean
Britain and the United States: General
Canada and the United States
Carter, Jimmy
Central Intelligence Agency
China and the United States
Cold War, Origins of
Cuba and the United States
Cuban Missile Crisis, 1962
Dulles, John Foster
Eisenhower, Dwight
Foreign Policy: General
Foreign Policy: Financial and Economic
    Aspects
Foreign Policy since 1945: General
Foreign Policy since 1945: Special Aspects:
    1) Relations with Asia
    2) Relations with China
    3) Relations with Europe
    4) Relations with Israel and the Middle
        East
    5) Relations with the Soviet Union
    6) Relations with the Western Hemisphere
Foreign Trade
Investment: Foreign Investment in the
    United States
Investment: United States Investment Abroad
Isolationism
Johnson, Lyndon Baines
Kennedy, John F.
Kissinger, Henry A.
Korean War, 1950–1953: Military and
    Diplomatic History

Foreign Relations and Foreign Policy: 4) Relations with Other Nations or Regions

Government and Government Agencies

Ideas, Ideology, and Social Commentary

Paine, Thomas
Penn, William
Pilgrim Fathers
Pragmatism
Progressivism
Puritanism
Race
Reform Movements, 1820s–1850s

Republicanism
Revivalism
Second Great Awakening
Sectionalism/Regionalism
Slavery: Proslavery Thought
Social Darwinism
Social Gospel
Socialism and Communism

States Rights
Tocqueville, Alexis de
Transcendentalism
Utopian and Communitarian
    Movements
Veblen, Thorstein
Washington, Booker T.
Wright, Frances

Labor History

American Federation of Labor
Colonial History: Slavery and Indentured
    Servitude
Congress of Industrial Organizations
Debs, Eugene V.
Gompers, Samuel
Industrial Workers of the World
Knights of Labor

Labor History: General
Labor History: Legal and Political
    Framework
Labor Unions
Lewis, John L.
New Deal: Legislation and Agencies
    2) Public Works, Social Security, and
    Labor

Perkins, Frances
Reuther, Walter
Slavery entries
Socialism and Communism
Strikes
Women's History: Women at Work
Working Classes

Media and Communications

Advertising
Bell, Alexander Graham
Bennett, James Gordon
Communications and Media: General
Computers and Data Processing
Edison, Thomas A.
Film

Greeley, Horace
Hearst, William Randolph
Lippmann, Walter
Mencken, H.L.
Morse, Samuel F.B.
Muckrakers
Newspapers and Magazines

Pulitzer, Joseph
Radio and Television
Technology and Invention
Webster, Noah
White, William Allen

Military and Naval History

Armed Services
British-French Rivalry in North America
Civil War: Campaigns
    1) Eastern theatre
    2) Western theatre
Civil War: the Common Soldiers
Civil War: Naval War
Cuban Missile Crisis, 1962
Custer, George A.
Draft/Conscription
Eisenhower, Dwight
Frémont, John C. and Jessie Benton
    Frémont
Grand Army of the Republic
Grant, Ulysses S.
Jackson, Thomas J. ("Stonewall")
Japan: Matthew Perry and the Reopening
    of, 1853–1854
Jones, John Paul

Korean War, 1950–1953: Military and
    Diplomatic History
Lee, Robert E.
Lost Cause/Southern Memories of the Civil
    War
MacArthur, Douglas
McClellan, George B.
Marshall, George C.
Mexican War: 1846–1848, Campaigns
Military History: General
Militia/National Guard
Native Americans: Indian Wars
Nimitz, Chester
Pacifism
Patton, George S.
Pearl Harbor, 1941
Pershing, John J.
Reconstruction: Policy and Politics
    1) 1861–1869

    2) 1869–1877
Scott, Winfield
Sherman, William Tecumseh
Space Policy and Program
Spanish-American War, 1898
Vietnam War: Military and Diplomatic
    History
War of 1812: Course and Consequences
War of Independence, 1775–1783: Military
    History
Washington, George
World War I: the United States at War,
    1917–1918
World War II, United States and
    1) Campaigns in Europe
    2) War Against Japan
    3) Naval War
    4) Air Power
    5) Atomic Bomb

Native American History

Boone, Daniel
Carson, Kit
Colonial History: Colonies, settlement and
    growth
    1) Chesapeake Bay
    2) New England
    3) Middle Atlantic
    4) Carolinas and Georgia

Colonial History: Relations with Native
    Americans
Colonial History: Westward Expansion
Custer, George A.
Great Plains
Jackson, Andrew
Lewis, Meriwether and William
    Clark

Native Americans: General
Native Americans: White Encounter
    with
Native Americans: Federal Policy
    towards
Native Americans: Indian Wars
Native Americans: Recent History (since
    1960s)

Native Americans: Chiefs, biographies
Native Americans: Cultures
  1) Northeast
  2) Southeast
  3) Great Plains
  4) Southwest
  5) Far West and Pacific Northwest
Pacific Northwest
Race
Seven Years' War, 1754–1763
Smith, John
Southwest
Westward Expansion
Women's History: Women in Ethnic
  Minority Groups

Reform and Protest Movements
[for Antislavery Movement, see under Slavery and Antislavery below]

Addams, Jane
Agrarian Discontent, 1865–1896
Anthony, Susan B.
Antimasonry
Beecher Family
Bellamy, Edward
Bethune, Mary McLeod
Black Power
Bryan, William Jennings
Catt, Carrie Chapman
Civil Rights Movement, 1950s–1960s
Debs, Eugene V.
Dix, Dorothea Lynde
Douglass, Frederick
Du Bois, W.E.B.
Feminism
Finney, Charles Grandison
Friedan, Betty
Garvey, Marcus
Gay and Lesbian Movements, since 1960s
George, Henry

Gilman, Charlotte Perkins
Goldman, Emma
Greeley, Horace
Hamer, Fannie Lou
Jackson, Jesse
Kelley, Florence
King, Martin Luther, Jr.
La Follette, Robert M.
Malcolm X
Mann, Horace
Marshall, Thurgood
Muckrakers
Municipal Government: Corruption and
  Reform, 1865–1917
Nation, Carry
National Association for the Advancement
  of Colored People
New Nationalism and New Freedom
Pacifism
Paine, Thomas
Populism (People's Party)

Progressivism
Prohibition
Reform Movements, 1820s–1850s
Roosevelt, Eleanor
Sanger, Margaret
Settlement House Movement
Social Gospel
Social Work/Social Reform
Socialism and Communism
Stanton, Elizabeth Cady
Temperance
Transcendentalism
Utopian and Communitarian
  Movements
Washington, Booker T.
Wells-Barnett, Ida B.
Willard, Frances
Women's History: Women's Liberation
  Movement
Woodhull, Victoria
Wright, Frances

Religion

African American History: Religion
Anti-Evolution Crusade (1920s)
Beecher Family
Bushnell, Horace
Catholic Church
Church and State
Colonial History: Religion
Eddy, Mary Baker
Edwards, Jonathan
Finney, Charles Grandison
Fundamentalism
Graham, Billy
Great Awakening

Hutchinson, Anne
Judaism
King, Martin Luther, Jr.
Malcolm X
Mather, Cotton and Increase Mather
Moody, Dwight L.
Mormons (Church of Jesus Christ of Latter-
  Day Saints)
Morse, Samuel F.B.
Nativism
Penn, William
Pilgrim Fathers
Protestantism: General

Protestantism: Denominational Histories
Puritanism
Religion: General
Revivalism
Second Great Awakening
Slavery: Slave Culture and Community
Social Gospel
Transcendentalism
Truth, Sojourner
Utopian and Communitarian Movements
Williams, Roger
Winthrop, John
Young, Brigham and Joseph Smith

Slavery and Antislavery

Abolitionism/Antislavery Movement
Adams, John Quincy
African American History: General
African American History: Colonial
  Beginnings to 1860
African American History: Civil War,
  Emancipation, and Reconstruction
African American History: Religion
Beecher Family
Brown, John
Buchanan, James
Calhoun, John C.

Chase, Salmon P.
Child, Lydia Maria
Civil War, Approach to
  1) 1846–1854: Wilmot Proviso,
    Compromise of 1850, and fugitive
    slaves
  2) 1854–1860: Kansas-Nebraska Act,
    "Bleeding Kansas," and Dred Scott
  3) 1854–1860: Political realignment,
    North and South; rise of Republican
    party
  4) 1860–1861: Secession crisis and

outbreak of war
Civil War: Debate on Causes
Colonial History: Colonies, settlement and
  growth
  1) Chesapeake Bay
  4) Carolinas and Georgia
Colonial History: Slavery and Indentured
  Servitude
Confederate States of America: General
Crandall, Prudence
Davis, Jefferson
Douglas, Stephen A.

Southern History

Sports, Entertainment, and Leisure

Urban History

African American History: 1870s–1954, the
  North
Boston
Chicago
Immigration and Ethnicity: General
Immigration: Acculturation and
  Americanization
Los Angeles

Mumford, Lewis
Municipal Government: Corruption and
  Reform, 1865–1917
New Orleans
New York City
Olmsted, Frederick Law
Philadelphia
Riots

San Francisco
Settlement House Movement
Small Towns
Suburbs
Urban History: General
Urban History: Government and Politics
Urban History: Economic and Social Aspects
Washington DC

Western History

Agrarian Discontent, 1865–1896
Agriculture, to 1860
Agriculture, since 1860
Asian Americans
Astor, John Jacob
Benton, Thomas Hart
Boone, Daniel
Brown, John
Bryan, William Jennings
Burr, Aaron
California
Carson, Kit
Cattle Kingdom
Chicago
Civil War: Campaigns
  2) Western theatre
Clark, George Rogers
Clay, Henry
Colonial History: Westward Expansion
Conservation
Cowboys, Cowgirls, Gunfighters, and
  Western Heroes: Individual Biographies
Custer, George A.
Erie Canal

Expansionism
Frémont, John C. and Jessie Benton
  Frémont
Gold Rushes
Great Plains
Jackson, Andrew
La Follette, Robert M.
Lewis, Meriwether and William Clark
Los Angeles
Louisiana Purchase, 1803
McCormick, Cyrus
Manifest Destiny, 1840s–1850s
Mexican War: 1846–1848, Campaigns
Mexican War: 1846–1848, Politics and
  Diplomacy
Midwest
Missouri Compromise, 1819–1821
Mormons (Church of Jesus Christ of Latter-
  Day Saints)
Muir, John
National Parks
Native Americans: General
Native Americans: White Encounter with
Native Americans: Federal Policy towards

Native Americans: Indian Wars
Native Americans: Recent History (since
  1960s)
Native Americans: Chiefs, biographies
Native Americans: Cultures
  3) Great Plains
  4) Southwest
  5) Far West and Pacific Northwest
Northwest Ordinances, 1784–1787
Pacific Northwest
Pinchot, Gifford
Populism (People's Party)
Powell, John Wesley
Public Land Policy
Rocky Mountains
San Francisco
Sectionalism/Regionalism
Southwest
Texas, Annexation of
Westward Expansion
World War II, United States and
  7) Economic Impact
  8) Home Front
Young, Brigham and Joseph Smith

Women's History

Adams, Abigail
Addams, Jane
Anthony, Susan B.
Barton, Clara
Beecher Family
Bethune, Mary McLeod
Birth Control
Carson, Rachel
Catt, Carrie Chapman
Child, Lydia Maria
Cowboys, Cowgirls, Gunfighters, and
  Western Heroes: Individual
  Biographies
Crandall, Prudence
Dix, Dorothea Lynde
Eddy, Mary Baker
Equality
Family
Feminism
First Ladies
Frémont, John C. and Jessie Benton
  Frémont

Friedan, Betty
Gay and Lesbian Movements, since 1960s
Gender
Gilman, Charlotte Perkins
Goldman, Emma
Grimké, Angelina and Sarah Grimké
Hamer, Fannie Lou
Homosexuality
Hutchinson, Anne
Kelley, Florence
Kennedy Family
Legal History: Special Aspects
Marriage and Divorce
Mott, Lucretia
Nation, Carry
Native Americans: Recent History (since
  1960s)
Paul, Alice
Perkins, Frances
Prostitution
Roosevelt, Eleanor
Sanger, Margaret

Settlement House Movement
Slavery: General
Social Welfare/Social Security
Social Work/Social Reform
Stanton, Elizabeth Cady
Truth, Sojourner
Tubman, Harriet
Wells-Barnett, Ida B.
Willard, Frances
Women's History: General
Women's History: Education
Women's History: Suffrage
Women's History: Women at Work
Women's History: Women in Ethnic
  Minority Groups
Women's History: Women's Liberation
  Movement
Woodhull, Victoria
World War II, United States and
  8) Home Front
Wright, Frances

A

Abolitionism/Antislavery Movement

Barnes, Gilbert Hobbs, *The Antislavery Impulse, 1830–1844*, New York: Appleton Century, 1933

Duberman, Martin (editor), *The Antislavery Vanguard: New Essays on the Abolitionists*, Princeton: Princeton University Press, 1965

Essig, James D., *The Bonds of Wickedness: American Evangelicals Against Slavery, 1770–1808*, Philadelphia: Temple University Press, 1982

Filler, Louis, *The Crusade Against Slavery, 1830–1860*, New York: Harper, 1960; revised as *The Crusade Against Slavery: Friends, Foes, and Reforms, 1820–1860*, Algonac, MI: Reference Publications, 1986

Friedman, Lawrence J., *Gregarious Saints: Self and Community in American Abolitionism, 1830–1870*, Cambridge and New York: Cambridge University Press, 1982

Jacobs, Donald M. (editor), *Courage and Conscience: Black and White Abolitionists in Boston*, Bloomington: Indiana University Press, 1993

McKivigan, John R., *The War Against Proslavery Religion: Abolitionism and the Northern Churches, 1830–1865*, Ithaca, NY: Cornell University Press, 1984

Magdol, Edward, *The Antislavery Rank and File: A Social Profile of the Abolitionists' Constituency*, Westport, CT: Greenwood Press, 1986

Perry, Lewis, *Radical Abolitionism: Anarchy and the Government of God in Antislavery Thought*, Ithaca, NY: Cornell University Press, 1973

Quarles, Benjamin, *Black Abolitionists*, New York: Oxford University Press, 1969

Walters, Ronald G., *The Antislavery Appeal: American Abolitionism after 1830*, Baltimore: Johns Hopkins University Press, 1976

Wyatt-Brown, Bertram, *Lewis Tappan and the Evangelical War Against Slavery*, Cleveland: Case Western Reserve University Press, 1969

Yellin, Jean Fagan and John C. Van Horne (editors), *The Abolitionist Sisterhood: Women's Political Culture in Antebellum America*, Ithaca, NY: Cornell University Press, 1994

BARNES began modern historical scholarship on abolitionism, and is still worth reading both for what he has to say about abolitionism's roots in revivalism and for his rescue from obscurity of non-Garrisonian abolitionists, particularly Theodore Weld, whose recently discovered papers he exploited. Within the context of the Second Great Awakening, he linked immediatist abolitionism to other moral reforms, and credited Weld with autonomously mobilising a western antislavery movement which, with the work of the Tappan circle in New York, came to constitute the abolitionist mainstream. In reaction against earlier identifications of abolitionism with William Lloyd Garrison he attributed too little significance to the Bostonian. He has, however, continued to influence scholarship on religion and reform and, in emphasising evangelical abolitionism and the beginnings of political action, he laid the bases for a more balanced treatment of abolitionism and antislavery.

A useful overall account is FILLER. He provides sketches of individual reformers in their contexts with plenty of detail. He is fullest on the 1830s and offers a more basic narrative of unfolding events and responses to them for the later period when antislavery sentiment was more widespread in the North. DUBERMAN's collection, appearing at the height of Civil Rights activity, was proclaimed as the first full statement of a "neo-abolitionist" perspective on antislavery. It is true that the essayists present opposition to slavery as substantially a rational cause rather than a form of maladjustment, but there are significant differences of tone and approach between, say, Zinn's sketch of Garrison as a radical hero who speaks directly to the 1960s, Thomas's ironic appreciation of the utopian strain in antislavery and Duberman's and Tompkins's subtle reflections on the psychology of reform commitment.

WYATT-BROWN not only provides a full contextualization for Tappan and his associates, for many years at the centre of the "benevolent empire" of missionary and moral reform activities, but offers also a sensitive psychological exploration of Tappan's evangelical temperament expressed through the ideals of the Christian self-made man and of the moral stewardship of wealth. The book is the best approach to the evangelical wing of antislavery

PERRY takes seriously the thinking of the New England radicals and follows out its various implications. He begins with the subtlest appreciation of the meanings of immediatism that we have, and shows how the doctrine could lead to an antinomian outlook and, in the case of some reformers, communitarian activity. Yet the reader is finally left with a strong sense, exemplified in the fascinating treatment of Adin Ballou and the Hopedale community, that the left wing of moral reform often combined intellectual daring and practical circumspection.

For the purposes of structural analysis WALTERS's influential book takes abolitionism after 1830 as a single phenomenon. He distinguishes what shaped the form and style of abolitionism through emphasizing how the society and culture made some modes of change seem feasible and others not. He adds a brilliant dissection of underlying abolitionists' perceptions and anxieties about America, many of which, he argues, abolitionists held in common with, though more intensely than, their fellow citizens. He thus presents reformers primarily as part of a generation and culture rather than as simply alienated from American society. FRIEDMAN is the most sophisticated internal study of abolitionism and antislavery. He traces the differences and inter-group relations between the Boston Clique, the Tappanites in New York, and the Gerrit Smith group in upstate New York, and studies the internal dynamics of each. He suggests that, to a greater or lesser degree, they all registered tensions between personal piety and the pull of group membership, though over the years the cohesion of the groups declined. Friedman complements rather than builds on Walters's orientation towards the larger culture.

Evangelical opposition to slavery did not begin in the 1820s and ESSIG provides the best study of an earlier phase in the late 18th century that emerged from the first Great Awakening and blended with the natural rights ideology of the Revolution. He is less convincing on the reasons for the weakening of the reform impulse by 1800 but ends with a useful comparison of this earlier phase with the militant abolitionism of the 1830s.

McKIVIGAN looks at abolitionist efforts to win over Northern churches to immediate emancipation in the expectation that success would help to end slavery peacefully through the leverage that denominations could bring to bear on members. The reformers failed, but McKivigan argues that it was a qualified failure by showing the spread of abolitionist commitment in Northern churches through adaptability of tactics. There is, though, little discussion of whether the project of peaceful change through church influence was ever realistic.

Analyses of the social bases of popular antislavery have, until recently, been sparse. MAGDOL's value arises from his own hypotheses based on analysis of abolitionist petitions correlated with other community data in Massachusetts and upstate New York, as well as from relating these to other scattered work in the field. The importance of labouring men and women, artisans and small businessmen in petitioning emerges strongly for the 1830s, and Magdol speculates that antislavery was an expression of their republican values. Methodists and Baptists and some immigrants, despite "transitory" nativism, were important to antislavery third parties later. This is a regionally limited but useful start.

QUARLES produced a pioneer work on black abolitionists, most useful for an outline narrative, with biographical information and some of the detail necessary for later, more interpretative literature. JACOBS's collection enables close focus on the relations of black abolitionists with white reformers through a study of Boston. White and black reformers were clearly mutually dependent, and yet African Americans also pursued distinctive courses of action – on desegregation, for example – which whites sometimes followed later.

The sixteen essays in YELLIN and VAN HORNE together provide an excellent overview of women in antislavery and of antislavery in the development of a women's public sphere and political culture. The essays reveal that there was no single line of development from women's antislavery to women's rights but rather dialogue and tension between different groups of white and black women over the proper limits of their action. While the strategy, tactics, language and ideology of antislavery white feminists command most attention in the book, women abolitionists are successfully placed in a variety of different contexts.

DAVID TURLEY

See also Reform Movements

Acheson, Dean 1893–1971
Secretary of State and presidential adviser

Acheson, Dean, *Present at the Creation: My Years in the State Department*, New York: Norton, 1969; London: Hamish Hamilton, 1970

Brinkley, Douglas, *Dean Acheson: The Cold War Years, 1953–1971*, New Haven: Yale University Press, 1992

Brinkley, Douglas (editor), *Dean Acheson and the Making of US Foreign Policy*, New York: St. Martin's Press, and London: Macmillan, 1993

Isaacson, Walter and Evan Thomas, *The Wise Men: Six Friends and the World They Made: Acheson, Bohlen, Harriman, Kennan, Lovett, McCloy*, New York: Simon and Schuster, and London: Faber, 1986

McLellan, David S., *Dean Acheson: The State Department Years*, New York: Dodd Mead, 1976

Smith, Gaddis, *Dean Acheson*, New York: Cooper Square, 1972

Dean Acheson is remembered as the major architect of America's Cold War containment policies. He served as under secretary of state under James F. Byrnes and George C. Marshall between 1945 and 1947 and as secretary of state during Truman's second administration between January 1949 and January 1953. His middle-class upbringing in a mix of British, Canadian and New England traditions encouraged him to enter the legal profession. Educated at Groton, Yale University and the Harvard Law School, Acheson joined the law firm of Covington and Burling in 1921. SMITH, a professor of history at Yale, was perhaps the natural choice to write the "official" account of Acheson as Truman's secretary of state. Smith describes Acheson as pro-British, pro-Atlanticist, an able statesman, a competent administrator and a realistic politician. Above all, he was a diplomat who was determined to deal with the Soviet Union from a position of strength based on America's military power. Acheson was therefore bound to clash with George Kennan's intellectualism and his limited version of containment policy, since Acheson wanted global containment and American rearmament. Although Smith's book was published more than twenty years ago, it remains the classic and definitive account of Acheson as secretary of state.

McLELLAN is a substantial biography of Acheson, which is rather more detailed than Smith. McLellan suggests that, although Acheson was successful in Europe, he failed to formulate a sufficiently constructive foreign policy in the Far East, and especially towards China. Of course, this was an area where Acheson was attacked by many Republicans for being "soft" on communism, and having "lost" China to the Chinese communists. Both Smith and McLellan show that Acheson played a significant role in promoting the Truman Doctrine, the Marshall Plan, the formation of the North Atlantic Treaty Organization, West German rearmament and the conclusion of the peace treaty with Japan in 1951, and also in engaging in delicate diplomatic manoeuvring with European and oriental allies during the Korean War. Acheson's years in the State Department after 1945 were filled with the events and crises which led to the outbreak and development of the Cold War and countless books have been written on this subject. This may partly explain why studies focusing specifically on Acheson are fewer than one might expect of such a pivotal figure.

BRINKLEY (1993) is a volume of essays on Acheson during the Truman years, based on the proceedings of a two-day conference held in Washington in April 1989, to mark the fortieth anniversary of Acheson's secretaryship. The contributors, who include Kaplan, Hogan, Kuniholm, Pogue, Tucker and Leffler, provide an authoritative account of Acheson as a major policymaker in the Truman administration; each writer re-appraises the role and political philosophy of Acheson in particular areas. For instance, Acheson's Anglophile leanings were reflected in his desperate efforts to arrange the destroyer-bases agreement between the United States and Great Britain in September 1940. However, after 1945, in face of the need to integrate Western Europe in resistance to the Soviet threat, and given that the decline of Britain as world power had become unmistakable by the time of the devaluation of the pound in 1949, Acheson encouraged Britain to play a more active role in furthering European integration, rather than in seeking to forge the Anglo-American "special relationship."

Similarly, the Marshall Plan was regarded by Acheson as a means of preventing a communist takeover of Western Europe rather than as a method of reinvigorating the economies of Western Europe, and thereby stimulating the world economy and expanding the American market. Acheson's policy towards China is interpreted as being flexible and moderate, at least until the outbreak of the Korean War, which froze American-Chinese relations for twenty years. None of the contributors has attempted any radical departure from the interpretations of Smith and McLellan. The overall effect of the volume is to confirm that Acheson was a realist, a pragmatic statesman, and a skilful diplomat, who contributed significantly to Truman's overall foreign policy goals.

ACHESON's own account of his years in the State Department under Truman is not merely a memoir, but a serious examination of his policy, based on the documentary records. Acheson wrote elegantly and lucidly, enlivening his descriptions of events with perceptive comments and judgments. His admiration for Truman comes across clearly, and demonstrates that Acheson was perfectly aware that his influence over policymaking was dependent upon his loyalty to Truman, and his maintenance of cordial relations with the president.

Acheson's memoir will remain one of the most scholarly and substantial autobiographical accounts ever written by a 20th-century American secretary of state.

ISAACSON and THOMAS offer a readable account of the background and careers of the powerful Eastern elite during and after World War II and down to 1968 – Dean Acheson, Robert Lovett, John McCloy, George Kennan, Charles Bohlen and Averell Harriman. The authors convey a vivid impression of the earlier Cold War years as seen through the eyes of this elite group. There is little analysis of Acheson's thinking or policies, but the book includes fascinating accounts of his relations with Kennan, Dulles, Kennedy, Johnson, and Nixon. In the process it sheds new light on Acheson's activities after he left the State Department in January 1953.

BRINKLEY (1992) is a much needed scholarly examination of Acheson's career between 1953 and 1971, when he occasionally served three presidents as an adviser, albeit in an unofficial capacity – to Kennedy on the Berlin and Cuban crises, to Johnson between 1964 and 1968 on the Vietnam War, and to Nixon on Southern African affairs. Brinkley sees Acheson as a tough negotiator and a staunch Cold War diplomat, who regarded the Cold War as the central factor in the international system and who sought to deal with America's adversary from a position of strength. Brinkley thus reinforces the view fostered by Smith and McLellan, and as a result, Acheson has now emerged as an even more staunch Cold Warrior than John Foster Dulles.

SAKI DOCKRILL

See also Cold War; Foreign Policy since 1945 entries

Adams, Abigail   1744–1818
First lady, writer and political activist

Akers, Charles W., *Abigail Adams: An American Woman*, Boston: Little Brown, 1980

Gelles, Edith B., *Portia: The World of Abigail Adams*, Bloomington: Indiana University Press, 1992

Keller, Rosemary, *Patriotism and the Female Sex: Abigail Adams and the American Revolution*, New York: Carlson, 1994

Levin, Phyllis Lee, *Abigail Adams: A Biography*, New York: St. Martin's Press, 1987

Nagel, Paul C., *The Adams Women: Abigail and Louisa Adams, Their Sisters and Daughters*, New York and Oxford: Oxford University Press, 1987

Withey, Lynne, *Dearest Friend: A Life of Abigail Adams*, New York: Free Press, and London: Collier Macmillan, 1981

One of the most remarkable women in Revolutionary and early national America, Abigail Adams, among her other achievements, set the pattern for those presidential wives who were also fascinating and significant historical figures in their own right. Two recent studies use opposite assumptions to analyze her letters and behavior. GELLES contends that all previous biographers merged Adams's story so completely with John's that the real Abigail has yet to appear. Taking an episodic approach, she ties various incidents in Adams's life to broader trends in American culture. The result is an insightful look into topics as various as marriage, gossip, domestic patriotism, and the conventions of letter writing. Adams emerges from this exercise as a fascinating and complex woman who, though careful to observe the gender conventions of her times, was often forced to act independently. As a result, she discovered her talent for business, her ability to meet a crisis, and most importantly her capacity to change and grow. In her first chapter, entitled "The Abigail Industry," Gelles examines the historiographical issues at stake and, not surprisingly, concludes that Adams has often been stereotyped by previous scholars. Innovative and provocative, this study breaks new ground not only for Adams, but for biography as a genre.

Taking issue with some of Gelles's assumptions, KELLER reaches more conventional conclusions. She argues that, as an adult, Adams defined herself in terms of her husband's life and career, implying that Gelles perhaps took on an impossible task when she tried to eliminate John from much of her story. Nevertheless, Keller also believes that Adams understood that women's roles were historically constructed – not ordained by God. Even though she accepted her place as wife and mother, Adams admired women such as Mercy Otis Warren who assumed less traditional roles as well. Keller also shows that, as a result of the Revolution, Adams changed and developed as a writer and thinker and as a woman concerned with gender issues. Keller concludes, however, that Adams best represents a model of feminism that is evolutionary rather than revolutionary in its approach.

Three more conventional modern biographies recount the life of Abigail Adams. Though lacking in original analysis, LEVIN offers a detailed narrative of Adams's experiences. She sees her subject as the embodiment of traditional female qualities and relies on conventional views of the Adams marriage. By quoting extensively from Adams's correspondence, she gives the reader many opportunities to appreciate the literary quality of her letters as well as the information they offer on culture in 18th- and early 19th-century America. Although at times Adams's life disappears into that of her husband or oldest son, Levin still writes with a journalist's eye for a good story, full of detail and admiration for her subject. WITHEY often falls into the same trap as Levin – confusing the story of Abigail with that of John and John Quincy so thoroughly at times that we lose sight of the main character for several pages at a stretch. Pursuing Adams from her years as a revolutionary to her later life as a conservative, Withey ultimately contends that Adams was really a conservative all along. Adams emerges as a moderate feminist who accepted her domestic role in life. Withey also interprets her as a woman who failed to understand the complexities of the revolutionary economy despite her successes in it, who encouraged independence in her children while she tried to manipulate them, and who was "prone to strong views and exaggeration."

Adopting a more analytical approach than Levin or Withey, AKERS focuses on Adams's concern with politics and world affairs but also sees her as someone who was interested in traditional women's issues such as female education, childbirth, health, and religion. Though he notes Adams's solid religious foundation, he views her life primarily through the lens of republican motherhood. One of many scholars who have emphasized the partnership quality of her marriage, Akers points out that her reading in the works of James Fordyce, a Scottish Presbyterian minister who encouraged women to realize their potential, and also Samuel Richardson's novels, reinforced her belief that men and women played complementary but equal roles in their lives together. He also offers the insight that not only did Adams's life shape her letters (Adams's chief literary outlet), but letter-writing conventions of the day also affected the way she lived her life. Akers contends that Adams saw daily events connected together as a narrative with highlights and a rhythm of their own, and she organized herself accordingly.

Seeking a new perspective on Adams, NAGEL places her in the context of two generations of her close female relatives. The first four of sixteen chapters focus on Adams and her sisters, illuminating both their lives and their relationships with one another. This generation of Adams women shared a philosophy of gender relations that idealized marriage as a necessity for men, desirable for women, and an equal partnership for both. Four additional chapters feature Adams in a secondary role, describing her influence on the next generation and their children. For example, Nagel offers compelling analysis to suggest that Adams had a strained relationship with her daughter. Sophisticated, yet readable and entertaining, Nagel's book reveals the complexity of Adams's life from a unique perspective.

ELIZABETH E. DUNN

See also First Ladies

Adams, Henry 1838–1918
Historian and social commentator

Contosta, David R., *Henry Adams and the American Experiment*, Boston: Little Brown, 1980

Dawidoff, Robert, "Henry Adams: The First American Tocquevillian," in his *The Genteel Tradition and the Sacred Rage: High Culture vs. Democracy in Adams, James, and Santayana*, Chapel Hill: University of North Carolina Press, 1992

Decker, William Merrill, *The Literary Vocation of Henry Adams*, Chapel Hill: University of North Carolina Press, 1990

Dusinberre, William, *Henry Adams: The Myth of Failure*, Charlottesville: University Press of Virginia, 1979

Hochfield, George, *Henry Adams: An Introduction and Interpretation*, New York: Barnes and Noble, 1962

Jordy, William H., *Henry Adams: Scientific Historian*, New Haven: Yale University Press, 1952

Levenson, J.C., *The Mind and Art of Henry Adams*, Boston: Houghton Mifflin, 1957

Samuels, Ernest, *The Young Henry Adams*, Cambridge, MA: Harvard University Press, 1948

Samuels, Ernest, *Henry Adams: The Middle Years*, Cambridge, MA: Harvard University Press, 1958

Samuels, Ernest, *Henry Adams: The Major Phase*, Cambridge, MA: Harvard University Press, 1964

Simpson, Brooks D., *The Political Education of Henry Adams*, Columbia: University of South Carolina Press, 1996

Henry Adams once explained that he wrote *The Education of Henry Adams* to shield him from biographers after he was dead. As a practitioner of the art and science of biography, he well knew what might happen to his life once commentators got their hands on him: indeed, he once likened biography to murder. To a large extent, he succeeded: *The Education of Henry Adams* has set the agenda for much of the writing about its author and continues to manipulate lines of inquiry. A large number of literary scholars have offered lengthy explications and explanations of the *Education*; not a few have fallen into the trap of assuming that it is indeed autobiography, a shortcoming shared by some historians and biographers. Moreover, some writers find attractive Adams's pose of disillusionment with American society, and a few even share it and embrace the role of alienated intellectual, producing studies that are as much autobiography as literary criticism. Only when the reader realizes the unique nature of the *Education* – part autobiography, part cultural and political criticism, part philosophy, part self-delusion, and part pure contrariness – can it be used to shed more revealing light on the actual Henry Adams.

SAMUELS remains Adams's foremost biographer: his three-volume study traces Adams the political reformer, the historian, and the idiosyncratic critic and writer. Of the three volumes, the first one, completed before many of Adams's papers were available to the public, is the weakest, bringing Adams through the 1870s. Samuels treats his subject sympathetically and favorably, and is most attracted to his later years. Aware of the distorting lens offered by the *Education*, Samuels sometimes overlooks the fact that Adams's times as well as his life are subject to that volume's warping influence. In 1989 Harvard University Press published a one-volume revised version of the biography that suffers from compression and fails to shore up the shortcomings of the initial volume of the trilogy.

Two short studies present readers with a good overview of Adams's life and works. In his concise biography, CONTOSTA views his subject in the context of American political and social ideology, and suggests that Adams was in some ways a throwback to the era of classical republicanism. HOCHFIELD's deceptively slim volume is rich with insight about Adams's writings, assessing them in the context of his life. It provides an excellent introduction to the entire body of Adams's work, revealing that many of the themes in the *Education* had long been topics of concern.

LEVENSON's lengthier explication of Adams's writings is part intellectual biography, part literary criticism, part commentary. Fiction, history, the *Education*: each represented a different way through which Adams sought to make sense of himself and his world. The entire corpus of his works represents a continuous, evolving effort at exploring and defining self, a process of discovery and education. JORDY also offers links between Adams's work and life, suggesting that his quest for scientific laws of human development was in fact little more than another means of offering social criticism under the guise of making objective inquiry. Levenson remains perhaps too fond of his subject, sometimes skimming over less attractive

aspects of Adams's life, such as his antisemitism (rather virulent, even for its time); Jordy points out his flaws and contradictions. DECKER also offers an overview of Adams's writings, noting that he experimented with various forms of prose and poetry in an effort to find an audience willing to discuss the possibilities and failings of modern American politics and society. Like other scholars who find Adams an attractive subject, Decker wants to render him relevant for present-day readers: this search for a usable Adams as social critic serves as a surrogate for Decker's own interest in assessing the strengths and weaknesses of American society.

Adams's account of his adventures in politics in the *Education* has long provided historians with plenty of quotable material about Ulysses S. Grant and other prominent politicians. In his examination of Adams's career as a reform journalist who aspired to advise those in power, SIMPSON suggests that much of his supposed failure in American political life was directly attributable to himself. His acerbic writings were as likely to offend as to persuade; his erratic commitment to political activity eroded his effectiveness and influence. Unlike other scholars who see Adams's foray into politics as some sort of mistake or a half-hearted attempt to follow the family's heritage, Simpson argues that Adams sought political influence through means that reconciled personal inclinations and the Adams heritage of public service.

The theme of failure – real and imagined – pervades both Adams's writings and writings about Adams. DUSINBERRE argues that Adams intentionally sought to divert attention from his personal failures, most notably the suicide of his wife in 1885, as well as his abortive political career, by suggesting that he was most disappointed with his failure as a historian – although Dusinberre argues that Adams in fact was a great historian despite his inability to attract the same kind of wide audience that George Bancroft had achieved. Of course, Adams did fail in politics, and he was bitter about it; his account of that failure in the *Education* was an effort to cast aside any personal responsibility for it. That he sought to conceal the tragedy of his personal life (through omitting any mention of it in the *Education*) has long been a staple of Adams biography. Nevertheless, readers will find Dusinberre's treatment of Adams the historian worth pondering.

Perhaps the most stimulating essay about Adams to appear in recent years is DAWIDOFF's witty and insightful examination of Adams's ambivalence toward American democracy. After being rebuffed in his efforts to reshape the republic by advising its leaders, Adams struck the pose of critical observer, unable to conceal his growing alienation from his world. One wonders, however, how much Adams's later writings were spurred by his early disillusionments and failures.

In all these studies one finds that Adams has set the terms of the debate over his life – a sign of the ultimate triumph of the *Education*.

BROOKS D. SIMPSON

Adams, John 1735–1826

Leader of the Revolution and 2nd President of the United States

Brown, Ralph Adams, *The Presidency of John Adams*, Lawrence: University Press of Kansas, 1975

Chinard, Gilbert, *Honest John Adams*, Boston: Little Brown, 1933

Ellis, Joseph J., *Passionate Sage: The Character and Legacy of John Adams*, New York: Norton, 1993

Ferling, John E., *John Adams: A Life*, Knoxville: University of Tennessee Press, 1992

Haraszti, Zoltán, *John Adams and the Prophets of Progress*, Cambridge, MA: Harvard University Press, 1952

Howe, John R., Jr., *The Changing Political Thought of John Adams*, Princeton: Princeton University Press, 1966

Kurtz, Stephen, *The Presidency of John Adams: The Collapse of Federalism, 1795–1800*, Philadelphia: University of Pennsylvania Press, 1957

Shaw, Peter, *The Character of John Adams*, Chapel Hill: University of North Carolina Press, 1976

Smith, Page, *John Adams*, 2 vols., New York: Doubleday, 1962

None of the founding fathers played a larger role in establishing the American republic than John Adams. This "Atlas of the Revolution" participated directly in every important American political crisis – the Constitutional Convention of 1787 alone excepted – from 1764 until 1801. But following defeat in the presidential election of 1800, Adams passed quickly from the world stage to obscurity. His lamentation in retirement proved all too accurate: "Mausoleums, statues, monuments will never be erected to me." While the public lionized George Washington, Benjamin Franklin, Thomas Jefferson and other Revolutionary heroes, Adams languished half-forgotten in the shadows of American history, the most complex and least understood of the founders. Then rather suddenly in the 1950s Adams was rediscovered. Granted access finally to the rich Adams family papers at the Massachusetts Historical Society, scholars began to produce a number of excellent monographs and biographies which rescued the second president from undeserved oblivion.

In the first modern biography of Adams, CHINARD prepared the way for this outpouring of Adams scholarship. Drawing upon a rich French tradition of popular scholarship, Chinard offers a sensitive and sympathetic picture of Adams. He focuses less on Adams's public life than on his personality, character, and the ideas and principles that shaped his politics. What emerges is a richly textured portrait of a man whose vanity, stubbornness, and perversity were balanced by profound learning coupled with wisdom, great moral courage, and a willingness to sacrifice personal interest for the public good. Writing soon after World War I, Chinard portrays his subject as the Clemenceau of his time, the "most realistic statesman of his generation in America," an intensely honest and resolute patriot who deserves a prominent place in the Pantheon of great Americans.

SMITH is a meticulously detailed two-volume narrative study of Adams's life and times which champions the subject as a beacon and preceptor for a nation caught up at mid-20th century in the throes of the Cold War. The first biography to draw on the voluminous Adams family papers, it is a sympathetic but balanced treatment. It firmly places Adams center-stage, playing a noble role during the great age of revolution. Rich in detail, these carefully crafted and gracefully written volumes rely heavily on Adams's own words to tell his story.

The most recent of the modern Adams biographies, FERLING is a comprehensive life-and-times narrative which focuses largely on Adams's public career. It portrays Adams as a single-minded man who sacrificed family and personal interests in the relentless but elusive pursuit of recognition and fame. No other biographer to date traces so deftly or explains so cogently his public life. In these pages Adams emerges as a man of action whose moral rectitude and stubborn independence served his country well and entitle him to the public monument he never received. The author's careful use of the documentary record and his mastery of a large body of secondary literature on the American Revolution published since 1960 make this an excellent single-volume biography suitable for scholars and general readers alike. Its shortcoming is that it does not explain and interpret the private man nearly as well as it does the public Adams.

SHAW is a penetrating personality study, a psycho-intellectual biography which analyzes Adams's writings in order to understand his mind, personality, and motives. Shaw argues that Adams was driven by a need to be recognized as a great man. He sacrificed financial security, family life, and even his personal health in pursuit of this end, only to be disappointed when the measure of fame and recognition which he achieved were not commensurate with the sacrifices which he made. His disappointment seemed only to magnify his vanity and, in the public mind, diminish the importance of his achievements. An earlier pioneering work that attempts to fathom Adams's mind is HARASZTI. This unusual study assumes the form of a series of dialogues between Adams and certain books in his library. An avid book collector, Adams was a vigorously creative reader who filled the margins and fly-leaves of his volumes on philosophy, history, and theology with lively and pungent comments. By analyzing these marginalia, Haraszti succeeds in shedding light on the mind and thought of Adams, whom he considers to be one of America's greatest political thinkers.

Adams's ideology is expertly examined in HOWE, a concise and well-written study which relates the subject's political ideas to his personal and political experience and to his moral and social assumptions. This experiential approach of analyzing Adams's political ideas as they evolved over time and placing them in the context of his experience and his understanding of American society provides an excellent vehicle for understanding Adams's deeply tormented mind. The author maintains that Adams invariably equated his own personal interest with the well-being of American society.

The two best general treatments of Adams's presidency are Kurtz and Brown. Despite its age, KURTZ remains a reliable and readable study which portrays the second president as a man of integrity and principle, who sacrificed his political career to avoid war with France. BROWN draws heavily on existing scholarship to give the general reader what is primarily, but not exclusively, a work of synthesis. It is sympathetic to Adams, who is portrayed as a strong executive who worked sacrificially to serve the public good. The volume treats

Adams's foreign policy more fully than other aspects of his presidency.

ELLIS focuses on Adams's life and work after his retirement in 1801. In a perceptive and well-written study, he argues convincingly that, despite the long-held view that the staid New Englander's abstract political theories were irrelevant to democratic America, his political ideas are indeed relevant to the contemporary United States. This is an excellent, readable analysis of the Adams legacy suitable for the general reader as well as the specialist.

CHARLES D. LOWERY

Adams, John Quincy 1767–1848

Secretary of State and 6th President of the
United States

Bemis, Samuel Flagg, *John Quincy Adams and the
    Foundations of American Foreign Policy*, New York:
    Knopf, 1949
Bemis, Samuel Flagg, *John Quincy Adams and the Union*,
    New York: Knopf, 1956
Hargreaves, Mary W.M., *The Presidency of John Quincy
    Adams*, Lawrence: University Press of Kansas, 1985
Howe, Daniel Walker, *The Political Culture of the American
    Whigs*, Chicago: University of Chicago Press, 1979
Ketcham, Ralph, *Presidents above Party: The First American
    Presidency, 1789–1829*, Chapel Hill: University of North
    Carolina Press, 1984
May, Ernest R., *The Making of the Monroe Doctrine*,
    Cambridge, MA: Belknap Press of Harvard University
    Press, 1975
Parsons, Lynn H., *John Quincy Adams: A Bibliography*,
    Westport, CT: Greenwood Press, 1993
Perkins, Bradford, *Castlereagh and Adams: England and the
    United States, 1812–1823*, Berkeley: University of
    California Press, 1964
Richards, Leonard L., *The Life and Times of Congressman
    John Quincy Adams*, New York: Oxford University Press,
    1986
Russell, Greg, *John Quincy Adams and the Public Virtues of
    Diplomacy*, Columbia: University of Missouri Press, 1995
Saxton, Alexander, *The Rise and Fall of the White Republic:
    Class Politics and Mass Culture in Nineteenth Century
    America*, London and New York: Verso, 1990
Weeks, William Earl, *John Quincy Adams and the American
    Global Empire*, Lexington: University Press of Kentucky,
    1992

John Quincy Adams is both an attractive and a daunting subject for a biographer. The manuscript diary that he left represents the greatest account of an American political life written by the participant himself, and yet it conceals or omits as much as it tells. Adams comes to us filtered through his son, Charles Francis Adams, whose mammoth edition of the *Memoirs* (12 vols., 1874–77) has been the version generally used, and yet it omits about one-third of the original diary. Thankfully, the Adams Papers project has made the original manuscript available on microfilm and is now slowly producing a complete edition of the diary (1981 onwards).

For a century after Adams's death there was no adequate, full-length biography. Then, after World War II, interest burgeoned, as foreign policy became central once more to national life. The fruits of that interest, down to 1990, are recorded in PARSONS's comprehensive, critical listing of works relevant to the career of the second Adams.

The great modern biography, to which all students must turn, is by BEMIS, the first professional historian to have access to Adams's manuscripts. The two volumes are divided by both theme and period, representing Adams's two careers, which meet and overlap during his presidency, 1825–29. The first volume, which won the Pulitzer prize, contains an appreciation, by the dean of American diplomatic historians, of Adams's contribution to American foreign policy; the second represents an equally shrewd investigation of Adams's remarkable, and less coherent, second career as a domestic politician. The chapters of each volume have a topical focus that includes informative brief introductions to the problem in hand.

According to Bemis's diplomatic volume, Adams's great achievement was not only to establish the United States as a transcontinental power, but to define the basic principles of American foreign policy: freedom of the seas, non-involvement in European affairs, no further European colonization in the Western hemisphere, and a manifest destiny to acquire adjacent territory in North America. In particular, as secretary of state (1817–25), he exploited the newly favorable, if still occasionally menacing, international circumstances that followed the War of 1812, and was directly responsible for the Monroe Doctrine. These judgments were echoed in the third volume of PERKINS's monumental trilogy on Anglo-American relations between 1795 and 1823, which demonstrated Adams's skill in restoring cooperative relations after the War of 1812 and withstanding the menaces that led ultimately to Monroe's famous message in December 1823.

Bemis's nationalistic celebration of Adams's achievements proved unpalatable to revisionists of the 1960s, but they produced no major work specifically on Adams. However, MAY argued that the Monroe Doctrine was more a product of Adams's political needs in the 1824 presidential election campaign than a necessary response to the diplomatic crisis of 1823. Adams apparently needed to demonstrate that he was no friend of Britain in order to protect himself against the charge of former Federalism, though May does not explain why other candidates who had no such political need agreed with his policy in cabinet.

WEEKS has recently reconsidered what he sees as Adams's greatest achievement – the Adams-Onís (or Transcontinental) Treaty of 1819. Drawing on Adams's upbringing and the "republican synthesis" to understand Adams's mentality, Weeks demonstrates his commitment to the notion of the United States as a redeemer nation spreading the benefits of republicanism around the world. Driven by a moralistic understanding of the country's and his own duty, Adams compromised classical republican virtue by cheating, lying, and endorsing violence in order to accomplish his ends. Ignoring Weeks, RUSSELL is more interested in the philosophical bases of Adamsonian foreign policy than in the realities. Drawing on ancient and Christian roots for his view of human nature and public ethics, Adams wrestled with the duty of expressing America's national purpose and commitment to liberty in her foreign policy.

A similar interest in ideas has led some modern students of Adams's second, domestic career to regard him as a principled exponent of the traditional "republican" ideology. In particular, KETCHAM's brief chapter on Adams argued that the sixth president endeavoured to embody all the traditional virtues of the ideal "Patriot King" – and so neglected to further his own re-election. This picture is confirmed to some extent by HARGREAVES, whose thorough but dull study of Adams's presidency is highly informative, especially on secretary of state Henry Clay's diplomacy, but at times becomes overwhelmed by operational detail. Focusing on the solid achievement of the government and its commitment to internal improvement, she emphasizes Adams's concern with "policy-oriented leadership" rather than with expanding and reinforcing his electoral support.

Yet many historians have recognized in Adams a tension between duty and ambition, between philosophical purpose and political necessity. Bemis's second volume recognised how Adams reconciled his conscience with playing politics and doing deals, seeing, for example, the political advantage that underlay his apparently high-minded flirtation with Antimasonry.

HOWE's chapter on Adams offers the most insightful analysis, recognizing the intensity of the personality, the impact of classical humanism and liberal religion, and the changing political pressures. Insisting that Adams was a self-conscious politician, perfectly capable of doing deals, Howe too stresses the role of antipartyism in his career and the way in which it influenced both his presidency and his relationship to the new major parties of the 1830s. However, by 1840, as Adams became more committed to an antislavery standpoint, he also emerged as a more self-consciously partisan Whig. RICHARDS's lively, readable study of Adams's career after 1829 challenges the view of Adams as an independent, non-partisan statesman, and insists that this image was the creation of his descendants. In practice Adams behaved in a deeply partisan fashion, always bitterly committed against the Jacksonians and constantly voting with the opposition parties. In taking up the cudgels against slavery and its expansion after 1835, he was supported by most northern Whigs in defining a northern sectionalist point of view.

In contrast to more orthodox treatments, but in keeping with contemporary correctness, SAXTON has used Adams as an exemplar of northern upper-class racial attitudes. This highly selective and over-interpretative study of National Republican-Whig ideology is provocatively revealing of Adams's views on Indians and blacks, which Saxton relates to the needs of nation-building, westward expansion, social improvement, and the maintenance of a beneficial class hierarchy.

DONALD J. RATCLIFFE

See also Monroe Doctrine

Adams Family

Burleigh, Anne Husted, "The Family Adams," *Modern Age*, 25(2), 1981

Musto, David F., "Continuity Across Generations: The Adams Family Myth," in *New Directions in Psychohistory: The Adelphi Papers in Honor of Erik H. Erikson*, edited by Mel Albin, Lexington, MA: Lexington Books, 1980

Musto, David F., "The Adams Family," *Massachusetts Historical Society Proceedings*, 93, 1981

Nagel, Paul C., *Descent from Glory: Four Generations of the John Adams Family*, New York: Oxford University Press, 1983

Nagel, Paul C., *The Adams Women: Abigail and Louisa Adams, Their Sisters and Daughters*, New York: Oxford University Press, 1987

Russell, Francis, *Adams: An American Dynasty*, New York: American Heritage, 1976

Shaw, Peter, "All in the Family: A Psychobiography of the Adamses," *American Scholar*, 54(4), 1985

Shepherd, Jack, *The Adams Chronicles: Four Generations of Greatness*, Boston: Little Brown, 1975

The Adams family's long tenure in domestic politics, diplomacy, historical writing, and the public imagination affords it a place of high distinction in American historiography. Together the family constitutes the closest thing to an intellectual and political dynasty that America offers. As the family's key figures are discussed in their own entries, this review centers on general works about the family.

Two works offer useful descriptions of the family's public life. Both were early attempts to exploit the mass of material in the Adams Family Papers that were made available on microfilm in 1951 by the Massachusetts Historical Society. As a result, both tend to be more anecdotal than analytic. RUSSELL begins with John Adams, who served in the Continental Congress, and overseas as an American diplomat, became the first vice-president, and finally the second President of the United States (1797–1801). John Quincy Adams succeeded to his father's place as a remarkable diplomat, and served as a United States senator and secretary of state before his election to the Presidency (1825–29), and distinguished service in the House of Representatives (1831–48). His son, Charles Francis Adams (1807–86), served as a congressman and later held the important post of minister to Great Britain during the crucial years of the American Civil War. His sons, Charles Francis, Jr. (1835–15), Henry (1838–1918), and Brooks (1848–1927) turned their attention from politics to the intellectual world. Charles Francis, Jr., grew wealthy as President of the Union Pacific Railroad, while his historical writings confirmed his standing as a gentleman scholar. Henry and Brooks distinguished themselves as historians and social critics. The 20th-century Adamses in Russell's book were marked less by interest in public office than by public service as business executives and archivists. SHEPHERD ends with the fourth generation of Adamses, following the course of their history through the death of Brooks in 1928. Written in the celebratory era of the American bicentennial, the work suffers from an overly exuberant tone. Nonetheless, its use of the private family papers to write their public history had been unmatched in previous works and provided the basis for a Public Broadcasting System series on the family. Shepherd's collection of family portraits and supporting paintings and photographs furnishes the reader with a nuanced understanding of the family's place in American history. Both works attempt to forge a new appreciation of this family, whose history had been neglected since the era of early-20th-century progressivism.

NAGEL (1983) offers the first critical study of the Adams family's private life. A tradition of extreme drive and active political involvement threads its way through the lives of most of the major figures. Unlike previous works, this book reveals the darker side of the family's pre-eminence – particularly the marital problems, alcoholism, and suicide – that characterized each generation. Many family members suffered from depression and too large a dose of self-scrutiny. A few were able to overcome their bouts to work obsessively for the public good. Others failed to conquer the inner tensions and turned to alcohol. In all, Nagel assumes knowledge of the world outside the family and sticks closely to family documents, letters and diaries, to write an inside history.

BURLEIGH describes common traits that characterized each of the most prominent Adamses. She concludes that each was conscious of his role in national history, especially as defined by his role in the family's history. Each dedicated himself to virtue and duty in this familial-national sense. Cognizant of the clan's role in creating the nation, each Adams feared the effects of democracy, which they felt encouraged wealth without responsibility and the political rule of the uneducated.

MUSTO (1980) underscores the sense of an intergenerational stream of identity. Emphasizing the shared quest for family identity and continuity, he argues that a "family myth" developed during the political stress of the American Revolution. Later generations sought to reconstruct the myth for their own times, as American society seemed to conform less and less to their ideals. MUSTO (1981) further examined the mental outlook, or "family mind," which remained remarkably consistent over four generations. For those who could meet the challenge of the myth, life proved full and fruitful. For others, namely for John's son Charles and for John Quincy's son George Washington Adams, the myth proved too burdensome – Charles died an early death due to alcoholism and George Washington committed suicide at 28.

SHAW agrees that both those who succeeded and those who failed measured themselves against their ancestors, particularly their fathers. He argues for polar-opposite Adams types, both governed by the same family imperatives. The "self-deniers" hardly deviated from family duty, while the "self-indulgers" fell short of expectations. Employing recent psychological theory, Shaw claims that the mechanism beneath the common patterns of Adams behavior was a shared "construction of reality" that was formed early in the family's history. While most families rediscover an ethos during times of crisis, the Adamses seemed to live in perpetual crisis, which caused explicit rules that govern thought and behavior to become the family model. It was not, then, superior abilities that led to success, but faithfulness to the lineal paradigm – measuring oneself by ancestors and remaining true to family history. The immense Adams Papers indicate this common responsibility to test one's actions against the record of those who had gone before, and to pass on to the next generation a record to use as their litmus test. Successful Adamses achieved success through sheer persistence, despite dreamy impracticality and an inwardly romantic nature. The latter evinced itself in the marriages of even the successful family members, whose wives were often overly emotional and depressive.

NAGEL (1987) offers a contradictory view of "the Adams women," namely John's wife Abigail and John Quincy's wife Louisa Catherine, with daughters and sisters as supporting characters. Less about the Adams women than those who married Adams men, the work traces the difficult private lives of those who put up with the men's idiosyncratic genius and drive. Alternating theses result: these women add to the mystique of a fascinating family, but they seem surprisingly indistinct from many other women of their day. Though Abigail Adams impressed statesmen by her letters, her relationships and her complaints to her sisters reveal that she had much in common with other 18th-century women. Louisa Catherine Adams was pessimistic about American democracy, and she also wrote passionately about women's sacrifices to achieve even minimal happiness in marriage. Overall, the book lacks deep analysis and allows the women's letters and diaries to dictate the narrative, but it offers the fullest inside history of the Adams women through the first two generations.

PHILIP K. GOFF

Addams, Jane 1860–1935
Pioneer of settlement house movement

Davis, Allen F., *American Heroine: The Life and Legend of Jane Addams*, New York: Oxford University Press, 1973
Deegan, Mary Jo, *Jane Addams and the Men of the Chicago School, 1892–1918*, New Brunswick, NJ: Transaction, 1988
Farrell, John C., *Beloved Lady: A History of Jane Addams' Ideas on Reform and Peace*, Baltimore: Johns Hopkins Press, 1967
Lasch, Christopher, *The New Radicalism in America, 1889–1963: The Intellectual as a Social Type*, New York: Knopf, 1965; London: Chatto and Windus, 1966
Levine, Daniel, *Jane Addams and the Liberal Tradition*, Madison: State Historical Society of Wisconsin, 1971
Linn, James Weber, *Jane Addams: A Biography*, New York: Appleton Century, 1935
Tims, Margaret, *Jane Addams of Hull House, 1860–1935: A Centenary Study*, New York: Macmillan, and London: Allen and Unwin, 1961

Jane Addams has received considerable attention from both historians and popular writers, but a good deal of it has been so adulatory that it verges on hagiography. Indeed, Addams's own autobiography, *Twenty Years at Hull-House* (1910), offers a more critical analysis of her life than do some of the early biographies.

LINN is more a celebration of Addams's life than a critical analysis of it. Written by Addams's nephew, it offers some useful insights into the early influences upon her and the way in which she was regarded by her family. It also provides some personal details which were not available to earlier biographers. Linn emphasizes Addams's strong commitment to democracy and her belief that social reform should be motivated by the desire for higher moral standards in industrial and social life. Since Linn's biography provides a referral point for all later biographies, its influence has been significant, but it has many of the problems often associated with biographies written by adoring relatives. TIMS is also very much a celebration of Jane Addams's life, written for the centennial of her birth. Addams is portrayed as a secular saint and a standard bearer for a generation which had lost its moral worthiness. Addams's creation, Hull House, is seen as a response to human need. Whether practical, moral or aesthetic – Hull House took care of all these needs. Tims provides little analysis either of Addams's motives or her achievements. The work suffers from being based only on Addams's published writings and Linn's biography, and the text contains a number of factual errors. Although it provides a useful introduction to Addams's life for the general reader, it has few pretensions to scholarship.

In contrast, FARRELL is more thoroughly researched. It concentrates upon Addams's ideas and convictions, offering new insights into the intellectual grounds for the foundation of Hull House. Farrell suggests that Addams's ideas on social reform and peace owed more to her experiences of living in Hull House than to any underlying theory. Her ideas were constantly developing throughout her life. She also continued to work for reforms which, she believed, would promote economic and social justice even during the 1920s when her main emphasis was on her work for peace. Not intended as a fully-fledged life, this is a competent intellectual biography which seeks to explain the origins and relevance of Addams's ideas. It performs this task well.

LEVINE sees Jane Addams within the Progressive intellectual framework, as a social thinker who exercised an important influence in America's transition from laissez-faire to the welfare state. The result is a very uneven biography, marred by ill-informed remarks, especially about her early life. Ultimately it offers few new insights into Addams's ideas or motives, nor does it fully explain the context within which she was working. While most of what Levine has written is competent enough, he never satisfactorily proves his main contention – that Addams was a radical and critical part of the liberal tradition in America. In the essay on Addams in his book on the New Radicalism, LASCH offers some interesting insights into her motives for establishing Hull House. He sees Addams's struggles to find a role for herself after college as part of a wider cultural crisis. Her long struggles over religion, revealed through her correspondence with Ellen Gates Starr, suggest that the settlements were ultimately a secular outlet for what in an earlier age would have been religious energies. By seeing intellectuals as a social type, Lasch places Addams in a class of people who were products of cultural fragmentation. In conjunction with his essay on "Woman as Alien," Lasch's essay on Addams is considerably more perceptive than some of the longer biographies.

Addams was portrayed by many of her early biographers as a secular saint, acting from admirable humanitarian impulses. DAVIS argues that Addams herself took considerable trouble to create this myth. Indeed, she was a skilled myth-maker and, according to Davis, even something of a hypocrite. He suggests that much of Addams's life can be explained by her need for approbation, and her wish to present herself as a symbol of Americanism. Davis is at his most persuasive in writing about the events of Addams's life. Indeed, to date his is probably the most accurate account of her life. However, he places too much emphasis on what he sees as her need to create an identity for herself as a symbol, and does her less than justice as a complex human being. The facts of Addams's life, especially during World War I and the first half of the 1920s, simply do not bear out Davis's thesis. Ultimately, though this is a book of considerable scholarship, it misunderstands Addams.

DEEGAN's purpose is quite different from that of Addams's earlier biographers. She seeks to rehabilitate Addams as one of the pioneers in American sociology, and one of the early influences on, and founders of, the Chicago School of Sociology. Deegan charts Addams's involvement with and influence on some of the male academics of the Chicago School. She makes a persuasive case. However, in attributing Addams's omission from the academic tradition of sociology purely to the sexism and conservatism of the academy, Deegan is not so persuasive. She argues from the perspective of the late 20th century, rather than placing Addams in the context of her time and explaining the constraints upon women's involvement in academia in the early 20th century. While Deegan's aim is admirable, and her argument is intriguing, the book is poorly written and doctrinaire in its approach.

ELIZABETH J. CLAPP

See also Settlement House Movement; Social Work/Social Reform

Advertising

Applegate, Edd (editor), *The Ad Men and Women: A Biographical Dictionary of Advertising*, Westport, CT: Greenwood Press, 1994

Fox, Stephen R., *The Mirror Makers: A History of American Advertising and Its Creators*, New York: Morrow, 1984; revised as *The Mirror Makers: A History of American Advertising*, London: Heinemann, 1990

Gunther, John, *Taken at the Flood: The Story of Albert D. Lasker*, New York: Harper, and London: Hamish Hamilton, 1960

Hower, Ralph M., *The History of an Advertising Agency: N.W. Ayer & Son at Work, 1869–1939*, Cambridge, MA: Harvard University Press, 1939, revised as *The History of an Advertising Agency: N.W. Ayer & Son at Work, 1869–1949*, 1949

Lears, T. Jackson, *Fables of Abundance: A Cultural History of Advertising in America*, New York: Basic Books, 1994

Marchand, Roland, *Advertising the American Dream: Making Way for Modernity, 1920–1940*, Berkeley: University of California Press, 1985

Mayer, Martin, *Madison Avenue U.S.A.: The Inside Story of American Advertising*, New York: Harper, and London: Bodley Head, 1958

Norris, James D., *Advertising and the Transformation of American Society, 1865–1920*, Westport, CT: Greenwood Press, 1990

Pease, Otis, *The Responsibilities of American Advertising: Private Control and Public Influence, 1920–1940*, New Haven: Yale University Press, 1958

Pope, Daniel, *The Making of Modern Advertising*, New York: Basic Books, 1983

Schudson, Michael, *Advertising, The Uneasy Persuasion: Its Dubious Impact on American Society*, New York: Basic Books, 1984; London: Routledge, 1993

Strasser, Susan, *Satisfaction Guaranteed: The Making of the American Mass Market*, New York: Pantheon, 1989

Tedlow, Richard S., *New and Improved: The Story of Mass Marketing in America*, New York: Basic Books, and Oxford: Heinemann, 1990

APPLEGATE's biographical dictionary brings together a selection of past and present copywriters and other major contributors to the American advertising industry. Of the 54 biographies in the dictionary, eight are of women. Through this collection of biographies of creative personalities, Applegate believes that he can help to provide a greater understanding of how and why creativity occurs. The dictionary includes biographies of some of the founders of the major American advertising agencies, which are especially useful for purposes of comparing the origins of these businesses. The best of the biographies in this book have sizable bibliographies, as aids to further reading and research.

Most of the histories of the American advertising industry tend to focus on discrete periods. FOX is the only recent comprehensive history of the industry. It traces its history from the mid-19th century to the beginning of the 1980s. The British edition has a new introduction which looks at developments in the 1980s. Although Fox draws on the work of previous advertising histories, his book contains important new material, for example on aspects of the history of the J. Walter Thompson and Young & Rubicam advertising agencies. Fox also provides some useful illustrations but not as many as some of the other advertising histories.

The development of American advertising between 1865 and 1920 is traced in NORRIS's illustrated volume, which relates advertising to the broader economic development of the United States during this period. He traces the history of probably the most important advertising medium of the period – popular magazines and journals – and analyzes the emergence of trademarks and brand names, using the examples of clothing, food and beverages. He also has several case studies looking at the advertising of soap, cigarettes, motor cars and consumer household appliances.

POPE emphasizes changes occurring in American advertising before the 1920s – in particular, he concentrates on the Gilded Age and the Progressive Era. He places advertising in a wider context, by relating it to the development of branded goods, and changes in the structure of retailing, and by examining its relationship with industry. He also has an interesting section on the early 20th century "truth in advertising" movement.

The principal weakness of this book is that it has no illustrations. STRASSER covers a similar period, roughly speaking from the beginning of the 1890s to the end of the 1920s. Her book contains numerous useful illustrations. Strasser's definition of advertising is much broader than that of Pope. In addition to display advertising for consumer goods, she traces the development of advertising through expositions, trade cards, free gifts for retailers and consumers, trading stamps and competitions for grocers. Advertising is placed in the wider context of the evolution of distribution and marketing. Strasser also deals with the wider social dimensions of advertising, for example, looking at the politics of packaged goods and the background to the Pure Food and Drug Act of 1906.

MARCHAND provides a masterly survey of the development of advertising during the inter-war years. His book is especially useful because it contains examples from the period of advertisements in colour, in addition to examples of monochrome advertisements. Marchand looks at both the internal history of the inter-war advertising industry and at its broader economic and social context. There is a comprehensive bibliographical essay. PEASE also looks at the inter-war years, although he begins with a useful survey of the growth of American advertising. Marchand considers Pease's book to be a pioneering study of the history of the industry in its wider cultural and political contexts. Pease considers the limits of self-regulation of American advertising, the industry's interaction with the consumer movement, the growth in government regulation of advertising and the reaction of the industry's trade associations to the consumer movement and to government regulation. He also examines the development of advertising copy in this period.

MAYER provides a contemporary survey of the state of advertising in the late 1950s. Although this is not an academic study, it provides an important insight into the history of early post-World War II American advertising – in particular the development of television advertising and, for example, the role played by the A.C. Nielsen Company. There are also several interesting case studies, for example, the advertising campaign for the unsuccessful Ford Edsel.

In spite of the important role which advertising agencies have played in the development of American industry and popular culture, business historians have paid very little attention to them. The exception is HOWER's comprehensive history of N.W. Ayer & Son, originally commissioned as a memorial to the founder of the agency. The first part traces the history of the agency from its foundation to 1939; the second part analyzes different aspects of the agency's business from a historical perspective. As with the advertising agencies themselves, surprisingly little work has been done on biographies of leading figures in the industry. Hence the importance of GUNTHER's biography of Albert D. Lasker. A journalistic rather than an academic work, it covers every aspect of Lasker's career, not just his involvement in advertising. A Jewish-American, Lasker worked at the Chicago advertising agency of Lord & Thomas from 1898 to 1942. He was responsible for the popularization of numerous American products and trademarks. The first person to see the potential of radio as an advertising medium, he was the originator of the "soap opera".

SCHUDSON seeks to place advertising within the context of American consumer culture. He draws on the history of advertising in the first half of his exposition. In the second half, there is a chapter on the historical roots of consumer culture followed by a case study of the contribution made by advertising to the success of the cigarette. Schudson also considers whether advertising is capitalist realism.

TEDLOW differs from the other studies because it traces the development of mass marketing in the United States down to the present time. This is a particularly important study and, unlike most of the advertising histories, not only has a bibliography, but a very useful and comprehensive one. Within a carefully constructed theoretical framework, Tedlow examines four case studies: Coca-Cola and Pepsi Cola; Ford and General Motors; the Great Atlantic and Pacific Tea Company (A&P); and Sears, Montgomery Ward and their more recent rivals.

A recent study by LEARS offers both a challenging reinterpretation of many issues and a wide-ranging analysis of the role of advertising in the history of American culture. Moving elegantly from the role of 19th-century peddlers to modern advertising agencies working for corporate clients, he sees advertising as being at the very heart of the contest within American culture between "control and release, stability and sorcery." This provocative study opens up fresh perspectives – and no doubt fresh debates – on the history of advertising in the United States.

RICHARD A. HAWKINS

See also Marketing and Distribution

African American History: General

Berry, Mary Frances and John W. Blassingame, *Long Memory: The Black Experience in America*, New York and Oxford: Oxford University Press, 1982

Foner, Philip S., *History of Black Americans*, 3 vols., Westport, CT: Greenwood Press, 1975–83

Franklin, John Hope, *The Color Line: Legacy for the Twenty-First Century*, Columbia: University of Missouri Press, 1993

Franklin, John Hope and Alfred A. Moss, Jr., *From Slavery to Freedom: A History of African Americans*, 7th edition, New York: McGraw Hill, 1994 (originally published, by Franklin only, as *From Slavery to Freedom: A History of American Negroes*, New York: Knopf, 1947)

Franklin, V.P., *Black Self-Determination: A Cultural History of the Faith of the Fathers*, Westport, CT: Lawrence Hill, 1984, 2nd edition, 1992

Harding, Vincent, *There Is a River: The Black Struggle for Freedom in America*, New York: Harcourt Brace, 1981

Hine, Darlene Clark (editor), *The State of Afro-American History: Past, Present, and Future*, Baton Rouge: Louisiana State University Press 1986

Jones, Jacqueline, *Labor of Love, Labor of Sorrow: Black Women, Work, and the Family from Slavery to the Present*, New York: Basic Books, 1985

Levine, Lawrence W., *Black Culture and Black Consciousness: Afro-American Folk Thought from Slavery to Freedom*, New York: Oxford University Press 1977

Meier, August and Elliott M. Rudwick, *From Plantation to Ghetto: An Interpretive History of American Negroes*, New York: Hill and Wang, 1966, 3rd edition, 1976; London: Constable, 1970

Meier, August and Elliott M. Rudwick, *Black History and the Historical Profession, 1915–1980*, Urbana: University of Illinois Press, 1986

Myrdal, Gunnar, *An American Dilemma: The Negro Problem and Modern Democracy*, 2 vols., New York: Harper, 1944; condensed by Arnold Rose as *The Negro in America*, 1948

Nalty, Bernard C., *Strength for the Fight: A History of Black Americans in the Military*, New York: Free Press, and London: Collier Macmillan, 1986

Thorpe, Earl E., *Negro Historians in the United States*, New York: Morrow, 1958, revised as *Black Historians: A Critique*, 1971

White, John, *Black Leadership in America, 1895–1968*, London and New York: Longman, 1985, 2nd edition, as *Black Leadership in America: From Booker T. Washington to Jesse Jackson*, 1990

Once the Cinderella of American historical scholarship, African American (previously and variously termed black, Negro or Afro-American) historiography has, since the civil rights movement of the 1960s, moved to centre stage, with an impressive array of specialized monographs (by black and white authors) on practically every aspect of the African American experience. Fewer in number, more general studies and published symposia have also reflected the concern of scholars and educators to redress the neglect (benign or otherwise) of overviews and interpretations of black history since the pioneering work of George Washington Williams who published *A History of the Negro Race in America* in 1883, and Carter G. Woodson, founding father of the Association for the Study of Negro Life and History (1915) and the *Journal of Negro History* (1916). The seminal work on the African American experience down to the New Deal remains MYRDAL's monumental study. With support from the Carnegie Foundation, the Swedish economist and his American collaborators synthesized existing historical and social science scholarship to produce an account and interpretation of the disjunction between "the American creed" and American practices as they affected white-black relations. Essentially optimistic in its predictions – it appeared during the social ferment and promises of the New Deal and American involvement in World War II – Myrdal's work inspired a generation of liberals to work for the resolution of what was called, in the terminology of the day, "the Negro problem." Subsequent events have only partially justified Myrdal's belief that America would resolve its racial "dilemma", but his book remains a major contribution to an understanding of its historical origins.

John Hope Franklin, the most distinguished of contemporary black historians (and the biographer of George Washington

Williams) produced the first edition of a now-classic and best-selling text in 1947. He observed in his Preface: "The history of the Negro people in America is essentially the story of the strivings of nameless millions who have sought adjustment in a new and sometimes hostile world," and offered a history with "a proper consideration for anonymous as well as outstanding people." Written with confidence, clarity and remarkable objectivity, FRANKLIN and MOSS, now in its co-authored 7th edition, and adopting the currently fashionable designation "African Americans" in its subtitle, is the most comprehensive, engaging and informed one-volume text available. With notable sections on African American women and popular culture, it also includes splendid colour photographs of African artefacts and 20th-century African American art, and is both a synthesis of, and a discrete contribution to, African American historiography.

BERRY and BLASSINGAME offer a thematic treatment of the "enduring institutions" (notably the family and the church) of black Americans, as well as sex and racism, wars, politics, and the forms of black nationalism, in an interpretive survey which begins and ends in Africa. Their emphasis throughout (in sometimes purple prose) is on African American adaptability, resilience, and strategies for survival and advancement, as revealed in such under-utilized sources as "poetry, song, folklore, novels, cartoons, plays, speeches, autobiographies and magazines."

Although it concludes in 1865, the trilogy by FONER is significant as an invigorating Marxist analysis of the African American experience to the mid-19th-century. Uneven in quality and with too many broadsides at academic adversaries, Foner's ambitious work, encyclopedic in scope and inclusiveness, and unfinished (at least two further volumes were planned) at the time of his death, is a monument to his engaged scholarship.

A colleague of Martin Luther King, Jr., HARDING – who is also cited in Berry and Blassingame as an advocate of retaliatory violence against whites in the 1960s – offers, in the first of two projected books, an evocative and often fervent "narrative, analytical, and celebratory history of the freedom struggle of black people" from their African homeland to their American emancipation in the Civil War. He applauds slave rebellion, the determination of northern blacks to prevent enforcement of the fugitive slave laws, and 19th-century forms of black separatism. His reflections on the integrationist objectives of the civil rights struggles of the 20th century are awaited with interest. V.P. FRANKLIN, another "black nationalist" historian, initially intended to provide "a more satisfactory explanation for the response of the Afro-American masses to the appeals of Marcus Garvey in the post-World War I era." It broadened into an attempt – through the examination of folklore and religion, slave resistance, the Great Migration and the rise of all-black institutions (churches, schools, businesses and independent black townships) – to prove that a sustained struggle for self-determination has been the hallmark of the African American historical experience. He maintains – unconvincingly – that such major African American leaders as Frederick Douglass, Booker T. Washington, and W.E.B. Du Bois failed to comprehend the values of "average black citizens" who have consistently desired to stand apart from the white majority. Washington,

and Du Bois – together with Marcus Garvey, Martin Luther King, Jr., Malcolm X, and Jesse Jackson – receive more considered (and sympathetic) treatment from WHITE, in a general survey of African American strategies for racial advancement in the 20th century.

"The ways in which historians came to do their scholarly work in the history of American blacks," and the reasons why that history, "originally a Jim Crow specialty ignored by nearly the entire profession, became legitimated into one of the most active fields of study in American history," prompted and informs an unusual study by MEIER and RUDWICK (1986). With incisive portraits of major African American and white historians, they trace succeeding generational perspectives on slavery and race, the indifference or hostility of the profession to black historians who routinely encountered discrimination in southern libraries and archives, and the post-1945 emergence of a cohort of southern white liberal historians, who had already begun to reassess the black historical record in the light of their own disenchantment with southern white bigotry. Themselves – singly and jointly – prolific interpreters of African American history, Meier and Rudwick observe that "as black history achieved legitimacy in the white academic world, the job opportunity structure in the field functioned to inhibit research into African-American history by white scholars."

That African American historians have themselves made signal contributions to the field is the persuasive contention of THORPE. In a critical survey of the literary merits, methodology, objectivity and impact of their work, he discusses the contributions of four generations of black historians from "The Justifiers of Emancipation" in the 19th century to "The New School: Modern Scholars, 1930–1960." Among those considered are George Washington Williams, Carter G. Woodson, W.E.B. Du Bois, Benjamin Quarles, and John Hope Franklin. Individually and collectively, Thorpe concludes, they have "uncovered and ordered the facts of the Negro's past, and published them to the eternal edification and enlightenment of all mankind."

From the "white" perspectives of, respectively, a historian and a sociologist. MEIER and RUDWICK (1966, 1976) offered a good introduction (subsequently revised and updated) to the formative stages in the evolution of black life in America, with a focus "less on what whites were doing to Negroes than what Negroes themselves were doing." The antebellum plantation, and its post-Civil War successor, the urban ghetto, are posited as the twin poles of the African American experience.

Reflecting changing attitudes in the profession, the American Historical Association, in 1983, sponsored a conference at Purdue University on the study, teaching and dissemination of African American history. HINE edited the published proceedings – which focus primarily on the issues of slavery, emancipation and urbanization. John Hope Franklin provides a masterly synthesis and explication of African American historiography; Kenneth L. Kusmer presents a valuable piece on those internal and external forces which produced considerable variety in the black urban condition, North and South; while Hine herself echoes and amplifies the conviction of all contributors that the roles of black women have, until recently, been slighted by historians. Her suggestion that the involvement of African-American women in Marcus

Garvey's Universal Negro Improvement Association, A. Philip Randolph's March on Washington Movement, and in the civil rights coalition of the 1950s and 1960s needs further investigation is a point to be taken. Many of the contributors to this useful but uneven symposium on African-American history "past, present, and future" receive "intellectual biographies" in Meier and Rudwick (1986).

Soon after the Purdue conference, JONES published her provocative assessment of the experiences of black women in 19th-century and 20th-century America. With a sharp focus on the primacy of race, and drawing on an impressive array of sources, she contends that, whether slave or free, black women "in their powerlessness and vulnerability" have experienced life "in fundamentally different ways compared to whites, regardless of class." Devoted to their traditional roles as wives and mothers, slave women worked in the cotton fields as well as in the cabins. After emancipation, as domestic workers or in other menial and poorly-paid jobs, they were doubly disadvantaged in a labour market segmented by gender and race. If labour unified the lives of black women, their struggle to maintain their families was "a labour of love" and often one of "sorrow" in an African American world as determinedly patriarchal as its white counterpart. Despite some over-generalization and a reluctance to recognize the similarities in the experiences of white and black women – for example, as sharecroppers or industrial workers – this is an important attempt to portray the distinctive history of African American working women.

Equally ambitious is LEVINE's outstanding book on the processes of continuity, adaptation and change in "the orally transmitted culture of Afro-Americans" from the slavery era to the 1940s. During slavery, black consciousness was manifested by an oral tradition which provided blacks with a sense of communal and individual identity and worth, as revealed, for example, in the spirituals, which afforded a metaphysical escape from bondage. After emancipation African American musical forms persisted, in gospel songs, and changed, with "the rise of a more personalized, individual-oriented ethos" as reflected in the blues. With highly enjoyable analyses of the components and targets of African American humour, the persistence of animal-trickster and slave-hero tales and contrasting images of black boxers, Jack Johnson ("bad") and Joe Louis ("good"), both celebrated in black folklore, Levine's book is at once an elucidation and celebration of the vibrancy and complexities of African-American popular culture. It is a truly remarkable piece of work.

The involvement of African Americans in all of their country's domestic and foreign conflicts from the colonial period to the present is ably charted by NALTY. In the Revolutionary War, which established American independence, African Americans (with freedom as their objective) rallied to both the patriotic and the British causes. During the Civil War, the Confederacy made use of black manpower, while ex-slaves and free blacks contributed to the final victory of northern arms. With the Union restored, black leaders and protest organizations pressed for an end to segregation and discrimination in America's armed forces – which offered mirror images of the endemic racism in American society at large. Nalty's persuasive thesis is that, at some periods, if out of expediency rather than morality, the "American armed forces have been powerful agents in effecting change in race relations." The Korean and Vietnam conflicts receive particularly acute analysis, and Nalty detects a reverse *Catch-22* irony in the fact that black Americans, having earlier pressed for the right to bear arms in defending their country, by the time of the Vietnam War "had begun complaining that too many of their race were receiving combat assignments."

In 1903, W.E.B. Du Bois forecast that "the problem of the color line" – in America, Asia and Africa – would be the greatest issue of the 20th century. In three incisive essays (originally given as lectures), FRANKLIN (1993) offers a critical review of the policies initiated by Ronald Reagan and continued by his successor, George Bush. Together with the larger conservative reaction of the 1980s and 1990s, they verify and extend Du Bois's prophecy to suggest that in America, "the problem of the 21st century will be the problem of the color line." From a historical perspective, Franklin reminded his audience that the "color line" had survived earlier attempts to eradicate it – emancipation without equality in the North after the Revolutionary War and in the South following the Civil War, and the only partially-realised objectives of the civil rights movement of the 1950s and 1960s. In contrast to these deferred promises of racial advancement, Reagan's call for a "new beginning" in his first inaugural address was, in fact, a "false start" – based on the assumption that American society had already achieved a "color blind" condition, and that public policy should no longer be directed to the needs of a growing black underclass. These sobering reflections from the doyen of African American historians suggest that an informed understanding of African American history, and its relevance to the present – and future – might yet help resolve what Gunnar Myrdal memorably termed "An American Dilemma."

JOHN WHITE

See also Race

African American History: Colonial Beginnings to 1860

Berlin, Ira, *Slaves Without Masters: The Free Negro in the Antebellum South*, New York: Pantheon, 1974; Oxford: Oxford University Press, 1981

Berlin, Ira, "Time, Space, and the Evolution of Afro-American Society on British Mainland North America," *American Historical Review*, 85, 1980

Blassingame, John W., *The Slave Community: Plantation Life in the Antebellum South*, New York: Oxford University Press, 1972, revised, 1979

Elkins, Stanley M., *Slavery: A Problem in American Institutional and Intellectual Life*, Chicago: University of Chicago Press, 1959; 3rd edition, 1976

Frey, Sylvia R., *Water from the Rock: Black Resistance in a Revolutionary Age*, Princeton: Princeton University Press, 1991

Genovese, Eugene D., *Roll, Jordan, Roll: The World the Slaves Made*, New York: Pantheon, 1974; London: Deutsch, 1975

Kolchin, Peter, *American Slavery, 1619–1877*, New York: Hill and Wang, 1993; London: Penguin, 1995

Levine, Lawrence W., *Black Culture and Black Consciousness: Afro-American Folk Thought from Slavery to Freedom*, New York: Oxford University Press, 1977

Litwack, Leon F., *North of Slavery: The Negro in the Free States, 1790–1860*, Chicago: University of Chicago Press, 1961

Parish, Peter J., *Slavery: History and Historians*, New York: Harper, 1989

Stuckey, Sterling, *Slave Culture: Nationalist Theory and the Foundations of Black America*, New York and Oxford: Oxford University Press, 1987

BERLIN (1980) distinguishes three different and evolving colonial black societies according to economic structure, the nature of the slave trade, and racial demographics. Northern non-plantation cereal agriculture and urban trade and industry required relatively few slaves, dictating a high degree and rapid rate of black acculturation to Euro-American society. Acculturation continued but with stronger African influence through significantly increased slave importations between 1732 and 1754. Early Chesapeake tobacco plantations relied heavily on white indentured servants, which again meant rapid acculturation for heavily outnumbered blacks. As slavery and racism solidified, however, African American society and culture became more distinct and yet bifurcated between Africans and Creoles in the early 18th century, although planter paternalism and the eventual decline of slave importation increased acculturation and cultural cohesion by the Revolutionary period. West Indian importation and frontier egalitarianism also meant high acculturation in the early Lower South, but the introduction of plantation staples, particularly rice, caused a massive increase of black population, especially through African imports, who, in the relative autonomy afforded by owner absenteeism and the task system of labour, developed a very distinct African American culture. Yet a light-skinned, relatively privileged, and highly acculturated urban black elite also meant an increasingly bifurcated black society.

FREY assesses the disruptions and transformations of African-American life caused by the Revolution. Large numbers of blacks were separated from loved ones and further enmeshed in the slave system by the disruptions of the War of Independence and the subsequent spread of slavery in the West. On the other hand, some blacks achieved freedom either by fleeing slavery during the war, or fighting for a side which offered freedom as a reward – or being manumitted by masters touched by Revolutionary principles of liberty. Even those who remained enslaved absorbed Revolutionary egalitarian ideals which, combined with a distinctive Afro-Christianity developed during the Great Awakening, sustained black people and even encouraged them to resist slavery until emancipation.

Northern slavery was gradually abolished after the Revolution, but LITWACK demonstrates the palpable limits to northern black freedom caused by a popular racism institutionalized in federal, state, and local authorities. Northern blacks suffered restricted freedom of movement, disfranchisement, curtailed legal rights, segregation, and poverty through restriction to menial labour. BERLIN (1974) shows how the liberties of southern free blacks were similarly limited and even endangered because they represented a threat and an anomaly in a society based on racial slavery. He also distinguishes an Upper South free black society which developed out of post-Revolution manumissions and a smaller Lower South one, resulting to some extent from paternity manumissions, which was lighter skinned, more materially privileged and protected, and had less contact with local enslaved black society.

The next five books concentrate on antebellum slavery and, Levine excepted, perhaps offer too static a portrayal of African-American history, although in each case notions of change over time are implied in the way the authors treat 19th century black culture. ELKINS argues that the trauma of the Atlantic Middle Passage cut blacks off from their African heritage and the plantation regime's "closed system", seen as comparable in some respects to Nazi concentration camps, produced the "Sambo" personality: childishly deceitful, dependent, and docile. The idea that blacks were "infantilized", with the implied denigration of their culture, has been heavily criticised. Using ex-slaves' autobiographies as well as traditional white sources, BLASSINGAME argues for a wider range of slave personalities from "Sambo" (which was often only self-protective dissembling anyway), to the much more common truculent but reliable "Jack", to the occasional incendiary "Nat". Most significantly, he argues that slaves were allowed sufficient autonomy for the development of strong families and communities in which they created a thriving culture most clearly seen in the distinctive theology and practices of Afro-Christianity. STUCKEY goes further still, making a case for the "essential Africanity" of black culture throughout American history. For the slave period he concentrates on the preponderance of circles in West African and American black culture, most notably manifest in the "ring shout", a counter-clockwise religious dance and song ritual.

These works have been criticised for their unchanging models of society and culture and for depicting black society and culture as so vibrant that it is easy to forget that most blacks were enslaved, and those who were not were far from free. LEVINE emphasizes the strength of African American culture under slavery, especially as seen in spiritual songs and folk tales. He notes, however, that culture is not static but dynamic and is adapted by people to suit their changing circumstances. Thus he argues that black culture was neither wholly African nor American but was a new African American culture based on a blend of African traits which survived (though often with new meanings) because they remained useful, adoptions or adaptations of white cultural traits necessary for survival, and invention in the face of the novelties and changing circumstances of American slavery. GENOVESE, who is also insufficiently sensitive to change over time, places a Marxist stress on the importance of master-slave relations. He argues that slaves accommodated to the paternalistic hegemony of masters but in doing so, because paternalism recognised the humanity of its victims, they thereby resisted the potential for total dehumanization inherent in slavery. He also notes that Afro-Christianity, while it undermined potential political resistance, mitigated the harshness of slavery by giving African Americans self-worth and spiritual strength.

KOLCHIN is the most up-to-date synthesis of all aspects of slavery, and of many of the diverse approaches to the subject. While recognizing slaves' remarkable social and cultural achievements, he stresses the extent of masters' power. He also acknowledges the varying geography and changing nature of African American life over two and a half centuries. PARISH is similar in spatial and temporal scope and offers an excellent historiographical introduction not only to slavery but all aspects of African American history before the 1860s.

STEVEN J. SARSON

See also Slavery entries

African American History: Civil War, Emancipation, and Reconstruction

Berlin, Ira, Barbara J. Fields, Steven F. Miller, Joseph P. Reidy and Leslie S. Rowland, *Slaves No More: Three Essays on Emancipation and the Civil War*, Cambridge and New York: Cambridge University Press, 1992

Brewer, James H., *The Confederate Negro: Virginia's Craftsmen and Military Laborers, 1861–1865*, Durham, NC: Duke University Press, 1969

Cornish, Dudley Taylor, *The Sable Arm: Negro Troops in the Union Army, 1861–1865*, New York: Norton, 1956; as *The Sable Arm: Black Troops in the Union Army*, Lawrence: University Press of Kansas, 1987

Fields, Barbara J., *Slavery and Freedom on the Middle Ground: Maryland During the Nineteenth Century*, New Haven: Yale University Press, 1985

Foner, Eric, *Reconstruction: America's Unfinished Revolution, 1863–1877*, New York: Harper, 1988, abridged as *A Short History of Reconstruction*, 1990

Glatthaar, Joseph T., *Forged in Battle: The Civil War Alliance of Black Soldiers and White Officers*, New York: Free Press, and London: Collier Macmillan, 1990

Kolchin, Peter, *First Freedom: The Responses of Alabama's Blacks to Emancipation and Reconstruction*, Westport, CT: Greenwood Press, 1972

Litwack, Leon F., *Been in the Storm So Long: The Aftermath of Slavery*, New York: Knopf, 1979; London: Athlone Press, 1980

Mohr, Clarence L., *On the Threshold of Freedom: Masters and Slaves in Civil War Georgia*, Athens: University of Georgia Press, 1986

Morris, Robert C., *Reading, 'Riting, and Reconstruction: The Education of Freedmen in the South, 1861–1870*, Chicago: University of Chicago Press, 1981

Quarles, Benjamin, *The Negro in the Civil War*, Boston: Little Brown, 1953

Ripley, C. Peter, *Slaves and Freedmen in Civil War Louisiana*, Baton Rouge: Louisiana State University Press, 1976

Rose, Willie Lee, *Rehearsal for Reconstruction: The Port Royal Experiment*, Indianapolis: Bobbs Merrill, 1964; with introduction by C. Vann Woodward, New York: Oxford University Press, 1976

Williamson, Joel, *After Slavery: The Negro in South Carolina During Reconstruction, 1861–1877*, Chapel Hill: University of North Carolina Press, 1965

There is no single recent overview which covers the African American experience throughout the period of the Civil War and Reconstruction. The best starting point is probably BERLIN *et al.* which brings together the introductory essays from the first three volumes of the massive *Freedom: A Documentary History of Emancipation* series, also edited by Berlin *et al.* As introductions to the subjects of the Civil War's immediate impact on slavery, the development and expansion of a free labour system in the South, and the wartime experiences of African American troops, these essays are unsurpassed. However, in their desire to rescue the slave from the role of victim they do occasionally come dangerously close to presenting an overly optimistic picture of the emancipation process. QUARLES's much earlier study (now available in a paperback reprint), manages to emphasize, with less obvious effort, that African Americans took an active part in the emancipation process and were not simply the grateful recipients of it. Quarles covers a wide variety of themes and subjects which, since his work first appeared, have had full-length studies devoted to them, for example: the role of African Americans in the military; the Port Royal experiment; and the Emancipation Proclamation. Throughout, Quarles never allows the reader to forget that, in the Civil War and beyond, the African American played "a role that was both heroic and significant," although, at the same time, the limitations placed on that role are never far from sight.

LITWACK, likewise, manages to keep the African American experience firmly in focus and yet not underestimate the problems that the freedmen encountered. This massive work covers the war years – it is particularly useful for the study of African American troops – before moving on to the early Reconstruction period. By staying very close to the primary sources, and thus letting the former slaves speak for themselves wherever possible, Litwack's study is extremely thorough and movingly evocative. It offers no simple, neatly-packaged conclusions, but is unsurpassed in revealing the range and the complex nature of the immediate responses to freedom.

Some of the best work on African American history in this period appears in local studies. There are many to choose from, but for the border states the best is FIELDS's study of Maryland, which, in common with the other border states, was specifically excluded from the Emancipation Proclamation. However, after 1863 it was evident that slavery there was doomed to extinction. Outstanding among studies of the Confederate states, MOHR traces the disintegration of the "peculiar institution" in Georgia, and the attempts of both the white and African American population to find a viable, and sustainable, alternative to a way of life that was clearly over. From 1861 onwards slavery and the social system that had sustained it were, as Mohr shows, increasingly undermined in Georgia, as in much of the Confederacy, by the steady deterioration of white authority, and the concomitant growth of African American autonomy in all areas of the state. Another excellent, although less detailed, study is RIPLEY, who uncovers in Louisiana a similar pattern of slavery's collapse, as both slaves and free blacks, either on their own account or as a result of white pressure, moved away from those routines and norms that had sustained the antebellum social structure, and towards a future which was, at best, uncertain, but was at least free.

The importance of African Americans to the Confederate war effort is the subject of BREWER's study of Virginia, which examines the wide range of African American – both free and slave – skilled labour that the Confederacy sought, not always successfully, to utilize. This a carefully researched, extremely detailed study, covering the use of African American labour in all parts of the Confederate army, including the Quartermaster and Commissary departments, the navy, and hospitals. As such, Brewer's work may be considered rather specialized for some readers. However, as he points out, compared to "Johnny Reb" and "Billy Yank" the Confederate African American remains something of a historical enigma, and this study serves more generally to remind us that there was much more to the African American military experience than serving in the Massachusetts 54th.

As far as service in the Union army is concerned, CORNISH remains the standard work. First published only two years after the *Brown v. Board of Education* ruling, Cornish's study represents a determined and vigorous attempt to move beyond the confines of Jim Crow history. It is both comprehensive and balanced in its analysis of the many military activities undertaken by African American troops, the victories they achieved and the discrimination they encountered. Among more recent works, GLATTHAAR is a lively and accessible study covering such topics as the breaking down of Northern resistance to black regiments, their recruitment and training, the relations between white officers and black troops under their command, the experience of battle, and the prejudice which, despite the military successes of African American troops, continued long after the war was over.

On the Reconstruction period, FONER's magisterial study provides the most comprehensive and authoritative overview. One of the central themes of his account of Reconstruction is that African Americans were active and important participants in the whole Reconstruction process. His broad treatment can be supplemented by a variety of local studies including KOLCHIN on Alabama and WILLIAMSON who examines African American political and social advances, and setbacks, in South Carolina. On the subject of the education of the freedmen, MORRIS is particularly instructive on the role of African American teachers, as well as on the work of the Freedmen's Bureau. Outstanding among all the local studies is ROSE's superb and beautifully-written account of the sea islands of South Carolina during the Civil War itself. Coming under Union control early in the war, the islands were very quickly abandoned by the white population, leaving the slaves behind to construct for themselves a new way of life. This "rehearsal for reconstruction" was fraught with difficulties, both economic and social, and one of the biggest battles at Port Royal, as elsewhere, was over land ownership. However, like Foner, Rose shows that it was not the land issue alone, but a far more general disorganization, and an unwillingness or inability on the part of the federal government to perceive what the freedmen required, that helped to undermine not only the Port Royal experiment but Reconstruction as a whole.

S-M. GRANT

See also Reconstruction entries

African American History: 1870s–1954, the North

Du Bois, W.E.B., *The Philadelphia Negro: A Social Study*, Philadelphia: University of Pennsylvania, 1899; reprinted, New York: Schocken, 1967

Franklin, John Hope and Alfred A. Moss, Jr., *From Slavery to Freedom: A History of African Americans*, 7th edition, New York: McGraw Hill, 1994 (originally published, by Franklin only, as *From Slavery to Freedom: A History of American Negroes*, New York: Knopf, 1947)

Greenberg, Cheryl Lynn, *"Or Does It Explode?": Black Harlem in the Great Depression*, New York: Oxford University Press, 1991

Grossman, James R., *Land of Hope: Chicago, Black Southerners, and the Great Migration*, Chicago: University of Chicago Press, 1989

Huggins, Nathan Irvin, *Harlem Renaissance*, New York: Oxford University Press, 1971

Kusmer, Kenneth L., *A Ghetto Takes Shape: Black Cleveland, 1870–1930*, Urbana: University of Illinois Press, 1976

Nielson, David Gordon, *Black Ethos: Northern Urban Negro Life and Thought, 1890–1930*, Westport, CT: Greenwood Press, 1977

Osofsky, Gilbert, *Harlem: The Making of a Ghetto: Negro New York, 1890–1930*, New York: Harper, 1966

Spear, Allan H., *Black Chicago: The Making of a Negro Ghetto, 1890–1920*, Chicago: University of Chicago Press, 1967

Thomas, Richard W., *Life for Us Is What We Make It: Building Black Community in Detroit, 1915–1945*, Bloomington: Indiana University Press, 1992

Watts, Jill, *God, Harlem USA: The Father Divine Story*, Berkeley: University of California Press, 1992

Weisbrot, Robert, *Father Divine and the Struggle for Racial Equality*, Urbana: University of Illinois Press, 1983

Weiss, Nancy J., *The National Urban League, 1910–1940*, New York: Oxford University Press, 1974

Weiss, Nancy J., *Farewell to the Party of Lincoln: Black Politics in the Age of FDR*, Princeton: Princeton University Press, 1983

The demographic shift of African Americans from the South – the Great Migration – to the cities of the North and West began after the Civil War and persisted until the 1960s. The subsequent experiences of these migrants in their host communities – in particular their reception by whites – and the development of an adaptive and distinctive black urban culture, have long engaged the attentions of historians and sociologists. FRANKLIN and MOSS treat these and other issues in the several relevant chapters of their authoritative history of the African American experience. In a pioneering and still valuable study, DU BOIS, a historian and sociologist, wrote primarily as a sociologist who, despite his sympathies, criticized Philadelphia's blacks for their immorality, criminality, and neglect of education, and the inattention of the city's middle class to its leadership responsibilities. But Du Bois also confessed that, as a leading member of the "Talented Tenth," he had been unaware of the socioeconomic and racial problems faced by the black population, and "learned far more from Philadelphia Negroes than I taught them concerning the Negro problem".

By the 1930s, most commentators viewed the growth of black northern urban ghettos – with their attendant problems of conflict and adjustment – as the most significant aspect of race relations outside the South. With some exceptions, earlier accounts (like that of Du Bois) stressed the debilitating effects and the bleakness of urban black life. However, later scholarship was more attuned to the complexity, creativity and dynamics of African American communities in the North, from the end of Reconstruction to the onset of the civil rights movement, which protested against racial segregation and discrimination – on both sides of the Mason-Dixon line.

NIELSON's announced and ambitious purpose is to trace the experiences of "the ordinary black American" living in an urban environment between 1890 and 1930. The first general survey of the period, it anticipated more recent scholarship in its stress on the variety among black urban concentrations, noting that "each related differently to the dominant white community" – for example, the black ghettos of Chicago and New York. Lacking a clear focus and occasionally self-contradictory, Nielson does, however, include an informative discussion of the vexed issue of the "color complex" among African Americans. But he is less persuasive – or consistent – in his assertion that, during the years surveyed, "the ordinary Negro became inherently nationalistic while at the same time he retained his American identity".

The rise and decline of America's most famous black community receives detailed attention from OSOFSKY, but he fails to compare and contrast the disabilities of Harlem's African American and West Indian populations with those faced by other immigrant groups in the same period. HUGGINS offers a trenchant cultural/intellectual analysis of the "Capital of the Black World" in the 1920s, with portraits of such major figures as writers Langston Hughes, Nella Larsen and Jean Toomer, and perceptive remarks on black contributions to American music and theatre. The responses of Harlem's labour organizers, black nationalists, ministers, cult leaders and communists to the sufferings of the Great Depression and the advent of the New Deal are ably treated by GREENBERG, in the fullest account of Harlem in the 1930s. She devotes attention to the Harlem riots of 1935 and 1943, suggesting plausibly that both were effective – if destructive – "extensions of political activity".

Father Divine (George Baker, Jr.) was the most charismatic of Harlem's black separatist leaders in the 1930s. Avoiding the sensationalist tone of earlier accounts, WEISBROT stresses that Divine's Peace Mission movement had a sincere concern for the welfare of its members and was committed to the struggle for racial equality. Father Divine instructed his followers in the virtues of thrift and industry, urged them to economic self-sufficiency, and criticized the New Deal's Works Progress Administration for sapping the work ethic. WATTS's sensitive study devotes more attention to Father Divine's origins and religious ideas, an amalgam of Pentecostalism, positive thinking and New Thought, and stresses his denial of racial differences and encouragement of interracial membership.

The black experience in other major northern cities has also received searching examination. SPEAR demonstrates that Chicago's "physical ghetto" was already in existence before World War I, and was "primarily the product of white hostility" rather than of the desire of African Americans to congregate together. Subsequent black arrivals faced discrimination in employment, public accommodations and welfare agencies. Their response was to create the "institutional ghetto" – in an attempt to organize a semi-autonomous community, providing services for its members. Despite a growth in black political power by 1920, Chicago's blacks received only "formal and ceremonial" concessions from the white power structure, while the race riot of 1919 "destroyed whatever hope remained for a peacefully integrated city". GROSSMAN's splendid book, partly based on oral testimonies, offers an original interpretation of the agencies and individuals who actively encouraged black migration from the South to Chicago. Although he offers little on the innovative musical traditions of black Chicagoans, Grossman discusses the complex and ambiguous relationship between the migrants and established residents, their impact on race relations, work experiences in the city's stockyards, and the interplay between class and race.

KUSMER's important book is offered as an exercise in "comprehensive comparative history" and describes the changing patterns of relations between the races, as well as change (including class divisions) within the black community itself in Cleveland over a 60-year period. Rejecting the pathological and negative connotations of the term "ghetto", Kusmer analyzes the roles of black Clevelanders as participants rather than ciphers in the unfolding of their distinctive urban experience.

THOMAS adopts the concept of "the community building process" to examine the ways in which "change agents" – social and industrial workers, ministers, politicians, business and professional workers, housewives and community activists – established Detroit as a major black urban centre by the end of World War II. His discussion of the Detroit Urban League complements and refines WEISS (1974), a narrative and organizational history of a major (and interracial) civil rights organization primarily concerned to aid blacks in their adjustment to urban life in the North. During the Depression and New Deal, the Urban League concentrated on securing relief benefits for blacks, and guaranteeing them the few low level jobs they held, but was unable to prevent their transformation "from an enslaved agricultural peasantry to an oppressed urban proletariat". The political consequences of the growing African American presence in northern cities (where they could vote) and the effects of the New Deal on their aspirations are ably summarized in WEISS (1983). Although they did not benefit from the New Deal measures to the degree warranted by their economic plight, the fact that they were included in its relief programmes swung the historic loyalties of African Americans from the Republican "party of Lincoln" to that of Franklin D. Roosevelt – and subsequent Democratic administrations. As Weiss concludes, "the black embrace of the Democratic party" was a considered reaction to the crisis of the Depression and the hopes of the New Deal. If persistent white racism, discrimination and poverty were the determining factors in African American life in the northern states from the 1870s to 1954, the responses of blacks themselves, as the books cited collectively illustrate, were active rather than passive, varied and not uniform.

JOHN WHITE

African American History: 1870s–1954, the South

Anderson, James D., *The Education of Blacks in the South, 1860–1935*, Chapel Hill: University of North Carolina Press, 1988

Brundage, W. Fitzhugh, *Lynching in the New South: Georgia and Virginia, 1880–1930*, Urbana: University of Illinois Press, 1993

Higgs, Robert, *Competition and Coercion: Blacks in the American Economy, 1865–1914*, Cambridge and New York: Cambridge University Press, 1977

Kelley, Robin D.G., *Hammer and Hoe: Alabama Communists During the Great Depression*, Chapel Hill: University of North Carolina Press, 1990

McMillen, Neil R., *Dark Journey: Black Mississippians in the Age of Jim Crow*, Urbana: University of Illinois Press, 1989

Meier, August, *Negro Thought in America, 1880–1915: Racial Ideologies in the Age of Booker T. Washington*, Ann Arbor: University of Michigan Press, 1963

Montgomery, William E., *Under Their Own Vine and Fig Tree: The African-American Church in the South, 1865–1900*, Baton Rouge: Louisiana State University Press, 1993

Palmer, Robert, *Deep Blues*, New York: Viking, and Harmondsworth, Middlesex: Penguin, 1981

Rabinowitz, Howard N., *Race Relations in the Urban South, 1865–1890*, New York: Oxford University Press, 1978

Ransom, Roger L. and Richard Sutch, *One Kind of Freedom: The Economic Consequences of Emancipation*, Cambridge and New York: Cambridge University Press, 1977

Williamson, Joel, *The Crucible of Race: Black-White Relations in the American South since Emancipation*, New York: Oxford University Press, 1984; abridged as *A Rage for Order*, 1986

The period between Reconstruction and the civil rights movement is the most underdeveloped in African American historiography, especially for the South. No comprehensive surveys of the subject are limited to this time period. Many important relevant works start with emancipation, and most focus on a single theme or topic. An exception is McMILLEN, a lucid work outstanding in its comprehensiveness and depth of research. McMillen's title suggests his theme, though readers should keep in mind that Mississippi was arguably the single most racially repressive state in the United States.

Commodity agriculture dominated the Southern economy and the working lives of most African Americans in the segregation era. RANSOM and SUTCH is a study by two economists of the place of blacks in the South's cotton regions. Using a large set of quantitative data, the authors stress the racial and institutional barriers to black economic progress and argue that these barriers contributed mightily to the South's relative poverty after the Civil War. HIGGS, shorter but in many ways more comprehensive, is a more optimistic analysis by an economist. He argues that racism, though powerful, was to some extent counterbalanced by the normal operations of the market. He concludes that, despite racism, and considering that they had begun in 1865 with virtually nothing in the way of property, education, and skills, blacks did make significant economic progress in the fifty years after the Civil War.

RABINOWITZ is by far the best study of the South's small but important urban population. Focusing on five cities – Atlanta, Montgomery, Nashville, Raleigh, and Richmond – chosen to represent a cross-section of the urban South, Rabinowitz covers the most important institutional, economic, and political developments. Rabinowitz's argument that segregation represented in many ways an improvement for blacks when compared to their earlier exclusion from access to education and other public services has played a significant role in our understanding of the development of segregation.

WILLIAMSON is an interpretation of the rise of particularly virulent forms of racism – or what Williamson calls "radicalism" – in the South after 1890. This is more a study of whites than blacks, but he includes interesting chapters on African American life and thought. His Freudian explanation for the rise of racial radicalism will not convince every reader, but no one has given us a more powerful account of the violence and irrationality faced by the South's blacks in this period. Among a number of recent studies of one manifestation of racial violence – lynchings – BRUNDAGE is the best. Using a more accurate set of data than any previously available, in a study of two states, he stresses the complexities of the phenomenon of lynching, including the fact that these extra-legal executions could vary significantly in motivation and style. Brundage also includes excellent chapters on African American responses to lynchings.

MEIER is a classic work on the more general black ideological response to rising white racism. Though national in scope, it naturally gives much attention to southerners, especially Booker T. Washington of Alabama, the single most influential African American public figure at the turn of the 20th century. Meier includes not only intellectuals, but also professionals, educators, and other elite blacks in his account. He is especially adept at tracing the inconsistencies and complexities in the thought and behavior of his subjects.

African American churches became the most important institutions under the control of black communities in the segregated South. The rise of an autonomous African American religious establishment in the South after emancipation is the theme of MONTGOMERY. He traces, in roughly chronological fashion, the ways in which blacks rejected most white proselytizers and established, instead, their own Protestant denominations. One result was a form of Christianity heavily influenced by African spiritual traditions. Montgomery also effectively discusses the many social roles of the churches and the powerful influence of their ministers in African American life.

Although all southern states severely discriminated against black public education, schools were perhaps second in importance to churches among black institutions. ANDERSON is the best survey of black education in the segregated South. He focuses on what he sees as a long-term conflict between the educational goals of African Americans and the policies of northern philanthropists who subsidized much black education. The book convincingly shows how the latter followed the lead of Booker T. Washington (and Washington's mentor, the white Samuel Armstrong) in trying to force black education into a mould appropriate to a permanent subordination of African Americans. While it includes important data on all aspects of formal education for blacks, Anderson's account pays little attention to the significant role of state and local governments in black education.

Another development in African American life during this period, with great long-term influence, was the rise of a new musical form, the blues. Among many books on the blues, PALMER is perhaps the best historical account. He has interviewed many of the musical pioneers, and he has an encyclopedic command of the music itself; his book has the special merit of placing the rise of the blues into the social and economic context of the area where many of the pioneers originated, the Mississippi-Yazoo Delta.

As will be clear even from the titles of most of the books discussed here, the mid-20th century is the most neglected period of all in the history of southern African Americans. An important exception is KELLEY. The Communist party in Alabama in the 1930s managed to build a significant presence among blacks in both urban and rural areas. Kelley may exaggerate the specific importance of what remained a relatively small group of black activists. More important, though, is his demonstration that communist successes built upon a widespread, if often invisible, folk culture of resistance to racism.

J. WILLIAM HARRIS

See also Jim Crow

African American History: since 1954

Edsall, Thomas Byrne and Mary D. Edsall, *Chain Reaction: The Impact of Race, Rights, and Taxes on American Politics*, New York: Norton, 1991

Garrow, David J., *Bearing the Cross: Martin Luther King, Jr., and the Southern Christian Leadership Conference*, New York: Morrow, 1986; London: Cape, 1988

Lawson, Steven F., *Running for Freedom: Civil Rights and Black Politics in America since 1941*, Philadelphia: Temple University Press, 1991

Lemann, Nicholas, *The Promised Land: The Great Black Migration and How It Changed America*, New York: Knopf, and London: Macmillan, 1991

Marable, Manning, *Race, Reform, and Rebellion: The Second Reconstruction in Black America, 1945–1982*, Jackson: University Press of Mississippi, and London: Macmillan, 1984; 2nd edition, as *Race, Reform, and Rebellion: The Second Reconstruction in Black America, 1945–1990*, 1991

Sitkoff, Harvard, *The Struggle for Black Equality, 1954–1992*, New York: Hill and Wang, 1993

Van Deburg, William L., *New Day in Babylon: The Black Power Movement and American Culture, 1965–75*, Chicago: University of Chicago Press, 1992

Weisbrot, Robert, *Freedom Bound: A History of America's Civil Rights Movement*, New York: Norton, 1990

Wilson, William Julius, *The Declining Significance of Race: Blacks and Changing American Institutions*, Chicago: University of Chicago Press, 1978

African American history since 1954, the year Chief Justice Earl Warren declared segregated public schools unconstitutional in the case of *Brown* v. *Board of Education*, has attracted the attention of numerous scholars, many of them inevitably concerned with the progress and achievements of the civil rights movement. There are a number of useful general surveys, including MARABLE, a readable and passionately argued study written from the perspective of a black socialist. Critical of the civil rights movement for targeting segregation instead of social and economic injustices rooted in the capitalist system, the book contains some provocative insights as well as a valuable account of events after 1970. Its value as a student textbook, however, is marred by its cursory treatment of major civil rights campaigns and its rather blinkered treatment of individuals like Martin Luther King and Lyndon Johnson. SITKOFF is another useful introduction to the main developments of the later 20th century. Written by a white liberal scholar, it is broadly sympathetic to King and optimistic about the capacity of mass protest to reform the social order in the United States. Like Marable, however, the book lacks depth. The final chapter on developments after 1970 is particularly thin and unconvincing.

LAWSON has the edge over both Marable and Sitkoff in that it emphasizes the importance of community-driven protest as well as high-profile national campaigns and federal legislation. While local voter registration campaigns served to liberate African Americans from the thraldom of Jim Crow, congressional voting rights legislation finally enabled them to participate in the political process, North as well as South. The book's overriding focus on politics, however, means that scholars must look elsewhere for an adequate treatment of themes such as movement ideology, black cultural nationalism and the growth of the so-called underclass. WEISBROT is the best single-volume survey of the civil rights movement in spite of the fact that it is rather error-prone and flawed by its lack of a substantial primary source base. The book is especially good on the interrelationship between civil rights organizations and the federal government. Disappointing, however, is its cursory treatment of the late 1950s.

For all his faults, Martin Luther King was unquestionably the most important black leader of his generation. GARROW is an epic biography of the famous civil rights leader, thoroughly researched and encyclopedic in scope. Unfortunately the blow-by-blow narrative, indispensable reading though it is for all historians of this topic, lacks a strong analytical drive, and the reader is left to wade through a mass of detail with little or no help from the author.

LEMANN is a very readable account of how the Great Society programmes of the 1960s failed to deliver social and economic justice to African Americans north or south of the Mason-Dixon line. A white liberal journalist, Lemann provides a damning indictment of the way local power elites such as the Daley machine in Chicago were allowed to co-opt federal welfare projects such as the Community Action Program, but is rightly insistent that the federal government remains best equipped to deal with the enormous problems of the ghetto.

Black Power is an important topic poorly dealt with by historians. The fullest scholarly account is probably VAN DEBURG which makes a brave effort to highlight the diversity of black nationalist sentiment in the late 1960s and early 1970s. The work is marred, however, by an annoying tendency to celebrate all aspects of this ambiguous phenomenon which had as many conservative as progressive roots.

The quarter century since the demise of the civil rights movement has not been well covered by historians, who have tended to leave the field open to political scientists, sociologists, and journalists. Among the most provocative works is WILSON, a highly controversial account of black progress in modern America, emphasizing the salience of class rather than race as an explanatory concept for the ills confronting the black community in post-industrial America. EDSALL argues persuasively that race remains the most critical factor in United States politics, providing the focus for a variety of cultural and interest group conflicts within the American electorate. By successfully linking popular prejudice against high taxation, big government and putatively welfare-dependent (and criminally-inclined) blacks, the Republicans succeeded in creating a conservative coalition capable of dominating national politics during the Reagan-Bush years. Although the book lacks a solid source base, it nonetheless helps to explain the symbolic power of race-freighted issues such as Affirmative Action and welfare.

ROBERT COOK

See also Civil Rights Movement

African American History: Religion

Baer, Hans A. and Merrill Singer, *African American Religion in the Twentieth Century: Varieties of Protest and Accommodation*, Knoxville: University of Tennessee Press, 1992
Cone, James H., *Speaking the Truth: Ecumenism, Liberation and Black Theology*, Grand Rapids, MI: Eerdmans, 1986
George, Carol V. R., *Segregated Sabbaths: Richard Allen and the Emergence of Independent Black Churches, 1760–1840*, New York: Oxford University Press, 1973
Gregg, Robert, *Sparks from the Anvil of Oppression: Philadelphia's African Methodist and Southern Migrants, 1890–1940*, Philadelphia: Temple University Press, 1993
Higginbotham, Evelyn Brooks, *Righteous Discontent: The Women's Movement in the Black Baptist Church, 1880–1920*, Cambridge, MA: Harvard University Press, 1993
Lincoln, C. Eric, *The Black Muslims in America*, Boston: Beacon Press, 1961; 3rd edition, Grand Rapids, MI: Eerdmans, 1994
Lincoln, C. Eric and Lawrence H. Mamiya, *The Black Church in the African-American Experience*, Durham, NC: Duke University Press, 1990
Montgomery, William E., *Under Their Own Vine and Fig Tree: The African-American Church in the South, 1865–1900*, Baton Rouge: Louisiana State University Press, 1993
Raboteau, Albert J., *Slave Religion: The "Invisible Institution" in the Antebellum South*, New York: Oxford University Press, 1978
Swift, David E., *Black Prophets of Justice: Activist Clergy Before the Civil War*, Baton Rouge: Louisiana State University Press, 1989
Watts, Jill, *God, Harlem USA: The Father Divine Story*, Berkeley: University of California Press, 1992

Religion has played a crucial role in the development of African American life and culture, and the independent black church has consistently provided spiritual and material sustenance to a people not allowed to participate fully in the American promise.

In their scholarly overview of the seven major black denominations, LINCOLN and MAMIYA provide an ideal starting point for those interested in the black church. Noting the importance of the black church in understanding the American religious experience, they supplement their historical survey of the denominations with statistical data and analysis. Lincoln and Mamiya examine topics such as the religious world-view and the theology of the black churches, the historical role of black ministers, the influence of politics and economics, the role of music, and the effects of migration and urbanization. The authors also develop a model for future study that emphasizes the dialectical tensions experienced within the black church.

Examining the dialectical convergence of protest and accommodation, BAER and SINGER achieve their stated goal of providing a useful introduction to 20th century African American religion. The authors emphasize the significance of American capitalism, the often contradictory interplay between religion and politics, and the diversity of African American religion – a diversity that makes the term "black church" seem misleadingly monolithic. Baer and Singer also offer a "typology of black sectarianism" and examine the history, beliefs, and social organization of black churches in four distinct, but often overlapping, categories.

Those interested in the beginnings of African American religion and the black church should refer to RABOTEAU's ground-breaking study of slave religion, the "invisible institution." He explores the spread of Christianity to Africans in America, emphasizing the syncretism of African religion and Christianity to form a unique folk religion. He also analyzes the influence of evangelism, conjure and magic, and slave spirituals. Using slave narratives, autobiographies, and black folklore, Raboteau strips away the cloak of invisibility to reveal many of the attitudes, values, and aspirations of American slave men and women.

Equally important for scholars is GEORGE's classic study of the emergence of independent black churches. With a strong emphasis on the development of black theology, George examines the life of Richard Allen, one of the founders and first bishop of the African Methodist Episcopal Church, and conditions among urban black northerners that initiated and sustained the drive toward separation from white control.

George also analyzes the social and political actions of free African Americans in their attempts to survive and prosper in a hostile American society. SWIFT focuses on the social and political activism of six ministers of independent black Presbyterian and Congregational churches in antebellum America. He examines the development of black churches, and of a liberation theology within predominantly white denominations that had liturgies and doctrines different from those normally associated with black Baptists and Methodists. Against a backdrop of protest and reform, Swift analyzes the influence of Puritan and revolutionary traditions, denominational emphasis on education and intelligence, and the unique position of clergy who were unapologetic black Christian Americans in white denominations.

The freedom of four million African Americans after the Civil War led to unprecedented organization, expansion, and consolidation of independent black churches in the South. MONTGOMERY gives an excellent account of that development, analyzing the role of black and white Northern missionaries, but especially of black southerners themselves. Most interesting is the conflict which Montgomery reveals between established denominations and persistent folk religion. He also examines conditions and attitudes in the South, and the influence of the Reconstruction period, and of black nationalism, on church development.

In his study of African Methodists and southern migrants in Philadelphia, GREGG examines the influence of migration and ghettoization upon the development of urban black churches. Focusing on the problems and attitudes of the "middling group" of black migrants, in the context of the formation of the ghetto, Gregg discusses the changing theology and ideology, and diminishing political influence, of African Methodism within the black community. He also furnishes useful statistical information on black ministers and migrants.

HIGGINBOTHAM's analysis of the interplay of gender, race, and class within the black Baptist church helps to compensate for the neglect of the role of women in the development of black churches. She explores the political activism of women in the formation of the National Baptist Convention, USA, and in their own regional and state conventions. Most compelling and illuminating is Higginbotham's examination of a unique feminist theology and gender perspective on black religion.

Two studies focus on black religious movements that emerged from the depression years of the 1930s. WATTS examines the career of Father Divine, self-proclaimed God, and his Peace Mission movement. Offering insight into black religious thinking outside mainstream black churches, Watts maintains that Divine drew heavily on the 19th-century ideology of New Thought, and positive thinking, to provide social, political, and economic programs to aid the poor of Harlem. LINCOLN (1961, revised 1994) provides an excellent analysis of the conditions that helped to foster the rise of the Nation of Islam, which he describes as the foremost black nationalist organization. Lincoln examines the ideology and doctrines of the Nation, and seeks to explain why it appealed to such large numbers of black Americans, and repelled such large numbers of white Americans. In the most recent edition, Lincoln also analyzes changes since the death of leader Elijah Muhammad.

Since the 1960s, scholars have considered the influence of a unique and often controversial black theology on the development of black churches and the African American community. In a series of brief polemical essays, CONE delves into the meaning, use, and historical context of black theology. Especially useful to historians are Cone's essays that trace and analyze the black theological themes of liberation, justice, love, suffering, and hope, from the time of slavery to the 1960s.

LAWRENCE S. LITTLE

Agrarian Discontent, 1865–1896

Clanton, Gene, *Populism: The Humane Preference in America, 1890–1900*, Boston: Twayne, 1991

Goodwyn, Lawrence, *Democratic Promise: The Populist Moment in America*, New York: Oxford University Press, 1976; abridged as *The Populist Moment: A Short History of the Agrarian Revolt in America*, 1978

Hahn, Steven, *The Roots of Southern Populism: Yeoman Farmers and the Transformation of the Georgia Upcountry, 1850–1890*, New York: Oxford University Press, 1983

Hicks, John D., *The Populist Revolt: A History of the Farmers' Alliance and the People's Party*, Minneapolis: University of Minnesota Press, 1931

Hofstadter, Richard, *The Age of Reform: From Bryan to FDR*, New York: Knopf, 1955; London: Cape, 1962

McMath, Robert C., Jr., *American Populism: A Social History, 1877–1898*, New York: Hill and Wang, 1993

Ostler, Jeffrey, *Prairie Populism: The Fate of Agrarian Radicalism in Kansas, Nebraska, and Iowa, 1880–1892*, Lawrence: University Press of Kansas, 1993

Palmer, Bruce, *"Man over Money": The Southern Populist Critique of American Capitalism*, Chapel Hill: University of North Carolina Press, 1980

Pollack, Norman, *The Populist Response to Industrial America: Midwestern Populist Thought*, Cambridge, MA: Harvard University Press, 1962

Scholarship on late 19th-century agrarian discontent has concentrated on the "Populist" movement of the 1880s–90s; much less has been written on the earlier Grange movement. HICKS's classic study offers a largely economic interpretation of the causes of Populism. He emphasizes pressure on land brought by the closing of the frontier, the long-term crisis in agricultural commodity prices in the quarter-century after the Civil War, and high levels of debt among small farmers. Largely sympathetic to the Populists, he portrays the Free Silver movement as a fatal compromise of the Populists' agricultural base, even if a politically expedient one. But he is also ultimately optimistic about the long-term impact of the Populists on American society and politics, and emphasizes their role in hastening the adoption of reforms such as agricultural price supports, the Federal Reserve system, and federal regulation of railways.

HOFSTADTER's highly influential interpretation was very different, concentrating on the psychological underpinnings of Populism. Viewing the movement as part of a longer "Age of

Reform," he saw the Populists as essentially backward-looking and even reactionary traditionalists. They were motivated less by economic conditions and more by "status anxiety" as their imagined place in American society as the "yeoman farmer" bedrock of the nation was eroded by the emergence of urban industrial capitalism and commerce. His generally unsympathetic assessment is accentuated by a focus on the alleged anti-semitism, xenophobia, and reactionary nature of the movement's rhetoric. The earliest counter to Hofstadter came from POLLACK, who mounted a brief, forceful, but not altogether convincing, defence of Populist ideology and policy. In particular, he claimed that, far from being a retreat into the past, Populism presented a set of serious answers to the problems of urbanizing and industrializing America.

GOODWYN's mammoth study (usefully abridged as *The Populist Moment*) was at its appearance the first comprehensive history of the Populists since Hicks, and it still dominates much of the debate despite subsequent criticism. Goodwyn's prodigious research into the lives of the foot-soldiers of the Populist movement – the farmers who flocked to the National Farmers' Alliance – emphasizes the economic roots of the movement, especially the monetary deflation of the post-Civil War era, and the crisis in cotton and wheat prices. He develops a model of "movement-building," identifying a "movement culture" in the farmers' meetings and political campaigns. For Goodwyn the central experience of the movement was in these meetings, lectures and other gatherings, an example of radical self-activity which led in turn to radical proposals for economic reform. The cooperatives and sub-treasury plan above all represent for Goodwyn the apogee of the movement's economic radicalism. His concentration on the Texas Farmers' Alliance leads him to set its distinctive ideas on economics and the currency – radical anti-monopolism and greenbackism – as a benchmark for the radicalism and effectiveness of the movement elsewhere. Thus Free Silver and indeed the People's Party itself represented a pernicious "shadow movement" that essentially hijacked the "mid-roader" mainstream of the farmers' movement, and imposed a narrow, compromised national electoral strategy, doomed to fail in the person of William Jennings Bryan. He is also much less sanguine about the Populists' long-term impact than Hicks, and sees in their defeat a blow to economic and political democracy, with long-lasting effects.

The overall impact of the many monographs appearing since Goodwyn has been to emphasize the wide variations between Populism in different states and regions. CLANTON offers the best single-volume comparison of the movement in different states. He rejects Goodwyn's thesis of a "shadow movement" around silver, seeing race in the South and prohibition in the North as the main obstacles to the success of the People's Party. He offers many examples of important variations in Populist opinion and support between different states, such as northern and western support for woman suffrage and southern opposition to it. He judges the West generally to have been more radical than the South. He analyzes Populism overall in more ideological than economic or political terms, seeing it as the last gasp of an older "humane preference," a valuation of human rights over property rights that was destroyed by industrial capitalism.

Among regional monographs on midwestern Populism, one of the best recent studies is OSTLER. He focuses on the differences between the political strategies of Farmers' Alliances in states that developed third parties, like Kansas, and those in states that did not, such as Iowa, where Populism is thus traditionally assumed to have "failed." He is strongly critical of Goodwyn's distinction between a "real" farmers' movement and the "shadow movement." He ultimately concludes that the decentralized American federal system created too many local divisions for Populism to spread further than it did. The southern movement has also attracted much scholarship, of which HAHN is one of the most important and original studies. He emphasizes the centrality of economic transformation to the social and political upheavals of the late 19th-century. The Georgia upcountry's economy and society before the arrival of the cotton-based commodity market was one based on "habits of mutuality" and essentially pre-capitalist notions of obligation and justice. The commodification of agriculture and the rise of share-cropping, what Hahn calls "the vortex of the cotton economy," sucked in these social relations as well as the economic arrangements that underlay them. The upcountry small farmers were only lukewarm to the planter-led secession and Civil War, and their antagonism to the planter class mounted after the war as they were driven into debt and off their land. Populism emerged as a movement of traditionalist but quasi-class resistance by smallholders to the planters and merchants.

In contrast, PALMER approaches southern Populism almost as intellectual history. He situates southern Populist thought within a matrix of 19th-century egalitarian ideas, in particular "republicanism," or what he prefers to call "producerism." This was a morally-based ideology with Jeffersonian roots, yet also infused with Lockean self-interest and, more importantly, with an acceptance of the basic tenets of capitalism. Ultimately, despite its sophistication, anti-monopoly/greenbackist populism was not a class ideology. Moreover, most Populists were smallholders with little sympathy for or understanding of industrial workers, their potential allies.

Finally, McMATH is a brief and useful synthesis of much of the literature to date, presenting the Populists primarily within the broader context of changes in rural society.

ANDREW NEATHER

See also Populism

Agriculture, to 1860

Atack, Jeremy and Fred Bateman, *To Their Own Soil: Agriculture in the Antebellum North*, Ames: Iowa State University Press, 1987

Chaplin, Joyce E., *An Anxious Pursuit: Agricultural Innovation and Modernity in the Lower South, 1730–1815*, Chapel Hill: University of North Carolina Press, 1993

Danhof, Clarence H., *Change in Agriculture: The Northern United States, 1820–1870*, Cambridge, MA: Harvard University Press, 1969

Gates, Paul W., *The Farmer's Age: Agriculture, 1815–1860*, New York: Holt Rinehart, 1960

Gray, Lewis C., *History of Agriculture in the Southern United States to 1860*, 2 vols., Washington, DC: Carnegie Institution, 1933

Henretta, James A., *The Origins of American Capitalism: Collected Essays*, Boston: Northeastern University Press, 1991

Kulikoff, Allan, *The Agrarian Origins of American Capitalism*, Charlottesville: University Press of Virginia, 1992

Lemon, James T., *The Best Poor Man's Country: A Geographical Study of Early Southeastern Pennsylvania*, Baltimore: Johns Hopkins Press, 1972

North, Douglass C., *The Economic Growth of the United States, 1790–1860*, Englewood Cliffs, NJ: Prentice Hall, 1961

Rothenberg, Winifred Barr, *From Marketplaces to a Market Economy: The Transformation of Rural Massachusetts, 1750–1850*, Chicago: University of Chicago Press, 1992

Schlebecker, John T., *Whereby We Thrive: A History of American Farming, 1607–1972*, Ames: Iowa State University Press, 1975

The idea that antebellum Americans tended to work the land even when manufacturing pursuits may have been more profitable has proven one of the most enduring themes in American economic and social history. Consequently, farmers' apparent loyalty to the agrarian ideal and its rational and irrational tendencies has provided much of the focus and impetus for historical writing on antebellum agriculture.

Some of the earliest treatments are also the most comprehensive. GRAY's two-volume work, though focused on the antebellum South, is perhaps the most thorough treatment available. While stressing the scientific agricultural practices of large planters, Gray was equally sensitive to the subsistence economy of the majority of small southern farms. While some of the findings presented in this substantial work have been called into question by later and largely econometric historians, Gray's history of southern agriculture is the most catholic still available.

Broader in geographic range is GATES. Here the emphasis is on American agriculture generally with most regions coming in for even-handed treatment. Highlighting divisions within the nation's farming communities, not just between North and South, Gates draws attention to the problems of credit and markets faced by farmers and tenants, problems that often turned creditors against debtors, large landowners against small, and growers of one staple against those of another. More generally, and important regional variations notwithstanding, the American farmer is characterized as a "creator of capital and an investor," someone who emphasised production for market first and self-sufficiency second. Despite more recent emphases on the autarkic nature of American farming in the antebellum period, Gates has rightly become something of a classic on the subject.

In his brief but sweeping history, SCHLEBECKER examines the social, economic, technological, and business aspects of America's agricultural history since 1607. A little over one third of the work covers the period to 1860 and provides very useful synopses of the main trends and events in the evolution of the nation's agriculture. Broad though it is in temporal scope, the work covers all the main regions and serves as a useful introduction to a sometimes unwieldy topic. By its own definition, this work is "a history of commercial farming." Yet the rather restricted definition of the term as "what the farmer actually did, not what he thought he was doing or wanted to do" gives the book a rather dated appearance in the light of more recent work.

Although it has been the subject of some penetrating and damaging critiques, NORTH's compact but important and wide-ranging work has proven important for an economic and regional assessment of antebellum American agriculture. Positing a model of regional specialization with the southern agricultural economy at its centre, North looked at regional trade flows and argued that the Midwest provided the South with foodstuffs, so enabling the latter to devote more of its resources to cotton cultivation. While he may have understated the self-sufficiency of many southern farms and plantations, his work helped profile the importance of regional analysis in the writing of the history of American agriculture.

More recently, KULIKOFF has kept alive the tradition of grand histories of pre-1860 American agriculture. From a Marxist standpoint, he emphasizes the importance of America's agricultural development in explaining the nation's capitalist development. While some may find his insistence on rural class antagonisms rather reductionist and determinist, the book does much to restore agriculture and the class relations which it fostered to its critical importance in American history. At times very nuanced and subtle, the work successfully interweaves theory and narrative to ask a number of important questions about the relationship between America's rural classes from the 17th through to the 19th century. Although one ultimately wonders whether yeomen, capitalist farmers, and large planters were sometimes as distinct and class-conscious as Kulikoff seems to think, the book is one of the more recent and useful attempts to place the history of agriculture in its rightful economic, political, and social context.

Agricultural development in the North has come in for particular attention. Building on Percy Wells Bidwell and John I. Falconer's 1925 study, *History of Agriculture in the Northern United States, 1620-1860*, and in many ways prefiguring later writing on the evolution of northern agriculture, DANHOF suggests that net gains in northern agricultural productivity are not discernible until the 1840s and 1850s. He focuses on the intricate process of continuing change, and teases out the interdependencies of farmers' attitudes towards agricultural innovation, an equally powerful resistance to such innovations, and the pivotal role played by the expansion of the market economy and northern urban-industrial society. On the basis of this analysis, he seeks to explain both the timing and the reasons for increased northern agricultural productivity. Danhof's emphasis on community-sanctioned modern production methods, the increasing importance of farmers' entrepreneurship, and how these were related to larger historical changes in the North seems to have informed more recent studies which also stress the interdependency of these forces.

Having correctly identified the 1970s and early 1980s as a relatively lean period for historical monographs on northern agriculture, ATACK and BATEMAN have recently reopened the question of northern agricultural efficiency and productivity from the quantitative perspective of the New Economic

History. Drawing on census data and stressing farming as both a market-oriented pursuit and a reflection of a way of life, this 1987 work does much to flesh out earlier studies. Most importantly, Atack and Bateman show that northern antebellum rates of return were higher for manufacturing than for agriculture. However they also reinforce the view that preference for working the land and the attendant Jeffersonian, agrarian ideal were persistent and attractive in the antebellum agricultural North. By splicing concerns about profit with a traditional dream of agrarian paradise, antebellum northern farmers apparently remained optimistic about their future by 1860.

The willingness or reluctance of northern farmers to enter the market economy has become the subject of some debate among historians. Since the 1970s, several have addressed the question of whether colonial farmers in particular engaged in the market economy and, if so, why. LEMON's study of southeastern colonial Pennsylvania argues that by the middle of the 18th century roughly 80 per cent of farmers had some agricultural surplus to sell and, on average, only 60 per cent of their farm output was for self-sufficiency. From this, Lemon concludes that Pennsylvania's colonial farmers were beginning to embrace capitalist, market-oriented production by the 1750s. This position is given further support by ROTHENBERG who has applied the methods of the New Economic History to a detailed examination of farm account books in colonial and antebellum Massachusetts. Her evidence suggests that as early as 1750, farmers made long-distance trips of 150 miles and more to market their crops despite the high cost of transportation. Such activities point to the colonial origins of commercial agriculture. HENRETTA, however, has rejected the idea that such behaviour constituted a capitalist impulse among colonial farmers. Their *mentalité*, he argues in the third chapter of his collected essays, placed a premium on self-sufficiency; goods were marketed only once this precondition had been met.

Recent work by CHAPLIN on a different region, the lower South, tries to yoke together questions of *mentalité* and agricultural innovation. By charting the responses of southern planters to philosophical, Enlightenment ideals and detailing their concrete, agricultural innovations, in the period 1730–1815, she explains that although lower South planters were conservative in their social relations, their willingness to adapt mechanization to plantation agriculture constituted an experiment with modernity that laid the basis for their agricultural success in the antebellum period. This meticulously researched book contains copious information on many southern staples and offers as much insight into the planters' philosophical *Weltanschauung* as it does into the methods of cultivating lower South crops.

Mark M. Smith

See also Market Revolution

Agriculture, since 1860

Clarke, Sally H., *Regulation and the Revolution in United States Farm Productivity*, Cambridge and New York: Cambridge University Press, 1994

Daniel, Pete, *Breaking the Land: The Transformation of Cotton, Tobacco, and Rice Cultures since 1880*, Urbana: University of Illinois Press, 1985
Fitzgerald, Deborah, *The Business of Breeding: Hybrid Corn in Illinois, 1890–1940*, Ithaca, NY: Cornell University Press, 1990
Hamilton, David E., *From New Day to New Deal: American Farm Policy from Hoover to Roosevelt, 1928–1933*, Chapel Hill: University of North Carolina Press, 1991
Neth, Mary C., *Preserving the Family Farm: Women, Community and the Foundations of Modern Agribusiness in the Midwest, 1900–1940*, Baltimore: Johns Hopkins University Press, 1995
Olmstead, Alan L., "The Mechanization of Reaping and Mowing in American Agriculture, 1833–1870," *Journal of Economic History*, 35, 1975
Saloutos, Theodore, *The American Farmer and the New Deal*, Ames: Iowa State University Press, 1982
Woodman, Harold D., *New South, New Law: The Legal Foundations of Credit and Labor Relations in the Postbellum Agricultural South*, Baton Rouge: Louisiana State University Press, 1995
Wright, Gavin, *Old South, New South: Revolutions in the Southern Economy since the Civil War*, New York: Basic Books, 1986

There is no single general survey of agriculture since 1860. It is conventional for economists to give competition the central role in accounting for economic developments in the farm sector. But the various factors implicit in a model of competition are more complex than theory allows. Historians have drawn out these complexities, by addressing different analytical questions including the role of the family, the state, and, especially in the South, race relations and labor markets. By doing so, these studies have used the experience of agriculture to speak to theoretical issues about economic growth.

WOODMAN reviews the legal evolution of sharecropping and crop lien laws in southern states after the Civil War. The original intent of the lien laws, he reasons, was to provide a means whereby landowners could obtain credit. The laws had unanticipated consequences, however, resulting in several parties competing for the first claim to the crop. Redeemer governments quickly rewrote the laws to give priority to landowners. In this way, croppers often had no say in the management of the farm. Further, by obtaining their wages at the end of the harvest, they were compelled to give an interest-free loan to the landowner; and yet, they paid interest on loans to buy the supplies necessary to see them through the year.

WRIGHT argues that, once southern farmers who lacked assets – freedmen and many small farmers – became indebted, they were under pressure to plant cotton, because this was the one crop that supplied the cash to pay their bills. Ironically, then, the region became more tied to cotton as more families lost their independence. This low-wage economy, Wright argues, persisted until it was inadvertently undermined by New Deal policies – policies often written by southerners themselves. As the Agricultural Adjustment Administration set its payments for restricting production, it gave landowners the incentive to displace sharecroppers. Landowners began to consolidate land

and mechanize pre-harvest operations. African American laborers became "foot loose" and, though many remained in the South during the 1930s, they were free to migrate to other places, as demand for labor began to rise during World War II. DANIEL compares cotton farming with prairie rice and flue-cured tobacco cultures in the years since 1880. The three crops were mechanized at different times, starting with rice as early as the 1880s, and tobacco not until the 1960s. Daniel argues that wealthier farmers in cotton and rice were able to cut their labor bills drastically. Despite protests over the terms of government assistance, the exodus of thousands of the South's smaller and poorer farmers proved to be distinctly "quiet."

In contrast to the South, numerous family operators on midwestern farms initiated the process of mechanization. Yet OLMSTEAD argues that, in the case of the mechanical reaper, competition among individual operators did not dictate the pace of change. Rather because a few farmers could share a machine, families often pooled their resources in order to purchase reapers. NETH has elaborated the role of family networks for farming in the Corn Belt. In the early 20th century, she argues that women were critical to establishing local networks in which families exchanged assistance. These activities included obvious examples such as butchering animals, but also sharing horses and labor for critical stages of farm production. In these ways, families avoided out-of-pocket expenditures and protected themselves against the effects of harsh weather or unusually low prices. Like Olmstead, she argues it was not competition but cooperation that permitted many family farms to survive and prosper in the early 20th century.

Sources of technology became far more complex during the 20th century. FITZGERALD uses one example, that of hybrid corn, to draw out important ideas about the role of land grant colleges and the extension service. Advice from public officials, she maintains, helped small private companies develop commercial varieties by the 1930s. But in the process authority shifted from public to private institutions. This had important implications for the nature of farming. For, unlike the extension service which taught farmers various ways to boost yields, private officials urged farmers to follow the firm's instructions for buying hybrid seed. In this sense, once again, authority shifted from farmers to corporations.

HAMILTON employs agriculture as a case study intended to assess the political economy of Herbert Hoover's administration. As Hoover attempted to contain economic "waste" but avoid state coercion, such as price controls, he promoted the use of marketing cooperatives intended to manage the distribution of crops and smooth out prices. Though this approach satisfied Hoover's political concerns, it never survived the tremendous collapse in prices after 1929. The state became far more involved in the farm sector during the 1930s. SALOUTOS offers a general survey of New Deal programs. He covers the best known agency, the Agricultural Adjustment Administration, in detail, along with critical issues such as the electrification of rural communities, the role of the Farm Security Administration, and the New Deal's impact on the Great Plains. Saloutos concludes that electrification and the Shelterbelt were important legacies of the New Deal, and argues that the New Deal could not have preserved small family

operations, given the effects of competition and the introduction of capital-intensive machinery.

CLARKE examines the long-term consequences of regulation for changes in farm productivity. Looking at the Corn Belt, she finds that despite competition, farmers, prior to 1930, hesitated to adopt expensive machinery. They feared the risks inherent in commodity and credit markets and preferred the safety which they found in their own family-run operations. During the 1930s, as New Deal policies altered their markets, the programs encouraged farmers to respond to competition by investing in productivity-enhancing equipment. These programs continued long after the crisis had passed. Ironically, as long as farm prices tended to fall, regulation contributed to a stable financial climate and the "quiet" exodus of thousands of farmers. But once prices met the intent of the New Deal legislation and rose in the 1970s, many commercial farmers found themselves vulnerable to a new crisis.

SALLY H. CLARKE

Alabama Claims and Treaty of Washington, 1869–1872

Campbell, Charles S., *The Transformation of American Foreign Relations, 1865–1900*, New York: Harper, 1976

Cook, Adrian, *The Alabama Claims: American Politics and Anglo-American Relations, 1865–1872*, Ithaca, NY: Cornell University Press, 1975

Donald, David, *Charles Sumner and the Rights of Man*, New York: Knopf, 1970

Duberman, Martin, *Charles Francis Adams, 1806–1886*, Boston: Houghton Mifflin, 1961

Jenkins, Brian, *Fenians and Anglo-American Relations During Reconstruction*, Ithaca, NY: Cornell University Press, 1969

Nevins, Allan, *Hamilton Fish: The Inner History of the Grant Administration*, New York: Dodd Mead, 1936

Smith, Goldwin, *The Treaty of Washington, 1871: A Study in Imperial History*, Ithaca, NY: Cornell University Press, 1941

Stacey, C.P., *Canada and the Age of Conflict: A History of Canadian External Policies, 1867–1921*, Toronto: Macmillan, 1977

Stuart, Reginald C., *United States Expansionism and British North America, 1775–1871*, Chapel Hill: University of North Carolina Press, 1988

When the Civil War ended, Anglo-American relations did not revert to the relatively harmonious state that had existed during the decade of the 1850s. The United States held Britain accountable for the depredations of the C.S.S. *Alabama* and her sister ships, which had been built in British shipyards or manned by British crews. This dispute, which carried with it the threat of reprisals and possible descent into hostilities, was not settled until the Treaty of Washington in 1871 and the Geneva Arbitration Tribunal in 1872. CAMPBELL offers an excellent short account of the whole controversy, but the most extensive scholarly monograph on the issues and their settlement is COOK. This well researched study begins in 1865 with the unsuccessful attempts of the diplomats to negotiate a settlement, and moves on to the elaborate efforts of Secretary of State Hamilton Fish to resolve the matter. Cook argues that the British government refused to accept responsibility for the claims immediately after the war, when the Americans would have accepted a modest gesture. However, as time passed, American resentments and demands grew.

Canada also became linked to this ongoing dispute as a result of its actions during the Civil War, through the desire of many Americans to see either the annexation of British North America or its independence, and as a consequence of a disagreement over fisheries prompted by the attempts of the Dominion of Canada to exclude American fishermen from using Canadian ports and inshore waters. These Canadian issues were the central focus of SMITH's study of the Treaty which, although published more than fifty years ago, still remains useful. More recently STACEY has looked at the Canadian context of the Treaty negotiations, and concluded that the Canadians may have placed too high a value on the inshore fisheries as a means to extract a renewal of reciprocity from the United States. Another issue was the possible complicity of the United States government in the attempts of the Fenian Brotherhood to organize a revolution in Ireland against the British and to aggravate Anglo-Canadian-American relations by invading Canada. The complicated affairs of the Fenians, in this context, have been skilfully analyzed by JENKINS.

Several individuals were prominent in the attempts to resolve these problems. NEVINS is still the only substantial study of Hamilton Fish, and provides a very solid account of the *Alabama* claims controversy from 1868 onwards. Nevins saw Fish as the crucial figure who picked up the pieces of the earlier failed attempts at settlement, and, by exercising great patience, political skill, and diplomatic finesse, managed to bring the parties to an accommodation. Although prepared to be more generous to Fish than Cook, Nevins did admit that Fish allowed ambiguities into the Treaty of Washington that nearly wrecked the Geneva Arbitration. Unquestionably Fish had as many problems with the leaders of the Senate and his own president as he did with the British. Charles Sumner, chairman of the Senate Foreign Relations Committee, had been a dominant figure in American foreign affairs throughout the 1860s, and his peroration in 1869 on Britain's injuries to the United States inflated American expectations on the *Alabama* claims to a virtually unresolvable level. Fish and President Grant were able to have Sumner removed as chairman of the Senate committee, ostensibly to clear the way for a settlement with Britain. In his biography of Sumner DONALD suggests that the senator's removal was an effort by the executive branch to regain control of foreign affairs from the Senate, rather than merely a tactical move to assure acceptance of a settlement of the *Alabama* claims. The fact that Sumner voted for the Treaty in the end would seem to support Donald's conclusion.

Nevins saw Grant's attitude as a further obstacle to Fish's attempts to reach an accommodation with the British, although recent biographies of Grant have concluded that the president was much more flexible on the questions of annexation of Canada, the Fenians, and the language of the American claims

against Britain than most earlier historians have acknowledged. Another key figure was Charles Francis Adams, first as Minister to Britain and then as American member of the Arbitration Tribunal. DUBERMAN's biography of Adams is particularly illuminating on Adams's role in working out a means through which the British could agree to participate in the Arbitration proceedings after the United States had jeopardized the whole enterprise by including in their argument the indirect claims for the cost of the war after 1863. By contrast, Campbell concluded that the initiative in this crisis came rather more from the British delegation at Geneva.

All historians, especially Campbell, Cook, Smith, and Nevins, saw the Treaty of Washington as a major international settlement which normalized Anglo-American relations after the Civil War, and served as an example of conflict resolution through arbitration. However, only STUART, and to a lesser extent Stacey, developed the equally important points that the American government, by dropping its commitment to the annexation of Canada and by accepting the Prime Minister of Canada as a member of the British High Commission, had reached a major turning point in foreign policy – a rejection of territorial expansion into British North America and a practical acceptance of the Dominion of Canada.

FRANCIS M. CARROLL

See also Britain and the United States; Canada and the United States

Alien and Sedition Acts, and Virginia and Kentucky Resolutions, 1798–1799

Berns, Walter, "Freedom of the Press and the Alien and Sedition Laws: A Reappraisal," *Supreme Court Review 1970*, 1971, pp.109–59
Brant, Irving, *James Madison: Father of the Constitution, 1787–1800*, Indianapolis: Bobbs Merrill, 1950
Koch, Adrienne, *Jefferson and Madison: The Great Collaboration*, New York: Knopf, 1950
Levy, Leonard W., *Legacy of Suppression: Freedom of Speech and Press in Early American History*, Cambridge, MA: Belknap Press of Harvard University Press, 1960; revised as *Emergence of a Free Press*, New York and Oxford: Oxford University Press, 1985
Malone, Dumas, *Jefferson and the Ordeal of Liberty*, Boston: Little Brown, 1962
Miller, John C., *Crisis in Freedom: The Alien and Sedition Acts*, Boston: Little Brown, 1951
Sharp, James Roger, *American Politics in the Early Republic: The New Nation in Crisis*, New Haven: Yale University Press, 1993
Smith, James Morton, *Freedom's Fetters: The Alien and Sedition Laws and American Civil Liberties*, Ithaca, NY: Cornell University Press, 1956

In the wake of the deepening crisis with France and the revelations of the XYZ affair in early 1798, while Congress considered a declaration of war, the Federalists passed a spate of preparedness legislation. This included strengthening the navy and army, providing new federal taxes to pay for this expenditure, passing a new Naturalization Act, two acts to control aliens, and a Sedition Act that among other things punished "false, slanderous and malicious" criticism of the federal government and its officials. The Republican leadership responded to the Federalist "Reign of Terror" by encouraging the passage of resolutions in the state legislatures of Kentucky and Virginia asserting the compact theory of the nature of the Union and the right of the states to determine the constitutionality of federal legislation.

It was not until the Red Scare following World War II that historians focused upon the Alien and Sedition Acts in a detailed and critical fashion. MILLER emphasizes the political nature of the Federalist legislation and the equally political response of the Republican party's leaders in their appeal to states rights. He assumes that the acts were unconstitutional and stood in violation of the best American ideals. This well-written brief study was designed for a popular audience, and characterized by a presentist perspective on the state of party development as well as freedom of the press. In his nearly definitive study of the legislative history and the enforcement of the Alien and Sedition laws, SMITH surveyed the arguments on both sides in Congress and the courts. While the scope of the book is more limited than that of Miller, it contains a far more detailed and sophisticated analysis of the constitutional and legal aspects of the Federalist legislation.

While reviews pointed out that Smith's easy assumption of the unconstitutionality of the Alien and Sedition acts was debatable, LEVY went much further and placed the question of seditious libel in a broad historical framework that further challenged the libertarian assumptions of the Republicans' defenders. He emphasized that the Sedition law incorporated the then radical ideas that the jury be allowed broad discretion in determining the guilt of the accused and that truth could stand as a defense. Levy argued that the response to the Alien and Sedition acts led some lesser known Jeffersonians, such as George Hay, to advance for the first time truly modern conceptions of freedom of expression, but that Jefferson himself was basically concerned with battling "consolidation," and was more than willing to use the state courts to silence his political opponents.

The main problem posed by the Virginia and Kentucky resolutions for the biographers of Jefferson and Madison involves their relationship to nullification and secession, both of which were justified by appeals to this sacred source. In her chapter on the resolutions – based on an earlier article co-authored by Harry Ammon – KOCH unraveled questions of the contribution of each man to the various documents, and included a previously unpublished letter from Jefferson to Madison in which he considered grounds under which "we" might "sever ourselves from the union." But Koch emphasized that in judging the intent of the resolutions, historians should ignore the "slogans employed, 'states' rights' particularly" and acknowledge that "they were intended primarily as a defense of civil liberties. It must be remembered that this defense was liberal and forward looking, not conservative or literalistic."

BRANT ended volume three of his masterful biography of Madison with a clear discussion of Madison's role in writing the Virginia Resolutions and the Report to the Virginia House of Delegates defending them against northern critics. He emphasized the political intent and moderate nature – relative to Jefferson's desires at the time – of these arguments that stood in tension both with Madison's own earlier words and with Brant's general interpretation of the Virginian as a consistent nationalist.

In the third volume of his own magisterial biography of Madison's friend and neighbor Jefferson, MALONE included the most authoritative discussion of the Kentucky Resolutions (of both 1798 and 1799) extant. He too emphasized the political situation and Madison's moderating influence, but confronted directly the question of Jefferson's private thoughts about nullification and secession. He built an extensive case that historians should emphasize Jefferson's defense of basic human rights rather than focus on "the weapon he used" – an appeal to states' rights. "In the end therefore this campaign which Jefferson had inspired boiled down to an appeal to public opinion against the offensive acts and the trend of the general government."

Among modern scholars only the conservative political scientist BERNS develops a defense of the Federalists and credits Hamilton with originating the liberal view of freedom of speech in the Croswell case that involved a New York editor who was charged with libeling Jefferson. He argues that even Hay, the most liberal of the Jeffersonian pamphleteers, "concedes" that the states could punish seditious libel. For Berns the Jeffersonian argument was basically a constitutional defense of state sovereignty; the federalist legislation was "the occasion more than the cause of Madison and Jefferson's famous resolutions." Jefferson and his colleagues were "inhibited" in developing a liberal view of freedom of expression, because of their "attachment to the institution of slavery."

Although neither conservative nor pro-Federalist, SHARP puts forward a similar argument in his superb synthetic study of the 1790s. He emphasizes the importance of the distrust of "faction" that was embedded in the Republican ideology and warns against portraying either the Federalists or the Republicans as modern political parties. Thus, neither the Alien and Sedition acts nor the Virginia and Kentucky resolutions can be viewed in the context of modern partisan conflict, as so many commentators have done. Sharp sees the Republican resolves as signaling a shift to a "new defensive enclave strategy" emphasizing protection of "their section . . . and its institutions" and warns that the "emphasis on the 'national' and 'liberal' aspects of Madison and Jefferson and their resolutions . . . has hindered many historians from appreciating the strongly sectional character of Jeffersonian Republicanism and from recognizing the real potential for violence in the 1790s."

WILLIAM G. SHADE

American Federation of Labor

Cobble, Dorothy Sue, *Dishing It Out: Waitresses and Their Unions in the Twentieth Century*, Urbana: University of Illinois Press, 1991
Commons, John R. and others, *History of the Labor Movement in the United States*, 4 vols., New York: Macmillan, 1918–35

Foner, Philip S., *History of the Labor Movement in the United States*, 8 vols., New York: International, 1947–88

Hattam, Victoria C., *Labor Visions and State Power: The Origins of Business Unionism in the United States*, Princeton: Princeton University Press, 1993

Kaufman, Stuart Bruce, *Samuel Gompers and the Origins of the American Federation of Labor, 1848–1896*, Westport, CT: Greenwood Press, 1973

Kazin, Michael, *Barons of Labor: The San Francisco Building Trades and Union Power in the Progressive Era*, Urbana: University of Illinois Press, 1987

Montgomery, David, *The Fall of the House of Labor: The Workplace, the State and American Labor Activism, 1865–1925*, Cambridge and New York: Cambridge University Press, 1987

Moody, Kim, *An Injury to All: The Decline of American Unionism*, London: Verso, 1988

The history of the American Federation of Labor (AFL) started to be written fairly early in the organization's own history, by the man usually regarded as the father of American labor history, John R. Commons. His views are set out most clearly in Volume IV of COMMONS's massive history, covering the period 1890–1920, and while his praise for the AFL's mostly narrow, conservative craft unionism is nowadays unfashionable, he lucidly draws important, broad conclusions. He stresses the differences between American and Western European trade unions, above all what he sees as the relative lack of class consciousness in the United States. For Commons, the AFL recognised the essentially craft- or job-based consciousness of the American working class, and accordingly concentrated on bargaining agreements and similar practical goals. Explicitly criticizing Marxist, class-based alternatives, he characterizes the AFL's strategy under Gompers as a pragmatic response to the failure of more radical strategies in the 1880s.

In contrast, FONER's even longer multi-volume history, which only ever got up to 1920, explicitly rejects the AFL's strategies as unacceptable capitulations to capitalism. But Foner, a lifelong communist, paradoxically shared Commons's strongly institutional focus. All but one volume of the *History* concentrates in encyclopedic detail on the actions of the AFL's mostly conservative craft unions rather than on more radical currents. Foner's real contribution was to focus on struggle and class conflict, in contrast to Commons's and his followers' stress on the AFL's moderation and bargaining achievements. But his work is lengthy, dull, and rarely draws explicit or broader conclusions.

KAUFMAN was one of the first of a generation of so-called "New Labor Historians" emerging from the early 1970s. While, like most of them, critical of the AFL's eventual conservatism, Kaufman is notable for his emphasis on the complexity of Gompers's early background and the volatility and contingency of the labor and radical world of the 1880s and 1890s. He stresses the compatibility of many of the AFL's demands in the 1880s with Marxist strategies of the day, for example noting Gompers's support for Henry George. From such positions and from Gompers's extensive contact with the exiled First International in New York in the 1870s, Kaufman concludes that the AFL in fact came "tantalisingly short" of a much more radical position. Among the numerous studies

of AFL unions, mostly focused on a single city, that appeared during the 1980s, KAZIN's fine monograph may be taken as a representative example. Kazin seeks to revise the (by-then) accepted Left, "New Labor History" view that the AFL was cautious, bureaucratic and conservative, by examining its use of political power in one of its greatest strongholds, San Francisco. He concludes that voluntarism was usually rejected at local level. The AFL formed pragmatic and effective political alliances with socialists and across craft lines – a phenomenon ended by the conservative and business victories following World War I.

MONTGOMERY represents in part an effort to sum up the "New Labor History" re-assessment of the early AFL. Montgomery deploys his vast knowledge of the period to argue that the American labor movement was essentially defeated by the outcome of the struggles at the end of World War I. While incorporating research on workers outside the AFL, craft unions like the machinists are the main focus of this dense but rewarding study. He argues that although their strategy was often narrow, many AFL unionists were feeling their way towards a more radical response to the savage business offensives of the pre-1914 era. This was particularly true during World War I and its immediate aftermath, when Montgomery believes the AFL unions were close to a breakthrough of the kind that eventually came in the 1930s. The dates covered by Montgomery point up a curiosity in the literature on the AFL: how little has been written about the period between the death of Gompers in 1924 and the merger with the Congress of Industrial Organizations (CIO) in 1955. The AFL's lacklustre leadership and blinkered strategy in this period seem to have deterred historians. But MOODY takes up the story in 1945, offering a damning critique of postwar business unionism under both the AFL and AFL-CIO. He argues lucidly that the relative stability in industrial relations between the late 1940s and early 1970s was achieved by conservative union bureaucracies stifling rank-and-file militancy in exchange for monetary rewards through collective bargaining. But the peace was really only a truce at the convenience of capital, and since the 1970s, especially from 1980 onwards, the true conflictual nature of workplace relations has re-emerged. The only remedy for the current weakened state of the unions, he argues, is a resurgence of 1930s-style militancy.

Both Cobble and Hattam illustrate newer directions emerging in the historical treatment of the AFL. Like a growing number of labor historians, one of COBBLE's main areas of interpretative emphasis is gender. Using a fairly traditional institutional focus, she examines waitresses' struggle against male domination within their unions. She concludes that the Hotel and Restaurant Employees' female-only waitress locals were more effective than gender-mixed locals, a positive example of proto-feminist separatism. She sees them as an example of both a radical craft union consciousness and a distinctive women's work culture. This led to about 25 per cent of waitresses being unionized in the 1950s; why the union declined disastrously after 1960 is less clear from this study. HATTAM examines another area at present generating great interest among historians of the early AFL: the law. She argues brilliantly that "a strong judiciary created a politically weak labor movement." The AFL was not an exception to the European pattern of union and political development, but the American judicial system was exceptional. She shows that the anti-union conspiracy cases of the late 19th century, and the use of injunctions from the 1880s onwards, made political reform ineffective. Thus the judiciary both blocked the labor movement's immediate progress, and stunted it in the long term by making the early-20th-century AFL disillusioned with political action, turning it towards voluntarism.

ANDREW NEATHER

See also Gompers; Labor Unions

American Party see Know Nothings

American Revolution: General

Bailyn, Bernard, *The Ideological Origins of the American Revolution*, Cambridge, MA: Belknap Press of Harvard University Press, 1967, revised 1992

Cappon, Lester J. (editor), *Atlas of Early American History: The Revolutionary Era, 1760–1790*, Princeton: Princeton University Press, 1976

Countryman, Edward, *The American Revolution*, New York: Hill and Wang, and London: Tauris, 1985

Greene, Jack P., *Peripheries and Center: Constitutional Development in the Extended Polities of the British Empire and the United States, 1607–1788*, Athens: University of Georgia Press, 1986

Greene, Jack P. and J.R. Pole (editors), *The Blackwell Encyclopedia of the American Revolution*, Oxford and Cambridge, MA: Blackwell, 1991

Heimert, Alan, *Religion and the American Mind: From the Great Awakening to the Revolution*, Cambridge, MA: Harvard University Press, 1966

Henretta, James A. and Gregory H. Nobles, *Evolution and Revolution: American Society, 1600–1820*, Lexington, MA: Heath, 1987

Jensen, Merrill, *The Founding of a Nation: A History of the American Revolution, 1763–1776*, New York: Oxford University Press, 1968

Jones, Alice Hanson, *Wealth of a Nation to Be: The American Colonies on the Eve of the Revolution*, New York: Columbia University Press, 1980

Main, Jackson Turner, *The Social Structure of Revolutionary America*, Princeton: Princeton University Press, 1965

May, Henry F., *The Enlightenment in America*, New York: Oxford University Press, 1976

Middlekauff, Robert, *The Glorious Cause: The American Revolution, 1763–1789*, New York and Oxford: Oxford University Press, 1982

Morgan, Edmund S., *The Stamp Act Crisis: Prologue to Revolution*, Chapel Hill: University of North Carolina Press, 1953; revised, with Helen M. Morgan, New York: Collier, 1963

Nash, Gary B., *The Urban Crucible: Social Change, Political Consciousness, and the Origins of the American Revolution*, Cambridge, MA: Harvard University Press, 1979

Tucker, Robert W. and David C. Hendrickson, *The Fall of the First British Empire: Origins of the War of Independence*, Baltimore: Johns Hopkins University Press, 1982

Wood, Gordon S., *The Creation of the American Republic, 1776–1787*, Chapel Hill: University of North Carolina Press, 1969

Wood, Gordon S., *The Radicalism of the American Revolution*, New York: Knopf, 1992

MIDDLEKAUFF has written the best single volume narrative history of the American Revolution. He focuses principally on the political and public events of the period between 1763 and 1789, and conveys a sense of the passion that infused the Revolutionary movement. His description of the experiences of common soldiers during the War of Independence, reflecting some of the work that he and his students have produced over the past fifteen years, is especially good in this regard. Middlekauff also argues convincingly that the millennial hopes and republican commitments of the Americans made their Revolution truly radical.

Different in scope and execution from Middlekauff is the volume edited by GREENE and POLE. A comprehensive tome involving more than 90 scholars and incorporating some 75 separate essays, the *Blackwell Encyclopedia* offers a veritable feast of ideas. Each of the substantive essays is eight to ten pages in length and summarizes much of the recent work pertaining to the context, concepts, course of events, and consequences of the Revolution. Topics include such mainstays as the structure of politics in the late 18th century, religion, ideology, political mobilization, loyalism, the Articles of Confederation, and state constitution-making. Also included, however, are discussions related to population growth, family structure, medicine, poverty and insanity, and the impact of the Revolution on the British Caribbean colonies.

Those interested in cartographical depictions of the political, economic, and cultural activities of the Revolutionary era will want to consult CAPPON. Easily one of the most important and useful books published during the American bicentennial, Cappon's *Atlas* contains 286 maps with accompanying text, and covers the period immediately before, during, and after the War of Independence. A superb selection of maps depicts, among other things, population distribution, Native American settlements, tobacco and rice exports, and British customs districts; the location of sugar refineries, silversmiths, religious congregations, and homes of members of the American Philosophical Society; and the spatial structure of the War, loyalist activities, and Confederation land ordinances.

Early in this century, Carl Becker noted that the American Revolution must be understood as a struggle not only for "home rule" but also over "who should rule at home." Becker's conceptualization of the dual nature of the Revolution is a useful way of approaching the vast body of monographs on Revolutionary America. Historians who view the Revolution primarily as a contest for "home rule" focus on various aspects of the imperial crisis. Central to their interpretations is an understanding of the nature of the relationship between the colonies and the mother country in the dozen years after the French and Indian War. JENSEN describes the complex political history of this period. In setting forth the principles espoused and political decisions taken on both sides of the Atlantic, he is careful to distinguish among the resistance movements in the thirteen colonies and between groups of Revolutionaries within each colony.

Jensen's study is intended to illuminate the actions of the colonists rather than their doctrines. The MORGANS pay closer attention to the constitutional quarrel between the colonies and England. In a highly readable account of the Stamp Act crisis, they demonstrate that colonial ideas of parliamentary power were surprisingly consistent throughout the entire period of the imperial controversy. Colonial radicals did not switch from one constitutional position to another as the occasion arose; they did not posit a distinction between "internal" and "external" taxes in 1765 only to reject all taxation in the aftermath of the Townshend duties. Instead, from the time of the Sugar Act, the colonists distinguished between taxation and general legislation, and rejected all claims of Parliament's right to tax them.

TUCKER and HENDRICKSON offer a different reading of the constitutional positions taken by the colonists. In a provocative analysis somewhat reminiscent of the interpretations of the imperial school of historians, they are critical of studies that have been too quick to condemn the actions of Parliament and the ministry after 1764. The crucial issue in the imperial debate was not taxation versus legislation, but sovereignty. And by 1774, colonial assertions amounted to a repudiation of parliamentary sovereignty. As such, imperial officials were forced either to meet the novel challenge posed by the Americans or to grant them de facto independence.

Tucker and Hendrickson assume that there was only one valid interpretation of the constitutional arrangement of the empire, and that officials in London best voiced that interpretation. GREENE disagrees. He reviews the relationship between the colonies and the mother country from the beginnings of colonization and contends that by the 1760s there were two competing definitions of the constitutional situation of the empire. Colonial arguments, based on a traditional application of the doctrine of consent, were constitutionally sound. Imperial arguments, based on a comparatively new and still evolving doctrine of parliamentary supremacy, were not unambiguously legitimate.

Since the mid-1960s, some historians have argued that the contest for "home rule" involved more than reasoned responses to constitutional challenges. BAILYN sees the essence of the Revolution embodied in the emotional rhetoric of the radicals – their ready use of "slavery," "corruption," and "conspiracy" to account for the crisis of empire. Rejecting earlier interpretations which dismissed such heated language as simply propaganda, Bailyn contends that the Revolutionaries, inspired by the writings of the radical Whig and opposition politicians of 18th-century England, subscribed to an anxious set of assumptions about human nature, abuses of power, and the survival of liberty in the body politic. In this perspective, parliamentary and ministerial actions after 1763 triggered real fears about corruption among rulers in England and conspiracies against liberty in the colonies.

Wood demonstrates that the radical Whig conceptualization of the dangers posed by power and corruption affected the entire history of the Confederation. WOOD (1969) traces the evolution of political thought among the founding fathers. In 1776, with the specter of British tyranny fresh in their minds, Revolutionary leaders sought to avert future threats against liberty by restraining the actions of executive officers and shifting the locus of power from a central authority to the states. However, the self-interested actions of the various state legislatures and their licentious constituents in the 1780s convinced an increasingly disillusioned leadership that the system needed still to be perfected. All power – executive and legislative, local and federal – had to be checked. The Federalist remedy for the vices of the republic involved an extension of the separation of powers doctrine and an understanding that sovereignty resided not in any body or level of government but only in the people at large.

The relationship between religion and politics, in particular between the Great Awakening and the American Revolution, has been the subject of a substantial number of studies. MAY discusses the context of religious and political thought in 18th-century America. He identifies four major categories of Enlightenment thought – Moderate, Skeptical, Revolutionary, and Didactic – and describes their impact on American Protestantism and Revolutionary ideas about human nature, liberty, order, and contractual government. May relates the fragmentation of the Enlightenment tradition in America to the Revolutionary generation's commitment to radical Whiggism and republicanism. May suggests that the Revolutionary Enlightenment featured both popular enthusiasm and religious radicalism. HEIMERT develops this theme more fully. Contrary to the conventional view, Heimert argues, the champions of liberal rational religion were not in the forefront of the independence movement; rather they were profoundly conservative politically and socially and, therefore, continued to hope well into the 1770s that the "multitudes" might be kept in check, and that some compromise might resolve the lamentable controversy between the colonies and England. It was left to the evangelicals, then, especially the ultra-Calvinists of the Great Awakening, to spearhead the rebellion. Radically communitarian in their social philosophy and convinced that the purpose of public discourse was to drive men and women into action, evangelical preachers inspired the movement toward nationhood and continued to affect the shape of American democracy well into the early 19th-century.

Historians concerned with the question of "who should rule at home" tend to interpret the Revolution as an integral part of the social development of the colonies. HENRETTA and NOBLES incorporate some of the recent findings of the "new" social historians in their short account of the evolution of American society from 1600 to 1820. They trace the roots of the Revolution to the cumulative impact of social divisions and political strife that transformed colonial society and predisposed a destabilized people to seek independence. COUNTRYMAN, more than Henretta and Nobles, concentrates on the period from the 1760s to the 1780s and presents a complex portrait of the Revolution as a multi-faceted movement. The American Revolution bound together many separate changes – social and intellectual – and thus meant different things to different participants. Countryman summarizes recent scholarship on the role of crowds in 18th-century politics and expertly integrates the experiences of ordinary farmers and artisans, women, and blacks into his account of the Revolutionary era.

Some historians focus on the social divisions that animated ordinary men and women to join the independence movement. NASH, the most influential historian in this group, examines the evolution of Boston, New York, and Philadelphia from 1685 to 1776 in making a case for the social origins of the Revolution. By 1776, as a result of demographic trends, economic changes, and the dislocations of intermittent warfare, colonial wealth was less equally distributed and colonists more class-conscious than they had been earlier in the century. Social distress coupled with religious awakening and growing popular participation in politics energized the poor of these port cities to see in the Revolution an opportunity to remake society.

Those who interpret the Revolution as an internal struggle over "who should rule at home" must confront two relevant questions. First, how rigid was the social order of colonial America? MAIN insists that Americans recognized the existence of class distinctions, but that colonial society was so fluid and opportunities for advancement so numerous that class-based resentments could not develop among the lower social orders. The pervasiveness of property ownership and the incidence of social and geographical mobility, especially in "frontier" regions, sustained an unusually egalitarian society in America. JONES attempts to answer a second question confronting scholars who view the Revolution as an internal struggle: how much wealth, regional and individual, had been accumulated by Americans on the eve of independence? Jones applies modern statistical techniques in her examination of 919 sample inventories from 21 counties in ten colonies in 1774. Included in her analysis are estimates of regional differences in wealth distribution, per capita wealth holdings according to age, sex, and occupation, aggregate domestic debts and assets, and comparative colonial inequality. Jones concludes that a composite portrait of the thirteen colonies indicates that wealth inequality rose during the century before independence, but not as dramatically as Nash and others have suggested.

Finally, how revolutionary was the American Revolution? Historians have addressed this question in its various manifestations since the conclusion of the War of Independence. One of the most important and challenging recent assessments is to be found in WOOD (1992) which examines prevailing perceptions of the social and political order in the years before and after independence, and concludes that the American Revolution was as radical as any in history. The Revolution altered the relationships that bound individuals together, undermined the role of social authority in politics, popularized the idea of gentility, released the entrepreneurial energies of ordinary people, redefined the virtues of the masses, and set American society unalterably on its course toward egalitarian democracy. Perhaps the surest measure of the radicalism of the Revolution lies in the anxiety, uneasiness, and growing pessimism of the founding fathers in the decades after independence. They were bewildered by the very forces which they had unleashed in 1776.

Melvin Yazawa

See also War of Independence entries

American Revolution: Causes

Alden, John R., *A History of the American Revolution: Britain and the Loss of the Thirteen Colonies*, New York: Knopf, and London: Macdonald, 1969

Bailyn, Bernard, *The Ideological Origins of the American Revolution*, Cambridge, MA: Belknap Press of Harvard University Press, 1967, revised 1992

Bancroft, George, *History of the United States of America, from the Discovery of the Continent*, 10 vols., Boston: Little Brown, 1834–74; revised (6 vols.), New York: Appleton, 1885

Bonwick, Colin, *The American Revolution*, London: Macmillan, and Charlottesville: University Press of Virginia, 1991

Bridenbaugh, Carl, *The Spirit of '76: The Growth of American Patriotism Before Independence, 1607–1776*, New York: Oxford University Press, 1975

Christie, Ian R. and Benjamin W. Labaree, *Empire or Independence, 1760–1776: A British-American Dialogue on the Coming of the American Revolution*, New York: Norton, and Oxford: Phaidon, 1976

Countryman, Edward, *The American Revolution*, New York: Hill and Wang, and London: Tauris, 1985

Egnal, Marc, *A Mighty Empire: The Origins of the American Revolution*, Ithaca, NY: Cornell University Press, 1988

Gipson, Lawrence Henry, *The Coming of the Revolution, 1763–1775*, New York: Harper, 1954

Jensen, Merrill, *The Founding of a Nation: A History of the American Revolution, 1763–1776*, New York: Oxford University Press, 1968

Maier, Pauline, *From Resistance to Revolution: Colonial Radicals and the Development of American Opposition to Britain, 1765–1776*, New York: Knopf, 1972; London: Routledge, 1973

Middlekauff, Robert, *The Glorious Cause: The American Revolution, 1763–1789*, New York and Oxford: Oxford: Oxford University Press, 1982

Miller, John C., *Origins of the American Revolution*, Boston: Little Brown, 1943

Morgan, Edmund S., *The Birth of the Republic, 1763–89*, Chicago: University of Chicago Press, 1956; 3rd edition, 1992

Nash, Gary B., *The Urban Crucible: Social Change, Political Consciousness, and the Origins of the American Revolution*, Cambridge, MA: Harvard University Press, 1979

Tucker, Robert W. and David C. Hendrickson, *The Fall of the First British Empire: Origins of the War of Independence*, Baltimore: Johns Hopkins University Press, 1982

The Revolution had two principal components: separation from Britain, which many (perhaps most) historians consider to be the more fundamental, and the founding of the republic. This article is concerned principally with the former, and in particular with those processes and immediate events in America which precipitated the outbreak of war and Congress's declaration of independence. Few writers commence their narratives before the end of the Seven Years' or French and Indian War in 1763, but many attach treatment of the war and the establishment of government to narratives of the coming of independence. Although their reasons vary considerably, virtually all historians implicitly agree that the colonies were sufficiently mature to make separation inescapable by the late 18th century.

Nineteenth-century historians took a Whiggish view which celebrated certain principles of progress and ratified their own present day convictions. BANCROFT, a nationalist and Democratic politician, wrote narrative exposition on the grand scale, with emphasis on military and political processes. He interpreted the Revolution as the grand climax of colonial growth and a classic struggle for liberty against British interference in American affairs. Arguing that Americans enjoyed an environment especially favourable to the growth of freedom, he insisted that Americans were God's chosen people and that the hand of Providence was at work in the Revolution. Its success would take mankind further along the road of progress. Begun in the 1830s and revised and extended later, his interpretation is recognised as a major contribution to the development of American culture. Although the details are not always reliable and many judgments have been overtaken by academic scholars, the work remains a masterpiece of imaginative history and literature. A tincture of Bancroft's Whig interpretation remains evident in much modern American scholarship.

The tide turned during the first half of the 20th century. The so-called "imperial school" of historians accepted that the long-term effects of physical environment, historical growth and cultural development made a clash inevitable, but interpreted the Revolution within the framework of a benign imperial administration. Viewing the crisis as much from London as from the colonies, they argued that British officials were intelligent and well-intentioned men faced with an acutely difficult problem. GIPSON, the only scholar so far to match Bancroft's broad sweep, succinctly articulates the argument developed in his fifteen-volume study of the mid-century empire. British officials failed to realise that the old system of imperial control was inappropriate to a sophisticated society after 1763, and colonial radicals failed to realise that their words and actions were provocative of coercion, which in turn suited those who wished to overturn the old system in favour of a new one. Yet Gipson's treatment of the 1770s is very brief and discussion of the outbreak of war and decision to declare independence sketchy and very insufficient.

MORGAN takes the opposite view. In a brief but elegantly written study, he argues that the Revolutionary crisis revolved round political principles which came to a successful conclusion in the federal Constitution. Though loyal members of the empire, Americans were obliged to defend their freedom against successive threats from incompetent and increasingly authoritarian British governments. Responsibility for the Revolution lay in London.

Many historians of the 1950s, writing at the same time as Morgan, were influenced by Progressive economic and social theories. For some the Revolution became an act of economic emancipation; others argued that the Revolution should also be seen as an internal class conflict. Economic interpretations generally came to a climax with independence, but social interpretations usually did so in conflicts over establishing new governments. This work is mostly located in specialised literature, but to a considerable extent the various threads are incorporated in MILLER. The principal themes of the defence of American liberty, economic interest and internal social conflict are traced in a firm and well-balanced narrative exposition, which though somewhat traditional in its judgment on Britain is by no means coarsely unsympathetic. It stands up remarkably well in spite of the prodigious expansion of writing during the decades that followed, and in some ways remains the broadest discussion of its subject.

JENSEN is a detailed political narrative of the intricate events during the crucial period between 1763 and 1776 which deliberately avoids any search for "causes" and "principles". It is dispassionate and trustworthy in its description of worsening Anglo-American relations, but ignores social, economic and intellectual processes. By focussing so consistently on political narrative it implies that the founding of the nation was coincident with the crisis in imperial relations. Yet, as other historians were conclusively demonstrating, the process was far more complex than that.

ALDEN, who covers the war as well as the coming of the Revolution, is disappointingly traditional in his approach. He rejects Bancroft's thesis of divine intention, but nevertheless describes the unfolding of an ineluctable process. The colonies were already mature by 1763, and it was British pressure which drove them to unity and independence. However, his discussion of British politicians and their policies is shallow and gauche; to that extent he diminishes the work of the revolutionary generation and creates little sense that difficult decisions were required.

CHRISTIE and LABAREE end their book in 1776, and create a far greater sense of men wrestling with difficult problems. Their analysis is unusually well balanced, in good measure because the British historian traces the government's side entirely separately from the American scholar's exposition of the colonial side. The outcome is a successful collaboration in which the balance significantly changes from heavy concentration on the British side in the early stages to preponderant attention to America as the crisis moves towards independence. They tentatively attribute the collapse of the first British empire to the inadequacy (among Americans and British alike) of those human powers of mind and will necessary to grasp the full implications of political situations and thus discover peaceful evolutionary solutions to the problems they pose.

TUCKER and HENDRICKSON examine the loss of the empire as a political problem confronting successive British governments. However, the focal point of their argument remains the colonies, for they argue that the imperial collapse, like its expansion, was the consequence of a series of profound upheavals and challenges on the periphery, not the product of a new attitude towards empire in the metropolis. Colonial expectations grew after 1763 to the point where they wished to be free from external control. In the end the crisis boiled down to a question of sovereignty, and opposition politicians had a solution no more convincing than the government's instrument of coercion. As political scientists, Tudor and Henderson are less concerned with continuous narrative than hard-headed analysis, and given their assumptions their argument possesses great power.

MIDDLEKAUFF starts at the same point but continues to 1789. About two-fifths of the book is a narrative of events leading to war. As part of a general history intended for a non-professional audience, the style is popular and the approach traditional: events unfold until they reach their inevitable climax. Treatment of successive British governments is simplistic, occasionally to the point of caricature, and the explanation of the Revolution is found in the structure of colonial society and its intellect. Middlekauff makes relatively little use of the extensive monographic literature on social, economic and even intellectual developments.

Both Countryman and Bonwick also cover domestic affairs after 1776, but each devotes attention to the coming of the Revolution. COUNTRYMAN is the first general exposition drawing on recent social scholarship and written from the perspective of the "New Left". He is less concerned with the details of political disputes with Britain than many writers, and, without advancing a reductionist thesis of class conflict, demonstrates that the Revolution was the work of common people as well as elites. BONWICK provides broad coverage. He discusses long-term processes and social relationships but pays attention to the activities of elites and details of the worsening political crisis. He argues that, although separation was virtually certain in the very long run, it was not inevitable in 1776, but he also interprets it primarily as a necessary prerequisite to the central process of founding the republic.

Among the rich monographic literature a number of books stand out by virtue of offering general theories. All have aroused great controversy. BAILYN dominates the field to the extent that virtually everything published since either develops or attacks his thesis. Preferring causal analysis to systematic narrative, his interpretation restores the defence of liberty to the heart of the process, and has been labelled "Neo-Whig" even though it lacks the crude conviction of progress and American virtue which characterised earlier writing. Drawing on the extensive pamphlet literature of the dispute, he argues that the colonists were convinced that the disposition of power lay at the heart of every political controversy and that liberty was its natural victim. As the imperial crisis worsened, Americans became increasingly convinced that they were victims of a British conspiracy to destroy their liberty. Inflamed sensibilities and the consequent sense of the need to defend their liberty – and not economic or social forces – gave American resistance its distinctive cast.

His student, MAIER, takes Bailyn's argument about libertarian ideology and incorporates it into an analysis of social and economic movements and the growing sense of disillusionment with Britain. She demonstrates how and why opposition to British policy in America slowly became transformed into armed resistance and finally into republicanism. She also extends his concern with intellectual arguments expressed through the printed word to riotous behaviour and other forms of popular political action. To a considerable extent the two books match each other.

BRIDENBAUGH stands outside the mainstream of contemporary American scholarship, partly because he takes a far longer timespan. Both his methodology, which is impressionistic and predominantly literary, and his thesis are unfashionable, and can also be described as "Neo-Whig". In a brief and highly stimulating book, he paints a broad picture of cultural processes which had begun with the first settlements and which he argues had already produced a distinctly American society by 1760; a sense of patriotism and nationalism had emerged in a mature society possessed of an increasingly strong sense of unity. In his view the Revolution had taken place well before the outbreak of war, and the Spirit of '76 was the culmination of everything that had gone before.

NASH's study challenges the traditional view of virtually automatic social progress in an overwhelmingly rural society by arguing that the Revolution was also a social upheaval in which seaport towns were at the leading edge. Class divisions and growing political consciousness among the labouring classes made them crucibles of revolutionary agitation and shaped the coming of the Revolution. The book's great merit is that it recognises artisans as autonomous actors and places them at the heart of the Revolution.

EGNAL reverts to an economic interpretation, though one which differs markedly from earlier explanations of the break from Britain. He challenges the "Neo-Whig" thesis on the ground of excessive concentration on political and intellectual issues as the driving force. But he also challenges the "New Left" thesis that the lower classes played a determining initiating role by pointing out that in no colony did they gain control of the revolutionary movement. Instead, he argues that in each colony the rebellion was led by an upper-class faction whose commitment to fostering America's rise to greatness was evident well before 1763. The struggle within America was between expansionists with a continental vision for the future, and those who were less confident and emphasized a continuing need for close ties with the mother country.

Historians towards the end of the 20th century still generally neglect grand comprehensive analysis in favour of close examination of micro-processes. Their scholarship is often superb, but too many imply that general conclusions can be confidently inferred from particular circumstances and specialized arguments.

COLIN BONWICK

American Revolution: Development of a Crisis, 1763-1770

Bullion, John L., *A Great and Necessary Measure: George Grenville and the Genesis of the Stamp Act, 1763–1765*, Columbia: Univerity of Missouri Press, 1982

Christie, Ian R. and Benjamin W. Labaree, *Empire or Independence, 1760–1776: A British-American Dialogue on the Coming of the American Revolution*, New York: Norton, and Oxford: Phaidon, 1976

Knollenberg, Bernhard, *Origin of the American Revolution, 1759–1766*, New York: Macmillan, 1960, revised 1961

Langford, Paul, *The First Rockingham Administration, 1765–1766*, Oxford: Oxford University Press, 1973

Maier, Pauline, *From Resistance to Revolution: Colonial Radicals and the Development of American Opposition to Britain, 1765–1776*, New York: Knopf, 1972; London: Routledge, 1973

Morgan, Edmund S., *The Stamp Act Crisis: Prologue to Revolution*, Chapel Hill: University of North Carolina Press, 1953; revised, with Helen M. Morgan, New York: Collier, 1963

Thomas, P.D.G., *British Politics and the Stamp Act Crisis: The First Phase of the American Revolution, 1763–1767*, Oxford: Clarendon Press, 1975

Thomas, P.D.G., *The Townshend Duties Crisis: The Second Phase of the American Revolution, 1767–1773*, Oxford: Clarendon Press, and New York: Oxford University Press, 1987

Tucker, Robert W. and David C. Hendrickson, *The Fall of the First British Empire: Origins of the War of Independence*, Baltimore: Johns Hopkins University Press, 1982

Historians continue to debate the precise causes and timing of the First British Empire's collapse. Although Jack P. Greene and others trace the origins of the troubles to Lord Halifax's reform programme of the late 1740s, KNOLLENBERG sees the years 1759 to 1764 as pivotal. During that period, he argues, a series of provocative British measures brought the colonies to the brink of rebellion. Each of these steps was irksome enough individually; their concentration in the brief span of five years transformed irritation into revolt. In ascribing blame for the ensuing crisis, Knollenberg therefore fixes his eye firmly on the arbitrary and unwise actions of the British. He indicates, however, that they resulted less from a calculated plot to destroy colonial liberties than from the "distracted state of British politics" and the inexperience of George III's new ministers.

For Knollenberg, then, the Stamp Act touched off the colonial outburst of 1765–66 but did not cause it. Most scholars, however, attribute more importance to that controversial measure. A readable and instructive work, MORGAN and MORGAN is an essential starting-point for understanding this critical phase of the breakdown in imperial-colonial relations. The authors convincingly show how the events of 1765 put Britain and America on a collision course. In the wake of the Stamp Act, most colonial leaders categorically denied to Parliament the right to levy external revenue duties as well as internal taxes. However, because the American position was misrepresented by both the Rockingham ministry and Benjamin Franklin in order to secure the measure's repeal, it was misunderstood initially by many British politicians and subsequently by historians.

Several works focus on the formulation of imperial policy during the mid-1760s. In a well-written monograph, BULLION carefully outlines the origins and development of George Grenville's American programme and how he steered it through Parliament. Using essentially familiar materials such as the papers of Charles Jenkinson, he concentrates on developing a more complete understanding of the motives of the first lord of the Treasury from Lord Bute's resignation to the Rockingham ministry's formation. To his credit, these events are located firmly against the backcloth of the first decade of George III's reign. LANGFORD attempts a re-interpretation of the Rockingham administration. While acknowledging his basic incompetence, inarticulateness, and general unworthiness for the post of prime minister, Langford concedes that his strategy of repealing (not modifying) the Stamp Act and buying off conservative opposition with the Declaratory Act was judicious. Indeed, he lauds it as "the most sensible colonial policy of any statesman of those years."

Providing one of the most cogent analyses to date, THOMAS (1975) also looks at the British background to the Stamp Act in a thoroughly-researched study. He insists that the Rockingham ministry never intended to enforce the measure. Instead, its strategy was to persuade Parliament to repeal the act by highlighting its disastrous economic consequences. However, Thomas ignores the Morgans' suggestion that the Declaratory Act was far more significant than the Stamp Act. Instead, he accepts the standard but debatable interpretation that it was a necessary preliminary to the latter measure's repeal.

THOMAS (1987) examines the middle period of the pre-Revolutionary crisis, from the demise of the Stamp Act to the Boston Tea Party. Once again he concentrates almost exclusively on Westminster and Whitehall politics. But, within these self-imposed limits, Thomas provides a full and convincing account of the ministerial maneuverings shaping American policy. Though no clear thesis develops out of this essentially narrative account, two telling points emerge. First, Thomas confirms that the main objective of the Townshend duties was political rather than fiscal: to create a civil list and so weaken the power of the assemblies. Second, according to Thomas, the differences among parliamentary factions over colonial policy were minor compared to their shared insistence upon Parliamentary sovereignty over America. In other words, there was little hope of a peaceable rapprochement between Britain and its colonies.

MAIER reinforces this conclusion. Weaving narrative and analysis, she traces the escalating opposition to imperial authority beginning with the Stamp Act crisis. Whereas initially American "radicals" remained loyal subjects and attempted to organize an ordered resistance, their perception changed over time. They came to oppose British sovereignty itself, not merely certain aspects of imperial legislation. Maier concentrates principally on the colonial leadership and the organizations they created, notably the Sons of Liberty. However, she also looks at their relationship with their popular following. What bound them together more than anything else was the Real Whig tradition. Drawing on Bernard Bailyn's influential work, Maier shows how this ideology played a crucial role in shaping American perceptions of British actions.

Among the more interesting overviews of the revolutionary crisis are CHRISTIE and LABAREE and Tucker and Hendrickson. The former is a collaborative venture between two prominent scholars, one British and one American. While acknowledging the importance of personality and contingency, Christie shows how notions of empire incompatible with American aspirations were so pervasive in Parliament before 1776 that very few statesmen could transcend them. For his part, Labaree provides a balanced, if conventional, appraisal of the colonists' motives. In particular, he shows how economic considerations became overshadowed by the constitutional implications of parliamentary taxation and later by "the basic issue of legislative power within the Empire and its limitations". The juxtaposition of the two individual contributions has the added advantage of starkly revealing the fundamental incompatibility of ministerial and "patriot" perceptions of the imperial crisis.

Written by two political scientists, TUCKER and HENDRICKSON challenges some earlier major interpretations of events. According to them, Whig scholars were mistaken because they sought the causes of the Revolution in conspiracies among ill-disposed politicians. Both the imperial school and the Namierists erred in searching for the origins of the crisis at the empire's heart. Economic determinists were wrong because the real reasons for the Revolution were political, even narrowly constitutional. Instead the authors insist that the First British Empire's breakdown emerged not out of a change in perception in London, but out of new attitudes, challenges, and capacities in the colonies themselves.

KEITH MASON

American Revolution: Development of a Crisis, 1770-1775

Ammerman, David L., *In the Common Cause: American Response to the Coercive Acts of 1774*, Charlottesville: University Press of Virginia, 1974

Brown, Richard D., *Revolutionary Politics in Massachusetts: The Boston Committee of Correspondence and the Towns, 1772–1774*, Cambridge, MA: Harvard University Press, 1970

Donoughue, Bernard, *British Politics and the American Revolution: The Path to War, 1773–1775*, London: Macmillan, and New York: St. Martin's Press, 1964

Fischer, David Hackett, *Paul Revere's Ride*, New York: Oxford University Press, 1994

Gross, Robert A., *The Minutemen and Their World*, New York: Hill and Wang, 1976

Marston, Jerrilyn Greene, *King and Congress: The Transfer of Political Legitimacy, 1774–1776*, Princeton: Princeton University Press, 1987

Nash, Gary B., *The Urban Crucible: Social Change, Political Consciousness, and the Origins of the American Revolution*, Cambridge, MA: Harvard University Press, 1979

Thomas, P.D.G., *Tea Party to Independence: The Third Phase of the American Revolution, 1773–1776*, Oxford: Clarendon Press, and New York: Oxford University Press, 1991

Scholars have approached the final descent into war and revolution from a variety of angles. Some authors understandably concentrate on the British background. A readable and detailed account, DONOUGHUE provides a reliable introduction to imperial policy from the Boston Tea Party to the outbreak of hostilities. However, his main conclusions are not startlingly original. He merely reiterates arguments that have been long familiar to historians: the Anglo-American quarrel was by 1774 a struggle over sovereignty; the opposition to the North ministry was both divided and inhibited by Rockingham's commitment to the Declaratory Act; the Quebec Act was not, whatever its consequences, designed as a coercive measure; British merchants were no longer an effective lobby against restrictive legislation; and the elections of 1774 were fought mainly on local issues and were only to a very small extent a barometer of opinion on the American question.

Completing his trilogy on the breakdown of relations between Britain and the colonies from the end of the Seven Years' War to the Declaration of Independence, THOMAS inevitably covers similar ground. This volume's most striking characteristic is its almost glowing portrayal of the North government. According to Thomas, the ministry was initially resourceful in its quest for solutions to the crisis and he commends it for its moderate yet resolute defense of Parliamentary supremacy in the wake of the Boston Tea Party: of the so-called Coercive Acts only the Port Act merited such a description. And, in an interesting reversal of orthodox historical judgment, Thomas even compares the statesmanship of these measures favourably with the folly of the Quebec Act. But just why the British government should be applauded for moderation while the colonists are condemned for rigidity is hard to understand. On the basis of Thomas's own evidence both sides were locked into irreconcilable positions. North was as reluctant to breach the principle of parliamentary sovereignty as the colonists were to endorse it.

Other historians focus on political developments within the restless colonies. BROWN examines the focal point of American resistance, Massachusetts. The study provides an excellent account of the Boston Committee of Correspondence and its relationship with neighbouring communities. Drawing on minute books and correspondence, it sheds light both on the committee's actual proceedings and on the ideological context in which it functioned. Brown highlights its moderate, cautious, almost self-effacing stance, while arguing that the "Radical Whig" rhetoric of the Revolution overlapped with earlier communitarian ideals and hence buttressed traditional values without significantly altering them.

A slim, well-written volume, AMMERMAN concentrates on a single year, March 1774 to April 1775, in order to ascertain what moved the bickering colonists, after the battle of Lexington, to confront Britain with "remarkable unanimity". Striving to catch the action at both levels, he moves easily from individual colonies to the Continental Congress and back again. Perhaps the most rewarding section is on the local committees. In analyzing their numerical expansion, Ammerman uncovers surprising breadth in the Revolutionary movement. Strikingly, large numbers of activists came from the hitherto passive middle classes and obtained an education in political and social consciousness through their participation. His analysis therefore has obvious implications for the debate over the Revolution's internal dimension.

As its sub-title suggests, MARSTON carefully and methodically outlines the "transfer of political legitimacy" to the Continental Congress during the years 1774–76. This began when the king became directly implicated in the British response to the American resistance movement, thereby loosening the last thread binding the colonies to the metropolis. Noting that the revolutionaries might then have moved in a variety of directions as they established a new political entity, she concludes that "they virtually remade the resistance organization of 1774, the Continental Congress, into a true continental government by molding it into as close a replica as circumstances would allow of the old imperial executive".

Social historians also provide considerable insight into the forces propelling the colonists towards independence. Some highlight the importance of internal tensions. NASH, for example, examines the struggle for political control among the various social groups protesting English rule in the cities of Philadelphia, New York, and Boston. For him, this contest was marked by "the rise of a radical political consciousness ... the crumbling of the elite's cultural hegemony, and the final assaults on the old political order". Nash has uncovered significant manifestations of lower-class consciousness. More important, he has related them successfully to political behaviour and thereby enriched our understanding of the American Revolution's complexity. But, as the urban gentry lost control only in Philadelphia, his characterization of pre-revolutionary struggles within the cities as a "profound social upheaval" perhaps seems exaggerated.

GROSS attempts to re-create the world of late 18th-century Concord, a community that holds a key place in accounts of the outbreak of the Revolution. Combining a detailed narrative with a quantitatively-based new social history, he argues that factional, religious, and generational conflicts racked the town due to the growing scarcity of land. The mounting hostility between the colonies and Great Britain simply intensified the strain on the inhabitants. The Revolution itself, Gross suggests, had a paradoxical effect. The minutemen fought to protect an older world from imperial and commercial encroachments, but only succeeded in creating a forward-looking, modern community. He concludes by tracing the transformation of Concord from the home of the minutemen to the domicile of Henry David Thoreau.

FISCHER is a lively, lavishly-illustrated, and gripping account of a familiar event that successfully highlights the importance of contingency and individual choice in the coming of the War of Independence. But in describing the respective roles of Paul Revere and General Thomas Gage, he also sheds light on the deep-seated clash of cultural values that helped to provoke the imperial crisis.

KEITH MASON

American Revolution: Character, Scope, and Significance

Andrews, Charles M., *The Colonial Background of the American Revolution*, New Haven: Yale University Press, 1924

Bailyn, Bernard, *The Ideological Origins of the American Revolution*, Cambridge, MA: Belknap Press of Harvard University Press, 1967, revised 1992

Bancroft, George, *History of the United States of America, from the Discovery of the Continent*, 10 vols., Boston: Little Brown, 1834–74; revised (6 vols.), New York: Appleton, 1885

Beard, Charles A., *An Economic Interpretation of the Constitution of the United States*, New York: Macmillan, 1913; with new Introduction, New York: Free Press, 1986

Becker, Carl L., *The Declaration of Independence: A Study in the History of Political Ideas*, New York: Harcourt Brace, 1922

Countryman, Edward, *The American Revolution*, New York: Hill and Wang, and London: Tauris, 1985

Greene, Jack P. (editor), *The American Revolution: Its Character and Limits*, New York: New York University Press, 1987

Jameson, J. Franklin, *The American Revolution Considered as a Social Movement*, Princeton: Princeton University Press, 1926

Kramnick, Isaac, *Republicanism and Bourgeois Radicalism: Political Ideology in Late Eighteenth-Century England and America*, Ithaca, NY: Cornell University Press, 1990

Morgan, Edmund S., *The Birth of the Republic, 1763–89*, Chicago: University of Chicago Press, 1956; 3rd edition, 1992

Pocock, J.G.A., *The Machiavellian Moment: Florentine Political Thought and the Atlantic Republican Tradition*, Princeton: Princeton University Press, 1975

Wood, Gordon S., *The Creation of the American Republic, 1776–1787*, Chapel Hill: University of North Carolina Press, 1969

Opinion on the character of the Revolution has often depended on assessments of the motives of participants, and opinion on the Revolution's scope and significance has depended on whether it was seen as a united colonial revolt or whether and to what extent it entailed economic, social, and political conflicts and transformations within the colonies. BANCROFT portrayed the Revolution as an uprising by selfless patriots, undivided by varying interests and rivalries, against an overbearing Britain and, written during the slavery controversy, presented this in "Whig" fashion as a defence of liberty against tyranny.

With growing industrial and urban poverty and burgeoning American imperialism at the turn of the century, however, historians challenged this view in two ways. First, ANDREWS, of the "imperial school," argued that far from imposing tyranny, the British tax measures which sparked conflict were perfectly reasonable exactions designed to defray the enormous debt legacy of the French and Indian War (1754–63). Far from preserving liberty, then, the colonists, the principal beneficiaries of that war, were little more than ungrateful tax evaders. The second challenge was to the "consensus" view of colonists as a united people. BEARD, of the "Progressive" school, argued that upper-class Americans served their own economic self-interests not only at the expense of Britain but also of other colonists. For him, the Constitution of 1787, providing for a strong government and a controlled economy, was the means whereby the wealthy could revalue their investments in government bonds, many of which they had purchased from ordinary soldiers who had received them as wages, but relinquished them at depreciated rates to pay their debts during the post-war depression. The Constitution was thus a betrayal of the principles of liberty and equality represented by the Declaration of Independence of 1776. BECKER further developed this theme, claiming that the Revolution was not only about American independence, or "home rule," but was also an internal political conflict over "who shall rule at home," in which many ordinary people challenged the economic, social, and political dominance of local elites and for the first time laid their own claims to equal political representation within America. JAMESON took this point further still, arguing that internal social pressures were part of the causes of the Revolution and that economic, social, and political advancements for ordinary people were the most significant consequences. Much more than a colonial revolt, then, he portrayed a "social revolution" comparable to that of France, though obviously less bloody.

In the economic abundance of the 1950s, and following the World War II defeat of Nazi tyranny but facing the Cold War threat of Soviet tyranny, MORGAN resurrected the Whig view of united colonists resisting overseas oppression. He and others successfully refuted Beard's claim that the Founding Fathers received direct economic gain from the Constitution, and, through emphasizing the works of Revolutionary pamphleteers, once again made imperial affairs the focus of the Revolution. BAILYN revised this Neo-Whig interpretation, though, arguing, like the "imperial" scholars, that Britain was merely seeking recompense for colonial wars and administration. Yet colonists were ideologically pre-disposed to interpret British measures as tyrannous because they were influenced by a number of streams of thought, most particularly 18th-century English country party opposition thought, as represented by Trenchard and Gordon. In what amounted to a renewed Whig interpretation of history, they viewed the world as a battle-ground of always endangered liberty and ever lurking tyranny. WOOD views colonists as even more tradition-minded than Bailyn does, arguing that 18th-century ideology was "essentially medieval." His work inspired the "republican synthesis" view of the Revolution as a battle of American public or civic "virtue," the selfless pursuit of the common weal, against British "corruption," the pursuit of individual betterment often at the expense of the public interest. POCOCK, the exemplar of this school, traces "republicanism" to ancient Greece and Rome, sees it revived by Machiavelli, and thus views the American Revolution as "the last great act of the renaissance."

KRAMNICK criticizes this interpretation for its emphasis on the backward-looking conservatism of "classical republicanism," and sees the Revolution as characterized more by the forward-looking, materialistic, and individualistic Lockean "liberal" thought common to the ascendant bourgeoisie in the market-oriented Atlantic world. COUNTRYMAN criticizes the Neo-Whigs for their "consensus" interpretation, and presents a "neo-Progressive" view that the Revolution was actuated by internal colonial social divisions. He sees it as partly caused by, and its consequences as largely determined by, a struggle of the "lower sort" and some "middling" people, whose "traditional corporatism" privileged the greater good over individual property rights, against some middling and many of the "better sort" of people who were more involved in Atlantic trade, and who held to an ideology which emphasized private property rights and the free market. Thus the Revolutionary struggle was entangled in the conflicts of the "transition to capitalism." While capitalism became ascendant it was resisted by ordinary people, including the poor, free and enslaved blacks, native Americans, immigrants, and many women, all of whom made some political gains by using their demographic preponderance which was crucial to the achievement of independence.

Through "crowd actions" and involvement in popular committees throughout the Revolution, people who had previously been uninvolved in politics established their own liberties and political rights. They thereby created a tradition through which other groups, notably women and blacks, have since laid further claims to civil rights and political equality so that the scope and significance of the American Revolution was perhaps even greater than that of the French. GREENE sees the Revolution as animated more by a liberal consensus, and views the gains made by ordinary people as either minimal or as caused by longer-term developments. But his collection of 22 essays contains the differing viewpoints of a great range of people, and perhaps shows above all that the Revolution's character, scope, and significance varied greatly according to the class, race, ethnicity, gender, locality, place of origin, and ideological disposition of particular participants.

STEVEN J. SARSON

See also Constitution entries; War of Independence entries

Anthony, Susan B.   1820-1906
Campaigner for women's rights

Anticaglia, Elizabeth, *Twelve American Women*, Chicago: Nelson Hall, 1975
Barry, Kathleen, *Susan B. Anthony: A Biography of a Singular Feminist*, New York: New York University Press, 1988
Buhle, Mari Jo and Paul Buhle (editors), *The Concise History of Woman Suffrage: Selections from the Classic Work of Stanton, Anthony, Gage, and Harper*, Urbana: University of Illinois Press, 1978
Burnett, Constance, *Five for Freedom: Lucretia Mott, Elizabeth Cady Stanton, Lucy Stone, Susan B. Anthony, Carrie Chapman Catt*, New York: Abelard Press, 1953
Edwards, Thomas G., *Sowing Good Seeds: The Northwest Suffrage Campaigns of Susan B. Anthony*, Portland: Oregon Historical Society Press, 1990
Flexner, Eleanor, *Century of Struggle: The Woman's Rights Movement in the United States*, Cambridge, MA: Harvard University Press, 1959, revised 1975
Gurko, Miriam, *The Ladies of Seneca Falls: The Birth of the Woman's Rights Movement*, New York: Macmillan, 1974.
Harper, Ida, *Life and Work of Susan B. Anthony*, 3 vols., Indianapolis: Bowen Merrill, 1898–1908; reprinted, 1 vol., New York: Arno Press, 1969
Kugler, Israel, *From Ladies to Women: The Organized Struggle for Woman's Rights in the Reconstruction Era*, New York: Greenwood Press, 1987
Lutz, Alma, *Susan B. Anthony: Rebel, Crusader, and Humanitarian*, Boston: Beacon Press, 1960

To many, Susan B. Anthony was the cornerstone of the United States' woman suffrage movement. In over half a century of service to that cause, she provided motivation and leadership for an untold number of woman suffragists. Still, as with so many women leaders, scholarly writing about Anthony remained sparse until well into the 1960s. Renewed interest in women's history in recent years has served her well, however, and sparked re-evaluation of Anthony both in terms of modern feminist theory and women's history.

For decades, HARPER's three volumes provided the most complete biography of Anthony. As a close friend and reform colleague, Harper originally envisioned her work as a collaborative effort designed to help Anthony produce an autobiography. Although Harper eventually took the lead role in writing the text, the first two volumes were not only written during Anthony's life, but produced while the author lived with her subject on the Anthony homestead. This led to an account that is less than objective, but one that provides valuable insight from the perspective of an Anthony intimate.

The first comprehensive examination of Anthony's life to be finished after her death was LUTZ. Published in 1960, this work embodies much of the compensatory spirit common in women's histories of that decade. Nevertheless, it provided the first, much needed, one-volume account of Anthony's life. In all, Lutz is a very readable condensation of the extensive detail provided by Harper and has been an important resource on which a number of authors have drawn.

There are chapter-length essays on Anthony in both Burnett and Anticaglia. BURNETT admits that her motive for writing her book stemmed from her belief that the efforts of women leaders deserved wider notice. In a group of essays on Anthony and her reform colleagues – Lucretia Mott, Lucy Stone, Elizabeth Cady Stanton, and Carrie Chapman Catt – Burnett emphasizes Anthony's success in transforming woman suffrage from an eccentric campaign whose leaders were ostracized, into a socially acceptable reform movement. Burnett communicates this message in a chapter divided into sixteen short narratives on various aspects of Anthony's life. When taken together, these vignettes appear as snapshots of a developing reformer and reform movement. ANTICAGLIA names Anthony among twelve women whom she describes as having a lasting impact on American civilization. She explores the lives of these women, ranging from post-American Revolution educator Emma Willard to 20th-century anthropologist Margaret Mead, in short biographical chapters that concentrate on recounting outstanding women's lives rather than providing analytical insight into their characters. In her chapter on Anthony, Anticaglia draws heavily on Lutz. As such, she provides a compact retelling of information found in other sources. Her work is suitable for readers seeking a concise review of Anthony's life that can easily be read at one sitting.

A more wide-ranging study that places Anthony in the context of other women reformers is GURKO. In addition to a chapter-length biography of Anthony, she offers extensive analysis of Anthony's relationship with other key suffrage reformers. Focusing on the women who participated in the 1848 Woman's Rights Convention in Seneca Falls, New York, Gurko shows how that meeting motivated Anthony and others. Although she acknowledges that Anthony did not attend the Seneca Falls session, Gurko identifies that gathering as a crucial factor in spurring Anthony to become involved in suffrage reform. FLEXNER, and BUHLE and BUHLE, two seminal texts on the American woman suffrage movement, offer thorough explanations of Anthony's role in winning the franchise for women. Neither book has a chapter devoted specifically to Anthony, but both are helpful in providing a general understanding of the suffrage movement, and in describing Anthony's role as one of its major leaders.

Among the books most critical of Anthony is KUGLER, who portrays her as radical, ruthless, and in many cases anti-male. Concentrating on the woman's rights movement of the post-Civil War years, Kugler emphasizes the growing rift in the movement, a split eventually formalized in the establishment of the National Woman Suffrage Association led by Anthony and Elizabeth Cady Stanton and the rival American Woman Suffrage Association led by Lucy Stone. Additionally, Kugler incorporates an appraisal of Anthony's involvement with women's organized labor in the 1870s. In Kugler's view, this aspect of Anthony's reform efforts has been played down by Flexner and others.

EDWARDS concentrates upon Anthony's activities in the Northwest on behalf of women's suffrage. In his estimation, Anthony's trips to Oregon, Washington, Victoria, and British Columbia in 1871, 1896, and 1905 were turning points in her career because they marked her first full-fledged suffrage campaign outside her home state of New York. Among the most appealing aspects of Edwards is his ability to show the daily drudgery of suffrage campaigning by describing the fear, sickness, problems of travel, and emotional anguish which Anthony experienced on her trip. His work aptly documents the difficulty of local suffrage work in the West, while showing Anthony as a developing leader in the national woman suffrage movement.

BARRY portrays Anthony as a woman who renounced her era's social prescriptions of womanhood to create a self-image based on egalitarianism. Acknowledging her gratitude to radical feminism for creating an ideological context for her study, Barry argues that Anthony's decisions to remain unmarried, and to focus her efforts primarily on woman suffrage in an era when a number of different reform movements vied for attention, were political choices designed to establish the possibility of women's independence. Barry argues forcefully that Anthony rejected the roles of both wife and old maid, creating instead an autonomous identity supported by a fulfilling reform career. This is the only work to employ modern feminist theory in assessing Anthony's life.

EMILY WALKER COOK

See also Women's History: Suffrage

Anticommunism

Donner, Frank, *Protectors of Privilege: Red Squads and Police Repression in Urban America*, Berkeley: University of California Press, 1990

Heale, M.J., *American Anticommunism: Combating the Enemy Within, 1830–1970*, Baltimore: Johns Hopkins University Press, 1990

Higham, John, *Strangers in the Land: Patterns of American Nativism, 1860–1925*, New Brunswick, NJ: Rutgers University Press, 1955, corrected reprint, 1963; 2nd edition, 1988

Kovel, Joel, *Red Hunting in the Promised Land: Anticommunism and the Making of America*, New York: Basic Books, 1994

Murray, Robert K., *Red Scare: A Study in National Hysteria, 1919–1920*, Minneapolis: University of Minnesota Press, 1955

Navasky, Victor S., *Naming Names*, New York: Viking, 1980, London: Calder, 1982; revised, New York: Penguin, 1991

Schrecker, Ellen W., *No Ivory Tower: McCarthyism and the Universities*, New York: Oxford University Press, 1986

In view of the powerful influence that anticommunism has exerted in modern American life, it remains surprisingly little studied. Most relevant historical works focus on a particular period or instance of anticommunism, most notably 1950s McCarthyism; very few examine the wider phenomenon over time. Studies of either type generally fall into either "rational" or "irrational" explanations for anticommunism.

In the former group, one of the earliest case studies of anticommunism was MURRAY. Pointedly appearing soon after the height of McCarthyism, Murray is a straightforward but thorough narrative of America's first real "Red Scare," the wave of anticommunist repression and hysteria that swept the country in the aftermath of World War I. He blames wartime propaganda for much of the atmosphere of tension. However, he never really explains why such virulent anticommunism surfaced when it did, attributing it somewhat vaguely to a snowballing hysteria propelled largely by fear of the Russian October Revolution. He ends with a liberal plea for civil liberties clearly aimed at contemporary McCarthyites.

Navasky and Schrecker are two of the more interesting examples of the fairly large and growing literature on the anticommunism of the McCarthy era. NAVASKY's focus is on Hollywood during the highly publicised hearings of the House Committee on Un-American Activities (HUAC), and especially on those who "named names," or informed on friends, acquaintances and colleagues connected to the Communist Party. Navasky examines what he calls the "degradation ceremonies" of HUAC's inquisitional hearings, and their development of an "informer principle" by which naming names became the greatest proof of patriotism. But most of all, this fastidiously even-handed study is what Navasky calls a "moral detective story" to uncover why the informants broke societal norms of loyalty even when they knew it would destroy the careers of innocent people. He concludes that most did so simply to protect or advance their own careers. He also blames the cowardice of Americans for Democratic Action (ADA) and American Civil Liberties Union (ACLU) liberals desperate to avoid charges that they themselves were communist sympathisers.

SCHRECKER lays even more blame on quiescent liberals in her important study of university life under McCarthyism. Backed by massive research, she targets the complicity of university administrators and faculty, above all in carrying out the more devastating stage of the HUAC process – firing those who would not name names. Despite the fact that no academic was ever charged with any crime under the various anti-subversion laws of the era, and the fact that most leftists were critical of the Communist Party, the universities fired hundreds

of them. She sees these failings as irretrievably damaging both research and the moral integrity of the academy as well as individual lives.

Anticommunism has proved harder to analyse as a phenomenon in itself, in part perhaps because it was for so long such a normal part of American life, a political philosophy embraced by almost all public figures. Nevertheless, HIGHAM's pathbreaking and still indispensable study of nativism appeared during the McCarthy era. Higham sees nativism as one of the main roots of American nationalism, and anti-radicalism in turn as one of the three principal strands of nativism (the other two are racism and anti-Catholicism). Stemming principally from a distrust of the anti-republican Old World, fear of European political currents was boosted massively by the events of the Paris Commune in 1871. Anti-radicalism grew through the violent industrial upheavals and strikes of the 1880s and intensified in the "nationalist '90s." Higham finds a psychological explanation, in the shape of periodic bouts of national insecurity over America's future, both for nativism in general, and for the anti-radicalism and the specific anticommunism into which it developed towards the end of his chosen period. By the time of the early 1920s, he concludes, anticommunism had eclipsed anti-Catholicism and become the main ingredient of nativist nationalism.

DONNER focuses on the mechanics of state anticommunist repression. Although he begins with a useful chapter on the origins of modern anticommunism in the Tompkins Square riot of 1874, the Haymarket affair of 1886, and the 1919–20 Red Scare, he focuses mostly on the 1960s. Then, he argues, the chief concern of police forces switched from public order to an obsession with "intelligence" on radical groups, African Americans, and critics of the police. An ACLU official, Donner sees anticommunism as a more-or-less rational (even if deplorable) response by capital to the potential threat posed by the Left.

Among recent synthetic studies, HEALE is the most ambitious and successful – concise, broadly researched and with a wealth of detail and wider insights. Heale notes the strong identification of Americanism with anticommunism, something which he believes has its roots in republican traditions of property-based individualism and citizenship. Through the 19th century, class conflict in the emerging industrial capitalist economy was the main motor for ruling-class and state anticommunism. From the earlier obsession with anarchism, fear of radicalism shifted decisively to Bolshevism after the Russian Revolution. After World War II, the interplay between anticommunism at home and in foreign policy became more significant. Heale sees anticommunism emerging largely out of rational rather than irrational reactions to foreign and anticapitalist threats.

On the other hand, KOVEL emphasizes the irrational and psychological roots of anticommunism. He examines in turn the ideas of a group of prominent 20th-century anticommunists including J. Edgar Hoover, John Foster Dulles, and Ronald Reagan. He distinguishes between *anticommunism*, a loathing of all forms of communism, and *anti-communism*, merely an intellectual opposition to communism. The former is his subject, involving a Manichaean logic dividing the world into absolute (American) good and absolute (communist) evil that became a "black hole anticommunism." He concentrates on his subjects' "personal deployment of desire and fear" in their anticommunism, a projection of internal psychological conflict and guilt on to an external enemy which he dates back to the Puritans' demonization of Native Americans. By 1877, fear of "Red Indians" had been transposed to "red" working-class radicals. But Kovel's ambitious argument is ultimately unconvincing. He divorces anticommunism from its social and political roots, leaving it to float free with a logic of its own. His sweeping generalizations are often based on thin research and do little to explain why so many Americans joined in the anticommunist hysteria of various periods.

ANDREW NEATHER

See also McCarthyism; Red Scare

Anti-Evolution Crusade (1920s)

Furniss, Norman F., *The Fundamentalist Controversy, 1918–1931*, New Haven: Yale University Press, 1954

Garson, Robert, "Political Fundamentalism and Popular Democracy in the 1920's", *South Atlantic Quarterly*, 76(2), 1977

Gatewood, Willard B., Jr., *Preachers, Pedagogues, and Politicians: The Evolution Controversy in North Carolina, 1920–1927*, Chapel Hill: University of North Carolina Press, 1966

Ginger, Ray, *Six Days or Forever? Tennessee v. John Thomas Scopes*, Boston: Beacon Press, 1958

Hofstadter, Richard, *Anti-Intellectualism in American Life*, New York: Knopf, and London: Cape, 1964

Larson, Edward J., *Trial and Error: The American Controversy over Creation and Evolution*, New York: Oxford University Press, 1985, revised 1989

Marsden, George M., *Fundamentalism and American Culture: The Shaping of Twentieth-Century Evangelicalism, 1875–1925*, New York and Oxford: Oxford University Press, 1980

Sandeen, Ernest R., *The Roots of Fundamentalism: British and American Millenarianism, 1800–1930*, Chicago: University of Chicago Press, 1970

Szasz, Ferenc Morton, *The Divided Mind of Protestant America, 1880–1930*, University: University of Alabama Press, 1982

The trial at Dayton, Tennessee, of John Thomas Scopes who was accused of contravening the state's Butler Act (1925) by teaching Darwin's theory of evolution in the classroom, has significance for two schools of historical writing. For historians of the decade of the 1920s it illustrates how the era was a crucial juncture in the modernization process. By pitting modernists against traditionalists and science against religion the trial served to illustrate the fault lines of cultural change. Many historians of American religion have reacted to dramatic renderings of the Scopes Trial, which represent evangelicals as intolerant reactionaries of a residual order, and which distort or misrepresent their principal concerns.

GINGER remains the most thorough account of the trial itself. The links between Scopes, Dayton and the anti-evolution movement are forged in the joint efforts of civic boosters and the American Civil Liberties Union (ACLU) who, effectively, engineered a contentious and highly-publicized trial. The roles and beliefs of the two real protagonists in the trial, William Jennings Bryan who served the prosecution, and Clarence Darrow, acting for the defence, are examined, and a detailed account is presented of the narrative of the trial which culminated in Darrow's cross-examination of Bryan. Scopes's conviction, Bryan's death, and the reversal of the earlier verdict upon appeal conclude the book's chronology. Little sympathy is displayed for the anti-evolutionists' case. While the author concedes that censorship of the curriculum was based on broad popular support he berates fundamentalist leaders for allowing the democratic genie to escape the bottle.

Tennessee was not the only state to enact anti-evolution legislation during the decade, and the movement was strong even in states like North Carolina where it was ultimately unsuccessful. GATEWOOD shows how fundamentalist publicists and revivalist preachers found a receptive audience in a state accustomed to moral regulation and in which socio-economic change had caused unease. Led by orthodox Presbyterians and Baptists, the anti-evolution movement targeted prominent liberal ministers, and in 1925 began a drive to prohibit by law the teaching of any evolutionary theory in state schools. However, no legislation was enacted, partly because the press and the colleges opposed censorship, and partly because many North Carolinians had learnt from Tennessee that a progressive image and anti-evolution statutes were incompatible, but mostly because, while most North Carolinians subscribed to fundamentalist theology, they were too concerned with the constitutional protection of religious liberty and freedom of speech to support repressive measures.

The intolerance of anti-evolutionists has been variously explained by historians. HOFSTADTER claims that the campaign against evolution contributed to the "anti-intellectual impulse" in American life and speculates about the links between fundamentalism and the postwar radical Right. GARSON is less judgmental, regarding fundamentalist extremism as a response to cultural marginalization. He claims that the militancy of the fundamentalists, like the growth of the Ku Klux Klan during the 1920s, reflected the concerns of "rural-minded" Americans about the erosion of local community and a determination to make public institutions accountable to the popular will. FURNISS locates the sources of the fundamentalist controversy of the 1920s in the xenophobia and insecurity spawned by World War I, which influenced much of the crusading character of the movement. Germany was associated with modernism, and its war aims with the evolutionary doctrine of the survival of the fittest, and both the Bolshevik Revolution and the Red Scare heightened anxieties and strengthened religious commitment. Furniss examines the development of anti-evolution legislation in the states, surveys the organizations and leaders who promoted the movement and explores the impact of militant fundamentalism on the established Protestant churches. Bryan's death, the distractions of the depression, and the enlightenment provided by the growth of the mass media are offered as reasons for the subsequent decline of militant fundamentalism.

Writing in the 1980s, LARSON appreciates that the conflict between fundamentalism and modernism was not resolved by the Scopes Trial. While he concedes that the ACLU triumphed by establishing the popular image of the anti-evolutionists as intolerant, bigoted and parochial, this did not entail a "mortal defeat" for the movement. In the short term, the ACLU failed to secure a ruling by the Supreme Court, and Bryan's death inspired his southern supporters to greater efforts to secure the passage of anti-evolution statutes. The controversy also had a lasting impact on the contents of high school biology textbooks which continued to neglect evolution up until the 1960s. Rather than going into decline, the anti-evolution movement observed a "thirty-year truce" which was broken only after a series of Supreme Court decisions restricted the teaching and observance of religion in schools, and when, in 1959, the National Science Foundation funded the revision of high school biology texts. The advent of creation science and the upsurge of the equal time movement in the 1970s amounted to a counteroffensive against modernism which suggests that as long as the issue remains contentious in public opinion it cannot be settled by law.

A growing number of historians of religion do not accept that fundamentalism was merely a reactive social phenomenon and do not regard anti-evolution as a salient aspect of evangelical Christianity before the 1920s. MARSDEN believes that the marginalization of evangelical Christians from the mainstream of American life since the Civil War resulted in the formation of an Anglo-Saxon sub-culture which became politicized only after World War I because of a concern that traditional Christianity was losing its authority. SANDEEN disputes that evangelicals were parochial, anti-intellectual and populistic. He does not regard the fundamentalist "controversy" of the 1920s as a "definitive part" of the movement itself because millenarianism, its most distinctive characteristic, did not accept that legislation could determine pure morals and because the anti-evolution campaign was concentrated in the South, not a traditional stronghold of the millenarians themselves. SZASZ believes that the evolution controversy of the 1920s revived an issue long dormant. During the late 19th century conservatives were more exercised about the challenges posed by the "higher criticism" to scriptural authority, and later they became concerned about the rise of the Social Gospel movement. Although the War galvanized conservatives against modernism, it was Bryan who was responsible for promoting the issue of evolution which came to "overshadow" all other aspects.

STUART KIDD

See also Fundamentalism

Antimasonry

Benson, Lee, *The Concept of Jacksonian Democracy: New York as a Test Case*, Princeton: Princeton University Press, 1961
Bullock, Steven C., *Revolutionary Brotherhood: Freemasonry and the Transformation of the American Social Order, 1730–1840*, Chapel Hill: University of North Carolina Press, 1996
Formisano, Ronald P., *The Transformation of Political Culture: Massachusetts Parties, 1790s–1840s*, New York: Oxford University Press, 1983
Goodman, Paul, *Towards a Christian Republic: Antimasonry and the Great Transition in New England, 1826–1836*, New York: Oxford University Press, 1988
Holt, Michael F., "The Antimasonic and Know Nothing Parties," in *History of US Political Parties*, edited by Arthur M. Schlesinger, Jr., New York: Chelsea House, 1973
Lipson, Dorothy Ann, *Freemasonry in Federalist Connecticut*, Princeton: Princeton University Press, 1977
Ludlum, David M., *Social Ferment in Vermont, 1791–1850*, New York: Columbia University Press, 1939
McCarthy, Charles, "The Antimasonic Party: A Study of Political Antimasonry in the United States, 1827–1840," *American Historical Association: Annual Report*, 1902
Ratner, Lorman, *Antimasonry: The Crusade and the Party*, Englewood Cliffs, NJ: Prentice Hall, 1969
Vaughn, William Preston, *The Anti-Masonic Party in the United States, 1826–1843*, Lexington: University Press of Kentucky, 1983

Scholars agree that the Antimasonic movement began with the reaction to the 1826 abduction and possible murder of former Masonic brother William Morgan by upstate New York Freemasons after he threatened to reveal the fraternity's secret rituals. The deeper causes and implications of the subsequent public outcry, however, continue to be debated. The growing interest in the attack on Masonry over the past generation centers on its place at the intersection of two key antebellum developments. The Antimasonic party, the first popularly-based third party in American history, helped shape the Jacksonian-era political system. Antimasonic agitation also provided personnel and inspiration for later reform movements such as abolitionism.

McCARTHY provided the first full-scale history of the party, looking most fully at New York and Pennsylvania. Like later scholars, McCarthy sees social and religious attitudes as the basis of Antimasonry. Although most adherents were conservatives, the movement itself expressed "the democratic spirit of the age." The political party that emerged out of the movement, however, failed to remain focused on Masonry for long. By 1832, shrewd politicians more concerned with defeating Andrew Jackson than the Masonic fraternity had taken over the party, creating the original foundation for the Whig coalition. LUDLUM connects the movement more directly to antebellum reform. The chapter on Antimasonry in this study of Vermont reform movements argues that not only did the movement draw upon pre-existing democratic and religious beliefs, but the Morgan episode served to intensify a long-standing opposition to the fraternity expressed most consistently by the Baptists. They and other religious groups provided the backbone of the new movement, whose true legacy, Ludlum suggests, lay in nurturing abolitionist leaders and newspapers. The introduction to RATNER depicts the 1950s view of Antimasonry as an example of the paranoid fear of subversion that later inspired McCarthyism. Ratner presents Antimasonry as a "crusade," a movement driven by moral and religious passion. Following Richard McCormick's discussion of the second party system, Ratner suggests that Antimasonry grew strongest politically where party divisions were still being created. His selection of documents includes a variety of New York materials.

BENSON offers an influential discussion of New York politics that assigns the Antimasonic party an important role in creating what he calls the Age of Egalitarianism. Antimasons extended political equality to include equal opportunity in all parts of life and "dramatically changed the style and substance of American politics." Tracing the history of New York's political parties, he argues that the Antimasons took the significant step of suggesting that the people's will should always prevail – making them, not the Jacksonians, the true founders of Jacksonian democracy.

In his explanatory comments on a broad range of documents, HOLT links the party to the feeling of boundless opportunity characteristic of the period. But Holt also sees the party as an expression of the anger of poor farmers against wealthy urban dwellers. Antimasonry's legacy lay not only in its rehearsing of the key themes of later 1830s political debate but also in its influence on the Whigs. The influx of former Antimasons made the Northern wing of the party more egalitarian and evangelical. A somewhat different perspective on the politics of Antimasonry is supplied by VAUGHN who traces the activities of its leaders in deal-making, conventions, platforms, and elections. While this approach offers little insight into the movement's broader significance, it helps to show more systematically that the emerging Whigs were not the only group to seek Antimasonic support, nor the only political destination for its voters. Masonry's dramatic (but temporary) decline, Vaughn argues, represents the movement's primary success.

In a sophisticated study of the political culture of the early national period, FORMISANO includes a chapter on Massachusetts Antimasonry. In his view, the Antimasonic party played an important part in creating America's first modern political system, challenging the control of the political process by state elites (particularly in expressing the orthodox Congregationalist resentment against the Unitarian establishment). The movement against the fraternity, however, was not an uprising of the dispossessed or marginal. Rather, Antimasonry formed a "middle-class moral populism" that politicized voters who were not very different from the adherents of other parties. In the end, the state's anti-Jackson forces were more willing to heed Antimasonic concerns and thus attracted most Antimasonic voters. GOODMAN provides a broader look at the party in New England, focusing on both cultural issues and the sources of political support. According to Goodman, Antimasons represented a "social paranoia" that viewed Masonry as a central symbol of their fears about the secularism, class divisions, and declining community cohesion of modern society. The book's second half examines biographical studies and local election returns to argue that Antimasonic support characteristically came from areas of religious conservatism touched by intense economic change.

Two books make Masonry itself the focus of their examination. LIPSON studies post-Revolutionary Connecticut Freemasonry. The book argues that the fraternity formed a counterculture to political and religious conservatism, providing adherents with male conviviality and a new acceptance

of pleasure in leisure time as well as easing the problems of mobility. The fraternity's vague religiosity, however, made it unacceptable to orthodox Christians. Her discussion of Antimasonry argues that the movement was of greater importance (and achieved greater success) than the party. BULLOCK takes a broader look at American Freemasonry from its beginnings in the 1730s through the Antimasonic movement. It argues that many post-Revolutionary Americans considered the increasingly popular fraternity the public embodiment of their central cultural and religious values. In turn, Americans in the 1820s who wanted to purify society in the name of democracy and evangelicalism saw the fraternity as a central symbol of a corrupt older order that rejected the sovereignty of public opinion and individual conscience. These Antimasons pioneered new means of mobilizing support that later political and reform movements would use to express and shape public attitudes. The book concludes with the 1840s revival of Freemasonry, arguing that the fraternity regained its former levels of membership but not its earlier significance.

STEVEN C. BULLOCK

See also Jacksonian Era; Third Parties

Antitrust Legislation and Court Cases, 1880s–1920s

Dewey, Donald, *Monopoly in Economics and Law*, Chicago: Rand McNally, 1959

Freyer, Tony Allan, *Regulating Big Business: Antitrust in Great Britain and America, 1880–1990*, Cambridge and New York: Cambridge University Press, 1992

Himmelberg, Robert F., *The Origins of the National Recovery Administration: Business, Government, and the Trade Association Issue, 1921–1933*, New York: Fordham University Press, 1976

Kolko, Gabriel, *The Triumph of Conservatism: A Reinterpretation of American History, 1900–1916*, New York: Free Press, and London: Collier Macmillan, 1963

Letwin, William, *Law and Economic Policy in America: The Evolution of the Sherman Antitrust Act*, New York: Random House, 1956

Neale, A.D. and D.G. Goyder, *The Antitrust Laws of the United States: A Study of Competition Enforced by Law*, Cambridge and New York: Cambridge University Press, 1980

Sklar, Martin J., *The Corporate Reconstruction of American Capitalism, 1890–1916: The Market, the Law, and Politics*, Cambridge and New York: Cambridge University Press, 1988

Thorelli, Hans Birger, *The Federal Antitrust Policy: The Origination of an American Tradition*, Baltimore: Johns Hopkins University Press, 1955

During the first two decades of the 20th century the "trust question" was arguably the most important issue in American political debate. It is, therefore, not surprising that many historians have studied the origins and development of antitrust policy. THORELLI provides the fullest examination of the factors that led to the passage of the Sherman Act, the first and most important antitrust statute. He shows that there was substantial public concern about the threat posed by industrial monopolies during the late 1880s and early 1890s. He also argues convincingly that the authors of the Sherman Act were themselves committed to defending competition, and were not simply seeking to placate public opinion. His work also includes an examination of the first few years of antitrust enforcement. Unfortunately, because the book's coverage of events ends in 1903, it sheds no light on the increasingly intense debate about antitrust that followed Theodore Roosevelt's successful prosecution of the Northern Securities Corporation in 1904.

LETWIN also looks at the origins of the Sherman Act. Like Thorelli, he highlights public enthusiasm for the measure, and traces the long tradition of popular anti-monopolism. Moreover, Letwin also provides an excellent account of how the law was treated by the courts, Congress and the executive between 1890 and 1914. In particular, he examines why the federal government initially failed to enforce the statute vigorously, and draws attention to the disagreements among members of the judiciary as to the precise meaning of the act's provisions. In addition, he lucidly discusses the antitrust policies of Roosevelt, Taft and Wilson. Overall, his work provides the most balanced and accessible introduction to the early development of policy.

A number of writers have focussed on antitrust policy during the Progressive era. KOLKO argues that, far from being committed to rigorous antitrust enforcement, most Progressives were determined to protect the interests of big business. Most controversially, he claims that Wilson's antitrust reforms of 1914 were designed to enhance the ability of large firms to dominate industry. Kolko's analysis has proved to be highly influential, but the evidence adduced in support of his thesis is not totally convincing. While he proves that policy makers welcomed the existence of large firms, he is less successful in showing that they also accepted that these firms should be allowed to wield monopolistic power. In his subtle and elegant study, SKLAR also questions Progressive commitment to the restoration of competition. He suggests that, rather than attempting to restore perfect competition, most policy makers accepted that large firms would continue to dominate industrial markets. However they did not believe that these companies should enjoy total freedom to exercise their economic power. Instead they insisted that large firms must be subject to some form of governmental control. The author is particularly effective in examining the different ways in which Roosevelt, Taft and Wilson approached the trust issue, showing how their beliefs about antitrust policy were influenced by their wider political philosophies. Parts of Sklar's analysis are not totally convincing: in particular, he occasionally appears to overestimate the economic sophistication of Progressive politicians. But, overall, this is an impressive and important piece of scholarship.

Although arousing less debate than the Progressive era, federal antitrust policy in the 1920s has attracted the attention of several historians. The fullest account is HIMMEL-BERG which focuses on the impact of the business campaign for the relaxation of antitrust restrictions, a campaign that was to culminate with the National Industrial Recovery Act in 1933. He shows that during the 1920s the federal government and the courts allowed firms to engage in a range of cooperative activities but refused to condone cartellistic behaviour. It was only after the onset of the Great Depression that policy makers began to consider suspending the antitrust laws.

In addition to these detailed monographs, a number of more general studies shed light on the early development of antitrust. In his extremely ambitious and wide-ranging work, FREYER attempts to locate the development of British and American antitrust policies within the context of the two countries' economic, social and political histories. Much of the book is suggestive and insightful, in particular in showing how the antitrust ideal can be seen as part of America's republican tradition. But the breadth of the work proves to be a weakness, as well as a strength. In such a broad survey, the author is forced frequently to rely upon some rather suspect generalizations about the character of American society. Moreover, he does not always have time to explore fully the economic and legal complexities that lie at the heart of antitrust.

Two other helpful introductions to the subject have been written by non-historians. NEALE and GOYDER elucidate some of the legal and economic issues faced by the makers of American antitrust policy. Their primary purpose is to introduce readers to the legal complexities of contemporary policy, rather than to provide a comprehensive historical analysis. But they do spend considerable time in charting the evolution of antitrust policy, detailing many of the key court cases of the late 19th and early 20th centuries. They also help to clarify the legal concepts used by legislators and the courts in defining policy. DEWEY, a distinguished member of the Columbia economics faculty, provides a lucid and largely non-technical introduction to the economic implications of antitrust policy. He highlights some of the weaknesses of antitrust enforcement, drawing attention, for instance, to the failure of the courts and enforcement agencies to recognise the threat posed by oligopolistic firms. But his analysis is generally favourable towards the laws, suggesting that they have had a salutary impact upon both business conduct and public opinion.

PHILIP CULLIS

See also Business History: Big Business; Gilded Age and Progressive Era

Appalachia

Corbin, David Alan, *Life, Work, and Rebellion in the Coal Fields: The Southern West Virginia Miners, 1880–1922,* Urbana: University of Illinois Press, 1981

Dunn, Durwood, *Cades Cove: The Life and Death of a Southern Appalachian Community, 1818–1937,* Knoxville: University of Tennessee Press, 1988

Eller, Ronald D., *Miners, Millhands, and Mountaineers: Industrialization of the Appalachian South, 1880–1930,* Knoxville: University of Tennessee Press, 1982

Inscoe, John C., *Mountain Masters, Slavery, and the Sectional Crisis in Western North Carolina,* Knoxville: University of Tennessee Press, 1989

McKinney, Gordon B., *Southern Mountain Republicans, 1865–1900: Politics and the Appalachian Community*, Chapel Hill: University of North Carolina Press, 1978

Mitchell, Robert D., *Commercialism and Frontier: Perspectives on the Early Shenandoah Valley*, Charlottesville: University Press of Virginia, 1977

Mitchell, Robert D.(editor), *Appalachian Frontiers: Settlement, Society and Development in the Preindustrial Era*, Lexington: University Press of Kentucky, 1991

Shapiro, Henry D., *Appalachia on Our Mind: The Southern Mountains and Mountaineers in the American Consciousness, 1870–1920*, Chapel Hill: University of North Carolina Press, 1978

Shifflett, Crandall A., *Coal Towns: Life, Work, and Culture in Company Towns of Southern Appalachia, 1880–1960*, Knoxville: University of Tennessee Press, 1991

Waller, Altina L., *Feud: Hatfields, McCoys and Social Change in Appalachia, 1860–1900*, Chapel Hill: University of North Carolina Press, 1988

Whisnant, David E., *Modernizing the Mountaineer: People, Power, and Planning in Appalachia*, Boone, NC: Appalachian Consortium Press, 1980; revised, Knoxville: University of Tennessee Press, 1994

The past two decades have seen Appalachia emerge as a major area of historical rediscovery and reinterpretation. The result has been the abandonment of traditional views of the southern mountains as an isolated, static and largely undifferentiated region, divorced from the American mainstream. These stereotypes were exposed by SHAPIRO in an influential study as in part fabrications of late 19th and early 20th century missionaries, educators and local color writers who construed "Appalachia", the naming of which they pioneered, as a society and culture apart, a throwback to the country's frontier past.

The unreliability of traditional views was demonstrated by MITCHELL (1977) who described the early penetration of commercial values and activity into Virginia's Shenandoah Valley, the main immigrant pathway into the uplands. He also revealed the Valley's ethnic diversity, evidence that the mountains were not immune from the cultural pluralism characteristic of early American society as a whole. Equally significant in pioneering the revision of long-held beliefs was McKINNEY's study of mountain politics in the post-Civil War period. McKinney explained the Republican party's success in terms of its ability to respond to local needs, and its deliberate fostering of a distinctive mountain political image derived from the war. By the 1890s, however, issues of race and the changes resulting from industrialization helped reorientate mountain Republicanism; now, local identities and allegiances were increasingly subordinated to the wider imperatives of American national politics.

The transformation of mountain society after 1880 through the exploitation of Appalachia's abundant coal and timber reserves was the subject of ELLER's major synthesis. Eller was keen to refute the argument that mountain underdevelopment arose from the region's isolation and persistent traditionalism. Instead, he argued that poverty and dependency were caused by enforced integration into an externally directed industrial system. Modernization itself, that is, and not the mountain people's resistance to it, produced the depressed socio-economic conditions that had come to characterize much of Appalachian life in the 20th century.

The view of southern Appalachia as an internal colony was reinforced by CORBIN's dramatic reconstruction of the struggles of the southern West Virginia miners between 1880 and 1920. Corbin's study stressed the class solidarity of mountain workers in this area, which lagged behind that of other coal producers in embracing unionism. Miners' opposition to the often ruthless regimes of the coal companies, and to the local and statewide political interests that sustained them, occasioned a series of bitter labour conflicts that culminated in the violent struggles in Mingo and Logan counties in the immediate aftermath of World War I. A second volume pursuing the story through the depression and into the modern era is in preparation.

In contrast, the recent study of company towns by SHIFFLETT offers a more ambivalent view of the relationship between miners and their employers. Shifflett does not deny that exploitation was rife, but takes exception to the class conflict model posed by Corbin and suggests that coal towns acted as social and cultural communities that broadly benefited the miners and their families who inhabited them. Coal company paternalism was double-sided: miners could profit from employer beneficence even as they struggled to resist the efforts to restrict worker freedom.

The internal colonialism model also formed the basis of WHISNANT's critique of modern – and in his view, often disastrous – efforts to remedy Appalachia's economic deficiencies through governmental intervention. Whisnant argued that state and federal development programmes such as the Tennessee Valley Authority, the Area Redevelopment Administration and, most significantly, the Appalachian Regional Commission, failed because they perpetuated the misapplied values of earlier generations of missionaries. Whisnant's book has recently been reissued, testimony to its highly influential role in shaping contemporary debates on Appalachian development.

The revision of accepted views on the causes of modern Appalachian dependency has also prompted re-examination of the pre-industrial era and a determination to relocate mountain society, economy and politics back into the American (and southern) mainstream. INSCOE challenges the view that antebellum mountain communities were isolated from the slave South and its dominant labour and caste system. In western North Carolina on the eve of the Civil War the peculiar institution was far from moribund, with local slaveholding elites benefiting from increased accessibility to regional and national markets. In particular, the area's developing commercial links with the plantation South help to explain its political responses during the secession winter of 1860–61. Sectional issues were thus not irrelevant to western North Carolinians whose responses to attacks upon southern liberty and autonomy mirrored those of much of the rest of the upper South.

The integration of pre-industrial Appalachia into the wider society is further investigated in an important and wide-ranging collection of essays edited by MITCHELL (1991), which provide abundant evidence of the dynamic, differentiated character of early Appalachian development. Among the more significant chapters are those by Mary Beth Pudup on class and economic development in southeastern Kentucky and the final contribution by an economic historian, Paul Salstrom, who traces the agricultural origins of modern Appalachian dependency.

Two important studies have examined continuity and change in Appalachia from a local perspective. DUNN's longitudinal reconstruction of Cades Cove, Tennessee in the heart of the Great Smoky Mountains demonstrates the value of testing the larger generalizations about Appalachian society against local evidence. With its highly fertile soil, for example, Cades Cove's development was conspicuously different from that of many other mountain communities. Above all, Dunn stresses the deeply communal life of Cades Cove's farm inhabitants, which shaped every aspect of their daily activities, but which ultimately failed to protect them from the combined assault of state and federal governments anxious to establish the new national park. WALLER provides another valuable micro-perspective, still rooted in place, the Tug Valley region of the West Virginia-Kentucky border, but here focusing upon a well-known series of events that have played a key role in shaping traditional stereotypes of Appalachian behaviour. In a detailed and sophisticated analysis, Waller interprets the Hatfield-McCoy feud not as a classic manifestation of mountain violence but in the context of the transformation in local and regional economic relations caused by industrialization.

MARTIN CRAWFORD

Armed Services

Clodfelter, Mark, *The Limits of Air Power: The American Bombing of North Vietnam*, New York: Free Press, 1989

Coffman, Edward M., *The Old Army: A Portrait of the American Army in Peacetime, 1784–1898*, New York and Oxford: Oxford University Press, 1986

Futrell, Robert Frank, *Ideas, Concepts, Doctrine: A History of Basic Thinking in the United States Air Force*, Maxwell Air Force Base, AL: Aerospace Studies Institute of Air University Press, 1971, revised, 2 vols., 1989

Ganoe, William A., *A History of the United States Army*, New York: Appleton, 1924; revised, New York: Appleton Century, 1942

Hagan, Kenneth J., *This People's Navy: The Making of American Sea Power*, New York: Free Press, 1991

Howarth, Stephen A., *To Shining Sea: A History of the United States Navy, 1775–1991*, New York: Random House, and London: Weidenfeld and Nicolson, 1991

Isely, Jeter A. and Philip A. Crowl, *The US Marines and Amphibious War: Its Theory and Its Practice in the Pacific*, Princeton: Princeton University Press, 1951

Love, Robert W., Jr., *History of the US Navy*, 2 vols., Harrisburg, PA: Stackpole, 1992

Mackin, Thomas E., *US Air Power: Ascension to Prominence*, Maxwell Air Force Base, AL: Aerospace Studies Institute of Air University Press, 1974

Millett, Allan R., *Semper Fidelis: The History of the United States Marine Corps*, New York: Macmillan, 1980

Moskin, J. Robert, *The US Marine Corps Story*, New York: McGraw Hill, 1977, revised 1987

Skelton, William B., *An American Profession of Arms: The Army Officer Corps, 1784–1861*, Lawrence: University Press of Kansas, 1992

Weigley, Russell F., *History of the United States Army*, New York: Macmillan, 1967; revised, Bloomington: Indiana University Press, 1984

In the 20th century, academic interest in the individual armed services has been concerned with these bodies as institutional entities, rather than perpetuating their image as patriotic symbols of American military glory. Hence to historians, the wartime tasks of the military are incidental to preparation for war, the promulgation of doctrine and the development of bureaucratic organization. This type of inquiry began with GANOE. Concerned primarily with the process of change in the United States Army, Ganoe charted the agendas and influence of reformers throughout the army's history. His analysis also gave rise to a long-lived and ultimately erroneous perception that the army operated largely in a social vacuum, isolated physically and intellectually from society at large.

Far more incisive in analysis and broader in scope is WEIGLEY, which stands as the most complete and scholarly general study of the army to date. Weigley identifies two competing American military ethics – one connected to a traditional reliance on the militia, and the other based on the Uptonian vision of a wholly professionalized army. The army's mission, and its relationship to society and to policy-makers, says Weigley, has been shaped by the ebb and flow of these two dichotomous ideals. His central thesis is strengthened by charting the development of other institutional dynamics, such as command, organization, training, and tactical and strategic thought.

More specific and detailed accounts of the growth of army professionalism, as well as the experience of everyday life in its ranks, have recently become available. The first of these, COFFMAN, examines the army as a discrete society during the 19th century. Although there were important elements of continuity throughout this period, Coffman notes that individual wars – the Revolution, War of 1812 and Civil War – produced strikingly different patterns of thought and professional behavior within the army during each subsequent stage of peace. Because each conflict created new social and political imperatives, army life and the army's mission reflected the changing attitudes and ambitions of the nation. In essence, Coffman's work is a lengthy rebuttal of Ganoe's theory of army isolation.

While Coffman examines all varieties of army society, including officers, enlisted men, non-commissioned officers and their wives and children, SKELTON limits his inquiry to the officer corps prior to the Civil War. In addition to concentrating on this circle as a society unto itself, Skelton charts a strong reforming bent among its members. He argues that the years between the War of 1812 and the Civil War were among the most critical for the growth of army professionalism. In advancing the concept of a closely-knit subculture among officers that regulated behavior and embraced positive change, Skelton notes that the essentials of its modern organization were already in place by 1861. Sadly, single-volume works similar to Coffman and Skelton that deal broadly with the 20th-century army are non-existent.

Because of American fears of a standing army, and the supposed threat which it posed to a democracy, historians have taken pains to understand and explain its relationship to civilian society. This is not the case with the navy, which has traditionally been considered a more "republican" arm. Instead, because of the navy's greater material demands, and its ability to project American power abroad, historians have been attracted to theories of sea power, the navy's part in the American military-industrial complex, and its relationship to American diplomacy. A particularly rich source of information on these topics is LOVE. Comprehensive in every sense of the word, Love's overriding theme is the use of the United States Navy in pursuit of foreign policy goals. He therefore views shipbuilding and naval strategy as components of diplomacy, and the wartime use of ships simply as an intensive application of that role. Although Love recognizes the importance of Mahanian "command of the sea" battle-oriented doctrine, he finds its historical impact less central to the navy's mission than its less glamorous political tasks.

HOWARTH is shorter than Love and written for a general audience. As a survey it broadly covers many of the issues treated by Love. Howarth emphasizes the combat role of the navy rather than its diplomatic role, although he never ignores the importance of the latter. His character sketches of various naval leaders are particularly illuminating. Unlike Love, Howarth accepts uncritically the Mahanian "big navy" doctrine as a prerequisite to the application of American power abroad. His handling of the navy during World War II is excellent, but his analysis of the post-war era flags. Less satisfying is HAGAN, whose one-volume survey is as much polemic as history. Hagan's thesis is decidedly anti-Mahanian in tone, arguing that United States naval strategy in the modern age has been wrong-headed. He rejects the use of the navy as a tool in international politics, and condemns rationales for a large navy, evidently preferring one that enforces American isolation.

Compared to the army and navy, far less has been written about the Marine Corps and Air Force, the one because of its small size, the other because of its relative youth. The single outstanding one-volume history of the Marines is MILLETT, which is highly institutional in scope. Millett's thesis turns on the Corps' search for legitimacy and a mission in a defense establishment dominated by the army and navy. Much space is devoted to administrative and organizational matters rather than combat operations, although Millett does discuss the evolution of Marine combat doctrine.

MOSKIN, on the other hand, is oriented toward the general reader, and spends considerable time describing the heroic actions of Marines in battle. Basing his general thesis on the notion of America as an imperialistic power, he argues that all such nations, the United States included, have found invaluable a rapidly-deployable amphibious force to secure and maintain physical control over its foreign possessions. While not a survey of the Corps, ISELY and CROWL is an invaluable companion that exhaustively describes the evolution of Marine amphibious doctrine and its application in World War II. Rather than offer any particular theme, the authors are content to provide expert analysis of the assumptions, requirements and operational features of amphibious warfare.

The Air Force seems to be the forgotten child of American military history, and to date no single-volume comprehensive scholarly work on the subject has been published. An excellent guide to the development and application of Air Force theory is FUTRELL. Although written for a professional audience, it describes clearly the evolution of air power theory in America, and its various turns under the test of combat. Given his focus, Futrell does not include descriptions of actual combat, nor does he deal with the Air Force as an institution. A serviceable overview is MACKIN, which concentrates heavily on American air power at war, particularly World War II. Its weakness is a general disregard for the internal, more political, developments of Air Force organization. Finally, although very narrow in scope, CLODFELTER offers a thoughtful critique of the use of American air power as an instrument of political coercion. He concludes that Air Force strategy in Vietnam was misdirected in its search to impair the enemy's will and ability to fight a conventional war, rather than apply itself to the kind of guerrilla war which North Vietnam was actually waging. His general argument is that air power is not a blanket weapon, and must instead be directed with great care, if its unique qualities are to have any political or military effect.

T.R. BRERETON

See also Military History; Militia/National Guard

Articles of Confederation

Brown, Roger H., *Redeeming the Republic: Federalists, Taxation and the Origins of the Constitution*, Baltimore: Johns Hopkins University Press, 1993

Ferguson, E. James, *The Power of the Purse: A History of American Public Finance, 1776–1790*, Chapel Hill: University of North Carolina Press, 1961

Fiske, John, *The Critical Period of American History, 1783–1789*, Boston: Houghton Mifflin, 1888

Gross, Robert A. (editor), *In Debt to Shays: The Bicentennial of an Agrarian Rebellion*, Charlottesville: University Press of Virginia, 1993

Jensen, Merrill, *The Articles of Confederation: An Interpretation of the Social-Constitutional History of the American Revolution, 1774–1781*, Madison: University of Wisconsin Press, 1940

Jensen, Merrill, *The New Nation: A History of the United States During the Confederation, 1781–1789*, New York: Knopf, 1950

McDonald, Forrest, *E Pluribus Unum: The Formation of the American Republic, 1776–1790*, Boston: Houghton Mifflin, 1965; 2nd edition, Indianapolis: Liberty Press, 1979

Main, Jackson Turner, *Political Parties Before the Constitution*, Chapel Hill: University of North Carolina Press, 1973

Marks, Frederick W. III, *Independence on Trial: Foreign Affairs and the Making of the Constitution*, Baton Rouge: Louisiana State University Press, 1973

Morris, Richard B., *The Forging of the Union, 1781–1789*, New York: Harper, 1987

Onuf, Peter S., *The Origins of the Federal Republic: Jurisdictional Controversies in the United States, 1775–1787*, Philadelphia: University of Pennsylvania Press, 1983

Wood, Gordon S., *The Creation of the American Republic, 1776–1787*, Chapel Hill: University of North Carolina Press, 1969

The Articles of Confederation have had rough going in the writing of the history of the United States. They are America's failed first experiment with the creation of a central government, and their limitations and inadequacies are usually emphasized. This was especially true during the 19th century, and particularly after the Civil War, when the Articles were invariably evaluated from the perspective of those who favored the adoption of the United States Constitution. A good example of this is FISKE, a philosopher and popular lecturer, who, in a book that had a wide circulation and remained influential for many years, pictured the 1780s as a "critical period" of economic stagnation, bankruptcy, anarchy and disintegration. He claimed that the country was rescued by the unselfish patriots who created the United States Constitution.

JENSEN (1940) is a sharply argued book that questions the relationship of the Constitution to the development of democracy in America. He sees independence in 1776 coming about as a consequence of an "internal revolution" whereby the small farmers, artisans and laborers overthrew not only British rule but also that of the colonial elite. Examining the debates over the drafting of the Articles, he claimed that the Articles were the constitutional expression of the democratic and egalitarian principles of the Declaration of Independence, while the Constitution represented a successful counter-revolution by conservative merchants, planters and lawyers, and a repudiation of these principles. JENSEN (1950) forcefully develops this argument in a general treatment of the 1780s, which stresses the development of democratic policies on the local level, the continuance of social and economic cleavage and the determination of the upper classes to overthrow the Articles. Jensen has been criticized for viewing the period too exclusively from an Antifederalist perspective and for not sufficiently appreciating the economic difficulties or foreign threats facing the country.

More recent general surveys of the period include McDonald and Morris. McDONALD is very lucid in its treatment of economic problems, upon which it focuses almost exclusively. The book has been severely criticized for its vague documentation, outlandish generalizations, and cavalier treatment of some incidents. In the most recent synthesis, MORRIS highlights the impact of the post-war depression, diplomatic problems, sectional tensions and secessionist threats in revealing the inadequacies of the Articles. He believes that the 1780s are best viewed as a period of trial and experimentation, culminating in the adoption of the Constitution which provided a bold and successful solution to the country's seemingly intractable problems. This is a competent and useful book, rather than a challenging one.

In his highly esteemed book, WOOD offers a penetrating analysis of American constitutional and ideological thought during the Confederation era. He stresses its dynamic and protean nature, and is especially good on changing attitudes toward the legislative, executive and judicial branches of the government. On the other hand, he gives relatively little attention to the framing of the Articles of Confederation and to the nature of federal-state relations during the 1780s.

There are a number of very valuable special studies that focus on important aspects of the 1780s. FERGUSON untangles the complicated issues involved in public finance and demonstrates their close relationship to the movement to create a stronger national government. He also has the best treatment of the unsuccessful nationalist attempt, under the leadership of Robert Morris, to strengthen the central government during the 1781–83 period. BROWN focuses on state taxation policy. He argues that popular opposition to taxes effectively prevented the establishment of responsible fiscal systems on the state and federal levels, and that this propelled wealthy merchants, financiers, lawyers and planters to support the movement for the Constitution. Although somewhat biased against those who favored "relief," it offers an authoritative discussion of taxation and monetary policy during the 1780s, and provides some useful new information.

Political developments on the state level are examined in an impressively researched book by MAIN. Using roll-call analysis of votes in state legislatures, and stressing social, economic and geographical tensions, he argues that a clear and consistent division existed between two groups that he terms "localists" and "cosmopolitans." He further argues that this division foreshadowed the fight between Antifederalists and Federalists over the adoption of the Constitution in 1787–88.

MARKS is a concise and useful analysis of the often neglected topic of American foreign relations during the Confederation period, and their effect upon the movement toward the Constitution. Writing mainly from a Federalist point of view, he explains how such issues as national defense, the problem of dealing with foreign trade restrictions and the sensitivity of national pride played key roles in the creation of a stronger national government.

The causes, the nature and the consequences of Shays' rebellion have been the subject of much controversy among scholars. The subject is well treated in GROSS, a collection of essays by different authors, originally delivered as papers at two bicentennial conferences convened in 1986.

ONUF is an attempt to understand the development of a federal system of government in the United States. He deals with the meaning of statehood and how it related to the broader problem of union by examining jurisdictional conflicts between and within different states, especially Pennsylvania, Virginia and New York during the Confederation period, and links it up with the broader issue of constitutional reform in 1787–88. This is a good account of a minor subject that has usually been ignored, although Onuf claims too much, perhaps, for its significance.

RICHARD E. ELLIS

See also Constitution: Philadelphia Convention, 1787; Continental Congress

Asian Americans

Chan, Sucheng, *This Bittersweet Soil: The Chinese in California Agriculture, 1860–1910*, Berkeley: University of California Press, 1986

Chan, Sucheng, *Asian Americans: An Interpretive History*, Boston: Twayne, 1991

Daniels, Roger, *Asian America: Chinese and Japanese in the United States since 1850*, Seattle: University of Washington Press, 1988

Daniels, Roger, *Prisoners Without Trial: Japanese Americans in World War II*, New York: Hill and Wang, 1993

Freeman, James M., *Hearts of Sorrow: Vietnamese-American Lives*, Stanford, CA: Stanford University Press, 1989

Jensen, Joan M., *Passage from India: Asian Indian Immigrants in North America*, New Haven: Yale University Press, 1988

Kitano, Harry H.L. and Roger Daniels, *Asian Americans: Emerging Minorities*, Englewood Cliffs, NJ: Prentice Hall, 1988, 2nd edition, 1995

Leonard, Karen I., *Making Ethnic Choices: California's Punjabi Mexican Americans*, Philadelphia: Temple University Press, 1992

Patterson, Wayne, *The Korean Frontier in America: Immigration to Hawaii, 1896–1910*, Honolulu: University of Hawaii Press, 1988

Takaki, Ronald T., *Strangers from a Different Shore: A History of Asian Americans*, Boston: Little Brown, 1989

Tamura, Eileen, *Americanization, Acculturation, and Ethnic Identity: The Nisei Generation in Hawaii*, Urbana: University of Illinois Press, 1993

Welaratna, Usha, *Beyond the Killing Fields: Voices of Nine Cambodian Survivors in America*, Stanford, CA: Stanford University Press, 1993

The 1990 census enumerated some 6.8 million Asian Americans who represented 2.8 percent of the population. There were more than a million each of Chinese and Filipino Americans, more than 800,000 Japanese and Asian Indian Americans, nearly as many Korean Americans, more than 600,000 Vietnamese Americans and about 500,000 other Southeast Asian Americans. Given both continued relatively heavy immigration and the birth rates typical of first-generation immigrants, Asian Americans will probably constitute four percent or more of the population in the 2000 census. Although nearly two-thirds of 1990's Asian Americans were foreign-born, most of them having arrived after the immigration liberalization of 1965, some Asian Americans, mostly Chinese and Japanese, had immigrated in the 19th and early 20th centuries. Not surprisingly much of the historical literature focuses on them.

Three works survey a variety of ethnic groups. KITANO and DANIELS has discrete chapters on eight ethnic groups, and topical chapters on immigration law, present status, and adaptation. CHAN (1991) tells the story "from a perspective that treats Asian immigrants and their descendants as creators of their own history" and organizes the material in nine chapters treating emigration, immigration, hostility and conflict, social organization, resistance to oppression, women and families, the period 1941–65, new immigrants and refugees, and

current status. TAKAKI has created a coherent narrative history which contains much less about the newer groups and a great deal more about Hawaii than the other two. A fourth work, DANIELS (1988) is a comparative history of the two earliest Asian immigrant groups, Chinese and Japanese Americans, with particular emphasis on the crucial era of World War II. He argues that the different pace of Chinese American and Japanese American family and community development in the United States was due more to the divergent policies of the American government, which resulted in vastly different demographic profiles, than to any inherent differences between the two communities. All four books have detailed bibliographies; that in Daniels is the most extensive.

CHAN (1986) is not only the best single volume written about Chinese Americans, but it also marks an important demarcation point in the literature. Before then, the emphasis of the serious scholarship was on what was done to Asian immigrants; after Chan, the emphasis has been on what they have accomplished, although no one can ignore the discrimination which they suffered in the past, and continue to encounter. Chan demonstrates, through archival evidence in both English and Chinese, that there was an important Chinese entrepreneurial presence in California agriculture, and that Chinese workers were not just hewers of wood and drawers of water.

Works about Japanese Americans still tend to focus on the wartime incarceration of the West Coast Japanese regardless of their citizenship, age, or gender. The most recent summary is DANIELS (1993), which synthesizes previous work and carries the story forward to include an account of the successful struggle for "redress," whereby the government formally apologized for its wartime "mistake" and awarded $20,000 to each survivor of the wartime camps. More representative of the newer trend is TAMURA whose work focuses on the pre-war struggle of the Hawaiian Nisei (second generation) to achieve first-class schooling, and the attempts of the islands' white establishment to exclude them. In the process she gives an insightful account of that generation's aspirations and achievements.

The best work now available on Asian Indian Americans treats their experience when they were a far-western minority of a few thousand persons, almost all male, early in this century with a profile very different from that of today's immigrant community from India. JENSEN tells the story of the tiny group of largely-Sikh Indian nationalists who formed the "Hindu conspiracy," a doomed and quixotic attempt to overthrow the Raj from a San Francisco base with German government help during World War I. LEONARD, an anthropologist, analyzes astutely and sensitively the family relationships of Punjabi men – again largely Sikhs – who settled in California's Imperial Valley, became agricultural proprietors, and formed unions with Mexican and Mexican American women.

Similarly, the best historical work on Koreans examines their settlement phase. PATTERSON studies that settlement from what is a mid-Pacific standpoint: that is, he pays attention to the forces existing in Korea which impelled Koreans to emigrate as well as the forces in Hawaii – largely the need for labor – which pulled them there. After the brief "window" examined here, Korea's Japanese overlords put a halt to significant Korean emigration to the New World. It did not resume until after the Korean War. Patterson also explains why the Korean migration had a different demographic and religious profile from that of its Asian immigrant contemporaries.

Traditional historical work on Southeast Asian Americans, whose migration began during the latter part of the war in Vietnam, has barely started. But the development of the tape recorder and the discipline of oral history have given those who want to tell the immigrant generation's stories a way of doing so. Had such technology, and the social foresight to utilize it, existed in the late 19th and early 20th centuries, we would know much more about the lives and thoughts of the immigrants of that era. Dramatic, trauma-filled refugee stories have proved particularly attractive. Two of the best of a number of good such histories are FREEMAN and WELARATNA. Each interviewed recent refugees resident in central California, one of the major loci for Southeast Asian Americans.

ROGER DANIELS

Astor, John Jacob 1763–1848

Fur trader, speculator and businessman

Chittenden, Hiram Martin, *The American Fur Trade of the Far West*, New York: Harper, 1902; edited by Stallo Vinton, Lincoln: University of Nebraska Press, 1986

Haeger, John Denis, *John Jacob Astor: Business and Finance in the Early Republic*, Detroit: Wayne State University Press, 1991

Irving, Washington, *Astoria; or, Anecdotes of an Enterprise Beyond the Rocky Mountains*, Philadelphia: Carey Lea and Blanchard, 1836; edited by Richard Dilworth Rust, Boston: Twayne, 1976 (The Complete Works of Washington Irving, vol. 15)

Lockwood, Charles, *Manhattan Moves Uptown: An Illustrated History*, Boston: Houghton Mifflin, 1976

Parton, James, *Life of John Jacob Astor*, New York: American News Company, 1865

Porter, Kenneth Wiggins, *John Jacob Astor, Business Man*, 2 vols., Cambridge, MA: Harvard University Press, 1931

Ronda, James P., *Astoria and Empire*, Lincoln: University of Nebraska Press, 1990

Sinclair, David, *Dynasty: The Astors and Their Times*, London: Dent, 1983; New York: Beaufort, 1984

Stokes, Isaac Newton Phelps, *The Iconography of Manhattan Island, 1498–1909*, 6 vols., New York: R.H. Dodd, 1915–28; reprinted, New York: Arno Press, 1967

John Jacob Astor was the founder of one of the great American fortunes. He has claims to be regarded as the first American big businessman, and, as a penniless young immigrant from Germany who left some $40 million on his death in 1848, he exemplifies the classic rags-to-riches story. Fiercely competitive and relentlessly acquisitive, and with a remarkable eye for an opportunity, he made large sums from the fur trade and the China trade, and then invested the profits in Manhattan real estate, at a time when New York City was about to expand dramatically.

Early works on Astor and his enterprises depended heavily on personal acquaintance or on the reminiscences of those who knew him. PARTON wrote biographies of a number of prominent 19th-century figures, and he was acquainted with many people who had known Astor personally. His biography remains useful as a reflection of contemporary opinion of Astor, and fostered the picture of a greedy and miserly figure who, unlike many other Americans of great wealth, left very little of his huge fortune for charitable or philanthropic causes. IRVING is a history of Astor's one great business failure – the trading post on the Oregon coast which, characteristically, he named for himself. While anything written by Washington Irving deserves respect, it must be remembered that this was not only an authorized history – Irving and Astor were long-time friends – but it was commissioned and paid for by Astor.

Other older works provide useful background on Astor's business activities. Although it is now nearly a century old, CHITTENDEN remains a useful source of information about the history of the fur trade in which Astor made his first fortune. The six large volumes of STOKES represent one of the monuments of American scholarship. They are the basic reference work on the physical history of Manhattan. A more recent work, on a more manageable scale, is LOCKWOOD, which provides a splendid and highly readable history of the physical development of Manhattan in the 19th century. It is indispensable for understanding the economic and urban milieu in which Astor turned the very considerable fortune which he had made in the fur trade into a far larger one based on real estate.

It was PORTER who, in two large volumes, including some 350 pages of documents to supplement the text, produced the first serious scholarly study of Astor. It is essentially a business history, with little attention to the personal life of the man himself. The first volume deals with his involvement in the fur trade and in the China trade. The second volume continues with these themes, but also covers Astor's investment in real estate in the Midwest, before moving on to his huge investments in Manhattan. There is also information on his interests in such fields as insurance, banking, hotels, canals and railroads. This is a work of careful, competent scholarship, packed with useful information, but cautious, limited, and sometimes ambivalent in its judgments.

There was a gap of sixty years between Porter's work and further serious scholarship on Astor. The gap was filled less than adequately by various popular accounts, dwelling more on the family and its spending of a vast fortune than on the man who amassed it. One of the more substantial of these is SINCLAIR, which is more of a gossipy family history than a serious study, and which has no footnote references and only a slender bibliography. It is highly critical of Astor's alleged dishonesty, meanness and ruthlessness.

Two recent books indicate a welcome, if belated, scholarly interest in Astor and his business ventures. HAEGER sees Astor as a central figure in the economic growth of the early republic. He writes from the perspective of recently fashionable entrepreneurial and modernization theories, and sees Astor in the context of the business revolution, described by Thomas Cochran and others. He challenges the conventional wisdom of the Chandler school that the great breakthrough in business methods and organization came with the railroads. Haeger sees the process starting earlier with developments in the form and structure of corporations, and in the promotion of urban development, in which Astor was a key figure. He also discusses Astor's political connections with Jefferson, Madison, Monroe and Gallatin, and his role in helping to finance the War of 1812, and in chartering the Second Bank of the United States. According to Haeger, "no individual of his time, perhaps, better exemplified the union of capitalism and the new liberal state." Haeger's fresh perspective is illuminating, even if some critics may feel that the less admirable features of Astor and his career are not given their due.

RONDA is mainly a detailed and revealing account of the Astoria venture in the Pacific Northwest, but it serves to highlight Astor's wider vision, as well as his business instincts and his determination. Less well-disposed than Haeger towards Astor, Ronda claims that, in his relentless pursuit of wealth, Astor "embodied all that was calculating and pragmatic in American capitalism." Astor, he says, ran his affairs with "a unique combination of thoughtful caution and stunning audacity." But it is also clear that Astor saw the wider geopolitical implications of what he was attempting. His Astoria venture was envisaged as the germ of a great American political and commercial empire in the far Northwest, and the center of a trading network stretching from western Europe to the wide Pacific. Despite its short-term failure, Astoria provided, in Jefferson's eyes, the basis for the entire United States claim to lands west of the Rockies. By their combined efforts, and their different approaches and interpretations, Haeger and Ronda have added breadth and depth to the assessment of Astor's role in the history of finance, business, urban development, politics and expansionism in the early republic.

JOHN STEELE GORDON

See also Business History entries; Pacific Northwest

Aviation and Aerospace

Bailey, Elizabeth E., David R. Graham and Daniel B. Kaplan, *Deregulating the Airlines*, Cambridge: Massachusetts Institute of Technology Press, 1985

Bilstein, Roger E., *Flight in America, 1900–1983: From the Wrights to the Astronauts*, Baltimore: Johns Hopkins University Press, 1984; revised (without dates in title), 1994

Carter, Dale, *The Final Frontier: The Rise and Fall of the American Rocket State*, London: Verso, 1988

Lewis, W. David and Wesley Phillips Newton, *Delta: The History of an Airline*, Athens: University of Georgia Press, 1979

Miller, Ronald, and David Sawers, *The Technical Development of Modern Aviation*, London: Routledge, 1968; New York: Praeger, 1970

Sampson, Anthony, *Empires of the Sky: The Politics, Contests and Cartels of World Airlines*, London: Hodder and Stoughton, and New York: Random House, 1984

Sherry, Michael S., *The Rise of American Air Power: The Creation of Armageddon*, New Haven: Yale University Press, 1987

Simonson, G.R. (editor), *History of the American Aircraft Industry: An Anthology*, Cambridge: Massachusetts Institute of Technology Press, 1968

The airplane was, of course, invented in the United States. Indeed its impact on that nation is probably greater than in any other country. Yet its history remains a strangely neglected subject, especially when compared with the volumes written on the automobile and the railroad. The original pioneers – the Wrights, Lindbergh, and Earhart for example – have received their fair share of attention, but no truly impressive and comprehensive study has yet been produced on the more general effect that aviation has had on everyday life in the United States.

SAMPSON provides a good introduction. Although his specific topic is the rise of international airlines, those in the United States inevitably play a major part in the story. Sampson provides a clear and highly accessible account of the airlines' role in the development of an entire travel product that incorporates hotels, travel agencies and other tourist services. For many, the experience of air travel changed from one of adventure to one bordering on the mundane. This was not without problems, and Sampson discusses these matters in a way that helps to simplify quite complex issues.

There have been several historical works on individual airlines, the best of which is perhaps LEWIS and NEWTON. Delta Air Lines has been one of the success stories among American airlines, and the book is a useful study in the growth of the operation. It is particularly strong on the decision-making processes behind the introduction of new types of aircraft and the pursuit of new routes. It also situates Delta's rise skilfully within the correspondent growth of Atlanta, its home base, and the rise of the South in general. However, there are some criticisms. First, the book often reads too much like an official history, and is too uncritical. Second, there is little mention of the contribution made by Delta's workforce, and especially of the company's far from progressive policy regarding the employment of African-Americans. Lastly, it badly needs updating to take into account the airline's performance during the turbulent 1980s.

The Airline Deregulation Act of 1978 overshadows recent American airline history. Its ramifications, and the arguments over those ramifications, are still going on, and thus it is difficult to take a strictly historical view of the matter. However, knowledge of the act is essential, and BAILEY, GRAHAM and KAPLAN provide an excellent overview. In Part One they provide a detailed background to the act, particularly the increasing tension between old regulatory statutes and new technology (especially the introduction of the jets). Part Two attempts an assessment of the impact of the act and provides an excellent study of the questions of pricing, competition, route provision and productivity which all airlines have had to face. While the language of the book is not difficult, some of the concepts may be confusing for those not well versed in economic or business history.

Those interested in the earlier, pre-World War II growth of American aviation need look no further than SIMONSON. This collection of informative essays covers the teething problems of the industry: the lack of airfield facilities, the antitrust scandals of the period, the various attempts at federal regulation, the role of the Air Mail and the establishment of a recognizable route structure. Particularly stressed is the importance of military concerns to the industry's growth. Only those manufacturers who received government military contacts were able to survive. Underpinning the work is a stress on the relationship between aviation, the government, and the military.

These themes are taken to a different level by CARTER. This is a highly unusual work that oscillates between the very funny and the very frightening. Loosely entwined around the novels of former Boeing engineer Thomas Pynchon, Carter's book ties post-1945 American culture to the dreams of the space race, while planting its economy very firmly in the manufacturing plants of military establishments. Those looking for a straightforward narrative may well be put off by Carter's expansive range of sources and argument, but anyone who perseveres will find reward in this highly original and well written book.

Impressive in the depth and cogency of its argument, SHERRY charts the rise of United States air power up to the dropping of the atomic bombs on Japan in 1945. He argues that military policy could never escape from a confusion that viewed the strategic bomber both as liberator and also as harbinger of doom. While his own views are not hidden, Sherry successfully navigates the fine line between loaded moralism and cool detachment. The detail of his arguments is impressive, but may deter those without a knowledge of the military history of the period.

BILSTEIN provides a useful general introduction, which charts a fairly comprehensive story from the early flights of the Wright Brothers up to the Voyager space probes. One advantage is his coverage of general aviation (which incorporates such aspects as private aircraft, business jets, and even crop sprayers). This is a largely neglected area which has had a sizable impact on the geography and economy of the United States. Typical of such broad surveys, the book is informative, if sometimes superficial.

Finally, despite its age, MILLER and SAWERS remains a classic. It is not strictly confined to the United States, but, in language that does not alienate those without technological or economic expertise, it explains the intricate details of improvements in airliner technology (especially in the crucial 1930s) and their relationship to the operating demands of the airlines. The issues that are raised by Miller and Sawers have not changed to the present day, and understanding of them is fundamental to any student of airline operations.

DREW WHITELEGG

B

Barton, Clara 1821–1912

Civil War nurse and founder of American Red Cross

Barton, William Eleazar, *The Life of Clara Barton*, 2 vols., Boston: Houghton Mifflin, 1922

Burton, David H., *Clara Barton: In the Service of Humanity*, Westport, CT: Greenwood Press, 1995

Dulles, Foster Rhea, *The American Red Cross: A History*, New York: Harper, 1950

Massey, Mary Elizabeth, *Women in the Civil War*, Lincoln: University of Nebraska Press, 1966

Oates, Stephen B., *A Woman of Valor: Clara Barton and the Civil War*, New York: Free Press, 1994

Pryor, Elizabeth, *Clara Barton: Professional Angel*, Philadelphia: University of Pennsylvania Press, 1988

A tiny, determined woman from Massachusetts, Clara Barton loathed inactivity and was at her best when confronted with a crisis, whether in the midst of battle, flood, or epidemic. Known as "The Angel of the Battlefield" and "The American Nightingale", Barton, saving grace to thousands of soldiers during the Civil War and founder of the American Red Cross, remains one of the most accomplished, and the most complex, women in American history. In spite of the magnitude of her accomplishments, or perhaps because of them, Barton's life has only recently begun to receive the close analysis that it deserves.

Much was written by and about Barton during her lifetime. Though an official biography, written by Percy Epler, appeared soon after her death in 1915, more than forty boxes of Barton's manuscripts were made available only after the book's publication. It was not until the dense, two-volume BARTON, written by a close friend and relative, that a more comprehensive biography was made available. Drawing heavily on her papers and letters, and interviews with friends and family, this is, as might be expected, a highly sympathetic and laudatory account of Clara Barton's life. Strictly a chronological narrative, it provides little or no objective analysis or sense of historical context, and the sources are poorly documented and thus unhelpful to the reader. However, BARTON closely traces Clara Barton's involvement in the Civil War in the first volume, and documents her successful establishment of the American Red Cross in the second. This substantial biography remains a useful source for strictly factual information about Barton's life and, more importantly, it gives the reader a clear sense of how the popular legend of Clara Barton was created.

It is this "legend" that more recent studies attempt to discuss at greater length. While several Barton biographies were published in the 1940s and 1950s, studies that attempt to explore the true complexity of Barton's life and personality have appeared only within the last ten years. One of the first attempts to wade through the Barton legend is PRYOR. Using Barton's 35-volume personal diary, this well-written book explores the conflicting images of Barton's personal and public life. Pryor explores the powerful forces that often pulled at Barton, including descriptions of her troubled family, and the bouts of deep depression and ill-health that led to her two-year sojourn in a sanatorium in the late 1870s. She also delves into the passionate side of Barton, providing new evidence that she engaged in an affair with a married Union officer in 1863. Though the author's admiration for her subject is evident, she achieves a major revision of the popular image of Barton as a pure and selfless philanthropist. Pryor reveals Barton as a complex, contradictory woman who, although deeply committed to her work, tended to exaggerate her own accomplishments, was wholly intolerant of any imagined ingratitude from those whom she assisted, and who became so autocratic and unyielding in her interactions that Red Cross workers sometimes referred to her as "the Queen".

Barton earned the name of "Angel of the Battlefield" for her role in the Civil War, during which she tirelessly collected and distributed supplies to Union soldiers, and later went to the front to administer to the wounded directly. This subject is given the most comprehensive treatment in OATES, in an extensively researched work which carefully traces the circumstances leading to Barton's involvement in the war. When fighting broke out, Barton at first stayed on the sidelines, unwilling to incur a reputation as a camp follower, but she soon decided that she would be more useful at the front. Oates gives an interesting, detailed account of Barton's efforts to gain access to the battlefield and of the dangers she encountered there. He is successful in setting the Civil War stage, although there is little exploration of the complexity of women's roles at this time. Oates tends to present Barton as a somewhat isolated figure, although she was only one of many women who worked extensively with both Union and Confederate soldiers.

MASSEY fills that gap by providing a more in-depth discussion of women's activities during the Civil War. This highly readable study documents the efforts of a number of women, including Barton, to organize and administer aid to soldiers and their families, nurse the wounded, and work toward creating and reforming government agencies designed for those purposes. Massey devotes substantial attention to Barton, while placing her work squarely within the larger context of the Civil War and the contributions of women in general. Most importantly, she explores the motivations of women war workers, and how women's perceptions changed in the mid-19th century as a result of their efforts.

The most recent biography is BURTON, who attempts the same kind of interpretative history as Pryor. However, it is neither as interesting nor as well-written as the earlier work, and, on the whole, it has little that is new to say about Barton. However, Burton does devote more attention to the circumstances surrounding Barton's removal from her position as head of the American Red Cross in 1904. Her "fall" was due in part to her personal rigidity and haphazard business practices, but Burton also shows that changing attitudes toward business management, political interests, and unfounded rumors about her integrity had at least as much to do with Barton's forced resignation.

Because she headed the organization for the first four decades of its existence, Barton's life and career can be better understood by a closer exploration of the history of the American Red Cross. DULLES does provide such a history, but this is a dated account which does not adequately place Barton's work, and the growth of the Red Cross, within the context of political and social changes occurring in the late 19th and early 20th centuries. However, it is one of the few available studies of the history of the Red Cross, and allows the reader a closer look at the details of the organization, and of the life of the woman who created it.

ROBIN L.E. HEMENWAY

Baseball

Goldstein, Warren, *Playing for Keeps: A History of Early Baseball*, Ithaca, NY: Cornell University Press, 1989

Rader, Benjamin G., *Baseball: A History of America's Game*, Urbana: University of Illinois Press, 1992

Riess, Steven A., *Touching Base: Professional Baseball and American Culture in the Progressive Era*, Westport, CT: Greenwood Press, 1980

Rogosin, Donn, *Invisible Man: Life in Baseball's Negro Leagues*, New York: Macmillan, 1983

Seymour, Harold, *Baseball*, 3 vols., New York: Oxford University Press, 1960–90

Voigt, David Quentin, *American Baseball*, vols. 1–2, Norman: University of Oklahoma Press, 1966–70; vol. 3, University Park: Pennsylvania State University Press, 1983

Most accounts of baseball's past fall into one of two groups. First, there are works of baseball history narrowly defined, voluminous in their detail of the game's competitive development, written by enthusiasts for enthusiasts. Second, there are historical accounts which try to place the story of the game's growth in a social, economic and even political context. Examples from the second category are discussed here, although professional sports historians may also be enthusiasts.

The multi-volume works of Voigt and Seymour may be said to represent the pioneering work that has made possible and encouraged subsequently much more specific work. These are works of narrative history. Nonetheless, VOIGT is at pains to discuss theories of leisure, and the "leisure revolution". He emphasizes that sport generally, and baseball particularly, demonstrate a degree of organization and a rational approach to the use of leisure. Baseball also shows how organization, rationality and commercialization can combine to create a mass spectator sport. SEYMOUR is keen to emphasize the impact of baseball on American society. In his narrative he demonstrates how, even before the end of the 19th century, the game became the country's national game and embedded itself in the vocabularies and consciousness of Americans. Both writers discuss the way in which the game, in an organized form, went from being a game for gentlemen to one played at the highest levels by professionals.

RADER is a single-volume study aimed at introducing interested readers to the history of the game. The author is a well-established and influential historian of sport, whose schematic approach to the whole of American sports history is usefully applied to baseball. He talks of An Age of Folk Games (1607–1800), the Rise of Organized Sports (1800–1890), The Ascendancy of Organized Sports (1890–1950), and The Age of Televised Sports. Rader draws on the work of many recent scholars, and discusses specific moments of crisis, including the Black Sox scandal, the ending of the colour line and the extraordinary impact on the game of Marvin Miller, the man who transformed the incomes and life styles of the top players. He also offers a readable and concise narrative.

Among the more specialized studies which underpin Rader's work are those of Goldstein, Riess and Rogosin. In his history of early baseball, GOLDSTEIN reminds readers that cricket preceded baseball as the first American team sport before being superseded by it during the 1850s. Once established, those who organised baseball were determined to uphold its respectability. Inevitably, the "sporting underworld" overlapped with baseball, but the game's defenders endeavoured to keep the game untainted. The presence of women as spectators was considered to be one positive development, as was the high profile of Harry Wright as player, manager and entrepreneur. Henry Chadwick, the game's first leading journalist and defender, also brought a battery of justifications for the game, emphasizing its manliness and honesty. Both Chadwick and Wright were English immigrants. Indeed, Goldstein maintains that one of the ironies of the game's history is that while its apologists have always maintained that baseball encouraged and still encourages a democratic mix of classes and ethnic and racial groups, these same apologists were among those working hard to enforce a standard of conduct of games based on respectability and the standards of the genteel white middle class. Goldstein also observes that Chadwick was happy to argue that baseball's paternity lay in "rounders". In contrast, the game's best known publicist, Albert G. Spalding, insisted on its uniquely American origins. Like Voigt and Seymour, Goldstein dismisses the "Cooperstown Story" as a serious explanation for the origins of the game, while recognising its mythic importance. He never ceases to emphasize that there has long been a strong historical consciousness about baseball in the United States, a consciousness that has been both chronological and emotional. The Baseball Hall of Fame at Cooperstown, New York, is an important element in how many Americans feel about "the national pastime".

Until Jackie Robinson's breakthrough, many Americans were not able to hope for a career in major league baseball or, in some cases, to sit where they wished in the stands. Making extensive use of oral history techniques, ROGOSIN discusses the realities of baseball's Negro Leagues. He notes that in the inter-war period the Leagues were among the largest black businesses and that some of the more prominent teams became important focal points for black communities. In these leagues, the relationship between gambling and racketeering and the teams was a close one. Rogosin delineates the business practices of the owners to emphasize this point. He also discusses the way in which black teams went on tours to try to drum up support and extra income, and the ways in which the Negro Leagues were linked to Latin America.

RIESS represents an attempt to integrate sports history into a study of the changing nature of American culture in the Progressive era. Again, one of his major themes is the desire of promoters to emphasise the moral worth of the game. He is particularly informative on the question of playing on the Sabbath, where a desire for respectability came up against the desire to maximize income. Different towns and cities had different approaches. By the 1890s, western clubs were playing on Sundays, while eastern clubs did not. Interestingly enough, there was player opposition to playing on the Sabbath. As baseball became more widely played on Sunday, working-class people were more likely to be able to watch it. In Riess's view, this enabled more and more Americans, from a variety of ethnic backgrounds, to internalize a great deal of the old American value system. He goes so far as to say that baseball, "America's secular religion", would eventually succeed where voluntary pietistic organizations had failed. Riess is quite clear that implicit in the rhetoric of baseball were values associated with a traditional, bourgeois, small-town society.

Riess also has much to say about the way in which the professional game was a source of upward social mobility for some young men. Most professional ballplayers came from a farming or white-collar background, but a significant minority came from blue-collar homes. Most retired players went on to reasonably prosperous careers, although this does not seem always to have been linked to their careers in baseball. Overall, baseball continued to be an urban sport which convinced its adherents of its rural origins and the values associated with them.

S.J.S. ICKRINGILL

See also Sport

Basketball

Axthelm, Pete, *The City Game: Basketball in New York from the World Champion Knicks to the World of the Playgrounds*, New York: Harper's Magazine Press, 1970

George, Nelson, *Elevating the Game: Black Men and Basketball*, New York: HarperCollins, 1992

Halberstam, David, *The Breaks of the Game*, New York: Knopf, 1981

Hult, Joan S. and Marianna Trekell (editors), *A Century of Women's Basketball: From Frailty to Final Four*, Reston, VA: National Association for Girls and Women in Sport, 1991

Isaacs, Neil D., *All the Moves: A History of College Basketball*, Philadelphia: Lippincott, 1975; revised, New York: Harper, 1984

Joravsky, Ben, *Hoop Dreams: A True Story of Hardship and Triumph*, Atlanta: Turner, 1995

Naismith, James, *Basketball: Its Origin and Development*, New York: Association Press, 1941

Peterson, Robert W., *Cages to Jump Shots: Pro Basketball's Early Years*, New York: Oxford University Press, 1990

Since its creation in 1891 by James Naismith, basketball has steadily developed into one of the most popular sports in America. In spite of this, scholars have virtually ignored the game, resulting in a dearth of analytical works on basketball history. In view of this gap, NAISMITH's own account of the game's initial development is still the best discussion of basketball's early years. He recounts the circumstances which led to his "invention" at the International YMCA Training School in Springfield, Massachusetts. In addition to these recollections, Naismith describes how the game became a full-scale spectator sport after it had spread to athletic clubs, high schools and colleges. Moreover, the book also contains useful information on the early administrative and physiological debates over basketball.

The history of the college game is covered by ISAACS, which chronicles the major players, coaches and teams throughout the century. Isaacs touches upon areas where college basketball has experienced lingering problems, such as gambling and recruiting. However, this work is mainly a season-by-season account of the top teams in the game and provides little comment on basketball's larger significance. Despite this deficiency, the book is still a good source of information on college basketball's on-court evolution up through the mid-1970s.

Developments in professional basketball during the first half of the 20th century are covered by PETERSON. Based on dozens of interviews, this work includes fascinating material on the early professional game. Peterson reveals that the contests were usually slow-moving, marred by violence, and often played on a court surrounded by a wire cage. With the help of numerous quotations, Peterson recalls the players and their experiences in the early leagues. There is also discussion of the black teams and Jewish teams which often dominated the game in the 1920s and 1930s. Peterson describes the business aspects of basketball, explaining that early pro teams frequently faced financial difficulties, while the college game, in contrast, soared in popularity. Although lacking footnotes, this is one of the most valuable works on the history of basketball.

HALBERSTAM discusses more recent developments in the professional game. He bases his book on the 1979–80 season which he spent traveling with the Portland Trail Blazers. From this experience, Halberstam describes in detail the grinding pace of a full year in the National Basketball Association. The book is not limited to the Trail Blazers however, as it also provides insights into the business and racial aspects of the league as part of an in-depth look at the NBA of the late 1970s. Throughout the work, Halberstam develops his main argument that commercialism and its corrupting effects are ruining this once great game. Writing in 1981, before Magic Johnson, Larry Bird and Michael Jordan revitalized the league and its popularity, Halberstam's gloomy forecast appears to have been exaggerated. However, his work is packed with revealing information about the modern NBA.

In addition to the college and professional games, there are several other areas of basketball history which warrant discussion. For example, women's basketball is a significant part of the game's overall history. HULT and TREKELL is a collection of essays on this subject – and Hult is also an important contributor. Many of the chapters are well-researched and informative, highlighting previously neglected aspects of basketball's past. The essays explore a variety of topics in the women's game, covering players, coaches and administrators at the high school and college levels. There is also a brief history of gender perceptions in sport to provide a general context for the essays. Although informative, the essays vary in quality and lack an overall theme to draw together the diverse discussions.

The impact of race is another significant aspect of basketball history. In what is the best examination of African American men in the game, GEORGE is especially concerned with exploring basketball's relation to African American culture. He shows how black players have embodied the modern black athletic aesthetic, and asserts that African Americans are largely responsible for transforming basketball into the "flying, faking, blocking, and dunking" game of today. In the discussion of black professional and college teams, he provides useful information about many early African-American players who have not been widely written about before. George concludes with a sober commentary on how basketball has been an unreliable avenue of escape from poverty, leaving thousands of urban kids with little hope after their NBA aspirations fail.

Exploration of this topic of inner-city basketball is essential to an understanding of the game's larger significance. AXTHELM was one of the first to examine basketball's role in the city. In his study of New York, he explains that poor education and racism prevent most black ghetto players from reaching college, leading many of them to turn to drugs and alcohol. He also describes the professional game in New York City, tracing the Knicks and their climb to the top, and including player profiles and an account of their 1970 world championship season. Although Axthelm's work is mainly descriptive, it remains a classic in basketball literature.

The most insightful discussion of basketball's place in urban life is JORAVSKY. Based on the critically acclaimed documentary, *Hoop Dreams*, this book traces the lives of two inner-city Chicago teenagers, Arthur Agee and William Gates, who hope eventually to play in the NBA. Joravsky vividly portrays the harsh realities of ghetto life on Chicago's West Side, describing the hardships and aspirations of the people who live there. He also reveals the exploitative nature of the current basketball recruiting system, which often places the goal of winning ahead of the players' overall welfare. Joravsky's interviews with the athletes and their families enabled him to explore their backgrounds thoroughly. In recounting the stories of Agee and Gates, as well as those around them, this work transcends the game of basketball, and offers profound insights into American urban society.

KENT M. KRAUSE

See also Sport

Beecher Family

Boydston, Jeanne, Mary Kelley, and Anne Margolis (editors), *The Limits of Sisterhood: The Beecher Sisters on Women's Rights and Woman's Sphere*, Chapel Hill: University of North Carolina Press, 1988

Caskey, Marie, *Chariot of Fire: Religion and the Beecher Family*, New Haven: Yale University Press, 1978

Clark, Clifford E., Jr., *Henry Ward Beecher: Spokesman for a Middle-Class America*, Urbana: University of Illinois Press, 1978

Hedrick, Joan D., *Harriet Beecher Stowe: A Life*, New York: Oxford University Press, 1994

McLoughlin, William G., *The Meaning of Henry Ward Beecher: An Essay on the Shifting Values of Mid-Victorian America, 1840–1870*, New York: Knopf, 1970

Rugoff, Milton, *The Beechers: An American Family in the Nineteenth Century*, New York: Harper, 1981

Sklar, Kathryn Kish, *Catharine Beecher: A Study in American Domesticity*, New Haven: Yale University Press, 1973

Stowe, Lyman Beecher, *Saints, Sinners, and Beechers*, Indianapolis: Bobbs Merrill, 1934

Waller, Altina L., *Reverend Beecher and Mrs. Tilton: Sex and Class in Victorian America*, Amherst: University of Massachusetts Press, 1982

Perhaps no other American family symbolizes 19th-century American culture as clearly as the Beechers: Henry Ward Beecher, Catharine Beecher, and Harriet Beecher Stowe were household names in the fields of religion, education, and literature. Their father, Lyman Beecher, was a powerful and popular preacher of evangelical Congregationalism and a direct descendant of the Puritans. A strong and domineering man, it was against his influence and thought that his children defined themselves, and their work would mirror America's transformation, as some have characterized it, from Puritan to Victorian America. The Beechers were American society, writ large. As such, they have been an attractive subject for biographers and historians.

There are two good general works on the family which provide a starting point. Much the older of the two, STOWE is the work of a direct descendant of Harriet Beecher Stowe, which offers an idiosyncratic and occasionally amusing account of the clan from the inside, including a number of anecdotes. It merits attention for this "inside knowledge" as well as for being the first biography of the family as a whole. But the most impressive and thorough work on the Beechers is RUGOFF. Highly readable as well as scholarly, Rugoff excels in analysis and discussion of the careers of Lyman Beecher, his children, and succeeding generations. Following in the footsteps of other scholars, Rugoff expanded upon the notion of the Beechers as symbolic of the nation and the century, and placed the stories of the various family members within their historical context. Once they are viewed in this way, the reader will be hard-pressed to imagine 19th-century America without the Beechers, and the Beechers without 19th-century America. Had the Beechers not existed, the United States would have had to invent them.

CASKEY is an admirable study of the clan and religion, the one factor that ineluctably informed the lives and careers of all Beechers. Lyman Beecher was a charismatic and stern minister, whose angry and unbending God alternately cowed his children into "appropriate" behavior and incited them to rebellion. In later life, Henry, who had followed his father into the ministry, withdrew from the pulpit because of his disbelief in a literal hell and his advocacy of evolution. Catharine became first a Unitarian and later an Episcopalian, and may have advocated women's moral role in the home as an antidote to the influence of male clergy. Harriet, too, would come to reject her father's Calvinism and champion radical abolitionism and women's rights. Caskey explores the spiritual conflicts between Lyman and his children in depth, and points out their significance in the careers of the various Beechers.

The Limits of Sisterhood, a collection of primary documents written by Catharine Beecher, Harriet Beecher Stowe, and Isabella Beecher Hooker (who was active in the women's rights movement), has useful introductory essays by BOYDSTON *et al.* at the start of each chapter. The authors sometimes rely on feminist analysis to an exaggerated degree, but, as the only volume specifically devoted to the women in the Beecher family, this is essential reading.

Catharine Beecher, the eldest of Lyman Beecher's children by his first wife, was a pioneer in the field of women's education and "domestic economy." An advocate of women's role in the home, she advised women to refrain from participation in the public and political sphere in favor of exercising a nurturing, moral influence on their families. She herself did not follow these prescriptions for female behavior. The one indispensable work on this formidable woman is SKLAR, a standard text in many college courses. Her book, although intended for an academic audience, is lucid and well-written and can be read with pleasure and comprehension by students and general readers. Sklar places both Catharine and the field of women's education within the 19th-century concept of a "woman's sphere" and analyzes its significance in the lives of male and female Americans.

Harriet Beecher Stowe is known to most Americans as the author of the most influential piece of American fiction, *Uncle Tom's Cabin*. Until recently there was no good biography of this woman whose reputation in later years suffered from her attacks on Lord Byron (which ironically have been borne out by the historical record). HEDRICK fills this gap, in an authoritative, well-written and exhaustively researched work, which tells Harriet's story in a sympathetic yet subjective style, and shows how her life and work influenced each other. She also gives Stowe's husband, Calvin, the acknowledgment which he deserves for his role in his wife's work.

Henry Ward Beecher became an even more influential clergyman than his father. Known for the eloquence of his sermons, Beecher influenced Americans' religious and political views, taking an active and radical stand on the events leading up to and during the Civil War. He himself became the center of controversy later in life when he was accused of adultery with the wife of a parishioner, and his influence waned thereafter. There are a number of books available on him, the best of which are McLoughlin's analytical work, Clark's biography, and Waller's more specialized study. McLOUGHLIN broke new ground in showing that Henry should be remembered for much more than the Tilton adultery scandal and that his influence on American society was far-reaching. This approach was a refreshing change from previous studies, which had often been heavily biased. CLARK furthered McLoughlin's work in a persuasive interpretive biography of Henry, which is probably the best starting point for a study of the man and his life. WALLER is an academic yet eloquent study which presents a political and social explanation for the eruption of the Beecher scandal, and shows, once again, how his life and the lives of his family intersected with their era and their country.

JEAN V. BERLIN

Bell, Alexander Graham 1847–1922
Inventor

Bruce, Robert V., *Bell: Alexander Graham Bell and the Conquest of Solitude*, London: Gollancz, and Boston: Little Brown, 1973

Eber, Dorothy, *Genius at Work: Images of Alexander Graham Bell*, New York: Viking, 1982

MacKenzie, Catherine, *Alexander Graham Bell*, Boston: Houghton Mifflin, 1928

Parkin, J.H., *Bell and Baldwin: Their Development of Aerodromes and Hydrodomes at Baddeck, Nova Scotia*, Toronto: University of Toronto Press, 1964

In view of Alexander Graham Bell's stature and the importance of his inventive work, the serious scholarly literature about him is disappointingly thin. Similarly, there has been only limited attention to the telephone either in the context of the history of technology and invention or in terms of its social consequences. It may be a revealing comment on attitudes on both sides of the Atlantic to the history of technology and the lives of the great inventors that most of the books on Bell published in the last decade have been addressed to children.

There was an early account of Bell's life, published six years after his death, by MacKENZIE, who was Bell's secretary. Like many such works by former colleagues or associates of the subject, it remains useful for its personal insights, and as a source of basic information.

BRUCE is the only major scholarly examination of Bell, and it is likely to stand for many years as the best and most comprehensive study of this fascinating and complex inventor. At almost 600 pages in length and packed with interesting detail, it offers a substantial yet sensitive and extremely readable description and assessment of the life of its subject. The work is based on research that Bruce conducted in the Bell papers held at the National Geographic Society in Washington, and the accompanying notes, for the most part, refer to this material. In all his work Bruce demonstrates his capacity to write extraordinarily well, but in Bell he has a subject worthy of his prose style.

The work is divided into three sections. The first covers the period from Bell's birth on 3 March 1847 up to his departure for Canada in 1870. The second focuses on the years in which Bell developed not only the telephone but also his abilities in teaching the deaf to speak. During this middle phase, he also became a professor at Boston University, taught first at the Boston School for Deaf Mutes (later the Horace Mann School) and then at Clarke School, and met his wife, Mabel Hubbard. The third part of the book covers the years following Bell's filing of Patent 174,465, which was to establish both his reputation and his fortune, and examines his later experiments into flight (the search for a stronger wing for airplanes) and into the hydrofoil, and his research into genetics. As Bruce puts it, "[n]o one word covers all [Bell's] activities, but the one that covers most is the word 'communication.' It applies to his work as a young teacher of speech, as a phonetician, as an advocate and teacher of speech for the deaf, as inventor of the telephone, as an organizer and collaborator in the development of the phonograph and the airplane, as a frequent and masterful public speaker, and as backer and adviser of key journals in the fields of general science, deafness, and geography." Yet, for all this, as Bruce shows, Bell was a strangely isolated individual, particularly in his later years. His life was not without tragedy: both his brothers had died of tuberculosis and, much later, his son died of breathing difficulties when Bell himself was in Washington trying to save the life of President Garfield. Such events may have contributed to Bell's solitary inclinations, but the overpowering sense that one gets from Bruce's work is of a man who was continuously involved with others and who did much to improve their lives.

Apart from Bruce, the only other significant studies of Bell are those by Parkin and Eber. PARKIN is an older study of the later part of Bell's career with special reference to his work on hydrofoils and aircraft in Baddeck. Very different in concept, EBER offers an insight into Bell as an individual through its combination of photographs and personal reminiscences from those who knew Bell, including members of his family, Helen Keller, and others. This is a large-format work, and the photographs which chart Bell's life from his early work for the deaf in Boston through to his kite-flying days at Baddeck are beautifully reproduced. Used in conjunction with Bruce, these two studies provide further fascinating material on Bell's life and work.

As already indicated, the dearth of significant scholarly work on Bell since the publication of Bruce's book is in sharp contrast to the steady stream of books for children about Bell and the telephone, which have been published during the 1990s. Examples include books by Andrew Dunn (1990), Richard Tames (1990), Steve Parker (1994) – and probably the best of the group for adult readers seeking a quick introduction to the subject, Michael Pollard (1991).

It may well be true that the lives of the great inventors are not a currently fashionable route into the history of technology, but it is a matter for regret that such work should be confined to school books aimed at young readers. One must be grateful

that the life and work of Alexander Graham Bell have inspired at least one scholar worthy of the subject, in the person of Robert V. Bruce.

S-M. GRANT

See also Telegraph and Telephone

Bellamy, Edward 1850–1898
Utopian thinker and social critic

Bellamy, Edward, *Looking Backward, 2000–1887*, Boston: Ticknor, 1888; edited by Cecelia Tichi, New York and Harmondsworth: Penguin, 1982; edited by Daniel H. Borus, New York: Bedford Books of St. Martin's Press, 1994

Bowman, Sylvia, *Edward Bellamy*, Boston: Twayne, 1986

Kumar, Krishan, *Utopia and Anti-Utopia in Modern Times*, Oxford: Blackwell, 1987

Lipow, Arthur, *Authoritarian Socialism in America: Edward Bellamy and the Nationalist Movement*, Berkeley: University of California Press, 1982

Patai, Daphne (editor), *Looking Backward, 1988–1888: Essays on Edward Bellamy*, Amherst: University of Massachusetts Press, 1988

Pfaelzer, Jean, *The Utopian Novel in America, 1886–1896: The Politics of Form*, Pittsburgh: University of Pittsburgh Press, 1984

Roemer, Kenneth M., *The Obsolete Necessity: America in Utopian Writings, 1888–1900*, Kent, Ohio: Kent State University Press, 1976

Thomas, John L., *Alternative America: Henry George, Edward Bellamy, Henry Demarest Lloyd and the Adversary Tradition*, Cambridge, MA: Belknap Press of Harvard University Press, 1983

Edward Bellamy's relatively short career as a journalist, novelist and utopian writer spanned a period of extremely rapid industrialization and social change in the United States. With antecedents in the Puritan clergy and spending much of his life in a small Massachusetts town that itself became dominated by factories, Bellamy can be seen as representative of the cultural and moral dilemmas that the 19th century posed to members of the Yankee middle class. His utopian novel *Looking Backward, 2000-1887*, published in 1888, briefly gave Bellamy public prominence, inspired a political movement, and led to an outpouring of writing (much of it imitative) that gave a new lease of life to the utopian literary tradition. Though it was never accepted into the "great tradition" of works taught in academic literature departments, the political interest and inherent utopian fascination of its vision of a future American society has kept *Looking Backward* in print, and kept Bellamy from the obscurity into which most comparable New England writers of his period have since sunk.

Though he worked as a journalist and helped found an important regional newspaper, the Springfield (Massachusetts) *Daily News*, Bellamy became chiefly absorbed by the challenge of writing fiction. He barely broke away from the conventions of contemporary romantic writing, but, as Thomas shows in his biographical essay, Bellamy's early work began to engage the political, social and moral problems that he saw besetting post-Civil War America, particularly its greed, waste and industrial conflict. Too young to fight in the Civil War, and rejected as an applicant to West Point in 1867, Bellamy was fascinated by the war and by the military as instances of collective, altruistic action in an otherwise divided and selfish society. In an unpublished essay, "The Religion of Solidarity," written in 1873–74, he set out ideas about the moral bases for social action that would strongly influence his later work. PATAI discusses the other themes which Bellamy explored in short stories and longer works of the 1870s and early 1880s – a fascination with the interplay between past, present, and future; the potential of time-travel, dreams and memory as devices for commenting on the present state of society; and the moral and psychological implications of his characters' translation from one period to another.

BELLAMY's *Looking Backward* brought together these themes of solidarity, the military example, social commentary, time-travel, dreams, and psychological tension in the romance of Julian West, who awakes to find himself in the Boston of the year 2000 in a society stripped of the inequalities, competitiveness, labor strife, political corruption, waste and poverty of the late 19th century. Critical introductions by Tichi (1987) and Borus (1994) to their editions of the novel provide good biographical material, and link Bellamy's most famous work to its wider context. Bellamy imagined a new society of efficiency, equality and material abundance, made possible in part by technological advances, but mainly an achievement of organizational reform, in which all activity is nationalized, incomes are guaranteed, work is done by an industrial army of the under-45s, and politics replaced by administrative co-ordination. Painting the contrasts between present faults and the future ideal, Bellamy coined some of the most striking and eloquent images of late-19th century social criticism. Employing his character, Julian West, as the emissary of the past in his future world, Bellamy indicated the possibilities of moral redemption through social action.

Looking Backward's combination of political tract and romantic story contributed to its influence. Bellamy found himself, reluctantly at first, at the head of a middle-class political movement based on so-called Bellamy Clubs or Nationalist Clubs that flourished briefly in the late 1880s and early 1890s. Dozens of writers were inspired to mimic, extend or criticize the book by producing utopian fiction of their own. Bellamy himself before the end of his life published a sequel, *Equality*, which traced Julian West's further experiences in the new society in a lengthy tract only very thinly wrapped in a novelistic plot. ROEMER and PFAELZER each trace the rise and limitations of this phase of utopian writing in America; KUMAR traces Bellamy's wider influence on the 20th century utopian tradition, not least through the work of the English writer William Morris, who was provoked by *Looking Backward* to write his own utopian novel, *News from Nowhere*, in 1890.

Inevitably *Looking Backward*, which far outstripped his other writings in its influence, has been a major focus for evaluations of Bellamy's life. BOWMAN, the most recent book-length biography, is principally concerned with the strengths and weaknesses of the ideas presented in the novel, and also discusses Bellamy's influence on 20th-century Progressives and liberals. But this legacy is much debated, and interpretations of Bellamy's politics run in at least three different directions. THOMAS locates him in a liberal/socialist tradition that explored the potential of political action to secure radical social change in an unjust society, though his stress on the parallels between Bellamy and others in this tradition has been criticized by some scholars. Writing just before Thomas, LIPOW associated Bellamy's vision with the late 19th-century "turn" in European socialist thought that would lead to authoritarianism and the excesses of Stalinism, an association that would no doubt have shocked the gentle minister's son from Chicopee Falls. More recent accounts have linked the authoritarian strands in Bellamy's thought to a basic conservatism evident, according to Pfaelzer, in his fictional style as well as his overt opinions. Essays in the Patai volume, in particular, note the paternalistic implications of a vision that saw social transformation emerging from peaceful change, not revolution; as the apotheosis of monopoly capitalism, not its overthrow; and as a future in which the bourgeoisie would find itself comfortably at home, not threatened or expropriated. Bellamy, in this view, was not really a socialist at all but the longest-lasting of the Mugwumps. We still need a full-length biographical study that could evaluate these conflicting interpretations.

CHRISTOPHER CLARK

See also Utopian and Communitarian Movements

Bennett, James Gordon   1795-1872
Newspaper editor

Carlson, Oliver, *The Man Who Made News: James Gordon Bennett*, New York: Duell, Sloan and Pearce, 1942

Crouthamel, James L., *Bennett's New York Herald and the Rise of the Popular Press*, Syracuse: Syracuse University Press, 1989

Fermer, Douglas, *James Gordon Bennett and the New York Herald: A Study of Editorial Opinion in the Civil War Era, 1854–1867*, New York: St. Martin's Press, and London: Royal Historical Society, 1986

Pray, Isaac C., *Memoirs of J.G. Bennett and His Times: By a Journalist*, New York, Stringer and Townsend, 1855; reprinted, New York: Arno Press, 1970

Schiller, Dan, *Objectivity and the News: The Public and the Rise of Commercial Journalism*, Philadelphia: University of Pennsylvania Press, 1981

Schudson, Michael, *Discovering the News: A Social History of American Newspapers*, New York: Basic Books, 1978

Seitz, Don C., *The James Gordon Bennetts, Father and Son: Proprietors of the New York Herald*, Indianapolis: Bobbs Merrill, 1928

A pioneer among publicists, James Gordon Bennett has been the subject of a number of biographies and studies of the press in the United States. Best known as the founder and long-time editor of the *New York Herald*, Bennett was also one of the most renowned and active figures in 19th-century American politics. The earliest useful study of Bennett is PRAY, who claimed, usually against Bennett's denials, to be a close associate of the editor. Drawn mostly from Bennett's own editorials recounting his personal history, this memoir provides the richest account available of the editor's youth in Scotland and his first years in the United States. This is a highly sympathetic biography with little organization and not much analysis of Bennett's motivations. The work was published in 1855, and thus is of little value to those curious about Bennett's activities in the critical period before and during the Civil War.

Little work on Bennett appeared in the late 19th century. The first full-length biography was SEITZ. The author, a journalist himself, was primarily interested in Bennett's career as an editor. The narrative is quite readable, but it is patchy, and omits Bennett's involvement in numerous events of the mid-19th century. Like many biographies of its period, the book substitutes long passages of original texts – particularly from the *New York Herald* – for substantive analysis. The work is a rich source for Bennett's editorial opinion, but it uses little source material besides the *Herald*. The last two-fifths of the book follows the career of Bennett's son, James Gordon Bennett, Jr., who also chose the newspaper profession. Unfortunately, the author makes little attempt to explore the personal connection between the two men.

CARLSON is a much more thorough biography, though it is also primarily occupied with telling lively tales about Bennett's entertaining and cavalier approach to newspaper work. Although this is not a scholarly work – there are no citations and only a small bibliography – the author quotes extensively from Bennett's paper to make the good point that the editor was one of the first in his profession to take independent political positions rather than serving the interests of a party machine. Bennett emerges here as a purveyor of information rather than consistent opinion. While the biography gives a comprehensive account of the editor's life up to the end of the Civil War, it is notably thin on Bennett's attitudes and experiences during Reconstruction.

Two recent studies of Bennett have offered a more rigorous analysis of the editor's attitudes and career. FERMER concentrates on Bennett's editorial positions during the era of sectional conflict, specifically 1854 to 1867. This is the first study to use manuscript collections, both of Bennett himself (unfortunately, the two main sets of Bennett papers are rather skimpy) and of his contemporaries. The author tracks the editor's sometimes rather unpredictable stances, from his defense of the Know Nothings in New York to his support for John C. Frémont in 1856 to his opposition to Abraham Lincoln in the early years of the Civil War. This is the earliest work to probe with some depth Bennett's rampant racism, but it fails to connect the editor's racial views satisfactorily with his other political stances. While this is the most analytical and well-researched study, one is left wanting to know what threads, if any, connected Bennett's opinions during these important years.

This is also a problem in CROUTHAMEL, which admittedly does not purport to be a study of Bennett's attitudes or his personal life, but rather an examination of his place in the rise of the popular press during the middle decades of the 19th century. The early chapters present the author's case that Bennett was the first truly modern editor, but the chapters on the 1850s and 1860s are less about newspapers than about

the *Herald*'s engagement with major events of the day. Much more compact and well-organized than its predecessors, it gives little attention, however, to Bennett's post-war years, when he curiously dropped his support of Andrew Johnson, and then turned against the radical Republicans.

Many general histories of journalism also give Bennett his due as an innovator, but two are particularly worth noting. SCHUDSON properly places Bennett's early years at the *Herald* in the context of the development of the penny press in Jacksonian America. The editor's ability to transform news into entertainment and his attention to the economic realities and profitable potential of running a newspaper emerge as a natural outgrowth of the market revolution transforming Jacksonian society. Bennett's journalism, then, emerges as a product of new middle-class values. This approach is critically examined and qualified by SCHILLER. A literary analysis of commercial journalism in the 19th century, this work contends that the claim of Bennett and other editors to objectivity was not necessarily a natural product of the development of an amorphous middle class. Rather, Bennett and his associates were opportunistically and consciously responding to the belief of a specific group – working-class tradespeople – that knowledge, like any other commodity, should be made easily available. Bennett's particular skill was in manipulating the republican rhetoric of egalitarianism into usable language for tradespeople.

MICHAEL VORENBERG

See also Newspapers and Magazines

Benton, Thomas Hart   1782–1858
Politician, United States Senator

Chambers, William N., *Old Bullion Benton: Senator from the New West*, Boston: Little Brown, 1956
Feller, Daniel, *The Public Lands in Jacksonian Politics*, Madison: University of Wisconsin Press, 1984
Herr, Pamela, *Jessie Benton Frémont: A Biography*, New York: Watts, 1987
McCandless, Perry, *A History of Missouri*, volume 2: *1820–1860*, Columbia: University of Missouri Press, 1973
Nagel, Paul C., *Missouri: A Bicentennial History*, New York: Norton, 1977
Smith, Elbert B., *Magnificent Missourian: The Life of Thomas Hart Benton*, Philadelphia: Lippincott, 1958

Despite the longevity of Thomas Hart Benton's political career and his prominence as a Jacksonian stalwart, he has not received the scholarly attention enjoyed by some of his rivals. In comparison with figures such as Henry Clay, John C. Calhoun and Daniel Webster, there is a relative paucity of interest in the Missouri Senator. Benton has fewer modern biographies than these figures, and the more general histories of the Jacksonian era seldom provide extended treatment of his role in the various controversies of the period.

The most authoritative and valuable study is CHAMBERS, which portrays Benton as the most distinctive representative of the democratic movement, excepting only Andrew Jackson himself. Chambers sees Jacksonian Democracy as adding social and economic equality to the older Jeffersonian idea of political equality, and argues that Benton, as evidenced by his commitment to a cheap land policy and his hard-money stance during the Bank War, was fully in tune with this shift of emphasis. He suggests that Benton's attitude to political parties differed from that of contemporaries such as Martin Van Buren in that, while he valued their usefulness, he regarded them more as a means to an end rather than an end in themselves. Moreover, Chambers contends, Benton was not tied down to specific class interests as were his senatorial rivals, Clay, Calhoun and Webster. Ultimately, therefore, he believes that Benton, as a sincere and forthright advocate of the interests of the nation's small farmers and working men, stands out as one of the foremost champions of an egalitarian Jacksonian Democracy.

The other major biography is SMITH, which was published shortly after Chambers. This too offers a favourable interpretation of the "undauntable" senator from Missouri as the title of the book itself readily indicates. Benton's public career is outlined as an ongoing attempt to provide equality of opportunity for the majority of white, male Americans, and the major events of the Jacksonian era in which he played a leading role are evaluated from that perspective. Thus, his attitudes towards land policy and the Bank of the United States as well as his support for direct, popular election of the president are offered as clear evidence of his faith in democracy. Smith also makes much of Benton's status as spokesman for the West and as a statesman with a national vision. Combining the brash self-confidence of the frontier with a conscious emulation of Roman senatorial grandeur and dignity, Smith's Benton at times takes on near-heroic proportions, not least in his courageous campaigning against pro-slavery forces in Missouri towards the end of his career. Though overstating its case somewhat, this study remains a useful and important account of Benton's political career, and the overall picture of the bombastic Benton as an unshakeable democrat, if not an egalitarian radical, is a persuasive one.

Although primarily concerned with the remarkable life and times of Jessie Benton Frémont and her relationship with the colourful John C. Frémont, HERR nevertheless provides some useful insights into the personality and private life of Thomas Benton. Suggesting that Jessie Benton's abundant energies and talents were diverted into making a success of her husband's career because of the limited opportunities available to her as a woman, Herr explores the support and encouragement which Benton gave his daughter, and offers a fresh analysis of the importance of his family relationships.

FELLER returns to older interpretations of Jacksonian Democracy, stressing economic divisions in an attempt to revise what he sees as the "new orthodoxy" of ethno-cultural histories. Arguing that politics underwent a fundamental transformation from sectional self-interest to partisan conflict when parties formed in the 1830s around the critical economic issues of tariffs, internal improvements, banking and, most importantly, land policy, this concise, well-written study assigns Benton the key role in leading the cheap land forces. A consistent and formidable defender of the rights of the people to settle the new lands of the West with minimal interference and at low cost, Benton championed various strategies – the cession of federally-owned lands to the states, pre-emption, graduation – by which this crucial aim might be achieved. Feller is not entirely convincing in his assessment of land policy as the central component of the Jacksonian creed, but his analysis of Benton's leadership of the "Sagebrush rebellion" contributes greatly to our understanding of a vitally important aspect of Benton's career.

General histories of the state politics of Missouri are helpful in achieving a more rounded appreciation of Benton's political career as a whole. McCANDLESS provides an informative basic history of the state during the ante-bellum era which pays considerable attention to the triumph of Jacksonian Democracy in the 1820s and 1830s, and the controversies over the slavery issues in the 1840s and 1850s, both areas of interest to Benton scholars. NAGEL offers a standard narrative of Benton's political activities in Missouri in the context of a wider history. A lively account, this offers little that is new or challenging on Benton, but it does allow a clear focus on the political heritage of the state in which he functioned so effectively and is interesting as a study of the lingering influence of Jeffersonian political ideals in the emergent frontier states of the West.

NEIL CURTIN

See also Public Land Policy

Bethune, Mary McLeod 1875–1955

African American educator and civil rights campaigner

Collier-Thomas, Bettye, "National Council of Negro Women," in *Black Women in America: An Historical Encyclopedia*, 2 vols., edited by Darlene Clark Hine and others, New York: Carlson, 1993

Holt, Rackham, *Mary McLeod Bethune: A Biography*, New York: Doubleday, 1964

Ross, B. Joyce, "Mary McLeod Bethune and the National Youth Administration: A Case Study of Power Relationships in the Black Cabinet of Franklin D. Roosevelt," in *Black Women in United States History*, vol. 8, edited by Darlene Clark Hine, New York: Carlson, 1990

Smith, Elaine M., "Mary McLeod Bethune and the National Youth Administration," in *Clio Was a Woman: Studies in the History of American Women*, edited by Mabel E. Deutrich and Virginia C. Purdy, Washington, DC: Howard University Press, 1980

Smith, Elaine M., "Mary McLeod Bethune," in *Black Women in America: An Historical Encyclopedia*, edited by Darlene Clark Hine and others, 2 vols., New York: Carlson, 1993

Sterne, Emma, *Mary McLeod Bethune*, New York: Knopf, 1957

Despite the impressive contributions of Mary McLeod Bethune over the 80 years of her life, little has been written about this extraordinary African American educator and leader. The earliest book-length biographies of Bethune bordered on hagiography. As a young girl, STERNE met Bethune and was smitten by "her charm, her wit and humor, her oratory, and her indefinable quality of leadership." At several points this volume's use of Bethune's success as a way of extolling the virtues of American democracy and urging others to replicate her success becomes tiresome. However, Sterne does provide a great deal of background information about Reconstruction and the advent of Jim Crow in the South. Another rather idealized biography of Bethune is HOLT. Although it presents a very romanticized version of Bethune's impoverished childhood, it does include a great deal of detail about Bethune's long educational career and various national leadership roles. However, although Holt at times gives the reader glimpses into the role which gender played in Bethune's life and leadership positions, that discussion is cursory at best. The reader is left wondering if Bethune ever felt restricted by the gender role expectations of her time. In short, Holt and Sterne both focus on Bethune's race to the exclusion of her gender.

It is not until the revival of women's history that Bethune reappears in historical literature. SMITH (1980) is an important contribution since it is one of the first works to focus on Bethune's position in the New Deal's National Youth Administration, first as a member of the Advisory Board and later as Director of the NYA's Division of Negro Affairs. This article serves as a vehicle for examination not only of Bethune's work during the NYA's existence, but also of her role in bridging the gap between President Franklin Roosevelt, a personal friend, and members of the black political community. Unfortunately, Smith falls prey to the same problem that faced Sterne and Holt; the analysis of Bethune continues to revolve solely around race with no consideration of gender.

Yet another piece dealing with Bethune's career in the National Youth Administration is ROSS, who places Bethune in the context of the other African Americans who held administrative posts in New Deal agencies. The members of this so-called "Black Cabinet" became unofficial spokespersons for African American interests within the Roosevelt Administration. As an important member of this cabinet, Bethune was sometimes in the position of having to make conciliatory and self-effacing remarks to white or biracial organizations that did not reflect her own strong racial pride. Ross places these remarks in the context of the New Deal and compares Bethune's leadership style to that of other members of the "Black Cabinet."

Most recently, both Collier-Thomas and Smith provide excellent articles on Bethune and her organization, the National Council of Negro Women. COLLIER-THOMAS's treatment of the National Council of Negro Women, an organization founded by Bethune in 1935, provides information on her long service as president of the group. In a brief, 13-page sketch, SMITH (1993) provides an excellent overview of Bethune's life, which avoids the excessively laudatory tone of Sterne and Holt. It includes a discussion of Bethune's work as an educator, her tenure as a member of the NYA and her vast voluntary activities, as well as a brief bibliography for further information.

VANESSA L. DAVIS

Bill of Rights, 1789–1791

Brant, Irving, *The Bill of Rights: Its Origins and Meaning*, Indianapolis: Bobbs Merrill, 1965
Conley, Patrick T. and John P. Kaminski (editors), *The Bill of Rights and the States: The Colonial and Revolutionary Origins of American Liberties*, Madison, WI: Madison House 1992
Dumbauld, Edward, *The Bill of Rights and What It Means Today*, Norman: University of Oklahoma Press, 1957
Hall, Kermit L. (editor), *By and for the People: Constitutional Rights in American History*, Arlington Heights, IL: Harlan Davidson, 1991
Hall, Kermit L. and others (editors), *The Oxford Companion to the Supreme Court of the United States*, New York and Oxford: Oxford University Press, 1992
Hickok, Eugene W., Jr. (editor), *The Bill of Rights: Original Meaning and Current Understanding*, Charlottesville: University Press of Virginia, 1991
Kukla, Jon (editor), *The Bill of Rights: A Lively Heritage*, Richmond: Virginia State Library and Archives, 1987
Levy, Leonard W. and Kenneth L. Karst (editors), *Encyclopedia of the American Constitution*, 4 vols., New York: Macmillan, and London: Collier Macmillan, 1986
Levy, Leonard W. and Kenneth L. Karst, *Encyclopedia of the American Constitution: Supplement 1*, New York: Macmillan, 1992
Rutland, Robert Allen, *The Birth of the Bill of Rights, 1776–1791*, Chapel Hill: University of North Carolina Press, 1955
Schwartz, Bernard, *The Great Rights of Mankind: A History of the American Bill of Rights*, New York: Oxford University Press, 1977; revised, Madison, WI: Madison House, 1992

Interest in the first ten amendments to the United States Constitution, or the Bill of Rights as they are better known, is a fairly recent development. Until about forty years ago they were considered as something that was tacked onto the Constitution at the end of the ratification struggle, and generally did not receive much attention from scholars. For the seventy years following the adoption of the Constitution the central question was the debate over the origin and nature of the union and the issue of how power should be distributed between the central government and the states. For almost a century thereafter, constitutional discourse focused on the power of the national government, under the Constitution, to regulate the economic life of the country. Only in the 20th century, and especially during its second half, have civil liberties and civil rights emerged as a central concern. Indeed, for many people, the Bill of Rights is the Constitution today. As a consequence, there has, in recent years, developed a substantial if disconnected literature on the Bill of Rights, much of which tends to be informed by contemporary ideological and political concerns.

Modern scholarship on the Bill of Rights begins with RUTLAND who was the first scholar to study it as an entity apart from the Constitution itself. His emphasis is on how and why the first ten amendments were adopted. For Rutland, James Madison is the central figure in the movement to create a bill of rights, and he was motivated mainly by political concerns: to get elected to the House of Representatives and to head off Antifederalist efforts to call a second Constitutional Convention. The book contains some valuable details but is weak on interpretation and analysis.

DUMBAULD covers much the same ground as Rutland but contains more material on the roots and meaning of the specific amendments. Legalistic in his approach and weak on historical context, Dumbauld plunders the past for various English, colonial and state precedents for the Bill of Rights. He also places primary emphasis on the role played by Madison in their adoption.

A much fuller treatment of the origins and meaning of the Bill of Rights is to be found in BRANT. His book is particularly useful for the information it provides on the English and colonial background of the individual amendments. He also adopts a broader definition of the Bill of Rights than his predecessors, including a discussion of such rights as the prohibition against bills of attainder and *habeas corpus* that are contained in the Constitution itself. He argues that Madison was motivated by more than political considerations and was genuinely committed to the rights protected by the first ten amendments. However, the book is in many ways a tract for its times. It is written from a strongly liberal point of view that stresses the dangers of arbitrary government. SCHWARTZ is the best of the general treatments of the Bill of Rights because it is the most knowledgeable, analytical and systematic of the studies of how the first ten amendments were added to the Constitution. It traces the English, colonial and revolutionary antecedents of the Bill of Rights, the relationship of the issue of judicial review to individual liberties during the Confederation period, the debate over the Bill of Rights during the drafting and ratification of the Constitution, its legislative history during the first Congress, and its ratification by the states, although on this last point the sources are quite recalcitrant.

There also exists a large and disparate literature on the individual amendments that make up the Bill of Rights. It takes the form of articles in historical, legal and political science journals and essays in encyclopedias, anthologies and various books. Help in tracking them down can be obtained from an extensive bibliographical essay by Gaspare J. Saladino in CONLEY and KAMINSKI. This book also contains essays on the development of civil rights and liberties in the different colonies and states in the years before the adoption of the Bill of Rights. This provides a comparative dimension and shows how varied and complex it is as a subject.

LEVY and KARST (1986, 1992) are particularly valuable. This high quality reference work contains brief essays on almost every aspect of the United States Constitution, including the Bill of Rights in general, each of the first ten amendments, and various parts or clauses of these amendments. The essays are arranged in alphabetical order, are appropriately cross-referenced, have bibliographical references, and are indexed, which makes the volumes easy to use. The different entries are by professional scholars and are generally authoritative. These same virtues are also to be found in HALL (1992) where the essays are even more succinct.

KUKLA is another valuable starting point for studying the individual amendments. It contains carefully documented essays by various authors on each of the different amendments.

Some are mainly concerned with the English and colonial background, while others stress how they have been interpreted by the courts and how their meanings have evolved since their adoption in 1791. HALL (1991) provides an unusually clear and comprehensible introduction to the study of the individual amendments. HICKOK contains a wide variety of essays of uneven quality on the different amendments, and a number of their clauses. It is a particularly good introduction to the interpretive problems that are raised when one attempts to apply the concept of original intent to contemporary decision-making.

RICHARD E. ELLIS

See also Constitution: Ratification

Birth Control

Chesler, Ellen, *Woman of Valor: Margaret Sanger and the Birth Control Movement in America*, New York: Simon and Schuster, 1992

Easterlin, Richard A., "Population Change and Farm Settlement in the Northern United States," *Journal of Economic History*, 36, 1976

Gordon, Linda, *Woman's Body, Woman's Right: A Social History of Birth Control in America*, New York: Grossman, 1976, Harmondsworth: Penguin, 1977; revised, New York: Penguin, 1990

Kennedy, David M., *Birth Control in America: The Career of Margaret Sanger*, New Haven: Yale University Press, 1970

McFalls, Joseph, Jr., and George S. Masnick, "Birth Control and the Fertility of the US Black Population, 1880–1980," *Journal of Family History*, 6, 1981

Mohr, James C., *Abortion in America: The Origins and Evolution of National Policy, 1800–1900*, New York: Oxford University Press, 1978

Reed, James, *From Private Vice to Public Virtue: The Birth Control Movement and American Society since 1830*, New York: Basic Books, 1978

Wells, Robert V., "Family History and Demographic Transition," *Journal of Social History*, 9, 1975

Our understanding of the history of birth control in America is still incomplete. In the past, notions of privacy and propriety have limited the sources available to historians for determining how and why Americans prevented conception and birth. However, historians have been able to throw light on some elements of the story. Demographic historians have identified a dramatic decline in birth rates after 1800, finding that white marital fertility dropped from an average of 7.04 births per woman around 1800 to 3.56 births by 1900. Other historians using more traditional methods have been able to outline the development of birth control techniques and technology, while still others have chronicled the history of the various organized movements for and against birth control.

EASTERLIN exemplifies the attempt by demographic historians to understand the revolutionary 19th-century drop in fertility. As historians and demographers eliminated physiological causes of the fertility decline, they speculated that this widespread employment of birth control was the result of forces attending industrialization and urbanization. Easterlin and others, however, have challenged this causal relationship by demonstrating a significant decline in the birth rate of women in rural, pre-industrial regions of the country. But the search for an adequate alternative explanation has proven difficult. Easterlin argues that a growing shortage of land and an increase in the capital costs of farming led parents to curtail the number of children born to them, in order to guarantee adequate property for children when they reached adulthood. However, this argument does not account for variations in regional patterns, nor does it explain fertility decline in urban areas. In a revised version of the modernization theory, WELLS has suggested that the decreasing fertility rates can be ascribed to the development of a modernized world view. As Americans internalized the idea of control over one's own destiny, they began to manipulate family size. However, the sources of this attitudinal shift and how it came about cannot be adequately explained by Wells's demographic approach.

More recent work by demographic historians has included study of the fertility rates of ethnic and racial groups. These studies show that some groups began practicing birth control later than others. McFALLS and MASNICK argue that, although African American slave folklore included knowledge of contraception and abortion, it was not until the decades following Reconstruction, when they acquired knowledge of the birth control methods used by white Americans, that African American fertility dropped. Although this argument implies a comparison between pre- and post-emancipation birth control, there is still a need for a study of the impact of emancipation on this major shift in African American fertility.

Historians using more traditional methods and sources have also sought to understand why and how this shift in fertility came about. One of these is MOHR's excellent study of the legal history of abortion in America. He charts the changes in legal policy from the unrestricted access to abortion before "quickening," or about the fourth month of gestation, in the early 19th century, to the outlawing of abortion at any stage, by 1900. Mohr suggests that, though it was increasingly condemned by public opinion and especially by the medical profession, American middle-class women in the mid-19th century frequently resorted to abortion, to limit their fertility. However, this claim, based on speculation and anecdotal evidence, is the weakest part of the book.

One of the best studies of the development of birth control technology is REED. Examining the birth control movement from its initial stages in the early 1800s through the development of oral contraceptives in the 20th century, Reed makes it clear that Americans used a variety of devices before 1900, including douches, pessaries, and condoms. In the bulk of the book Reed uses the biographies of three reformers, Margaret Sanger, gynecologist Robert L. Dickson, and population control advocate Clarence J. Gamble, to illustrate what he sees as the three primary motivations of the birth control movement: a desire for female autonomy, the promotion of marital harmony, and a fear of the growing lower-class population. However, this focus on the movement's leaders does tend to overemphasize the actions of the few at the expense of the contributions of the many.

KENNEDY also combines biography and social history to tell the story of the early birth control movement. Focusing on Margaret Sanger and the organized birth control movement from 1912 to World War II, he argues that Sanger, who started her career as a radical anarchist, used liberal, Progressive Era techniques to garner public support for pro-birth control legislation. In a portrayal of Sanger which is less sanguine than Reed's, Kennedy argues that, though Sanger contributed much to the movement, she also hindered its progress through her emotionalism and her strong desire to assert control. CHESLER's lengthy biography of Sanger presents a more positive view of the reformer. Utilizing the full range of archival material left by Sanger, Chesler writes a biography that celebrates and deepens our understanding of her personality and her role in the birth control movement. Of particular importance are her portrayal of Sanger's contributions after 1945, and her endeavors to link the American movement with international birth control efforts.

One of the few works to describe birth control from a woman-centered view, and perhaps the best social history of the subject, is GORDON. Most societies in the past had effective forms of birth control, argues Gordon, but by the 19th century, men's attempt to regulate female reproduction (through the state and the medical establishment) had forced birth control underground. Thus, the movement of the 19th and 20th centuries should be seen as a movement for women's "sexual and reproductive self-determination." Gordon remains constantly aware of class and race as important factors in the history of birth control, and she is particularly effective when illuminating the relationship between the birth control movement and feminism.

SHAWN JOHANSEN

See also Sanger

Black Power

Aptheker, Herbert (editor), *One Continual Cry: David Walker's Appeal to the Colored Citizens of the World*, New York: Humanities Press, 1965

Brown, Elaine, *A Taste of Power: A Black Woman's Story*, New York: Pantheon, 1992

Carmichael, Stokely and Charles V. Hamilton, *Black Power: The Politics of Liberation in America*, New York: Random House, 1967; London: Cape, 1968

Clarke, John Henrik, *Marcus Garvey and the Vision of Africa*, New York: Vintage, 1974

Eure, Joseph D. and James G. Spady (editors), *Nation Conscious Rap*, New York: PC International Press, 1991

McCartney, John T., *Black Power Ideologies: An Essay in African-American Political Thought*, Philadelphia: Temple University Press, 1992

Pearson, Hugh, *The Shadow of the Panther: Huey Newton and the Price of Black Power in America*, Reading, MA: Addison Wesley, 1994

Scott, Robert L. and Wayne Brockriede (editors), *The Rhetoric of Black Power*, New York: Harper, 1969

Seale, Bobby, *Seize the Time: The Story of the Black Panther Party and Huey P. Newton*, New York: Random House, 1991

Van Deburg, William L., *New Day in Babylon: The Black Power Movement and American Culture, 1965–75*, Chicago: University of Chicago Press, 1992

The phrase "Black Power" has long been subject to a number of interpretations within both its general reference as a tradition within African American history, and its specific reference to the Black Revolution of the 1960s. Though used by novelist Richard Wright and politician Adam Clayton Powell, Jr. along with others earlier in the 20th century, its birth as a significant slogan is usually attributed to Student Nonviolent Coordinating Committee activists Willie Ricks and Stokely Carmichael during the march to Jackson, Mississippi in June 1966. CARMICHAEL and HAMILTON might be looked on, therefore, as a primary source in its articulation of a political framework and ideology which the authors regarded as the last reasonable opportunity for revolutionary action in the United States that could still possibly stay short of violence. However, the book also seeks to place Black Power in terms of its historical roots, its relationship to the Civil Rights movement, and its economic and social implications within American society. Thus, the book works as a bridge between the general and specific references of the phrase "Black Power."

McCARTNEY takes the general view, and provides a broad and systematic survey of various instances and interpretations of Black Power ideologies in the United States from colonial times until the 1970s. He includes discussion of colonization, abolition, accommodation, Garveyism, King and moralism, the Black Panthers, the Black Muslims, electoral politics, separatism, the place of Malcolm X, and an overall assessment of the significance, contributions, and effectiveness of Black Power ideologies. He seeks to place the specific Black Power Movement of the 1960s in the broader context of both African American and Western political thought in order to demonstrate that it was hardly unique in American history.

With a similar objective, but very different approach, APTHEKER focuses on David Walker as the initial articulator of Black Power ideology in published form, and includes the full text of his 1829 *Appeal* along with a valuable interpretive essay discussing its context, meaning, and influence. Although published immediately prior to the popular adoption of the Black Power slogan, this book also seeks to contextualize a long tradition of African American protest and assertion, and to counter the then widely-shared view among European-Americans that the uprisings of the 1960s were surprising or something new. CLARKE chooses Marcus Garvey as a central figure both in time and in ideology in the Black Power tradition in the United States, and his work links together numerous essays and interpretations, along with examples of Garvey's own writing. The book is very wide-ranging and intellectually stimulating, reaching back to 19th-century figures such as Martin Delany and Bishop Henry McNeal Turner along with Caribbean antecedents, and also projecting forward to Marxist thought, and independence and liberation movements. In the Garvey materials themselves, the reader can sense the slight restraining influence of Clarke's necessary dependence on Amy Jacques Garvey, the widow of Marcus, for access to essential

information, a bargain that was well worth making in order to achieve the depth and fascinating interpretive variety of the overall volume.

SCOTT and BROCKRIEDE provide a valuable rhetorical analysis of the various postures and interpretations of Black Power in the discourses of Stokely Carmichael, Martin Luther King, Jr., and Hubert Humphrey. Their critical approach illustrates the ambiguities and inconsistencies inherent in organizing a complex and controversial social movement around a simplified "soundbite" phrase. The authors clearly acknowledge the revolutionary nature of the ideology and its bold challenge to established patterns of social, political, and economic power in the United States, while seeking to assess the nature of its rhetorical intervention in American public rhetoric.

Writing with a strong sense of immediacy, SEALE offers an immediate history of the Black Panther Party for Self-Defense, perhaps the single entity most closely associated with the phrase Black Power. His book gives dramatic articulation to the attempt to deploy the ambiguous phrase in a clear and full-blown revolutionary political movement grounded in the thinking of Malcolm X, Mao, and Fanon, and strategized by Huey Newton, Seale himself, and other members of the party. Under the tremendous pressure of the official backlash to the rhetoric, symbolism, and thought of the Black Panthers, Seale provides a bracing view of the attempt not only to discuss, formulate and understand, but to enact the ideology of Black Power and run with it. At a further distance, BROWN, another chair of the Black Panther Party, provides a fuller and broader perspective on the Black Power movement of the 1960s and 1970s from a woman's viewpoint. McCartney is the only other author who looks deeply at the positioning and participation of women in Black Power, in his section on Shirley Chisholm. In her book, Brown does not so much debate the meaning of the phrase as problematize the whole issue of power while looking back on her own experiences in a movement that sought to make Black Power and socialist revolution realities. The stress and the contradictions eventually led to her own nervous breakdown and departure from the party, which she came to regard as both admirable and abusive. PEARSON also arrives at an ultimately negative view of the Panthers and Black Power, as movements that were too immediately burdened with the sort of sensational rhetoric and imagery that ultimately prevented much effective movement towards liberation. Unlike Brown, he locates this problem not so much in the corrupting and deranging effects of power, but in the confining stereotypes of a powerful sense of public fear and expectation of black disorderliness, into which he feels the Panthers too readily fell.

VAN DEBURG takes a cultural approach to the decade of Black Power's high tide, and asserts that Black Power is best understood as a flexible and encompassing cultural term that both connects and inflects the various ideological orientations of movement activists and their supporters. His volume identifies different groups of participants and their ideologies and then discusses and interprets in depth the expressions of Black Power in African American culture of the time. He pays particular attention to manifestations of soul in style, music, rhetoric, belief, and the literary and performing arts. While acknowledging and giving a clear history of the political movement and its significant figures, Van Deburg locates the power in

Black Power within cultural expressions, and calls for their redeployment for change. EURE and SPADY pay attention to a similar location for Black Power in their examination of the Hip Hop Vision of the Black Power heritage in rap culture. One key facet of black scholarship is the often sophisticated analysis which takes place outside of academic institutions and traditional publishing. This book provides access to the serious contemporary theorists of Black Power and its history who express themselves articulately and with passion through the poetic, musical, and graphic media of the hip hop world.

ANDREW THOMPSON MILLER

See also African American History: General; African American History: since 1954; Civil Rights Movement

Boone, Daniel   1734–1820
Frontiersman and folk hero

Bakeless, John Edwin, *Daniel Boone: Master of the Wilderness*, New York: Morrow, 1939

Brown, John Mason, *Daniel Boone: The Opening of the Wilderness*, New York: Random House, 1952

Elliott, Lawrence, *The Long Hunter: A New Life of Daniel Boone*, New York: Reader's Digest Press, 1976

Faragher, John Mack, *Daniel Boone: The Life and Legend of an American Pioneer*, New York: Henry Holt, 1992

Filson, John, *Discovery, Settlement, and Present State of Kentucke*, Wilmington, DE: James Adam, 1784; reprinted, New York: Corinth, 1962

Flint, Timothy, *Biographical Memoir of Daniel Boone, the First Settler of Kentucky*, Cincinnati: George Conclin, 1833; edited by James K. Folsom, New Haven: Yale University Press, 1967

Lofaro, Michael A., *The Life and Adventures of Daniel Boone*, Lexington: University Press of Kentucky, 1978

Peck, John M. and Francis Bowen, *Lives of Daniel Boone and Benjamin Lincoln*, Boston: Little Brown, 1847

Thwaites, Reuben Gold, *Daniel Boone*, New York: Appleton, 1903

Perhaps more than any other person, Daniel Boone became the symbol of the American frontier in the area east of the Mississippi River. Numerous novels, movies and television portrayals have testified to the enduring strength of the Boone legend. He has been used frequently to point up the conflict between wilderness and civilization. Boone was the natural man, the child of nature, who loved the freedom and beauty of the wilderness but whose explorations and exploits helped open the frontier and destroy the life he loved.

FILSON, considered to be the first history of Kentucky, is more of a travel account than a history. Its purported "Autobiography" of Boone was obviously written by Filson, but it is important because Filson interviewed Boone at some length. Published in Europe as well as the United States, this exaggerated biographical sketch gave European recognition to the frontiersman. Among several modern reprints, the Corinth edition is one of the latest.

The pre-Civil War biographies were all hero-worshipping accounts that depended upon the authors' imaginations as major sources. The most useful are FLINT and PECK, for both authors had interviewed the elderly Boone. Their factual information was often incorrect, and Boone was depicted as a great Indian fighter who almost single handedly saved the early Kentucky settlements. THWAITES was the first biography to make substantial use of the splendid Draper Manuscript Collection in the State Historical Society of Wisconsin, the most important source of information on Boone and his frontier. Lyman C. Draper left five manuscript volumes on his proposed but never completed biography of Boone in addition to the great mass of Boone information that he had collected. Thwaites accepted at face value some of the most interesting Boone stories that had little basis in fact, but his was the most accurate portrayal of Boone to that time.

BAKELESS became the standard biography of Boone when it was published in 1939. It more fully exploited the riches of the Draper collection and other sources available elsewhere. It discarded some of the more fanciful tales that had become part of the Boone legend, and Daniel Boone began to emerge as a real person. The continued interest in Boone was demonstrated by the appearance of other studies, notably Brown and Elliott. BROWN emphasized the role of Boone in the transmontane frontier by focusing on the opening of the Wilderness Trail and the establishment and defense of Boonesboro. ELLIOTT, a better-written book, was designed for a popular audience that had little interest in a scholarly account of the frontier. Both were more realistic than the 19th-century biographies had been, but they depended heavily upon secondary sources. They displayed a lack of familiarity with the history of the period in which their subject lived, and some of their facts were suspect.

Modern developments in the study of the frontier and of social and cultural history have influenced the most recent Boone biographies. LOFARO was a serious attempt to separate legend from reality and to present Boone as a believable character rather than a mythical hero. The author made extensive use of both primary and secondary sources, and he had an excellent prose style. He was handicapped by the assigned length of his study, a volume in the *Kentucky Bicentennial Bookshelf* of 47 titles in a compact format. While Lofaro lacked space to examine many aspects of Boone's life in detail, he indicated clearly the dilemma in the pioneer's life. As he advanced to escape the civilization he enjoyed much less than the frontier, Boone blazed the pathways that others followed to destroy his wilderness. More than any previous study, Lofaro discussed the legends as an essential element in the Boone mystique, even if they were inaccurate.

FARAGHER is a full-length study, and the most recent and best biography of Boone. It is also based on extensive research in a wide variety of sources, including revisionist frontier studies. More attention is paid to the role of Rebecca Boone, who held the family together during her husband's long absences from home, and to Boone's relations with the Indians who fought to halt the intrusion of the whites into some of their favorite hunting grounds. Instead of being a relentless Indian killer, Boone enjoyed their way of life and was often on good terms with them. One of the happiest interludes in his life was the period when the captive Boone was the adopted son of Shawnee Chief Blackfish. Faragher studies both Boone the man and Boone the legend, because, in his view, the legends are a vital part of the story. This decent, courageous, likable character, the author writes, was "a man of contradictions" whose story reflects the thoughts and feelings of the diverse people on the frontier: he was one of them.

LOWELL H. HARRISON

See also Westward Expansion

Boston

Farrell, Betty G., *Elite Families: Class and Power in Nineteenth-Century Boston*, Albany: State University of New York Press, 1993

Formisano, Ronald P. and Constance K. Burns (editors), *Boston, 1700–1980: The Evolution of Urban Politics*, Westport, CT: Greenwood Press, 1984

Knights, Peter R., *Yankee Destinies: The Lives of Ordinary Nineteenth Century Bostonians*, Chapel Hill: University of North Carolina Press, 1991

Nash, Gary B., *The Urban Crucible: Social Change, Political Consciousness, and the Origins of the American Revolution*, Cambridge, MA: Harvard University Press, 1979, abridged as *The Urban Crucible: The Northern Seaports and the Origins of the American Revolution*, 1986

Pleck, Elizabeth H., *Black Migration and Poverty: Boston, 1865–1900*, New York: Academic Press, 1979

Rutman, Darrett B., *Winthrop's Boston: Portrait of a Puritan Town, 1630–1649*, Chapel Hill: University of North Carolina Press, 1965

Ryan, Dennis P., *Beyond the Ballot Box: A Social History of the Boston Irish, 1845–1917*, Rutherford, NJ: Fairleigh Dickinson University Press, 1983

Thernstrom, Stephan, *The Other Bostonians: Poverty and Progress in the American Metropolis, 1880–1970*, Cambridge, MA: Harvard University Press, 1973

Trout, Charles H., *Boston, The Great Depression, and the New Deal*, New York: Oxford University Press, 1977

Warden, G.B., *Boston, 1689–1776*, Boston: Little Brown, 1970

Warner, Sam Bass, *Streetcar Suburbs: The Process of Growth in Boston, 1870–1900*, Cambridge, MA: Harvard University Press, 1962

Given the complexities of urban development, it is perhaps unsurprising that there is no good single-volume history of Boston. However, the history can be pieced together through a number of more specialized works. The standard text outlining the 1630 settlement and early physical and institutional development is still RUTMAN, who, within a strong narrative framework, establishes some recurring themes in Boston's historiography. He finds that, from the beginning, tensions undermined the founders' ideal of a homogeneous community dedicated to spiritual and secular godliness. He sees a steady decline of the collective ethic, fragmenting in the face of theological schism, weak social structure and the acquisitive materialism of a commercial culture. In the first generation of settlement, Rutman describes the growth of a heterogeneous trading centre at odds with less cosmopolitan rural New England.

Two main works battle over the ground of late colonial Boston. In a comparative study which, in some respects, follows in the steps of Rutman, NASH views an uneasy town of growing poverty and social division. Perhaps rather overstating his case, Nash sees the formation and consciousness of class as central to the era. This stands in contrast to WARDEN who pictures a homogeneous community, united around traditional values of the harmony of responsible independent men, potently symbolised in the town meeting, asserting claims to self-government against imperial outsiders. However, the two studies complement each other, with Warden giving detailed evidence which often supports Nash's case rather more than his own. Whereas Warden is essentially a political history and Nash's approach is more quantitative, both works offer valuable introductions into the era of deep social and ideological change that culminated in the Revolution.

In contrast to the complex debates of the colonial era, historians of the 19th and 20th centuries divide more evenly into those who stress the primacy of class in explaining Boston's development, and those who emphasise the central role of ethnicity. To the fore of the latter group is the valuable collection of essays edited by FORMISANO and BURNS. In spite of the title, the focus is overwhelmingly on the incorporated city after 1822. The dominant theme which emerges from essays stretching through to the busing controversy of the 1970s is one of political conflict and coalition building between native and immigrant groups. This focus on ethnicity is inherent in RYAN's determinedly non-political short history of Boston's Irish community. He finds an insular group, unified by a collective identity, based in its own institutions and rhythms of social behaviour, sharing interests which conflicted with those of Protestant Yankee inhabitants. Ryan's accessible work also deals with the everyday experience of women, and with such topics as leisure and education. He includes a useful bibliography.

The class/ethnicity debate has been broadened by the quantitative historians, without being brought to a conclusive end. PLECK describes a divided post-bellum African American community. She finds, on one hand, a group with deep Northern roots aspiring to white middle-class values, and, on the other, Southern migrants who maintained a more insular, collectivist outlook. Whatever the aspirations, Pleck finds that both groups felt the effects of urban poverty stemming from racial prejudice, and she argues that the issue of race was the key determinant in the daily experience of the black community.

The ambiguities which Pleck discovers, of class aspirations mixing with ethnic determinism, are also found in THERNSTROM's wider-ranging study. Drawing upon research concerning some 8,000 "anonymous Americans", Thernstrom focuses upon themes of demographic growth, patterns of migration and mobility and the influence of ethnicity and class upon the life expectations of his sample. He finds that ethnic/racial background did significantly affect the experience of individuals. Among certain groups, however, particularly the native born, there was a class structure of lasting endurance. Within it, Thernstrom sees substantial mobility among middling sections, but rigidity at the very top and bottom.

These conclusions are supported by FARRELL, the most interesting and wide-ranging of a number of recent works examining the establishment and consolidation of the 19th-century Brahmin aristocracy. Dealing with a substantial amount of material in a brief study, Farrell seeks to explain the continuity of elite social and economic hegemony after the loss of political power. She focuses on the elaborate web of kinship ties and business institutions, and stresses the central importance of Brahmin women in maintaining social cohesion. In detailing the class strength of the elite, Farrell has added a new dimension to a growing area of historical research.

WARNER suggests some of the ways that this hegemony might have been maintained. His focus is on the development of Boston from a crowded peninsula to a metropolitan sprawl. Warner sees class identities working to reduce ethnic and religious tensions among a middle class sharing the aspiration of genteel rural living. Aware of, and commenting upon, events before and after his period, he sees 20th-century inner city decay as the flipside of 19th-century suburbanization.

The most interesting quantitative history is KNIGHTS. Drawing on earlier works, here he traces the life fortunes of nearly 3,000 native-born white males active in the mid-19th-century. It is an idiosyncratic work that illuminates many aspects of Boston life in this period. Knights makes clear that the poor and the well-to-do could expect very different lifetime experiences, and that economic fortune and social behaviour were closely linked. While providing some detailed evidence, the work does rather leave conclusions to the reader. Implicit within it, however, is the view of an emerging stable middle class more comfortable with the leadership of the Brahmins than of Irishmen. Knights provides a useful guide to further reading.

A number of these writers deal with aspects of the 20th-century, but much of this history has yet to be written. TROUT has made a useful start in his wide-ranging study of Boston between the wars. Looking at the political, social and economic developments within this Democratic stronghold, he finds substantial obstacles preventing more than modest change arising from New Deal legislation. Fittingly, he sees at the heart of these barriers deep and bitter divisions of ethnicity and class.

ANTHONY MANN

See also Class; Immigration and Ethnicity

Brandeis, Louis D. 1856–1941
Lawyer, reformer and Supreme Court justice

Baskerville, Stephen W., *Of Laws and Limitations: An Intellectual Portrait of Louis Dembitz Brandeis*, Rutherford, NJ: Fairleigh Dickinson University Press, 1994

Dawson, Nelson L. (editor), *Brandeis and America*, Lexington: University Press of Kentucky, 1989

Gal, Allon, *Brandeis of Boston*, Cambridge, MA: Harvard University Press, 1980

Konefsky, Samuel J., *The Legacy of Holmes and Brandeis: A Study in the Influence of Ideas*, New York: Macmillan, 1956

Lief, Alfred, *Brandeis: The Personal History of an American Ideal*, Harrisburg, PA: Stackpole, 1936

Mason, Alpheus T., *Brandeis: A Free Man's Life*, New York: Viking, 1946

Murphy, Bruce Allen, *The Brandeis/Frankfurter Connection: The Secret Political Activities of Two Supreme Court Justices*, New York: Oxford University Press, 1982

Paper, Lewis J., *Brandeis*, Englewood Cliffs, NJ: Prentice Hall, 1983

Strum, Philippa, *Louis D. Brandeis: Justice for the People*, Cambridge, MA: Harvard University Press, 1984

Strum, Philippa, *Brandeis: Beyond Progressivism*, Lawrence: University Press of Kansas, 1993

Urofsky, Melvin I., *Louis D. Brandeis and the Progressive Tradition*, Boston: Little Brown, 1981

Biographers of Louis D. Brandeis have had to confront three major problems in telling his story. First, during his long lifetime he was a prominent Boston attorney, one of the most effective progressive reformers in the United States, a presidential adviser, the leader of American Zionists, and, for 23 years, a distinguished justice of the United States Supreme Court. These diverse activities have put unusual demands on his biographers – some feeling comfortable with one facet of his multi-faceted life, others more at home with another. Second, by the time he died Brandeis was so highly revered that many early biographers had difficulty breaking loose from the tone of veneration that surrounded him. Finally, Brandeis, who first defined "the right to privacy," placed a very high value on his own, and biographers have had difficulty uncovering the private life of the figure behind the public façade of statesman, reformer, and judge.

LIEF is perhaps the best example of the early attempts to write Brandeis's biography. Writing while Brandeis was still on the Court and without any help whatever from him, Lief presents Brandeis as an American hero, and his opponents more often than not as villains. Lief's great advantage was that he could interview those who knew Brandeis and his work personally; his great disadvantage was that he had no access to private papers – his sources, besides the interviews, are all published documents. Now, almost sixty years later, Lief's book appears badly flawed by its worshipful tone and limited source material.

For three decades, the definitive work on Brandeis was the massive study by MASON. The Princeton professor had written, during the 1930s, several careful and complimentary monographs on episodes in Brandeis's reform career. Having resigned from the Supreme Court in 1939, Brandeis was willing to discuss aspects of his career with Mason – something he had refused to do with others. Mason also had access to papers and letters related to Brandeis's reform career and some letters that touched upon his personal life. He sprinkles his highly sympathetic study with long quotations from these papers. For the pre-Court years, Mason's study is still an excellent, richly detailed account. The book, however, has two weaknesses. Mason has little feel for Brandeis's Zionism, and the animosity of Brandeis's friend Felix Frankfurter cost Mason access to papers from the Court years. Since his final chapters rely entirely on the public record, they are less valuable than the earlier ones.

It is precisely those Court years that provide the focus for KONEFSKY. He argues that while Brandeis and Oliver Wendell Holmes, the Supreme Court's two great "dissenters," often joined in eloquent dissent from the Court's conservative majority, they were actually very different from each other. Holmes was philosophic, a social conservative, sceptical, and rather ignorant of the world; Brandeis was practical, an avid student of facts and figures, and passionately committed to liberal causes. Konefsky's work is an early attempt to analyze these two great judges, but his discussion of Brandeis is sometimes over-simplified and incomplete; for example, he seriously underestimates Brandeis's commitment to judicial restraint.

UROFSKY is one of the recognized authorities on Brandeis in the post-Mason period. Both the principal strength and the principal weakness of his biography is its brevity. For readers desiring a quick, smoothly written, but nevertheless scholarly and expert introduction to Brandeis's life, Urofsky's work is a good choice. Those wishing for details and documentation will be served better by more substantial works.

By intelligently and meticulously studying Brandeis's pre-Court professional and social life, GAL illuminates two important questions. How did a businessman's lawyer become a leading reformer, and how did one so indifferent to religion become the leader of American Zionism? Gal argues that Brandeis was excluded from Boston society because he was "an outsider, successful, and a Jew," and that, as a consequence, he fell into friendships and alliances that shaped his mature political and intellectual commitments.

The most controversial scholarly work about Brandeis is MURPHY's thorough, well-documented, and engrossing study of the extra-judicial activities of Brandeis and Frankfurter. The book attracted much attention because it detailed a questionable financial arrangement between the two men – Brandeis provided funds for Frankfurter, who undertook various political, legislative, and journalistic tasks in response to Brandeis's suggestions. Other historians had noted this arrangement before Murphy, but it was so sensationalized by the author's "now-it-can-be-told" tone and by his publisher's dubious advertising campaign, that the book's genuine merits were obscured in a flood of spirited attacks upon, and spirited defenses of the two justices.

The full biography by PAPER is based on sound but not exhaustive scholarship. It has little new to say about Brandeis's public career. But Paper was the first biographer to use a batch of family letters that shed important light on Brandeis's personal side. The fact that it is written with considerable verve makes the book, in general, a pleasure to read.

STRUM (1984) is a fully rounded and highly acclaimed successor to Mason. Basing her work on very extensive research in primary and secondary sources, she draws a superb portrait of both the public and the private man. She thoughtfully analyzes Brandeis's intellectual and political assumptions, but does not ignore the details of his crusades. Her account of the Supreme Court years is perhaps the best among the Justice's biographers. If one could only read a single work on Brandeis, this would be a sound choice. In a second work, STRUM (1993) attempts an analysis of Brandeis's thought.

This is also a thorough and worthwhile study, but in no sense a biography. While some have written as though Brandeis's ideas were largely fixed early in his life, Strum convincingly reveals the evolution of Brandeis's thought. The figure who emerges from this study may be a little more radical than others have portrayed him.

Like Strum's second book, BASKERVILLE also tries to explore Brandeis's mind, and, again like Strum, his work will also be more useful to readers who already know something of Brandeis's career. Baskerville emphasizes the fact that his subject was primarily a lawyer, accustomed by his profession to think and decide in particular ways, and that these habits of mind touched not only his judicial decision-making, but his reform activities and personal life as well.

DAWSON brings together six papers by leading scholars from a conference on Brandeis held in 1987. While not a biography, these six thoroughly-documented papers illuminate the latest scholarship on various aspects of his life and thought.

DAVID W. LEVY

See also Supreme Court

Britain and the American Colonies, 1651–1763

Barrow, Thomas C., *Trade and Empire: The British Customs Service in Colonial America, 1660–1775*, Cambridge, MA: Harvard University Press, 1967

Bliss, Robert M., *Revolution and Empire: English Politics and the American Colonies in the Seventeenth Century*, Manchester: Manchester University Press, 1990

Hall, Michael G., *Edward Randolph and the American Colonies, 1676–1703*, Chapel Hill: University of North Carolina Press, 1960

Henretta, James A. *"Salutary Neglect": Colonial Administration under the Duke of Newcastle*, Princeton: Princeton University Press, 1972

Johnson, Richard R., "The Revolution of 1688–89 in the American Colonies" in *The Anglo-Dutch Moment: Essays on the Glorious Revolution and Its World Impact* edited by Jonathan I. Israel, Cambridge and New York: Cambridge University Press, 1991

Katz, Stanley N., *Newcastle's New York: Anglo-American Politics, 1732–1753*, Cambridge: Belknap Press of Harvard University Press, 1968

Olson, Alison Gilbert, *Making the Empire Work: London and American Interest Groups, 1690–1790*, Cambridge, MA: Harvard University Press, 1992

Sosin, J.M., *English America and the Restoration Monarchy of Charles II: Transatlantic Politics, Commerce and Kinship*, Lincoln: University of Nebraska Press, 1981

Steele, Ian K., *The English Atlantic, 1675–1740: An Exploration of Communication and Community*, New York and Oxford: Oxford University Press, 1986

Webb, Stephen Saunders, *The Governors-General: The English Army and the Definition of the Empire, 1569–1681*, Chapel Hill: University of North Carolina Press, 1979

The relationship between the mother country and the American colonies has mainly been discussed in terms of how the authorities in London tried to control the colonial economies for the benefit of first English and then, after 1707, British interests. WEBB is therefore eccentric in his concept of the empire as a system of "garrison government" in which strategic rather than commercial considerations were uppermost in the policies of the "imperial executive." Nevertheless, while his thesis has not been widely accepted, his notion that military concerns were central to decision makers in Whitehall cannot be ignored. Indeed it carries conviction for some periods if not for others. It might not fit the reign of Charles II but there can be little doubt that James II's Dominion and Territory of New England was primarily strategic in purpose. Although Webb has yet to publish his account of them, his thesis is also persuasive for the war years under William III and Queen Anne, albeit not for the interval of peace between 1713 and the 1740s.

Most historians, however, stress instead the centrality of commerce. Thus BARROW provides a narrative of the customs service from the Restoration of Charles II to the outbreak of the Revolution. "The central theme in the story" he concludes "was its total inadequacy for the assignment with which it was entrusted." Barrow discerns two distinct epochs in the period: one from 1673 to about 1720 during which the government tried to superimpose a system of control which was stubbornly resisted in America; the second from the rise of Walpole to 1763 which was marked by "salutary neglect."

The actual chronology of the relationship has become a matter of debate. BLISS sees crucial developments in the Interregnum (1649–60), when parliament assumed the overview of colonial policy, particularly with the Trade and Shipping Act of 1650, to which he attaches more significance than to the Navigation Act of 1651. This leads him to insist that "the view that the Restoration marked a central turning point (or a useful starting point) for imperial history must be abandoned." Somehow this does not prevent him from starting or ending four of his nine chapters in 1660. His main theme is that the dynamic force behind the development of English America must be sought in the "politics of empire." Bliss examines the political forces in England which moulded settlements both on the American mainland and in the Caribbean. SOSIN has also investigated the interaction of English politics and colonial trends in a trilogy starting with a volume on the Restoration. His main thesis is that the English government had no overarching policy towards its American possessions but reacted to events as they occurred. Although his treatment is more detailed than that of Bliss it is less convincing, for Bliss is more authoritative on the tortuous politics of late Stuart England.

Edward Randolph, appointed customs officer in Massachusetts in 1675, appears in Bliss as a client of Lord Treasurer Danby, while he is given full biographical treatment by HALL. Randolph emerges as a totally dedicated indefatigable zealot for the Crown, who tried to close every loophole in the navigation system in colonial North America, starting with the charter colonies of New England and ending with the proprietary colonies of New Jersey and Pennsylvania in a career which spanned nearly thirty years.

Where Randolph epitomized the interventionist approach of the English government under the later Stuarts, the duke of Newcastle presided over the so-called period of "salutary neglect" under the early Hanoverians. HENRETTA concludes that it was more like culpable negligence, indicting the duke for treating the colonies as an appendage to his English political empire. This perpetuates an image of Newcastle as an incompetent minister which American historians, such as KATZ, tend to share, but which British historians have increasingly tended to reject. Certainly in his concern for imperial defence after 1740 the duke was not guilty of neglect, but on the contrary initiated the strategic intervention in American affairs which Grenville was to inherit.

OLSON, an authority on the connexions between English party politics and colonial America, investigates the informal rather than the formal interaction of the mother country with the colonies. Her study concentrates not on institutions but on interest groups – mercantile, ecclesiastical and ethnic, for example. Despite its subtitle her short book surveys the years 1640 to 1790, raising again the chronological issue. The development of colonial lobbies to some extent offset the alleged administrative neglect of the years 1721 to 1754, which Olson sees as "the high point of cooperation." After the death of Henry Pelham, however, the informal contacts broke down, with ultimately disastrous results.

One of the constant factors in the relationship between Britain and America was the Atlantic ocean and the state of communications over it. This milieu has tended to be taken for granted by historians. In a pioneering work, however, STEELE explores the physical environment in which the interaction between the two sides of the ocean took place. This Braudellian approach pays handsome dividends. For example Steele is able to cast fresh light on the Glorious Revolution in America, which has attracted much attention of late (the best brief account is JOHNSON). One problem which has puzzled previous historians is whether events in America were a reaction to or an anticipation of revolutionary events in England. By careful plotting of how news travelled across the ocean Steele is able to show that the insurgents in Massachusetts and New York were fully aware that William of Orange had triumphed over James II. The physical constraints of a 3000-mile sea crossing in the days of sail must now be taken into account in any study of Britain and the American colonies.

W.A. SPECK

Britain and the United States: General

Allen, H.C., *Great Britain and the United States: A History of Anglo-American Relations, 1783–1952*, London: Odhams, 1954; New York: St. Martin's Press, 1955

Allen, H.C., *The Anglo-American Relationship since 1783*, London: A. & C. Black, 1959

Bourne, Kenneth, *Britain and the Balance of Power in North America, 1815–1908*, London: Longman, and Berkeley: University of California Press, 1967

Dimbleby, David and David Reynolds, *An Ocean Apart: The Relationship Between Britain and America in the Twentieth Century*, London: Hodder and Stoughton/BBC, and New York: Random House, 1988

Dunning, William Archibald, *The British Empire and the United States*, London: Allen and Unwin, and New York: Scribner, 1914

Nicholas, H.G., *The United States and Britain*, Chicago: University of Chicago Press, 1975

Russett, Bruce M., *Community and Contention: Britain and America in the Twentieth Century*, Cambridge: Massachusetts Institute of Technology Press, 1963

Watt, D. Cameron, *Succeeding John Bull: America in Britain's Place, 1900–1975*, Cambridge and New York: Cambridge University Press, 1984

Willson, Beckles, *America's Ambassadors to England, 1785–1928*, London: Murray, 1928; reprinted, Freeport, NY: Books for Libraries Press, 1969

The overwhelming majority of general works on the British-American relationship have confined themselves to the 20th century and, indeed, most of these have concentrated upon the post-1945 era. There has also been a change from the optimism of earlier works to identification of difficulties and to scepticism about the relationship.

It is perhaps a reflection of shifting historical interests that ALLEN's (1954) survey of forty years ago remains the only substantial account to cover the whole period from 1783 to the mid-20th century. Part I, which comprises about a third of his study, provides an extremely valuable analysis of different types of ties, while the remaining three parts of this 1000-page volume are devoted essentially to diplomatic relations. The tone of the book is revealed by the author's words in the preface: "I have written it because I believe in the necessity of cordial Anglo-American relations". In his final chapter he adds: "In the building of the future, whatever it might hold, the Anglo-American partnership would plainly be of decisive importance". ALLEN (1959) then revised the first part of his longer study, and added a summary of the other three parts on diplomatic relations. In this shorter work the emphasis is very much on analysing the connections. The diplomatic interactions are taken up to 1958 and so show some of the contemporary anguish over the Suez crisis. Nevertheless, Allen's confidence re-surfaces because, he says, of the repairs to the relationship performed by Harold Macmillan. So he concludes: "Never perhaps before in history, has there been such correspondence, almost identity, of fundamental interests and intentions between two sovereign nations. Thus the 20th-century cordiality of Anglo-American relations is solidly based on a foundation of similar, even common, policies".

Allen acknowledged DUNNING as the most notable historical survey of British-American relations before his own. It covers the century up to 1914, and was written to mark the centenary of the treaty of Ghent which "secured to Great Britain and the United States one hundred years of unbroken peace". It is clearly written, and there is some attempt to analyse. Dunning's concluding chapter closes on an optimistic note: "There seems no reason, therefore, to suppose that the next hundred years will show less progress than the last in cordial relations among the English-speaking nations".

WILLSON spans 143 years in his collection of portraits of America's ministers and ambassadors to Britain (and 139 years in his companion volume on British envoys to America). He declares that his aim in this series of portraits is "to present, in all its significant fluctuations, the life of a relationship, racial, political, intellectual, moral and social, altogether without parallel in history". Nevertheless, his work is essentially a collection of sketches of the ambassadors which are long on character and narrative but short on analysis. In tone and language, and in their findings, these two studies are rather dated. Yet they provide a handy summary of many diplomatic issues between the two countries, about which information is not so readily available elsewhere.

BOURNE is a more recent study, written from a different perspective. While Allen, Willson, and Dunning all emphasized the cordiality of relations, Bourne has much more to say on Anglo-American hostility and mutual suspicion. In a work of considerable scholarship, he does not seek to dismiss as wrong the emphasis placed by other historians on the common features of British and American politics and society, the importance of their economic relations, and their interchange of ideas, culture and people. Rather, he notes that statesmen are preoccupied with power and that for a very long time British statesmen, like their counterparts on the other side of the Atlantic, tended to see a special danger and a special hostility in Anglo-American relations. He then examines the long and difficult process by which this attitude was eventually reversed. He adduces as the key to this change the recognition on both sides of the uncertainty of winning any conflict between the two countries: "a war in which even the militarists on both sides are unable to forecast total victory is singularly unlikely to occur".

There are a number of studies that concentrate on the 20th-century relationship. Pre-eminent among them is DIMBLEBY and REYNOLDS. Written as a companion to a television series, it stands on its own as a work of lucid narrative and analysis, based on extensive research and oral testimonies. Although principally concerned with political developments in peace and war, and so with the diplomatic and military dimension, it devotes a good deal of attention to economic relations, and it also stops to scrutinize the social and cultural links.

WATT has produced a work of great scholarship which is characteristically inquisitive and persistent in pursuit of awkward questions. It is not primarily a survey of the relationship, but rather an examination of the foreign policy elites, and indeed a commentary on their perceptions and attitudes. Watt stresses in particular the impact of new generations who, every decade or so, arrive at positions of responsibility in sufficient numbers to alter the balance, the emphasis, the flavour of activity on either side of the Atlantic. He concludes that the "special relationship" ended in 1970 or thereabouts, though there remains a residual pre-disposition in each country towards the other. Moreover, he feels that American policy-makers played a major part in bringing about British decline, although those who saw that decline consummated did not understand what they were doing, and regretted it when they realised what they had done.

RUSSETT ranges over the period from 1890 to the early 1960s in order to examine how each nation responded to the other. He constructs a model for analyzing the relationship and proposes different ways in which the two countries might be drawn closer together. The result is a distinctive and suggestive analysis of cultural and economic relations by a political scientist, seeking to determine the "mutual responsiveness" of the two societies.

Although Allen still remains the most useful large-scale survey, NICHOLAS offers a readable, more up-to-date but briefer book on the two centuries since 1776. It emphasizes the common bonds rather than problems in ties between the two countries, and is probably the best short introduction covering the years since independence.

MICHAEL F. HOPKINS

British Americans

Andrews, K.R., Nicholas P. Canny, and P.E.H. Hair (editors), *The Westward Enterprise: English Activities in Ireland, the Atlantic, and America, 1480–1650*, Liverpool: Liverpool University Press, 1978; Detroit: Wayne State University Press, 1979

Bailyn, Bernard, *Voyagers to the West: A Passage in the Peopling of America on the Eve of the Revolution*, New York: Knopf, 1986; London: Tauris, 1987

Bailyn, Bernard and Philip D. Morgan, *Strangers Within the Realm: Cultural Margins of the First British Empire*, Chapel Hill: University of North Carolina Press, 1991

Berthoff, Rowland T., *British Immigrants in Industrial America, 1790–1950*, Cambridge, MA: Harvard University Press, 1953

Burchell, R.A. (editor), *The End of Anglo-America: Historical Essays in the Study of Cultural Divergence*, Manchester: Manchester University Press, 1991

Ekirch, A. Roger, *Bound for America: The Transportation of British Convicts to the Colonies, 1718–1775*, Oxford: Clarendon Press, and New York: Oxford University Press, 1987

Erickson, Charlotte (editor), *Invisible Immigrants: The Adaptation of English and Scottish Immigrants in Nineteenth-Century America*, London: London School of Economics/Weidenfeld and Nicolson, 1972

Erickson, Charlotte, *Leaving England: Essays on British Emigration in the Nineteenth Century*, Ithaca, NY: Cornell University Press, 1994

Fischer, David Hackett, *Albion's Seed: Four British Folkways in America*, New York and Oxford: Oxford University Press, 1989

Horn, James, *Adapting to a New World: English Society in the Seventeenth-Century Chesapeake*, Chapel Hill: University of North Carolina Press, 1994

Karras, Alan L., *Sojourners in the Sun: Scottish Migrants in Jamaica and the Chesapeake, 1740–1800*, Ithaca, NY: Cornell University Press, 1992

Landsman, Ned C., *Scotland and Its First American Colony, 1683–1765*, Princeton: Princeton University Press, 1985

McFarlane, Anthony, *The British in the Americas, 1480–1815*, London and New York: Longman, 1992

Thistlethwaite, Frank, *The Anglo-American Connection in the Early Nineteenth Century*, Philadelphia: University of Pennsylvania Press, and London: Oxford University Press, 1959; as *America and the Atlantic Community: Anglo-American Aspects, 1790–1850*, New York: Harper, 1963

Thistlethwaite, Frank, *Dorset Pilgrims: The Story of West County Pilgrims Who Went to New England in the 17th Century*, London: Barrie and Jenkins, 1989

The recent scholarship in American history is finally beginning to correct what had been a persistent problem – the neglect of British Americans as an identifiable ethnic group in the American experience. But it is only a beginning. More literature is emerging on the distinctive and lasting presence of British influence as a result of the numerical strength of the British in America and the hegemony of British American cultural forces. Most of these new works, however, continue to focus upon the early role of the British in the transfer of culture within the Atlantic world. There are still few works which examine British Americans as a distinct ethnic group in America, and none which covers the entire period from colonization until the present.

One recent work which aims to provide a "brief, integrated account of British involvement in the Americas," is McFARLANE, which draws upon a host of secondary sources to explore the background and first three centuries of the Anglo-American world, and place it in the broader context of colonialism in the New World. It is a useful starting-point for an examination of British Americans, but it should be viewed as a survey, concerned with the American colonial experience, rather than a work which focuses on the British Americans as an ethnic entity. It is marred by some worrying factual and bibliographic errors.

The resurgence of interest in the exploration of the migration and mobility of British Americans, and in the process of cultural transmission, has been greatly stimulated by BAILYN's major contribution to the subject. In the second volume of a projected three-volume work (preceded by *The Peopling of British North America*), he uses formidable research to follow the lives of more than 9,000 emigrants who left Britain between 1773 and 1776. He identifies a dual migratory process in which one group, mainly of young men, left London and the south of England, and the second, mainly consisting of families, left the north of England and the Scottish Highlands. These were contrasting movements which he labels "metropolitan" and "provincial." He notes that the differences between the peoples at home, culturally and geographically, manifested themselves in the way they entered into American life, and made their impact upon it.

FISCHER's controversial work on the concept of regional migration and transfer of identity, has received praise and criticism in equal measure. He advances the notion of four distinct waves of migration from England which resulted in the emergence of four unique cultures or "folkways," each distinctly British American – Puritans from East Anglia in Massachusetts, migrants from southern and western England in Virginia, those from the English north Midlands in the Delaware valley; and those from the north of England, from Scotland and from Ulster in the western back country. This is a bold and ambitious work, which offers a wealth of information along with much uninhibited interpretation and speculation. Fischer hopes that his approach of "braided history" will resurrect ideas of synthesis that have been too long pushed aside.

There are a number of valuable case studies of the process of migration and cultural transmission in the colonial period.

THISTLETHWAITE (1989), one of the most influential histo-rians of Atlantic migration, offers a striking portrait of a Dorset community which emigrated to Massachusetts, and later moved, again as a community, to the Connecticut River valley. He explores the "contrasts and discontinuities" between the two moves, and claims – against the trend of much recent scholarship – that the experience of this group illustrates the progressive influence of England upon New England and New England upon the rest of the United States. On the other hand, in another outstanding recent work addressing the cultural adaptation and assimilation theme, HORN focuses on the Chesapeake region – in contrast to what he sees as an exces-sive preoccupation with the New England colonies. After a close analysis of two English locales from which migrants came, Horn examines the process by which their material circumstances changed dramatically in the Chesapeake, but their attitudes and values did not. He presents a powerful – perhaps an exaggerated – case for the Englishness of the Chesapeake in the 17th century, but finally gives ground to the extent of describing it as a "new and distinctive English province."

Two thoughtful and illuminating works focus on the Scots in America. Concentrating his study on the Scots in New Jersey, LANDSMAN posits that the European socio-cultural back-ground was just as vital to the direction taken by the Scots' settlement in the New World as the environment into which they migrated. Those who emigrated to America were a mixture of highland and lowland Scots with diverse class and religious backgrounds. Once in New Jersey they formed a Scottish enclave which was "distinctive but not isolated" and preserved their ethnic and national identity while they inter-acted with others who were, albeit slightly, different. KARRAS bases his account of the Scots on a cache of letters which detail the life of Scottish migrants in the Americas. Comparing two vastly different colonial regions, the Caribbean and the Chesapeake, he finds a great deal of sojourning – transitory migration and remigration – and thus links, skillfully, the history of the three regions. His focus on the process of remi-gration is one which is long overdue.

In another work which explores transitory or temporary migrants, though of a very different category, EKIRCH explores a culturally distinct cross-section of transported felons. This group was, he notes, the second largest body of immigrants compelled to go to America. The ability of American society to assimilate these felons into its midst, he claims, allows a historian the means to measure opportunity in early America, based on the ability of the convicts to move up from the bottom of the social scale. In keeping with more recent trends in the scholarship, he investigates the convicts who eventually returned to Britain, and thus furthered the cultural exchange between the two societies.

Two collections of essays, edited respectively by BAILYN and MORGAN, and ANDREWS, CANNY and HAIR, explore the role and presence of British Americans within the context of the larger British empire. Both collections contain essays which explore not just the transfer of English people to the colonies but also English ideas and practices. Each focuses on America in the broadest sense, including the Caribbean and Canada, and encounters with immigrants of other nationali-ties and races in the New World.

In contrast to the extensive literature on the colonial period, much less has been written on the more elusive subject of British Americans in the 19th-century United States. There is a revealing and superbly edited selection of English and Scottish emigrant letters in ERICKSON (1972), the work of the leading authority in the field. Her substantial editorial introductions to each part, which are models of their kind, discuss such matters as the motivation of the emigrants and their economic and social adjustment to American life. ERICKSON (1994) is a collection of seven of her essays, including two hitherto unpublished. Based on painstaking research in census records, passenger lists, and immigrant letters, the essays seek to examine both ends of the migration story – both the society from which migrants came (and the consequences of their departure for that society), and their impact on American society (and its impact upon them). She also sets out to present a more balanced view of the subject by giving proper atten-tion to immigrants in the Midwest, to the experience of women emigrants, and to the later 19th century.

In a much earlier study, BERTHOFF addresses some of the same issues, and asks what made British immigrants "different." On the whole, he argues, they were somewhat better off than most other emigrants, included a significantly higher proportion of industrial workers whose skills were much in demand in the United States, and found the process of economic and cultural adaptation rather easier. Both Berthoff and Erickson provide answers to the question of how and why British Americans did not generally remain in enclaves or ghettos, but merged into the wider community.

If the study of British Americans is extended beyond the migration of individuals and communities to include cross-cultural influences and connections, two volumes of essays, dealing with the early republic and the first half of the 19th century, offer a variety of insights. THISTLETHWAITE (1959, 1963) consists of a series of elegant essays, based on lectures, which examine aspects of the Anglo-American connection – economic, political, humanitarian, antislavery, and educational – that were distinctive to this period. BURCHELL has edited essays by several different authors on the theme of continuity and change in the political, economic, social, religious, literary and cultural life of "Anglo-America." Most of them highlight the process of increasing American divergence from the British model. Both volumes include discussion of the role of women in the Anglo-American connec-tion, and in the process of divergence.

JEROME D. BOWERS II

See also Colonial History: Colonies, settlement and growth

British-French Rivalry in North America

Black, Jeremy, *Natural and Necessary Enemies: Anglo-French Relations in the Eighteenth Century*, London: Duckworth, 1986; Athens: University of Georgia Press, 1987

Brewer, John, *The Sinews of Power: War, Money and the English State, 1688–1783*, London: Unwin Hyman, and New York: Knopf, 1989

Gipson, Lawrence Henry, *The British Empire Before the American Revolution*, revised edition, 15 vols., New York: Knopf, 1958–70

Graham, Gerald S., *Empire of the North Atlantic: The Maritime Struggle for North America*, Toronto: University of Toronto Press, 1950, 2nd edition, 1958

Haffenden, Philip S., *New England in the English Nation, 1689–1713*, Oxford: Clarendon Press, 1974

Kennedy, Paul, *The Rise and Fall of the Great Powers: Economic Change and Military Conflict from 1500 to 2000*, New York: Random House, 1987; London: Unwin Hyman, 1988

Leach, Douglas E., *Arms for Empire: A Military History of the British Colonies in North America, 1607–1763*, New York: Macmillan, 1973

Parkman, Francis, *France and England in North America*, 9 vols., Boston: Little Brown, 1865–92

Peckham, Howard H., *The Colonial Wars, 1689–1762*, Chicago: University of Chicago Press, 1964

Savelle, Max, *The Origins of American Diplomacy: The International History of Angloamerica, 1492–1763*, New York: Macmillan, and London: Collier Macmillan, 1967

Epic events generate epic histories. That at least appears to have been the case with the two multi-volume accounts of the struggle for the domination of North America. PARKMAN provided the first major treatment in what has become a classic of American historical literature, fully or partly reprinted on several occasions subsequently. Beginning with the first French presence in North America, Parkman went on to chart the growing competition between Britain and France and their colonists. This led almost inexorably to the eventual defeat of the French, memorably personalised by Parkman as the outcome of the individual struggle between Wolfe and Montcalm. Both in the detail, and in its broad sweep, Parkman's narrative still provides a sense of drama and the immediacy of unfolding events.

A major part of GIPSON's massive study of the British empire prior to the American Revolution concerns the importance of Anglo-French rivalry and its impact. While his main focus is on the Seven Years' War, Gipson provides useful information on the state of the British and French colonies during the earlier part of the 18th century. He analyses the "zones of international friction" which developed as the struggle came to a head. Although the length of Gipson's work may appear intimidating, the very full list of contents make it an easily usable source of information.

The more recent, single-volume, accounts of Anglo-French rivalry tend to deal with particular aspects or stages of the struggle. SAVELLE approaches the subject from the perspective of diplomacy, stressing the interplay of European and colonial policies, and showing how each affected the other. The balance of power in Europe was thought to depend, in large measure, on the balance of the colonial empires. Savelle pays due attention to the whole span of international relations as they affected the colonies, not just to the more familiar final stages, indicating the importance of the Treaty of Utrecht (1713) as well as that of the Treaty of Paris (1763).

While there is no completely satisfactory single treatment of the European diplomatic context, BLACK is useful because of its concentration on the bilateral relationship. Black warns against overstating the degree of animosity between the two countries. He draws attention to the significant period during which Britain and France were at peace between 1716 and 1739, and in alliance up to 1731. He devotes relatively little attention to the competition for trade and colonies, where hostility was more constant. However, this approach does highlight the fact that Britain might possibly have pursued an alternative policy to that involving the ending of French control over Canada.

Several works focus on the military aspects of the struggle for continental control. LEACH underlines the impact of war on colonial life, pointing out that in more than a third of the years between 1607 and 1763 there was war somewhere in the colonies. He suggests that the broader struggle among a number of powers for territory and resources had, by the 18th century, resolved itself into a single struggle between Britain and France, decided by the four great wars fought between 1689 and 1763. Leach deals mainly with the experience of war in the colonies, and useful maps are provided to assist the understanding of specific engagements.

Whatever the causes of conflict, the main theatre of war was the colonies themselves. A general account of the direct experience of war in the colonies, and its consequences, is provided by PECKHAM. One facet of this experience which has interested historians is the effect which the demands of war had on relations between Britain and her colonies. Generally the verdict has been a negative one. In his study of New England during the years between 1689 and 1713 HAFFENDEN paints a more positive picture. He outlines the way in which prominent New Englanders saw the struggle against the French as involving their own interests as much as those of the mother country, and regarded their contribution to the war as a part of their contribution to the Glorious Revolution. Given the general concentration on the later phases of the struggle, Haffenden's exploration of the earlier stages is also valuable.

While British control of North America was won primarily through fighting in North America, that was not the complete story. The broader dimensions of Britain's rise as a world power were also important. As GRAHAM outlines, command of the seas was both an objective of the Anglo-French struggle and a means by which territorial command could be achieved and maintained. BREWER shows how the British state developed the ability to mobilise its resources effectively to achieve this command. By examining institutional changes within Britain he provides essential information on the means by which the British were able to defeat the apparently more powerful French and to oust them from North America. By 1763 Britain had become a major international power, one whose dominance was feared by its competitors.

KENNEDY's broad analysis of the general causes of the rise and fall of great powers covers much more than the specific events in North America during the colonial period, but it helps to illuminate them nonetheless. Through its general approach and its specific discussion of the developments of the 17th and 18th centuries it provides a broad background against which to consider the ultimate success of British efforts.

At this point Britain had a claim to be the dominant world power, though its triumph in the specifically American sphere proved to be, in the eyes of some at least, surprisingly short-lived.

MALCOLM F. MORRISON

Brown, John 1800–1859
Militant abolitionist

Boyer, Richard O., *The Legend of John Brown: A Biography and a History*, New York: Knopf, 1973

Du Bois, W.E.B., *John Brown*, Philadelphia: G.W. Jacobs, 1909; reprinted New York: International, 1962

Malin, James C., *John Brown and the Legend of Fifty-Six*, Philadelphia: American Philosophical Society, 1942

Oates, Stephen B., *To Purge This Land with Blood: A Biography of John Brown*, New York: Harper, 1970

Quarles, Benjamin, *Allies for Freedom: Blacks and John Brown*, New York: Oxford University Press, 1974

Rossbach, Jeffery, *Ambivalent Conspirators: John Brown, the Secret Six, and a Theory of Slave Violence*, Philadelphia: University of Pennsylvania Press, 1982

Scott, Otto J., *The Secret Six: John Brown and the Abolitionist Movement*, New York: Times Books, 1979

Villard, Oswald Garrison, *John Brown, 1800–1859: A Biography Fifty Years After*, Boston: Houghton Mifflin, 1910; revised, New York: Knopf, 1943

Wilson, Hill Peebles, *John Brown, Soldier of Fortune: A Critique*, Lawrence, KS: H.P. Wilson, 1913

Woodward, C. Vann, *The Burden of Southern History*, Baton Rouge: Louisiana State University Press, 1960, 3rd edition, 1993

Herbert Aptheker once observed that "to fully master" the career of John Brown "remains one of the greatest challenges in United States historiography." Accounts of few lives in American history are marked by more extremes in partisanship. Beginning with contemporary biographies published just weeks after Brown's execution, there has been a steady stream of literature dealing with Brown and his attack on the United States arsenal at Harpers Ferry in 1859. Almost all of these works either praise or condemn Brown for his employment of violent tactics in the emancipation cause. They portray Brown as either a saint-like abolitionist martyr or a wild-eyed fanatic intent on sparking a bloody civil war. Rare among studies of Brown is a work that sees the abolitionist as neither divinely inspired nor dangerously insane.

Three early studies of Brown – biographies by Redpath, Hinton and Sanborn – were the work of associates in the Harpers Ferry plot. All three characterize Brown as a modern-day Cromwell, a stern Puritan warrior guided by Old Testament principles in battling slavery. This eulogistic portrayal dominated the published literature on Brown well into the 20th century. Two noteworthy books marked the fiftieth anniversary of Harpers Ferry in 1909. Mainly interested in indicting the institution of slavery, the noted African American historian DU BOIS recapitulates the traditional heroic image of Brown, but the work contains numerous factual errors.

VILLARD is a more carefully researched biography, featuring interviews with surviving Harpers Ferry plotters. Unfortunately, long quotations clutter its text. Villard concedes that Brown had important character flaws, and bungled the Harpers Ferry raid, but still offers a basically positive assessment of Brown's motivation.

The popular praise which Villard received provoked the widow of one of Brown's political enemies in Kansas to commission a rebuttal, written by WILSON. In this book, Brown is accused of numerous business frauds before his arrival in Kansas, and a host of criminal activities once he settled there. The more hostile portrayal of Brown received scholarly endorsement in MALIN. Focusing on the abolitionist's Kansas career, he minimizes Brown's contribution to free state military successes there. Viewing Brown as habitually dishonest, Malin charges that he participated in the sectional skirmishing there mainly as a cover for horse thievery and other criminal acts. He even characterizes Brown's Harpers Ferry attack as an effort to extend the scale of his plundering. Malin also endorses contemporary accusations that Brown suffered from inherited insanity. Much of the historical literature of the 1950s and 1960s on the coming of the Civil War – including the work of major authorities such as Allan Nevins and David Potter – broadly follows Malin in questioning Brown's mental stability. These works are concerned to identify Brown as a symbol of the destructive wave of sectionalism, which was threatening to overwhelm American institutions in the 1850s. In a famous and influential collection of his own essays, WOODWARD includes a piece on John Brown which broadly shares this view, but also offers an interesting analysis of the repercussions, in both North and South, of the Harpers Ferry raid.

The best modern biography of Brown is OATES, which manages a balanced appraisal of Brown's complex personality, as well as a thoroughly documented account of his activities. Oates identifies New Light Calvinism as the source of Brown's uncompromising antislavery creed. He refutes point-by-point the accusations by Malin and others that the desire for either financial gain or personal vengeance had guided the abolitionist's actions in Kansas. Oates also debunks the contemporary evidence for Brown's mental instability, and the amateurish misapplication of psychological theories by many of his modern critics. Dismissing the sanity issue, Oates declares Brown to have been a dedicated revolutionary, whose religious principles guided him to employ whatever means were required, including violence, to eradicate the unholy institution of slavery.

While Oates focuses mainly on Brown's last decade, BOYER provides a detailed examination of his pre-Kansas career. Not a conventional biography, this is an analysis of the social, economic and intellectual trends that shaped Brown's commitment to black emancipation. Boyer sees Brown not as a solitary fanatic but as a man of his times.

Besides the biographies of Brown, there is an additional literature focusing on the Harpers Ferry raid. Most of the books on the subject by non-academic authors, aimed at a popular reading audience, are highly charged by their moral appraisal of either the institution of slavery or the raiders' violent tactics. Other, more scholarly, studies of the Harpers Ferry conspiracy shed valuable light on Brown's activities.

While SCOTT appears more interested in castigating Brown and his backers as "terrorists" of the order of the Red Brigade, he does explore Brown's ability to forge, and conceal, a conspiracy of this kind. QUARLES examines how Brown attracted support from free blacks in Canada and the northern United States. By far the most helpful work on Brown's followers is ROSSBACH, which examines how Brown overcame the doubts which many conspirators harbored about the willingness of the slaves to revolt.

It remains true that any account or interpretation of the coming of the Civil War has to reckon with John Brown, and the shock waves which his raid on Harpers Ferry set off in both North and South.

JOHN R. McKIVIGAN

See also Abolitionism/Antislavery Movement; Civil War: Approach to War 3

Bryan, William Jennings 1860-1925
Political campaigner, presidential candidate and Secretary of State

Ashby, LeRoy, *William Jennings Bryan: Champion of Democracy*, Boston: Twayne, 1987

Cherny, Robert W., *A Righteous Cause: The Life of William Jennings Bryan*, Boston: Little Brown, 1985

Clements, Kendrick A., *William Jennings Bryan: Missionary Isolationist*, Knoxville: University of Tennessee Press, 1982

Coletta, Paolo E., *William Jennings Bryan*, 3 vols., Lincoln: University of Nebraska Press, 1964–69

Glad, Paul W., *The Trumpet Soundeth: William Jennings Bryan and His Democracy, 1896–1912*, Lincoln: University of Nebraska Press, 1960

Glad, Paul W., *McKinley, Bryan, and the People*, Philadelphia: Lippincott, 1964

Hofstadter, Richard, *The American Political Tradition and the Men Who Made It*, New York: Knopf, 1948; London: Cape, 1962

Koenig, Louis W., *Bryan: A Political Biography of William Jennings Bryan*, New York: Putnam, 1971

Levine, Lawrence W., *Defender of the Faith: William Jennings Bryan: The Last Decade, 1915–1925*, New York: Oxford University Press, 1965

William Jennings Bryan's life spanned the era when the United States was transformed from a rural to an urban nation. His long political career, including three unsuccessful campaigns as the Democratic Party's presidential candidate, coincided with the country's political adjustment to industrialization. Bryan's interest for historians has been in the way that his progressive political ideas were coupled with conservative moral values derived from his mid-western background. As such, he exemplifies the tensions of societal change, and biographers have tended to regard him as a transitional figure. Yet they recognize that he wielded an enormous influence over America's political development despite the brief periods he spent in elective or appointive office during his political career.

However, the tone of HOFSTADTER's appraisal of Bryan, "The Democrat as Revivalist", is reminiscent of the scorn heaped upon "The Great Commoner" by H.L. Mencken during the 1920s. Underlying his descriptions of Bryan's "simple emotions", "simple ideas", and "political primitivism" is a contempt for a politician who did not so much lead the people as embody their instincts. The essay focuses upon the way in which Bryan seriously oversimplified complex economic and social issues in his "free silver" campaigns of 1896 and 1900; his aggressive policies as Secretary of State towards Latin America and the Caribbean which contradicted his principled anti-imperialism at the time of Spanish-American War; and his championing of militant fundamentalism during the 1920s which constituted an ignoble attempt to compensate for his declining political power. Registered, but not explored, are Bryan's contributions to the achievement of a federal income tax, currency reform, direct democracy at state and national levels, and numerous other reforms.

Echoes of this viewpoint appear in COLETTA's three-volume biography, the most authoritative study of Bryan, in which he is described as "a symbol rather than a leader of reform", "a diagnostician rather than a healer", and a romantic who distrusted expertise and science and confused majority rule and liberty. Bryan's early emphasis on "free silver" is criticized, as Secretary of State he is berated for allowing moral principle rather than realpolitik to determine his actions, and his record is further criticized for excessive political partisanship, inconsistency and racism. Nevertheless, the ultimate verdict is favourable, for Bryan was an outstanding champion of political and economic democracy and "the world was better because he had lived".

GLAD (1960, 1964) describes Bryan as a "son of the middle border" whose struggles against the Cleveland wing of the Democrats to commit his party to progressive reform belied his own innate conservatism. Even in 1896 when Republican campaign propaganda depicted Bryan as a dangerous radical, he shared more in common with William McKinley than with genuine radicals of the day. Essentially, the source of Bryan's progressivism was the rural culture in which he was raised, and if his policies were progressive, his principles remained those of the "agrarian myth".

The tendency of most recent historical writing has been to understand Bryan rather than to judge him. When LEVINE adopted this approach to examine Bryan's controversial later career, it produced valuable results. Levine refuses to accept that Bryan went into decline after losing control of the Democratic Party to Woodrow Wilson in 1912. His progressive commitment remained constant, although it assumed new forms. Always a sensitive monitor of the pulse of reform, Bryan championed militant fundamentalism after 1920 as a response to the growing conservative mood of post-war America. He became the fundamentalists' principal spokesman, not out of personal self-interest, but in order to pursue reform through extra-governmental channels. Bryan did not share the political conservatism of the fundamentalists he led, for he believed that Christianity was the only sure source of the secular reforming impulse and sought to make the church "an instrument of reform". Earlier, as Secretary of State, Bryan's conduct of foreign policy had also been conditioned by idealistic aspirations for his country. His efforts to promote world peace through intergovernmental arbitration and his resignation over the neutral rights issue in 1915 expressed his belief that peace was in the best interests of American progress.

CLEMENTS believes that the confusions and contradictions of Bryan's views on America's foreign relations reflect those of the people he represented and indicate the difficulties of charting new directions for American foreign policy. Significant shifts in Bryan's world-view occurred during his career. An "ultra-nationalist" in 1896 due to his support of unilateral bimetallism, after 1900 Bryan became an "idealistic isolationist" who was not opposed to a world role for the United States, but sought influence without imperialism. The same Bryan who was prepared to avoid intervention in World War I by sacrificing America's neutral rights, came to accept the need for a League of Nations after the war's end. Bryan's stance was contradictory as well as inconsistent for, as Secretary of State, his missionary sense of America's international destiny resulted in policies of cultural imperialism in the southern hemisphere which were as hegemonic as the "big stick" or "dollar diplomacy" of his Republican predecessors. Such were the problems of a strategy which sought to balance the United States' traditional position of non-alignment with an idealistic ambition to use American influence to create a better world.

Bryan's contribution to domestic politics was more significant, and biographers have emphasized his influence on the development of the Democratic Party and his impact on national political life as a whole. In his substantial biography, KOENIG describes Bryan as a charismatic leader and an extraordinary orator who possessed "contagious optimism" and "translucent sincerity". However, he was no innovator, deriving his ideas from the Populists and other progressives. He was also slow to take up issues such as prohibition and women's suffrage and would back-pedal on controversial issues such as public ownership which outraged conservative opinion within his party. Nevertheless, Bryan's influence in the Democratic Party, most visible in his campaigning and determined work on convention resolutions committees, helped to establish the Party's progressive character. CHERNY believes that Bryan had more influence on public policy than most presidents during his lifetime. Neither an intellectual nor an innovator, his importance was as a popularizer of reform who used his speaking ability and political contacts to great effect.

ASHBY also credits Bryan with playing a pivotal role in identifying the Democratic Party with reform. He is concerned to rebut the claims of some historians of the Populist Movement that fusion in support of Bryan's candidacy in 1896 betrayed the movement's radical promise. Although Bryan did not subscribe to the principles of the Omaha Platform he related to its "soul" and, moreover, his candidacy offered the Populists the opportunity to revive a movement which was weakening in some states. Ultimately, both Bryan's strengths and weaknesses are attributed to his 19th century republican convictions and his evangelical faith. His principled commitment to "the People" and a consistent hostility towards the special interests reflected his commitment to fairness and justice and his distaste for cultural change in equal degrees.

STUART KIDD

See also Anti-Evolution Crusade; Imperialism and Anti-Imperialism; Populism; World War I: American Neutrality

Bryce, James 1838-1922
British historian, diplomat and commentator on the United States

Brogan, D.W., *The American Political System*, London: Hamish Hamilton, 1933

Fisher, H.A.L., *James Bryce*, 2 vols., London: Macmillan, 1927

Ions, Edmund, *James Bryce and American Democracy, 1870–1922*, London: Macmillan, 1968

Jensen, Richard J., *The Winning of the Midwest: Social and Political Conflict, 1888–1896*, Chicago: University of Chicago Press, 1971

Kleppner, Paul, *The Third Electoral System, 1853–1892: Parties, Votes and Political Cultures*, Chapel Hill: University of North Carolina Press, 1979

Laski, Harold, *The American Democracy*, New York: Viking Press, 1948; London: Allen and Unwin, 1949

Tulloch, Hugh, *James Bryce's American Commonwealth: The Anglo-American Background*, Woodbridge, Suffolk: Boydell Press, 1988

The Americanist's interest in James Bryce derives from his authorship of *The American Commonwealth* (1888), generally considered one of the most authoritative interpretations of the republic by a non-American, which can be compared in range and insight with Tocqueville's *Democracy in America* of fifty years earlier. Bryce also made important practical contributions to fostering Anglo-American relations throughout his life, and especially during his period as ambassador at Washington (1907–13). There are three biographies of Bryce and a multiplicity of references to him in historical works on the Gilded Age usually repeating one or two classic quotes from *The American Commonwealth*: Bryce on the similarities of the two parties, Bryce on municipal government as the one conspicuous failure in American politics.

FISHER, like Bryce a liberal academic and politician, provided the obligatory and respectful two-volume biography typical of the period. It is elegantly written and comprehensively deals with every aspect of Bryce's multifarious life in law, politics and academia. It quotes extensively from his letters and travel journals in Egypt, India, South Africa, Australia and elsewhere. It is especially good at placing Bryce firmly within the context of the Gladstonian Liberal party and his important role in attempting to resolve the Irish question (often with reference to America's achieved federalism), which dominated domestic politics in the latter years of the 19th century. Fisher devotes one chapter to *The American Commonwealth*, two to Bryce's ambassadorship and six to his reflections on the critical period leading up to World War I and the complex fate of Anglo-American relations up until Bryce's death in 1922. Fisher observes that, because of his British roots, Bryce had an advantage over the Frenchman, Tocqueville, as interpreter of America, but fails to consider that this might, in turn, have led Bryce to exaggerate Anglo-American continuities and the essential "Englishness" of the United States.

IONS is a highly competent study which concentrates on Bryce's long association with America, and is especially good on the details of Bryce's American travels. Ions was the first to utilize the vast collection of Bryce papers in the Bodleian Library, Oxford, particularly the 33 volumes of American correspondence to which were added the family papers, including Bryce's first American journal of 1870, and the complete manuscript of *The American Commonwealth*. But full use is not always made of this plethora of materials. In an appendix listing American friends who assisted in the composition of *The American Commonwealth*, for example, Ions gives only nineteen names while Bryce himself listed 23 in his introduction alone, and Tulloch lists 54.

TULLOCH is narrower in range and is essentially an intellectual history of those elements, both British and American, which went into the shaping of *The American Commonwealth*. However, this includes a wide range of subject matter stretching from Bryce's incorporation of Darwinian concepts of evolution and adaptation into his historical thinking, to his conversations with E.L. Godkin and Theodore Roosevelt concerning the best strategies for reforming a corrupt party system. Three chapters discuss these various formative influences, two chapters survey Bryce's analysis of the formal constitution and the informal party system respectively, and an epilogue charts Bryce's continued dedication to a "special relationship", and the posthumous reputation of *The American Commonwealth* itself. Its thesis is to suggest that the book effected a fundamental realignment in the British understanding of the United States. In stressing the essential unity of the Anglo-American race and, through comparative analysis, emphasizing the conservatism and stability of the American constitutional order, Bryce argued that, rather than posing a threat to the future existence of Britain and her empire, the American republic was in reality an ally and friend whose growing world influence could only add to, and in no substantial way diminish, Britain's future global role. Bryce was also the first scholar – native or foreign – to study comprehensively America's party system. Tulloch concludes that, for all its "mugwump" bias, *The American Commonwealth*, along with Henry George's *Progress and Poverty* (1879) and Henry Demarest Lloyd's *Wealth and Commonwealth* (1894), signaled the end of Gilded Age complacency, and gave an enormous fillip to progressive reformism in the United States.

There are two classic critiques of Bryce's conclusions. The first, by BROGAN, reacted against the late-Victorian's moralistic tone, which emphasized political salvation through patrician leadership and civil service reform. Bryce's villain, the professional politician, became, in part, Brogan's hero, and the concessions and compromises of the party process, so deplored by Bryce, the means by which America's endemic sectional and ethnic diversity was overcome and nationalized. Brogan also accused Bryce of naiveté in failing to appreciate the close economic links between machine bosses and businessmen. The socialist LASKI naturally attacked the laissez-faire liberal Bryce for underplaying class struggle and economic determinism in American history, and in particular for neglecting the struggles of labour and trade unionism in their fight against a prevailing capitalist ethos of worker exploitation. Oddly there has been no major reassessment of Bryce by an American scholar, though "new" political historians, such as JENSEN and KLEPPNER have accused *The American Commonwealth* of contributing to a false image of Gilded Age dullness and sterility, and have criticized Bryce for concentrating excessively on political elites and issue-oriented politics, while neglecting the seething ethno-cultural subcultures and high voting turnouts of the period. This is not entirely fair, for Bryce's more informal chapters, though morally censorious, are alive with the infinite variety of urban ethnic political activity. *The American Commonwealth* remains a wonderfully rich and analytically penetrating survey of late 19th century America.

HUGH TULLOCH

See also Britain and the United States; Gilded Age and Progressive Era

Buchanan, James 1791–1868

Secretary of State and 15th President of the United States

Auchampaugh, Philip G., *James Buchanan and His Cabinet on the Eve of Secession*, Lancaster, PA: Lancaster Press, 1926

Binder, Frederick Moore, *James Buchanan and the American Empire*, Selinsgrove, PA: Susquehanna University Press, 1994

Klein, Philip S., *President James Buchanan: A Biography*, University Park: Pennsylvania State University Press, 1962

Nevins, Allan, *The Emergence of Lincoln*, volume 1: *Douglas, Buchanan and Party Chaos, 1857–1859*, New York: Scribner, 1950

Nevins, Allan, *The Emergence of Lincoln*, volume 2: *Prologue to Civil War, 1859–1861*, New York: Scribner, 1950

Nichols, Roy F., *The Disruption of American Democracy*, New York: Macmillan, 1948

Smith, Elbert B., *The Presidency of James Buchanan*, Lawrence: University Press of Kansas, 1975

Stampp, Kenneth M., *America in 1857: A Nation on the Brink*, New York: Oxford University Press, 1990

Summers, Mark W., *The Plundering Generation: Corruption and the Crisis of the Union, 1849–1861*, New York: Oxford University Press, 1987

When James Buchanan left office in March 1861 his name was reviled and his policies cursed. The opinion of historians may have been modified since then but it has not been reversed. AUCHAMPAUGH was one of the first modern studies that attempted to refute the claims that Buchanan was criminally negligent in his duties or turned a blind eye to the traitorous activities of his Southern-dominated cabinet. He certainly includes a lot of useful material, but argues a case for Buchanan much too aggressively. It takes a measure of considerable historical perversity, not to say effrontery, to judge John B. Floyd one of the great Secretaries of War.

KLEIN is a much better, more balanced and scholarly biography. But it is a biography and not a general study. The strength of this approach is that Klein brings out clearly Buchanan's long record of public service as exemplified in the nickname, "Old Public Functionary". Buchanan appeared an impressive and experienced candidate for the presidency in 1856 and seemed an improvement on Franklin Pierce's compliant vacuousness. The weakness of Klein's biographical method is that sympathy for his subject leads him to be too indulgent towards Buchanan. He neglects the structural weaknesses of the Democratic Party in the 1850s, and the disastrous consequences for Northern Democrats of Buchanan's policy of maintaining party unity by placating Southern Democrats. BINDER extends our knowledge of Buchanan's successful career as a diplomatist, and his account contains much useful information. Yet, he does not tackle broader issues (such as the influence of interest groups), and the effect of his arguments is reduced by a somewhat rhetorical prose style.

While Buchanan's pre-presidential career has received only limited attention, there are a number of important works that cover the period of his presidency and which advance influential interpretations of it. NICHOLS is a superb narrative history, strongly recommended reading for the secession crisis and the confrontation at Fort Sumter in 1861. The style is trenchant and elegantly shaped, and resonates with strong judgments and the telling phrase. But the least convincing part of Nichols's account of the Buchanan years is his portrayal of Buchanan himself. He views Buchanan as obstinate, psychologically maladjusted, and weak – and overawed by his cabinet, though he resented it. He was a fussy old bachelor, who was petulant and petty. But Nichols fails to explain why he retained control of the patronage, and how Buchanan retained the respect of his cabinet members. He also signally fails to account for Buchanan's outmanoeuvring of the most dynamic politician of the age, Stephen A. Douglas, after his repudiation of the Lecompton Constitution in 1857–58.

The two volumes of NEVINS's monumental history are dedicated to charting the tussle between Buchanan and Douglas for the soul of the Democratic Party, and the duel between Douglas and Lincoln for the Senate in Illinois, and then ultimately for the presidency in 1860. Nevins's history is one of the great achievements of American historiography. It is written on a grander scale than Nichols, and is more olympian in tone, though the style is less trenchant. Nevins (like Nichols), was writing in the immediate post-World War II period, when it was received wisdom to condemn "appeasement". In Nevins's view, Buchanan was an object lesson in the follies of appeasing political adversaries. He sees Buchanan as characteristic of a mediocre generation of presidents who were incapable of rising to the challenge posed by the political crisis of the 1850s. They put self, and party, before country. Nevins was certainly right in arguing that Buchanan was dedicated to maintaining the unity of the Democratic Party, and that he was foolishly optimistic in thinking that it could be restored in 1861, if only the Missouri Compromise line was reaffirmed as demarcating those territories into which slavery could expand. But he was a much more aggressive party-manager than Nevins allowed for in his portrayal of a quivering chief executive, putty in the hands of the Southern "Directory" of cabinet members, who actually ran the federal government.

SMITH's study of the Buchanan presidency is much more sympathetic than the work of historians of the immediate postwar generation. He brings out Buchanan's skill as a political tactician, and his sheer industry in attending to intractable difficulties. His powers were undimmed, and he was most certainly not a psychological cripple or an exhausted husk of a man. Smith is surely right, too, in claiming that Buchanan was used as a convenient scapegoat for the secession crisis. Smith also pays welcome attention to foreign affairs, and claims that, but for the political crisis of the 1850s, Buchanan would have been one of the most consistent imperialists in American history. But his priorities in internal affairs were not clearly adumbrated. Smith contends that Buchanan failed not because he was supine or indecisive, but because he was deluded in "his profound emotional attachment to the South". He thus contributed to latent Northern fears of a malign "slave power" while failing to secure Southern loyalty to the Union.

Smith's account also underrates the extent to which the Buchanan administration was riddled by corruption. An extended treatment of the corroding effect of corruption can be found in Part 4 of SUMMERS. Buchanan was not personally corrupt, though he connived in the Secretary of the Navy, Isaac Toucey's, action in awarding shipbuilding contracts to companies that would enlarge their work force and ensure votes for Democratic candidates. Such abuses became an issue exploited effectively by the Republicans. Summers does not exaggerate the influence of corruption but he does demonstrate its debilitating effect both on the process of government and the degree of respect accorded to the president.

A sense of the inevitability of fratricidal conflict as a result of Buchanan's policies is conveyed by STAMPP's study of 1857–58. Stampp stresses that Buchanan's crucial, initial blunder was admitting at his inaugural that he would retire after serving a single term. Stampp's fluent and well-crafted survey covers the main crises of Buchanan's term, the Dred Scott decision, Kansas, the Lecompton Constitution and the Panic of 1857. But Stampp argues that even if Buchanan had resolved the Kansas crisis successfully, other disruptive sectional confrontations would have followed. Buchanan, in short, searched for the unobtainable.

BRIAN HOLDEN REID

See also Civil War: Approach to War 3 & 4

Burr, Aaron 1756–1836

Politician, adventurer and Vice-President of the United States

Abernethy, Thomas Perkins, *The Burr Conspiracy*, New York: Oxford University Press, 1954

Adams, Henry, *History of the United States of America During the Administrations of Jefferson and Madison*, 9 vols., New York: Scribner, 1889–91; edited by Earl N. Harbert, 2 vols., New York: Library of America, 1986

Lomask, Milton, *Aaron Burr*, 2 vols., New York: Farrar Straus, 1979–82

McCaleb, Walter Flavius, *The Aaron Burr Conspiracy*, New York: Dodd Mead, 1903; revised, New York: Wilson-Erickson, 1936

Nolan, Charles F., Jr., *Aaron Burr and the American Literary Imagination*, Westport, CT: Greenwood Press, 1980

Parmet, Herbert S. and Marie B. Hecht, *Aaron Burr: Portrait of an Ambitious Man*, New York: Macmillan, and London: Collier Macmillan, 1967

Parton, James, *The Life and Times of Aaron Burr*, 2 vols., New York: Mason, 1857, revised 1864

Philbrick, Francis S., *The Rise of the West, 1754–1830*, New York: Harper, 1965

Schachner, Nathan, *Aaron Burr: A Biography*, New York: Stokes, 1937

Smelser, Marshall, *The Democratic Republic, 1801–1815*, New York: Harper, 1968

Wandell, Samuel H. and Meade Minnigerode, *Aaron Burr: A Biography Compiled from Rare, and in Many Cases Unpublished, Sources*, 2 vols., New York: Putnam, 1925

Aaron Burr achieved in his own lifetime the unenviable popular reputation that has pursued him ever since of deceiver, murderer, traitor, and sexual predator. By 1980, as NOLAN's brief study points out, Burr had figured in 33 plays and 49 novels and stories, customarily as an embodiment of evil: the cold-hearted, ambitious Machiavellian who tried to cheat Thomas Jefferson of the presidency, killed Alexander Hamilton, and plotted to disrupt the Union. More recently he has been cast as victim, notably in Gore Vidal's excellent novel *Burr* (1973), which subverts the American pantheon by raising Burr above small-minded and self-centred rivals like Hamilton and Jefferson.

Modern biographers have repeatedly claimed to be rescuing Burr's reputation, without recognising that relatively few serious historians have been inclined to condemn him. The first accomplished biographer, PARTON – who as a child played marbles outside Burr's house and later spoke to many who knew him – exonerated Burr from the most serious charges, in what *Harper's Weekly* hailed at the time as "the most successful biography ever published in America." For example, Parton printed all the evidence he could find concerning Burr's supposed intrigue against Jefferson in the disputed election of 1800–01 in order to show how flimsy that evidence was. Burr, he insisted, acted throughout the crisis with "the strictest honor and consistency." Similarly, Burr was not "the greatest monster of licentiousness" in American history, but behaved towards women in a gallant, polite, and considerate fashion. Accused of being too generous to his subject, Parton had to spell out in the preface to the second, expanded edition that he saw Burr as "gifted and unwise, generous and unprincipled, amiable and deadly." The conscienceless Burr, he concluded, failed in public life because he lacked moral principle and consistency.

The major 20th-century biographies have portrayed Burr with equal sympathy. WANDELL and MINNIGERODE's leisurely and detailed biography offered an understanding appraisal of the public life and captured something of Burr's ability to captivate those who met him in private life. PARMET and HECHT's spritely, colourful narrative concentrated on Burr's public career, exempting him from charges both of underhand intrigue and, in particular, of deliberately premeditating Hamilton's death in the notorious duel of 1804. SCHACHNER's extensive research further exonerated Burr at all critical points, but many critics dismissed his book as an "apology" for Burr.

Ultimately, historical attitudes to Burr have depended largely on interpretation of the famous "conspiracy" of 1806–07. Parton considered the evidence contradictory; he suspected that Burr's real aim was to become the "Napoleon of Spanish America," though Burr would not have rejected the allegiance of the western states if they had seceded from the United States. ADAMS, ever eager to condemn his forefathers' enemies, portrayed Burr as an outrageous self-seeker willing to betray his country; and he found evidence in European archives of Burr's dealings with foreign governments, though Adams did not believe that the plots represented a serious threat to the Union. In the 1890s, however, McCALEB discovered in archives in Mexico and Texas evidence that the Spanish authorities believed that Burr was conspiring to invade and conquer their colonies, and he concluded that Burr's apparently treasonable correspondence had been designed to lever money from European governments. Convinced of Burr's innocence, McCaleb – like Parton earlier and Schachner later – criticized President Jefferson for trying to pressure Chief Justice Marshall into convicting Burr of treason.

ABERNETHY, by contrast, writing in a period more prone to suspect public men of un-American activities, had no doubt that Burr's intentions were indeed treasonous. Using a range of new evidence, notably the notes taken by a juryman at the treason trial, and taking the paranoia of the contemporary press seriously, Abernethy insisted that Burr's aim was not only to invade neighboring Spanish colonies, but to seize New Orleans and Louisiana and encourage the western states to secede from the Union. In view of the weakness of national bonds at the time, the tradition of western intrigue with Spain, and the uncertain international situation, Abernethy came to the conclusion that Burr's Conspiracy was the most dangerous threat to the integrity of the Union before the Civil War.

The continuing debate was reflected during the next decade in different volumes in Harper's *New American Nation* series. SMELSER accepted Abernethy's case, and waxed sarcastic about Burr's defenders. PHILBRICK countered that Abernethy's evidence was based on gossip, contained internal contradictions, and would not pass muster – as indeed it had not – in a court of law. Philbrick insisted that no hard evidence existed that Burr was ever involved in a "conspiracy," or that he ever believed that the West could be revolutionized, in view of its obvious loyalty to the Union.

By the late 1970s such scepticism gained support when the New-York Historical Society collected all Burr's papers together from more than two hundred depositories. The result was a comprehensive microfilm edition of the manuscripts on 27 reels, and the publication of his political correspondence and public papers by Princeton University Press in 1983. In the process the editor, Mary-Jo Kline, established that the so-called "cipher letter," which had previously been considered especially damning of Burr's behavior during the "conspiracy," had been written not by Burr but by a collaborator, Jonathan Dayton.

This discovery was first reported by LOMASK, in the fullest modern biography. Lomask describes Burr as taking to politics for "fun and honor and profit" rather than out of any sense of solemn duty; consequently Burr lacked deep commitment to any political cause, refused to break off relations with those on the other side, and enjoyed intrigue of all kinds. Hence both associates such as Jefferson and enemies like Hamilton came to regard him as entirely untrustworthy, and wished to be rid of him. Besides portraying Burr as victim, Lomask revealed new dimensions of his personality. Apparently Burr delighted in acting as "paterfamilias," especially in his last years following his return from Europe in 1812, gathering about him hordes of children, often of uncertain relationship to himself. Overall, Lomask sees Burr as a Chesterfieldian gentleman of great accomplishments, but too reasonable, considerate, generous, and improvident to succeed in the game of embittered partisan politics as it was developing in the new democratic republic.

DONALD J. RATCLIFFE

Bushnell, Horace 1802–1876
New England minister, author and critic

Adamson, William R., *Bushnell Rediscovered*, Philadelphia: United Church Press, 1966

Archibald, Warren Seymore, *Horace Bushnell*, Hartford, CT: E.V. Mitchell, 1930

Barnes, Howard A., *Horace Bushnell and the Virtuous Republic*, Metuchen, NJ: Scarecrow Press, 1991

Cheney, Mary Bushnell, *Life and Letters of Horace Bushnell*, New York: Harper, 1880

Crosby, Donald A., *Horace Bushnell's Theory of Language, in the Context of Other 19th-Century Philosophies of Language*, The Hague: Mouton, 1975

Cross, Barbara M., *Horace Bushnell: Minister to a Changing America*, Chicago: University of Chicago Press, 1958

Duke, James O., *Horace Bushnell: On the Vitality of Biblical Language*, Chico, CA: Scholars Press, 1984

Gray, Joseph M.M., *Prophets of the Soul*, New York: Abingdon, 1936

Johnson, William A., *Nature and the Supernatural in the Theology of Horace Bushnell*, Lund, Sweden: Gleerup, 1963

Munger, Theodore T., *Horace Bushnell: Preacher and Theologian*, Boston: Houghton Mifflin, 1899

Myers, A.J. William, *Horace Bushnell and Religious Education*, Boston: Manthorne and Burack, 1937

Connecticut-born Congregational minister Horace Bushnell is generally credited with leading the revolt against the dry rationalism and lingering implications of predestination that characterized mid-19th century American reformed theology. In its place, Bushnell elaborated romanticized doctrines that emphasized intuition, God's manifestation in nature, and Christian nurture, from his Hartford, Connecticut, North Church pulpit and in his many treatises and articles. At least a dozen book-length accounts of Bushnell's life and contributions have appeared since 1880, along with more than two dozen dissertations and countless popular and scholarly articles.

CHENEY collected and edited her father's letters soon after his death and wrote an adoring biography that has become the standard by which all others have been measured. The Cheney interpretation, heavily laden with correspondence, established Bushnell's reputation as the inspiring and courageous 19th-century liberal who led the revolt against the stifling remnants of Calvinism. Cheney's determination to fix her father's unblemished reputation in history has been largely successful, as successive generations of scholars have struggled

to free themselves of the Cheney legacy. This has been a difficult endeavor because very little of Bushnell's correspondence and personal papers has survived, aside from the edited versions which Cheney included in her biography. It seems likely that Cheney destroyed her father's papers soon after she completed her own biography in 1880. Only a few letters are extant in widely scattered collections. Thus Cheney's work represents not only the premier biography, but also the single most important primary source of Bushnell's life and work.

The only other 19th-century biography is MUNGER. It relies heavily on Cheney for its basic assessment of Bushnell's character, but scholars have taken issue with Munger for projecting his own naturalistic theology on to Bushnell. Bushnell was not a naturalist who identified God with nature to the extent that Munger suggests. Nevertheless, Munger argues that Bushnell's own evolutionary thinking might have led him to appreciate the full implications of his own naturalistic tendencies. Munger probably did more to distort Bushnell's ideas than did Cheney's efforts to disguise her father's blemishes, but both works established the framework within which much Bushnell scholarship developed.

Thirty years passed before a second group of works on Bushnell appeared, largely derived from published works and designed for admiring popular audiences. ARCHIBALD, who was pastor at Hartford's South Congregational Church, makes no pretense of originality, but rather seeks to glorify Bushnell's liberating accomplishments and offer him as an inspiration for the modern age. His short biographical treatment contains no notes or bibliography. GRAY also offers an appreciative and uncritical biography that closely follows Munger's lead. He credits Bushnell with destroying the old separation between spiritual and natural realms while maneuvering deftly between conservative and more liberal parties. MYERS is an enthusiastic gloss on Bushnell's influential *Christian Nurture,* with practical suggestions for application of Bushnell's notions of Christian education. One reviewer described this uncritical work as little more than a "cut and paste job," with the author acting as cheerleader.

More reflective and critical interpretations appeared during the 1950s and 1960s, as a new group of academics began to reassess Bushnell's contributions. The short intellectual biography by CROSS, based on her Harvard University dissertation, relies heavily on Cheney and other published sources. Nonetheless, it diverges from the older interpretations by suggesting that Bushnell's ideas were more conservative than previously portrayed, and constituted an attempt to devise a theology that could encompass all groups, especially the emerging middle class. He was a minister to a changing world, in Cross's words, who sought to harmonize his preaching with contemporary sentiments, even as he heeded to an age of home-spun Puritan family values. In contrast, JOHNSON's dissertation emphasizes Bushnell's liberalism, which he argues provided a coherent pattern of theological assumptions based on the notion that God's presence could be apprehended intuitively. While calling Bushnell the greatest American theologian of his time, Johnson also censures him for an over-reliance on intuition, a lack of interest in discourse and rational scrutiny, and a weak understanding of historical Christianity. Appended bibliographies of Bushnell's writings and secondary sources are more useful than most.

Recent works have focused more narrowly on particular aspects of Bushnell's writings. ADAMSON includes a short biographical sketch in the Cheney tradition, but his work emphasizes Bushnell's original contributions to Christian education. CROSBY examines Bushnell's theory of language, which was a romantic formulation based on the argument that the formal definitions of words were insufficient to express spiritual matters, but were rather suggestive of deeper truths. DUKE provides a sophisticated analysis of Bushnell's hermeneutics and includes a thorough and up-to-date bibliography.

BARNES is a modern interpretation that attempts to place Bushnell's life in the context of contemporary society. He suggests that Bushnell can be best understood as a cultural and intellectual elitist who represented the values of an ideal society of virtuous gentry elite. Bushnell's theology evolved from a confident optimism akin to Unitarianism early in his life to a disenchantment with man's goodness in his later years. Bushnell ended up with a hard dualistic Deity who sometimes had to deal harshly with his recalcitrant creations, reminiscent of the Calvinist God from whom Bushnell and others had striven to escape. Barnes includes a useful bibliographic essay on secondary sources that discusses both books and notable articles.

Emil Pocock

Business Cycle

Berry, Brian J.L., *Long-Wave Rhythms in Economic Development and Political Behavior*, Baltimore: Johns Hopkins University Press, 1991

Easterlin, Richard A., *Population, Labor Force, and Long Swings in Economic Growth: The American Experience*, New York: National Bureau of Economic Research, 1968

Fellner, William John, *Trends and Cycles in Economic Activity: An Introduction to Problems of Economic Growth*, New York: Holt, 1956

Frickey, Edwin, *Economic Fluctuations in the United States: A Systematic Analysis of Long-Run Trends and Business Cycles*, Cambridge, MA: Harvard University Press, 1942

Gordon, Robert J., *American Business Cycles: Continuity and Change*, Chicago: University of Chicago Press, 1986

Hansen, Alvin H., *Business Cycles and National Income*, New York: Norton, 1951

Jerome, Harry, *Migration and Business Cycles*, New York: National Bureau of Economic Research, 1930

Kondratieff, Nikolai, *The Long Wave Cycle*, translated by Guy Daniels, New York: Richardson and Snyder, 1984

Lee, Maurice, *Macroeconomics: Fluctuations, Growth and Stability*, Homewood, IL: Richard D. Irwin, 1955, 5th edition, 1971

Mitchell, Wesley Clair, *Business Cycles: The Problem and Its Setting*, New York: National Bureau of Economic Research, 1927

Mitchell, Wesley Clair, *Business Cycles and Their Causes*, New York: National Bureau of Economic Research, 1941

Schumpeter, Joseph, *Business Cycles: A Theoretical, Historical, and Statistical Analysis of the Capitalist Process*, 2 vols., New York: McGraw Hill, 1939

Solomou, Solomos, *Phases of Economic Growth, 1850–1973: Kondratieff Waves and Kuznets Swings*, Cambridge and New York: Cambridge University Press, 1987

Thomas, Brinley, *Migration and Economic Growth: A Study of Great Britain and the Atlantic Economy*, Cambridge: Cambridge University Press, 1954, 2nd edition, 1973

Thomas, Brinley, *Migration and Urban Development: A Reappraisal of British and American Long Cycles*, London: Methuen, 1972

Tylecote, Andrew, *The Long Wave in the World Economy: The Present Crisis in Historical Perspective*, London and New York: Routledge, 1992

Zarnowitz, Victor (editor), *Business Cycles: Theory, History, Indicators and Forecasting*, Chicago: University of Chicago Press, 1992

Business cycle history and analysis is an area in which economists and economic historians have had little difficulty in working together, albeit for different reasons. Wesley C. Mitchell played a crucial role in establishing the methodology of business cycle research, both in his own exemplary work and in his role as first Director of the National Bureau of Economic Research (NBER), the headquarters of work in the subject. He insisted on the accumulation of masses of statistical data, to be followed by their systematic analysis. "New" economic history or "cliometrics" is at least as old as the NBER. MITCHELL (1927) was written in response to the postwar depression; in the end policy formulation was always the objective of business cycle study. Mitchell's stamp was left on all subsequent publications of the NBER, and he continued the same methodology in his own later books, including MITCHELL (1941).

The opening chapters of LEE provide a clear exposition of the methodology and concepts used by Mitchell and the NBER, while the closing chapters are concerned with policy. The book was intended as an introduction to economic theory and provides an excellent starting point for further study of the subject. Lee shows that, instead of the assumption in the 1920s that there was one economic phenomenon generally called the business cycle, other analysts have identified four types of cycle; the "old" business cycle of 9 to 10 years, or the Juglar cycle, usually punctuated by crises in the banking system; a shorter cycle of about 40 months, the Kitchen cycle; the Kuznets cycle with an average length of about 20 years; and the "long swing" of about 50 years, the Kondratieff (or Schumpeterian) cycle. For earlier generations of students both FRICKEY and FELLNER offered textbook style surveys of American business cycle history, concentrating mainly on the "old" (Juglar) business cycle. Fellner later became a member of the council of three economic advisers to the president.

JEROME is a characteristic NBER production, as important to students of migration as it is to those of cyclical fluctuations. The relationship he showed was fairly straightforward: that, with a time-lag, immigrants entered the USA when times were good and held back when times were bad. This finding of a time-lag between downturns in the American economy and a slackening in the arrival of immigrants has become an article of belief among most subsequent historians of migration.

In two major works, Brinley THOMAS (1954, 1972) explores in great statistical detail the transatlantic interconnections between movements of population, movements of capital and large innovative investment in the USA (especially railroad building and urbanisation). He adds the suggestion (which other writers such as Cairncross have also made) that European economies were often in a reverse cyclical phase to that in America. This approach explores the view that 19th-century economic cycles were international rather than simply national in their origins and progress.

No survey of business cycle literature would be complete without reference to SCHUMPETER's massive work, though much of it may be of more interest to economists than to historians, many of whom have challenged his reading of the historical record. In recent decades economic experience in many countries has attracted attention to the long-wave phenomenon, the view originally associated with the name of KONDRATIEFF and also developed by Schumpeter. The long-wave hypothesis is based on the proposition that periods of major expansion result from large innovative investments and are then followed by periods of consolidation or relative stagnation. The stagnation hypothesis was very attractive to economic analysts in the 1930s and figured prominently in HANSEN's interpretation of the depression of the 1930s, a theme which he pursued in his later writings on cycles.

EASTERLIN's view of long swings introduces a highly sophisticated and complex analysis of the impact of population trends resulting from differential birth rates of native and immigrant Americans. While similar to Brinley Thomas in methodology, his work concentrates largely on internal factors in the USA. This work is as valuable in studies of population history as in those of economic fluctuations.

Most recently, the subject has increasingly been the domain of economists, and economic historians have paid less and less attention to cycles, particularly in their textbooks. In the NBER volume of 1986, edited by GORDON, the question was explicitly asked, has the business cycle changed? As one reviewer observed, "this volume provides the most useful summary currently available to those strands of research in empirical macroeconomics of relevance to issues in economic history."

The long period of economic optimism and expansion after World War II, and the subsequent years of seemingly intractable stagnation, again drew attention to theories of long swings. SOLOMOU examined the empirical evidence for the Kondratieff and Kuznets cycles, setting both in a transatlantic context. The author rejects any generalized view of such long swings, insisting that specific circumstances, particularly unique technological developments, were the main determinants. This interpretation is extended to the long post-war boom that created such economic optimism for two or more decades after World War II.

By contrast, BERRY sees confirmation of Kondratieff long waves in American 19th-century wholesale price movements, but also argues for the existence of Kuznets cycles within the longer trends. His not particularly novel conclusion that growth engenders optimism which in turn leads to excessive speculation, does little to explain the time scale. TYLECOTE is also more amenable to acceptance of a Kondratieff interpretation, but like Solomou emphasizes the "clustering" of technological innovations. His analysis leads him to a set

of firm policy recommendations for international economic expansion.

ZARNOWITZ edited a collection of essays, some reprints, some new, but all in the NBER tradition. Although this is very much an economist's book, historians may gain much from its approach and its findings.

JIM POTTER

See also Economic Growth; Population

Business History: General

Blackford, Mansel G., *A History of Small Business in America*, New York: Twayne, 1991

Blackford, Mansel G. and K. Austin Kerr, *Business Enterprise in American History*, Boston: Houghton Mifflin, 1986, 3rd edition, 1994

Chandler, Alfred D., Jr., *Strategy and Structure: Chapters in the History of the Industrial Enterprise*, Cambridge: Massachusetts Institute of Technology Press, 1962

Chandler, Alfred D., Jr., *The Visible Hand: The Managerial Revolution in American Business*, Cambridge, MA: Belknap Press of Harvard University Press, 1977

Cochran, Thomas C., *Business in American Life: A History*, New York: McGraw Hill, 1972

Galambos, Louis, and Joseph Pratt, *The Rise of the Corporate Commonwealth: US Business and Public Policy in the Twentieth Century*, New York: Basic Books, 1988

McCraw, Thomas K., *Prophets of Regulation: Charles Francis Adams, Louis D. Brandeis, James M. Landis, Alfred E. Kahn*, Cambridge, MA: Belknap Press of Harvard University Press, 1984

Pusateri, C. Joseph, *A History of American Business*, Arlington Heights, IL: Harlan Davidson, 1984

Sobel, Robert, *The Age of Giant Corporations: A Microeconomic History of American Business, 1914–1970*, Westport, CT: Greenwood Press, 1972, revised as *The Age of Giant Corporations: A Microeconomic History of American Business, 1914–1984*, 1984

Strasser, Susan, *Satisfaction Guaranteed: The Making of the American Mass Market*, New York: Pantheon, 1989

Tedlow, Richard S., *New and Improved: The Story of Mass Marketing in America*, New York: Basic Books, and Oxford: Heinemann, 1990

Trachtenberg, Alan, *The Incorporation of America: Culture and Society in the Gilded Age*, New York: Hill and Wang, 1982

Zunz, Olivier, *Making America Corporate, 1870–1920*, Chicago: University of Chicago Press, 1990

In spite of its central place in American history, business history has been the subject of serious inquiry for scarcely more than a generation. To be sure, a handful of scholars published biographies of businessmen in the 1940s and 1950s, most notably the multi-volume studies of John D. Rockefeller and of the Ford Motor Company. The vast majority of books published in the field were biographies of individual business leaders or companies produced by writers from starkly opposing camps. At one extreme were the laudatory chronicles churned out by company apologists and insiders (often retirees or public relations staffers), hagiographic tomes peppered with illustrations of buildings and executives, and lacking any critical analysis. From the opposite point of view came works in the muckraking "robber baron" tradition. Livelier than their corporate-sponsored distant cousins because of their journalistic origins and their focus on entrepreneurial misdeeds and machinations, these works were rarely grounded in primary research.

Two distinguished historians, Thomas Cochran and Alfred Chandler, were largely responsible for legitimizing the study of United States business history. Between 1942 and 1985, Cochran published scores of articles and essays, several of them highly influential, and wrote, co-wrote, or jointly edited thirty books, including company histories, textbooks, regional and international studies, sociological studies of business leadership, and works of synthesis. His primary interest was business and culture: how deeply imbedded values shaped the American business system, and how American society was transformed by the rise of giant enterprise. Change came slowly, according to Cochran, and the ultimate triumph of big business posed a salient threat to American initiative, individualism, republicanism, and liberty. In his dense 1972 work, COCHRAN synthesizes an enormous secondary literature and his own primary research to explore the relations between business and government, law, education, religion, and labor, among other topics.

While Cochran's work often lacks a strong central thesis, this was never a problem with Chandler's writings. Along with many edited volumes, Chandler wrote a half dozen books, two of which (listed above) became highly influential not merely in the field of history but also in business administration, economics, sociology, political science, and related disciplines. CHANDLER (1962), with its revealing title, *Strategy and Structure*, charted a new direction in business history that has dominated for three decades. Shifting away from Cochran's concern with social and cultural matters, Chandler focuses on the internal organization and dynamics of the giant industrial firm and its strategic adaptation to changing markets and new technology. He analyzes the early histories of General Motors, Du Pont, Standard Oil of New Jersey, and Sears, Roebuck to argue that a firm's organizational structure (for example, multidivisional) should follow from its competitive strategy. CHANDLER (1977) (which won the 1978 Pulitzer Prize in history) carries this further – though for a somewhat earlier period of American history. In this book he synthesizes hundreds of company and industry studies to chart the rise of a new class of middle managers who carried out crucial coordinating functions hitherto performed by what Adam Smith deemed the "invisible hand" of the marketplace. Chandler's model, which he later extended to other industrial nations, carries important implications about competitive strategy and the key role of "core" firms and industries as wellsprings of technological innovation and economic growth.

Still, Chandler spawned his critics, including those who suggest that his focus on giant firms slighted the importance of, for example, small business, public policy, and labor.

Several other general works help to fill these gaps. There is now a move to restore the small firm to its place in American business history, although inevitably the task of research into such companies is problematic, both in terms of ensuring that the historian has examined a representative cross section and because many smaller firms were at best transient. However, there is a very short study by BLACKFORD of the small firm in American business history, from colonial days to the present. This emphasizes the crucial role played by small firms within the American economy, and is illustrative of a more recent approach to business history.

A large number of scholars in recent years have addressed the important subject of business-government relations in America. McCRAW followed Chandler with his own Pulitzer prize-winning study of the history of regulation in America. McCraw's graceful prose, and his reliance on biographical case studies framed by contextual bridge chapters, ease the reader through this potentially stultifying topic. Influenced heavily by Chandler, McCraw generalizes from regulatory history only cautiously, yet suggests that regulation works best when policymakers (typically those trained in economics) understand the internal economics of their industries. Accordingly, McCraw lauds Charles Francis Adams, one of the first to comprehend the operating dynamics of American railroads, while criticizing Louis Brandeis – to the chagrin of many Brandeis scholars – for the highly politicized nature of his advocacy.

GALAMBOS and PRATT offer a cogent and well-informed overview of business-government relations in the 20th century. They chart the major transformations in the ways that firms have balanced three fundamental needs – to control risk, to innovate, and to increase efficiency – and emphasize correctly that these functions are carried out in shifting political as well as market environments. This largely optimistic work, which emphasizes the adaptability of the distinctively American "corporate commonwealth," nevertheless criticizes business leaders and policymakers for failing to respond well to changes such as global competition and energy scarcity that followed the heyday of corporate capitalism in the 1950s and 1960s.

BLACKFORD and KERR also highlight business-government relations in their solid and well-balanced textbook, which in more recent editions includes useful sections on slighted subjects such as business and gender, minorities in business, and 1980s mergers and corporate restructuring. These subjects received scant attention in the increasingly dated textbook by PUSATERI, which nevertheless remains attractive for its crispness and clarity. SOBEL explores the winners and losers in key industries in his microeconomic study of business since World War I, an intermittently insightful account by America's most prolific business historian that is strongest in its treatment of 1960s conglomerates and of the 1980s.

The social and cultural approach to the study of business history exemplified by Cochran, and the institutional focus made prominent by Chandler, have been carried on by historians of mass marketing. The institutional dimensions of STRASSER's study plainly reflect Chandler's influence, yet Strasser moves further into the analysis of advertising content, the role of gender in the rise of the mass market, and the propensity of promoters to change buying habits in ways that are not always socially beneficial. On this point she differs from TEDLOW, whose case studies of heroic marketing battles

(Ford versus GM, Coke versus Pepsi, to name two) carry lessons about sound business practices. Tedlow provides a useful overall framework that builds on Chandler's work, as well as some conservative conclusions about the limits of corporate promotionalism.

For readers sharing Cochran's cultural bent, TRACHTENBERG offers a concise interpretative synthesis of the Gilded Age that emphasizes the transformative impact of corporate ascent. But this work by a professor of American Studies is pre-eminently a study of literary form and content, architecture, the symbolism and myths that accompanied wholesale industrialization, and related subjects rather than a study of business itself. ZUNZ, whose book is grounded in archival research, is much stronger on this point. His somewhat idiosyncratic study of the emerging white-collar middle class between the Civil War and World War I emphasizes the diversity of these workers, and the large hand which they took in shaping the contours of change within their behemoth organizations. In this way, his work points in a promising direction: toward the melding of cultural and institutional approaches in American business history.

DAVID B. SICILIA

See also Advertising; Manufacturing Industry entries; Marketing and Distribution

Business History: Big Business

Chandler, Alfred D., Jr., *The Visible Hand: The Managerial Revolution in American Business*, Cambridge, MA: Belknap Press of Harvard University Press, 1977

Chandler, Alfred D., Jr., *Scale and Scope: The Dynamics of Industrial Capitalism*, Cambridge, MA: Belknap Press of Harvard University Press, 1990

Cochran, Thomas C. and William Miller, *The Age of Enterprise*, New York: Macmillan, 1942; revised, New York: Harper, 1961

Gunderson, Gerald, *The Wealth Creators: An Entrepreneurial History of the United States*, New York: Dutton, 1989

Lamoreaux, Naomi R., *The Great Merger Movement in American Business, 1895–1904*, Cambridge and New York: Cambridge University Press, 1985

Livesay, Harold C., *Andrew Carnegie and the Rise of Big Business*, Boston: Little Brown, 1975

McCraw, Thomas K. (editor), *The Essential Alfred Chandler: Essays Toward a Historical Theory of Big Business* by Chandler, Boston: Harvard Business School Press, 1988

Tedlow, Richard S., *The Rise of the American Business Corporation*, Chur, Switzerland, and Philadelphia: Harwood Academic, 1991

In examining the history of business within the United States, one very significant trend has been the rise of very large corporations, often denoted by the phrase "big business." Early interpretations were suspicious of the results of this concentration of power and saw it as reflecting the greed and ruthlessness of individual businessmen. The "robber barons", as they are often called, exercised political as well as economic influence.

In their survey of the social history of industrial America, COCHRAN and MILLER generally take this approach to the history of the period 1800–1940. Writing in the immediate aftermath of the New Deal, the authors clearly support government intervention and regulation of the economy as a curb upon big business.

This approach has been challenged by the doyen of American business history. Showing a mastery of the available sources, Alfred D. Chandler, Jr. has published a wide range of books and articles, with particular reference to larger corporations. His prime focus of interest is the organizational structure of American business, and how that changed over time, rather than the examination of individual entrepreneurs and their achievements. Chandler's works are crucial to an understanding of American business history, as so many authors either work within the framework of his ideas or react against them. He explains how, in the period from about 1850, the structure of American business gradually changed, partly in response to advances in transportation and communication, towards systems of mass production and mass distribution, organized around vertical integration. This prompted the development of larger business units, encapsulating speed and economies of scale. Increasingly, the profile of successful American businesses moved away from the owner-proprietor model, to a structure in which direction of policy lay in the hands of professional managers rather than owners. This encouraged an efficient, diverse administrative structure, with the emphasis upon competition and management. Those companies that survived and prospered were those which adapted best to the new circumstances. CHANDLER (1977) traces this process, arguing that the visible hand of managers replaced the invisible hand of the market. CHANDLER (1990) compares American managerial practice to that pertaining in Germany and Great Britain; in Britain, personal management through the family firm still predominated and hence the edge of competitiveness was lost. In the case of Germany, there was more reliance upon management as divorced from ownership, together with an awareness of the advantages of bigness, but here strong cartels reduced the level of competitiveness. McCRAW has also brought together a number of Chandler's most significant articles in a valuable book containing a good introduction describing Chandler's ideas.

TEDLOW employs Chandler's emphasis upon the organizational model in his short but informative study covering the whole period from colonial times to the present. In tracing the development of the private corporation, he stresses how technology, innovation and mass markets fostered development of large-scale corporate structures that were fully in place by the 1920s. The development of "bigness" in business was assisted by the ambivalent, sometimes directly helpful, attitude of American courts, and state and federal governments, towards large corporations.

LAMOREAUX looks closely at the merger movement around the turn of the century. In part, this study marks a reaction against Chandler's model, for which it acts as a useful corrective, although certainly not a refutation. She argues that the massive mergers in this period were driven by a desire for market control, rather than by technological progress or superior administrative efficiency. In this context, Lamoreaux emphasizes horizontal consolidation – that is, the merger of companies performing similar functions – rather than vertical integration (where one company carries out all functions, from acquiring the raw materials to distributing the finished product). She uses a combination of case studies and economic theory to argue her case, and readers unaccustomed to economic terminology might find some sections of her book difficult to follow.

GUNDERSON on the other hand emphasizes the role of individual entrepreneurs, although he rejects the notion of the robber baron, preferring instead to present them as wealth creators, who through their energy and innovation were crucial to sustaining economic development. LIVESAY takes a similar approach, stressing the importance of entrepreneurial individuals rather than organizational structures. He argues that massive companies could develop and succeed under the guidance of an individual owner; a view reflected in his biographical study of Andrew Carnegie, drawing upon the Carnegie papers in the Library of Congress. Livesay does emphasize the importance of new systems of industrial management in developing Carnegie's company, but also stresses that individual entrepreneurs could continue to play a crucial role.

FIONA VENN

Business History: Individual Corporations

Cheape, Charles W., *Family Firm to Modern Multinational: Norton Company, a New England Enterprise*, Cambridge, MA: Harvard University Press, 1985

Chernow, Ron, *The House of Morgan: An American Banking Dynasty and the Rise of Modern Finance*, New York: Atlantic Monthly Press 1990

Continental Oil Company, *Conoco: The First One Hundred Years: Building on the Past for the Future*, New York : Dell, 1975

Cortada, James W., *Before the Computer: IBM, NCR, Burroughs, and Remington Rand and the Industry They Created, 1865–1956*, Princeton: Princeton University Press, 1993

DeLamarter, Richard Thomas, *Big Blue: IBM's Use and Abuse of Power*, London: Macmillan, and New York: Dodd Mead, 1986

Fisher, Franklin M., James W. McKee and Richard B. Mancke, *IBM and the US Data Processing Industry: An Economic History*, New York: Praeger, 1983

Nevins, Allan with Frank Ernest Hill, *Ford*, 3 vols., New York: Scribner, 1954–63

Standard Oil Company, *History of Standard Oil Company (New Jersey)*
1. Hidy, Ralph W. and Muriel E. Hidy, *Pioneering in Big Business, 1882–1911*, New York: Harper, 1955
2. Gibb, George Sweet and Evelyn H. Knowlton, *The Resurgent Years, 1911–1927*, New York: Harper, 1956
3. Larson, Henrietta M., Evelyn H. Knowlton, and Charles S. Popple, *New Horizons, 1927–1950*, New York: Harper, 1971

4. Wall, Bennett H., *Growth in a Changing Environment: A History of Standard Oil Company (New Jersey), 1950–1972, and Exxon Corporation, 1972–1975*, New York: McGraw Hill, 1988

Tilley, Nannie M., *The R.J. Reynolds Tobacco Company*, Chapel Hill: University of North Carolina Press, 1985

There have been many histories of individual corporations, and only an illustrative sample are discussed here. Of least value to the historian in most cases are those produced "in house" without an academic author. Useful as providing some basic information, and often profusely illustrated, they offer little or no analysis. A widely available example of this genre is the history of the CONTINENTAL OIL COMPANY.

Many of the studies of individual corporations are in the form of articles in the specialized press, often inaccessible to the general reader. In order to discuss a particular corporation at book-length, it is usually necessary to have access to the archives and/or employees of that corporation. Many companies have explicitly commissioned, or co-operated with, a scholarly company history, undertaken by recognised business historians, as a way of diverting pressure from other researchers for access to their archives. From the 1950s through to the 1970s, a large number of very thorough and detailed business histories were produced.

There are two particularly impressive multi-volume series, produced by highly regarded historians (usually aided by research assistants and associate authors) which examine the history of two of the United States' largest companies: Standard Oil (New Jersey) and the Ford Motor Company. The history of STANDARD OIL concentrates upon the company, rather than individuals within it, and provides a useful, exceptionally detailed survey of all aspects of the corporation's operations, including, for example, technical discussion of advances in exploitation techniques and refining. It presents a graphic picture of the expansion and vertical integration of a large corporation and the management structures thus required. However, the level of detail and length of each volume may well deter the general reader. The company co-operated with the production of the volumes, but guaranteed complete editorial freedom.

The history of Ford Motor Company, which was dominated for far longer by its original owner, has necessarily to include a study of the individual (Henry Ford) as well as the firm. Despite its length, therefore, it is of greater interest to the non-specialist. NEVINS and HILL criticize Ford for trying to retain a personal style of management for too long; he was a gifted innovator, but an industrial autocrat. By the 1930s, Ford had lost his edge upon the rest of the automobile industry and was now merely a competitor among equals, and Ford's unsuccessful attempt to continue to run his company single-handed brought it into crisis. The Ford Motor Company helped to fund this three-volume history by means of a grant to Columbia University, which assumed responsibility for the academic management and direction of the project.

CHEAPE is another study written with access to company records, and was published under the aegis of the Harvard Studies in Business History series. He looks at a particular example of the way in which an individual company managed to develop into a strong multinational while retaining family ownership and control. Cheape emphasizes the self-financed nature of much of the company's business, which allowed it a substantial measure of self-control. However, in later years its products lagged behind in competitiveness, and the company had to resort to the recruitment of professional managers. The author made good use both of company archives and of interviews with employees and family members.

TILLEY was also given access to the company archives without apparent restriction, but in this case she was paid by the company. In her painstaking study of the Reynolds Tobacco Company from 1875 to the 1950s, in which she emphasises the crucial role played by a single entrepreneur, the original R.J. Reynolds, Tilley takes a very positive view of the company. In addition to highlighting its economic success, she points to its commitment to local education, and the economic and social improvement of North Carolina. She presents an extremely detailed account of the company's history; but without a more independent study as a basis for comparison, it is difficult to assess the level of objectivity.

There was a close relationship, of course, between American business and the large banking houses, and, in his massive volume, CHERNOW examines the best known of all, the House of Morgan. In this widely researched study, Chernow combines a deep knowledge of high finance with a lively command of anecdotes to produce an excellent study of how the House of Morgan adapted to the changing nature of global finance. The essential change was from a relationship based upon personal interaction and knowledge to the modern competitive strategies based on the offering of new products and services at competitive prices.

One way of overcoming the difficulty of sustaining discussion of particular companies at book length, without relying too heavily upon company co-operation, is to write a comparative study of several similar firms. One example is CORTADA who writes extensively upon the history of the computer industry. He explores the history of the information-handling industry in some detail, looking at the problems and process of transition from an electric and mechanical office to one dominated by the electronic computer. However, coverage of the history of the four companies is uneven, in part as a result of difficulties with sources. Moreover, by focusing on those companies which successfully bridged the transition, Cortada does not tackle the no-less-interesting question of why some companies survived while others proved incapable of managing the changeover to an electronic age.

One source for individual company histories not yet mentioned is the evidence and testimony in antitrust cases brought against large, potentially monopolistic companies. One particularly dramatic case is that of IBM, against whom a suit was brought in 1969 by the antitrust division of the Department of Justice. The case lasted until 1982, and as a consequence a very large number of documents and testimonies by involved witnesses entered the public domain. The evidence thus produced has been used in several books. One, by FISHER, McKEE and MANCKE, three expert economist witnesses called by IBM, provides a lengthy factual narrative (prepared by the authors during the case, for background) that seeks to be objective in its survey of the historical development of IBM. Clearly aware of possible charges of bias, the book is almost tediously factual in its approach, but it does provide a useful account of the development of the computer industry.

As against this can be set DeLAMARTER, who, as a lawyer in the Department of Justice, worked on the case. He perceives IBM as a monopoly and has written a highly critical study of the company's history, making clear from the beginning his disappointment at the decision to abandon the case. The extensive references demonstrate that this author too has made good use of the trial documentation. Until more companies are prepared to open their archives to researchers, historians have reason to be grateful for the light thrown by such cases upon the history of individual corporations.

FIONA VENN

See also Computers and Data Processing; Manufacturing Industry entries

C

Calhoun, John C. 1782–1850
Southern political leader

Bartlett, Irving H., *John C. Calhoun: A Biography*, New York: Norton, 1993

Capers, Gerald M., *John C. Calhoun, Opportunist: A Reappraisal*, Gainesville: University of Florida Press, 1960

Coit, Margaret L., *John C. Calhoun: American Portrait*, Boston: Houghton Mifflin, 1950

Current, Richard N., *John C. Calhoun*, New York: Twayne, 1963

Hofstadter, Richard, "John C. Calhoun: The Marx of the Master Class," in his *The American Political Tradition and the Men Who Made It*, New York: Knopf, 1948; London: Cape, 1962

Hunt, Gaillard, *John C. Calhoun*, Philadelphia: G.W. Jacobs, 1908

Meigs, William M., *The Life of John Caldwell Calhoun*, 2 vols., New York: Neale, 1917

Niven, John, *John C. Calhoun and the Price of Union*, Baton Rouge: Louisiana State University Press, 1988

Peterson, Merrill D., *The Great Triumvirate: Webster, Clay, and Calhoun*, New York: Oxford University Press, 1987

Spain, August O., *The Political Theory of John C. Calhoun*, New York: Bookman Associates, 1951

Von Holst, Hermann, *John C. Calhoun*, Boston: Houghton Mifflin, 1882

Wiltse, Charles M., *John C. Calhoun*, 3 vols., Indianapolis: Bobbs Merrill, 1944–51

In an era marked by deep political attachments and animosities, no man inspired greater reverence and loathing than John C. Calhoun. Unexceptionable in private character, he proclaimed and finally came to personify the most controversial of American political causes. Opinion on the South, states rights, and slavery has divided historians as it divided contemporaries. In consequence, most Calhoun studies exalt or condemn him, with few finding, or even seeking, neutral ground.

A nationalistic and antislavery viewpoint underwrote the first important works on Calhoun. VON HOLST's volume in the classic "American Statesmen" series is rather more of a critical commentary than a biography. It shows Calhoun as slavery's great champion, sinking all his brilliant talents in futile defense of a "doomed and unholy cause." Though dated in style and detail, Von Holst is still worth reading for its arresting judgments. Broader in coverage and less critical than Von Holst,

HUNT sees Calhoun more as a creature of circumstance than a mastermind of reaction. But he concurs in censuring Calhoun's states rights theories and considers him "the slavery cause incarnate." MEIGS is the first full biography. Thoroughly researched, it recounts Calhoun's private as well as public life in great detail, with long quotations from letters and speeches. While striving for detachment, Meigs affirms the legitimacy of southern grievances and the leniency of slavery in light of "ineradicable" black inferiority. Though not uncritical, Meigs's portrait is far more sympathetic than Von Holst's or Hunt's.

The next scholarly generation carried Calhoun's rehabilitation further. SPAIN's analytical treatise expounds Calhoun's constitutional doctrines and pronounces him a high-minded statesman, a "seeker after philosophical truth," and an original political thinker of lasting importance. COIT's colorful Pulitzer Prize-winning biography humanizes Calhoun with lively anecdotes and character sketches, not always reliably authenticated. Coit finds the key to Calhoun in his Puritan temperament. She is weakest in her grasp of politics, a grave handicap for a Calhoun biographer. Coit's Calhoun is the champion of an elevated "Southern way of life" against rapacious industrial capitalism, and of pure republicanism against the vulgar democracy of numbers.

WILTSE's thoroughly researched, scholarly three-volume portrayal has a similar thrust. Wiltse sees Calhoun much as he saw himself: a model statesman defending the Union and republican principle against Jacksonian despotism, knavish partisans, and abolitionist fanatics. Wiltse's Calhoun is nearly an inversion of Von Holst's – a "giant figure . . . towering over most of his contemporaries," and "the supreme champion of minority rights and interests everywhere." Wiltse, Coit, and Spain all find enduring worth in Calhoun's fight against majoritarian tyranny. They see the sectional struggle as driven by northern economic and ideological aggression. Slavery, in this light, shrinks from a paramount injustice to an almost morally neutral point of conflict between an industrial North and agricultural South. Spain speaks of slavery's "customs and manners, pleasures and joys." Without defending slavery, Wiltse and Coit, like Meigs, downplay its harshness and characterize blacks in terms that today seem condescending.

Its well-grounded narrative and wealth of detail make Wiltse the standard biography. But less admiring historians, disenchanted with economic explanations and newly attuned to issues of racial justice, have challenged its perspective. The first responses came in short, sharp retorts. In his psychological biography, CAPERS debunks Calhoun's reputation for disinterested and consistent statesmanship, and depicts him as driven by presidential ambition, political expediency, and self-deceiving egotism. HOFSTADTER is a brilliant sketch which reaffirms Calhoun as an apostle of reaction. CURRENT takes a similar view in his brief volume, which contains essays on Calhoun's life, political thought, and contemporary relevance. Re-asserting the centrality of slavery in Calhoun's world, Hofstadter and Current recast him from Wiltse's sage for the ages into a mouthpiece for Von Holst's doomed, ignoble cause. They view Calhoun's states rights doctrine as a contrivance to sustain the sway of slaveholders, the only minority which he ever cared about. Charging Calhoun with elementary moral inconsistency, Hofstadter says his order to whip a slave revealed more of his principles than all his constitutional dialectics. Current finds Calhoun's "true spirit" surviving among die-hard white supremacists.

Recent studies accept these critical assessments, but subdue them by subordinating moral argument to biographical narrative and psychological explanation. PETERSON is an epic traditional account of antebellum politics framed around the intertwining careers of Calhoun and his contemporaries Henry Clay and Daniel Webster. While sure in execution and rich in anecdote and vignette, it slights theme and analysis for storytelling. Peterson declines to judge his principals, but his text quietly stresses Calhoun's ambition, proslavery expediency, and blinding self-righteousness.

Drawing on the ongoing publication of Calhoun's complete papers, NIVEN's mid-length biography highlights his private and familial side. In politics Niven sets off the resolutely anti-party Calhoun against Martin Van Buren, the quintessential party man. While finding some enduring value in Calhoun's ideas, Niven sees him fitting principle to purposes in an obsessive search for stability. Fears for his section's future, compounded by personal insecurities and frustrated ambition, drove Calhoun knowingly to defend the "morally indefensible."

BARTLETT's biography, similar to Niven's in scope and coverage, likewise portrays Calhoun as more controlled than controlling, driven by impulses of ambition and self-justification he never understood. Bartlett finds the wellspring of Calhoun's political style in the frontier culture of his youth and the commanding example of his father. Unquestioningly accepting slavery and high-toned republican notions of duty and honor, Calhoun practised an elitist politics increasingly outmoded in a democratic age.

Portrayal of Calhoun as creature rather than master of his character and circumstances allows Niven and Bartlett to downplay moral judgment. Respecting the man without espousing his views, they portray Calhoun as neither demi-god nor evil genius, but a man of extraordinary talents directed by ordinary impulses. Thus detached from the cause he embodied, Calhoun appears a more approachable human figure, but also a less significant one. Lacking the urgency of conviction that drove previous scholarship, the newest biographies also lack thrust. Studies that judge Calhoun may persuade only readers who share their premises; but studies that mute judgment may seem to have little of importance to say.

DANIEL FELLER

See also Slavery: Proslavery Thought; South: Colonial Period to Civil War

California

Bancroft, Hubert Howe and Henry L. Oak, *History of California*, 7 vols. (i.e., vols. 18–24 of Bancroft's *Works*), San Francisco: History Company, 1884–90

Daniel, Cletus E., *Bitter Harvest: A History of California Farmworkers, 1870–1941*, Ithaca, NY: Cornell University Press, 1981

Lotchin, Roger W., *Fortress California, 1910–1961: From Warfare to Welfare*, New York: Oxford University Press, 1992

Pisani, Donald J., *From the Family Farm to Agribusiness: The Irrigation Crusade in California and the West, 1850–1931*, Berkeley: University of California Press, 1984

Rawls, James J. and Walton Bean, *California: An Interpretative History*, 6th edition, New York: McGraw Hill, 1993

Starr, Kevin, *Americans and the California Dream, 1850–1915*, New York: Oxford University Press, 1973

Starr, Kevin, *Inventing the Dream: California Through the Progressive Era*, New York: Oxford University Press, 1985

Starr, Kevin, *Material Dreams: Southern California Through the 1920s*, New York: Oxford University Press, 1990

Although BANCROFT was not the first to produce a history of California, the size and scope of his undertaking, together with its frequent and intensive quotation from primary sources, makes it the most rewarding place to begin reading the history of the state. Readers should be aware, however, that Hubert Howe Bancroft wrote only volumes six and seven of the work and that the first five and superior volumes were written by Henry L. Oak, whom Bancroft employed for the purpose but never publicly acknowledged. Together the volumes cover the period 1542 to 1890.

RAWLS and BEAN is one of the best single-volume textbooks. The first edition, published in 1968 by Walton Bean, remains evident in the sixth, but James Rawls has added chapters to cover the years since the 1970s, deliberately, as he says, increasing coverage of southern California and the history of women. As this last remark may suggest, the work is somewhat self-consciously politically correct and liberal in tone. One of its strengths is the breadth of its coverage, which encompasses social, cultural, and economic as well as political history.

STARR's three volumes, which may be followed by two others, explore the notion of the California Dream which has been behind much of the state's phenomenal growth since 1848. The author is happiest when using literary texts and figures to illustrate arguments, and adopts such an encyclopedic approach that the volumes may be better consulted than read consecutively. Not surprisingly, given the amount of detail offered, there is some repetition and argument sometimes struggles under the weight of fact. The volumes are based on readings of secondary rather than primary sources, but together go far to explain the hold which California has had on the American imagination.

Since Starr has not yet written much on the period after 1930, LOTCHIN provides a useful supplement. Though this work is primarily an investigation of the relationship between war and defence on the one hand, and urbanization and urbanism on the other, and is addressed primarily to urban historians, rather than to historians of California, the examination of its subject is so minute that readers will gain a good understanding of the dynamics of California's growth and development in the period. The work is distinguished by its use of many hitherto untapped primary sources.

Daniel and Pisani look at some of the realities behind the California Dream. DANIEL shows how California agriculture has always been characterized by a small class of wealthy landowners and a large class of itinerant farm labourers, who have never been able to proceed up the ladder from tenancy to ownership, save potentially in one instance, that of the Japanese, whose threatened progress, however, was deliberately made impossible by white racism. Daniel writes in the critical tradition first systematically established by Henry George in the 1870s, to produce an intricate and subtle analysis of the interplay of economic and ideological forces which destroyed the hope that California would become an egalitarian commonwealth. Though he ends his survey in 1941, his analysis could easily be extended to explain patterns of work and ownership in subsequent decades.

PISANI shows how the ever-growing gap between a small number of landowners, 310 of whom held over 4,000,000 acres of first-class farmland in 1916, and the rest of the farming community, was created in large measure by control over the state's water supply. His study, however, extends beyond the politics of water to the social and economic institutions of his period. He examines the way in which supporters of the family farm attempted to break up the large estates of California's early American period, diversify agriculture and establish a stable rural population which could practise the values of Jeffersonian liberalism, and thereby cleanse society of the evils of monopoly and inegalitarianism. But as he shows, both general and particular policies failed to achieve these goals. All these works help to explain that, if the California Dream exists today, it is one of steady employment in a service or industrial occupation and suburban home-ownership and lifestyle.

R.A. BURCHELL

See also Agriculture, since 1860; Los Angeles; San Francisco

Canada and the United States

Bothwell, Robert, *Canada and the United States: The Politics of Partnership*, Toronto: University of Toronto Press, and New York: Twayne, 1992

Brebner, John Bartlet, *North Atlantic Triangle: The Interplay of Canada, the United States and Great Britain*, New York: Columbia University Press, 1945

Granatstein, J.L. and Norman Hillmer, *For Better or for Worse: Canada and the United States to the 1990s*, Toronto: Copp Clark Pitman, 1991

Jones, Howard, *To the Webster-Ashburton Treaty: A Study in Anglo-American Relations, 1783–1843*, Chapel Hill: University of North Carolina Press, 1977

Stewart, Gordon T., *The American Response to Canada since 1776*, East Lansing: Michigan State University Press, 1992

Stuart, Reginald C., *United States Expansionism and British North America, 1775–1871*, Chapel Hill: University of North Carolina Press, 1988

Thompson, John Herd and Stephen J. Randall, *Canada and the United States: Ambivalent Allies*, Athens: University of Georgia Press, 1994

The historical literature of the relations between Canada and the United States has been dominated for the past fifty years by the impressive 25 volumes commissioned by the Carnegie Endowment for International Peace. The final volume in the series was BREBNER's overview that built on the detailed scholarly work of the earlier studies. The assumption of his book, and to some extent the whole series, was that the triangular relationship between Great Britain, Canada, and the United States, while not without periodic crisis, was the story of rational peoples who worked out processes of political stability, economic prosperity, and mutually beneficial neighborly relations. While some of Brebner's assessments seem dated, his analysis of the triangular relations among the three countries, particularly in the 19th century, remains crisp, informative, and insightful. His specific incorporation of British affairs into the discussion of events is particularly valuable.

There were few attempts to supersede Brebner until the 1980s. THOMPSON and RANDALL is a study of Canada and the United States that begins in the 1770s, although the emphasis of the book is on the 20th century. Thompson and Randall take the view that the affairs of the two countries have been characterized by the asymmetry of their population and power, and that relations between them have generally been uncomfortable, even if not actually hostile. The subtitle "Ambivalent Allies" is an accurate assessment of their understanding of the relationship. The ambivalence grows out of Canada's historic determination to pursue its own course without being absorbed by the larger and more powerful United States.

It has often been pointed out that Canadian-American studies are generally written from a Canadian point of view. The relationship is perceived in Canada as vital, whereas it is often ignored by Americans who are more likely to take it for granted. STEWART attempts to revise this view in a study which gives equal emphasis to the broad span of events from the 1770s to the 1980s. This certainly contributes to his analysis of the American perspective on relations with Canada and Great Britain. Throughout the late 18th century and perhaps until after the Civil War, United States policy is described as being defensive when dealing with the British presence in Canada, whatever the public rhetoric might suggest. In the 20th century different circumstances prevailed, but the relations were neither as co-operative nor as exploitative as many assert. Stewart concludes that Canadian-American relations in the 20th century were essentially pragmatic, but different from relationships between most modern countries.

There has been a growing body of monographic literature dealing with specific events or crises in early Canadian-American relations. STUART is a particularly useful study of the border culture, with its shared community, as well as its tensions. He describes American expansion in the Canadian context, and interprets it as largely a defensive reaction to British policies until 1815, and as largely rhetorical after that date. Commercial expansion, which can be dated from at least the 1850s, was more or less congruent with British practices and therefore not basically disruptive or threatening. Stuart identifies a border community of conservative Loyalists and Federalists drawn together in their hostility to Reformers and Jeffersonians, respectively. By the Treaty of Washington in 1871 the United States accepted the permanence of the self-governing British Dominion.

Whatever might be said for the view of the border community, there remained the fact of serious disagreement about the eastern boundary from 1783 to 1842. Several recent studies have examined the periodic border crises and the attempts to achieve a settlement. The most comprehensive of these studies is JONES, which, after a good general chapter that surveys the historic issues, focuses on the events from the 1830s that led to the Webster-Ashburton Treaty in 1842. The treaty is seen as an equitable compromise that settled the matter and ended the growing tension and fear of a third Anglo-Canadian-American war.

The study of these 19th-century crises has proved less compelling than the rapidly changing relationships between Canada and the United States in the 20th century. Clearly the decline of Great Britain and the corresponding rise of the United States, as well as the two World Wars and the Cold War, are key elements here. Not surprisingly this course of events has fascinated many historians. For example, much of the emphasis of Thompson and Randall is on the 20th century. GRANATSTEIN and HILLMER begin their survey with a chapter that runs from 1860 to 1903, but the focus of the book is on the cultural, economic, diplomatic, and military history of the 20th century. It is particularly useful in analysing the Canadian background of events and people, although less so for the United States. The book represents a fatalistic, although not hostile, Canadian view of the process that has drawn Canada and the United States closer together in the 20th century. In his study of Canadian-American relations since 1945, BOTHWELL focuses on the economic theme of American investment in Canada, the National Energy Policy, and the Free Trade Agreement, and on the diplomatic and military implications of the Cold War for Canadian-American relations. The emphasis is on the logic and the harmony of this relationship.

FRANCIS M. CARROLL

Carnegie, Andrew 1835–1919
Industrialist and philanthropist

Bridge, James H., *The Carnegie Millions and the Men Who Made Them, Being the Inside Story of the Carnegie Steel Company*, London: Limpus Baker, 1903; as *The Inside Story of the Carnegie Steel Company: A Romance of Millions*, New York: Aldine, 1903

Hacker, Louis M., *The World of Andrew Carnegie, 1865–1901*, Philadelphia: Lippincott, 1968

Hendrick, Burton J., *The Life of Andrew Carnegie*, 2 vols., New York: Doubleday, Doran, 1932

Livesay, Harold C., *Andrew Carnegie and the Rise of Big Business*, Boston: Little Brown, 1975

Wall, Joseph Frazier, *Andrew Carnegie*, New York: Oxford University Press, 1970

Andrew Carnegie seems to encapsulate the extremes of the American experience: the humble origins in Dunfermline, Scotland; the emigration and early problems involved in making his own way; his remarkable business career (through telegraphy, railways, sleeping cars, oil, bridge-building, iron manufacture, and finally steel); his hand in the formation of the world's first billion-dollar corporation; and then the lengthy "retirement" to devote himself to philanthropy and good causes. This is to say nothing of his work in the peace movement, his involvement with British and American politics, and his journalism, books and speeches. It is a career that has also evoked extremes in interpretation from historians and biographers.

Interestingly, the first account to document Carnegie's business career was written by a journalist, BRIDGE, in the aftermath of the formation of the United States Steel Corporation. The book developed from a magazine article and is essentially a company history of Carnegie Steel, rather than a biography of the leading protagonist. Bridge had assisted Carnegie for several years in the preparation of Carnegie's *Triumphant Democracy*, but his own book is not a commissioned work, and by focusing on the company he was able to maintain his distance from the leading subject. His book can still be read with profit by those interested in the development of the organisation of the Carnegie Steel Company. Indeed Bridge's view accords with many recent business historians, when he writes that Carnegie's company was "not the creation of any man, nor indeed of any set of men. It is a natural evolution; and the conditions of its growth are of the same general character as those of the 'flower in the crannied wall'".

It was more than a decade after Carnegie's death before the first major biography appeared. Characteristically, by then Carnegie had already had his say with the publication of his autobiography in 1920, in which he presented a benign and not always scrupulous account of his business career. HENDRICK, whose writings include various books eulogizing American captains of industry, presents the first really detailed account of Carnegie's life. In a two-volume work of more than 800 pages, he tells a straightforward chronological story. It has the merit of drawing on Carnegie's personal papers and other primary sources, but it is somewhat marred by its uncritical view of its subject. Carnegie's main personal attribute was his "deeply affectionate nature" – to his parents, to his business associates – which was unsullied by any envy or jealousy. Hendrick's biography makes an interesting counterpoint to Matthew Josephson's study of the American business class (published only two years later), which in its title – *The Robber Barons* – fixed in the American mind a rather different and perhaps more enduring view of Carnegie and his fellow business leaders.

The standard life of Carnegie, by WALL, appeared in 1970. Self-consciously in the Nevins tradition of grand industrial biography, this book covers broadly the same ground as Hendrick, though in much greater detail and with a more critical approach. Finance and technology are covered in straightforward fashion; while the famous events in Carnegie's career – such as the Homestead Strike and the struggles with Frick – are described authoritatively. Wall, too, evinces a grudging admiration for Carnegie, though his more detailed approach allows him to emphasize some of the complexities of the man, so that a more critical portrait emerges. Here we see Carnegie denouncing speculation once his own fortune was made; using collusion and dubious business practices to amass his fortune; and stooping to discreditable methods to cheat Henry Clay Frick. Here, too, is the radical dissenter in Britain, who was an arch-conservative in America; the follower of Herbert Spencer, whose ideas he disregarded when it suited him; and the advocate of laissez faire, who fought for state intervention to control the Pennsylvania Railroad.

Other books have attempted to place Carnegie in the economic and social context of the times. Only a quarter of HACKER is devoted to Carnegie himself; the rest includes chapters on agriculture, railroads, the banking system, education, and life in the cities. The broadly-based approach enables the author to defend the "Robber Barons" as not only creators of wealth, but also restorers of order and rationality in an anarchic market. In a similar vein, LIVESAY looks at Carnegie's business career and relates it to key organizational and technological changes in 19th-century American industry. Livesay's description of the cohesive Pittsburgh Scottish community of Carnegie's formative years echoes Oscar Handlin's *The Uprooted*. But an even greater influence on Livesay is fellow business historian, Alfred D. Chandler, Jr., who emphasized the major trends in business structure and control that underpinned the development of the great American corporations before 1914. In describing Carnegie's personality, Livesay follows Wall in describing him as a man who was full of paradoxes – ruthless and loyal, greedy and generous, violent and peace-loving, brash and shy. But much more important was Carnegie's business genius in the control of statistical data, costs and technology. Livesay shows how, in building his great steel works, Carnegie responded to the emergence of the urban market that followed the creation of the national railroad system (indeed, it is emphasized that Carnegie drew directly on his own experience with the railroads to create his business). In this view, not too different from that of Bridge, Carnegie's key contribution was organisational. Livesay (like Chandler) believes that entrepreneurs like Carnegie and others were successful because they correctly analyzed the economic situation and responded in a creative manner. This view, emphasizing how Carnegie played an important role in the dramatic growth of the economy and in the creation of an affluent society, is a favourable one, and shows that the old idea of the robber barons is now very much in eclipse.

GEOFFREY TWEEDALE

See also Business History: Big Business; Manufacturing Industry: Individual Industries

Carson, Kit 1809–1868
Frontiersman and mountain man

Blackwelder, Bernice, *Great Westerner: The Story of Kit Carson*, Caldwell, ID: Caxton Printers, 1962
Carter, Harvey L., *"Dear Old Kit": The Historical Christopher Carson*, Norman: University of Oklahoma Press, 1968
Estergreen, M. Morgan, *Kit Carson: A Portrait in Courage*, Norman: University of Oklahoma Press, 1962
Guild, Thelma S. and Harvey L. Carter, *Kit Carson: A Pattern for Heroes*, Lincoln: University of Nebraska Press, 1984
Kelly, Lawrence C., *Navajo Roundup: Selected Correspondence of Kit Carson's Expedition Against the Navajo, 1863–1865*, Boulder, CO: Pruett, 1970
McKee, James R., *Kit Carson: Man of Fact and Fiction*, New York: Arno Press, 1982
Sabin, Edwin L., *Kit Carson Days (1809–1868)*, Chicago: A.C. McClurg, 1914; reprinted as *Kit Carson Days: Adventures in the Path of Empire*, Lincoln: University of Nebraska Press, 1996
Smith, Henry Nash, *Virgin Land: The American West as Symbol and Myth*, Cambridge, MA: Harvard University Press, 1950
Steckmesser, Kent Ladd, *The Western Hero in History and Legend*, Norman: University of Oklahoma Press, 1965
Trafzer, Clifford E., *The Kit Carson Campaign: The Last Great Navajo War*, Norman: University of Oklahoma Press, 1982
Vestal, Stanley, *Kit Carson: The Happy Warrior of the Old West*, Boston: Houghton Mifflin, 1928

In 1946 the noted Meso-American scholar Edgar L. Hewett succinctly addressed the state of the scholarship on Christopher Carson: "I [have] read everything I could get about Kit, and have continued to do so. It amounts to a good many volumes, most of them worthless or worse. I have yet to read a good life of Kit Carson." Hewett knew of what he spoke. The Carson biographies published before this year were poorly researched eulogies with flawed chronologies and purpled prose. VESTAL may be the worst of these works. A University of Oklahoma English professor and Rhodes scholar, Vestal eschewed the Carson memoirs then available, and penned an epic based seemingly on a loose reading of bad biography and his own sense of dramatic license. Of the early biographies only SABIN stands in any measure the test of time. While minor flaws compromise Sabin's chronology, he provides a more level-headed narration and the photographs that grace the first edition (1914) are as near a complete set as any available.

In the early 1960s Carson biography became a cottage industry. Two residents of Taos, Carson's home town cum artist community, launched independent treatments of Kit's life. ESTERGREEN and BLACKWELDER are both ably written and well-researched, and cleave as closely as possible to the known facts of Carson's career. But both works tend to be overly trusting of the reminiscences of Carson and his descendants and fail to eliminate some of the fanciful elements that had stolen into his chronology. CARTER corrected these problems and more. The first rigorously academic treatment of Christopher Carson the man, Carter's work stands as the most reliable reference work yet published. In his introduction Carter gives a short synopsis of the Carson literature, showing how myriad errors had stolen into the record. He then provides a thoroughly annotated version of the memoirs Carson dictated to John Mostin in 1856. Finally, Carter provides a well-researched treatment of Carson's life after the dictation of the memoirs and before his death in 1869. With its elaborate attention to the finer points of the Carson timeline, Carter's work was well-received by academics but is now out of print. Somewhat disgruntled by this fact, Carter collaborated with retired school teacher Thelma Guild to write *A Pattern for Heroes*, a work that splices the chronological rigor of *Dear Old Kit* with the methods of popular biography. Contributing nothing new to our understanding of Christopher Carson, GUILD and CARTER has been ill-received in academic circles, but stands as the most trustworthy biography available.

While Guild and Carter give a clear account of Carson the man, none of the biographies is even vaguely satisfactory in its attempt to come to grips with Kit Carson the legend. Like Daniel Boone, Davy Crockett, and "Buffalo Bill" Cody, Christopher Carson lived a life so fraught with meaning for his countrymen that the mythologizing began even before he was comfortably under the ground. The first objectively to track the myths and symbols of the Carson legend was SMITH, who isolated two equally fanciful Carsons that graced the pages of 19th-century fiction. A genteel Carson was supposed by his fictionalizers never to have sworn or drank, never to have gambled or chased the ladies, and only to have killed out of a sense of noblesse oblige. A blood-and-thunder Indian killer provided the other pole of the Carson legend. The genteel version, seemed, to Smith at least, an attempt to civilize the West with wishful thinking, to give Victorian readers a disinfected version of their country's energetic origins; the two-guns version, made possible by new printing technologies and rising literacy rates, satisfied a more popular appetite for stories of physical adventure. Both versions, however, had their roots in the contradictory symbol system of the American West – garden and desert, paradise and purgatory. The settling of the virgin west epitomized simultaneously the advance of civilization and the descent into savagery. STECKMESSER fleshed out this Smith thesis with an in-depth examination of the lives and legends of Kit Carson, Billy the Kid, Wild Bill Hickok, and George A. Custer. The work of earlier authors was ably summarized in McKEE, whose dissertation was published under the auspices of Arno Press's Dissertations in American Biography series. McKee did not go much beyond these authors, though he did make an attempt to deal with the juvenile literature other scholars have all but ignored.

By the 1970s researchers were beginning to ask questions about the native societies that had done so much to provide Carson, man and myth, with his foil. KELLY is an extremely well edited and annotated collection of the correspondence concerning the Carson expedition against the Navajo from 1863 to 1865. Using this correspondence, but not pushing much beyond it in terms of research materials, TRAFZER has told the relatively familiar, though still quite compelling, story of this last great Navajo war. Though the task of fleshing out

our sense of how Native Americans perceived the westering of Euro-Americans is hardly complete, the Carson scholarship in this area stands at an interesting crossroads. A pattern for heroes or a remorseless agent of genocide, the Carson that emerges in this literature proves that, 150 years later, the symbolic significance of the American West is still fraught with the kind of contradiction that makes for energetic debate.

STEPHEN W. BERRY

See also Westward Expansion

Carson, Rachel 1907–1964
Environmentalist pioneer and publicist

Brooks, Paul, *The House of Life: Rachel Carson at Work*, Boston: Houghton Mifflin, 1972; London: Allen and Unwin, 1973

Dunlap, Thomas R., *DDT: Scientists, Citizens and Public Policy*, Princeton: Princeton University Press, 1981

Gartner, Carol B., *Rachel Carson*, New York: Ungar, 1983

Graham, Frank, *Since "Silent Spring,"* Boston: Houghton Mifflin, and London: Hamish Hamilton, 1970

Hynes, H. Patricia, *The Recurring Silent Spring*, New York: Pergamon Press, 1989

Lear, Linda, "Rachel Carson's *Silent Spring*," *Environmental History Review*, 17(2), 1993

Lutts, Ralph H., "Chemical Fallout: Rachel Carson's *Silent Spring*, Radioactive Fallout, and the Environmental Movement," in *The Recent Past: Readings on America since World War II*, edited by Allan M. Winkler, New York: Harper, 1989

Norwood, Vera, *Made from This Earth: American Women and Nature*, Chapel Hill: University of North Carolina Press, 1993

Despite Carson's reputation as pioneer environmentalist, eminent marine biologist, best-selling popular science writer and celebrated author of the book hailed as "*The Uncle Tom's Cabin* of the environmental movement," she has been comparatively neglected by historians. In the absence of an adequate biography, one must resort to a variety of more provisional and sometimes shorter treatments. These often take the form of a chapter within studies of prominent American women, leading conservationists and non-fiction nature writing, or of the problems of toxic chemicals before and after her most famous book, *Silent Spring* (1962), often acclaimed in lists of "books that changed America."

Given that Carson died in the 1960s and relatively young, most writers have been able to draw on those who knew her. Her talents as writer and scientist – and the highly effective manner in which she blended these skills – are broadly acknowledged, just as there is consensus on *Silent Spring*'s role in galvanizing modern environmentalism. Not least, the legitimacy of her charges against the chemical industry are generally upheld.

BROOKS intersperses commentary on her professional life and times – much of it based on unpublished correspondence

– with chapters consisting of selections from her writings, published and unpublished. Overlooking Graham's earlier book, the original edition's dust jacket claims this as the first study based on her papers. Brooks was Carson's editor at Houghton Mifflin – the publisher of *Silent Spring* – as well as a close personal friend and dedicated environmentalist. Yet this is the nearest that we have to a reliable biography, and Brooks's insider status produces a particularly revealing account of the researching, writing and publishing of *Silent Spring*. GARTNER focuses on Carson's literary persona and achievements. As such, she is mainly concerned with literary style and technique. Yet she does place *Silent Spring* within the muckraking tradition alongside Lincoln Steffens and Upton Sinclair. Gartner gives previous award-winning bestsellers, *The Sea Around Us* and *The Edge of the Sea*, as much space as *Silent Spring*, reminding us that Carson was already a famous author when it appeared.

Silent Spring has attracted as much attention as Carson herself. GRAHAM was the first to situate her life and book (to which he devotes a third of his study) within a broader context. A reporter and conservationist, Graham wrote specifically for the non-scientist and based his book on her then unprocessed papers and correspondence. This remains the most detailed and reliable study of the impact of *Silent Spring*. Graham brings to bear the evidence that has emerged since 1962 to bolster Carson's case against the chemical industry, but does not make excessive claims for the book's influence. DUNLAP serves partly as an update of Graham but its main focus – in line with the author's interest in the social history of science – is a fully fledged investigation of the relationships among science, government, industry, university research and concerned citizenry. Only one out of ten chapters is allotted to Carson, and this is mostly about *Silent Spring*. While acknowledging the book's impact and literary merits, Dunlap (who had a background in chemistry before turning to history) is mildly revisionist in emphasizing that *Silent Spring* was not the product of original research, and offers Robert L. Rudd's *Pesticides and the Living Landscape* (1964) as a superior scientific treatment. Dunlap also adds a fresh dimension by suggesting that the debate over the harmful effects of radioactive fallout that dominated the 1950s created a public mood predisposed to the reception of *Silent Spring*.

LUTTS states this more elaborately, arguing that the opening chapter ("A Fable for Tomorrow"), in which Carson evokes a small town rendered silent and lifeless by a "strange blight," drew on countless resonant images of nuclear holocaust. Lutts plays on the comparability of pesticides and radioactive compounds. He examines the various atomic incidents of the decade, and the fears which they aroused as expressed through media such as novels and film, and speculates on their influence over Carson.

The most up-to-date assessment is in an article by LEAR, an environmental historian, who is currently completing a critical biography of Carson. The article was conceived as the script for a Peace River Films documentary, "*Rachel Carson's Silent Spring*," aired on PBS in 1993. More authoritatively than any earlier treatment, Lear locates Carson and *Silent Spring* within the history of the environmental movement. Carson, as most writers point out, was a reluctant radical, and certainly no overt feminist. But apart from noting how rare female scientists were in the 1930–50 era, no one prior to Hynes, and then Norwood, devoted significant attention to gender. Norwood's chapter on Carson in her study of the role of women in American nature writing and conservation and Hynes's chapter in her roving critique of male-constructed science and technology, are the most gender-conscious treatments.

Rather than focus on Carson as an extraordinary, isolated female figure in a male-dominated world of science and conservation, NORWOOD stresses the extent of her supporting network of relations with other female scientists inside and outside government, with female nature writers and journalists, and various women's groups and clubs involved in conservation and animal welfare causes. This serves to highlight the hitherto underappreciated contribution of American women to conservation. Norwood also argues that Carson's writings had a special message for and appeal to women. In addition, she provides a gender-informed analysis of the responses to *Silent Spring*. HYNES, an environmental engineer, similarly contends that Carson seized the initiative for women, opening up a new era of environmental activism for previous "helpmates." She also attacks the received, male-constructed wisdom on Carson's personality, which, she claims, cast her as a lonely, retiring spinster who was professionally fulfilled but unfulfilled in her private life.

PETER A. COATES

See also Environment

Carter, Jimmy 1924–
39th President of the United States

Abernathy, M. Glenn, Dilys M. Hill, and Phil Williams (editors), *The Carter Years: The President and Policy Making*, New York: St. Martin's Press, and London: Pinter, 1984

Dumbrell, John, *The Carter Presidency: A Re-Evaluation*, Manchester: Manchester University Press, and New York: St. Martin's Press, 1993

Germond, Jack W. and Jules Witcover, *Blue Smoke and Mirrors: How Reagan Won and Why Carter Lost the Election of 1980*, New York: Viking, 1981

Glad, Betty, *Jimmy Carter: In Search of the Great White House*, New York: Norton, 1980

Hargrove, Erwin C., *Jimmy Carter as President: Leadership and the Politics of the Public Good*, Baton Rouge: Louisiana State University Press, 1988

Jones, Charles O., *The Trusteeship Presidency: Jimmy Carter and the United States Congress*, Baton Rouge: Louisiana State University Press, 1988

Kaufman, Burton I., *The Presidency of James Earl Carter, Jr.*, Lawrence: University Press of Kansas, 1993

Rosenbaum, Herbert D. and Alexej Ugrinsky, *Jimmy Carter: Foreign Policy and Post-Presidential Years*, Westport, CT: Greenwood Press, 1994

Rosenbaum, Herbert D. and Alexej Ugrinsky, *The Presidency and Domestic Policies of Jimmy Carter*, Westport, CT: Greenwood Press, 1994

Smith, Gaddis, *Morality, Reason, and Power: American Diplomacy in the Carter Years*, New York: Hill and Wang, 1986

Witcover, Jules, *Marathon: The Pursuit of the Presidency, 1972–76*, New York: Viking, 1977

Jimmy Carter's election as president in 1976 and his rather tumultuous four years in the nation's highest elective office have inspired a number of books on both his life and political career. While many of the early works lacked historical perspective and were often characterized by excessive animosity or uncritical adulation of the 39th president, recent studies have been more substantive and rigorous. The opening of the Carter presidential papers in 1987 has greatly facilitated new scholarship as well. While the scholarly canon remains somewhat limited in quantity, the quality of recent works provides readers with a sound basis for assessment of the public life, and especially the presidency, of Jimmy Carter.

Although a definitive biography of Carter has yet to be written, GLAD remains the best published thus far. Relying heavily on numerous interviews of Carter associates, acquaintances, and political foes, Glad traces the life of the president from birth and childhood in Plains, Georgia through the Democratic primaries of 1980. She devotes particular attention to the exposition of Carter's personality and its effect on his public actions. She argues that Carter's unending quest for mastery and control over his life and the presidency, coupled with his unyielding desire for victory, enabled him to win elections but greatly impaired his ability to govern effectively and successfully.

Several recent works have provided excellent overviews of the Carter presidency. Of these, KAUFMAN presents the most lucid, concise, and well-researched history of Carter's four years in office. He argues that while Carter possessed a keen intellect and a firm, technical grasp of a variety of issues, he failed to establish the public support necessary for successful leadership. Kaufman acknowledges the disastrous series of events in 1979 and 1980 might have debilitated any president, but contends that Carter's actions served only to make things worse. Carter's leadership of the country, Kaufman concludes, was at best mediocre.

DUMBRELL challenges the notion of mediocrity, in his revisionist history of the Carter presidency. Using a selective topical rather than chronological approach, Dumbrell examines Carter's policies on civil rights, women's rights and foreign relations with the Soviet Union, Northern Ireland, Nicaragua and Iran. This largely sympathetic account of the Carter presidency contends that Carter came to power at a time when post-war liberalism had disintegrated, and been replaced by a new era of limits. Although he notes that Carter failed to chart a successful new course for the nation during this period, he adds that the president nevertheless had considerable accomplishments to his credit, during a particularly turbulent period in American history. Dumbrell provides an almost perfect counterpoint for Kaufman's highly critical appraisal of Carter. In a vein similar to Dumbrell, HARGROVE argues that Carter came to power at a time of transition when liberalism was on the wane and the Democratic party was divided. Utilizing the extensive oral interview collection at the White Burkett Miller Center of Public Affairs, Hargrove uses chapters on Carter's domestic, economic, and foreign policies to illustrate the president's leadership style. He concludes that Carter saw himself as the custodian of the public good, sought to avoid actions that would ally him with special interest groups, and attempted to find comprehensive solutions that would benefit the entire national community. Hargrove's perceptive and thought-provoking analysis of Carter's leadership style, and the external challenges which he faced in a time of transition, contributes much to a more substantive understanding of his presidency.

JONES also uses interviews conducted by the White Burkett Miller Center for his study of Carter's relationship with Congress. Selective rather than comprehensive in his approach, Jones focuses on a number of significant policy issues and argues that Carter saw himself as a "trustee" president who acted independently and focused on national leadership. As a result Carter eschewed the traditional wheeling and dealing with Congress. Jones illustrates his findings with numerous tables and charts that allow the reader to grasp more firmly the intricacies of Carter's relationship with the legislative branch.

Carter's handling of foreign affairs receives excellent treatment in SMITH. Beginning with the vast series of foreign policy reforms and initiatives which Carter undertook in 1977, Smith gracefully traces Carter's foreign policy efforts through the end of his presidency. Paying particular attention to the shift in Carter's policy from human rights and conciliation to hard-line containment, Smith seeks to position Carter's foreign policy choices within the larger context of the history of American foreign policy. Although Smith gives too little attention to obstacles created by domestic events, and the changing status of the United States in the world, he provides the most comprehensive and judicious account of Carter's foreign policy written to date.

There are several volumes of essays which provide informative and detailed studies of more specific issues. Of particular note are the two volumes edited by ROSENBAUM and UGRINSKY that contain papers and comments from Hofstra University's conference on the Carter presidency. Although the quality of the essays varies, the series offers some of the most up-to-date interpretations of the Carter years. Also, the volume on foreign policy contains two essays on Carter's post-presidential activities. Another collection of essays which students of the Carter presidency may find useful is ABERNATHY *et al*. Using essays on both specific policy issues and Carter's relationships with Congress, the Democratic Party, and the federal bureaucracy, the ten contributors to the book seek to offer insight into Carter's defeat at the polls in 1980.

Although most of the books already discussed do at least touch on Carter's performance in the elections of 1976 and 1980, none provides the detail of the campaigns found in WITCOVER, and in GERMOND and WITCOVER. Written by veteran newspaper reporters, both books are organized chronologically and provide an excellent reference source for specific events in the two campaigns. Lacking adequate in-depth analysis of the elections, they nevertheless provide lively coverage of the events that signalled the beginning and the end of the Carter presidency.

JOHN C. BARROW III

Catholic Church

Abell, Aaron I., *American Catholicism and Social Action: A Search for Social Justice, 1865–1950*, Garden City, NY: Hanover House, 1960

Allitt, Patrick, *Catholic Intellectuals and Conservative Politics in America, 1950–1985*, Ithaca, NY: Cornell University Press, 1993

Billington, Ray Allen, *The Protestant Crusade, 1800–1860: A Study of the Origins of American Nativism*, New York: Macmillan, 1938

Crosby, Donald F., *God, Church, and Flag: Senator Joseph R. McCarthy and the Catholic Church, 1950–1957*, Chapel Hill: University of North Carolina Press, 1978

Cross, Robert D., *The Emergence of Liberal Catholicism in America*, Cambridge, MA: Harvard University Press, 1958

Dolan, Jay P., *The American Catholic Experience: A History from Colonial Times to the Present*, New York: Doubleday, 1985

Ellis, John Tracy, *American Catholicism*, Chicago: University of Chicago Press, 1956; revised edition, 1969

Gleason, Philip, *Keeping the Faith: American Catholicism, Past and Present*, Notre Dame, IN: University of Notre Dame Press, 1987

Greeley, Andrew M., *The American Catholic: A Social Portrait*, New York: Basic Books, 1977

Hennesey, James, *American Catholics: A History of the Roman Catholic Community in the United States*, New York: Oxford University Press, 1981

Kane, Paula M., *Separatism and Subculture: Boston Catholicism, 1900–1920*, Chapel Hill: University of North Carolina Press, 1994

O'Brien, David J., *American Catholics and Social Reform: The New Deal Years*, New York: Oxford University Press, 1968

Shannon, James P., *Catholic Colonization on the Western Frontier*, New Haven: Yale University Press, 1957

Writings on the history of the Catholic church in the United States have reflected the successive stages of the evolution of the church itself. They also mirror the tensions within a growing and diversifying religious community, and between that community and the larger American society. In the United States, a substantial Catholic population lived for the first time in a voluntary church, within a strongly Protestant society and culture. This generally poor and often unwelcome minority maintained a defensive posture at least until the mid-20th century. Catholic historians reflected – and indeed reinforced – this defensive or apologetic mentality. Many of them were themselves priests, and they tended to write institutional and often inward-looking history, with the emphasis on the work and the achievements of the clergy. An irreverent critic might suggest that many of their books could bear the sub-title of "The Invisible Layman" – and, even more, the invisible laywoman. Despite the important early French and Spanish contributions to North American Catholicism, Catholic history was presented essentially as the history of an immigrant church – and above all the history of Irish Americans. Catholicism and Irish-Americanism became almost synonymous, and the church appeared as an Irish fiefdom.

In the 1920s and 1930s, the presidential campaign of the Catholic Al Smith, and then the Great Depression and the New Deal, all helped to stimulate new thinking about the place of the Catholic church in American society. World War II and its aftermath brought about major adjustments in traditional Catholic obedience, discipline and outlook. In terms of higher standards of living and greater educational opportunities, Catholics benefited disproportionately from the welfare state. Moving into professional occupations and middle-class lifestyles, Catholics demanded a more sophisticated, inclusive and varied history of their community, and not just of an institution and its clerical leadership.

Overviews of American Catholic history reflect changing attitudes and assumptions. Writing in the 1950s, ELLIS, the most prominent Catholic historian of his day, produced a concise, accurate institutional history, which celebrated the acceptance of the Catholic church within American society, and professed the church's devotion to American principles. This was still primarily church history written by and about clerics, although the balance was redressed somewhat in the revised edition. It may be significant that Ellis was the author of biographies of Cardinal Gibbons and other Catholic bishops, which, with hindsight, may be seen as scholarly obituaries for a passing clericalism, written at a time when lay people were emerging into a more active role.

Written a generation later, HENNESEY describes itself as a "people's history," and, if it does not always live up to that description, it marks an important step in that direction. Seeking to place the history of the Catholic church in the context of the American experience as a whole, Hennesey divides that history into three main phases: the basic "American" period running from colonial beginnings to the early 19th century; the period of the "immigrant church" from the 1830s to the 1960s; and the years since the 1960s, when Catholics wrestled with upheavals in the wider American society and with fissures in their own ranks. This is a thorough and reliable survey, cautious in its judgments, particularly in dealing with the recent history. DOLAN, published a few years after Hennesey, has a stronger claim to be regarded as a history of the Catholic community, rather than the institutional history of a church. Dolan is a prolific historian of American Catholicism; his earlier work included an important study of the immigrant church in New York from 1815 to 1865, and he later edited two volumes of studies of the church at the level of the local parish. In his general history, he examines the whole American Catholic culture, and is equally at home in writing about the ethnic composition and the spiritual life of the church. His account gives noticeably greater attention to hitherto "submerged" ethnic groups, as well as to women and to African Americans.

Greeley and Gleason offer two very different interpretative assessments, rather than general surveys. GLEASON is a volume of judicious and thoughtful essays by a distinguished Catholic scholar, which examine various facets of the transformation of the Catholic church in the United States over a long period, and the adjustment of the church to an American society, itself in constant change. Topics discussed include the heritage from the medieval church, issues of immigration and

Americanisation, the school question, and the changes of the 1960s. GREELEY, a prolific author and tireless publicist, has himself been a major contributor to the re-shaping of Catholic self-perception and understanding in recent decades. In this portrait of the American Catholic written in the 1970s, he challenges stereotypes of American Catholics as narrow, rigid, anti-intellectual, morally authoritarian, politically corrupt, economically unsuccessful and racially prejudiced, and suggests that they lagged in occupational prestige only because of persistent forms of social discrimination at the upper levels of business, the professions, the foundations and the great private universities. He writes of the emergence of the "communal Catholic," loyal to the Catholic collectivity and its heritage, but often rejecting the teaching authority and leadership of the church.

There are many more specialised studies which focus on particular periods or on particular issues in American Catholic history. Some older works have remained very influential. In his classic study of nativism in the antebellum decades, BILLINGTON identified anti-Catholic feeling as its driving force. Later studies have modified his interpretation, but the weight of his evidence remains impressive. CROSS examines the efforts of more liberal church leaders in the late 19th century to adapt the Catholic church to American ways. In the process, he reveals the diversity within the church over such matters as Americanisation, education, labor unions and the use of English – and tensions with reactionary papal authority. SHANNON is an account of well-meaning, but ultimately not very successful efforts to settle poverty-stricken Irish men and women in rural, "dry" communities in Minnesota during the 1880s. Despite such efforts, American Catholics remained predominantly urbanised, and indeed became more so. Rather than escaping from the hardships and injustices of urban-industrial society, Catholics would have to do battle with them. ABELL is an informative study of Catholic social action and demands for social justice in the later 19th century and the first half of the 20th century.

Some more recent studies deal with Catholic reactions to various 20th-century political movements. O'BRIEN examines in detail a wide range of Catholic responses to the Great Depression and the programmes of the New Deal. CROSBY is a useful study of the tangled relationship between the Catholic church and Senator McCarthy and his -ism, but it should be used in conjunction with more recent work on the McCarthy phenomenon. He finds no unanimity or solidarity in the Catholic response to McCarthy, either among the leadership or among rank-and-file members who often remained indifferent. On an altogether higher intellectual plane is ALLITT's searching analysis of Catholic conservative thinkers who have been so influential in the broader conservative movement since the 1950s and 1960s. He shows the close interrelationship between their involvement in church politics, especially during and after Vatican II, and their role in the evolution of the conservative political tradition in America.

Some of the best work on the Catholic community is to be found in studies of large Catholic communities in such cities as Boston and Chicago. One outstanding recent community study of this kind is KANE's examination of Catholics in Boston during the first two decades of this century. She traces the struggle of Irish middle-class Catholics in particular to establish themselves in the wider American society, while being urged by a conservative church leadership to cultivate and maintain a separate Catholic identity. Her study ranges over issues of Americanisation, class, gender, material success, education, and even literary activity and architecture. According to Kane, the church pursued a policy of "separatist integration"; the Catholic church in Boston sought a position as an autonomous mediator between state and people. Although Kane may underestimate the extent to which ordinary working men and women managed to live their lives successfully both as members of their local parish and as citizens of Boston, this is an impressive and illuminating study.

BERNARD ASPINWALL

See also Religion: General

Catt, Carrie Chapman   1859–1947
Campaigner for women's suffrage

Catt, Carrie Chapman and Nettie Rogers Shuler, *Woman Suffrage and Politics: The Inner Story of the Suffrage Movement*, New York: Scribner, 1923; reprinted with introduction by T.A. Larson, Seattle: University of Washington Press, 1969

Degen, Marie Louise, *The History of the Woman's Peace Party*, Baltimore: Johns Hopkins Press, 1939; reprinted with introduction by Blanche Wiesen Cook, New York: Garland, 1972

Fowler, Robert Booth, *Carrie Catt: Feminist Politician*, Boston: Northeastern University Press, 1986

Kraditor, Aileen S., *The Ideas of the Woman Suffrage Movement, 1890–1920*, New York: Columbia University Press, 1965; 2nd edition, New York: Norton, 1981

Peck, Mary Gray, *Carrie Chapman Catt: A Biography*, New York: Wilson, 1944

Schneider, Dorothy and Carl J. Schneider, *American Women in the Progressive Era, 1900–1920*, New York: Facts on File, 1993

Van Voris, Jacqueline, *Carrie Chapman Catt: A Public Life*, New York: Feminist Press, 1987

For almost fifty years, Carrie Chapman Catt was the great women's organiser. In 1900, she inherited an un-coordinated, respectable body, the National American Woman Suffrage Association (NAWSA). During her two periods as president, from 1900 to 1904 (effectively only until 1902 because of her own and her second husband's ill-health), and between 1915 and 1920, she transformed NAWSA into a well-disciplined organisation, solely concerned with the achievement of votes for women. Between 1905 and 1915, as the leading figure in the International Woman Suffrage Association (IWSA), she gained a broader perspective on the same issue. She was a highly effective publicist who reinforced support for the movement through her oratory, her pamphlets and leaflets, and latterly through her monthly magazine, *The Woman Citizen*. She made the most of photo opportunities, and of such highly publicised events as a woman suffrage car journey carrying half a million signatures from California to Washington.

Her shrewd organisational, political and lobbying skills have not always received the attention and the credit which they deserve from more recent historians of the women's movement. Her single-minded concentration on pursuit of the vote, at the expense of broader issues, may have made good tactical sense at the time, but may have limited her appeal to later feminist historians with their own different agenda, or to other social historians preoccupied with the role of social scientists and social workers in the Progressive era.

Catt's earlier biographers are disappointing, but the best of them is PECK, which contains much detailed information of value to later scholars. These accounts written in her lifetime are generally uncritical; they dwell at length on Catt's ceaseless activity and her exhausting travels, and include substantial quotations from her speeches. Her essential conservatism on many matters is clearly revealed in CATT and SHULER. In this personal account, written in the heyday of "normalcy" in the early 1920s, the Protestant, nativist and even racist undercurrents of the woman suffrage movement emerge clearly. Un-American and corrupt political machines, and liquor and big business interests loom large – but, with the help of Catt, traditional American virtue eventually prevailed. T.A. Larson's introduction to the 1969 reprint provides valuable context.

KRADITOR convincingly shows Catt's contempt for ideological purity. Elizabeth Cady Stanton's *Woman's Bible*, Margaret Sanger's contraception, Florence Kelley's socialism and Alice Paul's militancy were, for her, distractions from the main issue: the vote. To that end, Catt was able to accommodate even those with nativist or southern racist inclinations in her membership. Anything which hastened enfranchisement was good; anything divisive was bad. Once the goal was achieved, learning how to use the vote effectively could be the key to progress in other areas – hence the importance of the League of Women Voters, of which she was a founder.

The few modern studies specifically devoted to Catt reinforce the image of her business-like feminism. Despite three opening chapters tracing her life, FOWLER is not a biography but essentially a scholarly study of Catt as a political leader and a political visionary. Claiming that Catt was one of the ablest politicians in American history, Fowler describes how she built a "potent suffragist machine," but he also stresses her vision of a society in which women and men were united in a community of free, equal and dignified persons. He justifies her strategy of concentration on a single-issue campaign for the vote, on the ground that the vote was crucial to wider objectives. Her split with Alice Paul arose from fears that Paul's more militant approach would upset her own strategy. Fowler depicts Catt as a strong, activist leader, determined to maintain her centralised control of NAWSA, which she took away from the realm of meetings of respectable middle-class women in church halls into the wider world of political reality. He places her firmly in the context of that wing of the Progressive movement which stressed the need for organised reform. There was a strong streak of conservatism, and a concern for social control, in such an approach to reform.

VAN VORIS captures many facets of Catt's character and her career, including her early determination in face of her father's resistance, her competitive nature, and her drive to succeed after the tragic deaths of two husbands. Catt's campaigning travels across many parts of the nation, including the South, demonstrated her iron constitution, her emotional toughness and her intellectual conviction. Her own inherited wealth increased her self-confidence, and gave NAWSA much-needed financial muscle. Van Voris also breaks out of the confines of the American suffrage movement, and integrates into her study discussion of Catt's endeavours as president of the IWSA, and also her role as a peace advocate.

DEGEN had earlier drawn attention to Catt's neglected pacifist concerns as president of IWSA – and the introduction to the 1972 reprint by Blanche Wiesen Cook is helpful. Lobbying against war, she played a leading role in founding the Women's Peace Party. However, disillusioned with pacifism, she resigned from the party in 1917 – and, as it happened, American participation in the war advanced the cause of votes for women. In their study of women in various progressive reform movements, SCHNEIDER and SCHNEIDER also place Catt in the wider international perspective, and discuss her involvement in the peace movement. But, like many others, they stress above all her contribution as an organiser of the movements and groups with which she was associated.

Some historians seem too eager to dismiss her as a mere organisation woman, but, in many ways, Carrie Chapman Catt was an archetypal Progressive – principled, non-partisan, and conservative in many of her basic instincts. Her skills and her single-mindedness responded to the concerns of a great many American women. A fully-rounded study of her life and work is needed.

BERNARD ASPINWALL

See also Women's History: Suffrage

Cattle Kingdom

Atherton, Lewis E., *The Cattle Kings*, Bloomington: Indiana University Press, 1961

Cronon, William, *Nature's Metropolis: Chicago and the Great West*, New York: Norton, 1991

Dale, Edward Everett, *The Range Cattle Industry: Ranching on the Great Plains from 1865 to 1925*, Norman: University of Oklahoma Press, 1930

Dary, David, *Cowboy Culture: A Saga of Five Centuries*, New York: Knopf, 1981

Dykstra, Robert R., *The Cattle Towns*, New York: Knopf, 1968

Gressley, Gene M., *Bankers and Cattlemen*, New York: Knopf, 1966

Osgood, Ernest Staples, *The Day of the Cattleman*, Minneapolis: University of Minnesota Press, 1929

Pelzer, Louis, *The Cattlemen's Frontier: A Record of the Trans-Mississippi Cattle Industry from Oxentrains to Pooling Companies, 1850–1890*, Glendale, CA: A.H. Clark, 1936

Slatta, Richard, *Cowboys of the Americas*, New Haven: Yale University Press, 1990

Walker, Don D., *Clio's Cowboys: Studies in the Historiography of the Cattle Trade*, Lincoln: University of Nebraska Press, 1981

Ramon F. Adams's bibliography, *The Rampaging Herd*, lists 2651 books and pamphlets relating to the United States cattle industry – and that was in 1959. Many of these concern the post-1865, open range cattle kingdom, a phenomenon lasting little more than a generation. This fleeting epoch was memorialized almost overnight. Epic narratives of cattle trade and cowboy life had already begun to appear in the 1870s, and were followed by a flood of reminiscences. The first studies that qualify as serious history, however, emerged between 1929 and 1936.

Osgood, Dale and Pelzer explicitly disavowed the hallowed romantic approach and promised scientific detachment. This "new" range history dealt in statistics of production and associative ventures rather than tales of rugged individuals, stampedes and whoop-ups. DALE is the most overtly economic, packed with tables of figures for market receipts, shipments, the price of land and feed, and volume of beef exports. Yet a distinct quality of affection and respect for a tough breed of entrepreneur shines through. PELZER is also ostensibly concerned with profits, wages, dividends and herd size. Yet he writes poignantly about a history "picturesque and tragic in its ending." And perhaps the strongest message to emerge from OSGOOD is that the cattle industry breathed life into the vast, unproductive wasteland of the plains, Indians and buffalo yielding in the face of historical destiny. All three accounts are tinged with nostalgia for the old days before fences.

Notable books from the 1960s sought to distance the cattle kingdom further from historical tradition by unearthing aspects "buried in the mush of sentimentality" (Gressley). The cattle industry serves here as a point of entry into larger issues and these reappraisals had ramifications for the wider history of the American West frontier. ATHERTON contended that cattlemen are both more important and exciting to study than cowboys (both of whom were virtually absent from the earlier wave of economic histories). He looked at areas such as the group's motivations, values, culture, business practices, and relations with labour (i.e., cowboys) – his thrust being that despite diverse social and national origins, cattlemen shared a common outlook and identity. Integral to his elevation of the cattleman is the debunking of the cowboy and his mystique. As such, Atherton relocates rather than denies the cattle kingdom's heroism. This may be primarily a business history but the closing sentiment is that the cattle industry represents the values that America was defending in the ideologically polarized world in which Atherton wrote.

GRESSLEY plugged a gaping hole by exploring the seminal role of the financiers, a group that left virtually no memoirs (let alone glamorous ones). He aimed to inject economics and the outside world into western American history, and his book opens on Wall Street instead of under big western skies. He draws on copious amounts of hitherto unexamined manuscript collections, to produce an economic history with a human face. Gressley provides an absorbing discussion of topics such as the appeal of the cattle trade, the intermediary role of the western attorney and the financier's response to the waning of the industry. His book set a fine example in correcting the often overly parochial approach to cattle kingdom history.

DYKSTRA raised the study of cowtowns to the level of scholarly respectability through his study of five Kansas settlements between 1867 and 1885. He is interested in the role of the cattle trade in urban growth and his book belongs to the history of rural-urban conflict, cities and social development as much as to the cattle kingdom. The drives in this book involve not cattle but crusades to quash the urban vices associated with the cattle trade. This is also the first serious dissection of fabled cowtown violence. Having scrutinized statistics in local newspapers, Dykstra reports a low incidence of homicide and the general effectiveness of law enforcement.

CRONON engages with the cattle trade in a study of Chicago's commercial and ecological conquest of the western hinterland. His vantage point is metropolitan – the Chicago stockyards and packing houses; the subtitle of his chapter on livestock is "meat." Cronon's focus on environmental transformation – the conversion of "nature" into "commodity" – is novel, yet we still await a history from the standpoint of the cow or the range it grazed.

Like many cattle kingdom historians, WALKER is closely roped to his subject in terms of personal history, but he calls for less emotional treatment. His brisk tour of the historical and novelistic literature is sprinkled with beguiling musings on the nature of history and on such intriguing questions as the failure to recognize cowboys as a rural proletariat. As for the cowboys themselves – and they were overwhelmingly male – the task of separating the real from the fictional and mythological has proved absorbing over recent decades. Historians are now more inclined to see the cowboy as wage worker rather than unfettered individualist. Walker emphasizes accounts of cowboy life that describe them as often overworked, underpaid (and undersexed).

SLATTA, who approached the Great Plains specimen of cowboy within a comparative, hemispheric framework, performed a great service in restoring the Hispanic dimension emphatically to centre stage in cattle kingdom cowboy history. Making effective use of first-hand accounts, this gorgeously illustrated social history reconstructs their lives and work in realistic fashion. DARY (a professor of journalism) places the cattle kingdom's cowboy in the widest historical and cross cultural perspective. This multiple prize winner, which combines a good journalist's prose with sound attention to both detail and broader issues, is intended for a general readership and also distinguished by fidelity to first-hand accounts, from which many extracts appear. One of Dary's stated aims is to "erase misconceptions," but what he has done toward this end is not at all clear.

PETER A. COATES

See also Great Plains

Central Intelligence Agency

Berkowitz, Bruce D. and Allan E. Goodman, *Strategic Intelligence for American National Security*, Princeton: Princeton University Press, 1989

Currey, Cecil B., *Edward Lansdale: The Unquiet American*, Boston: Houghton Mifflin, 1988

Grose, Peter, *Gentleman Spy: The Life of Allen Dulles*, Boston: Houghton Mifflin, and London: Deutsch, 1994

Jeffreys-Jones, Rhodri, *The CIA and American Democracy*, New Haven: Yale University Press, 1989

Johnson, Loch K., *America's Secret Power: The CIA in a Democratic Society*, New York: Oxford University Press, 1989

Kent, Sherman, *Strategic Intelligence for American World Policy*, Princeton: Princeton University Press, 1949

Marchetti, Victor and John D. Marks, *The CIA and the Cult of Intelligence*, New York: Knopf, and London: Cape, 1974

Pisani, Sallie, *The CIA and the Marshall Plan*, Lawrence : University Press of Kansas, 1991

Prados, John, *President's Secret Wars: CIA and Pentagon Covert Operations since World War II*, New York: Morrow, 1986

Smist, Frank J., Jr., *Congress Oversees the United States Intelligence Community, 1947–1989*, Knoxville: University of Tennessee Press, 1990

Woodward, Bob, *Veil: The Secret Wars of the CIA, 1981–1987*, New York: Simon and Schuster, 1987; London: Headline, 1988

Much of the history of the Central Intelligence Agency has been written by an extraordinary mixture of enthusiasts, defectors, apologists, polemicists and paranoids. However, there are a number of books which, though written from a variety of perspectives, do manage to avoid the extremes of either demonology or heroic myth. Historians and political scientists have much information about the CIA on which to draw. (Considerably more is known in the public domain about the CIA than, for example, about that probably equally influential Cold War intelligence body, the National Security Agency.) The problem is, however, not only that evidence is often unreliable, but that so much of it relates to particular aspects of the CIA's work. Somewhat paradoxically, we know more about covert operations than about intelligence analysis. Particular episodes in CIA history (such as the 1954 Guatemalan intervention) are well documented. Other areas, notably the CIA's role in direct US-Soviet relations, are, despite the ending of the Cold War, only just emerging from the bureaucratic shadows. The historian is at the mercy of the declassification process. Much information also relates to *causes célèbres* – the 1962 Cuban missile crisis, Watergate, Iran-contra – rather than to the Agency's day-by-day activity. Much also has come forth by means of leaks, whether from the CIA leadership or from internal dissidents, and inevitably tell only a partial story.

The two most readable and reliable general studies are those by Jeffreys-Jones and by Johnson. Both organise their material in relation to the central question of accountability: how can a clandestine governmental organisation operate in a democratic, open society? Both illustrate the degree to which the CIA, contrary to its founding charter, became involved in domestic as well as foreign surveillance. JEFFREYS-JONES is balanced and thoughtful, accepting the need for some kind of Cold War foreign intelligence agency. He is strongest on the pre-1965 period, on episodes such as the 1948 Italian election intervention, the U-2 flights and the 1961 Bay of Pigs invasion. JOHNSON, a former staffer on Congressional intelligence committees, focuses on the need for oversight of the CIA. He

concludes that abuses of CIA power have tended to thrive in circumstances where neither Congress nor public opinion have been inclined to set limits. Rather than a "rogue elephant" beyond Presidential control, the CIA has often been used by Presidents, against a background of Congressional and public insouciance, as part of the strategy of "plausible deniability". Johnson's "seven sins of strategic intelligence" (from "failure to provide policymakers with objective, uninhibited intelligence" to "indiscriminate use of covert action" and "inadequate accountability in the intelligence chain of command") constitute a valuable contribution to the tradition of intelligence literature inaugurated by Sherman Kent. As the head of the CIA Board of National Estimates, KENT mapped out a role for the Agency, and identified the need to utilize and integrate social science and the study of technology, in order to create the "big picture" of Soviet strength. Kent underlined the need to erect barriers between intelligence analysts and consumers. BERKOWITZ and GOODMAN is a conscious updating of Kent, applying his arguments to Reagan's "second" Cold War, while still recognizing the claims of post-Vietnam arguments for legislative accountability. The winding down of the Cold War in the later Reagan years made their work seem rather prematurely dated.

Several disaffected intelligence officers have committed their criticisms of the CIA to print. MARCHETTI and MARKS is a lively example of the genre. In a text replete with gaps relating to passages deleted following federal court orders, they attack CIA interventions (such as the undermining of President Allende in Chile in the early 1970s) and "paramilitary" activities. They also criticise the CIA's record in estimating Soviet and Chinese military capabilities and intentions. The book evokes the passions of the Vietnam War and Watergate years; yet Marchetti and Marks's close knowledge of CIA practice, including arcane areas like signal intelligence, makes this more than a period piece.

The literature on covert operations is huge. PRADOS provides one of the best surveys, especially good on CIA operations in Cambodia and Laos during the Vietnam War. WOODWARD offers a detailed narrative of illegal CIA involvement in the Central American conflicts of the early Reagan period. His sources are not cited, and the style occasionally teeters into journalistic sensationalism. Yet his indictment of the conduct of the CIA under William Casey (Director, 1981–87) is persuasive. Spurred by Casey's open contempt for legislative oversight, SMIST argues that it is both possible and desirable for Congress to play a substantive role in shaping intelligence policy. His book is a detailed and carefully documented study of legislative control of the CIA, primarily in the post-Vietnam War period. The work of the Senate Committee chaired by Frank Church (1975–76), the House Committee chaired by Otis Pike (1975–76), the Senate intelligence committees chaired by Barry Goldwater (1981–84) and the House committees led by Edward Boland (1977–84) is carefully appraised. Smist's book provides a good starting point from which to consider issues of CIA accountability and purpose after the Cold War.

The early Cold War period has produced many excellent monographs. We now know a great deal about CIA involvement in organisations such as the Congress for Cultural Freedom. PISANI traces the clandestine work of the Office of

Policy Coordination, which complemented the Marshall Plan in Europe by channelling funds to various political and labour organisations. CURREY's study of Edward Lansdale is rather gossipy, and far too uncritical, but is also fascinating, especially on the role of the CIA in 1950s Vietnam. GROSE's biography of Allen Dulles (CIA Director, 1953–61) also strains excessively to be sympathetic to its subject. Nevertheless, Grose examines the way in which Dulles misled Eisenhower over the U-2 flights, and countenanced various coups, assassinations and drug experiments.

JOHN DUMBRELL

See also Cold War; Foreign Policy since 1945 entries

Chase, Salmon P.   1808–1873
Secretary of the Treasury and Chief Justice of the Supreme Court

Blue, Frederick J., *Salmon P. Chase: A Life in Politics*, Kent, OH: Kent State University Press, 1987

Donald, David (editor), *Inside Lincoln's Cabinet: The Civil War Diaries of Salmon P. Chase*, New York: Longmans Green, 1954

Finkelman, Paul, *An Imperfect Union: Slavery, Federalism, and Comity*, Chapel Hill: University of North Carolina Press, 1981

Foner, Eric, *Free Soil, Free Labor, Free Men: The Ideology of the Republican Party Before the Civil War*, New York: Oxford University Press, 1970

Gerteis, Louis S., *Morality and Utility in American Antislavery Reform*, Chapel Hill: University of North Carolina Press, 1987

Hart, Albert Bushnell, *Salmon Portland Chase*, Boston: Houghton Mifflin, 1899

Kutler, Stanley I., *Judicial Power and Reconstruction Politics*, Chicago: University of Chicago Press, 1968

Niven, John, *Salmon P. Chase: A Biography*, New York: Oxford University Press, 1995

Schuckers, Jacob W., *The Life and Public Service of Salmon Portland Chase*, New York: Appleton, 1874; reprinted, Miami: Mnemosyne, 1969

Sewell, Richard H., *Ballots for Freedom: Antislavery Politics in the United States, 1837–1860*, New York: Oxford University Press, 1976

Warden, Robert B., *An Account of the Private Life and Public Services of Salmon Portland Chase*, Cincinnati: Wilstach Baldwin, 1874

Competition between Salmon P. Chase's private secretary, SCHUCKERS, and his prospective biographer, WARDEN, resulted in the division of Chase's private papers into two large collections and in the publication of two largely laudatory biographies the year after his death in 1873. Both biographers incorporated lengthy extracts from Chase's speeches and correspondence that continue to be useful for researchers.

HART's 1899 biography offered the first critical view of Chase. Broadly complimentary towards Chase's antislavery reform career, he offered a carefully balanced analysis of

Chase's presidential ambitions, his Democratic party ties, and his conflicts with President Abraham Lincoln that led to his 1864 resignation from the cabinet. On one point, however, Hart was sharply critical. As Lincoln's Treasury Secretary, Chase had supported the issue of federal notes, or "greenbacks," to finance the Union war effort. Later, as Chief Justice of the United States, Chase reversed himself and briefly succeeded, in the Supreme Court decision of *Hepburn* vs. *Griswold* (1870), in partially barring greenbacks as legal tender. The appointment of new members to the Court soon helped to secure the reversal of the Hepburn decision. Hart judged Chase's behavior in the legal tender controversy "unfortunate" for the country's financial health, for Chase's reputation for principled consistency, and for the dignity of the Court which became highly politicized over the issue.

A long gap in serious studies of Chase during the present century was partly filled by the excellent introduction to DONALD's edition of Chase's Civil War diaries, which provided a thorough but concise summary and assessment of Chase's career as antislavery politician, Treasury Secretary, and Supreme Court chief justice. By the mid-20th century, historical scholarship had consciously moved beyond earlier denunciations of abolitionist "fanaticism" and the "radicalism" of Reconstruction. As historians focused fresh attention on the antislavery upheaval in antebellum politics and on a related transformation in constitutional thought, Chase emerged as a figure of central importance.

KUTLER demonstrated Chase's activist role as Chief Justice and put to rest the older charge that Radical Republicans had ridden roughshod over the Supreme Court and its ability to protect constitutional liberties. FONER's pioneering study of the ideological origins of the Republican party found Chase to be a central figure in the free-soil tendencies of the northern Democratic party and in the Republican party's identification of a "slave power" threat to free labor interests. SEWELL's systematic history of antislavery politics established Chase's central role in the transition from the abolitionist Liberty party to the more broadly based Free Soil coalition, a role that placed Chase among the leaders of the antebellum Republican party.

In the realm of constitutional thought, FINKELMAN gave close scholarly scrutiny to Chase's argument against the federal fugitive slave law, an argument that insisted upon the municipal limits of state laws enforcing slavery. It was the prominence of this argument that prompted Chase's friends to describe him, while a young lawyer in Cincinnati, as the "attorney general of the fugitive slaves." GERTEIS, whose earlier work established Chase's importance in the development of federal policy toward southern blacks during the Civil War, identified linkages between Chase's antislavery thought and action and the triumph in the United States of legal formalism and utilitarian political economy.

Modern biographies followed these acknowledgments of Chase's historical significance. BLUE came to Chase through his previous study of the Free Soil party and treats Chase as a man consumed by politics. Elements of an older Whig distrust of Chase's Democratic ties (particularly in his coalition with Democrats to win election to the United States Senate in 1849) persist in Blue's biography. Chase's continuing ambition to become president, even after his appointment as Chief Justice, strikes Blue as unseemly. NIVEN provides the most comprehensive treatment of Chase's life, with a diligent and close reading of the voluminous and far-flung Chase Papers. In this respect, Niven's work is definitive. To the extent that Chase revealed his personal life in his correspondence and diaries, it is recorded in Niven's biography. However, Chase's private self remains elusive in the midst of these details. As a public figure, Niven describes Chase as "pre-eminently a representative nineteenth-century man." Absent, however, is an evaluation of Chase's sophistication as an antislavery ideologue, and of the extent to which antislavery ideology shaped Chase's sense of self. Niven carefully chronicles Chase's efforts to protect fugitive slaves and to extend equal rights to freedmen, but his overall picture of Chase presents him as an isolated, frustrated, "tragic figure," brought low by his "insidious ambition."

In some respects, Blue offers more clues than Niven to Chase's personality and character. He describes Chase's grief over the death of three wives, and four of his six children, and his anguish over the troubled marriage of his vivacious elder daughter Kate. But, whatever frustrations Chase encountered as an ambitious politician, whatever anguish he suffered as a grieving husband and father, the ideological struggle for emancipation and equal rights was clearly central to his sense of self.

LOUIS S. GERTEIS

See also Civil War: Approach to War entries; Civil War: the North 1; Supreme Court

Chicago

Biles, Roger, *Richard J. Daley: Politics, Race, and the Governing of Chicago*, DeKalb: Northern Illinois University Press, 1995

Cronon, William, *Nature's Metropolis: Chicago and the Great West*, New York: Norton, 1991

Einhorn, Robin L., *Property Rules: Political Economy in Chicago, 1833–1872*, Chicago: University of Chicago Press, 1991

Hirsch, Arnold R., *Making the Second Ghetto: Race and Housing in Chicago, 1940–1960*, Cambridge and New York: Cambridge University Press, 1983

Holli, Melvin G. and Peter d'A. Jones (editors), *Ethnic Chicago: A Multicultural Portrait*, Grand Rapids, MI: Eerdmans, 1977; 4th edition, 1995

Mayer, Harold M. and Richard C. Wade, *Chicago: Growth of a Metropolis*, Chicago: University of Chicago Press, 1969

Pierce, Bessie Louise, *A History of Chicago*, 3 vols., New York: Knopf, 1937–57

Spear, Allan H., *Black Chicago: The Making of a Negro Ghetto, 1890–1920*, Chicago: University of Chicago Press, 1967

Chicago has been blessed with a rich historiography, but because of the city's size and complexity scholars have almost always opted to write about it in carefully delimited monographic studies rather than comprehensive surveys. In one of the notable exceptions to this pattern, the Social Science Research Committee at the University of Chicago in 1929 invited PIERCE to prepare a comprehensive urban biography of the city. With research assistants and financial support from the university and private foundations, she produced three volumes that detailed Chicago's transformation from Indian trading post to modern metropolis at the time of the 1893 World's Columbian Exposition. Copiously researched and encyclopedic in their detail, if not consistently analytical, these volumes carefully explored the political, economic, and social changes in the city's development and remain the best source on Chicago's early years.

MAYER (a geographer) and WADE (a historian) also paint on a broad canvas, tracing Chicago's growth and development forward from its time of origin, but are concerned primarily with the physical expansion of the city. Although the book occasionally discusses population diversification, economics, and politics, the emphasis remains on how the city spread across the landscape and why it is configured in a certain way. The heart of the book is an extraordinary array of illustrations, including over one thousand photographs, prints, panoramas, sketches, and engravings, as well as fifty maps. Although the text does not always adequately develop the human dimension of the story, pictures of working-class bungalows and palatial estates, the central business district and neighborhood shopping centers, and elevated trains and multi-lane expressways, depict in a series of stunning visual images how Chicago became a modern metropolis.

CRONON brings his insights as an environmental historian to an examination of how Chicago developed economically in the 19th century. As the book's subtitle suggests, the author is principally concerned with the relationship of the city with its surrounding hinterlands. Relying heavily on the insights of historical geographers, he details how Chicago's entrepreneurs forged a series of links with raw material producers on the American frontier and thereby dominated a vast region of the mid-continent. Although his lengthy and richly detailed chapters on meat packing and grain commodity markets are largely derivative, a chapter on the lumber industry is original and useful.

Also concerned with Chicago's rapid growth from backwater settlement to commercial metropolis in the 19th century, EINHORN focuses on the interplay between political and economic institutions. As typical Jacksonian-age urban boosterism induced rapid population growth, the author posits, Chicagoans demanded more public works and changed the nature of city government to facilitate their provision. The result, a "segmented system" of service delivery, taxed the real-estate interests that would benefit from municipal improvements. Because only these property owners could exercise the political franchise, the city's municipal government became decentralized and responded primarily to propertied interests. Sectionalism in the 1850s and 1860s resuscitated party politics, segmentation vanished, and, by the Gilded Age, centralized government and machine politics predominated. The author's provocative interpretation of how Chicago's infrastructure materialized challenges traditional views of urban politics in the 19th century.

HOLLI and JONES edit a collection of original essays, recently revised and updated, that consider the ethnic and racial makeup of one of America's most heterogeneous cities. The most recent edition is divided into two parts, the first on "Ethnic Groups" and the second on "Ethnic Institutions." The richly detailed portraits of the social structures and cultural institutions of the Irish, Jewish, Greek, Ukrainian, Italian, Polish, German, Latino, French-Indian, African American, Japanese, Chinese, Asian-Indian and Korean communities constitute the best source on Chicago's constantly changing population mosaic.

Studies by Spear and Hirsch deal with Chicago's black population, a group whose numbers remained relatively small during the 19th century but increased dramatically during the 20th. In a model community study, SPEAR traces the metamorphosis of the city's minuscule black residential enclave into one of the nation's largest ghettos, and describes the concomitant change from a relatively fluid pattern of race relations to a rigid system of Jim Crow segregation. The book examines both the mechanics of the Great Migration of southern blacks to a northern city, and the development of the nascent community institutions that made Chicago's South Side a vital, sustaining neighborhood for African Americans.

HIRSCH analyzes the expansion of Chicago's Black Belt in the World War II years and after, carefully describing the means by which a second ghetto on the city's west side accommodated the dramatic African American population increase. The author shows how the perpetuation of segregation resulted from the creation of new means to circumvent legal restrictions against restrictive covenants. Although the book fully documents the incidence of violence in which white, working-class neighborhoods fought to preserve their homogeneity, Hirsch's greatest contribution is in demonstrating the central role of government in curtailing black residential mobility. Through the creative use of state- and federally-funded redevelopment and urban renewal programs, as well as the location of public housing projects in existing ghetto areas, the local government safeguarded the property interests of big business and white homeowners.

In a political biography of Mayor Richard J. Daley, BILES examines the last of America's big city bosses, and the powerful political machine over which he presided from 1955 to 1976. As an influential member of the Democratic party's national leadership, Daley exploited his ties with the Kennedy and Johnson presidential administrations to bring precious federal funds to Chicago, and presided over an unprecedented building boom that remade the face of the city's central business district. Adjudged a financial wizard for making Chicago "the city that works" when other American metropolises suffered severe financial crises, the mayor enjoyed less success in mitigating growing racial tensions and aligned himself with conservative whites against civil rights groups. His death and the subsequent dissolution of the Democratic machine unleashed forces of change long held in check, resulting in the election of Chicago's first black mayor, Harold Washington, in 1983.

ROGER BILES

See also African American History: 1870s–1954, the North; Immigration and Ethnicity; Urban History entries

Chicanos *see* Mexican Americans

Child, Lydia Maria 1802–1880
Abolitionist and writer

Baer, Helene Gilbert, *The Heart Is Like Heaven: The Life of Lydia Maria Child*, Philadelphia: University of Pennsylvania Press, 1964

Clifford, Deborah Pickman, *Crusader for Freedom: A Life of Lydia Maria Child*, Boston: Beacon Press, 1992

Karcher, Carolyn L., *The First Woman in the Republic: A Cultural Biography of Lydia Maria Child*, Durham, NC: Duke University Press, 1994

Meltzer, Milton, *Tongue of Flame: The Life of Lydia Maria Child*, New York: Crowell, 1965

Mills, Bruce, *Cultural Reformations: Lydia Maria Child and the Literature of Reform*, Athens: University of Georgia Press, 1994

Osborne, William S., *Lydia Maria Child*, Boston: Twayne, 1980

Venet, Wendy H., *Neither Ballots nor Bullets: Women Abolitionists and the Civil War*, Charlottesville: University Press of Virginia, 1991

Yellin, Jean Fagan, *Women and Sisters: The Antislavery Feminists in American Culture*, New Haven: Yale University Press, 1989

Lydia Maria Child, an author, editor, reformer, and antislavery activist, was one of the best known Americans in the 19th century. After a long period of historical neglect, she has again begun to be appreciated for her multiple talents and her far-reaching impact on society and culture. Strangely, there were no biographies of Child until BAER in 1964. This is a breezily written volume designed for popular audiences as much as for scholars (there are no footnotes though there is a short bibliography). The narrative contains some spicy gossip and is rich in romance, but the author does not take seriously enough Child's public endeavors, particularly her work as a reformer, for which the author seems to have little admiration. Although this is an important volume for those interested in Child's private life, particularly her marriage, the work gives perhaps too much attention to her relationship with her husband and gives excessive weight to that relationship as the source of Child's inspiration.

Less concerned with Child's private life is MELTZER, a non-scholarly book written for young adults. This thin volume gives an admiring if uncritical account of Child's often heroic struggles in various reform movements. Her antislavery activities emerge as the main focus of the book, and throughout she is portrayed as a genuinely passionate and persuasive reformer. Although the book is highly readable, it lacks any sustaining argument and is slim on interpretation. These are understandable shortcomings considering the target audience, and the monograph will probably have little use for serious students of Child's life.

CLIFFORD provides the best combination of good writing and fine scholarship in a book of reasonable length (just over 300 pages). The tightly woven narrative does not try to compartmentalize Child's life but instead makes connections between her family life, her literary efforts, and her activities in improving the lot of Native Americans, women, and African

Americans. The writer is careful not to pigeonhole Child either as a militant radical or as a consistent compromiser. Instead, the work notes the contradictions in Child's life (such as her early fervor in the antislavery movement followed by a ten-year hiatus) and allows the reader to make the judgments. As a result, the study offers no single explanation for Child's motivations and style, and it neither rationalizes nor condemns Child's occasional decision to succumb to popular tastes instead of abiding by pure principle. Although this is a scholarly work, it is nearly devoid of the feminist theory and literary criticism that would come in later studies of Child. The absence may disappoint some scholars but it helps to create a highly readable text.

KARCHER is a longer and more sophisticated work. This is a scholarly and sprawling book – more than 600 pages of text – which will long be regarded as the definitive study of Child even though its prose is at times impenetrable and its arguments occasionally tenuous. The author is much more interested than her predecessors in Child as a writer of fiction, and she uses the themes and subjects that appear in Child's early short stories to shed light on the subject's marriage and her attitudes towards reform. Also, the work attempts a psychological portrait of Child. The young Lydia's experience of her mother's untimely death, and the older Lydia's unhappiness in marriage, inclined her towards lobbying for the rights of the victims of inequality, through both her fiction and her political writing. But this is not just the story of a single life. Karcher takes pains to detail the cultural environment that gave rise to Child's works. In connecting her subject to the literary and political movements of the 19th century, the author draws on literary criticism and feminist theory of recent decades. Ultimately, however, the study does not portray Child as a purely 19th-century personality but rather as a woman whose setbacks and triumphs made her akin to women of the 20th century.

Literary critics in recent years have begun to turn their attention to Child. Although OSBORNE is purely a literary analysis, the work is easily approachable for non-specialists. It emphasizes a fundamental difference between Child's fictional and non-fictional writing, and is highly critical of the former. Child the author of fiction appears here as a copy-cat sentimentalist whose amateurish narrative structures did an injustice to the progressive ideas contained within. Child the editor and pamphleteer, however, was effective and innovative in her literary style. It was this difference in her authorial talents, it would seem, that accounts for her legacy as a reformer rather than a writer.

In contrast, MILLS sees no essential division between Child's fiction and non-fiction works. This is a sophisticated, highly abstract, and occasionally jargon-filled study which incorporates many recent literary theories. The author finds in Child's fiction and non-fiction a strain of conservatism, rooted in her upper-class Boston upbringing, which allowed her to reach both traditional and more progressive audiences. Child's tales as well as her reform pamphlets both emerge from cultural "boundaries" or "negotiations" between acceptance and critique of sentimental culture. By staying mostly within the confines of social norms, Child's work represented a distinct though not less effective agent of change than the writing of a more unconventional author like Harriet Beecher Stowe.

While Osborne and Mills locate Child almost exclusively in a literary world, YELLIN, which also employs literary analysis, is more effective in recognizing Child's role in the larger cultural and reform movements of the 19th century. This short but dense study examines the rise and fall of a distinctive women's culture, as expressed through literary and graphic imagery, in which white and black women were portrayed as equals with common interests but then, over time, distinguished by race. A chapter is devoted to Child, especially her creation of the figure of the "Tragic Mulatto" in the American imagination. Child is praised for her work for women's rights and abolitionism, but she is censured for helping to undermine the ideal of complete sisterhood between white and black women. By portraying female African Americans as dependent on white women's benevolence, Child helped to drive black women from white women's consciousness as full peers deserving all the benefits to come from the realization of social and gender equality. And by popularizing the image of the "Tragic Mulatto," particularly in her story "The Romance of Reunion," Child did further harm by perpetuating the idea of an essential difference between darker and lighter skinned African Americans.

VENET is more favorable towards Child and focuses almost exclusively on her political rather than her literary endeavors. The first and currently the only work to concentrate on female abolitionists during the Civil War, this study argues that the war opened the way for female reformers to become political leaders. As female abolitionists urged northern women to use their position in the domestic sphere to aid the war effort, they encouraged women to use their power in the political sphere as well. Although Child was not as renowned a war-time abolitionist as Anna E. Dickinson, she appears often in the work as the most important "literary recruit" for the antislavery movement. The author concedes that Child and her allies were somewhat naive in their methods, but she credits these women for helping to drive President Lincoln towards his support of emancipation and freed people's rights.

MICHAEL VORENBERG

Children and Youth

Calvert, Karin, *Children in the House: The Material Culture of Early Childhood, 1600–1900*, Boston: Northeastern University Press, 1992

Fass, Paula S., *The Damned and the Beautiful: American Youth in the 1920's*, New York and Oxford: Oxford University Press, 1977

Handlin, Oscar and Mary Flug Handlin, *Facing Life: Youth and the Family in American History*, Boston: Little Brown, 1971

Kett, Joseph F., *Rites of Passage: Adolescence in America, 1790 to the Present*, New York: Basic Books, 1977

Modell, John, *Into One's Own: From Youth to Adulthood in the United States, 1920–1975*, Berkeley: University of California Press, 1989

Slater, Peter Gregg, *Children in the New England Mind: In Death and in Life*, Hamden, CT: Archon, 1977

Wishy, Bernard, *The Child and the Republic: The Dawn of Modern American Child Nurture*, Philadelphia: University of Pennsylvania Press, 1968

Zelizer, Viviana A., *Pricing the Priceless Child: The Changing Social Value of Children*, New York: Basic Books, 1985

The publication in 1960 of Philippe Ariès's pathbreaking study of the history of European childhood, *Centuries of Childhood*, has had a profound influence upon the way in which historians have studied children and youth. Since the 1960s historians of American young people have produced a profusion of works, many of them very specialised, dealing with various aspects of child life and attitudes towards childhood.

WISHY examines ideas about child nurture in 19th-century American didactic writing and children's books. Clearly influenced by Ariès's work, but also a revision of it, Wishy explores the ways in which American nurture writers saw child-rearing in peculiarly American and republican terms. He argues that in the early 19th century nurture reformers began to reject ideas that the child was inherently sinful and to suggest instead that the child's character was flexible and open to possibilities for good or evil. By the second half of the 19th century writers were suggesting that the child was somehow better than the adult and that the best standards of life were those of the innocent child. Though Wishy's approach does have some limitations, and the differences between ante- and post-Civil War thinking are, perhaps, overdrawn, this is an insightful and often provocative work.

SLATER covers some of the same ground, but his coverage is much more concentrated. Structured as four essays, his study is concerned with ideas about children in the adult mind in New England between the 17th and mid-19th centuries. The first two essays are on attitudes towards the death of infants, the latter two on the rearing of young children. Within this structure Slater charts some of the changes in attitudes towards young children, influenced first by Calvinist theology and later by Enlightenment ideas and the more liberal attitudes resulting from the Great Awakening. Although, as a result of his concentration on religious and philosophical questions, Slater does not consider some of the other major changes in attitudes towards children, this is a significant contribution to the history of childhood. The structure of the book does lead to some repetition, but the essays are clear and well-argued.

In an examination of attitudes towards childhood in a rather different context, ZELIZER charts the profound transformation in the economic and sentimental value attached to children between the 1870s and the 1930s. She traces the emergence of the economically "worthless" but emotionally "priceless" child, through a study of children's insurance, laws relating to compensation for the accidental death of children, and attitudes towards adoption. Zelizer argues that this change in cultural attitudes towards children occurred first among the middle classes and later among the working classes. This is an imaginative study, giving a very different perspective upon adult attitudes towards children. Although the arguments are not always entirely convincing, this is generally well-argued and persuasive. CALVERT also explores changes in attitudes towards childhood, but through a close examination of material culture rather than ideas. Analysing portraiture, clothing and artefacts, she argues that the material culture of childhood reflected changes in ideas about children, and concludes that as attitudes towards childhood changed over time, three distinct chronological time periods may be identified. Each had its own vision of rearing children – those of the "inchoate adult", the "natural child" and the "innocent child". This is a fascinating study drawing upon evidence which has been little used by historians, but there are limitations. Almost inevitably, given the nature of the evidence, this is very much a study of upper-middle-class white childhood, which tends to ignore class and racial differences, as well as the wider context of social and economic change, which affected ideas about child-rearing.

A number of studies focus on adolescence and youth, rather than childhood. HANDLIN and HANDLIN focuses upon historical trends in the way in which youth has prepared for adult life, and explores the growth in education at all levels, apprenticeship and the lengthening in the growing-up process as young people remained at home longer. There is also a clear subtext through which the authors seek to explain the student protests of the 1960s. This is a highly opinionated and often eccentric study, which relies heavily on description with a minimum of analysis. Though it may be of interest to the general reader, this is not a work of scholarship. KETT covers much of the same ground as the Handlins but in a much more scholarly fashion. The influence of Ariès is clear. Kett shows the transformation of the life cycle and the evolution of adolescence as a concept, while exploring the way in which young people behaved and created a culture of their own. In a study which covers such a broad expanse of time, there is a tendency towards generalization. However, Kett uses a wide range of primary and secondary materials and his synthesis is a stimulating contribution to the study of adolescence in America. There are some limitations, the most notable of which is its concentration on male youth with only occasional reference to young women. While there is some discussion of class, there is little acknowledgment of racial differences.

Two further studies concentrate upon young people in the 20th century. In a study of college youth in the 1920s, FASS looks at the behaviour of young people themselves, as well as reaction to them by adults. She argues that the youth of the 1920s were both the products and the agents of social change. They were the first generation of young people who created a distinct youth culture, and whose lives were influenced more by their peer group than by family members or the wider society. This is, however, the study of a distinct minority – white, middle-class, college youth. Despite some bold generalizations, which are not always fully sustained by the evidence, this remains a fascinating specialized study. MODELL focuses on trends in the transitions of young people from high school to work, and from dating to marriage and parenthood. Though much of his evidence is based upon the statistical analysis of demographic trends, he also utilises more literary sources, including magazines aimed at the youth market. He explores the growth of a youth culture of dating, and suggests that this occurred both at college and high school level. This study covers a fairly long time-span which included periods of economic crisis and war, as well as major social change, all of which affected the lives of young people. Modell presents a sophisticated, if at times highly statistical, analysis of these changes.

ELIZABETH J. CLAPP

See also Family

China and the United States

Cohen, Warren I., *America's Response to China: A History of Sino-American Relations*, New York: Wiley, 1971; 3rd edition, New York: Columbia University Press, 1990

Etzold, Thomas H. (editor), *Aspects of Sino-American Relations since 1784*, New York: New Viewpoints, 1978

Fairbank, John K., *The United States and China*, Cambridge, MA: Harvard University Press, 1949, 4th edition, 1979

Hunt, Michael H., *The Making of a Special Relationship: The United States and China to 1914*, New York: Columbia University Press, 1983

Iriye, Akira, *Across the Pacific: An Inner History of American-East Asian Relations*, New York: Harcourt Brace, 1967

Schaller, Michael, *The United States and China in the Twentieth Century*, New York and Oxford: Oxford University Press, 1979, 2nd edition, 1990

China and the United States have bulked large in each other's perception of the outside world. In the 19th century, Americans saw China as a promising source of profit through trade and as a fruitful field of spiritual activity through the missionary effort. The Chinese hoped that the Americans would be a useful counter against the depredations of the European powers, while peasants in southern China sensed economic opportunities through emigration to California and beyond. Neither set of hopes of the other was fully realized. In the 20th century American-Chinese relations have oscillated violently. The United States experienced difficulties with Chinese nationalism in the 1920s, but in the 1930s and up to 1949 there was friendship, support and finally alliance at least with Nationalist China. The communist victory, and then the Korean War, made hostility and confrontation the order of the day, until a more amicable relationship emerged in the 1970s. For the United States at least, the relationship with China has not been a simple affair of bilateral dealings between two states, for relations with China decisively shaped United States relations with other powers in East Asia and frequently had a significant impact upon American domestic politics.

FAIRBANK was the towering figure in Chinese historical studies in the United States from World War II until his death. His *The United States and China* ran through four editions from its first appearance in 1949, and it is a minor classic of American historical writing. Fairbank believed that many of the problems which the United States encountered in its relations with the Chinese were a result of woeful ignorance about China, and consequently his work concentrated heavily upon the Chinese dimension of Sino-American relations. Fairbank wrote his accounts of China and the United States without regard to the prevailing political and intellectual climate in America, and his work remains a reliable guide to the subject written by a fine and honourable scholar. It was the trauma of Vietnam which stimulated widespread and critical reappraisal of the history of the relationships between the United States and east and southeast Asia. One of the keys to United States involvement in the region was widely seen as America's relations with China. As a result, from the late 1960s there has been a steady flow of scholarly works reviewing and revising the history of that relationship. The fruits of this new, involved but remarkably objective scholarship can be seen in works such as COHEN which is arguably the best general history of Sino-American relations. Skilfully weaving together the political, economic, social and cultural dimensions of the relationship, he takes the reader from the journey of the *Empress of China* to Canton in 1784 through the roller-coaster of admiration and disdain, friendship and hostility, love and hate to the normalization of American-Chinese relations in the 1970s.

ETZOLD is a collection of essays, and does not provide a connected history of Sino-American relations. It focuses on some of the key periods and themes of the relationship, including the Open Door, the three-way relationship between the United States, China and Japan in the crucial time immediately after World War I, and the breakdown of Sino-American relations in the late 1940s. The collection also helps to make the point that the history of Sino-American relations involves not only the story of Americans in China but also of Chinese in the United States.

Two works provide an overlapping chronological account of American-Chinese relations. HUNT's outstanding account of that relationship before World War I goes a long way towards explaining the emergence and nature of the American idea that there was a special empathy between the United States and China. Hunt's ability to use Chinese sources means that he is able to penetrate both sides of the relationship, through the coverage which he gives to the Chinese side of it, both in China and within the Chinese emigrant communities in the western United States. SCHALLER provides a short account of Sino-American relations from the beginning of the 20th century to American recognition of the People's Republic of China in 1979. His narrative is resolutely informed by the revisionist scholarship on American-East Asian relations which emerged from the Vietnam era. Thus he is consistently critical of United States policy towards China, at times to the point of cynicism, on issues such as American support for Chiang Kai-shek and the Nationalist regime, and constant American hostility to the Chinese communists. Both Hunt and Schaller successfully highlight the impact of China policy upon American politics.

The American relationship with China did not exist in an international vacuum. In the first half of the 20th century China was central to the emerging conflict between the United States and Japan. After World War II, China had a key role in the onset of the Cold War and the sharp deterioration in American-Soviet relations. These fateful triangular relationships between the United States, China and other Pacific powers, notably Japan and the Soviet Union, have never been better described and analyzed than in the work of the Japanese American scholar IRIYE. His brilliant and thought-provoking account places American-Chinese relations firmly in their wider international context.

DENNIS B. SMITH

See also Foreign Policy since 1945: Special Aspects 2

Church and State

Bradley, Gerard V., *Church-State Relationships in America*, New York: Greenwood Press, 1987

Cord, Robert L., *Separation of Church and State: Historical Fact and Current Fiction*, New York: Lambeth Press, 1982

Curry, Thomas J., *The First Freedoms: Church and State in America to the Passage of the First Amendment*, New York: Oxford University Press, 1986

Handy, Robert T., *Undermined Establishment: Church-State Relations in America, 1880–1920*, Princeton: Princeton University Press, 1991

Howe, Mark A. De Wolfe, *The Garden and the Wilderness: Religion and Government in American Constitutional History*, Chicago: University of Chicago Press, 1965

Levy, Leonard W., *The Establishment Clause: Religion and the First Amendment*, New York: Macmillan, 1986; revised, Chapel Hill: University of North Carolina Press, 1994

Pfeffer, Leo, *Church, State, and Freedom*, Boston: Beacon Press, 1953, 2nd edition, 1967

Stokes, Anson Phelps, *Church and State in the United States*, 3 vols., New York: Harper, 1950; revised by Leo Pfeffer, 1 vol., 1964

The First Amendment to the United States Constitution begins with the expression, "Congress shall make no law respecting an establishment of religion, or prohibiting the free exercise thereof." Prohibiting at least the establishment of a national religion and protecting Americans' freedom to hold and express their religious beliefs, these phrases form the basis for the relationship between the government and religious groups in American society. Until the 20th century, this relationship was governed by what one legal historian has described as a "de facto Protestant establishment." Favoring no denomination in particular, federal and state governments nevertheless supported Protestant social and cultural mores, believing that religion was necessary for a civilized society. The separation of church and state existed at the institutional level only. Beginning in the 1940s, the Supreme Court, reflecting a more diverse and secular American society, began to dismantle the partnership between government and Protestant religion and to erect a "wall of separation" between church and state.

STOKES provides the most comprehensive early examination of the relationship between church and state in America. A pathbreaking exploration to which all subsequent studies of the subject refer, the three massive volumes appeared shortly after the old patterns of church-state relations had begun to be reshaped by the Supreme Court. Combining documentary and interpretive material, Stokes examines the interplay between church and state from the colonial era to the mid-20th century, giving careful attention to the disputes and landmark cases of the 1940s.

HOWE is an original and thoughtful essay on the interaction between the "garden" of the church and the "wilderness" of the state. The wall between them, he argues, was erected to advance the interests of religion. Howe rightly points out that, from the passage of the First Amendment until the United States Supreme Court applied it to the states through the Fourteenth Amendment, state governments developed their own doctrines regarding the church-state relationship. In the 19th century, they developed a non-preferential system of general support for religion. Howe insists that government can aid religion without infringing the liberties of the irreligious. Protecting the rights of the irreligious belongs not to the religion clauses, Howe declares, but to the speech and press provisions of the First Amendment and to the equal protection and due process clauses of the Fourteenth Amendment.

CURRY presents an excellent historical treatment of the interaction of church and state in the American colonies during the 17th and 18th centuries. What he describes is a complex variety of experiences from the established church in some colonies to bold experiments in religious pluralism in others. The context of the framing of the First Amendment therefore emerges as ambiguous – Americans opposed the establishment of a national religion, but many believed in the social utility, or necessity, of religion in public life.

HANDY is a much-needed analysis of church-state relations during a part of the understudied period between the passage of the First Amendment and the Supreme Court's decisions of the mid-20th century. This period is important for an understanding of both the historical application of church-state doctrine at the state and federal level and the transformation of America into a more religiously diverse and more secular society. Handy explores the ways in which new or newly powerful religious groups such as Catholics and Mormons began to challenge the Protestant establishment late in the 19th century. He also demonstrates how immigrant religions altered the American spiritual landscape. These and other changes undermined the Protestant establishment in the early decades of the 20th century by forcing the state into a more neutral position among America's religious groups in what Handy terms a "second disestablishment."

Recent controversy among historians, political scientists, and legal scholars over the meaning of the First Amendment has produced a considerable body of scholarship. In a broad overview of the American experiment in church-state relations, PFEFFER declares that the principle of religious liberty and the separation of church and state constitute one of America's most important contributions to civilization. The First Amendment, in Pfeffer's view, must be read as requiring a divorce of church and state "as absolute as could be achieved," forbidding even non-monetary government aid to religion generally and non-preferential support of various religious groups. Pfeffer, who has argued many of the establishment cases before the Supreme Court, insists that all practices to the contrary are neither constitutional nor wise public policy. CORD contends that Pfeffer's "absolute separatism" interpretation is antithetical to the historical position of the founders. In his view, the Supreme Court has interpreted the establishment clause much too broadly. Instead of an absolute separation, Cord declares that non-discriminatory government aid to religion is constitutional and fulfils the founders' intention of supporting religion generally without establishing one sect.

Drawing on his examination of colonial and state establishments, LEVY insists that at the time the Bill of Rights was framed, establishment was equated with any support of religion by the government. Therefore, the establishment clause must be interpreted broadly as prohibiting Congress from acting in the field of religion in any manner. Levy forcefully criticizes the narrow interpretation of conservatives that the First Amendment prohibits federal support for a specific establishment while allowing congressional aid and support to religion in general. BRADLEY effectively critiques the Supreme Court's misuse of history in supporting the idea that the First Amendment requires the erection of a wall of separation between church and state. Drawing on the experience of the American colonies and early states and on federal governance of the territories, Bradley maintains that the First Amendment prohibited federal rather than state action. Furthermore, both federal and state law in the 19th and early 20th century proceeded on the basis of a general government promotion of religion with no preference for particular sects.

Simultaneously historical and polemical, the last four works present competing interpretations of the American past and prescriptions for the American future. Readers should consult Pfeffer or Levy *and* Cord or Bradley for a better understanding of the relationship between church and state in America.

DANIEL W. STOWELL

See also Religion

Cinema *see* Film

Cities *see* Urban History

Citizenship

Collins, Donald E., *Native American Aliens: Disloyalty and the Renunciation of Citizenship by Japanese Americans During World War II*, Westport, CT: Greenwood Press, 1985

Fehrenbacher, Don E., *The Dred Scott Case: Its Significance in American Law and Politics*, New York: Oxford University Press, 1978; abridged as *Slavery, Law, and Politics: The Dred Scott Case in Historical Perspective*, 1981

Kaczorowski, Robert J., *The Nationalization of Civil Rights: Constitutional Theory and Practice in a Racist Society, 1866–1883*, New York: Garland, 1987

Karst, Kenneth L., *Belonging to America: Equal Citizenship and the Constitution*, New Haven: Yale University Press, 1989

Kettner, James H., *The Development of American Citizenship, 1680–1870*, Chapel Hill: University of North Carolina Press, 1978

Nelson, William E., *The Fourteenth Amendment: From Political Principle to Judicial Doctrine*, Cambridge, MA: Harvard University Press, 1988

Shklar, Judith N., *American Citizenship: The Quest for Inclusion*, Cambridge, MA: Harvard University Press, 1991

Sinopoli, Richard C., *The Foundations of American Citizenship: Liberalism, the Constitution, and Civic Virtue*, New York: Oxford University Press, 1992

Surprisingly, in view of the importance of the subject, solid, comprehensive, and readable accounts of the history of American citizenship are in short supply. SHKLAR is a succinct, lecture-style discourse on the evolution of the meaning of American citizenship. For Shklar, there was always a gap between professed American ideals of equal citizenship and the idea of standing, which depends upon exclusion. She argues that lower status was particularly tied to exclusion from two activities: voting and earning. While in the past wealth, race, and gender had been used to disfranchise certain citizens and make them less equal, Shklar believes that earning money has become central to one's standing as an American citizen at the present day. She contends that the quality of citizenship is intimately concerned with earning, which, in her view, determines the quality of citizenship and shapes one's actual social standing.

KARST focuses on the ways in which contemporary law expresses the nation's commitment to an ideal of equal citizenship, but he does offer a discussion of how the idea of equal citizenship evolved from slavery to the *Brown* v. *Board of Education* decision (1954). Sharing Shklar's argument that inequality in citizenship exists, Karst argues that equal citizenship means full inclusion in the polity. But he stresses the notion of inclusion as having a primarily psychological basis: to be an equal citizen is to feel included in the national community, and to be unequal is to feel excluded. He recognizes that the psychological state of inclusion requires some material preconditions, and as a result he treats problems of poverty as at least in part problems preventing realization of full equal citizenship. Although Karst respects cultural diversity in a nation, he stresses that equal citizenship entails a certain degree of assimilation to the dominant culture.

Written not primarily for historians, SINOPOLI is essentially a textualist study of the interrelations between the understanding of citizenship, liberalism, and republicanism during the period of constitution-making. He specifically addresses the role of citizenship as perceived by the Federalists and Antifederalists. Challenging the traditional belief in dichotomies between republicanism and liberalism, Sinopoli contends that Federalist-Antifederalist debates over the Constitution, which were conducted under the general influence of the liberal view of government of John Locke, reflected not so much conflicting views of the just state, but rather competing solutions to the practical problem of how to instil in citizens sentiments of allegiance and the willingness to discharge civic duties. In Sinopoli's view, the founders' debates were ultimately concerned with the political psychology of citizenship, on which they disagreed, with the Federalists possessing a political view close to that of David Hume and Adam Smith and the Antifederalists sharing more that of Francis Hutcheson.

KETTNER's prize-winning book is a superb study of the development of the law of citizenship in America before 1870. Covering such important events as the War of Independence, the War of 1812, and the Dred Scott case, he examines the key factors that affected the evolution of American understanding and practice of citizenship before 1870. According to

Kettner, although the original idea of American citizenship followed the concept of English law, Americans, especially after independence, viewed citizenship in a way quite different from English tradition. While the English regarded citizenship as a ruler-subject bond, Americans saw it as a fundamentally volitional and contractual mutual agreement between an individual and a community that consented to adopt him as a subject. Very much in line with Bernard Bailyn's plea for a cross-Atlantic approach to such studies, Kettner presents an excellent social-intellectual history of American citizenship.

The most thorough and perceptive study of the landmark Dred Scott case (1857), the Pulitzer-winning FEHREN-BACHER offers a detailed discussion of the issue of citizenship in relation to the federal-state structure, the rights of free blacks, and sectional politics over the expansion of slavery as reflected in the Supreme Court's decision on the case. Fehrenbacher analyzes the major arguments of Chief Justice Taney regarding the historical origins of American citizenship, and the reasons why black Americans (free or enslaved) could not be granted citizenship. He concludes that Taney's arguments were legally erroneous, and were a politically motivated attempt to graft his extreme anti-black citizenship views authoritatively on to American law.

KACZOROWSKI examines the making and enforcing of the Civil Rights Act of 1866 and the Fourteenth Amendment, which first defined United States citizenship and prescribed federal responsibility for the protection of the privileges and immunities of United States citizens. On the basis of a study of the congressional debates between 1865 and 1868, Kaczorowski argues that the motivation behind the congressional program to establish national citizenship and national protection of United States citizens' civil rights lay in the Republicans' desire to protect the freedom and safety of both blacks and white Unionists in the South, and ultimately to assert the primacy of national authority over states rights. The change in the northern political and legal climate, as reflected in the *Slaughterhouse Cases* (1873) opinion, marked the retreat of the North from the enforcement of national protection of civil rights and black freedom.

Focusing on the constitutional and intellectual sources of the Fourteenth Amendment, the making of the amendment, and its consequences, NELSON presents an argument different from Kaczorowski. Nelson believes that the Fourteenth Amendment was designed as a simultaneous commitment to federal protection of black rights and to preservation of the existing balance of federalism. In his view, despite the changes wrought by the Civil War and their party's political agenda (to protect black rights), the Republican lawmakers of the Fourteenth Amendment still seriously respected the historical practice of state legislative freedom. The principles set out in the amendment (equality, individual rights, and local self-rule) came into inevitable conflict with each other only at the end of the century. Nelson also argues that the amendment was drawn up as a rhetorical venture designed to persuade people to do good, rather than as a bureaucratic initiative intended to establish precise legal rules and enforcement mechanisms.

COLLINS provides an in-depth analysis of why 5,589 Japanese-American citizens of Japanese descent, confined in Tule Lake Segregation Center, renounced their United States citizenship during the winter of 1944 and 1945. He examines the sociological structure of the Japanese American community on the West Coast, the wartime segregation policy of the federal government, anti-Japanese public opinion before the war, the internal convulsions and disagreements among the segregated camp inmates, and persecution by the federal authorities (including loyalty tests). Collins concludes that unjust discrimination and imprisonment strained the loyalty of the frightened and frustrated Japanese-Americans in Tule, and pushed them to renunciation, which was made possible constitutionally by the 1944 amendment of the Nationality Act of 1940.

Xi Wang

Civil Rights Acts, 1950s–1960s

Belz, Herman, *Equality Transformed: A Quarter-Century of Affirmative Action*, New Brunswick, NJ: Transaction, 1991

Berger, Morroe, *Equality by Statute: Legal Controls over Group Discrimination*, New York: Columbia University Press, 1952; revised as *Equality by Statute: The Revolution in Civil Rights*, New York: Doubleday, 1967

Berman, William C., *The Politics of Civil Rights in the Truman Administration*, Columbus: Ohio State University Press, 1970

Brauer, Carl M., *John F. Kennedy and the Second Reconstruction*, New York: Columbia University Press, 1977

Burk, Robert Fredrick, *The Eisenhower Administration and Black Civil Rights*, Knoxville: University of Tennessee Press, 1984

Graham, Hugh Davis, *The Civil Rights Era: Origins and Development of National Policy, 1960–1972*, New York: Oxford University Press, 1990

Harrison, Cynthia, *On Account of Sex: The Politics of Women's Issues, 1945–1968*, Berkeley: University of California Press, 1988

Lawson, Steven F., *Black Ballots: Voting Rights in the South, 1944–1969*, New York: Columbia University Press, 1976

Lawson, Steven F., *In Pursuit of Power: Southern Blacks and Electoral Politics, 1965–1982*, New York: Columbia University Press, 1985

Thernstrom, Abigail M., *Whose Votes Count? Affirmative Action and Minority Voting Rights*, Cambridge, MA: Harvard University Press, 1987

Whalen, Charles and Barbara Whalen, *The Longest Debate: A Legislative History of the 1964 Civil Rights Act*, Cabin John, MD: Seven Locks Press, 1985

During the first half of the 20th century the elected branches of the United States government had almost no involvement in passing or enforcing civil rights laws. By 1900 most of the civil rights statutes passed by Congress during Reconstruction had been ruled unconstitutional by the United States Supreme Court. The institutionalized caste system of racial segregation in the southern and border states was protected from federal interference by conservative federal courts, established practices and procedures in Congress (the committee system, southern seniority, the Senate filibuster, the House Rules committee), and a national tradition of state and local control of social policy.

For these reasons, liberal reformers in the post-war era concentrated on new forms of civil rights legislation in the northern industrial states. BERGER describes the development of state and municipal anti-discrimination statutes, pioneered in New York under the leadership of Senator Robert Wagner, a New Deal Democrat who sponsored the National Labor Relations Act of 1935. New York's State Law Against Discrimination of 1945, modeled on the Wagner Act, created an independent regulatory commission to police discrimination on account of race, religion, and national origin. By 1960 the state antidiscrimination agencies, commonly called fair employment practice commissions (FEPC), had spread to most industrial states and covered a majority of the American population. Berger's study, first published in 1952 and updated in 1967, reflects the belief of American liberals during the post-war generation that a national FEPC was needed to end discrimination in the South.

The political barriers to national civil rights legislation, unchallenged by President Franklin Roosevelt or his predecessors, were tested during the late 1940s by Roosevelt's successor, Harry Truman. BERMAN's study of Truman's civil rights initiatives is the first history of modern civil rights policy based primarily on documents in the presidential libraries. He emphasizes the symbolic politics of policy under Truman, whose re-election depended on black voters in the northern cities, but whose legislative proposals, which included a national FEPC, could not win in Congress.

Following the Berman model of civil rights policy-making reconstructed from presidential archives, Burk and Brauer have provided politics-of-civil-rights studies for the Eisenhower and Kennedy presidencies, respectively. Resisting the tide of revisionist scholarship favorable to Eisenhower, BURK criticizes him for failure to support the Warren Court with strong executive or legislative leadership. Similarly, BRAUER criticizes Kennedy for excessive presidential caution as the civil rights crisis intensified during 1961–63. But he praises Kennedy's decisiveness, following the violence in Birmingham triggered by demonstrations led by Martin Luther King, in sending Congress a bill to ban racial segregation.

Kennedy's bill became the Civil Rights Act of 1964, the watershed event of post-war American domestic history. WHALEN and WHALEN, in their Congress-makes-a-law account of the Civil Rights Act's perilous journey through the House and Senate during 1963–64, give credit to the firm presidential leadership of John Kennedy and Lyndon Johnson. However, the Whalens concentrate on the political bargaining and procedural manipulations of Congress, where Charles Whalen represented Ohio's third district from 1967 to 1979. The 1964 law reflected a national consensus – excluding white southerners – that public policy should be blind to race, religion, and national origin.

Presidential monographs like those of Berman, Burk and Brauer, typically stemming from doctoral dissertations in history, based on research in presidential libraries, provided cumulative case studies of policy formulation and enactment.

They lacked, however, the continuity needed to understand the crucial process of implementation. In his two-volume study of voting-rights policy, Lawson provides continuity over nine presidencies by reconstructing the development of federal policy from the Supreme Court's 1944 ruling against the all-white party primary to the voting-rights revisions signed by President Ronald Reagan in 1982. LAWSON (1976) begins with congressional passivity in voting-rights policy, moves through the ineffective, court-centered reforms enacted by Congress in 1957, and concentrates on the passage in 1965 of the Voting Rights Act, which led with surprising speed to equal voting participation by southern blacks. LAWSON (1985) describes the radical shift in federal policy goals from equal voting rights to proportional electoral results, as reflected in the voting-rights amendments of 1982.

Like most scholars writing about American civil rights issues, Lawson generally approves of the policy development he describes. THERNSTROM, on the other hand, does not. A political scientist, she criticizes the shift in voting-rights policy from equal access to the ballot box, the explicit goal of the 1965 law, to proportional electoral results, the implicit goal of the 1982 amendments. Whereas Lawson looks only at southern blacks, Thernstrom includes language-based voting rights, added by Congress in 1975 primarily to extend federal protection to Latino citizens. Her book sparked controversy by criticizing as racial gerrymandering the efforts by Justice Department officials under presidents Carter and Reagan to win court orders requiring states and cities to draw "minority-majority" electoral districts.

The controversial shift in federal civil rights policy generally from non-discrimination to affirmative-action requirements based on minority preferences is the focus of GRAHAM's study of the Kennedy, Johnson, and Nixon presidencies. In explaining this shift, he locates civil rights reform at the cutting edge of the new social regulation of the 1960s, where social movements formed advocacy groups and demanded new protections from government. African Americans led the way, followed by feminists, environmentalists, Hispanics and other racial and ethnic minorities, consumer-rights advocates, the physically and mentally disabled, the elderly, and others. Graham emphasizes the role of federal courts and enforcement agencies, following the urban riots of the late 1960s, in accelerating the redistribution toward minorities of jobs, promotions, and school admissions. In the late 1960s, the court-ordered shift to school busing in the interests of racial balance was followed by requirements from newly created federal enforcement agencies (the Equal Employment Opportunity Commission, Office of Federal Contract Compliance, Office for Civil Rights) that the distribution of jobs and other benefits should reflect the minority share of the workforce.

In his study of affirmative action from 1961 through the Reagan administration, BELZ condemns the shift to minority preference policies as betraying the ban on discrimination enacted in 1965. Concentrating on enforcement agencies and federal court rulings, Belz approves of the Reagan administration's attempts to restrict affirmative-action requirements. In his view, however, most Reagan efforts were defeated by the civil rights coalition, well entrenched by the 1980s in "iron triangle" alliances between advocacy organizations, congressional committees, and agency bureaucracies.

Civil rights policy includes equal opportunity for women as well as for minorities. Comparing policies to combat sex as well as race discrimination, Graham concludes that although the feminist movement largely modeled itself after the successful black civil rights movement, the two social movements developed in opposite policy directions during the 1960s. Between 1960 and 1972, he argues, government policy on race discrimination responded to demands by minority rights groups by shifting from color-blind policies to minority preference policies. During the same period, however, government policy on sex discrimination responded to demands by feminist groups by shifting from special protective policies for women to the sex-blind requirements of the Equal Rights Amendment.

Grounding her study of national policy and women's issues in the Kennedy and Johnson libraries, HARRISON documents the effective, bi-partisan insurgency of a "second-wave" feminist movement led by well-educated, affluent, white women. Her book, covering the years 1945–68, describes the difficult shift by women leaders, especially Democratic women associated with organized labor, from the special-protection tradition of Eleanor Roosevelt and the AFL-CIO to the radical challenge of equal-rights liberalism – a position previously associated with Republican women.

Harrison's study includes the prohibition of sex discrimination in Title VII of the Civil Rights Act. Historians have contributed relatively little to the literature on women's issues during the 1970s, when the feminist movement won congressional passage of the Equal Rights Amendment, enactment of Title IX of the education amendments of 1972, and Supreme Court approval for a widening range of equal-protection claims on behalf of women's rights. Most of this literature reflects social science scholarship based on published documents and interviews, not historical research in the archives. It is one of the ironies of recent history in the United States that just as social movements led by minority and women insurgents were forcing breakthrough civil rights legislation during the 1960s, the new generation of historical researchers, shifting their interest toward the "bottom-up" drama of social history, largely turned away from the study of public policy itself.

HUGH DAVIS GRAHAM

See also African American History: since 1954; Feminism; Women's History: Women's Liberation Movement

Civil Rights Movement, 1950s–1960s

Bass, Jack, *Unlikely Heroes: The Dramatic Story of the Southern Judges of the Fifth Circuit Who Translated the Supreme Court's Brown Decision into a Revolution for Equality*, New York: Simon and Schuster, 1981

Branch, Taylor, *Parting the Waters: America in the King Years, 1954–63*, New York: Simon and Schuster, and London: Macmillan, 1988

Carson, Clayborne, *In Struggle: SNCC and the Black Awakening of the 1960s*, Cambridge, MA: Harvard University Press, 1981

Cecelski, David S., *Along Freedom Road: Hyde County, North Carolina, and the Fate of Black Schools in the South*, Chapel Hill: University of North Carolina Press, 1994

Chafe, William H., *Civilities and Civil Rights: Greensboro, North Carolina, and the Black Struggle for Freedom*, New York and Oxford: Oxford University Press, 1980

Colburn, David R., *Racial Change and Community Crisis: St. Augustine, Florida, 1877–1980*, New York: Columbia University Press, 1985

Dittmer, John, *Local People: The Struggle for Civil Rights in Mississippi*, Urbana: University of Illinois Press, 1994

Eagles, Charles W., *Outside Agitator: Jon Daniels and the Civil Rights Movement in Alabama*, Chapel Hill: University of North Carolina Press, 1993

Fairclough, Adam, *To Redeem the Soul of America: The Southern Christian Leadership Conference and Martin Luther King, Jr.*, Athens: University of Georgia Press, 1987

Fairclough, Adam, *Race and Democracy: The Civil Rights Struggle in Louisiana, 1915–1972*, Athens: University of Georgia Press, 1995

Garrow, David J., *Protest at Selma: Martin Luther King, Jr., and the Voting Rights Act of 1965*, New Haven: Yale University Press, 1978

Garrow, David J., *Bearing the Cross: Martin Luther King, Jr., and the Southern Christian Leadership Conference*, New York: Morrow, 1986; London: Cape, 1988

Greene, Melissa Fay, *Praying for Sheetrock: A Work of Nonfiction*, Reading, MA: Addison Wesley, 1991

King, Richard H., *Civil Rights and the Idea of Freedom*, New York: Oxford University Press, 1992

Kluger, Richard, *Simple Justice: The History of Brown v. Board of Education and Black America's Struggle for Equality*, New York: Knopf, 1975; London: Deutsch, 1977

Lawson, Steven F., *Running for Freedom: Civil Rights and Black Politics in America since 1941*, Philadelphia: Temple University Press, 1991

Meier, August and Elliott M. Rudwick, *CORE: A Study in the Civil Rights Movement, 1942–1968*, New York: Oxford University Press, 1973

Morris, Aldon D., *The Origins of the Civil Rights Movement: Black Communities Organizing for Change*, New York: Free Press, 1984

Norrell, Robert J., *Reaping the Whirlwind: The Civil Rights Movement in Tuskegee*, New York: Knopf, 1985

O'Reilly, Kenneth, *Racial Matters: The FBI's Secret File on Black America, 1960–1972*, New York: Free Press, and London: Collier Macmillan, 1989

Payne, Charles M., *I've Got the Light of Freedom: The Organizing Tradition and the Mississippi Freedom Struggle*, Berkeley: University of California Press, 1995

Powledge, Fred, *Free at Last? The Civil Rights Movement and the People Who Made It*, Boston: Little Brown, 1991

Raines, Howell, *My Soul is Rested: Movement Days in the Deep South Remembered*, New York: Putnam, 1977

Ralph, James R., Jr., *Northern Protest: Martin Luther King, Jr., Chicago, and the Civil Rights Movement*, Cambridge, MA: Harvard University Press, 1993

Sitkoff, Harvard, *The Struggle for Black Equality,*
    1954–1992, New York: Hill and Wang, 1993
Weisbrot, Robert, *Freedom Bound: A History of America's*
    Civil Rights Movement, New York: Norton, 1990

The burgeoning scholarship on this subject reflects a growing
agreement among historians that the civil rights movement was
one of the most unusual, idealistic, democratic, and – overall
– successful efforts for social change in the history of the United
States. Many of the early books focused on the movement's
preeminent leader, Martin Luther King, Jr., and on the organizations that promoted dramatic demonstrations and confrontations in the Deep South during the period 1960–65. However,
as historians delve into the origins of the movement, its organizational diversity, and its broad popular base, the old
"Montgomery-to-Selma" narrative is being modified by a more
complex view that employs a longer chronological framework
and places a greater emphasis on the strength and continuity
of black protest at the state and local level. The role of litigation, long criticized as ineffective, is being reassessed; so too
is the role of that strategy's principal exponent, the NAACP.
Historians are also exploring the ways in which the federal
government – presidents, judges, the Congress, the Federal
Bureau of Investigation – affected and responded to black
protest.

The first scholarly synthesis to present an overall view of
the civil rights movement, SITKOFF is a concise and lively
narrative that is the most widely assigned textbook on the
subject in American universities. Its brevity, however, limits
the depth of analysis, as does its general reliance upon
secondary rather than primary sources. Although it has been
revised, the book is now somewhat dated. It is a useful if rather
superficial introduction to the subject. WEISBROT provides a
good alternative to Sitkoff. Also a well written narrative, it is
more analytical, delves into individual topics more deeply, and
devotes more attention to events in the North after 1965. Like
Sitkoff, it is drawn mainly from secondary sources and journalistic accounts, and its view of the movement does not go
far beyond how it was perceived by contemporary commentators. LAWSON provides a succinct account of the civil rights
movement and a rather fuller discussion of its political repercussions. The author of two previous books treating black
efforts to gain political representation in the South, Lawson
focuses on the struggle for the ballot and the history of black
political participation since 1965. He incorporates recent scholarship, is particularly informative on electoral politics, and his
judgments are sober and sound.

Two other surveys of the movement, both written by men
who reported it for the press, are based on interviews with
former participants, opponents and observers. RAINES is a
compilation of interview extracts with little editorial interpretation; but some of the interviews illuminate events and personalities in a way that conventional histories often fail to do.
However, it is too limited and anecdotal to provide anything
more than a bare introduction to the subject. POWLEDGE has
balanced his interview extracts with extended passages of narrative and interpretation; the result is a more substantial and
coherent work. Neither Raines nor Powledge, however, pays
adequate attention to the origins of the civil rights movement,
or to its decline, and neither analyzes its long-term effects.

Although rather schematic and thinly researched, MORRIS
provides another handy introduction to the subject. Wider in
scope than its title implies, it illustrates how the civil rights
movement grew out of existing community institutions and
networks – especially black churches and black colleges – in
the segregated South. Morris also shows how new organizations, assisted by older, more experienced groups, welded localized protest campaigns into a unified regional movement.

Most early civil rights scholarship focused on the major
organizations that appeared to dominate the movement, and
on the leadership of Martin Luther King, Jr. CARSON has
written a concise history of the Student Nonviolent Coordinating Committee (SNCC), which spearheaded the civil rights
movement in Mississippi and played an important role in
Georgia, Alabama and elsewhere. It is still the standard work
on SNCC, although, because of its its relative brevity, it does
not do full justice to such an important subject. MEIER and
RUDWICK's history of the Congress of Racial Equality
(CORE), an organization that operated in both the North and
the South, is a much more deeply researched and solid book.
An impressive work of scholarship, its very comprehensiveness
sometimes weakens its narrative drive, threatening to overwhelm the reader with detail. It is more successful as an institutional history than as a study of black insurgency in the
South. In its treatment of the Southern Christian Leadership
Conference (SCLC) FAIRCLOUGH (1987) stresses the flexibility and tactical flair of this organization, and its success in
mobilizing ordinary black southerners in dramatic and effective campaigns of nonviolent direct action. While acknowledging the contributions of colleagues and advisers, it depicts
Martin Luther King, Jr. as the principal architect of SCLC's
victories in Birmingham and Selma – actions that helped
produce the 1964 Civil Rights Act and the 1965 Voting Rights
Act.

The latest biographies of King also explore the political and
institutional context in which this leader operated. GARROW
(1986) displays astonishing depth of research and is the fullest
and most accurate account of King's civil rights career. No
hagiography, this work depicts King as a reluctant and often
indecisive leader from whom the burdens of leadership exacted
a heavy psychic toll. Compared to Fairclough, Garrow downplays King's importance to the civil rights movement. The first
volume of a projected two-part work, BRANCH is a biography of King, and also a wider study of the civil rights movement that deals at length with other key figures (Bob Moses,
John F. Kennedy, Robert F. Kennedy). A sprawling narrative
based on solid research, Branch brings history to life in
sparkling prose. This is old-fashioned narrative history at its
best, but it cannot transcend the limitations of that form;
Branch can be faulted for overwhelming the reader with unnecessary detail and for failing to provide a clear interpretation
of the events he narrates so skillfully.

When so much attention had been devoted to the regional
and national dimensions of the civil rights movement – events,
organizations and leaders – it was logical for historians to turn
next to the largely unwritten story of the movement at the
state and local level. Studies that deal with a single city or
rural county have the advantage of allowing greater depth
of research and a longer chronological perspective. They
also effectively illuminate the complex patterns of protest,

resistance and compromise that characterized relationships between blacks and whites.

NORRELL focuses on the black struggle for voting rights and political power in Macon County, Alabama, from the 1930s to the 1970s. One man, Charles G. Gomillion, dominates the narrative, exemplifying the strong element of continuity that underpinned the civil rights struggle in many communities. In what is the best account of the civil rights struggle in a large city, CHAFE analyzes the complexities and paradoxes of race relations in Greensboro, North Carolina, from the 1950s to the 1970s. Both works conclude that the real achievements of the civil rights movement cannot mask the fact that true integration and equality remain elusive goals. COLBURN comes to the more pessimistic conclusion that blacks in the Florida tourist town of St. Augustine are still poor, segregated and politically powerless – despite King's presence there in 1964, the civil rights movement brought about little positive change.

State studies, by combining breadth with depth, offer a promising way of analyzing the broad popular base of the civil rights movement, the relationships between local movements and national organizations, and the connections between local, state and federal power. DITTMER provides a well-crafted narrative of the civil rights struggle in Mississippi – widely regarded as the most oppressively racist state in America – from the end of World War II to the late 1960s. Dittmer describes the crucial role of SNCC between 1961 and 1966, but stresses that local activists, women as well as men, provided core support and much of the dynamism for the civil rights struggle. He also effectively analyzes the political strains and conflicts both within the civil rights movement and within the Democratic Party.

FAIRCLOUGH (1995) covers an even longer period, and argues that the civil rights movement in Louisiana had its origins in the labor, left-wing and NAACP activism of the 1930s, and grew to the proportions of a fully-fledged movement during the 1940s, when World War II fostered a massive increase in black militancy. He concludes that the National Association for the Advancement of Colored People (NAACP), an organization based in New York but rooted in local black communities, provided essential leadership from the 1930s to the 1970s.

Although not strictly speaking a state study, PAYNE's study of the civil rights movement in the Mississippi Delta complements Dittmer and Fairclough by providing a richly textured account of how the young organizers of SNCC linked up with local inhabitants – many of them long-time activists – and how between them they created a new kind of political movement. Payne is the best study that we have of the social networks that underpinned black activism, and of the community organizing efforts that gave such a strong foundation to the civil rights movement of the 1960s.

Among books about white participants in the civil rights movement, EAGLES is outstanding. A moving account of a young Episcopalian minister from the North who was shot dead in Lowndes County, Alabama, it is at one and the same time a biography, a portrait of the Deep South, and an analysis of a judicial system that allowed a white murderer to go free.

The relationship between the civil rights movement and the federal government is a complex subject, full of ambiguities and contradictions. BASS is essential reading for an understanding of the vital role of the federal judiciary in sometimes hampering, but more usually assisting, the struggle against racial discrimination between 1954 and 1970. O'REILLY recounts the very different story of how the Federal Bureau of Investigation regarded the civil rights movement as a threat to American institutions, and conducted a covert effort to impede its operations and discredit key leaders. In a careful analysis of the relationship between the civil rights movement, the news media and the political system, GARROW (1978) shows how President Johnson and the Congress responded to the Selma protests of 1965. He reaches the striking conclusion that the central goal of King's non-violent demonstrations was to elicit the kind of violent white reaction that would generate favorable publicity, and hence political support, for the civil rights movement.

The struggle to integrate southern schools is another large topic that has spawned an extensive literature, although an adequate overview has yet to be written. KLUGER traces the NAACP's campaign, prosecuted in federal courtrooms by lawyers Charles Houston and Thurgood Marshall, against the South's system of segregated schools and universities. This sweeping and marvellously written narrative recounts a heroic story that culminated in a magnificent victory, the pivotal Supreme Court decision, *Brown* v. *Board of Education* (1954). CECELSKI, on the other hand, analyzes some of the unfortunate consequences of school desegregation as it was actually implemented by the white school board in one North Carolina county: the closure of black schools, the demotion of black principals, and the firing of black teachers. The ensuing campaign – ultimately successful – to keep the schools open underlined the fact that integration was rarely a clear-cut gain for the black community. Throughout the South, many blacks mourned the loss of schools that they had regarded as community institutions.

GREENE also describes the impact of the civil rights movement in microcosm, telling how blacks in rural McIntosh County, Georgia, assisted by upstate civil rights lawyers, challenged the power of the local sheriff, who had erected and maintained a not-so-benevolent dictatorship. Deservedly praised for its fine prose, it is full of finely-limned and realistic portraits of individual people, blacks and whites. This is not a conventional historical study, but it is a fascinating story of political change in one small community – a story that is probably typical of what happened, and is still happening, throughout the rural South.

KING provides the only extended discussion of how participants in the civil rights movement elaborated the concept of "freedom" in their speeches and writings. Stressing the uniqueness of the period 1955–65, King argues that the creation of a new, democratic, political community lay at the heart of what movement activists meant by "freedom." The civil rights movement thus supplied more than inspiring rhetoric: it also made an important contribution to the theory and practice of democracy.

The dispiriting story of how the civil rights movement failed to take root in the North is skilfully told by RALPH. This incisive and balanced analysis of SCLC's protests in Chicago shows that entrenched conservatism and pervasive racism among white northerners, rather than egregious errors by King and his allies, accounted for the defeat and disintegration of the civil rights coalition pieced together by King between 1965 and 1967. King's failure in Chicago ensured that black rioting and white backlash would continue to polarize the races, dooming efforts to eliminate poverty and segregation.

ADAM FAIRCLOUGH

Civil Service

Heclo, Hugh, *A Government of Strangers*, Washington, DC: Brookings Institution, 1977

Rourke, Francis E., *Bureaucracy, Politics, and Public Policy*, Boston: Little Brown, 1969, 3rd edition, 1984

Seidman, Harold, *Politics, Position, and Power: The Dynamics of Federal Organization*, New York: Oxford University Press, 1970; 4th edition, as *Politics, Position, and Power: From the Positive to the Regulatory State*, 1986

Stillman, Richard J., *The American Bureaucracy*, Chicago: Nelson Hall, 1987

Van Riper, Paul P., *History of the United States Civil Service*, Evanston, IL: Row Peterson, 1958

White, Leonard D., *The Federalists: A Study in Administrative History*, New York: Macmillan, 1948

White, Leonard D., *The Jeffersonians: A Study in Administrative History, 1801–1829*, New York: Macmillan, 1951

White, Leonard D., *The Jacksonians: A Study in Administrative History, 1829–1861*, New York: Macmillan, 1954

White, Leonard D., *The Republican Era, 1869–1901: A Study in Administrative History*, New York: Macmillan, 1958

This essay deals not only with the Civil Service, its history, development and role, but with the broader federal bureaucracy and its relationship with the wider political system. For an authoritative and detailed historical perspective on administrative arrangements in the United States, readers should turn to WHITE's four volumes of American administrative history from 1789 to 1901. These are an indispensable source and represent the first systematic analysis of American ideas about public administration. White provides a clear picture of how the pattern of national administration was formed and established. His books are not a dry record of institutional evolution but rather an illuminating interpretation of bureaucracy in the context of the key personalities and unfolding events and issues. White firmly establishes that administrative arrangements and procedures have been shaped by political and historical influences, and he authoritatively weaves the themes together in these classic works.

The 20th century history of the civil service was taken up by VAN RIPER, whose book both supplements White's analysis of the period up to 1901 and then takes the story forward to the late 1950s. Van Riper shares White's perspective that the civil service should be understood as a political institution, but he is more interested in the mechanics of the administrative process. His claim is that his analysis offers a view of the American ship of state less from the quarterdeck

and more from the engine room. He shows clearly how and why the American civil service differs from its European counterparts, by identifying both the lateness of the civil service reform movement and its limited and partial impact on the diverse American bureaucracy.

More recent analyses, notably those of Rourke, Seidman and Heclo, have focused directly on the political and policy aspects of bureaucratic activity. ROURKE rejects the view that public organizations are like private organizations, for the important reason that public agencies have a unique function as instruments of the state intimately involved in the development and execution of public policy. Rourke's book is centrally concerned to explore the role of the federal bureaucracy in the policy process, and he identifies as almost distinctively American the way in which government agencies seek to create and to nourish a constituency. He concludes that, in practice, public policy is ultimately determined by the bargaining, negotiation and conflict among appointed civil servants and officials, rather than elected politicians.

SEIDMAN was for 25 years a senior official in what was then called the Bureau of the Budget, and his book is that of a perceptive and reflective practitioner who offers an insider's view of the realities of government and administration since the 1960s. He analyzes how the civil service has been shaped by the competition for power and political advantage. He argues that the choice of bureaucratic institutions and procedures involves decisions which have profound political implications, and he points to the dangers of allowing political expediency to dictate the design of administrative systems. Seidman offers a timely warning that there is a real risk that American bureaucratic structures will become, not a reflection, but a caricature, of America's pluralist society.

HECLO gives his book the sort of compelling title that both provokes readers to think and encapsulates the essential argument of the author. His focus is on the relations between the fleeting and the enduring forces in government, the political appointees and the civil servants, in an effort to understand how the dual need for change and continuity in policies and procedures can be reconciled. His conclusion is that many of the problems related to the interaction between political leadership and bureaucratic power in the United States are structural rather than personal. He points out that the problems frequently ascribed to unresponsive civil servants are commonly due to the inadequacies of the leadership shown by temporary political appointees who neither know each other nor how the Washington system really works.

The reader who wants to compress his study into a single volume should consult STILLMAN, whose book covers the rise of the bureaucracy in the United States, its modern characteristics, current trends and future prospects. It identifies the sources, structures and variety of public bureaucracies in the United States, as well as the major sources of growth, decline and stability. Stillman analyzes what the civil service does, the means it employs and how it can best be made to serve, and be responsive to, the public interest. His book is aimed at the student market and it helpfully defines key concepts, summarizes important points and, for the reader inspired to go further, provides guides to supplementary reading on every topic.

ROBERT WILLIAMS

Civil War, 1861–1865: General

Barney, William L., *Battleground for the Union: The Era of the Civil War and Reconstruction, 1848–1877*, Englewood Cliffs, NJ: Prentice Hall, 1990

Bensel, Richard Franklin, *Yankee Leviathan: The Origins of Central State Authority in America, 1859–1877*, Cambridge and New York: Cambridge University Press, 1990

Brock, William R., *Conflict and Transformation: The United States, 1844–1877*, Harmondsworth: Penguin, 1973

McPherson, James M., *Ordeal by Fire: The Civil War and Reconstruction*, New York: Knopf, 1982; revised, New York: McGraw Hill, 1993

McPherson, James M., *Battle Cry of Freedom: The Civil War Era*, New York and Oxford: Oxford University Press, 1988

McPherson, James M., *Abraham Lincoln and the Second American Revolution*, New York and Oxford: Oxford University Press, 1990

Nevins, Allan, *The War for the Union*, 4 vols., New York: Scribner, 1959–71 (vols. 5–8 of his *Ordeal of the Union*)

Nichols, Roy F., *The Stakes of Power, 1845–1877*, New York: Hill and Wang, 1961

Parish, Peter J., *The American Civil War*, New York: Holmes and Meier, and London: Eyre Methuen, 1975

Pressly, Thomas J., *Americans Interpret Their Civil War*, Princeton: Princeton University Press, 1954

Randall, J.G. and David Donald, *The Civil War and Reconstruction*, Boston: Heath, 1961, revised 1969 (original edition, by Randall only, 1937)

Ransom, Roger L., *Conflict and Compromise: The Political Economy of Slavery, Emancipation, and the American Civil War*, Cambridge and New York: Cambridge University Press, 1989

Sewell, Richard H., *A House Divided: Sectionalism and Civil War, 1848–1865*, Baltimore: Johns Hopkins University Press, 1988

The Civil War remains for many Americans the most important sequence of events in their country's history between the Revolution and the New Deal. The fighting itself has been studied in legions of books and articles. Political studies have proliferated. The social impact of the war has been less systematically examined, although much exciting work on the South and the collapse of slavery has appeared in recent decades. The war's economic impact has been hotly debated, yet relatively little explored in depth or detail. The attempt to make sense of all this therefore becomes a considerable challenge. What we know most about with precision – the battles themselves and the political process in Washington – are least controversial in their outcomes: the Confederacy lost the war and the Republicans fulfilled their political agenda. Our knowledge is less wide-ranging, or simply very patchy, concerning the larger questions of whether the war transformed or "modernized" the American economy, accelerated social change and re-cast American culture. If economic, social and cultural life were indeed transformed by the war, did such turbulent changes have a lasting effect or were they followed by a return to

"normalcy"? And looking behind much discussion of these broader issues lies the often implicit question, "Was the war necessary?" The more the achievements of the war are viewed as long-lasting, profound and unlikely to have been attained without the crushing of the Confederacy, the more unambiguous the answer to that question becomes.

PRESSLY is not a general account of the period but an invaluable analysis of the intellectual context in which we study the subject. He examines the historiography of the Civil War in the first half of this century, focusing especially on James F. Rhodes's linking of the Northern cause with the national cause and the reaction by historians of many different ideological persuasions against that view. He concludes by emphasizing the revival of the nationalist strain in historical writing of the late 1940s and early 1950s. That revival, with modifications, has been dominant ever since.

A leading proponent of the nationalist perspective was NEVINS. His four-volume history of the war years, *The War for the Union*, has won less respect from scholars than his earlier, four-volume history of the coming of the war. But it offers a very clear and full narrative of a wide range of wartime experience, political, economic, and social as well as military. It dramatically brings to life all the excitement and uncertainty of the war years. Nevins argued that the war transformed Americans from an improvising people in 1861–62 into "a shaped and disciplined nation, increasingly aware of the importance of plan and control." He concluded by underscoring the possibilities, opportunities, and sense of a potential world role which the war opened up for the United States.

For many years, RANDALL and DONALD (1961, 1969), itself a major revision by Donald of Randall's 1937 text, stood pre-eminent as the best single-volume history. Many readers may dislike its restrained tone, limited probing into social attitudes, lack of attention to African American perspectives, and general complaisance in the "compromise" of 1877. Yet Randall and Donald consider a vast array of issues with clarity, good sense and a commendable desire to disseminate understanding rather than stimulate passion. If *some* – but by no means all – of their perspectives seem anachronistic to contemporary readers, that is no bad thing; the whole point of examining the past is to comprehend assumptions and approaches different from our own.

A major challenge to Randall and Donald's volume as the leading general textbook was mounted by PARISH in 1975. His account is relatively brief on Reconstruction and focused more fully on the war years than did Randall and Donald. Its particular strengths are a superb prose style, a persistent focus on the significance of events or developments, judicious assessments of conflicting interpretations, and careful analysis of wartime politics and policy-making. After placing slavery at the heart of his explanation of the war's origins, Parish also traces the various ways in which slavery shaped the war's outcome, notably in weakening the Confederacy's quest for international recognition. Similarly, the centrality of slavery in the conflict underscored the importance of Lincoln's handling of slavery issues and of Grant and Sherman's practice of war in hitting the Confederates' home front. Parish concludes by emphasizing that the war prevented a disruptive, conservative revolution and maintained the continuity of America's pursuit of liberty and equality. He is more positive about the war's outcome than Randall and Donald, but sees the war as less revolutionary in its impact than Nevins does.

The next commanding and large-scale work of synthesis and interpretation to appear was McPHERSON (1982). This is a very fine textbook, setting out topics adeptly and step-by-step and supported, especially on the war years, by excellent maps. The tone is less analytical than Parish, but what is lost in rumination is made up for by sheer pace. McPherson makes a vigorous case for the extent of pre-war sectional differences and pushes his conclusion, briefly, to the 1880s and early 1890s and the disappointments of the "New South". McPHERSON (1988) has established itself as the dominant text of recent years. It covers a briefer period than Randall and Donald, and Parish, stopping in 1865, but it is on a similar scale. In a formidable achievement, McPherson has produced the best single-volume history of the war itself, providing a compelling narrative with ample detail on individual engagements, while maintaining a clear sense of strategic imperatives. While the book focuses most powerfully on the fighting, tying political developments to the conduct of war, it does not ignore interpretative themes. Throughout his account of the war, McPherson considers the extent to which the conflict marked a struggle to disseminate capitalist free labor values more widely. He brings out far more forcefully than probably any other general account has done the impact of the war upon African Americans; they participate in the struggle for freedom and are not simply acted upon by white society, North and South. Finally, McPherson argues repeatedly for the importance of contingency in the conflict. We are dealing here not with general historical forces or the balance sheets of manpower and resources but with events shaped by, and in turn influencing, real people subject to sometimes rapid fluctuations of morale and will.

For larger questions of the war's impact as the Second American Revolution, readers should turn to McPHERSON (1990), a collection of his essays which offers an excellent introduction to a number of debates on the Civil War's significance. Easily readable, they cast the war in a longer perspective as a profoundly revolutionary experience for those engaged in it.

RANSOM usefully supplements McPherson's large-scale narrative study. His focus on political economy, and analysis of the structures of politics and economics, offer a real advance on earlier works of synthesis. Over half the book deals with the origins of the war, mostly following familiar themes. But the chapter on the economics of slavery helpfully explores the relationship between the prices of land, slaves and cotton, the higher productivity of western lands in cotton, and the impulse of slavery to extend westwards. While Ransom rightly emphasizes the importance of territorial policy, he is less sure in the weight which he gives to constitutional and legal issues. On the period of the war itself, Ransom is perhaps more impressive, providing clear, broad, up-to-date discussions of major themes. Yet his conclusion that the Confederacy failed not through lack of resources but through lack of the will to continue to fight seems to contradict much of the available evidence. Ransom ends his book with an assessment of the war's economic impact. He does not find the revolutionary transformations often discerned by others. He is sceptical about data on growth rates in the 1860s, arguing that the war did not stimulate economic growth. The Republicans' wartime economic programme is portrayed as being more expedient than visionary and as yielding limited results. We are left with a sense, by 1877, of a failed revolution.

Another stimulating, but more specialized, general study is BENSEL, which explores the linkage between the growth of government power and the establishment of some form of national social and economic order. While this is not a textbook, it is not a detailed monograph either. It ranges over the sectional crisis, wartime mobilization and then the impact of war on government financial, economic and Reconstruction policies. It depicts the emergence of federal government power as the principal development of the 1860s and 1870s. Bensel argues that the compromise of 1877 – far from being the necessary conclusion of a turbulent era welcomed by Randall and Donald – inaugurated a debilitating period in national politics; the federal government lost an opportunity of spreading genuine reconstruction in the South and promoting social democracy in the North, and instead became absorbed in disputes flowing essentially from the separatist agenda pursued by the South, under restored Confederate officials and politicians in the 1880s and 1890s. If Bensel may exaggerate the scale and scope of the federal leviathan that forms the centre of his analysis, he offers refreshing scepticism on the nature of Northern victory by 1877 and reflects dispassionately – though perhaps too briefly – on the possible consequences of Confederate success either in securing secession without war or winning independence through fighting. For far too long historical writing has simply assumed or asserted that the United States without the states which formed the Confederacy was unimaginable or unacceptable. Bensel at least offers some reasoned analysis of that issue.

For readers seeking accounts of this period which are shorter than 800 pages but still intellectually probing, one might note four surveys from among many stimulating and respectable contenders. NICHOLS is a very brief survey – strongly analytical in approach – of this crisis-ridden period. It has little on the war itself, but it is good on the sectional balance of political power and the interconnections between party programmes, sectional interests, national consciousness, and economic development. Although research in the last thirty years has deepened our understanding of many issues discussed by Nichols, the way in which he links economic developments across the mid-19th century provides a fruitful framework for considering the whole era. BROCK is similar to Nichols in subordinating the war itself to an extended discussion of the pattern of political change over the whole period from the mid-1840s to the end of Reconstruction. It excels at portraying the shifting states of mind of the Northern political elite and those intellectuals who concerned themselves with the changing political economy of the nation. Brock's approach reflects the values of high-minded liberal Republicans and his clear, fluent analysis provides a stimulating guide to the national policy-making of that particular group. His comments on the war are often perceptive, but, as with Nichols, the fighting itself and the fabric of social relations do not concern him in detail. A more recent short synthesis is SEWELL, which offers a reliable, thoughtful analysis of the state of historical understanding in the 1980s, and therefore provides a secure basis from which to examine particular issues more deeply. It does a good job for the reader not wishing to be overwhelmed by narrative detail. BARNEY is a vivid and lively textbook covering the same period as Nichols and Brock, and similarly portrays the history of an era rather than of the war alone. Again, like Nichols, Barney analyses economic change and the policies flowing from economic developments. He gives far more attention to the differential impact of such developments upon various social groups; the social dimension is both more fully and more grittily portrayed, and the political impact of religious sentiment is also considered. While African Americans receive more attention than is the case in older accounts, Barney retains a strong narrative command over the making of national policy throughout the period. He concludes with a sharply drawn view of the crisis of the 1870s. Facing large-scale immigration, urbanization and economic depression, the wealthy in both sections sought to retreat from expanding government power and resorted to simpler notions of stability and authority. Optimistic Republicanism of the 1850s – based on ideas of free labor and small-scale entrepreneurship – faded in the altered economic circumstances of the 1870s. Barney is clearer and sharper in his depiction of the class dynamics of the era's politics than are most recent general histories of the period. Although his emphasis on a sense of political retreat and failure in 1877 scarcely differs from Nichols's, the precise character of that political failure is differently explained.

The Civil War thus continues to stimulate varied approaches to understanding the impact of sectional crisis and war upon Americans of different racial, class and regional backgrounds, and to provoke debate over its impact.

BRUCE COLLINS

See also African American History: Civil War, Emancipation, and Reconstruction

Civil War: Approach to

1) 1846–1854: Wilmot Proviso, Compromise of 1850, and fugitive slaves

Campbell, Stanley W., *The Slave Catchers: Enforcement of the Fugitive Slave Law, 1850–1860*, Chapel Hill: University of North Carolina Press, 1970

Cooper, William J., Jr., *The South and the Politics of Slavery, 1828–1856*, Baton Rouge: Louisiana State University Press, 1978

Foner, Eric, "The Wilmot Proviso Revisited," *Journal of American History*, 56(2), 1969

Freehling, William W., *The Road to Disunion: Secessionists at Bay, 1776–1854*, New York: Oxford University Press, 1990

Gara, Larry, *The Liberty Line: The Legend of the Underground Railroad*, Lexington: University Press of Kentucky, 1961

Hamilton, Holman, *Prologue to Conflict: The Crisis and Compromise of 1850*, Lexington: University Press of Kentucky, 1964

Holt, Michael F., *The Political Crisis of the 1850s*, New York: Wiley, 1978

Morris, Thomas D., *Free Men All: The Personal Liberty Laws of the North, 1780–1861*, Baltimore: Johns Hopkins University Press, 1974

Morrison, Chaplain W., *Democratic Politics and Sectionalism: The Wilmot Proviso Controversy*, Chapel Hill: University of North Carolina Press, 1967

Nevins, Allan, *Fruits of Manifest Destiny, 1847–1852*, New York: Scribner, 1947 (vol. 1, part 1 of his *Ordeal of the Union*)

Nye, Russel B., *Fettered Freedom: Civil Liberties and the Slavery Controversy, 1830–1860*, East Lansing: Michigan State University Press, 1949, revised 1963

Potter, David M., *The Impending Crisis, 1848–1861*, completed by Don E. Fehrenbacher, New York: Harper, 1976

Any reader wholly unfamiliar with the events which placed America on "the road to Civil War" should begin with one of the single-volume works on the war itself, which will provide the necessary background to more detailed study. Such suitable starting points may be found in the earlier chapters of one of the following: Peter J. Parish, *The American Civil War* (1975); James M. McPherson, *Ordeal By Fire: The Civil War and Reconstruction* (1982) or his *Battle Cry of Freedom: The Civil War Era* (1988). From there, the reader can choose from a wealth of material, since the Wilmot Proviso, the Compromise of 1850, and the effects of its fugitive slave clause are covered, to a greater or lesser extent, in many studies of the antebellum and Civil War periods.

Of all the general works available, POTTER offers the most accessible account and analysis of political events in the decade preceding the American Civil War, and chapters four through six concentrate on the Wilmot Proviso, the Compromise of 1850, and reactions to its fugitive slave clause. The great strength of Potter's study, which was completed by Don E. Fehrenbacher after Potter's death, is that his interpretation of events is supported by a wealth of detail, both in the text itself and in the accompanying notes, which will prove invaluable for anyone seeking to pursue further any of the specific topics.

HOLT's study of political disintegration in this period is essential reading for anyone hoping to disentangle the various threads of party allegiance and the shifting sectional balance. It deals very lucidly with the impact of the Fugitive Slave Act on Northern Whigs in particular, and consequently on the Second Party system in general. Both Potter and Holt concentrate on the political arena, but the first volume of NEVINS's older, although recently reprinted, eight-volume study places equal emphasis on political, social and cultural change in the aftermath of the Mexican War. The Wilmot Proviso, the Compromise debate, and the Fugitive Slave Law are placed firmly in the context of the sweeping changes that America was undergoing at this time.

There are several broader studies of antebellum politics and society, particularly on the South, which give close attention to the Compromise of 1850 in particular. Emphasizing the primacy of the slavery issue in Southern politics, COOPER examines territorial expansion and reactions to the Wilmot Proviso from a Southern perspective. In his view, Southerners identified the Proviso "as a potentially lethal assault on their political power." FREEHLING is broader in scope and more controversial in its arguments. The final two sections (Parts VI and VII) cover the Southern reaction to the Wilmot Proviso, the Compromise and its fugitive slave clause. On all these issues, as on many others, Freehling argues, the South was divided, a fact which did much to undermine the effectiveness of what Freehling, following Potter, calls "The Armistice of 1850."

Among studies of particular topics, the only book devoted specifically to the Wilmot Proviso is MORRISON, which examines both shifting Democratic loyalties and white supremacist ideology in order to explain Northern Democratic support for Wilmot's proposal. It is detailed and, in many ways, persuasive in its arguments. However, it is worth supplementing Morrison with FONER, written two years later, which takes issue with some of Morrison's conclusions. On the Compromise of 1850, the standard work is HAMILTON. This is an extremely detailed study which, in its own words, "contains a reevaluation of celebrated and half-forgotten figures, provides a perspective for what they did and said, and reassesses the strategy and tactics of Northerners and Southerners, Easterners and Westerners, Democrats and Whigs in that great debate of 1850." In this it succeeds very well, offering vignettes of the politicians involved, close analysis of most of the major speeches, and a detailed breakdown of the voting on all parts of the bill. Throughout Hamilton stresses the significance of the role played by the House, the relative unimportance of Clay and Webster compared to "the primary Democratic direction of the adjustment forces," and reminds us that, but for several absentees, the outcome might have been very different in September 1850. The Compromise of 1850, Hamilton concludes, not only failed to do all that was expected of it, but its most infamous component, the Fugitive Slave Act – "enforced for the first time when only one week old" – succeeded only in exacerbating tensions that were beginning to threaten the Union.

The Fugitive Slave Law of 1850, and its repercussions, have attracted a good deal of attention. GARA's study of the underground railroad is both balanced and comprehensive, cutting through many of the myths surrounding the extent of this particular escape route for fugitive slaves. Both MORRIS and NYE focus on aspects of the Northern reaction to the slavery issue over a broad time-span. Nye concentrates mainly on the abolitionists, while Morris offers a detailed examination of the impact of the various personal liberty laws passed in some of the Northern states, both on the states themselves and on North-South relations, particularly after the Compromise of 1850. Both regard the Fugitive Slave Act as, in Nye's words, "a major factor in the growth of antislavery opinion in the north." Morris sees sustained opposition to the law, as expressed in the enactment of personal liberty laws, as a major contributory factor to Northern fears of Southern domination. In this he differs somewhat from CAMPBELL, who provides the most substantial examination of all aspects of the Fugitive Slave Law, from its passage in 1850 through to its disintegration, as the Civil War began the destruction of the institution which the law was designed to protect. Campbell's thesis is that "while most citizens residing in the North were opposed to the institution of slavery, only a few in isolated communities engaged in active opposition to enforcement of the Fugitive Slave Law," although, after the passage of the

Kansas-Nebraska Act in 1854, he detects a shift in public sentiment. From the outset Campbell stresses both the constitutionality and the effectiveness of the Fugitive Slave Law, and he shows that, in the majority of cases, "slaves were remanded to their owners or were returned to the South at government expense," although most slaveholders at the time did not think this was the case. Opposition to, as well as enforcement of, the law is examined, with many individual cases isolated for specific analysis. The effectiveness and implications of the personal liberty laws are also considered, and the study concludes with an examination of the way in which the contention that fugitive slaves were "contraband of war" effectively undermined the implementation of the law after 1860.

S-M. GRANT

2) 1854–1860: Kansas-Nebraska Act, "Bleeding Kansas," and Dred Scott

Cole, Arthur Charles, *The Irrepressible Conflict, 1850–1865*, New York: Macmillan, 1934

Fehrenbacher, Don E., *The Dred Scott Case: Its Significance in American Law and Politics*, New York: Oxford University Press, 1978; abridged as *Slavery, Law, and Politics: The Dred Scott Case in Historical Perspective*, 1981

Gienapp, William E., *The Origins of the Republican Party, 1852–1856*, New York: Oxford University Press, 1987

Hopkins, Vincent C.S., *Dred Scott's Case*, New York: Fordham University Press, 1951

Huston, James L., *The Panic of 1857 and the Coming of the Civil War*, Baton Rouge: Louisiana State University Press, 1987

Nevins, Allan, *A House Dividing, 1852–57* (volume 1, part 2 of *The Ordeal of the Union*), New York: Scribner, 1947

Nevins, Allan, *The Emergence of Lincoln: Douglas, Buchanan and Party Chaos, 1857–1859* (volume 2, part 1 of his *Ordeal of the Union*), New York: Scribner, 1950

Potter, David M., *The Impending Crisis, 1848–1861*, completed by Don E. Fehrenbacher, New York: Harper, 1976

Rawley, James A., *Race and Politics: "Bleeding Kansas" and the Coming of the Civil War*, Philadelphia: Lippincott, 1969

Stampp, Kenneth M., *America in 1857: A Nation on the Brink*, New York: Oxford University Press, 1990

Wolff, Gerald W., *The Kansas-Nebraska Bill: Party, Section, and the Coming of the Civil War*, New York: Revisionist Press, 1980

Many of the excellent single-volume studies of the American Civil War will offer some introduction to the respective roles played by the Kansas-Nebraska Act of 1854, the ensuing violence in Kansas following the March 1855 election there, and the Dred Scott decision of 1857 in the coming of the war itself. In such volumes the attention afforded each issue will, of necessity, be relatively brief. However, convenient places to start include the opening chapters of Peter J. Parish's *The*

American Civil War (1975) and, more recently, James M. McPherson's *Battle Cry of Freedom: The Civil War Era* (1988). From there it is best to move on to a selection of general studies of the antebellum period before turning to the few works devoted specifically to each topic.

The most authoritative introduction to the complex events of these years is to be found in POTTER. He explains with great clarity and care the intricate political manoeuvring that lay behind the whole issue of territorial expansion in the 1850s, including both congressional legislation on slavery and the Supreme Court decision in the Dred Scott case. On the specific subjects of the Kansas-Nebraska Act and "Bleeding Kansas," Potter's combination of close attention to the sources and clarity of analysis results in a comprehensive yet comprehensible account both of the events themselves as they occurred, and the later historical assessment of them. This approach derives its impetus from Potter's desire to mitigate the distorting effects of hindsight when applied to the antebellum period.

NEVINS is a classic multi-volume study of the Civil War years, the first two (original) volumes of which cover the subjects of Kansas-Nebraska, "Bleeding Kansas" and Dred Scott. It has recently been republished in a four-volume paperback edition. There is still much to be learned from Nevins, although it is more narrative than interpretative in orientation, and many will be intimidated by its sheer size. However, Nevins's broad sweep over the whole antebellum period does serve to place particular topics in context. COLE is another, much older, work that has recently been reprinted. Late-20th-century readers will find his style and approach dated, but he provides a clear and well-balanced narrative account of the antebellum and Civil War years. It is based on a wide range of primary and older secondary material, some of which will be unfamiliar to the modern reader. Any reader embarking on a more rigorous study of any aspect of this period will doubtless find some hidden gems in Cole.

The contrast between these older works and more recent scholarship is illustrated by GIENAPP's study of the origins and development of the Republican party up to its first election campaign in 1856. He offers an intricate and perceptive analysis of the role which the Kansas-Nebraska question played in the disintegration and realignment of parties during this period, and is particularly effective in his assessment of growing northern hostility toward the South after the Kansas-Nebraska Act and the subsequent violence in Kansas. Rigorously, indeed exhaustively, researched, with a helpful index and bibliographical essay, Gienapp analyzes with great skill the role that anti-Nebraska and, eventually, anti-Southern, sentiment played in the formation of the Republican party and the coming of the Civil War.

There are more specialized studies which focus on the Kansas-Nebraska Act and the Dred Scott case. The best, and the most methodologically sophisticated, study of anti-Nebraska sentiment and its repercussions is provided by WOLFF, who focuses on the "reactions of the rank and file members of Congress toward the Nebraska question." Wolff employed the technique known as Guttman scalogram analysis, in order to "expose a sophisticated and systematic set of attitude patterns on many issues, against which party and sectional variables could be tested." Wolff's close analysis of roll calls

on issues relating to the Nebraska Act – in particular the Homestead Bill of 1854 – failed to identify any clear sectional tendencies, even following the passage of the act, leading him to conclude that historians may "have exaggerated the role played by the Kansas-Nebraska Act in crystallizing the sectional hostility that eventually resulted in civil war." Readers who are confident with pages of noughts and crosses can check Wolff's conclusions for themselves in the detailed Appendix to this impressive study.

The subject of "Bleeding Kansas" and its relationship to the exclusion not only of slavery but of black Americans from the territory is examined in an early work by RAWLEY. Between 1854 and 1858, Rawley argues, Kansas "was the keynote of United States politics," but it only "outwardly" dominated events; racial prejudice was what lay at the heart of attitudes towards the territorial issue in the 1850s. Given the huge amount of research and publication on the subject of slavery and racism in 19th-century America since 1969, Rawley's contention that "the ordeal of the Union was among other matters a racial ordeal" is unlikely to have the impact that it had on first publication. In any event, Rawley's study is less about "race" and "Bleeding Kansas" than about "politics" and the Civil War. In this regard it remains useful for its assessment of the personalities involved, although here, too, its "blundering generation" interpretation of the causes of the Civil War is, in the light of recent scholarship, somewhat dated.

The event which, even more than "Bleeding Kansas," underlined the importance of race throughout America in the 1850s was, of course, the Dred Scott decision of 1857. There is an early study of this case by HOPKINS, which provides an adequate, if limited, assessment of the background to, and implications of, the 1857 decision. However, it has been overtaken by the work of the now-acknowledged expert on the subject, FEHRENBACHER, whose authoritative and substantial study of the case is available in two versions. The earlier of the two is the more comprehensive, with an impressive amount of supporting documentation, but the abridged version, *Slavery, Law, and Politics*, retains all the main arguments of the original without sacrificing essential detail. Fehrenbacher reminds us that although Taney's decision "defended a minority section," in fact "the racial theory underlying his opinion was majoritarian." From a straightforward appeal in 1846, Dred Scott's case increased in complexity as it moved through the American judicial system on its way to the Supreme Court. In order to explain this escalation, Fehrenbacher looks at much more than the 1857 ruling itself. He traces the development of slavery as an institution from the colonial period onwards, and by examining such related subjects as the Wilmot Proviso, the Lincoln-Douglas debates, specifically Douglas's Freeport Doctrine, and the Lecompton Constitution, Fehrenbacher places the case firmly in its broad, legal and historical context.

The actual year in which the Dred Scott case was decided by the Supreme Court is the subject of works by Huston and Stampp. HUSTON's study of the economic and political repercussions of the panic of 1857 refers to Dred Scott only in passing, although it does contain some interesting assessment of the differences between North and South at this time. In contrast, STAMPP includes substantial analysis of the Dred Scott decision and the threat which it posed to Republicans, for whom, Stampp argued, "the Dred Scott decision was the last in a chain of sinister events beginning with the annexation of Texas and including the War with Mexico, the passage of the Fugitive Slave Act of 1850, and the adoption of the Kansas-Nebraska Act." Stampp, however, concurs with Fehrenbacher's conclusion that the decision itself did not perceptibly increase support for the Republicans although, in a more general sense, it "lent credence to the charge of abolitionists and Republicans that the southern Slave Power conspired to make slavery a national institution."

S-M GRANT

3) 1854–1860: Political realignment, North and South; rise of the Republican Party

Anbinder, Tyler, *Nativism and Slavery: The Northern Know Nothings and the Politics of the 1850s*, New York: Oxford University Press, 1992

Foner, Eric, *Free Soil, Free Labor, Free Men: The Ideology of the Republican Party Before the Civil War*, New York: Oxford University Press, 1970

Formisano, Ronald P., *The Birth of Mass Political Parties: Michigan, 1827–1861*, Princeton: Princeton University Press, 1971

Gienapp, William E., *The Origins of the Republican Party, 1852–1856*, New York: Oxford University Press, 1987

Holt, Michael F., *Forging a Majority: The Formation of the Republican Party in Pittsburgh, 1848–1860*, New Haven: Yale University Press, 1969

Holt, Michael F., *The Political Crisis of the 1850s*, New York: Wiley, 1978

Mayer, George H., *The Republican Party, 1854–1966*, 2nd edition, New York: Oxford University Press, 1967

Nichols, Roy F., *The Disruption of American Democracy*, New York: Macmillan, 1948

Potter, David M., *The Impending Crisis, 1848–1861*, completed by Don E. Fehrenbacher, New York: Harper, 1976

Silbey, Joel H., *The Partisan Imperative: The Dynamics of American Politics Before the Civil War*, New York: Oxford University Press, 1985

Thornton, J. Mills III, *Politics and Power in a Slave Society: Alabama, 1800–1860*, Baton Rouge: Louisiana State University Press, 1978

Political realignments are rare in the United States; so rare that the realignment of the 1850s, which resulted in the rise of the Republican Party, established a two party system that has remained, at least nominally, intact to the present day. Given the longevity of the Republican-Democratic rivalry, it is perhaps natural to underestimate the contingencies involved in the system's creation. For generations, studies of the antebellum period fell victim to such error, often reducing a muddled political process with an uncertain outcome to an inevitable and dramatic confrontation over the question of slavery. Only during the last 25 years has a sophisticated, and sometimes contentious, body of historical literature emerged to remedy this problem.

No modern scholar has captured the complexities of the realignment process better than GIENAPP in his outstanding work on the origins of the Republican Party. His strength lies in his formidable research which extends across several Northern states and employs a variety of sources. In a field which often pits "new political historians" against "traditionalists," Gienapp manages to embrace both approaches with equally impressive competence. He contends that the realignment proceeded in two stages. First, he argues that the nativists or Know Nothings offered a plausible alternative to the Republicans for Northerners who were frustrated by the inability of the old parties – Whigs and Jacksonian Democrats – to address the slavery problem, and who were anxious over the influx of European immigrants into Northern towns and cities. Then, he demonstrates on a state-by-state basis how the Republicans managed to overcome and co-opt the nativists with superior political management and a more compelling message.

None of the ground covered by Gienapp is entirely new. The rise of the Republican Party has long been a staple of antebellum surveys. What has been in dispute, however, is the motivation underlying the new partisan alignments of the 1850s. POTTER represents a tightly argued response to earlier generations of revisionists who regarded antebellum politicians with some contempt. Potter reasserts the moral conflict over slavery as the dynamic behind the political realignment. Yet he does so while recognizing that the participants occasionally lost sight of the larger issues and acted out of self-interest and political ambition. The result is a multi-layered yet cogent narrative that succeeds in making a turbulent decade accessible to the modern student.

Nevertheless, HOLT (1978) offers a provocative and brilliant challenge to the insistence on the primacy of antislavery sentiment in the politics of the 1860s. While not denying the importance of the moral conflict over slavery, Holt argues vigorously for a broader, more nuanced view of the period. Rejecting the tendency of Potter and others to date the rise of the Republican Party from the passage of the Kansas-Nebraska Act of 1854, he describes instead how the Second Party System of Whigs and Democrats began to collapse prior to that landmark controversy. Holt attributes much of the antebellum political dynamic, in both North and South, to the ideology of republicanism and to anxieties about the future of the American experiment in self-government. According to Holt, what resulted from these anxieties was a new, more polarized party system that led to the breakdown of political debate and ultimately to Civil War.

Holt's critique opens the door for SILBEY to postulate that nativism, or anti-immigrant sentiment, was an even more salient cause of the realignment than slavery. Silbey not only argues, as other new political historians have done, that ethnocultural factors have been overlooked by traditionalists, but also that the Civil War has been overemphasized as a political dividing point. He contends that the realignment of American politics was driven by ethnic and religious concerns which originated during the Jacksonian era and remained relevant throughout most of the 19th century.

While many scholars have written on the coming of the Civil War, far fewer have addressed the specifics of antebellum party organizations. Among several works on the Republican Party,

FONER's study of the ideology of the movement remains the most influential. His principal contribution is to show how the antebellum Republicans were strong free labor advocates, not just antislavery critics. He also presents a compelling picture of the way in which the free soil platform of the Republicans succeeded in attracting the support of a wide range of varied, and sometimes conflicting, groups and factions, ideals and interests, fears and aspirations. Foner's perspective harmonizes to a degree with Potter's, and provides an important counterpoint to both Holt and Gienapp.

The standard histories of the Republican Party are generally inadequate. Of these, MAYER is the most reliable, but he devotes only the first two chapters of his work to the pre-Civil War era. The Democrats have attracted even less attention than the Republicans. NICHOLS remains the most complete examination of the break-up of the antebellum Democratic Party, both in the North and South. Although his approach has become dated, Nichols's narrative still makes good reading and remains a useful source.

Despite the wealth of attention showered upon the nativist movement during the last 25 years, ANBINDER is the first detailed study of the actual workings of the Know Nothing or American Party. In contrast to Silbey and others, however, Anbinder attributes a large measure of the nativists' success to their willingness to participate in the slavery debate. He considers their decline evidence of the greater relevance of slavery to most antebellum Northerners.

Since antebellum political parties were really little more than loose associations of state organizations, one cannot study the realignment of the 1850s without examining developments at the state and local level. HOLT (1969) is a detailed study of the Republican Party in Pittsburgh, which broke new ground when it first appeared and still offers a good introduction to the nature of the Republican movement in the Middle Atlantic region. Holt argues here for the influence of socioeconomic factors over antislavery beliefs in the make-up of the party's leadership and membership. FORMISANO's exhaustive study of antebellum Michigan opens a revealing window on to the realignment in the Northwest. His work also employs a variety of statistical techniques later emulated by a number of historians examining other states. In a fascinating look at the realignment in a Southern state, THORNTON offers a complicated portrait of life in antebellum Alabama. He concludes that the realignment, while less dramatic across the South, was nonetheless as important in the coming of the Civil War as the rise of the Republican Party in the North, because changing Southern political perceptions increased the likelihood of conflict.

MATTHEW PINSKER

See also Republican Party

4) 1860–1861: Secession crisis and outbreak of war

Barney, William L., *The Secessionist Impulse: Alabama and Mississippi in 1860*, Princeton: Princeton University Press, 1974
Channing, Steven A., *Crisis of Fear: Secession in South Carolina*, New York: Simon and Schuster, 1970
Crofts, Daniel W., *Reluctant Confederates: Upper South Unionists in the Secession Crisis*, Chapel Hill: University of North Carolina Press, 1989
Dumond, Dwight Lowell, *The Secession Movement, 1860–1861*, New York: Macmillan, 1931
Johnson, Michael P., *Toward a Patriarchal Republic: The Secession of Georgia*, Baton Rouge: Louisiana State University Press, 1977
Potter, David M., *Lincoln and His Party in the Secession Crisis*, New Haven: Yale University Press, and London: Oxford University Press, 1942
Stampp, Kenneth M., *And the War Came: The North and the Secession Crisis, 1860–1861*, Baton Rouge: Louisiana State University Press, 1950
Thornton, J. Mills III, *Politics and Power in a Slave Society: Alabama, 1800–1860*, Baton Rouge: Louisiana State University Press, 1978
Wooster, Ralph A., *The Secession Conventions of the South*, Princeton: Princeton University Press, 1962

Rather surprisingly, the secession crisis of 1860–61 has yet to receive comprehensive treatment in a modern study. DUMOND, the only work that treats the crisis from the perspective of all the Southern states, is on the thin side but does offer a concise overview of the process of secession. Strongest on constitutional issues and weakest on the social and economic factors behind secession, Dumond stresses the organizational skills of the seceders and what he views as the aggressive intent of an antislavery Northern majority that had coalesced behind the incoming Lincoln administration.

WOOSTER also examines secession throughout the South but focuses almost exclusively on the type of men elected to the secession conventions. After analyzing county voting results and constructing a statistical profile of immediate secessionists, cooperationists, and conditional unionists, he concludes that a strong relationship existed between slaveholding and secession. He shows that the immediate secessionists were wealthier and more likely to be Democrats than their opponents and that counties with large numbers of slaves were much more prone to back secession than those with low slave populations.

Much of the best work on secession has come out of specialized state studies. CHANNING argues that secession in South Carolina was "an affair of passion." Beginning his narrative with the reaction to John Brown's raid at Harpers Ferry in October 1859, he shows how hysteria and suspicion gripped South Carolina whites fearful of losing racial control over their slaves. By exploiting this fear, one magnified by the growing power of the antislavery Republican Party, the radicals were able to discredit moderate political sentiment and drive the state to secession. BARNEY also sees the fear of racial unrest as a factor motivating secession in Alabama and Mississippi but, unlike Channing, suggests that the slaveholding class was divided from within. Older, more established planters, he argues, were more conservative than younger, lesser slaveholders. Secession was attractive to the younger planters as a means of keeping open paths of social mobility that the Republicans threatened to block with their stand against the expansion of slavery.

JOHNSON pushes the theme of internal class conflict the furthest in his study of Georgia. He sees two revolutions occurring in Georgia in 1861. The first was directed against the external threat of the Republicans and took the form of secession. The concern of planters that the non-slaveholding white majority would provide the basis for an antislavery party built around Republican offers of patronage triggered the second revolution, one aimed at forestalling this internal threat to planter hegemony. The revised Georgia constitution of 1861, according to Johnson, was drafted with the explicit goal of shoring up the power of planters at home, especially the old Whig planters.

For THORNTON, the key to secession rests not in class or political structures but in the obsessive fear of common white Southerners over a loss of their independence and autonomy to encroaching centers of outside power. He places secession in the context of Jacksonian ideology and argues that white Alabamians used that ideology to lash out at any potential source of corrupting power that threatened to "enslave" them. Although small farmers in Alabama were generally opposed in the 1850s to state support for commerce and industry that was favored by planters, the power they most feared came from outside the state in the shape of the abolitionists and the "black" Republicans. Convinced that white liberties could rest only on the bedrock of slavery for blacks, these farmers readily followed the lead of planters in taking Alabama out of the Union.

CROFTS provides the best treatment of secession in the Upper South. He focuses on Virginia, Tennessee, and North Carolina, the three states which, in addition to Arkansas, seceded in the aftermath of the Fort Sumter crisis. Relying on a sophisticated statistical analysis of electoral returns, Crofts shows how and why the Unionists were temporarily able to stem the secessionist tide. He explains the success of the Unionists in building popular majorities against secession in terms of two factors lacking in the Lower South. Upper South Unionists were able to operate from the base of a competitive two-party system, and they could rely on the Unionist sympathies of an upcountry yeoman class that was much larger than in most areas of the slave-dominated Lower South. Non-slaveholding Whig farmers were the backbone of the Unionist coalition that came together during the February elections of 1861. Nonetheless, and as stressed by Crofts, their Unionism was conditional on the conferral of additional constitutional guarantees for Southern rights, and on the absence of any coercive policy by the federal government toward the states that had already seceded. Had Lincoln adhered to these conditions, Crofts suggests, the Civil War could have been averted and the Upper South kept in the Union.

POTTER also emphasizes the possibility of a voluntary reunion in the spring of 1861. The Lincoln that he depicts was a conciliatory leader who believed that secession could still be peaceably reversed when he took office in March 1861. In Potter's view, Lincoln and his fellow Republicans rejected compromise so as not to cave in to the demands of the secessionists and strengthen them at the expense of Southern Unionists. Where they erred was in overestimating the extent and depth of Unionist sentiment in the South. In deciding to reprovision Fort Sumter, Lincoln was not deciding on war, a conclusion that Potter insists can be reached only with the advantage of hindsight. Instead, he was taking the only action consistent with his pledge not to abandon the Union.

STAMPP is the other major study that concentrates on Lincoln and his party during the secession crisis. In contrast to Potter, he sees Lincoln as more willing to take a firm stand against the seceders and more willing to accept the possibility of war. For Stampp, Republican talk of a voluntary reunion was more a political strategy to disarm the Democratic opposition clamoring for compromise than a viable policy alternative. Stampp's Lincoln never wavered from his commitment to uphold the Union through enforcing the laws, and, though he did not want war, he was quite prepared to accept it over Fort Sumter as long as the Confederacy had to carry the burden of opening hostilities.

WILLIAM L. BARNEY

Civil War: Debate on Causes

Beard, Charles A. and Mary R. Beard, *The Rise of American Civilization*, volume 2, New York: Macmillan, and London: Cape, 1927, revised (in 1 vol.), 1930, and (in 2 vols.), 1933

Craven, Avery O., *The Growth of Southern Nationalism, 1848–1861*, Baton Rouge: Louisiana State University Press, 1953

Foner, Eric, *Politics and Ideology in the Age of the Civil War*, New York: Oxford University Press, 1980

Freehling, William W., *The Road to Disunion: Secessionists at Bay, 1776–1854*, New York: Oxford University Press, 1990

Holt, Michael F., *The Political Crisis of the 1850s*, New York: Wiley, 1978

Levine, Bruce, *Half Slave and Half Free: The Roots of Civil War*, New York: Hill and Wang, 1991

Luraghi, Raimondo, *The Rise and Fall of the Plantation South*, New York: New Viewpoints, 1978

Moore, Barrington, Jr., *Social Origins of Dictatorship and Democracy: Lord and Peasant in the Making of the Modern World*, Boston: Beacon Press, 1966; London: Allen Lane, 1967

Nevins, Allan, *Ordeal of the Union*, 8 vols., New York: Scribner, 1947–71; reprinted, 4 vols., New York: Maxwell Macmillan, 1992

Potter, David M., *The Impending Crisis, 1848–1861*, completed by Don E. Fehrenbacher, New York: Harper, 1976

Pressly, Thomas J., *Americans Interpret Their Civil War*, Princeton: Princeton University Press, 1954

The literature on the coming of the Civil War is enormous and PRESSLY offers a very useful guide to material that appeared before 1950. This basic work in Civil War historiography begins with contemporary interpretations of the conflict and is particularly strong in showing how shifting intellectual currents associated with America's participation in World Wars I and II were reflected in the very sharp debates between those who saw the war as irrepressible and those who viewed it as avoidable.

The opening two essays in FONER discuss more recent trends in the historiography and are especially useful as a critique of ethnocultural and modernization interpretations. As the title of the collection suggests, Foner emphasizes the primacy of politics and ideology as unifying themes for understanding how race and slavery intersected in producing the sectional crisis of the 1850s.

BEARD and BEARD explain the Civil War in terms of a fundamental and irrepressible conflict between two competing economies, one based on industrial capitalism in the North and the other on plantation agriculture in the South. They downplay slavery as a moral issue dividing the sections and insist that impersonal forces of divergent economic interests determined the breakup of the Union. The war itself they view as "the Second American Revolution," one that decisively placed power in the hands of industrial capitalists and so marked the divide between an agricultural and industrial America.

The Beards' economic interpretation was immensely influential during the depression decade of the 1930s. The main dissenters were the revisionists, those who believed that sectional differences were negotiable and that therefore the war was an unnecessary tragedy. CRAVEN makes the case for the "needless war" by arguing that clumsy politicians and sectional extremists, most notably the northern abolitionists, so emotionalized otherwise manageable differences as to cause a breakdown in the political means of achieving a consensus. Abstract questions of right and wrong made it impossible to engage in any rational political discourse, and the nation drifted into war.

In his multi-volume history of mid-19th-century America, NEVINS attempts to strike a balance on Civil War causation. Although he rejects the economic determinism of Beard and holds that the war "should have been avoidable," he argues that sectional differences were divisive enough to produce war. In his slavery-cultural interpretation, these differences were rooted in slavery and its accompanying problem of "race-adjustment." The refusal of the South to take any steps toward placing slavery on the road to extinction, combined with the refusal of the North to accept the moral responsibility of assisting the South in dismantling the institution and offering meaningful freedom to African Americans, made the war virtually inevitable.

MOORE agrees with Nevins that economic factors alone could not have produced the Civil War and indeed stresses how complementary was much of the economic development in the North and South. However, he also resurrects a Beardian framework by insisting that any moral differences over slavery were grounded in the growing divergence between the values and interests of two different capitalist societies in the North and South. Specifically, he argues that the alliance forged by the 1850s between northern industrialists and western farmers employing family labor precluded any need for a coalition between conservative elites in the North and South. Without such a coalition, sectional compromise grew increasingly difficult and finally collapsed in a power struggle over whether free labor or slave labor would dominate the federal territories. Like Moore, LURAGHI sees a basic conflict between a bourgeois North and a quasi-aristocratic South dominated by a landholding elite. He places the coming of the war in the worldwide context of 19th-century developments in which the industrial bourgeoisie integrated premodern and agricultural societies into consolidated national states and markets.

HOLT departs from the slavery-cultural interpretation by shifting attention back to the theme of political behavior so highlighted by the revisionists. Although granting the importance of sectional antagonisms over slavery, Holt insists that the issue became politicized only because of the calculated decisions of politicians. In his view, divisions over slavery led to war only after politicians acting out of partisan motives badly miscalculated the consequences of keeping slavery at the center of national political debate. Party competition fed sectional hostilities until the very success of the new and sectionalized Republicans in 1860 provoked the southern response of secession.

Politics also figure heavily in POTTER's masterly survey of the 1850s. Contrary to Holt, however, Potter is more sensitive to the unintended consequences of political acts, and his analysis of the process of sectional polarization concentrates on the ironic twists of the political decisions taken in the decade. As he deals with the problems of slavery, expansion, and sectionalism, he shows how the growing fulfilment of liberal nationalism in America also released forces of sectional discord that came to be symbolized by the status of slavery in the territories. More than any other factor, slavery isolated the North from the South and raised the stakes in politics to the point where secession and war seemed logical responses to the negative stereotypes which each section had of the other.

FREEHLING sounds a cautionary note against viewing the South as a monolithic unit. He emphasizes political differences over slavery within the white South, especially those running along a fault line between the Upper South and the Lower South, the area of the region's heaviest concentration of slaves. These differences, he argues, exacerbated the fears of radicals in the Lower South over the safety of slavery within the Union and drove them to make ever escalating political demands that culminated in secession and war.

LEVINE offers the most up-to-date survey of the coming of the war. Superb at explicating the social basis of political action, he shows how a popular basis for the Civil War developed out of the contradictions inherent in America's incomplete revolution of 1776, a revolution that enshrined freedom for white males at the expense of racial enslavement for African Americans.

WILLIAM L. BARNEY

Civil War: Campaigns

1) Eastern theatre

Adams, Michael C.C., *Our Masters the Rebels: A Speculation on Union Military Failure in the East, 1861–1865*, Cambridge, MA: Harvard University Press, 1978; as *Fighting for Defeat: Union Military Failure in the East, 1861–1865*, Lincoln: University of Nebraska Press, 1992

Catton, Bruce, *Mr. Lincoln's Army*, New York: Doubleday, 1951

Catton, Bruce, *Glory Road: The Bloody Route from Fredericksburg to Gettysburg*, New York: Doubleday, 1952

Catton, Bruce, *A Stillness at Appomattox: The Army of the Potomac*, New York: Doubleday, 1953

Catton, Bruce, *Grant Takes Command*, Boston: Little Brown, 1969; London: Dent, 1970

Coddington, Edwin B., *The Gettysburg Campaign: A Study in Command*, New York: Scribner, 1968

Freeman, Douglas Southall, *Lee's Lieutenants: A Study in Command*, 3 vols., New York: Scribner, 1942–44

Hennessy, John J., *Return to Bull Run: The Campaign and Battle of Second Manassas*, New York: Simon and Schuster, 1993

Rhea, Gordon C., *The Battle of the Wilderness, May 5–6, 1864*, Baton Rouge: Louisiana State University Press, 1994

Sears, Stephen W., *Landscape Turned Red: The Battle of Antietam*, New York: Ticknor and Fields, 1983

Sears, Stephen W., *To the Gates of Richmond: The Peninsula Campaign*, New York: Ticknor and Fields, 1992

Woodworth, Steven E., *Davis and Lee at War*, Lawrence: University Press of Kansas, 1995

For an overview of military operations in the Eastern theatre of the American Civil War, one could not do better than to turn to two three-volume studies, each by a master. Catton's trilogy on the Army of the Potomac takes it from the first battles of the war to the surrender at Appomattox. Although CATTON (1951) bears the title *Mr. Lincoln's Army*, it is in fact an account of George McClellan's army, as that general built a professional force from naive volunteers but then failed to use it to gain victory. CATTON (1952) recounts how Union soldiers bore up under incompetent leadership and secured victory at Gettysburg. CATTON (1953) shifts the focus to the interaction between Ulysses S. Grant and the army as both fought a war devoid of romance but ending in victory. These skilfully composed volumes feature several of the themes that are often attributed to later studies, including the political dimensions of the conflict, the experiences of the common soldier, and how war transforms those who experience it. Although FREEMAN's volumes on the Army of Northern Virginia cover the same campaigns from the Confederate side, they do so from the perspective of command relationships, providing perhaps the finest study available of military leadership below the army level.

Two single-volume studies provide provocative analysis of the rival armies. ADAMS argues that the Army of the Potomac suffered from an inferiority complex. Officers believed that their Confederate counterparts were more dashing, more determined, and better fighters; generals overestimated rebel numbers, grew anxious in the presence of Lee and his commanders and worried about what would happen next. Some of these themes build on Catton's trilogy; only with Grant, according to Adams, was someone able to overcome these handicaps. However, Adams fails to note that Grant shared some of the characteristics which he identifies as crippling the Army of the Potomac, including a tendency to overestimate enemy numbers and to assume that the Confederacy stood solidly behind its armies. In other ways, his account of Grant's experiences echoes that offered by Catton in his trilogy and elsewhere. WOODWORTH's title contains a double meaning that is at the heart of his volume. As Jefferson Davis and Robert E. Lee waged war against the Yankee invader, they disagreed on the best way to do so, with Lee's preference for the offensive winning out over Davis's desire to remain on the defensive whenever possible. Other chapters trace disputes between the Confederate president and other generals prior to Lee's taking command in June 1862.

Although every engagement in the Eastern theatre is the subject of at least one and usually more books – studies of Gettysburg alone could fill several bookcases – several stand out for the general reader. In a pair of studies covering McClellan's major campaigns, SEARS (1983, 1992) offers a rather damning indictment of the Union commander as lacking the temperament of a successful military leader. His account of the Antietam campaign makes clear what was at stake politically as well as militarily in September 1862, and he integrates debates about foreign intervention and emancipation into the narrative. Although Sears credits Lee with daring, he also reveals the Confederate leader's flaws, especially during the Peninsula campaign. Lee's triumph over blustering John Pope at Second Bull Run receives long-overdue attention from HENNESSY, who demonstrates how, even in the best of circumstances, it was virtually impossible to destroy an opposing army.

Readers looking for a single account of the Gettysburg campaign will find it in CODDINGTON's justly acclaimed study. Reflecting a great deal of research and thought, this volume offers measured assessments and well-reasoned conclusions on the whys and what-ifs of the single most studied battle of the war. Most refreshing is the author's realization that the Yankees had something to do with the outcome of the battle in contrast to those studies which focus on the Confederate high command and attempt to discover what went wrong and who was to blame.

For some reason the confrontation between Grant and Lee has not received quite the same attention as other campaigns in the East. However, in addition to the third volume of his trilogy, CATTON (1969), the second of his two volumes on Grant and the Civil War, examines how the Union general-in-chief approached his task, and reminds readers of the political as well as military limits on his freedom of action. The initial clash between the two generals in the Wilderness is the subject of RHEA's fine battle study, which clarifies much about this confusing firefight in the woods. While giving full weight to the problems of command, and the incomplete and incorrect information available to commanders, Rhea discusses lucidly how Grant, Lee and their generals directed operations, and refutes popular notions of the battle as a blind grapple. Those readers who want to explore how the Confederates responded to Grant's offensive should first turn to the final volume of the Freeman trilogy.

BROOKS D. SIMPSON

2) Western theatre

Castel, Albert, *Decision in the West: The Atlanta Campaign of 1864*, Lawrence: University Press of Kansas, 1992

Catton, Bruce, *Grant Moves South*, Boston: Little Brown, 1960

Connelly, Thomas L., *Army of the Heartland: The Army of Tennessee, 1861–1862*, Baton Rouge: Louisiana State University Press, 1967

Connelly, Thomas L., *Autumn of Glory: The Army of Tennessee, 1862–1865*, Baton Rouge: Louisiana State University Press, 1971

Cooling, Benjamin Franklin, *Forts Henry and Donelson: The Key to the Confederate Heartland*, Knoxville: University of Tennessee Press, 1987

Cozzens, Peter, *No Better Place to Die: The Battle of Stones River*, Urbana: University of Illinois Press, 1990

Cozzens, Peter, *This Terrible Sound: The Battle of Chickamauga*, Urbana: University of Illinois Press, 1992

Cozzens, Peter, *The Shipwreck of Their Hopes: The Battle of Chattanooga*, Urbana: University of Illinois Press, 1994

Fellman, Michael, *Inside War: The Guerrilla Conflict in Missouri During the American Civil War*, New York: Oxford University Press, 1989

Glatthaar, Joseph T., *The March to the Sea and Beyond: Sherman's Troops in the Savannah and Carolinas Campaigns*, New York: New York University Press, 1985

Josephy, Alvin M., Jr., *The Civil War in the American West*, New York: Knopf, 1992

Sword, Wiley, *Shiloh: Bloody April*, New York: Morrow, 1974

Sword, Wiley, *Embrace an Angry Wind: The Confederacy's Last Hurrah: Spring Hill, Franklin, and Nashville*, New York: HarperCollins, 1992

Williams, Kenneth P., *Lincoln Finds a General: A Military Study of the Civil War*, vols. 3–5, New York: Macmillan, 1956–59

Woodworth, Steven E., *Jefferson Davis and His Generals: The Failure of Confederate Command in the West*, Lawrence: University Press of Kansas, 1990

In light of the critical importance of the western theatre of operations to the outcome of the American Civil War, it is surprising that scholars have not always given it due attention. Critical campaigns such as Vicksburg have been relatively neglected, and there are far fewer studies of battles in the West than in the East. Nevertheless, aspects of the war in the West have attracted the talents of several skilled historians.

WOODWORTH provides readers with the most complete overview of Confederate strategy in the West. Focusing on the relationships between Jefferson Davis and his generals, Woodworth explores how friction between the president and his military leaders affected the conduct of operations. He questions claims that Davis shielded Braxton Bragg and offers substantial evidence to show that continual discord between commanders hindered efforts at defending the region or exploiting opportunities to take the offensive. Lack of coordination and cooperation and the failure to develop an overall approach to strategy proved crucial, especially as the Confederacy had little margin for error. However, it is not clear what exactly could have been done differently, especially as one cannot expect perfection in either human relationships or the execution of military plans. CONNELLY's two volumes about the primary Confederate fighting force, the Army of Tennessee, offers a comprehensive discussion of that army's activities.

Neither the overall Union war effort in the West nor that theatre's most successful Union army, the Army of the Tennessee, has received the treatment which Woodworth and Connelly offer for their Confederate counterparts. Perhaps the best overview of Union operations through September 1863 is to be found in the three volumes of WILLIAMS's unfinished study. His detailed treatment of military operations emphasizes Ulysses S. Grant's rise to prominence, but offers what remains, despite shortcomings, the best available discussion of Don Carlos Buell's performance. At times Williams's pro-Grant bias is too pronounced. Equally compelling is CATTON's examination of Grant's career from the beginning of hostilities through the surrender of Vicksburg. Tracing Grant's development as a commander, Catton casts an eye beyond the battlefield proper to explore the escalation of the conflict, the issues raised by slavery, emancipation, and the enlistment of blacks, and command relationships. Readers looking for coverage of Grant's Vicksburg campaign should consult one of these sources in the absence of a first-class, comprehensive study of that classic and crucial campaign.

For the campaigns in West Tennessee that first brought Grant to the attention of the public, two studies prove most helpful. COOLING brings readers the story of the capture of Forts Henry and Donelson, reflecting that Confederate mismanagement and some good fortune as well as Grant's initiative secured the Union victory that opened up several avenues of invasion. Two months later, Confederate general Albert Sidney Johnston sought to regain what was lost when he launched an attack on Grant's army encampment next to Pittsburg Landing: the resulting battle of Shiloh is chronicled in detail in SWORD (1974). As he suggests, Shiloh revealed that Grant had much to learn about generalship, but his performance in rallying his dispirited men and in establishing a defensive line that gave ground grudgingly while he awaited the arrival of reinforcements and nightfall made up for his earlier errors.

In three volumes COZZENS relates the efforts of the Union's Army of the Cumberland to complete the conquest of Tennessee, climaxing in the battles of Stones River, Chickamauga, and Chattanooga. In offering detailed descriptions of small-unit actions that integrate soldier recollections as well as the reports of officers and generals, Cozzens's narratives suggest something of the chaos and confusion of combat; readers are cautioned that as a result the narrative sometimes becomes hard to follow. Although he treats both sides, the Union forces receive somewhat more attention.

Two campaign studies offer readers a comprehensive treatment of the major campaigns of 1864. CASTEL's lengthy and detailed narrative of the Atlanta campaign offers a much more critical view than most of the generalship of William T. Sherman, suggesting that the Union commander was not particularly adept at, or eager to wage, battle. With the campaign in Virginia between Grant and Lee reaching a stalemate by the summer of 1864, the contest in northern Georgia became decisive; the capture of Atlanta by Sherman's forces at the beginning of September played a large role in securing the re-election of Abraham Lincoln two months later. Under Joseph E. Johnston, the Confederates retreated when it might have been better to fight; under John Bell Hood, they fought when it might have been better to hold their ground. SWORD (1992) tells the story of Hood's ill-fated offensive into Tennessee in the fall of 1864, culminating in the Confederate disasters at Franklin and Nashville.

GLATTHAAR is a study of Union soldiers who participated in Sherman's marches in 1864 and 1865, and it offers a revealing look at the attitudes and actions of the Union fighting man in these controversial campaigns. Readers learn something of the change that war had wrought in the common soldier, as well as gaining a better awareness of what they thought the war was all about, and how these understandings shaped their attitudes and their actions toward white civilians, escaped slaves, and their treatment of property.

The trans-Mississippi West receives short shrift in many histories of the war, largely because, to most historians, operations there appear tangential to the outcome of the conflict. Nevertheless, several studies reveal that what happened in these areas had a profound impact on the people who lived there. JOSEPHY's wide-ranging volume offers overviews of several Civil War operations, notably the Red River campaign in Louisiana and the Confederate invasion of New Mexico, as well as conflicts between Native Americans and whites. It serves as a solid introduction to events in the region. FELLMAN offers a rather disturbing account of the war in Missouri, which quickly degenerated into a nasty guerrilla conflict that ripped through the social fabric of the state. Such a struggle melted distinctions between combatant and noncombatant, and resulted in a society at war against itself.

BROOKS D. SIMPSON

Civil War: the Common Soldiers

Barton, Michael, *Goodmen: The Character of Civil War Soldiers*, University Park: Pennsylvania State University Press, 1981

Glatthaar, Joseph T., *The March to the Sea and Beyond: Sherman's Troops in the Savannah and Carolinas Campaigns*, New York: New York University Press, 1985

Kennett, Lee, *Marching Through Georgia: The Story of Soldiers and Civilians during Sherman's Campaign*, New York: HarperCollins, 1995

Linderman, Gerald F., *Embattled Courage: The Experience of Combat in the American Civil War*, New York: Free Press, and London: Collier Macmillan, 1987

McPherson, James M., *What They Fought For, 1861–1865*, Baton Rouge: Louisiana State University Press, 1994

Mitchell, Reid, *Civil War Soldiers: Their Expectations and Their Experiences*, New York: Viking, 1988

Robertson, James L., Jr., *Soldiers Blue and Gray*, Columbia: University of South Carolina Press, 1988

Wiley, Bell Irvin, *The Life of Johnny Reb: The Common Soldier of the Confederacy*, Indianapolis: Bobbs Merrill, 1943

Wiley, Bell Irvin, *The Life of Billy Yank: The Common Soldier of the Union*, Indianapolis: Bobbs Merrill, 1952

Wilkinson, Warren, *Mother, May You Never See the Sights I Have Seen: The Fifty-Seventh Massachusetts Veteran Volunteers in the Army of the Potomac, 1864–1865*, New York: Harper, 1990

Despite roomfuls of regimental histories and narratives of the Civil War, the values, interests, and experiences of the common soldiers during the war received scant scholarly attention until WILEY (1943) shifted the gaze from officers to the ranks with his study of Johnny Reb. Basing his work chiefly on soldiers' diaries and letters, he looked as closely at camp life as at combat to determine the character of Confederate soldiers and concluded that, though drawn from varied backgrounds, they shared an aversion to discipline, reeked of class prejudices, fought hard, grew hardened to suffering and sin, and hardly understood or cared much about ideological or constitutional issues, viewing the war instead as a defense of home.

WILEY (1952) followed with a composite biography of Billy Yank. Using the same kinds of materials and the same approach as in his previous book, he reached similar conclusions about the ways in which Billy Yank became inured to war's cruelties and the soldier's lot. But contemporary studies of World War II soldiers that showed them as indifferent to ideological issues inclined Wiley to see Billy Yank also as not much interested in elusive abstract ideals. Loyalty to one's own unit and survival counted most. Race, however, did matter in Wiley's estimations of Billy Yank's values.

Wiley's copious readings of soldiers' lives almost closed discussion, for many scholars assumed there was little left to say. Indeed, no one else has since essayed the common soldier so fully. The most recent synthesis by ROBERTSON adopts Wiley's basic methodology and conclusions, and seeks only to supplement and enrich the accounts with new material. Like Wiley, he eschews theory and principally lets the soldiers tell their own stories.

New insights into the common soldier came with the emergence of the "new military history," emphasizing the cultural, ideological, and social contexts in which soldiers acted. A vigorous debate about motivation spurred one phase of inquiry. BARTON relied on neo-Freudian psychological theory and statistical analysis to conclude that northern soldiers particularly fought to maintain self-control over themselves and restore it to the Union. The war was a test of masculinity in its demand to subscribe to Victorian codes of conduct, which Barton insists weighed more heavily on southerners.

With a post-Vietnam sensitivity to combat and military discipline informing his work, MITCHELL finds that both Rebs and Yanks evinced a higher level of ideological commitment to their respective causes than most scholars assumed, and that Victorian masculinity defined the common soldiers' responses to military life and battle. The slave issue aside, soldiers shared many common reasons for fighting, including appeals to the American Revolution, political freedom, loyalty to region and race, fear of God, and family honor. Increasingly, the face of battle, a concept borrowed from British historian John Keegan, became the focal point in considering how war changed soldiers. Like Mitchell, LINDERMAN suggested that wartime experience altered homefront expectations about how soldiers should act. Impersonal death and piles of amputated body parts ended any Victorian sentimentality which soldiers might have brought to the war, and alienated soldiers from the folks at home. Combat recast courage into less noble forms for soldiers who prized survival over ideology or romantic notions of bravery.

McPHERSON demurs from the emphasis on primary group loyalty as the principal characteristic of common soldiers and the reason why they fought. Acknowledging a bias toward literate men likely to think in ideological terms, he insists that soldiers on both sides were well-informed on politics, conscious of historical obligations to uphold republicanism and political liberty, and committed to order. Matters of race separated northerner from southerner, with the former overcoming objections to emancipation once it became evident that black freedom was essential for Union victory. McPherson suggests that the mass destruction of the war was due in large part to the soldiers' ideological convictions.

Close examination of one particular army became another important approach to studies of the common soldiers. The bias of Wiley's and others' work toward eastern armies led GLATTHAAR to examine Sherman's western army, itself a subject of growing historical scrutiny. In looking at the health, hardships, racial attitudes, values, and daily lives of Sherman's men, he concluded that the veteran character of the army gave it the grit to wage "total war" in the march to the sea and the almost missionary zeal to end the war on its terms. KENNETT discounts hatred of southerners as the driving force of Sherman's men, and sees little evidence that the war degenerated into a warfare of terror as soldiers hardened to suffering. From the beginning soldiers acted both nobly and cruelly toward their enemies, soldier or civilian, as much from whim as from morality or policy. Day-by-day he follows the soldiers, and civilians, in an almost anthropological effort to recreate the total community of the army.

The study of the war as the soldiers experienced it received significant boosts from new-style unit histories which examined the sub-culture of a regiment. Knowing each soldier in each unit became the ideal, as exemplified by WILKINSON, who built on John J. Pullen's *The Twentieth Maine: A Volunteer Regiment in the Civil War* (1957) to track the daily lives of the 57th Massachusetts from recruitment through training, camp life, and battle. With a roster of individual biographies and attention to ethnic, racial, and class conflicts, he established the model for modern unit histories and the recognition that no single "type" will stand for the common soldier in the Civil War.

RANDALL M. MILLER

Civil War: Naval War

Beringer, Richard E., Herman Hattaway, Archer Jones, and William N. Still, Jr., *Why the South Lost the Civil War*, Athens: University of Georgia Press, 1986

Bradford, James C. (editor), *Captains of the Old Steam Navy: Makers of the American Naval Tradition, 1840–1880*, Annapolis, MD: Naval Institute Press, 1986

Canney, Donald L., *The Old Steam Navy*, 2 vols., Annapolis, MD: Naval Institute Press, 1990–93

Durkin, Joseph T., *Stephen R. Mallory: Confederate Navy Chief*, Chapel Hill: University of North Carolina Press, 1954

Hayes, John D. (editor), *Samuel Francis Du Pont: A Selection from His Civil War Letters*, 3 vols., Ithaca, NY: Cornell University Press, 1969

Niven, John, *Gideon Welles: Lincoln's Secretary of the Navy*, New York: Oxford University Press, 1973

Reed, Rowena, *Combined Operations in the Civil War*, Annapolis, MD: Naval Institute Press, 1978

Roland, Alex, *Underwater Warfare in the Age of Sail*, Bloomington: Indiana University Press, 1978

Silverstone, Paul H., *Warships of the Civil War Navies*, Annapolis, MD: Naval Institute Press, 1989

Still, William N., Jr., *Confederate Shipbuilding*, Athens: University of Georgia Press, 1969; revised, Columbia: University of South Carolina Press, 1987

Still, William N., Jr., *Monitor Builders: A Historical Study of the Principal Firms and Individuals Involved in the Construction of USS Monitor*, Washington, DC: National Parks Service, 1988

Wise, Stephen R., *Lifeline of the Confederacy: Blockade Running During the Civil War*, Columbia: University of South Carolina Press, 1988

The naval dimension of the Civil War is best approached through one of the better general histories. Most accounts of the naval war itself have tended to isolate the subject from the strategic situation, from the politics of the war, and in particular from the technical, tactical and strategic developments in naval capability demonstrated during the Crimean War (1854–56). However, these issues are all addressed in HAYES's exemplary study of Admiral Du Pont through the secession crisis, when many of his friends in the officer corps "went south", and through a two-year period of active duty in command of the South Atlantic Blockading Squadron. This began in triumph, with the seizure of Port Royal, and ended in controversy with the repulse of his half-hearted attack on Charleston. In this turbulent period, Du Pont made many enemies, notably the ambitious Assistant Secretary of the Navy Gustavus Vasa Fox, who, he believed, had become party to a conspiracy to force Ericsson's monitor concept on to the Navy. Du Pont demonstrated the value that professional officers had gained from a close study of Anglo-French operations in the Crimean and Chinese Wars.

BRADFORD studies twelve senior naval officers who fought in the war, revealing the underlying themes of pre-war doctrine, particularly the tactics required for ships to engage forts. Here it is necessary to distinguish between operations that required ships to pass forts, as happened at New Orleans, and those that required the ships to batter the forts into submission, such as those that failed at Charleston. NIVEN and DURKIN examine the careers, respectively, of the Northern and Southern Secretaries of the Navy, providing an insight into the politics of the naval war, and the relative lack of weight given to naval considerations in the political direction of the conflict.

The strategic role of seapower, often shaped by geography, is admirably handled in REED. As conceived in General Winfield Scott's initial strategy, the South was eventually cut in half along the Mississippi, and opened up to riverine and coastal operations, which further reduced the opportunities for overseas contact. Reed shows that experience from the Crimean War had a major impact on General George McClellan. Having studied the war at first hand, he recognized the strategic value of large-scale amphibious operations that would allow him to combine the strategic offensive with powerful defensive positions, based around fieldworks and heavy artillery. Riverine logistics, as much as railways, proved critical to Northern victory.

In contrast, WISE has argued that the blockade, once cited as a model of its type, was in fact porous throughout the war. It was not so much the blockade which created serious shortages in the Confederacy, as the Southern laissez-faire approach, which was prepared to leave to the private sector the choice of cargoes for blockade-running vessels. This hands-off approach wasted an opportunity to compensate for Southern industrial weakness. Fast, British-built steamships, often commanded by Royal Navy officers on half-pay, constantly evaded capture at sea, and it was only by taking the main Confederate ports that the Union could impose an effective blockade. In BERINGER *et al.*, William N. Still stresses that the failure of the blockade provided the Southern economy with a breathing space in which to build some kind of industrial base. By the time access to the sea was lost, it was no longer critical.

Of more significance to the outcome of the war was the inability of the South to create an adequate naval defence for the major rivers. STILL (1969, 1987) demonstrates the limitations on Southern shipbuilding resources: lack of skilled labour, seasoned timber and steam engineering resulted in the construction of simple, unseaworthy craft of limited combat potential. Attempts to import warships or key equipment, including engines and armour, were unsuccessful, through capture, or because of the cost of transport.

In contrast, CANNEY shows how the United States Navy of 1861 was already well equipped for coastal operations, and traces the development of armoured and unarmoured warships during the war. He supports Du Pont, as portrayed in Hayes, arguing that the Monitor concept was not the most effective use of northern resources. It was a weapons system with severe limitations, including inadequate firepower and dubious seaworthiness. He also lays to rest the myth of "Yankee ingenuity", demonstrating the derivative nature of the Federal ironclad effort.

In detailing the various types of vessels used – warships, purchased steamers, river craft and transports – SILVER-STONE shows the scale of naval mobilization. By contrast, STILL (1989), a pioneering study of great significance, provides a specific case study of industrial mobilization by examining the engineering resources deployed to construct the *Monitor* in one hundred days, and also the political links of the companies concerned. Underwater warfare also made great strides during the war. ROLAND links this development to earlier work in America and Russia, while showing that countermeasures involving the use of mines were largely based on British experience.

ANDREW D. LAMBERT

Civil War: International Aspects

Adams, Ephraim Douglass, *Great Britain and the American Civil War*, 2 vols., New York: Longmans Green, and London: Longman, 1925

Bernath, Stuart L., *Squall Across the Atlantic: American Civil War Prize Cases and Diplomacy*, Berkeley: University of California Press, 1970

Case, Lynn M. and Warren F. Spencer, *The United States and France: Civil War Diplomacy*, Philadelphia: University of Pennsylvania Press, 1970

Crook, David Paul, *The North, the South, and the Powers, 1861–1865*, New York: Wiley, 1974

Ferris, Norman B., *Desperate Diplomacy: William H. Seward's Foreign Policy, 1861*, Knoxville: University of Tennessee Press, 1976

Ferris, Norman B., *The Trent Affair: A Diplomatic Crisis*, Knoxville: University of Tennessee Press, 1977

Jenkins, Brian, *Britain and the War for Union*, 2 vols., Montreal: McGill-Queen's University Press, 1974–80

Jones, Howard, *Union in Peril: The Crisis over British Intervention in the Civil War*, Chapel Hill: University of North Carolina Press, 1992

Owsley, Frank Lawrence, *King Cotton Diplomacy: Foreign Relations of the Confederate States of America*, Chicago: University of Chicago Press, 1931, revised 1959

Warren, Gordon H., *Fountains of Discontent: The Trent Affair and Freedom of the Seas*, Boston: Northeastern University Press, 1981

Winks, Robin W., *Canada and the United States: The Civil War Years*, Baltimore: Johns Hopkins Press, 1960

The international aspects of the American Civil War have been the subject of a number of excellent studies. The best single-volume survey is CROOK which attempts to put the conflict in its larger international context. Working primarily from printed sources, Crook provides a solid account of the relations of both the Union and Confederate governments with the major European powers. Both sides in the war quickly realized that the rending of the Union opened the door to Great Power intervention, with possibly decisive consequences for the results of the war. Great Britain was the most important European power in this respect, thanks to her naval and maritime resources, as well as her industrial and financial capacities, although Crook never loses sight of the role and influence of such countries as France, Spain, or Russia.

Because of her crucial position, Britain has been the subject of several major studies of Civil War diplomacy. The classic 1925 work by ADAMS was based on extensive original research in Britain, and attempted to explain the relationship as seen from London. Adams stood for almost fifty years until the publication in 1974 of the first of Jenkins's two volumes. His work provides an important second look at the war from Britain's perspective. However, as JENKINS had access to many collections of documents in the United States that were not available when Adams started his project, this study is much more balanced. Jenkins shows a divided Britain, uncertain whether its interests would best be served by a Northern or a Southern victory, anxious alike about Yankee bluster and genuine northern economic strength, nervous about the security of Canada, uncomfortable with southern slavery, and worried about what too great a commitment in North America might allow the French or the Russians to do in Europe. A third major Anglo-American study is JONES, who focuses extensively on the mediation crisis of the autumn of 1862. British motivation and eventual hesitation have long been a topic of controversy. Jones gives a plausible analysis of the factions within the British Cabinet and how they came almost to the point of decision on intervention, only to postpone and then never raise the issue again.

The Civil War seriously affected relations with several other countries. WINKS presents a careful and extensive examination of both public opinion and official attitudes in Canada to the war. Canadians opposed slavery, but did not approve of coercing the southern states to stay within the Union. Incidents like the Trent affair left them caught in the middle between Britain and the United States, and the St. Alban's, Vermont, raid placed them between the Union and the Confederacy. Winks traces Canadian views on these pitfalls. A third country with a vital interest in the war was France. In a lengthy and exhaustively researched book, CASE and SPENCER explain how the loss of cotton and tobacco, as well as export markets, affected the French economy. France was also caught up in the Trent affair and the possibility of joint intervention with the British in America. The French intervention in Mexico caused further serious complications. While focused on French diplomacy, Case and Spencer give a fresh European perspective on the now familiar sequence of events.

A number of special studies of the international aspects of the Civil War are particularly useful. FERRIS (1976) attempts to explain the seemingly contradictory policy of Secretary of State William H. Seward during 1861. Did he want to provoke an incident with the European powers or not? FERRIS (1977) tries to explain why the Trent affair escalated into such a major international crisis. Public opinion on both sides of the Atlantic certainly aggravated the issue which, Ferris concludes, both sides were anxious to settle. WARREN also examines the Trent crisis and concludes that Lord Palmerston and others were much more willing to be driven to the brink of war by public opinion than Ferris had suggested. Warren argues that Seward's belligerent statements earlier in 1861, together with alarmist despatches from Lord Lyons, the British Minister, had led the Cabinet to think that Seward probably wanted to provoke a war. Even after the release of Mason and Slidell, the British were not certain what American intentions were. A major weapon used by the Union in the war was the blockade of the Confederate ports, although this action had the potential for a clash with Great Britain, the major shipper in and out of those ports. BERNATH examines the legal issues surrounding the blockade, analysing the key cases to come before the Admiralty Courts, which had profound naval and maritime implications for both countries.

Most of the books looking at the international dimensions of the Civil War make at least some reference to Confederate foreign policy, although generally they focus on the diplomacy of Washington. OWSLEY's 1931 study of Confederate foreign relations, revised in 1959, remains the most thorough monograph on Confederate policy, based on extensive research in Europe as well as in Britain and the United States. It goes beyond an examination of the southern attempt to engage

Britain in the war by withholding cotton from the market, and thereby provoking a world crisis. Britain was the primary hope of the Confederacy until 1863 for recognition, for intervention, for a supply of ships, and for credit. Owsley shows the flawed logic of the southerners in presuming that a shortage of cotton would force Europe to intervene in the war on their behalf. Events did not unfold as the Confederates expected, in Britain, France, or even Mexico. Owsley concludes that neither cotton nor any other asset the Confederacy had to offer was sufficient to induce the Europeans to intervene in the war.

FRANCIS M. CARROLL

Civil War: the North

1) Wartime government and politics

Baker, Jean H., *Affairs of Party: The Political Culture of Northern Democrats in the Mid-Nineteenth Century*, Ithaca, NY: Cornell University Press, 1983

Baum, Dale, *The Civil War Party System: The Case of Massachusetts, 1848–1876*, Chapel Hill: University of North Carolina Press, 1984

Bensel, Richard Franklin, *Yankee Leviathan: The Origins of Central State Authority in America, 1859–1877*, Cambridge and New York: Cambridge University Press, 1990

Bogue, Allan G., *The Earnest Men: Republicans of the Civil War Senate*, Ithaca, NY: Cornell University Press, 1981

Curry, Leonard P., *Blueprint for Modern America: Non-Military Legislation of the First Civil War Congress*, Nashville: Vanderbilt University Press, 1968

Paludan, Phillip S., *"A People's Contest": The Union and Civil War, 1861–1865*, New York: Harper, 1988

Silbey, Joel H., *A Respectable Minority: The Democratic Party in the Civil War Era, 1860–1868*, New York: Norton, 1977

Zornow, William Frank, *Lincoln and the Party Divided*, Norman: University of Oklahoma Press, 1954

Like the general study of American politics, interpretations of Civil War politics have moved beyond the chronicles of who won and who lost elections to engage matters of political culture and public administration. ZORNOW is a study of the divisions within the Republican party that culminated in the competition for that party's nomination in 1864. It is a worthy example of the leader-focused, episode-laden traditional approach to wartime politics. Zornow concludes that Lincoln was not only responsible for winning the war on the battlefield. The 16th president also held the Republican party together despite its factionalism, fought off competitors for its leadership, and ultimately won reelection.

CURRY also uses traditional methodology to investigate the evolution of legislation in the crucial 37th Congress. Covering slavery, private property, public lands, taxation, and internal improvements (especially the controversy over subsidies to the Pacific Railroad), Curry focuses, from committee to final vote, on bills which created "a blueprint for modern America."

Writing with a nod to the present, Curry reaches the controversial conclusion that in the process of passing legislation of enduring social significance, Congress established dominance over both judiciary and executive. A less effective politician than Zornow's Lincoln, the president, according to Curry, allowed his executive prerogatives to be absorbed by Congress.

In an excellent example of the new quantitative political history, BOGUE analyzes the Republicans in the Civil War Senate, and probes the nature of a term casually attached to the wartime Republicans – "radicalism." First examining the personal and partisan backgrounds of these "earnest men," Bogue uses senatorial votes as benchmarks for ideological positions. Through roll-call analysis and scaling, he creates a voting spectrum extending from the moderates to the radicals. Not surprisingly, a senator's perception of race and constitution determined his policy preference in the Civil War senates.

Taking a different approach to northern Civil War politics, but also using sophisticated quantitative procedures, BAUM uses Massachusetts as a case study. He views wartime politics in Massachusetts as part of a system of party competition, not just a series of public episodes occurring from 1861 to 1865. Employing regression analysis and the decomposition of variance method for comparing electoral change, the author follows state voting patterns from 1848 to 1876 with data that show changes and continuities over time. Unlike older interpretations, Baum, along with Baker, Silbey, and Bensel, sees Civil War politics as part of a longitudinal process that neither begins nor ends with the war. Also unlike other historians, Baum downplays the importance of nativists in the Republican party.

While in the past historians concentrated on the majority Republicans, recently the Democrats have attracted scholarly attention. SILBEY covers the minority party as they searched for a role during the Civil War. Using statistical measures of competition and state electoral percentages, Silbey offers a comprehensive view of a loyal opposition which, after nearly disappearing in the early days of the war, revived in the 1862 congressional elections. Silbey divides party members into purists and legitimists, and is less interested in evaluating their loyalty than in viewing the Democrats as a political organization.

BAKER also concentrates on the Democrats, and, like Baum and Silbey, she sees that party as part of a political system. Baker uses the Democrats as a means to investigate public life in the United States, not from the perspective of elections and voting patterns, but from the point of view of political education, thought and behavior. She uses culture and party ritual as a means of probing their wartime views. During the Civil War, according to Baker, Democrats revived certain views of republicanism and based their opposition to change in the status of black slaves on an intense racism and "conservative naturalism."

BENSEL has written a comparative study of the Union and Confederate governments during the Civil War that is grounded in modernization and state administration theory. His focus is on the wartime transformation of a weak antebellum state apparatus that in the process of confronting Southern secession sought state-centered solutions. As the Republicans became the major agent of economic and political development, the party fostered the formation of national markets for commercial activity. Bensel contends that, by means of a national debt created by the war, the state shaped a dependency by financiers and capitalists on the central government.

PALUDAN includes literature, the economy and military events in his coverage of the North during the Civil War. Four chapters deal exclusively with wartime politics as do parts of others. Paludan provides a synthesis of recent scholarship, emphasizing the importance of the survival of the North's competitive politics along with the congressional achievement of "a second American system."

JEAN H. BAKER

2) Home Front

Bernstein, Iver, *The New York City Draft Riots: Their Significance for American Society and Politics in the Age of the Civil War*, New York: Oxford University Press, 1990

Gallman, J. Matthew, *Mastering Wartime: A Social History of Philadelphia During the Civil War*, Cambridge and New York: Cambridge University Press, 1990

Gallman, J. Matthew, *The North Fights the Civil War: The Home Front*, Chicago: Dee, 1994

Geary, James W., *We Need Men: The Union Draft in the Civil War*, DeKalb: Northern Illinois University Press, 1991

McKay, Ernest A., *The Civil War and New York City*, Syracuse, NY: Syracuse University Press, 1990

Paludan, Phillip S., *"A People's Contest": The Union and Civil War, 1861–1865*, New York: Harper, 1988

Venet, Wendy H., *Neither Ballots nor Bullets: Women Abolitionists and the Civil War*, Charlottesville: University Press of Virginia, 1991

Vinovskis, Maris A. (editor), *Toward a Social History of the American Civil War: Exploratory Essays*, Cambridge and New York: Cambridge University Press, 1990

Until recently, the Northern home front remained one of the few relatively unexplored areas in the historiography of the American Civil War. This situation has changed considerably, and the heightened interest in the subject is epitomized by the publication in 1988 of PALUDAN, which, the author notes, is the first comprehensive treatment of the war's impact on Northern society since 1910. Paludan examines Northerners' motives for fighting; the internal conflicts they faced; and the changes which the war wrought in their society. These themes singly or together are at the core of all subsequent histories of the Northern home front. Paludan finds that fighting the war impelled Northerners towards the collective discovery of a profound – if not always well articulated – purpose for defending the Union that centered upon a millennial vision of the United States as the fulfilment of God's promise of liberty to themselves, their communities, and all humankind. The wartime experience transformed the relationship of northern Americans to their government, which expanded its role in their lives by introducing new financial systems, expanding its powers of taxation, supporting innovations in higher education, and providing for transcontinental transportation.

Both of Gallman's works address the question of whether or not the Civil War effected significant political, economic, and social changes in the North. In contrast to other studies, he finds that both in Philadelphia (GALLMAN, 1990) and in the region as a whole (GALLMAN, 1994), continuity rather than change characterized the war's impact on Northern society. He does acknowledge that the conflict established precedents for the future expansion of federal authority, especially in the areas of civil rights and taxation. He also concludes, however, that the war brought few permanent changes in economic development, women's roles in society, and race relations. Northerners fought not in order to promote change but to defend established principles of local democracy and individual freedom, which they had personally experienced in both small and large communities throughout the region. The outcome of the conflict therefore fulfilled the expectations of Northerners who fought the war for conservative ends, above all for the preservation of the Union.

McKAY finds that New Yorkers interpreted the war differently from most other Northerners. Overpopulation, class friction, ethnic and racial tensions, poverty, and other urban problems combined in New York City to create ideological conflicts largely non-existent elsewhere. Like most other Northerners, the majority of New Yorkers remained committed to the Union, but many also exhibited an uncharacteristic sympathy for Southern grievances as well as a deep fear of war. Devout Unionists and unrepentant Copperheads constantly struggled to win the political support of the bulk of New Yorkers whose loyalties seemed to shift with every Union victory or defeat. The city's inability to reconcile its multitude of internal conflicts contributed to the intensity of the July 1863 riots sparked by Federal conscription.

Although racism or public opposition to conscription are typically cited as causes for New York's draft riots, BERNSTEIN believes that there is another explanation for the violence that struck the city. He argues that the riots must be viewed as part of two decades of resistance by New York's working classes, that originated in the early 1850s, against efforts to usurp their economic and political autonomy by elitist reformers and Republicans. The riots served their participants as a communal challenge to an increasingly intrusive federal government controlled by their enemies. The inevitable association of the riots with treason after the war prevented them from becoming part of workers' heritage which later generations of laborers might have used to resist further encroachments on their independence.

GEARY challenges the idea that conscription inaugurated in 1863 intensified class conflict in the North. He notes that the initial $300 commutation fee, traditionally viewed as unfair to poor workers, did not discriminate against them and favor the wealthy. Instead, it prevented substitutes from charging higher free market prices for their services and allowed most workers who wanted to escape the draft to do so through their own resources, community contributions, loans, and insurance pools. The end of commutation the following year resulted in both a commensurate increase in the price and decrease in the availability of men willing to work as substitutes. This effectively raised the proportion of professionals, property owners, and white-collar workers brought into the army. Geary argues that although relatively few men were actually conscripted, the draft succeeded because the bounties offered in its wake encouraged significant numbers of men to enlist. Conscription also strengthened federal authority over the states, and thus contributed to Northerners' psychological transition from localism to nationalism.

The efforts of female abolitionists on behalf of African Americans during the war are discussed in VENET, who sees the conflict as a watershed for modern feminism. Many feminists worked for emancipation because they believed that the abolition of slavery would also lead to suffrage for women. These women used what were for them innovative tactics, such as public speaking, petition drives, and lobbying politicians, to advance abolition. Their experiences provided feminists with the organizational and oratorical skills that enabled them to promote suffrage vigorously in the public sphere over the decades that followed the war.

In a collection of essays by various authors, VINOVSKIS addresses the social history of the North during the Civil War. The editor's "Have Social Historians Lost the Civil War? Some Preliminary Demographic Speculations" observes that the war's military history is extremely well studied but that historians know very little about the everyday lives of Northerners. Thomas R. Kemp provides some insights on this subject in "Community and War: The Civil War Experience of Two New Hampshire Towns." Reid Mitchell's "The Northern Soldier and His Community" chronicles the divergence of convictions that developed between the men who fought the war and the communities that sent them. J. Matthew Gallman's "Voluntarism in Wartime: Philadelphia's Great Central Fair" and Robin L. Einhorn's "The Civil War and Municipal Government in Chicago" investigate public life in those urban environments. Stuart McConnell and Amy E. Holmes contribute essays on the aftermath of war, dealing respectively with veterans' organizations and widows' pensions.

DAN R. FROST

Civil War: The South *see* Confederate States of America

Clark, George Rogers   1752–1818
Military leader in War of Independence

Bakeless, John Edwin, *Background to Glory: The Life of George Rogers Clark*, Philadelphia: Lippincott, 1957

Barnhart, John D., *Henry Hamilton and George Rogers Clark in the American Revolution*, Crawsfordville, IN: Banta, 1951

Bodley, Temple, *George Rogers Clark: His Life and Public Services*, Boston: Houghton Mifflin, 1926

English, William Hayden, *Conquest of the Country Northwest of the River Ohio, 1778–1783, and Life of Gen. George Rogers Clark*, 2 vols., Indianapolis: Bowen Merrill, 1896

Harrison, Lowell H., *George Rogers Clark and the War in the West*, Lexington: University Press of Kentucky, 1976

Havighurst, Walter, *George Rogers Clark: Soldier in the West*, New York: McGraw Hill, 1952

James, James Alton, *The Life of George Rogers Clark*, Chicago: University of Chicago Press, 1928

Thwaites, Reuben Gold, *How George Rogers Clark Won the Northwest and Other Essays in Western History*, Chicago: McClurg, 1931

Waller, George Macgregor, *The American Revolution in the West*, Chicago: Nelson Hall, 1976

George Rogers Clark's reputation is based largely upon his activities in Kentucky and the Old Northwest during the years of the American Revolution. The war in the West was fought on a small scale when compared to the conflict along the eastern seaboard, but it was a war of survival for the settlers who had ventured across the mountains. More than any other man, Clark saved Kentucky by taking the war to the British and their Indian allies north of the Ohio River. He became a legendary figure, especially to those living in the West, but, despite his heroic stature, no biography appeared until near the end of the 19th century. Clark's declining years after his 1778–79 expedition dimmed the lustre of his reputation, and for various reasons several would-be biographers never wrote their intended work. Leonard Bliss, a New Englander who had moved to Louisville, had written a chapter before he was killed in 1842 because of some antislavery remarks. Lyman C. Draper was fascinated by Clark, but Draper was such an avid collector of data that he died before completing the biographies of his two frontier heroes, Clark and Daniel Boone. The Clark Papers are the largest segment of the Draper Manuscript Collection in the State Historical Society of Wisconsin. All scholarly studies of Clark have depended heavily upon this collection.

ENGLISH, the first reasonably complete biography, was based on considerable research, and it included a number of documents, such as Clark's two personal accounts of his expedition, that were not easily found elsewhere. It was too sympathetic to its subject, and Clark was sometimes credited with greater success than he deserved. Written in an old-fashioned style, this study seems outdated now. Two major biographies appeared in the 1920s. BODLEY was a full-scale study based upon extensive research, including the Draper Collection. It devoted more attention than its predecessor to Clark's career before and after the 1778–79 campaign. Convinced that Clark had been maligned and neglected, Bodley wrote to rehabilitate Clark's reputation. JAMES, published three years later, was a more objective study that is still the best biography of its subject. He had edited the two volumes of Clark's papers, and he was knowledgeable on all aspects of Clark's career. While he praised Clark's Revolutionary accomplishments, he was critical of Clark's alcoholism and his acceptance of a French commission in the 1790s for an attack on Spanish possessions in the lower Mississippi Valley. THWAITES was a useful essay on the campaign in the Northwest, but it gave Clark too much credit for the American acquisition of the Old Northwest in the peace treaty.

Interest in Clark continued into the 1950s. BARNHART added a new dimension to the story by including the journal of Henry Hamilton, Clark's British opponent in the Northwest. Barnhart was more critical of Clark than were the authors of earlier studies. HAVIGHURST, a well-written biography, added little to what had already been written about Clark, and it exaggerated his role in obtaining the Old Northwest for the United States. It contained little information on Clark after about 1785. BAKELESS was the best of the new studies. Well-researched and well-written, it used a number of foreign sources from Great Britain, France and Spain. Bakeless identified too closely with his subject when he asserted that but for Clark much of the United States in the 20th century would be quite different from what it is.

The bicentennial of the American Revolution sparked another revival of interest in Clark. HARRISON praised Clark, but warned that his exploits should not be exaggerated. He also defended Clark against the charges of some Kentucky leaders that he neglected the stations in central Kentucky by pointing out that Clark was also responsible for protecting the French settlements in Illinois. WALLER contended that Clark was "a major figure in the Revolution as a whole" and compared him favorably with George Washington. Both studies concentrated on the war years in the West which the authors believed had been neglected in general histories of the war. Clark deserves a new full-length study that would use the insights drawn from the new approaches to the history of the frontier, and the relationship between the new westerners and the Indians whom they encountered.

LOWELL H. HARRISON

See also War of Independence: Military History

Clark, William *see* Lewis, Meriwether and William Clark

Class

Abernethy, Thomas Perkins, *Three Virginia Frontiers*, Baton Rouge: Louisiana State University Press, 1940

Bailey, Fred Arthur, *Class and Tennessee's Confederate Generation*, Chapel Hill: University of North Carolina Press, 1987

Baltzell, E. Digby, *The Protestant Establishment: Aristocracy and Caste in America*, New York: Random House, 1964; London: Secker and Warburg, 1965

Bloom, Jack M., *Class, Race, and the Civil Rights Movement*, Bloomington: Indiana University Press, 1987

Cecil-Fronsman, Bill, *Common Whites: Class and Culture in Antebellum North Carolina*, Lexington: University Press of Kentucky, 1992

Escott, Paul D., *After Secession: Jefferson Davis and the Failure of Confederate Nationalism*, Baton Rouge: Louisiana State University Press, 1978

Foner, Philip S., *Labor and the American Revolution*, Westport, CT: Greenwood Press, 1976

Hahn, Steven, *The Roots of Southern Populism: Yeoman Farmers and the Transformation of the Georgia Upcountry, 1850–1890*, New York: Oxford University Press, 1983

Jameson, J. Franklin, *The American Revolution Considered as a Social Movement*, Princeton: Princeton University Press, 1926

Lipsitz, George, *Rainbow at Midnight: Labor and Culture in the 1940s*, Urbana: University of Illinois Press, 1994

McMath, Robert C., Jr., *American Populism: A Social History, 1877–1898*, New York: Hill and Wang, 1993

Main, Jackson Turner, *The Social Structure of Revolutionary America*, Princeton: Princeton University Press, 1965

Owsley, Frank Lawrence, *Plain Folk of the Old South*, Baton Rouge: Louisiana State University Pres, 1949

Pessen, Edward, *Riches, Class, and Power Before the Civil War*, Lexington, MA: Heath, 1973

Shugg, Roger W., *Origins of Class Struggle in Louisiana: A Social History of White Farmers and Laborers During Slavery and after, 1840–1875*, Baton Rouge: Louisiana State University Press, 1939

Sydnor, Charles S., *Gentlemen Freeholders: Political Practices in Washington's Virginia*, Chapel Hill: University of North Carolina Press, 1952; as *American Revolutionaries in the Making: Political Practices in Washington's Virginia*, New York: Macmillan, 1962

Turner, Frederick Jackson, *The Frontier in American History*, New York: Holt, 1920

Wade, Richard C., *The Urban Frontier: Pioneer Life in Early Pittsburgh, Cincinnati, Lexington, Louisville, and St. Louis*, Chicago: University of Chicago Press, 1959

Zinn, Howard, *A People's History of the United States*, New York: Harper, and London: Longman, 1980

The theme of class, class consciousness, and class conflict has been a controversial topic among 20th century American scholars. One school, the consensus historians, argues that American egalitarian ideology, prosperity, and social mobility militate against class consciousness. They see broad themes in American culture that have produced a largely seamless society unified by a faith in a capitalistic ideal which offers to the hard-working masses comfort and to the ambitious few wealth, and in a political and social system which is expansive enough to encompass all religions, races, and nationalities. Conflict historians, however, point to class consciousness as a major stress factor in the evolution of American society. Along with ethnic and gender frictions, it has seasoned the American experience with an emphasis on struggle, as clearly identifiable groups contested for their fair share of the national weal.

Conflict historians seldom produce volumes dedicated to the entire scope of American history, preferring instead to focus on specific epochs which lend themselves to a discussion of class interaction. ZINN is a rare exception. A shipyard worker and labor organizer before he turned to academe, he brings to his craft a working-class viewpoint not shared by consensus scholars. From Columbus to the collapse of Richard Nixon, Zinn explores the American panorama from the perspective of the underside. His version of American history is the repeated story of Native Americans, indentured servants, African slaves, exploited laborers, disenchanted farmers, and others struggling against an entrenched aristocracy grounded upon the pillars of wealth, education, and social connections.

Sydnor, Jameson, Foner and Main constitute a sampling of works explicating class themes during the American Revolutionary era. Not to be counted among conflict historians, SYDNOR is a defender of aristocratic virtue. Noting that 18th-century Virginia produced such stellar leaders as George Washington, Thomas Jefferson, James Madison, and many others, he argues that a clearly defined upper class possessed the ability to place the most qualified people into positions of authority and influence. Well-written and easy to read, his work describes how Virginia's first families maintained their closed society of wealth, education, and family connections, how they dominated most of the local offices, and how they limited democracy's influence to insure that only the "best people" moved up to positions of political and military influence during and after the Revolution.

First given as a series of four lectures in 1925, JAMESON is an early contribution to the theme of class struggle during the Revolutionary era. More than a war for independence from England, Jameson saw the events from 1775 to 1783 as a crusade of the less privileged – small farmers, laborers, debtors – to democratize a society long dominated by a colonial aristocracy of merchants, planters, and government officials. He postulated that "the relations of social classes to each other, the institution of slavery, the system of land-holding, the course of business, the forms and spirit of the intellectual and religious life, all felt the transforming hand of revolution." To him the strength of the Revolution "lay most largely in the plain people" who pushed for social changes "in the direction of levelling democracy." FONER's examination of urban workers during the American Revolution is a classic example of writing history from the bottom up. In the events leading to the conflict, he theorizes that while "all classes in America suffered from British policies and practices, . . . the artisans, mechanics, seamen, and day laborers suffered most intently." According to Foner, laboring Americans led the fight to secure home rule, but lost out in the contest over who should rule at home. The Revolution, he explains, "accelerated the trend toward the consolidation of wealth and a deterioration of the condition of the lower classes." Nonetheless, workers emerged from years of conflict "with a greater class consciousness and a greater ability to voice their grievances." This Foner sees as the genesis of the American labor movement.

MAIN selected the period from 1763 to 1788 to make a thorough analysis of the meaning and importance of class in early American society. While conditions varied extensively from the North to the South and between rural and urban neighborhoods, he essentially concludes that the United States possessed an "economic class structure which can be identified and described." At bottom was a dependent mass owning no land and little personal property; above these was a class of small independent property holders (the largest element of the population) who lived on a social equality with urban artisans and shop keepers; and ensconced at the top were large landholders and affluent merchants who constituted only one-seventh of the population but who held just under half the total wealth. In spite of this glaring economic inequality and an ever increasing number of poor, Main concludes that the potential for social mobility, especially along the frontier, muted class consciousness.

Historians of the American frontier have long debated the role of class in the westward movement. Published in 1920, TURNER is a collection of his principal essays, the most important of which is "The Significance of the Frontier in American History." First presented as a paper before the American Historical Association in 1893, it postulates ideas that to this day divide scholars into pro- and anti-Turnerians. In it, he argues that, while the more settled eastern regions fostered an aristocratic establishment, the wilder frontier domain mandated social leveling. Thus the frontier – "the meeting point between savagery and civilization" – created the uniquely American institutions of democracy. There, the basic struggle for survival made irrelevant social distinctions based upon education and ancestry and instead created a spirit of egalitarianism that held individual worth as its highest virtue.

A Turner student at Harvard, ABERNETHY inverts his mentor's essential themes, proclaiming that aristocracy and not democracy dominated the frontier. The scion of southern patricians, Abernethy shared with Sydnor an admiration for elite rule. As he traced the westward movement of Virginia culture from the Tidewater to the Piedmont to the Kentucky country, he notes that government policies favored aristocratic interests, and offered them a congenial land distribution policy. As men of wealth, political influence, and entrepreneurial courage, eastern planters not only possessed the mettle necessary to conquer the frontier, but also had the strength to protect their class interest against the uneducated and uncouth masses who demanded a more democratic society.

WADE traces the evolution of social life in the principal frontier cities of Pittsburgh, Cincinnati, Lexington, Louisville, and St. Louis. To a great extent, he explains, democracy and social leveling characterized the culture of each city's initial settlers. However, a stratification developed as these communities matured, "lines sharpened, class divisions deepened, and the sense of neighborliness and intimacy weakened." Some social mobility existed between the merchants and the vast underclass, but the rungs of the class ladder gradually grew further and further apart.

Although the "Age of Jackson" (essentially the decade of the 1830s) is popularly associated with common-man democracy, PESSEN concludes from his study of upper-class families in Boston, New York, Brooklyn, and Philadelphia that reform hardly threatened the status of these elites. Examining both the quantifiable data base of tax and census records and contemporary literary sources, he concludes that wealth remained concentrated into a few hands, that urban elites married within their own class, and that in spite of "democratic reforms" they easily retained their control over local governments.

More than any other section of the United States, the American South lends itself to a class analysis. Acknowledging the obvious existence of a sharply articulated society, consensus historians nonetheless assert that conflict between the classes rarely existed. A classic work published in 1949, OWSLEY succinctly articulates this view. In his South, there were important forces that diminished the feeling of class stratification and helped in the creation of a sense of unity between the common people and the aristocracy. From the wealthy to the impoverished, southerners resided in the same neighborhoods, worshipped at the same churches, and studied at the same schools. Through such associations the "rich and poor" developed "frequent ties of blood kinship" and any jealousy over differences in wealth was moderated by "the generally folkish and democratic bearing of the aristocracy."

A contemporary of Owsley, SHUGG strongly disagreed with his interpretation. He argues that in Louisiana wealthy planters dominated every aspect of the state's social, economic, and political life. Antebellum Louisiana was, he wrote, "a slave state policed by gentlemen; and the masses, having no real voice in government, received from it no benefit." Discontent arising from the pre-Civil War class struggles fueled the agrarian protests of the 1880s and the Populist Party crusade of the 1890s.

Bailey, Cecil-Fronsman, Escott and Hahn are among recent works that more closely agree with Shugg's interpretation of the southern class structure. An analysis of more than 1,200 biographical questionnaires filled out by Tennessee's Confederate veterans between 1915 and 1923, BAILEY not only delineates significant class differences in the old soldiers' housing, working environments, educational opportunities, etc., but he also reports strong expressions of class consciousness and class discontent among the impoverished, the small farmers, and the planters. In his examination of common whites in antebellum North Carolina, CECIL-FRONSMAN contends that while "class conflict was a regular feature of antebellum North Carolina life," prior to the Civil War there was at this time only "an undeveloped form of class consciousness." Essentially, common whites formed their own cultural attachments built around songs, stories, and other traditions that gave meaning to their lives. Focusing on the Confederate era, ESCOTT argues that a "quiet rebellion of the common people" is a major factor leading to the South's defeat. Impoverished by the exactions of war, the region's common folk "encountered such indifference to their plight among the wealthy, [that] they felt frustration and anger." Throughout the war, he writes, "the conditions of life for the common people deteriorated, and at the same time class resentments sapped the loyalty of non-slaveholding soldiers and civilians". HAHN demonstrates that in Georgia class discontent, born prior to the Civil War, grew with the resurgence of aristocratic power following Confederate defeat, and led directly to the small farmers' support for the Populist crusade to overthrow the South's aristocratic leaders.

The Populist movement of the 1890s may be depicted as one more chapter in the class struggle in American history. McMATH argues that the Populists represented a discontented class of producers (small farmers) who identified the railroads and banks of the Midwest and the merchants and large landholders of the South as their oppressors. Small farmers – black and white – allied in a campaign to overthrow the elites that had long dominated in the South and to regulate railroads and banks which threatened their economic survival.

BLOOM chronicles the southern aristocrats' successful employment of anti-Negro rhetoric to break up the Populist alliance of white and black small farmers. To prevent any future alliance of under-class whites and southern blacks, patrician-dominated state governments passed laws segregating the races, and enacted legislation disenfranchising the vast majority of blacks and significant numbers of whites. Protected in their class status, aristocratic whites would dominate southern society until again challenged during the civil rights campaigns of the 1950s and 1960s.

Two works illustrate the continuing importance of class as a seminal element of American society. LIPSITZ explores variations on the theme of class consciousness as it relates to the labor movement in the 1940s. In addition to labor strikes and political protests, he finds significant expressions of working-class consciousness in movie scripts and song lyrics. BALTZELL sketches the existence of a white, Anglo-Saxon, Protestant establishment, which, isolated in its country clubs and elite colleges, tries to maintain a caste system keeping Catholics, Jews, and African Americans out of seats of power. Writing shortly after the assassination of John F. Kennedy, he hoped that the election of a Catholic president would breach the wall of class.

FRED ARTHUR BAILEY

See also Equality; Middle Classes; Social Mobility; Wealth; Working Classes

Clay, Henry   1777–1852
Politcal leader, orator and presidential candidate

Baxter, Maurice G., *Henry Clay and the American System*, Lexington: University Press of Kentucky, 1995

Brown, Thomas, *Politics and Statesmanship: Essays on the American Whig Party*, New York: Columbia University Press, 1985

Colton, Calvin, *The Life, Correspondence, and Speeches of Henry Clay*, 6 vols., New York: Barnes, 1857

Howe, Daniel Walker, *The Political Culture of the American Whigs*, Chicago: University of Chicago Press, 1979

Peterson, Merrill D., *The Great Triumvirate: Webster, Clay, and Calhoun*, New York: Oxford University Press, 1987

Poage, George Rawlings, *Henry Clay and the Whig Party*, Chapel Hill: University of North Carolina Press, 1936

Remini, Robert V., *Henry Clay: Statesman for the Union*, New York: Norton, 1991

Schurz, Carl, *Life of Henry Clay*, 2 vols., Boston: Houghton Mifflin, 1887

Van Deusen, Glyndon G., *The Life of Henry Clay*, Boston: Little Brown, 1937

Henry Clay's contribution to American political history rests on his half-century career of leadership in public life, his numerous but unsuccessful efforts to gain the presidency, his formulation of a sweeping plan for economic development known as the "American System", his leadership of the Whig party, and his authorship of three great "Compromises" which brought temporary abatements of the disputes between slave-holding and non-slaveholding states in the decades before the Civil War. His role as the "Great Pacificator" in these disputes underlies his reputation as a statesman devoted to the Union. Clay is also famous for his brilliant oratory, his magnetic personality, the devoted admiration of his followers, and the bitter animosity of his enemies. In the words of one eulogist, he was one of America's "most eminent citizens and statesmen and . . . its greatest genius", but Andrew Jackson condemned him as "the bases[t], meanest, scoundrel, that ever disgraced the image of his god [*sic*]". For the most part, Clay's biographers have been more temperate in their praise and their criticism, but all have struggled with the diversity of talents, accomplishments, and personality traits that made Henry Clay one of the more complex characters in antebellum politics.

Clay's place in historiography began to take shape in the works of campaign biographers and journalists. Of these, COLTON was the most prominent and influential, producing large collections of letters and speeches as well as a laudatory "Life and Times" while Clay was yet alive. He completed these materials in a final six-volume edition of 1857, which long remained the standard compilation of Clay sources. At the end of the 19th century, SCHURZ drew on these volumes to compose a balanced and judicious biography that grappled seriously with Clay's fierce ambition and rash impulses, and above all, with the moral ambiguity of his fabled compromises.

Clay was a slaveholder himself who professed to deplore slavery and served for many years as the president of the American Colonization Society. As a centrist on the slavery issue, Clay seized the opportunity to propose sectional compromises when the question of slavery threatened to split the union. In 1820, Missouri applied for admission as a slave state, arousing the opposition of northeastern representatives who objected to the endless expansion of an infamous institution and a perpetuation of the slaveholders' political advantages under the Constitution's "three-fifths compromise". Twelve years later, South Carolina "nullified" the federal tariff and prepared to go to war to defend its plantation economy from the burden of a protective tariff. Finally, in 1850, southern states threatened secession unless they were given full opportunity to extend the system of slavery to the territories conquered from Mexico, while northern representatives insisted on the principles of free soil embodied in the Wilmot Proviso. In all three cases, Clay devised compromises that preserved the union by making partial concessions to the slaveholders' demands, without resolving the fundamental issues of the debate.

A Republican political leader who took great pride in his party's emancipationist record, Schurz agonized over the morality of Clay's evasive policies, but concluded that his measures had bought time while the antislavery forces had gained strength and maturity. A generation later, revisionists had softened the prevailing view of slavery and blamed the bloodshed of the Civil War on the stubborn refusal of sectional hot-heads to compromise their differences. In this environment, VAN DEUSEN gave Clay a much more enthusiastic appraisal. While admitting Clay's impetuosity and lapses of judgement, Van Deusen gave the Kentuckian high marks for vision, patriotism, and conservative instincts. In the same decade POAGE's monograph examined a less flexible Clay, paying special attention to his role as an intransigent party leader who fought to impose a Whig economic platform over the opposition of President John Tyler, whom he regarded as an apostate.

A pair of essays in the 1970s took a fresh look at Clay as part of a growing interest in political culture and ideology. HOWE paid serious attention to Clay's advocacy of tariffs, internal improvements, distribution, and colonization and gave him credit for "a vision of America as economically diverse, commercially powerful, and politically integrated". Properly locating Clay in the company of his fellow Whigs, Howe and BROWN praised the party as the champion of a Victorian sense of decency and ordered self-improvement that compared favourably to the violence and the cult of liberty that verged on license which their Democratic opponents exemplified. For these authors, Clay's love of compromise was not a matter of equivocation or opportunism, but an honourable principle which recognized the great and enduring interests of the nation as morally superior to the Democrats' reliance on fickle public opinion in the construction of public policy. In their view, Clay believed in the fundamental harmony of diverse interests in society and strove to establish that harmony within a structure of balanced order and gradual adjustments.

Three important biographical studies have followed Howe's and Brown's analyses of Clay's role as a defender of compromise. PETERSON followed his lengthy life of Jefferson with a consideration of three leaders, Webster, Clay, and Calhoun, who dominated national affairs in the generation after Jefferson's death. He concludes with sadness at their collective failure to silence the Founding Fathers' famous "firebell in the night". REMINI followed his own massive life of Jackson, Clay's greatest adversary, with a biography which was inspired by personal affection and by the desire for a more rounded knowledge of the period. His work succeeds in capturing Clay's sparkling wit and personality, and explaining the details of Clay's life and programme. BAXTER neglects almost all personal details for a careful explication of Clay's economic programme. His work is very valuable for its analysis of Clay's contribution to the political economy of development in antebellum America. Future studies of Clay will all be indebted to the generous selection of papers and correspondence which has now been completed by the University Press of Kentucky.

HARRY L. WATSON

See also Jacksonian Era

Cold War, Origins of

Alperovitz, Gar, *Atomic Diplomacy: Hiroshima and Potsdam: The Use of the Atomic Bomb and the American Confrontation with Soviet Power*, New York: Simon and Schuster, 1965, London: Secker and Warburg, 1966; revised, New York and Harmondsworth: Penguin, 1985; 2nd revision, London: Pluto, 1994

Gaddis, John Lewis, *The United States and the Origins of the Cold War, 1941–1947*, New York: Columbia University Press, 1972

Harbutt, Fraser J., *The Iron Curtain: Churchill, America, and the Origins of the Cold War*, New York and Oxford: Oxford University Press, 1986

Isaacson, Walter and Evan Thomas, *The Wise Men: Six Friends and the World They Made: Acheson, Bohlen, Harriman, Kennan, Lovett, McCloy*, New York: Simon and Schuster, and London: Faber, 1986

Leffler, Melvyn P., *A Preponderance of Power: National Security, the Truman Administration, and the Cold War*, Stanford, CA: Stanford University Press, 1992

Reynolds, David (editor), *The Origins of the Cold War in Europe: International Perspectives*, New Haven and London: Yale University Press, 1994

Spanier, John W., *American Foreign Policy since World War II*, New York: Praeger, 1960, 8th edition, New York: Holt Rinehart, 1980

Williams, William Appleman, *The Tragedy of American Diplomacy*, Cleveland: World, 1959; revised, New York: Dell, 1972

Until the mid-1960s, scholarship on the origins of the Cold War was dominated by the orthodox or traditional school. As with the majority of Americans who lived through the late 1940s, these historians argued that Soviet expansionism, particularly in Eastern Europe, was the root cause of the Cold War, and that the development of the containment policy by President Harry Truman and his advisers was a necessary response. Representative of this viewpoint is SPANIER. Traditional Russian goals and Marxist-Leninist ideology combined, Spanier argued, to generate an aggressive Soviet foreign policy that threatened the international balance of power. Truman, although no Franklin Roosevelt, was to be commended for responding vigorously to that challenge.

The first challenge to this approach came from WILLIAMS. More a polemic than a weighty piece of scholarship, this work has exerted more influence on the entire field of United States foreign relations than anything written since. In his treatment of the coming of the Cold War, Williams argues that Soviet leader Joseph Stalin, in taking control of Eastern Europe, was doing no more than implementing the "percentage" agreement that he had made with Winston Churchill in the autumn of 1944. Instead of focusing on Soviet aggression, Williams concentrates on American economic expansion. American foreign policy under Truman and Roosevelt (and other presidents) had been aimed primarily at extending the overseas markets for American trade. Hence, Washington did not accept Soviet policy in Eastern Europe simply because it reduced the number of potential markets for commercial penetration. The United States, moreover, could have used its vast resources to help the Soviet Union regenerate its war-shattered economy, but failed to do so.

Two factors ensured that historians would develop the arguments made by Williams. The first was that he had trained a group of talented young scholars who would go on to write important works. The second was the general change in climate during the 1960s. As Americans began to question various aspects of their own society (such as the status of blacks) and their government's policies abroad (especially in Vietnam), so historians began to adopt a more critical approach to the role played by the United States in the coming of the Cold War. The result was the birth of the revisionist school, a group of scholars who regarded the United States as more responsible than the Soviet Union for the Cold War.

The most provocative of these revisionist studies is ALPEROVITZ. The official explanation that Truman dropped atomic bombs to save American lives that would be lost in an invasion of Japan was a fallacy, according to Alperovitz. Instead, the decision was influenced by anti-Soviet considerations, namely a desire to end the war before Stalin took control of Manchuria. The Truman administration also hoped that the atomic bomb could be used as a diplomatic weapon to intimidate the Soviets into accepting American objectives in Central and Eastern Europe.

In the 1970s, revisionism was replaced by post-revisionism, which sought to provide a more balanced, eclectic interpretation. Responsibility for the Cold War was apportioned fairly equally (although the Soviet Union was typically blamed more than the United States), and the overall approach was more moderate and restrained. The classic work of this genre is GADDIS. Both superpowers, he argues, helped to bring about the Cold War, but the Soviet Union was the more culpable. Unlike American leaders, Stalin was not subject to the restraints imposed by a critical Congress, public opinion, and the press. The Soviet leader thus had a greater capacity than his American counterparts to take steps that would have generated goodwill between the emerging superpowers and perhaps have prevented the onset of the Cold War.

One of the most important trends in recent years has been a move away from a Washington-dominated view of the part played by the West to an interpretation that takes into account other powers, especially Britain. The most prominent of these works is HARBUTT. He argues that in the transformation of American policy from cooperation to confrontation with Moscow in early 1946, Britain, and especially Winston Churchill, played an influential role in convincing Truman of the need to counter Soviet ambitions. REYNOLDS presents a number of stimulating essays that, in addition to exploring the American role, examine how various European powers helped to shape, and were shaped by, the onset of the Cold War.

The most impressive recent study of American policy in this period is LEFFLER. In what is unquestionably the best-researched book on the subject, he succeeds in crafting an interpretation that, although clearly influenced by the thinking of previous generations of historians, is distinctive and sophisticated. "Fear" and "power," according to Leffler, were the key factors underpinning the Truman administration's foreign policy. American leaders were confident at the end of World War II that they possessed the economic and military strength, in short, the power, to maintain a stable world order. The fear that a sensible world balance of power would be disrupted was due not only to Soviet ambitions, but also the threats posed by such developments as the British decline and the indigenous popularity of communism in countries like France and Italy.

In addition to works which provide general coverage of the origins of the Cold War, there are a number of relevant biographical studies, of which the most stimulating is ISAACSON and THOMAS. Examining the lives of key American policymakers, such as George Kennan, Dean Acheson, and Averell Harriman, Isaacson and Thomas shed light on the social and intellectual values of the American Establishment figures who dominated United States foreign policy during these years. Perhaps rather uncritical in its evaluation of their ideas, this is none the less a richly detailed, eloquently written volume.

MARK J. WHITE

See also Foreign Policy since 1945 entries; World War II: United States and 5 & 6

Colonial History: General

Bailyn, Bernard, *The Peopling of British North America: An Introduction*, New York: Knopf, 1986

Bailyn, Bernard, *Voyagers to the West: A Passage in the Peopling of America on the Eve of the Revolution*, New York: Knopf, 1986; London: Tauris, 1987

Boorstin, Daniel J., *The Americans: The Colonial Experience*, New York: Random House, 1958; Harmondsworth: Penguin, 1965

Fischer, David Hackett, *Albion's Seed: Four British Folkways in America*, New York and Oxford: Oxford University Press, 1989

Greene, Jack P., *Pursuits of Happiness: The Social Development of Early Modern British Colonies and the Formation of American Culture*, Chapel Hill: University of North Carolina Press, 1988

Greene, Jack P., *The Intellectual Construction of America: Exceptionalism and Identity from 1492 to 1800*, Chapel Hill: University of North Carolina Press, 1993

Greene, Jack P. and J.R. Pole (editors), *Colonial British America: Essays in the New History of the Early Modern Era*, Baltimore: Johns Hopkins University Press, 1984

Hofstadter, Richard, *America at 1750: A Social Portrait*, New York: Knopf, 1971; London: Cape, 1972

Kammen, Michael G., *People of Paradox: An Inquiry Concerning the Origins of American Civilization*, New York: Knopf, 1972

Katz, Stanley N. (editor), *Colonial America: Essays in Politics and Social Development*, Boston: Little Brown, 1971; 3rd edition, with John M. Murrin, 1983; 4th edition, with Murrin and Douglas Greenberg, New York: McGraw Hill, 1993

McCusker, John J. and Russell R. Menard, *The Economy of British America, 1607–1789*, Chapel Hill: University of North Carolina Press, 1985; revised 1991

Meinig, D.W., *The Shaping of America: A Geographical Perspective on 500 Years of History*, volume 1: *Atlantic America, 1492–1800*, New Haven and London: Yale University Press, 1986

Nash, Gary B., *Red, White, and Black: The Peoples of Early America*, Englewood Cliffs, NJ: Prentice Hall, 1974, 3rd edition, 1991

Wells, Robert V., *The Population of the British Colonies in America Before 1776: A Survey of Census Data*, Princeton: Princeton University Press, 1975

A good place to begin a survey of general works on Colonial America is with BOORSTIN. This first volume of Boorstin's three-volume history of "The Americans," reflects the emphases of much of the historical scholarship produced between World War II and the early 1960s. Boorstin, like other historians of the so-called consensus school, saw in the colonial period the beginnings of American exceptionalism. The newness of the physical environment in which the immigrants found themselves unsettled Old World plans, made a virtue of accommodating the unexpected, and resulted in the development of a distinctively American set of institutions, viewpoints, and expectations. Having experienced on a personal level the disadvantages of Old World knowledge in New World circumstances, Boorstin's colonists quickly shed whatever reverence they may have held for philosophical dogma and outside authorities, dissolved European distinctions, and moved steadily toward a society of undifferentiated persons.

Recent interpreters of the colonial period have found much to criticize in Boorstin. His unsympathetic treatment of Quakers and Native Americans, in particular, has been supplanted by more balanced accounts. But essential parts of Boorstin's argument remain in place, albeit in modified form. GREENE (1993) examines the idea of American exceptionalism from the time of first contact to the establishment of the Revolutionary republic. Contrary to the assertions of some of its critics, Greene argues, the notion of American distinctiveness was not a creation of chauvinistic scholars intent on promoting national allegiance. Rather, contemporary testimony had established by the end of the 16th century the principal tenets of the concept of America as a special place. Even as visions of communal utopias faded, the pursuit of individual material betterment intensified. And for 18th-century British Americans, Greene notes, what is most remarkable about their experiences is how well they succeeded in realizing their dreams.

KAMMEN highlights the shortcomings of Boorstin's two main assumptions: that there was an identifiable and static "European" culture out of which the immigrants came; and that the American environment into which they arrived was so alien to them that they quickly abandoned Old World plans. Kammen accepts the idea, however, that there developed over the course of the 17th and 18th centuries a uniquely American "national style," a style rooted not in successive adaptations to the physical environment, but in a complex of factors related to the multi-dimensional pluralism of the immigrants themselves, and to their prolonged quest for personal and institutional legitimacy on the periphery of the British empire.

If historians have, as Kammen suggests, rejected the sort of simple environmental determinism encapsulated in Boorstin's description of the origins of the American character, they have by no means overlooked the significance of the physical setting in colonial history. MEINIG synthesizes most of the important work done by historical geographers over the past thirty years. His book is notable in at least three ways. First, Meinig reminds us that the colonial period cannot be described solely or even primarily in terms of discovery and the transfer of Europeans to American shores. Second, he manages to discuss the experiences not only of the thirteen colonies that became the United States but of the British island colonies, Canada, Louisiana, and Florida. Third, he offers a sensitive assessment of the geographical and cultural impact of ongoing contact among Europeans, Native Americans, and Africans in the New World.

Meinig's appreciation of the multiplicity of cultural and regional patterns in the "reshaping" of America, like Kammen's earlier rejection of the notion of a generalized European background for the immigrating populations, is a reflection of the manner in which the study of colonial America has been transformed since Boorstin's study first appeared. Impressed by the methods and insights of the French "Annales" school, colonial social historians began in the 1960s to produce detailed studies of small communities and everyday life. Two useful surveys that appeared in the early 1970s incorporated some of the initial findings of these historians. HOFSTADTER describes the social and demographic conditions that prevailed in mid-18th-century America. His discussion of the process of immigration and population growth in the 17th century and the development of a middle-class world in the 18th century is finely drawn. Hofstadter's portrayal of the conditions of servitude – white and black – although surpassed by more recent treatments, remains a good introduction to the subject of unfree labor in the colonial period.

Eager to shed any semblance of a Eurocentric bias in his survey of the peoples of early America, NASH demonstrates that Indians and slaves were active participants on the historical stage. The evolving patterns of Indian-European conflict and diplomacy, for example, were shaped by calculations of self-interest on the part of each group. Nash also effectively argues that the nature of European interaction with Native Americans and African Americans was more likely conditioned by local demographic characteristics than by religious persuasion, racial attitudes, or institutional inertia.

The advent and impact of the new social history movement can be followed in the successive editions of KATZ, arguably the best anthology for students of the period. From 1971 to 1993, the publication dates of the first and fourth editions of the book, innovative research on the colonial period made it, as Katz observed, the most dynamic field of American history. Katz's volume underwent successive transformations that mirrored changes affecting the field as a whole. The most notable alteration made by Katz, who was joined by MURRIN and later by GREENBERG, was to down-play political history. Eight of the 22 essays in the first edition deal with politics or aspects of the imperial relationship; only four of the 24 selections in the fourth edition do so. In place of politics, the editors chose to emphasize various aspects of social history. But because the field of social history itself was not static from 1971 to 1993, the selections continued to vary from edition to edition. Ten of the 22 essays in the second edition were new; 17 of the 25 in the third were new; and 14 of the 24 in the fourth were new. In 1971, much of the best work available in the new social history vein dealt with New England; consequently, Katz chose for his first edition essays on the demography of witchcraft in Salem, family structure in Andover, domestic life in Plymouth, town government in Dedham, cultural persistence in Hingham, and wealth distribution in Boston. Indeed, 13 of his 22 selections dealt exclusively with New England. By 1993, the focus of many social historians had shifted away from New England and been broadened to encompass a more diverse population. Eight essays in the fourth edition deal with Native Americans, African Americans, or women; only five of the 24 selections center on New England.

The very dynamism which distinguishes the field of colonial history and which inspired Katz to produce the first edition of his anthology makes it difficult for even the most avid readers to keep abreast of the literature. Fortunately, GREENE and POLE have edited a superb volume that sums up the state of our knowledge. Fourteen substantive essays, each written by an expert in the field, identify an array of social, economic, and political questions that have occupied the attention of early American historians since the 1960s. The essays provide excellent historiographical overviews, offer assessments of prevailing interpretations, and together suggest a framework for understanding the British-American world as a coherent whole.

The need for a unifying theme for the numerous and seemingly discordant regional and topical histories of the early modern period is the note that BAILYN sounded in his 1981 American Historical Association presidential address. His contribution to the quest for coherence is a sophisticated analysis of the processes involved in the British migration to and occupation of the lands of the New World. *The Peopling of British North America* is, as its subtitle indicates, an introductory essay on the nature and scope of the transatlantic migration. Most importantly, Bailyn argues that after the initial phase of colonization, two distinctive patterns of migration emerged. The first involved isolated young men from London and southern England who responded to the needs of the colonial labor market and arrived in the colonies as indentured servants. The second involved families from northern England and Scotland that were lured to America by the prospect of owning land. In *Voyagers to the West*, Bailyn develops this argument more fully. Based on an examination of more than nine thousand persons who left England between 1773 and 1776, he describes the composition of the dual migration in terms of the emigrants' geographic origins, recruitment, motivation, social backgrounds, occupations, conditions of transport, and destinations.

Bailyn's call for a general framework for the myriad of new social histories underscores an effort made a decade earlier by WELLS, who took the view that the burgeoning interest in demographic history, while commendable, was making it increasingly difficult to generalize about the population of the colonies. His study, which is intended to facilitate intercolonial comparisons, covers all of the British colonies for which census data are available and contains a wealth of information pertaining to the colonial population: size, growth, and distribution; racial and ethnic composition; age profile; and sex ratios and marital status. Wells conveys a sense of change over time within specific localities, categorizes colonial regions according to population characteristics, and discusses the significance of demographic variations among the colonies.

In a work that usefully complements Wells's survey, McCUSKER and MENARD contend that early American historians are only beginning to investigate the links between demographic and economic processes. The authors discuss the ways in which economic developments seem to have affected immigration, settlement, population growth, wealth distribution, and labor organization. Their regional and topical approach to the subject of economic growth allows them to review recent studies for all of British America from Canada to the Caribbean, draw instructive interregional comparisons, and indicate the directions in which historical scholarship is headed. For the truly indefatigable, McCusker and Menard provide a 75-page bibliography of published materials.

Finally, two senior historians have developed sweeping reinterpretations of the colonial period based on the work of a generation of new social historians. While contending that the 1960s initiated a revolution in the writing of history, FISCHER nevertheless resurrects as his organizing concept a modified version of the 19th-century "germ theory." He argues that four large waves of English-speaking immigrants – Puritans from East Anglia, Royalists from the south of England, Quakers from the North Midlands, and Scots and Scotch-Irish from North Britain – established four distinct regional cultures in the colonies between 1629 and 1775, and thereafter shaped the entire cultural history of America. Fischer's discussion of speech ways, building ways, family ways, marriage ways, gender ways, and so forth (he systematically examines 24 of these "ways" in each of the four regions), is a single-minded search for British antecedents to New World patterns.

Like Fischer, GREENE (1988) attempts to describe the process by which a general American culture emerged out of several regional cultures. Unlike Fischer, however, he examines the dynamics of internal colonial developments rather than the persistence of cultural tradition. Greene makes two points especially well. First, he demonstrates that New England communities, the focus of most of the early work of the new social historians, were atypical and, therefore, inappropriate exemplars for analyzing the social development of British America. Second, he makes a compelling case for cultural convergence in the century after 1660 as all of the regions of British America, save one, became more cohesive, stable, and harmonious, while New England, the lone exception, became less so. Readers wishing to assess the dimensions of the "revolution" in historical writing that began in the 1960s might begin by contrasting *Pursuits of Happiness* with Boorstin's *Colonial Experience*.

MELVIN YAZAWA

Colonial History: Colonies, settlement and growth

1) Chesapeake Bay

Beeman, Richard R., *The Evolution of the Southern Backcountry: A Case Study of Lunenburg County, Virginia, 1746–1832*, Philadelphia: Temple University Press, 1984

Carr, Lois Green, Philip D. Morgan, and Jean B. Russo (editors), *Colonial Chesapeake Society*, Chapel Hill: University of North Carolina Press, 1988

Clemons, Paul G.E., *The Atlantic Economy and Maryland's Eastern Shore: From Tobacco to Grain*, Ithaca, NY: Cornell University Press, 1980

Craven, Wesley Frank, *White, Red, and Black: The Seventeenth-Century Virginian*, Charlottesville: University Press of Virginia, 1971

Kulikoff, Allan, *Tobacco and Slaves: The Development of Southern Cultures in the Chesapeake, 1680–1800*, Chapel Hill: University of North Carolina Press, 1986

Menard, Russell R., *Economy and Society in Early Colonial Maryland*, New York: Garland, 1985

Morgan, Edmund S., *American Slavery, American Freedom: The Ordeal of Colonial Virginia*, New York: Norton, 1975

Perry, James R., *The Formation of a Society on Virginia's Eastern Shore, 1615–1655*, Chapel Hill: University of North Carolina Press, 1990

Rutman, Darrett B. and Anita H. Rutman, *A Place in Time: Middlesex County, Virginia, 1650–1750*, 2 vols., New York: Norton, 1984

Sheehan, Bernard W., *Savagism and Civility: Indians and Englishmen in Colonial Virginia*, Cambridge and New York: Cambridge University Press, 1980

Steiner, Bernard C., "The Protestant Revolution in Maryland", in *American Historical Association Annual Report ... 1897*, Washington, DC: American Historical Association, 1898

Wertenbaker, Thomas J., *The Shaping of Colonial Virginia*, New York: Russell and Russell, 1958

The first modern studies of Chesapeake foundation and settlement, written in the late 19th and early 20th centuries, concentrated on personal and political conflicts between the Virginia Company of London, Stuart monarchs, and early settlers (particularly Captain John Smith) and, in the case of the Maryland Proprietorship, the personal and political difficulties of the Lords Baltimore. In a compilation from three volumes first published between 1910 and 1922, WERTENBAKER went beyond this to examine conflicts between slaveholders and non-slaveholders in Virginia. STEINER, especially while editor of the *Archives of Maryland*, explored relations between rich and poor and Catholics and Protestants in Maryland. The interests of these historians remained essentially political, however, and, in Whiggish fashion and in the post-Reconstruction spirit of positively revising southern history, they emphasized the development of liberty and representative government in these colonies.

More recent Chesapeake scholarship has drawn attention to the economic, social, and cultural dimensions of settlement, particularly issues of class, race, and gender, and whereas more traditional studies celebrated the material and political successes of European settlement of New World "virgin" lands, recent works have counted the horrifying costs. CRAVEN's book was the culmination of decades of pioneering study of encounters with Native Americans, the social structure and developing economy of Virginia, and the development of slavery and African American culture. SHEEHAN shows how Native Americans' societies and cultures, which Chesapeake settlement decimated, were much more complex than was previously thought. Particular attention is drawn to their practice of communal landholding and agriculture, misinterpreted as idleness and savagery by Europeans who practised and idealised individual ownership. Native Americans could offer only temporary and spasmodic resistance to the military power of the Europeans, and their voracious appetite for land.

MORGAN shows how the Virginia Company aimed less to settle America than to establish military outposts from which to exploit local peoples and resources, and possibly find a route to Asia, in the fashion of 16th-century Spanish *conquistadors*. This partly explains the disasters of early imperial enterprises. Indeed, the first attempt at English colonisation of the Chesapeake, Sir Walter Raleigh's Roanoke Colony, mysteriously disappeared in the 1580s, probably destroyed by, or its settlers absorbed into, local Indian communities. Even at the second attempt at Jamestown from 1607, death by disease or Indian attack, the excesses of labour exploitation, and neglect of food production in the rush for tobacco profits, rendered life "nasty, brutish, and short" for the earliest "adventurers". Nevertheless, tobacco made Virginia a permanent settlement and once the market eased into steady growth in the 1620s settlers established more coherent societies.

In his in-depth local study, PERRY revises the view that Chesapeake settlement was chaotic and early society so extremely atomistic, and emphasizes that migrants settled contiguously, interacted frequently, and formed bonds of friendship and kinship deliberately to form ties of economic and social interdependence, thereby rapidly constructing an ordered and coherent society. He borrowed his methodology from the RUTMANs' pioneering "network analysis"; a prosopographical "record stripping" and reconstruction of the multifarious "nodal points" of settlers' social interaction. But in emphasizing community ties these Virginia scholars perhaps lose sight of the essential individualism and dynamism of this rapidly developing society. The relentless expansion of settlement and conflicting economic and social aims of migrating planters and yeomen are explored in BEEMAN's study of a western community from the late colonial period. Beeman shows that while Chesapeake society aspired to order and cohesion it retained elements of fluidity and conflict.

While recognizing the interconnections which inevitably tied settlers to one another, MENARD, of the Maryland school, never loses sight of the dynamic qualities of the Chesapeake economy or the individualistic nature of its society. His detailed yet wide-ranging work also covers social change over time, arguing that migrants, notwithstanding their arrival in the colony as indentured servants, often succeeded in their aspirations to landownership at least until the 1660s. About then, however, available land became scarcer and more expensive, leading to a relative decline in the wealth of poorer Marylanders and gentrification among the wealthy. Increased economic and social differentiation were also effected by the transition from indentured servitude to slavery caused by a decreasing supply of white servants and an increasing supply of black slaves. Menard ties all these social developments to the crests and troughs of the tobacco economy. CLEMONS also analyzes the international tobacco economy and its effects on everyday Chesapeake life, but is especially useful for detailing the increasing economic diversity and decreasing dependence on slavery caused by the switch to grain agriculture, which, by the mid-18th century, made the northern and western Chesapeake economically and socially resemble Pennsylvania.

The continued development of tobacco society is explored in Morgan, who argues that black slavery helped to create white freedom through the equality of status among whites afforded by its replacing of indentured servitude as the principal means of labour exploitation, and the caste unity it inspired in the face of fear of a racial "other". KULIKOFF's detailed study of three Chesapeake counties argues for continuing white social tensions caused by the material advantages which slaveholders had over non-slaveholders and the patriarchalism that slavery inculcated in masters. These works also examine slavery in its own right, not just its effects on white society. Kulikoff is especially useful for his explorations of slave life and master-slave relations. He recognizes the appalling injustices and cruelties of enslavement, but at the same time portrays paternalistic regimes which permitted enough social space for the development of vibrant African American communities and culture in which African inheritances were adapted to New World circumstances.

Much seminal work on Chesapeake foundation and settlement has been published as articles and essays rather than books. They have appeared in a wide variety of journals but the *William and Mary Quarterly*, *The Virginia Magazine of History and Biography*, and the *Maryland Historical Magazine* are perhaps the most fruitful sources. CARR, MORGAN, and RUSSO contains superb relevant essays and a comprehensive historiographical introduction by the editors.

STEVEN J. SARSON

2) New England

Allen, David Grayson, *In English Ways: The Movement of Societies and the Transferral of English Local Law and Custom to Massachusetts Bay in the Seventeenth Century*, Chapel Hill: University of North Carolina Press, 1981

Anderson, Virginia De John, *New England's Generation: The Great Migration and the Formation of Society and Culture in the Seventeenth Century*, Cambridge and New York: Cambridge University Press, 1991

Cressy, David, *Coming Over: Migration and Communication Between England and New England in the Seventeenth Century*, Cambridge and New York: Cambridge University Press, 1987

Cronon, William, *Changes in the Land: Indians, Colonists, and the Ecology of New England*, New York: Hill and Wang, 1983

Demos, John, *A Little Commonwealth: Family Life in Plymouth Colony*, New York: Oxford University Press, 1970

Greven, Philip J., *Four Generations: Population, Land, and Family in Colonial Andover, Massachusetts*, Ithaca, NY: Cornell University Press, 1970

Lockridge, Kenneth A., *A New England Town, the First Hundred Years: Dedham Massachusetts, 1636–1736*, New York: Norton, 1970; revised 1985

Martin, John Frederick, *Profits in the Wilderness: Entrepreneurship and the Founding of New England Towns in the Seventeenth Century*, Chapel Hill: University of North Carolina Press, 1991

Morgan, Edmund S., *The Puritan Dilemma: The Story of John Winthrop*, Boston: Little Brown, 1958

Salisbury, Neal, *Manitou and Providence: Indians, Europeans, and the Making of New England, 1500–1643*, New York: Oxford University Press, 1982

The study of the foundation and settlement of New England has produced a plethora of works. Early studies tended to focus on high politics and religion during the period of settlement. The 1970s saw a transformation of the region's historiography with a flurry of local town studies that provided a focus on the demographic forces shaping society. Recent work has seen the focus of research shift further to the broader influences on New England's unique culture and society, with special attention paid to the nature of migration.

MORGAN is an excellent and readable, though now a little dated, introductory text to the issues surrounding the settlement of New England. By focusing on the problems that beset John Winthrop, arguably the most important individual in early New England, Morgan provides an insight into the broader experiences of the early settlers. In particular, Morgan examines Puritan concerns over how Godly men and women

should behave in an immoral world – whether they should remain in the world or separate themselves from it. The work also provides a good discussion of the specific problems encountered by the early settlers, their motives for migration, and the difficulties they faced upon arrival, especially the difficulties of establishing a functioning society, economy, and government.

In a more recent study of the motivations for settlement, ANDERSON uses seven surviving passenger lists of emigrants to New England in the mid-1630s to explore their experiences. Focusing on the experiences of individuals, rather than an entire community, Anderson examines in detail these people's motives for migrating, their difficulties in travelling to New England, and their experiences after arrival. Unlike many other historians, she argues that religious motives were the most important single reason in determining an individual's decision to move to New England. She also examines the ways in which the Great Migration of the 1630s shaped New England society and became part of the mythology of colonial America. CRESSY is another investigation of motivations for migration to New England. Studying migration patterns throughout the 17th century, he stresses that the shaping of New England's society depended largely upon the English origins of the emigrants. He argues that religious motivation was not the crucial reason determining whether an individual migrated. Instead, migrants came for a variety of reasons, economic and personal as well as religious. In addition, kinship and personal ties between Englishmen had a central role in encouraging settlement. Unlike other historians, Cressy also shows the impact that New England had upon England, and discusses the two-way flow of information and people across the Atlantic.

In an influential study of family life in 17th century New England, DEMOS combines demographic information, showing the fecundity of the colonial family and high life expectancy, with archaeological evidence, revealing the material culture of life in Plymouth Colony. Demos argues that the family was central to shaping the nature of colonial society. He thus looks closely at family structure, and examines the relationship not only between parents and children, but also husbands and wives, and masters and servants.

In a community study of the town of Dedham, Massachusetts LOCKRIDGE examines the nature of social change within the community over the course of a century. He portrays early Dedham as a tightly knit community with low migration rates. Lockridge claims that the main drive behind settling the town was a utopian communitarianism, and this was reflected in the nature of the town in the mid-17th century. However, by the early 18th century the town had fragmented and become more socially diverse. In another town study, GREVEN examines the town of Andover, and comes to conclusions quite similar to those of Lockridge. However, Greven pays rather more attention to how the experience of family life changed through the generations, and discusses the impact of demographics on the experiences of later generations. In particular he stresses how the longevity of the first generation increased the control that they exercised over later generations.

MARTIN provides a rather different interpretation of the nature of New England towns. In an analysis of the foundation of 63 New England towns in the 17th century, he attacks the communitarian thesis of town life and argues instead that the founding of towns was from the beginning an economic and commercial exercise that quickly became dominated by a small group of powerful and experienced men. ALLEN examines the origins of New England society and local government institutions. Focusing on five particular New England towns, he compares societies on both sides of the Atlantic. Allen stresses that New England towns had differing social and governmental structures depending upon the region of England from which the settlers had migrated. As the settlers sought to recreate the life which they had left behind in England, they consciously copied the society of their home towns.

SALISBURY examines New England's foundation from a very different perspective, that of the Native Americans. In a lively narrative covering 150 years, Salisbury demonstrates that contact between Europeans and Indians began a century before colonization. He argues that there were two phases of interaction between Native Americans and Englishmen: contact with explorers and traders, then contact with settlers themselves. The first was as destructive as the second because of the dislocation of native society which created a state of dependency upon trade with Europeans. Salisbury also demonstrates how demographic changes in both England, with increasing population pressure, and in North America, where epidemics reduced native population by up to 90 percent, led to the establishment and success of English settlements.

CRONON provides another different approach, from the perspective of environmental history. He uses the different attitudes of Native Americans and English settlers towards the environment to illustrate distinctive traits of their societies. Unlike many other historians, he shows how Native Americans shaped their environment as much as later settlers, by burning the underbrush, and damming the rivers and streams. However, this was very different from English colonists who built fences and walls to control and mark their property, and built roads and cleared fields to conquer the environment.

MATTHEW C. WARD

3) Middle Atlantic

Bonomi, Patricia U., *A Factious People: Politics and Society in Colonial New York*, New York: Columbia University Press, 1971

Bonomi, Patricia U., "The Middle Colonies: Embryo of the New Political Order" in *Perspectives on Early American History: Essays in Honor of Richard B. Morris*, edited by Alden T. Vaughan and George Athan Billias, New York: Harper, 1973

Bronner, Edwin B., *William Penn's "Holy Experiment": The Founding of Pennsylvania, 1681–1701*, Philadelphia: Temple University Press, 1962

Landsman, Ned C., *Scotland and Its First American Colony, 1683–1765*, Princeton: Princeton University Press, 1985

Lemon, James T., *The Best Poor Man's Country: A Geographical Study of Early Southeastern Pennsylvania*, Baltimore: Johns Hopkins Press, 1972

Levy, Barry, *Quakers and the American Family: British Settlement in the Delaware Valley*, New York: Oxford University Press, 1988

Pomfret, John Edwin, *The Province of West New Jersey, 1609–1702: A History of the Origins of an American Colony*, Princeton: Princeton University Press, 1956

Rink, Oliver A., *Holland on the Hudson: An Economic and Social History of Dutch New York*, Ithaca, NY: Cornell University Press, 1986

Ritchie, Robert C., *The Duke's Province: A Study of New York Politics and Society, 1664–1691*, Chapel Hill: University of North Carolina Press, 1977

Tully, Alan, *Forming American Politics: Ideals, Interests, and Institutions in Colonial New York and Pennsylvania*, Baltimore: Johns Hopkins University Press, 1994

Zuckerman, Michael (editor), *Friends and Neighbors: Group Life in America's First Plural Society*, Philadelphia: Temple University Press, 1982

The Middle Atlantic colonies comprised New York, New Jersey, Pennsylvania, and Delaware. Although some historians have expressed scepticism about the coherence of these, pointing out for example vital differences between the history of colonial New York and the others, most have seen them as a distinct entity between the New England and Chesapeake colonies. By contrast with the northern and southern settlements they were planted later and as a result of conquest from another European power, the Dutch.

The Dutch presence in New Netherland has attracted growing attention of late. Among the more scholarly contributions to this revival of interest is RINK, who shows that the efforts of the West India Company were never likely to make the colony profitable. However, its encouragement of private investment by Amsterdam merchants led to the creation of substantial landed estates in the Hudson River valley and the development of a lively trans-Atlantic trade. Thus, on the eve of its conquest by the English, New Netherland was on the point of becoming viable.

The conquest of New York from the Dutch in the 1660s looms large in all accounts of its early history. RITCHIE argues that it was undertaken partly to overawe New England but also to consolidate the eastern coastline for the English empire, which, with the acquisition of territory from the Hudson to the Delaware rivers, stretched in an unbroken line from Maine to the Carolinas. It meant that the newly acquired colonies contained a heterogeneous European population which provided another distinction between them and the predominantly English colonies to the north and south. Ethnic diversity was a key to the early political history of New York, where Dutch aspirations, especially following the reconquest of "New Netherland" during 1672 and 1673, clashed with the English aim of anglicising the colony. These tensions underlay Leisler's rebellion in 1689 and, as BONOMI (1971) demonstrates, reverberated for years in New York politics.

LANDSMAN adds another nationality to the clash of cultures in the Middle Colonies with his study of the Scots in East New Jersey. Many of the original settlers of this area came from northeast Scotland, to be joined later by Scots from the southwest and "Scotch Irish" from Ulster. These groups developed into unified ethnic settlements with Scottish social practices. Although Quakers and Episcopalians were prominent among the early settlers, East New Jersey became staunchly Presbyterian. At the same time the Scots "established a national and secular rather than sectarian colony". This was in sharp contrast with West New Jersey which, as POMFRET narrates, became a Quaker colony soon after its acquisition. Pomfret also untangles the complex web of proprietary rights, whereby the overall proprietor of New Jersey, James, Duke of York and, after 1685, king of England, ceded his rights to the territory – not to the government but to Lord John Berkeley and Sir George Carteret. Berkeley sold his share, West New Jersey, to Quakers, who turned West New Jersey into a haven for persecuted Friends.

Among the Quaker proprietors of West New Jersey was William Penn. In 1681 he obtained the largest proprietorial grant ever made by the Crown, the colony of Pennsylvania. The early history of the "holy experiment," as Penn dubbed his new venture, has led historians to concentrate on the religious features of the settlement. Thus LEVY analyses the migration of Quaker families from Wales and the English Midlands to the Delaware valley. While clearly these regions contributed significantly to the development of Pennsylvania, the contribution of first purchasers of land in the colony, who came from London, has tended to be downplayed in recent accounts of the transference of "folkways" from Britain to the Delaware.

Whether Penn's experiment was a success has prompted debate. The propensity of the Friends to engage in acrimonious political debate, and even religious schism, proved a great disappointment to Penn himself. It led the predominantly Anglican three lower counties which ultimately became the state of Delaware to secede from Pennsylvania in 1703. It also leads BRONNER to conclude that by and large the experiment failed. While there might be dispute about the successful launching of Pennsylvania from Penn's viewpoint, there can be little doubt about its economic success, which some see as undermining his pious intentions. Philadelphia grew rapidly to become the biggest seaport on the east coast. Its hinterland contained some of the most fertile agricultural soil on the continent, and, as LEMON argues in his survey of its historical geography, developed an economy which led to Pennsylvania achieving the reputation of being "the best poor man's country" on earth.

The characteristics which gave it this image were largely shared by the other Middle Colonies, and this has led historians such as BONOMI (1973) and ZUCKERMAN to suggest that they were quintessentially embryonic American states. Where others have seen the crucible of American society in New England, or even Virginia, they point out that, in their ethnic diversity, religious pluriformity and partisan politics, the Middle Colonies had much more in common with the future United States. Where the northern and Chesapeake settlements were settled largely from England, those between the Hudson River and Delaware Bay were peopled by Europeans from Scandinavia, the Netherlands and Germany as well as from the British Isles. In this regard the Middle Colonies were the first melting pot. Again, where Congregationalism predominated in New England and Anglicanism in Virginia, there was a profusion of sects in between, of which the Dutch Reformed, Lutheran, Moravian, Mennonite, Presbyterian, and Quaker were but the most prominent. Finally, political parties first emerged in New York and Pennsylvania, with the Leislerians and anti-Leislerians in the former, the proprietary and anti-proprietary in the latter. Thus TULLY concludes, in a detailed narrative of the political history of New York and Pennsylvania in the colonial era, that the "First Party System" was largely an extension to other states of many of the features of the political cultures of these two colonies.

W.A. SPECK

4) Carolinas and Georgia

Abbot, W.W., *The Royal Governors of Georgia, 1754–1775*, Chapel Hill: University of North Carolina Press, 1959

Alden, John R., *John Stuart and the Southern Colonial Frontier: A Study of Indian Relations, War, Trade, and Land Problems in the Southern Wilderness, 1754–1775*, Ann Arbor: University of Michigan Press, 1944

Crane, Verner W., *The Southern Frontier, 1670–1732*, Durham, NC: Duke University Press, 1928

Davis, Harold E., *The Fledgling Province: Social and Cultural Life in Colonial Georgia, 1733–1776*, Chapel Hill: University of North Carolina Press, 1976

Ekirch, A. Roger, *"Poor Carolina": Politics and Society in Colonial North Carolina, 1729–1776*, Chapel Hill: University of North Carolina Press, 1981

Kay, Marvin L. Michael and Lorin Lee Cary, *Slavery in North Carolina, 1748–1775*, Chapel Hill: University of North Carolina Press, 1995

Littlefield, Daniel C., *Rice and Slaves: Ethnicity and the Slave Trade in Colonial South Carolina*, Baton Rouge: Louisiana State University Press, 1981

Meriwether, Robert L., *The Expansion of South Carolina, 1729–1765*, Kingsport, TN: Southern Publishers, 1940; reprinted Philadelphia: Porcupine, 1974

Merrens, H. Roy, *Colonial North Carolina in the Eighteenth Century: A Study in Historical Geography*, Chapel Hill: University of North Carolina Press, 1964

Sirmans, M. Eugene, *Colonial South Carolina: A Political History, 1663–1763*, Chapel Hill: University of North Carolina Press, 1966

Weir, Robert M., *Colonial South Carolina: A History*, Millwood, NY: KTO Press, 1983

Wood, Betty, *Slavery in Colonial Georgia, 1730–1775*, Athens: University of Georgia Press, 1984

Wood, Peter H., *Black Majority: Negroes in Colonial South Carolina from 1670 Through the Stono Rebellion*, New York: Knopf, 1974

Until comparatively recently historians displayed little interest in the colonies of the Lower South, with the result, that unlike colonies in the Chesapeake and New England, the new social history made less impact on the region than elsewhere. The poverty of the region's surviving records provides a partial explanation for this relative neglect but so too does the modest role in colonial afffairs that historians attributed to the Lower South.

Much the best studied of the three colonies is South Carolina which enjoyed spectacular economic growth in the second quarter of the 18th century as exports of slave-produced rice and indigo soared to meet the demands of expanding European markets. Less interest has been shown in North Carolina than the size of its population at the time of the Revolution would seem to warrant. The fourth most populous of the colonies, it was also distinct among southern colonies in that it was not tied to staple crop agriculture, had a low proportion of non-whites in its population, and few men of wealth except in the Cape Fear region where South Carolina merchants acquired large tracts of land. Viewed in its first decades as "small, poor and weak", Georgia, the last of the English colonies to be founded, was nonetheless fully integrated into the mainstream of colonial political development by 1775. Two themes have tended to dominate the colony's history: the viability of the policies adopted by the trustees and the extent to which Georgia replicated the development of other colonies in half the time.

Imperial perspectives and a concern with British politics and administration have shaped much of the work on the Lower South. The excellent studies of CRANE and ALDEN explored successive periods in the tortuous and violent history of the southern frontier, a zone of intercolonial as well as international contacts, where the competing interests of European powers, indigenous peoples, South Carolina traders and rival colonial land claimants came into conflict. While Crane's eminently readable work focused largely on South Carolina and the repercussions which stemmed from the activities of its Indian traders, Alden looked to British policy and British politics.

The growth and development of these colonies have been examined from a variety of perspectives in a number of works. Published over fifty years ago and republished in 1974, MERIWETHER's immensely detailed study of the systematic attempt to promote settlement in South Carolina's "middle country" remains the standard work on Governor Johnson's township scheme, the impetus behind which lay in the perception of provincial leaders that settlement by groups of Europeans was the "only available remedy" to the prospect of domination by African slaves. More readable is MERRENS's exploration of the economic development of North Carolina in the last quarter of the colonial period. Undertaken from the perspective of a historical geographer, this study is accessible to the non-specialist reader, though the title might suggest a longer study than that actually undertaken. Based on Merrens's doctoral dissertation, this work analysed regional variations in the economy, and the rate and direction of change: the influx of immigrants who entered the colony from the north determining the rate of change, while environmental factors, and to some extent cultural factors, shaped its direction. He focused on what made North Carolina unique: the absence of staple agriculture and dependence on naval stores and wood products, cattle raising among the highland Scots and intensive agriculture among the Moravians. Particularly interesting was his explanation of the pattern and importance of the colony's small urban settlements.

In his discussion of the social and cultural forces that shaped life in Georgia, DAVIS challenges the view that the colony remained a crude frontier during the colonial period, "a primitive spot on a barely developed shore". In a broad-ranging analysis, Davis discussed not only the material conditions of peoples' lives, but also the public festivities and government-supported ceremonies which sustained communal life and loyalty. Despite the advent of slavery, it was also, in comparison with other colonies, a more open and less differentiated society at the end of the colonial period.

Conflict between governors and assemblies and the growth of political stability are the major themes of colonial political history. Stylishly, even elegantly written, ABBOT is a short account of developments in Georgia during the royal period when, under the tutelage of royal governors, this previously young and weak colony, menaced on three sides by hostile French, Spanish and Cherokee, developed into a thriving province.

Still the standard work on colonial South Carolina politics is the comprehensive analysis by SIRMANS, usefully supplemented by WEIR. For much of the colonial period South Carolina was driven by factionalism, caught in a cycle of chaotic disputes generated by religious, political, economic and social tensions, and of compromise settlements which resolved nothing. Sirmans divided South Carolina politics into three distinct periods: 1670 to 1712 when former Barbadian settlers, "Goose Creek Men", sought to establish their ascendancy over the government of the Proprietors; 1712 to 1743 when political turmoil raged despite the overthrow of proprietary rule in 1719 and growing prosperity after 1729; and 1743 to 1763 when social harmony finally prevailed. EKIRCH, too, characterizes the politics of North Carolina as chaotic and unstable but, unlike its more powerful neighbours, the colony failed to achieve stability before the end of the colonial period, a state of affairs which Ekirch attributed to the weaknesses of the ruling group among whom corruption was endemic. His concern with corruption led him to an interpretation of the Regulator Movement which was very different from earlier sectional and class interpretations. When violence broke out in the 1760s, what galvanized the backcountry population was a commitment to "country" ideology.

Interest in slavery reflects more recent concerns. Peter WOOD's pathbreaking study, notable for its interdisciplinarity, set new standards for the study of slavery. His work attested to the larger role played by Africans in the development of the economy of South Carolina, and the relative freedom of black Carolinians in the early decades before rice and indigo came to dominate the economy and delimit black experience. Wood's insights were carried a stage further by LITTLEFIELD, whose research indicated the degree to which traders, merchants and planters were familiar with the cultural regions of Africa and bought selectively. In the first scholarly study of slavery in colonial Georgia, Betty WOOD shows that, unlike other colonies, Georgia's adoption of slavery was not "an unthinking decision," but rather the product of extensive debate. Slavery came relatively late to North Carolina which was why many of the colony's slaves were African rather than native born. In their long-awaited book, KAY and CARY emphasize the degree of autonomy retained by slaves over aspects of their lives in a society where masters, lacking the confidence of more established slave societies, ruthlessly exploited the structures of power in order to control them.

GWENDA MORGAN

Colonial History: Government and Politics

Bonomi, Patricia U., *A Factious People: Politics and Society in Colonial New York*, New York: Columbia University Press, 1971

Bushman, Richard L., *King and People in Provincial Massachusetts*, Chapel Hill: University of North Carolina Press, 1985

Daniels, Bruce C. (editor), *Power and Status: Officeholding in Colonial America*, Middletown, CT: Wesleyan University Press, 1986

Ekirch, A. Roger, *"Poor Carolina": Politics and Society in Colonial North Carolina, 1729-1776*, Chapel Hill: University of North Carolina Press, 1981

Greene, Jack P., *The Quest for Power: The Lower Houses of Assembly in the Southern Royal Colonies, 1689-1776*, Chapel Hill: University of North Carolina Press, 1963

Greene, Jack P., *Peripheries and Center: Constitutional Development in the Extended Polities of the British Empire and the United States, 1607-1788*, Athens: University of Georgia Press, 1986

Labaree, Leonard W., *Royal Government in America: A Study of the British Colonial System Before 1783*, New Haven: Yale University Press, 1930

Morgan, Edmund S., *Inventing the People: The Rise of Popular Sovereignty in England and America*, New York: Norton, 1988

Nobles, Gregory H., *Divisions Throughout the Whole: Politics and Society in Hampshire County, Massachusetts, 1740-1775*, New York: Cambridge University Press, 1983

Purvis, Thomas L., *Proprietors, Patronage, and Paper Money: Legislative Politics in New Jersey, 1703-1776*, New Brunswick, NJ: Rutgers University Press, 1986

Sydnor, Charles S., *Gentlemen Freeholders: Political Practices in Washington's Virginia*, Chapel Hill: University of North Carolina Press, 1952; as *American Revolutionaries in the Making: Political Practices in Washington's Virginia*, New York: Macmillan, 1962

Tully, Alan, *William Penn's Legacy: Politics and Social Structure in Provincial Pennsylvania, 1726-1755*, Baltimore: Johns Hopkins University Press, 1977

Weir, Robert M., *"The Last of American Freemen": Studies in the Political Culture of the Colonial and Revolutionary South*, Macon, GA: Mercer University Press, 1986

Zemsky, Robert, *Merchants, Farmers, and River Gods: An Essay on Eighteenth-Century American Politics*, Boston: Gambit, 1971

The classic interpretation of colonial government in British North America is LABAREE. He argued that there was a ratchet effect as the provincial assemblies extended their control over royal government, converting themselves into sovereign bodies modelled on the House of Commons. This process was not confined to continental North America but occurred in the British West Indies too. Labaree's thesis remained popular with conservative historians who believed that the independence of the United States was both inevitable and desirable. Most contemporary scholars see such an interpretation as too determinist and too simple, because it ignores the numerous internal struggles for power that occurred during the provincial period.

Labaree's thesis was further explored by GREENE (1963) in his study of the southern provincial assemblies. He too found a similar pattern of colonial encroachment on the royal prerogative. But though more detailed, Greene essentially added little to Labaree's interpretation. Nevertheless GREENE (1986) returned to this theme of mutual hostility, and argued that the essential dynamic of colonial politics was the metropolitan insistence that everything be subordinated to the interests of the mother country. Changing attitudes to America's place in the world induced Greene to be more sympathetic to the imperial point of view.

Since Greene's 1963 study, historians have tended to concentrate on the study of individual colonies, leading to different foci and conclusions. Most notable has been the emphasis on colonial diversity and the fact that political power lay mainly with the local elites. Among the first to acknowledge these factors was BONOMI in her study of New York, where she emphasized that the key to understanding the province's politics was its lack of homogeneity. Hence political battles were less a case of crown versus assembly than of faction against faction, based on religious antagonism, the differing demands of commerce and agriculture, and rivalry between Albany and New York City. Surprisingly, New Jersey, with similar ethnic and religious divisions to New York, suffered less disruption, according to PURVIS. Several factors kept its politics relatively harmonious: the need to combine against powerful neighbours; the readiness of the governing elite to keep taxes low; the lack of an exposed frontier; and the absence of an established church. The customary concord was only seriously threatened in the 1740s when the old issues of paper money and land titles resurfaced. The same argument that consensus rather than contention was the rule is the theme of TULLY's study of Pennsylvania. There were periods of tension between Quakers and Proprietors, which were exacerbated by the need to accommodate the influx of Germans and Scots-Irish from 1720 onwards. But for most of the time the political system functioned in an orderly and effective manner.

But not all the colonies enjoyed such harmony. North Carolina experienced serious regional conflict, as EKIRCH shows. For much of the period its government was bedevilled by divisions between the northern and southern parts of the province, the result of differing economies. The Albemarle Sound region was basically a tobacco growing area, the Cape Fear area being devoted to rice. The first looked towards Virginia, the second to South Carolina. In contrast, WEIR argues that South Carolina's politics were relatively free of conflict during the period 1720-63, though disputes did occur between the provincial council and assembly when the latter attempted to exclude royal officials from the legislative process. Provincial harmony was induced by the need for unity against the large African American slave population. The threat of hostility from the adjacent Native American peoples and neighbouring French and Spanish settlements was another spur to unity.

If colonial politics were driven by hostility between crown and assembly, as Labaree and Greene argued, Massachusetts seemingly provides the best example, at least for the first four decades of the 18th century, when disputes broke out over the selection of a speaker, payment of the governor's salary, and the right of the assembly to adjourn without royal assent. However, as ZEMSKY shows, politics in Massachusetts was not simply a matter of hostility between crown and people. The governor enjoyed substantial support from a court party which on occasion comprised a majority in the House of Representatives. Even the country party was ready to work with royal government, following the emergence of a class of semi-professional politicians, anxious for influence if not power.

Support for this interpretation is provided by Nobles and Bushman. NOBLES concentrates on the towns of the Connecticut river in Western Massachusetts. These were controlled by local elites who invariably supported the governor, though their authority was weakened after the ferment caused by the Great Awakening. BUSHMAN similarly argues that the people of Massachusetts were essentially loyal, though monarchy shaped the form rather than the content of provincial politics. So long as the monarchy conformed to the stereotype of the good ruler, the people were content. However the attachment to the crown was little more than a sentimental veneer, though few realized this before 1760.

There has been no recent study of Virginia's politics and government. The best analysis is still SYDNOR who argued that harmony was the norm, especially for the period after 1720. Sydnor was one of the first writers to emphasize the importance of local elites. Britain's empire worked in Virginia because the large planters helped to control its government. Before 1760 this harmony was only broken occasionally through the incompetence of the governor.

The importance of elites in colonial politics and government is also the theme of DANIELS. Town selectmen, county justices, assemblymen, or members of the council were all appointed largely because of their wealth and social status, though as a creole population developed, it became an advantage to be native-born.

Colonial politics were always underpinned by ideology. Most important in the period 1689–1763 was the colonists' belief in their rights as Englishmen. However, as MORGAN points out, the concept of a sovereign people was unknown even in England until the mid-17th century. By 1763 it was so endemic to the colonial perspective that little difficulty was experienced in changing from a monarchical to a republican system of government in 1776.

RICHARD MIDDLETON

Colonial History: Economic Development

Carr, Lois Green, Russell R. Menard, and Lorena S. Walsh, *Robert Cole's World: Agriculture and Society in Early Maryland*, Chapel Hill: University of North Carolina Press, 1991

Chaplin, Joyce E., *An Anxious Pursuit: Agricultural Innovation and Modernity in the Lower South, 1730–1815*, Chapel Hill: University of North Carolina Press, 1993

Doerflinger, Thomas M., *A Vigorous Spirit of Enterprise: Merchants and Economic Development in Revolutionary Philadelphia*, Chapel Hill: University of North Carolina Press, 1986

McCusker, John J. and Russell R. Menard, *The Economy of British America, 1607–1789*, Chapel Hill: University of North Carolina Press, 1985; revised 1991

Perkins, Edwin J., *The Economy of Colonial America*, New York: Columbia University Press, 1980, 2nd edition, 1988

Shepherd, James F. and Gary M. Walton, *Shipping, Maritime Trade, and the Economic Development of Colonial North America*, Cambridge and New York: Cambridge University Press, 1972

Walton, Gary M. and James F. Shepherd, *The Economic Rise of Early America*, Cambridge and New York: Cambridge University Press, 1979

Despite the field's obvious importance, colonial economic history has traditionally been regarded as something of a poor relation. Most of the work done on British America has instead focused on political, social, and intellectual issues, seen as less mundane and more exciting. Recently, however, there has been a renewed and welcome interest in both the external and internal dimensions of the colonial economy. SHEPHERD and WALTON (1972) concentrate on the role of trade in a detailed, yet lucid, monograph. At the heart of their analysis is a considerable amount of quantitative material relating to shipping and distribution costs in the 17th and 18th centuries, as well as a set of balance-of-payment accounts for the main colonial regions for the years 1768 to 1772. Drawing extensively on this evidence, they argue convincingly that technological change was less important in fostering colonial economic growth than were improvements in economic organization and increasing regional specialization.

The same authors' undergraduate textbook, WALTON and SHEPHERD (1979), also concentrates on commercial developments in British North America. After a short introduction, they take the reader quickly through the period of discovery and conquest. The next five chapters contain the core of their analysis and deal with colonization, the "ascent of foreign trade", and economic progress. A final section deals briefly with some economic aspects of the American Revolution and its results. Re-using the statistics derived from their earlier work, the authors argue that the colonists' wealth and standard of living grew, especially in the 17th century, due primarily to the trading sector. But they do not neglect the relationship between the rise of commercialism and increasing social and economic inequalities.

A short, well-organized overview, PERKINS begins with a discussion of foreign trade and population, but moves on to explore the economic lives of individual types of colonists. He then turns his attention to money and taxes, and concludes with a survey of the scholarship on early American income and wealth. The book offers several interesting points of comparison with Shepherd and Walton (1979). Not only does Perkins synthesize more of the scholarly literature, he defines the field of economic history more broadly to include writings on colonial society. He is at his best when discussing changes in early American agriculture, whereas Shepherd and Walton are strongest on commercial developments. Finally, Perkins tries to downplay the evidence of increasing economic inequality and polarization in colonial society. Instead, the picture painted is of a growing economy characterized by a buoyant agriculture sector, no deep class divisions, low taxes, and a high and slowly improving standard of living.

McCUSKER and MENARD stands out as the most rounded and sophisticated analysis of the colonial economy. It is a major work of synthesis that weaves together the manifold conclusions of a diffuse literature within a strong theoretical framework. The authors argue persuasively that the best interpretive structure stems from a combination of two models, the staples approach and the so-called Malthusian tradition. The former emphasizes the importance of external markets; the latter, the significance of internal population growth. Though these models have often been seen as incompatible, McCusker and Menard suggest that colonial economic history can best be understood in terms of "the interaction between the pull of external markets and the push of internal population pressures", with the former dominating during the early years of settlement and the latter becoming increasingly important over time.

Other valuable recent studies concentrate on particular localities and see economic processes within the wider social context. CARR, MENARD, and WALSH is a carefully researched and astutely nuanced study of rural life in early Maryland that concentrates on one successful middling planter's estate. It challenges the standard depiction of 17th-century Chesapeake planters as wasteful, slovenly, and resistant to innovation. Instead, the authors argue, they made "creative adaptations" to New World circumstances. Also, they suggest that neither the export sector nor the domestic market was the principal dynamic force in the growth of Robert Cole's plantation. Rather, wealth increased primarily because of the high ratio of savings and investment to income, a process of capital accumulation made possible less by constricting consumption than by limiting leisure. Economic success was therefore achieved at a cost in a harsh, exploitative environment.

CHAPLIN turns the spotlight on to the large planters of the 18th-century Lower South. Combining economic, social, and intellectual history approaches, she shows how their distinctive mentality and ideology influenced the major economic decisions they took from 1730 to 1815. Their self-image as enlightened individuals, according to Chaplin, shaped their behaviour as entrepreneurs and slaveowners. Receptive to contemporary European thought, the planters of the Lower South tried to maintain humane relationships with their laborers while developing successful estates that continually adjusted to volatile market conditions. Neither does she ignore how the slaves themselves played an active role in shaping the evolving social order and larger history of the region.

DOERFLINGER examines the Philadelphia merchant community during the Revolutionary era in order to understand their entrepreneurial inventiveness and to assess their role in the growth of the American economy. He argues that ease of entry, diversity, high turnover, and relative lack of cohesion account for the dynamism of the city's traders. The result is a challenging, analytically rigorous, and controversial

book. Some might dispute his emphasis on entrepreneurship as the motor of economic development, while others might object to his celebration of merchants and his easy dismissal of the costs of growth. Certainly his thesis dwells on only one aspect of a complex problem. Other factors – the role of the hinterland, the education and mobility of the labour force, the impact of capital flows – all require further attention. However significant their activities, northern merchants did not build prosperity on their own.

KEITH MASON

Colonial History: Society

Bailyn, Bernard, *The Peopling of British North America: An Introduction*, New York: Knopf, 1986

Bailyn, Bernard, *Voyagers to the West: A Passage in the Peopling of America on the Eve of the Revolution*, New York: Knopf, 1986; London: Tauris, 1987

Boorstin, Daniel J., *The Americans: The Colonial Experience*, New York: Random House, 1958; Harmondsworth: Penguin, 1965

Brown, Richard D., *Modernization: The Transformation of American Life, 1600–1865*, New York: Hill and Wang, 1976

Eggleston, Edward, *The Transit of Civilization from England to America in the Seventeenth Century*, New York: Appleton, and London: Hirschfeld, 1901; with new Introduction, Gloucester, MA: Peter Smith, 1972

Fischer, David Hackett, *Albion's Seed: Four British Folkways in America*, New York and Oxford: Oxford University Press, 1989

Greene, Jack P., *Pursuits of Happiness: The Social Development of Early Modern British Colonies and the Formation of American Culture*, Chapel Hill: University of North Carolina Press, 1988

Greene, Jack P. and J. R. Pole (editors), *Colonial British America: Essays in the New History of the Early Modern Era*, Baltimore: Johns Hopkins University Press, 1984

Hartz, Louis, *The Founding of New Societies: Studies in the History of the United States, Latin America, South Africa, Canada, and Australia*, New York: Harcourt Brace, 1964

Henretta, James A. and Gregory H. Nobles, *Evolution and Revolution: American Society, 1600–1820*, Lexington, MA: Heath, 1987

Meinig, D. W., *The Shaping of America: A Geographical Perspective on 500 Years of History*, volume 1: *Atlantic America, 1492–1800*, New Haven and London: Yale University Press, 1986

Miller, Perry, *Errand into the Wilderness*, Cambridge, MA: Belknap Press of Harvard University Press, 1956

EGGLESTON began modern discussion of the character of colonial society with his "germ theory" contention that American social (and other) institutions were outgrowths of European ones, stressing the English origins of American social and political liberty and democracy. BOORSTIN, on the other hand, is probably, for the colonial period, the staunchest exponent of American "exceptionalism," contrasting a static, almost feudal, Old World society with a New World environment of abundance and opportunity. As in Frederick Jackson Turner's "frontier thesis," Europeans were transformed into characteristically American practical, anti-authoritarian, "rugged individualists" who created a uniquely egalitarian, free, and dynamic but consensual society. HARTZ falls on both sides of this issue. While portraying American society as created out of European "fragments," he also depicts a "traditionalizing" process whereby American society was cut off from Europe's feudal past and socialist future. Thus America was and remained exceptional for its equality, fluidity, dynamism, freedom, and liberal consensus.

Probably the most influential of the older characterizations of colonial society and social development was MILLER's portrayal of the "declension" of Puritan utopian communities in the face of the economic temptations of the American wilderness. This prefigured the traditional-to-modern interpretations favoured by historians influenced by the social sciences in the 1960s and 1970s. HENRETTA and NOBLES, a revised edition of a volume first published in 1973, depicts movement from stable, ordered, pre-market, communities to a more conflicted, fluid, individualistic, capitalistic, liberal society reminiscent of Ferdinand Tönnies's *gemeinschaft-gesellschaft* (community-society) model. BROWN employs the similar concept of modernization but reverses many of the value judgments to emphasize movement from an undemocratic, unequal, superstitious, and traditional world to a democratic, egalitarian, rational, enlightened, and progressive one.

Much "new history" scholarship from the 1960s onwards, however, revealed that colonial society was more complex and variegated than these interpretations allow. GREENE and POLE contains fourteen essays directly or indirectly addressing the variations among colonial societies based on differences of politics, religion, geography, economics, labour organisation, and so on. While this kind of work made our understanding of colonial societies much more sophisticated it also, as the editors bemoaned, meant such a degree of "fragmentation" of research and opinion that there was no longer any general agreement on the fundamentals of colonial society or social development. GREENE answered his own call for a new "synthesis" of colonial history by assimilating an enormous amount of disparate research into a coherent "developmental model" of colonial America. The Chesapeake, Lower South, and Middle Colonies (and the island colonies and Ireland in an expansive conception of the British-Atlantic world) underwent a common pattern of "simplification" of English social institutions and practices at the moment of settlement, followed by their "elaboration" over time, leading eventually to social "replication." New England was exceptional, moving, as it did, from stability, coherence, relative equality, and communitarianism; the reverse direction of all other British Atlantic societies, including what British revisionists had found to be the dynamic, materialistic, and individualistic society of the Mother Country. New World "experience" and Old World "inheritance" both played roles in a gradual British-Atlantic social and cultural "convergence."

BAILYN differentiates colonial societies into New England, the Hudson and Delaware river valley regions, the Chesapeake,

and the Carolinas, and migrants into those from a "metropolitan" (mostly "betterment migrants") and those from "provincial" (mostly "subsistence migrants") European background. What migrants had in common were aspirations for "independence" through opportunity provided by colonial land and labour markets. What the regions had in common was belonging to a world in great demographic, social, economic, and political flux. As a "primitive" periphery of the European "core" culture, colonial America was characterised by violence and exploitation. Bailyn is less definite about social development than Greene, and tends more towards increasing regional divergence than convergence, though he does delineate pockets of "growing civility." In *The Peopling of British North America*, Bailyn overviews what will be a multi-volume interpretation, of which *Voyagers to the West* is a part, based mainly on the exhaustively researched fates of 9,364 emigrants who left Britain between 1773 and 1776.

MEINIG is more spatially and temporally expansive than Bailyn and even Greene, and is part of an ongoing multi-volume project which will extend to the present. Within the overarching "geopolitical theme" of the interactions among the "Atlantic system" of Europe, Africa, and the Americas, Meinig considers the settlement and development of thirteen regions, from Newfoundland to the lower Rio Grande, distinguished by their "spatial systems," (connections binding a region together), "cultural landscapes" (adaptations to varying environments), and "social geographies" (particular configurations of demographic and social groups, institutions, and relations). A geographer, Meinig emphasizes the effects of two particular New World conditions, the physical environment and racial and ethnic heterogeneity, and thus tends even more than Bailyn to a view of colonial and inter-regional divergence over time (despite imperial attempts to control colonies). But, also recognizing the continuing if diminishing importance of European inheritances, he places social diversification on a "distance decay spectrum."

In contrast, FISCHER returns to "germ theory" in a depiction of the transit of East Anglian society to Massachusetts, southern and western England to Virginia, the north Midlands to the Delaware Valley, and English, Scottish, and Ulster borderlands to the western backcountry. Using anthropological methods, Fischer identifies these regions by their particular configurations of 24 folkways, including power, wealth, religion, family, speech, and sport. His "cultural diffusion" model incorporates a brief post-migration period of "cultural crisis" followed by an elite-led "cultural consolidation" in which British regional folkways were recreated wholesale in the respective colonial "cultural hearths." Although uncovering a massive wealth of information, this controversial work has been criticized for overly selective and inaccurate depictions of British social and cultural traits, ignoring certain colonial regions, insensitivity to change over time, and overlooking the influence of the American environment and Native Americans, Africans, and other Europeans.

STEVEN J. SARSON

Colonial History: Education

Axtell, James, *The School upon the Hill: Education and Society in Colonial New England*, New Haven: Yale University Press, 1974

Bailyn, Bernard, *Education in the Forming of American Society: Needs and Opportunities for Study*, Chapel Hill: University of North Carolina Press, 1960

Calhoun, Daniel, *The Intelligence of a People*, Princeton: Princeton University Press, 1973

Cremin, Lawrence A., *American Education: The Colonial Experience, 1607–1783*, New York: Harper, 1970

Greven, Philip J., *The Protestant Temperament: Patterns of Child-Rearing, Religious Experience, and the Self in Early America*, New York: Knopf, 1977

Lockridge, Kenneth A., *Literacy in Colonial New England: An Enquiry into the Social Context of Literacy in the Early Modern West*, New York: Norton, 1974

Middlekauff, Robert, *Ancients and Axioms: Secondary Education in Eighteenth-Century New England*, New Haven: Yale University Press, 1963

Morison, Samuel Eliot, *The Puritan Pronaos: Studies in the Intellectual Life of New England in the Seventeenth Century*, New York: New York University Press, 1935; as *The Intellectual Life of Colonial New England*, Ithaca, NY: Cornell University Press, 1960

Robson, David W., *Educating Republicans: The College in the Era of the American Revolution, 1750–1800*, Westport, CT: Greenwood Press, 1985

Yazawa, Melvin, *From Colonies to Commonwealth: Familial Ideology and the Beginnings of the American Republic*, Baltimore: Johns Hopkins University Press, 1985

The field of education history has undergone a fundamental transformation in the last three decades. The most influential instigator of this change has been BAILYN. In his pathbreaking 1960 essay, Bailyn argued that earlier historians were prone to adopt a definition of education too narrowly focused on formal instruction and public institutions. For historians of the colonial period in particular, such an approach often amounted to a search for the antecedents of the modern system of public schooling. Bailyn suggests a broader definition, one that concerns itself with the entire process of cultural transmission. Under this definition, the most important agents of education for the colonists were the family, church, and community. Although Bailyn's conclusions about the impact of the American environment on the nature and development of early American families and communities have been modified by more recent studies, the best histories of education have adopted his approach to the subject.

CREMIN has written the best single-volume history of colonial education. Employing a definition of education nearly as broad as Bailyn's, Cremin describes the ways in which colonial families, churches, schools, and communities transmitted knowledge, values, attitudes, and skills from one generation to the next. For Cremin, the late 17th century marks a watershed in colonial educational history because of the intellectual changes associated with that era. Colonial culture, which had been overwhelmingly derivative, became more and more creative, as provincial intellectuals disseminated the potentially liberating ideas of Isaac Newton and John Locke among an increasingly literate populace. By the time of the American Revolution, a combination of economic growth, widespread political participation, expansive schooling, and a free press had prepared the American colonists for independence.

The best of the regional histories of education focus on New England. AXTELL offers a wide-ranging analysis of the ways in which children were prepared for life in New England society. Because he is particularly interested in the habits of thought and behavior that adults attempted to instil in the young, Axtell examines the experiences of infants and adolescents in a variety of settings. He also offers an engaging discussion of the patterns of discipline that prevailed in families, schools, and colleges.

Two older studies of education in colonial New England may be used to supplement Axtell's work. MORISON devotes a chapter each to elementary schools, public grammar schools, and 17th-century colleges. Of equal importance, however, is his description of what he terms the flowering of intellectual life in early New England. Morison's survey of colonial printing, bookselling, library holdings, sermons, and literary and scientific activities is a good introduction to some of the topics Cremin covers in greater detail. MIDDLEKAUFF adds to Axtell's analysis by focusing more narrowly on students and the curricula of secondary schools in 18th-century New England. He is at his best in describing systems of schooling that prevailed in the late colonial period and the alteration of those systems necessitated by the American Revolution.

Middlekauff's study of secondary education is itself usefully complemented by ROBSON's examination of the relationship between politics and higher education before, during, and after the Revolution. Paying especially close attention to curricular changes and library holdings, Robson argues that American colleges were politicized in the 1760s and became agents of revolution in the 1770s. Faculty members, steeped in the ideology of the radical Whigs of the 18th century, energized students already predisposed to support the movement toward independence and thus furthered the patriots' cause.

YAZAWA employs a broader definition of education than Robson used in order to assess the relationship between politics and education in the Colonial and Revolutionary eras. Colonial parents and schoolmasters were intent on promoting habits of disciplined obedience in communal settings modeled after the well-ordered family. The imperial crisis and the final break with the mother country resulted in the replacement of the familial model with the republican ideal. The mode of education adopted by independent Americans reflected this fundamental shift from subjectship to citizenship.

Under Bailyn's inclusive definition, child-rearing is an essential part of education. GREVEN, whose study is among the most imaginative we have, identifies three patterns of child-rearing in colonial America: the evangelical, in which the will of the child is broken; the moderate, in which the will of the child is bent; and the genteel, in which the wilful child is indulged. Greven effectively describes the interaction between these patterns and such variables as parental authority, household structure, discipline, domestic affection, and perceptions of human nature.

Two other studies have addressed difficult subjects related to education. LOCKRIDGE examines the social context of literacy in colonial New England. Taking as an indicator of literacy the percentage of testators who signed their names to their wills, Lockridge concludes that between the 1650s and 1790s New England evolved from a society little more than half-literate to a society of about 90 per cent male literacy. He attributes this improvement to sharp increases in literacy among rural farmers, artisans, and laborers – increases made possible by the triumph of the Puritan educational tradition in America.

CALHOUN asks whether there was a significant change in the general intelligence of the American people in the century after 1750. In answering this difficult and controversial question, Calhoun offers an intriguing analysis of what he terms displays of intelligence. What Americans expected and produced, he argues, may be interpreted as expressions of intelligence. Calhoun's discussions cover topics as varied as child-rearing attitudes, preaching styles, shipbuilding, and antebellum bridge-building. Viewed as a response to Bailyn's call for studies of education that reach beyond the narrow confines of curricular and institutional surveys, Calhoun's work is without peer.

MELVIN YAZAWA

Colonial History: Religion

Ahlstrom, Sydney E., *A Religious History of the American People*, New Haven: Yale University Press, 1972

Bonomi, Patricia U., *Under the Cope of Heaven: Religion, Society, and Politics in Colonial America*, New York: Oxford University Press, 1986

Bremer, Francis J., *The Puritan Experiment: New England Society from Bradford to Edwards*, New York: St. Martin's Press, 1976

Bridenbaugh, Carl, *Mitre and Sceptre: Transatlantic Faiths, Ideas, Personalities, and Politics, 1689–1775*, New York: Oxford University Press, 1962

Butler, Jon, *Awash in a Sea of Faith: Christianizing the American People*, Cambridge, MA: Harvard University Press, 1990

Demos, John, *Entertaining Satan: Witchcraft and the Culture of Early New England*, New York and Oxford: Oxford University Press, 1982

Hall, David D., *Worlds of Wonder, Days of Judgment: Popular Religious Belief in Early New England*, New York: Knopf, 1989

Handy, Robert T., *A History of the Churches in the United States and Canada*, Oxford: Clarendon Press, and New York: Oxford University Press, 1976

Lovejoy, David S., *Religious Enthusiasm in the New World: Heresy to Revolution*, Cambridge, MA: Harvard University Press, 1985

McLoughlin, William G., *New England Dissent, 1630–1833: The Baptists and the Separation of Church and State*, Cambridge, MA: Harvard University Press, 1971

Trinterud, Leonard J., *The Forming of an American Tradition: A Re-Examination of Colonial Presbyterianism*, Philadelphia: Westminster Press, 1949; reprinted Freeport, NY: Books for Libraries, 1970

Woolverton, John Frederick, *Colonial Anglicanism in North America*, Detroit: Wayne State University Press, 1984

There are a number of ways of approaching the broad topic of colonial religion, ranging from general surveys, regional narratives, and denominational histories, to studies of specific topics, such as the relations between church and state, and the development of specific genres, such as popular religion.

General surveys fall into a variety of types. The more traditional focus primarily on organised religion. The colonial period is usually given considerable coverage in broad overviews of the history of the American religious development. AHLSTROM is the outstanding example of this sort of broad introduction, blending both denominational and regional perspectives. In rather briefer compass, HANDY provides additional coverage of Canada. Both describe the early impact of Catholicism in America, before going on to discuss the Protestant experience which was more central to the English colonial settlements. Both look at the role of religion in motivating the early settlers; at the variety of beliefs, institutions, and practices which the colonists established during the early settlement; and at the changes which accompanied the development of more complex societies. While not ignoring the continued influence of Europe, these histories tend to concentrate on what was taking place within the English mainland settlements. They deal with both the religion of America and the characteristics of American religion.

More recent surveys have moved in a number of different directions. As well as covering many aspects of the development of institutionalised religion, BUTLER seeks to pay due attention to popular religion and to religion as culture. He suggests that less emphasis needs to be paid to Puritanism as the major force in shaping religion in America; that the 18th century may have been more significant for its religious tradition than the 17th; and that religion operated throughout the colonial period along with non-Christian or quasi-Christian beliefs that were part of the general culture. This is a wide-ranging and authoritative book, which also contains a wealth of reference to further, more detailed reading.

The nature and emphasis of BONOMI's survey are rather different. She approaches the religious history of the colonies from the viewpoint of the relationship between religion and society and politics. She is interested, for example, in religion as a prime determinant of political loyalties. Her focus is very much on the 18th century, though she provides a sound introduction to aspects of the 17th century. In particular, she both describes and contributes to the discussion of the linkage between the Great Awakening and the American Revolution.

Perhaps surprisingly, it is not always easy to find good, up-to date, denominational histories of the colonial period. TRINTERUD still has merits as the best single account of Presbyterianism, and certain aspects of its influence in the middle colonies, though his main concern was to establish how a specifically American Presbyterianism came to emerge. WOOLVERTON provides a full and up-to date description of the role of the Anglican church, looking at the way in which it expanded throughout the colonies from its initial Virginia base, in particular through the efforts of the missionary society, the Society for the Propagation of the Gospel. The fact that the influence of Anglicanism was on the increase should encourage a certain caution about the effects of religious belief on national character.

The clash between Anglicans and the dissenting denominations dominant in many of the colonies was transatlantic in scope, as BRIDENBAUGH makes clear. He surveys the struggle between the denominations to establish predominance, and thereby their specific form of church government and view of the relationship between church and state. McLOUGHLIN is also concerned with the issue of relations between church and state. He covers a broad time period and, although his main concern is with the challenge of the Baptists to the Congregationalists of New England, he also takes in the contributions made by the Quakers and the Anglicans. In a sense McLoughlin provides an account of the development of religion in New England from the point of view of some of those who dissented from the accepted way. While the studies of Puritanism and the dominant Congregational churches are legion, BREMER may be mentioned as just one introductory regional survey which covers a lot of ground in a concise narrative.

An alternative approach to that which stresses the importance of denominations or regions is one which emphasises characteristics or themes which cut across denominational lines. In a valuable example of this approach, LOVEJOY examines a variety of groups and individuals who were regarded as religious extremists within their own times or localities, and were therefore described by the pejorative title of "enthusiast". They diverged radically in thought and practice from many of their fellows. Their experience is an important part of colonial religious history in its own right. It also helps to highlight many of the features of the more orthodox principles and practices which they confronted. As with many others, Lovejoy also sees these dissenters as contributing significantly to the wider developments within America which gave rise to the movement for independence.

Recent studies of colonial religion have sought to move away from the churches and the ministers to examine lay attitudes and responses. HALL provides a useful introduction to this approach, and to the types of concerns which give rise to it. His concern is to recover some sense of religion as lay men and women knew and practised it, and to give some account of the meaning which they ascribed to specific religious rituals and practices. Religion was one factor which helped to provide ordinary people with their perception of their community and their world. That perception of course included a place for the supernatural, as well as the natural, and left room for a variety of quasi-religious or non-religious beliefs and practices. DEMOS provides an effective and accessible starting point for the study of the role of magic and witchcraft.

MALCOLM F. MORRISON

See also Puritanism

Colonial History: Slavery and Indentured Servitude

Galenson, David W., *White Servitude in Colonial America: An Economic Analysis*, Cambridge and New York: Cambridge University Press, 1981

Jordan, Winthrop D., *White over Black: American Attitudes Toward the Negro, 1550–1812*, Chapel Hill: University of North Carolina Press, 1968

Kulikoff, Allan, *Tobacco and Slaves: The Development of Southern Cultures in the Chesapeake, 1680–1800*, Chapel Hill: University of North Carolina Press, 1986

McManus, Edgar J., *Black Bondage in the North*, Syracuse, NY: Syracuse University Press, 1973

Menard, Russell R., *Economy and Society in Early Colonial Maryland*, New York: Garland, 1985

Morgan, Edmund S., *American Slavery, American Freedom: The Ordeal of Colonial Virginia*, New York: Norton, 1975

Salinger, Sharon V., *"To Serve Well and Faithfully": Labor and Indentured Servants in Pennsylvania, 1682–1800*, Cambridge and New York: Cambridge University Press, 1987

Wood, Betty, *Slavery in Colonial Georgia, 1730–1775*, Athens: University of Georgia Press, 1984

Wood, Peter H., *Black Majority: Negroes in Colonial South Carolina from 1670 Through the Stono Rebellion*, New York: Knopf, 1974

GALENSON's study of the origins of 20,000 English indentured servants bound for the labour-hungry Americas finds that in the 17th century they were predominantly young, male, and neither mostly of the "middling" nor the "common sort", as previously debated, but evenly divided between the yeomen classes, craftsmen, unskilled labourers, and youths. In the 18th century servant migrants were equally young, even more predominantly male, and, owing to increased use of slaves in agricultural labour, more often skilled craftsmen. The general terms of indenture were bondage for seven years in return for transportation, food, clothes, and housing, although the "custom of the country" and status of redemptioner caused variations. SALINGER, a localized study, concentrates less on servant origins than on their experience of servitude and after. The predominantly English servants of the first forty years were treated relatively benignly and, although few made fortunes after their service, most did better than their successors. From the 1720s servitude became more harsh and conflictual as servants, more often of Scotch-Irish and German birth, were treated more as commodities. Furthermore, servants, especially women, fared poorly after completion of their terms. The second half of the 18th century saw a transition from servitude to free wage labour, although this did not necessarily improve standards of living, as evidenced by increasing urban poverty.

MENARD also concentrates on one colony and depicts a decline of fortune over time. Before 1660, Maryland ex-servants often become owners of land and even servants and slaves, but increasing monopoly of scarcer land by wealthy planters progressively restricted economic opportunity. Menard also analyzes the transition from servitude to slavery between 1680 and 1720, noting a declining supply of servants and rising supply of slaves. Also, while slaves were initially more expensive, they made better long-term investments as they were enslaved for life (as were their children), cheaper to feed, clothe, and house, and could be forced to work harder. KULIKOFF covers the same economic ground for a wider range of the Chesapeake region, but two-thirds of his study concentrates on social history. He depicts a patriarchal gentry increasingly dominating Chesapeake society in collusion with the yeomanry at the expense of poor whites, including those who were or had been servants, who were forced into either ever greater poverty or westward migration. On black society he analyzes the increasing strictures of paternalism, but also the development of strong, stable, distinctive African American family, community, and culture.

MORGAN stresses the improvement of conditions for whites resulting from the introduction of slavery. He depicts a chaotic early Virginia in which the headright system (whereby planters received fifty acres of land per indenture purchased as a reward for contributing to population and settlement) and the tobacco boom caused brutal and often fatal servant exploitation. The easing of the tobacco boom moderated conditions, although white Virginians remained deeply divided by class until the later 17th century. Until then white servitude and black slavery had not been sharply differentiated: servants and slaves often worked in the fields together and the latter were often freed after seven years. From 1660, however, legislation made slaves and their offspring chattels for life, made the condition inheritable, established separate codes of behaviour and punishment, and restricted all kinds of interracial social intercourse. As blacks became more numerous and increasingly identified with slavery, whites united around fears of rebellion and a white supremacist conception of freedom. JORDAN also addresses the relationships of freedom, slavery, and race, arguing that rather than slavery causing racism or vice versa, they developed together and reinforced each other. Elizabethan Englishmen already projected negative images on to Africans in establishing their self-identity and then had these perceived polarities, black-white, savage-civilized, free-unfree, confirmed by their perspective of blacks as slaves. Less convincing, perhaps, given already widespread slavery in the Americas caused by huge New World labour demand, is Jordan's notion that the introduction of slavery to North America resulted from an "unthinking decision."

Betty WOOD deals with the unique introduction of slavery to Georgia, whose colonial Trustees hoped to create a utopian society by limiting landownership and banning slavery, as well as providing a white population to safeguard against the threats of Spanish Florida and South Carolina's black majority. A proslavery coalition, resenting restrictions on potential prosperity, forced the Trustees to accede to slavery in 1750 and by the time of independence Georgia's population was 40 per cent black. Peter WOOD, like Kulikoff, is concerned with slave society and culture, but distinguishes South Carolinian from Chesapeake slavery by the initial familiarity between masters and slaves, who often migrated together from Barbados, and the "sawbuck equality" established in primitive frontier conditions. Staple plantation agriculture increasingly differentiated the races, however, and rice in particular caused such demand

for labour that by the early 18th century blacks formed a majority of the South Carolina population. Harsher labour and black majority were, as the Stono Rebellion showed, an explosive combination, but blacks still mitigated the severities of slavery. African knowledge and skill in rice cultivation, for example, contributed to adoption of the task system of labour which, unlike Chesapeake sunup-to-sundown gang labour, left slaves leisure time once tasks were completed. This, combined with their large population, especially of African-born, and relatively high owner absenteeism, helped them create a uniquely strong and distinct African American culture. Northern colonial slavery was also a distinct system, as McMANUS shows in his depiction of uniquely variegated slave labour in agriculture, commerce, and industry. He also demonstrates that while this was a non-plantation system, slavery was still important to the demography and economy of the North, particularly in ports such as New York where trade and shipbuilding created the largest urban concentration of slaves outside Charleston, South Carolina. Also, while northern, unlike southern, colonies never became "slave societies", racial fears and prejudices were nevertheless deep, causing harsh slave codes and oppression and segregation after emancipation.

Steven J. Sarson

Colonial History: Non-English Settlements in North America

Dahlgren, Stellan and Hans Norman (editors), *The Rise and Fall of New Sweden: Governor Johan Risingh's Journal, 1654–1655, in Its Historical Context*, translated by Marie Clark Nelson, Stockholm: Almqvist & Wiksell, 1988

Eccles, W.J., *France in America*, New York: Harper, 1972; revised, East Lansing: Michigan State University Press, 1990

Hall, Gwendolyn Midlo, *Africans in Colonial Louisiana: The Development of Afro-Creole Culture in the Eighteenth Century*, Baton Rouge: Louisiana State University Press, 1992

Meinig, D. W., *The Shaping of America: A Geographical Perspective on 500 Years of History*, volume 1: *Atlantic America, 1492–1800*, New Haven and London: Yale University Press, 1986

Rink, Oliver A., *Holland on the Hudson: An Economic and Social History of Dutch New York*, Ithaca, NY: Cornell University Press, 1986

Usner, Daniel H., Jr., *Indians, Settlers, and Slaves in a Frontier Exchange Economy: The Lower Mississippi Valley Before 1783*, Chapel Hill: University of North Carolina Press, 1992

Weber, David J., *The Spanish Frontier in North America*, New Haven: Yale University Press, 1992

Recent interest in multiculturalism has triggered renewed study of the non-English settlement of North America. Although victory in the Seven Years' War assured British imperial dominance over the continent, several other powers had rivaled the

British for their mastery over the previous two centuries. Spain, France, Sweden, and the Netherlands all sought to carve out colonial enclaves in the New World in the hopes of obtaining raw materials for their national economies and geopolitical bases to counter their enemies' movements. The story of the non-English colonies is, therefore, tied intimately to questions of mercantilist economics and imperial strategy. In addition to these larger issues, historians are beginning to look beyond politics and economics to explore what types of cultures grew out of the non-English colonies, and how they have survived to the present.

Overviews of the colonial scramble for North America are often more conspicuous for their oversights than for their substantive contributions. However, MEINIG combines the synchronic concerns of history with the spatial concerns of geography in an exemplary history of colonization. Three models explain the very different composition, purpose, and fate of European colonization. The English expelled native peoples from their settlements and maintained a frontier to separate themselves from the Indians. In contrast, the French, with few exceptions, preferred to enter amicable trade and military alliances with the Indian population. The Spanish, however, attempted to create a stratified colonial society based upon a hierarchical ordering of republics, or estates, made up of different ethnic groups. Although Meinig's models describe accurately the larger colonial efforts, neither the Swedes nor the Dutch fit neatly into one model; instead they combined elements of English and French imperialism.

Born of commercial ambitions, the Swedish colony was only as successful as its financial parent, the New Sweden Company. Built in 1638 by traders, Fort Christina was the economic, political, and social center of the colony. The trading post rivaled English and Dutch outposts in the Indian fur trade and exacerbated tensions between the three countries. Despite the success of Swedish traders, substantial problems imperiled the colony. These causes, DAHLGREN and NORMAN show, led to the utter collapse of New Sweden in the face of a Dutch invasion in 1655. Included in this volume is the journal of Johan Risingh, the colony's last governor, which provides a unique perspective on colonial politics, diplomacy, and the struggle to build a viable and long-lasting colonial presence, something the Swedes failed to do.

New Netherland sat squarely in the middle of the English settlements, and the colony competed with the English in the deerskin trade during the first half of the 17th century. RINK argues that trade dominated colonial affairs to the detriment of government and settlement. While the West India Company concerned itself with other matters, the colony fell under the control of a few private traders whose refusal to share wealth and power hindered the development of conditions that might have attracted more settlers. As was often the case, imperial wars decided the fates of the non-English colonies. After a series of Anglo-Dutch wars, the English overpowered New Netherland in 1664.

Unlike the Swedes and the Dutch, the Spanish Empire withstood English aggression throughout the colonial period. WEBER's masterful survey of the Spanish effort to colonize North America emphasizes their dependence on Native Americans to defend and support their colonies. Spain armed Indians with guns and mounted them on horses to harass their imperial rivals. Around Spanish settlements, colonists organized Indian populations as a peasant workforce that would provide food, labor, and other essential services. Despite some success, the Spanish lacked the economic and political resources to develop fully their North American settlements. Missionaries, settlers, and hispanicized Native Americans, nevertheless, left an enduring legacy in North America. Weber forcefully argues that historians have too long overlooked Spanish North America, and this volume goes a long way towards correcting that oversight.

Quebecois separatism and Cajun music and cuisine are prominent reminders of the French settlement of North America. ECCLES's fine narrative history details the growth of France's North American empire. The French developed colonies both to the north and south of the English, to exploit natural resources and to cut off English expansion. Traders, clergymen, and the royal government blended capitalistic business incentives and feudal political and social prerogatives to populate the region and create a viable colony. But, as happened with the Dutch, the inability of France to defend its colonies against the English led to the loss of New France at the conclusion of the Seven Years' War.

The development of non-English cultures in North America is perhaps the most interesting aspect of this colonial history. In addition to Weber, both Usner and Hall have traced the emergence of a unique colonial culture in the Louisiana colony. USNER argues that Indians, settlers, and slaves interacted daily in an exchange economy of foodstuffs, material items, and services. The influence of one culture upon the other led to a variety of cultural innovations. HALL details the African component of this colonial melange. She asserts that the laxity of the French slaveholding regime made possible the spread of a generalized African culture. Whether through music, housing styles, foodways, or oral history, the crucible of colonization produced new cultures for the new world.

Studies like Hall and Usner reveal colonization as an individual endeavor that produced results unforeseen by planners, financiers, and government agents in the home countries. As studies of the non-English settlement of North America come to focus on cultural issues, historians will gain a greater appreciation of life in the colonies than studies such as Rink and Eccles are able to deliver. Knowing what life was like for non-English colonists begs the question of how they responded to English control once it was established, and, moreover, what sort of legacy these people left behind that can be seen today in foodways, popular music, political activism, and regional life.

JAMES TAYLOR CARSON

Colonial History: Relations with Native Americans

Axtell, James, *The Invasion Within: The Contest of Cultures in Colonial North America*, New York: Oxford University Press, 1985

Jennings, Francis, *The Invasion of America: Indians, Colonialism, and the Cant of Conquest*, Chapel Hill: University of North Carolina Press, 1975

Merrell, James H., *The Indians' New World: Catawbas and Their Neighbors from European Contact Through the Era of Removal*, Chapel Hill: University of North Carolina Press, 1989

Nash, Gary B., *Red, White, and Black: The Peoples of Early America*, Englewood Cliffs, NJ: Prentice Hall, 1974, 3rd edition, 1991

Richter, Daniel K., *The Ordeal of the Longhouse: The Peoples of the Iroquois League in the Era of European Colonization*, Chapel Hill: University of North Carolina Press, 1992

Salisbury, Neal, *Manitou and Providence: Indians, Europeans, and the Making of New England, 1500–1643*, New York: Oxford University Press, 1982

Steele, Ian K., *Warpaths: Invasions of North America*, New York: Oxford University Press, 1994

White, Richard, *The Middle Ground: Indians, Empires, and Republics in the Great Lakes Region, 1650–1815*, Cambridge and New York: Cambridge University Press, 1991

Many works have studied the relationship between European colonists and Native Americans. During the 1970s this field was transformed by the combination of anthropological and historical techniques to produce "ethnohistory" – the study of cultural change and exchange between Native Americans and colonists. Many recent works have used ethnohistory to provide detailed studies of how individual native peoples responded to contact with Europeans.

NASH is the best introductory text to the topic. The work characterizes colonial American history in terms of the interaction between European colonists, African slaves, and Native Americans. Nash shows how each of the peoples actively contributed to the creation of American society and stresses the common experiences of each group. The work also provides a good synthesis of the colonization of America until the Seven Years' War. In a chronological narrative, extending from the pre-Columbian era to the Seven Years' War, Nash analyses how the balance of power between Europeans and Indians shifted as a result of trade, disease, and war.

JENNINGS is a provocative work that portrays relations between colonial Americans and Native Americans in terms of the resettlement of native peoples, the "invasion" of America by a new people. Like Nash, Jennings seeks to show that Native Americans played an active role in the history of colonial America. In the first half of the work Jennings examines the impact of disease, trade, and missionary activities upon native populations. He also illustrates the fraudulent methods used to deprive the Indians of their lands. The second half of the work provides a chronological narrative of the expansion of southern New England in the 17th century, paying particular attention to the Pequot War in the 1630s and King Philip's War of 1675.

STEELE provides a chronological overview of relations between Native Americans and Europeans from the Spanish explorations in the 16th century to the Seven Years' War. Even more than Jennings, Steele portrays the colonization of North America in terms of armed conflict, examining the history of warfare between the two peoples. Steele argues that the early colonies should be viewed not as the precursor to the inevitable overrunning of the continent but rather as a precarious foothold, made possible in part by the acquiescence and involvement of the native peoples. Indeed, Steele stresses that European technological superiority was largely a myth during the early phases of colonization, and that the Indian peoples were quite capable of resisting and defeating their European opponents, and did so on many occasions.

With a different emphasis, AXTELL depicts relations between Europeans and Native Americans in the 17th century, not in terms of an armed struggle – for as he points out most of the colonial era was a period of declared peace – but rather in terms of European efforts to educate and convert the Indian peoples. Axtell examines how and why French Jesuit missionaries were much more successful than English Puritan missionaries. He stresses that a key to French success was the acceptance of an element of cultural relativism, adopting and adapting native traditions to the Roman Catholic Church. Axtell also discusses the often neglected success of the native peoples in converting Europeans into Native Americans.

Cultural relativism is also stressed by WHITE. In a study of cultural change in the Ohio Valley and Great Lakes region, covering almost two centuries, White argues that Europeans did not have the power to impose their will upon Native Americans and had to conform to native demands. He explains how the needs of trade, warfare, and diplomacy led to the creation of what he terms "the middle ground," a culture neither European nor Indian. For over a century Europeans, at first Frenchmen but then Englishmen, were forced to adapt to Native American society and behave as Native Americans expected. Only with the American Revolution did American settlers begin to gain the strength to ignore the concerns of the Indian peoples and the "middle ground" slowly eroded and disappeared.

SALISBURY also examines cultural change, studying the impact of trade upon the native peoples of New England. He demonstrates that contact between Europeans and Indians began a century before the beginnings of colonization. He sees two phases of interaction between Native Americans and Englishmen: contact with explorers and traders, then contact with settlers themselves. The first phase was as destructive as the second because trade dislocated native society by making the native inhabitants dependent upon European goods. Salisbury also demonstrates how demographic changes in both England, with increasing population pressure, and in North America, where epidemics reduced the native population by up to 90 percent, led to the establishment and success of English settlements.

Among various local case studies, one of the best is MERRELL. He examines the forces that transformed native life in the North Carolina Piedmont from first contact with Europeans, in the mid-16th century, to the period of Indian removal in the mid-19th century. Focusing particularly on the impact of disease, trade and white settlement in the 18th century, Merrell explains how the native peoples responded and adapted to these forces, effectively creating the Catawba Nation. The work is a study of cultural change drawing upon, in addition to traditional historical sources, anthropological and archaeological resources. Merrell stresses that the Catawbas were able to "survive" by gaining an understanding of the working of the white society that surrounded them.

Another fine case study is RICHTER. He examines the reactions to European settlement of the Iroquois Confederacy, possibly the most important native group in colonial British North America. Like other studies Richter stresses the importance of disease and trade dependency in undermining the integrity of the Iroquois. However, he also examines Iroquois politics, and the way in which the confederacy became enmeshed in European conflicts. He asserts that the political structure of the league should be regarded more as a series of factions, at most five separate nations, rather than a united confederacy. In assessing the success of the league he argues that the keys to its survival were its geographic location, between the French and English, and the diversified economic basis of many of its communities.

MATTHEW C. WARD

Colonial History: Westward Expansion

Alden, John R., *John Stuart and the Southern Colonial Frontier: A Study of Indian Relations, War, Trade, and Land Problems in the Southern Wilderness, 1754–1775*, Ann Arbor: University of Michigan Press, 1944

Alvord, Clarence Walworth, *The Mississippi Valley in British Politics*, 2 vols., Cleveland: Arthur H. Clark, 1917

De Vorsey, Louis, *The Indian Boundary in the Southern Colonies, 1763–1775*, Chapel Hill: University of North Carolina Press, 1966

Egnal, Marc, *A Mighty Empire: The Origins of the American Revolution*, Ithaca, NY: Cornell University Press, 1988

McConnell, Michael, *A Country Between: The Upper Ohio Valley and Its Peoples, 1724–1774*, Lincoln: University of Nebraska Press, 1992

Sosin, J.M., *Whitehall and the Wilderness: The Middle West in British Colonial Policy, 1760–1775*, Lincoln: University of Nebraska Press, 1961

Steele, Ian K., *Warpaths: Invasions of North America*, New York: Oxford University Press, 1994

White, Richard, *The Middle Ground: Indians, Empire, and Republics in the Great Lakes Region, 1650–1815*, Cambridge and New York: Cambridge University Press, 1991

The topic of the westward expansion of the American colonies is one that attracted much attention from the historians of the British Empire writing before the 1960s. However, it is a topic which was then much neglected until revived by the recent historiographical interest of ethnohistorians in Indian-White relations.

ALVORD is the classic, but dated, work on this topic. In this two-volume study, written from the perspective of an imperial historian, Alvord examines the development of British policy in the West from the Seven Years' War through to the American Revolution. He sees British policy as being the creation of the President of the Board of Trade, the Earl of Shelburne, and resulting from the factional disputes over the Treaty of Paris in 1763. Alvord's great contribution was to place western issues firmly in the discussion of British colonial policy before the American Revolution, and to argue that the West was central to British policymakers throughout the period.

Studying British policy over the same period, SOSIN sought to update Alvord's work by using sources not available to him. He portrays British western policy not as the result of conscious policy decisions, but rather as an ad hoc development as British ministers sought to resolve individual issues as they arose. Unlike Alvord, Sosin argues that while the West was important to British policy immediately after the Treaty of Paris, it declined in importance after 1765. Sosin justifies British policy by claiming that the quest for security on the western frontier was the prime motive of ministers. Consequently, they sought to restrain westward expansion and sought funds to contribute to the cost of administering the interior, with the resulting, disastrous, consequences. Despite its age, this is probably still the best overall discussion of the development of British western policy during the period.

DE VORSEY also examines the development of British policy, but focuses on the Southeast and the development of one specific policy: the evolution of the boundary-line separating Native Americans from colonists. De Vorsey maintains that the concept of a boundary-line had developed as early as the Treaty of Paris, but examines the manner in which the concept evolved over the following years. Like Sosin, he portrays the development of the policy as the result of ad hoc decisions by British officials, but he also pays attention to the actions of colonial officials. The work stresses the extent to which the decision to halt western expansion marked a major shift in policy, for previously settlers had been encouraged to move West. ALDEN is another important study of the development of British western policy in the South during the period between the Seven Years' War and the Revolution. He argues that in the South diplomatic rather than military affairs dominated colonial relations with Native Americans. He claims that British policy was initially shaped by the success of the French in winning Indian support. This led to the centralization of Indian policy with the development of the Indian superintendents. In the years after the Seven Years' War John Stuart, the Superintendent of the Southern Department, played a central role in shaping government policy. Stuart's primary goals were to establish a boundary between colonists and Indians to prevent future conflict, and to regulate trade in order to prevent abuses by white traders. This policy failed largely because of the impossibility of preventing the westward migration of the colonists.

EGNAL examines how western expansion and British policies towards the West affected the politics of the five important colonies of Massachusetts, New York, Pennsylvania, Virginia and South Carolina. Covering the 18th century before the Revolution, but focusing especially on the period after the Seven Years' War, Egnal argues that the split between expansionist and non-expansionist factions was central in creating colonial political factions. According to Egnal, the expansionists became increasingly frustrated with British western policy in the years after the Seven Years' War, and hence supported the Revolutionary movement.

McCONNELL is a detailed study of how the Indian peoples of the upper Ohio Valley, present day Ohio and western

Pennsylvania, responded to the westward expansion of the colonists from the 1720s to the eve of the American Revolution. He shows how the Native Americans who populated the region by the mid-18th century had already been pushed there from the East by British colonial expansion. Their central concern was the maintenance of their independence, both from Europeans and other Indian peoples, in particular the Iroquois. This desire explains their shifting allegiances. McConnell shows how, after the removal of the French from North America in the Seven Years' War, it became increasingly difficult for the Ohio Indians to prevent encroachment on their lands by white settlers. Once the American colonies had broken from Britain, the Ohio Indians were unable to halt the tide of western expansion.

In a broader but similar study, WHITE examines how the peoples of the Ohio Valley and Upper Great Lakes region responded to European expansion into their homelands. He argues that until the late 18th century Europeans were not able to impose their will upon the Native Americans of the region but rather were forced to come to terms with native wishes. This created what he terms a "middle ground" a culture which was neither Indian nor European. Expansion into the Ohio Valley and Great Lakes was not therefore inevitable but took over one hundred years.

In contrast to more specialized works, STEELE provides an overview of the expansion of the European colonies, British, French and Spanish, throughout the colonial period. In a sweeping survey of relations between colonists and Native Americans, Steele examines the processes of expansion from first settlement through to the era of the American Revolution. He argues that Native Americans were capable of resisting the expansion of European colonies throughout the 17th and into the 18th centuries. Indeed, he argues that the early settlement of North America should be viewed as no more than a precarious foothold on a hostile continent which could easily have been wiped out and, as he illustrates, often was.

MATTHEW C. WARD

Communications and Media: General

Blondheim, Menahem, *News over the Wires: The Telegraph and the Flow of Public Information in America, 1844–1897*, Cambridge, MA: Harvard University Press, 1994

Czitrom, Daniel J., *Media and the American Mind: From Morse to McLuhan*, Chapel Hill: University of North Carolina Press, 1982

Dégh, Linda, *American Folklore and the Mass Media*, Bloomington: Indiana University Press, 1994

Douglas, Susan J., *Inventing American Broadcasting, 1899–1922*, Baltimore: Johns Hopkins University Press, 1987

Marchand, Roland, *Advertising the American Dream: Making Way for Modernity, 1920–1940*, Berkeley: University of California Press, 1985

May, Lary, *Screening Out the Past: The Birth of Mass Culture and the Motion Picture Industry*, New York: Oxford University Press, 1980

Udelson, Joseph H., *The Great Television Race: A History of the American Television Industry, 1925–1941*, University: University of Alabama Press, 1982

Wasserman, Neil H., *From Invention to Innovation: Long-Distance Telephone Transmission at the Turn of the Century*, Baltimore: Johns Hopkins University Press, 1985

Over the last century and a half, American society has been influenced, and even shaped, by constant changes in methods of communication. Telegraph and telephone, radio and television, the movies and the advertising business, have revolutionized the communication of news and information, and patterns of mass consumption. In the varied literature on the subject, some work focuses on technological innovation and development, while other studies examine the broader economic, social and cultural consequences of the continuing media revolution. This essay can only discuss one sample study of each of the main branches of the media, along with one or two more general works on the impact of the mass media.

BLONDHEIM examines the introduction of the telegraph, its impact on news reporting, and its larger social consequences during the latter half of the 19th century. Central to the telegraph's acceptance by the public and the press was its usefulness in a rapidly commercializing society. By the late 1840s, the major northeastern newspapers discerned material advantages in pooling resources and formed the Associated Press. The subsequent Republican partisanship in reporting inspired a hostile public reaction to biased news. The telegraph and its role in news reporting demonstrated an ability either to divide the nation, demonstrated in the years prior to the Civil War, or to unify it, as Blondheim indicates was the case by the late 19th century.

WASSERMAN examines American Telephone and Telegraph's attempt to develop a technology that would allow long-distance telephone transmission in the late 19th century. However, the new technology needed to be compatible with the existing local networks so as not to disrupt service. Wasserman's main strength lies in his examination of the interaction of corporate interests and technological development. However, his model, which depicts technological development as emerging from a scientific base, has been questioned by other historians of technology, most notably Hugh Aitken. Additionally, some readers may lament the lack of attention to the larger social and cultural framework in which innovation took place.

MAY situates the emergence of the motion picture industry at the crossroads of Victorian society's decline, Progressivism's attempt to reconcile modern industrial society with traditional values, and, ultimately, the general acceptance of modernity. Correspondingly, perceptions of movies alternate as potential corrupters of values (and therefore in need of regulation), tools to "uplift" and "civilize" the masses, and finally as an accepted form of mass entertainment and popular culture. At times, May relies too heavily on using the movies to explain the general society in what is otherwise an engaging book.

Using a "social construction" approach, DOUGLAS traces radio's development into an entertainment medium as opposed to another form of the telegraph or telephone. Highlighting the larger social trends that influenced radio's evolution through 1922, Douglas explains why certain alternative paths were not taken. Radio came to maturation in a burgeoning middle-class consumer culture during an era when advanced technology came increasingly under corporate control, and demand grew for government to undertake a regulatory role. Most intriguing is Douglas's account of popular perceptions and representations of radio technology over the course of its development.

UDELSON places television's development in the context of precedents set by the closely related radio industry and the consumer demand for high definition technology. The greatest advancements in television technology occurred after the incorporation of movies and radio into popular culture. Consequently, improvements in the medium were made with an eye toward a mass audience. Low quality transmission and regulatory problems needed to be surmounted before the eagerly anticipated television could enter mainstream culture. The components were in place and ready for widespread use by 1941, only to be delayed by World War II. The book is a good technological history of television, and useful parallels are drawn with radio. Udelson nicely elucidates the corporate and political dynamics of television development. However, some readers may prefer greater attention to the audience in a broader social and cultural context.

Advertising assumed a prominent place in these new forms of communication and media as they became incorporated into the developing culture of consumption. MARCHAND examines how a new group of professionals, the advertising men, perceived their role in the modernizing society of the 1920s and 1930s. These "mediators of modernity" promoted the culture of consumption as a way to counter the loss of community and feelings of alienation produced by the new consumer society. The "personal touch" could be restored by promoting items of various styles and colors to suit individual tastes. Advertisements offered "professional" advice on functioning in modern society. Advertising men often saw themselves as agents of "uplift" and "civilization" for the masses. Marchand analyzes assumptions of society and gender depicted in the advertisements. A chapter on the way in which perceptions of radio moved away from regarding it as a potential tool of "uplift" is especially useful in emphasizing both the outlook of the advertisers and the power of consumers.

For those readers most interested in breadth of coverage, CZITROM provides a comprehensive two-part survey that studies both media development and the theories concerned with its role in society. Underscoring the development of the telegraph, movies, and radio between 1838 and 1940, the first part examines, in less detailed fashion, the various forms of the media discussed in more specialized monographs. Czitrom emphasizes each new technology's departure from the past, the popular expectations of, and responses to, the new forms, and the eventual evolution toward corporate control. The second part is devoted to discussion of various theorists concerned with media, including John Dewey, Walter Lippmann, and Harold Innis. The questions that each theorist asked of the media are framed within the context and concerns of their day. In an epilogue, Czitrom highlights the continual inability of the new media to meet utopian expectations as a unifier of all peoples.

For those readers concerned with contemporary society, DÉGH offers a study examining the evolution of traditional folk narrative into mass culture. Using anthropological and ethnographic methods, Dégh charts how folklore adapted to modern communications technology, reached out to larger groups, and increased its ability to sustain tradition. Traditional perceptions of magic are visible in marketing techniques. The content and gender assumptions of classic folktales manifest themselves in mass entertainment. The tape recorder becomes a tool to "enhance the variation and dissemination of folklore in an unprecedented way." Dégh sketches the evolution of death and mourning rituals into the modern day practice of submitting memoriams to the local newspaper. The book suggests how the content of mass media is paradoxically limited by tradition, while it also acts as an agent of change.

MICHAEL A. KRYSKO

See also Advertising; Film; Radio and Television; Telegraph and Telephone

Communism *see* Socialism and Communism

Compromise of 1877

Benedict, Michael Les, "Southern Democrats in the Crisis of 1876–1877: A Reconsideration of *Reunion and Reaction*," *Journal of Southern History*, 46, November 1980

De Santis, Vincent P., "Rutherford B. Hayes and the Removal of the Troops and the End of Reconstruction," in *Region, Race, and Reconstruction: Essays in Honor of C. Vann Woodward*, edited by J. Morgan Kousser and James M. McPherson, New York: Oxford University Press, 1982

Gillette, William, *Retreat from Reconstruction, 1869–1879*, Baton Rouge: Louisiana State University Press, 1979

Hoogenboom, Ari, *The Presidency of Rutherford B. Hayes*, Lawrence: University Press of Kansas, 1988

Peskin, Allan, "Was There a Compromise of 1877?" *Journal of American History*, 60, June 1973

Polakoff, Keith Ian, *The Politics of Inertia: The Election of 1876 and the End of Reconstruction*, Baton Rouge: Louisiana State University Press, 1973

Rable, George C., "Southern Interests and the Election of 1876: A Reappraisal," *Civil War History*, 26, December 1980

Simpson, Brooks D., "Ulysses S. Grant and the Electoral Crisis of 1876–77," *Hayes Historical Journal*, 11, Winter 1992

Woodward, C. Vann, *Reunion and Reaction: The Compromise of 1877 and the End of Reconstruction*, Boston: Little Brown, 1951

Woodward, C. Vann, "Yes, There Was a Compromise of 1877," *Journal of American History*, 60, June 1973

Until 1950 most historians accepted that the Compromise of 1877, which resolved the disputed presidential election of 1876, consisted of a political deal whereby Republican presidential candidate Rutherford B. Hayes confirmed his claim to the White House in exchange for various concessions to Southern Democrats, including the withdrawal of federal military support from the remaining Republican regimes in the South, thus marking in the popular mind the end of Reconstruction. WOODWARD (1951) challenged this interpretation in a provocative revisionist work. According to Woodward, federal intervention was already doomed: moreover, the real compromise involved a series of negotiations involving railroad magnates, newspaper reporters, Republican leaders, and former Whigs-turned-Southern Democrats, in which federal aid for internal improvements and the building of a Southern transcontinental railroad would provide the foundation for a new bi-sectional Republican coalition grounded on issues of economic development. For Woodward the real compromise was to be found in these negotiations, and not in the process whereby Congress sought to resolve the awarding of disputed electoral votes through the establishment of an electoral commission, followed by the political deal to assure the conclusion of that process.

Woodward's thesis quickly won acceptance among American historians, and dominated explanations of the Compromise of 1877 for two decades. However, in 1973 two challenges appeared. PESKIN argued that as most of the components of Woodward's compromise never came to pass, perhaps there was no firm agreement in the first place. In response to this criticism, WOODWARD (1973) insisted that simply because the compromise was never realized, it did not mean that one was not made, even if it was later violated. More compelling was POLAKOFF's reassessment of the entire electoral crisis. He argued that neither Republican nor Democratic leaders possessed sufficient control over the party organization to exercise the control necessary to reach a binding agreement and execute it. It was precisely because of the problems of party leadership that newspaper reporters and businessmen could inject themselves into the process, although they too did not possess the ability to deliver on their promises.

Seven years later two articles questioned Woodward's conclusions by examining the behavior of Southern politicians. RABLE reminded readers that the primary issue in the minds of most Southern Democrats was an end to federal intervention in the South and the resumption of what they called "home rule." Using quantitative methods of roll-call analysis, BENEDICT called into doubt Woodward's description of how Southern Democrats voted, and suggested that the Northern Democrats contributed as much to the settlement of the crisis through their inadequate support for the effort to obstruct the counting of the electoral votes through filibuster. Neither historian questioned whether the negotiations described by Woodward took place; they doubted that those negotiations proved very influential in shaping the outcome of the crisis. De SANTIS offered a concise summary of the scholarly discussion, although his conclusion that Woodward's thesis had essentially weathered these assaults was not quite persuasive. It is much closer to the truth to observe that, in their attempts to refute Woodward's argument, historians passed over other ways to examine the crisis, and overlooked key elements of it.

Several other studies, even as they moved away from the agenda of inquiry established by Woodward, also cast doubt upon his interpretation of events. GILLETTE argued that the Grant administration had already abandoned its policy of intervention, so that the concessions supposedly made by Republicans in fact served only to confirm the abandonment of the remaining Southern Republican regimes in Louisiana and South Carolina. In recounting Hayes's actions during the election of 1876 and the resolution of the electoral crisis, HOOGENBOOM reminds readers that, long before the disputed election, the Ohio Republicans had already decided to embark upon a different course of action toward the South, including the construction of a new Southern wing of the Republican party based upon a common economic agenda. Indeed, Hayes thought that only by replacing race with economic development as the primary issue of southern politics would whites be induced to respect the right of blacks to vote. This vision never came to pass. SIMPSON focuses on the actions of Ulysses S. Grant during the electoral crisis, revealing that the outgoing president was no lame duck. He encouraged a peaceful resolution in ways that increased Hayes's chances for victory even as they allowed Grant to maintain a neutral posture in the interest of preserving American political institutions. His account barely touches upon the negotiations that are at the heart of Woodward's story. Instead he concentrates on the electoral commission and Grant's careful handling of affairs in Louisiana and South Carolina as he refused either to abandon or to recognize Republican claimants until Southern Democrats abandoned their filibuster, which was blocking the completion of the count in the House.

BROOKS D. SIMPSON

See also Reconstruction entries

Computers and Data Processing

Aspray, William, *John von Neumann and the Origins of Modern Computing*, Cambridge: Massachusetts Institute of Technology Press, 1990

Austrian, Geoffrey D., *Herman Hollerith: Forgotten Giant of Information Processing*, New York: Columbia University Press, 1982

Ceruzzi, Paul, *Reckoners: The Prehistory of the Digital Computer, from Relays to the Stored-Program Concept, 1935–1945*, Westport, CT: Greenwood Press, 1983

Cortada, James W., *Before the Computer: IBM, NCR, Burroughs, and Remington Rand and the Industry They Created, 1865–1956*, Princeton: Princeton University Press, 1993

Flamm, Kenneth, *Creating the Computer: Government, Industry and High Technology*, Washington, DC: Brookings Institution, 1987

Manes, Stephen and Paul Andrews, *Gates: How Microsoft's Mogul Reinvented an Industry–and Made Himself the Richest Man in America*, New York: Doubleday, 1993

Metropolis, Nick, Jack Howlett, and Gian-Carlo Rota (editors), *A History of Computing in the Twentieth Century: A Collection of Essays*, New York: Academic Press, 1980

Pugh, Emerson W., Lyle R. Johnson, and John H. Palmer, *IBM's 360 and Early 370 Systems*, Cambridge: Massachusetts Institute of Technology Press, 1991

Rodgers, William, *Think: A Biography of the Watsons and IBM*, New York: Stein and Day, 1969; London: Weidenfeld and Nicolson, 1970

Stern, Nancy, *From ENIAC to UNIVAC: An Appraisal of the Eckert-Mauchly Computers*, Bedford, MA: Digital Press, 1981

Watson, Thomas J., Jr., and Peter Petre, *Father, Son & Co.: My Life at IBM and Beyond*, New York: Bantam, 1990

If one confines oneself to the commercial development of the electronic digital computer, then the history of the subject only covers the last forty years or so, and it would not be surprising to find that the number of books on the subject is limited. In practice, however, the number and diversity of books on American computer history is wider than one might suppose. There are three main reasons: first, the history of the computer in America really goes back to the 19th century, with the appearance of tabulators and punched-card machinery; second, the rapid growth of computing has generated a parallel interest in its history; and finally, America since the 1940s and 1950s has been easily the world's most successful computer manufacturer and developer of computer programmes (software).

AUSTRIAN covers the first major development in American data-processing by looking at the career of Herman Hollerith, the United States census special agent, whose punched-card machinery transformed the tabulation of the American census of 1890. Besides being a first-rate biography, Austrian is important because it emphasizes the crucial nature of data-processing to the census, experience which was immediately utilized by American industry.

Had it not been for the computer revolution of the 1950s and 1960s, however, Austrian's book would probably not have been written (or at least, no one would have thought the subject important). The same might have been true of CORTADA who examines the information-handling industry from its origins in the late 19th century up to the emergence of the data-processing computer in the 1950s. Like many American business historians, Cortada adopts the thesis that information processing was one of the key organizational changes that enabled the development of American large-scale enterprise in the Gilded Age. The book describes the development of the office-machine industry from 1865 to 1920; examines the mature office-machine industry (with the emphasis on punched-cards) between the wars; and, finally, takes up the story of the emergence of practical business computers in the mid-1950s.

The initial push towards the electronic digital computer, however, did not come from the business world (which was often sceptical of computers). Before the 1950s, calculators and computers were mainly seen as scientific tools for mathematicians and engineers, who received most of their funding from scientific and military sources. This is demonstrated by CERUZZI, who covers the work of the early pioneers, such as the Harvard mathematician Howard Aiken, the physicist George Stibitz at the Bell Telephone Laboratories, and the electronics engineers J. Presper Eckert and John Mauchly at the University of Pennsylvania.

The fact that the emergence of the digital computer is so recent has meant that some of the history has been written by participants, as well as by professional historians. A fine mirror of the times is the volume edited by METROPOLIS, HOWLETT and ROTA, which records the proceedings of a conference on the history of computing at Los Alamos Scientific Laboratory in June 1976. Many of the American presenters of papers at the conference – John Backus (on the creation of FORTRAN programming), Eckert and Mauchly (on the design of the ENIAC) – were directly involved with the developments they describe. Besides providing a rough narrative of events, the volume provides interesting (though not unimpeachable) source material for future historians.

The development of the first successful American stored-program computer, the ENIAC, generated much controversy after the event, especially concerning the rival claims of Eckert and Mauchly and the mathematical genius, John von Neumann. In a fine scholarly study, STERN goes a long way towards settling these matters, besides providing a standard history of the development of America's first business computer – the UNIVAC. A key member of the ENIAC team – some would say *the* key member – was von Neumann. ASPRAY's study provides a detailed examination of his career in computing. It is not written as a biography, though it comes close to being the standard life of the subject, as von Neumann's interest in computing occupied much of his professional career. Aspray concentrates on the wider impact of computers by following von Neumann's pioneering interests in automata, analogies between the brain and the computer, weather forecasting, and the theory of complicated information-processing systems.

By the 1960s, business computing (data-processing) had really come into its own. In America, one company – International Business Machines (IBM) – cast a very long shadow over its competitors, a situation that is mirrored in the historiography. Three books on IBM computers in the MIT Press series on the history of computing, launched in 1984, fill nearly two thousand pages – as much as all the other seven books in the series combined! One of the most ambitious of those books, by PUGH, JOHNSON and PALMER, provides a detailed technological history of IBM's System/360, which by launching a "compatible" family of third-generation computers marked a watershed in the industry. Although the authors were IBM employees, this has not prevented them from writing a critical history.

Readers interested in other aspects of IBM's history can choose from a wide range of books: business histories, autobiographies, and muckraking accounts that attack some of IBM's allegedly dubious selling tactics. One of the best of the first crop of books on IBM was RODGERS, who focuses on the career of company president Tom Watson, Sr. Characteristically, IBM tried to hinder its publication, though, as Tom Watson, Jr. later admitted, Rodgers does a good job (despite his slightly journalistic approach) of catching the paternalistic spirit of the company. WATSON himself (with PETRE) has written a remarkably candid account of his own presidency at IBM, which brings Rodgers's account up to date.

Few historians have attempted a general synthesis of the history of the computer industry, though FLAMM is close to being a standard text. Not only does he provide a succinct, but admirably-referenced historical account of the development of the American computer industry, he also sets that industry in an international context by looking at computing overseas. The economic roots of US computing are analyzed, revealing the enormous extent to which the computer was a child of World War II and the Cold War.

As yet, the focus of most of the literature on the history of computing and data- processing is on the great pioneers and their machines. This is even true of more recent books on software, such as MANES and ANDREWS, a biography of Bill Gates, president of Microsoft and the dominant figure in the American software industry. The wider impact of computing on American society and the technology's social repurcussions are still largely unexplored topics. But then, computer historiography, like the industry itself, is still in its infancy.

GEOFFREY TWEEDALE

See also Business History: Individual Corporations; Technology and Invention

Confederate States of America: General

Beringer, Richard E., Herman Hattaway, Archer Jones, and William N. Still, Jr., *Why the South Lost the Civil War*, Athens: University of Georgia Press, 1986

Davis, William C., *"A Government of Our Own": The Making of the Confederacy*, New York: Free Press, 1994

Escott, Paul D., *After Secession: Jefferson Davis and the Failure of Confederate Nationalism*, Baton Rouge: Louisiana State University Press, 1978

Faust, Drew Gilpin, *The Creation of Confederate Nationalism: Ideology and Identity in the Civil War South*, Baton Rouge: Louisiana State University Press, 1988

Rable, George C., *The Confederate Republic: A Revolution Against Politics*, Chapel Hill: University of North Carolina Press, 1994

Ramsdell, Charles W., *Behind the Lines in the Southern Confederacy*, Baton Rouge: Louisiana State University Press, 1944

Thomas, Emory M., *The Confederacy as a Revolutionary Experience*, Englewood Cliffs, NJ: Prentice Hall, 1971

Thomas, Emory M., *The Confederate Nation, 1861–1865*, New York: Harper, 1979

Three general questions provide a framework for general studies of the Confederacy. First, was the Confederate experience truly a "revolution" in the sense that its founders sought a radical break with antebellum American traditions? Second, did southerners create a fully functioning nation, or did the manifest internal disagreements among its own citizenry fatally hamper the Confederate enterprise from the outset? Third, exactly why did the Confederacy lose the Civil War?

THOMAS (1971) takes the first question as its central theme, and argues that the new southern nation was created by secessionist radicals in a paroxysm of revolutionary fervor. These radicals very quickly lost control of their own revolution, however, as southern moderates were elevated to positions of power in the Confederacy. According to Thomas, a second sort of "revolution" occurred after 1861, as southerners were compelled to jettison cherished principles of states rights and individual autonomy in the name of waging a modern war. This succinct statement of his point of view was both developed and modified in THOMAS (1979). The organizing idea of an unexpected wartime revolution remains, but is discussed within the framework of a comprehensive narrative of the Confederacy. Whether one agrees or disagrees with Thomas's approach, this is probably the best single-volume history of the Confederacy. Part of the New American Nation series, it fulfils the central purpose of that series by synthesizing large amounts of secondary source material in a readable yet challenging form, deftly combining military, political, economic and social issues. The bibliographic essay, while somewhat dated by now, is nevertheless very useful.

RABLE argues that southerners shared a common political value system based on a version of republicanism which rejected the factionalism of party politics and instead called for absolute southern unanimity on political values and goals (especially in support of slavery). For Rable the Confederate experience was a revolution in that it was a rebellion against what was perceived to be the very un-republican beliefs and practices of antebellum America, and against northern political culture. Like Thomas, Rable argued that wartime developments surprised and shocked many Confederates, who discovered that their new nation's citizenry was far from unanimous on the sensitive political issues of government centralization, states rights and the peculiar institution. Rable's book is thoughtful, perceptive, and clearly written; but it is a sophisticated study, intended for an audience which is already well-versed in the basics of Confederate history.

DAVIS offers another perspective on the Confederate revolution. Where Thomas and Rable present closely reasoned arguments for viewing the establishment of a southern nation as a revolutionary event, Davis takes a more narrative-based approach, focusing on the personalities and relationships of the men who were the founding fathers of this new nation. He provides a detailed, almost day-by-day history of the first months of the Confederate government, including the opening sessions of the Confederate Congress and the drafting of a constitution. In this lively and colorful account, Jefferson Davis, Alexander Stephens and other Confederate leaders come vividly to life. While not as analytically sophisticated as Thomas or Rable's books, Davis offers a fascinating and highly readable narrative of the establishment of the Confederacy.

Historians posed the question of whether the South was able to create a truly viable nation only when they were able to look past the battlefield, and examine life on the home front. One of the first to do so was RAMSDELL who suggested that the internal weaknesses of the Confederacy, particularly the collapse of its fledgling economy, undermined its ability to wage war successfully. Now more than fifty years old, Ramsdell's book is a classic which has withstood the test of time well and offers important insights into daily life in the Confederacy. In a searching examination of the political flaws of the South at war, ESCOTT argues that the Confederate experiment was weakened from the outset by the limitations of its president and its political pedigree. The pervasive states rights mentality of southerners, and Davis's inability to articulate a persuasive national agenda meant that Confederates were never really able to overcome disagreements and squabbles among themselves. This fatally handicapped both the Confederate war effort and attempts to foster feelings of commonality among southerners.

In a brief but penetrating analysis, based on her Fleming Lectures, FAUST offers a thoughtful challenge to this school of thought. She points out that southerners created a strong sense of a unique Confederate cultural identity, and that this helped to nourish and sustain a real sense of Confederate-ness during most of the war. Faust's book provides an important counterbalance to Escott; both are essential reading for serious students of the Confederacy.

Among the many works which have attempted to answer the question of why the Confederacy lost the Civil War, one book above all is indispensable. In BERINGER *et al.* four distinguished scholars of the Confederacy collaborated in an exhaustive examination of this issue. In many respects, they echo Ramsdell and Escott, by arguing that a lack of internal social and political cohesion, and the consequent decline in morale, were the primary factors in the Confederacy's demise. They also devote much attention to rebuttal of competing theories and even manage to provide a fairly complete chronicle of the war itself. The result is a large, somewhat daunting but valuable book.

BRIAN DIRCK

Confederate States of America: Constitution, Government, and Politics

Alexander, Thomas B. and Richard E. Beringer, *The Anatomy of the Confederate Congress: A Study of the Influences of Member Characteristics on Legislative Voting Behavior, 1861–1865*, Nashville: Vanderbilt University Press, 1972

Beringer, Richard E., Herman Hattaway, Archer Jones, and William N. Still, Jr., *Why the South Lost the Civil War*, Athens: University of Georgia Press, 1986

Davis, William C., *Jefferson Davis: The Man and His Hour*, New York: HarperCollins, 1991

Davis, William C., *"A Government of Our Own": The Making of the Confederacy*, New York: Free Press, 1994

Escott, Paul D., *After Secession: Jefferson Davis and the Failure of Confederate Nationalism*, Baton Rouge: Louisiana State University Press, 1978

Faust, Drew Gilpin, *The Creation of Confederate Nationalism: Ideology and Identity in the Civil War South*, Baton Rouge: Louisiana State University Press, 1988

Owsley, Frank Lawrence, *State Rights in the Confederacy*, Chicago: University of Chicago Press, 1925

Rable, George C., *The Confederate Republic: A Revolution Against Politics*, Chapel Hill: University of North Carolina Press, 1994

Schott, Thomas E., *Alexander H. Stephens of Georgia: A Biography*, Baton Rouge: Louisiana State University Press, 1988

Thomas, Emory M., *The Confederate Nation, 1861–1865*, New York: Harper, 1979

Compared to the innumerable military studies, the number of works on Confederate political history is fairly small. In this comparatively neglected field OWSLEY was a pioneer. Taking a cue from many Confederates themselves, he argues that states rights was an inherent flaw in a political system that ultimately led to the collapse of the fledgling southern nation. Owsley describes in detail how states withheld military and financial support from the Confederate government and specifically how constitutional objections to conscription and the suspension of habeas corpus – with governors Joseph E. Brown of Georgia and Zebulon Vance of North Carolina as the chief obstructionists – hamstrung the war effort.

The Owsley thesis survived for over half a century without serious challenge, but in recent decades, various scholars have raised some serious questions about its validity. THOMAS points out that despite the rancorous wartime disputes over states rights, a remarkable degree of centralization occurred in the Confederacy. Public policy questions are nicely integrated with military events, though the coverage is sometimes uneven. By taking increasing control over arms production and transportation, for example, the national government by the end of the war was able adequately to supply the soldiers in the field. For Thomas, the real weakness of Confederate nationalism lay in a commitment to slavery and in the shifting and often competing definitions of revolution. The absence of a political party system and the ambitions of mediocre politicians further undermined the political structure – a contention that until very recently has gone largely unchallenged.

BERINGER *et al.* reject Owsley, build on Thomas, but also emphasize the inherent weaknesses of Confederate nationalism. Because many Southern whites felt guilty about slavery and ambivalent about secession, their commitment to a southern nation was tenuous from the beginning. As for constitutional questions, states rights became more an asset than a liability to the political system. Suffering from what Beringer *et al.* term "cognitive dissonance" and a fear that God had abandoned them, Confederates ultimately lacked sufficient commitment to the cause. By paying too little attention to morale, Confederate leaders failed to rally their people to what in any case was an ill-defined and feeble nationalism.

For ESCOTT, a more fundamental problem was the loyalty of non-slaveholders. Jefferson Davis devoted considerable energy to establishing unity by emphasizing a defense of liberty and fear of northern subjugation. His centralizing measures stirred up furious opposition and their financial burdens alienated many ordinary citizens. Escott was the first historian to use the thousands of letters and petitions sent by civilians to the Confederate government to examine common problems on the home front. These documents revealed how class divisions eroded patriotism, and how belated welfare measures by both state and national governments failed to stem the tide of disaffection that ultimately defeated the Confederacy.

FAUST broadens the discussion of Confederate nationalism by examining the relationships between ideology, culture, religion, and society. In three concise essays, she describes Confederate nationalism as a complex mixture of elitism and democracy with strong appeals to both Christian and American revolutionary traditions. The course of the war prompted jeremiads against the sin of avarice and calls for reforming the institution of slavery. For Faust, official ideology contained both notable strengths and fatal weaknesses, and the history of the Confederacy embodied persistent tensions between public ideals and people's lives.

Many of these conflicts were played out in the Confederate Congress. In a path-breaking quantitative study, ALEXANDER and BERINGER meticulously analyze congressional voting behavior. Their work dissects the chaotic factionalism of Confederate politics and shows how members from districts under Union military occupation were the strongest supporters of strong war measures such as conscription and the suspension of habeas corpus.

Both the personal and public aspects of political conflict are chronicled in two excellent biographies. In a study that splendidly integrates personality and politics, SCHOTT presents a sympathetic yet critical portrait of Alexander H. Stephens as a reluctant Vice President who was determined to keep the southern revolution a safely conservative one. Sharing with Jefferson Davis traits of stubbornness and vanity along with a strong commitment to political principles, Stephens eventually broke with the headstrong President and helped encourage opposition to the administration in Georgia. DAVIS (1991) offers a remarkably judicious and easily the best biography of the always controversial Jefferson Davis. The key to understanding Davis was his fundamental sense of insecurity. He also manifested many personal and political traits, whether for good or for ill, to an extreme degree, including such contradictory characteristics as stubbornness and indecisiveness. Thus Davis proved to be a capable but also seriously flawed chief executive.

Many problems described in these works appeared early in the Confederacy's history, and receive full treatment in DAVIS (1994), a recent narrative of the birth of the Confederate government. This book takes readers inside the Montgomery convention and is especially effective on the physical setting and the personalities. Included are descriptions of streets, rooms, and weather along with pungent sketches of the delegates with all their idiosyncrasies and foibles. Davis offers a useful account of the decision to fire on Fort Sumter and presents far and away the most thorough account of Jefferson Davis's election as Confederate president.

RABLE offers the most recent comprehensive narrative and analysis of Confederate political culture. Seeking to understand the Confederate experiment on its own terms, he presents the southern nation's founding fathers as conservative (and sometimes reactionary) reformers seeking to restore a mythical political purity rooted in 18th-century republicanism. In their new constitution and in their new government, Confederates attempted to turn their backs on years of electioneering, patronage, and political wirepulling; they were especially determined to create a political system without the evils of political parties. During the war itself, a basic counterpoint between these high ideals and the realities of political ambitions, pettiness, and prejudice played itself out in the churches and the schools as well as the political arena. Some politicians stressed national unity while others emphasized individual, community, and state liberty.

GEORGE C. RABLE

Confederate States of America: Home Front

Beringer, Richard E., Herman Hattaway, Archer Jones, and William N. Still, Jr., *Why the South Lost the Civil War*, Athens: University of Georgia Press, 1986

Channing, Steven A. and the Editors of Time-Life Books, *Confederate Ordeal: The Southern Home Front* (The Civil War series), Alexandria, VA: Time-Life Books, 1984

Clinton, Catherine and Nina Silber (editors), *Divided Houses: Gender and the Civil War*, New York: Oxford University Press, 1992

Current, Richard N. (editor), *Encyclopedia of the Confederacy*, 4 vols., New York: Simon and Schuster, 1993

Escott, Paul D., *After Secession: Jefferson Davis and the Failure of Confederate Nationalism*, Baton Rouge: Louisiana State University Press, 1978

Kenzer, Robert C., *Kinship and Neighborhood in a Southern Community: Orange County, North Carolina, 1849–1881*, Knoxville: University of Tennessee Press, 1987

McMillan, Malcolm C., *The Disintegration of a Confederate State: Three Governors and Alabama's Wartime Home Front, 1861–1865*, Macon, GA: Mercer University Press, 1986

Massey, Mary Elizabeth, "The Confederate States of America: The Homefront," in *Writing Southern History: Essays in Historiography in Honor of Fletcher M. Green*, edited by Arthur S. Link and Rembert W. Patrick, Baton Rouge: Louisiana State University Press, 1965

Rable, George C., *Civil Wars: Women and the Crisis of Southern Nationalism*, Urbana: University of Illinois Press, 1989

Ramsdell, Charles W., *Behind the Lines in the Southern Confederacy*, Baton Rouge: Louisiana State University Press, 1944

Thomas, Emory M., *The Confederate Nation, 1861–1865*, New York: Harper, 1979

Wiley, Bell Irvin, *The Plain People of the Confederacy*, Baton Rouge: Louisiana State University Press, 1943

Woodward, C. Vann (editor), *Mary Chesnut's Civil War*, New Haven: Yale University Press, 1981

In recent years, the South has received rather less attention than the North in studies of the home front during the Civil War. CHANNING, the best synthesis, is a book written for a popular audience as part of a Civil War series, and devotes as much space to evocative illustrations as to narrative and analysis. Channing is a master historian of the South in the Civil War era, and this neglected book suggests many themes and issues relating to the Confederate home front.

MASSEY pioneered scholarly work on the subject, and her 1965 essay mourns the dearth of historical research on the Confederate home front. She maintains that the everyday experience of men and women on the home front, when understood in its proper social and economic context, can help to explain the war's outcome, and can cast new light on the ways in which warfare transforms the lives of non-combatants.

Subsequent historians focusing on the question of why the Confederacy lost the Civil War have indeed looked at the home front. Revisionist studies, notably THOMAS, recognize that the Confederate government was much more of a centralizing force than had previously been thought. Starting in the crucial spring months of 1862, and continuing throughout the war, a series of executive directives and national legislation regarding conscription, suspension of habeas corpus, impressment of supplies and slaves, and tithing of agricultural production was implemented to bring about a more efficient and balanced use of home front resources, and to foster a greater unity of purpose. In some respects, the policy worked, and, in spite of the North's overwhelming economic, technological and demographic advantages, the South was able to sustain its rebellion for four long years.

Despite this apparent Confederate success, studies since Thomas have provided an entirely new perspective on the South during the Civil War. Recent scholars attribute the Confederate defeat to internal – and sometimes intangible – factors, such as economic self-interest, loss of the will to win, and declining morale on the home front. They emphasize the inability of the Confederacy to create a unified southern society in response to the war. ESCOTT argues that the activities of the Confederate government created (or at least aggravated) a class conflict that alienated both yeomen and planters from the government and the war effort. BERINGER *et al.* favor a multi-causal explanation of southern defeat, but give particular attention to religion and war guilt. They single out a deficient nationalism, stimulated by a "cognitive dissonance" over Confederate war aims, and they identify problems on the home front as the basic reason why the South lost.

Such emphasis on disillusionment with the war effort was not a new theme for historians of the Confederacy. In the published version of his 1937 Fleming Lectures, RAMSDELL anticipated much of the recent scholarship, particularly the emphasis on disaffection and discontent. Quoting extensively from letters and documents that convey a sense of the disintegration and pain of the home front, he stresses the inability of the Confederate nation, or state or local government, to cope with problems of financial hardship and economic distress faced by the common people. His thesis that the collapse of the home front was a major cause of Confederate defeat has been echoed by more recent studies.

As with Ramsdell, WILEY's book, based on his Fleming Lectures, is now somewhat dated, but it has greatly influenced subsequent scholars. Wiley wrote in reaction against the prevailing view of an aristocratic American South. Some of the themes of his earlier work on the common soldiers and on African Americans during the Civil War are summarized in this study. Wiley was also an early proponent of the now popular argument that internal social factors are a crucial part of the explanation of the collapse of the Confederacy.

Before the appearance of recent studies of the internal history of the Confederacy, a number of scholars were contributing editions of source material which looked at the home front through the words of participants. A prime example is WOODWARD's Pulitzer Prize-winning edition of *Mary Chesnut's Civil War*, hailed by historian Joe Gray Taylor as the "most important source about the Confederate home front." Woodward's introduction and annotations are essential to an understanding of this diary of an astute, if opinionated, aristocratic South Carolinian, who, through her husband, was privy to central decision-makers of the Confederacy, and who offers shrewd insights into life in wartime Richmond. Once believed to be a primary source for the Civil War home front, her observations are in reality a literary expansion and re-casting of her actual wartime diary.

Renewal of interest in the social history of the Civil War has inspired recent work on a variety of subjects. In a fascinating study of Alabama's three wartime governors and their insoluble home front problems, McMILLAN reinforces Ramsdell's earlier argument that the imposition of sacrifices for the war effort greatly increased disaffection. Governors had to find ways to recruit soldiers, maintain a state militia, feed soldiers' families, obtain supplies of salt, impress planters' slaves, regulate alcohol distillation, control crop selection and production, and protect citizens from outlaws and deserters. McMillan argues that, if elections had been held in 1865, the Peace party would have prevailed.

RABLE casts new light on the ways in which warfare transformed the lives of southern white women of all classes, who both supported, and ultimately undermined, southern nationalism and the war effort. His insightful analysis follows the changes wrought on the home front, and is an excellent overview of crucial issues of patriarchy, class tensions, patriotism – and survival itself. CLINTON and SILBER offer a wide variety of essays, of varying quality, covering both North and South. Several important essays on the Confederacy argue that the Civil War broke down the traditional Southern patriarchy, as women assumed roles customarily performed by men. Especially important in this volume is Drew Gilpin Faust's influential article, "Altars of Sacrifice: Confederate Women and the Narratives of War." She argues that men at the battlefield failed their home front gender responsibilities, and women thus became disenchanted with a prolonged war, and helped to undermine the war effort.

Recent reference works contain essays on the Confederate home front, and provide important bibliographies, especially of the relevant community studies. See, for example, Burton's essay and bibliography on "Society" in CURRENT. Most studies of 19th-century southern communities, states or regions relate in some way to the Confederate home front. Experience varied widely, often in accordance with proximity to, or distance from, the actual fighting. North Carolina has received some of the best coverage. One outstanding example is KENZER's study of Orange County, which examines relief efforts, the problems of refugees, and the economic hardship suffered by the community. Kenzer suggests that the war shattered the isolation of each local community, as neighborhoods began to look to county and state governments for aid. In his view, one of the lasting effects of the war was the breakdown of the self-sufficiency of local neighborhoods.

Many more studies of various aspects of the internal life of the Confederacy, including further local community studies, are likely to appear in the next few years.

ORVILLE VERNON BURTON

Congress

Alexander, Thomas B., *Sectional Stress and Party Strength: A Study of Roll-Call Voting Patterns in the United States House of Representatives, 1836–1860*, Nashville: Vanderbilt University Press, 1967

Bacon, Don, Roger H. Davidson, and Morton Keller (editors), *The Encyclopedia of the United States Congress*, 4 vols., New York: Simon and Schuster, 1995

Benedict, Michael Les, *A Compromise of Principle: Congressional Republicans and Reconstruction, 1863–1869*, New York: Norton, 1974

Bogue, Allan G., *The Congressman's Civil War*, Cambridge and New York: Cambridge University Press, 1989

Brady, David W., *Critical Elections and Congressional Policy-Making*, Stanford, CA: Stanford University Press, 1988

Cooper, Joseph, *The Origins of the Standing Committees and the Development of the Modern House*, Houston: Rice University Press, 1970

Fite, Gilbert, *Richard B. Russell, Jr., Senator from Georgia*, Chapel Hill: University of North Carolina Press, 1991

Hamilton, Holman, *Prologue to Conflict: The Crisis and Compromise of 1850*, Lexington: University Press of Kentucky, 1964

Silbey, Joel H. (editor-in-chief), *Encyclopedia of the American Legislative System*, 3 vols., New York: Scribner, 1994

Sinclair, Barbara, *The Transformation of the US Senate*, Baltimore: Johns Hopkins University Press, 1989

Stewart, Charles H. III, *Budget Reform Politics: The Design of the Appropriations Process in the House of Representatives, 1865–1921*, Cambridge and New York: Cambridge University Press, 1989

Thompson, Margaret Susan, *The "Spider Web": Congress and Lobbying in the Age of Grant*, Ithaca, NY: Cornell University Press, 1985

Historical scholarship about Congress has been extensive, largely descriptive, and quite episodic. Few volumes cover its whole history and none is of recent vintage. Researchers have traditionally focused on dramatic moments and outstanding leaders, primarily seeking to discover how external political matters played out in the congressional environment. Evidence for this has largely been drawn from surviving manuscripts, newspapers, speeches, and memoirs. One example of this approach is HAMILTON's study of the Compromise of 1850, which closely follows the debates on the floor of both Houses, delineates the pressures on the members, and carefully describes how they emerged from the significant sectional confrontation of the late 1840s. Congress served two functions in his view, one, to echo the forces at play outside of its halls, and, second, to provide a place where those external problems could be resolved by the actions of astute political leaders.

Dealing largely in the same manner with matters a century later, FITE provides an excellent biography of an important senatorial leader of the conservative coalition during the New Deal and civil rights eras, when the nation's policy agenda and the relative importance of the President and Congress were both significantly transformed. The work is drawn largely from Russell's papers, newspapers, and congressional printed material. The method is similar to Hamilton's (and much other work as well) in that its main emphasis is on detailing the facts of a career (or a crisis), and describing how, in this case, Russell dealt with the vast pressures for change present in the political environment, from his seat on the Senate floor.

A different approach to studying Congress has been taken by a group of historians, heavily influenced by their interaction with political scientists, who, since the 1960s, have revolutionized the study of the contemporary Congress by moving beyond events and personalities to focus on processes and patterns. Their methods are different as well, incorporating the systematic measurement of a large range of actions taken on the floor, rather than relying on methods that did not catch the totality of congressional behavior. Although description is important, the essential focus is analytic, while usually remaining topic-specific rather than encompassing large blocks of time.

Some of these scholars look to settle persistent historiographic conflicts. Through the use of computer technology and sophisticated quantitative methods, ALEXANDER measures a more extensive range of activity than anyone before him, the full roll-call record of the House of Representatives across more than twenty years, in order to assess the different elements – party identification, sectional loyalty, sensitivity to constituency – that determined individual voting decisions in the middle of the 19th century. He stresses the prime importance of party identification in shaping how congressmen reacted to events and issues, but also notes that there were serious shifts in their loyalties when sectional pressures impinged on their world. In Alexander's precise delineation, congressmen, in short, continued to reflect the pressures and realities of the external political world.

BENEDICT similarly uses roll-call analysis to describe the nature of intra-party differences among Republican congressmen as they dealt with emancipation and the reconstruction of the South. Historians have battled constantly over the sources and nature of the different blocs and what they stood for. As with Alexander, Benedict's attempt to clarify these matters has the virtue of incorporating more evidence (the reactions of all of the Republican representatives rather than a few "representative" ones) in a more systematic way than those who had preceded him and establishing, thereby, some claim to completeness and precision.

Congressmen's actions are also shaped by each chamber's institutional arrangements: its leadership and committee structure, as well as the members' notions (or norms) of proper behavior, function and role. A number of historians, influenced by the way political scientists have delineated these matters in the contemporary world, have looked at facets of these at different points in time. Thus, BOGUE takes us into the House chamber and its meeting rooms to paint a picture of the congressional world in the Civil War era as the members viewed it, and tried to work their way through it. He includes a range of elements in his analysis: who congressmen were, and where they came from, how they organized themselves, their relationship with the President, and the way that they used their investigative power to assert their place and role during the war. It is a textured portrait of the House and its members in an unprecedented era involving a unique range of policy initiatives and a workload previously unknown.

THOMPSON has a similar purpose, dealing with Congress at a time of vast changes and the confusion that ensued among its members as they found themselves besieged by new forces, demands, and pressures, stemming from the urban and industrial revolutions and the policy needs that followed, with a set of institutions singularly undeveloped and inadequate to their tasks. As a result, congressmen turned to lobbyists for information and guidance, and took short cuts through the complex, obsolete maze they inhabited. Thompson stresses the importance of understanding the widening corruption of the era as not simply the result of the venality of the members, but the product of societal transformation and institutional inadequacies.

Some political scientists have turned from the contemporary scene to reach back into the past to illuminate current patterns and behavior. In doing so, they have made some major contributions to understanding the history of the institution as well. The committees of Congress are critical to House and Senate operations. COOPER's examination of their origins emphasizes that, despite their critical importance, even indispensability, as controllers of the business of the House, they did not emerge without difficulty. They were shaped by shifts in the external political environment, and in the understandings and assumptions of congressmen, about how to get things done. Politics at the time were beset by managerial inexperience and consumed by elaborate fears of the power of small groups to dominate the world for their own selfish purposes, factors that had to be overcome before an effective committee system could emerge.

STEWART examines one of the key committees of the House across a fifty-year span almost a century later. In the beginning, in the 1860s, budget making was a highly decentralized process involving a large number of members, reflecting the decentralized nature of the House and of the country more generally. But, faced with massive changes in the external environment, and responding to individual electoral needs and the shifting interaction between Congress and the President, the process grew increasingly centralized and controlled by the House leadership. These patterns were reflected elsewhere in the government apparatus over the same period.

Significant changes across time have characterized Congress in the 20th-century, as well, and some of the best historical scholarship by political scientists has dealt with this century. In covering the years from the 1950s to the present, SINCLAIR emphasizes how much the Senate moved from an earlier pattern established early in the 1900s, dominated by the leadership, deference by the membership to the institution's elders, and to each other's particular needs and issues, to a more freewheeling, highly individualistic, uncontrolled and unpredictable situation. Older Senate norms have frayed into impotence as the massive force of a media revolution, the disintegration of political parties, and the loss of respect for authority in the post-World War II era have directly affected senators. It is a compelling and chilling description which sets the scene for analyses of chaos, gridlock and decline in the contemporary world.

Elections are the primary external pressure on congressmen, never far from their minds. BRADY examines the way in which massive electoral realignments, that may profoundly change the American political landscape, work their way through the House of Representatives, regenerating its activities, particularly in the appearance and enactment of new policy agendas. New members thrown up by realigning changes in the electorate, with stronger electoral bases than their predecessors (at least at first) overcome existing inertia to change committee make-ups and leadership patterns, in order to force through policies that were previously resisted. The truth of this at three scattered moments in our history is a strong affirmation of the power of electoral politics and the external environment to affect congressional behavior directly.

Any listing of some of the important scholarship about Congress across two centuries should include two recently published encyclopedias. The essays in BACON, DAVIDSON and KELLER, on one hand, and in SILBEY, on the other, include a range of textured historical descriptions, details about institutions, policy making, internal dynamics, and the pressures manifested at different moments. The essays in Silbey are longer and more thematic, than those in Bacon *et al.*, which, in turn, cover more items. Each encyclopedia contains essays that specifically cover distinct chronological eras. If these essays were to be published separately, they would comprise an excellent, scholarly, up to date, history of the first branch of government, something which, as noted at the outset, is regrettably lacking at present.

JOEL H. SILBEY

Congress of Industrial Organizations

Bernstein, Irving, *Turbulent Years: A History of the American Worker, 1933–1941*, Boston: Houghton Mifflin, 1970

Dubofsky, Melvyn and Warren Van Tine, *John L. Lewis: A Biography*, New York: Quadrangle/New York Times, 1977

Foster, James C., *The Union Politic: The CIO Political Action Committee*, Columbia: University of Missouri Press, 1975

Fraser, Steven, *Labor Will Rule: Sidney Hillman and the Rise of American Labor*, New York: Free Press, 1991

Levenstein, Harvey A., *Communism, Anti-Communism, and the CIO*, Westport, CT: Greenwood Press, 1981

Lichtenstein, Nelson, *Labor's War at Home: The CIO in World War II*, Cambridge and New York: Cambridge University Press, 1982

Lichtenstein, Nelson, *The Most Dangerous Man in Detroit: Walter Reuther and the Fate of American Labor*, New York: Basic Books, 1995

Zieger, Robert H., *The CIO, 1935–1955*, Chapel Hill: University of North Carolina Press, 1995

ZIEGER is the only scholarly history of the CIO that covers the full period of its separate existence. Since the CIO was always a creature of the powerful international unions that provided its funding and leadership, students of its history must consult the extensive literature relating to its affiliated unions, notably the United Mine Workers of America, the Amalgamated Clothing Workers, the United Automobile

Workers, and the United Steelworkers. The large body of works dealing with these and other affiliates, and with racial, ethnic, gender, legal, and other aspects of the CIO's history is traceable through the bibliography and citations in this book.

BERNSTEIN remains standard on the CIO's early development. Written from a New Deal-liberal perspective, it combines a vivid narrative account of a wide range of organizing campaigns, strike actions, and personalities with authoritative discussions of developments in labor law, collective bargaining, and union formation. It is marked by arresting vignettes, personality profiles, and thorough familiarity with the New Deal era.

DUBOFSKY and VAN TINE, FRASER, and LICHTEN-STEIN (1995) are outstanding biographies of 20th-century labor leaders, respectively John L. Lewis, Sidney Hillman, and Walter Reuther. Strong on the social history of industrial America, they explore authoritatively the dynamics of the labor movement, the development of collective bargaining, and the politics of the CIO era. Taken together, they provide a rich and textured picture of the CIO's origins and of the ideological and political conflicts that rocked it in the World War II period. Each parts company with the triumphant liberalism characterizing Bernstein, and stresses the problematic nature of the political and economic order in which the CIO was born and carried through its initial development.

LICHTENSTEIN (1982) highlights the politicization of the CIO and the long-term consequences of policies adopted to meet wartime exigencies. Provocative in its interpretation, this book provides a spirited and challenging account of the explosive industrial union scene during the period 1939 to 1946. Assessing positively the widespread strike action of CIO members during the war, Lichtenstein, in common with Fraser, is sharply critical of CIO leaders such as Hillman and Philip Murray for cooperating with government agencies in suppressing shop floor activism. In Lichtenstein's view, many of the post-war tribulations of organized labor are directly attributable to the wartime choices of the CIO leadership.

FOSTER traces the emerging importance of political action, from the beginnings of the CIO's Political Action Committee in 1943 through the merger of the industrial union body with the American Federation of Labor in 1955. Based on archival research, it presents a balanced view of the narrow options available to CIO leaders in the changed post-World War II environment. It clearly explicates the CIO's liberal political agenda while providing a careful account of the then-innovative mechanisms by which the CIO attempted to implement it and of the constraints under which post-war liberalism labored.

The best work on the contentious and decisive issue of Communism in the CIO is LEVENSTEIN. It reflects the favorable post-1960s historiographical assessment of the contributions of pro-Soviet elements in union building and race relations. Levenstein acknowledges the Stalinist context in which the activities of such CIO affiliates as the United Electrical Workers and the International Longshoremen's and Warehousemen's Union were conducted but he is even more critical of the CIO's anti-Communists, notably UAW, and later-CIO, president Walter Reuther and secretary-treasurer James B. Carey. There is extensive coverage of this issue and related matters of foreign policy and political action in Zieger. The latter also provides substantial treatment of the

CIO's postwar collective bargaining, organizing, and political action programs, as well as a detailed account of the merger of the CIO with the AFL.

ROBERT H. ZIEGER

See also Labor Unions

Conscription *see* Draft/Conscription

Conservation

Coates, Peter, *In Nature's Defence: Conservation and American Studies*, Keele: British Association for American Studies (Pamphlet 26), 1993
Fox, Stephen R., *John Muir and His Legacy: The American Conservation Movement*, Boston: Little Brown, 1981; as *The American Conservation Movement: John Muir and His Legacy*, Madison: University of Wisconsin Press, 1985
Hays, Samuel P., *Conservation and the Gospel of Efficiency: The Progressive Conservation Movement, 1890–1920*, Cambridge, MA: Harvard University Press, 1959; with new preface, New York: Atheneum, 1969
Koppes, Clayton R., "Efficiency, Equity, Esthetics: Shifting Themes in American Conservation," in *The Ends of the Earth: Perspectives on Modern Environmental History*, edited by Donald Worster, Cambridge and New York: Cambridge University Press, 1988
Merchant, Carolyn (editor), *Major Problems in American Environmental History: Documents and Essays*, Lexington, MA: Heath, 1993
Nash, Roderick (editor), *American Environmentalism: Readings in Conservation History*, 3rd edition, New York: McGraw Hill, 1990 (originally published as *The American Environment*, 1974)
Reiger, John, *American Sportsmen and the Origins of Conservation*, Norman: University of Oklahoma Press, 1975, revised 1986
Strong, Douglas, *Dreamers and Defenders: American Conservationists*, Lincoln: University of Nebraska Press, 1988 (revised edition of *The Conservationists*, Menlo Park, CA: Addison Wesley, 1971)

Conservation is defined here as ideas of natural resource husbandry and nature protection and their political expression, especially through the turn-of-the-century conservation movement. There are grounds for treating conservation and environmentalism as separate entities but as these terms are often used interchangeably, this entry does not exclude the post-1945 period when conservation was transformed by environmentalism. However, it does not cover studies primarily concerned with the environmental movement of the past three decades. See separate entries for material on general attitudes to nature, leading conservationists, the environment itself and specific categories of conservation such as national parks.

Older studies of conservation were overwhelmingly of a political and administrative nature, dominated by federal natural resource policies and controversies such as the damming of Hetch Hetchy, the Ballinger-Pinchot conflict and the confrontation between conservation's utilitarian and preservationist wings symbolized by the clash between Gifford Pinchot and John Muir. Earlier commentators (in line with the conventional approach to Progressivism) had portrayed conservation as a bid to secure a more equitable distribution of natural resources and approached it as part of a public crusade to fulfil American democracy. In sharp contrast, HAYS argued that conservation was the apolitical, technocratic initiative of a scientific and engineering elite pursuing more efficient natural resource management and utilization, and definitely not hostile to corporate interests. In view of this book's influence, it is ironic, as Hays explained in the preface to the 1969 edition, that he was less concerned with "the substance of conservation" than "the realm of political structure"; conservation simply epitomized the era's centralizing and modernizing tendencies.

The assumption of a sharp dichotomy between this dominant, so-called utilitarian strand and aesthetic conservation (or preservationism) became a convention. Whereas most historians studied forestry, reclamation and public land, soil and mineral policies, and those interested in the preservationist camp wrote about national parks and wilderness preservation, REIGER drew attention to a neglected component of conservation – sports hunters. A sports hunter himself, Reiger attacked with gusto what he considered the anti-hunting bias of conservation scholars. He claimed that concern for dwindling wildlife rather than fears for forests or interest in reclamation or parks marked the origins of conservation. Having attempted to dethrone both utilitarians and preservationists, Reiger also broke with orthodoxy by claiming that a conservation ethic and organized movement (in the shape of sportsmen) predated the Progressive era, and went back to the 1870s. Moreover, whereas most have characterized conservation as middle class, Reiger identifies these upper-crust sportsmen as "the real spearhead." His partisan treatment places sportsmen in the vanguard of all three major late 19th-century conservation activities: forests and national parks as well as wildlife. The unconvinced have queried the extent to which wildlife protection and sportsmen were representative of Progressive era conservation.

FOX is the most comprehensive, thoughtful and scholarly full-scale study of conservation. The opening biographical section on Muir himself serves as a prelude to a history of conservation from national park formation in the 1890s to anti-nuclear protest in the 1970s. All influential organizations, individuals and issues feature in the detailed, finely nuanced and intensively documented narrative. Fox claims that "the radical amateur" – a type typified by Muir – as distinct from professional conservationists in government bureaucracies, supplied conservation with its main drive and vision. The final section reflects on the salient themes and larger meaning of conservation, characterizing it as "a religious protest against modernity." The role of women and ethnic exclusivity also receive welcome attention. As the subtitle suggests, Muir's presence is pervasive – unlike studies such as Hays, in which preservationism and Muir are firmly subordinate to utilitarian conservation and Pinchot.

The NASH compilation has been catering to proliferating undergraduate history courses on American environmentalism since the early 1970s. The most recent (and revised) edition ranges from extracts of seminal historical works (such as Reiger and Hays) to selections from prominent conservationist writings. Two of the five parts are devoted to the past three decades. As a stimulating introduction to the history of conservation – Nash's introductions are engaging and informative – this item is now rivalled to some degree by MERCHANT. Though Merchant's brief is environmental history as an entire field, conservation and environmentalism merit about a third of the available space. There is inevitably a fair amount of overlap with Nash, but Merchant includes urban issues and reforms as well as highlighting gender and race. Merchant also differs in appending an essay section to each chapter that features state-of-the-art commentary.

Another highly accessible point of entry into conservation history is provided by STRONG in a revised and expanded version of a work first published as *The Conservationists* in 1971. Three of the four new chapters deal with post-1945 environmentalists and, in the cases of Rachel Carson and Barry Commoner, address problems of pollution and industrialization associated with environmentalism rather than conservation. Strong deftly recounts "the development of a more enlightened attitude toward the land" through the lives and times of eleven male conservationists and a lone female.

KOPPES is a snappy and easily digestible guide to the broad features of conservation. Identifying three major themes – efficiency, equity and esthetics/ecology – he traces their relationship and relative strengths between 1900 and environmentalism's onset in the early 1960s. A particular strength is the effective communication of a sense of the forces in American life that shaped conservation's identity. COATES is a crisp overview especially geared to the needs of a non-American readership and written with the uninitiated in mind. Besides the Progressive era movement and conservation's fortunes down to the 1950s, Coates examines American Indian antecedents, colonial precedents, and earlier 19th-century anticipations. He concludes with the transition to modern-day environmentalism.

PETER A. COATES

See also Environment

Conservatism

Allitt, Patrick, *Catholic Intellectuals and Conservative Politics in America, 1950–1985*, Ithaca, NY: Cornell University Press, 1993

Diggins, John Patrick, *Up from Communism: Conservative Odysseys in American Intellectual History*, New York: Harper, 1975

Dorrien, Gary, *The Neoconservative Mind: Politics, Culture, and the War of Ideology*, Philadelphia: Temple University Press, 1993

Dunn, Charles W. and J. David Woodard, *American Conservatism from Burke to Bush: An Introduction*, Lanham, MD: Madison, 1991

Genovese, Eugene D., *The Southern Tradition: The Achievement and Limitations of an American Conservatism*, Cambridge, MA: Harvard University Press, 1994

Gottfried, Paul, with Thomas Fleming, *The Conservative Movement*, Boston: Twayne, 1988, revised 1993

Himmelstein, Jerome L., *To the Right: The Transformation of American Conservatism*, Berkeley: University of California Press, 1991

Hoeveler, J. David, Jr., *Watch on the Right: Conservative Intellectuals in the Reagan Era*, Madison: University of Wisconsin Press, 1991

Judis, John B., *William F. Buckley, Jr.: Patron Saint of the Conservatives*, New York: Simon and Schuster, 1988

Kirk, Russell, *The Conservative Mind*, London: Faber, 1954; 7th edition, as *The Conservative Mind from Burke to Eliot*, Washington, DC: Regnery, 1993

Lienesch, Michael, *Redeeming America: Piety and Politics in the New Christian Right*, Chapel Hill: University of North Carolina Press, 1993

Nash, George H., *The Conservative Intellectual Movement in America since 1945*, New York: Basic Books, 1976

Until recently the history of American conservatism has been left largely to conservatives, but this has changed with the growing political power of self-proclaimed conservatives. However, works on conservatism – no matter who writes them – struggle with definition. What is a conservative? Does the label apply to an ideology or a disposition regarding the status quo? Is there such a thing as a conservative movement in the United States? Anyone who writes on conservatism must begin by defining the kind of conservatism under investigation.

DUNN and WOODARD is a helpful, and brief, introduction to the many strains of conservative beliefs. Like the vast majority of books on this subject, they emphasize the development of a conservative movement since 1945, but, very helpfully, they connect the principles (or "canons") of modern conservatives with a historical tradition that extends back to Edmund Burke. However, the most important contribution of this book lies in the way in which its authors compare and contrast the many definitions provided by conservatives and scholars alike – a sort of taxonomy of conservative beliefs. The best introduction to the pre-1945 period is KIRK, which surveys conservatism through both American and British history from Edmund Burke to T.S. Eliot. Equally important, Kirk is more than a history, it is a defense (or construction) of a tradition that helped to reinvigorate conservative thought in the 1950s. Because of the astonishing success of this book, the author is regarded by many as the father of modern conservatism – or at least the traditionalist strain of it. The book is therefore both a history of conservative thought and an introduction to a dominant strain of conservatism in the post-1945 era.

The most interesting overview of the conservative movement since 1945 is GOTTFRIED. This brief survey, written by a traditionalist conservative, chronicles the shifting power relationships within the movement, with special attention to the rise of the "neoconservatives" in the 1970s and 1980s. HIMMELSTEIN provides a more social scientific analysis of the movement in the same period. It maintains a greater distance from its subject, with all the advantages and disadvantages that go with this.

For an understanding of the intellectual evolution of the movement in its formative years (the 1950s and 1960s) four books are especially useful. NASH is an excellent and almost encyclopedic intellectual history, especially important for an understanding of the complex relationships between different wings of the intellectual conservative movement. DIGGINS examines the transition of four intellectuals from communism to conservatism. He helps to clarify the role which former leftists – most of whom did not accept the religious beliefs of the dominant conservatives – played in the evolution of a vigorous anticommunist element of the conservative movement in the 1950s and 1960s. Key to the integration of the various conservative factions into a coherent reactionary front was William F. Buckley, Jr., whose life, beliefs, and career are admirably detailed in JUDIS. He describes how Buckley galvanized the movement through his spirited, if sporadic, editing of the *National Review*, which became the most influential political journal on the right, and which did more than anything else to create a responsible conservatism. Although Buckley brought together traditionalists, libertarians, and former communists in a common cause against liberalism, his own views were very much forged in the Catholic conservative tradition which is traced brilliantly in ALLITT. The special contribution of Allitt's work is to examine the development of Catholic conservatives in the context of the ongoing debates within the Catholic church, with special attention to Vatican II. Thus, Allitt helps to deepen our understanding of the dynamics of the conservative movement, by demonstrating the relationship between church politics and the political views of Catholic conservatives who dominated the intellectual conservative movement in the 1950s and 1960s.

Understanding the conservative movement has become more difficult with the introduction of the largely Jewish "neoconservative" wing and the largely Christian fundamentalist "religious right" wing. The most obvious effect of the infusion of these groups is the decline of the so-called "paleoconservatives" – which usually refers to Catholic traditionalists and their "southern traditionalist" allies. The brief study of the latter by GENOVESE, a fascinating and unpredictable marxist, suggests that the anti-corporate and anti-consumerist conservatism of neo-confederates like Richard Weaver and Mel Bradford was a product of a southern way of life fast passing away.

The complex relationships of the various conservative groups, especially since the election of Ronald Reagan in 1980, are still largely unexplored by scholars. In the best effort so far to understand the intellectuals of the Reagan era, HOEVELER emphasizes the generic connections between various kinds of conservative intellectuals in an effort to identify a common conservatism linking traditionalists with neoconservatives. A more thorough, though less balanced, examination of neoconservatives is DORRIEN, which focuses on Irving Kristol, Norman Podhoretz, Michael Novak, and Peter Berger. The rise of the religious right since the late 1970s has produced a great deal of literary heat but precious little light. LIENESCH is a particularly commendable attempt to understand the ideas and underlying cosmology of the evangelical right. More importantly he has helped to place this group in both the conservative camp (to which they are late-comers) and in the larger evangelical tradition from which they came. By so doing Lienesch has helped to explain the fervency of this group, and the reason why these populists became part of a conservative movement that had heretofore been a largely elitist, intellectualized reaction to liberal America. What is unclear is how the confusing and overlapping ideological commitments of various conservatives will work out in the political arena.

TED V. McALLISTER

Constitution: the Document

Adler, Mortimer J., *We Hold These Truths: Understanding the Ideas and Ideals of the Constitution*, New York: Macmillan, and London: Collier Macmillan, 1987

Bickel, Alexander M., *The Least Dangerous Branch: The Supreme Court at the Bar of Politics*, Indianapolis: Bobbs Merrill, 1962; 2nd edition, New Haven: Yale University Press, 1986

Corwin, Edward S., *The Constitution and What It Means Today*, Princeton: Princeton University Press, 1920, revised by Harold W. Chase and Craig R. Ducat, 1978

Corwin, Edward S. and Jack W. Peltason, *Understanding the Constitution*, New York: Sloane, 1949; 11th edition, New York: Holt Rinehart, 1988

Fisher, Louis, *Constitutional Dialogues: Interpretation as Political Process*, Princeton: Princeton University Press, 1988

Kammen, Michael G., *A Machine That Would Go of Itself: The Constitution in American Culture*, New York: Knopf, 1986

Levy, Leonard W., *Original Intent and the Framers' Constitution*, New York: Macmillan, and London: Collier Macmillan, 1988

Lieberman, Jethro, *The Enduring Constitution: An Explanation of the First 200 Years*, New York: Harper, 1987

Rakove, Jack N. (editor), *Interpreting the Constitution: The Debate over Original Intent*, Boston: Northeastern University Press, 1990

Tribe, Laurence H., *Constitutional Choices*, Cambridge, MA: Harvard University Press, 1985

Tushnet, Mark V., *Red, White, and Blue: A Critical Analysis of American Constitutional Law*, Cambridge, MA: Harvard University Press, 1988

Wechsler, Herbert, "Toward Neutral Principles of Constitutional Law," *The Harvard Law Review*, 73(1), 1959

One does not have to agree with William Gladstone's assertion that "the American Constitution is . . . the most wonderful work ever struck off at a given time by the brain and purpose of man" to admit its importance both in American history and as a statement of applied political philosophy. The role of the Constitution is essential to any understanding of much of the political, legal and intellectual history of the United States. One of the greatest authorities on the document was Edward S.

Corwin, for nearly thirty years the McCormick Professor of Jurisprudence at Princeton. His numerous works on the Constitution repay attention, but two are essential to understanding its meaning. Believing that the Constitution is what the courts, and especially the Supreme Court, says it is, he compiled and summarized the key decisions of the Supreme Court in order to elucidate the meanings of key phrases as interpreted by the judicial branch. CORWIN and PELTASON is aimed at a more general audience while CORWIN, revised by CHASE and DUCAT, is more scholarly, and assumes a greater knowledge of law. Peltason's stylistic clarity makes this a book particularly useful for the general readership (and even for scholars), while Chase and Ducat offer longer and more detailed commentaries.

The meaning of the Constitution has become a matter of constant political dispute, notably since the 1960s. In earlier days, the Constitution often came to public notice, mainly as an object of assumed public veneration. KAMMEN shows that even this was not always the case. He professes to be surprised by the public ignorance of the document even when there was a strong belief in "constitutionalism". In his view, Americans have taken "too much pride and proportionately too little interest" in their Constitution. Kammen has produced an unusual and original book – certainly not a conventional constitutional history, but rather a cultural history of the fluctuating relationship of the American people with their fundamental constitutional document. Kammen's exploration is judicious, balanced and full of fresh insights. How legal elites see the document and understand its meaning is, however, a rather different matter.

Throughout the 19th and early 20th centuries most jurists and commentators believed that the document had one meaning and judges simply divined that meaning and applied it to the cases before them. Even in the late 19th century, however, sophisticated observers, such as James Bryce, knew that this was not the whole of the matter. In his *Common Law*, Oliver Wendell Holmes, Jr., argued that law was organic and changed with conditions over time. Out of this view developed "sociological jurisprudence" which became the new orthodoxy. "Settling" one argument led to another one. Although all admitted that the courts' reading of the Constitution changed in reaction to societal change, the question was how much was proper and what was the value of precedent? It is on these points that much of the debate now turns. Clearly, that debate is also affected by the dominant political and social issues of the time when an author is writing.

The Warren Court (1953–69) inspired many Americans, and the majority of authors have supported its interpretive structure. They see the Supreme Court as an appropriate agency to achieve social justice and to adjudicate disputes previously seen as beyond the judicial ambit. Some commentators, including BICKEL, feared that the Warren Court's activism would undermine popular acceptance of the Court as a final arbiter of all legal matters. WECHSLER suggested that constitutional adjudication could be taken out of the political sphere, through the application of politically neutral standards. He tried to show how and where these might be found but, as his title suggests, he could not offer a set of them. He triggered a lengthy debate on the issue that lasted through the 1960s and beyond. Although widely criticized, his view remains a part of that debate.

Constitutional interpretation has thus become a political minefield, and there appears to be no limit to the entrants to the debate. ADLER offers a useful volume for anyone seeking a background to the controversy. He covers ground that other authors assume "everybody knows". He discusses the philosophical and intellectual framework behind the Constitution, and much of the later political controversy surrounding it. LIEBERMAN bridges the gap between the general and scholarly reader with an insightful text that is arranged by broad topic area (e.g., Structure of Government, Liberty, Business) but still covers the whole of the Constitution's history. This is a volume full of the specifics of history, in contrast to Adler's more social science and philosophical view.

More typical of recent constitutional scholarship are attacks on the assumptions of much of the public and the elite alike, that the courts are the sole and final arbiters of constitutional matters, and can use a single interpretive scheme to reach just decisions. TUSHNET analyzes the Constitution and constitutional law as well as constitutional theory and the relationship of the document to major institutions in American society. He concludes that, in a liberal society, constitutional law is necessarily messy, or as he puts it, "necessary and impossible". It is necessary because of the restraints it imposes on the governors, but impossible because some body, either the legislature or judiciary, has to have the final decision in a constitutional dispute. Seen in another way, the unsolvable problem lies in trying to formulate a balance between the rights or privileges of majorities and minorities. FISHER offers a salutary reminder that, in a constitutional system, all components have to be concerned with constitutional controversies, and not just the courts. He includes numerous examples of occasions when the other branches were involved, and when they ought to have been. He shows instances when society "overruled" the courts, and argues that the country still needs the "constitutional dialogues" of his title, as government has to be a cooperative process if it is to act for the best in society.

TRIBE is a, if not the, leading left-of-centre commentator writing on these issues today. He argues that no normative system of constitutional adjudication, can, in any final sense, be preferred to any other, and he implicitly suggests that all, whether of the left or the right, are reduced to social policy choices in considering constitutional questions. He wants those involved in the process to be aware of the nature of the choices they are making. Tribe participates in the controversy started by Attorney General Edwin Meese and others close to the Reagan administration, who argued that judges ought to be guided by the opinions and intentions of the drafters of the Constitution and its amendments. This appeal for a return to what is called "original intent" set off a substantial debate in the late 1980s. RAKOVE edits a collection of readings on this subject, including essays setting out the terms of the debate (including Wechsler's essay noted above), and essays on related issues, for example the completeness and reliability of the records of the Constitutional Convention. Although Rakove shows that he is unsympathetic to those who call for the use of "original intent", he includes contributions from a number of different perspectives. LEVY presents the detailed case for those who find the "original intent" view either wrong in terms of the current political debate or simply impossible. As Mr. Justice Robert H. Jackson (1941–1954) said "Just what our

forefathers did envision, or would have envisioned had they foreseen modern conditions, must be divined from materials almost as enigmatic as the dreams Joseph was called on to interpret for Pharaoh". With wit and verve, Levy not only argues his case persuasively, but shows that in important areas, such as foreign relations, there is much evidence to suggest that the Founding Fathers planned a much weaker Executive than that favoured by the Reagan administration. It is more likely, he asserts, that the drafters wanted an "imperial" Senate than an "imperial" presidency.

GEORGE CONYNE

See also Legal History entries; Supreme Court

Constitution: Philadelphia Convention, 1787

Beard, Charles A., *An Economic Interpretation of the Constitution of the United States*, New York: Macmillan, 1913
Bernstein, Richard B. with Kym S. Rice, *Are We to Be a Nation? The Making of the Constitution*, Cambridge, MA: Harvard University Press, 1987
Brown, Robert E., *Charles Beard and the Constitution: A Critical Analysis of "An Economic Interpretation of the Constitution"*, Princeton: Princeton University Press, 1956
Lynd, Staughton, *Class Conflict, Slavery, and the United States Constitution: Ten Essays*, Indianapolis: Bobbs Merrill, 1967
McDonald, Forrest, *Novus Ordo Seclorum: The Intellectual Origins of the Constitution*, Lawrence: University Press of Kansas, 1985
Rossiter, Clinton, *1787: The Grand Convention*, New York: Macmillan, 1966
Wood, Gordon S., *The Creation of the American Republic, 1776–1787*, Chapel Hill: University of North Carolina Press, 1969

BEARD remains the obvious starting-point for any review of the voluminous literature on the framing of the United States Constitution. Written against the backcloth of the Progressive Era, this controversial and iconoclastic study argued that the Constitution was an "economic document" drafted by holders of a certain kind of property – personalty ("money, public securities, manufactures, and trade and shipping") – to gratify both their own and their supporters' material interests. Its adoption, Beard claimed, was opposed by realty, principally small farmers, similarly motivated by self-interest. While earlier authors had shown some awareness of the economic dimension to the constitutional debate, what gave Beard's book its sensational quality was his detective work into its authors' motives. Drawing upon United States Treasury records, he constructed financial profiles of the framers which purported to show how they would benefit financially from the various clauses they wrote into the Constitution. Beard demonstrated, to his own satisfaction, that in drafting the document they were "immediately, directly, and personally interested in, and derived economic advantage from the establishment of the new government."

Initially denounced as Marxist and subversive, Beard's book nevertheless became the standard text on the Constitution's origins during the 1930s and 1940s. By the mid-1950s, however, many studies of individual states had cast doubt on his basic assumptions: that the contest over the document was one that pitted realty against personalty, that late 18th-century society was undemocratic, and that the Constitution was the result of a minority coup. Written during this period, BROWN is a devastating frontal assault on Beard. In a systematic chapter by chapter dissection of *An Economic Interpretation of the Constitution*, Brown contended that his predecessor had done "great violence" to historical methods, that he manipulated evidence to fit his preconceived notions, used inapplicable statistics, deliberately misquoted sources, and committed logical fallacies.

The consensus school's attack on Beard – culminating in Brown's work – cleared the way for the re-emergence of a more positive view of the Constitution's framers. This is exemplified by ROSSITER. Viewing the Convention of 1787 as *the* defining moment in American history, he puts the Founding Fathers back on their pedestal. Power and economic interest may have played some part in their deliberations, but they were guided principally by their determination to create a political framework commensurate with the national potential for greatness. The framers succeeded in their objectives, Rossiter argues, because they were essentially good conservatives and avoided doctrinaire solutions and simple-minded idealism. The Constitution, then, reflected their essential pragmatism: it was definitively nationalist but did not threaten the states' viability. Though not inherently democratic, it remained responsive to the popular tide already flowing in the republic. And far from being a reaction to the Revolution, it was the logical fulfilment of it.

Not all scholars writing in the 1960s adopted such a positive view. Even while abandoning the tendency of Progressive historians to find conspiracies behind the Constitution and to equate economic causation with the pursuit of self-interest, LYND saw deep forces at work. He moves slavery from the wings to centre stage in an echo of the earlier 19th-century abolitionist critique. Writing from a New Left position, he argues that differences between northern capitalists and southern slaveholders produced some of the most important divisions in the Confederation Congress and the Constitutional Convention. The Northwest Ordinance and the Constitution represented an accommodation between these two interests – a compromise which provided protection for both and seemed to offer to each the hope of future supremacy by winning the allegiance of the West. Though this coalition of "property" broke down in the 1790s, Lynd feels that not until the Civil War was the question of who should rule at home decided in favour of northern capitalists.

The most influential work on the subject since Beard, WOOD is an imposing study. Though rejecting Beardian economic determinism, he continues to emphasize social conflict. The framers, he asserts, intended "to confront and retard the thrust of the Revolution with the rhetoric of the Revolution." There were, he explains, "partisan and aristocratic purposes that belied the Federalists' democratic language". The makers of the Constitution were alarmed by the strength of the democratic forces and irrepressible social mobility unleashed by the Revolution, which manifested themselves in the vicious conduct of many state legislatures during the Confederation period. The goal of the framers became to control this ebullient democracy; to do this, they relied on the strategy, later explained in Federalist 10, of monopolizing national offices for the "natural aristocracy" by enlarging the electoral districts in which they ran. By bringing the "natural aristocracy of the country back into dominance in politics" the nation's problems would be solved. The Constitution, Wood concludes, "was intrinsically an aristocratic document designed to check the democratic tendencies of the period."

Another strand in the historiography concentrates on the ideas animating the delegates to the Philadelphia Convention. McDONALD provides a useful, if slightly idiosyncratic, critical commentary of this work. His principal target is Bernard Bailyn and the "ideological school" whose approach he finds "ultimately unsatisfying". According to McDonald, they failed to distinguish between the several kinds of republicanism espoused by various Americans, which largely reflected regionally different socio-economic norms. Also, the influence of Scottish thinkers and John Locke was downplayed; the role of legal traditions and institutions disregarded. Finally, Bailyn and his followers failed to address adequately the tensions between communitarian consensus and possessive individualism, between the liberty to participate in the governing process and liberty from unlimited government. Given this detailed analysis of intellectual currents, McDonald's conclusion is surprising. Ultimately he argues that, although the framers brought a variety of ideological positions to bear upon their task, they were guided primarily by their own experience, wisdom, and commonsense. He therefore goes some way towards confirming Rossiter's view of the Founding Fathers as cautious pragmatists.

BERNSTEIN does not engage explicity with these historiographical debates, but it is a useful introduction for those new to the subject. The book provides an extremely lucid, up-to-date narrative account of the Convention's proceedings, deals extensively with political culture, and makes excellent use of the published editions of the papers of the Founding Fathers. Moreover, the volume consistently cites and discusses the newest literature on women, free blacks and slaves, and immigrants in Revolutionary America.

KEITH MASON

Constitution: Ratification

Beard, Charles A., *An Economic Interpretation of the Constitution of the United States*, New York: Macmillan, 1913

Beeman, Richard R., Stephen Botein, and Edward C. Carter (editors), *Beyond Confederation: Origins of the Constitution and American National Identity*, Chapel Hill: University of North Carolina Press, 1987

Brown, Robert E., *Reinterpretation of the Formation of the American Constitution*, Boston: Boston University Press, 1963

Ferguson, E. James, *The Power of the Purse: A History of American Public Finance, 1776–1790*, Chapel Hill: University of North Carolina Press, 1961

Jensen, Merrill, *The New Nation: A History of the United States During the Confederation, 1781–1789*, New York: Knopf, 1950

Kaminski, John P. and Patrick T. Conley (editors), *The Constitution and the States: The Role of the Original Thirteen in the Framing and Adoption of the Federal Constitution*, Madison, WI: Madison House, 1988

Levy, Leonard W. (editor), *Essays on the Making of the Constitution*, New York: Oxford University Press, 1969, 2nd edition, 1987

Libby, Orin Grant, *The Geographical Distribution of the Vote of the Thirteen States on the Federal Constitution, 1787–88*, Madison, WI: The University, 1894; reprinted, New York: Franklin, 1969

Main, Jackson Turner, *The Antifederalists: Critics of the Constitution, 1781–1788*, Chapel Hill: University of North Carolina Press, 1961

Main, Jackson Turner, *Political Parties Before the Constitution*, Chapel Hill: University of North Carolina Press, 1973

Morgan, Edmund S., *The Birth of the Republic, 1763–89*, Chicago: University of Chicago Press, 1956; 3rd edition, 1992

Wood, Gordon S., *The Creation of the American Republic, 1776–1787*, Chapel Hill: University of North Carolina Press, 1969

Wood, Gordon S. (editor), *The Confederation and the Constitution: The Critical Issues*, Washington, DC: University Press of America, 1979

Wright, Benjamin F., *Consensus and Continuity, 1776–1787*, Boston: Boston University Press, 1958

The adoption of the Constitution in 1787–88 is one of the defining events in American history. As a consequence, a great deal has been written about it. This literature is generally of very high quality, but it is also controversial. This was not always the case. In the late 19th century, just when professional historians began to write, the Constitution, which had been sanctified by the result of the Civil War, was a revered document. But then scholars discovered that the fight over its ratification was both bitter and close. The debate among scholars that followed has generally revolved around two main points. First, what is the relationship between the forces of democracy and equality unleashed in 1776 and the adoption of the Constitution? Second, to what extent can the ratification struggle be explained by underlying social, economic and sectional tensions existing in late 18th-century America?

A significant early attempt to explain why some people supported the adoption of the Constitution, and others opposed it, is LIBBY. A student of Frederick Jackson Turner, he placed considerable emphasis on geography. Plotting the areas of Federalist and Antifederalist strength on a map, he argued that support for the Constitution came from creditor and mercantile centers near the coast and navigable waterways, while the opposition came from debtors who were found mainly in the back country. Although many of Libby's generalizations are in need of refinement, his interpretation has proved to be a powerful and resilient one that re-emerged in a more sophisticated form later on.

BEARD offered a more dramatic interpretation in what was to be one of the most influential and controversial books ever published in American history. In a deliberate attempt to strip away the "demi-god" status that many people had accorded to the founding fathers, he argued that the dynamic element in the movement for the Constitution was a group of self-interested merchants and financiers who speculated in government securities, and who expected to make substantial profits if a government committed to paying off the national debt was created. Opposition to the adoption of the Constitution came from owners of land, mainly small farmers, who represented a majority of the people, but many of whom were disfranchised, disorganized and otherwise politically ineffective. Although not accepted by everyone, Beard's thesis dominated American historiography during the first half of the 20th century.

This rapidly changed in the 1950s. Fueled by the Cold War, many American scholars became critical of any interpretation that stressed class divisions, or appeared to be influenced by Marxism. The assault on Beard was led by Robert E. Brown and Forrest McDonald, who found his scholarship deeply flawed and his conclusions unsustainable. Criticizing Beard turned out to be fairly easy, but providing an alternative explanation of what occurred in 1787–88 has proved to be more difficult. The scholars who dominated the 1950s came to be known as consensus historians because they stressed the fundamental agreement that existed between Americans on most important issues, and believed that the American political experience was characterized by compromise and continuity. Three notable attempts were made to fit the ratification of the Constitution into this framework. Building upon the findings of a number of his earlier works, BROWN argued that despite the existence of property qualifications for voting, the great majority of white males owned enough land to be able to participate in the political process, and that the Constitution was essentially a victory for middle-class America. Both MORGAN and WRIGHT argued that it was a recognition of the inadequacies of the Articles of Confederation, and that nationalism rather than economic self-interest lay behind the drive to create a stronger central government. In their view, the Constitution represented the fulfilment, and not the repudiation, of the principles of the American Revolution. They have been criticized for minimizing divisions in American society in the 1780s, and for failing to explain the strength of the opposition to ratification of the Constitution.

At the same time, a number of scholars continued to examine the ratification struggle from a position sympathetic to Beard's general approach. JENSEN regarded as misleading Federalist claims that the country was on the verge of economic disaster, political disintegration and even anarchy. He paints a too rosy picture of the 1780s as a period of economic adjustment and growth, and argues that the small farmers and artisans, empowered by the democratic thrust of the Revolution, were generally content with conditions under the Articles, and were winning many key struggles on the state level. Instead, it was a coalition made up of merchants, lawyers, senior military officers and other established elites, who were losing control on the state level, that wanted the Constitution. Jensen has been effectively criticized for a tendency to view the period too much from the perspective of the Antifederalists.

More successful is the work of FERGUSON, one of Jensen's students. In a very impressive piece of scholarship he unravels the role played by public securities in the movement for the adoption of the Constitution. He downplays the role of self-interest, but does demonstrate how the desire for financial responsibility and the need to pay off the national debt were the driving issues in the creation of the new government. Also of great significance is the work of MAIN (1961 and 1973), another Jensen student, who uncovers a great deal of information on the sectional, social and economic divisions that existed at the time of the ratification struggle. He also effectively demonstrates that alignments at the state level on such issues as paper money, taxes, debtor relief legislation and the treatment of loyalists (which in many cases involved the confiscation and redistribution of property) were the same as in the struggle over ratification. He concludes by resurrecting, in a more sophisticated form, Libby's argument that the basic division in the fight over the ratification of the Constitution was between "cosmopolitans" who were part of the market economy and "localists" who were outside or on the periphery of it.

Many scholars consider WOOD (1969) to be the best book ever written about the adoption of the Constitution. It is an elegant and penetrating analysis of evolving American political and constitutional thought between 1776 and 1788. It is perhaps best known for its emphasis on the influence of radical Whig ideas upon the development of republican thought. The book can be confusing, however, since it begins as a form of consensus history, stressing the importance of ideas as an independent variable, as well as fundamental agreement among Americans upon the principles of republicanism, but ends up much closer to a progressive interpretation, when it argues that the sharp debate between Federalists and Antifederalists in 1787–88 had deep roots in social, economic and sectional differences. Still, along with Main and Ferguson, Wood is absolutely essential reading for understanding the movement that led to the ratification of the Constitution.

For a good introduction to the critical issues involved in the debate among scholars on the struggle over the Constitution's adoption there are two useful books. LEVY discusses the controversy around Beard. WOOD (1979) deals with the intellectual and constitutional issues. Both volumes contain relevant excerpts from the most significant writings on their subjects and include the best material to be found in the periodical literature. The bicentennial of the adoption of the Constitution produced an overabundance of work on the ratification struggle. Two collections of essays are worth noting. BEEMAN et al. is the result of a conference sponsored by the Institute of Early American History and contains important but conflicting essays on the nature and legacy of Antifederalism, and the role of James Madison in creating and implementing the Constitution. Also useful is KAMINSKI and CONLEY which traces the struggle over ratification in each of the states and includes a good bibliography of the relevant monographic and periodical literature.

RICHARD E. ELLIS

Constitutional History: General

Bodenhamer, David J. and James W. Ely, Jr., *The Bill of Rights in Modern America: After 200 Years*, Bloomington: Indiana University Press, 1993

Ely, James W., Jr., *The Guardian of Every Other Right: A Constitutional History of Property Rights*, New York and Oxford: Oxford University Press, 1992

Fausold, Martin L. and Alan Shank (editors), *The Constitution and the American Presidency*, Albany: State University of New York Press, 1991

Hall, Kermit L. and James W. Ely, Jr. (editors), *An Uncertain Tradition: Constitutionalism and the History of the South*, Athens: University of Georgia Press, 1989

Kelly, Alfred H. and Winfred A. Harbison, *The American Constitution: Its Origins and Development*, New York: Norton, 1948; 7th edition, with Herman Belz, 2 vols., 1991

Morgan, Donald, *Congress and the Constitution: A Study of Responsibility*, Cambridge, MA: Belknap Press of Harvard University Press, 1966

Ollman, Bertell and Jonathan Birnbaum (editors), *The United States Constitution: 200 Years of Anti-Federalist, Abolitionist, Feminist, Muckraking, Progressive and Especially Socialist Criticism*, New York: New York University Press, 1990

Read, Conyers, *The Constitution Reconsidered*, New York: Columbia University Press, 1938; revised by Richard B. Morris, New York: Harper, 1968

Thelen, David P. (editor), *The Constitution and American Life*, Ithaca, NY: Cornell University Press, 1988

Books on the history of the U. S. Constitution often read like histories of the United States Supreme Court. They do overlap extensively, but not quite so far as Charles Evans Hughes suggested, when he claimed that the Constitution is what the Supreme Court says it is. This view has been reflected in the vast literature on the subject as well as in much of the political debate on constitutional matters. In recent years, however, this narrow view has begun to change, and the almost innumerable conferences, books, articles and collections marking the bicentenary of the Constitution in 1987–89 and the Bill of Rights in 1991 both reflected, and acted as a catalyst for, this change of view.

One of the dominant texts of the post-war period, KELLY, HARBISON and BELZ, has reflected this change. The first two authors, now deceased, published it in 1948. It was a relatively simple tale focused on the rise of the Court throughout American history, with the post-Civil War Courts rendering the best and most logical constitutional decisions in history. By 1983, when Belz took over the revisions, legal historians no longer supported so simple a view of constitutional development. Belz introduced much more material on extra-judicial constitutional influences and corrected some of the Whiggish judgments of the earlier versions. His perspective reflected the reaction to the Court's increasingly rightward swing since the early 1970s, and these changes also appear in the seventh edition, the first in two volumes. Regardless of variations in the points of view of the earlier and later editions, the popularity of this text, and its extensive bibliography make it a vital overview of the subject.

An earlier attempt to take a broader view of constitutional development was made in READ's collection, as revised by MORRIS. Although written in the late 1930s, many of these essays have withstood the test of historical judgment; they present material which is not easily found elsewhere, and maintain their power to provoke. Many scholars, for example, disagree with Charles Beard but all have to answer his views, at least as they were modified. Hamilton's piece on the history of the due process clause to 1937 is the best short study on the subject, and the essays by Henkin and Roche for the new edition offer useful and more modern insights.

THELEN edited a more recent collection of essays by very distinguished authors who try to put the Constitution in context. Where Read had focused on the Constitution's origins and its influences on American and overseas thought, Thelen's authors write on the Constitution's relation to broad areas of American society (such as the economy and foreign relations) and also on the components of American "rights consciousness", an aspect of American thought too often overlooked. Read and Thelen's compilations are valuable because they convey something of the work of this century's best constitutional commentators.

Rights lie at the centre of BODENHAMER and ELY's collection. After two general essays on constitutional "rights consciousness", a fine list of authors review the current controversies over specific parts of the Bill of Rights. These include such areas as free speech, religion, arms, property, the rights of the accused, and inter-governmental rights, which have assumed special interest in view of the activism of an increasingly conservative Court in the 1990s. Regardless of how long conservatives remain dominant on the Court, these essays will comprise a useful introduction to the debates over these key elements of the Constitution.

ELY, who wrote the essay in this collection on property rights, explores the topic at greater length in his own brief volume. This is a particularly useful contribution, as the Court shows greater solicitude for private property claims. Ely does not offer any startling views and rightly sees Justice Harlan Fiske Stone's opinion for the Court in U.S. v. Carolene Products (1938), after the "court-packing" controversy, as the turning point, when the Court ceased its stout defence of private property.

FAUSOLD and SHANK offer a collection divided into two parts. In the first half, leading authorities recount the status of the Constitution on issues concerning the presidency under Jefferson and during the Jacksonian era, the later 19th century, the Progressive era, the 1930s, and the Truman period. In the second half, political scientists write on major constitutional issues concerning the presidency, raising points, on the power of the purse and foreign relations among others, that students of history will find useful. MORGAN looks at the Constitution in relation to the legislature. He decries what he calls "judicial monopolism" which he sees as prevailing during the mid- to late-20th century. He describes this as the view that the courts will settle all constitutional matters, and he argues that it replaced the earlier view that all branches had a voice in these areas. Although Morgan was writing in the mid-1960s,

his research and conclusions are still relevant, if not more relevant to the 1990s, when the Court is reconsidering so many doctrines thought settled.

Dissenters to the constitutional mainstream received relatively little attention until the 1960s. HALL and ELY collected a series of pieces on southern dissent from the dominant trends. This is more than a study of states rights, as minorities, women's treatment before the law and property rights receive consideration. The contributors conclude that the South has a distinctive and coherent tradition, descended from a view held in both North and South in the colonial and early national periods. The book projects an important and frequently overlooked view of constitutional development. OLLMAN and BIRNBAUM have collected criticism of the mainstream from angles very different from those presented by Hall and Ely. As their title suggests, they have compiled an anthology of what can broadly be described as left-wing criticism of the Constitution. They include a wide selection from contemporary critics and modern scholars, as well as pieces from such possibly surprising sources as Franklin Roosevelt, Woodrow Wilson, Gore Vidal, and Ralph Nader. This is a useful compendium of views that challenge the norms in various ways.

GEORGE CONYNE

See also Supreme Court

Constitutional History, 1789–1877

Billikopf, David Marshall, *The Exercise of Judicial Power, 1789–1864*, New York: Vantage Press, 1973

Fehrenbacher, Don E., *The Dred Scott Case: Its Significance in American Law and Politics*, New York: Oxford University Press, 1978; abridged as *Slavery, Law, and Politics: The Dred Scott Case in Historical Perspective*, 1981

Hyman, Harold M., *A More Perfect Union: The Impact of the Civil War and Reconstruction on the Constitution*, New York: Knopf, 1973

Hyman, Harold M. and William M. Wiecek, *Equal Justice under Law: Constitutional Development, 1835–1875*, New York: Harper, 1982

Kutler, Stanley I., *Judicial Power and Reconstruction Politics*, Chicago: University of Chicago Press, 1968

Kutler, Stanley I., *Privilege and Creative Destruction: The Charles River Bridge Case*, Philadelphia: Lippincott, 1971

Mitchell, Broadus and Louise Pearson Mitchell, *A Biography of the Constitution of the United States*, New York and Oxford: Oxford University Press, 1964, 2nd edition, 1975

Newmyer, R. Kent, *The Supreme Court under Marshall and Taney*, New York: Crowell, 1968

Warren, Charles, *The Supreme Court in United States History*, 3 vols., Boston: Little Brown, 1922, revised, 2 vols., 1926

Wiecek, William M., *The Sources of Antislavery Constitutionalism in America, 1760–1848*, Ithaca, NY: Cornell University Press, 1977

Any study of the Constitution must include, if not indeed start with, WARREN's massive study. Although this three-volume work covers the history of the Supreme Court until 1916, the commentary for the period after 1888 declines in both quantity and quality, and becomes little more than the listing of key cases. But it is still vital to the student of constitutional history, as distinct from the history of the Supreme Court, because it became the standard work of its time, and reflects the dominant jurisprudential views of the era before the New Deal ushered in sociological jurisprudence. It remains a work of great scholarship and can give the reader important insights, not least on the dominant legal thinking of the early 20th century. Volumes I to VII of the Holmes Devise (discussed in the entry on the Supreme Court) have replaced Warren as the magisterial study of the Supreme Court's first century. Their authors' insights on the Constitution are of essential importance, and must be consulted for a complete understanding of American constitutional history.

NEWMYER offers another excellent, if much briefer, example of a study of the Supreme Court which also has much to say on wider constitutional issues. Chief Justices John Marshall and Roger Brooke Taney knew that their decisions shaped the Constitution, and were well aware of the centrality of their roles. Newmyer argues that the Marshall and Taney Courts, when viewed as a whole, established a system of American constitutional law which was more important than the Dred Scott case or than their differing views of state-federal relations. Their decisions expanded the federal judicial power and created a truly co-equal branch of government in a way that the Founding Fathers may well never have envisaged.

BILLIKOPF examines that power in detail. The book arose, the author tells us, from a decision that an "entertaining" way of passing a quiet winter in Chile would be to read the opinions of the Supreme Court during the years 1789–1864. While one might question his preferences in amusements, what he produced was a work, both readable by a general audience and useful to scholars, which examines the real and unglamorous basis of judicial authority in the United States. The text is arranged by subject and stays close to the cases, as might be expected from its origins. It is valuable as a reminder that the other components of government did not always defer to the Court on such matters. These chapters are very important to the story of constitutional development, as they represent the "technical side" of judicial power.

MITCHELL and MITCHELL write for the general reader and, in spite of the title, concentrate on the framing of the Constitution, and on constitutional history under John Marshall. After his tenure, the account becomes too compressed to cover more than a few important cases. However, the book is a useful introduction to the early years of constitutional history, although it ought to be read with caution. Occasionally the authors' judgments on political and social history are simplistic, or no longer reflect modern scholarship.

WIECEK traces the collapse of what he calls the "federal consensus" on slavery. This held that the "peculiar institution" was subject to state, and not federal, control, and it lasted from the 1780s until approximately 1838. The abolitionists then managed to destroy that consensus over the following ten years. The author argues that, contrary to the normal pattern of American constitutional history, the breaking of the

consensus came directly from extra-judicial forces. The book is particularly effective in showing the interaction between constitutional and socio-political trends in American history. It draws together a mass of interesting and diverse material, and it should help to demystify various aspects of constitutional history for the non-specialist.

KUTLER (1971) is a fascinating and provocative study which uses one famous case to tackle the key problem of the Constitution and change. The Charles River Bridge Case had long been seen as a great setback for the progress of Marshallian nationalism. Although he was not the first to dispute this view, Kutler demonstrates very effectively what the case means in the broad sweep of American political and constitutional history, and shows how the Taney Court sought to balance technological change and the rights of property. Kutler does not offer simple answers as to how a balance between the two ought to be achieved. His discussion of the issue has relevance for other periods of American history, and it also succeeds in its narrower purpose, to place the case in the context of antebellum legal and political development.

In any narrative of mid-19th century constitutional history, the Dred Scott case looms large. Fortunately FEHRENBACHER's Pulitzer Prize-winning study places it in broad historical context, and, unlike earlier accounts, does not treat it just as an appalling aberration. He goes deeply into the history of slavery under the Constitution, and traces Scott's quest for freedom over many years. Fehrenbacher explains that Taney wanted to increase the Court's authority and use it to settle the questions relating to the status of African Americans, the status of the territories, and slavery itself. He examines closely all the opinions in the case, and assesses its many-sided legacy.

KUTLER (1968) is also concerned with the legacy of Dred Scott in his provocative and ground-breaking study on judicial power. He demonstrates that the Republicans were not implacably hostile to the Court and Constitution, and, particularly after Lincoln's appointments to the Court, they contributed to the expansion of its powers. In fact, Kutler argues that the Civil War and Reconstruction period was characterized by continuity in judicial development. The Supreme Court showed flexibility and a commonsense willingness to swim with the tide, and emerged from Reconstruction ready to play a very active role in the later 19th century.

HYMAN refines and expands Kutler's argument by showing the continuity in constitutional thought before and after the Civil War. He discusses both the growth and the limitations of national power in many areas of national life, in a rich and detailed book. HYMAN and WIECEK's contribution to the New American Nation Series is a distinguished synthesis of the constitutional and legal changes during the four decades of the title. Inevitably, this study is dominated by slavery and the Civil War and, while they offer no startling or controversial insights, the authors do show how this critical period brought out new strength and greater resilience in the Constitution. They give consideration to the development of commercial law under the Constitution, and its relationship to 19th century attitudes to property. The coverage of Reconstruction weaves constitutional developments into the complex fabric of the new society that was emerging. All in all, this is the most wide-ranging and authoritative treatment of the complex constitutional issues of the Civil War and Reconstruction periods.

GEORGE CONYNE

See also Supreme Court

Constitutional History, since 1877

Beth, Loren P., *The Development of the American Constitution, 1877–1917*, New York: Harper, 1971

Cortner, Richard C., *The Supreme Court and the Second Bill of Rights: The Fourteenth Amendment and the Nationalization of Civil Liberties*, Madison: University of Wisconsin Press, 1981

Jackson, Percival E., *Dissent in the Supreme Court: A Chronology*, Norman: University of Oklahoma Press, 1969

Mason, Alpheus T., *The Supreme Court from Taft to Warren*, Baton Rouge: Louisiana State University Press, 1958; 3rd edition as *The Supreme Court from Taft to Burger*, 1979

Meyer, Howard, *The Amendment That Refused to Die*, Radnor, PA: Chilton, 1973; revised, Boston: Beacon Press, 1978

Murphy, Paul L., *The Constitution in Crisis Times, 1918–1969*, New York: Harper, 1972

Swindler, William F., *Court and Constitution in the Twentieth Century*, 3 vols., Indianapolis: Bobbs Merrill, 1969–74

No single volume covers the whole of American constitutional history after Reconstruction. The parts of the Holmes Devise so far published include only three that cover parts of this period. They are: Charles Fairman, *Reconstruction and Reunion* 2 vols. (New York: Macmillan, 1971–87), which covers the story to 1888; Owen M. Fiss, *Troubled Beginnings of the Modern State, 1888–1910* (New York: Macmillan, 1993); and Alexander M. Bickel and Benno C. Schmidt, Jr., *The Judiciary and Responsible Government, 1910–21* (New York: Macmillan, 1984), which covers the tenure of Chief Justice White.

Notable books dealing with parts of this long period include BETH, who offers a clear narrative of the years from 1877 to 1917, as, in his words, the country changed "from a democracy to a republic". Beth sees the period as a time when new legal and judicial principles developed in state and federal courts, in an attempt to keep pace with demographic and technological change. The complexity of that task, and the requirements of the New American Nation Series of which this book is a part, mean that it does not have a strong interpretive view. Beth takes the uncontroversial view that American society was dominated by an increasingly prosperous middle-class with a classical liberal or laissez-faire attitude. This set the tone for what the Courts could do.

MURPHY weaves constitutional development and social and political history together in his worthy successor to Beth's volume. He does it, however, in a very different way. His study concentrates far more on the Supreme Court, which he sees as a "legal-political agency" that has an important role in settling the (largely domestic) crises of the title. Murphy is more inclined than Beth to argue and interpret, and sees the Warren Court as having fulfilled that role well. Focusing on the Court and writing in the early 1970s, he is able to give a fair, if rather Whiggish, account of the period under discussion. Although this cannot be the last word on the subject, it remains a valuable study, not least for its extensive bibliography, which, though inevitably out-of-date, is still very useful.

SWINDLER's massive and thorough study covers a substantial part of the whole period in great detail, and draws on a wide range of sources. He, too, adopts a "pro-Warren" line in common with most writers who have written broad syntheses of the Court's history. Writing in the late 1960s, he rightly suspected that a change was in the wind, with Warren's retirement and Nixon's election, but he saw the accomplishments of the Warren Court as fixed – which may turn out not to be so, as the Rehnquist Court reconsiders the legacy.

Shorter than the Swindler or the Beth/Murphy treatment is MASON, who covers the years 1921–78. This is a readable and learned account by one of the leading scholars in the field, and it has benefited from two re-writings. Mason agrees with the general "pro-Warren" view of other authors, but sees the Court's history as having more than its share of irony. For example, he finds it ironic that the justices appointed by Richard Nixon were labelled "strict constructionists" by their supporters; in his view, they wanted to change the principles of constitutional law in place when they arrived on the Court. This, he says, exemplifies the inappropriate labels that politicians give justices, and he sees the history of the Court as strewn with such examples.

JACKSON does dissent from the mainstream and disagrees with the thrust of the Warren Court's jurisprudence. His extensive use of quotations from a wide variety of sources and different periods makes this a useful book, even for those who may not share the author's view. Although the title suggests a general review of dissent, Jackson devotes approximately half of the book to the years of the Warren Court. This does not do justice to the long, and too often overlooked, history of dissent on the Court, but as Jackson is mainly interested in writing a critique of the modern Court, this is of secondary importance to him. His writing on the earlier period, while brief, is useful, and will introduce the reader to important aspects of the Court's work.

The most important change which draws a line between the years before and after the 1870s is the passage of the 13th, 14th, and 15th Amendments, the so-called "Second Bill of Rights". From the perspective of subsequent constitutional history, the most significant words are to be found in Section 1 of the 14th Amendment. This vital text is the subject of the studies by Cortner and Meyer. CORTNER is a solid, careful overview of the evolution of the 14th amendment from an element of the Republican Reconstruction programme after the Civil War into the bulwark of many different minorities in their attempts to exercise their civil rights. Cortner explains the nationalization of liberties in the complex American federal system. This is an essential part not only of American constitutional history, but of American history in general, as a contribution to the development of the more united and interconnected framework of the country in the late 20th century. Cortner approves of the shedding of the looser arrangements of the earlier period, but does not use his book as a platform to advocate one view to the exclusion of others. For MEYER, advocacy is important. He believes American society has to continue traveling down the road started by the Warren Court, if the country is ever going to achieve the promise of liberty in the Declaration of Independence and the Constitution. His book is a call to achieve what he calls the "Third American Revolution" which will eradicate all the discriminations of the post-war era. He writes in a more popular and less narrow and scholarly style, but offers interesting insights and discusses material not used elsewhere.

GEORGE CONYNE

See also Supreme Court

Continental Congress

Ammerman, David L., *In the Common Cause: American Response to the Coercive Acts of 1774*, Charlottesville: University Press of Virginia, 1974

Burnett, Edmund Cody, *The Continental Congress: A Definitive History of the Continental Congress from Its Inception in 1774 to March, 1789*, New York: Macmillan, 1941

Henderson, H. James, *Party Politics in the Continental Congress*, New York: McGraw Hill, 1974

Marston, Jerrilyn Greene, *King and Congress: The Transfer of Political Legitimacy, 1774–1776*, Princeton: Princeton University Press, 1987

Rakove, Jack N., *The Beginnings of National Politics: An Interpretive History of the Continental Congress*, New York: Knopf, 1979

Silbey, Joel H. (editor), *The Congress of the United States: Its Origins and Early Development*, New York: Carlson, 1991

The Continental Congress was the United States' original governing body and yet, surprisingly, a relatively small number of studies has appeared on the subject. Moreover, only a few books dealing with the institution have appeared in the last fifteen years, thereby prolonging the value of the earlier works.

One of the first scholarly examinations of the Continental Congress was BURNETT's chronological study of the institution. He presents the Congress as the central fixture of the Revolutionary period, the single place where the political, economic, and military aspects of the war merged. This is an exhaustively detailed account of Congress that describes its origins as a deliberative body of delegates organized to allow Americans a means to voice common grievances. Burnett traces the development of the institution to its replacement in 1789. Although somewhat dated, this study still contains a wealth of valuable information.

Through a quantitative analysis of congressional voting, HENDERSON maintains that Congress witnessed the formation of contentious partisan alignments that arose from regional differences rather than from personal loyalties or family connections. The primary division developed between the New England states and the South, with the middle states varying their position depending on the particular issue. According to Henderson, these were not mature, modern political parties, nor the seed of the first party system of the 1790s, but rather coalitions that displayed similar voting patterns throughout the Confederation period. Regionalism was not the only factor that determined divisions among delegates; social position and wealth also contributed to factionalism. Yet, despite these divisions, Congress functioned reasonably well. The representatives instituted a plan for settlement of western lands, kept an army in the field (at times in spite of themselves), and they took the not so small step of declaring independence.

RAKOVE offers a revisionist history of the Continental Congress that differs from Henderson's description of a contentious institution. Although he acknowledges the existence of militant and moderate factions, Rakove shows that Congress's decisionmaking was driven more by events, such as the battle at Bunker Hill, than by sectionalism or ideological conflicts. "Congressional factions were too fluid in composition, small in size, and primitive in function" to have hindered the legislative process. Further, he demonstrates that the representatives initially accepted the 1787 Constitutional Convention as a means to address the nation's governmental problems and revise the Articles of Confederation, not as an effort by nationalists to institute a more centralized system of government. Henderson's study is impressive in its breadth as well as its writing, and is essential to grasp the workings of the Continental Congress.

AMMERMAN's study of the American colonists' response to the Coercive Acts of 1774 focuses on the First Continental Congress. Like Rakove, he finds little evidence of factionalism among the delegates, and in fact maintains that they were of one mind on the question of grievances and the means of redress. Ammerman also traces the development of the Continental Association, the method adopted by Congress to keep the public informed, and to enforce compliance with nonimportation, nonexportation, and nonconsumption. Ammerman's account is well-organized and concise, a valuable source for understanding the Continental Congress's first year of existence.

The "transfer of political legitimacy" from George III to what in 1774 was little more than a resistance organization is the focus of MARSTON. The author recounts the transformation of Americans' attitudes from 1774 to 1776 as they gradually rejected the king's authority to govern, and accepted the Continental Congress as their legitimate institution of government. Congress took on powers formerly held by the king and exercised a surprising number of functions normally associated with the executive, such as the conduct of military and foreign affairs, and establishing policy on Native Americans. Congress delegated legislative powers to the states, permitting local governments to establish tax laws and regulate trade. The rather poor governmental record produced by this arrangement forced the further evolution of American constitutional thought and eventually contributed to support for a constitutional convention in 1787. Marston provides insightful analysis, clearly demonstrating how Americans came to accept Congress as their legitimate institution of government and how that institution exercised its authority.

SILBEY's edited collection of essays addresses Congress's early years and contains a series of articles dealing specifically with the Continental Congress. Jack Rakove examines the national legislature in light of the perceptions of Madison and other revolutionaries of what the Constitution was to accomplish. He argues that many of their expectations did not come to fruition, particularly their belief that the elective process would provide a "filtration of talent" and ensure that only the natural elite would gain public office. Rick K. Wilson and Calvin Jillson explore the role of leadership in the Continental Congress and find that institutional procedures prevented the development of strong legislative leaders. The office of president of Congress and the committee system were designed to inhibit the accumulation of power in the hands of individuals or factions. The failure of Congress to develop stable leadership demonstrated the effectiveness of the design. In a further essay, Wilson and Jillson use a social choice model developed by political scientists to explain the decline and failure of the Continental Congress. They argue that constrained decision making led to a deadlock in the legislative process, thus inhibiting the ability of the delegates to govern. As in their earlier essay, they argue that institutional design inhibited the formation of coalitions necessary to carry out effective lawmaking. Although neither exhaustive nor definitive, the articles in Silbey's collection bring together the results of recent work, and enhance understanding of the Founding Fathers' political philosophy and the Continental Congress's origins, development, and demise.

HARRY S. LAVER

Conventions, Political

Byrne, Gary C. and Paul Marx, *The Great American Convention: A Political History of Presidential Elections*, Palo Alto, CA: Pacific Books, 1976

Chase, James S., *Emergence of the Presidential Nominating Convention, 1789–1832*, Urbana: University of Illinois Press, 1973

David, Paul Theodore, *The Politics of National Party Conventions*, Washington, DC: Brookings Institution, 1960; condensed version, with Ralph M. Goldman and Richard C. Bain, 1964

Davis, James W., *National Conventions in an Age of Party Reform*, Westport, CT: Greenwood Press, 1983

Jeffrey, Thomas E., *State Parties and National Politics: North Carolina, 1815–1861*, Athens: University of Georgia Press, 1989

Shafer, Byron E., *Bifurcated Politics: Evolution and Reform in the National Party Convention*, Cambridge, MA: Harvard University Press, 1988

Smith, Larry David and Dan Nimmo, *Cordial Concurrence: Orchestrating National Party Conventions in the Telepolitical Age*, New York: Praeger, 1991

Thornton, J. Mills III, *Politics and Power in a Slave Society: Alabama, 1800–1860*, Baton Rouge: Louisiana State University Press, 1978

Party nominating conventions have been an important part of the political apparatus which Americans have devised to convert the provisions of the Constitution into an operative system of government. The origins of national party conventions are discussed by CHASE. He details the demise of "King Caucus," which seemed increasingly at odds with developing notions of democracy, and traces the use of conventions at the local and state level back into the 18th century. Finally in 1831 the Antimasons and the National Republicans, and Democrats the next year, adopted the convention to choose their presidential candidates. Chase is particularly strong on the central role of Antimasons in urging the adoption of the convention instead of the caucus. He maintains that conventions depended on the actuality of stable parties (not vice versa), and reflected an existing consensus. He concludes that although the chief contemporary argument for replacing the caucus with the convention was that the latter would be more democratic, this was not always true, particularly with the advent of professional party managers who gave the convention an appearance of spontaneity but actually manipulated events behind the scenes.

Most studies of party development in the antebellum period devote at least some attention to the role of conventions. Two of the best that examine state and local, rather than simply national conventions are Thornton and Jeffrey. JEFFREY outlines the development of mass political parties and the importance of conventions in maintaining a reliable organization. He also discusses the widespread mood of distrust and latent hostility toward conventions and political "cliques," sentiments that reflected the dominant republican heritage. THORNTON provides a more detailed, point by point account of party organization and the evolution of local, county, district, and state conventions. He further recounts how party organizers had difficulty in arousing much interest in these gatherings, which often failed to attract many delegates. State meetings had to be coordinated with legislative sessions or county meetings with court day, to insure any meaningful attendance.

The classic, nearly encyclopedic treatment of party conventions is DAVID, GOLDMAN and BAIN. This massive study, sponsored by the Brookings Institution, focuses on the nomination process and behavior of delegates in convention from the antebellum period through 1956. The authors review party leadership, candidates, apportionment and selection of delegates, and functions of the convention other than nominations. They popularized the orthodox view that nomination in convention is often more important than the general election that follows. The authors offer penetrating, subtle discussions of many debates about the nature of conventions, such as whether it represents popular influence (or "democracy") or simply the will of party leaders and machine bosses. A principal drawback is the book's age – it considers nominations before many of the modern reforms in delegate selection. Thus, some of the arguments will be outdated, although it remains useful as a reference tool. In some respects the "updated version" of David, Goldman and Bain is DAVIS. He covers most of the same ground, but from a post-reform perspective. Davis believes that national conventions functioned better before the so-called "progressive" or "democratizing" reforms of the 1960s. He argues forcefully against further changes, such as a national primary, and urges the need to re-establish the independence of delegates in the nominating process, which would increase their effective role. His discussion of the probable effects of such modifications, particularly the relationship between nominated and elected officials and party regulars, is insightful.

In a slender volume, BYRNE and MARX analyze the presidential nominating conventions of major parties from 1864 to 1972. The authors argue that the convention, its form and style, or degree of unanimity, typically determine whether the party's nominee will win the general election (a theory first propounded by David, Goldman, and Bain). They focus on two factors as decisive: the percentage of votes cast for the eventual nominee on the first ballot; and whether or not the party currently occupies the White House. Based on these two determinants, Byrne and Marx offer a predictive model that classifies every convention on a scale, ranking each in descending likelihood of success from "conciliatory" to "incumbent failure." While the model is rather mechanistic (although generally accurate), the authors provide a succinct account of the conventions encompassed by their study.

SHAFER explores national conventions since World War II, using them as a "window" on to more pervasive political trends. He maintains that they are part of a general "nationalization of American politics," due to a universal media, especially television, and partisan independence among better educated voters, which has left state and local parties failing and ineffective. Primary reform in the 1960s and early 1970s accentuated the power of interest groups and ideologues, Shafer contends, while isolating party regulars from the nomination of a presidential candidate. As the convention lost this function, party leaders focused more and more on the outside audience – using their national meeting as a springboard for the autumn campaign. The result, he says, is really two conventions ("bifurcated"): one that the ever-shrinking television audience sees; and one that happens backstage, where the nominee and his closest advisers make many of the meaningful decisions, such as choosing a Vice President and resolving a platform. In addition to this provocative thesis, Shafer contributes an exhaustive history of post-war conventions.

As Shafer and others point out, conventions have become as much a television happening as a political event. SMITH and NIMMO examine how party leaders create solidarity behind a predetermined candidate. They also show how party resources are coordinated through the media, especially television, and combine with other institutional forces (a "cordial concurrence"). The authors main focus remains, however, the creation and management of a television spectacle, its purpose to unify party regulars and to inspire, and sometimes confuse, the viewers. Smith and Nimmo's narrative, which uses opera as a metaphor for the "orchestration" of political resources, is entertaining, although a little strained.

CHRISTOPHER J. OLSEN

See also Elections entries

Coolidge, Calvin 1872–1933
30th President of the United States

Hawley, Ellis W., *The Great War and the Search for a Modern Order: A History of the American People and Their Institutions, 1917–1933*, New York: St. Martin's Press, 1979, 2nd edition, 1992

McCoy, Donald R., *Calvin Coolidge: The Quiet President*, New York: Macmillan, 1967; reprinted Lawrence: University Press of Kansas, 1988

Murray, Robert K., *The Politics of Normalcy: Governmental Theory and Practice in the Harding-Coolidge Era*, New York: Norton, 1973

Russell, Francis, *A City in Terror: 1919, The Boston Police Strike*, New York: Viking, 1975

Silver, Thomas B., *Coolidge and the Historians*, Durham, NC: Carolina Academic Press, 1982

White, William Allen, *A Puritan in Babylon: The Story of Calvin Coolidge*, New York: Macmillan, 1938

His name a byword for executive-branch passivity and business-friendly conservatism, Calvin Coolidge has not inspired a large scholarly literature from American historians, who have preferred to focus on the activist Democratic presidents who preceded and followed him. Along with Warren Harding and Herbert Hoover, Coolidge languished in the textbooks for decades as a man who fiddled (or slept) while the Great Depression loomed. During the last thirty years, however, scholars have reconsidered old stereotypes of the "Roaring '20s," and have crafted a more nuanced portrait of the decade, well beyond images of flappers, bootleggers, and jazz. Readers looking for an introduction to Coolidge and his era, then, would do well to start with recent surveys of the 1920s.

One of the best of these works of synthesis is HAWLEY. Balanced and judicious, this study traces New Era attempts to rationalize and organize all facets of American life, from foreign policy to the home. A central theme of the 1920s, Hawley argues, is the development of bureaucratic organizations, managed by technical elites who hoped to coordinate governmental and private efforts to achieve an efficient, stable society. The reader can take from Hawley a sophisticated interpretive framework in which to place Coolidge and his presidency.

Another useful source on the Coolidge years is the recent scholarship on his Secretary of Commerce, Herbert Hoover. Along with general reconsiderations of the 1920s have come fresh appraisals of the executive branch, in which Hoover has fared well. No one should miss the important insights that much of the Hoover literature throws on the personality and administrative style of Coolidge. Hoover has won new respect for what Hawley terms his "vision of an associative state," formulated in the often undervalued Harding-Coolidge cabinet. Such reappraisals have not yet redeemed Coolidge, who sardonically termed Hoover "the wonder boy," and never warmed to Hoover's bustling, expansive administrative style.

As with most presidents, Coolidge was the subject of a number of campaign and other contemporary biographies, both laudatory and critical, none of which need detain modern readers for long. The earliest solid study, and one that helped to fix the image of Coolidge as a laconic New Englander out of place in the 20th century and in Washington, DC, was WHITE. In this full-length biography, the noted Kansas newspaperman argues that Coolidge was temperamentally unfit to meet the demands of the rapidly changing years of his presidency. White presents a highly readable account of an upright man, albeit one who was a "Yankee throw-back to McKinley's era". But, unlike Harding, Coolidge was untainted by personal scandal. Rich in details of Coolidge and such contemporaries as Henry Cabot Lodge and Andrew Mellon, White's study remains valuable for the insights into American politics that his years covering presidents and the presidency gave him. However, White should be read in conjunction with more recent works to give a balanced vision of broader political and social trends in the Coolidge years.

The best study of Coolidge remains McCOY. Admiring yet judicious, this biography argues that Coolidge brought restraint, dignity, and simplicity to the presidency. An able administrator, Coolidge achieved the rebuilding of public confidence in the presidency after the scandalous revelations following Harding's death. McCoy reminds us as well that Coolidge's probity and patience were highly popular among a public generally satisfied with a less activist government. "For a nation that was tired of having the ship of state rocked," writes McCoy, "he was a reassuring skipper." No hagiographer, though, McCoy does not see Coolidge's restraint as always in the country's best interest. Coolidge's strict reading of his responsibilities led him too often to unimaginative approaches to pressing issues, such as his determination that the European nations be held to their war debts. The reprint edition contains a valuable bibliographical essay surveying recent literature on Coolidge and his times.

Less valuable than McCoy is SILVER. This brief essay seeks to redeem Coolidge from a half century of criticism at the hands of such partisans of Democratic presidents as Arthur Schlesinger, Jr. In tune with the Coolidge mini-revival during the Reagan years (Ronald Reagan replaced Thomas Jefferson's portrait in the White House Cabinet Room with one of Coolidge), Silver's study is an unabashed and strident attack on the scholarship of the historians who have, in his estimation, systematically undervalued Coolidge, distorting the historical record in the process. Reading more like a lawyer's brief than a historian's monograph, Silver's study fails to convince through its overstatement.

Apart from the biographies, one of the few solid studies of Coolidge is MURRAY. Best known for his work on the Harding administration, Murray argues that Harding's policy of "normalcy" came to fruition under Coolidge. A needed transition from post-war anxieties, "normalcy," a belief that limited, restrained government was what the nation generally should have, provided a foundation for the decade's political life. Not a full study of Coolidge's presidency, Murray is best on Coolidge's transition from vice president to election in his own right. Applauding the achievements of "normalcy," Murray points to the creation of the Budget Bureau and efforts at disarmament, among other measures. Some readers will, however, find that Murray is too generous in finding programmatic coherence in Harding's "normalcy."

Those interested in Coolidge's rise to national prominence should not miss RUSSELL. As governor of Massachusetts,

Coolidge called out the National Guard to put down a strike by the Boston police, proclaiming that "there is no right to strike against the public safety by anyone, anywhere, anytime." Russell's study is a readable introduction to this event.

As historians continue to turn away from presidential personalities and toward larger issues of the structure of the executive branch and its administration, Coolidge may well begin to excite more attention. But he is unlikely ever to reach the "great" or "near-great" status in social scientists' presidential rankings which consistently favor colorful personalities and activist policies.

TRENT A. WATTS

See also Nineteen-Twenties

Counterculture, 1960s

Burns, Stewart, *Social Movements of the 1960s: Searching for Democracy*, Boston: Twayne, 1990

Cluster, Dick (editor), *They Should Have Served that Cup of Coffee*, Boston: South End Press, 1979

Dickstein, Morris, *The Gates of Eden: American Culture in the Sixties*, New York: Basic Books, 1977

Farber, David, "The Counterculture and the Anti-War Movement" in *Give Peace a Chance: Exploring the Vietnam Antiwar Movement*, edited by Melvin Small and William D. Hoover, Syracuse, NY: Syracuse University Press, 1992

Gitlin, Todd, *The Sixties: Years of Hope, Days of Rage*, New York: Bantam, 1987, revised 1993

Kessler, Lauren, *After All These Years: Sixties Ideals in a Different World*, New York: Thunder's Mouth Press, 1990

Podhoretz, Norman, *Breaking Ranks: A Political Memoir*, New York: Harper, 1979; London: Weidenfeld and Nicolson, 1980

Reich, Charles A., *The Greening of America*, New York: Random House, 1971

Roszak, Theodore, *The Making of a Counterculture: Reflections on the Technocratic Society and Its Youthful Opposition*, New York: Doubleday, and London: Faber, 1970

Rubin, Jerry, *Do It! Scenarios of the Revolution*, New York: Simon and Schuster, and London: Cape, 1970

Steigerwald, David, *The Sixties and the End of Modern America*, New York: St. Martin's Press, 1995

Wells, Tom, *The War Within: America's Battle over Vietnam*, Berkeley: University of California Press, 1994

Defining the Counterculture remains as much an issue now as it was in the 1960s. Participants, historians (and participants-now-historians) can agree that the Counterculture posed a challenge to the American establishment, but how much of a challenge, with what cohesion, direction, and result is still debated. As a descriptor (probably dating from 1968), the term "Counterculture" itself is broad, most often considered synonymous with a generality of New Left and anti-war protests, civil rights and Black Power, Yippies and hippies, youth culture and music, acid and psychedelia. Therefore, the histories of Black culture, feminism, and anti-war protest are all interwoven into any discussion, but as the other common alternative term of the time – "the Movement" – implies, the question of what unity existed between these groupings is problematic.

As a set of social movements which came together in the mid-1960s possessing at least a common umbrella of oppositions, the issue of what it all meant, and how it fitted together – if indeed it did – occupied the Counterculture from the beginning. Writing at the close of the 1960s, RUBIN offers a sweeping denunciation of "Amerika" in words, cartoons and images, but the leader of the Youth International Party – the Yippies – was also staking a claim against the "old politics" (including the New Left), and for the transcendental unity of a new lifestyle, centred on youth, drugs, and "the Moment." Such transcendentalism was common; ROSZAK argued for a transformational unity, but unlike Rubin, saw it as incorporating a new politics of the Left, and, as the full title suggests, promising the overthrow of industrial capitalism. REICH offered a hybrid prognosis, explaining the Movement in terms of evolutionary categories of Consciousness I, II, and III, with a utopian vision of future youth liberation – though it now reads as marred by overpraise for items such as bell-bottom jeans.

Roszak, Reich, and Rubin remain valuable as early attempts to argue historical and theoretical underpinnings for the Counterculture. All notably dwelt upon transcendental American unities, though with different constituents. When, in the post-Vietnam, post-Watergate America of the 1970s, transcendent unity failed to arrive, assessment of the past decade began. DICKSTEIN is perhaps the first major analysis of the 1960s overall, and, again, the text argues for unity in a cultural shift, the revolutionary and utopian character of the Movement (fundamentally described as millennial). As such, Dickstein is chiefly useful as testament to the legacy that the Counterculture created, and its questioning in the climate of the 1970s. By the late 1970s and early 1980s, the common strategy for re-evaluation was reminiscence. CLUSTER provides a set of essays from activists who recall the anti-war movement, civil rights, feminist and campus protests. The Counterculture is recognized as divided, although Cluster does contribute a conclusion entitled "So What?", arguing the value and durability of its gains. A decade later, KESSLER offers further oral recollections, including statements by Angela Davis and Tom Hayden, but also less-remembered activists. It is notable that Kessler feels obliged to detail where the contributors stood, in terms of their radicalism, in 1989.

In contrast, PODHORETZ provides a scathing account of disillusioned radicalism. He locates the Movement in the anti-establishment politics of the Left in the late 1950s, the result of self-loathing and contempt by the white liberal intelligentsia. Offering multiple ironies on the eve of Reagan's election, Podhoretz regards the Counterculture as triumphant, having achieved its unity in the comprehensive destruction of the values of liberalism. Eight years on under Reagan, GITLIN, a former leader of the Students for a Democratic Society (SDS), wrote his own comprehensive account of the era. Unlike Podhoretz, he does not reject the radicalism of his youth, but he is nevertheless critical of the Movement in general (and the New Left in particular). He attributes its failures to a

bankrupt ideology, and the effects of its own sectarianism and self-aggrandizement – if there was no unity, then it was the movement's own fault in imagining it could be taken as a transcendental given.

In the 1990s, those too young to have participated have begun to offer analysis. BURNS provides a dispassionate history, divided into sections on civil rights, the New Left, feminism, and other topics, and arguing for a unity in the grass roots democracy of the Movement. WELLS takes the other tack, providing an ultra-comprehensive history of the anti-war movement, looking at both protesters and their opponents in government. Wells details factional in-fighting, but gives credit to the resilience and courage of those active in the trenches of the protest movement. In the excellent collection edited by Small and Hoover, the most valuable essay in this context is FARBER's, which analyses the uneasy relationship between the New Left, the anti-war movement and the Counterculture, arguing that common ground was quite sparse – just as Rubin evidenced in 1970.

Finally, STEIGERWALD is a recent text which successfully attempts to avoid stale discussion of Left vs. Right, Old Left vs. New Left, or New Left vs. Counterculture. His innovative aim is to characterise the 1960s as a transition from modernism to postmodernism; in this he apparently echoes the grand unities of Roszak and Reich, but argues that it is only in the postmodern consumerization of everything – including protest and radical lifestyles – that a commonality for the Counterculture can be found. It is a convincing argument, and one which provides a construction of the Counterculture and the 1960s which will challenge future writing.

ALASDAIR SPARK

See also Black Power; Civil Rights Movement; Vietnam War: Political and Social Consequences; Women's History: Women's Liberation Movement

Cowboys, Cowgirls, Gunfighters, and Western Heroes: Individual Biographies

Dary, David, *Cowboy Culture: A Saga of Five Centuries*, New York: Knopf, 1981

DeArment, Robert K., *Bat Masterson: The Man and the Legend*, Norman: University of Oklahoma Press, 1979

Durham, Philip and Everett L. Jones, *The Negro Cowboys*, New York: Dodd Mead, 1965

Frantz, Joe B. and Julian Ernest Choate, Jr., *The American Cowboy: The Myth and the Reality*, Norman: University of Oklahoma Press, 1955

Furman, Necah Stewart, *Caroline Lockhart: Her Life and Legacy*, Seattle: University of Washington Press, 1994

Lake, Stuart N., *Wyatt Earp, Frontier Marshal*, Boston: Houghton Mifflin, 1931

Riley, Glenda, *The Life and Legacy of Annie Oakley*, Norman: University of Oklahoma Press, 1994

Roach, Joyce Gibson, *The Cowgirls*, Houston: Cordovan, 1977; revised, Denton: University of North Texas Press, 1990

Rosa, Joseph G., *They Called Him Wild Bill: The Life and Adventures of James Butler Hickok*, Norman: University of Oklahoma Press, 1964, revised 1974

Rosa, Joseph G., *The Gunfighter: Man or Myth?*, Norman: University of Oklahoma Press, 1969

Settle, William A., Jr., *Jesse James Was His Name; or, Fact and Fiction Concerning the Careers of the Notorious James Brothers of Missouri*, Columbia: University of Missouri Press, 1966; reprinted, Lincoln: University of Nebraska Press, 1977

Steckmesser, Kent Ladd, *The Western Hero in History and Legend*, Norman: University of Oklahoma Press, 1965

Utley, Robert M., *Billy the Kid: A Short and Violent Life*, Lincoln: University of Nebraska Press, 1989

Throughout western history, a variety of heroes appeared whose lives and contributions became obscured as they obtained legendary status. Whether arising from folk culture or depicted in literature and film, popular images determined how audiences understood the historical roles of individuals. STECKMESSER follows this premise in analyzing the heroic status of Kit Carson, Billy the Kid, Wild Bill Hickok, and George A. Custer. He gives a historical account of each, then shows how dime novelists, biographers, and Hollywood altered or invented facts to portray them as legends. Once stories had been established that encouraged a legendary image, writes Steckmesser, they became "extremely difficult to correct" because repetition enforced their veracity.

The mythic image of cowboys began in the literature of the 19th century, and it served to obscure their historical roles. Cowboys, write FRANTZ and CHOATE, were the embodiment of "all the virtues and vices of the Anglo-American in one folk type." They could be ranch hands or rustlers. Defined by their distinctive clothing and horsemanship, but primarily by their guns, cowboys increasingly attracted attention as gunfighters or outlaws. The authors explain this transformation in discussing both the world of working cowboys and their literary counterparts.

More concerned with the historical cowboy than the literary one, DARY's award-winning book traces the development of cattle ranching and the culture associated with it. He describes the clothing, terminology, and techniques of cowboys, beginning with the 16th-century vaqueros, and chronicles life on the cattle trails and in the cowtowns, on the open range and in the bunkhouse. The cowboy, he writes, "was colorful because he was not typical" and evoked a romantic image. Despite its glamour to easterners, cattle raising was a business and cowboys were laborers. This point becomes apparent, as Dary suggests, in realizing the impact of barbed-wire fences or the decorum expected of members at the exclusive Cheyenne Club.

DURHAM and JONES provide an important contribution to western history by drawing attention to the many African American cowboys, from the slave Big-Mouth Henry to rodeo showman Bill Pickett, who participated in the cattle industry. After the Civil War, black cowboys joined cattle drives moving north from Texas or worked the open range at ranches throughout the West. Other African Americans found employment in stockyards, served as cooks, or worked in cowtown saloons. Durham and Jones believe that ability and the need for experienced cowhands tempered the racial prejudice of white co-workers, but recognize that it existed for both African American and Hispanic cowboys.

Among the many personalities of the West the best known were the gunfighters, who shared one characteristic – a willingness to kill. Though ROSA (1969) acknowledges the contribution of literature and movies in creating legendary gunmen, he believes that the lives of some, like Wild Bill Hickok and Bat Masterson, resembled their legends. He discusses various historical circumstances that produced such men, or outlaws like Sam Bass, and of these, the prevalence of guns in a turbulent society seemed the primary reason. Rosa overstates the violent character of the West, but he offers a lively and thoughtful look at one of the popular themes in western history.

Much of Rosa's understanding of gunfighters stems from his study of James Butler Hickok, the famous Wild Bill. ROSA (1964, 1974) depicts Hickok as a "man of action, cool, reserved, ruthless, and at times unscrupulous" who earned his legendary status. While separating the historical Hickok from the imagined hero, Rosa shows how these two identities merged.

Like Hickok, William Barclay Masterson led an exciting and colorful life. A buffalo hunter, army scout, law officer, gambler, and, later, a newspaperman, his western experience encouraged journalists and biographers to embellish his many exploits. Using these stories as his starting point, DeARMENT devotes his study to separating the legendary Bat Masterson from the historical person. In the process, DeArment admirably recounts life in the cattle towns and on the Great Plains, clarifies the role of Wyatt Earp in Dodge City's history, and discovers that Bat Masterson, the gunfighter and lawman, never killed anyone.

Another of the most famous Western "heroes" is Wyatt Earp, and LAKE remains Earp's only official biography. It traces Earp's life from birth, following his travels West and his years as a farmer, buffalo hunter, and then lawman of towns such as Dodge City and Tombstone. Based primarily on a series of personal interviews with Earp, who died in 1929, Lake is at times an overly simplistic narrative that provides little objective analysis of its subject. However, though dated, this is still the most comprehensive account of Earp's life to date, and gives some clues to the process of converting him into a legendary hero.

Because the lives of western heroes have been obscured by pulp literature and oral folk culture, biographers find themselves trying to isolate a legendary figure's factual past. But SETTLE is interested as much in the legend of Jesse James as in the person. For sixteen years Jesse James, along with his brother Frank and their gang, robbed banks and trains, yet despite numerous killings associated with the group, he became a folk hero. Settle associates much of James's heroic status with the Civil War's impact on Missouri. As a symbol for the Lost Cause, James became a kind of Robin Hood who challenged the economic and political power represented by banks and railroads after the war.

By the time of Henry McCarty's death in 1881 at age 21, he had become the legendary William H. Bonney, Billy the Kid of New Mexico Territory. UTLEY recounts Henry's life and shows how the young rustler earned his notorious image. Focusing on the bloody Lincoln County War, Utley views the Kid as a soldier in a struggle between local elites for economic superiority. When the smoke cleared, the mythic Billy the Kid had been created, and the legend never waned. Utley presents a complex portrait and argues that the Kid sustained, yet contradicted, the stories and tales about his life.

Finally, the role of women in the American West is a subject that has only recently begun to receive the attention which it deserves. Riley and Furman are two of the best biographies of female western figures, Annie Oakley and Caroline Lockhart, respectively. RILEY is an in-depth study of Oakley as both a legendary western heroine and as a woman making her way in a man's sport. Riley not only provides a sensitive and objective analysis of Oakley's life, but also skilfully places Oakley's accomplishments in the context of attitudes toward women in the 19th century, and in the context of the folklore of the American West. FURMAN is an objective but fascinating account of the life of cattlewoman and writer Caroline Lockhart, who, after pursuing a career as a journalist in the East, moved to Wyoming to begin ranching at the age of 33. Lockhart was well-known not only for her work as a journalist and investigative reporter, but also for her colorful tales of the West, such as *The Fighting Shepherdess*.

While substantial biographies of other western women such as Calamity Jane and Wyoming's "Cattle Kate" have yet to be written, ROACH is one of the few broader studies of cowgirls in the American West. She explores the experiences of rodeo queens, cowgirls, and women ranchers in the late 19th and early 20th centuries. She also examines the portrayal of the cowgirl or ranch woman in song, literature, film, and folklore, and successfully challenges the stereotypical portraits of Western women and the perception of the American West as a male-dominated sphere.

ROBIN L.E. HEMENWAY
J. THOMAS MURPHY

Crandall, Prudence 1803–1890
Pioneer in African American education

Foner, Philip S., *Three Who Dared: Prudence Crandall, Margaret Douglass, Myrtilla Miner: Champions of Antebellum Black Education*, Westport, CT: Greenwood Press, 1984
Fuller, Edmund, *Prudence Crandall: An Incident of Racism in Nineteenth-Century Connecticut*, Middletown, CT: Wesleyan University Press, 1971
Strane, Susan, *A Whole-Souled Woman: Prudence Crandall and the Education of Black Women*, New York: Norton, 1990
Welch, Marvis Olive, *Prudence Crandall: A Biography*, Manchester, CT: Jason, 1983

Though now a largely-forgotten woman, Prudence Crandall was at the center of the controversy over slavery, emancipation, and the education of blacks in antebellum Connecticut.

While slavery was illegal in Connecticut in 1832 when her story begins, most citizens did not want free blacks in their state and did not want to give those already there basic civil rights or provide them with an education. Abolitionists, on the other hand, argued strenuously that free blacks should be welcomed and given whatever basic civic and educational tools they needed to make their way in the world. It was in this climate of tension and racial intolerance that Crandall, a 29-year-old Quaker schoolteacher, would advertise in William Lloyd Garrison's abolitionist paper *The Liberator* that she was opening a high school for young black women in Canterbury, Connecticut.

The ensuing debate over black education led, on the state-wide level, to the passage of a notorious "Black Law," forbidding the education of out-of-state blacks in Connecticut. Clearly aimed at Crandall and her school (the legislation was sponsored by a state legislator from Canterbury), this legislation was typical for its time. Crandall was jailed and eventually found guilty when a judge ruled that blacks were not citizens, a precedent that would be cited in the Dred Scott case. The case was thrown out on appeal on a minor technicality, and Crandall returned to her school. It was burned down soon after. Now married, to a Baptist minister, Crandall gave up education and returned to private life. In the late 1880s, the state of Connecticut awarded her an annuity of $400 per year as recompense for her experience. In an interesting footnote to her story, her younger brother Reuben, a doctor, also became an abolitionist martyr when he was arrested in Washington, DC in 1835 and charged with possessing and distributing abolitionist literature, which he claimed his sister had placed among his belongings. His arrest, a product of the fear caused by a slave's attempt to murder his female owner, was one of the causes of a major riot in the city in August 1835. The restless crowds in the capital sought to lynch him and the slave in question. Although eventually acquitted, Crandall contracted tuberculosis during his jail stay and died two years later.

With the rising interest in the history of women and blacks in America, Crandall has become a minor topic of interest to historians and biographers. Although most mentions of her in works on black education and female educators are cursory, there have been four works to focus on her, all of which are worthy of perusal. The first of these, FULLER, was the work of a literary scholar rather than a historian, and a product of white Americans' search for role models in the struggle for black civil rights. Women such as Crandall, who had placed themselves in jeopardy in order to secure basic rights for blacks in the 19th century, were ideal heroes. Fuller relies on the transcripts of the trial, which had been published, and various records in the Connecticut state archives, to flesh out a picture of the shadowy Crandall. He offers a succinct and well-organized account of the conflict in Connecticut, Crandall's role in it, her trial, and the aftermath. He was acute enough to see that Crandall had never been in danger of spending any significant amount of time in prison and that her conviction was symbolic rather than actual, as indicated by the flimsy pretext used to overturn her conviction. Rather, a certain segment of Connecticut society wished to use her prosecution to send a strong message to others who might wish to follow in her footsteps, not turn her into a martyr. Perhaps the most moving portion of Fuller's book is a reprint of an interview with Crandall toward the end of her life, published in a book about cycling through America in the late 1880s. Crandall, now a widow and living in a small town in Kansas, remained defiant and revolutionary-minded to the end, reading extensively in the debate on Social Darwinism and angrily recalling her husband's attempts to censor her reading material. Fuller's account is probably the best place to start for an overview of Crandall's life.

WELCH is an admirable attempt to flesh out Fuller's picture of Crandall, and to see her as more than just an "incident" in 19th-century racism. More facts and stories about her can be found in this work, but for a sustained effort to place her in the nexus of 19th-century reform, women's activism, and education, readers should consult FONER, which was published only one year after Welch's book, but offers a more advanced scholarly thesis. By comparing Crandall with two other pioneers in the antebellum education of blacks, Foner is able to show Crandall's place in this important movement, which scholars have examined with increasing care after the growth of black and women's studies. Foner's work is invaluable to any student, teacher, or scholar, who wants to see where Crandall belongs in 19th-century America.

But most important of all is STRANE which takes advantage of the works published since Foner's 1984 book to offer a more sophisticated discussion of Crandall and the movement to educate black women. She argues for the inclusion of Crandall in the pantheon of 19th-century female abolitionists, such as Lydia Maria Child and the Grimké sisters. To Strane, Crandall is an important and unrecognized figure in the American struggle to end slavery and include blacks in society. However, the fact remains that despite her important role in the controversy over black rights in the 1830s, Crandall soon disappeared from the American stage, largely, one can infer, because of her husband. While this makes her typical of American women in a sad sense, it does not permit her to be considered the equal of lifelong reformers whose actions had far more impact.

JEAN V. BERLIN

Crime and Punishment

Abelson, Elaine S., *When Ladies Go A-Thieving: Middle-Class Shoplifters in the Victorian Department Store*, New York: Oxford University Press, 1989

Ayers, Edward L., *Vengeance and Justice: Crime and Punishment in the 19th-Century American South*, New York: Oxford University Press, 1984

Friedman, Lawrence M., *Crime and Punishment in American History*, New York: Basic Books, 1993

Hindus, Michael Stephen, *Prison and Plantation: Crime, Justice, and Authority in Massachusetts and South Carolina, 1767–1878*, Chapel Hill: University of North Carolina Press, 1980

Hoffer, Peter C. and N.E.H. Hull, *Murdering Mothers: Infanticide in England and New England, 1558–1803*, New York: New York University Press, 1981

Masur, Louis P., *Rites of Execution: Capital Punishment and the Transformation of American Culture, 1776–1865*, New York: Oxford University Press, 1989

Monkkonen, Eric H. (editor), *Crime and Justice in American History: Historical Articles on the Origins and Evolution of American Criminal Justice; The Colonies and Early Republic*, 2 vols., Westport, CT: Meckler, 1991

Rise, Eric W., *The Martinsville Seven and Southern Justice: Race, Rape, and Capital Punishment in Virginia, 1949–1951*, Charlottesville: University Press of Virginia, 1993

Walker, Samuel A., *Popular Justice: A History of American Criminal Justice*, New York: Oxford University Press, 1980

The history of crime and of criminal justice are often characterized as neglected and underdeveloped areas in comparison with other "new fields" such as women's history and labor history. However, the past three decades have witnessed increased scholarly attention to crime, punishment, and justice as historical problems, facilitating the emergence of a pioneering body of literature on, for example, the Americas, Europe, and Australia. Nevertheless, with regard to the United States, significant gaps remain.

WALKER made the first attempt to integrate the historical research on crime and criminal justice of the 1960s and 1970s into a coherent interpretative framework. This is a concise historical overview of the development of the U.S. criminal justice system from colonial times to the late 1970s that focuses on the constant struggle to balance the rule of law with the demands of "popular justice." The strengths of this work are in the discussions of prisons and police. Walker is rather overshadowed by FRIEDMAN's impressive history of a "working" criminal justice system, written from a social science perspective, that runs chronologically from colonial beginnings to the first Rodney King trial in 1992. It is extremely reader-friendly and comprehensive in scope, covering a wide range of topics from prosecution of Puritan morality offenses to organized crime, but the emphasis is on societal reaction to crime from, for example, the courts, police, juvenile agencies, and reformers, rather than on offenders. Friedman argues that the shape of the American criminal justice system is defined by social structure and cultural norms, and that criminal behaviour is rooted in culture, thus calling into question the overall effectiveness of the justice system.

Friedman is more attentive to 19th- and 20th-century issues, yet considerable scholarly attention has been devoted to developments during the colonial period, particularly in the form of studies of individual colonies, which focus on property crime and/or interpersonal violence. MONKKONEN's invaluable two-volume collection of essays illuminates the contours of a lively discourse on the scope and meaning of crime, deviance, discipline, and authority in the colonial and early republican periods.

MASUR provides a penetrating analysis of the cultural and social origins of the northeastern anti-gallows movements, and the context of experimentation with new forms of punishment including the penitentiary in the period between the Revolution and the Civil War. He uses the debates over public executions and the role of capital punishment in a nascent republican society as the medium through which to explore the impact on American culture of an emerging middle class which valued privacy and self-control, and found the spectacle and rituals of public hanging repugnant and threatening to the social order. At the core of these debates were competing visions of "man and society"; the sinful and depraved individual versus the moral, reasonable and savable person, reflecting the challenge to Puritanism posed by Enlightenment ideals and liberal theology.

Recent works on crime and punishment emphasize how class, race, ethnicity, and gender shape the commission of offenses, and the attitudes of the courts and of reformers, as well as forms of discipline and long-term incarceration. In an extremely well-written and meticulously documented work HINDUS compares notions and structures of authority, patterns of crime and prosecution, and the state prison and the plantation as dominant institutions of penal policy, in Massachusetts and South Carolina in the late 18th and 19th centuries. Hindus argues that different economic systems – a growing urban-manufacturing base and a rural slave-based economy – as well as political realities, account for the evolution of dissimilar systems of criminal justice, the one pursuing legal rationalization and the other showing a high tolerance of extra-legal violence. Yet, these dissimilar systems of law and authority served similar ends: to preserve order and social cohesion by controlling those elements in the population, specifically foreign-born and African American, which were perceived to be the most threatening to the social order.

AYERS places southern responses to crime before and after the Civil War in a broad social, economic, and cultural context, while focusing intensively on three diverse Georgia counties. One of the strengths of this superb book is the way in which Ayers examines the influence of the market economy on southern crime and punishment, for example, the visible growth in vagrancy, and the development of the convict lease system as the southern social order became increasingly tied to the national market in the post-war period.

Crime is usually assumed to be a masculine phenomenon, yet constructions of gender and gendered notions of "women's place" have had a powerful impact on the perception and treatment of women offenders and victims at all levels of the criminal justice system. HOFFER and HULL's challenging socio-legal study of the domestic crimes of infanticide and child-murder on both sides of the Atlantic over 250 years is significant for its use of pioneering quantification techniques to chart the shift from severe punishment of infanticide suspects, typically young unmarried women accused of murdering their new-born children, in the late 16th century to increased leniency by the late 18th century, as a result of environmental factors and changing social values.

ABELSON's intriguing study examines how a burgeoning 19th-century consumer culture and the urban department store gave rise to a new category of criminal offender: the middle-class female kleptomaniac. She discusses the ensuing characterization of kleptomania by doctors and lawyers as a female behavioral disorder connected to the female life cycle.

Until very recently, rape was a gender-specific offense, and perhaps because of this, still suffers from trivialization and neglect as a historical issue. RISE's revealing study of seven young African American men executed in the Virginia electric chair in 1951, two years after their conviction for the rape of a white women, has much to commend it. He examines the southern legal process, efforts of the NAACP and Civil Rights Congress to secure due process and leniency in an era of heightened black expectations and of xenophobic anti-communism, and notions of "proper" female behavior in the South.

VIVIEN M.L. MILLER

See also Legal History entries; Violence

Cuba and the United States

Benjamin, Jules R., *The United States and the Origins of the Cuban Revolution: An Empire of Liberty in an Age of National Liberation*, Princeton: Princeton University Press, 1990

Bethell, Leslie (editor), *Cuba: A Short History*, Cambridge and New York: Cambridge University Press, 1993

Gillespie, Richard (editor), *Cuba after Thirty Years: Rectification and Revolution*, London: Cass, 1990

Marshall, Peter, *Cuba Libre: Breaking the Chains?*, London: Gollancz, 1988

Morley, Morris H., *Imperial State and Revolution: The United States and Cuba, 1952–1986*, Cambridge and New York: Cambridge University Press, 1987

Pérez, Louis A., Jr., *Cuba: Between Reform and Revolution*, New York: Oxford University Press, 1988

Smith, Wayne S. and Esteban Morales Dominguez (editors), *Subject to Solution: Problems in Cuban-U.S. Relations*, Boulder, CO: Lynne Rienner, 1988

Thomas, Hugh, *Cuba: The Pursuit of Freedom*, London: Eyre and Spottiswode, and New York: Harper, 1971; abridged as *The Cuban Revolution*, New York: Harper, 1977; London: Weidenfeld and Nicolson, 1986

The complex and often hostile relationship between Cuba and the United States has generated a vast and varied historical literature. Most studies of Cuban history necessarily involve consideration of the role of its powerful neighbour to the north. Authors immersed in a Cold War mentality are largely ahistorical, focusing on the extent of communist influence on Castro and giving little consideration to its background. Their utility to this study is therefore limited. More rewarding texts adopt the concept of American imperialism and reflect a much stronger sense, albeit critical, of the history of imperial dominance of Cuba. Finally a significant number of writers have attempted, with varying degrees of success, to avoid either of these approaches and rely on personal interpretation. Many of the selections given here offer further bibliographic guidance.

THOMAS produced an extraordinarily comprehensive history of Cuba. Running to more than 1600 pages, in terms of sheer size alone this is undoubtedly the definitive work on the subject. Thomas covers two centuries from the British capture of Havana in 1762 to the Missile Crisis of 1962. With the exception of a brief epilogue which touches on the 1960s, this is largely an event-driven history in which the author relies upon a narrative description of the events together with some limited analysis. At times the discussion of topics is rather fragmented, and judicious use of the index is necessary. The narrative is somewhat dense, and this, coupled with its length, makes the book as a whole rather overwhelming. This was partially solved by the subsequent publication of a portion of the main text, dealing with the period from 1952 to 1962, as a separate volume. In recent years Thomas's work has attracted some criticism from more radical authors who focus upon the negative effects of the American presence in Cuba. None of these criticisms is sufficient to undermine the position of this text as the most complete examination of Cuban history to date.

MARSHALL takes a much lighter, more journalistic, approach. While, in terms of its scholarly importance, this book is not on a par with other selections, it is a useful starting point for more in-depth study. Beginning from a statement of sympathy, Marshall sets out to assess Castro's revolution in the light of Cuban history. The chapters on social and cultural issues are worth consulting. Four major scholars, including Thomas, are brought together in BETHELL's collection of extracts from *The Cambridge History of Latin America*. Each author contributes a chapter together with a bibliographic essay. The conciseness of the text makes it useful as a single source, but is rather at the expense of referencing. It makes a worthwhile contribution to a survey course on Latin America but offers only a limited insight into the overall study of Cuba-U.S. relations. In a number of works PÉREZ has made a significant contribution to an understanding of the subject of Cuba. In this book he seeks to answer the question of why the 1959 Revolution occurred, yet devotes only a single chapter to socialist Cuba. Pérez makes extensive use of Cuban sources to provide an explanation for Castro's rise and to place him within the Cuban revolutionary tradition. The author makes Cuban writers, not yet translated into English, accessible to non-Spanish speakers, and this is a strength. Pérez's regard for the geography of the island and his consideration of social issues are both valuable. This single-volume summary of a wide time period, from pre-Columbian Cuba to the 1980s, can be used to identify areas worthy of further reading.

BENJAMIN provides a well written and generally insightful analysis of the Cuban-American relationship. He is especially strong on the 20th century. He presents a "study in the nature of hegemony" which, while taking a self-proclaimed North American approach, could have been further strengthened by greater reference to Cuban sources. This author is not so much concerned with how American imperial dominance was established, but with its effects. In pointing to the tragedy of the disparity between American policy intentions and outcomes Benjamin's debt to William Appleman Williams is clear, but this is not a wholly derivative analysis and deserves independent attention. The author's decision to close his discussion in the early 1960s is disappointing.

MORLEY's analysis is challenging in that he takes an openly Marxist approach to his assessment of American policy on Cuba. He interprets the course of United States-Cuban relations since 1952 as evidence that the United States is an imperial state, the nature of which he details in a highly theoretical opening chapter. His identification of capitalist interests as the key to the American reaction to the Cuban Revolution could conceivably be seen to ignore other relevant and more justifiable concerns. But while it is possible to fault his conclu-

sions, Morley's research and referencing are exemplary and there is much of value in his detailed observations.

Smith and Morales, and also Gillespie, provide collections of essays which cover many subjects of interest. Both selections are drawn from conferences and both are slightly undermined, but certainly not made obsolete, by the subsequent collapse of the Soviet Union. SMITH and MORALES springs from a series of meetings held between Cuban and American scholars to address solutions to particular problems in United States-Cuban relations. Their identification of the obstacles to accommodation between the two nations provides an alternative perspective from which to view the previous history of the relationship. Their conclusion that both nations could gain more from discussion than confrontation remains trenchant. Although only one essay in the collection is provided by authors based in Cuba, GILLESPIE edits a selection more closely concerned with the Cuban perspective. The fact that the authors produce diverse conclusions reflects the range of opinion on the subjects covered. The contributors to Gillespie's collection focus on the pressure for change within the revolution and on its foreign policy. The collection is particularly strong on Cuba's place within Latin America, and links are drawn between the Cuban experience and that of other revolutionary traditions. Additionally José Martí's influence is considered and the film essay is a useful comment on culture's place within the Revolution.

JULIA L. OATHAM

See also Latin America and the United States

Cuban Missile Crisis, 1962

Abel, Elie, *The Missile Crisis*, Philadelphia: Lippincott, 1966, with new Introduction, New York: Bantam, 1968; as *The Missiles of October: The Story of the Cuban Missile Crisis, 1962*, London: MacGibbon and Kee, 1966, revised 1969

Allison, Graham T., *Essence of Decision: Explaining the Cuban Missile Crisis*, Boston: Little Brown, 1971

Blight, James G., Bruce J. Allyn, and David A. Welch, *Cuba on the Brink: Castro, the Missile Crisis, and the Soviet Collapse*, New York: Pantheon, 1993

Brugioni, Dino A., *Eyeball to Eyeball: The Inside Story of the Cuban Missile Crisis*, edited by Robert F. McCort, New York: Random House, 1991

Detzer, David, *The Brink: Cuban Missile Crisis, 1962*, New York: Crowell, 1979; London: Dent, 1980

Garthoff, Raymond L., *Reflections on the Cuban Missile Crisis*, Washington, DC: Brookings Institution, 1987, revised 1989

Paterson, Thomas G. (editor), *Kennedy's Quest for Victory: American Foreign Policy, 1961–1963*, New York: Oxford University Press, 1989

Thompson, Robert Smith, *The Missiles of October: The Declassified Story of John F. Kennedy and the Cuban Missile Crisis*, New York: Simon and Schuster, 1992

White, Mark J., *The Cuban Missile Crisis*, London: Macmillan, 1996

Most of the early writing on the Cuban missile crisis defined the episode in narrow chronological terms. The question of why Soviet leader Nikita Khrushchev decided to deploy nuclear missiles in Cuba received some attention. For the most part, however, interest centred on the thirteen days from 16 October 1962, when John Kennedy learned about the presence of nuclear weapons in Cuba, until 28 October, when a settlement to the crisis was achieved. The best example of this approach is ABEL. Without access to documents that would later be declassified, Abel relied on interviews with various policy-makers for his source materials. The work is ostensibly a factual narrative rather than an interpretive study, but the language which the author employs subtly conveys the sense that he admires Kennedy's performance during the crisis far more than Khrushchev's. As for Soviet motives for putting missiles in Cuba, Abel stresses the importance of Kennedy's failure to use sufficient force to ensure the success of the invasion attempt made by Cuban exiles at the Bay of Pigs in April 1961, and his inability to hold his own with Khrushchev at the Vienna summit a few weeks later. Both furnished the Soviet leader with the impression that Kennedy was weak and hence would not respond with vigour to a missile deployment in Cuba.

Of the early works ALLISON is without doubt the most important. In a work of immense analytical sophistication, Allison presents three models for understanding the confrontation over Cuba. One, the "Rational Actor Paradigm," is based on the idea that decisions are made when policymakers select the best option after a careful cost-benefit analysis of all the alternatives. The second, the "Organizational Process Paradigm," postulates that bureaucracies have their own agendas, usually the furthering of their own interests, which affect policy. The "Governmental (Bureaucratic) Politics Paradigm" recognises that final policy choices are the result of a competitive debate, a bargaining process that takes place between various officials. Allison uses these models to shed light on many of the key decisions made before and during the missile crisis. The work continues to exert a great influence on those who adopt a theoretical approach to the crisis. For historians, though, it is less a focus of debate.

The general trend in the 1970s toward a more critical view of the Kennedy presidency was also evident in the literature on the missile crisis. DETZER is a case in point. A 1975 Senate investigation revealed that in the period preceding the October 1962 confrontation the CIA had tried not only to oust Cuban leader Fidel Castro through a programme of covert sabotage known as Operation Mongoose, but even to assassinate him. Whereas previous authors had been unable to use that sort of information because it was simply unavailable, Detzer could. Although he thought State Department officials had performed admirably during the missile crisis, his praise of Kennedy was more restrained. He argued that Kennedy was excessively concerned with the enhancement of his own prestige both before and during the crisis.

One of the major developments in the recent literature has been a greater emphasis on the roles played by the Soviet Union and Cuba. Earlier studies had been forced to rely on Khrushchev's memoirs and a few other sources for their analysis of Soviet policy, but with the period of *glasnost* in the Soviet Union during the late 1980s and the increasing availability of former Soviet officials for interviews, it became possible to provide a more substantial account of the policy-making process in Moscow; and this is what GARTHOFF succeeds in doing. Garthoff had been a Kennedy administration official at the time, and in its evaluation of American policy before and during the crisis, his study comes across as an uncritical memoir. On the Soviet side, however, he managed to produce a work of unparalleled richness. A similar interest in the Cuban role has been evident in the 1990s. Basing their work on a 1992 Havana conference on the missile crisis in which many former officials, including Castro himself, participated, BLIGHT, ALLYN and WELCH argue that an understanding of the Cuban role is essential for a full appreciation of the events of 1962.

A number of other important books were also published in the late 1980s and early 1990s. In a forcefully argued and prodigiously researched essay, in the volume which he himself edited on Kennedy's foreign policy, PATERSON argues that Khrushchev would not have put missiles into Cuba, and hence there would have been no missile crisis, had Kennedy not tried through policies such as Mongoose, economic sanctions, and diplomatic pressure to overthrow Castro in 1961 and 1962. BRUGIONI provides an exceedingly detailed narrative of the crisis, one which sheds light in particular on the role played by American photographic interpreters. THOMPSON, like Paterson, is highly critical of Kennedy. He argues that Kennedy's desire to appear tough shaped his policies toward Cuba before and during the missile crisis. The resolution of the crisis is portrayed as a victory for Khrushchev and a defeat for Kennedy because the United states had failed to achieve its goal of overthrowing Castro.

WHITE is an attempt to provide a balanced, even-handed account. It is highly critical of the policies of Kennedy and Khrushchev in the months leading up to the missile crisis, but generally positive in its appraisal of their performance during the crisis itself. Khrushchev's deployment of missiles in Cuba was a mistake, but in trying to oust Castro and by extending and boasting of American's vast nuclear superiority over the Soviet Union, Kennedy may have put the Soviet leader in a position where he felt compelled to make that decision. In the missile crisis, both leaders made important contributions to the forging of a settlement; and by the time the crisis was resolved Kennedy seemed determined to do all that he could to avoid the sort of military confrontation that some of his advisers thought inevitable.

MARK J. WHITE

See also Kennedy, John F.

Custer, George A. 1839–1876
Civil War soldier and Indian fighter

Connell, Evan S., *Son of the Morning Star: Custer and the Little Bighorn*, Berkeley, CA: North Point Press, 1984; London: Pavilion, 1985

Dippie, Brian W., *Custer's Last Stand: The Anatomy of an American Myth*, Missoula: University of Montana Press, 1976

Hutton, Paul Andrew (editor), *The Custer Reader*, Lincoln: University of Nebraska Press, 1992

Leckie, Shirley A., *Elizabeth Bacon Custer and the Making of a Myth*, Norman: University of Oklahoma Press, 1993

Monaghan, Jay, *Custer: The Life of General George Armstrong Custer*, Boston: Little Brown, 1959

Rosenberg, Bruce A., *Custer and the Epic of Defeat*, University Park: Pennsylvania State University Press, 1974

Urwin, Gregory J.W., *Custer Victorious: The Civil War Battles of General George Armstrong Custer*, Rutherford, NJ: Fairleigh Dickinson University Press, 1983

Utley, Robert M., *Cavalier in Buckskin: George Armstrong Custer and the Western Military Frontier*, Norman: University of Oklahoma Press, 1988

Since the death of George Armstrong Custer in 1876, contemporaries and scholars have debated his experience as a Civil War commander, his skill as an Indian fighter, the controversy surrounding his final battle, and his role as a mythic figure. Early accounts of Custer's career, particularly those written by his wife, Elizabeth Bacon Custer, praised him as a fallen hero, but in 1934, Frederic F. Van de Water's *Glory-Hunter: A Life of General Custer* challenged this perception by accusing Custer of recklessness, incompetence, and vanity. MONAGHAN's treatment, though friendly to Custer, offers a more thorough and level-headed appraisal than his predecessors. Custer appears as a cheerful, daring, and prankish youth with a strong sense of family loyalty, and this profile defined him as an adult. Because of his daring, Monaghan argues, Custer became a successful Civil War commander. Fifteen of the book's 28 chapters discuss the war years and reflect the importance of this period to Custer's heroic stature. Only seven chapters cover his time in the West following Reconstruction. Describing this period, Monaghan passes over Custer's intrigues with politicians and businessmen, and he is unwilling to speculate on events at the Little Bighorn beyond what is supported by creditable testimony. He concludes by discussing Elizabeth Custer's efforts to protect her husband's image and the impact of paintings of the last stand in preserving Custer in the public memory.

Because of the popular association of Custer with the Indian-fighting army of the American West, and particularly the Little Bighorn battle, writers have based their judgment of his career on that period of his life. URWIN disagrees with this narrow assessment and, expanding on Monaghan's position, argues that Custer established his abilities as a soldier and attained a legendary status during the Civil War. Urwin describes Custer's rise from West Point cadet to "Boy General" whose courage and exploits attracted the attention of commanding officers and inspired the loyalty of his troopers. "With Custer as a leader," wrote a cavalryman, "we are all heroes and hankering for a fight." Custer benefited from his association with George B. McClellan, Alfred Pleasonton, and Philip H. Sheridan, but his fearlessness and tactical skill made him an effective leader worthy of praise.

One of the premier historians of the American West, UTLEY presents an insightful look at Custer's life, focusing primarily on his post-Civil War career. Early chapters of this award-winning book reflect the influence of Urwin and Monaghan as Utley describes Custer's exemplary Civil War record. But "the essential man," Utley writes, "remained to be developed – or revealed." The tedium facing the post-war army tested Custer's leadership abilities and he fared poorly. According to Utley, Custer suffered an identity crisis that was ultimately resolved by the modest success of the Washita campaign. Fame sustained his ego and his confidence as a commander returned, but more importantly, a new image emerged. Custer assumed the posture of a plainsman and Indian fighter – a "cavalier in buckskin." Tracing the remainder of Custer's life, Utley descibes the Battle of the Little Bighorn and demonstrates his knowledge of the event and its historiography. He speculates about tactics and criticizes decisions, and his engaging style makes this a thoughtful and readable biography.

In discussing Custer's western career and retelling the story of the Little Bighorn battle, CONNELL lacks Utley's perceptive understanding of military life and battlefield tactics, but he writes with a literary flair that inspired a television mini-series. A novelist, Connell describes the personalities of soldiers, scouts, and Native Americans as if developing characters for fiction. This approach, along with his reliance on a variety of sources, including testimony by Native Americans, gives credence to Connell's interpretation of Custer's life and final battle.

Because of the circumstances of Custer's death, writes the folklorist ROSENBERG, "an aura of sublime glory" surrounded his name and shaped his image as a martyred hero. To become a legend, Rosenberg contends, requires an audience, and by examining popular responses to Custer's defeat, he finds that Custer's heroic status became comparable to other legendary heroes. DIPPIE argues that because Custer's reputation has vacillated in the public mind, the "Last Stand myth is larger than Custer's personal legend" and, indeed, "subsumes" it. Like Rosenberg, Dippie studies popular attitudes. In poetry and paintings concerning the Last Stand, Custer and his troopers face death with no hope of escape. This heroic depiction, Dippie suggests, is central to the pervasive myth of the West. Rosenberg views the image more personally. "Our hero of epic defeat," he writes, "is what we would want to be ourselves as long as we couldn't win."

For readers wanting a synopsis of the Custer historiography, HUTTON incorporates a collection of scholarly articles and photographic essays with a mix of reminiscent accounts by Custer and his contemporaries, both soldier and Native American, to present a thoughtful and thorough portrayal of Custer as a man and legend. His anthology offers a good sampling of the historical literature and includes essays by Urwin and Monaghan on Custer's Civil War career. Assessing Custer's post-war experience in Kansas, Minnie Dubbs Millbrook sees a "reluctant warrior" whose many impetuous acts led to his court-martial. Custer's impact on popular culture is considered in several essays. Two are by Hutton on Custer's image in film and literature, and others examine the legacy of the Battle of the Little Bighorn as depicted in paintings. In the anthology's final essay, Rosenberg argues that the Custer myth retains its power despite the changing popularity of the historical Custer.

Any discussion of Custer must include the contribution of Elizabeth Bacon Custer in shaping and guarding his image for public memory. LECKIE's biography is significant for examining both the Custer mystique and the role of middle-class women in 19th-century society. She portrays Elizabeth Custer as bright, wilful, and a conscious manipulator of social conventions concerning domesticity and death. In books, articles, and lectures, Elizabeth Custer presented herself as a devoted wife and model widow, while idealizing Custer's character and promoting him as a national hero. To reinforce her own efforts, she encouraged favorable accounts of Custer's career, such as Frederick Whittaker's *Life of Custer*, initiated plans for a battlefield museum in Montana, and stifled all critics until her death in 1933.

J. THOMAS MURPHY

See also Native Americans: Indian Wars

D

Darrow, Clarence 1857–1938
Lawyer and sceptic

Jensen, Richard J., *Clarence Darrow: The Creation of an American Myth*, New York: Greenwood Press, 1992

Livingston, John C., *Clarence Darrow: The Mind of a Sentimental Rebel*, New York: Garland, 1988

Ravitz, Abe C., *Clarence Darrow and the American Literary Tradition*, Cleveland: Case Western Reserve University Press, 1962

Stone, Irving, *Clarence Darrow for the Defense*, New York: Doubleday, 1941

Tierney, Kevin, *Darrow: A Biography*, New York: Crowell, 1979

Weinberg, Arthur and Lila Weinberg, *Clarence Darrow: A Sentimental Rebel*, New York: Putnam, 1980

The essential elements of Clarence Darrow's life are outlined in STONE. One of the most celebrated of all American lawyers, Darrow was born and grew up in small-town Ohio. He went to Allegheny College in Meadville, Pennsylvania, but left without taking a degree. After an undistinguished year in law school in Ann Arbor, Michigan, he studied in a law office and was admitted to the Ohio bar. After three years of reasonably successful practice as a small-town lawyer, he moved to Chicago where, at first, he failed to make an impression. But, aided by a successful speech at the Henry George Club, with George himself in the audience, he had a succession of posts in the government of Chicago, ending as the city's corporation counsel. Moving to private employment with a railroad, Darrow was rapidly becoming a successful corporation lawyer when the Pullman strike intervened. The strike, according to Stone, was the turning-point in his career. It led him to re-evaluate his priorities. Resigning from his railroad job, he defended the President of the American Railroad Union, Eugene V. Debs, when Debs was arrested for criminal conspiracy, thereby beginning a long career as attorney for the defense.

The major incidents in Darrow's career as a labor lawyer are outlined by Stone in a fairly uncritical way: the woodworkers' conspiracy trial in Wisconsin (1898); his role in the arbitration of the anthracite coal strike (1902–03); the trial for conspiracy to murder of William D. Haywood and other officials of the Western Federation of Miners in Boise, Idaho (1907); the case of the McNamara brothers accused of blowing up the Los Angeles *Times* building (1911). In most trials, apart from the last (he pleaded the McNamaras guilty in order to save their lives and was himself later twice tried for attempting to bribe a juror in the case), Darrow eventually secured the acquittal of his clients.

Stone showed how Darrow's personal interests brought him to participate in a number of celebrated cases. He took on the defense of Leopold and Loeb, accused of murder, in 1924 because of his abhorrence of capital punishment. His life-long agnosticism led him to face William Jennings Bryan in the celebrated "monkey trial" at Dayton, Tennessee, a year later, defending the right to teach Darwinism in the schools. His commitment to aiding African Americans drove him to defend them in many cases, including the Sweet trials in Detroit of 1926–27. According to Stone, Darrow's success as a defense counsel stemmed from his ability to explain social realities rather than legal points to juries, and his skill in examining witnesses.

TIERNEY challenges Stone's hagiographical account in a number of crucial areas. Although Darrow's altruism was genuine, he believes, it was only part of the story. Darrow was highly ambitious, and spent a good deal of time during the early part of his career cultivating political connections, including John Peter Altgeld, whom he helped to the governorship of Illinois. The distaste which Darrow himself expressed for politics was mostly pretended: he served a term in the state legislature and, if he had not been narrowly defeated in a congressional race in 1896, he would have abandoned the law for a career in politics. Seeking fame and admiration, he came dangerously close at times to soliciting clients, often selected cases on the basis of their capacity to attract attention, and published the addresses made to juries in key cases (often in greatly revised and improved form). He could be both abrupt and dictatorial, his legal partnerships never lasted, and he found it hard to operate as part of a team. Most interesting of all, since Tierney writes as a lawyer as well as historian, is his assessment of Darrow's performance in court. Tierney sees his cases as argued on the basis of theory and principle. Evidence itself was only incidentally reviewed. This meant that Darrow had an excuse for not preparing himself for trials. His success as a lawyer – in particular as a labor lawyer – was based on a highly confrontational style, his ability to spot weak points in the prosecution's case, and his capacity to manipulate the emotions of jury members. Reviewing the evidence in the jury bribery cases, Tierney sees it as inconclusive in determining Darrow's guilt – or his innocence.

WEINBERG and WEINBERG, longtime Darrow admirers, defend his record in spirited fashion. They analyze his legal career in considerable detail. Around a quarter of their book, indeed, concentrates on the McNamara case and Darrow's own subsequent trials. Their book is much less critical than Tierney's.

LIVINGSTON is a study of Darrow's intellectual life as expressed in his writings and speeches as well as his courtroom performances. It emphasizes the paradoxes and contradictions in his political and philosophical ideas. Many of these occurred because Darrow's thought did not evolve in tune with changing circumstances. He remained a Jeffersonian individualist in an era of huge corporations, a believer in the Darwinian struggle for existence in a world in which competition was disappearing, and a Cleveland Democrat who endured into the era of the New Deal. Though Livingston discusses the impact of Henry George and John Peter Altgeld, he makes it plain that the main influences on Darrow's intellectual development were free thought (which was his link to social reform), deism, and Darwin.

JENSEN looks at Darrow's rhetorical strategies in the context of his contribution to public address. He argues that, both as a lawyer and a speaker/debater, Darrow relied on a range of stock arguments repeated as occasion demanded. Jensen believes that Darrow helped to create a myth out of his life and career. His style of argument and the "studied theatricality" of his courtroom appearances were important factors – together with the help of a cooperative media – in the growth of that myth.

RAVITZ shows that, in addition to his legal career, Darrow was also an important writer and an exponent of realistic fiction. He published many short stories, together with two novels: *Farmington* (1904), a fictionalized account of his early life which (in the tradition of Ed Howe and Hamlin Garland) criticized small town existence, and *An Eye for an Eye* (1905), a polemic against capital punishment loosely based on a famous trial for murder in Chicago.

Melvyn Stokes

See also Anti-Evolution Crusade

Davis, Jefferson   1808–1889
President of the Confederate States of America

Beringer, Richard E., Herman Hattaway, Archer Jones, and William N. Still, Jr., *Why the South Lost the Civil War*, Athens: University of Georgia Press, 1986
Beringer, Richard E., Herman Hattaway, Archer Jones, and William N. Still, Jr., *The Elements of Confederate Defeat: Nationalism, War Aims, and Religion*, Athens: University of Georgia Press, 1988
Davis, William C., *Jefferson Davis: The Man and His Hour*, New York: HarperCollins, 1991
Dodd, William Edward, *Jefferson Davis*, Philadelphia: G.W. Jacobs, 1907
Eaton, Clement, *Jefferson Davis*, New York: Free Press, 1977
Escott, Paul D., *After Secession: Jefferson Davis and the Failure of Confederate Nationalism*, Baton Rouge: Louisiana State University Press, 1978
Hendrick, Burton J., *Statesmen of the Lost Cause: Jefferson Davis and His Cabinet*, Boston: Little Brown, 1939
Strode, Hudson, *Jefferson Davis*, 3 vols., New York: Harcourt Brace, 1955–64
Woodworth, Steven E., *Jefferson Davis and His Generals: The Failure of Confederate Command in the West*, Lawrence: University Press of Kansas, 1990
Woodworth, Steven E., *Davis and Lee at War*, Lawrence: University Press of Kansas, 1995

While most early biographies of Jefferson Davis reflected contemporary sectional prejudice, DODD worked hard to maintain impartiality. He conceded that Davis could be haughty, rigid, and contemptuous toward associates, traits which alienated even close friends and made it nearly impossible for him to compromise with enemies. Dodd blamed the Confederate congress, stacked with "bitter, provincial" men, and long-time rivals such as Henry Foote for disrupting the president's well-conceived nationalist policies. The author criticized Confederate military leaders, even Robert E. Lee, for glaring tactical errors, while acknowledging Davis's unfortunate tendency to interfere in military strategy, where he considered himself an expert. On balance, Dodd's work was clearly favorable toward Davis, although he recognized the psychological limitations that made Davis a poor compromiser and thus a poor politician.

The three-volume biography by STRODE is an obsequious tribute that lacks meaningful analysis or an historical framework. The author portrays Davis as noble, saintly, beset by intriguers and betrayed by enemies whose self-serving obstinacy and egotism sapped the Confederate war effort. The work's principal contribution is volume three, which traces Davis's post-war struggles, tragedy, and finally enshrinement as southern icon and beloved, unreconstructed rebel. Strode also uncovered previously unused personal letters, although scholars will find his lack of documentation frustrating.

Unmistakable in the work of EATON (but noted by other scholars) are the inauspicious character traits – overly sensitive to criticism, inflexible, opinionated, proud, and haughty – that created tension with subordinates. Eaton compliments Davis for recognizing, sooner than most southerners, the need to pursue nationalistic policies at the expense of states rights, but recalcitrant congressmen and governors undermined the president's efforts. Davis himself hurt the war effort with poor military strategy and bad appointments to please political enemies, while showing too much loyalty to incompetent friends. Eaton also blames Davis for his failure to stimulate Confederate nationalism, which stemmed from his cold, aloof manner and uninspired speeches. The work suffers from its traditionalist view of southern history, and unfamiliarity with the previous thirty years of relevant historical scholarship.

The most recent, and best, biography of the Confederate president is from DAVIS. This lengthy book is a penetrating psychoanalysis that reveals the nuances of his often conflicting personality, and the subtle consequences of those characteristics. Like others, author Davis portrays his subject as acutely sensitive to criticism, meddling, and unwilling to compromise.

The author notes the formative significance of his father's early death and Davis's own military training, but emphasizes in particular the tragic death of his first wife – an event that burdened Davis with suppressed guilt and caused him to insist on the infallibility of his own judgment. Finally, the author maintains that Confederate military leadership was truly dismal, and concludes that president Davis performed as well as any other potential leader could have. The book includes little on Davis's policies on the home front, and virtually nothing on his post-war life.

Works that assess Confederate policy and southern defeat naturally focus on Davis as president. ESCOTT concentrates on civil policy and Davis's inability to create an effective nationalism which all southerners could embrace. There is a careful examination of many of Davis's most far-reaching programs, including conscription, legislated crop production, impressment, and tax-in-kind. Escott blames Davis for underestimating the consequences of these plans, which alienated rich and poor alike, and neglecting relief for lower-class men and women hurt by Richmond's aggressively nationalist strategy. The author commends Davis, however, for recognizing the imperative of such programs – indeed earlier than Lincoln. Escott also argues that Davis largely succeeded, and that states rights devotees did not undermine the Confederate war effort to any significant degree.

Among the myriad of older works on Davis and the Confederacy, HENDRICK presents much information on the often neglected presidential cabinet, but is very outdated in its approach and its basic assumptions. The book also exemplifies the thesis that states rights obstructionists undermined Davis's nationalist policies and had a crippling effect on the war effort. The author further contends that Confederate defeat hinged on the new nation's inability to produce "statesmen" of the caliber that characterized the "Virginia dynasty." Davis, in contrast, represented the "crude, parvenu" South characteristic of the cotton frontier, and was not a "gentleman."

The immense body of literature that assesses southern defeat is summarized in two works by Beringer and his collaborators. BERINGER et al. (1986) is longer and more fully documented, while BERINGER et al. (1988) synthesizes even further. Both books cover many areas of Confederate history, but they are not, of course, biographies of Davis himself. The authors range over military, social, political, and intellectual history, encompassing themes from battlefield strategy and tactics to the religious foundations of Confederate nationalism and the pro-slavery notions of southern "Manifest Destiny." Davis and other leaders are criticized for failing to address problems of morale. Overproduction of cotton, and the necessities of orienting a great portion of remaining resources toward the army, put an especially heavy burden on civilian morale; when that sank it was relayed to soldiers through newspapers and personal letters. Davis and his government knew civilian morale was a problem, but it was one which they failed to solve. The authors conclude that this was a major factor in eventual defeat.

Hundreds of books cover nearly every aspect of Confederate military strategy, tactics, and leadership. In two separate volumes, Woodworth focuses on Davis's relationship with many of his generals, and studies the interplay of personalities. Unlike the majority of scholars who have criticized Davis

for interfering too much in military strategy, and for overconfidence, WOODWORTH (1990) maintains that he actually lacked self-confidence and failed to take decisive action under pressure. A "more assured" leader might have won the war in the West, and ultimately southern independence. Like most Davis critics, the author censures him for being too loyal to bungling friends such as Leonidas Polk. Woodworth concludes that if every southern general had performed as well as Davis, the Confederacy would probably have won the war. However, he also criticizes the president for a number of relatively minor mistakes, any of which could have been decisive since the South's margin for error was so very thin. WOODWORTH (1995) pursues some of the same themes in a study of the crucial relationship between Davis and Robert E. Lee (and Lee's predecessors in command in the Virginia theatre). Woodworth places considerable emphasis on the contrast between Davis's more cautious and defensive approach, and Lee's greater inclination to seize the initiative and take the offensive.

CHRISTOPHER J. OLSEN

See also Confederate States of America entries; Civil War: Campaigns entries

Debs, Eugene V. 1855–1926
Labor leader and socialist presidential candidate

Coleman, McAlister, *Eugene V. Debs: A Man Unafraid*, New York: Greenberg, 1930

Ginger, Ray, *The Bending Cross: A Biography of Eugene Victor Debs*, New Brunswick, NJ: Rutgers University Press, 1949

Kraditor, Aileen S., *The Radical Persuasion, 1890–1917: Aspects of the Intellectual History and the Historiography of Three American Radical Organizations*, Baton Rouge: Louisiana State University Press, 1981

Laslett, John H.M., *Labor and the Left: A Study of Socialist and Radical Influences in the American Labor Movement, 1881–1924*, New York: Basic Books, 1970

Painter, Floy Ruth, *That Man Debs and His Life Work*, Bloomington: Indiana University Press, 1929

Salvatore, Nick, *Eugene V. Debs: Citizen and Socialist*, Urbana: University of Illinois Press, 1982

Shannon, David, *The Socialist Party of America: A History*, New York: Macmillan, 1957

Eugene Debs is the closest approximation to a true folk hero that the American left has ever produced. Until recently his biographers have approached him with a reverence usually reserved for demigods. With greater or lesser skill, all his early biographers treated his ideological peregrinations – from conservative craft unionist to militant industrial unionist, from apolitical defender of the status quo to perennial Socialist Party presidential candidate – as though they were chronicling the life of a saint. Although more recent historians are more sophisticated in their approach, Debs himself remains central to key issues in American labor and radical history.

The first hagiography was published just three years after Debs's death. And while there is little in PAINTER by way of information or interpretation that has not been superseded, the stated purpose of the book set the tone for several other studies that followed. On the one hand Painter intended to make a "scientific investigation" of Debs's life, to provide a factual account based on available sources. But on the other hand she did not want to ignore the intangibles, to lose sight of "the great heart of the man." The result is a portrait of a "great man" without flaws, a humanitarian idealist who preached evolutionary rather than revolutionary socialism.

COLEMAN is equally reverent, although his biography is more thorough and readable. The text is a fine example of journalistic history, and the author captures some of the drama of the major capital-labor confrontations of the 1890s and the burgeoning socialist movement of the early 20th century. Coleman remains useful because of the engaging account of the Pullman strike and the early efforts of the Socialist Party, but students of Debs should use this work only with caution since the author did not have access to all of Debs's private papers. Undoubtedly the best hero-biography is GINGER. Thoroughly researched and richly detailed, it offers a blow-by-blow account of Debs's life from his childhood in Terre Haute, Indiana, to his imprisonment for opposing America's participation in World War I. He argues that Debs underwent a sudden conversion to socialism while in prison after the Pullman strike of 1894, a transforming moment when he realized that only the collective ownership of industry would guarantee a democratic society and individual rights. While it acknowledges Debs's faults, including his weakness as a theoretician, the overall tenor of the book is that of a man who gave a voice to the downtrodden and therefore suffered persecution at the hands of capitalists and statesmen.

SALVATORE is not only far and away the best biography of Debs, it is arguably the best biography in the fields of American labor and radical history. Winner of the Bancroft and Dunning prizes, it firmly sets Debs within the cultural and political milieu of his times. The author demonstrates that Debs's ideological transformations to a large extent mirrored the changes in his home town. Whereas the small town of his youth exhibited neighborliness and humane economic enterprise, during his early adulthood the town (and Debs) embraced the new values of industrialism, and by the time Debs matured the town had become another industrial outpost at the mercy of distant decision makers. Above all, Debs is shown to be a product of his environment and a reflection of mainstream American values. His turn to socialism was not so much a sudden conversion as a growing realization after years of labor strife that industrial capitalism was undercutting personal freedom and economic security. Salvatore also portrays the man with all his blemishes – his massive ego, his racist tendencies, his lack of ideological consistency. All scholars interested in Debs should consult this book.

Readers who wish to study Debs in the context of American socialism in general should begin with SHANNON, one of only two general histories of the movement. This remains the most succinct and readable history of Debs's party. Like most scholars of the subject, Shannon is especially concerned with the demise of the party after World War I and whether the failure of the left marks America as unique within the western world. A conservative's discussion of the same issues can be found in KRADITOR. Her answer to the famous question posed by German sociologist Werner Sombart in 1906 ("Why is there no socialism in the United States?") is simple: socialists like Debs failed because they were wrong. Their ideology was muddled because they failed to appreciate the capacity of America's democracy to ameliorate capitalist abuses. She views Debs as the leader of a rag-tag minority of misfits who held wrong-headed views on class and culture-bound views on gender and race.

Those readers interested in the connections between socialism and trade union activity can start with LASLETT, a collection of essays on socialist strength within individual unions. Not only does the author provide a detailed analysis of Debs's appeal to working people in various occupations, he also offers his own explanation for the ultimate failure of socialism. Arguing that trade union commitment to socialist politics weakened its ability to achieve higher pay and better working conditions for its members, Laslett believes that, as trade unions became more successful, fewer and fewer unionists found socialism attractive.

CRAIG PHELAN

See also Labor History entries; Socialism and Communism; World War I: the United States at War

Declaration of Independence, 1776

Becker, Carl L., *The Declaration of Independence: A Study in the History of Political Ideas*, New York: Harcourt Brace, 1922

Boyd, Julian P., *The Declaration of Independence: The Evolution of the Text as Shown in Facsimiles of Various Drafts by its Author*, Washington, DC: Library of Congress, 1943

Dumbauld, Edward, *The Declaration of Independence and What It Means Today*, Norman: University of Oklahoma Press, 1950

Fliegelman, Jay, *Declaring Independence: Jefferson, Natural Language, and the Culture of Performance*, Stanford, CA: Stanford University Press, 1993

Friedenwald, Herbert, *The Declaration of Independence: An Interpretation and an Analysis*, New York: Macmillan, 1904; reprinted, New York: Da Capo Press, 1974

Hawke, David Freeman, *A Transaction of Free Men: The Birth and Course of the Declaration of Independence*, New York: Scribner, 1964

Hazelton, John H., *The Declaration of Independence: Its History*, New York: Dodd Mead, 1906; reprinted, New York: Da Capo Press, 1970

Head, John M., *A Time to Rend: An Essay on the Decision for American Independence*, Madison: State Historical Society of Wisconsin, 1968

Malone, Dumas, *The Story of the Declaration of Independence*, New York: Oxford University Press, 1954, Bicentennial edition, 1975

Pole, J.R., *The Decision for American Independence*, Philadelphia: Lippincott, 1975; London: Arnold, 1977

Wills, Garry, *Inventing America: Jefferson's Declaration of Independence*, New York: Doubleday, 1978; London: Athlone Press, 1980

The Declaration of Independence is discussed in every study of the coming of independence and the work of the Continental Congress, every analysis of the philosophy and political ideas of the Revolution, and in biographies of its principal author, Thomas Jefferson. Specialised studies can be divided into three overlapping groups: narrative, technical and philosophical.

The earliest narrative to retain some value is FRIEDEN-WALD. His scholarship is meticulous, but his 1904 analysis is seriously outdated. Half the book is a narrative of the conflict with Britain in which the growing authority of Congress and the resultant strengthening of the union are seen as inseparable from the advance toward inevitable independence. In social terms, this sits in the tradition of Progressive scholarship which argues the centrality of rivalry between the "patriotic" people and the more conservative and cautious upper classes. The most useful section is the discussion of the disparity between the names of the signers and the names of those known to have been present or absent on the day. The book ends with a brief defence of the Declaration against 19th-century critics and a short exposition of the grievances listed in it.

HAWKE is a general popular narrative based predominantly on secondary literature which includes a bibliographical essay in place of annotation. It balances Thomas Jefferson's familiar role by crediting John Adams for his contribution to independence and contrasting their philosophical disagreements, especially in later years. Much of the text is taken up by tracing their respective careers, and there is relatively little on the immediate circumstances of the debate over independence. A useful, if limited, chapter traces the fluctuating reputation of the Declaration in later years; when taken with the accompanying bibliographical survey it goes some way towards meeting the important need for a systematic monograph on the subject.

POLE is a brief essay tracing the transformation of the colonists' initial desire for redress of grievances at the First Continental Congress into an imperative for independence in 1776. It considers the social and economic background and the influence of public opinion, but its greatest strength lies in its treatment of the hesitancy and conflict in debate on the issue. A number of major documents are printed to illustrate the process, and there is a useful survey of the literature. Discussion of philosophical issues is very limited, but this is one of the best introductions to the politics of the subject. HEAD is an extended scholarly essay which complements Pole and also focuses on the decision for independence rather than the document, on which there is very little indeed. It stresses the disagreements in Congress on the issue. While not taking a simplistically determinist view, it attributes them primarily to the social and economic differences within and among the colonies. Though written by Jefferson's most distinguished modern biographer, MALONE is no more than a short popular narrative expressing standard values supplemented by brief biographies and excellent illustrations.

HAZELTON is a technical study that focuses closely on the events immediately surrounding the Declaration's composition, issue and signing, and its immediate publication and reception. It carefully sifts the sometimes conflicting evidence from the records of Congress and other participants, and incorporates extensive quotations, including variant readings from its sources, thus demonstrating among other things the extent to which there was an active debate throughout the colonies as to the desirability of declaring independence at that point. The appendix includes a variorum text. Though dating from the early 20th century it remains the most detailed study. BOYD is a preparatory essay for his edition of Jefferson's writings and can be regarded as the definitive description of the drafting process, including Congress's amendments, but it does not discuss the signers of the engrossed copy. To a considerable extent it covers similar ground to Hazelton, but its range is narrower; consequently it does not entirely supplant it. Nor does it consider philosophical issues, preferring to rely largely on Becker. It usefully includes facsimiles of the drafts and some relevant preliminary documents.

Published more than seventy years ago, BECKER still stands pre-eminent among analyses of the thought contained in the Declaration. Its scholarship, literary elegance and irony make it a masterpiece of American historical writing, all the more so since the discussion is rooted in the European enlightenment as well as American thought. It traces the political context and drafting of the Declaration, but above all is known for its intellectual analysis. For many years it has been accepted as the standard exposition of the Declaration's philosophy in spite of its brevity, although some modern scholars consider the judgments outdated. Becker insists that the Declaration is thoroughly English in ideology and that its thesis was drawn predominantly from John Locke's theory of social contract. His assessment of Jefferson's mind is cool though not unsympathetic.

DUMBAULD is in effect a legal reference work, since it offers a commentary on the meaning of each phrase in the document, including the list of grievances. In spite of its title and its insistence that its principles remain the foundation of American political philosophy, it interprets the Declaration in historical terms rather than linking it to the concerns of the mid-20th century. In particular, the document is set in the context of international law, and its legal as well as political origins are traced. Much of the treatment retains its value after fifty years of fresh scholarship.

The commanding modern discussion is WILLS which traces the historical and symbolic context, but is principally a sustained discussion of Jefferson's original draft rather than the amended version published by Congress. It takes a rich and expansive view of the philosophy of the Declaration, by examining it as an expression of Jefferson's scientific, moral and psychological sensibilities. Often brilliant and always challenging, Wills correctly argues that Becker's study was not the last word on the subject, and vigorously attacks it. His central conclusion that the document's philosophy derived principally from the Scottish enlightenment rather than Locke is substantially overstated, but nevertheless the book is immensely valuable.

FLIEGELMAN defines independence as a rhetorical problem as much as a political one. In place of historical narrative and philosophical analysis the Declaration is set in a cultural and literary context. Jefferson is discussed less as an autonomous subject and more as a witness to and participant in, a new affective understanding of the operations of language. The author argues that the Declaration was written to be spoken as well as read; instead of being confined to formalized discourse among the elite, it marked a change towards addressing a socially much broader audience.

COLIN BONWICK

See also American Revolution entries; Continental Congress; Jefferson

Democracy

Bailyn, Bernard, *The Ideological Origins of the American Revolution*, Cambridge, MA: Belknap Press of Harvard University Press, 1967, revised 1992

Bailyn, Bernard and others, *The Great Republic*, 2 vols., Lexington, MA: Heath, 1977, 4th edition, 1992

Beer, Samuel H., *To Make a Nation: The Rediscovery of American Federalism*, Cambridge, MA: Belknap Press of Harvard University Press, 1993

Benedict, Michael Les, *The Blessings of Liberty: A Concise History of the Constitution of the United States*, Lexington, MA: Heath, 1996

Degler, Carl N., *Out of Our Past: The Forces That Shaped Modern America*, New York: Harper, 1959; 3rd edition, New York: Harper, 1984

Hartz, Louis, *The Liberal Tradition in America: An Interpretation of American Political Thought since the Revolution*, New York: Harcourt Brace, 1955

Hofstadter, Richard, *The American Political Tradition and the Men Who Made It*, New York: Knopf, 1948; London: Cape, 1962

Kazin, Michael, *The Populist Persuasion: An American History*, New York: Basic Books, 1995

McKenna, George (editor), *American Populism*, New York: Putnam, 1972

Pole, J.R., *The Pursuit of Equality in American History*, Berkeley: University of California Press, 1978, revised 1993

Tocqueville, Alexis de, *Democracy in America*, translated by Henry Reeve, 4 vols., 1835–40; translated by George Lawrence and edited by J.P. Mayer and Max Lerner, 2 vols., New York: Harper, 1966

Wiebe, Robert H., *Self-Rule: A Cultural History of American Democracy*, Chicago: University of Chicago Press, 1995

Wood, Gordon S., *The Radicalism of the American Revolution*, New York: Knopf, 1992

Democracy is especially important to Americans. It is not a central or even necessary component of most nationalities, but for Americans it is a defining part of their national identity. When comparing Americans to Europeans, Tocqueville wrote, "The great advantage of the Americans is, that they have arrived at a state of democracy without having to endure democratic revolution; and that they are born equal, instead of becoming so." So, when historians of the United States write about democracy, they explore the very core of American history. It is hardly surprising that nearly every textbook of general American history bears a title or sub-title conveying the fact that the United States is a republican democracy of a sovereign people.

The most common approach of textbooks to telling the story of the American people is to follow the continuities and discontinuities of their democratic experience. For the student approaching a study of American democracy for the first time, it follows that the obvious place to start is with a good general American history text. BAILYN *et al.* is one very appropriate example, but a number of others would do as well. Bailyn and his colleagues provide extensive and helpful suggestions for further reading at the end of each chapter. DEGLER's more interpretative work – more a commentary than a textbook – now in its third edition, is a model of clarity and accessibility. One of its great services to readers at all levels is the valuable reporting and comparison throughout the book of the interpretations which different historians have placed on events. This is reinforced by a lengthy and critical bibliographical essay.

The next step might be a study of American constitutional history. The United States possesses the world's oldest written constitution in continuous use, and from its beginning, America has been a federal, constitutional republic based on binding contractual agreements among its citizens. Non-Americans, who are usually accustomed to the entity of The State in their national lives, often find it difficult to comprehend the American concept of a political contract among citizens in place of one between the citizens on the one hand and the state and its institutions on the other. BENEDICT is the best and most up-to-date historical treatment of the constitutional story. In one indispensable volume, he provides a thorough survey from the British and colonial backgrounds through almost four centuries to the state of the Union in the 1990s. He addresses himself at length to the inherent blemishes and eventual obstacles that the Republic has grappled with over the centuries in seeking to achieve its democratic ideal. Probably the most important single fact about American democracy is its basis in popular sovereignty. The story of American democracy is very much the story of the American people and the development of their idea of inclusive and sovereign citizenship, in the context of principles which have remained immutable since the foundation of the Republic. Again, Benedict provides a good introduction.

TOCQUEVILLE has been continuously in print for 160 years for good reason. His profoundly perceptive observation of the young Republic's democratic precepts and practices provides ample evidence that a strong democratic political tradition was already well entrenched by 1832. More startling for the late 20th century reader is the continuing relevance of the great majority of these observations after sixteen decades of expansion, civil war, mass multi-ethnic immigration and development from post-colonial experiment to world super power. Tocqueville provides the archetypical description of American democracy against which all subsequent evolution and variations can be measured and illuminated. He is particularly adept at explaining the nature of fundamental characteristics in the American democratic ethos, such as popular sovereignty, independence, individualism, community, voluntarism, constitutionalism, federalism, republicanism, nationalism and patriotism. The first volume concentrates on the nature and structure of American democracy, its origins, and the forces and traditions that maintain it. The second volume is devoted to the influence of democracy in the United States on intellectual life, religion, business culture and industry, sexual equality and social and political mores.

WOOD offers a modern historian's view of the America Tocqueville experienced. Wood rejects the view, often fashionable, that the American Revolution was a conservative event, hardly revolutionary at all. Instead, he finds that the Revolution produced within a few decades a radical transformation from a hierarchical society with patrician republican impulses to the popular liberal democracy Tocqueville described and that we can recognise today. "Almost overnight," Wood writes, Americans became "the most liberal, the most democratic, the most commercially minded, and the most modern people in the world."

If there is a weakness in Wood's highly influential work, it is his relative inattention to political and institutional history and the central issues of the organization of government during the gestation of American democracy. BEER does much to restore the balance. Ideally, Beer and Wood should be read together, for they complement each other so well. However, most students will find Beer more approachable after studying at least the first four chapters of Benedict, and reading Tocqueville and Wood. Beer's book is the authoritative result of sixty years' study of American and British political theory and history. He has produced a seminal work that identifies the crucial issue dividing American from British democracy as the location of sovereignty. Americans chose popular sovereignty in preference to Britain's hierarchical system of institutional sovereignty. Beer shows why, as early as the 18th century, the British attachment to parliamentary sovereignty made impossible a solution to American dissatisfaction short of revolution and separation. He thus finds the kernel of American popular sovereignty and democracy in American national identity and federalism. He explores the historic wellsprings of liberal democratic thought in order to understand the design of American institutions. Ultimately, Beer explains in great detail the nature and significance of popular sovereignty and federalism as the twin guarantors of American liberty and democratic union. Unlike Wood, Beer does not view republicanism as a paternalistic antecedent to popular democracy in America. Instead, he considers that the federalist republicanism of the 1789 Constitution, embracing the principle of popular sovereignty, strengthened rather than impeded popular liberal democracy. Regardless of the reader's standpoint on this argument, Wood provides an invaluable and convincing historical context in which to set Beer's profound insights.

BAILYN (1967, 1992) is a prize-winning intellectual history of the revolutionary period. It is not the history of an intellectual elite, although Bailyn provides an interesting description of the reading and references used by leaders of rebel and loyalist opinion. Bailyn studied many hundreds of pamphlets and other documents to synthesize a record of the substance of revolutionary and democratic debate in the 18th century up to and including (in the enlarged edition) the debate over ratification of the Federal Constitution. Like Wood, Bailyn finds the Revolution a profoundly transforming event. He also discovers a strong strain of anti-authoritarianism inherited from the English Civil War and a fear of anti-democratic conspiracy which he sees as a characteristic Anglo-American response to perceived elite threats to individual liberty and democracy. The concept of sovereignty is again identified as crucial, and Bailyn states that its redefinition in reaction to Parliament's authority was "the central intellectual problem that confronted the leaders of the American cause".

Armed with an understanding of the foundations and principles of democracy in America, the reader may wish to move on to a study of its historical development in a more interpretative fashion than Benedict can afford. HOFSTADTER is still a very good place to start. It may well be the most popular post-1945 learned work on American history. From the first chapters on the Founding Fathers, Jefferson and Jackson to the last, on Franklin D. Roosevelt, Hofstadter presents iconoclastic portraits of democratic heroes that have always intrigued and engaged undergraduates and other readers. Hofstadter saw himself as writing from a viewpoint somewhat outside the political tradition that he was describing. He was thirty when he wrote the book, but nearly half a century later, and 25 years after his death, the book seems much more the work of a youthful American squarely located within that tradition, and employing scepticism to cleanse it of myth, in order to embrace its real substance and optimism.

HARTZ has worn rather less well. His central thesis, that the key explanation of American democracy is its lack of a feudal past, was greeted in the 1950s as a major insight. Today, historians such as Wood have largely vitiated Hartz's impact by showing that feudal and aristocratic influences did exist prominently in the colonial period but were overwhelmed in the Revolution by an inherent popular democratic radicalism. Hartz nevertheless remains relevant to an understanding of American democracy's resistance through the generations to aristocratic values, patrician whiggery and the varieties of Marxism and socialism.

"Within decades following the Declaration of Independence," writes Wood, "the United States became the most egalitarian nation in the history of the world, and it remains so today, regardless of its great disparities of wealth." POLE critically examines this proposition and the consequences of other disparities. Dedicated to Hofstadter, Pole's book does not take sides or preach at the reader, but provides a sound guide to the imperfections in the dream and the strivings to realise the promise of equality in American democracy. Starting with an examination of the meaning of the "self-evident truth" of human equality asserted in the Declaration of Independence, Pole proceeds to consider the pursuit of an equal democracy through American history over the hurdles built upon religion, slavery, race, immigration, gender and wealth distribution.

To this list WIEBE adds class, industrialization and the growth of centralizing corporate and government hierarchies in the 20th century. Wiebe begins his review in the 1820s with an appreciation of the self-ruling democracy of "the People" described by Tocqueville and Wood. He claims that tension within the democratic system increased during the 19th and into the 20th century as a result of technological change, and the persistent and successful demands of immigrants, women and non-whites to be part of "the People." Between 1890 and 1920, in response to these pressures, a centralized hierarchical structure took shape, and this disrupted democratic relations among the people. American democracy's individual and majoritarian strands separated, says Wiebe, coming into conflict in the 1960s ("democracy at war with itself"). He believes that the power structure "resists popular participation" and "operates in tension with individualist democracy," but he expresses some optimism for a renewal of democracy based on the American people's traditional distrust of exclusive power centres and self-perpetuating authority, their insistence on their liberties and their attachment to federalism and decentralization of democratic power.

More confidence in the continuity of "the People" as the most essential element of American popular liberal democracy may be found in studies of American populism by both McKenna and Kazin. McKENNA confidently postulates the identification of populism as the American "ism" and produces intelligently selected readings from Thomas Jefferson to the 1970s to support his thesis of the essential continuity of American democracy's populist spirit. He shows how it permeates the political process and the whole spectrum of political opinion, left to right.

Acknowledging McKenna among others as indispensable to his understanding of American populism, KAZIN concentrates on post-1890 exponents from Samuel Gompers to George Wallace and Ronald Reagan. Writing as a disappointed liberal intellectual trying to make sense of the decline of the American Left, Kazin finds populism a major strand of American democracy that intellectuals, instinctively an anti-populist elite, must recognise and respect. He does not quite say that American intellectuals should identify with "the common people," but he advises them to differentiate between the constructive and meaner aspects of populism and accept that, without it, mass democracy cannot be revitalized and "we are lost." Kazin's book displays his own intrinsic if unconscious left-wing populism – an example that suits McKenna's thesis. Readers may find McKenna's less self-involved and more wide-ranging treatment more convincing. Both books reward the serious student, and belong to a tradition of sympathetic historical analysis of contemporary American democracy which runs from Tocqueville to the present day.

DOUGLAS EDEN

See also American Revolution entries; Constitution entries; Equality

Democratic Party

Burner, David, The Politics of Provincialism: The Democratic Party in Transition, 1918–1932, New York: Knopf, 1968; reprinted Cambridge, MA: Harvard University Press, 1986

Craig, Douglas B., After Wilson: The Struggle for the Democratic Party, 1920–1934, Chapel Hill: University of North Carolina Press, 1992

Edsall, Thomas Byrne and Mary D. Edsall, Chain Reaction: The Impact of Race, Rights, and Taxes on American Politics, New York: Norton, 1991

Key, V.O., Jr., Southern Politics in State and Nation, New York: Knopf, 1949

Kovler, Peter B. (editor), Democrats and the American Idea: A Bicentennial Appraisal, Washington, DC: Center for National Policy Press, 1992

Rutland, Robert Allen, The Democrats: From Jefferson to Carter, Baton Rouge: Louisiana State University Press, 1979

Savage, Sean J., Roosevelt: The Party Leader, 1932–1945, Lexington: University Press of Kentucky, 1991

Shafer, Byron E., Quiet Revolution: The Struggle for the Democratic Party and the Shaping of Post-Reform Politics, New York: Russell Sage Foundation, 1983

Silbey, Joel H., A Respectable Minority: The Democratic Party in the Civil War Era, 1860–1868, New York: Norton, 1977

Watson, Harry L., Jacksonian Politics and Community Conflict: The Emergence of the Second American Party System in Cumberland County, North Carolina, Baton Rouge: Louisiana State University Press, 1981

Wesser, Robert F., A Response to Progressivism: The Democratic Party and New York Politics, 1902–1918, New York: New York University Press, 1986

The Democratic Party is the oldest political organization in the United States. Its origin dates back to Andrew Jackson's presidency, if not earlier. There has been no single volume overview of the party's history since RUTLAND. This is a useful and readable survey, which seeks to identify elements of basic continuity in the party's history, despite internal divisions, fluctuating electoral fortunes, and major switches of policy and direction.

There are plenty of studies of the party at particular stages of its history. On the early stages, WATSON provides a first-class introduction to Jacksonian politics, the formation of the Democratic Party, and the accompanying historiographical debates. He examines one county, Cumberland County, North Carolina from 1824 to 1848, to uncover the birth of political parties, which he calls "arguably the largest social movement of its day." Watson takes a middle ground in the scholarly debates. He contends that social and cultural issues mattered in the formation of the Democrat and Whig parties. However, questions of political economy, such as banks and internal improvements, predominated, and Democrats tended to oppose active government involvement in the economy.

Watson studied the party at the grass-roots, during its origins and early triumphs. In contrast, SILBEY considers the national party's fate during the 1860s, a time of despair. In the North, Republicans painted their Democratic opponents as disloyal. Indeed, the Democrats would not win the presidency again until 1884 and would not become a consistent majority party again until the 1930s. Silbey wonders why the party did not implode and simply disappear. Instead, after a period of "confusion and adjustment, [it] forcefully challenged the government's policies" during the Civil War and afterwards. Silbey attributes the party's capacity to survive internal dissent and Republican attacks to a "partisan imperative" – a kind of psychological, social, and cultural adherence to "the party of their fathers." Democrats continued to fight against government intrusion into all aspects of life. They also opposed the racial and sectional policies of the Republicans.

Reconstruction and the Civil War shaped the political fortunes of the Democratic Party. This was especially true in the South, which remained solidly Democratic for the next century. KEY is a magisterial and massive study of southern politics (and therefore the Democratic Party) in the first half of the 20th century. The starting point for all subsequent studies of southern politics, Key considers each of the former Confederate states. He found differences (personal factionalism predominated in Alabama; a political oligarchy ran Virginia) between and within states, which helped break the idea of the monolithic South. Race dominated southern politics, however, entrenching the one-party system. The single-party system, Key averred, created an "issueless politics" based on personal factionalism and demagogic appeals. It harmed southern development. Key expected southern urbanization and the liberalizing of the policies of the national Democratic Party to create fissures in Democratic predominance. He was right.

Democrats in the North, unlike the South, belonged to a minority party. In a study of the Democratic Party in New York state from 1900 to 1918, WESSER examines how party leaders sought to recapture power. His story of politicians' efforts to win votes and elections has several important lessons. First, Wesser paints the Democrats as reformers, noting that their actions "helped redefine and broaden progressivism so as to lay the foundations on the state level" for the New Deal. The appeal to ethnic minorities and the urban masses also shifted Democratic policies away from personal liberty and negative government to social reform, economic regulation, and the protection of cultural diversity.

BURNER is an authoritative study of the divisions in the party during the 1920s, emphasizing deep political and cultural differences between its electoral support in urban and rural areas, which were clearly exposed in the elections of 1924 and 1928. CRAIG, however, contends that northeastern economic conservatives retained control of the national Democratic Party throughout the 1920s, an era of constant electoral defeat. Craig rejects both the "new" political history, which focuses on voter behavior, and cultural interpretations of the era. His old-fashioned, but not dated, study examines the ideological bickering among political elites. National Democrats retained a faith in conservatism, that is an anti-statism that promoted individualism and business development, and opposed government intervention, planning, and bureaucracy. The conservative reaction to the New Deal, Craig adds, showed the tenacity of these ideas.

The Great Depression and Franklin D. Roosevelt ushered in a new era for the nation and the Democratic Party. SAVAGE offers no radical new interpretations of the period or the party; instead he relies on the conclusions of a vast literature. Savage provides a brief but useful summary of Roosevelt the party leader. He argues that Roosevelt placed the Democratic Party's achievement of electoral success ahead of his own ambitions. Moreover, Roosevelt sought to transform the Democrats into a liberal/reformist party. He believed that government intervention to solve the nation's economic problems would unite the northern and southern Democrats. He succeeded for a while, and Roosevelt's election in 1932 began a thirty-year period of dominance for the party. Nonetheless, the New Deal coalition began to crumble after World War II.

Craig's study of elites assumed that party policy flows from the top down. SHAFER's consideration of reforms in the presidential nominating process between 1968 and 1972 shows how changes in party rules and organization affected the party's future. Shafer, who seems to assume that history began in 1968, explains how grass-roots activity transformed a national organization, which in turn had dramatic effects on both the national and local levels. Shafer, who at times provides a minute-to-minute history of the party, maintains that the rules changes ushered in (and then institutionalized) new ruling elites with differing political agendas. The "regular" party, with its blue-collar constituency, was one casualty of the altered rules.

Current political observation often analyzes the ongoing battle for disaffected former Democrats – alternately referred to as Reagan Democrats, Joe Sixpack, or Bubba (in the South). Although not a party history, EDSALL and EDSALL suggests why post-war Democratic policies helped break apart the New Deal coalition during the Johnson administration. "The post-1965 liberal agenda had engendered fundamental conflict over values, rights, and taxes," Edsall writes, "and race was driving the process in many complex ways." In particular, liberalism (or government intervention) began to come under increasing attack.

Observers have declared the Democratic Party dead or obsolete many times. Recent electoral catastrophes – especially the emergence of a solid Republican presidential majority in the South – have reinvigorated that chorus. KOVLER, a collection of essays by academics and pundits, offers a sobering counterpoint. The essays, which consider the triumphs and pitfalls in the party's past, highlight the Democrat's tenacity. In addition, Kovler serves as a useful single-volume introduction to the study of the party's uneven history.

CHRISTOPHER MACGREGOR SCRIBNER

See also Parties and Political Movements

Depression, Great *see* Great Crash and Great Depression

Dewey, John 1859–1952
Educational theorist and philosopher

Campbell, Harry M., *John Dewey*, New York: Twayne, 1971

Coughlan, Neil, *Young John Dewey: An Essay in American Intellectual History*, Chicago: University of Chicago Press, 1975

Dykhuizen, George, *The Life and Mind of John Dewey*, Carbondale: Southern Illinois University Press, 1973

Feffer, Andrew, *The Chicago Pragmatists and American Progressivism*, Ithaca, NY: Cornell University Press, 1993

Garrison, Jim (editor), *The New Scholarship on Dewey*, Dordrecht, Netherlands: Kluwer, 1995

Hook, Sidney, *John Dewey: An Intellectual Portrait*, New York: Day, 1939

Rorty, Richard, *Philosophy and the Mirror of Nature*,
Princeton: Princeton University Press, 1979
Rorty, Richard, *Consequences of Pragmatism: Essays,
1972–1980*, Minneapolis: University of Minnesota Press,
1982
Westbrook, Robert B., *John Dewey and American
Democracy*, Ithaca, NY: Cornell University Press,
1991

As the founding father of the philosophy of pragmatism, and as a prolific author on many subjects, John Dewey is a figure of enormous influence, not only in the history of American thought, but in other fields too. He was always concerned to relate his ideas to contemporary American concerns, for example in the field of education and in the character of American democracy. HOOK produced a study that – over half a century later – remains an excellent introduction to Dewey's social and philosophical thought. Since Hook himself was one of Dewey's most faithful followers, the tone of his book was by no means critical. Indeed, the only point at which he seemed to disagree with Dewey was in the latter's use, in some of his later works, of the term "God" in reference to the subjective projection of man's own ideas. Hook criticized this usage as liable to misinterpretation, by traditional theists, as restoring a transcendental view of life and existence. After a brief survey of Dewey the man at the beginning of his work, Hook went on to analyze Dewey's principal ideas in thematic fashion. He believed, in general, that Dewey had demonstrated how the ideals of American democracy, born in a simpler, agrarian world, could be adapted to the needs of a corporate industrial society.

CAMPBELL's book is mainly devoted to the part of Dewey's career beginning in 1925 with the publication of *Experience and Nature*. It summarizes his early attempts to combine Christianity and Hegelianism – an effort abandoned in the 1890s – and the subsequent development of his experimental naturalism. This became more and more caught up in a romanticism which prophesied the attainment of a millennium when the scientific method could be applied to aesthetic and moral as well as natural phenomena. Campbell argues that Dewey acted as prophet of a new religion combining science and nature, and based on democracy as a way of life. He takes Dewey to task for the ambiguity of much of his thought, his repetitiveness, his dogmatism, his habit of stating as fact what was merely his own *ex cathedra* opinion, and – from the opposite side of the debate to Hook – his refusal to admit that any case could be made for the existence of either an immanent or a transcendent Deity.

DYKHUIZEN's intention was to write a biography of Dewey and at the same time to outline the major aspects of his thought. His book provides a useful guide to Dewey's career: his Vermont boyhood and youth, his education at the University of Vermont and Johns Hopkins, his time spent as a high school teacher, his appointments at Michigan, Minnesota, Chicago, and Columbia universities, his family life, and his travels in Europe and the Far East. Although some parts of Dewey's social thought (his ideas on education, for example) are made much clearer by their explanation in the context in which they evolved, there was much more "life" than "mind" in his book.

COUGHLAN attempted, with greater success, to profile Dewey's intellectual growth. He sees it as shaped by two contexts: that of a crisis in 19th-century evangelical Protestant culture and the emergence of the modern American university. But his study has severe limitations: although Coughlan claims to have discerned the emergence of Dewey's pragmatism by the mid-1890s, and there is a final chapter dealing briefly with his later life and thought, most of the rest of his book is concerned with that early period during Dewey's career in which he was most accurately identified with neo-Hegelian idealism. Oddly, the longest chapter deals not with Dewey but with the evolution of the ideas of George Herbert Mead, who would become Dewey's colleague at Michigan and Chicago universities.

After his death in 1952, Dewey's reputation plummeted. Some of the radicals of the 1960s endeavored to utilize his ideas for their own purposes: the Port Huron Statement of 1962, issued by the Students for a Democratic Society, was strongly Deweyan at times in its language. The single greatest influence in the revival of Dewey's influence in recent years, however, has been Richard Rorty. RORTY (1979) asserts that Dewey, Wittgenstein, and Heidegger were "the three most important philosophers of our century." RORTY (1982), while repeating this assertion of Dewey's importance, also insists that there was little real difference between Dewey and Foucault. This claim ignores differences in the two men's attitudes to grand theory, the possibility of improvements in the human condition brought about by reason, the relation between society and the individual and that between natural science and social science. It was not only the parallels between Deweyan pragmatism and French post-structuralism, however, that Rorty distorted. Much of his account of Dewey's thought is more Rortyan than Deweyan. Yet his use of Deweyan pragmatism gives him a powerful weapon in his attempt to create a new philosophy remote from traditional metaphysical and epistemological preoccupations.

GARRISON presents the fruits of the new scholarship which has evolved on Dewey's ideas on education over the last decade. One theme of this new work is to place Dewey's ideas on aesthetics closer to the center of his vision. Several of the contributors to this volume of essays maintain that an education built on the expressiveness and creativity of aesthetics and the arts generally may actually be more basic than the so-called "basics" of E.D. Hirsch and other conservative critics of "progressive" education with their emphasis on memorizing by rote. Another major concern of the book is to compare and contrast Deweyan pragmatism with critical theory (Habermas), post-structuralism (Lyotard, Foucault), and present-day feminism.

Although WESTBROOK denied that his work was a "full intellectual biography," it is the best and most detailed study of Dewey now available. In preparing it, he examined all of Dewey's writings – no inconsiderable task in view of their size (37 published volumes) and habitual lack of clarity (Justice Holmes famously remarked that Dewey wrote as "God would have spoken had He been inarticulate but keenly desirous to tell you how it was"). Westbrook analyzes the evolution of Dewey's thought in the context of his own time and culture. He argues that at the core of Dewey's philosophy was a belief in participatory democracy. This distinguished him from mainstream 20th-century American liberalism, which preferred to place its faith in decision-making by bureaucratic or scientific elites. Dewey took the radical position of wanting the public to be involved in democratic policymaking.

FEFFER is very skeptical of the attempt by contemporary writers – including Rorty, Westbrook, Richard J. Bernstein, and Cornel West – to revive Dewey-type pragmatism in order to promote a new approach to democratic politics. Dewey was at the heart of Feffer's book on the Chicago pragmatists from the 1890s to World War I, though he also included material on Jane Addams, George H. Mead, James H. Tufts, and Ella Flagg Young. Feffer credits the Chicago group with considerable success in their attempts to deal with the immediate problems – particularly those to do with education – of their city. They had failed, however, to create a truly democratic community. One reason for this was the backward-looking nature of much of Dewey's philosophy, which Feffer sees in terms of the restatement – in new scientific language – of older concepts drawn from 19th-century Protestantism, Hegelian thought, and traditional American artisanal republicanism. A second reason (here Feffer followed the line Reinhold Niebuhr had argued against Dewey in the 1930s) derived from the naiveté of the pragmatists over issues of class and power, and their failure to understand that their advocacy of reasonableness and cooperation hid an elitism that made them unwitting allies in the advance of corporate capitalism.

MELVYN STOKES

See also Pragmatism

Disfranchisement *see* Jim Crow

Distribution *see* Marketing and Distribution

Dix, Dorothea Lynde 1802–1887
Social reformer and campaigner for the mentally ill

Brooks, Gladys, *Three Wise Virgins*, New York: Dutton, 1957

Lowe, Corinne, *The Gentle Warrior: A Story of Dorothea Lynde Dix*, New York: Harcourt Brace, 1948

Marshall, Helen E., *Dorothea Dix: Forgotten Samaritan*, Chapel Hill: University of North Carolina Press, 1937

Schlaifer, Charles and Lucy Freeman, *Heart's Work: Civil War Heroine and Champion of the Mentally Ill: Dorothea Lynde Dix*, New York: Paragon House, 1991

Schleichert, Elizabeth, *The Life of Dorothea Dix*, Frederick, MD: Twenty-First Century Books, 1992

Tiffany, Francis, *Life of Dorothea Lynde Dix*, Boston: Houghton Mifflin, 1891; reprinted, Ann Arbor, MI: Plutarch Press, 1971

Wilson, Dorothy Clarke, *Stranger and Traveler: The Story of Dorothea Dix, American Reformer*, Boston: Little Brown, 1975

Dorothea Lynde Dix spent a great deal of her adult life crusading throughout the United States and Europe for improved treatment of the insane and for adequate facilities for the mentally disturbed. Remarkably successful in her efforts – more than 123 insane asylums and hospitals were built through her efforts – Dix was completely committed to her cause. Biographers have lauded Dix's public victories, but few have dissected her personal ambitions and other philanthropic work. Dix turned her personal papers over to a literary executor to be used after her death in the preparation of a biography. TIFFANY, a Unitarian minister, wrote a highly complimentary biography with particular attention to Dix's influential Boston friends, such as William Ellery Channing and Charles Sumner, who assisted in her efforts. Tiffany also collected many of Dix's other letters and secured anecdotes and testimonials from friends and pupils that might otherwise have been lost. Since only a portion of these letters were sent to archival repositories, Tiffany's publication of these sources has been invaluable to later biographers.

Almost fifty years later, MARSHALL produced the first biography of Dix using historical analysis. She emphasized Dix's role in the United States reform movement of the mid-19th century, and she singled out Dix for pioneering a field of reform that attracted few female advocates. Marshall incorporates an important chapter on the treatment of the mentally ill in the 19th century which helps explain Dix's motivations. Throughout the biography Marshall documents thoroughly the evolution of methods used in caring for mental patients. She also dedicates a chapter to Dix's significant but controversial work as Superintendent of United States Army Nurses during the American Civil War. LOWE's biography of Dix is a ghastly mix of truth and melodrama. Dix is portrayed as a saint with no foibles, even though most biographers have expounded on her stiff and inflexible personality. BROOKS is another brief treatment of a similar kind, but does provide information about Dix's motivations, including her familial background and the religious zeal of the reformers.

To date the best analysis of Dix's life is WILSON whose biography is based upon far greater access to primary and secondary sources than previous biographers. Because publishers were particularly interested in women's history and issues during the 1970s, Wilson was able to exploit a particular collection of letters between Dix and her friend Anne Heath housed at Harvard University. Using these letters, Wilson was able to portray Dix as a highly motivated woman, but one not without frailties. The letters also paint a desolate picture of travel and of the rest facilities available during Dix's numerous journeys. Wilson thoroughly documents Dix's miserable childhood as well as the methods Dix employed to present her pleas for funds to numerous state legislatures.

Two later biographies lack Wilson's scholarship. SCHLEICHERT offers little interpretation, and concentrates almost exclusively on Dix's childhood and her philanthropic work with the insane. SCHLAIFER and FREEMAN is a very readable biography with lengthy quotations from Dix's correspondence. It includes a state-by-state examination of Dix's work for the insane, provides coverage of other reforms that Dix advocated, and applauds her Civil War work.

JONATHAN JEFFREY

See also Prisons and Asylums

Douglas, Stephen A.   1813–1861
Political leader and presidential candidate

Baker, Jean H., *Affairs of Party: The Political Culture of Northern Democrats in the Mid-Nineteenth Century*, Ithaca, NY: Cornell University Press, 1983

Capers, Gerald M., *Stephen A. Douglas: Defender of the Union*, Boston: Little Brown, 1969

Jaffa, Harry V., *Crisis of the House Divided: An Interpretation of the Issues in the Lincoln-Douglas Debates*, New York: Doubleday, 1959

Johannsen, Robert W., *Stephen A. Douglas*, New York: Oxford University Press, 1973

Johannsen, Robert W., *The Frontier, the Union, and Stephen A. Douglas*, Urbana: University of Illinois Press, 1989

Johnson, Allen, *Stephen Douglas: A Study in American Politics*, New York: Macmillan, 1908

Milton, George Fort, *The Eve of Conflict: Stephen A. Douglas and the Needless War*, Boston: Houghton Mifflin, 1934

Sigelschiffer, Saul, *The American Conscience: The Drama of the Lincoln-Douglas Debates*, New York: Horizon Press, 1973

Wells, Damon, *Stephen Douglas: The Last Years, 1857–1861*, Austin: University of Texas Press, 1971

Zarefsky, David, *Lincoln, Douglas, and Slavery: In the Crucible of Public Debate*, Chicago: University of Chicago Press, 1990

Throughout most of his lifetime, Stephen Douglas was infinitely better known than his local rival Abraham Lincoln. The irony is that ever since the reverse has been true. Despite an impressive career and remarkable life story, Douglas would be practically unknown without reference to Lincoln. His most authoritative biographer, JOHANNSEN (1973), demonstrates the injustice of this development by showing how Douglas was pre-eminently a "man of his times" who embodied the expansionism and nationalism of his age better than Lincoln or any other antebellum political figure. Johannsen carefully surveys Douglas's life, from his early years in Vermont through his spectacular political career in Illinois and Washington, DC. By pursuing critical, but elusive, information about Douglas's early years and personal life, Johannsen succeeds in presenting an understanding portrait of a rambunctious personality and shrewd political strategist. All judgments on Douglas must come to terms with questions about his motivations. Johannsen exhibits especially sound judgment on these controversial issues, concluding that Douglas was neither immoral, nor amoral, as his detractors argue, but rather an ambitious leader deeply committed to the vision of an ocean-bound republic.

Other Douglas biographies are less impressive. JOHNSON produced the first significant academic biography of the Illinois senator. However, lacking access to many of the documents later employed so expertly by Johannsen, he settles for a discussion more limited to Douglas's political career, particularly during the 1850s. Still, Johnson occasionally offers interesting insights into Douglas's political and personal habits, mainly as a result of his rather extensive use of recollections from Douglas's peers. Yet, the account fundamentally lacks

sympathy for its protagonist and too easily dismisses Douglas as uninterested in the moral issues of his day. MILTON more than makes up for Johnson's ambivalence and writes a sometimes breathless account of Douglas's humble origins and political achievements. Writing from the revisionist perspective, Milton depicts Douglas as a tragic hero unable to prevent a needless conflict, but loyal to the Union once the fighting began. Although practically hagiography, this monograph relies upon a greater variety of sources than any other work except Johannsen's.

Writing a *Library of America* biography designed for the general reader, CAPERS lacks both the fire of Milton and the occasional insight of Johnson, but nevertheless produces a readable summary of Douglas's life. Capers eschews footnotes and focuses almost exclusively on the political battles of the 1850s where he emphasizes Douglas's importance to the national Democratic party.

Two other specialized studies of Douglas's life are worth mentioning. In a concentrated look at Douglas's final years, WELLS disagrees sharply with Milton and attempts to present a more balanced appraisal of Douglas's evolution as a nationalist. Wells believes that prior to 1861 Douglas had to appease southern interests and thus never had the freedom to support a consistent set of national beliefs. He also asserts, unlike Johannsen, that Douglas was fundamentally out of harmony with his times, because he was a nationalist during a period of sectional strife, and a compromiser during an age of conflict.

JOHANNSEN (1989) is a collection of essays, and an important supplement to his earlier biography, which spells out in more forceful terms the wide-ranging nature of Douglas's views. Johannsen not only explains how Manifest Destiny influenced Douglas's approach to the Oregon territory and the western frontier, but also how this basic tenet of expansionism provides the key to understanding Douglas's approach to the slavery question. In addition, the collection includes a memorable essay on Douglas's political philosophy as well as a provocative – and rare – examination of Lincoln's convictions from the perspective of a Douglas scholar.

Since the Lincoln-Douglas Debates of 1858 might well represent Douglas's most lasting contribution to American history, studies of the contest offer some insight into Douglas's political character. The seven extended debates that occurred between Lincoln and Douglas during the course of the 1858 Illinois legislative elections (the outcome of which would determine which man would be elected to the US senate) brought out the best in both combatants. JAFFA remains the finest exposition of the political ideas at stake in the Lincoln-Douglas contest. Using a rigorous philosophical approach, Jaffa offers a lucid, although occasionally dense, analysis of Douglas's doctrine of popular sovereignty. Anticipating Johannsen's argument, Jaffa emphasizes the expansionist motivation behind Douglas's positions, but he also links that desire with what he terms Douglas's belief in "white supremacy." The result leads Jaffa to the disturbing – and dubious – conclusion that Douglas represented a totalitarian threat to the American republic.

SIGELSCHIFFER offers a less demanding account of the debates which he presents in dramatic fashion. Out of several possibilities, Sigelschiffer's version is probably the best narrative of the campaign, although it relies upon few primary sources other than extended quotations from the speeches themselves. ZAREFSKY examines the text of the debates, less for philosophical purposes as Jaffa does, than for insights into the methods of two great communicators. The result is an accessible and well-documented study of what Zarefsky considers to be the four principal patterns of argument used by Lincoln and Douglas: conspiracy, legal, historical, and moral. Zarefsky also demonstrates in an impressive manner how both politicians used surrogate contentions to position themselves against their opponents.

Since Douglas played a role in almost every major political development in the United States between 1850 and 1861, he can be encountered in numerous ways through the general historical literature on the period. BAKER offers one of the most rewarding examples in her well-regarded study of the political culture of the antebellum Northern Democratic party. She connects antebellum Democratic sensibilities to several strands of American life and shows how various institutions and practices nurtured those values. Douglas assumes a prominent role in this account, and his ideas receive sophisticated and thoughtful attention. In particular, Baker suggests revealing connections between Douglas and Edmund Burke on issues of community and natural law.

MATTHEW PINSKER

See also Civil War: Approach to War entries

Douglass, Frederick 1818–1895

African American spokesman and leader

Blight, David W., *Frederick Douglass's Civil War: Keeping Faith in Jubilee*, Baton Rouge: Louisiana State University Press, 1989

Foner, Philip S., *Frederick Douglass: A Biography*, New York: Citadel Press, 1964

Holland, Fredric May, *Frederick Douglass: The Colored Orator*, New York: Funk and Wagnalls, 1891

Huggins, Nathan Irvin, *Slave and Citizen: The Life of Frederick Douglass*, Boston: Little Brown, 1980

McFeely, William S., *Frederick Douglass*, New York: Norton, 1991

Martin, Waldo E., Jr., *The Mind of Frederick Douglass*, Chapel Hill: University of North Carolina Press, 1984

Miller, Douglas T., *Frederick Douglass and the Fight for Freedom*, New York: Facts on File, 1988

Preston, Dickson J., *Young Frederick Douglass: The Maryland Years*, Baltimore: Johns Hopkins University Press, 1980

Quarles, Benjamin, *Frederick Douglass*, Washington, DC: Associated Publishers, 1948

Washington, Booker T., *Frederick Douglass*, Philadelphia: G.W. Jacobs, and London: Hodder and Stoughton, 1907

Any student of Frederick Douglass should start by examining his three autobiographies: *Narrative of the Life of Frederick Douglass, an American Slave* (1845); *My Bondage and My Freedom* (1855); and *Life and Times of Frederick* Douglass (1881; revised edition, 1892). The *Narrative* is by far the most

widely read and available, in large measure due to Douglass's vivid depiction of the psychological as well as physical depravity found in slavery. *Bondage and Freedom* is the most detailed autobiographical account of Douglass's experiences as a slave and contains interesting commentary on his early career as an abolitionist. In the last autobiography, Douglass clearly was trying to define what he felt was his legacy as a leader of his race during the 19th century.

Of the earliest biographies of Douglass, the best is HOLLAND. Douglass granted the author access to his personal collection of published speeches and essays. Unfortunately Holland incorporates extremely long quotations from this material which clutters an otherwise dramatic narrative. In 1906, WASHINGTON hired a ghost writer to prepare a Douglass biography, which largely abridges *Life and Times*.

The first scholarly biography of Douglass was written by QUARLES in 1948. Sixteen years later, FONER published a second well-researched biography by consolidating the introductions to his multi-volume, *The Life and Writings of Frederick Douglass*, which also provides the texts for several hundred of Douglass's speeches, letters, and writings. Both Quarles and Foner rely heavily on Douglass's autobiographies, especially for the slave years. The two authors generally accept Douglass's self-assessment and fail to delve deeply into his personality. Quarles, an African American scholar, underlines Douglass's claims to have been an exemplary self-made man. The white Marxist Foner portrays Douglass as a revolutionary proponent of racial equality and exaggerates Douglass's concern for labor issues. HUGGINS largely follows Quarles's interpretation of Douglass's public career and adds little new information about the inner Douglass. MILLER is a is well-written account, but it is aimed at a juvenile audience.

PRESTON shows the contribution that can be made to the study of history by dedicated non-professional writers – in this case a retired journalist. His thorough research through manuscripts, tax records, genealogical materials, and local histories enables him to recreate the milieu of Douglass's childhood on an Eastern Shore plantation as well as in the bustling port city of Baltimore. Preston traces Douglass's genealogy back through several generations of Maryland slaves, and establishes his year of birth as 1818 not the generally accepted 1817. He also discusses sympathetically Douglass's relations with his master's family not just in slavery but for decades afterwards. This detailed information on Douglass's childhood and adolescence casts invaluable light on the psychological formation of the later public figure.

MARTIN is an exhaustive examination of Douglass's intellectual development as reflected in fifty years of public speaking and writing. Organizing this material topically, Martin discovers a remarkable level of consistency in Douglass's views despite the rapid transformation of his own and his race's status. He also uses Douglass's thought as a mirror to illuminate the broader African American reception of the many intellectual trends of those years. Martin finds Douglass ambivalent about his African heritage. Douglass's faith in democracy, progress, and a Christian-based social ethic, however, caused him to believe that racism and all forms of ethno-centrism would steadily diminish and that consequently all groups would be absorbed into a *composite* rather than a *compound* American nationality.

Martin's lead in examining Douglass as an intellectual figure is followed by BLIGHT who focuses more narrowly on the black leader's view of the Civil War's causes, goals, and consequences. Douglass viewed the Civil War as the central event of 19th century United States history. He lobbied hard to make emancipation and equal rights for blacks the war's mission. Blight explains that Douglass was bitterly disappointed not to receive the officer's commission promised him by Lincoln, and refused to serve as an enlisted man. Nonetheless, he supported the Union cause by employing his powerful oratorical tools as a military recruiter of fellow African Americans. After the war, Douglass's lectures and writing sought to keep alive the memory of the struggle's highest purposes. As a valued Republican stump-speaker, Douglass vainly resisted the trend toward reconciliation with the white ex-Confederates at the price of abandoning federal protection of black rights.

While these various studies have uncovered much detail about Douglass's activities and thoughts, McFEELY contributes a valuable psychological assessment of the African American leader. He perceptively explores the cultural influence of each successive residence on Maryland's Eastern Shore, Baltimore, New Bedford, Rochester, Washington, DC, and Great Britain which he visited on three occasions. McFeely demonstrates the complex psychological relationship between Douglass and his master Thomas Auld, who the author speculates was the young slave's unacknowledged father. He argues that this relationship caused a blurred racial identity in Douglass. Once he escaped slavery, Douglass attempted to locate himself in both the white and black communities. McFeely also pays close attention to the interaction of race, class and gender issues on Douglass. He feels that Douglass sought intellectual and probably sexual gratification with educated white women. McFeely does not ignore his subject's weaknesses, noting that Douglass's desire for appointed political office after the Civil War caused him to mute his criticism of the Republican party's retreat from the protection of black civil rights. McFeely also chides Douglass for forgetting his southern black roots when he condemned the Exoduster movement in the late 1870s. Thanks to the efforts of Ida Wells-Barnett, Douglass recovered his earlier mission as a civil rights spokesperson in his final years.

JOHN R. McKIVIGAN

See also Abolitionism/Antislavery Movement; African American History: Civil War, Emancipation, and Reconstruction

Draft/Conscription

Bernstein, Iver, *The New York City Draft Riots: Their Significance for American Society and Politics in the Age of the Civil War*, New York: Oxford University Press, 1990

Chambers, John Whiteclay II, *To Raise an Army: The Draft Comes to Modern America*, New York: Free Press, and London: Collier Macmillan, 1987

Clifford, J. Garry and Samuel R. Spencer, Jr., *The First Peacetime Draft*, Lawrence: University Press of Kansas, 1986

Flynn, George Q., *The Draft, 1940–1973*, Lawrence: University Press of Kansas, 1993

Geary, James W., *We Need Men: The Union Draft in the Civil War*, DeKalb: Northern Illinois University Press, 1991

Kohn, Stephen M., *Jailed for Peace: The History of American Draft Law Violations, 1658–1985*, Westport, CT: Greenwood Press, 1986

Millett, Allan R. and Peter Maslowski, *For the Common Defense: A Military History of the United States of America, 1607–1983*, New York: Free Press, and London: Collier Macmillan, 1984; revised, Free Press, 1994

O'Sullivan, John, *From Voluntarism to Conscription: Congress and Selective Service, 1940–1945*, New York: Garland, 1982

Useem, Michael, *Conscription, Protest, and Social Conflict: The Life and Death of a Draft Resistance Movement*, New York: Wiley, 1973

Weigley, Russell F., *The American Way of War: A History of United States Military Strategy and Policy*, New York: Macmillan, 1973

A general introduction to the linked topics of the draft and conscription may be found in one of the general histories of the American armed forces and the American military tradition. One of the best, and most readily available, is WEIGLEY. Among many other topics, he assesses the changing manpower requirements of the United States, as well as the various draft measures, such as the system of Universal Military Training and Service (UMT), brought in following World War II. More recently, MILLETT and MASLOWSKI have provided quite a detailed discussion of the introduction of national conscription to America during the Civil War. For the North, this was the first time that the conscription procedure bypassed the states in favour of the federal government, a change that was by no means universally welcomed. Later administrations attempted to approach this issue more cautiously, and the various acts that were introduced during and following World War I are comprehensively covered in this volume.

There are a number of specialized studies of the draft, but most of them deal with particular periods, or focus on opposition to the draft. The exception to this is CHAMBERS, which is in many ways the best starting-point for study of the subject. He breaks down American military development into six distinctive stages, and provides a useful framework in which to place other studies. Throughout, the emphasis is on non-military factors as determinants of change in military policy, and on the political, demographic, economic and social factors which lay behind the introduction of national conscription. The development of the draft, Chambers argues, was a natural result of the modernization of America, and the increased power of the state in its citizens' lives. However, since an analysis of the 1917 draft and the introduction of the Selective Service System during World War I is by far the most detailed part of the work, this is a less comprehensive study than it might first appear.

There are two very good studies of the introduction of the draft during the Civil War, although both deal only with the Union side. As its title suggests, BERNSTEIN focuses on opposition to the draft in New York City, and considers its economic, social and political context, as well as its impact on northern society. Bernstein's is an extremely well-researched study, which abounds in detail. From his examination of the political crisis of the 1850s through to the strikes of 1872, Bernstein argues that the draft riots were at the very "center of a contentious era, an era of politicized social conflict." Opposition to conscription, he shows, "merged with a much broader debate over the definition of justice in mid-century New York," as both workers and elites struggled to come to terms with the changes that urbanization and industrialization had brought not just to their city but to the North as a whole.

GEARY focuses on the northern recruitment drive during the Civil War, which he sees as a time of "transition from localism to the nascent nation-state." The draft exemplified this transition, and Geary examines its impact on those involved. In the North's move toward conscription as a solution to its manpower problems after two years of fighting, Geary finds parallels with President Lincoln's general approach to the conflict, in particular his approach to the emancipation issue. As he describes it, although both conscription and emancipation were "revolutionary" concepts, each resulted from "evolutionary" forces. Geary's concluding chapter offers some thoughts on conscription – and opposition to it – in the 20th century. He shows how class issues – the notion of a "rich man's war and a poor man's fight" – have constantly accompanied the draft. Both Bernstein's and Geary's studies contain extremely valuable guides to further reading on this subject. Bernstein has a comprehensive bibliographical essay, and Geary has voluminous and detailed notes.

The most up-to-date study of conscription in more recent times is FLYNN, who examines the period between the introduction of the Selective Training and Service Act and the Vietnam Peace Agreement. Flynn focuses on the dual nature of the draft. While its implementation represented the centralization of authority in the post-1940 period, the means by which it was conducted – via local draft boards – ensured that localism remained strong, thus hopefully both minimizing objections to it and ensuring that local peer pressure ensured enforcement. By the time of Vietnam the localized nature of the draft was no longer effective in encouraging enforcement, since "community consensus on the Vietnam War had broken down." Flynn concludes his study with an assessment of the rather unsuccessful All Volunteer Force (AFV) which was introduced after Nixon had dismantled the draft in 1973.

An extremely detailed analysis of the introduction of the Selective Training and Service Act in the immediate pre-World War II period is provided in CLIFFORD and SPENCER. Although essential for America's later involvement in World War II, the act was the result of neither military nor presidential pressure, but was rather "conceived, written, and lobbied through Congress by a determined group of private citizens who had no formal connection with the government." What the authors are concerned with, therefore, is "the story of a pressure group," and in particular the story of its leader, Grenville Clark. In a wider sense they examine America's changing approach to military preparedness and the move away from an isolationist position which was seen to be no longer sustainable in a world made smaller by technological change.

O'SULLIVAN is a detailed and well-written study of the implementation, the impact and the limitations of the Selective Training and Service Act of 1940, and of the "process by which most Americans came to accept the draft as part of the nation's political culture." It does, to some degree, reflect the period in which it was written – it was completed in 1971. However, for anyone wishing to pursue this topic the notes and bibliography, and the "New Preface" composed in 1981, offer an invaluable guide, especially to primary material.

Finally, opposition to the draft is examined by both Kohn and Useem. KOHN covers opposition to conscription into the armed forces from the colonial period through to the late 20th century. Draft resistance, Kohn argues, "is one of the largest, longest, and most successful campaigns of civil disobedience in American history," and draft resisters themselves "have made significant and lasting contributions to civil and religious liberty." Throughout, Kohn draws parallels between pacifism and other types of social, and political, reform movements, such as abolitionism and the civil rights movement. In some ways this approach results in rather a cursory assessment of what were, and are, complex issues. USEEM, likewise, offers an assessment of the collective attempt to oppose military mobilization, although his focus is firmly on opposition to the Vietnam War. Useem covers the impact of conscription during the Vietnam era on the draftees themselves and on society as a whole, and examines both its emotional and its economic repercussions. Based on a wide selection of first-hand interviews, this work is, again, very much a product of its time, but one which offers a unique insight into the turbulent era of late 1960s/early 1970s America.

S-M. GRANT

Du Bois, W.E.B. 1868–1963
African American leader, author and civil rights campaigner

Andrews, William L. (editor), *Critical Essays on W.E.B. Du Bois*, Boston: Hall, 1985

Broderick, Francis L., *W.E.B. Du Bois: Negro Leader in a Time of Crisis*, Stanford, CA: Stanford University Press, 1959

De Marco, Joseph P., *The Social Thought of W.E.B. Du Bois*, Lanham, MD: University Press of America, 1983

Horne, Gerald, *Black and Red: W.E.B. Du Bois and the Afro-American Response to the Cold War, 1944–1963*, Albany: State University of New York Press, 1986

Lewis, David L., *W.E.B. Du Bois: Biography of a Race, 1868–1919*, New York: Holt, 1993

Marable, Manning, *W.E.B. Du Bois: Black Radical Democrat*, Boston: Twayne, 1986

Moore, Jack B., *W.E.B. Du Bois*, Boston: Twayne, 1981

Rampersad, Arnold, *The Art and Imagination of W.E.B. Du Bois*, Cambridge, MA: Harvard University Press, 1976

Rudwick, Elliott M., *W.E.B. Du Bois: A Study in Minority Group Leadership*, Philadelphia: University of Pennsylvania Press, 1960

The earliest substantial publications on W.E.B. Du Bois occurred while he was still alive and in control of his papers. He was a controversial figure throughout his career, and, when the first books on him appeared during the Cold War, he was the target of an indictment by a federal grand jury as the result of his hostility to American foreign policy and sympathy for the Soviet Union, China and anti-imperialist movements in the Third World. These circumstances have influenced the character of some of the literature on Du Bois.

BRODERICK's use of Du Bois's papers for his career up to 1910 provides a sound and nuanced account for that period. The later career is documented largely from already published material. The book provides the chronological framework and initial lines of analysis of Du Bois's writings which have since been taken up by others. While the conflict with Booker T. Washington is interpreted as disguising the elements they had in common, it is Du Bois's involvement in the NAACP which Broderick sees as symbolizing a new alliance against racism and Jim Crow, between a new educated African American elite and white liberals. Yet the book argues that, beginning in the 1920s, Du Bois's significance declined as his developing socialist, Pan-Africanist and separatist ideas strained to breaking point his relation to the NAACP's integrationism. The final phase of his public activity, concerned with peace politics and anti-imperialism, and revealing a sympathy for the Soviet Union, Broderick regards as a rupture with many of his earlier commitments.

RUDWICK's major interest is in race leadership and in conflicts over the direction which the race should take, as expressed in controversy over education, and competition between race and civil rights organizations. He devotes space to the Tuskegee versus Atlanta models of education, and Washington's efforts to resist the challenge of the NAACP. Yet because he believes Du Bois had little capacity for organizational leadership, Rudwick treats him primarily as a sociologist and propagandist editor of *The Crisis*. However, he argues that the propaganda role was vitiated by the contradiction between Du Bois's championing of separate black cultural and even (by the 1930s) economic development, and his rage against the colour line. The focus of the book leads to a cursory treatment of the years after 1934 when Du Bois left the NAACP.

A literary scholar alert to historical context, RAMPERSAD has produced the best survey of the whole range of Du Bois's writing. He is interested in his subject's use of the language, linking it to intellectual changes in his career, especially through detailed readings of *Souls of Black Folk* (1903), *Darkwater* (1920) and his novels. He adds to earlier writers' discussion of Du Bois's editorship of *The Crisis* through a consideration of the magazine's role in promoting African American literary and artistic work, especially in the 1920s. MOORE is a useful introduction to Du Bois as a writer, through a series of analyses of his books in chronological order, concentrating on their ideas and "verbal strategies". While the large question of Du Bois's possible inconsistencies is reduced, in pursuit of the "essential" man, to the notion of "harmonious contradiction," the discussion of the texts is always sensible and in particular provides a positive evaluation of *Black Reconstruction* (1935). The multi-author collection edited by ANDREWS is of more marginal interest to the historian, since most of the essays deal with Du Bois's fiction.

However, there is a useful sampling of contemporary reaction to his books among both educated blacks and liberal whites. Some of the essays illuminate the non-fictional work by illustrating how Du Bois often blurred categories of writing, for example when his historical scholarship also offers moral commentary on American society.

DE MARCO's interests are in philosophy and intellectual history. Charting Du Bois's intellectual development, he emphasizes the lasting imprint on him of the philosophical pragmatism which he encountered at Harvard. In later decades, however, he is impressed by the growing significance which Du Bois attributed to the economic forces underlying cultures, culminating in an engagement with Marxism understood in terms of economic determinism and class struggle. In De Marco's view, Du Bois's activism follows from his ideas, rather than contributing anything significant to the intellectual changes which Du Bois underwent.

The energy and sweep of MARABLE's book make it the liveliest entry of moderate length into Du Bois's intellectual world. He pays more attention than other writers to Du Bois's concern with Africa and his role as a socialist theorist. The continuous thread which he discerns running through his subject's long career as a public intellectual is his commitment as a radical democrat to advancing the democratic rights of peoples of African descent, and ultimately of all workers worldwide. Marable seeks to dissolve the much discussed contradiction between Du Bois's separatism and racial egalitarianism, by presenting him as a misunderstood cultural pluralist, who prefigures a contemporary multicultural American democracy.

In a study of the last twenty years of Du Bois's life, HORNE seeks to refute the argument of earlier scholars that these were decades of marginality and departure from earlier achievements in race leadership. Du Bois is located within a group of other politically dissident black figures who stood out against the Cold War consensus in the United States. Intellectually, Horne argues that Du Bois's socialism and anti-imperialism are continuous with his earlier career, and that his long concern with class and race remained relevant to his analysis of the conditions of war and peace in the Cold War era. The book is a forceful work of advocacy.

LEWIS's volume is the first based on full examination of Du Bois's papers. It provides the most complete account of Du Bois's formation and intellectual and political development to the end of the Red Summer of 1919. As the subtitle suggests, the individual life is richly contextualized. Du Bois's German years during which he further encountered philosophical idealism and, for the first time, historical political economy are given greater significance by Lewis than by others. A long, nuanced narrative of the Washington-Du Bois relationship avoids shorthand reliance on different notions of race leadership or organisational rivalry. The full exploration of tensions among NAACP leaders in the early years reveals the complexity of relationships reflected in, but not reducible to, different policy emphases. While the full range of the role which Du Bois envisaged for *The Crisis* does not emerge, the concluding chapters underscore the editor's passionate identification, despite his elitist reputation, with the rage and aspirations of ordinary African Americans at the time of the racial brutalities of 1919. Lewis's is the major achievement in interpretation of Du Bois.

DAVID TURLEY

Dulles, John Foster 1888–1959
International lawyer and negotiator, and
Secretary of State

Gerson, Louis L., *John Foster Dulles*, New York: Cooper
  Square, 1964
Goold-Adams, Richard, *John Foster Dulles: A Reappraisal*,
  New York: Appleton Century Crofts, 1962; as *The Time
  of Power: A Reappraisal of John Foster Dulles*, London:
  Weidenfeld and Nicolson, 1962
Guhin, Michael A., *John Foster Dulles: A Statesman and
  His Times*, New York: Columbia University Press, 1972
Hoopes, Townsend, *The Devil and John Foster Dulles*,
  Boston: Little Brown, 1973; London: Deutsch, 1974
Immerman, Richard H. (editor), *John Foster Dulles and the
  Diplomacy of the Cold War: A Reappraisal*, Princeton:
  Princeton University Press, 1990
Marks, Frederick W. III, *Power and Peace: The Diplomacy
  of John Foster Dulles*, New York: Praeger, 1993
Pruessen, Ronald W., *John Foster Dulles: The Road to
  Power*, New York: Free Press, and London: Collier
  Macmillan, 1982
Toulouse, Mark G., *The Transformation of John Foster
  Dulles: From Prophet of Realism to Priest of
  Nationalism*, Macon, GA: Mercer University Press, 1985

As Secretary of State in the Eisenhower Administration from
January 1953, until his death in May 1959, John Foster Dulles
was one of the central figures of American history in the Cold
War era. His austere manner and moralistic rhetoric gave him
a reputation as a self-righteous Cold War ideologue who advocated dangerously confrontational policies. Many of the historical studies of Dulles place much emphasis on these aspects of
his personality and policies. Other studies suggest that Dulles
was broader and more complex in personality than the image
of a narrow-minded moralist would suggest, and that his policies were much more subtle than simplistic confrontation.

HOOPES provides the fullest discussion of Dulles as a
dangerously self-righteous moralist, although he qualifies this
portrayal to some extent. In a lengthy, lively biography which
covers Dulles's entire career, he emphasizes the role of religion
in Dulles's life as the son of a Presbyterian minister who acted
as an adviser to the Federal Council of Churches of Christ in
America, and whose rhetoric was full of religious references.
Hoopes argues that Dulles viewed the Cold War in terms of
moral absolutes, with the United States leading the West in a
holy crusade against godless communism. Hoopes suggests that
despite appearances Dulles was politically shrewd, and engaged
in hyperbole in his rhetoric partly for the domestic political
reasons of appealing to right-wing Republicans and to East
European ethnic groups. Overall, however, Hoopes is very critical of Dulles's policies such as brinkmanship, liberation and
massive retaliation, which, it is argued, gravely imperiled the
prospects for peace in the 1950s.

IMMERMAN is a collection of chapters on various aspects
of Dulles's policies by distinguished historians, including John
Lewis Gaddis, William Roger Louis and George C. Herring.
There are differences of viewpoint among the different authors,
but the overall conclusion tends toward a rehabilitation of
Dulles's reputation. The authors suggest that, on such issues
as relations with the Soviet Union, the European Defense
Community, the Suez Crisis, Indo-China and Formosa, Dulles
was more flexible than he has generally been portrayed. Most
of the authors show that he was professionally very competent, with a great knowledge of world affairs and an appreciation of the nuances and subtleties in many of the situations
with which he had to deal. The point is also made that Dulles
served as a useful lightning rod for Eisenhower, deflecting criticism from the president, who took the major decisions in
foreign policy and pursued a moderate course.

GERSON is a volume in the multi-volume series, The
American Secretaries of State and Their Diplomacy, edited by
Robert H. Ferrell. It is a mainly factual account, with little
discussion of controversial issues. A book of substantial length
, it provides basic information on issues during Dulles's time
as Secretary of State, but offers only limited interpretation.

MARKS is a spirited, somewhat controversial defense of
Dulles's record. Marks argues that Dulles's image as an ogre
is based on myth rather than on reality and on an uncritical,
literal interpretation of such phrases as brinkmanship, rollback
and massive retaliation rather than on an examination of such
concepts in their proper context. Marks has engaged in a
considerable amount of archival research, especially on the way
in which Dulles was viewed by his colleagues and fellow diplomats. Marks argues that Dulles was an outstanding, able negotiator whose position on most issues, such as relations with
the Soviet Union, was much more moderate than most historians have suggested. Although Marks may overstate his
case somewhat, his book is a stimulating, thought-provoking
interpretation.

GOOLD-ADAMS is an earlier rehabilitation of Dulles by a
British journalist. Dulles was reviled by leading British contemporary statesmen and public opinion even more than in the
United States. Goold-Adams seeks to present a more balanced
view than that which prevailed in Britain in the 1950s.
Although he wrote before archival evidence was available, his
study is a useful, and fairly comprehensive study of the issues
during Dulles's tenure of office.

GUHIN examines the mind of Dulles and the influences
upon his thinking, rather than details of policy. He explores
the early influences on Dulles and argues that, while religion
was of considerable importance, his training in law and his
involvement in politics influenced him in the direction of pragmatic statesmanship. Guhin emphasizes that Dulles's rhetoric
has been interpreted too literally, and that there has been a
failure to appreciate the domestic political motives for the
extravagance of his rhetorical expression. Guhin also attempts
to place Dulles's thought in the context of the international
situation in which he operated, and he seeks to demonstrate
the limitations of American power, as well as the possible
opportunities for the exercise of that power.

PRUESSEN is a detailed study of Dulles's life up to 1952,
which depicts it as a long preparation for the office of Secretary
of State, which he attained at the age of 64. The grandson of
one Secretary of State, John W. Foster, and the nephew of
another, Robert Lansing, Dulles was involved in the negotiations at Versailles in 1919, acted as foreign policy adviser to
Thomas Dewey in the 1940s and negotiated the Japanese Peace
Treaty in 1950–51. Pruessen, like Guhin, argues that, while

religion was an important influence on Dulles, his legal training and involvement in politics were also of considerable significance. Pruessen stresses, for example, the sharp impact on Dulles of Dewey's unexpected defeat in the election of 1948, which robbed him of the opportunity to become Secretary of State in a Dewey administration.

TOULOUSE is also a study of Dulles before his tenure of office as Secretary of State. Whereas Pruessen is biographical and chronological, Toulouse is a study of ideas. He suggests that Dulles was drawn toward internationalism in his early career, partly due to religion and partly due to the influence of Wilsonian internationalism. By the time of World War II, he had moved towards a position of more hard-headed realism. In the late 1940s, Toulouse suggests, Dulles had become much less an internationalist and much more a nationalist, yet his religious views and his conception of America's leading moral role in world affairs pushed his nationalist position towards advocacy of an internationalist role for the United States.

PETER G. BOYLE

Du Pont Family

Burk, Robert Fredrick, *The Corporate State and the Broker State: The Du Ponts and American National Politics, 1925–1940*, Cambridge, MA: Harvard University Press, 1990

Chandler, Alfred D., Jr., *Strategy and Structure: Chapters in the History of the Industrial Enterprise*, Cambridge: Massachusetts Institute of Technology Press, 1962

Chandler, Alfred D., Jr., and Stephen Salsbury, *Pierre S. Du Pont and the Making of the Modern Corporation*, New York: Harper, 1971

Chandler, Alfred D., Jr., and Richard S. Tedlow, *The Coming of Managerial Capitalism: A Casebook on the History of American Economic Institutions*, Homewood, IL: Irwin, 1985

Colby, Gerard, *Du Pont: Behind the Nylon Curtain*, Englewood Cliffs, NJ: Prentice Hall, 1974 (as Gerard Colby Zilig); revised as *Du Pont Dynasty*, Secaucus, NJ: Lyle Stuart, 1984

Du Pont, Bessie Gardner, *E.I. Du Pont de Nemours and Company: A History, 1802–1902*, Boston: Houghton Mifflin, 1920

E.I. du Pont de Nemours & Company, *Du Pont: The Autobiography of an American Enterprise*, Wilmington, DE: E.I. du Pont de Nemours, 1952

Hounshell, David A. and John Kenly Smith, Jr., *Science and Corporate Strategy: Du Pont R & D, 1902–1980*, New York: Cambridge University Press, 1988

Kerr, George H., *Du Pont Romance: A Reminiscent Narrative of E.I. du Pont de Nemours and Company*, Wilmington DE: Du Pont Printing Division, 1938

Merrill, James M., *Du Pont: The Making of an Admiral: A Biography of Samuel Francis Du Pont*, New York: Dodd Mead, 1986

Wall, Joseph Frazier, *Alfred I. du Pont: The Man and His Family*, New York: Oxford University Press, 1990

Wilkinson, Norman B., *Lammot du Pont and the American Explosives Industry, 1850–1884*, Charlottesville: University Press of Virginia, 1984

Members of the Du Pont family have exerted a significant influence over American business and political life for nearly two hundred years. Studies of the family fall into two broad categories. Some, written from the perspective of business history, examine the family firm and its transition into one of the world's leading corporations. Others are concerned with the biographies of particular members of the family, or with the dynasty more generally, and give the firm a more cursory treatment. There is a rich vein of family and business sources, now deposited at the Hagley Museum and Library in Wilmington, Delaware.

Early studies of the family's business activities – Du PONT (1920), KERR (1938), du PONT & CO. (1952) – offer largely uncritical, eulogistic "in house" accounts. A major leap forward in serious historical study of the subject came in CHANDLER (1962) which puts the Du Ponts' business activities into the centre of the author's compelling thesis about the development of managerial capitalism in the United States. Chandler selected four companies – General Motors, Standard Oil, Sears, and Du Pont – as being among the very first, shortly after World War I, to devise the "decentralised" structure. In time the organisational innovations became models for similar changes in many American corporations. There is a revised version of Chapter 2 in CHANDLER and TEDLOW.

CHANDLER and SALSBURY show how Pierre S. Du Pont (1870–1954) was the single most important executive in two of the nation's largest and most powerful business corporations during the most critical periods in their existence. Under his guidance, E.I. du Pont de Nemours & Co. became the largest explosives, and then chemical, enterprise in America; and the General Motors Corporation the largest manufacturer of cars. The authors attempt to tell the story from the inside, as events and opportunities unfolded, showing how Pierre, the corporation builder, facilitated the introduction of modern administrative controls, financial techniques and administrative structures. His non-business activities are mentioned only when they had a direct bearing on his career.

In his biography of Lammot du Pont (1831–84), who was the grandson of the founder of the firm, WILKINSON provides a largely descriptive account of the inventive role played by his subject in powder-making technology. The author's claims for the strategic role played by Lammot in making the firm the leading producer in United States are perhaps exaggerated, and would need to be counter-balanced by a study of the senior partner, Henry du Pont.

The scholarship of Chandler and others tends to emphasize Du Pont's contribution to general management. In their highly detailed study of the company's research and development, HOUNSHELL and SMITH identify the roles of R&D and internal growth in Du Pont's development up to 1980. The book's two main themes are the tension between centralization and decentralization of R&D in the company and the long-term impact of the phenomenal success of a single product – nylon – on Du Pont's subsequent approach to R&D. The denseness of the text makes this a hard but rewarding read: a work to be consulted and sampled rather than read straight through.

The family histories are generally less satisfactory than the business histories. COLBY offers a radical critique of the family's political interventions and employee relations based largely on published sources and interviews. The author was debarred from all post-1933 manuscripts at the Hagley Museum and Library – which limits the depth of coverage. MERRILL offers an interesting biography of Samuel Francis Du Pont (1803–65), the admiral, who was chairman of the Blockade Board, which mapped out the strategy for the Union's naval effort in the Civil War, and who also commanded the South Atlantic Blockading Squadron. The account is largely descriptive and its value is reduced by the author's failure to supply footnote references to the sources which he consulted at the Hagley Museum. WALL's study of Alfred I. du Pont (1864–1935) makes full use of the family papers to provide a rounded biography which weaves together the different strands of Alfred's life. It is readable but sometimes opinionated.

BURK is the most important study to date of the Du Ponts' interventions in national politics. He shows how the family tried in their business careers to centralize and magnify their own power while they struggled to keep their opponents – rival firms, labour unions and political adversaries – decentralized, fragmented and weak. The family therefore advocated the "corporate" state and resisted bitterly but unsuccessfully the New Deal broker state. This convincing and well-documented thesis offers an exemplary study in 20th-century political economy.

GEOFFREY CHANNON

See also Business History entries

E

Early Exploration of North America

Axtell, James, *Beyond 1492: Encounters in Colonial North America*, New York: Oxford University Press, 1992

Briceland, Alan Vance, *Westward from Virginia: The Exploration of the Virginia-Carolina Frontier, 1650–1710*, Charlottesville: University Press of Virginia, 1987

Hoffman, Paul E., *A New Andalucia and a Way to the Orient: The American Southeast During the Sixteenth Century*, Baton Rouge: Louisiana State University Press, 1990

Hudson, Charles, *The Juan Pardo Expeditions: Exploration of the Carolinas and Tennessee, 1566–1568*, Washington, DC: Smithsonian Institution Press, 1990

Ingstad, Helge, *Westward to Vinland: The Discovery of Pre-Columbian Norse House-Sites in North America*, translated by Erik J. Friis, New York: St. Martin's Press, and London: Cape, 1969

Simmons, Marc, *The Last Conquistador: Juan de Oñate and the Settling of the Far Southwest*, Norman: University of Oklahoma Press, 1991

Steele, Ian K., *Warpaths: Invasions of North America*, New York: Oxford University Press, 1994

Trudel, Marcel, *The Beginnings of New France, 1524–1663*, translated by Patricia Claxton, Toronto: McClelland and Stewart, 1973

The quincentenary of Christopher Columbus's discovery of America renewed popular and scholarly interest in the exploration of North America. Formerly historians had cast explorers as fearless stars in an epic drama of discovery, but scholars have begun more recently to consider exploration as an encounter between Europeans and Native Americans. The approach has stripped the age of discovery of much of its mythic bravado, and instead revealed exploration to be a mutual process of conflict, accommodation, and change whereby Europeans and Indians created a "New World."

The Norse made the first verifiable exploration of North America around the 10th century AD. After years of searching, INGSTAD located the remains of a Viking settlement at Lance aux Meadows, Newfoundland as well as several associated sites scattered along the Canadian coast that indicate other Norse attempts to explore and settle the region. Native hostility and the collapse of the nearby Greenland colony hastened the Norse departure from North America. At the time of its publication, Ingstad's combination of historical and archaeological research marked it as a pathbreaking study of the first documented European exploration of North America.

After Columbus's voyage of 1492 European attention focused on the New World, and both Steele and Hoffman discuss the initial post-Columbus exploration of North America. STEELE focuses on the military aspects of exploration. From the outset he considers exploration as an invasion, and uses examples from Spanish Florida, French Canada, and English Jamestown and Plymouth to show the brutal conflicts that erupted when Indians challenged European expansion. According to Steele, exploration was far from the triumphant success that the mythmakers and apologists of later generations had lauded. HOFFMAN concurs, for he argues that while each explorer contributed information to the growing body of European knowledge of North America, much of that information was inaccurate. Thus, in the 1520s when Spanish sailors reported the existence of a fabulously wealthy Indian civilization in the southeast called Chicora, each of the European powers scrambled to explore the continent and find it. From ill-fated Spanish settlements on the South Carolina coast to the English debacle at Roanoke, the search for a land that did not exist proved fatal to early colonial ambitions.

The Spanish first undertook a comprehensive exploration of North America, and Hudson and Simmons chronicle two of the more inauspicious efforts to follow up earlier explorations. HUDSON examines two expeditions led by Juan Pardo, who was charged with finding a path to Mexico through the southeastern interior first visited by Hernando de Soto some twenty years earlier. Hudson brings together archaeology, anthropology, and history to show the myriad implications of exploration and contact, from the introduction of epidemic diseases to the collapse of Native American societies. SIMMONS argues that Juan de Oñate was the last conquistador. Armed with the same feudal privileges and prerogatives as his predecessors Cortés and Pizarro, Oñate departed from Mexico City in 1598 to explore and settle the American southwest. Like Pardo, Oñate never found the wealth he sought, but the power of myth held firm in his mind. In 1601 he set out to find the legendary golden city of Quivira that Hernando de Coronado had reported during his trek through the region some years earlier. Oñate reached the grassy plains of Kansas before his men convinced him that Quivira, like Chicora, did not exist.

In 1524 Giovanni da Verrazano sailed under the fleur de lys to find a passage to the Orient. While the Florentine navigator found no such passage, Hoffman argues that his inaccurate charts nonetheless provided the first comprehensive look at the eastern seaboard. TRUDEL contends that the initial failures and subsequent successes of the Frenchmen who followed Verrazano were linked to domestic politics, international affairs, and the uncertain support of the Iroquois. Between 1534 and 1542 Jacques Cartier explored the Gulf of St. Lawrence, but a permanent settlement was not built until Samuel de Champlain founded Quebec in 1608. Much like Spain, France's initial exploration of North America was marred by failed settlements and disappointed dreams. However, unlike the Spanish who struck no gold and founded only a handful of settlements, the French harvested a wealth of furs from the North American interior and this trade spurred a more systematic exploration of the continent.

While Oñate searched in vain for Quivira and Champlain oversaw the construction of Quebec, the English recovered from the Roanoke disaster and explored Virginia in search of either gold or a passage to India. They found neither, but Jamestown served as a center of early English exploration of North America. BRICELAND scrutinized the diaries of several English explorers who fanned throughout the eastern half of the continent, and he found that their achievements had been overstated because few traveled as far and wide as previously thought. Briceland further concludes that the Occanneechee trail, which several explorers had touted as a road to the interior, did not even exist at the time they made their explorations. Thomas Batts and Robert Fallam, however, did cross the Appalachian mountains, but they, like so many other explorers, found neither the legendary gold mines nor the South Sea.

More than any other scholar, AXTELL has been at the forefront of reinterpreting the legacy of exploration and contact in North America. In a collection of his essays he considers exploration as an evolving process. He views exploration from the perspectives of the Indians and Europeans and offers insightful interpretations of the intercultural contact that followed exploration. Furthermore, Axtell assesses current understanding of the age of exploration, and he reveals numerous errors in the treatment of the period in American college textbooks. Factual errors and historical sleight of hand, he argues, have created a biased account of exploration which has sacrificed the richness and complexity of the period to the sacred cow of Anglo-American exceptionalism.

Historians like Hudson, Simmons, Hoffman and Briceland have begun to correct the deficiencies that Axtell noted. Their sophisticated and imaginative interpretations of the era reflect a growing awareness that exploration was a long and arduous process that built upon the combined achievements of explorers and Native Americans.

JAMES TAYLOR CARSON

Early National Period, 1789–1815: General

Appleby, Joyce, *Capitalism and a New Social Order: The Republican Vision of the 1790s*, New York: New York University Press, 1984

Banning, Lance, *The Jeffersonian Persuasion: Evolution of a Party Ideology*, Ithaca, NY: Cornell University Press, 1978

Bowers, Claude G., *Jefferson and Hamilton: The Struggle for Democracy in America*, Boston: Houghton Mifflin, 1925

Buel, Richard, Jr., *Securing the Revolution: Ideology in American Politics, 1789–1815*, Ithaca, NY: Cornell University Press, 1972

Cott, Nancy F., *The Bonds of Womanhood: "Woman's Sphere" in New England, 1780–1835*, New Haven and London: Yale University Press, 1977

Cunliffe, Marcus, *The Nation Takes Shape, 1789–1837*, Chicago: University of Chicago Press, 1959

Gray, Ralph D. and Michael A. Morrison (editors), *New Perspectives on the Early Republic: Essays from the Journal of the Early Republic, 1981–1991*, Urbana: University of Illinois Press, 1994

Krout, John Allen and Dixon Ryan Fox, *The Completion of Independence, 1790–1830*, New York: Macmillan, 1944

Larkin, Jack, *The Reshaping of Everyday Life, 1790–1840*, New York: Harper, 1988

Lewis, Jan, *The Pursuit of Happiness: Family and Values in Jefferson's Virginia*, Cambridge and New York: Cambridge University Press, 1983

Lipset, Seymour Martin, *The First New Nation: The United States in Historical and Comparative Perspective*, New York: Basic Books, 1963; London: Heinemann, 1964

Matthews, Jean V., *Towards a New Society: American Thought and Culture, 1800–1830*, Boston: Twayne, 1990

Miller, Perry, *The Life of the Mind in America: From the Revolution to the Civil War*, New York: Harcourt Brace, 1965; London: Gollancz, 1966

Nye, Russel B., *The Cultural Life of the New Nation, 1776–1830*, New York: Harper, and London: Hamish Hamilton, 1960

Watts, Steven, *The Republic Reborn: War and the Making of Liberal America, 1790–1820*, Baltimore: Johns Hopkins University Press, 1987

Wiebe, Robert H., *The Opening of American Society: From the Adoption of the Constitution to the Eve of Disunion*, New York: Knopf, 1984

Wood, Gordon S., *The Radicalism of the American Revolution*, New York: Knopf, 1992

Young, Alfred F. (editor), *Beyond the American Revolution: Explorations in the History of American Radicalism*, DeKalb: Northern Illinois University Press, 1993

For nearly three decades after World War II, the early republic seemed a historical backwater – either the period between the more exciting era of the Revolution and the age of Jackson or the period dominated by the lengthened shadow of Thomas Jefferson (and perhaps his rival Hamilton), a central exhibit in the role of big events (and even bigger great men). Over the past two decades, however, historians have revisited the period, seeing it once again as one where some of the central shifts in American history took place.

Early 20th-century "Progressive" historians made the early republic central to their vision of American development. BOWERS offers a lively expression of these views. He sees the 1790s as a battle between the forces of democracy and of aristocracy, symbolized by Jefferson and Hamilton respectively. Bowers does not emphasize the other major side of the progressive view, however – the Charles Beard theory that the Jeffersonians represented agricultural and the Federalists commercial and financial interests.

LIPSET offers one of the more provocative discussions coming out of the post-World War II breakdown of this Progressive synthesis. Like other scholars of the time, the sociologist Lipset considers values and institutions more important than economic interests. He focuses first on the way the period raised problems for political legitimacy and then on the formative influence of this revolutionary break upon a national character and style that would shape American institutions. Finally, the book compares America with the structure and experience of democratic politics in other Western nations. CUNLIFFE provides a brief introduction to the basic facts of the period's public life for the general reader. The book shows its age particularly in its discussion of culture, where, for example it focuses upon national character (a mid-20th century obsession) and completely ignores religion. By looking at such themes as the creation and consolidation of government, the pattern of foreign relations, the process of westward expansion, and the relationship between nationalism and sectionalism, over a period of half a century, it attempts to break free from the conventional division of the early republic into the Federalist 1790s, the Jeffersonian ascendancy, and the Era of Good Feelings.

The recovery of the early republic's importance began in the 1970s as historians inspired by work on republicanism in the Revolutionary period began to apply these concepts to the years after the Constitution. BUEL looks at public discussions about policy in the period 1789–1815, focusing primarily on the 1790s. For him, the important issue was neither democracy nor party, but ideology – the different views of post-Revolutionary leaders about the best way to help the new republic survive and flourish. This disagreement finally revolved around the degree to which the national government should respond to public pressure. Although these differences were apparent right from the start of the new government, the international upheaval created after 1794 by the French Revolution prevented compromise and escalated the quarrel. Only with the end of the War of 1812 would the question of "securing the republic" be finally resolved.

BANNING also highlights the importance of ideas, but he places the Jeffersonian Republicans (and by extension the entire politics of the early republic) more systematically within the tradition of republican ideology. He traces Jeffersonian ideas back to the 17th-century English Civil War and through the American Revolution, suggesting that the Jeffersonian Republicans saw Federalist policies as a conspiratorial attempt to reverse the Revolution and restore a British system of government. Like their ideological predecessors, the Jeffersonians focused on the dangers of growing executive power, the corruption of Congress and the public, and the repression of liberty. The turbulent 1790s added new issues to the Jeffersonian critique, but its core remained the same. Like Buel, Banning also sees Jeffersonian rule after 1801 as an expression, not a repudiation, of earlier values.

APPLEBY provides the most sustained case against the "republican" interpretation of the period, by introducing into the debate the idea of liberalism – an ideology that emphasized people's freedom to do as they wished rather than the republican emphasis on the freedom to participate independently in government. Rather than seeing both political groups as operating within this earlier tradition, she argues that Federalists continued to adhere to these republican ideas while the Jeffersonians broke free from their limitations to imagine a bright future. These optimistic Americans, buoyed by the growth of commercial agriculture, envisioned a society of free and equal individuals progressing economically and participating fully in the political realm.

WATTS further expands this theme of a transition from republicanism to liberalism by tying it even more closely to the rise of capitalism. For Watts, this development was not the bold breakthrough portrayed by Appleby. Rather, Americans felt anxious and ambivalent about these changes, which in any case emerged more as an extension of their older views than a repudiation of them. Like Buel and Banning, Watts portrays the end of the War of 1812 as a turning point. But he suggests that the war itself is important primarily because the common idea of war as a movement to restore civic commitment enabled people to accept liberal values without guilt. The book consists largely of a series of polished biographical sketches of Jeffersonian Republicans, an approach that perhaps allows too easy a linkage between personal neuroses and social tensions, but also provides powerful immediacy and drama.

WOOD provides the fullest and most sophisticated statement of this theme of the early republican years as a transition. Like Watts, he sees an entire way of life in transformation, not just politics. The book begins with a colonial past portrayed as highly monarchical in its social outlook and progresses through a Revolution inspired by republican values. Virtually by the time the war ended, however, these ideals of enlightenment, natural social harmony, and self-denying civic activity began to give way. Americans below the level of the Revolutionary elites began to demand the right to participate in government and to seek their own economic interests. The result was a "middle-class order" where labor, equality, and public opinion were celebrated, and the individual pursuit of self-interest became the means of holding society together. The Revolution therefore was radical because it destroyed the traditional concept of aristocratic rule and made common people the focus of thinking about society.

A challenging collection of essays, edited by YOUNG, suggests that the Revolution was not radical enough. Focusing on the marginalized Americans that Wood and others tend to slight in their larger vision of the period, the authors look at people on the margins of both the old and the new order, African Americans, women, and small farmers (and, although they are not discussed in detail, Indians). For these people, the ideals of liberty and equality held out by the Revolution intertwined with their earlier traditions to inspire resistance to their subordinate position. Young himself concludes by arguing that these groups would seldom experience the fulfillment of the Revolutionary promise, but their diverse reactions helped shape the revolutionary settlement by forcing elite Americans to take notice of their concerns.

A less critical, but still enlightening, reading of many of the period's changes is presented in GRAY and MORRISON, a collection of essays from the *Journal of the Early Republic*, the leading scholarly journal of the era. Although many of the pieces focus on the years after 1815, others offer specific studies of issues like labor, literature, internal improvements, and changing views of society and its leaders that play important roles in larger changes. Wood's opening article presents a particularly valuable account of the ways historians have viewed the period.

WIEBE offers an alternative reading of the early republic in a difficult but ultimately rewarding argument that extends from the Revolution to the Civil War. Rather than the now conventional categories of republicanism and liberalism, the book focuses on the power of national leaders (whom he calls the gentry) and the way in which their position declined in the midst of both attempts to reconstruct society on a comprehensive basis and also of expanding opportunities for a wide range of Americans. Wiebe seems to argue that the most important transition in the years after the Revolution took place in the Jacksonian era.

NYE provides a traditional cultural history of the early republic that is encyclopedic rather than sharply interpretive. He suggests that the period from the Revolution to the Age of Jackson represents an extended transition between the Enlightenment and Romanticism. Covering a wide range of topics, Nye looks at science, nationalism, social activities, education, religion, literature, art, and architecture. MATTHEWS presents a more recent overview of the period's cultural history that draws upon newer studies of the intellectual context of political life. Like Nye, she portrays a complex cultural transition in the period but she sees republican ideals as intertwined with neoclassical literary style and with Enlightenment religion and science. She also presents democracy and Evangelical Christianity as part of the Romantic view. Matthews looks at the traditional cultural history topics examined in Nye but gives attention also to strains within republican values and to changing thinking about race and gender. Like Wiebe, she sees the 1820s (not the 1790s) as the key period of transition.

MILLER is the last, unfinished work of one of the century's greatest intellectual historians. Conceived as a comprehensive interpretation of the period from the Revolution to the Civil War, Miller completed only the lengthy sections on religion and the law, and the start of a discussion of science, before his death in 1963. Revivalistic religion, Miller argues, provides the central theme in America during this period. His discussion of legal ideas looks primarily at the attempts to pull together an American view of the law and the increasing cultural significance of lawyers. Overall, Miller seems to be emphasizing a continuing battle between the heart and the head, between emotions and freedom on the one hand and rationality and control on the other.

COTT provides perspective on the period's changing gender roles. Building upon documents written by women as much as attempts to define their place theoretically or morally, Cott presents a rich picture of a growing distinction between home and the world, rooted largely in the increasing location of male work outside the household. Women gained a new significance in this transformed domestic setting, taking on the responsibility to anchor society through the home. As the result of this new ideal of domesticity, women gained new opportunity for education and religious leadership and increasingly valued friendship among themselves. Although Cott's work looks only at New England, its themes have wide applicability to middle- and upper-class Americans elsewhere. Like Cott, LEWIS examines a particular region (in this case Virginia), but her view of changing cultural and emotional ideals provides a similarly broad perspective on early republican culture. Her study of the new centrality of family and home stresses the importance of sentimental (often evangelical) religion and republican values as well as ideas about domesticity. The increasing importance of private life for both men and women helped to create a world that emphasized emotions, personal expression, and individualism.

KROUT and FOX provide an old-fashioned social history based on anecdote and example rather than theory and counting. This is a vast and sprawling but also panoramic and vivid book. Looking at different geographical settings, occupations, and activities, the book covers important areas that often get squeezed out of syntheses built around political, economic, or cultural changes. Its substantial bibliography offers a dated but still useful guide to materials on the more private and social side of life. LARKIN is a more recent look at many of these same issues that is more focused on everyday activities. Bringing together a substantial but scattered and technical literature on material culture into a readable synthesis, Larkin examines a wide range of activities from the architecture of houses to music and cleanliness. He suggests that, despite many continuities, Americans created "a sweeping reformation of social ways" during the early republic – becoming less rough, less dirty, and more disciplined, but also more socially divided.

STEVEN C. BULLOCK

Economic Growth

Baumol, William J., Sue Anne Batey Blackman, and Edward Wolff, *Productivity and American Leadership: The Long View*, Cambridge: Massachusetts Institute of Technology Press, 1989

David, Paul A., "The Growth of Real Product in the United States Before 1840: New Evidence, Controlled Conjectures", *Journal of Economic History*, 27(2), 1967

Denison, Edward F., *Accounting for United States Economic Growth, 1929–1969*, Washington, DC: Brookings Institution, 1974

Engerman, Stanley L. and Robert E. Gallman, "U.S. Economic Growth, 1783–1860," *Research in Economic History*, 8, edited by Paul Uselding, 1982

Kendrick, John W., *Productivity Trends in the United States*, Princeton: Princeton University Press, 1961

Weiss, Thomas, "U.S. Labor Force Estimates and Economic Growth, 1800–1860," in *American Economic Growth and Standards of Living Before the Civil War*, edited by Robert E. Gallman and John Joseph Wallis, Chicago: University of Chicago Press, 1992

Williamson, Jeffrey G. and Peter H. Lindert, *American Inequality: A Macroeconomic History*, New York: Academic Press, 1980

Economic growth, that is the increase in a nation's wealth usually measured in per capita national income, has exercised the scholarly efforts of economic historians for many decades. A great deal of research has concentrated on the roots of American economic growth in the antebellum period. During the 1950s and 1960s some historians searched for a break or discontinuity in the growth rate which could be described as a "take off" or an industrial revolution. Others were convinced that either a gradual acceleration or long cycles of growth was the most likely explanation of American economic progress.

In a pioneering article, DAVID claimed that the onset of modern economic growth in the first half of the 19th century was not preceded by a decisive break in the long run trend. David's calculations pointed to a consistent and steady growth between 1790 and 1860. However, there was also strong evidence of a structural transformation in the economy in the form of a shift of labour into non-farm occupations where productivity was relatively high. These structural changes were regionally important but they were not felt throughout the economy until after the Civil War. Although this remains an authoritative study, problems, for example with the quality of the data, have not left it immune from challenge. ENGERMAN and GALLMAN address some of the most crucial issues in the debate on economic growth in the early 19th century. For example, they recognise that the different regions are so important that one has to consider whether one or more separate economies should be analysed. They opt for the national picture, but they also highlight the geographic composition of the economy as one of the key factors in the structural change which took place in the antebellum economy. In this crisply written essay, Engerman and Gallman find that the rate of economic growth was not only high between 1783 and 1860, it was also increasing. A full explanation for this pattern of growth, however, remains elusive, partly because of the difficulty in weighting the various social and economic forces which contributed to the expansion and partly because of data imperfections, especially in the earlier years of the study.

The search continues for better quality data in order to explain and to quantify the beginning of economic and social modernisation in America, and recently WEISS has provided a telling contribution to the debate. Not only are his income estimates the most robust of those available, he also worked with two alternative concepts of national product, one of which can be used to make international comparisons while the other includes economic activities, such as the value of home manufacture, which are usually excluded. Examining the period 1800–60, he finds that while growth was most rapid in the two decades before the Civil War, during the years 1800–40 per capita income was much higher than was previously supposed. The antebellum economy saw more labour being absorbed by the most highly productive parts of the economy, industry and commerce, for example, and also more of the capital stock moving to areas of relatively high productivity. Weiss's findings will no doubt lead to a renewed interest in the roots of economic growth in the 18th century.

The rate at which an economy generates wealth is important, but so is the distribution of that wealth. WILLIAMSON and LINDERT, in a provocative and challenging volume, grapple with the issue of inequality. One of the strengths of this book is that it tackles fully the problems of definition and measurement before posing key questions such as how does one account for inequality within and between regions? The 19th century was a time of great wealth inequalities despite the abundance of natural resources and the widespread view that the United States was a country where the poor could prosper. On the other hand, the four decades after 1929 saw a considerable equalisation of wealth and income. Williamson and Lindert find no simple explanations for these long-run trends, but suggest that movements in the supply of labour and in the rate of technological progress are among the most likely causes. Some readers may find that the quantification of variables such as technology, demography and capital accumulation, together with the construction of general equilibrium models adds up to an intimidating text. It is possible, however, even for readers who are unhappy with graphs and equations to extract a great deal of interesting information on inequality over the long period from colonial times until the 1970s.

BAUMOL et al. are rightly convinced that nothing is as important for economic welfare as the rate of productivity growth. Moreover, as even small disadvantages in productivity can have a pronounced effect over a long period, the authors take a more historical view in their analysis than do most economists. Indeed, this book gives the clear message that the examination of a short period can lead to a serious misunderstanding of productivity movements and also to policy error. The authors explain how productivity is measured, what are its determinants and why it is so crucial, and they cite many historical examples. One finding which is of interest to modern historians is that, contrary to popular belief, there is no evidence that U.S. productivity fell below its historical trend between 1965 and 1980. The book also raises a number of related analytical issues in a way which historians will welcome.

Those who wish to pursue the study of productivity further can do so by consulting KENDRICK. This detailed, scholarly study is a rich source of information on the national economy and also on individual industries from the late 19th century until the 1950s. DENISON, too, has produced a detailed reference work which the modern historian cannot ignore. In it annual growth estimates are provided for the period 1947–69 and the years 1929, 1940 and 1941. Denison's work is particularly imaginative in its analysis of the productivity effects of rising educational levels and also in its estimates of potential output, which is the gap between actual output and what the economy could have produced. Potential output is a particularly useful concept in calculating the effect of depressions.

PETER FEARON

See also Business Cycle; Economic History

Economic History: General

Atack, Jeremy and Peter Passell, *A New Economic View of American History: From Colonial Times to 1940*, New York: Norton, 1994

Callender, Guy S., *Selections from the Economic History of the United States, 1765–1865*, Boston: Ginn, 1909

Coats, A.W. and Ross M. Robertson (editors), *Essays in American Economic History*, New York: Barnes and Noble, and London: Arnold, 1969

Conference on Research in Income and Wealth, *Trends in the American Economy in the 19th Century*, Princeton: Princeton University Press, 1960

Davis, Lance E. and others, *American Economic Growth: An Economist's History of the United States*, New York: Harper, 1972

Dillard, Dudley, *Economic Development of the North Atlantic Community: A Historical Introduction to Modern Economics*, Englewood Cliffs, NJ: Prentice Hall, 1967

The Economic History of the United States (projected vols. 1. and 10 never published)

2. Nettels, Curtis P., *The Emergence of a National Economy, 1775–1815*, New York, Holt Rinehart, 1962

3. Gates, Paul W., *The Farmer's Age: Agriculture, 1815–1860*, New York: Holt Rinehart, 1960

4. Taylor, George Rogers, *The Transportation Revolution, 1815–1860*, New York: Rinehart, 1951

5. Shannon, Fred A., *The Farmer's Last Frontier: Agriculture, 1860–1897*, New York: Farrar and Rinehart, 1945

6. Kirkland, Edward C., *Industry Comes of Age: Business, Labor, and Public Policy, 1860–1897*, New York: Holt Rinehart, 1961

7. Faulkner, Harold U., *The Decline of Laissez Faire, 1897–1917*, New York: Holt Rinehart, 1951

8. Soule, George Henry, *Prosperity Decade: From War to Depression, 1917–1929*, New York: Rinehart, and London: Pilot Press, 1947

9. Mitchell, Broadus, *Depression Decade: From New Era Through New Deal, 1929–1941*, New York: Rinehart, 1947

Faulkner, Harold U., *American Economic History*, New York: Harper, 1924, 9th edition, with Harry N. Scheiber and Harold G. Vatter, 1976

Kilby, Peter (editor), *Quantity and Quiddity: Essays in US Economic History*, Middletown, CT: Wesleyan University Press, 1987

Kirkland, Edward C., *A History of American Economic Life*, New York: Crofts, 1932; 4th edition, New York: Appleton Century Crofts, 1969

Nash, Gerald D., *Issues in American Economic History*, Boston: Heath, 1964, 3rd edition, 1980

North, Douglass C., *The Economic Growth of the United States, 1790–1860*, Englewood Cliffs, NJ: Prentice Hall, 1961

Olson, James S. and Susan Wladaver-Morgan, *Dictionary of United States Economic History*, Westport, CT: Greenwood Press, 1992

Parker, William N., *Europe, America and the Wider World: Essays on the Economic History of Western Capitalism*, volume 2, Cambridge and New York: Cambridge University Press, 1991

Ratner, Sidney, James H. Soltow, and Richard Sylla, *The Evolution of the American Economy: Growth, Welfare and Decision Making*, New York: Basic Books, 1979; 2nd edition, New York: Macmillan, 1993

Robertson, Ross M., *History of the American Economy*, New York: Harcourt Brace, 1955; 4th edition, with Gary M. Walton, 1979; 6th edition, rewritten by Gary M. Walton and Hugh Rockoff, San Diego: Harcourt Brace, 1990

Temin, Peter, *Causal Factors in American Economic Growth in the 19th Century*, London: Macmillan, 1975

Weiss, Thomas and Donald Schaefer, *American Economic Development in Historical Perspective*, Stanford, CA: Stanford University Press, 1994

Economic history developed much later as a separate discipline in the United States than in many European countries. Although the American Economic Association and the American Historical Association both date from the 1880s, the Economic History Association was not founded until 1940. Two major historians whose work made important contributions to the study of economic history, Frederick Jackson Turner and Charles A. Beard, will not be considered in this survey, partly because their work is discussed elsewhere in this Guide, but also because they cannot be regarded, and would not have regarded themselves, as economic historians. Similarly, business histories are not included here.

The writer with the best claim to be regarded as the first American economic historian is CALLENDER. Although his book is primarily a collection of source materials (useful in themselves), Callender's importance lies in the short introductions to each section, which in a quite remarkable way identify the questions to be asked, and in effect set the agenda for succeeding generations. His main Introduction provides a working definition that, consciously or unconsciously, writers in recent decades have themselves adopted: "The economic historian ought to apply the science of economics to past conditions and past problems in exactly the same way that it is ordinarily applied to current conditions and current problems." Callender's immediate impact was slight and early comprehensive economic histories, many of them excellent works on their own terms, were generally written in descriptive style by historians who were not also economists. By the 1940s university economics departments were interesting themselves in economic history, and trained economists increasingly made contributions to the subject.

The advent of the computer brought increased emphasis on quantification, with the rise of the so-called "new" economic history, or "Cliometrics", or econometric history. This may be dated from the 1957 Williamstown CONFERENCE on Research in Income and Wealth and the publication of *Trends in the American Economy* with William Parker as Conference Editor. In its simplest form, "new" economic history insisted on the use of accurate statistics wherever available, and the rigorous application of economic theory in their analysis; in its more advanced form, it applied econometric interpretation to the data, producing texts with algebraic equations which were troublesome to the non-mathematical reader.

The works discussed here have been chosen to represent the main phases in the development of the subject. One of the earliest descriptive "textbooks" was FAULKNER, still being published in its 8th edition in 1960, and subsequently rewritten in a 9th edition by two like-minded historians Scheiber and Vatter and published in 1976. The eight published volumes in *The Economic History of the United States*, appearing at dates between 1945 and 1962, contain some of the best examples of "narrative" economic history, including such classics as Curtis P. Nettels's *The Emergence of a National Economy, 1775–1815*, Paul W. Gates's *The Farmer's Age: Agriculture, 1815–1860* and Fred A. Shannon's *The Farmer's Last Frontier: Agriculture, 1860–1897*. The other authors are George Rogers Taylor, Edward C. Kirkland, George Henry Soule, Harold U. Faulkner, and Broadus Mitchell.

Of the many "textbooks" by single authors published during this phase, KIRKLAND is comprehensive and well balanced in outlook. While he is most at home in dealing with transport and industry (his volume in the Rinehart series was entitled *Industry Comes of Age: Business, Labor and Public Policy, 1860–1897*), Kirkland's expertise, and not least his writing skill, are evident in every section of the book. ROBERTSON was a professional economist who turned to academic work in economic history. His background with the Federal Reserve Bank of St. Louis shows in the strength of his sections on monetary history. Gary WALTON, the editor of the posthumous fourth edition, pays tribute to the detailed knowledge and interpretive understanding he derived from the book and above all to its "clarity and readability". NORTH, with Robert Fogel one of the two recipients of the Nobel Prize in Economic History, places strong emphasis on the significance of foreign trade in early American economic development. This book caused a major revision in the economic history of the antebellum period.

A marked trend to multi-authored works is well exemplified by the recent second edition of RATNER, SOLTOW and SYLLA, the work of three authors who combine expertise over a very wide range of subject matter. Starting with a long section on the colonial period, the authors bring the story right up to date with a final chapter on "Deficits, Debts and Defaults, 1980–1992". Several works since the 1960s have specifically set out to incorporate the findings of "new economic history" into their texts. The volume by DAVIS *et al.* (most of the collaborators themselves being practitioners) is a very usable textbook without any problems for the non-mathematical reader. Recently ATACK and PASSELL rewrote an earlier work by Susan Lee and Passell with a similar purpose in mind. Another recent overview is provided by WEISS and SCHAEFER.

TEMIN is the author of numerous works on specific aspects of American economic history, including his ingenious treatment of the Jacksonian economy and his analysis of the causes of the Great Depression. In this short 80-page general work in the Economic History Society's series *Studies in Economic and Social History*, he too seeks to appraise the main reinterpretations of the previous two decades: the measurement of growth, and the contributions of land abundance, technology, railroads, banking and, inevitably, slavery. The book

summarizes extremely complicated arguments without undue oversimplification and also provides a valuable reading list.

Among the various volumes of collected essays, COATS and ROBERTSON seek to present articles with especial emphasis on economic theory and quantitative method, with an introduction entitled "Aspects of Quantitative Research in Economic History" by Lance Davis, Jonathan T. Hughes and Stanley Reiter. In his volume of essays, NASH usefully juxtaposes differing views of the same topic: for example, land speculation (Gates v. Bogue); Jackson and the Second Bank (Schlesinger v. Hammond); and the effect of the Civil War on the economy (Cochran v. Salsbury). The 1980 edition has an entry on the "new" economic history (Fogel v. Redlich). A collection of essays in honour of Stanley Lebergott, KILBY is appropriately a collection of commissioned "new economic history" essays, with an extremely distinguished list of contributors including Paul David, Gavin Wright, Claudia Goldin, Thomas Weiss, Robert Gallman, Jeremy Atack and Lance Davis, and with a historiographical introduction by William Parker. In contrast OLSON and WLADAVER-MORGAN's Dictionary is a purely factual compilation, aiming to be a "ready reference of basic information". The listing includes persons, artefacts, events, legislation, and relevant political movements.

Most textbooks of American economic history are confined largely to the domestic economy, with the outside world considered only incidentally in such obvious contexts as foreign trade. DILLARD is an ambitious attempt to survey the economic development of western civilization from the late middle ages to the present, increasingly shifting its emphasis to North America in its later section (but regrettably neglecting Canada). It seeks to investigate the common features in economic life and to establish what generalizations can be made about economic behaviour, at the same time giving constant reminders of the different environmental, human, institutional and intellectual pre-conditions to be found.

Most of the chapters in the two volumes by PARKER are reprints of lectures, articles, and occasional papers from his long career. Unlike many American economic historians, the author is as familiar with European economic experience and literature as with American. The first volume deals largely with Europe, the second with the United States. The three main sections of volume 2 are: on the South, including seminal essays on the economics of slave plantations and on "Capitalism: Southern Style"; on the rural North (including "The True History of the Northern Farmer"); and on the industrialization of the North, with a long chapter on "The Industrial Civilization of the Midwest". The final three chapters and two "Annexes" are both a *tour d'horizon* and a *tour de force* in their survey and analysis of the economic development of the western world. Parker incorporates quantitative precision and analytical rigour enough to satisfy the most fastidious of cliometricians, but does so with a wealth of literary references, citations and allusions that betray his early beginnings as a student of literature. Parker's two volumes represent American scholarship at its very finest.

JIM POTTER

See also Business History entries; Economic Growth; Financial History entries; Manufacturing Industry entries

Economic Thought

Barber, William J. (editor), *Breaking the Academic Mould: Economists and American Higher Learning in the Nineteenth Century*, Middletown, CT: Wesleyan University Press, 1988

Conkin, Paul Keith, *Prophets of Prosperity: America's First Political Economists*, Bloomington: Indiana University Press, 1980

Dorfman, Joseph, *The Economic Mind in American Civilization*, 5 vols., New York: Viking, 1946–59

Fine, Sidney, *Laissez Faire and the General-Welfare State: A Study of Conflict in American Thought, 1865–1901*, Ann Arbor: University of Michigan Press, 1956

Furner, Mary O., *Advocacy and Objectivity: A Crisis in the Professionalization of American Social Science, 1865–1905*, Lexington: University Press of Kentucky, 1975

Gruchy, Allan G., *Modern Economic Thought: The American Contribution*, New York: Prentice Hall, 1947

Ross, Dorothy, *The Origins of American Social Science*, Cambridge and New York: Cambridge University Press, 1991

Sobel, Robert, *The Worldly Economists*, New York: Free Press, 1980

Stoneman, William E., *A History of the Economic Analysis of the Great Depression in America*, New York: Garland, 1979

DORFMAN remains, without doubt, the most scholarly, exhaustive and judicious history of American economic thought. The work contains a great deal of detailed information about major economists, covering their careers and characters as well as their major contributions to economics. In addition to looking at specific writers, the author lucidly highlights the dominant trends in the discipline's development, showing how these trends were the product, in part, of wider political, social and economic forces. He also examines how a broader public viewed economic issues, and analyzes sermons, political rhetoric and philosophical treatises as well as economic texts. Inevitably, even a work on this scale is not comprehensive. Its coverage of particular periods is uneven: for instance, the single volume on the five decades between 1865 and 1918 is far less thorough than the two volumes on the period 1918 to 1933. Regrettably, too, Dorfman's account ends with the start of the New Deal. Nevertheless, whatever its flaws, this is one of the great works of American intellectual history.

There are a large number of more specialized studies of economic thought. CONKIN discusses the development of economic science in the antebellum era, looking in detail at major writers including Henry Carey, John Taylor, George Tucker and Daniel Raymond. As well as describing their careers, Conkin incisively analyses their major ideas and theories. He makes little attempt to identify any common themes running through the work of these writers: indeed, he suggests that diversity was one of the defining characteristics of economic thought in the antebellum era. Although Conkin concedes that these writers failed to exert much influence either upon government policy or upon the subsequent development of economic thought, he argues that they were grappling with many of the same problems and dilemmas that trouble economic policymakers today.

Many historians have looked at the development of economics in the late 19th and early 20th centuries. FINE focuses on the fierce disagreements among the intellectual leaders of the Gilded Age concerning the government's proper economic role. This extremely ambitious book contains detailed examination of the ideas of a large number of theorists. It discusses how not only professional economists but other groups, including clerics, jurists, and political scientists, interpreted economic change and viewed government intervention. Published forty years ago, Fine's analysis remains consistently elegant, accurate and lucid. In her study of the evolution of American social science, ROSS examines how intellectual and social developments between the Civil War and the eve of the Great Depression helped to shape the distinctive character of American economic thought. The continuing strength of American exceptionalism, she suggests, made social scientists reluctant to acknowledge that economic, social and political changes were threatening American ideals of economic opportunity, democracy and social mobility. By adopting an essentially ahistorical methodology, economists and other social scientists were able to ignore the discomforting reality of economic and social change. Ross's narrative is dense and highly nuanced, and parts of the book are extremely difficult, but this is an impressive work, combining rigorous scholarship with sophisticated analysis.

Several studies focus on the growth in the professional status of economists during the late 19th century. The essays edited by BARBER also examine the professionalisation of economics in the decades after the Civil War. The essays describe how a number of universities established departments of economics, recognising the subject as a distinctive and important discipline rather than as a minor branch of theology or moral philosophy. The contributors also examine how the institutionalisation of economics was accompanied by debates about the discipline's character and about the importance of academic freedom. The latter issue is examined in greater detail by FURNER. She examines a series of cases in which conservative university authorities attempted to dismiss "radical" professors such as Richard Ely and Edward Bemis. In the long term, she argues, these incidents served to enhance academic freedom, and made university authorities more reluctant to discipline heretical members of staff. However, Furner also suggests that such incidents led economists themselves to act with greater restraint, and increasingly to focus on technical questions rather than controversial ethical issues.

Economic thought during the 20th century has predictably commanded much attention. GRUCHY looks closely at the economists, including Thorstein Veblen, John Maurice Clark and Wesley Mitchell, who challenged neoclassical orthodoxy in the first few decades of the century. The author suggests that, in attempting to re-shape existing methodology, these writers had a decisive impact on the subsequent development of economic thought. Gruchy's discussion of these economists' work is largely uncritical, and his assessment of their significance appears grossly exaggerated. But, despite its flaws, the book remains a valuable account of an important chapter in the history of American economics. STONEMAN highlights the critical impact of the Great Depression on economic thought in the United States. He argues that, in trying to explain the Depression, writers began to reject many of their old economic assumptions. In particular, he suggests that, although initially putting the blame on the sinister machinations of business leaders, economists increasingly began to accept that cyclical changes in demand and other impersonal economic forces were responsible for the nation's economic problems. SOBEL provides a superb account of the development of economic thought since World War II. He focuses on a number of outstanding economists, including J.K. Galbraith, Arthur E. Burns and Paul Samuelson. Sobel describes the character of these men, the dominant themes in their writings, and their influence over economic policy. After the war, he argues, economists increasingly occupied important positions within government, and, even if they proved unable to solve America's problems, they still enjoyed a high public profile and real political power.

PHILIP J. CULLIS

See also Intellectual History

Eddy, Mary Baker 1821–1910
Founder of Christian Science

Cather, Willa (ghostwriter) and Georgine Milmine, *The Life of Mary Baker G. Eddy*, New York: Doubleday Page, and London: Hodder and Stoughton, 1909; as *The Life of Mary Baker Eddy and the History of Christian Science*, edited by David Stouck, Lincoln: University of Nebraska Press, 1993

Parker, Gail Thain, *Mind Cure in New England: From The Civil War to World War I*. Hanover, NH: University Press of New England, 1973

Peel, Robert, *Mary Baker Eddy: The Years of Discovery*, New York: Holt Rinehart, and Boston: Christian Science Publishing Society, 1966

Peel, Robert, *Mary Baker Eddy: The Years of Trial*, New York: Holt Rinehart, 1971

Peel, Robert, *Mary Baker Eddy: The Years of Authority*, New York: Holt Rinehart, 1977

Powell, Lyman P., *Mary Baker Eddy: A Life Size Portrait*, New York: Macmillan, and London: Nisbet, 1930

Smaus, Jewel Spangler, *Mary Baker Eddy: The Golden Days*, Boston: Christian Science Publishing Society, 1966

Thomas, Robert David, *"With Bleeding Footsteps": Mary Baker Eddy's Path to Religious Leadership*, New York: Knopf, 1994

As founder and leader of the Church of Christ Scientist, Mary Baker Eddy has provided inspiration to generations of Christian Scientists, and is a notable leader among 19th-century American women. It is, therefore, unfortunate that historians and other scholars have largely overlooked Eddy as a topic of study. Despite the renewed interest in her that is evidenced by the 1993 reprint of Willa Cather's 1909 volume about her and Thomas's recently published biography, most books on Eddy seem dated, behind modern scholarship, and in need of revision. Consequently, readers interested in this religious leader and social reformer are likely to find limited materials about her.

Perhaps the earliest biography of Eddy was CATHER and MILMINE, which was first serialized in *McClure's Magazine*, of which Cather was the editor, before being published as a book in 1909. The work has been controversial since its first appearance. When initially published, the writing was attributed only to Milmine. Since that time, however, much of it has been identified as Cather's, causing today's publishers to add her name to the work. The picture of Eddy that the account offers is full and unapologetically honest, showing both what was positive and negative about the subject. The candidness of the volume, Cather's prose, and the excellent introduction written by David Stouck that was added to the 1993 reprint edition make it interesting and informative reading.

One of the leading publishers of works about Eddy is the Christian Science Publishing Company, associated with the church that she founded. POWELL is among the numerous biographies of Eddy which this press has produced. Rich with religious language and scriptural references, Powell provides a comprehensive re-telling of Eddy's childhood, the development of her religious beliefs, and the latter days of her life. But, while Powell's book is both informative and entertaining, its objectivity must be questioned. His biography is highly complimentary of Eddy, and, although Powell was not a Christian Scientist, the prologue of the book includes an endorsement from the Christian Science Board of Directors.

SMAUS provides a more objective, although less comprehensive, account based on a wider variety of sources. It focuses on Eddy's childhood and youth in an attempt to reconstruct the small-town New England experience that shaped Eddy's early life. Intended to be a popularly appealing book for young people rather than a scholarly work, Smaus's account paints a colorful picture of the childhood of a great 19th-century leader. Smaus engaged in seemingly exhaustive local research, and took up residence for two years in Bow, New Hampshire, where Eddy was born and spent her childhood years. There Smaus sought out local residents who harbored in their attics and closets documents pertaining to Eddy's family. Her research efforts resulted in the discovery of a wealth of documents and new information not previously known to exist. For that reason, Smaus's detailed footnotes would be of interest to even the most sophisticated researcher.

Of all the accounts of Eddy's life, Peel is by far the most comprehensive. His three volumes on Eddy, published at approximately five-year intervals, complement each other, producing a complete, detailed account. PEEL (1966) deals with Eddy's life up to the publication of her *Science and Health* in 1875, and gives particular attention to the development of Eddy's beliefs and the birth of Christian Science. PEEL (1971) covers the middle years of Eddy's career, a time Peel describes as Eddy's years of "trial," and he focuses on early challenges to Christian Science. PEEL (1977) covers the last twenty years of Eddy's life, the period he describes as her most productive. An in-depth study of Eddy's life and beliefs, Peel's account seems objective and well-researched, and will appeal to those who desire comprehensive knowledge. For the more casual reader, however, the detail may be overwhelming.

PARKER offers a perspective quite different from other authors. Her study is not a biography, but rather an examination of the ideas behind Christian Science healing and Eddy's role in their development. She confronts head on the lingering question of the originality of Eddy's beliefs and writings, and challenges the claims of Eddy's 19th-century colleagues Julius and Annetta Dresser, who said that Eddy essentially plagiarized the works of their religious teacher, Phineas P. Quimby. Parker's account is, on the whole, interesting, informative, and well balanced. She devotes one long chapter specifically to Eddy, but sections throughout the book relate her to the development of Christian Science beliefs about healing.

However, by far the most professional, scholarly and insightful work about Eddy is THOMAS, who deploys considerable expertise in both history and psychoanalysis in his recent ground-breaking biography. Although not a Christian Scientist, Thomas had remarkable access to the holdings of the Christian Science archives. Using materials stored there, he examines the social and psychological circumstances surrounding the emergence of Christian Science. Claiming that personal illness and deaths in her family prepared Eddy psychologically for the role of religious leader and healer, Thomas connects Eddy's career to her early years. Thus he describes a continuity of personal development in Eddy's life, linking her experiences to her religious beliefs, and giving credence to American writer Mark Twain's claim that Eddy was "the most interesting woman that ever lived."

EMILY WALKER COOK

Edison, Thomas A. 1847–1931

Inventor and entrepreneur

Conot, Robert, *A Streak of Luck*, New York: Seaview, 1979

Friedel, Robert and Paul Israel, with Bernard S. Finn, *Edison's Electric Light: Biography of an Invention*, New Brunswick, NJ: Rutgers University Press, 1986

Hughes, Thomas P., *Networks of Power: Electrification in Western Society, 1880–1930*, Baltimore: Johns Hopkins University Press, 1983

Josephson, Matthew, *Edison: A Biography*, New York: McGraw Hill, 1959; London: Eyre and Spottiswoode, 1961

Millard, Andre, *Edison and the Business of Innovation*, Baltimore: Johns Hopkins University Press, 1990

Passer, Harold C., *The Electrical Manufacturers, 1875–1900: A Study in Competition, Entrepreneurship, Technical Change, and Economic Growth*, Cambridge, MA: Harvard University Press, 1953

Wachhorst, Wyn, *Thomas Alva Edison: An American Myth*, Cambridge: Massachusetts Institute of Technology Press, 1981

The world's most famous inventor, and one of its most renowned individuals, Thomas Edison has inspired innumerable biographies since his rise to celebrity in the 1870s. But surprisingly few of these works penetrate the mythology that has long shrouded the "wizard of Menlo Park" by looking rigorously at the man, his methods, and his place in American industrial history. Fortunately, the hagiography that dominated for a century has given way in recent years to scholarship characterized by new research, new questions, and exciting new findings.

Most of Edison's early biographers rehashed apocryphal stories about a puckish boy who grew into a rough-hewn, quirky individualist with a superhuman gift for problem-solving. A few first-hand accounts by Edison assistants added little precision to our understanding of Edison's methods as a creator, manager, and promoter of technology. As WACHHORST points out in his fascinating study of Edison's evolving legend, the inventor's public image *du jour* – whether "wizard," "Professor," "Great Inventor," or "Great American" – bore little relationship to the course of Edison's career.

JOSEPHSON, working with papers at the Edison Laboratory at West Orange (run by the National Park Service), produced the first well-grounded, comprehensive biography of Edison in 1959. A solid first step toward debunking the myth that Edison spurned science, Josephson's book was reasonably balanced in its treatment of Edison's genius, promotionalism, and shortcomings, although subsequent research challenges many of its interpretations.

Two decades later, CONOT foraged in the growing mass of available Edison documents to produce a richly-detailed revisionist biography. Conveying the vast spectrum of Edison's endeavours – in telegraphy and telephony, mimeography and phonography, motion pictures, automobiles and railroads, cement and ore separation, and electric light, power, and storage batteries, and early electronics (the so-called "Edison effect") – Conot nevertheless seeks to puncture the Edison mystique by portraying him as "lusty, crusty, hard-driving, opportunistic and occasionally ruthless," an "ingenious" technician and promoter "but a bumbling engineer and businessman." This assessment has not been supported by the work of specialists in business and technology history.

Those who have focused on Edison's professional life – especially his unparalleled contributions to the development of electric light and power – have found a shrewder and more reasoned "engineer-entrepreneur," who adroitly combined technical and commercial expertise. In his still-valuable 1953 study, PASSER shows how Edison and the other pioneers of the electrical manufacturing industry developed commercially viable systems – in Edison's case, direct current isolated plants and central stations producing incandescent light and motor power. Edison founded a constellation of enterprises, some devoted to the development and control of his technology, others (including the predecessor to General Electric) to manufacturing key system components, still others for promoting electric utilities.

HUGHES, a leading historian of technology, elaborates the notion of Edison as a "system builder," and traces the evolution and diffusion of Edison's (and other leading) electrical systems across time and space. Hughes broadens the definition of electrical system to encompass economic, technical, geographical, social, and cultural components; and analyzes the social construction of these technological systems by contrasting the electrification of Chicago, London, and Berlin.

The Thomas A. Edison Papers Project at West Orange – an ambitious, on-going effort to process some 3.5 million pages of drawings, letters, notebooks, and other documents – has given rise to new, well-researched, monographs with fresh conclusions. Returning to the subject that originally intrigued Edison-watchers – how Edison invented – FRIEDEL and ISRAEL chronicle a single invention, Edison's incandescent light, to reveal more about this process. With the inclusion of dozens of sketches from Edison's notebooks, their book accords proper attention to the non-linear, visual nature of the inventor's thinking. Friedel and Israel also challenge the notion (emphasized by Passer, Hughes, and others) that Edison was driven in his electrical work first and foremost by a "system approach."

Along with Friedel and Israel, MILLARD helps to put to rest the misguided notion that Edison was a super-pragmatic "cut and try" tinkerer, a loner who thrived on flashes of brilliance. Rather, Edison assembled first-rate technicians, state-of-the-art equipment, and one of the best technical libraries in the industrialized world; and he worked intensely alongside machinists and model-builders in the "machine shop culture" of his West Orange Laboratory. By studying Edison's activities within that larger and better financed "invention factory" (rather than its predecessor at Menlo Park), Millard brings a new insight into Edison as a manager of innovation and manufacturing.

Rather than diminishing Edison's stature, the recent, more clear-eyed scholarship has given authenticity and perspective to his towering achievements. Hardly a lone "heroic" inventor, Edison brilliantly melded business and technology, and was a pivotal figure in the coming of modern, institutional research and development.

DAVID B. SICILIA

Education: General

Bailyn, Bernard, *Education in the Forming of American Society: Needs and Opportunities for Study*, Chapel Hill: University of North Carolina Press, 1960

Cremin, Lawrence A., *American Education*, 3 vols., New York: Harper, 1970–88

Cubberley, Ellwood P., *Public Education in the United States: A Study and Interpretation of American Educational History*, Boston: Houghton Mifflin, 1934

Katz, Michael B., *Reconstructing American Education*, Cambridge, MA: Harvard University Press, 1987

Perkinson, Henry J., *The Imperfect Panacea: American Faith in Education, 1865–1990*, 3rd edition, New York: McGraw Hill, 1991

Ravitch, Diane, *The Troubled Crusade: American Education, 1945–1980*, New York: Basic Books, 1983

Spring, Joel, *The American School, 1642–1993*, 3rd edition, New York: McGraw Hill, 1994

In 1960, BAILYN severely criticized the historiography of American education for its uncritical and narrow focus upon educators and institutions. He argued that educational historians unquestioningly trumpeted the democratic development of public schools and their supposed triumph over ignorance, privilege, and sectarianism. Academic historians had surrendered the field to professors of education who maintained a professional interest in convincing the American public of the achievements of their discipline. Bailyn called for a new approach to the history of American education that would place its development within an economic, political, and social context thus far absent from the field. He also encouraged historians to look beyond the schoolhouse for the sources of Americans' educational experience. In his own work on the colonial era, Bailyn noted that people received their educations from institutions other than the schools, especially from the family, church, and community.

The type of educational history that Bailyn laments is exemplified by CUBBERLEY who views the history of the public schools as a series of hard fought but invariably successful "battles" waged throughout American history by virtuous educators against their unenlightened opponents. These epic struggles include the "battle for tax support," the "battle to eliminate sectarianism," and the "battle to establish the American high school." Public schools, Cubberley argues, evolved out of Americans' desire for democratic institutions needed to sustain the republic. They were the nation's most effective tool for solving social problems, including the assimilation of immigrants into American society and juvenile delinquency.

CREMIN embraces the broader educational history espoused by Bailyn. His monumental three-volume work attempts to cover American education in its entirety by encompassing the varied means by which Americans have educated themselves. He argues that they have been confronted by numerous "configurations" of educational opportunities apart from schools that through time have included almanacs, bookstores, libraries, lyceums, magazines, mechanics' institutes, museums, newspapers, pamphlets, sermons, and television. Individuals interact with these "configurations" to create their own unique educational experiences. Schools played a socializing role by attempting to equip Americans with common values in the 19th century and by preparing them for societal change in the 20th. Conflicts over the goals of formal public education represent the competing ideological visions of various groups of individuals, for example those of evangelicals and modernists, in their efforts to construct an American national identity.

Some historians disagree with Cremin's unwieldy inclusion of virtually all social and cultural agents as educational institutions, and continue to focus on educators and schools. Among these is KATZ, who also rejects Cremin's analysis of the clashes over formal education as primarily ideological. Katz believes that historical disagreements over how and what is taught in American schools are rooted in social conflicts which have resulted from economic and political inequality. The author dismisses the traditional historical model that ties the development of public education to liberal democracy. Instead, Katz identifies the origins and growth of public schools with the expansion of capitalism and the formation of the working class. Political and economic elites allowed for the creation of public schools that would teach workers industrial discipline. These elites also sought to destroy the cultural diversity of immigrants through the imposition of Anglo-American values in order to win obeisance to their authority from otherwise resistant cultures. Scholastic oppression persists into the present because educators refuse to recognize the continuing authoritarian nature of their institutions which discriminate against the poor, ethnic and racial minorities, and females.

Katz and others have coalesced into a school of radical revisionists who unapologetically call upon historians to censure American education in an effort to help end what they believe is a legacy of inequality. The basic principles of revisionist historiography are synthesized in SPRING. He finds that public schools emerged in the antebellum period as an elitist means of governing society by unifying diverse cultural, ethnic, and linguistic groups through the creation of a common education centered upon capitalism, nationalism, and Protestantism. Unassimilated peoples, or the "dominated cultures" of African Americans, Asians, Hispanics, and Native Americans, have been historically segregated and provided with inferior educations in order to exploit them economically. The 20th century, Spring argues, witnessed the ascendancy of educational bureaucrats who attempted to shape the career choices of ever increasing numbers of students through differentiated curricula. Professional educators received the support of corporate and government elites who used the schools to serve their own purposes. In recent decades, federal involvement in public education, which previously concerned only state and local governments, has created a struggle over who should control the public schools. Racial and ethnic minorities, feminists, religious groups, and teachers have sought the support of the federal government in order to enhance their authority. Students, however, remain within an educational system that legitimizes social inequality through graded competition that stresses individual and not cooperative achievement.

Criticisms of education, however, have not come only from radical revisionists. Conservative historians have their own critique of the public schools. RAVITCH is representative of those who argue that the current national dissatisfaction with the schools results from the educational establishment's perpetual obsession with the problem of inequality at the expense of the pursuit of excellence. The author finds that Progressive-era educators abandoned the original goal of earlier proponents of public schools, who sought to better society by improving individuals, in favor of adjusting students to the existing social order. Concerns over Soviet advances in science in the 1950s led to a reaction against "progressive education" which critics blamed for a supposed decline in the quality of instruction that left American youth academically behind their Russian counterparts. Nevertheless, a "new progressivism" emerged during the mid-1960s and its adherents blamed the schools for racial and social inequities, but yet sought to use them to remedy historical injustices. Ravitch argues that the progressive tradition continues to influence public education and has moved its curriculum from an earlier focus on academic values, character, and standards to one that emphasizes utility, conformity, and accommodation.

PERKINSON disapproves of the politicization of educational history. He notes that public education served a social structure dominated by white middle-class men until television exposed inequalities which inspired women and various minorities to demand equal status. Disadvantaged groups instinctively turned to education as the means by which to accomplish this task because it is the "panacea" Americans have traditionally used in attempting to solve national problems. These include the preservation of republican government, the transformation of an agricultural society into an industrial nation, and the assimilation of immigrants. The habit of Americans (including their historians) of looking to public education for solutions to social difficulties stems from their misconception that schools are either the sole or primary transmitters of knowledge while ignoring family, media, peers, and other sources. The conflict between the old order and new interests eliminated the consensus that sustained middle class control of public education for over a century. These groups, however, have been unable to build a new consensus capable of finding a solution to the problem of inequality.

DAN R. FROST

See also Schools entries; Universities and Colleges entries

Edwards, Jonathan 1703–1758
Theologian, preacher and author

Cherry, Conrad, *The Theology of Jonathan Edwards: A Reappraisal*, New York: Doubleday, 1966; revised, Bloomington: Indiana University Press, 1990
Conforti, Joseph A., *Jonathan Edwards, Religious Tradition, and American Culture*, Chapel Hill: University of North Carolina Press, 1995
Delattre, Roland André, *Beauty and Sensibility in the Thought of Jonathan Edwards: An Essay in Aesthetics and Theological Ethics*, New Haven: Yale University Press, 1968
Fiering, Norman, *Jonathan Edwards's Moral Thought and Its British Context*, Chapel Hill: University of North Carolina Press, 1981
Guelzo, Allen C., *Edwards on the Will: A Century of American Theological Debate*, Middletown, CT: Wesleyan University Press, 1989
Holbrook, Clyde A., *Jonathan Edwards, the Valley and Nature: An Interpretive Essay*, Lewisburg, PA: Bucknell University Press, 1987
Lee, Sang Hyun, *The Philosophical Theology of Jonathan Edwards*, Princeton: Princeton University Press, 1988
McDermott, Gerald R., *One Holy and Happy Society: The Public Theology of Jonathan Edwards*, University Park: Pennsylvania State University Press, 1992
Miller, Perry, *Jonathan Edwards*, New York: Sloane, 1949
Smith, John E., *Jonathan Edwards: Puritan, Preacher, Philosopher*, London: Geoffrey Chapman, and Notre Dame, IN: University of Notre Dame Press, 1993
Stout, Harry S., *The New England Soul: Preaching and Religious Culture in Colonial New England*, New York: Oxford University Press, 1986
Tracy, Patricia J., *Jonathan Edwards, Pastor: Religion and Society in Eighteenth-Century Northampton*, New York: Hill and Wang, 1980

Regarded by many as the greatest American theologian, Jonathan Edwards has long attracted scholarly attention for his interpretation of Calvinist theology, his role in the revivals sometimes known in their entirety as the First Great Awakening, and his influence on later schools of American thought as diverse as New Divinity theology and transcendentalism. Modern scholarship on Edwards begins with MILLER. This intellectual biography cast an enduring image of Edwards as a hero who sought to reconcile elements of the Puritan inheritance like biblicism and an overwhelming sense of God's presence with parts of the new learning like Lockean empiricism and Newtonian science, which a young Edwards encountered at Yale College. Lockean influences directed Edwards's attention to the phenomenology of religious experience, which reveals in history successive insights into God's great design for humankind, including the work of redemption. Among the most influential ever propounded by an American academic, Miller's views have been criticized and, in some quarters, dismissed.

The major study of Edwards's Calvinism is CHERRY. Examining faith, this work shows that Edwards's deity was a covenanting God. Faith is an opportunity, offered in a covenant by God, for the union of the human heart with the glorious, transcendent ruler of the universe. Two works open a wonderful view of the language of ethics and aesthetics which Edwards used. Ranging far beyond Locke and Calvin, FIERING finds Edwards's sources and affinities in British and continental moral philosophers. This work asks how Christian is an ethics based on Edwards's standard of disinterested benevolence. DELATTRE extends Miller's insight that the faithful find God and the divine design beautiful. The divine nature and the divine work in history (the creation and governance of the world and the redemption of humankind) are relished by the faithful, who perceive their beauty with the aid of a sense of the heart. Reacting against a 20th-century "process theology" that slights God's transcendence and prior existence, LEE argues that Edwards mediated a theology based on a transcendent God and a theology based on a deity revealed in the events and structure of the world. Faith and the sense of the heart appear here in a religious habit that allows an organic integration of experience and fuller encounters with God.

After great successes in the 1730s and 1740s in starting individuals on the road to conversion in his revival preaching, Edwards debated the efficacy of such sermonizing with Charles Chauncy, a liberal Boston minister. STOUT shows that the two ministers were shoulder to shoulder in using the bible to support their positions, the Calvinist emphasizing God's work in religious affections formed in the revivals, and the liberal denouncing orgiastic enthusiasm in revivalistic excesses. This debate fired Edwards's literary imagination (in the creation of durable images and metaphors), but it also led him to philosophize about the nature of true religion (the holy affections). Despite his successes in revivals, Edwards was dismissed in 1750 by his Northampton congregation. TRACY explains the dismissal as resulting from a general rejection in New England of ministers' authority and from Edwards's personal and family background. Edwards's inspiring sermons sustained him in a congregation only temporarily in the absence of more developed preacherly skills and a general deference to ministers. One comment which Edwards made about the possibility that the millennium would occur in America has led many to view him as a kind of proto-American nationalist. McDERMOTT argues against this view by noting Edwards's beliefs in a global

millennium and in a public ethics demanding a charitable concern for the weak and the poor. Although Edwards was optimistic about God's providence, he was a pessimistic Jeremiah in his views of sinful America, where disinterested benevolence was rare.

One of the central theological issues for the 18th and the early 19th century was the role of the will in conversion. Disbelieving in the freedom of the will, Edwards and the New Divinity men saw individuals as incapable of initiating their own salvation. Indeed, even self-centered desire to be saved, according to Samuel Hopkins, leader of the New Divinity, was a sure sign of depravity, since true converts love God without regard for the self and any of its concerns. GUELZO shows that this view of the freedom of the will troubled moderate Calvinists, who sought to preserve the value of human striving for salvation. Only the "New Haven Theology," articulated by Timothy Dwight and Nathaniel William Taylor between the end of the 18th century and the middle of the 19th, replaced the Edwardsean view of the will. In addition to the freedom of the will, nature was a characteristic concern of American thinkers in the century after Edwards's death in 1758. HOLBROOK argues that Edwards, among the many American writers deeply affected by the beauty of nature, progressed from an immediate experience of Connecticut Valley landscapes, to a sense of God's hand at work in the order and harmony of nature, and to an expressive use of images and metaphors in theology.

SMITH revisits the classic themes of Edwardsean scholarship: Lockean empiricism, revivalism, the phenomenology of religious experience, the freedom of the will, the nature of virtue, and the idea of a sovereign God who works in the world as creator, sustainer, ruler, and redeemer of humankind. CONFORTI surveys the entire tradition of modern Edwards scholarship, pinpointing its origins in the theological persuasion of pro-Edwardseans like Joseph Haroutunian and H. Richard Niebuhr, and arguing that Edwards survived as a vibrant figure in popular culture in a way few of his 20th-century interpreters have recognized. All readers of Edwards benefit from the monumental Yale University Press edition of his writings, which began appearing in 1957.

JOHN SAILLANT

See also Colonial History: Religion; Great Awakening; Puritanism

Eisenhower, Dwight   1890–1969
Military commander and 34th President of the United States

Alexander, Charles C., *Holding the Line: The Eisenhower Era, 1952–1961*, Bloomington: Indiana University Press, 1975

Ambrose, Stephen E., *Eisenhower*, 2 vols., New York: Simon and Schuster, 1983–84; London: Allen and Unwin, 1984

Brendon, Piers, *Ike: His Life and Times*, New York: Harper, 1986; London: Secker and Warburg, 1987

Burk, Robert Frederick, *Dwight D. Eisenhower: Hero and Politician*, Boston: Twayne, 1986

Divine, Robert A., *Eisenhower and the Cold War*, New York: Oxford University Press, 1981

Greenstein, Fred I., *The Hidden-Hand Presidency: Eisenhower as Leader*, New York: Basic Books, 1982

Pach, Chester J., Jr. and Elmo Richardson, *The Presidency of Dwight D. Eisenhower*, Lawrence: University Press of Kansas, 1991

Parmet, Herbert S., *Eisenhower and the American Crusades*, New York: Macmillan, 1972

Pickett, William B., *Dwight David Eisenhower and American Power*, Wheeling, IL: Harlan Davidson, 1995

Dwight Eisenhower's career as Supreme Allied Commander in World War II and as President of the United States, 1953–61, marks him as one of the major figures of American history in the 20th century. Historians have judged his record as military leader favorably, with relatively minor reservations. The judgment of his political career has been more varied. Through the 1950s and 1960s, intellectuals derided Eisenhower as an inept president who accomplished almost nothing in domestic affairs, while in foreign affairs his allegedly weak leadership was held to have allowed his Secretary of State, John Foster Dulles, to pursue a dangerously confrontational course. Since the early 1970s, "revisionist" historians have argued that this portrayal of Eisenhower as weak and naive is a false caricature and that Eisenhower was in fact an intelligent, shrewd, effective and successful leader, both as military commander and as president.

AMBROSE provides the most complete account of the "revisionist" interpretation of Eisenhower. It is a lengthy two-volume biography, the first volume covering Eisenhower's early life, his military career and his campaign for president in 1952, while the second volume covers his presidency and his years in retirement. Ambrose is full of praise for Eisenhower as a military leader, with emphasis on his professional skills as an organizer of troops and supplies, his outstanding ability to achieve relatively harmonious co-operation among allies and among prima donna generals, and his willingness to make difficult decisions when necessary. Ambrose makes some criticisms of Eisenhower as president, such as a poor record on civil rights and a reluctance to stand up to Senator Joseph McCarthy. But, on the large issues of maintaining peace, prosperity and a national mood of good will, Ambrose argues that Eisenhower was extremely successful.

PICKETT presents a similar interpretation in much briefer form. His small book of less than 200 pages incorporates scholarship on Eisenhower up to the early 1990s. Each aspect of his career is treated succinctly, including a discussion of the cycles of historical interpretation of Eisenhower. The brevity of the book does not permit analysis of any issues in great depth or detail. The interpretation, while not wholly uncritical, is very favorable to Eisenhower.

PACH and RICHARDSON deals mainly with Eisenhower as president. Ostensibly a revised edition of an earlier work by Richardson, this is effectively a new book written by Pach. The interpretation, in Pach's phrase, is "post-revisionist", that is, while Pach broadly accepts the "revisionist" view, he suggests that the pendulum should not swing too far in

Eisenhower's favor. Pach is quite severely critical of various policies of Eisenhower's administration, in both domestic and foreign affairs, including anti-poverty measures, the environment, Formosa and Cuba.

Although largely superseded by later works, PARMET was the first major "revisionist" account. He made very good use of archives which had only recently been opened in the Eisenhower Library in Abilene, Kansas. Also, it is a lengthy study of more than 500 pages which permits discussion of issues in considerable detail. The approach, moreover, is analytical, which brings out different sides to arguments on various issues of Eisenhower's presidency. Although the overall assessment is very favorable to Eisenhower, Parmet presents a fair-minded discussion of differing points of view.

Another earlier account and interpretation, ALEXANDER, provides a bridge between negative assessments of the Eisenhower presidency and the full-blown revisionist view. In a carefully balanced appraisal, he modifies, without completely overturning, the old stereotype of a dull do-nothing administration, headed by an inactive president. He gives Eisenhower credit for ending the Korean War, avoiding involvement in other conflicts, restraining the demands of the military establishment, and generally creating a calmer atmosphere. On the other hand, he is very critical of the president's weakness in dealing with Senator McCarthy, blames him for involving the United States much more deeply in Southeast Asia, and attacks his lack of enthusiasm for racial justice. "Holding the line" is very much the theme of the book – holding it against expansion of the welfare state, settling for containment of the Soviet threat (despite the rhetoric of liberation), resisting Cold War pressures to expand the size and cost of the military establishment, and avoiding fundamental and divisive issues.

GREENSTEIN is a detailed study by a political scientist of Eisenhower's political methods and strategy. Greenstein argues that Eisenhower acquired considerable political skills during his military career and that he developed these skills further when he entered the political arena. According to this view, Eisenhower was in no way a political innocent or an amateur in politics. On the contrary, he deliberately cultivated and projected this image since it had appeal to the general public, while behind the scenes he was a shrewd, calculating politician.

DIVINE is a relatively brief study of certain aspects of Eisenhower's foreign policy – specifically, policy towards the Soviet Union, the Middle East and Asia. Arguing that Eisenhower, not Dulles, took the major decisions in foreign policy, Divine defends Eisenhower's record in virtually every aspect. He believes that in an extremely dangerous and unstable world situation Eisenhower provided strong, steady and sensible leadership which enabled the West to build up its strength at an affordable cost, while the war in Korea was brought to an end, and the United States was kept out of war in Indo-China and elsewhere.

BURK is a relatively brief biography, covering Eisenhower's entire career. Although the author does not use the term, his book displays the first signs of the "post-revisionist" interpretation of Eisenhower. While taking a very positive view overall, Burk does devote more attention to Eisenhower's shortcomings and limitations than, for example, Ambrose or Divine. He describes approvingly Eisenhower's rise from the humble origins of a rural background in Abilene to become a successful military commander, but suggests that, as president, Eisenhower failed to build the institutional framework that might have sustained the values which he tended simply to extol in homilies. Moreover, although Eisenhower's skills as a political tactician were considerable, as Greenstein showed, Burk suggests that he was less effective as a longer-term political strategist – as illustrated by his inability to build up a Republican party of moderate conservatism with broad electoral appeal.

BRENDON is out of the mainstream of trends in historical writing on Eisenhower. A British journalist who has engaged in research in the archives of the Eisenhower Library, he is harshly critical of Eisenhower, and arrives at rather different conclusions from most other historians who have worked in the same sources, and is often harshly critical in his judgments. Brendon's view of Eisenhower is not dissimilar from the perspective of intellectuals of the 1950s and 1960s, although he approaches his subject from the standpoint of a British conservative rather than an American liberal. The book is of reasonable length and is fully documented, and it offers a perspective on Eisenhower different from most other recent works.

PETER G. BOYLE

Elections: General

Burnham, Walter Dean, *Critical Elections and the Mainsprings of American Politics*, New York: Norton, 1970

Clubb, Jerome M. and Howard W. Allen (editors), *Electoral Change and Stability in American Political History*, New York: Free Press, 1971

Clubb, Jerome M., William H. Flannigan, and Nancy H. Zingale (editors), *Partisan Realignment: Voters, Parties and Government in American History*, Beverly Hills, CA: Sage, 1980

Congressional Quarterly's Guide to US Elections, Washington, DC: Congressional Quarterly, 1975, 2nd edition, 1985, 3rd edition, 1994

Kleppner, Paul and others, *The Evolution of American Electoral Systems*, Westport, CT: Greenwood Press, 1981

Kleppner, Paul, *Who Voted? The Dynamics of Electoral Turnout, 1870–1980*, New York: Praeger, 1982

Lichtman, Allan J., "The End of Realignment Theory: Toward a New Research Program for American Political History," *Historical Methods Newsletter*, 15, 1982

Schlesinger, Arthur M., Jr., with Fred L. Israel (editors), *History of American Presidential Elections, 1789–1968*, 4 vols., New York: Chelsea House, 1971; 9-volume edition, 1985; supplemental volume, 1972–1984, 1986

Shafer, Byron E. (editor), *The End of Realignment? Interpreting American Electoral Eras*, Madison: University of Wisconsin Press, 1991

The history of American voting behaviour, from the Jacksonian Era at least up to about the 1960s, seems to reveal long periods in which the aggregate partisan preference of the electorate was remarkably consistent, punctuated by occasional episodes of more intense change. These "critical elections," or "critical realignments," have been a central concern of historians and political scientists engaged in the study of electoral history. CLUBB and ALLEN include several of the most important essays published between 1952 and 1969, including V.O. Key, Jr.'s pioneering articulation of the theory of critical elections, a series of attempts by writers like Angus Campbell, Gerald Pomper and Charles G. Sellers to refine both the theory and its application to American political history, and a number of essays dealing with the election of 1928 and the New Deal realignment. The collection offers a useful picture of the state of the field at the beginning of the 1970s.

BURNHAM is probably the most influential and imaginative statement of realignment theory. In particular, he relates the cycle of electoral stability and instability more explicitly to the political process as a whole. Critical realignments were associated with periods of intense political excitement and ideological polarisation, during which large blocks of the electorate shifted their allegiance from one party to another, resulting in a new alignment between the parties and, often, important changes in policy. Indeed, according to Burnham, in view of the inherent rigidities of the American political system, it was only at such moments of electoral realignment that popular impulses had a major impact. But the progressive decline of partisan loyalties in the 20th century made the political system even less susceptible to such influences than in the past.

Electoral historians, using a variety of definitions and a variety of statistical techniques, have found it extraordinarily difficult to pin down exactly when realignments occurred. Recognising this, CLUBB et al. insist that the key to partisan realignment lay not in electoral behaviour alone but in the way in which political leaders seized the opportunity offered by periods of electoral instability to forge a new dominating coalition by innovations in policy. Much of the book consists of an attempt to trace linkages between periods of electoral change and periods of policy innovation. As critics of realignment theory, like LICHTMAN, have pointed out, such linkages are, with one or two obvious exceptions like the New Deal, remarkably hard to find. This volume, therefore, both sums up the argument to date and clearly demonstrates its intrinsic difficulties. KLEPPNER (1981) is a collection of essays organised around the now conventional model of five successive party systems. Ronald P. Formisano, William G. Shade, Paul Kleppner, Walter Dean Burnham and Richard Jensen deal with these in turn, with a commentary by Samuel P. Hays. Interestingly, the authors, each a specialist in his field, offer different, sometimes conflicting, views of the realignment process as a whole.

Burnham has done more than anyone else to direct scholarly attention to the marked decline in electoral turnout since the turn of the century. KLEPPNER (1982) is the most comprehensive and detailed examination of trends in turnout, using multiple regression techniques. He attributes the high turnouts of the 19th century to powerful ethnocultural rivalries which mobilised voters in large numbers, and the lower polls of this century to the unscrambling of linkages between ethnocultural groupings and political parties during the realignment of the 1890s. Kleppner understates the importance of other factors, such as the lessening of party competition, changes in election laws and new campaigning techniques, commonly adduced to explain the phenomenon.

SHAFER presents contributions to a recent symposium which focused on the apparent failure of realignment theory to explain recent electoral trends. The historians Joel H. Silbey and Samuel T. McSeveney and the political scientist Byron E. Shafer believe that whereas realignment theory was useful for explaining past elections, the political system has now moved beyond realignment. The political scientist Everett Carll Ladd questions its applicability to either past or present conditions, while only Burnham seems willing to contemplate the possibility of a realignment occurring in the foreseeable future.

The CONGRESSIONAL QUARTERLY *Guide* is an easily usable collection of election results, covering state and congressional as well as national elections. Another useful work of reference is SCHLESINGER and ISRAEL, which, for each presidential election from 1788 to 1984, provides a brief and informative essay by a leading scholar, state-level election results and a number of key documents.

ROBERT HARRISON

See also Parties and Political Movements

Elections

1) 1789–1860

Baker, Jean H., *Affairs of Party: The Political Culture of the Northern Democrats in the Mid-Nineteenth Century*, Ithaca, NY: Cornell University Press, 1983

Benson, Lee, *The Concept of Jacksonian Democracy: New York as a Test Case*, Princeton: Princeton University Press, 1961

Gienapp, William E., *The Origins of the Republican Party, 1852–1856*, New York: Oxford University Press, 1987

Kleppner, Paul and others, *The Evolution of American Electoral Systems*, Westport, CT: Greenwood Press, 1981

Schlesinger, Arthur M., Jr., *The Age of Jackson*, Boston: Little Brown, 1945; London: Eyre and Spottiswoode, 1946

Watson, Harry L., *Jacksonian Politics and Community Conflict: The Emergence of the Second American Party System in Cumberland County, North Carolina*, Baton Rouge: Louisiana State University Press, 1981

Williamson, Chilton, *American Suffrage: From Property to Democracy, 1760–1860*, Princeton: Princeton University Press, 1960

Winkle, Kenneth J., *The Politics of Community: Migration and Politics in Antebellum Ohio*, New York: Cambridge University Press, 1988

Scholars have expended a great deal of energy describing and analyzing the frequent and intense election activity that characterized American politics in the first three-quarters of a century under the Constitution. The early essays in KLEPPNER integrate and summarize this scholarship, extend its findings, and delineate the larger patterns present. After an initial period of intermittent involvement, shallow commitment to the emerging, but incompletely formed, political parties, and great volatility at the polls from year to year, the electorate settled down by the 1830s into well marked channels. As the political parties overcame early resistance to their presence, and matured into powerful organizations, they successfully mobilized voters to follow them on election day. Turnout at the polls soared under the spur of the minute organization of the electorate to fight closely contested elections in which much seemed to be at stake. As a result, from the 1830s onward, continuity characterized American popular voting behavior. High involvement, intense commitment, and unflinching loyalty were what mattered, with each voter a member of a disciplined army facing the enemy across the electoral barricades.

Undergirding this pattern was the increasing number of eligible voters. WILLIAMSON details how much 19th-century Americans believed that political democracy meant the extension of suffrage to almost all white males. Colonial era restrictions wasted away in this climate, and the bitter political battles to control the new nation stimulated political leaders to seek out new supporters among those who had not hitherto participated. A large pool of eligibles emerged by 1840, with little challenge to their participation on election day. Such rights and opportunities did not extend to women, African Americans or other outsider groups, however, all of whom remained constrained by ideological and cultural prejudices against their political participation.

The second foundation of the era's electoral behavior concerned the reasons behind each voter's decision to choose one party over the other, a decision rooted in group, not individual, predispositions and definitions. A number of specific examples may be used to illustrate different schools of thought and different approaches to this key question. Following the dominant Progressive explanatory paradigm of the first half of the 20th century, SCHLESINGER argues that the basis of voter choice lay in the persistent clash of different economic interests which usually divided people along class lines in 19th-century America. The unequal distribution of wealth in the nation, combined with the desire to use government to promote and protect specific class interests, created the environment of election contests. Each major party represented a different part of the class system. On one side, the Federalists, then the Whigs and Republicans organized the upper classes and the more affluent behind a conservative perspective, while a liberal party, the Jeffersonians and, later, the Jacksonian Democrats, represented society's have nots on election day.

BENSON offers a different perspective, arguing that Schlesinger's economic determinism does not stand close examination. Benson was among the first scholars to utilize, in systematic fashion, a wide array of election returns, correlating them with the social make-up of New York state's townships in the 1840s, rather than relying, as most earlier analysts had, on less direct sources and less systematic use of evidence. On the basis of such methods, he pointed out that popular voting cut across class lines and reflected common group experiences and particular contexts, rather than always revealing an economic orientation. Economics does not disappear from his explanation, but, as the prime shaper of party choice, he stresses the importance of deeply rooted, and always relevant, tensions between the many ethnic and religious groups that uneasily existed with one another on the local landscape. He introduces the sociological concept of reference groups to help explain partisan choice – that voters did not always react directly to specific policy arguments but, rather, acted in reference to the presence and behavior of other groups, friends, or enemies.

This kind of ethno-religious explanation of voting behavior has become well established in political history scholarship, but has never been unchallenged by those who continue to stress economic influences as the main source of human behavior at the polls. A refinement of the Progressive paradigm emphasizes not so much class or interest group conflict but, rather, the clash between distinct orientations toward economic development. Utilizing a range of election returns in a sophisticated manner, WATSON argues that in the South, at least, voters split ideologically between those who accepted vigorous economic development and the use of government power to promote market capitalism, and those who resisted such changes in the name of preserving pre-market societal virtues, free of the intense and deleterious pressures unleashed by development.

Whatever the specific socio-economic sources of voter choice, BAKER underlines the great importance of powerful communitarian transmission of political values to its members. Arguing that the absorption of cultural norms precedes behavior, she suggests that the learning, by the large mass of individual Americans, of their community's particular values through family, church, education, and social associations, included their political values and commitments, especially association with a political party. She traces the story of such transmission through such conveyors of societal norms as textbooks, popular literature and sermons. Her focus is on Democrats in the Northern states. However, she argues that whether one was a Democrat or not, loyalty to the party's stances and candidates was internalized as part of a set of outlooks, values and realities planted in the minds of future voters from an early age.

To WINKLE, the important feature of popular voting behavior was its continuity at the local level from election to election, despite the extraordinary amount of population movement across antebellum America and the consequent instability of individual communities. Closely linking census records to surviving poll books which specifically listed those who cast votes in a given election, he found voter turnover on a massive scale from one year to the next. Most voters cast ballots in a particular place only once or twice over the course of a decade and then disappeared from the record. Yet, the communities remained relatively stable in their turnout numbers and in their commitment to a political party, as if the same people were voting in each election. Winkle suggests that such cross-cutting elements have to be explained by focusing on the significant role played by those who were always present and who controlled elections and transmitted local values, and how party identification was awakened or refreshed among new groups of voters each year.

The pre-Civil War years concluded in a major political crisis in which voters and elections played significant roles. Through a sophisticated use of quantitative methods, GIENAPP examines the sudden disruption of the prevailing, apparently rock-like, electoral patterns usually present, by a massive voter realignment in which some dropped out of the political system entirely, and new voters appeared, while others changed their party allegiances. Such realignments have been rare phenomena in American electoral history, the one in the mid-1850s leading to the creation of a major new party out of the wreckage of the existing two party system. He argues that this disruption originated in ethnic and religious confrontation unleashed by the wave of Catholic immigration that flooded the North from the mid-1840s onwards, leading to a massive backlash against the existing parties. But the electoral transformation continued. Other elements – economic interests, antislavery, and resistance to Southern expansionism – became part of the electoral brew as well. Republican party leaders brilliantly weaved together the various strands of anger, discontent and resentment into a new party that effectively mobilized voters by reorganizing a wide range of commitments, interests, values and outlooks into a different and appealing configuration that combined frustration, prejudice, morality and economics.

JOEL H. SILBEY

2) 1864–1928

Austin, Erik W., *Political Facts of the United States since 1789*, New York: Columbia University Press, 1986

Congressional Quarterly's Guide to US Elections, Washington, DC: Congressional Quarterly, 1975, 2nd edition, 1985, 3rd edition, 1994

Kleppner, Paul, *Who Voted? The Dynamics of Electoral Turnout, 1870–1980*, New York: Praeger, 1982

Martis, Kenneth C., *The Historical Atlas of United States Congressional Districts, 1789–1983*, New York: Free Press, 1982

Martis, Kenneth C., *The Historical Atlas of Political Parties in the United States Congress, 1789–1987*, New York: Macmillan, and London: Collier Macmillan, 1989

Petersen, Svend, *A Statistical History of the American Presidential Elections*, New York: Ungar, 1963

Porter, Kirk H. (editor), *National Party Platforms*, New York: Macmillan, 1924; 4th edition, as *National Party Platforms, 1840–1968*, with Donald Bruce Johnson, Urbana: University of Illinois Press, 1972

Schlesinger, Arthur M., Jr., with Fred L. Israel (editors), *History of American Presidential Elections, 1789–1968*, 4 vols., New York: Chelsea House, 1971; 9-volume edition, 1985

After the secession of the strongly Democratic southern states in 1861, and then the ultimate defeat of the Confederacy in 1865, the national American elections from 1864 through 1928 were mostly dominated by Republicans and northern business interests. Political and economic interests that had once so dominated and defined elections and ideology in the antebellum period were increasingly forced to change in the years after the Civil War. In this period there was a transition away from local and smaller-scale economic entities and towards larger-scale entities which increasingly pursued regional and national activities, and as such helped to redefine America's political and economic landscape. Because of many new and alternative economic and social issues, the American political system evolved along with the changes in its economy and society. As the United States became more urban than rural and more industrial than agrarian, its elected politicians and the policies they advocated began to reflect these changes. Out of the seventeen contested quadrennial presidential elections from 1864 to 1928, Republicans won thirteen. Democratic candidates won the other four elections but there were only two Democratic Presidents: Grover Cleveland in 1884 and 1892, and Woodrow Wilson in 1912 and 1916. Until Wilson's election, every winning candidate in this period called a northern state home and three out of four came from the states of Ohio and New York.

Summaries of election results and analyses of specific campaigns can be found in a variety of sources. One of the most useful and comprehensive sources of data on national, state, and congressional elections is the CONGRESSIONAL QUARTERLY *Guide*. It is an extensive and well-organized account of the history and statistics of American elections. The *Guide* provides not only absolute and relative statistics for general and primary elections but also summaries of pluralities and explanations of odd and unusual events. It also includes a concise and informative narrative on the origins of American political parties, along with a chronology of their nominating conventions dating back to 1832. Among the more practical features of the book are the indexes of candidates for presidential, gubernatorial, senate, and house elections from 1789 through 1975. AUSTIN is a concise and comprehensive guide to the statistics of America's political history. It provides data on electoral and popular votes by states, along with the names and dates of service of senators, representatives, and cabinet officers. Austin also provides data apportionment of seats in the House of Representatives, votes cast in congressional races, and estimates of the costs of conducting presidential campaigns dating back to 1860. PETERSEN provides statistics on presidential elections by state and political parties. It lists not only vote totals and percentages but examines such questions as the notion that certain states or regions can be used to gauge political trends.

SCHLESINGER and ISRAEL is a valuable multi-volume guide to the trends and details of American political and social history. Each of the nine volumes in this fine and comprehensive series contains essays and documents that lucidly define the issues and the context of each of these elections. Volume 2 analyzes the elections from 1848 to 1896, and Volume 3 covers the elections from 1900 to 1936. The essays in these volumes are written by distinguished historians and social scientists, and are accompanied by contemporary speeches, letters, and editorials. There are detailed descriptions and thoughtful interpretations of the issues, and the positions advocated by candidates and parties in each of these elections.

Formal platforms were first espoused by American political parties in 1840, and PORTER outlines each of the major and principal minor party platforms from 1840 through 1968. As formal statements of policy, these platforms are useful in a historic sense as indicators of what parties perceived as the basis of their popular appeal. They are interesting both for what they say and what they do not say. Porter asserts that these official position statements were more than empty words, and did to some extent reflect political trends.

Among the more interesting and detailed reference works available on American elections and political parties are two historical atlases. MARTIS (1982) is a quarto-sized volume that maps, defines, and describes all of the congressional

districts of the United States from 1789 through 1983. It is a thorough, detailed, and well-organized guide to the structure and transformation of the American political landscape. MARTIS (1989) is also a quarto-sized volume, and is a similarly remarkable study that graphically outlines the fortunes of political parties in more than 31,000 congressional contests from 1789 through 1989. It explains much about the development, organization, purpose, and evolution of American political parties. It also displays clearly the geographic pattern of political affiliation, and suggests how this can reflect and define both local and regional concerns and national policies.

KLEPPNER is a scholarly study of the level and degree of American political participation from the mid-19th century to the 1980s. It uses longitudinal data to portray and explain patterns of voter turnout in American presidential and off-year congressional elections. Kleppner concludes that the strong partisanship of the late 19th century was due to the power of institutional organizations and strong ethnocultural loyalties.

TIMOTHY E. SULLIVAN

3) Since 1932

Allswang, John M., *The New Deal and American Politics: A Study in Political Change*, New York: Wiley, 1978

Black, Earl and Merle Black, *The Vital South: How Presidents Are Elected*, Cambridge, MA: Harvard University Press, 1992

Campbell, Angus and others, *The American Voter*, New York: Wiley, 1960

Drew, Elizabeth, *Portrait of an Election: The 1980 Presidential Campaign*, New York: Simon and Schuster, and London: Routledge, 1981

Ladd, Everett Carll, Jr., with Charles D. Hadley, *Transformations of the American Party System: Political Coalitions from the New Deal to the 1970s*, New York: Norton, 1975, revised 1978

Lubell, Samuel, *The Future of American Politics*, New York: Harper, 1952, 3rd edition, 1965

Roseboom, Eugene H., *A History of Presidential Elections*, New York: Macmillan, 1957

Schlesinger, Arthur M., Jr., with Fred L. Israel (editors), *History of American Presidential Elections, 1789–1968*, 4 vols., New York: Chelsea House, 1971; 9-volume edition, 1985; supplemental volume, 1972–1984, 1986

Sundquist, James L., *Dynamics of the Party System: Alignment and Realignment of Political Parties in the United States*, Washington, DC: Brookings Institution, 1973, revised 1983

White, Theodore H., *The Making of the President 1960*, New York: Atheneum, 1961; London: Cape, 1962

White, Theodore H., *America in Search of Itself: The Making of the President, 1956–1980*, New York: Harper, 1982; London: Cape, 1983

American elections are often as much the register of deeper changes in politics as their progenitor; thus to understand them one needs to discern the forces that shaped their outcome as well as examining the individual contest. Among these forces, some are of only transient importance, while others have enduring significance. Long-term patterns may be more illuminating than short-term results.

ALLSWANG is a clearly written 130 page commentary on the changing politics of the 1930s. It is partly derived from a massive, systematic, quantitative data base, including voting statistics and census returns for all the then 3100 or so counties of the United States. He charts the formation of the Roosevelt coalition that made the 1932 election a genuine turning point in American politics.

LUBELL is a classic of political reporting. Originally written just before Eisenhower's capture of the presidency, it attempted "to take the mystery out of present-day American politics" by identifying "eight prime forces" which shaped them: the coming of age of various urban minorities; the rise of a new middle class; the migration of black Americans; the economic revolution in the South; the abrupt upheaval in world strategy and its effects on American isolationism; the changing relationship of the farmer to the town; the growth of organized labour; and the impact of the Cold War upon the welfare state. A particular strength of the book is its readiness to swing the spotlight largely away from Washington out into the country. "It is there, among the people themselves, that the real drama of political realignment is being acted out". Lubell postulates a sun and moon theory of American politics: "It is within the majority party that the issues of any particular period are fought out; while the minority party shines in reflected radiance of the heat thus generated."

CAMPBELL *et al.* is a pioneering study. Its aim is "to understand the voting decisions of the national electorate in a manner that transcends some of the specific elements of historical circumstance." The data collected spans the period 1948 to 1956, though it is fuller on the two Eisenhower campaigns; in some 550 pages the authors discuss such issues as voter perception, turnout, party identification, social class and personality factors. It is very much a book for psephologists. LADD and HADLEY is a similar comprehensive study which aims "to help clarify the reordering which has been imposed upon political life by societal change since the New Deal." With more than 60 figures and tables, it is based heavily on Gallup Polls, "the longest continuous stream of survey information on the American public – covering the entire span since the New Deal," supplemented by biennial election studies since 1952 and other opinion polls and surveys. A work of political science, its main theme is a detailed examination of the unravelling of the Roosevelt coalition at a time when the outlines of a substitute were difficult to discern.

Another example of the same genre, SUNDQUIST is a study of how the American two-party system is periodically reshaped. Though it also examines earlier re-alignments to construct a theory of the process, half the book, over 200 pages in its revised format, is devoted to the period 1932 to 1982. Sundquist writes clearly and is not engulfed by his material. He records the arrival of the Reagan revolution but is in two minds as to its long-term import, which was to take another decade to mature.

BLACK and BLACK explore the phenomenon of how the centre of American political gravity has shifted. The once solid Democratic South completely reversed its allegiance as early as the presidential election of 1972 – a trend confirmed in the

1980s. The region's electoral weight is such that it now has over half the votes needed to win a majority in the electoral college.

The elections of the last four decades have inspired some journalistic accounts of very high quality. WHITE (1961) is a celebrated work that initiated a series of individual studies. He captures the drama and excitement of the presidential election process and was to repeat his success with similarly titled books on the 1964, 1968, and 1972 elections. Yet he never quite succeeded in recreating the élan of the original work, in part because Johnson and Nixon never had for White the glamour of John Kennedy, clearly the hero of the book. Indeed White may have unwittingly helped burnish the image of "the Imperial Presidency" as he follows the campaign from the early primary elections through the conventions to the White House. The 1960 contest was important too for the role of television which was to transform American elections. White excels at immensely readable historical journalism, a clever blending of narrative and analysis. WHITE (1982) is in part a distillation of some of the themes that underlay his previous individual studies, but is also designed to elucidate the context of the 1980 election, to which half the book is devoted. Written when the high hopes of the early 1960s had turned to disillusionment and national self-doubt, it is a sober epitaph.

DREW is another journalistic study of a significant election. An accomplished reporter, she is perceptive, good on background detail, and more critical in approach than White. Although the book is a kind of mosaic, Drew contends that "as the story unfolds the election can be seen not as a succession of isolated and inchoate events but as a total picture". There are some eye-opening appendices containing campaign memoranda drawn up by Reagan's and Carter's respective pollsters. They are not for the idealistic.

Relevant sections of more general histories of presidential elections may serve as useful introductions, at least to the earlier part of this period. ROSEBOOM is a broad survey, now somewhat out-dated, but a convenient source of basic information. SCHLESINGER and ISRAEL is a much more substantial work of reference. Each presidential election from 1932 to 1968 is discussed by a specialist historian, with some entries as long as forty or fifty pages. There is a supporting chapter on "Financing Presidential Campaigns".

JOHN KENTLETON

Eliot, Charles W. 1834–1926
Educator; president of Harvard University

Hawkins, Hugh, *Between Harvard and America: The Educational Leadership of Charles W. Eliot*, New York: Oxford University Press, 1972

Hofstadter, Richard and Walter P. Metzger, *The Development of Academic Freedom in the United States*, New York: Columbia University Press, 1955

James, Henry, *Charles W. Eliot: President of Harvard University, 1869–1909*, 2 vols., Boston: Houghton Mifflin, and London: Constable, 1930

Krug, Edward A., *The Shaping of the American High School, 1880–1920*, Madison: University of Wisconsin Press, 1969

Morison, Samuel Eliot, *The Development of Harvard University since the Inauguration of President Eliot, 1869–1929*, Cambridge, MA: Harvard University Press, 1930

Morison, Samuel Eliot, *Three Centuries of Harvard, 1636–1936*, Cambridge, MA: Harvard University Press, 1936

Saunderson, Henry Hallam, *Charles W. Eliot, Puritan Liberal*, New York: Harper, 1928

Smith, Richard Norton, *The Harvard Century: The Making of a University to a Nation*, New York: Simon and Schuster, 1986

Story, Ronald, *The Forging of an Aristocracy: Harvard and the Boston Upper Class, 1800–1870*, Middletown, CT: Wesleyan University Press, 1980

Synnott, Marcia Graham, *The Half-Opened Door: Discrimination and Admissions at Harvard, Yale, and Princeton, 1900–1930*, Westport, CT: Greenwood Press, 1979

Veysey, Laurence R., *The Emergence of the American University*, Chicago: University of Chicago Press, 1965

Arguably the most influential man in the history of American higher education, Charles W. Eliot presided over Harvard University for forty years (1869–1909) through what is often labelled "the Age of the University." During his presidency the nation's oldest college translated its heritage into a new status as America's most prestigious university. The architect of that successful transition was, not surprisingly, lauded in a series of biographies and institutional histories published shortly after his death in 1926.

Two years later, SAUNDERSON wrote a hero-worshipping hagiography that portrayed Eliot following in the footsteps of Channing, Emerson, and Parker as the apotheosis of the New England Puritan tradition. Defending Puritanism in a decade when the term had become a pejorative, Saunderson portrayed Eliot's Unitarian liberalism and tolerance as the true Puritan heritage. The depiction of Eliot as deeply religious no doubt surprised many who had seen him as a secularizer. Two years later, JAMES (not the novelist but a son of one of Eliot's faculty members and an alumnus) wrote a two volume "life and letters" biography. Less florid than Saunderson, it is similarly uncritical. Both are elegant period pieces of little modern use.

Fortuitously, planning for Harvard's 300th anniversary began soon after Eliot's death and resulted in Morison's magisterial multi-volume history of America's first institution of higher education. MORISON (1930) is a collection of accounts by leading Harvard administrators and faculty who uniformly characterised Eliot as far-sighted and wise, particularly praising him for augmenting and upgrading professional and graduate work. In MORISON (1936), the author's esteem for Eliot is reflected in his title for the chapter on post-1869 Harvard, "The Olympian Age". He portrayed pre-1869 Harvard as a stagnant institution facing new rivals and suffering a leadership vacuum which was filled perfectly by Eliot. Morison lauds Eliot's wisdom and courage in reforming the graduate and professional schools and the undergraduate curriculum, although he notes that Eliot's tactlessness complicated the task. There is also criticism of him for excessive faith in curricular liberty, particularly for dropping the Greek entrance requirement and encouraging electives in high school that undermined classical education. Otherwise, Morison lionizes Eliot.

The next generation still held Eliot in high regard. Defending academic freedom and university values in the midst of McCarthyism, HOFSTADTER and METZGER applauded Eliot's defense of educational liberty. In VEYSEY's definitive work, Eliot is the leading figure, placed above the other university builders. He is portrayed as the archetypal Mugwump, defending laissez-faire and tolerance while promoting utilitarian education in its best sense. Although laudatory, Veysey draws a complex picture in which Eliot's legacy is complicated by unintended consequences; his championing of university values and student liberty promoted academic specialization and a student culture with which he was very uncomfortable.

Eliot's elevated reputation was enhanced by the only modern biography. Avowedly writing from a liberal-progressive perspective, HAWKINS was troubled by the implications of the liberal corporatism represented by Eliot's Harvard but was more worried by the threat to university values of student protests. The result was high praise for Eliot as a mediator between industrial capitalists and universities who effectively promoted an ideal of universities that provided specialized expertise while giving refuge to higher values threatened by materialism. Eliot's ethno-religious and racial tolerance was commended by Hawkins and also by SYNNOTT. His openness to diversity at Harvard resulting from a Jeffersonian vision of creating a natural aristocracy was rare in the period. Eliot's benign neglect of collegiate life permitted the co-existence of an elite "Gold Coast" along with talented students from groups shunned at many other universities.

More than any other figure in higher education, Eliot participated in and influenced debates over secondary education. Indicatively, he served as President of the National Education Association, and Honorary President of the Progressive Education Association. His role, particularly as chairman of the Committee of Ten, is well described in KRUG, who portrays him as an important curricular modernizer though one whose belief in a similar curriculum for all students was rapidly outpaced by the realities of mass secondary education and the comprehensive high school.

No other figure in American higher education has emerged with such a flattering historical reputation. On the whole, his strict adherence to 19th-century liberalism stood him in good stead during the half century after his death. For two decades Eliot was the central actor, and often hero, in a succession of works from Hofstadter and Metzger to Hawkins, that still dominate the historiography of American higher education. But recently Eliot has received little attention, as historians' interest and sympathy have shifted away from the university. Indicative of changing sensibilities, STORY questions the meaning of Eliot's liberal reputation by highlighting his relationship to the Boston elite. Story maintains that Eliot's 19th-century religious "liberalism" has blinded historians to his social conservatism. He paints Eliot as the ultimate Boston Brahmin who intertwined Harvard with the Boston business establishment which he courted assiduously. Whereas Hawkins worried about liberal corporatism but was generally comfortable with Eliot's legacy, Story represents the recent work of historians who are more deeply troubled by Eliot's Harvard, and who have turned their attention away from long-established universities to less elite institutions of higher education.

Harvard's 350th anniversary in 1986 presented an opportunity to re-interpret Harvard and Eliot within the debate over corporatism. That did not happen and, unlike 1936, little useful history emerged from the anniversary celebration. SMITH provided a breezy and engaging account that uncomfortably mixed high praise of Eliot's accomplishments with sardonic comments on his personal rigidity. This very readable book adds nothing new. Thus Eliot's reputation stands intact and formidable. It is a sign of his eminence that, in order to win acceptance, a long overdue new synthesis of the history of American higher education would have to come to grips with Eliot's looming legacy.

W. BRUCE LESLIE

See also Universities and Colleges entries

Emancipation Proclamations, 1862–1863

Belz, Herman, *A New Birth of Freedom: The Republican Party and Freedmen's Rights, 1861 to 1866*, Westport, CT: Greenwood Press, 1976

Berlin, Ira, Barbara J. Fields, Steven F. Miller, Joseph P. Reidy, and Leslie S. Rowland, *Slaves No More: Three Essays on Emancipation and the Civil War*, Cambridge and New York: Cambridge University Press, 1992

Cox, LaWanda, *Lincoln and Black Freedom: A Study in Presidential Leadership*, Columbia: University of South Carolina Press, 1981

Donald, David Herbert, *Lincoln*, New York: Simon and Schuster, and London: Cape, 1995

Foner, Eric, *Nothing but Freedom: Emancipation and Its Legacy*, Baton Rouge: Louisiana State University Press, 1983

Franklin, John Hope, *The Emancipation Proclamation*, New York, Doubleday, and Edinburgh: Edinburgh University Press, 1963

Gerteis, Louis S., *From Contraband to Freedman: Federal Policy toward Southern Blacks, 1861–1865*, Westport, CT: Greenwood Press, 1973

Litwack, Leon F., *Been in the Storm So Long: The Aftermath of Slavery*, New York: Knopf, 1979; London: Athlone Press, 1980

McPherson, James M., *The Struggle for Equality: Abolitionists and the Negro in the Civil War and Reconstruction*, Princeton: Princeton University Press, 1964; with new preface, 1995

Paludan, Phillip S., *The Presidency of Abraham Lincoln*, Lawrence: University Press of Kansas, 1994

Quarles, Benjamin, *Lincoln and the Negro*, New York: Oxford University Press, 1962

Voegeli, V. Jacque, *Free but Not Equal: The Midwest and the Negro During the Civil War*, Chicago: University of Chicago Press, 1967

Wood, Forrest G., *Black Scare: The Racist Response to Emancipation and Reconstruction*, Berkeley: University of California Press, 1968

The historic importance of the Emancipation Proclamations is not matched by the number of books specifically devoted to the documents themselves, or to the circumstances which produced them. The only modern work devoted specifically to the evolution and impact of the two proclamations is FRANKLIN. This brief study, written by the most distinguished of black American historians to mark the centenary of emancipation, examines the mounting, if conflicting, pressures on Lincoln, the formulation of the documents, and the reactions to the proclamations in both North and South as well as abroad.

QUARLES covers some of the same ground in a thoughtful and generally sympathetic study of the "Great Emancipator." He traces the development of Lincoln's thinking about slavery and the broader issues of race, from the ambivalence of his earlier years, through his interest in colonization and gradual emancipation, to the approach embodied in the proclamations, and on to his powerful support for a constitutional amendment to end slavery once and for all. Quarles praises Lincoln's extraordinary sensitivity to what would be acceptable to the people at large. He also shows how the attitude of northern blacks towards Lincoln moved from initial coolness to considerable hostility during the earlier stages of the war, and then to hero-worship toward the end of the conflict.

More recent accounts of the pressures on Lincoln, and his eventual decision for emancipation, may be found in various general works on Lincoln as president, or on the North in the Civil War. These benefit from recent scholarship on the subject. One of the best is PALUDAN, which places the problems of emancipation very clearly in the context of turbulent northern politics, the demands of the war effort, and the racial feelings and prejudices of northern whites. In his recent magisterial biography of Lincoln, DONALD incorporates the evolution of the president's policy on emancipation into his basic thesis that Lincoln was essentially a pragmatist, and a man who reacted to events rather than one who sought to shape them. Perhaps for this reason, the Emancipation Proclamations figure less prominently in his account than one might have expected.

Among the most vocal of the pressure groups pushing Lincoln towards emancipation were the abolitionists. In what was, in its day, a path-breaking book, McPHERSON demonstrated that, far from receding into the background when the war came, the abolitionists continued to press hard for the ending of slavery, and then for equal rights for black Americans. They were leading champions of the economic, social, and educational interests of the former slaves. As the conscience of the radical Republicans, they provided a moral basis for policies initiated primarily for political or military reasons.

On the other hand, pressures against emancipation and hostility to its effects often stemmed from racial fears and prejudices. VOEGELI is a revealing study of the evolution of midwestern attitudes during the Civil War from abhorrence at the idea of freedom for the slaves to acceptance of emancipation, as long as it was not followed by mass migration of former slaves into the North. Lincoln was so sensitive to midwestern opinion, according to Voegeli, because he himself so often epitomized it. WOOD is a broader, but less judicious, treatment of racially-inspired hostility to emancipation and its aftermath, which covers both the war years and Reconstruction. However, it is richer in lurid detail and eye-catching quotations than in penetrating analysis.

GERTEIS examines the methods used by the federal authorities to deal with the problems of the freed slaves during the war years. Emancipation was essentially a war measure, and responses to its effects on the ground were dictated by the requirements of the war effort. As Gerteis sees it, federal policy was mainly directed towards the mobilization of black labour and of black soldiers, and the avoidance of violent or revolutionary change (including mass migration to the North). This is a challenging study of post-emancipation policy and its implementation, and not a social history of the transition from slavery to freedom.

BELZ is also concerned with the consequences of emancipation, but he places the subject in a different context and takes a more positive view. Having dealt briskly with emancipation itself, he uses an examination of black military service, the Freedmen's Bureau, the Thirteenth Amendment, and the earlier phases of Reconstruction to press the point that, whatever the limitations of Republican policy in other respects, the establishment of the principle of equality before the law was of the highest importance. Indeed, according to Belz, this was a genuinely radical policy in a society that had not yet arrived at a belief in basic equality between the races.

One of Lincoln's staunchest defenders is COX, who sees him as a consistent champion of black freedom. The firmness of his commitment to the principle of equal rights was often masked by his political pragmatism, his need to respond to a variety of pressures, and the limits of presidential power in matters of this kind. The force of Cox's challenge to more critical assessments of Lincoln is weakened somewhat by over-concentration on the tangled story of his Reconstruction policy in Louisiana.

The most important thrust of recent work on emancipation has been its emphasis on the active participation of African Americans in the process of their own liberation. The classic study of the experience of the mass of southern blacks in the transition from slavery to freedom is LITWACK, a huge, sprawling book, packed with fascinating detail and based on a vast array of source material. For Litwack, these four million African American men and women were the principal actors in the drama. Always aware of the enormous variety and ambiguity of individual reactions to the experience of emancipation, Litwack finds it difficult to arrive at firm conclusions or broad generalizations. The book presents a wonderfully intricate mosaic rather than one coherent and sharply-defined image.

Two much briefer books which also place the slave, or ex-slave, at the centre of the picture are Foner and Berlin et al. In a book derived from a series of lectures, FONER briefly explores comparisons between the ending of slavery in the South and in the Caribbean. He then discusses the reshaping of class relations in the South in the wake of emancipation, and finally examines the implications of a strike of workers

on rice plantations in South Carolina in 1876. One of his key points is that, uniquely in the history of post-emancipation societies, former slaves in America gained the right to vote within a few years, and were thus able to participate, however briefly, in the political struggles of the period.

Three long essays by BERLIN and his colleagues deal respectively with the destruction of slavery, the wartime genesis of free labor, and the black military experience. The essays are a by-product of their superb editorial work on *Freedom: A Documentary History of Emancipation*, a multi-volume project of outstanding quality and importance, which is still in progress. Berlin and his team are steeped in the raw materials of the subject, and their essays are the best possible demonstration that the Emancipation Proclamations were but the public ratification of an underlying process which ran right through the Civil War.

PETER J. PARISH

Energy

Barger, Harold and Sam H. Schurr, *The Mining Industries, 1899–1939: A Study of Output, Employment and Productivity*, New York: National Bureau of Economic Research, 1944

Borenstein, Israel, *Capital and Output Trends in American Mining Industries, 1870–1914*, New York: National Bureau of Economic Research, 1954

Castle, Emery N. and Kent A. Price (editors), *US Interests and Global Natural Resources: Energy, Minerals, Food*, Washington, DC: Resources for the Future, 1983

Cuff, David J. and William J. Young, *The United States Energy Atlas*, 2nd edition, New York: Macmillan, and London: Collier Macmillan, 1986

Johnson, Arthur Menzies, *The Development of American Petroleum Pipelines: A Study in Private Enterprise and Public Policy, 1862–1906*, Ithaca, NY: Cornell University Press, 1956

Lambie, Joseph T., *From Mine to Market: The History of Coal Transportation on the Norfolk and Western Railway*, New York: New York University Press, 1954

Passer, Harold C., *The Electrical Manufacturers, 1875–1900: A Study in Competition, Entrepreneurship, Technical Change, and Economic Growth*, Cambridge, MA: Harvard University Press, 1953

Schurr, Sam H. and others, *Energy in the American Economy, 1850–1975: An Economic Study of Its History and Prospects*, Baltimore: Johns Hopkins Press, 1960

Williamson, Harold F. and others, *The American Petroleum Industry*, 2 vols., Evanston, IL: Northwestern University Press, 1959–63

Despite its significance for economic development, energy is rarely treated in the literature as a discrete subject, though there are ample industrial and business histories of its separate parts (coal, electricity, petroleum). A complete survey would start with human and animal muscular energy derived from products of the soil and waterways, propellent energy derived from wind and water, the forest used as wood fuel and then as coal, coal used for steam and then for electricity generation, hydro-electricity and wind used for power stations, oil and gas in all their uses, and finally nuclear power.

The most comprehensive historical study of the subject is the 1960 study by SCHURR *et al.* It endeavours to quantify the respective contributions of the main energy sources, though the 1850 starting date involves the omission from consideration of the importance of water and wind in the early economy. Nevertheless, it makes very clear the relatively short reign of coal as the major power source, roughly from the mid-1880s to the mid-1920s, and assesses the importance of the arrival of gas and oil and the use of all three (and water) in electricity production.

LAMBIE is as much a contribution to railroad history as to the study of energy. The production, distribution and use of coal symbolize much of the achievement of the American economy in the half-century after the Civil War. Lambie demonstrates the total dependence of coal development on railroad building and operation, for providing access to coal and making possible its distribution, not least to the iron and steel industry, on a scale far beyond the capabilities of canals. The book examines the role of the Norfolk and Western Railway from the early 1880s, when the all-important West Virginia coalfield (which still in 1950 produced almost half of all US bituminous coal) was first opened up. The industrial history of coal has been chronicled in many volumes and from varying viewpoints, particularly by BORENSTEIN in a characteristic National Bureau of Economic Research volume, and in an earlier study by BARGER and SCHURR. Similarly, PASSER's business history of electrical manufacturers examines the importance and organisation of the early development of all the industries ancillary to power generation in the last quarter of the 19th century.

There are numerous studies of individual oil companies, some of them, like Ida Tarbell's muck-raking *History of Standard Oil*, highly tendentious. By contrast, the two volumes by WILLIAMSON *et al.* provide a general economic and social history of the oil industry in all its aspects. The first volume shows how kerosene – that is, oil for lighting – at first accounted for 80 per cent (falling to 60 per cent) of output. Oil was marketed in a competitive environment, partly because sales were uncharacteristically dependent on exports where Russian oil began to create competition in the 1880s, and partly because of the rise of alternative means of illumination – that is gas and electricity – in the domestic market. The second volume carries the story into the 20th century, with the manifold demands for oil for transport and industry. The rise of petro-chemicals is explained in terminology understandable to the layman. The role of, and policy problems created by, the development of oil pipe-lines is examined by JOHNSON.

Since the OPEC crisis of 1973, attention has turned to world energy supplies, and oil has entered the realm of international relations more than ever. CUFF and YOUNG give a geographical assessment of America's mineral resources while CASTLE and PRICE is one of many studies of the international resource problem.

JIM POTTER

See also Oil and Natural Gas

Environment

Cowdrey, Albert E., *This Land, This South: An Environmental History*, Lexington: University Press of Kentucky, 1983
Cronon, William, *Changes in the Land: Indians, Colonists, and the Ecology of New England*, New York: Hill and Wang, 1983
Cronon, William, *Nature's Metropolis: Chicago and the Great West*, New York: Norton, 1991
Petulla, Joseph M., *American Environmental History: The Exploitation and Conservation of Natural Resources*, San Francisco: Boyd and Fraser, 1977; 2nd edition, Columbus, OH: Merrill, 1988
Simmons, I.G., *Environmental History: A Concise Introduction*, Oxford and Cambridge, MA: Blackwell, 1993
Worster, Donald, *Dust Bowl: The Southern Plains in the 1930s*, New York: Oxford University Press, 1979
Worster, Donald (editor), *The Ends of the Earth: Perspectives on Modern Environmental History*, Cambridge and New York: Cambridge University Press, 1988
Worster, Donald, *Under Western Skies: Nature and History in the American West*, New York: Oxford University Press, 1992
Worster, Donald, *The Wealth of Nature: Environmental History and the Ecological Imagination*, New York: Oxford University Press, 1993

Environmental history has emerged as an important field of American history over the past 25 years. Environmental historians seek to integrate the natural world into the study of the past; to examine how humans have adjusted to and transformed the natural world around them. There are currently several worthwhile introductory studies available, as well as studies dealing with environmental history on local, regional, national, and international levels. Some deal with the more traditional fields of political and intellectual history, seeking to discover the ways in which Americans have thought about and managed their environment, while others delve into deeper cultural and ecological aspects.

PETULLA is a comprehensive and accessible introduction to American environmental history. Written in textbook fashion, it takes a chronological approach to examining the human impact on the North American environment from the pre-colonial past to the present. As with most textbooks, its subject matter is broad and its depth is limited. It examines the environmental impact of Native Americans and early European settlers, and then continues up to the present day with sections on agriculture, mining, forestry, and industrialization, all the while attempting to integrate environmental change into the broader field of American history. Petulla is particularly adept at examining the linkages between economic, technological, and environmental factors; however, political and cultural attitudes toward the environment also receive attention with sections on the early 20th century conservation movement and more recent environmental thought. Overall, Petulla's work serves as a valuable introduction and a useful reference source.

SIMMONS, a British geographer, has also written a useful introduction to the field of environmental history. Unlike Petulla, however, Simmons's work is thematic and interpretive rather than chronological and narrative in its approach. Although it does not focus specifically on the United States, dealing instead with world history, it does discuss issues such as the conservation movement, the environmental impact of irrigation, and changing attitudes toward wilderness. It is more useful, however, as an introduction to the aims and method-ology of environmental history and it illustrates these with some fascinating case studies drawn from all over the world. It also contains a helpful discussion of basic ecological concepts which are vital to an understanding of American environmental history.

WORSTER (1988) contains a series of diverse articles that illustrate the range and varieties of environmental history. Worster himself contributes an essay that examines the origins of the field, reviewing literature from disciplines that have influenced environmental historians, such as ecology and anthropology. He also delineates what he considers to be the most important aims of the discipline, and outlines three major levels on which environmental historians should concentrate their efforts: first, understanding changes in nature over time; second, how the socio-economic realm interacts with the environment; and third, explaining the impact of human intellectual and cultural perceptions of the environment. The volume also contains essays by Alfred Crosby on the biological exchanges that occurred when Europeans came into contact with the Americas; by Carville Earle on the environmental impact of agriculture in the South; and by Clayton Koppes on shifting themes and ideas in American conservation history.

There are excellent environmental histories of most regions of the United States, though the Northeast and the West seem to have drawn the most attention. CRONON (1983) is a compact, elegant work, which examines how various peoples interacted with their environment in New England, and how they changed the region's landscape and ecology. Cronon argues that the shift from Indian to European dominance entailed major changes, not only in how various peoples organized their lives, but also in the way the region's plants and animals reorganized theirs. He contrasts the pre-colonial and colonial eco-systems, and is especially interested in the differing views of Indians and colonists on land ownership, which helped shape the pattern of the landscape.

COWDREY is a significant contribution to both environmental and Southern history. Taking a *longue duree* approach, it begins with the pleistocene age, and works its way purposefully toward the present. Along the way, Cowdrey manages to describe and explain the processes of change and interaction between the region's topography, geology, ecology, economy, and society. The book is organized along roughly chronological lines with most chapters containing sections on ecological change and on the interaction between people and their environment. Eschewing the Civil War, a rare thing for a work that purports to explain southern uniqueness, Cowdrey nevertheless manages to deal with ecological exchanges resulting from the migration of flora and fauna (including humans); with the development of tobacco and cotton agriculture and its ecological and socio-economic consequences; and the impact of ideology and politics on the southern environment, especially the New Deal, which Cowdrey sees as a major watershed in southern history as it helped cement human control over the environment.

The finest work of environmental history dealing with the Midwest is arguably CRONON (1991), a pioneering and magisterial work that attempts to show how "first nature" (the pre-European environment) was modified and commodified into "second nature" (nature that has been transformed by human activity). In the process, Cronon quite brilliantly shows how the city of Chicago, as the major city in the region, helped to transform the environment into "second nature" and in return was itself shaped and fueled by this process.

In the quintessential environmental history of the southern Great Plains, WORSTER (1979) argues that the Dust Bowl of the 1930s was largely a human-made disaster created by an economic culture that emphasized constant growth and quick profits. Farmers moving west into Texas, Oklahoma, and Kansas in the 19th century brought with them the "culture of capitalism and attempted to get the most out of the land as quickly as possible." In the semi-arid, ecologically delicate short-grass prairie eco-system, the practice of capitalist agriculture was a recipe for disaster. In a collection of his own essays, WORSTER (1992) offers another fine introduction to the environmental history of the West. It tackles most of the familiar themes in Worster's work, including the environmental impact of capitalism, the attempt to dominate nature and to view it as a commodity, and the effects of irrigation and agriculture on the western landscape and eco-system. There is also a lengthy essay on Alaska and how it fits into the broader environmental history of the West. WORSTER (1993) is a still more recent study of many of his familiar themes by one of the most influential and prolific scholars in American environmental history.

FRANK ZELKO

See also Conservation; Nature

Equality

Cohen, Marshall, Thomas Nagel, and Thomas Scanlon (editors), *Equality and Preferential Treatment: A Philosophy and Public Affairs Reader*, Princeton: Princeton University Press, 1977

Foner, Eric, *Nothing but Freedom: Emancipation and Its Legacy*, Baton Rouge: Louisiana State University Press, 1983

Gans, Herbert J., *More Equality*, New York: Pantheon, 1973

McPherson, James M., *The Struggle for Equality: Abolitionists and the Negro in the Civil War and Reconstruction*, Princeton: Princeton University Press, 1964; with new preface, 1995

Montgomery, David, *Beyond Equality: Labor and the Radical Republicans, 1862–1872*, New York: Knopf, 1967

Morgan, Edmund S., *The Birth of the Republic, 1763–89*, Chicago: University of Chicago Press, 1956; 3rd edition, 1992

Morgan, Edmund S., *Inventing the People: The Rise of Popular Sovereignty in England and America*, New York: Norton, 1988

Paludan, Phillip S., *A Covenant with Death: The Constitution, Law, and Equality in the Civil War Era*, Urbana: University of Illinois Press, 1975

Pole, J.R., *The Pursuit of Equality in American History*, Berkeley: University of California Press, 1978, revised 1993

Redenius, Charles, *The American Ideal of Equality: From Jefferson's Declaration to the Burger Court*, Port Washington, NY: Kennikat Press, 1981

Verba, Sidney and Gary R. Orren, *Equality in America: The View from the Top*, Cambridge, MA: Harvard University Press, 1985

Equality is a word with a variety of meanings and it appears in many different historical contexts. For an introduction to the American concept of "equality," however, two works by Morgan – neither of which includes any reference to equality in its title – offer an appropriate starting point. MORGAN (1956, 1992) is a relatively brief student text on the period of the American Revolution. It provides a useful introduction to the American discovery of "the principle of human equality" during the Revolutionary era, a principle that was eventually asserted most notably in the Declaration of Independence. Despite their sincere belief in it, Americans "were not prepared to follow the principle of equality to its logical political conclusion," says Morgan – for example in the establishment of their state legislatures. From the start, the principle of equality was constrained by the attitude toward property. An affirmation of their equality with Englishmen, rather than total equality *per se*, was what most 18th-century Americans had in mind, and glaring contradictions of the principle – most obviously the existence of slavery in American society – were not likely to be easily or speedily resolved.

Pursuing the subject in more depth, MORGAN (1988) examines the expansion of the American idea of equality through the growth of "popular sovereignty," and the limitations of the idea in social, political and economic practice. Inevitably, the subject of equality figures prominently in many other studies of the Declaration of Independence, the making of the Constitution, and, more generally, of 18th-century political thought, not all of which can be covered here. Among the most useful and important are Gordon S. Wood, *The Creation of the American Republic, 1776-1787* (Chapel Hill: University of North Carolina Press, 1969), on the political interpretation and application of the concept of equality; and another work by Morgan, *American Slavery, American Freedom: The Ordeal of Colonial Virginia* (New York: Norton, 1975), on its social and racial implications.

POLE is the main – indeed, the only – sustained study of equality in American history. It is an impressive and broad-ranging work, which traces the American approach to, and understanding of, the idea of equality from the 18th century through to the present day. From the earliest days of the republic, Pole reminds us, "equal rights meant equal claims rather than equal obligations." The idea of equality has had, Pole reminds us, "since the nation's founding hours a tenacity which afforded a peculiar glamor to American claims and

pretensions." In practice, and often in principle, however, the ideal was limited only to certain groups in American society, and was far from inclusive in application. In the course of his analysis of this topic, Pole covers such subjects as: religious tolerance, emancipation, immigration, assimilation and the nature of citizenship, female suffrage, and civil rights. In short, this is a major study of a multi-faceted subject, richly stimulating if not always an easy read. It does not, unfortunately, include any guide for further reading on the topic.

Apart from Pole, other works on equality vary greatly in approach and also in quality. GANS is a sociological rather than a historical study, but, for some purposes, may prove of interest. (It does include a useful, if now rather dated, bibliography, which does cite more "historical" material.) The work comprises a collection of the author's essays on the theme of "equality of results," some of which originally appeared elsewhere – such as in the *American Journal of Sociology* and the *New York Times Magazine* – and some of which were composed specifically for this volume. Gans approaches his subject by subdividing it into three main sections, within which he covers such topics as the demands for change that came from African American and women's groups in the 1960s and 1970s; the rising expectations of the American middle classes; and the importance of economic and political equality. Inevitably, as a work which was, for the most part, a response to debates conceived in the 1960s, both its arguments and its conclusions have been overtaken by more recent work on the "underclass debate," and on the social and economic problems facing late 20th century America.

Among more recent works, REDENIUS is a study of the "ideal" (rather than the "idea") of equality, which emphasizes the uniqueness of the American experiment as far as equal rights are concerned. Equality as understood by Americans, he argues, is an aspirational ideal, which seeks to level upwards. Many of the main points made in this study are better made, and more comprehensively debated, in Pole – particularly the argument that equality in America is more concerned with individualism than with collectivism. There is a sustained discussion of the role played by the immigrant, whom Redenius sees as "pragmatic," with an "open bent of mind, one that was predisposed to cast old ideas into new moulds," and of the role played by the "common man" and also by America's presidents in the development of the principle of equality. The work includes a useful, if short, bibliography on the subject.

VERBA and ORREN examine the contradictions that exist in America between political equality and economic inequality. As the authors themselves put it, this work is "both practical and theoretical." It begins by comparing the American political and economic system with that of other democratic nations, and identifies four distinctions to be kept in mind when assessing the nature and extent of equality in America: between economics and politics, the reality and the ideal, the individual and the group, and the opportunity and the result. Equality, Verba and Orren remind us, is a constantly recurring theme in American history, and one which has been especially relevant at various times, including the Revolutionary era, the Jacksonian period, the Civil War and in the 1960s and 1980s. It is unclear why the decade between these two last examples, which saw so much women's rights activity, is neglected, but perhaps it is because the assessment here, as the title suggests, concentrates on the concept of equality as espoused by America's 20th-century leaders (up to and including Ronald Reagan), and on how they developed, and promulgated, their views on the subject.

Several works focus on the Civil War and Reconstruction periods of American history, and on the changes that emancipation brought to American society and to the practice of equality. These include McPherson, Montgomery, Paludan and, more recently, Foner. In a book originally published more than thirty years ago, McPHERSON analyzes northern abolitionist attitudes towards emancipation and equal rights from the outbreak of the Civil War through to the passage of the Fifteenth Amendment in 1870. Although he warns in his new (1995) preface that the perspective of the work reflects the period in which it was composed – the civil rights era – this in no way detracts from what remains an extremely useful and important study of ideas about equality, and the often ambivalent attitude that Americans have expressed both toward the ideal and toward those who espoused it most strongly.

PALUDAN comprises a series of case studies of individuals such as Francis Lieber and Sidney George Fisher, and aims to "answer important questions about the struggle for equality and the disunion crisis which gave that struggle hope." The growth of hostility toward slavery and the South, the impact of racism, and the revolutionary nature of what has been termed the "Second American Revolution" are just some of the issues that Paludan addresses in what is an extremely detailed and in-depth consideration of the "ability of law to adapt" to the changes brought about in American society by the Civil War. Ultimately, Paludan concludes, it was another case of an opportunity, if not exactly missed, then certainly mishandled. Unable to justify the expense (be it economic or social) of guaranteeing to the freedmen the full equal rights to which they were entitled, the federal government failed either to test the limits or to implement the full weight of its authority. Concluding that, in strict constitutional terms, equality could not be enforced, the government relegated the problem of equal rights for African Americans to the South.

The latter part of this turbulent period is the focus of MONTGOMERY's study of the process whereby "capitalism eliminated slavery and redefined the relations between citizen and state." By connecting the issues of Reconstruction to the activities of the labor movement during this same period, he raises important issues about the meanings of liberty and equality. In a short book derived from his 1982 Fleming Lectures, FONER synthesizes a large amount of material in the course of three distinct, but linked, chapters, covering "The Anatomy of Emancipation," "The Politics of Freedom," and "The Emancipated Worker." Foner's work also enjoys the benefit of the comparative approach. He examines the emancipation process in the British Caribbean, Haiti and, to a lesser extent, southern and eastern Africa before turning to the American case. Throughout, Foner's focus is not on equality *per se*, but rather on the construction of a new social order in which equality was not achieved and which offered the African American "nothing but freedom."

The collection of essays edited by COHEN *et al.* focuses on the position of African Americans and women in American society. There are essays on such topics as: "Equal Treatment and Compensatory Discrimination"; "Justifying Reverse Discrimination in Employment; and "School Desegregation". As a slightly older text, some of its arguments do now seem somewhat dated, but it offers useful insights into various strands of the equality debate.

S-M. GRANT

Era of Good Feelings, c. 1815–1824

Ammon, Harry, *James Monroe: The Quest for National Identity*, New York: McGraw Hill, 1971

Dangerfield, George, *The Awakening of American Nationalism, 1815–1828*, New York: Harper, 1965

Freehling, William W., *The Road to Disunion: Secessionists at Bay, 1776–1854*, New York: Oxford University Press, 1990

Hammond, Bray, *Banks and Politics in America, from the Revolution to the Civil War*, Princeton: Princeton University Press, 1957

Hargreaves, Mary W.M., *The Presidency of John Quincy Adams*, Lawrence: University Press of Kansas, 1985

Moore, Glover, *The Missouri Controversy, 1819–1821*, Lexington: University Press of Kentucky, 1953

Peterson, Merrill D., *The Great Triumvirate: Webster, Clay and Calhoun*, New York: Oxford University Press, 1987

Remini, Robert V., *Andrew Jackson and the Course of American Empire, 1767–1821*, New York: Harper, 1977

Remini, Robert V., *Andrew Jackson and the Course of American Freedom, 1822–1832*, New York: Harper, 1981

Rothbard, Murray, *The Panic of 1819: Reactions and Policies*, New York: Columbia University Press, 1962

Sellers, Charles, *The Market Revolution: Jacksonian America, 1815–1846*, New York: Oxford University Press, 1991

Turner, Frederick Jackson, *Rise of the New West, 1819–1829*, New York: Harper, 1906

The decade from the end of the War of 1812 to the collapse of Jeffersonian hegemony and the emergence of the Jacksonians to power in the elections of 1824 and 1828 is often referred to as the "Era of Good Feelings." The term makes some sense for the beginning of the period, which was characterized by peace, prosperity and political harmony, but not for the second half, which was dominated by a depression, sectionalism and sharp political division. It was also a decade in which the way most people lived and earned their livings was fundamentally altered. Given the significance of these developments, the quality of the existing historical literature tends to be disappointing.

Now almost a century old, TURNER still remains one of the most important books ever written about the 1820s. It is organized around the concept of sectionalism and concisely lays bare the geographical, social and economic differences that characterized the various regions of the United States: New England, the Middle Atlantic states, the South and the West. He examines the views of these different areas on what he considers to be the great issues of the day, the tariff, a federal program of internal improvements, public land policy and the slavery question. For Turner, it is the emergence of the West to a position of dominance, as signified by Jackson's victory in 1828, that is the dynamic element of the decade. For all its virtues, however, the book pays insufficient attention to class and other conflicts to be found within regions, and it does not deal adequately with such developments as urbanization, the emergence of a labor movement, the proliferation of banks, and the nature of the Jeffersonian heritage against which the Jacksonians rebelled.

DANGERFIELD is a major synthesis of the period, and a wonderful example of narrative history. Its central theme is the struggle between the nationalism of the American System advocated by Henry Clay and John Quincy Adams and the democratic nationalism espoused by Jackson's partisans. Dangerfield also delineates the economic rivalry that emerged during these years between the United States and Great Britain. While the book is a delight to read, the analysis, reflecting in many ways the inadequacies of the secondary literature available at the time it was written, does not go very far below the surface.

Much more recent is SELLERS, a sweeping, penetrating and controversial analysis of the entire Jacksonian era. It stresses the connection between the social and economic changes transforming America and political developments. The chapters dealing with the 1815–28 period are especially good, even brilliant. The main thesis is that democracy developed in tension with capitalism in the United States. Sellers has been criticized for using the concept of the Market Revolution to explain too much, and for adopting a Marxist point of view, which is hostile to the development of middle-class values, and romanticizes America's agrarian and pre-capitalist past.

There are also a number of valuable studies that deal with specific aspects of the period. The problems created by the spread of banking institutions are well treated in HAMMOND. It is a complex subject, but Hammond's erudition and skill as a writer make it accessible, although he is better in explaining the function of banks than he is on politics. He also does not sufficiently appreciate the hold that the agrarian ideal had upon the psyche of many Americans. The Panic of 1819 and the problems unleashed by it are examined in ROTHBARD. He deals with such issues as debtor-creditor relations, monetary reform and expansion and the movement for a protective tariff. Although competent in handling economic issues, he fails to put them in a social context or examine their political implications.

The standard treatment of the Missouri crisis is MOORE. The book is well-researched and presents a clear and detailed narrative, but its viewpoint is dated and somewhat cynical when dealing with the motivations of the anti-slavery forces. A broader and more thoughtful treatment of the emergence of slavery as a political issue may be found in FREEHLING. It is especially good in describing the complex and diverse nature of the Old South, but does not always meaningfully connect the politics of slavery to the other issues of the Jefferson-Jackson era.

Biographies are a useful way of looking at developments in the 1815–28 period. PETERSON treats the period from the vantage point of Henry Clay, Daniel Webster and John C. Calhoun in his well-crafted joint examination of the lives of these three important figures. The book is knowledgeable, thoughtful, and sensible, but does not break new ground. James Monroe presided over much of the Era of Good Feelings, and AMMON's competent and careful biography is generally as quiet and unexciting as its subject. It paints a largely sympathetic portrait of a president in tune with the nationalist mood of the times, but often restrained by constitutional scruples and political pressures. REMINI is now the standard biography of Jackson whose emergence as a political figure put an end to the so-called Era of Good Feelings. The book is an unusually lively account that makes full use of the existing sources and the current secondary literature, and is full of wonderful anecdotes. However, some scholars believe its breezy writing style tends to an oversimplification of complex events. The first two volumes of this three-volume work cover this period, as well as much else. The fullest treatment of John Quincy Adams's troubled presidency is to be found in HARGREAVES. It is a solid account of the interlude between the end of the Virginia dynasty and Jackson's triumph in 1828. It does not deal adequately with the more impersonal social and economic forces which shaped politics at that time, and also views events too exclusively through the eyes of Adams and Clay.

RICHARD E. ELLIS

Erie Canal

Bourne, Russell, *Floating West: The Erie and Other American Canals*, New York: Norton, 1992

Condon, George E., *Stars in the Water: The Story of the Erie Canal*, New York: Doubleday, 1974

Miller, Nathan, *The Enterprise of a Free People: Aspects of Economic Development in New York State During the Canal Period, 1792–1838*, Ithaca, NY: Cornell University Press, 1963

Shaw, Ronald E., *Erie Water West: A History of the Erie Canal, 1792–1854*, Lexington: University Press of Kentucky, 1966

Shaw, Ronald E., *Canals for a Nation: The Canal Era in the United States, 1790–1860*, Lexington: University Press of Kentucky, 1990

Wyld, Lionel D., *Low Bridge! Folklore and the Erie Canal*, Syracuse, NY: Syracuse University Press, 1962

Stretching 363 miles from Albany on the Hudson to Buffalo on Lake Erie, the Erie Canal, completed in 1825, was one of the most important and successful internal improvements undertaken by Americans during the first half of the 19th century. Its success demonstrated for the first time that canals could do as much to promote industry, trade, and travel in America as they had done in England. There are two excellent surveys by Bourne and by Shaw of American canals and the canal-building era before the Civil War. BOURNE has three good chapters devoted to the Erie Canal's history, construction, and social impact, and includes illustrations and engineering and technical drawings showing how the canal was constructed and how it operated. It is a well-written account suitable for the general reader. SHAW (1990) is a general history of the canal-building era which reflects the influence of economic studies that have emphasized the dual role of mixed enterprise and government in canal building. Shaw sees canal building in the United States as an expression of 19th-century nationalism, a very important aspect of which was the preservation of republicanism. Canals linked the newly developing West to the original states and, by thus binding the Union together, ensured the expansion of republican government and institutions. He sees canals as "audacious achievements" of engineering and construction, often in seemingly impossible terrain. The narrative is filled with detailed information about construction problems, engineering achievements, labor relations, financing, politics, and social history. The volume's comprehensive and detailed treatment of canal building will appeal more to the specialist than to the general reader.

SHAW (1966) is an engaging and readable study that focuses entirely on the Erie Canal, beginning with the inception of the idea in 1792 and tracing the canal's construction and operation until 1854, when the transition from canal to railroad transportation was far advanced. It is a balanced study that deals with the full scope of the canal's history, including at the outset its advocates and opponents, its construction and operation, the transfer of canal engineering technology, travel and commerce, and its social and cultural significance. It successfully shows the place the Erie Canal played in the lives of the people who planned, built, and first traveled on it. An important focus is on the politics of canal construction, culminating in a major political showdown in 1854 between Whigs and Democrats over the canal's enlargement.

Shaw's history of the canal complements MILLER, an essentially economic study of the impact of the canal's financing on the fiscal operations of New York's banking institutions, and on the state government itself. The volume demonstrates just how much the canal contributed to the economic development of the towns along the route and how it played a major role in making New York the "Empire State." The canal was immensely profitable. Revenues generated by canal traffic were deposited at interest in various banks along the canal route. These funds, used by the banks in their lending operations, promoted economic growth. In times of crisis, such as the Panics of 1834 and 1837, the Canal Commission was able through its control of these deposits to exercise functions of a central bank. Its control of bank reserves enabled the Commission, for example, to promote fiscal responsibility during the Panic of 1837 by compelling the speedy resumption of specie payment. While the study is, for the most part, too specialized and narrow in focus to appeal to the general reader, it contains background information about the operations of banks and other investment agencies of the day that will be of interest to all.

WYLD is a popular treatment of the Erie Canal which the author aptly describes as "a kind of a folklorist's tour on the one hand and a literary history on the other." Drawing on a wide variety of sources, including gazettes, diaries, journals, memoirs, newspapers, and folklore, it recounts the folktales and songs of the canallers and relates stories and experiences about life and travel on the canal. Following a brief summary of the canal's planning and construction, and the grand celebration of its triumphal opening, the volume examines the language and colloquialisms, or "canalese," that the people working on the canal developed. It sketches the towns and villages along the route and describes folk characters who lived there. An interesting chapter on canal songs and ballads includes the words and music of such well-known songs as "Low Bridge" and "The Erie Canal." The place of the Erie Canal in tall tales, poetry, drama, and novels is also examined. The interesting cultural mosaic which this book offers will appeal to the social historian, the folklorist, and the general reader.

CONDON is another popular history written for the general reader. It offers sketches of a series of places and people linked to the Erie Canal. Places include such cities as Albany, Rochester, Syracuse, and Buffalo, cities which grew and flourished, according to Condon, because of the Erie Canal. The people include famous men such as DeWitt Clinton, who sponsored the canal, and President William McKinley, who was assassinated at its western terminus. Men not so well known, such as the faceless Irish workers who dug the canal and the immigrants who rode it westward, are included as well. Lively and entertaining though it is, its failure to document the source of its stories and statistics will disappoint the specialist but will not limit its broader appeal.

CHARLES D. LOWERY

See also Internal Improvements; Rivers and Canals

Expansionism

Drinnon, Richard, *Facing West: The Metaphysics of Indian-Hating and Empire-Building*, Minneapolis: University of Minnesota Press, 1980

Horsman, Reginald, *Race and Manifest Destiny: The Origins of American Racial Anglo-Saxonism*, Cambridge, MA: Harvard University Press, 1981

LaFeber, Walter, *The New Empire: An Interpretation of American Expansion, 1860–1898*, Ithaca, NY: Cornell University Press, 1963

May, Ernest R., *Imperial Democracy: The Emergence of America as a Great Power*, New York: Harcourt Brace, 1961

Merk, Frederick with Lois Bannister Merk, *Manifest Destiny and Mission in American History: A Reinterpretation*, New York: Knopf, 1963

Pletcher, David M., *The Diplomacy of Annexation: Texas, Oregon, and the Mexican War*, Columbia: University of Missouri Press, 1973

Stephanson, Anders, *Manifest Destiny: American Expansionism and the Empire of Right*, New York: Hill and Wang, 1995

Welch, Richard, *Response to Imperialism: The United States and the Philippine-American War, 1899–1902*, Chapel Hill: University of North Carolina Press, 1979

The rise of the United States to the role of superpower is due in large part to American expansion. The first major period of growth occurred between the start of the 18th century and the climax of the sectional crisis. In this period, Americans sought to conquer the land west of the original thirteen colonies on the mainland of British North America. The second wave of American expansion lasted from the 1860s to the early 20th century. In these years, the United States sought to spread its influence and power across the seas to Europe, Asia, and Latin America. Though American expansion predates the start of the 19th century and extends beyond the onset of the 20th century, the periods 1803–48 and 1860–98 comprise the major eras for historians of American expansionism.

Historians studying this subject have utilized various frameworks. One group, typified by Drinnon, Horsman and Welch, use intellectual and cultural explanations to define United States expansionism. Others, such as LaFeber, focus on economic motivations of American growth, while Pletcher, on the other hand, evaluates American expansion in political and diplomatic terms. Merk and May offer somewhat more diverse and synthetic evaluations of American expansion.

DRINNON is concerned with racism and its role as a motivating factor in the expansion of America. The first three sections, nearly one-half the book, explore the relationship between Indians and white Americans from the 1630s to 1840s. Using mostly literary sources, Drinnon focuses primarily on individuals as he crosses the spectrum from the Puritan-Pequot War of 1630 to William Gilmore Simms and Robert Montgomery Bird in the 1830s and 1840s. By tracing white attitudes toward the Indian from the 1630s, Drinnon persuasively argues that American racism as a cultural phenomenon far predates the appearance of scientific racism in the mid-19th century. Heavily influenced by Freudian theory, Drinnon finds this cultural racism embedded in the sexual and psychic repression of white colonists. The second half of his book discusses the theory and practice of United States expansion in the late 19th and 20th centuries. He explains the growth during this period as not being very different from the 1630s or 1840s. The United States Army treated Filipinos at the turn of the 20th century much as white Americans had treated Indians. This later section focuses particularly on individuals and, in his discussion of the Vietnam war, for example, he engages in a lengthy examination of CIA agent Edward Lansdale.

HORSMAN offers a more substantial look at the origins and effects of scientific racism in mid-19th century North America. Like Drinnon, Horsman traces the theory of American exceptionalism – which both authors contend is the major intellectual driving force behind American expansionism – to the Puritans. The Puritans, convinced that their social institutions had allowed them to survive and succeed in the New World, concluded that Providence had bestowed upon them an obligation to export those institutions to less fortunate races, like Indians. By the 1830s, Horsman explains, American scientists – phrenologists for example – began to offer physiological explanations for the superiority of the Anglo-Saxon race. After explaining the origins of American racial Anglo-Saxonism, Horsman uses literary and historical source material to demonstrate how American racialism motivated the United States' drive for expansion, especially during the Mexican-American War.

In his analysis of the politics and diplomacy of this period, PLETCHER argues that power, not culture, dictated the course of American expansionism in the mid-19th century. He focuses on the Anglo-American dispute over Oregon and the Mexican-American dispute over Texas to argue that the United States went to war over the Southwest, and not Oregon, because the Mexicans were much weaker than the British, not necessarily because the Mexicans were non-white. Power politics, Pletcher asserts, dictated the form that American expansion took in the mid-19th century. He also argues that President James K. Polk took the initiative in beginning the Mexican-American War.

Though LaFEBER agrees that American exceptionalism provided the impetus for American expansion during the latter 19th century, he argues for the primacy of economic motives. After devoting a large part of his introduction to a study of the industrial revolution in the United States, LaFeber concludes that "It was not accidental that Americans built their new empire at the same time their industrial complex matured." He argues that America's expansion abroad, especially into Latin America and Asia, represented a desire for markets. Using more traditional historical sources than Drinnon or Horsman, LaFeber places a major focus on the American business community during this period of American expansion.

WELCH focuses on the American domestic response to the Spanish-American War of 1898. Specifically, he traces the history of the Anti-Imperialist League's efforts to stop the United States' course of expansion at the end of the 19th century. He pays particular attention to individual groups and their attitudes to the war and the American acquisition of the Philippines. These groups include many New Englanders, Methodists, Catholics, and black Americans. This method of inquiry provides a very useful analysis of how Americans viewed their nation's course of expansion.

Though MAY, who focuses on the Spanish-American War, and MERK, who discusses the Mexican-American War, primarily concern themselves with public opinion, each takes up issues discussed by the other authors. For example, May disagrees with LaFeber and argues that an over-hysterical public pressured the American business community into supporting the Spanish-American War. By analyzing Congressional speeches and editorial writing during the 1830s and 1840s, Merk contends that public hysteria moved the administration of James K. Polk to war against Mexico.

There is a recent brief survey of the whole history of American expansionism, from colonial times to the 1980s, in STEPHANSON, who argues that political, religious, social, and economic factors contributed to a powerful expansionist ideology.

PETER K. PARIDES

See also Imperialism and Anti-Imperialism; Manifest Destiny; Westward Expansion

F

Family

Cashin, Joan E., *A Family Venture: Men and Women on the Southern Frontier*, New York: Oxford University Press, 1991

Demos, John, *A Little Commonwealth: Family Life in Plymouth Colony*, New York: Oxford University Press, 1970

Gutman, Herbert G., *The Black Family in Slavery and Freedom, 1750–1925*, New York: Pantheon, and Oxford: Blackwell, 1976

Hawes, Joseph M. and Elizabeth I. Nybakken, *American Families: A Research Guide and Historical Handbook*, New York: Greenwood Press, 1991

Levy, Barry, *Quakers and the American Family: British Settlement in the Delaware Valley*, New York: Oxford University Press, 1988

Mintz, Steven, *A Prison of Expectations: The Family in Victorian Culture*, New York: New York University Press, 1983

Mintz, Steven and Susan Kellogg, *Domestic Revolutions: A Social History of American Family Life*, New York: Free Press, and London: Collier Macmillan, 1988

Ryan, Mary P., *Cradle of the Middle Class: The Family in Oneida County, New York, 1790–1865*, Cambridge and New York: Cambridge University Press, 1981

Skocpol, Theda, *Protecting Soldiers and Mothers: The Political Origins of Social Policy in the United States*, Cambridge, MA: Belknap Press of Harvard University Press, 1992

Smith, Daniel Blake, *Inside the Great House: Planter Family Life in Eighteenth Century Chesapeake Society*, Ithaca, NY: Cornell University Press, 1980

The best overview of American family history is MINTZ and KELLOGG. Accessible to students, and useful to specialists, this survey covers the colonial period to the 1980s. The very readable narrative avoids jargon, and includes two appendices to explain methodology and basic terminology. For specialists, an important source of information and guidance on many aspects of the subject is HAWES and NYBAKKEN.

The chronological emphasis of the literature on the family discussed here runs from the colonial period through the 19th century. Although there are monographs on the 20th-century family, that historiography is less well developed at this stage. Colonial historians facilitated the birth of family history, as a cluster of community studies from the early 1970s opened up this new field. Using quantitative demographic data and borrowing methods from anthropology and psychology, DEMOS (and other scholars) have described a colonial family that was tightly bound, strictly supervised by the state, and vigorously patriarchal. Colonial New Englanders, it seemed, socialized their children into strict obedience to church, state, and father. Nor did reaching adulthood end the obedience and respect demanded from children by their parents. By withholding transfer of property until their deaths, fathers maintained control over their sons long after they had reached adulthood.

By the early 1980s, historians had recognized that class, race, and region were important variables in the discussion of "the family." In fact, there were so many variations that there was no such thing as "the family." GUTMAN, for example, examined the impact of slavery on African American families. He argued that slavery did not destroy slave families, but instead slaves maintained strong families bolstered by kinship ties that stretched far beyond the nuclear family. These extended kinship systems drew upon West African traditions while confronting New World conditions. The family was the source of support for individuals, and the transmitter of culture for the slave community.

SMITH found that whites in the colonial Chesapeake had dramatically different demographic trends from those of New England, trends which helped produce a very different familial ethos from that of Puritan New England. Planter class families desired to raise independent, self-reliant adults, and used a permissive parenting style to achieve that goal. Chesapeake parents permitted far more rebelliousness and indiscipline in their children than New Englanders would have found acceptable. Moreover, these families appear quite "modern": they were affectionate, child-centered, and very private. During the 18th century, patriarchal authority softened, and affectionate relations between spouses grew. At the same time, the separate spheres for men and women grew more distant, as slave-produced wealth allowed planter class women to withdraw into a more purely domestic role.

While Smith and others examined families within discrete classes, RYAN went further and suggested that in fact the family was the essential building block for the making of the middle class. In a sophisticated local study of antebellum Utica, New York, Ryan found that artisan and shopkeeping families began developing a new set of family relations, gender norms, and social mores. "Domesticity," combined with evangelicalism, helped to define the values and the culture which made the new middle class distinct and cohesive. LEVY suggested that "domesticity" originated even earlier, with the Quaker inhabitants of 17th century Pennsylvania. Under the pressure of a religious ideal which attempted to spiritualize marriage and family relations, colonial Quakers developed an early version of domesticity which came to dominate their culture and even influenced their economic decisions. Colonial Quaker families, then, were also very "modern."

Scholars have often suggested that the modern family is not only affectionate, it is also extremely private, isolated from the outside world, and resistant to intrusion from the state. MINTZ rejected the view that the Victorian family was a "haven in a heartless world," and argued instead that the Victorian family socialized its members properly to prepare them for life in the outside world. The family was in effect a microcosm of the world, where children learned to negotiate, battle, and debate with adults, where adult gender roles were acquired, and where class values were learned. The outside world was brought in, to be learned and adopted in small doses, in the protective environment of the home.

Other recent scholars have challenged the view that the 19th-century family successfully resisted state intervention. SKOCPOL, for example has pointed out numerous ways in which the state attempted to intervene in family life in order to bolster the institution. Veterans pensions, public schooling, protective labor legislation, and mothers pensions were some of the ways in which governments at various levels acted to prop up precariously balanced families.

Another recent trend, incorporating insights from women's history, has been the examination of the family through the lens of gender. CASHIN, for example, considered the impact that western migration had on antebellum planter class families. She found that planter class males and females experienced migration and frontier settlement quite differently. Men looked on the westward migration as a positive challenge, a place to prove their masculinity, and a means of escaping the repressive kinship obligations of the established seaboard planter class. Women, however, found themselves bereft of the female kinship network that was so important to their physical and emotional survival. Migration meant more work for women, with less help, fewer educational opportunities, and an increased dependence on their husbands. The southwest frontier may have been a place where men gained independence, but women did not.

ELNA C. GREEN

See also Children and Youth; Marriage and Divorce

Federal Bureau of Investigation

Cook, Fred, *The FBI Nobody Knows*, New York: Macmillan, 1964; London: Cape, 1965
Donner, Frank, *The Age of Surveillance: The Aims and Methods of America's Political Intelligence System*, New York: Knopf, 1980
Garrow, David J., *The FBI and Martin Luther King, Jr.: From "Solo" to Memphis*, New York: Norton, 1981

Keller, William, *The Liberals and J. Edgar Hoover: Rise and Fall of a Domestic Intelligence State*, Princeton: Princeton University Press, 1989
Lowenthal, Max, *The Federal Bureau of Investigation*, New York: Sloane, 1950; London: Turnstile Press, 1951
O'Reilly, Kenneth, *Hoover and the Un-Americans: FBI, HUAC, and the Red Menace*, Philadelphia: Temple University Press, 1983
O'Reilly, Kenneth, *Racial Matters: The FBI's Secret File on Black America, 1960–1972*, New York: Free Press, and London: Collier Macmillan, 1989
Powers, Richard Gid, *G Men: Hoover's FBI in American Popular Culture*, Carbondale: Southern Illinois University Press, 1983
Preston, William, *Aliens and Dissenters: Federal Suppression of Radicals, 1903–1933*, Cambridge, MA: Harvard University Press, 1962; 2nd edition, Urbana: University of Illinois Press, 1994
Summers, Anthony, *Official and Confidential: The Secret Life of J. Edgar Hoover*, New York: Putnam, and London: Gollancz, 1993
Theoharis, Athan and John Stuart Cox, *The Boss: J. Edgar Hoover and the Great American Inquisition*, Philadelphia: Temple University Press, 1988; London: Harrap, 1989

Much as the figure of J. Edgar Hoover dominated the FBI during his long tenure as Director (1924–72), so the ethos which he created has influenced the nature of published works on the Bureau. The secrecy of the agency, its defensiveness in the face of criticism, and the burial of information in a labyrinthine filing system ensured that most of the early works on the FBI were either propaganda efforts by favoured journalists or attempts to discredit and expose clandestine activities by concerned whistleblowers.

However, in 1950, LOWENTHAL, former head of the National Agency for Law Enforcement, published a closely argued and densely documented 500-page account of the history of the FBI. This was a groundbreaking study, an insider's view, based on thirty years' experience in civil service, and meticulous sourcing from government documents. While the anti-Bureau bias is clear and the language sometimes impenetrable, it offers a rich source of information on the origins of domestic surveillance, and the introduction and spread of wiretapping. Discredited and "killed" on publication as Communist-inspired, it enjoyed a resurgence in the 1970s and remains a standard early source.

The activities of the Bureau in World War I and its aftermath, and in particular its role in the campaign against enemy aliens, are examined in PRESTON. Using Bureau files since lost to the public (cleansed by the agency after Preston's publication), he shows convincingly the origins of later covert action in the early career of Hoover and Bureau agents. It gives the best account of these seminal years of Bureau activity.

COOK exposed the "hidden" agenda of the Bureau, and, for all his journalistic tone, has provided subsequent scholars with a rich source of inside information. He has pointed investigators toward the unauthorized political surveillance of major figures, and the role of the Director in controlling and determining the structures and operations of the Bureau. The book was seen as a severe indictment of an uncontrolled and dangerously unaccountable agency, and was harshly attacked in the press by FBI defenders.

Hoover's death in 1972, the strengthening of the Freedom of Information Act in 1974, and the Congressional investigations of the mid-1970s, opened up new possibilities for scholars seeking access to FBI records. Under the auspices of the American Civil Liberties Union, DONNER's comprehensive study provides impressive detail on the origins and development of a crusade against nonconformity, and the rationale developed by the Bureau to defend internal surveillance and intelligence gathering. It is essential reading for an understanding of how, why and when the brief for national security became transposed into covert action, and of the central role played by the Bureau in legitimising "spying" on Americans.

The workings of the FBI in the Cold War era have been exhaustively dealt with in O'REILLY (1983). This is a fascinating look at the relations of the Bureau with the House Un-American Activities Committee, in particular, and with agencies of government in general, in the era of McCarthyism. The uncovering of a close relationship between FBI agents and McCarthy, to whom they fed continual information despite public denials, establishes the FBI as central in the anti-Communist purges of the era.

The FBI's operations against civil rights activists, and Martin Luther King in particular, are revealed in Garrow and O'Reilly (1989). GARROW's short study emerged from his biography of King, and focuses upon the FBI's attempts to discredit the civil rights leader in the 1960s. He uses FBI files to show the successive stages of a campaign which variously sought to undermine King for his Communist associations, his radical politics, and his sexual activities. Garrow shows the strong personal animosity felt by Hoover toward King, and how this influenced the sustained attacks by the Bureau, including bugging and extensive disinformation. O'REILLY (1989) covers much wider territory, examining campaigns against a variety of civil rights organizations, and the more radical groupings of the Black Panthers and white supremacy organizations. This is an excellent study of the contrast between the public rhetoric of the New Frontier and the Great Society, and the private operations which sought to discredit both moderate and radical activists. It sheds important light on the FBI attitude toward race and civil rights.

KELLER presents the argument that liberal elements in the United States, and in public office, have been instrumental in furthering the work of the Bureau. He claims that the extension of the FBI's powers from the 1930s onward could not have occurred without the support of the "liberal state", indeed that the contradictions and tensions in liberalism ensured the creation of a "state within a state" for the needs of national security. This is a thought-provoking study of the sources and structures of repression in a democratic society, and Keller's conclusions are likely to remain controversial.

The FBI relationship with the public and the media has received attention in POWERS. He illustrates how the image of the Bureau and its agents was distilled into the archetypal G-man, through the popular press, the radio and the cinema. The creation of the myth of the FBI is an important part of understanding the public approval which supported the Bureau in its law enforcement role. This is an excellent study both of

the influence of the FBI propaganda machine on public attitudes, and of the FBI as part of the history of American popular culture.

Biographies of J. Edgar Hoover have proliferated in recent years, with four published between 1987 and 1993. All have been critical studies of the Director's private and public life, and rely on extensive releases under the Freedom of Information Act. THEOHARIS is arguably the most scholarly, and certainly provides the greatest insight into the extraordinary Bureau files. The interrelationship between the Director's private prejudices and the character of Bureau activities is revealed, and no doubt can remain of his power to control events through the contents of his confidential files. It is an impressive work, well written and accessible, which acknowledges both the dangerous obsessions and the bureaucratic achievements of this extraordinary figure. It will remain the benchmark scholarly biography for the forseeable future.

As a counterbalance to this rather cautious study, SUMMERS presents the image of a corrupt and salacious man in a controversial study, which will stimulate much debate. It may tempt scholars into areas which, because of their "secret" nature, and difficulties of documentation, have too often deterred academic researchers. It is in the nature of the FBI and its Director that "holding" information was the source of power, and Summers raises unanswered questions about the history of the FBI, including its lack of attention to the problem of organized crime.

KATHRYN CASTLE

Federal Government: Establishment of, 1789–1793

Bell, Rudolph M., *Party and Faction in American Politics: The House of Representatives, 1789–1801*, Westport, CT: Greenwood Press, 1973

Bonwick, Colin, *The American Revolution*, London: Macmillan, and Charlottesville: University Press of Virginia, 1991

Buel, Richard, Jr., *Securing the Revolution: Ideology in American Politics, 1789–1815*, Ithaca, NY: Cornell University Press, 1972

Elkins, Stanley and Eric McKitrick, *The Age of Federalism: The Early American Republic, 1788–1800*, New York: Oxford University Press, 1993

Freeman, Douglas Southall, *George Washington: A Biography*, vol. 6: *Patriot and President*, New York: Scribner, and London: Eyre and Spottiswoode, 1954

McDonald, Forrest, *The Presidency of George Washington*, Lawrence: University Press of Kansas, 1974

Miller, John C., *The Federalist Era, 1789–1801*, New York: Harper, 1960

Rutland, Robert Allen, *The Birth of the Bill of Rights, 1776–1791*, Chapel Hill: University of North Carolina Press, 1955

Sharp, James Roger, *American Politics in the Early Republic: The New Nation in Crisis*, New Haven: Yale University Press, 1993

White, Leonard D., *The Federalists: A Study in Administrative History*, New York: Macmillan, 1948

The years immediately following inauguration of the Federal Constitution in 1789 coincided with Washington's first administration and were as crucial to the development of the United States as the 1780s, yet the period has received less attention than it deserves. The Constitution had set out basic principles, sometimes in detail, sometimes in general terms, sometimes with gaps for the new regime to fill; otherwise the new system started almost from scratch. During these years all three branches of government were established, and lasting and important precedents set. A Bill of Rights was ratified and the meaning of the Constitution fleshed out, particularly through the doctrine of implied powers. Simultaneously important issues of policy were resolved.

The period is usually considered only as the opening of a fresh stage in the narrative of American development. BONWICK argues that these processes can also be regarded as part of the Revolutionary settlement. By creating a muscular system in the form of the government itself and a directing nervous system in the form of the party system, they gave life to the skeleton of the Constitution.

Establishment of the federal government is mostly treated as part of broader coverage of the 1790s. A lot of material can be found in biographies of major figures such as Madison, Jefferson and Hamilton, and studies of party formation. MILLER is a narrative coverage of the decade. Its grand theme is the growth of strong national government, and thus it focuses on national politics. There is an undertow of economic interest, but the background of American social and economic development is largely taken for granted. It treats the issues in a much more even-handed form than had been customary in earlier work, particularly on the disputes between Jefferson and Hamilton. Nevertheless, the Federalists occupy the foreground and Hamilton emerges as the man of the future. It is somewhat outdated by recent scholarship, especially concerning race and ethnicity, gender, class, ideology and party growth, but for all these limitations remains the standard systematic treatment of the period.

BUEL's approach a decade later marks a sea change. More limited in range and much narrower in its treatment of Washington's first administration than Miller, it focuses on politics but its analytical stance is inverted. It claims that party formation, not Hamiltonian policy, was the core of politics; insists that ideas and perceptions mattered; and argues that public opinion was the single most crucial ingredient in formation of the first party system.

SHARP recognises that the new regime had to confront many acute problems, including the disjunction between the Founders' ideas and the realities they faced, and argues that the birth of the new regime was far from painless. His analysis takes account of the extensive scholarship of the 1970s and 1980s on American ideology, and challenges the consensual model. He insists that the greatest single problem confronting the new government was establishing its legitimacy as a national authority in a society which had conflicting expectations about the future, and he argues that the old elitist-deferential relationship was being challenged by democratic dissatisfaction. His approach is necessarily analytical rather than narrative or descriptive.

About half of ELKINS and McKITRICK, a work which discusses the entire decade at considerable length, is devoted to the early years. Their approach is largely narrative, but they also provide extensive analysis, and in so doing they differ markedly from Miller, and are more comprehensive than Buel and Sharp. The book's concern is with the emergence of the new nation, and its perspective is ideological; moreover, it takes its lead primarily from the classical republican school of interpretation. Although the principal features of political debate are discussed, no attempt is made to be comprehensive in treatment. Many of the matters omitted by Miller are by design also excluded here, and in that respect the discussion is a little old-fashioned.

McDONALD discusses the establishment of the new government at some length with a sharp eye for the illuminating illustration and detail. Unlike the previous works he demonstrates awareness of the socio-economic context. His discussion has great clarity in that his analysis is couched largely in terms of the rivalry of competing interest groups. Washington's personal contribution is downgraded; McDonald argues that he was important for who he was and as a symbol, not for what his administration achieved, which was largely the work of others. Not all scholars would agree, but this is the best treatment of the subject currently available.

The problems created by starting almost from scratch are described by WHITE. In a deceptively simple study in administrative history, he describes the mechanics of constructing a new government, and demonstrates the importance of humdrum details and the degree to which Washington established commanding precedents which quickly became incorporated into American political behaviour and constitutionalism. He also shows how the federal government began to establish its political hegemony over the states.

FREEMAN focuses steadily and with virtually no deviation on Washington, whose day-by-day, and sometimes hour-by-hour activities are described in elegant and detailed narrative. Although a professionally trained historian as well as a journalist, he provides little extended analysis and assumes that his readers will share his view of Washington as an heroic figure.

RUTLAND is still useful for the narrative of events which led to the attachment of the Bill of Rights to the Constitution, although in other respects the book is rather narrow in its concerns. It traces the background and early precedents for the Bill of Rights, particularly in the first state constitutions, but only one chapter deals with its drafting in Congress and ratification; there is no analysis of its provisions and terms. In so far as it deals with principles it has been overtaken by later work.

BELL uses statistical analysis of voting records to trace sectional, factional and party alignments. His discussion is illuminating, but his highly technical methodology is directed towards professional scholars, particularly political scientists, rather than the general reader.

COLIN BONWICK

See also Early National Period

Federalism

Bryce, James, *The American Commonwealth*, 3 vols., London and New York: Macmillan, 1888

Clark, Jane P., *The Rise of a New Federalism: Federal-State Cooperation in the United States*, New York: Columbia University Press, 1938

Derthick, Martha, *The Influence of Federal Grants: Public Assistance in Massachusetts*, Cambridge, MA: Harvard University Press, 1970

Gelfand, Lawrence E. and Robert J. Neymeyer (editors), *Changing Patterns of American Federal-State Relations During the 1950s, the 1960s, and the 1970s*, Iowa City: University of Iowa Press, 1985

Gelfand, Mark I., *A Nation of Cities: The Federal Government and Urban America, 1933–1965*, New York: Oxford University Press, 1975

Karl, Barry, *The Uneasy State: The United States from 1915 to 1945*, Chicago: University of Chicago Press, 1983

Patterson, James T., *The New Deal and the States: Federalism in Transition*, Princeton: Princeton University Press, 1969

Reagan, Michael D., *The New Federalism*, New York: Oxford University Press, 1981

Sundquist, James L., *Making Federalism Work: A Study of Program Coordination at the Community Level*, Washington, DC: Brookings Institution, 1969

Wright, Deil S., *Understanding Intergovernmental Relations: Public Policy and Participants' Perspectives in Local, State, and National Governments*, North Scituate, MA: Duxbury Press, 1978

Zimmerman, Joseph F., *Contemporary American Federalism: The Growth of National Power*, New York: Praeger, and Leicester: Leicester University Press, 1992

The first students of federalism dealt with the constitutional separation of national and state authority. BRYCE, for example, explains the distinct functions and powers of the federal and state governments in the late 19th century. In the 1930s definitions of federalism shifted to reflect the blurring of governmental activity in the 20th century. CLARK highlights the trend toward shared power, or cooperative federalism, in public administration. Increasing government action (especially in response to the Great Depression) and the concentration of economic power in Washington altered traditional governance. The responsibilities of both state and federal governments grew, according to Clark, and the various levels of government worked together. In particular, Washington used state officials to implement its grant-in-aid (funding) programs for relief, scientific research, and welfare, among others.

The constant tension between local and national authority forms the central motif in KARL's first-rate history of the period from 1915 to 1945. Karl offers a caveat: centralization had not been accomplished by 1945 as some historians had suggested. The New Deal did change political relationships, and people now looked to Washington to solve everyday problems, but it aided local power as well. Karl contends that Americans continued to cling to the dominant political ideology, which stressed independence, individualism, and local autonomy. Karl's interpretation built upon the work of PATTERSON. who examines the New Deal's effect on state governments and finds a mixed legacy. New Deal reforms promoted cooperation and improved the efficiency of state government administration, expanded social legislation, aided political participation, and increased federal spending. Change was modest, however. The 1930s was an era of achievement, but also of confusion and ineffectiveness. The lack of a reform tradition, a shortage of funds, and institutional and political barriers blocked dramatic change, which came in the 1950s and 1960s.

DERTHICK's case study of public assistance in one state underlines the slow pace of reform. Yet significant changes did occur as federal grant-in-aid programs became institutionalized in Massachusetts from 1935 to 1970. Federal intervention liberalized public assistance benefits – making more people eligible for grants and standardizing requirements. In addition, policymaking became centralized, professionalized, and bureaucratized, and less subject to political pressures. The power of program administrators exceeded that of state legislators. In a word, uniformity reigned. Derthick hesitates to attribute this solely to federal influence, but she notes that Washington's role accelerated each transition.

Federalism had entered a new phase by the mid-1960s, according to SUNDQUIST. The number and scope of national programs exploded. Indeed a new term appeared: intergovernmental relations. More than mere academic jargon, it described a now established pattern of federal-state relationships. Sundquist's survey, which originated as a government study of the problems of coordinating various grant-in-aid programs, examines several urban and anti-poverty programs as models. Great Society-era programs, he reports, reflected a new national purpose. Policymaking power had shifted to Washington. New policies were now federal programs, not state programs funded by federal dollars as before, and federal oversight increased. Paradoxically, these new federal programs also attempted to encourage and support community action.

The commitment to community action underscored the complexity of grant delivery in an expanded federalism. Cities as well as community and private interest groups joined the states as actors in an evolving intergovernmental system. GELFAND uncovers the emerging relationship between Washington and city governments. This is a clearly-written but somewhat dry account of the formation of national urban policy. It is not, like Derthick or Sundquist, a study of policy implementation. GELFAND and NEYMEYER, which includes three essays by political scientists, summarizes three eras of federalism: 1935 to 1960, the 1960s, and the 1970s. (It is political scientists, in fact, who have written most widely on federalism.) Intergovernmental relations took root in the first era; they deepened during the 1960s. In the 1970s, Derthick argues, the interdependence among governments grew. Increasing spending by Washington brought chaotic results that did not always increase federal power. States became more dependent on federal funding sources and Congress became more committed to social policy, using its regulatory power in such diverse fields as environmental protection and racial relations. Simultaneously, Washington's power loosened as Congress less clearly defined its policy goals, and policymaking authority fragmented.

By the 1970s, academics and politicians rarely discussed federalism as a static constitutional abstraction. They considered it as a dynamic system of inter-related governments. REAGAN provides a concise account of historical shifts in federalism through the 1970s. He highlights the different types of federal aid and how they worked. WRIGHT covers much of the same material in more detail. It stands as the best textbook of federalism, especially strong in explaining fiscal and tax policies among the national and state governments.

Reagan, like Derthick and Sundquist for example, highlights the benefits of intergovernmental cooperation. Sundquist, in particular, argues that with minor adjustments, grant programs could solve ongoing economic and social problems of the day. A decade-and-a-half later ZIMMERMAN offers a more pessimistic account of recent trends in federalism. He views with trepidation the declining policymaking authority of state and local governments. Ironically, as local power declined, Zimmerman reports, their share of spending – proportional and absolute – increased.

Zimmerman calls the post-1965 era coercive federalism. Revolutionary changes brought unfortunate consequences. Coercive federalism reduced democracy, according to this analysis, by shifting power from ordinary citizens to less representative and accountable special interests. In his book, Zimmerman considers the historical dimensions of federalism – in particular, the constitutional basis of separation of powers, the shifting fiscal relationships among governments, the growing power of the federal judiciary, and the practice of congressional preemption. (This last point refers to the attachment to federal grants of increasingly stringent conditions and regulations which have reduced state power.) This, he argues, had ominous implications in the 1980s when Congress reduced its financial assistance but increased its rule-making power. These issues remain important; questions about the proper reach of federal power continue to provoke fierce and divisive debates in American politics.

CHRISTOPHER MACGREGOR SCRIBNER

See also States Rights

Federalist Papers

Dietze, Gottfried, *The Federalist: A Classic on Federalism and Free Government*, Baltimore: Johns Hopkins Press, 1960

Engeman, Thomas S. (editor), *The Federalist Concordance*, Middletown, CT: Wesleyan University Press, 1980

Epstein, David F., *The Political Theory of The Federalist*, Chicago: University of Chicago Press, 1984

Kesler, Charles R. (editor), *Saving the Revolution: The Federalist Papers and the American Founding*, New York: Free Press, 1987

Millican, Edward, *One United People: The Federalist Papers and the National Idea*, Lexington: University Press of Kentucky, 1990

Ostrom, Vincent, *The Political Theory of a Compound Republic: A Reconstruction of the Logical Foundations of American Democracy*, Blacksburg, VA: Public Choice

Society, 1971; 2nd edition, as *The Political Theory of a Compound Republic: Designing the American Experiment*, Lincoln: University of Nebraska Press, 1987

Rossiter, Clinton (editor), *The Federalist Papers*, New York: New American Library, 1961

White, Morton, *Philosophy, The Federalist, and the Constitution*, New York: Oxford University Press, 1987

In late 1787 and early 1788, James Madison, Alexander Hamilton, and John Jay, writing under the pen name of Publius, crafted a series of 85 essays collectively known as *The Federalist*, to support ratification of the Constitution. Their purpose was not only to counter the arguments of opponents, but to persuade them that the proposed system of government would ensure the nation's survival and the ideals of the Revolution.

ROSSITER's edition of *The Federalist* is perhaps the most accessible and useful of the numerous available editions. Following a brief introduction that establishes the context in which the essays were written, Rossiter includes an annotated table of contents and an appendix that collates the essays with the Constitution. Readers will find this edition especially useful when used in conjunction with Ralph Ketcham's *The Anti-Federalist Papers* (1986) which cross-references the two sets of essays. Of invaluable aid to those performing extensive research on *The Federalist* is ENGEMAN's *Concordance*. This exhaustive reference guide lists citations for key words, providing essay number, page, and line for Jacob E. Cooke's edition of *The Federalist* (Middletown, CT: Wesleyan University Press, 1961). Further, Engeman goes so far as to note whether the entry appears in italics, boldface, a quotation, or parenthesis, and whether in the text or footnote.

DIETZE analyzes the writing of Madison, Hamilton, and Jay by focusing on their political philosophy and the context in which they drafted their arguments. He finds that Publius offered three primary observations in defense of the proposed plan for government: the Constitution would protect the individual from governmental interference; it would moderate conflicts among the states; and it would allow the development of an effective system of national defense. According to Dietze, *The Federalist* outlined two original theories that revolutionized political and constitutional thought: the notion that federalism could protect individual rights, and the introduction of the doctrine of judicial review. Although somewhat dated, this remains a useful introduction to *The Federalist*.

OSTROM, a political theorist, attempts to recover the philosophical underpinnings of American government by way of the Founding Fathers' constitutional theories, especially those of Hamilton and Madison. Through analysis of the writings of Publius, Ostrom attempts to demonstrate the continuing relevance of the essays. He identifies federalism as the critical theory of *The Federalist*, and upon this foundation the Revolutionaries built a compound republic, meaning a division of powers between systems of government and a separation of powers within these systems. Ostrom presents a liberal, Hobbesian interpretation of the essays and maintains that Hamilton and Madison offered a view of human nature characterized by self-interest and individualism. Apparently Ostrom finds little evidence that civic virtue was to play a part in the new republic, an interpretation that many historians will find questionable. Although it is intended primarily for political scientists and constitutional theorists, historians will still find the analysis informative.

In contrast to Ostrom, MILLICAN argues that nationalism, not federalism, is *The Federalist*'s ideological cornerstone. While Millican acknowledges that Publius did assign the states authority over local matters and the role of monitor to prevent the national government from becoming oppressive, he argues that the Founders placed the greatest emphasis on the central government. *The Federalist*'s overarching theme, according to Millican, is that Americans comprised "a national community with a distinct interest." Federalism, separation of powers, popular sovereignty, and representation were vital issues, but, according to the author, these were secondary to the creation of a national government that incorporated Americans' similar values, concerns, and ideals. Millican's focus on nationalism prevents a comprehensive analysis of Publius's political philosophy. His contention that federalist theory played only a minor part in Publius's political theory does not convincingly counter the findings of a number of historians who have successfully demonstrated the centrality of federalism to the *The Federalist*.

EPSTEIN provides a clear and lucid analysis of *The Federalist*, demonstrating that the essays incorporated elements of both liberal *and* republican ideologies. His stated purpose is not only to analyze what the writers wrote, but to discover their understanding of political theories. Epstein argues that Madison and Hamilton defended a governmental structure that sought the liberal goal of protecting individual rights, while concurrently promoting the concept of a common good associated with republicanism. By dividing *The Federalist* into two sections, volume 1 (nos.2–36) that address theories, and volume 2 (nos.37–85) that address application of theories, Epstein shows how Publius successfully created a liberal/republican philosophy. This book is essential to understanding the political theory of *The Federalist* and will be of value to political scientists as well as historians.

WHITE approaches *The Federalist* from the perspective of a philosopher and is little concerned with political and constitutional theories. Instead, he seeks to analyze the writings of Madison, Hamilton, and Jay to establish the philosophical foundation of their ideas. White approaches this formidable task by examining such issues as moral philosophy, ideas of knowledge, and theories of psychology, action, and metaphysics. This is an impressive study, yet historians may come away unsatisfied. White interprets *The Federalist* as a philosophical text, paying little attention to the reality of Publius's immediate concern with gaining ratification of the Constitution.

The essays collected in KESLER will prove useful to those not wishing to plumb the depths of Locke, Hobbes, and political theories. Although Kesler does not ignore these topics, he includes a number of articles that specifically address other issues such as *The Federalist*'s relationship to foreign policy, Americans' acceptance of the essays in the years immediately following ratification of the Constitution, and the Progressive era's apparent neglect of *The Federalist*. Contributors also address the usual political topics of separation of powers, the role of the executive, and federalism, as well as a variety of other issues.

HARRY S. LAVER

See also Constitution: Ratification

Federalist Party

Banner, James M., Jr., *To the Hartford Convention: The Federalists and the Origins of Party Politics in Massachusetts, 1789–1815*, New York: Knopf, 1970

Buel, Richard, Jr., *Securing the Revolution: Ideology in American Politics, 1789–1815*, Ithaca, NY: Cornell University Press, 1972

Elkins, Stanley and Eric McKitrick, *The Age of Federalism: The Early American Republic, 1788–1800*, New York: Oxford University Press, 1993

Fischer, David Hackett, *The Revolution of American Conservatism: The Federalist Party in the Era of Jeffersonian Democracy*, New York: Harper, 1965

Hofstadter, Richard, *The Idea of a Party System: The Rise of Legitimate Opposition in the United States, 1780–1840*, Berkeley: University of California Press, 1969

Kerber, Linda K., *Federalists in Dissent: Imagery and Ideology in Jeffersonian America*, Ithaca, NY: Cornell University Press, 1970

Livermore, Shaw, *The Twilight of Federalism: The Disintegration of the Federalist Party, 1815–1830*, Princeton: Princeton University Press, 1962

Miller, John C., *The Federalist Era, 1789–1801*, New York: Harper, 1960

Sharp, James Roger, *American Politics in the Early Republic: The New Nation in Crisis*, New Haven: Yale University Press, 1993

White, Leonard D., *The Federalists: A Study in Administrative History*, New York: Macmillan, 1948

The formation of political parties in the early years of the Republic has evoked considerable interest among historians, and the role of the Federalist Party, both as a protagonist in the nascent first American party system and as a promoter of a distinctive governmental ideology, has attracted widespread attention. Much of the debate has been between two main schools of thought. On the one hand, there are scholars who emphasize the ferocity of partisan rivalry between Federalists and Republicans; on the other, those who detect, beneath the sound and the fury, a shared belief in fundamental principles. The idea that the fierceness of partisan rhetoric in the 1790s belied a more fundamental consensus on the basic premises of American government is articulated most persuasively in HOFSTADTER, which is particularly interesting on the reaction of the Federalists to their defeat in 1800. He suggests that the absence of any plan for violent resistance or disunion may be taken as an indication that the Federalists, reconciled to their defeat at the polls, had, however unwittingly, gone some way towards advancing the notion of a legitimate opposition.

This view is challenged in SHARP, who contends that, while consensus may be apparent to historians, it was not widely recognised among contemporaries who were still a long way from accepting the formal existence of a party system. Arguing that "proto-parties" emerged "almost in spite of themselves", Sharp sees the Federalists as occupying a pro-commercial position centred particularly around what he describes as the "moralistic republicanism" of New England. An up-to-date and readable study of the political turbulence of the 1790s, this also contains a detailed analysis of the Federalists' role in the contentious aftermath of the 1800 election. Acute ideological and sectional differences are also stressed in BUEL, who portrays the Federalists as fearful elitists alarmed by the radicalism of the French Revolution and the threat posed to the domestic stability of the United States by the democratic sentiments and tactics of their Republican opponents. Buel argues that much of the Federalists' anxiety, particularly in the northern states, stemmed from basic feelings of insecurity about their leadership status, which they believed to be less stable than that of propertied, slave-owning, aristocratic southern Republicans.

Of the more general histories of the period, one of the most accessible is MILLER. This concise study gives a lucid and cogent reading of the major events leading to the formation of parties, such as Hamilton's Reports on Credit and Manufactures, and the French Revolution. Miller concludes that the Federalists, while honest and efficient administrators, were inept and vindictive party politicians. A more recent and much more detailed account and analysis of the same period is ELKINS and McKITRICK. This is a comprehensive treatment of the era based on a prodigious amount of research which offers fascinating insights into a wide range of policies and personalities. The sustained readability of such a lengthy work is a refreshing feature and the well-informed evaluation of diplomacy and politics benefits greatly from a succession of vivid biographical sketches of both leading and secondary figures. Some of the book's major strengths include its appreciation of subtle differences within the Federalist Party hierarchy beyond the conventional division into Hamilton and Adams factions, and its frank recognition of the relatively unimportant diplomatic status afforded the United States by the British and French governments. It is also illuminating on less widely treated subjects such as the implications of siting the national capital on the Potomac.

WHITE is an important and largely sympathetic study of the Federalists' philosophy of government and administrative practice. Identifying the main aims of the Federalist Party as sound credit and strong government, White shows how a clear and consistent doctrine of public administration was formulated which emphasized national over state government, vigorous executive leadership, energetic administration, and the maintenance of high standards of public service. In view of the scale of the task confronting them in the first twelve years of the newly constituted republic, especially given the strident opposition of the emergent Republican Party, White concludes that the Federalists performed creditably and efficiently.

There are several important works exploring the nature of the Federalist Party in opposition. One of the most impressive is FISCHER which charts the rise to prominence of a new breed of young Federalist politicians who rejected the gentlemanly ethics of the old guard, and adopted instead the organizational skills and party techniques recently used with such success by the Republicans. Abandoning the aloof disdain of older leaders both for the discipline of the party and the need to make populist appeals to the mass of voters, these young Federalists, according to Fischer, ensured that a competitive two-party system came into operation in many states. He suggests that the keener electoral competition engendered by the acceptance of modern tactics by younger Federalists played

a major role in the erosion of long-standing patterns of deference in American society, and was thus crucial to the emergence of democracy in the United States.

KERBER offers an interesting analysis of cultural differences between Federalists and Republicans in this era. She argues that the Federalists did not confine themselves to expressions of bitterness at electoral defeat, but frequently voiced dismay at what they perceived to be the "dangerously naive" Republican approach to politics in general, as well as the impracticality of their preferred social system.

An examination of the Federalist mentality in the key state of Massachusetts is provided in BANNER, which explores the social and religious influences on leading Federalists in the state as well as evaluating the long-term intellectual heritage. The book also contains a searching analysis of the Hartford Convention of 1814, which Banner sees as an attempt by moderate Federalists to deflect extremist calls for disunion, during a phase of intense New England opposition to the war with Great Britain. The final disintegration of the Federalist Party in the years after 1815 is discussed in LIVERMORE. This seeks to prove that while the Federalists no longer constituted a credible national opposition to the Republicans by this time, their continued strength in areas such as New England, as well as the seeming acceptance of many of their policies by Republican administrations, sustained their influence into the 1820s and beyond, when prominent Federalists were to be found in the ranks both of the Jacksonian coalition and its opponents.

NEIL CURTIN

See also Parties and Political Movements

Feminism

Buechler, Steven M., *Women's Movements in the United States*, New Brunswick, NJ: Rutgers University Press, 1990

Cott, Nancy F., *The Grounding of Modern Feminism*, New Haven: Yale University Press, 1987

DuBois, Ellen Carol, *Feminism and Suffrage: The Emergence of an Independent Women's Movement in America, 1848–1869*, Ithaca, NY: Cornell University Press, 1978

Epstein, Barbara Leslie, *The Politics of Domesticity: Women, Evangelism, and Temperance in Nineteenth-Century America*, Middletown, CT: Wesleyan University Press, 1981

Flexner, Eleanor, *Century of Struggle: The Woman's Rights Movement in the United States*, Cambridge, MA: Harvard University Press, 1959, revised 1975

Gabin, Nancy F., *Feminism in the Labor Movement: Women and the United Auto Workers, 1935–1975*, Ithaca, NY: Cornell University Press, 1990

Hooks, Bell, *Ain't I a Woman: Black Women and Feminism*, Boston: South End Press, and London: Pluto, 1982

Sharf, Lois, *To Work and to Wed: Female Employment, Feminism, and the Great Depression*, Westport, CT: Greenwood Press, 1980

Yellin, Jean Fagan, *Women and Sisters: The Antislavery Feminists in American Culture*, New Haven: Yale University Press, 1989

One of the basic issues which students of American feminism must resolve is why the feminist movement emerged at the times it did. Many factors should be taken into account, including religious sentiment, economic and demographic change, and the American political context. It is possible to see a progression in women's participation in activities outside the household in the 19th century from church-based Bible and mission societies to temperance reform, abolitionism and the campaign for women's rights. Not all women followed this progression and not all who became active in their churches went on to participate in other reform movements, but many did.

The first feminist movement in the United States built upon several earlier reform movements. Women, no less than men, were caught up in the reform fervor which swept over the United States in the 1820s, 1830s, and 1840s. Religious revivals emphasized the role of the individual conscience and the need to act in accordance with one's beliefs. Women, especially from Protestant Evangelical churches, founded moral reform societies, and worked together in church mission societies, and charity organizations. The temperance and abolitionist movements of the 1830s and 1840s attracted many female supporters who had begun to worry about the impact of the outside world on the home itself. EPSTEIN documents the interrelationships between evangelical religion, temperance, and domestic feminism. She finds that women's special responsibilities acted as a platform for female activism, but does not see women as a unified group.

FLEXNER situates the rise of feminism in the 19th century in the context of the abolitionist movement, rising levels of education, labor union activism, and the westward movement. This is the classic account of the woman's suffrage and feminist movements. It treats the struggle for women's rights as part of the reformist spirit of the mid-19th century. Flexner pioneered a model of inclusive history which examined the rise of a complex movement from a variety of perspectives. This work encompasses the efforts of slave and free, farmer and factory worker, middle and working class women on behalf of women's rights and even includes a chapter on those opposed to women's suffrage.

YELLIN concentrates upon the role of the anti-slavery movement in prompting women to speak and act in public, thereby transgressing the narrowness of the female sphere. She explores the iconography of the anti-slavery movement, the gender and racial symbolism of the early 19th century, the uses of literature as part of the anti-slavery and feminist struggles, and the extent to which the category of "woman" was racially defined. Yellin documents four women's battle against slavery: Angelina Grimké, the daughter of southern slave owners; Lydia Maria Child, a writer who incorporated the plight of slaves into her fiction; Sojourner Truth, a former slave whose words come down to us only through transcriptions of her speeches; and Harriet Jacobs, another former slave whose narrative *Incidents in the Life of a Slave Girl* powerfully portrayed the sexual exploitation of slave women.

Focusing upon a shorter chronological period, DuBOIS's examination of the emergence of the women's movement also sees women's activism as part of the reform movements of their age, particularly abolitionism. By concentrating on the antebellum and Civil War eras, she gives primacy to the racial and gendered dynamics of American life, particularly the conflict between some abolitionists and feminists over the wording of the Fourteenth and Fifteenth amendments. The Fourteenth Amendment provided civil rights to all former slaves, but the effect of the Fifteenth Amendment was to extend suffrage rights only to black men. The argument over whether it was "the Negro's hour" ignored the obvious fact pointed out by Sojourner Truth that women accounted for about half the African American population, but did not benefit from the expansion of the franchise. The battle over these amendments split the old abolitionist movement and fragmented the suffrage movement through the remainder of the 19th century.

Studies of African American women activists emphasize their challenges to the race/gender hierarchies of American life. HOOKS's analysis of feminism in the black community specifically confronts the historiographical tradition which equates feminism with white women and the Civil Rights Movement with black men. She analyzes and indicts racism within the feminist movements of both the 19th and 20th centuries and the sexism of the African American liberation movements. She calls upon feminists to reject all ideologies of oppression, whether based on race, gender, or class.

The feminist struggle altered in the 20th century as COTT notes in her examination of the women's rights movement between 1900 and 1930. As a growing number of women joined the battle for the vote, worked outside the home, undertook higher education, and became sexually aware, the character of the movement changed. More women subscribed to its goals, but after the passage of the women's suffrage amendment those became diverse and diffuse. By exploring the continued discrimination which women encountered in public life (whether in employment or politics) Cott underscores the limitations of legal reform without attitudinal shifts.

Feminism is conventionally regarded as existing in two waves, the first lasting from the 1840s until 1920 and the second from the 1960s onwards. BUECHLER investigates the connections and parallels between the first and second waves of feminism, providing an overview of feminist activism in the United States from the 1840s to the present, from a sociological perspective. He explores the relationship between social change and social movements, comparing the two movements' origins, ideologies, and outcomes as well as their class and racial compositions. Examining the two peaks of feminism, he omits the period from 1920 through 1960, which some historians regard as the trough of organized activity on behalf of women's rights. Some of this gap is filled in SHARF's examination of women's employment and activism in the 1930s. She explores the significance of rising levels of labor force participation among married women and the implications of this for the women's rights movement. She also investigates how the Great Depression affected feminist values and women's opportunities, and finds that it blighted both, despite some advances by women into the higher ranks of federal government employment.

While most studies of feminism concentrate on middle-class women, GABIN shifts the area of investigation to working-class women during the Great Depression and the post-World

War II period. Her study of women in the United Auto Workers investigates the ways in which feminist sentiment sparked women's participation in industrial unions, the response of the UAW to women's demands, and the contribution of union women to organized feminism, especially in the 1960s. Her thesis is that the role of working-class women in the feminist movement has been neglected, and that in fact black and white women trade unionists contributed significantly to the movement.

S.J. KLEINBERG

See also Women's History entries

Film

Anger, Kenneth, *Hollywood Babylon*, Phoenix: Associated Professional Services, 1965; London: Century Hutchinson, 1986 (originally published in French, 1959)

Balio, Tino, *United Artists: The Company Built by the Stars*, Madison: University of Wisconsin Press, 1976

Balio, Tino, *Grand Design: Hollywood as a Modern Business Enterprise, 1930–1939*, New York: Scribner, 1993

Bowser, Eileen, *The Transformation of Cinema, 1907–1915*, New York: Scribner, 1990

Cripps, Thomas, *Slow Fade to Black: The Negro in American Film, 1900–1942*, New York: Oxford University Press, 1977

Dyer, Richard S., *Stars*, London: British Film Institute, 1979

Hampton, Benjamin B., *A History of the Movies*, New York: Covici Friede, 1931; London: Douglas, 1932

Haskell, Molly, *From Reverence to Rape: The Treatment of Women in the Movies*, New York: Holt Rinehart, 1974, London: New English Library, 1975; 2nd edition, Chicago: University of Chicago Press, 1987

Jacobs, Lea, *The Wages of Sin: Censorship and the Fallen Woman Film, 1928–1942*, Madison: University of Wisconsin Press, 1991

Jacobs, Lewis, *The Rise of the American Film: A Critical History*, New York: Harcourt Brace, 1939

Jewell, Richard B. with Vernon Harbin, *The RKO Story*, New York: Arlington House, and London: Octopus, 1982

Koszarski, Richard, *An Evening's Entertainment: The Age of the Silent Feature Picture, 1915–1928*, New York: Scribner, 1990

Musser, Charles, *The Emergence of Cinema: The American Screen to 1907*, New York: Scribner, 1990

Ramsaye, Terry, *A Million and One Nights: A History of the Motion Picture*, 2 vols., New York: Simon and Schuster, 1926; London: Frank Cass, 1964

Sarris, Andrew, *American Cinema: Directors and Directions, 1929–1968*, New York: Dutton, 1968

Sklar, Robert, *Movie-Made America: A Cultural History of American Movies*, New York: Random House, 1975, London: Chappell, 1978; revised, New York: Vintage, 1994

Staiger, Janet, *Interpreting Films: Studies in the Historical Reception of American Cinema*, Princeton: Princeton University Press, 1992

Since World War I, much of the world market for movies has been dominated by the United States. Inhabitants of other countries who went to the cinema absorbed American culture together with their own. In the boom year of 1946, in the United States itself, 80 million people went to the movies each week. Despite the cultural impact of Hollywood both at home and abroad, however, it took a long time for movie history to establish itself as a serious subject in its own right. Several reasons explain this: film, as popular entertainment, was regarded as too frivolous a subject for serious scholarship; sources, apart from the material produced by studio publicity departments and gossip about stars and leading industry figures, were limited; Hollywood's own reputation as a center of scandal and excess (a theme well covered in ANGER) discouraged sober historians from showing any real interest.

Early histories of the American motion-picture industry, therefore, were usually by insiders. RAMSAYE's study reflected both his experience of the various sectors of the industry – production, distribution, and exhibition – and his journalistic training. His 81-chapter work, fascinating in its way, was highly impressionistic and anecdotal. It analyzed at length the movie industry's business and technological giants – Thomas A. Edison emerged as a particular hero. By using the "great men" approach, of course, Ramsaye largely excluded other factors – aesthetic, social, and economic – from his treatment of film history.

HAMPTON approached the history of the movies from the perspective of an independent producer squeezed out of the industry by a large conglomerate. His work was primarily a business history of the movie industry. It dealt with business operations – the defeat of the Edison Trust, the battle for movie theaters – to the point where films themselves seemed largely to disappear, save as commodities. Hampton was greatly concerned about the implications of corporatization in the movie business both for Hollywood itself and for the entire democratic process – his book was apparently written in response to a suggestion from John Dewey, the philosopher of democracy.

Appearing near the end of the Depression decade, Lewis JACOBS (1939) saw the movies as socially useful, and defended their right to be made without excessive interference. It divided the history of the movie industry into six parts and analyzed the main elements of the industry at each stage. Much of the book, however, was little more than a directory of "significant" films produced during these stages of the industry's growth. In answering some of the key questions to do with American movies – who made them and why – Jacobs emphasized the importance of individual pioneers, particularly Edwin S. Porter, D. W. Griffith, and Walt Disney.

As a discipline, film history really began in the late 1960s and 1970s. It followed in the wake of a veritable explosion in film studies during that period. In recent years, it has also reflected the increasing salience of cultural issues in general historical writing. Modern film historians have not only developed new approaches to their discipline, they have also been fortunate enough in some cases to have access to newly-available documentation.

One approach to the history of the movies came through the auteur theory. This grew out a political stance taken by a group of French film critics, including François Truffaut, who wanted to establish film as an art form, and argued that individual movies should be regarded as artistic expressions of the director's vision. Auteurism was converted into a theory by SARRIS. His book maintained that the best films were those in which – despite a production system that hampered the expression of a single vision – the director had succeeded in impressing his personality on the work. Sarris then proposed a ranking of directors according to their degree of success as auteurs, starting at the top with a "pantheon" of fourteen directors, including Ford, Hitchcock, and Welles.

One response to auteurism as a historical method reflected the New Social History which began to appear from the end of the 1960s. This was primarily concerned with the attempt to construct a past in which working people, women, and racial minorities struggled for control of their own lives – in sharp distinction to the preoccupation of earlier historians with elites. SKLAR, for example, interpreted the history of the movie industry, from early struggles over censorship to the later Hollywood blacklist, as one of struggle between a dominant native middle-class culture and working class and/or immigrant ideas and behavior.

HASKELL, a pioneer in feminist writing about the cinema, perceived American movies as helping to perpetuate a stereotype of women's basic inferiority. The narrative of most films required even the most intelligent and capable of female characters to submit themselves in the end to men. Haskell saw such screen images as an accurate reflection of male attitudes towards women in society at large. CRIPPS agreed that society's most deep-seated values found expression in film as a popular art. But he argued that this was not an automatic process. The image of blacks on screen between 1900 and 1942 was, he maintained, mediated by the almost wholly non-black film industry, itself responding to perceived pressure from audiences and from particular social groups. After 1942, according to Cripps, Hollywood was influenced by growing pressure from civil rights groups – rather than any change in public sentiment – to improve the image of blacks on film.

New approaches to the writing of film history also influenced the perception of stardom. More has probably been written about "stars" than any other issue arising out of Hollywood. Much of it, however, has been essentially frivolous gossip arising from their personal lives. Stardom itself has long been perceived as a creation. Historians have traditionally explained it either as basically a democratic phenomenon, with moviegoers selectively "voting" for their favorite actors and actresses, or as a product of conscious manipulation (through publicity and fan magazines, for example) on the part of the studios. DYER, writing from a Marxist perspective, argued that most stars played an ideological role: they reconciled conflicts and divergences in society through the medium of their own images, and thereby helped maintain the status quo and the dominant ideology of Western capitalism.

Among new materials that have recently been utilized by scholars working in film history have been a number of studio archives and the records of the Hays Office – Hollywood's self-censorship agency. BALIO (1976) was an account of United Artists as a financial and bureaucratic institution. It was the first book to cover the history of a major studio on the basis of extensive primary documentation. JEWELL also wrote his history of RKO – though it was considerably more film-oriented – on the basis of newly-available studio records. Exploiting the files of the Hays Office, Lea JACOBS (1991) argued that censorship was a process of constant negotiation over how explicit films could be in sexual terms. The aim was to maximize the use of filmic material produced while at the same time minimizing the danger of outside interference. Before 1934, films which belonged to the "fallen woman" genre were more explicit, often concerned with women who used men to become rich, and often had endings that were arbitrary because they largely reflected censorship requirements. After 1934, according to Jacobs, the pursuit of wealth by such women and the moral imperatives of the Hays Code began to be brought together in a far more integrated narrative form.

STAIGER began with the assumption that changes and variations in the critical interpretation of movies are linked to social, economic, and political conditions. She also believed them to be influenced by "constructed identities" (including sexual preference, gender, race, class, and nationality). Taking these factors into account, she analyzed interpretive strategies on a number of critical questions – including how genres are constructed and read, or spectators persuaded to identify with stars and narrative stories – together with those evolved in relation to individual films from *Uncle Tom's Cabin* (1903) to *Zelig* (1983).

During the last few years, as if to recognize the coming-of-age of historical scholarship on the cinema, a detailed history of the American film industry has begun to appear. When the series is completed, in a projected ten volumes each dealing with a period of approximately a decade, it will be the most comprehensive account of the movie industry yet available. Each of the four volumes so far published – by MUSSER, BOWSER, KOSZARSKI and BALIO (1993) – has combined the analysis of film style and aesthetics, social and economic conditions, and technology to give an impressive overview of its own period.

MELVYN STOKES

Financial History, 1780s–1930s

Board of Governors of the Federal Reserve System, *The Federal Reserve System*, Washington DC: Government Printing Office, 1st edition, 1939, with frequent reprints and revisions thereafter

Burns, Helen M., *The American Banking Community and New Deal Banking Reforms, 1933–1935*, Westport, CT: Greenwood Press, 1974

Carosso, Vincent P., *Investment Banking in America: A History*, Cambridge, MA: Harvard University Press, 1970

Chandler, Lester V., *American Monetary Policy, 1928–1941*, New York: Harper, 1971

Friedman, Milton and Anna Jacobson Schwartz, *A Monetary History of the United States, 1867–1960*, Princeton: Princeton University Press, 1963; chapter 7 reprinted as *The Great Contraction, 1929–1933*, 1965

Hammond, Bray, *Banks and Politics in America, from the Revolution to the Civil War*, Princeton: Princeton University Press, 1957

Livingston, James, *Origins of the Federal Reserve System: Money, Class, and Corporate Capitalism, 1890–1913*, Ithaca, NY: Cornell University Press, 1986

Meyer, Richard H., *Bankers' Diplomacy: Monetary Stabilization in the Twenties*, New York: Columbia University Press, 1970

Myers, Margaret G., *A Financial History of the United States*, New York: Columbia University Press, 1970

Redlich, Fritz, *The Molding of American Banking: Men and Ideas*, New York: Johnson Reprint Corporation, 1968 (reprint of *History of American Business Leaders*, vol. 2, 1951)

Rockoff, Hugh, *The Free Banking Era: A Re-examination*, New York: Arno Press, 1975

Sylla, Richard, *The American Capital Market, 1846–1914: A Study of the Effects of Public Policy on Economic Development*, New York: Arno Press, 1975

Temin, Peter, *Did Monetary Forces Cause the Great Depression?*, New York: Norton, 1976

Timberlake, Richard H., Jr., *The Origins of Central Banking in the United States*, Cambridge, MA: Harvard University Press, 1978

West, Robert Craig, *Banking Reform and the Federal Reserve, 1863–1923*, Ithaca, NY: Cornell University Press, 1977

White, Eugene Nelson, *The Regulation and Reform of the American Banking System, 1900–1929*, Princeton: Princeton University Press, 1983

For more than two hundred years, the history of American money and banking has been surrounded by controversy, and, moreover, highly politicized controversy. From Hamilton's 1790 Report on the Public Credit, the establishment of the First Bank of the United States in 1791, his Report on the Establishment of a Mint in 1792 and the subsequent Coinage Act, to the latest variation in interest rates by the Federal Reserve Board, this has been true. In the interim lay the Jacksonian "Bank War" and Specie Circular, the period of "free banking", the apparently inadvertent omission of the plural ending "s" from the word "office" in the 1864 revision of the Bank Act of 1863, thereby prohibiting national banks subsequently from establishing branch offices, the "Crime of '73", the Free Silver Movement and Populism, the frequent bank panics, both national and local, the drawn-out discussion of where to site the Federal Reserve Banks during the preliminaries to the Federal Reserve Act of 1913 (resulting in two Banks, of Kansas City and St. Louis, being allocated to one state) the role of the "Fed," under the *de facto* direction of Benjamin Strong, and of the banking system in general, in the years preceding the Wall Street crash of 1929, FDR's "bank holiday" and subsequent banking legislation, and the academic and political debates surrounding Milton Friedman's "monetarist" doctrines. Inevitably these controversies have been reflected in the historiography of the subject. The literature on the subject is vast, and only selected items can be discussed here.

One book that attempts to remain detached is MYERS, who was already well known for her classic *History of the New York Money Market to 1913*. She commits herself to no single theoretical interpretation. Keynes is mentioned, but only as head of the British delegation to Bretton Woods; Friedman is present, in the bibliography. Nevertheless, with the healthy disdain of American economic historians towards formerly accepted interpretations, she calls for constant re-examination and re-formulation of the accepted clichés. The demonetization of silver, the so-called "crime of '73" is shown not as a coup but as the result of prolonged deliberation and debate in which the issues were carefully considered. The story of the tariff, as she sees it, suggests that "the Trust was mother to the Tariff" as often as *vice versa*.

A very different approach was taken by HAMMOND in a survey of banking history up to the Civil War which at the time of publication (1957) was highly iconoclastic. The approach is an economist's, sharply at variance with the view of the events presented by most political historians. Nevertheless the author shows deep understanding of the period of which he writes and displays great narrative skill. Although attention should be paid to the whole book, its centre-piece is the Jackson-Biddle conflict over the Second Bank of the United States in which both these characters appear very differently from their normal portrayal. The outcome of the struggle was victory indeed, but victory for the financiers of Wall Street (New York) who could thereafter operate without the restraining hand of Chestnut Street (Philadelphia) – home of Biddle's bank – a view which was eventually to gain readier acceptance than at the time of publication.

Taking up the story where Hammond ends is another economists' work, by FRIEDMAN and SCHWARTZ. This comprehensive study examines in detail all aspects of both fiscal and monetary policy, interpreted from the point of view of their own monetarist theories. If any work can be described as "essential reading" then this is it. The chapter which deals with the years 1929–33 is also published separately as *The Great Contraction*. REDLICH is a monumental if less analytical survey of the evolution of banking in the United States by a highly respected scholar, and includes detailed accounts of the personalities and problems involved. The main emphasis of this work, "old" economic history at its best, is on the second half of the 19th century.

A neglected period in monetary history is that between the demise of the Second Bank and the restoration of federal influence over banking practices in the National Banking Acts of 1863 and 1864. However, interest is beginning to be shown, now that some economists in Europe as well as in America are beginning to think the unthinkable and query the necessity for central banking controls. ROCKOFF offers an examination of the American experience of "free banking" in the late 1830s and the 1840s.

Inevitably the banking panics of 1873 and 1893, with the subsequent economic downturns and the growing acceptance of the need for banking reforms, have attracted the attention of both historians and economists. Following a further panic in 1907 the Aldrich-Vreeland Act of 1908 among other things set up the National Monetary Commission, the eventual findings of which appeared in multiple volumes that themselves provide a monetary history not merely of the United States but also of most countries of western Europe. The Commission's Report relevant to American problems appeared in 1912 and drew attention to the many weaknesses in the structure of American banking. The prolonged discussions and politicking which followed eventually produced the Federal Reserve Act and the Federal Reserve System. Four separate studies WEST, TIMBERLAKE, WHITE, and LIVINGSTON all deal with these events from differing ideological viewpoints.

The Federal Reserve Bank faced its first trials during the financing of World War I, followed immediately by the "normalcy" of the 1920s. White continues his account into the 1920s and Friedman and Schwartz give it great prominence in their analysis. The main debate has concerned the Fed's management of the money supply in the 1920s: whether domestic or international considerations predominated; how far the Fed can be held responsible for the 1929 inflation on Wall Street; indeed what members of the Board had any knowledge or experience of banking either in practice or in theory. The tensions between international considerations and the goal of internal economic stability are discussed by MEYER. The role of Benjamin Strong, the governor of the Federal Reserve Bank of New York, has received particular attention and, in the interpretation of many authors, his death in October 1928 left the system leaderless at a critical juncture. Following an earlier (1958) biography of Strong, CHANDLER surveys the Wall Street Crash, the Depression and the New Deal legislation. TEMIN's short analysis of the causal relationship between decisions in the field of banking and the Depression challenges some of the Friedmanite interpretation.

Most general accounts of the New Deal examine the banking reforms then undertaken. BURNS deals with the less political aspects of these reforms, looking at the topic from the point of view of the reactions of the bankers themselves. Starting in 1939, the BOARD of GOVERNORS of the Federal Reserve System published a series of useful booklets designed to instruct the public about its functions and methods of operation. These have been regularly up-dated in line with legislative and other changes.

Two further aspects of the subject need also to be mentioned. SYLLA writes with great authority in his survey of the development of the capital market in America through the second half of the 19th century and to the World War I. CAROSSO examines another, and extremely important, aspect of the subject in his history of the significance of banks in providing direct investment for American economic development.

JIM POTTER

Financial History, since 1940s

Degen, Robert A., *The American Monetary System: A Concise Survey of Its Evolution since 1896*, Lexington, MA: Lexington Books, 1987
Galbraith, John Kenneth, *Money: Whence It Came, Where It Went*, Boston: Houghton Mifflin, and London: Deutsch, 1975; revised, Houghton Mifflin, 1995
Geisst, Charles R., *Visionary Capitalism: Financial Markets and the American Dream in the Twentieth Century*, New York: Praeger, 1990
Rose, Peter S., *The Changing Structure of American Banking*, New York: Columbia University Press, 1987
White, Lawrence J., *The S & L Debacle: Public Policy Lessons for Bank and Thrift Regulation*, New York: Oxford University Press, 1991

DEGEN is probably the best place to begin a study of financial history since the New Deal. Although he discusses the entire period from 1896, about half his book concerns the years after 1939. This is a very clear and measured account of the banking system, occasionally technical but never obscured by too much theory. The essentials of theoretical debates are explained simply and well. The approach is pragmatic and Degen argues that the banking system, and the regulatory regime governing it, have evolved steadily rather than undergone convulsive change. Degen effectively relates the policymaking of the Federal Reserve Board to major economic shifts and to political developments. Those running the Board were aware of the multiple objectives which they were expected to pursue. The contrast between the banking system's relative stability from the mid-1940s to the late 1960s and its far more challenging existence from 1968 is well developed. Degen stresses the importance of decisions taken in 1979–80, before Ronald Reagan's election to the presidency, for the cause of monetarism and deregulation.

One irony about money is that something so pleasurable to possess should be so unenjoyable to read about. Irony and pleasure are always, however, to be found in the works of GALBRAITH. His book on money is the most readable general account of this highly technical subject. As long as one realises that Galbraith is trying to enlighten us as to the culture of capitalism, and to the political choices we should exercise once we have understood that culture, then his work is to be commended. But Galbraith does not seek to assess the range of theoretical issues at stake, nor does he write from the premise that economic policymaking might actually be a difficult task.

To counter-balance Galbraith's approach, GEISST offers an example of a general book on financial history that is favourable to the market system: it is a readable and non-polemical account of developments since 1929. It examines commercial banking and the main areas of credit-provision for mortgages, farm credits, and higher education. This wider view of the system of financial credit emphasizes the sheer reach and scale of financial intermediaries. Geisst also describes the main developments in financial markets since the early 1970s, with brief accounts of, for example, international loans and junk bonds. The least satisfactory part of the book is probably the last chapter on the stock market. While recognizing that the stock market's behaviour results from a wider range of factors than the party allegiance of the occupant of the White House, Geisst explores that relationship at greater length than seems necessary in a general work. He concludes, however, by stressing that the relationship is a myth.

A dramatic episode in the 1980s was the collapse of Savings and Loan associations (equivalent to old-style building societies in Britain), following a period of deregulation and rapid growth. WHITE describes and analyses this sorry saga in a first-rate, detailed study which is technical without being econometric. The S and L crisis of the second half of the 1980s offers a field-day for those wishing to expose the excesses of "casino capitalism", and the corrupt opportunities opened up by a looser regulatory order for deals to be struck between state politicians and financial entrepreneurs. But White sets the developments of the 1980s in a broader and less emotive or polemical framework. The S and L sector absorbed about 30 per cent of all deposit liabilities in banks, S and Ls, and credit unions in 1989; corruption did not grip the entire sector. White argues that deregulation should have occurred much earlier. When it came, it coincided with changes in tax laws and in oil prices (important especially in Texas, where so many S and Ls crashed) which accentuated the turbulence of a system undergoing reform. A fall in property prices, notably in the Southwest, fuelled the crisis after 1985. The Federal Home Loan Bank Board in 1983 did not accept advice that it should restrain S and Ls' risk-taking practices more tightly. Far from the financial system being evolutionary as Degen would have it, the S and L crash illustrated the dangers of partial reforms being introduced in a period of rapid change. White spells out a carefully reasoned case for not over-reacting to the crisis, and suggests a range of regulatory changes. Among many defects of the new set-up that emerged in the early 1980s were a reliance on historic-cost, rather than current market-value, inadequate accounting procedures, and a failure to relate insurance premiums to levels of risk. These, and other issues, are major questions of practice in accountancy and insurance, the subjects of prolonged professional debate and of professional associations' competing claims.

ROSE provides a more general analysis of banking institutions and the banking system since 1945. His book is technical without being mathematical, and introduces the reader to a wide range of scholarly material. Rose's methodology is that of an economist rather than a historian. He discusses issue after issue by reference to academic papers in the field. This approach underscores the richness of research on the subject and the variety of interpretations concerning it. But the book does not offer a strong chronological analysis in its own right. Rose examines important questions concerning regulation and enters a wise cautionary note about the extent to which deregulation might be pressed.

The technical demands of the subject probably explain why so little is written by historians on this vital topic. There is also a sense that the financial system remained fairly uncontroversial in the 1950s and 1960s, when other political and social questions exploded into public prominence and later commanded the attention of historians. But the turbulent financial events of the 1980s will require and attract the close scrutiny of historians. The studies noted here include only a few works in a large and impressive technical literature. They open the subject for further exploration, with Rose in particular making wider comparisons with deregulation in other sectors in this period. Gradually, we will see the financial history of the 1970s and 1980s woven into a more general debate over deregulatory impulses and institutional changes, both political and economic, in that era of economic uncertainty.

BRUCE COLLINS

Finney, Charles Grandison 1792–1875
Revivalist preacher and educator

Fletcher, Robert S., A History of Oberlin College from Its Foundation Through the Civil War, 2 vols., Oberlin, OH: Oberlin College, 1943

Hardman, Keith J., Charles Grandison Finney, 1792–1875: Revivalist and Reformer, Syracuse, NY: Syracuse University Press, 1987

Hewitt, Glenn A., Regeneration and Morality: A Study of Charles Finney, Charles Hodge, John W. Nevin, and Horace Bushnell, New York: Carlson, 1991

McLoughlin, William G., Modern Revivalism: Charles Grandison Finney to Billy Graham, New York: Ronald Press, 1959

Sweet, Leonard I., The Minister's Wife: Her Role in Nineteenth-Century American Evangelicalism, Philadelphia: Temple University Press, 1983

Wright, G. Frederick, Charles Grandison Finney, Boston: Houghton Mifflin, 1891

Charles Finney, Connecticut-born evangelical revivalist, professor of theology, college president, and midwife to reform movements, was a controversial figure in his own day and remains so among recent historians. Finney's Presbyterian and Congregational co-religionists were divided over his rejection of traditional Calvinism in favour of an emphasis on human ability in conversion, and also over his "new measures" revivalism which encouraged such practices as women praying in public and the use of the "anxious bench." Conservatives North and South blamed Finney for fomenting abolitionism, while radicals condemned him for putting the salvation of souls above the freeing of slaves. Some historians have seen Finney as a key figure in the emergence of reform movements, especially abolitionism, during the 1830s, while others have argued that his brand of revivalism, by diverting energies from more radical politics, became an instrument of social control and a means of conservative politicization for the Whig party. Many of these issues are addressed more pointedly in the general literature dealing with antebellum revivalism and social reform.

The first three chapters of McLOUGHLIN are still the best introduction to the career of Finney, whom it considers the creator of modern revivalism. During his most active period as a revivalist, from about 1825 to 1835, Finney developed the Arminianized (that is, emphasizing human ability) Calvinism of such New Divinity luminaries as Lyman Beecher and Nathaniel Taylor into a practical set of techniques that tamed the wilder aspects of frontier evangelicalism and institutionalized it within mainstream Protestantism. McLoughlin provides a close reading of Finney's writings on the techniques of revivalism and also a lucid discussion of the relationship to social reform of three important aspects of antebellum evangelicalism, namely, benevolence, perfectionism, and millennialism, that influenced Finney. His revivalism may have been forward-looking for its day, but, according to McLoughlin, its attempt to make reform hinge upon the conversion and reformation of individuals was bound to have limited results, becoming, with the failure of millennial expectations, increasingly inward-looking and mechanistic.

Although a number of biographies of Finney, mostly popular accounts by evangelicals, have appeared over the years, the definitive life has yet to be written. For many years the standard biography was by WRIGHT, a professor of theology at Oberlin College. Strongly defending his revivalism as a catalyst for reform, it still has the merit of first-hand acquaintance with the milieu where Finney spent the last four decades of his life and with people who knew him. Wright also has a useful, if over-systematized, section on Finney's theology.

For most purposes, however, the standard life is now HARDMAN, a scholarly and informed account of Finney's career, which, however, slights his personal life and fails to reach the wellsprings of his character and personality. It is better at elucidating Finney's relations with a plethora of preachers, reformers, and philanthropists, such as Lyman Beecher, Theodore Dwight Weld, and Arthur and Lewis Tappan, than in interpreting its subject within the larger cultural and social setting. Still, it provides good critical discussions of the influence of Finney's legal training on his religious life, the events surrounding his conversion in 1821, the great revival successes such as Rochester in 1831, his role in the establishment of Oberlin Institute (later College) where he became professor of theology in 1835 and president from 1851 to 1865, and, finally, his two great tours of England and Scotland during the 1850s. Hardman offers a particularly good account of the Tappan brothers' growing impatience with Finney's subordination of abolition to the saving of souls and his willingness to tolerate racial discrimination.

For the Oberlin setting of Finney's career the best place to turn is FLETCHER, a detailed and thoroughly researched, if overly laudatory, history of the college, which was nonetheless unique in that it accepted students without regard either to sex or race. Oberlin supported a variety of movements, including abolitionism, temperance, dietary reform, and peace, all of which, in Fletcher's view, were nurtured by Finney's revivalism. Even so, under Finney's influence the college by the 1840s placed more emphasis on turning out evangelists than reformers.

HEWITT, which will be of primary interest to students of 19th century religious ideas, is concerned with the way a theologian's doctrine of conversion and regeneration affects his understanding of ethics and morality. It compares Finney with three other American theologians whose backgrounds were also in the reformed (Calvinist) tradition but who reached quite different conclusions. Finney's emphasis with respect both to regeneration and ethics was on voluntarism. What God required us to do, He must have given us the ability to do. Perfection for Finney, unlike Wesley's sanctification through divine grace, involved consistently making the right choices. Of the four theologians, Finney was the only one who had no formal training and it showed in the inconsistencies and contradictions in his thought. Yet Finney's belief that a perfected society could be achieved through the actions of perfected individuals was, Hewitt argues, fully in accord with his revival methods that emphasized individual decision.

SWEET defines four models of the minister's wife between the Reformation and the 19th century: the companion, the sacrificer, the assistant, and the partner. Finney's first two (of three) wives, Lydia Ford Andrews and Elizabeth Atkinson, are taken as the principal case studies for the last two models

respectively. Lydia assisted her husband, shared many of his responsibilities, and became active in reform movements, such as the Female Moral Reform Society. Elizabeth, according to Sweet, became a true partner, developing, especially during their two tours in Britain, a ministry among women alongside her husband's ministry. Providing keen insight into Finney's domestic relations, this goes well beyond other studies in relating Finney's ministry to the changing role of women and issues of gender.

FREDERICK A. BODE

See also Reform Movements; Revivalism

First Ladies

Anthony, Carl Sferrazza, *First Ladies: The Saga of the Presidents' Wives and Their Power, 1789–1961* and *1961–1990*, 2 vols., New York: Morrow, 1990–91

Boller, Paul, Jr., *Presidential Wives: An Anecdotal History*, New York and Oxford: Oxford University Press, 1988

Caroli, Betty, *First Ladies*, New York and Oxford: Oxford University Press, 1987

Furman, Bess, *White House Profile: A Social History of the White House*, Indianapolis: Bobbs Merrill, 1951

Gould, Lewis L. (editor), *American First Ladies: Their Lives and Their Legacy*, New York: Garland, 1996

Gutin, Myra G., *The President's Partner: The First Lady in the Twentieth Century*, Westport, CT: Greenwood Press, 1989

Kellerman, Barbara, *All the President's Kin*, New York: Free Press, 1981; London: Robson, 1982

Means, Marianne, *The Woman in the White House: The Lives, Times and Influence of Twelve Notable First Ladies*, New York: Random House, 1963

Smith, Nancy Kegan and Mary C. Ryan (editors), *Modern First Ladies: Their Documentary Legacy*, Washington, DC: National Archives and Records Administration, 1989

The analysis of first ladies in the United States has been a fast-growing sub-field in presidential studies since the early 1980s. As interest in women's studies has burgeoned, the spouses of presidents have attracted more attention as public symbols of the role of women in society. Research on individual first ladies such as Eleanor Roosevelt, Mary Todd Lincoln, and Jacqueline Kennedy has also contributed to the emergence of a body of literature about first ladies and their contributions to national issues. Popular fascination with presidents and their families seems likely to expand the literature on first ladies in the immediate future.

FURMAN was a well-connected Washington reporter who wrote a social history of the White House that drew on her own extensive research into the lives of presidents and their families. Largely anecdotal, the book nonetheless contains a wealth of information that has been incorporated into subsequent non-scholarly treatments of first ladies. In the early 1960s, MEANS also brought the perspective of a national reporter to the treatment of selected first ladies. She did some initial work in a presidential library for her chapter on Bess

Truman. Selective in its coverage, Means's pioneering book made her work an indispensable starting point for the writers who turned to examining first ladies during the 1980s. KELLERMAN examined the role of presidential families in a book that drew primarily on published sources and newspapers, though she made some use of oral history interviews at the John F. Kennedy Library. Although it does not focus exclusively on presidential wives, it offers a good indication of where general scholarship on the subject stood at the beginning of the 1980s.

The first effort to synthesize what had been written about all of the first ladies was CAROLI. She investigated how the wife of the president had evolved from a ceremonial figure to an individual with worldwide fame and celebrity such as Jacqueline Kennedy or Eleanor Roosevelt. Caroli used primary sources for first ladies before 1961, but did not explore the extensive files in modern presidential libraries on the role of the wife of the president. As the first serious scholarly treatment of this important institution in the national government, Caroli's book will have enduring importance.

BOLLER represented a reversion to the older method of dealing with first ladies. As its title suggests, it treats these women in anecdotal fashion and is undiscriminating about the veracity of the stories that are recounted in the text. More a compilation of trivia than a serious contribution to the field, Boller's book attracted a wide audience among the general public but had no serious impact on how first ladies have been studied.

In contrast, SMITH and RYAN used a collection of essays on the primary source materials about first ladies to indicate how much information about these women and their impact on society can be found in the collections at the Library of Congress and at individual presidential libraries. The essays vary in quality, of course, but they all point the way to significant research information. Two essays by Lewis L. Gould explore the institutional development surrounding the first lady in the White House, and the way in which wives of the presidents have become political celebrities.

GUTIN is a monograph on first ladies in the 20th century that draws on the author's research into sources at the presidential libraries in order to examine how presidents have employed their wives to advance the political and policy aims of their administrations. Gutin is sensitive to changes in the public personae of the presidential wives, and her findings trace the enhanced role of the first lady as policy advocate, political surrogate, and individual actor on the national stage.

ANTHONY is a popularizing author who has produced an extensive two-volume narrative of the evolution of the role of the first lady in American history. He depicts them as influential forces in the administrations of their husbands and advances that thesis throughout his text. The chronological organization means that he deals with a number of first ladies within each chapter. As a result, the focus of the books often shifts quickly from one personality to another. The treatment is more anecdotal than analytic, but the books do contain an abundance of information.

GOULD contains 38 essays on each woman who has served as first lady while her husband was in the White House. The thirty authors present an interpretation of these women that reflects the latest scholarship, and bibliographical essays supply information about primary sources and previous writings. For the student initially coming to the subject with research questions, this book will be the most accessible and useful of the volumes listed. With the activist role of Hillary Rodham Clinton during the mid-1990s, interest in the historical contributions of presidential wives has further intensified. Biographies of individual first ladies are constantly appearing, and this aspect of the history of women in the United States is likely to gain in sophistication and importance in the near future.

Lewis L. Gould

See also Presidency, and entries on individual presidents

Food

Belasco, Warren James, *Appetite for Change: How the Counterculture Took on the Food Industry, 1966–1988*, New York: Pantheon, 1989; revised, Ithaca, NY: Cornell University Press, 1993

Brumberg, Joan Jacobs, *Fasting Girls: The History of Anorexia Nervosa as a Modern Disease*, Cambridge, MA: Harvard University Press, 1988

Cowan, Ruth Schwartz, *More Work for Mother: The Ironies of Household Technology from the Open Hearth to the Microwave*, New York: Basic Books, 1983; London: Free Association, 1989

Cummings, Richard Osborn, *The American and His Food: A History of Food Habits in the United States*, Chicago: University of Chicago Press, 1940, revised 1941

Levenstein, Harvey A., *Revolution at the Table: The Transformation of the American Diet*, New York and Oxford: Oxford University Press, 1988

Levenstein, Harvey A., *Paradox of Plenty: A Social History of Eating in Modern America*, New York and Oxford: Oxford University Press, 1992

Root, Waverley and Richard de Rochemont, *Eating in America: A History*, New York: Morrow, 1976

Strasser, Susan, *Never Done: A History of American Housework*, New York: Pantheon, 1982

American historians have trailed their English and French counterparts in studying food. In France, whether due to cultural proclivities or to the *histoire totale* of the *Annales* school, there is a rich tradition in the field as demonstrated in Robert Forster and Orest Ranum's translated anthology *Food and Drink in History* (1979). Although part of a less distinguished culinary tradition, English historians have produced a range of works that take food seriously, as exemplified by John Burnett's *Plenty and Want* (1966, revised 1979).

American coverage has been more limited and recent. But Levenstein's two volumes now provide a solid treatment of the subject for the period since 1880. The volumes examine the forces that established a national food consensus, one that was created by 1930 and remains essentially intact. LEVENSTEIN (1988) maintains that the Victorian upper class relished multi-course French meals, a taste exemplified by Delmonico's, the first grand restaurant. The Victorian middle class, assisted by one or two servants, struggled to emulate that style. However a "new nutrition" that urged choosing food more on chemical content (protein, for example) emerged from the new profession of home economics and it spread among a middle class increasingly faced with the loss of servants, health fears, progressive reformers, food faddists, and mass producers. Its victory was symbolized by the victory of wafer-thin Woodrow Wilson over William Howard Taft, the last bulky president. In the process, Americans returned to their long tradition of an Americanized English cuisine, though its roots were often unacknowledged, as suggested by the "American as apple pie" aphorism about an English dish.

The army, public schools, mass producers, and growing affluence spread the new diet among often resistant working-class and ethnic cultures. In the 1920s, perhaps two-thirds of Americans shared it. Prohibition finished off most of the remaining grand old French-style restaurants, and strengthened the trend towards a uniform pattern of food consumption.

According to LEVENSTEIN (1992), the Depression and World War II further disseminated the meat (especially beef) and potatoes preferences through America. The combined forces of large food processors and the Federal government spread its hegemony. The period from the 1920s to the 1960s stands as a time of a homogeneous and uninventive but remarkably egalitarian diet. Although critical of the food industry, Levenstein also questions the arguments of food reformers about malnutrition, and maintains that the food industry has provided remarkably inexpensive and plentiful food even though it has been less nutritious and healthy than it should have been.

The last three decades have produced two changes. One, dubbed "negative nutrition" by Levenstein, was a new fear of some foods and additives. The second was the re-emergence of class distinctions, with the "yuppie" interest in foreign and health foods, while much of the population swelled the lines of McDonald's and Burger King.

Levenstein's depiction of a food industry that is duplicitous and profit-centred, yet responsive to consumers, draws on BELASCO for the 1970s and 1980s. Arising in the late 1960s as a respectable alternative to the self-defeating racial and anti-war politics, an ecological movement conscious of food issues transformed the food scene. A moral panic made "organic" and "natural" widely recognized and valuable labels. Belasco effectively analyzes the remarkably rapid change in public and corporate behaviour and the eventual corporate response to new concerns. Between them, Belasco and Levenstein have given food an up-to-date history lacking in many other fields.

Although Levenstein provides the benchmark, his sweeping search for national trends and his concentration on economic and political causation leave room for further study and dissenting views. CUMMINGS's classic history, written at the end of the Depression, took the fears about malnutrition more seriously and praised the efforts of food reformers. Similarly, modern scholars may challenge Levenstein's dismissal of hunger scares, and his scepticism about the accuracy, if not the motives, of food reform's heroes and heroines.

ROOT and de ROCHEMONT is a more recent survey of American eating from the early Native Americans to the 1970s. It stresses the continuing dominance of Anglo food, a choice that confounds them. Unlike Belasco and Levenstein, Root and de Rochemont do not address professional historical debates, but provide an intelligent and readable work that is a good starting point and reference for professional historians.

None of these works has much to say on the relationship of food preparation to the division of labour inside the household. Strasser and Cowan provide competing versions of the gender dynamics of housework, including food preparation. Although acknowledging the satisfaction of home-cooked meals, STRASSER essentially portrays housework as an oppressive trap. Her depiction of a battle between corporate power and occasional consumer resistance is less convincing than Cowan's greater emphasis on human agency. COWAN conceptualizes choices in household management in terms of family strategies which, combined with technological developments that repeatedly reduced the jobs traditionally performed by men and children, made women more productive but bound them to higher standards. Communal and cooperative alternatives to family-centred meals repeatedly floundered on the desire of couples to control their own environment; the desire for privacy overcame inefficiency.

BRUMBERG explores another aspect of a primarily female relationship with food: anorexia. Although she traces the history of female self-starvation back to medieval saints, she confirms the conventional wisdom that the modern epidemic is unprecedented. She rejects the case that anorexics are merely victims of cultural emphases on the female body. While such pressures contribute, Brumberg also blames family choices such as the decline of family meals and individual self-defeating attempts to use eating as a form of control. Thus anorexics are not simply victims, and food is often the symptom rather than the cause.

All of the above works delineate broad national trends and modal behaviour. Historians need to turn to less common practices and greater diversity in eating habits, as anthropologists and literary scholars have done in Linda Keller Brown and Kay Mussell (editors), *Ethnic and Regional Foodways in the United States* (1984). The history of food in America is still at an early stage.

W. BRUCE LESLIE

Football

Brown, Paul E. with Jack Clary, *PB: The Paul Brown Story*, New York: Atheneum, 1979

Carroll, John M., *Fritz Pollard: Pioneer in Racial Advancement*, Urbana: University of Illinois Press, 1992

Harris, David, *The League: The Rise and Decline of the NFL*, New York: Bantam, 1986

Lester, Robin, *Stagg's University: The Rise, Decline, and Fall of Big-Time Football at Chicago*, Urbana: University of Illinois Press, 1995

O'Brien, Michael, *Vince: A Personal Biography of Vince Lombardi*, New York: Morrow, 1987

Oriard, Michael, *Reading Football: How the Popular Press Created an American Spectacle*, Chapel Hill: University of North Carolina Press, 1993

Smith, Ronald A., *Sports and Freedom: The Rise of Big-Time College Athletics*, New York: Oxford University Press, 1988

Sperber, Murray, *Shake Down the Thunder: The Creation of Notre Dame Football*, New York: Holt, 1993

Despite football's prominent place in American society, scholars have generally neglected the study of the sport and its larger significance. However, recent works covering the rise of the college game give some indication of progress. In his study of early intercollegiate athletics, SMITH examines the development of football in the latter half of the 19th century. He argues that the students originally controlled their own sports, but the increasing emphasis placed on winning caused a shift in power, depriving them of this freedom. Eventually, the alumni and professional coaches took total control, bringing an early end to amateurism in college athletics. Smith also believes that football, with its violent element, became the dominant college sport because it best reflected the prevailing American values of that time. With impressive archival research, especially with respect to Harvard and Yale, this work effectively documents the politics surrounding the organizational development of early college football, prior to the formation of the NCAA in 1906.

ORIARD also studies the early college game, but his treatment of football as a "cultural text" provides a different perspective. He develops the thesis that the late 19th century press "created" intercollegiate football as a popular spectacle. According to Oriard, since most Americans first learned about the game through the newspapers, journalistic accounts of the contests became instrumental in defining football's significance to the country. Those who wrote about football offered a variety of interpretations, making the game meaningful to the general public and increasing its popularity. Oriard's analysis of the game is sophisticated, and his book, although difficult, provides the best study of football as an American cultural phenomenon.

In the absence of a comprehensive historical treatment of 20th century football, two individual case studies offer the best accounts of the game's development prior to World War II. In his study of the University of Chicago and its coach Amos Alonzo Stagg, LESTER presents a fascinating insight into college football's evolution through the first three decades of this century. Thoroughly analyzing how the program was built, Lester views Stagg as a pioneer in the development of football into a mass entertainment industry by the 1920s. Documenting the coach's relationship with university administrators, the author also explores the lengthy debate over football's role at an institution of higher learning. Lester traces this controversial issue up through 1939, when the University of Chicago finally abolished its football program.

In contrast to the University of Chicago, Notre Dame went on to become the premier college gridiron power of this century. SPERBER examines the rise of this program, giving specific attention to coach Knute Rockne and the creation of the Notre Dame legend. After delving into the university's archives, Sperber assaults several myths surrounding the famed success of the Fighting Irish. He argues that, instead of winning only because of inspired determination, Notre Dame rose to prominence by carefully manipulating a variety of factors to its advantage. For example, Rockne routinely employed the standard recruiting violations of the era, hired friendly officials to work his games and influenced the press to ensure a favorable national image for his team. Sperber's account of Rockne's stormy relationship with school administration also provides a revealing look into the university politics which often accompany a successful football program.

In addition to these case studies, a few biographies are noteworthy sources of information on football history. CARROLL's study of Fritz Pollard gives insights into the college game as well as the early professional leagues of the 1920s. Since Pollard was the first black to play in the Rose Bowl, as well as the first black quarterback and head coach in the National Football League, this work provides an important description of race relations in football's earlier years. Although Carroll's discussion focuses on the career of an overlooked but important "racial pioneer" in American sports, the descriptive account of Pollard's life is excessively detailed at times and his overall significance is not always brought out clearly.

Biographies are especially important in compensating for the paucity of scholarly histories covering professional football. BROWN's autobiography is among the most informative works in this area. A successful coach in the high school, college and professional ranks, Paul Brown pioneered many developments in the game. His account contains useful information about these football innovations which have become the standard practice of today. Although this book is not a balanced scholarly study of football and its larger significance, Brown's discussion of the post-World War II development of the NFL is still a source of profitable material. While Paul Brown was the dominant coach in professional football during the 1950s, Vince Lombardi's teams ruled the 1960s. O'BRIEN is a substantial biography, packed with details about the life of this legendary coach. Thoroughly researched, this book not only covers Lombardi's career but examines his attitudes and beliefs as well. O'Brien reveals a driven man whose intense leadership methods have been widely praised and criticized. Particularly interesting is the book's discussion of the vast range of emotions that Lombardi inspired in those around him, including his great Green Bay Packer teams. The biography is generally balanced in its assessments, but O'Brien's work is mainly descriptive and does not satisfactorily analyze Lombardi's larger historical significance.

HARRIS is the best work on the recent history of the NFL. Based on scores of interviews, court documents and the minutes of NFL board meetings, it provides a behind-the-scenes look into the business history of professional football since the 1960s. Stretching to over 600 pages of text, the book features a revealing description of Commissioner Pete Rozelle's lengthy battle with Raider's owner Al Davis. Harris also profiles the activities of the other owners in the league including their handling of the increasing labor agitation of the 1970s and 1980s. While this book is unmatched in the wealth of information it presents about the NFL in the Rozelle era, its value is limited somewhat by a lack of footnotes and a tendency toward hyperbole.

KENT M. KRAUSE

See also Sport

Ford, Henry   1863–1947

Industrialist and pioneer of assembly line production

Arnold, Horace Lucien and Fay Leone Faurote, *Ford Methods and Ford Shops*, New York: Engineering Magazine, 1915

Beynon, Huw, *Working for Ford*, London: Allen Lane, 1973; 2nd edition, Harmondsworth: Penguin, 1984

Chandler, Alfred D., Jr., *Scale and Scope: The Dynamics of Industrial Capitalism*, Cambridge, MA: Belknap Press of Harvard University Press, 1990

Greenleaf, William, *Monopoly on Wheels: Henry Ford and the Selden Automobile Patent*, Detroit: Wayne State University Press, 1961

Hounshell, David A., *From the American System to Mass Production, 1800–1932: The Development of Manufacturing Technology in the United States*, Baltimore: Johns Hopkins University Press, 1984

Kraft, Barbara S., *The Peace-Ship: Henry Ford's Pacifist Adventure in the First World War*, New York: Macmillan, 1978

Lacey, Robert, *Ford, the Men and the Machine*, Boston: Little Brown, and London: Heinemann, 1986

Lewchuk, Wayne, *American Technology and the British Vehicle Industry*, Cambridge and New York: Cambridge University Press, 1988

Meyer, Stephen III, *The Five Dollar Day: Labor Management and Social Control in the Ford Motor Company, 1908–1921*, Albany: State University of New York Press, 1981

Nevins, Allan with Frank Ernest Hill, *Ford*, 3 vols., New York: Scribner, 1954–63

Tolliday, Steven and Jonathan Zeitlin (editors), *The Automobile Industry and Its Workers: Between Fordism and Flexibility*, Cambridge: Blackwell/Polity Press, 1986; New York: St. Martin's Press, 1987

Wilkins, Mira and Frank Ernest Hill, *American Business Abroad: Ford on Six Continents*, Detroit: Wayne State University Press, 1964

Henry Ford is probably the most written-about industrialist of the 20th century. In addition to Ford's autobiography and numerous biographies, he features prominently in many business and economic histories, either as a case study or as an exemplar of the rise of corporate America and the primacy of mass production. On the latter point alone Ford permeates a very broad literature, ranging from sociology to urban geography, as "Fordism" and "Post-Fordism" have been successively proposed and debated as forms of modern society.

NEVINS and HILL remains the most comprehensive, standard account. Exhaustively researched, these three volumes contain comprehensive details of Ford's rise and fall, from the pioneering years of engineering and financial struggles, to the designing and building of the world's most popular car and the factory systems to produce it, and on to the decline of fortunes in the face of competition from other corporate giants like General Motors, and the succession crisis, ending in the take-over by grandson Henry Ford II. These books are very well written, containing an admirable balance of the industrial and the personal. Ford's heroic persona comes through very vividly in a story of battles over restrictive patents, predatory Wall Street financiers, and the quest to provide the American citizen (and particularly the farmer) with an affordable and reliable car. One also gets a picture of Ford's less than heroic side, with inept political interventions, increasingly autocratic and paternalist management techniques, debates over alleged anti-semitism and quirky fascinations – for example, his obsession with soya bean production, carried to the extent of wearing a suit woven from soya cloth. (Some of these issues are covered in monographs such as GREENLEAF and KRAFT.) Ford's family life is adequately covered by Nevins and Hill, particularly the close working relationship with son, Edsel, and later the controversial introspective working partnership with Harry Bennett, leader of the "servicemen" at Ford factories, charged with resisting unionisation and generally intimidating the workforce during the 1930s. Personal details are also given extensive coverage in LACEY, a populist account for the general biography or "lives of the rich and famous" market.

On the industrial side the classic study of its kind is ARNOLD and FAUROTE – a contemporary tour through the Ford Highland Park factory, which is yet to be bettered by historical scholarship. Full details of plant layout, production methods (including the original moving assembly line) and observations of Ford's manufacturing philosophy are covered in exacting technical detail. The best recent treatment of the industrial aspect, though in a book covering a wider history, is HOUNSHELL. Based on secondary and archival sources, the three chapters devoted to Ford outline his pivotal position in the transition from the American system of manufacture to mass production. Similarly CHANDLER locates Ford as playing a part in establishing a new system of corporate control, engendering the visible hand of the rationalized, multi-divisional large-scale American enterprise. For a very full account of the evolution and extent of the Ford empire in global terms WILKINS and HILL should be consulted.

As noted Ford and Fordism have drawn attention from a wider academic sphere. BEYNON, a sociological study focusing on Britain, nevertheless contains a useful historical introduction, particularly to industrial relations practices. One notable example of Ford's quixotic (or pragmatic, depending on one's point of view) industrial relations exercises is given full coverage in MEYER. The "$5 dollar day" was introduced by Ford in the face of rising labour turnover and was aimed at tying labour to a high-wage high-effort bargain by more than doubling the prevailing wage-rate in 1914. A short-lived experiment, it coincided with a paternalist "Sociological Department" – established to oversee the moral rectitude of employees – at work and at home. Developments such as these led visionary contemporaries as disparate as Antonio Gramsci and Aldous Huxley to posit a new form of society based on mass production and consent. Apocalyptic visions aside, the international spread of, and limits to, Ford methods are impressively outlined in LEWCHUK. Discussions of the eventual failure of Ford methods and their replacement by flexible specialization or mass customization currently feature in much economic history literature. Probably the most comprehensive and theoretically robust account is that of TOLLIDAY and ZEITLIN.

RICHARD COOPEY

See also Business History entries

Foreign Policy: General

Bailey, Thomas A., *A Diplomatic History of the American People*, New York: Crofts, 1940; 10th edition, New York: Appleton Century Crofts, 1980

Cole, Wayne S., *An Interpretive History of American Foreign Relations*, Homewood, IL: Dorsey Press, 1968, 2nd edition, 1974

Combs, Jerald A., *American Diplomatic History: Two Centuries of Changing Interpretation*, Berkeley: University of California Press, 1983

DeConde, Alexander, *A History of American Foreign Policy*, 2 vols., New York: Scribner, 1963, 3rd edition, 1978

Jones, Howard, *The Course of American Diplomacy: From the Revolution to the Present*, New York: Watts, 1985; 2nd edition, New York: McGraw Hill, 1994

LaFeber, Walter, *The American Age: United States Foreign Policy at Home and Abroad since 1750*, New York: Norton, 1989; 2nd edition, 1994

Paterson, Thomas G., J. Garry Clifford, and Kenneth J. Hagan, *American Foreign Policy*, Lexington, MA: Heath, 1977; 4th edition, as *American Foreign Relations*, 1995

Thompson, Kenneth W., *Traditions and Values in Politics and Diplomacy: Theory and Practice*, Baton Rouge: Louisiana State University Press, 1992

Older histories of American foreign policy tended to be nationalistic in interpretation and narrowly diplomatic in methodology. More recent studies have become much more critical of the United States, and have explored the deeper forces within American society which have helped to shape American foreign policy, as well as examining the diplomatic record of relations between the United States and foreign governments.

PATERSON, CLIFFORD and HAGAN provides a chronological account of major issues of American foreign policy from the colonial period to the present, incorporating the most recent scholarship on the subject and utilizing the most recent methodology. Although originally published in 1977, the 4th edition is completely revised. The change in title from *American Foreign Policy* in earlier editions to *American Foreign Relations* in the latest edition indicates the attempt to develop an approach which covers the myriad interactions of peoples, cultures and economies, rather than a more superficial coverage merely of diplomatic exchanges. Environmental issues, popular images, cultural relations, race and gender are integrated with the more traditional issues of foreign policy such as war and peace treaties. The book is of sufficient length to allow a reasonable depth of analysis, while it is sparing in detail. A useful up-to-date bibliographical essay is provided after each chapter.

A new edition of a book first published in 1985, JONES draws upon the most recent scholarship. Chapters are organized chronologically on the major issues such as the American War of Independence, the War of 1812, the Mexican War, American imperialism, intervention in World War I, isolationism, intervention in World War II, the origins of the Cold War, Korea, Vietnam, and the end of the Cold War. Jones emphasizes the interrelationship between foreign and domestic policy, and also between ideals and interests, in the pursuit of American foreign policy. Although not quite so up-to-date as Paterson *et al.* or Jones, DeCONDE is a very good, well-organized synthesis. Volume 1 covers in succeeding chapters the major developments in American foreign policy from the colonial period to the Spanish-American War. Volume 2 covers American foreign policy in the 20th century. DeConde provides narrative detail of the various episodes in the history of American foreign policy, but his approach is largely analytical and interpretative. He emphasizes the pursuit of self-interest in American policy at least as much as the pursuit of idealism.

In an interpretation that leans towards a New Left, revisionist position, LaFEBER places heavy emphasis upon economic considerations as a determining force in the shaping of American policy. The overall interpretation offers a somewhat jaundiced view, with considerable attention given to the darker side of American policy. The organization is chronological, covering in a fairly broad sweep the major episodes in American foreign policy from the mid-18th century to the present. Extensive use is made of maps and illustrations throughout the book, and a useful guide to further reading is given at the end of each chapter.

BAILEY is a classic in the historiography of American foreign policy. First published in 1940, with its 10th edition forty years later, this book has been enormously influential and can still be read with profit. Bailey emphasizes the importance of public opinion in the formulation of American foreign policy, though his methodology in analyzing public opinion is somewhat superficial in comparison to analyses in works by later historians. He makes extensive use of political cartoons. The book is written in a lively style and its judgments are well-argued, even though its overall approach may now seem old-fashioned.

In contrast to textbook surveys of the subject, COMBS offers a history of historical writing on American foreign policy. He suggests that the first comprehensive account of American foreign relations was written by Theodore Lyman in 1826, and shows how Lyman's pro-Federalist interpretation came to be challenged by pro-Republican historians such as William H. Trescot and George Tucker. In succeeding chapters, Combs traces the development of historical writing on foreign policy through the 19th and 20th centuries. From an early stage, many episodes in American foreign policy aroused both immediate controversy and later historiographical argument. Combs elaborates on the development of differing interpretations of such issues as the origins of the War of 1812, American imperialism in the 1890s, intervention in World War I and World War II, the origins of the Cold War and American involvement in Vietnam.

In an interpretative analysis with relatively little narrative detail, COLE has had a seminal influence in giving greater depth to the study of the history of American foreign policy by focusing on the forces which shaped America's policy rather than on a factual narrative of events. His innovative methodology was to divide the history of American foreign policy into six chronological periods, and then to deal with each period, first with a chapter discussing the external influences on the United States, then with a chapter analyzing the domestic conditions affecting American foreign relations, and third with several chapters tracing America's foreign policy in that period in terms of the interplay of external and internal influences.

The more theoretical ideas and concepts which have helped to shape American foreign policy are the concern of THOMPSON. For example, the book includes discussion of classical and Christian traditions which were of fundamental importance in the formulation of American policy. Thompson then examines both the concepts with which American policymakers have needed to deal, such as realism, power, freedom and equality, and the application of those traditions and concepts to such issues as human rights and arms control. Finally, Thompson selects the foreign policy of a number of presidents to illustrate the conflict of values and traditions in the actual practice of American foreign policy.

PETER G. BOYLE

Foreign Policy: Financial and Economic Aspects

Aldcroft, Derek, *From Versailles to Wall Street, 1919–1929*, Berkeley: University of California Press, and London: Allen Lane, 1977

Becker, William H. and Samuel F. Wells, Jr. (editors), *Economics and World Power: An Assessment of American Diplomacy since 1789*, New York: Columbia University Press, 1984

Bhagwati, Jagdish, *The World Trading System at Risk*, Princeton: Princeton University Press, 1991

Block, Fred L., *The Origins of International Economic Disorder: A Study of United States International Monetary Policy from World War II to the Present*, Berkeley: University of California Press, 1977

Clauder, Anna C., *American Commerce as Affected by the Wars of the French Revolution and Napoleon, 1793–1812*, Philadelphia: privately printed, 1932; reprinted, Clifton, NJ: Kelley, 1972

Costigliola, Frank, *Awkward Dominion: American Political, Economic, and Cultural Relations with Europe, 1919–1933*, Ithaca, NY: Cornell University Press, 1984

Devlin, Patrick, *Too Proud to Fight: Woodrow Wilson's Neutrality*, New York: Oxford University Press, 1974

Kennedy, Paul, *The Rise and Fall of the Great Powers: Economic Change and Military Conflict from 1500 to 2000*, New York: Random House, 1987; London: Unwin Hyman, 1988

LaFeber, Walter, *The American Search for Opportunity, 1865–1913* (The Cambridge History of American Foreign Relations, volume 2), Cambridge: Cambridge University Press, 1993

Lake, David A., *Power, Protection, and Free Trade: International Sources of US Commercial Strategy, 1887–1939*, Ithaca, NY: Cornell University Press, 1988

Milner, Helen V., *Resisting Protectionism: Global Industries and the Politics of World Trade*, Princeton: Princeton University Press, 1988

Thistlethwaite, Frank, *The Anglo-American Connection in the Early Nineteenth Century*, Philadelphia: University of Pennsylvania Press, and London: Oxford University Press, 1959; as *America and the Atlantic Community: Anglo-American Aspects, 1790–1850*, New York: Harper, 1963

Until the 20th century at least, continental scale and geographical remoteness combined to make the United States very strong in the Americas, but not necessarily elsewhere. The major problem for United States foreign economic policy in the 19th century was therefore to secure open access for trade and safe passage for American citizens overseas. In the 20th century, the United States adopted the additional role of creating a stable and open economic and political environment for trade and development in Europe and Asia. The central problem has always been how to secure these objectives in distant areas at reasonable cost.

Foreign trade was particularly important in the early republic, before the West developed. Though an old book, CLAUDER is a good introduction to the complex economic diplomacy of the period. From 1783 to 1793, the United States government was powerless to help American merchants excluded from many European and colonial markets. The onset of the French wars in 1793 suddenly presented them with huge opportunities. Clauder describes how American merchants attempted to exploit their neutrality, but were often themselves caught up in the conflict. At first they made huge profits, but after 1806 they were increasingly trapped in British and French regulatory systems. The United States government was generally too weak to help except when the European belligerents were closely balanced. Eventually, under Jefferson and then Madison, the government felt obliged to resort, first to embargoes on foreign imports, and then war.

BECKER and WELLS is a useful collection of articles on American foreign economic policy, including Field on the period 1783–1815, and Brauer on the period 1821–1860. In his article, Brauer demonstrated the limited support which American administrations gave to overseas commerce. Fortunately for the United States, a conscious foreign economic policy was hardly necessary. The westward impulse was so powerful that the United States was able to brush aside weak British opposition to Manifest Destiny. Britain did successfully protect Canada, but was divided on a more general North American policy. THISTLETHWAITE shows how the economic complementarity – of cotton, wheat, manufactures and capital – and the growth of mutual liberal sympathies, forged the transatlantic rapprochement of the 1850s, and dissipated potential mercantilist rivalries between Britain and the United States.

Northern victory in the Civil War confirmed that the United States would develop as a consolidated industrial nation overwhelmingly dominant in its own hemisphere. LAKE demonstrates that the United States soon learned that, overseas, America could get a "free ride on British free trade" – exploiting British markets for cotton and grain but protecting American industries without fear of retaliation. LaFEBER was a student of the New Left historian William Appleman Williams who argued that late 19th-century United States imperialism was a function of American economic power. LaFeber's book in the useful Cambridge History of American Foreign Relations series summarizes the literature on the outward thrust of American foreign economic policy. Pletcher's essay in Becker and Wells covers similar ground.

The United States had supported international attempts to develop neutral rights on the high seas into a generally accepted doctrine. To take one example from the huge literature on the subject, DEVLIN argues that World War I soon demonstrated how frail this assertion was in face of the conflicting interests of European belligerents. American intervention came at a point in the war when the United States could influence the outcome at relatively small cost.

Official foreign economic policy in the 1920s was a reaction against Wilsonian internationalism, but COSTIGLIOLA argues that American political and economic leaders did unofficially exercise an effective economic policy which attempted to promote economic stabilization in Europe. However, ALDCROFT argues that lack of American cooperation with Europe in the 1920s led to the Great Depression and indirectly to World War II.

BLOCK describes how, after World War II, the United States attempted to establish a post-war economic system incorporating America's long-term aims. The key features were Bretton Woods and the Marshall Plan. Both attempted to establish stable international structures to protect American interests abroad at minimum cost. In the short run these polices were very successful. The United States managed to re-establish liberal capitalism in Europe and to restore a rules-based system of international trade. Europe and Japan were tied into the American trading system. American companies expanded safely over nearly the whole globe and world trade grew enormously. However, in Block's view, the effort proved too great. Military expenditure overseas and concessions made to lubricate the system gradually eroded the American trade surplus. Eventually, in 1971, the United States was forced to renege on vital elements in the Bretton Woods system.

KENNEDY develops this theme of "imperial overstretch" in a broader historical context – and sees the military costs of opposing Russia as the long-term cause of the weakening of the American economic position. However, his case rests too heavily on the military costs of hegemony. What is more surprising is that, despite abandonment of the Bretton Woods parities, the essential American economic bargain with Europe and the Far East continued. Successive GATT (General Agreement on Tariffs and Trade) rounds took tariffs even lower. MILNER argues that the United States continued the free trade policy through the 1970s because of the increasing influence of multinational companies with vested interests in open international trade.

Although the American trade balance deteriorated even more rapidly in the 1980s, the administration preserved its free trade policy. The Reagan boom gave a huge fillip to America's trading partners and possibly thereby completed the demoralization of the eastern bloc. However, many economists, such as BHAGWATI, suggest that even though the United States has continued to support GATT, it is now reneging on other aspects of the post-war bargain. He argues that the United States is gradually moving from internationalism towards "aggressive unilateralism" by increasingly managing American trade with Europe and Japan. It seems more likely that, since the American government no longer has large trade and budget surpluses to finance overseas subsidies like the Marshall Plan, it has reverted to managing access to its own huge market as a lever in foreign economic policy. The fundamental aim however remains the same – to consolidate the North American market – hence NAFTA – and to gain access for American traders in distant markets.

JOHN R. KILLICK

See also Economic History; Financial History entries; Foreign Trade; Investment: United States Investment Abroad

Foreign Policy, 1865–1918

Anderson, Stuart, *Race and Rapprochement: Anglo-Saxonism and Anglo-American Relations, 1895–1904*, Rutherford, NJ: Fairleigh Dickinson University Press, 1981

Campbell, Charles S., *The Transformation of American Foreign Relations, 1865–1900*, New York: Harper, 1976

Grenville, John A.S. and George Berkeley Young, *Politics, Strategy, and American Diplomacy: Studies in Foreign Policy, 1873–1917*, New Haven: Yale University Press, 1966

Hagan, Kenneth J., *American Gunboat Diplomacy and the Old Navy, 1877–1899*, Westport, CT: Greenwood Press, 1973

Knock, Thomas J., *To End All Wars: Woodrow Wilson and the Quest for a New World Order*, New York and Oxford: Oxford University Press, 1992

LaFeber, Walter, *The New Empire: An Interpretation of American Expansion, 1860–1898*, Ithaca, NY: Cornell University Press, 1963

Langley, Lester D., *Struggle for the American Mediterranean: United States-European Rivalry in the Gulf-Caribbean, 1776–1904*, Athens: University of Georgia Press, 1976

McCullough, David, *The Path Between the Seas: The Creation of the Panama Canal, 1870–1914*, New York: Simon and Schuster, 1977

Offner, John L., *An Unwanted War: The Diplomacy of the United States and Spain over Cuba, 1895–1898*, Chapel Hill: University of North Carolina Press, 1992

Perkins, Bradford, *The Great Rapprochement: England and the United States, 1895–1914*, New York: Atheneum, 1968; London: Gollancz, 1969

Historians now see the period between the end of the Civil War and the end of World War I as critical to the development of the United States' approach to the world. How did the U.S. become part of the developing capitalist "world system" in the 19th century? Was U.S. foreign policy imperialistic during this era, or was the Spanish-American War a "Great Aberration"? Was there was a significant difference between continental expansionism before 1898 and extra-hemispheric imperialism after 1898? What were the economic, political, social, and psychological components of American policy? Why did the United States go to war with Spain in 1898? Was President William McKinley a weak leader pressured by congress, the public, the press, or his party? To what extend did he exhaust diplomacy before taking his nation to war? What were the reasons for American entry into World War I and why did the United States refuse to join the League of

Nations? Most general surveys treat the period from 1865 through 1900. Typically, World War I is covered separately.

An excellent basic introduction to the period is CAMPBELL, a sophisticated and balanced synthesis that emphasizes intellectual trends such as Social Darwinism rather than economics as a cause of expansion. Major topics include: the rapprochement with Great Britain; the Panama Canal; Pacific expansion; relations with Latin America; and Cuba and the war with Spain. The book also has an extensive bibliography.

A valuable topical study is GRENVILLE and YOUNG, which examines some of the major navalists, politicians, lobbyists, and statesmen of the era. The insights into Henry Cabot Lodge, Stephen B. Luce, Benjamin Harrison, and Grover Cleveland are particularly useful. The book also makes a compelling case that President McKinley's policy toward Cuba and Spain was careful and coherent and that the president chose war only after concluding that it was the only way to produce Cuban independence. The authors also demonstrate a good understanding of the strategic (military and naval) factors involved in American policy.

A classic example of the economic-determinist interpretation of the period is LaFEBER. He offers a readable narrative portraying politicians, intellectuals, navalists, and business interests as reacting to the depression of the 1890s with an energetic search for overseas markets and investments. While some earlier historians had argued that the business community opposed war in 1898, LaFeber suggests that some favored war. This work is stimulating, but the reader must carefully evaluate LaFeber's use of sources.

No examination of this period would be complete without some study of the navy, the main agent of American foreign policy. The standard work is HAGAN, which sees naval policy and operations in the context of the search for markets, and describes a generally consistent and coherent policy being implemented by naval commanders. A readable work, the book provides a good analysis of the navy's basic role, and a good summary of fundamental diplomatic-naval events.

Aside from the war with Spain and World War I, the development during this period with greatest implications for American foreign policy was the "rapprochement" between the United States and Great Britain. A century of strained relations ended in the 1890s, setting the stage for the "special relationship" between the two nations during the 20th century. It is a well-known story, but the standard work on the subject, PERKINS, is a graceful and detailed account. A significant supplement is ANDERSON, which evaluates the extent to which "Anglo-Saxonism" contributed to the development of transatlantic understanding.

The Spanish-American War ushered the United States on to the world stage. Unfortunately, there is still no single volume that includes political, diplomatic, and military details. On the other hand, OFFNER is a solid and up-to-date general history of the diplomacy leading up to the war. Offner says that both the United States and Spain tried to resolve the Cuban situation peacefully, but that Cuban nationalists and "powerful domestic forces" in the United States and Spain made the conflict inevitable. McKinley had firm control over American policy, but mistakenly hoped for peace because of misconceived advice from diplomatic officials. Ultimately, Republicans made war on Spain because of domestic political calculations rather than expansionism, markets and investments, the sensational press, or national security interests. In the end, Offner argues, the United States took a moderate course in not seizing Spain's Atlantic, Mediterranean, or African colonies.

Latin America and the Caribbean have long been regions of special interest to most United States foreign policy makers. LANGLEY provides a solid synthesis of the rivalry between the United States and European powers in that region, and finds the roots of 20th-century United States intervention in the 19th-century. The work is particularly useful for its "international" perspective and its understanding of issues of American security.

The culmination of United States policy toward Latin America can be seen in the building of the Panama Canal. McCULLOUGH is the most accessible work, a multiple-prize-winner written for a popular audience, yet based on solid research and considered reflection. This is a big book, but McCullough tells a good story. He is particularly good on social and technological history, but he covers the political and diplomatic side thoroughly too.

Virtually every aspect of American involvement in World War I has been researched and written about, and there are dozens of excellent volumes on the subject to select. One of the most recent, and also one of the most comprehensive and readable, is KNOCK. The book provides an excellent overview of Wilson's "internationalism" – throughout his career as an academic and as president – and explores the logical connections between domestic reform and foreign policy. In particular, Knock sees a United States that was decidedly "internationalist," not isolationist, but that rejected Wilson's League of Nations treaty because of competing visions of internationalism.

KENNETH J. BLUME

See also Imperialism and Anti-Imperialism; Open Door Policy; Spanish-American War; World War I entries

Foreign Policy, 1919–1941

Adler, Selig, *The Uncertain Giant, 1921–1941: American Foreign Policy Between the Wars*, New York: Macmillan, 1965

Costigliola, Frank, *Awkward Dominion: American Political, Economic, and Cultural Relations with Europe, 1919–1933*, Ithaca, NY: Cornell University Press, 1984

Dallek, Robert, *Franklin D. Roosevelt and American Foreign Policy, 1932–1945*, New York: Oxford University Press, 1979; with new afterword, 1995

Divine, Robert A., *The Reluctant Belligerent: American Entry into World War II*, New York: Wiley, 1965, 2nd edition, 1979

Gellman, Irwin F., *Good Neighbor Diplomacy: United States Policies in Latin America, 1933–1945*, Baltimore: Johns Hopkins University Press, 1979

Hoff, Joan, *American Business and Foreign Policy, 1920–1933*, Lexington: University Press of Kentucky, 1971

Iriye, Akira, *The Origins of the Second World War in Asia and the Pacific*, London and New York: Longman, 1987

Kaufman, Robert Gordon, *Arms Control During the Pre-Nuclear Era: The United States and Naval Limitation Between the Two World Wars*, New York: Columbia University Press, 1994

Reynolds, David, *The Creation of the Anglo-American Alliance, 1937–1941: A Study in Competitive Co-Operation*, London: Europa, 1981; Chapel Hill: University of North Carolina Press, 1982

Williams, William Appleman, *The Tragedy of American Diplomacy*, Cleveland: World, 1959; 2nd revised edition, New York: Dell, 1972

Wood, Bryce, *The Making of the Good Neighbor Policy*, New York: Columbia University Press, 1961

The period between the end of World War I and the outbreak of World War II has been the subject of much debate among historians. Initial opinion tended to be critical of American unwillingness to engage in collective security through the League of Nations. Although a little outdated, and based predominantly upon secondary rather than primary sources, ADLER remains a useful introduction to interwar foreign policy. He presents a clear interpretation of events in those crucial two decades, arguing that the United States should have played a larger role in international affairs, and attacking the isolationists for clinging to 19th-century opinions. Adler points to an articulate minority who recognized that the United States had to take on responsibilities commensurate with its new world position. Conflict between the two views resulted in an unfortunate uncertainty in foreign policy.

Originally published in 1959, WILLIAMS covers the first half of the 20th century, but is worth reading for its classic exposition of the concept of the "legend of isolationism". According to Williams, the United States government pursued an activist policy of defending American economic interests overseas through the use of diplomacy and government action, even though it refused to participate in the League of Nations. This policy of economic intervention was based upon support for the "open door", in line with an assumption that domestic economic interests were best served by a policy of foreign expansionism. This is a thought-provoking, stimulating book that presumes a prior level of knowledge.

One important theme that runs through the entire period – or at least until the mid-1930s – is that of disarmament, a cause espoused by the United States as it combined morality in foreign affairs with financial and strategic priorities. In a carefully researched work, KAUFMAN discusses the various attempts at negotiating international agreements on naval arms control, in the Washington treaty of 1922 and the London Naval Treaties of 1930 and 1936. He draws a clear distinction between the 1920s, when international conditions made agreement on naval limitation politically possible, and the 1930s when the Japanese in particular were determined upon their expansionist policy in the Pacific.

HOFF's excellent study of Republican foreign policy in the interwar period demonstrates how it gave explicit support to American businesses wishing to expand abroad through a judicious combination of advocating the "open door" in areas (such as the Middle East) in which American business had as yet little representation, while seeking to maintain a "closed door" in areas where the United States already had a strong commercial presence – notably Latin America. She categorizes American foreign policy in the period as "independent internationalism", with the United States refusing to undertake any formal commitments, but nonetheless internationalist in its outlook.

COSTIGLIOLA's superb study of American relations with Europe, solidly rooted in archival research, is an example of the corporatist interpretation of the 1920s. He argues that Harding and Coolidge, in part under the guidance of Secretary of Commerce Herbert Hoover, tried to use economic diplomacy to achieve peace through prosperity, without having to undertake the kind of military or political commitments encapsulated in the Treaty of Versailles. Government and business shared common assumptions about the best policies to pursue.

The area of most immediate concern to American policymakers was that closest to home, Latin America. The policy most commonly identified with the interwar period is that of the "good neighbor", a phrase coined by Franklin Roosevelt. In his thorough study of United States policy in Latin America from 1926 to 1943, WOOD locates the origins of the policy in the preceding Republican administrations, particularly that of Herbert Hoover, where he traces signs of a more conciliatory policy, less reliant upon military interventionism. GELLMAN, on the other hand, identifies the policy very firmly with Roosevelt himself, as a response to the Depression, and he rejects notions of Republican influence. Both agree, however, that during World War II hemispheric co-operation provided a useful tool for Roosevelt, enabling him to use a regional base to underpin some of his policies.

Although books on Franklin Roosevelt's foreign policy inevitably concentrate upon the period of American belligerency, general works on his presidency are worth consulting. DALLEK provides the most judicious and comprehensive study of Roosevelt's foreign policy, drawing upon the wealth of archival material available by the 1970s, and giving due weight to the pre-Pearl Harbor period. He presents the president as a man who was by inclination an internationalist, and well aware of the pressing importance to the United States of a policy of support for Britain. However, he was also very conscious of the constraints upon his policy. Thus, he recognised the need to carry congressional and public opinion with him, a factor which Dallek emphasizes.

After war broke out in the Far East in 1937, to be followed two years later by European conflict, the United States government had to steer an uneasy course aimed at defence of American interests while avoiding involvement in war. DIVINE has examined this period in a number of works, of which the one cited here is the best. In his discussion of the entry of the United States into World War II, he emphasizes American reluctance to become a belligerent, and the slow process by which its involvement steadily increased.

The same period is explored in some detail by REYNOLDS in his comprehensive and thoroughly researched study of Anglo-American relations in the four years before American belligerency. He emphasizes not only the forces drawing the United States and Great Britain into ever greater co-operation but also the continuing conflicts between the two powers. It was the war, rather than any cosy transatlantic harmony or particularly close relationship between the leaders of the two nations that brought the countries together. Like Divine, Reynolds stresses Roosevelt's continuing hope that the United States would not have to enter the war as a belligerent, but could use Britain and France as a first line of defence.

Although much of the president's attention was devoted to events in Europe, American entry into World War II came initially as a result of events in the Far East and the Japanese attack upon Pearl Harbor. IRIYE's book on the origins of the war in the Pacific and the Far East clearly covers more than just the Japanese-American conflict, but is a succinct and readable survey based on the latest scholarship as well as his own research. It also illustrates the importance of the wider context in understanding American opinion towards European affairs.

FIONA VENN

See also Isolationism; World War I: American Neutrality

Foreign Policy since 1945: General

Cohen, Warren I., *America in the Age of Soviet Power, 1945–1991* (The Cambridge History of American Foreign Relations, volume 4), Cambridge and New York: Cambridge University Press, 1993

Gaddis, John Lewis, *The Long Peace: Inquiries into the History of the Cold War*, New York and Oxford: Oxford University Press, 1987

Hunt, Michael H., *Ideology and US Foreign Policy*, New Haven: Yale University Press, 1987

Kunz, Diane B. (editor), *The Diplomacy of the Crucial Decade: American Foreign Relations During the 1960s*, New York: Columbia University Press, 1994

LaFeber, Walter, *The American Age: United States Foreign Policy at Home and Abroad since 1750*, New York: Norton, 1989, 2nd edition, 1994

Leffler, Melvyn P., *A Preponderance of Power: National Security, the Truman Administration, and the Cold War*, Stanford, CA: Stanford University Press, 1992

McCormick, Thomas J., *America's Half Century: United States Foreign Policy in the Cold War*, Baltimore: Johns Hopkins University Press, 1989

The end of the Cold War offers great opportunities for the diplomatic historian. The collapse of the Soviet Union has coincided with a resurgence in the field, reinvigorated by scholars with innovative conceptual and analytical approaches. Recent works reflect concern for issues once ignored, such as race, culture, ideology, gender, psychology, and world systems theory. At the same time, traditional archival-based research has flourished. Scholars have taken advantage of the thousands of documents, including materials from Eastern Europe and the Soviet Union, declassified in recent years. This combination of new approaches and intensive archival research has produced a clearer and more complete understanding of U.S. foreign policy since 1945.

Calling historians to understand the role of ideas in diplomacy, HUNT offers a provocative survey of the impact of ideology on United States foreign policy. He finds three "core ideas" that have shaped American diplomacy from the Revolution through the 20th century. In this view, United States foreign policy has been driven by a desire to achieve national greatness based on the promotion of liberty, Anglo-Saxon racial superiority, and a conservative response to political and social change. Influenced by anthropologist Clifford Geertz, Hunt looks to culture and shared systems of beliefs and values to find the ideas that have undergirded and directed American diplomacy. Through a detailed examination of the public rhetoric of foreign policy elites, Hunt demonstrates how his three "core ideas" influenced American foreign policy during the Cold War. Traditional visions of America's role in the world as defender of liberty and freedom, as well as a longstanding fear of radical social and political change, help to explain policies as various as containment in Europe and involvement in Vietnam. Hunt's most striking contribution lies in his discussion of the impact of race on diplomacy. Development theory in the Cold War, he argues, drew on the historical tradition of viewing the peoples of the world in terms of a racial hierarchy. He traces the racism of modern American foreign policy elites, revealing the attitudes behind the condescending and paternalistic policies directed towards the Third World in the 1950s and 1960s. Although Hunt fails to deal with the changing attitudes towards race that occurred within American culture during this same period and the implications of that change, his work offers an intriguing interpretation.

In his survey of foreign policy since 1945, McCORMICK draws upon world systems theory to explain the hegemonic rise of the United States and its subsequent decline. World system theory offers a model for understanding global capitalism. The world is divided into geographic and functional zones of center, semi-periphery, and periphery. At the center, the United States emerged from World War II as the dominant capitalist nation and sought to create a world order conducive to its interests. In order to maintain its economic pre-eminence, American leaders sought to integrate Western economies and to spark economic development in the Third World through political agreements and, in some cases, military force. According to McCormick, the militarization of foreign policy resulted in heavy defense spending which weakened the American economy in the 1970s and 1980s. Without a strong economic base, the United States could not maintain its political and military hegemony. However, McCormick's assertion that the relative economic decline of the United States is solely attributable to military overspending ignores a variety of other causal factors related to specific changes within the American economy. Although compelling, world systems theory is too rigid and deterministic to explain American foreign policy. According to McCormick, the actions of individual policymakers nearly always emerge from a desire to perpetuate American economic dominance. He discounts ideologies, ideas, and motivations that might be contrary to the systemic workings of his model. Despite these criticisms, McCormick's book is written with great skill and challenges historians to understand American foreign policy as part of a larger system.

Although the term "national security" is commonly used by diplomatic historians, LEFFLER breaks new ground by building an interpretive framework around the concept. In this meticulously researched study of the Truman administration, Leffler argues that policymakers after World War II wisely perceived that Soviet exploitation of social and political chaos in Western Europe and growing Third World nationalism had dangerous implications for the economic prosperity and national security of the United States. In Leffler's national security framework, Truman administration officials recognized that a communist takeover of Western Europe, or advances in the Third World, would deprive the United States of needed markets and raw materials, and force the United States to restructure its economy and political order. Communist advances would turn the United States from a prosperous, liberal society to a "garrison state" forced to ration its resources. Integrating revisionist and realist approaches, Leffler's model demonstrates the complex interrelationship between economic concerns and national security. Leffler argues that policymakers acted prudently to counter the Soviet threat through the re-building of Germany and Japan, the implementation of the Marshall Plan, and the creation of NATO. Secretary of State Dean Acheson sought to bring America's "preponderance of power" to bear in order to ensure the creation of an international system that would support American economic interests and protect its long-term security. Yet, Leffler argues, these policymakers made serious errors in their attempts to deal with the communist threat in the Third World. A tendency to see all communist movements as inspired and directed by Moscow rather than as independent forms of anti-colonial nationalism led to disastrous support of right-wing regimes, as well as unpopular and corrupt governments. Despite a lack of attention to domestic politics, Leffler's work stands out as one of the most sophisticated and thoughtful studies on the origins of the Cold War.

In the first survey written after the collapse of the Soviet Union, COHEN reflects on the origins, evolution, and consequences of the Cold War. In this sweeping overview, he devotes great attention to both the domestic and international contexts of United States foreign policy, as he traces the spread of the conflict from Europe to the Third World. He argues that the dynamics of the two superpowers' political systems played a crucial role in intensifying Cold War tensions. The brutal and paranoid nature of the Soviet system prevented open dialogue and encouraged hostility. At the same time, the structure of the American political system contributed to the conflict. In order to win public and congressional support for foreign policy initiatives, the executive branch had to exaggerate the dangers which the Soviet Union posed to American interests and national security, or had to subvert the political process. Cohen's survey incorporates Leffler's argument that a "security dilemma" prolonged and intensified the Cold War – each side believed that, in order to protect itself from the other's arms build-up, it had to increase its own defenses. Cohen uses his expertise in American-East Asian relations to bring a global perspective to this survey. He uses Soviet and Chinese sources to enhance his discussion of the Korean War, the Quemoy and Matsu crises, and the Cuban Missile crisis. His conclusion also offers some tentative insights into the impact of the Cold War on American society. On a global level, United States foreign policy has promoted the pervasive spread of American culture and values. Although in relative decline as an economic power, the United States achieved the goal of creating a liberal-capitalist world order. As Cohen concludes, it is a better world than the one Joseph Stalin might have created.

In his collection of eight essays, GADDIS traces the relationship between the Soviet Union and United States. Rich in detail and documentation, these essays reconstruct the policy-making process in the first decade of the Cold War. Gaddis examines American perceptions of the Soviet Union after World War II, the debate between George Kennan and Charles Bohlen over European strategy, the formation of the defensive perimeter strategy in East Asia, and Truman's and Eisenhower's rejection of the use of nuclear weapons in response to crises in Korea, Indochina, and the Taiwan Straits. In "Dividing Adversaries," Gaddis argues that the nation's foreign policy leaders possessed remarkable vision. With his discovery of a 1953 briefing in which John Foster Dulles calls for the United States to exploit Sino-Soviet tensions, Gaddis demonstrates the value of careful archival research. Although the United States did not wholeheartedly pursue this "wedge strategy" until the Nixon administration, Gaddis debunks the notion that foreign policy elites ever saw communism as monolithic. In his last and most theoretical essay, Gaddis raises provocative questions about how scholars should understand the Cold War. He argues that future historians may look back on it as "the long peace." Although the era was not free of armed conflict, Gaddis marvels that a cataclysmic war was somehow averted. Influenced by the thinking of political scientist Kenneth Waltz, he argues that the bi-polar structure of the world order reinforced stability and prevented crises from spiraling out of control. Reliance on nuclear weapons encouraged such caution. If one can accept his definition of "peace" as avoidance of war between the two superpowers, Gaddis's argument is compelling and will serve as a starting point for further discussion of this critical question.

Recent release of archival material has allowed historians to address critical aspects of American foreign policy in the "crucial decade" of the 1960s. KUNZ brings together an impressive array of scholars who discuss U.S. foreign policy towards Western Europe, the Middle East, Asia, Latin America, and Africa. In these essays, historians such as David Kaiser explore elements of continuity and change between the Kennedy and Johnson administrations. Escalation in Vietnam came to dominate the attention of both administrations, and Robert D. Schulzinger skilfully analyzes the evolution of United States policy in that area. The historians in Kunz's anthology are sensitive to the impact of Vietnam on other aspects of foreign policy. Michael Schaller argues that the Vietnam War helped transform U.S.-Japanese relations, and created conditions for Japan's emergence as an economic superpower. In his appraisal of Kennedy's and Johnson's policies towards Western Europe, Thomas Alan Schwartz demonstrates how the Kennedy and Johnson administrations resolved a number of potentially dangerous security issues and stabilized conditions in Europe. Like other contributors to this collection, Schwartz shows how the United States sometimes found itself caught between the goals and policies of other nations, especially in the Third World, where countries were often able to resist American pressure. In the 1960s, policymakers viewed the world through the prism of the Cold War, and, as Douglas Little, Gerald E. Thomas, and William O. Walker III demonstrate, this worldview resulted in disastrous policies in the Middle East, Africa, and Latin America. Using Soviet and Eastern European sources, Vladislav M. Zubok explores the thinking of Soviet policymakers and gauges to what extent the Soviet Union posed a threat to American interests in the 1960s. The global perspective of Kunz's anthology illuminates a number of important issues and demonstrates the importance of multi-national archival research.

Including a new chapter on the end of the Cold War, LaFEBER's revised textbook offers students an introduction to the history of U.S. diplomacy from the American Revolution to the Clinton administration. A rare example of a textbook in which the author's judgments – generally from a New Left perspective – are not watered down, LaFeber entertains as well as educates. He draws the reader in with anecdotes, political cartoons, and illustrations, and skilfully integrates the best of recent historical findings with his own interpretations. LaFeber also includes a helpful bibliographic guide to various themes and subjects. A strength of his text is his attention to the domestic context of American foreign policy, and he explores the tensions between the legislative and the executive branch over the formation of foreign policy. He also is sensitive to the interrelationship between culture, society, and diplomacy.

MICHAEL G. DAVIS

See also Cold War

Foreign Policy since 1945: Special Aspects

1) Relations with Asia

Borden, William, *The Pacific Alliance: United States Foreign Economic Policy and Japanese Trade Recovery, 1947–1955*, Madison: University of Wisconsin Press, 1984

Brands, H.W., *Bound to Empire: The United States and the Philippines, 1890–1990*, New York: Oxford University Press, 1992

Cullather, Nick, *Illusions of Influence: The Political Economy of United States-Philippines Relations, 1942–1960*, Stanford, CA: Stanford University Press, 1994

Dower, John W., *Empire and Aftermath: Yoshida Shigeru and the Japanese Experience, 1878–1954*, Cambridge, MA: Harvard University Press, 1979

Hess, Gary R., *The United States' Emergence as a Southeast Asian Power, 1940–1950*, New York: Columbia University Press, 1987

McMahon, Robert J., *Colonialism and Cold War: The United States and the Struggle for Indonesian Independence, 1945–1949*, Ithaca, NY: Cornell University Press, 1981

McMahon, Robert J., *The Cold War on the Periphery: The United States, India, and Pakistan*, New York: Columbia University Press, 1994

Merrill, Dennis, *Bread and the Ballot: The United States and India's Economic Development, 1947–1963*, Chapel Hill: University of North Carolina Press, 1990

Schaller, Michael, *The American Occupation of Japan: The Origins of the Cold War in Asia*, New York: Oxford University Press, 1985

The war in Vietnam shattered the consensus in Cold War historiography in the United States. The waves of revisionism and post-revisionism that followed continue to transform the study of American relations with Asia. The literature still lacks a coherent synthesis, but in the 1980s the focus of scholarship expanded beyond the primary battlefields of the Cold War to encompass the broader framework of Asian history and politics, and to integrate areas that once seemed peripheral.

The process of document declassification has yielded some surprises, including the revelation of the extent to which Japan occupied a central position in American planning from the earliest days of the Cold War. DOWER exploits extensive American and Japanese sources for his biography of statesman and postwar prime minister Yoshida Shigeru. Almost half of this major study is devoted to the reform and reconstruction of postwar Japan, including the politics and diplomacy of the treaty negotiations. Dower's attention to Asian sources and perspectives as well as the critical edge to his analysis are characteristic of the best recent work in the field.

Taking advantage of an expanding, multi-archival documentary base, Dower's biography and SCHALLER's monograph shed new light on Japan's importance in postwar strategy and diplomacy. Both authors reject conventional views about the idealism of American occupation policy, and argue that its liberal reform phase was shortlived. Schaller uses the "reverse course" in occupation policy – the 1947–48 shift in emphasis from reform to rehabilitation and economic recovery – to mark the onset of the Cold War in the Far East. Dower documents a complex two-way relationship, and a balancing act in occupation policy that served the interests of each side. Both studies advance our understanding of how peripheral nations like Vietnam and Korea assumed such importance in United States strategy; providing "workshop Japan" with access to Southeast Asian markets and resources was deemed vital for securing both areas as Cold War assets.

Schaller emphasizes the strategic calculations governing relations with Japan. BORDEN's wide-angle focus on American economic strategy shows that Japanese recovery was part of a broader plan for bringing Asia and the Pacific into the American orbit. The "fall" of China and invasion of South Korea mobilized plans that included the economic integration of Japan with Southeast Asia and the economic containment of China. Without quibbling over the relative weight of strategic and economic concerns, Borden asserts that calculations of the economic balance of power were central to American policy.

The American role in decolonization in Asia initially attracted interest in relation to the Cold War in Europe and the pre-history of the Vietnam War. McMAHON (1981) establishes the Indonesian case as important in its own right. Illustrating the cross-currents of anti-colonialism and anti-communism in United States policy, McMahon's monograph locates the Truman administration's response to the Indonesian independence movement in the context of emerging strategies for containment, first in Europe and secondarily in Asia.

McMahon criticizes the Truman administration for subordinating colonial policy to the requirements of European reconstruction, and for allowing a Cold War frame of reference to shape its response to Indonesian nationalism and neutralism. HESS treats Indonesian policy as part of a broader regional study. He replaces the usual timeline based on World War II with one that reflects the steady accretion of American interest and influence in Southeast Asia between 1940 and 1950. Focusing narrowly on the decolonization debates at the top of the policy-making process in Washington, Hess reveals the strategic alchemy that transformed Southeast Asia from a diplomatic backwater into a vital national interest in less than a decade.

The Philippines offer the best perspective on the American model for decolonization. The literature on the Philippines is extensive, but few books duplicate the full-length narrative of the century-old relationship found in BRANDS. His highly readable synthesis of the primary and secondary literature traces the development of an alliance between United States policymakers and the Philippine elite that survived the colonial period. Economic ties assumed relatively greater importance as political ties weakened, but Brands argues that American control of the Philippines was scarcely diminished by independence.

With a better balance of Philippine and American sources, CULLATHER looks closely at the post-independence relationship between Washington and Manila. He rejects the conventional patron-client and dependency models in favor of a more complex relationship based on mutual interests and reciprocal leverage. By the 1950s Philippine elites were experienced at manipulating relations with Washington, particularly at using American strategic interests and military basing needs to achieve Philippine economic goals. Cullather finds American influence in Manila more illusory than real.

There was seldom even the illusion of American influence in New Delhi, as MERRILL's monograph on the United States aid program for India demonstrates. The aid was less a response to Indian needs than an instrument of containment and Washington's "hegemonic ambitions." The resulting programs were frequently inappropriate and ineffective. Merrill suggests that the Truman administration missed an opportunity to avoid the subsequent tragedy of Vietnam when it chose to build Asian policy around a military commitment in Southeast Asia rather than the political and economic commitment to democratic India which it had contemplated. Nothwithstanding India's nonalignment in the Cold War, ties with the United States steadily improved until the Kennedy administration's naive diplomatic and developmental initiative collided with Indian interests and opinion.

Updating the strange career of containment in the subcontinent, McMAHON (1994) argues that historians have underestimated the "limitations and inconsistencies" of American planning. He finds the Truman and Eisenhower administrations shortsighted and misdirected in their designs for establishing Pakistan as the keystone in a "Northern Tier" strategy for containment in South and Southwest Asia. The resulting Baghdad Pact alienated India, aggravated local tensions, and had scant military value. McMahon and Merrill depict successive administrations imposing a Cold War framework on regional policy and pursuing contradictory goals; a military relationship with Pakistan was incompatible with the economic and political ties sought with India.

DANIEL P. GREENE

See also Cold War

2) Relations with China

Chang, Gordon H., *Friends and Enemies: The United States, China, and the Soviet Union, 1948–1972*, Stanford, CA: Stanford University Press, 1990

Cohen, Warren I., *America's Response to China: A History of Sino-American Relations*, New York: Wiley, 1971; 3rd edition, New York: Columbia University Press, 1990

Cohen, Warren I. and Akira Iriye (editors), *The Great Powers in East Asia, 1953–1960*, New York: Columbia University Press, 1990

Fairbank, John K., *The United States and China*, Cambridge, MA: Harvard University Press, 1949, 4th edition, 1979

Garson, Robert, *The United States and China since 1949: A Troubled Affair*, London: Pinter, 1994

Harding, Harry, *A Fragile Relationship: The United States and China since 1972*, Washington, DC: Brookings Institution, 1992

Harding, Harry and Yuan Ming (editors), *Sino-American Relations, 1945–1955: A Joint Reassessment of a Critical Decade*, Wilmington, DE: SR Books, 1989

Shambaugh, David, *Beautiful Imperialist: China Perceives America, 1972–1990*, Princeton: Princeton University Press, 1991

Arguably historians of Sino-American relations since 1945 do not simply write about the recent past, but actually shape the present through their activity. They have actually played an important role in shaping national images and so their work presents a quite special interest. A dearth of Chinese sources has inevitably created problems, but the array of books on the subject is nevertheless impressive.

A number of good studies cover the whole period. Others deal with particular issues or narrower time scales. COHEN covers the period from the first significant contacts in the 1830s. He shows that until the imperialist 1890s American policy consisted of a series of ad hoc reactions to events in China and responses to requests from merchants, missionaries and diplomats. American policies were of little benefit to China. Indeed Chinese resentment simmered throughout the 19th century and shaped the destructive hostility that erupted after World War II. America's interests were not vital in China, but the United States used its resources to ensure equal treatment for Americans. By 1945 the United States had become a major player in China, though in the overall scheme of things China was something of a sideshow for Washington. Relations deteriorated rapidly after the communist revolution. The mishandling of minor issues and events in 1949–50 played straight into the hands of the opponents of contact in both countries. Cohen's last two chapters deal with the period up to American recognition of China in 1979. While the bulk of the book deals with the period prior to 1945, it provides information that is crucial to a sophisticated understanding of the postwar years.

No review of the literature on Sino-American relations should omit the contribution of John K. Fairbank, who ranks as the dean of historians of China in the United States. FAIRBANK (1979) is seminal; it is not a survey but an interpretation of Chinese history for an American readership. It covers the expanse of the Chinese experience in the last two centuries and bemoans the fact that the United States has never understood the essence of that experience. The communist revolution, Fairbank argues, did not really invent a new order, but drew older political traditions together. China's hostility to the United States has to be understood in the context of the West's exploitation of China. Sino-American relations can only be understood if China is seen as a victim. Fairbank's special strength lies in the richness of his insights rather than in any detail in the narrative of historical events.

Other studies cover a narrower time span. HARDING and YUAN MING have edited a volume of essays that constitute the best introduction to the Sino-American relationship in the years before and immediately after the communist revolution. Essays cover the failure of the United States to understand the meaning of the communist victory, and the disastrous effect, at least on United States relations with the People's Republic of China, of America's tenacious loyalty to Chiang Kai-shek. The Korean War, it is shown, ensured that the rift survived for two decades. Much of the best research in the field is in essay form. COHEN and IRIYE have edited an outstanding collection of essays, focusing on the post-Korean War period. In this volume Nancy Tucker demonstrates how China policy was ossified by the preponderance of pro-Chiang loyalists in the State Department. He Di shows that conflicts over the offshore islands of Jinmen and Mazu served to invigorate the People's Republic of China. Other essays cover trade sanctions and the impact of America's ostracism on its western allies.

CHANG takes the story further forward and is particularly good on the 1960s for which there is still very little detailed historical scholarship. Chang argues that American policy was more discriminating than many historians have acknowledged. He shows that few American policymakers assumed that communism was monolithic, and he indicates that the United States did try to nurture a Sino-Soviet split. It was a matter of finding the weak point in the communist partnership. In the early 1960s China's development of an atomic bomb dominated American thinking. Kennedy hoped that a test ban treaty would somehow inhibit further Chinese research and development and that it would certainly drive a wedge between China and the Soviet Union. Nixon's visit in 1972, therefore, represented the culmination of the evolution of American policy over two decades.

That visit also marked a turning point in the Sino-American relationship, and is something of a threshold in the historiography of that relationship. HARDING traces the course of Sino-American relations since 1972. He argues that the relationship went through an oscillating pattern of progress and stagnation, and crisis and consolidation, in which the vicissitudes of the relationship depended on the domestic and international context. It cannot be divorced from the state of detente with the Soviet Union nor from the emphasis placed by successive administrations on human rights issues. Harding examines the impact of the relationship on relations with Taiwan, student and cultural exchanges, trade, technology transfer, and tourism. The book is very well informed and its judgments finely balanced.

SHAMBAUGH does not deal with diplomacy but with the ideological forces that constituted the intellectual framework through which China dealt with the United States. He examines the role played by China's "America Watchers" since 1972 and the image of America that was projected through scholarship and the media in China. He shows that the new climate of intellectual inquiry, fuelled by travel and scholarly exchanges, resulted in the emergence of a positive and identifiable non-Marxist mode of analysis. Beijing began to present a more sophisticated analysis of how the American polity functions, and Shambaugh implies that the academy's tendency to view America through a pluralist lens eased the process of detente and cooperation.

GARSON is an introductory survey and synthesis covering the entire postwar period. It tries to show that the Sino-American relationship was conditioned both by internal politics and by the broad spectrum of international affairs.

ROBERT GARSON

3) Relations with Europe

Costigliola, Frank, *France and the United States: The Cold Alliance since World War II*, New York: Twayne, 1992

Duignan, Peter and L.H. Gann, *The United States and the New Europe, 1985–1992*, Palo Alto, CA: Hoover Institution Press, 1992; 2nd edition, as *The United States and the New Europe*, Oxford and Cambridge, MA: Blackwell, 1994

Grosser, Alfred, *The Western Alliance: European-American Relations since 1945*, London: Macmillan, and New York: Continuum, 1980

Hanrieder, Wolfram F., *Germany, America, Europe: Forty Years of German Foreign Policy*, New Haven, CT: Yale University Press, 1989

Kaplan, Lawrence S., *The United States and NATO: The Formative Years*, Lexington: University Press of Kentucky, 1984

Paxton, Robert O. and Nicholas Wahl (editors), *De Gaulle and the United States: A Centennial Reappraisal*, Oxford: Berg, 1994

Powaski, Ronald E., *The Entangling Alliance: The United States and European Security, 1950–1993*, Westport, CT: Greenwood Press, 1994

Smith, Michael, *Western Europe and the United States: The Uncertain Alliance*, London and Boston: Allen and Unwin, 1984

Smith, Steven K. and Douglas A. Wertman, *US-West European Relations During the Reagan Years: The Perspective of West European Publics*, London: Macmillan, and New York: St. Martin's Press, 1992

The complex and at times troubled postwar relationship between the United States and Europe has received much attention from historians and political scientists. Not surprisingly, most works in this field tend to focus on America's relations with Western European countries and usually on NATO/EC members. One of the earliest and most wide-ranging introductory texts is GROSSER. Though somewhat dated now, it offers a distinctly European perspective on the transatlantic relationship. It also highlights the fact that uncertainties in the Alliance predated 1945, and stresses both the continuities and changes in the relationship. While not neglecting other countries, Grosser concentrates largely on French and German relations with the United States, and emphasizes how these two nations have followed divergent policies. While the French wished to be as independent as possible, the Germans saw the American alliance as essential for their security and their recovery of world status. Grosser sees this divergence as being at the root of the lack of solidarity prevalent in Western Europe during this whole period.

In his short study, SMITH (1984) agrees with the "continuity and change thesis" and argues that, despite the seemingly permanent links between the United States and Western Europe, the most enduring characteristic of the relationship has been its uncertainty. He develops this theme through an examination of the substance of United States-European relations, and its conduct on a number of levels – institutional, bilateral and multilateral. This is a succinct, well-written introduction to the major issues and debates.

A feature of more recent works is concern over the future of the Atlantic alliance after the end of the Cold War. For example, in their comprehensive and highly readable survey, DUIGNAN and GANN, unashamedly Atlanticist by conviction, not only trace the development of the innumerable links between Europe and the United States but also argue that despite disagreements their interests coincide in the long run. This work is particularly illuminating on the post-1985 period, and includes a chapter on Eastern Europe's "great transformation" and one on recommendations for future American foreign policy.

POWASKI focuses on America's postwar military commitment in Europe and is largely a work of synthesis. It summarizes the reasoning behind the original and continuing military commitment, and outlines the recent decline in the United States military presence in Europe. It also chronicles the major disagreements that have confronted NATO since 1950, for example over the rearmament of West Germany, burden sharing, and the pace and extent of detente. However, Powaski does not adequately back up his assertion that the United States is likely to remain committed militarily to Europe in the foreseeable future.

Acknowledging the importance of America's strategic commitment to an Atlantic alliance, which was in contrast to its long tradition of non-alignment, KAPLAN offers a detailed and informed analysis of NATO's origins and early years through a set of separate but related essays. The rationale of the Truman administration, and the lengthy negotiations surrounding the decision to join a multilateral military alliance, are fully documented, as are the changes to NATO's structure after the Korean War. Kaplan is rather generous in his appraisal of NATO and of American intentions in joining it. Rejecting revisionist interpretations of American foreign policy that see economic imperialism as the driving force behind American entanglement in European affairs, he stresses European – especially British and French – requests for American involvement.

While Anglo-American relations have received much attention, studies of United States relations with the other key European nations are relatively few. On German-American relations a substantial, scholarly work from a pro-German angle is HANRIEDER. He puts forward the stimulating, if not entirely original thesis, that the United States placed the Federal Republic at the centre of its post-war foreign policy by following a plan of "double containment" – containment of both the Federal Republic and the Soviet Union. The economic and political reconstruction of West Germany by way of integration into the post-war economic and strategic institutions, made the United States' physical and political containment of the Soviet Union much easier. This policy proved too successful, however, as West German economic strength had by the 1960s begun to place strains on German-American relations. West Germany began to see her interests as being different from those of the United States, and Hanrieder skilfully conveys the Federal Republic's dilemma of desiring both Atlantic and European unity.

Among books dealing with United States relations with France, COSTIGLIOLA is the best. The fluctuating nature of this relationship is shown through a well-written narrative of the major diplomatic and political events, including disputes over Indochina in 1954, Suez in 1956 and France's withdrawal from the military structure of NATO in 1966. This is never a dull story largely because of the infusion of cultural and psychological analysis. Clashes of personality and culture often impacted on the diplomatic relations.As a complementary work, PAXTON and WAHL offer insights into the De Gaulle years through an excellent series of essays covering Franco-American relations from 1945 to the late 1960s. They are particularly strong on the general's personal feelings towards America, and on his relationships with Presidents Roosevelt, Truman, Kennedy and Johnson.

SMITH and WERTMAN is an in-depth, quantitative analysis of the Reagan administration's relations with Western Europe. They show that Reagan placed greater emphasis on Western European public opinion than previous administrations, partly because some of his foreign policies required Western European support, particularly in relation to arms control discussions. Utilizing telephone and personal interview surveys carried out by the United States Information Agency's Office of Research, they conclude that much of the Western European public remained broadly in support of key United States-Western European policies such as NATO. Contrary to the beliefs of the Reagan administration and the mass media, anti-Americanism did not sweep Europe in the 1980s, although there was much public dissatisfaction with particular United States policies. This is a useful reference work but is difficult to digest in one reading.

SYLVIA ELLIS

See also Cold War

4) Relations with Israel and the Middle East

Ball, George W. and Douglas B. Ball, *The Passionate Attachment: America's Involvement with Israel, 1947 to the Present*, New York: Norton, 1992

Brands, H.W., *Into the Labyrinth: The United States and the Middle East, 1945–1993*, New York: McGraw Hill, 1994

Freedman, Lawrence and Efraim Karsh, *The Gulf Conflict, 1990–1991: Diplomacy and War in the New World Order*, Princeton: Princeton University Press, 1992; London: Faber, 1993, updated 1994

Grose, Peter, *Israel in the Mind of America*, New York: Knopf, 1983

Kaplan, Robert D., *The Arabists: The Romance of an American Elite*, New York: Free Press, 1993

Neff, Donald, *Warriors at Suez: Eisenhower Takes America into the Middle East*, New York: Linden Press/Simon and Schuster, 1981

Neff, Donald, *Warriors for Jerusalem: The Six Days that Changed the Middle East*, New York: Linden Press/Simon and Schuster, 1984

Quandt, William B., *Decade of Decisions: American Policy Toward the Arab-Israeli Conflict, 1967–1976*, Berkeley: University of California Press, 1977

Quandt, William B., *Camp David: Peacemaking and Politics*, Washington, DC: Brookings Institution, 1986

Rubin, Barry, *Paved with Good Intentions: The American Experience in Iran*, New York and Oxford: Oxford University Press, 1980

Sick, Gary, *All Fall Down: America's Tragic Encounter with Iran*, New York: Random House, 1985

Spiegel, Steven L., *The Other Arab-Israeli Conflict: Making America's Middle East Policy, from Truman to Reagan*, Chicago: University of Chicago Press, 1985

Stookey, Robert W., *America and the Arab States: An Uneasy Encounter*, New York: Wiley, 1975

Yergin, Daniel, *The Prize: The Epic Quest for Oil, Money, and Power*, New York: Simon and Schuster, 1991

The literature on American relations with the Middle East since 1945 is as episodic and disjointed as those relations themselves have often been. American dealings with the region have focused on two topics – Israel and oil – and the literature has tended to follow suit. Thus there are many books on American relations with Israel, and by extension on American connections to the Arab-Israeli conflict; and also a sizable number of works on relations with the states that have oil, particularly those that border the Persian (in the customary American usage) Gulf. Other topics, however, have frequently fallen by the wayside. The Arab states with neither oil nor a front-line position against Israel have received relatively little attention from either policymakers or their chroniclers. Turkey, after being brought into NATO in the early 1950s, was accorded the European status the Turks usually desired; rarely has it been considered in the context of the Middle East, and then as sui generis (which, admittedly, it is).

This skewing has resulted in the fact that there are very few books that deal comprehensively with United States-Middle East relations. The leading work in this small field is BRANDS, which carries the story close enough to the present to include the Gulf War of 1991 but not the ongoing Israeli withdrawal from the territories occupied during the June (Six Day) War of 1967. (The rapidly changing circumstances in the Middle East are doubtless another reason for the dearth of recent overviews.)

Among the books on the United States, Israel, and the Arab-Israeli conflict, GROSE affords a sympathetic look at the perceptions and emotions that caused nine American administrations (until now!) to take Israel under the U.S. wing as something slightly less but at the same time considerably more than an official ally. BALL and BALL, by contrast, is unsympathetic and often impatient; the authors contend that whatever the arguments in favor of U.S. support for Israel, these arguments have not warranted the disruption in U.S.-Arab relations they have caused. The elder Ball (George) speaks as a former undersecretary of state who felt the influence of Israel's friends from within the institutions of policy. STOOKEY leans more explicitly toward the Arabs, rather than merely away from Israel; though now a bit dated, it is still insightful on the first generation of the postwar period. SPIEGEL is the single most thorough scholarly account of the pulling and hauling within the U.S. government on the issue of Israel and the Arabs. KAPLAN looks askance at a subgroup of those doing the pulling and hauling.

The frequent wars that have punctuated the Arab-Israeli dispute have regularly captured the attention of international observers, including historians and their intellectual kin. NEFF (1981 and 1984) are the most readable books in the genre; the author strikes an unusually felicitous and persuasive balance between the immediacy of journalism and the meticulousness of scholarship. The books are doubly useful because they afford a window on to the interests and activities of other big powers besides the United States in the Middle East.

Peacemaking has consumed almost as much American energy in the Middle East as warmaking, and substantially more time. The most satisfactory retelling of the most successful American initiative to date is QUANDT (1986), the work of an American official who was closely involved with the Camp David accords. QUANDT (1977) applies this same expertise to a broader study of American policy towards Israel and the Arabs during the late 1960s and the first half of the 1970s.

For an entire generation, even while Washington refused to commit itself formally to the defense of Israel, American leaders cozied up to Iran – in particular, to the Shah of Iran. The Shah was deemed a bulwark against the southward expansion of communism and, no less significant, a crucial custodian of the oil which the West required; accordingly he received large amounts of both covert and acknowledged American assistance. Until the late 1970s, this assistance helped to ensure the Shah's continued control of Iran. After Iranian revolutionaries, notwithstanding all the aid, swept the Shah away, the erstwhile intimacy of the Washington-Tehran axis helped to ensure the enmity of the revolutionaries toward the United States. RUBIN provides an uncomplimentary survey of the United States-Iranian relationship to the period just after the Shah's overthrow. SICK is less sparing still (of an administration of which he was a part) in explaining what, from the American perspective, went wrong.

Most of the world would not have noticed that the Shah was missing, had his demise not sent shudders through the international oil markets. The same could be said of Kuwait following Saddam Hussein's 1990 invasion of that country. YERGIN covers much more than the Middle East, but his saga (the "epic" of the subtitle is not an exaggeration) goes far toward explaining why so many people, including Americans, have paid so much attention – and so much money – to the Middle East for the last half-century. On the war that followed the Iraqi takeover of Kuwait, the early entry into this field of instant history that is most likely to last is FREEDMAN and KARSH.

H.W. BRANDS

See also Oil and Natural Gas

5) Relations with the Soviet Union

Boyle, Peter G., *American-Soviet Relations: From the Russian Revolution to the Fall of Communism*, London and New York: Routledge, 1993

Crockatt, Richard, *The Fifty Years War: The United States and the Soviet Union in World Politics, 1941–1991*, London and New York: Routledge, 1995

Gaddis, John Lewis, *Russia, the Soviet Union, and the United States: An Interpretive History*, New York: Wiley, 1978; 2nd edition, New York: McGraw Hill, 1990

Hyland, William G., *The Cold War is Over*, New York: Random House, 1990

Killen, Linda, *The Soviet Union and the United States*, Boston: Twayne, 1989

LaFeber, Walter, *America, Russia, and the Cold War, 1945–1966*, New York: Wiley, 1967; 7th edition, as *America, Russia, and the Cold War, 1945–1992*, New York: McGraw Hill, 1993

Paterson, Thomas G., *Meeting the Communist Threat: Truman to Reagan*, New York and Oxford: Oxford University Press, 1988

Stevenson, Richard W., *The Rise and Fall of Detente: Relaxations of Tensions in US-Soviet Relations, 1953–84*, Urbana: University of Illinois Press, and London: Macmillan, 1985

America's relations with the Soviet Union constituted by far the most important single issue of U.S. foreign policy in the post-World War II era. America's rivalry with the Soviet Union in this period consisted not only of an ideological contest between capitalism and communism but also of a potentially deadly competition between two nuclear superpowers. The unexpectedly sudden end of the Cold War, with the collapse of the Soviet Union in 1991, has made possible historical treatments of the Cold War from beginning to end, while it has also significantly influenced historical judgments on issues relating to U.S.-Soviet relations throughout the entire period of the Cold War. The origins of the Cold War have been the subject of a long-standing debate between traditionalist historians who defend American policy as a necessary response to Soviet expansionist ambitions, "revisionist" historians who place as much responsibility for the onset of the Cold War on the United States as on the Soviet Union, and "post-revisionists" who largely agree with the traditionalist interpretation but who accept a number of the revisionist points. The end of the Cold War has created debate between conservatives who argue that the confrontational policies of Ronald Reagan brought down the Soviet Union and liberals who argue that the Soviet collapse was the consequence of internal Soviet developments which occurred in spite of as much as because of hard-line American policies. Historians have examined a large number of issues in the course of the Cold War, such as the Berlin Blockade, the Korean War and the Cuban missile crisis both as issues in themselves and as issues related to the origins, the end and the basic nature of the Cold War.

BOYLE is a comprehensive treatment of American policy towards the Soviet Union from the Russian Revolution in 1917 to the collapse of the Soviet Union in 1991. The first few chapters cover the period 1917–45, which is important background for a better understanding of the post-1945 period. Succeeding chapters provide a relatively succinct analysis of the major topics in U.S.-Soviet relations, 1945–91. These topics, which are covered in chronological order, include: the origins of the Cold War; the communist revolution in China; the Korean War; the Eisenhower era; Kennedy and Khrushchev; Johnson, Vietnam and Czechoslovakia; Nixon, Kissinger and detente; the demise of detente in the 1970s; Reagan and the new Cold War, 1981–85; Reagan and Gorbachev, 1985-89; the Bush era and the end of the Cold War, 1989–91. In the final chapter, "The Lessons of History", Boyle draws together the main themes which have run through American policy towards the Soviet Union. Throughout the book he emphasizes the importance on the shaping of American policy towards the Soviet Union of internal political, economic and psychological influences. Boyle suggests that American policy towards the Soviet Union was determined partly by rational concern for American national interests and partly by irrational concerns which arose from some of the internal influences within the United States. On the particular issues of the Cold War and in his overall interpretation, Boyle takes a balanced approach, raising the main questions which historians have debated and presenting an analysis of the differing viewpoints, leaving readers to reach their own conclusions. The book is of sufficient length to provide an overall survey of the period in reasonable depth and detail, while it is not overly long as an introduction to the subject.

GADDIS briefly covers America's relations with Russia in the pre-1917 period as well as 1917 to 1945 before his treatment of U.S.-Soviet relations since 1945, which makes up the bulk of the book. The inclusion of the pre-1917 period shows that some of the issues in relations between the United States and the Soviet Union predated the Russian Revolution and were concerned with geopolitics and great power rivalry as much as with ideology. The book deals largely with American policy, but also discusses the Soviet side of the relationship in some detail. Gaddis is the leading proponent of the "post-revisionist" interpretation. His account is largely defensive of American policy throughout the Cold War period. In particular, Gaddis argues that the policy of containment was the most reasonable policy for the United States to pursue in the circumstances which arose from the Soviet threat after World War II. Yet he also demonstrates that containment was not a simplistic doctrine but was subject to varying interpretations in application. Hence, Gaddis is critical, for example, of alleged over-reaction to the Korean War by an excessive increase in U.S. arms spending, which was provocative to the Soviet Union. The book was published before the downfall of the Soviet Union, and it is a second edition of a book first published in 1978, so that it slightly lacks the overall sweep of the entire period. The book is a sophisticated analysis, yet it is suitable in length and depth for an introduction to the subject.

CROCKATT is a much lengthier study than either Boyle or Gaddis, and it is methodologically more complex. The book is better-suited, therefore, for more advanced students who have a reasonable prior knowledge of the subject. Crockatt uses the work of international relations theorists as much as historians and attempts to blend the two together. He examines the Soviet side of the relationship as well as the American side, although the American side receives fuller treatment. Crockatt tries to set the U.S.-Soviet relationship into its wider context in world politics and to explore transnational processes and pluralist theories rather than to deal only with the narrow bilateral relationship between the two superpowers. The approach is broadly chronological but partly topical, treating as separate topics, for example, the arms race, the Third World and the war in Vietnam. Crockatt begins in 1941, so that the post-1945 period is provided with the background of the World War II U.S.-Soviet relationship. As the book was published after the downfall of the Soviet Union, it covers the entire Cold War period from a post-Cold War perspective.

LaFEBER was first published in 1967, covering the years 1945–66, and subsequent editions have been brought out every few years, with the addition of a new chapter and some other revisions to update the book. The 7th edition covers the years 1945–92 and therefore deals with the entire Cold War period, but, in contrast to Boyle and Crockatt, its perspective reflects the fact that it is an updated account which was first written in the midst of the Cold War. For the most part, LaFeber presents the "revisionist" view, though he takes an independent position on particular issues and does not unfailingly accept the "revisionist" interpretation. He is highly critical of many aspects of American foreign policy, especially the influence of economic interests on shaping that policy and American interference in Third World countries. The book is of comparable length to Boyle and Gaddis.

HYLAND is a brief, lively survey of the issues of the Cold War from 1945 to 1989. To some extent, Hyland brings the perspective of an insider, since he was a participant in events as well as a commentator. He served as a CIA analyst of Soviet affairs from the 1940s to the 1960s and as deputy to Henry Kissinger in the National Security Council in the Nixon and Ford administrations. He strongly advocates detente as the most promising approach in relations with the Soviet Union. The brevity of the book does not permit discussion of issues in detail, but the book provides a stimulating, comprehensive brief survey. As it was published before the collapse of the Soviet Union in 1991, Hyland did not have the opportunity to round out his account, and to present more complete conclusions, in the light of that event.

STEVENSON also focuses on the key concept of detente. He discusses the thaws and freezes in the Cold War from Stalin's death in 1953 to the end of the new Cold War of Ronald Reagan's first term. The book consists of chapters which in chronological order analyze the various episodes of detente, in particular: the aftermath of Stalin's death in 1953; the summit meeting and the "spirit of Geneva" in 1955; Khrushchev's visit to the United States and the "spirit of Camp David" in 1959; the post-Cuban missile crisis detente in 1963;

the Nixon-Kissinger era of detente, 1969-74. Stevenson analyzes the meaning and nature of detente and brings out its ambiguities. The book does not cover the period 1945–52 or the period since 1985, but it is, like Hyland, a brief, stimulating discussion of the major issues.

PATERSON is not a comprehensive treatment of American policy towards the Soviet Union, but a selection of particular topics from the Truman to the Reagan years. Nine of the topics are from the period 1945–60 and five from the period 1960–88. Paterson presents a "revisionist" viewpoint. The thesis which is developed in discussion of particular topics is that, while the Soviet Union and its Communist allies did indeed pose a threat to American interests and principles, American policymakers and American public opinion greatly exaggerated and distorted the threat. Paterson illustrates this thesis in chapters on such topics as the manipulation of public opinion by the Truman administration in shaping a Cold War mentality; Eisenhower's Middle East policy; and Reagan's policy towards Nicaragua.

KILLEN is a brief study which is for the most part topical and chronological. The first chapters deal with American diplomatic recognition of the Soviet Union in 1933 and the United States-Soviet Union alliance during World War II. The book then provides only a bare chronology of events for the post-1945 period, with discussion in a little more depth of selected topics, such as the arms race, Yugoslavia, and the Middle East. The book examines the Soviet side of the relationship to some extent as well as the American side. Killen ends in 1989, and does not therefore cover the collapse of the Soviet Union in 1991.

PETER G. BOYLE

See also Cold War

6) Relations with the Western Hemisphere

Blasier, Cole, *The Hovering Giant: US Responses to Revolutionary Change in Latin America, 1910–1985*, Pittsburgh: University of Pittsburgh Press, 1976, revised 1985

Cobbs, Elizabeth Anne, *The Rich Neighbor Policy: Rockefeller and Kaiser in Brazil*, New Haven: Yale University Press, 1992

Immerman, Richard H., *The CIA in Guatemala: The Foreign Policy of Intervention*, Austin: University of Texas Press, 1982

LaFeber, Walter, *Inevitable Revolutions: The United States in Central America*, New York: Norton, 1983, revised 1993

Martz, John D. (editor), *United States Policy in Latin America: A Quarter Century of Crisis and Challenge, 1961–1986*, Lincoln: University of Nebraska Press, 1988

Pastor, Robert A., *Whirlpool: US Foreign Policy Toward Latin America and the Caribbean*, Princeton: Princeton University Press, 1992

Paterson, Thomas G., *Contesting Castro: The United States and the Triumph of the Cuban Revolution*, New York: Oxford University Press, 1994

Rabe, Stephen G., *Eisenhower and Latin America: The Foreign Policy of Anticommunism*, Chapel Hill: University of North Carolina Press, 1988

Smith, Gaddis, *The Last Years of the Monroe Doctrine,*
   1945–1993, New York: Hill and Wang, 1994
Wood, Bryce, *The Dismantling of the Good Neighbor
   Policy*, Austin: University of Texas Press, 1985

During the 1980s and 1990s, scholars have critically analyzed
United States relations with Latin America since 1945. They
have focused on the disparities in wealth, power, and prestige
that exist between the United States and its southern neighbors. They have also examined questions of economic development, political reform, and revolution in Latin America and
how the United States has responded to these persistent desires
for change. Historians have concluded that national security
concerns and the imperatives of the Cold War have shaped
U.S. hemispheric policies.

Writing in a breezy, entertaining style, SMITH provides a
solid overview of United States policies during the Cold War
and the key historiographic issues. He argues that policymakers
transformed the hoary Monroe Doctrine from a defense of
democracy and national self-determination into a justification
for excluding the Soviet Union and "international communism" from the region. Under the aegis of this new Monroe
Doctrine, the United States embraced a series of military dicta-
tors who professed to be anti-communist.

WOOD also sees a decline in United States idealism. He
had previously written an influential study of the Good
Neighbor Policy under which President Franklin D. Roosevelt
had pledged not to intervene in the internal affairs of Latin
American republics. The Eisenhower administration, however,
dismantled the Good Neighbor Policy when, in 1954, it
covertly intervened in Guatemala. In both studies, Wood limits
his definition of being a good neighbor to questions of military intervention and ignores trade and investment issues.

The central role of the Eisenhower administration in formulating the Cold War policies of the United States is highlighted
in RABE. He argues that President Eisenhower and his advisers
interpreted inter-American relations almost solely within the
context of the Soviet-American confrontation and dramatically
expanded the list of what actions the United States might take
to preserve national security and defeat communism. In waging
Cold War, the United States repeatedly intervened in Latin
America. Perhaps the most dramatic account of such an intervention to overthrow an allegedly communist government can
be found in IMMERMAN. He demonstrates that the decision
of the United States to destroy the Guatemalan government
was motivated not by a decision to rescue the economic interests of the United Fruit Company but by an erroneous conviction that the government of Jacobo Arbenz Guzmán would
establish a Soviet beach-head in the hemisphere.

The Latin American communist who most obsessed the
United States was Fidel Castro. In a richly documented study,
PATERSON outlines the response of the United States to
the anti-Batista movement and the triumph of the Cuban
Revolution. Despite its professions of neutrality, the United
States constantly schemed to block Castro's road to power and
laid the foundation for the long, bitter hostility between Cuba
and the United States.

After 1959, Washington worried that Castro's brand of
revolutionary nationalism would spread throughout Latin
America. BLASIER, a political scientist, formulates explanatory
models in categorizing United States responses to Latin
American reformist and revolutionary movements. He concludes that the United States, although adamantly opposed to
economic nationalism, would negotiate terms of trade and
investment, providing Latin American nationalists did not align
their movement with a great power rival of the United States.
Additional analyses by social scientists of the policy of the
United States can be found in the collection edited by MARTZ.
Federico Gil reiterates Blasier's point that the United States has
constantly sought to exclude from the hemisphere extra-conti-
nental powers and to secure its dominant politico-economic
presence in the region. Michael Francis develops a heuristic
schema that reveals how perceptions of disputes influence the
level of decision making and the type of policy implemented.
This collection also contains useful essays on interventions in
the Dominican Republic (1965) and Chile (1970–73).

During the latter stages of the Cold War, the United States
focused on turmoil in Central America. LaFEBER provides a
provocative history of the role of the United States in the five
small countries of the area. Although not disputing the anticommunist thesis in accounting for United States hostility
to revolutionary movements in Nicaragua and El Salvador,
LaFeber asks readers to consider how the security and commercial interests of the United States made revolution "inevitable,"
by combining to create a system of poverty, injustice, dictatorship, and dependency in Central America.

For insight into how the United States might interact with
Latin America in the post-Cold War era, PASTOR should be
consulted. The author, who served on the National Security
Council during the Jimmy Carter presidency, analyzes what he
dubs the "whirlpool," the alternating cycle of fixation and inattention toward Latin America that has characterized United
States policy. He predicts that, despite the passing of Soviet
power, the United States will still have regional security
concerns and therefore must engage Latin Americans on issues
of democracy, free trade, and economic integration.

Although historians of post-1945 United States foreign
policy have concentrated on the exercise of political and military power in Latin America, they have not ignored the roles
played by private institutions and individuals in inter-American
relations. In an award-winning study, COBBS examines how
North American entrepreneurs tried to shape the socio-
economic development of Brazil. Readers will also find that
Cobbs offers a thorough discussion of the vital theoretical
and historiographic issues in the field of United States relations with Latin America.

STEPHEN G. RABE

Foreign Trade

Albion, Robert Greenhalgh with Jennie Barnes Pope, *The
   Rise of New York Port, 1815–1860*, New York: Scribner,
   1939
Ashworth, William, *A Short History of the International
   Economy since 1850*, 3rd edition, London: Longman,
   1975

Chandler, Alfred D., Jr., *The Visible Hand: The Managerial Revolution in American Business*, Cambridge, MA: Belknap Press of Harvard University Press, 1977

Chapman, Stanley, *Merchant Enterprise in Britain: From the Industrial Revolution to World War I*, Cambridge and New York: Cambridge University Press, 1992

Condliffe, J.B., *The Commerce of Nations*, New York: Norton, 1950; London: Allen and Unwin, 1951

Destler, I.M., *American Trade Politics*, 2nd edition, Washington, DC: Institute for International Economics/New York: Twentieth Century Fund, 1992

Evans, John W., *The Kennedy Round in American Trade Policy: The Twilight of the GATT?*, Cambridge, MA: Harvard University Press, 1971

Hidy, Ralph Willard, *The House of Baring in American Trade and Finance: English Merchant Bankers at Work, 1763–1861*, Cambridge, MA: Harvard University Press, 1949

Morison, Samuel Eliot, *The Maritime History of Massachusetts, 1783–1860*, Boston: Houghton Mifflin, 1921; London: Heinemann, 1923

North, Douglass C., *The Economic Growth of the United States, 1790–1860*, Englewood Cliffs, NJ: Prentice Hall, 1961

Pastor, Robert A., *Congress and the Politics of U.S. Foreign Economic Policy, 1929–1976*, Berkeley: University of California Press, 1980

Perkins, Edwin J., *Financing Anglo-American Trade: The House of Brown, 1800–1880*, Cambridge, MA: Harvard University Press, 1975

Thomas, Brinley, *Migration and Economic Growth: A Study of Great Britain and the Atlantic Economy*, Cambridge: Cambridge University Press, 1954, 2nd edition, 1973

Williamson, Jeffrey G., *American Growth and the Balance of Payments, 1820–1913: A Study of the Long Swing*, Chapel Hill: University of North Carolina Press, 1964

Woodman, Harold D., *King Cotton and His Retainers: Financing and Marketing the Cotton Crop of the South, 1800–1925*, Lexington: University Press of Kentucky, 1968

Yonekawa, Shin'ichi and Hideki Yoshihara (editors), *Business History of General Trading Companies*, Tokyo: University of Tokyo Press, 1987

Foreign trade was the "engine of economic growth" for many countries in the 19th century, but its relative importance in the United States has never been clear. Foreign trade was rarely more than 5 per cent of American GNP, but it is still possible to argue that this was sufficient to stimulate growth in the early 19th century. Most historians agree that after about 1850 exports were obviously overshadowed by growing domestic demand. In the early 19th century, cotton was the chief export, but after 1865 the United States exported a huge variety of commodities mostly to Britain and Europe, such as cotton, grain, processed food, oil and high technology manufactures. However as late as 1910 cotton was still providing about 30 per cent of U.S. exports and grain, 15 per cent.

NORTH contains the clearest exposition of the Export Base thesis. He argues that the cotton trade not only drove southern development but also, through internal trade, the economic growth in the Midwest and Northeast. Southern plantations, he argues, specialized in cotton and imported western food for the slaves. In fact for most of the late antebellum period in most of the South, later studies have shown that the large plantations were more nearly self-sufficient. However it is possible that plantation demand from the deep South in the 1820s and 1830s did have a substantial effect on western development higher up the Mississippi valley.

WOODMAN, which is based on planter records, is the best study of domestic cotton marketing, but conveys no feel for the riverine geography of the South, or the trade beyond the ports. He shows how in the early 19th century the planters sold cotton direct to the coastal factors who then consigned it to Liverpool merchants. After 1865 the plantations were replaced by small sharecropping tenancies, and the cotton was purchased locally through landlords and country stores, for sale by telegraph to large Liverpool firms, and shipped by rail to the coast.

North also argues that the newly liberated American economy was stagnant after 1783 until the European wars of 1793–1815 opened up huge possibilities for neutral trade. Undoubtedly the American seaport cities gained greatly from the wars, although the wider effects have been disputed. ALBION describes how New York after 1815 captured most of the European import trade from its east coast rivals, and also captured the coastal cotton and wholesale trades. Philadelphia and Baltimore both lost out to New York. The southern ports like New Orleans relied almost entirely on exporting staples, mostly cotton. MORISON is the best study of how the New England ports, especially Boston, preserved their deep water trades until about 1870. Despite their age, Albion and Morison remain the best introductions to their respective subjects.

In the early 19th century most American trade was controlled by large merchants. CHAPMAN is primarily a study of British trade, but he lists the largest Anglo-American trading firms and demonstrates how American trade was organized by complex networks originating in Liverpool and London. Two of the largest firms in the North Atlantic trade were the Barings and Browns. HIDY's long chronological study of the former is complemented by PERKINS's more recent study of the Browns. CHANDLER shows how after about 1860 the great merchants who had dominated traditional American commerce declined, and were eventually replaced by the modern corporation. By 1900 huge firms like Standard Oil were marketing substantial parts of American exports.

YONEKAWA and YOSHIHARA is a report of a conference comparing American, European and Far Eastern trading organizations. It includes useful essays on the organization of American manufactured exports by Porter, and on the cotton trade by Killick. In the former, manufacturers like Baldwins (locomotives) or Singer (sewing machines) controlled sales of complex producer and consumer goods or established overseas branches. In the latter, relatively small shippers, such as Anderson Clayton, hedging on the futures exchanges, exported huge volumes of cotton to Europe. It was their advanced marketing techniques – and similar methods in the grain trade

– that kept the United States ahead of its agricultural rivals in the British market.

Trade, migration and financial flows, taken together, were usually sufficiently strong to link economic conditions in the United States intimately with those in the old world. THOMAS and other historians have suggested that it was not just that certain critical years – 1819, 1837, 1856, 1873, 1894, 1907, 1921, and 1929, for example – were common to both sides of the Atlantic, but that the whole ten- to twenty-year trade-cycle was part of one uniform system involving trade, foreign investment, migration, frontier settlement, and railroad building, all driven by European demography and migration. Other historians such as WILLIAMSON accept the twenty-year periodicity, but place greater emphasis on the trade cycles in the United States as providing the driving force. Obviously as the United States grew at the expense of Europe, so American events increasingly dominated the cycle, but deter-mination of the exact causes and proportions is subject to endless debate.

In the 20th century, United States foreign trade was still influenced by protectionist and neo-mercantilist attitudes, at least until 1934, when Franklin D. Roosevelt's Reciprocal Trade Agreements Act pointed to a policy of free trade and open markets. This trade policy has continued to the present time, despite protests and interruptions from protectionists. The major study of this change from a protectionist to a more liberal, free trade vision is DESTLER. A careful examination of the problems of the "Kennedy Round" of GATT negotia-tions is provided by EVANS. In 1993, President Clinton inau-gurated a North American Free Trade Area (NAFTA) with Canada and Mexico – a kind of projected common market in the western hemisphere. Because it is a vehicle for expressing the views of so many local and regional interests, Congress has a loud and sometimes influential voice in shaping trade policy. PASTOR is a specialized study of this topic for the period 1929–76, while a more recent appraisal is provided in Destler.

More specialized studies of the volume, content and direction of the overseas trade of the United States may be better appreciated if placed in the context of older surveys of international economic relations. Two good examples are CONDLIFFE, a classic which has stood the test of time, and ASHWORTH, a textbook which may still be found extremely useful.

JOHN R. KILLICK
PETER D'A. JONES

See also Foreign Policy: Financial and Economic Aspects

France and America, 1763–1815

Commager, Henry Steele, *The Empire of Reason: How Europe Imagined and America Realized the Enlightenment*, New York: Doubleday, 1977; London: Weidenfeld and Nicolson, 1978

DeConde, Alexander, *Entangling Alliance: Politics and Diplomacy under George Washington*, Durham, NC: Duke University Press, 1958

DeConde, Alexander, *The Quasi-War: The Politics and Diplomacy of the Undeclared War with France, 1797–1801*, New York: Scribner, 1966

Echeverria, Durand, *Mirage in the West: A History of the French Image of American Society to 1815*, Princeton: Princeton University Press, 1957

Egan, Clifford L., *Neither Peace nor War: Franco-American Relations, 1803–1812*, Baton Rouge: Louisiana State University Press, 1983

Elkins, Stanley and Eric McKitrick, *The Age of Federalism: The Early American Republic, 1788–1800*, New York: Oxford University Press, 1993

Higonnet, Patrice, *Sister Republics: The Origins of French and American Republicanism*, Cambridge, MA: Harvard University Press, 1988

Hill, Peter P., *French Perceptions of the Early American Republic, 1783–1793*, Philadelphia: American Philosophical Society, 1988

Kaplan, Lawrence S., *Jefferson and France: An Essay on Politics and Political Ideas*, New Haven: Yale University Press, 1967

Kennedy, Roger G., *Orders from France: The Americans and the French in a Revolutionary World, 1780–1820*, New York: Knopf, 1989

May, Henry F., *The Enlightenment in America*, New York: Oxford University Press, 1976

Palmer, R.R., *The Age of the Democratic Revolution: A Political History of Europe and America, 1760–1800*, 2 vols., Princeton: Princeton University Press, 1959–64

Spurlin, Paul Merrill, *The French Enlightenment in America: Essays on the Times of the Founding Fathers*, Athens: University of Georgia Press, 1984

Americans have long been ambivalent about France, and the period of the American Revolution and the early years of the republic display a characteristic mixture of admiration, suspicion and ignorance in full measure. However, France was second only to Britain in its influence upon the formation of American politics and culture. Before 1763, France had been regarded as the great enemy, but the Treaty of Paris in that year removed the French "threat," and the traditional hostility began to subside. French diplomatic and military support in the Revolutionary War completed the transformation from enemy to ally, but enthusiasm for France did not last. By 1793 and 1794, the radical turn of events in France's own revolution had begun to alienate many conservative Americans. Divided American reactions to the French Revolution played a crucial role in the development of political parties in the 1790s, and the French Revolutionary and Napoleonic Wars caused a series of foreign policy crises over a period of twenty years.

Studies of Franco-American relations in this period fall into several different categories. Some consider the influence of the French Enlightenment on American culture and institutions, while others focus on the influence of the French Revolution on American domestic politics. There are a number of polit-ical and diplomatic histories of the alternating cordiality and hostility of relations between the two governments – and their domestic American political repercussions. The shifting images which each society had of the other are discussed in a quite different group of studies.

Writing at the time of the bicentennial of the Revolution, COMMAGER sees America as representing the fulfilment of the Enlightenment. The European *philosophes* were able to formulate their ideas of liberty and human progress, but were incapable of achieving them in practice. Unencumbered by the weight of the old regime, America was capable of creating the more just society envisaged by the *philosophes*. The triumphalist tone, and the picture of a classless, strifeless civil society in America, have incurred much criticism. MAY provides a cooler appraisal of the Enlightenment in America. Exploring the conflict of Enlightenment ideas with America's Calvinistic Protestantism, he identifies four main phases in the American Enlightenment: a moderate phase, marked by an accommodation between religion and the Newtonian view; a sceptical phase in which the influence of Voltaire and Hume began to undermine the earlier truce; a revolutionary phase, culminating in the French Revolution's attempts to regenerate mankind; and a final phase in which the Enlightenment went down to defeat, borne under by a rising tide of religiosity.

SPURLIN is much less concerned with grand themes in his collection of essays which focus specifically on the literary presence of French authors in America, and on questions of diffusion and availability of texts and ideas. He discusses the influence of Buffon, Voltaire, Diderot and Condorcet, and the precision of his analysis is a welcome contrast to vague generalities about the "climate of opinion." KENNEDY's approach to the question of French influence in America takes as its unifying theme the arrival of French architects and engineers in the United States between 1783 and 1820. However, this is not a book primarily about architecture; Kennedy takes the physical evidence of buildings as a way of exploring the interrelationship of Franco-American business, politics, and culture. In a fascinating glimpse into a relatively neglected area, he takes the opportunity to discuss, among other topics, the exchange of aesthetic ideas, technology, and farming techniques.

In an influential, wide-ranging, if now somewhat outdated, study, PALMER sees the American and French Revolutions as part of a general democratic movement in the Atlantic world of the later 18th century. He finds evidence of a broad attack on privilege and inequality in the political and constitutional turmoil which affected many parts of Europe, as well as North America. The leaders of these movements often knew each other, either personally or by reputation, and they drew on a common fund of ideas inspired by the Enlightenment. Palmer's broad and inclusive approach is obviously vulnerable to criticism on many fronts, but he does not ignore the conditions which are specific to each revolutionary outbreak – although he is not perhaps at his most authoritative when discussing America.

HIGONNET focuses on the differences between the American and French Revolutions. While the American Revolution led to the creation of a pluralist, federal government, the French Revolution resulted in a dictatorial Republic of Virtue. Higonnet traces these very different outcomes back to French and American attitudes to the individual and the community in the 17th and 18th centuries. The greater emphasis on the individual in American religion, culture, and political experience helped to produce a better balance between the rights of the individual and the interests of the community. This argument may sound excessively abstract, but Higonnet marshals a good deal of evidence in its support.

The related topics of diplomatic tensions between France and the United States in the 1790s, and the impact of the French Revolution on American domestic politics, have been the subject of various detailed studies, some of them now rather outdated. In two substantial volumes, DeConde provides a detailed and authoritative account of the interaction between foreign policy and domestic politics. DeCONDE (1958) covers the period of the Washington presidency, and confronts the questions of how and why the French alliance, the cornerstone of American foreign policy in 1789, had become a dead letter by 1796, by which time the United States was virtually at war with France. He finds answers in partisanship, sectionalism, and the shortcomings of Washington's leadership at home, and American weakness abroad. The alliance increasingly lacked a clear basis in the common interest of both countries. DeCONDE (1966) examines the "undeclared war" with France which dominated so much of the presidency of John Adams. Once again, he skilfully interrelates international and domestic politics, gives much credit to Adams's restraining influence, and portrays the whole story as an example of a nation going to the brink without finally falling over the edge.

A much more recent account and evaluation of the impact of France on the early American republic can be found in relevant sections of ELKINS and McKITRICK. In their long and detailed political history of the Federalist era, they give full weight throughout to French influence, and Chapter 8 on "The French Revolution in America" is invaluable. The excellent account of the extraordinary mission of Edmond Genet to the United States underscores the role of mutual incomprehension in the tensions and crises of the Franco-American relationship in this period.

EGAN carries the story of that relationship into the period from the Louisiana Purchase (1803) to the eve of the War of 1812. Jefferson and Madison never understood the extent to which American prosperity – the product of neutrality – infuriated both Britain and France. The United States was in increasing danger of being crushed between the ever tougher policies of the two belligerents. France's American policy from 1807 was to involve the United States in war against Britain, but the policy was pursued in an erratic and unpredictable way. The French role in the coming of the War of 1812, Egan argues, owed less to diplomatic duplicity than to capricious enforcement of the Continental system, and attacks on American shipping, which bewildered Americans and intensified their nationalist feelings.

There is a very different literature on the images which France and America had of each other, during this whole period. The basic theme of ECHEVERRIA is conveyed by its evocative title. In an attractive, if rather old-fashioned, study, he suggests that, in France, the "American dream" reached its peak in the years from 1784 to 1794, and then collapsed into hostility, suspicion and disillusionment – and eventually into cultural condescension. In a much more recent and more modest study, HILL claims that the erosion of Franco-American amity began earlier, in the 1780s, for a variety of reasons, including commercial friction and the clash of values between the two societies. In a study based on French consular reports from America, Hill identifies one of the main themes as "French chagrin at American ingratitude." KAPLAN is a thoughtful essay on Jefferson's relations with France, which challenges the notion that he was a slave to French ideas, and that his affinities with France drew him into subservience to Revolutionary and Napoleonic France, in the embargo policy and in the approach to the War of 1812. For Kaplan, Jefferson emerges as the tolerant and even patronising teacher of the French as they groped towards democracy and true liberty.

ROBERT L. DIETLE

See also: American Revolution: General; Early National Period

Frankfurter, Felix 1882-1965

Jurist and Supreme Court Justice

Baker, Leonard, *Brandeis and Frankfurter: A Dual Biography*, New York: Harper and Row, 1984

Freedman, Max, William M. Beaney, and Eugene V. Rostow, *Perspectives on the Court*, Evanston, IL: Northwestern University Press, 1967

Murphy, Bruce Allen, *The Brandeis/Frankfurter Connection: The Secret Political Activities of Two Supreme Court Justices*, New York: Oxford University Press, 1982

Parrish, Michael E., *Felix Frankfurter and His Times: The Reform Years*, New York: Free Press, and London: Collier Macmillan, 1982

Silverstein, Mark, *Constitutional Faiths: Felix Frankfurter, Hugo Black, and the Process of Judicial Decision Making*, Ithaca, NY: Cornell University Press, 1984

Simon, James F., *The Antagonists: Hugo Black, Felix Frankfurter and Civil Liberties in Modern America*, New York: Simon and Schuster, 1989

Urofsky, Melvin I., *Felix Frankfurter: Judicial Restraint and Individual Liberties*, Boston: Twayne, 1991

Writings about Felix Frankfurter may be clustered into four categories: biographies (all one-volume and brief), studies of his relationship with Louis D. Brandeis, studies of his relationship with Hugo Black, and a few works devoted to specific doctrinal aspects of his judicial career. (To these might be added a fifth category, books "by" Frankfurter: an oral history interview, excerpts from his diaries, notes which he made, off-the-bench essays, a collection of his early opinions, as well as actual books which he wrote.) The lack of a large-scale biography of Frankfurter is surprising. He died in 1965, leaving a massive volume of papers, many of which are available on microfilm. Many of his numerous clerks, protégés, friends, and acquaintances survive and are thus available for oral history interviews. He wrote extensively off the bench as well as on it, and he was not reticent about expressing his opinions. Yet to date, only a handful of slender biographies has appeared.

PARRISH covers Frankfurter's life up to his appointment to the Supreme Court in 1939. He treats of such disparate subjects as the Lower East Side cultural world of *fin de siècle* Jewish immigrants, the politics of Zionism, and the intellectual milieu of the Harvard Law School, which impresses him less than it did his subject, who as student and teacher extolled its supposedly pure meritocracy. Parrish does an excellent job of tracing Frankfurter's labyrinthine network of connections and influence, and of explaining legal issues that Frankfurter

confronted. A specialist might wish for more extensive treatment of such involvements as the Sacco-Vanzetti trial, but most readers will find in this book ample coverage of Frankfurter's pre-judicial career. The writing is clear and vigorous. Parrish expects that a second volume, covering Frankfurter's career on the Court, will appear "eventually".

UROFSKY is the best of the one-volume biographies, which unfortunately is faint praise since there is so little competition, and it is already dated. Urofsky is wide-ranging and interpretive, but its principal shortcoming is its brevity – a mere 179 pages of text. In such a brief compass, the author's judgments about major issues of such a long and contentious career can only be thinly substantiated or qualified.

The warm affiliation between Frankfurter and Justice Louis D. Brandeis had long been public knowledge, as had the behind-the-scenes political involvements of both men. Yet MURPHY's book stirred a storm of criticism when it appeared in 1982, for two reasons. First, Murphy assiduously traced their political influence and machinations, revealing that these had been more extensive than any but a few insiders realized. Both judges, he contended, "wielded, in camera, enormous political influence through their extensive off-the-bench political activities." Second, Murphy was explicitly critical of both, referring to Frankfurter as "a bit of a hustler, angling for power" – strong words, even for those distanced from the Justice. The portrait of Brandeis in this book does not much tarnish the halo; the portrayal of Frankfurter is unflattering, but not unfair.

BAKER, a writer of popular biographies and histories, began his work before Murphy's work appeared, but it reads as if it were an attempted rehabilitation of the two judges' reputations. Not quite apologetic, Baker's book is nevertheless uncritical, as in his treatment of Frankfurter's wartime refusal to accept the reality of the Holocaust, with whatever consequent measure of responsibility he bore for the Roosevelt Administration's indifference to the plight of Europe's Jews. Subtitled *A Dual Biography*, Baker's book is just that, two brief biographical surveys packaged together.

Frankfurter was as anxious about how he would appear in historical writing as his idol Justice Holmes had been, and he went so far as to withdraw his letters to Brandeis from the University of Louisville archives, and apparently to destroy them. He selected the journalist and *Atlantic Monthly* writer Max Freedman as his authorized biographer. Frankfurter need not have worried that his chosen chronicler would disappoint him, if we are to judge by the one brief adulatory sketch that FREEDMAN composed in the 1965 Rosenthal Lectures. Historians cherish an instinctive aversion to the very idea of an "authorized biography", and particularly to restrictions imposed on access to a subject's papers or, much worse, to the destruction of those papers. Frankfurter's determination to control his historical reputation did not serve his cause well.

Studies of the Frankfurter-Black relationship have been more successful. There is some irony here, since the animosity between them had a more corrosive effect, at least within the Court, than any baneful results of the Frankfurter-Brandeis collaboration had outside it. For most of the quarter-century that Frankfurter and Black served together on the Court, their personal relationship was acrimonious to the point of being disruptive, while their ideological competition polarized the court, the set-piece confrontation being *Adamson* v. *California* (1947). Acolytes of one or the other, most notably Wallace Mendelson, a disciple of Frankfurter, have promoted partisan positions extolling their hero. Only recently have scholars achieved a scholarly distance from the debate and the disputants. SILVERSTEIN adopts the approach of a political scientist concerned with role orientation, seeking to explain the divergent views of both men in terms of their differing solutions to what they perceived to be the core dilemma of judging, the conflict between majority rule and judicial review.

SIMON, a lawyer who worked as a legal journalist and wrote several prize-winning books on the Court and Justice Douglas, stresses the late reconciliation of the two men and the commonalities of their outlook. He tends to downplay Frankfurter's pettiness and Black's vituperation, giving the impression that their personal relations on the court were more amicable than in fact they were. The book reads well, however, and if specialists do not find its analysis of specific cases, like *Dennis* v. *United States*, innovative or penetrating, the general reader will find Simon's treatment more than adequate.

WILLIAM M. WIECEK

Franklin, Benjamin 1706–1790
Scientist, inventor, writer, politician and diplomat

Aldridge, Alfred Owen, *Franklin and His French Contemporaries*, New York: New York University Press, 1957

Aldridge, Alfred Owen, *Benjamin Franklin and Nature's God*, Durham, NC: Duke University Press, 1967

Breitwieser, Mitchell Robert, *Cotton Mather and Benjamin Franklin: The Price of Representative Personality*, Cambridge and New York: Cambridge University Press, 1984

Bridenbaugh, Carl and Jessica Bridenbaugh, *Rebels and Gentlemen: Philadelphia in the Age of Franklin*, New York: Reynal and Hitchcock, 1942

Cohen, I. Bernard, *Benjamin Franklin's Science*, Cambridge, MA: Harvard University Press, 1990

Conner, Paul W., *Poor Richard's Politicks: Benjamin Franklin and His New American Order*, New York: Oxford University Press, 1965

Crane, Verner W., *Benjamin Franklin and a Rising People*, Boston: Little Brown, 1954

Dull, Jonathan R., "Franklin the Diplomat: The French Mission," *American Philosophical Society Transactions*, 72(1), 1982

Hanna, William S., *Benjamin Franklin and Pennsylvania Politics*, Stanford, CA: Stanford University Press, 1964

Hutson, James H., *Pennsylvania Politics, 1746–1770: The Movement for Royal Government and Its Consequences*, Princeton: Princeton University Press, 1972

Lemay, J.A. Leo (editor), *Reappraising Benjamin Franklin: A Bicentennial Perspective*, Newark: University of Delaware Press, 1993

Lemay, J.A. Leo and P.M. Zall (editors), *Benjamin Franklin's Autobiography: An Authoritative Text, Backgrounds, Criticism*, New York: Norton, 1986

Lopez, Claude-Anne, *Mon Cher Papa: Franklin and the Ladies of Paris*, New Haven: Yale University Press, 1966

Seavey, Ormond, *Becoming Benjamin Franklin: The Autobiography and the Life*, University Park: Pennsylvania State University Press, 1988

Stourzh, Gerald, *Benjamin Franklin and American Foreign Policy*, Chicago: University of Chicago Press, 1954, 2nd edition, 1969

Tourtellot, Arthur B., *Benjamin Franklin: The Shaping of Genius: The Boston Years*, New York: Doubleday, 1977

Van Doren, Carl, *Benjamin Franklin*, New York: Viking, 1938; London: Putnam, 1939

Wright, Esmond, *Franklin of Philadelphia*, Cambridge, MA: Harvard University Press, 1986

Scholars continue to be fascinated by the extraordinary life of Benjamin Franklin, prototypical self-made man, internationally famous scientist, and Revolutionary leader involved with the Declaration of Independence, the Great Seal, the peace treaty, and the Constitution. Not surprisingly, making sense out of such an immense range of activities (and an immense span of years that allowed Franklin contact with both the Puritan Cotton Mather and the antislavery John Quincy Adams) has proved difficult.

Despite continued interest in the oldest founding father, the 60-year-old VAN DOREN remains the fullest biography. He covers Franklin's numerous activities with remarkable consistency and depth. For Van Doren, Franklin was a classic great man, someone who succeeded in almost every field and who would have been great regardless of his circumstances. In the closing words of the some 800 pages, Franklin was "a harmonious human multitude." While Van Doren presents a model comprehensive biography, CRANE provides a model of comprehensible compactness, presenting in 200 pages the best introduction to Franklin's career. While he devotes most of the book to Franklin's Revolutionary experiences, Crane also portrays a Franklin who was neither a simple moralist concerned solely with making money nor a theoretically-minded thinker. WRIGHT occupies the biographical middle range, shorter than Van Doren by almost half, twice as long as Crane. He too covers Franklin's entire career solidly, focusing most fully on Franklin's Revolutionary experience and on his role in establishing American values and identity. Wright does not attempt to prove an overall thesis about Franklin's personality, but tends to stress his ability to put on different characters and different masks – even to become the roles that he created or took on.

Such attention to Franklin's different modes of presentation has become a central theme of discussions about the man. Franklin's *Autobiography*, his own attempt to present his image, remains the primary text for this work and it has received extensive attention. LEMAY and ZALL provide the best introduction to the *Autobiography*. Not only do they include a trustworthy text (not as common as might be expected), but they also offer extensive notes that identify Franklin's references as well as all the individuals mentioned in the text. They also include a guide to literary discussions of the work and excerpts from important critics over the past two centuries, including the influential comments of Max Weber and D.H. Lawrence.

SEAVEY is a stimulating discussion of the *Autobiography* that considers 18th-century cultural models as well as structure and language. Because it also focuses on the ways that Franklin viewed his own development, it has the additional virtue of being insightful on Franklin himself. For Seavey (as for Wright), Franklin's public roles are the center of his life and provide the basis for understanding the man. Seavey argues that Franklin made a concerted attempt (in the *Autobiography* and elsewhere) to fix a particular image of himself, a set of qualities which he portrayed as the essence of his success.

BREITWIESER provides another attempt to make sense out of Franklin. Like Cotton Mather, the subject of the other part of this book, Franklin in Breitwieser's estimation carefully shaped his life to conform to a vision of the self. While Mather attempted to annihilate self-assertion in the name of God and the example of his fathers, Franklin created a self that resisted such external coercion without sliding into complete lack of control. This complex but ultimately rewarding book thus suggests that Franklin's self-presentation as an unattached, dispassionate individual represented a deliberate project that allowed him to take up widely different disguises and activities without ever wholly becoming them.

Specialized studies of particular parts of Franklin's life and activities are also numerous. TOURTELLOT is a valuable look at Franklin's early years in Boston, providing an extensive examination of the context that shaped his first seventeen years. Although not deep or original in its arguments, the book offers full pictures of Franklin's family (including his deeply religious father and his anti-establishment brother), his Boston education, and contemporary religious developments that suggest how deeply Franklin was shaped by his original environment.

LEMAY is a valuable collection of essays that covers a wide range of topics about Franklin in the years after he moved to Philadelphia in 1723. Particularly useful are discussions of Franklin as a publisher and bookseller, as a diplomat and influential member of the Constitutional Convention, as a writer and book collector, and as the subject of a wide range of portraits.

ALDRIDGE (1967) provides the fullest study of Franklin's religious attitudes. Looking at his writings and his interactions with a wide range of religious folk rather than his intellectual influences or the ways his attitudes fit contemporary religious ideas or movements, the book convincingly refutes the stereotypes of Franklin as a self-seeking materialist or an unthinking pragmatist. Franklin still emerges as a deistic opponent of dogma and a supporter of ethical growth, but Aldridge also presents a Franklin who is more Anglican than normally suspected and more caught in a tension between deism and orthodox Christianity. Aldridge also shows that Franklin engaged in serious thinking about classic theological issues.

CONNER suggests that Franklin also had a particular vision of American society. Arguing against a stereotype of Franklin as a simple pragmatic materialist, Conner shows that Franklin envisioned a country where concern for the public good (encompassing both equality and cohesion) would allow people to thrive in a "happy mediocrity," a state where neither poverty nor luxury, neither aristocracy nor complete leveling,

predominated. Within this harmonious system, a vision fed by Franklin's intellectual, social, and psychological experiences, America would engage in continual economic, demographic, and geographic expansion.

BRIDENBAUGH and BRIDENBAUGH discusses the cultural context of Philadelphia during Franklin's pre-Revolutionary life. Although it provides an overly genial view of Philadelphia, and its distinction between English-leaning gentlemen and more Americanizing elements has not withstood further scrutiny, the book still provides the fullest picture of the surrounding figures in Franklin's intellectual activities – and, to a great extent, his social life. It offers lively portraits of education, books and printing, art and literature, science and medicine, as well as some account of the rise of benevolent organizations and a colonial aristocracy.

COHEN surveys Franklin's scientific activities in more detail, summarizing the author's half-century of pioneering scholarly work on the subject. The leading expert on Franklin's science, Cohen reveals a thinker and experimenter who was not simply a mechanic who played with gadgets. He was instead a serious and highly influential scientist. Franklin's electrical experiments not only invented much of the terminology used today (including positive and negative charges) but discovered many of the basics of the subject (including the distinction between conductors and insulators).

While Franklin's science still receives short shrift in most general accounts, his Pennsylvania political activities, the other focus of his life after 1748, have received even less attention. HANNA is the fullest look at this complex subject. After tracing Franklin from his entry into politics, when he operated as an independent between the Quaker party and the proprietary group that supported the Penn family as the proprietors of the colony, the book then examines Franklin's subsequent split with the proprietor and his attempt to establish royal control of the colony, despite the growing imperial crisis with Britain. Hanna offers a more negative portrait of Franklin than is usual in other areas of his life, portraying the movement against the proprietor as motivated largely by Franklin's personal pique. His involvement in provincial politics, Hanna argues, was virtually a complete failure.

HUTSON examines in more detail Franklin's attempt to end the Penn family's proprietary role, and covers more fully than Hanna Franklin's English lobbying activities and the sources of his political support. Although Hutson sees the movement for royal government as essentially a precursor of the Revolution (another movement against arbitrary government from the outside), rather than the result of Franklinian peevishness, he too uncovers a less than perfect Franklin. Not only was he finally unsuccessful, he also could be disingenuous and even foolish.

Franklin's more successful activities as a Revolutionary diplomat are covered in two works. STOURZH offers an analytical intellectual history of Franklin's view of American foreign policy interests, suggesting that he was not simply a pragmatic or small-minded politician. Stourzh argues that Franklin struggled with the tension between morality, including his essential desire for peace, and the demands of national interest. He believed that enlightened mutual self-interest, rather than gratitude or treaties, formed the only lasting basis of international relations. For America, such a course would require freedom of action (but not isolationism) and expansion as a means of both ensuring security and meeting the demands of a growing population. DULL is a study of the working diplomat that complements Stourzh's view of the theorist. Franklin was not a professional diplomat (an amateurishness seen in his lack of concern for security), but he grew into the role and became enormously successful. His earlier English missions had involved constant activity. In France, he deliberately waited, trusting in the essential harmony of French and American interests. Although he sometimes seemed lazy, his tactfulness, reserve, and common sense proved perfectly suited to the situation.

Although Dull suggests that Franklin's French celebrity was not central to that country's policy, his enormous popularity there as an embodiment of the Enlightenment and American ideals was extraordinary and has been the subject of two important works. LOPEZ looks at the more social and private side of Franklin in a delightful book that examines his interactions with the leading women of French society. Franklin was particularly popular with the influential leaders of salon circles not only because he was an accomplished flirt but also because he believed women had a particular contribution to make.

The larger French reaction to Franklin, particularly expressed in literary works, is the subject of ALDRIDGE (1957). By looking at his evolving reputation as a scientist and an economist before he became well-known as a moralist and diplomat, the book shows how Franklin became a legendary figure in French culture. Aldridge examines descriptions of Franklin's French experience in both his own and his friends' works, and also traces Franklin's image as a mythical rural sage in French belles lettres. He concludes with a study of the French eulogies that commemorated Franklin after his death in 1790.

STEVEN C. BULLOCK

Frémont, John C. 1813–1890 and
Jessie Benton Frémont 1824–1902
Soldier, explorer, and presidential candidate; political activist

Bancroft, Hubert Howe and Henry L. Oak, *History of California*, 7 vols. (i.e., vols. 18–24 of Bancroft's *Works*), San Francisco: History Company, 1884–90
Bartlett, Ruhl Jacob, *John Charles Frémont and the Republican Party*, Columbus: Ohio State University Press, 1930
Gienapp, William E., *The Origins of the Republican Party, 1852–1856*, New York: Oxford University Press, 1987
Harlow, Neal, *California Conquered: War and Peace on the Pacific, 1846–1850*, Berkeley: University of California Press, 1982
Herr, Pamela, *Jessie Benton Frémont: A Biography*, New York: Watts, 1987
Herr, Pamela and Mary Lee Spence (editors), *The Letters of Jessie B. Frémont*, Urbana: University of Illinois Press, 1993
Jackson, Donald and Mary Lee Spence (editors), *The Expeditions of John Charles Frémont*, 3 vols., Urbana: University of Illinois Press, 1970–80
Nevins, Allan, *Frémont, The West's Greatest Adventurer*, 2 vols., New York: Harper, 1928
Nevins, Allan, *Frémont, Pathmarker of the West*, New York: Appleton Century, 1939; revised, New York: Longmans Green, 1955
Rolle, Andrew, *John Charles Frémont: Character as Destiny*, Norman: University of Oklahoma Press, 1991
Royce, Josiah, *California from the Conquest in 1846 to the Second Vigilance Committee in San Francisco: A Study of American Character*, Boston: Houghton Mifflin, 1886; reprinted, New York: Knopf, 1948

John Charles Frémont gained national recognition in the 1840s by his exploits as explorer and surveyor of the mountain West. With the considerable assistance of his wife, Jessie Benton Frémont, he produced lively, readable reports of his adventures that quickly became best-selling popular reading matter. Jessie then further publicized his exploits as the supposed "conqueror of California" in 1846. Frémont first became the subject of biographies, however, when he won the nomination of the Republican party as its first presidential candidate. The campaign biographies of 1856 by John Bigelow and Charles Wentworth Upham were both eulogistic in tone, and rather dull and undistinguished. Otherwise the main contemporary accounts were the memoirs published by himself and Jessie in 1887.

In his last years Frémont's reputation came under attack from historians of California, notably the debunking ROYCE and the distinguished historian BANCROFT. They criticized Frémont for the rash and unnecessary Bear Flag revolt, which prevented a peaceful transfer of the province to the United States. In his search for glory, they claimed, Frémont acted without orders, displayed irresponsible bloodthirstiness against the native population, and exaggerated both the Indian menace and the British threat to California.

NEVINS (1928) reversed the picture, not by presenting an *apologia*, but by seeing things through Frémont's chauvinist eyes. Nevins's dramatic narrative showed Frémont at his best as an explorer, and insisted that the urgencies of the situation and a lack of information justified his attempts to seize power during the Bear Flag revolt. Nevins also acknowledged Frémont's failures as a Civil War general, but insisted that his controversial Missouri Proclamation of 1861, freeing captured slaves, was not a selfish political manoeuvre. Far from trying to enhance his personal prospects by attracting abolitionist support, Frémont had been trying to solve the pressing problem of what to do with slaves fleeing to his army. Overall, however, Nevins saw Frémont as impulsive and lacking in practical judgment, never quite making the most of the brilliant opportunities offered him, and repeatedly suffering from his own improvidence.

Eleven years later NEVINS (1939) offered a more serious and critical look at Frémont, based on fresh research and new materials. Stronger in its presentation of the general background, the new single volume was actually longer than the more popular two-volume work of the previous decade. Yet in many ways the book was much the same, still offering "a wonderfully variegated and romantic story of adventure," and defending the hero at the critical points in his public life. Its treatment of Frémont's political career was not particularly perceptive, even though Nevins could now draw upon BARTLETT's solid if limited monograph.

After 1945, historians showed relatively little interest in Frémont's career, except where it touched other concerns. Frémont's exploration of the West has been the subject of a magnificent three-volume reprint of his notebooks, edited by JACKSON and SPENCE, while HARLOW has critically reconsidered his role in the acquisition of California in the spirit of Royce and Bancroft. GIENAPP's definitive study of the Republican party's first presidential campaign includes detailed and authoritative coverage of Frémont's nomination as its presidential candidate.

Most recently, ROLLE has combined thorough biographical research with a "relatively cautious psychiatric approach" to explain Frémont's character deficiencies. Aloof, secretive, and impervious to criticism, Frémont so often threw away the advantages that celebrity gave him. In addition, Rolle exposes not only the questionable nature of Frémont's business transactions but also his growing indulgence in extramarital affairs after 1861.

Frémont's celebrity owed much to his marriage to Thomas Hart Benton's daughter, who has frequently attracted attention in her own right. Jessie's writings are now regarded as unreliable, especially those relating to her husband, but she has long been recognized as one of the few women who achieved mainstream political influence in the mid-19th century. Most biographies have been sentimentalized or semi-fictional accounts, but HERR's distinguished biography has brought her to life and located her firmly in social and cultural context. Repeatedly bursting into the public sphere, she was yet confined to a woman's role and had to channel her ambition, imagination, and energy through her husband's career.

Thus Herr's account becomes also the history of a marriage, which turns out to be more complex and troubled than had been appreciated. In this most sensitive treatment, John Frémont appears glamorous, extravagant, vainglorious, distant, and unreliable. As the excellent summaries and private letters published in HERR and SPENCE confirm, Jessie's tragedy was that the "compelling yet elusive man" to whom she so fiercely committed her life was simply not worthy of such single-minded devotion.

DONALD J. RATCLIFFE

French and Indian War *see* Seven Years' War

Friedan, Betty 1921–
Feminist campaigner and writer

Barker-Benfield, G.J. and Catherine Clinton (editors), *Portraits of American Women: From Settlement to the Present*, New York: St. Martin's Press, 1991

Blau, Justine, *Betty Friedan*, New York: Chelsea House, 1990

Cohen, Marcia, *The Sisterhood: The True Story of the Women Who Changed the World*, New York: Simon and Schuster, 1988

Meyerowitz, Joanne, "Beyond the Feminine Mystique: A Reassessment of Postwar Mass Culture, 1946–1958," *Journal of American History*, 79(4), March 1993

Miller, John N. (editor), *A World of Her Own: Writers and the Feminist Controversy*, Columbus, OH: Merrill, 1971

Mompullan, Chantal, *Voice of America: Interviews with Eight American Women of Achievement*, Washington, DC: Voice of America, United States Information Agency, 1984

Reynolds, Moira Davison, *Women Champions of Human Rights: Eleven US Leaders of the Twentieth Century*, Jefferson, NC: McFarland, 1991

Betty Friedan is often billed as the mother of the modern women's movement. Since her 1963 book *The Feminine Mystique* energized a generation of women and fueled the growth of groups like the National Organization for Women (NOW), which Friedan helped to found, Friedan has devoted her life to the struggle for women's rights. Today she stands, just as she has for decades, at the forefront of women's quest for equality, inspiring a level of scholarly interest in her life that attests to her impact on society. Although books about Friedan remain limited in number, those studies which are available reveal much of the life and work of a remarkable social leader.

Foremost among biographies of Friedan is BLAU. Published as part of the American Women of Achievement series, Blau is among the best sources of information about Friedan's life, work, family, and professional achievement. There is also a concise, but comprehensive, section on the founding of NOW and Friedan's role as the organization's first president. Also of note are the photographs of Friedan reproduced in the book. Taken from news archives and Friedan's private papers, which are now housed in Radcliffe College's Schlesinger Library, these photographs provide a pictorial history of Friedan's childhood and family as well as the women's marches and public rallies she has organized.

Another informative study of Friedan's life is REYNOLDS, who describes Friedan's work from her years at Smith College through her current efforts, and provides a complete, compact, and accessible account, but one that lacks analytical insight. A more penetrating biographical essay on Friedan is contained in BARKER-BENFIELD and CLINTON. The portrait of Friedan included in this collection of essays couples a chronological overview of Friedan's life with discussion of her motives, illustrations of how personal experiences inspired her writing, and an exploration of the tensions that developed between Friedan and some other women's movement leaders. Overall, this is both an objective and an informative assessment.

Possibly the best discussion of Friedan and her efforts on behalf of women is contained in COHEN. This book, which includes chapters on both *The Feminine Mystique* and the founding of NOW, is scholarly and professional, but also easy to read and entertaining. Cohen focuses her writing on the activities of Friedan and two of her feminist associates,

Germaine Greer and Kate Millett, in the years 1966–82. Described as "an intimate history of the women's movement," Cohen's work is an enjoyable, and authoritative account of the women's movement in those years.

MOMPULLAN's publication of a transcript of her 1984 Voice of America interview offers Friedan's perspective on various topics including women's history, Ronald Reagan, aging, and the Equal Rights Amendment. Grouped with interviews of seven other outstanding American women scientists, artists, and writers, the conversation between Mompullan and Friedan stands out as the most interesting. The responses which the interviewer elicited are classic Friedan – frank, straightforward, and logical. The text is delight to read.

Although Friedan enjoys considerable fame for her role as a women's leader, it is for her writings that she is most widely known. Both Miller and Meyerowitz seek to analyze Friedan's literary efforts. In an examination of the chapter from *The Feminine Mystique* entitled "The Happy Housewife Heroine," MILLER evaluates Friedan's style, and subject matter, and the impact of her writing, and thus provides a short cut to an understanding of Friedan as an author as well as women's leader. Unlike Miller, who gives most attention to an assessment of her writing style, MEYEROWITZ challenges Friedan's contention in *The Feminine Mystique* that, in the 1950s and early 1960s, a conservative promotion of domesticity prevailed in widely read popular magazines. Meyerowitz, who duplicated the survey of periodicals which Friedan conducted to undergird the argument in her book, claims that both domesticity and women's success in non-traditional careers were equally encouraged in post-World War II journals. Extensive and well-documented research provides impressive support for Meyerowitz's critique, which launches the most direct challenge so far to Friedan's thesis.

EMILY WALKER COOK

See also Feminism; Women's History: Women's Liberation Movement

Fulton, Robert 1765–1815
Inventor and steamboat pioneer

Dickinson, H.W., *Robert Fulton, Engineer and Artist: His Life and Works*, London and New York: John Lane, 1913

Evans, Dorinda, *Benjamin West and His American Students*, Washington, DC: Smithsonian Institution Press, 1980

Flexner, James Thomas, *Steamboats Come True: American Inventors in Action*, New York: Viking, 1944; with new Foreword, Boston: Little Brown, 1978

Morgan, John S., *Robert Fulton*, New York: Mason/Charter, 1977

Owen, Cynthia Philip, *Robert Fulton: A Biography*, New York: Watts, 1985

Parsons, William Barclay, *Robert Fulton and the Submarine*, New York: Columbia University Press, 1922

Sutcliffe, Alice Crary, *Robert Fulton and the Clermont*, New York: Century, 1909

Sutcliffe, Alice Crary, *Robert Fulton*, New York: Macmillan, 1915

There is less current historical work available on Robert Fulton than most other prominent Americans of his age, reflecting recent historians' lack of interest in the history of American technology. Episodes in this explosion of inventions, such as the development of the cotton gin, looms, and steamboats, have been examined, but historians have failed to explore the context of early 19th-century inventiveness, spurred by the establishment of a national patent office and the rise of a national business establishment. But there is enough work of value on Fulton and his inventions to present a good picture of the man and his times. Trained as a painter, Fulton turned to inventions only when he failed to establish himself as an artist. While his name is synonymous with steamboats, he also made significant contributions to the field of canal technology and naval engineering, and his first invention was a machine for cutting and polishing marble. His most controversial assertion was that an inventive genius combined previously existing concepts to create new and improved mechanisms, rather than come up with completely new ideas, a philosophy that would place him at odds with other inventors throughout his life and leave him embroiled in litigation from the time of the *Clermont*'s success in 1807 until his death.

OWEN is probably the best starting-point for the study of Fulton's life. While perhaps she identifies too closely with her subject, she has nonetheless produced an accessible and thorough lifestudy of this difficult man. Owen used both new and old sources to illuminate Fulton and analyze his personality and motivations, including colorful anecdotes about his private life during his sojourn in France designing submarines. Fulton's rivalries and litigation with other inventors, his seemingly never-ending troubles with the United States Patent Office and its obstreperous superintendent, William Thornton, and his complicated business and personal relationships with the wealthy and powerful Livingston family of New York, are all carefully documented and analyzed. Owen also does her best to place Fulton at the forefront of the history of American ingenuity. Certainly in his attempts to market his inventions as well as create them, Fulton showed himself to be a prototype of later business tycoons who attempted to control all aspects of the production of, and market for, particular goods or services.

Although over 80 years old, DICKINSON is still a serviceable reference point. It has worn well because the author relied heavily on primary sources and wrote in a clear and plain style, eschewing the verbal efflorescence of the time. Dickinson is weak on the analysis of Fulton's character, not surprising in the age before Freudian analysis changed the writing of history. But he included a good characterization of the important business and personal partnership between Fulton and Robert R. Livingston.

The other biographies are suitable only as complementary sources to Owen and Dickinson. SUTCLIFFE (1915) is a pedestrian and hagiographic account by Fulton's great-granddaughter, enlivened only by the inclusion of otherwise-unknown family anecdotes about the inventor. These stories have made Sutcliffe a standard source on Fulton, but many of them can be found in other accounts. MORGAN is adequate but pedestrian, lacking the *gravitas* of Dickinson and the analytical flair and research of Owen. The brief flowering of interest in American technology in the 1970s inspired his look back at the inventor, who had not been the subject of a full-scale biography for more than sixty years, but in spite of his best efforts, Morgan was not able to offer any new information about Fulton.

There are a number of good studies of Fulton's technological accomplishments. Most interesting and lively is FLEXNER, an engaging account of the race to build a functional steamboat in America. Flexner, perhaps better known for his four-volume biography of George Washington, here displays his grasp of the history of American inventiveness. His main theme is that the realization of the dream of steam-driven boats plying the waterways of America would be an essential factor both in the growth of a national economy by means of easy and relatively cheap transportation of goods, and the strengthening of bonds between regions by means of the easy and fast transportation of passengers. He also portrayed the pioneers of American steam technology, including John Fitch, William Thornton, and John Stevens, as well as Fulton, not only as visionaries, but also as pragmatists who hoped to become rich from their exertions. SUTCLIFFE (1909) is useful on Fulton and the *Clermont*, because she drew on private family papers and stories to construct this account of his steamboat operations on the Hudson River. PARSONS contains interesting material on Fulton and the submarine. Although his innovations in the field of marine technology, particularly on submarines and torpedoes, are not as well known as his work on steam engines, they were just as significant. Parsons's book remains the only accessible introduction to Fulton and his role in this field.

EVANS is illuminating on Fulton as an aspiring artist.. He arrived in London in 1786 to study painting with Benjamin West, the American-born master of 18th-century historical painting and portraiture. He and West forged a close private as well as professional relationship, ably delineated by Evans, who explores Fulton's failure as an artist. Understanding this disappointment in Fulton's life is critical to any explanation of why he turned to technology instead of art, as did many 19th-century inventors. They hoped that the wide range of skills often attributed to artists would enable them to find success in other, perhaps more lucrative, fields. But none would succeed as well as Fulton.

JEAN V. BERLIN

See also Technology and Invention

Fundamentalism

Ammerman, Nancy, *Bible Believers: Fundamentalism in the Modern World*, New Brunswick, NJ: Rutgers University Press, 1987

Bendroth, Margaret, *Fundamentalism and Gender, 1875 to the Present*, New Haven: Yale University Press, 1993

Boyer, Paul S., *When Time Shall Be No More: Prophecy Belief in Modern American Culture*, Cambridge, MA: Belknap Press of Harvard University Press, 1992

Brereton, Virginia Lieson, *Training God's Army: The American Bible School, 1880–1940*, Bloomington: Indiana University Press, 1990

Marsden, George M., *Fundamentalism and American Culture: The Shaping of Twentieth-Century Evangelicalism, 1870–1925*, New York and Oxford: Oxford University Press, 1980

Marsden, George M., *Reforming Fundamentalism: Fuller Seminary and the New Evangelicalism*, Grand Rapids, MI: Eerdmans, 1987

Numbers, Ronald L., *The Creationists: The Evolution of Scientific Creationism*, New York: Knopf, 1992

Sandeen, Ernest R., *The Roots of Fundamentalism: British and American Millenarianism, 1800–1930*, Chicago: University of Chicago Press, 1970

Fundamentalism, a conservative religious movement which emerged out of mainstream American Protestantism in the early 20th century, has attracted a great deal of scholarly attention in recent decades. Before 1970, historians of fundamentalism generally portrayed the movement as a product of the social changes in America around the turn of the 20th century. Fundamentalists were typically seen as predominantly southern obscurantists dedicated to rural ways of life in opposition to the values of the city and modern scientific inquiry, the latter symbolized by the theory of evolution. As the last gasp of an older way of life, fundamentalism was believed to be "afloat on a receding wave of history," in the words of the eminent historian Richard Hofstadter.

This interpretation of fundamentalism came under attack in the 1960s, largely as a result of the work of SANDEEN, who observed that the movement's early constituency was largely northern and urban in make-up. Eschewing social definitions, Sandeen portrays fundamentalism as primarily a theological movement generated by and devoted to the doctrine of premillennialism. While 19th-century American Protestants had typically been "postmillennial" in that they believed Jesus Christ would return to earth after Christians had transformed society into the Kingdom of God, premillennialists believed that society would grow continually worse until Christ returned suddenly to establish his kingdom on earth. This led fundamentalists to bypass social reform in favor of individual soul-winning, and to attempt to purge modernist heretics from the Protestant church. Intertwined with this belief in premillennialism was the fundamentalist doctrine of biblical inerrancy, the idea that the original manuscripts of the Bible were literally true in all matters of faith, science, and history.

Sandeen's book corrects previous interpretations of fundamentalism that failed to take seriously its theological dimensions, but errs to the opposite extreme in viewing the movement in narrowly ideological terms. The interpretation of fundamentalism that has won general assent among historians is that of MARSDEN (1980), who saw worthwhile elements in both Sandeen and his predecessors. Marsden portrays fundamentalism as a complex amalgamation of historic Protestant groups including, in addition to premillennialists and biblical inerrantists, "Higher Christian Life" proponents, revivalists, and conservatives within Protestant denominations. All of these groups were united by an antipathy to theological modernism.

Thus, while religious and theological elements were central to fundamentalism, it was the cultural changes of the turn of the 20th century that galvanized these various groups into a single movement. Like immigrants in a strange new land, 19th-century orthodox Protestants awoke in the 20th century to find themselves aliens in a culture that had come to regard many of their beliefs as nonsense. The result was paradoxical: fundamentalists alternated between retreating into a subculture of their own making and fighting to return America to its Protestant moorings.

MARSDEN (1987) continues the story of certain second-generation fundamentalists in the mid-20th century who sought to rid the movement of its anti-intellectual and combative temper. He uses Fuller Seminary, founded in 1947 by fundamentalists, as a case study of how fundamentalism evolved into the broad, irenic, socially-concerned "new evangelicalism" best represented in the figure of Billy Graham, himself a graduate of a fundamentalist Bible college.

Two crucial elements in fundamentalism – its intense piety and institutional framework – receive little attention in Marsden but are brought to the fore in BRERETON. Fundamentalists were vitally concerned with educating young people for Christian work and instilling in them a fervent spirituality. These elements, Brereton explains, were nurtured in Bible schools, which formed the institutional core of fundamentalism and assumed the role that denominations had typically played in historic American Protestantism.

An aspect of fundamentalism that has received attention recently is the role of women in the movement. In a concise, comprehensive, and balanced treatment of the subject, BENDROTH argues that fundamentalism has historically harbored a sense of ambivalence toward the role and status of women. On the one hand, fundamentalists have taken literally the New Testament passages which exclude women from leadership roles in church; on the other hand, the urgent imperative to win the world for Christ has meant that public roles as missionaries, evangelists, and preachers have remained open to fundamentalist women. Bendroth chronicles the ways that fundamentalists have sought to mediate the tensions between theology, practical necessity, and changing roles of women in the surrounding culture.

Despite predictions from earlier scholars that it was dying out, fundamentalism has displayed a remarkable vitality in modern American culture. Two painstaking but readable books explore fundamentalism's trademark ideas and their popularity today. BOYER demonstrates in exhaustive detail that belief in the literal second coming of Jesus Christ, a bedrock doctrine of fundamentalism, is rampant in present-day America, and he explores the causes and consequences of this surprising development. NUMBERS charts the fate of another idea central to fundamentalism – the belief in the literal, six-day creation of the world by God in the not-too-distant past. Contrary to previous scholarly opinion, the celebrated Scopes Monkey Trial of 1925 did not signal the demise of anti-evolutionism among American Protestants. Rather, Numbers tells the fascinating story of how a Seventh Day Adventist teaching of the origin of the world evolved into "scientific creationism," a belief that has come to acquire wide assent among rank and file fundamentalists. Both Boyer and Numbers testify to the continuing vitality of fundamentalism in modern America: Hal Lindsey's *The Late Great Planet Earth*, a popular exposition of premillennialism, was the best-selling book of the 1970s, while according to a 1991 Gallup poll 47 per cent of Americans believed in biblical creationism.

Those interested in getting behind fundamentalist ideas and institutions to the people themselves will find AMMERMAN rewarding reading. Ammerman, a sociologist, spent a year among a middle-class fundamentalist congregation in suburban Boston. Her work explores the fundamentalists' experience in the modern world – their sense of separation, their emphasis on personal holiness, and their concept of family relationships and child-rearing. The book illustrates the ways in which fundamentalists have erected a "sacred canopy" to preserve their beliefs and lifestyles in modern America.

RICHARD OSTRANDER

G

Gallatin, Albert 1761–1849
Secretary of the Treasury, diplomat, and banker

Adams, Henry, *The Life of Albert Gallatin*, Philadelphia: Lippincott, 1879; reprinted, New York: P. Smith, 1943

Balinky, Alexander, *Albert Gallatin: Fiscal Theories and Policies*, New Brunswick, NJ: Rutgers University Press, 1958

Merk, Frederick, *Albert Gallatin and the Oregon Problem: A Study in Anglo-American Diplomacy*, Cambridge, MA: Harvard University Press, 1950

Nelson, John R., Jr., *Liberty and Property: Political Economy and Policymaking in the New Nation, 1789–1812*, Baltimore: Johns Hopkins University Press, 1987

Stevens, John Austin, *Albert Gallatin*, Boston: Houghton Mifflin, 1884

Walters, Raymond, Jr., *Albert Gallatin: Jeffersonian Financier and Diplomat*, New York: Macmillan, 1957

Albert Gallatin was the Republican Alexander Hamilton. As a United States Congressman and later Secretary of the Treasury under Presidents Jefferson and Madison, he more than anyone else articulated and structured Republican fiscal policies. Best remembered for his political economy, the Swiss-born immigrant also played an important role in moderating the Whiskey Rebellion, helped to negotiate the Treaty of Ghent ending the War of 1812, served in various other diplomatic missions, and in his old age wrote several important works on Native American ethnography. Yet, while Hamilton has long fascinated American historians, they have written very little on Gallatin.

Gallatin's earliest biographer was a young Henry ADAMS. His full-scale biography has held up well over the years, but the modern reader may be irritated by his inclusion of Gallatin's letters and other documents within the body of the text. Adams portrays Gallatin as an equal partner in the Republican "triumvirate" along with Madison and Jefferson, and as the creator of the Republican emphasis on discharging the national debt at the expense of military expenditures. He praises Gallatin's abilities highly but criticizes the doctrinaire inflexibility of the Republican program, arguing that their efforts to avoid military spending led to the disastrous Embargo of 1807, a policy about which, he adds, Gallatin was ambivalent at best.

STEVENS's biography of Gallatin is far less critical although more succinct. He praises Gallatin's opposition to the national debt, and somewhat misleadingly celebrates Gallatin as a free trader and an opponent of the American System, when in fact Gallatin was a strong proponent of federally funded internal improvements. Stevens also makes much of Gallatin's opposition to the Embargo and denies Adams's implicit charges that his debt reduction came at the expense of military preparedness.

WALTERS is the only modern scholarly biography. A clearly written full-scale treatment of Gallatin's public and private life, it is admiring of Gallatin but not uncritical. Walters makes much of Gallatin's Swiss birth, arguing that his "Genevan heritage" influenced his conservative fear of debt. As an immigrant, Gallatin was also able to rise above petty sectional differences and become a true nationalist, according to Walters. He argues that Gallatin stood between Hamilton and Jefferson as a strong nationalist whose fiscal policies tended to favor the small farmer.

Gallatin's role in Anglo-American negotiations over the northwest border of the United States is the subject of MERK's short monograph. In a thorough diplomatic history of the London Conference of 1826–27, at which Gallatin served as the American minister to Great Britain, Merk credits Gallatin with almost single-handedly saving the negotiations. Thanks to his diplomacy, Britain backed down from earlier more belligerent proposals, and this made possible a continuation of Anglo-American joint occupation of Oregon. Merk praises Gallatin for his diplomatic skills and his "internationalist" outlook, which allowed him to avoid bellicose nationalism.

Gallatin's political economy is sharply criticized in BALINKY's monograph, although at times the author's true target appears to be then-President Dwight D. Eisenhower. Writing from the perspective of an economist, he stresses the similarity between the Republican fiscal programs of 1800 and 1958, focusing specifically on Gallatin's efforts to reduce government spending, decrease the public debt, and lower taxes. In a close study of Gallatin's budgets during his years as Secretary of the Treasury, Balinky portrays him as an enemy to large government who pursued a policy of economy at any cost that ultimately failed by emasculating the nation's defense in the years prior to the War of 1812.

Gallatin appears as more of a friend to active government in NELSON. In a series of stimulating revisionist essays on Federalist and Republican political economy, Nelson argues that, contrary to common wisdom, the Republicans (and especially Gallatin) wanted government assistance for manufacturing, while Hamilton cared little for it, supporting it only as a means of attracting merchant capital into the federal coffers. Nelson skillfully uses Gallatin's writings calling for government support of manufactures and internal improvement to support his thesis. Unlike previous authors, he also portrays Gallatin as a manufacturer (he owned a glass factory and, briefly, a munitions factory, but he rarely oversaw these businesses in person). However, Nelson's argument is partially undermined by his failure to differentiate between the policies of Gallatin and those of the other Republicans. In particular, he argues that the Embargo was a logical outcome of Gallatin's political economy, when in fact Gallatin was clearly ambivalent about this policy.

LAWRENCE A. PESKIN

Garrison, William Lloyd 1805-1879
Abolitionist campaigner and publicist

Kraditor, Aileen S., *Means and Ends in American Abolitionism: Garrison and His Critics on Strategy and Tactics, 1834–1850*, New York: Pantheon, 1969

Merrill, Walter McIntosh, *Against Wind and Tide: A Biography of William Lloyd Garrison*, Cambridge, MA: Harvard University Press, 1963

Nye, Russel B., *William Lloyd Garrison and the Humanitarian Reformers*, Boston: Little Brown, 1955

Rogers, William B., *"We Are All Together Now": Frederick Douglass, William Lloyd Garrison and the Prophetic Tradition*, New York: Garland, 1995

Stewart, James Brewer, *William Lloyd Garrison and the Challenge of Emancipation*, Arlington Heights, IL: Harlan Davidson, 1992

Thomas, John L., *The Liberator: William Lloyd Garrison, A Biography*, Boston: Little Brown, 1963

William Lloyd Garrison remains the most prominent and controversial of the abolitionist leaders. The eradication of slavery was only one of his numerous reform causes. It is hardly surprising that such a turbulent and many-sided figure should have attracted much attention – and lively debate – among historians and biographers.

The format of the series in which NYE appeared required the treatment of a significant theme in American history through tracing the career of an individual. The book thus provides a useful survey of abolitionism and antislavery generally, though Nye devotes less attention to Garrison's other reform interests. The view of Garrison is also shaped by the debate, still current in the 1950s, over how central he was to abolitionism as compared to Weld, Birney and the political abolitionists. The answer provided is that although he neither originated abolitionism nor played a major organizational role, he was at his most influential in the 1830s when, through effective propaganda, he lodged slavery as an issue in the public mind. Thereafter he is portrayed as a diminishing asset. The context of the Second Great Awakening is sketched but the links between religion and reform are not explored in detail.

MERRILL is still the most detailed biography of Garrison, and is based upon the author's work as an editor of the Garrison letters, a project completed in the following years. Merrill's attention is devoted primarily to Garrison the man, his character and how his personality was displayed in his relations with his family and closest associates. Merrill also distributes his space relatively equally between different stages of Garrison's life. His emotionally deprived and unstable childhood and the pressure of his mother's rigorous piety are seen as the psychological bases for Garrison's self-assertiveness and moral authoritarianism. Merrill has no doubt of his subject's importance in abolitionism and other moral reforms as someone who dramatized himself in order to dramatize social evils. However, the attempt to integrate the personal story with a narrative of antislavery is only partially successful.

In a number of respects THOMAS remains the major interpreter of Garrison within a brilliantly developed account of the intellectual and emotional culture of moral reform and moral radicalism before the Civil War. Although Thomas offers a psychological sketch of Garrison not dissimilar to Merrill's, and shrewdly links it to the adolescent's sense of social displacement and later drive to achieve recognition, the study is above all the story of the evolution of an outsider's attitudes to a sinful world, and how to transform it by transforming the individuals within it. Thomas's key to Garrison is the perfectionist stance which he adopted by the later 1830s, the logic of which pointed to universal reform, disunion and Christian anarchism. This emphasis also allows the exploration, both within Garrison himself and between Garrisonians and other reformers, of the tension between individual piety and the social ethics which demanded a greater recognition of the complexities of social organization and power than Garrison was willing to acknowledge.

If Thomas's account of antebellum culture reveals powerful elements of fantasy and irrationality in the visions of Garrison and other moral radicals, KRADITOR implies a much more shrewdly calculating culture of reform. She seeks to clarify what she sees as the often sophisticated and complex debates over strategy and tactics within abolitionism, and thus to remove misconceptions about Garrison and the radicals, and thereby to vindicate them. She presents an ethos of reform in which vigorous debate expressed a sense of fluid but usable institutions, and more flexibility on the part of the Garrisonians than their opponents. Instead of seeing Garrison's perfectionism as limiting his methods to moral persuasion and denunciation in the search for purity, she insists that he consistently tolerated a broad variety of outlooks, provided that his associates accepted the sinfulness of slavery and the need for immediate emancipation. The analysis of debate is lucid and formidably documented, but Kraditor can account for opponents' critical perceptions of Garrison only by attributing to them deliberate misrepresentation.

The objective of STEWART's study is similar to Nye's, but he has the advantage of being able to build on Thomas, Kraditor and a number of excellent, more general studies of abolitionism. The result is a concise and well integrated synthesis in which Garrison's romantic individual perfectionism is given due weight, but he is shown to be able to qualify its relentless logic in successfully becoming a self-made man, within a neatly sketched world of journalism and reform networks. While ROGERS is often weakly written, repetitive and distracted by the need to justify a rather arbitrarily constructed "prophetic tradition" he does eventually provide a useful summary of some of the similarities and differences between Frederick Douglass and Garrison as reformers, which may stimulate more sophisticated future analysis.

DAVID TURLEY

See also Abolitionism/Antislavery Movement; Reform Movements

Garvey, Marcus 1887–1940
Black nationalist leader

Burkett, Randall K., *Garveyism as a Religious Movement: The Institutionalization of a Black Civil Religion*, Metuchen NJ: Scarecrow Press, 1978

Cronon, Edmund D., *Black Moses: The Story of Marcus Garvey and the Universal Negro Improvement Association*, Madison: University of Wisconsin Press, 1955

Garvey, Amy Jacques, *Garvey and Garveyism*, Kingston, Jamaica: A.J. Garvey, and New York: Collier, 1963

Martin, Tony, *Race First: The Ideological and Organizational Struggles of Marcus Garvey and the Universal Negro Improvement Association*, Westport, CT: Greenwood Press, 1976

Stein, Judith, *The World of Marcus Garvey: Race and Class in Modern Society*, Baton Rouge: Louisiana State University Press, 1986

Tolbert, Emory J., *The UNIA and Black Los Angeles: Ideology and Community in the American Garvey Movement*, Los Angeles: Center for Afro-American Studies, University of California, 1980

Vincent, Theodore G., *Black Power and the Garvey Movement*, Berkeley, CA: Ramparts Press, 1972

The black nationalism of Marcus Garvey and the Universal Negro Improvement Association (UNIA) has received considerable attention from historians, who have reached differing conclusions about their subject and the American phase of Garvey's world-wide movement in the 1920s. In the first full-length monograph, CRONON arrived at a mixed verdict. On the one hand, he found Garvey to have been an inept leader with such personal deficiencies that they "overbalanced the sounder aspects of his program." On the other, Cronon conceded that the Jamaican-born Garvey was essentially an honest man, vilified by the black and white American establishment, which was determined to rid the country of a dangerous subversive, who yet managed to inspire his followers (numbered in many thousands) with a pride in blackness and dreams of going "Back to Africa." Yet Cronon also typified the UNIA as a movement of the extreme right espousing an emotive and chauvinistic nationalism under a centralized leadership with decidedly fascist tendencies.

Garvey's widow (and second wife) Amy Jacques GARVEY offered a partisan but fascinating version of her husband's chequered career, which includes a valuable account of their stay in London in the late 1920s, where Garvey established an office of the UNIA. She also insists that the Black Star Line, Garvey's most ambitious venture, was never conceived as the agency for the mass transportation of black Americans to Africa, but rather as a commercial operation which would "transport our people on business and pleasure," in suitable accommodations.

Reflecting the resurgence of black separatism which (ironically) followed the legislative victories of the civil rights movement, VINCENT depicts Garvey as the inspiration of later leaders of independent African states and as the Founding Father of 20th-century black nationalism in America. The UNIA, Vincent demonstrates, was a heterogeneous movement of cultural and political nationalists, pacifists and militants, supporters of women's liberation, opponents of organized religion, Democrats and Republicans, united in their desire for black liberation. Its Declaration of Rights "might well pass for the pronouncement of a contemporary black power organization." Vincent asserts that Cronon had displayed a "negative attitude" toward the UNIA, since he was unable to "visualize a black nationalism that was neither reactionary nor demagogic." The opposition of the European colonial powers to Garvey's schemes of "African redemption" is seen as the basic cause of his ultimate failure. Vincent also discusses Garvey's differences with W.E.B. Du Bois and A. Philip Randolph, as well as factionalism within the UNIA itself.

Despite his use of materials denied to Vincent – the papers of Garvey's widow, documents in the British Public Records Office and the files of the American Department of Justice – MARTIN offers a polemical, erroneous and often confusing account of Garvey and Garveyism. Martin claims unconvincingly that Garvey was a "revolutionary" nationalist who, apart from the mismanagement of the Black Star Line, made no serious tactical blunders – conveniently ignoring his disastrous meeting with the leader of the Ku Klux Klan. Martin also blames Garvey's imprisonment and deportation on his African American critics – notably Du Bois and other leaders of the National Association for the Advancement of Colored People – yet unwittingly demonstrates and documents the campaign waged against Garvey by the young J. Edgar Hoover which pre-dated Du Bois's criticisms of Garvey as at best, misguided or at worst, a charlatan. Martin's claim that Garvey was perhaps "the greatest black figure in the 20th century" is open to question; the suggestion that after his American downfall, Du Bois simply appropriated Garvey's ideas of voluntary segregation and "Pan-Negroism" is patently absurd.

Fresh insights into the Garvey phenomenon are provided by BURKETT, who examines the implicitly and explicitly religious language, symbols and rituals of the UNIA, and concludes that "the religious ethos of the UNIA was pervasive, embracing nearly every facet of its organizational life." Well-written and persuasively argued, Burkett's largely neglected exegesis of the religious dimensions (and appeal) of Garveyism substantiates his contention that Garvey "articulated a remarkably well developed and internally consistent theological framework by which to interpret the meaning of his people's history and their destiny under a God who was working on their behalf."

Garvey's wider American influence is ably examined by TOLBERT, who demonstrates that the first American chapters of the UNIA were in southern California in 1920 – by 1926 there were 16 divisions of the organization in the state. Rank-and-file members in Los Angeles were politically experienced, with a real interest in African and African American history, and did not "engage in the open ideological warfare" that characterized relations between the UNIA and the NAACP in Harlem. Tolbert also offers informative collective profiles of the respective memberships of the NAACP and the UNIA in California. While the black middle class comprised the bulk of the NAACP's members, Garveyites were a more diverse group, and included a large proportion of homeowners. There were, however, differences between the California branches of the UNIA and its parent body – notably over the issue of accepting white financial assistance – which was opposed by the New York division. After Garvey's conviction, brief imprisonment and deportation for mail fraud in 1927, the UNIA in Los Angeles remained intact. But the advent of the Great Depression brought the rapid decline of Garveyism in the city and after 1934 "local Garveyites no longer stalked Central Avenue with their cries for a free Africa."

The petit bourgeois spirit of Garveyism, exemplified in the Black Star Line and Garvey's other American business enterprises, the functioning of the UNIA as a fraternal organization and the class structure of African American communities, receive detailed treatment by STEIN. Like Vincent and Martin, she agrees that Garveyism did not represent "an escape to a psychological or real Africa," but does not accept that "the UNIA's militance and black nationalism were earlier versions of the racial politics of the 1960s." Placed in geographical and comparative context, the UNIA was no more (and no less) than an "historical movement anchored in specific class and race relationships and ideologies." Reassessments of Garvey will undoubtedly be stimulated by the on-going publication by the University of California Press of *The Marcus Garvey and Universal Negro Improvement Association Papers*, edited by Robert A. Hill – a major enterprise in African American historiography.

JOHN WHITE

Gay and Lesbian Movements, since 1960s

Adam, Barry D., *The Rise of a Gay and Lesbian Movement*, Boston: Twayne, 1987, revised 1995

D'Emilio, John, *Sexual Politics, Sexual Communities: The Making of a Homosexual Minority in the United States, 1940–1970*, Chicago: University of Chicago Press, 1983

Duberman, Martin, *About Time: Exploring the Gay Past*, New York: Gay Presses of New York, 1986; revised, New York: Meridian, 1991

Duberman, Martin, *Stonewall*, New York: Dutton, 1993

Faderman, Lillian, *Odd Girls and Twilight Lovers: A History of Lesbian Life in Twentieth-Century America*, New York: Columbia University Press, 1991; London: Penguin, 1992

Although gay and lesbian studies has recently emerged as a burgeoning field, a great deal of current research and writing is either highly theoretical or deals with the emergence of homosexuality as an identifiable category in the late 19th century. As a result, there is scant literature on the rise of the gay, lesbian and bisexual movement since the 1960s. However, D'EMILIO provides a useful starting-point. Although a great deal of his seminal study focuses on the years prior to the 1960s, approximately half of the volume is devoted to the 1960s and beyond. A major focus of D'Emilio's work is his attempt to explain why an identifiable and vocal gay liberation movement emerged in the 1970s. To this end, D'Emilio attempts to place the post-1960s gay, lesbian and bisexual movement into a historical context that analyzes the emergence of a gay consciousness and self-identity as well as a "distinctly new culture of protest." The concluding section of the book discusses the rationale and the rhetoric surrounding the emergence of a gay liberation movement in the 1970s.

Perhaps one of the best known works on gay and lesbian history is DUBERMAN (1986, 1991), a collection of annotated primary documents and essays which was one of the first gay and lesbian history books. A 1991 revised edition expands upon the first and adds several new essays. The essays in part two of the book are of particular interest. Although at times these are not historical accounts in the traditional sense of the term, they provide an enlightening window on to the development of a gay and lesbian movement in the 1970s. The final essay, "Hidden from History: Reclaiming Gay/Lesbian History, Politics and Culture," is a good critique of the problems involved in constructing and publishing gay and lesbian history. Unfortunately, there is a decidedly white male bent to this study.

As with D'Emilio, much of DUBERMAN (1993) is concerned with providing the historical context for the 1969 rioting which, it is widely believed, marked the beginning of the gay liberation movement. However, Duberman skilfully chronicles the emergence of several of the most important gay and lesbian organizations which sprang up in the wake of the Stonewall riots. Because of his reliance on interviews with six of the major figures involved in the riots and the political movement they spawned, the human faces behind the movement are more clearly seen in Duberman's account than in D'Emilio's.

For the reader interested in lesbian history and the role of lesbians in the gay liberation movement, FADERMAN remains the best monograph. Although, like the other works discussed here, its scope pre-dates the 1960s and 1970s, close to half of the monograph deals with lesbian history since the 1960s. Faderman offers a particularly useful account of the tensions between lesbians and gay men in the 1970s gay liberation movement and 1980s gay rights movement, as well as the sometimes hostile relationship between lesbians and feminist organizations in the 1960s and 1970s. Unfortunately, although Faderman attempts to include women of color and various class backgrounds, she has only limited success; the subjects of her work are largely white, middle to upper class women.

Like several other books, ADAM's account extends back to the beginning of the 20th century. However, his is the only book to deal with the gay and lesbian movement in a comparative framework. Although mainly concerned with the United States, Adam also includes some discussion of parallel events in Great Britain, France, Germany (including a section on the Holocaust), Eastern Europe, Asia, Africa, and Latin America. He pays particular attention to the development of New Right conservative politics in the United States and its effect on the gay and lesbian movement of the late 1970s and 1980s. Finally, Adam is perhaps the only history which attempts to trace and explain the relationship between the gay and lesbian movement, civil/human rights, electoral politics, and "queer" politics in the age of AIDS. Of particular note are his brief discussions of pornography and censorship, AIDS, and radical "queer" political groups such as Queer Nation and ACT-UP.

VANESSA L. DAVIS

Gender

Braude, Anne, *Radical Spirits: Spiritualism and Women's Rights in 19th-Century America*, Boston: Beacon Press, 1989

Carnes, Mark C., *Secret Ritual and Manhood in Victorian America*, New Haven and London: Yale University Press, 1989

Carnes, Mark C. and Clyde Griffen (editors), *Meanings for Manhood: Constructions of Masculinity in Victorian America*, Chicago: University of Chicago Press, 1990

Cogan, Frances B., *All-American Girl: The Ideal of Real Womanhood in mid-Nineteenth-Century America*, Athens: University of Georgia Press, 1989

Cott, Nancy F., *The Bonds of Womanhood: "Woman's Sphere" in New England, 1780–1835*, New Haven and London: Yale University Press, 1977

Glenn, Susan A., *Daughters of the Shtetl: Life and Labor in the Immigrant Generation*, Ithaca, NY: Cornell University Press, 1990

Karlsen, Carol F., *The Devil in the Shape of a Woman: Witchcraft in Colonial New England*, New York: Norton, 1987

Kerber, Linda K., *Women of the Republic: Intellect and Ideology in Revolutionary America*, Chapel Hill: University of North Carolina Press, 1980

May, Elaine Tyler, *Homeward Bound: American Families in the Cold War Era*, New York: Basic Books, 1988

Russett, Cynthia Eagle, *Sexual Science: The Victorian Construction of Womanhood*, Cambridge, MA: Harvard University Press, 1989

Ryan, Mary P., *Cradle of the Middle Class: The Family in Oneida County, New York, 1790–1865*, Cambridge and New York: Cambridge University Press, 1981

Ryan, Mary P., *Women in Public: Between Banners and Ballots, 1825–1880*, Baltimore: Johns Hopkins University Press, 1990

Stansell, Christine, *City of Women: Sex and Class in New York, 1789–1860*, New York: Knopf, 1986

Ulrich, Laurel Thatcher, *Good Wives: Image and Reality in the Lives of Women in Northern New England, 1650–1750*, New York: Knopf, 1982

White, Deborah Gray, *Ar'n't I a Woman? Female Slaves in the Plantation South*, New York: Norton, 1985

Although gender has been a subject of considerable historical interest for the past two decades, there are few good general surveys of the topic. Instead, numerous excellent studies exist which explore particular aspects of women's experience and the construction of femininity and masculinity in American society.

Several important works examine the role of women in the colonial and revolutionary period. ULRICH analyzes the construction of gender among the Puritan settlers of 17th-century New England. She rejects the notion of the invisibility or the marginality of women in Puritan culture, and overturns the stereotype of the submissive, passive Puritan goodwife. Drawing upon a wealth of cultural artifacts and written evidence, Ulrich demonstrates that New England Puritans conceived of women's role as incorporating such diverse biblically-sanctioned models of behaviour as Deborah (helpmeet, housekeeper, and good neighbour), Eve (wife, mother, and sexual partner), and Jael ("political" protester and defender of the home and family). Ulrich's work takes an even-handed view of Puritan culture and is the best overall study so far of the lives of Puritan women in America.

KARLSEN takes a somewhat different view of the role of women and ideals of womanhood in Puritan New England. Employing both a statistical and a case study approach, she examines in depth several famous cases of witchcraft accusations in an attempt to discover why charges of witchcraft were disproportionately levelled against women. Karlsen concludes that such accusations were a tool used to control and assert authority over those women who deviated significantly from Puritan models of womanhood – women who wielded authority or eschewed male guidance. While Karlsen's study is interesting and provocative in its conclusions, it is rather too polemical and takes an unduly negative view of Puritan society.

KERBER examines the emergence of socially sanctioned public and political roles for women during and following the American Revolution. She argues that the Revolution presented American women with their first opportunity to participate in the public and political life of the nation. In Kerber's view, women reinterpreted their traditional roles as wives and mothers in order to justify their entrance into the public sphere and to create a political role for themselves as educators of future generations of American citizens and guardians of republican "virtue". This work is a classic in American women's history and provides the best study to date of the development of the concept of the "republican mother".

Many of the works addressing the topic of gender in American history focus on the 19th century and are concerned with the impact of industrialization on women, and the role played by women in the construction of middle-class values and ideologies. COTT studies the growth of the middle class "cult of domesticity" and the development of the notion of "separate spheres" for men and women. She argues that the coming of industrialization and the destruction of the home-based economy created a situation in which white, middle-class women were excluded from American public and economic life, and relegated to the home and the private sphere. Instead of regarding this as evidence of female disempowerment, Cott interprets this new conception of women as guardians of piety and morality in a materialistic world as a source of social and cultural power for middle-class women. Cott's work is the classic, book-length study of the development of the cult of domesticity in 19th-century America.

RYAN (1981) expands upon the argument that the needs of a rapidly industrializing society wrought great changes in the roles of women and the conception of womanhood. Ryan describes how, despite being consigned to the economic fringes of a newly industrial society, women, through their roles as educators of children and arbiters of morality, were instrumental in the formulation, inculcation, and perpetuation of those values, attitudes, behaviours, and lifestyles which were necessary for success in 19th-century industrial society, and which came to be regarded as "middle class".

While Cott and Ryan are concerned with the role played by the 19th-century industrial order and women's economic marginality in the construction of ideals of womanhood, RUSSETT studies another element in the creation of middle-class conceptions of femininity in the 19th century. Examining the (male) scientific construction of womanhood, she describes how late 19th-century scientific paradigms based on the theory of evolution replaced an earlier conception of women as *different* from men (but still capable of being "elevated" to their level through the manipulation of their environment). The new "scientific" model defined women as less evolved than men and thus innately and permanently *inferior*, both physically and mentally. Russett also explores the connection between this new scientific evaluation of women's potential and changes in the economic, social, and legal status of women in 19th-century Europe and America.

While many works consider the social and cultural ramifications of the 19th-century conception of women as pure, pious, spiritual, and weak, other works focus on alternative constructions of femininity. RYAN (1990) rejects the argument that 19th-century women occupied an exclusively private sphere, separate from and diametrically opposed to the public sphere occupied by men. She argues instead that women's lives had public as well as private components. Their concerns influenced events taking place within the public sphere and their behaviour was governed by social codes which determined acceptable public presentations of femininity. In developing her argument, Ryan examines women's use of public space, their role in the formulation of public discourse and public policy, and the uses of female images in public ceremonies to symbolize patriotism, ethnicity, and political affiliation. This outstanding study provides a thought-provoking analysis of American political culture and the meaning of "politics" and "public discourse".

In a similar vein, BRAUDE analyzes the manner in which women involved in the spiritualist movement of the mid-to-late 19th century drew upon cultural constructions of women as innately pure, pious, and spiritual to create powerful public roles for themselves. Braude describes how female mediums and spiritualists used their position as public speakers, and the authority derived from their communion with a higher sphere, to advocate support of such radical causes as women's rights, dress reform, temperance, and "irregular" (non male-dominated) methods of healing.

In her study of 19th-century popular women's literature, COGAN highlights its rejection of the cultural ideal of submissive, passive, domestic women enshrined in the middle-class cult of domesticity. Her analysis of popular novels reveals an

alternative model of femininity which emphasized courage, independence, strength, intelligence, and physical hardiness. For all its merits, this study suffers from its failure to provide examples of women who did in fact adopt this alternative ideal of womanhood as a real model for behaviour.

All of the works consider the construction of gender primarily in terms of how it affected white, middle-class women. However, other historians have examined the lives and roles of women excluded from this relatively privileged group. STANSELL, for example, argues that white, working-class women did not participate in the 19th-century, middle-class "cult of domesticity", and had little or no conception of separate spheres for men and women. She analyzes instead the nature of the dual roles of worker and housewife-mother forced upon working-class women by the rise of industrialization and the destruction of the home economy. She also studies the creation of female networks among working-class women, and shows how the dual role of wife and worker alienated working-class women from both men of their own class and women of the middle class. Stansell's work is much the best and most thorough examination of the lives of American working-class women in the 19th century.

In a study of the lives of Jewish immigrant women in turn-of-the-century New York, GLENN argues in similar fashion that conceptions of womanhood and notions of women's proper sphere in Jewish immigrant households differed radically from the standards of femininity upheld by the native-born middle class. She contends that Jewish women's poverty and immigrant status, together with *shtetl* traditions of wives working to support impoverished and/or scholarly husbands, pushed Jewish women in the world of work and also into an active life in the public sphere. Glenn describes the home and work lives of these women and examines how their position as family breadwinners, the discrimination they faced as recent immigrants, and traditions of socialist activity in their homelands, encouraged them to assume public roles as union organizers and public speakers.

WHITE studies the influence of sex, the work experience, West African traditions, and slave status on the construction of gender and conceptions of womanhood among southern slave women. Their role as labourers under slavery combined with West African traditions regarding the importance of women to give black women great power within the family and the slave community, and substantial equality in their dealings with slave men. White also explores how the frequent segregation of slave women in all-female work environments, the reality of violence and sexual exploitation by both white and black men, and women's skill in such areas as healing and witchcraft led to strong feelings of solidarity among slave women and made their experience profoundly different from that of either slave men or white women. Gray's work is the most useful study to date of the lives of African American slave women.

In contrast to the volume of work on the subject of gender in earlier periods, fewer historians have addressed the specific topic of gender in the 20th century. Most studies of 20th-century women's history tend to focus almost exclusively on political developments and the growth of feminism. However, MAY is concerned with the construction of gender and, in that context, studies women's roles and societal perceptions of womanhood in the Cold War era. She describes how the economic crisis of the 1930s, the social disruptions caused by World War II, and the threat of nuclear warfare in the Cold War era profoundly affected cultural conceptions of marriage, the family, and femininity in the postwar period. She suggests that, in an attempt to reassert their authority in a society which granted increased social and economic power to women, and to reestablish control over an increasingly unstable world, American men upheld an informal policy of "domestic containment" which reaffirmed the importance of home, family, and traditional gender roles.

While much attention has been given to the changing meanings and constructions of "womanhood" and "femininity" in American society, much less work has been devoted to a parallel examination of the construction of "manhood" and "masculinity". CARNES and GRIFFEN have compiled a valuable group of essays which explore the construction of masculinity in Victorian America. Among the topics covered are the inculcation and development of ideas of masculinity in childhood, the relationship between work and notions of masculinity, and the ways in which men participated in the cult of domesticity. CARNES (1989) argues that middle-class men in 19th-century America felt profoundly threatened by the feminizing influence which women were exerting on all aspects of society, including such former bastions of male power as the church and the family. He examines the creation of all-male fraternal orders which stressed the importance of male bonding, and which emphasized secret ceremonies and rituals through which men reaffirmed their masculinity and underwent symbolic (re)birth in an atmosphere free from feminine influence. While Carnes's premise is interesting and the book makes fascinating reading, its thesis is somewhat weakened by a failure to consider adequately alternative explanations of the popularity of fraternal orders.

ANN KORDAS

George, Henry 1839–1897
Economic theorist and social critic

Aaron, Daniel, *Men of Good Hope: A Story of American Progressives*, New York: Oxford University Press, 1951

Andelson, Robert V., *Critics of Henry George: A Centenary Appraisal of Their Strictures on Progress and Poverty*, Rutherford, NJ: Fairleigh Dickinson University Press, 1979

Barker, Charles Albro, *Henry George*, New York: Oxford University Press, 1955

Blaug, Mark (editor), *Henry George, 1839–1897*, Aldershot, Hampshire: Elgar, 1992

Geiger, George Raymond, *The Philosophy of Henry George*, New York: Macmillan, 1933

George, Henry, Jr., *The Life of Henry George*, 2 vols., New York: Doubleday and McClure, 1900

Hellman, Rhoda, *Henry George Reconsidered*, New York: Carlton Press, 1987

Jones, Peter d'A., *The Christian Socialist Revival, 1877–1914: Religion, Class, and Social Conscience in Late-Victorian England*, Princeton: Princeton University Press, 1968

Jones, Peter d'A., *Henry George and British Socialism*, New York: Garland, 1991

Lawrence, E.P., *Henry George in the British Isles*, East Lansing: Michigan State University Press, 1957

Post, Louis F., *The Prophet of San Francisco: Personal Memories and Interpretations of Henry George*, New York: Vanguard Press, 1930

Rose, Edward J., *Henry George*, New York: Twayne, 1968

Thomas, John L., *Alternative America: Henry George, Edward Bellamy, Henry Demarest Lloyd and the Adversary Tradition*, Cambridge, MA: Belknap Press of Harvard University Press, 1983

Henry George was a leading critic of the emerging industrial capitalism of the late 19th century, and, in his major book, *Progress and Poverty*, he argued that, because economic and population growth led to soaring land values and monopoly power, a more just and equitable economic order could be achieved by means of a tax on the market value of land. He engaged himself directly in reform and labor movements, and was only narrowly beaten in the election for Mayor of New York in 1886. His influence waned thereafter, but he retains significance as a champion of the causes of antimonopoly and economic and social equality.

His son, Henry GEORGE Jr., who helped to collect his father's writings in ten volumes, also wrote the first survey of his life in America and beyond, in a two-volume biography, based on memories of an intimate association with his father's activities. Personal conversations, unpublished documents and family reminiscences are features of this biography.

A number of reassessments of George appeared between the 1930s and the 1950s. POST, a one-time co-worker of George, and a strong advocate of the Georgist taxation of land values, wrote a book full of personal memories of the single tax movement. GEIGER provided a full discussion of George's ideas, including his semi-religious convictions on the "First Cause," and, of course, the single tax. AARON places George skilfully in the context of American progressivism. He portrays George, along with other Progressives, standing out against the trend of late 19th century laissez-faire, big business conservatism and oligopoly. Aaron gained critical distinction for himself by bravely resisting the pressures of McCarthyism in the 1950s, and his stand on behalf of progressivism retains its value, even if the excitement of George's ideas has not always stood the test of time very successfully.

Scholarship on George took a major step forward in the mid-1950s with the publication of BARKER's substantial biography. Based extensively on George's own published and unpublished writings, it gives detailed attention to George's earlier life in California, and the shaping influence of that experience on *Progress and Poverty*. Strongly sympathetic to his subject, Barker makes large claims for the national and international influence of George's major work, and defines the basic axioms of his thought as the Jeffersonian and Jacksonian principles of destroying economic monopolies, and advancing freedom and economic opportunity for all.

George's international influence – especially in Britain, where he made a very successful tour in 1881–82 – has attracted a good deal of attention. The pioneer in this field is LAWRENCE, who published various articles on George before his book on George in the British Isles. JONES (1968) places George and the Georgists in Britain squarely in the midst of the economic and social furore which led to the rebirth of Christian Socialism in England. JONES (1991), a revision of a thesis written almost forty years earlier, tells the story of George's across-the-board influence on British socialism.

THOMAS is the major modern reassessment of George, but, in a study which deals also with Edward Bellamy and Henry Demarest Lloyd, the argument is not always as clear or cogent as it might be. Thomas has some difficulty in riding three horses at once, and the reader can be distracted by the frequent switching from one to another. The book mixes biography and intellectual history, and includes extensive exposition of the major texts of all three authors. In discussing George, Thomas inevitably highlights his emphasis on land as the key factor in the production of wealth, and rent as its equivalent in the distribution of wealth. Rejecting collectivist or centralized solutions to the problem, George found his solution in the single tax on land. In later chapters, Thomas describes George's subsequent political experiences and his attempts to propagate his ideas, and he concludes with a downbeat evaluation of George's limited and relatively short-lived legacy. Whatever its shortcomings – and Thomas has been criticized for depicting all three of his subjects as backward-looking pastoralists – this remains an important study of "alternative" voices in late 19th century America.

ROSE is a very brief study, of only 160 pages but offers a useful introduction to George and his ideas. HELLMAN is an enthusiastic, if rather unsophisticated, study, and defence, of George and his ideas. It includes a brief account of his life and career, a very positive assessment of his influence, both during his lifetime and later, and an attempt to analyze why the land tax idea has been so widely disregarded. George's inadequate articulation of his own ideas receives its share of the blame.

Two collections of essays and readings provide a range of estimates of George's influence and importance. ANDELSON is a collection of 27 short essays by a variety of authors who discuss the views of numerous critics of George and his ideas. BLAUG includes a wide selection of 26 essays and articles, originally published between 1969 and 1988. Editorial comment is minimal, and goes little beyond asking the question: who reads Henry George?

PETER D'A. JONES

German Americans

Conzen, Kathleen Neils, *Immigrant Milwaukee, 1836–1860: Accommodation and Community in a Frontier City*, Cambridge, MA: Harvard University Press, 1976

Keil, Hartmut (editor), *German Workers' Culture in the United States, 1850–1920*, Washington, DC: Smithsonian Institution Press, 1988

Keller, Phyllis, *States of Belonging: German-American Intellectuals and the First World War*, Cambridge, MA: Harvard University Press, 1979

Levine, Bruce, *The Spirit of 1848: German Immigrants, Labor Conflict, and the Coming of the Civil War*, Urbana: University of Illinois Press, 1992

Luebke, Frederick C., *Germans in the New World*, Urbana: University of Illinois Press, 1990

Nadel, Stanley, *Little Germany: Ethnicity, Religion, and Class in New York City, 1845–1880*, Urbana: University of Illinois Press, 1990

Rippley, La Vern J., *The German Americans*, Boston: Twayne, 1976

Shore, Elliott, Ken Fones-Wolf, and James P. Danky (editors), *The German American Radical Press: The Shaping of a Left Political Culture, 1850–1940*, Urbana: University of Illinois Press, 1992

Trommler, Frank and James McVeigh (editors), *America and the Germans: An Assessment of a Three-Hundred-Year History*, 2 vols., Philadelphia: University of Pennsylvania Press, 1985

Wyman, Mark, *Immigrants in the Valley: Irish, Germans, and Americans in the Upper Mississippi Country, 1830–1860*, Chicago: Nelson Hall, 1984

German American invisibility in contemporary society and in history is an anomaly deserving attention. By standard statistical measurement, the Germans were the largest immigrant group. Yet historians have been far more interested in Italian, Irish, Polish, and Eastern European Jewish immigration and culture. Irish bars, Italian restaurants, and Jewish humor abound. German language is rarely studied in high schools or colleges and German restaurants are an endangered culinary species. The blending of so many millions into the American mainstream with barely a trace is one of the major untold stories in American history.

Recent years have produced a modicum of scholarship on the subject and the creation of the German-American Historical Institute in Washington provides a new focus for scholars. Recent studies reject earlier filiopietism and conceptions of national character in order to examine the ethnic group with more detachment. There is now a considerable range of studies of German Americans, especially for the period from the great immigrations of the mid-19th century to the trauma of World War I.

A new one-volume survey is needed, but RIPPLEY, two decades old, is still usable. It provides even-handed coverage well based in demographic data and with particularly good coverage of cultural and linguistic developments. He maintains that Germanness was strong only when connected with religious uniqueness (as with the Amish) or an outside threat (for example Prohibition), and accepts assimilation with less regret than the previous generation of historians.

LUEBKE's work traces the intellectual journey of one of the few historians to address the subject regularly since the 1950s. Although raised in a German-American culture, he criticizes its leaders' ethnocentrism and even partially blames their exploitation of cultural chauvinism for the World War I attacks on Germanness. Leubke punctures other balloons by questioning whether the great icon Carl Schurz was truly an ethnic leader, and by doubting the extent to which such a diverse group as German Americans can truly be described as an ethnic group. This book provides a model for an insider's affectionate yet critical understanding of an ethnic group. The articles in TROMMLER and McVEIGH exhibit debts to the few historians, like Carl Wittke and Luebke, who worked steadily in the field after World War II. Some of the contributors to this two-volume collection of conference papers are represented in the works reviewed here. The papers represent a new generation of work that tends to view cultural diversity sympathetically, but with scholarly detachment. Influenced by the social history of the 1970s, these studies approach this most varied ethnic group with much greater specificity than was possible for earlier historians.

One of the earliest fruit of the "new" social history was CONZEN's study of German Americans arriving in Milwaukee while it was still a frontier community and becoming its dominant ethnic group. She found a group that quickly and confidently shaped its own culture and exerted its power; this was not a disoriented "uprooted" group. But its community was based on a surface commonality and language that would easily erode across a few generations. WYMAN examined the impact on the upper Mississippi Valley of recently arrived Germans fleeing the aftermath of the 1848–49 revolutions and Germany's lesser-known potato blight. Like Conzen, Wyman rejects the "uprooted" model, depicting an assertive group that barely missed a step in immigration, and quickly emerged to play a major role in the Civil War.

Although the leaders of the 1848 revolution have received considerable attention, LEVINE, in contrast, focused on craftsmen and workers. By tracing immigration back to economic troubles in southern Germany, he provides the context for the spirited involvement of early German Americans in trade unionism and radical politics, and their success in dominating many of the crafts. He also examines the long-standing controversy over whether German Americans crucially swung the 1860 vote to Lincoln. Levine concludes that they did not, but the myth was powerful, and roughly 10 per cent of the Union army was German-born.

The various writers contributing to KEIL carry the study of German American workers, particularly in Chicago, through the postbellum years to World War I. The essays combine ethnic and working-class history and examine the intersection of radical German traditions with indigenous American conditions. Several authors examine the surprising extent to which the German American working class participated in high culture, thus continuing an aspect of German social democratic culture. The essays in SHORE, FONES-WOLF, and DANKY explain this phenomenon in their study of the radical German American press. They suggest that radicals often saw themselves as defending high culture from the middle-class popularizers and assimilationists. German Americans were the most prolific newspaper creators among the immigrant groups and they played a major role up to World War I in maintaining the culture, radical and otherwise.

NADEL provides a much needed account of Kleindeutschland on the Lower East Side of New York City, the city with the third largest German-speaking population in the world after Berlin and Vienna. In a rich multi-faceted cultural and social interpretation Nadel found that German regionalism structured Kleindeutschland in the 1850s and 1860s; religion operated within those lines. But class increasingly divided Kleindeutschland in the 1870s, drawing the affluent into uptown neighborhoods, and destroying the former multi-class diversity. Yet regionalism continued to play a surprising role through the second generation. Only then did a broader German ethnicity, divided by class and religion, emerge.

KELLER examined three leading German American intellectuals (Hugo Munsterberg, George Sylvester Viereck, and Hermann Hagedorn) during the trying years of World War I. Surprisingly, the most assimilated was the leader of the pro-German faction, while the least assimilated led the pro-Allied sentiment among German American activists. Intriguingly she suggests that, because of World War I, ethnicity, for most German Americans, conflicted in a unique way with being American, and most felt they had to choose one or the other.

In recent years, a small but growing body of work has expanded our understanding of this neglected topic. The concept of "German American" has been enriched by studies of regional, class, and religious divisions, leading to the portrayal of "Germanness" as a later construction. The "uprooted" model has been largely destroyed by depictions of rapid cultural and political adaptation. Using these specialized studies as a base, historians may be ready to come to grips with the process by which a huge ethnic group was merged into the mainstream.

W. BRUCE LESLIE

Gilded Age and Progressive Era, 1877–1917: General

Buenker, John D. and Nicholas C. Burckel (editors), *Progressive Reform: A Guide to Information Sources*, Detroit: Gale, 1980

Buenker, John D., John C. Burnham, and Robert M. Crunden, *Progressivism*, Cambridge, MA: Schenkman, 1977

Buenker, John D. and Edward R. Kantowicz (editors), *Historical Dictionary of the Progressive Era, 1890–1920*, Westport, CT: Greenwood Press, 1988

Chambers, John Whiteclay II, *The Tyranny of Change: America in the Progressive Era, 1890–1920*, New York: St. Martin's Press, 1992

Cooper, John Milton, Jr., *The Pivotal Decades: The United States, 1900–1920*, New York: Norton, 1990

De Santis, Vincent P., *The Shaping of Modern America, 1877–1916*, Boston: Allyn and Bacon, 1973; 2nd edition, as *The Shaping of Modern America, 1877–1920*, Arlington Heights, IL: Forum Press, 1989

Ginger, Ray, *Age of Excess: The United States from 1877 to 1914*, New York: Macmillan, 1965

Gould, Lewis L., *The Progressive Era*, Syracuse, NY: Syracuse University Press, 1974

Hays, Samuel P., *Response to Industrialism, 1885–1914*, Chicago: University of Chicago Press, 1957

Hofstadter, Richard, *The Age of Reform: From Bryan to FDR*, New York: Knopf, 1955; London: Cape, 1962

Link, Arthur S. and Richard L. McCormick, *Progressivism*, Arlington Heights, IL: Harlan Davidson, 1983

Mann, Arthur (editor), *The Progressive Era: Liberal Renaissance or Liberal Failure?*, New York: Holt, Rinehart, 1963

Painter, Nell Irvin, *Standing at Armageddon: The United States, 1877–1919*, New York: Norton, 1987

Trachtenberg, Alan, *The Incorporation of America: Culture and Society in the Gilded Age*, New York: Hill and Wang, 1982

Wiebe, Robert H., *The Search for Order, 1877–1920*, New York: Hill and Wang, and London: Macmillan 1967

These terms of periodization, originated by contemporaries and utilized by most historians, encompass United States history from the end of Reconstruction in 1877 to American participation in World War I. Some historians have treated those years as a conceptual whole, characterized by the emergence of, and response to, the evolution of the United States as a modern, urban, industrial, multi-ethnic world power. Others have chosen to regard the era as two reasonably distinct periods, separated by the serious economic depression of 1893–97. The term "Gilded Age" was popularized by novelists Mark Twain and Charles Dudley Warner as a designation for a period in which the thin gilt of technological progress and exponential increases in wealth barely concealed vast inequality, the ruthless pursuit of profit, political corruption, conspicuous consumption, and vulgarity in taste and manners. The "Progressive Era" designation also originated with contemporaries who were energized by the possibilities for "progress" provided by technological and organizational advances, if they could be managed by science and reason, tempered by morality and humanism. Although historians have generally acquiesced in the usefulness of the Progressive Era as a periodization device, they have disagreed, profoundly and vigorously, over the period's duration, origins, nature, accomplishments, decline, and legacy.

The first significant attempt to interpret the entire period as a unit is GINGER, who divides it into three parts: first, 1877–93, characterized by rapid and massive industrialization; second, 1893–98, the time of depression and imperialism; and third, 1898–1914, the era of ultimately futile attempts to curb industrial capitalism and its consequences. He entitles the first period "wherein questions are posed", the second "wherein some questions are answered; others evaded", and the third, "wherein Americans go to live in the clouds." As befits the sympathetic biographer of Eugene V. Debs, Ginger finds the material progress of the period "awe-inspiring", but containing a "faulted core." The dynamic of mass production and consumption generated extravagant military expenditures, transmuted the traditional society of independent workers into a world of bureaucracy, and facilitated the capture of representative government and politics by corporations. The pursuit of wealth and social mobility for their own sakes destroyed traditional values, relationships and institutions, fostering changes so swift and so basic that "nobody could grasp more than a fraction of what was happening"

Equally pessimistic is TRACHTENBERG, who emphasizes the "emergence of a changed, more tightly structured society with new hierarchies of control", and the impact of that "incorporation of America" on "culture, on values and outlooks, on the way of life". He asserts that economic incorporation during the period "wrenched American society from the moorings of its familiar values", and that the process "proceeded by contradiction and conflict." In successive chapters, Trachtenberg deals with the impact of that process first upon the West, as land, natural resource and myth; second upon the machine as social metaphor; third on the growing gulf between capital and labor; fourth upon the "mystery" of city life; then on politics; and on literature; and finally upon the imagery of the "White City" at the Chicago World's Columbian Exposition of 1893. In Trachtenberg's view, the Gilded Age set in motion an ongoing conflict between the corporation's promise of unlimited material wealth and the reality of large-scale deprivation, a dichotomy which a century of reformers has failed to reconcile.

WIEBE concurs with both Ginger and Trachtenberg that the massive socioeconomic changes of the Gilded Age almost completely destroyed traditional values and institutions, leaving America "a society without a core", afflicted by "a general splintering process." Into this void, Wiebe postulates, stepped a "new middle class" of professionals, intellectuals, technicians and bureaucrats, who were dynamic and optimistic, and who sought to impose a new set of values, such as "continuity and regularity, functionality and regularity, administration and management" on a "distended society", in order to create a new social and moral order. Triumphant in the private sector by the turn of the century, this new middle class embraced "the need for a government of continuous involvement", one dominated by executives who planned, regulated, and administered nearly every aspect of life. "The Progressive moment", Wiebe concludes, "was the triumph of this new middle class with its bureaucratic mentality."

Diametrically opposed to Wiebe's interpretation is PAINTER. The truly dynamic force during the late 19th century, according to Painter, consisted of the groups most dislocated and disadvantaged by industrialization, urbanization and modernization: industrial workers, farmers, women, and racial and ethnic minorities. Between 1877 and 1897, those people who bore the brunt of "hard times" responded by organizing, demonstrating, striking and rioting, instilling deep and widespread fear among more comfortable Americans that class revolution and violent revolts would lead to an "Armageddon", which would bring down the entire system. This fear, in turn, motivated a sizable segment of the middle and upper classes to sponsor and support the myriad ameliorative reforms that characterized the Progressive Era. Throughout the entire period, Painter asserts, "different groups advocated conflicting interpretations of how society works", with one proclaiming the "persuasive idiom of prosperity" and the essential unity of interest among all Americans, and the other speaking "the equally positive language of democracy", which stressed equal access to life, liberty and property. Although Painter clearly concedes that "prosperity" emerged victorious, she insists that "democracy" won its share of victories and survived to continue the struggle.

Far less ideological than Ginger, Trachtenberg, Wiebe or Painter, DeSANTIS presents the entire period as the era that established "the foundations of modern America." DeSantis's book is a model of solid narrative history, informed by an impressive grasp of the best scholarship available, but contains a minimum of interpretation. It constitutes the best introduction to the entire period for anyone who wants to acquire a good working knowledge of the period's history before venturing into the interpretive thicket.

Drawing a road map through the topography of Progressive Era historiography is a truly daunting task. Those seeking to immerse themselves in that protean literature should begin by consulting BUENKER and BURCKEL, a selective, annotated bibliography of 1656 items, including books, journal articles and dissertations, organized around thirteen subject categories. Those desiring to familiarize themselves with the period's most important people, organizations, events, publications, and concepts should utilize the historical dictionary edited by BUENKER and KANTOWICZ.

The modern historiographical debate on the Progressive era began with the publication of HOFSTADTER. He was the first to stress the urban origins of progressive reform, challenging the prevailing view that it was essentially an outgrowth of the agrarian-based movements begun by the Grangers, Alliances and Populists. He locates the reformist impulse precisely in the "old middle class" of intellectuals, ministers and civic leaders, who responded to a "status revolution" wrought by industrialization, urbanization, modernization and immigration. Caught between the voracious upper classes of industrialists and financiers, on the one hand, and the restive, militant lower classes, on the other, the old middle class embraced a reform agenda in an energetic effort to reclaim their declining status. Fatally flawed in motivation and conception, and essentially defensive and reactive in nature, Hofstadter contends, progressivism failed to survive World War I and enjoyed little or no continuity with "the new departure" and the "new opportunism" of the New Deal. Testing the validity of the status revolution thesis, and challenging its assumptions and conclusions, set the agenda for an entire generation of scholars.

Less celebrated at the time, but more lasting in influence, is HAYS. Although he makes no mention of Hofstadter's work, his interpretation directly challenges the status revolution thesis by interpreting the Progressive Era as a broad-based response, on the part of people from many walks of life, to the dislocations engendered by industrialism, urbanism, sectionalism, modernism and imperialism. The social, economic and political movements of those thirty years, Hays argues, constituted a reaction "against industrialism and the many ways in which it affected the lives of Americans", and an attempt "to cope with industrial change in all its ramifications". By clearly identifying the complexity, diversity, and sometimes internally contradictory nature of Progressive Era reform, Hays provides a potential framework for the inclusion of most other interpretations.

By the mid-1970s, the debate over the Progressive Era had produced a variety of conflicting interpretations and several attempts at synthesis. MANN's anthology provides a wide spectrum of interpretations by sixteen prominent historians, beginning with an excerpt from DeWitt's *Progressive Movement*. Mann's anthology includes essays on the origins of progressivism by George E. Mowry, Michael P. Rogin and John L. Shover, and David P. Thelen, on economic regulation by G. Cullom Davis and Gabriel Kolko, on political reform by Hays and Buenker, on welfare by James Weinstein and Robert L. Buroker, on race by Nancy J. Weiss and Gilbert Osofsky, and on World War I and its aftermath by Hofstadter, Allen F. Davis, Arthur S. Link, and Mann himself. The editor provides an incisive introduction which places the various essays in an understandable context.

GOULD seeks the same goal through the device of original, interpretive essays by eight prominent scholars. He himself supplies an insightful and integrative introduction, as well as an essay on the evolution of the Republican party during the Progressive years. He also includes essays by Stanley P. Caine on the origins of progressivism, by R. Laurence Moore on progressive thought, by John J. Broesamle on the Democratic party, by James Penick, Jr. on the conservation movement, by Melvin G. Holli on urban reform, by Wilton G. Fowler on diplomacy, and by Thomas K. McCraw on the progressive legacy. Each essay is replete with historiographical information, as well as with synthesis and interpretive analysis.

More directly confrontational is BUENKER, BURNHAM and CRUNDEN. Each author not only provides his own synthesis of the existing literature and his own interpretive framework, but also contributes a specific rejoinder to the essays of his two collaborators. Generally speaking, Burnham and Crunden each set forth their own arguments in favor of the proposition that there was a reasonably unified "progressive movement" and a reasonably coherent body of thought deserving the designation "progressivism". Buenker stresses the complexity and diversity of the reformist impulse, the tendency for different groups to support the same measure for different, or even conflicting reasons, and the need for groups to form "shifting coalitions" around specific issues.

During the 1980s, several scholars produced new syntheses that attempted to incorporate many of the insights gained from the vast outpouring of Progressive Era studies during the previous quarter century. Much the best brief synthesis is LINK and McCORMICK, which packs an incredible amount of information and interpretation into 120 pages of text. Link and McCormick, both distinguished Progressive Era historians in their own right, succeed in striking a delicate and rational balance between the era's often bewildering complexity of groups, motives and programs, and the common characteristics infused in the period's myriad reform efforts. After a perceptive discussion of the identity, origins, character and spirit of "progressives" and "progressivism", Link and McCormick provide a highly persuasive interpretive analysis of the transformation of politics and government, the interaction between social justice and social control, and the decline and endurance of progressivism. They conclude that "the essence of progressivism lay in the hopefulness and optimism which the reformers brought to the tasks of applying science and administration to the high moral purposes in which they believed."

CHAMBERS offers a more highly interpretive and considerably more detailed synthesis of the impressive outpouring of scholarship which appeared in the previous two decades. He stresses the variegated nature of Progressive Era reform efforts in response to the bewildering changes wrought during the Gilded Age. He contends that rapid, widespread socioeconomic alterations spawned a "new interventionism", in which newly organized segments of society abandoned their faith in the workings of impersonal, immutable natural laws and embraced the practice of purposeful management according to the tenets of science and morality. Chambers also documents the growing importance of government as an instrument of interventionism, as well as the application of the "new interventionism" to international relations.

COOPER is the most recent effort to provide a comprehensive synthesis of the Progressive Era. A renowned interpreter of Theodore Roosevelt and Woodrow Wilson, Cooper views the first two decades of this century as a period in which "a political, economic, social and cultural agenda was set that still dominates American life as we enter the century's final decade." He pronounces it "a second golden age of American politics – second only to the generation of the founders of the American republic." Significantly, Cooper almost completely eschews any description of the period as "the Progressive Era", and asserts that "his aim has been to construct a comprehensive narrative and not to argue an overreaching interpretation of the period." Whether this represents a growing consensus to forgo the frequently contentious ideological and interpretive debates which have characterized Progressive Era historiography for the past forty years remains to be seen.

JOHN D. BUENKER

See also Progressivism

Gilman, Charlotte Perkins   1860–1935

Feminist and social critic

Allen, Polly Wynn, *Building Domestic Liberty: Charlotte Perkins Gilman's Architectural Feminism*, Amherst: University of Massachusetts Press, 1988

Degler, Carl N., "Charlotte Perkins Gilman on the Theory and Practice of Feminism," *American Quarterly*, 8, Spring 1956

Hill, Mary A., *Charlotte Perkins Gilman: The Making of a Radical Feminist, 1860–1896*, Philadelphia: Temple University Press, 1980

Karpinski, Joanne B. (editor), *Critical Essays on Charlotte Perkins Gilman*, New York: G.K. Hall, 1992

Kessler, Carol Farley, *Charlotte Perkins Gilman: Her Progress Toward Utopia, with Selected Writings*, Syracuse, NY: Syracuse University Press, 1995

Lane, Ann J., *To "Herland" and Beyond: The Life and Work of Charlotte Perkins Gilman*, New York: Pantheon, 1990

Meyering, Sheryl L. (editor), *Charlotte Perkins Gilman: The Woman and Her Work*, Ann Arbor, MI: UMI Research Press, 1989

Scharnhorst, Gary, *Charlotte Perkins Gilman*, Boston: Twayne, 1985

Charlotte Perkins Gilman, a member of the culturally influential Beecher family, was one of the leading thinkers and writers on the social condition of women in the late 19th century. Gilman's social and economic analyses have earned her the designation of "feminist," a term which she herself rejected in favor of "humanist." She is best known for her important book *Women and Economics* (1898) and for her chilling short story "The Yellow Wallpaper" (1892). In addition to her fictional and utopian writings, she was a prolific author of works on history, sociology, and ethics. Her attempts to reconcile her intellectual beliefs about the role of women in society with her own private life have made her an attractive subject for feminist and literary scholars.

Gilman's reputation stood very high in her own lifetime, but declined considerably thereafter until the modern women's movement revived interest in her work; all her major works have now been reprinted. Critical attention has largely focused on Gilman's well-known works, and has been characterised by a dominant tendency towards biographical criticism, while critical analyses of the formal and strategic properties of her work have been rare.

DEGLER's article was the first critical assessment of Gilman to be published after her death in 1935, and marked the beginning of the rediscovery of Gilman as an important turn-of-the-century American writer. The article is an appreciative overview of her main ideas, and acts as a valuable introduction to her work. While keen to promote the value of Gilman's contribution, Degler also analyzes some inconsistent elements in her thinking. He describes some contradictions in the relation between theory and practice in her work as follows:

> Her freedom from preconceptions and traditions allowed her to make fresh and often penetrating examinations of the human institutions around her. But that same attitude of mind prevented her from appreciating the tenacious hold which prejudice, tradition and sentiment had upon most of the men and women she was trying to convince. Hence when she came to offer means to attain goals she set, her rationalism and radicalism, so incisive in analysis, merely served to vitiate her realism.

Degler's focus is very much on Gilman's work rather than her life – a perspective which is passed over by most ensuing Gilman scholars.

SCHARNHORST is an account of Gilman through her literature, and is an indispensable contribution to the study of her work. Scharnhorst provides a useful chronology at the start of the book, and although choosing not to focus on her private life, shows Gilman's writing as vital and relevant to the society in which it was written and to which it is addressed.

KESSLER centers her study on Gilman's utopian writings, which she argues still have relevance for women today. Analyzing Gilman within the framework of cultural studies, Kessler combines literary criticism with the text of some of Gilman's shorter works, and also includes a solid biographical chapter. ALLEN focuses on Gilman's attempt to abolish women's subordinate status by restructuring traditional housework through a "socialized neighborhood architecture" in order to ease the double duty faced by many women who worked for wages and performed housekeeping duties. Her analysis ties Gilman to material feminism and to the progressive movement.

HILL concentrates on Gilman's attempt to reconcile her career with her private life. This biography, which covers Gilman's life through 1896, makes extensive use of correspondence from the Gilman collection at the Schlesinger

Library, including letters from Gilman to her first and second husbands. She discusses Gilman's relationship with her parents, her female friends, and other important characters, and analyzes the relationship between her life and her work. Hill proposes that Gilman's early struggle for independence, self-assertion, and self-respect provided the groundwork for her later radical feminism; her views are detailed, thoughtful, and highly informative.

LANE, following in the dominant bio-critical tradition of Gilman scholarship, presents Gilman's work in relation to and against the backdrop of her life. She analyzes Gilman's personal life and its development, and as such the book is structured around her central relationships: with her father and mother, with her three intimate women friends, with her two husbands, with the neurologist who treated her, and with her only daughter Katharine. This is a significant work not only because of its comprehensive account of Gilman's life and work, but also because it is an example of the standard scholastic approach to Gilman, in terms of its emphasis on the influence of Gilman's heterosexual relationships (rather than that of her relationships with women); in its use of the public-private conflict as the analytical framework for Gilman's life and work; and in its neglect of the formal and aesthetic aspects of Gilman's writings. Overall, the book, which is the first part of a projected two-volume biography, is comprehensive, lively, and accessible.

Karpinski and Meyering have both edited collections of scholarly articles about Gilman and her work. KARPINSKI includes a useful introduction written by Carol Ruth Berkin, and the book is divided between contemporary and modern criticism of Gilman's work. MEYERING's collection was the first edition of critical essays on Gilman, and aims to "do justice to the enormous range and amount of imaginative work Gilman left us. Each article maps a way for readers to approach such a large body of fiction and poetry." Meyering begins her collection with a reprint of Degler's pioneering article, followed by Mary A. Hill's insightful "Charlotte Perkins Gilman: A Feminist's Struggle with Womanhood." While "The Yellow Wallpaper" and *Herland* are well covered, there are also articles on Gilman's verse, on her connections with Walt Whitman, and her novel *What Diantha Did*. Christopher R. Wilson's analysis of *Herland*'s literary devices and its implicit commentary on art, gender, and property is noteworthy: Wilson shows how Gilman's attempts to challenge what she saw as a bourgeois and masculine aesthetic often produces an elusive and paradoxical outcome.

THERESA KAMINSKI

See also Feminism

Gold Rushes

Fahey, John, *Hecla: A Century of Western Mining*, Seattle: University of Washington Press, 1990

Greever, William S., *The Bonanza West: The Story of Western Mining Rushes, 1848–1900*, Norman: University of Oklahoma Press, 1963

Holliday, J.S., *The World Rushed in: The California Gold Rush Experience*, New York: Simon and Schuster, 1981; London: Gollancz, 1983

Kelley, Robert L., *Gold v. Grain: The Hydraulic Mining Controversy in California's Sacramento Valley: A Chapter in the Decline of the Concept of Laissez Faire*, Glendale, CA: Arthur Clark, 1959

King, Joseph E., *A Mine to Make a Mine: Financing the Colorado Mining Industry, 1859–1902*, College Station: Texas A & M University Press, 1977

Parker, Watson, *Gold in the Black Hills*, Norman: University of Oklahoma Press, 1982

Paul, Rodman, *Mining Frontiers of the Far West, 1848–1880*, New York: Holt, Rinehart, 1963

Smith, Duane A., *Mining America: The Industry and the Environment, 1800–1980*, Lawrence: University Press of Kansas, 1987

Spence, Clark C., *British Investments and the American Mining Frontier, 1860–1901*, Ithaca, NY: Cornell University Press, 1958

Unruh, John D., Jr., *The Plains Across: The Overland Emigrants and the Trans-Mississippi West, 1840–1860*, Urbana: University of Illinois Press, 1979

PAUL remains the best general survey of the gold and other mineral rushes, but is limited to the period 1848 to 1880. The rushes to California, Colorado, the Dakotas and Nevada are given particular treatment. There is also a very useful account of the technologies used in the gold and other mines, understandably since the author was a member of the faculty of the California Institute of Technology. The rushes are generally interpreted as occurring in the context of a developing industrialism, which governed the world in which the miners moved, especially influencing relations between capital and labour. As one of a series of studies of America's frontiers, the work has to take Frederick Jackson Turner's frontier thesis as its point of departure, but it argues that the rushes disrupted the regular pattern of frontier settlement rather than fitting into the Turnerian frame.

GREEVER covers a longer period, extending into the 20th century. At once a more detailed and less analytic work than Paul, it is based on a wide reading in secondary sources, and is deliberately aimed at the general reader. It also covers the rush to the Klondike. The author came from a generation not interested in questions of gender, ethnicity or race, but he does provide a well-paced and wide-ranging narrative. PARKER is open to the same qualification. Originally published in 1966, the book now seems old-fashioned in tone, celebratory rather than critical, and lacking an overall analytic frame. It is, however, based on extensive knowledge of the primary sources and provides a good introduction to one gold rush.

Holliday and Unruh each describe the way in which the gold-seekers reached the Californian mines by the overland route, which the majority took. HOLLIDAY is unusual in being constructed around the diary and letters of a single gold-seeker, William Swain, who left Youngstown, New York, in April 1849 to go to California. The addition of hundreds of excerpts from the diaries and letters of other Argonauts, however, helps to make this seem an account of the typical gold-seeker. Holliday is much helped by the fact that Swain had a keen eye for detail and wrote very expressively. As his story makes clear, the vast majority of those participating in the gold rushes were to return east disappointed, for few found gold easily and the great majority lacked the capital necessary to work underground gold deposits. UNRUH puts the story of the overland migration into a perspective of twenty years, offering a clear picture of the problems faced in reaching the gold fields.

By and large only the very earliest arrivals found gold easily. Later arrivals were forced into wage labour, usually working for absentee mine-owners. SPENCE gives an excellent account, based on work in British sources, of the way in which British capital was attracted to American mines. His coverage of investments in Colorado mines is particularly thorough. FAHEY is useful in showing how Ohio, Illinois and Minnesota capitalists financed an Idaho mining company. Although the Hecla mine produced mainly lead and silver, Fahey's discussion of its history over more than a century reveals much about the world of corporate management which quickly came to structure the society into which gold-seekers moved. KING looks at the way in which the Colorado mines were financed, and suggests that many capitalists as well as many miners failed to realise expectations in the gold rushes.

Two works deal with the impact of the rushes on the environment. KELLEY is not primarily concerned with environmental damage but his discussion of the struggle between landowners and mine-owners and the attempt of the former to curtail the hydraulic mining of the latter, shows how mining debris was harmfully affecting the lower Sacramento Valley by the late 1850s. Here the results of the gold rush may have been unexpected but they went equally uncontrolled. SMITH shows that, apart from the controversy over hydraulic mining, there was little discussion before the 1960s of the environmental impact of the rushes and the subsequent development of mining industries. Argonauts who largely intended to return east with their "pile" were as uninterested as any in the long-term effects of their mining activities.

Few who participated in the gold rushes expected their outcomes, especially the early development of wage labour and the concomitant, if slightly later, emergence of labour unions, both suggesting limits to the acquisitive individualism which drove miners to participate in the rushes in the first place. But as Fahey, Holliday and Paul in particular show, the rushes helped bring about that highly capitalized, market-oriented American West which was to emerge within a decade of the first gold rush to California in 1848–49, and to endure thereafter.

R.A. BURCHELL

Goldman, Emma 1869-1940
Anarchist and feminist

Avrich, Paul, *Anarchist Voices: An Oral History of Anarchism in America*, Princeton: Princeton University Press, 1995

Drinnon, Richard, *Rebel in Paradise: A Biography of Emma Goldman*, Chicago: University of Chicago Press, 1961

Falk, Candace, *Love, Anarchy, and Emma Goldman*, New York: Holt Rinehart, 1984

Haaland, Bonnie, *Emma Goldman: Sexuality and the Impurity of the State*, New York: Black Rose, 1993

Morton, Marian J., *Emma Goldman and the American Left*, Boston: Twayne, 1992

Shulman, Alix Kates (editor), *Red Emma Speaks: Selected Writings and Speeches by Emma Goldman*, New York: Random House, 1972

Solomon, Martha, *Emma Goldman*, Boston: Twayne, 1987

Waldstreicher, David, *Emma Goldman*, New York: Chelsea House, 1990

Wexler, Alice, *Emma Goldman: An Intimate Life*, New York: Pantheon, and London: Virago, 1984

Wexler, Alice, *Emma Goldman in Exile: From the Russian Revolution to the Spanish Civil War*, Boston: Beacon Press, 1989

Any discussion of American labor and political dissent is incomplete without mention of international anarchist Emma Goldman. During her three decades of activism in the United States, Goldman and her associate Alexander Berkman became possibly the most notable anarchists in American history. A controversial figure long before her deportation from the United States in 1919, Goldman remains at the center of debate over class strife, workers' rights, and anarchism. Thus, although the late 19th and early 20th century American public harbored a general dislike for Goldman, she has been the subject of intense study, inspiring a number of high quality biographies as well as books about her political beliefs and activism.

Among the best early biographies of Goldman was DRINNON. Although he admits at the outset that he is sympathetic to Goldman, his book is analytically insightful and even-handed. The longevity of Drinnon's work attests to its quality. First published over three decades ago, the book is still in print today. Concentrating on Goldman's professional life, but including some information on her family and childhood as well, Drinnon's volume would be of interest to the reader seeking a complete and non-judgmental assessment of Goldman's career.

Complementing Drinnon's work is FALK, who tells a fascinating story of Goldman's private life. Relying on long hidden private letters written by Goldman, Falk exposes the amorous but stormy relationship between Goldman and her professional associate Dr. Ben Reitman, a Chicago gynaecologist. Falk's happenstance discovery of the cache of letters on which she based her book inspired her to seek out former colleagues of Goldman. With their eventual blessing and assistance, she has reconstructed the details of a dynamic social reformer's love life in a volume that reads as much like a romance novel as a history.

Building on both Falk and Drinnon, WEXLER (1984) brings together the scholarship of her predecessors, and adds further information on both Goldman's private and public lives. This is a substantial and comprehensive piece of work, which deals with her personality, her career and her writings in a well-rounded account. WEXLER (1989) is a more specialized study, which focuses on Goldman's life and work after she was deported from the United States. The book gives an in-depth description of Goldman's work in Europe and her activities relating to the Spanish Civil War. Thus it covers an area of Emma Goldman's life that is often overlooked by American biographers.

Readers seeking a briefer biography of Goldman should find that SOLOMON meets their needs. She condenses the work of Falk, Drinnon, and others into a concise volume and also includes a useful bibliography of both primary and secondary material about Goldman and the causes which she espoused. WALDSTREICHER also provides a readable, interesting, short biography of Goldman, which includes a number of excellent photographs of Goldman and her colleagues. This is another good starting-point for readers not already familiar with Goldman and her activities.

MORTON concentrates on Goldman's political activities. A volume in Twayne's Twentieth Century American Biography series, this compact text offers a clear and compelling account of Goldman, anarchism, and the American left in this period. After a succinct explanation and history of anarchism, it traces the story of Goldman and her emergence as a political leader of the American left, and concludes with a bibliographic essay that describes materials relating to all aspects of the topic.

Also focusing on Goldman's public life and writings is HAALAND, who examines Goldman's advocacy of living an "emancipated" life through the unbounded expression of personal "instincts." Haaland discusses these ideas as they relate to modern feminist theories, especially concepts of sexual liberation. Her book is, therefore, much more analytical and theoretical than the conventional biographies. It is the most important study of Goldman's ideas insofar as they relate to modern feminist thought.

Shulman and Avrich introduce a variety of primary materials relating to Goldman. AVRICH includes transcripts of more than two hundred interviews conducted with anarchist leaders, or others related to the anarchist movement. One entire chapter of his book, which includes extensive explicatory comments, is devoted to interviews with colleagues of Goldman. Both Avrich's introduction to this chapter and the comments of the interviewees offer a unique perspective. SHULMAN focuses on Goldman's own writings. Although she provides only limited commentary and background information, she does bring together Goldman's disparate writings, organizing them into subject headings that make them more accessible to the reader. By letting Emma Goldman speak for herself, she conveys some sense of the ideas of an intriguing and important international figure

EMILY WALKER COOK

Gompers, Samuel 1850–1924
Labor leader

Dick, William M., *Labor and Socialism in America: The Gompers Era*, Port Washington, NY: Kennikat Press, 1972

Harvey, Rowland H., *Samuel Gompers, Champion of the Toiling Masses* , Stanford, CA: Stanford University Press, 1935

Kaufman, Stuart Bruce, *Samuel Gompers and the Origins of the American Federation of Labor, 1848–1896*, Westport, CT: Greenwood Press, 1973

Laslett, John H.M., "Samuel Gompers and the Rise of American Business Unionism," in *Labor Leaders in America*, edited by Melvyn Dubofsky and Warren Van Tine, Urbana: University of Illinois Press, 1987

Livesay, Harold C., *Samuel Gompers and Organized Labor in America*, Boston: Little, Brown, 1978

Mandel, Bernard, *Samuel Gompers: A Biography*, Yellow Springs, OH: Antioch Press, 1963

Thorne, Florence C., *Samuel Gompers, American Statesman*, New York: Philosophical Library, 1957

While Samuel Gompers is universally acknowledged as the single most important figure in the American labor movement during the critical years of the late 19th and early 20th centuries, there has been little agreement on his legacy since his death in 1924. Until recently, scholarly interpretations fluctuated between extremes: to some he was a prophet who accurately diagnosed the nature of the American working class and created a "pragmatic" movement – the American Federation of Labor (AFL) – that improved the lives of millions; to others he was little more than a sellout who, enticed by power and fame, abandoned the socialism of his youth, betrayed the interests of the working class, and constructed a movement that all but excluded the unskilled, women, and racial minorities.

Among those in the first camp is THORNE, his one-time research assistant, whose biography is valuable as a glowing example of the art of hagiography and a demonstration of Gompers's charismatic hold over his underlings. Thorne was more concerned with her boss's enduring image than with historical accuracy. More sophisticated is HARVEY, but this work is flawed because the author lacked access to all of Gompers's private papers. Although written in colorful prose and full of interesting anecdotes, the book does little to explain the motivation of the man or the dynamics of his era. By far the best hero-biography is LIVESAY, a short study which at least mentions Gompers's faults while chronicling his numerous achievements. Livesay is adept at belaboring the obvious: in an age when business practices went largely unchecked by government regulation, and when working people struggled against both capital and the state to create their own means of protecting their rights and interests, Gompers cultivated ideas and created an institution to safeguard at least a portion of the working class. While many organizations were set up at this time to champion the cause of workers, the AFL was the only one that withstood the test of time.

Of Gompers's numerous detractors, the only one to write a full-length biography is MANDEL. This is also the first attempt to provide a truly comprehensive portrait of both the man and the leader, and the first study based on a thorough examination of Gompers's letters and speeches, and all published material pertaining to the AFL. It is above all a relentless condemnation of Gompers for his knee-jerk opposition to socialism, political action, and industrial unionism. Mandel faults Gompers for pandering to business leaders, for failing to support militant activity during the Pullman strike and other key struggles, and for refusing to challenge the segregationist policies of individual unions. While Mandel, at points, tends to oversimplify the issues, to portray the labor struggle exclusively as "good guys" versus "bad guys," this biography is still a highly useful account of Gompers's public and private life.

More recent analyses attempt to transcend the praise-or-scorn dichotomy by exploring the work culture that gave rise to his early radicalism, the shift in his outlook in the 1890s, and the myriad economic and political forces that led him to jettison notions of working-class unity and embrace a narrow vision of trade unionism for skilled workers only. In one slim volume, DICK provides a cogent interpretation of Gompers's career, the relationship between socialists and the labor movement, and the evolving trade union philosophy of the mainstream American Federation of Labor. The narrative that holds these themes together is the enmity between Gompers and socialists that began in the 1890s and burned at a fever pitch until his death. Dick suggests that Gompers's departure from the socialism of his youth did not lead him to embrace capitalism (and therefore hatred of the socialists), but rather to syndicalism. Believing that the government was firmly under the control of large corporations and Wall Street financiers, Gompers had even less faith in the American political system than his socialist opponents. Gompers pegged his hopes on the economic muscle of labor to win concessions through strikes and collective bargaining. This book was one of the first to explore in depth the transition of Gompers's thought in the 1890s, and it remains a useful overview of the Gompers era.

An indispensable study of Gompers's early radicalism and his transition in the 1890s is KAUFMAN. The author is both scholar-in-residence at the AFL-CIO archives and editor of *The Samuel Gompers Papers* (several volumes of which have already been published by the University of Illinois Press, with more to follow). Based on painstaking research in a wide variety of sources, this book chronicles Gompers's intellectual development from his years as an immigrant apprentice in the cigar shops of New York City, where he first encountered Marxism, to his maturity in the 1890s. Above all Kaufman demonstrates that Gompers never completely abandoned Marxist ideas, and that from the 1870s onward he was consistently attempting to apply the Marxist tradition to what he perceived to be the special industrial conditions of the U.S. By the 1890s Gompers had become convinced that class struggle in America must take place in the economic and not the political arena.

While there is no modern, sophisticated biography of the man and the leader, the closest approximation is LASLETT. This thirty-page essay provides a succinct analysis of Gompers's intellectual influences and the emergence of a narrow craft union outlook in the United States. The late 1880s struggle between cigar makers in the reform-minded Knights of Labor and the "pure and simple" Cigar Makers International Union, Laslett contends, was the key episode that led Gompers away from socialism and inclusive unionism.

CRAIG PHELAN

See also American Federation of Labor

Government and the Economy: Promotion and Regulation

Goodrich, Carter, *Government Promotion of American Canals and Railroads, 1800–1890*, New York: Columbia University Press, 1960

Gunn, L. Ray, *The Decline of Authority: Public Economic Policy and Political Development in New York, 1800–1860*, Ithaca, NY: Cornell University Press, 1988

Handlin, Oscar and Mary Flug Handlin, *Commonwealth: A Study of the Role of Government in the American Economy: Massachusetts, 1774–1861*, revised edition, Cambridge, MA: Belknap Press of Harvard University Press, 1969

Hartz, Louis, *Economic Policy and Democratic Thought: Pennsylvania, 1776–1860*, Cambridge, MA: Harvard University Press, 1948

Hawley, Ellis W., *The New Deal and the Problem of Monopoly: A Study in Economic Ambivalence*, Princeton: Princeton University Press, 1966

Hurst, James Willard, *Law and the Conditions of Freedom in the Nineteenth-Century United States*, Madison: University of Wisconsin Press, 1956

Keller, Morton, *Regulating a New Economy: Public Policy and Economic Change in America, 1900–1933*, Cambridge, MA: Harvard University Press, 1990

McCormick, Richard L., *The Party Period and Public Politics: American Policy from the Age of Jackson to the Progressive Era*, New York: Oxford University Press, 1986

McCraw, Thomas K. (editor), *Regulation in Perspective: Historical Essays*, Cambridge, MA: Harvard University Press, 1981

McCraw, Thomas K., *Prophets of Regulation: Charles Francis Adams, Louis D. Brandeis, James M. Landis, Alfred E. Kahn*, Cambridge, MA: Belknap Press of Harvard University Press, 1984

Scheiber, Harry N., *Ohio Canal Era: A Case Study of Government and the Economy, 1820–1861*, Athens: Ohio University Press, 1969; with new preface, 1987

Skowronek, Stephen, *Building a New American State: The Expansion of National Administrative Capacities, 1877–1920*, Cambridge and New York: Cambridge University Press, 1982

Young, James Harvey, *Pure Food: Securing the Federal Food and Drugs Act of 1906*, Princeton: Princeton University Press, 1989

Although it is unwise to draw too categorical a distinction between a 19th-century regime of government promotion of business activity and a 20th-century regime of regulation and control, there is no doubt that the overall complexion of government intervention changed markedly around the turn of the century. That American government policy was never wholeheartedly devoted to the principle of laissez-faire is clearly shown by HURST. The author, a legal historian, reveals with admirable brevity and lucidity how the pattern of 19th-century American lawmaking, in courts as much as in legislatures, was committed to the release of entrepreneurial energy and the freeing of resources for economic development. He also shows how the rise of big business, the development of a more integrated economy and the growth of an urban society encouraged a greater degree of calculation and control in the last quarter of the century. This short analytical study offers a useful and stimulating overview of the relationship between law and the economy during the 19th century.

The 1940s and 1950s saw a profusion of monographic studies of economic policy in the states, all of which demonstrated how varied and extensive public support for economic development was during the 19th century. HANDLIN and HARTZ are two of the more ambitious and influential of these works. Perhaps, in their determination to explode the "laissez faire cliché," they overstate the extent of government support for enterprise, focusing as they do on ideas about political economy rather than actual practice, and they are too ready to accept that laissez-faire principles took command after mid-century, if not before. Nevertheless, these are imaginative and stimulating studies which have contributed greatly to our present understanding of 19th-century economic policy.

GUNN's study of New York is the outstanding recent contribution to the analysis of state promotion of economic development. Until the 1830s, an essentially distributive policy of subsidy and regulation had generally prevailed, but eventually the public authority which had helped to create an expanding market came to be regarded as the chief hindrance to its smooth operation. Gunn identifies a major transformation in the structure and function of state government around the mid-19th century. Government authority declined, as the state withdrew from interventionist economic policies, and a new state constitution prohibited most promotional activities. New York, he argues, exemplified wider trends towards political democratization on the one hand, and the removal of large areas of social and economic life from the reach of democratic power on the other.

Transportation was one of the principal areas of government promotional activity, at both the federal and the state level, during the 19th century. GOODRICH summarises the findings of a large number of monographic studies of the government promotion of canals and railroads, culminating in the grandiose federal railroad subsidies of the Civil War era. Goodrich shows, among other things, how extensive public support for government investment in transportation was, virtually throughout the century, and how large a proportion of the funds for canal and railroad-building was drawn from the public sector. A very useful case study of public support at the state level for improvements in transportation may be found in SCHEIBER's account of the Ohio canal system. The ambitious programe of public enterprise in Ohio was eventually weakened by the pressure of conflicting local interests within the state, and then overtaken by the development of the railroads.

McCORMICK is a collection of essays and articles on the history of political parties and governance since the Jacksonian Era. It includes in particular an influential article which relates the promotional, or "distributive," policies of the 19th century to the structure of party politics, and a later essay which explains the surge of regulatory legislation after 1905 as the aftershock of a series of revelations of the corrupting effect of business influence on politics. Other essays examine the growth of regulation in the context of the politics of the Progressive Era.

The development of regulatory policy in the Progressive Era, specifically railroad regulation, is one of the aspects of state-building studied in SKOWRONEK. The author, a political scientist, demonstrates how early attempts at regulation were hampered by a lack of administrative capacity, a deficiency which was only partially overcome by later legislation. Here, too, changes in economic policy are placed firmly in the context of changes in political institutions.

KELLER provides a full conspectus of government regulatory activity, state as well as federal, during the first thirty years of this century. It is a remarkable repository of information about almost every conceivable aspect of economic policy, made all the more valuable by recurrent reference to the experience of comparable industrial nations, particularly Britain and Germany. The reader is immersed in details of legislation and court cases, at the expense of general explanations, which the author carefully avoids. Instead he sees policy as shaped by persistence and pluralism: the influence of pre-existing values and institutions and the interplay of a complex array of competing ideals and interests. Surprisingly, the account terminates in 1932, on the eve of the New Deal.

Keller is one of the contributors to McCRAW (1981). His essay anticipates many of the themes of his later book. The other contributions are a stimulating case-study by Ellis Hawley of Herbert Hoover's "associationalist" approach to government-business relations during the 1920s; a study by Vogel of the "new regulation" of the 1960s and 1970s, which was designed to protect the interests of consumers and the environment, rather than those of competing economic interest groups, as in earlier periods of regulatory activity; a critique by Thomas McCraw of Louis Brandeis's flawed comprehension of the economics of antitrust; and a more abstract discussion by Samuel P. Hays. McCRAW (1984) uses the careers of its four subjects as points of departure for an analysis of the development of regulatory ideas and practice, and the conditions under which they operated most effectively. Successful regulators, McCraw argues, were those, like Adams or Landis, who adapted to economic realities rather than seeking, like Brandeis, to impose inappropriate ideas upon them. Though too tightly locked into a consideration of the economic, rather than the political and social, dimensions of regulation, this is still perhaps the most informative general study of the history of regulation.

Several more detailed studies of federal promotion and regulation are discussed elsewhere in this book, particularly in the various entries on progressivism and the New Deal. However, two excellent examples may be noted here. YOUNG is a fascinating study of the politics of pure food which also presents a balanced and considered analysis of the many factors contributing to regulatory legislation in the Progressive Era. HAWLEY is a thorough and clearly-articulated examination of the New Deal's shifting relationship with the business community. Both are models of their kind.

ROBERT HARRISON

See also Antitrust Legislation and Court Cases, 1880s–1920s; Internal Improvements; Railroads: Legislation and Court Cases; Rivers and Canals

Graham, Billy 1918–

Evangelist

Frady, Marshall, *Billy Graham: A Parable of American Righteousness*, Boston: Little Brown, and London: Hodder and Stoughton, 1979

High, Stanley, *Billy Graham: The Personal Story of the Man, His Message, and His Mission*, New York: McGraw Hill, 1956; Kingswood, Surrey: World's Work, 1957

McLoughlin, William G., *Billy Graham: Revivalist in a Secular Age*, New York: Ronald Press, 1960

Martin, William, *A Prophet with Honor: The Billy Graham Story*, New York: Morrow, 1991; London: Hutchinson, 1992

Pollock, John, *Billy Graham: The Authorized Biography*, New York: McGraw Hill, and London: Hodder and Stoughton, 1966

Pollock, John, *Billy Graham: Evangelist to the World*, San Francisco: Harper, 1979

Pollock, John, *To All The Nations: The Billy Graham Story*, San Francisco: Harper, 1985

Billy Graham's life as evangelist and national Christian leader in the post-World War II period has inspired a lively and quite diverse group of biographies. Some are the work of insiders who see Graham as a heroic figure, while to others he exemplifies some of the worst sides of modern America.

HIGH is an admirer of Graham, and his book, published only seven years after Graham became a national figure at a Los Angeles revival meeting in 1949, shows clear signs of the work of an insider. Nonetheless, it introduces themes for subsequent scholarship. It argues that Graham was far more significant as a powerful revival preacher than as a religious thinker, that he owed his basic religious outlook to a southern evangelical tradition which stressed the centrality of conversion, the spoken word, and revivalism, and that Graham made extraordinary use of the modern media. High also stresses that Graham maintained a high standard of propriety in his personal and economic life and thus avoided the mistakes that have scarred the reputations of many evangelists.

A much more academic and less positive analysis is provided by McLOUGHLIN, the leading historian of the American revival tradition. He deftly shows how Graham fits into a long history of American religious leaders who claimed that the nation had a special religious mission which it could only uphold with a religious renewal. Such changes occurred, he argues, in times of shifts in Protestant theology. He describes the events of post-World War II America as a fourth American revival, following those of the mid-1700s, the early 1800s, and the Social Gospel movement, that stressed the role of mankind in helping to establish the Kingdom of God. Graham was part of a fundamentalist movement which alleged that the Social Gospel movement had denied the basic sinfulness of humanity and the literal truth of the Bible. His generation faced numerous issues in the 1930s and 1940s that suggested the imperfectibility of humanity and the apparent falsehood of the idea of a heaven on earth. Graham stressed the need for personal conversion and a regeneration of society which would involve personal morality, hard work, and traditional gender roles.

McLoughlin's harshest criticism is that Graham's message of conversion is too simple to allow people to cope successfully with difficult issues of either theology or social ethics.

In three volumes, POLLOCK (1966, 1979, 1985) has produced the authorized and extremely positive account of Graham's life. These have the strength of a wealth of details that come with access to Graham's papers, but they have the weakness of claiming that the career of the evangelist has been an almost unchallenged success story. Pollock argues that Graham's greatest achievement has been his ability to provide the inspiration for millions of people throughout the world to have conversion experiences. Graham's use of mass media and his extensive preparation of crusade locations are successful means of spreading his message. Rather than seeing Graham as fundamentally conservative, Pollock argues that the crusades helped to overcome social conflict by bringing together groups, both in the United States and throughout the world, that had long been enemies. A conference of evangelicals in Lausanne, Switzerland in 1974 is seen as one of the most important signs of the growing world-wide importance of Graham and his message.

Applying some of the arguments of McLoughlin to a post-Watergate America, FRADY interprets Graham as an example of the tragic consequences of American innocence. Critical and often harsh, it argues that Graham's insistence on the conversion of individuals makes religion too easy, offers no critique of basic power relations in society, and substitutes respectability for any other moral goal. The first to describe Graham's boyhood in detail, Frady sees him as a wide-eyed Billy Budd, incapable of believing that things will not work out for the best in a Christian America. He criticizes Graham for avoiding the issues of the Civil Rights movement and the Vietnam War and, especially, for supporting Lyndon Johnson and Richard Nixon.

In many ways the best biography is MARTIN, a long narrative study written at Graham's request but not as an authorized work by an insider. It agrees with all previous scholars that Graham's primary interest has been the saving of souls, but it does not follow McLoughlin and Frady in arguing that Graham's message avoided social issues. Martin agrees that Graham represents the latest stage in American revivalism, but stresses with Pollock the importance of Graham in taking an evangelical message throughout the world. He sees the strong component of personal morality in Graham's message as a social statement about changing society through individual transformations, and he argues that, after a sluggish beginning, Graham became a clear spokesman for racial desegregation. A forgiving book, it generously explains numerous gaffes as the work of a wide-eyed Carolina farm boy still amazed to find himself on a world stage. Martin is most critical in detailing the depth of Graham's support for Richard Nixon – support that included an unpublished and previously unknown article which Graham wrote to endorse the presidential candidate in 1960. One of the advances which Martin makes on past scholarship is to detail the tension between Graham as a "New Evangelical" and a fundamentalist movement critical of his ecumenical approach toward non-fundamentalists.

TED OWNBY

See also Revivalism

Grand Army of the Republic

Beath, Robert B., *History of the Grand Army of the Republic*, New York: Bryan Taylor, 1888

Davies, Wallace Evan, *Patriotism on Parade: The Story of Veterans' and Hereditary Organizations in America, 1783–1900*, Cambridge, MA: Harvard University Press, 1955

Dearing, Mary R., *Veterans in Politics: The Story of the GAR*, Baton Rouge: Louisiana State University Press, 1952

Glasson, William H., *Federal Military Pensions in the United States*, New York: Oxford University Press, 1918

Heck, Frank Hopkins, *The Civil War Veteran in Minnesota Life and Politics*, Oxford, OH: Mississippi Valley Press, 1941

McConnell, Stuart, *Glorious Contentment: The Grand Army of the Republic, 1865–1900*, Chapel Hill: University of North Carolina Press, 1992

Skocpol, Theda, *Protecting Soldiers and Mothers: The Political Origins of Social Policy in the United States*, Cambridge, MA: Belknap Press of Harvard University Press, 1992

As the largest and most powerful Union veterans' organization, the Grand Army of the Republic (GAR) was at once a fraternal order, a pension lobby, a Republican political club, a historical and memorial organization, and a patriotic society. The earliest work devoted entirely to the GAR was the official history of BEATH, a prominent Philadelphia businessman who was among the order's founders in Pennsylvania. Beath's book is a standard 19th-century compendium, more useful now as a source than as an interpretation. It recounts the proceedings of each GAR national encampment up to the date of publication, includes capsule biographies of GAR national leaders, and provides statistical information on Grand Army membership and charity practices. But Beath was an organization man, seriously obfuscating the GAR's early Republican partisanship while emphasizing its charitable works.

A much more critical early voice was that of GLASSON, who devoted considerable portions of his history of the military pension system to descriptions of GAR politicking. Writing just as the United States was about to pay millions of dollars in benefits to veterans of World War I, Glasson was scornful of the 19th-century pension system, which he viewed as a series of wasteful give-aways. In this he simply echoes genteel opinion of the Progressive Era. Glasson's overall tone is scholarly and judicious, however, and all subsequent historians have relied on the valuable legislative and statistical information which he gathered on Civil War pensions.

HECK focuses heavily on Minnesota politics, with whole chapters devoted to intra-party factions and to "The Veteran as a Political Worker." His is the only book to result from a decade in which state-level GAR history was a common dissertation topic (unpublished studies of Missouri, New York, and Ohio also exist), and reflects the strengths and limitations of the genre. By treating a single GAR department, Heck is able to show the intricacies of veteran politics in an era when most political activity remained concentrated at the state level. But

beyond Minnesota, the questions asked of this material are very dated, fixating chiefly on the problem of whether the GAR was a Republican party front.

As DEARING would soon show, it was. Her life's work, which began as a 1938 dissertation, was the first comprehensive history of the Grand Army and remains unequaled as a political history of the order. Beginning with the recruitment of the "soldier vote" during the Civil War, Dearing traces veteran political activity through the bitter election of 1868, the machinations of pension attorneys and Republican bloody shirt-wavers, the opposition of Grover Cleveland, and the GAR's patriotic crusades in the 1890s. Throughout, the source base is both wide and deep, with many excursions into state-level political controversies, especially in the pivotal Midwest. In many ways an old-fashioned political narrative, Dearing's book is concerned with who wins elections and why. As a student of William Hesseltine, Dearing was sceptical about the GAR's patriotic rhetoric, but she also had a family connection with the order that tended to make her sympathetic. She was not interested in the social and cultural sides of the order – charity, fraternalism, historical memory – though her concluding chapters address the GAR's "crusade against anarchy" in the 1890s.

DAVIES concentrates on the social side of the GAR, albeit as part of a general history of patriotic societies, veteran and civilian, over two centuries. There are bows to "the rise of the city" as an analytical concept (Davies was a student of Arthur Schlesinger), but in general his book is more descriptive than analytical, with little formal or theoretical attention to ideology, ritual, gender, and social class. Davies does address the problem of race relations within the GAR, which previous authors had neglected. He is also quite informative on the social linkage between the GAR and other patriotic orders (notably the Sons of Veterans, and the Sons and Daughters of the American Revolution) and on the veteran press. But the overall tone of the book is pedestrian.

Between Dearing's work and the most recent comprehensive analysis of the GAR – that of McCONNELL – lie four decades of rapid methodological change. Instead of focusing on the GAR's maneuvers in electoral politics, McConnell offers what is essentially an ethnography of the order. The analysis combines social history techniques – such as a membership analysis of three typical GAR posts – with concepts drawn from intellectual history and cultural anthropology. Separate chapters treat the order's social composition, its rituals, its pension politics, and its members' ideas about history and memory. A concluding chapter explores the relationships between these facets of GAR membership and the American nationalism that exploded on to the scene in the 1890s. Like Dearing, Heck and Davies, McConnell ends his narrative in 1900, after which date the GAR was clearly in decline.

The GAR's central role in the development of the pension system is a central subject for all students of the order, but the subject is most broadly and explicitly explored by SKOCPOL. Her history of 20th-century social policy begins with an extended analysis of the 19th-century pension system and the politics that produced it. Skocpol argues that fixation on European models has kept Americans from seeing the 19th-century veterans' benefit system for what it really was: the origin of the American welfare state. The GAR offered a particular definition of entitlement that continued to influence policy debates even after 1900. On the pension issue, at least, Skocpol makes connections between the 19th and 20th centuries that previous authors left implicit.

STUART McCONNELL

Grant, Ulysses S. 1822–1885

Civil War general and 18th President of the
United States

Catton, Bruce, *U.S. Grant and the American Military Tradition*, Boston: Little Brown, 1954

Catton, Bruce, *Grant Moves South*, Boston: Little Brown, 1960

Catton, Bruce, *Grant Takes Command: The Vital Years of the American Civil War*, Boston: Little Brown, 1969; London: Dent, 1970

Fuller, J.F.C., *The Generalship of Ulysses S. Grant*, New York: Dodd Mead, and London: Murray, 1929

Garland, Hamlin, *Ulysses S. Grant: His Life and Character*, New York: Doubleday McLure, 1898

Hesseltine, William B., *Ulysses S. Grant: Politician*, New York: Dodd Mead, 1935

Lewis, Lloyd, *Captain Sam Grant*, Boston: Little Brown, 1950

McFeely, William S., *Grant: A Biography*, New York: Norton, 1981

Simpson, Brooks D., *Let Us Have Peace: Ulysses S. Grant and the Politics of War and Reconstruction, 1861–1868*, Chapel Hill: University of North Carolina Press, 1991

Wilson, James Grant, *General Grant*, New York: Appleton, 1897

As the foremost Union Civil War general and 18th president of the United States, Ulysses S. Grant has been an important subject in countless books and has attracted generations of biographers. No work, however, can be considered a definitive assessment of the man, and none has won acclaim comparable to Grant's *Personal Memoirs* (1885, 1886), written while the hero was dying from throat cancer.

Wilson and Garland typify accounts written by Grant's contemporaries. Both present Grant in laudatory terms, and much of their value lies in personal recollections of contact with Grant and reminiscences by Grant's military compatriots and friends. WILSON emphasizes Grant's battlefield accomplishments and looks to personal history primarily for clues to his stirring success as a commander. GARLAND writes a full and sympathetic biography that is particularly insightful on Grant's financial disaster late in life. These works either ignore or gloss over Grant's much debated bouts with the bottle.

FULLER, a British general and military thinker, was a key figure in the revival of Grant's reputation in the 20th century. He subjects Grant's military prowess to systematic analysis and concludes that as a subordinate commander, general-in-chief, and peacetime general he ranks high among the roll of leaders, from the ancient world to World War I. Grant receives particular accolades for his determination, strategic grasp, and bold

tactical maneuvers. He realized that the best course was to keep the Confederate armies continuously engaged on all fronts, giving play to the superior Union resources in men and supplies while preventing the enemy from shifting troops between active and inactive theaters. Grant's only notable flaw was an inclination towards frontal attacks that showed too little regard for the killing power of the rifled musket. On the whole, however, he ably adapted new technologies to the battlefield.

A newspaperman turned historian, LEWIS inaugurated a projected multi-volume military biography of Grant with an engaging narrative of his life up to his taking a Civil War field command. Every anecdote of Grant's boyhood, career at the United States Military Academy, army post life, Mexican War service, and civilian misadventures finds its place. Grant emerges as a likable man with an earnest and loving concern for his responsibilities as husband and father. He is willing to face new experiences, to work hard, to make sacrifices, and to recover from disappointments. The suggestion is that these traits will serve him well as a wartime commander.

CATTON (1960, 1969) added two further volumes to the full-scale biography begun by Lewis. The first of his two volumes deals with Grant's remarkable Vicksburg campaign, while the second focuses on Grant's role as commander-in-chief in 1864–65. The combined efforts of Lewis and Catton remain the most authoritative detailed account of Grant's Civil War record. Those readers deterred by the scale of these three volumes may turn to CATTON (1954), a very much briefer, and earlier, sketch of his generally favorable view of Grant as a person and military leader. Rising above the pettiness of army politics so much enjoyed by so many Civil War generals, Grant proved his detractors wrong with striking successes in the field, an energetic approach to every undertaking, and elevation to command of the army, which he led to victory. By war's end, he personified determination, directness, and competence. More than a brilliant general, Grant also displayed an acute sense of the political realities and complexities inherent in a civil war, but he could not transfer his leadership qualities from commander of the army to president. Partly because of poor tutelage under President Andrew Johnson and partly because of his own temperament, Grant simply could not assert the powers and prerogatives of the president for the good of the nation and finally fell victim to the worst sort of partisan politics. The great general deserved better than having his name associated with a period of gross materialism and scandal.

In a lengthy study which centers on Grant's presidency, HESSELTINE begins with the position that more literate political enemies stacked the historical deck against a fair assessment of Grant's two administrations. Even after re-evaluation, however, Grant still seemed "peculiarly ignorant of the Constitution and inept in handling men." Grant's obstinacy, central to his military success, proved a hindrance in the political arena. Rather than emerging as a dignified statesman, Grant developed into nothing more than a party hack aligned with the most conservative elements in the Republican party.

Praise and prestigious awards – and some sharp criticism – came to McFEELY for what is the first modern one-volume biography of Grant. Perhaps influenced by the Vietnam-era bias against the military, this somewhat dense book portrays

Grant as disengaged and unfeeling. He responds to situations rather than asserting his own will or sense of direction. As a general, Grant is successful but too often willing to butcher his troops to achieve victory; as a politician and president, he is clumsy, picking the wrong issues to press and being too trusting of his friends. Similar bad judgment leads him to financial ruin. He returns his family to financial solvency by writing his *Memoirs* while gravely ill, and in the process of overcoming this intensely personal challenge becomes "a man." Such credit is not given to Grant for overcoming earlier trials, especially his difficult civilian years as a farmer in St. Louis and as a clerk in his father's leather shop in Galena, Illinois, or his weakness for whiskey. McFeely's distaste for matters military makes his treatment of Grant's generalship the least satisfactory part of the book, and he is too eager at times to use Grant as a case study to illustrate some broader speculation on mid-19th-century American society.

SIMPSON presents a more perceptive and dynamic Grant. He understood "the political role of the soldier" and during the Civil War deftly directed military operations in a manner that anticipated and eased political strains. Grant's position on black troops showed how smoothly he made the transition from a limited war to preserve the Union to a more destructive war to establish freedom as a guiding national principle. After securing a magnanimous peace at Appomattox, he proved an island of stability – resolutely working to preserve the fruits of victory and building upon emancipation through a commitment to black suffrage and civil equality – in the turbulent sea of Johnson's presidency. While Grant lagged in pursuing economic reforms beneficial to blacks, such as land redistribution, he boldly issued military orders and framed congressional legislation to guarantee civil rights. This provocative analysis ends abruptly with Grant's election as president, a time when his political skills faced more formidable tests.

Recent works on Grant have benefited from John Y. Simon (editor), *The Papers of Ulysses S. Grant* (Carbondale: Southern Illinois University Press, 1967–, 25 vols. projected). This outstanding editorial production promises to assist future studies by bringing together for the first time all significant Grant writings, in their historical contexts.

WILLIAM M. FERRARO

Great Awakening

Bushman, Richard L., *From Puritan to Yankee: Character and the Social Order in Connecticut, 1690–1765*, Cambridge, MA: Harvard University Press, 1967

Crawford, Michael J., *Season of Grace: Colonial New England's Revival Tradition in Its British Context*, New York and Oxford: Oxford University Press, 1991

Gaustad, Edwin Scott, *The Great Awakening in New England*, Gloucester, MA: P.Smith, 1965

Gewehr, Wesley M., *The Great Awakening in Virginia, 1740–1790*, Durham, NC: Duke University Press, 1930

Griffin, Edward G., *Old Brick: Charles Chauncy of Boston, 1705–1787*, Minneapolis: University of Minnesota Press, 1980

Harlan, David, *The Clergy and the Great Awakening in New England*, Ann Arbor, MI: UMI Research Press, 1980

Heimert, Alan, *Religion and the American Mind: From the Great Awakening to the Revolution*, Cambridge, MA: Harvard University Press, 1966

Isaac, Rhys, *The Transformation of Virginia, 1740–1790*, Chapel Hill: University of North Carolina Press, 1982

Rutman, Darrett B., *The Great Awakening: Event and Exegesis*, New York: Wiley, 1970

Stout, Harry S., *The Divine Dramatist: George Whitefield and the Rise of Modern Evangelism*, Grand Rapids, MI: Eerdmans, 1991

Trinterud, Leonard J., *The Forming of an American Tradition: A Re-Examination of Colonial Presbyterianism*, Philadelphia: Westminster Press, 1949; reprinted Freeport, NY: Books for Libraries, 1970

Westerkamp, Marilyn J., *Triumph of the Laity: Scots-Irish Piety and the Great Awakening, 1625–1760*, New York: Oxford University Press, 1988

The Great Awakening was one of the few events which affected the whole of Anglo-America, both mainland colonies and mother country. It has been seen both as a culmination of trends in the development of colonial religion, and, perhaps too readily, as a precursor to the American Revolution. There are a number of brief introductory guides to the Awakening. One of the most useful is RUTMAN, which provides a selection of writings on the Awakening as well as some documentary extracts.

Among regional studies, GAUSTAD provides a clear and comprehensive guide to the main features of the Awakening as it developed in New England. However, the New England pattern was not universal, and other studies have helped to illustrate that diversity. TRINTERUD describes the impact of the Awakening in the middle colonies and on the Presbyterians in particular. GEWEHR's account describes three phases of revivalist activity, associated with the Presbyterians, the Baptists and the Methodists. Both studies show that the Awakening started earlier in certain other colonies than in New England, and also continued later. While these older works retain their value, they need to be supplemented by more recent accounts, such as those of Westerkamp or Isaac. Much of the more recent work has tried to set the religious elements of the Awakening in the context of social, economic, and political developments in the colonies. In the context of a wider study of Virginia, ISAAC gives a clear picture of the rise of revivalism, particularly that associated with the Baptists, and emphasizes its challenge to established religious institutions and forms of authority. BUSHMAN also describes how the Awakening was a key element in shaping changes in the character of the people of Connecticut and their responses to law, authority, and established institutions.

Many historians of the Awakening have been concerned to elucidate the connection between the Awakening and the American Revolution. The most ambitious of these attempts is HEIMERT, who suggests that the Awakening revealed a clear-cut religious division within American Protestantism which transcended the specific consequences in terms of fragmented denominations and the proliferation of sects. It created two "parties" – those who supported the revivals and those who opposed them. The first part of Heimert's book examines this conflict of ideas, and contains a considerable depth of material both on the Awakening and the response of its opponents. The second part argues more controversially that these ideas exerted a strong influence on the crisis of the American Revolution, and in particular that it was from the beliefs of the evangelical supporters of the Awakening that the ideas which fuelled the Revolution came. Further research has suggested that Heimert's thesis cannot be fully maintained in its broad sweep, but his book is still informative and stimulating.

Many problems still remain in disentangling the causes and consequences of the Awakening in general, and its relation to the Revolution in particular. Not the least of these is the extent of the revivals. Just as New England was not the only site of revivalism in the colonies, so the colonies were themselves only one region within Britain and Europe where such movements occurred. As CRAWFORD indicates, the religious culture of the colonies was still part of the general culture of the mother country. Seeing the various revivals as similar in cause and mutual in influence, Crawford focuses on the ideas behind them and on the language through which these were expressed. He sees these as not just American but transatlantic, not rooted in particular social circumstances but in more general ones.

Perhaps the key figure in expanding the revivals through Britain and the colonies was George Whitefield. There is no entirely satisfactory comprehensive study of Whitefield's role. STOUT emphasises Whitefield's role as a great communicator, claiming him as "Anglo-America's first modern celebrity", comparable to the evangelists of the electronic age. His biography does, however, cover the full range of Whitefield's activities in Britain and America.

One of the claims made by much writing on the Awakening is that American religion was split into two polarized groups, each led or represented by prominent figures, such as Jonathan Edwards and Charles Chauncy. HARLAN argues against the view that the Awakening divided the New England ministry into two opposing "armies". He seeks to describe the response of the ministers who he sees as occupying the middle ground – the Old Calvinists or "Regular Lights" who saw themselves as defending the traditional balance of the New England way, often against both Old Lights and New Lights. In his study of the career of Charles Chauncy, GRIFFIN offers a similar approach to the Awakening, from the perspective of those who were ambivalent or hostile towards it. Griffin broadly agrees with Harlan on the existence of a middle group among the New England ministers, though he sees Chauncy as a member of it. Chauncy was one of the strongest critics of the Awakening as it developed and intensified. He was not, however, unambiguously a spokesman for any "liberal" position, but rather a member of the "supernatural rationalist" tradition and a staunch defender of the New England Way. While Chauncy may have anticipated the coming of Unitarianism, he was not part of it.

In a valuable recent study WESTERKAMP brings many of these themes together, with a specific focus on the middle colonies, rather than New England, and the role of figures like the Tennents, rather than Edwards or Whitefield. She provides a concise summary of the main elements of the historiography of the Awakening, restating many of its key features. Her account of the revivals focuses on changes in religious practices brought about by the application of traditional practices and expectations to new cultural circumstances. By showing that lay immigrants from Scotland and Northern Ireland provided the pressure to change in the direction of what had been familiar to them back home, Westerkamp again emphasises that the Awakening was not a uniquely American phenomenon.

MALCOLM F. MORRISON

See also Edwards; Revivalism; Second Great Awakening

Great Crash and Great Depression, 1929–1939

Bernstein, Michael A., *The Great Depression: Delayed Recovery and Economic Change in America, 1929–1939*, Cambridge and New York: Cambridge University Press, 1987

Chandler, Lester V., *America's Greatest Depression, 1929–1941*, New York: Harper, 1970

Fearon, Peter, *War, Prosperity and Depression: The US Economy, 1917–45*, Deddington, Oxfordshire: Philip Allan, 1987

Friedman, Milton and Anna Jacobson Schwartz, *A Monetary History of the United States, 1867–1960*, Princeton: Princeton University Press, 1963; chapter 7 reprinted as *The Great Contraction, 1929–1933*, 1965

Galbraith, John Kenneth, *The Great Crash: 1929*, Boston: Houghton Mifflin, and London: Hamish Hamilton, 1955

Kindleberger, Charles P., *The World in Depression, 1929–1939*, Berkeley: University of California Press, and London: Allen Lane, 1973

Temin, Peter, *Did Monetary Forces Cause the Great Depression?*, New York: Norton, 1976

Thomas, Gordon and Max Morgan-Witts, *The Day the Bubble Burst: A Social History of the Wall Street Crash of 1929*, New York: Doubleday, and London: Hamish Hamilton, 1979

Wicker, Elmus R., *Federal Reserve Monetary Policy, 1917–1933*, New York: Random House, 1966

The great depression, which began in 1929, and the dismal decade which followed, have captured the attention of more modern economic historians than any other topic. There is still sharp disagreement over both the cause of the depression and the reasons for its severity. Much of the literature is now highly technical, as this debate is dominated by scholars who use the techniques of modern economics in their exegesis, thus excluding those who have no training in economics from part of the intellectual battle. Popular opinion has always placed great emphasis on the Wall Street Crash which is seen as the harbinger of national misfortune. The most readable account of this financial panic is still GALBRAITH's slim volume, which has become a classic. Elegant and witty, Galbraith guides the reader through the financial labyrinth with skill. THOMAS and MORGAN-WITTS have written a lively and entertaining narrative of the crash as seen through the lives of many of the individuals, both in the United States and abroad, who were deeply affected by the sudden fall in stock market values. However, while both these volumes are excellent descriptions of the events surrounding the crash, neither is strong on the causes or on the long-run effect of the collapse.

It should be remembered that the fall in stock prices in 1931 and 1932 was more precipitous than 1929. FEARON's wider ranging analysis enables the reader to follow the fluctuations of the market over two decades and to place these movements in perspective. His conclusion is that the stock market responded to events rather than led them, and therefore we should not over-emphasize the impact that it had on the worsening economy. The movements of the key economic variables during the depression are illustrated by CHANDLER. By the use of tables and graphs which accompany a clear text, he is able to show not only the national economic decline and recovery throughout the 1930s, but also the performance of individual industries and even regions. The problems experienced by the farmer can be contrasted with those of the industrialist, the banker and even the unemployed. The clarity of the text is aided by a careful division into short chapters which themselves are further divided into sections. Rather than being overwhelmed by the material, the reader can locate relevant information quickly.

Two of the most important groups locked into conflict over their differing analysis of the economic collapse are monetarists and Keynesians. FRIEDMAN and SCHWARTZ remains the bible for monetarists. They seek to demonstrate the key role that money has played in economic fluctuations in the United States since the Civil War. In this rigorous critique, the Federal Reserve is blamed for the severity of the depression. Inept action led to bank failures and to a catastrophic decline in the quantity of money in the economy. Although this book is aimed at the economically literate reader, it is not cluttered with jargon and is so well written that sections will be intelligible to those who are ready to persevere.

TEMIN has produced a vigorous critique of the monetarist thesis. In a carefully argued, though at times highly technical book, he analyzes the claims of the monetarists, and remains unconvinced of their explanation of the depression's severity. Temin finds little evidence of money as a leading factor before the autumn of 1931 and even after that date he believes that non-monetary factors played a vital role in bringing about economic collapse. In a meticulously researched work which examines the action of the Federal Reserve, WICKER reaches a different conclusion from Friedman and Schwartz. Monetarists are critical of the actions of the Fed during the years 1928 to 1933, which they believe to have been at variance with the expansionary action taken by the monetary authorities during the recessions of 1924 and 1927. Wicker, however, is able to show that the Federal Reserve acted rationally in response to the economic collapse, even though one can see, with the benefit of hindsight, that a different monetary policy might well have moderated economic decline. Those who are wary of economics should consult Fearon where these arguments, and others, are explained in language which is aimed at the general reader. In addition, this book contains extensive bibliographical information for historians and economic historians who might want to pursue this lively debate.

Some scholars view the monetarist - non-monetarist battle as insular. KINDLEBERGER, for example, emphasizes international events in his explanation of the great depression. In a volume which attempts to integrate politics with economics, he argues, in language intelligible to the general historian, that surplus commodities played a crucial role in a world-wide depression which engulfed the United States. Indeed one of the strengths of this book is its constant reminder that the savage economic decline after 1929 affected most of the world. Another strength is its readability.

Finally, in a particularly imaginative contribution to the debate, BERNSTEIN provides a wealth of detail on the variable performance of the manufacturing sector. While his methodical disaggregation is a refreshing approach, it does not make for easy reading. Nevertheless this volume is an invaluable reference work for the history of those troubled years.

PETER FEARON

See also Business Cycle

Great Plains

Bader, Robert Smith, *Hayseeds, Moralizers, and Methodists: The Twentieth Century Image of Kansas*, Lawrence: University Press of Kansas, 1988

Hurt, R. Douglas, *The Dust Bowl: An Agricultural and Social History*, Chicago: Nelson Hall, 1981

Limerick, Patricia Nelson, *The Legacy of Conquest: The Unbroken Past of the American West*, New York: Norton, 1987

Miner, Craig, *West of Wichita: Settling the High Plains of Kansas, 1865–1890*, Lawrence: University Press of Kansas, 1986

Ostler, Jeffrey, *Prairie Populism: The Fate of Agrarian Radicalism in Kansas, Nebraska, and Iowa, 1880–1892*, Lawrence: University Press of Kansas, 1993

Turner, Frederick Jackson, *The Significance of the Frontier in American History*, Madison: State Historical Society of Wisconsin, 1894; edited by Harold P. Simonson, New York: Ungar, 1963

Webb, Walter Prescott, *The Great Plains*, Boston: Ginn, 1931

West, Elliot, *The Way to the West: Essays on the Central Plains*, Albuquerque: University of New Mexico Press, 1995

White, Richard, *"It's Your Misfortune and None of My Own": A New History of the American West*, Norman: University of Oklahoma Press, 1991

In 1893 TURNER delivered his now famous essay, "The Significance of the Frontier in American History," in which he argued that the process of westward expansion had defined both American history and the unique character of the American people. According to Turner's "thesis," the frontier was a process whereby the inexorable tide of American civilization had rolled westward and uprooted all that was "uncivilized." The thesis came to dominate the subsequent historiography of the Great Plains for many years. WEBB is a western classic, very much in the Turnerian tradition, but wide-ranging in its treatment of the Plains environment, and hinting at some of the approaches by more recent historians of the region. However, champions of the "New Western History" have now mounted a major challenge to the basic assumptions of the Turner interpretation.

Foremost among the revisionist scholars is LIMERICK who argues that western history ought to focus on the frontier as a place rather than as a process. In so doing, historians will be better able, she argues, to give due attention to those peoples whom Turner had overlooked – women, Native Americans, Hispanics, and other ethnic groups. The inclusiveness of Limerick's call for a New Western History has created a history far more complex than that which Turner had envisioned in 1893. Nevertheless, proponents of both the Turnerian and New West approaches continue to debate the merits of each school of thought.

In an important collection of essays, WEST reveals the great strengths of New Western History. His use of environmental and ethnohistorical methods enables him to tell a complex and troubling story of competition between Native Americans and Anglo-Americans for the land. West examines Plains history from a number of perspectives, from the fortunes of the American bison herd to the changes that occurred in Native American and Anglo-American family structures. Perhaps his most persistent theme is the continual decline of the Great Plains environment, a theme which resonates well with the region's later history.

After the United States government had wrested control of the Plains away from its native inhabitants, homesteaders streamed across the region. They brought with them the technological wherewithal to bust the tough sod and create prosperous farms in what earlier generations of Americans had considered the "Great American Desert." Writing in a Turnerian vein, MINER shows that irregular rain and grasshopper plagues made life difficult for farmers and their families. His adroit use of settlers' journals and letters nicely personalizes the pioneer experience and suggests the profound impact which the environment had on those who staked out homesteads on the Kansas plains.

In addition to local hardships, Plains settlers found them-selves confronted with a national economic crisis in the early 1890s. As grain prices plummeted, farmers banded together first in the Farmers' Alliances and then in the Populist party. OSTLER argues, however, that the panic was not the sole force behind the emergence of Plains Populism. He examines the rise of Populism in Nebraska and Kansas, and its absence in Iowa, and concludes that the political structures of each state, more than the extent of the crisis, influenced the formation of the Populist party. On the one hand, Iowa had a vigorous two-party system, and agrarian discontent was channeled through both the Republican and Democratic parties. On the other hand, Nebraska and Kansas were virtually one-party Republican states, where, in the absence of a Democratic party to voice their concerns, disgruntled farmers formed Populist parties. Despite the unfulfilled promises of Populism, the move-ment enjoyed its greatest successes in the Plains states.

The hard times that had helped give rise to Populism had eased by the turn of the century. World War I brought an increased global demand for wheat, and Plains farmers obliged by bringing more and more land into cultivation. This expan-sion, HURT shows, coincided with the beginning of a drought cycle that had last hit the region between 2000 and 600 BC. Consequently, commercial agriculture depleted the Plains envi-ronment. When the soil lost its cohesiveness, strong winds peeled back the earth, and the dust clouds that rolled across the region created the enduring image of the "Dust Bowl."

According to BADER, the association of the "Dust Bowl" with the Great Plains transformed popular conceptions of the prairie states. First known as freedom's dark and bloody ground, Kansas entered the national consciousness as a battle-field on which abolitionists and pro-slavery men fought tooth and nail to secure their different ways of life. The abolition-ists' victory, Bader believes, earned for the state a stern and Puritanical reputation, and its prominent role in the temper-ance movement of the 1920s did little to disabuse the American public of this notion. After the hard times of the Great Depression had passed, however, Kansas's image failed to rebound. The crisis effectively transformed the state, in the popular mind, from America's bountiful heartland to its barren hinterland, an image which, Bader argues, has lasted to the present.

The above-mentioned books discuss various issues relevant to both the New Western and the Turnerian schools. In terms of synthetic works, however, New West scholars have domi-nated the literature. Like Limerick, WHITE offers a compre-hensive interpretation of the region that considers it a place where Native Americans, Europeans, Americans, and Asians created together a complex multi-ethnic history. If a central theme is to be found, White locates it in the important role of the federal government. With a light and ironic touch, he juxtaposes the individualism that is popularly regarded as characteristic of the region with the ever-present influence of Washington's bureaucracy. From organizing territorial govern-ments to funding much of its economic development, the federal government still plays a crucial role in the life of the region.

The vigorous debate that has accompanied the development of New Western History suggests that as historians struggle over whether to interpret Great Plains history as either a place or a process, our understanding of the region will change considerably over the next few decades. Recent advances in ethnohistory and environmental history in particular will place Great Plains history in a wider and deeper context.

JAMES TAYLOR CARSON

Great Society

Aaron, Henry J., *Politics and the Professors: The Great Society in Perspective*, Washington, DC: Brookings Institution, 1978

Califano, Joseph A., Jr., *The Triumph and Tragedy of Lyndon Johnson: The White House Years*, New York: Simon and Schuster, 1991

Chalmers, David M., *And the Crooked Places Made Straight: The Struggle for Social Change in the 1960s*, Baltimore: Johns Hopkins University Press, 1991

Ginzberg, Eli and Robert M. Solow (editors), *The Great Society: Lessons for the Future*, New York: Basic Books, 1974

Katz, Michael B., *The Undeserving Poor: From the War on Poverty to the War on Welfare*, New York: Pantheon, 1989

Levitan, Sar A., *The Great Society's Poor Law: A New Approach to Poverty*, Baltimore: Johns Hopkins Press, 1969

McPherson, Harry M., *A Political Education: A Washington Memoir*, Boston: Little Brown, 1972

Matusow, Allen J., *The Unraveling of America: A History of Liberalism in the 1960s*, New York: Harper, 1984

Moynihan, Daniel Patrick, *Maximum Feasible Misunderstanding: Community Action in the War on Poverty*, New York: Free Press, and London: Collier Macmillan, 1969

Murray, Charles, *Losing Ground: American Social Policy, 1950–1980*, New York: Basic Books, 1984

Quadagno, Jill, *The Color of Welfare: How Racism Undermined the War on Poverty*, New York: Oxford University Press, 1994

Schwarz, John, *America's Hidden Success: A Reassessment of Twenty Years of Public Policy*, New York: Norton, 1983, revised as *America's Hidden Success: A Reassessment of Public Policy from Kennedy to Reagan*, 1988

Scholarship on 1960s American liberalism can usefully be divided into two categories, on the understanding that there exists a considerable degree of overlap between the two. First are those works which attempt to evaluate the effectiveness of such Great Society initiatives as the Economic Opportunity Act, Medicare/Medicaid, the Model Cities program and the Elementary and Secondary Education Act. Second are those which treat the *politics* of liberalism during the Johnson era, relating the Great Society vision to the wider travail of the New Deal order during a period of acute political dislocation.

In the first category, three works of social science are particularly notable. AARON, a Brookings Institution economist who worked for the Johnson Administration, is good on the mixture of intellectual hubris and political calculation which underpinned the ambitious legislative agenda of 1964–65. Chapters on poverty, race, education and economic policy each reveal how policy failure and new challenges stimulated new perspectives on social policy as the decade progressed. The GINZBERG and SOLOW collection contains essays by some notable social scientists, and constitutes an invaluable introduction to many of the same themes treated by Aaron. It also treats some additional themes, notably housing, health and manpower. LEVITAN – who has written numerous standard texts on social policy from an unabashedly liberal perspective – provides a useful title-by-title evaluation of the Economic Opportunity Act, the centerpiece of Lyndon Johnson's War on Poverty.

All three books are sympathetic to the goals of the Great Society, but modestly sceptical about its legacy. Insufficient expenditures, rhetorical excess, and conceptual naivety lie at the heart of their limited criticisms. Scepticism is considerably more ascendant in MOYNIHAN, who believes that Johnson should have stressed income and jobs, rather than a speculative and sometimes politically destabilizing melange of rehabilitative services. Like Levitan and Aaron, Moynihan was an active participant in the events which he describes.

More recent work has a dramatically polarized character. On the one hand, SCHWARZ provides an unequivocally favourable analysis of the Johnson programs, supporting his unfashionable view with a welter of useful statistics. On the other hand, MURRAY – in a highly influential book published at around the same time – argues that they promoted self-destructive behavior on the part of the poor, whose work ethic was undermined by federal largesse with disastrous consequences. From the left, the most impressive critical evaluation comes from MATUSOW. He sees public policy during these years as being emblematic of a "corporate liberal" ideology which failed to recognize – let alone challenge – the structural inequities of the American economy. Sometimes struggling to find the right balance between depth and breadth, his account remains an illuminating analysis of the mounting crisis of liberalism during the Vietnam/civil rights era. Like Matusow, CHALMERS sees the Great Society agenda as a necessary response to a maelstrom of destabilising, threatening, but also energising social change. (This contrasts strikingly with the approach of Moynihan, who sees Johnson's programs as the autonomous product of elite deliberation.) In both works, and others of their type, the politics of centrist liberalism appear irredeemably squalid when juxtaposed with the idealism of the various insurgent movements which the author elevates.

On occasion, the rush to moral judgement prevents these authors from considering some harsh political realities which Lyndon Johnson had no option but to respect. Herein lies the value of two excellent political memoirs by prominent Johnson staffers: McPHERSON writes beautifully and is particularly insightful on the impact which Vietnam and the radicalization of black protest had upon the reform coalition. In a more recent book, CALIFANO makes good use of his own papers, currently unavailable to other scholars. While sympathetic to Johnson, neither work is a hagiography in the Sorensen/Schlesinger tradition.

The relationship between race and social policy is incisively explored by KATZ, who provides the most thoughtful account of the Moynihan Report controversy and its consequences. Also noteworthy is his sophisticated explanation for the guaranteed income movement, which gained momentum after 1966 as Johnson's service-oriented antipoverty strategy faltered. Like Katz, QUADAGNO is concerned to place Great Society programs in a broad historical context. To a still greater degree, she believes that racial considerations have dominated social policymaking ever since the 1930s. Quadagno views the Great Society agenda as an attempt to create an "equal opportunity state" in place of the racist welfare state which had come into effect during the New Deal era. Hers is the most important work on 1960s liberalism to have appeared in some years, and opens up fruitful possibilities for future research in this rich field of study.

GARETH DAVIES

See also Johnson, Lyndon Baines

Greeley, Horace 1811–1872
Newspaper editor and presidential candidate

Hale, William Harlan, *Horace Greeley: Voice of the People*,
New York: Harper, 1950
Isely, Jeter A., *Horace Greeley and the Republican Party,
1853–1861*, Princeton: Princeton University Press, 1947
Linn, William Alexander, *Horace Greeley, Founder and
Editor of the New York Tribune*, New York: Appleton,
1903; reprinted, New York: Chelsea House, 1981
Lunde, Erik S., *Horace Greeley*, Boston: Twayne, 1981
Reavis, L.U., *A Representative Life of Horace Greeley, with
an Introduction by Cassius M. Clay*, New York:
Carleton, 1872
Ritchie, Donald A., *Press Gallery: Congress and the
Washington Correspondents*, Cambridge, MA: Harvard
University Press, 1991
Summers, Mark W., *The Press Gang: Newspapers and
Politics, 1865–1878*, Chapel Hill: University of North
Carolina Press, 1994
Van Deusen, Glyndon G., *Horace Greeley: Nineteenth-
Century Crusader*, Philadelphia: University of
Pennsylvania Press, 1953

Best known as the world-famous founder and editor of the
New York Tribune, Horace Greeley, a shaper and constant
object of public opinion, exerted a massive influence on culture,
society, and politics in the 19th-century United States. His life
and thought have been the subject of many popular and scholarly works. Many of Greeley's associates and contemporaries
wrote biographies of the notable publicist. Of these early
works, the most valuable is REAVIS. This is a long and highly
sympathetic treatment of Greeley; indeed, it was used as a
campaign biography for the editor's presidential bid in 1872.
But the book contains a wealth of primary materials unavailable elsewhere, including letters written by Greeley prior to his
founding of the *Tribune*. Obviously intended as a popular
work, it has no particular interpretive slant, other than a
predisposition towards viewing the subject as the most important intellectual of his time.

LINN is more balanced and analytical. As a one-time writer
for the *Tribune*, the author was particularly interested in
Greeley's day-to-day management of that paper. The editor's
ability to master every aspect of the modern newspaper, from
writing quick but pointed editorials to building subscription
lists, was responsible for his success. This short book also
offers one of the first attempts to make sense out of Greeley's
constantly evolving attitudes on slavery, contending that his
devotion to strengthening the Union always kept him disposed
towards abolishing slavery but wary of taking a hard-line
abolitionist stance.

An outburst of Greeley biography occurred after World War
II. ISELY is the first serious, full-length scholarly work on
Greeley, though it concentrates only on the editor's years in
the decade before the Civil War. Like many books of its time
on the coming of the Civil War, this study tends to envision
Greeley as a member of a "blundering generation" willing to
put principle above well-reasoned compromise, even at the cost
of disunion. Greeley often emerges here as a public figure who

feeds on attention from the people, and whips up support for
his position without fully considering the consequences. But
this lively book still has some sympathy for Greeley, and it
remains the best available work on the editor's role in the
formation of the Republican party and on the connection
between Greeley's thinking – on labor, on poverty, on slavery,
and on sectionalism – and his political actions.

HALE is aimed at a popular audience, and it delivers one
of the fullest and most readable accounts of Greeley's life. An
unprecedented and massive amount of research reveals rich
new material on the editor's personal as well as his political
life. Especially valuable here are the chapter on Greeley's experiments in and attitudes towards utopianism, and the chapter
on the last months of his life. Usually the publicist appears as
a champion of common people – hence the title. Yet, perhaps
because Greeley's life is treated as a series of episodes, a more
meaningful and convincing theme connecting all aspects of his
intellect and experience fails to surface with any impact.

This is not so with VAN DEUSEN, the most thorough and
interpretive work on Greeley to date. A richly documented
study of Greeley's personality as well as his politics, the biography shows how moral fervor pervaded every aspect of
the editor's life. But Van Deusen sees a conservative side to
Greeley's commitment to popular causes. Consistently, the
editor was ready to abandon his struggle for an ideal as soon
as the effects of that struggle threatened to subvert the
minimum state authority necessary for social progress. This
book remains the definitive volume on Greeley's life.

Surprisingly, there has been a paucity of recent biographies
about Greeley. LUNDE is a slim volume, one in a series on
United States authors. A work devoted to Greeley's writings,
it makes no claim to be a full-life study. This breezy and highly
sympathetic work gives an excellent synthesis of the themes
running through Greeley's writing throughout his career. The
unifying thread is a contention that the editor, in all his phases
and inclinations, was one of the most articulate and influential champions of a distinct, American democratic culture.

Greeley figures prominently in a number of works on
American journalism and its influence. RITCHIE, an essential work for understanding the interdependent and ever-
changing relationship between newspaper correspondents and
Washington politicians, devotes a chapter to Greeley and the
correspondents of the *New York Tribune*. Here Greeley
appears as a man "addicted to politics" who learned to temper
his partisan leanings at times in order to collect information
from all sides. Yet the editor, ambitious himself for political
office, could never maintain the distance from partisan haggling
needed to preserve objectivity. At the same time, to his credit
as a reformer, but to his downfall as a politician, his passion
crept too much into the pages of his newspaper.

SUMMERS takes the reader on a rollicking romp through
the Reconstruction years by examining the unraveling of the
symbiotic relationship between the press and politicians. While
highly readable, this is also a serious, scholarly work with
exhaustive documentation. Greeley appears throughout as one
of many newspeople wishing to expand their roles as news
providers to become news makers. Included in the study is a
chapter providing one of the most thorough and enlightening
examinations of Greeley's 1872 run for the presidency. The
author demonstrates how difficult it was for Greeley, always

derisive of the mechanics of politics, to switch course and manipulate the political system for himself. Hoping that a third-party bid would capitalize on the ideal of independence in the press, Greeley instead faced the insurmountable obstacle of a lingering partisanship which aligned many of his former allies with Ulysses Grant.

MICHAEL VORENBERG

See also Newspapers and Magazines

Grimké, Angelina 1805–1879 and
Sarah Grimké 1792–1873
Abolitionists and campaigners for women's rights

Bartlett, Elizabeth Ann (editor), *Letters on the Equality of the Sexes and Other Essays*, by Sarah Grimké, New Haven: Yale University Press, 1988

Bartlett, Elizabeth Ann, *Liberty, Equality, Sorority: The Origins and Interpretation of American Feminist Thought: Frances Wright, Sarah Grimké, and Margaret Fuller*, New York: Carlson, 1994

Birney, Catherine H., *The Grimké Sisters: Sarah and Angelina Grimké: The First American Women Advocates of Abolition and Woman's Rights*, Boston: Lee and Shepard, 1885; reprinted, Westport, CT: Greenwood Press, 1969

Ceplair, Larry (editor), *The Public Years of Sarah and Angelina Grimké: Selected Writings, 1835–1839*, New York: Columbia University Press, 1989

Hersh, Blanche Glassman, *The Slavery of Sex: Feminist-Abolitionists in America*, Urbana: University of Illinois Press, 1978

Lerner, Gerda, *The Grimké Sisters from South Carolina: Rebels Against Slavery*, Boston: Houghton Mifflin, 1967; as *The Grimké Sisters from South Carolina: Pioneers for Women's Rights and Abolition*, New York: Schocken, 1971

Lumpkin, Katharine Du Pré, *The Emancipation of Angelina Grimké*, Chapel Hill: University of North Carolina Press, 1974

Nies, Judith, *Seven Women: Portraits from the American Radical Tradition*, New York: Viking, 1978

Yellin, Jean Fagan, *Women and Sisters: The Antislavery Feminists in American Culture*, New Haven: Yale University Press, 1989

The Grimkés' pioneering crusades against slavery and patriarchy – twin pillars that structured the society of their native South – have attracted the attention of biographers, feminist theorists, and historians of antebellum reform alike. An early biography by BIRNEY, who befriended the sisters during their stay at the Raritan Bay community, is highly sympathetic and impressionistic. Birney's references to her personal exchanges with the sisters as well as extensive quotations from their diaries and correspondence – some of which would otherwise have been lost to posterity – give this book the quality of a primary document.

There are two modern biographies of the Grimkés. LERNER's sweeping narrative traces the emergence of the diffident Sarah and her more self-assured and brilliant younger sister Angelina from Charleston's slaveholding elite to become the first Southern white female advocates of abolitionism, racial egalitarianism, and an original brand of feminism rooted in scriptural authority. Lerner pays careful attention to the interplay among the Grimkés' deep spirituality, their inner struggles, the changes in their thinking, and the shifting contexts of the divergent worlds through which they moved. By no means uniformly laudatory, Lerner points out Sarah's obsession with martyrdom, and the crisis in her relationship with Angelina brought on by her domination of her sister's household after 1838. Despite its traditional approach, this thoroughly researched book remains the definitive biography of the Grimkés.

LUMPKIN's engaging portrait of Angelina Grimké differs from Lerner chiefly in its emphasis on the younger Grimké's eventual personal triumph over the self-doubt that prompted her to withdraw from public life for a dozen years after her marriage to the abolitionist Theodore Dwight Weld. In this quasi-psycho-historical biography, Lumpkin makes imaginative use of sparse documentary evidence to speculate on the dynamics of intra-familial relationships in the Grimké-Weld household. She argues that charges of intellectual vanity and ambition levelled by a rivalrous sister and a subconsciously envious husband induced the guilt-ridden Angelina to retire into domesticity in order to deliver herself from the "bondage of sin". It was by winning this private battle against her family's judgments, and her own fears, to resume her campaign for human rights that Angelina Grimké achieved true emancipation.

NIES is a collective biography of seven women in the American radical tradition which offers the non-specialist reader a lively and passionate introduction to Sarah Grimké. However, it suffers from an uncritical tone, a polemical style and a lack of documentation. The Grimkés are among the 51 abolitionist-feminists surveyed in HERSH's study of the experiential and ideological connections between antislavery and women's rights. The broad scope of this book precludes an in-depth treatment of the Grimkés, but does lend their story comparative and contextual perspective. Hersh examines the impact of the sisters' writings on the development of 19th-century feminist ideology, as well as their influence on the lives and work of other reformers of their day. In a chapter on the role of husbands in the women's movement – more creative than any other in the book – she suggests that the failure of the Grimké-Weld marriage to sustain the public careers of the couple may have discouraged other feminists from getting married.

YELLIN brings a refreshingly original and interdisciplinary perspective to the familiar theme of the abolitionist-feminist relationship. She employs the insights of contemporary literary criticism to study the changing interpretations of the antislavery-feminist emblem of the kneeling female slave in a diverse range of visual icons as well as written texts from the 1830s to the 1850s. In this context, she analyzes the career and writings of Angelina Grimké – together with the lives and works of Lydia Maria Child, Sojourner Truth and Harriet Jacobs – in an attempt to resurrect the silenced discourse of these antislavery feminists. In a novel approach to the emancipation of Angelina Grimké, Yellin shows how, in Grimké's texts, the figure of woman structured by the visual symbol of the enchained female slave, evolves from a prostrate, powerless victim into an erect self-liberated reformer of the world. Despite its broad scope and larger concern, this study provides the most thoughtful and imaginative textual analysis of Grimké's writings.

Both Ceplair and Bartlett (1988), are useful additions to the body of published primary source material on abolitionism and women's rights, which contain informative editorial introductions. CEPLAIR is a collection of selected documents written by the Grimkés during their brief years in the spotlight of public attention from 1835 to 1839. A general prologue provides a succinct account of the abolitionist movement and the sisters' family background, while introductions to each chapter complement the annotated documents in charting their path to reform. The strength of Ceplair's commentaries lies in their concise exposition of the Grimkés' public activities rather than in a searching critique of their ideas.

By contrast, the introduction to BARTLETT (1988), an anthology of Sarah Grimké's writings on the "woman question," probes the ideological and social roots of Grimké's thinking. Her discussion of Grimké's intellectual debt to the four traditions that inspired 19th-century feminism – enlightenment liberalism, romanticism, utopian socialism and Anglo-American radical sectarianism – is enlightening. Bartlett traces the evolution of Grimké's feminism from a male-defined vision of equality into a woman-centered world view based on the affirmation of female beauty, moral autonomy, and solidarity. Her attempt to relate this transition, as well as other aspects of Grimké's thinking, to the "minimalist/maximalist" debate over gender differences and other issues in contemporary feminist theory is, however, strained, revealing less about Grimké's age than our own. In a similar vein, BARTLETT (1994), an intellectual history of 19th-century feminism, argues that the dynamic relationship between the concepts of liberty, equality and sorority in the thought of three women, including Sarah Grimké, resonates in the tensions within modern feminism. Bartlett's examination of the ways in which the outlook of her historic subjects departed from the western political tradition is fresh and original. On the other hand, the presentist prism of her analysis makes this book a provocative statement on contemporary feminism, rather than a work of pure history.

GUNJA SENGUPTA

See also Abolitionism/Antislavery Movement; Feminism; Weld

H

Hamer, Fannie Lou 1917–1977
Civil rights campaigner

Collum, Danny, "Stepping Out into Freedom: The Life of Fannie Lou Hamer," in *Sojourners*, 12 December 1982

Crawford, Vicki L., Jacqueline Anne Rouse, and Barbara Woods (editors), *Women in the Civil Rights Movement: Trailblazers and Torchbearers, 1941–1965*, New York: Carlson, 1990

Garland, Phyl, "Builders of a New South: Negro Heroines of Dixie Play Major Role in Challenging Racist Traditions," *Ebony*, 21, August 1966

Grant, Jacquelyn, "Civil Rights Women: A Source for Doing Womanist Theology," in *Women in the Civil Rights Movement* (see Crawford, above)

Locke, Mamie, "Is This America? Fannie Lou Hamer and the Mississippi Freedom Democratic Party" in *Women in the Civil Rights Movement* (see Crawford, above)

Mills, Kay, *This Little Light of Mine: The Life of Fannie Lou Hamer*, New York: Dutton, 1993

Peterson, Franklynn, "Sunflowers Don't Grow in Sunflower County," *Sepia*, February 1970

Peterson, Franklynn, "Mother of Black Women's Lib," *Sepia*, December 1972

Reagon, Bernice Johnson, "Women as Culture Carriers in the Civil Rights Movement: Fannie Lou Hamer," in *Women in the Civil Rights Movement* (see Crawford, above)

In the early 1960s, when the Student Nonviolent Coordinating Committee (SNCC) went into the rural Deep South to challenge existing racial structures, they hoped to create opportunity, or spaces, in which local grassroots black leadership might grow and develop. Testimony to SNCC's faith in this approach to combating institutionalized racism was provided by the emergence of Fannie Lou Hamer, who became one of the most inspirational and influential figures of the black freedom movement. The twentieth child of poor Mississippi Delta sharecroppers, herself a sharecropper and timekeeper for many years on a local plantation, Hamer went on to become a voter registration worker; a SNCC field secretary; a founder, vice-chair, and candidate for office of the Mississippi Freedom Democratic Party; and a welfare rights activist.

Over the years, reference has been made to Hamer in numerous works, and she has been the focus of several articles, both in popular magazines and in scholarly journals.

However, until recently, there existed little in the way of substantial treatment. As a woman working in the local community, Hamer was penalized twice over. For some time the mainstream historiography of the civil rights movement concentrated on national leaders and organizations at the expense of local groups and activities, and on male leaders and activists to the exclusion of women. But there has been a shift of emphasis in more recent years.

Published in 1993, MILLS is the first (and to date only) major full-length biography of Hamer. Well-researched and lucidly written, it is basically a chronological narrative of Hamer's life, from the dismal early years in Sunflower County, on to the arrival of civil rights organizers and Hamer's immediate decision to register to vote, and then to her attempts to secure political change, working within the Mississippi Freedom Democratic Party. Mills describes Hamer's attempts to ameliorate the economic condition of poverty-stricken local blacks and whites, and her dream of community self-reliance through the Freedom Farm Cooperative. Mills also captures well Hamer's untiring efforts outside the Mississippi Delta to rouse people in the struggle against all forms of oppression, and gives an insightful account of her later years, dogged by poverty and ill-health.

This is a sympathetic but not uncritical study, which concedes that Hamer was not without her detractors. There was considerable conflict between Hamer and some of the local black community, and resentment inspired by Hamer's insistence on maintaining a high public profile. Mills is also clear about Hamer's failures, including the collapse of the Freedom Farm. But Mills concludes that Fannie Lou Hamer was a remarkable woman, an inspiring figure who fought to bring light into the darkness of Mississippi. Uneducated in the formal sense, yet intellectually sharp, and with a well-developed sense of humour, she saw clearly a sickness pervading the nation, and in her inimitable style urged Americans to eradicate it.

Useful material on Hamer can be found also in CRAWFORD *et al*. The seventeen essays in this volume were originally papers presented at a 1988 conference in Atlanta entitled: "Women in the Civil Rights Movement: Trailblazers and Torchbearers, 1941-1965". Hamer is the subject of three of these seventeen essays. Grant, Locke and Reagon all delineate the degrading conditions that southern rural blacks such as Hamer were forced to endure, and recount the transforming effect of her civil rights movement activism. They then focus on various aspects of Hamer's life. GRANT deals with the religious philosophy that guided Hamer throughout her life, and how she related her religious faith to the black freedom struggle. LOCKE focuses on Hamer's political activism, her major role in the formation and life of the Mississippi Freedom Democratic Party, and her several attempts to run for public office as a Freedom Democrat. Most of the political challenges mounted by Hamer and the MFDP failed, but Locke makes the point that these efforts had far-reaching results in terms of local, state and national party politics. REAGON focuses on the importance of the oral tradition in African American culture generally, and the civil rights movement in particular. She sees Hamer as contributing to that tradition in terms of her particular gifts for story-telling and song. Reagon discusses how Hamer's vocal ability was crucial in terms of creating an environment which sustained people in struggle.

COLLUM offers a concise overview of Hamer's life and also notes her growing awareness of wider issues – for example, her opposition to the Vietnam War and her belief in the basic injustice of the nation's economic system. This article also includes a short piece on Hamer by Chuck McLaurin, a SNCC organiser who worked closely with her in Ruleville. McLaurin remembers Hamer chiefly for the stirring power and calming effect of her singing voice.

GARLAND is one of several pieces on Hamer which are useful for their contemporaneity. Although Fannie Lou Hamer is not the sole focus of this magazine article, a substantial part of it covers her struggle and offers some interesting insights into her work. The narrative of Hamer's life is interspersed with some poignant testimony from Hamer herself.

In the first of two articles, PETERSON (1970) discusses the cycle of deprivation and intimidation experienced by the black people of Hamer's local community, most of them impoverished farmers ousted from employment by two factors; racism, and the arrival in the Delta of mechanised farming. The author presents an optimistic assessment of the various strategies employed by the community in the freedom struggle. He writes particularly enthusiastically on Hamer's dedicated and energetic work with several local anti-poverty programmes. PETERSON (1972) presents another rather sanguine look at the community self-help programmes instigated by Hamer. He concludes with Hamer's hopeful vision that the 1980s would bring racial harmony and economic prosperity to the people of Sunflower County.

MAUREEN CRESSEY-HACKETT

Hamilton, Alexander 1755–1804
Political leader and first Secretary of the Treasury

Cooke, Jacob Ernest, *Alexander Hamilton*, New York: Scribner, 1982

Emery, Noemie, *Alexander Hamilton: An Intimate Portrait*, New York: Putnam, 1982

Flexner, James Thomas, *The Young Hamilton: A Biography*, Boston: Little Brown, and London: Collins, 1978

Lodge, Henry Cabot, *Alexander Hamilton*, Boston: Houghton Mifflin, 1882

McDonald, Forrest, *Alexander Hamilton: A Biography*, New York: Norton, 1979

Miller, John C., *Alexander Hamilton: Portrait in Paradox*, New York: Harper, 1959

Miroff, Bruce, *Icons of Democracy: American Leaders as Heroes, Aristocrats, Dissenters, and Democrats*, New York: Basic Books, 1993

Mitchell, Broadus, *Alexander Hamilton*, 2 vols., New York: Macmillan, 1957–62

Rossiter, Clinton, *Alexander Hamilton and the Constitution*, New York: Harcourt Brace, 1964

Schachner, Nathan, *Alexander Hamilton*, New York: Appleton Century, 1946

Sumner, William Graham, *Alexander Hamilton*, New York: Dodd Mead, 1890

Alexander Hamilton was the youngest of the founding fathers and framers of the Constitution. Unlike the others, he was also, as his political opponents often noted, a bastard and an immigrant, having been born in the West Indies of the illegitimate union of a Scottish father and a mother of French descent. A thinker, essayist, soldier, lawyer, politician, administrator, and statesman of uncommon skill and "energy" (one of his favorite words), Hamilton – from the time of his arrival as a precocious teenager in the early 1770s until Jefferson's election in 1801 – was involved in most of the key events that launched the United States. Talleyrand considered him the greatest public figure of that era, ahead of Napoleon and Pitt; later writers, including a 20th-century United States senator in a book so titled, thought him to be "the greatest American." But others have regarded him as an "evil genius" (Noah Webster's phrase), obsessed with aristocracy, capitalism, militarism, centralized power, and order – an enemy of the common people and democracy. While a cabinet member, he had a notorious affair with a woman; when the affair was revealed to the public a few years later, he published a long essay about it. His life ended in a duel, at the hands of his political arch-enemy Aaron Burr, who happened at the time to be the sitting Vice President of the United States. It is no surprise, then, that biographies and other Hamiltoniana are extensive; the subject is both fascinating and well documented.

In a recent study of democratic leadership, MIROFF has a penetrating essay, "Alexander Hamilton: The Aristocratic Statesman and the Constitution of American Capitalism," that analyzes the various cross-currents of his career. Many Americans, Miroff argues, still prefer leaders with Hamilton's class, strength, energy, and goals – as long as they are clothed in obligatory democratic disguises. The two Roosevelts and John F. Kennedy are possible examples. Given Hamilton's origins, the fact that his interpreters persist in identifying him with aristocracy remains one of the many paradoxes surrounding his life. A possible resolution of the paradox could be that Hamilton's career illustrates that a true statesman becomes in some ways an aristocrat, and not that leadership should always be drawn from a pre-existing aristocracy.

Not much was written about Hamilton in the decades after his death. His ideological and political antagonists were in power, and he was not a popular subject. Moreover, Hamilton's widow outlived him by half a century, and it was only around the time of her death in the 1850s that their son,

John C. Hamilton, brought out editions of Hamilton's writings and a history of his times as seen through them. Those editions, along with the political changes wrought by the Civil War, led to a revival of interest in Hamilton, the great advocate of national power and diminisher of states rights. An example is the short biography by LODGE, later a prominent senator from Massachusetts; in it Hamilton is seen as fierce nationalist, equalled in that respect perhaps only by Washington, working to overcome the weaknesses and divisions of the original confederation of states. Less adulatory among the Hamilton studies from that era is the work of SUMNER, a Yale professor of social science notable for being a champion of Social Darwinism. Sumner looked favorably on Hamilton's contributions to the union in overcoming "the turbulent, anarchistic elements" of the revolutionary era, but he often faults Hamilton on his political tactics and even on his celebrated financial policies, which were filled with fallacies in the eyes of Sumner's late 19th-century financial orthodoxy.

Until the Great Depression, 20th-century studies of Hamilton tended to be adulatory and unoriginal; he was the great statesman who recognized that the business of America was business. The Depression and the New Deal cast aspersions on business, and Hamilton went into eclipse as a subject. Since World War II, however, there have been many biographies. The earlier ones appeared before the 27-volume collection of Hamilton's papers was published during the 1960s and 1970s. They include SCHACHNER, which is a detailed, straightforward, unexciting narrative account, but has little interpretation. Still more encyclopedic is MITCHELL's two-volume study that runs to some 1500 pages. Mitchell is able to explain and interpret Hamilton's economic theories and policies in better fashion than most of the other biographies. For overall sophistication, however, the best of these early postwar biographies is MILLER, who explores many of the paradoxes associated with Hamilton: for example, his birth outside of the American colonies, yet his fierce nationalism; his major contributions to the development of the United States as a nation, yet his feeling late in his life that he did not belong to "this American world;" and his attempts to unite the states that resulted in a factionalization of American politics.

Among the rather more recent biographies, the most scholarly is McDONALD, which is strong on the intellectual influences on Hamilton as well as on the three areas of his greatest contributions: finance, economics, and the law. EMERY focuses more on the psychological dimensions of its subject, and devotes more attention than most to Hamilton's later life. In contrast, FLEXNER says almost nothing about Hamilton's life after age 26; Flexner is also heavy on psychology, and, in this study of the young Hamilton, the child is not so much the father of the man as the man himself. COOKE, for many years editor of the Hamilton Papers, presents a concise and authoritative account of all the phases of Hamilton's brief but varied life. He seeks to interrelate Hamilton's personality and private life with his dramatic and sometimes erratic public career. Cooke provides what is probably the most accessible introduction to this complex and controversial figure.

ROSSITER, a distinguished political scientist, gives us not a biography but an extended meditation on Hamilton and the Constitution. Its basic message is that, in virtually every important respect but one (namely, leadership of the convention that drafted the document), Hamilton, not Madison, should be regarded as the father of the Constitution.

RICHARD SYLLA

Hamilton, Alexander: Financial and Economic Program, 1789–1795

Elkins, Stanley and Eric McKitrick, *The Age of Federalism: The Early American Republic, 1788–1800*, New York: Oxford University Press, 1993

Ferguson, E. James, *The Power of the Purse: A History of American Public Finance, 1776–1790*, Chapel Hill: University of North Carolina Press, 1961

Hammond, Bray, *Banks and Politics in America, from the Revolution to the Civil War*, Princeton: Princeton University Press, 1957

McDonald, Forrest, *The Presidency of George Washington*, Lawrence: University Press of Kansas, 1974

McDonald, Forrest, *Alexander Hamilton: A Biography*, New York: Norton, 1979

Mitchell, Broadus, *Alexander Hamilton*, 2 vols., New York: Macmillan, 1957–62

Otenasek, Mildred, *Alexander Hamilton's Financial Policies*, New York: Arno Press, 1977

Perkins, Edwin J., *American Public Finance and Financial Services, 1700–1815*, Columbus: Ohio State University Press, 1994

Swanson, Donald F., *The Origins of Hamilton's Fiscal Policies*, Gainesville: University of Florida Press, 1963

When the federal government established by the Constitution formed in 1789, it had a huge overhang of debt left from the Revolution. Under the previous Confederation, lack of revenue led to arrears in servicing the debt that were met by issuing more debt. The new government had as yet no revenue, but unlike its predecessor it at least had the power to generate a revenue. Still, the various instruments that formed the debt were selling at from 15 to 25 per cent of par value. The country lacked a functioning Treasury and had no national currency or coinage. It had no organized money and capital markets. There were only three isolated banks, none more than a decade old, and no semblance of a banking system.

In just a few years after 1789, all that had changed. A newly structured federal debt sold in thriving capital markets at or above par, and was rapidly being bought up by European investors. The federal government had ample hard-money revenues to service its debt, mostly from duties on imports but also from domestic excise taxes. A Bank of the United States, far larger than any of the other banks, had been created to serve as a handmaiden of government finance as well as a commercial bank; it formed the core of an emerging United States banking system. Provisions had been made for a national mint and coinage. And a thriving capital market emerged, fueled by the high credit of the new federal securities, the shares of the Bank, and the shares of other corporations that were formed under state charters. This remarkable turnabout in the finances of the United States was largely the work of Alexander Hamilton, the first Secretary of the Treasury, who served in that capacity from 1789 to 1795. Hamilton essentially created a financial system where none had been, but, unsurprisingly, he aroused fierce political opposition in the process. His system persisted, with changes to be sure, and became the first key element of the economic infrastructure of the country.

In a work of synthesis covering a period of more than a century, PERKINS provides a fairly comprehensive account of the context of Hamilton's financial program and its effects in creating an articulated financial system. Hamilton's report on coinage and the creation of a mint are the only elements neglected. There are a few inconsistencies in Perkins's treatment, but they are more than offset by his detailed coverage of the circumstances leading up to Hamilton's appearance on the stage and the very different circumstances that resulted from his work. Erosion of the program set in almost as soon as it was in place, Perkins argues, but the deviations led to further problems that prompted a return to it. Perkins carries the history only to 1815, but his point about deviations from and returns to Hamiltonian principles could well be applied to much of subsequent American financial history.

The remarkable success of Hamilton's program led scholars to investigate the practical and intellectual origins of his ideas. Hamilton's political enemies at the time, and later scholarly critics, accused him of basing the program on British precedents, an example of his allegedly excessive fondness for British institutions. SWANSON, among others, demonstrates that Hamilton was well aware of British financial theories and practices, and seemingly modeled key parts of his program on them, for example, the Bank of the United States on the Bank of England model. But, Swanson argues, there was more originality to Hamilton than others perceived; making his program look rather British was really a ploy on Hamilton's part to assure British and European capitalists of its essential soundness, so that they would respect the new federal government and be more likely to support it and the country by investing in American securities. That, of course, is exactly what happened.

In a 1939 dissertation published much later, OTENASEK is more convinced that Hamilton's program was based on European precedents rather than on original ideas. That, however, in no way detracts from Hamilton's true achievement which, Otenasek argues, was in implementing the program in a most effective manner against great odds, to the benefit of the new government and the country.

Of the many Hamilton biographies, two go into considerable detail on the financial program. MITCHELL's extensive account in the second of his two volumes is mainly factual yet also laudatory. Equally if not more laudatory, McDONALD (1979) devotes more attention to the intellectual influences on Hamilton's economic and financial ideas, but he argues that Hamilton's greatest achievements were not in formulating the program in his celebrated reports of 1790–91, but in implementing the program politically and then administratively. Similar points are made in McDONALD (1974), a study of the Washington presidency which treats Washington himself as little more than a figurehead, who provided a valuable "shield" for Hamilton against his political opponents. Washington approved the nationalist thrust of Hamilton's

program, even if he had reservations about it (or did not fully understand it). The politics of Hamilton's financial program were exceedingly controversial, which makes all the more interesting the fact that the administrative operations of the Treasury Department, which Hamilton essentially built from scratch, were remarkably uncontroversial.

There are a number of more general works on the financial and political history of the period, which provide useful background, and help to place Hamilton's policies in context. FERGUSON is an authoritative treatment of public finance from the Revolutionary War to the approval of Hamilton's funding program. He sees financial problems as an important factor in the demands for a stronger national government, and follows earlier interpretations which emphasized the stake of financial speculators in the redemption of the public debt. In his earlier chapters, HAMMOND describes the origins and history of the Bank of the United States, and has many astringent comments on the politics of banking in the early republic. In their monumental study of the Federalist age, and especially in the second, third and seventh chapters, ELKINS and McKITRICK offer an elegant and discursive treatment of Hamilton's financial and economic program. They stress the centrality of the public credit, and they focus particularly on the political storms which Hamilton's policies provoked – and their role in his break with Madison and Jefferson. From their various perspectives, these works testify to the fundamental importance of Hamilton's program for the infant United States, and to the depth and bitterness of the political divisions which they caused.

RICHARD SYLLA

See also Early National Period; Federal Government; Financial History, 1780s–1930s

Harding, Warren G. 1865–1923
29th President of the United States

Means, Gaston B., *The Strange Death of President Harding*, New York: Guild, 1930

Mee, Charles L., *The Ohio Gang: The World of Warren G. Harding*, New York: Evans, 1981.

Murray, Robert K., *The Harding Era: Warren G. Harding and His Administration*, Minneapolis: University of Minnesota Press, 1969

Russell, Francis, *The Shadow of Blooming Grove: Warren G. Harding in His Times*, New York: McGraw Hill, 1968; as *President Harding: His Life and Times, 1865–1923*, London: Eyre and Spottiswoode, 1969

Sinclair, Andrew, *The Available Man: The Life Behind the Masks of Warren Gamaliel Harding*, New York: Macmillan, 1965

Trani, Eugene P. and David L. Wilson, *The Presidency of Warren G. Harding*, Lawrence: Regents Press of Kansas, 1977

White, William Allen, *Masks in a Pageant*, New York: Macmillan, 1928

In every poll of leading American historians conducted since the 1950s, the name of Warren Harding is placed last in the ranks of United States presidents. Given the notoriety of his administration, the literature on Harding is surprisingly sparse. Few major biographies exist. Accounts of his presidency are most usually found in historical narratives of the 1920s, in which Harding himself is an ephemeral figure. Most works seem unusually preoccupied with the president's personal character, his tormenting self-doubt and adulterous liaisons, and with the dubious morals of his "cronies". Early works in particular are often condescending or sensationalized in style. Despite the opening of the Harding papers in 1964, few serious scholarly evaluations of this underrated president have emerged.

WHITE contributed an early version of such impressionistic and exaggerated portrayals. The Ohioan stands condemned, along with his successor, for his essential ordinariness in a work which includes portraits of early 20th-century giants such as Theodore Roosevelt and Woodrow Wilson. The author's "pageant" captures the drama of the times while missing many of the underlying tensions and problems which gave birth to the Harding-Coolidge era. White's judgement of Harding himself is relentlessly condescending, superficial and at times almost bitter (White, a Kansas progressive, attended the 1920 Republican Convention and opposed Harding's nomination). No observations or explanations of administration policy are offered. White's treatment served as a template for Harding literature down to the 1960s.

A modern, tongue-in-cheek representation of this style is offered by MEE. The primary objective of this "historical entertainment" is to document the corruption of "The Ohio Gang", led by Attorney-General Harry Daugherty and his sidekick, Jess Smith. Mee plays to the galleries with lighthearted accounts of bribery and fraud in the Veterans Bureau and Department of the Interior. Harding once again takes the stage as the well-meaning dupe. Highly unreliable reminiscences come from the discredited self-publicist Gaston B. Means, whom Mee denounces but utilizes for added colour. The work is a romp, and the complete lack of serious reflection on Harding's personality or policies should not surprise. Its significance lies in demonstrating that, after nearly sixty years, Harding's era is recalled chiefly for its entertainment value. MEANS contributes one of the oldest and most notorious works in the Harding literature. A former Justice Department investigator, he claimed to have worked directly for Mrs. Harding in an effort to "protect" the President from the designs of his mistress and corrupt associates. The prose is lurid and self-congratulatory, and the content largely fictitious (Means was twice imprisoned for conspiracy and larceny). The impact of his work was to reinforce unsubstantiated but persistent rumours that Harding was murdered by his wife to save him from impeachment.

With the opening of the Harding papers, the 1960s yielded three new, more carefully considered texts. While not particularly sympathetic to some administration policies, and at times oversimplifying them, SINCLAIR finally explodes the myth of the President as a tool of Harry Daugherty, citing new evidence of Harding's independence and political acumen. Sinclair identifies political expediency as a root cause of the President's lamentable posthumous reputation. Republican

anxiety to sweep the dead leader, along with Teapot Dome, under the carpet in order to bask in "Coolidge prosperity" helped to ensure that Harding's personal weaknesses would carry the burden of blame for what was essentially a systemic problem. Additionally, he regards the contemporary penchant for deriding "Main Street" America, its values and personalities, as a vital factor in undermining Harding. Authors and historians habitually succumb to the Menckenesque habit of lampooning the Ohioan's grammar, eating habits and social connections in order to prove his unsuitability for high office. This persistent "Babbitt in the White House" theme predominates in Harding literature and assists in obscuring the president's personal and political abilities.

RUSSELL's heavyweight treatment of Harding's life clearly seeks to move as much as to inform. Policy outlines are present but disappointingly thin. The textual focus is more or less firmly upon Harding's personality, marital problems, extramarital affairs and racial lineage. This last factor – allegations that the 1920 Republican nominee had negro blood in his family – is somewhat overplayed. Descriptions of his early Ohio and later senatorial careers and of the 1920 Chicago Convention are impressively detailed, but again personalities overshadow substantive political discussion. The style is journalistic, at times reading almost like a novel. Like Mee, Russell borrows substantially from a less-than-reliable source – a book by Harding's infatuated young lover Nan Britton. As a representation of Harding's intimate life and of the personalities most closely involved in the unfolding tragedy of his presidency, this book is unmatched and immensely readable. By comparison, the political content of the work – the treatment of Harding's cabinet meetings and policy decisions together with his evolving executive style – is rather light and results in an incomplete portrait of the man as president. Despite the author's evident sympathy for his subject, Harding's reputation as befuddled philanderer and incompetent party hack is, perhaps unwittingly, reinforced.

MURRAY's revisionist text presents a refreshing break from stereotype, finally disposing of the "amiable dunce" perspective. The author offers a complex portrayal of a limited but capable politician presiding with reasonable competence over a difficult era of transition. The building of the "Best Minds" Cabinet demonstrates the Harding's partisan dexterity and accounts of its meetings reveal Harding's "board chairman" approach and his willingness to permit Cabinet secretaries to pursue their own initiatives. The president's image becomes almost heroic in the confrontations with industry over the eight-hour day and with the veterans lobby over the issue of the soldiers' bonus. Murray's view is of a president daunted by his office, often agonizing over complex decisions but growing increasingly sure-footed and determined to overcome his own intellectual limitations. The much-neglected presidential speeches made during the final, fatal, tour of the western United States in July 1923, are used by the author to demonstrate Harding's growing antipathy towards the isolationists in Congress and his own stiffening resolve to reassert executive authority. His decision to risk splitting his own party over the issue of the World Court is presented as evidence of the President's new-found assertiveness. Despite the perhaps exaggerated claim that Harding's 882-day presidency set the political tone for the rest of the decade, this work remains the weightiest, most detailed and balanced study yet produced on the 29th president.

TRANI and WILSON's review is concise and policy-oriented. Evidently influenced by Murray's ground-breaking work, it acknowledges Harding's political guile and credits him, rather than Daugherty, with the success of the long-shot 1920 nomination campaign. Nevertheless, the overall tone remains largely negative, for example the description of Harding as a small-town politician of limited education and vision who failed to provide effective policies or moral leadership. The Naval Disarmament Conference is seen as merely a "stopgap" solution and the eight-hour day as only a small first step in improving workers' conditions. At times, the authors appear to criticize Harding for lacking the advantage of hindsight and for taking actions or stances entirely appropriate for the political era in which he governed. Some concluding evaluations are disappointingly rooted in post-1933 concepts of presidential leadership. The book remains, however, a concise and useful introduction to the Harding presidency.

NIALL ANDREW PALMER

Harlan, John M. 1833–1911

Supreme Court justice and civil rights defender

Beth, Loren P., *John Marshall Harlan: The Last Whig Justice*, Lexington: University Press of Kentucky, 1992

Canfield, Monte, Jr., "'Our Constitution is Color-Blind': Mr. Justice Harlan and Modern Problems of Civil Rights," *University of Missouri at Kansas City Law Review*, 32, Summer 1964

Gordon, James W., "Did the First Justice Harlan Have a Black Brother?" *Western New England Law Review* 15, 1993

Porter, Mary Cornelia Aldis, "John Marshall Harlan the Elder and Federal Common Law: A Lesson from History," *Supreme Court Review*, 1972

Przybyszewski, Linda C.A., "Mrs. John Marshall Harlan's Memories: Hierarchies of Gender and Race in the Household and the Polity," *Law and Social Inquiry*, 18, Summer 1993

Watt, Richard F. and Richard M. Orkiloff, "The Coming Vindication of Mr. Justice Harlan," *Illinois Law Review*, 44, 1949

Westin, Alan F., "John Marshall Harlan and the Constitutional Rights of Negroes: The Transformation of a Southerner," *Yale Law Journal*, 66, April 1957

Westin, Alan F., "Mr. Justice Harlan," in *Mr. Justice*, edited by Allison Dunham and Philip B. Kurland, revised edition, Chicago: University of Chicago Press, 1964

White, G. Edward, "John Marshall Harlan I: The Precursor," in his *The American Judicial Tradition: Profiles of Leading American Judges*, New York: Oxford University Press, 1976, revised 1988

Yarbrough, Tinsley E., *Judicial Enigma: The First Justice Harlan*, New York: Oxford University Press, 1995

Although John Marshall Harlan was a well-known judicial figure in his lifetime, he remained a relatively neglected historical subject until the Supreme Court decision of *Brown v. Board of Education* in 1954. WATT and ORKILOFF had predicted the coming vindication of his broad interpretation of the Thirteenth, Fourteenth, and Fifteenth Amendments, but little attention had been paid him. Suddenly Harlan's dissents from the *Civil Rights Cases* (1884) and *Plessy v. Ferguson* (1896) – decisions which allowed the states to segregate blacks despite the guarantees of the Civil War Amendments – seemed prophetic, especially because of the righteous tone in which Harlan had spoken. A flurry of law review articles followed *Brown*; the Spring 1958 issue of the *Kentucky Law Journal* was devoted to Harlan.

Yet it was another forty years before a book-length study appeared. The long delay in the deposit of Harlan's private papers in public archives made true biographical work difficult for a time and resulted in many articles which merely surveyed Harlan's published decisions. In fact, the conventions of legal studies and political science encouraged such pieces even after the papers became available in the 1970s. Having sole access to Harlan's papers, WESTIN (1957) was the best of the early articles. He narrated Harlan's pre-war political career and attributed Harlan's transformation from slaveholder to Republican politician to a revulsion from white terrorism. Westin then traced Harlan's line of civil rights decisions, but unlike Watts and Orkiloff, he criticized Harlan's readings of the Thirteenth and Fourteenth Amendments as misinterpretations of their wording and of the intent of their writers. Harlan had rejected the state action doctrine which holds that the Fourteenth Amendment can only be used against states and not against violent individuals. But Watt and Orkiloff and CANFIELD show that the rules of constitutional draftsmanship and interpretation are less helpful in understanding Harlan's jurisprudence than a recognition of the historical evils which he believed the amendments must have addressed, and the precedents which they must have overturned. Harlan understood the abolition of slavery to have also entailed the end of second-class citizenship for free blacks.

Overlapping with this first wave of interest in Harlan as a champion of civil rights was a second which turned towards his economic decisions. WESTIN (1964) expanded his work to include Harlan's decisions in the economic sphere. He characterized him awkwardly as a "premature New Dealer" because of his dissents in favor of pro-labor laws and government regulation of corporations. Writing in the same vein, WHITE is the more satisfying in its depth of analysis and in the specificity of its definitions. White laid out three competing views of judicial behavior, each containing an understanding of the relationship between government and the economy: Jacksonianism, laissez-faire, and paternalism. He concluded from Harlan's civil rights and economic decisions that he was a paternalist opposed to the theory of laissez-faire. Hence his support of the federal income tax and federal regulation of the economy.

PORTER turns her eye beyond the two well-rehearsed areas of civil rights and economic rights to focus on Harlan's dubious contribution to the doctrine of the federal common law. She is meticulous in her analysis of the doctrinal record on municipal bond repudiation. Like Westin, White and others, she concludes that Harlan's objectives were generally good ones but that his legal reasoning and precedents were unsound.

The first book-length study of Harlan finally appeared in 1992. BETH uses southern Whig nationalism as a recurring motif but he moves quickly over many issues both personal and doctrinal without great analysis. The book contains numerous and lengthy quotations upon which little comment is made. In his desire to praise Harlan, Beth overplays the Harlan family's alleged aversion to slavery. He is also slightly uncomfortable in his final judgment on Harlan's contribution to judging. He concludes that Harlan was a great judge, yet must acknowledge that he was not known for his judicial craftsmanship.

This being a generally admitted fact, it is perhaps not surprising that interest has turned more recently from a focus on the decisions and towards the personal and social sources of Harlan's thought. In some ways, these studies take up the issues raised by Watt and Orkiloff and Canfield because they try to make sense of Harlan by going beyond strictly doctrinal issues. PRZYBYSZEWSKI uses the previously neglected memoirs of Harlan's wife in order to explore the paternalist ideal of the Harlan men. She argues that the paternalism which was supposed both to protect and to subordinate slaves and white women lies at the root of Harlan's civil rights thought. GORDON indicates that the Harlans dealt in slaves more actively than previously supposed, but he speculates with less care than have other historians upon the possibility of Harlan's having had a black half-brother and the effect which such a person might have had on his decision-making.

YARBOROUGH is the second full-length narrative biography of Harlan. This is better written than Beth, but Yarborough has no particular line of argument of his own, save that Harlan remains an enigma, as his title suggests. He draws especially on Gordon's work for information about Harlan's possible black half-brother, and, on this topic as well as on several others, he indulges in speculation in the absence of hard evidence. Yarborough tries to juxtapose material in an unusual manner, in an attempt to relate Harlan's personal relations with his legal positions. The results are often awkward – for example, when he tries to make a connection between Harlan's position on applying the Bill of Rights to the insular possessions, and his relationship with his alcoholic brother. While Yarborough's descriptions of Harlan's brother, and of Harlan's own financial situation, provide more detail than earlier accounts, he adds little to the analysis and interpretation of Harlan's life and judicial record.

LINDA C.A. PRZYBYSZEWSKI

See also Supreme Court

Hearst, William Randolph 1863–1951
Newspaper publisher

Carlisle, Rodney P., *Hearst and the New Deal: The Progressive as Reactionary*, New York: Garland, 1979

Carringer, Robert L., *The Making of Citizen Kane*, Berkeley: University of California Press, 1985

Davies, Marion, *The Times We Had: Life with William Randolph Hearst*, Indianapolis: Bobbs Merrill, 1975

Leonard, Thomas C., *News for All: America's Coming-of-Age with the Press*, New York: Oxford University Press, 1995

Liebling, A.J., *The Press*, New York: Ballantine, 1961, revised 1975

Littlefield, Roy Everett, *William Randolph Hearst: His Role in American Progressivism*, Lanham, MD: University Press of America, 1980

Lundberg, Ferdinand, *Imperial Hearst: A Social Biography*, New York: Modern Library, 1936

O'Donnell, James F., *100 Years of Making Communications History: The Story of the Hearst Corporation*, n.p.: Hearst Professional Magazines, 1987

Older, Mrs. Fremont, *William Randolph Hearst, American*, New York: Appleton Century, 1936

Robinson, Judith, *The Hearsts: An American Dynasty*, Newark: University of Delaware Press, 1991

Swanberg, W.A., *Citizen Hearst: A Biography of William Randolph Hearst*, New York: Scribner, 1961; London: Longman, 1962

Lincoln Steffens conducted the most penetrating interview with William Randolph Hearst in 1906 and concluded that he was "The Man of Mystery." Decades of observation and scholarship have not dispelled that mystery. As a politician, as a publisher, and as a personality Hearst has been difficult to pin down.

His erratic political career has many chroniclers. SWANBERG tells this story without the vitriol of Hearst's contemporaries who, often with good reason, called him variously a populist, an anarchist, a socialist, a communist and a reactionary during his five decades as a major player in national politics. Swanberg finds a man of so much color and vigor that moral judgments seem almost beside the point. LUNDBERG, sounding the alarm from the left, is the best example of heretic hunting by a contemporary. This early biography disclaims interest in Hearst's personal life, but delivers the thundering judgment that he was "the most influential American fascist." In his preface to Lundberg, the historian Charles A. Beard said that "Hearst's fate is ostracism by decency in life, and oblivion in death." OLDER is the hagiographic counterpoint with a progressive Californian's loyalty to a native son. Hearst is "the most misunderstood man in America" and an indefatigable reformer. Older, the biographer of the publisher's father, was on easy terms with the remarkable Hearst clan, and her generous reprinting of correspondence as well as her feel for the West are the best parts of this contemporary profile.

Hearst was a life-long Democrat, and LITTLEFIELD and CARLISLE are the most recent scholars to show his love-hate relationship with that party. They both used sources not available to Swanberg and add to the picture of Hearst's shifting agenda. These recent monographs are conventional political histories, however, and are not good places to look for an understanding of his role in the wider culture. This is the dimension missing in all the literature, the link between Hearst's role as impresario of popular culture for a new urban America and his erratic political dreams.

LIEBLING's acidic essays sum up the contempt that many working journalists had for Hearst by the end of his life, and suggest a simple explanation for his power: no one before Hearst threw a great American fortune into media. The story of how the mining wealth of the first industrial era was transformed into the business of information and entertainment has not been fully told. As might be expected, the authorized business history by O'DONNELL treads lightly over corporate reverses and faltering editorial judgments, but he also corrects errors in Swanberg about the corporation. Until this private corporation opens its files to business historians, there will be much guesswork. Historians who keep an eye on marketing are opening up new perspectives. LEONARD, for instance, notes that the broad reach of the Hearst papers stemmed in part from the organization's ignorance about who was in fact buying their papers in New York.

Hearst's character traits are not so much analyzed as they are enumerated by Swanberg, the best of the biographers. "This does not pretend to be definitive biography," he warns. Swanberg's is a considerable achievement, however, for while Hearst lived, reliable information was rare. Older, for example, mentions Marion Davies only once (as a screen actress) and says nothing about her central role in Hearst's life for more than three decades. The film *Citizen Kane* (1941), written by Orson Welles and Herman Mankiewicz, colors every view of Hearst, and critics who have shown how the film was put together have made a signal contribution to biography. CARRINGER, continuing the pioneering work of the journalist Pauline Kael, has shed more light on Hearst than many other writers in recent decades. His imaginative scholarship on the culture of celebrityhood and the myth-making power of film shows the limitations of authors who would fit Hearst into a single political tradition. Since Hearst had a role in creating these narrative forms, both as a publisher and a filmmaker, Hollywood is an important vantage point on the man. DAVIES, with a gracious and disingenuous preface by Welles, is also essential reading on this world. These works put to rest the notion that Hearst was a victim of emotional trauma or that he suffered anguish over his abuses of power. ROBINSON makes careful use of new Hearst papers and helps to restore the strong role of women in shaping the future tycoon, but this family portrait stops with the 1920s and does not supplant Swanberg, even for the Hearst journey to middle age.

THOMAS C. LEONARD

See also Newspapers and Magazines

Hispanic Americans

Acuña, Rodolfo, *Occupied America: The Chicano's Struggle Toward Liberation*, San Francisco: Canfield Press, 1972; 3rd edition, as *Occupied America: A History of Chicanos*, New York: Harper, 1988

De León, Arnoldo, *They Called Them Greasers: Anglo Attitudes Toward Mexicans in Texas, 1821–1900*, Austin: University of Texas Press, 1983

Deutsch, Sarah, *No Separate Refuge: Culture, Class, and Gender on an Anglo-Hispanic Frontier in the American Southwest, 1880–1940*, New York: Oxford University Press, 1987

Dolan, Jay P. and Jaime R. Vidal, *Puerto Rican and Cuban Catholics in the US, 1900–1965*, Notre Dame, IN: University of Notre Dame Press, 1994

García, Mario T., *Desert Immigrants: The Mexicans of El Paso, 1880–1920*, New Haven: Yale University Press, 1981

Griswold del Castillo, Richard, *The Treaty of Guadalupe Hidalgo: A Legacy of Conflict*, Norman: University of Oklahoma Press, 1990

Hinojosa, Gilberto Miguel, *A Borderlands Town in Transition: Laredo, 1755–1870*, College Station: Texas A & M University Press, 1983

Moore, Joan and Harry Pachon, *Hispanics in the United States*, Englewood Cliffs, NJ: Prentice Hall, 1985

Pitt, Leonard, *The Decline of the Californios: A Social History of the Spanish-Speaking Californians, 1846–1890*, Berkeley: University of California Press, 1966

Portes, Alejandro and Robert L. Bach, *Latin Journey: Cuban and Mexican Immigrants in the United States*, Berkeley: University of California Press, 1985

Sanchez Korrol, Virginia E., *From Colonia to Community: The History of Puerto Ricans in New York City*, Westport, CT: Greenwood Press, 1983; revised Berkeley: University of California Press, 1994

The history of the Hispanics in the United States is both a relatively new and a disputatious field. Inasmuch as it largely began as a result of the war with Mexico which led to the acquisition by conquest of a large non-Anglo population, GRISWOLD DEL CASTILLO provides a good starting point. The author looks not only at the events surrounding the treaty but also at how it has been viewed, both in Mexico and in the United States, especially since 1960. Thus this work also serves as an introduction to discussions over the place of the acquired populations in the United States. There is a short but interesting chapter on the Chicano Movement and the treaty and another on the way the Supreme Court has interpreted it over the years. The author argues very strongly that the failure of the United States to live up to both the letter and the spirit of the treaty, in particular in ensuring the fullest civil and property rights for the acquired populations, leaves much to be desired.

ACUÑA's third edition is less polemical than earlier ones, but its title still suggests the main thrust. It is therefore very useful in also introducing readers to the often barely disguised anger that pervades much of the writing on the subject of Hispanics in the United States. Its discussion of the vexed subject of nomenclature is helpful, for, as the book titles listed above clearly show, writers are not all agreed on how Hispanics should be defined. Since Acuña is writing about the Southwest and since he approves of the Chicano political movement he is comfortable with the term. The opening chapters deal with the colonization of Mexico's Northwest, from the first movements of United States citizens into Texas to the dispossessions that followed the Treaty of Guadalupe Hidalgo in Arizona, California and New Mexico. Part Two examines the creation of a Mexican American underclass in the early 20th century and then continues the story to the present. Acuña argues that the present and future history of the Chicanos reflects, and will be created by, developments and transformations in the national economy, producing an increasingly centrifugal community, the wealthier profiting, the poorer suffering from the changes. There is no bibliography, but the endnotes show the author's familiarity with a wide range of sources. The level of commitment occasionally leads to overstatement but never to equivocation.

MOORE and PACHON is a study of the situation of Hispanics in the early 1980s, which stresses the diversity of Hispanic groups – a term with which they are comfortable, though their view that it refers to men and women of ultimately Spanish origin would annoy those who would accent the mestizo. Many of the tables in this work are based on the census of 1980, so would need updating to take account of the findings of the 1990 census. The authors provide what is essentially a study of Hispanic culture – that is attitudes and behaviour – examining school attendance, income and occupation, poverty, homeownership, class and family values, including exogamy. They also examine attitudes to religion and have an interesting section on the growth of Hispanic Protestantism. They look at language and other cultural retentions and also at attitudes to immigration, though this section suffers from having been written before the passage of the 1986 act. The final chapter examines Hispanic political participation to explain why it is weaker than it might be. There are a few references to African Americans but no systematic account of relations between the communities. There is no bibliography but the footnotes are useful for suggesting further reading.

PORTES and BACH look at two Hispanic communities, the Cuban and the Mexican. Though their data is largely taken from the 1970s, their work is useful because of its theoretical concerns which help to suggest answers to general questions on migration. Some of their research consisted of interviews with newly-arrived immigrants and their conclusions, if accepted, would modify more traditional accounts of migration. Portes and Bach believe that immigrants are drawn to the United States as their local societies become drawn into the international economy, of which the United States is so much a part. They also point out that much migration is circular, rather than final, and that the groups they studied seemed to discount rates of unemployment in the United States when making the decision to move. Cuban immigrants benefited from having a multi-layered community into which they moved, while Mexicans, lacking this, have experienced less upward mobility. Unusually, the authors argue that the more educated members of their communities were the more aware of prejudice in the host society and therefore the more critical of it. There is a bibliography, but the latest work cited dates from 1984.

Although PITT wrote a generation ago, he should be read for his lucid and full account of the way in which the Californio elite lost their lands after 1848, through a combination of ignorance and inexperience and the determined acquisitiveness of the incoming Anglos. The work opens with an overview of California before 1846 and continues with an account of the war, of which the author does not approve. It discusses the way in which the Gold Rush destroyed previous arrangements, both by ensuring that the Californios became a small minority in their own region, and by exposing them to the harmful effects of the hostile prejudices of many of the Argonauts. The levels of ensuing violence lead Pitt to entitle one of his chapters "Race War in Los Angeles." Californios were helped by a relatively strong Catholic Church but found it difficult to retain teaching in Spanish. The 1860s saw natural catastrophe, drought and flood, add to their difficulties and their dispossessions. The glossary of ethnic terms is interesting inasmuch as it does not include "Hispanic" – which suggests how recently the word has been generally adopted.

DE LEÓN has been a very influential work. Based on much work among primary sources, it has become the definitive study of the interaction of Hispanics and Anglos on one frontier during the 19th century. Since it is a study in attitudes and images it has little to say on socio-economic conditions. It has been criticized for its undifferentiating attitude to Anglos, often merely referred to as whites, and it does provide a good example, probably inadvertent, of the need to demonize the other "side." There are few half-tones, but this is a book that cannot be ignored.

HINOJOSA looks at one Texas town, but over a longer time-span than is often the case. It is primarily a demographic study and based in part on census materials. With a better sense of the socio-economic frame than De León, Hinojosa is led to argue that there was less ethnic and more class conflict in the town than elsewhere, though the smallness of the Anglo population must have helped to diminish possible tensions. The work is unusual in almost completely ignoring communal strife. GARCÍA deals with another Texan town and covers a different period. El Paso began to grow once the railroad arrived and allowed the mines and ranches to expand. Mexican immigrants provided the labour for ensuing enterprises. Here occupation and ethnicity combined to lead to an ethnically stratified society, with the Mexican immigrants relegated to unskilled and semi-skilled positions. They were also hindered in any attempts to take advantage of economic growth and development by the public policy of segregated schools, which taught a limited curriculum, readying the children for their restricted place in society. The town's geographical position, on the boundary with Mexico, ensured that ties with the homeland would remain the tightest and led to doubts as to how far the newcomers wished to assimilate. It also allowed frequent returns south of the border and the maintenance of Mexican culture in the United States. The work is based on a wide range of primary and secondary sources and has a good bibliography.

DEUTSCH has rightly taken its place as one of the foremost investigations of not only ethnicity but also gender in the Southwest, more particularly northern New Mexico and southern Colorado. The author is interested in the ways in which women helped to maintain Hispanic culture in the face of the need to move to work, and the resultant fragility of uprooted settlements. The work positions itself between those who would see ethnicity deeply eroded by the need to join the Anglo-dominated economy, and those who would argue that ethnic identity was too strong to be endangered. Deutsch distinguishes between village life, where Hispanic women in particular had a freedom to adopt defensive strategies aimed at preserving local custom, and the settlements attached to mines and agri-business which often gave Hispanics few means through which to act. The author also suggest that the New Deal had its destructive effects, since its interventionism limited the freedom of the Hispanics to pursue their own strategies. The work may be read either as a contribution to the New Western History with its investigation of gender, or as an example of the history of ethnicity. Either way it is to be recommended. There are 93 pages of notes and a 38 page bibliography.

Originally published in 1983, SANCHEZ KORROL has recently been updated with a new preface and a new final chapter. It also contains an additional bibliography covering the period between the editions which will suggest further reading. The author's description of the present-day Puerto Rican community in New York City adds weight to Acuña's conclusions that the de-industrialization of the American economy is undermining its poorer, blue-collar sections. Indeed, many recent years have seen more Puerto Ricans return to the island than leave. The bulk of this work, however, is concerned with the transplanting of Puerto Rican culture to the mainland and particularly the associational forms this took. As is often the case in writing on ethnicity, the author has to choose between the optimistic and the pessimistic, but in a conclusion which speaks of empowerment and achievement appears to prefer the first. There is a chapter on political behaviour which makes the valid point that little is known of voting behaviour and, presumably, to judge from the author's silences on such matters, of registration and turnout.

The close connection between ethnicity, culture and religion is explored in a work edited by DOLAN and VIDAL, but in fact written by Vidal and Lisandro Perez. This is part of a continuing series on the History of Hispanic Catholics in the United States, produced by the University of Notre Dame. The two companion volumes published so far are *Mexican Americans and the Catholic Church, 1900–1965* and *Hispanic Catholic Culture in the U.S.: Issues and Concerns*. Vidal heads his chapters "Citizens Yet Strangers" and shows through an examination of Puerto Rican Catholicism how very little desire there is on the part of the islanders to acculturate very far, even to the point of rejecting multiculturalism, on the grounds that its acceptance would give value to cultural practices of which they disapprove. Perez's survey of Cuban Catholicism suggests that it was weak well before the Revolution of 1958, and has always contained strong African elements. This inhibits connection to the wide Catholic world. Whereas Vidal suggests a strong desire on the part of Puerto Ricans for Spanishlanguage services, Perez implies a weaker demand among Cubans. This may serve to identify one important distinction between two branches of the Hispanic community, one which is composed of citizens of the United States, the other comprising in large part refugees. Their disparate histories, not to mention those of the acquired and immigrant populations of the Southwest, help to explain the variety and the controversies within this area of United States historiography.

R.A. BURCHELL

Historical Geography

Brown, Ralph H., *Historical Geography of the United States*, New York: Harcourt Brace, 1948

Clark, Andrew Hill, *Acadia: The Geography of Early Nova Scotia to 1760*, Madison: University of Wisconsin Press, 1968

Earle, Carville, *Geographical Inquiry and American Historical Problems*, Stanford, CA: Stanford University Press, 1992

Gibson, James R. (editor), *European Settlement and Development in North America: Essays on Geographical Change in Honour and Memory of Andrew Hill Clark*, Toronto: University of Toronto Press, 1978

Jordan, Terry G., *Trails to Texas: Southern Roots of Western Cattle Ranching*, Lincoln: University of Nebraska Press, 1981

Lemon, James T., *The Best Poor Man's Country: A Geographical Study of Early Southeastern Pennsylvania*, Baltimore: Johns Hopkins Press, 1972

Meinig, D.W., *The Shaping of America: A Geographical Perspective on 500 Years of History*, 2 vols., New Haven: Yale University Press, 1986–93

Sauer, Carl O., *The Early Spanish Main*, Berkeley: University of California Press, 1966

Historical geography is the fruitful offspring of shared methodologies and historiographical ferment. Geography's concerns with spatial and ecological factors which shape landscape and place, and history's commitment to rigorous archival research, and a searching inquiry into human action, are combined in the modern study of historical geography.

The founder of modern American historical geography was Ralph H. Brown. Through a fresh and innovative survey of regional settlement from colonization to the turn of the 20th century, BROWN illustrated how generations of frontiersmen shaped their local environment, and ultimately settlement patterns, with the technological equipment available to them as they settled, occupied, and ordered the landscape around them. Based on rigorous manuscript research and decades of field work, Brown's analysis is lucid, and his ability to portray the landscape through the eyes of the settler is second to none.

Although North America was only rarely the focus of his superb scholarship, it is impossible to write of American historical geography without reference to the towering figure of Carl O. Sauer. His ability to utilize broad historical and anthropological methodologies in analyzing the long-term cultural transformation of the landscape under colonization and initial European settlement is exemplified in SAUER. He is scathingly critical of Columbus and the entire colonial administration during the twenty years following initial Spanish contact in 1492. The Spaniards, he states, decimated the native population, destroyed the local ecology, and established a tragic precedent for European colonization in the Caribbean.

While Sauer's focus was largely ethnographic, Andrew Clark returned to Brown's paradigm of regional settlement and development. To Clark, historical geography required intensive empirical research in the field and the archives and a thorough familiarity with the larger patterns of geography and history. Only a finely woven tapestry of local studies, he believed, might collectively reveal the geography of regional change. Clark's own work and that of his graduate students characterizes this approach. In one good example of his work, CLARK carefully analyzes a cross section of geographical change in the settlement, population, and economy of Nova Scotia and New Brunswick up to 1760. A festschrift, edited by GIBSON and produced by Clark's former students, bears the indelible stamp of their mentor's style. Although the subject matter varies widely, each essay in this brief though coherent collection exemplifies Clark's fine-grained analytical approach to regional geography. Particularly stimulating are the essays by Cole Harris on the disintegration of the "ancien regime" in Quebec, Mitchell's analysis of early American culture regions, McQuillan's discussion of Mennonite settlement in Kansas, and Hilliard's examination of the antebellum rice industry in South Carolina.

Another Clark student, LEMON investigates the agrarian origins of liberalism in southeastern Pennsylvania. Rural settlers, he contends, preserved a liberal, bourgeois, yet ultimately conservative ideology that shaped and molded early Pennsylvanian history and geography. Settlers of every ethnic stripe shared this ideology and consequently rejected Penn's model of organized farms and public interest in favor of an individualistic and dispersed settlement pattern. Lemon challenges the notion that ethnic origins defined regional patterns of settlement and economic behavior.

JORDAN attempts to explain the cultural origins of the Great Plains Cowboy. He challenges Webb's environmental determinism and argues that the Texas cowboy culture derived not from Mexico but rather from cattle ranching in colonial South Carolina. Through a first-rate methodological application of cultural diffusion, Jordan delineates sixteen cultural traits that diffused along two routes from the "culture hearth" in South Carolina to east Texas in the 19th century. Rather than emphasizing the formative influence of the frontier, Jordan sees the migrant male as fashioning the landscape around him. In this he differs fundamentally from Frederick Jackson Turner and Walter Prescott Webb.

While Clark and his students wrote extensively on regional geography, they did not attempt the broad macro-geographical sweep of continental change and world system development. Unquestionably, the most ambitious exponent of this approach is Meinig who has thus far published two of the four projected volumes of his *magnum opus*. Anyone seeking to understand American historical geography and broad historical trends must address Meinig's work. MEINIG (1986) defines the settlement and expansion of the New World as a product of limitless European imperialism. Hailing from northern and southern Europe, the settlers fashioned a network of transatlantic links, swept aside native peoples, drove toward the interior of the continent, and finally re-ordered their domestic and international geopolitical positions with Britain, France, and Spain. Particularly useful is Meinig's schematic approach to the Revolutionary War. MEINIG (1993) explains American territorial expansionism in imperial terms and suggests that "capitalist-imperialist" forces were at work shaping the frontier and integrating the nation into the world economy. The same kind of imperialism explains the wartime destruction of the Old South and the imposition of northern culture during Reconstruction.

Broad scale geographic and historical themes are also the hallmarks of EARLE, who uses two main theoretical models to explain economic, historical, and geographical change. His commitment to staple theory and to Kondratieff's long wave economic cycles underlie his firm belief that agrarian processes have shaped American history over the past four hundred years. Whether he addresses labor unrest in the 1880s or agricultural improvement in the cotton South, Earle consistently brings the reader back to his methodological formula. Although his essays are strenuous reading, they stand as a benchmark of modern geographical inquiry into history.

RICHARD J. FOLLETT

Historiography

Bassett, John Spencer, *The Middle Group of American Historians*, New York: Macmillan, 1917

Benson, Lee, *Turner and Beard: American Historical Writing Reconsidered*, Glencoe, IL: Free Press, 1960

Cartwright, William H. and Richard L. Watson, Jr. (editors), *The Reinterpretation of American History and Culture*, Washington, DC: National Council for the Social Studies, 1973

Cunliffe, Marcus and Robin W. Winks (editors), *Pastmasters: Some Essays on American Historians*, New York: Harper, 1969

Foner, Eric (editor), *The New American History*, Philadelphia: Temple University Press, 1990

Gatell, Frank Otto and Allen Weinstein, *American Themes: Essays in Historiography*, New York: Oxford University Press, 1968

Higham, John, *History: Professional Scholarship in America*, New York: Harper, 1965; revised, Baltimore: Johns Hopkins University Press, 1989

Hofstadter, Richard, *The Progressive Historians: Turner, Beard, Parrington*, New York: Knopf, 1968; London: Cape, 1969

Kammen, Michael G. (editor), *The Past Before Us: Contemporary Historical Writing in the United States*, Ithaca, NY: Cornell University Press, 1980

Kraus, Michael and Davis D. Joyce, *The Writing of American History*, revised edition, Norman: University of Oklahoma Press, 1985 (earlier editions, by Kraus only, as *A History of American History*, 1937, and *The Writing of American History*, 1953)

Novick, Peter, *That Noble Dream: The "Objectivity Question" and the American Historical Profession*, Cambridge and New York: Cambridge University Press, 1988

Wish, Harvey, *The American Historian*, New York: Oxford University Press, 1960

American history has been dominated over the past century by a few great historiographic schools. The sequence of patrician, progressive, consensus, and new history forms the backbone of any treatment of American historiography. These schools of thought are peculiar to the American experience and grew up largely uninfluenced by historical writing in the rest of the world. American historians have generally steered clear of theory and ideology as well. They remain wary of Marxist modes of analysis and the grand scope of the *Annalistes*, for example, even as they borrow heavily from the insights and visions of these European modes of thought. Similarly, standard surveys and critiques of American historiography tend to take a parochial point of view that makes greater reference to American history itself, and to contemporary politics, than to particular theories or philosophies of history.

The best comprehensive account of American historiography is probably KRAUS and JOYCE. First published under a different title in 1937 and revised twice since, this chronological survey spans the late 16th century to the early 1970s. It opens with a brief review of the contemporary historians of exploration and colonization and continues with the nationalists and romantics of the early republic. These first half-dozen chapters set the stage for discussion of the remainder of the 19th century, from the rise of the scientific school to the late-19th-century nationalists and imperialists. The 20th century is covered through the traditional succession of progressive, consensus, and new history schools. The strong biographical organization of each chapter provides brief, almost encyclopedic, accounts of dozens of historians, many of them neglected in other studies. Kraus and Joyce are less successful in discussing the larger historiographic issues and falter in accounting for the post-consensus writing of the 1960s and 1970s.

Several collections of essays survey history written since the 1950s and thus pick up where Kraus and Joyce lapse. GATELL and WEINSTEIN is a collection of distinguished historiographic review articles published in prominent American scholarly journals. Twenty-two essays cover each of the traditional time periods in American history, from colonization to the post-World War II era. Those by Jack P. Greene, Gordon Wood, David Brion Davis, Frank Freidel, and others have become standard accounts of American historical writing through 1960. A separate bibliography of historiographic works, divided by historical time period, is dated but still useful. The 25 original essays in CARTWRIGHT and WATSON were addressed to history teachers who were revising their curricula to reflect recent historical interpretations, but they still make a useful resource, even for specialists. Two introductory chapters provide an overview of writing in the 1960s, a period of transition from the dominant consensus school to the wide-ranging interests of the new history, with its renewed focus on social issues. Individual chapters on such topics as African Americans, immigrants, ethnic groups, women, and the city reflect the emerging trends. About half the chapters focus on traditional time periods. Bibliographic references are in footnotes.

KAMMEN neatly fills a gap between Cartwright and Watson (1973) and Foner (1990). Twenty essays by distinguished American historians survey the state of historical writing in the United States during the 1970s from various topical perspectives. The thirteen chapters that deal with American history cover such traditional areas as political, social and labor history, but there are separate essays on the newly emerging fields of community, women and the family, psychohistory, and African Americans, among others. Extensive footnotes provide ample bibliographic references. Excellent surveys of the new American history can be found in FONER, a collection of thirteen original essays by prominent historians in their respective fields. This project was initiated by the American Historical Association, which wanted a series of pamphlets on recent historiography for use by secondary school teachers. The original conception was broadened to address the more sophisticated needs of college students and academics, and the essays were published in this single-volume edition. Seven chapters cover traditional time periods, but six others reflect the concerns of the new history. Thus separate chapters are devoted to social history, women, ethnicity and immigration, and labor. Selected bibliographies of the monographic literature from the 1970s and 1980s are included with each chapter.

NOVICK provides an exhaustive analysis of modern historiography structured around the long-standing debate over the nature of historical truth. His account begins in the 1880s, when the first currents of scientific history and its appeal to objective truth began to be felt in the United States. Many historians, just then struggling to gain status as professionals in an age of scientific optimism, eagerly grasped the notion that their discipline could discover the unaltering and objective truths that constituted history. By the second decade of the 20th century the debate was joined when a new generation began to question many of the stringent assumptions of the objectivists. Although frankly dubious about claims for historical truth, Novick explores with a great deal of sensitivity and nuance – and plentiful references to individual historians and particular schools of thought – a question that has permeated much of American historical thinking. It is not the only issue that has animated historiographic debate over the past century, but Novick demonstrates that it is one that has engendered a good deal of passion among historians. "What has been at issue," Novick observes, "is nothing less than the meaning of the venture to which they have devoted their lives, and thus, to a very considerable extent, the meaning of their own lives." He views with some dismay the fragmentation and confusion that have afflicted the American historical profession during the last thirty years.

Three works provide retrospective analysis of particular periods of American historiography. BASSETT remains the standard account of the mid-19th-century gentlemen historians, exemplified by Jared Sparks and George Bancroft. Bassett provides a brief discussion of colonial history by way of background, but focuses on what he terms the middle ground, from 1826 to 1884 – the founding year of the American Historical Association. The emergence of the association marked the transition to the modern era of professional historians. HIGHAM picks up with the development of professional writing of history in the United States at the turn of the century and continues to the 1950s. This intellectual history considers historians working in all fields, not just American history, but the historiographic trends and the closely related professional issues involved transcend the parochialism that often characterizes American historiography. WISH is an intellectual history concerned with the social conditioning of American historians from William Bradford to Allan Nevins. Each of fifteen chapters considers a different historian representative of his time or historiographic school. These discussions are quite useful in demonstrating the relationship between historical writing and the historian's own social milieu, even though Wish measures historiographic progress primarily in terms of movement toward greater objectivity.

Specialized studies of influential American historians from Francis Parkman to C. Vann Woodward can be found in the collection of thirteen essays edited by CUNLIFFE and WINKS. Each essay is an analytical portrait of a pastmaster – an exemplar of a particular historiographic school or period, including such notables as Henry Adams, Perry Miller, Daniel Boorstin, and Richard Hofstadter. Five of the essays are written by British historians. Taken together, they constitute a history of the writing of American history from the mid-19th century to the 1960s.

The overwhelming influence of the progressive historians, Frederick Jackson Turner, Charles Beard, and Vernon Parrington, on American historiography has prompted numerous specialized studies. BENSON's critique of the venerable Turner and Beard was designed to show that their ideas were influenced by the Italian economist Achille Loria, and so were not solely the home-grown products of the American experience. Loria argued that the availability of free land governed the pace and direction of economic progress. An abundance of free land, as existed in the United States and other frontier societies, conditioned men to be independent. Benson argues that Beard and Turner absorbed Loria's economic determinism and applied it to the American condition. HOFSTADTER reconsidered the role of the progressive historians in his own searching work. He criticized the progressives for their over-reliance on geographic and economic determinism, their tendency to see conspiracies in history, and their habit of imputing base motives to all those whom they placed on the wrong side of important issues.

EMIL POCOCK

Holmes, Oliver Wendell, Jr. 1841–1935
Supreme Court Justice

Baker, Liva, *The Justice from Beacon Hill: The Life and Times of Oliver Wendell Holmes*, New York: HarperCollins, 1991

Bowen, Catherine Drinker, *Yankee from Olympus: Justice Holmes and His Family*, Boston: Little Brown, 1944; London: Benn, 1949

Frankfurter, Felix, *Mr. Justice Holmes and the Supreme Court*, Cambridge, MA: Harvard University Press, 1938

Gordon, Robert W. (editor), *The Legacy of Oliver Wendell Holmes, Jr.*, Stanford, CA: Stanford University Press, 1992

Howe, Mark A. De Wolfe, *Justice Oliver Wendell Holmes*, 2 vols., Cambridge, MA: Harvard University Press, 1957–63

Konefsky, Samuel J., *The Legacy of Holmes and Brandeis: A Study in the Influence of Ideas*, New York: Macmillan, 1956

Monagan, John S., *The Grand Panjandrum: The Mellow Years of Justice Holmes*, Lanham, MD: University Press of America, 1988

Novick, Sheldon M., *Honorable Justice: The Life of Oliver Wendell Holmes, Jr.*, Boston: Little Brown, 1989

White, G. Edward, *Justice Oliver Wendell Holmes: Law and the Inner Self*, New York: Oxford University Press, 1993

Oliver Wendell Holmes was the kind of man about whom it was easy to create legends. The son of a famous writer, he was raised in a Boston environment of high intelligence and aristocratic manners. He was wounded three times in the Civil War and earned considerable admiration because of his bravery under fire. After the war he turned to the study of the law and soon developed into a nationally recognized legal scholar and writer. And then he embarked upon a judicial career that lasted for fifty years, the last thirty as perhaps the most distinguished Associate Justice in the history of the United States Supreme Court. By the time he died, he was a virtual symbol of imperturbable wisdom, intellectual courage, and careful judgment. If all this were not enough, he was also tall and ruggedly handsome, irresistibly charming and gallant, a marvelous conversationalist and correspondent, and one of the greatest literary stylists ever to sit upon the bench. He had an unrivaled talent for transforming acquaintances into loyal disciples. The heroic, almost godly stature and reputation of Holmes have been the chief problem that his biographers have had to confront. Not surprisingly, therefore, much of the writing about him during the last quarter century has been partly a process of demythologizing, of making this extraordinary man more ordinary, of exploring and analyzing aspects of his life and thought that were not always entirely admirable.

One of Holmes's most loyal admirers was FRANKFURTER, a law professor at Harvard and, four years after his idol's death, himself a member of the Supreme Court, nominated to that position by his friend Franklin Roosevelt. Frankfurter's book on Holmes as a constitutional thinker attempts to argue that the great Justice was also a liberal, one who would have been in warm sympathy with the various experiments in social engineering that the federal government, under Roosevelt, embarked upon in the 1930s. It was one of many efforts by constitutional and legislative liberals to claim Holmes as a predecessor and ally.

BOWEN's biography – which encompasses the story of the entire family – is both the most widely read book about Justice Holmes and perhaps the best example (as her title suggests) of the godlike Holmes. The figure that emerges is a paragon of every virtue, a loving husband and warm-hearted and compassionate friend of those less privileged than himself. Her beautifully written story is undocumented, and she invents conversations – so that the work is partly a fictionalized account of Holmes's life.

For the task of writing Holmes's scholarly biography, Frankfurter, who had hoped to do it himself until his Court duties made it impossible, hand-picked Mark Anthony De Wolfe HOWE, one of Holmes's former clerks and a professor of law at Buffalo and then at Harvard. Howe immersed himself in Holmes's papers, but completed only two volumes of the biography, carrying his subject only up through his work as a legal scholar and ending with his appointment to the Massachusetts Supreme Judicial Court in 1882. Thus, although these two volumes provide an excellent account of Holmes's youth, military service, and scholarly labors, the most interesting and important part of his life, his work as a judge, was left for others.

The picture of Holmes typified by Frankfurter and Bowen – a liberal-minded judicial philosopher and a model of virtue – reached its climax in the 1930s and 1940s, but fell under serious questioning after World War II. The attack on Holmes's judicial and philosophic views surfaced first in law review articles, but much of it was summarized by KONEFSKY, who compares Holmes with his fellow-dissenter Louis D. Brandeis and finds them very different minds. To Konefsky, Holmes was backward looking, pessimistic about the human prospect, and unworldly – a man whose extreme scepticism led him to a tolerance of legislative experimentation and enabled him to appear as a liberal.

After a second failed attempt to obtain an "official" biography of Holmes after Howe's death, Harvard opened his personal papers to the general scholarly community in 1985. The first result of this decision was the charming study by MONAGAN. It focuses on Holmes's final years, and on his personal life. While far from adequate as regards Holmes's scholarly and judicial work, the book gives a fine sketch of the man in his nineties. Monagan is also the first to reveal Holmes's long and passionate love affair with Lady Clare Castletown, a married Irish aristocrat.

The opening of the Holmes papers has also resulted in three splendid and substantial biographies by Baker, Novick and White. The modern reader can scarcely go wrong in choosing any of these three. Each is comprehensive, accurate, and nicely written. All three authors, moreover, have legal as well as historical credentials: Novick is a lawyer himself; Baker has written an able biography of Frankfurter; and White is a professor of law and a distinguished scholar of the American judicial tradition. Each of the three looks squarely at Holmes's intellectual quirks and personal flaws. BAKER is probably the best at describing the boyhood and early life; NOVICK stands out for his account of the Civil War experience. But WHITE, the last of the three, is easily the best on the judicial career and more than adequate on the other aspects of Holmes's life. He also makes the most serious attempt to plumb the inner man. White has the added benefit of a fine bibliographical essay which summarizes much of the enormous journal literature. If one were limited to a single book, White would be a very sound choice.

For a taste of the recent scholarship, the articles collected by GORDON, after a 1985 Stanford symposium, might be consulted. The eight papers vary widely in interest and technicality, and the book will be more useful to those who have already read one of the three modern biographies. Along with Gordon's own introduction, particularly helpful are the articles by J.W. Burrow and Morton Horwitz, each of whom tries to place Holmes in intellectual context. The piece by David Hollinger, explaining why Holmes was so profoundly attractive to a rising generation of Jewish lawyers and intellectuals, is also fascinating.

DAVID W. LEVY

See also Supreme Court

Homosexuality

Berube, Allan, *Coming Out under Fire: The History of Gay Men and Women in World War Two*, New York: Free Press, 1990

Cahn, Susan K., *Coming on Strong: Gender and Sexuality in Twentieth-Century Women's Sport*, New York: Free Press, 1994

Chauncey, George, *Gay New York: Gender, Urban Culture, and the Making of the Gay Male World, 1890–1940*, New York: Basic Books, 1994; London: Flamingo, 1995

D'Emilio, John, *Sexual Politics, Sexual Communities: The Making of a Homosexual Minority in the United States, 1940–1970*, Chicago: University of Chicago Press, 1983

D'Emilio, John and Estelle B. Freedman, *Intimate Matters: A History of Sexuality in America*, New York: Harper, 1988

Duberman, Martin, Martha Vicinus, and George Chauncey (editors), *Hidden from History: Reclaiming the Gay and Lesbian Past*, New York: New American Library, 1989; London: Penguin, 1991

Faderman, Lillian, *Odd Girls and Twilight Lovers: A History of Lesbian Life in Twentieth-Century America*, New York: Columbia University Press, 1991; London: Penguin, 1992

Williams, Walter L., *The Spirit and the Flesh: Sexual Diversity in American Indian Culture*, Boston: Beacon Press, 1986

Perhaps the best place to start for a reader interested in the history of homosexuality in America is with D'EMILIO and FREEDMAN. This work, a comprehensive history of sexuality in the United States, provides a good general discussion of the history of homosexuality in America from the period of colonization to the 1980s. Among the topics covered are Puritan attitudes toward "sodomy," the tradition of "romantic," same-sex friendships among 19th-century women and men, the development of the concept of "homosexuality" at the turn of the century, and the birth of the movement to protect homosexual rights in the 1960s and 1970s.

Another excellent starting point is the collection of essays edited by DUBERMAN, VICINUS, and CHAUNCEY. While this work does not focus exclusively on America, many of the essays concern such topics as the role of lesbians in various American Indian societies, "romantic friendship" among men in early 19th-century American fiction, female transvestism in the United States, and the gay subculture of Harlem in the 1920s. Especially noteworthy are George Chauncey's "Christian Brotherhood or Sexual Perversion?," an examination of the construction of homosexual identity before World War I, and Carroll Smith-Rosenberg's "Discourses of Sexuality and Subjectivity," a study of the connections drawn between feminism, gender inversion, and female sexuality in late 19th and early 20th century America.

Homosexuality in America from the colonial period to the present is explored in a different context by WILLIAMS. In this unique work, he studies conceptions of homosexuality in various American Indian cultures and the role played by homosexual men and women in these societies. Williams examines the effect which contact with white Americans had on these traditions and also provides a fascinating chapter on homosexuality among white men on the American frontier.

The majority of works on the history of homosexuality in the United States focus on the 20th century. Of these works, the best by far is CHAUNCEY, which studies in depth the lifestyle and culture of male homosexuals in New York City in the early 20th century. Chauncey argues that gay men in late 19th- and early 20th-century New York created a broad social world which, far from being hidden from the heterosexual world, was highly visible and generally tolerated by the dominant society. Among the elements of the gay cultural scene which receive attention are the differences between working- and middle-class homosexual men; the gay presence in saloons, restaurants, nightclubs, and bathhouses; drag queen balls; and gay life in bohemian Greenwich Village and African American Harlem. Chauncey also examines differences in the conceptions and definitions of homosexuality held by working- and middle-class men, and discusses how a rigid adherence to gender roles on the part of the working class led the men of this class not only to tolerate but to engage freely in sexual relations with other men. Chauncey's book is well-written and fascinating to read. It is the best history of homosexuality in the United States yet written.

Also of high quality is BERUBE, a study of gay life in the American military during World War II. He argues that World War II was a pivotal event which both brought large numbers of gay men and lesbians together for the first time and led to the official labelling of such men and women as "deviant." Berube studies the role played by psychiatrists in convincing the military that homosexuality was not a criminal offense involving inappropriate sexual behavior, but was instead a disease; he argues that, as a result of this change in policy, homosexuals, for the first time, were classified by the army as "deficient" personality "types" whose innate mental and physical make-up rendered them unfit for service. This work also provides the reader with a fascinating look at many aspects of gay life in the military during the war, including patterns of sociability among gay soldiers, the special roles adopted by homosexual men in army units, and the generally supportive and tolerant attitude toward gay soldiers on the part of heterosexual comrades.

D'EMILIO focuses primarily on the formation of societies committed to securing civil rights for gay men and lesbians in the post-World War II period. He examines such early organizations as the Mattachine Society and the Daughters of Bilitis, their role in promoting homosexual rights in the homophobic climate of the Cold War, and their influence on the gay rights movement of the 1970s. Although not always the most exciting reading, it nevertheless provides information crucial to an understanding of the homosexual experience during the Cold War era.

For those interested primarily in lesbian history, FADERMAN provides an excellent overview of the lesbian experience in the United States in the late 19th and 20th centuries. She examines changes in the conception of lesbianism in 20th-century America, from the acceptance of lesbianism as a component of a chic, bohemian lifestyle in the 1920s, to its redefinition as a form of deviancy and disease during the Depression and the World War II-Cold War period, and its

emergence as a symbol of female power and unity during the women's rights movement of the 1960s and 1970s. Faderman also explores the similarities and differences among working-, middle-, and upper-class lesbians and between white lesbians and lesbians of color.

CAHN is a history of women's involvement in sports in 20th-century America, which examines the connection between women's sports and lesbianism, both in reality and in the popular mind. She argues that because strength, aggression, and competitiveness have always been perceived by American society as masculine qualities, female athletes have often been regarded as "lesbian" by the American public. Cahn examines the intersection of such popular perceptions with cultural stereotypes of race and class, as she studies the dominance of black and working-class women in sports regarded as especially competitive and "masculine," and the efforts made by the promoters of female athletes to present them as "feminine" and heterosexual.

ANN KORDAS

See also Gay and Lesbian Movements

Hoover, Herbert   1874–1964
31st President of the United States

Barber, William J., *From New Era to New Deal: Herbert Hoover, the Economists, and American Economic Policy, 1921–1933*, Cambridge and New York: Cambridge University Press, 1985

Best, Gary Dean, *Herbert Hoover, The Postpresidential Years, 1933–1964*, 2 vols., Stanford, CA: Hoover Institution Press, 1983

Burner, David, *Herbert Hoover: A Public Life*, New York: Knopf, 1979

Fausold, Martin L., *The Presidency of Herbert C. Hoover*, Lawrence: University Press of Kansas, 1985

Nash, George H., *The Life of Herbert Hoover*, 2 vols., New York: Norton, 1983–88

Romasco, Albert U., *The Poverty of Abundance: Hoover, the Nation, and the Depression*, New York: Oxford University Press, 1965

Schwarz, Jordan A., *The Interregnum of Despair: Hoover, Congress, and the Depression*, Urbana: University of Illinois Press, 1970

Wilson, Joan Hoff, *Herbert Hoover: Forgotten Progressive*, Boston: Little Brown, 1975

Herbert Hoover's historical reputation has improved with the passage of time. The earliest books written about him took a very partisan tone. Blamed for the Great Depression, the Herbert Hoover written about in the years after 1933 appeared as a conservative reactionary with little understanding of the needs and requirements of the modern economy. On the other hand, Hoover did also have his partisan defenders. Thus, an equally unobjective body of work emerged that parroted the explanations which Hoover and his administration had given in the early 1930s for the economic catastrophe that had beset the nation. Not until the 1960s did Hoover scholarship take a more penetrating line of inquiry. Two events combined to produce a spate of serious works on Hoover and his times. New Left historians, frustrated with the liberal politics of their own era, had challenged the wisdom and commitment of much of Franklin D. Roosevelt's New Deal, thus characterizing Hoover and his ideas as a favorable alternative to the modern liberal state. Furthermore in 1966 the Hoover Presidential Library in West Branch, Iowa opened for research. Previously scholars had little in the way of primary source material for study of the 1920s and early 1930s. The availability of Hoover's papers and those of people who served with him encouraged research by scholars of varying ideological perspectives.

ROMASCO, who published his analysis of Hoover and the Depression before the opening of the library in West Branch, foreshadowed much of the research in Hoover's personal papers, since he presented a much more balanced portrait of the 31st president. Romasco argued that Hoover provided an intermediate level of presidential involvement in national affairs, and he stressed Hoover's commitment to voluntary cooperative action as a solution to the Depression, which had produced poverty among abundance. Yet the author also argued that private charity could not ameliorate the economic catastrophe in a complex industrial economy. Furthermore, Romasco suggested that Hoover's failed recovery program proved to the country that only a more extensive national effort could correct the national crisis.

After extensive manuscript research, SCHWARZ analyzed Hoover's relationship with congress. He provides an in-depth study of the politics of the period and demonstrates the relationship among various factors including ideology, party identity, and personality in the making of public policy. Schwarz portrays a president who preferred to chart his own course, and a congress initially receptive to Hoover's program, but by 1932 ready for independent action. In a study which both political and economic historians will find useful, Schwarz provides useful background and context on the policy-making environment of the Hoover presidency.

WILSON fits squarely into the New Left critique that a corporate desire to thwart genuine reforms has been a constant feature of 20th-century American history. In a tightly-written analytical synthesis, she argues that Hoover's concept of a decentralized yet technological and corporate society provided an alternative and progressive course for the development of the modern state. While she places Hoover's career in a more favorable light, she also rebukes Hoover's lack of intellectual flexibility and his tendency to internal contemplation. One of the book's strengths lies in its treatment of Hoover's ideas about economic organization. Despite little attention to his career before 1921, this is one of the more important books on Hoover for both students and more specialist scholars.

BURNER's biography emphasizes Hoover's Quaker religion as a central feature of his character. He explores why and how Hoover could on the one hand achieve great success in business and on the other be responsible for economic crisis. While searching for a middle course in his assessment of Hoover, Burner does not, however, provide a balanced narrative. The bulk of his attention is devoted to the years 1914–21 and 1928–32, while he skips over Hoover's career

as Secretary of Commerce (1921–28) – years important to any assessment of Hoover's contribution to modern economic organization – and also his post-presidential years. Still, Burner has written an important, if incomplete, account of Hoover's life before the New Deal that stresses the continuity in Hoover's intellectual outlook on society and government throughout his life.

Nash has so far published the first two volumes of a multi-volume Hoover biography. NASH (1983) is a thorough account of Hoover's life before he entered public service in 1914. The author discounts the significance of Hoover's Quaker heritage and argues that the distinguishing factor in Hoover's progressivism was his faith in the public accountability of modern professional organizations. Business historians will find much of value in this initial volume, which recounts Hoover's successes in the mining industry, but the general reader may be daunted by the amount of detail. In another thoroughly documented account, NASH (1988) deals with Hoover's involvement with the Commission for the Relief of Belgium between 1914 and 1917. The author suggests that Hoover's mental attitude toward the Depression was conditioned in part by his own success in business and in part by his participation in Belgian relief, which worked because of private charitable contributions. It remains to be seen what Nash will make of the remainder of Hoover's career, but one may be sure that the work will be thorough.

BEST's two-volume account of Hoover's life after the presidency provides a useful corrective to the notion that he had little influence on public affairs after Franklin D. Roosevelt's election. It deals with Hoover's campaign to reinvigorate the Republican party and to offer a sharply defined alternative to an interventionist foreign policy. Not everyone will be convinced by Best's arguments, but he has provided an important yet sympathetic analysis of Hoover's years after the White House, that has portrayed a man much more nuanced and interesting than previous authors have conceded.

BARBER is the first economist to write about the new economics of the 1920s and its similarity with post-World War II Keynesianism. He uses the works of contemporary economists to shed light on Hoover's ideas about business-government relations, and then argues that Hoover was an active president. While Barber believes that the new economics had promise and in fact formed the basis for the New Deal, he suggests that Hoover's failure to combat the Depression stemmed from a lack of political acumen. Barber is at his best in describing the arguments which economists put forward in the first few years of the Depression, but he never explains how – or indeed whether – economists affected the formation of public policy in the Hoover years.

FAUSOLD is a one-volume account of Hoover's years in the White House, in the Kansas series on the history of the presidency. Making good use of the relevant secondary literature on Hoover as well as primary sources, he does not always reconcile conflicting interpretations. Having examined Hoover's reform policies in the months before the market crash, Fausold explains the president's earliest efforts to combat the Depression with counter-cyclical procedures, and moves on to explore the confines of Hoover's economic intervention. The author concludes that Hoover failed to combat the Depression effectively because the crisis highlighted his weaknesses as a leader. Fausold is the best single volume yet published on the Hoover presidency, and will serve as a good introduction to the subject.

NANCY BECK YOUNG

See also Great Crash and Great Depression

Hughes, Charles Evans 1862–1948

Secretary of State, presidential candidate, and Chief Justice of the Supreme Court

Danelski, David J. and Joseph S. Tulchin (editors), *The Autobiographical Notes of Charles Evans Hughes*, Cambridge, MA: Harvard University Press, 1973

Glad, Betty, *Charles Evans Hughes and the Illusion of Innocence: A Study in American Diplomacy*, Urbana: University of Illinois Press, 1966

Hendel, Samuel F., *Charles Evans Hughes and the Supreme Court*, New York: King's Crown Press, 1951

Hughes, Charles Evans, *The Supreme Court of the United States: Its Foundations, Methods, and Achievements*, New York: Columbia University Press, 1928; reprinted, New York: Garden City Publishing, 1936

Hyde, Charles Cheney, "Charles Evans Hughes", in *American Secretaries of State and Their Diplomacy*, volume 10, edited by Samuel Flagg Bemis, New York: Cooper Square, 1963

Lovell, S.D., *The Presidential Election of 1916*, Carbondale: Southern Illinois University Press, 1980

McIlwain, Edwin, "The Business of the Supreme Court as Conducted by Chief Justice Hughes," *Harvard Law Review*, 63(1), 1949

Perkins, Dexter, *Charles Evans Hughes and American Democratic Statesmanship*, Boston: Little Brown, 1956

Pusey, Merlo, *Charles Evans Hughes*, New York: Macmillan, 1951

Vinson, John Chalmers, "Charles Evans Hughes", in *An Uncertain Tradition: American Secretaries of State in the Twentieth Century*, edited by Norman A. Graebner, New York: McGraw Hill, 1961

Wesser, Robert F., *Charles Evans Hughes: Politics and Reform in New York, 1905–1910*, Ithaca, NY: Cornell University Press. 1967

The remarkable public career of Charles Evans Hughes covered the years 1905 to 1941, during which he was involved in various ways with almost every major political issue of the period. As a crusading prosecutor against the "interests" in New York City, Governor of New York (and elected in the race fictionalized in Orson Welles's *Citizen Kane*), Associate Justice of the Supreme Court, Republican presidential nominee in 1916, Secretary of State, Judge of the International Court of Justice at the Hague, and Chief Justice of the United States throughout the turbulent 1930s, he displayed a vast capacity for work, an encyclopedic mind, a tremendous dignity, great personal charm, and what most saw as a natural ability for leadership.

The "standard" biography is PUSEY, who interviewed Hughes extensively in his last years. Long and detailed, it suffers from the typical problem of an "authorized" biography – that the author revered his subject too much. As no one else has published an account that attempts to be as authoritative, it must be read, but read carefully.

PERKINS's very much briefer work appeared in the Library of American Biography, and traced the theme of Hughes as a mediator in the American political arena. There is little explicit argument here, much of the perspective is advanced by implication, and the reader is left looking for more explication and elaboration, which the format of the series prevented.

The incomplete attempt by Hughes to tell his own story is published in DANELSKI and TULCHIN's edition. *The Autobiographical Notes* are important, but show that Hughes was a product of his age in this regard. They are discreet and self-effacing, passing over many of the controversial parts of his career. Hughes adopts a matter-of-fact tone throughout and rarely reflects on the context of his life or the history about him. The editors give important background, but little, if any, interpretation.

There are various studies covering periods or aspects of his life. WESSER's study started as a doctoral thesis and it still has that air. He covers the gas and insurance investigations as well as the governorship and concludes that, although Hughes compiled a solid progressive record as governor, he never fully defeated the "Old Guard" in New York politics, and cannot be considered a great holder of that office. This remains the only study specifically devoted to the earlier phases of Hughes's public life.

HENDEL covers both of Hughes's periods of service on the Supreme Court. He is quite complimentary towards Hughes's first period on the Court, and slightly less enthusiastic over his Chief Justiceship. This may reflect the fact that Hendel, writing in 1951, was still very suspicious of the Court's power to invalidate congressional acts. There is a valuable and detailed chapter on the stormy confirmation debate over President Hoover's nomination of Hughes as Chief Justice. Its reliance on a close paraphrasing of the debate gives the reader a clear sense of the arguments. In general, Hendel argues his points effectively and the book is persuasive, although occasionally it shows signs of its age.

The most thorough account of Hughes's administration of the Supreme Court is by McILWAIN who argues that Hughes was a great Chief Justice – a point with which few, if any, would disagree – on the basis of his running of the Court alone. This is a more controversial stance, but McIlwain's view may have been coloured by his awareness of the administrative troubles of Hughes's successors, Harlan Stone and Fred Vinson, and before the success of Earl Warren as an administrator.

HUGHES himself gave a series of lectures on the Supreme Court at Columbia University in between his periods of service on the bench. They were published and repay very careful reading. They conceal insightful comment and argument about how the Court should act, behind a veneer of cautious and safe observation. The book is valuable as an exposition of Hughes's attitudes to the law, which are not easily discerned from his opinions. However, his major opinions are skilful expositions of a brilliant legal mind addressing the major political issues of the day, and ought to be consulted when reading any study of Hughes's career on the high bench.

Hughes's least successful venture in public life – the 1916 campaign for the presidency – is recorded with care and detail by LOVELL. He goes a long way towards disproving the common assumption that Wilson beat Hughes with the slogan "He kept us out of War", but never quite reaches an unequivocal conclusion on this point. Apart from a few minor errors, Lovell has painstakingly assembled a mass of information, gleaned from a vast array of sources, yet declines to interpret and shape his evidence. For all its usefulness, it is also a frustrating book, because it could say so much more. However, Lovell does treat Hughes fairly throughout the narrative – a welcome change from most studies of the 1916 campaign, in which Hughes often disappears in Wilson's shadow.

There are three specialized treatments of Hughes as Secretary of State, and they are more critical of him than those who have written on other phases of his career. VINSON, the first of them, identified Hughes's main difficulty as his assumption that the world's problems would respond to the application of order and reason. Expanding on Vinson's article in a book-length assessment, HYDE recognized the same failing in Hughes, but suggests that his efforts were a logical reaction to the collapsed world which he confronted in 1921. In Hyde's view, Hughes's failed attempts to impose order deserve some credit. In a sympathetic portrayal of Hughes, GLAD argues that he was both a product and a captive of his time, and that he probably could not have done more in the light of the domestic political situation which he faced.

GEORGE CONYNE

See also Foreign Policy, 1919–1941; Supreme Court

Hutchinson, Anne 1591–1643
New England religious leader

Battis, Emery, *Saints and Sectaries: Anne Hutchinson and the Antinomian Controversy in Massachusetts Bay Colony*, Chapel Hill: University of North Carolina Press, 1962

Hall, David D., *The Antinomian Controversy, 1636–1638: A Documentary History*, Middletown, CT: Wesleyan University Press, 1968; 2nd edition, Durham, NC: Duke University Press, 1990

Huber, Elaine C., *Women and the Authority of Inspiration: A Re-examination of Two Prophetic Movements from a Contemporary Feminist Perspective*, Lanham, MD: University Press of America, 1985

Koehler, Lyle, *A Search for Power: The "Weaker Sex" in Seventeenth-Century New England*, Urbana: University of Illinois Press, 1980

Lang, Amy Schrager, *Prophetic Woman: Anne Hutchinson and the Problem of Dissent in the Literature of New England*, Berkeley: University of California Press, 1987

Lewis, Mary Jane, "Anne Hutchinson," in *Portraits of American Women: From Settlement to the Present*, edited by G.J. Barker-Benfield and Catherine Clinton, New York: St. Martin's Press, 1991

Anne Hutchinson, Puritan controversialist, holds a central place in the Antinomian controversy which wracked the Massachusetts Bay Colony from 1636 to 1638. Her subsequent exile to Rhode Island and death at the hands of Indians in New York was seen by the Bay authorities as justification for their decision to expel her from Massachusetts. The charge against her was one of antinomianism, being in opposition to the law. The law was bound up with the covenant of works, which she denied. This was seen as a threat to both the theological and social orders.

The debate surrounding the role of Hutchinson has been studied from several perspectives; social, political, feminist and theological. In social terms the controversy brought into question the liberties of the individual. Politically it involved a struggle for power between the supporters of John Cotton, who included Hutchinson, and Governor Winthrop. The feminist outlook articulates the gender debate through the theological argument and literary comparisons. The theological point of view embraces the debate about the relative efficacy of the covenant of works and free grace. All of these views converge on one basic point – the challenge to authority and the response of the state to that threat. This in itself, as Withington and Schwartz asserted, is timeless ("The Political Trial of Anne Hutchinson," *New England Quarterly*, vol. 51, 1978, pp. 226–40). Hence the fascination with this 300-year-old episode.

The socio-political approach adopted by both Battis and Koehler places discussion of the trial of Hutchinson in the context of the liberty of the individual. BATTIS puts Hutchinson in the class of those men, her contemporaries, who challenged the hierarchy. Where radicals such as Lilburne gave impetus to the English radical movement, Hutchinson carried these ideas across the Atlantic. Moreover, she can be seen as a link between the radicalism of the century before and the following century with the emergence of Quakerism which Lilburne and Hutchinson's protégée, Mary Dyer, embraced. Her espousal of the inner light and direct revelation anticipated the similar philosophy of the Quakers.

KOEHLER extends the social implication of the Hutchinson case by setting her up as the model for a redefinition of women's roles in society. Through Hutchinson, women were able to challenge the system by way of theological debate. Although Koehler points out that proof of Hutchinson's activities as a social reformer can be seen in her later involvement over the land allotment controversy in Rhode Island, the gender issue is crucial. The reaction of Winthrop, who accused her of acting in a manner inappropriate to her sex, seems to be proof of the significance of the gender argument.

The feminist line is expanded by HUBER, who connects the situation in 1636–38 with present-day gender crises in what she sees as, at the most basic level, a sexist society. She compares Hutchinson's movement with Montanism, a 2nd-century heresy which also involved women playing a conspicuous part in challenging the hierarchy by appealing to the authority of inspiration. It is this appeal, she contends, which links Hutchinson's activities with the feminist argument. Thus in the first four chapters of the book, the author seeks to answer three main questions relating to the question of authority. The final chapter links up the historical episodes with the contemporary movement of the Christian feminists.

Where Huber analyses the relationship between antinomianism and inspiration, LANG investigates that between antinomianism and sentimentalism. She explores this relationship through the study of literature, highlighting works which stress the emotions. Thus Cotton Mather's *Magnalia Christi Americana* shifts the focus of antinomianism from doctrinal debates to the question of character. The debate, as Lang points out, was based on a conflict between reason, seen to be masculine, and enthusiasm, which had female attributes. In her examination of Nathaniel Hawthorne's comparison of Hester Prynne, in *The Scarlet Letter*, to Anne Hutchinson, Lang draws a literary link between the two "rebels" in sentimental terms: they were rebels for the sake of "heart." Consequently Lang's work rests less on the historical than the literary record.

HALL's study of the antinomian controversy depicts Hutchinson in a broader setting. The episode took place in a period of spiritual depression brought on by the rise in material expectations, and the consequent decline of piety. The second edition brings together essential documents including five previously unpublished. Thus the work is an expansion of, and a departure from, Charles Francis Adams's collection a century earlier which emphasized the significance of the controversy in terms of a power struggle. Hall approaches the debate from a theological standpoint, in which John Cotton was the key figure. Of the twelve documents edited by Hall only three pertain directly to Hutchinson herself, a fact which illustrates Hall's aim. He contends that Cotton's differences with the ministers were at the heart of the controversy. Anne, who was inspired by Cotton, was the catalyst which produced what became a crisis in the colonists' religious ideas. Hall also diverges from Perry Miller's work concerning the message of salvation. Whereas Miller promoted the idea of "preparation for salvation," Hall emphasizes the assurance of salvation as the central issue in the controversy, noting that almost nothing was said about preparation in the debate.

Biographies of Hutchinson are limited due to the sparse documentation, and add little to the usual picture of her. LEWIS is a brief sketch which draws on information given in the trial in order to give a glimpse of Hutchinson as an individual. However, the main purpose of the outline is to put Hutchinson in the framework of the overall concept of the book, which is the American woman.

MARY K. GEITER

Hutchinson, Thomas 1711–1780
Colonial governor, author and Loyalist

Bailyn, Bernard, *The Ordeal of Thomas Hutchinson*, Cambridge, MA: Belknap Press of Harvard University Press, 1974

Freiberg, Malcolm, *Prelude to Purgatory: Thomas Hutchinson in Provincial Massachusetts Politics, 1760–1770*, New York: Garland, 1990

Hosmer, James K., *The Life of Thomas Hutchinson: Royal Governor of the Province of Massachusetts*, Boston: Houghton Mifflin, 1896

Norton, Mary Beth, *The British-Americans: The Loyalist Exiles in England, 1774–1789*, Boston: Little Brown, 1972; London: Constable, 1974

Pencak, William, *War, Politics, and Revolution in Provincial Massachusetts*, Boston: Northeastern University Press, 1981

Pencak, William, *America's Burke: The Mind of Thomas Hutchinson*, Washington, DC: University Press of America, 1982

Shipton, Clifford K., *Biographical Sketches of Those Who Attended Harvard College*, volume 8, Cambridge, MA: Harvard University Press, 1951

The early career of Thomas Hutchinson seemed to represent a model for the way in which an able colonial could prosper as a servant of the British empire. Rising through positions as representative and councillor, to chief justice and lieutenant-governor, he ultimately succeeded Francis Bernard as royal governor of Massachusetts. By the early 1770s, however, Hutchinson had become a feared and detested figure, not just in his own province, but throughout the American colonies. His debate with the General Court early in 1773 served to highlight the differences between the Tory and the Patriot views of the power of Parliament over the American colonies. The publication in June of his letters to British ministers seemed to his opponents to provide clear evidence of a conspiracy against American liberty led by Hutchinson and his associates. This destroyed the last hope that Hutchinson, as governor, could restore peace to the tumultuous colony, and he left for England in June 1774.

Hutchinson's absence during the climax of the movement towards independence may be one reason for the relative lack of study of his life and career. Since the victors wrote the history there was little interest in Hutchinson or the Loyalists in general during the 19th century, as Bailyn's useful survey of the historiography of loyalism makes clear. HOSMER was the only biography, written when the wish to emphasise a common Anglo-Saxon unity led to efforts to stress those things which united Americans and British, and to downplay those which might once have divided them. It attempts to exonerate Hutchinson and the Loyalists, viewing them as worthy Americans, mistaken only in underestimating the degree to which the Patriots were truer to the defence of Anglo-Saxon liberties than was the Hanoverian George III. While Hosmer recognises the similarities between Patriots and Loyalists, the insight is limited by the fact that it is predetermined by his broad overall view of the development of history.

The modern assessment of Hutchinson begins with SHIPTON's "sketch" in the Harvard Graduates series. This provides a rather olympian view of Hutchinson, who is seen as having a rather simple or naive attitude to the problems with which he became involved. FREIBERG's account of his early career up to 1770 is a reprint of his doctoral dissertation of 1950. Because it ends before the revolutionary struggle was fully under way, this account pictures Hutchinson as the embattled colonial official, as opposed to the Loyalist exile. It shows, however, the degree to which the personal and specifically Massachusetts-based quarrels into which Hutchinson was drawn came to be related to, and affected by, the broader problems of imperial relations.

In his general study of Massachusetts politics during the 18th century, PENCAK (1981) outlines the context within which Hutchinson had to operate. He shows the development of the factional conflicts that helped shape Hutchinson's own career and political style, and which contrasted with the ideological conflicts of the revolutionary years. His chapter comparing and contrasting the Patriot and Loyalist leadership groups within the province provides a composite sketch to set beside the more detailed portraits of Hutchinson himself.

Neither of the two major studies of Hutchinson's role during the revolution is a full biography, and each provides contrasting prespectives on, and versions of, Hutchinson's personality and actions. In the more ambitious and wide-ranging of the two, BAILYN focuses on the way in which Hutchinson, as an individual in a key position, responded to the intensifying crisis in imperial relations, a crisis which his temperament and experience left him ill-equipped to handle, both in political and personal terms. As a pragmatist, as someone familiar with the problems of government, as someone used to working within the limits of normal politics, he was unable to understand the passion of those who felt that the times were abnormal, and that the colonists were facing a momentous crisis. Bailyn does not discount the existence of definite principles underpinning Hutchinson's actions, but describes the anguish with which he faced the fact that his principles were increasingly rejected by his neighbours, and his actions came to be interpreted in a most negative light. Bailyn provides a dramatic and sympathetic picture of the way in which Hutchinson faced his "ordeal", trying to confront "the furies" – the harassment of his enemies – and the forces which threatened to overturn the world with which he was familiar.

Bailyn describes Hutchinson as the politician and administrator, as a man engaged in dealing with practical problems under intense stress. PENCAK (1982) outlines his role as a man of thought and of reflection, looking less at Hutchinson's actions in the public sphere and more at the explanations and justifications for these actions which Hutchinson prepared in private. His study is based on such materials as the manuscript memoir which Hutchinson left, on his correspondence, and on his history of the Massachusetts colony. He describes Hutchinson as judge, as historian, and as political theorist. He challenges Bailyn's view of Hutchinson as a pragmatist, instead claiming him to be a consistent conservative thinker, showing considerable originality in the positions which he worked out on fundamental issues of morality and political philosophy. As his title suggests, he compares Hutchinson with Edmund Burke, arguing that they shared a respect for tradition, and an unwillingness to tamper with institutions and practices which had stood the test of time in favour of some blueprint or theoretical prescription.

Pencak provides an overview of the various aspects of Hutchinson's intellectual identity. He is less concerned than Bailyn with mapping the unfolding of events. The bitterness of Hutchinson's last years in exile in England, for example, are covered effectively by Bailyn, whereas Pencak reflects Hutchinson's own attempts to stand back dispassionately from the events themselves. Hutchinson's experiences in London can be linked in with the more general view of the Loyalist experience of exile provided by NORTON. Bailyn is able to portray what Hutchinson lost as an individual, while Norton documents the way in which the Loyalists as a group were the losers from the Revolution.

MALCOLM F. MORRISON

See also American Revolution: Development of a Crisis entries; Loyalists

I

Immigration and Ethnicity: General

Archdeacon, Thomas J., *Becoming American: An Ethnic History*, New York: Free Press, 1983

Bodnar, John, *The Transplanted: A History of Immigrants in Urban America*, Bloomington: Indiana University Press, 1985

Daniels, Roger, *Coming to America: A History of Immigration and Ethnicity in American Life*, New York: HarperCollins, 1990

Debouzy, Marianne (editor), *In the Shadow of the Statue of Liberty: Immigrants, Workers, and Citizens in the American Republic, 1880–1920*, Urbana: University of Illinois Press, 1992

Fuchs, Lawrence, *The American Kaleidoscope: Race, Ethnicity and the Civic Culture*, Hanover, NH: University Press of New England, 1990

Gabaccia, Donna R., *From the Other Side: Women, Gender, and Immigrant Life in the US, 1820–1990*, Bloomington: Indiana University Press, 1994

Jones, Maldwyn A., *American Immigration*, Chicago: Chicago University Press, 1960, 2nd edition, 1992

Nugent, Walter T.K., *Crossings: The Great Transatlantic Migrations, 1870–1914*, Bloomington: Indiana University Press, 1992

Thernstrom, Stephan (editor), *Harvard Encyclopedia of American Ethnic Groups*, Cambridge, MA: Belknap Press of Harvard University Press, 1980

Vecoli, Rudolph J. and Suzanne M. Sinke (editors), *A Century of European Migrations, 1830–1930*, Urbana: University of Illinois Press, 1992

Yans-McLaughlin, Virginia (editor), *Immigration Reconsidered: History, Sociology and Politics*, New York: Oxford University Press, 1990

The first two generations of historians of American immigration, whose chief exemplars were Marcus Lee Hansen (1892–1938) and Oscar Handlin (b. 1915), usually subscribed to a monocausal acculturation model for which the shorthand term "Melting Pot" is appropriate. Handlin also created, with the publication of *Boston's Immigrants* (1941), the prototypical format still used by most historians of American immigration, the investigation of a single ethnic group, or a segment of it, in a particular locale, usually a city. Contemporary immigration historians usually pay a great deal more attention to the cultural traits that immigrants retain and sometimes contribute to the general culture, which is increasingly seen as involving some kind of cultural pluralism as opposed to the so-called "Anglo-conformity" which once was paramount. The outpouring of monographs in the very recent past makes any attempt to focus on a small number of books all but impossible; instead of making an arbitrary selection of monographs, the analysis here will focus on works which survey either the entire field or at least the European aspects of it.

THERNSTROM, which identified 106 ethnic groups without, admittedly, exhausting the possibilities, was a monumental – 1101 large double-columned pages – summation of the "state of the art" as it existed in the late 1970s. Its major entries were of two sorts: those on individual ethnic groups and "thematic essays." Most of the entries on ethnic groups are of substantial length – the longest runs to some 50,000 words – and written by the most eminent scholars in the field, for example Theodore Saloutos on Greeks, and Maldwyn Jones on Scotch-Irish. The thematic essays are more problematic, as many cover topics that are quite controversial. Three separate essays by five authors, for example, treat various aspects of "prejudice" from points of view ranging from traditional liberal to neo-conservative. All but a few essays of both kinds have bibliographies. This splendid if somewhat aging monument is still an ideal place to start any study of race and ethnicity in American life.

Of the four comprehensive treatments, JONES is both the oldest and the most recently revised. It was the first survey that can be called modern, and the first general work even to consider treating African Americans as immigrants and to acknowledge the slave trade as a major contributor to the peopling of America. The revised edition recognizes most of the major shifts in emphasis since 1960, such as the inclusion of a wider range of immigrants, a greater appreciation of the significance of "blacks and Native Americans as well as immigrants," the greater complexities of assimilation and ethnic pluralism, and the "mid-Atlantic" stance of many historians of immigration in early American history.

ARCHDEACON represents a distinctly social science approach, and is fully aware of the complexities of the questions of assimilation and acculturation. More than any of its predecessors, it views immigration as a world-wide phenomenon, comparing the American experience to that of Australia, Canada, and, to a lesser degree, Argentina and Brazil, but not South Africa. It devotes significant space to the slave trade and African Americans, but is surprisingly fragmentary in its treatment of individual American ethnic groups.

BODNAR represents the most overtly ideological approach characteristic of the "new social history" and is as much or more concerned with class as with ethnicity in its focus "on the common experience of confronting capitalism." More than other surveys it pays attention to immigrant churches and other aspects of immigrant culture, especially the cultures of immigrants from central, eastern and southern Europe. There is an extended treatment of what the author calls "the culture of everyday life."

DANIELS devotes more space to Asian and Latin American immigrants and to immigration policy than do the others. Like Bodnar, it disputes the traditional "old" and "new" immigrant dichotomy and in addition makes more sustained comparisons between ethnic groups from different regions. Alone of the surveys discussed here, it is self-consciously multicultural. Its major divisions are "Colonial America," "The Century of Immigration (1820–1924)," and "Modern Times."

FUCHS ranges widely over American ethnic history but is highly present-minded, devoting nearly half the text to the period since 1970. Strongly policy-oriented, it hypothesizes "a strong civic culture that permits and protects expressions of ethnic and religious diversity based on individual rights" and which "inhibits and ameliorates conflict among religious, ethnic and racial groups ... unites Americans and protects their freedom." To analyze the "civic culture" Fuchs develops concepts called "tribal pluralism," "caste pluralism" and "sojourner pluralism." The events of the decade since it was written call the essential optimism of this text into question, but it may well be justified in the long run.

NUGENT aims to construct a "demographic mosaic of the transatlantic region from 1870 to 1914" and erects a tripartite schema – "The Atlantic Region and Its Population," "The European Donors," and "The American Receivers" to do so. The first treats fertility and mortality, general patterns and motives; the second has discrete chapters on Britain, Ireland, Scandinavia, the German Empire, Austria-Hungary and Russia, Jews and Poles, Italy, and Spain and Portugal; while the third examines Argentina, Brazil, Canada, and the United States. Nugent is greatly influenced by social science, and no other work is so consistently comparative, particularly in part three. This highly allusive, terse, almost epigrammatic, work – its text is just 162 pages – ends with a nine-paragraph conclusion pondering "Modernization, Transition, and Exceptionalism."

Three anthologies, taken collectively, provide an excellent epitome of the best kinds of work now going on in the field. DEBOUZY emanated from a 1986 Paris colloquium that was part of the centennial of the Statue of Liberty. Fifteen of its nineteen contributors were Europeans – seven French, none British – reflecting the attention that continental scholars outside of Scandinavia are finally beginning to pay to the departure of some sixty million Europeans since 1600. The emphasis here, as in Bodnar, is on the intersection between labor and immigration history. Its four sections focus on "The Image of the Model Republic and Its Metamorphoses," "The Immigrant Experience," "The Transatlantic Perspective," and "A Nation Intended for a Race of Free Men."

Similarly YANS-McLAUGHLIN grew out of a 1986 conference in New York City sponsored by the Statue of Liberty/Ellis Island Foundation. More catholic in content than the other anthologies, it brings together contributions from sociologists as well as from historians, and is concerned not only with European immigrants but also with Third World immigrants from Africa, Asia, Latin America, and the Caribbean. All of its eleven contributors teach at American universities. Its five general topics are "Migration Patterns in World History," "Ethnicity and Social Structure," "The Study of Immigration," "New Approaches to the Study of Immigration," and "The Politics of Immigration." Of particular utility are three essays that are both comparative and bibliographical: Philip D. Curtin, "Migration in the Tropical World;" Sucheng Chan, "European and Asian Immigration into the United States in Comparative Perspective, 1820s to 1920s;" and Ewa Morawska, "The Sociology and Historiography of Immigration."

VECOLI and SINKE developed from a 1986 conference in Minnesota that celebrated both the centennial of the Statue of Liberty and the twentieth anniversary of the Immigration History Research Center at the University of Minnesota. Its 43 participants – 24 from the United States – came from ten nations. The topics of the sixteen published papers – nine by Americans – were somewhat broader than the volume's subtitle: one focused on the "re-peopling of British America, 1600-1790" and another considered emigration from Quebec. The volume begins with Frank Thistlethwaite's seminal 1960 essay on "Migration from Europe Overseas ..." and includes a postscript which he delivered at the conference. Both Vecoli and Sinke and Nugent elaborate the themes that Thistlethwaite first set forth in his paper, read at the eleventh International Congress of Historians in Stockholm.

None of these works says very much about women, and until very recently there were simply no sophisticated monographs about women immigrants. Similarly there was not even an entry on "women" in Thernstrom. A scattering of such monographs has appeared in recent years, and GABACCIA has pioneered in producing a necessarily brief, allusive and somewhat impressionistic survey of women immigrants. That is the case because it was written without the kind of broad monographic base that will someday exist. It deals with the special legal, economic and social problems that faced immigrant women. It is at its best on those groups of European women – Irish, Jewish and Italian – about whom some monographic scholarship exists, and significantly weaker on other European groups, and on Asian, Middle Eastern, African and Latin American women.

As these studies indicate, the study of American immigration has evolved from a field with a relatively narrow focus on European immigrants, American exceptionalism and a model of cultural conformity imposed by a core group, to one that is increasingly world-oriented and aware of multi-causal and complex forces of assimilation, acculturation and even cultural persistence. Once a subject which concerned only American scholars, it is now practised by increasing numbers of European academics and a small but growing number from Asia.

ROGER DANIELS

Immigration: Federal Policy towards

Divine, Robert A., *American Immigration Policy,
    1924–1952*, New Haven: Yale University Press, 1957

Higham, John, *Strangers in the Land: Patterns of American
    Nativism, 1860–1925*, New Brunswick, NJ: Rutgers
    University Press, 1955, corrected reprint, 1963; 2nd
    edition, 1988

Hutchinson, E.P., *Legislative History of American
    Immigration Policy, 1798–1965*, Philadelphia: University
    of Pennsylvania Press, 1981

McClain, Charles J., Jr., *In Search of Equality: The Chinese
    Struggle Against Discrimination in Nineteenth-Century
    America*, Berkeley: University of California Press, 1994

Reimers, David M., *Still the Golden Door: The Third World
    Comes to America*, New York: Columbia University
    Press, 1985, 2nd edition, 1992

Salyer, Lucy, *Laws Harsh as Tigers: Chinese Immigrants and
    the Shaping of Modern Immigration Law*, Chapel Hill:
    University of North Carolina Press, 1995

Modern scholarship on American immigration policy begins
with HIGHAM's trenchant intellectual analysis of the nativist
impulses which have been and continue to be one of its
major shaping forces. Higham was generally unsympathetic to
nativism but explicated its arguments well. He coined the
phrase "tribal twenties" to describe the ethnocultural struggles
between an old-stock, Protestant, small town-rural America
and an immigrant-stock, Catholic and big-city America.
Higham remains a modern classic, indispensable for anyone
concerned with the topic.

DIVINE took up the story where Higham ended, but his
approach was more policy-oriented and generally sympathetic
to the notions of the congressional majority which sought to
maintain restriction. His narrative and analysis end with the
passage of the 1952 McCarran-Walter Act, which he described
as enforcing "an immigration policy which sought to protect
the internal strength of the nation." Although he recognized
that it continued a policy which in effect "discriminated against
people of Asia and southeastern Europe," he insisted that
"there is little evidence to show that racial prejudice was the
primary reason for [its] passage."

Both Higham and Divine, along with almost all of the early
practitioners of the relatively new field of immigration history,
which had its birth in the mid-1920s, shared the mistaken
assumption that immigration as a major factor in shaping
American life had run its course. By the time HUTCHINSON
wrote, the erroneousness of that assumption was plain to see,
and it is now clear that the era of restriction which began with
the first Chinese Exclusion Act (1882) had begun to relax in
1943 with the repeal of Chinese exclusion. The 1952 restrictions, which seemed so substantial to Divine, had been totally
swept away by 1965. Hutchinson's work is bipartite. Part I
analyses congressional action, congress by congress, for nearly
400 often tedious but informative pages. It is meant to be
consulted rather than read. Part II spends nearly 300 pages
treating the development of immigration policy in a series
of chronological-topical chapters, such as "Selection by
Exclusion," "Selection by Deportation," and "Restriction of

Admissions." The result is a valuable if bureaucratic narrative
wholly appropriate for one who had been a longtime employee
of the Immigration and Naturalization Service.

REIMERS begins with a 60-page account of immigration
restriction, and 30 pages on the landmark 1965 Act which he
characterizes as "A Cautious Reform." Since it had consequences unintended by its drafters – the great subsequent
inflow of Asians and Latin Americans who now dominate
immigration to the United States – it might also be called an
inadvertent reform. Later chapters focus more on immigrant
groups than on policy, but Reimers always takes pains to show
how policies and peoples interacted and how the laws actually worked. Individual chapters treat post-1965 immigrants
from Asia, and from Latin America; and "The Unwanted:
Third World Refugees," and "Undocumented Aliens: People
and Politics." A brief coda considers the ongoing debate about
immigration policy. Reimers is clearly positive about the effects
of revitalized immigration to the United States: "the new third
world immigrants ... have already contributed to the
American society. In the near future they will no doubt
continue to do so."

Both McClain and Salyer approach immigration policy from
an entirely different angle, that of legal history, but a legal
history oriented to the social history currents so strong in the
American academy in recent decades. Where the historians
previously discussed utilized chiefly congressional documents
and journalistic accounts, they use court decisions, legal briefs,
and, in the case of Salyer, administrative documents. Both focus
on Chinese immigrants, who, although they composed only a
minute fraction of the immigrant population, were crucial in
the development of American immigration law and policy as
they were the first, and for decades the only, ethnic or racial
group excluded. Legal scholars had long been aware of this
but the special contribution of McCLAIN is his perception that
"the willingness of Chinese litigants to confront the government in a succession of cases gave rise to sharper delineations
of limits on governmental authority and the rights of citizens
and non-citizens. In defining these limits and rights, they
contributed far more to the ideals of democracy and republicanism upon which their adopted country was based than did
their antagonists." The first half of McClain is devoted to the
period before 1882 when the federal courts largely protected
Chinese immigrants' rights against state and municipal persecution, while the second half deals with cases stemming from
the 1882 exclusion act and its sequelae. The rich and detailed
analysis in McClain makes it an important book: it has settled,
at least for this generation, the formal legal history of the 19th
century California Chinese.

SALYER focuses on the transition from an almost wholly
judicial enforcement of the Chinese exclusion laws to the rise
of what she describes as "bureaucratic tyranny." She makes
the quite persuasive argument that the tripartite conflict
between Chinese immigrants and their attorneys, the growing
federal immigration bureaucracy, and the federal courts was
crucial in the creation of "Executive Justice," in which officers of the executive branch increasingly exercised judicial functions. One of the side effects of the work of McClain, Salyer
and others has been to move the Chinese and the litigation
they generated from a peripheral to a central place in the
history of immigration policy.

On a subject of such intense current interest, it is hardly surprising that further work is in progress, for example by Daniels on immigration policy since 1924, and by Reimers on late 20th century nativism.

ROGER DANIELS

Immigration: Acculturation and Americanization

Bodnar, John E., *The Transplanted: A History of Immigrants in Urban America*, Bloomington: Indiana University Press, 1985

Glazer, Nathan and Daniel Patrick Moynihan, *Beyond the Melting Pot: The Negroes, Puerto Ricans, Jews, Italians, and Irish of New York*, Cambridge: Massachusetts Institute of Technology Press, 1963

Gordon, Milton M., *Assimilation in American Life: The Role of Race, Religion, and National Origins*, New York: Oxford University Press, 1964

Handlin, Oscar, *The Uprooted: The Epic Story of the Great Migrations That Made the American People*, Boston: Little Brown, 1951; *The Uprooted: From the Old World to the New*, London: Watts, 1953

Luebke, Frederick C. (editor), *Ethnicity on the Great Plains*, Lincoln: University of Nebraska Press, 1980

Morawska, Ewa, *For Bread with Butter: The Life-Worlds of East Central Europeans in Johnstown, Pennsylvania, 1890–1940*, Cambridge and New York: Cambridge University Press, 1985

Mormino, Gary R. and George E. Pozzetta, *The Immigrant World of Ybor City: Italians and Their Latin Neighbors in Tampa, 1885–1985*, Urbana: University of Illinois Press, 1987

Thernstrom, Stephan (editor), *Harvard Encyclopedia of American Ethnic Groups*, Cambridge, MA: Belknap Press of Harvard University Press, 1980

Early 20th century scholarship on the subject of American immigration, influenced as it was by the "Melting Pot" theory of ethnic interaction, tended to assume that the acculturation and Americanization of immigrants were both desirable and inevitable. (The term "Americanization" is employed here in its generic sense, that is meaning roughly the same as assimilation, rather than in its more specific sense as the name given to the historical movement of the period 1900–1920). Writing shortly after World War II, HANDLIN rejected the view that adjustment to American society was smooth or easy, but affirmed that immigration was a profoundly acculturating experience. Uprooted from their homelands by forces beyond their control, immigrants were at a stroke separated from all that previously had given their lives meaning – family, community, culture – and then thrust as atomized individuals into an unfamiliar, threatening environment. However, the trauma of acculturation was worth it, if not for the immigrants themselves then for their children as, freed from the bonds of peasant tradition, the ethnic second generation successfully adapted to American society.

Although masterfully written and highly suggestive, Handlin's study suffered from limitations and flaws that were to be exposed by the next generation of immigration scholars. During the 1960s and 1970s, when the melting pot was increasingly challenged by cultural pluralism as the ideal paradigm of American society, a host of young historians began questioning long-held assumptions about the desirability and actuality of acculturation and Americanization, and emphasizing instead the role of cultural survival, and ethnic persistence. An important theoretical stimulus to this revision of immigration history was provided by two social science studies. After analyzing patterns of group cultural identity among various ethnic communities in New York City, GLAZER and MOYNIHAN concluded that the melting pot "did not happen." One year later, GORDON, in a work that exerted considerable influence over historical writing, stressed the growing significance of "structural pluralism" among ethnic groups.

BODNAR is a sophisticated and immensely useful synthesis of the revisionist studies of the 1960s and 1970s. Immigration, Bodnar argues, did not involve as drastic a break with the past as Handlin supposed. The immigrants had already encountered the effects of modernization in their homelands, and their decision to emigrate was usually based on rational calculations of economic advantage. Typically, the transatlantic passage followed established patterns laid down by migration traditions. After their arrival in the New World, immigrants constructed ethnic communities around familiar institutions, most important of which was the family. These communities duplicated many of the characteristics – including the class divisions and conflicts – of the originating societies. Moreover when immigrants came to deal with American institutions, they often did so on their own terms. In sum, Bodnar depicts the immigrants as neither acculturated nor Americanized.

One of the most interesting findings of revisionist scholarship concerns immigrants' deployment of "peasant ways" in America. Handlin had perceived traditional homeland beliefs and practices as obstructing the successful progress of immigrants in the New World. Several recent works have revealed how in fact peasant ways, far from hindering, often helped the new arrivals as they struggled to adapt to American society. For example, in her study of East Central Europeans living in the industrial centre of Johnstown, Pennsylvania, MORAWSKA shows how Slavic immigrants coped with poverty and dismal living conditions by utilizing peasant skills and traditional family and ethnic networks. Morawska's study is also notable for its command of a wide range of primary sources in a variety of languages, its grasp of complex sociological theory, and its excellent illustrations.

Despite their emphasis on ethnic resilience, Bodnar and Morawska do not propose that immigrants were completely unchanged by their experiences. Cultural persistence occurred, they believe, only when old traditions retained their usefulness in the new environment; otherwise such traditions were discarded, and new ones adopted, in a process of selective adaptation, or "syncretism." Indeed, the last decade has seen a renewal of scholarly interest in acculturation. However the concept is handled differently from in the past. In several works, attention has focused on a hitherto unexplored dimension of the phenomenon, acculturation by other immigrant groups. MORMINO and POZZETTA, for example, use oral history to document the interactions between Spanish, Cuban and Italian residents of Ybor City, Florida, concluding that in time a common Latin identity emerged, based on the experience of shared residence, institutions, and adversity. However, in spite of this partial resurrection of acculturation, the term Americanization is used only rarely, except when referring to the movement of the early 20th century.

The essays contained in LUEBKE represent another interesting application of this more complex model of cultural adaptation, here to the history of ethnic groups in the American West. Earlier scholarship, influenced by the Turnerian view of the Frontier as an agent of acculturation and Americanization, downplayed the significance of immigrant ethnicity on the Great Plains. The contributors to Luebke seek to show that not only were European immigrants present in large numbers in the West, they also constructed ethnic communities there, hence ensuring a high degree of cultural persistence, especially language maintenance. Change did occur; those who failed to modify their farming practices to suit the Plains environment faced extinction, and the steady rise of national communications networks during the 20th century inevitably made for a degree of acculturation. Nonetheless this did not amount to the absolute Americanization postulated by Turner.

Finally, students of immigrant adaptation might wish to refer to the very stimulating theoretical essays on "American Identity and Americanization" and "Assimilation and Pluralism" in THERNSTROM. The former, by Philip Gleason, includes a useful brief section on the Americanization movement.

HUGH WILFORD

Imperialism and Anti-Imperialism, 1890–1914

Beisner, Robert L., *Twelve Against Empire: The Anti-Imperialists, 1898–1900*, New York: McGraw Hill, 1968; with new preface, Chicago: University of Chicago Press, 1985

Healy, David, *US Expansionism: The Imperialist Urge of the 1890s*, Madison: University of Wisconsin Press, 1970

Hunt, Michael H., *Ideology and US Foreign Policy*, New Haven: Yale University Press, 1987

LaFeber, Walter, *The American Search for Opportunity, 1865–1913* (The Cambridge History of American Foreign Relations, volume 2), Cambridge and New York: Cambridge University Press, 1993

Rystad, Göran, *Ambiguous Imperialism: American Foreign Policy and Domestic Politics at the Turn of the Century*, Lund, Sweden: Esselte Studium, 1975

Tompkins, E. Berkeley, *Anti-Imperialism in the United States: The Great Debate, 1890–1920*, Philadelphia: University of Pennsylvania Press, 1970

Williams, William Appleman, *The Tragedy of American Diplomacy*, Cleveland: World, 1959; 2nd revised edition, New York: Dell, 1972

The issue of imperialism became directly relevant to the United States in the 1890s with the discussion of the implications of a policy of overseas expansion. It is possible to point to two schools of thought on the debate. The two can be defined as the traditionalist approach, which focuses on the formation of official policy, and the revisionists, who arose largely as a critical reaction to this and focus on the effects of this policy. The second school gained particular prominence in the 1960s when the war in Vietnam helped to stimulate retrospective interest in the first great imperialism debate. Writers drawn from the revisionist school receive greater attention here.

LaFEBER, one of the most prominent revisionists working today, provides a useful volume which explores the issues and events surrounding the imperialism debate. He concentrates on the belief that the United States quest for power and influence outweighed any consideration of the effects of expansion. Indeed, he suggests that the demands of the American economic system subsumed concerns over revolutions sparked abroad. Further, he discusses the growth of presidential power facilitated by the acquisition of overseas interests at the turn of the century.

HUNT advances a strong case for ideology as a key motivation behind American foreign policy and surveys the continuities that this approach exposes. This is a refreshingly well written and accessible book. While he considers a broad sweep of history, Hunt's contention is that at the turn of the century the crux of the ideology that sustains American foreign policy became established, and the critics' arguments were decisively defeated. The major elements of this ideology are, Hunt argues, the need to go abroad to seek "national greatness", a conception of a racial hierarchy and a conviction that revolution, despite America's own example, is a danger to international stability. Of the three aspects, his work on the issue of race is perhaps the strongest, and it is usefully supported by cartoons. This is a critical work in which the author suggests that it is now time to replace the dominant ideology with a more constructive approach to the world which, he argues, may still be drawn from American history. Some more worthwhile aspects of America's ideological heritage can be discovered, he suggests, in the arguments of the anti-imperialists.

WILLIAMS has been so hugely influential that it demands consideration despite the reductionist tendency toward history identified by Hunt. Much of the book covers a much wider period, and this is an interpretive essay rather than a conventional work of scholarship, but Williams's basic line of argument is powerfully articulated and remains provocative. Taking a self-professed "radical point of view", he claims that the resolution of the debate between the imperialists and anti-imperialists shaped 20th-century American foreign policy. Williams sees the great debate of 1898–1901 as a three-cornered fight between imperialists, anti-imperialists and a third camp of those promoting the Open Door policy. The Open Door provided a means to create an informal empire, a form of anti-colonial imperialism which preserved the myth of an anti-imperial America. In briefly considering the major personalities of the debate, Williams stresses the consensus in favour of expansion but gives little space to, and indeed rejects any need for, in-depth consideration of the differences between the policies advocated. To Williams, the question of whether actually to acquire colonies was the only issue that separated the camps.

RYSTAD puts forward an analysis of American policy at the turn of the century which ties foreign and domestic issues together. By focusing mainly on the election campaign of 1900, he is able to present an analysis of the arguments, which may not provide any strikingly new conclusions but, in its detailed discussion and supporting evidence, adds a good deal to the debate. Taken together, Beisner and Tompkins provide a comprehensive examination of the arguments of the anti-imperialists. Of the two, BEISNER has greater analytical depth. He rejects the idea, advanced by the New Left, that the two sides of the debate were essentially similar, and in only a few cases does he find evidence to justify their argument that the anti-imperialists supported expansion on economic grounds, with the sole qualification that they opposed the acquisition of colonies. The 1985 edition of the book is worth consulting for the new preface added. But Beisner's self-confessed "somewhat arbitrary" exclusion of the contribution of the Democrats to the debate, together with his rather idiosyncratic choice of the twelve men on whom he focuses, leaves gaps in overall consideration of the question, which Tompkins helps to fill. TOMPKINS's analysis is neither particularly insightful nor original, and he adopts an essentially descriptive approach to the events of 1890–1920, with a structure that is dictated more by chronology than ideas. While his research is undoubtedly voluminous, he relies rather heavily on published sources and too little on the private papers of the key participants in the debate. Tompkins does have the virtue of staying with the anti-imperialists until 1920, but his work may be most useful as a starting point for more advanced reading. More critical work on this aspect of the debate remains to be done.

HEALY adds further to an understanding of the great debate. In line with Beisner and Tompkins, he reflects an awareness of the strength of the issues dividing the camps yet does not neglect the similarities. He sees the 1890s and the policy of imperialism as far removed from the "aberration" that it has been conveniently labelled. In Healy's analysis, this was in fact the decade in which American expansion opened the way for the nation's development into a world power. Taking a multi-faceted approach, the author examines five schools of thought and focuses on the individuals who supported them. He concludes with an examination of the anti-imperialist argument which, while brief in comparison to the two previous authors, is nevertheless trenchant.

JULIA L. OATHAM

See also Expansionism; Open Door Policy

Industrial Workers of the World

Brissenden, Paul F., *The IWW: A Study of American Syndicalism*, New York: Columbia University Press, and London: King, 1919; 2nd edition, 1920

Conlin, Joseph R., *Bread and Roses Too: Studies of the Wobblies*, Westport, CT: Greenwood Press, 1969

Conlin, Joseph R. (editor), *At the Point of Production: The Local History of the IWW*, Westport, CT: Greenwood Press, 1981

Dubofsky, Melvyn, *We Shall Be All: A History of the Industrial Workers of the World*, Chicago: Quadrangle, 1969; 2nd edition, Urbana: University of Illinois Press, 1988

Dubofsky, Melvyn, *"Big Bill" Haywood*, Manchester: Manchester University Press, and New York: St. Martin's Press, and Manchester: Manchester University Press, 1987

Foner, Philip S., *History of the Labor Movement in the United States*, vol. 4: *The Industrial Workers of the World*, New York: International, 1965

Gambs, John S., *The Decline of the IWW*, New York: Columbia University Press, 1932

Haywood, William D., *Bill Haywood's Book: The Autobiography of William D. Haywood*, New York: International, and London: M. Lawrence, 1929

Kornbluh, Joyce L. (editor), *Rebel Voices: An IWW Anthology*, Ann Arbor: University of Michigan Press, 1964; revised, Chicago: Charles H. Kerr, 1988

Renshaw, Patrick, *The Wobblies: The Story of Syndicalism in the United States*, New York: Doubleday, and London: Eyre and Spottiswoode, 1967

Thompson, Fred, *The IWW: Its First Fifty Years, 1905–1955*, Chicago: IWW, 1955, revised as *The IWW: Its First Seventy Years, 1905–1975: The History of an Effort to Organize the Working Class*, 1976

Winters, Donald E., Jr., *The Soul of the Wobblies: The IWW, Religion and American Culture in the Progressive Era, 1905–1917*, Westport, CT: Greenwood Press, 1985

The Industrial Workers of the World (IWW) – the "Wobblies" – were founded by a combination of breakaway radical unions, like the Western Federation of Miners, and dissident socialists like Eugene Debs, Daniel DeLeon and Bill Haywood. Between 1905 and 1925 it challenged the American Federation of Labor by trying to organize that 90 per cent of the American working class that was unorganized into industrial unions which would overthrow the capitalist system and provide the basis for a socialist commonwealth. While such revolutionary aims were largely confined to IWW propaganda, it did manage to establish unions for migratory farm, lumber and dockside workers, and led notable textile strikes at Lawrence, Massachusetts and Paterson, New Jersey in 1912–13. Fiercely attacked and prosecuted during World War I, the IWW became a full-time legal defence organization between 1917 and 1921 when 101 leading members were jailed for up to 20 years and heavily fined. Comintern attempts to take over the IWW exacerbated its internal conflicts, and the union also suffered the decline that all unions experienced during the 1920s. However, its satirical songs and parodies, such a lively feature of its appeal, survived to inspire workers who successfully established strong industrial unions during the 1930s and after.

Various participants in the story of the IWW wrote their own first-hand accounts, but the first serious academic treatment came from BRISSENDEN. Although he was concerned largely with internal, institutional questions, based on close reading of union records, this was an impressive pioneering study which is still useful today. None of the early books, however, could explain IWW disunity and decline, since they were written before this had occurred. The autobiography of HAYWOOD, the most prominent figure in the movement, was composed when he was a political refugee in the Soviet Union, where he fled on jumping bail in 1921. Published shortly after his death in 1928, it did discuss the decline of the IWW, but failed to confront the devastating effect which his own defection had had on rank-and-file sentiment, and in any case it was ghosted to fit the Communist party line. However, it still provides invaluable information on Haywood's early life. DUBOFSKY (1987) is an authoritative modern study of Haywood.

GAMBS attempted a fuller explanation of the decline of the IWW. It contained some vivid descriptions of violent faction fighting in the 1920s, but was essentially unsympathetic to the Wobblies and minimised the decisive part played by government repression in destroying them. After this, historians neglected the subject for a generation. However, THOMPSON, who had served many years in jail because of his beliefs, remained completely true to them and wrote the IWW's official 50th anniversary history in 1955. By then anticommunism was rampant in the United States and organizations like the IWW appeared completely discredited, if not treasonable. Nevertheless, Thompson argued loyally that the IWW had not failed but was still alive, waiting its opportunity. In a bibliographical sense at least, this proved to be true. For, with the publication in 1964 of KORNBLUH's comprehensive, lively and lavishly illustrated book of readings and extracts from other historians and Wobblies themselves, the floodgates opened. During the great social and political upheaval of the 1960s, a whole generation strove eagerly to recover the truth about the history of the American left.

In some respects, RENSHAW can be said to have begun this task, as far as the Wobblies were concerned. When it appeared in 1967 it was not only the first complete account by an objective historian, but also the first by a British one. In his own work, Dubofsky described it as "a spritely, engaging and readable general history." DUBOFSKY (1969, 1988) is a large-scale study, based on formidable scholarship, which remains the most authoritative history of the IWW. Hitherto, labour historians like Selig Perlman and Philip Taft (a former Wobbly himself) had explained the IWW as being largely a product of the unique circumstances of America's western frontier. Dubofsky places it much more firmly within the harsh realities of American industrial capitalism. With the monopolistic power and wealth of the trusts ruthlessly exploiting labour, the IWW was simply trying to organize a monopoly of labour power in self-defence. However, despite its comprehensive coverage, Dubofsky's book largely neglected the international dimension of IWW activity, in Australia, Britain, South Africa, South America and elsewhere, which Brissenden had sketched and Renshaw discussed more fully. FONER's study, longer even than Dubofsky's, made full use of union records, but failed to explain the IWW's origins or end satisfactorily, and is in any case somewhat distorted by a Marxist analysis peculiarly ill-suited to such a free-wheeling movement.

The essays collected in CONLIN (1969) failed to explain the movement satisfactorily. However, the essays by various historians in CONLIN (1981) provide not only the most useful and comprehensive account of the IWW at the local level, but by the far the fullest IWW bibliography in print. Finally, WINTERS has written a thoughtful study of the seriously neglected subject of religion and the IWW. This is important not simply because Wobbly song writers often parodied Christian hymns, nor even because evangelicals like the Salvation Army and the Social Gospel movement aimed at recruiting the same workers as the IWW, but because labour historians have failed to confront properly the whole subject of religion and the American labour movement.

PATRICK RENSHAW

See also Labor Unions

Industrialization

Chandler, Alfred D., Jr., *The Visible Hand: The Managerial Revolution in American Business*, Cambridge, MA: Belknap Press of Harvard University Press, 1977

Clark, Victor S., *History of Manufactures in the United States*, 3 vols., New York: McGraw Hill, 1929

Cochran, Thomas C., *Frontiers of Change: Early Industrialism in America*, New York: Oxford University Press, 1981

Cochran, Thomas C. and William Miller, *The Age of Enterprise: A Social History of Industrial America*, New York: Macmillan, 1942; revised, New York: Harper, 1961

George, Peter James, *The Emergence of Industrial America: Strategic Factors in American Economic Growth since 1870*, Albany: State University of New York Press, 1982

Hays, Samuel P., *The Response to Industrialism, 1885–1914*, Chicago: University of Chicago Press, 1957, 2nd edition, 1995

Higgs, Robert, *The Transformation of the American Economy, 1865–1914: An Essay in Interpretation*, New York: Wiley, 1971

Hounshell, David A., *From the American System to Mass Production, 1800–1932: The Development of Manufacturing Technology in the United States*, Baltimore: Johns Hopkins University Press, 1984

Kirkland, Edward C., *Industry Comes of Age: Business, Labor, and Public Policy, 1860–1897*, New York: Holt Rinehart, 1961

Licht, Walter, *Industrializing America: The Nineteenth Century*, Baltimore: Johns Hopkins University Press, 1995

Mayr, Otto and Robert C. Post (editors), *Yankee Enterprise: The Rise of the American System of Manufactures*, Washington, DC: Smithsonian Institution Press, 1981

Vatter, Harold G., *The Drive to Industrial Maturity: The US Economy, 1860–1914*, Westport, CT: Greenwood Press, 1975

In view of industry's great impact upon American society, politics and culture, it is not surprising that many historians have studied the dynamics and impact of industrialization. CLARK's monumental study provides an exhaustive account of industrial growth in America from the colonial era through to 1929. The first volume, which charts the growth of industry between 1607 and 1860, is particularly important, because it includes a great deal of material on the limited development of manufacturing during the colonial era. More generally, the work contains a huge amount of information about the growth of a wide range of industries. Unfortunately, the sheer mass of descriptive material ensures that parts of the study lack sparkle and analytical vigour. But the thoroughness and care of Clark's scholarship ensures that it remains an invaluable reference work.

COCHRAN and MILLER also provide a wide-ranging discussion of industrialization from the beginning of the 19th century through to the 1930s. The authors give a straightforward account of America's industrial growth. Maintaining that "business" was the single most important factor shaping American life, they also describe how industrial growth revolutionised the social, political and intellectual life of the United States. It is impossible to do justice to all the complexities of industrialization in a one-volume study, and, inevitably, parts of Cochran and Miller's narrative now seem dated and simplistic. For instance, in place of a full analysis of the role played by America's industrial leaders, the authors merely list a few examples of corporate greed and misconduct. However, despite such shortcomings, this remains an extremely informative and highly readable introduction to the topic. LICHT is a recent, highly-compressed, survey and interpretation of 19th-century industrial development which sees industrialization as both consequence and cause of dramatic economic and social transformation. In a skilful sythesis, he examines industrialization in the context of the pervasiveness of the market economy in 19th-century America.

There are surprisingly few specialised works on industrialization in the antebellum period. In the most recent and accessible of these studies, COCHRAN gives an elegant account of the emergence of industry, and analyzes how its development affected American society. He also discusses the factors that underlay America's achievements in manufacturing, placing particular emphasis upon the nation's distinctive culture. Having migrated to a new continent, Cochran suggests, Americans were naturally more disposed to try new productive techniques, to experiment and to tinker. In the collection of essays edited by MAYR and POST, a number of distinguished historians of technology, business, and labour relations discuss the development and impact of the American system of manufactures – the heavily mechanized productive techniques that facilitated the nation's industrial growth. While a few essays look at technological developments during the late 19th and early 20th centuries, most contributors focus on mechanisation during the antebellum period.

The literature on the development of industry in the years after the Civil War is extensive. HAYS provides a good, brief overview of the major results of America's Industrial Revolution. The author is not an economic historian and his discussion of the dynamics of industrialization is cursory, but he does highlight very effectively the myriad ways in which the rise of manufacturing affected American society and culture. He also discusses how politicians and the public responded to, and tried to shape, the process of industrial growth. Several studies provide more detailed analysis of the economics of industrialization after the Civil War. KIRKLAND emphasises the benefits of industrial growth, providing examples of the achievements of individual firms and arguing that

the growth of manufacturing led to a substantial rise in the standard of living of American workers. Kirkland's account is clearly written, well-organised and completely free of economic jargon. But, not surprisingly in a book written more than three decades ago, much of the analysis now appears rather dated. There is little use of the theoretical models and statistical techniques that have recently been employed so extensively by practitioners of the "New Economic History." Kirkland also appears too prepared to accept business leaders' optimistic claims about the beneficial impact of industry.

HIGGS is a much more incisive examination of the dynamics of industrialization, which emphasizes the central role played by changing patterns of consumer demand in the growth of industry. But he also stresses the importance of technological innovations and the emergence of a more skilled workforce, in the great surge in America's industrial productivity. He concludes by analyzing how industrial growth affected various groups in American society, including farmers, immigrants and workers. An interpretive essay rather than a comprehensive overview, Higgs is informative and stimulating. In particular, although drawing upon sophisticated theory, he succeeds in making his argument accessible even to those with little background in economics. VATTER covers many aspects of industrialization in his ambitious survey of economic change in the five decades after the Civil War. Although putting particular emphasis upon the role of changing patterns of demand in the growth of industry, Vatter also explores the impact of structural and technological developments upon industrial production. He draws heavily upon the quantitative and theoretical techniques of the New Economic History, but, like Higgs, he presents his arguments in an extremely lucid manner.

A number of specialised studies supplement these general accounts of industrialization after the Civil War. GEORGE highlights the principal sources of America's industrial growth between 1860 and 1930. In a series of nine thematic essays, he discusses the significance of various causal factors, including technological innovation, business organisation and entrepreneurship. In his study of mass production HOUNSHELL also discusses the causes of industrialization. He argues that, until the early 20th century, firms generally continued to employ time-consuming and labour-intensive techniques of production. The success of America's industrial giants in the late 19th century was, he suggests, primarily the result of effective marketing, rather than efficient production. CHANDLER examines how America's corporate leaders shaped, and responded to, the nation's industrial growth. The study is most famous for its pellucid analysis of the development of modern corporate management structures, but, more generally, Chandler also provides a compelling account of the role that the giant corporations played in transforming America into the world's pre-eminent industrial power.

PHILIP J. CULLIS

See also Business History entries; Manufacturing Industry entries

Intellectual History: General

Appleby, Joyce, *Liberalism and Republicanism in the Historical Imagination*, Cambridge, MA: Harvard University Press, 1992

Diggins, John Patrick, *The American Left in the Twentieth Century*, New York: Harcourt Brace, 1973; revised as *The Rise and Fall of the American Left*, New York: Norton, 1992

Hollinger, David A., *In the American Province: Studies in the History and Historiography of Ideas*, Bloomington: Indiana University Press, 1985

Hollinger, David A. and Charles Capper (editors), *The American Intellectual Tradition: A Sourcebook*, 2 vols., New York and Oxford: Oxford University Press, 1989, 2nd edition, 1993

Jacoby, Russell, *The Last Intellectuals: American Culture in the Age of Academe*, New York: Basic Books, 1987

Matthiessen, F.O., *American Renaissance: Art and Expression in the Age of Emerson and Whitman*, New York and London: Oxford University Press, 1941

Miller, Perry, *The New England Mind: The Seventeenth Century*, New York: Macmillan, 1939

Miller, Perry, *The New England Mind: From Colony to Province*, Cambridge, MA: Harvard University Press, 1953

Parrington, Vernon L., *Main Currents in American Thought: An Interpretation of American Literature from the Beginnings to 1920*, 3 vols., New York: Harcourt Brace, 1927–30

Pells, Richard H., *Radical Visions and American Dreams: Culture and Social Thought in the Depression Years*, New York: Harper, 1973

Pells, Richard H., *The Liberal Mind in a Conservative Age: American Intellectuals in the 1940s and 1950s*, New York: Harper, 1985

Perry, Lewis, *Intellectual Life in America: A History*, New York: Watts, 1984

Tallack, Douglas, *Twentieth-Century America: The Intellectual and Cultural Context*, London and New York: Longman, 1991

Trachtenberg, Alan, *The Incorporation of America: Culture and Society in the Gilded Age*, New York: Hill and Wang, 1982

A quick and convenient introduction to American intellectual history is available in the form of the headnotes that preface each document in HOLLINGER and CAPPER. In addition to vivid thumb-nail portraits of individual intellectuals, these contain helpful advice on further reading. Also useful are the "Chronologies" at the end of Volume II. The best recent book-length survey of the field is PERRY. Over eight chronologically arranged chapters this work traces changes in both the position of intellectuals and conceptions of the intellect in America from the colonial period to the present day. Although quite conventional in his choice of themes and subject matter, Perry nonetheless achieves a freshness of tone which, combined with his impressive knowledge of the whole area, make him at once authoritative and accessible. Particularly welcome is

his sensitivity to the changing institutional context of American intellectual life.

American intellectual history has always been marked by a tension between scholars who are principally concerned with the formal analysis of isolated texts and those interested mainly in the historical circumstances in which texts are produced. Like many other so-called "Progressive" historians, PARRINGTON preferred the latter approach. In his classic three-volume account of the main currents of American thought, yet to be surpassed as the most comprehensive guide to pre-20th century American intellectual history, he chose to follow (in his own words) "the broad path of our political, economic, and social development, rather than the narrower belletristic." Volume I, 1620-1800, *The Colonial Mind*, takes his account from the colonization of New England to the presidential election of 1800; Volume II, 1800-1860, *The Romantic Revolution in America*, explores the intellectual consequences of the rise of industrial capitalism and the influence of French Romanticism; and Volume III, 1860-1920, *The Beginnings of Critical Realism in America*, addresses the effects of further industrialization, mechanization, and growing opposition to the middle class. This privileging of the historical over the aesthetic was not unrelated to Parrington's leftist politics which, as he readily confessed, inclined him to take a more sympathetic view of liberal and "Jeffersonian" than of conservative and "Federalist" movements and individuals. His veneration for Roger Williams, Benjamin Franklin and, of course, Jefferson himself is evidence of this bias. So too is his portrayal of Puritanism as an absolutist and reactionary theology obstructing the importation into colonial New England of liberal European ideologies such as the doctrine of natural rights.

MILLER could not accept this view of Puritanism. He also rejected the Progessive scholars' materialist interpretation of early American intellectual history as crudely determinist, and favored instead a formalist or "literary" methodology. Consequently, in his two-volume study of the New England mind, he set out to portray the Calvinist theology of the Puritan divines in all its complexity, difficulty, and strangeness. For example, the second volume contains minutely detailed reconstructions of doctrinal disputes concerning the Half-Covenant, inoculation, and witchcraft. In performing this task Miller both disproved the dominant academic view of the New England mind as a set of gloomy superstitions, and corrected the popular confusion, perpetuated by H.L. Mencken, of Puritanism with repressive Victorian morality. However, it is arguable that he went too far in the formalist direction, abstracting Puritan doctrines from their social and economic context, and thereby rendering his analysis ahistorical. Recently such scholars as Sacvan Bercovitch have challenged central aspects of his work, and attempted to reintegrate Puritanism into the history of national development. It has also been pointed out that Miller tended to project his own philosophical preoccupations on to the Puritan divines, for example misrepresenting Jonathan Edwards as a precursor of modern existentialist theology.

Recent scholarship concerning the intellectual history of the American Revolution has also tended to fall into one of two camps, depicting ideas as either historically determined or relatively autonomous. "Republican" historians such as Bernard

Bailyn, Gordon Wood, and J.G.A. Pocock have located the intellectual origins of the Revolution in 18th-century British opposition thought. APPLEBY in contrast bases her explanation of Revolutionary ideology in economic changes affecting the American colonies. She argues that the spread of market economics during the 1700s produced a new middle class intellectual tradition, distinct from and sometimes rival to the British "country" position. This, she claims, inspired colonial resistance to imperial policy, and eventually culminated in the optimism, pluralism and liberalism of the Jeffersonian Republicans. Despite some faults – for example its failure to explain the party conflicts of the early national period – this thesis has proved a highly influential interpretation of the ideas of the Revolutionary movement. It is presented here in the form of thirteen essays written over the course of the 1970s and 1980s, all notable for their clarity and elegance.

As for the 19th century, the most stimulating examination of intellectual life during the antebellum period is still MATTHIESSEN. It has been suggested that Perry Miller's investigation of the New England mind was partly prompted by a desire to define the essence of the American national character. One of the declared aims of Matthiessen's study (published on the eve of American entry into World War II) was to identify the "common denominator" in the work of five writers – Emerson, Thoreau, Whitman, Hawthorne, and Melville – in the half-decade 1850–55, a period which saw the United States "coming to its first maturity and affirming its rightful heritage in the whole expanse of art and culture." Whatever its motivation, the book was soon recognized as a masterpiece of literary scholarship, and in the years after the war was adopted as a founding text of the American Studies movement. Matthiessen attempted to steer a middle course between the extremes of formalism and contextualism. It is significant that the impulse which he identified as the common denominator in the work of his five chosen authors was political – that is, "their devotion to the possibilities of democracy." Still, he does not avoid the trap of aestheticism altogether, often seeming rather less interested in the democratic potentiality of American literature than in complex questions of literary technique.

One book that does avoid the pitfalls of either excessive formalism or excessive determinism is TRACHTENBERG's study of American society and culture in the Gilded Age. The scope of this work is not limited to intellectual history – rather it sets out to evaluate the impact on all parts of the national culture of such characteristic developments of the era as the rise of corporations – but it nonetheless offers the best description of late 19th-century American intellectuals available (Parrington is less good on this period than on earlier ones, and in any case the final volume of his trilogy was not complete at the time of his death). In the course of seven brilliant essays on subjects such as mechanization and urbanization, all containing excellent syntheses of recent mainstream historical scholarship, Trachtenberg touches on such aspects of Victorian intellectual life as the rise of Social Darwinism, genteel culture, great cultural institutions, and literary realism. His grasp of historical context combined with his appreciation of the formal dimension of cultural texts make this work a model of interdisciplinary American Studies. Finally, the concluding bibliographical essay is extraordinarily wide-ranging.

Two works serve well as accounts of 20th-century American intellectual history. Part Two of TALLACK, "The Culture of Politics," consists of a chronological survey of movements and individuals, starting with William James and Pragmatism and ending with Richard Rorty and Postmodernism. In between are discussions of the Greenwich Village Rebels of the 1910s, the Lost Intellectuals of the 1920s, and the Southern Agrarians; of the Old Left, the New York Intellectuals, and the New Left; and of two groups regrettably missing from most general works on American intellectual history, African American and feminist intellectuals. Perhaps inevitably in a work of this scope and ambition there are omissions: conservative intellectuals are conspicuous by their absence, as is reference to contemporary debates concerning intellectual professionalization and multiculturalism. Still, this is the best available introduction to 20th-century American intellectuals. Not the least of its virtues is its command of recent developments in critical theory; the sections on Feminism and Postmodernism are especially good in this regard. Also, the extensive appendices, including a chronology, bibliography, and potted biographies, are impressive.

Second, DIGGINS, while not strictly speaking a work of intellectual history, nevertheless provides an illuminating commentary on leftist thought in 20th-century America. Distinguishing between four distinct and separate radical movements, (the "Lyrical Left" of the 1910s, the Old Left, the New Left, and the "Academic Left" of the 1980s), Diggins interweaves his historical narrative with perceptive portraits of leading leftist thinkers (such as Sidney Hook and Richard Rorty) and lively discussions of the theories they have propounded (such as Marxism and Post-Structuralism). One is left in no doubt where his sympathies lie: with the Lyrical and New Lefts, not the Old and Academic Lefts. His hostility to the last does result in the occasional over-simplication or distortion. For the most part, though, this is an admirably fair and even-handed treatment of a controversial subject. Ironically it is Diggins's major weakness as a historian of the Left – that is, his tendency to concentrate on leaders and theoreticians at the expense of ordinary, rank-and-file activists – that makes his book so valuable as intellectual history.

There are a number of works dealing with specific groups and periods in the 20th century. Outstanding among these are Pells's two volumes. PELLS (1973) deals with the 1930s, when many American intellectuals, confronted by the human catastrophe that was the Great Depression, rejected liberalism in favour of radicalism; while PELLS (1985) deals with the 1940s and 1950s, when those same intellectuals reverted from radicalism to liberal anti-Communism. In neither case, though, were these developments straightforward or clear-cut, and Pells does full justice to the complexities and nuances of intellectual life in both eras, for example emphasizing the underlying conservatism of many radical utterances during the 1930s, and highlighting continuities between the supposedly conformist 1950s and rebellious 1960s. The structure of both books is broadly chronological, with the focus lingering on particular problems, movements, and individuals. The effect is fresh and engaging. Admittedly both accounts have gaps. For example, given Pells's interest in the ways in which 1950s intellectuals influenced the New Left and Counterculture, his failure to treat Critical Theorists like Herbert Marcuse or sexual radicals like

Norman O. Brown is puzzling. These flaws notwithstanding, Pells's two books add up to an excellent record of American intellectual history between 1930 and 1960.

For a provoking, indeed polemical, view of American intellectuals from the 1950s to the 1980s readers may turn to JACOBY. The central claim of this work is that America's intellectual life is in a state of disastrous decline. Before the 1950s "public intellectuals," institutionally non-affiliated critics like Edmund Wilson and Dwight Macdonald, communicated regularly with a large audience about matters of general concern in an easily understandable style. As the postwar period unfolded however a number of factors, including suburbanization and the decline of the inner city, forced such intellectuals out of the public sphere and into institutional employment, chiefly of course in the universities, with the result that today's intellectuals, if they can be called that, communicate only with each other about obscure academic issues in an arcane jargon. As he develops this thesis Jacoby offers some extremely acute observations about several public intellectuals of the 1950s (including C. Wright Mills, Lionel Trilling, and Richard Hofstadter), about the Beats, and about certain New Leftists. More importantly, his argument about the institutionalization of oppositional intellectuals is well documented and highly convincing. That said, his picture omits a group of prominent contemporary public intellectuals, namely the Neo-Conservatives. More problematic still is his assumption that professionalization is a disaster from which American intellectual life will never recover. A great deal of recent work by such academics as Andrew Ross and Bruce Robbins has been devoted to showing how professional intellectuals like themselves can and should operate in the public sphere.

Finally, HOLLINGER (1985) is an important collection of essays written during the 1970s and 1980s, some dealing with particular aspects of 20th-century American intellectual history, such as the philosophy of William James, the impact of Eastern European Jewish intellectuals, and the canonization of Modernist literature, others with methodological issues, like the ideas of Michel Foucault, Richard Rorty, and Thomas Kuhn. These essays were not originally designed for publication together, and the work consequently lacks cohesion and unity when viewed as a whole. Still, it has two very significant merits. The author is a leading contemporary intellectual historian, and several of the older essays reproduced here, particularly the ones on Pragmatism and Cosmopolitanism, have a prophetic quality when read in light of subsequent developments in the discipline. Also, Hollinger is extremely adept at simplifying complex theories and ideas without misrepresenting them. The essay on Pragmatism, for example, is a masterpiece of synopsis.

HUGH WILFORD

Internal Improvements

Fishlow, Albert, *American Railroads and the Transformation of the Antebellum Economy*, Cambridge, MA: Harvard University Press, 1965

Goodrich, Carter, *Government Promotion of American Canals and Railroads, 1800–1890*, New York: Columbia University Press, 1960
Handlin, Oscar and Mary Flug Handlin, *Commonwealth: A Study of the Role of Government in the American Economy: Massachusetts, 1774–1861*, revised edition, Cambridge, MA: Belknap Press of Harvard University Press, 1969
Hartz, Louis, *Economic Policy and Democratic Thought: Pennsylvania, 1776–1860*, Cambridge, MA: Harvard University Press, 1948
Hill, Forest Garrett, *Roads, Rails, and Waterways: The Army Engineers and Early Transportation*, Norman: University of Oklahoma Press, 1957
Scheiber, Harry N., *Ohio Canal Era: A Case Study of Government and the Economy, 1820–1861*, Athens: Ohio University Press, 1969; with new preface, 1987
Taylor, George Rogers, *The Transportation Revolution, 1815–1860*, New York: Rinehart, 1951

Despite the prominence of the internal improvements issue in 19th-century America, the topic has elicited few book-length studies of high quality. Of course, historians have spent much time on specific developments in transportation improvement, but the ideological conflicts over internal improvements remain a fertile, but under-cultivated, field for study. For example, the most important work to date on the subject is still TAYLOR. In his overview of the antebellum era, Taylor described – indeed, was the first to define – the transportation revolution which, as part of the market revolution, has become recognized as a central element in 19th-century American history. His original research into labor wages and improvement costs, and his synthesis of the multitude of secondary monographs produced in the 1940s, make Taylor's work indispensable. Yet Taylor underemphasized the ideological tensions over internal improvements, in order to highlight the actual mechanisms of improvement programs and the degree of government involvement.

HILL took as a major theme the centrality of the federal government in internal improvements. Although he recognized the importance of private investments, Hill argued that the need for engineers to survey roads, canals and railroads, to design waterway improvements, and to explore the trans-Mississippi West was fulfilled only through the United States Army engineers. As a historian of technology, Hill explored the development of the engineering profession, in light of the demand for transportation which accompanied American expansion into the West.

GOODRICH, like Hill, examined the connections between the national government and the economy. The era of the canals, so crucial to the development of the trans-Appalachian West, arose from the combined efforts of public and private enterprises. Goodrich concluded that, in comparison to private investments in improvements, the government's role proved minor and indirect. The pattern of substantial government promotion but minimal government investment continued into the railroad era, thereby guaranteeing that the development of the trans-Mississippian West would be shaped more by individual and corporate interests than by coherent government programs.

While Taylor and Goodrich shared interests in the role and degree of government participation in internal improvements, FISHLOW offered a more quantitative approach which emphasized the consequences of technological change for mid-19th century America. Fishlow's concern was the relationship between improvements and economic development. His conclusions overturned the traditional notion of interconnectedness between railroads and industrial growth. Rather, Fishlow suggested that agriculture, not industrial development, benefited most from the expansion of the railroad. Thus, he challenged the connection between improvements and industrialization, which was so central to Taylor's and Goodrich's views of internal improvements.

While the majority of studies of internal improvements approach the topic on a regional or national scale, several fine studies illuminate the intricate workings of improvements at the state level. One of the best examples is HARTZ, who argued that attention to the national level had led to neglect or distortion of internal improvements at the state level. In Pennsylvania, activity by the state was more pervasive and intense than federal action. Through analysis of the legal and economic regulations of the era, Hartz found that the antebellum period witnessed state government intervention in many areas of local development. Not until the post-bellum years, when corporate interests besieged state government, did the state relinquish much of its influence over internal improvements.

Another excellent state study is HANDLIN and HANDLIN. In their analysis of Massachusetts' state laws concerning economic development, the Handlins likewise found the state active in internal improvements, although in a less overt manner than in Pennsylvania as described by Hartz. While private investment created improvements, the state government successfully used charters to dictate the terms of improvement. Towns and villages unwillingly became heirs to poorly improved roads, bridges, and waterways when charters expired. Along with its activities in poor relief, education, and immigration, the state's role in internal improvements was one of regulation, rather than peripheral participation.

In another state-level study, SCHEIBER examined Ohio's internal improvements. The state government promoted, financed, constructed and operated canals. Scheiber concluded, however, that even the state level may be too large to make possible a full understanding of the impetus behind internal improvements. The local level, where entrepreneurial spirit and egalitarianism merged, became the arena in which the battle over improvements was fought. By the 1840s, local demands contributed to a canal-building boom, which offered freight rate reductions and set the stage for competition with the railroads in the 1850s.

In view of modern preoccupation with the question of the role of government in the economy, it is rather surprising that there has not been more recent scholarly attention to 19th-century internal improvements. Some of that attention has shifted to the legal framework within which economic development took place, which has been the subject of influential studies by J. Willard Hurst, Morton Horwitz, William Nelson and others.

CRAIG THOMPSON FRIEND

See also Government and the Economy; Rivers and Canals; Roads entries; Transport

Investment: Foreign Investment in the United States

Adler, Dorothy R., *British Investment in American Railways, 1834–1898*, Charlottesville: University Press of Virginia, 1970

Burk, Kathleen, *Britain, America and the Sinews of War, 1914–1918*, London and Boston: Allen and Unwin, 1985

Davis, Lance E. and Robert J. Cull, *International Capital Markets and American Economic Growth, 1820–1914*, Cambridge and New York: Cambridge University Press, 1994

Edelstein, Michael, *Overseas Investment in the Age of High Imperialism: The United Kingdom, 1850–1914*, New York: Columbia University Press, and London: Methuen, 1982

Hidy, Ralph Willard, *The House of Baring in American Trade and Finance: English Merchant Bankers at Work, 1763–1861*, Cambridge, MA: Harvard University Press, 1949

Jenks, Leland H., *The Migration of British Capital to 1875*, New York: Knopf, and London: Nelson, 1927

Lewis, Cleona, *America's Stake in International Investments*, Washington, DC: Brookings Institution, 1938

Michie, R.C., *The London and New York Stock Exchanges, 1850–1914*, London and Boston: Allen and Unwin, 1987

Organisation for Economic Cooperation and Development, *Economic Surveys of the United States*, Paris: OECD, 1961–

Platt, D.C.M., *Britain's Investments Overseas on the Eve of the First World War: The Use and Abuse of Numbers*, London: Macmillan, and New York: St. Martin's Press, 1986

Wilkins, Mira, *The History of Foreign Investment in the United States to 1914*, Cambridge, MA: Harvard University Press, 1989

The classic work on foreign investment in the United States and American investment overseas is LEWIS, which was based on numerous 19th- and early 20th-century surveys. In the 19th century, the United States absorbed large amounts of foreign capital. A substantial proportion of this was repatriated in the years 1914–18, but the inward flow was renewed in the 1920s, and again after 1960. Now the flow once more outweighs American investment overseas. In a book containing 625 pages of text and 350 pages of notes and bibliography, WILKINS provides the fullest and most detailed modern survey of the period up to 1914. A 20th-century sequel is promised. DAVIS and CULL is a short analytical survey of inward and outward investment.

Both Lewis and Wilkins show that the federal government was the chief long-term borrower in the period 1783–1815, but from 1815 to 1860 federal government debt fell, relative to GNP. JENKS's classic study of British overseas lending includes two colourful chapters on American state government borrowing in the 1830s. Many southern and western states defaulted on these debts during the financial crises between 1837 and 1843, and Jenks quotes the Paris Rothschilds' comment that henceforth the United States could not borrow "a dollar, not a dollar". Short-term commercial credits were almost as important as long-term loans in the pre-1860 period. HIDY's long and detailed study of the Barings shows how British credit was advanced to East Coast importers and southern planters. Such credits contracted after 1839, but recovered in the 1850s.

American railroads attracted an increasing proportion of the total flow after 1850. ADLER is the most detailed study of British investment in American railroads. Both Lewis and Wilkins also survey Dutch, French and German investments. Wilkins argues that European capital provided a substantial share of American railroad investment, thus releasing American resources for use in manufacturing and other services. While Jenks had argued that most American railroads were efficient and profitable enough to attract foreign capital without ceding control, Adler shows that foreign investors did attempt to protect their interests by such means as forming investment trusts, and sending their own accountants across the Atlantic. By 1900, however, the great Wall Street investment bankers such as J.P.Morgan had assumed this role, disciplining the more unruly entrepreneurs, amalgamating railroad systems, and re-assuring the foreign investors.

Substantial amounts of foreign capital went into other areas. Wilkins chronicles foreign investments in a wide variety of American industries – food, drink and tobacco, textiles, leather, chemicals, banking and financial, commercial and communication services. An increasing proportion of this investment was of the modern multinational kind – in directly controlled branches of European firms. Companies making these direct investments tended to be large operators in the more advanced scientific industries such as chemicals, or engaged in a global marketing strategy, as in oil. They aimed to avoid American tariffs, and to control sales and servicing in the United States.

Hidy's account of the Barings shows that in the early 19th century, the leading Anglo-American merchant houses purchased American canal, bank and state securities in the US and marketed them in Britain. In the 1840s, Barings financed shipments of railroad iron to American railroads, by selling the companies' securities in London, or even direct to the ironmasters. The merchant houses however were soon superseded. MICHIE describes how well-organized stock exchanges listing the most important domestic railroad stocks were created during the 1840s and 1850s railroad booms in Britain and America. By 1870 the London and New York Stock exchanges had been linked by telegraph. By 1900 arbitrage operations using the telegraph, telephone and ticker tape had reduced international stock price differentials to virtually zero. Regional stock exchanges in Europe and North America linked in with London and New York to create a well organized international system. Wilkins shows how many other European financial institutions such as life insurance companies made substantial investments in America, or contributed important financial services. For instance, nearly all of the leading American accounting firms – such as Deloittes, Peat Marwick, Price Waterhouse – originated in Britain.

PLATT has suggested that the generally accepted figures for British investment in the United States are too large. They rely ultimately either on aggregating sales of American stocks in London, or on aggregating residuals in the balance of payments. But the former, for instance, makes no allowance for resales of American stocks from London to other European countries, or back to the United States. The argument partly turns on how much was sold during World War I. BURK discusses how the Allies used American investments to finance their war effort.

EDELSTEIN argues that the United States did indeed need vast increases in capital formation to develop the West and build eastern cities, but that most of this was found by huge increases in American domestic saving from about 10 per cent of GNP in the 1830s to 28 per cent of GNP by 1900. The net foreign contribution was marginal (about 1 per cent of GNP), and most important relative to domestic savings in the 1830s, the early 1870s and the 1880s. In contrast, Wilkins argues that gross European investment remained quantitatively important all through the 19th century, and was especially useful in important sectors such as the railroads, many new industries, and some essential services.

Large-scale foreign investment in the United States did not recover from the Depression and war until the 1960s, but since 1980 has reached huge proportions. The regular OECD SURVEYS on the United States track the macro-economic variables that control the inflow, and provide references to the most recent government reports and academic research on the subject. The Reagan boom sucked in massive overseas resources. Foreign individuals, banks and multinational companies now hold American assets in many forms – in short-term dollar claims, in government and corporate bonds, in American real estate, and in commercial and industrial plant. The size of the capital inflow is determined not only by linked American factors such as the foreign trade deficit, the government deficit, and shortfalls in domestic savings, but also by varying foreign demand for American assets.

JOHN R. KILLICK

Investment: United States Investment Abroad

Chandler, Alfred D., Jr., *Scale and Scope: The Dynamics of Industrial Capitalism*, Cambridge, MA: Belknap Press of Harvard University Press, 1990

Chapman, Stanley, *The Rise of Merchant Banking*, London and Boston: Allen and Unwin, 1984

Gilpin, Robert, *US Power and the Multinational Corporation: The Political Economy of Foreign Direct Investment*, New York: Basic Books, and London: Macmillan, 1975

Lewis, Cleona, *America's Stake in International Investments*, Washington, DC: Brookings Institution, 1938

Servan-Schreiber, J. J., *The American Challenge*, translated by Ronald Steel, London: Hamish Hamilton, and New York: Atheneum, 1968

Strange, Susan, *Casino Capitalism*, Oxford: Blackwell, 1986

Vernon, Raymond, *Sovereignty at Bay: The Multinational Spread of US Enterprises*, New York: Basic Books, and London: Longman, 1977

Wilkins, Mira, *The Emergence of Multinational Enterprise: American Business Abroad from the Colonial Era to 1914*, Cambridge, MA: Harvard University Press, 1970

Wilkins, Mira, *The Maturing of Multinational Enterprise: American Business Abroad from 1914 to 1970*, Cambridge, MA: Harvard University Press, 1974

Woodruff, William, *America's Impact on the World: The Role of the United States in the World Economy, 1750–1970*, New York: Wiley, and London: Macmillan, 1975

Yannopoulos, George N. (editor), *Europe and America, 1992: US-EC Economic Relations and the Single European Market*, Manchester: Manchester University Press, 1991

WOODRUFF is a straightforward account of America's impact overseas to about 1970. The chapter on finance compares U.S. and foreign overseas investment, and is well supported by convenient tables. The annual *Statistical Abstract* extends the statistics to the present. Rudimentary calculations of the value of United States assets overseas did not begin until 1843. All through the 19th century, the United States was the recipient of far more capital than it sent overseas. However by 1900 American wealth had grown so much that there was a net surplus to invest, and American overseas investment grew rapidly. During World War I, much foreign capital in the United States was liquidated. After the war, the United States overtook Britain and, in the 1920s, became the world's largest overseas investor. After World War II, there was a renewed flood of American investment overseas. Since 1960 there have been huge flows of capital in the opposite direction, into the United States, which have redressed the balance to some extent, but America still retains immense overseas assets.

American firms first made their mark overseas in the early 19th century. CHAPMAN deals mainly with British merchant bankers, but he shows that there were a few Americans such as George Peabody and J.S.Morgan among the many foreign firms attracted to Liverpool, Manchester and London in the early 19th century. He lists a good deal of basic information about leading foreign merchant firms. The United States had little surplus capital at this time. The Americans came to sell staples, buy British goods and raise British capital for American projects. What little capital was sent was used to provide support and collateral for overseas branches so that they could borrow more readily in Europe. In the late 19th century firms such as Morgan Grenfell, the British branch of the Wall Street Morgans, became major conduits for capital flows from Britain to America.

American manufacturing firms began to establish themselves in Britain and other countries, from the middle-to-late 19th century onwards. LEWIS made the first detailed survey of American investment overseas, but the best recent survey is WILKINS (1970). In a relatively short but very informative book, she shows how American firms first exported their new high technology products through agents, then, when these failed, through branches, and then finally established their own manufacturing plant overseas. Singer (sewing machines) provides an excellent example of this process. Singer established a factory near Glasgow in 1868, which later exported machines to many parts of the British Empire, and created similar branches elsewhere in Europe, including Russia. Singer's British operations lasted until the 1970s when they were undercut by Far Eastern competition. Wilkins details many other American companies operating overseas before 1914, including Edison, Ford, Gillette, Heinz, Kelloggs, and Westinghouse.

WILKINS (1974) shows how American direct foreign investment spread in the late 1920s, declined after the Great Crash, recovered during the years 1933–39, survived the war, and then expanded dramatically in the postwar period. Most American investment overseas was by branches of existing American firms. Advanced manufacturing industries predominated in Europe, extractive industries in the Third World. Although powerful at home, these companies had to struggle for access against well entrenched interests in European colonies, or make compromises with communist and Nazi regimes or corrupt Third World dictatorships. Wilkins attempts to summarize the impact of American outwards investment on the receiving countries and on the United States itself, and she relates her detailed narrative to the existing theoretical explanations of corporate growth and multinational investment. This is a very detailed study, based on massive research in government records and company archives.

Overseas investment had become so large and invasive by the 1960s and 1970s that it was possible to imagine a world economy dominated by a small number of very large, mostly American, global corporations. Overseas publicists such as SERVAN-SCHREIBER naturally described American investment as a potential threat. Many political economists such as GILPIN explained multinational investment as a form of hegemony. In the short to medium term, these firms were an instrument of American interests overseas. In the longer run however, American power may have been eroded by these huge exports of capital and technology. Some commentators have tried to arrive at a more balanced assessment. Economists such as VERNON attempted to assess the costs and benefits of American overseas investment to the host nation and to the United States. Business historians such as CHANDLER explained multinational expansion overseas as one more phase in the growth of the modern corporation, and compared the leading characteristics of American, British and German firms.

Since 1975 United States investment overseas has continued, despite the growing American payments deficits. YANNOPOULOS includes essays by Dunning and Zupnick on the likely impact of the European Single Market on transatlantic trade and investment. Zupnick concludes that American companies are well placed to benefit from closer European integration. Dunning shows that the growth of American investments in Europe was stimulated *inter alia* by the formation, extension and consolidation of the European Community. By 1987 sales by American multinationals *in* Europe were six times greater than American exports *to* Europe. European firms similarly have made huge inroads into the American market since 1975. American multinationals are now organising their production and strategic alliances to take account of growing European and Japanese competition.

After World War II, the United States established the leading international monetary institutions such as the International Monetary Fund, and the dollar became the key currency in most international dealings. STRANGE shows how, since the

1960s, persistent American payments deficits have gradually undermined this role and created a very unstable "Casino Capitalism", in which surges of short-term international investment can generate great financial crises and de-stabilize many smaller economies. Since 1980 these deficits have grown to huge proportions. Strange argues that the United States should attempt to "cool the casino" by stabilizing the central markets dealing in dollars. Kaufman's essay in the Yannopoulos volume shows how the German mark has gradually been displacing the dollar as the key international currency in Europe, potentially offering regional stability, but posing critical economic and political problems.

JOHN R. KILLICK

Irish Americans

Brown, Thomas N., *Irish-American Nationalism, 1870–1890*, Philadelphia: Lippincott, 1966

Carroll, Francis M., *American Opinion and the Irish Question, 1910–23: A Study in Opinion and Politics*, Dublin: Gill and Macmillan, and New York: St. Martin's Press, 1978

Diner, Hasia R., *Erin's Daughters in America: Irish-American Women in the Nineteenth Century*, Baltimore: Johns Hopkins University Press, 1983

Leyburn, James G., *The Scotch-Irish: A Social History*, Chapel Hill: University of North Carolina Press, 1962

McCaffrey, Lawrence J., *Textures of Irish America*, Syracuse, NY: Syracuse University Press, 1992

Miller, Kerby A., *Emigrants and Exiles: Ireland and the Irish Exodus to North America*, New York: Oxford University Press, 1985

Shannon, William V., *The American Irish*, New York: Macmillan, 1966; 2nd edition, as *The American Irish: A Political and Social Portrait*, Amherst: University of Massachusetts Press, 1989

Ward, Alan J., *Ireland and Anglo-American Relations, 1899–1921*, London: Weidenfeld and Nicolson, 1969

There are a number of well-written and well-researched studies of Irish Americans. In some ways, SHANNON provides the best introduction to the subject. He begins with a brief sketch of the history of Ireland and the causes of emigration, and then proceeds to several chapters on settlement in the United States and on Irish American politics in the larger cities. The heart of the book, however, is a series of portraits of notable Irish-Americans – athletes, clergymen, writers, and politicians – that give a broad picture of those figures within the community who have become famous or infamous, or have risen to positions of leadership. McCAFFREY's study of the Irish in America is more scholarly than Shannon, and develops a more articulated central thesis that the experience of the Irish in the United States has been one of social progress from the ghetto, where the Irish made up the first identifiable community of the urban poor, to the prosperous suburb, where they shared increasingly the values of the American middle class. McCaffrey, the author of many books on Irish history, does not ignore the historical circumstances in Ireland, but his main focus is on the experience of the immigrants in the United States. The book is very strong in its analysis of the Irish in politics, the role of the Catholic Church, and the contemporary dilemma of the successfully integrated Irish American community. One advantage of McCaffrey is that his observations extend right up to the present.

MILLER concentrates on the degree of alienation that the Irish have experienced. Even more than McCaffrey, Miller is a close study of the forces in Irish culture which led to the phenomenal level of out-migration that created Irish émigré communities all over the world. Miller argues that the Irish land tenure system, together with the fragility of a colonial economy, made it almost impossible for the lower ranks of Irish society, Protestant or Catholic, to make a satisfactory living. The result was that from the 17th century to the 20th, Irish peasants and artisans were increasingly marginalized in their own country and driven to emigration. Once abroad, the Irish endured a great sense of cultural loss, did not fit readily into North American life, and remained uncomfortable exiles. Pushed as far as it is by Miller, this is a provocative thesis. Based on massive research, Miller's book gains strength from the fact that it deals with both Catholic and Protestant migration to the United States and Canada.

The theme of alienation is not altogether new in the study of the Irish in the United States. BROWN suggested that much of the motivation for Irish American political nationalism arose from a rejection by the American establishment and an expectation that an independent and prosperous Ireland would win respect and acceptance for those immigrants who, however successful materially, were still regarded as people of no consequence. In Brown's view, this impulse, as much as the practical desire to see political change in Ireland, enlisted the support of thousands of Irish Americans for the Fenians, the Clan na Gael, the Land War, and Parnell's Irish Parliamentary Party. Irish American political nationalism reached a high point during the years of the Irish War for Independence, 1919 to 1921. Ward and Carroll both analyze Irish American involvement in these events in Ireland. WARD focuses on how Irish affairs interfered with Anglo-American diplomatic relations from the Boer War through 1921, while CARROLL examines how nationalist groups worked to influence the United States government on Ireland's behalf, first in support of home rule and then independence.

One of the distinctive features of post-famine Irish emigration was that single women out-numbered single men in leaving the country. DINER studied social conditions in 19th-century Ireland where, without opportunities for marriage (no marriage for women without dowries) or for employment (few jobs in a declining rural economy), emigration offered women a chance to escape from conditions of poverty, eroding social status, and increasing marginalization. Migration, even with its pitfalls, offered the hope of material improvement and the possibility of a respectable marriage. Domestic service was the principal occupation of Irish immigrant women, but by the end of the 19th century factory work and school teaching became better paying alternatives.

Protestant Irish seem often to be left out of a discussion of immigration, although they moved in large numbers to the American colonies in the 18th century and to Canada in the 19th century. LEYBURN attempted to look at the

Ulster-Scots, or Scotch-Irish as he called them, in the larger context of their move to Ulster in the 17th century and their subsequent migration to North America. Between 1717 and the end of the century, Leyburn pointed out, perhaps as many as 250,000 emigrated, a substantial proportion of the Protestant population of Ireland. The first settlers came in large numbers to Pennsylvania, but by mid-18th century they migrated to the frontier regions of Virginia and the Carolinas as well. Leyburn suggested that life in both Scotland and Ulster provided a social heritage that particularly fitted these people for the state of semi-warfare and subsistence agriculture that characterized life on the frontier in North America. The reader is left wishing that this study of the Ulster-Scots had been carried further into the 19th century.

The study of Irish Americans can be followed in at least two other areas, too detailed and too voluminous to enumerate here. One is the role of the Irish in local history, for example, the Irish in New York, Philadelphia, or San Francisco, in either social or political history categories. A second area is the role of the Irish in Catholic Church history in America, for example, the Irish both as parishioners and as clergy.

Francis M. Carroll

See also Catholic Church; Immigration and Ethnicity

Isolationism

Adler, Selig, *The Isolationist Impulse: Its Twentieth-Century Reaction*, London and New York: Abelard Schuman, 1957

Beard, Charles A, *The Idea of National Interest: An Analytical Study in American Foreign Policy*, New York: Macmillan, 1934; revised by Alfred Vagts and William Beard, Chicago: Quadrangle, 1966

Cole, Wayne S., *America First: The Battle Against Intervention, 1940–1941*, Madison: University of Wisconsin Press, 1953

Cole, Wayne S., *Roosevelt and the Isolationists, 1932–1945*, Lincoln: University of Nebraska Press, 1983

Divine, Robert A., *The Illusion of Neutrality*, Chicago: University of Chicago Press, 1962

Gilbert, Felix, *The Beginnings of American Foreign Policy to the Farewell Address*, Princeton: Princeton University Press, 1961

Graebner, Norman A., *The New Isolationism: A Study in Politics and Foreign Policy since 1950*, New York: Ronald Press, 1956

Jonas, Manfred, *Isolationism in America, 1935–1941*, Ithaca, NY: Cornell University Press, 1966

Jonas, Manfred, "Isolationism", in *Encyclopedia of American Foreign Policy: Studies of the Principal Movements and Ideas*, edited by Alexander DeConde, 3 vols., New York: Scribner, 1978

Lubell, Samuel, *The Future of American Politics*, New York: Harper, 1952; 3rd edition, 1965

Osgood, Robert E., *Ideals and Self-Interest in America's Foreign Relations: The Great Transformation of the Twentieth Century*, Chicago: University of Chicago Press, 1953

Rossignol, Marie-Jeanne, "Early Isolationism Revisited: Neutrality and Beyond in the 1790s," *Journal of American Studies*, 29(2), 1995

The defining statement for most theories about America's foreign relations is Washington's "Farewell Address," delivered to the Congress on 17 September 1796 and persuasively analyzed by GILBERT. Appealed to by scholars of different persuasions, and invoked rhetorically by politicians of all parties, it has been used to legitimate both isolationism and internationalism. Statements can rapidly become doctrines, but Washington's message was an unambiguous analysis of the best interest of the nation in the context of the circumstances of the time. Factors of geography and politics distinguished the interest of the United States from those of Europe, and he therefore warned against letting emotions rule the head, leading to unnecessary involvement in other people's vicissitudes and politics. He understood the legitimacy of neutrality, being haunted by the spectre of the French alliance of 1778 but, while denouncing permanent alliances, was prepared to accept the legitimacy of temporary alliances when the interest of the United States so demanded. He did not, therefore, advocate uncompromising unilateralism.

ROSSIGNOL briefly reviews the controversy over whether the term isolationism can be applied to the policies of the early Republic, and emphasizes the contemporary conviction that political engagement with Europe should be excluded. But she also subscribes to recent scholarship that places Amerindian issues in the ambit of foreign relations, and stresses the expansionist ambitions of the West that necessarily brought the United States into contact with European imperial nations.

Preoccupation with the traditions of American foreign policy necessarily infuses the literature on isolationism – a word which entered the discourse in 1922. Before that date, unilateralism, non-intervention and neutrality had been descriptive terms applied to American policies. As JONAS (1978) notes in his authoritative and well referenced essay, there is a significant difference between geographical and political isolation, and doctrinal isolationism. The traditional policy, as Secretary of State Seward declared in 1863, was one of non-intervention. In this, of course, there is no trace of exceptionalism: intervention is not normally characteristic of state policy. Following Woodrow Wilson's assertion that American isolation had been ended by history rather than by choice, Jonas argues persuasively that isolationism was more a particular phenomenon of the 1930s than a matter of tradition. However, he accepts that its proponents firmly believed that they shared the realism of the statesmen of the early Republic. This ambiguity has surrounded the historical debate over isolationism. The experience of World War I and its aftermath created profound disillusionment with Europe. This did not deter limited international commitments, as witnessed by the treaties of 1922, but it led to cynicism, mistrust, and the development of conspiracy theories. Revisionist historical writing about the reasons for intervention in 1917, stimulated by reactions to the debt issue, the Bolshevik revolution and the rise of fascism, encouraged political isolationism. Identifying five varieties of isolationists – those with ethnic or ideological sympathies with certain foreign powers, strict unilateralists, those prepared to surrender some of the traditional rights of neutrals to keep out of war, radical progressives and old order conservatives – JONAS (1966) carried his analysis forward to the "new isolationism" of the post-1945 era that had been identified and described by GRAEBNER.

In his confident and indeed assertive study of isolationism, ADLER has no hesitation in regarding isolationism as the traditional policy of the Republic. This "complex mass of sentiment and policy" was challenged and set back, but not obliterated, by the tensions of the 1930s and the resulting war. Adler is less Eurocentric than some other writers on the subject, and appreciates the Far Eastern dimension to the crisis of American thinking in the 1930s.

All writers agree in varying degrees on the significance of ethnicity in the complex factors underlying isolationalism. In a provocative discussion of "the myth of isolationism," LUBELL dismisses the suggestion that isolationism was strongest in the Midwest because of "the insularity of the American interior", and defines it as ethnic and emotional rather than geographical. It was Irish Americans, Scandinavian Americans and pre-eminently German Americans who made the Midwest isolationist. The thesis is vulnerable but suggestive.

Agrarianism has always been a visible force in American history, and it would be surprising if it were not a factor in isolationism. Midwesterners traditionally invoked the machinations of the eastern money power, foreign entanglements and the "merchants of death" who somehow manipulated affairs to their detriment. COLE (1983), who has devoted his career to analysis of the many facets of isolationism, suggests that agrarianism has been the life force of the movement, and that it has been deeply rooted in rural and small town America challenged by rapid socio-economic change. Although questions arise about the distribution of support for neutrality and non-intervention in the 1930s, when some rural areas were clearly interventionist and some urban politicians isolationist, Cole's thesis must be respected. In an earlier work on the America First Committee, COLE (1953) provides a classic study of an interest group that sought to keep the United States out of World War II. His analysis of the ethnic and ideological support for the Committee is powerfully presented.

Most writers agree that isolationism emerges as a strong and identifiable political force in the inter-war years and that, as the counterpoint to internationalism, it is capable of subtle definitions. DIVINE sees the battle over neutrality legislation as the high tide of 20th-century isolationism. He explores in considerable detail congressional battles over bills that sought to isolate the United States from war by, in effect, abandoning some of the traditional rights of neutrals. He portrays Roosevelt as a reluctant realist.

In an important contemporary study, BEARD, a leading progressive historian, focused on the concept of national interest as fundamental to the proper evolution of external policies. His wide-ranging analysis, suggesting the desirability of a policy of continentalism, is less polemical than some of his other writings. On Beard, and for the general debate on isolationism and internationalism, OSGOOD continues to provide the most sophisticated discussion.

DAVID ADAMS

See also Foreign Policy: General; Foreign Policy, 1919–1941

Italian Americans

Alba, Richard D., *Italian Americans: Into the Twilight of Ethnicity*, Englewood Cliffs, NJ: Prentice Hall, 1985

DeConde, Alexander, *Half Bitter, Half Sweet: An Excursion into Italian-American History*, New York: Scribner, 1971

Eula, Michael J., *Between Peasant and Urban Villager: Italian-Americans of New Jersey and New York, 1880–1980: The Structures of Counter-Discourse*, New York: Peter Lang, 1993

Foerster, Robert F., *The Italian Emigration of Our Times*, Cambridge, MA: Harvard University Press, 1919

Iorizzo, Luciano J. and Salvatore Mondello, *The Italian-Americans*, Boston: Twayne, 1971, revised 1980

Mangione, Jerre and Ben Morreale, *La Storia: Five Centuries of the Italian American Experience, 1492–1992*, New York: HarperCollins, 1992

Mormino, Gary R. and George E. Pozzetta, *The Immigrant World of Ybor City: Italians and Their Latin Neighbors in Tampa, 1885–1985*, Urbana: University of Illinois Press, 1987

Pozzetta, George E. and Bruno Ramirez (editors), *The Italian Diaspora: Migration Across the Globe*, Toronto: Multicultural History Society of Ontario, 1992

Vecoli, Rudolph J., "Italian-American Ethnicity: Twilight or Dawn?" in *The Italian Immigrant Experience*, edited by John Potestio and Antonio Pucci, Thunder Bay, Ontario: Canadian Italian Historical Association, 1988

The larger context of the history of Italian Americans is the diaspora which scattered some 26 million Italians across the globe over the course of a century (1876–1976). Although written contemporaneously with the exodus, FOERSTER remains the most satisfactory treatment of this mass migration. Based primarily on Italian governmental sources, it contains detailed analyses of the causes of the emigration as well as of the experience of Italians in various countries of arrival. Foerster's characterization of the immigrants is on the whole positive and sympathetic, no small thing at a moment of intense nativism in the United States.

A recent collection of essays, POZZETTA and RAMIREZ, advances a world history (rather than nation-state) perspective of the Italian emigration. While introducing new topics, such as women and radicals in the emigration, and case studies of Italians in North and South America, France and Australia, the volume lacks the depth and range of Foerster. An essay by Donna Gabaccia places Italian labor migration within the workings of an international economy, and seeks to explain the differing encounters of Italian workers with labor movements in various countries.

Although scores of monographs and hundreds of articles have appeared in the past two decades, there is no satisfactory one-volume history of the Italian Americans. MANGIONE and MORREALE is the most recent attempt at a comprehensive account of the Italian American experience. Encyclopedic in character, ranging from Columbus to Cuomo, and written in an accessible style, it is attractive to the casual reader. The serious scholar, however, will find it less than satisfactory. While incorporating recent scholarship with its emphasis on the common immigrants, the work is episodic and anecdotal, lacking an interpretive structure. The authors focus on southern Italians whom they portray as oppressed, first by northern Italians, then by Americans, but who nonetheless overcome obstacles to become successful Italian Americans.

DeCONDE is a synthetic account of the relationship between Italy and the United States from 1621 to 1970. Although the Italian immigration is given considerable attention, it is treated as one of the several strands, cultural, political, and economic, which make up the fabric of Italo-American relations. Emphasizing American perceptions of the Italian immigrants, DeConde characterizes the ambiguity of the latter's status as half-sweet, half-bitter. Tracing their gradual assimilation and ascent to the middle class, he concludes that the relationship became sweeter over time. De Conde is recommended for its comprehensive overview, organizational coherence, and thorough scholarship.

Although dated, IORIZZO and MONDELLO remains the most reliable concise treatment of the history of Italian Americans. Devoting only a few pages to "adventurers and pioneers," the text moves quickly to a consideration of the mass migration and its consequences. With topical chapters devoted, for example, to Little Italies, religion, organized crime, and fascism, the work is strongest in its detailed factual narrative. However, it is weak on interpretation. Essentially Italian immigrants and their descendants are portrayed as active participants in all spheres of modern American society and, in the process, becoming Americans.

Recent studies of Italian Americans have most often taken the form of community histories. There are probably over a hundred such studies which vary greatly in scholarly quality. One of the best of these is MORMINO and POZZETTA. A history of Italians in Ybor City, Florida, this monograph details their backgrounds in particular Sicilian villages and the distinctive conditions of their employment in the cigar industry. Its unique contribution is the analysis of how the interaction among Cuban, Spanish, and Italian cigar workers in the work place and in labor movements resulted in the creation of a pan-Latin radical culture. Through extensive oral histories as well as documentary sources, the authors depict the varied responses of the workers to strikes, ethnic organization, outmigration, and individual enterprise. The work is notably successful in marrying immigration and labor history, and thus dealing with both class and ethnicity.

In recent years, much writing about Italian Americans has focused on questions of assimilation, ethnicity, and identity, particularly of the second, third, and successive generations. In a historical-sociological study, ALBA argues that Italian Americans are approaching the twilight of their ethnicity. Discounting the idea of an ethnic revival, he portrays them rather as undergoing rapid assimilation into a general American population. After tracing the actual migration and the enclave settlements of the immigrants, the monograph identifies the post-World War II decades as the time when their descendants experienced accelerated social mobility and acculturation. Based on census and survey data, it cites cultural and structural indices of assimilation, such as increased rates of intermarriage, which indicate a merging with other Americans. Surviving manifestations of ethnicity become voluntary, private, lifestyle activities (Herbert Gans's symbolic ethnicity) rather than being an authentic, communal way of life.

EULA maintains to the contrary that the lives of working-class Italian Americans (in the New Jersey/New York metropolitan area) into the third and fourth generations are distinguished by cultural continuities which link them to their peasant forebears. Drawing on ethnographic and sociological studies, as well as literary works and original sources, the work traces the persistence of southern Italian cultural values in the spheres of adolescence, family dynamics, and Roman Catholicism. From a Gramscian perspective, Eula analyzes what he terms the "counter-discourse" by which the peasant-workers resisted Anglo-American middle-class hegemony.

While agreeing with Alba about the increasing assimilation and mobility among Italian Americans, VECOLI finds with Eula that certain basic cultural values continued to be transmitted from generation to generation. The essay analyzes the economic, cultural and political factors which over the course of a century brought about transitions in collective identity from *campanilismo* (parochialism) to Italian nationalism, to an Italian American identity. Arguing for the continuing viability of that identity, Vecoli conceives of ethnicity (a shared sense of peoplehood) not as primordial, but as invented, capable of adapting to new conditions. Given the heightened pluralism of American society, he concludes that self-interest will make for enhanced ethnic solidarity among Italian Americans.

RUDOLPH J. VECOLI

See also Immigration and Ethnicity

J

Jackson, Andrew 1767–1845
Military leader and 7th President of the United States

Bassett, John Spencer, *The Life of Andrew Jackson*, 2 vols., New York: Doubleday Page, 1911; reprinted, Hamden CT: Archon, 1967

Cole, Donald B., *The Presidency of Andrew Jackson*, Lawrence: University Press of Kansas, 1993

Curtis, James C., *Andrew Jackson and the Search for Vindication*, Boston: Little Brown, 1976

Hofstadter, Richard, "Andrew Jackson and the Rise of Liberal Capitalism," in his *The American Political Tradition and the Men Who Made It*, New York: Knopf, 1948; London: Cape, 1962

James, Marquis, *Andrew Jackson: The Border Captain* and *Andrew Jackson: Portrait of a President*, 2 vols., Indianapolis: Bobbs Merrill, 1933–37

Latner, Richard B., *The Presidency of Andrew Jackson: White House Politics, 1829–1837*, Athens: University of Georgia Press, 1979

Parton, James, *Life of Andrew Jackson*, 3 vols., New York: Mason, 1859–60

Remini, Robert V., *Andrew Jackson and the Course of American Empire, 1767–1821*; *Andrew Jackson and the Course of American Freedom, 1822–1832*; and *Andrew Jackson and the Course of American Democracy, 1833–1845*, 3 vols., New York: Harper, 1977–84; condensed in 1 vol. as *The Life of Andrew Jackson*, 1988

Rogin, Michael Paul, *Fathers and Children: Andrew Jackson and the Subjugation of the American Indian*, New York: Knopf, 1975

Schlesinger, Arthur M., Jr., *The Age of Jackson*, Boston: Little Brown, 1945; London: Eyre and Spottiswoode, 1946

Ward, John William, *Andrew Jackson: Symbol for an Age*, New York: Oxford University Press, 1955

It is not surprising that Andrew Jackson has attracted the attention of so many historians. A strong man of honor, and the only president to fight a duel, he salvaged American self-esteem in the War of 1812 by his victory at the battle of New Orleans. He was the first westerner and the first common man to become president, and he helped to build the first mass political party. As the dominant figure at a time when the nation began to take on its modern style and shape, he is the only American for whom an era has been named. Generation after generation of historians have been drawn to Old Hickory, hoping to gain from his life and times a better understanding of America.

The earliest and still one of the most perceptive of Jackson biographers is PARTON, who also wrote popular narrative lives of Benjamin Franklin, Thomas Jefferson, Aaron Burr and Horace Greeley. In preparing his life of Jackson, Parton sought much information from Old Hickory's surviving allies, but unfortunately many of them – including Martin Van Buren, Roger B. Taney and Francis P. Blair – failed to cooperate, leaving Parton with the memories of lesser figures such as Sam Houston and William B. Lewis. Writing in the North on the eve of the Civil War, Parton portrayed Jackson as a strong nationalist who, a generation earlier, had saved the Union from the machinations of South Carolinians. Although Parton admired Jackson for his contributions to nationalism and democracy, he could not forgive him for starting the political spoils system, which, he believed, corrupted all American society.

The first 20th-century study of Jackson was BASSETT, written during the age of Theodore Roosevelt. Bassett presented a progressive interpretation of Jackson, portraying him as a democratic advocate of the common man. One of the leading historians of his time, Bassett made good use of manuscript sources, especially the Jackson and Van Buren papers, which had been acquired by the Library of Congress. Bassett's biography quickly became the definitive life of Jackson, but his rather dull writing style kept it from being a popular success. JAMES filled this gap with a dramatic, prize-winning masterpiece, glorifying Jackson as a military hero, but his work was too one-sided to be considered sound scholarship.

It remained for SCHLESINGER to offer a study that combined scholarship and popular appeal. Writing during World War II, Schlesinger compared Jackson and Jacksonian Democracy with Franklin Roosevelt and the New Deal. A partisan Democrat, he depicted Jackson as a heroic liberal, protecting the public against the Bank of the United States. With dozens of vivid sketches of Jacksonian politicians and intellectuals, Schlesinger described Jacksonian Democracy as a class movement against the business interest.

The Age of Jackson provoked a controversy that lasted for several decades. The most influential attack on the book came from HOFSTADTER, who agreed that Jackson was a liberal, but placed him on the side of business rather than labor. In Hofstadter's eyes, Jackson was a well-to-do planter who profited from land speculation and cotton growing. Inspired by Hofstadter, a new school of historians reflecting the entrepreneurial ethos of the Eisenhower years began to see Jacksonian Democracy as but one chapter in the triumph of American capitalism.

WARD viewed Jackson as a champion of neither labor nor capital, but as a symbol. Drawing skilfully on the literature of the period, he described Jackson as a mirror for Americans, the embodiment of what his fellow countrymen considered the ideal American – a man of nature, a man of God, and a man of iron will. Although recognizing the contradictions in these images, Ward did not fully explore them.

After the Vietnam War, a new generation of historians, less sympathetic towards Jackson and his age, took another look at Jackson's personality. In a provocative piece of psychological-historical writing that sometimes strains in developing its thesis, ROGIN finds the symbolic roots of American racism in Jackson's unhappy childhood. Angry at his early loss of childhood bliss, Jackson projected his rage on to the American Indians, who seemed to live as perpetual children. He carried out a racist policy of infantilization and removal that cleared the way for the westward movement. By shifting attention from the Bank War to Indian removal, Rogin addressed social and psychological questions that had been neglected in the debate inspired by Schlesinger's work. CURTIS also finds the roots of Jackson's policies in his childhood, which left him so insecure that his career became a constant "search for vindication." Following no firm political creed, Jackson was motivated by intensely personal considerations. As a result, he had a difficult presidency, destroying his cabinet in the Peggy Eaton affair and splitting his party in the nullification crisis.

Amid these negative assessments, REMINI was laying the groundwork for his three-volume life of Jackson. In his earlier studies of the origins of the Democratic party, the election of 1828, and the Bank War, Remini had developed a deep appreciation of Jackson's devotion to American nationalism, republicanism and democracy. Remini produced a dramatic, powerful biography, the only full-length treatment of Jackson since World War II, and a sturdy defense of the Old Hero against his detractors.

The two modern studies of Jackson's presidency present conflicting interpretations. LATNER believes that Jackson was a staunch republican, committed to restoring the principles of Thomas Jefferson. If Jackson at times seemed to support the South, it was only because many southerners shared his ideals. According to Latner, the strongest influence on Jackson came from western republicans Amos Kendall and Francis P. Blair. COLE, on the other hand, sees Jackson as a non-ideological, often uncertain, president, struggling ineffectually against the forces of the market revolution. He considers Van Buren, not Kendall or Blair, to have been Jackson's most important adviser, and he regards the formation of the Democratic party, not Indian removal or the Bank War, as his greatest achievement.

DONALD B. COLE

Jackson, Jesse 1941–

African American political leader and civil rights campaigner

Barker, Lucius J. and Ronald W. Walters (editors), *Jesse Jackson's 1984 Presidential Campaign: Challenge and Change in American Politics*, Urbana: University of Illinois Press, 1989

Collins, Sheila D., *The Rainbow Challenge: The Jackson Campaign and the Future of US Politics*, New York: Monthly Review Press, 1986

Faw, Bob and Nancy Skelton, *Thunder in America: The Improbable Presidential Campaign of Jesse Jackson*, Austin: Texas Monthly Press, 1986

Frady, Marshall, *Jesse: The Life and Pilgrimage of Jesse Jackson*, New York: Random House, 1996

Gurin, Patricia, Shirley Hatchett, and James S. Jackson, *Hope and Independence: Blacks' Response to Electoral and Party Politics*, New York: Russell Sage Foundation, 1989

Hatch, Roger D., *Beyond Opportunity: Jesse Jackson's Vision for America*, Philadelphia: Fortress Press, 1988

Hertzke, Allen D., *Echoes of Discontent: Jesse Jackson, Pat Robertson, and the Resurgence of Populism*, Washington, DC: Congressional Quarterly Press, 1993

House, Ernest R., *Jesse Jackson and the Politics of Charisma: The Rise and Fall of the PUSH/Excel Program*, Boulder, CO: Westview Press, 1988

Landess, Thomas H. and Richard M. Quinn, *Jesse Jackson and the Politics of Race*, Ottawa, IL: Jameson, 1985

Reed, Adolph L., Jr., *The Jesse Jackson Phenomenon: The Crisis of Purpose in Afro-American Politics*, New Haven and London: Yale University Press, 1986

Reynolds, Barbara A., *Jesse Jackson: The Man, the Movement, the Myth*, Chicago: Nelson Hall, 1975

Although Jesse Jackson has ranked among the most dynamic and visible of America's political figures over the past thirty years, the literature on his life and career is surprisingly thin and often partisan. There are signs, however, that scholars are beginning to dig below the surface and connect the work of this fascinating man with the deeper impulses and currents of modern America.

REYNOLDS – the first major study of Jackson – remains essential. A lively biography by a black Chicago journalist, it is heavy on anecdotes, generally free of psycho-biographical posturing, and hardly uncritical. Reynolds explores Jackson's youth in segregated Greenville, South Carolina, but she focuses on his Chicago years, especially his work with Operation Breadbasket and then his leadership of Operation PUSH after he broke with SCLC in 1971. The many excerpts from interviews with Jackson himself and his associates are one strength of this biography, although a reliance on oral history explains why the book is not free from factual errors. While recognizing Jackson's charisma and accomplishments – chiefly his crusade for black economic power and cultural pride – Reynolds exposes Jackson's inattention to administration, his sense of self-importance, and his conflicts with other black leaders. (It should be noted that Reynolds penned a warm introduction to a 1985 reprint of her biography that was revealingly retitled, "Jesse Jackson: America's David".)

Reynolds stood as virtually the only detailed source about Jackson until an outpouring of studies in the aftermath of the activist's first campaign for the presidency in 1984. FAW and SKELTON provide an engaging narrative of that campaign. The book captures the spirit of this historic run by a black candidate, the controversies it spawned, and the diverse reaction of the electorate. LANDESS and QUINN offer a skeptical view of the candidate. Though overwritten, heavily indebted to Reynolds for its profile of the early Jackson, and unreliable in places, this study nevertheless presents a provocative perspective on the African American leader, especially during his command of Operation PUSH, his overseas adventures, and his turn to politics since the early 1970s. While duly acknowledging Jackson's identification with the dispossessed, Landess and Quinn argue that Jackson is a charismatic black populist who plays the politics of race to energize supporters, but who ultimately lacks a coherent program to improve their lot.

HATCH presents Jackson in a far more favorable light. Written by a former Jackson aide, this brief book forgoes extended commentary on the black leader's personality for close explication of his ideas. To counter charges of Jackson's essential opportunism, Hatch stresses the consistency of his thought over his public career, especially his insistence on racism as a deep, formidable problem in American life, on a moral vision of a pluralist, progressive America (shaped by his exposure to the black church and the civil rights movement), and on the value of coalitions to promote social change.

COLLINS moves beyond Jackson the individual and identifies the rise of the Rainbow Coalition as the central accomplishment of Jackson's 1984 presidential campaign. Although at times a plea for progressive politics, this rambling study, written by an inspired Jackson campaign worker, is nonetheless rewarding. Jackson's candidacy, according to Collins, was the catalyst behind a broader movement to rally the dispossessed and to inject a moral voice into American politics. Collins explores the precursors to the Rainbow Coalition, chronicles the efforts to bring diverse peoples together, discusses the achievements of grassroots Rainbow activists in places like Alabama and Vermont, and details the formidable obstacles to success, including the Democratic party.

BARKER and WALTERS have edited a collection of sympathetic essays on the 1984 campaign ranging from broad overviews to detailed discussions of Jackson's impact in individual states. GURIN, HATCHETT and JACKSON is a dense but important analysis of the response of the black electorate to Jackson's candidacy based on a detailed survey of the black voter. They develop the argument that Jackson voters sought to demonstrate their independence in order to foster a more responsive federal government.

The most widely discussed and controversial book about the 1984 campaign is REED. Less interested in Jackson himself than in the type of politics which he exemplifies, this brief, but weighty, book laments the ascendancy of charismatic leadership at the expense of regularly elected officials. The Jackson phenomenon is deleterious for black America, Reed contends, because this kind of leadership is undemocratic, lacks accountability, and stresses style over content. Reed questions the prevailing view of the black church as a fountain of progressive politics and argues that Jackson's candidacy obstructed rather than advanced a left-liberal agenda.

Little attention has been paid specifically to the many projects in which Jackson has been involved, outside of his quest for the presidency. HOUSE is an exception. This study analyzes the short history of the PUSH/Excel program to motivate black youth. While House points to the fickleness of the federal government and the intransigence of school officials as the principal culprits for the fall of the program, he also stresses the limitations of Jackson's brand of leadership.

HERTZKE is an insightful study of Jackson, despite its unlikely pairing of the African American leader with Pat Robertson of the Christian Right. Hertzke places Jackson, along with Robertson, within the broad populist tradition which historically has championed the common American. Jackson, according to Hertzke, defies the conventional political labels of liberal and conservative. Instead Jackson offers a critique of liberal modernity as he blends a message of egalitarian economics, collective responsibility, and traditional values that resonates not only with black Americans but with others distressed by trends in American life. Hertzke also shows how the black church was central to Jackson's crusade for the presidency in 1984 and 1988.

FRADY is the richest and most comprehensive study of the black leader. In more than 500 packed pages, this sympathetic, episodic and explanatory biography not only traces Jackson's remarkable ascent from obscurity to international renown, but also searches for the deeper motivations of this complicated man. With confidence based on several years of close study of the subject – but heavily indebted to personal observations and interviews with Jackson and his colleagues – Frady argues that Jackson is best understood as a perennial outsider, "a kind of American version of Ishmael," even though he represents an American success story. No other book about Jackson explores so fully his life after 1970, especially the expansion of his social ministry beyond the United States to reach across the world, his mastery of the mass media, which also ironically imprisons him at times, his difficulties in developing his role as a social reformer during his relentless pursuit of the presidency, and his recent confusion over the direction of his mission as an inspirational leader.

JAMES RALPH

See also African American History: since 1954

Jackson, Thomas J. ("Stonewall")
1824–1863
Confederate general

Chambers, Lenoir, *Stonewall Jackson*, 2 vols., New York: Morrow, 1959

Farwell, Byron, *Stonewall: A Biography of General Thomas J. Jackson*, New York: Norton, 1992

Freeman, Douglas Southall, *Lee's Lieutenants: A Study in Command*, 3 vols., New York: Scribner, 1942–44

Henderson, G.F.R., *Stonewall Jackson and the American Civil War*, 2 vols., London: Longman, 1898; reprinted London and New York: Longman, 1961

Jones, Archer, *Civil War Command and Strategy: The Process of Victory and Defeat*, New York: Free Press, 1992

Luvaas, Jay, *The Military Legacy of the Civil War: The European Inheritance*, Chicago: University of Chicago Press, 1959; revised edition, Lawrence: University Press of Kansas, 1989

Royster, Charles, *The Destructive War: William Tecumseh Sherman, Stonewall Jackson, and the Americans*, New York: Knopf, 1991

Selby, John, *Stonewall Jackson as Military Commander*, London: Batsford, and Princeton: Van Nostrand, and London: Batsford, 1968

Vandiver, Frank E., *Mighty Stonewall*, New York: McGraw Hill, 1957

"Stonewall" Jackson is one of the most famous of all Confederate generals, but the quality of the literature about him does not match the exalted levels of his fame. The earliest books on Jackson were slavishly pious and uncritical; indeed the Jackson "legend", stimulated by his sudden death in 1863, pre-dates that of Robert E. Lee. But, like Lee, he has not engaged the attention of academic historians overmuch since 1970. It may be that his character does not appeal to late 20th century scholars. Jackson was dogmatic, self-righteous and revealed an unrelenting spirit that could degenerate into vindictiveness. He was eccentric and unpredictable. He was the kind of man that comes alive in war – in peace he stumbled through life unregarded and ridiculed. Beneath his shy, unassuming and retiring surface there lay a cold, impenetrable sheet of steel. Jackson was a harsh, secretive man who benefited from his unshakable conviction that he was right.

Such qualities appealed to 19th-century historians. Jackson owes his high standing as a commander, not to an American historian, but to a British writer, HENDERSON, author of the most important book written about Jackson. He exaggerated his abilities, but successfully conveyed his qualities as a general. Henderson attempted to establish a theoretical model for future British commanders of fast-moving, semi-professional armies; he was not interested in the political, social and economic sources of strategy. A lot of Henderson's book can still be read with profit. He was a skilled narrator with an eye for colour and telling detail. His discussion of Jackson's technique of command has not yet been bettered. Henderson's Jackson was first and foremost a dynamic man of action, and in this regard, Stonewall's undoubted strengths are given a fulsome treatment.

The influence of Henderson's model of Jackson is sensitively traced in LUVAAS. He explores Henderson's methods and the nature of his research, including correspondence with members of Jackson's staff, such as his topographical engineer, Major J. Hotchkiss. Luvaas also brings out Henderson's appeal and assesses the cult of Jackson in the British Army. This did a great deal to give substance to, and provide justification of, claims made by Confederate apologists for Jackson's preeminent genius. Luvaas was heavily influenced by Captain Sir Basil Liddell Hart, who was highly critical of Henderson's obsession with Jackson. Henderson's methods, by stressing the collection of "facts", did lead to the abuse of military history and arid antiquarianism. SELBY, a readable if derivative, semipopular book by a Sandhurst lecturer, and based too heavily on Henderson and Freeman, shows that the spirit of Jackson was still thriving in the British Army in the 1960s. Otherwise, the Jackson "legend" has not been systematically investigated by any historian, a curious oversight.

The result of Henderson's book was to give Jackson an undue prominence in Confederate historiography. FREEMAN's classic study redresses the balance and shows that Lee was the master and Jackson the prime executor of the designs of the Army of Northern Virginia. Freeman's book is a model of how to treat the operational level of war – that which is concerned with the fighting and winning of campaigns – viewed as a single, organic sequence rather than a miscellaneous series of tactical actions. His approach is rather narrow by the standards of the 1990s, but none can doubt Freeman's mastery of military operations. He brings out Jackson's excellence as an operational executor at the corps level of command.

The later accounts are rather disappointing. CHAMBERS is a highly detailed tribute to Jackson which verges on hagiography. VANDIVER is the best modern biography based on manuscript sources. It is scholarly (and, like Chambers, very detailed), but the style relies on graphic description and rhetorical flourishes in the absence of analysis and assessment. "The greyclads had been checked" is the way a tactical rebuff is dressed up in extravagant language. This kind of over-writing is not to everybody's taste. The book lacks a conclusion, even though Vandiver attributes to Jackson most of the credit for audacious moves, such as the out-flanking manoeuvre at Chancellorsville in 1863. FARWELL is the most recent biography by a non-specialist, professional writer, but adds little to our knowledge. JONES is a more satisfactory attempt to place Jackson in the overall context of Civil War command problems. In a book worth consulting on a whole range of other issues, Jones suggests that Jackson's tactical skills were not of the same order as his operational insight. He was also slow to adopt entrenchments and was too keen on dynamic but unprotected pursuits that sustained heavy Confederate casualties. ROYSTER explores aspects of Jackson's thinking on the punitive character of the war. He includes some interesting material, though he might have interpreted it too literally; moreover, his book is diffuse, and a far from systematic treatment. Clearly, Jackson's generalship will have to be assessed within the context of recent interpretations of the Civil War. That task has yet to be discharged.

BRIAN HOLDEN REID

See also Civil War: Campaigns 1

Jacksonian Era, 1824–1848: General

Benson, Lee, *The Concept of Jacksonian Democracy: New York as a Test Case*, Princeton: Princeton University Press, 1961

Feller, Daniel, *The Jacksonian Promise: America, 1815–1840*, Baltimore: Johns Hopkins University Press, 1995

Fish, Carl Russell, *The Rise of the Common Man, 1830–1850*, New York: Macmillan, 1927

Meyers, Marvin, *The Jacksonian Persuasion: Politics and Belief*, Stanford, CA: Stanford University Press, 1957

Pessen, Edward, *Jacksonian America: Society, Personality, and Politics*, Homewood, IL: Dorsey Press, 1969, revised 1978

Schlesinger, Arthur M., Jr., *The Age of Jackson*, Boston: Little Brown, 1945; London: Eyre and Spottiswoode, 1946

Sellers, Charles, *The Market Revolution: Jacksonian America, 1815–1846*, New York: Oxford University Press, 1991

Tocqueville, Alexis de, *Democracy in America*, translated by Henry Reeve, 4 vols., 1835–40; translated by George Lawrence and edited by J.P. Mayer and Max Lerner, 2 vols., New York: Harper, 1966

Turner, Frederick Jackson, *The United States, 1830–1850: The Nation and Its Sections*, New York: Holt, 1935

Van Deusen, Glyndon G., *The Jacksonian Era, 1828–1848*, New York: Harper, 1959

Watson, Harry L., *Liberty and Power: The Politics of Jacksonian America*, New York: Hill and Wang, 1990

Wiebe, Robert H., *The Opening of American Society: From the Adoption of the Constitution to the Eve of Disunion*, New York: Knopf, 1984

The Jacksonian era has long been a focus of intense historiographic controversy. Its interest stems from the fact that commentators from that day to this have seen it as the point at which the United States tore loose from its European and colonial roots and embarked on a new, original course. If, as is often said, this era encompassed the birth of modern America, then what was uniquely Jacksonian remains uniquely American. While agreeing thus far, historians have disputed widely over wherein lies Jacksonian and American distinctiveness, and have organized their treatments of the era around a multitude of discordant and even flatly contradictory themes. The opaque label of "Jacksonian era" itself stands less as an interpretive guidepost than a surrogate for interpretive controversy. Historians have found it easier to unite on Andrew Jackson as a symbol for the age than to agree on what he represents.

The association of Andrew Jackson and his era with American distinctiveness began with a contemporary Frenchman who visited the United States in 1831–32 and discovered there "the image of democracy itself." TOCQUEVILLE found the "primary fact" in America to be "the general equality of condition among the people." Together, equality and democracy shaped every facet of national existence, from law, politics, and the press to manners, relations between the sexes, science, philosophy, literature, and art. Tocqueville invoked Americans' religiosity, participatory voluntarism, and institutions of local self-government to explain how their society held together without aristocratic bulwarks of hierarchy and tradition. At the same time he pointed up what he believed to be democratic dangers of atomizing individualism (a word he coined), mediocrity, conformity, and submission to the tyrannical sway of public opinion. Tocqueville's penetrating though often abstract analysis remains the most influential assessment ever

offered of American society and character. In identifying equality and democracy as salient national traits and locating them historically in the Jackson years, Tocqueville fixed an image on the era with which period scholars have contended ever since.

FISH's lucid volume in the landmark History of American Life series supplied specifics to Tocqueville's generalizations, tracing the influence of Jacksonian Americans' spirit of millennial optimism, self-confidence, equality, and individualism upon their society and culture. Though outmoded in some areas and governed by a descriptive approach now out of fashion, it wears surprisingly well as a summary view of the Jacksonian scene. TURNER's sprawling, unfinished general history mediated Tocquevillian themes through a regionalist lens. Turner saw Jacksonian America as composed of geopolitical sections demarcated by economy, ethnoreligious makeup, social structure, and cultural attributes. A survey of sectional characteristics provided a platform for Turner's political narrative, in which sectional interests, fortified or crossed by partisan allegiances, vied for national power. Turner traced both the national traits noted by Tocqueville and the political movement headed by Andrew Jackson to origins in "pioneer democracy."

Fish and Turner are rarely read today. Not so SCHLESINGER, which remains, a half century after publication, the best-known (and best-written) general history of the era and the starting-point for discussions of Jacksonian politics. Challenging Turner's frontier emphasis, Schlesinger argued that the era's new political parties – Andrew Jackson's Democrats and the opposing Whigs – reflected a root class division between laboring people and the business community. Schlesinger traced ramifications of this struggle in philosophy, religion, reform, and literature, but the center of his monumental work was an exciting, richly textured, and frankly partisan political narrative. Schlesinger's Democrats drew their ideas and core following from eastern wage-earners, not frontiersmen. Thus the birth of industrial capitalism, not the rise of the West, was the era's distinguishing feature. Harking back to the Federalist period and forward to the New Deal, Schlesinger depicted a continuing contest for ascendancy between the Hamiltonian-Whig-Republican business aristocracy and recurrent movements for economic democracy headed by Jefferson, Jackson, and Franklin Roosevelt. This ongoing battle for political power Schlesinger saw as salutary, providing the only sure foundation for freedom in a state both democratic and capitalist.

Though assailed in many particulars, Schlesinger's framework for understanding Jacksonian society through its politics dominated scholarship for a generation. VAN DEUSEN's volume in the New American Nation series codified the thesis by tempering its excesses. Incorporating themes of social consensus stressed by Schlesinger's critics, Van Deusen modulated his picture of Whigs and Democrats as representatives of opposing class interests. Though stripped of partisan cheerleading, Van Deusen's approach was still essentially Schlesingerian: Democrats were popular and "liberal," Whigs elitist and "conservative." In keeping with the premise that Jacksonian America's essence was expressed in its politics, nearly the whole book narrated party warfare on the national scene.

Dissenters challenged Schlesinger's class thesis. Interpreting Jacksonian social and political discourse in a series of tantalizing essays, MEYERS found Americans divided by temperament more than circumstance. Some held confident hopes for the future, while others suffered anxieties, misgivings, and nostalgic longings. Parties reflected these attitudes, though more in style and rhetoric than policy. Forward-looking Whigs unreservedly embraced the free pursuit of self-interest, while backward-glancing Democrats sought to encompass it within the moral values of a vanishing yeoman republic. Jackson's celebrated struggle against the Second Bank of the United States was thus less a genuine assault on business than a psychological purgation, a way for Democrats suffering pangs of conscience over their own striving to regain a sense of righteousness. All Americans pursued the main chance, but some less guiltily than others.

Meyers's approach to political rhetoric was literary and evocative. BENSON's case study of political practice in New York State was determinedly matter-of-fact, quantitative, and "scientific." Scrutinizing Whig and Democratic leaders, voters, principles, and policies, Benson found no evidence of class differentiation between the parties. Americans were consensually democratic and enterprising in what Benson dubbed the "Age of Egalitarianism." Differing only over means, not ends, in their approach to political economy, parties instead mustered ethnic and religious constituencies through contrasting cultural and moral appeals. Benson's suggestion of an "ethnocultural" rather than socioeconomic basis for Jacksonian (and subsequent) party affiliations proved widely influential. Like Meyers, Benson also pictured Whigs as optimistic and forward-looking in temperament, Democrats as conservative and traditionalist.

Meyers, Benson, and other revisionists warned against taking Jacksonian class-war rhetoric at face value: social and political realities were not what Democratic party publicists made them seem. Scepticism about the substance in Jacksonian politics climaxed in PESSEN's far-reaching indictment of Andrew Jackson, his party, his era, and his scholarly admirers. Commentators since Tocqueville had disputed whether egalitarian impulses pervaded all of Jacksonian society or came only from certain sections, classes, or parties. Pessen went further and questioned their existence altogether. He saw the era not as the fount of American equality and democracy, but as the source of an enduring myth about them.

Proceeding topically, Pessen depicted Jackson's America as a class society, firmly inegalitarian and quickly becoming more so. Gross disparities of wealth, power, and status divided the moneyed elite from the laboring masses. Blacks, women, Indians, and immigrants suffered degradation and exploitation. Politicians of neither party addressed growing social and economic injustice. Rather they disguised it, paying lip-service to the common man to mask their own self-interested pursuit of pelf and perquisites. While both parties were hypocritical, the Democrats were the greater humbugs. Jackson's Bank War, the centerpiece of Schlesinger's heroic narrative, revealed to Pessen little more than the craving of one greedy clique to unseat another. Party battles over political economy, which had furnished the main plot line for previous chronicles, Pessen found containing so little substance as to be not worth recounting. Politicians served themselves, not their constituents. Yet both shared traits of ambition, vulgarity, and overriding materialism. Jacksonian America was the land not of opportunity, but of opportunism.

Overturning all the old verities, Pessen cast a jaundiced eye on Jacksonian America and all it bequeathed. Subsequent scholarship generally seconded his grim view of the Jacksonian legacy while contesting the particulars of his analysis. Studies of political ideology and state and local practice uncovered new depths of differences between the parties, while social and cultural historians explored themes of conflict and loss in the period they now labelled as marking America's "transition to capitalism" or "market revolution."

SELLERS incorporated these trends into a comprehensive history designed to supplant Schlesinger's master narrative. Like Pessen, Sellers challenged Tocqueville, but in a very different way. Andrew Jackson, Pessen's chief villain, was Sellers's hero. Sellers saw Jacksonian America as an epic battleground between Jackson's traditionalist, egalitarian, communal, agrarian majority and the self-aggrandizing, socially repressive, market-oriented Whig entrepreneurial elite. Into this thesis Sellers wove developments in law, politics, religion, and reform. The result was a highly textured and subtly nuanced account, though one marred by turgid, at times nearly impenetrable prose.

Sellers combined and accentuated two previously opposed elements: Schlesinger's class-based political analysis and Pessen's disaffection with capitalist America. Where Schlesinger had sketched a sustaining political tension between Whig business and Democratic popular elements, Sellers saw a basic antagonism – not an ongoing contest for control of a capitalist democracy, but a determinative Jacksonian struggle between democracy and capitalism themselves. Though Democrats won some battles, democracy lost the war, and Americans have suffered the consequences of "bourgeois hegemony" ever since. Sellers thus saw Jackson and his party confronting the evils of capitalism, where Pessen saw them shielding them. Yet despite this difference, both accounts breathed repugnance for the era's legacy to modern America as surely as Schlesinger's had exuded patriotic pride. Tocqueville had been stood upside down: instead of denoting the triumph of equality and democracy, the Jacksonian era now seemed to mark their demise.

Disengaging from the historiographic debate surrounding Schlesinger and his successors, WIEBE offered a sweeping interpretive survey of American social and cultural evolution from the Constitution to the Civil War, with the Jacksonian transformation at its heart. Echoing Tocqueville and Turner, Wiebe traced Jacksonian distinctiveness to the plethora of American resources. Spatial expansion underwrote a "revolution in individual choices" in all walks of life, freeing citizens to decide things for themselves and thus toppling elite direction of the country's affairs. Systematic development under centralized control gave way to opportunity, enterprise, democracy, diversity, and diffusion.

Two brief works introduce the era and summarize the current state of Jacksonian scholarship. WATSON updates, or supersedes, Van Deusen's standard political narrative by incorporating new findings on political ideology and partisan activity in states and localities. Watson's thesis is a more tempered, even-handed variant of Sellers's. Whigs promoted and Democrats resisted the "market revolution," yet both practiced democratic techniques and avowed republican values.

Like Sellers, Watson stresses the anxieties and resentments that economic development evoked as much as the hopes it buoyed. Andrew Jackson bespoke small producers' fear of dependence and corruption, not their thirst for opportunity.

Challenging the declensionist thrust in recent scholarship, FELLER's topical portrait emphasizes consensual elements in Jacksonian society. In terms reminiscent of Tocqueville and Fish, he argues that a common optimism and energy underlay the era's myriad innovations in business, politics, religion, and reform. Americans considered themselves a favored people and confidently envisioned a perfected future. Their open society invited novelty and experiment, but fissures appeared when citizens organized to implement competing plans of national progress.

Surely no other era in American history has been invoked to signify so many things – the rise of the common man and the reign of the businessman, the spread of opportunity and the entrenchment of hierarchy, the flowering of America's hopes and the death of its dreams. Themes of conflict versus consensus, change versus continuity, and progress versus declension evolve and permutate endlessly as historians find new vantages for assessing Jacksonian society and politics. Controversy over the import of the Jackson era and the reality behind its emblems of equality and democracy is certain to continue.

DANIEL FELLER

Japan: Matthew Perry and the Reopening of, 1853–1854

Cosenza, Mario Emilio (editor), *The Complete Journal of Townsend Harris: First American Consul-General and Minister to Japan*, New York: Doubleday, 1930; revised, New York: Tuttle, 1959

Crow, Carl, *He Opened the Door of Japan: Townsend Harris and the Story of His Amazing Adventures in Establishing American Relations with the Far East*, New York: Harper, 1939

Ibe, Hideo, *Japan, Thrice-Opened: An Analysis of Relations Between Japan and the United States*, translated by Lynne E. Riggs and Manabu Takechi, New York: Praeger, 1992

Morison, Samuel Eliot, *"Old Bruin": Commodore Matthew C. Perry*, Boston: Little Brown, 1967; Oxford: Oxford University Press, 1968

Szczesniak, Boleslaw (editor), *The Opening of Japan: A Diary of Discovery in the Far East, 1853–1856*, by George Henry Preble, Norman: University of Oklahoma Press, 1962

Wiley, Peter Booth with Korogi Ichiro, *Yankees in the Land of the Gods: Commodore Perry and the Opening of Japan*, New York: Viking, 1990

Given the significance of the expedition of Commodore Matthew Calbraith Perry in bringing about the re-opening of Japan, it is surprising that there is so little in the recent historiography. WILEY's illustrated narrative history is the only one which deals exclusively with this theme. His book consists of a chronological account of Perry's visit to Japan and his negotiations with the Japanese authorities. Wiley also puts these events in a broader context of Japanese history.

MORISON is a comprehensive biography of Commodore Perry, illustrated with pictures, maps, plans and charts. "Old Bruin" was a nickname given to Perry by his men. About a third of the book covers Perry's Japan Expedition. Morison shows that until he embarked upon the expedition Perry had never sailed in the Pacific. His previous experience had been in the Caribbean, West Africa and Europe. This is a popular rather than an academic biography and has no footnotes, although it does have a bibliography.

George Preble served on the U.S.S. *Macedonian*, one of the ships that formed part of Perry's Japan Expedition. SZCZES-NIAK has edited Preble's diaries of the expedition and added a short biography of Preble, a bibliography, some illustrations and footnotes. The diaries give a valuable insight into mid-19th century Japan through the eyes of a senior member of Perry's expedition, who participated in all of its important activities.

IBE is a translation of a revised 1990 Japanese-language edition of the original 1988 book *Kaikoku* [Opening of the Country], which is a survey of relations between Japan and the United States from the mid-19th century to the beginning of the 1990s. Unlike Morison or Wiley, Ibe's approach is analytical. He provides a Japanese perspective on the re-opening of Japan by Commodore Perry, and places it in the context of the subsequent history of United States-Japanese relations. Ibe also shows that although Perry was responsible for the re-opening of Japan, it was actually Townsend Harris, the first American Consul-General to Japan, who succeeded in negotiating the first commercial treaty between the two countries in 1858.

CROW argues that Harris's achievement was greater than that of Perry, because the former, unlike the latter, actually had to live among the Japanese and did not have a well-armed fleet, support staff, or sufficient funds to meet his daily expenses. This is a popular biography of Harris, the greater part of which concentrates on his diplomatic posting in Japan, and his triumph in achieving one of the original goals set by the American government for Perry's earlier expedition, a commercial treaty. COSENZA edited the first complete version of Harris's surviving journals. They cover the period May 1855 to February 1858. No journals have survived for the remainder of Harris's tour of duty in Japan, March 1858 to May 1862. Cosenza's book is an important primary source for the study of the beginning of United States-Japanese diplomacy.

RICHARD A. HAWKINS

Jefferson, Thomas 1743–1826
Revolutionary leader, political thinker and 3rd
President of the United States

Adams, Henry, *History of the United States of America
During the Administrations of Jefferson and Madison*,
9 vols., New York: Scribner, 1889–91; edited by
Earl N. Harbert, 2 vols., New York: Library of America,
1986

Becker, Carl L., *The Declaration of Independence: A Study
in the History of Political Ideas*, New York: Harcourt
Brace, 1922

Boorstin, Daniel J., *The Lost World of Thomas Jefferson*,
New York: Holt, 1948

Brodie, Fawn M., *Thomas Jefferson: An Intimate History*,
New York: Norton, and London: Eyre Methuen, 1974

Chinard, Gilbert, *Thomas Jefferson: The Apostle of
Americanism*, Boston: Little Brown, 1929, revised 1939

Cunningham, Noble E., Jr., *In Pursuit of Reason: The Life
of Thomas Jefferson*, Baton Rouge: Louisiana State
University Press, 1987

Huddleston, Eugene L., *Thomas Jefferson: A Reference
Guide*, Boston: Hall, 1982

Koch, Adrienne, *The Philosophy of Thomas Jefferson*, New
York: Columbia University Press, 1943

Levy, Leonard W., *Jefferson and Civil Liberties: The Darker
Side*, Cambridge, MA: Belknap Press of Harvard
University Press, 1963

McDonald, Forrest, *The Presidency of Thomas Jefferson*,
Lawrence: University Press of Kansas, 1976

McLaughlin, Jack, *Jefferson and Monticello: The Biography
of a Builder*, New York: Holt, 1988

Malone, Dumas, *Jefferson and His Time*, 6 vols., Boston:
Little Brown, and London: Eyre and Spottiswoode,
1948–81

Matthews, Richard K., *The Radical Politics of Thomas
Jefferson: A Revisionist View*, Lawrence: University Press
of Kansas, 1984

Miller, Charles A., *Jefferson and Nature: An Interpretation*,
Baltimore: Johns Hopkins University Press, 1988

Miller, John C., *The Wolf by the Ears: Thomas Jefferson
and Slavery*, New York: Free Press, and London: Collier
Macmillan, 1977

Nock, Albert Jay, *Jefferson*, New York: Harcourt Brace,
1926

Onuf, Peter S. (editor), *Jeffersonian Legacies*, Charlottesville:
University Press of Virginia, 1993

Peterson, Merrill D., *The Jefferson Image in the American
Mind*, New York: Oxford University Press, 1960

Peterson, Merrill D., *Thomas Jefferson and the New Nation:
A Biography*, New York: Oxford University Press, 1970;
Oxford: Oxford University Press, 1975

Peterson, Merrill D. (editor), *Thomas Jefferson: A Reference
Biography*, New York: Scribner, 1986

Risjord, Norman K., *Thomas Jefferson*, Madison, WI:
Madison House, 1994

Sheehan, Bernard W., *Seeds of Extinction: Jeffersonian
Philanthropy and the American Indian*, Chapel Hill:
University of North Carolina Press, 1973

Sheldon, Garrett Ward, *The Political Philosophy of Thomas
Jefferson*, Baltimore: Johns Hopkins University Press,
1991

Shuffelton, Frank, *Thomas Jefferson: A Comprehensive
Annotated Bibliography of Writings about Him,
1826–1980*, New York: Garland, 1983, supplemented
with *1981–1990*, 1992

Tucker, Robert W. and David C. Hendrickson, *Empire of
Liberty: The Statecraft of Thomas Jefferson*, New York
and Oxford: Oxford University Press, 1990

Wills, Garry, *Inventing America: Jefferson's Declaration of
Independence*, New York: Doubleday, 1978; London:
Athlone Press, 1980

Wiltse, Charles M., *The Jeffersonian Tradition in American
Democracy*, Chapel Hill: University of North Carolina
Press, 1935

Thomas Jefferson's life was long, diverse, and fruitful. He is
widely seen as the father of American democracy and has
remained a major figure in public ideology until the present
day. Many early biographers were so concerned with his
posthumous importance to American ideology that the historical person was often obscured.

Shifts in Jefferson's reputation from his own day to the years
after 1945 are brilliantly and sensitively traced in PETERSON
(1960). In a major intellectual study, he traces the emergence
of a national hero while drawing out the inconsistencies in
Jefferson's thought and illuminating the changing character
of American society. He shows how successive generations
deployed his memory on both sides of party conflict until
in recent years Jefferson's public reputation has become less
contentious albeit remaining a key reference point for political
debate. Peterson also separates Jefferson the historical figure
from Jefferson as symbol by providing a helpful guide to
the principal biographies and interpretations, beginning
with family compilations, through the gentlemanly and journalist writers of the 19th and early 20th centuries to modern
academic scholars. Since much early history was written by
hostile Federalist sympathisers, 19th-century biographers were
defensive.

As Peterson ably demonstrated, 20th-century authors
remained influenced by the concerns of their contemporary
generation and dominated by Jefferson's personality and position in public affection. During the 1920s, for example,
Bowers, a journalist active in Democratic party politics, interpreted Jefferson as a libertarian, leveller, and humanitarian
leader without peer, and a master of men. Seldom read now,
his biography met the needs of the depression decade and
was the dominant exposition for a time. NOCK wrote an
extended essay focusing particularly on the 1790s rather than
a complete biography, but his analysis rested on a more secure
theoretical basis. Explicitly working from Beard's thesis that
economic interests lay at the heart of political behaviour, and
personally attached to Herbert Spencer's laissez-faire individualism, he reluctantly criticized Jefferson's failure to grasp the
centrality of economics to political behaviour, and argued that
like other politicians he shifted ground in response to the interests of those whom he represented. Instead, he insisted,
Jefferson's primary contribution was to civilised philosophy
and conduct; harmony and order, rather than politics.

CHINARD, a French scholar resident in the United States, broadened his treatment to offer a cultural as well as political discussion, and saw Jefferson as the Apostle of Americanism: Jeffersonian and American culture were coincident. Yet surprisingly he followed the tradition of placing politics at the core of his biography, and insisted that Jefferson's principles originated in the Anglo-Saxon American tradition not in French principles. His thesis was that Jefferson was an American nationalist with a distinctive programme as party leader. Chinard's well-balanced and sensitive book was the reigning single-volume text into the 1960s and still has value.

Jeffersonian scholarship underwent three major developments in the mid-20th century. The full surviving corpus of Jefferson's writings became available, partly in a comprehensive but as yet incomplete letter-press edition and partly on microfilm. This replaced the limited collections available to earlier authors and became the basis for all later work. Second, Jeffersonian writing was largely professionalized. Earlier authors had been generally independent gentlemen-scholars or journalists; from then on Jeffersonian scholarship has become dominated by academically trained authors. They self-consciously attempted to be scientific and dispassionate, but although the grinding of partisan axes is muted, their writing remains tinged with concern for Jefferson's contemporary ideological significance. Third, the literature became more specialized and narrower in focus. Previous authors had often set their exposition in an international as well as American context, but this broad perspective was largely abandoned, even by the major biographers. The research and writing improved, but the loss of a comparative dimension weakened the light and shade of the analyses, and to that extent the understanding of Jefferson became shallower.

MALONE's six volumes are the grand climax of a generation of Jeffersonian scholarship and unquestionably rank as one of the great American biographies. Taking full advantage of the newly available material, Malone covers the full range of Jefferson's activities and his narrative is rich in public and private detail alike; his study is virtually a reference work. Unlike many predecessors, he does not focus disproportionately on the battle with Hamilton: a volume is devoted to each term of Jefferson's presidency, and a final volume traces his long retirement at Monticello. The judgments are measured if somewhat over-sympathetic. To Malone, Jefferson was a high-minded public servant who was also a conspicuous symbol of republicanism but uncomfortable as a party leader. He insists that Jefferson's conduct as president was broadly consistent with his earlier beliefs.

PETERSON (1970) amply fulfilled the promise of his earlier work. Aimed at the general reader and lacking in scholarly apparatus, it immediately established itself as the major single-volume biography of its generation. Scholarly and dispassionate in approach, substantial in length, and broad in its treatment of the many aspects of Jefferson's interests, it provided a detailed narrative interweaving three recurrent motifs: democracy, nationality and enlightenment. It is particularly good on high politics and grand themes.

Although it is somewhat shorter, CUNNINGHAM complements Peterson by balancing his material differently and making rather grittier judgments. Having written extensively on Jeffersonian party formation and politics and government

administration, he pays more attention to those aspects in his biography. Although covering the broad ground and stressing Jefferson's Enlightenment conviction that reason could be applied as much to human politics as to the natural world, his strength lies in treatment of daily political activity and in particular the development and functioning of parties and elections, as well as the formulation of policy and the handling of crises. Perhaps surprisingly he also demonstrates that Jefferson was a highly efficient administrator.

RISJORD is a brief political biography which provides a useful general introduction. He handles the scholarly argument over the relationship between Jefferson's principles and his conduct in office by arguing that he never developed a fully coherent ideology.

BRODIE challenges the conventionally favourable treatment by subordinating Jefferson's public and intellectual life to a highly controversial psychological study. The portrait illuminates his emotional stress and ambivalence, but its centrepiece is an extended argument that he had children by a slave concubine, Sally Hemings. The evidence is circumstantial and sometimes strained, but though the thesis is not proven, it has not been completely demolished. McLAUGHLIN combines a study of Jefferson's architectural activities with a graceful and sensitive exploration of his domestic life by tracing the constantly altering building works at Monticello. He is cautious about the Brodie thesis and in many respects more perceptive.

PETERSON (1986) is an excellent collection of essays by leading scholars on different aspects of Jefferson, including those such as his religion, political economy, constitutionalism and republicanism which are not always easily accessible in other works. ONUF is a more specialized collection of essays which, by reflecting modern scholarly concerns, illuminate more perhaps than they intend. Thus three discuss aspects of race and slavery, and others deal with Jefferson's domestic life and civil liberties; there is relatively little on the West, the presidency, or natural science, for example.

The monographic literature on Jefferson is immense. His intellectual life has been widely analysed. BOORSTIN attempts to reconstruct the mind-set of the Jeffersonian circle rather than Jefferson's individual intellect. Now somewhat unfashionable in its approach, it focuses on the Enlightenment world of nature and reason and their application to political science. More recently, Charles MILLER critically yet sympathetically and at length analyses Jefferson's sense of nature and argues that it was central to Jefferson's mind – from his understanding of God to his political system.

KOCH concedes that Jefferson was not an original, speculative thinker, but insists that he was a disciple of scientific method. What marked him out was his concern for the application of ideas and principles to social and public life. Avoiding chronology in favour of thematic analysis, she discusses Jefferson's ethics, philosophy and ideology before developing his theory of society and government, and concludes that he had a conscious programme of action, and believed that American political procedures represented something novel in the history of civilization. MATTHEWS is confined to political philosophy and proposes a provocatively radical revision of current orthodoxy. He denies that Jefferson was backward looking, insists that he offered an optimistic humanist democratic alternative to market-oriented liberalism and possessive individualism, and argues that his political system explicitly called for mass participatory democracy and permanent revolution, in order to adapt to changing circumstances and to keep humanity and society healthy.

SHELDON traces the chronological development of Jefferson's political ideas and relates them to concepts found in the classics of political theory. This contextual discussion is particularly helpful, both in relation to the sources of Jefferson's ideas and recent historiographical debate. It is more balanced than Matthews and concludes with a brief statement of Jefferson's sense of freedom, democracy, equality and rights. WILTSE, though older, retains some usefulness in that it offers a description of Jefferson's political science and his views on the structure of government, before devoting half the book to tracing its adaptation by later generations down to the New Deal.

For many years the classic analysis of the Declaration of Independence was BECKER, who described the document's textual structure, and argued that its philosophy derived from the natural rights theory of the Enlightenment and Locke's theory of compact. WILLS challenges this at greater length, places it in a more extended context, and substitutes the Scottish Enlightenment for its intellectual underpinnings; his thesis has in turn been severely criticized.

The classic study of Jefferson's presidency remains ADAMS, albeit extensively revised by later historians, and largely supplanted by Malone. Rich in irony as well as detail, it stressed the disjunction between Jefferson's theories and the modifications necessitated by the imperatives of office, and in particular the irony that a policy dedicated to peace and democracy led the country to the edge of war and his departure from office in great unpopularity. McDONALD is a brief but characteristically fresh survey which discusses the presidency as well as the president, and argues that the Jeffersonians unsuccessfully resisted the modern world, and failed to reverse the tide largely because of a bankrupt foreign policy.

The preeminent analytical study of Jefferson's foreign policy is now TUCKER and HENDRICKSON. As political scientists they move beyond the narratives contained in the historical biographies to identify what they argue are its central principles. They declare that it differed little from the statecraft of the *ancien regimes*: what he regarded as the necessities of the state and nation overrode the principles that appeared to jeopardise these necessities, including principles that otherwise commanded his undeviating allegiance, the only distinguishing difference being Jefferson's reluctance to use force.

LEVY challenges the validity of his reputation as the apostle of liberty by arguing, in what he admits is a lawyer's brief, that Jefferson's conduct in office diverged considerably from the principles customarily associated with him. He argues that Jefferson endorsed the doctrine that the ends justify the means, flouted the Constitution, urged prosecutions for seditious libel and supported loyalty oaths. Though overheated, his arguments have some substance.

John Chester MILLER analyzes Jefferson's attitude towards race and slavery. In a dispassionate discussion which explores his mind set as well as the many occasions on which he had to confront the institution, Miller concludes that there was an irreconcilable inconsistency between his principles and his behaviour. SHEEHAN similarly discusses Jefferson's attitude towards Native Americans.

HUDDLESTON and SHUFFELTON are both helpful annotated bibliographies of Jeffersonian scholarship.

Colin Bonwick

Jeffersonian Republican Party

Adams, Henry, *History of the United States of America During the Administrations of Jefferson and Madison*, 9 vols., New York: Scribner, 1889–91; edited by Earl N. Harbert, 2 vols., New York: Library of America, 1986

Appleby, Joyce, *Capitalism and a New Social Order: The Republican Vision of the 1790s*, New York: New York University Press, 1984

Banning, Lance, *The Jeffersonian Persuasion: Evolution of a Party Ideology*, Ithaca, NY: Cornell University Press, 1978

Buel, Richard, Jr., *Securing the Revolution: Ideology in American Politics, 1789–1815*, Ithaca, NY: Cornell University Press, 1972

Cunningham, Noble E., Jr., *The Jeffersonian Republicans: The Formation of a Party Organization, 1789–1801*, Chapel Hill: University of North Carolina Press, 1957

Cunningham, Noble E., Jr., *The Jeffersonian Republicans in Power: Party Operations, 1801–1809*, Chapel Hill: University of North Carolina Press, 1963

Elkins, Stanley and Eric McKitrick, *The Age of Federalism: The Early American Republic, 1788–1800*, New York: Oxford University Press, 1993

Hofstadter, Richard, *The Idea of a Party System: The Rise of Legitimate Opposition in the United States, 1780–1840*, Berkeley: University of California Press, 1969

Sharp, James Roger, *American Politics in the Early Republic: The New Nation in Crisis*, New Haven: Yale University Press, 1993

White, Leonard D., *The Jeffersonians: A Study in Administrative History, 1801–1829*, New York: Macmillan, 1951

The nature and character of the Jeffersonian Republican party, both in opposition and in government, has provoked a lengthy and lively debate among historians. There are a number of works tracing the emergence of the Republican party as an opposition faction in the 1790s. Among the more recent interpretations of this process are Sharp, and Elkins and McKitrick, both of which place heavy emphasis on sectional and ideological divisions between national leaders. SHARP sees the main strength of the Republican party deriving from the coherence of the agrarian philosophy of its Virginian leaders, who were themselves sincerely committed to the ideals of classical republicanism and genuinely fearful for the safety of the republic in the hands of a Federalist party seemingly infused with monarchism and commercialism. In their monumental study of the 1790s, ELKINS and McKITRICK discern an identifiable "Virginia mentality" personified by Thomas Jefferson and James Madison, which, while it did not exactly replicate the tradition of the "country" opposition in English politics, did retain many of its characteristic features, such as a suspicion of cities and a resistance to central power. At the same time, they stress, these leaders displayed a staunch Anglophobia. Complex political issues are subjected to detailed and subtle evaluation, but the book maintains an accessible narrative style throughout.

HOFSTADTER considers how leading Republicans such as Jefferson, Madison and James Monroe constructed the Republican party as an opposition vehicle in a political and cultural atmosphere hostile to parties, and once in power sought to achieve party consolidation by an accommodation with some of the principles of Federalism, if not with the Federalists themselves. According to Hofstadter, it was only with the rise to prominence of a second generation of political leaders – such as Martin Van Buren – following the "misnamed Era of Good Feelings" that the notion of a party system as beneficial in itself achieved credibility and acceptance.

There has been considerable interest in the underlying ideology of the Jeffersonian Republicans. BUEL makes a strong case for the central role of ideas in shaping the actions of Republican politicians, and credits them with a much deeper faith in the republic and the people than their Federalist opponents. Buel attributes the Republicans, commitment to popular rights to the greater sense of security of their southern leaders in their social leadership roles. The most persuasive exponent of the view that Jeffersonian Republicanism represented a revision of the English "country" tradition is BANNING. This influential study maintains that the Jeffersonians have too often been interpreted anachronistically and should properly be understood on their own intellectual terms. Accordingly, Banning explores the influence of 17th- and 18th-century English opposition thought on American politics in the years of the early republic, and concludes that the country tradition, with its emphasis on the corrupting influence of executive power, was the primary motivation behind Republican opposition to Federalist measures of the 1790s. This perhaps makes less of the social and economic context than it might, but is nonetheless a soundly-reasoned and forceful analysis.

APPLEBY offers an alternative interpretation of Jeffersonian ideology, which rejects the notion that the politics of the 1790s, and beyond, can be explained in terms of a "court" versus "country" struggle. Rather, Appleby believes that the Republicans, deriving more inspiration from Lockean liberalism than from classical republicanism, sought an expansive society based on commercial agrarianism where individuals could advance according to their merits. She contends that the Republicans' optimistic faith in prosperity laid the basis for the future success of American capitalism. A challenging and well-formulated thesis, this argument nonetheless depends on a revised and somewhat specialized definition of capitalism.

More concerned with the mechanisms of party organization, CUNNINGHAM (1957) shows how the Republicans consistently took the initiative in developing party machinery and innovative electoral campaigning techniques. Cunningham argues that the Republican party initially developed on the national stage as a result of the opposition of Jefferson and Madison to Alexander Hamilton's economic measures. Then,

as party lines hardened in the wake of the French Revolution, the Jay Treaty and the election of 1796, party organization radiated outwards to the states. He concludes that the peaceful transfer of power to the Republicans after the election of 1800 constituted proof that political parties had "come of age" in the United States. CUNNINGHAM (1963) provides a valuable assessment of the operation of the Jeffersonian party in power, focusing on party machinery, the press, campaign methods and patronage. Although primarily a study of the national party, the book also contains a brief review of the Republican party organization in each of the states, which displayed varying levels of party unity and efficiency depending in part on the effectiveness of the Federalist opposition. Overall, Cunningham gives a sympathetic appraisal of the strength of the Republican party organizations, and is more appreciative of Jefferson's political skills than many other commentators.

A balanced consideration of the Jeffersonian operation of government is given in WHITE, which contends that the Republicans, lacking as coherent a theory of government and administration as the Federalists, and in any case restricted by their inheritance of an already fully functioning administration, were content to maintain the Federalist structure more or less intact for nearly three decades. White, indeed, believes that, in terms of both his politics and administration practices, the last Republican president John Quincy Adams, was "more nearly Federalist" than Republican.

Still the most comprehensive treatment of the Republican ascendancy after 1800 is ADAMS. This elegant multi-volume work, dealing extensively with the diplomatic wrangles which culminated in the War of 1812, takes as one of its central themes the claim that the Jeffersonians, and Jefferson in particular, secured power and popularity largely through an abandonment of principle. Adams's indictment of Jefferson's hypocrisy in this regard is at least partly explicable by family animus – he was the great-grandson of Jefferson's erstwhile rival John Adams – and despite its eloquence is hampered by inconsistency, since Adams identifies a stubborn adherence to outmoded principles as chiefly responsible for the conflict with Great Britain.

NEIL CURTIN

See also Early National Period; Parties and Political Movements

Jewish Americans

Cohen, Naomi, *Jews in Christian America: The Pursuit of Religious Equality*, New York: Oxford University Press, 1992

Dinnerstein, Leonard, *Antisemitism in America*, New York: Oxford University Press, 1994

Feingold, Henry L. (general editor), Jewish People in America series, 5 vols., Baltimore: Johns Hopkins University Press, 1992:
   1. Faber, Eli, *A Time for Planting: The First Migration, 1654–1820*
   2. Diner, Hasia R., *A Time for Gathering: The Second Migration, 1820–1880*

3. Sorin, Gerald, *A Time for Building: The Third Migration, 1880–1920*

4. Feingold, Henry L., *A Time for Searching: Entering the Mainstream, 1920–1945*

5. Shapiro, Edward S., *A Time for Healing: American Jewry since World War II*

Feingold, Henry L., *Bearing Witness: How America and Its Jews Responded to the Holocaust*, Syracuse, NY: Syracuse University Press, 1995

Goren, Arthur A., *New York Jews and the Quest for Community: The Kehillah Experiment, 1908–1922*, New York: Columbia University Press, 1970

Heinze, Andrew, *Adapting to Abundance: Jewish Immigrants, Mass Consumption and the Search for American Identity*, New York: Columbia University Press, 1990

Howe, Irving with Kenneth Libo, *World of Our Fathers: The Journey of the East European Jews to America and the Life They Found and Made*, New York: Harcourt Brace, 1976; as *The Immigrant Jews of New York*, London: Routledge, 1976

Markowitz, Ruth Jacknow, *My Daughter, the Teacher: Second-Generation Jewish Teachers in the New York City Public School System, 1920–1940*, New Brunswick, NJ: Rutgers University Press, 1994

Moore, Deborah Dash, *To the Golden Cities: Pursuing the American Jewish Dream in Miami and LA*, New York: Free Press, 1994

Morawska, Ewa, *Insecure Prosperity: Small-Town Jews in Industrial America, 1890–1940*, Princeton: Princeton University Press, 1996

Orleck, Annalise, *Common Sense and a Little Fire: Women and Working-Class Politics in the United States, 1900–1965*, Chapel Hill: University of North Carolina Press, 1995

Rischin, Moses, *The Promised City: New York's Jews, 1870–1914*, Cambridge, MA: Harvard University Press, 1962

Urofsky, Melvin I., *American Zionism from Herzl to the Holocaust*, New York: Anchor Press, 1975

Urofsky, Melvin I., *We Are One! American Jewry and Israel*, New York: Anchor Press, 1978

The mass immigration of East European Jews and their settlement in New York City's Lower East Side district dominates historical study of American Jews. RISCHIN captures the dreams and dynamism of that epic migration which brought almost a third of East European Jewry to the banks of the Hudson river. There they created the largest Jewish settlement in history. His ground-breaking study locates the stimulus for American progressive reform politics with New York Jews, and suggests that their contributions extended well beyond the city's boundaries.

GOREN's classic account picks up the story of immigrant Jews where Rischin left off, but focuses on communal politics and an ambitious effort to transplant and democratize Jewish communal institutions in the new world. He charts the complex relationships among different ideological groups of Jews, including socialists and capitalists, orthodox and reform, nationalists and universalists. But his flawed heroes are clearly the Zionists who valued ethnic solidarity and political compromise above ideological purity.

A masterful summary that integrates American Yiddish culture into its compelling narrative is provided by HOWE, whose personal vision as the son of immigrant parents informs his writing. He argues that secular Jewishness, *yidishkayt*, shaped immigrants' collective and individual dreams as well as their culture. Unlike Rischin and Goren, Howe's massive volume has a nostalgic edge as he pays tribute to a world that has disappeared, leaving no heirs to appreciate a rich heritage. Perhaps because it offers such a seemingly complete history, *World of Our Fathers* immediately stimulated historians of American Jews to revisit the Lower East Side to see what Howe had missed. It turned out that he had missed a great deal – women and consumer culture, for example. HEINZE remedied the latter with an interpretation of Americanization that emphasizes consumption rather than production as the critical process. Thus women, not men, transform immigrant Jews into Jewish Americans by cooking the family's food, buying their clothes, and purchasing that symbol of success: a piano for the parlor.

If New York City typified immigrant adjustment, Johnstown, Pennsylvania represents the atypical experiences of Jewish immigrants and their children who settled in small cities. MORAWSKA deliberately contrasts the choices of this select group, Jews coming from small towns in eastern Europe and seeking to replicate their situation in America, with the predominant New York paradigm. She discovers that their lives lacked the sense of possibilities characteristic of most big city American Jews, and that the lack of sufficient numbers to support an ethnic economy constrained their prosperity.

The possibility of effecting social change and gaining control over one's life motivates the immigrant Jewish women who feature in ORLECK's rewarding study. Although familiar figures for a brief moment when they grabbed the limelight as union activists and political leaders, this quartet of women – Rose Schneiderman, Fannia Cohn, Pauline Newman, and Clara Lemlich Shavelson – continued to champion change and struggle for a more just society, even when historians were not paying attention. Orleck chronicles their aspirations and accomplishments, and in the process radically revises Howe's emphasis upon immigrants as men and Heinze's focus on women as consumers.

Women also make up half of the second generation, the children of immigrant Jews. MARKOWITZ stays within the boundaries of New York City in her account of Jewish teachers, but she shows how gender restricted occupational choices and the dreams of thousands of Jewish women during the interwar years. These women also faced antisemitic prejudice – and, during the Cold War era, political persecution, too – as anticommunists attempted to rid the public schools of their ideological opponents.

The subject of antisemitism is acknowledged in all histories of Jewish Americans but few emphasize its impact. DINNERSTEIN makes it his focus. He examines discrimination against Jews in education and occupations; he explores political prejudice, including the infamous Leo Frank case – the only lynching of an American Jew on record – and he discusses social and cultural biases. Antisemitism peaked during World

War II and then declined precipitously, though small pockets still exist among radical right-wing fringe groups and African Americans. Jews consistently fought antisemitism, although they rarely agreed upon tactics or philosophy. COHEN sets Jewish efforts to create a genuinely neutral public political space in historical context, looking at different strategies designed to guarantee Jews equal citizenship. Although she does not examine the question of race and whiteness, and how its changing definition relates to Jews, she does treat the complex issue of religion. Jews are dissenters from the Christian majority, a potential vanguard for other non-Christians.

By contrast, Jewish nationalism has often followed precedents established by such groups as Irish Americans. In his narrative of American Zionism UROFSKY (1975, 1978) reveals how a minority movement among Jews achieved widespread acceptance, even becoming the touchstone of Jewish identity. Another recent touchstone of identity for Jewish Americans is the Holocaust. Recrimination and guilt over Jewish failure to rescue European Jewry from destruction dominates most historical interpretations. FEINGOLD's (1995) collection of essays stands out for its rigorous historical honesty and unwillingness to succumb to moralism.

Perhaps the best way to gain an overview of American Jewish history is to read the five volumes produced under FEINGOLD's editorial direction. Each historian synthesizes several decades of scholarship. A model of gender sensitivity, Diner's history of 19th century German Jewish immigrants seamlessly integrates women into her account. Faber covers the colonial era thoroughly and Sorin pays attention to politics in his interpretation of East European immigration. Shapiro faces the greatest challenge in covering the decades since 1945 because most historians have ignored the period.

MOORE is one of the few exceptions. Her book invites a shift in focus away from New York City and immigrants, to the emerging sunbelt cities of Los Angeles and Miami. She examines the results of internal Jewish migration within the United States and how it produces new communities. Although the immigrant era will continue to attract new scholarship – studies that pay attention to sexuality, for example – the future will surely see more attention directed to the past half century when Jewish Americans achieved security and respect.

DEBORAH DASH MOORE

See also Immigration and Ethnicity; Judaism

Jim Crow: Segregation and Disfranchisement in the South, 1870s–1917

Ayers, Edward L., *The Promise of the New South: Life after Reconstruction*, New York: Oxford University Press, 1992

Brundage, W. Fitzhugh, *Lynching in the New South: Georgia and Virginia, 1880–1930*, Urbana: University of Illinois Press, 1993

Cell, John W., *The Highest Stage of White Supremacy: The Origins of Segregation in South Africa and the American South*, Cambridge and New York: Cambridge University Press, 1982

Fredrickson, George M., *The Black Image in the White Mind: The Debate on Afro-American Character and Destiny, 1817–1914*, New York: Harper, 1971

Grossman, James R., *Land of Hope: Chicago, Black Southerners, and the Great Migration*, Chicago: University of Chicago Press, 1989

Kirby, Jack Temple, *Darkness at the Dawning: Race and Reform in the Progressive South*, Philadelphia: Lippincott, 1972

Kousser, J. Morgan, *The Shaping of Southern Politics: Suffrage Restriction and the Establishment of the One-Party South, 1880–1919*, New Haven: Yale University Press, 1974

Meier, August, *Negro Thought in America, 1880–1915: Racial Ideologies in the Age of Booker T. Washington*, Ann Arbor: University of Michigan Press, 1963

Rabinowitz, Howard N., *Race Relations in the Urban South, 1865–1890*, New York: Oxford University Press, 1978

Rabinowitz, Howard N., *Race, Ethnicity, and Urbanization: Selected Essays*, Columbia: University of Missouri Press, 1994

Williamson, Joel, *After Slavery: The Negro in South Carolina During Reconstruction, 1861–1877*, Chapel Hill: University of North Carolina Press, 1965

Williamson, Joel, *The Crucible of Race: Black-White Relations in the American South since Emancipation*, New York: Oxford University Press, 1984; abridged as *A Rage for Order*, 1986

Woodward, C. Vann, *Origins of the New South, 1877–1913*, Baton Rouge: Louisiana University Press, 1951, updated by Charles B. Dew, 1971

Woodward, C. Vann, *The Strange Career of Jim Crow*, New York: Oxford University Press, 1955, 3rd revised edition, 1974

Conditions for blacks in the South noticeably worsened during the late 19th and early 20th centuries. But although it is common to link segregation, disfranchisement, and mob violence against blacks under the rubric of Jim Crow due to their overlap in terms of timing and causation, each of these three phenomena had its own timetable and motivation. WOODWARD (1951, 1971) was largely responsible for the linkage. The most influential historian of the South in his time, Woodward argued that a new generation of post-Civil War Democratic white leaders, whom he called Redeemers, overthrew the Republican-controlled Reconstruction governments and, following a transitional period of fluidity, supervised the comprehensive subjugation of the region's blacks. WOODWARD (1955, 1974), a brief overview of southern race relations based on a set of lectures in 1954, sought to demonstrate that the *Brown* v. *Board of Education* Supreme Court decision would mean less of a break with "southern folkways" than white southerners feared. The book initiated what became after the mid-1950s an ongoing debate over the origins of segregation after the Civil War. Noting the relatively late appearance of laws enforcing segregation in public conveyances and public accommodations, and basing his work almost entirely on conditions in Virginia and the Carolinas, Woodward maintained that segregation did not become the rule in the South until after 1890. And although he blamed the North, southern poor whites and Redeemers for the onset of disfranchisement and segregation, he seemed to assign the greatest blame to the poor whites.

A number of case studies of the same states initially supported what was almost immediately dubbed "the Woodward Thesis." However, WILLIAMSON (1965) criticized Woodward for relying so heavily on forms of legal discrimination, and he documented extensive segregation both by custom (*de facto*) and by law (*de jure*) in South Carolina even during Reconstruction. Once the battle was joined, historians jumped in on both sides of the debate. Some have continued to support Woodward, but others report findings for the immediate postwar period similar to those of Williamson, while still others have appeared to undermine Woodward by revealing the existence of widespread segregation in the antebellum North and South. In subsequent editions which brought his survey into the 1970s, Woodward acknowledged these criticisms, but essentially maintained his original position.

RABINOWITZ (1978) however, noted that, even though segregation in both its *de jure* and, especially, *de facto* forms appeared earlier than Woodward had claimed, the more interesting point was that it replaced a system of exclusion rather than integration, and thus marked an improvement rather than a setback in the lives of southern blacks. For that reason it was generally supported by blacks and their white Republican allies, especially since separate treatment was to be equal treatment. Several of the articles in RABINOWITZ (1994) trace post-1890 developments, and assess the subsequent historiographical debate which has too often exaggerated both the extent of fluidity prior to 1890 and uniformity afterward. Although using "segregation" and "Jim Crow" interchangeably, CELL accepts the exclusion-to-segregation framework, while expanding on the role of racial moderates in bringing it about, and providing a useful comparative framework for the study of southern race relations.

A number of other works reveal the range of white attitudes towards blacks. WILLIAMSON (1984) is a moving though often repetitive *tour de force* that divides white southerners into three mentalities – Liberal, Conservative, and Radical – in an effort to explain the triumph of white racism and separate but unequal treatment at the end of the 19th century. Unfortunately Williamson's terminology is confusing and his psychosexual explanation for the Radicals' white racism is unpersuasive. Less ambitious, but more compelling than Williamson, FREDRICKSON originated the term "herrenvolk democracy" to describe white support for discrimination against blacks.

Williamson's discussion of lynching is particularly insightful and impassioned. However, it should be supplemented by BRUNDAGE's more complex statistical examination of how the legacies of slavery and Reconstruction combined with variations in regional, social, and economic contexts, to help make mob violence a pervasive and semi-official institution in the South, while it declined in frequency elsewhere in the country. Distinguishing among "mass mobs," "terrorist mobs," "private mobs," and "posse lynchings," and focusing on two states, Brundage avoids simplistic answers, but the applicability of his findings for the rest of the South remains an open question.

Most of the segregation and disfranchisement statutes were enacted during the so-called progressive era, while lynching did not crest until 1919. Thus Woodward's depiction of progressivism as "for whites only," has been more widely accepted than his assessment of segregation. Nevertheless under the impact of the civil rights movement and the Vietnam War, more recent scholarship has been even more critical of these "reformers" and has seen the racism of white progressives as central to their movement. It has also been less ready to blame lower-class whites for the increase in racial discrimination. KOUSSER sees disfranchisement preparing the way for progressivism in some states, while being the tool of the progressives themselves in others. Relying heavily on sophisticated quantitative methodology, he also convincingly takes issue with Woodward by arguing that elites rather than poor whites were the primary disfranchisers, but is on less secure ground when arguing that their targets were as much poor whites as blacks. KIRBY emphasizes the ways in which progressivism embraced and expanded the racial settlement of the 1890s.

The emphasis on the black dimension of progressivism is part of a recent body of work, ably synthesized in Williamson (1984) and in AYERS, that has sought to view black life during these years as something more than simply the product of white oppression. Even though whites set the ground rules, blacks themselves helped create their own institutions and culture within the larger segregated society. In the process, as subjects rather than simply objects of history, ordinary blacks were able to maintain a degree of autonomy and sense of self-respect previously unrecognized. MEIER's encyclopedic account, however, remains the best introduction to alternatives proposed by black leaders to the increasing discrimination. Although W.E.B. Du Bois and Booker T. Washington justly receive the major share of attention, lesser figures are amply treated. Meier examines the alternatives of protest and accommodation, as blacks debated the merits of remaining in the South as against leaving for the West, the North or Africa and accepting segregation or pressing for integration. GROSSMAN is the most balanced of the growing number of studies which chronicle the most significant response of southern blacks, that is the "Great Migration" out of the South into northern cities during World War I, primarily for economic reasons. Although such studies tend to exaggerate the degree of continuity between the pre- and post-migration lives of blacks, they are useful corrective to the earlier emphasis on the great gap between their institutional and working lives in the urban North and rural South.

HOWARD N. RABINOWITZ

See also African American History, 1870s–1954; South: since 1865

Johnson, Andrew 1808–1875

17th President of the United States

Beale, Howard K., *The Critical Year: A Study of Andrew Johnson and Reconstruction*, New York: Harcourt Brace, 1930

Benedict, Michael Les, *The Impeachment and Trial of Andrew Johnson*, New York: Norton, 1973

Bowen, David Warren, *Andrew Johnson and the Negro*, Knoxville: University of Tennessee Press, 1989

Castel, Albert, *The Presidency of Andrew Johnson*, Lawrence: Regents Press of Kansas, 1979

Cox, LaWanda, and John H. Cox, *Politics, Principle, and Prejudice, 1865–1866: Dilemma of Reconstruction America*, New York: Free Press, 1963

McKitrick, Eric, *Andrew Johnson and Reconstruction*, Chicago: University of Chicago Press, 1960

Milton, George Fort, *The Age of Hate: Andrew Johnson and the Radicals*, New York: Coward McCann, 1930

Sefton, James E., *Andrew Johnson and the Uses of Constitutional Power*, Boston: Little Brown, 1980

Trefousse, Hans L., *Andrew Johnson: A Biography*, New York: Norton, 1989

The historical reputation of Andrew Johnson has fluctuated in direct response to shifts in scholarly interpretations of Reconstruction. The predominance of the so-called Dunning school of Reconstruction historiography, with its critical treatment of Republican policy and scepticism about the viability of racial equality, led historians during the first decades of the 20th century to portray the 17th president as a defender of constitutional prerogatives and an advocate of sectional reconciliation against vengeful Radicals bent upon political domination. BEALE went so far as to argue that the real issues at stake concerned economic policy, with Republicans pushing for protective tariffs and fiscal policies to build a new industrial order. In his account, Reconstruction and racial equality before the law were mere side issues, used by Republicans to obscure their economic agenda. Johnson not only failed to reveal the true thrust of Republican initiatives, but also met his opponents on their chosen ground. MILTON, in contrast, insisted that Reconstruction was the central issue of Johnson's presidency. Presenting a sympathetic treatment of the president, Milton characterized his impeachment as a Republican grab for power and celebrated Johnson's acquittal as a vindication of the American constitutional order. These two studies provide the most scholarly versions of this once-dominant perspective; subsequent work demonstrated that Beale's representation of Republican economic priorities did not reflect intra-party divisions over tariff and fiscal policy, and suggested that federal policy toward the defeated South was the primary cause of friction between the president and his Republican opponents.

Historians who came of age during the civil rights movement of the 1950s endorsed the Republican crusade for racial equality, and treated Johnson critically, if not with hostility. McKITRICK's influential study of Johnson and the congressional Republicans suggests that the president's unwillingness to reach a compromise with moderate Republicans cast aside an opportunity to divide moderates from radicals, and secure an agreement that would have stopped short of large-scale black enfranchisement. Johnson, McKitrick claims, was an "outsider" and a "loner" who was not pre-disposed to work with others, and thus nullified whatever chance existed for negotiation and compromise. COX and COX offered a different explanation, suggesting that the president was bent upon building a coalition in which Democrats would play a large role: his decision to emphasize issues of race played upon the prejudices of the American electorate. These decisions precluded cooperation with Republican moderates. Criticism of Johnson, evident in several reassessments of Reconstruction during the 1960s and early 1970s, reached a high point with BENEDICT's reassessment of the president's impeachment. According to Benedict, Johnson deserved impeachment and conviction for obstructing the execution of congressional legislation. However, a flawed indictment and prosecution, constitutional reservations, and the concerns of some Republicans about the economic policy preferences of the man who would take over the presidency upon Johnson's conviction – Senator Benjamin F. Wade of Ohio – persuaded just enough Senate Republicans to vote for acquittal. Even more than McKitrick, Benedict emphasized divisions among Republicans and demonstrated how constitutional concerns restrained their actions, and he repudiated earlier characterizations of them as a unified group that trampled over the Constitution to achieve their ends.

Early biographies of Johnson proved superficial; historians most often treated him within the context of the Reconstruction debate during his presidency. Several recent biographies offer different ways to place Johnson's presidency in the context of his entire life and political career. SEFTON's concise portrait harkens back to Milton in its insistence that Johnson acted upon Jacksonian conceptions of the Constitution and executive power. Of all modern studies, this book comes closest to accepting Johnson on his own terms, resulting in a most sympathetic treatment. It plays down the impact of white supremacist behavior against blacks in the postwar South – behavior which Johnson either condoned, or blamed on Republican agitators or blacks themselves. TREFOUSSE's full-scale biography is far more critical of its subject, emphasizing his racial attitudes, his intransigence, and his inability to grow and change in response to the transformations wrought by the Civil War. Like Benedict, Trefousse stresses that Johnson's exercise of presidential power did much to determine the outcome of Reconstruction. His decision to return plantations to their pre-war owners short-circuited any hope of their redistribution to the freedpeople, and his battles against Congress absorbed Republican political energies that might well otherwise have been directed to overseeing a more far-reaching reform program in the South. The best study currently available of the 17th president, it is also representative of the broad indictment of him drawn up by many American historians since 1960. At times Trefousse seems more anxious to judge than to understand Johnson. Both Sefton and Trefousse provide excellent coverage of Johnson's pre-presidential career, including his rise to prominence as an antebellum Democrat, his fierce unionism during the secession crisis, and his performance as military governor of Tennessee, which led to his becoming Abraham Lincoln's running mate in 1864 and thus his successor as president.

Two studies offering a somewhat more dispassionate assessment of Johnson are by Bowen and Castel. In his detailed examination of Johnson's racial attitudes, BOWEN sets them in the context of discussions about slavery in the antebellum South, as well as his Jacksonian beliefs. To Johnson, slavery and slaveholding were a matter of class as well as race, for he was troubled that those whites who owned large numbers of slaves dominated southern politics and society, threatening to transform a democracy into an aristocracy. Slavery itself never seemed to trouble his conscience, and he was a fierce believer in white supremacy. Emancipation threatened the latter belief, and he opposed Republican initiatives in part because he believed that they gave blacks opportunities denied to those whites (such as himself) who had always struggled to get ahead. CASTEL examines Johnson's exercise of presidential power, finding that his performance was uneven because he did not always possess a firm grasp of his options or the tools of his office. However, his obstructionism went far to frustrate the very measures that it inspired; during the impeachment trial Johnson demonstrated that he was willing to do what was necessary to retain his office.

BROOKS D. SIMPSON

See also Reconstruction: Policy and Politics 1

Johnson, Lyndon Baines 1908–1973
36th President of the United States

Berman, Larry, *Lyndon Johnson's War: The Road to Stalemate in Vietnam*, New York: Norton, 1989
Califano, Joseph A., Jr., *The Triumph and Tragedy of Lyndon Johnson: The White House Years*, New York: Simon and Schuster, 1991
Caro, Robert A., *The Years of Lyndon Johnson: The Path to Power*, New York: Knopf, 1982; London: Collins, 1983
Caro, Robert A., *The Years of Lyndon Johnson: Means of Ascent*, New York: Knopf, and London: Bodley Head, 1990
Clifford, Clark M. with Richard Holbrooke, *Counsel to the President: A Memoir*, New York: Random House, 1991
Conkin, Paul Keith, *Big Daddy from the Pedernales: Lyndon Baines Johnson*, Boston: Twayne, 1986
Dallek, Robert, *Lone Star Rising: Lyndon Johnson and His Times, 1908–1960*, New York and Oxford: Oxford University Press, 1991
Divine, Robert A. (editor), *The Johnson Years*, volume 3: *LBJ at Home and Abroad*, Lawrence: University Press of Kansas, 1994
Goodwin, Richard N., *Remembering America: A Voice from the Sixties*, Boston: Little Brown, 1988
Kearns, Doris, *Lyndon Johnson and the American Dream*, New York: Harper, and London: Deutsch, 1976
McNamara, Robert S. with Brian VanDeMark, *In Retrospect: The Tragedy and Lessons of Vietnam*, New York: Times Books, 1995
Redford, Emmette S. and Richard T. McCulley, *White House Operations: The Johnson Presidency*, Austin: University of Texas Press, 1986
Welborn, David M. and Jesse Burkhead, *Intergovernmental Relations in the American Administrative State: The Johnson Presidency*, Austin: University of Texas Press, 1989

In one of the worst depression years, 1931, Lyndon Johnson began his lengthy career in Democratic politics as aide to a Texas legislator in Washington, DC. From that time on, political life was his profession, from the U.S. House of Representatives (1937–48), the Senate (1949–60), where he climbed to be Democratic majority leader in 1954 under Republican President Eisenhower, to the office of Vice President (1961–63) under Kennedy, and the 36th President (1963–68). Johnson was dogged to the end of life by the contrast between, on the one hand, the successes of his domestic policy, the extended-New Deal reforms of America, and the Great Society; and, on the other hand, the tremendous failure of his foreign policy in the Vietnam War. These concerns have been the subject of most of the biographical studies of Johnson, together with the personal Johnson technique – alternately flattering, fawning, bullying and blackmailing – for securing whatever he wanted in his political career.

In addition to all the records of Johnson and his administration, for instance the *Public Papers of the Presidents of the United States* (Washington, DC, 1964–69), Johnson published his own rather unexciting and unrevealing memoirs in 1971, under the title of *The Vantage Point*. The first biography of note was KEARNS, based on her knowledge as a White House insider, and on follow-up conversations with LBJ in Austin, Texas. Kearns tells the reader what Johnson has told her; she writes a great deal about his early "childhood trauma" and his love for his mother, and nothing at all new about his dramatic rise to power in the Democratic party. But, for all that, the book is entertainingly written, most of all when it paraphrases the words of Johnson himself.

CARO is a relentlessly hostile biographer of LBJ. In his first two volumes (1982, 1990), he carries the story only as far as the disreputable victory in the battle for the Texas senate seat in 1948, with a "fixed" 87-vote margin over Coke Stevenson. As Caro sees it, LBJ's radio station became the basis of the Johnson fortune. The Brown and Root construction firm, allied to the Johnson camp, won fat government contracts and provided campaign funds for LBJ in the 1940s. Johnson armed himself with politically expedient anti-union and anti-civil rights votes, until the late 1950s; he was a tool of Texan oil and gas billionaires. Caro exposes LBJ's most disturbing faults: his lust for wealth and power, his stupendous ambitions – LBJ always wanted to become President, according to Caro – his selfish exploitation of his cronies and opponents, and his unnerving dishonesty. Johnson becomes a cartoon-like character, in Caro's portrait. At the same time, Caro acknowledges Johnson's role in the passage of liberal social and civil rights legislation for the poor, the young and the underprivileged.

In the first volume of a projected two-volume study, DALLEK interprets Johnson in a less critical, more cautious way. To Dallek, LBJ was domestically a moderate social reformer, a Texan imbued with the idea of the resurgent New

Deal "New South" integrating into mainstream America at last. Vulgar, greedy and spiteful as he sometimes was, he had a liberal vision. Even though he was involved in campaign-law violations, influence peddling and pirated elections, LBJ was a friend of the downtrodden and the underdog. In 1957 as Senate majority leader, he pushed through the first civil rights legislation since Reconstruction. In his long congressional career, LBJ had not intended to make a bid for the U.S. presidency. Volume Two of Dallek s biography is yet to appear; it will deal with LBJ as vice president and president, and his wrestling with the problem of Vietnam. Whether or not Dallek can maintain the story of LBJ the "liberal internationalist" remains to be seen.

In contrast to these large-scale biographies, CONKIN is a relatively short book covering the whole of LBJ's life in 300 pages. He locates Johnson somewhere in the middle of the ideological spectrum of American life, always willing to move either right or left to meet the needs of one constituency or another. An unremarkable, non-partisan account of LBJ s domestic policy, the Great Society, is accompanied by a valuable description of the Vietnam War, as Johnson experienced it. In that disastrous war, he sees Johnson as being at the mercy of his foreign policy advisers. Some other writers, like Richard Goodwin, Clark Clifford and Robert McNamara, blame Johnson for promoting the war in Vietnam. According to them, "Win the war !" was LBJ's message. Conkin takes a different point of view. For him, the war in Vietnam was a failure of post-1945 American foreign policy, not attributable to any one president. Not so, according to BERMAN, who says that LBJ was chief architect of the Vietnam War, and so responsible for the "failure" of the United States to "win" the war.

REDFORD and McCULLEY and WELBORN are both studies of the administrative history of the Johnson administration, sponsored by the University of Texas. They deal with the "subpresidency" and domestic policy initiatives on the regional level. There are a number of accounts of the Johnson administration – some more revealing than others – by members of his cabinet or his White House staff. GOODWIN, a talented adviser and speechwriter in turn to John F. Kennedy, Lyndon Johnson and anti-war activist Eugene McCarthy, praised LBJ's Great Society program for "commitment to the cause of black equality." But in 1965, when Johnson first resolved to deploy American forces in Vietnam, a "dangerous change" came over the president – a change to "escalation." From that time on, in Goodwin's view, Johnson's behavior went to the extreme and took "a huge leap into unreason."

CALIFANO, a top aide for domestic affairs from 1965 to 1969, stood in "awe and admiration" of LBJ, even though he looked askance at the president's "bizarre" behavior, cruelty to his staff (especially Vice President Hubert Humphrey) and ribald, scatological harangues. Johnson was proud of his many Great Society laws and programs; he thought that legislation would fix everything, and "ached" over the lack of general appreciation of his legislative achievement, according to Califano. Much more frustrating is CLIFFORD's autobiography. The author served as temporary Secretary of Defense for a few months in 1968, when McNamara resigned. Clifford worked as a Washington lawyer for 46 years, and served as an unofficial adviser to several presidents, but was actually in government service for only six years. After the Tet Offensive,

Johnson was finally convinced of the need for de-escalation in Vietnam. Clifford compromised with a limited bombing halt, instead of persuading LBJ to stop American bombing totally. The complete bombing halt was not called until 31 October 1968, even though by 31 March LBJ had already announced that he would not stand for re-election as president. Clifford's weakness at this time left a bitter residue, in the minds of some critics.

In 1995, McNAMARA surprised the American public with his confession of culpability over Vietnam. He was responsible for the conduct of the war as Secretary of Defense, from 1961 to 1968; the war was called by some: "McNamara's War." He was picked by JFK from Ford Motor Company at the age of 44, to run the Department of Defense with his modern management techniques, and to shift United States military strategy away from reliance on the nuclear response to greater emphasis on conventional warfare. Now, at the age of almost 79, he confesses that he was mistaken about Vietnam, two decades after the United States sustained a defeat, the first major defeat in its history. Why did he not resign long before 1967? He gives the somewhat lame excuse: "I was loyal to the presidency." Almost three decades after the event, McNamara effectively blames the long-dead President, Lyndon Johnson.

DIVINE has brought together a collection of essays by a varied and distinguished group of contributors – including Divine himself – who examine different aspects of the Johnson presidency, and review the literature on LBJ. For anyone seeking to strike a balance between his achievements in domestic policy, and his frustrations and failures in Vietnam, this may be the place to start.

PETER D'A. JONES

See also Great Society; Vietnam War entries

Jones, John Paul 1747–1792
Sailor, naval commander and adventurer

Bradford, James C. (editor), *The Papers of John Paul Jones*, 10 reels, Cambridge and Alexandria, VA: Chadwyck-Healey, 1986 (printed guide and microfilm)

Buell, Augustus C., *Paul Jones: Founder of the American Navy*, 2 vols., New York: Scribner, 1900

De Koven, Mrs. Reginald [Anna], *The Life and Letters of John Paul Jones*, 2 vols., New York: Scribner, 1913

Golder, F.A., *John Paul Jones in Russia*, New York: Doubleday, 1927

Lorenz, Lincoln, *John Paul Jones: Fighter for Freedom and Glory*, Annapolis, MD: Naval Institute Press, 1943

Mackenzie, Alexander Slidell, *The Life of Paul Jones*, 2 vols., Boston: Hilliard Gray, 1841; condensed version, under pseudonym Edward Hamilton, Aberdeen: Clark, 1848

Morison, Samuel Eliot, *John Paul Jones: A Sailor's Biography*, Boston: Little Brown, 1959; London: Faber, 1960

Sands, Robert, *Life and Correspondence of John Paul Jones, Including His Narrative of the Campaign of the Liman*, New York: Fanshaw, 1830

Sherburne, John Henry, *The Life and Character of John Paul Jones, A Captain in the United States Navy, During the Revolutionary War*, New York: Vanderpool, 1825

John Paul Jones's conduct of operations in British waters during the American War for Independence – particularly his capture of the *Serapis* while captain of the *Bonhomme Richard* (1779) – made him a hero in the United States and France, hated in Great Britain, and a role model for American naval officers for two centuries. During the early 19th century dozens of chapbooks and biographical sketches vilified Jones in England and held him up for emulation in America. On the fiftieth anniversary of the founding of the Continental Navy, SHERBURNE, Register of the United States Navy, published the first full-length biography of Jones. Based on primary sources, it set the tone for Jones biographies to follow by depicting him as a patriot whose self-education, bravery, determination, and victories made him worthy of a place in the pantheon of American heroes. SANDS added detail to Sherburne's portrait by reproducing numerous extracts from papers in the possession of Jones's niece and heir. MACKENZIE, a naval officer, produced a much more readable volume by substituting narrative for the long quotations of both Sherburne and Sands.

The rise of navalism at the beginning of the 20th century, the return of Jones's body to America from France, and its enshrinement in the crypt beneath the chapel at the United States Naval Academy in Annapolis caught the general public's imagination and renewed its interest in Jones. BUELL cashed in with a potboiler portraying Jones not only as a dashing hero but also as a visionary proto-professional naval officer, the latter feat accomplished by Buell's fabrication of documents which he attributed to Jones.

During the same era, De KOVEN produced a much more accurate "life and letters" biography of Jones, but one that retained many of the legends which developed about Jones during the 19th century. Though romantic and hagiographic, De Koven's work advanced scholarship on the subject of Jones. The public's fascination with Jones led to publication of over a dozen biographies based directly on Buell's and De Koven's during the next quarter century. Titles such as *The Splendid Renegade*, *The Sailor Whom England Feared*, and *Knight of the Seas* are indicative of their contents, and none merits reading as an aid to understanding the man or his times. The next advance in Jones scholarship was made by GOLDER who reproduced documents which he discovered in Russian archives, and, making good use of them, wrote a concise, factual account of Jones's service in the Russian navy during the Russo-Turkish War in 1788. It remains the standard treatment of the topic.

There are two notable more recent biographies of Jones. LORENZ is the longer at 846 pages, and portrays Jones as the ideal naval officer with few faults. Though shorter than De Koven's two volumes, it is more comprehensive in its coverage and its analysis, and also adheres more closely to the documentary record. In 1959 MORISON, himself a sailor, produced the finest biography of Jones to date, one so magisterial that even the Bicentennial of American Independence which spawned hundreds of books on the Revolution, and the publication of BRADFORD's comprehensive edition of Jones's papers, failed to produce a rival. The many merits of Morison include explanations of events, descriptions of people and places, and apt analogies drawn between 18th- and 20th-century figures and events. Though rejecting most of the lore that had encrusted Jones, especially his early life about which little is known, Morison does include "stories" concerning Jones which he considers "intrinsically probable," even if there exists no contemporary source for them. Morison provides somewhat vague bibliographical paragraphs for each chapter, rather than specific footnotes, and the result can be annoying and sometimes baffling to scholars, but most readers have little interest in sources and are simply entertained by the lively writing. Morison's portrait of Jones as a self-made man, a consummate sailor, an intrepid fighter, and an inspiring leader, is balanced by the recognition that he was also vain, short-tempered, and self-serving. More narrowly focused studies of Jones's ideas, battles, and relations with other individuals may supplant parts of Morison, but few writers, if any, will match Morison's evocation of Jones the mariner, his emotions, and his character.

JAMES C. BRADFORD

See also War of Independence: Military History

Judaism

Eisen, Arnold M., *The Chosen People in America: A Study in Jewish Religious Ideology*, Bloomington: Indiana University Press, 1983

Fishman, Sylvia Barack, *A Breath of Life: Feminism in the American Jewish Community*, New York: Free Press, 1993

Glazer, Nathan, *American Judaism*, Chicago: University of Chicago Press, 1957, 2nd edition, 1972, revised 1987

Gurock, Jeffrey S., *The Men and Women of Yeshiva: Higher Education, Orthodoxy, and American Judaism*, New York: Columbia University Press, 1988

Jick, Leon A., *The Americanization of the Synagogue, 1820–1870*, Hanover, NH: University Press of New England, 1976

Joselit, Jenna Weissman, *The Wonders of America: Reinventing Jewish Culture, 1880–1950*, New York: Hill and Wang, 1994

Sarna, Jonathan, *JPS: The Americanization of Jewish Culture, 1888–1988*, Philadelphia: Jewish Publication Society of America, 1989

Sklare, Marshall, *Conservative Judaism: An American Religious Movement*, Glencoe, IL: Free Press, 1955; revised, New York: Schocken, 1972

Wertheimer, Jack (editor), *The American Synagogue: A Sanctuary Transformed*, New York and Cambridge: Cambridge University Press, 1987

Wertheimer, Jack, *A People Divided: Judaism in Contemporary America*, New York: Basic Books, 1993

Judaism has not received the attention it deserves from historians as opposed to social scientists. Religious innovation characterizes American Judaism, yet only recently have historians started to research the changes that produced Jewish denominationalism. Judaism's unusual diversity in the United States reflects American religious organization as a voluntary activity of individual citizens. WERTHEIMER (1987), a collection of essays on the American synagogue, is perhaps the first book to draw the attention of modern Jewish historians to Judaism as a subject of study. In addition to three long interpretive essays on each of the major Jewish denominations – Reform, Conservative and Orthodox Judaism – the volume includes excellent original case studies on various aspects of synagogue development from suburbanization to mixed seating of men and women.

The theme of denominational differentiation and growth pervades GLAZER's influential account. His second edition sounds an optimistic note regarding possibilities for Judaism's survival under conditions of American religious freedom and pluralism, but his third edition returns to the original's more gloomy conclusions. Glazer sees steady decline in Jewish observance, with Orthodoxy becoming increasingly marginalized. None of the alternatives – including Reform and Conservative Judaism – represent more than accommodations to American norms and way stations for Jews assimilating into American society.

SKLARE's classic study of Conservative Judaism, written during the heyday of the movement's growth after World War II, presents a more optimistic assessment of religious readjustment. Although critical of Conservatism's lack of theological innovation to accompany its organizational creativity, Sklare accepts the movement's premise that it occupies the middle ground of American Judaism. Its appeal derives from its encouragement of the expression of Jewish ethnic identity under religious auspices. Conservative Jews may belong to a religious denomination, but they neither identify themselves nor behave according to Jewish religious norms.

JICK locates in the 19th century the process of accommodation and Americanization that Sklare sees as typifying 20th-century Jewish Americans, and credits Jewish immigrants from the German states with creating in Reform Judaism a genuine American Judaism. Although a Reform rabbi's son like Felix Adler left Judaism and its particularism to found the Ethical Culture Society, most American Jews accepted Reform's blend of rationalism and radically reduced rituals. Jick argues that Reform theology, such as its rejection of a personal messiah and Jewish return to the land of Israel, mattered mostly to rabbis. Reform's concept of a special Jewish mission as a light to the nations, however, appealed to rabbis and laymen.

The establishment of denominationalism and its divisive impact on Jewish Americans forms the central theme of the account of contemporary Judaism in WERTHEIMER (1993). In addition to Reform, Conservatism and Orthodoxy, he looks at Reconstructionism, an indigenous American form of Judaism based on the pragmatic philosophy and naturalist theology of Mordecai Kaplan, and Hasidism, pietist orthodox sects transplanted from Europe in the wake of Nazi persecution. Like Glazer, Wertheimer emphasizes the corrosive inroads of assimilation on all forms of Judaism. In his view, even feminism with its imaginative innovations exacerbates discord among American Jews. Understandably, FISHMAN approaches feminism more positively, emphasizing how it invigorates American Judaism today. She explores its influence on ritual innovation. For example, feminists popularized *bat mitzvah* for girls to correspond to *bar mitzvah* for thirteen-year-old boys (the ritual actually was pioneered by Reconstructionism which emphasizes the equality of women and men within the synagogue). She also credits feminists for developing baby-naming ceremonies to initiate infant daughters into the covenant, as circumcision does for eight-day-old sons. But she weighs the pros and cons of gender inclusive language in prayer and feminist theology.

Theological reflection is not among American Judaism's strong suits, especially in contrast to organization and ritual experimentation. Nevertheless, rabbis continue to struggle to balance Jewish perspectives with those beliefs held sacred by most Americans. The concept of the chosen people intensifies potential conflict because it is central to Judaism, but many Americans either reject chosenness as undemocratic or arrogate it to the American people. EISEN explores this difficult issue. Rabbis coped in various ways, from affirming Jews as God's chosen people to rejecting the idea as undemocratic – the latter iconoclastic view taken by Kaplan. For Eisen, some measure of dissent from American norms is critical for Judaism's persistence.

In the perspective of history, Judaism's flexibility appears less threatening. Perhaps because they take a long view of religious change, historical treatments of Judaism stress continuity. Certainly this characterizes the institutional studies by Gurock and Sarna. Both historians analyze remarkable and enduring American Jewish inventions: Yeshiva University and the Jewish Publication Society, respectively. The former yokes traditional modes of Jewish religious learning with secular academic study. The latter creates a non-profit organization to disseminate Jewish knowledge, comparable to the many religious publishing houses in America. GUROCK chronicles the changes involved and even the criticisms leveled at such a compromise as a Yeshiva University (what critics might call an oxymoron), but he never discounts its viability or the legitimacy of its synthesis. SARNA notes the tensions between elite cultural goals and popular demands bedeviling the Jewish Publication Society, yet he rarely criticizes the inevitable compromises. Both historians suggest that these institutions reflect the maturation of American Judaism, especially in relation to European religious culture.

A similar non-judgmental tone pervades JOSELIT's account of popular Judaism – the foods and objects, rituals and ceremonies that distinguished American Judaism during the first half of the 20th century. Following the life cycle provides the best way to understand Jewish religious culture, she argues, because Judaism acquires most salience at such crucial junctures as marriage, birth, coming-of-age, and death. At these important moments, American Jews want to acknowledge the relevance of Judaism to their lives. Joselit urges a close reading of Jewish material culture for insight into the playfulness and inventiveness of American Jews. For example, what counts in *bar mitzvah* is less the religious ceremony of reading from the sacred Torah scroll in the synagogue than the lavish birthday party celebration that follows. Joselit asks why *bar mitzvah* has become so important a ritual in American Judaism when it was relatively insignificant in Europe. Such questions frame the old issues of assimilation and accommodation in a new context.

DEBORAH DASH MOORE

See also Jewish Americans

Judiciary

Barrow, Deborah J. and Thomas G. Walker, *A Court Divided: The Fifth Circuit Court of Appeals and the Politics of Judicial Reform*, New Haven: Yale University Press, 1988

Bass, Jack, *Unlikely Heroes: The Dramatic Story of the Southern Judges of the Fifth Circuit Who Translated the Supreme Court's Brown Decision into a Revolution for Equality*, New York: Simon and Schuster, 1981

Carp, Robert A. and C.K. Rowland, *Policymaking and Politics in the Federal District Courts*, Knoxville: University of Tennessee Press, 1983

Carp, Robert A. and Ronald Stindham, *The Federal Courts*, Washington, DC: Congressional Quarterly Press, 1985

Frederick, David C., *Rugged Justice: The Ninth Circuit Court of Appeals and the American West, 1891–1941*, Berkeley: University of California Press, 1994

Howard, J. Woodford, Jr., *Courts of Appeals in the Federal Judicial System: A Study of the Second, Fifth, and District of Columbia Courts*, Princeton: Princeton University Press, 1981

Posner, Richard A., *The Federal Courts: Crisis and Reform*, Cambridge, MA: Harvard University Press, 1985

Schick, Marvin, *Learned Hand's Court*, Baltimore: Johns Hopkins University Press, 1970

Smith, Christopher E., *Courts and Public Policy*, Chicago: Nelson Hall, 1993

Yarbrough, Tinsley E., *Judge Frank Johnson and Human Rights in Alabama*, Tuscaloosa: University of Alabama Press, 1981

The Supreme Court rests at the apex of the federal judiciary. Despite its obvious importance, the Court is just one element of a vast national legal system that includes almost one hundred district courts, twelve circuit courts of appeals, and hundreds of judges. CARP and STINDHAM offer a comprehensive introduction to the federal judiciary. The book, written in jargon-free prose, provides an entry into a sprawling literature about the federal courts. It covers basic topics, including the organization and roles of the various courts, the selection of judges, how judges reach decisions, and the policy impact of those decisions. A reader might become overwhelmed by the endless facts, but will close the book knowing how the federal courts operate.

SMITH, like Carp and Stindham, contends that the public role of federal judges has expanded in the past half-century. He seeks to "synthesize scholars' arguments and findings about judicial policy-making." In less than 150 pages, Smith reviews a range of issues, such as school desegregation, education financing, and abortion, to show how judges have accumulated power. In the section on school desegregation, Smith highlights the limits of judicial policymaking and the interrelationship between judicial decision-making and politics, from national elections to grass-roots protest. Smith, a political scientist, avoids comment on the merits of the growth of judicial authority. POSNER, an appellate judge, believes his brethren should practice judicial restraint. He opposes over-reaching forays into public policy and believes federal courts have accumulated too much power. As a result court dockets have become overloaded. This insider's view of judicial administration proposes reforms to limit the role of federal judges.

Legal scholars have long sought coherent explanations of how judges reach their decisions. CARP and ROWLAND acknowledge that, in most cases, it is the strongest arguments backed by law and precedent that persuade judges. They seek, however, to expand that commonsense definition. They analyze thousands of decisions in the *Federal Supplement* to discover what effect the party affiliation of the judges as well as the presidents who appointed them, and other factors such as geography, had on the process. The results were inconclusive. They did find, however, that Democratic judges tended to be more liberal (especially if they were appointed by Democratic presidents) than their Republican counterparts and that there was an identifiable North-South split in rulings in certain cases.

HOWARD follows another method to reveal how judges reach their decisions. He made a detailed study of rulings in three of the twelve federal circuit courts of appeals. Unlike the generalizations of the Carp and Rowland study, Howard puts a human face on the courts. His conclusions are less abstract. His extensive interviews of sitting judges provide clear insights, such as his assertion of a period of socialization (marked by infrequent opinion-writing and tentativeness) at the start of most judicial tenures. Howard built upon the work of SCHICK, the first in-depth consideration of a single federal court. Schick examined the Second Court of Appeals (based in New York City) from 1941 to 1951. The dates coincided with the leadership of Learned Hand, the best-known judge never appointed to the Supreme Court. This collective biography of the court's judges, which relies heavily on one judge's personal papers, tears down the imposing black-robed barrier separating the public from the judiciary. It offers behind-the-scenes glimpses of the judges at work. Schick provides vivid examples of the philosophy of each judge and how they reached decisions.

Schick professes ambivalence about the legacy of the esteemed Judge Hand and the Second Circuit Court of Appeals. BASS, on the other hand, makes a bold claim for the significance of the Fifth Circuit Court of Appeals, serving Alabama, Georgia, Mississippi, Louisiana, Florida, and Texas, in the 1950s and 1960s. Bass calls the court the key to racial change in the South, declaring it the "institutional equivalent of the civil rights movement itself." The book begins with short biographies of four judges crucial to the court's reforms, and then shows the court's role at critical moments of the civil rights era in the South, from Montgomery through Birmingham. The journalistic style which the author adopts is both the strength and the weakness of a book that entertains but at times lacks sufficient context to explain events. However, Bass emphasizes a key point: lower federal courts often pushed ahead of the Supreme Court on issues of racial fairness.

Studies of single courts can provide insights into broader historical issues. FREDERICK seeks to show how the Ninth Circuit Court of Appeals influenced the development of the West. He examines the court's first fifty years, from 1891 (when congress created the appellate courts) to 1941. He touches on issues of railroad regulation and the use of public lands, among others. Nevertheless, the book focuses more on legal issues than economic or social history. It is most successful in exploring the court's institutional development, how its judges reached decisions, and the growth of federal judicial authority.

BARROW and WALKER use the Fifth Circuit Court to illuminate a significant aspect of judicial history. They tell the story of the attempt to split the Fifth into two circuits. The authors breathe drama into this seemingly dry story of judicial administration. Some reformers saw the split, first proposed in 1963 and approved by Congress in 1981, as a way to relieve burdensome caseloads; others imagined it as an effort to derail the court's history of social reform. The story proves Barrow and Walker's contention that the judicial and legislative branches constantly interact (what they inelegantly call "interinstitutional politics"). Judicial administration includes controversial battles over legal philosophy, personal antagonism, partisan opportunism, and interest group lobbying.

The federal district courts, numbering almost one hundred, contain fascinating stories as well. YARBROUGH provides a competent biography of Judge Frank M. Johnson, Jr., who served more than twenty years as district court judge in Alabama. Johnson ruled first on many epochal issues, such as the Montgomery bus boycott, political reapportionment, and school desegregation. Yarbrough details Johnson's role in fostering social and legal change in the South. The book highlights the issues facing Johnson's court more than it illuminates the judge's personality or judicial philosophy. The stories emphasize one man's impact on a broader social movement. In doing so, Yarbrough reiterates the importance of the federal judiciary and the law in American history.

CHRISTOPHER MACGREGOR SCRIBNER

See also Legal History entries; Supreme Court

K

Kelley, Florence 1859–1932

Social reformer and head of the National Consumers' League

Blumberg, Dorothy Rose, *Florence Kelley: The Making of a Social Pioneer*, New York: A.M. Kelley, 1966

Chambers, Clarke A., *Seedtime of Reform: American Social Service and Social Action, 1918–1933*, Minneapolis: University of Minnesota Press, 1963

Goldmark, Josephine Clara, *Impatient Crusader: Florence Kelley's Life Story*, Urbana: University of Illinois Press, 1953

Hart, Vivien, *Bound by Our Constitution: Women, Workers, and the Minimum Wage*, Princeton: Princeton University Press, 1994

Sklar, Kathryn Kish (editor), *The Autobiography of Florence Kelley: Notes of Sixty Years*, Chicago: Kerr, 1986

Sklar, Kathryn Kish, *Florence Kelley and the Nation's Work: The Rise of Women's Political Culture, 1830–1900*, New Haven: Yale University Press, 1995

Florence Kelley's career as a campaigner for social welfare reforms for women and children has elicited only a limited number of biographies and, until recently, there have been few other studies which focus on her work. This is, perhaps, more a reflection of the general invisibility of women in the historical record, than a reflection of Kelley's importance in the reform movements of the Progressive Era. Kelley did produce an autobiography, originally written as four articles which appeared in *The Survey* magazine in 1926–27. As SKLAR (1986) points out in her edition of the autobiography, these articles appeared in response to right-wing attacks on Kelley as the "chief conspirator for Moscow". They therefore played down Kelley's life-long participation in a variety of socialist organisations and did not always tell the full story. Sklar's introductory essay is a helpful commentary both on Kelley's life and the problems of using autobiography as a historical source.

GOLDMARK also glosses over Kelley's involvement with socialism – no doubt a reflection of the McCarthyite Red Scares which formed the context in which she was writing. This is a personal account of Kelley's life, written by one of her associates in the National Consumers League. Goldmark's admiration for Kelley emerges clearly in a very sympathetic biography which presents its subject in glowing terms. It does not probe very deeply into Kelley's motivations, and is very cautious in dealing with the more controversial aspects of Kelley's work. The failure to use Kelley's letters and papers very extensively makes for a somewhat lifeless biography, which gives the reader little sense of Kelley's compelling personality or her intellectual powers. Nor does it really give much sense of the context within which Kelley was operating.

BLUMBERG concentrates on Kelley's life up to her appointment as secretary of the National Consumers League. It only briefly sketches in her later life and her involvement in the social welfare reforms of the Progressive Era. It is based on painstaking research into sources which had not previously been available. This is a useful account of the intellectual, social and personal factors which shaped Kelley's thought and actions in the formative period of her career. The chapters on her involvement with the socialist party in New York and her connections with international socialism, are especially interesting. However, there are no adequate explanations for some of the transformations in Kelley's ideals and actions, and broader questions about Kelley's historical role and her significance in shaping social welfare reform are left unanswered. This is then, essentially a chronicle, informative but not very analytical.

There is some mention of Kelley in a number of more general works on progressive reform, or on women reformers, but only one or two of these have shed important new light on Kelley's career. CHAMBERS examines Kelley in the context of the continuity of reform between the Progressive Era and the New Deal. He argues that voluntary organisations such as the settlement houses and the National Consumers League kept progressivism alive during the conservative years of the 1920s. Reformers such as Kelley continued with the work they had always done, even if they did not triumph. The New Deal was heavily influenced by the moral purpose and methods of analysis of these reformers. Although Chambers's main focus is not upon Kelley's individual career, there are substantial sections on her. Kelley is placed in the context of the other female reformers of the period, and this helps to illustrate the obstacles which women reformers faced because of their gender. Although less eulogistic than some earlier work on Progressive social reformers, Chambers does tend to take them at their face value.

Until very recently there has been no substantial book-length study of Kelley since the 1960s. HART's work on the minimum wage broke new ground in examining Kelley's involvement in agitating for minimum wage legislation. Hart's main concern is with the evolution of minimum wage policies in the United States and Britain. However, since Kelley played a conspicuous role in developing protective legislation for women workers in the early 20th century, she naturally features prominently in this study. Hart examines the constraints within which Kelley and other female reformers worked, and the contradictions and inconsistencies which this produced. Basing her analysis on primary research and drawing upon recent scholarship in gender history, Hart places Kelley's career in a meaningful context.

The first of two volumes, SKLAR (1995) examines Kelley's career until she became secretary of the National Consumers League. Although covering much of the same ground as Blumberg, this is a much more analytical and nuanced work. Sklar explores both aspects of Kelley's personal life and the dynamics of social reform in the late 19th century. She examines the tradition of female activism among earlier generations of women, and the way in which this set the stage for women's central role in the 1890s. Against this background, Sklar explores Kelley's search for a meaningful place within American political culture. Thus, she uses Kelley's career to illustrate the way in which women were able to offer an effective response to the social problems engendered by mass immigration, industrialisation and urbanisation. Some of the more theoretical aspects of this work assume a fairly extensive background knowledge which may prove daunting to the general reader, but it is generally written with great clarity and persuasion. It illustrates well the way in which gender history can help to shed new light on certain aspects of mainstream history – in this case on Progressivism.

ELIZABETH J. CLAPP

See also Progressivism; Social Welfare/Social Security

Kennedy, John F. 1917–1963
35th President of the United States

Bernstein, Irving, *Promises Kept: John F. Kennedy's New Frontier*, New York and Oxford: Oxford University Press, 1991

Beschloss, Michael R., *The Crisis Years: Kennedy and Khrushchev, 1960–1963*, New York: Burlingame, and London: Faber, 1991

Giglio, James N., *The Presidency of John F. Kennedy*, Lawrence: University Press of Kansas, 1991

Hamilton, Nigel, *JFK: Reckless Youth*, New York: Random House, and London: Century, 1992

Parmet, Herbert S., *JFK: The Presidency of John F. Kennedy*, New York: Dial Press, 1983

Paterson, Thomas G. (editor), *Kennedy's Quest for Victory: American Foreign Policy, 1961–1963*, New York: Oxford University Press, 1989

Reeves, Thomas C., *A Question of Character: A Life of John F. Kennedy*, New York: Free Press, and London: Bloomsbury, 1991

Schlesinger, Arthur M., Jr., *A Thousand Days: John F. Kennedy in the White House*, Boston: Houghton Mifflin, and London: Deutsch, 1965

Sorensen, Theodore C., *Kennedy*, New York: Harper, and London: Hodder and Stoughton, 1965

Wills, Garry, *The Kennedy Imprisonment: A Meditation on Power*, Boston: Little Brown, 1982

John F. Kennedy's short life and brief presidency have generated a literature of vast dimensions. Most of the early works were panegyrics, influenced by the sense of loss and tragedy felt after his assassination in November 1963. The two most popular and substantial of these favorable accounts were SCHLESINGER and SORENSEN. As with later authors, they concentrated primarily on his presidential years. Both had been members of the Kennedy administration, Schlesinger as special assistant to the president, and Sorensen as special counsel. The overall impression conveyed in these works is of a man of immense talent who matured continuously. Specifically, Kennedy is credited for his promotion of high-minded civil rights reforms (such as his introduction of the 1963 civil rights bill), and for expertly defusing two of the most dangerous episodes in the Cold War – the 1961 Berlin crisis and the 1962 Cuban missile crisis. Kennedy comes across as a man blessed with a highly effective blend of idealism and pragmatism. Although Schlesinger and Sorensen succeeded in producing richly detailed, highly readable accounts, their interpretations were clearly less than dispassionate. In fact, they helped to create the "Camelot" mythology that caused many to regard Kennedy as a flawless hero.

Ordinarily, books of this kind would have been regarded as memoirs, primary source materials that were important but which did not constitute scholarly work. However, Schlesinger's background as a brilliant and prolific historian and the fact that Sorensen had crafted so many of Kennedy's famous speeches meant that their books became part of the scholarly literature on JFK.

The positive interpretation offered by Schlesinger, Sorensen, and others, was not effectively challenged until the 1970s. The disaster of American involvement in Vietnam, public revelations about Kennedy's sexual indiscretions, and a 1975 Senate investigation into CIA assassination attempts on foreign leaders (some of which JFK may have endorsed) produced a change in climate that encouraged a more disparaging view of Kennedy. Up until the present day, there has been a flood of works that, in seeking to demolish the gushingly positive Sorensen-Schlesinger model, are just as skewed in the opposite direction. Of these works, WILLS and REEVES have been particularly influential. In their studies, the gap between the image and reality of Kennedy as man and as leader is stressed. Kennedy is portrayed as a hawkish Cold Warrior, who helped create the dangerous international crises of the early 1960s, and deepened American involvement in Vietnam. He is also depicted as a lukewarm liberal, whose support for civil rights was excessively cautious. Kennedy's obsession with image and his manipulation of the press are stressed, as are the juicier aspects of his personal life, such as the infidelities and drug-taking. Reeves, in particular, pulls no punches, arguing that JFK was an individual who lacked any real sense of personal or political morality.

Fortunately, there are a couple of works which have sought to provide the sort of judicious, balanced treatment of JFK that has been conspicuously lacking, both in the earlier studies and in many of the later more critical works. Parmet was the first attempt to adopt a more evenhanded approach, one which Giglio has duplicated to good effect. PARMET is critical of Kennedy's leadership, noting his belligerence on many international issues and his caution on important domestic issues. Still, he credits JFK with several significant successes, including the test ban treaty which he signed with the Soviet Union in 1963, his American University speech in which he argued with such eloquence for a lessening of Cold War tensions, and the commitment that he finally made to civil rights. GIGLIO praises JFK for his handling of the crises in Berlin and Cuba, but assails his approach to the problem of Vietnam; he commends Kennedy's economic policies but is unimpressed by his legislative record generally. For its conciseness and balance, Giglio is perhaps the book worth consulting first, when embarking on a journey through the Kennedy literature.

A number of books on specific aspects of Kennedy's life and presidency have also been written. For his early years, the definitive study is HAMILTON. Based on immense research and written with great élan, this study examines JFK's life up until his election to the House of Representatives in 1946. The book sparked tremendous controversy, partly because of its unflattering portrayal of Kennedy's family, and especially his parental, background. What many critics have missed is the fact that Hamilton goes on to credit JFK with a growing maturity, stressing *inter alia* his intellectual evolution and his general ability to move beyond the rather narrow mind set that characterized the outlook of both his father and elder brother.

For foreign policy, the two best studies are Beschloss and Paterson. The essays collected in PATERSON's volume make it the more comprehensive of the two, as they cover a wide variety of topics – including for example Kennedy's policies towards Africa and the Middle East. BESCHLOSS, who focuses on JFK's relationship with Soviet leader Nikita Khrushchev, provides a more even-handed account than those offered by the sharply critical essays in the Paterson volume. Beschloss also presents material previously unavailable, such as the records of the discussions between Kennedy and Khrushchev at the June 1961 Vienna summit.

BERNSTEIN has emerged as the standard work on JFK's domestic policies. The accepted wisdom has been that, whatever the merits of his approach to international affairs, Kennedy's domestic programme was timid, cautious, rather conservative, and generally unsuccessful, especially when compared to the achievements of his successor, Lyndon Johnson. Bernstein provides detailed coverage of Kennedy's domestic policies in order to challenge that view. He points out that the majority of the bills which JFK sent to Congress were passed. He also argues that had Kennedy lived he would have managed to secure the passage of various key items of his legislative programme, including civil rights, that were still under debate at the time of his death.

MARK J. WHITE

Kennedy, John F.: Assassination of

Belin, David W., *Final Disclosure: The Full Truth about the Assassination of President Kennedy*, New York: Scribner, 1988

Clarke, James W., *American Assassins: The Darker Side of Politics*, Princeton: Princeton University Press, 1982, revised 1990

Davison, Jean, *Oswald's Game*, New York: Norton, 1983

Epstein, Edward J., *Inquest: The Warren Commission and the Establishment of Truth*, New York: Viking, and London: Hutchinson, 1966

Henggeler, Paul R., *In His Steps: Lyndon Johnson and the Kennedy Mystique*, Chicago: Dee, 1991

McMillan, Priscilla Johnson, *Marina and Lee*, New York: Harper, 1977

Mailer, Norman, *Oswald's Tale: An American Mystery*, New York: Random House, and London: Little Brown, 1995

Manchester, William, *The Death of a President: November 20–November 25, 1963*, New York: Harper, and Harmondsworth: Penguin, 1967

Posner, Gerald, *Case Closed: Lee Harvey Oswald and the Assassination of JFK*, New York: Random House, 1993; London: Warner, 1994

Sparrow, John, *After the Assassination: A Positive Appraisal of the Warren Report*, New York: Chilmark Press, 1967

US Congress, House, Select Committee on Assassinations, *Investigation of the Assassination of President John F. Kennedy: Final Report* (95th Congress, 2nd session), Washington, DC: Government Printing Office, 1979

Warren Commission, *Report of the President's Commission on the Assassination of President John F. Kennedy* (Warren Report), Washington, DC: Government Printing Office, 1964

Since 1964, more than 450 books have been published about the assassination of President Kennedy, making it one of the most written-about events in American history. Quantity, however, should not to be confused here with quality. There are but an armful of reliable books on the assassination and its aftermath, and the vast literature chiefly underscores H.L. Mencken's famous observation about "the virulence of the [American] national appetite for bogus revelation."

Any guide must begin with the *Report* of the President's Commission on the Assassination of President Kennedy, more commonly referred to as the *Warren Report* after then Chief Justice Earl WARREN, who presided over the investigation. The Commission mounted the largest criminal fact-finding inquiry ever seen in the United States, and the *Report* provides copious evidence of that effort. Despite three decades of unrelenting scrutiny, the accuracy of the Commission's essential finding remains unimpeached, and the *Report* stands as testimony to the Commission's fundamental integrity and skill.

However, its sheer mass of detail makes the Report difficult reading. It was mainly written by lawyers, and as one critic noted at the time, it had a telling defect stemming from lawyers' adversarial training: omnivorous inclusiveness. Although nearly everyone harbors an opinion about it, few people have actually read the 888-page *Report*. A more accessible account of what happened in Dallas on 22 November 1963 can be found in Belin or Posner. BELIN is the work of a lawyer who, as a member of the Commission's staff, sifted through the evidence collected by the FBI and other federal agencies. He presents a compelling account of the utterly damning case assembled against Lee Harvey Oswald. Belin also gives some insight into the process by which the staff derived its conclusions from the evidence, and the level of cooperation that the Commission received from other government agencies, most significantly the FBI and CIA. Despite its presidential mandate the Commission encountered difficulties from entrenched bureaucracies protecting their own reputations or Cold War secrets. A more recent exploration of the assassination in Dallas is POSNER. Hailed as the definitive work when it was published on the thirtieth anniversary of the assassination, Posner more correctly represents a thorough re-write of the Warren Report. It takes into account some ingenious methods of testing the evidence not available to the Commission. Perhaps its chief importance is that it persuasively rebuts three decades of every manner of allegation leveled by critics of the Warren Commission.

McMillan and Davison are the most reliable biographers of Oswald, a callow, ex-Marine who found solace in Marxist rhetoric. McMILLAN emphasizes the psychological and familial elements of Oswald's deeply-rooted alienation, while DAVISON stresses the peculiar brand of politics that may have motivated Oswald's violent act. MAILER's study uses recently available Soviet sources to describe in detail, in fact literally to eavesdrop on, Oswald's time in Russia. As a work that compares and contrasts Oswald with other assassins in American history, CLARKE stands out. He traces the history of assassination from the first attempt against Andrew Jackson in 1835. Though one may differ with the categories he develops (he classifies assassins into four psychological types), no work comes close to being as scholarly or thoughtful about the peculiarities of presidential assassinations in America. Especially illuminating is Clarke's discussion of how political biases have tended to brand all assailants as deranged or deluded individuals.

Widespread doubt about Oswald's culpability despite overwhelming evidence as to his guilt is itself a significant phenomenon associated with the Kennedy assassination. No guide would therefore be complete without some bow to the critics of the official version of events. EPSTEIN cannot withstand serious scrutiny and employs precisely the tactics which it accuses the Warren Commission of using. Still, it has long been regarded as the "respectable" critique, and the critique is widely believed to this day. SPARROW is perhaps the most effective rebuttal of Epstein, and other, even more disingenuous critics.

Although MANCHESTER's account was undertaken at the behest of the Kennedys, the family tried but failed to stop publication in 1967. Painstakingly researched, it stands out as the best narrative of four wrenching days in November, and the political passions which raged between Kennedy and Johnson partisans just below the surface, (and sometimes not even beneath it). HENGGELER is a scholarly and extended treatment of this same rivalry, the most immediate political consequence following the assassination. The rivalry cast a pall over Lyndon Johnson's presidency, and helped to unhinge the Democratic party in 1968.

In the mid-1970s unprecedented congressional investigations of the CIA and FBI revealed, among many other things, that these agencies had been less than totally forthcoming with the Warren Commission. The FBI withheld information that would have tended to damage the Bureau's public image, while the Agency denied the Commission access to highly classified information about its efforts to overthrow the Castro regime. Neither instance materially affected the Warren Commission's essential findings, but these revelations further eroded the public's already low regard for the Report. Analysis of this controversy is contained in the *Final Report* of the House Select Committee on Assassinations, which re-investigated the murder of President Kennedy after the Watergate scandal.

With the end of the Cold War the federal government began to release tens of thousands of secret documents generated as a result of its investigations into the Kennedy assassination. The present writer is using these new materials to write a narrative history of the Warren Commission, and a portrait of the government at work after a national trauma. It is hoped that this will fill one conspicuous gap in a vast but uneven literature.

MAX HOLLAND

Kennedy Family

Burner, David and Thomas R. West, *The Torch is Passed: The Kennedy Brothers and American Liberalism*, New York: Atheneum, 1984

Burns, James MacGregor, *Edward Kennedy and the Camelot Legacy*, New York: Norton, 1976

Davis, John H., *The Kennedys: Dynasty and Disaster, 1848–1983*, New York: McGraw Hill, 1984; London: Sidgwick and Jackson, 1985

Giglio, James N., *The Presidency of John F. Kennedy*, Lawrence: University Press of Kansas, 1991

Hamilton, Nigel, *JFK: Reckless Youth*, New York: Random House, and London: Century, 1992

Leamer, Laurence, *The Kennedy Women: Saga of an American Family*, New York: Villard, and London: Bantam, 1994

McGinniss, Joe, *The Last Brother*, New York: Simon and Schuster, 1993

Newfield, Jack, *Robert Kennedy: A Memoir*, New York: Dutton, 1969; London: Cape, 1970

Reeves, Thomas C., *A Question of Character: A Life of John F. Kennedy*, New York: Free Press, and London: Bloomsbury, 1991

Schlesinger, Arthur M., Jr., *Robert Kennedy and His Times*, Boston: Houghton Mifflin, 1978

Whalen, Richard J., *The Founding Father: The Story of Joseph P. Kennedy*, New York: New American Library, 1964; London: Hutchinson, 1965

The rise of the Kennedy family cannot be understood without an examination of the remarkable life of Joseph P. Kennedy, the patriarch of the dynasty. It was his ambition, talent, and money that built the foundations from which three of his four sons, John, Robert, and Edward, were able to launch their astonishingly successful and painfully tragic political careers.

The basic work on Joseph Kennedy is WHALEN. Published shortly after JFK's assassination, and reprinted since, this is a balanced but sobering biography. It describes the mechanics of how Joseph Kennedy acquired his fortune, and explains how he instilled a deep sense of competitiveness into his children. Whalen also makes clear that Joe Kennedy's involvement in JFK's election campaigns and political career in general was far greater than many had thought to be the case at the time of his election as president in 1960.

Another book which provides fascinating coverage not only of Joe Kennedy, but Rose as well, is HAMILTON. The focus of this 1992 work is JFK's early life and the start of his political career. In telling that story, though, the author obviously sheds light on the role played by his parents. One of the most striking features of Hamilton's book is its portrayal of Rose. Many observers had regarded Joseph Kennedy for some time as a ruthlessly ambitious, personally insufferable individual. Rose, however, was generally viewed as the model mother, who patiently tolerated her husband's infidelities and other shortcomings and guided her children in the right direction. In Hamilton's book, however, Rose comes across as an inadequate, distant parent.

John Kennedy has obviously been the subject of many studies. REEVES is an exciting, highly readable, although rather uncharitable, biography of JFK. Arguing that he lacked character, a prerequisite, Reeves says, for good leadership, the author goes on to stress the gap between the glowing and moral image which he conveyed to the American people and the dissolute private life that he led. JFK's womanizing, drug-taking, and other personal shortcomings receive extensive coverage. For his years as president, the most balanced, judicious treatment is provided by GIGLIO. This work praises Kennedy for some of his policies, such as his economic strategies and handling of the Berlin crisis, but gives him low marks for others, such as his involvement in Vietnam and his legislative record.

The two most popular books on Robert Kennedy, attorney general, senator for New York, candidate for the Democratic party's presidential nomination in 1968 before his assassination, are SCHLESINGER and NEWFIELD. Both authors knew Robert Kennedy personally, and their coverage of him is very favourable. They stress, in particular, the capacity which he revealed to change and mature through the experiences of his life. Narrowly conservative at the outset of his political career, he became by the time of his death a compelling voice for the underprivileged, while maintaining an ability to appeal to a broad cross-section of the American public. More than mere hagiography, that view of Robert Kennedy's life is probably an accurate, certainly defensible one. Of the two books, Schlesinger's is the more scholarly, being based on extensive research in Robert Kennedy's papers.

With a career in the United States Senate spanning over three decades and a legislative record that some regard as one of the most impressive in American political history, it is appropriate that Edward Kennedy, despite his well-publicized personal shortcomings and his failure to win the presidency, should be the subject of some substantial biographies. Burns and McGinniss offer two contrasting views. BURNS, published

as early as 1976, is not an authorized biography, but the senator did supply the author with research material for the book. Burns had written a glowing biography of John Kennedy before his bid for the presidency in 1960, and although this is more balanced – for example, it does talk openly about the seamier side of Edward Kennedy's personal life – a generally positive tone permeates the work. This study includes an analysis of how Edward Kennedy might perform if elected president.

McGINNISS, who focuses on Edward Kennedy's experiences in the 1960s, is more critical, though not unsympathetic. The author stresses how Edward Kennedy's career was hampered by the way in which he was expected to match up to the mythologized view of John and Robert Kennedy. This is certainly a lively, exciting read. Controversy erupted at the time of the book's publication, however, over whether the author borrowed excessively from the works of other writers, and over the accuracy of some of the dialogue that is presented.

There are a number of works that provide general coverage of the rise of the Kennedys as America's leading political dynasty. Vast in scope, DAVIS examines the Kennedy family from their roots in Ireland to their political exploits in the 1960s and beyond. In a richly detailed and entertainingly written book, Davis, despite being related to Jacqueline Kennedy, presents a critical view of the Kennedys. Such issues as the assassination attempts on Castro and the marital infidelities are not avoided.

BURNER and WEST is a sensible and illuminating work, which focuses on John, Robert, and Edward Kennedy. Through an examination of their political careers, the authors examine how the three brothers redefined the meaning of liberalism in America, explaining how Robert moved to the left of the sort of politics embraced by JFK, and how Edward maintained that commitment to liberal-left ideas.

A recent book that represents an important contribution is LEAMER. The glittering political careers of the Kennedy brothers have attracted most attention, but Leamer adds to the story by concentrating on the role played by the wives and sisters and mothers of consecutive generations of Kennedy men. Paying particular attention to Rose Kennedy, Leamer succeeds in producing a detailed, substantial, and well-researched account.

MARK J. WHITE

King, Martin Luther, Jr. 1929–1968
Civil rights leader, preacher and orator

Baldwin, Lewis V., *There is a Balm in Gilead: The Cultural Roots of Martin Luther King, Jr.*, Minneapolis: Fortress Press, 1991

Branch, Taylor, *Parting the Waters: America in the King Years, 1954–63*, New York: Simon and Schuster, and London: Macmillan, 1988

Fairclough, Adam, *To Redeem the Soul of America: The Southern Christian Leadership Conference and Martin Luther King, Jr.*, Athens: University of Georgia Press, 1987

Garrow, David J., *The FBI and Martin Luther King, Jr.: From "Solo" to Memphis*, New York: Norton, 1981

Garrow, David J., *Bearing the Cross: Martin Luther King, Jr., and the Southern Christian Leadership Conference*, New York: Morrow, 1986; London: Cape, 1988

Hanigan, James P., *Martin Luther King, Jr., and the Foundations of Nonviolence*, Lanham, MD: University Press of America, 1984

Lewis, David L., *King: A Critical Biography*, New York: Praeger, 1970

Lischer, Richard, *The Preacher King: Martin Luther King, Jr., and the Words That Moved America*, New York and Oxford: Oxford University Press, 1995

Miller, Keith D., *Voice of Deliverance: The Language of Martin Luther King, Jr., and Its Sources*, New York: Free Press, 1992

Oates, Stephen B., *Let the Trumpet Sound: The Life of Martin Luther King, Jr.*, New York: Harper, 1982

Smith, Kenneth L. and Ira G. Zepp, *Search for the Beloved Community: The Thinking of Martin Luther King, Jr.*, Valley Forge, PA: Judson Press, 1974

Despite the current emphasis of many historians on the "local people" who constituted the broad social foundation of the civil rights movement, the continuing scholarly interest in Martin Luther King, Jr. testifies to his enduring reputation as the most important leader and powerful symbol of that movement.

Of the early biographies that were based primarily upon newspaper accounts, LEWIS is by far the best. Written in ornate but compelling prose, Lewis presents a level-headed and generally reliable account of King's life which, while broadly sympathetic, brings a critical intelligence to bear upon its subject. For a work published so soon after King's death it stands up remarkably well. The next major biography, OATES, is a throwback to the hagiographic portraits that appeared during King's lifetime. Despite the fact that he utilized primary sources unavailable to Lewis, the author's determination to underline King's greatness, and his relative unfamiliarity with the history of the civil rights movement, resulted in a disappointing work that fails to illuminate either King's personality or the subtleties of his leadership. While it may serve the needs of a general reader who wants an accessible overview of King's life, it is too superficial and unreliable to be anything more than that.

GARROW (1986) is by far the best biography. Without peer as a researcher, Garrow not only mined virtually all the available written sources, but also undertook an extensive oral history project. In addition, GARROW (1981) drew upon voluminous files obtained through the Freedom of Information Act, to document the FBI's determined underhand effort to discredit King. This research also prompted Garrow to discuss, with a frankness that no previous biographer had displayed, the undeniable fact of King's sexual promiscuity. Although Garrow (1986) tries to eschew overt interpretation, the picture that emerges is that of a guilt-ridden, gloomy and frequently indecisive man who was more of a reluctant symbol than an assertive leader. Rather surprisingly, Garrow plays down the significance of King's contribution to the civil rights movement. While one can take issue with his overall assessment, Garrow is the most reliable authority on the details of King's life.

BRANCH is the first volume of a projected two-part history of King and his times. An expert story-teller, Branch skilfully shifts his narrative viewpoint in time and place so that the reader shares the perspectives of other protagonists – Bob Moses, John Kennedy, Robert Kennedy – and learns about the origins of, for example, Dexter Avenue Baptist Church and Morehouse College. Although the book is not as well-researched as Garrow, Branch is better-written – his vignettes are marvellously readable and he is able to sustain a sense of dramatic tension – and his portrait of King is subtler and more rounded. However, in his sprawling narrative Branch tends to get bogged down in irrelevant detail, is excessively verbose, and sometimes allows the exuberance of his prose to substitute for hard analysis.

FAIRCLOUGH presents an interpretation of King's leadership within the institutional context of the organization which he founded and led. Weighing the contributions of colleagues, staff workers and advisers, he concludes that King dominated the Southern Christian Leadership Conference (SCLC) through moral commitment, tactical brilliance and sheer force of personality, and that his leadership proved crucial to the success of the civil rights movement. Fairclough dwells on King's talents as a strategist of nonviolent direct action, as a mobilizer of ordinary men and women, and as a builder of biracial and bipartisan coalitions in the world of secular politics. He has been criticized, however, for neglecting the role of the black church and the importance of King's own religious convictions.

King's roots in the black church, and his grounding in the traditions of black preaching, are at last being explored in a systematic way. In a boldly original analysis, MILLER examines the actual textual sources of King's sermons and speeches and provides clear evidence of extensive "borrowing" from the published sermons of other preachers. Disputing King's own claim that he was strongly influenced by Gandhi, Hegel, Marx, Rauschenbusch, Niebuhr, and other philosophers and theologians, Miller asserts that his social ethics grew out of the liberation theology of the black church and the individual example of his own father. The power of King's words, Miller claims, stemmed from his mastery of a preaching tradition that relied heavily upon the repetition of familiar phrases and examples. While he rightly faults white historians for their ignorance of the black Christian tradition, Miller errs in the other direction, by dismissing the "Great White Thinkers" (his phrase) as marginal influences. An extreme statement of one trend in King scholarship, Miller verges on an uncritical celebration of the black church, and displays an anti-intellectualism that underestimates King's breadth of mind and intellectual eclecticism. LISCHER offers an informed alternative analysis of King's sermons, although his work lacks the originality and critical edge of Miller's.

Neither a full-dress biography nor an intellectual treatise, BALDWIN discusses King's personality and ethical outlook in the context of the black community from which he came. Like Miller, Baldwin argues that the black Christian tradition moulded King far more profoundly than did the white philosophers and theologians that he cited in his famous essay "Pilgrimage to Nonviolence." Baldwin also stresses the importance of King's family background and cultural roots, influences that made him a quintessentially *southern* black leader.

If many scholars have overemphasized King's significance as an original thinker – ignoring the role of ghostwriters and over-looking evidence of extensive plagiarism – it is nonetheless evident that the philosophers and theologians whom he studied at the seminary and university influenced him. The most careful and thoughtful analyses of King's intellectual development and social philosophy – specifically, of the ideas that he derived from *outside* the black religious tradition – are HANIGAN, and SMITH and ZEPP. Both discuss King's ideas about nonviolence and social justice with subtlety and insight, placing them within the intellectual framework that he acquired at Morehouse College, Crozer Theological Seminary, and Boston University. Clearly, King was a man who straddled cultures, and his ethic has a universal relevance.

ADAM FAIRCLOUGH

See also Civil Rights Movement

Kissinger, Henry A. 1923–

Presidential adviser and Secretary of State

Hersh, Seymour, *The Price of Power: Kissinger in the Nixon White House*, New York: Summit, 1983; as *Kissinger, the Price of Power*, London: Faber, 1983

Isaacson, Walter, *Kissinger: A Biography*, New York: Simon and Schuster, and London: Faber, 1992

Kalb, Marvin and Bernard Kalb, *Kissinger*, Boston: Little Brown, 1974

Kissinger, Henry A., *Nuclear Weapons and Foreign Policy*, New York: Harper, 1957

Kissinger, Henry A., *White House Years*, Boston: Little Brown, and London: Weidenfeld and Nicolson, 1979

Kissinger, Henry A., *Years of Upheaval*, Boston: Little Brown, and London: Weidenfeld and Nicolson, 1982

Kissinger, Henry A., *Diplomacy*, New York: Simon and Schuster, 1994

Schulzinger, Robert D., *Henry Kissinger: Doctor of Diplomacy*, New York: Columbia University Press, 1989

Valeriani, Richard, *Travels with Henry*, Boston: Houghton Mifflin, 1979

Anyone trying to understand Henry Kissinger has first to grapple with the individual revealed in his voluminous writings. Kissinger was a student of diplomacy for years before becoming a practitioner. Not surprisingly, many of the ideas that he developed during his researches colored his policies as national security adviser and secretary of state. Contemporary Kissinger-watchers often called him the "American Metternich," a simultaneous reference to his pragmatic – critics said cynical – style of diplomacy, and to the subject of his Harvard doctoral dissertation, later published as *A World Restored*. Kissinger later felt compelled to declare that Metternich was not his hero; perhaps not, but numerous passages in the book, complimentary to the Austrian statesman, bore a decided resemblance to the diplomat that Kissinger was evidently attempting to be.

While the book on Metternich aroused interest principally among historians, KISSINGER (1957) attracted the attention of civilian and military government officials – and the much larger group worried about the course of evolution of nuclear strategy. Written under the auspices of the Council on Foreign Relations, the book challenged the strategy of "massive retaliation" that passed for orthodoxy in the Eisenhower administration. Kissinger contended, with others at the time, that massive retaliation was unrealistic and unworkable, since no American president would really risk general nuclear war over peripheral interests, such as Korea and Indochina. Kissinger argued instead for a more flexible approach that tailored the degree of response to the severity of the aggression. The book became a surprise bestseller, conferring credibility and name recognition on its author. The ambitious Kissinger connected with Nelson Rockefeller and, eventually, with Richard Nixon. This latter link afforded Kissinger the entrée to power which he sought. He became candidate Nixon's chief foreign policy adviser and, following Nixon's 1968 election, his national security adviser. Chronic tension between Kissinger and the State Department during Nixon's first term caused the president to name Kissinger secretary of state in 1973. Kissinger survived Nixon's 1974 Watergate-triggered downfall and remained secretary of state under Gerald Ford.

KISSINGER (1979, 1982), a two-volume account of his years in office, ranks with the best of American diplomatic memoirs. Not as acerbic as Dean Acheson's nor as funny as George Ball's, Kissinger's ballast-bricks (2800 pages together) are more thorough than either. This is the world – almost literally, considering the scope of his travels, actions and ambitions – according to Kissinger. Objectively, he is hardly less defensive than his co-conspirator and fellow memoirist Nixon, but subjectively he sounds less so, partly because he is a much better writer. Kissinger gives his side of issues both mundane and controversial. There is more here than almost anyone would want to know about the negotiations that led to the 1973 Paris accords on Vietnam, and less about the doubts that even as tortoise-backed a realist as Kissinger must have felt at a settlement that had cost so much and was so transparently flimsy. Kissinger the policymaker comes through quite clearly; Kissinger the man is more elusive. The book is valuable for providing substantial extracts of documents generated contemporaneously with events, but also suspect on precisely the same ground. As Kissinger once told an interviewer, "What is written in diplomatic documents never bears much relation to reality." He added, "I could never have written my Metternich dissertation based on documents if I had known what I know now."

Biographers have had marginally better luck in finding the man beneath the memos. An early celebratory school succumbed to Kissinger's surprising but undeniable charm. VALERIANI tells the tale of how reporters queried the new secretary of state about his preferred form of address. Should it be Mr. Secretary, Dr. Secretary or what? In his thick German accent – which seemed to get only thicker with passing years – Kissinger replied that if reporters simply called him "Excellency," everything would be fine. KALB and KALB are slightly less smitten by the Kissinger charm, and somewhat more objective.

Kissinger never captured the loyalty of everybody on the press plane; no one who was involved in Vietnam, Watergate, detente and other lesser controversies could possibly have done so. HERSH despised Kissinger for his Indochina policies, and generalized his distaste into a very hostile account. If Hersh heads the prosecution; the Kalbs and Valeriani can be summoned for the defense.

Alternatively, the reader impatient with adversarial history can turn to the rather more balanced judgments delivered by Schulzinger and Isaacson. Diplomatic historian SCHULZINGER is the more impressive of the two in his assessment of the significance and context of Kissinger's geopolitical maneuvering. He respects Kissinger's achievements in injecting greater realism into American policy and recognizing the limits of American power, but deplores the unscrupulous and ruthless means to which he often resorted. Journalist ISAACSON excels anecdotally and is at his best in his portrayal of Kissinger as a shrewd and tough operator in the corridors of power. The reader who can spare time for only one readable, and not too demanding, book on Kissinger, should probably turn to Isaacson.

Yet the last (as of mid-1995) word on Kissinger might well be a couple of hundred thousand more of his own. KISSINGER (1994) is an apologia parading as a history of international relations since the Peace of Westphalia. The author treats three centuries of diplomacy as a primer in what national leaders can reasonably hope to accomplish and what is fatuousness and folly. Kissinger comes down hard on the side of limited aims, the balance of power and a clear-eyed pragmatism – which, amazingly enough, is the side he consistently adhered to during his own active participation. The book makes for lively, if lumpy, history – and also revealing, if elliptical, autobiography.

H.W. BRANDS

See also Foreign Policy since 1945 entries; Nixon

Knights of Labor

Fink, Leon, *Workingmen's Democracy: The Knights of Labor and American Politics*, Urbana: University of Illinois Press, 1983

Grob, Gerald N., *Workers and Utopia: A Study of Ideological Conflict in the American Labor Movement, 1865–1900*, Evanston, IL: Northwestern University Press, 1961

Kealey, Gregory S. and Bryan D. Palmer, *Dreaming of What Might Be: The Knights of Labor in Ontario, 1880–1900*, Cambridge and New York: Cambridge University Press, 1982

Laurie, Bruce, *Artisans into Workers: Labor in Nineteenth-Century America*, New York: Hill and Wang, 1989

Levine, Susan, *Labor's True Woman: Carpet Weavers, Industrialization, and Labor Reform in the Gilded Age*, Philadelphia: Temple University Press, 1984

Oestreicher, Richard Jules, *Solidarity and Fragmentation: Working People and Class Consciousness in Detroit, 1875–1900*, Urbana: University of Illinois Press, 1986

Rachleff, Peter J., *Black Labor in the South: Richmond, Virginia, 1865–1890*, Philadelphia: Temple University Press, 1984

Ware, Norman J., *The Labor Movement in the United States, 1860–1895: A Study in Democracy*, New York: Appleton, 1929

Although the Noble Order of the Knights of Labor was a powerful force on the industrial relations scene for only a few years in the mid-1880s, it has spawned a long and fruitful historical debate that is likely to continue for some time to come. Not only were the Knights the largest and most democratic labor organization in the 19th century, with a progressive record on the organization of African Americans, women, and the unskilled, but the competition between the reform-minded Knights and the apparently "pragmatic" American Federation of Labor offers labor historians a battleground for their debates on such seminal issues as American exceptionalism, the role of the state in labor affairs, and the nature of working-class culture.

GROB is a good starting-point for a journey into the literature of the Knights. It is an admirable example of the "Wisconsin School" of labor history that was initiated by John R. Commons in the Progressive Era. While Grob was not a student of Commons, he asks the same questions and reaches similar conclusions. He views the Knights of Labor and the American Federation of Labor as polar opposites that struggled for ideological control of the labor movement. The Knights represented the last gasp of the utopian traditions of the early 19th century which, he believes, were unsuited to economic realities, plagued by meddling middle-class cranks, and hamstrung by their attraction to third party activities. The American Federation of Labor, on the other hand, represented a "pure and simple" craft unionism that focused on bread and butter issues such as wages, hours and working conditions. The AFL's survival and the Knights' decline offer proof that the former was better suited to American conditions.

WARE is a classic labor history study that still deserves attention. It remains the best overall history of the Knights at the national level. Although the author was a socialist who rejected the notion that craft unionism was somehow inevitable, he accepts the "Wisconsin School" notion of a fundamental ideological cleavage between the Knights and the AFL. In his view, the Knights were originally a trade union movement reflecting the class consciousness of American workers. By 1880, however, middle-class meddlers interfered, and the Knights were transformed from a working-class economic organization into a middle-class reform society. Also in line with the "Wisconsin School" is his relentless focus on the institution rather than the lives of workers on and off the job.

FINK is a superb study of the Knights' political activities in five communities. As such it represents the dominant trend in labor historiography since the 1970s: community studies that strive toward a holistic portrayal of both organized and unorganized workers rather than national studies of institutions. While Fink identifies several stages of Knights' political action, he focuses on the various grass-roots insurgent movements that flourished between 1885 and 1887. In these years of intense labor unrest, often referred to as the Great Upheaval, local labor parties supported by the Knights made impressive showings across the nation. This promising development was cut short by a variety of factors, including the failure of the Knights' national leadership to endorse the campaigns and a ruthless employer offensive that destroyed local Knights' assemblies and undercut the power base of insurgent politics.

Numerous other local studies of the Knights which appeared in the 1980s serve to undermine the simplistic assertions of earlier scholars. Through painstaking research, OEST-REICHER reconstructs the lives of typical Knights on the shop floor and in the political arena. Because of the Knights' quick growth and diverse membership, he argues, the organization lacked cohesion and eventually collapsed due to internal factionalism exacerbated by the Great Upheaval. KEALEY and PALMER provide an admirable analysis of the political and cultural activities of the Knights' membership in Ontario. They point the way to an understanding of the Knights as a cultural as well as an economic movement. RACHLEFF looks at the Knights from the perspective of the black membership in Richmond. While he found much to applaud in the economic cooperation between white and black Knights, he concludes that there were few instances when the cultural activities of the organization were able to overcome the color line. LEVINE analyzes female textile workers in the North to uncover the source of the Knights' positive record on organizing women workers. The Knights accepted traditional notions of female piety and moral superiority, she argues, but they found these ideals compatible with their reform goals and thus actively recruited women members. Because of their domestic role as household consumers, "Lady Knights" proved key players in the numerous employer boycotts conducted by the Order. Levine is also the best source of information on the Knights in the 1870s.

The most useful brief introduction to the Knights is LAURIE. Although this is a survey of labor in the 19th century as a whole, one of its major concerns is the rise and fall of the Knights and the emergence of what the author dubs the "prudential unionism" of the American Federation of Labor. Laurie views the Knights as the last significant flowering of a labor reform tradition based on radical republicanism. The principal reason for its downfall lay not in ideological flaws or middle-class interference, but rather in ruthless resistance from industrialists and government. Repression destroyed the Knights and steered the American Federation of Labor, out of necessity, into a cautious position designed to ensure its survival in a hostile environment.

CRAIG PHELAN

See also American Federation of Labor; Labor Unions

Know Nothings

Anbinder, Tyler, *Nativism and Slavery: The Northern Know Nothings and the Politics of the 1850s*, New York: Oxford University Press, 1992

Baker, Jean H., *Ambivalent Americans: The Know Nothing Party in Maryland*, Baltimore: Johns Hopkins University Press, 1977

Billington, Ray Allen, *The Protestant Crusade, 1800–1860: A Study of the Origins of American Nativism*, New York: Macmillan, 1938

Carwardine, Richard J., *Evangelicals and Politics in Antebellum America*, New Haven: Yale University Press, 1993

Gienapp, William E., *The Origins of the Republican Party, 1852–1856*, New York: Oxford University Press, 1987

Holt, Michael F., *The Political Crisis of the 1850s*, New York: Wiley, 1978

Mulkern, John R., *The Know-Nothing Party in Massachusetts: The Rise and Fall of a People's Movement*, Boston: Northeastern University Press, 1990

Overdyke, W. Darrell, *The Know Nothing Party in the South*, Baton Rouge: Louisiana State University Press, 1950

For many years after the Civil War the American or Know Nothing party's meteoric rise and fall during the mid-1850s were subsumed by discussions of the developing sectional conflict between North and South. In the 1920s and 1930s, however, Professor Richard Purcell at Catholic University supervised a number of state studies which brought the party to the attention of professional historians. BILLINGTON follows the Purcell students in depicting the Know Nothing party as a vehicle for anti-Catholic bigotry in the United States and is predictably critical of this initially secret and shadowy organization. Although the work lacks balance, it rightly highlights the importance of the slavery question to the party's development. Less convincing is the assertion that the party's decline was inevitable.

HOLT contains a much more sophisticated and persuasive account of the Know Nothings. Drawing on his own research on Pittsburgh and the work of more mainstream ethnocultural historians like Ronald Formisano, he contends that nativism rather than arguments over slavery was to blame for the demise of the second party system in the first half of the 1850s. The Know Nothings, in his view, were not so much bigots as patriotic reformers who sought to capitalize on a profound grass-roots antipathy towards professional politicians and parties. By persuasively locating the Roman Catholic church as a major threat to republican institutions, the Know Nothings rapidly emerged as the main opposition to the Democrats. Holt follows Billington in suggesting that the Know Nothing party declined primarily because it failed to accomplish its objectives in office.

GIENAPP adheres to the Holt line on the significance of political nativism to the break-up of the established party system, but moves beyond this to examine in detail the realigning state elections of 1854 and 1855. His sophisticated regression analysis of state-level voting returns and exhaustive mining of contemporary political correspondence reveal the complexity and diversity of the fusion process between nativists and antislavery Republicans. Gienapp stresses the close correlation between support for temperance and the Know Nothings (especially in rural areas) and emphasizes the impact of sectional issues on the party's decline.

ANBINDER constitutes the fullest and most up-to-date study of the American party. Insisting that the sectional conflict played a fundamental role in the collapse of the second party system, he contends that northern Know Nothings owed their success as much to their opposition to the Kansas-Nebraska Act as to their anti-Catholic rhetoric and policies. Significantly, Anbinder also argues that economic factors were not critical to the rise of the party as had been claimed by Holt and others. He views intra-party factionalism over slavery as a chief cause of the party's demise.

CARWARDINE follows Holt and Gienapp in arguing that the Know Nothing appeal lay not primarily in unionism or economic nativism but in the party's manipulation of anti-Catholicism, and its call for social and political reforms to protect Protestant republicanism. He demonstrates that the party's mass membership evinced a significant evangelical orientation, with Methodists, Baptists, Presbyterians, and Congregationalists particularly evident in the nativist ranks. However, he also suggests that many evangelicals resisted the Know Nothings because they perceived the latter to be a threat to republican and Christian values. Secrecy, xenophobia, and encouragement of street violence were all associated with Americanism, and as such provided good reasons for many antebellum Protestants to oppose the order.

There are two good state studies of the Know Nothing party. The better of the two is MULKERN which, while it argues tendentiously that nativism was primarily a product of strains induced by modernization, contains a wealth of important information on the labyrinthine politics of antebellum Massachusetts, a state controlled by the Know Nothing party during the mid-1850s. Mulkern highlights the organization's reformist dynamic and the effective way in which free-soil politicians like Henry Wilson sectionalized the party from within. BAKER is less satisfactory, partly because of its tight thematic structure, but it remains the best study of the Know Nothing party in a border state where unionism was as significant a factor in the party's appeal as nativist bigotry. Efforts to analyze the social composition of Know Nothing lodges in Maryland are hampered by the fragmentary nature of the evidence.

OVERDYKE is still the only general account of southern political nativism. Although seriously dated and providing fewer insights than one might hope, it nonetheless highlights the extent to which southern Know Nothings were hampered by their opponents' claims that they were allies of northern abolitionists. It is, however, unconvincing on the class and partisan make-up of the American party in a region containing relatively few immigrants.

ROBERT COOK

See also Civil War: Approach to War 3; Nativism

Korean War, 1950–1953: Military and Diplomatic History

Cumings, Bruce, *The Origins of the Korean War*, 2 vols., Princeton: Princeton University Press, 1981–90

Foot, Rosemary, *The Wrong War: American Policy and the Dimensions of the Korean Conflict, 1950–1953*, Ithaca, NY: Cornell University Press, 1985

Hastings, Max, *The Korean War*, London: Joseph, and New York: Simon and Schuster, 1987

James, D.Clayton with Anne Sharp Wells, *Refighting the Last War*, New York: Free Press, 1993

Kaufman, Burton I., *The Korean War: Challenges in Crisis, Credibility, and Command*, Philadelphia: Temple University Press, 1986

Lowe, Peter, *The Origins of the Korean War*, London: Longman, 1986

MacDonald, C.A., *Korea: The War Before Vietnam*, London: Macmillan, 1986

Rees, David, *Korea: The Limited War*, London: Macmillan, and New York: St. Martin's Press, 1964

Whelan, Richard, *Drawing the Line: The Korean War, 1950–1953*, London: Faber, and Boston: Houghton Mifflin, 1990

All wars of reasonable proportions provoke vast literatures. When they involve the invocation of ideological imperatives, they also attract controversies. Korea was the first hot war of the Cold War, and as such it flared into life as a major topic throughout its three-year duration and for a few years afterwards. Its unresolved armistice seemed to produce a similar response in students of the conflict. By the early 1960s it came to be almost forgotten, as Vietnam emerged as the major war involving East-West tension. Not until the late 1970s was there a substantial renewal of interest in Korea – partly due to the availability of documents and partly due to the decline of interest in Vietnam.

The first academic books, written at a certain distance from the passions of the time, appeared periodically in the 1960s and 1970s. REES produced the first valuable survey of the war, paying attention to both combat operations and the domestic political debate in the United States. As its subtitle suggests, it seeks to place the conflict in the context of the development of American thinking about a limited war in the nuclear era. Though a reliable outline of contemporary knowledge of events, it does not offer an especially penetrating explanation of either the causes of the fighting or of the place of the war in East-West relations.

On the origins of the war the outstanding study is CUMINGS. His two volumes, running to nearly 1500 pages, are a tour de force of scholarship. He does not blame Soviet expansionism for the conflict, but instead emphasizes the domestic Korean factors: "It was more ... that the Americans and the Soviets arrayed themselves around existing Korean cleavages ... than that Koreans chose sides in American-Soviet conflicts." A short, readable summary can be found in LOWE, the result of considerable work in both American and British archives.

The voluminous official histories of the war provide exhaustive coverage of the conflict, including the air and naval war, as well as the land fighting, and also the strategic direction of the war, and the decision-making processes involved. However, the sheer weight of detail may be too much for all but the most determined and tireless readers.

Since the mid-1980s there has been a major increase in studies of the war. From the American perspective, one of the most useful is KAUFMAN. He explores the problems posed by United States involvement in what began as an internal struggle in Korea, and became part of a world-wide confrontation. He focuses on questions of international relations, geopolitics and grand strategy, rather than on the military operations, and he expresses reservations about the way in which the United States became drawn so deeply into a widening conflict.

MacDONALD has written a very readable account, based on considerable research in American, British and Canadian public and private archives. The first section, comprising about two-thirds of the book, addresses the impact of the war on the Americans and their allies as it affected high politics and strategy. The second part concerns military operations on the ground and in the air. MacDonald has a good feel for the essentials of tactics and strategy, but he is more concerned with the problem of conducting a limited war. Unlike most general studies, which are produced principally by Americans, he looks at the contribution of other nations, particularly the British. In his conclusion he stresses that Korea marked a new phase in the relationship between the United States and its major allies. He adds that the war helped shift American attention to the Far East, and to a recognition that China could no longer be ignored as a power factor. HASTINGS appeared at almost the same time and enjoyed much greater popularity, being published in paperback in 1988. The higher public profile of the author helped, as did his easy prose style, honed as a journalist. Good though it is in many respects, it nevertheless shows signs of haste, for example in a number of factual errors.

WHELAN is a clear, well-arranged account based on a wide range of secondary sources and selected printed American government sources. He makes the astute observation that Korea became neglected as a subject because it was wrongly perceived as a failure – "Americans tend to regard the Korean War as an embarrassment best forgotten, as 'the first war we lost.'" Perhaps this explains why there was a resurgence in interest in it after the undoubted failure in Vietnam. Americans were now willing to examine an Asian war that they could claim to have won.

FOOT has concentrated not upon a detailed history of the war, but rather on its impact on American thinking about possible conflict with China. She takes her title from the words of Omar Bradley, chairman of the Joint Chiefs of Staff, who wanted hostilities confined to Korea and not expanded into China: "the wrong war, at the wrong place, at the wrong time, and with the wrong enemy." She makes her point effectively in a clear and fluent study, grounded in extensive research in American private and government archives and the Public Record Office, London. Foot suggests that this "limited" war of most interpretations came close to a "wider and more dangerous Far Eastern conflict, in which the United States contemplated the use of atomic weapons against an Asian nation once again." The war remained limited in military terms but not in policy terms. She stresses the thinness of the dividing line between a limited and expanded conflict, and how that line was crossed in the spring of 1953.

JAMES and WELLS is in two parts. First they examine five key decision-makers – Truman and the military chiefs – giving a vivid portrait of them and of the circumstances in which they were operating. Second, they consider six major command decisions – from opting to intervene to the commitment, after the large-scale Chinese involvement, to keep the war a limited one. This is a hugely informative and perceptive study, replete with insights, the product of mature judgement. It is written in a trenchant, penetrating, and well-focused style. It is pointed out that, in contrast to World War II, Acheson and his lieutenants heavily influenced military policy, military strategy and even their operational implementation.

Though not designed as a narrative history of the conflict, it draws out the main progress of the war. It explains how this so-called limited war had two main phases. The first was war against North Korea alone, June–October 1950, which

tended to become, by that autumn, a refighting of World War II, with the American forces pursuing total war, decisive victory and unconditional surrender. In the second phase, with the entry of the communist Chinese, gradually there arose on both sides unspoken and unwritten agreements to place significant restraints on their own conduct of the war. The theme of the book is that the war began as a refighting of World War II, but soon changed into a limited conflict, as the strategic value of Korea was reassessed. These are nuances that are too often omitted in other studies; they help to make this the best single volume on the Korean War.

MICHAEL F. HOPKINS

See also Foreign Policy since 1945: Special Aspects 3; MacArthur

Korean War, 1950–1953: Political and Economic Impact

Caridi, Ronald J., *The Korean War and American Politics: The Republican Party as a Case Study*, Philadelphia: University of Pennsylvania Press, 1968

Donovan, Robert J., *Tumultuous Years: The Presidency of Harry S. Truman, 1949–1953*, New York: Norton, 1982

Hamby, Alonzo L., *Beyond the New Deal: Harry S. Truman and American Liberalism*, New York: Columbia University Press, 1973

Heller, Francis H. (editor), *The Korean War: A 25-Year Perspective*, Lawrence: Regents Press of Kansas, 1977

Marcus, Maeva, *Truman and the Steel Seizure Case: The Limits of Presidential Power*, New York: Columbia University Press, 1977

Mueller, John E., *War, Presidents, and Public Opinion*, New York: Wiley, 1973

Spanier, John W., *The Truman-MacArthur Controversy and the Korean War*, Cambridge, MA: Belknap Press of Harvard University Press, 1959

Westerfield, H. Bradford, *Foreign Policy and Party Politics: Pearl Harbor to Korea*, New Haven: Yale University Press, 1955

The effects of the Korean War on American politics, economy, and society were profound, but the literature specifically devoted to the subject is limited and somewhat dated. The only study focusing exclusively on the domestic impact of the Korean War on the United States is CARIDI, who examines only the narrow issue of partisan politics. He contends that the Republicans chose opposition to Democratic President Harry S. Truman's handling of the Korean conflict only to gain political advantage. Without presenting any consistent and viable foreign policy alternatives, the Republican party was able to exploit public discontent to seize control over Congress and the presidency in the 1952 elections. This study elaborates on WESTERFIELD, who examines politics throughout the decade of the 1940s. His conclusion asserts that, when an opposition party favors specific foreign policy alternatives, it risks damaging American interests in world affairs. Both works rely heavily on published materials, rather than research findings in manuscript collections, in their assessment of the behavior of top political leaders.

Caridi identifies political expediency as the motive behind the Republican party's enthusiastic support for General Douglas MacArthur's strategy to achieve a military victory in the Korean War. But according to SPANIER, it was the problem of waging limited war, rather than partisanship, which was at the root of this political dispute, and which made internal political divisions inevitable. While exploring the divisive impact of the Communist triumph in China on American politics, this carefully argued and balanced study probes how the frustrating stalemate in the Korean War raised questions for many Americans about the wisdom of the principle of civilian control over the military. In a broader study focusing on the post-World War II fate of liberal reform, HAMBY, like Spanier, applauds Truman's courage in protecting his presidential prerogatives. He advances the perceptive and persuasive argument that the decisions to save South Korea and later to invade North Korea were reflections of a re-fashioned liberalism that had emerged during Truman's presidency. While Spanier lists as sources mainly published government documents and magazine articles, Hamby is based on archival research.

Hamby demonstrates that the Korean War helped to discredit political liberalism among American voters. MUELLER provides an empirical explanation for this conservative revival, using public opinion poll data. He finds that opposition to the war in Korea grew steadily after the "rally-round-the-flag" effect disappeared, and continued fighting brought mounting casualties. Mueller concludes that the conflict in Korea inflicted much more damage on Truman's popularity as president than did the Vietnam War as an independent factor on President Lyndon Johnson. This fascinating study, utilizing the behavioral mode of political analysis, shows how public support for the Korean War declined in a pattern that closely resembled domestic reaction to the conflict in Vietnam. Though not nearly as vocal as Vietnam War dissenters, opponents of the Korean conflict came from the same sectors of society. Surprisingly, the most consistent support for both wars came from young and well-educated Americans. Mueller discusses frankly the limits on analysis of polling data, but offers conclusions that, while speculative, have great value.

It is unfortunate that there has been no study thus far which covers in detail the impact of the Korean War on the American economy. MARCUS provides a narrowly focused but useful substitute. This volume explores the reasons behind Truman's decision to seize the steel plants in April 1952. Like Spanier, Marcus stresses the problems of fighting a limited war as a major factor, but exposes other complexities. Tracing the events leading to the Supreme Court's unexpected decision to declare Truman's action unconstitutional, she praises the justices for reaffirming the limits of executive authority and strengthening the principle of separation of powers. Marcus combines exhaustive research in manuscript collections with cogent analysis to produce this authoritative study. While American soldiers were dying in Korea, Congress and the press were denouncing Truman as a dictator, the general public was worrying about inflation far more than steel production, and union members were hailing the president as a hero.

Marcus exposes how shallow was the domestic support for economic mobilization during the undeclared Korean "police action." American society in fact experienced little change as a result of the conflict in Korea. Unfortunately, only John E. Wiltz's impressive article in HELLER explores this subject directly and in detail. "The Korean War and American Society" is judicious and perceptive, while the rest of the volume, with a couple of exceptions, adds very little new to knowledge on the Korean War. Wiltz accurately describes the conflict as "not a particularly traumatic interlude" in the everyday affairs of most Americans. He argues, however, that the war educated the public about the need to set limits on the application of military power in the nuclear age. Desegregation of military units also had a significant impact on weakening racial barriers at home. Wiltz believes that the Korean War had a positive impact on the American economy, but provides no comprehensive or detailed analysis of this issue.

There is useful coverage of the Korean War's effects on American politics, economy, and society in various studies of the Truman and Eisenhower presidencies. One of the best is DONOVAN, although he follows Heller in overstating the positive domestic impact of the war in Korea. A veteran journalist, Donovan has the ability to convey material from archival and manuscript collections in colorful language that the non-specialist reader will find enjoyable and entertaining. This study describes how the Korean War diverted public attention away from domestic reform, enhanced the appeal of McCarthyism, and established troublesome economic patterns. While rich in interesting facts and anecdotes, this popular history offers an uncritical assessment of Truman. Because Donovan still accepts a Cold War conceptual framework, his analysis of the domestic impact of the conflict in Korea is now in many ways inadequate. More comprehensive studies exploring the effects of the Korean War on American politics, economy, and society remain to be written.

JAMES I. MATRAY

See also MacArthur; Truman

Ku Klux Klan

Alexander, Charles C., *The Ku Klux Klan in the Southwest*, Lexington: University of Kentucky Press, 1965

Chalmers, David M., *Hooded Americanism: The First Century of the Ku Klux Klan, 1865–1965*, New York: Doubleday, 1965; 3rd, revised edition, as *Hooded Americanism: The History of the Ku Klux Klan*, Durham, NC: Duke University Press, 1981

Goldberg, Robert A., *Hooded Empire: The Ku Klux Klan in Colorado*, Urbana: University of Illinois Press, 1981

Horn, Stanley F., *Invisible Empire: The Story of the Ku Klux Klan, 1866–1871*, Boston: Houghton Mifflin, 1939; 2nd edition, Cos Cob, CT: J.E. Edwards, 1969

Jackson, Kenneth T., *The Ku Klux Klan in the City, 1915–1930*, New York: Oxford University Press, 1967

Lay, Shawn (editor), *The Invisible Empire in the West: Toward a New Historical Appraisal of the Ku Klux Klan of the 1920s*, Urbana: University of Illinois Press, 1992

Lay, Shawn, *Hooded Knights on the Niagara: The Ku Klux Klan in Buffalo, New York*, New York: New York University Press, 1995

MacLean, Nancy, *Behind the Mask of Chivalry: The Making of the Second Ku Klux Klan*, New York and Oxford: Oxford University Press, 1994

Moore, Leonard J., *Citizen Klansmen: The Ku Klux Klan in Indiana, 1921–1928*, Chapel Hill: University of North Carolina Press, 1991

Trelease, Allen W., *White Terror: The Ku Klux Klan Conspiracy and Southern Reconstruction*, New York: Harper, 1971; London: Secker and Warburg, 1972

Wade, Wyn Craig, *The Fiery Cross: The Ku Klux Klan in America*, New York: Simon and Schuster, 1987

Founded in Tennessee shortly after the end of the Civil War, the original Ku Klux Klan eventually became one of the most powerful white-supremacist organizations in American history. Launching a campaign of terror against African Americans and white Republicans, the Klan spread to all the states of the former Confederacy before being suppressed by the federal government in the early 1870s. The story of this violent secret society is best told in TRELEASE, a well-researched and splendidly written volume that stresses the KKK's close links with the Democratic party in the South and the group's role in undermining Reconstruction; Trelease also emphasizes the decentralized nature of the original Klan, presenting a state-by-state account that demonstrates the local variation that characterized the organization. Although it is an older work influenced by the Dunning school of Reconstruction, HORN also provides valuable information concerning the first Klan, especially in regard to its secret rituals and nightriding activities. Brief but useful accounts of the Reconstruction Klan can additionally be found in the early sections of both Chalmers and Wade, but the first resort for both scholars and general readers should be Trelease.

First founded as a secret men's fraternity in Georgia in 1915, a second Ku Klux Klan rapidly evolved into a powerful political and social movement during the first half of the 1920s. Far larger than the original Klan – membership estimates vary from three to six million – the revived KKK stressed the themes of strict law enforcement, traditional morality, and Protestant solidarity in scoring political triumphs across the nation. CHALMERS provides the best general survey of the second Klan, utilizing a detailed state-and-community approach that focuses upon KKK-sponsored violence and political activity. Clearly more concerned with condemning the Klan than with understanding the complex motivations of the group's membership, the author frequently lapses into moralizing, but the sheer wealth of information presented in his book makes it an invaluable resource. A more recent but less successful survey, WADE, examines the Klan's alleged association with Protestant fundamentalism and the secret order's experiences in the state of Indiana. There is some useful material here, but Wade's shallow analysis and reliance on gross stereotypes severely mar the volume.

Because it was a huge grassroots organization that lacked strong central control, the Klan of the 1920s is most effectively assessed at the regional, state, and community level.

ALEXANDER, the best regional study to date, discusses the KKK in the southwestern states of Texas, Louisiana, Arkansas, and Oklahoma. Although heavily influenced by Theodor Adorno's psychosocial concept of "moral authoritarianism," Alexander notes that Klansmen were reacting to very real and legitimate problems of crime and social disorder; he also shows that the secret order was far more preoccupied with the transgressions of fellow whites than those of African Americans.

Surveying the second KKK in cities across the nation, JACKSON stresses the predominant role of urban residents in the Klan movement, both as leaders and as approximately half of the total membership. Presenting occupational-status distributions for KKK members in five cities, Jackson concludes that the organization found its greatest strength among lower-middle-class Americans who were alarmed by the social and economic advancement of African Americans and immigrants from southern and eastern Europe. Despite an uncritical commitment to the concept of status anxiety, the book lends strong support to the view that the large majority of Klansmen were rational citizens responding to real problems – albeit in an inappropriate and counterproductive manner.

Building upon the work of Alexander and Jackson, GOLDBERG presents a superb case study of the 1920s Klan in Colorado, focusing on the city of Denver and four other communities. Making use of rare membership data and other sources, the author demonstrates that Colorado Klansmen were drawn from a balanced cross section of the white Protestant population and for the most part were ordinary citizens motivated by a sincere desire to improve local society. He also notes that the nature of the Klan's activities varied from community to community, arguing that the organization cannot be accurately assessed outside of its local context.

Several other examinations of the Klan in western communities have arrived at conclusions very similar to those of Goldberg, and much of this work is brought together in LAY (1992). Composed of detailed essays on the KKK in Denver, Colorado; El Paso, Texas; Anaheim, California; Salt Lake City, Utah; and Eugene and La Grande, Oregon, this anthology emphasizes the mainstream nature of the second Klan and its role as a medium of corrective civic action. Similar themes are developed in MOORE, which looks at the huge Indiana Klan of this period, and LAY (1995), a detailed examination of the secret order in a northern industrial city; both of these studies utilize rare KKK membership lists.

A harsher assessment of the Klan is rendered in MacLEAN, who has applied feminist and Marxist theory to probe the appeal of the secret order in northern Georgia during the 1920s. Claiming that the Klan represented a form of "reactionary populism," the author asserts that the organization proved most attractive to middle-class men who felt threatened by economic recession, feminism, a new youth culture, and growing assertiveness among African Americans. This argument is undermined at crucial points by a shortage of documentation and MacLean's unsure use of statistics, but the book's treatment of Klan ideology is the best yet presented.

Since the late 1940s, a number of new Klan organizations have appeared in the United States, but none of these groups has constituted a mass movement. Chalmers and Wade examine the vehemently racist Association of Georgia Klans, U.S. Klans, United Klans of America, and White Knights of the Ku Klux Klan of Mississippi of the 1950s and 1960s, detailing the violent activities of these small and marginal groups; Wade additionally provides a solid survey of Klan activity in the 1970s and early 1980s. While these treatments are competent, it is clear that much work remains to be done on the various Klans of this era.

SHAWN LAY

L

Labor History: General

Baron, Ava (editor), *Work Engendered: Toward a New History of American Labor*, Ithaca, NY: Cornell University Press, 1991

Brody, David, *In Labor's Cause: Main Themes in the History of the American Worker*, New York: Oxford University Press, 1993

Commons, John R. and others, *History of the Labor Movement in the United States*, 4 vols., New York: Macmillan, 1918–35 (see especially volume 4)

Foner, Philip S., *History of the Labor Movement in the United States*, 8 vols., New York: International, 1947–88

Gutman, Herbert G., "Work, Culture, and Society in Industrializing America, 1815–1919," in his *Work, Culture, and Society in Industrializing America: Essays in American Working-Class and Social History*, New York: Knopf, 1976; Oxford: Blackwell, 1977

Laurie, Bruce, *Artisans into Workers: Labor in Nineteenth-Century America*, New York: Hill and Wang, 1989

Montgomery, David, "To Study the People: The American Working Class," in *Labor History*, 21, Fall 1980

Montgomery, David, *The Fall of the House of Labor: The Workplace, the State and American Labor Activism, 1865–1925*, Cambridge and New York: Cambridge University Press, 1987

Moody, J. Carroll and Alice Kessler-Harris (editors), *Perspectives on American Labor History: The Problems of Synthesis*, DeKalb: Northern Illinois University Press, 1989

Roediger, David R., *Towards the Abolition of Whiteness: Essays on Race, Politics and Working Class History*, London and New York: Verso, 1994

Wilentz, Sean, "Against Exceptionalism: Class Consciousness and the American Labor Movement," *International Labor and Working-Class History*, 26, Fall 1984

American labor history is generally agreed to have begun as a distinct field with John R. Commons of the University of Wisconsin. Commons was himself a historic figure of the early 20th century: he was a prolific writer on labor and social issues and a friend of many prominent contemporary trade union leaders. Of the sprawling, erratic *History of the Labor Movement*, compiled by COMMONS and noted students and collaborators including Selig Perlman and David Saposs, it is volume 4, covering the period 1890–1920, which best illustrates Commons's methodology and interpretative emphasis. Like all his work, it has the institutional focus that became a hallmark of his so-called "Wisconsin school" of labor history. He praises the American Federation of Labor's cautious craft unionism and voluntarist political strategy, seeing them as a pragmatic response to the failure of previous more radical strategies.

Commons's influence lived on in the "Wisconsin school" until the late 1960s, its main challenger the extraordinarily prolific communist historian Philip Foner. While highly critical of the AFL's ideological and institutional conservatism, Foner paradoxically shared the Wisconsin school's strongly institutional focus. In his multi-volume history, FONER concentrates in encyclopedic detail on the actions of unions, most of them conservative craft organisations. His contribution was to focus on struggle and class conflict, in contrast to the stress of contemporary Wisconsinites such as Philip Taft on the AFL's moderation – a contrast heightened by the publication of the early volumes during the McCarthy era, when such ideas were generally unacceptable and the Wisconsinites were firmly anticommunist.

In the late 1960s a new generation of so-called "New Labor Historians" emerged, part of a wider "New Social History" that emphasised the history of workers, women, African Americans and other marginalized members of society. Slightly ahead of the trend, with publications beginning in the early 1960s, GUTMAN went on to be the mentor of many of the new labor historians. His work focused especially on immigrant and African American workers, and above all concentrated on workers' culture. "Work, Culture and Society," first published in 1973, is a typical and highly influential piece. Emphasising the largely immigrant composition of the American working class by the turn of the 19th/20th century, Gutman theorises that each wave of immigration resulted in the working class constantly being "re-made," as each group of Old World peasants and artisans was proletarianized in industrial jobs. But they gave up old work habits and culture slowly, and fought back, even when ignored by established trade unions.

By 1980 American labor history seemed to have reached a crossroads, addressed by David Montgomery, the doyen of the field since Gutman's untimely death, in a highly influential essay. MONTGOMERY (1980) praises the new labor history's highlighting of the prolonged and patchy transition to industrial mass production – of which his own work on the struggle over "workers' control" of the shop floor is an example. But he urges a further fleshing out of this expanded vision of working-class history to create a synthesis encompassing the full range of working-class social experience and consciousness as well as production.

The challenge of writing a synthetic history was already being taken up by younger historians such as WILENTZ. In an important essay he examines the old and thorny question of explaining the differences between the mostly conservative United States and mostly socialist European labor movements. Wilentz denies that the American case is "exceptional": he points to the long record of militancy of American workers, and to the complexity of European working-class consciousness. American workers *have* been class conscious, he argues, even if not in stereotypical European social-democratic or Marxist ways.

A useful, well-written, brief synthesis of some of the new approaches to labor history, at least for the 19th century, may be found in LAURIE. It includes both a lucid historiographical introduction, and a valuable bibliographic essay. MONTGOMERY (1987) takes up his own challenge to put into practice a broader view of labor and working-class history, in a widely-acclaimed study of the late 19th and early 20th centuries. Packed with detailed examples drawn from many different situations, Montgomery's work discusses varying patterns of work and diverse strands of labor activism. He insists that the history of the period can and must be analyzed in terms of conflicting social classes, but stresses that there were many different views, not always in accord with one another, within the ranks of the working class.

The collection of papers edited by MOODY and KESSLER-HARRIS from the landmark 1984 conference on synthesis in American labor history captures much of the growing disagreement over the field's direction at that time. The collection is most notable for the unflinching post-mortem of the acrimonious and frustrating meeting, written by leading women's labor historian Kessler-Harris. One of the major causes of disagreement was the criticism by feminists and women's historians of the field's inattention to gender; the relative lack of serious attention to race was also a contentious issue. Kessler-Harris reiterates and elaborates this criticism here, and calls for a gendered analysis of class.

While the experience of women has since become one of the fastest-growing sub-fields in American labor history, the dispute over the significance of gender and race has continued. A collection of ROEDIGER's seminal essays on race and class includes his critique, "The Crisis in Labour History." He focuses on race, lamenting the continued failure of historians of working-class African Americans and other ethnic minorities to break into the labor history mainstream. He blames the mainstream's inability to integrate race with class in its analysis, and especially the lack of interest in slavery from labor historians. He calls not only for such integration, and for more work on race and gender, but for studies of working-class "whiteness," a construct which he sees as the nefarious counterpart to black working-class racial identity.

BARON's pathbreaking collection represents a major effort at analytical integration of gender and class. Challenging essays by leaders in the field of women's labor history are augmented by an introductory essay by Baron herself in which she decries the "ghettoization" of women's labor history. She calls for greater attention to gender, including consideration of *male* workers' gender.

However, the most recent collection of essays by BRODY, one of the most respected figures in the field, demonstrates the continuing importance of issues like collective bargaining and union politics. Brody, prominent since his pioneering 1960 study of 19th-century steelworkers, is still trying to advance the project of synthesis that he and others have been calling for since the late 1970s. These essays synthesise the enduring importance and ironies of older issues in labor history while inadequately addressing race or gender. But Brody's time-frame is sweeping and he offers many new insights. For instance, he asserts provocatively that post-World War II business unionism, with its concentration on legally-enforceable bargaining, or "workplace contractualism," emerged very early, from early 20th century work practices and power relations in the workplace.

ANDREW NEATHER

Labor History: Legal and Political Framework

Dubofsky, Melvyn, *The State and Labor in Modern America*, Chapel Hill: University of North Carolina Press, 1994

Forbath, William E., *Law and the Shaping of the American Labor Movement*, Cambridge, MA: Harvard University Press, 1991

Gross, James A., *The Making of the National Labor Relations Board, 1933–1937*, Albany: State University of New York Press, 1974

Gross, James A., *The Reshaping of the National Labor Relations Board, 1937–1947*, Albany: State University of New York Press, 1981

Orren, Karen, *Belated Feudalism: Labor, the Law, and Liberal Development in the United States*, New York: Cambridge University Press, 1991

Roediger, David R., and Philip S. Foner, *Our Own Time: A History of American Labor and the Working Day*, Westport, CT.: Greenwood Press, and London: Verso, 1989

Skocpol, Theda, *Protecting Soldiers and Mothers: The Political Origins of Social Policy in the United States*, Cambridge, MA: Belknap Press of Harvard University Press, 1992

Tomlins, Christopher L., *The State and the Unions: Labor Relations, Law and the Organized Labor Movement in America, 1880–1960*, Cambridge and New York: Cambridge University Press, 1985

Tomlins, Christopher L., *Law, Labor and Ideology in the Early American Republic*, Cambridge and New York: Cambridge University Press, 1993

Trattner, Walter I., *Crusade for the Children: The National Child Labor Committee and Child Labor Reform in America*, Chicago: Quadrangle, 1970

Vittoz, Stanley, *New Deal Labor Policy and the American Industrial Economy*, Chapel Hill: University of North Carolina Press, 1987

Yellowitz, Irwin, *Labor and the Progressive Movement in New York State, 1897–1916*, Ithaca, NY: Cornell University Press, 1965

Some of the works discussed here examine the development of state legislation on the subject of wages, hours and conditions of employment, while others focus upon the evolution of government policy relating to labor relations and the status of trade unions. Among studies of the first topic, YELLOWITZ examines the progress of labor legislation during the Progressive Era in New York State. Its focus is the troubled relationship between elite reformers, particularly through the medium of the American Association for Labor Legislation, and local trade union leaders, who were far less committed to the principle of "voluntarism" than the national leadership of the American Federation of Labor. Another illuminating monographic study is TRATTNER, which examines the campaign against child labor during the same period. The author demonstrates the difficulties attending regulation of child labor, which was inextricably linked to the problems of economic security for working-class families. Two later chapters take the story to the New Deal and beyond.

SKOCPOL is an immensely detailed analysis of social policy in the Progressive Era, which, among other things, examines the reasons why legislation to regulate the conditions of male employment was mostly unsuccessful, whereas many states passed laws covering the hours and wages of women workers. It offers perhaps the fullest and most considered recent analysis of labor legislation in this period. The author, a historical sociologist, adopts a state-centred approach which gives preference to explanations based on political institutions and structures rather than social forces.

ROEDIGER and FONER provide a detailed account of the movement for shorter hours since the early 19th century. They present a comprehensive survey of campaigns and legislation. The movement for shorter hours, the authors argue, was categorically different from struggles for higher wages, involving as it did workers' claims to full citizenship and control of their lives, and, in effect, it gave birth to the organized labor movement.

Whereas most scholars have seen the 19th-century American law of labor relations as embodying the ideals of laissez-faire individualism, ORREN argues that it was firmly based upon English common law principles and therefore essentially feudal in character. American workers enjoyed only a "relative liberty." In the workplace they owed their employers unconditional loyalty and obedience. Judges consistently applied common law principles, argues Orren, until the legislature took over the regulation of labor relations during the 1930s. This is a controversial but in many ways a convincing interpretation.

A separate body of work deals with the legal status of trade unions. Understanding of this subject has in recent years been greatly informed by the work of legal historians. TOMLINS (1993), like the author's earlier work, is strongly influenced by the Critical Legal Studies movement in legal history. Drawing similar conclusions to Orren regarding the unequal character of the master-servant relationship in the early Republic, Tomlins also demonstrates how the legal understandings of the day operated to cripple the growth of labor movements, principally through the articulation of the doctrine of criminal conspiracy. A similar contribution is made by FORBATH. On the basis of an examination of the development of labor law during the late 19th and early 20th centuries, the author argues that judicial condemnation of union boycotts and most forms of picketing, along with the growing resort to labor injunctions, not only curtailed the numerical strength of unions but forced them into a narrow legalistic frame of action, forsaking radical alternatives for less provocative options. Though overstated, this is a vigorous and challenging argument.

Although the first third of the book traces the development of legal doctrines relating to labor organizations from the late 18th century to the 1920s, the core of TOMLINS (1985) is an analysis of the impact of New Deal labor policy. Before the 1930s, it is noted, trade unions were seen as purely voluntary organisations with no power to compel their members or anybody else, a condition which greatly hampered their capacity to operate effectively. From the 1930s they were regarded as government-sanctioned bargaining agents. However, the privileges conferred by this status were offset by responsibilities which greatly constrained the unions' freedom of action. Though largely reflecting an AFL critique of New Deal labor policy, this is a stimulating and informative analysis.

GROSS (1974, 1981) are two recent studies of the development of labor law during the heroic age of the 1930s and 1940s. They focus narrowly on the history of the National Labor Relations Board (NLRB). The first volume is a painstaking and tightly-woven account of the work of the agency during the life of the National Industrial Recovery Act and the first two years of the National Labor Relations Act, while the second traces in similarly exhaustive detail the progression from the Supreme Court's ratification of the Wagner Act in 1937 to the passage of the Taft-Hartley Act ten years later. Although this is a narrow institutional study, so many of the forces influencing New Deal labor policy operated through or upon the NLRB that an account of the agency encapsulates much of the history of labor legislation and its enforcement during two crucial decades.

VITTOZ is one of a number of attempts to explain New Deal labor policies in "corporate liberal" terms. He argues that, in certain industries at least, business interests saw government-sponsored trade unions as a way of stabilising intolerably competitive conditions. Such a claim can be made much more strongly for the NRA (National Recovery Administration) than for the Wagner Act, which virtually all industrialists roundly condemned, and for highly competitive industries such as soft coal and textiles than for mass-production industries. This therefore is a provocative rather than a wholly convincing interpretation.

The best introduction to the subject is DUBOFSKY, an up-to-date synthesis of the history of government policy towards trade unions since the late 19th century. Like many recent writers on labor history, he believes that the state and the law have been of paramount importance in shaping the development of labor organizations in the United States. Though in some ways a rather lifeless account, descriptive rather than analytical in approach, it is thorough, well-researched and has an excellent bibliography.

ROBERT HARRISON

See also Legal History entries

Labor Unions

Brody, David, *In Labor's Cause: Main Themes on the History of the American Worker*, New York: Oxford University Press, 1993

Cobble, Dorothy Sue, *Dishing It Out: Waitresses and Their Unions in the Twentieth Century*, Urbana: University of Illinois Press, 1991

Commons, John R. and others, *History of the Labor Movement in the United States*, 4 vols., New York: Macmillan, 1918–35 (see especially volume 4)

Foner, Philip S., *History of the Labor Movement in the United States*, 8 vols., New York: International, 1947–88

Gerstle, Gary, *Working Class Americanism: The Politics of Labour in a Textile City, 1914–1960*, Cambridge and New York: Cambridge University Press, 1989

Laslett, John H. M., *Labor and the Left: A Study of Socialist and Radical Influences in the American Labor Movement, 1881–1924*, New York: Basic Books, 1970

Moody, Kim, *An Injury to All: The Decline of American Unionism*, London and New York: Verso, 1988

Perlman, Selig, *A Theory of the Labor Movement*, New York: Macmillan, 1928

Tomlins, Christopher L., *The State and the Unions: Labor Relations, Law and the Organized Labor Movement in America, 1880–1960*, Cambridge and New York: Cambridge University Press, 1985

Van Tine, Warren, *The Making of the Labor Bureaucrat: Union Leadership in the United States, 1870–1920*, Amherst: University of Massachusetts Press, 1973

John R. Commons, the father of labor history in the United States, began collecting trade union documents and writing the unions' history at the turn of the century, as the modern trade union movement first took shape. In his *History of the Labor Movement*, compiled together with noted collaborators including Selig Perlman and David Saposs, COMMONS covers the formative period (1890–1920) of America's most enduring trade union confederation, the American Federation of Labor (AFL). In outlining the AFL's evolution, Commons sees a fundamental difference in European and American working-class consciousness leading to different union structures and ideologies. Above all, Commons portrays American workers as having a much stronger craft- or job-based consciousness than class consciousness. This both resulted in and justified the AFL's cautious craft unionism and voluntaristic rejection of political action or state intervention in the labor market.

Written in the conservative atmosphere of the 1920s, with the AFL cowed by business, PERLMAN's classic study famously elaborates the idea of American "job consciousness," and the resulting absence of strong industrial unions and socialist political parties. Starting from a conviction that trade unionism is essentially pragmatic and pro-capitalist and that radicalism instead emanates from the middle class, Perlman uses a lengthy comparison of labor relations in the United States with those of Britain, Germany and Russia to prove the "exceptionalism" of the American case. His theory concludes that the AFL of the 1920s, like the "welfare capitalism" within which it operated, was "mature" and "stable."

Commons's and Perlman's influence lived on in the "Wisconsin school" of labor history until the 1960s, unchallenged by the contemporary focus in the discipline of industrial relations on corporatist and collective bargaining issues. In the atmosphere of McCarthyism, one of this orthodoxy's few challengers was the communist historian Philip Foner. The originality of FONER's work lay in his emphasis on struggle and class conflict, especially in the extended coverage which he gave to the anarcho-syndicalist Industrial Workers of the World. He rejected the emphasis of contemporary Wisconsinites like Philip Taft, unchanged since Perlman, on the maturity of AFL strategy. His encyclopedic – indeed dull – examination of mostly conservative craft unions is highly critical of their failure to spawn European-style socialist parties.

BRODY's pioneering work from 1960, however, introduced a new subtlety to trade union history, still visible in this collection of his most recent essays. While concentrating on trade union subjects dear to the Wisconsinites – collective bargaining, union leadership, and the role of the state – he offers long perspectives on their development, and a more positive view of state intervention. Particularly striking is his examination of what he calls "workplace contractualism," the legalistic collective bargaining approach of the post-World War II period. While usually criticized by leftists, Brody sees workplace contractualism as a legitimate expression of rank-and-file radicalism, and one emerging from decades before the Congress of Industrial Organizations (CIO)'s rightward turn of the late 1940s.

The late 1960s and early 1970s saw the emergence of the so-called "New Labor Historians," mostly leftists who generally paid more attention to radical influences in trade unions. LASLETT is a good example, concentrating on left influence in half a dozen unions. He presents the rise and fall of socialist influence in many late 19th/early 20th century unions as a function more of external pressures in American society than of any inherent conservatism in the structure of the unions.

Although now dated by its narrowly institutional focus, VAN TINE is a fascinating and detailed examination of the mechanics of early trade union formation, operation and leadership. From extensive union evidence he shows convincingly that the pressures of organizational growth and the increasingly complex superstructure of unions caused a professionalization and bureaucratization of their officialdom.

Since the 1970s, trade union history has expanded in major new directions. The industrial unionism of the CIO has attracted a growing number of community-based studies. GERSTLE is one of the finest of these, a detailed examination of the growth of the Independent Textile Union (ITU) in Woonsocket, Rhode Island. Gerstle shows how the ITU, unlike most AFL craft unions, was built from an ethnic working class, yet also drew on potent symbols of "working class Americanism." He concludes that their unprecedented degree of control over the shop floor at the height of their power in the 1940s represented the closest that American unions had yet come to a socialist strategy.

COBBLE is part of another area of massive growth in 1980s and 1990s trade union history: gender. Her study is unusual among women's histories in that it employs a fairly traditional institutional focus on a particular union over a considerable period – the waitresses, a division of the Hotel and Restaurant Employees (HERE). She concludes that HERE's female-only waitress locals were more effective than gender-mixed locals, a positive example of proto-feminist separatism. More importantly for the issue of craft versus industrial organisation, she concludes that their craft union consciousness did not impede radicalism or militancy.

TOMLINS illustrates another new direction: the law. He stresses the lack of recognition which plagued unions before the 1930s, and the judiciary's powerful influence in stunting the potential of early American unions. But his main focus, paradoxically, is a critique of the much more liberal National Labor Relations (or Wagner) Act of 1935. Tomlins sees Wagner as re-defining – and ultimately constraining – the unions' function. It ensured that business unionism in the post-World War II era would concentrate on collective bargaining gains in a stable atmosphere, abandoning the mass shop-floor militancy of the 1930s. In other words, the state granted unions legal recognition in exchange for their cooperation in an industrial pluralism aimed at maximising the accumulation of capital.

MOODY's view of postwar AFL-CIO business unionism is similarly pessimistic, although aimed at transforming the fortunes of today's labor movement. He sees the burgeoning, conservative union bureaucracies from the 1950s onwards as stifling rank-and-file militancy and internal democracy. Their principal gains were in collective bargaining, but even those have disappeared with capital's return to the offensive since the late 1970s. The only salvation for today's shrinking trade union movement, he argues, is an end to contract concessions, redoubled organizing, and improved internal democracy.

ANDREW NEATHER

See also American Federation of Labor; Congress of Industrial Organizations; Industrial Workers of the World; Strikes

La Follette, Robert M. 1855–1925
Reformer and progressive political leader

Barton, Albert O., *La Follette's Winning of Wisconsin (1894–1904)*, Madison: University of Wisconsin Press, 1992

Caine, Stanley P., *The Myth of a Progressive Reform: Railroad Regulation in Wisconsin, 1903–1910*, Madison: State Historical Society of Wisconsin, 1970

Greenbaum, Fred, *Robert Marion La Follette*, New York: Twayne, 1975

La Follette, Belle Case and Fola La Follette, *Robert M. La Follette, June 14, 1855–June 18, 1925*, 2 vols., New York: Macmillan, 1953

La Follette, Robert M., *Robert La Follette's Autobiography: A Personal Narrative of Political Experience*, Madison: University of Wisconsin Press, 1960

Maxwell, Robert S., *La Follette and the Rise of the Progressives in Wisconsin*, Madison: State Historical Society of Wisconsin, 1956

Thelen, David P., *The Early Life of Robert M. La Follette, 1855–1884*, Chicago: Loyola University Press, 1966

Thelen, David P., *The New Citizenship: Origins of Progressivism in Wisconsin, 1885–1900*, Columbia: University of Missouri Press, 1972

Thelen, David P., *Robert M. La Follette and the Insurgent Spirit*, Boston: Little Brown, 1976

Weisberger, Bernard A., *The La Follettes of Wisconsin: Love and Politics in Progressive America*, Madison: University of Wisconsin Press, 1994

From the 1880s through the 1920s, "Fighting Bob" La Follette was a major figure on the political scene. Over those four decades he evolved from regular Republican Congressman to nationally celebrated progressive governor and promoter of the "Wisconsin Idea", to leader of the Insurgent coalition in the United States Senate, then to the most influential opponent of American involvement in World War I and in the League of Nations, and finally to presidential candidate of the resurrected Progressive Party in 1924. An icon in his home state of Wisconsin, La Follette has attracted surprisingly little scholarly attention outside its borders.

The indispensable starting point is La FOLLETTE (1960). In his foreword to this 1960 edition, historian Allan Nevins contends that "for an understanding of Bossism, Reform, and Progressivism as they were known in the United States between 1890 and 1912, this book is the most illuminating as well as the most interesting work in existence". The *Autobiography* personifies the crusading moralism, faith in democracy, science and reason, and "the people versus the special interests" orientation that animated so much of Progressive Era reform. There can be even less doubt that it reveals the inner La Follette – courageous, sincere, dedicated, honest, righteous, vindictive, humourless, self-centred and arrogant – far better than any third-person analysis ever could.

A careful reading of the autobiography is a required introduction for anyone hoping to understand its author's role in the Progressive Era, but it must be counteracted immediately with a healthy dose of more objective and critical analyses. Before proceeding to that task, however, one should look for further insight into the La Follette aura, provided by La FOLLETTE (1953), the work of his wife Belle Case La Follette and their daughter Fola. Although almost as obviously biased as the *Autobiography*, the biography is far richer in detail, carries the story through to the end of La Follette's life, contains extensive references and features a bibliography that includes several manuscript collections, personal interviews, public documents, periodical and newspaper articles, and unpublished manuscripts. The last three-quarters of the book, completed by Fola after her mother's death in 1931, often attains a surprising degree of scholarly detachment. It also provides numerous glimpses into La Follette's private and family life, dimensions which are lacking entirely in the *Autobiography*.

More objective, but essentially laudatory, is BARTON, a contemporary account by a journalist. An astute and experienced analyst of Wisconsin politics, Barton supplies a wealth of insider detail on La Follette's struggle to gain the governorship, to win control of the Republican party, and to enact his legislative programme. Like the La Follettes themselves, Barton generally casts his subject in the role of champion of economic and political democracy in the fight against the entrenched forces of "machine" Republicans and "reactionary" Democrats. He painstakingly guides the reader through the maze of party caucuses and conventions, and through the machinations involved in the passage of La Follette's landmark legislative programme.

Most of the other books written about La Follette prior to the 1960s were equally positive and uncritical; none were penned by trained historians. The key figure in scholarly revisions of La Follette is David P. Thelen. THELEN (1966) emphasizes that the pre-Progressive era La Follette was "clearly a man on the make", who "never questioned his devotion to the party" and who had profound faith in the Republican legislative programme". Thelen pronounces La Follette "mainly a seismograph of the tremors which were moving political parties, schools, churches, local government, farm and labor organizations into increasingly progressive directions," and asserts that La Follette's later legislative agenda "was borrowed root and branch from many Wisconsin groups and individuals". His future greatness, the author concludes "was that he listened to the will of the people". THELEN (1972) carries his investigations up to La Follette's election as governor in the "harmony campaign" of 1900, and finds further evidence that La Follette was far more a remarkably adaptive politician than he was a progressive innovator. The strongest impetus for the impressive outpouring of reform legislation that made Wisconsin the nation's primary progressive model was provided by a variety of urban-based civic associations, professional organizations, social scientists, social gospel clergy, labor unions and agrarian groups. Only when these grassroots activists had generated an apparently irresistible groundswell of support for the progressive reform agenda did La Follette and his band of ambitious young followers embrace those issues, as the most productive path to the power and benefits of political office. THELEN (1976) presents La Follette as a prototype for the author's paradigmatic belief that progressive reform evolved from "insurgency" (grassroots, angry, largely unorganized campaigns by consumers, taxpayers and citizens against the power and privilege of concentrated wealth) into "modernization" (organized movements by self-conscious "pressure groups" to seek help from government). He sees La Follette as an ambitious politician bent on destroying corporate control of society and government, who gradually moved from insurgency to interest group politics in order to further his ultimate agenda. His most enduring attribute, according to Thelen, was "his special kind of courage" that enabled him, once convinced that he spoke for the majority, to defy entrenched corporate and political power. La Follette's career, Thelen concludes sadly, "had truly encompassed the rise and fall of insurgency".

GREENBAUM focuses more tightly and conventionally on La Follette himself. Acknowledging that it took La Follette twenty years in politics before he embraced his first true reform issue, Greenbaum nevertheless insists that "once he made his commitment his career was characterized by a consistency of purpose, and he emerged as the acknowledged leader of the national progressives". That consistency of purpose resided in an abiding faith in political, economic and social democracy, and in a corresponding aversion to corporate domination and special privilege, an analysis which he applied to both domestic and foreign affairs. Greenbaum candidly admits that La Follette was "enormously ambitious" and plagued with a "savage suspiciousness" which was frequently turned against friends and supporters. He also acknowledges that La Follette's career was "essentially marked by failure". Far more sceptical, at least of La Follette's role in statewide reform, is CAINE. The first scholar to explore seriously the perspective of La Follette's chief adversaries – the Stalwart Republicans – Caine also subscribes to the theory that government regulation of business eventually facilitated corporate takeover of the governing process. Like Thelen, Caine sees the real authors of railroad regulation as civic reformers and agrarian radicals, and La Follette as an opportunist who pushed the issue when it suited his political strategy and ignored it when courting business support in 1900. In Caine's view, La Follette "hitched a ride on a reform train which stretched far into the past, then made it look like he was the engineer". La Follette then allegedly compounded his duplicity by accepting a watered-down version of the railroad regulation bill and by appointing pro-industry people to the commission. Caine infers that the weaknesses displayed by La Follette on railroad regulation were generic to his whole programme, and that he was an ineffectual legislative leader. As his title suggests, MAXWELL is primarily concerned with the phenomenon of Wisconsin Progressive Era reform, but he acknowledges that the "personality of Robert M. La Follette cast a long shadow over the events and problems of the era". Like Thelen, Maxwell presents La Follette and his political organization as only one faction in a progressive reform coalition, one who arrived late and frequently subordinated issues to political expediency. Particularly insightful is his discussion of continuity and change in Wisconsin progressivism after La Follette left for the United States Senate in 1906, and of how and why La Follette became the personification of such a complex and variegated phenomenon.

The most recent attempt to provide a comprehensive interpretation of the elder La Follette, is WEISBERGER. This study is distinguished by its multi-generational focus and by its effort to weave together the La Follettes' public and family life into a conceptual whole. Weisberger's point of departure concurs with Greenbaum's observation that La Follette was a "devoted husband and father" who raised his children "to continue the progressive tradition". Although these two orientations occasionally come into conflict with one another, Weisberger asserts that, more frequently, "the line between their inner selves, their identities within the family, and their public lives seemed to be nearly non-existent". He asserts that La Follette deserves to be honoured, not for any particular programme or accomplishment, but for his courage and devotion to democracy.

JOHN D. BUENKER

See also Progressivism

Latin America and the United States

Bemis, Samuel Flagg, *The Latin American Policy of the United States: An Historical Interpretation*, New York: Harcourt Brace, 1943

Connell-Smith, Gordon, *The United States and Latin America: An Historical Analysis of Inter-American Relations*, London: Heinemann, and New York: Wiley, 1974

Dozer, Donald M., *Are We Good Neighbors? Three Decades of Inter-American Relations, 1930–1960*, Gainesville: Florida University Press, 1959

Kryzanek, Michael J., *US-Latin American Relations*, New York: Praeger, 1985, 2nd edition, 1990

Lowenthal, Abraham F., *Partners in Conflict: The United States and Latin America*, Baltimore: Johns Hopkins University Press, 1987; revised, 1990

Molineu, Harold, *US Policy Toward Latin America: From Regionalism to Globalism*, Boulder, CO: Westview Press, 1986

Niess, Frank, *A Hemisphere to Itself: A History of US-Latin American Relations*, London: Zed, 1990

Shurbutt, T. Ray (editor), *United States-Latin American Relations, 1800–1850*, Tuscaloosa: University of Alabama Press, 1991

Smith, Gaddis, *The Last Years of the Monroe Doctrine, 1945–1993*, New York: Hill and Wang, 1994

Smith, Joseph, *Illusions of Conflict: Anglo-American Diplomacy Toward Latin America, 1865–1896*, Pittsburgh: University of Pittsburgh Press, 1979

The classic historical account of relations between the United States and Latin America is BEMIS. Published in 1943 by the doyen of American diplomatic historians, this is a work of traditional diplomatic history which provides a scholarly overview of the Latin American policy of the United States from 1776 to 1942. Like the vast majority of writers on this subject, Bemis is primarily concerned with the attitudes and actions of the United States and, in emphasizing American goodwill and idealism, he expressed the mind-set of a confident generation, who saw their country's policy as motivated by the desire to promote not only hemispheric security but also freedom and democracy. The thesis was cogently argued and well-documented, but its overly sympathetic portrayal of United States intentions and deeds was never revised by the author to take account of events after World War II.

From the 1950s onwards, the growing disenchantment with United States policy towards Latin America stimulated the publication of several works which were critical of Bemis. A prominent example was the British historian, CONNELL-SMITH, whose survey of inter-American relations goes beyond Bemis's cut-off date of 1942, as far as 1973, and was therefore able to include some of the more controversial events in Latin America during those years, such as the 1954 Guatemala crisis and the rise to power of Fidel Castro in Cuba. Connell-Smith's theme is that the United States has historically sought to establish its hegemony over Latin America. By exposing the flaws and contradictions in American foreign policy, he concludes that the image of the United States as a benevolent neighbour was largely a myth.

Originally published in German in 1984, NIESS is even more critical of the United States. This concise and tightly-written study of just over 200 pages emphasizes the crucial importance of economic factors, especially the drive for overseas markets, in shaping the Latin American policy of the United States. The book is informative but highly polemical. The author's sympathies are clearly on the side of the Latin Americans whom he regards as the unfortunate victims of ruthless United States imperialism.

The policy of the United States towards Latin America is perceptively analyzed and dissected in two textbooks which have considerable value for historians and political scientists. Both works contain only brief historical introductions and concentrate most on developments since 1945. MOLINEU is particularly lucid and informative. The work is organised into sections with clear chapter headings and subheadings. The author identifies the pursuit of national power and security as the main motives of American policy. This has led, however, to direct intervention in the affairs of Latin American countries, which, in Molineu's view, has been counter-productive and mistaken. KRYZANEK is a straightforward text. Like Molineu, it is primarily concerned with relations during the period of the Cold War. A notable difference, however, is the close attention given to analyzing the making of United States foreign policy. He explains the role not only of the President and Congress but also of non-governmental participants such as business, the church and the media.

The establishment of relations between the United States and the new independent nations of Latin America at the beginning of the 19th century was once considered an attractive topic for diplomatic historians. But these works are now regarded as old-fashioned and out of date. A modern study is the collection of articles in SHURBUTT which provides several interesting case studies of American diplomatic relations with individual Latin American countries during the first half of the 19th century. The result is not a comprehensive history, but the book is particularly useful because it carries the story up to 1850, and is not limited to dealing only with the period of the Wars of Independence.

During the 19th century Britain was the leading rival of the United States in Latin America. The Anglo-American relationship from 1865 to the Venezuelan Boundary Dispute in 1895–96 is carefully examined in a monograph by Joseph SMITH, which acknowledges that Britain and the United States were economic competitors in Latin America, but concludes that perceived diplomatic rivalries were illusory.

Of the huge literature on specific periods of United States relations with Latin America during the 20th century, DOZER provides a valuable corrective to Bemis by highlighting the tensions inherent in the relationship during the 1930s and 1940s. In a thoughtful and provocative study, Dozer questions the official rhetoric and describes how the generous intentions of the Good Neighbor policy were replaced by the national security objectives arising from World War II and the ensuing Cold War.

Although the principal aim of Gaddis SMITH is to explain the demise of the Monroe Doctrine, in doing so he also provides a well-informed and readable survey of United States policy towards Latin America from 1945 to 1993. The author does not conceal his personal sympathies, and deplores what he describes as the duplicity and anti-democratic nature of this diplomacy, especially that pursued by the Reagan administration in Central

America. LOWENTHAL agrees that American policymakers and diplomats became too fixated by fear of communism and did not appreciate the scale of the economic and political changes that transformed Latin America during the 1960s and 1970s. This scholarly study offers many insights into the state of inter-American relations towards the close of the 20th century. Lowenthal convincingly argues that the United States is no longer so dominant in the western hemisphere, and should seek to pursue a Latin American policy based on co-operation rather than conflict.

JOSEPH SMITH

See also Cuba and the United States; Foreign Policy since 1945: Special Aspects 6; Mexico and the United States; Monroe Doctrine

League of Nations *see* Versailles, Treaty of, and League of Nations

Lee, Robert E. 1807–1870
Confederate general

Connelly, Thomas L., *The Marble Man: Robert E. Lee and His Image in American Society*, New York: Knopf, 1977

Dowdey, Clifford, *Lee: A Biography*, Boston: Little Brown, 1965; London: Gollancz, 1970

Fishwick, Marshall W., *Lee after the War*, New York: Dodd Mead, 1963

Flood, Charles B., *Lee: The Last Years*, Boston: Houghton Mifflin, 1981

Freeman, Douglas Southall, *R.E. Lee: A Biography*, 4 vols., New York: Scribner, 1934–35, abridged by Richard Harwell, 1 vol., 1961

Fuller, J.F.C., *Grant and Lee: A Study in Personality and Generalship*, London: Eyre and Spottiswoode, 1933; Bloomington: Indiana University Press, 1957

Jones, Archer and Thomas L. Connelly, *The Politics of Command: Factions and Ideas in Confederate Strategy*, Baton Rouge: Louisiana State University Press, 1973

Maurice, Frederick, *Robert E. Lee: The Soldier*, London: Heinemann, and Boston: Little Brown, 1925

Nolan, Alan T., *Lee Considered: General Robert E. Lee and Civil War History*, Chapel Hill: University of North Carolina Press, 1991

Thomas, Emory M., *Robert E. Lee: A Biography*, New York: Norton, 1995

Woodworth, Steven E., *Davis and Lee at War*, Lawrence: University Press of Kansas, 1995

Robert E. Lee's very success as a field commander of dazzling skill has itself proved an obstacle to an authoritative and convincing discussion of his military merits. Lee emerged from the Civil War as the symbol of all that was admirable about the Old South. He was the quintessential Virginia gentleman. According to the British military historian, Colonel G.F.R. Henderson, he was the greatest general who ever spoke the English language. The influence of British commentators in shaping Lee's reputation has been profound. Another example is MAURICE who began research before 1914 for his study of Lee which appeared more than a decade later. He believes that Lee's offensive dispositions before the Seven Days Battles (1862) and Chancellorsville (1863) were models for an offensive campaign. Equally, in defence, Lee's skill in manoeuvre and shrewd insight into the value of entrenchments were portents for the future, ignored by generals of 1914–16. Maurice's discussion is didactic, based on limited sources, but lucidly presented. He provides the essential, authoritative, conceptual structure for the civilian historians that followed him.

By far the most important of these is FREEMAN. Although he set out with the specific objective of not glorifying war, Freeman (at a time when the United States was consumed by one of its periodic bouts of disillusionment with war) certainly succeeds in demonstrating the nobility of Lee's character. His book is a magnificent achievement, and must be considered as among the front rank of biographies written in the English language. It is presented in a beautiful, flowing style worthy of Lee's own manoeuvres. The evidence is marshalled with a sharp eye, and a mastery of the *Official Records* of Lee's campaigns. But the book is by no means perfect. Lee is invariably acquitted of blame for errors, and because the evidence is always interpreted through Lee's eyes and what he knew at any given moment, he tends to appear in the most favourable light. The style now has a slightly anachronistic ring. Freeman's Lee is too perfect, and other writers have sought to cut him down to size.

This process was already under way before Freeman had completed his biography. FULLER, another British writer, found the Confederate model of generalship wanting, after the experience of World War I. He provides the conceptual case for the prosecution. He thought Lee a poor strategist and incompetent logistician, though a tactician of great, if uneven quality. He criticizes Lee's loose command system, which delegated the direction of battles to subordinates, once they started. Above all, he considers Lee parochial and obsessed with Virginia. Lee failed to grasp the importance of the war in the West.

There are modern writers, like DOWDEY, another Virginian, who develop Freeman's approach and reject Fuller's strictures as false or exaggerated. But though Dowdey was a popular writer of great ability, his approach was narrow and rather partisan. His biography is written in a graphic and attractive style, but lacks any scholarly apparatus. It does not directly contradict Fuller's criticisms, and gives an impression – like Freeman – of special pleading. Nonetheless, it stood until recently as the best biography since Freeman. Writing of Lee in the context of the postwar years of Reconstruction, FISHWICK (another Virginian), suggests that Lee's parochialism was a source of strength. His book has great charm and lightness of touch, but FLOOD is now to be preferred on Lee's last years. It is more considered, less committed to a Virginian standpoint, and has absorbed the insights of recent Reconstruction scholarship, which rejects Dowdey's prejudices as unhistorical.

The Virginian "Lee tradition" has exerted a tenacious hold over historians. Nonetheless, it would be mistaken to suggest that it has dominated the views of professionals. It has not. Lee has been the subject of a strongly critical literature over the last fifty years – much of it appearing in works that consider Lee indirectly, or in passing. He has not excited much interest among academics. Freeman and Dowdey (but not Fishwick) were journalists. The exception that proves the rule is CONNELLY. He is convinced of the strategic importance of the West and critical of Lee's neglect of it. He shows how Virginians, like Jubal A. Early, sought to protect themselves by elevating Lee. The first part of the book is more persuasive than the second. His judgments are often hasty and accusatory, and rely on innuendo rather than evidence. This is even more true of the second chapter of JONES and CONNELLY(written by Connelly), than of Connelly's own book. It is an interesting undertaking to check the quotations from Freeman and other historians which he uses, and compare them with the gloss that he puts on them. Connelly often shows himself to be as committed and polemical as those he criticizes, and no more convincing. Furthermore, he confuses "mythology" with historiography; they are by no means the same.

Similar criticisms can be made of NOLAN, which is essentially a series of rather superficial essays on aspects of Lee's career. He has strong opinions and advances them cogently. The audacity of his view, however, is in inverse proportion to its originality. He challenges the traditional view of Lee's unimpeachable integrity, but his case is far from proven. As for Lee's generalship, he considers Lee's offensive strategy disastrous, risky and self-defeating, because it wore down the Confederacy's manpower. Nolan has warmed up Fuller's views in his boiling pot and added the piquant sauce of post-Vietnam abhorrence of casualties not shared by the 19th century. Somehow the spirit of his subject eludes him. The "Gray Fox" has yet to be cornered by a biographer.

Two recent reappraisals bear witness to continuing fascination with Lee the commander and the man. WOODWORTH provides a judicious assessment of the crucial relationship between Lee and the Confederate president. He contrasts Lee's inclination to seize the initiative and take the offensive, with Davis's more cautious approach and preference for remaining on the defensive.

The most recent biography, and the most successful attempt to delineate the features of Lee's enigmatic personality, is THOMAS. He takes as his central theme the underlying frustrations that disfigured Lee's life, and his stoic response to them. Thomas detects a paradox in Lee's life between the control which he sought over his emotions and the freedom which he simultaneously struggled to gain from the many disappointments that he confronted. Although there is little that is new here about Lee's conduct during the Civil War, the figure that emerges is much more human, and less saintly, than that portrayed in earlier biographies.

BRIAN HOLDEN REID

See also Civil War: Campaigns 1

Legal History: General

Bodenhamer, David J. and James W. Ely, Jr. (editors), *Ambivalent Legacy: A Legal History of the South*, Jackson: University Press of Mississippi, 1984
Friedman, Lawrence M., *A History of American Law*, New York: Simon and Schuster, 2nd edition, 1985
Friedman, Lawrence M., *Crime and Punishment in American History*, New York: Basic Books, 1993
Hall, Kermit L., *The Magic Mirror: Law in American History*, New York: Oxford University Press, 1989
Hoffer, Peter C., *Law and People in Colonial America*, Baltimore: Johns Hopkins University Press, 1992
Horwitz, Morton J., *The Transformation of American Law, 1780–1860*, Cambridge, MA: Harvard University Press, 1977
Horwitz, Morton J., *The Transformation of American Law, 1870–1960: The Crisis of Legal Orthodoxy*, New York: Oxford University Press, 1992
Hurst, James Willard, *The Growth of American Law: The Law Makers*, Boston: Little Brown, 1950
Hurst, James Willard, *Law and the Conditions of Freedom in the Nineteenth-Century United States*, Madison: University of Wisconsin Press, 1956
Hyman, Harold M. and William M. Wiecek, *Equal Justice under Law: Constitutional Development, 1835–1875*, New York: Harper, 1982
Nelson, William E., *Americanization of the Common Law: The Impact of Legal Change on Massachussetts Society, 1760–1830*, Cambridge, MA: Harvard University Press, 1975
Salmon, Marylynn, *Women and the Law of Property in Early America*, Chapel Hill: University of North Carolina Press, 1986

Any investigation of the history of American law must begin with James Willard Hurst. The founding father of modern legal history, Hurst offered in the 1950s two broad propositions for legal historians. First, he suggested that social, cultural and economic forces have shaped, as much as they have been shaped by, the development of American law; prior to this, historians had concentrated almost exclusively on the development of abstract legal reasoning and analysis, with almost no attention given to larger socioeconomic contexts. Second, Hurst formulated a model for understanding 19th-century American law as having been designed to provide a legal space for economic entrepreneurship, or what he termed capitalism's "release of energy." In this sense, the law played an active role in defining both the shape of economic developments and the parameters of Americans' response to those developments.

Of his many books, HURST (1956) is the most succinct and eloquent expression of his viewpoint. An earlier book, HURST (1950) is longer and more eclectic, touching upon a variety of legal issues in the 19th and early 20th centuries. Both are useful introductions to Hurst's approach to legal history, an approach which has exercised a profound influence on all subsequent scholarship.

HALL built on the insights offered by Hurst's first proposition to produce an effective study of the interaction between society and the law. He is more concerned with the social underpinnings of the law and the development of an American legal culture, rather than with statutes, court opinions, and other formal legal trappings. Hall argued that the law is in effect a "mirror" which both reflects and refracts the everyday concerns of American people. Particularly strong in its analysis of private law doctrines in the 20th century, this is a comprehensive narrative of American law which also includes a useful bibliographic essay.

The heightened awareness of the interaction between society and the law has predictably spurred the interest of legal historians in gender and race, although these areas remain relatively underdeveloped. Two studies are particularly noteworthy in this regard. BODENHAMER and ELY is an excellent collection of essays which address a variety of legal issues, particularly the interaction of southern law with race and slavery. SALMON charts the development of women's legal status and property rights from the colonial era through the early 19th century.

Morton Horwitz and William Nelson expanded upon Hurst's second proposition by focusing on the law's relationship to the profound economic changes wrought by the market and industrial revolutions. HORWITZ (1977) examined the changing function of the law in the American economy from the Revolution through the antebellum era, stressing the importance of the courts and legal doctrines in distributing both the costs and the burdens of a rapidly growing market economy. Horwitz stressed the instrumental purposes for which the law was utilized by capitalist entrepreneurs to further their economic interests, often at the expense of the American laboring classes. HORWITZ (1992) extends these themes into the modern era, but suggests that the law's instrumentalist complicity with capitalism changed during the early 20th century, as many jurists and legal thinkers came to understand the social costs of industrial development and demanded that legal institutions police as well as facilitate capitalist growth. Horwitz's scholarship is intellectually sophisticated and sometimes difficult to follow; nevertheless, it is highly influential (and controversial), and deserves careful scrutiny by serious students of American legal history.

From a standpoint somewhat similar to Horwitz, NELSON argues that the law played a crucial role in the profound social and economic transformations which took place in Massachusetts after the Revolution. Before the war, the law was designed to reinforce patterns of deference and class hierarchy, and therefore discouraged economic mobility or capitalistic entrepreneurship. In the last decades of the 18th century, however, Americans who embraced the new Market Revolution used the law to encourage a greater degree of social mobility and economic flexibility. Although concerned with a relatively narrow time and subject, Nelson's study is both readable and highly significant, and has wide implications for our understanding of early American legal thought. Those seeking a broader survey of the legal developments of the colonial period will find HOFFER very useful, and his bibliography offers a helpful guide to further study.

Some constitutional historians have utilized the insights offered by Nelson, Horwitz and other Hurstian scholars, and HYMAN and WIECEK offer perhaps the best example. While primarily concerned with the evolution of constitutional issues such as federalism and civil rights in the era of the Civil War and Reconstruction, they do not neglect the courts or the legal profession, and their effect on the course of American constitutionalism. Hyman and Wiecek are particularly adept at analyzing the legal and jurisprudential background of the Reconstruction amendments, and they tie these events to the larger social and economic milieu of the 19th century.

The work of the last four decades, which has re-shaped our understanding of legal history, is ably synthesized in FRIEDMAN (1985) which is so far the only complete, modern, one-volume study of the history of American law. It is an impressive book, although in the first edition Friedman slighted 20th-century legal developments. The second edition, published in 1985, redressed the balance to some extent (while still giving precedence to 19th-century matters). FRIEDMAN (1993) is likewise the only modern history of the development of American criminal law. This is another thorough scholarly treatment of a complex subject, and once again Friedman displays a rare skill for summarizing enormous amounts of primary and secondary source materials in a form which is both comprehensive and comprehensible.

BRIAN DIRCK

See also Constitutional History entries

Legal History: Special Aspects

Bergstrom, Randolph E., *Courting Danger: Injury and Law in New York City, 1870–1910*, Ithaca, NY: Cornell University Press, 1992

Dubofsky, Melvyn, *The State and Labor in Modern America*, Chapel Hill: University of North Carolina Press, 1994

Forbath, William E., *Law and the Shaping of the American Labor Movement*, Cambridge, MA: Harvard University Press, 1991

Freyer, Tony Allan, *Forums of Order: The Federal Courts and Business in American History*, Greenwich, CT: Jai Press, 1979

Freyer, Tony Allan, *Producers Versus Capitalists: Constitutional Conflict in Antebellum America*, Charlottesville: University Press of Virginia, 1994

Glendon, Mary Ann, *The Transformation of Family Law: State, Law and Family in the United States and Western Europe*, Chicago: University of Chicago Press, 1989

Grossberg, Michael, *Governing the Hearth: Law and the Family in Nineteenth-Century America*, Chapel Hill: University of North Carolina Press, 1985

Hoff, Joan, *Law, Gender, and Injustice: A Legal History of US Women*, New York: New York University Press, 1991

Horwitz, Morton J., *The Transformation of American Law, 1780–1860*, Cambridge, MA: Harvard University Press, 1977

Hurst, James Willard, *Law and the Conditions of Freedom in the Nineteenth-Century United States*, Madison: University of Wisconsin Press, 1956

Hurst, James Willard, *Law and Markets in United States History: Different Modes of Bargaining among Interests*, Madison: University of Wisconsin Press, 1982

Riley, Glenda, *Divorce: An American Tradition*, New York: Oxford University Press, 1991

Rosenberg, Norman, *Protecting the Best Men: An Interpretive History of the Law of Libel*, Chapel Hill: University of North Carolina Press, 1986

Salmon, Marylynn, *Women and the Law of Property in Early America*, Chapel Hill: University of North Carolina Press, 1986

Steinfeld, Robert J., *The Invention of Free Labor: The Employment Relation in English and American Law and Culture, 1350–1870*, Chapel Hill: University of North Carolina Press, 1991

Teeven, Kevin M., *A History of the Anglo-American Common Law of Contract*, Westport, CT: Greenwood Press, 1990

Tomlins, Christopher L., *Law, Labor and Ideology in the Early American Republic*, Cambridge and New York: Cambridge University Press, 1993

White, G. Edward, *Tort Law in America: An Intellectual History*, New York: Oxford University Press, 1980

Legal historians have attended closely in recent decades to the interaction between law and other social institutions. The relationship between law and economic development has received the most attention. In seminal works, HURST (1956, 1982) discusses how Americans shaped law so as to develop and allocate resources. In the 19th century, he writes, they framed law in a way that encouraged "the release of [entrepreneurial] energy" – making resources available to developers as widely as possible, eliminating monopolies and legal rules that inhibited development, allowing individuals to frame contracts free of most restrictions and supervision. In the 20th century, public policy demanded regulation and limitations, balanced by a continued recognition that individual initiative was the most effective engine of economic development. HORWITZ argues that judges and lawyers consciously reshaped the law to serve entrepreneurial interests. FREYER (1994) discusses how antebellum constitutional issues reflected conflict between small producers and larger corporate capitalism, while in an earlier book, FREYER (1979), he explains how the federal court system promoted the development of the modern commercial economy.

The history of contract law is closely linked to the broader question of the relationship between law and the economy. The early chapters of TEEVEN are rather technical, but the discussion in later chapters of how contract doctrines were modified first to promote economic development and then to deal with the excesses of the free market is accessible. The history of tort law is also closely related to the history of law and the economy. WHITE presents a history of tort doctrine in the context of social and economic change, although he concentrates on the intellectual contributions of leading jurisprudents. BERGSTROM, in contrast, analyzes how tort law responded to change at the turn of the 20th century, arguing that trial court judges resisted progressive reforms, and paying special attention to how law really was applied at the trial-court level. An area of law not so intimately connected to commerce is libel. ROSENBERG's history pays special attention to its relationship with developments in the media.

The legal history of American labor is also closely linked to the general history of law and the economy. STEINFELD takes his study of free and unfree labor back to medieval and early modern England. He describes how the concept of free labor undermined indentured servitude in the late 18th and early 19th centuries and made slavery untenable. TOMLINS describes the law governing labor organization and employer-employee relations in the early republic. He argues that jurists refused to devise legal doctrines that would have reinforced republican preference for basic egalitarianism. Instead, they reinforced traditional common-law doctrines that promoted a liberal, individualistic economic system, the tenets of which promoted economic inequality by insisting on an ever-more fictional legal equality. FORBATH argues that Gilded Age and Progressive Era legal doctrines determined both the aspirations of American labor and the way in which it organized. In a detailed narrative of labor law and legislation from the Gilded Age to the present, DUBOFSKY challenges the notion that governmental institutions have been as unremittingly hostile as most historians of law and labor allege.

Legal historians have also studied how legal developments affected women and the family. HOFF provides a trenchantly critical look at the history of women, gays, and the law, arguing that the law has always subjected women and gays to "pluralist male standards of justice and equity". SALMON is a seminal work on women and property in colonial America, explaining both the limitations which the common law placed on women's legal rights and the protections and benefits that both common law and equity law provided. GLENDON provides a comparative overview of American and European family law over the centuries, with special attention to recent developments. GROSSBERG is the standard analysis of the history of American family law in the 19th century, describing both increasing rights for women and growing judicial intrusion into family life. RILEY explains how the character of American society and its individualistic values contributed to the victory of those who advocated broad access to divorce over those who advocated its strict limitation.

M. LES BENEDICT

See also Judiciary; Labor History: Legal and Political Framework

Legal Thought/Jurisprudence

Boorstin, Daniel J., *The Mysterious Science of the Law: An Essay on Blackstone's Commentaries*, Boston: Beacon Press, 1941

Hart, Henry M., Jr., and Albert M. Sacks, *The Legal Process: Basic Problems in the Making and Application of Law*, edited by William N. Eskridge, Jr., and Philip P. Frickey, Westbury, NY: Foundation Press, 1994

Herget, James E., *American Jurisprudence, 1870–1970: A History*, Houston: Rice University Press, 1990

Horwitz, Morton J., *The Transformation of American Law, 1870–1960: The Crisis of Legal Orthodoxy*, New York: Oxford University Press, 1992

Summers, Robert S., *Instrumentalism and American Legal Theory*, Ithaca, NY: Cornell University Press, 1982

Twining, William, *Karl Llewellyn and the Realist Movement*, London: Weidenfeld and Nicolson, 1973; Norman: University of Oklahoma Press, 1985

White, G. Edward, *Patterns of American Legal Thought*, Indianapolis: Bobbs Merrill, 1978

White, Morton, *Social Thought in America: The Revolt Against Formalism*, New York: Viking, 1949

Until recently, American jurists and lawyers have not been conspicuous for systematization or sustained jurisprudential speculation. There has been no American Descartes, Locke, Kant, Mill, Marx, Weber, or Durkheim. Nor is there a body of disciplined American jurisprudential thought or even any original contributions comparable to the writings of English thinkers like Bentham, Austin, Maine, or Hart, or continental jurists like Savigny, Ihering, and Kelsen. (The only significant exception would be Oliver Wendell Holmes's *The Common Law* [1881], substantively revised if not repudiated by his 1897 lecture, "The Path of the Law".) American lawyers have merited their reputation for being both parochial and practical. Seldom fluent in any language but English, they have found continental legal thought inaccessible unless translated, while their practical bent has channelled their systematizing impulses into treatises on particular legal subjects.

Nevertheless, Americans have written extensively in a practical vein in treatises and law reviews – to say nothing of judicial opinions, lawyers' briefs, and other legal instruments – and implicit in these writings are sets of coherent assumptions about political philosophy and legal theory. While these *nebulae* of belief do not rise to the level of jurisprudential schools, they have made important contributions to legal thought. Prominent 19th-century examples are Joseph Story's *Commentaries on the Constitution* (1833) and Thomas M. Cooley's *Treatise on Constitutional Limitations* (1868). Eminent 20th-century legal theorists include Roscoe Pound, Lon Fuller, Felix Cohen, Morris Cohen, Karl Llewellyn, and J. Willard Hurst. Recently, the work of John Rawls, Ronald Dworkin, and arguably Richard Posner constitutes America's belated entry into the lists of jurisprudential contention.

HERGET provides the only survey of all American legal thought up to the 1970s. He eschews conventional classifications such as formalism or Legal Realism, mimicking his subject by reorganizing it in functional categories. These include classification, universal principles, evolutionary development, social-science methods, and natural law, among others. His treatment of difficult subjects is clear and accessible to the lay reader. He is particularly adept at tracing lines of influence among legal thinkers, pointing out, for example, the debt that Yale's Wesley Hohfeld owed to the Anglo-Australian jurisprude John Salmond.

G. Edward White, who was trained originally as an intellectual historian, has written about jurisprudential subjects extensively in his prolific career. Some of his most penetrating essays are collected in G. Edward WHITE. His article, "The Path of American Jurisprudence", is both a jurisprudential contribution in its own right and a survey of the development of legal theory. Later writings, especially his intellectual biography of Justice Holmes, *Justice Oliver Wendell Holmes: Law and the Inner Self* (1993), explore other jurisprudential themes so extensively that the body of his writings taken as a whole constitutes an extensive review of American legal theory.

BOORSTIN's study of Blackstone's *Commentaries* is broader than its subject might suggest. The author captured the book's thesis and scope in its subtitle: "showing how Blackstone, employing 18th-century ideas of science, religion,

history, aesthetics, and philosophy, made of the law at once a conservative and a mysterious science". Much of the explanation for the persistently conservative inclination of American law may be found here.

Morton WHITE is an enduring classic, which is surprising considering that its subject is essentially negative: he describes not a body of legal thought so much as the rejection of that thought, which he labelled formalism, a judicial outlook dominant among the elite of the bar and the bench from approx-imately 1886 to 1930. Morton White located the legal component of this movement of repudiation within a broader intellectual tradition, usually but not altogether accurately referred to as "pragmatism". He described the affinities among such Progressive-era thinkers as John Dewey, Charles A. Beard, and Thorstein Veblen. His insights have retained their validity, and all subsequent writers on the subject have to some extent at least followed the trails he blazed.

HORWITZ surveys the same period as Herget, but with more focus and concentration on selected trends and figures. He devotes one chapter to formalism, which he terms "legal orthodoxy". Most of the remainder of the book, six chapters, considers the Progressive and Legal Realist challenge to that orthodoxy. Horwitz reinterprets Realism, evaluating its weaknesses as well as its strengths. He is particularly effective in tracing the influence of the Realist tradition into the postwar world.

TWINING's is the most useful of the various studies of Legal Realism, not because others are inferior or less interesting – Laura Kalman's *Legal Realism at Yale* (1986) is insightful and a model institutional study – but because Twining's focus is Karl Llewellyn, that astonishingly gifted giant of the Realist enterprise. Because Realism was so diffuse and heterogeneous, intellectual biography offers as useful a vehicle as any for exploring its content and development, and none of the men associated with the movement is as rewarding to the writer and reader of biographies as Llewellyn.

SUMMERS contends, contrary to the arguments of sceptics on the subject, that Americans *have* created one significant school of jurisprudential thought, which he labels "pragmatic instrumentalism", their "only indigenous legal theory". He numbers it one of the four great schools produced by Western thought, the others being the natural law tradition, analytical positivism, and historical jurisprudence. Summers identifies Holmes, Pound, Dewey, John Chipman Gray, Walter Wheeler Cook, Felix Cohen, and Llewellyn as exemplars of this body of thought. Summers cautions that he has not written a history of the subject, but his treatment is as historical as it is analytical.

An ill-tempered reaction against Legal Realism set in during World War II, and by 1950 the movement, such as it was, had disintegrated. Filling the vacuum was an equally amorphous tendency of thought usually termed Legal Process. Its bible was a casebook never conventionally published, known by the names of its editors as "HART and SACKS", which had been pioneered at the Harvard Law School. In recognition of the movement's and the book's great though short-lived influence, Eskridge and Frickey provided a scholarly introduction to the book's post-mortem appearance as a published museum-piece. That introduction provides the best review and evaluation of Legal Process to date.

WILLIAM M. WIECEK

Lewis, John L.   1880–1969

Labor leader

Alinsky, Saul, *John L. Lewis: An Unauthorized Biography*, New York: Putnam, 1949

Brody, David, "Market Unionism in America: The Case of Coal," in his *In Labor's Cause: Main Themes in the History of the American Worker*, New York: Oxford University Press, 1993

Brophy, John, *A Miner's Life: An Autobiography*, Madison: University of Wisconsin Press, 1964

Dubofsky, Melvyn and Warren Van Tine, *John L. Lewis: A Biography*, New York: Quadrangle/New York Times, 1977

Finlay, Joseph, *The Corrupt Kingdom: The Rise and Fall of the United Mine Workers*, New York: Simon and Schuster, 1972

Hume, Brit, *Death and the Mines: Rebellion and Murder in the United Mine Workers*, New York: Grossman, 1971

Zieger, Robert H., *John L. Lewis: Labor Leader*, Boston: Twayne, 1988

Zieger, Robert H., *The CIO, 1935–1955*, Chapel Hill: University of North Carolina Press, 1995

Most historical works on John L. Lewis are strong on Lewis's public career, especially his lengthy leadership of the United Mine Workers and central role in the labor upsurge of the 1930s. Scholars have been unable, however, to explore the private and paradoxical sides of Lewis, and to explain fully his motivation at certain key points in labor history. Despite a colorful and extravagant public persona, Lewis was an intensely private individual, who explained his motives to few confidants and failed to leave any real written record. As a result, biographies of Lewis are not as close-grained and penetrative as might be wished.

Despite these limitations, Lewis has been the subject of some excellent historical scholarship. The most detailed and exhaustive biography is DUBOFSKY and VAN TINE, who promise a "warts and all" treatment of Lewis, and duly deliver it in a portrait that emphasizes Lewis's opportunism and "possessive individualism." The book is not an unfavorable account, however, but is well-balanced throughout, describing Lewis's genius for timing and stressing the constraints under which he operated. Dubofsky and Van Tine are particularly perceptive at looking beyond many of the unsubstantiated myths that have surrounded Lewis. They convincingly explain Lewis's famous split with Roosevelt in 1940 as based more on differences over foreign and domestic policy issues than on a personality clash. The book is also enhanced by its authors' complete honesty about the shortcomings of the sources in providing answers to particular questions. Overall, Dubofsky and Van Tine clearly stands as the authoritative work on Lewis.

For many years the standard work on Lewis was ALINSKY. Because of its claim to be based on "unlimited interviews" between Lewis and Alinsky, this book enjoyed considerable authority for some years. However, it has now been discredited as flimsy and unreliable, especially after Dubofsky and Van Tine demonstrated that Alinsky may well have created many of his "interviews" out of thin air. Apart from these problems, Alinsky, himself a labor organizer and radical thinker, tends to eulogize Lewis and exaggerate his role in the conflicts of the 1930s and 1940s. Alinsky's work now remains useful more as a document than a scholarly account.

As a volume in a series intended to provide readable, brief studies of influential Americans, ZIEGER (1988) is considerably shorter and more accessible than Dubofsky and Van Tine. It is a well-written, lucid account that identifies and develops a number of key themes in Lewis's life. While Zieger reiterates many of Dubofsky and Van Tine's arguments, his work has the advantage of incorporating the considerable amount of scholarship that has been written on Lewis, the UMW, and the Congress of Industrial Organizations since the publication of Dubofsky and Van Tine's work. Less discursive than Dubofsky and Van Tine, Zieger argues that Lewis was a paradoxical figure who lacked a "consciously articulated creed" and wished to be judged by the public record.

In his much-needed recent history of the CIO, ZIEGER (1995) also incorporates a wide variety of scholarship and primary research about Lewis. This history puts Lewis's role in the union upsurge of the New Deal era in clear perspective, stressing his central role in the unionization of the automobile and steel industries. As Lewis left the CIO in 1941, the value of this account as far as Lewis is concerned lies mainly in its coverage of his central role in the formation and turbulent early years of the CIO.

Given the lack of first-hand evidence pertaining to Lewis, BROPHY, a UMW and CIO official who worked alongside Lewis, offers a valuable account, especially in providing detailed inside information for the 1920s and 1930s. Despite Brophy's closeness to the events, this account is also relatively unbiased. Brophy indeed provides some valuable insights into Lewis's character, although it does not deal with important events of the postwar period such as the 1946 coal strike.

Although Lewis is best-known for his role in the formation of the CIO, his ascendancy as a national labor leader was much shorter than his leadership of the UMW. Lewis was president of the miners' union for more than forty years, and any assessment of Lewis must explore his record in the coal industry. BRODY is a detailed essay that provides an overview of Lewis's presidency of the UMW and analyzes the economic ideas that guided him throughout this time. It is a perceptive account that suggests that Lewis thought primarily in economic terms and sought to apply marketplace economics to the coal industry. Brody also shows that the miners' union was Lewis's power-base throughout his career.

Lewis's legacy has been a question that has attracted a considerable amount of scholarship. The accounts of Zieger, and Dubofsky and Van Tine, point out how Lewis silenced all voices of dissent within the UMW, and showed scant regard for union democracy. In the postwar years, moreover, Lewis co-operated with coal operators in implementing contracts that caused job losses. These aspects of Lewis's presidency are reviewed by HUME and by FINLAY, both of whom argue that Lewis's legacy was a corrupt and weak UMW that failed to fight for workers' rights in the 1960s and 1970s. Both of these works contain useful material on Lewis, although they are too heavily reliant on secondary sources.

TIM MINCHIN

See also Congress of Industrial Organizations; Labor Unions

Lewis, Meriwether 1774–1809 and
William Clark 1770–1838

Leaders of transcontinental expedition, 1804–06

Allen, John Logan, *Passage Through the Garden: Lewis and Clark and the Image of the American Northwest*, Urbana: University of Illinois Press, 1952

Bakeless, John Edwin, *Lewis and Clark: Partners in Discovery*, New York: Morrow, 1947

Cutright, Paul Russell, *Lewis and Clark: Pioneering Naturalists*, Urbana: University of Illinois Press, 1969

De Voto, Bernard, *The Course of Empire*, Boston: Houghton Mifflin, 1952; as *Westward the Course of Empire*, London: Eyre and Spottiswoode, 1953

Dillon, Richard H., *Meriwether Lewis: A Biography*, New York: Coward McCann, 1965

Furtwangler, Albert, *Acts of Discovery: Visions of America in the Lewis and Clark Journals*, Urbana: University of Illinois Press, 1993

Lavender, David, *The Way to the Western Sea: Lewis and Clark Across the Continent*, New York: Harper, 1985

Ronda, James P., *Lewis and Clark among the Indians*, Lincoln: University of Nebraska Press, 1984

Steffen, Jerome O., *William Clark: Jeffersonian Man on the Frontier*, Norman: University of Oklahoma Press, 1977

Despite the passage of almost two centuries since Meriwether Lewis and William Clark led the Corps of Discovery across the uncharted northwest to the Pacific Ocean and back, both popular and scholarly interest in the great American epic remains strong. BAKELESS, the first satisfactory modern account of the great adventure, is a collective biography whose principal focus is not on the men themselves but on the expedition. The narrative retells a dramatic story with energy and clarity. Although it limns the personalities of Lewis and Clark only poorly and is weak on analysis and interpretation, for the general audience it remains a readable if dated history of the expedition.

De VOTO allocated a major section of the third volume of his great trilogy on the West to Lewis and Clark. In tracing the path of the two explorers across the Northwest, De Voto is at his storytelling best, producing a lively and perceptive account of daring and adventure. But he delivers more. He gives the expedition context and meaning by maintaining that it was part of Jefferson's grand design for establishing his empire for liberty. A necessary step in defending the United States against expanding, rival empires in the Western Hemisphere, it was more than a daring western tour or a scientific expedition, it was a quest for continental power. De Voto made another important contribution to Lewis and Clark studies in 1953, when he condensed into a single volume the eight volumes of the explorers' journals originally published by Reuben G. Thwaites in 1904–05. His introduction to that volume is especially helpful in evaluating the objectives, achievements, and international context of the expedition.

The discovery in the 1950s of important documentary sources, and the 1962 publication of *Letters of the Lewis and Clark Expedition with Related Documents, 1783–1854*, edited by Donald Jackson, intensified interest in the explorers.

A veritable renascence of Lewis and Clark studies followed, producing some first-rate scholarly monographs.

CUTRIGHT is one of the best of these. A biologist, he offers a careful assessment of the expedition's scientific accomplishments, focusing on botany, zoology, geography, anthropology, and medicine. Each chapter concludes with a summary of discoveries. The medical aspects of the expedition are of particular interest, as is the chapter describing the fate of the botanical, zoological, and ethnological material collected on the journey. Beyond demonstrating the magnitude of the expedition's scientific accomplishments, Cutright provides a well-wrought chronological narrative of the trip that omits no major occurrences. It is one of the most important secondary works on the Voyage of Discovery.

Cutright is representative of the tendency since De Voto to play down the journey as an epic of human courage and endurance and to look instead at the captains as pioneer western naturalists, ethnologists, cartographers, and diplomats. ALLEN, a geographer, exemplifies this trend. He probes the nature of the exploratory process, shows how prevailing ideas of geography affected the explorers' decision-making, and offers a systematic analysis of expedition cartography. The prevailing Jeffersonian images of the American West – as a passage to India and garden of the world – were images that influenced Lewis and Clark, but were in turn modified and reshaped by them as a result of their discoveries. Allen is an intriguing study in conceptual geography which, though occasionally burdened with social science jargon, is a solid intellectual history of the expedition.

RONDA focuses on one of the least understood aspects of the expedition, the party's relations with the Indians. Borrowing from archaeology, anthropology, and linguistics, he reminds us that the Corps of Discovery was simply another dimension of the ongoing culture clash between Euro- and Native Americans. Linguistically and culturally, Lewis and Clark were ill-equipped to understand and deal with the Indians. They could collect artefacts and describe Indian manners but did not comprehend the complexities of native culture. For this reason, they failed in their diplomatic mission to establish peace among the tribes and win them as allies and trading partners. Objective and sensible in its judgments, Ronda's thoughtful monograph treats the subject from both the white and Indian points of view.

In the best American studies tradition, FURTWANGLER examines the Lewis and Clark journals as history, literature, and science. He argues that the journals are a neglected American literary classic whose features compare favorably with works by such writers as William Wordsworth and Mark Twain. The explorers, he asserts, not only carried out but surpassed Jefferson's enlightened instructions. They gathered important new natural history information with extraordinary perception and intelligence and were thereby responsible for helping to achieve a new understanding of the continent that would radically alter America's image of itself.

LAVENDER is a popular narrative which covers in great detail the day-to-day passage but fails to incorporate much recent scholarship. Its failure to offer new insights and interpretations or to analyze the expedition as an important scientific endeavor is disappointing. Even so, it is a standard narrative account of the journey.

For all the important new insights of recent Lewis and Clark literature, the expedition leaders themselves have had surprisingly little biographical attention. Older biographies of Lewis are woefully inadequate. More recent studies, such as DILLON, which is the latest and best, do not satisfy the canons of modern biographical scholarship. Dillon attempts a full reappraisal of Lewis who, he argues, was much more important than Clark to the success of the expedition. The prose is heavy, the documentation weak, and the interpretation of both the man and the journey less than satisfying. Clark has fared no better than Lewis. STEFFEN looks only at Clark's post-1806 career in what is really a thematic study rather than biography. Steffen uses his subject, whom he sees as an 18th-century enlightenment figure, as a vehicle for tracing changes in American society from the age of Jefferson to the age of Jackson. While it is a thoughtful and stimulating study, it does not fill the need for a good, comprehensive biography.

The revival of scholarly interest in Lewis and Clark since mid-century shows no signs of abating. It is likely, indeed, that the publication of the superb new edition of the explorers' journals under the skillful editorship of Gary Moulton will intensify that interest and encourage scholars to accelerate their efforts to define and interpret the great expedition.

CHARLES D. LOWERY

Liberalism

Appleby, Joyce, *Liberalism and Republicanism in the Historical Imagination*, Cambridge, MA: Harvard University Press, 1992

Berman, William C., *America's Right Turn: From Nixon to Bush*, Baltimore: Johns Hopkins University Press, 1994

Brinkley, Alan, *The End of Reform: New Deal Liberalism in Recession and War*, New York: Knopf, 1995

Diggins, John Patrick, *The Lost Soul of American Politics: Virtue, Self-Interest, and the Foundations of Liberalism*, New York: Basic Books, 1984

Greenstone, J. David, *The Lincoln Persuasion: Remaking American Liberalism*, Princeton: Princeton University Press, 1993

Hamby, Alonzo L., *Liberalism and Its Challengers: From F.D.R. to Reagan*, New York: Oxford University Press, 1985, 2nd edition, as *Liberalism and Its Challengers: From F.D.R. to Bush*, 1992

Hartz, Louis, *The Liberal Tradition in America: An Interpretation of American Political Thought since the Revolution*, New York: Harcourt Brace, 1955

Hofstadter, Richard, *The American Political Tradition and the Men Who Made It*, New York: Knopf, 1948; London: Cape, 1962

Matusow, Allen J., *The Unraveling of America: A History of Liberalism in the 1960s*, New York: Harper, 1984

Wood, Gordon S., *The Creation of the American Republic, 1776–1787*, Chapel Hill: University of North Carolina Press, 1969

Two books published during the first decade of the Cold War described the nation's political tradition as being hostile to foreign ideologies and broadly liberal – that is, grounded in a consensus on individual liberty, private property, and a representative government with limited powers. HARTZ traced these notions to America's lack of a feudal past. In his view the generation of political theorists who fought the American Revolution and wrote the Constitution found John Locke's notions of natural rights attractive primarily because they confirmed American economic and social conditions. Liberalism was a "natural" philosophy because it accorded with observed reality. During the 19th century and through the 1930s, democracy and capitalism, while seemingly in conflict, in fact expressed a similar impulse rooted in the pervasive spirit of individualism and entrepreneurial independence.

In what is essentially a series of biographical essays, HOFSTADTER likewise argued that their commonalities set Americans apart from the citizens of other more divided societies. Beginning with a chapter stressing the realistic and non-ideological world-view shared by the Founding Fathers, he went on to emphasize how the public lives of political leaders, including presidents Jefferson, Jackson, Lincoln, Cleveland, the two Roosevelts, Wilson and Hoover exemplified the individualist and capitalist liberal consensus shared by Americans.

Given the synthetic nature of their books, Hartz and Hofstadter did not provide an intellectual history of the political discourse that shaped the American political tradition from the colonial period to the New Deal. During the 1960s and 1970s, numerous studies of early American history, notably WOOD, questioned the influence of liberalism and developed a "republican synthesis" which explains American political culture as originating more in classical antiquity, Renaissance humanism, and Enlightenment rationalism than in American economic and social conditions. According to republicanism, the protection of virtue, not the pursuit of self-interest, provides the master key to early American political thought. APPLEBY takes issue with the republican argument and chides its practitioners for claiming more for their theory than their evidence allows. In thirteen sharply focused essays based on analysis of 17th- and 18th-century economic and political treatises in the context of changes in the Atlantic political economy of the time, she reasserts the importance of liberal, as distinct from republican, ideology to the Revolutionary generation.

DIGGINS affirms the significance of liberalism in a persuasive intellectual history that ranges widely across the 18th and 19th centuries and encompasses a variety of thinkers, including Jefferson, Madison, and John Adams, as well as Emerson, Thoreau, Melville, Abraham Lincoln, and Henry Adams. The lost soul of the title refers to the strain of Calvinist or Puritan moralism that provided the Revolutionary generation with the wherewithal to practice selfish individualism, without losing sight of the importance of community or the need for a transcendent national purpose. The decline of Christian values coincident with national expansion after the War of 1812 fostered a critique of amoral liberalism that has marked American intellectual history ever since.

Abraham Lincoln occupies a prominent place in GREENSTONE as well as in Diggins. Both writers regard Lincoln's attack on slavery as an expression of characteristic tensions associated with 19th-century liberalism. Diggins attributes Lincoln's position to his religious conscience; thus the president's commitment to ending the peculiar institution represented a critique based on Christian morality external to amoral liberal self-interest. Greenstone, however, regards Lincoln's stance as rooted in a tension between two views within liberalism itself. Lincoln rejected the dominant view that sought satisfaction solely in the pursuit of material interests and embraced a reformist view that emphasized the need to link material success to the development of human potentialities, an endeavor obviously denied the victims of slavery.

What Greenstone characterizes as reformist liberalism provided the rationale for some of the social reforms of the Progressive Era and New Deal. BRINKLEY concludes that the reformist version of liberalism associated with the experiments of Franklin D. Roosevelt's first administration was under siege well before the Democratic party landslide of 1936 and suffered further defeats after the recession of 1937, the formation of the conservative coalition between Republicans and southern Democrats, and the pressures of fighting a two-ocean world war. In an epilogue, he describes how liberalism was reconstructed by the end of World War II. Theories of government planning and control of the economy were replaced by a determination to accept and foster the growth of corporate productivity; utopian schemes of social engineering were rejected in favor of a limited welfare state.

MATUSOW chronicles the history of liberalism as it was transformed by its largely Democratic party proponents during the 1960s. Because the liberals exaggerated the affluence of the nation and could not predict President Johnson's decision to finance the war in Vietnam, they committed the government to a broad array of programs to rid the nation of unemployment, racism, and poverty. They failed for several reasons, in addition to the strength of conservative opposition. Their definitions of the nation's problems were flawed by naivete and their solutions were marred by faulty assumptions about the process of social change. Sixties liberalism also failed because it suffered attacks from the new left, from black power advocates, and from anti-war protesters. By the end of the decade, the nation's social fabric had begun to unravel, and an era of pessimism and divisiveness was under way.

Adopting a biographical approach, HAMBY provides a reliable survey of those presidents – Roosevelt, Truman, Kennedy and Johnson – who set themselves the task of leading the nation along the lines of Democratic party liberalism, as well as those presidents – Eisenhower, Nixon, and especially Reagan – who challenged such an agenda. Hamby also profiles other political figures who influenced the national debate on liberalism, including Robert Taft, Joseph McCarthy, Martin Luther King, Jr., and Robert Kennedy. While more sympathetic to the challengers than to the challenged, his survey is a reliable and indispensable account of liberalism since the New Deal and an excellent guide to its decline since the 1970s. In a brief account intended for classroom use, BERMAN provides the best political history of how the Democratic and Republican parties both contributed to and reacted to the demise of liberalism and the revival of conservatism in the electorate, in the period after the 1960s.

WILLIAM ISSEL

See also Republicanism

Lincoln, Abraham 1809–1865

16th President of the United States

Baker, Jean H., *Mary Todd Lincoln: A Biography*, New York: Norton, 1987

Boritt, Gabor S., *Lincoln and the Economics of the American Dream*, Memphis, TN: Memphis State University Press, 1978; reprinted, Urbana: University of Illinois Press, 1994

Boritt, Gabor S. (editor), *Lincoln the War President*, New York: Oxford University Press, 1992

Burlingame, Michael, *The Inner World of Abraham Lincoln*, Urbana: University of Illinois Press, 1994

Cox, LaWanda, *Lincoln and Black Freedom: A Study in Presidential Leadership*, Columbia: University of South Carolina Press, 1981

Current, Richard N., *The Lincoln Nobody Knows*, New York: McGraw Hill, 1958

Donald, David, *Lincoln Reconsidered: Essays on the Civil War Era*, New York: Knopf, 1956; 2nd edition, New York: Vintage, 1961

Donald, David Herbert, *Lincoln*, New York: Simon and Schuster, and London: Cape, 1995

Fehrenbacher, Don E., *Prelude to Greatness: Lincoln in the 1850s*, Stanford, CA: Stanford University Press, 1962

Fehrenbacher, Don E., *Lincoln in Text and Context: Collected Essays*, Stanford, CA: Stanford University Press, 1987

Greenstone, J. David, *The Lincoln Persuasion: Remaking American Liberalism*, Princeton: Princeton University Press, 1993

Herndon, William H. and Jesse W. Weik, *Herndon's Lincoln: The True Story of a Great Life*, 3 vols., Chicago: Belford Clarke, 1889, and later reprints; abridged edition, edited by David Freeman Hawke, Indianapolis: Bobbs Merrill, 1970

Jaffa, Harry V., *Crisis of the House Divided: An Interpretation of the Issues in the Lincoln-Douglas Debates*, New York: Doubleday, 1959

Johannsen, Robert W., *Lincoln, the South, and Slavery*, Baton Rouge: Louisiana State University Press, 1991

Long, David E., *The Jewel of Liberty: Abraham Lincoln's Re-Election and the End of Slavery*, Mechanicsburg, PA: Stackpole, 1994

McPherson, James M., *Abraham Lincoln and the Second American Revolution*, New York and Oxford: Oxford University Press, 1990

Neely, Mark E., Jr., *The Abraham Lincoln Encyclopedia*, New York: McGraw Hill, 1982

Neely, Mark E., Jr., *The Fate of Liberty: Abraham Lincoln and Civil Liberties*, New York: Oxford University Press, 1991

Neely, Mark E., Jr., *The Last Best Hope of Earth: Abraham Lincoln and the Promise of America*, Cambridge, MA: Harvard University Press, 1993

Nicolay, John G. and John Hay, *Abraham Lincoln: A History*, 10 vols., New York: Century, 1890; 1-volume abridgment, edited by Paul M. Angle, Chicago: University of Chicago Press, 1966

Oates, Stephen B., *With Malice Toward None: The Life of Abraham Lincoln*, New York: Harper, 1977; London: Allen and Unwin, 1978

Paludan, Phillip S., *The Presidency of Abraham Lincoln*, Lawrence: University Press of Kansas, 1994

Peterson, Merrill D., *Lincoln in American Memory*, New York: Oxford University Press, 1994

Randall, J. G., *Lincoln the President*, 4 vols. (vol. 4 with Richard N. Current), New York: Dodd Mead, and London: Eyre and Spottiswoode, 1945–55

Sandburg, Carl, *Abraham Lincoln*, New York: Harcourt Brace: *The Prairie Years*, 2 vols., 1926; *The War Years*, 4 vols., 1939; 1-volume abridgement, as *Abraham Lincoln: The Prairie Years and The War Years*, 1954

Strozier, Charles B., *Lincoln's Quest for Union: Public and Private Meanings*, New York: Basic Books, 1982

Thomas, Benjamin P., *Abraham Lincoln: A Biography*, New York: Knopf, 1952; London: Eyre and Spottiswoode, 1953

Thomas, John L. (editor), *Abraham Lincoln and the American Political Tradition*, Amherst: University of Massachusetts Press, 1986

Wills, Garry, *Lincoln at Gettysburg: The Words that Remade America*, New York: Simon and Schuster, 1992

From time to time, leading Lincoln authorities, having had their own say, have suggested that the Lincoln theme was at or near the point of exhaustion. But the tide of books, essays and articles on Lincoln shows no signs of ebbing. In this highly selective discussion of Lincolniana, the emphasis will be on classic works which have shaped much of the subsequent historiography, and then on notable recent studies of various aspects of his life and career.

A number of the dominant myths of the American national past – all of them containing a measure of historical truth – converge on the figure of Abraham Lincoln. The embodiment of the log-cabin-to-White House legend, he also stands as the saviour/martyr of the Union cause, and as the Great Emancipator of four million slaves, who gave new meaning to the promise of liberty and equality expressed in the Declaration of Independence. One of the enduring challenges to his biographers has been to separate reality from myth, and to distinguish the historical Lincoln from the folk-hero, the icon, and the member, along with Washington and Jefferson, of the great American secular trinity of household gods. Another problem has lain in the difficulty of striking the right balance between the frontier obscurity of the first forty years of his life and the high drama of his last seven years, on the national stage – barely one-eighth of his whole life – which coincided with the greatest crisis of the Union.

PETERSON is an illuminating and comprehensive guide to changing interpretations and images of Lincoln at the hands of generations of biographers, historians, artists, dramatists and novelists. He shows how different groups of Americans, including African Americans, have shaped and re-shaped the Lincoln image, and how his reputation has fluctuated with many of those groups.

Lincoln biographies began with works written by close associates. Two sharply contrasting accounts have had an enduring influence on all subsequent Lincoln studies. William H. Herndon, who was Lincoln's close confidant and law partner in Springfield, Illinois, later traded on his knowledge of Lincoln's earlier life, and his unshakable belief in his own psychological insights into the great man's character and personality. HERNDON and WEIK is not a carefully structured biography but an amalgam of reminiscences, anecdotes, gossip and speculation about Lincoln's pre-presidential life. Neither Herndon's memory nor his critical judgment is to be taken on trust, and his imagination was very active. However, despite its unreliability, Herndon's work, as recorded by his collaborator Weik, is the main, sometimes the only, source for many episodes in Lincoln's early life, and has been much used, especially by some of Lincoln's modern psycho-biographers.

In contrast, NICOLAY and HAY is a massive, multi-volume study with its main emphasis on the Civil War years. The authors, who acted as Lincoln's private secretaries during the White House years, laboured long and hard to produce what is not so much a biography as a history in which the president is the central figure, indeed the hero. The style is formal and unexciting, and the tone almost uniformly laudatory, but there is little on the private Lincoln. Among many other sources, the authors had access to the Lincoln Papers, jealously guarded by his son, Robert Todd Lincoln, and included substantial extracts from the sources in their work. Extensively mined by later authors, this monumental work is now more widely respected than read.

Two major multi-volume Lincoln biographies appeared during the first half of this century. Once again, they could scarcely have been more different from each other. SANDBURG, poet, storyteller, and troubadour for the common man, presented a Lincoln who was not a larger-than-life superman, but rather the personification of the American democratic spirit, born out of the frontier experience. Colourful and imaginative in their style – some critics regard Sandburg's prose as more poetic than his poetry – the first two volumes on the "prairie years" are evocative and atmospheric, but not to be treated as a precise record of Lincoln's early life. The human interest of a good anecdote often took precedence over its reliability as historical evidence. In the four volumes on the war years, Sandburg paid a little more respect to the conventions of historical study, but adhered to the same method of piecing together an intricate mosaic made up of countless anecdotes and eye-catching details, without much attempt at sustained analysis or explanation. A popular and literary success, Sandburg's volumes have not found great favour among professional historians.

On the other hand, in his four volumes RANDALL set new standards of historical scholarship for Lincoln biographers. Concentrating mainly on the Lincoln presidency, he examined the great issues meticulously but often inconclusively. A sympathetic critic of Lincoln, he found himself drawn towards some of those men with whom Lincoln most notably crossed swords. Stephen A. Douglas emerges almost as a hero in the first volume, and General McClellan is presented in a surprisingly favourable light. Randall was a leading proponent of the "revisionist" school of Civil War historians, who regarded the war as unnecessary, and blamed it on a blundering generation of politicians. He is sternly critical of radical Republicans and abolitionists, and sees them as the cause of many of Lincoln's difficulties. After Randall's death, the final volume was completed with great skill and good judgment by Richard Current, himself destined to become a major Lincoln scholar.

Single-volume biographies are numerous but not many are equally at home in dealing with the earlier life and the presidential years. Somewhat surprisingly, the work of an English peer, Lord Charnwood, published in 1916, was widely regarded for some decades as the best available. It retains some interest now, more for its literary grace than for its historical weight. It was largely supplanted by Benjamin THOMAS, who was not an academic, and dispensed with much of the scholarly apparatus, but who was completely immersed in the sources, including the recently-opened Robert Todd Lincoln Papers. His richly textured book carries great authority, and, although on such matters as race, for example, it is seriously outdated, it remains one of the best of the briefer biographies. Thomas's attitude to Lincoln is sympathetic but not blindly so, his judgments are balanced and careful, and his informal style occasionally tends towards folksiness.

Three more recent single-volume biographies all benefit from the mass of recent specialised work on Lincoln and the Civil War, and from changing perspectives, particularly on questions of slavery and race. OATES is the work of a professional biographer rather than a historian, and his mastery of historical context is not always assured. On a larger scale than Thomas, but always very readable, this might be regarded as the first post-civil rights study of Lincoln. (Oates moved on to a study of Martin Luther King). He sees Lincoln as close to the radical Republicans, and presents him as strongly committed to freedom and civil rights for the slaves. The most important modern biography is DONALD (1995), the work of the leading Civil War and Lincoln scholar of his generation. His mastery of the sources is clear, and there is enormous technical virtuosity in his control of a detailed chronological narrative. This is a warts-and-all portrait of a very practical politician, with a strong streak of fatalism, and there is only occasional reference to the great moral issues at stake in the war for the Union. If, for all its many strengths and virtues, Donald's biography leaves the reader less than fully satisfied, it may be because he adopts as his central theme the notion that Lincoln was essentially a passive figure, reacting to events. This is hardly the most promising or productive standpoint for the biographer of a major figure. It is also a very questionable interpretation; pragmatism, patience and a shrewd sense of timing are not the same as passivity or fatalism.

Those seeking a much briefer, but highly perceptive, study of Lincoln, based on recent scholarship, may turn to NEELY (1993), which packs a great deal of sense into less than 200 pages of text. After a brief discussion of the pre-presidential years, the fuller treatment of the war years is arranged topically in chapters on Lincoln in relation to the conduct of the war, slavery, emancipation and race, the home front, and wartime politics. Although it assumes a certain amount of knowledge in the reader, this is much the best study of Lincoln for those seeking a concise interpretative overview.

One of the best recent insights into the troubled private and domestic life of Abraham Lincoln is provided by BAKER's superb biography of Mrs. Lincoln. Despite straining too hard occasionally to use Mary Lincoln's tragic life to explore some of the wider preoccupations of women's history, Baker paints a convincing picture of the troubled relationship of the Lincolns. The strains of wartime leadership often made Lincoln a depressed, exhausted and increasingly remote figure to his volatile, high-tempered and lonely wife.

Baker has been more willing than many historians to draw upon the work of the growing number of psycho-biographers of Lincoln. Some of the earlier work in this field – for example by Dwight Anderson and George Forgie – was highly speculative and often very hostile. Strozier and Burlingame are somewhat more circumspect, and also rather more sympathetic to Lincoln. STROZIER concentrates on Lincoln's pre-1860 life, and includes a thoughtful chapter on Mary Lincoln. He sets out to relate Lincoln's search for "inner coherence" in the face of many personal and family problems to his public commitment to the great issue of slavery and the Union. BURLINGAME discusses a variety of topics, including Lincoln's depressions, his attitude towards women, his temper and his ambition, and his relations with his sons and his wife. His portrait of the Lincoln marriage is extremely bleak, and his judgment on Mary Lincoln very severe. In an intriguing picture of a complex personality, Burlingame offers insights into Lincoln's transformation from run-of-the-mill politician to major statesman. Although many mainstream historians remain sceptical about the work of the psycho-biographers, they are bound to influence future studies of Lincoln.

The great feature of the last forty years has been the proliferation of detailed studies of particular aspects of Lincoln's career, particularly as president. Many of them reflect the concerns of America in the second half of the 20th century, with civil rights, racial equality and the exercise of presidential power. On the crucial years from the Kansas-Nebraska Act of 1854 to the presidential election of 1860, FEHREN-BACHER (1962) remains a valuable guide, despite its age. He portrays with sympathetic insight the evolution of Lincoln's antislavery ideas, and his emergence on to the national stage. Dating from a similar period, JAFFA is a detailed discussion of the political ideas of the two protagonists in the Lincoln-Douglas debates – and a powerful counterblast to the "revisionist" claim that there was little to choose between their respective positions on slavery and its further extension. In sharp contrast, JOHANNSEN, distinguished biographer of Douglas, uses his Fleming Lectures to argue that political calculation and opportunism played a larger part than moral conviction in shaping Lincoln's increasingly antislavery and anti-Southern stance.

Studies of wartime politics had earlier been dominated by fierce debate over the internal divisions within the Republican party between radicals and conservatives, and where Lincoln stood in relation to them. That has now largely subsided, with a growing recognition that the party, like all major American parties, was a shifting and unstable coalition of various groups and interests. By far the most important recent work on the Lincoln presidency is PALUDAN, a masterly and comprehensive discussion of all the main aspects of the Lincoln record in the White House, except perhaps his role as commander-in-chief. Paludan's basic contention is that, for Lincoln, the goals of saving the Union and freeing the slaves were not separate questions or competing priorities but were closely and crucially interrelated. Certainly, his treatment of Lincoln's handling of the issues of emancipation and reconstruction is particularly impressive.

Among the plethora of works on particular aspects of the Lincoln presidency, three important examples may be cited. COX is a powerful re-statement – some critics might say an over-statement – of the case for Lincoln's strong and positive presidential leadership in the cause of black freedom, which focuses particularly on the complex story of wartime Louisiana. NEELY (1991) cuts down to size much earlier discussion of Lincoln's record on civil liberties – especially on arbitrary arrests – by concentrating on political realities and on the practical implementation of his policy. He finds much evidence of confusion and inefficiency, but little to support allegations of presidential dictatorship. LONG is a vigorous account of the election of 1864, with a strong emphasis on Lincoln's leadership. Seeking to make good his claim that this was the most important election in American history, Long emphasises the extent to which the future of the Union and freedom for the slaves depended upon the outcome. Unlike some earlier historians, he takes seriously the threat of Copperhead disloyalty, and he paints a grim picture of what might have happened if Lincoln had been defeated.

Lincoln's ideas have attracted increasing attention in recent years. In a challenging study, BORITT (1978) examines the economic emphasis of the young Lincoln's beliefs, and shows how his thinking increasingly focused on the American citizen's "right to rise". This is an important point, which surely relates to social and political as much as economic aspirations, and Boritt runs into difficulty in trying to apply Lincoln's "economic" thinking to his presidential leadership, even to his role as commander-in-chief. Boritt is always stimulating, even when he is not convincing. GREENSTONE is a highly abstract discussion of American liberalism by a political scientist, who makes little reference to historical context or political reality. He seeks to show that Lincoln synthesised, or at least reconciled, two strands of the American liberal tradition – the "humanist" liberalism of Jefferson and Jackson and the "reform" liberalism of the Adamses. The discussion is thoughtful, but historians will find it difficult to see the likes of Martin Van Buren and Stephen A. Douglas – and Abraham Lincoln for that matter – as systematic political thinkers, apparently unconcerned with how to win the next election.

In his widely-acclaimed and controversial analysis of the origins, context, language and meaning of the Gettysburg address, WILLS contends that, by accepting Lincoln's concept of a people dedicated to the proposition that all men are created equal, "we live in a different America." Wills argues that Lincoln saw the Declaration of Independence as both a founding national document and as the statement of a transcendent ideal. American history, from the Constitution onwards, became a constant struggle to approximate to that ideal. This is not an entirely original argument, and Wills is not given to understatement of his case, but he has stimulated fresh debate on Lincoln's fundamental ideas and ideals.

One way to come to terms with the unending historical debate on Lincoln is to turn to various collections of essays. One generally reliable guideline is that the selected essays of one distinguished scholar are often more illuminating than collections of essays by several different authors, often thrown together hastily after a conference or symposium. Two outstanding earlier examples of the former category are DONALD (1956, 1961) and CURRENT which provide

critical evaluation of Lincoln controversies of their time. Two more recent, and equally distinguished, examples of this genre are provided by Fehrenbacher and McPherson. FEHRENBACHER (1987) offers wise reflections on a variety of topics – including an influential essay on Lincoln's attitude to slavery and race – and adds some judicious assessments of the Lincoln literature. McPHERSON begins with two essays which develop the theme stated in his title, that the Civil War was the second American Revolution. However, more enduring value may attach to two later essays which discuss Lincoln and liberty, particularly his role in shifting the emphasis from negative liberty (freedom *from*) to positive liberty (freedom *to*).

One superior collection of essays by a variety of authors is edited by John L. THOMAS. It includes important contributions by Robert Wiebe, William Gienapp and Don Fehrenbacher, and a typically combative piece by Michael Holt, as well as an earlier outing for McPherson on the second American Revolution. Gabor Boritt, Director of the Civil War Institute at Gettysburg College, and generator of much activity in Civil War studies, is a tireless and enterprising editor of various collections of essays on Lincoln. BORITT (1992) has a distinguished group of contributors, including James McPherson, David Brion Davis, Kenneth Stampp, Carl Degler, Arthur Schlesinger and Robert V. Bruce, who discuss various aspects of Lincoln as war president.

Those seeking brief but authoritative explanations of many different episodes and aspects of Lincoln's life may turn with confidence to NEELY (1982), an invaluable work of reference. But however much we may know, or think we know about Abraham Lincoln, he remains in many ways an elusive and enigmatic figure.

PETER J. PARISH

Lippmann, Walter 1889–1974
Journalist and publicist

Blum, Steven B., *Walter Lippmann: Cosmopolitanism in the Century of Total War*, Ithaca, NY: Cornell University Press, 1984

Diggins, John Patrick, *The Promise of Pragmatism: Modernism and the Crisis of Knowledge and Authority*, Chicago: University of Chicago Press, 1994

Forcey, Charles, *The Crossroads of Liberalism: Croly, Weyl, Lippmann and the Progressive Era, 1900–1925*, New York: Oxford University Press, 1961

Kloppenberg, James, *Uncertain Victory: Social Democracy and Progressivism in European and American Thought, 1870–1920*, New York: Oxford University Press, 1986

Riccio, Barry D., *Walter Lippmann: Odyssey of a Liberal*, New Brunswick, NJ: Transaction, 1994

Steel, Ronald, *Walter Lippmann and the American Century*, Boston: Little Brown, 1980

Syed, Anwar Hussain, *Walter Lippmann's Philosophy of International Politics*, Philadelphia: University of Pennsylvania Press, 1963

Weingast, David Elliott, *Walter Lippmann: A Study in Personal Journalism*, New Brunswick, NJ: Rutgers University Press, 1949

Wellborn, Charles, *Twentieth-Century Pilgrimage: Walter Lippmann and the Public Philosophy*, Baton Rouge: Louisiana State University Press, 1969

Wright, Benjamin F., *Five Public Philosophies of Walter Lippmann*, Austin: University of Texas Press, 1973

Two large questions dominate the literature on Walter Lippmann's career and legacy: did he remain true to his liberal, progressive principles? and was he as much a political philosopher as he was a journalist? Whatever their verdicts might be on these matters, scholars have no such dispute as to the political and historical significance of America's most renowned columnist and political commentator. STEEL tells superbly the story of a man involved in the most pressing political matters of this, the American, century. This biography is a masterpiece of storytelling that avoids addressing the two dominant questions without losing the sense of importance that surrounded Lippmann. Although Steel interweaves the life of Lippmann with the political fabric of most of the 20th century, he is unable to uncover this very hidden man – his book lacks psychological depth.

Much of the interest in Lippmann's career has concentrated on his early years as the enfant terrible of the Progressives. FORCEY is a somewhat dated book that examines Lippmann (along with Herbert Croly and Walter Weyl) during his days with the *New Republic*. The author placed a special burden on the editors of *New Republic* as the founders of a new form of liberalism that Forcey feared was fatally flawed. His book was an effort to uncover its flaws, and, despite the reductionist and tendentious nature of the argument, Forcey provides a very illuminating history of the foundation of this very influential journal, and the thinkers who shaped it.

The young Lippmann is placed in a much larger historical and philosophical context by KLOPPENBERG. In this impressive and substantial work the author traces a transatlantic philosophical movement in which thinkers sought ways of living in an open-ended and disenchanted universe. According to Kloppenberg, Lippmann, as heir of American pragmatists like William James and John Dewey, sought to move from theory to politics. DIGGINS agrees with Kloppenberg that Lippmann was a product of pragmatic philosophy, but he discusses Lippmann in terms of his coming to grips with the failure of pragmatism to live up to its promise to give some direction to politics in an age without normative principles. Diggins concentrates on the mature Lippmann to demonstrate how much the changes in his views indicate a more fundamental problem with his earlier philosophical commitments. Kloppenberg wrote his book in defense of the beliefs held by the early Lippmann; Diggins wrote his to argue that Lippmann's life proved those beliefs problematic.

It is the oft-noted shifts in Lippmann's philosophical views that WRIGHT emphasizes in his effort to prove that Lippmann was a poor philosopher – so poor as to be no philosopher at all. Wright finds no fewer than five distinct philosophical arguments in Lippmann's work, which suggests, the author argues, that Lippmann lacked the analytical rigor to be considered an important philosophical thinker. Others have sought to emphasize an underlying continuity in Lippmann's thinking. Both Wellborn and Riccio emphasize Lippmann's "liberalism." RICCIO's is the richer and more nuanced study that deals lucidly – if not always persuasively – with the numerous "contradictions" in Lippmann's behavior (support for Alf Landon in 1936, for instance) and connects them with the tensions inherent in American liberalism. WELLBORN deals more with Lippmann as a moral thinker. In a similar vein, BLUM emphasizes that Lippmann's thought was not only coherent and reasonably consistent, but also serious political philosophy. Blum argues that Lippmann's views were a product of his "cosmopolitanism" – that he saw all important matters in the context of the interdependence of the modern world. This theme not only pervaded many of his most important books, Blum argued, but is one of the most useful insights that Lippmann offered to his readers, most of whom lived in provincial bliss.

Many of the books written about Lippmann's philosophy emphasize his liberal credentials or lament his failure to live up to those credentials – either he was a traitor or he has been misunderstood. In short, most of the work on his political philosophy tends to be by liberals on behalf of something they call "liberalism." Others – whatever their ideological views – have focused on other aspects of his career. Arguably, Lippmann's greatest political impact was felt in foreign affairs, a subject to which he turned often in his columns (and he had a hand in policymaking from World War I through the early Cold War). SYED explores the way in which Lippmann approached international affairs, with particular attention to the problem of seeking to apply substantive theories in a world where the struggle for power motivates most international behavior. However useful Syed may be in understanding this part of Lippmann's thinking, it is hardly the last word on Lippmann's involvement in foreign policy. That book is still to be written. Similarly, the role of Lippmann as a journalist (and on journalism) is not well explored. WEINGAST is a fine study on Lippmann the journalist, but it was written in the middle of Lippmann's career and before some of his more controversial contributions.

TED V. McALLISTER

Lodge, Henry Cabot 1850–1924
Political Leader and Senator

Garraty, John A., *Henry Cabot Lodge: A Biography*, New York: Knopf, 1953

Groves, Charles Stuart, *Henry Cabot Lodge, the Statesman*, Boston: Small Maynard, 1925

Lawrence, William, *Henry Cabot Lodge: A Biographical Sketch*, Boston: Houghton Mifflin, 1925

Schriftgiesser, Karl, *The Gentleman from Massachusetts: Henry Cabot Lodge*, Boston: Little Brown, 1944

Washburn, Charles G., *Henry Cabot Lodge*, Boston: Massachusetts Historical Society, 1925

Widenor, William C., *Henry Cabot Lodge and the Search for an American Foreign Policy*, Berkeley: University of California Press, 1980

Henry Cabot Lodge was long portrayed as one of the great controversial figures of American politics, not only because he was a thorough party-line figure, but mostly because, as a close friend of Theodore Roosevelt and the chairman of the Senate Foreign Relations Committee, he had great influence on major decisions relating to the Spanish-American War, the United States rejection of the League of Nations, and the nomination of Warren Harding in 1920. The earliest biographies of Lodge, mostly written by his friends and associates, generally highlighted Lodge's contribution to American politics and were largely personal tributes. WASHBURN is a brief recollection, delivered as a memorial at the Massachusetts Historical Society shortly after Lodge's death in 1924. It was not a scholarly piece, but it focused particularly on a series of landmark events in Lodge's career. Following the same pattern, LAWRENCE portrayed Lodge as a favorite son of Massachusetts who had made an enormous contribution to American political life. He concentrated mostly on Lodge's later career, especially his role in the making of American foreign policy from the 1890s to the 1920s. In contrast, GROVES offered a more detailed picture of Lodge, which included his early life, his acquaintance with many important political figures in Massachusetts, including Charles Sumner, and his fight for the Federal Election Bill of 1890, in addition to his senatorial career. But his assessment of Lodge differed little from that of Washburn and Lawrence. These early biographies are friendly and largely uncritical.

The first fully-fledged critique of Lodge and his career was SCHRIFTGIESSER. Although a journalist, Schriftgiesser treated his subject with great caution and careful research. Using mostly available printed sources, including the correspondence between Theodore Roosevelt and Lodge, Schriftgiesser's study covers the whole story, from the beginning of the Lodge family in America in 1700 to Lodge's death. He portrays Lodge as a shrewd, conservative partisan in domestic politics and, in terms of foreign policy, an unequivocal imperialist. Although he gives Lodge credit for leading the fight for federal protection of black suffrage in 1890, he incorrectly finds Lodge's motivation in his ambition to be the heir to the senate seat of Charles Sumner. Again, in evaluating Lodge's role in promoting restriction of child labor in the District of Columbia in 1907, Schriftgiesser believed that Lodge was not motivated by genuine humanitarian concern. His sharpest criticism of Lodge is directed at the latter's theories and decisions on immigration, national security, commercial expansion of the United States, and, most of all, Lodge's firm opposition to Wilson's policy. Schriftgiesser argues that it was the Republican defeat of the Wilson peace plan that planted the seeds of World War II – and the reason for the defeat lay purely in the partisanship exploited by Lodge. Although comprehensive, Schriftgiesser's study is marred by his own partisanship which was as extreme as that of his subject – as well as by the lack of primary sources, because at this time the Lodge papers were unavailable for his use.

Substantive, coherent, and critical, GARRATY remains the definitive biography of Lodge. The first Lodge biographer to use the Lodge papers in the Massachusetts Historical Society, Garraty disclaims any notion that his work is an official biography. Garraty documents major events in Lodge's early life – his involvement with the reform-minded Liberal Republicans, his editorship of the *North American Review*, his brief teaching career at Harvard, and his association with the Mugwumps in 1884 – so as to trace the evolution of Lodge's political character, and to explain how and why Lodge decided to abandon political independence and become a devoted party leader. Compared to Schriftgiesser, Garraty presents a more accurate and convincing picture of the early Lodge, particularly the foundations of his intellectual and political mentality. A substantial portion of the book is devoted to Lodge's later career in Washington, and his impact on the foreign policy making of the United States. Here Garraty offers a more detailed analysis of Lodge's motivations. He examines Lodge's anti-immigrant policy and concludes that his opposition to further European immigration was based on "nationality" rather than on biological race. Although Garraty admits that Lodge's foreign policy contained elements of imperialism, he argues that Lodge developed his imperialistic outlook only after 1899, when the United States had taken the Philippines, and new vistas opened for American economic expansion. The China policy – the Open Door and suppression of the Boxer Rebellion – was the turning point in the development of Lodge's vision of imperialism.

WIDENOR provides an in-depth analysis of the ideological and historical foundations of Lodge's foreign policy. Using principally Lodge's published writings and private papers, Widenor corrects the traditional image of Lodge as a personally vindictive Republican partisan and a ruthless imperialist. In Widenor's view, Lodge was a Federalist intellect who was deeply concerned with exploring the proper relationship between foreign policy and the domestic political structure. Claiming that Lodge was no less idealistic than Wilson, Widenor sees the way in which Lodge formulated and conducted foreign policy as consistent with his historical and ideological thinking, which he believes grew out of Lodge's search for an appropriate foreign policy under American democratic conditions.

XI WANG

See also Foreign Policy, 1865–1918 and 1919–1941

Long, Huey

1893–1935
Louisiana politician and campaigner

Brinkley, Alan, *Voices of Protest: Huey Long, Father Coughlin and the Great Depression*, New York: Knopf, 1982

Graham, Hugh Davis (editor), *Huey Long*, Englewood Cliffs, NJ: Prentice Hall, 1970

Hair, William Ivy, *The Kingfish and His Realm: The Life and Times of Huey P. Long*, Baton Rouge: Louisiana State University Press, 1991

Jeansonne, Glen, *Messiah of the Masses: Huey P. Long and the Great Depression*, New York: HarperCollins, 1993

Sindler, Alan P., *Huey Long's Louisiana: State Politics, 1920–1952*, Baltimore: Johns Hopkins Press, 1956

Williams, T. Harry, *Huey Long*, New York: Knopf, and London: Thames and Hudson, 1969

Elected governor of Louisiana in 1928 and United States senator in 1930, Huey Pierce Long consolidated his power base through one-man ("Kingfish") rule in Lousiana and by 1935 was attacking President Franklin Roosevelt for failure to end the Depression. Long's presidential ambition, based on a soak-the-rich appeal to the angry masses, was stilled by an assassin's bullet in September 1935. The high drama of Long's meteoric career was captured in the driven figure of Willie Stark, protagonist in Robert Penn Warren's Pulitzer Prize-winning novel *All the King's Men* (1946).

Warren's Willie Stark humanized a man whose flamboyant style and dictatorial practices in Louisiana persuaded most contemporary writers that he combined the qualities of southern demagoguery and Mussolini-style fascism. GRAHAM's edited biography provides representative interpretations, few of them favorable, from the pre-1960s literature – including journalist Raymond Gram Swing, "Forerunner of American Fascism"; Louisiana publisher Hodding Carter, "American Dictator"; political scientist V.O. Key, Jr., "The Seamy Side of Democracy"; and historian Arthur Schlesinger, Jr., "Messiah of the Rednecks."

Key's essay, drawn from the chapter on Louisiana in his classic study of 1945, *Southern Politics*, acknowledges the ruthless nature of Long's political machine, fueled by involuntary "deducts" from state worker paychecks and enforced by heavy-handed state police. But Key explained Long as a product of an impoverished state dominated by privileged elites. SINDLER, like Key a political scientist, expanded Key's argument that Democratic party rivalry between the Long and anti-Long factions gave Louisiana a semblance of two-party competition lacking in other southern states. This provided hope for escape from the South's crippling political legacy of racial segregation, disfranchisement, malapportionment, and the one-party system.

In the 1960s, as in the 1930s, American political sympathies shifted toward the left, and writers searching for a usable past re-evaluated Long's legacy. Unlike most American politicians, Long had called for radical redistribution of income. Unlike most southern demagogues, Long had largely avoided racial scapegoating. In 1969 WILLIAMS, a historian at Louisiana State University, published his Pulitzer Prize-winning biography of Long. In the absence of a substantial body of Long manuscripts, Williams based his 876-page book on almost 300 interviews. In an era of insurgent social movements on behalf of African Americans, women, the poor and disadvantaged, Williams acknowledged Long's warts, but saw him as a "good mass leader," crusader for social justice against the power and wealth of reactionary elites.

Challenging the view that associated Long with modern social reform, BRINKLEY compared the protests led by Long and by the Roman Catholic "radio priest" from Detroit, Father Charles E. Coughlin. In Brinkley's view, Long and Coughlin were not precursors of rational, forward-looking social mobilization. Rather, they were manifestations of a powerful impulse common to the Great Depression and many decades before it: "the urge to defend the autonomy of the individual and the independence of the community against encroachments from the modern industrial state." Theirs was a protest of nostalgia, rooted in an idealized past.

Brinkley's association of Long with the politics of memory in national history, reacting against the sympathetic portrayal of Williams, found parallels in studies of Long that emphasize the shaping force of Louisiana's unique history. In the first full-length study of Long since the Williams biography, HAIR emphasizes Long's unbridled lust for power. Conceding Long's formidable mental acuity, his mesmerizing capabilities and his impish wit, Hair nonetheless describes the emphasis on expediency in the career of a crude, sarcastic, egotistical bully, without redeeming qualities of social sincerity or political integrity. Hair emphasizes the raw, bizarre, burlesque traditions of Louisiana politics. In national politics, he saw Long's Share Our Wealth scheme as economic absurdity, his attitude toward international relations as unreflective isolationism and protectionism. To Hair, Long's political solution for the country in 1935 was cynically self-serving: split the Roosevelt coalition, elect a Hooverite Republican, and profit from four more years of economic disaster by offering to save the country in 1940.

JEANSONNE, like Hair, acknowledges Long's modest positive accomplishments in Louisiana, mostly of the road-paving and bridge-building variety. In his slim interpretive biography, Jeansonne observes that Long failed to institutionalize his revolution. Moreover, Louisiana's Long-centered bi-factionalism faded after 1960, when racial issues dominated state politics. Like Brinkley, Jeansonne sees Long as an adept politician whose populist nostrums represented a protest against modernism. "On the state level he furnished works without ideology," Jeansonne concludes; "on the national level he provided ideology without works."

HUGH DAVIS GRAHAM

See also New Deal: Political and Constitutional Issues

Los Angeles

Baldassare, Mark (editor), *The Los Angeles Riots: Lessons for the Urban Future*, Boulder, CO: Westview Press, 1994

Banham, Reyner, *Los Angeles: The Architecture of Four Ecologies*, London: Allen Lane, and New York: Harper, 1971

Davis, Mike, *City of Quartz: Excavating the Future in Los Angeles*, London: Verso, 1990

Fogelson, Robert M., *The Fragmented Metropolis: Los Angeles, 1850–1930*, Cambridge, MA: Harvard University Press, 1967

George, Lynell, *No Crystal Stair: African-Americans in the City of Angels*, London: Verso, 1992

Jencks, Charles, *Heteropolis: Los Angeles, the Riots and the Strange Beauty of Hetero-Architecture*, London: Academy, and New York: St. Martin's Press, 1993

McWilliams, Carey, *Southern California Country: An Island upon the Land*, New York: Duell, Sloan, and Pearce, 1946

Rieff, David, *Los Angeles: Capital of the Third World*, New York: Simon and Schuster, 1991; London: Cape, 1992

Soja, Edward W., *Postmodern Geographies: The Reassertion of Space in Critical Social Theory*, London: Verso, 1989

Starr, Kevin, *Inventing the Dream: California Through the Progressive Era*, New York: Oxford University Press, 1985

Starr, Kevin, *Material Dreams: Southern California Through the 1920s*, New York: Oxford University Press, 1990

The study of Los Angeles has been a relatively recent phenomenon, and it is only since 1985 that there has been a surge of critical attention. Several factors have fuelled this interest: a sense of Los Angeles as the home of the postmodern condition; its significance as a paradigm for the American city of the future; and, since the riots of 1992, an interest in the ethnic composition of the city and its portents for identity politics in both the city and the United States as a whole. Similarly, in this short period, several different types of analysis have also developed: archaeologies of the city's culture and politics; studies of ethnicity; and studies of Los Angeles as the future city of postmodernity.

Three important books published prior to this period do not fit readily into any of these categories but have helped to set the ground for recent study. Ex-District Attorney McWILLIAMS's history of pre-war Los Angeles is the first notable study of the city. It documents Los Angeles in the first half of the century and focuses on concerns that are still very relevant to the city today: for example, Los Angeles' sense of cultural and demographic rootlessness and the culture of puritanism and health fostered by the city's Boosterist pioneers at the turn of the century. FOGELSON is a sound, conventional work of urban history which synthesizes much of the earlier work on Los Angeles, and remains useful although inevitably somewhat outdated. It traces the process of urbanization from small beginnings in the mid-19th century to the sprawling city of the inter-war period. It combines economic, social and political history in its account of the evolution of the "fragmented metropolis" of its title.

The third important book published before 1985 is BANHAM, a study of Los Angeles architecture written at the end of the 1960s which offers a utopian vision of the city and also identifies broad cultural movements. Banham argues that the culture and built environment of Los Angeles are constructed around four different "ecologies": a nostalgic and romanticized Spanish past; a technological "autopian" vision of the city based around the freeways; individuality and elitism; and the rootless homogeneity of the suburbs. The result is a contradictory city, but one where internal differences create an eclectic and plural society.

The utopian view of Los Angeles has not, however, been shared by recent commentators, particularly those who present an archaeology of the city in order to understand how the city's past has shaped the present. DAVIS is the key critic of the city in this respect. His concern is to demythologize the dominant "sunshine" images of the city by reference to the economic and political realities that have kept large groups (mainly non-white) perpetually marginalized, and to show the disparity between utopian representation (in the *LA 2000* report) and dystopian actuality (the criminalization of black youth). His analysis of the city is the outstanding study of Los Angeles, its range of concerns (civic politics, suburbanism, riot architecture, postmodern enclaves, images of Los Angeles in film and fiction, gangs, demography, ethnic history, religion, cults, and failed utopias). The rigorous and critical way in which history is related to contemporary trends makes this the essential book on Los Angeles.

Starr offers a similar demythologization of Los Angeles, but does so by reference to the period of the city's rise to national importance between 1890 and 1930. Although his two volumes cover Southern California as a whole, it is Los Angeles that forms the main focus. Covering the settlement of Los Angeles from 1880 to 1920, STARR (1985) discusses the settlement of the city in imagination and symbol (as a desert turned into a garden) as well as in historical reality. STARR (1990) continues this theme by studying the 1920s and deals with the way in which the city was represented as a paradigm for the materializing of dreams in this decade, not only through its material growth (engineering projects, architecture, development of suburban landscape), but also as an image of material success and freedom. The two volumes together provide an important account of the city's earlier history. They present both a cogent account of the ideas that dominated the city's social and cultural life, and a wealth of examples and details not matched in any other works on the city.

The continued dominance of Anglo-American images of Los Angeles is something that is also considered by RIEFF whose focus is on Anglo representations of Hispanic and African American groups in the city. This book began as an account of Rieff's stay in Los Angeles, but becomes more than this in his analysis of white paranoia in contemporary Los Angeles, particularly with respect to the growing Hispanic population. As a consequence, Rieff generates a powerful critique of stereotypes and images of the city and presents a strong sense of the lived experience of Los Angeles.

Since the 1992 riots several books on ethnicity in Los Angeles have appeared. Of these probably the strongest is BALDASSARE, a collection of essays which historicizes the Los Angeles riots, by reference to wider ethnic concerns and conflicts in the city, particularly in terms of the displacement of tensions away from the white-black axis on to conflicts between Asian, Hispanic and African American groups. The reader will find strong historical and sociological analysis, including a wealth of useful statistical tables and maps as well as details of the city's ethnic politics both before and after the riots.

Specific treatment of the African American experience in the city can be found in GEORGE's excellent collection of essays which deal with the everyday experience of racism, ethnic tension, and marginality through a study of individual struggles for justice within the African American areas of the city. The book combines these attempts to represent African American politics and culture with a series of essays in the final section which offer a wider social and political analysis of ethnicity and marginality in the city.

The study of Los Angeles comes full circle with Jencks and Soja who both follow Banham in focusing primarily on contemporary trends. They concentrate on the "postmodern" facets of the city and its future, and argue for a positive vision. Written before the 1992 riots, SOJA presents an optimistic account of the postmodernization of society, and he focuses on Los Angeles' cosmopolitanism in the last two chapters because of the city's apparent cultural diversity and political plurality. JENCKS offers a more double-edged and original argument. He argues that the cosmopolitan discourses that characterize the city's politics and culture have actually produced an apartheid version of heterogeneity in which Anglos sample or consume non-white cultures (in the form of ethnic cuisine), but socially, economically and institutionally wall out these same cultures. The result is the fragmentation, ethnic conflict, privatization of space, and defensive architecture that helped to cause the 1992 riots. Jencks looks instead for a properly postmodern and "heteropolitan" hybridization of Los Angeles through the reclamation of public space which, he believes, will produce meaningful contacts between ethnic groups and allow real cross-fertilization of cultures.

FRAN MASON

See also California

Lost Cause/Southern Memories of the Civil War

Connelly, Thomas L., *The Marble Man: Robert E. Lee and His Image in American Society*, New York: Knopf, 1977

Connelly, Thomas L. and Barbara L. Bellows, *God and General Longstreet: The Lost Cause and the Southern Mind*, Baton Rouge: Louisiana State University Press, 1982

Foster, Gaines M., *Ghosts of the Confederacy: Defeat, the Lost Cause, and the Emergence of the New South, 1865–1913*, New York: Oxford University Press, 1987

Neely, Mark E., Jr., Harold Holzer, and Gabor S. Boritt, *The Confederate Image: Prints of the Lost Cause*, Chapel Hill: University of North Carolina Press, 1987

Osterweis, Rollin G., *The Myth of the Lost Cause, 1865–1900*, Hamden, CT: Archon, 1973

Piston, William Garrell, *Lee's Tarnished Lieutenant: James Longstreet and His Place in Southern History*, Athens: University of Georgia Press, 1987

Royster, Charles, *The Destructive War: William Tecumseh Sherman, Stonewall Jackson, and the Americans*, New York: Knopf, 1991

Warren, Robert Penn, *The Legacy of the Civil War: Meditations on the Centennial*, New York: Random House, 1961

Weaver, Richard M., *The Southern Tradition at Bay: A History of Postbellum Thought*, edited by George Core and M.E. Bradford, New Rochelle, NY: Arlington House, 1968

Wilson, Charles Reagan, *Baptized in Blood: The Religion of the Lost Cause, 1865–1920*, Athens: University of Georgia Press, 1980

Woodward, C. Vann, *The Burden of Southern History*, Baton Rouge: Louisiana State University Press, 1960, 3rd edition, 1993

"Lost Cause," originally and often still used to describe the South's war for independence, is now primarily employed by

scholars to describe the white South's celebration and memory of the Civil War. WARREN, a novelist's extended essay on the tragic nature of the war, argues that its memory still captivates the American and, especially, the southern mind. The Confederacy became immortal at Appomattox, Robert Penn Warren maintains, and southerners used their defeat as a "Great Alibi," blaming all subsequent shortcomings on it. Essays in WOODWARD also explore the persisting burden of defeat, which along with guilt, poverty, and other frustrations, could have led southerners to a deeper sense of the past, and an escape from Americans' perception of their innocence. These arguments for a unique southern perspective shaped by defeat remain central to conceptions of the Lost Cause, at least among intellectuals. Warren and Woodward should be read for that reason alone, but also because both provide powerful, evocative essays. Other books, however, offer more systematic examinations of the Lost Cause.

WEAVER provides the most extensive analysis available of various genres of late 19th century southern writing on the war. He finds in them a pattern of thought rooted in agrarian ways and characterized by scepticism toward science and technology, deep spirituality, and a hierarchical vision of society. He shares these values, believes the South was fundamentally right, and wields the southern tradition against modern society.

Studies of the postwar images of Confederate leaders provide useful insights. In a reinterpretation of Robert E. Lee based on a critical analysis of earlier treatments, CONNELLY carefully documents how various Virginia Confederates made Lee a southern idol. They portrayed him as having a perfect character and, by blaming James Longstreet for the Confederate debacle at Gettysburg, rendered him an unequaled military leader. The resulting Lee cult eased the pain of defeat and provided southerners with a saint whose purity alone justified their cause. Re-examining the Gettysburg controversy from Longstreet's point of view, PISTON adds a few details to Connelly's account of the Virginians' efforts, but reaches similar conclusions about their role. NEELY, HOLZER, and BORITT provide a marvelous collection of photographs and pictures from and about the Confederacy, along with brief essays on the images of Lee, Jefferson Davis, Stonewall Jackson, and other rebel leaders. ROYSTER furnishes a more substantial evaluation of the nature and use of Jackson's postwar reputation. A widely researched, well-written, and wise exploration of the meaning of the Civil War for Americans of both regions, it offers other occasional insights into the Lost Cause as well.

Four books focus specifically on the Lost Cause. OSTERWEIS traces the influence of Romanticism within the Lost Cause. Short and superficial, it has been superseded by the other three, each of which has particular merits. Based on extensive research, especially in southern magazines and the personal papers of southern ministers, WILSON derives much of its interpretive power from its portrayal of the Lost Cause as a civil religion, which gave the region a special, and in its mind superior, cultural identity. After the war, Wilson shows, southern churches, colleges, and rituals perpetuated this civil religion. It centered on a myth of crusading Christian Confederates, including certain sainted leaders, and interpreted defeat as part of God's plan for the future vindication of the South. It also buttressed white supremacy and segregation but offered a critique of the materialism of the New South. By the end of World War I, the South had once again embraced an American nationalism, but according to Wilson, its special sense of identity persisted as well.

CONNELLY and BELLOWS also stress the tie between the Lost Cause and evangelical piety. Defeat brought alienation and estrangement, its authors contend, which was then eased by an "Inner Lost Cause," characterized by a belief that the Confederates had been the more moral men in the war and by a providential view of history. Connelly and Bellows argue that by the end of the century a "National" Lost Cause had emerged, as Virginia became synonymous with the Confederacy. Here and in other places, they stress the importance of Lee's image and draw heavily on Connelly's earlier work. But, as no other book does, Connelly and Bellows take the story of the Lost Cause up to the present. Echoing themes developed by Woodward, they contend that the Lost Cause mentality does not celebrate the Confederacy but recalls defeat. It persists in a distinctive morality, sense of estrangement, and acknowledgment of failure that they find expressed in 20th-century southern literature and, especially, in modern country music.

Based, more than are other studies, on an interpretation of organizational behavior and a "reading" of Memorial Day celebrations, the erection and unveiling of monuments, and veterans' reunions as well as writings, speeches, and personal papers, FOSTER also analyzes the traumatic effect of defeat upon white southerners, and finds an initial response similar to that presented in Wilson and in Connelly and Bellows. It too traces the role of the Virginians but questions their influence on southern society at a time when most white southerners sought only to memorialize the Confederacy. In the 1890s and under new leaders, a popular celebration of the Confederacy soothed the persisting pains of defeat and eased the tensions that social change brought. This celebration vindicated the South's conduct in the war, supported the emergence of a New South, and facilitated national reconciliation. In perhaps the most direct challenge to the view of Warren and Woodward, Foster concludes that the public memory of the Confederacy lost power and specificity as the 20th century progressed, and claims that defeat did little to create a special southern sense of the past.

GAINES M. FOSTER

See also South: since 1865

Louisiana Purchase, 1803

Adams, Henry, *History of the United States of America During the Administrations of Jefferson and Madison*, 9 vols., New York: Scribner, 1889–91; edited by Earl N. Harbert, 2 vols., New York: Library of America, 1986

Dangerfield, George, *Chancellor Robert R. Livingston of New York, 1746–1813*, New York: Harcourt Brace, 1960

DeConde, Alexander, *This Affair of Louisiana*, New York: Scribner, 1976

Lyon, E. Wilson, *Louisiana in French Diplomacy, 1759–1804*, Norman: University of Oklahoma Press, 1934

Lyon, E. Wilson, *The Man Who Sold Louisiana: The Career of François Barbé-Marbois*, Norman: University of Oklahoma Press, 1942

Tucker, Robert W. and David C. Hendrickson, *Empire of Liberty: The Statecraft of Thomas Jefferson*, New York and Oxford: Oxford University Press, 1990

Whitaker, Arthur Preston, *The Mississippi Question, 1795–1803: A Study in Trade, Politics, and Diplomacy*, New York: Appleton Century, 1934

There is an abundance of literature on the Louisiana Purchase but few satisfactory modern, scholarly studies. Associated with the centennial of the Purchase was a spate of narrative histories, including such standard accounts as James K. Hosmer, *The History of the Louisiana Purchase* (1902), James Q. Howard, *History of the Louisiana Purchase* (1902), and Curtis M. Geer, *The Louisiana Purchase and the Western Movement* (1904), which are now too dated to be of much real value. A number of popular accounts, such as Donald B. Chidsey's *Louisiana Purchase* (1972) and Marshall Sprague's *So Vast, So Beautiful a Land: Louisiana and the Purchase* (1974), are too poorly documented and inaccurate to satisfy the serious reader.

Of the older treatments of the Purchase, ADAMS alone meets the canons of modern scholarship. The first and third volumes of his nine volumes on the presidencies of Jefferson and Madison contain an excellent general account of the Purchase. Drawing heavily upon both American and European archives, he gives greater weight to European than to American causes for the sale. According to Adams, Napoleon's military and diplomatic situation, and not expansionist pressures from the United States, explain the decision to sell Louisiana.

Two books by Lyon detail the history of the Purchase from the French point of view. LYON (1934) is the more comprehensive and important account, which draws upon French as well as Spanish archives to trace French diplomacy relating to Louisiana, from the time the region was divided between Great Britain and Spain in 1763 down to the transfer of the territory to the United States in 1803. He explains fully how the French used Louisiana to exploit Spain, thwart Britain, and befriend the United States. He skilfully describes the Directory's complicated manoeuverings and explains how the failure of Napoleon's plans for a new empire in America, coupled with his desire to gain American support against Britain, prompted him to sell Louisiana. An excellent supplement to this volume is LYON (1942), a very readable biography of François Barbé-Marbois, the French civil servant who negotiated the sale of Louisiana. Barbé-Marbois, a career diplomat whose service spanned more than fifty years, was a skilful negotiator whom Napoleon trusted to secure for France the best bargain possible. The biography amplifies and reinforces aspects of Lyon's 1934 study, showing that, after the debacle in Santo Domingo, Napoleon read correctly the handwriting on the wall: France could not hold on to Louisiana. His best strategy was to win the good will of the virile young American republic, whose restless frontier inhabitants would soon flood into Louisiana. Napoleon instructed Barbé-Marbois to hold out for fifty million francs; the shrewd horse-trader asked the American commissioners for a hundred million and settled for eighty.

What Lyon accomplishes for the French side of the story, WHITAKER does for the Spanish side. His account, which draws heavily on Spanish archival sources, is more than just a treatment of the diplomatic issues that grew out of the Treaty of San Lorenzo. He covers the commercial, political, and frontier developments in both the United States and Louisiana while, at the same time, he examines and analyzes Spanish, French, and American policy toward Louisiana. He treats fully and thoughtfully the four-year period following the Treaty of San Lorenzo when the United States, fully aware of France's attempts to regain Louisiana, supported various filibustering efforts to seize the province rather than allow it to fall into French hands. During this time both countries, he says, "hovered on the brink of war". Spain gladly retroceded Louisiana to France in 1800 because it could no longer afford the cost of defending it. The "Mississippi Question" was solved only by the Louisiana Purchase. Taken together with Whitaker's earlier work, *The Spanish-American Frontier, 1783–1795: The Westward Movement and the Spanish Retreat in the Mississippi Valley* (1927), it gives a full account of the clash of Spanish and American interests along the Mississippi Valley frontier and thus offers an excellent background to the Louisiana Purchase itself.

The American side of the story is best told by DANGERFIELD, whose superb biography of Robert Livingston, the United States minister to France and purchaser of Louisiana, sheds light on personal and psychological aspects of the negotiations, and presents a balanced, judicious, and skilfully written life of an important diplomatic player. TUCKER and HENDRICKSON complement Dangerfield in an excellent, succinct study of Jefferson's foreign policy. It details how Jefferson, in creating his "empire of liberty", pursued the ambitious ends of territorial expansion and commercial reformation through peaceful means, renouncing the military and financial system that characterized the great powers of Europe. The chapters treating the Louisiana Purchase incorporate the latest scholarship and offer an insightful account of the background, the course of negotiations, and the significance of the Purchase.

The best comprehensive modern treatment is DeCONDE, a chronological narrative which analyzes and interprets the Purchase within the larger framework of manifest destiny. He sees the acquisition not as an isolated incident, but rather as a phase of Anglo-American expansionism which, already several centuries old, would culminate in the imperialism of the late 19th century. DeConde covers a good deal of familiar ground, already explored three-quarters of a century earlier by Henry Adams. No new light is cast on Napoleon's motives for selling Louisiana; he upholds the conventional view that Napoleon, disappointed by his inability to crush the Haitian insurgents of Toussaint L'Ouverture and distressed by the devastation wrought by tropical diseases on General Charles Leclerc's army, decided to sell Louisiana to the rising American republic while it was still advantageous to do so. DeConde minimizes the role of the frontiersmen in exerting pressure first on Spain, then on France, to sell Louisiana to the United States. He does occasionally make claims which the documentary record simply does not support. For example, he asserts that a bellicose President Jefferson was prepared to seize New Orleans by force if he could not acquire it by purchase. There

is nothing in the record to document this claim. Jefferson did not regard French occupation of New Orleans as a *casus belli*. Both the president and his secretary of state, James Madison, drew a clear distinction between mere French occupation of New Orleans, on the one hand, and on the other hand, denial to the United States of free navigation of the Mississippi River with the right of deposit. The latter could not be tolerated. This cavil aside, DeConde is a thoughtful, well-written narrative account of the Louisiana Purchase which both the specialist and general reader may read with benefit.

CHARLES D. LOWERY

Loyalists

Bailyn, Bernard, *The Ordeal of Thomas Hutchinson*, Cambridge, MA: Belknap Press of Harvard University Press, 1974
Brown, Wallace, *The King's Friends: The Composition and Motives of the American Loyalist Claimants*, Providence, RI: Brown University Press, 1965
Calhoon, Robert M., *The Loyalists in Revolutionary America, 1760–1781*, New York: Harcourt Brace, 1973
Nelson, William H., *The American Tory*, Oxford: Clarendon Press, and New York: Oxford University Press, 1961
Norton, Mary Beth, *The British-Americans: The Loyalist Exiles in England, 1774–1789*, Boston: Little Brown, 1972; London: Constable, 1974
Potter-MacKinnon, Janice, *While the Women Only Wept: Loyalist Refugee Women*, Montreal: McGill-Queen's University Press, 1993

History has not been kind to the Loyalists. With some notable exceptions such as Lorenzo Sabine and Claude H. Van Tyne, 19th- and early 20th-century scholars generally ignored or condemned them. Even those who had some interest in emphasizing their role and significance – imperial historians like Lawrence H. Gipson and Charles M. Andrews and, arguably, Progressives such as J.F. Jameson and A.M. Schlesinger, Sr. – viewed them through the prism of their particular theories concerning the character of the American Revolution. They failed, as a result, to provide a rounded view of Loyalism as a social and intellectual movement.

Arguably, the first nuanced and balanced study to appear was NELSON. In this slim, compact work, he departs from his predecessors by arguing that the Loyalists did not come exclusively from the ranks of imperial officials, clergymen, and wealthy merchants. Instead, according to Nelson, the movement was socially heterogeneous and drew popular support from conscious minorities and from peripheral or vulnerable geographical areas. Despite the thrust of his argument, however, he still falls into the trap of seeing Loyalist ideology exclusively in terms of the attitudes espoused by prominent colonial administrators and Church of England luminaries. Their values, which can be dubbed as Anglican High Toryism, were almost certainly atypical. Still, in other respects, Nelson did anticipate the agenda of the next quarter century of scholarship in relation to the central issues of Loyalist motivation, social background, and treatment.

Among the sources neglected by Nelson were the Loyalist compensation claims at the Public Record Office in London. They form the basis of BROWN's work. He analyzes almost three thousand claims, and then compares his findings with data from other material in an attempt to find out who the Loyalists were and why they adopted the stance they did. The core of his study is an impressive series of tables for each state providing a statistical breakdown of the claimants' national origins, the dates of their arrival, their occupations, the amounts of their claims, their service to the British government, and their geographical distribution. In his commentary, however, he loses sight of the fact that his findings do not apply to all Loyalists but rather only to the select band of Tories who found their way to Nova Scotia or London to file their claims. Obviously this reduces the book's utility and raises questions about the extent to which his principal source can provide a genuine foundation for a general study of Loyalism.

Using Loyalists' correspondence and government papers, NORTON concentrates on the British authorities' response to the appeals of prominent émigrés for pensions, compensation, and financial aid. She also looks at the exiles' personal lives, thoughts on the war, criticisms of the government's efforts, and dispersal throughout the empire. What emerges strongly is their marginal status and position. The émigrés were displaced persons who could not return to the newly-independent United States, yet obviously did not feel entirely at ease in English society or at one with the British authorities.

In many ways, CALHOON remains the most ambitious, comprehensive, and insightful study of the subject. The problem is that the book is rather unwieldy. It comprises 48 chapters in all, grouped in six sections. The first three examine the growing imperial crisis in various colonies more or less chronologically from the early 1760s to the outbreak of war. The last three parts describe the Revolution's development in New England, the Middle Colonies, and the South. As a result, the narrative is marred by both discontinuities and an unfortunate degree of unnecessary repetition. Throughout, Calhoon's underlying concern is Loyalist motivation, examined principally through a collage of intelligently drawn biographical portraits and situational vignettes. However, Calhoon seldom offers meaningful generalizations based on these discrete studies. Nor does he attempt to assess the extent to which his chosen examples are representative of wider currents.

There have been several major biographies of individual Loyalists. BAILYN is perhaps the best-known. He provides an excellent intellectual portrait of Thomas Hutchinson during the last two decades of his life and stresses the anguish which he felt over his inability to mediate between his superiors in London and his fellow citizens in Massachusetts. Ultimately, however, it is difficult for the reader to evaluate all the influences operating on Hutchinson because Bailyn devotes very little attention to his subject's first 54 years and chooses throughout to emphasize ideological considerations at the expense of social and economic factors.

Recently Loyalist women have received welcome attention. In her study of northern New York, POTTER-MACKINNON argues that these wives and daughters of close-knit minority frontier communities contributed more to the war effort than their Patriot counterparts. They also suffered more from the stress of losing their homes and from their subsequent exile in eastern Ontario. But, in a classic example of women being denied their rightful place in history, their contribution was minimalized as early as the 1780s and this distorted view of the past was then passed down to subsequent generations.

KEITH MASON

M

MacArthur, Douglas 1880–1964
Military commander

Higgins, Trumbull, *Korea and the Fall of MacArthur: A Précis in Limited War*, New York: Oxford University Press, 1960

James, D. Clayton, *The Years of MacArthur*, 3 vols., Boston: Houghton Mifflin, and London: Leo Cooper, 1970–85

Long, Gavin, *MacArthur as Military Commander*, London: Batsford, and Princeton: Van Nostrand, 1969

Manchester, William, *American Caesar: Douglas MacArthur, 1880–1964*, New York: Dell, 1978; London: Hutchinson, 1979

Rovere, Richard H. and Arthur M. Schlesinger, Jr., *The General and the President*, New York: Farrar Straus, 1951; as *General MacArthur and President Truman*, New Brunswick, NJ: Transaction, 1992

Schaller, Michael, *Douglas MacArthur: The Far Eastern General*, New York and Oxford: Oxford University Press, 1989

Spanier, John W., *The Truman-MacArthur Controversy and the Korean War*, Cambridge, MA: Belknap Press of Harvard University Press, 1959

Whitney, Courtney, *MacArthur: His Rendezvous with History*, New York: Knopf, 1956

Few figures in 20th-century America have been more powerful – both in terms of the control which they exercised and the strength of the aura which surrounded them – than Douglas MacArthur. Studies of him have been influenced not only by available records and the natural cycles of historical reputation, but also by the fierce controversies surrounding his activities.

JAMES has produced by far the best biography, a standard reference work the influence of which subsequent writers have found it hard to escape. His three volumes, totalling 2,500 pages, are a model of scholarship, detailed scrutiny of the important questions, incisive analysis, and judicious and fair assessment. He has captured both the stature and the awfulness of MacArthur – "Like me, you the reader will probably find yourself alternately admiring and despising MacArthur." For all its massive scale, the biography is written in an easy, fluent, clear style. James is restrained in making judgments, observing how many people who never met MacArthur in life and research speak with great certainty about his traits as a commander and as a man. Volume I covers his early life and career in the army, culminating in his appointment as its youngest chief of staff and then, in 1935, as military commander of the Philippines, a post he held when Japan attacked in 1941. The next volume examines his generalship in the Pacific War. The third volume covers his aloof, autocratic rule over Japan; his command in the Korean War – from the daring Inchon invasion to the blunders which contributed to the disaster and crisis of November 1950 to January 1951 – and, finally, his challenge to the president's authority, resulting in his recall and the attendant, short-lived uproar in the United States.

There is no entirely satisfactory single-volume study. Manchester and Schaller might be cited as the cases for the defence and the prosecution, respectively. MANCHESTER is a vivid and gripping account which is perhaps the most enjoyable read of any MacArthur biography. Although it identifies the paradoxes and complexities of the general, it does not probe to the heart of his personality. Moreover, its coverage concentrates upon the war, giving rather too little attention to his post-1945 career. It draws on a variety of sources but does not pay enough attention to a number of official collections. Manchester needs to be used with caution and should be checked against the more reliable James.

SCHALLER's angle of approach is to view MacArthur as a gauge of the nature of United States-Far Eastern relations. If his writing lacks the zest of Manchester, the contents are absorbing enough, and he does scrutinize MacArthur's character more fully, even quoting comments on his sex life – "he's a buck private in the boudoir", asserted his first wife. It may be that both authors attribute too much influence to questions of personality, and too little to broader forces such as the shape of contemporary opinion or the nature of the international scene. The case for the prosecution seems overstated. In some degree, Schaller is a reverse image of Manchester; while one cites mainly sources favourable to MacArthur, the other uses material injurious to his reputation. Schaller almost dismisses the general's achievements in the Pacific War, in Japan, and in Korea. Neither writer adequately addresses those aspects of the general's character and career that are out of keeping with his own perspective. Manchester does not quite explain MacArthur's fall, while Schaller does not succeed in explaining his high reputation up to that time.

A flavour of contemporary and near contemporary opinion is conveyed in a sympathetic vein by WHITNEY, a general close to MacArthur, and in a disapproving way by ROVERE and SCHLESINGER. The latter is a critical assessment written in the heat of the drama of his recall from Korea in April 1951. As the Harriman Papers reveal, it was prepared by Schlesinger (a friend of Harriman and his former aide on the Marshall Plan) and Rovere to support the President's case against MacArthur. As such it concentrates its focus on the general, stressing his failure to prepare for the Chinese offensive of November 1950, and taking an unfavourable view of his opinions on foreign policy. Though not intended as a rounded account but as a sustained argument, it is nevertheless honest – it does not manipulate the facts. This is reinforced by Schlesinger's introduction to the 1992 edition, which reflects frankly on its strengths and weaknesses as seen at a distance from the controversies. It is not based on archival research, yet contains many useful insights. The writing is cool, compelling and elegant, spiced with a judicious blend of irony and aphorism. This tone is admirably complemented by the inclusion of a number of Herblock's penetrating and pungent cartoons.

Two other studies focus on Korea. Both HIGGINS and SPANIER concentrate on the debate between MacArthur and the Truman administration over conduct of the war, detailing the attitudes of both sides towards limited war. Both are thorough works of scholarship, based on extensive use of printed government documents and newspapers, but Spanier is the more impressive. It is less an assessment of MacArthur than of the controversy about the conduct of the Korean War, for, unlike most other studies, he does not see MacArthur as the main cause of the crisis. Instead, he suggests that the heart of the crisis lay in the lack of adequately developed mechanisms for civil-military co-operation in such a limited war. In a total war, for which the government had planned, there would be subordination of partisan politics to the war effort. But in the limited Korean war party politics continued and deepened the Truman-MacArthur crisis. Spanier illustrates these problems of civil-military relations by analysing the eight major decisions that US policymakers had to make during the war.

MacArthur's military record in both the Korean War and World War II are treated in LONG's candid Australian assessment which devotes a good deal to issues concerning the Australians. Based on memoirs, official histories and other secondary accounts, it provides a thorough survey of MacArthur at war plus a brief outline of his early life. In the last chapter Long seeks to weigh two conflicting impressions. First is the self-confident, commanding figure with breadth and depth in his thinking who could inspire his subordinates and others. The second is the lucky general who escaped dismissal after the Philippines debacle of 1942 and who was lucky again at Inchon. He opts for the inspirational and courageous patriot, a more generous judgment than those found in recent accounts of issues touching on MacArthur.

MICHAEL F. HOPKINS

See also Korean War entries; World War II, United States and 2

McCarthy, Joseph R. 1908–1957
Senator and anticommunist agitator

Bayley, Edwin R., *Joe McCarthy and the Press*, Madison: University of Wisconsin Press, 1981

Bell, Daniel (editor), *The New American Right*, New York: Criterion, 1955; revised as *The Radical Right*, New York: Doubleday, 1963

Buckley, William F., Jr., and L. Brent Bozell, *McCarthy and His Enemies*, Chicago: Regnery, 1954

Crosby, Donald F., *God, Church, and Flag: Senator Joseph R. McCarthy and the Catholic Church, 1950–1957*, Chapel Hill: University of North Carolina Press, 1978

Fried, Richard M., *Nightmare in Red: The McCarthy Era in Perspective*, New York and Oxford: Oxford University Press, 1990

Oshinsky, David M., *A Conspiracy So Immense: The World of Joe McCarthy*, New York: Free Press, and London: Collier Macmillan, 1983

Reeves, Thomas C., *The Life and Times of Joe McCarthy: A Biography*, New York: Stein and Day, and London: Blond and Briggs, 1982

Rogin, Michael Paul, *The Intellectuals and McCarthy: The Radical Specter*, Cambridge: Massachusetts Institute of Technology Press, 1967

Rovere, Richard H., *Senator Joe McCarthy*, New York: Harcourt Brace, 1959; London: Methuen, 1960

In view of the highly controversial nature of his senatorial career, it was inevitable that Joseph McCarthy would quickly attract the attention of – and occasion fierce disagreement among – American scholars. BUCKLEY and BOZELL was an early instance of such interest, and was unusual for taking a sympathetic, even apologetic, attitude towards its subject. Although containing some useful factual data, for example concerning the Tydings Committee hearings of 1950, its main value now is that of an indicative historical document rather than an authoritative interpretation of events. More typical of the viewpoint adopted by McCarthy's early biographers is ROVERE, who depicts the senator as an entirely disreputable figure. A journalist who covered congressional anticommunist investigations during the early 1950s, Rovere provides an extremely vivid, if sometimes impressionistic, account of McCarthy's rise and fall. Although relying heavily on anecdotal evidence, this book remains in many respects the most compelling and insightful portrait of its subject yet written.

In addition to this biographical literature there also rapidly sprang up a host of studies seeking to identify the social bases of McCarthy's political support. The most influential of these was a collection of essays edited by BELL, including contributions by Bell himself, Richard Hofstadter, David Riesman and Nathan Glazer, Peter Viereck, Talcott Parsons, and Seymour Martin Lipset. This volume portrays McCarthyism as a mass movement, irrational, even hysterical in tone, and targeted at the authority of the country's ruling elites. McCarthy, it proposes, owed his political success to his skill at exploiting popular grievances, such as those of marginalized rural groups. In this regard he was reminiscent of the demagogic leaders of the late 19th-century agrarian protest movement, Populism.

As might be expected, this interpretation was subjected to searching scrutiny by later generations of scholars. Most notably ROGIN questioned the claim that McCarthy was a latter-day Populist, pointing out that the issues with which he was associated, and the geographical sources of his popular support, were different from those of earlier agrarian leaders. Moreover, Rogin argues, McCarthy did not in fact derive his main strength from mass elements, but rather from political elites, precisely those groups Bell *et al.* had supposed were his targets. Following Rogin's lead, during the 1960s and 1970s a number of revisionist historians explored the roots of McCarthyism in traditional partisan politics, some emphasizing the part played by the Republican party in protecting and nurturing McCarthy, others the part played by the Democrats in creating an ideological atmosphere congenial to reckless and destructive anticommunism. Despite these differences of emphasis, the revisionists all tended to relegate McCarthy himself to a secondary role in the origins of McCarthyism.

Nevertheless, a fascination with McCarthy the individual remained, and the 1970s and 1980s witnessed the publication of a number of new biographies. The most important of these, Reeves and Oshinsky, share many features in common. Both are formidably well researched and thorough in their coverage. Also, both are concerned to present as rounded a picture of their subject as possible. OSHINSKY, for example, challenges the dominant liberal perception of McCarthy by emphasizing his political talents, and claiming that his anticommunism was sincere rather than opportunistic. REEVES, faintly echoing Buckley and Bozell, attempts a partial rehabilitation of McCarthy's character. He is particularly intent on refuting liberal allegations of lying and recklessness based merely on anecdotal evidence – he is very critical of Rovere on this score. However, neither study denies that McCarthy was guilty of improper and irresponsible behavior, and the senator's various transgressions are documented with the same meticulous attention to detail that characterizes both works throughout. Finally, a common weakness is a marked reluctance to speculate about McCarthy's larger historical significance.

In addition to these biographies, the last two decades have seen the publication of numerous monographs dealing with specific aspects of McCarthy's career, such as his relations with particular institutions and organizations. One example of this genre is CROSBY, which examines McCarthy's links with the Catholic Church, reaching the conclusion that there was no unified response by Catholics to the senator's activities, with Church elites divided down the middle, and the mass of laity indifferent. Another is BAYLEY, an exhaustively thorough analysis of the coverage given to McCarthy by American television and over one hundred newspapers, supplemented by extensive personal interviews with editors and reporters – like Rovere, Bayley was a practising journalist during the McCarthy era – which finds that, although the senator succeeded in manipulating substantial elements of the press, there was also significant opposition to him from several quarters.

Finally, FRIED represents a very valuable synthesis of the findings of the recent monographic literature. One of the many virtues of this volume is that it places McCarthyism in an extremely wide historical context, tracing the roots of post-World War II anticommunism as far back as the post-World War I Red Scare, and its consequences forward into the 1960s and 1970s. However Fried also pays McCarthy himself due attention, treating him in an admirably judicious and fair-minded manner.

HUGH WILFORD

McCarthyism

Bell, Daniel (editor), *The New American Right*, New York: Criterion, 1955; revised as *The Radical Right*, New York: Doubleday, 1963

Bennett, David H., *The Party of Fear: From Nativist Movements to the New Right in American History*, Chapel Hill: University of North Carolina Press, 1988

Caute, David, *The Great Fear: The Anti-Communist Purge under Truman and Eisenhower*, New York: Simon and Schuster, and London: Secker and Warburg, 1978

Fried, Richard M., *Nightmare in Red: The McCarthy Era in Perspective*, New York and Oxford: Oxford University Press, 1990

Haynes, John Earl (editor), *Communism and Anti-Communism in the United States: An Annotated Guide to Historical Writings*, New York: Garland, 1987

Heale, M.J., *American Anticommunism: Combating the Enemy Within, 1830–1970*, Baltimore: Johns Hopkins University Press, 1990

Hixson, William B., Jr., *Search for the American Right Wing: An Analysis of the Social Science Record, 1955–1987*, Princeton: Princeton University Press, 1992

Kovel, Joel, *Red Hunting in the Promised Land: Anticommunism and the Making of America*, New York: Basic Books, 1994

Rogin, Michael Paul, *The Intellectuals and McCarthy: The Radical Specter*, Cambridge: Massachusetts Institute of Technology Press, 1967

Theoharis, Athan, *Spying on Americans: Political Surveillance from Hoover to the Huston Plan*, Philadelphia: Temple University Press, 1978

Anticommunism has a long tradition in America, dating from the earliest period in which communism in any of its forms was bruited as a possible societal arrangement. Its potency and virulence peaked during the Red Scare of 1919–20, then subsided, only to revive gradually through the 1930s as the New Deal challenged orthodox views of the federal government's role in the economy, and as foreign communist and fascist threats multiplied and conflated. Domestic anticommunism grew to maximum strength as the nation settled into the Cold War. As that struggle evolved into a stable system marked by fits of détente, the popularity of more fervid forms of anticommunism shrank.

The roots of the extreme form of anticommunism associated with Senator Joseph R. McCarthy, the Wisconsin Republican, have been described in varied ways. Early biographers stressed McCarthy's many political skills and none-too-burdensome ethical sense. In 1949–50, the USSR's detonation of an atomic bomb, the "fall" of China to communism, and revelations of pro-Soviet spying induced an atmosphere of anxiety. Other explanations arose. Social scientists identified socio-psychological traits which predisposed certain sectors of American society to support McCarthy and his populist, anti-elitist brand of politics. This interpretation was countered by scholars who found McCarthy's power rooted in the normal functioning of the American party system. New Left revisionists found President Harry S. Truman and the Democratic party complicit because they conceded the premises of extremist anticommunism through their anti-Soviet foreign policy, adopted anticommunist measures at home like the federal loyalty program, and used provocative rhetoric to defend such programs. Some authors have examined other institutional sources of anticommunism such as the Federal Bureau of Investigation, Congress, the judicial system, and various interest groups. The House Un-American Activities Committee has received ample attention. Interpretations differ on other issues, such as whether extreme anticommunism had its primary basis in traditional American ideology or stemmed from the self-interest of various groups or institutions.

In McCarthy's heyday, intellectuals naturally groped to discern the sources of his strength. Several social scientists published essays in a collection edited by BELL, which remains the most important source for this primarily sociological interpretation of McCarthy's power and appeal. With varying emphases these authors suggested, frighteningly, that McCarthy tapped deep wells of anti-elite, "populist" angst among a number of disgruntled groups, including Irish and German Americans and Catholics generally, those who were "status-deprived," and those with isolationist backgrounds.

This collective view, published soon after McCarthy was censured and faded from influence, exaggerated support for the senator and the extent to which he could harness it. A number of political scientists (and historians of a more political bent) took aim at this view. ROGIN offered a telling critique with his quantitative analysis of electoral support for McCarthy and McCarthyite candidates in several states of the Midwest. He found little empirical evidence for the theories in Bell and concluded, as had others, that McCarthy's strength was rooted in the principal institutions of American politics and the customary workings of the two-party system.

HIXSON provides a valuable critical guide to these social-science interpretations and those at odds with them. He locates McCarthyism as the first in a series of manifestations of conservatism. The others were the 1958–64 "radical right" phase (the emergence of the John Birch Society and the Barry Goldwater presidential candidacy), the George Wallace phenomenon (1964–72), and the rise of the "new right" culminating in the election of Ronald Reagan in 1980.

In his earlier work, Theoharis stressed Truman's and the Democrats' culpability in tilling the soil for McCarthyism by accepting most of its premises. However, his later work, notably THEOHARIS (1978), focused more on the role of J. Edgar Hoover and the Federal Bureau of Investigation in giving an often concealed but powerful impetus which drove the federal government and the political culture toward anticommunism. Thus, along with the public anticommunism of the loyalty programs and congressional probes, Hoover worked covertly to sway public opinion from behind the scenes, and to conduct surveillance and various provocations against communists and others on the left.

Critiques of the "radical right" approach did not foreclose the search for long-term patterns of which McCarthyism was a part. Tracing the long history of nativism from its colonial-era roots, BENNETT finds it in sharp decline after World War II and thus not important in the rise of McCarthy or that era's anticommunism; these must be understood, he argues (along with many others), in the context of rising Cold War tensions. HEALE also takes a long view of anticommunism in America. He provides a valuable analysis of the role of deep-rooted ideational formulations, such as America's republican ideology and the power of evangelical Protestantism, and a good sense of the interests of a broad array of economic groups, entities such as patriotic and veterans organizations, and government agencies which gave energy to various phases of anticommunism.

CAUTE is the most detailed, broadest description of the second Red Scare's depredations. It describes the impact on employees of government at all levels, union members and workers, teachers and entertainers – and on occupations that ranged from diplomat to professional wrestler. The chief virtue is the comprehensiveness of his taxonomy of victims. The main shortcoming is an explanatory scheme which combines, not always consistently, a New Left and sociological interpretation.

FRIED depicts both the political culture and the political structures in which McCarthyism flourished and assesses local as well as national influences. A less chronologically encompassing view of anticommunism than Bennett's or Heale's, his book stresses the development of the political milieu of the late 1930s and World War II – a generalized fear, rhetoric and program of counter-subversion – in producing the anticommunist politics of a decade later.

KOVEL critiques anticommunism in brief studies of such disparate exemplars as Father Charles Coughlin, J. Edgar Hoover, Joe McCarthy, George F. Kennan, John Foster Dulles, and Hubert H. Humphrey. He finds in anticommunism a pathology deeply rooted in American culture. He argues that anticommunism is not so much "about Communism" as it is "a way of being American that proceeds from a deep historical wound." This is revisionism with a psycho-cultural twist and metaphoric overstretch best illustrated, perhaps, in the claim that American Indians were victims of the "first red scare."

HAYNES provides a useful bibliography, albeit one that merits updating.

RICHARD M. FRIED

See also Anticommunism

McClellan, George B. 1826–1885
Union general in Civil War and presidential candidate

Adams, Michael C.C., *Our Masters the Rebels: A Speculation on Union Military Failure in the East, 1861–1865*, Cambridge, MA: Harvard University Press, 1978; as *Fighting for Defeat: Union Military Failure in the East, 1861–1865*, Lincoln: University of Nebraska Press, 1992

Hagerman, Edward, *The American Civil War and the Origins of Modern Warfare: Ideas, Organization and Field Command*, Bloomington: Indiana University Press, 1988

Hassler, Warren W., *General George B. McClellan: Shield of the Union*, Baton Rouge: Louisiana State University Press, 1957

Myers, William Starr, *A Study in Personality: General George Brinton McClellan*, New York: Appleton Century, 1934

Reed, Rowena, *Combined Operations in the Civil War*, Annapolis, MD: Naval Institute Press, 1978

Sears, Stephen W., *George B. McClellan: The Young Napoleon*, Boston: Ticknor and Fields, 1988

Williams, Kenneth P., *Lincoln Finds a General: A Military Study of the Civil War*, vols. 1-2, New York: Macmillan, 1949–52

Williams, T. Harry, *McClellan, Sherman, and Grant*, New Brunswick, NJ: Rutgers University Press, 1962

George B. McClellan has been aptly described as the "problem child" of Civil War historiography. A man of great talent, he was brought down by his own weaknesses. He was an American example of Voltaire's aphorism on Charles XII, namely, that his virtues were cancelled out by their corresponding vices. The judgments made by historians for and against McClellan have been dogmatic and shrill. They have also focused on perceived flaws in his personality. His admirers have been equally strident in his defence. Discussion has also evolved around McClellan's image of himself as a professional soldier. McClellan's early biographers found much to admire in the latter, and presented the general as a Christian gentleman who was the victim of fanatical and unpleasant politicians, especially his critics on the Joint Committee on the Conduct of the War, whose meetings were a "curse" on the Union cause. Such is MYERS's approach. He condemns the lack of warmth and sympathy between McClellan and the Lincoln administration. He takes McClellan's side in criticizing the president's "interference" and justifies some of McClellan's more controversial decisions, such as his failure to renew the Union attack on 18 September at the Battle of Antietam, on spurious military grounds. Myers's stress on McClellan as the embodiment of truthfulness and integrity no longer convinces.

HASSLER's discussion of McClellan is even narrower. He is concerned with McClellan's military career in the Civil War, and a biographical context is kept to the bare minimum. He makes a strong case for McClellan's indirect strategy of transferring the Army of the Potomac to the Peninsula, and advancing on Richmond from the east. He also scores some debating points in demonstrating the difficulties that McClellan confronted in maintaining and sustaining his advance. However, he shows no understanding of Lincoln's immense difficulties, and his account is written in a military vacuum without reference to the crucial political context. Hassler also contributes to an interpretation which sees Lincoln and McClellan in an adversarial relationship. If McClellan was right, Lincoln was automatically wrong, and vice versa.

Historians who admired Lincoln offer an interpretation which was the opposite of McClellan's admirers. McClellan's inability to perceive the true mettle of his head of state is increasingly criticized. Lincoln was the true military genius of the Civil War, and his conceptual thinking – especially in understanding that it was the enemy's army which was the true decisive point – was far in advance of McClellan's, which focused around geographical points. Both T.H. WILLIAMS and K.P. WILLIAMS stress McClellan's conceit and vainglory, his fatal hesitation and over-caution, his obsessive fussing over logistical detail, and the extraordinary contrast between his vaulting military ambition, and his inability to win great victories in the field.

ADAMS explores these psychological questions with flair and imagination. He argues that McClellan's military failings – his over-caution and tendency to exaggerate Confederate strength, while underestimating his own, had social and psychological roots which he communicated to his subordinates. McClellan found much to admire in southern society, was in awe of its "military tradition", and approved of slavery as a means of maintaining black subordination in America. His cautious strategy could be interpreted as a means of preserving the southern social structure intact. Adams's thesis explains many, but by no means all, of the reasons for McClellan's hesitation. It ignores the basic structural problems that McClellan faced and overcame, and assumes that war is merely the business of giving orders and seeing that they are carried out – which it is not.

By far the most cogent analysis of McClellan's structural problems in attaining strategic mobility is HAGERMAN. He dissects authoritatively the difficulties of organizing and moving an army of 100,000 men through difficult terrain, when levels of staff training, as well as tactical and command training, were so rudimentary. The logistical demands were voracious. Hagerman pays just tribute to McClellan's gifts as a trainer and organizer, and the subtlety of his strategic appreciations. The book arrives at a fair assessment of McClellan's professionalism, but never becomes an apologia. The weakness of Hagerman's book is its rather dull style, but this is more than compensated for by its range and penetration.

McClellan's strategy has also found its defenders, among whom REED is by far the most sophisticated. She finds much to complain about, because Union generals, with the conspicuous exception of McClellan, failed to take advantage of their virtually unchallenged command of the sea and rivers. McClellan emerges as the hero of her book, and Reed argues forcefully that McClellan was the only Union general who developed a coherent grand strategical view. He wished to exploit Union sea power to land forces on the Confederate littoral and advance on pivotal Confederate communication centres. Once these were threatened, he could stand on the defensive, entrench, and force southern armies to attack him, whereupon they would be decimated by defensive firepower. This strategy was frustrated by myopic Union commanders, especially Halleck, and by Lincoln and other politicians, who preferred attritional overland campaigns. Reed's argument is more subtle than Hassler's, though she exaggerates McClellan's consistency; but in her attacks on McClellan's peers and on the politicians, she has much in common with Hassler.

For the best, most recent account of McClellan's life and career, the reader should turn to SEARS's well-controlled and lucid biography. It is consistently critical (though not wholly unappreciative, as, for instance, of his period as general-in-chief), and is especially damning on McClellan's fatal hesitancy during battle itself, when he effectively abandoned command. It also effectively demolishes the view that McClellan was a political innocent; the full extent of his mendacity and political manoeuvring, and disloyalty to the Lincoln administration, is clarified. This book, however, is not a work of strategic analysis, and tends to describe rather than explain both McClellan's views and his methods. For example, it does not explain McClellan's hold over his staff and his soldiers – an affection which survived so many setbacks. No doubt General McClellan will continue to intrigue, frustrate and irritate historians.

BRIAN HOLDEN REID

See also Civil War: Campaigns 1

McCormick, Cyrus 1809–1884
Inventor and businessman

Ardrey, Robert L., *American Agricultural Implements: A Review of Invention and Development in the Agricultural Implement Industry of the United States*, Chicago: privately printed, 1894; reprinted, New York: Arno Press, 1972

Atack, Jeremy and Fred Bateman, *To Their Own Soil: Agriculture in the Antebellum North*, Ames: Iowa State University Press, 1987

Bidwell, Percy W. and John I. Falconer, *History of Agriculture in the Northern United States, 1620–1860*, Washington, DC: Carnegie Institution, 1925

Bogue, Allan G., *From Prairie to Corn Belt: Farming on the Illinois and Iowa Prairies in the Nineteenth Century*, Chicago: University of Chicago Press, 1963

Casson, Herbert Newton, *Cyrus Hall McCormick: His Life and Work*, Chicago: McClurg, 1909; reprinted, Freeport, NY: Books for Libraries Press, 1971

Danhof, Clarence H., *Change in Agriculture: The Northern United States, 1820–1870*, Cambridge, MA: Harvard University Press, 1969

Hounshell, David A., *From the American System to Mass Production, 1800–1932: The Development of Manufacturing Technology in the United States*, Baltimore: Johns Hopkins University Press, 1984

Hutchinson, William Thomas, *Cyrus Hall McCormick*, 2 vols., New York: Century, 1930

McCormick, Cyrus, *The Century of the Reaper: An Account of Cyrus Hall McCormick, the Inventor of the Reaper*, Boston: Houghton Mifflin, 1931

Rogin, Leo, *The Introduction of Farm Machinery in Its Relation to the Productivity of Labor in the Agriculture of the United States During the Nineteenth Century*, Berkeley: University of California Press, 1931

Cyrus Hall McCormick was born in rural Rockbridge County, Virginia in 1809. He was an inventor and entrepreneur and helped to revolutionize American farming during the mid-19th century. McCormick first built a mechanical reaper in 1831 and received a patent for it in 1834. In 1840 he sold his first machine, but did not achieve significant sales until after the opening of his Chicago-based factory in 1849. By the time of his death in 1884, the business begun by McCormick had long since begun to diversify its product line and was one of the best known and most successful manufacturing firms in the United States. In 1902, the McCormick Harvesting Machine Company merged with the Deering Harvester Company along with three other implement firms to form the International Harvester Company.

In a biography written by his grandson, McCORMICK praises the life and work of Cyrus Hall McCormick and provides a history of the agricultural implement industry. Written by a family member, it makes extensive use of personal and associated recollections as well as McCormick's own diaries, and as such provides a sense of the man himself that other biographers might have some difficulty recreating. Notable among the other McCormick biographies are Hutchinson and Casson. HUTCHINSON is a thorough and scholarly study that has become in essence the authoritative biography of McCormick. It deals with the invention of the reaper, the organization and management of the family business, and its many patent disputes, along with other aspects of McCormick's public and private life. It portrays McCormick as a tireless and driven entrepreneur dedicated to promoting and expanding his business and influence. Hutchinson describes how McCormick also later devoted his considerable energies to his philanthropic work, the Presbyterian Church, the Democratic party, and his other varied commercial interests. CASSON outlines more concisely the history of the man, his machine, and the context in which he established, operated, and expanded his business. Both biographies are sympathetic and portray McCormick and his contributions as pivotal in the economic history and industrial transformation of the United States.

A standard and useful guide to the design, adoption, and impact of farm machinery during the 19th century is ARDREY. The relative impact of farm implements on the productivity of American labor is extensively outlined in ROGIN. He provides specific estimates not only of the utilization of farm implements and work rates, but also of the resulting labor savings that were derived from the use of these mechanical devices. Despite the public's sometimes ambiguous use of the term harvester, Rogin helps to clarify the differences and effectiveness among the many variations of farm implements in the 19th century. His study is extensively documented, and contains several specific references to the reapers and harvesting machinery manufactured by Cyrus McCormick and his brothers. BOGUE examines the processes of change on midwestern farms during the mid- to late 19th century, in a study which is particularly useful because the adoption and relative impact of reapers were largely geographically concentrated in the American Midwest. The adoption of mechanized production had very important consequences and repercussions which Bogue examines in detail.

BIDWELL is a well-organized guide to the early history of American agriculture. Beginning in the colonial era and continuing through the mid-19th century, Bidwell provides very useful and detailed descriptions, tables, and diagrams that clearly demonstrate and define changes within the American agricultural sector. DANHOF focuses on northern agriculture in the early to mid-19th century in a well-organized and thorough study. He explains that, since the cutting of grains and grasses was the most difficult and costly task facing northern farmers, they would obviously benefit from the development of mechanical harvesters. Danhof goes on to argue that developments in the American agricultural sector, along with growth in its manufacturing sector, were often shaped by specific events and individuals. McCormick and the development of a mechanical reaper helped to change the agricultural sector. ATACK and BATEMAN provide a detailed and scholarly study of the organization and operation of northern farms and rural households, and the agricultural economy. Based on an extensive data base drawn from agricultural and population censuses, Atack and Bateman give quantitative estimates of such things as crop yields, self-sufficiency and marketable surpluses, mechanization, and productivity change on northern antebellum farms. Along with Bogue and Danhof, Atack and Bateman provide a comprehensive and insightful view of the many and pervasive consequences of technological change – and McCormick and his company were major participants in that process.

McCormick and the company which he founded are also significant as a model or case study of large-scale 19th century manufacturing and marketing. The conventional wisdom holds that the McCormick Harvesting Machinery Company was at the forefront of mass production technology. In his study of the development of manufacturing technology in the United States, HOUNSHELL concludes that the diffusion and adoption of mass production technology was not as pervasive nor as rapid as has often been assumed. Using the McCormick Harvesting Machinery Company as one of his case studies, Hounshell presents compelling evidence that despite being one of the most prominent manufacturers in the United States, the company resisted many changes and was slow to adopt new production techniques.

TIMOTHY E. SULLIVAN

McGuffey, William H. 1800–1873
Educator and compiler of schoolbooks

Glad, Paul W., *The Trumpet Soundeth: William Jennings Bryan and His Democracy, 1896–1912*, Lincoln: University of Nebraska Press, 1960
Minnich, Harvey C., *William Holmes McGuffey and His Readers*, New York: American Book Company, 1936
Mosier, Richard D., *Making the American Mind: Social and Moral Ideas in the McGuffey Readers*, New York: King's Crown Press, 1947
Nash, Roderick, *The Nervous Generation: American Thought, 1917–1930*, Chicago: Rand McNally, 1970
Sullivan, Dolores P., *William Holmes McGuffey: Schoolmaster to the Nation*, Rutherford, NJ: Fairleigh Dickinson University Press, 1994
Westerhoff, John H. III, *McGuffey and His Readers: Piety, Morality, and Education in Nineteenth-Century America*, Nashville: Abingdon, 1978

The historical significance of William Holmes McGuffey lies in his creation of the *Eclectic Readers* which appeared in later editions as *McGuffey's Eclectic Readers* and which have had a profound impact upon American popular culture. First published in 1836, they reign as the most often adopted textbooks in the American chronicle. By the early 1920s more than 122,000,000 volumes had been sold, several thousand copies are still purchased each year, and they remain the textbook of choice for extremely conservative private academies that emphasize "traditional" American values of family, church, and patriotism. Writing in 1978, WESTERHOFF reflected that McGuffey "represents an anomaly in history. He remains one of those persons whose influence is still testified to by great numbers of average citizens, but whose life and work are more often than not neglected or shunned by scholars."

Westerhoff establishes the importance of the *McGuffey Readers*, a six-volume set consisting of a primer and five graded readers (William McGuffey compiled the primer through the fourth reader, his younger brother Alexander created the fifth). As 19th-century Americans developed their extensive public school system, educators sought textbooks which would establish a cultural norm reflective of the prevailing religious and republican values. McGuffey's work not only proved an admirable pedagogical instrument for teaching literacy, but it also inculcated into young people an unquestioning acceptance of Calvinistic Christianity, an intense spirit of patriotism, and a stern view of family responsibilities.

Little is known of the author of these readers. Raised on the Ohio frontier, McGuffey grew up in the presence of an authoritarian, hardworking Presbyterian father and a loving mother who nurtured his interest in religion and scholarship. In youth, he matriculated at several private academies taught by Presbyterian clergymen, often boarding with the minister and thereby absorbing the familial piety of his hosts. Graduating with honors from Washington College in western Pennsylvania in 1826, he was appointed professor of languages at Miami University, Oxford, Ohio, where he conceived and developed his famous readers. Resigning this post in 1836, he briefly served as president of Cincinnati College and Ohio University before assuming the chair of moral philosophy at the University of Virginia in 1845. He remained there until his death in 1873. An ordained Presbyterian minister, McGuffey was as conservative in demeanor as he was in theology and he assiduously avoided the often virulent religious and political controversies of his day. Westerhoff argues that religion played the dominant role in McGuffey's thinking and that he saw his books as an evangelistic tool urging young Americans to seek salvation above all; after his death newer editions of the *McGuffey Eclectic Readers* softened its theological emphasis stressing instead themes of civil religion and ethical morality.

An older biography, MINNICH is a panegyric celebrating McGuffey as an icon of the American spirit. In spite of its effusiveness, however, it remains an excellent compendium of general information on McGuffey and the thematic evolution of his readers. Minnich praises McGuffey's innovations in selecting reading materials appropriate for graded levels of ability, for his standardization of pronunciation useful in a nation populated by immigrants trying to master the American tongue, and for his emphasis upon spiritual and moral lessons suited to an agrarian nation. The inclusion of high quality illustrations, Minnich observes, elevated McGuffey's work above his competitors and assured its success. Given McGuffey's constant praise of rural society, the dedication of Minnich's study to the wealthy industrialist and conservative reactionary Henry Ford, "life long devotee and patron of his boyhood Alma Mater, the McGuffey Readers," seems ironic.

MOSIER examines the impact of the *McGuffey Eclectic Readers* on American culture. Although at first glance they appear to be hymns to an Arcadian ideal, he argues that they taught values best suited to the mores of an aggressive capitalistic society characterized by rapid industrialization and accumulation of wealth. McGuffey and his textbooks epitomized the peculiar American interpretation of Calvinistic contract theology: God blesses with material abundance those who are honest and work hard; he curses with poverty the indolent. Generations succored on McGuffey lessons thus saw as ideal Americans such captains of industry as John D. Rockefeller, Andrew Carnegie, and Henry Ford.

Glad and Nash see in McGuffey's teachings the foundation philosophy motivating William Jennings Bryan and Henry Ford, representatives of two distinctly different aspects of early 20th century American society. GLAD explains that Bryan – self-styled champion of the common man and three times Democratic Party nominee for president – symbolized the aspirations of a fading rural America. He was the product of and later the spokesman for a farming society characterized by a distinctive *volksglaube* (folk religion). The *McGuffey Readers* constituted its sacred texts, creating a faith built upon the basic virtues of honesty, thrift, charity, and courage combined with the dignity of labor and the sanctity of private property.

NASH finds in Henry Ford the dynamic tensions which seized American society during the 20th century's first three decades. More than any other individual, he created the industrial system which gave rise to the modern city, and he manufactured the automobiles which enabled village Americans to migrate to the metropolis. Raised on McGuffey homilies, Ford was appalled at the sins he associated with urban life, and he dedicated his wealth to the dissemination of McGuffey's ideas. He not only collected one of the few complete sets of all the editions of the *McGuffey Eclectic Readers*, but he also published and distributed thousands of copies of *Old Favorites of the McGuffey Readers* (1926), an anthology of the textbooks's most cherished stories. Nash notes with irony that the work "dispensed an ideal of individualism and self-reliance at the same time that Ford's assembly lines were making men cogs in an impersonal machine."

SULLIVAN is an engaging biography and an excellent summary of the scholarship on McGuffey and his *Eclectic Readers*. In a modern age when contemporary reading books represent a flaccid compromise between the demands of liberal and conservative partisans, his readers remain the standard for moral fortitude and literary quality. With the continuing sale of more than 200,000 volumes annually, the *McGuffey Readers* attest, Sullivan writes, to the "general conservative trend" in the United States, and "a simmering discontent with current educational methods."

FRED ARTHUR BAILEY

McKinley, William 1843–1901
25th President of the United States

Dobson, John M., *Reticent Expansionism: The Foreign Policy of William McKinley*, Pittsburgh: Duquesne University Press, 1988

Gould, Lewis L., *The Presidency of William McKinley*, Lawrence: Regents Press of Kansas, 1980

Gould, Lewis L., *The Spanish-American War and President McKinley*, Lawrence: University Press of Kansas, 1982

Grenville, John A.S. and George Berkeley Young, *Politics, Strategy, and American Diplomacy: Studies in Foreign Policy, 1873–1917*, New Haven: Yale University Press, 1966

LaFeber, Walter, *The New Empire: An Interpretation of American Expansion, 1860–1898*, Ithaca, NY: Cornell University Press, 1963

Leech, Margaret, *In the Days of McKinley*, New York: Harper, 1959

May, Ernest R., *Imperial Democracy: The Emergence of America as a Great Power*, New York: Harcourt Brace, 1961

Morgan, H. Wayne, *William McKinley and His America*, Syracuse, NY: Syracuse University Press, 1963

Morgan, H. Wayne, *America's Road to Empire: The War with Spain and Overseas Expansion*, New York: Wiley, 1965

Offner, John L., *An Unwanted War: The Diplomacy of the United States and Spain over Cuba, 1895–1898*, Chapel Hill: University of North Carolina Press, 1992

Olcott, Charles S., *The Life of William McKinley*, 2 vols., Boston: Houghton Mifflin, 1916

William McKinley's central role in the coming of the Spanish-American War of 1898 and his historical image as the last of the older style presidents of the late 19th century defined biographical appraisals of him until the mid-1960s. Recent scholarship has shown McKinley to have been a forceful and effective chief executive whose leadership in the crisis with Spain showed greater resolution and power than his initial biographers understood.

OLCOTT was the official biographer who used McKinley's papers under the supervision of George B. Cortelyou, the president's secretary and literary executor. The book offers an overview of McKinley's life but gives the greatest attention to the impact of the war with Spain. Until the McKinley papers became available for research, the Olcott volumes had value as a source. The analysis was always inadequate, and this biography is now very dated. More than forty years later, LEECH won the Pulitzer Prize for her interpretation of the president and his administration. She was the first scholar to have access to the Cortelyou Diaries, and she used them effectively to develop a winning portrait of McKinley as a president and a husband. Stronger on the personal and social aspects of the McKinley era, the book did contribute to a revival of interest in his presidency.

MAY represented a return to the critical interpretation of McKinley's leadership that had been fashionable since the 1930s. In May's well-written pages, McKinley was depicted as irresolute and prone to expediency. Although May's evidence sometimes revealed a more forceful president than the narrative realized, the thrust of the book reinforced older impressions of McKinley's failures during the crisis with Spain over Cuba in 1898. Two years later, LaFEBER's analysis of the roots of American expansionism found McKinley to be the agent of the business community, but one who pursued the agenda of capitalism with a higher degree of skill than previous historians had recognized. Like other historians who were influenced by William Appleman Williams, LaFeber disliked the results of what McKinley and his administration accomplished, but he asserted that the president had been a skilful leader in accomplishing his goals. The important result of LaFeber's work was to take McKinley seriously and to examine in detail what the record of foreign policy had been during his term of office.

MORGAN (1963) published the first full biography of McKinley, based on primary sources, in four decades. The book benefited from Morgan's impressive command of the political scene during the late 19th century. His account of McKinley's foreign policy was more thorough and balanced than any previous treatment. On the issue of the coming of the war with Spain, however, Morgan conceded a good deal to the critics of the president and there was an apologetic tone to the narrative of the events of 1898. Morgan's work remains the standard biography. In 1965, in his contribution to a series of books about significant episodes in American foreign policy, MORGAN (1965) returned to the issue of McKinley's leadership in 1898. His brief narrative adopted a much more positive tone toward the president's decision-making, and the book provides a more plausible account of how McKinley and his advisers had reached key decisions. By the mid-1960s, Morgan's second book on McKinley became a key element in the revival of the president's reputation.

In a book of essays on American foreign policy during the late 19th century GRENVILLE and YOUNG included two essays about McKinley that sought to rehabilitate his historical image as a foreign policy leader. Their discussion of the coming of the war with Spain and the decision-making with regard to United States acquisition of the Philippines proved important in convincing historians during the 1960s that McKinley's historical reputation deserved to be reappraised.

GOULD (1980) is a volume in the Kansas series on the individual presidents, and the assignment gave him the chance to distil the findings of other historians about McKinley, along with his own research in the recently opened papers of George B. Cortelyou about the war with Spain. Gould contended that McKinley was the first of the modern presidents. In his use of experts, manipulation of public opinion, relations with Congress, and use of the war power of the president to conduct foreign policy, he anticipated the powerful presidents, Theodore Roosevelt and Woodrow Wilson, who followed him. To reach a wider audience of non-professional historians, GOULD (1982) extracted the chapters about the war with Spain from the study of McKinley's presidency to focus on the major foreign policy issue of the administration. As the most accessible study of McKinley, widely used in diplomatic history courses, the book served its purpose well as a supplemental text, and enhanced the assessment of McKinley as an effective president.

At the end of the 1980s, DOBSON returned to a more traditional view of McKinley's role in foreign policy. While conceding the impact of the revision that occurred during the 1960s, Dobson called McKinley a lazy president who was often lacking in "energy and decisiveness." Dobson made some use of primary sources in the United States and England, but the absence of material from the McKinley or Cortelyou Papers at the Library of Congress limits the scope of his analysis.

OFFNER wrote his doctoral dissertation on McKinley and the coming of the war with Spain, and then returned to the topic many years later. Based on exhaustive research in foreign archival sources and personal papers in the United States, the book depicts McKinley as a chief executive in control of American foreign policy, but also advances some perceptive criticisms of his conduct during the crisis with Spain in 1898. In many respects, Offner offers the best synthesis of the decades of McKinley revisionism in his re-examination of the decisive moment in the administration of this important president. A modern biography of McKinley remains the most pressing need to draw together the analysis and findings about his life and impact on the history of the United States.

Lewis L. Gould

See also Spanish-American War

Madison, James   1751–1836
Leader of the Revolution, constitutionalist, and 4th President of the United States

Banning, Lance, *The Sacred Fire of Liberty: James Madison and the Founding of the Federal Republic*, Ithaca, NY: Cornell University Press, 1995

Brant, Irving, *James Madison*, 6 vols., Indianapolis: Bobbs Merrill, 1941–61

Ketcham, Ralph, *James Madison: A Biography*, New York: Macmillan, 1971

Koch, Adrienne, *Jefferson and Madison: The Great Collaboration*, New York: Knopf, 1950

McCoy, Drew R., *The Last of the Fathers: James Madison and the Republican Legacy*, Cambridge and New York: Cambridge University Press, 1989

Matthews, Richard K., *If Men Were Angels: James Madison and the Heartless Empire of Reason*, Lawrence: University Press of Kansas, 1995

Meyers, Marvin (editor), *The Mind of the Founder: Sources of the Political Thought of James Madison*, Indianapolis: Bobbs Merrill, 1973; revised, Hanover, NH: University Press of New England, 1981

Rakove, Jack N., *James Madison and the Creation of the American Republic*, Glenview, IL: Scott Foresman/Little Brown, 1990

Rutland, Robert Allen, *James Madison: The Founding Father*, New York: Macmillan, 1987

Rutland, Robert Allen, *The Presidency of James Madison*, Lawrence: University Press of Kansas, 1990

Rutland, Robert Allen (editor), *James Madison and the American Nation, 1751–1836: An Encyclopedia*, New York: Simon and Schuster, 1994

James Madison is arguably the most important of the Founding Fathers, for he somehow managed to be on the winning side of every crucial political struggle that took place in the young republic: the movement for independence, the debate to establish religious freedom, the battle over the adoption of the United States Constitution, the triumph over Alexander Hamilton and the Federalists in the election of 1800, the fierce intraparty struggle that preoccupied the Republican party during the first decade of the 19th century, and the fight over the War of 1812. Since the revolutionary generation defined the kind of country America was to become, and Madison was the most successful of the Founding Fathers, it is essentially his view of the kind of country America should become that has triumphed. Yet, despite his very real accomplishments, Madison has never received the public esteem that he seems so richly to deserve. There are many reasons for this: a small, shy and retiring figure, he was an ineffective public speaker and an undistinguished writer, who was not much inclined to promote himself. He was, therefore, easily overshadowed by more charismatic and aggressive contemporaries like George Washington, Thomas Jefferson and Alexander Hamilton. It is precisely this need to give Madison his due, combined with the recent bicentennial of his greatest accomplishment, the Constitution, that has been the driving force behind the recent upsurge in writing about Madison.

BRANT is the essential starting place for the ever-accelerating attempt to re-establish Madison as the pre-eminent founding father. It consists of six sizable volumes and is clearly a labor of love. It is by far the most detailed and comprehensive biography of Madison that exists. Sprightly in style and vigorous in argument, it is also highly partisan, and fails to deal adequately with Madison's failures, limitations and inconsistencies. Further, its vague and at times eccentric documentation has made a number of scholars wary of some of Brant's bold assertions.

KETCHAM is another major biography, but in one long volume, and therefore more accessible than Brant's massive work. It stresses Madison's commitment to union and liberty. While definitely sympathetic to its subject, it is nonetheless sensible and balanced in its judgments. Certainly an adequate biography, it does not break new ground in what it ultimately explains. There are two brief modern biographies of Madison. RUTLAND (1987) is authoritative, making good use of the material which he helped to publish as editor-in-chief of the monumental *The Papers of James Madison* at the University of Virginia. Although knowledgeable about Madison, Rutland's biography is not very analytical. He does not deal adequately with the knottier problems of Madison's career or effectively place him within the context of his times. In particular, he fails to explain how and why Madison shifted from being a nationalist in the 1780s to a proponent of states rights during the 1790s only to have his nationalism undergo a resurgence after 1800. In fact, his treatment of Madison's career as secretary of state, president and retired sage at Montpelier is superficial. RAKOVE is more perceptive and analytical. It is on top of the interpretive problems that have been raised by the current monographic literature for the early national period. Concise and well-written, it is a particularly good introduction to Madison for undergraduates.

Very useful and innovative is RUTLAND (1994), a reference book containing some four hundred brief essays on every aspect of Madison's life, and every person connected with him. They are arranged in alphabetical order and this, along with appropriate cross-references and an index, make this volume easy to use and accessible. The entries are by professional scholars and are knowledgeable and succinct.

Much can be learned from the treatment of particular aspects or phases of Madison's life. KOCH examines the close relationship that existed between Madison and Jefferson. The two shared much in common, but they also differed on how to deal with specific problems. Koch examines the two men's views on federal-state relations, the public debt, the French Revolution, the development of a political opposition during the 1790s, the Supreme Court and the Louisiana Purchase. Of particular and enduring value is her treatment of the influence which they had on each other during the drafting of the Virginia and Kentucky Resolutions.

For a useful history of the Madison presidency see RUTLAND (1990). He successfully takes issue with the long dominant view promulgated by Henry Adams that Madison was a confused, vacillating and ineffective leader. Although Rutland has provided a good beginning, he has not produced a very penetrating work, and the Madison presidency still needs more attention from scholars than it has so far received.

McCOY is a fascinating and thoughtful examination of the last years of Madison's life. Because he lived for such a long time following his retirement from the presidency in 1817 (until 1836), Madison had an opportunity to observe and comment on a number of significant developments that affected the next generation of Americans: the Missouri Compromise, the great decisions of the Marshall Court and the Nullification Crisis. The book has an extended discussion of Madison's views on race and on the slavery issue which was becoming an increasingly important issue during the 1830s. How the leading member of one generation tried to impress upon his younger countrymen the lessons of the Revolution and his understanding of the Constitution makes for fascinating reading.

Madison's political thought has been examined in three very different books. The first is MEYERS which is a selection of Madison's writings, with a perceptive and probing introduction that touches on a number of subtle issues. MATTHEWS is a rigorously argued interpretation written from a Marxist perspective. He appreciates Madison's significance, but is critical of the liberal and capitalist values of the society Madison helped to create. He also makes too much of the differences between Jefferson and Madison and does not do justice to their broadly shared values. BANNING is very favorable to Madison. His main point, which not everyone will find convincing, is that Madison's political thought was much more consistent during the important transition from the 1780s to the 1790s than many scholars have generally recognized.

RICHARD E. ELLIS

Mahan, Alfred Thayer 1840–1914
Naval officer and strategic thinker

Livezey, William E., *Mahan on Sea Power*, Norman: University of Oklahoma Press, 1947, revised 1980

Puleston, W.D., *Mahan: The Life and Work of Captain Alfred Thayer Mahan*, New Haven: Yale University Press, and London: Cape, 1939

Seager, Robert II, *Alfred Thayer Mahan: The Man and His Letters*, Annapolis, MD: Naval Institute Press, 1977

Seager, Robert II, and Doris D. Maguire (editors), *Letters and Papers of Alfred Thayer Mahan*, 3 vols., Annapolis, MD: Naval Institute Press, 1975

Taylor, Charles Carlisle, *The Life of Admiral Mahan, Naval Philosopher*, New York: Doran, and London: Murray, 1920

Turk, Richard W., *The Ambiguous Relationship: Theodore Roosevelt and Alfred Thayer Mahan*, New York: Greenwood Press, 1987

West, Richard S., Jr., *Admirals of American Empire: The Combined Story of George Dewey, Alfred Thayer Mahan, Winfield Scott Schley and William Thomas Sampson*, Indianapolis: Bobbs Merrill, 1948

As a historical figure, Alfred Thayer Mahan is inseparable from his writings. Following the publication of *The Influence of Sea Power upon History, 1660–1783* (1890) and *The Influence of Sea Power upon the French Revolution and Empire, 1793–1812* (1892), Mahan became a well-known proponent of a more powerful navy and the acquisition of the coaling stations and bases which such a navy required. He published articles in most of the major journals and reviews during the next decade and a half. These articles, as well as Mahan's books, are listed as an appendix to LIVEZEY, which is a readable introduction to the main lines of Mahan's thinking. Livezey sets Mahan's views in the context of his times, as well as in the context of his career.

TAYLOR provides a more complete account of Mahan's background and personal affairs. Authors on Mahan tend to be fans; Taylor is merely more explicit than most in calling his work "the overflow of an English heart full of admiration" for Mahan. Thus forewarned, Taylor's reader is scarcely surprised at the praise that the author lavishes on his subject, but by the end of the book it becomes a little tiresome.

Some relief, though not much, is afforded by PULESTON, whose resource base of letters and other documentary evidence is larger than Taylor's. In addition, at a greater distance in time from his subject, he provides a perspective which was beyond Taylor's reach. Yet he concurs that Mahan bequeathed great things to America; he cites approvingly an editor who eulogized the admiral with the words: "The superdreadnoughts are his children, the roar of the 16″ guns are but the echoes of his voice." Puleston volunteers the opinion that Mahan's principles apply almost as well to air power, just coming into play at the time of writing, as to sea power.

More objective still is SEAGER (1977) who describes Mahan as a man of his times, and of those times' limitations. Mahan, he says, was a "historian, strategist, tactician, philosopher, Episcopalian, theologian, diplomat, imperialist, mercantilist, capitalist, Anglophile, patriot, Republican, racist, Social Darwinist, journalist, polemicist, naval reformer, adviser to presidents and legislators, teacher, academic administrator, social climber, egoist, introvert, swain, husband, and father." Readers who stuck to Taylor and Puleston would have no idea that their subject was so well rounded. Yet Seager would probably not have devoted a large part of his own career to Mahan had he not admired him, and his admiration shows – and is the more convincing for its greater objectivity.

The student of Mahan who desires to form his or her own opinions can turn to SEAGER with MAGUIRE. As these editors acknowledge, their collection is by no means the whole story; they estimate that of the letters, as many as three-quarters have been lost or destroyed. But the reader of these volumes can readily gain insight into what was, if not necessarily the best, certainly the most influential mind ever to write about American naval affairs.

Neither WEST nor TURK add very much to our knowledge of Mahan himself which is not available in other accounts, but they do help to position him among his professional and political contemporaries and peers.

H.W. Brands

See also Imperialism and Anti-Imperialism

Malcolm X 1925–1965
Black nationalist leader

Breitman, George, *The Last Year of Malcolm X: The Evolution of a Revolutionary*, New York: Merit, 1967

Carson, Clayborne, *Malcolm X: The FBI File*, New York: Carroll and Graf, 1991

Clarke, John Henrik (editor), *Malcolm X: The Man and His Times*, New York: Macmillan, 1969

Cone, James H., *Martin & Malcolm & America: A Dream or a Nightmare*, Maryknoll, NY: Orbis, 1991; London: Fount, 1993

Friedly, Michael, *Malcolm X: The Assassination*, New York: Carroll and Graf, 1992

Goldman, Peter, *The Death and Life of Malcolm X*, New York: Harper, 1973, London: Gollancz, 1974; revised, Urbana: University of Illinois Press, 1979

Malcolm X, with Alex Haley, *The Autobiography of Malcolm X*, New York: Grove Press, 1965; London: Hutchinson, 1966

Perry, Bruce, *Malcolm: The Life of a Man Who Changed Black America*, Barrytown, NY: Station Hill Press, 1991

Wolfenstein, Eugene Victor, *The Victims of Democracy: Malcolm and the Black Revolution*, Berkeley: University of California Press, 1981

Spike Lee's controversial motion picture *Malcolm X* (1992), Hollywood's first epic treatment of an African American leader, and the orchestrated sales of X baseball caps, jackets and T-shirts brought what one commentator has called the "commodification" of its eponymous hero to a generation that had only the vaguest knowledge of the man or his significance. Yet there is readily available a substantial – and proliferating – amount of scholarly, polemical and popular literature (including

Malcolm's speeches) which provides alternative references for assessments of the apostate Black Muslim who predicted his own violent end.

Lee's film is based very much on the autobiography retailed by Malcolm to HALEY and which, on every count, is a remarkable document. It contains graphic (if exaggerated) descriptions of Malcolm's early years in Omaha, Nebraska, and Lansing, Michigan, his subsequent criminal activities, prison experiences, entry into to the Nation of Islam and conversion to the true Muslim faith on his journey to Mecca. Throughout, Malcolm presents himself as a man constantly in motion, engaged in a quest for self-discovery that had seen his metamorphosis from a ghetto hoodlum to a "responsible" race leader. Haley's foreword, a valuable essay in its own right, is also basic to an understanding of Malcolm's personality, style and intellectual growth.

Writing from a Trotskyist perspective, BREITMAN claims plausibly that Malcolm was "one of the most slandered and misunderstood Americans of our time," but argues, less convincingly, that by the end of his life Malcolm had embraced revolutionary socialism – a verdict at odds with the more considered opinions of other commentators. CLARKE asserts that Malcolm "had the greatest leadership potential of any person to emerge directly from the black proletariat in this century" and provides a collection of African American estimates of Malcolm (including those of his widow, Betty Shabazz, and the actor, Ossie Davis), which are either elegiac or eulogistic, as well as a useful selection of his speeches and interviews.

A white journalist and senior editor of *Newsweek* magazine, GOLDMAN focuses on Malcolm's later years in a sympathetic but overblown biography. It contains a detailed account of Malcolm's assassination, an analysis of "the Malcolm legend" and some astute comparisons between Malcolm and his great contemporary rival, Martin Luther King, Jr. Goldman admits that he has, unavoidably, viewed Malcolm "from a white perspective," but notes that "Malcolm addressed himself to white people too" and is "large enough to survive being seen and written about from a white as well as a black point of view."

Another white point of view is offered by WOLFENSTEIN, a political scientist and practising psychoanalyst, who places Malcolm on the couch in a difficult but rewarding study grounded in Marxian and Freudian theory. In an attempt to map the processes by which Malcolm both represented and mobilized the aspirations of the black underclass, Wolfenstein offers a series of "meditations" on the "critical moments" in his life: the destruction of the Little family's house by Klansmen, the influence of his father, a proselytizer for Marcus Garvey, and surrogate father Elijah Muhammad, the "conscious decision" to become a Muslim, the wrenching but liberating break with the Nation of Islam, and Malcolm's subsequent relationship with Alex Haley which "provided a mirror in which he could see the meaning of his life history."

Like Goldman, CONE rejects the romantic notion that had they lived, Malcolm and Martin Luther King would have joined forces, given a "mutual unwillingness to denounce their respective commitments to self-defence and nonviolence." But Cone, a leading black theologian, also argues that Malcolm's spiritual beliefs – like those of King – deserve serious consideration. In a series of chronologically-ordered chapters alternating between the two men, Cone illuminates their vastly differing experiences which led them to view the struggle for African American liberation "with contrasting temperaments and personality traits." Each was to transcend the provinciality of his respective environment and, at the end of his life, each was attempting to reach the other's constituency. This is a passionate and largely convincing monograph which concludes that the "internationalism" of Malcolm and Martin "was their most important contribution to the African American struggle for freedom in the United States."

Even before his assassination at the Audubon Ballroom in upper Manhattan on 21 February 1965 it was widely known that the Federal Bureau of Investigation (FBI) and the Nation of Islam (NOI) were both increasingly concerned with Malcolm's activities as, initially, the most prominent Muslim minister, and subsequently, after his break with Elijah Muhammad, the independent leader of the Muslim Mosque, Inc. (MMI) and the Organization of Afro-American Unity (OAAU). CARSON's selection of FBI materials on Malcolm, marred by misspellings and typographical errors, does not include any reference to the agency's files on the MMI and OAAU or on Muhammad and the NOI. Their inclusion might have illuminated the circumstances surrounding and the individuals involved in Malcolm's murder. His five assassins were identified as members of the NOI Temple No. 25 in Newark, New Jersey. FRIEDLY's study (originally an undergraduate thesis) adds little to the account provided by Goldman, but correctly remarks that although the available evidence does not directly implicate Elijah Muhammad, the NOI's newspaper, *Muhammad Speaks* "did everything but order the Muslim faithful to kill Malcolm X." What still remains unclear is the possible culpability of the FBI and the intelligence service of the New York Police Department in failing to anticipate – and prevent – Malcolm's murder.

The detailed account of Malcolm's life in PERRY's exhaustively-researched biography attempts to identify the selective and didactic devices of Malcolm's autobiography that were uncritically accepted by Haley and Spike Lee. Based on interviews with Malcolm's surviving relatives, friends and acquaintances, it offers important correctives to the Lee/Haley portraits. It is difficult to dissent from Perry's conclusion that "Malcolm's greatness was not his ego-boosting attempt to counteract white ethnocentrism with black ethnocentrism, but an enormous capacity for intellectual, moral, and political growth" that transformed "the pseudo-masculine criminal Malcolm into the manly political Malcolm." The best study to date of "one man's struggle to liberate himself inwardly by liberating his people politically," Perry's book deserves a wide readership.

JOHN WHITE

Manifest Destiny, 1840s–1850s

Adams, Ephraim Douglass, *The Power of Ideals in American History*, New Haven: Yale University Press, 1913

De Voto, Bernard, *The Year of Decision: 1846*, Boston: Little Brown, 1943; London: Eyre and Spottiswoode, 1957

Graebner, Norman A., *Empire on the Pacific: A Study in American Continental Expansion*, New York: Roland Press, 1955

Hietala, Thomas R., *Manifest Design: Anxious Aggrandizement in Late Jacksonian America*, Ithaca, NY: Cornell University Press, 1985

Horsman, Reginald, *Race and Manifest Destiny: The Origins of American Racial Anglo-Saxonism*, Cambridge, MA: Harvard University Press, 1981

Merk, Frederick with Lois Bannister Merk, *Manifest Destiny and Mission in American History: A Reinterpretation*, New York: Knopf, 1963

Stephanson, Anders, *Manifest Destiny: American Expansionism and the Empire of Right*, New York: Hill and Wang, 1995

Van Alstyne, Richard W., *The Rising American Empire*, New York: Oxford University Press, 1960

Ward, John William, *Andrew Jackson: Symbol for an Age*, New York: Oxford University Press, 1955

Weinberg, Albert K., *Manifest Destiny: A Study of Nationalist Expansionism in American History*, Baltimore: Johns Hopkins Press, 1935

The term Manifest Destiny is generally credited to the Democratic publicist, John L. O'Sullivan. It initially appeared in the debate over Oregon, but quickly expanded to encompass and to legitimate the entire expansionist enterprise. Northern Whigs denied the divinity of these Democratic policies and argued that expansion was dictated primarily by an aggressive slavocracy that wished to expand the peculiar institution.

ADAMS takes issue with these views and those of "materialistic historians" who explained American expansionism in the 1840s in terms of the desire to enhance "the gross comforts of material abundance". In contrast, he argues, its impetus lay in a popular sentiment to expand American institutions that combined the ideal of democracy and the "inspiration of nationality". The South particularly coveted Texas, but "the hearts of all our Western people beat responsive to the cry". Americans shared a "general profession of faith in the inevitable progress of democratic institutions and "Anglo-Saxon" ideals, destined to triumph over monarchical principles and "inferior races". It was only the "anti-slavery faction" – a "conservative minority" – that opposed this glory in American power and territorial greatness.

WEINBERG expands this interpretation and insists that Manifest Destiny was an expression of the broadly held conviction that the United States had a special mission to extend its way of life and institutions across the country. The purpose of American expansion was the fulfilment of the idea of democracy. He examines the interplay of certain elements in the idea that emphasized the "destined use of the soil" as a justification for Indian Removal and the "extension of the area of freedom" to sustain Texas annexation, the Mexican War, and the acquisition of New Mexico and California. The weak and the corrupt would be pushed aside and vast new lands opened to the exploitation of the white Anglo-Saxon Protestant people who would thus be enabled to exercise their natural rights and liberties to the fullest.

DE VOTO's study maintains that in the 1840s Americans realized their "identity to spread our free and admirable institutions by action as well as by example by occupying territory as well as by practising virtue". He dismisses "those historians" who emphasized southern interest, or the land hunger of the midwestern farmers, or "the blind drive of industrialism", asserting that the "fundamental reality" was that "hard-handed, hard-minded Americans seeking a new home in the West" took up the challenge to tame the continent. The victory of Polk made possible the filling out of the country's natural boundaries, but expansion was primarily the achievement of those heroic pioneers whose poet was Walt Whitman and whose exemplar was adventurer John Charles Frémont.

WARD joined Weinberg and De Voto with a powerful analysis of how Andrew Jackson symbolized the themes of Nature, Providence, and Will that expressed both the spirit of the age and essential elements of the American character. Expansion was a central aspect of Jacksonian Democracy and the exponents of Manifest Destiny are pictured as the agents of human progress.

Such idealistic and symbolic treatments of American expansionism were challenged by scholars who were either committed to the older economic interpretation or who embraced the newer emphasis on "realism" in their analysis of American foreign policy. VAN ALSTYNE portrays expansionism in the 1840s as an aspect of "the rising American empire" which reflected the desires of eastern commercial groups to gain their economic ends through the extension of foreign trade. GRAEBNER explicitly denies the adequacy of Manifest Destiny as "a description of American expansionism in the forties" and argues that historians have "exaggerated the urge of the American people to expand". Their emphasis on pioneers and public opinion cannot explain the specific geographical "objectives of American officials from Adams to Polk". American policy was the result of efforts by commercial interests and agrarian expansionists who wished to profit from the Pacific trade by gaining control of the major ports in the Oregon Country and California.

MERK distinguishes between Manifest Destiny and the idea of mission, associating the former with imperialism in the 1840s, and the latter with American idealism. Analyzing the press, personal correspondence, and congressional voting, he clearly identifies both the partisan nature of expansionist policies and those aspects which were the specific by-products of the slaveholders' desire to protect and expand slavery. Merk associates expansion with the Democratic party and sees Manifest Destiny as party "propaganda" created to justify the policies of the Polk administration in terms of the Jeffersonian conception of the United States as an empire of independent republics.

In the wake of the Vietnam debacle, historians took an even more critical look at Manifest Destiny. HORSMAN contrasts the different outcomes of the controversies over Texas and Oregon. In the latter case, compromise was possible because the Americans not only respected British power, but also accepted the British as fellow Anglo-Saxons. The idea of Manifest Destiny combined ethnocentrism with an ancient sense of mission that drew on the Puritan heritage. Initially this racist ideology justified the dispossession of the Indians and the enslavement of African Americans. When Anglo

Americans encountered the Mexicans, they increasingly defined them as "a mongrel race" infused by "considerable Indian and some black blood". They assumed that for this reason the Mexican government was weak and would yield in the face of American resolve. Gradually Americans came to believe that "the peoples of large parts of the world were incapable of creating efficient, democratic and prosperous governments" and that a stable world could only be achieved by American commercial dominance.

HIETALA agrees with Horsman "that racial prejudice was a basic determinant of American domestic and foreign policy during the Jacksonian period". He focuses more specifically on the "myths" of Manifest Destiny that have continued to influence Americans' impressions about their history and to affect the nation's foreign policy. He challenges those who have repeated the arguments of the Jacksonian Democrats, who portrayed American expansion as "accidental and innocent", and insists that expansion expressed American anxiety to "preserve the vulnerable nation from enemies foreign and domestic". The advocates of Manifest Destiny were "neo-Jeffersonians" who lauded romantic agrarianism, but feared industrialization, urbanization, and modernization.

STEPHANSON is a recent, highly compressed overview of Manifest Destiny as a national ideology, which, despite its brevity, extends its coverage from the colonial period all the way to Ronald Reagan. He analyzes the process by which a variety of ideas, religious and secular, political, commercial and racial, were fused into a national ideology.

WILLIAM G. SHADE

See also Expansionism

Mann, Horace 1796–1859
Educational reformer and politician

Compayre, Gabriel, *Horace Mann and the Public Schools in the United States*, New York: Crowell, 1907

Culver, Raymond B., *Horace Mann and Religion in the Massachusetts Public Schools*, New Haven: Yale University Press, 1929

Downs, Robert B., *Horace Mann: Champion of Public Schools*, New York: Twayne, 1974

Kaestle, Carl F. and Maris A. Vinovskis, *Education and Social Change in Nineteenth-Century Massachusetts*, Cambridge and New York: Cambridge University Press, 1980

Messerli, Jonathan, *Horace Mann: A Biography*, New York: Knopf, 1972

Monroe, Paul, *Founding of the American Public School System: A History of Education in the United States*, 2 vols., New York: Macmillan, 1940

Nasaw, David, *Schooled to Order: A Social History of Public Schooling in the United States*, New York: Oxford University Press, 1979

Tharp, Louise Hall, *Until Victory: Horace Mann and Mary Peabody*, Boston: Little Brown, 1953

Welter, Rush, *Popular Education and Democratic Thought in America*, New York: Columbia University Press, 1962

Williams, E.I.F., *Horace Mann: Educational Statesman*, New York: Macmillan, 1937

The *Dictionary of American Biography* describes Horace Mann as an "educator," a description which, however accurate, hardly does justice to Mann's work in various fields. For although Horace Mann is best remembered for his role as Secretary of the Board of Education of Massachusetts and for the educational reforms he encouraged, in fact his influence extended far beyond the sphere of education. This emphasis on his role as "educator" at the expense of his other contributions in the political arena in particular is noted by MESSERLI, whose 1972 biography remains the most comprehensive and detailed study of Mann to date. As Messerli notes, although in "terms of biographers, Horace Mann has been fortunate, both in their number and good will," it is nevertheless the case that in their attempt to "establish and make secure Mann's reputation as the founder of public education. these numerous hagiographers have unwittingly circumscribed the true significance of his career." Anyone interested in Mann's efforts in the field of law, as a member of the Massachusetts State Legislature, and especially in his anti-slavery activities in the House of Representatives between 1848 and 1852, will need to use Messerli's study. It would be an over-simplification to say that, as far as the others are concerned, once you have read one you have read them all, but it would not be too far from the mark. In short, Messerli offers the only comprehensive assessment of a figure who was an educator in the broadest sense of the term, and no other study comes close to it.

Other biographies of Mann include Compayre, Williams and, more recently, Downs. All three focus on his educational reform activities and are designed to praise Mann, not to assess him. COMPAYRE – a notable writer on educational matters in his own right – provides a relatively straightforward narrative of his subject's life and work. WILLIAMS's biography offers a rather more substantial overview of Mann's work in Massachusetts and his influence elsewhere. Somewhat surprisingly in a more modern work, DOWNS fails to utilize the readily available primary material. As the title suggests, the focus is almost wholly on Mann's work in education, and it does have some useful analysis of his twelve *Annual Reports*, but it sheds little light on those other aspects of Mann's life which were influenced by, and in turn influenced, his views on the importance of education in a republic.

Two studies of Mann adopt a slightly different approach to their subject. THARP is useful for her emphasis not just on the role that Mary Peabody Mann played in her husband's life but also for her treatment of Mann's work in other fields. An earlier study by CULVER takes Mann's attitudes to religion as its focus, in particular the question of how far Mann was actually responsible for the secularisation of schools in Massachusetts. Clearly, as an early study it is somewhat dated in style, but it is also strangely legalistic in tone and in approach. For example, "we conclude," he writes, "that the traditional view which holds Horace Mann responsible for the taking of religion out of the public schools of Massachusetts, and which regards him as the great protagonist of secularism in education is untrue." Culver's careful consideration of all the "evidence" which lies behind this conclusion, however, means that his remains a useful, if rather unusual, study of Mann.

Several of the more general works on education in 19th-century America have more important things to say on Mann than some of the biographies. Such studies often have the merit of taking a rather less laudatory approach to Mann, which, without diminishing him, serves to provide a more rounded and considered assessment of his ideas and his impact. They do not, of course, offer much on his work beyond education. Mann's role as an anti-slavery activist still demands some serious, and much needed, reappraisal. Almost all studies of American education include some reference to Mann. MONROE is now outdated, but as an introduction to some of the themes and issues surrounding Mann's activities it remains useful. Monroe considers, albeit relatively briefly, the impact of changes in communication technology, economic and political conditions, and the dramatic rise in population in the 19th century, on the perceived educational requirements of the nation. A more recent study, by KAESTLE and VINOVSKIS, is essentially a statistical analysis of the impact of social change on education, and *vice versa*, during the 19th century. Supported by an impressive range of figures, this study manages to cut through some of the "myths" surrounding educational reform, in particular the "illusion that there was little schooling prior to 1840 in the American Northeast," a misconception which the authors argue "can be traced to reformers like Horace Mann."

WELTER adopts a very broad approach to the subject of American education, and is particularly good on the growing need, as many 19th-century Americans perceived it, "to make their educational system match their democratic hopes," a view that crossed the political spectrum to the extent that "the attitudes of leading conservatives very nearly duplicated those of liberal Democrats" in the years before the Civil War. Mann, Welter argues, was "one of the country's leading social theorists," a description that does greater justice to his activities than "educator." However, as Welter shows, Mann was not alone in his views, many of which were shared by other leading figures of the day, such as Thaddeus Stevens and William H. Seward.

The centrality of education to social thought and reform is the theme of NASAW, who isolates Mann as representative of his generation of school reformers, all of whom held firmly to "the American dream of unlimited material progress for the society at large, of upward mobility for all." For Mann, Nasaw argues, "hard work was the key to the kingdom of riches, power, and personal glory because that had been his own experience." Mann's "republican solution to a universal problem" was to regard education as "a moral testing ground" which would lay the groundwork for future economic independence, although Nasaw shows that certain aspects of this "solution" were not as benign as Mann, and others, suggested. The textbooks selected took a very definite Whig/Federalist line, thereby ensuring that "the catalogue of republican/American virtues sounded curiously like a Whig one." The wider implications of this argument for the history of antebellum America deserve further consideration. Nasaw's study reveals that, as an educator and as a social reformer, Mann had an agenda

that was both more considered and more complex than some of his biographers would have us believe.

S-M. GRANT

See also Schools: from the Revolution to 1900

Manufacturing Industry: General

Bishop, James Leander, *A History of American Manufacturers from 1608 to 1860*, 2 vols., Philadelphia: Young, and London: Sampson Low, 1861–64

Chandler, Alfred D., Jr., *The Visible Hand: The Managerial Revolution in American Business*, Cambridge, MA: Belknap Press of Harvard University Press, 1977

Clark, Victor S., *History of Manufactures in the United States*, 3 vols., New York: McGraw Hill, 1929

Depew, Chauncey M. (editor), *1795–1895: One Hundred Years of American Commerce*, 2 vols., New York: Haynes, 1895

Dertouzos, Michael L. and others, *Made in America: Regaining the Productive Edge*, Cambridge: Massachusetts Institute of Technology Press, 1989

Fabricant, Solomon, *The Output of Manufacturing Industries, 1899–1937*, New York: National Bureau of Economic Research, 1940

Hounshell, David A., *From the American System to Mass Production, 1800–1932: The Development of Manufacturing Technology in the United States*, Baltimore: Johns Hopkins University Press, 1984

Niemi, Albert W., Jr., *State and Regional Patterns in American Manufacturing, 1860–1900*. Westport, CT: Greenwood Press, 1974

Piore, Michael J. and Charles F. Sabel, *The Second Industrial Divide: Possibilities for Prosperity*. New York: Basic Books, 1984

Porter, Glenn, *The Rise of Big Business, 1860–1920*, 2nd edition, Arlington Heights, IL: Harlan Davidson, 1992

Rosenberg, Nathan (editor), *The American System of Manufactures: The Report of the Committee on the Machinery of the United States 1855, and the Special Reports of George Wallis and Joseph Whitworth 1854*, Edinburgh: Edinburgh University Press, 1969

A sprawling topic, the history of American manufacturing has inspired few general treatments in spite of its importance in American economic history. The best starting place for pre-1930s developments remains CLARK's classic three-volume study. Although Clark draws broad-gauged and thought-provoking conclusions in the first and third volumes, the real strengths of this work are its rigorous primary research and inclusive approach. Clark comprehensively addresses topics ranging from household production, to demographic and market shifts, to manufacturing wages and working conditions, and the impact of government policies (from the Navigation Acts to modern antitrust). The study ostensibly ends in the mid-1920s, but post-World War I coverage is thin, and Clark generally favors traditional industries (textiles, woollens, iron and steel, and the like) over modern ones such as automobiles, chemicals, and aircraft manufacturing.

Two other sources are older and less useful, although rich in detail. BISHOP chronicles colonial industries in volume 1; and gives a year-by-year summary of developments between 1789 and 1860, as well as brief histories of key industries and leading firms, in volume 2. DEPEW is a collection of 100 historical essays by industry leaders. In spite of the book's title, most of these chapters pertain to manufacturing.

The state of American manufacturing in the mid-19th century is portrayed vividly in the contemporary reports compiled and introduced by ROSENBERG. A reprint of the Special Reports written by two British commissioners (Joseph Whitworth and George Wallis) assigned to the New York Exhibition in 1853, this volume offers an extremely detailed and reliable account of state-of-the-art manufacturing techniques. The commissioners gave special attention to industries (most notably, firearms) that employed specialization and interchangeable parts – the so-called "American System of Manufactures". The long introduction by Rosenberg, a leading historian of technology, is itself a small masterpiece.

The American System opens HOUNSHELL's definitive study of American manufacturing technology in the 19th and early 20th centuries. He astutely traces the diffusion and evolution of manufacturing methods through the manufacture of firearms, sewing machines, furniture, reapers, and bicycles, culminating in automotive mass production. Hounshell aptly contrasts Fordism with the flexible production pioneered by General Motors, the latter a crucial progenitor of modern automobile manufacturing.

Not surprisingly, the era of rapid, large-scale industrialization in America between the Civil War and World War I has garnered the most attention from historians of manufacturing and related subjects. Although CHANDLER's central concern is the rise of bureaucracy and professional management in big business during this period, his book includes a great deal on manufacturing firms and methods, and he argues for the central importance of economies of scale and vertical integration in corporate strategy-making and economic growth. With high fixed costs, manufacturers and transportation companies were driven to merge with competitors and to take over distribution and primary processing functions from independents. PORTER's concise, popular survey has carried Chandler's key insights to a wide audience, while adding on business-labor relations and social attitudes toward giant enterprise. The "trust" problem is central to Porter's well-written treatment.

NIEMI brings an economist's perspective to the Gilded Age by analyzing data on national, regional, and state patterns of manufacturing. By adjusting for census data classification problems, this study finds that non-mobile factors of production (such as resources and demand) were more important than mobile factors (capital and labor) in determining regional patterns; and that manufacturing in most industries spread from the Northeast to the South and West (especially Ohio and Illinois) after 1860, and at an accelerated pace after 1900. Niemi thus offers quantitative support for many of the patterns identified decades earlier by Clark. FABRICANT's older but more comprehensive study of manufacturing output in the early 1900s, completed for the National Bureau of Economic Research, analyzes aggregate data as well as sixteen specific industries.

Most studies of post-World War II manufacturing in the United States have grappled with the problem of declining American international competitiveness. A leading example is the study published by DERTOUZOS and the other fifteen members of the Commission on Industrial Productivity at the Massachusetts Institute of Technology. Taking a microeconomic and firm-level approach, these experts report on eight key manufacturing industries: automobiles; chemicals; commercial aircraft; consumer electronics; machine tools; semiconductors, computers and copiers; steel; and textiles. Concluding that the problem of the fall (relative) in manufacturing productivity is serious but reversible, the Commission calls for longer-term thinking, greater commitment to technology, human resources, and education, and more cooperation between business and government – common themes in this literature.

Other scholars, most notably PIORE and SABEL, question more fundamentally the wisdom of American manufacturing's continuing reliance on the kind of standardized mass production that brought it greatness in the previous century. Using history to illuminate comparative dimensions of industrial relations and technology change, these authors suggest a shift toward flexible "craft production" at the current "industrial divide". This work challenges Chandler on some fundamental issues – particularly whether the late 20th century should be seen as an extension of the 19th or as a new age demanding new strategies and structures. But both works engage the largest questions in this sweeping story of the rise and decline of American manufacturing prowess.

DAVID B. SICILIA

See also Business History: General; Industrialization; Technology and Invention

Manufacturing Industry: Individual Industries

Baron, Stanley Wade, *Brewed in America: A History of Beer and Ale in the United States*, Boston: Little Brown, 1962

Flink, James J., *The Automobile Age*, Cambridge: Massachusetts Institute of Technology Press, 1988

Haynes, Williams, *American Chemical Industry*, 6 vols., New York: Van Nostrand, 1945–54

Hidy, Ralph W., Frank Ernest Hill, and Allan Nevins, *Timber and Men: The Weyerhaeuser Story*, New York: Macmillan, 1963

Liebenau, Jonathan, *Medical Science and Medical Industry: The Formation of the American Pharmaceutical Industry*, Baltimore: Johns Hopkins University Press, 1987

Panschar, William G., *Baking in America*, volume 1: *Economic Development*, Evanston, IL: Northwestern University Press, 1956

Passer, Harold C., *The Electrical Manufacturers, 1875–1900: A Study in Competition, Entrepreneurship, Technical Change, and Economic Growth*, Cambridge, MA: Harvard University Press, 1953

Rae, John B., *The American Automobile Industry*, Boston: Twayne, 1984

Scranton, Philip, *Proprietary Capitalism: The Textile Manufacture at Philadelphia, 1800–85*, Cambridge and New York: Cambridge University Press, 1983

Scranton, Philip, *Figured Tapestry: Production, Markets, and Power in Philadelphia Textiles, 1885–1941*, Cambridge and New York: Cambridge University Press, 1989

Skaggs, Jimmy M., *Prime Cut: Livestock Raising and Meatpacking in the United States 1607–1983*, College Station: Texas A & M Press, 1986

Temin, Peter, *Iron and Steel in Nineteenth-Century America: An Economic Inquiry*, Cambridge: Massachusetts Institute of Technology, 1964

Wall, Joseph Frazier, *Andrew Carnegie*, New York: Oxford University Press, 1970

Williamson, Harold F. and Arnold R. Daum, *The American Petroleum Industry: The Age of Illumination, 1859–1899*, Evanston, IL: Northwestern University Press, 1959

Williamson, Harold F., Ralph L. Andreano, Arnold R. Daum, and Gilbert C. Klose, *The American Petroleum Industry: The Age of Energy, 1899–1959*, Evanston, IL: Northwestern University Press, 1963

The goods that have flowed out of American shops and factories from the early 17th century to the present span dozens of industries. But historians have paid scant attention to many of these manufacturing businesses. Rather, they have favored industries that turn out ubiquitous consumer products (such as automobiles and computers); those that were built up by powerful and often colorful entrepreneurs (Carnegie in steel, Rockefeller in oil); industries with relatively complex manufacturing processes; and those dominated by large firms, especially when concentrated into oligopolies (instead of, for example, furniture making or boot and shoe production – major industries with large numbers of relatively small producers). No scholar, for instance, has written the history of the construction industry – for centuries the leading business in America – because it comprises tens of thousands of small firms, and arguably is less glamorous than most high-tech and advertising-driven businesses. Even so, the meteoric and now concentrated computer industry has also not been chronicled in a satisfactory way. Fortunately, however, there are sound historical treatments of most key manufacturing industries.

The first significant industry in the United States was textile manufacture. Many old company and industry studies tell a story about the emergence and diffusion of the Lowell system (named for Francis Cabot Lowell) in New England. These spinning and weaving mills employed farm girls under well-supervised living and working conditions in the early 19th century, then turned to European immigrant labor. Recent scholarship has complicated this picture, particularly the work of SCRANTON, whose two sequential volumes about Philadelphia textile firms portray an alternative path toward textile-driven early industrialization. Rather than Lowell-style mass production corporations, Scranton's producers were proprietary, relatively small, and oriented toward flexible batch production – an approach that worked well until it confronted competition from southern mills in the early 20th century.

The concentration and technological advance that transformed heavy industries in the late 19th and early 20th centuries did the same in lumber and food processing. There are no satisfactory general studies of the former, although HIDY *et al.* shed some light on broad developments (such as legislative milestones) through their competent history of the industry leader, Weyerhaeuser. Covering the century from the 1850s to the 1950s, and laudatory toward the firm's managers – three generations of Weyerhaeusers and the professionals who succeeded them – this treatment seems from today's perspective rather thin on environmental issues. SKAGGS is a crisp survey of livestock and meatpacking from 1607 to 1983. The industry changed little before the Civil War, then consolidated under the likes of Swift and Armour. After World War II, competition and westward population shifts led to a profound shake-out; by the 1980s, only half the number of firms in 1945 were still operating.

In baking, as surveyed by PANSCHAR, methods evolved slowly prior to the mid-1980s, when the business began to commercialize rapidly. But the most significant change came between 1900 and 1930, when single baking shops – up to then the vast majority of producers – were eclipsed by a much smaller number of large-scale industrial operations. Panschar is strong on technology, distribution, and industry-wide data, but weak in his treatment of leading firms, with the exception of Continental Baking. As for brewing, BARON begins his colorful story in the mid-19th century, focusing on regional differences and manufacturing processes, with reasonable attention to broader developments such as the Prohibition movement. This survey, too, gives inadequate attention to the strategies and rivalries of key firms, and it pays scant attention to developments after 1945.

Among 19th-century heavy industries, iron and steel have been the subject of numerous useful works. The best remains TEMIN, which uses economic analysis to explain the timing and diffusion of developments in coked iron and steel by linking long-term trends (growing sophistication with heat, and rising demand) with sudden developments (the discovery of low-sulphur bituminous coal deposits, a surge in demand for rails, and the development of the Bessemer process). Another useful perspective on this story, and on the rise of big steel late in the century, can be gleaned from WALL's magisterial biography of the industry leader, Andrew Carnegie, who transformed the industry with cost accounting, modern plant logistics, and other new methods before selling out to J.P. Morgan's United States Steel combination in 1901.

Most histories of the petroleum industry focus on its leading figure, John D. Rockefeller, and his Standard Oil Company. The notable exception is the industry-wide study by WILLIAMSON *et al.* Sponsored by the American Petroleum Institute, these two rigorously researched volumes (each roughly 800 pages) offer a comprehensive picture of technical change (especially in chemistry and cracking techniques), macro-economic trends, demand and distribution, and politics. Supported by hundreds of useful exhibits, it is the definitive industry study. The history of the closely related chemical industry from colonial times through the 1930s is told masterfully and in glorious detail by HAYNES. An industry insider with training in chemistry and a gift for lively prose, Haynes fashioned this definitive work from exhaustive primary research when there was little secondary literature. After surveying the period from 1607 to 1911 in the first volume, Haynes delves deeply into the 1920s and 1930s in volumes 2–5. The final volume is a valuable compilation of short company histories. There is no similar treatment for the post-World War II era.

LIEBENAU concisely, yet thoughtfully, examines the pharmaceutical industry for a century following its modern origins in Philadelphia. Focusing on the nexus of relationships among companies and the medical community in research, Liebenau also explores key regulatory changes and debates over ethics. The transformative period was 1890–1930, when doctors and medical laboratories played a growing role.

Electrical equipment manufacturing also emerged as a big business in the late 19th century, with General Electric and Westinghouse at its center. Those firms still await good histories, but the founding era of the industry is treated masterfully in PASSER. He looks at the relations among competing forms of light, heat, and power (gas, arc and incandescent lighting, direct and alternating current, electric motors and traction) and rivalries among leading "inventor entrepreneurs" such as Charles Brush, Frank Sprague, Thomas Edison, and George Westinghouse. Recent studies have revised some of Passer's conclusions, but none offers better coverage of this crucial formative period.

Automobiles are a favorite subject in business history, although surprisingly few studies concentrate on the manufacturing side. RAE's short overview, which incorporates some of the research from his related earlier studies, is the best general treatment of business issues. Sprinkled amid the competent narrative are interesting interpretations: of the regional shift of the industry from New England to Detroit, the response of the Big Three manufacturers (General Motors, Ford, and Chrysler) to the energy crisis, and other subjects. FLINK, another leading automotive historian, takes a much broader view of automobility as a global and cultural phenomenon, but his synthetic book still includes plenty on the business of making and selling cars. Its post-World War II chapters fill a gap that is too common in studies of leading American manufacturing industries.

DAVID B. SICILIA

See also Business History: Individual Corporations; Technology and Invention

Market Revolution, 1815-1850s

Clark, Christopher, *The Roots of Rural Capitalism: Western Massachusetts, 1780–1860*, Ithaca, NY: Cornell University Press, 1990
Horwitz, Morton J., *The Transformation of American Law, 1780–1860*, Cambridge, MA: Harvard University Press, 1977
Innes, Stephen, *Creating the Commonwealth: The Economic Culture of Puritan New England*, New York: Norton, 1995
Larkin, Jack, *The Reshaping of Everyday Life, 1790–1840*, New York: Harper, 1988

Rogin, Michael Paul, *Fathers and Children: Andrew Jackson and the Subjugation of the American Indian*, New York: Knopf, 1975
Rose, Anne C., *Voices of the Marketplace: American Thought and Culture, 1830–1860*, New York: Twayne, 1995
Rothenberg, Winifred Barr, *From Marketplaces to a Market Economy: The Transformation of Rural Massachusetts, 1750–1850*, Chicago: University of Chicago Press, 1992
Sellers, Charles, *The Market Revolution: Jacksonian America, 1815–1846*, New York: Oxford University Press, 1991
Stokes, Melvyn and Stephen Conway (editors), *The Market Revolution: Social, Political, and Religious Expressions, 1800–1880*, Charlottesville: University Press of Virginia, 1996
Watson, Harry L., *Liberty and Power: The Politics of Jacksonian America*, New York: Hill and Wang, 1990
Wilentz, Sean, "Society, Politics, and the Market Revolution, 1815–1848," in *The New American History*, edited by Eric Foner, Philadelphia: Temple University Press, 1990

The first half of the 19th century in the United States has long been associated with rapid and profound economic and social change. Recently the term "market revolution" has emerged in the literature to encapsulate these processes and to link them with parallel political and institutional developments. The creation of national markets in goods, capital and labour, it is argued, was such a powerful force in this period that it embraced deep patterns of change at all levels of American experience. ROGIN was one of the first scholars to use the "market revolution" concept. He applied it to material changes that, in his view, underpinned the broader cultural and psychological shifts necessary to explain the process of Indian removal in the Jacksonian period. Over a decade after he wrote in the mid-1970s, the concept was being applied to general interpretations of Jacksonian society and politics, as a tool for synthesizing the vast array of findings that had emerged from recent scholarship. Like any effort at synthesis it is controversial and, many would argue, inadequate. But this is part of its value; the debate over the "market revolution" itself prompts scholars to rethink the connections between apparently disparate topics and themes, and even to recast their assumptions about the trajectories of change in early America.

As WILENTZ suggests in his essay, one of the best brief introductions to the topic, the concept of "market revolution" captures the connections between growing productive and commercial activity, the emergence of new forms of transportation and manufacturing, social shifts associated with urbanization, industrialization and immigration, the political implications of new party systems, struggles over slavery and native American land, and the legal and juridical doctrines that underpinned private economic development. It stresses the role of conflicts over economic and social change in shaping politics at state, sectional and federal levels, and has the potential to recast the traditional periodization of the early 19th century, based on presidential politics.

Still, it is to the Jacksonian period that the term is most frequently applied. WATSON's fine survey of Jacksonian politics notes the prominence of economic issues in national political debates, and traces these to the changes taking place in agriculture, commerce and industry. Economic change entailed more than the extension of transportation or new technologies; farmers and artisans were becoming increasingly dependent on markets for their livelihoods, though this followed different patterns in different regions. A focus on class conflict and cultural struggles underpins the discussion in SELLERS, the single most influential exponent of the market revolution thesis. He argues that the Jacksonian movement represented the climax of a confrontation between groups in American society aligned, on the one hand, with the market and its commercial, religious and cultural advocates and, on the other, with the land, the repository of older, subsistence-oriented, democratic values, that rejected the incursion of market culture and made the Jacksonian Democratic party the instrument of resistance to the market's powerful onslaught.

Debate over the market revolution thesis is taking two distinct but connected forms. First, were conditions in the early 19th century as novel as the thesis would imply? A long-standing tradition holds that America was a capitalist society from the start of white settlement, so that markets, and market-orientation, were always intrinsic to its evolution. Powerfully restating this view, INNES focuses on New England, often seen as the most economically "backward" region of colonial North America, to imply that there was no "market revolution" to take place in the 19th century because it had already happened. This complements the findings of ROTHENBERG, who uses detailed empirical evidence from farm account books to argue that a crucial shift towards market production took place in the Massachusetts countryside during the 18th century.

However, in the view of other scholars, it was not just the existence of markets and commerce, but the increasing depth of their influence on the conduct of life and politics that marked the changes of the early 19th century. Evidence for these changes is presented in a variety of studies, though none restrict their analysis to the Jacksonian period alone. In a lively and readable account, LARKIN examines the range of cultural and material change in the American countryside and small towns during the period, with a particular but not exclusive focus on New England. CLARK traces the shift from household-based to increasingly commercialized capitalist production in rural Massachusetts, suggesting that this was an extended process of evolution, rooted in cultural expectations and demographic conditions, that pressed rural people towards new ways of earning their livelihoods. The market was not just imposed on the countryside by outside forces. Even so it led to new inequalities and divisions in rural society. In a pioneering study of judicial decision-making, HORWITZ argued that the courts in many states actively promoted economic development during the first half of the 19th century. His work has been a particularly important influence on studies, like that of Sellers, on the market revolution and politics.

Parallel to the debate over the extent and timing of economic change has been a series of critiques of the political implications of the market revolution thesis. Of several symposia on Sellers's work the most accessible in book form is STOKES and CONWAY which includes assessments by a number of scholars of the relationships between social, religious or cultural divisions and the patterns of 19th-century political allegiance. As one scholar has commented, it has not been possible for Sellers or others to demonstrate a direct connection between economic position and the voting activities of any individual during the Jacksonian period. However, this may be seeking to oversimplify the links between class and political allegiance. Politics is not the only arena of cultural expression, and voting not the sole activity in the political sphere. The patterns of social conflict and political change operated at different levels under different circumstances. The notion of "market revolution" is likely to continue to shape discussions of the early 19th century for some time to come.

Not least, the actual experience of markets and the consequences of living in a society where commercial activities were becoming prominent in individuals' lives affected the production, distribution and reception of information. In a powerful, fresh interpretation of antebellum culture, ROSE demonstrates the interconnectedness of commercial and communications revolutions with the evolution of democracy, Christianity and capitalism, and their influence on intellectual, literary and artistic life. Rose's work demonstrates that if markets were not new, their influence was increasingly profound.

CHRISTOPHER CLARK

See also Jacksonian Era

Marketing and Distribution

Atherton, Lewis E., *The Frontier Merchant in Mid-America*, Columbia: University of Missouri Press, 1971

Barger, Harold, *Distribution's Place in the American Economy since 1869*, Princeton: Princeton University Press, 1955

Chandler, Alfred D., Jr., *The Visible Hand: The Managerial Revolution in American Business*, Cambridge, MA: Belknap Press of Harvard University Press, 1977

Clark, Thomas Dionysius, *Pills, Petticoats, and Plows: The Southern Country Store*, Indianapolis: Bobbs Merrill, 1944

Cochran, Thomas C., *200 Years of American Business*, New York: Basic Books, 1977

Emmet, Boris and John E. Jeuck, *Catalogues and Counters: A History of Sears, Roebuck and Company*, Chicago: University of Chicago Press, 1950

Horowitz, Daniel, *The Morality of Spending: Attitudes Towards the Consumer Society in America, 1875–1940*, Baltimore: Johns Hopkins University Press, 1985

Hower, Ralph M., *History of Macy's of New York, 1858–1919: Chapters in the Evolution of the Department Store*, Cambridge, MA: Harvard University Press, 1985

Kowinski, William Severini, *The Malling of America: An Inside Look at the Great Consumer Paradise*, New York: Morrow, 1985

Larson, Henrietta M., *The Wheat Market and the Farmer in Minnesota, 1858–1900*, New York: Columbia University Press, 1926

Lebhar, Godfrey Montague, *Chain Stores in America, 1859–1950*, New York: Chain Store Publishing, 1950, 3rd edition, as *Chain Stores in America 1859–1962*, 1963

McAusland, Randolph, *Supermarkets – 50 Years of Progress: The History of a Remarkable American Institution*, Washington, DC: Food Marketing Institute, 1980

Marchand, Roland, *Advertising the American Dream: Making Way for Modernity, 1920–1940*, Berkeley: University of California Press, 1985

Olney, Martha L., *Buy Now, Pay Later: Advertising, Credit and Consumer Durables in the 1920s*, Chapel Hill: University of North Carolina Press, 1991

Pope, Daniel, *The Making of Modern Advertising*, New York: Basic Books, 1983

Porter, Glenn and Harold C. Livesay, *Merchants and Manufacturers: Studies in the Changing Structure of Nineteenth-Century Marketing*, Baltimore: Johns Hopkins Press, 1971

Strasser, Susan, *Satisfaction Guaranteed: The Making of the American Mass Market*, New York: Pantheon, 1989

Tedlow, Richard S., *New and Improved: The Story of Mass Marketing in America*, New York: Basic Books, and Oxford: Heinemann, 1990

Twyman, Robert W., *History of Marshall Field & Co.*, Philadelphia: University of Philadelphia Press, 1954

The description and analysis of industrial production, concentrated as it is at the location of manufacturing, is relatively easier for historians than the widely spread and highly diverse activities involved in distribution and marketing. There has to be physical carriage of the final products from the centre of production to the myriad final points of consumption. Without transport there can be no distribution and without information there can be no marketing. Several writers have attempted to systematize and rationalize these multifarious activities; others have isolated and described particular aspects or particular organisations. For many years BARGER (author of a number of valuable studies) remained the only general work on the subject of distribution. In 1971 PORTER and LIVESAY provided a very wide-ranging and more analytical survey of the field that can also be read as a general economic history of the 19th century.

In his many writings on business history, CHANDLER has underlined the significance of marketing in the furtherance of economic efficiency. In the work cited here he describes the changes in the organization of marketing brought about by the rise of large-scale productive enterprises. A similar line of investigation was pursued by COCHRAN, another celebrated business historian, though one less favourably disposed to big business than Chandler. Cochran wrote prolifically and the work cited here is only one of many in which he examines the interplay between production and distribution.

However, the earliest specialized study of marketing, by that pioneer of business studies, Henrietta LARSON, dealt with agriculture. This now sadly neglected work is as much an agricultural and railroad history as a study of marketing. Well documented and splendidly related, the book refutes many of the Populist stereotypes about the interplay between farmers and railroads, at least so far as Minnesota is concerned.

Two writers, Clark and Atherton, may be regarded as the historians of the early country stores, those institutions much revered as tourist curiosities but not taken particularly seriously by historians. CLARK shows the dependence of rural communities on these stores in the South, which relied (like latter-day supermarkets) on the customers' provision of their own transport. ATHERTON's focus was on the Midwest, about which he has written several books. The picture that he presents of country stores is similar in some respects to Clark's, although there are important regional differences.

The marketing of such major items as barbed wire, McCormick reapers, and Singer sewing machines each has its separate story. But the most far-reaching innovation was the mail-order catalogue, and mail-order distribution. Backed by the Grangers, Montgomery Ward was the first, established in Chicago as early as 1872. The firm dealt directly with farmers and small townspeople across the country, going some way at least towards breaking the total reliance of customers on, and therefore monopolistic position of, the small country stores. Sears Roebuck followed, at first selling watches by mail, but rapidly expanding to supply most of the goods available in the country stores. As Chandler relates, Sears developed mechanisms to speed up transactions, and by the end of the century was handling as many in one day as "most traditional merchants in pre-railroad days handled in a lifetime". The story of Sears Roebuck is related in EMMET and JEUCK in a work which examines the social significance of the mail-order catalogue, and the expanding range of Sears Roebuck's enterprise.

Almost in parallel, chain stores began to spread across America. The prototype was the Great Atlantic and Pacific Tea Company (A & P), founded in 1859. In 1879 Frank Winfield Woolworth opened his first 5-cent store in Utica, New York. This failed, but his second venture, at Lancaster, Pennsylvania, started the business which thirty years later had three hundred stores and brought the first example of Gothic skyscraper architecture to Manhattan, the 57-storey Woolworth building, opened in 1913. Such changes in the 1880s as the growth of town populations, the increasing use of electricity for street and shop lighting, and improvements in packaging, all assisted the spread of large urban stores. But, as with mail-order, the first decade of the new century saw the most rapid and widespread development. LEBHAR chronicles the history of chain stores in vivid detail.

Urban department stores such as Macy's in New York and Marshall Field's in Chicago were also established in this same period and rapidly became American institutions. HOWER and TWYMAN respectively depict their progress in detail. Such "palaces of consumption" with ostentatious decor both inside and out aimed to make shopping a pleasure rather than a chore, while at the same time keeping prices down. They led the way in the use of electricity, not only for lighting (Wanamaker's in Philadelphia was the first in the world to introduce window lighting in 1878), but also for heating and for elevators.

Marketing received a further boost in the 1890s with the associated proliferation of newspapers and advertising, a development which also presupposed literacy. As new, previously unknown, commodities came on to the market, advertising became an essential channel of information as well as a means to enhance sales. In the 20th century, all the new technologies, above all radio and later the cinema, television and even airplanes were called into service. POPE and MARCHAND provide good sources for the study of these developments.

Concern about dishonesty in advertising led to deeper concern about the morality of "consumerism" voiced by such social commentators as Thorstein Veblen. The growth and influence of such social critics of spending, recalling some of the older American traditions of Puritanism, are examined in HOROWITZ.

The 1920s saw a vast new range of products on the markets and these were no longer limited to provision of the primary needs of simple foodstuffs and shelter. Automobiles and the new household equipment associated with the electrification of the home were more expensive than could generally be met out of the weekly wage packet, but also had the characteristic of durability. The notion of a "consumer durable goods revolution" has been challenged by some writers, but OLNEY has no such doubts. As food prices fell and other "single-use goods" came to absorb a smaller fraction of household incomes, expensive, indivisible purchases seemed ever more desirable. Instalment buying became a very significant, and largely new, feature of life in the 1920s. "Buy Now, Pay Later", is indeed the title of Olney's book. These two features of the new goods – fractional payments and postponable replacement – came to constitute a source of general economic weakness when prosperity began to fade.

The concept of "mass marketing" is obviously linked with that of "mass production". Despite the huge setback of the 1930s, both processes are best seen as continuous through most of the 20th century. Even in the depressed 1930s, improved (that is, cheapened) packaging and distribution permitted increases in per capita consumption of many consumables. Both STRASSER and TEDLOW examine the factors involved in the changes in the very nature of retailing in the second half of the 20th century, while McAUSLAND and KOWINSKI respectively discuss the manifestations of these changes in the growth of supermarkets and shopping malls. The groundwork was already laid before World War II, but it was the still further spread of car ownership and general affluence after the war that transformed not only domestic life but the very concepts of urbanization and suburbanization. As the electrification of the home had advanced female emancipation from the 1920s onwards, entirely new and much expanded shopping facilities changed the routines of domesticity and allowed the expansion of labour force participation. But was this to become the American Dream of Marchand's title or the Great Consumer Paradise of Kowinski's or is it to turn into some kind of American nightmare?

JIM POTTER

See also Advertising

Marriage and Divorce

Basch, Norma, *In the Eyes of the Law: Women, Marriage, and Property in Nineteenth-Century New York*, Ithaca, NY: Cornell University Press, 1982
Blake, Nelson Manfred, *The Road to Reno: A History of Divorce in the United States*, New York: Macmillan, 1962

Griswold, Robert L., *Family and Divorce in California, 1850–1890: Victorian Illusions and Everyday Realities*, Albany: State University of New York Press, 1982
Gutiérrez, Ramón A., *When Jesus Came, the Corn Mothers Went Away: Marriage, Sexuality, and Power in New Mexico, 1500–1846*, Stanford, CA: Stanford University Press, 1991
Gutman, Herbert G., *The Black Family in Slavery and Freedom, 1750–1925*, New York: Pantheon, and Oxford: Blackwell, 1976
Lystra, Karen, *Searching the Heart: Women, Men, and Romantic Love in Nineteenth-Century America*, New York: Oxford University Press, 1989
May, Elaine Tyler, *Great Expectations: Marriage and Divorce in Post-Victorian America*, Chicago: University of Chicago Press, 1980
Mintz, Steven and Susan Kellogg, *Domestic Revolutions: A Social History of American Family Life*, New York: Free Press, and London: Collier Macmillan, 1988
Morgan, Edmund S., *The Puritan Family: Religion and Domestic Relations in Seventeenth-Century New England*, Boston: Public Library, 1944, 2nd edition, 1956; revised, Westport, CT: Greenwood Press, 1966
Riley, Glenda, *Divorce: An American Tradition*, New York: Oxford University Press, 1991

Of these two related topics, divorce has the better comprehensive overviews. A still readable introduction to divorce in America is BLAKE's narrative legal history. Beginning with the roots of divorce in the ancient world, and touching on key changes in the law up to the easy Nevada divorce of the 1950s, the book argues that the conservative policy in states like New York led to the rise of "divorce colonies" – states with lenient residency requirements and liberal divorce laws. Its dated material and its assumptions about the representativeness of New York limit the book's value, but it still provides a good, brief introduction to the topic. In a more recent overview, RILEY combines social and legal history in a well researched volume. She presents the thesis that the "conflict between anti-divorce and pro-divorce factions has prevented the development of effective, beneficial divorce laws, procedures and policies." Although Riley's interpretation of links between national identity and attitudes to divorce may be questioned, the book shows the necessity of seeing divorce as more than a legal institution. The book concludes with suggestions for future divorce policy.

Both Griswold and May focus on limited geographical areas and time periods, but both use divorce to explore the larger issue of marriage. GRISWOLD's study of court records in post-Gold Rush California suggests that the rise in divorce rates in the second half of the 19th century must be seen as a logical consequence of the decline of the patriarchal family and the emergence of the domestic, "companionate" marriage system. He argues that in these new marriages men as well as women had duties to fill and ideals to uphold. However, Griswold's interpretation exaggerates the egalitarian nature of this new marriage system and probably over-emphasizes cross-class adherence to the domestic ideal.

MAY is a brief social history of marital breakdown and rising divorce from 1880 to 1920. Using 1000 Los Angeles divorce cases from this period, May argues that the domestic, Victorian values that dominated marriage in the late 19th century were increasingly being challenged and replaced in the early 20th century by new attitudes based on consumerism, sexual gratification and personal fulfilment. When these great expectations of self-fulfilment were not met, marriages failed. Although May perhaps infers too much from her limited evidence, the book takes a provocative look at the intersection of marriage, divorce, sexuality and consumerism.

While an adequate historical overview of marriage in the United States has yet to be written, MINTZ and KELLOGG provide a good introduction to the subject in their social history of the family. A synthesis of much of the recent work in family history, the book touches on the marriage and divorce patterns of Americans in different classes and ethnic groups from the Puritans to the present. Although the scope of the book prevents the authors from doing justice to complex Native American and immigrant marriage practices, this is still a valuable account of a large and daunting subject.

Although it comprises only a portion of his early study of the Puritan family, MORGAN is in many ways still the best treatment of colonial New England marriage. In laying out the rights, privileges and duties of women and men in a society dominated by Calvinism, Morgan rescues the Puritans from the stereotype of prudishness and austerity. He gives us a complex and earthier picture of Puritan marriage that includes love and sexuality as well as duty and responsibility.

LYSTRA is a path-breaking study of romantic love and intimacy in 19th-century America. Relying mostly on the letters and journals of white middle-class Americans, she finds that the relations of these men and women were deeply emotional, sometimes intensely erotic, and built on a mutual identification that stretched gender conventions and occasionally bridged divisions based on gender. A few of Lystra's claims (cooperative birth control and sexual experimentation before marriage, for example) are not sufficiently documented, but this book deepens our understanding of marriage as a personal relationship shaped by emotion, ritual and the negotiation of roles.

BASCH provides a valuable discussion of the history of married women's property rights. The first part of the book gives a detailed analysis of coverture, showing how this notion of marital unity persisted long after the Revolution. The second portion describes the lobbying efforts that led to changes in New York law that gave married women greater legal control of their own property. Basch's exploration of the alliance of propertied men seeking to protect family property and feminists fighting for legal equality, though at times somewhat dry, is a valuable discussion of the politics of power and legal change.

One of the most significant developments in the history of marriage is the study of the family systems of particular ethnic and racial groups. GUTMAN's pioneering study remains the most important work on the African American family. Written in part as a response to political and academic attacks on the black family, the book affirms that the dyadic marriage remained a key characteristic of the black family throughout this period. Attitudes shaped by an adapted African culture led slaves to condemn most adultery, polygamy and desertion. Separation and single parenthood were more often the result of sale during slavery, and a high death rate in a discriminatory

society after emancipation. Gutman's evidence is less than convincing at times, particularly for the post-emancipation period, but scholars have since corroborated several of the book's main points.

GUTIÉRREZ uses marriage to explore themes of domination, acculturation and assimilation through three centuries of Spanish, Mexican and Native American contact. The book has two parts. The first uses marriage as a window to reveal the cultural differences and conflicts between the Pueblo Indians and the Spanish conquerors before 1693. The second half analyzes the ways in which elite Spaniards and Mexicans used marriage to perpetuate racial and class hierarchies in 18th- and 19th-century New Mexican society. Though at times uneven in its assessment of women and gender, the book effectively weaves together the stories of religious conquest with marriage and sexuality.

SHAWN JOHANSEN

See also Family

Marshall, George C.   1880–1959
Military commander, Secretary of State and Secretary of Defense

Cray, Ed, *General of the Army: George C. Marshall, Soldier and Statesman*, New York: Norton, 1990

Ferrell, Robert H., *George C. Marshall*, New York: Cooper Square, 1966

Parrish, Thomas, *Roosevelt and Marshall: Partners in Politics and War*, New York: Morrow, 1992

Payne, Robert, *The Marshall Story: A Biography of General George C. Marshall*, Englewood Cliffs, NJ: Prentice Hall, 1951; as *General Marshall: A Study in Loyalties*, London: Heinemann, 1952

Pogue, Forrest C., *George C. Marshall*, 4 vols., New York: Viking Press, 1963–87; vols. 1–3 published London: MacGibbon and Kee, 1964–73

Stoler, Mark A., *George C. Marshall: Soldier-Statesman of the American Century*, Boston: Twayne, 1989

George C. Marshall's unique role as Army Chief of Staff throughout World War II, then subsequently presidential envoy, secretary of state and of defense in the troubled years of the early Cold War make him a major figure in America's rise to world power, which the span of his life neatly matches. To Henry Stimson, Marshall was "the finest soldier I have ever known"; to Dean Acheson he was invariably "in command of himself"; to Harry Truman he was simply "the greatest living American". Yet Marshall, self-contained to the point of remoteness, reserved and intensely private, has inspired his biographers as a public figure yet often eluded them as a man. Perhaps it was the price of his achievement that the two facets of his personality should be merged; that, as Winston Churchill grandiloquently suggested, Marshall was "the greatest Roman of them all".

PAYNE is less a straight biography than a biographical study, sometimes overwritten, at others impressionistic and speculative. It is, however, readable, relatively short, and interesting as a period piece appearing in Marshall's lifetime, just at the end of his public career. It is not a work of scholarship, can indeed be inaccurate on detail, and received no help from its subject. It does nonetheless try to pierce the enigma of the man and, while not always uncritical, its general tone is one of admiration.

POGUE is magisterial, almost as lofty as its subject, and absolutely indispensable to an evaluation of Marshall's career. As the Director of the Research Center of the George C. Marshall Foundation, the author had access to all Marshall's papers, the benefit of a series of taped interviews with his subject running to some 125,000 words, plus the recollections of more than three hundred friends and associates. Typically the only stipulation which Marshall made was that the Director chosen for the project should be appointed without reference to him and that any profits accruing should go to the Foundation. Yet even so, as Pogue concedes, "the General was not an easy man to interview. Possessed of a strong personal reserve, he considered it unseemly to talk too much about himself and felt that family history was a personal matter". The four volumes, however, though a long time in gestation, more than compensate by their comprehensively detailed treatment of every aspect of Marshall's public life. The author makes no concessions to a general readership but is concerned to provide the linchpin for all subsequent Marshall historiography.

If the first volume necessarily examines the General's long-maturing army career, the subsequent volumes are also contributions to the history of World War II and the Cold War thereafter. The picture that emerges is of a selflessly dedicated public servant, recognizing the constitutional constraints and obligations of his respective positions, and, at all times, concerned only for the nation's good. If he held aloof from Roosevelt, it was to preserve the integrity of his judgment, a position that the president respected, so that he truly deserved the soubriquet of the third volume's subtitle, "Organizer of Victory". Although one might regret that this is seen as the European War, with the conclusion of the Pacific War included as background to Marshall's China Mission in the fourth volume, the biography overall gathers strength with Marshall. By the concluding volume one can see how the soldier with "the civilian mind" works for restraint and moderation both in the deployment of America's power and in the breaking down of the relationship with her former wartime ally, the Soviet Union. The four volumes collectively provide an authoritative exposition of that dramatic immersion in world affairs by the United States that Marshall's career served and reflected.

STOLER is a work of compression and synthesis, under two hundred pages of text, aimed at the student market and interested general reader. The first scholarly one-volume biography, it has as its theme the emergence of the United States as an international power and Marshall's place therein, blending biography with military and diplomatic history. It is well-written and admiring of its subject. CRAY is narrative history at its best. Immensely readable, well-researched, balanced in judgment, it is the outstanding one-volume work, though substantial in length. The author follows the main contours of Marshall's career and is more content to recount events than raise questions about them. The Marshall that emerges is still the hero without feet of clay, but the book

provides a useful source of reference for those daunted by the detail found in Pogue. It benefits from research and publication since the appearance of Pogue's volumes, and fills a gap in the literature.

PARRISH explores a fascinating if more specialized topic. It is a comparative study of a subject of great importance, when the American Constitution makes the president the Commander-in-Chief to insure civilian control of the military, and events conspired to make him fight the greatest war in history. Clearly Roosevelt's relationship with his Army Chief of Staff was vital yet difficult to delineate, because both men masked their deepest thoughts, and their interaction was inevitably not immediately easy to discern. Based on wide research, Parrish's study contends that the success of the relationship and the effectiveness of their co-operation lay in each man's willingness to adopt the methods of the other's profession. Roosevelt became a strategically active Commander-in-Chief, while Marshall, surprisingly, became a "political" soldier. Marshall's refusal to be enveloped in Roosevelt's customary geniality reflected a professional distance-keeping that, as the author demonstrates, strengthened a partnership that nonetheless raised concerns about civilian-military relationships for the future. Here, perhaps, even the god-like Marshall may have a question mark set against him.

FERRELL is part of an on-going series on the American secretaries of state, and appeared well before the relevant volume of Pogue. It is scholarly but now inevitably somewhat dated in approach. It is, however, clearly written and gives a narrative overview of the principal issues of Marshall's secretaryship in a little over two hundred pages.

JOHN KENTLETON

Marshall, John   1755–1835
Chief Justice of the Supreme Court

Baker, Leonard, *John Marshall: A Life in Law*, New York: Macmillan, and London: Collier Macmillan, 1974

Beveridge, Albert J., *The Life of John Marshall*, 4 vols., Boston: Houghton Mifflin, 1916–19

Corwin, Edward S., *John Marshall and the Constitution: A Chronicle of the Supreme Court*, New Haven: Yale University Press, 1919

Faulkner, Robert K., *The Jurisprudence of John Marshall*, Princeton: Princeton University Press, 1968

Haines, Charles Grove, *The Role of the Supreme Court in American Government and Politics, 1789–1835*, Berkeley: University of California Press, 1944

Haskins, George Lee and Herbert A. Johnson, *Foundations of Power: John Marshall, 1801–15*, New York: Macmillan, 1981

Newmyer, R. Kent, *The Supreme Court under Marshall and Taney*, New York: Crowell, 1968

Shevory, Thomas C., *John Marshall's Law: Interpretation, Ideology, and Interest*, Westport, CT: Greenwood Press, 1994

Stites, Francis N., *John Marshall, Defender of the Constitution*, Boston: Little Brown, 1981

Warren, Charles, *The Supreme Court in United States History*, 3 vols., Boston: Little, Brown, 1922, revised, 2 vols., 1926

White, G. Edward, *The Marshall Court and Cultural Change, 1815–35*, New York: Macmillan, 1988; abridged New York: Oxford University Press, 1991

History has been very good to John Marshall. It is his nationalist views of the origins and nature of the United States Constitution, vigorously criticized by many of his contemporaries, that have, as a consequence of the North's victory in the Civil War, come to dominate the way we interpret the federal government's powers today. Undoubtedly, Marshall would also be very pleased to learn that today the United States Supreme Court is viewed as the final arbiter in constitutional questions, a claim much contested in his own day. As a consequence, almost all constitutional history written in the 20th century has had a nationalist bias and has been written from a point of view extremely favorable to the Supreme Court. Further, Marshall has been elevated to the status of the single most important interpreter of the Constitution in American history.

This trend was firmly established in the first full-length scholarly biography of Marshall, that by BEVERIDGE, an important Progressive and United States Senator from Indiana, who also wrote a distinguished biography of Abraham Lincoln. Simply put, it is a magnificent, full-scale biography of Marshall's life and times. It is wonderfully written and the research is impressive in scope, if at times erratic. It ranges over the Chief Justice's entire life as a Virginian, a soldier, a lawyer, a politician, a diplomat and finally as a judge. Rich in detail, it contains much valuable background material on the cases that led to Marshall's greatest decisions. To be sure, it is excessively partisan towards the Chief Justice's point of view and overly dramatizes his confrontations with Thomas Jefferson. Nonetheless, it remains the essential starting point for all modern treatments of Marshall.

BAKER is the only other full-scale treatment of Marshall's life. It tends to be journalistic and anecdotal in its approach, and is best when dealing with Marshall's personality and his relationship with his family and many of the other leading figures of his day. On the other hand, his treatment of Marshall's constitutional philosophy and his numerous decisions tends to be very conventional and does not go very far below the surface. More impressive are two brief treatments of Marshall's life. CORWIN was probably the greatest American constitutional scholar to write during the first half of the 20th century. Some of his interpretations are now dated, but he presents many of the complex issues involved in Marshall's most important decisions with an authority and clarity that have enduring value. STITES is more recent and, therefore, more up-to-date in its interpretations. Concise and balanced in its treatment of a number of controversial issues, it provides an admirable introduction to Marshall, particularly appropriate for undergraduates.

Marshall's legal philosophy has received attention from two political scientists. FAULKNER stresses the importance of Lockean liberalism as central to Marshall's understanding of constitutional issues. SHEVORY, on the other hand, emphasizes the role of classical republicanism. This difference is a reflection of a much fuller debate among scholars of the founding era over the ideological sources of late 18th and early 19th century American political and constitutional thought. This is a rapidly accelerating debate and both these books are soon likely to be dated.

A rich source of information about Marshall is to be found in standard histories of the Supreme Court. One of the earliest and still one of the best is WARREN. Based on extensive research in primary sources, it contains much useful information about popular reaction to the Court's decisions. It is, however, very partial to Marshall's point of view. HAINES is less well-researched, but is useful as one of the few treatments of Marshall and the Court to look at the issues from the points of view of their Jeffersonian and Jacksonian critics. It raises a number of important questions about Marshall's impartiality and his use of the law to further certain partisan and economic interests. NEWMYER is a brief and measured introduction to many of these same developments and more up-to-date in its interpretations.

Two volumes of the monumental History of the Supreme Court of the United States, under the general editorship of Paul Freund, are devoted to the Marshall Court. The first volume by HASKINS and JOHNSON is not a joint effort, but really two different books in the same volume. Haskins is a conventional history of the institutional development of the Court and its most important early cases: *Marbury* v. *Madison*, Aaron Burr's treason trial, and *United States* v. *Peters*. It contains very little that is really new. Johnson capably examines the Court's rulings on a variety of topical issues: prize cases, marine insurance, international law, public land policy and the problem of a federal Common Law of Crimes. Among other things, he makes it clear that Marshall's legal expertise extended beyond constitutional questions.

WHITE treats the period 1816–35, when Marshall handed down the great majority of his most famous decisions. White ably describes how the Court operated, and usefully explicates the content of Marshall's most important decisions: *Dartmouth College* v. *Woodward*, *McCulloch* v. *Maryland*, *Cohens* v. *Virginia*, *Gibbons* v. *Ogden* and *Worcester* v. *Georgia*. However, White's attempt to explain these decisions in terms of a rapidly changing culture is less successful. In particular, there is too much emphasis on the so-called "republican synthesis," an organizing theme that has undergone rapid disintegration in recent years

Ironically, all of these works were written before the appearance of the excellent collection of Marshall papers that is currently in progress, under the editorship of Charles F. Hobson. Over the long run it will probably stimulate a good deal of revisionist history.

RICHARD E. ELLIS

See also Supreme Court

Marshall, Thurgood 1908–1993
Civil rights campaigner and Supreme Court justice

Bland, Randall W., *Private Pressure on Public Law: The Legal Career of Justice Thurgood Marshall*, Port Washington, NY: Kennikat Press, 1973; revised, Lanham, MD: University Press of America, 1993

Brennan, William J. and others, "A Tribute to Justice Thurgood Marshall," *Harvard Law Review*, 105, 1991

Davis, Michael D. and Hunter R. Clark, *Thurgood Marshall: Warrior at the Bar, Rebel on the Bench*, New York: Birch Lane Press, 1992

Greenberg, Jack, *Crusaders in the Courts: How a Dedicated Band of Lawyers Fought for the Civil Rights Revolution*, New York: Basic Books, 1994

Kluger, Richard, *Simple Justice: The History of Brown v. Board of Education and Black America's Struggle for Equality*, New York: Knopf, 1975; London: Deutsch, 1977

Rosenberg, Gerald N., *The Hollow Hope: Can Courts Bring about Social Change?*, Chicago: University of Chicago Press, 1991

Rowan, Carl T., *Dream Makers, Dream Breakers: The World of Justice Thurgood Marshall*, Boston: Little Brown, 1993

Tushnet, Mark V., *The NAACP's Legal Strategy Against Segregated Education, 1925–1950*, Chapel Hill: University of North Carolina Press, 1987

Tushnet, Mark V., *Making Civil Rights Law: Thurgood Marshall and the Supreme Court, 1936–1961*, New York: Oxford University Press, 1994

The full story of Thurgood Marshall's extraordinary life and career has yet to be written. The existing biographies are all in some ways inadequate, and the scholarly treatments of Marshall's legal career do not constitute rounded biographies. Nevertheless, for all their shortcomings, the existing studies nearly all point to the conclusion that in the long perspective of the struggle for civil rights, Marshall was a figure of comparable stature and importance to Martin Luther King, Jr.

For many years the only judicial biography of Marshall, BLAND provides a useful summary of Marshall's legal career, including an assessment of his four years as a federal appeals court judge, two years as Solicitor General, and 24 years as an associate justice of the United States Supreme Court. Bland is too brief, however, to furnish more than a superficial overview. Moreover, it is based almost entirely upon published court decisions and does not adequately explore Marshall's role as an activist and organizer, as well as a lawyer, in the NAACP. Bland gives little insight into Marshall's personality.

DAVIS and CLARK is the closest that we have to a rounded biography. A readable narrative, it places its subject in the context of the civil rights movement, discusses Marshall's role in the NAACP, and provides interesting glimpses into his life outside the courtroom. Its principal shortcoming is superficiality. Based largely upon secondary sources, it betrays unfamiliarity with the voluminous records of the NAACP, neglect of which will seriously flaw any study of Marshall.

ROWAN provides the best portrait of Marshall's private and semi-public sides. America's foremost black journalist, Rowan knew Marshall personally, and also possessed unrivalled knowledge of America's black leadership. The result is a gossipy book that includes many quotations and anecdotes from a man who was famous for his plain speaking, razor wit, and storytelling skill. Rowan also shows a sophisticated knowledge of internal NAACP politics. However, although the author obtained access to the records of the NAACP Legal Defense and Educational Fund, the book lacks depth of research. Based largely upon interviews with Marshall, the many ill-digested quotations betray evidence of a hastily-written book. Still, Rowan has more depth than either Bland or Davis and Clark, and is consistently readable.

KLUGER tells the complex story of *Brown* v. *Board of Education* (1954), the greatest triumph of Thurgood Marshall and the NAACP. It is a long but beautifully-written book that is deservedly considered a classic. The story is a multi-layered one, and the large cast of characters includes judges, lawyers, psychologists, politicians, and plaintiffs. The sprawling narrative ranges over many topics in order to provide depth and context – it uses one hundred pages, for example, to summarize the legal and social status of blacks between the Declaration of Independence and the 1920s. In a story with many heroes, Kluger succeeds admirably in highlighting, but not exaggerating, Marshall's role in the *Brown* decision. Although lawyers and judges crowd the narrative, Kluger gives due weight to the ordinary men and women who challenged Jim Crow in the first instance.

Although Marshall never wrote his memoirs, GREENBERG partially fills that void. Marshall's longtime deputy, and his successor as head of the NAACP Legal Defense and Educational Fund (the "Inc. Fund"), Greenberg presents a thoughtful and detailed account of the many cases in which he and Marshall collaborated. He is particularly helpful in explaining the distinction – and growing antagonism – between the "Inc. Fund" and the NAACP proper. He is also illuminating on the aftermath of the *Brown* decision (when the NAACP became the object of harsh repression by state authorities in the South), Marshall's attitude to the Communist party, and his relationship with local black attorneys. The book gives an excellent account of the inner workings of the "Inc. Fund" and adds considerably to our knowledge of Marshall's personality and his methods as a lawyer.

Along with Greenberg, TUSHNET (1994) is essential reading for any serious study of Marshall's contribution to the civil rights movement. Although Tushnet pays attention to Marshall's role as an organizer as well as a lawyer, this is an analysis of his record as a civil rights lawyer, not a conventional biography. A legal historian and a former law clerk of Marshall's, Tushnet is well placed to write what promises to become the definitive account of Marshall's legal career. He has thoroughly mined the relevant papers of the NAACP, and he provides both a careful analysis of the NAACP's courtroom battles, and an informed appraisal of the political and organizational dynamics that moulded and influenced Marshall's strategy of litigation. Although an admirer of his subject, Tushnet does not indulge in hero-worship and scrupulously assesses the limitations and shortcomings of Marshall's reliance upon the federal judiciary. The book ends with Marshall's appointment to the federal bench; a second volume is promised. In an earlier work, TUSHNET (1987) provided a more detailed account of the origins of the NAACP's strategy of litigating in federal courts to equalize, and then to desegregate, public schools and universities. The book describes the crucial role of Marshall's predecessor, Charles Hamilton Houston, and goes on to analyze the decisive shift that took place in NAACP strategy, between 1946 and 1950, from the goal of equalizing facilities to that of abolishing segregation completely.

When Marshall retired from the Supreme Court, a group of former law clerks, NAACP colleagues, and federal judges paid tribute to his life and career. Although the nature of the occasion made criticism inappropriate, BRENNAN and the other contributors offer useful insights into Marshall as man, lawyer and judge.

While saying little about Marshall directly, ROSENBERG forcefully challenges the efficacy of the NAACP's litigation strategy by arguing that the *Brown* decision did little to bring about school integration or advance the cause of civil rights generally. Although he grossly overstates his case, Rosenberg offers a useful reminder to both activists and historians that they should not attribute too much influence to the federal courts when it comes to bringing about, or explaining, social change.

ADAM FAIRCLOUGH

See also Civil Rights Movement; Judiciary; National Association for the Advancement of Colored People

Marshall Plan, 1947–1951

Dulles, Allen W., *The Marshall Plan*, edited by Michael Wala, Providence, RI, and Oxford: Berg, 1993

Fossedal, Gregory A., *Our Finest Hour: Will Clayton, the Marshall Plan, and the Triumph of Democracy*, Stanford, CA: Hoover Institution Press, 1993

Gimbel, John, *The Origins of the Marshall Plan*, Stanford, CA: Stanford University Press, 1976

Hogan, Michael J., *The Marshall Plan: America, Britain, and the Reconstruction of Western Europe, 1947–1952*, Cambridge and New York: Cambridge University Press, 1987

Maier, Charles S. and Günter Bischof (editors), *The Marshall Plan and Germany: West German Development Within the Framework of the European Recovery Program*, New York and Oxford: Berg, 1991

Milward, Alan S., *The Reconstruction of Western Europe, 1945–1951*, Berkeley: University of California Press, and London: Methuen, 1984

Pelling, Henry, *Britain and the Marshall Plan*, London: Macmillan, 1988

Pogue, Forrest C., *George C. Marshall: Statesman, 1945–1959*, New York: Viking, 1987

The Marshall Plan was initiated by General George C. Marshall, the American secretary of state in the Truman administration, in a speech to the Harvard alumni on 5 June 1947. He wanted the United States to provide dollars to help the postwar recovery of Europe. The Marshall Plan, or the European Recovery Program as it was later called, operated between 1948 and 1952 ($13 billion in total) and was administered by the Organization for European Economic Cooperation (OEEC), which was formed in 1948 by 16 Western European nations (no Communist countries participated). Based on material in the United States and in Germany, which was declassified in the early 1970s, GIMBEL is a detailed and balanced account of the origins of the Marshall Plan. Unlike both traditionalist and new left historians of the Cold War, he argues that it was France, not the Soviet Union, which was the major obstacle to American efforts to revive the Western European economies, and especially the economy of a defeated and occupied Germany, after World War II. Gimbel emphasizes that the Marshall Plan was not the result of any long-range American planning in response to the Soviet "threat." Marshall's speech at Harvard was based on a combination of ideas and plans floated in the State Department by Will Clayton, George Kennan, Dean Acheson, and Robert Lovett, who all participated in the formulation of the Marshall Plan. Although published in 1976, Gimbel's masterly monograph on the Marshall Plan remains the most authoritative account of the subject.

Various essays in MAIER and BISCHOF volume follow Gimbel in stressing that the Marshall Plan originated in Germany's economic distress. However, the contributors differ in their assessments of the economic impact of the Marshall Plan. Werner Abelshauser, a German historian, argues that the recovery of the German economy was already under way by 1948 and concludes that the Marshall Plan helped in the reorganisation of the German economic system, rather than in effecting the recovery itself. Alan Milward, a British historian, shows that the Marshall Plan did succeed in expanding America's exports to Europe and that it laid the foundations for America's burgeoning market in Germany. In his own book, MILWARD shows in greater detail that the effect of the Marshall Plan was exaggerated by the Americans, and that the successful European recovery owed more to the efforts made by the Europeans themselves than to American financial intervention. Thus, more recent work suggests that historians are now concerned less with the ideological implications of the plan, and more with its practical impact upon the political and economic systems of Western Europe.

HOGAN looks at the Marshall Plan from a wider perspective and places it in the context of America's efforts to reconstruct war-ravaged Europe after World War I. He argues that the driving force behind the Marshall initiative was the American conviction that the recovery of the European economy, and the adoption throughout Europe of American management techniques, were essential to America's long-term interests. The Cold War and the ensuing tensions with the Soviet Union made the success of the European Recovery Program even more important, but, like Gimbel, Hogan does not believe that the Cold War was the cause of the Marshall Plan. He also shows that the success of the Marshall Plan depended upon the Europeans' willingness to help themselves. Consequently, the recipients retained considerable discretion in the application of the Plan and, in this context, Hogan discusses Anglo-American differences over European integration and the role which Washington expected Britain to play in the process.

In a more extended treatment of Anglo-American relations in connection with the Marshall Plan, PELLING, like a number of other historians, emphasizes that Britain's decline did not result from her sacrifices during World War II, but was part of a long process during the first half of the 20th century. After 1945, Britain continued to suffer from the burden of maintaining substantial military forces overseas. Although Britain became the second largest financial contributor (after the United States) to the OEEC during its initial years, Britain and the United States differed over methods of achieving an economically prosperous and politically stable Western Europe.

The personalities and values of the major actors are of course crucial to an understanding of the origins of the Marshall Plan. The fourth and final volume of POGUE, the official biography of George C. Marshall, covers the years from 1945 to 1959. Pogue lucidly chronicles the events leading up to Marshall's speech at Harvard. Marshall, frustrated by the futile negotiations with the Russians at the Council of Foreign Ministers in Moscow in the spring of 1947, was even more distressed to learn from his French and British colleagues that little progress had been made in the recovery of the European economies. He appreciated that poor economic conditions there would make Western Europe even more vulnerable to communist encroachments. His concern was to address the problem at the right time and before the right audience, in order to overcome congressional opposition to assisting Europe financially. He turned his Harvard address into an appropriate opportunity. In formulating the Marshall Plan, the secretary of state relied on the advice of a number of State Department officials, who called for an urgent American initiative to rescue what appeared to be an economically crumbling Europe. FOSSEDAL shows that William Clayton, the under secretary of state for Economic Affairs played a major part in promoting the Marshall Plan.

However, Marshall's speech marked only the beginning of the State Department's effort to sell the Plan to a sceptical American public and a reluctant Congress. Allen Dulles was a founding member of the "Committee for the Marshall Plan to Aid European Recovery", which was set up on 1 October 1947, and chaired by Henry Stimson, the former secretary of war. The Committee was meant to be an unofficial body, but in fact it became a vehicle for State Department publicity. Largely for this purpose, DULLES wrote a monograph on the Marshall Plan, but its publication in 1948 was abandoned in the face of rising Cold War tensions and the subsequent congressional approval of the European Recovery Program. Nearly 45 years later, Michael Wala edited Dulles's monograph and published it. Dulles argued that unless the United States took over from a declining Britain the responsibility for restoring Western Europe economically, Western Europe would be at the mercy of the Soviet Union. Dulles confirms that, while the Marshall Plan was not conceived as part of America's long-range Cold War policy, the Truman administration skilfully maximized Cold War rhetoric in an effort to convince Congress of the need for America's economic intervention in Europe. By 1948, Truman's Cold War rhetoric appeared to be substantiated by a series of Stalinist coups in Eastern and Central Europe.

SAKI DOCKRILL

See also Foreign Policy since 1945: Special Aspects 3

Mather, Cotton 1663–1728 and
Increase Mather 1639–1723
New England Puritan ministers and authors

Bercovitch, Sacvan, *The Puritan Origins of the American Self*, New Haven: Yale University Press, 1975

Breitwieser, Mitchell Robert, *Cotton Mather and Benjamin Franklin: The Price of Representative Personality*, Cambridge and New York: Cambridge University Press, 1984

Hall, Michael G., *The Last Puritan: The Life of Increase Mather*, Middletown, CT: Wesleyan University Press, 1988

Levin, David, *Cotton Mather: The Young Life of the Lord's Remembrancer, 1663–1703*, Cambridge, MA: Harvard University Press, 1978

Lovelace, Richard, *The American Pietism of Cotton Mather: Origins of American Evangelicalism*, Grand Rapids, MI: Christian University Press, 1979

Lowance, Mason I., Jr., *Increase Mather*, New York: Twayne, 1974

Middlekauff, Robert, *The Mathers: Three Generations of Puritan Intellectuals, 1596–1728*, New York: Oxford University Press, 1971

Miller, Perry, *The New England Mind: From Colony to Province*, Cambridge, MA: Harvard University Press, 1953

Silverman, Kenneth, *The Life and Times of Cotton Mather*, New York: Harper and Row, 1984

As central clerical figures in the development and transformation of the New England Puritanism that Increase's father Richard helped create, Increase Mather and his son Cotton have been difficult figures to comprehend, a task made more difficult by the immense range of their activities, their reading, and their writing. Historians have often used the Mathers as a means of understanding – and judging – Puritan New England. The numerous studies of their lives and ideas suggests the contested nature of early New England history.

The starting point for recent work on the Mathers is MILLER, the final volume of his brilliant study of "the New England Mind." Miller largely celebrates early Puritanism as a tough-minded attempt to unite rigorously-reasoned faith and action. But he made Cotton, and to a lesser extent Increase, an emblem of later Puritan decline (what Miller calls declension), arguing that its carefully-wrought synthesis proved unable to meet new circumstances. Cotton, portrayed as fevered and unbalanced, receives the harshest criticism, becoming the symbol both of the attempt to compel small-town conformity through piety and of the surrender to rationalism that together marked the end of Puritanism.

MIDDLEKAUFF provides the most comprehensive attempt to revise Miller. Studying Richard as well as Increase and Cotton, the book examines the ministers as intellectuals involved in a clerical culture, a perspective that excludes the key political role played by Increase (and to a lesser extent Cotton). The Mathers attempted to unite piety and intellect. They struggled intellectually with a changing society that increasingly sundered religious and secular life – but without, as Miller suggested, giving up their principles or their commitment to reason. Thus they represented a vital continuation of New England Puritanism, not its death throes. Middlekauff devotes nearly half the book to Cotton, providing a rich, multi-faceted picture of his personality and ideas. Cotton, the book argues, went even further than Increase in revising Puritanism, engaging with American and international issues, preaching a simplified gospel, and helping to start the expectations of the millennium that would be influential through the next century, but eventually letting the synthesis of piety and intellect collapse in favor of heart-oriented religion.

Subsequent works tend to focus on either Increase or Cotton. HALL uses Increase's extensive unpublished diaries to provide the only full picture of his life. Hall portrays the elder Mather as the central figure in the high-water mark of Puritanism in the 1670s and its most prominent defender afterwards. The book is particularly useful on Increase's role in the political developments of the 1680s and 1690s. Besides helping to create the myth of New England's founders, Hall suggests, Increase negotiated the new Massachusetts charter that destroyed the foundations of the Puritan state and society. He then aided the transition to the new circumstances of 18th-century New England. LOWANCE provides a study of Increase as author that complements Hall's emphasis on his personal and political life. Lowance offers introductions to each of Increase's major works, as well as an examination of his different types of sermons, both as literary texts and as expressions of his generation's religious ideals.

As the more prolific author (including an almost painfully revealing diary), Increase's son Cotton has received greater attention. SILVERMAN is a rich psychologically-informed biography that devotes particular attention to Cotton's early stutter as an expression of his anxieties and a precursor to his distinctive personality and modes of expression. Nonetheless, Silverman generally stresses the ambivalence of Cotton's reactions to events and ideas, and sees less internal consistency than other historians. LEVIN provides a full study of Cotton's first forty years that stresses his internal development. The book tends to be more sympathetic to the Mathers than Silverman (and certainly more than Miller), seeing Cotton as relatively healthy and resilient – and as a vital part of the Mather and the Puritan tradition. Levin also devotes greater attention to Cotton's literary achievements.

BREITWIESER presents a complex and intriguing argument that considers Cotton's personality as a coherent whole. He suggests that Cotton attempted to make himself an exemplary figure that represented the heart of New England piety. Despite a persistent desire to assert himself, he tried to imitate his fathers (literal and religious) and to annihilate his own self-will. In turn, Cotton projected his own internal tension upon his relationship with the world, seeing himself as the representative of pious tradition and his society as the embodiment of the self-assertion he attempted to destroy within himself. LOVELACE attempts to connect Cotton to his context in a different way. Studying theological ideas, he sees Mather at the center of a major shift. On one hand, resisting Miller's attempt to separate Mather from his Puritan inheritance, Lovelace sees in him an attempt to distill the vast Protestant tradition dating back to the Reformation. Just as important, partly through his connection with European pietists like the

German August Hermann Francke, Mather also played a central role in creating what would become American Evangelicalism. So, rather than the end of an old tradition, Mather's attempt to simplify his religious messages, to create voluntary associations and ecumenical ties, and to encourage the coming millennium, can be seen as the precursor to the Great Awakenings.

BERCOVITCH presents yet another side of Cotton in a book that looks closely at the biography of John Winthrop in Mather's huge collection of New England history, the *Magnalia Christi Americana* (1702). Bercovitch highlights Mather's literary artistry, arguing that it helped create a myth that has shaped Americans' views of themselves and their country. Drawing upon central traditions in Renaissance and Reformation literature, Mather went further to describe America itself (implicit in his view of New England) as a Christian saint making progress towards salvation. American heroes in turn would be viewed as the embodiment of America. Mather is thus the crucial link in American's views of themselves that would again be reshaped by Emerson in the following century. Bercovitch perhaps pushes too hard to see long-term rhetorical continuities, but he also makes clear Mather's literary skill and his importance within an intellectual tradition that extended beyond religion.

STEVEN C. BULLOCK

See also Puritanism

Mellon, Andrew 1855–1937
Businessman, financier and Secretary of the Treasury

Folsom, Burton W., *The Myth of the Robber Barons*, Herndon, VA: Young America's Foundation, 1991

Hersh, Burton, *The Mellon Family: A Fortune in History*, New York: Morrow, 1978

Holbrook, Stewart H., *The Age of the Moguls*, New York: Doubleday, 1953; London: Gollancz, 1954

Koskoff, David E., *The Mellons: The Chronicle of America's Richest Family*, New York: Crowell, 1978

Love, Philip H., *Andrew W. Mellon: The Man and His Work*, Baltimore: F. Heath Coggins, 1929

Mellon, William Larimer, *Judge Mellon's Sons*, Pittsburgh: privately printed, 1948

Murray, Lawrence L., "Bureaucracy and Bi-Partisanship in Taxation: The Mellon Plan Revisited," *Business History Review*, 52, Summer 1978

O'Connor, Harvey, *Mellon's Millions – The Biography of a Fortune: The Life and Times of Andrew W. Mellon*, New York: Day, 1933

Rader, Benjamin G., "Federal Taxation in the 1920s: A Re-Examination," *The Historian*, 33, May 1971

Ratner, Sidney, *American Taxation: Its History as a Social Force in Democracy*, New York: Norton, 1942

Despite Andrew Mellon's historical importance as a venture capitalist and influential shaper of national economic policy during the 1920s, the literature on him has remained sparse. A biography commissioned by the family was not published, and a doctoral dissertation done at Michigan State University has yet to appear as a book. Consequently, the available literature still consists chiefly of muckraking exposés, uncritical defenses, and journalistic chronicles, although in recent years the attack on the progressive historical interpretation has led some scholars to reconsider both Mellon's business career and the tax measures enacted while he was secretary of the treasury. Some conservative interpreters now see him not as a malefactor of great wealth whose sabotage of progressive reform helped to bring on the Great Depression but as a builder of great business and philanthropic institutions who was ahead of his time in understanding how appropriate tax reductions could stimulate economic growth and increase total revenue.

Appearing at the height of liberal efforts to discredit Mellon and Mellonism, O'CONNOR still stands as the best of the muckraking accounts of Mellon's life and work. Although unabashedly progressive in its interpretation and overly zealous in its prosecutorial stance, it is written with force and verve, reflects some admirable spadework in uncovering details about the Mellon holdings, and excels in pulling together the indictment emerging from congressional investigations. In it Mellon appears as a sorry figure with few virtues and much responsibility for the country's plight in 1933, but he is also a more complex, believable, and tragic figure than the villainous caricature that would become a staple of liberal political rhetoric.

O'Connor's interpretation has also had a strong influence on what more scholarly historians have written and taught about Mellon. It became the standard interpretation in textbooks and surveys written from a progressive point of view as well as in sections on Mellon in works dealing with the building of large American fortunes and their role in shaping public policy. In the latter category, HOLBROOK accepts the O'Connor interpretation, but also goes beyond it to see Mellon as one of the "new giants" to appear in the second wave of fortune-building, and to stress how atypical he was in his penchant for acquisition by stealth and his success in combining the roles of promoter, banker, and industrialist.

Still another body of work featuring negative portrayals of Mellon has been that dealing with the history of American taxation. The classic in the field, long regarded as definitive in its scholarship and exemplary in its narration, is RATNER, a work in which three chapters cover in detail the politics of taxation during the period when Mellon was secretary of the treasury. The theme of the book as a whole is one of progressive heroes trying to make the American tax system an instrument for promoting economic and social justice, and in this larger story the Mellon era appears as a time of retrogression and setbacks in which the forces of conservatism and privilege mobilized behind the Mellon Plan and were temporarily successful in defeating their progressive adversaries.

Early defenses of Mellon appeared in what is still the only book-length biography and in works produced by members of the Mellon family. The biography is LOVE, which in general is an uncritical eulogy extolling Mellon's prodigious achievements in business and public affairs and quoting extensively from his speeches and statements. Its value today is primarily as an indicator of how he was viewed in some quarters in the late 1920s. Of the family works, the most informative and useful is MELLON. Written by Andrew's nephew, it defends the secretary's point of view on the issues of the day and is

in other ways biased and uncritical. But readers can glean from it much interesting information about family affairs and Mellon's interactions with other business and political figures.

Two other works in which Mellon appears as the central figure in a larger family story are HERSH and KOSKOFF, both the result of journalistic projects that culminated in 1978. Both are lengthy works of popular history, relying heavily on interviews as well as a reading of published sources, and tending to eschew interpretation and analysis in favor of colorful anecdotes and catchy quotations. Both linger unduly over such matters as Mellon's sensational divorce proceedings in 1911 and Congressman Wright Patman's colorful attempts to have him impeached in the early 1930s. But both have also earned praise as goldmines of information, and both offered some rehabilitation of Mellon's tarnished image. Of the two, Koskoff is less breathless and pretentious in its prose, better at guiding the reader through the complexities of Mellon's dealings, and more restrained in its assessments of Mellon's business acumen and political influence.

The recent rehabilitation of Mellon in scholarly circles has been led by conservative revisionists critical of progressive historical interpretation and in search of a history that helps to justify the tax reductions and deregulatory measures of the 1980s. An example is FOLSOM, which began as a book bent upon turning "robber barons" into "great competitors" but was subsequently revised to include a chapter on Andrew Mellon, his program of cutting taxes to raise revenue, and the lies told about him in progressive history. One center for this effort to reinterpret the policies of the 1920s and 1930s has been the journal *Continuity*, of which Folsom is the editor.

Two revisionist articles that have also become part of the current debates about Mellon are MURRAY and RADER. Both note the continuity in policy between Mellon and his predecessors in the Wilson administration, and Rader offers persuasive evidence to show that, while the Mellon tax system of 1929 allowed the growth of greater income inequity, it was not the mechanism by which this occurred. On the contrary, it actually imposed a greater relative tax burden on the rich than had the system of 1921, primarily because rate reductions had been accompanied by increased personal exemptions which allowed most Americans to escape the payment of any income taxes.

ELLIS W. HAWLEY

Mencken, H.L. 1880–1956
Journalist, author and social critic

Angoff, Charles, *H.L. Mencken: A Portrait from Memory*, New York: Yoseloff, 1956

Bode, Carl, *Mencken*, Carbondale: Southern Illinois University Press, 1969

Dorsey, John (editor), *On Mencken: Essays*, New York: Knopf, 1980

Douglas, George H., *H.L. Mencken: Critic of American Life*, Hamden, CT: Archon, 1978

Goldberg, Isaac, *The Man Mencken: A Biographical and Critical Survey*, New York: Simon and Schuster, 1925

Manchester, William, *Disturber of the Peace: The Life and Riotous Times of H.L. Mencken*, New York: Harper, 1951, 2nd edition, Amherst: University of Massachusetts Press, 1986; as *The Sage of Baltimore: The Life and Riotous Times of H.L. Mencken*, London: Melrose, 1952

Nolte, William H., *H.L. Mencken: Literary Critic*, Middletown, CT: Wesleyan University Press, 1966

Any attempt to summarize the life and works of Henry Louis Mencken will be difficult, and will depend very much on the standpoint of the commentator. This journalist, lay philosopher, and critic of both America and "ideas" in general maintained a fairly consistent set of beliefs, which resonated with the young and progressive in the 1920s, but sounded hopelessly reactionary during the Depression. Time has not done any favours to Mencken's philosophy (a sort of Nietzschean evolutionism in a naively progressive world), but his observations of the American scene are unparalleled. As one observer noted, Mencken lies halfway between Mark Twain and Woody Allen.

Some recent commentators have tended unfairly to dismiss Mencken's work as sexist, racist or reactionary, although no one has yet attempted a revisionist account. While his work is clearly not politically correct, his actions and voluminous writings do not substantiate these claims. Instead, Mencken should be seen as a consistent thinker whose intellectual rebellion against "Puritanism" and the middle-class values of his time inspired and stimulated some of the major American writers of the early 20th century. Theodore Dreiser, Sherwood Anderson, Sinclair Lewis and F. Scott Fitzgerald all expressed their respect for the role that Mencken played in their careers, and in American letters as a whole.

GOLDBERG was the first biographer, writing just after Mencken's tenure at the magazine *Smart Set*, and in the midst of Mencken's most popular period as editor and moving force behind the magazine *American Mercury*. His book conveys some idea of the intellectual climate of the 1920s from someone who had intimate and friendly contact with Mencken. The manner in which it is written, with metaphors as long as Mencken's but without the glitter, may lead those with limited stamina to give up, but it remains worthwhile nonetheless. There is a naive Nietzschean philosophy informing Goldberg's account appropriate to Mencken's work, with its innocent espousal of a natural elite, that most would now find dated. However, it remains readable, and it offers the bonus of a wonderful collection of Menckeniana in the appendix.

In contrast, DOUGLAS offers a much harder and more unsympathetic portrayal. His examination of Mencken's ideas focuses on his alleged disgust with democratic ideals. None of the fun that Mencken obviously had from the American political system is evident; rather an acerbic Mencken is portrayed, to the detriment of the Mencken that most readers find attractive. Veiled (and not so veiled) references to the intellectual problems created by "women libbers" and "student protesters" at the time of this book's writing reveal more about its author than about Mencken.

ANGOFF, co-editor of the *American Mercury*, begins and ends with a description of Mencken urinating, descriptions which are in tune with the goal of this book. Angoff, an underemployed Harvard graduate who was lifted to one of the most envied intellectual positions in the 1920s, might have been expected to show a little more gratitude than this book offers. Iconoclastic, vulgar, but well documented, the book offers a point of view very different from other writers. Angoff's focus on Mencken's vulgarity may be more a reflection of his subject's desire to shock a representative of the "professors" whom he so often railed against, than an accurate depiction of Mencken.

A very readable collection of essays by most of Mencken's biographers, edited by DORSEY, stands out as the best introduction to Mencken for newcomers to the subject. Possibly handicapped by the fact that almost all were his friends, essays by Manchester, Cairns, Cooke, Fecher, Moos, Nolte, Bode, and Knopf offer diverse approaches to the many facets of Mencken, but hardly in a critical manner. However, they do not, on the whole, praise him without reservation, and the selections present a good sample of the self-named prejudices that made Mencken both incredibly popular and unpopular at the same time.

One of the contributors to Dorsey, MANCHESTER makes a comprehensive attempt to portray Mencken to "the future" from the perspective of the early 1950s. The author is guided by a sense of critical nostalgia particularly effective in showing Mencken at odds with his own time, but unsurprisingly (given the time when it was written) less successful in examining Mencken from any illuminating revisionist viewpoint. The references to other Menckeniana and other commentators are useful. Written with genuine warmth, the book is enjoyable to read and is enhanced by Manchester's close friendship with Mencken.

BODE, also a contributor to Dorsey, has written a scholarly and detailed tome on Mencken. This book is far and away the most "academic" thus far, but due perhaps to its genre, it lacks some of the excitement of the other books. Its critical and largely fair evaluation of his whole life makes it required reading for anyone deeply interested in Mencken. In particular, Bode's attempt to reveal more of Mencken than he wished to reveal is very skilfully executed, without seeming iconoclastic. In fact, this is probably the most balanced and considered evaluation of Mencken thus far, although issues of Mencken's perceived racism and sexism, while mentioned, are rather skimmed over.

An attempt to look at Mencken's career as a literary critic, NOLTE is so faithful to his subject's views that we find Menckenisms paraphrased into Nolte's own words. He has a useful account of Mencken's *Smart Set* period, which he believes was a very important and mostly undervalued phase of Mencken's life. Nolte effectively echoes Mencken's polemic against academic criticism, although some critical distance might be lost by his wholesale embrace of these views. This study is valuable for its discussion of Mencken's relationship with, and critical evaluation of, many early 20th century writers.

DAVID J. MIKOSZ

Mexican Americans (Chicanos)

Acuña, Rodolfo, *Occupied America: The Chicano's Struggle Toward Liberation*, San Francisco: Canfield Press, 1972; 3rd edition, as *Occupied America: A History of Chicanos*, New York: Harper, 1988

Blea, Irene I., *La Chicana and the Intersection of Race, Class, and Gender*, New York: Praeger, 1992

Chávez, John R., *The Lost Land: The Chicano Image of the Southwest*, Albuquerque: University of New Mexico Press, 1984

García, Mario T., *Mexican Americans: Leadership, Ideology, and Identity, 1930–1960*, New Haven: Yale University Press, 1989

McWilliams, Carey, *North from Mexico: The Spanish-Speaking People of the United States*, edited by Louis Adamic, Philadelphia: Lippincott, 1949; revised by Matt S. Meier, New York: Greenwood Press, 1990

Meier, Matt S. and Feliciano Rivera, *The Chicanos: A History of Mexican Americans*, New York: Hill and Wang, 1972, revised as *Mexican Americans/American Mexicans: From Conquistadors to Chicanos*, 1993

Montejano, David, *Anglos and Mexicans in the Making of Texas, 1836–1986*, Austin: University of Texas Press, 1987

Muñoz, Carlos, Jr., *Youth, Identity, and Power: The Chicano Movement*, London: Verso, 1989

The genre of Mexican American (Chicano) history is a recent phenomenon. In 1969 one observer was moved to write that "no history of a people has been more obscure, more apocryphal, and so utterly misapprehended by the majority of Anglo-Americans than the history of Mexican-Americans, for they continue to exist in the United States as an 'invisible minority'".

McWILLIAMS was the first to offer a significant general history of the group. McWilliams was fêted as "the Anglo foster father of Chicano historical studies", and his work stood alone in the field for some twenty years before the subject was revived in the late 1960s. Appreciative of the group's diverse cultural heritage and potential, it takes as its starting point "The Spanish Prologue" and follows the history through until the mid-1940s, acknowledging as it proceeds that the history of the Mexican American can be understood only within the wider context of both Mexican and United States history. The account tends to become more episodic as it details events which the author himself experienced, but to this day it remains a classic. In its updated form three chapters have been added, picking up the story with the impact on the Chicano of World War II.

As it was Meier who updated that text, it is not surprising that the history which he has co-authored with Rivera follows in McWilliams's footsteps. A revised version of an earlier publication, MEIER and RIVERA is an excellent general history, concise, comprehensive and easily accessible to the reader. It is particularly valuable for its coverage of the Indo-Hispanic period, during which the cultural mestizaje (blending) began. The bulk of the book deals with the confrontation of the Mexicans and Anglo Americans over the last two hundred years, but a chapter on the Chicano cultural renaissance and a glossary of the more commonly used Spanish terms are also useful features.

The titles chosen by both Acuña and Chávez clearly indicate a development of the idea that the Anglo American has established for the Chicano a pattern of internal colonialism. ACUÑA moderates this theme in the third edition, but this remains an impassioned account of the history of the Chicano from the conquest of Mexico's northern territory onwards. Dismayed at the conservatism that has accompanied the "graying" of the United States since the youthful exuberance of the 1960s, Acuña is clearly disdainful of the propensity of middle-class Chicanos to distance themselves from poor Chicanos. Following a chronological framework, the book has eleven clearly indexed chapters and is a good source of detailed information about any given event. CHÁVEZ follows the changes in the Chicano perception of the Southwest, contending that the 1848 Treaty of Guadalupe Hidalgo occasioned a "loss" of the homeland. While some of the assertions may be challenged as oversimplifications, it is particularly informative about the concept of Aztlán which in the late 1960s became a collective symbol and focus for Chicano nationalism. As stated in its introduction, the desire to recover a lost homeland is allied to the desire for cultural, political and economic self-determination. The belief that Chicanos are indigenous to and dispossessed of the Southwest is thus one that has an abiding influence on the Chicano mind, and for this reason the book is worthy of attention.

In a study which won the Frederick Jackson Turner prize in 1988, MONTEJANO applies a sociological dimension to his exploration and analysis of the history of Mexican and Anglo relations in Texas since the Alamo. Inspired by personal curiosity as a fourth generation native, he posits race as a socially defined sign, and provides a fascinating study of the political, economic and cultural dimensions of four broad periods in Texas history. In spite of its regional focus, this ranks as an important race-class analysis of the whole Chicano experience.

The political history of the Chicano is at its most apparent in relation to the Chicano Movement of the late 1960s and early 1970s. As a major participant in the events of the time, MUÑOZ provides the first full-length work on the subject. Drawing on first-hand and primary material, the text mirrors the author's own concerns in its chapters on the student movement and La Raza Unida party, and the struggle to establish Chicano Studies. In contradistinction to other comments on the 1960s, it stresses the importance of the involvement of Mexican American youth in the politics of the time. A source of great detail about Chicano activism during this era, it is also informative about the generationally political distinctions between the labels Mexican American and Chicano. Lamenting the return to prominence of the "old-guard pro-assimilationist and liberal reformist" groups of the 1930s and 1940s, GARCÍA reveals Muñoz to be on shaky ground in his dismissive treatment of that "Mexican-American" generation. Based on extensive archival research presented in the form of separate case studies, this is the first work to take the political history of this generation as its specific focus. Also utilising the concept of the political generation, it contends that it was the Mexican Americans and not the Chicanos who organised their first significant civil rights movement and thereby challenges the impression that the generation was "accommodationist".

García asserts that he made a conscious effort to locate material on the role of women but found only scant reference. It is only recently that the absence of the Chicana from the historical text has begun to be addressed. Only in 1986 did the National Association of Chicano Studies publish a work devoted exclusively to the Chicana experience. As national chair of the Chicana Caucus of the Association, BLEA is ideally placed to offer a history of the Chicana. Divided into ten chapters and covering a variety of angles, her study examines the social reality of the Chicana, and considers the intersection of race, class and gender. Regrettably, the text amounts to a simplistic review, and too often relies on conviction instead of consideration, but it does at least offer a starting point for further study.

CANDIDA N. HEPWORTH

Mexican War, 1846–1848: Campaigns

Alcaraz, Ramón, *The Other Side; or, Notes for the History of the War Between Mexico and the United States*, edited and translated by Albert C. Ramsey, New York: Wiley, 1850

Bauer, K. Jack., *The Mexican War, 1846–1848*, New York: Macmillan, 1974

Bill, Alfred H., *Rehearsal for Conflict: The War with Mexico*, New York: Knopf, 1947

Eisenhower, John S.D., *So Far from God: The US War with Mexico, 1846–1848*, New York: Random House, 1989

Henry, Robert Selph, *The Story of the Mexican War*, Indianapolis: Bobbs Merrill, 1950

Singletary, Otis A., *The Mexican War*, Chicago: University of Chicago Press, 1960

Smith, Justin H., *The War with Mexico*, 2 vols., New York: Macmillan, 1919

Weems, John Edward, *To Conquer a Peace: The War Between the United States and Mexico*, New York: Doubleday, 1974

The most reliable brief introduction to the Mexican War is still SINGLETARY. He provides an excellent brief overview of the war's causes and highlights the rivalry between the principal United States field generals, Zachary Taylor and Winfield Scott. Moreover, Singletary analyzes the antagonisms between those generals and their highly-partisan commander-in-chief, Democratic President James K. Polk. Singletary provides incisive characterizations of Scott and Taylor, calling Scott the "ablest American commander between the Revolution and the Civil War." In Singletary's view, Taylor was intuitive and aggressive, winning a well-publicized series of battles along the Rio Grande early in the war that set the tone for the direction of the conflict. Polk then designated Scott to lead the campaign to capture Mexico City, which he did in "decisive" and "brilliant" fashion. Meanwhile, the United States campaign to take control of California undermined Mexican national defenses, but also demonstrated the lack of cooperation between American army and navy officers, especially Brigadier General Stephen W. Kearny and Commodore Robert F. Stockton.

As comprehensive as Singletary is brief, SMITH has long been noted both for his remarkable research and strident anti-Mexican viewpoint. Winner of the Pulitzer Prize in 1920, Smith's two volumes may never be equaled in research on their subject, but sometimes his confusing endnotes make it impossible to know what sources he actually used. Considering the Rio Grande campaign (battles of Palo Alto and Resaca de la Palma), Smith emphasizes how the encounters showed that the United States fielded superior infantry and artillery to the Mexicans, but that Taylor was lacking in the qualities of a great commander. Later, at Buena Vista, Taylor personally selected poor dispositions for his forces and, again, according to Smith, demonstrated that he "knew little about the art of war." Instead, Taylor's main contribution was his dynamic, inspiring personality, not any astute leadership or direction of units on the battlefield. High-quality, well-led American artillery units played a major part in overcoming the bravery of the sturdy Mexican soldados, who suffered at the misdirection of their own inadequate senior officers, including their President-General, Antonio López de Santa Anna. By contrast, Smith maintains that Scott was a "great general" who led one of the 19th-century's great campaigns, the one that resulted in the American capture of Mexico City, and thus brought about the end of the war. Scott's skills in army organization, staff selection, and operational art were all meritorious. Smith provides a detailed treatment of the Vera Cruz-Mexico City campaign.

In his contribution to the prestigious series, the Macmillan Wars of the United States, BAUER lauds Scott's generalship and his audacious campaign to take Mexico City, giving the general high marks for strategic vision and operational skill. By his measured march toward the capital, careful evaluation of the enemy dispositions and forces, and unfailing self-confidence, Scott left his imprint on campaign leadership. General Taylor comes across as a tough field officer who had no qualms in giving hard orders to his regular soldiers in the war's early battles at Palo Alto and Resaca de la Palma. In contrast, most of his units at the Battle of Buena Vista were comprised of volunteer soldiers. Taylor gave scant direction to most of his subordinates, who led their units in disconnected engagements to repel the Mexican thrusts. Bauer also judiciously reprises the successful United States effort to acquire California, which he had covered in a separate volume, *Surfboats and Horse Marines: U.S. Naval Operations in the Mexican War* (1969).

Two works are notable for their lucid writing supported by copious maps and illustrations. EISENHOWER gives a comprehensive treatment of all the war's campaigns. In Eisenhower's view, both Taylor and Scott were exceptional leaders, though each had his foibles and made his share of mistakes. Their competence and military skills eventually won out in campaigns against forces led by inferior commanders. WEEMS selects ten individuals and follows the course of the war from their perspective. His list of personalities is headed by President Polk and General Santa Anna, but also includes less senior army officers and a navy lieutenant who held posts at crucial scenes of action – for example, U.S. Grant, Robert E. Lee, Ethan Allen Hitchcock, and John C. Frémont.

Two older studies are worthwhile references. BILL portrays Polk as an intense and assertive commander-in-chief who developed a grand strategy of what the military campaigns should accomplish for the United States. Although a poor index hampers Bill's book, he presents good descriptions of the battle action, giving most of the credit for Taylor's victories to his soldiers and subordinates. Bill contends that, for many officers, the Mexican War turned out to be a rehearsal or preparation for the Civil War of the 1860s. HENRY pictures Polk as a stern and demanding president, determined to gain all the new territories possible for the United States. Taylor and Scott each brought valuable qualities to their commands and were responsible for hard-earned victories in campaigns in which they were usually outnumbered by the Mexican forces.

A valuable complement to all of the foregoing books is the work of ALCARAZ. Although a contemporary apologia filled with second guessing, it provides recollections, translated into English, of the campaigns from the Mexican view. Written mostly by officers who participated in the action, its chapters are supplemented by good maps.

JOSEPH G. DAWSON III

Mexican War, 1846–1848: Politics and Diplomacy

Bauer, K. Jack, *The Mexican War, 1846–1848*, New York: Macmillan, 1974

Brack, Gene M., *Mexico Views Manifest Destiny, 1821–1846: An Essay on the Origins of the Mexican War*, Albuquerque: University of New Mexico Press, 1975

Griswold del Castillo, Richard, *The Treaty of Guadalupe Hidalgo: A Legacy of Conflict*, Norman: University of Oklahoma Press, 1990

Pletcher, David M., *The Diplomacy of Annexation: Texas, Oregon, and the Mexican War*, Columbia: University of Missouri Press, 1973

Price, Glenn W., *Origins of the War with Mexico: The Polk-Stockton Intrigue*, Austin: University of Texas Press, 1967

Singletary, Otis A., *The Mexican War*, Chicago: University of Chicago Press, 1960

Weems, John Edward, *To Conquer a Peace: The War Between the United States and Mexico*, New York: Doubleday, 1974

Between 1846 and 1848, the United States fought a war with Mexico that secured the annexation of Texas and acquired the vast Western territories that would become the states of New Mexico, Arizona, Nevada, Utah, Wyoming, and California. Although this territorial expansion marks the Mexican War as one of the most important conflicts in the history of the United States, scholars have yet to address the war with the sophistication that they have devoted to other American wars.

While the Mexican War has never been given its due, numerous historians have devoted their attention to this conflict.

One of the best short accounts of the Mexican War is SINGLE-TARY. Analyzing the conflict from a strictly American perspective, Singletary argues that the United States became burdened with a number of "hidden" conflicts: military leaders against politicians and diplomats, regular soldiers against the volunteer troops, and the navy against the army. Only the superiority of the American military, Singletary believes, prevented the failure of the first American war on foreign soil. Although scholars may find his account somewhat dated, and even sketchy, it still serves as a useful introduction to the Mexican War.

A general readership will welcome WEEMS's blending of political, diplomatic, and military history. Weems avoids the typical listing of facts and dates by telling the story through the perspective of ten characters. This approach helps him to portray the feelings and emotions of the Mexican War in a way not often seen in historical works. He argues that the Mexican War was needless but inevitable, and that the most important effect of the war was to hasten the coming of the Civil War. Although Weems – who almost completely ignores the Mexican perspective – adds nothing new to the historiography, the general reader will find his story dramatic, rewarding and accessible.

BAUER has no peer as an authoritative military history of the conflict. Laced with detailed maps, clear discussions of battles, evaluations of military leadership, and descriptions of naval operations, Bauer is likely to stand the test of time among military historians. However, he spends very little time on wider historical issues, and bases much of his discussion of the origins of the conflict upon the oft-repeated but shallow assertion that the war was inevitable, given United States territorial ambitions and Mexican pride. While military historians will applaud his work, other scholars will have to look beyond Bauer for serious discussion of the important political and diplomatic questions posed by the Mexican War.

Those interested in the origins of the Mexican War will discover two opposing schools of interpretation. One argues that the United States was justified in going to war with Mexico, while the other contends that President Polk conspired to provoke the Mexicans. This latter "plot thesis" has recently been revised by PRICE who has attempted to substantiate the claim by Anson Jones, one-time President of Texas, that representatives of Polk asked Jones to join in a conspiracy to provoke Mexico into a war with Texas. Although Price demonstrates that an attempt to provoke hostilities probably did occur on the Texas border almost a year before the start of the Mexican War, he does not show conclusively that Polk knew of, and authorized, the actions on the border. One finds in Price strong evidence to be suspicious of Polk but little direct evidence of the "plot thesis."

While most American historians, including Price, have concentrated on the origins of the United States entry into the Mexican War, BRACK investigates the Mexican political scene. He argues that the Mexican public simultaneously admired and distrusted their northern neighbors in the early 19th century. When trouble with Texas immigrants emerged in the 1830s, however, Mexican ambivalence hardened into dislike, fear and contempt. By the time of the 1846 confrontation, years of hard feelings compelled Mexican leaders to fight. Brack's thorough research in Mexican sources fills an important gap in the historiography.

While these monographs will interest specialists, readers seeking a comprehensive study should turn to PLETCHER, the definitive account of United States foreign policy in the 1840s. His even-handed account both revises and synthesizes all of the previous historical literature on Manifest Destiny. He contends that previous historians of the era have failed to appreciate the significance and importance of European diplomacy in Texas, Oregon, and Mexico. Pletcher also dismisses the "plot thesis" and argues, instead, that Polk drifted into the Mexican War under the mistaken impression that a forceful American policy would cause the Mexican position to crumble. The peaceful acquisition of California, Pletcher believes, might have been diplomatically possible, but Polk's blundering reduced the Mexican options to capitulation or war. In breadth and importance, Pletcher stands alone in the scholarly literature on Manifest Destiny and the Mexican War.

Unlike Pletcher, GRISWOLD DEL CASTILLO concentrates on the legacy of the Mexican War. After three unremarkable chapters on the war and its background, the heart of the book lies in five chapters that discuss the effect of the Treaty of Guadalupe Hidalgo on 140 years of United States-Mexican relations. One of the more important ramifications of the treaty was the dispossession of Mexican landholders in the newly acquired territories. In the original treaty, Article 10 allowed Mexican landholders to acquire a clear title from the Mexican government after ratification. When that passage was deleted by the United States Senate in favor of more ambiguous language, the path lay open for American settlers to acquire the lands of Mexican residents. Although poorly edited, Griswold del Castillo offers an important perspective on the diplomatic and political legacy of war.

Although the United States gained the vast lands of the West in the conflict, there are no reading groups, no documentary specials, and no big-budget movies on the Mexican War. Americans have found it difficult to memorialize a war in which the United States aggressively attacked a weaker nation for the ignoble purpose of a land grab.

WILLIAM CARRIGAN

See also Manifest Destiny

Mexico and the United States

Bauer, K. Jack, *The Mexican War, 1846–1848*, New York: Macmillan, 1974

Cline, Howard F., *The United States and Mexico*, Cambridge, MA: Harvard University Press, 1953

Langley, Lester D., *Mexico and the United States: The Fragile Relationship*, Boston: Twayne, 1991

Pastor, Robert A. and Jorge G. Castañeda, *Limits to Friendship*, New York: Knopf, 1988

Pletcher, David M., *Rails, Mines, and Progress: Some American Promoters in Mexico, 1867–1911*, Ithaca, NY: Cornell University Press, 1958

Pletcher, David M., *The Diplomacy of Annexation: Texas, Oregon, and the Mexican War*, Columbia: University of Missouri Press, 1973

Quirk, Robert E., *An Affair of Honor: Woodrow Wilson and the Occupation of Vera Cruz*, Lexington: University Press of Kentucky, 1962

Schmitt, Karl M., *Mexico and the United States, 1821–1973: Conflict and Coexistence*, New York: Wiley, 1974

Smith, Justin H., *The War with Mexico*, 2 vols., New York: Macmillan, 1919

Smith, Robert Freeman, *The United States and Revolutionary Nationalism in Mexico, 1916–1932*, Chicago: University of Chicago Press, 1972

Despite the fact that more books have been written on aspects of United States relations with Mexico than with any other single Latin American country, there are few comprehensive historical overviews. Although CLINE is a useful introduction to the subject, the title of the book is misleading. It actually contains little on relations between the two countries, and is largely a very informative but descriptive account of internal Mexican political history since 1910. SCHMITT is more directly relevant, and provides an excellent and balanced survey of United States-Mexican relations from the colonial period to 1970. Aimed at teachers and students, it is less than 300 pages in length, and provides a summary and synthesis of the modern historical literature on the subject. Although Schmitt often criticizes American policy for being too forceful and aggressive, he attempts to be objective and explains that Mexico has simply been vulnerable to the superior economic and military power of the United States.

During the 19th century the most notable example of the exercise of American power was the Mexican War which lasted from 1846 to 1848. The excitement and drama of the conflict were captured in the two volumes of J.H. SMITH. This detailed work was based upon massive research, and its erudition and lively style earned the award of the Pulitzer Prize in 1920. The causes of the war are examined with impressive thoroughness, and the blame for the conflict is mainly assigned to inept and corrupt Mexican leaders. The war itself is presented as a triumph for President Polk and the American Army. Smith's work has remained a classic, but its patriotic appeal has not proved so attractive to later generations of Americans, disillusioned by the traumatic experience of wars in Korea and Vietnam. This is evident in BAUER, which recognises the successes achieved in the Mexican War, but also points out the many logistical problems of mounting a military campaign in a foreign country. Although Bauer concentrates on military operations, he evokes parallels with later wars in his discussion of broader issues such as the existence of tensions between the government in Washington and its commanders in the field, and the growing public discontent when the anticipated quick and bloodless victory was not forthcoming. The traditional interpretation of Smith is also effectively challenged in a scholarly monograph by PLETCHER (1973) which sees more merit in Mexican diplomacy, and marshals impressive documentary evidence to argue that President Polk's forceful and uncompromising attitude made war unavoidable. In contrast to Smith, however, Pletcher is not so easy or entertaining to read.

A later intervention which greatly soured relations between Mexico and the United States was President Woodrow Wilson's decision to send marines to seize the port of Vera Cruz in 1914. In a finely written and researched study, QUIRK brings the incident to life and perceptively links it to the clash between myth and reality that so often occurs in American diplomacy. While he acknowledges Wilson's idealism and desire to act honourably, Quirk condemns the president's patronizing attitude towards the people of Mexico. The book presents an instructive lesson by demonstrating that intervention not only failed in 1914 but was also counter-productive in that it stimulated anti-American feeling in Mexico.

Awkward diplomatic relations were offset by the marked growth of commercial links during the late-19th century. The significance of American business skills and investment for the development of the Mexican economy during the period from 1867 to 1911 is ably examined in PLETCHER (1958). This work offers a series of case studies of seven American entrepreneurs, the most famous of whom was Ulysses S. Grant. Pletcher's mini-biographies reveal, however, that the schemes of these entrepreneurs enjoyed little financial success, primarily because local difficulties and obstacles were either over-simplified or ignored. The protection of American economic interests in Mexico later became a major diplomatic issue as a result of the Mexican Revolution and its declared intention to expropriate foreign companies. The issue is explored in R.F. SMITH. Although Smith is personally sympathetic to Mexico, his main concern is not to explain either Mexican history or that country's political and economic relations with the United States, but to stress the allegedly excessive influence of American mining and oil companies upon American policy. The work is very specialized and narrowly conceived, but it is useful in directing attention to an important and neglected period of United States-Mexican relations.

The closing decades of the 20th century have seen the United States and Mexico draw more closely together than at any point in their respective national histories. This significant development is addressed in two competent studies of contrasting lengths. LANGLEY consists of just over 130 pages. Based on secondary sources, it is written mainly for students and general readers. Langley lucidly explains that the reality of economic interdependence in the second half of the 20th century has reversed a century of political and economic divergence. The work is useful in highlighting the dramatic growth of economic activity in the border region, and the increasing evidence of political co-operation between the two governments. PASTOR and CASTAÑEDA is a more substantial study. At 500 pages in length it is almost four times the size of Langley. Of particular value is the fact that the work is jointly written, and consequently reflects both an American and a Mexican perspective. Although there is some discussion of the historical background, the book is mainly concerned with seeking to identify and explain contemporary developments, and to suggest courses of action that will lead to an improvement of relations in the future.

JOSEPH SMITH

Middle Atlantic States

Bliven, Bruce, Jr., *New York: A Bicentennial History*, New York: Norton, 1981

Bodnar, John, Roger Simon, and Michael P. Weber, *Lives of Their Own: Blacks, Italians, and Poles in Pittsburgh, 1900–1960*, Urbana: University of Illinois Press, 1982

Brugger, Robert J., *Maryland: A Middle Temperament, 1634–1980*, Baltimore: Johns Hopkins University Press, 1988

Cochran, Thomas C., *Pennsylvania: A Bicentennial History*, New York: Norton, 1978

Downey, Dennis B. and Francis J. Bremer, *A Guide to the History of Pennsylvania*, Westport, CT: Greenwood Press, 1993

Ellis, David Maldwyn, *New York: State and City*, Ithaca, NY: Cornell University Press, 1979

Fleming, Thomas, *New Jersey: A Bicentennial History*, New York: Norton, 1977

Gerber, David A., *The Making of an American Pluralism: Buffalo, New York, 1825–60*, Urbana: University of Illinois Press, 1989

Hoffecker, Carol E., *Delaware: A Bicentennial History*, New York: Norton, 1977

Klein, Philip S. and Ari Hoogenboom, *A History of Pennsylvania*, New York: McGraw Hill, 1973; 2nd edition, University Park: Pennsylvania State University Press, 1980

Munroe, John A., *History of Delaware*, Newark: University of Delaware Press, 1979; 3rd edition, 1993

Pencak, William and Conrad Edick Wright (editors), *New York and the Rise of American Capitalism: Economic Development and the Social and Political History of an American State, 1780–1870*, New York: New-York Historical Society, 1989

Shaw, Douglas V., *Immigration and Ethnicity in New Jersey History*, Trenton: New Jersey Historical Commission, 1994

Thompson, Donald G.B., *Gateway to a Nation: The Middle Atlantic States and Their Influence on the Development of the Nation*, Rindge, NH: R.R. Smith, 1956

Wright, William C., *The Secession Movement in the Middle Atlantic States*, Rutherford, NJ: Fairleigh Dickinson University Press, 1973

The Middle Atlantic states have never acquired the same strong sense of distinctive regional identity as their neighbors to the north and south, New England and the Old South. This may be partly explained by the domination of the region by two of the largest and most powerful states in the Union – and two of the great cities of the nation, which have played their own major part in American history. It is also explained partly by the very diversity, ethnic, social, religious and economic, of the region – a diversity, ironically, which has given the Middle Atlantic states a special position as a seeding ground, and a model, for the nation as a whole.

Authoritative treatments of the history of the region as a whole are conspicuous by their absence. For the most part, it is necessary to turn to histories of individual states – first to brief introductions and then to more substantial histories of each state. THOMPSON is one of the very few works to treat the region as a whole. Now forty years old, and inevitably out-of-date, it still retains value as an introduction to the whole region, and for the overall perspective which it provides. In its focus on the influence of the Middle Atlantic states upon the development of the nation, it offers a theme which deserves closer examination in a more up-to-date history, and perhaps one rather less celebratory and more critical in its approach. Even in studies of shorter periods or specialised subjects, the Middle Atlantic states are seldom treated as a whole. One exception is WRIGHT, a study of support for secession in the region in 1860–61. Wright describes all the Middle Atlantic states as border states, to a greater or lesser degree. He casts the secessionist net wide, by including not only the small minority who wanted actually to join the Confederacy, but also those who favored a separate middle states confederacy, and the larger group who were simply inclined to let the southern states go in peace. However, as Wright points out, the Confederate firing on Fort Sumter and the outbreak of war ruled out the idea of peaceable secession.

A very brief introduction to the history of each of the states is provided in the appropriate volumes of the Bicentennial History series, published on behalf of the American Association of State and Local History. These slender volumes, of around 200 pages each, are little more than extended essays, and they are extremely variable in coverage, emphasis, and approach – and also in quality. BLIVEN on New York is the least satisfactory of the four, and provides a somewhat disjointed mixture of politics, economics, culture and personalities. One-third of the brief text is devoted to the period up to the Revolution, and it is very sketchy on the 20th century – there are only eight pages on the period since the Great Depression. COCHRAN on Pennsylvania is the work of an immensely distinguished economic historian, who writes what is largely an economic history of the state during the 19th century. According to Cochran, Pennsylvania's main contributions to the nation derived from its natural resources, its business institutions and its manufacturing role, which made the state pre-eminent in the 19th century. By the 20th century, as the rest of the nation industrialised, Pennsylvania had become less distinctive – and this period is covered in one chapter.

It is probably somewhat easier to write a brief history of a smaller state rather than a larger one. Certainly, both Fleming and Hoffecker provide more even-handed coverage of their respective subjects. FLEMING is a balanced, if rather breathless, narrative history of New Jersey, with the emphasis on politics, in what is described as a "fractured and fractious commonwealth." It points to religious, ethnic, racial and economic divisions, as well as the domination of much of the state by two great cities beyond its borders – New York to the north and Philadelphia to the south. HOFFECKER faces a similar problem of influential forces from beyond the boundaries of the tiny state of Delaware. Claiming that Delaware may be seen as a microcosm of the United States, she adopts a mainly thematic approach. The first part of the book deals with the land and its use, and weighs economic development against environmental concerns. The second part deals with peoples and cultures, including concerns over race relations, and the third part is devoted to political history.

Those seeking more substantial and comprehensive histories of states in the Middle Atlantic region will find some states better served than others. ELLIS is a more balanced and authoritative history of New York than Bliven, but it is still quite brief. It tackles such themes as the peoples of the state, its economy and politics, and its "mind and spirit." As its title implies, there is a good deal of attention to the tense relationship between New York City and the upstate area. The ten essays by different authors in PENCAK and WRIGHT range over economic, social and political aspects of New York history, with a good deal of emphasis on New York City. Its main theme is the relationship between public authority and economic development, and contributors debate the merits of laissez-faire as against government as facilitator.

For Pennsylvania, DOWNEY and BREMER provide a valuable bibliographical guide, in a series of essays by leading authorities on particular periods and topics, and a final section on research and archival collections throughout the state. KLEIN and HOOGENBOOM provide a solid, substantial and mildly celebratory history of the state, packed with detailed information on economic, social, political and cultural history. It tends to divide its treatment rather rigidly between politics and everything else, especially in the later chapters, but it offers an overall chronological perspective on the history of the state, and there are useful bibliographies at the end of each chapter. MUNROE performs a similar function for the history of Delaware, in a straightforward, heavily factual narrative from the colonial period to the second half of the 20th century. He describes how changes in the American corporate world – with a shifting of industry and wealth from local hands to the control of international companies – has had important repercussions for Delaware and its identity. The final chapter on "the suburban state" underlines the influence upon Delaware of its more populous neighbours. Munroe also includes a valuable bibliographic essay.

Paradoxically, one of the best state histories emphasizing the "middling" characteristics of the region focuses on Maryland, which may or may not be regarded as one of the mid-Atlantic states. Once a border slave state, Maryland in its modern history has been aligned more and more with the mid-Atlantic group. BRUGGER is a large and comprehensive history, some 800 pages long, which blends political, economic and social history and much else besides from Chesapeake Bay crustaceans to baseball in Baltimore. It pays more attention to ethnic groups, to women, and to the substantial African American population than many state studies. As his subtitle implies, Brugger sees the moderation and the middle-state ethos of Maryland as the distinctive feature of its history and character. Maryland lies close to the median of the fifty states according to many of the significant statistical indicators. Despite its bulk, this is a very readable book, and those who wish to dip into it as a work of reference will be helped by excellent maps and tables, a useful chronology, a variety of illustrations and a superb bibliographical essay.

There are numerous more specialised studies of particular communities in the Middle Atlantic states, or of issues of class, gender, race, urbanisation and industrialisation in the region. Immigration and ethnicity provide one obvious unifying theme. A good example is GERBER's thoughtful study of "social pluralism" in antebellum Buffalo, which examines the formation of ethnic groups and the interaction of class and ethnicity. Bodnar is one of the major historians of the immigrant experience, and, in their study of Pittsburgh during the first half of the 20th century, BODNAR *et al.* compare both ethnic and racial experiences in a major industrial city. SHAW is a brief survey of immigration and the reception of immigrants in New Jersey, from the early Dutch and Swedish settlers to recent Asian and Hispanic arrivals. He sees New Jersey as an overflow area for numerous immigrants who arrived in New York. Perhaps the ethnic and racial pluralism of these states might provide a starting-point for a new attempt at a synthesis of the history of the whole region.

JEROME D. BOWERS II

See also Colonial History: Colonies 3; New York City; Philadelphia

Middle Classes

Aron, Cindy Sondik, *Ladies and Gentlemen of the Civil Service: Middle-Class Workers in Victorian America*, New York: Oxford University Press, 1987

Baritz, Loren, *The Good Life: The Meaning of Success for the American Middle Class*, New York: Knopf, 1988

Blumin, Stuart M., *The Emergence of the Middle Class: Social Experience in the American City, 1760–1900*, Cambridge and New York: Cambridge University Press, 1989

Gilkeson, John S., Jr., *Middle-Class Providence, 1820–1940*, Princeton: Princeton University Press, 1986

Halttunen, Karen, *Confidence Men and Painted Women: A Study of Middle-Class Culture in America, 1830–1870*, New Haven: Yale University Press, 1982

Johnson, Paul E., *A Shopkeeper's Millennium: Society and Revivals in Rochester, New York, 1815–1837*, New York: Hill and Wang, 1978

Mills, C. Wright, *White Collar: The American Middle Classes*, New York: Oxford University Press, 1951

Ryan, Mary P., *Cradle of the Middle Class: The Family in Oneida County, New York, 1790–1865*, Cambridge and New York: Cambridge University Press, 1981

Stock, Catherine McNicol, *Main Street in Crisis: The Great Depression and the Old Middle Class on the Northern Plains*, Chapel Hill: University of North Carolina Press, 1992

Zunz, Olivier, *Making America Corporate, 1870–1920*, Chicago: University of Chicago Press, 1990

That America is a middle-class society has been a frequent observation by foreign visitors and an often proud self-identification for Americans. Even after a decade of Depression, in a 1940 Roper poll 79 per cent labelled themselves "middle class." In normal times over 90 per cent of Americans typically identify with that label. Yet few American historians have systematically examined the middle classes *per se.* The concept is so pervasive that it discourages study. Ethnic, religious, and racial identities, and gender divisions within them are more specific and consonant with the American inclination to avoid class categorization. Historians most likely to use class as a framework, those influenced by Marxian thought, usually view middle class as a false category.

Post-World War II "consensus" historians appeared to chronicle the middle class, but too often failed to distinguish it from the elite. In reaction to this presumably middle class history, the "new" social historians of the late 1960s and 1970s sought to craft a "history from the bottom up." Others continued to study the powerful and famous. The result has been relative historical invisibility of arguably the most pervasive cultural and social force in American society.

In the 1980s historians began to produce a body of work that systematically delineated the origins of the middle class and delineated distinctions within what had often been portrayed as a relatively undifferentiated group. Studies of Utica and Rochester, New York and Providence, Rhode Island sketched the family and political strategies of small proprietors and professionals finding common cause and trying to shape their rapidly changing world. Both RYAN and JOHNSON found the Second Great Awakening to be a defining event shaping shopkeepers, farmers, and artisans into a self-conscious middle class. The religious revival provided the energy for taming the rough elements of new urban cultures through voluntary associations based on its values. Economic forces increasingly separated these families from those of industrial workers and farm laborers. New cultural models from England and East Coast cities offered lifestyles compatible with the growing separation of home and work. These centered on the home as a refuge presided over by women living within "the cult of true womanhood" that kept children away from industrial chaos and humanized their fathers.

GILKESON found similar patterns in Providence. Echoing Johnson and Ryan, he located the origins of middle class consciousness in the desire of antebellum small producers to separate themselves from the values and behavior both of workers and of traditional gentlemen. A victim of its own success and of economic change, the Providence middle class increasingly fragmented into a variety of voluntary organizations. In the Progressive Era, a self-concept of the disinterested negotiator for the public interest led to a broader consolidation of middle-class consciousness based on a shared identity as consumers. Thus Providence's "old" middle-class origins eventually blended into a pervasive "new" middle-class culture by World War II. MILLS had created the old/new distinction in his sociological classic, a distinction that remains fundamental but has been given greater specificity in recent scholarship.

HALTTUNEN tackled the old charge, dating at least from Dickens, of Victorian middle-class hypocrisy. An examination of conduct manuals and other antebellum advice literature convinced her that early Victorian middle-class sentimentality was based on a deep commitment to sincerity. The social forms that helped to create a middle-class culture were shaped by sincere expression of inner feelings. This culture of sentimentality declined after the Civil War, leading to the later more hollow sentiments of Horatio Alger, Dale Carnegie, and the world of salesmanship.

All of these works contributed to BLUMIN, the dominant synthesis on the formation of the middle class. Like most of them, he locates the emergence of a middle class in the Jacksonian period, but emphasizes economic developments more than most other writers. In Blumin's view, the crucial cause was an economic change that hoisted many "middling folk" over the manual/non-manual barrier that dichotomized earlier urban society. The growing numbers of clerks, salesmen, and small businessmen increasingly occupied income levels and residences which clearly separated them from artisans and industrial workers. The occupational change was accompanied by a sentimental Victorian culture which fostered new images of mothers, fathers, and children. Blumin effectively ends his account in the 1870s, with the label "middle class" coming into common usage, and reflecting an established self-conscious group based on non-manual work and recognized social conventions. Glancing past 1880 he perceived new developments which threatened to divide the new class. As clerical and sales jobs tripled in the 1880s and 1890s, a higher paid set of "white collar" jobs developed in corporations and government demanding higher educational credentials and threatening to bifurcate the middle class.

ARON traced this growing division within the civil service. Mid-century government clerical jobs had involved responsibility and a surprising commonality between male and female work. But in the late 1800s a division developed between routinized and managerial positions, the latter occupied mainly by males. In a study of corporate managerial development, ZUNZ also found rising barriers between manual and non-manual workers, and within the ranks of non-manual workers, based on credentials and qualifications, and reinforced by professional culture and skyscraper architecture. Zunz detected the same patterns of professionalization among new upper middle class professions such as engineers, managers and accountants that earlier historians had found in the traditional professions.

Thus in the early 1900s, there had emerged a largely salaried, professional and managerial upper middle class with national connections and common professional styles. In a study of the Dakotas in the 1930s, STOCK found deep tensions between the upper end of this "new" middle class and the "old" middle class when the New Deal brought them into contact. While Dakotans wanted federal aid they resented the professionals who delivered it and quickly re-established control over their communities when the crisis passed.

BARITZ returns to the large lens, seeking to understand middle-class culture as a whole, with little attention to internal divisions. With broad strokes he paints a voracious middle-class culture that envelops most Americans, exemplified by the astonishing absorption of the descendants of southern and eastern European immigration within a century. The price of admission is loss of sense of place and intimacy.

In conclusion, there has been long overdue work in recent years on understanding the origins and evolution of the middle classes. However the stages after 1880, where Blumin's study ends, await a synthesis.

W. BRUCE LESLIE

See also Class; Professions

Midwest

Bogue, Allan G., *From Prairie to Cornbelt: Farming on the Illinois and Iowa Prairies in the Nineteenth Century*, Chicago: University of Chicago Press, 1963

Cayton, Andrew R.L. and Peter S. Onuf, *The Midwest and the Nation: Rethinking the History of an American Region*, Bloomington: Indiana University Press, 1990

Cronon, William, *Nature's Metropolis: Chicago and the Great West*, New York: Norton, 1991

Curti, Merle, *The Making of an American Community: A Case Study of Democracy in a Frontier County*, Stanford, CA: Stanford University Press, 1959

Faragher, John Mack, *Sugar Creek: Life on the Illinois Prairie*, New Haven: Yale University Press, 1986

Gjerde, Jon, *The Minds of the West: Ethnocultural Evolution of the Rural Middle West, 1830–1917*, Chapel Hill: University of North Carolina Press, 1997

Shortridge, James R., *The Middle West: Its Meaning in American Culture*, Lawrence: University of Kansas Press, 1989

Smith, Henry Nash, *Virgin Land: The American West as Symbol and Myth*, Cambridge, MA: Harvard University Press, 1950

Turner, Frederick Jackson, *The Frontier in American History*, New York: Holt, 1920

Weber, Ronald, *The Midwestern Ascendancy in American Writing*, Bloomington: Indiana University Press, 1992

The Midwest or Middle West is a region of the United States that defies precise definition. Not only are other American regions – the "South," the "East" and the "West" – associated with cardinal directions, but they are typically connected to peculiar characteristics: the South, for example, is inextricably identified with a past of racial slavery. The Midwest, in contrast, is qualified by being midway between something else and, as such, its boundaries have lacked a constant and clear precision. Even the origins of the term are in doubt. Whereas many assume that the Midwest originated as a middle border – a region of settlement that displaced the frontier West as it moved westward – Shortridge notes that the term derived originally as the middle region differentiated from the Northwest and Southwest.

By the early 20th century, however, the Midwest had come to be defined as a twelve-state bloc in the north-central United States, and it was at this time, as Shortridge, Cayton and Onuf, and Weber note, that the region was culturally ascendant. Leading literary figures, such as Willa Cather, Sherwood Anderson, and Sinclair Lewis, as well as prominent historians, such as Turner, were sons and daughters of the middle border. TURNER's influential "frontier thesis," which cast a long shadow over American historiography, also serves as an appropriate starting point for the discussion of the Midwest. For Turner, the frontier was central to understanding the distinctive characteristics of America; it was the environment that removed the influence of Europe and fashioned the American traits of independence, democracy, and ingenuity, among others. As Cayton and Onuf argue, moreover, Turner's interpretation stemmed from his middle western perspective, one that connected free land to unprecedented economic opportunity and the possibility of democracy.

Turner's thesis and the study of the Midwest were a victim of their own early success. Given Turner's belief that the western, and by implication American, history was the story of the Midwest, there was dismay when the region was perceived in subsequent decades as only one part of America, and one of decreasing significance at that. It is true that, in a pioneering case study of a Wisconsin county, CURTI attempted to revive the notion that Turnerian freedom and democracy did indeed take root in the Midwest. Using new quantitative techniques, Curti argued that Turner's principal implications connecting the frontier to democracy were valid. Yet most historical works rejected middle western exceptionalism and attempted to set the region into the larger story of the United States. In a path-breaking work of cultural history, SMITH had already drawn attention to the myth of the Garden, the symbol of the "domesticated" West. One reason that BOGUE wrote his significant work on the transition from wilderness to settled farming in Iowa and Illinois, he explained, was the increasing urban orientation of American historians. Whereas Curti's book revived old myths that Smith had earlier surveyed, Bogue's revealed a more troubling reality: the study of the Midwest (as well as the importance of regionalism) seemed in decline.

After some decades of neglect, there occurred a revival of interest in the Midwest in the 1980s and 1990s. Some studies focused on the region as exemplary of larger processes occurring throughout the United States. In a detailed case study of a region in central Illinois, FARAGHER explored the transformation of society from a frontier community to one of settled agriculture and family-based farms. CRONON wrote a compelling environmental history of the region centered on Chicago and its hinterland. Hewing to a neo-Turnerian tradition, he showed how capitalist development of the city and the country surrounding it were inextricably linked. GJERDE focused on the diverse ethnocultural patterns that took root in the Midwest. Juxtaposing the opportunity which the region presented to European immigrants to enjoy an improved standard of living and the preservation of traditional ways of life, with cultural changes encouraged by the political and economic pressures in the region, he illustrated the tensions in the immigrant narrative as they played out in the rural Midwest.

Whereas some recent scholars placed the Midwest in the larger American story, others from a variety of disciplinary perspectives analyzed how the region was distinctive. For geographer, SHORTRIDGE, the key characteristic of the Midwest was Americans' attachment to a pastoral myth. The Midwest was mythically connected to promising traits associated in the American mind with pastoralism: morality, independence, and egalitarianism. As a reservoir of rural virtue, the mythic Midwest continued to serve a purpose for Americans. Its geographical boundaries, as a result, were constantly redefined to conform to the pastoral myth. For literary critic WEBER, the narrative of the Midwest was the breathtaking speed at which it was developed. The ascendancy of the Midwest occurred during an era of ambivalence when the awareness of lost innocence and of human limitations were set in the context of a rapidly transformed middle western landscape. For historians CAYTON and ONUF, the defining feature of the Midwest was its thorough identification with capitalism, which resulted in the triumph of bourgeois culture in the region. Immediately associated in the United States with free land and the illegality of slavery, the territory that would become the Midwest was quickly transformed into republican states that developed commercial agriculture. For celebrants of the region during its era of ascendancy, and especially among an increasingly dominant middle class, the Midwest demonstrated the possibility of commercial capitalism and cultural conformity. It was from this world that Turner emerged, connecting the possibilities of the frontier to the distinctiveness – indeed, the exceptionalism – of the American nation. Whether they viewed the Midwest as pastoral myth, as a landscape rapidly developed, or as an arena of commercial capitalism, then, scholars continued to return to Turner's observation about the informing power of "free" land.

JON GJERDE

Military History: General

Carroll, John M. and Carroll F. Baxter, *The American Military Tradition: From Colonial Times to the Present*, Wilmington, DE: SR Books, 1993

Doughty, Robert A., Ira D. Gruber, and others, *American Military History and the Evolution of Warfare in the Western World*, Lexington, MA: Heath, 1996

Esposito, Vincent J. (editor), *The West Point Atlas of American Wars*, 2 vols., New York: Praeger, 1959; revised, New York: Holt, 1995

Huntington, Samuel P., *The Soldier and the State: The Theory and Politics of Civil-Military Relations*, Cambridge, MA: Harvard University Press, 1957

Leckie, Robert, *The Wars of America*, New York: Harper and Row, 1967, revised 1992

Millett, Allan R. and Peter Maslowski, *For the Common Defense: A Military History of the United States of America*, New York: Free Press, 1984, revised 1994; London: Collier Macmillan, 1984

Millis, Walter, *Arms and Men: A Study in American Military History*, New York: Putnam, 1956

Perret, Geoffrey, *A Country Made by War: From the Revolution to Vietnam – The Story of America's Rise to Power*, New York: Random House, 1989

Upton, Emory, *The Military Policy of the United States*, Washington, DC: Government Printing Office, 1904; reprinted, New York: Greenwood Press, 1968

Weigley, Russell F., *The American Way of War: A History of United States Military Strategy and Policy*, New York: Macmillan, 1973

Writing on the American military has been a particularly rich endeavor for historians. The subject has almost universal appeal in both lay and professional circles. The limits of inquiry seem boundless, interpretations have waxed and waned, and interest through the years has shown little sign of flagging. The diversity and wealth of material on the subject can be, therefore, daunting to all but the most dedicated reader.

The role of the military in a democratic society has long drawn the attention of academics and servicemen. The first thoughtful examination of American military policy, written in 1876 but not published until 1904, is UPTON. Combining history, critical commentary and special pleading for enlightened military leadership, Upton despaired at what he saw as persistent civilian interference and mismanagement in military affairs. His solution was an end to the militia system of self-defense and the creation of a politico-military apparatus on the Prussian model. Although Upton's army has long since vanished, his frustration with civilian authority and a national infatuation with volunteer armies accentuates the political discrepancies still extant between the assertion of military authority and politically-motivated, non-military, democratically-elected oversight.

Upton's extreme conservatism and distrust of civilian rule prompted HUNTINGTON to hypothesize that the military were historically a closed community, isolated from society, in pursuit of a professional ethic that was out of step with the American political tradition. That isolation produced an officer corps that was insular, conservative and antagonistic toward American liberalism. Civilians, he argues, reciprocated that hostility and only grudgingly tolerated any military presence in the United States except in time of war. As a political scientist writing in the 1950s, Huntington was more interested in constructing a model that would explain contemporary attitudes about military intellectualism, than in writing a bona fide history. The result is a series of sweeping and sometimes unsubstantiated generalizations which nonetheless were accepted as fact by the academic community for some years. Starkly contrasting with Huntington is MILLIS, which appeared at much the same time. Millis concentrates on the effect of internal developments and reforms within the military on civilian policy, rather than any ideological struggle between the two. Here there is little, if any separation between military and civilian. Millis draws attention to the military's fundamental and positive role in society, noting the exchange of ideas between one and the other. Although he did not directly challenge Huntington's position, Millis's views have largely been corroborated and augmented, while Huntington's have been overturned.

It is the conduct of war to which most military histories turn, and certainly the most influential work in this arena is WEIGLEY. This brilliant endeavor seeks and convincingly finds a uniquely American way of warfare, forged in the combat of the Civil War, that Weigley calls the strategy of annihilation. According to this account, American military strategy since 1865 has been dedicated to the total destruction of the enemy's ability and will to resist. What began as Ulysses S. Grant's strategy of sustained confrontation became, particularly during and after World War II, a national policy that sought to apply all of America's physical resources towards the goal of total exhaustion of the enemy. A brief but excellent companion volume to Weigley is CARROLL and BAXTER which, through a series of well-written essays, charts the development and application of American armed force since the colonial era. Although the book offers no over-arching theme, its topical essays are highly interpretive, often thought-provoking, and provide a useful alternative to more traditional, sequential histories of the military in the United States. Each chapter

distils the findings of a large array of recent, specialized works, and thus may serve as a convenient point of departure for closer reading.

General works should not be eschewed, and numerous such volumes are available. Recently revised, ESPOSITO offers concise, if terse, battle histories of all major American wars through Vietnam. Although it offers no interpretation and scant analysis, its numerous detailed maps provide a visual complement that is vital to understanding the flow of battle. The traditional, textual variety of military history is well-served in MILLETT and MASLOWSKI. Conceived as a college-level textbook, this comprehensive work examines nearly all aspects of the American military heritage, with heavy emphasis on the institutional and policy aspects of the varied armed services. From this perspective, the actual phenomenon of war is less important than how the military has prepared for it, and what intellectual assumptions have been employed in waging it. Although the authors proceed from a number of discrete themes, perhaps the most important is the interaction between the armed forces and civilian authority in the planning and projection of national strategy in wartime. Moreover, they are careful to distinguish between political and military objectives, noting that in a democracy the two may not always coincide and may even conflict. Hence political considerations that have an impact upon the military – in peacetime and in war – play a central role in this account.

Another textbook, DOUGHTY and GRUBER, is far less concerned with military policy than with wartime strategy and tactics, and takes a distinctly operational approach. Here the emphasis is on how the American military has waged war, and how its means of doing so have matured over time. Tactics, driven by technological change, is a central issue pursued throughout the text, and the authors devote appreciable space to the effect of increasingly powerful and sophisticated weaponry of warfare. In addition, Doughty and Gruber treat their topic in the context of military developments in European armies, and spend much time discussing conflicts to which the United States was not a party. Their point is that the history of American arms is merely a part of the wider evolution of western warfare, and cannot be viewed simply in a narrower, nation-centered context.

Both Millett and Maslowski, and Doughty and Gruber, are highly analytical and critical, and scholarly in tone. A work for popular audiences that has stood the test of time is LECKIE. Although somewhat dated and drawn entirely from secondary sources, it deftly unites a wide range of published material into a smooth, very readable narrative. The writing is often florid, even melodramatic, and is strong on human interest – which no doubt explains much of its appeal. Leckie reminds the reader that the United States has largely been created and preserved through war rather than by non-violent means. This point is elaborated by PERRET, who identifies an American love-hate relationship with things military by noting the dissonance of a peace-loving and traditionally anti-military nation that has accrued a remarkably successful record in war. As in Leckie, writ large in this account are the actions of well-known military and political leaders, whom Perret describes with sharp, often sardonic wit. Neither Leckie nor Perret is very concerned with institutional or technical developments in the military, nor in its political role in a republic, but both achieve a satisfactorily comprehensive overview of the nation and its armed forces in wartime.

T.R. BRERETON

See also Armed Services

Militia/National Guard

Cooper, Jerry, *The Militia and the National Guard in America since Colonial Times: A Research Guide*, Westport, CT: Greenwood Press, 1993

Derthick, Martha, *The National Guard in Politics*, Cambridge, MA: Harvard University Press, 1965

Fogelson, Robert M., *America's Armories: Architecture, Society, and Public Order*, Cambridge, MA: Harvard University Press, 1989

Jacobs, Jeffrey A., *The Future of the Citizen-Soldier Force: Issues and Answers*, Lexington: University Press of Kentucky, 1994

Johnson, Charles, Jr., *African American Soldiers in the National Guard: Recruitment and Deployment During Peacetime and War*, Westport, CT: Greenwood Press, 1992

Kreidberg, Marvin A. and Merton G. Henry, *History of Military Mobilization in the United States Army, 1775–1945*, Washington, DC: Department of the Army, 1955

Krenek, Harry, *The Power Vested: The Use of Martial Law and the National Guard in Texas Domestic Crisis . . . 1912–1932*, Austin, TX: Presidial Press, 1980

McConnell, Roland C., *Negro Troops of Antebellum Louisiana: A History of the Battalion of Free Men of Color*, Baton Rouge: Louisiana State University Press, 1968

Mahon, John K., *History of the Militia and the National Guard*, New York: Macmillan, and London: Collier Macmillan, 1983

Riker, William H., *Soldiers of the States: The Role of the National Guard in American Democracy*, Washington, DC: Public Affairs Press, 1957

Shea, William L., *The Virginia Militia in the Seventeenth Century*, Baton Rouge: Louisiana State University Press, 1983

Singletary, Otis A., *Negro Militia and Reconstruction*, Austin: University of Texas Press, 1971

Stone, Richard G., Jr., *A Brittle Sword: The Kentucky Militia, 1776–1912*, Lexington: University Press of Kentucky, 1977

COOPER's research guide provides the only complete bibliography for serious students of the American militia and National Guard. It is organized topically and chronologically and recommends future research areas. MAHON has produced the best overall study of the history of the militia and National Guard to 1983. It is narrative in form with little critical interpretation. Although it recognizes militia shortcomings, it is very sympathetic on the whole to the National Guard, and rejects the thesis of Active Army Major General Emory Upton.

In their study of the American mobilization experience through World War II, KREIDBERG and HENRY give insight into the Active Army's interpretation of the militia and National Guard history. The work is influenced by Upton's severely critical view of the militia. Nevertheless, it is important in understanding not only mobilization, but also Active Army and National Guard conflict.

There are a number of specialized studies of the militia and National Guard in particular states and particular periods, and only a few examples are cited here. SHEA describes the Virginia colonial militia from the founding of Jamestown through King William's War. He portrays its shift from a mass, inclusive force to an elite, exclusive institution that evolved with its success in establishing absolute military supremacy in the Tidewater region. STONE examines the Kentucky militia from the American Revolution to the beginning of the 20th century. He believes that frontier necessity ensured an effective force until the end of the War of 1812 when the system floundered. Increased federal funding with the Dick Act of 1903 revived it. KRENEK studies the Texas Army National Guard during the 1920s and 1930s, arguing that the institution served largely as the state's police force until the formation of the Department of Public Safety in the mid-1930s. In this role, the Guard broke strikes, quelled racial riots, and enforced martial law in the oil fields.

Derthick, Jacobs and Riker all use the militia and National Guard for case studies of the political relationship between the state and federal government. RIKER argues that the states failed to sustain their part in the federal structure when dealing with militia and National Guard issues. In the 19th century when federal support came only in the form of annual weapons allotments, the states did not support the militia systems. In the 20th century as the Guard assumed a more important reserve role, the states expected federal financial support of the Guard. Embracing Upton's view, Riker believes that the Guard's voluntary nature encouraged support of elite and property interests. FOGELSON supports this thesis, arguing that the commanding armory architecture that appeared in the eastern United States during the Gilded Age served as fortresses in the defense of capitalism from a restless proletariat. DERTHICK examines the political influence of the National Guard Association of the United States from its inception in the 1880s to the 1960s. She suggests that the NGAUS pursued mainly a defensive strategy to counter efforts by the Active Army to undermine its position as a first reserve in the National Security Strategy. This is an important work for an understanding of the NGAUS's lobbying effort in Congress.

JACOBS attempts to determine the future shape of the reserve components of the United States Army. In practice if not policy, the Army is three separate services: the active Army, the Army National Guard, and the Army Reserve. The National Guards are hybrid organizations, part state and part federal with a perception of Active Army leadership engaging in political maneuvers to snub them. In peacetime, there are 54 separate National Guards, one for each state, the District of Columbia, Puerto Rico, the Virgin Islands, and Guam. The major distinctions between the active Army and the reserves create various stumbling blocks to reserve readiness – state control of the National Guard, geographic separation and distances, ineffective use of training time, and politics.

Three very different studies shed light on the African American experience as Guardsmen. JOHNSON provides a broad view of the black experience from 1877 to the integration of the United States military in the late 1940s. McCONNELL's analysis of the free black battalion of Louisiana spans the French colonial and early American experience. The frontier environment, and the difference between French and American cultures encouraged its development, but statehood led to its demise. SINGLETARY is the major work on the black militia during the Reconstruction period, when units were sometimes integrated. These units disappeared quickly following the Compromise of 1877 and the white "redemption" of the southern states.

BRUCE A. OLSON

See also Armed Services

Missouri Compromise, 1819–1821

Brown, Everett S., *The Missouri Compromises and Presidential Politics, 1820–1825: From the Letters of William Plumer, Jr., Representative of New Hampshire*, St. Louis: Missouri Historical Society, 1926

Brown, Richard H., "The Missouri Crisis, Slavery, and the Politics of Jacksonianism," *South Atlantic Quarterly*, LXV, Winter, 1966

Dangerfield, George, *The Era of Good Feelings*, New York: Harcourt Brace, 1952

Dixon, Susan Bullitt, *The True History of the Missouri Compromise and Its Repeal*, Cincinnati: Robert Clarke, 1899

Fehrenbacher, Don E., *The South and Three Sectional Crises*, Baton Rouge: Louisiana State University Press, 1980

Livermore, Shaw, *The Twilight of Federalism: The Disintegration of the Federalist Party, 1815–1830*, Princeton: Princeton University Press, 1962

Moore, Glover, *The Missouri Controversy, 1819–1821*, Lexington: University of Kentucky Press, 1953

Shoemaker, Floyd, *Missouri's Struggle for Statehood, 1804–1821*, Jefferson City, MO: Hugh Stephens, 1916

Sydnor, Charles S., *The Development of Southern Sectionalism, 1819–1848*, Baton Rouge: Louisiana State University Press, 1948

In view of its importance, the Missouri Compromise (actually a set of congressional measures passed in 1820 and 1821 which determined the future pattern of admission of free and slave states) has been the subject of a remarkably limited amount of serious historical study. Originally hailed as a signal southern victory, the principal compromise, which stipulated that Missouri would enter the Union with slavery but that states created out of the Louisiana Purchase north of the line 36° 30 would be free, came to be viewed by southerners as a fatal obstacle to their goal of maintaining legislative parity with the North. The deliberate obfuscation used by the architects of the Compromise in order to secure its passage has been faithfully reflected in the confusion and inaccuracy in many

modern studies. The task of reconstructing its origins, goals, and ultimate impact remains an uncompleted aspect of basic historical research.

E. S. BROWN, an edited collection of letters from William Plumer, Jr., a New Hampshire senator, is the place to start. Plumer's letters capture the high drama of the controversy, painting indelible portraits of its chief combatants, including Henry Clay, Rufus King and William Lowndes, and providing first-hand information on the strategy of the antislavery party. Plumer's reflections lend weight to the view of the Compromise as a setback for antislavery. By the 1850s, that view had been superseded, and the 36° 30 line was regarded in the North as nearly sacrosanct. The repeal of the Missouri Compromise in 1854 prompted Abraham Lincoln's return to politics, and provided the theme for several of his most important writings, in particular the Peoria speech of October 1854. DIXON, the widow of the Kentucky senator who authored the repeal, supports the interpretation of the Compromise as a defeat for slavery and for the South; her work, suffused with a remarkable bitterness, is a tendentious 600-page vindication of her late husband's fateful legislative course. The chapters on the passage of the Compromise, drawn largely from published congressional debates and other public documents, are unreliable and anachronistic.

Much better in capturing contemporary southern attitudes before and after the Missouri controversy is SYDNOR. Though a far more general work, it correctly identifies the debate as the pivot on which the history of the South as a self-conscious region turns. Though dated in some respects, it remains an excellent introduction to the impact of the Missouri episode on the course of southern society and politics.

DANGERFIELD, bravura in style and sweeping in scope, is deeply evocative of the period of the Missouri controversy and disquieting in its suggestions of the deeper meaning of the episode. The author is particularly strong in placing the Compromise in the context of international relations and diplomacy, though weak in his analysis of the detailed political maneuvering. His judgments are highly personal, but well-considered; he convincingly disproves contemporary charges (given historical weight by the endorsement of Jefferson) that Federalists fomented the Missouri agitation for the purpose of regaining power.

SHOEMAKER remains the definitive work on the role of Missourians in the controversy. Well-researched and engagingly written, it is an essential source for territorial politics. Shoemaker is especially informative in his description of the strong-arm tactics used to silence Missourians opposed to slavery and to elect proslavery delegates to the state constitutional convention, whose final document (including provisions barring emancipation or the entry of free blacks and mulattos) precipitated the crisis of 1821.

MOORE is the most comprehensive study of the Compromise; he has tapped nearly every relevant archive and read virtually every significant source. Unfortunately, such thoroughness has scared off later researchers from revising a badly dated work which uncritically propounds the traditional southern interpretation of the entire controversy as a Federalist-Clintonian plot to seize the presidency and dominate the South. The book too often seems more like a contribution to the political pamphleteering of the Missouri debate than a work of history. Above all, Moore's contempt for advocates of anti-slavery – and more particularly for defenders of the rights of blacks – colors every judgment and undergirds every interpretation. For its exhaustiveness (and its thorough bibliography), Moore is essential, but should not be used uncritically.

LIVERMORE is a valuable corrective to Moore, whose allegations against the Federalists are confronted directly. Although the Missouri Compromise is tangential to Livermore's subject, his focus on the final years of Federalism proves to be a far clearer vantage point from which to view the episode, rather than the implicit Jacksonian bias of most modern histories. Livermore argues that rather than narrowly averting a Federalist grab for power, northern Republican leaders capitulated to southern intimidation over Missouri, and adopted the notion of a Federalist plot as a "cover story," in order to quell their constituents' anger over the extension of slavery.

In a frequently republished essay, R.H. BROWN extends Livermore's insight into a sweeping reinterpretation of antebellum American history. According to Brown, southern control of the federal government constituted the "central fact" of American political history before the Civil War, with the purpose of the Republican party of Jefferson and Madison being to perpetuate that control. The challenge to southern dominance caused by the Missouri uproar led to the creation by Martin Van Buren and others of the "second party system," designed to thwart the northern challenge to slavery by inculcating party loyalty as a check to the development of sectional identity. Although Brown's brief, unfootnoted article inevitably oversimplifies complex developments and adds nothing new to the documentary history of the Missouri episode, it is unmatched in placing the controversy in a broader context and assessing its larger significance in the structure of antebellum politics.

FEHRENBACHER's chapter on the Missouri Compromise (originally delivered as a Fleming Lecture at Louisiana State University) is among the most succinct and intelligent discussions of the subject, placing it in the context of two other political crises, the Nullification controversy of 1831–33 and the Compromise of 1850. Particularly valuable is Fehrenbacher's analysis of sectional divisions within the South revealed by House votes on the Compromise's individual measures.

ROBERT P. FORBES

"Money Question," 1865–1896

Bolles, Albert S., *The Financial History of the United States from 1861 to 1885*, New York: Appleton, 1886
Goodwyn, Lawrence, *Democratic Promise: The Populist Moment in America*, New York: Oxford University Press, 1976; abridged as *The Populist Moment*, 1978
Haynes, Frederick E., *James Baird Weaver*, Iowa City: State Historical Society of Iowa, 1919
Nugent, Walter T.K., *Money and American Society, 1865–1880*, New York: Free Press, 1968
Reitano, Joanne, *The Tariff Question in the Gilded Age: The Great Debate of 1888*, University Park: Pennsylvania State University Press, 1994
Sharkey, Robert P., *Money, Class, and Party: An Economic Study of Civil War and Reconstruction*, Baltimore: Johns Hopkins Press, 1959
Unger, Irwin, *The Greenback Era: A Social and Political History of American Finance, 1865–1879*, Princeton: Princeton University Press, 1964
Weinstein, Allen, *Prelude to Populism: Origins of the Silver Issue, 1867–1878*, New Haven: Yale University Press, 1970

The "money question" during the late 19th century took the form of a vigorous debate over inflationary currency and was a shorthand for concerns about the economic, social, political, and moral health of the nation. Sound money based on hard currency, particularly gold, stood for conservatism, stability, and integrity, while inflationary money – notably paper, like the celebrated "greenbacks," or silver coined without restriction – suggested boldness, fluidity, and depending on the point of view, desperation or democratic values. Without doubt, the money question raised passions.

To argue about money it was important to know its history in detail. BOLLES, a contemporary witness of the debate, supplies a compendium of dates and facts. Like a scorecard at a sporting event – only thicker and less colorful – this book imparts information on the financial players, strategies, and record.

Seven decades passed before historians provided serious and illuminating interpretations of the money question's well-established chronicle. In a "politico-economic history of the Civil War and Reconstruction," SHARKEY scrutinizes, with the aid of economic theory, the controversial Legal Tender Acts of 1862 and 1863 that expanded the money supply to meet unprecedented wartime demands, secretary of the treasury Hugh McCulloch's postwar efforts to contract the paper money supply, and the influence of manufacturers, farmers, labor, and bankers in the East and the West on the shifting fortunes of monetary policy. He pays close attention to divisions within the Radical Republicans in congress and factions within the Democratic party as well as the relationship between tariff policy – especially among those favoring protectionism – and ideas about money. In sum, this study chisels distinctive features on to the monolithic presentations of economic determinism by precursors like Charles and Mary Beard and Howard K. Beale.

Following this rich vein, UNGER provides a nuanced social and political analysis of monetary policy through the 1870s. After pointing out that financial questions had long sparked social conflict, he launches into an account of competing groups seeking to "identify the locus of control in emerging modern America." He departs from earlier interpretations by placing emphasis on ethics and conscience – the values and convictions of decision-makers – instead of economic self-interest, and adds precision to the labels "hard money" and "soft money" by linking the terms to attitudes toward the resumption of specie payment for paper currency. A graceful narrative – certainly a factor in this book winning a Pulitzer Prize – tells a complex story without confusion, and lends force to the conclusion that a powerful coalition of conservative interests little changed from antebellum America, and given direction by secretary of the treasury John Sherman, "the supple master of accommodation," finally prevailed in seemingly endless battles for specie resumption. This result, in 1879, emanated from an intricate process rather than being the triumph of one side over its total opposite.

NUGENT also sees the money question as a social and moral event but explores its dimensions within the context of international monetary developments. He argues cogently that debates on the proper standard of money mirrored thoughts on the proper moral standard of the society. Up to 1873, harmony and relative tranquillity predominated among groups on the money question; after this date "stress, conflict, and fragmentation" crumbled the consensus among politicians, bankers, and social commentators. Bickering over money finally led to a society oriented toward industrial values; its flawed ethos was the dubious legacy of the dispute over the money question. Chapters on the 1867 and 1878 International Monetary Conferences in Paris serve as poles for this interpretation of the postbellum world.

The silver aspect of the money question takes center stage in WEINSTEIN. From the legal demonetization of silver in 1873, through dreams and schemes for resumption or bimetallism, to the final partial victory of silver promoters in the Bland-Allison Act of 1877, the silver drama unfolds scene by scene. Many noteworthy political actors head the large cast that made this play a gripping public performance.

REITANO focuses another lens on the shifting financial and ideological landscape of the Gilded Age by looking carefully at the spirited tariff debate of 1888. She shows how exchanges over a bill – that ultimately failed to pass Congress – revealed concerns about the competency of government to manage the economy, the place of agriculture in an increasingly industrial society, growing inequities in income, tensions between workers and management, and the standing of the United States within the global economy. Protectionists and free traders are the *dramatis personae* of the debate, but the outcome affected styles of living across the country. The principal conclusion – that by examining "the relationship between humanitarianism, egalitarianism, and materialism," tariff debaters confronted the nation's "most fundamental dilemmas" – attempts to rehabilitate the reputation of the maligned Gilded Age.

The agrarian movement, also responsive to dilemmas of the period, had deep roots in the money question, and its most spectacular outgrowth was Populism. GOODWYN views Populism positively as a broad expression of cultural beliefs and values rather than a narrow protest ideology. The farmers and small townspeople who committed themselves to Populism wanted to dull the sharp competitive edges of capitalism with cooperative economic institutions and genuine communal mores. Unfortunately, the dams and eddies of monetary policy, and especially the lure of silver coinage, diverted the Populist current, and it dried up after the failed presidential candidacy of William Jennings Bryan in 1896. Colorful characters populate the annals of the money question. James B. Weaver, presidential candidate of the Greenback party in 1880 and the Populist party in 1892, comes to life in HAYNES, a biography which reveals much about the odd peregrinations of the people and ideas that made the money question a significant aspect of United States history during the late 19th century.

WILLIAM M. FERRARO

See also Financial History, 1780s–1930s; Gilded Age and Progressive Era

Monroe, James 1758–1831
5th President of the United States

Ammon, Harry, *James Monroe: The Quest for National Identity*, New York: McGraw Hill, 1971

Ammon, Harry, *James Monroe: A Bibliography*, Westport, CT: Meckler, 1991

Cresson, W.P., *James Monroe*, Chapel Hill: University of North Carolina Press, 1946

Gilman, Daniel C., *James Monroe*, Boston: Houghton Mifflin, 1898

Monroe, James, *Autobiography*, edited by Stuart Gerry Brown, Syracuse, NY: Syracuse University Press, 1959

Morgan, George, *The Life of James Monroe*, Boston: Small Maynard, 1921

Skowronek, Stephen, *The Politics Presidents Make: Leadership from John Adams to George Bush*, Cambridge, MA: Belknap Press of Harvard University Press, 1993

Styron, Arthur, *Last of the Cocked Hats: James Monroe and the Virginia Dynasty*, Norman: University of Oklahoma Press, 1945

Wilmerding, Lucius, Jr., *James Monroe, Public Claimant*, New Brunswick, NJ: Rutgers University Press, 1960

James Monroe, 5th president of the United States, is the least-studied of the so-called "Virginia dynasty" that included Washington, Jefferson and Madison. Known as the "last of the cocked hats," he has tended to be viewed – inaccurately – as something of an anachronism; an 18th-century figure in the 19th century. Despite one of the most extensive résumés of any president, including service in the Revolutionary War, elective office as Continental congressman, United States senator, and governor of Virginia, numerous important diplomatic postings and two cabinet appointments, Monroe has often been researched more for his ties to more famous figures and his proximity to important events than for his own somewhat ambiguous contributions. Reticent and shy, Monroe inspired no major biography by a contemporary; it is likely that no contemporary was in a position to write it. MONROE's own *Autobiography*, written after his retirement and first published more than a century after his death, illustrates this inaccessibility; a turgid and disappointingly unrevealing third-person account, it concludes well before Monroe's presidential career and adds almost nothing to the public record.

Prepared for John T. Morse's American Statesmen series, GILMAN is pedestrian and labored, and chooses simply to avoid certain of the more controversial episodes of Monroe's life. The author keenly felt the inaccessibility of the uncalendared Monroe papers in the Department of State, and perhaps his own limitations as an historian; in his preface to the revised edition, Gilman openly invites Henry Adams to continue his *History of . . . the Administrations of Jefferson and Madison* through the Monroe administration and so write the work that his own was not. Unfortunately, Adams declined to rise to the challenge, leaving it instead to MORGAN, whose biography, although the first to take advantage of the State Department calendar of Monroe papers and the seven volumes of Monroe's writings edited by S. M. Hamilton (1898–1903), is dated, breezy and superficial, and displays little real interest in its subject. Monroe's presidential years, in particular, appear almost as an afterthought, with the exception of a detailed discussion of the formation of the Monroe Doctrine, the centennial of which presented the occasion for the book's appearance.

STYRON is an even more extreme example of a biography uncaptivated by its subject. Monroe often seems like a mere bystander while the author engages in long and often dubious digressions into figures he finds more compelling, such as Jefferson and Napoleon. When he does focus on Monroe, moreover, Styron is apt to be inaccurate and shallow. The book is entertaining, but unreliable.

CRESSON is the first scholarly biography and perhaps the first relatively modern treatment which is interested in Monroe for his own sake, not simply because, like Mount Everest, he "is there." Unfortunately, the work, which remained unfinished at its author's death and was completed by numerous hands, perpetuates many traditional inaccuracies and introduces new ones. Although a former State Department officer, the author is perhaps weakest on Monroe's diplomatic career. Nonetheless, this is the first biography in which a distinctive Monroe personality begins to emerge.

A less flattering portrait is presented by WILMERDING, a strange work in which an economic historian in effect conducts a posthumous audit of Monroe's accounts, and finds many of his claims for expenses incurred in public service inflated, fanciful, or sometimes even fraudulent. This is a highly specialized study which displays a distinct but unexplained animus against the 5th president.

With AMMON (1971), Monroe at last obtained a study worthy of his remarkable career – not only the best book on Monroe, but a model presidential biography. Ammon's deep understanding of both Virginia and federal politics of the early republic enables him to present a convincing portrait of Monroe's gradual evolution from a die-hard, antifederalist Old Republican, more Jeffersonian than Jefferson, to a cautious but unequivocal nationalist, while striving with ever-increasing difficulty to maintain his local political base among Virginia's strict-constructionist gentry. Monroe's long and only passably successful diplomatic career is here shown to have been a valuable process of learning what works and what does not – lessons which Monroe applied with increasing effectiveness throughout his public life. Much of Monroe's seeming blandness, and apparently agonizing reluctance to act decisively, were dictated, in Ammon's view, by the necessity not to appear to exceed his constitutional prerogatives. Evaluated on the basis of actions, rather than appearances, Ammon's Monroe emerges as a talented, flexible and effective leader. AMMON (1991) is a comprehensive bibliography of works relating to Monroe; and an invaluable guide to more specialized research.

In the course of a structural study of presidential politics, SKOWRONEK has a chapter on Monroe, which helps to reconcile Ammon's activist president with the traditional passive, reactive portrait. He does so by placing the particular obstacles which Monroe faced within a broader theoretical framework of recurrent patterns in American political development. According to Skowronek, Monroe's method of consolidation and consensus, while building on his most important

personal strengths and political assets, precluded his enunciating a clear statement about the new and contentious nationalist direction in which he was leading the country. Although somewhat schematized and based exclusively on secondary research, Skowronek's structural approach throws unexpected light on a president whose legacy remains obscure.

ROBERT P. FORBES

See also Era of Good Feelings

Monroe Doctrine

Dozer, Donald M. (editor), *The Monroe Doctrine: Its Modern Significance*, New York: Knopf, 1965

May, Ernest R., *The Making of the Monroe Doctrine*, Cambridge, MA: Harvard University Press, 1975

Merk, Frederick, *The Monroe Doctrine and American Expansionism, 1843–1849*, New York: Knopf, 1966

Perkins, Bradford, *Castlereagh and Adams: England and the United States, 1812–1823*, Berkeley: University of California Press, 1964

Perkins, Dexter, *The Monroe Doctrine, 1823–1826*, Cambridge, MA: Harvard University Press, and London: Oxford University Press, 1927

Perkins, Dexter, *The Monroe Doctrine, 1826–1867*, Baltimore: Johns Hopkins Press, 1933

Perkins, Dexter, *The Monroe Doctrine, 1867–1907*, Baltimore: Johns Hopkins Press, 1937

Perkins, Dexter, *Hands Off: A History of the Monroe Doctrine*, Boston: Little, Brown, 1941; revised as *A History of the Monroe Doctrine*, 1955

Smith, Gaddis, *The Last Years of the Monroe Doctrine, 1945–1993*, New York: Hill and Wang, 1994

Webster, C.K.(editor), *Britain and the Independence of Latin America, 1812–1830: Select Documents from the Foreign Office Archives*, 2 vols., London: Oxford University Press, 1938

Dexter Perkins is the historian *par excellence* of the Monroe Doctrine. Indeed, readers could justifiably begin and end their study of this particular subject by consulting only his publications. Perkins earned his pre-eminent reputation by consecutively writing three volumes dealing with the origins and evolution of the Monroe Doctrine during the 19th century. In the first, PERKINS (1927) examines the events leading to Monroe's famous message in November 1823, and the immediate response that it evoked in high diplomatic circles in both Europe and Latin America. A notable feature of this compact monograph is its lucid discussion of diplomatic relations between the United States and the great powers of Europe. Perkins carefully avoids the temptation to glorify Monroe's action and notes that its actual impact upon diplomatic events in 1823 was slight. The remarkable evolution of the statement into a "doctrine" is described in PERKINS (1933). This covers the years from 1826 to 1867 and includes extensive discussion of the question of a Central American canal and the controversy arising from the French military intervention in Mexico. PERKINS (1937) deals with the period from 1867 to

1907. He skilfully describes the positive American diplomatic response to a succession of crises occurring in Panama, Venezuela and the Caribbean, and he convincingly portrays these years as the high point of the Monroe Doctrine. The two volumes covering the period from 1826 to 1907 are very detailed and, added together, consist of more than 1,000 pages. In effect, they provide not only a comprehensive history of the Monroe Doctrine but also, by virtue of the importance of the subject, a very informative account of American diplomacy during the 19th century. PERKINS (1941, 1955) is a one-volume study of the Monroe Doctrine. This is not a synthesis but an abridged version of the earlier three volumes with the significant addition of a lengthy survey on the development of the Doctrine during the first half of the 20th century. The new section is well-informed and thoughtful, but inevitably lacks the wealth of detail associated with Perkins's studies of the 19th century.

The four books by Perkins on the Monroe Doctrine illustrate traditional diplomatic history at its best. They are based upon mastery of the source material, and on extensive research in American and European archives. The narrative style is clear and easy to read. The interpretation is perceptive and well-supported by the evidence presented. Admittedly, Perkins does concentrate on the activities of the political and diplomatic elite and makes no specific mention of economic influences and social forces. Nevertheless, Perkins's scholarly authority has not been surpassed and has stood the test of time.

There is no other full-length study of the history of the Monroe Doctrine to rival the works of Perkins. The subject is of course covered in textbooks on American and Latin American history and in books devoted to related historical topics. For example, the introductory chapter in the first volume of WEBSTER (1938) is a readable exposition of British diplomacy towards the Latin American movements for independence, and places the events of 1823 in a European context. Webster also reprints a large number of key diplomatic documents. Further supplementary information on the significance of Anglo-American relations is contained in PERKINS (1964) which has a final chapter that persuasively interprets Monroe's action as the assertion of American diplomatic independence from Britain. Less convincing is MAY which discounts the impact of diplomatic events and suggests instead that the 1823 statement was the product of domestic political pressures arising from the presidential election scheduled for 1824. At first sight, there may be some plausibility in the idea of John Quincy Adams bent upon gaining personal political advantage by exploiting an alleged threat from overseas, but the documentary evidence offered by May is not conclusive.

Despite its prominent inclusion in the title, MERK's book does not specifically consider the history of the Monroe Doctrine. It is principally an account of the movement for Manifest Destiny during the 1840s, and how the concept of the Monroe Doctrine was deliberately manipulated by politicians to promote the territorial expansion of the United States.

An interesting and varied collection of 20th-century views of the Monroe Doctrine is provided by DOZER. The 25 extracts are all short pieces and are selected from books, articles and official government documents published between 1898 and 1964. The editor commendably chooses more contributors from Latin America than from the United States.

There are even articles from Canada and Japan. Dozer also includes an excellent introductory essay which outlines the history of the Monroe Doctrine from 1823 to 1965.

The emergence of the United States as a global superpower after 1945 has made the Monroe Doctrine appear redundant. This view is effectively dispelled in an informative and readable monograph by SMITH, which demonstrates that the Monroe Doctrine has been frequently used by successive presidents from Truman to Reagan to rationalize and justify an aggressive American policy towards Latin America. The end of the Cold War has resulted, however, in the removal of the threat of international communism to the security of the western hemisphere. Without an external danger, Smith logically concludes that the Monroe Doctrine is finally dead.

JOSEPH SMITH

See also Foreign Policy: General; Foreign Policy since 1945: Special Aspects 6

Moody, Dwight L. 1837–1899
Evangelist

Curtis, Richard K., *They Called Him Mister Moody*, New York: Doubleday, 1962

Findlay, James F., Jr., *Dwight L. Moody, American Evangelist, 1837–1899*, Chicago: University of Chicago Press, 1969

Gundry, Stanley N., *Love Them in: The Life and Theology of D.L. Moody*, Chicago: Moody Press, 1976

Kent, John, *Holding the Fort: Studies in Victorian Revivalism*, London: Epworth Press, 1978

McLoughlin, William G., *Modern Revivalism: Charles Grandison Finney to Billy Graham*, New York: Ronald Press, 1959

Moody, William R., *The Life of Dwight L. Moody*, New York: Revell, 1900

Moody, William R., *D.L. Moody*, New York: Macmillan, 1930

Pollock, John, *Moody: A Biographical Portrait of the Pacesetter in Modern Evangelism*, New York: Macmillan, 1963; as *Moody: The Biography*, Chicago: Moody Press, 1984

Weisberger, Bernard A., *They Gathered at the River: The Story of the Great Revivalists and Their Impact upon Religion in America*, Boston: Little Brown, 1958

During the last quarter of the 19th century, Dwight L. Moody was perhaps the most important religious leader in America. He refused ordination because of his lack of education, and began his religious career when he formed a Sunday school among the poor in Chicago. He was also an early leader in the Young Men's Christian Association (YMCA) movement. After two earlier trips to Great Britain to learn from Christian leaders there, Moody accepted an invitation to return in 1873. For the next two years, this dynamic layman and his singing partner, Ira D. Sankey, led urban revivals throughout England, Scotland, and Ireland, culminating in a four-month series of meetings in London attended by a total of 1.5 million people.

Returning to the United States a celebrity, Moody began a series of mass revivals in the country's major cities over the remainder of the decade. Later in his career he founded schools for girls and boys in Northfield, Massachusetts, and an institute to train Christian lay workers in Chicago. Preaching to thousands at a time, day after day, Moody proclaimed a simple message of personal salvation and Christian service to the affluent and the working classes. During his career, an estimated 100 million people heard or read his sermons.

Even during Moody's lifetime, amateur biographers capitalized on his success by offering the public brief sketches of the evangelist, often published together with some of his sermons. Shortly after he died, more unauthorized biographies began to appear, forcing his son William R. Moody to release the biography which his father had urged him to write. This hastily produced volume, MOODY (1900), and the more carefully prepared revision, MOODY (1930), offer important information about Moody's career from the perspective of one intimately associated with him. The revised version provides useful information on his career outside revivalism, but both volumes are filiopietistic in tone and make little attempt to place Moody's life in historical context.

Admiring biographies of Moody continued to appear for decades after his death. Two of the best are those by CURTIS and POLLOCK, which share many similarities. Both works rely extensively on the many anecdotes that Moody's career produced. Curtis effectively captures much of the excitement that Moody's revivals held for his contemporaries, though Pollock's overtly inspirational biography is more readable and offers the best overview of Moody's life for the general reader. Neither book offers a critical analysis of his career and accomplishments, nor do they adequately examine him in the social context in which he lived. Both authors consulted many of the primary materials available in both England and America. Curtis's volume is carefully referenced, but Pollock's 1984 volume lacks notes and contains only a limited bibliography.

WEISBERGER examines the revival as an institution and the traveling preachers who used it in 19th-century America, while McLOUGHLIN presents a broad interpretation of American revivalism in the 19th and 20th centuries. Both necessarily deal with Moody and successfully place him in a broader historical context. Both studies are also highly critical of Moody as the heir to Charles G. Finney, the mid-19th century revivalist, who insisted that revivals could be produced by the proper application of human means. Weisberger and McLoughlin argue that Moody refined Finney's ideas by applying the principles of business to revivals, thereby creating a sort of machinery of revival that Moody applied to British and American cities and which later revivalists inherited from him. In his determination to achieve results – converts – Moody employed whatever methods worked best, regardless of their theological implications. His appeal was largely to those who felt most threatened by the changes wrought by industrialization and urbanization, and who longed for a traditional, agrarian past.

In his larger study of British revivalism in the latter half of the 19th century, KENT includes three chapters on the team of Moody and Sankey, and their revival efforts in Britain. Finding Moody "vulgar," Kent argues forcefully that his British meetings relied for their success on thorough advance preparation by the evangelical subculture in the various cities that he visited. Moody manipulated British audiences with his showmanship, Kent maintains, but his evangelistic efforts produced few long-term results for British churches. In a chapter devoted to Moody's preaching, Kent describes the evangelist as a cruel exploiter of the fears and anxieties of Victorians, whom he harassed into making superficial conversion decisions.

FINDLAY is the definitive scholarly biography of Moody, and the best starting point for understanding his historical significance. Based on extensive research, it avoids both the harsh criticisms of Weisberger and McLoughlin and the uncritical admiration of many eulogistic biographers. With great skill, Findlay places Moody within both the "inner" context of evangelical Protestantism and the "outer" context of the Gilded Age. Although Findlay finds more to admire in Moody than other historians have done, he still trains a critical eye on the evangelist's career. The result is a judiciously balanced biography that respects Moody's personal faith, while evaluating the ways in which his social context shaped the formation and expression of that faith.

The best study of Moody's theology is GUNDRY. Although Moody had no formal theological training, Gundry examines his "implicit theology" as revealed in his sermons. In contrast to negative characterizations that Moody made professional revivalism into big business, Gundry insists that Moody used innovative techniques only within the boundaries of his theology, and that his methods did not determine his message. Gundry portrays Moody's theology as an unresolved tension between Arminianism and Calvinism. Although Moody was conservative in doctrine and disturbed by liberal theological trends, he was also ecumenical in his associations within a broad evangelical group. Gundry's analysis of Moody and his theology is rather uncritical, but he effectively challenges some of the harsher evaluations of Moody's theology and methods. Gundry's volume and Kent's chapter on Moody's preaching, read together, provide useful opposing viewpoints both on Moody's theology and on the revivalist himself.

DANIEL W. STOWELL

See also Revivalism

Morgan, J. Pierpont 1837–1913
Banker and financier

Allen, Frederick Lewis, *The Lords of Creation*, New York: Harper, and London: Hamish Hamilton, 1935

Allen, Frederick Lewis, *The Great Pierpont Morgan*, New York: Harper, 1949

Carosso, Vincent P., *The Morgans: Private International Bankers, 1854–1913*, Cambridge, MA: Harvard University Press, 1987

Chernow, Ron, *The House of Morgan: An American Banking Dynasty and the Rise of Modern Finance*, New York: Atlantic Monthly Press, 1990

Jackson, Stanley, *J.P. Morgan: A Biography*, New York: Stein and Day, 1983; as *J.P. Morgan: The Rise and Fall of a Banker*, London: Heinemann, 1984

Josephson, Matthew, *The Robber Barons: The Great American Capitalists, 1861–1901*, New York: Harcourt Brace, 1934

Satterlee, Herbert L., *J. Pierpont Morgan: An Intimate Portrait*, New York: Macmillan, 1939

Sinclair, Andrew, *Corsair: The Life of J. Pierpont Morgan*, London: Weidenfeld and Nicolson, and Boston: Little Brown, 1981

At the height of his influence around the turn of the century, J. P. Morgan was regarded as the personal symbol of the power of Wall Street. This was the man who, by his personal authority and the operations of his bank, ushered in a new era of finance capitalism, when much of the power of individual industrial pioneers passed into the hands of the investment bankers. Morgan master-minded major reorganizations of railroad companies and many other businesses; in 1901, he was instrumental in setting up the giant U.S. Steel Corporation; he twice rescued the United States government itself from financial crisis; he was a close associate of monarchs, heads of state and political and financial leaders around the world; and he used much of his great wealth to amass a private art collection of unprecedented size and scope.

It is hardly surprising that such a figure should have received a mixed press from biographers and historians. SATTERLEE, who was Morgan's son-in-law, set the tone, and provided much of the information, for the admiring, or at least always respectful, approach to his formidable subject. He provides what is indeed an intimate portrrait, based on observation from within the bosom of the family over a long period, and full of detail that is unavailable elsewhere. Equally, of course, it omits much that would have been unflattering to Morgan, and it can have no great claims to objectivity.

It was JOSEPHSON who set the tone for much of the opposing school of thought about Morgan, in his biographical study of a number of the prominent industrialists and financiers of the late 19th and early 20th centuries. The title conveys the basic message of fierce hostility to big business and businessmen, and few stones are left unturned in the effort to depict them as scoundrels. Written in a lively style, and finding a receptive audience in many quarters, Josephson has remained immensely popular since it was first published more than sixty years ago (in the depths of the Great Depression). However, business history has been transformed in the intervening period, and Josephson's evidence and his conclusions cannot now be taken at face value.

Most work on Morgan falls into one of two categories. On the one hand, there are a number of popular biographies, written with varying degrees of sympathy or hostility, but sharing a common fascination with great wealth and the power which it brings. On the other hand, there are a few large-scale, very detailed, scholarly studies of the House of Morgan, and its intricate web of banking and financial activities. ALLEN (1949) is one of the first of the popular accounts, and remains in many ways the best available – and the most attractively written – despite being now almost half a century old. He sees Morgan as typifying the American ideal of individualism, and as one of the architects of a transformation of the American economy. In an earlier work, ALLEN (1935) provides a wonderfully evocative picture of the rapid changes that the turn-of-the-century American economy was undergoing.

Among several more recent popular biographies of Morgan, two of the best examples are Sinclair and Jackson. SINCLAIR is in the same mould as Allen, with a lively and colorful style, a liberal supply of anecdotes, and coverage of both Morgan's business and personal life. Sinclair sees Morgan as a driven man, with a lust to accumulate and excel. But he also fulfilled a prominent role in American economic development, as "the midwife of the bourgeois revolution, the necessary stage of accumulation before provoking state intervention." Sinclair concludes that Morgan's work made possible "the economic transition from the farm belt to the conveyor belt: he died as he became unnecessary." The flamboyance of Sinclair's style and the boldness of his generalizations are sometimes at odds with the ambivalence of his attitude towards his subject – and his grasp of financial and economic history is not always as secure as it might be. JACKSON is a gossipy popular account, with much narrative detail of Morgan's travels, social contacts and actual or alleged womanizing. There is little attempt at sustained analysis, and only a limited grasp of Morgan's business operations. A good deal of the book is devoted to his earlier life, including some psychological speculation about the lasting consequences of his brief early marriage to his consumptive first wife, Mimi. According to Jackson, Morgan was a man of paradoxes – a good Christian who was guilty of all the seven deadly sins, except sloth – but no doubt the same could be said of many others.

At the other end of the scale of Morgan literature are the massive studies by Carosso and Chernow. CAROSSO's history of the Morgans, which carries the story to the year of J.P.Morgan's death in 1913, is business history of a very high order, authoritative, clearly written, and based on massive research, some of it in previously unavailable family and business records. (There are 215 pages of notes which take up around one quarter of the volume.) In tracing the banking operations of the Morgans, and demonstrating J.P. Morgan's huge international power, Carosso also sheds much light on the mechanics of international trade and finance in this period. Although this is essentially a work of business and financial history, some attention is given to other facets of J.P. Morgan's life, ranging from his health and his travels to his religious interests, his family network and his circle of friends. The tone of the book is generally sympathetic, but this is no hagiography, and Carosso treats seriously and sensibly the criticisms and the opprobrium which Morgan and his reputation have often encountered.

One of the central themes of Carosso is the kind of discreet, careful, conservative, private banking which was Morgan's milieu, where a man's word was his bond. His greatest assets were the people whom he knew, and the outstandingly able partners who worked with him. One of the main themes of CHERNOW's study of the House of Morgan over a longer period is the transition from this personal style of banking to a more modern, more corporate and more impersonal structure, with new competitive strategies for the provision of a range of services. Chernow matches Carosso in the massive scale of his work and the breadth of his research. His use of particular incidents and anecdotes gives an occasional lighter touch to what is inevitably a demanding study of the world of high finance and international banking. It remains to be seen whether some future author can combine the scholarship of a Carosso and a Chernow with the human interest and lively style of popular writers, to produce a fully-rounded biography of the formidable John Pierpont Morgan.

JOHN STEELE GORDON

See also Financial History, 1780s–1930s

Mormons (Church of Jesus Christ of Latter-Day Saints)

Allen, James B. and Glen M. Leonard, *The Story of the Latter-Day Saints*, Salt Lake City: Deseret Book Company, 1976, revised, 1992

Arrington, Leonard J. and Davis Bitton, *The Mormon Experience: A History of the Latter-Day Saints*, New York: Knopf, 1979; 2nd edition, Urbana: University of Illinois Press, 1992

Beecher, Maureen Ursenbach and Lavina Fielding Anderson (editors), *Sisters in Spirit: Mormon Women in Historical and Cultural Perspective*, Urbana: University of Illinois Press, 1987

Bushman, Richard L., *Joseph Smith and the Beginnings of Mormonism*, Urbana: University of Illinois Press, 1984

Foster, Lawrence, *Religion and Sexuality: Three American Communal Experiments of the Nineteenth Century*, New York and Oxford: Oxford University Press, 1981

Hansen, Klaus J., *Mormonism and the American Experience*, Chicago: University of Chicago Press, 1981

Hardy, B. Carmon, *Solemn Covenant: The Mormon Polygamous Passage*, Urbana: University of Illinois Press, 1992

Ludlow, Daniel H. (editor-in-chief), *Encyclopedia of Mormonism*, New York: Macmillan, 1992

O'Dea, Thomas F., *The Mormons*, Chicago: University of Chicago Press, 1957

Quinn, D. Michael (editor), *The New Mormon History: Revisionist Essays on the Past*, Salt Lake City: Signature, 1992

Roberts, Brigham H., *A Comprehensive History of the Church of Jesus Christ of Latter-Day Saints: Century I*, 6 vols., Salt Lake City: Deseret News, 1930

Shipps, Jan, *Mormonism: The Story of a New Religious Tradition*, Urbana: University of Illinois Press, 1985

Before 1950, virtually all Mormon history, or history written about the Church of Jesus Christ of Latter-Day Saints and its members, fell into one of two categories: apologetic or sceptical. Books written by believing Mormons bore witness to the divine nature of Joseph Smith's calling to restore Christ's church on earth, while works in the latter group sought to expose Smith as a fraud and charlatan. The efforts of these two camps resulted in numerous polemics full of emotion and opinion but short on sound historical research and writing. No early work escaped this constricting debate, but perhaps

the best is ROBERTS's six-volume centennial history of the church published in 1930. A prominent church leader in the early 20th century, Roberts wrote to affirm and bolster faith but still managed to avoid many of the pitfalls of this approach to history by making extensive use of primary sources and attempting to portray the Latter-Day Saints "warts and all." Although only partially successful in this objective, his work remains important for the breadth and depth of its treatment of the first 100 years of the church.

The two best among more recent comprehensive surveys of Mormon history continue the tradition of Roberts; both books are the work of Latter-Day Saint authors sympathetic to the church, who attempt to reconcile objectivity with a sensitivity to the faith of both their subjects and their Mormon readers. ALLEN and LEONARD is a narrative account, written primarily for a Mormon audience, and provides what is perhaps the most complete treatment of 20th-century Mormonism, though it sometimes becomes swamped in the details of administrative history. Designed for a more general readership, ARRINGTON and BITTON approach the Mormon experience thematically within a chronological sweep of church history. Both books introduce the "text" of Mormon history with a minimum of analysis.

The dichotomy of believer and non-believer still shapes the history being written about Mormons, but since 1950 professionally trained historians have shifted the focus away from proving or disproving the origins of the church, towards an analysis of its history. One of the first serious scholarly examinations by a non-Mormon was O'DEA's historical and sociological study, which suggests that, although Mormonism "manifested its own peculiarities," it primarily sprang from the evangelical revivalism of the early 19th century "Burned-over District." It shared the millennialist and ecumenical vision of the time as well as a strong communitarianism and belief in free will. O'Dea is most effective, however, in his insightful sociological examination of the stresses and conflicts within modern Mormonism.

Adopting a different standpoint, both Shipps and Bushman place 19th-century Mormonism in the larger context of American religious history, and see that it was more than just a product of its environment. Coming to her topic from religious studies, SHIPPS, perhaps the most sympathetic of all non-Mormon historians, suggests that, by appropriating and eventually transforming primary elements of the Judaic-Christian tradition, Mormonism developed quickly into an entirely new religious tradition. BUSHMAN, a Mormon and prominent historian of colonial New England, finds the most important influences on Joseph Smith coming from the Smith family's social situation and religious tradition. Both Bushman and Shipps seek to present events as the participants themselves experienced them, leaving room for divine intervention in the story of the Mormons. HANSEN adopts a more topical and multi-disciplinary approach to Mormon history. Though not always living up to the breadth indicated in its title, his work does address several of the thorny problems of Mormon history – the source of Joseph Smith's revelations, polygamy, the Mormon political Kingdom of God, and the church's racial views. Hansen's approach is not entirely effective, particularly in his use of speculative psychological theories as explanations of religious experience.

Although many of the important gender issues in the history of the church have yet to be adequately addressed, several historians have broached these subjects. In a remarkable book edited by BEECHER and ANDERSON, several Mormon women from a wide range of educational backgrounds illuminate "Mormon women's experience, present and past." Underlying the historical essays in the collection is a sometimes implied, sometimes explicit, theme of the social, doctrinal and political changes that have moved Mormon women from positions of relative freedom and power in the 19th century into primarily domestic roles in the 20th century. The one aspect of Mormon gender relations that has received considerable attention is polygamy. FOSTER's interdisciplinary study, which also contains a discussion of the Oneidan and Shaker communities, has long been the standard non-Mormon interpretation. Placing the Mormon practice of "plural marriage" in the context of 19th-century communitarianism, Foster sees Mormon polygamy as a key component of a serious attempt to re-structure social life and bring order to a rapidly changing world. Less concerned with origins, HARDY is a more recent examination of Mormon polygamy which fills important gaps in the literature, such as the role of sexuality in polygamous families, polygamy's contribution to the patriarchal orientation of the church, and most importantly, "post-Manifesto" polygamy (the practice of plural marriage after its official abrogation by the church).

Some of the best work on Mormons is in article form. The collection of previously published essays edited by QUINN provides a good overview of the "New Mormon history" – revisionist history that has attempted to rise above the biases of the celebratory and sceptical approaches to the subject. The collection shows the increasing professionalization of the field, but should have included more essays on gender and ethnicity. The encyclopedia edited by LUDLOW covers an impressive range of subject matter. There are around 150 history articles of variable quality, which often lean toward "faithful history," but, conveniently brought together in this form, they provide the reader with a wealth of information on a wide range of topics.

SHAWN JOHANSEN

See also Young, Brigham and Joseph Smith

Morris, Robert 1734–1806
Merchant and financier of the Revolution

Doerflinger, Thomas M., *A Vigorous Spirit of Enterprise: Merchants and Economic Development in Revolutionary Philadelphia*, Chapel Hill: University of North Carolina Press, 1986

East, Robert A., *Business Enterprise in the American Revolutionary Era*, New York: Columbia University Press, and London: King, 1938

Ferguson, E. James, *The Power of the Purse: A History of American Public Finance, 1776–1790*, Chapel Hill: University of North Carolina Press, 1961

Henderson, H. James, *Party Politics in the Continental Congress*, New York: McGraw Hill, 1974

Kohn, Richard H., *Eagle and Sword: The Federalists and the Creation of the Military Establishment in America, 1783–1802*, New York: Free Press, 1975

Oberholtzer, Ellis Paxson, *Robert Morris: Patriot and Financier*, New York: Macmillan, 1903; reprinted, New York: Franklin, 1968

Rakove, Jack N., *The Beginnings of National Politics: An Interpretive History of the Continental Congress*, New York: Knopf, 1979

Ryerson, Richard Alan, *The Revolution is Now Begun: The Radical Committees of Philadelphia, 1765–1776*, Philadelphia: University of Pennsylvania Press, 1978

Sumner, William Graham, *Robert Morris*, New York: Dodd Mead, 1892

Ver Steeg, Clarence L., *Robert Morris: Revolutionary Financier*, Philadelphia: University of Pennsylvania Press, 1954

With the possible exception of George Washington, Robert Morris probably did more than any other individual to bring about America's victory in the Revolution. Despite this, he has received only scant attention from scholars. It has been almost a hundred years since the last biography of him was written. In large part this was because he was not of the stuff from which heroes are made. There was nothing inspiring about him; as the country's chief financial officer during the Revolution, his main claim to fame was that he raised and spent money efficiently. He also had a darker side; frequently engaged in controversial activities, he used privileged information to further his own interests, and died a broken and poor man after spending several years in debtor's prison.

Still useful after more than a century, SUMNER reduces to a simple narrative form the material to be found in his fuller but idiosyncratically organized earlier work on *The Financier and the Finances of the American Revolution* (1891). Sumner was a strong advocate of fiscal responsibility, a sound monetary system and free trade, and his biography is implicitly very sympathetic to Morris. It is also very intelligent and contains a number of sharp insights. However, as most of Morris's papers were not available at the time when he wrote, the book is thin on details.

OBERHOLTZER is a more complete treatment of Morris's life, for by the time he wrote the Library of Congress had obtained the great bulk of Morris's private papers. However, it is inevitably dated in its interpretation and often weak in analysis. Oberholtzer wrote at a time when the supporting secondary literature was sparse and the interpretive problems associated with the Articles of Confederation were only beginning to be understood. A modern biography is needed – and would be greatly helped by *The Papers of Robert Morris*, currently being published by the University of Pittsburgh Press.

Morris's political career before 1776 is put into context by RYERSON in his study of the mobilization of popular support for the Revolution in Philadelphia. He demonstrates how Morris and his fellow merchants were on the "conservative" side of the movement that successfully overthrew British rule in America. They were fearful of sweeping social change, only reluctantly accepted independence and opposed the Pennsylvania Constitution of 1776.

VER STEEG examines Morris's career as Superintendent of Finance for the Continental Congress. He details his administrative reforms and financial program. This included the curtailing of federal expenditures, the introduction of a more efficient system for collecting revenue, a more regular system of accounting, the implementation of a private contracting system to provide supplies for the troops, Morris's use of his own private credit to shore up the government, the creation of the Bank of North America, and his failed plan to fund the national debt by giving Congress an independent income. What Ver Steeg fails to explore adequately are the political and constitutional ramifications of these measures, including Morris's relations with the military, especially the discontented officers at Newburgh, who talked about overthrowing the federal government.

The link between Morris's economic policies as Superintendent of Finance and his political and constitutional ideas is made explicit in FERGUSON, who examines the complicated issue of public finance during the Confederation era. He argues that Morris deliberately set out to create a strong central government in 1781–83. He was unsuccessful, but, by bloating the national debt, he created the economic conditions that made the constitutional revolution of 1787–88 necessary. Strong support for this interpretation comes from KOHN who focuses on the role of the army in the Confederation period and examines Morris's connections to the Newburgh conspiracy and the possibility of a *coup d'etat*. HENDERSON also considers Morris's role as Superintendent of Finance and his relations with the military. His approach is more cautious and he is unwilling to endorse a conspiracy theory. But he also does not offer any meaningful alternative interpretation. RAKOVE makes a more direct assault on the interpretation offered by Ferguson and Kohn, and denies the existence of anything resembling a conspiracy, but his view has found little support from other scholars.

Less controversial are two admirable studies of the American business community at the time of the Revolution. EAST places special emphasis on Morris and discusses his relationship to the other leading entrepreneurs, merchants, financiers and speculators of the day, especially Thomas Willing, William Bingham, William Duer, Silas Deane and Jeremiah Wadsworth. He then links their activities to the broader economic problems of the 1780s, the movement for the United States Constitution and the establishment of various banks. DOERFLINGER is a more recent and sophisticated economic study that focuses on the rise and role of the merchant community of Philadelphia, of which Morris was a leading member, from 1750 to 1789. He stresses the entrepreneurial origins of the city's economic growth and explains how its business enterprises, such as land speculation, banking and securities trading, laid the foundation for America's future industrial development. Among other things, Doerflinger argues for the connection between constitutional nationalism and the development of American capitalism.

RICHARD E. ELLIS

Morse, Samuel F.B. 1791–1872

Inventor, artist and anti-Catholic campaigner

Billington, Ray Allen, *The Protestant Crusade, 1800–1860: A Study of the Origins of American Nativism*, New York: Macmillan, 1938
Coe, Lewis, *The Telegraph: A History of Morse's Invention and Its Predecessors*, Jefferson, NC: McFarland, 1993
Kloss, William, *Samuel F.B. Morse*, New York: Abrams/Smithsonian Institution, 1988
Larkin, Oliver W., *Samuel F.B. Morse and American Democratic Art*, Boston: Little Brown, 1954
Mabee, Carleton, *The American Leonardo: A Life of Samuel F.B. Morse*, New York: Knopf, 1943
Prime, Samuel Irenaus, *The Life of Samuel F.B. Morse*, New York: Appleton, 1875; reprinted, New York: Arno Press, 1974
Staiti, Paul J., *Samuel F.B. Morse*, Cambridge and New York: Cambridge University Press, 1989

Renowned as an artist, an inventor, and, to a lesser degree, a political figure, Samuel F. B. Morse has been the subject of numerous popular and scholarly works, though few have attempted to weave together the divergent threads of his life.

PRIME offered the first full-length study of Morse. This is a massive effort, nearly 800 pages long, which promises to give equal attention to Morse's career as an artist in the early Republic, as the inventor of the telegraph in Jacksonian America, and as a celebrity in the last decades of his life. Instead, the book concentrates mostly on Morse's work with the telegraph, offering detailed descriptions of the invention and Morse's struggle to establish a reputation as the machine's primary inventor. The study is not annotated and it contains no bibliography. But because the author was chosen by the executors of Morse's will as the official biographer, he was the first to examine Morse's original letters and journals, long extracts of which are reprinted here. Since many of the original documents have since been reprinted elsewhere in their entirety, and since the book smacks of hagiography, this study may be less valuable than it once was. Also, little effort is made to connect Morse's artistic endeavors with his technological innovations, and Morse's social attitudes and political activities are almost wholly ignored.

A much more thorough, analytical and well-crafted work is MABEE, which remains the definitive biography of Morse. This scholarly book makes a convincing case that Morse was one of the leading creative geniuses of his age. Yet instead of devoting attention to the sources of that creativity, the author argues that creativity alone was not the source of Morse's accomplishments. Rather, it was a combination of imagination, self-promotion, and Puritanical persistence that established Morse's fame. Carefully weighing the complicated and controversial evidence on the question of whether Morse was indeed the father of the telegraph, the author gives his subject the lion's share of the credit, though he is careful to note the significant contributions of Morse's predecessors and competitors. This is the first biography to attend to Morse's political attitudes and views – his early nativism, his proslavery beliefs, and his anti-administration stance during the Civil War – but the discussion is disappointingly brief, no doubt because of the unpopularity of all of these positions.

LARKIN is a more recent but less satisfying biography. This is one of the slim volumes which formed part of the Library of American Biography series, and the author was less interested in fitting Morse's life into some analytical framework than in providing an easily readable digest of his achievements, for popular audiences and students. The subject matter of the work is skewed towards Morse's artistic career, and it is unusually full in discussing Morse's efforts to found the National Academy of Design. The decision to focus on Morse's years as an artist is purposeful: the author believes that the roots of Morse's scientific ideas and of his commitment to democratic principles in the young Republic are to be found in his formative years as a young artist. Unfortunately, few of the facts about Morse's personal and political life are woven into the narrative; only a concluding chapter on the inventor's last years, for example, mentions his role as the head of the Society for Diffusion of Political Knowledge, the leading opposition propaganda organization during the Civil War.

Other works concentrate on specific aspects of Morse's career. There have been many studies, for example, of Morse the artist, of which KLOSS is one of the best. A handsome volume which includes numerous plates reproducing Morse's best known works, this study treats Morse as a quintessential "history painter." The artist saw no difference between his creative renditions of historical figures and his efforts to popularize art; both sets of endeavors aimed at celebrating public life in the United States. There is not much attention to Morse's life outside his artistic career, however, though the author does suggest that his subject's failed bid for Congress in 1854 was a watershed event.

A much more thorough and scholarly work is STAITI, by far the best work on Morse's early career. This is a well researched and beautifully illustrated study, one which concentrates on Morse's paintings but integrates into the analysis the artist's work with the telegraph. The author successfully demonstrates Morse's essential conservatism by placing him in his proper contexts: as a communitarian in an era of Jacksonian individualism; as an advocate of social welfare in an age of self-realization; and as a defender of institutions in the midst of widespread challenges to bureaucracy. In his achievements Morse emerges as a truly modern American, but in his underlying philosophy he seems to reach back to Puritanical ideals. Although this work is the best of its kind, it offers almost no information on Morse's life after the 1840s, when he began to turn away from a career in painting.

For those interested solely in Morse's contributions to the field of telegraphy, a highly readable and informative work is COE. This small volume offers a chapter on Morse and explains in easily understandable terms how the inventor developed his machine and his telegraphic code. The remainder of the work traces the legacy of the invention.

Strangely, there has been no study concentrating exclusively on Morse's political career. Although a somewhat outdated study of nativism, BILLINGTON is one of the few works on the subject that traces Morse's career as a disseminator of anti-Catholic works, and as a candidate of nativist political parties. Sadly, the explanation of Morse's specific motivations is thin – it is suggested that Morse was provoked to act when a member of the papal guard tipped his hat off.

MICHAEL VORENBERG

See also Nativism; Telegraph and Telephone

Mott, Lucretia 1793–1880
Abolitionist and campaigner for women's rights

Bacon, Margaret Hope, *Valiant Friend: The Life of Lucretia Mott*, New York: Walker, 1980

Cromwell, Otelia, *Lucretia Mott*, Cambridge, MA: Harvard University Press, 1958

Hallowell, Anna Davis (editor), *James and Lucretia Mott: Life and Letters*, Boston: Houghton Mifflin, 1884; reprinted, New York: Russell, 1971

Hare, Lloyd C.M., *The Greatest American Woman: Lucretia Mott*, New York: American Historical Society, 1937

Hersh, Blanche Glassman, *The Slavery of Sex: Feminist-Abolitionists in America*, Urbana: University of Illinois Press, 1978

Riegel, Robert E., *American Feminists*, Lawrence: University of Kansas Press, 1963

Tolles, Frederick B., "Lucretia Coffin Mott", in *Notable American Women, 1607–1950: A Biographical Dictionary*, edited by Edward T. James, Janet Wilson James, and Paul S. Boyer, Cambridge, MA: Belknap Press of Harvard University Press, 1971

Lucretia Mott attracted admiration in her lifetime because she was a happily married woman and devoted mother as well as a notable preacher and reformer, whose opposition to the slavery of African Americans was inextricably linked to her disgust with the slavery of sex. Mrs. Mott's portraits do justice to her beauty and frail physique; they, together with the tributes showered upon her in old age and posthumously, tend to obscure the real woman. She has not attracted numerous biographers, but we are at last in a position to see the human being as well as the noble example.

Like Elizabeth Cady Stanton, who became her protegée and friend, Mott experienced the common lot of women. Unlike Stanton, however, her reform interests did not clash with her domestic duties, and the large and loving memoir of Mott by her granddaughter, Anna HALLOWELL, has served her rather better than her children's tribute served Stanton. For one thing, it was possible to present the Motts – unlike the Stantons – as an ideal married couple, with complementary characteristics, playing conventional roles within the home and unconventional roles only in the wider world. Unlike the Stantons, who drifted apart and divided their offspring in the process, the Motts remained devoted; and one of the services James Mott rendered his wife was to travel with her on the journeys she undertook as a Quaker minister: one such taking her away for 70 days and 2400 miles, requiring her to speak at 71 meetings. The *Life and Letters* pays tribute to Lucretia Mott's energy and cheerfulness, her quick perceptions and impatience with delay, her keen "sense of the ludicrous" and her "unswerving conscientiousness". Nor was family pride so great that Hallowell could not acknowledge Mott's lack of imagination and appreciation for "discriminating praise".

The title of HARE's biography confirms how lavish was the praise that came Mott's way – so much so that she uncomfortably described herself as a "much over-valued woman". Providing a full chronological account of her life, though without index or other scholarly apparatus, Hare takes as his theme Mott's role as a "social pioneer" and draws fully (as do his successors) on the *Life and Letters*. His judgment that her interest in the women's cause probably never equalled her concern for antislavery would be contested now, but his judgment that her influence was "always for harmony, good will, and the broadest charity" has stood the test of time. This does not mean that Mott managed to avoid controversy in the two campaigns that concerned her most. Rather it is the case that her Quaker upbringing and sense of proportion made her more suitable for the position of stateswoman (as during the post-Civil War split in the suffrage ranks) than for that of agitator.

CROMWELL provides a comprehensive account of Mott's life, which makes effective use of surviving primary evidence, and is particularly helpful on her intellectual development. Her progress was marked from a young age, not just because of Mott's sharp mind and fine memory but also because of her upbringing in Nantucket, where women's roles were enhanced by the frequent absences of the seafaring men of that island community. As Cromwell sees it, we may take seriously Mott's claim that "women's rights was the most important question of my life from a very early day", though the significance of the 1840 World Anti-Slavery Convention in strengthening her convictions is not denied.

TOLLES reaffirms the importance of James Mott's role in making his wife respectable without diminishing his own reform credentials, and he points out that Mrs. Mott remained an activist until her death, working in her later years for freedmen's aid, the provision of higher education and the peace movement. But his most important conclusion is that she was crucial in carrying the Hicksite Friends towards theological liberalism: a remarkable feat in an era when women ministers were unwelcome in all the major sects.

The brief studies by HERSH and RIEGEL allow us to measure Mott against her contemporaries. Hersh traces the emergence of both Motts from reform backgrounds and notes Mrs. Mott's unusual sensitivity on class and race issues. Riegel is unpersuaded of the early emergence of her feminism while expressing gratitude for her avoidance of assertions about female superiority.

The most recent scholarly biography of Mott is BACON, which has the great merit of disposing of the Victorians' saccharine version of this Quaker radical. Mrs. Mott, she contends, was a woman of stubbornness, temper, vanity, undue seriousness about herself, and a sharp tongue that led her mother to bestow the nickname of Long Tongue. Making a case for Mott's feminism dating from at least the time when she was discriminated against as a teacher, Bacon gives due space to the many aspects of Mrs. Mott's reform career and to her resilience in the face of accusations that she substituted "good causes for true religion". We are also left with an impression of a woman whose rare courage on the public platform did not desert her in the face of bereavements, illness and the resistance of many of her loved ones to her various

causes: a woman who even mellowed with age sufficiently to take a medicinal drink and come to terms with music and dancing.

CHRISTINE BOLT

Movies *see* Film

Muckrakers

Chalmers, David M., *The Social and Political Ideas of the Muckrakers*, New York: Citadel Press, 1964
Filler, Louis, *Crusaders for American Liberalism*, New York: Harcourt Brace, 1939
Filler, Louis, *Appointment at Armageddon: Muckraking and Progressivism in the American Tradition*, Westport, CT: Greenwood Press, 1976
Harrison, John M. and Harry H. Stein, *Muckraking: Past, Present, and Future*, University Park: Pennsylvania State University Press, 1973
Miraldi, Robert, *Muckraking and Objectivity: Journalism's Colliding Traditions*, Westport, CT: Greenwood Press, 1990
Regier, Cornelius C., *The Era of the Muckrakers*, Chapel Hill: University of North Carolina Press, 1932
Wilson, Harold S., *McClure's Magazine and the Muckrakers*, Princeton: Princeton University Press, 1970

It was Theodore Roosevelt's reference to the "man with the muckrake" in a speech warning of the dangers of sensationalism which gave the muckrakers a name, that they converted from an insult into an accolade. REGIER was the first full-length historical study of the muckraking journalism of the first years of the 20th century. He explained it as a consequence of the association of two things: dissatisfaction with the immoralities and illegalities accompanying American industrialization and the appearance of the cheap, mass-circulation monthly magazine. Though there were precedents for the literature of exposure, Regier believed that the muckraking era proper started with articles by Lincoln Steffens on urban corruption and Ida M. Tarbell on the Standard Oil Company in *McClure's Magazine* in the fall of 1902. Such exposure articles proved very popular and, for almost a decade, readers of approximately a dozen magazines were presented with denunciations of American conduct and institutions. Ultimately, Regier maintained, muckraking declined because of its growing sensationalism, business pressures (including the withdrawal of advertising), the satiation of the public, and the perception that – some objectives having been achieved – it was now unnecessary. He believed, in the end, that muckraking was a fad which offered little in the way of fundamental analysis of, or prescription for, national problems.

FILLER (1939) took a more favorable view of the muckrakers than Regier. He discussed the links between muckraking and the achievement of certain specific reforms, including the Pure Food and Drug Act and the Meat Inspection Act, both of 1906. Muckrakers could, he contended, be proud of the part they had played in producing insurance reform. They had also supported local reformers and helped the movement for the direct election of United States senators. Filler saw muckraking as something that changed and evolved in the period after 1900–02 (the first muckraker, he argued, was not Steffens or Tarbell but Josiah Flynt, who introduced the word "graft" into the discourse of the time). David Graham Phillips's "The Treason of the Senate" series, published in 1906, marked the high-point of the initial phase of exposure. After 1906, according to Filler, muckraking's focus shifted from exposure to reform. New issues – women working in industry, child labor, saloons, prostitution, and race relations – increasingly came to dominate the movement. It reached another peak of activity around 1910, but then succumbed very quickly to a systematic conspiracy organized by corporate interests.

On the whole, FILLER (1976) took a more critical view than in his earlier work. Analyzing the relationship between muckraking and progressivism, he noted that muckraking did not always (as in the attack on child labor) produce effective reform. It was often sober and accurate in its style of reporting, but at times was more inclined toward sensationalism (although Filler defended Phillips's "Treason of the Senate" series as "fair and representative"). Whatever their opponents believed, the muckrakers were very far from united as a group in what they were doing.

Filler's later reflections drew attention to the issue of how much the muckrakers themselves shared in terms of ideas, mode of approach, and what they hoped to achieve. Both Chalmers and Wilson found considerable unity of style and purpose underlying the work of the muckrakers about whom they wrote. CHALMERS analyzed in a systematic way the work of thirteen writers whom he considered the "core" of the muckraking movement. These journalists saw businessmen as the main source of corruption in American life. They perceived the process of corruption itself as the result of a gap between the long-established customs and institutions of society and new economic developments. The thirteen muckrakers studied, therefore, were in broad agreement in their perception of what was wrong. They differed widely, however, in the solutions they suggested – from having businessmen themselves turn their hand to public affairs (George Kibbe Turner), through the enforcement of existing law such as the Sherman Act (Christopher Powell Connolly) or the demand for new laws to reinforce competition (Alfred Henry Lewis, Will Irwin, and Ida Tarbell), to calls for a more thoroughgoing social reconstruction on the part of those who either endorsed socialism (Upton Sinclair, Charles Edward Russell) or came very close to doing so (Ray Stannard Baker, Lincoln Steffens, and David Graham Phillips).

WILSON explored the relationship between *McClure's Magazine* and the muckraking movement. His book covered the life and career of Samuel S. McClure and the first, pre-muckraking years of the magazine. It also drew attention to the fact that – even during its muckraking years – *McClure's* continued to publish a good deal of fiction and articles of general interest. In the last five chapters of the book, however, Wilson examined the thought of the principal *McClure's* muckrakers. He found it more coherent than other historians had believed. In their ideas on the state, the structuring of power in politics, and business and its operations, together with their view of social ethics and behavior, he argued that they shared a collective outlook. In many ways, indeed, the most prominent *McClure's* muckrakers perceived themselves as successors of the abolitionists, comparing the antebellum fight against slavery with their own struggle against privilege and corruption.

HARRISON and STEIN is a collection of essays by a number of authors. It revealed that some muckraking authors who examined race relations contributed to the formation of the NAACP. In race relations as in attitudes toward the judicial system, however, the needs of magazines catering to a predominantly white middle-class readership limited both the extent of muckraking and its radicalism. While most of the essays in the book concentrated on early 20th century muckraking in the popular magazines, some also dealt with muckraking-style fiction and extended the time-scale to cover what appeared to be a revival of muckraking across a range of media in the late 1960s and early 1970s. Whereas early 20th century muckraking aimed to stimulate reform, contemporary muckraking – it was argued – often seemed more concerned with entertainment and escapism.

MIRALDI was also primarily a study of Progressive Era muckraking, but it included chapters on the 1959 attempt (by television and newspaper journalists) to publicize the plight of migrant farm workers, and the 1974 crusade of reporter John L. Hess to expose scandalous conditions in New York nursing homes. Confining his analysis of the muckraking movement of 1902–12 to exposures in the magazines, and excluding works of fiction, Miraldi maintained that differences among the muckrakers in matters of style and purpose could best be explained by developments within journalism itself, as what had been an occupation matured into a profession. An older tradition of partisan or reform journalism was in the process of giving place to a newer ideal of objective reporting. Miraldi challenged Filler's account of muckraking's downfall as simplistic. While conceding that business pressures had existed – many magazines had been taken over by corporations hostile to muckraking and some advertisers had applied pressure of an economic type – there had been no actual conspiracy. A range of other factors – waning public interest, the more critical climate of opinion after Roosevelt's "man with the muckrake" speech, tougher libel laws, the emergence of a new profession of corporate public relations able to take the sting out of muckraking attacks, even the loss of motivation by many muckrakers themselves – all contributed to the movement's demise.

MELVYN STOKES

See also Newspapers and Magazines; Progressivism

Muir, John   1838–1914
Conservationist and naturalist

Cohen, Michael P., *The Pathless Way: John Muir and the American Wilderness*, Madison: University of Wisconsin Press, 1984

Fox, Stephen R., *John Muir and His Legacy: The American Conservation Movement*, Boston: Little Brown, 1981; as *The American Conservation Movement: John Muir and His Legacy*, Madison: University of Wisconsin Press, 1985

Miller, Sally M. (editor), *John Muir: Life and Work*, Albuquerque: University of New Mexico Press, 1993

Nash, Roderick, *Wilderness and the American Mind*, New Haven: Yale University Press, 1967, 3rd edition, 1982

Oelschlaeger, Max, *The Idea of Wilderness: From Prehistory to the Age of Ecology*, New Haven: Yale University Press, 1991

Turner, Frederick, *Rediscovering America: John Muir in His Time and Ours*, New York: Viking, 1985

Wolfe, Linnie Marsh, *Son of the Wilderness: The Life of John Muir*, New York: Knopf, 1945

Worster, Donald, *The Wealth of Nature: Environmental History and the Ecological Imagination*, New York: Oxford University Press, 1993

Of all American conservationists of the past, John Muir has attracted the most public and scholarly attention. Almost seventy books and articles were written about him between 1979 and 1990. Most of his writings – including unpublished journals – have been reprinted over the past twenty years and his personal papers are available as a major microfilm collection. In 1980, the California Historical Society voted him the greatest figure in the state's history.

Between Muir's death and the opening of his personal papers in the 1970s at the University of the Pacific's Holt-Atherton Library (Stockton, California), a number of biographies appeared, ranging within a narrow spectrum from the sympathetic to the reverential. Beyond the details of his life and personality, these studies focused on literary and scientific accomplishments and his influential role in conservation politics as champion of the national parks. WOLFE's Pulitzer prize-winning "official" biography was undertaken at the request of Muir's elder daughter. Wolfe was his literary executor and had previously edited many of his unpublished writings. It remains of enduring value not least due to the painstaking nature of her research, especially among those who knew Muir. His children apparently wanted their father to be presented in human terms as opposed to the saintly icon of previous narratives, and Wolfe (personally unacquainted with Muir) devoted much attention to his relations with family and friends. Her preface reports her failure to unearth anything damaging to Muir's reputation. As Muir left no proper autobiography, all subsequent Muir scholars acknowledge Wolfe's achievement in fashioning an ordered narrative out of his life's raw materials. Her work remains the definitive study of Muir's life. Later studies have added little in this respect. Instead, recent books broach matters hitherto largely unexplored, notably the larger significance of Muir's ideological legacy and his relevance to the concerns of contemporary environmentalism. As such, they not only underscore but amplify Muir's status in the pantheon of American conservationist "greats."

The cluster of biographies published since his papers became available – they were locked away after Wolfe finished her study – are markedly different both from each other and the older studies, but all are the work of avowed environmentalists. FOX functions as interpretative biography and history of the nature preservationist wing of conservation since Muir. As Muir's achievements are undisputed to date, debate revolves around the nature of his ideas. Whereas earlier biographers such as Wolfe did not question Muir's Christianity, Fox suggests that his intellectual progress toward a less anthropocentric view of the world involved a rejection of his religious heritage. Another of Fox's major claims is that Muir supplied the ideological impetus for an anti-modern "radical amateur tradition" of holistic conservation as distinct from the professional utilitarian tradition of the "resource" conservation establishment associated with Muir's contemporary and sometime rival, Gifford Pinchot.

COHEN (who has since written a history of the Sierra Club that Muir founded) is interested in reconstructing Muir's "spiritual journey" rather than writing another biography. In fact, this worshipful book is as much about Cohen's own spiritual journey (and that of what he calls "my generation"). The musings of the author (as avid a Sierran mountaineer as Muir) threaten to obliterate the ostensible subject and this study is not recommended for the Muir novice. On the subject of Muir's spirituality, Cohen goes further than Fox, casting him rather fancifully as a Western Taoist or Buddhist.

TURNER explains that he has written an intuitive biography which attributes to Muir "certain perceptions for which there is no documentary proof." For the gaps in the record, Turner substitutes his own imagination, views and experience of the places that featured in Muir's life. Nevertheless, Turner has carried out the most extensive research of the three new biographers discussed here and provides much firmer historical context and useful orientation than Cohen, with whom he takes issue on a few minor points but mostly ignores.

In his seminal study of American relationships with wilderness, NASH allocated a chapter to Muir, presenting him primarily as an effective publicist of transcendentalist ideas of nature associated with Emerson and Thoreau. By contrast, Cohen and Turner identify an avant garde "biocentric egalitarian" character in Muir's creed which, they assert, anticipated "deep ecology" with its emphasis on the intrinsic value and rights of non-human forms of nature. OELSCHLAEGER is a philosopher, and in the course of a far reaching (but essentially American) study of philosophical attitudes to wilderness offers perhaps the strongest and most ahistoricist endorsement of Muir as an original and anti-Christian thinker. Not content to see occasional or half-formed glimmers of modern environmental ethics in his thought, Oelschlaeger's chapter on Muir argues unhesitatingly for recognition of Muir's affinity with paganism, pantheism, "archaic peoples" and "the Paleolithic mind." While concurring with much of Fox's thrust concerning Muir's place in conservation history, Oelschlaeger diverges in casting Muir as a "constructive" postmodern rather than a "destructive" anti-modern – the former assessment being of far more utility (in Oelschlaeger's mind) as a path forward in human relations with the rest of nature.

The extent to which Muir's nature worship and aesthetic sensibility were rooted in Christianity as opposed to an acquired orientalism remains a live issue. WORSTER seizes on Muir as part of an imaginative attempt to identify a radical Protestant tradition within the history of American environmentalism. There are a number of important essays on this and other aspects of Muir in MILLER. Essays by Mark Stoll and Dennis Williams also re-emphasize his Christianity, however unconventional its content, and stress (as Turner did) how unacquainted Muir was with oriental thinking. Limbaugh argues that biblical stewardship theory most strongly influenced

Muir's relationship with nature. He is more persuasive than many recent commentators in that he locates Muir squarely within his times, preferring to approach him as a transitional figure between appreciation of wild nature for its aesthetic, spiritual and recreational value, and the emergence of a more modern perspective informed by scientific ecology and notions of the "rights of nature." Limbaugh, the director of the John Muir Center for Regional Studies at the University of the Pacific, casts Muir as a "weak" anthropocentrist rather than a fully-fledged biocentrist.

PETER A. COATES

See also Conservation; National Parks; Nature

Mumford, Lewis 1895–1990
City planner, and social and cultural critic

Carrithers, Gale, Jr., *Mumford, Tate, and Eiseley: Watchers in the Night*, Baton Rouge: Louisiana State University Press, 1991

Fried, Lewis F., *Makers of the City*, Amherst: University of Massachusetts Press, 1990

Goist, Park Dixon, *From Main Street to State Street: Town, City, and Community in America*, Port Washington, NY: Kennikat Press, 1977

Hughes, Thomas P. and Agatha C. Hughes (editors), *Lewis Mumford: A Public Intellectual*, New York: Oxford University Press, 1990

Krueckeberg, Donald A. (editor), *The American Planner*, New York: Methuen, 1983

Miller, Donald L., *Lewis Mumford: A Life*, New York: Weidenfeld and Nicolson, 1989

Novak, Frank G., *The Autobiographical Writings of Lewis Mumford: A Study in Literary Audacity*, Honolulu: University of Hawaii Press, 1988

Lewis Mumford belonged to a rare and declining species in 20th-century America: the public intellectual. He wrote on a staggering variety of topics, from American literature, to urban planning and the history of cities, to the history of technology and its influence on culture. Mumford, who lived midway into his tenth decade, published thirty books and thousands of essays. His longevity and prodigious output may have dissuaded, or at least delayed, full-scale considerations of his life and work – but no longer.

The first book-length biography of Mumford appeared shortly before his death. MILLER offers a detailed account of Mumford's personal and professional life. At its best the biography, which makes extensive use of Mumford's personal and private papers, provides clear synopses of Mumford's major work and informative sketches of members of his circle. The book, somewhat like its subject, is a loose, sprawling work, stretching to almost 600 pages. Mumford himself, however, often remains elusive despite the detail. Miller fails to capture his subject's essence. Mumford, the author concludes, remained something of a mystery even to his closest friends. Miller also equivocates about Mumford's lasting influence on American thought or culture.

In contrast, NOVAK discards any doubt about Mumford's place among 20th-century thinkers. In this brief survey of Mumford's three autobiographical works, Novak calls Mumford a major intellectual figure of the era. The book, often fawning and uncritical, highlights the consistency of Mumford's thinking (such as his themes of the organic unity of life and his faith in man's potential) as well as the evolution of his career. While Mumford's early writings included general considerations of American culture, his later works addressed broader global problems (such as the destructiveness of nuclear weapons).

CARRITHERS also considers Mumford a civic moralist. She, like Miller and Novak, finds him out of step with his times. This is a literary analysis of Mumford's major writings, in particular his four-volume "Renewal of Life" series (1934–51), *The City in History*, and the two-volume *The Myth of the Machine* (1967, 1971). It is part of a larger study of the rhetorical style of Mumford, Loren Eiseley, and Allen Tate. Carrithers considers all three writers, who partly embraced and partly shunned American culture, as practitioners of the prophetic essay. She seeks to illuminate the philosophical roots, assumptions and deeper meanings in Mumford's work. The dense prose, laced with the jargon of literary criticism, however, makes demanding reading. Carrithers focuses more on the presentation of ideas than the significance or impact of the ideas themselves.

Mumford's influence is clearer in the field of urban planning. He was a staunch advocate of regional planning and helped to form the influential Regional Planning Association of America in the 1920s. This did not reflect, according to GOIST, a nostalgia for small towns or anti-urban sentiment. Rather, Mumford, who lived his first forty years in New York City, thought planning could disperse and protect the benefits of urban life. His views on planning matched his thoughts on the subject of technology. Massive cities, like the mega-machines of the day, he feared, represented a dangerous abandonment of limitations in modern society. Goist provides a concise, readable summary of Mumford's ideas about the changing meanings of community in the first half of the 20th century.

Goist develops the broad themes of Mumford's thought more fully in KRUECKEBERG, a collection of short biographies of the leading figures in American planning in the first half of the 20th-century. The essay's title, "Seeing Things Whole," aptly summarizes Mumford's beliefs. Goist emphasizes his distrust of specialization, his search for holistic solutions, and his goals of renewal and balance in American culture. Again Goist emphasizes the interrelatedness of Mumford's thinking regarding planning and the effects of technology. He concludes that Mumford's thinking remained remarkably consistent from the 1920s until his death.

FRIED also demonstrates the connectedness of Mumford's ideas about cities and technology. In this study of four intellectuals who focused on the city as a cultural center, Fried, unlike Goist, detects a mid-life shift in Mumford's thinking. Totalitarianism, World War II, nuclear weapons, and McCarthyism, all helped to darken Mumford's perceptions about the past, and intensified his concern for the present and future. He even developed an ambivalence toward planning, although he remained committed to the idea that it represented the best way for culture to avoid being trampled by technology. Fried centers on the broad sweep of Mumford's thinking, comparing Mumford to Oswald Spengler as a historian of civilizations.

Historians of science and technology also see shifts in Mumford's outlook. The essays in HUGHES loosely conform to the three periods of Mumford's life identified by the editors. A sense of hope filled Mumford's work in the 1920s; creeping doubts appeared in the 1930s; despair marked the postwar years. The volume collects papers from a Lewis Mumford conference held at the University of Pennsylvania, which houses the Mumford Papers. The essays are of uneven quality, but they emphasize Mumford's astonishing range. Topics include Mumford's conceptions of regionalism, his views on how culture influences technology, his relationship to such diverse intellectuals as Howard Odum, Reinhold Niebuhr, and John Dewey, his architectural criticism, and his influence on modern sociology, among others.

Taken together the essays in Hughes highlight Mumford's role as a public intellectual. In exploring the breadth of his thinking and influences, the collection implies Mumford's central position in 20th-century intellectual life. Indeed, the editor claims that Mumford's rejection of liberalism and pragmatism foreshadowed the American shift away from optimism in the face of social evil in the 1940s and after. The recent burst of academic activity suggests continuing retrospectives about Mumford's life and influence. The Mumford canon should expand. The irony is rich, for Mumford himself derided the Ph.D., and spurned full-time academic appointments.

CHRISTOPHER MACGREGOR SCRIBNER

See also Technology and Invention; Urban History entries

Municipal Government: Corruption and Reform, 1865–1917

Allswang, John M., *Bosses, Machines, and Urban Voters: An American Symbiosis*, Port Washington, NY: Kennikat Press, 1977; revised, Baltimore: Johns Hopkins University Press, 1986

Callow, Alexander B., Jr., *The Tweed Ring*, New York: Oxford University Press, 1966

Holli, Melvin G., *Reform in Detroit: Hazen S. Pingree and Urban Politics*, New York: Oxford University Press, 1969

Miller, Zane L., *Boss Cox's Cincinnati: Urban Politics in the Progressive Era*, New York: Oxford University Press, 1968

Schiesl, Martin J., *The Politics of Efficiency: Municipal Administration and Reform in America, 1880–1920*, Berkeley: University of California Press, 1977

Teaford, Jon C., *The Unheralded Triumph: City Government in America, 1870–1900*, Baltimore: Johns Hopkins University Press, 1984

Traditional accounts viewed the clash between bossism and reform as a moral battle ranging the forces of corruption against the crusaders for good government. In a number of works published in the 1960s and 1970s, urban historians shifted the focus of study away from this moral clash and instead considered the causes of boss rule and the functions of the urban political machine.

For example, CALLOW offers a highly readable account of the most notorious of 19th-century political gangs, New York City's Tweed Ring. Examining its rise and fall, he draws a graphic portrait of William Marcy Tweed and his colleagues in corruption, presenting an enjoyable account of their various misdeeds and misadventures. Though his study is stronger on narrative than analysis, Callow does argue that the fragmented formal governing structure of New York City was conducive to the rise of a political machine which could profit from the prevailing disarray. As no single public official held sway over the destinies of the city, a party leader like Tweed could step in and benefit from the void in the power structure. Moreover, Callow claims that the Tweed Ring served the needs of the city's large immigrant population. Callow remains the standard work on the Tweed Ring, though it lacks the critical insight of some later studies of urban political machines.

ALLSWANG examines urban bosses from the 1860s to the second half of the 20th century. Among the political leaders discussed are two from the 19th and early 20th centuries, Boss Tweed and Charles Murphy, both chieftains of New York City's Tammany organization. Allswang discusses the electoral base of Tammany and uses statistical analysis to identify the social and economic status of those who voted for the political machine. He confirms the previously-held impression that the immigrant and working-class voters kept Tammany in power. According to Allswang, Tammany served the cultural and economic needs of the foreign born and less affluent, and they responded with loyal support at the polls. Relatively brief but packed with information and insight, Allswang's book offers a fine synthesis for anyone seeking an introduction to urban bossism in the United States.

MILLER presents a case study of Cincinnati and local "boss" George B. Cox. According to Miller, the distinction between boss and reformer was not so clear as previously assumed. Cox rose to power with the support of upper-middle-class leaders who lived on the periphery of the city and who sought to improve municipal rule. He also satisfied many of their demands, professionalizing the police, maintaining low taxes, and centralizing authority in the executive branch. Gradually, however, the base for Cox's political organization shifted from the middle-class periphery to the working-class core neighborhoods. Moreover, in middle-class minds, Cox came to represent the sickness of corruption rather than the cure of reform. In his detailed study, Miller thus charts the changing pattern of Cincinnati's government and politics from the 1880s through the first decade of the 20th century. Yet this work is basically an exercise in local history and not as illuminating about the general pattern of American city politics as some other studies.

HOLLI presents one of the most insightful accounts of reform in city government. Focusing on Detroit's Mayor Hazen Pingree, he shows how even a reformer might mobilize working-class followers, using some of the very techniques often associated with corrupt machines. Holli also distinguishes between structural reformers and social reformers. Structural reformers sought to ensure honest government through tinkering with the municipal charter or appointing "good" men to public positions. Social reformers endeavored to redistribute economic and political power in the city through municipal ownership of public utilities and other reforms aimed at improving the lot of the working class. Pingree began his career as a structural reformer but as mayor became a notable social reformer. Holli's classification of the two types of municipal reformers has been adopted by other scholars, and has definitely influenced the study of Progressive-era reform. Holli offers the best case study of a reform mayor, and this book deserves the attention of all students of the American city.

SCHIESL focuses on the structural reformers of the Progressive-era and their struggle to ensure efficient municipal administration. Unlike most other historians, Schiesl admirably chooses to study the efficiency movement nationwide rather than offering a case study of a single municipality. This is, then, an ambitious work which surveys efforts throughout America to rationalize public finances, strengthen the municipal executive, and create a professional city bureaucracy. Though not as engaging or readable as some of the studies of the corrupt scoundrels populating city hall, Schiesl's rather colorless survey of Progressive-era devotees of efficiency merits the attention of serious scholars.

TEAFORD offers an alternative to the traditional preoccupation with bosses and reformers. His study argues that late 19th century city government should not be viewed as simply a dichotomous battle between reform and the machine. Instead, it was a complex interplay of actors and interests. Professional experts in park design, library administration, water supply, and fire protection emerged during the late 19th century, and they had limited tolerance for interference from any elected official, no matter whether reformer or boss. Moreover, despite all the complaints about corruption, city governments accomplished a great deal, laying miles of sewers, paving hundreds of boulevards, and planning thousands of acres of parkland. And following the economic depression of the 1870s, American municipalities were models of fiscal conservatism rather than shameful spectacles of irresponsible profligacy. The long-standing emphasis on the political rhetoric of bossism and reform has distracted attention from the actual operations of urban government and the accomplishments of American municipal leaders. Just as the history of the Old West is not simply a tale of cowboys and Indians, so American city government of the late 19th century is not merely a story of bosses and reformers.

JON C. TEAFORD

See also Gilded Age and Progressive Era; Urban History entries

N

Nation, Carry 1846–1911

Temperance campaigner

Asbury, Herbert, *Carry Nation*, New York: Knopf, 1929

Bader, Robert Smith, *Prohibition in Kansas: A History*, Lawrence: University Press of Kansas, 1986

Blocker, Jack S., Jr., *Retreat from Reform: The Prohibition Movement in the United States, 1890–1913*, Westport, CT: Greenwood Press, 1976

Clark, Norman H., *Deliver Us from Evil: An Interpretation of American Prohibition*, New York: Norton, 1976

Sinclair, Andrew, *Prohibition: The Era of Excess*, London: Faber, and Boston: Little Brown, 1962; as *Era of Excess: A Social History of the Prohibition Movement*, New York: Harper, 1964

Taylor, Robert L., *Vessel of Wrath: The Life and Times of Carry Nation*, New York: New American Library, 1966

Carry Nation was a remarkable phenomenon. After passing her first fifty years in decent obscurity, she began her anti-saloon crusade in the Women's Christian Temperance Union (WCTU) in Medicine Lodge, Kansas, and rapidly moved through a series of state, national and international sensations from 1900 to her death in 1911. Her demolitions of illegal bars were extraordinary and newsworthy events – her "hatchetation" regularly made the headlines. To some, she seemed a ludicrous fanatic; to others, an astonishingly resilient woman in a male-dominated world. A one-woman course in self-assertion, she could be as self-righteous, outrageous and unctuous as any man.

There are few works devoted specifically to Nation, but she figures prominently in various studies of the temperance movement. Biographers and historians have not been kind to Nation, and have often dismissed her as a crank, lunatic, clown or bigot. Two amusingly scathing accounts represent the views of sophisticated East Coast or European authors, indulging their disdain for a stereotypical midwesterner from Populist Kansas. Nation offered an easy means of discrediting all temperance advocates. SINCLAIR's witty account of the prohibition era uses the evidence of Nation's own autobiography to show that nine of her family were mentally disturbed, and that her mother and her only child died in asylums. But recent studies suggest that frontier women were often deeply disturbed. ASBURY is a highly entertaining but destructive account. In his knockabout book, Nation emerges as a deranged figure of fun – a fanatical, deluded, obsessive woman. His interpretation combines popular Freudianism, a distaste for Methodism and a mixture of condescension and contempt for the earnest hypocrisy of prohibition. For Asbury, Puritanism threatened to destroy American life.

In these studies, a somewhat unhappy woman rages against a male-dominated world. Driven by megalomania, she listens as God speaks directly to her. In a difficult childhood, she moved from Kentucky to Missouri, Texas and finally to Kansas. She moved, too, from one religious commitment to another – Baptist, Campbellite, spiritualist, Methodist, and, finally, no formal church membership. Her two marriages were unfortunate. Her first husband died an alcoholic within a year of marriage; the second divorced her during her "smashing" campaign. Her campaigns deteriorated from drives against illegal saloons to bizarre visits to Ivy League schools, and appearances in music halls, and an eventful tour of Britain. She is depicted as a liability to her cause.

TAYLOR is another entertaining but unsympathetic account, written against the background of the laid-back mood of the permissive mid-1960s. He scoffs at Nation's moral pretensions and finds her arrogant certainty disconcerting. The Kansas of Wyatt Earp, Billy the Kid and "Sockless" Jerry Simpson was an appropriate setting for her. After an inadequate father and two inadequate husbands, she used her anti-alcohol, anti-tobacco and anti-pornography campaigns as a means of disciplining men. Her public correction of her preacher second husband in church was but one extreme manifestation of this approach. In Taylor's view, Nation lived a fantasy life, fed by family delusions, romantic novels and her divine visions, and thus found compensation for the harshness of the real world in which she lived.

In modern reassessments of the WCTU, the organisational skills of Emma Willard are commonly seen as more significant than Carry Nation's direct action. BLOCKER does stress the positive aspects of temperance reform – and, whatever her problems and shortcomings, Nation always sympathised with the poor, and with Catholics, Jews and African Americans. She did not share contemporary nativist prejudices. In his fine study, CLARK presses this same point, and takes a rather more generous view of Nation's role. Her concern for respectability and decency persuaded thousands to join her attacks on saloons. In Winfield, Kansas, some 2,000 men brought out 500 rifles and two cannon to defend anti-saloon churches. Despite being kicked, whipped and beaten almost to death, she persisted in her crusade. In this interpretation, she appears as more a tragic than a comic character, dedicated to her cause almost to the point of obsession.

In more recent studies, her influence at state level has been recognised, and BADER shows her remarkable influence in Kansas. If she was a poor organiser and a difficult associate, she still had local achievements to her credit, including a refuge for women, and a proposed college for women, run by women. She mobilised respectable, educated temperance men, most of them Republicans, and embarrassed them into taking direct action. Legislation followed her visit to the statehouse, and a reluctant national WCTU supported her. In Oklahoma, effective organisation for prohibition and for woman suffrage followed her visit.

As Bader shows, she clearly had a considerable impact on many women in Kansas, but most feminist historians have neglected her. She does not fit comfortably into contemporary agendas, but, like William Lloyd Garrison in the abolitionist movement, she would not, and could not, be ignored. An assertive woman in a male-dominated world, she adopted an exaggerated aggression which mirrored the behaviour of male society. Her attacks on pornography offer parallels with modern feminists, and her outspoken attacks on tobacco – a neglected aspect of progressive reform – have many modern parallels. She inspired a number of midwestern imitators, and she appealed to a radical strain that ran through midwestern populism to socialism: the enslavement and manipulation of man by irresponsible forces. Her unorthodox methods make a balanced assessment difficult; her whirlwind style was both an asset and a liability. Her wider impact on the prohibition movement, and on the eventual passage of the Eighteenth Amendment, cannot easily be measured, but was probably quite limited.

BERNARD ASPINWALL

See also Prohibition; Temperance

National Association for the Advancement of Colored People

Cortner, Richard C., *A Mob Intent on Death: The NAACP and the Arkansas Riot Cases*, Middletown, CT: Wesleyan University Press, 1988

Fairclough, Adam, *Race and Democracy: The Civil Rights Struggle in Louisiana, 1915–1972*, Athens: University of Georgia Press, 1995

Hine, Darlene Clark, *Black Victory: The Rise and Fall of the White Primary in Texas*, Millwood, NY: KTO Press, 1979

Kellogg, Charles Flint, *NAACP: A History of the National Association for the Advancement of Colored People*, volume 1: *1909–1920*, Baltimore: Johns Hopkins Press, 1967

Kluger, Richard, *Simple Justice: The History of Brown v. Board of Education and Black America's Struggle for Equality*, New York: Knopf, 1975; London: Deutsch, 1977

Lawson, Steven F., *Black Ballots: Voting Rights in the South, 1944–1969*, New York: Columbia University Press, 1976

Tushnet, Mark V., *The NAACP's Legal Strategy Against Segregated Education, 1925–1950*, Chapel Hill: University of North Carolina Press, 1987

Tushnet, Mark V., *Making Civil Rights Law: Thurgood Marshall and the Supreme Court, 1936–1961*, New York: Oxford University Press, 1994

Zangrando, Robert L., *The NAACP Crusade Against Lynching, 1909–1950*, Philadelphia: Temple University Press, 1980

In spite of its importance in the African American struggle for civil rights the National Association for the Advancement of Colored People (NAACP) still lacks a comprehensive overview. Although KELLOGG appears to offer an all-encompassing study, this is in fact misleading, not least because the promised second volume failed to appear. The first volume is in many ways a maverick text that contains a large amount of straightforward factual material about the NAACP from 1909 to 1920 but is lacking in rigorous analysis. By today's standards it appears very dated, and retains value more as a reference tool than as a source of illuminating in-depth insights on the subject.

Most studies of the NAACP focus on three main aspects of its work. A first area of interest has been the organization's campaigns against lynching and mob violence. ZANGRANDO studies this important field of early NAACP activity by focusing on three periods running from 1918 to 1923, 1934 to 1940, and 1946 to 1950. He argues that although the NAACP did not succeed in overcoming obstacles to get an anti-lynching bill through Congress during these campaigns, it did raise public awareness of the horrors of lynching, and thus contributed significantly to its demise in the first half of the 20th century.

CORTNER provides a detailed example of the kind of case which the NAACP dealt with in their early years. He examines the events leading up to the United States Supreme Court landmark ruling in *Moore* v. *Dempsey* (1923) which freed twelve African American prisoners handed the death sentence for their alleged part in a race riot at Elaine, Arkansas, in 1919, on the grounds that they had been convicted at a mob-dominated trial. Cortner foregrounds the importance of co-operation and co-ordination between local lawyers and national officials of the NAACP in winning one of their first major victories in the courts.

A second area of interest has been the NAACP's role in the struggle for voting rights. On the face of it, LAWSON might seem to have little direct connection with the NAACP. However, as he traces the struggle for African American participation in electoral politics in the South from *Smith* v. *Allwright* (1944) to the years following the Voting Rights Act (1965), it soon becomes clear that the NAACP had an integral part to play in that battle. Lawson demonstrates that through lobbying, voter registration drives, and litigation in the courts, at both local and national level, the NAACP played a pivotal role in gaining African American suffrage rights.

HINE concentrates exclusively on events leading to the landmark *Smith* v. *Allwright* case, in which the United States Supreme Court decreed that the use of the all-white Democratic party primaries – which had effectively disfranchised the African American population in a number of southern states – was unconstitutional. In an insightful account of early voting rights struggles, Hine traces *Smith* v. *Allwright* through a series of litigative triumphs, starting with the first challenge to the all-white primary in *Nixon* v. *Herndon* (1927). Throughout there is a strong emphasis on interaction between local people and national figures in the NAACP.

A third area of interest has been the NAACP's role in the battle for equal educational opportunities for African Americans. KLUGER provides a monumental account of the key United States Supreme Court decision in *Brown* v. *Board of Education* (1954). *Brown* overturned the earlier *Plessy* v. *Ferguson* (1896) which had ruled that "separate" facilities in the South could be provided for the races, so long as they were of an "equal" standard. Kluger places *Brown* in the context of an ongoing African American struggle for equality, looks in detail at the issues surrounding the case, and, finally, examines the implications and consequences of the Supreme Court decision.

In the first of two excellent works on the NAACP's fight for equal educational opportunities, TUSHNET (1987) looks in greater detail at the quarter century leading up to the decision to pursue the *Brown* case, from 1925 to 1950. He analyzes the planning and funding of a sustained attack on segregation in education during these years. Throughout, a central contention is that the consummate political skills and legal acumen of leading figures in the NAACP, such as Walter White, Charles Hamilton, and Thurgood Marshall, played an important role in the flexibility and creativity of legal tactics pursued, which brought about its tremendous successes. TUSHNET (1994) builds upon his earlier work, but this time with a different emphasis. At the center of this study is Thurgood Marshall, a chief architect of NAACP legal strategy, and his career in the NAACP Legal and Defense Fund from 1936 to 1961. This is not a straightforward biography, but rather, Marshall's work is placed within the context of a range of NAACP legal activities, mostly but not exclusively concerned with education, in what proved to be the halcyon days of the organization.

Most of these studies focus upon rulings of national importance, although, to varying degrees, they establish links with the local activism of the NAACP. In an examination of the NAACP within the context of the unfolding civil rights struggle in Louisiana, FAIRCLOUGH shifts the primary focus to a local level and provides the first sustained analysis of the organisation in one particular state. He indicates that the local NAACP formed the backbone of the civil rights movement there. He also paves the way for future scholarship to concentrate more intently on the work of the indigenous membership at town, city and state level, and on their relationship with, and attitudes toward, the national organization.

JOHN A. KIRK

See also Civil Rights Movement

National Guard *see* Militia/National Guard

National Parks

Albright, Horace M. (as told to Robert Cahn), *The Birth of the National Park Service: The Founding Years, 1913–33*, Salt Lake City: Howe, 1985

Bartlett, Richard A., *Yellowstone: A Wilderness Besieged*, Tucson: University of Arizona Press, 1985

Everhart, William C., *The National Park Service*, Boulder, CO: Westview Press, 1983

Foresta, Ronald A., *America's National Parks and their Keepers*, Washington, DC: Resources for the Future, 1984

Freemuth, John C., *Islands under Siege: National Parks and the Politics of External Threats*, Lawrence: University Press of Kansas, 1991

Ise, John, *Our National Park Policy: A Critical History*, Baltimore: Johns Hopkins Press, 1961

Runte, Alfred, *National Parks: The American Experience*, Lincoln: University of Nebraska Press, 1979, 2nd edition, 1987

Runte, Alfred, *Yosemite: The Embattled Wilderness*, Lincoln: University of Nebraska Press, 1990

Sax, Joseph L., *Mountains Without Handrails: Reflections on the National Parks*, Ann Arbor: University of Michigan Press, 1980

Swain, Donald C., *Wilderness Defender: Horace M. Albright and Conservation*, Chicago: University of Chicago Press, 1970

The high profile of national parks in the history of conservation in the U.S. and their special status in the nation's culture have been expressed through numerous studies of individual parks and a handful of biographies of influential directors of the National Park Service. But the former, with a few notable exceptions, are parochial, preoccupied with origins, and reveal little of the wider historical context, while the latter tell us more about people than parks. The first substantial overview was ISE, written under the auspices of Resources for the Future by an "active lover of the parks." It served as the basic reference for almost two decades, and remains unsurpassed for sheer weight of detail. The major portion of this massive tome is organized around the highlights of the seven park service administrations between 1916 and 1959. It concludes with a more thematic treatment of "special park problems" such as wildlife and concessionaires, which will form the most interesting part of the book for many readers today.

Studies prior to RUNTE (1979, 1987) – exemplified by Ise – dealt mostly with legislative and adminstrative affairs. Moreover, they were long on narrative and description and short on interpretation. In addition, they usually reflected unquestioning pride in a noble and altruistic American contribution to nature preservation and world civilization (though Ise is more critical than Runte allows). By contrast, Runte is interested in cultural and intellectual history and a more rigorous analysis of the values and motivations of those involved. Unearthing the more "negative" features of park history, he redirects discussion into fresh channels, such as the role of cultural nationalism in the founding of early parks.

Runte also stresses how nature preservation was compromised by economic considerations, and a "monumentalist" obsession with protecting scenic wonders. His so-called "worthless lands" thesis – that only territory unpromising from the standpoint of natural resource development was considered for park status – is extended to cover the Alaskan additions to the park system (1980) in the second edition. Though challenged by some in the specialist journals, this thesis has become the prevailing consensus.

Among studies of prominent park service officials, SWAIN covers the administration of the first director, Stephen Mather, as well as that of his successor, Horace Albright. Together with ALBRIGHT/CAHN, this provides a detailed narrative of the first twenty years of the service and the major controversies affecting the system, notably those concerning Jackson Hole (Grand Tetons) and Hetch Hetchy Valley (Yosemite).

Some of the problems afflicting the national parks today – chiefly over use and over commercialization – were evident when Ise was writing and received his attention. As such pressures have grown over the past thirty years and fresh challenges have appeared, the literature has shifted away from the formative era of the late 19th and early 20th centuries toward modern dilemmas. A staple theme is the conflict between the historically dominant anthropocentric management philosophy and a more radical biocentric approach. Published to coincide with Yosemite's centennial, RUNTE (1990) is a savage yet historically scrupulous and eloquent attack on management priorities since the original Yosemite grant of 1864. Runte does not hide his sympathies, and the heroes of his account are the dissenting voices of natural scientists who advocated putting earth first.

SAX is a trenchant attack on park management from the standpoint of the wilderness preservationist. Parks, according to Sax (a legal scholar), are special, undeveloped places where most modern, motorized recreational activities have no legitimate place: the book's title is a succinct statement of its purist case. Focusing on the post-1945 period, Sax urges a fundamental reorientation of park priorities, closing with "A policy statement: the meaning of national parks today," in which he argues that the park service has a missionary role: to cultivate a taste for "contemplative" recreation. Biocentric arguments receive no attention and Sax is critical of a park defence based on ecological grounds.

The main object of attention in FORESTA is "their keepers" – the National Park Service itself – rather than the parks it administers. Foresta, a geographer, traces the growing pains of the service and its system, examines the external pressures and larger economic, political, governmental and social world within which it operates, and looks at the conflicting demands made upon it. In doing so, he poses hard questions about the purpose, mission and functions of the service and its parks. Based on extensive interviews, this is the most comprehensive treatment of recent park problems – the period after 1960 receiving the bulk of attention. The nature parks of the trans-Mississippi West, understandably, have attracted far greater scholarly attention than the urban and battlefield parks, historic sites and recreation areas more recently added to the system. Foresta is distinctive in giving these newer units their due. His study is also noteworthy for discussing the emerging threats to the parks from beyond their boundaries.

Foresta is more in sympathy than Runte or Sax with the service's efforts to grapple with shifting and intensifying problems and competing constituencies. Sax and Foresta both place human interests first, though Foresta champions the mass of recreationists not the wilderness seekers, arguing for a return to the view that parks are for people – even motorized people. EVERHART is an insider's account (he worked for the park service for more than 25 years) that covers much of the same terrain as Foresta, if less rigorously. It contains a useful chapter on the problems posed by the new Alaskan parks, and is especially strong on the threat of politicization.

BARTLETT examines how the first American national park has fared since 1872 in an ever more complex world. In prose prone to quaintness, he chronicles the threats posed at various times by poachers, irrigationists, railroads, energy developers, visitors and the park service itself. Grounded in massive archival research, the bulk of the book concerns the visitor, revolving around expectations and impact. Only a third deals with the period since 1916 and by far the shortest section engages with post-1945 issues (the author declares his reluctance to advance too close toward the present). Bartlett's is the most patriotic and populist of recent studies, and certainly the most tolerant of past errors and mistakes, as well as the most sanguine about the future.

He identified geothermal developments just outside Yellowstone as one of the most pressing modern problems, and Foresta, as noted, gave external threats a chapter. But FREEMUTH is a direct, if selective discussion of what are increasingly identified as the critical challenges to the parks' integrity today. Freemuth (a natural resources policy specialist and sometime park ranger) first supplies a historical perspective to the evolution of such threats and the formulation of responses. He then concentrates on case studies from the 1970s and 1980s of what he sees as the most pressing forms of encroachment – air pollution and mineral extraction. He investigates these from a political-administrative angle within the so-called golden circle of desert parks on the Colorado Plateau (though his rationale for choosing this region over Alaska is not particularly convincing). Intended as a contribution to policy formulation, his story is one of frustrated corrective efforts, but critical of both the environmentalist community and the Reagan administration.

PETER A. COATES

Nationalism

Bensel, Richard Franklin, *Yankee Leviathan: The Origins of Central State Authority in America, 1859–1877*, Cambridge and New York: Cambridge University Press, 1990

Burbick, Joan, *Healing the Republic: The Language of Health and the Culture of Nationalism in Nineteenth-Century America*, Cambridge and New York: Cambridge University Press, 1994

Craven, Avery O., *The Growth of Southern Nationalism, 1848–1861*, Baton Rouge: Louisiana State University Press, 1953

Curti, Merle, *The Roots of American Loyalty*, New York: Columbia University Press, 1946

Dangerfield, George, *The Awakening of American Nationalism, 1815–1828*, New York: Harper, 1965

Faust, Drew Gilpin, *The Creation of Confederate Nationalism: Ideology and Identity in the Civil War South*, Baton Rouge: Louisiana State University Press, 1988

Greenfeld, Liah, *Nationalism: Five Roads to Modernity*, Cambridge, MA: Harvard University Press, 1992

Hall, Peter Dobkin, *The Organization of American Culture, 1700–1900: Private Institutions, Elites, and the Origins of American Nationality*, New York: New York University Press, 1982

Hess, Earl J., *Liberty, Virtue, and Progress: Northerners and Their War for the Union*, New York: New York University Press, 1988

Kohn, Hans, *The Idea of Nationalism: A Study in Its Origins and Background*, New York: Macmillan, 1945

Kohn, Hans, *American Nationalism: An Interpretative Essay*, New York: Macmillan, 1957

Lipset, Seymour Martin, *The First New Nation: The United States in Historical and Comparative Perspective*, New York: Basic Books, 1963; London: Heinemann, 1964

McCardell, John, *The Idea of a Southern Nation: Southern Nationalists and Southern Nationalism, 1830–1860*, New York: Norton, 1979

Niebuhr, Reinhold and Alan Heimert, *A Nation So Conceived: Reflections on the History of America from Its Early Visions to Its Present Power*, New York: Scribner, 1963; London: Faber, 1964

Potter, David M., *People of Plenty: Economic Abundance and the American Character*, Chicago: University of Chicago Press, 1954

Potter, David M., *The South and the Sectional Conflict*, Baton Rouge: Louisiana State University Press, 1968

Silber, Nina, *The Romance of Reunion: Northerners and the South, 1865–1900*, Chapel Hill: University of North Carolina Press, 1993

Taylor, William R., *Cavalier and Yankee: The Old South and American National Character*, New York: Braziller, 1961

Tuveson, Ernest Lee, *Redeemer Nation: The Idea of America's Millennial Role*, Chicago: University of Chicago Press, 1968

Wilson, Major L., *Space, Time, and Freedom: The Quest for Nationality and the Irrepressible Conflict, 1815–1861*, Westport, CT: Greenwood Press, 1974

Although the past few years have witnessed renewed interest in the subject of nationalism across many disciplines, its American variant has commanded only a small share of this attention. Social and political scientists have, for the most part, avoided the subject altogether, and historians usually approach it from a specific direction; for example, by concentrating on the Revolutionary period alone, or by examining the role which the Civil War played in the creation or consolidation of the American nation. This can be explained, at least in part, by the fact that the United States, as a nation of immigrants, is perceived to lack the ethnic and genealogical ties that some consider to be at the root of any national identity, but also because other "nationalisms" – in particular "Southern Nationalism" – have often been regarded as more valid and rewarding subjects for study. American nationalism, and its distinctive features, remain a challenging and elusive subject.

Kohn was the author of two of the earlier studies of American nationalism. In KOHN (1945), the American example is allocated only one chapter which focuses mainly on the revolutionary experience, and in particular on the question why the colonies broke away from the "mother country". The ideology that prompted the separation, Kohn argued, also lay at the root of American national consciousness, which "is based upon the conviction of being different from other nations." Americans, Kohn concluded, perceived themselves "as the first people with the greatest possible approximation to perfection." The threat to this idea, in the form of sectionalism, is explored further in KOHN (1957). Pointing to the evidence of internal improvements and the economic interdependence of the states, Kohn argues that "America became the first nation to develop the theory and to enforce the practice of modern economic nationalism." The threat to the stability of the nation, Kohn suggests, derived from the clash between New England and the South, although quite how southern and American nationalism fit together in his thesis is not entirely clear. Kohn perceives southern nationalism as a "nascent true nationalism, distinct from the original American nationalism," with the Civil War as the process whereby the latter re-defined itself. Given Kohn's emphasis on southern nationalism, however, the question of whether there was such a thing as "American nationalism" prior to the Civil War remains a moot one.

In recent work, as in older studies, the role of the Civil War remains central in debates about American nationalism. In her impressive study of the nationalist impulse in England, France, Russia, Germany and the United States, GREENFELD, like Kohn, emphasizes the importance of ideology in the construction of American nationalism, with the Civil War as the dividing "line between the dream of nationality and its realization." She also echoes Kohn's argument that "the promise of original English nationalism was carried much further toward its realization . . . by Englishmen on the other side of the Atlantic," but her examination of the American case goes much further both in its analysis of the growth of nationalism during the colonial and revolutionary periods and in the 19th century, and in its assessment of the importance of the "Union" to this process. Following the separation from Britain, Greenfeld points out, "Americans did not conceive of a nation, or a people, or a state, in terms of a unitary entity," but rather regarded it in "contractual" terms. With the "separatist impulse . . . inherent in the very conception of the Union," Greenfeld argues, "the forces that could . . . bring the United States to the brink of disintegration were at least as strong as those which fostered unity." Ultimately, Greenfeld concludes, the Civil War recommitted America to the roots of its own nationalism, the promise of democracy, but it was, and remains, a nation of "multiple allegiances."

Studies which focus more narrowly on the role of the Civil War in the creation of the American nation include Bensel and Hess. BENSEL argues that the war "created the American state by conferring upon it the fundamental attributes of territorial and governmental sovereignty." This is an important and controversial study of the nationalizing process in the United States up to the end of Reconstruction, particularly with regard to the northern states. For them, Bensel argues, the choice "was never between one nation and two but between one nation and many," a possibility that forced the promulgation of an "imperialistic nationalism" in order to counter the secessionist threat. One of the questions which Bensel asks in his study is why did the North fight? This is a question which HESS seeks specifically to address. Hess's argument is that Northern ideals and values lay "at the basis of American identity in the immediate antebellum period." Believing that southerners had "lost their grip on true republican principles," northerners perceived the Civil War "in terms of national character," with the future ideals of the nation dependent on the outcome of the conflict. In places Hess's argument is somewhat convoluted – particularly when he discusses culture and nationality – but this is a study which contains many insights into the process of constructing the nation in the mid-19th century.

WILSON is a more wide-ranging study covering the antebellum decades, which pursues some of the same themes as Hess. Wilson takes issue with Kohn, who, he asserts, failed to "deal with the pattern of tensions within the complex idea of freedom," a defect which Wilson seeks to correct by focusing, in particular, on the growth of what he terms "larger liberty," as the expanding nation sought some "order to the common life." In common with Hess, Wilson argues that certain elements in the northern states began to identify in the South a society antithetical to the ideals of liberty and progress which they perceived as defining the American nation, and thus set in motion "a pattern of creation by destruction," which culminated in the internecine conflict that was the American Civil War. Wilson's perceptive, if somewhat over-elaborate, analysis may be supplemented by DANGERFIELD's work on the years immediately following the War of 1812, when the economic nationalism of Henry Clay's "American System" vied with the democratic nationalism of Andrew Jackson. For America at this time, Dangerfield argues, "it was precisely the emergence of a common tradition that counted most." How this common tradition was achieved, and the forms that it took, are the subject of Dangerfield's detailed study, which covers topics such as the Missouri Compromise and the Monroe Doctrine, concluding with the Tariff of 1828 (the so-called "Tariff of Abominations"), which, Dangerfield argues, heralded the emergence of a new type of introspective nationalism. After 1828 many Americans, it is suggested, were prompted to reconsider what nationalism meant and what their nation stood for.

The South which, according to Hess and Wilson, prompted so much reassessment of the nature of American nationality, has received a great deal of attention in studies of nationalism. Some would argue that "Southern Nationalism" was merely sectionalism by another name, while others have, like Kohn, regarded southern nationalism as a "nascent true nationalism." The most sustained argument, and one of the most influential, on the differences between sectionalism and nationalism is presented by POTTER (1968). Chapter III, entitled "The Historian's Use of Nationalism and Vice Versa" is a classic and widely reprinted essay, which is essential reading for anyone seeking to clarify the terminology and understand the implications of the subject.

Studies specifically on southern nationalism include those by Craven, McCardell and Faust. Given his title, CRAVEN might be expected to show how southern sectionalism transmuted itself into southern nationalism after 1848, but, in an account of developments culminating in secession and civil war, it does no such thing. In a more recent and much more penetrating study, McCARDELL does argue for the emergence of southern nationalism as a detectable ideology between 1830 and 1860. As far as the sectionalism versus nationalism debate is concerned, McCardell is careful to explain his terminology in his introduction, and, along with Potter, offers useful guidance on controversial problems of definition. McCardell's major contribution is to synthesize a great deal of work which has a bearing upon the subject of southern nationalism, under such headings as: the southern economy; politics, education, religion and literature in the South; the southern perspective on territorial expansion, particularly after 1840; and, most importantly, the proslavery argument. He has, in addition, isolated several different strands of nationalism in the South, including literary, educational and proslavery movements. How these different elements interacted and, in time, merged to create a coherent southern nationalist ideology is the main focus of McCardell's work. FAUST focuses on the Civil War itself, by which time southern had become Confederate nationalism. In a brief compass, she covers a wide range of material, from an examination of the difficulties involved in defining what, exactly, constituted "Confederate nationalism," through detailed analysis of how this was constructed and what elements it comprised. Southerners, Faust argues, were "strikingly self-conscious about the need to undertake this introspection and to publicly define the foundations of their unity." Consequently, the debates over Confederate nationalism really "constituted a discourse about power and change," as southerners attempted both to define and defend their society and its beliefs.

The interaction of North and South in the American nation is examined in two outstanding studies. TAYLOR examines how the American national character was defined by the North-South relationship in the antebellum period. "By 1860," Taylor argues, "most Americans had come to look upon their society and culture as divided between a North and a South, a democratic commercial civilization and an aristocratic, agrarian one." How these two societies interacted is the focus of this study, but more specifically, how the "democratic commercial civilization" of the North came to identify in the South certain elements which were perceived to be lacking in its own. HALL sets out "to examine the evolution of American nationality," by focusing "on the social groups and institutions through which nationality was achieved." In particular it examines the rise of private organizations – most of which were located in the Northeast – which Hall credits with both formulating and sustaining "political, economic, and cultural nationality." In a complex and detailed analysis, he covers a great deal more than northern reactions to the South, although northern hostility to southern institutions is examined when Hall turns his attention to the discourse concerning republicanism and nationality in the immediate antebellum period. In terms of its approach, it is a deliberate, and on the whole successful, attempt to utilize "the theories and methods of the social sciences as tools of historical investigation," which concludes that, up to the 1940s, "the fulfilment of the promise of American life meant the full achievement of nationality," enabling all Americans "to put aside their differences in pursuit of a common goal."

The question of how successfully, and to what extent, North and South managed to put aside their differences after the Civil War is the subject of a recent study by SILBER. The emphasis here is on how northerners persuaded themselves to come to terms with the South, and, like Taylor, Silber has uncovered a certain degree of admiration for southern society among northerners who remained "unconvinced as to the unqualified benefits of the Union victory." Nevertheless, by the time of the Spanish-American War, Silber concludes, North and South had reached a new national consensus, although this was, in many cases, a white, male consensus, predicated on nostalgia for the past and opposition to an integrated society.

There are a number of further studies which, from a variety of perspectives, offer valuable insights into American nationalism, usually through examination of what lies behind, encourages, and helps to maintain American national sentiment. The earliest study of this type is CURTI, who assesses the extent, and limitations, of loyalty to the American nation, mostly in the 19th century, and pursues ideas similar to those found in Kohn, Greenfeld and Hess. TUVESON focuses on Kohn's idea that the United States perceives itself as essentially different from other nations, argues that the "myth of American millennialism is undoubtedly an example of nationalist ideology," and pursues examples of this ideology, in literature, poetry and sermons most of which are, again, drawn from the 19th century. Much the same idea is pursued in NIEBUHR and HEIMERT, which covers the 19th to early 20th centuries in its assessment of how American ideology shaped the American national character and how the nation's original sense of mission changed over time.

One of the most wide-ranging treatments of the American national character and the nation's sense of mission is to be found in POTTER (1954), a highly influential work in its day, but now curiously neglected. Potter examines how historians and behavioural scientists have analyzed national character, and he emphasizes economic abundance as a key factor in his discussion of such issues as the impact of democracy and Turner's "Frontier Hypothesis." The most comprehensive sociological study of America's search for a national identity and a national value system is provided by LIPSET, who, among other factors, emphasizes the role that religion plays in defining the American national character. Finally, and much more recently, BURBICK offers an original and stimulating addition to the debate on American nationalism with a study of writings on health, tracing how this literature both defined and supported "the enormous effort that went into inventing American nationalism" in the 19th century.

S-M. GRANT

Native Americans: General

Bolt, Christine, *American Indian Policy and American Reform: Case Studies of the Campaign to Assimilate the American Indians*, London and Boston: Allen and Unwin, 1987

Deloria, Vine, Jr., and Clifford M. Lytle, *The Nations Within: The Past and Future of American Indian Sovereignty*, New York: Pantheon, 1984

Fagan, Brian M., *The Great Journey: The Peopling of Ancient America*, New York and London: Thames and Husdon, 1987

Josephy, Alvin M., Jr., *500 Nations: An Illustrated History of North American Indians*, New York: Knopf, 1994; London: Hutchinson, 1995

Kehoe, Alice Beck, *The North American Indians: A Comprehensive Account*, Englewood Cliffs, NJ: Prentice Hall, 1981, 2nd edition, 1992

McNickle, D'Arcy, *Native American Tribalism: Indian Survivals and Renewals*, New York: Oxford University Press, 1973

Philp, Kenneth R., *John Collier's Crusade for Indian Reform, 1920–1954*, Tucson: University of Arizona Press, 1977

Prucha, Francis Paul, *The Great Father: The United States Government and the American Indians*, 2 vols., Lincoln: University of Nebraska Press, 1984

Ramenofsky, Ann, *Vectors of Death: The Archaeology of European Contact*, Albuquerque: University of New Mexico Press, 1987

Sheehan, Bernard W., *Seeds of Extinction: Jeffersonian Philanthropy and the American Indian*, Chapel Hill: University of North Carolina Press, 1973

Tilton, Robert S., *Pocahontas: The Evolution of an American Narrative*, Cambridge and New York: Cambridge University Press, 1994

Utter, Jack, *American Indians: Answers to Today's Questions*, Lake Ann, MI: National Woodlands Publishing, 1993

Waldman, Carl, *Atlas of the North American Indian*, New York: Facts on File, 1985

There are nearly two million Native Americans in the United States today, comprising just under 1 per cent of the population. This may be more than lived in the same territory before the coming of Europeans. Most Native Americans speak English today, but more than 100 Indian languages are still spoken as well. Only about 25 per cent of Native Americans live on reservations, but more than 500 tribes are officially recognised by the federal government. The Native American population is not in decline, but rather increasing rapidly. Such apparent paradoxes are sometimes hard to assimilate, given the popular perception of Indians as driven to extinction by the wars and skirmishes of the 19th century.

The subject of Native American history has a particularly long history of publication aimed at the non-specialist reader. There are plenty of sources, but many are as romanticised and inaccurate as they are outdated. For a very quick and sound orientation to a broad topic, the reader may find UTTER's wide-ranging almanac a valuable source. The questions that we ask about a particular topic change over time, as does the nature of the answers we expect. Utter has assembled hundreds of frequently asked questions, and has researched the primary and secondary sources to give some preliminary answers. The book could be useful to answer questions that arise in the course of specific historical research, but can also be used to provide an introductory orientation to particular topics. Questions posed range over treaties, common misinformation and stereotypes, legal status, health and education. Useful addresses for further information are given as well as a good bibliography and appendices which reproduce some interesting documents. WALDMAN's atlas is another indispensable and trustworthy companion. He has assembled a wide range of newly drawn maps, together with other materials which may be helpful for those coping with shifting place names and human movement over vast and unfamiliar terrritories. Waldman has included maps which indicate the shifting patterns of culture, military campaigns, demographic changes, migrations, land transfer, white settlement patterns, journeys of exploration and more. However, he reproduces only a few old maps. The atlas includes brief essays on many of the topics introduced by the maps. JOSEPHY is a beautiful and encyclopaedic volume which combines brief but up to date coverage of a huge range of historical and ethnographic material, with well-chosen illustrations and maps. The book is the culmination of a lifetime's interest in and research into Native American history. It will provide a careful guided introduction to Native America for readers with little previous familiarity with the subject. (A version of this volume was released as a CD-ROM for use with personal computers.) These three recent works are aimed at the general non-specialist reader, and assume little prior knowledge. The remaining works on the list will be found most useful for those needing detailed information on particular groups, regions and historical problems.

The history of the aboriginal peoples of the United States is surely one of the most complex subjects in North American history. There has been an informal, and seldom discussed, division of labour in covering the subject: the period before European contact has been allotted primarily to archaeologists, the history of particular nations or tribes most often discussed by anthropologists, the unfolding story of relationships between colonial and federal governments and the tribes, or of immigrants and their contact with indigenous communities, researched by historians. This is an oversimplification, but perhaps a useful one. It has often been noted that most of the available material was written by Euro-American scholars, without sufficient regard for the historical knowledge and analyses of Native American people themselves. In the past thirty years however, vigorous criticism of the existing literature by Native American specialists has helped to encourage an integrative ethnohistorical approach, which incorporates indigenous forms of history as well as the evidence of the historian, the anthropologist and the archaeologist. Readers aware of these patterns will find it easier to begin research into particular topics.

In the literature on pre-contact peoples there are discussions of hundreds of separate groups, culturally, linguistically and historically the products of complex individual circumstance. New readers will encounter a sometimes confusing proliferation of descriptive schemes, with shifting tribal names and terms used to describe archaeological cultures which cannot always be simply related to either historically known groups or contemporary tribes. With an increasing amount of evidence available from the archaeological record, and with much attention being paid to the analysis of traditional oral accounts of the past preserved among the people of the many tribes which still exist, the pre-contact historical record is rapidly being enriched by new discoveries. FAGAN offers a lively analysis of thought about early Native American prehistory. He has woven the scholarly research of thousands of archaeologists into a coherent and accessible narrative which tells the story of the peopling of North America over the past 15,000 years. The book also provides a brief and clear account of the changes in our thinking about pre-Columbian North America. Fagan demonstrates some of the perils of painting broad stroke portraits of prehistory based on a narrow range of evidence, but also indicates the range of views possible, given such evidence. He emphasises the evidence for migration over the Bering Strait, and the subsequent patterns of migration within North America, focusing on the relationship between climatic and environmental changes over time, and the availability of food resources, to explain some of the motives and activities of the palaeo-Indian bands which were the ancestors of contemporary Native Americans. Fagan also has a particularly useful section on further reading with comments and evaluations of the material included.

RAMENOFSKY's investigation into the archaeological evidence for the impact of European contact is a narrow, detailed and specialist work. It is however a particularly important one, being the best single source of information on the research into population figures before and after contact. Previous estimates have ranged from less than one million inhabitants of the continent before European exploration, to estimates as high as eighteen million. Ramenofsky has made a detailed study of these figures, on the basis of both the historical record and the archaeological evidence. The results challenge previous explanations and illuminate our understanding of the calamitous consequences that European-introduced diseases have had for American Indians.

For a more detailed introduction to the culture and history of the many individual groups which make up Native America, KEHOE offers a brilliant and succinct historical and anthropological survey. She organises her discussion around regional and historical linkages, centering her material in the Native American perspective, bringing the reader up to date, but not using the customary artificial break into prehistory and post-contact experience. She emphasises the dynamic nature of Native American polities and cultures over time. The brief and blunt advisory note to the reader which prefaces the book is a small masterpiece.

General issues relating to the attitudes of settlers to indigenous peoples and the gradual consolidation of earlier individual colonial policies towards Indians into national policies over the course of the past 200 years have been examined by many historians. Three of the most common analytical perspectives are highlighted in separate studies which not only document policymaking and implementation, but try to explain the shifting paradigms for thinking about Indians which have been adopted over time.

The single most useful and comprehensive work on the relationship between native peoples and the United States government is PRUCHA, who is the leading contemporary authority on this topic. This book summarizes his work over an entire career. It covers the period from the Revolutionary War down to 1980. Prucha systematically considers the importance of economic, social and political factors in shaping the attitudes and legislation of the dominant society towards Native Americans. He deals exclusively with the history of federal government-tribal relations, and his emphasis on federal relationships means that issues of treaty rights affecting the disposition of land, water and mineral rights, education and welfare programmes, reservation and social policy decisions are given prominence. There is however a particularly useful running discussion of the shifting philosophies which have shaped the attitudes of other Americans towards the Native American population over time. In Prucha's analysis the underlying theme of most federal policy has been a paternalistic perspective, embodied in schemes which seldom questioned the credentials of western European values.

The "assimilationist," or "Jeffersonian" policymakers are discussed by SHEEHAN. He argues that well-intentioned policymakers in the period 1775–1830 based their understanding of American Indians on sometimes perilous humanitarian generalizations born of the conjuncture between natural history and contemporary philosophy. He suggests that the apparently contradictory policy of removal, which saw the wholesale forced dislocation of reluctant tribes at the end of the period, was the inevitable consequence of ill-conceived benevolent assimilationist policy. The more broadly based study by BOLT, on the other hand, looks at the history of efforts to assimilate Indians into American society over a longer period of time. She compares the Native American experience with that of the Native community in Canada.

The proponents of "self-determination" are discussed by such leading authorities as McNickle, and Deloria and Lytle. McNICKLE's history of tribalism is a good starting point for any discussion of self-determination. DELORIA and LYTLE move beyond this to emphasise the arguments for sovereignty – a status which acknowledges not only the desirability of self-determination for Native Americans, but the right to be treated as domestic dependent nations. There is a particularly important discussion of the intentions behind the reform of Indian policy planned by John Collier during the presidency of Franklin Roosevelt, as well as of the subsequent effects of that policy. The history of legal issues surrounding the concept of sovereignty for native groups is a useful companion to the discussion of philosophical change.

Sometimes work with a very narrow focus helps to reveal broader patterns. Both Philp and Tilton can be recommended for this quality of illuminating the general by reference to the particular. PHILP has written a very good biography of John Collier, a key figure in the development of 20th-century Indian policy. Collier was Franklin Roosevelt's Commissioner of Indian Affairs, and drafted the Collier Bill, which was both the starting point for the eventual Indian Reorganization Act, passed in 1934, and a turning-point in the move from paternalism to ideals of self-determination in the rhetoric of policymakers. TILTON's excellent study of the uses of the past focuses on the historical figure of Matoaka, usually known as Pocahontas, the daughter of a key Indian leader in late 16th and early 17th century Virginia. Most Americans know that Powhatan's daughter married a colonist from the settlement at Jamestown, and that she lived in England after her marriage until her early death. Few realise how important the many versions of this sketchy story have become as an index of

shifting attitudes on race relations in the United States. Tilton's engaging account of legend exploitation thoroughly enriches Native American historical studies.

TERI F. BREWER

Native Americans: White Encounter with

Axtell, James, *The Invasion Within: The Contest of Cultures in Colonial North America*, New York: Oxford University Press, 1985

Gutiérrez, Ramón A., *When Jesus Came, the Corn Mothers Went Away: Marriage, Sexuality, and Power in New Mexico, 1500–1846*, Stanford, CA: Stanford University Press, 1991

Hurtado, Albert L., *Indian Survival on the California Frontier*, New Haven: Yale University Press, 1988

Jennings, Francis, *The Invasion of America: Indians, Colonialism, and the Cant of Conquest*, Chapel Hill: University of North Carolina Press, 1975

Merrell, James H., *The Indians' New World: Catawbas and Their Neighbors from European Contact Through the Era of Removal*, Chapel Hill: University of North Carolina Press, 1989

Salisbury, Neal, *Manitou and Providence: Indians, Europeans, and the Making of New England, 1500–1643*, New York: Oxford University Press, 1982

Usner, Daniel H., Jr., *Indians, Settlers, and Slaves in a Frontier Exchange Economy: The Lower Mississippi Valley Before 1783*, Chapel Hill: University of North Carolina Press, 1992

White, Richard, *The Middle Ground: Indians, Empires, and Republics in the Great Lakes Region, 1650–1815*, Cambridge and New York: Cambridge University Press, 1991

Before Jennings, historians had characterized contact between Europeans and Native Americans as a battle between cultures. Historians from Francis Parkman to Alden Vaughan had argued that inevitably the superior European culture had defeated the inferior Native American culture. JENNINGS, however, revolutionized historians' understanding and interpretation of such encounters; he asserted that nothing about the "invasion of America" was inevitable. The struggle for North America instead involved conscious decisions on both sides, and, on the part of the Puritan English, the promulgation of a myth of cities on hills and Edens in the wilderness that had justified the dispossession of the Indians. Jennings's acerbic prose and iconoclastic agenda may not please everyone, but his work redrew the historiographical picture of culture contact. Historians have since begun to look at missionaries as agents of contact, the structural processes of colonization, and the networks of mutual accommodation that linked Europeans and Indians, in order to understand better the history of encounters between Native Americans and Europeans.

Several recent studies have focused on European missionaries as agents of intercultural contact. In a provocative and hotly debated argument, GUTIÉRREZ asserts that Spanish Jesuits, appalled by the sexual rituals that patterned Navajo culture, successfully transformed the Navajos into a hispanized Christian society. According to AXTELL, English efforts to convert the Indians of New England likewise centered on a wholesale transformation of the Indians' culture. After defeating tribes in battle, the English endeavored to teach the surviving remnants to work, dress, live, and worship like Englishmen. In contrast, French Jesuits put conversion before conquest. Axtell argues that the Black Robes won converts by living among tribes such as the Huron, Iroquois, and Micmac, and by working with rather than against indigenous cultures. Although the difference between the Spanish, English, and French missionary experiences can be attributed to different approaches to the missionary endeavor, other factors influenced the course of contact as well.

Both Salisbury and Merrell have placed events like the missionary experience in the broader context of colonization and used a model of frontier sequences to explain and interpret contact between Europeans and Native Americans. SALISBURY attributes the failure of the English to convert the Indians to the speed of the settlement of New England. Ravaged by disease, weakened by economic dependency, and defeated militarily in quick succession, the region's Indians had little chance to recover from the effects of one disruption before facing the next. To the south, MERRELL applies a similar model to the history of the Catawbas of the South Carolina back country. Unlike the Indians of New England, the Catawbas experienced successive waves of disease, trade, and settlement over a much longer period of time. For this reason they adapted to the disruptions of each phase and coped with subsequent developments in a much more organized and successful fashion. Whether catching colonists' slaves, fighting for George Washington in the Revolutionary War, or enduring the pernicious racism of the 19th and early 20th centuries, the Catawbas have maintained a presence in the Palmetto state.

Merrell uses the metaphor of the "New World" to conceptualize the Catawba experience, arguing that Native Americans viewed the Columbian world with the same amount of awe and uncertainty as did the newly arrived Europeans. While the two peoples struggled for some sort of relationship, systems of cooperation and rivalry emerged all across the continent. In the Great Lakes Region WHITE locates a "middle ground" where French, British, and American traders, soldiers, and settlers worked with their Indian counterparts to coexist in relative peace. The bubble of the "middle ground" burst, however, on the swordpoints of imperial arms. Warfare and the use of trade to establish military alliances had threatened its stability over two centuries, and the War of 1812 finally tilted the balance of the "middle ground" to the Americans' advantage.

Much of what characterized the "new world" and the "middle ground" also occurred in the early 17th century French colony of Louisiana. USNER describes a frontier exchange economy in which Indians, French colonists, and African slaves exchanged foodstuffs, material goods, and services. In spite of French attempts to divert economic energies towards staple crop production, the frontier exchange economy thrived until the 1780s when the Spanish and British enacted a variety of laws to restrict intercultural action and exchange. Together, Merrell, White and Usner have argued persuasively that the early stages of contact between Europeans and Americans and Indians were as full of accommodation and cooperation as they were of violence and deceit, but that is only half of the story.

Violence and brutal exploitation did occur, and HURTADO chronicles this history in horrifying detail. After acquiring California in the Mexican War, American ranchers and farmers maintained the exploitative Spanish *encomienda* labor system. Despite its harshness, the system allowed Indians to retain traditional housing and settlement patterns, and cultural practices, as long as the Indians gave their labor to the landowner. Following the rapid expansion of the state's agriculture, migrant labor replaced the cumbersome *encomienda*. Uprooted Indian families scattered in search of seasonal work picking fruits and vegetables. The decline of the family structure, Hurtado argues, led to a collapse in fertility rates and subsequent demographic crisis. Agricultural mechanization drove what few Native Americans remained in the fields into the cities where some found work as domestics or menial laborers. By the middle of the 19th century, California's Indian population stood on the brink of extinction.

The history of contact between Indians and Euramericans, leading to the inevitable triumph of the latter, had been a dominant theme in American history until Jennings. Scholars who have followed in his footsteps have shown that on the contrary contact was a much more complex phenomenon. In addition to correcting previous historians' misconceptions about the past, the works of these scholars raises difficult questions about the nature of contact, and its role in the formulation of the values, assumptions and ideals that have defined the history of the United States.

JAMES TAYLOR CARSON

Native Americans: Federal Policy towards

Burt, Larry W., *Tribalism in Crisis: Federal Indian Policy, 1953–1961*, Albuquerque: University of New Mexico Press, 1982

Cornell, Stephen E., *The Return of the Native: American Indian Political Resurgence*, New York: Oxford University Press, 1988

Deloria, Vine, Jr., and Clifford M. Lytle, *The Nations Within: The Past and Future of American Indian Sovereignty*, New York: Pantheon, 1984

Fixico, Donald Lee, *Termination and Relocation: Federal Indian Policy, 1945–1960*, Albuquerque: University of New Mexico Press, 1986

Hauptman, Laurence M., *The Iroquois Struggle for Survival: World War II to Red Power*, Syracuse, NY: Syracuse University Press, 1986

Hoxie, Frederick E., *A Final Promise: The Campaign to Assimilate the Indians, 1880–1920*, Lincoln: University of Nebraska Press, 1984

Kelly, Lawrence C., *The Assault on Assimilation: John Collier and the Origins of Indian Policy Reform*, Albuquerque: University of New Mexico Press, 1983

Prucha, Francis Paul, *The Great Father: The United States Government and the American Indians*, 2 vols., Lincoln: University of Nebraska Press, 1984

For over two centuries federal policy has defined the relationship between the United States and Native Americans. Historians, however, have only recently begun to relate the formulation of policy at the federal level to its implementation and effect at the local level. Far from consistent in its application, the goals of federal policy have ranged over time from government intervention and Indian assimilation to native autonomy and segregation.

PRUCHA was the first historian to offer a comprehensive interpretation of federal policy. He asserts that it reflected the federal government's sincere intentions to help Native Americans. Born of a concern to preserve and "civilize" what contemporaries thought was a vanishing race, policy has continued, according to Prucha, to reflect the paternalism of policymakers. Other scholars have begun to revise Prucha's argument. Whereas he found little historical change in policy goals, Fixico, Kelly and Hoxie have all shown that federal policy mirrored broader, historical economic, cultural, and political trends. Furthermore, Burt, Cornell, Deloria and Lytle, and Hauptman have re-directed Prucha's national and federal focus by concentrating on the consequences of federal policy at the local level, and by acknowledging the important influence Native Americans have had on policy.

HOXIE examines the "allotment" policy that characterized federal policy from the Gilded Age to the Progressive Era. In the 1880s the federal government began a comprehensive program to end Native Americans' collective ownership of land, and to allot parcels of land to individual Indians. Land which went unclaimed, or which exceeded each tribe's allotment, was sold to Americans at bargain prices. Needless to say, railroad companies and timber, mining, and cattle concerns benefited tremendously from this windfall. Besides undercutting tribal self-sufficiency, allotment also abrogated the sovereignty of tribal governments. In theory the federal government hoped to force Indians to assimilate into American society as freeholders and citizens, but, as Hoxie shows, such ambitious expectations went unmet. By 1900, allotment had led to what Hoxie terms "peripheralization." Relegated to the margins of American society, economy, and culture, Indians, for the most part, faced lives of hardship and poverty with little hope for the future.

By all accounts allotment was a dismal failure. Special reports and commissions reported widespread bureaucratic bungling and corruption. In his biography of John Collier, head of the Bureau of Indian Affairs under Franklin D. Roosevelt, KELLY shows how, during the New Deal, the federal government abandoned allotment and emphasized instead economic assistance, social aid, and cultural revitalization. Collier's administration instituted a number of programs that provided relief to impoverished Indians. For example, the Indian Civilian Conservation Corps employed out-of-work Indians, built much needed bridges, roads, and other public works, and reforged strong bonds between the federal government and Native Americans. Although Collier's programs ameliorated desperate poverty and disillusionment, his more ambitious hopes for re-establishing Indian sovereignty foundered on political opposition, American as well as Indian, and unrealistic expectations.

The spectre of communism in the years after World War II led policymakers to reconsider Collier's collectivization and cultural revitalization program. According to FIXICO, the Eisenhower administration returned federal policy to the retrenchment that had characterized policy before the New Deal. The Republican administration substituted "termination" for allotment and attempted to sever ties between the federal government and Native Americans, in order to cut government costs as well as to force Native Americans to assimilate into American society. To facilitate this process, another program, "relocation," helped some Native Americans find housing and work in urban areas. Municipal and county governments, Fixico argues, opposed termination and relocation because they feared they would be left shouldering the cost of maintaining Indian populations.

Native Americans added to the protests that confronted termination, and their continued activity has led to the self-determination that characterizes today's policy. BURT shows that, by the 1950s, Native American activism had crystallized into an effective movement, and that this movement played an instrumental role in termination's ultimate defeat. In a broader study, CORNELL links Native American opposition throughout American history to the dialectical interplay of national economics, politics, and policy, and Native American activism. According to Cornell, the recent return to tribal self-determination has defused much of the radicalism that accompanied Native American protests, but has opened up new opportunities for change. In the view of DELORIA and LYTLE, self-determination may offer the only hope of solving the "Indian problem." If the federal government is to have any further role in Native American affairs, it should, Deloria and Lytle conclude, concentrate on creating economic stability for Native Americans and extending to them the kind of respect which has been conspicuously absent from over two centuries of policy.

HAUPTMAN draws together themes explored by other authors, and examines the effects and responses engendered by federal policy among the Iroquois of New York, Oklahoma, Wisconsin, and Canada from World War II to the 1970s. The Iroquois had contributed mightily to the war effort, and they deeply resented termination. Some Iroquois mobilized in the 1960s as part of the Red Power movement. Hauptman concludes, however, that the movement was as important as a force for cultural revitalization as it was for political self-determination. By the 1970s, political activism and cultural rejuvenation had polarized the tribe. Conservatives and progressives vied over control of the nation's future in a debate that has of late taken violent turns.

As studies of federal policy have moved from the rarefied concerns of the Founding Fathers to its impact on Native Americans, Prucha's generalizations have lost some of their force. At different times, policy has affected different segments of Native America in different ways. The return of self-determination may have restored a measure of control to Native Americans, but the history of federal policy is still imperfectly understood and far from over.

JAMES TAYLOR CARSON

Native Americans: Indian Wars

Gump, James O., *Dust Rose Like Smoke: Subjugation of the Zulu and the Sioux*, Lincoln: University of Nebraska Press, 1994

Horsman, Reginald, *Expansion and American Indian Policy, 1783–1812*, East Lansing: Michigan State University Press, 1967; with new preface, Norman: University of Oklahoma Press, 1992

Hutton, Paul Andrew, *Phil Sheridan and His Army*, Lincoln: University of Nebraska Press, 1985

Sword, Wiley, *President Washington's Indian War: The Struggle for the Old Northwest, 1790–1795*, Norman: University of Oklahoma Press, 1985

Utley, Robert M., *Frontiersmen in Blue: The United States Army and the Indian, 1848–1865*, New York: Macmillan, 1967

Utley, Robert M., *Frontier Regulars: The United States Army and the Indian, 1866–1891*, New York: Macmillan, 1973

Utley, Robert M., *The Indian Frontier of the American West, 1846–1890*, Albuquerque: University of New Mexico Press, 1984

Utley, Robert M. and Wilcomb Washburn, *The American Heritage History of the Indian Wars*, New York: American Heritage, 1977; as *The History of the Indian Wars*, London: Mitchell Beazley, 1977

Welch, James with Paul Stekler, *Killing Custer: The Battle of the Little Bighorn and the Fate of the Plains Indians*, New York: Norton, 1994

White, Richard, *The Middle Ground: Indians, Empires, and Republics in the Great Lakes Region, 1650–1815*, Cambridge and New York: Cambridge University Press, 1991

Wooster, Robert, *Nelson A. Miles and the Twilight of the Frontier Army*, Lincoln: University of Nebraska Press, 1993

Although there are a number of one-volume surveys of America's Indian wars, many recent ones taking a deliberately pro-Indian stance, UTLEY and WASHBURN remains an excellent departure point. Their work combines encyclopaedic knowledge with balanced judgement and has a way of illuminating the general through particularly well-chosen individual points. The work is also remarkable for its illustrations and for the quality of the captions, which frequently point to the distance between mythic representations of the wars and the historical realities. The work lacks footnotes and a bibliography, but the text is wholly reliable nonetheless. The first half covers the period to 1850 and includes coverage of Spanish, French and Dutch clashes with the Indians, as well as the English. The second half closes with the events surrounding the "battle" of Wounded Knee. There is only one notable omission, a lack of any discussion of Alaska, although treatment of events there would help to put those elsewhere into an interesting perspective.

WHITE does not centre on the wars but is essential all the same. He describes them as one of a number of interactions between whites and Indians during the period 1650–1815. In thought-provoking and pathbreaking ways he shows how wrong it is to see the white and Indian communities as separate and distinct, only communicating when they collided. There was mutual accommodation, though little acculturation, throughout the period, the fluctuating accommodation producing many forms of instability, of which war was only the most extreme. There is no bibliography, but the footnotes are copious and revealing.

White's insights have not yet been systematically applied to the 19th century, but SWORD, which deals with part of White's period, should be read in conjunction since it reveals a similar picture of white and Indian communities brought to states of tension in many ways. It also reminds the reader of the small size of the original American army, which received funding for 672 men in 1789, increased to support 1216 in 1790. Sword is overtly sympathetic to the Indians and sometimes appears to be writing as an act of personal expiation, but his study of the earliest Indian wars of the national period is an important one. If nothing else, it reminds readers of the chronic inefficiency of the earliest American armies.

HORSMAN was originally published in 1967 but has been reprinted as a paperback with a new preface. Though the work does not deal specifically with the wars of its period, it adds to understanding of how they came about, arguably somewhat inadvertently. The author defends United States government policy in the early national period, seeing it as coherent and rational but, as he also admits, of little final use, given the frontiersmen's lust for land and the unwillingness or inability of the government to prevent encroachment on lands not already ceded by the Indians. The work includes a short and succinct chapter on Jefferson's expectation that conflict could be avoided either through Indian adoption of white ways, especially sedentary agriculture, or through a government policy of distributing provisions, essentially producing a culture of dependency. Either way the Indians would not need to hunt and therefore would not need extensive lands. They could be persuaded to cede these and thus avoid war. The limitations of this way of thinking help explain the frequent conflicts of the 19th century.

UTLEY (1967, 1973, and 1984) remain unsurpassed in his description of the conflicts of the period 1848–91. The bibliographies necessarily need supplementing, but are well-chosen for their date. The bibliography in Utley (1984) includes new material, but would also need supplementing. In the works on the army, Utley deals with matters like the size of the army, the character of its men and officers, their pay and conditions, the command structures and the doctrines governing action in war and peace, and the public attitude to both. There are excellent summaries of events during particular wars, such as those against the Sioux. Overall, the three works become slightly less celebratory in tone over nearly two decades, but there is no doubt that Utley has always admired the resistance which the Indians put up to the white encroachments. He may also be read as suggesting that all Indian wars after 1848 were something of a coda, the Indians having little chance of determining their future after the whites had established a significant presence on the Pacific and decided to defend their transcontinental communications. Utley (1984) argues forcibly that the wars of the later 19th century all had one aspect in common in that they were a violent rejection by Indians of the reservation policy, which ironically friends of the Indians thought would be a means of Indian salvation. All in all, Utley shows how the wars were the result of the failure of the American government to establish a workable policy for Indian relations in the 19th century, though he also makes it clear that public opinion was very largely against funding any policy that might have made a difference. The 1984 work is also useful for its remarks, brief as they are, on the exceptionalism of Alaska where war was virtually unknown.

Some of the reasons for the victory of whites in the wars may be gathered from biographies of white military commanders. HUTTON's biography of Sheridan, who commanded the Department of Missouri from 1867 to 1869 and the Division of the Missouri (that is, most of what is normally thought of as the West of the day) from 1869 to 1883, underlines Utley's contention that fighting frequently erupted as Indians sought to leave reservations and the army sought to confine them. Hutton shows that while Sheridan was not, as he has often been portrayed, an inflexible and shallow-minded Indian-hater, he did have great difficulties in seeing why the Indians should have a say in their future. The study also shows something of the infighting within the army and something of the struggle with Washington, particularly with the Department of the Interior, which hampered the army militarily. Close reading of this work also shows the limited effects of force in comparison with starvation, exposure, stock and property losses and the constant insecurity that bedevilled the Indians. Hutton also suggests that the war against the Sioux in 1876–77 was the only conventional war that the army ever fought against the trans-Mississippi Indians.

WOOSTER looks at the career of the captor of Chief Joseph and Geronimo, the son-in-law of Senator Sherman and therefore the nephew-in-law of William T. Sherman. While he does not suggest that Miles married with an eye to the main chance, this biography again underlines the point that the American army of the late 19th century was riddled with rivalries between those in its highest ranks and that, if the serving men were not all lions, many of the officers were donkeys. Miles resembled the latter in his personal relations, but militarily his career is worth studying for the way in which he obtained results. Unlike some officers who wanted a reprise of the Civil War on the Plains, with set battles and European tactics, Miles adapted to the demands of western warfare, developing a good rapport with his men, using scouts sensibly, developing good transportation networks and being tenacious in pursuit of an enemy that often, perforce, did not wish to flee over large distances. Like his colleagues he had scant respect for the Indian way of life and believed that the Indian would be well served by the reservation system. Wooster also shows that Miles was one of the few who adopted new technologies in fighting the wars, while the army as a whole learned new strategies painfully slowly.

GUMP looks at two sets of wars which resulted from expanding imperialisms. He also shows how collaboration between whites and the "other" was apparent in South Africa as well as in the American West and that, at least initially, there was more inter-communication between communities than an inaccurate sense of continuous warfare would suggest. His work brings us back to White, inasmuch as he sees the wars between incoming whites and indigenous peoples as part of a complex series of contacts and confrontations which had many causes. The comparative approach fruitfully suggests that America's Indian wars were the results of decisions by imperial and later national governmental agents, indigenous mediators, the perceived imperatives of economic expansion, the mobility of populations, the instability of indigenous communities and the divide-and-rule tactics of white policymakers.

Although WELCH is not the work of an academically-trained historian, the end-notes show it does rely on the work of academic historians, and it has considerable value as a deliberate attempt to present an Indian view of what is arguably the most studied battle of the wars. The fact that the author is a member of the Blackfeet Nation explains why the first chapter deals with the Marias River Massacre of 1870 while the shape of the book stems directly from its connection with the film on the Battle of the Little Bighorn made for PBS by Paul Stekler. The author's readiness to rely on Indian sources is deliberate and helps provide an unusual perspective on a much-studied subject. One remark bears quoting here and gives the flavour of the work: "One of the common fallacies in regard to the Battle of the Little Bighorn is that there were no survivors. There were plenty of survivors – Sioux and Cheyennes." The work is well illustrated, many of the illustrations providing Indian memories of the Battle.

R.A. BURCHELL

Native Americans: Recent History (since 1960s)

Bahr, Howard, Bruce A. Chadwick, and Robert C. Day, *Native Americans Today: Sociological Perspectives*, New York: Harper, 1972

Brand, Johanna, *The Life and Death of Anna Mae Aquash*, Toronto: Lorimer, 1978

Deloria, Vine, Jr., *Behind the Trail of Broken Treaties: An Indian Declaration of Independence*, New York: Delacorte Press, 1974

Hauptman, Laurence M., *The Iroquois Struggle for Survival: World War II to Red Power*, Syracuse, NY: Syracuse University Press, 1986

Hertzberg, Hazel W., *The Search for an American Indian Identity: Modern Pan-Indian Movements*, Syracuse, NY: Syracuse University Press, 1971

Mankiller, Wilma and Michael Wallis, *Mankiller: A Chief and Her People*, New York: St. Martin's Press, 1993

Matthiessen, Peter, *In the Spirit of Crazy Horse*, New York: Viking, 1983; revised, Viking, and London: HarperCollins, 1991

Meredith, Howard L., *Dancing on Common Ground: Tribal Cultures and Alliances of the Southern Plains*, Lawrence: University Press of Kansas, 1995

Parman, Donald L., *Indians and the American West in the Twentieth Century*, Bloomington: Indiana University Press, 1994

Powers, Marla N., *Oglala Women: Myth, Ritual, and Reality*, Chicago: University of Chicago Press, 1986

Unger, Steven (editor), *The Destruction of American Indian Families*, New York: Association on American Indian Affairs, 1977

Weyler, Rex, *Blood of the Land: The Government and Corporate War Against the American Indian Movement*, New York: Everest House, 1982; revised as *Blood of the Land: The Government and the Corporate War Against First Nations*, Philadelphia: New Society, 1992

From the 1890 massacre of a Lakota village at Wounded Knee, South Dakota, to the tribal occupation and stand-off at Wounded Knee in 1973, to today's struggles with government and corporate interests, the experiences of Native Americans have remained imbued with a deeply emotional resonance. The long-standing trials of Native tribes throughout the centuries over stolen land, tribal disintegration, and the ever-present threat to their cultural identity have culminated, since 1960, in a political and cultural resurgence for many Native Americans. In recent years there has been a proliferation of new research on Native Americans. Many analyses are often highly charged, in both a political and socio-cultural sense – and it is sometimes difficult to separate fact from fiction. However, there are numerous studies available that adequately explore Native American history since 1960 and provide significant insights into this turbulent era.

Many early studies of recent Native history focus almost exclusively on the "Red Power" movements of the 1960s and 1970s. One of the most comprehensive of the earlier works, written at the height of the Red Power movement, is BAHR. This sociological study features writings by a diverse group of essayists, ranging from Vine Deloria to Senator Edward Kennedy. The essays cover a broad range of topics, exploring issues of racism, tribal termination policies practised by the United States government, cultural assimilation, urbanization, education, and crime and alcoholism among Native Americans. Though dated, Bahr is a useful introduction to the complex issues confronting Native Americans at the time it was written, and of the views held by prominent Native and non-Native figures on these issues.

Two other early works, Deloria and Weyler, also provide a useful history of the political and cultural shifts leading up to the Red Power movement and Native cultural resurgence in recent years. DELORIA, a well-known Native writer and activist, delineates the circumstances leading up to "The Trail of Broken Treaties", the movement organized by Native activists to reclaim land stolen from them, which culminated in November 1972 with the American Indian Movement occupation of the Bureau of Indian Affairs building in Washington DC, WEYLER elaborates on the "wars" waged between the federal government and corporate interests, on the one hand, and the American Indian Movement on the other, in the late 1960s and early 1970s, which led to the suspicious deaths of several activists and the arrests of other prominent AIM members such as Leonard Peltier.

Of the earlier studies, MATTHIESSEN stands out as the most extensively researched and realistic exploration of the "new Indian wars" of the 1970s, and specifically the suspicious circumstances surrounding the arrest, trial, and conviction of Peltier for the murder of two FBI agents in 1975. Highly readable, Matthiessen presents not only a solid history of the Native American struggles over land leading up to the Red Power movements, but also sets out a well-documented case for Peltier's re-trial.

Meredith, Hauptman and Parman each discuss specific issues confronting Native American tribes in different geographical regions. MEREDITH explores the traditions of Native dance and tribal alliances among the Southern Plains tribes, and places those traditions within the context of the contemporary struggle to maintain cultural identities. HAUPTMAN focuses on the recent history of the Iroquois tribe, documenting the long-standing fight between the Iroquois and corporate interests over land development in the Northeast. He also discusses the role of the Iroquois in the Red Power movements. Finally, PARMAN documents the history of Western tribes in the 20th century, specifically governmental policies relating to Western tribes and regional development before and after World War II.

While the battles between activists and the United States government raged on, Native American families and tribes were plagued by yet another bureaucratic assault on an even more personal level. Beginning with the BIA sponsored Indian Adoption Project in 1958 and extending into the late 1970s, thousands of Native children were removed from their families and tribes and adopted into white homes. Featuring essays by writers such as Native American attorney William Byler and Senator James Abourezk, who helped pass the Indian Child Welfare Act in 1978, UNGER explores the short and long term effects of child removal on Native families. There are also essays focusing on the effects of urbanization on Native American families, and on the shortcomings of family and child welfare services in assisting those families. While Unger is one of the few studies available that specifically addresses the disintegration of Native families, its lack of either an index or a bibliography makes it less than helpful in tracking down other sources on this subject.

Yet another subject that has only recently begun to receive sufficient attention in Native American studies is the history and status of Native women. While comprehensive approaches to this subject remain to be written, Hertzberg and Powers each discuss the roles of Native women as community leaders in specific areas. HERTZBERG provides extensive information on women's roles in the Pan-Indian movements of the 1960s and 1970s, and POWERS discusses Native women's tribal, community, and professional leadership among the Oglala tribes.

Brand and Mankiller are biographies of individual Native women, but the differing status of their subjects within the tribal community makes each study useful in its own way, for gaining an understanding of the issues confronting contemporary Native women. BRAND tells the story of murdered AIM activist Anna Mae Aquash whose death in 1976 remains, for many Native Americans, emblematic of the FBI targeting of AIM and other Red Power groups. Aquash was a prominent member of AIM who participated in the Wounded Knee occupation, and her mysterious murder at the height of the FBI crackdown on the group is still viewed with suspicion by many Native groups. MANKILLER is an autobiographical account of Cherokee Chief Wilma Mankiller, the first woman to be appointed to such an office within her tribe. An accomplished writer and speaker, she clearly delineates the struggles of Native American women, both within the tribe and within white society.

ROBIN L.E. HEMENWAY

Native Americans: Chiefs, biographies

Adams, Alexander B., *Geronimo: A Biography*, New York: Putnam, 1971

Eckert, Allan W., *A Sorrow in Our Heart: The Life of Tecumseh*, New York: Bantam, 1992

Hagan, William T., *Quanah Parker: Comanche Chief*, Norman: University of Oklahoma Press, 1993

Hartley, William and Ellen Hartley, *Osceola: The Unconquered Indian*, New York: Hawthorn, 1973

Howard, Helen Addison, *War Chief Joseph*, Caldwell, ID: Caxton, 1941; as *Saga of Chief Joseph*, 1965, reprinted Lincoln: University of Nebraska Press, 1978

Mankiller, Wilma and Michael Wallis, *Mankiller: A Chief and Her People*, New York: St. Martin's Press, 1993

Snow, Dean R., *The Iroquois*, Oxford and Cambridge, MA: Blackwell, 1994

Sweeney, Edwin R., *Cochise: Chiricahua Apache Chief*, Norman: University of Oklahoma Press, 1991

Utley, Robert M., *The Lance and the Shield: The Life and Times of Sitting Bull*, New York: Holt, 1993

All histories – and American history is no exception – are often made up of the stories of "heroes", accounts of those individuals who have come to be regarded as remarkable in some way. In recent years, the way in which the history of men and women of achievement is told has undergone some major shifts, and many historians have begun to redefine their conceptions of what constitutes a "hero". In the history of Native American leaders, these shifts have resulted in a re-assessment of the roles those leaders played, both among their own people and within the context of white/Native American relations. From the first contact with Europeans, through the "Indian Wars" of the 19th century, through the "Red Power" movements of the 1960s and 1970s, to the present day, Native American tribes have experienced assimilation, land loss and resettlement, and the loss of their cultural and political autonomy. Native American chiefs have led their tribes through extreme social, political, economic and cultural change. Both glamorized and demonized throughout history, Native American leaders were very often devoted tribespeople, courageous mediators, astute politicians, and sometimes fierce warriors. The lives of these men (and women) have long been a source of fascination to biographers, and only recently have historians begun a serious re-evaluation of their stories.

Many Native tribes, especially in the earliest years of white settlement, did not recognize the same codes of authority as white society. It is perhaps for this reason that there are very few studies documenting the lives of early Native American chiefs. However, one of the most prominent tribes in American history, the Iroquois, were forced to confront the threat of white domination during the first years of white settlement. Although it does not focus exclusively on any particular chiefs, SNOW nonetheless serves as a useful resource for examining the circumstances confronting early tribal leaders. His comprehensive account explores the history of the Iroquois tribe from 900 AD to the present day, focusing extensively on the lives of Iroquois tribespeople before and during white contact. Snow also examines the first "Indian Wars" between Natives and white colonists, including the well-known conflict dominated by the Mohawk chief King Philip, and the role of the Iroquois in these conflicts.

The life of Tecumseh, the famous Shawnee leader and warrior, is vividly portrayed in ECKERT. Born in 1768 during a period of rising tensions between whites and Natives, Tecumseh, although he was never a Shawnee Chief, nonetheless grew to be one of the most powerful Native warrior leaders during the Native/white conflicts of the late 18th and early 19th century. Renowned as a charismatic and highly spiritual tribesman among the Shawnee, Tecumseh fought to unite Native tribes against the threat of white domination. Eckert traces Tecumseh's life in a narrative style that is both informative and fascinating, and succeeds remarkably in re-evaluating mythologized perceptions of Tecumseh's experiences and accomplishments.

HARTLEY documents the life of one of the most legendary of the Native American chiefs: Osceola, a Seminole warrior chief who led the Seminoles in the early and mid-19th century. Like many of his contemporaries, Osceola played a prominent role in the Native/white conflicts of the 19th century, particularly in the famous "Seminole Wars", in which the vastly outnumbered Florida tribe fought the United States army to retain control of their land. These wars stand as the one of the strongest examples of Native resistance to white encroachment and governmental authority, and Osceola is largely remembered as an inspiring personification of this resistance. Hartley focuses primarily on Osceola's role in the Second Seminole War, which took place from 1835 to 1842, although he also attempts to reconstruct other phases of Osceola's life and experiences. Although the narrative is sometimes one-dimensional and the sources are often sketchy, Hartley nonetheless remains the only comprehensive biography of this great Seminole warrior.

SWEENEY's biography of Cochise, the 19th-century Apache chief known for his accomplishments in battle during the "Indian Wars", is well-written and extensively researched. During the long Native American resistance to white settlement in the 19th century West, Cochise was renowned throughout the Apache nation as a valiant warrior and a great leader. Known for his fierce hatred of all whites, Cochise led his tribe in battle from 1861 to 1872. He was often the aggressor in these battles, a fact which made him one of the most feared and vilified "Indian savages" among white settlers. Sweeney does an admirable job of separating the myth of Cochise from reality in this study. He situates Cochise in the context of his accomplishments as an Apache leader, rather than evaluating his life within the traditional historical view that held Cochise to be an "enemy" to whites. Sweeney explores Cochise's motives and ambitions, and documents the events occurring among Native American tribes in the 19th century that led to the creation of the Cochise "legend".

One of the best recent accounts of a Native chief is HAGAN, who documents the life of the Comanche chief Quanah Parker. The son of a Comanche warrior and a white captive, Parker acted as an intermediary between the Comanche and United States government officials from 1875 until his death in 1911. Well researched and highly readable, Hagan is especially useful for its account of the ways in which Parker and other Plains Indian leaders negotiated their dual roles as both tribal leaders and political diplomats, as Native Americans attempted to maintain their cultural identity and their commitment to their tribes, while working with white officials.

In his study of the life of Geronimo, ADAMS attempts to reassess the mythic image of its subject. Geronimo, an Apache chief from the 19th century and one of the most famous of the Native American chiefs, has often served as the model for many of the stereotyped portrayals of chiefs in literature, television, and film. Adams explores these portrayals and provides a good review of sources for further study of Geronimo's life. The narrative is somewhat dated, and Adams devotes too much attention to Geronimo's assistance to whites, rather than to an adequate exploration of Geronimo's position among the Apache, and within the larger Native American community.

Although HOWARD, first published in 1941, is a somewhat dated account of the Chief Joseph, the famous Nez Perce warrior chief and tribal diplomat, it nonetheless remains one of the only comprehensive studies of Chief Joseph's life. It focuses mainly on Chief Joseph's prominent role in the Nez Perce War of 1877, which was one of the last major open conflicts between Native tribes and United States forces. Sometimes called "The Red Napoleon of the West", Chief Joseph was often portrayed as a brilliant tactician in war, but Howard proposes a "new interpretation" of Joseph's role as warrior-chief. She explores, for example, his tireless diplomatic efforts to attain justice at the hands of whites. Howard stands out as one of the earliest accounts of a Native American chief that explores its subject within the context of both tribal life and the tensions between whites and Natives in the 19th century.

UTLEY is a substantial account of the life of Sitting Bull, one of the most well-known warrior chiefs of the 19th century. A Hunkpapa Sioux, Sitting Bull was the predominant leader of the "non-treaty" Lakota tribes, those Native bands who rejected compromise and resisted white domination in the face of great odds until the late 1800s. Utley tackles traditional perceptions of Sitting Bull, choosing to examine his actions and motivations not only within the context of the Sioux culture, but also within the context of his role as a man caught between the white threat he struggled against and the tribe he fiercely defended.

MANKILLER is an autobiographical account of Cherokee Chief Wilma Mankiller, the first woman to be appointed to an official position of leadership within her tribe. Wilma Mankiller was elected principal chief of the Cherokee Nation of Oklahoma in 1987, and was re-elected to that office in 1991. While her election as the first female chief brought much attention to her and her tribe, Mankiller has continued to work tirelessly to improve the lives of the Oklahoma Cherokee, and has proved to have a lasting influence on the tribe. One of the few available biographical portraits of a contemporary Native American leader, Mankiller not only delineates the struggles of Native American women within tribal culture and contemporary white society, but also the experiences of contemporary Native American leaders confronting persistent threats to cultural identity and political, social, and economic justice for Native tribes.

ROBIN L.E. HEMENWAY

Native Americans: Cultures

1) Northeast

Axtell, James (editor), *The Indian Peoples of Eastern America: A Documentary History of the Sexes*, New York: Oxford University Press, 1981

Barbour, Philip L., *Pocahontas and Her World: A Chronicle of America's First Settlement*, Boston: Houghton Mifflin, 1970; London: Hale, 1971

Brown, Jennifer S.H., *Strangers in Blood: Fur Trade Families in Indian Country*, Vancouver: University of British Columbia Press, 1981

Frazier, Patrick, *The Mohicans of Stockbridge*, Lincoln: University of Nebraska Press, 1992

Hauptman, Laurence M., *The Iroquois and the New Deal*, Syracuse, NY: Syracuse University Press, 1981

Hauptman, Laurence M., *The Iroquois in the Civil War: From Battlefield to Reservation*, Syracuse, NY: Syracuse University Press, 1993

Jennings, Francis, *The Invasion of America: Indians, Colonialism, and the Cant of Conquest*, Chapel Hill: University of North Carolina Press, 1975

Jennings, Francis, *The Ambiguous Iroquois Empire: The Covenant Chain Confederation of Indian Tribes with English Colonies from Its Beginnings to the Lancaster Treaty of 1744*, New York: Norton, 1984

Snow, Dean R., *The Iroquois*, Oxford and Cambridge, MA: Blackwell 1994

Trigger, Bruce G. (editor), *Handbook of North American Indians*, volume 15: *Northeast*, Washington, DC: Smithsonian Institution Press, 1978

Van Kirk, Sylvia, *Many Tender Ties: Women in Fur-Trade Society, 1670–1870*, Norman: University of Oklahoma Press, 1983

Wallace, Anthony F.C., *The Death and Rebirth of the Seneca*, New York: Knopf, 1969

The history of Native peoples of the northeastern United States necessarily records a series of complex cultural transformations in response to the influence of European contact. It also incorporates events and interactions of fundamental significance to the development of the United States and Canada, and to the development of the discipline of anthropology in both countries.

The most comprehensive, broad-ranging and detailed study of northeastern native peoples is the volume edited by TRIGGER. This handbook is the second published of a multi-volumed set which aims to give an encyclopaedic summary of what is known about the prehistory, history, and cultures of the aboriginal peoples of North America who lived north of the urban civilizations of central Mexico. Given that the concept of culture areas is considered problematic, the handbook's contributors have regarded the Northeast as an editorial convenience. It deals with the region's prehistory in four analytical segments and then discusses separate tribes within three geographical sub-divisions delineated by ecological boundaries: the Coastal Region, the Saint Lawrence Lowlands Region and the Great Lakes-Riverine Region. More than seventy separate essays, up to date as of the mid-1970s, describe the history, cultural background, and contemporary circumstances of the Native American peoples of the northeastern United States and southeastern Canada. Those Native American groups who live there and those who have lived there during the most significant or best-documented period of their history are discussed. These summaries are accompanied by an invaluable overview of the history of research on the region and an 84-page bibliography. The volume remains an excellent scholarly introduction to further study.

In contrast to Trigger's large tome, SNOW provides a highly readable and fresh account of perhaps the largest and best-documented group of Native peoples in the Northeast – the Iroquois. Beginning in 900 AD, and integrating modern archaeology, ethnohistory and anthropology, Snow traces the depth of change endured and initiated by the Mohawk, Oneida, Onondaga, Cayuga, Seneca and later Tuscarora peoples and their ancestors. He gives a concise reading of events surrounding the formation of the League of the Iroquois in the 16th century and its connection to the legendary Hiawatha. The text's final sections chronicle Iroquois revival and cultural continuity up to the present day. Although non-Indian, Snow has used his experience and field-based research to create a valuable insight into Iroquois history, and he is careful to categorize his text as a "book about the Iroquois, not about the non-Iroquois who interacted with them and who largely wrote their history as we now know it". He makes general inferences about the nature of human evolution, and uses the direct historic approach in this volume.

Earlier but more specific treatments of northeastern native peoples are provided by Jennings who describes his 1984 book as a "balancing supplement" to the material in his earlier study. JENNINGS (1975) is a useful introduction to the ideological and cultural complexities of early contact and interrelationship in New England. He attempts to strip away the myths of European conquest and to highlight the contributions of both colonists and natives to the creation of the United States. JENNINGS (1984) details an aspect of northeastern history which the Smithsonian handbook ignores – that is, what Jennings describes as "the history of the peoples who formed a Covenant Chain of formal cooperation between Indian tribes and British colonies." An iconoclastic writer whose work often stimulates heated debate and dissent, he has nonetheless brought new insight to definitions of the American frontier and brought a fuller "Indian" perspective to that history.

Although 20th-century Native American history has not to date received sufficient scholarly attention, Hauptman's contributions to the Syracuse University Press "The Iroquois and Their Neighbours" series has done much to bring modern Iroquoia into clearer focus. His acute knowledge of Iroquois history, attention to rich archival sources, and credibility within contemporary Iroquois communities makes his work incisive

and authoritative. HAUPTMAN (1981) illustrates both the successes and limitations of the Indian New Deal in Iroquoia, sheds new light on New Deal Indian policy and policymakers and highlights modern developments in Iroquois leadership. HAUPTMAN (1993) examines Iroquois military participation in the Civil War, details Iroquois attempts to retain autonomy and identity during this period and records the impact of the war upon Iroquois populations. This text usefully details "Grant's Indian", Ely S. Parker – the first Indian Commissioner of Indian Affairs – as well as lesser known Iroquois figures such as the military commander Cornelius C. Cusick (War Eagle) and the political spokesman Samuel George.

Studies of single Northeastern tribes include WALLACE's penetrating study of the late colonial and reservation history of the Seneca Iroquois, and FRAZIER's discussion of the Mohicans of Stockbridge, Massachusetts. Wallace usefully records the religious revitalization of Native American society which accompanied the rise of the prophet Handsome Lake around 1800. Although somewhat pedestrian, Frazier's text relates the 18th-century history of the Mohicans/Mahicans, a tribe immortalized and mythologized by the novelist James Fenimore Cooper.

European views of Northeastern Native American women receive a degree of attention in AXTELL, and Northeastern Native American women themselves are considered in some of the recent literature on the fur trade. One example is BROWN's excellent monograph, which highlights the economic and familial relationships that developed between Native American women and British and French fur traders. Native American female sexual and cultural alliances are also the focus of VAN KIRK who discusses "country marriages" and the impact of the products of those marriages on the Anglo-American frontier. BARBOUR's thorough study attacks the myths surrounding the early Northeastern Powhatan "heroine" Pocahontas, and remains a fruitful starting point for study of Northeastern women and their representation.

JOY PORTER

2) Southeast

Blitz, John, *Ancient Chiefdoms of the Tombigbee*, Tuscaloosa: University of Alabama Press, 1993

Braund, Kathryn E. Holland, *Deerskins and Duffels: The Creek Indian Trade with Anglo-America, 1685–1815*, Lincoln: University of Nebraska Press, 1993

Covington, James, *The Seminoles of Florida*, Gainesville: University Press of Florida, 1993

Finger, John R., *Cherokee Americans: The Eastern Band of Cherokees in the Twentieth Century*, Lincoln: University of Nebraska Press, 1991

McLoughlin, William G., *Cherokees and Missionaries, 1789–1839*, New Haven: Yale University Press, 1984

Martin, Joel, *Sacred Revolt: The Muskogees' Struggle for a New World*, Boston: Beacon Press, 1991

Merrell, James H., *The Indians' New World: Catawbas and Their Neighbors from European Contact Through the Era of Removal*, Chapel Hill: University of North Carolina Press, 1989

Williams, Walter L. (editor), *Southeastern Indians since the Removal Era*, Athens: University of Georgia Press, 1979

The mound sites that loom over the landscape of the Southeast today stand as mute reminders of the region's Native American past, but the region's Native American present is far from silent. Over five centuries southern Indians have responded in a variety of ways to the pressures of European colonization and American expansion. The moundbuilders may have long vanished, but their descendants today are still a part of southern society.

Between 700 and 1000 AD, the Mississippian cultural complex spread across much of the South and differentiated the region's peoples from other North American Indian cultures. Characterized by centralized, hierarchically organized polities known as chiefdoms, Mississippian societies raised corn on river floodplains, constructed impressive mound sites, and produced artwork of extraordinary beauty. Archaeologists like Blitz are now beginning to piece together what Mississippian life may have been like. BLITZ nicely balances narrative synthesis with archaeological site details, and explains how small simple chiefdoms differed from large complex ones, such as Moundville, in terms of economic and political organization. After the Spanish *entradas* of the 16th century these societies collapsed, and the people who confronted European settlement in the 17th century cast but a shadow of their Mississippian past.

MERRELL tells the remarkable story of some of these remnant peoples who struggled to reconstruct their lives and cultures in the new world. Like other southern tribes, the Catawbas of present South Carolina had not existed before contact. After successive waves of disease, trade dependency, and settlement pressures ravaged the region's tribes, the remnants pulled together as one people for purposes of subsistence and protection. Ever since, the Catawbas have always managed to find a niche in the region's economy, whether as colonial slavecatchers, revolutionary levies, or 19th century craftsmen and hunters.

The Creeks of present Georgia and Alabama experienced a history similar to that of their Catawba neighbors. But unlike the marginal Catawbas, the Creeks were major players in the English deerskin and slave trade. BRAUND tracks the impact of the trade on Creek traditions of reciprocity, communalism, and kinship, and concludes that despite the operation of market incentives, overhunting, and economic dependency, essential elements of Creek culture persisted. Nevertheless, economic dependency had undermined the tribe's autonomy. Pressed after the American Revolution by traders demanding payment of debts and aggressive settlers pushing for more land, the Creeks had to sell their greatest resource, their land.

They responded in two ways to settlement pressures and economic dependency. According to MARTIN, those who had profited from the deerskin trade, like William McIntosh, favored accommodation with the United States. Others, inspired by prophetic religious visions, resented the growing influence of the United States, and determined to resist it tooth and nail. These nativists, called Red Sticks, acted out their fears through what Martin considers the ritual of warfare. The Red Sticks' religious zeal sparked a Creek Civil War that spilled over into the War of 1812. The millenarian hopes of the Red Sticks, however, collapsed under the weight of several American assaults.

McLOUGHLIN argues that in response to problems similar to those faced by the Creeks, Cherokee chiefs led their people in a decidedly different direction. Rather than restoring traditions such as matrilineal descent, clan revenge, and political decentralization, Chief John Ross and his supporters enacted a variety of reforms designed to acculturate the Cherokees to American ways of life. The reform effort culminated in the drafting of a national constitution in 1829 that created a Cherokee government modeled after that of the United States. Charged with defending Cherokee sovereignty, the national government waged its struggle in newspapers and lawsuits rather than on the battlefield.

By 1840 the federal government had removed most of the Creeks, Cherokees, and other Southeastern Indians from their homes to Indian Territory, present Oklahoma. For those that remained life proved extremely difficult. Southern Indians belonged to neither the white nor the black castes of southern society, and, in many cases, lacked legal title to land. Impoverished and denigrated, they eked out a meager living on the margins of southern society.

Among the larger groups of Indians who remained in the South after removal were the Florida Seminoles. COVINGTON tracks the Seminoles from their genesis as a tribe in the 17th century to their present attempts to build a strong and prosperous tribe. Two major wars and a number of other conflicts with the federal government shaped a unique Seminole culture based on small family bands scattered throughout the state's swampy interior. In spite of Florida's expansion, interference from various benevolent organizations, and a reluctance to organize as a tribe, the Seminoles have been remarkably successful at coping with change. Covington shows that when given the opportunity to direct their own affairs, the tribe has skilfully invested in cattle ranching, construction, smokeshops, and gambling.

FINGER argues that much of the Cherokees' post-removal history has involved a struggle to retain their identity. Thanks to the work of Will Thomas, the Eastern Cherokees held title, albeit unsure, to land in western North Carolina that was not covered by the 1839 removal treaty. In the early 20th century, logging, the Appalachian railroad, and the World War I draft pulled these Cherokees into the American mainstream. Ever since, their greatest challenge has been to balance a tension between participation in the market economy and preservation of their distinct identity. Tourism, the tribe's leading economic activity throughout the 20th century, exacerbated this tension, and bitter factional disputes persist to the present as Cherokees debate how best to juxtapose modernization and tradition.

Other smaller tribes also continue to live throughout the South. WILLIAMS surveys several remnant groups that either escaped removal or were overlooked by the federal government. Unrecognized as tribes until recently, the Tunicas, Houmas, and Lumbees, as well as remnants of the Creeks and Choctaws have struggled for federal recognition, tribal services, and, most importantly of all, land.

Far from a vanished people, Native Americans still comprise a significant segment of the southern population. As the South confronts its legacy of racism, economic under-development, and political conservatism, Native Americans will continue their struggle to survive, and contribute their own vision to debate over the region's future.

JAMES TAYLOR CARSON

3) Great Plains

Anderson, Gary C., *Kinsmen of Another Kind: Dakota-White Relations in the Upper Mississippi Valley, 1650–1862*, Lincoln: University of Nebraska Press, 1984

Ewers, John, *The Blackfeet: Raiders on the Northwestern Plains*, Norman: University of Oklahoma Press, 1958

Foster, Morris W., *Being Comanche: A Social History of an American Indian Community*, Tucson: University of Arizona Press, 1991

Fowler, Loretta, *Arapahoe Politics, 1851–1978: Symbols in Crises of Authority*, Lincoln: University of Nebraska Press, 1982

Moore, John H., *The Cheyenne Nation: A Social and Demographic History*, Lincoln: University of Nebraska Press, 1987

Rollings, Willard H., *The Osage: An Ethnohistorical Study of Hegemony on the Prairie-Plains*, Columbia: University of Missouri Press, 1992

Wishart, David J., *The Fur Trade of the American West, 1807–1840: A Geographical Synthesis*, Lincoln: University of Nebraska Press, 1979

The past popularity of western movies, dimestore novels, and cowboy romances secured for the Plains Indians an important place in the mythology of the American West. According to the myth, the Plains Indians were nomads who rode horseback across the Great Plains in search of buffalo and who resisted violently the westward expansion of the United States. Historians, however, have been writing against such ingrained stereotypes for several years, and recent scholarly works on the Plains Indians have revealed a complex history of cultural change and ethnic persistence over the course of four centuries.

Spanish horses and European guns were by far the most profound agents of cultural change among the Plains Indians. EWERS is a classic work which compares the "dog days" of the Blackfeet, a nomadic tribe of hunters and gatherers that used dogs as beasts of burden, with their 17th century transformation into feared horseback warriors and hunters. Blackfeet dominance, however, waned as the tribe succumbed to epidemic diseases and became dependent on European manufactured goods. In the 19th century the U.S. army confined the Blackfeet to a reservation, and Ewers traces the difficulties which they faced in adjusting to the loss of their freedom and way of life.

Unlike the Blackfeet, the Osage inhabited a transitional zone between the western plains, where they hunted buffalo, and the eastern prairies, where they farmed corn and other crops. Though horses and guns dramatically changed their lives, ROLLINGS argues that their semi-sedentary lifestyle, mixed economy, complex kinship organization, and geographic location facilitated their rise as a major power in the 18th century. The Osage, Rollings shows, created a "plains-prairie hegemony" predicated on controlling the flow of trade goods that reached their western rivals. Numerous changes in the Osage's social and economic organization occurred as a result of their growing hegemony. The traditional political system, however, was incapable of keeping pace with the changes, and United States traders and agents began to exert a destabilizing influence on tribal affairs. By the 19th century the tribe had

fragmented into rival bands that were ill-prepared to confront the westward expansion of the United States.

To acquire the guns and horses that made them so powerful, tribes like the Blackfeet and Osage traded slaves, livestock, and, most importantly, animal skins. The importance of the Indians in the western fur trade had been overlooked until WISHART showed that the western trade was not a monolithic enterprise dominated by capitalist companies and American traders. Rather, the trade consisted of a buffalo hide trade in the Upper Plains and a beaver pelt trade in the Rocky Mountains. Whereas Indians played only a limited role in the expansion and profitability of the latter, they were crucial to the creation and expansion of the former. Wishart focuses on the structure of the fur trade, rather than on its impact on tribal cultures.

ANDERSON complements Wishart in a study which explores how fur traders affected the Dakota. French traders first married into the Dakota in the mid-17th century, and the tribe welcomed them into their families. As part of their reciprocal ethic, the Indians shared with the traders their food, shelter, and protection in exchange for manufactured goods and cloth. Over time, traders gained influence in the tribe's political councils, and they facilitated the maintenance of peaceful relations with whites. However, much as happened among the Osage, United States agents usurped the earlier traders' influence and meddled in tribal affairs. Decades of fraud and deceit exacerbated political tensions, and in 1862 the Dakota attacked surrounding American settlements, sparing only traders and their families. The Dakota war inspired similar conflicts across the Plains which erupted sporadically until the 1890 massacre at Wounded Knee.

In the aftermath of Wounded Knee, the federal government sought to confine Plains Indians on their reservations and to change them from nomadic hunters to farmers and stock raisers. The people, however, were reluctant to accept the admonitions of agents and missionaries to become "civilized." Among the Arapahoe for example, FOWLER shows how their culture, particularly their system of age-grades, enabled them to avoid the generational strife and political factionalization that occurred among other Plains reservation tribes as their earlier way of life vanished. Fowler uses Arapahoe myths and rituals to uncover the sources of this tribe's unique history and exceptional success, and she shows how Arapahoe culture has endured in spite of various economic, social, and political changes.

FOSTER argues that, among the Comanche, kinship and a shared need to gather in public places has preserved the tribe's distinct identity. To the Comanche one's public reputation or "face" determined one's identity as a Comanche and one's place within the tribe. Foster concludes that participation in 19th century Peyote ceremonies, early 20th century Christian congregations, and contemporary powwows ensured the persistence of a tribal identity despite several transformations of the tribe's political economy.

Like Fowler and Foster, MOORE is concerned with how Plains Indians have maintained their identities to the present. He focuses his attention not on the context of Cheyenne political adaptations or social gatherings, but on the sacred imagery of the circle that structured those gatherings. From the shapes of tipis to the circular pattern of seating at tribal councils, the circle has symbolic significance in Cheyenne society and history. In Moore's capable hands oral and documentary sources come together to describe Cheyenne ethnogenesis in the 16th century, their transformation from hunters and gatherers to nomadic buffalo hunters in the 17th and 18th centuries, and their subsequent confinement to reservations in the 20th century. Through it all, the symbolic circle has ensured a continuity in identity and in belief.

Sacred circles are a far cry from the feathered war bonnets that have been popularly associated with Plains Indian culture. From the "dog days" of the Blackfeet to the modern Cheyenne powwow, Plains Indian culture has changed considerably. In contrast the meaning of being Blackfeet, Osage, Dakota, Arapahoe, Comanche, or Cheyenne has changed little, and it is this sense of identity that binds together the past and the present of the Plains Indians

JAMES TAYLOR CARSON

4) Southwest

Bailey, Garrick and Roberta Glenn Bailey, *A History of the Navajos: The Reservation Years*, Santa Fe: School of American Research Press, 1986

Benedek, Emily, *The Wind Won't Know Me: A History of the Navajo-Hopi Land Dispute*, New York: Knopf, 1992

Cordell, Linda, *Prehistory of the Southwest*, Orlando, FL: Academic Press, 1984

Dozier, Edward P., *The Pueblo Indians of North America*, New York: Holt Rinehart, 1970

Fagan, Brian M., *Ancient North America: The Archaeology of a Continent*, New York: Thames and Hudson, 1991, revised 1995

Frazier, Kendrick, *People of Chaco: A Canyon and Its Culture*, New York: Norton, 1986

Horgan, Paul, *Great River: The Rio Grande in North American History*, 2 vols., New York: Rinehart, 1954; revised, 1 vol., Austin: Texas Monthly Press, 1984

McNitt, Frank, *The Indian Traders*, Norman: University of Oklahoma Press, 1962

Ortiz, Alfonso (editor), *Handbook of North American Indians*, volumes 9–10: *The Southwest*, Washington, DC: Smithsonian Institution Press, 1979–83

For purposes of this discussion the Southwest includes the present-day states of Arizona and New Mexico, southwestern Colorado, southeastern Utah and southern Nevada. The U.S.-Mexican border is an entirely artificial cultural demarcation, since some of the tribes discussed are closely linked to groups now resident in northern Mexico, but historically and politically its presence is significant in the experience of the Indian community. The Native American population of the southwest divides into the Pueblo communities of New Mexico, most of which are found along the Rio Grande; the more isolated pueblos of Acoma and Zuni in New Mexico; the Hopi Pueblos in northern Arizona; the Apache and Navajo tribes in Arizona and New Mexico; and the Uto-Aztecan people of southern Arizona: the O'otam (Papago), Pima, and Yaqui as well as the related Ute of southern Nevada and southeastern Colorado, and the Yuman peoples of the Colorado river. While there are

many reservations and other Native communities spread through the region, it is true that in the Southwest, as elsewhere, many people live in urban areas, and may actively participate in the traditional life of their pueblo or tribe only on special occasions.

A long human history is clearly written in the landscape of the greater Southwest. Evidence of hunting camps dating back more than ten thousand years, remains of impressive and complex ceremonial centres such as Chaco Canyon in New Mexico, the small farming villages of the Colorado Plateau, all contribute to the detailed view of Southwestern archaeology in CORDELL. Archaeologists can help interpret the early contact period by working together with contemporary Indians, historians and anthropologists. In the Southwest it has been possible to assemble the best documentation on pre-contact history available for any area of the United States. Most of the indigenous people of the Southwest have lived as farmers in well-constructed permanent communities known as pueblos (from the Spanish for town) for many centuries. The remains of long abandoned pueblos and cliff dwellings, and the evidence of social, economic and spiritual activity which they provide, are used in combination with the historical information available from their descendants.

In a lively study of the Chaco Canyon sites aimed at a general audience FRAZIER fleshes out the story of one particularly fascinating area. Patterns of migration, trade, settlement, and culture change are inferred from the combination of archaeological, historical, linguistic and environmental evidence evaluated in conjunction with recorded histories, myths and legends of individual living communities and groups. For those who need only a brief overview, a particularly lucid short summary of the complicated archaeological history of the Southwest is included in FAGAN.

While written accounts of the area date from as early as 1540 with the visit of the Coronado expedition, Spanish influence on and occupation of the Southwest really commenced in the late 16th century. For information on the period of Spanish and Mexican occupation the reader should turn to histories and ethnographies of individual tribes which had quite varying experiences of this occupation; some, such as the Yuman peoples were little affected by this initial colonization, while others, such as the Rio Grande pueblos were placed under great pressure. ORTIZ (1979, 1983) provides a scholarly introduction to the history and culture of the entire range of tribes and communities in the Southwest, and also to the literature on the subject. DOZIER has surveyed the history and culture of the Pueblo peoples in careful detail. BAILEY and BAILEY on the Navajo is a good example of the many long awaited tribal histories which have begun to appear.

The vast and sweepingly grand narrative human history of the Rio Grande region by HORGAN provides an exciting introduction to the interaction of the Native American, Hispanic and Yankee cultures which began in this era and continues today. Some of Horgan's analyses seem dated now, but it remains an illuminating and unusual history.

The Pueblo rebellion of 1680 saw the Spanish temporarily driven back into Mexico. Mexico briefly controlled most of the area from 1821 until 1846 when the United States took possession of the region. During the Civil War, the Apache and Navajo were seen as a threat to United States military interests, standing in the way of free travel to the Pacific Coast. Military campaigns resulted in the imprisonment of most of the Navajo in Fort Sumner in New Mexico for four years. The contemporary reservation system was established in the late 19th century. Southwestern historian McNITT has written a sympathetic and engaging study of the characters who ran trading posts among the Navajo during the period following Navajo resettlement. His book usefully examines the economic interactions between the Navajo and outsiders, which have played an important part in shaping culture change for many tribes.

Real reform of the reservation system did not begin until 1934, with the work of John Collier, who had a particular personal interest in the Indians of the Southwest. One of the most important problems in 20th-century Native American history has been competition over land, mineral rights and water rights in the Southwest. The Navajo-Hopi land dispute and its attendant issues have been particularly well documented. BENEDEK provides a journalist's history of the problem which has plagued the lives of many Navajo and Hopi, profoundly affecting relations between the two tribes, as well as their relations with state and federal officials and other residents of Arizona. Her account makes good use of interviews with those involved in the dispute.

TERI F. BREWER

5) Far West and Pacific Northwest

Cook, Sherburne F., *The Conflict Between the California Indian and White Civilization*. Berkeley: University of California Press, 1976

D'Azevedo, Warren L. (editor), *Handbook of North American Indians*, volume 11: *Great Basin*, Washington, DC: Smithsonian Institution Press, 1986

Hurtado, Albert L., *Indian Survival on the California Frontier*, New Haven: Yale University Press, 1988

Kehoe, Alice Beck, *The Ghost Dance: Ethnohistory and Revitalization*, New York: Holt Rinehart, 1989

Kroeber, Alfred L., *Handbook of the Indians of California*, Washington, DC: Smithsonian Institution, 1925

Laird, Carobeth, *Encounter with an Angry God: Recollections of My Life with John Peabody Harrington*, Banning, CA: Malki Museum Press, 1975

Ruby, Robert H. and John A. Brown, *A Guide to the Indian Tribes of the Pacific Northwest*, Norman: University of Oklahoma Press, 1992

Suttles, Wayne (editor), *Handbook of North American Indians*, volume 7: *Northwest Coast*, Washington, DC: Smithsonian Institution Press, 1990

Vane, Sylvia and Lowell John Bean, *California Indians: Primary Resources: A Guide*, Menlo Park, CA: Ballena Press, 1990

Weibel-Orlando, Joan, *Indian Country, L.A.: Maintaining Ethnic Community in Complex Society*, Urbana: University of Illinois Press, 1991

The peoples covered here include Native Americans resident in the present-day states of California, Oregon, Washington and Nevada as well as parts of Utah, Wyoming, and Idaho. This region is generally separated into geographical regions which correspond broadly to the different cultural styles and historical experiences of their respective peoples. Most of California from the western slope of the Sierra Nevada mountains to the Pacific Coast, with the exception of a few tribes on the northern coast of the state, forms one locus of discussion in the work of most historians and anthropologists. The "intermontane west", the sometimes desolate terrain of basin and range which runs from the crest of the Sierra Nevada east towards the western slopes of the Rocky Mountains, is divided into two distinct areas, the Great Basin, and the Columbia Plateau. Finally, the peoples of the Pacific Northwest are those who live along the coast from Humboldt County in Northern California northwards through Oregon and Washington to the Canadian border. It is worth noting that there is no cultural line to be drawn along the Mexican or Canadian border, although there is of course a difference in the historical experience of tribes which find themselves governed by different nations or whose original territory crosses current borderlines. The most extensive literature for the region overall is undoubtedly that for California, followed by the Northwest Coast. Most of the historical work on the Great Basin and the Columbia Plateau is still to be found only in specialist journals.

The Indians of California experienced successive waves of pressure from immigrant groups beginning with the early Spanish exploration and land claims of the 16th century, but significant influence did not begin until the late 18th century when a chain of Catholic missions was established as the precursor to the coming of military and civilian settlement from Spain. The evidence for this early period of colonization and missionary activity is extensively analysed by COOK, who also discusses the other critical period in California Indian history, the Gold Rush and subsequent American conquest of California, which took place in the mid-19th century. Cook based his work on the notion that the experience of colonization, conquest and re-settlement by immigrant populations from powerful and "advanced" nations could be analysed as a shift in human ecology. He applied a biologist's understanding to historical sources. Although somewhat dated, his work remains a classic and it contains much detailed material not easily available elsewhere. HURTADO re-studied the evidence available for the pressures on late 19th century California tribes, emphasizing the analysis of those cultures which survived the calamitous impact of American settlement, and the role played by the development of California's ranching and agricultural market economy in limiting the options for cultural and individual survival.

KROEBER remains the classic anthropological reference on the cultural and linguistic characteristics of the more than fifty nations which made up present-day California. This broadly historical work, often supplemented but never replaced, remains an essential handbook for a large region with an extensive literature, much of which is contained in academic journals and other periodicals. VANE and BEAN's excellent guide to primary resources provides indispensable information on the wealth of manuscripts, artifacts, photographs, drawings and paintings which document the native cultures of California, and which are now scattered throughout the United States and around the world. One of the best introductions to the history of native California in the early 20th century is available parenthetically in LAIRD. She has written a biography of John

Peabody Harrington, a linguist and ethnologist whose detailed studies of the fragile enclaves of Indian life which survived the 19th century in California are only now being gradually published, as his extensive hoards of notes are finally transcribed many years after his death. Perhaps the most surprising thing about the recent history of Native California is the substantial increase in Indian population over the course of the 20th century. Since World War II the native community has been split into two groups, the lively but small and primarily rural indigenous communities, and the large and increasingly coherent urban Indian populations, with most individuals originating from reservations outside California. There are now more than 75,000 Native Americans in the city of Los Angeles, for example, most of whom are from tribes in other states. They have come to California in pursuit of work and educational opportunities, and some introduction to the history of the urban Native American communities in the far west can be found in WEIBEL-ORLANDO.

The peoples of the Northwest Coast are so inextricably linked with coastal peoples of Canada and Alaska that few general histories of the region would treat them separately despite the borders which divide the region. The period of real contact with Europeans and Americans began at the opening of the 19th century as fur trappers and coastal traders made their presence felt. The sedentary and stratified societies of the region were soon engaged in the fur trade, but they were left relatively unprepared for the influx of later settlers who would seek land suitable for agriculture, and usurp and destroy much of the stock of fish and marine mammals which provided the basis of the pre-contact economy along the coast. The fundamental reference work on the culture, language and experience of individual tribes is SUTTLES's comprehensive and up to date handbook. It is usefully supplemented by RUBY and BROWN, which includes concise and useful recent histories of each tribe, detailed notes on the legal status of the various communities which do not have federal acknowledgement, and useful information on further sources. Both serve as basic references for tribes of the Columbia Plateau as well.

The historical experience of Great Basin tribes was somewhat different from that of the other groups discussed here, because their highly successful and sophisticated adaptation to the difficult high desert and basin environment was not challenged until later than many other Native Americans in the far west. There was no real immigrant competition for land and resources in the Great Basin until the 1850s when American settlers began to experiment with farming and mining. Reservations established in the 1860s were broken up or reduced by the passage of the Dawes Act. A basic sourcebook for the Great Basin is D'AZEVEDO, which reliably summarizes basic cultural, linguistic and historical knowledge for all tribes in this region. Perhaps the best known historical episode in the Great Basin was the development and spread of the Ghost Dance movement, a syncretic millenarian movement based on the vision and prophecy of the Paiute prophets Wodziwob and Wovoka, beginning in 1869. An excellent account of the history of this movement, which encouraged the revival of traditional religion throughout and beyond the Great Basin, can be found in KEHOE.

TERI F. BREWER

Nativism

Anbinder, Tyler, *Nativism and Slavery: The Northern Know Nothings and the Politics of the 1850s*, New York: Oxford University Press, 1992

Bennett, David H., *The Party of Fear: From Nativist Movements to the New Right in American History*, Chapel Hill: University of North Carolina Press, 1988

Billington, Ray Allen, *The Protestant Crusade, 1800–1860: A Study of the Origins of American Nativism*, New York: Macmillan, 1938

Higham, John, *Strangers in the Land: Patterns of American Nativism, 1860–1925*, New Brunswick, NJ: Rutgers University Press, 1955, corrected reprint, 1963; 2nd edition, 1988

Jackson, Kenneth T., *The Ku Klux Klan in the City, 1915–1930*, New York: Oxford University Press, 1967

Wallace, Les, *The Rhetoric of Anti-Catholicism: The American Protective Association, 1887–1911*, New York: Garland, 1990

Fear, suspicion and hostility towards immigrants and alien ideas and influences have been recurrent features of American history. This "nativism" has taken different forms and targeted different groups at various times, and some historians see it as an emotional release, or as a search for scapegoats, in times of social tension or national crisis.

Religious intolerance of Roman Catholics was the most prominent form of nativism in antebellum America. As BILLINGTON describes in great depth in his older, but still valuable work, anti-Catholicism was the focal point of nativist activity from colonial times to the years immediately preceding the Civil War. The leaders of this movement were prominent Protestant clergymen from numerous denominations bent on halting the perceived threat of papal domination in the United States. In this richly detailed book, Billington shows how the fear of papal designs to establish a Catholic base of power in America led clergymen and others to combat encroachments from Rome on American institutions. Nativists perceived Catholic plots for domination in the public schools, where Catholics actively fought against reading the King James version of the Bible, or lobbied state legislatures for a share of public funds for their own schools; in public office-holding, where they feared Catholics would use their power to institute papal orders; and in the flood of Irish and German Catholic immigrants who were seen as purposely sent to America to overpower native Protestants numerically. Through public debates, propaganda, the formation of numerous organizations, and, at times, violent confrontation, these anti-Catholic nativists sought to expose the papist conspiracy. From outright lies and condemnation to more subtle efforts to convert unknowingly-led Catholics, nativists fought to promote Protestant values and maintain Protestant political and social power. Billington charts the rise of anti-Catholic sentiment to its pinnacle with the formation of the Know Nothing Party in 1854.

ANBINDER's examination of the quick rise and equally swift demise of the Know Nothing Party in the mid-1850s is an interesting case study of the power and limits of nativist ideology in America. Toward the middle of the 19th century, dramatically increasing immigration rates combined with escalating tensions between Protestants and Catholics over educational and political patronage issues led to the formation of the secret nativist fraternal order popularly called Know Nothings. By 1854, Know Nothings would enjoy unprecedented electoral success. Although Anbinder acknowledges the important attraction of nativist ideals in Know Nothing political triumphs, the ultimate cause for such stunning success lay not in nativism's appeal but in the political realities of 1850s America. The political parties forged during the Jacksonian era lost much of their appeal among anti-Catholic voters concerned with immigration restriction, as well as to those who placed the temperance issue or the geographical restriction of slavery at the top of their political agenda. The combination of nativism, temperance, and anti-slavery made the Know Nothings an attractive alternative to the Whigs and Democrats. It explained both their success and their rapid demise. Know Nothings began to split by 1856 over their regional differences on slavery. As the newly formed Republican party was able to attract Know Nothings on the basis of their strong anti-slavery stance, the power of the Know Nothings receded. Nativism alone could not provide the basis for a lasting political party at a time when slavery dominated national debate.

Relying more on rhetorical criticism than historical analysis, WALLACE examines the continuation of the anti-Catholic strain of American nativism into the late 19th and early 20th century as manifested in the American Protective Association (APA). Anti-Catholicism rose again because of a combination of the ever-present, although sometimes dormant, Protestant tradition fearing papal authority, and renewed conflicts over public schools caused, in part, by a new wave of Catholic immigrants. The APA gave organizational form to resurrected nativism aimed at Catholics. Although the APA officially existed between 1887 and 1911, it was only truly powerful between 1893 and 1896. APA rhetoric centered around a number of related themes: fear of papal authority, Catholic militancy and political power, the diminished integrity of Protestant public education, immigration restriction, denigration of Catholics, and the patriotic duty of Protestants to resist Romanism. The APA declined after 1896 not because of Catholic resistance, but because of its own political failures. Wallace's book is hampered by his reliance on rhetorical criticism, which makes his prose clumsy and formulaic. Its value is in synthesizing and categorizing the major thrust of the speeches and writings of numerous APA members.

JACKSON provides another case study of nativist organization, the resurrected Ku Klux Klan of the 1920s, among whose main targets were Catholics and immigrants from southern and eastern Europe. By close examination of Klan organization and activity in a variety of cities in the 1920s, Jackson argues that the Klan was an expression of lower-middle-class dissatisfaction with the changing urban world. Rather than being a predominantly rural or small town movement, the Klan in the 1920s was strongest in urban areas that experienced the most dramatic changes caused by industrialization, immigration, and black migration. Although violence did exist, most Klansmen were not violent people. Jackson argues that the rapid rise of the movement is best explained by understanding how one group of people responded to modernism by looking backward and seeking to preserve what

to them were traditional social arrangements, now dramatically challenged by the perceived threats of immigrants and blacks.

Originally published in 1955, HIGHAM's work remains the standard examination of American nativism from the late 19th century to the passage of immigration restriction laws in the early 1920s. Higham describes nativism as a variant of nationalism, a constant force in American culture. The appeal of nativism, defined as an intertwining of anti-Catholic, anti-radical, and racist ideas, expands and contracts depending on political, economic, and psychological factors. Higham probes the extent to which nativism was a response to times of perceived or real crisis, and he dissects why certain nativist ideas were stronger than others during these crises. Nativist activity in the first two decades of the 20th century, however, was not just another outburst from a relatively powerless group of xenophobes. Nativists permanently changed American culture. Massive immigration to the United States was cut off, the validity of the idea of America as a sanctuary for the oppressed was greatly diminished, and the equation of national loyalty with conformity became a dominant and enduring idea.

BENNETT provides a comprehensive narrative of fear of foreigners and alien influences in American culture and politics. From the colonial era to the rise of the New Right in the 1980s, Bennett synthesizes numerous primary and secondary sources in examining nativist movements, why they grow, and why they recede. The decline of traditional nativism, comprising fear of alien ideas and ethnic minorities, beginning in the 1930s, is the most interesting argument in the book. The end of mass immigration, the impossibility of blaming the Great Depression on foreigners, the pluralism generated by the New Deal's emphasis on meritocracy, and the general discrediting of racism by anthropologists and other social scientists are given as evidence of the permanent decline of nativism in America. Bennett fails, however, to include the efforts of immigrants themselves in combating nativist sentiment. After the 1930s, the fear normally directed toward aliens was turned toward old-line elites, and, by the 1960s and 1970s, toward liberals, who were viewed by the New Right as destroyers of the traditional America which they were seeking to protect.

ALEXANDER URBIEL

See also Catholic Church; Immigration and Ethnicity; Know Nothings

Nature: Attitudes to

Cronon, William, *Changes in the Land: Indians, Colonists, and the Ecology of New England*, New York: Hill and Wang, 1983

Evernden, Neil, *The Social Creation of Nature*, Baltimore: Johns Hopkins University Press, 1992

Fox, Stephen R., *John Muir and His Legacy: The American Conservation Movement*, Boston: Little Brown, 1981; as *The American Conservation Movement: John Muir and His Legacy*, Madison: University of Wisconsin Press, 1985

Nash, Roderick, *Wilderness and the American Mind*, New Haven: Yale University Press, 1967, 3rd edition, 1982

Nash, Roderick, *The Rights of Nature: A History of Environmental Ethics*, Madison: University of Wisconsin Press, 1989

Oelschlaeger, Max, *The Idea of Wilderness: From Prehistory to the Age of Ecology*, New Haven: Yale University Press, 1991

Sale, Kirkpatrick, *The Green Revolution: The American Environmental Movement, 1962–1992*, New York: Hill and Wang, 1993

Worster, Donald, *Nature's Economy: A History of Ecological Ideas*, Cambridge and New York: Cambridge University Press, 1977, 2nd edition, 1994

There is a wealth of recent literature dealing with the way Americans have thought about the natural world throughout their history. Intellectual, environmental, and political historians, as well as philosophers, have descended on the field providing us with a wide variety of different studies and interpretations. Undoubtedly, such studies will continue to proliferate as Americans are increasingly forced to confront environmental degradation and to reevaluate their relationships with the natural world.

Readers interested in how ideas about nature have evolved in the broad context of western history would do well to begin with EVERNDEN, who examines how the concept of "nature" has developed from the ancient Greeks and Romans, through the Middle Ages, the Renaissance, the Enlightenment, and up to the more recent past in the United States and Europe. Evernden convincingly demonstrates that the idea of "nature" is a human invention, and one that has changed throughout history in response to broader intellectual and social changes. His fellow philosopher, OELSCHLAEGER, takes a similar approach to the idea of wilderness throughout history, effectively "deconstructing" it and examining the evolution of our dualistic view of ourselves as somehow existing outside of nature. Unlike Evernden, however, Oelschlaeger provides extensive coverage of how seminal American thinkers such as Thoreau, John Muir, and Aldo Leopold have influenced our ideas about nature, as well as examining the ideas of recent writers and philosophers such as Gary Snyder and Arne Naess.

NASH (1967, 1982) was a pioneering study of American ideas about wilderness, which is now somewhat dated, but its influence remains strong, despite the fact that writers such as Oelschlaeger have challenged some of its central arguments. Nash argues that wilderness, in both a material and symbolic sense, was the raw material from which American civilization was constructed. He delineates differing perceptions of nature over time, and argues that the change from viewing wilderness as a moral and physical wasteland to a valuable sanctuary constitutes one of the most profound changes in human thought about nature. The change was partly the result of the "scarcity theory of value" which came into operation as Americans began to realize that they might soon run out of wilderness altogether, though the vision of men such as Thoreau, Muir, and Leopold was also an important factor. In a more recent work, NASH (1989) has sought to trace the history of environmental ethics in America, beginning with the natural rights philosophers of the Enlightenment and

coming up to modern day Deep Ecologists and Animal Rights activists. Nash argues that our increasing concern with the "rights of nature" is part of an ongoing history of ethical extension, that has seen rights gradually extended from European nobles to American colonists, to peasants, slaves, women, laborers, native Americans, and, with the passage of the Endangered Species Act of 1973, to non-human life forms. Although this central thesis embodies a rather old fashioned liberal teleology, the book is nevertheless valuable for its discussion of modern environmental philosophy, and how it has operated in various strands of the environmental movement.

Although he is more concerned with ecological relationships than with conceptions of nature, CRONON's environmental history of New England is still one of the most useful, and most readable, introductions to how Native Americans thought about nature, and how their views contrasted with those of early colonists. For example, Indians preferred to resettle on a frequent basis in order to find the most abundant food sources through the minimum of labor and to reduce their impact on the land. Europeans, on the other hand, believed in stable settlements and were less interested in how their agricultural and hunting activities affected the local environment. Cronon brilliantly demonstrates how the different attitudes of the colonists and Indians toward animals helped change the New England landscape. Where Indians hunted their game and had no conception of it as their *property*, colonists sought to maintain maximum control over their livestock. As a result, land was fenced off, predators were exterminated, and new fields planted with grazing plants became a common sight.

The history of ideas about nature as viewed through the filter of science is the subject of WORSTER's wide-ranging study of ecological ideas. Following the theory that science is driven and shaped by broader social and cultural concerns, Worster traces the development of ecological thought over the past two centuries, including discussions of such key figures as Charles Darwin, Henry David Thoreau, and the English parson-naturalist, Gilbert White, as well as prominent 20th century American scientists such as Frederic Clements, Aldo Leopold, Rachel Carson, and Eugene Odum. According to Worster, late 19th century ecological ideas tended to reflect the dominant values of the period, particularly social Darwinism and rugged individualism. In the post-World War II period, when the Keynesian virtues of cooperation and interdependence became dominant, ecological theory moved from its earlier emphasis on independent and competitive organisms to a view of the natural world as interdependent. The recent influence of chaos theory in ecology is, according to Worster, a reflection of broader trends that are becoming evident in our increasingly postmodern culture. Scientific views of nature, in short, can never be separated from the dominant ideology of any particular period.

The history of conservation in the late 19th and 20th centuries is the main subject of FOX's study. Starting with a biography of John Muir, the great turn-of-the-century preservationist, Fox proceeds to examine how 20th century environmental attitudes were shaped by the conservationist-preservationist debate of the Progressive era. Conservationists, best represented by the figure of Gifford Pinchot, America's first chief forester, viewed nature as a commodity that needed to be conserved and managed in order to supply future human needs. The followers of Muir, however, rejected this utilitarianism and advocated the preservation of nature on ethical and aesthetic grounds. Fox studies several environmental organizations, examining their ideologies, organizing efforts, lobbying abilities, and their political effectiveness, and points to the tensions which developed, not just between conservation-minded and preservation-minded organizations, but among different groups within the same ideological faction. Government policies and attitudes toward conservation are also considered, with the Progressive era, the New Deal, and the 1960s as watershed periods.

The American environmental movement since the early 1960s is the main subject of SALE's compact volume. The early pages are taken up by a detailed and very useful timeline dealing with major organizations, events, and legislation. Sale's analysis of the environmental movement and the political reactions to it (especially during the Reagan years) provides us with an excellent example of how the idea of nature can be manipulated to suit the ideological requirements of a particular class or interest group. Sale sees modern environmentalism arising out of the postwar "affluent society": on the one hand, a greater number of people had attained the necessities of life and were thus able to turn their attention to enjoying the fruits of nature, while on the other hand these fruits were being spoiled by the very forces that had created the affluence – heavy industry, mining, logging, and industrial agriculture – as well as by the impact of affluence itself in the form of more automobiles and refrigerators, for example. This realization, combined with the impact of such environmental exposés as Rachel Carson's *Silent Spring*, created a fertile ground for the growth of environmentalism and a greater appreciation of "nature". Sale also provides a useful history of major environmental organizations as well as charting their popularity and political effectiveness throughout this period.

FRANK ZELKO

See also Conservation; Environment

New Deal: General

Badger, Anthony J., *The New Deal: The Depression Years, 1933–40*, London: Macmillan, and New York: Hill and Wang, 1989
Best, Gary Dean, *Pride, Prejudice, and Politics: Roosevelt Versus Recovery, 1933–1938*, New York: Praeger, 1991
Biles, Roger, *A New Deal for the American People*, DeKalb: Northern Illinois University Press, 1991
Brinkley, Alan, *The End of Reform: New Deal Liberalism in Recession and War*, New York: Knopf, 1995
Burns, James MacGregor, *Roosevelt: The Lion and the Fox*, New York: Harcourt Brace, and London: Secker and Warburg, 1956
Conkin, Paul Keith, *The New Deal*, New York: Crowell, 1967; 3rd edition, Arlington Heights, IL: Harlan Davidson, 1975
Freidel, Frank, *FDR: Launching the New Deal*, Boston: Little Brown, 1973

Hawley, Ellis W., *The New Deal and the Problem of Monopoly: A Study in Economic Ambivalence*, Princeton: Princeton University Press, 1966
Leuchtenburg, William E., *Franklin D. Roosevelt and the New Deal, 1932–1940*, New York: Harper, 1963
Patterson, James T., *Congressional Conservatism and the New Deal: The Growth of the Conservative Coalition in Congress, 1933–1939*, Lexington: University Press of Kentucky, 1967
Romasco, Albert U., *The Politics of Recovery: Roosevelt's New Deal*, New York: Oxford University Press, 1983
Schlesinger, Arthur M., Jr., *The Coming of the New Deal*, Boston: Houghton Mifflin, 1958; London: Heinemann, 1960
Schlesinger, Arthur M., Jr., *The Politics of Upheaval*, Boston: Houghton Mifflin, 1960; London: Heinemann, 1961
Schwarz, Jordan A., *The New Dealers: Power Politics in the Age of Roosevelt*, New York: Knopf, 1993
Watkins, T.H., *The Great Depression: America in the 1930s*, Boston: Little Brown, 1993
Wolfskill, George and John A. Hudson, *All But the People: FDR and His Critics, 1933–1939*, New York: Macmillan, 1969

Scholarship on the New Deal has been a growth industry for several decades. However, there are several important trends that exist within this vast body of literature. Many, but not all, of the early, serious works on the New Deal carried a partisan tone that praised Franklin D. Roosevelt for rescuing the country from the depression. Another school of thought, generally associated with the New Left and most dynamic in the 1960s and 1970s, criticized the New Deal for its fundamental conservatism. These scholars would have preferred much more aggressive reform. More recently scholars have moved beyond the paradigm of the welfare state and re-examined the developmental nature of New Deal economic programs. Against this large backdrop, other scholars have debated the relationship between the New Deal and the business community.

Two major large-scale works on Roosevelt and the New Deal have influenced much of the subsequent historiography. Schlesinger has written three volumes of what promised to be a multi-volume study of Roosevelt and the New Deal. The second and third volumes treat the New Deal through 1936 and portray much of its complexity. Schlesinger presents a powerful case for the separation of the period into two New Deals. SCHLESINGER (1958) covers the first two years of the New Deal. As with the later volume, it is elegantly written, based on an impressive amount of research, and maintains a position of unabashed support for Roosevelt and the New Deal. Schlesinger explains the president's flexibility, deceptiveness and real or apparent inconsistency as largely a matter of tactical political maneuver. He does not delve much below the upper echelons of political and bureaucratic elites, and generally relegates Congress to a minor role. The author describes Roosevelt as the savior of capitalism, and disputes arguments to the contrary that a more radical program of economic and social reform should have been enacted. Organized by topics, the book describes the passage of legislative programs but does not elaborate on their impact. SCHLESINGER (1960) covers the years 1935–36 and what he terms the second New Deal. Praising Roosevelt's pragmatism and adaptability, he discusses much of the reform legislation of 1935 as an adroit response to pressure from critics on the left, and outside mainstream politics. Schlesinger displays little tolerance towards Roosevelt's business critics, and finds few businessmen who supported the New Deal. However dated in some of their interpretations, Schlesinger's volumes are still required reading for scholars of the period since so many subsequent authors have challenged his portrait of Roosevelt and the New Deal.

The second work on the grand scale – and, like Schlesinger, uncompleted – is a biography of Roosevelt, and not a study of the New Deal. Indeed, it is only in the course of his fourth volume that FREIDEL reaches the election of Roosevelt to the White House and the first hundred days of the New Deal. This volume does help to place the first phase of the New Deal in broader historical context, and Freidel links Roosevelt's policy agenda to the heritage of regulation and national planning dating from the Progressive Era. Anyone interested in the relationship between the New Deal and the preceding Hoover administration should consult Freidel's explanation of why Roosevelt declined joint action in the months between his election and his inauguration.

Among earlier single-volume accounts, BURNS, writing in the 1950s, anticipates one major school of New Deal historiography. He criticizes Roosevelt for adopting an inherently conservative approach to the Great Depression, and contends that the New Deal functioned primarily as a broker between organized interests instead of reshaping the basic relationship between interests in society. Arguing that Roosevelt did not provide adequate leadership in 1935, he credits liberal voices in Congress with the reform legislation of that year. Furthermore, Burns finds fault with Roosevelt's half-way approach to Keynesian fiscal policies, and argues that more aggressive spending policies would have strengthened the New Deal. He is also critical of Roosevelt's failure to put fresh impetus into the New Deal after his 1936 re-election. While Burns's focus is essentially on Roosevelt as a political leader, the book also has much to say about the policies and programs of the New Deal.

There are several important, and more recent, single-volume accounts of the New Deal. LEUCHTENBURG has established itself as the classic in this group, whether for scholars or for the general reader. It combines original research with an authoritative synthesis of New Deal and Roosevelt literature up to the early 1960s. Leuchtenburg argues that the New Deal generated a revolution in many aspects of politics, society, and the economy, and that the biggest changes resulted from the inclusion of new groups in the political process, and an expanded role for the federal government in national affairs. Yet he recognizes that the New Deal revolution was not fundamental in that it preserved, rather than overthrew, the capitalist system.

CONKIN's account of the New Deal epitomizes the New Left critique of the 1960s. Written at a time when the very nature of government was under attack for its conduct of the Vietnam War and its failure to address issues of minority rights, it criticizes the New Deal for initiating a process which ended eventually in Lyndon Johnson's Great Society. Conkin laments what might have been, if New Dealers had not been insistent upon saving corporate capitalism. Far from being pragmatic in his approach to reform, Roosevelt sought to absorb radical measures into his own New Deal program, and thus head off genuine reform. Conkin's severe New Left critique is weakened by its faulty logic, and by the attempt to apply the ideas of the 1960s to the situation of the 1930s, but it remains a prime example of a particular school of thought on the New Deal.

BILES is a much more recent synthesis of New Deal scholarship, which does not however supplant older, more established accounts. He writes a taut narrative that mixes chronological coverage with topical organization. The book's major problems arise from its internal inconsistencies. On the one hand, Biles argues that the New Deal failed to reach its full potential because Roosevelt did not push hard enough for genuine liberal reform, while, on the other hand, he recognizes that the president's choices were limited by the conservative presence in Congress and in the courts. One strength of Biles's book lies in his attention to African Americans and women.

The most readable, authoritative and judicious of the single-volume histories is BADGER. Attractively written and lucidly organized, it adopts a mainly thematic approach, and skilfully synthesizes a mass of the more recent specialized literature on various aspects of the New Deal. Most notably, Badger encapsulates the recent trend to focus less on Washington politics and bureaucracy, and to give more attention to the impact of New Deal programs at the regional and local level, and to examine how the New Deal affected the lives of farmers, industrial workers and the unemployed, and various minority groups. Overall, he sees the New Deal as a "holding operation" for American society, and suggests that World War II ushered in more fundamental changes in the lives of Americans.

Aimed at the general reader, WATKINS is a deftly written and splendidly illustrated survey of the Great Depression and the 1930s. Published as a companion to a Public Broadcasting System television program on the depression, it helps to place the New Deal in the context of the social and economic concerns of the 1930s.

Only a small sample of the literature on special aspects of the New Deal can be discussed here. Among studies of the New Deal and business, ROMASCO seeks to explain the impact of early New Deal recovery programs on the business community. He finds that politics shaped much of the recovery program, and he focuses on the political struggles between and within the executive office, the Congress, and the business community. Romasco argues that Roosevelt needed business on his side in order to achieve recovery, and suggests that the New Deal did not want a hostile relationship with the business community. A different perspective is offered by BEST who criticizes Roosevelt and his administration for their failure to bring about recovery during his first two terms of office. Best depicts the New Deal as a guide on how not to combat a depression, and argues that the White House cut itself off from business and prevented early recovery. Citing the conservative business critics of the New Deal, Best overlooks scholars and sources that suggest a different and more nuanced picture of business-government relations during the 1930s.

In a work of impressive scholarship and major importance, HAWLEY examines the intersection of the antimonopoly crusade with depression-era politics and its impact on the New Deal. Hawley analyzes the widely varying proposals – from national planning to economic decentralization – put forward to address the economic crisis and the problems of big business, and finds less distinction than some other historians between the two great bursts of New Deal reform in 1933 and 1935–36. Hawley regards the National Industrial Recovery Act (NIRA) as a failure, and criticizes subsequent legislative measures as a patchwork full of inconsistencies. Pessimistic about the possibilities of coherent economic planning in a democratic political system, he nevertheless finds some redeeming features in the more ad hoc short-term approach of the New Deal. Hawley remains essential reading on the ideology of antimonopoly, and the relationship between business and government during the New Deal.

SCHWARZ makes a distinctive contribution to the immense body of literature on the New Deal. Instead of identifying Keynesianism and the development of the welfare state as the primary legacy of the New Deal, he contends that Roosevelt's economic proposals deserve attention because they instituted a system of "state capitalism," or public investment, that had as its aim bringing the South and the West, both impoverished regions, into the mainstream of the national economy. To achieve that aim, Schwarz argues, the federal government transformed itself into the nation's banker of last resort. The use of biographical vignettes to develop the story sometimes limits the effectiveness of Schwarz's argument, because the individual careers of his subjects occasionally compete with his main thesis. Yet Schwarz deserves attention for the way in which it recasts the interpretative arguments about the nature of the New Deal in a wholly fresh and creative manner.

Further insights into the New Deal are provided by studies of its critics and opponents. PATTERSON was among the first to recognize the central importance of Congress in New Deal politics and policy – in contrast to previous scholars who had all but suggested that the legislative branch abdicated in favor of Roosevelt. Patterson identifies who the conservatives were, explains what issues and concerns drew them together, and analyzes the reasons for increasing conservative strength in Congress as the New Deal wore on. By re-focusing attention on Congress during the New Deal, he opened up a fresh perspective on the whole subject. In their thorough account of Roosevelt's domestic critics between 1933 and 1939, WOLFSKILL and HUDSON highlight two different styles of criticism – the vicious personal attacks on Roosevelt himself, and the contention that Roosevelt purposefully sought the destruction of democracy in favor of dictatorship. The authors argue that Roosevelt never addressed all the problems resulting from the Great Depression, nor did he explain adequately the thinking behind the New Deal. Thematic in its coverage, the book is illuminating on the political alignments of the period.

BRINKLEY's recent addition to New Deal scholarship analyzes the transformation of New Deal liberalism during the 1937–38 recession and World War II. While acknowledging that the most active phase of reform had ended by 1937, Brinkley argues that the idea of New Deal liberalism continued into the next decade. However, he shows that the New Dealers abandoned necessary economic reforms, when faced with the need to reach an accommodation with business, as part of the challenge of responding to the military imperatives imposed by World War II. He points the way towards the shift of New Deal liberalism from a concern with economic issues such as antimonopoly before the war, to a concern in later years with rights for minorities and women. This is a well-written and stimulating analysis of the New Deal legacy.

NANCY BECK YOUNG

See also Great Crash and Great Depression; Franklin D. Roosevelt

New Deal: Legislation and Agencies

1) Business, Industry, and Agriculture

Bellush, Bernard, *The Failure of the NRA*, New York: Norton, 1975

Clarke, Sally H., *Regulation and the Revolution in United States Farm Productivity*, Cambridge and New York: Cambridge University Press, 1994

Gordon, Colin, *New Deals: Business, Labor, and Politics in America, 1920–1935*, Cambridge and New York: Cambridge University Press, 1994

Hawley, Ellis W., *The New Deal and the Problem of Monopoly: A Study in Economic Ambivalence*, Princeton: Princeton University Press, 1966

Irons, Peter H., *The New Deal Lawyers*, Princeton: Princeton University Press, 1982

Kirkendall, Richard S., *Social Scientists and Farm Politics in the Age of Roosevelt*, Columbia: University of Missouri Press, 1966

Olson, James S., *Saving Capitalism: The Reconstruction Finance Corporation and the New Deal, 1933–1940*, Princeton: Princeton University Press, 1988

Perkins, Van L., *Crisis in Agriculture: The Agricultural Adjustment Administration and the New Deal, 1933*, Berkeley: University of California Press, 1969

Saloutos, Theodore, *The American Farmer and the New Deal*, Ames: Iowa State University Press, 1982

Vittoz, Stanley, *New Deal Labor Policy and the American Industrial Economy*, Chapel Hill: University of North Carolina Press, 1987

Weinstein, Michael M., *Recovery and Redistribution under the NIRA*, Amsterdam: North Holland Publishing, 1980

Scholarship about business, industrial and agricultural legislation and agencies of the New Deal usually focuses on the theme of recovery from the depression. Older studies tend to the descriptive while newer works include more analysis and interpretation.

On the relationship between the New Deal and business and industry, HAWLEY is the most authoritative study, and it has been supplemented, rather than replaced, by more recent scholarship. He provides a judicious assessment of the National Recovery Administration (NRA), including the dominant influence of business in drawing up the industrial codes, the difficulty of enforcing them, and the reasons for the NRA's ultimate failure. Hawley is equally impressive on New Deal attempts to regulate business and industry after the NRA, and on the later anti-trust campaign. He generally inclines towards scepticism about the coherence and effectiveness of New Deal policies in this field.

There are other useful studies of the operation and eventual failure of the NRA. WEINSTEIN is an assessment of the immediate impact of the NRA codes in promoting recovery and redistributing income. He concludes that the codes were responsible for a dramatic increase in nominal wages and prices, and had significant effects on the distribution of income. On the other hand, they favored the larger and better organised companies, and, in many ways, contributed to economic stagnation and persistent high unemployment. BELLUSH is a brief examination of the reasons for the failure of the NRA, written from a position of strong pro-labor sympathy, and critical of the NRA's failure to help labor. Too much power was placed in the hands of a bureaucracy, which worked hand in glove with business interests. Interweaving discussion of politics and law with portrayal of many of the personalities involved, IRONS is an interesting study of the lawyers who worked for the NRA, the Agricultural Adjustment Administration (AAA), and the National Labor Relations Board (NLRB), and reveals much about the problems of carrying out, and defending, the responsibilities of these agencies.

VITTOZ looks at the intersections between labor policy and the industrial economy, under the New Deal. While the book would profit from more analysis of the evidence cited, Vittoz nevertheless makes an important contribution to this important subject. He shows that the response of industries to the National Industrial Recovery Act (NIRA) differed according to individual industrial circumstance. The majority of the book deals with the origins and the administration of the NRA. While sensitive to New Left arguments, Vittoz discounts the thesis that New Deal labor policy was shaped by corporate elites. Instead, he suggests that policies emerged out of the process of bargaining between contending interests.

OLSON argues that New Deal scholars have been remiss in overlooking the main agency of recovery, the Reconstruction Finance Corporation (RFC), which tried to revive the banking and credit system. The government's re-financing of credit institutions and homeowner mortgages was crucial to the prevention of complete economic disaster. Yet Olson makes clear that stimulation of credit was not sufficient in itself to combat the depression; stimulation of consumption was essential. However, he finds that the RFC achieved some success as an agent of state capitalism that provided for moderate government involvement in the economy. Olson argues that the RFC and the notion of state capitalism ranked among the major accomplishments of the New Deal.

GORDON looks at the American political economy through analysis of its three major components – business, labor, and politics. He finds that, at the onset of the Great Depression, each was disorganized because of various internal weaknesses and divisions. He argues that business interests needed the power of government to mitigate the effects of competition among themselves, and to achieve some measure of stability. Generally, business gained the upper hand in the struggle, and guided the course of New Deal reform to achieve its goals of industrial peace and increased national consumption. Gordon sees business opposition of the late 1930s not as a response to New Deal reforms, but as a reaction to the failure of these reforms to achieve the business community's goals. This is a subtle and complex – and at times controversial – treatment of a complicated subject. It may do much to set the terms of the next round of the debate.

SALOUTOS has written the standard account of New Deal agricultural policy. Unlike other studies that focus on a particular agency or a particular group of people, he places his treatment of Roosevelt's farm program in the context of the farm crisis that began in the 1920s. His assessments of the impact of the AAA and of New Deal policy generally are balanced and judicious. He sees both continuity and change in the legislative response to the agricultural depression.

PERKINS uses the AAA to study government involvement in the economy during the first year of the New Deal. He explains the competing visions of acreage reduction and agricultural exports as means of solving the farm crisis, and argues that Roosevelt had few other options. In a thoughtful narrative history of the AAA, Perkins assesses its impact, by gauging the amount of money that the program put into the economy, and he concludes that the agency achieved some success. KIRKENDALL's monograph, focusing on the professionally trained experts in farm policy, describes how social scientists acted as advocates for organized rural interests, in formulating the agricultural adjustment legislation of the New Deal. Agriculture, he suggests, offered these intellectuals the perfect venue for social science experimentation and policy development. Kirkendall is ambivalent about the results of their endeavors; while they altered the status quo, they did not generate radical change.

From a broader historical perspective, CLARKE examines the relationship between the regulatory farm programs of the New Deal and agricultural productivity. She argues that the New Deal programs increased productivity and efficiency. Aware of the importance of technology in these economic gains, Clarke appraises what government regulation meant for the farm economy and the larger national economy of which it was a part, in the years between World War I and the farm crisis of the 1980s. Her carefully balanced and ironic conclusion suggests that the kind of regulation initiated by the AAA helped to achieve a measure of financial stability while farm prices tended to fall, but, when prices rose in the 1970s (as the New Deal legislation had intended), many farmers were exposed to a new crisis.

NANCY BECK YOUNG

See also Agriculture, since 1860; Government and the Economy

2) Public Works, Social Security, and Labor

Bernstein, Irving, *Turbulent Years: A History of the American Worker, 1933–1941*, Boston: Houghton Mifflin, 1970

Bernstein, Irving, *A Caring Society: The New Deal, the Worker, and the Great Depression: A History of the American Worker, 1933–1941*, Boston: Houghton Mifflin, 1985

Brock, William R., *Welfare, Democracy and the New Deal*, Cambridge and New York: Cambridge University Press, 1988

Gordon, Colin, *New Deals: Business, Labor, and Politics in America, 1920–1935*, Cambridge and New York: Cambridge University Press, 1994

Lubove, Roy, *The Struggle for Social Security, 1900–1935*, Cambridge, MA: Harvard University Press, 1968; 2nd edition, Pittsburgh: University of Pittsburgh Press, 1986

Nelson, Daniel, *Unemployment Insurance: The American Experience, 1915–1935*, Madison: University of Wisconsin Press, 1969

Patterson, James T., *America's Struggle Against Poverty, 1900–1980*, Cambridge, MA: Harvard University Press, 1981, revised as *America's Struggle Against Poverty, 1900–1994*, 1994

Vittoz, Stanley, *New Deal Labor Policy and the American Industrial Economy*, Chapel Hill: University of North Carolina Press, 1987

The New Deal's efforts to use public works and social insurance to tackle poverty have attracted the attention of a large number of historians. BERNSTEIN (1985) provides the clearest and most informative examination of the principal social welfare measures of the 1930s. The book systematically discusses the major initiatives, looking at their origins and impact. The author draws attention to some of the limitations of the New Deal reforms: in particular, he notes that several brought few benefits to women and blacks. But his account is generally positive, and, as the title suggests, he believes that the measures were inspired by humanitarian motives. He also highlights the remarkable achievements of New Deal agencies in implementing such a complex and wide-ranging welfare system.

PATTERSON also provides a good introduction to the New Deal's social welfare measures. Rather than focussing specifically on the policies of the Roosevelt administration, the book provides a general history of welfare in the 20th century. As a consequence, its coverage of the reforms of the 1930s is necessarily brief. But it is very effective in highlighting the importance of New Deal measures in the development of the welfare state, showing how they set the pattern for subsequent reforms. It also skilfully illustrates the link between New Deal policies and changing American attitudes towards the causes and effects of poverty.

A number of writers have studied specific welfare measures in greater detail. BROCK looks at federal relief policy, focussing on the Federal Emergency Relief Administration and the Works Progress Administration. He is mainly interested in examining how political and constitutional considerations shaped the evolution of policy. He illustrates how fears about the future of local democracy prevented the creation of a fully-centralized and professionalized system of relief. The system that emerged relied, instead, upon the cooperation of federal, state and county officials, with local politicians battling against professional social workers for control. While the continued influence of local officials ensured that the welfare system remained under democratic control, it also undermined its effectiveness in tackling poverty.

Several studies focus on the introduction of the social security system, perhaps the New Deal's most enduring legacy. LUBOVE surveys the debates about social insurance that raged during the first part of the 20th century and which culminated in the passage of the Social Security Act of 1935. Although the author is mainly concerned with the period before 1933, the book is an invaluable source for those seeking to understand the New Deal. It shows how efforts to create an adequate welfare system were hampered before 1933 by prevailing fears about the impact of centralization and by the widespread preference for voluntarist solutions to social problems. Against this background, the book both highlights the ground-breaking character of the Social Security Act and helps to explain why the measure's aims were necessarily limited.

NELSON provides a detailed account of the origins of unemployment insurance, examining the debates about the policy during the two decades preceding the passage of the Social Security Act. He shows how supporters of unemployment insurance disagreed among themselves as to the purposes of reform. Some were primarily concerned with providing economic assistance to the unemployed, while others hoped that a well-designed insurance system would encourage firms to stabilise employment levels. Nelson concludes that the ideas of the latter group held sway during the 1920s and continued to influence the evolution of policy even after the Great Depression had focussed popular attention on the plight of the unemployed.

The labor reforms of the New Deal have also attracted a great deal of attention. BERNSTEIN (1970) provides an extremely comprehensive history of New Deal policy towards trade unions. Much of the book looks at the history of the unions themselves, highlighting their growth in size and power during the 1930s, but it also charts the evolution of New Deal policies towards collective bargaining. In fact, one of the book's great strengths is its ability to show the link between the struggles of workers and developments in Washington. Bernstein is not uncritical of Roosevelt, and in particular, he highlights the president's essentially opportunistic attitude towards the National Labor Relations Act of 1935. However, Bernstein's treatment of New Deal reforms is fundamentally sympathetic. He sees the 1930s as a period of great progress for American workers and stresses that the New Deal did much to improve their position.

Two recent studies are far more critical of the New Deal, questioning whether its labor reforms stemmed from a concern with the interests of workers. VITTOZ suggests that business was not solidly opposed to the labor reforms of the 1930s, and emphasizes that business leaders hoped that the measures would help them to reduce the severity of competition. He also shows that New Dealers' efforts to aid workers were, in part, inspired by their desire to revitalize American capitalism through increasing mass purchasing power. However, while much of its analysis is suggestive, the book fails to provide a wholly convincing account of labor policy. Its coverage of New Deal reforms is partial and fragmented. Moreover, Vittoz is far more effective in refuting claims that business leaders were uniformly opposed to the New Deal than he is in clarifying their precise role in shaping federal policy.

GORDON provides a more precise and systematic discussion of business attitudes to the New Deal's principal labor reforms. Like Vittoz, he shows that business leaders were not united in opposing these measures. He argues that many business leaders hoped that, by strengthening trade unions, New Deal reforms would help to eliminate their low-wage, marginal competitors. At times, he even implies that business leaders were the decisive force behind the passage of these measures. Overall, Gordon provides an important new perspective on the labor reforms of the 1930s. Admittedly, he never provides much convincing evidence that business leaders shaped New Deal policies, but he does undermine the assumption that the reforms of the 1930s simply represented a triumph of public over business interests.

PHILIP J. CULLIS

See also Social Welfare/Social Security

New Deal: Political and Constitutional Issues

Adams, David K., *Franklin D. Roosevelt and the New Deal*, London: Historical Association, 1979

Adams, David K., "The New Deal and the Vital Center: A Continuing Struggle for Liberalism," in *Franklin D. Roosevelt: The Man, the Myth, the Era, 1882–1945*, edited by Herbert D. Rosenbaum and Elizabeth Bartelme, Westport, CT: Greenwood Press, 1987

Allswang, John M., *The New Deal and American Politics: A Study in Political Change*, New York: Wiley, 1978

Kelly, Alfred H. and Winfred A. Harbison, *The American Constitution: Its Origins and Development*, New York: Norton, 1948; 7th edition, with Herman Belz, 2 vols., 1991

Leuchtenburg, William E., "Franklin D. Roosevelt's Supreme Court 'Packing Plan'," in *Essays on the New Deal*, edited by Harold M. Hollingsworth and William F. Holmes, Austin: University of Texas Press, 1969

Patterson, James T., *Congressional Conservatism and the New Deal: The Growth of the Conservative Alliance in Congress, 1933–1939*, Lexington: University Press of Kentucky, 1967

Patterson, James T., *The New Deal and the States: Federalism in Transition*, Princeton: Princeton University Press, 1969

Schlesinger, Arthur M., Jr., *The Crisis of the Old Order, 1919–1933*, Boston: Houghton Mifflin, and London: Heinemann, 1957

Schlesinger, Arthur M., Jr., *The Coming of the New Deal*, Boston: Houghton Mifflin, 1958; London: Heinemann, 1960

Schlesinger, Arthur M., Jr., *The Politics of Upheaval*, Boston: Houghton Mifflin, 1960; London: Heinemann, 1961

Schlesinger, Arthur M., Jr. (general editor), *History of US Political Parties*, volume 3: *1910–1945: From Square Deal to New Deal*, New York: Chelsea House, 1973

Not the least of the New Deal's achievements was to stimulate debate about the future of American politics and the viability of the Constitution. Adams's particular forte is in attempting to define Roosevelt's political philosophy. ADAMS (1979) is a pamphlet, but tries "to consider the general shape of the New Deal in terms of Franklin Roosevelt's vision of a just society". He detects an underlying consistency of purpose, "He seemed to tack with the winds, but the course steered was generally steady". Although a brief overview, Adams does set the New Deal within a loosely defined liberal context. ADAMS (1987) is a vignette of less than twelve pages, but the distillation of wide reading, as amply documented footnotes indicate. Adams argues "that the New Deal can best be seen as a whole, and that Franklin Roosevelt was deeply committed to a philosophical tradition that was recognisably 'liberal'". For Adams "FDR was not just a pragmatic politician but a more substantial thinker".

The fullest and strongest statement of how this worked in practice is Schlesinger's magnificent trilogy. Writing from an avowed liberal standpoint, with great verve and acute characterization, and using an enormous range of archival, published and oral sources, he provides a panoramic view of the New Deal and American politics. SCHLESINGER (1957) sets the genesis of the New Deal in the context of a tradition that went back to Theodore Roosevelt's New Nationalism and Woodrow Wilson's New Freedom. One sees how Roosevelt, personally and politically, was prepared for the greatest American crisis since the Civil War. For Schlesinger, 1933 is a watershed. SCHLESINGER (1958) examines how the New Deal evolved in its first two years, with different issues such as agriculture, industrial planning and relief discussed thematically. The last third of the book is devoted to the resurgence of conservatism and the evolution of the presidency. SCHLESINGER (1960) begins with an apparently indecisive Roosevelt after the 1934 elections, assailed by opposition forces that are expertly delineated in a 200-page section entitled "the Theology of Ferment", until he was goaded into the Second New Deal. The title of this volume is itself suggestive and it concludes with an examination of the problems arising from Supreme Court decisions, and the election campaign of 1936.

Schlesinger's concentration on presidential politics is balanced by PATTERSON (1967). He examines the development of congressional conservatism which was to frustrate further New Deal measures. Patterson demonstrates the unreliability of simple generalizations by close examination of individuals and their voting records. However certain patterns do emerge: conservatives did tend to come from safe seats; the more influential Democrats usually had committee seniority; after 1936 most, though not all, conservatives were from rural constituencies; different issues provoked different opposition; and early dissent coalesced not only as Roosevelt lost political prestige but as economic conditions improved and the urban, liberal nature of his support became more vociferous. Even so the opposition was never formally united, and the first obligation of many protagonists on both sides was not to a programme but to their state or district.

Indeed, notwithstanding its centralizing tendencies, the New Deal had to operate within a federal system. PATTERSON (1969) brilliantly examines this phenomenon which shadows but is distinct from conservatism *per se*. He argues that essentially American politics is the politics of the (then) 48 states; hence the fitful, unco-ordinated, unreliable nature of individual state responses to the New Deal. Achievements in some states were matched by failures in others; consistency of purpose rarely survived limited financial resources, while semi-autonomous, faction-ridden, local parties impeded an overall national policy.

SCHLESINGER (1973) provides a useful short introduction to the party politics of the period, with essays by Graham and Mayer respectively on the Democratic and Republican parties at national level, complemented by supporting documents such as party platforms and campaign speeches. It also includes a general overview by Harrington of the Socialist party, with a discussion of Norman Thomas and the 1930s.

ALLSWANG is the best commentary on the changing politics of the decade. It is partly derived from a massive, systematic quantitative data base including voting statistics and census returns for all the then-3,100 or so counties of the United States. Yet the author is never weighed down by his material (there are only 15 tables and no footnotes), and in just over 130 pages sustains a clear overview with separate chapters on such themes as the New Deal and the people, the cities, the states and national politics. This is a most skilful extrapolation from the particular to furnish evidence to support the general.

Meanwhile the flexibility of the American Constitution was also tested by the changes which the New Deal wrought. KELLY and HARBISON is still the standard work, as a 7th edition revised by BELZ amply testifies. Written originally from the vantage point of a welcoming acceptance of interventionist national government that the New Deal exemplified, its later up-dating also endeavours to reflect recent alternative conservative viewpoints. Thus the chapters on "The New Deal", and "The New Deal and the Emergence of a Centralized Bureaucratic State" provide a judicious 40-page summary of the major constitutional developments of the 1930s which also points up inherent changes such as "the transformation of the presidency into an instrument of virtually permanent emergency government". Hence the Executive Reorganization Act, albeit more restricted than Roosevelt wished, "laid the institutional foundation for the creation of the modern presidency," while "the effect of the Court packing plan, had it been approved, would have been to weaken the independence and integrity of the judiciary".

The Supreme Court battle is concisely recounted by LEUCHTENBURG in a masterly blend of narrative and analysis. It is an exciting story, arrestingly re-told, with an eye for the pertinent quotation. Leuchtenburg does not minimise "the fearful price," which Roosevelt paid in the retarding of reform, Democratic party divisions, loss of popularity, weakening of support and even distrust of his leadership in foreign policy that the Court-packing plan entailed. He does however, conclude that his one big success was "the legitimation of the vast expansion of the power of government in American Life".

JOHN KENTLETON

New Deal: Economic Impact

Bernstein, Michael A., *The Great Depression: Delayed Recovery and Economic Change in America, 1929–1939*, Cambridge and New York: Cambridge University Press, 1987

Chandler, Lester V., *America's Greatest Depression, 1929–1941*, New York: Harper, 1970

Fearon, Peter, *War, Prosperity and Depression: The US Economy 1917–45*, Deddington, Oxfordshire: Philip Allan, 1987

Friedman, Milton and Anna Jacobson Schwartz, *A Monetary History of the United States, 1867–1960*, Princeton: Princeton University Press, 1963; chapter 7 reprinted as *The Great Contraction, 1929–1933*, 1965

Gordon, Colin, *New Deals: Business, Labor, and Politics in America, 1920–1935*, Cambridge and New York: Cambridge University Press, 1994

Hawley, Ellis W., *The New Deal and the Problem of Monopoly: A Study in Economic Ambivalence*, Princeton: Princeton University Press, 1966

Romasco, Albert U., *The Politics of Recovery: Roosevelt's New Deal*, New York: Oxford University Press, 1983

Weinstein, Michael M., *Recovery and Redistribution under the NIRA*, Amsterdam: North Holland Publishing, 1980

An evaluation of the New Deal presents formidable problems for the economic historian, as the plethora of programmes make it virtually impossible to measure the impact of any single initiative. Moreover, the lack of a coherent economic strategy confuses those who try to assess the New Deal solely on economic grounds.

Most economic studies have concentrated on the attempts to achieve industrial recovery, especially in the context of planning. WEINSTEIN has attempted to quantify the impact of the National Industrial Recovery Act (NIRA) and has come to the conclusion that it had a harmful macro-economic impact which actually retarded recovery. He is especially critical of the inflationary impact of the National Recovery Administration (NRA) codes which he claims nullified the expansionary effects of the increase in the money supply between 1933 and 1935. This is an interesting attempt by an economist to evaluate the impact of a single New Deal agency, but it suffers, as do many such studies, from a narrow focus on a few years.

In an original contribution to the debate, BERNSTEIN suggests that the key issue which faced the United States at this time was the transition from the old declining industries to the new vibrant sectors which could have spearheaded a business revival. He sees planning, largely abandoned after 1935, as a way out of the Depression if it had been pursued in an enlightened manner. Unfortunately, New Deal planning was dominated by the power of the older, sluggish and relatively unprofitable enterprises. If planners had directed their efforts towards the stimulation of new fast-growing industries the elusive industrial recovery might have been achieved. Occasionally complex and detailed, this book is worth the time spent on absorbing its message.

One of the most effective contributions to this debate has been provided by HAWLEY, who covers the period 1933 to 1939. He notes that the Roosevelt administration was never fully committed to the detailed regulation of competition before 1935 or to the antitrust policies which followed. The difficulties facing policymakers are fully explored in this study and the ambivalence of public opinion highlighted. For example, while Americans favoured policies which protected the "little man" they were also conscious of the role played by big business in providing cheap consumer goods. As a result, any attempt to break up the big corporations into smaller units would have been met with vigorous consumer resistance. This carefully researched, closely argued, but readable volume provides many insights into a period when policy shifts could seem huge but proved in practice to be more moderate.

As GORDON's analysis commences in 1920 he is able to illustrate the linkages between the voluntary policies of business during the 1920s and the influence of employers on policymaking in the first and second New Deals. Gordon shows that, during the 1920s, businessmen tried to regulate competition through the establishment of trade associations and even by encouraging the development of trade unions. The relationship that existed between employers and unions was complex, and employers did not simply show blind hostility towards organized labour. Gordon not only examines the views of the business community on the NRA, but also shows that its influence in the origins and administration of the Wagner Act was more pervasive and diverse than previously thought. Even the Social Security Act is presented as a response to pressure from the leaders of some large companies. Indeed, Gordon's conclusion, in a volume which displays a refreshing clarity, is that New Deal policies were essentially business-friendly measures dressed in progressive clothing.

Although the president was given wide-ranging powers by Congress to inflate the economy, monetary policy during the New Deal period was weak and ineffective. FRIEDMAN and SCHWARTZ, in their polemical classic, argue that the Federal Reserve, which they blame for the severity of the Depression between 1929 and 1933, was also responsible for the severe 1937–38 recession. Although essential reading for the economic historian, this book does pose some problems for the non-economist.

The easiest way to confront New Deal monetary and fiscal policy, as well as the programmes on agriculture and unemployment, is to use some general texts. CHANDLER has a very full account of all New Deal economic initiatives. Presented in uncomplicated language and organized in a reader-friendly fashion, Chandler is able to provide a clear picture of both the problems and the attempted solutions. FEARON analyses the economic issues in a style that is directed at the non-economist. This book has especially useful critiques on the agricultural sector and on the stubborn refusal of unemployment to return to its 1920s level. Finally, one of the most interesting examinations of New Deal economic policies is offered by ROMASCO, who emphasizes the politics rather than the economics of Roosevelt's recovery plans. In this fascinating study, Romasco demonstrates that it was politics not economics which drove the New Deal. Indeed, the economic strategies that were employed can only be understood if one considers the political framework in which decisions were taken. It is the political economy of the New Deal, not just its economics, that deserves our closest attention.

PETER FEARON

See also Great Crash and Great Depression

New Deal: Social Impact

Badger, Anthony J., The New Deal: The Depression Years, 1933–40, London: Macmillan, and New York: Hill and Wang, 1989

Bernstein, Irving, A Caring Society: The New Deal, the Worker, and the Great Depression: A History of the American Worker, 1933–1941, Boston: Houghton Mifflin, 1985

Cooney, Terry A., Balancing Acts: American Thought and Culture in the 1930's, New York: Twayne, 1995

Gregory, James N., American Exodus: The Dust Bowl Migration and Okie Culture in California, New York: Oxford University Press, 1989

Saloutos, Theodore, The American Farmer and the New Deal, Ames: Iowa State University Press, 1982

Ware, Susan, Beyond Suffrage: Women in the New Deal, Cambridge, MA: Harvard University Press, 1981

Weiss, Nancy J., Farewell to the Party of Lincoln: Black Politics in the Age of FDR, Princeton: Princeton University Press, 1983

Recent writings on the New Deal's social impact appear to reflect a type of post-revisionism, emphasizing both the triumphs and failures of Roosevelt's policies and alphabetical agencies. Taken together, these works show how the New Deal affected Americans of differing socioeconomic status, race, and gender.

A good place to begin an examination of the New Deal's social impact is BADGER, which is perhaps the finest recent one-volume study of the New Deal, and which concentrates less on personalities and politics than on the impact of the New Deal nationwide. It starts with an intelligent historiographical introduction and ends with a well-reasoned conclusion. There are chapters devoted to workers and farmers, and there is coverage of issues of race, class, and gender. Despite its weaknesses, the New Deal provided many with the assistance needed to survive the Depression.

WEISS examines the assistance which the New Deal provided for blacks, and she answers a question that has intrigued historians who have looked at the relationship between the New Deal and African Americans. Why in 1936 did blacks abandon the Party of Lincoln to vote for the Party of Roosevelt? Weiss argues that they voted for Franklin D. Roosevelt as a result of a rational political calculation. Despite the discrimination in some New Deal programs, the Roosevelt administration after four years in office had provided many African Americans with enough economic assistance to garner political loyalty. In addition, FDR performed several symbolic acts in sympathy with black civil rights. Although the New Deal did not make civil rights a priority, blacks benefited from Roosevelt's presidency and thus moved into the Democratic party en masse.

Another critical element in Roosevelt's political coalition was labor. BERNSTEIN provides an excellent description of some of the relief and reform programs of the New Deal that affected workers. He focuses on the effectiveness of the Federal Emergency Relief Administration, the Works Progress Administration, and the Federal Arts Project. In addition, he details the Social Security, the Wagner Act, and the Fair Labor Standards Act. These New Deal reforms and agencies provided many urban workers with the means to survive the Great Depression, and gave organized labor a new status in American society. In addition, the New Deal created a federal support system to cushion the periodic economic recessions endemic to capitalism. In short, the New Deal went some way towards the creation of a "caring society," in which the federal government provided a safety net for workers.

SALOUTOS describes the New Deal's safety net for landowning farmers. The New Deal's agricultural policy went through three distinct phases which attempted to control production, raise prices, and provide relief to farmers. Although by 1939, farm prices had not risen above 1929 levels, the Agricultural Adjustment Administration helped to alleviate the hardships of the Depression. In addition, other Roosevelt agencies such as the Farm Security Administration, the Rural Electricification Administration, and the Farm Credit Administration stabilized and reshaped the agricultural sector of the economy. Saloutos recognizes the shortcomings of Roosevelt's farm policy such as the failure to assist African Americans and many other poorer farmers, and yet he sees the New Deal as the most innovative period in the history of American agricultural policy.

In his study of rural migrants from Arkansas, Missouri, Oklahoma, and Texas, GREGORY examines the New Deal's farm policy from a different angle, focusing on agricultural workers rather than landowners. During the Great Depression, millions moved from the middle Southwest to California to escape the economic hardships caused by mechanization, drought, erosion, insects, and the Agricultural Adjustment Administration (AAA) whose policies forced some tenant farmers from the land. Once in California, the "Okies" were helped by the Farm Security Administration during the 1930s and by the federal defense programs during the 1940s. The Roosevelt administration provided economic opportunities that allowed the Dust Bowl migrants to stay in California and form their own subculture that Gregory labels "Plain-Folk Americanism," a collection of values ranging from religious fundamentalism to neo-populist politics.

Gregory suggests some limitations of the New Deal in his description of the AAA. Another area where the New Deal fell short may be seen in the experiences of women during the Great Depression. The New Deal did not often specifically address the needs of women, and was not inspired by feminist ideas. Nevertheless, as WARE demonstrates, the Roosevelt administration created the conditions that allowed an important female network to develop in Washington, DC. Ware examines a network of 28 elite white women including Eleanor Roosevelt, Ellen Sullivan Woodward, Frances Perkins, and Mary "Molly" Dewson who were an instrumental part of the New Deal. Although the network women were not feminists, they struggled to help women through patronage and the shaping of social welfare policy. The network declined in power before World War II and ceased to exist by 1945. However, a few individual network members such as Eleanor Roosevelt continued to influence politics in Washington after the New Deal.

COONEY surveys the New Deal's cultural legacy. He argues that the economic depression and the introduction of economic planning and reform at the national level sparked various intellectual and cultural responses. While some accepted the New Deal, others rejected it. The Roosevelt administration had conservative critics, including Herbert Hoover, who sought to re-establish what they saw as traditional American values. Other opponents of the New Deal called for more radical solutions to the Great Depression. Both proponents and opponents of the New Deal utilized the new media of radio and film to convey their messages. Thus the 1930s provided Americans with a plurality of cultural responses and reactions to the Great Depression.

Collectively, these studies reflect more than a type of post-revisionism. Some of their authors, including Badger, Bernstein, and Gregory, expand the "New Deal" into the World War II era. An approach which sees at least part of the social history of the wartime home front as a New Deal by other means suggests one direction for further studies.

ANDREW E. KERSTEN

New England

Barron, Hal S., *Those Who Stayed Behind: Rural Society in Nineteenth-Century New England*, Cambridge and New York: Cambridge University Press, 1984

Brooke, John L., *The Heart of the Commonwealth: Society and Political Culture in Worcester County, Massachusetts, 1713–1861*, Cambridge and New York: Cambridge University Press, 1989

Brown, Richard D., *Massachusetts: A Bicentennial History*, New York: Norton, 1978

Clark, Charles E., *Maine: A Bicentennial History*, New York: Norton, 1977

Clark, Christopher, *The Roots of Rural Capitalism: Western Massachusetts, 1780–1860*, Ithaca, NY: Cornell University Press, 1990

Dalzell, Robert F., Jr., *Enterprising Elite: The Boston Associates and the World They Made*, Cambridge, MA: Harvard University Press, 1987

Dawley, Alan, *Class and Community: The Industrial Revolution in Lynn*, Cambridge, MA: Harvard University Press, 1976

Hall, Peter Dobkin, *The Organization of American Culture, 1700–1900: Private Institutions, Elites, and the Origins of American Nationality*, New York: New York University Press, 1982

Hansen, Karen V., *A Very Social Time: Crafting Community in Antebellum New England*, Berkeley: University of California Press, 1994

Kaufman, Martin, John W. Ifkovic and Joseph Carvalho III (editors), *A Guide to the History of Massachusetts*, Westport, CT: Greenwood Press, 1988

McLoughlin, William G., *Rhode Island: A Bicentennial History*, New York: Norton, 1978

Morison, Elizabeth Forbes and Elting E. Morison, *New Hampshire: A Bicentennial History*, New York: Norton, 1976

Pierson, George Wilson, "The Obstinate Concept of New England: A Study in Denudation," *New England Quarterly*, vol.28, 1955

Prude, Jonathan, *The Coming of Industrial Order: Town and Factory Life in Rural Massachusetts, 1810–1860*, Cambridge and New York: Cambridge University Press, 1983

Tager, Jack and John W. Ifkovic (editors), *Massachusetts in the Gilded Age: Selected Essays*, Amherst: University of Massachusetts Press, 1985

New England as a region of the United States has received nothing comparable to the intense scrutiny which historians have bestowed upon the New England colonies before the Revolution. The region has undergone massive transformation during the last two hundred years. The descendants of the Puritan Yankees are now but one element in a population made up of a rich ethnic mixture. In the 19th century, Massachusetts and Rhode Island became two of the most industrialised states in the Union, and, in the 20th century, more and more of Connecticut has been suburbanised as part of metropolitan New York. The northern tier of New England states, drained of much of their population in the 19th century by the lure of fertile western lands or new industrial employment nearer at hand, have become a vacationland, and a weekend retreat for affluent refugees from metropolitan pressures.

For all that, New England retains a strong sense of regional identity. No one has addressed this theme more eloquently and wittily than PIERSON, who insists in his famous 1955 essay that, despite all the changes, New England survives as a region of the mind. Its role on the national stage has often been as an exporter of people, institutions, ideas, religious faith, education and technological innovation. Surprisingly, there is no recent and comprehensive history of New England as a region of the United States. In consequence, the subject often has to be pursued at the level of the individual state or the local community. A brief introduction to the history of some of the states may be found in the relevant volumes of the Bicentennial History series, published on behalf of the American Association of State and Local History. These small volumes have a standardised format, and are all around 200 pages in length, but they vary enormously in method, emphasis and quality.

Perhaps because of his distinction as a historian of American religion, McLOUGHLIN is allowed to get away with a longer than average history of the smallest state. Almost half of his history of Rhode Island is devoted to the colonial and Revolutionary periods. In the three chapters on the national period, he pursues the story of the state's survival against heavy odds. He moves from industrialisation in the first half of the 19th century to the subsequent period of "prosperity, respectability, and corruption," and concludes with a chapter quizzically entitled "changing, surviving, hoping." Predictably, in his history of Massachusetts, BROWN also concentrates heavily on the colonial and Revolutionary periods. His later chapters tackle themes of industrialisation and ethnic and social

pluralism, and give some emphasis to the influence of the state on the rest of the nation. The last eighty years receive only cursory attention.

In one of the more attractive bicentennial histories, MORISON and MORISON on New Hampshire adopt a blend of chronological and thematic approaches, and emphasise social and economic, rather than political, history. In what is clearly a labour of love, they focus in later chapters on New Hampshire's struggle to adapt to the challenges of new technology and modern life in general. Charles E. CLARK often reads more like an elegy to the state of Maine than a conventional history. Treating Maine as a state of mind, he traces the history of successive images of the state from its frontier beginnings, and touches on such themes as economic growth, devotion to moral reform causes – New Deal and prohibition, for example – and the growth of tourism.

Inevitably, Massachusetts has commanded a large share of attention from historians of New England – and, in comparison, Connecticut, for example, has been ill-served. KAUFMAN *et al.* provide excellent guidance to students of Massachusetts history. There are historiographical essays by leading authorities on successive periods of the history of the state, as well as on such topics as urban history and women's history. These essays are complemented by useful brief descriptions of libraries and archives throughout the state. In contrast to the usual heavy emphasis on the years from the Revolution to the Civil War, the dozen or so essays by various authors collected in TAGER and IFKOVIC represent a deliberate attempt to stimulate interest in the relatively neglected period of the late 19th and early 20th centuries. They deal with aspects of social and economic change, in such areas as social reform, social mobility and ethnicity.

No other region has attracted so many local community studies as New England, and the best of them yield many insights into the wider New England experience. One outstanding example is BROOKE, which takes Worcester County as a middling area at the heart of the state of Massachusetts, and follows its evolution through the 18th century, the Revolutionary era and down to the antebellum years. He explores the interaction between republican and liberal ideology in the experience of the people as they lived through political revolution and industrial revolution. In contrast to those who treat republicanism and liberalism as opposite poles, he points to the achievement of a working synthesis between the two. Industrialisation and its consequences in one manufacturing town are examined in DAWLEY, an influential and controversial study of the shoe industry and the shoemakers of Lynn. Written from a Marxist perspective, it places a heavy emphasis on class struggle against capitalist exploitation.

From their different standpoints, both Prude and Clark analyse the consequences of the coming of capitalist enterprise and industrialisation to the rural and small town communities of Massachusetts. PRUDE uses his penetrating case study of three small Massachusetts communities – Dudley, Oxford and Webster – to establish important points about industrialisation in New England (and other areas). It took place not only in and around large cities but also – and more typically – in small towns and rural areas; and it was not a smooth and untroubled transition to a new age, but the cause of serious tension and conflict, between workers and employers, and also between the mills and the small town communities in which they were located. In his study of western Massachusetts, Christopher CLARK examines both agricultural and non-agricultural aspects of the local economy, and traces the gradual transition from household production to more complex relationships with the wider market. The move towards cash crops, the development of industry in the local towns, and the key role of local merchants are all features of his account.

There have been so many laments about the depopulation of large parts of rural New England – especially in Vermont and New Hampshire – that BARRON's study of "those who stayed behind" comes as a refreshing change. Focusing on the township of Chelsea, Vermont, he shows that the story is not simply one of decline and decay, but of the continuing existence of stable and well-ordered communities, which were spared much of the turmoil of industrialisation and urbanisation. In a recent study of the evolution of New England communities in the antebellum period, HANSEN highlights the social sphere within which working people lived, and sees it as a "third mediating category" between the private and the public spheres. She examines the function within the social sphere of such activities as social visiting, churchgoing, shopping, attending meetings, and joining voluntary political movements and voluntary organisations.

New England history must also encompass the wider Yankee influence in the United States. DALZELL is a fascinating study of the Boston Associates, the tightly-knit group of merchants (many of them not natives of Boston) who invested in the textile industry, and later used the profits to invest in railroads, banking, insurance and other businesses in New England and beyond, and who added to their economic and political influence by their support for philanthropic and educational causes. In doing so, they helped to change the face not only of New England but of American society generally. HALL does not describe itself as a book about New England at all, but one of its constant themes is the influence of New England institutions and elite groups on the shaping and ordering of American nationality. Hall argues that, by control of private corporations and charitable trusts, reinforced by evangelical missionary zeal, moral reform, professional societies and educational effort, New England's conservative leadership set out to tame and civilise the rapidly expanding United States.

In this wider view, New England is not just a group of six small states at the northeastern extremity of the country; rather, as Pierson claimed, it is more of a state of mind which resides in that "greater New England" which spreads far and wide across the land.

S-M. GRANT

See also Boston; Colonial History: Colonies 2

New Nationalism and New Freedom

Blum, John Morton, *The Republican Roosevelt*, Cambridge, MA: Harvard University Press, 1954, 2nd edition, 1977
Cooper, John Milton, Jr., *The Warrior and the Priest: Woodrow Wilson and Theodore Roosevelt*, Cambridge, MA: Belknap Press of Harvard University Press, 1983
Cooper, John Milton, Jr., *The Pivotal Decades: The United States, 1900–1920*, New York: Norton, 1990
Davidson, John Wells (editor), *A Crossroads of Freedom: The 1912 Campaign Speeches by Woodrow Wilson*, New Haven: Yale University Press, 1956
Gable, John Allen, *The Bull Moose Years: Theodore Roosevelt and the Progressive Party*, Port Washington, NY: Kennikat Press, 1978
Gould, Lewis L., *Reform and Regulation: American Politics, 1900–1916*, New York: Wiley, 1978; 2nd edition, as *Reform and Regulation: American Politics from Roosevelt to Wilson*, New York: Knopf, 1986
Link, Arthur S., *Wilson: The Road to the White House*, Princeton: Princeton University Press, 1947
Link, Arthur S., *Wilson: The New Freedom*, Princeton: Princeton University Press, 1956
Mowry, George E., *Theodore Roosevelt and the Progressive Movement*, Madison: University of Wisconsin Press, 1947
Watson, Richard L., Jr., *The Development of National Power: The United States, 1900–1919*, Boston: Houghton Mifflin, 1976

Historians have depicted the confrontation between Theodore Roosevelt's New Nationalism and Woodrow Wilson's New Freedom during the presidential election of 1912 as one of the defining moments in the development of modern liberalism in the United States. Writings about the issue, however, have tended to focus on the individual leaders and their separate doctrines rather than engaging the encounter directly, at least until the mid-1980s. With the ascendancy of conservatism in modern American politics since the 1970s, the importance of the Wilson-Roosevelt clash of philosophies has faded somewhat in significance. Nonetheless, the underlying tension between Roosevelt's articulation of a strong national government to oversee the economy and Wilson's reliance on the market to maintain equality has persisted in contemporary debates about the role of the federal government.

LINK (1947) and MOWRY presented the two major protagonists of the 1912 presidential contest in important books that established the broad outlines of what was at stake between Wilson and Roosevelt. Mowry's work has endured less well than Link's first volume of his magisterial Wilson biography. But Mowry indicated what Roosevelt owed to his presidential experience in shaping the New Nationalism after 1909, and Link examined the role of Louis D. Brandeis as the theoretician of the New Freedom.

BLUM's important work on Roosevelt as a president and politician showed how the New Nationalism grew out of his regulatory program during his second term in the White House. It demonstrated a continuity of ideas about the function of government in Roosevelt's mind that enhanced the credibility of his espousal of the New Nationalism in 1910. By restoring Roosevelt as a credible political leader, Blum emphasized the historical significance of Roosevelt's evolution away from an allegiance to Republicanism toward a third party in 1912.

GABLE is a history of the Progressive or Bull Moose party, and treats the New Nationalism as an element of that narrative. His analysis of the campaign and election of 1912 is very useful, and he provides the most detailed account of what happened to Roosevelt's own conception of the New

Nationalism during the period after November 1912. The footnotes are a rich guide to the extensive primary sources for this phase of Roosevelt's career.

LINK (1956) showed in masterful fashion how Wilson implemented the early stages of the New Freedom during 1913–14, and he also discussed the limits of Wilson's conception of reform by the end of 1914. The book provides the most thorough exploration of how the legislative program of the New Freedom made its way through Congress. All five volumes of Link's biography of Wilson illuminate issues relating to the New Freedom and the New Nationalism. An edited collection of Wilson's campaign speeches, DAVIDSON provides an essential basis for understanding what Wilson was arguing for in 1912 and how the debate with Roosevelt over the role of government in regulating the economy proceeded on the stump. The introductory materials and the notes to the texts of the speeches make this book an indispensable source for understanding what Wilson believed was the essence of the New Freedom.

Although designed as a text, WATSON's study of how government power grew during the Progressive Era is so thoroughly researched and so perceptive that his book has great utility for understanding how the clash between Wilson and Roosevelt developed. Watson also has the best brief account of how Wilson transformed his position, and moved toward the New Nationalism as the election of 1916 approached. Watson addresses the issue of whether Wilson acted out of expediency or political conviction. The book is now hard to locate outside of libraries, but remains an excellent overview of the entire subject.

COOPER (1983) is the most accessible way to see the complex interplay between Wilson and Roosevelt that arose from their presidential ambitions and their articulation of these two competing programs. The volume is very well-researched and thoughtful. More sympathetic to Wilson than to Roosevelt, Cooper nonetheless points out the extent to which Wilson's New Freedom gave way to an adoption of the New Nationalism and its implications during the presidential election of 1916. Cooper's work is the best single guide to the entire historical issue of the relationship between the New Nationalism and the New Freedom.

Like Watson's book, GOULD was written as a supplemental text for undergraduate survey courses in American history. It is now out of print and has become hard to obtain. The book draws on primary sources to place the confrontation between the New Freedom and the New Nationalism in the context of political developments since the beginning of the 20th century. COOPER (1990) is another authoritative survey of early 20th century American history, which places the New Nationalism and the New Freedom in a broader context.

The controversy over the New Nationalism and the New Freedom had a large impact on the way that undergraduates learned about the history of the United States during the years after World War II. Seeing the 20th century as the unfolding of liberalism, historians saw the battle between Roosevelt and Wilson as a foreshadowing of the ideological struggles of the New Deal and the Great Society. As a new century approaches with a powerful federal government under assault, the ascendancy of liberalism no longer seems to be the dominant feature of American politics. Nonetheless, the battle that began

between Roosevelt and Wilson in 1912 retains its fascination because of the abilities of the two combatants and the way in which they set the terms of American political debate for several crucial decades.

LEWIS L. GOULD

New Orleans

Asbury, Herbert, *The French Quarter: An Informal History of the New Orleans Underworld*, New York: Knopf, 1936; London: Jarrolds, 1937

Blassingame, John W., *Black New Orleans, 1860–1880*, Chicago: University of Chicago Press, 1973

Cable, George Washington, *The Creoles of Louisiana*, New York: Scribner, 1884; London: Nimmo, 1885

Federal Writers' Project, *New Orleans City Guide*, Boston: Houghton Mifflin, 1938; revised by Robert Tallant, 1952

Haas, Edward F., *DeLesseps S. Morrison and the Image of Reform: New Orleans Politics, 1946–1961*, Baton Rouge: Louisiana State University Press, 1974

Hirsch, Arnold R. and Joseph Logsdon (editors), *Creole New Orleans: Race and Americanization*, Baton Rouge: Louisiana State University Press, 1992

Jackson, Joy J., *New Orleans in the Gilded Age: Politics and Urban Progress, 1880–1896*, Baton Rouge: Louisiana State University Press, 1969

Lichtenstein, Grace and Laura Dankner, *Musical Gumbo: The Music of New Orleans*, New York: Norton, 1993

Rogers, Kim Lacy, *Righteous Lives: Narratives of the New Orleans Civil Rights Movement*, New York: New York University Press, 1993

Rose, Al and Edmond Souchon, *New Orleans Jazz: A Family Album*, Baton Rouge: Louisiana State University Press, 1967, 3rd revised edition, 1984

The city of New Orleans does not fit within the framework of scholarship on American urban studies. Yet, at the same time the peculiar cultural, social, racial, and political history of New Orleans has created a mystique about the city that has encouraged numerous studies of it. Although the FEDERAL WRITERS' PROJECT city guide published in 1938 under the auspices of New Deal legislation and revised in 1952 is dated, it still provides a good starting point for general information on New Orleans. The information concerning restaurants, hotels, night life and other aspects of city life at the time now has little value, but some sections, for example on geography and social and economic development, offer pertinent information on labor, transportation, education, religion, arts, literature, architecture, politics, and Mardi Gras, and even provide recipes from famous restaurants. This work also provides a good description of established neighborhoods like the Garden District, the French Quarter, Irish Channel, and Mid City.

New Orleans possessed a special class of people in the Creoles – the inhabitants who by reason of French or Spanish ancestry gained a higher social rank in society and who are considered the original settlers. CABLE traces the history of the Creole people and their crucial role in the exploration, founding, and control of the city. His work is marred by his refusal to concede that African American blood was a part of the Creole makeup, his contention that slavery had been the cause of the economic backwardness of the city, and his refusal to discuss the history of New Orleans during the Civil War and during the "bitter days of Reconstruction." Cable expresses deep concern in this 1884 book about the possibility that the Creole race would either lose control over the city or disappear entirely as a people because of the growing influence of Americans.

Because of its racial diversity and unique race relations, most studies of New Orleans address the issue of race, and HIRSCH and LOGSDON have edited a book of essays on the subject. The essays examine the evolution of race relations from the early days of the city to the post-World War II era. Hirsch and Logsdon claim that the "peculiarities" of New Orleans can be understood only in terms of its distinctive history of race relations.

According to BLASSINGAME, even African Americans living in New Orleans during the period from the beginning of the Civil War to the end of Reconstruction experienced an environment and lifestyle different from that of African Americans living in other southern cities. He concentrates on the social aspects of African American life and finds that, despite their relative political powerlessness, the members of the black community achieved considerable gains in education, business, and per capita wealth. Blassingame stresses that while segregation was the established cultural norm in New Orleans, there was some integration of transportation, public accommodations, and neighborhoods.

At the same time that the African American community was adjusting to changes in the post-Civil War era, the rest of New Orleans was also in flux. In her study of the changing political power structure and progressive responses to urban problems, JACKSON finds that, while ameliorative measures were taken to tackle long-standing problems, many of the antebellum social and cultural norms remained firmly in place. Jackson also argues that many of the reforms undertaken during the period from 1880 to 1900, in areas such as public improvements, transportation and fighting political corruption and gambling, and transportation, were diluted in practice because of the weakness of the city government. After 1896 a new breed of reformers emerged, advocating further reform measures.

HAAS provides an excellent insight into the more recent political culture not only of New Orleans but Louisiana as well, in a study of the political career of DeLesseps Morrison, a four-time mayor of New Orleans. Haas also traces the history of the powerful Democratic urban machine and places it in the context of conflict with the Long machine that dominated state government through the first half of the 20th century. Haas probes the political motives behind the urban reforms under Morrison's administration in such areas as slum clearance, recreation, municipal services, and commercial expansion.

Despite the appearance of a less restrictive attitude in New Orleans society toward racial mixing and the obvious racial "blending" of African Americans, Creoles, and white southerners, the institution of segregation remained firmly entrenched in the 20th century. Through the collective biography of

25 African American and white civil rights leaders, ROGERS examines the efforts of the 1950s and 1960s civil rights movement to combat massive resistance to change, the desegregation of the public schools and later public accommodations, and the struggle to create a new vision of an integrated society.

The history, legends and myths of the French Quarter have attracted much attention. ASBURY concentrates on the underworld of New Orleans, and the French Quarter and the adjoining area called Storyville provide the backdrop for much of his survey, which covers the period from the early 1700s to the early 1900s. The French Quarter was the original settlement of New Orleans, and Asbury traces the emergence of both the district and some of its more notorious inhabitants from around 1700 to 1803. He includes stories about riverboat men, river pirates, bandits, dueling, gambling, prostitution, and voodoo in a colorful popular account of the mystique that has surrounded both the French Quarter and New Orleans.

One of the cultural aspects of New Orleans that makes the city unique is its musical heritage. LICHTENSTEIN and DANKNER give an excellent overview of the various types of music found in New Orleans. They provide short biographies of major figures in traditional and contemporary jazz, Dixieland, rhythm and blues, brass bands, gospel, and even Cajun music. Another study focusing specifically on jazz is ROSE and SOUCHON. Combining photographs of musicians, musical events, and jazz funerals with brief biographies of the city's top jazz musicians, they effectively show how different styles of New Orleans jazz developed in different neighborhoods (Uptown, French Quarter, and Storyville, for example). They also provide a comprehensive listing of jazz and Dixieland bands, dance and novelty orchestras, and string and co-op bands.

CRAIG S. PASCOE

New York City

Bernstein, Iver, *The New York City Draft Riots: Their Significance for American Society and Politics in the Age of the Civil War*, New York: Oxford University Press, 1990

Bridges, Amy, *A City in the Republic: Antebellum New York and the Origins of Machine Politics*, Cambridge and New York: Cambridge University Press, 1984

Fitch, Robert, *The Assassination of New York*, London and New York: Verso, 1993

Gilfoyle, Timothy J., *City of Eros: New York City, Prostitution, and the Commercialization of Sex, 1790–1920*, New York: Norton, 1992

Homberger, Eric, *Scenes from the Life of a City: Corruption and Conscience in Old New York*, New Haven and London: Yale University Press, 1994

Jackson, Kenneth T. (editor), *The Encyclopedia of New York City*, New Haven and London: Yale University Press/New York: New-York Historical Society, 1995

Mollenkopf, John Hull (editor), *Power, Culture, and Place: Essays on New York City*, New York: Russell Sage Foundation, 1988

Newfield, Jack and Paul Du Brul, *The Abuse of Power: The Permanent Government and the Fall of New York*, New York: Viking, 1977; Harmondsworth: Penguin, 1978

Pye, Michael, *Maximum City: The Biography of New York*, London: Sinclair-Stevenson, 1991

Sleeper, Jim, *The Closest of Strangers: Liberalism and the Politics of Race in New York*, New York: Norton, 1990

Stansell, Christine, *City of Women: Sex and Class in New York, 1789–1860*, New York: Knopf, 1986

Starr, Roger, *The Rise and Fall of New York City*, New York: Basic Books, 1985

There is a rich and varied body of modern scholarly work on New York City in the 19th century, especially in the antebellum period, and a quite separate literature on the much-publicized problems and crises of recent decades. Few historians have been ready to face the daunting task of writing a history of the great American metropolis over a period of two centuries or more.

In the essays edited by MOLLENKOPF, the interactions between economic, cultural and political perspectives are used to illustrate the conflicts in different phases of New York's development: the mercantile, industrial and post-industrial. Despite the city's global reach and importance in finance, culture, and communications, economic and social inequality has grown apace. Mollenkopf contrasts current failures with the earlier and more successful manner in which party organizations built integrative class and ethnic coalitions offering opportunity to many. Reform swept away the old party bosses and weakened organization, so that now the dangers of under-representation are evident in a city where two-thirds of the controlling electorate, but less than one half of the city's residents, are white.

A wide historical canvas is painted by PYE in his informal historical biography which captures the city's many transitions, and the hopes and aspirations of its inhabitants – one chapter is entitled "audition city." Anecdotes abound, illuminating the history. The Dutch never paid the legendary $24 in 1626, as that was based on a 19th-century exchange rate that was 25 times too low! Money and markets drove development, but he notes "the real dirty story is always real estate."

Although they focus on different aspects of the subject, various studies of 19th-century New York all suggest something of the vitality and vibrancy – and sometimes the violence – of a city in the throes of mushroom growth and dramatic change. BRIDGES is a study of New York politics in the three decades before the Civil War, which analyzes the trend towards machine politics, with a new emphasis on party organization and the emergence of a new breed of politician. She relates political trends to wider social and economic change – the sheer pace of economic development; the rapid growth of population and wider suffrage which required new techniques for managing and manipulating a larger electorate; the influx of immigrants and the increase in numbers of the working classes, which stimulated a new politics based on ethnic and class loyalties. In her impressive study of the often bleak lives of working-class women, STANSELL adds gender to class and ethnicity as a shaping influence in the social structure of New York before the Civil War. She examines women's labor in the workplace, along with their burdensome roles in home and family life, and the connections and contacts among women themselves. The overall picture is one of an unrelenting struggle for survival.

BERNSTEIN provides a vivid account of the New York draft riots in July 1863 – but he does much more than that. He weaves the story of the riots inextricably into the complex social, economic and political history of mid-19th century New York, and draws out their longer term consequences for its future development. At a time when various groups were searching for order and coherence in a turbulent and fragmented city, the draft riots highlighted conflicts between rich and poor, blacks and whites, and Republicans and Democrats – and also between city and nation. According to Bernstein, outright winners and losers from the crisis precipitated by the riots are difficult to identify, but, by discrediting both radical Republicans and the more extreme Copperhead Democrats, the riots helped to pave the way for Tammany rule in the years that followed.

In his elegantly written study of the vice trade, GILFOYLE charts its rise and relative fall over 130 years. In the mid-19th century the business reached its apogee, second only to the garment trade in terms of revenue, and with links to corrupt Tammany politicians. Moral reformers from the 1870s onwards succeeded in controlling the trade, but the availability of better paid service sector jobs for women, declining immigrant numbers and the physical redevelopment of seedier parts of the city at the beginning of the 20th century all played a key role too.

Equally stimulating is HOMBERGER's study of mid-19th century Manhattan, focused on four interrelated narratives bursting with life and incident. He demonstrates how the traditional elite fought back against the forces of corruption epitomized by the abortionist "Madame Restell," who was hounded to the point of suicide by the moral reformer Comstock, and the fraudulent comptroller of the city and key member of the Tweed Ring, "Slippery Dick" Connolly. Conscience, personified by Dr. Smith and the middle class sanitary struggle against the cholera ridden "lower depths," was rewarded with the passing of the Metropolitan Health Act of 1866. Above all though, the triumph of civic betterment with the building of Central Park by the representative figure of Olmsted came to symbolize the possibility of re-creating a sense of community within a tainted and abused democratic order.

There is no shortage of investigations and analyses of the more recent problems of New York City. In his examination of decline since World War II, STARR reserves his scorn for the ruling liberal elite's mealy-mouthed attitudinizing: lacking a collective sense of moral responsibility, directionless and confused in trying to satisfy all, and thereby serving none. His admired role model from the 1930s was the autocratic but effective Robert Moses. NEWFIELD and DU BRUL castigate almost everyone involved in the governance of the city during the fiscal crisis of the mid-1970s when New York was "rescued" by its bankers, a key element in a governing (unelected) elite who helped precipitate the emergency by their earlier withdrawal of credit. The now familiar litany of job losses in manufacturing, swollen municipal pay-rolls and corruption of the county clubhouse Democrats, whose use of patronage and links to the Mob so exacerbated matters, are revealed with distaste.

FITCH concentrates on one particular banking and real estate dynasty, whose conspiratorial powers were instrumental in creating the city's predicament. The varied mass of small manufacturing plants that once absorbed new immigrants with relative ease peaked in 1951 when they provided employment for more than one million people. Powerful propertied interests (notably the Rockefellers and their foundations) building on earlier city beautification schemes, used the planning and zoning laws to sustain their own vested interests by forcing manufacturing to relocate out of Manhattan. They promoted office development at the expense of manufacturing, and diversity gave way to an over-planned single function economy based on finance, insurance and real estate which could never replace the prosperity and jobs of earlier days. Thus, newcomers today lack the higher level entry employment skills of office workers now commuting from the suburbs, and so add to the city's welfare rolls and falling tax base.

Yet another negative image of New York finds expression in its racial politics. SLEEPER examines the emerging liberal political agenda from the 1930s onwards, culminating in the election of its first black mayor. Few are spared in this catalogue of racial mistrust and stereotyping. The failures of white Democratic liberalism, the intransigence of white racism and economic exploitation, and the equally repugnant self-indulgence of black leaders exploiting situations for narrow sectional ends – such as the notorious Tawana Brawley rape case and its manipulation by the militant black nationalist Al Sharpton – are all exposed in Sleeper's coruscating analysis.

JACKSON is an indispensable reference work containing 4300 articles by 680 contributors on an astonishing variety of places, people, institutions, events, and topics, covering the entire area now occupied by the five boroughs from prehistory to the present. Most articles provide brief bibliographies, and the articles on "Histories" is a capsule bibliographical essay which is especially useful for its descriptions of 18th- and 19th-century publications. This is one encyclopedia that not only provides answers to innumerable questions but can also be read with pleasure.

RICHARD DE ZOYSA

Newspapers and Magazines

Baldasty, Gerald J., *The Commercialization of News in the Nineteenth Century*, Madison: University of Wisconsin Press, 1992
Cohn, Jan, *Creating America: George Horace Lorimer and the Saturday Evening Post*, Pittsburgh: University of Pittsburgh Press, 1989
Lutz, Catherine A. and Jane L. Collins, *Reading National Geographic*, Chicago: University of Chicago Press, 1993
Marzolf, Marion Tuttle, *Civilizing Voice: American Press Criticism, 1880–1950*, New York: Longman, 1991
Mott, Frank Luther, *A History of American Magazines*, 5 vols., Cambridge, MA: Harvard University Press, 1930–68
Schneirov, Matthew, *The Dream of a New Social Order: Popular Magazines in America, 1893–1914*, New York: Columbia University Press, 1994
Suggs, Henry Lewis (editor), *The Black Press in the South, 1865–1979*, Westport, CT: Greenwood Press, 1983
Summers, Mark W., *The Press Gang: Newspapers and Politics, 1865–1878*, Chapel Hill: University of North Carolina Press, 1994
Wood, James P., *Magazines in the United States*, New York: Ronald Press, 1949, 2nd edition, 1956, 3rd edition, 1971

Early American newspapers had intimate ties to politicians and their factions. By the close of the 19th century, however, newspapers had abandoned this advocacy and instead presented the news, including topics like crime, business, fashion, sports and the weather as well as politics, in a more detached style. According to BALDASTY, the commercialization of the news in the 19th century marked a major transformation in American history. In less than 150 pages, Baldasty explains the concurrent changes in the values of the American press. In the Jacksonian era editors "defined news as a political instrument intended to promote party interests." By the end of the century they imagined it "within a business context to ensure or increase revenues." Societal changes, such as technological innovation and urbanization and especially the rise of advertising, contributed to these shifts. This brief but rich book examines newspapers of large cities and small towns alike.

SUMMERS provides a more concentrated study of one aspect of mid-19th century American newspapers. This engaging work uncovers the press's political role during Reconstruction, a particularly turbulent era in American history. The story here, unlike the vast literature on individual publishers and newspapers, centers on the reporters. It was a confusing time in which journalists, participants (indeed "gladiators") in the debates they covered, shaped the political agenda. Summers fills the text with scores of entertaining vignettes that highlight his thesis. Summers also identifies a transition in the newspaper business at mid-century. Reporters became more independent and developed a sense of professionalism. Summers, unlike Baldasty, believes that the growing separation between politicians and the press improved news-gathering and reporting. The reading public benefited.

MARZOLF also see advantages in the rise of a "fair-minded" press. This book supplies a valuable counterpoint to the notion that economic and market forces alone contributed to changes in newspapers. Marzolf asserts that self-appraisal influenced the evolution of the modern press. Through a study of criticism of the press that appeared in popular, professional, and scholarly journals between 1880 and 1950, he suggests that, at least in a haphazard manner, values and standards did change during that period. Influential critics, who often sought to defend a perceived morality against the vulgarity of the masses, raised issues of accountability. This helped spawn professionalism, including journalism schools, and a greater sense of responsibility.

Marzolf argues that critics attacked shoddy journalism in order to safeguard American freedoms. Like other authors, he believes that newspapers serve a special role in a democracy, as a conduit between citizens and politicians. On the other hand, what was not in newspapers could be as important as what appeared in print. Editors often ignored African American communities, and in response a robust African American press emerged, especially in the South. SUGGS offers the first and the most comprehensive reference work about black newspapers. Individual chapters, of varying but often high quality, survey black newspapers in twelve southern states. There is a detailed bibliographic essay that suggests further avenues of study.

The study of American magazines has also engaged scholars and provoked bruising debates. Although now out of date, MOTT remains a mine of information on hundreds of titles, and a valuable reference work. In 1956, the year in which WOOD published the second edition of his general survey of American magazines, more than seven thousand titles were in print. Wood's examination of scores of various publications, including *The New Yorker*, *Reader's Digest*, women's magazines, and farm journals, and the rise of advertising, offers tantalizing glimpses of social change in American life. He asserts that magazines both "reflected and helped mould" American habits, public opinion, consumerism, and crusades for social and political reform.

SCHNEIROV "explores the cultural dreams of the American popular magazine" during the 1890s and 1900s. He offers a detailed account of one segment of the magazine market in an era of remarkable flux and change. In particular, he highlights the rise of, and writing in, mass circulation monthlies such as *Cosmopolitan*, *McClure's*, and *Munsey's*. The writers and editors participated in a shift in American culture. They no longer celebrated the past, but attempted to capture the excitement of the future.

Much of the writing about American magazines centers on the rise of a mass culture at the turn of the 20th century. Magazines had a special role in the cultural transformation because they were the only form of national communication. COHN seeks to understand how George Horace Lorimer used the *Saturday Evening Post*, which had the largest circulation of its day, to "create America." Whereas Schneirov emphasized that editors must appeal to their readers, Cohn contends that Lorimer (and one supposes by extension other influential editors) helped formulate a unified and complete culture of business that shaped the public's perception of rapid social and economic changes in the first three decades of the 20th century. The argument is complex and somewhat circular: "the *Saturday Evening Post* was not only a medium for the dissemination of ideology but in fact became itself an artifact of that ideology," Cohn writes. In addition to writing the history of American magazines, Cohn and Schneirov fight battles for cultural studies as well. The self-referential and unappealing academic jargon detracts from their work.

LUTZ and COLLINS, like Cohn, find that national magazines have exerted a conservative influence on American public opinion. The two anthropologists studied the photographs of nearly fifty years of *National Geographic*. They wanted to understand how those famous pictures have sculpted Americans' understanding of, and responses to, the outside world since World War II. Their reasoning is original and perceptive. Lutz and Collins maintain that as an institution *National Geographic* presents "a world of happy, classless people outside of history but evolving into it, edged with exoticism and sexuality." Even if one accepts their imaginative understanding of the uses of photography, their claims for institutional hegemony and the pervasive influence of *National Geographic* seem somewhat extravagant. Nonetheless, their

intensive study of magazine photographs underlines the complexity and conflict lurking behind the exchange of information. As vehicles of communication, newspapers and magazines (whatever their formats in an electronic age) will remain targets of scrutiny and comment.

CHRISTOPHER MacGREGOR SCRIBNER

Niebuhr, Reinhold 1892–1971
Theologian, and political and social commentator

Bingham, June, *Courage to Change: An Introduction to the Life and Thought of Reinhold Niebuhr*, New York: Scribner, 1961

Brown, Charles C., *Niebuhr and His Age: Reinhold Niebuhr's Prophetic Role in the Twentieth Century*, Philadelphia: Trinity Press, 1992

Clark, Henry B., *Serenity, Courage, and Wisdom: The Enduring Legacy of Reinhold Niebuhr*, Cleveland: Pilgrim Press, 1994

Fox, Richard Wightman, *Reinhold Niebuhr: A Biography*, New York: Pantheon, 1985

Kegley, Charles W. and Robert W. Bretall (editors), *Reinhold Niebuhr: His Religious, Social and Political Thought*, New York: Macmillan, 1956; 2nd edition, New York: Pilgrim Press, 1984

Lovin, Robin W., *Reinhold Niebuhr and Christian Realism*, Cambridge and New York: Cambridge University Press, 1995

Rice, Daniel F., *Reinhold Niebuhr and John Dewey: An American Odyssey*, Albany: State University of New York Press, 1993

Stone, Ronald H., *Professor Reinhold Niebuhr: A Mentor to the Twentieth Century*, Louisville, KY: Westminster/John Knox Press, 1992

A prolific author and popular speaker, Reinhold Niebuhr occupies a critical position in the shaping of the 20th-century religious mind. As "America's public theologian," Niebuhr forced audiences and readers to think critically about the relationship between religion and public life, and has therefore been the subject of a range of thoughtful books and essays, many of them written by close friends and former students. In the first substantial biography, BINGHAM provides a unique glimpse of Niebuhr's strength and power, without being excessively laudatory. Bingham attempted to interweave the story of Niebuhr's life with his ideas, by alternating chapters devoted to his life and to analysis of his thought. This approach introduces variety, but can cause the reader to lose focus. Published ten years before Niebuhr's death, Bingham's account is lively and well-written, but it is not footnoted, and obviously could not cover the writings or involvements of the last years of his life.

The standard narrative of Niebuhr's life is FOX. It provides the clearest and most in-depth account of Niebuhr's life, but does not adequately communicate the depth of the intellect and charisma which brought Niebuhr to public prominence. In his discussion of Niebuhr's life and family, Fox laces the account of the important relationship between Reinhold and his brother H. Richard with a clumsy psychological analysis. Despite the difficulties of the psychological examinations in which Fox engages and the brief consideration given to Niebuhr's later writings, this book remains the benchmark against which later monographs are measured.

Revisions of Fox began almost immediately after its publication, and were led by STONE. He emphasizes Niebuhr's vocation as a seminary professor dedicated to training ministers, and his critical accounts of Niebuhr's classroom lectures on Christian ethics do much to reveal a fuller picture of Niebuhr's thought and life beyond his published work. In an attempt to provide a balance to other biographies of Niebuhr, Stone emphasizes Niebuhr's life as a professor to the exclusion of the myriad of other activities in which he was involved and inevitably this is a less than full account of a very public figure.

Providing further context to Niebuhr's life is BROWN, which relates Niebuhr's thought and action to the course of world events. While not as informative as Fox on the details of Niebuhr's life, Brown sheds light on his power and persuasiveness. He portrays Niebuhr the public individual, in contrast to the extensive discussion of Niebuhr's private life in Fox, and he emphasizes the polemical nature of many of Niebuhr's writings.

The relationship between two of the 20th-century's most profound and influential thinkers, John Dewey and Reinhold Niebuhr, is skillfully analyzed by RICE. In the first book-length discussion of their relationship, Rice details the chronology of their interaction, which spanned the time between Niebuhr's arrival at Union Theological Seminary in 1928 and Dewey's death in 1953. These titans of democratic theory battled over the definition and meaning of the American political system in a myriad of academic and political contexts. Rice concludes with a discussion of the specific nature of their disagreements, concentrating on their differing views concerning naturalism, human nature, religion, liberalism, and democracy. Despite these critical differences, Rice finds a fundamental similarity between these two men through their common debt to pragmatism.

Niebuhr's writings continue to have an impact. The first major collection of essays about Niebuhr's thought, edited by KEGLEY and BRETALL, was published in 1956 and revised in 1984. While some of the work is dated, this volume contains a masterful collection of essays on Niebuhr's theology, political philosophy, and ideas about social welfare. Particularly important are the essays by Arthur Schlesinger, John C. Bennett, Emil Brunner, and Abraham Heschel. Also included are two pieces written by Niebuhr himself, an intellectual autobiography and a response to his critics. Despite its age this volume is particularly helpful because of the varied background of the authors who contributed and the many angles from which Niebuhr's thought is viewed.

The continuing legacy of Niebuhr's thought is the subject of CLARK. Written in an easy, readable style, it presents Niebuhr as a model of theological method and reflection. He addresses the major criticisms of Niebuhr's thought, and answers them in order to demonstrate Niebuhr's continuing relevance to the contemporary theological and philosophical climate. Focusing on the conjuncture of religious belief and social action, Clark stresses the importance of religion in understanding Niebuhr's thought, and its relevance to contemporary debates about social justice.

LOVIN is another attempt to relate Niebuhr's ideas to contemporary issues. In his discussion of Christian realism, he breaks it down into its distinctive elements – God, Ethics, Freedom, Politics, and Justice – in order to bring out its relevance to current issues and future debates. At the heart of this Niebuhrian realism lies the principle of love which serves to regulate our actions and allows us to act confidently, but with humility. Similar in scope to Clark, Lovin is a more intense theological and philosophical exposition, and is not for the faint of heart. Writing for an academic audience, Lovin seeks to develop a practicable Christian realism for the 21st century, based upon the ideas and writings of Niebuhr.

R.J. HEINIG

Nimitz, Chester 1885–1966

Naval commander

Baer, George W., *One Hundred Years of Sea Power: The US Navy, 1890–1990*, Stanford, CA: Stanford University Press, 1994

Barlow, Jeffrey G., *Revolt of the Admirals: The Fight for Naval Aviation, 1945–1950*, Washington, DC: Naval Historical Center, Department of the Navy, 1994

Isely, Jeter A. and Philip A. Crowl, *The US Marines and Amphibious War*, Princeton: Princeton University Press, 1951

James, D. Clayton, *The Years of MacArthur*, 3 vols., Boston: Houghton Mifflin, and London: Leo Cooper, 1970–85

Love, Robert W., Jr., *History of the US Navy*, volume 2: *1942–1991*, Harrisburg, PA: Stackpole, 1992

Potter, E.B., *Nimitz*, Annapolis, MD: Naval Institute Press, 1976

Potter, E.B. and Chester W. Nimitz (editors), *The Great Sea War: The Story of Naval Action in World War II*, New York: Bramhall House, 1960

Spector, Ronald H., *Eagle Against the Sun: The American War with Japan*, New York: Free Press, and London: Viking, 1985

Fleet Admiral Chester W. Nimitz was one of the few significant admirals of World War II not to write his memoirs, as a matter of deliberate and typical choice. Instead, the basic text is the fine and readable biography by POTTER. This is not strictly an academic work, since much of the material is based on interview, there are few references and it features much gossipy detail that is significant only for the light that it casts upon the character of the man and his circumstances. Nonetheless, the author taught naval history at the United States Naval Academy, and his book is an authoritative if somewhat admiring introduction to his subject. Nimitz emerges as a quiet, determined, clear-sighted man, with a particular gift for picking effective, loyal subordinates. He was Commander-in-Chief Pacific for virtually the whole of World War II exercising full command over all but the largely inactive South Pacific and General MacArthur's South-West Pacific area.

The same author, plus his colleagues, also collaborated with Nimitz in producing POTTER and NIMITZ, since they wanted a teaching text for use at Annapolis. The result is a notably clear and succinct survey of World War II, which, claimed Nimitz, "... was basically a naval war." Although two-fifths of the book focuses on the Atlantic campaign, rather than the Pacific where Nimitz was to make his mark, this volume provides a calm, clear and objective introduction to Nimitz's wartime career, and is particularly interesting for his association with its production.

Nimitz went to the Naval Academy at Annapolis in 1905, and his career spanned the period during which the United States Navy emerged from comparative obscurity to become the world's greatest navy. The context for Nimitz's naval career is provided by BAER, whose explanation of the forces militating for, and the constraints upon, America's rise to naval mastery is elegant and convincing. While the timing of his career may have made Nimitz one of the accidental personal beneficiaries of this rise to naval mastery, he was, at the very end of his time in the Navy from 1945 to 1947, to be its custodian, in a time of great stress and danger.

Nimitz was appointed Commander-in-Chief Pacific, CINC-PAC, on the last day of 1941, a few weeks after the disaster at Pearl Harbor. In what has become the standard single-volume text on the Pacific campaign, SPECTOR shows that Nimitz's first requirement was to rally his forces and, by a policy that mixed caution with a readiness, to take calculated risks, to build up his fleet's offensive spirit. For this reason he encouraged Admiral Halsey's hit-and-run tactics in early 1942. Profiting from the advantages provided by superior naval intelligence derived from effective code-breaking, Nimitz was able to provide the conditions that led to the battles of Coral Sea and Midway.

But for the remainder of the war Nimitz was in dispute with, and, in the public and political eye, sometimes overshadowed by, that other great commander of the Pacific War, General Douglas A. MacArthur. The differing strategic views of these two men started with a significant division of opinion about the best way to recapture Rabaul. It was soon to develop into a major and continuous conflict between MacArthur and Nimitz in the Pacific, and their superiors back in Washington, about the best route for the counter-offensive against Japan – a controversy that bedeviled American strategy-making and the overall conduct of the Pacific War. In his comprehensive and authoritative biography of MacArthur, JAMES shows the vehemence with which his subject objected to the Nimitz drive across the Central Pacific and the extent of the resources which he commanded. But, as Spector also shows, Nimitz sometimes agreed with MacArthur, rather than with Fleet Admiral King, the Chief of Naval Operations. Spector also provides examples of the way in which the quietly spoken but independently-minded Nimitz sometimes overruled the views of his subordinates.

Nimitz's strategy was heavily amphibious in its approach, and the semi-official ISELY and CROWL analyzes the lessons learned from the early landings and the changing nature of the Central Pacific War, as it approached the Japanese home islands. Appropriately, Nimitz represented the United States at the signing of the Japanese surrender on the battleship *Missouri* in Tokyo Bay, in the triumphant culmination of one of the major maritime campaigns of military history.

After the war, Nimitz was to claim that the Central Pacific campaign was largely won through the capacity of the United States Navy and Marine Corps to project decisive power ashore. This convincingly demonstrated the effectiveness of sea power, and its continued utility for the future. The instrument of this power was a balanced fleet, centred on fast carriers and ships suitable for amphibious warfare. All this became an issue on 15 December 1945 when Nimitz became Chief of Naval Operations. LOVE shows the extent of the problems that the postwar navy faced – most particularly the desperate need to reduce the size of the fleet to manageable proportions, without undermining America's naval mastery in an uncertain and dangerous era. There were many who argued that now there was no major adversary at sea, there was no need for a global navy.

BARLOW explores several of the most contentious and connected issues facing Nimitz in this his last, and perhaps most arduous, appointment. As Chief of Naval Operations, he had to deal with ferocious inter-service disputes about the prospective unification of the services, about the balance to be struck between the roles of sea power and air power in the atomic age, and about the comparative utility of land-based bombers and fleet carriers. Nimitz stood out against some of his naval colleagues in arguing for a separate air force and in advocating organizational integration between the services. But he was adamant that global naval power in general, and carrier aviation in particular, were essential to the future security of the United States. Although he was only partially successful in these difficult matters, Nimitz showed once again the qualities of determination and independence that had made him such an effective Commander in the Pacific.

GEOFFREY TILL

See also MacArthur; World War II: United States and 2 & 3

Nineteen-Twenties: General

Allen, Frederick Lewis, *Only Yesterday: An Informal History of the Nineteen-Twenties*, New York: Harper, 1931

Braeman, John, Robert H. Bremner, and David Brody (editors), *Change and Continuity in Twentieth Century America: The 1920s*, Columbus: Ohio State University Press, 1968

Dumenil, Lynn, *The Modern Temper: American Culture and Society in the 1920's*, New York: Hill and Wang, 1995

Hawley, Ellis W., *The Great War and the Search for a Modern Order: A History of the American People and Their Institutions, 1917–1933*, New York: St. Martin's Press, 1979, 2nd edition, 1992

Hicks, John D., *Republican Ascendancy, 1921–1933*, New York: Harper, 1960

Leuchtenburg, William E., *The Perils of Prosperity, 1914–1932*, Chicago: University of Chicago Press, 1958, 2nd edition, 1993

Lynd, Robert Staughton and Helen Merrell Lynd, *Middletown: A Study in Contemporary American Culture*, New York: Harcourt Brace, 1929

McCoy, Donald R., *Coming of Age: The United States During the 1920's and 1930's*, Baltimore and Harmondsworth: Penguin, 1973

Parrish, Michael E., *Anxious Decades: America in Prosperity and Depression, 1920–1941*, New York: Norton, 1992

Schlesinger, Arthur M., Jr., *The Crisis of the Old Order, 1919–1933*, Boston: Houghton Mifflin, and London: Heinemann, 1957

Soule, George Henry, *Prosperity Decade: From War to Depression, 1917–1929*, New York: Rinehart, and London: Pilot Press, 1947

The 1920s are still very much subject to the "Jazz Age" images created by F. Scott Fitzgerald – Fords, flappers, speakeasies, and sexual license. ALLEN's entertaining popular journalistic account, written from the perspective of the 1930s and a best-seller in its own day, reinforces such stereotypes. Although the emphasis is sometimes on the frivolous – the author expressly intended to record "fads and fashions and follies" – Allen established a view of the decade, albeit a superficial one based solely on newspapers and magazines, which subsequent historians either largely accepted or, increasingly, challenged. The absence of farmers, immigrant communities or African Americans from this account is all too obvious. Nonetheless, the focus on broad cultural issues has generally been followed by more recent writers.

The LYNDs' classic study of Muncie, Indiana, covers some of the same ground as Allen, but is based on first-hand observation and a social scientific approach, looking at "Getting a Living, Making a Home, Training the Young, Leisure, Religion, and Community Acivities." Political events do not feature, and social divisions are much more evident in this view of the decade. There is a wealth of detail on social and economic conditions, pointing up the mixture of modern consumerism and hardship which was the reality of Coolidge prosperity for many Americans.

In contrast SOULE provides a detailed economic survey of the decade which, despite its age, is still a reliable account which makes clear the main developments of the period in a readable narrative. Labor relations and standards of living are examined in two chapters. The fluctuations in economic growth which are described indicate some of the problems of over-generalization about the prosperity of the New Era.

SCHLESINGER's book was the first of four volumes which focused on the age of Franklin D. Roosevelt, and his survey of the period is entirely shaped by that concern – almost half the book deals with FDR and the mounting crisis after 1929. An old-fashioned emphasis on political biography dominates the writing, and hardly a name is mentioned without a brief thumbnail sketch being provided. The decade is judged almost entirely against the backdrop of Depression and, despite a generally sympathetic portrait of Hoover, it is predictably judged as a period of political failure.

Although published within a year of Schlesinger, LEUCHTENBURG's survey is altogether different in quality, emphasis and character. Combining Allen's style and coverage with Schlesinger's political commentary, the author's more judicious view sees the period as a time of questioning, of rural-urban conflict, and an attempt to come to terms with "a strong state, the dominance of the metropolis, secularization and the breakdown of religious sanctions, the loss of authority of the family, industrial concentration, international power politics, and mass culture."

HICKS is a solid, factual account of the decade based on considerable research in primary and secondary sources, other than the Hoover papers to which the author did not have access. The emphasis is on straightforward political narrative and a descriptive account of other developments; there is little on social matters – the Lynds, for example, merit only one brief reference for their "on-the-spot investigations," and social inequality, women, and African Americans fare little better.

These matters are much more fully explored in McCOY's broader study which has all the hallmarks of the 1960s on it. Where previous writers, implicitly or explicitly, tended to point to the contrasts between the 1920s and 1930s, McCoy emphasises continuity – "Despite the depression, the two decades had far more in common than they had separating them." The unifying elements were the broad political, economic, and social changes which marked the inter-war period as a transitional period between old and new.

The collection of essays in BRAEMAN *et al.* is a useful attempt at revisionism, although the various articles cover well-established areas such as 1919, political scandals, the plight of farmers and labor unions, welfare capitalism, religious fundamentalism, the Ku Klux Klan, prohibition, the city, and the "revolution in morals". Some of this work is itself now dated, and one has to look elsewhere for alternative views on the social history or politics of the era.

HAWLEY's succinct general survey rejects the established view of political reaction and business conservatism and establishes a line of continuity back to the progressive period and World War I. His emphasis is on the further development of the managerial and governmental systems which evolved into "the associative state" spearheaded by Herbert Hoover. Although ultimately Hawley judges the period as one of failure, he describes a move away from classical ideas on economics and government, which provided a basis for future development. While social and cultural issues are touched upon, they are not very fully examined, but an extremely useful bibliography is provided.

Like some others, including McCoy, PARRISH sees a unity in the period between World War I and the Great Depression. While he covers similar ground, he does so with a somewhat different emphasis and content. Reflecting the work of authors such as Jackson Lears, Parrish sees the two decades linked by the "virtues and vices of a consumer society." The emphasis on consumption and advertising is evident in more than one chapter. While standards of living do come under some examination, there is perhaps less on this topic than in some other accounts. Labor is dealt with in only a few pages, but racial groups and women each merit a separate chapter, and, unlike McCoy, Parrish also looks at literary and artistic developments in some detail.

While resembling Parrish in some respects – in providing a skilful synthesis of existing secondary works, rather than a study based on extensive primary research – DUMENIL's more focused, thematic work emphasizes the "erosion of community and personal autonomy," ethnic and racial diversity, and growing cultural pluralism, in an increasingly heterogeneous society. The experiences of blue and white collar workers, women, African Americans, and different ethnic and religious groups are compared and contrasted, in relation to both work and leisure, in order to show how different sections of society were affected by, and responded to, the development of mass production and mass consumption. American "culture" is seen as a contested terrain, in which different groups struggled to give shape and meaning to their lives in a period of rapid change. Not only are film and literature considered in separate sections of the book, but references to them are woven into the general text.

NEIL A. WYNN

Nixon, Richard M.   1913–1994
37th President of the United States

Aitken, Jonathan, *Nixon: A Life*, Washington, DC: Regnery, and London: Weidenfeld and Nicolson, 1993

Ambrose, Stephen E., *Nixon*, 3 vols., New York: Simon and Schuster, 1987–91

Brodie, Fawn M., *Richard Nixon: The Shaping of His Character*, New York: Norton, 1981

Haldeman, H.R., *The Haldeman Diaries: Inside the Nixon White House*, New York: Putnam, 1994

Hoff, Joan, *Nixon Reconsidered*, New York: HarperCollins, 1994

Kutler, Stanley I., *The Wars of Watergate: The Last Crisis of Richard Nixon*, New York: Knopf, 1990

Nixon, Richard, *RN: The Memoirs of Richard Nixon*, New York: Grosset and Dunlap, and London: Sidgwick and Jackson, 1978

Nixon, Richard, *In the Arena: A Memoir of Victory, Defeat and Renewal*, New York: Simon and Schuster, 1990

Parmet, Herbert S., *Richard Nixon and His America*, Boston: Little Brown, 1990

Richard Milhous Nixon was one of the most complex, puzzling and, to many people, loathsome figures in the political panorama of the last five decades, yet he is also the only man in American history ever to be elected twice as Vice President and twice as President. In the White House he achieved many major successes: the United States withdrawal from Vietnam, restored relations with China, the first major arms agreement with the Soviet Union, and much more. For good and for ill, he defined American politics and policy by his successes and failures. Historians have debated, and will continue to debate, his role and achievements, and Nixon will, undoubtedly, both fascinate and abhor them, as he did his contemporaries. Most certainly, he is, and will be, noted in the history texts as the first, and hopefully the last, President of the United States to resign because of scandal.

The well respected and exhaustively researched Nixon trilogy by AMBROSE is a frank look at Nixon's life which carefully dissects the words, private writings and tape-recorded conversations of Nixon and captures the man, the president, the scrutinized, the scorned, the private citizen, and finally, the respected elder statesman that he became during the latter stages of his life. With dispassionate objectivity and justice, the

first volume covers the tempestuous years of his youth, his legal education at Duke, his early political activities including support of the Truman Doctrine and the Marshall Plan, and his involvement in the House Committee on Un-American Activities, and his failed 1960 presidential bid, concluding with the deep low point of his 1962 defeat for the governorship of California. The second volume covers his interim recovery and rise to the top political seat in America with complex descriptions of his first term, including the Vietnam quagmire, relations with China and the USSR and, ultimately, the extra-legal pre-1972 campaign attacks on his enemies. With astute detail, Ambrose carefully charts the highs and lows as he follows each milestone in Nixon's life, creating a man with an intriguing early life and a ruthless political agenda, who emerges, in the third and final volume, as an arrogant Nixon who would risk everything if only to be revered for his dubious return to the political arena.

Like BRODIE a decade before him, PARMET adopts the "psycho-history" approach in his attempt to discover why Nixon has become an icon of sorts in American postwar history. Through in-depth interviews with Nixon himself, and access to Nixon's papers and White House files not available to others, Parmet explains how one man shaped a nation and its politics through his cunning Cold War policies and popular conservative campaign for the voice of the "silent majority". Though Parmet is revisionist in his viewpoint, and intent on presenting an amiable Nixon, he nonetheless portrays a man who is dangerously complex and unmanageably egocentric. In his concluding discussion of how the effects of the Nixon era continue to be felt today, as they embody the "thrust of our political future," Parmet reiterates his belief that, above all else, Nixon was a very powerful man.

In the same pro-Nixon vein falls AITKEN, a former Conservative party Member of Parliament. In his over sixty hours of interviews with Nixon, he seeks to fathom the "Nixon enigma" which has escaped so many biographers before him. His research included access to thousands of pages of previously sealed private Nixon documents. As an "outsider", Aitken does offer a different perspective on Vietnam and Watergate, but unfortunately his distorted convictions about the powers of the American presidency leave one with the realization that his unbiased opinions are often based on his ignorance of America. His conclusion that the forced resignation of Nixon was "a political overreaction, human injustice and mistake" and his portrayal of Nixon as a politician of conviction led astray by bad company, are oversimplifications which lead to serious distortions of American political realities.

No other Nixon scholar could disagree more vehemently than KUTLER. Although his book was published a few years before Aitken, Kutler admonishes revisionists who attempt a favorable re-evaluation of Nixon without condemning him, and his administration, for the most odious act of his presidency – Watergate. This is the impetus behind Kutler's stinging reply to Nixon's later attempts at political rehabilitation, with his character crushing discussions on ethics, ends and means and the dangers of an imperial presidency. Kutler contends that, while historians should and will disagree on the merits of Nixon's policies, all must conclude that Watergate was the most inexcusable breach of faith. This book may be the all-encompassing and definitive work on Watergate, but

Kutler's compelling synthesis is not without its shortcomings. Unfortunately, at the close of his more than 700 pages, the reader is left questioning why he never clearly evaluates any of the wide range of Watergate break-in theories. Nonetheless, this comprehensive endnotes, which all would do well to read carefully, give additional authority and credence to this exhaustive study of this most infamous American political event.

The anti-Nixon rhetoric, somewhat muted in his later years by his elder statesman activities, was kept at bay until Nixon's death. This was quickly followed by the controversial publication of the revisionist work of HOFF, which restored the subject to the forefront of hotly contested scholarly debate. She seeks to realign the order of the criteria by which Nixon is to be remembered, and assessed. Hoff is convinced that journalists and scholars have unfairly condemned Nixon's entire presidency because of Watergate, and have ignored what she considers to be his most important accomplishments in areas such as civil rights, the environment and welfare reform. Her book, which was held for release until just weeks after the 22 April 1994 death of Nixon, attempts to place domestic reform at the top of the evaluation list, followed by foreign policy and then Watergate. Hoff cautions that historians must not dwell on Watergate when evaluating Nixon's long and remarkable career, which needs to be placed in "balanced historical context." The book's inattentiveness to Nixon's foreign-policy accomplishments in China and the Soviet Union indicates Hoff's belief that they are egregiously overrated. She is exceptionally trenchant on the secret bombing of Cambodia and other Nixon administration actions that served to expand and, as she contends, prolong the war in Vietnam. Hoff concurs with many of the early Nixon biographers, that he was in fact guilty of obstructing justice, a crime for which, she admits, he should have been impeached.

However, the posthumously published diaries of HALDEMAN stalled the Nixon rehabilitation campaign begun by Hoff and other admirers who emerged after Nixon's death. The diaries attempt to lay to rest the claims that Haldeman "took to his grave" all he knew about Watergate and Nixon's role therein. With unembellished frankness, these diaries, which cover the crucial four years and three months that Haldeman was Chief of Staff for President Nixon, recreate with vivid detail such outstanding events as the Vietnam War, the 1972 election, the White House staff power struggles and the Watergate scandal. The key figure is the insecure, obsessive, manipulative Nixon who desperately needed to destroy his enemies and prove himself a worthy statesman. Nixon's less then scrupulous actions are given credence through Haldeman's startling accusations of set-ups, cover-ups and the need to locate a "fall guy" for Watergate.

But there is nothing quite like NIXON (1978 and 1990). Being the intensely self-conscious man he was, Nixon published his own memoirs twice. Although they are obviously attempts at self-justification and self-rehabilitation, they also provide remarkable insights into various phases of his career – notably some of his foreign policy decisions. There are many evasions and half-truths, but no apologies – and no answers to the questions about his character and motives which so many journalists and historians have sought in vain.

SHARI L. OSBORN

Northwest Ordinances, 1784–1787

Barnhart, John D., *Valley of Democracy: The Frontier Versus the Plantation in the Ohio Valley, 1775–1818*, Bloomington: Indiana University Press, 1953

Bloom, John Porter (editor), *The American Territorial System*, Athens: Ohio University Press, 1973

Jensen, Merrill, *The New Nation: A History of the United States During the Confederation, 1781–1789*, New York: Knopf, 1950

Onuf, Peter S., *Statehood and Union: A History of the Northwest Ordinance*, Bloomington: Indiana University Press, 1987

Philbrick, Francis S. (editor), *Laws of the Illinois Territory, 1809–1818*, Springfield: Illinois State Historical Library, 1950

Williams, Frederick D. (editor), *The Northwest Ordinance: Essays on Its Formulation, Provisions, and Legacy*, East Lansing: Michigan State University Press, 1989

The Northwest Ordinance, a document which some historians have ranked only behind the Declaration of Independence and the Constitution in importance, has attracted considerable scholarly attention over the years but has been the subject of very few books. Historical context for understanding the ordinance is provided by JENSEN, a good general study of the United States during the Confederation period. It details the history of the three separate ordinances passed by the Confederation Congress governing the Northwest Territory – the Ordinance of 1784, the Land Ordinance of 1785, and the Northwest Ordinance of 1787. Jensen challenges the conventional view that the Northwest Ordinance, which replaced the Ordinance of 1784 drafted by Jefferson, established a democratic government for the territory. The very opposite, he says, was true. Jefferson's ordinance providing for democratic self-government was abolished in 1787 when Congress, yielding to pressure from avaricious land jobbers anxious to secure their property against frontier lawlessness, passed the Northwest Ordinance. That document placed control of the Northwest solidly in the hands of Congress, and western settlers were compelled to endure a period of colonial subjection under the arbitrary rule of congressional appointees.

In a volume that focuses broadly on the laws of the Illinois Territory but includes important sections on the Northwest Ordinance, PHILBRICK agrees with Jensen. The 1787 ordinance, he asserts, was "utterly reactionary." It reversed the democratic thrust of the 1784 ordinance. By not providing settlers with representative government initially, it betrayed the principles underlying the Revolution. Like Philbrick and Jensen, BARNHART covers a broader subject than the Northwest Ordinance, but includes a good summary chapter describing and analyzing the three ordinances. Barnhart acknowledges that settlers living in the Northwest during the first territorial stage were subject to an unrepresentative and undemocratic government. There was no suffrage and no elections, and the people were governed by appointed officers, without their consent or participation. Even so, the undemocratic character of the government created by the Northwest Ordinance was temporary. In due time the people gained all the rights and privileges of the inhabitants of the original thirteen states.

BLOOM is a collection of papers written by specialists for a scholarly conference on the history of the United States territories sponsored by the National Archives and Records Service. It contains a section on the Northwest Ordinance with essays by Arthur Bestor and Robert F. Berkhofer, Jr. In his essay, Bestor shows how the new American nation, following independence, gradually shaped a constitutional policy for the western territories that fulfilled the promise of the Revolution. Jefferson led the way when he included in the Ordinance of 1784 a provision granting western settlers at the very outset virtually complete powers of self-government. Congress delayed implementing the ordinance but did not repudiate the constitutionalism that underlay it. In the end the Northwest Ordinance reaffirmed the nation's commitment to bring the territories into the Union on an equal footing with the original states. From this basic commitment there was never any real retreat. "Constitutionalism – the idea that the fundamental law could control even the process of expansion – remained somehow at the heart of the territorial system." In another chapter Berkhofer says that the 1787 ordinance grew out of America's general spirit of "innovative idealism." Americans were fully conscious of the need to make their institutions and actions conform to their republican ideals. The Northwest Ordinance was the "culmination of American thinking about the nature of a colonial system for a republican empire." This system allowed colonies to evolve from dependency to statehood. The innovative principle was that colonies ultimately would enjoy equality with the mother country. Both the provision for territorial evolution and the granting of equal statehood fulfilled the promise of the Revolution.

WILLIAMS is a collection of essays by five prominent scholars who participated in the bicentennial celebration of the Northwest Ordinance sponsored by Michigan State University. Utilizing the latest scholarship, each of its five chapters casts new light on some aspect of the ordinance. Jack N. Rakove describes the ordinance's ambiguous legacy, which on the one hand ensured republican self-government for the white settlers of the territory but on the other condemned resident Native Americans to subjugation and exile. Ruth Bloch examines the work of New England missionaries on the northwestern frontier, Jurgen Herbst treats the development of public universities in the territory, Gordon T. Stewart shows how the establishment of stable government in the western country tilted the balance of power in North America toward the United States, and Paul Finkelman examines the paradoxical situation in which slavery, despite being prohibited by the Northwest Ordinance, continued to exist in the territory.

ONUF is the most recent and best of the studies of the Northwest Ordinance. By that ordinance, which the author calls one of the most important documents of the founding period, Congress established a colonial government on the Ohio frontier to provide stability and to protect property interests. At the same time, however, it promised settlers that they would regain all the rights and privileges of self-governing citizens when new states were carved from the territory and admitted to the Union. The Ordinance was a blueprint for continental expansion, but it was more than that. Drafted at a time when the future of the Union was in doubt, it was an act of supreme faith. If the nation survived its constitutional crisis, the frontier could assume its rightful place in the revitalized Union, but only if law and order and stability were firmly established within its borders. Most of the nation's leaders saw the frontier as a lawless region where self-interested squatters, freebooters, speculators, and scofflaws pursued their private agendas without reference to governmental authority. The frontier must be transformed by the strong hand of the national government if republican institutions were to be preserved and expanded. The Northwest Ordinance was the vehicle for accomplishing this purpose. It was a realistic response to the social, political, and economic problems which the Northwestern Territory created for the young nation. Onuf is a carefully researched and well-written study suitable for both the general reader and the specialist.

CHARLES D. LOWERY

Nullification Crisis, 1832–1833

Ellis, Richard E., *The Union at Risk: Jacksonian Democracy, States' Rights, and the Nullification Crisis*, New York: Oxford University Press, 1987

Freehling, William W., *Prelude to Civil War: The Nullification Controversy in South Carolina, 1816–1836*, New York: Harper, 1966

Freehling, William W., *The Road to Disunion: Secessionists at Bay, 1776–1854*, New York: Oxford University Press, 1990

Hartz, Louis, "South Carolina vs. the United States," in *America in Crisis: Fourteen Crucial Episodes in American History*, edited by Daniel Aaron, New York: Knopf, 1952

Latner, Richard B., *The Presidency of Andrew Jackson: White House Politics 1829–1837*, Athens: University of Georgia Press, 1979

Peterson, Merrill D., *Olive Branch and Sword: The Compromise of 1833*, Baton Rouge: Louisiana State University Press, 1982

Remini, Robert V., *Andrew Jackson and the Course of American Democracy, 1833–1845*, New York: Harper, 1984

Wilson, Clyde N., Introductions to vols. 10–12 of *The Papers of John C. Calhoun*, edited by Robert L. Meriwether, W. Edwin Hemphill, and Clyde N. Wilson, 22 vols. to date, Columbia: University of South Carolina Press, 1959–

Wiltse, Charles M., *John C. Calhoun, Nullifier, 1829–1839*, Indianapolis: Bobbs Merrill, 1949

FREEHLING (1966) is the first and most comprehensive modern study of the nullification crisis, which occurred when South Carolina sought to nullify federal legislation on the tariff. In this path-breaking work the author took advantage of the vast amount of manuscript material that had become available since the last major work on the subject fifty years earlier, especially the letters uncovered by the editors of the Papers of John C. Calhoun. These new materials enabled Freehling to demonstrate for the first time that Calhoun was far more loyal to the Union than any of the other leading nullifiers. Freehling also challenges the standard economic interpretation of the crisis by arguing that the nullifiers were more interested in holding back abolitionism than in lowering the tariff. In his view the slaveholders supported nullification because they had over-reacted to the early antislavery movement, and wanted a weapon to defend their peculiar institution. Freehling looks ahead to the coming of the Civil War, and focuses his attention on the nullification movement in South Carolina rather than on the political crisis in Washington.

ELLIS, in contrast, looks back towards the American Revolution and deals primarily with the Democratic party, both in Washington and in the states of Georgia, Virginia, and New York. He explains the dilemma of the Jacksonians as they tried to defend the Union against nullification while remaining faithful to the states rights republican beliefs they had inherited from the Revolution. While Freehling agrees with earlier writers that Jackson emerged victorious in the crisis, Ellis argues that the victor, if any, was Calhoun. He considers Jackson the loser because he allowed his party to split over the issue of states rights. In coping with the crisis, he went too far in the direction of national rights and failed to express adequately the traditional states rights position of many Democrats.

In a recent major work on the coming of secession, FREEHLING (1990) has modified his emphasis on the role of slavery in nullification. He now concedes that the correlation between counties in South Carolina with heavy slave population and counties strongly committed to nullification is not as strong as he had originally thought. He also says that the slaveholders reacted more rationally than he had supposed. But he still maintains that fears over the future of slavery fueled the movement. Pointing to the differences between the upper and lower South, he believes that the nullifiers in South Carolina were deeply concerned that the upper South would give in to the antislavery movement in the North.

HARTZ attacks the nullifiers for illogical reasoning. If the states were as sovereign as they claimed, then the logical course for the South Carolinians would have been secession, not nullification. But they chose nullification, which, according to their theory, could be overturned by three-fourths of the states through the amendment process. If the nullifiers accepted this outcome, they would have relinquished state sovereignty. Hartz attacks Calhoun for threatening the Union, and then insisting that it would be strengthened by something as mechanical as nullification.

WILTSE, on the other hand, sees no such inconsistency. In the second of his three classic volumes on Calhoun he argues that Calhoun was justified in shifting from his early nationalism to states rights because the economic situation had changed and the South was being abused. Far ahead of his time, Calhoun recognized that American society had divided between the interests of manufacturing and agriculture. In such a society, nullification was the only way in which the interests of the South and the sovereignty of individual states could be protected.

Another defender of Calhoun is WILSON, the present editor of the Calhoun Papers. Pointing out, as the nullifiers had, that nullification could be overturned by three-fourths of the states, he argues that it was less radical than critics have maintained. Nullification was no more mechanical or unusual than judicial review, and was a logical outgrowth of the republican states rights tradition. Calhoun was simply following Thomas Jefferson, James Madison, and John Taylor in seeking to protect the rights of minorities against a corrupt national government. Nullification was not a step toward secession, but a step to avoid secession and save the Union.

LATNER places not only nullification but also the Jacksonian response to it in the republican tradition. Each side, he says, used the rhetoric of republicanism to justify its position. The South Carolinians insisted that they were resisting the abuses of a consolidated government; while the Jacksonians said that nullification violated the rights of the majority, which were implicit in the doctrine of republicanism.

In describing the way in which the nullification crisis was resolved in Congress, historians have generally approached the subject from the point of view of one of the major participants. In the final volume of his definitive three-volume biography of Jackson, REMINI concludes that the Old General saved the Union by isolating South Carolina and by talking tough, but all the while acting with moderation. Unlike Ellis he finds no fault with the president's behavior, and says that he was more of a hero after the crisis than before. Wiltse believes that Calhoun joined Henry Clay in the compromise measures because he sincerely wanted to restore peace. Both he and Clay feared the consequences if Jackson were allowed to resort to force, and both wanted to keep Jackson from getting credit for solving the crisis. The compromise tariff reduced rates sufficiently to save face for Calhoun, and the Force Bill saved face for Jackson.

The most detailed account of the compromise is by PETERSON, who presents the story from Clay's point of view. Badly defeated in the election of 1832, Clay saw the compromise as a way in which he could strengthen his political power. He would win southern votes by lowering the tariff, but would salvage the support of northern manufacturers by postponing the tariff cuts and by increasing the effective rate of protection through the policy of home valuation. Unlike most of the studies of the nullification crisis, Peterson keeps the focus on Washington and practical politics rather than on South Carolina and political theory.

DONALD B. COLE

See also Calhoun; States Rights

O

Oil and Natural Gas

Blair, John, *The Control of Oil*, New York: Pantheon, and London: Macmillan, 1977

Bromley, Simon, *American Hegemony and World Oil*, Cambridge: Polity Press, and University Park: Pennsylvania State University Press, 1991

Clark, John G., *Energy and the Federal Government: Fossil Fuel Policies, 1900–1946*, Urbana: University of Illinois Press, 1987

Larson, Henrietta M. and Kenneth Wiggins Porter, *History of Humble Oil and Refining Company: A Study in Industrial Growth*, New York: Harper, 1959

Randall, Stephen J., *United States Foreign Oil Policy, 1919–1948: For Profits and Security*, Kingston, Ontario: McGill-Queen's University Press, 1985

Vietor, Richard H.K., *Energy Policy in America since 1945: A Study of Business-Government Relations*, Cambridge and New York: Cambridge University Press, 1984

Williamson, Harold F., Ralph L. Adreano, Arnold R. Daum, and Gilbert C. Klose, *The American Petroleum Industry*, 2 vols., Evanston, IL: Northwestern University Press, 1959–63

Yergin, Daniel, *The Prize: The Epic Quest for Oil, Money, and Power*, New York: Simon and Schuster, 1991

The literature upon the oil and gas industries, and particularly oil, is a very extensive one, covering a number of different aspects. There are several studies of individual companies involved in the industry, of which LARSON and PORTER is a good example. Unlike some of the more laudatory, company-produced volumes, Larson and Porter's book is a thoroughly researched, exhaustive example of business history. It was written by two historians under the auspices of the Business Foundation Inc, (which received a gift from the company); they had the advantage of access to the company archives and employees, past and present, while retaining freedom over what to publish. There is a tremendous amount of factual and technical detail in this massive book, which takes a generally positive attitude towards the company's history and management.

WILLIAMSON *et al.* (1959 and 1963) remains the most accessible general survey of the first hundred years of the oil industry in the United States, although the books cover only the period to 1959, and they were published well over thirty years ago. Nonetheless, the period covered includes the setting up of the early American oil industry, the development of a strong international dimension, and the transformation of American transportation and industry through the use of oil. Although these books contain little research based upon primary sources, they provide a useful factual overview.

The United States government became involved in the oil and gas industries at a relatively early stage. An excellent study of government policies towards all fossil fuels (oil, gas and coal) is provided by CLARK, who has used government archives extensively in his very detailed – some might say too detailed – study of federal oil policies. He traces the story through government regulation in World War I to voluntarism in the inter-war period, and concludes that even in World War II there was no real threat to private control. In common with some of the studies of foreign oil policy, therefore, Clark concludes that private interests triumphed over attempts by the state to provide a coherent policy, although he perhaps tends to overlook the growing regulations imposed by government.

VIETOR continues the story beyond World War II. However, he clearly believes in the efficacy of market forces, and castigates federal government policy for interfering with those forces through a programme of price controls and regulatory measures. The policies thus imposed reduced economic efficiency, yet gained little in the way of improved economic stability and national security. Vietor does not advocate a complete return to a non-interventionist role for government, but this is a book written with a contemporary agenda very much in mind, although it does provide a lot of useful factual information.

No study of the United States oil industry would be complete without a study of the world oil industry, in which four of the so-called "seven sisters" are American companies. A readable and comprehensive survey of the international oil scene, albeit one rather tilted towards the anecdotal and biographical, is YERGIN, upon which a very successful television series was based. It draws upon a remarkably wide range of research, including a considerable number of personal interviews with important individuals. In particular, Yergin demonstrates the interplay between oil and international diplomacy, particularly with reference to the Middle East. His discussion of the domestic oil industry is less complete.

High domestic production meant that until the 1940s the United States government had little reason to adopt a foreign oil policy, beyond providing diplomatic support for American oil companies wishing to explore overseas. However, this was to change in World War II, as awareness of future vulnerability caused a reassessment. This is discussed in a number of works on foreign oil policy, of which one excellent example is RANDALL. On the basis of extensive archival research, Randall argues that the United States government saw private oil interests as important agents in pursuing foreign oil policy goals. Looking at various, abortive attempts by the state to gain direct control over parts of the oil industry, Randall concludes that while the private sector did not determine United States foreign oil policy entirely on its own, it nonetheless succeeded in defeating any thought of the state exercising a direct role in the international petroleum industry. The result was that the state did not develop a coherent foreign oil policy in this period, although it did seek to defend both strategic and economic interests in foreign oil, by maintaining the "Open Door" and opposing early signs of oil nationalism in other nations.

Randall completes his study in the 1940s. BROMLEY puts more emphasis upon the post- World War II period, in a book dominated by the use of international relations theory. In it he explores how the United States exercised hegemony through the structures of the world system, and how the development of oil policy should be set within that broader context. This is not a book for anyone unhappy with the use of theoretical models.

One concern of historians and political scientists has been the political influence exercised by oil companies. The nature of this influence, and of its concerns, have differed. The majors had extensive interests abroad and hence a concern over foreign policy, while the powerful independents within the domestic market were eager to safeguard their own position. Studies written in the aftermath of the oil crisis of 1973–74 are frequently critical of the oil industry's power to fix prices and work in conjunction to control production, and often adopt a historical approach to their investigations. A useful example of this trend is BLAIR. He is concerned to show that the oil industry has been largely successful in controlling production, distribution and pricing of petroleum, both internationally and domestically, often with the co-operation of government agencies. This is a campaigning book calling for government action, either through regulation or, preferably, by an antitrust approach to restore competition. Along with other books cited here, it demonstrates the difficulty of avoiding present-mindedness in discussing the oil industry.

FIONA VENN

See also Energy; Foreign Policy: Financial and Economic Aspects; for Standard Oil Company see Business History: Individual Corporations

Olmsted, Frederick Law 1822–1903
Travel writer and city planner

Fabos, Julius Gy., Gordon T. Milde, and V. Michael Weinmayr, *Frederick Law Olmsted, Sr.: Founder of Landscape Architecture in America*, Amherst: University of Massachusetts Press, 1968

Fein, Albert, *Frederick Law Olmsted and the American Environmental Tradition*, New York: Braziller, 1972
Graff, M.M., *Central Park/Prospect Park: A New Perspective*, New York: Greensward Foundation, 1985
Kalfus, Melvin, *Frederick Law Olmsted: The Passion of a Public Artist*, New York: New York University Press, 1990
McLaughlin, Charles Capen and others (editors), *The Papers of Frederick Law Olmsted*, 6 vols., Baltimore: Johns Hopkins University Press, 1977–92
Mitchell, Broadus, *Frederick Law Olmsted: A Critic of the Old South*, Baltimore: Johns Hopkins Press, 1924
Roper, Laura Wood, *FLO: A Biography of Frederick Law Olmsted*, Baltimore: Johns Hopkins University Press, 1973
Stevenson, Elizabeth, *Park Maker: A Life of Frederick Law Olmsted*, New York: Macmillan, and London: Collier Macmillan, 1977
White, Dana F. and Victor A. Kramer (editors), *Olmsted South: Old South Critic/New South Planner*, Westport, CT: Greenwood Press, 1979
Zaitzevsky, Cynthia, *Frederick Law Olmsted and the Boston Park System*, Cambridge, MA: Belknap Press of Harvard University Press, 1982

Frederick Law Olmsted was a man whose career was, to say the least, peripatetic. Starting out as, among other things, a cabin-boy and later a farmer, by the 1850s he had abandoned both in order to pursue a literary career, reaching a wide audience through his series of dispatches for both the *New York Daily Times* and the *New York Daily Tribune* on slavery and the antebellum South, many of which were republished as *A Journey in the Seaboard Slave States* (1856), *A Journey Through Texas* (1857), and *A Journey in the Back Country* (1860). He then went on to act as a publishing agent and to serve as managing editor of *Putnam's Monthly Magazine*, before taking up the position of superintendent, and then Architect in Chief, of Central Park. The Civil War saw him as acting secretary of the United States Sanitary Commission, then superintendent of a Californian mining estate, before he returned to Central Park and, finally, settled down to the career for which he is probably best remembered, landscape architecture.

Unsurprisingly, such an active life has provided a wealth of material for biographers and historians. The relative value of the various works on Olmsted will depend on whether the reader's interest is in Olmsted's life and work as a whole, or in a particular aspect of it. In the latter case, the best starting point would be one (or more) of the introductory essays in the six-volume series of Olmsted's papers, edited by McLAUGHLIN *et al.* These essays are substantial and detailed in their coverage, and each focuses on the particular aspect of Olmsted's career covered by that volume.

A useful collection of essays for those who wish to "dip into" Olmsted's career is edited by WHITE and KRAMER. As its title would indicate, the focus of this collection is upon Olmsted's relationship with the South, and the topics covered range from an assessment of him as a travel writer, through his work with the Sanitary Commission during the Civil War, to his influence on the development of Atlanta at the turn of the century. Although there is a greater emphasis on the "Old South Critic" part of the title, with more than half the essays devoted to some aspect of Olmsted's travels through, and writings on, the antebellum Cotton Kingdom, the aim of this collection is to "confront both the environment – physical and cultural – and the whole man – designer and social critic – within a sharply defined historical frame of reference." In short, the collection aims not only to present an integrated view of Olmsted's multifaceted career, but also to offer some new ideas on Olmsted's relationship with the postwar South, "an area thought to have been largely removed from the kind of physical planning he advocated." Overall, this volume offers an excellent introduction to virtually all aspects of Olmsted scholarship.

Biographies of Olmsted start with MITCHELL, which is rather dated now in terms of its approach and style, although still perfectly readable and an extremely good introduction to Olmsted as social critic of the antebellum South, in particular Olmsted's very mixed response to that region. Although, as Mitchell argues, Olmsted "had real sympathy with the South," he was nevertheless "alive to the violence – physical, economic, political – which underlay Southern life," a dichotomy of sentiment that informed much of his commentary on slavery and southern life.

Among more recent biographies, the most authoritative is ROPER, which covers every aspect of Olmsted's life and work in impressive detail. Readers new to the subject should not be deterred by its sheer size. At some 500 pages in length, it is a substantial and extraordinarily well-researched work, which is nevertheless written in a lively and approachable way. Roper's great strength is that she succeeds in integrating Olmsted's twin "roles" of social critic and landscape architect, places him firmly in the context of his times, and shows how Olmsted as an individual reflects the significance of 19th-century social and environmental change on America as a nation. Less unsure than Mitchell about some of Olmsted's ideas, Roper suggests that these can be summed up by the notion of "communicativeness," which "involved recognizing . . . that one had an essential community of interest with other human beings, regardless of regional, class, economic, color, religious, or whatever differences." "Translated into political terms," Roper argues, "communicativeness was the essence of democracy."

Two further biographies have appeared since Roper's, the first by STEVENSON and the second, and more recent, by KALFUS. Both differ in certain details from Roper's account of some aspects of Olmsted's life, in particular the degree to which Olmsted influenced the design of Central Park, and the nature of his relationship with his associate, Calvert Vaux. In brief, where these two biographies differ from earlier work lies in their attempt to move beyond what they perceive as the celebratory tone of much Olmsted scholarship towards a more "realistic" assessment of the man. In this regard Kalfus goes much further than Stevenson. In particular he finds in Olmsted's "troubled, sometimes tragic, childhood and adolescence," the seeds not only of his intellectual development but also "of the painful narcissistic wounds that fired his ambition."

As far as Central Park is concerned, Kalfus sees this as one of Olmsted's greatest and most lasting achievements, an enduring symbol for both his time and our own. In contrast, GRAFF, a vehement critic of Olmsted's impact on landscape architecture, argues that Olmsted was inherently unqualified for the task he undertook, and that "Central Park still suffers from the effects of his ignorance of the nature and habits of plant materials." Graff's work is not specifically about Olmsted, but is one of several studies of the construction of the city landscape in America, which include some analysis of Olmsted's contribution to landscape design and development. It is worth noting that there are also several edited editions of Olmsted's own writings on landscape architecture, many with useful introductions.

The best secondary works which focus on Olmsted specifically, however, include Fabos, Fein and Zaitzevsky. Of these the most recent and up-to-date is ZAITZEVSKY who places Olmsted's work on Central Park and Prospect Park in context. FABOS, with co-authors Gordon T. Milde and V. Michael Weinmayr, produced a lavishly illustrated volume to accompany a 1964 exhibition devoted to Olmsted's work in landscape architecture. Designed as a tribute, it is of course celebratory, but not overly so, and the illustrations do offer the reader some visual "evidence" against which to place Graff's criticisms of Olmsted's ability in a way that text alone cannot do. FEIN is also a volume with illustrations "selected and arranged so as to form a visual essay" on Olmsted's landscape work. With only some seventy pages of text to introduce the illustrations, Fein's study is unable to develop many of its ideas and arguments about Olmsted as a landscape architect. In order to get the best out of Fabos and Fein, it is probably advisable to use them in conjunction with one of the biographies of Olmsted by Stevenson, Kalfus or Roper.

S-M. GRANT

Open Door Policy

Anderson, David L., *Imperialism and Idealism: American Diplomats in China, 1861–1898*, Bloomington: Indiana University Press, 1985

Hunt, Michael H., *Frontier Defense and the Open Door: Manchuria in Chinese-American Relations, 1895–1911*, New Haven: Yale University Press, 1973

Hunt, Michael H., *The Making of a Special Relationship: The United States and China to 1914*, New York: Columbia University Press, 1983

Israel, Jerry, *Progressivism and the Open Door: America and China, 1905–1921*, Pittsburgh: University of Pittsburgh Press, 1971

McCormick, Thomas J., *China Market: America's Quest for Informal Empire, 1893–1901*, Chicago: Quadrangle, 1967

Varg, Paul A., *The Making of a Myth: The United States and China, 1893–1912*, East Lansing: Michigan State University Press, 1968

Young, Marilyn Blatt, *The Rhetoric of Empire: American China Policy, 1895–1901*, Cambridge, MA: Harvard University Press, 1968

The late 19th century saw the industrialized powers establish "spheres of influence" throughout a weakened China. These spheres discriminated against the economic activities of other countries. The United States, arriving late to the scene, opposed these foreign machinations. Based on two sets of notes that Secretary of State John Hay issued to the powers in 1899 and 1900, the Open Door Policy asserted the desire to protect China's integrity and foster free trade. Ultimately, it did little to help either, partly because the United States lacked both a sphere of influence and substantial commerce in China. The decision to issue the notes and the subsequent impact they had on American China policy have inspired considerable debate among historians.

VARG presents the traditionalist interpretation. The notes were issued with an understanding that the United States lacked concrete interests in China. However, certain vocal constituencies demanded an activist American policy. Set in this context, Varg points to the rhetorical quality of the notes that masked the intent of the "realists" to take no action on China's behalf. By 1909, a more activist group of policymakers emerged. Impressed with the age-old myth of the "China market" and interpreting the notes as a commitment to that country, these "idealists" adopted an ill-considered activist position. This stance compromised American China policy for years to come. While Varg's account demonstrates how the Open Door evolved, its lack of attention to the economic situation within the United States obscures one reason why the interest in China increased in the late 19th-century.

The claim that, at the end of the century, the United States had no substantial interests in China is challenged by McCORMICK. With the 1893 depression heightening fears of excess production, the "power elite" looked to China's potential market to solve the problem and sought to maintain a future stake in it. However, domestic politics exercised restraint on policy formulation. The notes, powerful in rhetoric but weak in specifics, reflected both the opportunities and constraints of American domestic politics. McCormick elucidates the alternatives open to the policymakers, and explains why certain options were chosen. However, the focus on economic factors obscures other social and cultural variables that equally influenced America's late-century involvement in China.

YOUNG combines many of the virtues found in the Varg and McCormick interpretations. According to Young, the Open Door assumed different meanings to different people. To some, the Open Door represented a commitment to free trade which could alleviate economic problems at home. To others, it was indicative of a "special friendship" between the two countries in which the United States assumed the role of paternalist defender. Some saw the notes as reflecting a duty to "civilize" China. The notes' appeal to a wide cross-section of American society lay in their lofty rhetoric devoid of specifics. However, this multitude of meanings ultimately rendered them meaningless. Young's use of Chinese sources allows for a much better presentation of the Chinese perspective, surpassing the more uncertain treatment it receives in Varg and McCormick.

ANDERSON casts doubts both on scholars like McCormick, who see the Notes as arising from a clear definition of economic interests, and on historians such as Young, who depict policymakers as lacking an understanding of both the situation in China and the notes' implications at home.

Focusing on the activities of the American ministers in China from 1861 through 1898, the author presents the notes as reflecting four decades of policy that sought to westernize China, but wavered between the extremes of idealism and imperialism. Faced with forty years of inconsistency, Hay simply tried to "make the best of a bad situation" and blended the ideals and interests inherent in American policy since 1861. Anderson's account is good at highlighting the freedom granted to individual ministers to formulate and implement policy. However, in a study centered in China, the absence of official Chinese sources prevents a truly comprehensive assessment of the various diplomats examined.

The protection of the economic Open Door in Manchuria is the focal point of HUNT (1973). Both the United States and China had mutual interests in preventing the region from being dominated by one power. Despite the low overall trade figures, Manchuria provided a significant market for American cotton and other select goods. For their part, the Chinese needed this resource-rich and strategically located region to counter imperialist designs. Recognizing shared interests in Manchuria, Chinese officials developed a policy to secure American assistance. That policy failed largely because of American racism, ethnocentrism, and a failure to appreciate the complexities of Chinese diplomacy. Hunt's extensive use of Chinese sources enables him to provide the best view of the Chinese perspective to be found in any of the studies of the Open Door policy.

Domestic factors always had a strong bearing on American policy, and ISRAEL examines how the interpretation and implementation of the Open Door evolved in the context of Progressive politics. The pursuit of Progressive economic and social objectives at home paralleled the development of a China policy seeking to remake that country in the American image. Anti-corruption campaigns, "muckraking," conservation efforts, and other hallmarks of Progressive politics are shown to have parallels in the articulation of the Open Door policy. Israel's linkage of the Open Door's evolution to the larger domestic context moves away from Varg's inclination to explain change by pointing to specific policymakers.

HUNT (1983), covering the period from 1784 to 1914, is the most comprehensive interpretive survey of American China policy. Interweaving political, diplomatic, economic, social, and cultural analysis, Hunt demonstrates that the two countries pursued policies based on mutual misperceptions. Hunt presents the Open Door ideology as expressing long held beliefs of westward expansion, moral and material uplift, and fears of excess production. However, diversity of interests at home and misperceptions abroad prevented that ideology from being translated into workable policy. Hunt manages to integrate the question of Chinese immigration and the Exclusion Acts into the larger framework of American China policy. As in his earlier work, Hunt's thorough examination of Chinese sources allows for an integrated presentation of both sides' policies and attitudes.

MICHAEL A. KRYSKO

See also Foreign Policy, 1865–1918; Imperialism and Anti-Imperialism

P

Pacific Northwest

Arrington, Leonard J., *History of Idaho*, 2 vols., Moscow: University of Idaho Press, 1994

Boag, Peter G., *Environment and Experience: Settlement Culture in Nineteenth-Century Oregon*, Berkeley: University of California Press, 1992

Jeffrey, Julie Roy, *Converting the West: A Biography of Narcissa Whitman*, Norman: University of Oklahoma Press, 1991

Loewenberg, Robert J., *Equality on the Oregon Frontier: Jason Lee and the Methodist Mission, 1834–43*, Seattle: University of Washington Press, 1976

May, Dean L., *Three Frontiers: Family, Land, and Society in the American West, 1850–1900*, Cambridge and New York: Cambridge University Press, 1994

Pomeroy, Earl, *The Pacific Slope: A History of California, Oregon, Washington, Idaho, Utah, and Nevada*, New York: Knopf, 1966

Ronda, James P., *Astoria and Empire*, Lincoln: University of Nebraska Press, 1990

Schwantes, Carlos A., *The Pacific Northwest: An Interpretative History*, Lincoln: University of Nebraska Press, 1989

Taylor, Quintard, *The Forging of a Black Community: Seattle's Central District, from 1870 through the Civil Rights Era*, Seattle: University of Washington Press, 1994

White, Richard, *Land Use, Environment, and Social Change: The Shaping of Island County, Washington*, Seattle: University of Washington Press, 1980

The Pacific Northwest, comprising the states of Oregon, Washington, and Idaho, was a 19th-century hinterland brought into the commercial, social and political mainstream of America by transportation, Pacific markets, high technology, higher education, and recreation. General histories of the region include Schwantes and Pomeroy. SCHWANTES describes the hinterland status of the region in the 19th century dominated by mining, lumber, fishing, and farming. Export linkages to Asia enabled the growth of Portland and Seattle, but World War II and increased industrial growth created metropolitan expansion, particularly in Seattle. High technology companies further expanded economic growth enabling Boise to gain population.

POMEROY puts the region in a broader context and uses comparative analysis to explain economic, social, and political change. Commercial ties to Asia fostered urban and industrial growth, but Asians in Oregon and Washington experienced long periods of discrimination, both legal and unofficial. The railroad brought manufactured goods to the region from the east and dominated the lumber industry and politics for much of the 19th and early 20th centuries. World War II reconfigured regional economics and society.

Among books on the earlier history of the region, RONDA details the American fur empire of John Jacob Astor, the creation of the Pacific Fur Company, and Astor's travail in the Oregon country. Astoria's existence and Astor's empire provided a basis for the United States claim to the Oregon country. JEFFREY focuses upon the life of Narcissa Whitman and the failed Christian mission to the Indians of Oregon. The Indian point of view is explicitly detailed, racial interaction analyzed, and the role of women on the frontier explored. LOWENBERG looks at Jason Lee and the Methodist mission to the Indians, finding Lee's mission to the Indians a failure, but his efforts to divide land among the settlers democratically far more important.

MAY compares the 19th-century experiences of settlers in Sublimity, Oregon, Alpine, Utah, and Middleton, Idaho. Oregon settlers built homes on the land and Idaho settlers thought land a medium for economic gain. Increasingly settlers were attracted to material acquisition, and preferred personal space and privacy, within the framework of civil society. TAYLOR closely details the growth and vitality of the African American residents of Seattle. Their small, centrally located community remained spatially and socially isolated until after World War II. Black leaders worked to increase community pride and established lasting institutions such as the African Methodist Episcopal (AME) churches. Civil rights and access to jobs increasingly became the focus of African Americans in the 1960s.

WHITE analyzes the impact of man on the environment in Island County, Washington. The Salish manipulated the environment to increase desired plant species such as bracken, nettles and camas, but with the aid of technology the white man drastically changed the land. White settlers plowed the land, drained the marshes, and cut the forests. These alterations reduced the moisture retention properties of some soils to the point that they were unable to produce crops. Donkey engines, saw mills, and railroads depleted natural stands of trees and enabled the invasion of hemlock and deciduous trees.

With agricultural expansion, wheat, cattle, and pigs dotted the land, but farming also brought new problems and pests, such as the Canadian thistle and rats. The Salish peoples viewed the land through spiritual lenses and followed mystical commands from nature. White settlers saw the land solely in terms of its economic usefulness, disregarding the environmental consequences of their actions.

BOAG focuses upon environmental change in the Willamette Valley of Oregon. The Kalapuya peoples maintained an ecological balance, using annual fires to clear brush. The white man altered the environment to favor livestock, crops and private property. The latter manipulation was by far the most disruptive. The influx of settlers pushed the Kalapuya from the Willamette Valley, and their environment was replaced by towns, farms, wheat fields, pastures, fences, private property and factories. White settlers maintained a garden image of their valley despite the destruction of the grasslands, the eradication of most of the wildlife habitat, the invasion of brush and weeds, and the loss of soil fertility. Logging and construction helped to pollute the streams and destroy fish populations.

ARRINGTON describes in extensive detail the history of Idaho. The state's history rightfully begins with Native American life, soon affected by explorers and fur trappers. Missionaries ministered to many Indian tribes, but the dramatic change in Native American life came with the emigrant. Settlers traveling to Oregon used Idaho's trails, but seldom stayed, until the discovery of gold and silver. Mormon pioneers moved into southern Idaho from Utah, creating their own communities and attracting hostility from Gentile neighbors. The railroad brought more settlers and enabled the expansion of the market economy, with agriculture and lumber dominant. World War I and World War II were major factors in the economic and social expansion during the 20th century. The maturation of community fostered arts, literature, and education, but environmental degradation accompanying the mining and lumbering industries had major consequences for water resources and the recreation industry.

GORDON MORRIS BAKKEN

Pacifism

Brock, Peter, *Pacifism in the United States: From the Colonial Era to the First World War*, Princeton: Princeton University Press, 1968

Chatfield, Charles, *The American Peace Movement: Ideals and Activism*, New York: Twayne, 1992

Curti, Merle, *The American Peace Crusade, 1815–1860*, Durham, NC: Duke University Press, 1929; reprinted New York: Octagon, 1965

DeBenedetti, Charles, *The Peace Reform in American History*, Bloomington: Indiana University Press, 1980

DeBenedetti, Charles with Charles Chatfield, *An American Ordeal: The Antiwar Movement of the Vietnam Era*, Syracuse, NY: Syracuse University Press, 1990

Heineman, Kenneth J., *Campus Wars: The Peace Movement at American State Universities in the Vietnam Era*, New York: New York University Press, 1993

McNeal, Patricia, *Harder than War: Catholic Peacemaking in Twentieth-Century America*, New Brunswick, NJ: Rutgers University Press, 1992

Marchand, C. Roland, *The American Peace Movement and Social Reform, 1898–1918*, Princeton: Princeton University Press, 1973

Small, Melvin and William D. Hoover (editors), *Give Peace a Chance: Exploring the Vietnam Antiwar Movement*, Syracuse, NY: Syracuse University Press, 1992

Wittner, Lawrence S., *Rebels against War: The American Peace Movement, 1941–1960*, New York: Columbia University Press, 1969; revised as *Rebels against War: The American Peace Movement, 1933–1983*, Philadelphia: Temple University Press, 1984

Ziegler, Valarie H., *The Advocates of Peace in Antebellum America*, Bloomington: Indiana University Press, 1992

Peace advocates are invariably among the first casualties of war, and their voices were drowned out amid the patriotic fervour generated by wars in 1861, 1898, 1917, 1941 and 1950. During the world wars of this century, pacifism was widely regarded as disloyal, if not treasonable, but the advent of nuclear weapons and the bitter divisions over the Vietnam war renewed positive interest in what has in fact been a long American tradition (albeit a minority tradition) of crusading against war. During the last 25 years, there has been a steady stream of historical writing on the peace movement – much of it, predictably, the work of sympathisers with, or activists in, the movement.

This is in sharp contrast to the situation in the 1920s when CURTI was a pioneer in a virtually unexplored field. His study focuses on the organised peace movement, and on such leading figures as William Ladd and Elihu Burritt, during the antebellum decades, and strongly emphasises the religious impulse behind it. Curti's work is now outdated, but it set the pattern for much subsequent study. BROCK covers a wider period in his truly massive and encyclopedic history of American pacifism, which runs to over 1000 pages. He gives an unusual amount of attention to the colonial and revolutionary periods, but his main concern is with the peace movements of the period from the early 19th century to 1865. By the standards of this huge tome, the coverage of the years from 1865 to 1914 is relatively slight.

More recent general surveys are, mercifully, much briefer – sometimes too brief, perhaps, to do full justice to the subject. The most popular is DeBENEDETTI (1980), a basically chronological account by an author who makes no attempt to hide his own commitment to the cause. In contrast to Curti, he brings out the multi-faceted character and diverse make-up of the peace movement. Dividing his history into eight periods, he labels each one as the phase of, successively, sectarian, revolutionary, humanitarian, cosmopolitan, practical, necessary, subversive and deferred reform. He adds some afterthoughts on the "failure" of the peace movement, and attributes it largely to its status as a minority reform, and a subculture opposed to the country's dominant power culture and power realities.

CHATFIELD is in one sense a sequel to DeBenedetti, and, after a brief survey of the earlier history, deals mainly with the campaigns against nuclear weapons and against the Vietnam war. It combines a historical and a sociological approach, and once again, the author's own sympathies are honestly declared and transparently obvious. In a thought-provoking final section, Chatfield argues that the peace movement has had some effect on the American people and government – and even some impact on the shaping of national security policy.

The peace movement before the Civil War has been re-examined by ZIEGLER. She distinguishes two main strands in the movement. One was a moderate, "respectable" group, organised in the American Peace Society, which chose to work within the existing framework of society; the other a much more radical group of Garrisonian "non-resisters" who rejected all existing state authority. Both based their ideas on a Christian "ethic of love," but, when the Civil War came – and with it the opportunity to get rid of slavery – the ethic of love gave way to an ethic of coercion. Each group justified the change, in the one case by the claim that this was not a war at all but a large-scale police action, and in the other by interpreting the war as God's judgment on the guilty South. Ziegler notes the irony of peace advocates who were brought "to support war in the name of peace." She presents her argument incisively, but, in her unswerving pursuit of her central theme, she repeats herself rather too often, and takes a restricted view of the peace movement.

In the late 19th and early 20th centuries, peace became a very respectable cause – even an establishment cause. MAR-CHAND is a skilful analysis of the interconnections of the peace movement with many of the other political trends and social reforms of the period. Both conservatives and reformers at home feared the consequences of international instability for their domestic concerns. In this sense, the peace movement became part of the search for order which characterised the period, and its highly respectable advocates turned their attention to such practical steps as international arbitration and the proposal for an international court.

WITTNER is a useful survey, which in its revised edition covers the half century from the 1930s to the 1980s. It began life as a more concentrated study of the period of World War II and its aftermath. After being brought to a very low ebb by the war, the movement was revived by the threat of nuclear destruction, and by the spread of the philosophy of non-violent resistance in other areas. Wittner sets out to refute the two common criticisms that the peace movement was unpatriotic or even subversive, and, on the other hand, that it was well-meaning but naive. The changing character and standing of the peace movement, as described by Wittner, are reflected in McNEAL's study of the transformation of American Catholic attitudes to the peace issue. She traces the transformation of the Catholic position from earlier support for the doctrine of the just war, which could co-exist with ardent patriotic support for particular wars, to the legitimation of a more clear-cut pacifism, as for example in the bishops' pastoral letter in 1983. Once again, nuclear weapons and Vietnam are seen as the crucial factors, but McNeal also gives due attention to various groups and individuals, from Dorothy Day to Pope John XXIII, and the Berrigan brothers.

Opposition to the Vietnam war has inspired a susbtantial literature, much of it written by erstwhile activists in – or very strong sympathisers with – the anti-war movement. Charles DeBenedetti died when he had almost completed a first draft of his study of the anti-Vietnam movement, and Charles Chatfield completed the project. In the resulting volume, DeBENEDETTI and CHATFIELD give close attention to the peak years of protest between 1965 and 1970, but they also examine developments in the years before and after. They stress the strong personal commitment of those involved, and their alarm at what they saw as the moral insensitivity and institutional near-madness of much of American society. There is some discussion of divisions within the movement, but the focus is almost entirely on activity at the national, rather than the local, level, and the role of women in the movement is strangely neglected. SMALL and HOOVER is a collection of essays based on papers delivered at a 1990 conference in memory of DeBenedetti. Variable in quality and coverage, the essays are of particular value for their focus on aspects of the movement often neglected elsewhere: the role of women and of Vietnam veterans, and the importance of developments after 1969, when both of these groups were particularly influential.

In his book on student involvement in the campaign, HEINEMAN seeks to get away from concentration on the prestigious private universities, and turns the spotlight instead on four state universities: Michigan State, Penn State, Kent State, and SUNY Buffalo. While stressing various divisions within the movement, Heineman draws his main distinction between working-class and lower-middle-class students at the state universities who generally adhered to a strategy of non-violence, and the more privileged students from private universities who often sought violent confrontation.

BERNARD ASPINWALL

See also Vietnam War: Political and Social Consequences

Paine, Thomas   1737–1809
Publicist, agitator and political thinker

Claeys, Gregory, *Thomas Paine: Social and Political Thought*, Boston and London: Unwin Hyman, 1989
Conway, Moncure Daniel, *The Life of Thomas Paine*, 2 vols., New York: Putnam, 1892
Foner, Eric, *Tom Paine and Revolutionary America*, New York and Oxford: Oxford University Press, 1976
Fruchtman, Jack, Jr., *Thomas Paine and the Religion of Nature*, Baltimore: Johns Hopkins University Press, 1993
Fruchtman, Jack, Jr., *Thomas Paine: Apostle of Freedom*, New York: Four Walls Eight Windows, 1994
Hawke, David Freeman, *Paine*, New York: Harper, 1974
Keane, John, *Tom Paine: A Political Life*, Boston: Little Brown, and London: Bloomsbury, 1995
Williamson, Audrey, *Thomas Paine: His Life, Work, and Times*, New York: St. Martin's Press, and London: Allen and Unwin, 1973

Thomas Paine's biographers have always faced a daunting task. Not only do they have to grapple with his complex personality in the absence of most of his correspondence and papers, they also need to immerse themselves in the history of America, England and France during the Age of Revolution simply in order to describe his varied career. A familiarity with 18th-century science, theology, political philosophy, and radicalism is also essential because of the stunning range of Paine's activities and interests. Given these many obstacles, it is perhaps not surprising that Paine has never had the sustained attention that he deserves.

Although Paine was one of the best-known Englishmen in the world at the end of the 18th century, no proper account of his life and writings appeared until a century later with the publication of CONWAY. This was an impressive, detailed, and generally reliable narrative biography and rightly became the standard work on its subject. Subsequent authors worked very much in its shadow and, until recently, none has significantly improved on its basic account of Paine's career.

WILLIAMSON is a worthy, if rather conventional, biography. Attempting to redress the American emphasis in Conway (who had been a 19th-century abolitionist), she concentrates on the English social and political background and their formative effect on Paine's character and outlook. Also, his French Revolutionary contacts and experience are analysed in considerable detail. Her underlying aim is obvious and explicit: to make clear to general readers, not just historians, how important a figure Paine was in the evolution of democratic thought.

HAWKE is more successful. He takes greater care to view Paine in the context of time and place and offers a more critical account. His Paine is no wild-eyed radical. Though early to propose American independence, quick to support the French Revolution, and keen to promote republican revolutions in England and elsewhere, he had, as Hawke makes clear, a conservative strain in his thinking. He was sensitive to the plight of ordinary people everywhere, but enjoyed associating with the influential and powerful. He opposed property qualifications for voting, but respected property rights. He favoured equality of opportunity, but did not expect equality of outcome. And the radical turn which the French Revolution took following the execution of Louis XVI left him disenchanted. Ultimately, for Hawke, Paine's principal achievement was to write about complex social and political ideas with "elegant simplicity" and make them accessible for the first time to the average citizen.

Perhaps of most interest to readers of this volume, FONER was "intended to be both more and less than another biography of Paine." Less, because there was no need to retrace with the biographer's detailed hand the chronology of his life or to explore his personality once again. More, because the book was an attempt to trace the relationships between an individual and his times and between a particular brand of radical ideology and the social and political history of revolutionary America. To accomplish these goals, Foner explores crucial moments in his subject's career while also investigating specific aspects of Paine's America. What was really significant about Paine, Foner concludes, was that he embraced the dual transformation that overtook America in those years – the emergence of mass political participation and the expansion of market relations in the economy and society.

CLAEYS provides a sophisticated analysis of Paine's most influential work – The Rights of Man. He is careful, however, to place this text in the context of the evolution of Paine's thinking from his early American writings, and against the background of natural law and natural rights teaching, republicanism and radicalism, and Paine's Quaker and deist beliefs. Indeed, what the book most clearly demonstrates is that his profound commitment to natural rights for all men was the pivot on which his many opinions turned.

FRUCHTMAN (1993) is a welcome addition to the corpus of Paine scholarship because it provides a novel perspective on the influence of religious traditions on his thought and approach. The author seeks to show how, in his role as the prophet of democratic republicanism, Paine borrowed and made use of an older homiletic style. Fruchtman also brings out how Paine treats his readers almost as a congregation, warning them of the evils that tarnished their lives (owing to the oppression of kings and aristocrats and, later, of Federalists) and exhorting them to undertake the task of reforming society without delay. Again, like a preacher, Paine spent considerable energy making his thought accessible to his audience, addressing the common man in language he could understand. He grasped an obvious lesson – for democratic politics to be feasible, politicians must master the art of speaking to the many.

Two recent biographies attest to a renewed interest in Paine's life and thought. Both attempt to locate Paine within the context of the long-standing debate over whether "Lockean liberalism" or "classical republicanism" held sway in the early American republic. KEANE identifies Paine with the Commonwealth tradition, but does see the differences: Paine "pushed and dragged republicanism firmly into the modern world" by means of a democratic populism alien to many of its spokesmen. By contrast, FRUCHTMAN (1994) is keen to establish his subject's debt to John Locke and his brand of liberalism. Beyond this disagreement these biographies have complementary strengths. Whereas Fruchtman provides insights derived from his background as a historian of political thought, Keane has uncovered some new biographical material. Both works, then, are fascinating, richly documented, and readable. On balance, however, Keane's book is more substantial than Fruchtman's and makes some fresher contributions to the historical record. The book is particularly enlightening on what have been, until now, the more obscure parts of Paine's career, namely the years in England before his departure for America and his decade in France from 1792 to 1802.

KEITH MASON

See also American Revolution: Character, Scope, and Significance

Panama Canal

Castillero Pimentel, Ernesto, Panamá y los Estados Unidos, Panamá City: Universidad de Panamá, 1953
Conniff, Michael, Panama and the United States: The Forced Alliance, Athens: University of Georgia Press, 1992
DuVal, Miles, Jr., Cadiz to Cathay: The Story of the Long Diplomatic Struggle for the Panama Canal, Stanford, CA: Stanford University Press, 1940, 2nd edition, 1947

DuVal, Miles, Jr., *And the Mountains Will Move: The Story of the Building of the Panama Canal*, Stanford, CA: Stanford University Press, and London: Oxford University Press, 1947

McCullough, David, *The Path Between the Seas: The Creation of the Panama Canal, 1870–1914*, New York: Simon and Schuster, 1977

Major, John, *Prize Possession: The United States and the Panama Canal, 1903–1979*, New York: Cambridge University Press, 1993

Padelford, Norman, Jr., *The Panama Canal in Peace and War*, New York: Macmillan, 1942

Richard, Alfred Charles, Jr., *The Panama Canal in American National Consciousness, 1870–1922*, New York: Garland, 1990

Books on the Panama Canal are legion, and, given the canal's significance as an emblem of United States hegemony over Latin America, many of them tend to be apologias for either American or Panamanian nationalism. One American historian, however, did not let his patriotism get in the way of his scholarship. Miles Du Val, a United States Navy officer and architect of an unconsummated plan for the modernization of the canal, published two works in the 1940s, both well-grounded in archival research, which have stood the test of time. Du VAL (1940) relates the history of the negotiations leading up to the United States-Panama canal convention of 1903, while Du VAL (1947) recounts the events of the construction decade of 1904–14. The treatment is a model of reliability, and one can only regret that a third volume, on the operation of the canal since its opening, has not yet gone into print.

Covering much the same ground, McCULLOUGH produced a highly readable bestseller, excellently illustrated with contemporary photographs. Its strengths lie in its exposition of the engineering problems entailed in the building of the canal, and in its descriptions of the personalities and the social ambience of both the French and the American projects. Completed at a time when the Canal Zone was about to be relinquished, it is an elegiac tribute to an accomplishment which Americans rightly regard as outstanding in their 20th-century history. While it does not go deeply into many features of United States government policy, it cannot be bettered for bringing out the flavour and the atmosphere of time and place.

RICHARD gives a graphic account of what the canal came to mean to American public opinion, as expressed in the newspapers and journals of the period. The attachment of most Americans to the canal as a symbol of the country's achievement, which endured down to the signing of the 1977 treaties, has its roots here, and no other work conveys it so well. The book is a testament to the pride which the canal evoked at a time when the United States was beginning to move towards the centre of the international stage, though the author is by no means uncritical of the possessiveness which often went with it.

PADELFORD contrived at one and the same time to be an uncompromising advocate of United States national interests and a professor of international law. His book, published soon after the United States entry into World War II, sets out the legal basis of the American position in relation to both the canal and the surrounding Canal Zone, in the light of the 1936 treaty whereby Franklin Roosevelt had modified the 1903 convention. Padelford's text was seen as a highly authoritative presentation of the United States case for its various rights in Panama, and remained an essential work of reference for anyone seeking guidance to the multitude of rules and regulations governing the administration of the waterway.

There are three general surveys of the history of the canal, each written from a different standpoint. CASTILLERO was an active Panamanian nationalist and co-leader of one of the earliest demonstrations against the Zone in 1959. His book is less a history than an extended statement of the case for Panama on the many issues which brought it into confrontation with the USA. If read in that light, it gives a valuable insight into the mentality of the Panamanian elite. The work is largely reliant on secondary sources, and a new interpretation is long overdue, founded on the hitherto inaccessible Panamanian primary material. A more recent examination of the United States-Panama relationship, written from an American liberal perspective, is provided by CONNIFF. An authority on the West Indian community in Panama, he knows the country well and provides a succinct account running from the 1820s to the 1990s. The book is part of the series The United States and the Americas, the object of which is to give a wider significance to inter-state relations by emphasizing the non-governmental dimension of economic and cultural exchanges, and the role of popular opinion in the formation of national responses to international affairs. It is a demanding assignment, and the volume should be seen as an attempt to pioneer this innovative approach, which subsequent historians can elaborate in more detail.

MAJOR is an archive-based analysis of key elements in the history of the Canal Zone: the Zone's administrative structure; the canal's labour force; canal defence; and Washington's handling of its political and commercial relations with Panama. Written by a British academic, it aims for an objectivity difficult to achieve from a United States or Panamanian perspective, and if acclaimed or denounced by both parties it will have served its purpose. While near-comprehensive as a study of American government policy, it falls short of being definitive in that the author could not gain access to Panamanian sources and did not explore the records of the Zonians – the United States community living and working in the Canal Zone. These reservations apart, it is the most thorough investigation of the subject to date.

JOHN MAJOR

Parties and Political Movements: General

Binkley, Wilfred E., *American Political Parties: Their Natural History*, New York: Knopf, 1943, 4th edition, 1962

Burnham, Walter Dean, *The Current Crisis in American Politics*, New York: Oxford University Press, 1982

Chambers, Walter Nisbet and Walter Dean Burnham (editors), *The American Party Systems: Stages of Political Development*, New York: Oxford University Press, 1967

Kleppner, Paul and others, *The Evolution of American Electoral Systems*, Westport, CT: Greenwood Press, 1981

Maisel, L. Sandy and William G. Shade (editors), *Parties and Politics in American History: A Reader*, New York: Garland, 1994

Schlesinger, Arthur M., Jr. (editor), *History of US Political Parties*, 4 vols., New York: Chelsea House, 1973

Silbey, Joel H., *The American Political Nation, 1838–1893*, Stanford, CA: Stanford University Press, 1991

Wattenberg, Martin, *The Decline of American Political Parties, 1952–1980*, Cambridge, MA: Harvard University Press, 1984; 5th edition, as *The Decline of American Political Parties, 1952–1994*, 1996

It is impossible to think about American political history without paying a great deal of attention to the many political parties that have been persistent participants in elections and government since the 1790s, organizing and shaping most of the important developments. Most dissenting political movements outside the reigning two-party consensus, ultimately took partisan form as well. As a result, American historians have devoted enormous attention to the party experience, describing and analyzing the history of individual parties, both major and minor, their leaders and supporters, significant episodes of party confrontation, and the range of important party factions that dot the record. A few scholars have addressed the totality of party history in overviews that provide context and understanding beyond the specific moment or episode.

BINKLEY presents a classic approach to such general overviews, narrating the story of American politics through the activities and maneuvering of the parties in election after election. He follows the party leaders and the factions they commanded, considers the policy arguments offered, and describes something about party organization. He focuses most of his attention on the social groups that supported each party – to him, the core element of party history. In doing so, he follows the dominant Progressive scholarly paradigm of the early 20th century, which believed that the root of partisan conflict lay in the persistent divisions between different economic interests and/or classes in America.

SCHLESINGER offers another classic descriptive approach to party history. Each essay in this multi-authored work is a detailed description of one of the individual parties on the scene since the 1790s. All of the authors focus on the party's campaigning, platforms, and behind-the-scenes factional maneuvering, as well as the distribution of the vote, and the way in which the parties behaved once in office. As with Binkley, election contests are the key. Each author suggests how central the parties have been in articulating what was at stake in presidential contests, and in providing guidelines which the voters largely followed. Some contributors remain sceptical about the parties' ideological commitment and consistency, others take partisan claims more seriously. Some continue to follow the Progressive account of political conflict, others find non-economic social tensions, such as differences between religious and nationality groups, to be the sources of party conflict.

Over time, studies of party history have become more analytic and precise in definition and categorization, more affected by the measuring techniques and theorizing aspects of the social sciences, more sensitive to exact patterns of continuity and change and the existence of a broad transformative pattern in party history. The essays in CHAMBERS and BURNHAM are organized around the notion that there has been a regular, cyclical pattern to the American party experience as seen in the behavior of the electorate at the polls. The individual authors map five distinct party systems since the 1790s, each containing a singular pattern of two-party confrontation energized by the intense and persistent loyalty of specific groups to each party in election after election. Each system was bounded by a sharp electoral disruption and voter realignment in which, due to a crisis, there was a break in the traditional partisan commitments of many groups, and the emergence of a rearranged pattern of electoral alignment to form a new party system.

Such cyclical patterns are a given of modern party history. But, as the authors of the essays in KLEPPNER argue, there is also great variation in that history. There were significant differences in party role and function, and in the level of commitment to them at different times. In the early Republic, Americans were fervently anti-party, since they greatly feared anything that threatened societal unity by promoting persistent, damaging conflict. As a result, the so-called first party system was incomplete in organization, and limited in acceptance, reach and authority. There followed a difficult and hesitant development from this non-party condition to the dominant party system that emerged by the 1840s, and commanded the scene thereafter. But variation continued as party history unfolded, culminating eventually in the decline of the parties over the course of the 20th century, as they lost their hold over the electorate and their prominence in the nation's politics.

The essays by different authors in MAISEL and SHADE combine the skills of political science with the talents of historians to summarize the breadth of recent scholarship about specific dividing moments in party history, the particular state of organizational maturity of the parties at different times, how leaders and followers interacted with one another over time, and the meaning and importance of the parties within the American polity in different eras. Although not so detailed as Binkley and Schlesinger, and rarely touching on the fortunes of individual parties, the work effectively offers an up-to-date scholarly portrait of the many complexities of American party history while also exploring some new interpretative ground.

As scholars have digested the notions of transformative shifts in party history, a number of them have focused on key eras. SILBEY's synthesis of the years from the 1830s to the 1890s, when the political parties dominated the political scene, pulls much of the relevant scholarship together in a generally sympathetic overview, which stresses the intense commitment to the parties by leaders and followers alike, the relatively advanced state of party organization, the sources of their voter support, and the coherence of their ideologies and policy agendas. Arguing that the parties were more than electoral machines, he notes the sharp differences in attitudes and interests between the voter groups that supported each party, the different perspectives about the world in general and specific policies in particular, that each party articulated in election after election, and, most tellingly, the different ways that each acted once in office.

BURNHAM, a political scientist deeply committed to utilizing historical evidence to help understand current political phenomena, paints a grim picture of party decline after the 1890s, and the impact of that decline on American politics more generally. He notes the occasional still potent ideological intensity between the different parties, but marks, as well, how limited party influence over the everyday course of political life has become over the course of the 20th century. He stresses the increased volatility, fragmentation and confusion that characterize so much of current politics, and the inability, in the absence of effective parties, to articulate what is at stake in elections and government debate. The result has been the growing disengagement of the voters, not only from the parties, but from an increasingly weakened political system, shorn of its major foundation.

In another analysis of popular voting behavior, WATTENBERG traces the way in which parties and loyalty to them have faded from the voters' minds in the second half of the 20th century, a fading which has become the dominant characteristic of American politics. While they retain their institutional structures and continue to organize and occasionally influence elections, parties in the late 20th century are no longer, in the minds of voters, the important organizers of their political education and the shaper of the directions which they follow – or even relevant to them at election time. To him, as to Burnham, the collapse of parties ordains a political future dominated by sudden intense flashes of popular anger, and the loss of belief, commitment, and the kind of political stability that the parties once provided.

JOEL H. SILBEY

See also Elections entries; Third Parties; entries on individual parties

Patronage/Spoils System

Hoogenboom, Ari, *Outlawing the Spoils: A History of the Civil Service Reform Movement, 1865–1883*, Urbana: University of Illinois Press, 1961
Josephson, Matthew, *The Politicos, 1865–1896*, New York: Harcourt Brace, 1938
McFarland, Gerald W., *Mugwumps, Morals, and Politics, 1884–1920*, Amherst: University of Massachusetts Press, 1975
Schlesinger, Arthur M., Jr., *The Age of Jackson*, Boston: Little Brown, 1945; London: Eyre and Spottiswoode, 1946
Sproat, John G., *"The Best Men": Liberal Reformers in the Gilded Age*, New York: Oxford University Press, 1968
Summers, Mark W., *The Plundering Generation: Corruption and the Crisis of the Union, 1849–1861*, New York: Oxford University Press, 1987
Summers, Mark W., *The Era of Good Stealings*, New York: Oxford University Press, 1993
Thompson, Margaret Susan, *The "Spider Web": Congress and Lobbying in the Age of Grant*, Ithaca, NY: Cornell University Press, 1985
White, Leonard D., *The Jacksonians: A Study in Administrative History, 1829–1861*, New York: Macmillan, 1954

The terms "patronage" and "spoils system" refer to awarding positions in government service to pay off personal or political debts, generally with an eye toward directing public funds into the pockets of cronies or building an electoral machine largely impervious to subsequent challengers. Even now, after 20th-century civil service systems have eliminated most features of the spoils system, there is little, short of outright corruption, which conjures up worse images of politics and politicians. Yet, while often bandied about in books and discussions concerning political activity, patronage and the spoils system have been only infrequent subjects for thoroughgoing study and analysis.

The election of President Andrew Jackson, often perceived as a victory of the common people over elites, brought the notion of political spoils to greater national prominence. The "mob" that descended on Washington for Jackson's inauguration in March 1829 allegedly came to seek government jobs more than to sing the praises of "Old Hickory." SCHLESINGER argues, with distressingly few details, that Jackson gladly obliged these supplicants and redistributed federal offices as "an invaluable means of unifying administration support." He continued the practices of wide patronage distribution and rotation-in-office as means of keeping government in close contact with the people and preventing it from becoming a preserve of lofty bureaucrats. Schlesinger's brief discussion of the spoils system, however, serves as a launching point for his influential evocation of the entire age. WHITE is a judicious and authoritative study of the practice of government in the Jacksonian era, which, among many other aspects, shows how political parties assumed a crucial role in the operation of the spoils system.

SUMMERS (1987) is mainly concerned with wider manifestations of political corruption in antebellum America, but he argues that the spoils system is the place to begin a study of the broader subject, because it was corrupting in its effects. While patronage helped to make government work, patronage politics set an unsatisfactory ethical tone at every level of government.

JOSEPHSON paints a vivid picture of patronage use and abuse and ineffectual attempts at reform during the heyday of the spoils system in the late 19th century. Examining first the political spoilsmen, such as United States Senator Roscoe Conkling of New York, and then reformers in and out of the federal government, and finally the captains of industry – notably Mark Hanna – who co-opted and updated the old spoils system for their own ends, Josephson offers a panoramic view, with more than a little penetrating analysis, of political parties and personalities, along with a history of patronage through the presidencies of Ulysses S. Grant, Rutherford B. Hayes, James A. Garfield, Chester A. Arthur, Grover Cleveland, and Benjamin Harrison. He closes by presenting the presidential campaign of William Jennings Bryan as a valiant but failed effort of the people to recapture government for their own purposes.

HOOGENBOOM is a superior history of the movement to reform patronage and the spoils system. He convincingly demonstrates the prominence of the issue of civil service reform, even during a time of patronage excess. He focuses on actual civil service reformers – especially George William Curtis, Thomas Allen Jenckes, and Edwin L. Godkin – and considers "the impact of reform upon politics and upon the civil service itself." While Garfield's assassination by a disappointed office-seeker brought the question of civil service reform to the forefront, Hoogenboom suggests that civil service reformers played a more continuous and important role during the years between 1865 and 1896 as a political faction able to frustrate presidents or spoilsmen with legislative initiatives or loud publicity; or, even more significantly, by holding the balance of power in presidential elections. In sum, civil service reform operated across a broad field and had many implications.

Sproat and McFarland probe more deeply the minds and motivations of those who advocated reform of patronage and the spoils system and desired a more elevated tone in political debate. SPROAT describes the "best men" of his book as "the intellectuals, the men of substance and breeding, the voters of independent political disposition" too often left out of Gilded Age accounts. Viewing men such as Curtis, Godkin, Edward Atkinson, Carl Schurz, and David Ames Wells as a distinct group, he tells a story with lessons "about the limited nature of reform in America and about the difficulty of maintaining standards of moral conduct in a society enchanted by 'progress.'" McFARLAND examines the internal diversity of the Mugwumps – those who bolted the Republican party in 1884 to vote for Cleveland – along socioeconomic lines, and compares them to regular Republicans, without resorting to simple dualistic portrayals. He also extends his analysis two decades into the 20th century. McFarland achieves a much more satisfying depiction of a group generally either dismissed as pompous, sour, and hypocritical, or celebrated as high-minded political dissidents. Appendices with lists of names and statistical summaries complement a readable text.

The great virtue of THOMPSON is her recognition of how lobbyists facilitated patronage – and much else about the legislative process of the 1870s – by providing overworked congressmen with crucial information about applicants and their likely impact on supporters. Through an examination of the patronage predicaments encountered by Garfield while a representative from Ohio and by Benjamin F. Butler of Massachusetts, she shows both the awkwardness and the delicacy inherent in making recommendations for appointment. The seemingly mundane appointments – postmasters in the small towns of the district – generally required the most information from trusted political lieutenants; foreign appointments, such as ministers and consuls, more readily supplied opportunities for settling old political scores or snubbing a personal enemy.

In a sequel to his earlier work, SUMMERS (1993) revisits the notorious political corruption of the Gilded Age in order to reassess the extent of its enormities. He concludes that prevailing notions about the "Great Barbecue" are somewhat overdone. Other periods had their scandals, and negligence or incompetence caused problems more than premeditated peculation (and such planned acts were "scattered rather than systemic"). Concern over the appearance of rampant corruption, however, prompted reform efforts, including attempts to curb patronage abuses and to establish a competent professional bureaucracy. Southern and racial aspects of this story receive welcome attention. Like other books addressing patronage and the spoils system, Summers offers plenty of colorful anecdotes and a definite feel for the many facets of late 19th-century political culture.

WILLIAM M. FERRARO

Patton, George S. 1885–1945
Military commander

Blumenson, Martin, *The Patton Papers*, 2 vols., Boston: Houghton Mifflin, 1972–74

Blumenson, Martin, *Patton: The Man Behind the Legend, 1885–1945*, New York: Morrow, 1985; London: Cape, 1986

Blumenson, Martin, *Battle of the Generals: The Untold Story of the Falaise Pocket*, New York: Morrow, 1993

D'Este, Carlo, *Patton: A Genius for War*, New York: HarperCollins, 1995

Essame, H., *Patton: A Study in Command*, New York: Scribner, 1974

Farago, Ladislas, *The Last Days of Patton*, New York: McGraw Hill, 1981

Nye, Roger H., *The Patton Mind: The Professional Development of an Extraordinary Leader*, New York: Avery, 1993

Patton, George S., Jr., *War as I Knew It*, Boston: Houghton Mifflin, 1947; London: W.H. Allen, 1948

Weigley, Russell F., *Eisenhower's Lieutenants: The Campaign of France and Germany, 1944–1945*, Bloomington: Indiana University Press, and London: Sidgwick and Jackson, 1981

The life and wartime contributions of General George S. Patton, Jr., one of the United States Army's greatest World War II commanders, have been, and look set to remain, a popular subject for military historians and the general reading public. The result has been the publication of a wealth of material on Patton's life, wartime record, and tragic death in 1945. Works relating to Patton tend to fall into three categories: biographies, examinations of his military leadership, and investigations of specific aspects of his life, most notably the events leading up to his death.

Patton did not have the opportunity to write his memoirs or autobiography. Such a work might well have become one of the great classics of World War II. Patton's interpretation of World War II, and his analysis of what happened during the war, will remain a mystery. Anyone seeking Patton's own words will have to depend primarily upon his edited diary, as presented in PATTON or in BLUMENSON (1972–74). His diary, originally published in 1947, remains extremely popular even though it has been heavily edited, and Patton's colourful language has been removed. Blumenson, a Patton historian for over fifty years, remains a leading authority. He allows Patton to speak for himself through his voluminous papers, but provides context where needed, and his approach offers invaluable insights into a complex man.

Patton biographies have appeared fairly regularly over the years, as the public's interest in the general has only increased with the passage of time. BLUMENSON (1985) updates and clarifies his earlier portrayal of Patton. He combines his vast knowledge of Patton with years of reflection and thought to provide a complete, readable biography in which the author incorporates his latest research. D'ESTE is the best, well-rounded biography currently available. A retired United States Army officer and leading authority on World War II, D'Este chronicles Patton's life and seeks to explain Patton's genius for war. This well-researched study, which synthesizes much earlier work, will stand as the definitive study of Patton for the foreseeable future.

Much of the work on Patton has focused on his wartime experience in an attempt to understand or evaluate his genius for war. ESSAME seeks to place him in his appropriate place within the pantheon of military greats, and concludes that, in the realm of mobile operations, Patton outshone his contemporaries and ranks with the great battlefield commanders such as Murat, Sherman and Rommel. BLUMENSON (1993) examines the issues related to the Falaise Pocket in World War II, and concludes that, of all the generals involved, Patton had the clearest understanding of what needed to be done, and was the best suited to deal with the situation. WEIGLEY provides both an extensive overview of the American Army at war in Europe, 1944–45, and a detailed examination of its leadership during this crucial period. This comprehensive work highlights both Patton's strengths and his faults, within the overall context of the war in Europe.

Other monographs cover diverse aspects of, or topics related to, Patton's life and death. FARAGO conducted the most comprehensive investigation to date into the accident which resulted in General Patton's death, and in the process examines the various conspiracy theories which have been presented over the years. He concludes that Patton's death was the result of an accident, not a conspiracy to eliminate him. NYE examines the professional development of Patton by examining his personal library and shows how he utilized it to educate himself on military matters. This assessment of Patton from the unique perspective of the books he acquired and read over the course of his career offers invaluable insights into the workings of an unusual military mind.

STEVE R. WADDELL

See also World War II, United States and 1

Paul, Alice 1885–1977
Campaigner for women's rights and women's suffrage

Becker, Susan D., *The Origins of the Equal Rights Amendment: American Feminism Between the Wars*, Westport, CT: Greenwood Press, 1981
Cott, Nancy F., *The Grounding of Modern Feminism*, New Haven: Yale University Press, 1987
Ford, Linda G., *Iron-Jawed Angels: The Suffrage Militancy of the National Woman's Party, 1912–1920*, Lanham, MD: University Press of America, 1991
Irwin, Inez Haynes, *The Story of the Woman's Party*, New York: Harcourt Brace, 1921; as *The Story of Alice Paul and the National Woman's Party*, Fairfax, VA: Denlinger's, 1964
Lunardini, Christine A., *From Equal Suffrage to Equal Rights: Alice Paul and the National Woman's Party, 1910–1928*, New York: New York University Press, 1986
Lunardini, Christine A., "Alice Paul (1885–1977)," in *Portraits of American Women: From Settlement to the Present*, edited by G.J. Barker-Benfield and Catherine Clinton, New York: St. Martin's Press, 1991
Stevens, Doris, *Jailed for Freedom*, New York: Boni and Liveright, 1920

Controversial in her own day, militant suffragist and architect of the Equal Rights Amendment (ERA), Alice Paul continues to evoke ambivalent feelings among historians. The elusiveness of the private Paul, and the apparent merger of her identity with the causes she championed, perhaps accounts for the relative dearth of the kind of full-scale psycho-historical biography that other public figures have inspired. Instead, most modern works emphasize her leadership style and the dynamics and impact of the movements that she led.

Stevens and Irwin are contemporary accounts of the militant minority wing of the suffrage movement institutionalized in 1917 in Paul's National Woman's Party (NWP). They stand in sharp contrast to most suffrage histories that accord the NWP's more genteel rival, the National American Woman Suffrage Association (NAWSA), by far the more significant role in winning the vote for women. STEVENS was an NWP Executive Committee member and organizer who brought to her memoirs the sympathetic bias of a committed participant. Her book excludes the battle over ratification, focusing instead on the radicals' confrontations with Woodrow Wilson, their dauntless resolve in the face of the horrors of imprisonment, and the slow attrition of the president's resistance to a federal suffrage amendment. Writing before she broke with Paul in the 1930s, Stevens portrayed the NWP Chair as a charismatic and inspiring "general" capable of commanding unquestioned loyalty.

Paul looms much larger in novelist and suffragist IRWIN's monumental official history of the NWP from 1913 through the adoption of the Anthony Amendment. This stirring narrative is as much a eulogy of Paul as it is a paean to the NWP. It tells how a "human dynamo" led a tightly knit legion of resolute activists in breathing life into a moribund movement and steering it to victory. Irwin did not go into Paul's difficulties with the NAWSA, choosing instead to ignore the mainstream suffrage group altogether. The chief strength of this book lies in its graphic descriptions of the pageantry, the picketing, the hunger strikes, and the harrowing prison experiences that so effectively publicized the militants' cause. Its celebration of the "Pan-American woman quality" of the suffrage movement, on the other hand, appears idealistic in the light of modern research on American feminism. Historians have drawn heavily upon the wealth of anecdotal and other details provided by Irwin and Stevens despite their obvious partisanship.

Most studies of women's movements written from the 1950s through the 1970s exhibited a marked NAWSA bias, and often marginalized the role of the NWP. To some degree, the microfilming of the NWP papers in 1979 rescued the organization and its leader from scholarly neglect, although some of the best work on the subject has dealt with the party's post-suffrage career.

BECKER is the first comprehensive modern history of the NWP. This solid work of scholarship on the party's struggle for the ERA after 1920 is slightly marred by its listless narrative style. Becker traces the failure of the NWP's quest for leadership of the national and international women's movements to opposition from the social feminist advocates of protective legislation, as well as to the party's internal conflicts, and a narrow, legalistic formulation of feminist ideology that appealed to few women. Paul's presence on the national stage appears as rather subdued. Her role in furthering the cause of international feminism receives greater attention.

Lunardini's overlapping works combine the fullest recent profile of Paul with a highly favorable assessment of her direction of militant suffragism and the ERA campaign. LUNARDINI (1991) is an essay in an anthology that seeks to relate the lives of selected American women to the larger world of which they were a part. A useful editorial introduction to the "age of transition" to which Paul belonged lends her story an historical context not found in more specialized studies. The essay itself integrates relevant biographical data on Paul with a discussion of her complex personality, her leadership, and the varied reactions she has evoked from critics and admirers, contemporaries and historians. Lunardini emphasizes her subject's ambivalence on the race issue, and argues that the NWP Chair's official decisions were motivated not so much by racism as by pragmatism.

LUNARDINI (1986) is a short monograph which provides fewer biographical details, and focuses primarily on Paul's political acumen and leadership powers. This book moves the NWP from the periphery to the center of the suffrage movement. Like Irwin, Lunardini attributes President Wilson's capitulation on the suffrage issue to the efficacy of NWP pressure tactics, including the controversial British-inspired political strategy of punishing the "party in power" (Wilson's Democratic party) for the failure of a federal suffrage amendment. A short chapter on the ERA debate disputes the charge that Paul engineered the cavalier dismissal of alternatives to a blanket ERA proposal, and blames the amendment's failure on relentless opposition from the champions of protective legislation, and the advent of the Great Depression, rather than on flaws in Paul's leadership.

COTT's interpretation of the ERA's fate offers a more penetrating and critical analysis of Paul's role. This general work on women's group consciousness between 1910 and 1930 includes a splendid study of the NWP's legacy for feminist political discourse. Cott argues that Paul's adherence to single-issue politics succeeded during the fight for suffrage by achieving a consensus among her heterogeneous followers. In the changed political and economic context of the 1920s however, the same sharp focus on the more ambiguous concept of "equal rights" contributed to the failure of the ERA. The single-minded pursuit of the "purely feminist," narrowly defined as opposition to women's legal disabilities, divorced

the NWP from broader issues of social reform that encompassed but were not confined to gender concerns, thus narrowing its constituency. Cott detects the dogmatic and authoritarian hand of Paul behind the elitist transformation of the NWP, and suggests that her insistence on working at the top rather than the grassroots hindered the mobilization of feminist consciousness in favor of the ERA.

FORD is more concerned with the suffrage phase of Paul's public life. Her book probes the evolution and ideological underpinnings of suffrage militancy. She skilfully traces the influence of the British suffragists as well as the Stanton-Anthony brand of female egalitarianism on Paul's thinking. Her attention to the gender symbolism embedded in the confrontation over suffrage is interesting. Ford demonstrates that feminist militancy, defined as non-violent civil disobedience, developed gradually as a logical response to a male-oriented government's obstinate indifference to women's political aspirations. She documents the sexist nature and language of the anti-suffragist reprisals. Her most original contribution, however, lies in her analysis of the social and political profile of imprisoned suffragists which suggests that Alice Paul's movement, notwithstanding its elite affiliations, attracted a diverse range of women.

GUNJA SENGUPTA

See also Women's History: Suffrage

Pearl Harbor, 1941

Lewin, Ronald, *The American Magic: Codes, Ciphers and the Defeat of Japan*, London: Hutchinson, and New York: Farrar Straus, 1982

Prange, Gordon W. with Donald M. Goldstein and Katherine V. Dillon, *At Dawn We Slept: The Untold Story of Pearl Harbor*, New York: McGraw Hill, 1981; London: Joseph, 1982

Prange, Gordon W. with Donald M. Goldstein and Katherine V. Dillon, *Pearl Harbor: The Verdict of History*, New York: McGraw Hill, 1986; Harmondsworth: Penguin, 1991

Stephan, John J., *Hawaii under the Rising Sun: Japan's Plans for Conquest after Pearl Harbor*, Honolulu: University of Hawaii Press, 1984

Toland, John, *Infamy: Pearl Harbor and Its Aftermath* New York: Doubleday, and London: Methuen, 1982

Wohlstetter, Roberta, *Pearl Harbor: Warning and Decision*, Stanford, CA: Stanford University Press, 1962

Pearl Harbor was certain to bring forth a tidal wave of books and, both because of the dimensions of Japan's military triumph and the implications of that success, it is still capable of attracting attention more than half a century after the Japanese navy's attack on the Pacific fleet's naval base on 7 December 1941. Works on Pearl Harbor deal with one or both of two basic themes: the military dimensions of the attack and who was responsible for the American debacle, and why. The doyen of Pearl Harbor studies was Gordon Prange whose two posthumously-published works cover in great detail almost every imaginable aspect of the Japanese attack. Militarily, the operation was a triumph for Japan and a disaster for the United States. It is unlikely that there will ever be a more comprehensive single account of the antecedents and details of the attack than PRANGE (1981). Beginning the story in 1940, Prange covers the Japanese planning for the attack, describes American military doctrine and practice which would make that assault more effective, and covers Japanese espionage in the Hawaiian islands. Through use of Japanese as well as American written and oral evidence, the personnel, the weaponry and the methods of the attack are brought to life and analyzed to the point where the reader is almost a spectator on that fateful Sunday morning when, with audacity and ingenuity, the Japanese naval air force was able to surprise and cripple the United States Pacific fleet. Prange's analysis goes beyond the attack to probe the reasons why the Japanese failed to exploit their initial success and launch a second strike, a move which would probably have turned a military disaster into a catastrophe.

Prange's account could be used profitably in conjunction with the first half of STEPHAN's excellent book, which should be read by anyone with an interest in Pearl Harbor and Japanese ambitions in the Hawaiian islands. Stephan is particularly revealing on two important aspects of the Pearl Harbor attack: the Japanese long- and short-term planning for operations against the Hawaiian islands, and the position and attitudes of the 40 per cent of Hawaii's population who were of Japanese extraction. Doubts about the latter's loyalty led American commanders into disastrous tactical errors in December 1941, which added to the scale of American defeat.

The greatest controversy over Pearl Harbor has swirled around the question of how the United States was taken unawares on 7 December. American cryptographers had broken some of the most important Japanese codes, and therefore had reasonable knowledge of the thrust of Japanese policies and intentions, and yet the surprise at Pearl Harbor was complete. Since the late 1940s, revisionist scholars had been arguing that the Roosevelt administration, anxious to lead the United States into World War II, had been unduly obdurate with the Japanese in 1941 in order to provoke them into war. Certain writers have tried to use evidence of American intelligence about Japanese intentions to take this interpretation a step further, by alleging that knowledge of an impending Japanese attack was suppressed by the Roosevelt administration, which was anxious to take a united nation into World War II on the side of the allies. An unprovoked, surprise attack by the Japanese would have been an ideal means of accomplishing this objective. They plead in evidence not only that codebreaking gave warning, but also that it could hardly be a coincidence that the United States Navy's aircraft carriers, the unit of seapower which was to be decisive in the Pacific War, were absent from Pearl Harbor when the Japanese attacked. This is the thrust of the interpretation offered by TOLAND, a leading proponent of the school of thought which emphasizes conspiracy, and argues that too much was known for the failure to act upon the knowledge to be seen as accidental.

In order to arrive at any assessment of the reasons why the United States was caught by surprise it is essential to know the extent to which intelligence and codebreaking did provide adequate warning of Japanese intentions. The details and technicalities of how (and how far) the American military gained access to Japanese diplomatic and other material are clearly described in LEWIN's account of American codebreaking and deciphering which went under the name of MAGIC. What was done with this material, and the failure to interpret and handle it to best effect, are analyzed by Lewin and, in greater detail, in WOHLSTETTER's fine forensic account of the run-up to the attack. The conclusions reached in both of these works are supported by PRANGE (1986) which is an exhaustive inquiry into how Pearl Harbor could have happened, and who was responsible. For them, there was no Rooseveltian conspiracy. In part, the Americans were surprised at Pearl Harbor because of the inherent problems involved in processing, assessing and using intelligence and cryptographical material. In part, Pearl Harbor happened because the United States navy and army fell into that most common of military errors, complacency. Until 7:50 a.m. on 7 December 1941 no senior American commander believed that Pearl Harbor could be attacked, let alone that Japan would be capable of mounting such an operation.

DENNIS B. SMITH

See also World War II, Approach to 2; World War II, United States and 2

Penn, William 1644–1718
Quaker founder of Pennsylvania

Bronner, Edwin B., William Penn's "Holy Experiment": The Founding of Pennsylvania, 1681–1701, Philadelphia: Temple University Press, 1962

Buranelli, Vincent, The King and the Quaker: A Study of William Penn and James II, Philadelphia: University of Pennsylvania Press, 1962

Dunn, Mary Maples, William Penn: Politics and Conscience, Princeton: Princeton University Press, 1967

Dunn, Richard S. and Mary Maples Dunn (editors), The World of William Penn, Philadelphia: University of Pennsylvania Press, 1986

Endy, Melvin B., Jr., William Penn and Early Quakerism, Princeton: Princeton University Press, 1973

Illick, Joseph E., William Penn the Politician: His Relations with the English Government, Ithaca, NY: Cornell University Press, 1965

Peare, Catherine Owens, William Penn: A Biography, Philadelphia: Lippincott, 1959

Wildes, Henry Emerson, William Penn, New York: Macmillan, and London: Collier Macmillan, 1974

William Penn, founder of Pennsylvania, Quaker, social philosopher, and politician, moved easily between the egalitarian world of the Quakers and the aristocratic world at Whitehall. He was, above all, an enigma. The literature about him illustrates the different facets of Penn's life, but also reveals an ultimate inability to solve some of the mysteries about his career.

For all the excellent qualities of the various studies of the life of William Penn, it has to be noted that, since they appeared, the five volumes of *The Papers of William Penn*, (together with the microfilm supplement) have significantly enhanced the availability of sources for fresh investigations of his career (*The Papers of William Penn*, general editors Richard S. Dunn and Mary Maples Dunn, Philadelphia: University of Pennsylvania Press, 1981–87). One aspect where work is still needed concerns Penn's early life before he became a Quaker. His experiences as a young man before his conversion require more attention. An examination of his training as a student of Amyraut at Saumur would provide a fuller understanding of his philosophy on toleration, and his political relationship with royalty during the period of the 1680s.

The most recent work by DUNN and DUNN, which tries to encapsulate the various aspects of Penn's life, does so through a series of essays. This is accomplished in four main sections: Penn's life, Penn's Britain, Penn's America, and the Quaker background to his business and religious legacy. Several of the essays, however, are merely shorter versions of books written on Penn. Mary Maples Dunn's essay is a summary of her book. Likewise Melvin Endy recounts Penn's development as a Quaker which he covers at length in his larger work. Edwin Bronner presents once again the "Holy Experiment" argument which he put forward in his 1962 study. However, there are some fresh insights into Penn's world. His business activity is discussed by Richard Dunn, who brings together evidence showing that in financial terms his success as an entrepreneur is questionable. Two essayists, Stephen Saunders Webb and J.R. Jones, give an imperial dimension to Penn's activities. Webb places the founding of Pennsylvania within an English military strategy which aimed at the consolidation of the English North American colonies. Jones deals with the impact of Quakerism upon Penn's life in Restoration politics. By becoming a successful intermediary in the English political world, Penn was able to further the cause of his persecuted brethren and eventually become proprietor of Pennsylvania.

The Irish connection is covered by Nicholas Canny who advances the case that Penn's overseas endeavors were based upon his experiences in England's first plantation, Ireland. As a young man sent to the family estates in Munster, Penn learned the financial importance of having suitable tenants. More importantly, perhaps, he learned that being a proprietor in residence was crucial to the development of a plantation.

There have been many biographies of Penn which reflect the period in which they were written and the religious background of the authors themselves. Primarily concentrating on his religious activities, these studies virtually ignore the personality of the man. The biographies by Peare and Wildes, although published two or three decades ago, are essential starting points for anyone who is interested in the man and his contributions to the larger world. PEARE does get the essence of the man. Penn is portrayed as a young man with an inquiring mind who through family contacts made his way into the world of Restoration politics. It was also through his father's contacts that he was saved from the consequences of his conversion to Quakerism.

WILDES is the most comprehensive and definitive account of Penn's private and public life. There is an in-depth approach to Penn's activities and relationships which succeed in rounding out the picture of the man. This is no doubt helped by

extensive use of Penn's correspondence, much of which was not previously available. However, major British manuscript repositories are overlooked.

Although three major works on Penn's political career attempt to reconcile his political and religious activities, they take different approaches. DUNN takes the broader approach by arguing that Penn's ability to straddle both worlds was due to his connections at Court and his firm belief in liberty of conscience. His ideas and actions are explained through an examination of his writings. Thus tracts such as *England's Present Interest Discovered* and *The Continued Cry of the Oppressed* were illustrations of his belief that liberty would not come from the prerogative but from Parliament. However, the study fails to explain why Penn received the charter for Pennsylvania, and treats it as a mystery.

BURANELLI stresses the interconnection of religious and political goals. His relationship with James as duke and later as king was based upon the mutual objective of religious toleration, albeit a short-term one on James's part. In Buranelli's view, this relationship explains Penn's success in holding on to the colony during the mid-1680s. ILLICK attempts to separate the two areas of religion and politics by viewing Penn as a pragmatist. He ably demonstrates Penn's ability to change with political currents in England and yet retain his credibility as a Quaker leader.

According to both Bronner and Endy, Penn's social and religious outlook permeated the other areas of his life. Both works interpret Penn's philosophy within the framework of 17th-century expansionism and experimentation. BRONNER particularly stresses Penn's interest in putting the tenets of his faith into practice through the formation of a colony devoted to religious toleration. This spiritual purpose was, in essence, an experiment to provide a model for the rest of the world. Bronner concludes that the experiment did not work, not least because the Quakers themselves broke down into factions. ENDY highlights Penn's spiritual purpose, which guided him in all aspects of his decision-making. His Quakerism is put into the context of earlier groups such as the Seekers, and Familists. From this spiritual foundation, with its emphasis on the inner light, Penn constructed his philosophy of toleration.

MARY K. GEITER

See also Colonial History: Colonies 3

People's Party *see* Populism

Perkins, Frances   1880–1965
Social reformer and first woman cabinet member

Colman, Penny, *A Woman Unafraid: The Achievements of Frances Perkins*, New York: Atheneum, 1993

Lawson, Don, *Frances Perkins: First Lady of the Cabinet*, New York: Abelard Schuman, 1966

Martin, George, *Madam Secretary: Frances Perkins*, Boston: Houghton Mifflin, 1976

Mohr, Lillian, *Frances Perkins: "That Woman in FDR's Cabinet!"*, Croton-on-Hudson, NY: North River Press, 1979

Perkins, Frances, *The Roosevelt I Knew*, New York: Viking, 1946

Severn, Bill, *Frances Perkins: A Member of the Cabinet*, New York: Hawthorn, 1976

Ware, Susan, *Beyond Suffrage: Women in the New Deal*, Cambridge, MA: Harvard University Press, 1981

Frances Perkins, the first woman Cabinet member in American history, was a distinguished advocate of progressive reform. Throughout her life she worked for social justice and fought for wages and hours legislation, health and safety at work policies and recognition of the rights of women. The Mine Workers leader in the 1930s, John L. Lewis, may have called her "woozy in the head", with as much knowledge of economics as a Hottentot, but the tribute of one of her successors as secretary of labor when she died more adequately recognized the depth of her convictions, her formidable persistence, and her political astuteness when he said that every working man and woman in America was in her debt.

LAWSON is a short life of Perkins, vigorously written, infectiously enthusiastic, well illustrated and belonging to the Homeric school. An editor and author of books for young readers, Lawson diligently traces her career from her early work for the Consumers' League. She witnessed the terrible fire at the Triangle Shirtwaist Company in New York City in 1911 in which 146 women died, became a member, later Commissioner, of the State Industrial Commission, and was appointed Secretary of Labor in the administration of President Franklin D. Roosevelt, serving throughout his twelve years in office. President Truman appointed her to the United States Civil Service Commission, from which she retired in 1953 with the comment "I'm the last tired leaf on the New Deal tree!"

Lawson tells the story well. Equally heroic are SEVERN and MOHR, who add more detail in their accounts. Socioeconomic conditions in the United States in the early 20th century were such that, as both Mohr and later Colman suggest, there was some point to Perkins's frequent citation of the poem "Little Toilers" by Sara N. Claghorn, in which little children at work in the mill look out at men playing golf! COLMAN, a professional writer who commands a good communicative style, has written a clear and straightforward biography that should be appealing to a wide readership. Her narrative is unassuming and informative. Her history is sound and she handles tactfully the illness of Perkins's husband Paul, who was never in the public eye but was always, with their daughter Susanna, the focus of her private commitment.

Generally, however, Perkins has been little memorialized, although numerous references inhabit general studies of reform and of the women's movement, including WARE. For detailed analysis of her career MARTIN remains essential. Comprehensive and well researched, without being tediously pedantic, Martin portrays in his substantial volume the life of an intensely practical and pragmatic woman, sceptical of visionary proposals and utopian demands, who continuously sought to ameliorate conditions through legislative and executive action that commanded the support of the communities involved. Martin's vignette of her initial conference with leaders of organized labor in Washington in March 1933 epitomizes her tough but conciliatory approach, but his balanced account of her career does not allow over-emphasis on particular aspects. This is true even of his discussions of her role as chair of the Committee on Economic Security that led to passage of the Social Security Act of 1935, which she herself regarded as the cornerstone of a security structure.

For PERKINS herself, this was a crowning achievement for both President Roosevelt and his Secretary of Labor. Perkins's formality, her commitment to individual privacy, and her customary tricorne hat camouflaged her passionate commitments. Her own study of the politician with whom she worked so closely, in both New York state and Washington, DC, also reveals herself. Her admiration for FDR was not uncritical, but she understood his instinctive sympathy for ordinary people, and it was this that drove her own career. Perkins has little doubt that the concept of "cradle to the grave" insurance was not the phrase of William Beveridge in the United Kingdom in 1942 but that of Roosevelt in 1934. Perkins was an intensely serious woman, who was not initially impressed by Roosevelt following his election to the state legislature, but came to admire both his political skills and his commitment to reform. Their careers became intertwined and their relationship that of trusted confidants with a shared agenda of social policy. Perkins's memoir must be interpreted, but it gives the best insight into her democratic faith and her public service.

DAVID ADAMS

See also New Deal: Legislation and Agencies 2

Pershing, John J. 1860–1948
Military commander

Bullard, Robert Lee, *Personalities and Reminiscences of the War*, New York: Doubleday, 1925

Coffman, Edward M., *The War to End All Wars: The American Military Experience in World War I*, New York: Oxford University Press, 1968

Liddell Hart, B.H., *Reputations, Ten Years After*, Boston: Little Brown, 1928; as *Reputations*, London: Murray, 1928

McCracken, Harold, *Pershing: The Story of a Great Soldier*, New York: Brewer and Warren, 1931

O'Connor, Richard, *Black Jack Pershing*, New York: Doubleday, 1961

Pershing, John J., *My Experiences in the World War*, New York: Stokes, 1931

Smythe, Donald, *Guerrilla Warrior: The Early Life of John J. Pershing*, New York: Scribner, 1973

Smythe, Donald, *Pershing: General of the Armies*, Bloomington: Indiana University Press, 1986

Trask, David F., *The AEF and Coalition Warmaking, 1917–1918*, Lawrence: University Press of Kansas, 1993

Vandiver, Frank E., *Black Jack: The Life and Times of John J. Pershing*, 2 vols., College Station: Texas A & M University Press, 1977

John J. Pershing remains among the more enigmatic personalities in American military history, due in large part to his outward reserve and uncompromising reputation. The overwhelming bulk of Pershing studies focuses on his activities as commander of the American Expeditionary Forces (AEF) during World War I, which is perhaps natural, given his significant role in that conflict. Only in recent years have historians delved into his personal life, or evaluated his effectiveness as a commander.

Memoir accounts by Pershing's lieutenants – Joseph T. Dickman, James G. Harbord, and Hunter Liggett – defend their chief against allegations that he was a prickly, mercurial ally who needlessly antagonized the army's chief-of-staff, Peyton C. March, over issues of readiness and training. These accounts are unanimous in their appraisal of Pershing as a commander with a fresh vision of how the war should be fought, and in their view that French and British generals had run out of ideas and were consumed with defeatism. They conclude that the AEF might have won the war by itself had the allies given Pershing a free hand. BULLARD is more candid, recognizing that Pershing's obstinacy hindered the war effort and contributed to American shortcomings. In his autobiography, PERSHING attacked his critics for being unable or unwilling to appreciate the special difficulties which he encountered with his French and British counterparts, and claimed that the AEF's deficiencies, especially in the Meuse-Argonne campaign, were not his fault.

In the first full-scale biography, McCRACKEN comes down heavily in Pershing's favor, with very little criticism of his military performance. While not quite a hagiography, it rosily portrays Pershing as a great captain who had to overcome extreme personal difficulties and wartime problems. Separated by thirty years is O'CONNOR, a biography heavily influenced by Pershing's own memoir. O'Connor includes some gentle criticism of his subject, noting that he was no diplomat and had little patience with the squabbling among his allies, but he prefers to concentrate on Pershing's strengths, particularly his indomitable will. As a comprehensive biography, however, the work is flawed by shallow research and perfunctory examination of the events that surrounded Pershing's command of the AEF.

Two modern biographies stand out for their exhaustive research on Pershing's life. In his two-volume study, VANDIVER is highly congratulatory and generally takes Pershing's side on troublesome issues. He takes special pains to reveal Pershing the man, and includes a remarkable amount of anecdotal material in order to put flesh on his subject. It is also at times distracting, as is the author's fascination with local color. Vandiver's extensive use of Pershing's voluminous papers, while granting the reader an unparalleled glimpse of Pershing's mind, tends to present a biased view of the general, with little analysis in between. Vandiver is more interested in explaining why Pershing acted as he did, rather than in criticizing his actions. As a result, this is more a personality study than anything else. The result convincingly demolishes the established view of Pershing as a stony, aloof individual, instead revealing a man of strong emotions and deeply-held convictions.

A shorter, but more probing, two-volume biography is SMYTHE, which takes a much more analytical approach than Vandiver or previous accounts. Smythe frankly discusses a number of controversies in which Pershing found himself embroiled early in his career, and fully discusses the unusual circumstances surrounding his rapid promotion to brigadier general. Smythe is at his most critical (and insightful) in appraising Pershing's leadership abilities during World War I, suggesting that his stubborn and protective personality led him to eschew delegation of authority to subordinates, and complicated the delicate issue of amalgamation. These tendencies, moreover, created confusion and enmity between the AEF in France and the American general staff. Rather than a tactical visionary, Pershing is described as grossly uninformed about the nature of the war in Europe, and his preferred remedy to the military stalemate there – open warfare – as a relic of a bygone era. Indeed, Smythe's image of Pershing depicts him as something of an anachronistic figure in an era of modern war, who could not see that times had changed.

Other works that examine Pershing's aptitude for inter-allied command, his strategic abilities and specific preferences regarding combat and training find him falling short on all counts. In a collection of essays on World War I generals, LIDDELL HART views Pershing as efficient, talented and ambitious but, in the end, inadequate to the test of the Western Front. Liddell Hart's early analysis helped ingrain the popular view of Pershing as a difficult, intractable commander. Despite Pershing's flaws, Liddell Hart recognizes him as the only American leader who could have tackled the military challenges facing the United States. COFFMAN broaches subjects upon which Smythe later elaborated, pointing out Pershing's most flagrant lapses of judgment and failings as an ally. However, because it is a general history of America's participation in the war, Coffman's analysis of these incidents is brief.

The most recent critical assessment of Pershing's capacity as General of the Armies is TRASK. In this study of inter-allied cooperation, Pershing is portrayed as a flawed commander who was nonetheless convinced of his own supreme competence. Although Trask is sympathetic to the fact that Pershing was forced to commit the AEF to combat before it was ready, he notes that the general failed to do those things which might have made the American presence more potent, particularly regarding the issues of amalgamation and training. Given the deficiencies, which Trask crisply identifies, the author suggests that Pershing might well have been relieved of command had the war continued into 1919.

T.R. BRERETON

See also World War I: the United States at War

Philadelphia

Baltzell, E. Digby, *Philadelphia Gentlemen: The Making of a National Upper Class*, Glencoe, IL: Free Press, 1958

Baltzell, E. Digby, *Puritan Boston and Quaker Philadelphia: Two Protestant Ethics and the Spirit of Class Authority and Leadership*, New York: Free Press, 1979

Hershberg, Theodore (editor), *Philadelphia: Work, Space, Family and Group Experience in the Nineteenth Century: Essays Toward an Interdisciplinary History of the City*, New York: Oxford University Press, 1981

McCaffery, Peter, *When Bosses Ruled Philadelphia: The Emergence of the Republican Machine, 1867–1933*, University Park: Pennsylvania State University Press, 1993

Morgan, George, *The City of Firsts, Being a Complete History of the City of Philadelphia from Its Founding in 1682 to the Present Time*, Philadelphia: Historical Publication Society, 1926

Oberholtzer, Ellis Paxson, *Philadelphia: A History of the City and Its People*, 4 vols., Philadelphia: Clarke, 1912

Scharf, J. Thomas, and Thompson Westcott, *A History of Philadelphia, 1609–1884*, 3 vols., Philadelphia: Everts, 1884

Warner, Sam Bass, *The Private City: Philadelphia in Three Periods of Its Growth*, Philadelphia: University of Pennsylvania Press, 1968, 2nd edition, 1987

Weigley, Russell F. (editor), *Philadelphia: A 300-Year History*, New York: Norton, 1982

Wolf, Edwin, *Philadelphia: Portrait of an American City*, Harrisburg, PA: Camino, 1976, revised with Kenneth Finkel, 1990

As the birthplace of the Revolution, and a former capital city, Philadelphia holds a special place in the nation's history. Its other distinctive features – as the linchpin of William Penn's Holy Experiment and as the nation's first major industrial city – have, in addition, meant that the city has been the subject of considerable scholarly enterprise. To such an extent, indeed, that life in the "City of Brotherly Love" has, from its inception in 1682, probably been documented to a degree at least equal to, if not greater than, any other city in the Union. Predictably, this scholarship has not been characterized by a uniform approach to the study of the city. On the contrary, most studies of Philadelphia tend to fall into one of three broad categories: "local histories" that have been produced with a view towards boosting the city's image; city biographies that have attempted to chronicle the city's growth and development; or case studies which have used the city as a local and particular test-case of broader national trends.

Among the works in the first category, MORGAN is, in essence, a collection of fragments of Philadelphia history; compiled by a local journalist in such a way – that is, by listing the hundreds of achievements in which Philadelphia has been a pioneer – as to bear testimony to the city's enterprise and initiative. Written in a lively and racy style, it also offers an informative, if uneven, account of the city's history from a partisan perspective.

WOLF, similarly, provides a benign and flattering portrait of the city; though, on this occasion, a handsomely illustrated one, compiled by the eminent librarian of the Library Company of Philadelphia to mark the 1976 Bicentennial celebration. It reflects the author's keen sense of the city's distinctive features, while it provides a chronological text that is rich in local lore and detailed vignettes.

Of the city's biographies, SCHARF and WESTCOTT is a three-volume work, much venerated among chroniclers of Philadelphia's past – and rightly so, as it is still arguably the most thorough and reliable account of the first 200 years of the city's history, although the narrative does run thinner as it approaches its terminus in 1884. OBERHOLTZER is another multi-volume study; one which provides a serious and scholarly analysis of Philadelphia's development from the vantage-point of 1912. It is particularly useful for its detailed coverage of many of the city's leading citizens.

WEIGLEY, by contrast, is a contemporary collaborative work by twenty scholars who, in conscious imitation of Scharf and Westcott's enterprise, attempt to cover a third as much again of the city's history (down to 1982) in the course of a single-volume study. It is an ambitious undertaking that, unfortunately, did not produce the definitive history of the city that its contributors had intended. On the contrary, the absence of a natural unity or coherence among its seventeen chapters – in addition to the dearth of maps and figures – deprives the reader of a balanced and systematic guide to the city's development. Nevertheless the contributions are both readable and well-illustrated, and the volume as a whole does supply at least some detail on most aspects of the city's history.

It is in fact the case-studies, rather than the city's biographies, which offer some interpretation, rather than simply a narration, of Philadelphia's past. As a result it is they which best convey an overall impression of the character and quality of life in the city. Not surprisingly perhaps, given that it was prompted by the "urban crisis" facing the nation in the late 1960s, WARNER provides a historical portrait that is sharply critical of the basic ("capitalist") mode of social organization in the city – specifically, the long tradition of excessive reliance on private institutions and private wealth. Well-written and persuasively argued, it also offers a critical insight into the city's development during three successive periods (1770–80; 1830–60; 1920–30) of urban growth.

No less polemical – in this case in its implicit advocacy of "affirmative action" for northern urban blacks – and just as rigorous in its methodology, HERSHBERG provides a quantitative exploration of the city's social, spatial and economic systems in the 19th century. A product of the federally-funded Philadelphia Social History Project, the fourteen essays that make up the collection are as much concerned with demonstrating the efficacy of a new, interdisciplinary approach to the study of urban history, and addressing matters of "public policy", as they are with identifying the distinguishing features of Philadelphia's development. It is an impressive work that not only meets its own set objectives, but which is also presented in a form which caters to the needs of the quantitative specialist and the general reader alike.

In contrast to Hershberg, BALTZELL (1958) is an impressive pioneering sociological study which focuses on the top, rather than the bottom, of Philadelphia's society. It too, like Warner, is critical of the role played by "Proper Philadelphians" in the development of the city, though in this case Baltzell, as a political and social conservative (if not an economic one), views their behaviour as cause for concern rather than anger.

This theme of abdication of social responsibility on the part of the upper class is developed further in BALTZELL (1979), a more substantial work, in which he traces the comparative history of the upper classes of Boston and Philadelphia, in order to determine why such contrasting class traditions emerged in the two cities. From Baltzell's own perspective, this is primarily a treatise on the need for upper class authority in an increasingly egalitarian political system. However, it is also a fine contribution to the continuing debate over the relationship between religious ideology and social change, and in this sense it offers a different, yet fascinating, framework within which to view the entire history of Philadelphia as well as Boston.

The abrogation of responsibility on the part of the city's elite, as identified by Baltzell, and the prevalence of "privatism" as depicted by Warner, are both themes that are integrated by McCAFFERY in his study of the emergence – and consequences – of Republican machine rule. He argues that the city was not served any better by the successive party bosses who had ousted the city's elite from public office.

PETER McCAFFERY

Philanthropy

Alexander, John K., *Render Them Submissive: Responses to Poverty in Philadelphia, 1760–1800*, Amherst: University of Massachusetts Press, 1980

Axinn, June and Herman Levin, *Social Welfare: A History of the American Response to Need*, New York: Dodd Mead, 1975; 2nd edition, New York: Harper, 1982

Brilliant, Eleanor L., *The United Way: Dilemmas of Organized Charity*, New York: Columbia University Press, 1990

Ginzberg, Lori D., *Women and the Work of Benevolence: Morality, Politics and Class in the Nineteenth-Century United States*, New Haven: Yale University Press, 1990

Holt, Marilyn Irvin, *The Orphan Trains: Placing out in America*, Lincoln: University of Nebraska Press, 1992

Huggins, Nathan Irvin, *Protestants Against Poverty: Boston's Charities, 1870–1900*, Westport, CT: Greenwood Press, 1971

Kunzel, Regina G., *Fallen Women, Problem Girls: Unmarried Mothers and the Professionalization of Social Work, 1890–1945*, New Haven: Yale University Press, 1993

Lubove, Roy, *The Professional Altruist: The Emergence of Social Work as a Career, 1880–1930*, Cambridge, MA: Harvard University Press, 1965

Neverdon-Morton, Cynthia, *Afro-American Women of the South and the Advancement of the Race, 1895–1925*, Knoxville: University of Tennessee Press, 1989

Pascoe, Peggy, *Relations of Rescue: The Search for Female Moral Authority in the American West, 1874–1939*, New York: Oxford University Press, 1990

Patterson, James T., *America's Struggle Against Poverty, 1900–1980*, Cambridge, MA: Harvard University Press, 1981, revised as *America's Struggle Against Poverty, 1900–1994*, 1994

Rothman, David J., *The Discovery of the Asylum: Social Order and Disorder in the New Republic*, Boston: Little Brown, 1971, revised 1990

AXINN and LEVIN provide an overview of the cultural responses to poverty, including philanthropy, in their examination of the range of charitable, philanthropic, and social welfare activities from the colonial period through the 1970s. In a text accompanied by selected documents, they offer a balanced account of the development of public and private aid to the poor. The book follows certain groups, such as African Americans and veterans, throughout, adding in new groups as they became objects of concern. The documents, drawn from official reports and investigations, tend to give the "official" view of poverty and the poor, rather than serving as the testimony of the objects of philanthropy. PATTERSON describes the development of charity in the United States in the 20th century. He examines private philanthropy as well as state responses to impoverishment and distress. The coverage is stronger on the later periods (New Deal and Great Society) than on the early years of the 20th century, but it nevertheless describes the growth in provision, especially at the federal level.

ROTHMAN concentrates upon the colonial era and early republic in his examination of charity and correction, noting how intertwined these issues were (and are). He roots attitudes towards the poor in the size and complexity of American society. As the United States grew more diverse, methods of assisting the poor and correcting antisocial or socially unacceptable behavior became more formalized, resulting in organized benevolence and the construction of institutions, frequently at state expense. Rothman focuses primarily on those institutions, giving a useful overview of the role of the state and of influential philanthropists in the construction of reformatories, prisons, and asylums.

Much of the work on philanthropy approaches the subject through study of a particular city. ALEXANDER, for example, charts the development of charity in Philadelphia in the late 18th century. He is concerned with how the poor lived, the growing anxiety and fear of the poor, and the attempts to control them. The American Revolution inspired reforms, including expansion of education and the right to vote regardless of wealth, although not of sex or race. Since the Revolution also led to a decline in the deference of the poor to the elite, the affluent responded by imposing more formal mechanisms of social control through institutions such as almshouses and through charity limited to those who behaved in an acceptable fashion. HUGGINS probes the impetus of charitable reform and charitable activity in Boston, reaching conclusions broadly similar to Alexander's. He finds Boston's charity workers to have been deeply conservative, looking for the roots of problems of the poor in the poor themselves. Organizations such as the Charity Organization Society tried to alter the behavior of the poor and to treat the supposedly underlying causes of poverty, which they believed to be drunkenness, shiftlessness, and immorality.

The important charity work done by women is the subject of GINZBERG's study of philanthropy in the 19th century. She writes gender into the history of charity by considering how changing role definitions for women led them to organize across a wide range of philanthropic and benevolent activities. She emphasizes the class basis of benevolence and the diversity of women's participation in social reform movements. This study enriches understanding of philanthropy through its exploration of the cultural, religious, and political dimensions of women's philanthropic endeavors.

PASCOE explores a similar set of concerns for women reformers in the West, taking an intercultural approach which incorporates the views of those acted upon, as well as the progenitors of philanthropic endeavors. She analyzes the limits of the social control approach to charity by questioning the passivity of the recipients of aid, while maintaining a sensitive approach to issues of race, class, and gender. This study looks at the cross-cultural issues of reform as it explores the relations between native-born white female reformers and their Indian, Chinese, and Mormon clients.

Work with dependent children was one of the main philanthropic endeavors in the 19th and early 20th centuries. HOLT places the orphan trains in their historical context through an critical analysis of the motives and methods used by those who shipped children from eastern cities to western farms and small towns for fostering, adoption, or unremitting hard labor. Unmarried mothers were another of the primary targets for the philanthropically minded in the late 19th and early 20th centuries. KUNZEL examines the motivation of genteel women who provided homes for unmarried mothers and the way in which social workers supplanted them from the 1910s onwards. As social workers sought to wrest control over philanthropy from people they stigmatized as "do-gooders" they substituted the language of professionalism for the sympathetic sisterhood of well-intentioned, if untrained, philanthropists.

By focusing upon self-help and race-specific philanthropy, NEVERDON-MORTON portrays the panoply of charitable activities within the southern African American community in the general context of racial uplift and the development of women's organizations. While not ignoring the vexed issue of inter-racial cooperation, this work concentrates upon the philanthropic ventures of better-educated and more affluent African American women across the South, setting their work in the national context. Special attention is paid to their work in Hampton, Tuskegee, Atlanta, Nashville, and Baltimore.

LUBOVE is the seminal work on the transition between philanthropy and social work. He documents the transition from impulsive do-gooding to organized benevolence and scientific social work. He investigates the ways in which professionals replaced volunteers, the growing complexity of charity administration, and the ways in which the professionalization of social work altered philanthropy. His analysis of the professional subculture of social workers and the rise of the case work methods of scientific philanthropists remains the standard account of the origins of social work.

BRILLIANT picks up many of the themes explored by these historians. She provides a brief historical overview of organized philanthropy, concentrating upon the large national organizations which ultimately made up the United Way, an amalgamation of philanthropic societies and business leaders which raised millions of dollars annually for charity in American cities. The United Fund's leadership came firmly from the business community, which sought to limit competition in fund raising, and also to limit distribution of the money raised to non-controversial, mainstream charities. This institutional history illuminates the internal workings of the United Way, the limited number of organizations which benefited from its allocations, and the way in which it eventually adjusted its funding allocations to take account of new organizations and complaints about racial bias.

S. J. KLEINBERG

See also Poverty; Prisons and Asylums; Social Work/Social Reform

Phillips, Wendell 1811–1884
Abolitionist, reformer and orator

Aptheker, Herbert, *Abolitionism: A Revolutionary Movement*, Boston: Twayne, 1989

Bartlett, Irving H., *Wendell Phillips: Brahmin Radical*, Boston: Beacon Press, 1961

Bartlett, Irving H., *Wendell and Ann Phillips: The Community of Reform, 1840–1880*, New York: Norton, 1979

Brown, Ira, *Mary Grew: Abolitionist and Feminist, 1813–1896*, Selinsgrove, PA: Susquehanna University Press, 1991

Korngold, Ralph, *Two Friends of Man: The Story of William Lloyd Garrison and Wendell Phillips and Their Relationship with Abraham Lincoln*, Boston: Little Brown, 1950

McInerney, Daniel J., *The Fortunate Heirs of Freedom: Abolition and Republican Thought*, Lincoln: University of Nebraska Press, 1994

Sherwin, Oscar, *Prophet of Liberty: The Life and Times of Wendell Phillips*, New York: Bookman, 1958

Sterling, Dorothy, *Ahead of Her Time: Abby Kelley and the Politics of Anti-slavery*, New York: Norton, 1991

Stewart, James Brewer, *Wendell Phillips: Liberty's Hero*, Baton Rouge: Louisiana State University Press, 1986

The several scholars who have chronicled and analyzed the life and career of Wendell Phillips, abolitionist and reformer, seem to agree on two aspects of his life – his great oratorical skills and devotion to the concept of liberty. Born within the Boston elite, Phillips used his knowledge, skills, and influence to champion the cause of reform in a career that spanned nearly fifty years until his death in 1884. Early biographers, including George Austin, Carlos Martyn and Lorenzo Sears, were sympathetic toward Phillips and the abolition movement in general, while noting some excesses of the more radical abolitionists. They provide some useful information on his efforts in the causes of abolition, temperance, women's rights, Irish immigrants, black suffrage, and labor and prison reform.

Examining the lives of Phillips, Garrison and Lincoln in brief biographies, KORNGOLD attempts to reveal how these three leaders influenced one another and the major events of the abolition movement. Sympathetic toward Phillips, and finding Lincoln years behind on racial issues, Korngold is nevertheless critical of Phillips's virulent attacks on Lincoln – attacks that even forced Garrison to take exception. Korngold also examines the views of the three men on controversial subjects such as colonization and compensated emancipation. SHERWIN describes Phillips as a philosopher of agitation who revolutionized oratory. Generally sympathetic and occasionally overly dramatic, Sherwin emphasizes the revolutionary traditions that influenced Phillips, but offers little analysis. Sherwin often finds abolitionists unreasonable, referring to Garrison as a natural autocrat, and he too is critical of Phillips's attacks on Lincoln. Still, he praises Phillips for his devotion to duty, reform, and nation.

Perhaps the most critical biography of Phillips and the abolition movement in general is BARTLETT (1961). While acknowledging him as the intellectual leader of the radical abolitionists, Bartlett maintains that Phillips lived in two worlds, the Brahmin world of Boston elites and the "bizarre world of crackpots, fanatics, cranks, and saints" of the abolitionists. Maintaining that the ideals of the American Revolution influenced Phillips, Bartlett examines many of the tensions and conflicts that surrounded his professional and personal life, and describes Phillips's continued struggle for reform after the Civil War as anachronistic. He asserts that Phillips had the ability to castigate public figures with seeming impunity, an ability which he attributes to Phillips's social status and oratorical skills rather than the message that he delivered. Bartlett was the first biographer to offer a detailed analysis of Phillips's life and career.

Beyond crediting Ann Greene Phillips with intensifying Wendell's already simmering interest in abolitionism, most of the above authors all but ignore the relationship between this wife and husband team of abolitionists and reformers. Suffering from long bouts of illness that confined her to home most of her life, Ann, nevertheless, profoundly affected every facet of Wendell's long career. Part of the neglect stemmed from lack of sources. Until found in a dusty corner in 1977, most of the correspondence between the two, along with other valuable papers, were assumed lost or destroyed. The discovery, the Blagden Papers, provided BARTLETT (1979) with an opportunity to revisit the Phillipses. He re-evaluated Wendell's relationship with his parents and family, and revised his attitude toward Ann. Rather than the neurotic invalid whom Bartlett described in his earlier work, Ann becomes "an intelligent, articulate, assertive wife, informed about public issues and determined to participate in his career." Bartlett also provides a sampling of the Blagden Papers that reveals a more personal side of Phillips.

The best biography of Wendell Phillips is STEWART. He makes extensive use of primary and secondary sources to analyze Phillips's contribution to the goals, strategies, and conflicts of the abolition as well as other reform movements. Stewart focuses on the theme of republicanism, and asserts that Phillips's humanistic sense of duty, virtue, and moral order not only inspired his actions but also anchored his ideological rationale, that demanded liberty and self-restraint in a nation that would be a republic. Spanning the entire life of Phillips, Stewart also explores Phillips's personal relationships with Ann and his family, and his relationships with friends and enemies within and outside of reform. Stewart's study is essential reading for any student of abolition, reform, or this era in American history.

Phillips appears in most of the biographies of the leading abolitionists and reformers, especially those centered in New England. Attracted to strong-minded women such as Ann, Phillips also championed women's rights, as revealed in recent biographies about Mary Grew and Abby Kelley, two women often neglected in the reform historiography. BROWN uses correspondence between Grew and her cousin Ann Greene Phillips and Wendell to examine the life of the Philadelphia-based abolitionist and early feminist. Brown offers insight into a personal side of Phillips and his relation with abolitionists outside the Boston circle. STERLING analyzes Phillips's relationship to one of his closest friends, the outspoken Abby Kelley whose husband was Stephen Foster, arguably the most radical of the radical abolitionists. Phillips's unwavering support and tolerance of this wing of abolition led to much conflict within the movement. Together these two biographies offer fresh interpretations of Phillips's role within the women's movement.

The rhetoric and actions of Phillips are often present in monographs on specific themes concerning the abolition movement. For instance, APTHEKER claims that Phillips's revolutionary consciousness and behavior in struggling for a complete overhaul of the nation's social order demonstrated the revolutionary character of abolitionism. Analyzing Phillips's speeches, articles, and essays, Aptheker notes his radicalism on such issues as racism, equality, capitalism, and education.

McINERNEY uses Phillips's works to support the thesis that abolitionists derived the language, logic, and legitimacy of the abolition movement from republican thought that emphasized the protection of liberty from tyranny through independence and virtue. McInerney examines Phillips's views on the marketplace, religion, American identity, and interestingly, on attempts to reconcile Saxon lore and racial equality. Both monographs provide unusual perspectives on the complexities of Phillips's life.

LAWRENCE S. LITTLE

See also Abolitionism; Reform Movements

Pilgrim Fathers

Abbott, John S.C., *Miles Standish: Captain of the Pilgrims*, New York: Dodd Mead, 1872

Blaxland, G. Cuthbert, *"Mayflower" Essays on the Story of the Pilgrim Fathers, as Told in Governor Bradford's MS History of the Plimoth Plantation*, London: Ward and Downey, 1896; reprinted, Freeport, NY: Books for Libraries Press, 1972

Brewster, Dorothy, *William Brewster of the Mayflower: Portrait of a Pilgrim*, New York: New York University Press, 1970

Kirk-Smith, H., *William Brewster, the Father of New England: His Life and Times, 1567–1644*, Boston, Lincolnshire: Kay, 1992

Plooij, D., *The Pilgrim Fathers from a Dutch Point of View*, New York: New York University Press, 1932

Sherwood, Mary B., *Pilgrim: A Biography of William Brewster*, Falls Church, VA: Great Oak Press, 1982

Smith, Bradford, *Bradford of Plymouth*, Philadelphia: Lippincott, 1951

Westbrook, Perry D., *William Bradford*, Boston: Twayne, 1978

Both historians and genealogical descendants have long been fascinated by those who traveled to America on the *Mayflower*. As a result, a great deal has been written about the Pilgrim fathers. Unfortunately, as Perry Westbrook observes, much of this is "rubbish." Even those biographies of William Bradford, William Brewster, and Miles Standish, the political, religious, and military leaders of the Plymouth colony, which are serious works suffer from a set of common faults.

The primary source of information about the colony, its experiences and leaders, is Bradford's *History of Plymouth Plantation*, written during his lifetime although not published until 1856. Most works either adhere closely to this account, or use background information to infer, guess, and fill in the gaps – or alternate between quoting and inventing. There are few hard facts about the lives, especially personal lives, of these three men for they did not leave papers other than the "History" itself. As a result, biographers frequently resort to such words as "must have" and "probably." Several of the books are the products of descendants, but even those which are not are generally laudatory, offering little criticism of their subjects. Readers seeking information on these early leaders of New England are advised to look at the biographies in conjunction with histories of Plymouth.

Despite the fact that he served as the governor of the Plymouth colony for most of its early years, and wrote its history, William Bradford was not the subject of a full biography until 1951. SMITH is definitive and the best of the Bradford biographies. However, it is both simultaneously enhanced and flawed by the author's use of his imagination to reconstruct feelings, events, and places out of what he refers to as "scattered hints and materials." By such devices the author pulls the reader into his story, but the source of some descriptions, and of dialogue in the book, is not clear.

After a dramatic opening, Smith follows Bradford's life chronologically. For him there is "no doubt" that this Pilgrim father "was Plymouth's greatest man," "a thinker and man of action, a writer of considerable charm, a linguist, diplomat and man of God." Smith also admires the Dutch, arguing that Holland rather than England is the real source of American political and social ideas – learned by the Pilgrims while they lived there. He analyzes Bradford's handwriting as an indication of his character, and uses psychology to explain the career failures of his son John. At the end of the book he discusses the *History* and other writings, including poems, left by Bradford. Although it is occasionally problematic, there is much of interest in this biography.

Bradford's "scribblings" are the main concern of two other works. BLAXLAND consists of four essays, the last on "William Bradford, as Author, Man, and Statesman." This chapter briefly examines the History as autobiographical text, comments on when the book was written, its style, and the author's life. Bradford, he concludes was "brave, indefatigable, public spirited, keen sighted . . . the ideal governor to watch over" the colony's "struggling infancy." WESTBROOK is also primarily concerned with *Of Plimmoth Plantation* as a literary work, as befits a book which is part of the Twayne series of brief biographies of American authors. He discusses Bradford's commitment to church and community, his dealings with the Indians, his other prose and poetry, and his style.

The first book to deal with William Brewster was Ashbel Steele's *Chief of the Pilgrims; or, The Life and Time of William Brewster* (1857). Long out of date, it contained little on his early life in England or Holland. This period is the main concern of both Plooij and Dorothy Brewster. PLOOIJ's work was originally presented in a series of lectures to celebrate the 300th anniversary of the Dutch Reformed Church in America. One chapter discusses William Brewster, the Pilgrim press used to publish forbidden texts in Holland, and the elder's subsequent hiding and then escaping from English authorities on board the *Mayflower*. Dorothy BREWSTER also traces the activities of her ancestor up to his departure for New England. As a university English teacher caught up in the net of McCarthyism in the 1950s, her interest was aroused by a man whose experiences had "contemporary relevance." He too had taught, discussed ideas deemed heretical, been summoned by the government, and refused permission to leave the country. In this short book she discusses his early life in England, probable experiences as a Cambridge student, and time in Amsterdam and Leiden. She is particularly interested in the press, and in his persecution.

More complete coverage of Brewster's life is offered by both Sherwood and Kirk-Smith. SHERWOOD states that she concentrated on the "story of one man and the world he saw" rather than a general history of the Pilgrims, but in fact both her work and Kirk-Smith's are often more about the times than the individual. Her Brewster was a "complicated man," the "single most important individual" among the settlers. When details of his life are lacking she uses background information to suggest his experiences – for example as a university student. Her style is often vivid and the book is interesting to read. There is a centerfold full of pictures of buildings, likenesses of Brewster, and pages from the books he owned. KIRK-SMITH is also laudatory in tone. His Brewster is "one of the greatest men in the early history of the American nation." He utilizes many sources, including recent works, to give an overview of Brewster's contributions to the religious, moral, and legal life of the colony. But this attempt to prove Brewster's "true place" is hindered by the fact that Brewster left almost no written record, by the author's use of too many long quotations, and by his romantic reading of the Pilgrims' mission.

ABBOTT's book on Miles Standish was part of a late 19th century series on American "pioneers and patriots," written for "entertainment and instruction." It follows the Pilgrims from England to Holland and on to America, ending with Standish's death. This soldier was "a gentleman born," a "gallant leader" who joined the Pilgrims because he loved adventure. He was in the thick of all military actions, which were always undertaken in self-defense. Much of this is based on Bradford's History, and there is little here on Standish's personal life. This is old-fashioned history, but in many ways its laudatory tone is similar to the other more recent biographies of the Pilgrim fathers. Ancestor worship and limited sources have inhibited biographers. The reader needs to consult the many good studies of the colony in order to gain a better understanding of its founders.

MAXINE N. LURIE

Pinchot, Gifford 1865–1946

Conservationist

Fausold, Martin L., *Gifford Pinchot: Bull Moose Progressive*, Syracuse, NY: Syracuse University Press, 1961

McGeary, M. Nelson, *Gifford Pinchot, Forester-Politician*, Princeton: Princeton University Press, 1960

Mason, Alpheus T., *Bureaucracy Convicts Itself: The Ballinger-Pinchot Controversy of 1910*, New York: Viking, 1941

Penick, James, Jr., *Progressive Politics and Conservation: The Ballinger-Pinchot Affair*, Chicago: Chicago University Press, 1968

Pinchot, Gifford, *Breaking New Ground*, New York: Harcourt Brace, 1947

Pinkett, Harold T., *Gifford Pinchot: Private and Public Forester*, Urbana: University of Illinois Press, 1970

Taylor, Bob Pepperman, *Our Limits Transgressed: Environmental Political Thought in America*, Lawrence: University Press of Kansas, 1992

Wister, Owen, *Roosevelt: The Story of a Friendship, 1880–1919*, New York: Macmillan, 1930; as *Theodore Roosevelt*, London: Macmillan, 1930

Gifford Pinchot, the pioneer American forester and Republican Progressive politician, and twice governor of Pennsylvania, was a close friend and associate of Theodore Roosevelt, and directed the first conservation movement as chief forester. Pinchot's Papers at the Library of Congress are formidable in size. In his autobiography, PINCHOT covers his running battles over how to care for the scientific management of the American forests, as well as personal conflicts inside the conservation movement, from 1889 to 1912. Although Pinchot's autobiographical style is sometimes vainly self-centred and tedious, this cannot reduce the true value of his life's work.

Owen WISTER, the noted Pennsylvania writer who followed the example of his Harvard classmate Theodore Roosevelt in heading for the West, and achieved success with *The Virginian* in 1902, left a picture of Pinchot (along with several other friends of TR). Pinchot was a Roosevelt "Rough Rider" – a tall, vigorous and handsome man who inspired loyal, if cranky, followers.

The standard, academic, judicious (but non-judgmental) biography of Pinchot to this date, is by McGEARY. The dispute over conservation of land in the public domain between Pinchot and Richard A. Ballinger in the Taft administration in 1910, which led Pinchot's dismissal from federal government service, is fully covered. In the barren 1920s, still speaking from the viewpoint of conservation, Pinchot directed an assault on the business giants who controlled the public utilities, from the state governor's office in Pennsylvania. He was again governor in the Great Depression years, and in 1940, aged in his mid-70s, was strongly interventionist in World War II, and firmly supported Franklin D. Roosevelt. Pinchot's political career traversed much of 20th-century American history, from the Republican and Progressive Theodore Roosevelt, to the Democratic and New Deal Franklin D. Roosevelt. Belief that he could have been president of the United States himself, if things had worked out rather differently, perhaps helped to keep him going.

More than fifty years ago, MASON was the earliest scholar to tackle the Ballinger-Pinchot controversy. The occasion for the book was an article by Harold L. Ickes, Secretary of the Interior, which resurrected the affair, and defended Taft from anti-conservation charges. Thirty years later, PENICK carefully re-examined the Ballinger-Pinchot quarrel, as a struggle between rival government bureaucratic agencies. FAUSOLD has a different emphasis. He focuses on Pinchot's political career, after his 1910 dismissal, as a "Bull Moose Progressive."

PINKETT is a brief, compressed biography of Pinchot as a forester – not as a general conservationist – and is valuable for its account of the forestry movement managed by Pinchot between the 1890s and the beginning of the 1920s. Pinchot's approach to American forestry was in one sense utilitarian; his aim was "to make the forest produce the largest amount of whatever crop or service will be most useful, and keep on producing it, for generation after generation of men and trees." His views were opposed by wilderness crusaders like John Muir, as well as bureaucrats and congressmen, homesteaders, miners and lumber interests.

Pinchot's place in American environmental history is well-known, and his role is considered in many general works on the subject. TAYLOR is a recent book on environmental political thought, which includes discussion of Pinchot's commitment to utilitarian conservation of natural resources, as a means of achieving distributive justice.

Peter d'A. Jones

See also Conservation

Police and Law Enforcement

Berman, Jay S., *Police Administration and Progressive Reform: Theodore Roosevelt as Police Commissioner of New York*, New York: Greenwood Press, 1987

Fogelson, Robert M., *Big-City Police*, Cambridge, MA: Harvard University Press, 1977

Harring, Sidney L., *Policing a Class Society: The Experience of American Cities, 1865–1915*, New Brunswick, NJ: Rutgers University Press, 1982

Johnson, David R., *Policing the Urban Underworld: The Impact of Crime on the Development of the American Police, 1800–1877*, Philadelphia: Temple University Press, 1979

Johnson, David R., *American Law Enforcement: A History*, St. Louis: Forum Press, 1981

Lane, Roger, *Policing the City: Boston, 1822–1885*, Cambridge, MA: Harvard University Press, 1967

Miller, Wilbur R., *Cops and Bobbies: Police Authority in New York and London, 1830–1870*, Chicago: Chicago University Press, 1977

Monkkonen, Eric H., *Police in Urban America, 1860–1920*, Cambridge and New York: Cambridge University Press, 1981

Morn, Frank, *"The Eye That Never Sleeps": A History of the Pinkerton National Detective Agency*, Bloomington: Indiana University Press, 1982

Prassel, Frank Richard, *The Western Peace Officer: A Legacy of Law and Order*, Norman: University of Oklahoma Press, 1972

Richardson, James F., *The New York Police: Colonial Times to 1901*, New York: Oxford University Press, 1970

Steinberg, Allen, *The Transformation of Criminal Justice: Philadelphia, 1800–1880*, Chapel Hill: University of North Carolina Press, 1989

Walker, Samuel A., *A Critical History of Police Reform: The Emergence of Professionalism*, Lexington, MA: Lexington Books, 1977

Walker, Samuel A., *Popular Justice: A History of American Criminal Justice*, New York: Oxford University Press, 1980

Since the end of the 1960s there has been considerable academic research and publication on the history of law enforcement in the United States. Much of this work has consisted of local studies, and understandably so, since policing in America remains essentially a local concern. The broader perspective, however, can be followed up in JOHNSON (1981) and WALKER (1980); the former providing a more detailed study of police development than the latter's survey of the whole criminal justice system.

Modern, bureaucratic police in the United States began in the cities of the East. LANE, RICHARDSON and JOHNSON (1979) chart respectively 19th-century police developments in Boston, New York and largely, but not exclusively, Philadelphia and Chicago. Lane and Richardson begin their studies with critical assessments of the legacy of the colonial period when the maintenance of law and order was in the care of a combination of part-time watchmen and constables. They stress the importance of popular disorder in encouraging the creation and development of police forces, though they also note the significance of the occasional sensational crime. Johnson's main focus is on crime and its importance in shaping police behaviour. Young cops soon recognised that it was best to concentrate on real or putative offenders from lower status groups, since these were the individuals who generated the most fear and the least sympathy. A good arrest toll was the way to advancement, while toughness, even brutality, were deemed necessary attributes. The carrying of guns began as a result of initiatives taken among the police ranks, rather than as a result of directives from their superiors. In an important comparative study, MILLER explores a similar theme by contrasting the difference between the personal authority of the New York cop, based on his courage, swagger, and personality, and the impersonal authority of London's "bobby" who was perceived much more as the physical personification of the law.

Early police reformers argued that the old system of watchmen and constables was corrupt and inefficient. While Lane, Richardson and others have drawn attention to the corruption of the new forces, they have also tended to accept the view that the new police were an improvement on the old. STEINBERG's important study of Philadelphia paints a rather different picture. Drawing on a variety of sources, and perhaps most notably on the fragments of three aldermen's notebooks, Steinberg shows that, while there was corruption in the old system, the citizens – even the poorest, blacks and immigrants – were in constant touch with it and did not hesitate to use the law for prosecuting minor criminal offences. For the first twenty years of their existence the new police in Philadelphia concentrated particularly on public order offences, while assaults and petty thefts continued to be taken before local, neighbourhood courts. Steinberg's work poses the question whether the new police served ultimately to make the system of criminal justice less accessible to the less well off.

Focusing on the period after the Civil War, and deploying a quantitative analysis, MONKKONEN has charted the adoption of police forces in new and smaller cities across the country. He suggests that it was rank and size which prompted this adoption rather than reaction to any specific incident. He also draws attention to the wide range of duties undertaken by the police, particularly with reference to the homeless and those in need of assistance, and how the role of crime fighter came to the fore in the 20th century, as the other tasks were taken over by other agencies.

An alternative view of police development is offered by HARRING. Focusing on the cities around the Great Lakes, and notably Buffalo, he emphasises the role of the police as the agents of capitalism in suppressing strikes and union activity. However, while Harring's work may be convincing in the case of the cities that he covers, it would be difficult to demonstrate that all police forces pursued such policies, and there were clearly other alternatives open to enforce the laws against trade union activities and to break strikes. While concentrating on the Pinkerton Detective Agency, MORN recognises that this was only the biggest and best known organisation which supplied a variety of watchmen, guards, informers, and strike-breaking thugs in the second half of the 19th century, and well into the 20th.

Scandals over police violence and corruption periodically brought investigations and reforms. The Progressive Era in particular witnessed such reforms, most colourfully perhaps in New York where Theodore Roosevelt cut a dash as Police Commissioner – the focus of BERMAN's study – but also in other major cities. FOGELSON begins with the reforms of the 1890s, moving on to explore developments into the 1930s and beyond. He emphasises how arguments about the control of the police reflect more general local conflicts between an established, native elite and new immigrants, whose political leaders saw the police as central to their power base, by providing employment for their supporters and protection for their interests. The poor reputation of policemen at the turn of the century also fostered reforms from within the police aimed at what the police themselves called "professionalization." These reforms are the subject of WALKER (1977).

Perhaps the most romantic of the law enforcement agents in American history were the peace officers of the Old West. PRASSEL sets out to separate the myth, originating in the dime novels and developed by Hollywood, from the reality. He describes a situation not greatly dissimilar from that outlined in studies of urban police, with peace officers commonly representing the interests of community wealth and authority, but, surprisingly, often going unarmed as they so rarely encountered violence. He concludes by noting that though at the time when he was writing, guns were now commonplace, poor standards of personnel and bureaucratic inefficiency among many western police departments were still apparently widespread.

CLIVE EMSLEY

See also Crime and Punishment

Polk, James K. 1795–1849
11th President of the United States

Bergeron, Paul H., *The Presidency of James K. Polk*, Lawrence: University Press of Kansas, 1987

Hietala, Thomas R., *Manifest Design: Anxious Aggrandizement in Late Jacksonian America*, Ithaca, NY: Cornell University Press, 1985

McCormac, Eugene I., *James K. Polk: A Political Biography*, Berkeley: University of California Press, 1922

McCoy, Charles A., *Polk and the Presidency*, Austin: University of Texas Press, 1960

Pletcher, David M., *The Diplomacy of Annexation: Texas, Oregon, and the Mexican War*, Columbia: University of Missouri Press, 1973

Sellers, Charles, *James K. Polk*, 2 vols., Princeton: Princeton University Press, 1957–66

Sellers, Charles, "The Election of 1844," in *History of American Presidential Elections 1789–1968*, vol. 1, edited by Arthur M. Schlesinger, Jr. and Fred L. Israel, New York: Chelsea House, 1971

Smith, Justin H., *The War with Mexico*, 2 vols., New York: Macmillan, 1919

The only modern scholarly biography of James K. Polk is SELLERS (1957, 1966), a magisterial study that carries Polk's life down to 1846 – part way through his presidency and three years short of his death. Sellers has never completed the biography. Deeply interested in Polk's personal development, Sellers sensitively portrays the frustrations and inner tensions of this rigid, determined, uncommunicative man, who accomplished almost every goal he set for himself as president.

In telling Polk's story Sellers brings to life many of the themes of early American history, including the westward movement, Jeffersonian Republicanism, Manifest Destiny, sectionalism, and especially Jacksonian Democracy. He compares the agrarian Jacksonianism of Polk with the entrepreneurial Jacksonianism of his brother-in-law James Walker to show the ambivalence of the movement, but considers it more the former than the latter. Emphasizing Polk's Jeffersonian upbringing, Sellers stresses his role in defeating the Second Bank of the United States, and calls him the first speaker of the House to try to carry out a party program. Sellers is sympathetic with Polk throughout the first volume.

The positive view continues in the early chapters of volume two as Sellers describes Polk's victory over Henry Clay in the election of 1844. He attributes the victory to Polk's clever handling of the tariff question and Clay's bungling of the Texas issue. A convenient condensed discussion of the election with much the same interpretation may be found in SELLERS (1971). Later in volume two of the biography,

Sellers's sympathy begins to wane. He calls Polk's agrarian philosophy anachronistic and accuses him of racism, chauvinism, and deception in leading the United States into the Mexican War. The biography ends in August 1846 with the congressional debate over the Wilmot Proviso to ban slavery in any land to be acquired from Mexico. The debate ushered in a decade and a half of controversy leading to the Civil War. Sellers concludes by saying that Polk would be the last president to have any hope of coping with the slavery issue, but was too old-fashioned to understand the violence of the emotions that had been aroused.

An older scholarly biography, McCORMAC, ignores Polk's personality and deals only with his political career. Convinced that Polk had been overlooked by historians because he lacked personal magnetism, McCormac set out to prove that he was a capable executive and a great statesman. The result is a long defensive work praising Polk for his legislative accomplishments and his territorial acquisitions. McCormac justifies Polk's policies in dealing with Mexico and Great Britain. Inevitably the book seems very dated today.

Students of Manifest Destiny have differed in assessing Polk. After the Civil War northern historians portrayed him as the tool of a slaveholder conspiracy to add new slave states to the Union, a view that is no longer held. During the surge of patriotism and nationalism following World War I, historians – like McCormac – were more inclined to trust Polk's motives. SMITH, whose two volumes are still the most comprehensive treatment of the Mexican War, calls Mexico the aggressor and applauds Polk for waging war honorably, and for securing both peace and territory from Mexico. This uncritical view has also been rejected.

The anti-war sentiments of the 1960s, and after, spawned attacks on Polk's foreign policy. The best example is HIETALA, who believes that Polk and the American people went to war against Mexico for imperialistic and racist reasons. They sought commercial profits and land for slavery. Southerners wanted to expand slavery; northerners wanted a place to drain off blacks so that they would not migrate to the north. According to Hietala the great myth of Manifest Destiny was that it was necessary in order to spread democracy. Instead, he argues, the United States brought racial discrimination to the new lands. This rather one-sided account has met some resistance.

The best-balanced treatment of Polk and Manifest Destiny is PLETCHER. Instead of considering what was right or wrong, Pletcher raises the question of whether Polk's diplomacy was the most appropriate policy that might have been followed to secure the best interests of the United States. On that basis he faults Polk for having no well-developed strategy in seeking his goals. By relying on bluff and a show of force, he stumbled from crisis to crisis and forced the country to pay a higher price for Manifest Destiny than was necessary. Polk, he believes, would have done better if he had proceeded more deliberately, avoided war, and allowed annexation of the Pacific coast to come gradually, as more and more Americans moved into California.

Two books deal exclusively with Polk as president. McCOY, a political scientist, argues that Polk succeeded as president because he insisted on taking personal control of the government. Although conceding that Polk could be devious, McCoy concludes that he was an excellent diplomat, commander-in-chief, legislator, and party head. BERGERON, a historian, is the latest to attempt to restore Polk's reputation. In a volume for the American Presidency series, he praises Polk for carrying out his vow to be a strong president and for achieving his ambitious goals. Even-handed in his treatment, he makes no attempt to hide Polk's personal limitations or his role in provoking war with Mexico. Although Bergeron depends mainly on secondary sources, he makes effective use of Polk's diary.

DONALD B. COLE

See also Manifest Destiny; Mexican War entries

Population

Acosta-Rodríguez, Antonio, *La población de Luisiana Española, 1763–1803*, Madrid: Ministerio de Asuntos Exteriores, 1979

Anderson, Margo J., *The American Census: A Social History*, New Haven: Yale University Press, 1988

Bean, Lee L., Geraldine P. Mineau, and Douglas L. Anderton, *Fertility Change on the American Frontier: Adaptation and Innovation*, Berkeley: University of California Press, 1990

Bogue, Donald J. with George W. Rumsey and others, *The Population of the United States: Historical Trends and Future Projections*, New York: Free Press, 1985

Cassedy, James H., *Demography in Early America: Beginnings of the Statistical Mind, 1600–1800*, Cambridge, MA: Harvard University Press, 1969

Chudacoff, Howard P., *Mobile Americans: Residential and Social Mobility in Omaha, Nebraska, 1880–1920*, New York: Oxford University Press, 1972

Coale, Ansley J. and Melvin Zelnik, *New Estimates of Fertility and Population in the United States: A Study of Annual White Births from 1855 to 1960*, Princeton: Princeton University Press, 1963

Dobyns, Henry F., *Native American Historical Demography: A Critical Bibliography*, Bloomington: Indiana University Press, 1976

Forster, Colin and Graham S.L. Tucker, *Economic Opportunity and White American Fertility Ratios, 1800–1860*, New Haven: Yale University Press, 1972

Glass, David V. and David E.C. Eversley, *Population in History: Essays in Historical Demography*, London: Arnold, and Chicago: Aldine, 1965

Greene, Evarts B. and Virginia D. Harrington, *American Population Before the Federal Census of 1790*, New York: Columbia University Press, 1932

Greene, Jack P. and J.R. Pole (editors), *Colonial British America: Essays in the New History of the Early Modern Era*, Baltimore: Johns Hopkins University Press, 1984

Greven, Philip J., *Four Generations: Population, Land, and Family in Colonial Andover, Massachusetts*, Ithaca, NY: Cornell University Press, 1970

Lathrop, Barnes F., *Migration into East Texas, 1835–1869: A Study from the United States Census*, Austin: Texas State Historical Association, 1949

Okun, Bernard, *Trends in Birth Rates in the United States since 1870*, Baltimore: Johns Hopkins Press, 1958

Schapiro, Morton O., *Filling up America: An Economic-Demographic Model of Population Growth and Distribution in the 19th-Century United States*, Greenwich, CT: Jai Press, 1985

Sutherland, Stella H., *Population Distribution in Colonial America*, New York: Columbia University Press, 1936

Thompson, Warren S. and P.K. Whelpton, *Population Trends in the United States*, New York: McGraw Hill, 1933

Vinovskis, Maris A. (editor), *Studies in American Historical Demography*, New York: Academic Press, 1979

Wells, Robert V., *The Population of the British Colonies in America Before 1776: A Survey of Census Data*, Princeton: Princeton University Press, 1975

Wells, Robert V., *Uncle Sam's Family: Issues and Perspectives on American Demographic History*, Albany: State University of New York Press, 1985

Yasuba, Yasukichi, *Birth Rates of the White Population in the United States, 1800–1860: An Economic Study*, Baltimore: Johns Hopkins Press, 1962

For about thirty years after the appearance in the mid-1930s of three major works on American population history – GREENE and HARRINGTON, in 1932, THOMPSON and WHELPTON, in 1933, and SUTHERLAND, in 1936 – so little research and writing appeared that in 1979 one writer, Vinovskis, could observe, "most of the work in this field has been done during the past fifteen years", after another, Easterlin, had commented in 1977 that "foreigners" – a Japanese, a Briton and two Australians – "are responsible for several of the most important research contributions in the last two decades". The "foreigners" referred to were Yasuba; Potter in Glass and Eversley; and Forster and Tucker.

One possible reason for this apparent neglect of population history by American historians may well be the excellence of the American Census itself, which sometimes seemingly leaves little for professional historians to do. It is therefore significant that much of the research mentioned was on the pre-Census colonial period. The many publications of the Census Bureau, including its monographs and atlases, are not discussed in detail in this survey.

As is well known, the First Census in 1790 originated in the political requirement in the Constitution for the apportionment of seats in the House of Representatives according to state population. It revealed the useful information that there were as many white males under 16 years as there were over, a fact of great significance for the size of the labour force. Continuous age structure can be found from as early as 1800, and from 1830 the age information enables a consistent series to be constructed to the present day. The 1820 Census began to show occupations and information on manufacturing. Following a special law passed to extend the enquiries, the 1850 Census provided the crucial datum of birthplace, state for native-born Americans, country for foreign-born. Data on agriculture, manufacturing, occupations, immigrant population, urbanization, literacy, religion, household size, amenities and structure, and personal assets, came to be collected and published in increasing quantity and presented with increasing sophistication. (A cartoon in 1860 depicted a census marshal confronting a genteel southern family with the words, "Ah jist wanna know how many av y'll is deaf dumb blind insane and idyotic-likewise how many convicts there is in the family – whaty'all's ages are, especially the old woman and the young ladies – and how many dollars the old gentleman is worth.")

With the appointment of Carroll D. Wright to head the Census Bureau, the 1890 Census became a landmark of great significance, not least for the use it made of an electrical tabulator designed by Dr. Herman Hollerith, able to count "combined facts" and allowing one clerk to tabulate up to 10,000 items per day, thus presaging the pioneering international role of the Census Bureau in the use of computers. The Census incorporated a special enumeration of Indians, and its reports ran to many volumes. Its findings were also presented in 1898 in the remarkable Atlas of the Census compiled by Henry Gannett, a publication astonishing for its detail, cartography, typography, diagrammatic techniques and statistical sophistication. In the late 1950s the Census Bureau commissioned the installation of the first computer designed for mass data-processing, UNIVAC 1, on the University of North Carolina campus at Chapel Hill (and in the process of construction brought the first non-segregated public toilets to that State).

The history of the Census itself has been told in several works, by A.R. Eckler in *The Bureau of the Census* (1972) and Dan Halacy in *Census: 190 Years of Counting America* (1980), and in others published by the Bureau itself, including one in 1900 by Carroll Wright. ANDERSON, a revised version of an earlier edition, is the most recent. The Census Bureau has been not merely a collector and recorder of historical data, but has increasingly become a powerful influence on events and opinions. The 1890 Census provides a good example with its laconic but famous footnote that "there can [now] hardly be said to be a frontier line. In the discussion of its extent and its westward movement it can not therefore any longer have a place in the census reports". Despite allegations to the contrary, the Bureau remained, in principle at least, strictly neutral on contentious issues. However, the persistent undercount of the black and Hispanic population has been one of the many contentious problems faced by the compilers – all the more so because Census findings have enormous effects on resource allocation and policy decisions.

The colonial period presented the greatest challenge to demographic historians because of the seeming lack of statistics. CASSEDY argued that Americans always had a high propensity to count, and that more statistical information is available for colonial America than for most parts of contemporary Europe. He attributed this first to religion but second to the very fact of colonial status; the government in Westminster regularly asked governors for information about colonial population, usually for military reasons. WELLS (1975) compiled and analyzed 124 censuses or counts held in the colonies between 1623 and 1775. He includes all the American colonies, providing information about Canada, Newfoundland, Nova Scotia and the West Indies, as well as

the thirteen colonies which achieved independence in 1783. The materials vary greatly from place to place, however, and bear no relationship to the size or importance of the colony. The worst gaps are for Virginia, with no counts between 1634 and 1669 and, after counts in 1701 and 1703, no more before the Revolution; and for Pennsylvania with no counts at all.

From about 1965 colonial social and demographic history became an extremely fruitful field of research and the outcome was a vast quantity of valuable published work. Much of the writing appeared as articles or as chapters in more general books. Potter's chapter in GREENE and POLE provides a summary of findings up to 1984 and, in footnotes, a detailed listing of the relevant works. Attention at first centred on New England, on which region GREVEN's study was one of the first and may be cited as exemplar. The New England evidence confirmed the view developed in GLASS and EVERSLEY that the natural growth rate of population was not far below Malthusian suppositions. From a quite early date the New England population was self-reproducing. Good food supplies were the key to rapid growth, allowing population to grow despite the rigours of climate and of pioneer life, above all sustaining the health of women of child-bearing age and thus keeping low the infant mortality rate.

The later findings about the Chesapeake area were in sharp contrast, revealing a much longer seasoning period and an appallingly heavy death toll due to climate and disease. It was not until well into the 18th century that this region became self-reproducing. Before that time, it relied for its growth on constant replenishment from outside. Mortality was high and life expectancy correspondingly low. VINOVSKIS offers a representative collection of essays on this region. The findings of ACOSTA-RODRÍGUEZ for the quite separate Spanish colonial development in the Mississippi Valley before the Louisiana Purchase show marked similarities with the Chesapeake experience.

Despite the wealth of Census evidence, no single volume adequately covers the national period, unless one goes back to Thompson and Whelpton. The later part of Potter's essay in Glass and Eversley briefly sets out the parameters and poses the problems. The first seventy years of the national period saw the maintenance of the same rapid rate of population growth as in the colonial period, averaging almost 35 per cent per decade (though with considerable differences between regions and states), a growth rate more than twice that of Britain in the same period. However, since immigration increased mightily in those years, the natural growth rate must have been declining. A regional pattern is clearly observable, with the highest growth rate, not surprisingly, in the areas of new settlement. Not all this differential can be accounted for by migration, and the conclusion must be that natural growth was more rapid at the frontier. This may be explained either negatively because fertility was lower and mortality higher in the longer-settled, sometimes urban, areas of the east, or positively because fertility was higher at the frontier, encouraged by land abundance.

After the Civil War, the growth rate fell to around 25 per cent per decade, despite the even higher level of immigration, indicating a continuing fall in the natural growth rate, but still remaining at a higher level than that in contemporary Europe.

Some of the literature has been greatly concerned, perhaps excessively so, with this fertility differential. Differing from Potter's emphasis on the negative influences of urbanization, YASUBA's highly sophisticated and elegant analysis stressed the positive aspects of frontier society, arguing that ease of access to land and high human fertility were causally connected, though acknowledging also that urbanization and industrialization brought higher social expectations, with postponement of marriage or restriction of family size within marriage. FORSTER and TUCKER came down firmly in support of the view that high frontier fertility was directly related to land abundance, resultant economic opportunity and early marriage. SCHAPIRO also supported the land availability argument. Frontier farmers continued to have relatively larger families, even though frontier birth rates did decline; at the same time an increasing share of the population was in more densely settled areas. The demographers COALE and ZELNIK also concur in the view that the birth rate was declining in these years in a work that will probably appeal to demographers rather than historians.

OKUN attempted to identify and explain the secular trends of birth rates for both white and black populations, and reaches different conclusions for each. He argues that, overriding the marked regional and state differences, the major cause of the declining trend differed for the two groups. For whites he found a change in reproductive habits within both urban and rural areas; for blacks it was the shift of habitation from country to town that was the decisive influence. Finally, and most recently, on this subject, BEAN, MINEAU and ANDERTON use the detailed data available from the Mormon Historical Demographic Project to analyze the fertility patterns in 19th- and early 20th-century Utah.

Internal migration and population mobility present problems of their own. LATHROP used the place of birth date of the 1850 and 1860 Censuses to trace the migration routes of the families which he examined in East Texas; by noting the birth places of parents and of subsequently born children he was able to map the families' westward movement. CHUDACOFF's study of Omaha is one of several to emphasize the very high volatility of migrant Americans, moving as often as at least once every ten years.

WELLS (1985) provides a concise introduction to the literature and to the main variables that have to be considered – fertility, migration and mortality – in a manner intended for an undergraduate readership interested in social history. BOGUE's encyclopedic volume is mainly concerned with the years since World War II and perhaps gives the best possible illustration of the starting point of this survey, that the United States Census is so comprehensive that it leaves little for the historian to do other than compile, analyze and reiterate.

Most of the works already discussed differentiate between the demographic history of the various ethnic groups making up American society. DOBYNS is one of several studies emanating from the Newberry Center which are transforming the understanding of the demographic history of the Indian tribes, postulating a tenfold larger native population at the time of Columbus than had generally been assumed.

JIM POTTER

Populism (People's Party)

Goodwyn, Lawrence, *Democratic Promise: The Populist Moment in America*, New York: Oxford University Press, 1976; abridged as *The Populist Moment: A Short History of the Agrarian Revolt*, 1978

Hicks, John D., *The Populist Revolt: A History of the Farmers' Alliance and the People's Party*, Minneapolis: University of Minnesota Press, 1931

Hofstadter, Richard, *The Age of Reform: From Bryan to FDR*, New York: Knopf, 1955; London: Cape, 1962

Jones, Stanley, *The Presidential Election of 1896*, Madison: University of Wisconsin Press, 1964

McMath, Robert C., Jr., *American Populism: A Social History, 1877–1898*, New York: Hill and Wang, 1993

Nugent, Walter T.K., *The Tolerant Populists: Kansas Populism and Nativism*, Chicago: University of Chicago Press, 1963

Palmer, Bruce, *"Man over Money": The Southern Populist Critique of American Capitalism*, Chapel Hill: University of North Carolina Press, 1980

Pollack, Norman, *The Populist Response to Industrial America: Midwestern Populist Thought*, Cambridge, MA: Harvard University Press, 1962

Pollack, Norman, *The Just Polity: Populism, Law, and Human Welfare*, Urbana: University of Illinois Press, 1987

Woodward, C. Vann, *Tom Watson: Agrarian Rebel*, New York: Macmillan, 1938

Despite the widespread interest which Populism has aroused, few historians have completed general accounts of the movement. For over four decades HICKS remained the only comprehensive history of the Populist crusade. Generally sympathetic in tone, it presents the movement as a rational reaction by farmers to the economic hardship that they faced. It also places Populism within the mainstream of American liberalism, suggesting that it helped to inspire some of the great reforms of the Progressive Era and the 1920s. Subsequent research has questioned several aspects of Hicks's thesis, including his emphasis upon the economic origins of agrarian discontent. But, six decades after its initial publication, it remains a highly informative and influential account.

GOODWYN was the second general history of the movement to appear. In a vigorous and well-researched narrative, it presents Populism as a dynamic and radical movement. Particularly informative about the origins of Populism in the South, it skilfully shows how the creation of the People's Party in these states was inspired, in part, by the failure of farmers' attempts to operate marketing co-operatives. It also shows why southern Populists were so committed to reforms such as the sub-treasury plan and the introduction of a fiat currency. The treatment of the western states is less satisfactory, and too much inclined to dismiss Populism in these areas as a sham movement which was largely to blame for the demise of the People's Party in 1896. But overall this is a superb study, which any serious student of Populism should consult.

More recently, McMATH has provided a succinct, clear and informative introduction to the history of agrarian protest in the late 19th century. Synthesizing much of the secondary literature that has appeared in the past two decades, he offers a balanced and judicious account of Populism, which, unlike Goodwyn, gives as much weight to the movement in the West as in the South. McMath also traces the social, political and cultural roots of Populism, rather than presenting it solely as the product of economic problems.

These general histories are supplemented by a large number of detailed works on specific aspects of the movement. Several scholars have focused on the character of Populist thought. HOFSTADTER provides a highly critical analysis in his lucid, elegant and insightful book. He points to some of the inconsistencies and contradictions in the Populists' economic complaints, and highlights the farmers' ambivalent attitude towards commercialism. More controversially, he argues that Populists were guilty of anti-semitism and nativism. Hofstadter's work should be read with a degree of caution. Although some of his conclusions appear rather impressionistic, and his entire account is based on a relatively limited range of sources, his analysis is both original and suggestive, and provides a valuable corrective to some of the less critical accounts.

NUGENT also focuses on Populist attitudes to ethnic minorities in his examination of the movement in Kansas. He argues that, far from being guilty of nativism, the Populists were more tolerant of foreign minorities than most Americans in the late 19th century. He also draws attention to the fact that many immigrants participated in the agrarian crusade. As the author is careful to emphasize, his conclusions relate solely to the movement in Kansas. But his work is a model of meticulous research which goes a long way to disproving the charges of nativism that have been levelled against the Populists.

Other writers focus on the character of the Populists' economic thought. POLLACK (1962) praises the Populists for formulating a radical critique of American capitalism, and argues that there were many similarities between Populist philosophy and Marxian socialism. He also draws attention to the sympathy with which Populists viewed the plight of industrial workers. However, POLLACK (1987) draws upon a close textual analysis of the writings of a few Populist leaders to give a revised interpretation. Rather than opposing capitalism, he suggests, Populists merely wanted to limit the power of monopolies and to secure a more democratic form of capitalism. PALMER, for his part, argues that the movement was fundamentally divided over economic policy. While a few recognised the need to replace capitalism, the majority of Populists were only prepared to support moderate financial reform. Palmer shows, in turn, how these intellectual differences undermined the movement in 1896, with many of the less sophisticated Populists foolishly believing that "Free Silver" would be sufficient to solve their economic problems. Overall, the book makes a valuable contribution to our understanding of southern Populism. It succeeds in highlighting and clarifying the key concepts in the movement's ideology, even if the author's emphasis upon providing a composite picture of Populist thought prevents him from discussing the views of specific leaders in great detail.

Other scholars have focused on prominent figures within the movement. WOODWARD's study of Tom Watson remains the most influential biography of a Populist leader. Not only a superb account of Watson's life, it also provides tremendous insight into the dynamics of southern Populism. The book was written over five decades ago and, as the author himself admits, some aspects of its argument now appear questionable: for instance, it takes the Populists' complaints about economic exploitation too much at face-value and exaggerates the farmers' commitment to biracial cooperation. But the book is a masterpiece of humane scholarship and remains an indispensable source on agrarian discontent.

Historians agree that the decision by the People's Party to support William Jennings Bryan, the Democratic nominee, in 1896 was one of the critical moments in the history of Populism. JONES provides the fullest and clearest account of that remarkable presidential election. He explains why "Free Silver" became the dominant issue in the campaign, and shows how its emergence led the Populists to throw in their lot with the Democrats. He also examines why Bryan lost, a defeat which effectively sealed the fate of Populism. More generally, in emphasizing the strengths of the Republicans and Democrats, Jones highlights the many obstacles that faced Populists and other third party movements during the Gilded Age.

PHILIP J. CULLIS

See also Agrarian Discontent

Poverty

Burton, C. Emory, *The Poverty Debate: Politics and the Poor in America*, Westport, CT: Greenwood Press, 1992

Chalfant, H. Paul, *Sociology of Poverty in the United States: An Annotated Bibliography*, Westport, CT: Greenwood Press, 1985

Dudley, William (editor), *Poverty: Opposing Viewpoints*, St. Paul: Greenhaven Press, 1988

Flynt, J. Wayne, *Poor but Proud: Alabama's Poor Whites*, Tuscaloosa: University of Alabama Press, 1989

Flynt, J. Wayne and Dorothy S. Flynt (editors), *Southern Poor Whites: A Selected Annotated Bibliography of Published Sources*, New York: Garland, 1981

Harrington, Michael, *The Other America: Poverty in the United States*, New York: Macmillan, 1962; Harmondsworth: Penguin, 1963

Jones, Jacqueline, *The Dispossessed: America's Underclasses from the Civil War to the Present*, New York: Basic Books, 1992

Mead, Lawrence M., *The New Politics of Poverty: The Nonworking Poor in America*, New York: Basic Books, 1992

Patterson, James T., *America's Struggle Against Poverty, 1900–1980*, Cambridge, MA: Harvard University Press, 1981, revised as *America's Struggle Against Poverty, 1900–1994*, 1994

Thomas, Susan L., *Gender and Poverty*, New York: Garland, 1994

The paradox of a land renowned worldwide for its prosperity but unable to solve the problem of intractable poverty has attracted considerable attention from scholars representing many disciplines. Two of the best surveys of poverty in America are by Jones and Patterson. JONES is the more recent and inclusive, covering the years from Civil War to the 1990s. She traces American poverty to the South in the aftermath of the Civil War. Landless blacks and whites were absorbed into the system of tenancy and sharecropping. Deprived of both property and alternative industrial employment, crippled by illiteracy, and quickly deserted by Congress, courts, and president, freedmen found their newly won freedom a chimera. Whites joined them in poverty in ever increasing numbers due to higher land taxes, fluctuations in demand for and prices of cotton, poor health and education, and lack of alternative jobs. Together southern poor whites and poor blacks experienced the longest downward economic cycle in American history, a plunge that lasted from the 1860s until the 1940s. Jones also discusses migration patterns that dispersed poor blacks and whites, thus nationalizing the problem. She discusses ghettos, homelessness, and the modern American "underclass." PATTERSON focuses exclusively on the 20th century and tends to emphasize welfare as a way of eliminating poverty more than the causes of indigence. His discussions of the origins of the welfare state and especially the New Deal in the 1930s and the War on Poverty in the 1960s are particularly illuminating. His description of the explosion of welfare clients during the 1970s and 1980s and the generational dependence on welfare are important in understanding the growing revulsion against the system among liberal and conservative intellectuals as well as the general public.

Two annotated bibliographies provide guidance to the extensive literature on the subject. CHALFANT takes a more sociological perspective, examining social stratification, ideology, economic and racial dimensions of poverty, status issues, poverty among ethnic minorities, alleviation and welfare strategies and correlates of poverty such as education, crime, law, family, housing, physical and mental health. Notations are lengthy. FLYNT and FLYNT focus their annotated bibliography on a single region and race. It is an important corrective to the stereotype that most poverty in America consists of ethnic minorities, particularly blacks, Hispanics, and Native Americans. Actually two-thirds of America's poor are whites – and they are disproportionately located in the South. Of the four major concentrations of poverty in America – Appalachia, the historic Black Belt and Delta regions, the Rio Grande Valley, and the western Indian reservations – the first three are in the South. Items annotated deal with economics, education, health, migration, urbanization, agriculture, race, religion, women, politics, folk culture, Appalachia, and the Ozarks.

The publication of HARRINGTON in 1962 was a seminal event in the politicization of the poverty debate in America. A socialist associated at various times with *The Catholic Worker* and the Workers Defense League, Harrington described an America seldom viewed either by other Americans or the world. The "other America" was a land of persistent poverty, hopelessness, and social disintegration. The poor were largely invisible and chronically unemployed or underemployed. This book is not so important for its data or analysis as for its timing and impact. Appearing shortly after John F. Kennedy took office as president, the book helped galvanize him into action. Shocked already by what he had seen in West Virginia during the 1960 Democratic primaries, he used the book to spark a national debate on poverty. After the president's

assassination in 1963, President Lyndon B. Johnson relied on the public debate and nationwide publicity generated by the book to launch his War on Poverty.

FLYNT (1989) is a study of Alabama poverty which explores the impact of poverty on a single ethnic group in one state over nearly two centuries. It examines the antebellum sources of poverty in landlessness and the way in which the Civil War compounded the problem. It also examines a series of occupations – tenant farming, iron and steel, coal mining, textile work – that absorbed most poor whites into the economy. Other chapters explore religion, folkways, family relations, racial views, the impact of the New Deal, and the War on Poverty.

THOMAS adds a gender component to the discussion of poverty. One of the most troubling aspects of poverty has been its feminization during the 1980s. This has had a particularly profound effect on children. Even though only one of seven Americans is poor, the proportion of poor children is one in five. Thomas explains why poverty most affects women and children and the long-range consequences of gender-based poverty.

BURTON provides a useful standard of measurement for poverty in America. Some countries use caloric intake to determine poverty rates, but the United States defines poverty by the extent of income necessary to provide minimal existence (food, housing, clothing, and other necessities). He also estimates the extent of poverty, the nature of the permanent underclass, homelessness, the so-called culture of poverty, the relationship between welfare and dependency, and theories of reform.

MEAD estimates the societal cost of the non-working poor. Welfare recipients refuse to take available jobs because of many factors: low wages, habitual dependency, and health and education inadequacies. He also explores the growing resistance to welfare among middle and upper classes and the prospects and strategies for welfare reform. DUDLEY's slim volume is part of a series that features conflicting viewpoints on urgent public policy issues. The work provides alternating expert views on rates of poverty, causes, societal attitudes, homelessness, ethnic over-representation, and the success and failure of intervention strategies.

WAYNE FLYNT

Powell, John Wesley   1834–1902
Explorer, geologist and regional planner

Darrah, William Culp, *Powell of the Colorado*, Princeton: Princeton University Press, 1951

Goetzmann, William H., *Exploration and Empire: The Explorer and the Scientist in the Winning of the American West*, New York: Knopf, 1966

Meadows, Paul, *John Wesley Powell: Frontiersman of Science*, Lincoln: University of Nebraska Press, 1952

Smith, Henry Nash, *Virgin Land: The American West as Symbol and Myth*, Cambridge, MA: Harvard University Press, 1950

Stegner, Wallace, *Beyond the Hundredth Meridian: John Wesley Powell and the Second Opening of the West*, Boston: Houghton Mifflin, 1954

Utah Historical Quarterly: John Wesley Powell and the Colorado River Centennial Edition, 37(2), 1969

Worster, Donald, *Rivers of Empire: Water, Aridity, and the Growth of the American West*, New York: Pantheon, 1985

Worster, Donald, *An Unsettled Country: Changing Landscapes of the American West* Albuquerque: University of New Mexico Press, 1994

John Wesley Powell is a central figure in the history of the American West. Raised by English Methodist parents in Wisconsin and Illinois, Powell fought in the Civil War (losing his right arm in the process) before leading several expeditions throughout the West. A geologist, naturalist, and pioneering ethnologist, Powell was perhaps above all else an expert organizer and administrator, and he demonstrated these traits in his time as head of the Bureau of Ethnology and the United States Geological Survey. Given his importance, the literature on Powell is rather sparse and scattered. Apart from the recent work of Donald Worster (who is currently working on a biography of Powell which is due to be published by 2000), one must rely mainly on a spate of publications from the 1950s and 1960s.

The best of the more extended biographies is STEGNER. He views Powell as a rational, scientific thinker who saw the West as a region that differed markedly from the rest of the nation and therefore required a different form of planning and settlement. He discusses Powell's opposition to extending the geometric, grid-like division of the land characterized by the Land Ordinance of 1785, which was unsuited to the arid region of the West. Instead, he proposed a settlement pattern that provided settlers with access to water and placed a limitation on acreage. For Stegner, Powell's vision was one that combined scientific rationalism with democratic idealism; one in which benevolent rational planning could help to create a Jeffersonian society within the environmental limits set by the arid West. It is a vision that replaced economic individualism and laissez-faire capitalism with cooperative, locally controlled democratic communities. Although Stegner's account verges on being hagiographic, crediting Powell with everything from the New Deal and the welfare state in America, to remaking cultural anthropology, it is an immensely readable work and provides by far the finest introduction to Powell and his historical significance.

Though impressively researched, DARRAH is less useful than Stegner, and gives short shrift to the historical context within which Powell's life took place. A geologist by training, Darrah gives a largely narrative account, with little analytical depth or historical insight. Somewhat melodramatic in style, he tends to portray Powell as a mythical, Daniel Boone-like character – a simple homespun man with boundless energy and an insatiable curiosity and sense of adventure. Nevertheless, it is a detailed, careful, and substantial work which gives a close-up view of Powell's life. For the reader unfamiliar with the history of the American West, however, it has severe limitations, and needs to be supplemented by Stegner and Worster.

Less ambitious than Darrah, MEADOWS does not attempt to be comprehensive, and concentrates on "the lesser goal of recounting Powell's work as a scientific trapper, as a restless and gifted frontiersman of American science." It is broken up by many lengthy quotations in an attempt to allow Powell to speak for himself or to see how his contemporaries viewed him. Meadows delves into some of the murkier depths of Powell's philosophical writing, but is rather reluctant to criticize some of its more cranky and bewildering manifestations. For those interested in some of the intricacies of Powell's intellect, however, Meadows provides a thoughtful and relatively accessible account.

Henry Nash Smith and William Goetzmann assign Powell a small but important part in their broader histories of the West. In his classic and still valuable study, SMITH casts Powell as a heroic realist, who stood against vociferous western boosters such as Horace Greeley, Frederick Jackson Turner, and Charles Dana Wilber (who dreamed that rain would follow the plow). GOETZMANN takes a similar position, arguing that Powell was an outstanding representative of a group of scientific and realistic men who "sought to put the explorer's experience to practical use in promoting the fair, efficient, and socially useful development of the West." Although Goetzmann's book, as the title implies, is redolent with the "great white men who conquered and tamed the wilderness" approach to western history, he provides an engaging and useful summary of Powell's life and the impact of his scientific achievements. He also views Powell and others of his ilk as the precursors of the Progressive movement, with its penchant for rational, scientific planning and its reformist ideals, most of which were propelled by middle-class values. This is reflected in Powell's plan for "civilizing" the Indians – a plan that was merely a sophisticated version of the 1887 Dawes Severalty Act which attempted to Americanize Indians by imbuing them with a Protestant work ethic, and giving them an individualistic rather than a communal orientation.

The UTAH HISTORICAL QUARTERLY's special issue devoted to Powell has several interesting articles, the most useful of them by Don and Catherine Fowler, who examine Powell's career as an anthropologist. As well as providing a narrative account of Powell's work among various Indian tribes in the Southwest, the Fowlers examine his influence as head of the Bureau of Ethnology, and his efforts to classify and analyze Indian languages. They argue that Powell's place in the history of anthropology, and of science in general, rests largely on his organizational capabilities rather than on any profound theoretical insights. The volume also contains a brief biography by Darrah and several articles which examine various expeditions and the geological surveys in more detail.

The most recent and most promising work on Powell has come from environmental historian WORSTER (1985, 1994) who picks up where Stegner left off, weaving Powell into the broader tapestry of 19th-century American history. He agrees with Stegner and others that Powell presented a more realistic, environmentally sensitive view of western settlement than the boosterism which dominated the era, and he sees in Powell's ideas much that is still relevant today. However, unlike earlier writers, Worster also sees the danger in a vision that involved the use of scientific and rational planning to control and exploit the natural environment of the West. Also, unlike Goetzmann,

Worster argues that Powell's vision was in many ways the very antithesis of Progressivism. Where Powell dealt with the West in local and regional terms, he was strongly opposed by such figures as Theodore Roosevelt and Gifford Pinchot, who felt that the West had to fit in with their grander national vision. Worster's relatively brief but insightful work on Powell is essential reading for anyone interested in Powell's significance for western history, and his forthcoming biography of Powell will be eagerly awaited.

FRANK ZELKO

Pragmatism

Ayer, A.J., *The Origins of Pragmatism: Studies in the Philosophy of Charles Sanders Peirce and William James*, London: Macmillan, and San Francisco: Freeman Cooper, 1968

Diggins, John Patrick, *The Promise of Pragmatism: Modernism and the Crisis of Knowledge and Authority*, Chicago: University of Chicago Press, 1994

Kuklick, Bruce, *The Rise of American Philosophy: Cambridge, Massachusetts 1860–1930*, New Haven: Yale University Press, 1977

Moore, Edward C., *American Pragmatism: Peirce, James and Dewey*, New York: Columbia University Press, 1961

Rorty, Richard, *The Consequences of Pragmatism: Essays, 1972–1980*, Minneapolis: University of Minnesota Press, and Brighton: Harvester Press, 1982

West, Cornel, *The American Evasion of Philosophy: A Genealogy of Pragmatism*, Madison: University of Wisconsin Press, 1989

White, Morton (editor), *Pragmatism and the American Mind: Essays and Reviews in Philosophy and Intellectual History*, New York: Oxford University Press, 1973

Critics of pragmatism seek to examine the term either in its manifestation as an American trend of philosophy in the late 19th century, or in its re-emergence as a dominant theoretical position in recent years, albeit in a slightly altered form. MOORE is "an examination of the basic doctrines of pragmatism", in which he stresses the differences between the three chief pragmatist thinkers, Charles Sanders Peirce, William James and John Dewey, as well as their collective importance. His detailed study of a particular aspect of each of the writers (Peirce's "theory of reality", James's "notion of truth" and Dewey's "concept of the good") is framed by sketching in three of the most profound areas of influence for the genesis and growth of pragmatism in America: science, religion and philosophy.

The British analytic philosopher AYER understands pragmatism to have "fairly deep roots in the history of [Western] philosophy." In this book he contrasts the "dynamic" thought of Peirce and James in his aim "to expound and criticize ... the central themes of pragmatism." Eschewing all secondary material relating to pragmatism, Ayer philosophically disputes certain areas of thought espoused by both thinkers, reserving particularly harsh criticism for James's theories of truth and radical empiricism.

The series of essays by WHITE combine philosophical analysis, intellectual history and cultural criticism in order to describe and evaluate the far-reaching implications of the "Golden Age" of American philosophy. White is sympathetic to the "historical spirit of the nineteenth century", stressing his kinship with the concerns of James, Dewey and George Santayana and reserving his criticism for those "narrower" philosophical studies which neglect the social and historical formation of ideas. The book falls into three parts: the first dealing with "general aspects of American intellectual history"; the second paying particular attention to pragmatism (including one essay which defends James against the criticisms of Ayer); and the third in which he attempts to link philosophical studies with "some important problems concerning the central institutions and disciplines" of American culture, including considerations of education, law and religion.

In his intellectual history of the Harvard philosophers (a group which includes all the major exponents of pragmatism except Dewey), KUKLICK "charts the history of philosophic thinking in the United States as typified and dominated by Harvard" between the years of his study. He begins by exploring the difficulties faced by these philosophers in their attempts to reconcile religious belief with the assault of Darwinian science. Not until the appointment of James and Josiah Royce at Harvard was such a reconciliation made, the truth of a belief understood by James as "a function of its practical significance." While Kuklick detects that the growth of pragmatism was indebted to the early thought of Peirce, the idealistic character of Harvard Pragmatism was a distinct development of it. He goes on to claim that the professionalization of philosophy at Harvard in the early years of the 20th century was at least partially connected with "the paradigmatic achievements of Harvard Pragmatism."

DIGGINS also explores pragmatism from the perspective of the intellectual historian, using "one author to interrogate another so that ideas speak to our condition as well as theirs", in an attempt to re-evaluate not only the early pragmatists (James, Peirce and Dewey), but also their predecessors and opponents. He explores the crisis of modernism which, according to the author, manifested itself as the "crisis of knowledge and authority" for the pragmatists, but he goes on to take issue with their tendency to subordinate reflective history to future-directed experience. In order to examine this tension, Diggins uses Henry Adams as a checking and restraining force to the pragmatist directive which promises "to relieve such anxiety by showing us not what to think but how to think and how to move confidently ahead." In the light of the catastrophic events of the 20th century Diggins suggests that historical memory can provide pragmatism with "a little more humility."

In the introduction to his collection of essays, RORTY states his purpose as an attempt "to draw consequences from a pragmatist theory about truth." Rorty understands the pragmatists to have broken from what he calls the "presuppositions of Philosophy" (the search for indubitable grounds for knowledge) in order to conceive of knowledge as "a tool for coping with reality." This line of argument is woven through a series of essays on American and European thinkers (including such luminaries as Dewey, Stanley Cavell, Martin Heidegger, Ludwig Wittgenstein and Jacques Derrida). Whereas vestiges of metaphysics can be detected in the work of the early prag-matists, he claims that the Post-Philosophy ethos of neo-pragmatism has surrendered all of its epistemological aspira-tions and instead seeks to play "vocabularies and cultures off against each other" in order to "produce new and better ways of talking and acting."

Motivated by his disenchantment with fellow American intellectuals in the 1980s, WEST reflects upon the pragmatist tradition in the hope that it can "reinvigorate our moribund academic life." He charts "the emergence, development, decline, and resurgence" of pragmatism, from what he discerns as its roots in the writings of Ralph Waldo Emerson through to "the diverse and heterogeneous tradition" of pragmatist writings, a tradition which includes, among others, W.E.B. Du Bois and W.V. Quine. West detects that "the evasion of epis-temology-centered philosophy" does not represent "an evasion of serious thought and moral action", but instead "results in a conception of philosophy as a form of cultural criticism" which is distinctly American in character. It is from within this American "progressive tradition", rather than through the adoption of European theorists, that West sees the possibility of regenerating "social forces empowering the disadvantaged, degraded and dejected."

MARTIN HALLIWELL

Presidency

Barber, James D., *The Presidential Character: Predicting Performance in the White House*, Englewood Cliffs, NJ: Prentice Hall, 1972, 4th edition, 1992

Corwin, Edward S., *The President: Office and Powers*, New York: New York University Press, 1940, 5th edition, revised by Randall W. Bland, Theodore T. Hindson, and Jack W. Peltason, 1984

Cunliffe, Marcus, *American Presidents and the Presidency*, New York: American Heritage, 1968; London: Eyre and Spottiswoode, 1969

Hess, Stephen, *Organizing the Presidency*, Washington, DC: Brookings Institution, 1976

Lowi, Theodore J., *The Personal President: Power Invested, Promise Unfulfilled*, Ithaca, NY: Cornell University Press, 1985

McDonald, Forrest, *The American Presidency: An Intellectual History*, Lawrence: University Press of Kansas, 1994

Neustadt, Richard E., *Presidential Power: The Politics of Leadership*, New York: Wiley, 1960; revised as *Presidential Power: The Politics of Leadership from Roosevelt to Reagan*, New York: Free Press, 1990

Pessen, Edward, *The Log Cabin Myth: The Social Backgrounds of the Presidents*, New Haven and London: Yale University Press, 1984

Rose, Richard, *The Postmodern President: The White House Meets the World*, Chatham, NJ: Chatham House, 1988, revised as *The Postmodern President: George Bush Meets the World*, 1991

Schlesinger, Arthur M., Jr., *The Imperial Presidency*, Boston: Houghton Mifflin, 1973, London: Deutsch, 1974; with new epilogue, Houghton Mifflin, 1989

Skowronek, Stephen, *The Politics Presidents Make: Leadership from John Adams to George Bush*, Cambridge, MA: Belknap Press of Harvard University Press, 1993

The presidency has attracted the attention of numerous histo-rians, biographers, political scientists and constitutional author-ities – as well as a steady stream of more popular and gossipy accounts. Only a few of the more distinctive and enduring works can be discussed here.

CORWIN has been accepted for many years as the stan-dard constitutional analysis of the office. He discusses the different conceptions of the office, the constitutional provisions regarding election, succession and impeachment, appointing and removal powers, and presidential prerogatives in foreign affairs and as commander-in-chief, as well as the constitutional basis of the president's relations with Congress.

Historians, and political scientists too, have examined the presidency in the long perspective of its evolution over two centuries. Surprisingly, there is no really satisfactory and up-to-date single-volume history of the presidency. McDONALD's stimulating study fills part of the gap, but, as he himself makes clear, this is essentially a "history of the idea of the presi-dency" – how it was born and implemented and how it has evolved. The first part deals with the roots of the presidency in earlier political, legal and constitutional thought, and the second deals with the establishment of the office – not only the drafting and ratification of the Constitution, but its shaping during the presidencies of Washington and Jefferson. The final part examines its evolution from Andrew Jackson to the present. Perhaps the least successful section of the book, it adopts a topical approach, and covers the presidency in rela-tion to the law, administration, Congress, and foreign affairs, and also the symbolic role of the office. McDonald's neo-conservative position comes through clearly, but, for all the flaws in its record, he pays tribute to the presidency as a great and successful institution.

In characteristically elegant and beguiling style, CUNLIFFE discusses the themes of both development and discontinuity in the history of the presidency. His account is enriched by extensive contemporary quotation, and by skilfully drawn pen portraits of presidential personalities. Most importantly, Cunliffe shows how the presidency is a contested office in the sense that there has never been unanimity about its scope.

PESSEN is concerned with the kind of men who have become president. Always sceptical about the degree of upward mobility in America, he sets out to puncture the log-cabin-to-White-House myth. After an examination of the social and economic circumstances of the presidents' families, and of their own pre-White House careers, he concludes that presidents have come predominantly from the upper reaches of American society. As successful products of the prevailing economic and social order, they have usually become defenders of that order, once they are in office. According to Pessen, even "liberal" presidents have been essentially conservative, in their aim to preserve the existing order by remedying its faults.

A very different picture emerges from SKOWRONEK, which is based on a very different methodology. This is the most ambitious and elaborate recent analysis of presidential leadership in its broad historical context. Skowronek is a political scientist, with strong historical leanings, and, although historians may find his approach too schematic for their tastes, and his prose dense and sometimes jargon-ridden, they should not ignore the importance of his work. In contrast to Pessen, he sees presidents as almost inevitable disturbers of the status quo, as each in turn seeks to undo or revise the work of his predecessor and to put his own stamp on the exercise of the office. Skowronek suggests that the most effective comparisons may not be between presidents from the same period. Why not, he says, compare Truman with Van Buren, Eisenhower with William Henry Harrison, Reagan with Andrew Jackson? He sets up an elaborate tripartite analytical model, based on the constitutional, organisational and political demands of the presidency, and tests the performance of a variety of presidents, "great" and not so great, against its criteria.

Political scientists – and some historians, too – have contributed to a distinct body of literature on the modern presidency. NEUSTADT demonstrates that understanding the constitutional powers of the presidency is not the most helpful way of explaining why some presidents enjoyed more success than others. He locates presidential success in a particular, persuasive style of leadership, which lays emphasis on the tactics necessary to overcome the constitutional constraints on the presidential office. Neustadt started a new trend in presidential analysis, moving away from legalism and placing a new emphasis on the realities of presidential behaviour. But he seemed to imply that presidents can exercise influence even when opposed by institutional and ideological vested interests. He also seems to assume that presidents were, almost by definition, guardians of the public interest, and he does not seem to have envisaged that less worthy individuals might be elected to office, and would seek to enforce their will by means far removed from Neustadt's conception of persuasion.

The concern with the tactics of presidential success also focused attention on the psychology of presidential leadership. BARBER highlights the importance of presidents' personalities as major influences on the style and effectiveness of their presidencies. He developed an influential typology of the personal traits of presidents and he uses it to predict success in office. Despite the crudities inherent in reducing complex personalities to fit a few broad categories, Barber has ensured that attention to individual character and personality form an important element in studies of the presidency.

The idea of a powerful, activist presidency has been widely accepted only during the last sixty years and, until the 1970s, scholars gave little attention to the problem of how to impose a presidential presence on an executive organisation which has grown too large for personal supervision. HESS produced the first systematic account of how modern presidents, from Roosevelt to Nixon, have organized themselves. He discusses how presidents tackle such common problems as personnel selection, gathering information, relations with Congress, and relations between the White House and the Cabinet departments and other agencies. Hess was among the first to link the expansion of the presidency as an institution to its malfunctioning.

The debacle of Vietnam encouraged a reappraisal of the presidency and its role in the political system. SCHLESINGER offered an interpretation of the office which traced its development from an institution apparently subordinate to Congress to an institution which assumed and accumulated power at a rapid rate in the 1960s and 1970s. Schlesinger's analysis is an indictment of both presidential duplicity and congressional subservience. He focuses on the conduct of foreign policy but many have drawn wider lessons from his argument. It has also been noted that, as a liberal Democrat and adviser to President Kennedy, Schlesinger's concerns about presidential abuses of power in the foreign policy field emerged after he left the White House, and increased when Kennedy's arch enemy, Richard Nixon, took office.

Writing in the 1980s, LOWI suggests that, in a sense, the American people have, since the 1930s, had an implicit understanding with the president. In exchange for getting more power and support from the people, the president is supposed to ensure that the people get what they want from the government. According to Lowi, the use of the mass media has allowed presidents to amass tremendous personal power directly from the people. Presidents tell voters what they think their needs are, and are judged directly by ballots and opinion polls. The "personal presidency" has a direct relationship with the electorate and is held accountable by it for the ills of the nation.

ROSE draws readers' attention to the reality that the age of American hegemony is over, and that, in an interdependent world, a president cannot always do what he wants. The persuasive skills that Neustadt thought so essential to the domestic policy arena are, in the late 20th century, equally relevant to the international arena. While the responsibilities of the presidency are larger than ever before, Rose reminds us that the capacity to discharge them is more limited, because of changes that have occurred outside the United States and outside any president's control.

ROBERT WILLIAMS

See also entries on individual presidents

Press *see* **Newspapers and Magazines**

Prisons and Asylums

Freedman, Estelle B., *Their Sisters' Keepers: Women's Prison Reform in America, 1830–1930*, Ann Arbor: University of Michigan Press, 1981

Grob, Gerald N., *The Mad among Us: A History of the Care of America's Mentally Ill*, New York: Free Press, 1994

Hirsch, Adam Jay, *The Rise of the Penitentiary: Prisons and Punishment in Early America*, New Haven: Yale University Press, 1992

Jimenez, Mary Ann, *Changing Faces of Madness: Early American Attitudes and Treatment of the Insane*, Hanover, NH: University Press of New England, 1987

Pisciotta, Alexander W., *Benevolent Repression: Social Control and the American Reformatory-Prison Movement*, New York: New York University Press, 1994

Rafter, Nicole Hahn, *Partial Justice: Women in State Prisons, 1800–1935*, Boston: Northeastern University Press, 1985

Rothman, David J., *The Discovery of the Asylum: Social Order and Disorder in the New Republic*, Boston: Little Brown, 1971, revised 1990

Rothman, David J., *Conscience and Convenience: The Asylum and Its Alternatives in Progressive America*, Boston: Little Brown, 1980

The problem of punishment has preoccupied Americans for centuries, and, as a result, there exists a large body of primary and secondary literature on this subject. Many historians see the late 18th and early 19th centuries as a period of great ideological innovation regarding incarceration and institutionalization in the United States. Similarly, eugenic prison science and psychological explanations for deviant behaviour influenced policies for inmates in the early 20th century.

Controversy surrounds the origins of the penitentiary, but the standard work for over two decades has been ROTHMAN (1971). This study explores the social context of the "invention" of penitentiaries, asylums, almshouses, orphanages, and reformatories after the 1820s, and the reform ideology of the Jacksonians, who were disillusioned with the deterrent approach adopted by penal reformers after the Revolution; their belief in the environmental causes of crime and delinquency; and their view of the penitentiary and the asylum as novel solutions to a crisis of disorder wrought by emergent capitalism, urban-industrial changes, and the rise of wage labour. Rothman locates the origins of the penitentiary movement in the debates over competing systems of incarceration: the Auburn or congregate system versus the Pennsylvania or separate system, both of which sought to reform their charges. Officials organized the penitentiary and the asylum around the doctrines of isolation, obedience and productive labour, resulting in a quasi-military routine permeating every aspect of institutional life. Rothman charts the failure of the reformers' utopian goals and the descent into custodialism in the second half of the 19th century. By the 1850s the institutions had become dumping grounds for lower-class and foreign-born "undesirables." Many valid criticisms have been levelled at Rothman over the years, for example, his failure to note the class and gender interests of the Jacksonian reformers.

ROTHMAN (1980) focuses on criminal justice, juvenile justice and mental health care, and, as in his earlier book, a central issue is the expanding power of the state over the individual. He explores the search for alternatives to incarceration by benevolent and philanthropic-minded Progressive reformers pursuing humanitarian and scientific objectives to cure crime, delinquency and insanity. The essential feature of the Progressive reform agenda is the concept of individual justice to effect reformation, as reflected in the innovations of probation, parole, and indeterminate sentencing for adult offenders; juvenile courts and reform schools for youthful offenders; and outpatient facilities for the mentally ill. What evolved however was "a highly discretionary system of justice," reflecting the failure of the reformers' goals and the triumph of administrative convenience.

Using the subdisciplines of legal, intellectual, social and economic history, while focusing on Massachusetts, HIRSCH offers a challenging new interpretation of the origins and development of the penitentiary system. He argues that the ideology of incarceration has its roots in 16th-century English ideas of punishment at hard labour, which had been adopted by Americans long before the Jacksonian period; and he finds in black slavery the ideological context for the penitentiary in America. Hirsch further offers a very different view of the Jacksonians, who "reared" rather than "invented" the penitentiary; they were much more practical and less misguided than Rothman would have us believe. While Hirsch raises important questions about the debate over prisons and the penitentiary, and suggests new research directions, this is not a definitive refutation of Rothman's analysis.

PISCIOTTA criticizes Rothman for ignoring the Elmira reformatory-prison for youthful male offenders and the influence of the adult reformatory movement or "third penal system", with its own social control agenda. This led to the creation of a new criminal type: the dangerous youthful offender. Adult reformatories promised benevolent reform, to transform the dangerous classes into law-abiding and economically productive citizens, but delivered repression and brutality. Pisciotta uses organizational and social systems theories to explain the failure of "total institutions" such as Elmira.

RAFTER's well-researched and persuasive work attempts to overcome the deficiencies of previous research which neglects female prisoners and issues of gender discrimination in conviction and punishment. "Partial justice" refers to the inferior care given to female inmates of prisons and reformatories. Rafter examines the emergence of two types of women's prison: "semi-autonomous" custodial institutions in the mid-19th century, and reformatories opening in the 1870s which concentrated on rehabilitation, but had significantly returned to custodialism by the 1930s. Using case studies of institutions in New York, Ohio, and Tennessee, she pays special attention to regional variations of punishment and inmate demography. The chapter on race and racism in state prisons with female inmates looks at the influence of gender and race on incarceration rates, and the treatment of black women in prison. FREEDMAN examines the origins and development of the women's prison reform movement in New York, Massachusetts, and Indiana. She analyses the response of white middle-class women, motivated by religious belief and growing gender-consciousness, to the plight of 19th-century women prisoners suffering overcrowding, lack of productive labour, sexual abuse and harsh treatment. She discusses the performance of the first state prisons run by and for women between 1840 and 1900, and the work of women criminologists and penologists in the first decades of the 20th century.

GROB's fifth and most comprehensive work on the care and treatment of America's mentally ill from colonial times to the present is largely a narrative history which draws heavily on his previous works, as well as much primary research and recent secondary works. The focus is on societal reaction and institutional response to the mentally disordered, from colonial family- and community-centred care to the institutionalization drive of the 19th century, and the shift to community psychiatry in the 1960s. Grob's discussion of colonial mental health care parallels much of JIMENEZ's insightful work on

Massachusetts. Jimenez contrasts two distinct social orders, colonial and post-revolutionary, and their reaction to madness. Because of the decentralized nature of colonial society, mentally disordered persons lived with family and friends unless they posed a violent threat to, or financial burden on, the community. In the early republic, insanity came under medical jurisdiction and the mentally ill were increasingly subject to incarceration.

VIVIEN M.L. MILLER

See also Crime and Punishment

Professions

Auerbach, Jerold S., *Unequal Justice: Lawyers and Social Change in Modern America*, New York: Oxford University Press, 1976

Bledstein, Burton J., *The Culture of Professionalism: The Middle Class and the Development of Higher Education in America*, New York: Norton, 1976

Haber, Samuel, *The Quest for Authority and Honor in the American Professions, 1750–1900*, Chicago: University of Chicago Press, 1991

Horwitz, Morton J., *The Transformation of American Law, 1780–1860*, Cambridge, MA: Harvard University Press, 1977

Horwitz, Morton J., *The Transformation of American Law, 1870–1960: The Crisis of Legal Orthodoxy*, New York: Oxford University Press, 1992

Johnson, William R., *Schooled Lawyers: A Study in the Clash of Professional Cultures*, New York: New York University Press, 1978

Kimball, Bruce A., *The "True" Professional Ideal in America: A History*, Cambridge, MA and Oxford: Blackwell, 1992

Ludmerer, Kenneth M., *Learning to Heal: The Development of American Medical Education*, New York: Basic Books, 1985

Novick, Peter, *That Noble Dream: The "Objectivity Question" and the American Historical Profession*, Cambridge and New York: Cambridge University Press, 1988

Scott, Donald M., *From Office to Profession: The New England Ministry, 1750–1850*, Philadelphia: University of Pennsylvania Press, 1978

Starr, Paul, *The Social Transformation of American Medicine: The Rise of a Sovereign Profession and the Making of a Vast Industry*, New York: Basic Books, 1982

Zunz, Olivier, *Making America Corporate, 1870–1920*, Chicago: University of Chicago Press, 1990

Early accounts of the professions and professionalization in America usually lauded the process, and the organizations which encouraged it, for raising standards and embracing rationality. After World War II, McCarthyite attacks on elites and the functionalist orientation of consensus history discouraged criticism. In the late 1960s, however, more critical perspectives emerged. By placing late 19th century professionalization within a broader re-ordering of American society and specifically connecting it to the emergence of the "new" middle class (adopting C. Wright Mills's term), Robert H. Wiebe's *The Search for Order* (1967) provided a conceptual framework for re-evaluating professionalization.

BLEDSTEIN developed Wiebe's concept, intertwining the professionalization of the 19th century with the rise of the research university, which he attributed to the forces seeking to promote professional authority. The symbiotic relationship enabled universities to live in a manner to which they wished to grow accustomed while the college-educated members of the professions gained control over credentialling and promoted their professional vision. The decades after the Civil War saw the proliferation of national professional associations that made the new middle class "guilded" as well as "gilded." Bledstein's pioneering work connected Wiebe's "search for order" to the mechanisms of professionalization.

Medicine has a long history of prestige which was converted into a model of professionalization. Early works relatively uncritically lauded the victories of "regular" doctors, and their ultimate mastery following the Flexner Report. LUDMERER provides a corrective that denotes the damaging social consequences of that victory. STARR provided the definitive work. He rejects the idea that scientific progress or an American fixation on health pre-ordained medical prestige. Rather he maintains that particular strategies combined with peculiar American circumstances to create the profession's immense cultural authority and political and economic power. Between 1850 and 1930 a breed of college-educated professionals attained almost complete control over American medicine. They were virtually unchallenged until the 1970s when hospitals, insurance companies, government, and other institutions began to contest their authority.

Law, the second most powerful profession, also began to face a more critical treatment in the late 1970s. HORWITZ (1977) comprehensively revised earlier works written either from a laissez-faire or New Deal perspective which, despite their contrasting ideologies, both accepted the neutrality of the law. Horwitz demonstrated that the legal transformation in the eighty years between the Revolution and Civil War was largely shaped by emerging commercial interests which, in turn, benefited from the emerging legal formalism.

JOHNSON examined the connection between education and legal professionalization from the antebellum heyday of judicial circuit law to the triumph of the law school model by 1930. Law schools were marginal in the 19th century, having a smaller educational role than law office apprenticeship and training on the legal circuit. Only after 1900 did the Harvard approach which treated law as a science, gain ground and law schools become more professional and more important. Their success was due as much to a desire to limit entry, especially by recent immigrants, as it was to a desire to raise academic standards. Johnson provides a sense of day-to-day law practice that supplements Horwitz's broader strokes. While Horwitz and Johnson fit power into their analyses and are ambivalent about the changes, AUERBACH depicts elite lawyers making a blatant power grab with few redeeming social virtues. HORWITZ (1992) concentrates on the struggle between "Classical Legal Thought" and "Progressive Legal

Thought" which was clearly joined with the *Lochner* case (1905), and saw dominance shift to the latter in the 1930s with the triumph of "legal realism," which mixed moral outrage with social scientific certainty.

Academic professionalization has naturally received plentiful attention, usually studied within the disciplinary lines that have channelled academic thought for a century. The discipline of history is blessed with a perceptive examination of its deep commitment to objectivity. Ranging from Ranke to the Abraham-Feldman controversy, NOVICK challenges the 19th-century belief in the possibility of objectivity that has been a central tenet of historians, and remains an important but more contested concept in the 1990s. As in other professions, the professionalization of historians combined guild-like self-protection and promotion with commitment to a set of ideals.

Although the ministry was arguably the first truly "learned profession" in America and shaped the dominant professional model based on high academic standards, journals, and meetings, it has been neglected in mainstream history. A good starting point is SCOTT's examination of the transformation of the ministry, which in the 1700s was a local "office" demanding a variety of community-based tasks and offering broad authority. By 1850 Scott depicts a transformation to a profession whose members increasingly looked to each other, rather than to the community and congregation, for identity and authority.

In the late 19th century, differentiation of function within the burgeoning new corporations created new specializations that soon turned to the traditional professions for models or organization. ZUNZ places this process within the framework of professionalization, demonstrating how engineers, accountants, and managers adapted models from the "learned professions" in order to create new professions.

There are specialized studies of other professions in the vast literature on the subject. However, this essay concludes by returning to overviews of professionalization. Most works written since the mid-1970s have been very critical, emphasizing the self-interested aspects of professionalization. HABER provides a more positive view, tracing professional senses of "authority and honor" not from modern concepts but from ideas originating with 18th-century English gentlemen. As people increasingly sold their labor rather than goods the professions sold their labor "but not their right to be commanded." Although they were responding to market forces with self-interest, Haber portrays professionalization as strongly motivated by a concern to defend higher values and old-fashioned autonomy.

True to history's literary turn in the 1990s, KIMBALL examines the word "profession" and its derivatives. He challenges the basic assumption of most writing on the subject, that the late 19th century was a gestation period for a professional model that has changed little. Kimball claims that continuity of language and the consternation of academics over their own declining prestige have blinded historians to changes hidden beneath rhetorical continuity.

W. BRUCE LESLIE

See also Middle Classes

Progressive Era *see* Gilded Age and Progressive Era

Progressivism

Buenker, John D., *Urban Liberalism and Progressive Reform*, New York: Norton, 1978

Chambers, John Whiteclay II, *The Tyranny of Change: America in the Progressive Era, 1890–1920*, New York: St. Martin's Press, 1992

De Witt, Benjamin Parke, *The Progressive Movement: A Non-Partisan, Comprehensive Discussion of Current Tendencies in American Politics*, New York: Macmillan, 1915

Ekirch, Arthur A., Jr., *Progressivism in America: A Study of the Era from Theodore Roosevelt to Woodrow Wilson*, New York: New Viewpoints, 1974

Faulkner, Harold U., *The Quest for Social Justice, 1898–1914*, New York: Macmillan, 1931

Frankel, Noralee and Nancy S. Dye (editors), *Gender, Class, Race, and Reform in the Progressive Era*, Lexington: University Press of Kentucky, 1991

Hofstadter, Richard, *The Age of Reform: From Bryan to FDR*, New York: Knopf, 1955; London: Cape, 1962

Huthmacher, J. Joseph, *Senator Robert F. Wagner and the Rise of Urban Liberalism*, New York: Atheneum, 1968

Kolko, Gabriel, *The Triumph of Conservatism: A Reinterpretation of American History, 1900–1916*, New York: Free Press, and London: Collier Macmillan, 1963

Link, Arthur S. and Richard L. McCormick, *Progressivism*, Arlington Heights, IL: Harlan Davidson, 1983

Rodgers, Daniel T., *Contested Truths: Keywords in American Politics since Independence*, New York: Basic Books, 1987

Sklar, Martin J., *The Corporate Reconstruction of American Capitalism, 1890–1916: The Market, the Law, and Politics*, Cambridge and New York: Cambridge University Press, 1988

Thelen, David P., *The New Citizenship: Origins of Progressivism in Wisconsin, 1885–1900*, Columbia: University of Missouri Press, 1972

Weinstein, James, *The Corporate Ideal in the Liberal State, 1900–1918*, Boston: Beacon Press, 1968

Wiebe, Robert H., *Businessmen and Reform: A Study of the Progressive Movement*, Cambridge, MA: Harvard University Press, 1962

Wiebe, Robert H., *The Search for Order, 1877–1920*, New York: Hill and Wang, and London: Macmillan, 1967

Yellowitz, Irwin, *Labor and the Progressive Movement in New York State, 1897–1916*, Ithaca, NY: Cornell University Press, 1965

DE WITT's pioneering book on progressivism portrayed it as a mass movement on the part of "the people" against "special interests." In what, after more than eighty years, is still the most thorough account of progressive sentiment in the various parties, he set out to summarize how, in the late 19th and early 20th centuries, reformers struggled to abolish political corruption, to make politics itself more democratic, and to mobilize the resources of government to improve social and economic conditions. Sixteen years later, FAULKNER filled in more of the background to progressivism: the personalities who led it, its concern for the poor and deprived, its non-political attempts at amelioration. His view of Progressive Era politics, however, was much the same as De Witt's, and based on the people-interests dualism which remained the prevailing interpretive paradigm for more than three decades.

As the result of a combination of factors, a more complex interpretation of progressivism finally began to appear. Events of the 1930s and 1940s – the Great Depression, the growth of fascism, World War II, the first use of nuclear weapons, and the onset of the Cold War – encouraged a growing sense of distance from the comparatively innocent concerns of the early 20th century. The conviction of a growing number of scholars that Americans shared a number of fundamental values – the outlook of the consensus school – had the effect of making many of the conflicts and much of the rhetoric of the Progressive Era seem exaggerated, at times even spurious. A distrust of mass movements, from fascism to the McCarthyite crusade, coupled with the decline of the "progressive" approach to history associated with Charles A. Beard and others, which had insisted on the primacy of economic considerations in causing political conflict, prompted the search for alternative means of explaining this conflict, and a new stress on such influences as irrational fears and status anxieties. At approximately the same time, social scientists began to show how industrialization, urbanization, and immigration in the 19th-century United States had brought about the decline of old elites, the fragmentation of political power, and the creation of a society based on many special-interest groups.

Many of these trends found expression in HOFSTADTER. As he frankly confessed, Hofstadter was writing "from the perspective of our own time." His account of the progressive tradition was more critical than would have been the case earlier, because it was influenced by McCarthyism and a conservative reaction that seemed to threaten the achievements of the New Deal. Accepting Lionel Trilling's dictum that American conservatism had no real thought but only "irritable mental gestures," he looked for McCarthyism's roots not in conservatism itself, but in the paranoid side of the pre-New Deal reform tradition. It was a deeply moralistic attempt to eradicate a "single conspiratorial force" in the same way as the progressives had tried to curb big business, attack political corruption, or eliminate the saloon. In his attempt to defend the New Deal, Hofstadter emphasized the break which it represented in the reform tradition. Whereas progressivism had been a mass movement, the New Deal operated politically as a series of adjustments between rival groups. In place of the moralistic demands of the Progressives, it offered a thoroughly pragmatic response to pressing human needs. In Hofstadter's account, therefore, it was the political machines – seen by the progressives as the prime agencies of urban political corruption – that emerged, with their real if calculated concern for local supporters, as the natural precursors of the New Deal. In another decisive break with earlier views, Hofstadter minimized the altruistic motivation of progressivism's middle-class leaders, seeing them as self-interested men who turned to political reform as a means of asserting themselves after experiencing a "status revolution" – a major decline in their social position compared to that of a rising corporate elite.

Early responses to Hofstadter's work included attempts to prove that a "status revolution" could not have been a major factor in encouraging a commitment to reform, since both the progressives and their "stand-pat" opponents came from a remarkably similar middle-class background. More interestingly, additional research began to reveal greater complexity in progressivism itself. Hofstadter had depicted it as a movement on the part of a declining middle-class, whereas WIEBE (1967) argued that it was led by an upwardly mobile elite of managers and new professionals. Other studies showed how progressive reforms were in fact enacted. WIEBE (1962), demonstrated that some reforms had business backing, while YELLOWITZ looked at the relationship between progressivism and labor and both BUENKER and HUTHMACHER wrote about the role of the urban political machine. Studies of the part played by African Americans and women, including the essays brought together by FRANKEL and DYE, have also begun to appear in recent years. One consequence of this work has been a new interpretation of progressivism, which is no longer widely viewed as a monolithic, middle-class movement so much as a swirling series of diverse and differing coalitions. The last few decades, therefore, have seen Hofstadter's pluralistic approach to New Deal politics applied to progressivism as well.

One response to this pluralistic interpretation has been the attempt to deny it. Thus, for example, KOLKO endeavored to reinterpret the history of the early 20th century not as a triumph for the forces of reform, but as an example of how business corporations influenced the political process in pursuit of their own interests. In contrast, THELEN, attempting to explain why different groups came together to struggle for reform at the same time, argued that the economic depression of the 1890s and the "corporate arrogance" of many large businesses during those years were decisive factors.

Some historians have placed the rising strength of corporations at the center of their interpretation of progressivism. Both WEINSTEIN and SKLAR, for example, have analyzed the events of the Progressive Era from the perspective of a Gramscian reinterpretation of Marx, in an attempt to show how a dominant corporate class consolidated its hegemonic power by co-opting the forces of protest and reform. In contrast, RODGERS, studying the rhetoric of progressive politicians, dismisses the notion of hegemony as "a single, class-based worldview" that minimizes the extent of conflict in American political life.

Attempts to synthesize the history of progressivism in a single volume include EKIRCH, who also discusses reformist parallels with Europe and foreign policy matters; LINK and McCORMICK, who offer an excellent summary of political developments, and CHAMBERS, who sees progressivism as one part of a general response to the emergence of modern urban, multi-ethnic, and industrial society.

MELVYN STOKES

See also Gilded Age and Progressive Era

Prohibition

Blocker, Jack S., Jr., *Retreat from Reform: The Prohibition Movement in the United States, 1890–1913*, Westport, CT: Greenwood Press, 1976

Blocker, Jack S., Jr., *American Temperance Movements: Cycles of Reform*, Boston: Twayne, 1989

Gusfield, Joseph, *Symbolic Crusade: Status Politics and the American Temperance Movement*, Urbana: University of Illinois Press, 1963

Hofstadter, Richard, *The Age of Reform: From Bryan to FDR*, New York: Knopf, 1955; London: Cape, 1962

Kerr, K. Austin, *Organized for Prohibition: A New History of the Anti-Saloon League*, New Haven: Yale University Press, 1985

Kyvig, David E., *Repealing National Prohibition*, Chicago: University of Chicago Press, 1979

Merz, Charles, *The Dry Decade*, New York: Doubleday, 1931

Rumbarger, John J., *Profits, Power, and Prohibition: Alcohol Reform and the Industrializing of America, 1800–1930*, Albany: State University of New York Press, 1989

Sinclair, Andrew, *Prohibition: The Era of Excess*, London: Faber, and Boston: Little Brown, 1962; as *Era of Excess: A Social History of the Prohibition Movement*, New York: Harper, 1964

Timberlake, James H., *Prohibition and the Progressive Movement, 1900–1920*, Cambridge, MA: Harvard University Press, 1963

Early scholarship on prohibition tended to ask whether it represented the fulfilment of a tradition of intolerance. After decades of patchy and generally negative treatment, most historians of the topics since the 1970s have reacted against a general public impression that temperance and prohibition advocates were grim, puritanical, and unrealistic, and have argued that they addressed real and potentially destructive problems. Recent scholarship also emphasizes the diversity of backgrounds and motives of both prohibition advocates and their opponents.

Surveying national prohibition in action, MERZ attributes the passage of the Eighteenth Amendment to the special circumstances of World War I. The Anti-Saloon League capitalized on the war by stressing the increased authority of the federal government, the need to save food and the widespread antipathy to everything German. By emphasizing the inability and unwillingness of state and federal government agencies to do anything about stills, illegal breweries, and smuggling, the book argues that, in practice, prohibition was a failure.

In the most influential five pages that a historian has written on the subject, HOFSTADTER judges that prohibition was a "pinched, parochial substitute for reform" that "was carried about America by the rural-evangelical virus". Home-grown evangelicals saw liquor as an upper-class luxury and an urban, lower-class, immigrant vice. Far from continuing the goals of the Progressive movement, the passage of the Eighteenth Amendment showed the efforts of alienated rural dwellers trying to regain lost status by forcing their outdated notions of propriety on the rest of America.

SINCLAIR is a colourful narrative depicting prohibition as the misguided work of rural religious extremists. It details the national pursuit of alcohol under prohibition and the failures of prohibition enforcement. TIMBERLAKE places prohibition in the context of the Progressive movement, arguing that its spokespeople saw opposition to alcohol as part of a larger movement against trusts – in their case the liquor business – for industrial efficiency through better workers, for democratic government through clear-minded voters, and against the poverty which drunkenness could cause. In an essential book, GUSFIELD follows Hofstadter in emphasizing the importance of status saving in the prohibition movement, but is far less harsh and does not view the movement as an empty substitute for more meaningful reform. A work of sociology, it is most interested in the functions which anti-liquor movements performed in the lives of different groups, and thus does not study economic or other power issues. In an argument that echoes Hofstadter, national prohibition advocates in the early 20th century are seen as rural Americans fearing loss of status in an increasingly urban country.

BLOCKER (1976) begins with an examination of the late 19th century prohibition movement as a middle-class campaign, with aspirations to adopt planks from the populists, labour, and women's suffrage movements in the 1890s. Fusion seemed possible until 1896, when realignments of the national party system and the obvious failures of the Prohibition party encouraged many prohibition supporters to adopt another strategy. The Anti-Saloon League emerged as a less extreme group with more support from corporate groups, a willingness to work within the two-party system, and no interest in fusion with leftists.

In an institutional history of the Anti-Saloon League, the organization that led the way to legal prohibition, KERR agrees with Timberlake in placing the movement in the context of Progressivism. Along with the anti-monopoly theme, his study emphasizes the goal of rationalization. The League was organized like a modern business operated by a small group of leaders who mobilized support, in contrast to many temperance groups which emerged from local organizations. Challenging other modern interpretations, RUMBARGER argues that wealthy industrialists were most responsible for prohibition laws. "Men of power," who wanted above all an orderly society and sober workers, orchestrated the variety of anti-liquor sentiment in their favour. He agrees with Blocker that the Anti-Saloon League represented a conservative alternative to the experimentation of the Prohibition party, but pushes his emphasis on the basic conservatism of temperance leaders back to the antebellum period.

In the best work on the repeal of national prohibition, KYVIG argues that sentiment for repeal came from three sources. First was the well-known national reaction against the problems of enforcement. Second was the Depression and the ensuing effort to direct the energies of government to solving its problems. Third were organized groups such as the Association Against the Prohibition Amendment, a conservative, corporate group hoping to end prohibition without bringing back saloons.

In what is by far the best synthesis of modern scholarship, BLOCKER (1989) emphasizes change and diversity within various forms of opposition to alcohol, in part as responses to changes in drinking habits. He identifies five "cycles of reform": three periods of 19th-century temperance activity, followed by the success and then failure of the Anti-Saloon League from the 1890s through the prohibition period, and then the emphases on medicine, safety, and treatment groups since 1933.

TED OWNBY

See also Temperance

Prostitution

Butler, Anne M., *Daughters of Joy, Sisters of Misery: Prostitutes in the American West, 1865–90*, Urbana: University of Illinois Press, 1985

D'Emilio, John and Estelle B. Freedman, *Intimate Matters: A History of Sexuality in America*, New York: Harper, 1988

Freedman, Estelle B., *Their Sisters' Keepers: Women's Prison Reform in America, 1830–1930*, Ann Arbor: University of Michigan Press, 1981

Gilfoyle, Timothy J., *City of Eros: New York City, Prostitution, and the Commercialization of Sex, 1790–1920*, New York: Norton, 1992

Goldman, Marion S., *Gold Diggers and Silver Miners: Prostitution and Social Life on the Comstock Lode*, Ann Arbor: University of Michigan Press, 1981

Hill, Marilynn Wood, *Their Sisters' Keepers: Prostitution in New York City, 1830–1870*, Berkeley: University of California Press, 1993

Hobson, Barbara Meil, *Uneasy Virtue: The Politics of Prostitution and the American Reform Tradition*, New York: Basic Books, 1987

Pivar, David J., *Purity Crusade: Sexual Morality and Social Control, 1868–1900*, Westport, CT: Greenwood Press, 1973

Rosen, Ruth, *The Lost Sisterhood: Prostitution in America, 1900–1918*, Baltimore: Johns Hopkins University Press, 1982

Although there have been many studies by scholars from other disciplines, prostitution is not a subject which has attracted many historians until relatively recently. The advent of the "new social histories", however, changed this situation dramatically. The earliest studies explored the campaigns against prostitution. PIVAR broke new ground in his work on the social purity reformers of the second half of the 19th century. He examines the involvement of former abolitionists and members of the women's movement in shaping the social purity movement after the Civil War. It was their influence which transformed the crusade against prostitution into an attempt to reform all segments of society by secularizing and converting religious values into standards of social behaviour, sometimes through coercion. Pivar bases his analysis upon impressive research, but some of his conclusions are strained, and his writing style is, at times, awkward.

FREEDMAN concentrates mainly on the women reformers who agitated for changes in the treatment of female prisoners. She argues that women were frequently incarcerated for crimes which violated the moral and sexual codes of the time. Female reformers often saw these "fallen women" as the victims of limited economic opportunities and sexual exploitation. Increasingly they blamed men for the sexual double standard which victimized these women. Although Freedman has little to say about the women criminals themselves, this is an invaluable study of the gender politics involved in the treatment of those women who violated society's codes of female sexual behaviour.

ROSEN studies both the Progressive Era campaigns against prostitution, and the lives of prostitutes themselves. She argues that the hysteria over prostitution and "white slavery" in the early 20th century was as much a reflection of middle-class anxieties about rapid social change, particularly changes in the position of women, as it was a reaction to the increasing commercialization of vice. Drawing upon a wide range of evidence, Rosen concludes that, although white slavery probably did exist, it explains only a small percentage of prostitution. The vast majority of women entered the profession voluntarily, some even perceiving it as a means to upward social mobility. By centring her analysis around class and gender, Rosen makes a significant contribution towards our understanding of early 20th century attitudes towards prostitution.

A more comprehensive study of the politics of prostitution from the early 19th century is provided by HOBSON, who highlights the highly volatile and divisive nature of prostitution reform. She is illuminating on both society's organization of class and gender, and on the state's role in regulating morals. In examining the lives of the prostitutes themselves, Hobson reveals that many women entered prostitution because of their limited access to the legitimate labour market – most employment available to women made prostitution seem an attractive alternative. Hobson draws on an impressive array of primary evidence, and also draws comparisons between policies in the United States and in Europe. Often provocative, this a helpful analysis of the great paradox in the views of female sexuality revealed by prostitution policy.

Whereas most work concentrates upon prostitution in the urban centres of America, there are two studies which examine prostitution on the American frontier. Both argue that the reality was quite different from the idealized myth of the frontier prostitute. GOLDMAN compares the lives of prostitutes on the Comstock Lode with those of respectable women, arguing that prostitution supported the social organization of courtship and marriage, and fulfilled a necessary function in frontier society. She examines who the prostitutes were, the organization of prostitution, and the relationships between prostitutes and respectable society. The study is based on thorough research and provides an interesting insight into the real lives of frontier prostitutes.

BUTLER also seeks to dispel the myth of the frontier prostitute as a noble, independent woman, supported by close friendships with other prostitutes and their clients. Butler, by contrast, paints a very bleak picture of the life of the frontier prostitute. She argues that women entered prostitution because of the limited scope for women's employment in the West, but that their lives as prostitutes were an unending stream of violence and grief. Marriage was often an exploitative arrangement with a pimp, and friendships among prostitutes could rarely overcome the competition between the women. Moreover, although prostitution was tacitly accepted by both the officers of the law and the military, prostitutes often had to pay a high price for this acceptance. This is an interesting and informative study, but it leaves many questions unanswered.

In his study of commercial sex in New York City, GILFOYLE paints a much more positive picture of the life of prostitutes. He argues that female prostitution challenged the sexual morality of the growing urban middle class. As an increasing number of women moved outside the family for financial reasons, prostitution presented an attractive alternative to the low wages offered by other female employment. Gilfoyle reconstructs the everyday life of commercialized sex with a detailed description of the subcultures of the prostitutes and their clients, the "sporting male". There are also examinations of the changing geographical location of commercialized sex in New York, and of the various attempts to control or eradicate prostitution from the city. This is a significant contribution to the history of popular culture in New York City, but the analysis is rather limited and some of the sources Gilfoyle has examined are questionable.

HILL's study of prostitution in New York City covers a much narrower period, and is also more firmly grounded in gender history. She argues that, during the period 1830–70, class and feminine identities were fairly fluid and consequently there were promising possibilities for women. One such possibility was prostitution. Drawing upon many previously unexploited archival sources, Hill examines the lives of prostitutes in mid-19th century New York. While prostitutes had to deal with "occupational hazards" such as disease, violence and social ostracism, they were also able to gain a considerable degree of autonomy and control over their lives. Hill does suggest, however, that as prostitution became increasingly commercialized this ceased to be the case. This is a very thorough study, but at times the conclusions seem a little overblown.

In their general history of sexuality in America, D'EMILIO and FREEDMAN place prostitution in the wider context of attitudes towards sex and sexuality. They make clear the relationship between prostitution and social change, and examine the anti-prostitution campaigns of the 19th and early 20th centuries. Although the subject plays only a relatively minor part in the book, the examination of attitudes towards sexuality helps to explain why prostitution has been such a constant factor in American life.

ELIZABETH J. CLAPP

Protestantism: General

Butler, Jon, *Awash in a Sea of Faith: Christianizing the American People*, Cambridge, MA: Harvard University Press, 1990

Handy, Robert T., *A Christian America: Protestant Hopes and Historical Realities*, New York: Oxford University Press, 1971, revised 1984

Hatch, Nathan O., *The Democratization of American Christianity*, New Haven: Yale University Press, 1989

Hudson, Winthrop S., *American Protestantism*, Chicago: University of Chicago Press, 1961

Marsden, George M., *Religion and American Culture*, San Diego: Harcourt Brace, 1990

Marty, Martin E., *Righteous Empire: The Protestant Experience in America*, New York: Scribner, 1970; as *Protestantism in the United States: Righteous Empire*, 1986

Mathews, Donald G., *Religion in the Old South*, Chicago: University of Chicago Press, 1977

Mead, Sidney E., *The Lively Experiment: The Shaping of Christianity in America*, New York: Harper, 1963

Moore, R. Laurence, *Selling God: American Religion in the Marketplace of Culture*, New York: Oxford University Press, 1994

Wuthnow, Robert, *The Restructuring of American Religion: Society and Faith since World War II*, Princeton: Princeton University Press, 1988

The history of religion in the United States has largely been the history of the Protestant tradition and its denominational manifestations. Protestantism shaped religious life in the United States for much of its history, and many Americans, despite the separation of church and state, embraced a distinctive Protestant sense of mission. Although in recent decades most Protestants have taken for granted religious diversity in a pluralistic society, many of them still believe that religious, even if not distinctively Protestant, values should continue to shape public life and policy. Although most historians once gave pride of place to the Puritan heritage of New England, more recent scholars have emphasized the diversity of Protestant traditions and practices.

There is no recent history of Protestantism as such, though most general histories of American religion effectively serve that purpose. The best brief introduction remains HUDSON whose coverage extends from the colonial period to about 1960. It is helpful for understanding the diversity of Protestantism, especially during the colonial era and the 19th century, and offers a good discussion of the origins of denominationalism. Hudson is less useful on the rise of Pentecostal, Holiness, and conservative evangelical movements and has almost nothing to say about black Protestantism. MARSDEN, a good general survey of American religion with bibliography, gives particular attention to religious "outsiders" and is helpful on the recent rise of tele-evangelists and the religious right.

MEAD is a master of the interpretative essay, and this first collection has been the most influential. Written in the "consensus" tradition of historiography, the book stresses the dominance of space over time in shaping Americans' experience of freedom as flight from constraint and commitment. Americans acknowledged both a religion of the republic grounded in Enlightenment rationalism and an increasingly ahistorical evangelicalism that relied less on theological distinctiveness than on techniques of persuasion. Fleeing from their rationalist-republican heritage, Protestants embraced an uncritical Americanism that made them ill-equipped to cope with the intellectual and social challenges of modernity.

While Mead explores the tensions between Enlightenment and pietism, HANDY argues that the aim of American Protestantism was to create a Christian civilization in its own image. At first voluntaristic evangelical revivalism sought to transform the nation's morals. By the end of the century a liberalized Protestantism became more complacent about the society it had helped to create and subordinated its religious vision to conceptions of historical progress, whether informed on the one side by social Darwinism and Anglo-Saxonism or on the other by the Social Gospel. Despite such renewal movements as neo-orthodoxy during the 1930s, the Protestant era, understood as embodying a more or less distinctive vision, was coming to an end.

In his richly textured interpretative history MARTY also laments the absence of a prophetic stance. He argues that the competitive ethos of post-revolutionary American society, which stimulated the growth of denominations and voluntary societies, encouraged Protestants to believe that through the saving of souls they could create a righteous empire. This was essentially an Anglo-Saxon imperial ambition that had little place for Native Americans and blacks, among others. After the Civil War it proved difficult to respond in a coherent way to the problems of immigration, industrialization, and new currents of thought. Broadly considered, a "two party system" that crossed denominational lines emerged. One side concentrated on saving the individual from the corrupting influences of society, while the other still believed in the possibility of social transformation but with the goal of saving souls often a secondary consideration.

Marty's two party model has been a fruitful source of hypotheses for students of 20th-century Protestantism, and is best exemplified in the work of WUTHNOW, a sociologist. He describes the post-World War II decline of denominationalism, which was a prerequisite for the restructuring of religion. The formation of "liberal" and "conservative" parties was a result of the enormous expansion of higher education in the 1960s and the growing liberalization of culture and society. Those who resented these changes found their way into the rapidly growing conservative camp which supported a network of special interest groups hostile to abortion, homosexuality and the ban on school prayer.

Breaking with the New England Puritan synthesis in religious history, two recent studies have shifted the debate about the defining characteristics of American Protestantism to a later period. BUTLER argues that American denominational pluralism owes little to the democratic and anti-institutional individualism stressed in most studies. Even though the first Great Awakening of the 1740s probably never happened and the regional and localized revivals that did occur had little to do with the coming of the Revolution, many of the key organizational innovations in American Protestantism can be traced to the 18th century. After the Revolution, an essentially secular event inspired by Enlightenment ideas, the denominations did succeed, through creative leadership and institutional innovation, in extending their authority and power over vast numbers of people and in recasting the meaning of the republic. This detailed and provocative study stresses the persistence of popular magic and occult practices and offers a controversial thesis on the 18th century destruction of African religious systems among slaves.

Like Butler, HATCH discounts the centrality of 17th-century Puritanism while stressing the diversity and vitality of the American religious tradition. Hatch, however, focusing on the period 1780–1840, emphasizes the role of popular and charismatic leaders who denied distinctions between clergy and laity and challenged the authority of established institutions in the name of democratic egalitarianism. This populist tradition continued to challenge Protestants whenever they succumbed to elitism and respectability. There are excellent sections on a host of obscure and well-known figures, including Lorenzo Dow, the black Methodist Richard Allen, and the Mormon prophet Joseph Smith. Both Butler and Hatch may overstate their respective arguments, but together they contribute to understanding the tension in American Protestantism between an individualistic piety and the impulse toward structure and discipline. Surprisingly, neither book explores the role of women, who comprised the majority of church members.

According to MOORE, the challenges of a pluralistic society dominated by the market account for the continuing vitality of religion. There has been no debasement of the Protestant tradition since the 19th century nor has it been overtaken by growing secularization. Religion and other cultural products have always been options competing in the marketplace. Despite obscuring the distinction between what is sold and how it is sold, the book provides a fascinating and thoroughly documented account of how evangelical Protestants have effectively exploited the media from the newspapers and tracts of the early 19th century to television and electronic gadgetry in the late 20th.

Finally, MATHEWS offers the best introduction to the religious ethos of the most Protestant region in America. The book traces the evangelical impulse from its lowly beginnings in the awakenings of the 18th century to its place at the center of southern society on the eve of the Civil War. Rejecting the view that white evangelicals' accommodation to slavery was mere hypocrisy, it analyzes the tensions within a religion that provided a sense of community and individual worth but also embraced and sought to influence the social order. In addition to an excellent section on black Christianity, which provided a measure by which white Protestantism could be judged, the book includes a sensitive exploration of the role of women in the churches.

FREDERICK A. BODE

See also Religion

Protestantism: Denominational Histories

Albright, Raymond W., *A History of the Protestant Episcopal Church*, New York: Macmillan, 1964

Balmer, Randall and John R. Fitzmier, *The Presbyterians*, Westport, CT: Greenwood Press, 1993

Brackney, William Henry, *The Baptists*, Westport, CT: Greenwood Press, 1988

Fitts, Leroy, *A History of Black Baptists*, Nashville: Broadman Press, 1985

Lincoln, C. Eric and Lawrence H. Mamiya, *The Black Church in the African-American Experience*, Durham, NC: Duke University Press, 1990

Norwood, Frederick A., *The Story of American Methodism: A History of the United Methodists and Their Relations*, Nashville: Abingdon Press, 1974

Robinson, David, *The Unitarians and the Universalists*, Westport, CT: Greenwood Press, 1985

Von Rohr, John, *The Shaping of American Congregationalism, 1620–1957*, Cleveland: Pilgrim Press, 1992

Youngs, J. William T., *The Congregationalists*, Westport, CT: Greenwood Press, 1990

In 1985 the Greenwood Press launched the inaugural volume of a new series of denominational histories, the first such collection since the 1890s. Synthetic works based on the most recent scholarship and including full bibliographical essays, the volumes in the series place denominational history and theological ideas within the context of wider religious and social developments. After a narrative first half, each book presents biographical sketches of key denominational figures. Brief chronologies of events are also included. Although the authors make strong efforts to include women in their coverage, they tend to neglect African-Americans and other minorities.

ROBINSON produced the first volume in the series. In a well-written and balanced work of intellectual history, he traces the changing nature of Unitarian and Universalist beliefs from their origins in the colonial era to the 20th century. He also outlines institutional developments. Robinson uses the sermons, publications and letters of key denominational figures to explore major issues. Although he notes that Unitarians and Universalists developed in opposition to Calvinism, he emphasises the social and theological differences between them and warns against treating their merger in 1961 teleologically.

If Robinson is concerned with emphasizing difference, BRACKNEY's assignment is to examine Baptist diversity within a coherent framework. He argues that Baptists have always emphasized the authority of the Bible, congregational autonomy and the necessity of religious witness. After an overview of Baptist history, Brackney presents five thematic chapters that address Baptist divisions and disagreements concerning biblical inerrancy, the nature of the church, sacraments and ordinances, denominational organization, and religious liberty. An excellent and extensive thematic bibliographical essay complements the analytical chapters. An American Baptist, Brackney tends to neglect those outside that tradition, particularly National Baptists and Southern Baptists.

In their study of Presbyterians, BALMER and FITZMIER take a more traditional narrative, chronological approach. They focus on the plethora of theological disputes that have marked Presbyterian history. In six chapters they examine the origins of Presbyterianism, its growth in America during the colonial era, the different development of 19th-century Northern and Southern Presbyterianism, and the nature of 20th-century Presbyterianism, especially in the context of ecumenicalism. Although the authors write clearly and concisely, their allotted space of 112 pages means that their work can only serve as an introduction to the topic.

YOUNGS upholds the emphasis of the Greenwood series on clear exposition of theological developments within American denominations. He focuses on the origins of Congregationalism in the colonial period, especially its connection with Puritanism.

Youngs adopts a biographical approach to illustrate the sense of religious need that spurred the development of Congregationalism. Although purportedly a full history of the denomination, the study gives the 20th century only scant attention. VON ROHR's study of Congregationalism is more balanced in its chronological coverage and hence superior as a denominational history. Its seven chapters are spatially even and structured to address developments in theology, polity, worship and mission. Von Rohr takes a narrative, synthetic approach, incorporating the latest scholarship in a lengthy study approaching 500 pages.

Although neither Greenwood nor another publishing house has yet produced new histories of Episcopalianism or Methodism, older studies by Albright and Norwood have retained their value. ALBRIGHT's study of Episcopalianism is a thorough, detailed and clearly written reference work of 366 pages. It pays as much attention to institutional history as to theological and liturgical developments. Albright supports his arguments with extensive footnotes based on primary and secondary sources. The bibliography is lengthy but necessarily dated. Although he discusses events into the mid-20th century, Albright disproportionately devotes more than a third of the book to the colonial and Revolutionary era. Women are also barely mentioned in the narrative.

NORWOOD's thorough and comprehensive study of Methodism integrates female, African American, Native American, Asian American and white ethnic Methodists throughout its coverage of the period between 1725 and 1970. Aimed at the general reader, with few footnotes and its bibliographical references contained within them, the book is nevertheless of considerable value for the scholar. The author's self-confessed status as "a committed Methodist" only occasionally detracts from the narrative. The book is particularly useful for its incorporation of every shade of Methodism.

FITTS, a black Baptist pastor, also writes from an insider's perspective but, unlike Norwood, makes no attempt to detach himself from the subject. A sound, detailed and populist narrative of events covering all the main black Baptist groups, Fitts's book is marred by its florid language and celebratory tone. Based on published primary and secondary religious history sources and some convention minutes and newspapers, the book ignores secondary academic works. Fitts argues that black Baptists formulated a social gospel as early as the 1840s and have continued that tradition through to the present. However, his appropriation of the term Social Gospel ignores its theological underpinnings and time-specific quality. Fitts also downplays differences between Baptists, such as Joseph L. Jackson's opposition to the direct action tactics of the civil rights movement.

In the absence of any recent, scholarly account of black denominations, LINCOLN and MAMIYA offer a fine introduction to the subject in their study of the seven largest historically-black denominations. They provide narrative overviews of each denomination, grounded in the latest secondary sources, and combine these with contemporary statistical information about the rural and urban black church, based on surveys conducted with nearly 1,900 pastors between 1978 and 1986. There are also thematic chapters examining the response of the black church in recent years to the civil rights movement, black consciousness, politics and economics, women, and young people. Lincoln and Mamiya reject the conventional wisdom that Protestant blacks are apolitical and otherworldly. By contrast, they argue that both clergy and lay people overwhelmingly support civil rights and political activity by the church. Reinforcing the theme, an additional chapter examines black church music from slavery to civil rights. The book has extensive footnotes and a comprehensive bibliography.

MARK NEWMAN

See also African American History: Religion

Public Land Policy

Cawley, R. McGreggor, *Federal Land, Western Anger: The Sagebrush Rebellion and Environmental Politics*, Lawrence: University Press of Kansas, 1993

Fairfax, Sally K. and Carolyn E. Yale, *Federal Lands: A Guide to Planning, Management, and State Revenues*, Washington, DC: Island Press, 1987

Feller, Daniel, *The Public Lands in Jacksonian Politics*, Madison: University of Wisconsin Press, 1984

Gates, Paul W., *History of Public Land Law Development*, Washington, DC: Government Printing Office, 1968

Johnson, Hildegard Binder, *Order upon the Land: The US Rectangular Land Survey and the Upper Mississippi Country*, New York: Oxford University Press, 1976

Opie, John, *The Law of the Land: Two Hundred Years of American Farmland Policy*, Lincoln: University of Nebraska Press, 1987

Rohrbough, Malcolm J., *The Land Office Business: The Settlement and Administration of American Public Lands, 1787–1837*, New York: Oxford University Press, 1968

Worster, Donald, *Rivers of Empire: Water, Aridity, and the Growth of the American West*, New York: Pantheon, 1985

There are a number of one-volume histories of public land policy but GATES is the most monumental. It was written for the Public Land Law Review Commission, which was set up in 1964, to provide it with a study of the public land laws, their administration, weaknesses and inadequacies. It is based on both secondary and primary sources and includes new material on the operation of the land laws in Tennessee, Indiana and Nebraska. It is also strong on what happened in Illinois, Oregon and California. There is an opening general survey, and this is followed by a series of chapters that take the history of public land policy from colonial land systems to the reclamation of arid lands in the 20th century. It also contains a chapter by Robert W. Swierenga on the legal aspects of mineral resource exploitation on the public lands. Gates attempts to be dispassionate on the operation of the land laws, refusing, for instance, to condemn land speculation outright, and is able to defend voluntary tenancy, but readers are very likely to come away with a strong impression of the inadequacies of public land policies, at least since the 18th century.

OPIE is unreservedly critical of the way in which land policy was created and implemented. His particular targets include the rectangular survey, which took no notice, he argues, of contours, soil quality or water courses; the national ideology, especially the belief in unrestricted ownership of private property for personal profit, which so often shaped policy; and what he sees as the mythology of family farming. Here he points to the tension between the idea of the family farm existing to support its owner, and the need of farmers to produce for distant and eventually global markets. Some readers may be irritated by his relish for cutting down to size major historical figures, including even Washington and Jefferson, and may wonder whether he is entirely successful in defining his alternative to the agricultural system that has grown up since 1785. However, this is a vigorous critique which will attract those eager to deplore the excesses of private enterprise. There is no bibliography.

JOHNSON is far less critical of the rectangular survey, pointing out that land agents would have found it difficult to operate with a survey system in which land parcels were identified ambiguously. Those who know the trouble caused in California where many of the land grants made during the Mexican period were never properly surveyed, would be likely to concede this point. Her survey covers the colonial as well as the national period, and includes comments on French Canada and Japan. It also points up the fact that despite the rectangular survey, irregularly shaped townships occurred in both Minnesota and Wisconsin, while no fewer than six systems were used in the survey of Ohio lands. Johnson does admit that the system had its drawbacks, but sees it as cost-effective – and successful in producing accurate surveys. There is no bibliography but the work is well illustrated.

ROHRBOUGH introduces the reader to the early 19th century world of land speculators, greedy bureaucrats, weak central government and a general disinclination to obey the land laws, whatever they said. There was from the first a close connection between those who made land policy, in Congress or in the Treasury, and those who administered it, often to their own and their associates' advantage. The work does not need to be overtly critical of policy, since it throws up so many examples of its failings. It also shows implicitly how 18th-century views on administration lasted long into the 19th century, allowing those employed by government the moral freedom to exploit their position. Speaking of the Jacksonian politicians, Rohrbough notes that they served themselves, and their party, and not the nation, in their administration of the land laws. The bibliography would need updating, but the work shows an outstanding knowledge of sources.

FELLER comes close to arguing that land policy was the central issue of the Jacksonian years, though he denies that any one issue can explain the political configurations of the period. The work revolves around congressional debates and roll calls, and shows how land legislation reflected the desires of the East, including the Southeast, rather than the West. The West failed to secure passage of a Graduation Act, allowing for the sale of land at reduced prices if it had been on the market and unsold for specified periods, and eventually Henry Clay managed to pass a short-lived act to distribute revenues from the sale of western lands to all the states. The work is very successful in showing how Congress made its land policy, and how there was no general political agreement on what that policy should be. The bibliography suggests that this work is the product of an interest in both political and land law history.

Although all unreserved lands in the public domain were withdrawn from all forms of entry in 1934 and 1935, save where there were existing rights of entry, debate over land policy has continued, and often very vehemently. FAIRFAX and YALE is a very factual study of present-day revenue-producing programmes on the public lands, which significantly was produced by the Western Office of the Council of State Governments. Western states have recently become very vociferous on the matter of who should control the public lands, arguing that control should be exercised by those states within which the lands lie. All states have found the federal government increasingly eager to pass financial burdens to the individual states, which in turn have become increasingly interested in ways of raising revenue. Present-day land policy is thus being debated in terms of control over revenues from resources, the proper relation between the federal and state governments, and the issue of who should determine and control land policy. The authors try not to enter these controversies. Their brief is to establish what revenues are raised from resources, something that proves more difficult than might be imagined. There are helpful tables and maps, and close analysis of two pieces of legislation and their results: the 1872 General Mining Act and the 1920 Mineral Leasing Act. This study is particularly useful for understanding recent land legislation.

CAWLEY looks at contemporary western feeling on the question of control of the public domain. It is an attempt to understand the perceptions and motivations of the Sagebrush rebels, rather than an assessment of the morality or legitimacy of their complaints. Sagebrush rebels were so-called to suggest that the movement, which began in 1979 in Nevada to assert state rather than federal control over the public lands, was supported by the less-educated and less-knowledgeable of the rural populations, but the term was taken up by the rebellion and made a badge of honour. The work shows how the debate over control is connected to other issues, such as the definition and control of the wilderness, administration of grazing, mining and recreational rights, and urban/suburban growth. It also shows contemporary difficulties in defining terms like conservation and environmentalism. Cawley shows that, even during the presidency of Ronald Reagan, thought to be very sympathetic to the rebels, they did not achieve their aim, partly because many of them were as hostile as their eastern enemies to the idea that the public lands should be privatized. The issues behind the rebellion are, however, still smouldering.

WORSTER's substantial and significant work takes up the question of public land policy in the 20th century, in relation to arid land. It is clear from the start that the author is unimpressed by the way in which land laws have created the present-day hydraulic society in the West, through the intensive, large-scale manipulation of water and its products in an arid setting. The work explicitly acknowledges the influence of Karl August Wittfogel who produced the "hydraulic society" thesis that, as irrigation systems become more complex, power flows into the hands of an elite, typically a ruling class of bureaucrats and their allies. As this thesis suggests, Marx and Weber can also be detected in the background. Worster believes that the thesis does apply to the American West, the flavour of his views apparent in his comment on the Newlands Act that it was both an evasion of, and a distraction from, the problems being produced by America's corporate monopoly. The case is

powerfully made that land policies have increasingly given resources to the few, and helped to create a rural proletariat. Corporate interests have also become increasingly dangerous to the majority inasmuch as they have reinforced profligate attitudes to resources and led to environmental hazards, such as increasing salinity in water supplies, sedimentation, and pesticide contamination, not to mention a series of aging, collapsing dams. The costs of decommissioning those dams will surely not be met by agribusiness. Like Opie and, to a lesser extent, Gates, Worster sees that land policy has ultimately failed because it has been geared to the accumulation rather than the redistribution of private property. It is certainly difficult to suppose that Thomas Jefferson would approve of the contemporary situation in California's Central Valley, often thought of as synonymous with agribusiness.

R.A. BURCHELL

Pulitzer, Joseph   1847–1911
Newspaper editor and publisher

Barrett, James W., *Joseph Pulitzer and His World*, New York: Vanguard Press, 1941

Hohenberg, John, *The Pulitzer Prizes: A History of the Awards*, New York: Columbia University Press, 1974

Juergens, George, *Joseph Pulitzer and the New York World*, Princeton: Princeton University Press, 1966

Leonard, Thomas C., *The Power of the Press: The Birth of American Political Reporting*, New York: Oxford University Press, 1986

Pfaff, Daniel W., *Joseph Pulitzer II and the Post-Dispatch: A Newspaperman's Life*, University Park: Pennsylvania State University Press, 1991

Rammelkamp, Julian S., *Pulitzer's Post-Dispatch, 1878–1883*, Princeton: Princeton University Press, 1967

Seitz, Don C., *Joseph Pulitzer: His Life and Letters*, New York: Simon and Schuster, 1924; London: Bles, 1926

Swanberg, W.A., *Pulitzer*, New York: Scribner, 1967

The combined efforts of Swanberg, Rammelkamp and Juergens have produced a clearer picture of Joseph Pulitzer than exists for any other major figure in the American press of the 19th century. They make use of the extensive Pulitzer papers at Columbia University and the shelf of reminiscences from his fellow journalists and his private secretaries. These modern works are vastly more sophisticated than the narratives stitched together by the publisher's newspaper associates, Barrett and Seitz. However, SEITZ is the handiest place to find the hammer blows in letters that Pulitzer used to shape family members and journalists to his will. BARRETT remains useful for treating the death of Pulitzer's greatest paper as part of the evaluation of the journalist.

SWANBERG brings Pulitzer more fully to life than any other author, and provides a key to all phases of his career – one unusual feature in this book is the word code to Pulitzer's correspondence, in which for example "Malaria" was the Republican party. Swanberg acknowledges his debt to two lucid monographs published at about the same time.

RAMMELKAMP shows how Pulitzer set down roots in the German political culture of St. Louis, and then transcended ethnic ties with his newspaper. In Rammelkamp's view, Pulitzer was a herald of urban progressivism. JUERGENS places Pulitzer on the national stage after the publisher's move to New York in 1883, and has a sharp focus on his successes both in revitalizing the content of the American daily, and in extending its reach to a vast urban public. Both scholars establish that Pulitzer trimmed his political beliefs to suit his markets, and that there were gaps in his fabled editorial integrity. Swanberg is the best place to look for information on Pulitzer's excesses in coverage of the Spanish-American War, an episode which Juergens downplays along with other familiar tales, such as the round-the-world trip by Pulitzer reporter Nellie Bly. Swanberg argues that the publisher's conduct, especially in his later life, is suggestive of manic depressive psychosis. Whether or not he is right about this, Swanberg richly illustrates the role of anxiety and neurosis in the making of this reformer.

No journalist tried harder to make American life more public, with exposés of corruption, gossip on the passing scene, and calls for citizen action. Pulitzer raised funds for the pedestal of the Statue of Liberty in New York harbor, welcoming diversity to American shores. Biographers must struggle to explain how badly cast Pulitzer was for this role, with his mind fixed on the classics and, by the 1890s, his nerves unable to stand life in the United States. To escape, he spent many of his most influential years sailing his yacht on distant seas. In his biography of Pulitzer's middle son, PFAFF turns up new documentation of the father's physical torment (bordering on hypochondria) and his anxiety about acknowledging his Jewish parentage. In an age when "Jewish Pulitzer" was fair comment in the trade press, the publisher's sensitivity is understandable. (As an adult, he joined the Episcopal church.) Pulitzer's ethnic politics, accommodating immigrants with native stock, is a wonder of his journalism that has yet to be fully explained.

Pulitzer was a 19th-century liberal (no matter what leveling schemes his papers might endorse to please working-class readers). Along with his reclusiveness in the last decades, this has made it difficult to link him with 20th-century reform movements. LEONARD re-examines the link to a modern age of social activism. For him, Pulitzer is the master of the provincial scandal, and this marks his work off from the muckrakers in national magazines who succeeded in placing corruption in the context of a new age of reform.

Neither the memoirs nor the critical histories of Pulitzer have succeeded in making his legacy problematic. Pulitzer is a patron saint of print journalism, not the confounding figure known to his contemporaries. HOHENBERG shows how the ancestor worship was arranged. Pulitzer's gift to Columbia University made him the most honored founder of journalism education and the icon of the working press (in the prizes, which are embossed with his profile). One irony of this celebration is that Pulitzer is seldom recognized as a pioneer who settled the wrong frontier. The number of dailies had peaked before his death and when his beloved New York World failed in the 1930s, the circulation of newspapers had reached their zenith in American homes. His rival, William Randolph Hearst, never enjoyed Pulitzer's reputation for genius, yet he made the moves into new media that insured continued influence on popular culture. Pulitzer had no vision beyond the daily and expressed no interest in the other media prospering at the beginning of the 20th century. Biographers, too, have assumed that the daily is the defining institution of the press, an increasingly doubtful assumption as these newspapers lost their share of the audience in the last third of this century. Future scholars, who free themselves of the newspaper paradigm for journalism, are likely to see both the strengths and weaknesses of Pulitzer differently.

THOMAS C. LEONARD

See also Newspapers and Magazines

Puritanism

Foster, Stephen, *The Long Argument: English Puritanism and the Shaping of New England Culture, 1570–1700*, Chapel Hill: University of North Carolina Press, 1991
Gura, Philip F., *A Glimpse of Sion's Glory: Puritan Radicalism in New England, 1620–1660*, Middletown, CT: Wesleyan University Press, 1984
Hall, David D., *Worlds of Wonder, Days of Judgment: Popular Religious Belief in Early New England*, New York: Knopf, 1989
Innes, Stephen, *Creating the Commonwealth: The Economic Culture of Puritan New England*, New York: Norton, 1995
Martin, John Frederick, *Profits in the Wilderness: Entrepreneurship and the Founding of New England Towns in the Seventeenth Century*, Chapel Hill: University of North Carolina Press, 1991
Miller, Perry, *The New England Mind: The Seventeenth Century*, New York: Macmillan, 1939
Miller, Perry, *The New England Mind: From Colony to Province*, Cambridge, MA: Harvard University Press, 1953
Morgan, Edmund S., *The Puritan Dilemma: The Story of John Winthrop*, Boston: Little Brown, 1958
Rutman, Darrett B., *American Puritanism: Faith and Practice*, Philadelphia: Lippincott, 1970
Stout, Harry S., *The New England Soul: Preaching and Religious Culture in Colonial New England*, New York: Oxford University Press, 1986

The best, though perhaps the most difficult, place to begin an examination of Puritanism is with Perry Miller. His two-volume exegesis of the New England mind has defined the nature and scope of Puritan studies for the last fifty years. MILLER (1939) is a topical study; its overriding concern is structural rather than chronological. Miller defines, classifies, and traces the interrelationship among Puritan ideas pertaining to piety, logic, human nature, conversion, and the God of the Covenant. MILLER (1953) is more strictly chronological, and in this volume he examines the repercussions of accommodating a coherent and highly articulated set of imported ideas to the American landscape. Miller's story is one of spiritual declension, of Puritans decrying the erosion of piety and purposefulness among the generations of New Englanders who came after the first. Such self-denunciations, which Miller termed jeremiads, became the dominant literary production of 17th-century New Englanders and reflected ultimately the tension that existed between the demands of establishing an ideal Bible commonwealth here on earth and the dictates of making a living here and now.

Among Miller's followers, none has been more influential than MORGAN. In a book which has been required reading for legions of undergraduates in the United States, Morgan adopts his mentor's concept of Non-separating Congregationalism in recounting the experiences of John Winthrop and his cohorts. Non-separatists felt obliged to remain in the world without becoming worldly, to confront the evils and temptations of the world rather than to withdraw from them. Even the decision to emigrate to Massachusetts was a means of addressing the problems posed by the so-called corruption of the Anglican Church. By moving across the Atlantic and dedicating themselves to creating a "city upon a hill" that would serve as a model of reform, Winthrop and others hoped to withdraw from England without thereby engaging in the errors of separatism.

Whereas Morgan elaborates on some of the ideas that Miller originally presented, other historians take issue with him. GURA is critical of the disposition to regard Puritanism as a homogeneous doctrine. Among the twenty thousand colonists who migrated to New England in the 1630s, many espoused beliefs that were not consistent with the tenets of Non-separating Congregationalism. Diversity and heterogeneity characterized the New England migrants. Therefore, New England Puritanism was not a coherent import but a by-product of the challenges lodged against official doctrine by separatists, antinomians, anabaptists, millenarians, familists, seekers, and other radical dissenters.

Employing a transatlantic approach, FOSTER modifies Miller's interpretation in two ways. First, he argues that Puritanism was above all a movement; therefore, it resists the sort of denominational taxonomy offered in Miller (1939). English Puritans constituted a loose alliance of progressive Protestants whose identity was shaped over time as they responded to successive challenges. Second, Foster insists that American Puritanism cannot be understood apart from its English context. Unlike Miller, who contends that Puritanism in New England became in the 1640s an isolated remnant of English Protestantism, and that this isolation contributed to the Americanization of inherited ideas, Foster sees the changes occurring in New England as a continuation of the pattern of conflict and accommodation that came to define Puritanism in England during the half century before the first ships set sail for Massachusetts.

STOUT argues that Miller's studies, which are based on a brilliant reading of published sermons, tell only half of the story, because published sermons constitute a select fraction of the total number of sermons preached and heard in New England. Published sermons were primarily sermons delivered on special occasions: election days, days of thanksgiving, and public fasts, for example. By contrast, the message of the unpublished sermons preached routinely on Sundays changed very little over the course of the 17th century. Not declension, but continuity of commitment to the ideals of the divine covenant in New England stands out in these everyday sermons.

In a 1970 essay on the analytical utility of the concept of Puritanism, RUTMAN criticizes earlier studies which describe Puritanism in terms of ministerial doctrines. What the preachers said about sin and salvation, and how lay members interpreted what they heard, were potentially at variance. Historians have devoted much time and energy to examining the ideas of the former, Rutman says, they need now to concentrate on the ideas and actions of the latter.

HALL focuses on the beliefs of lay men and women and offers two provocative propositions. The first is that the spectrum of popular beliefs in New England was so vast that it cannot be subsumed without distortion under a single definition of faith. The second is that lay men and women, for the most part literate and opinionated, could not be dominated by the clergy. Divisions within the ranks of the clergymen themselves made any hope of domination tenuous to begin with, but lay believers also knew enough to select among the doctrinal choices presented to them.

Miller argues that a principal cause of the decline of piety in Massachusetts was the Puritans' growing involvement in commerce. Recently, historians have begun to reconsider the relationship between commercial development and Puritanism. MARTIN examines the founding of 63 towns in 17th-century New England, and concludes that the desire for profit played an important role in the majority of cases. Martin argues that this finding is surprising only because historians have assumed that commercial motives were antithetical to Puritan designs. They were not.

INNES asserts that Puritanism not only condoned profit-seeking but encouraged it. At the very core of Puritanism was a dynamic tension between social ethic and spiritual conviction. Puritans were model Protestants when it came to the work ethic. They strove to be industrious, diligent, and frugal; they despised those among their ranks who were idle and indolent. At the same time, however, Puritans were predisposed by conviction to distrust the consequences of their actions. Industriousness and frugality led to the accumulation of personal wealth, which in turn seemed inevitably to lead to worldliness and spiritual decay. Paradoxically, the practice of piety undermined the "city upon a hill."

MELVIN YAZAWA

See also Colonial History: Religion

R

Race

Du Bois, W.E.B., *Souls of Black Folk: Essays and Sketches*, Chicago: McClurg, 1903, London: Constable, 1905; reprinted, New York: Johnson, 1973

Fredrickson, George M., *The Black Image in the White Mind: The Debate on Afro-American Character and Destiny, 1817–1914*, New York: Harper, 1971

Fredrickson, George M., *The Arrogance of Race: Historical Perspectives on Slavery, Racism, and Social Inequality*, Middletown, CT: Wesleyan University Press, 1988

Genovese, Eugene D., *Roll, Jordan, Roll: The World the Slaves Made*, New York: Pantheon, 1974; London: Deutsch, 1975

Gutman, Herbert G., *The Black Family in Slavery and Freedom, 1750–1925*, New York: Pantheon, and Oxford: Blackwell, 1976

Huggins, Nathan Irvin, *Harlem Renaissance*, New York: Oxford University Press, 1971

Jordan, Winthrop D., *White over Black: American Attitudes Toward the Negro, 1550–1812*, Chapel Hill: University of North Carolina Press, 1968; abridged, as *The White Man's Burden: Historical Origins of Racism in the United States*, New York: Oxford University Press, 1974

Lemann, Nicholas, *The Promised Land: The Great Black Migration and How It Changed America*, New York: Knopf, and London: Macmillan, 1991

Meier, August, *Negro Thought in America, 1880–1915: Racial Ideologies in the Age of Booker T. Washington*, Ann Arbor: University of Michigan Press, 1963

Morgan, Edmund S., *American Slavery, American Freedom: The Ordeal of Colonial Virginia*, New York: Norton, 1975

Myrdal, Gunnar, *An American Dilemma: The Negro Problem and Modern Democracy*, 2 vols., New York: Harper, 1944; condensed by Arnold Rose as *The Negro in America*, 1948

Phillips, Ulrich Bonnell, *American Negro Slavery: A Survey of the Supply, Employment and Control of Negro Labor as Determined by the Plantation Regime*, New York: Appleton, 1918

Stampp, Kenneth M., *The Peculiar Institution: Slavery in the Ante-Bellum South*, New York: Knopf, 1956; London: Eyre and Spottiswoode, 1964

Takaki, Ronald T., *Iron Cages: Race and Culture in Nineteenth-Century America*, New York: Knopf, 1979; London: Athlone, 1980

Woodward, C. Vann, *The Strange Career of Jim Crow*, New York: Oxford University Press, 1955, 3rd revised edition, 1974

The native peoples of North America were objects of racial description and discrimination in the United States as were successive waves of European, Asian, and Latin American immigrants. But it was primarily the dark-skinned peoples of sub-Saharan Africa (the "Negroes" and their descendants) who occupied the center of all discussion of race in America. The changing social status and economic condition of African Americans over time defined the general areas within which discussions of race took place, in the contexts of racial slavery, emancipation and segregation, and the emergence of urban "ghettos."

Two very influential studies examine the evolution of racial attitudes and their relationship to a system of racial slavery, in the colonial and Revolutionary eras. JORDAN focused his work on the racial dimension of slavery and traced the idea of racial hierarchy to the psycho-sexual realm of British and European encounters with sub-Saharan Africans. These encounters were, in Jordan's analysis, both exploitative and erotic, leading to a construction of race among whites that was not simply a justification for the control of a subject people's labor power, but an outlet for the deepest sexual fears and fantasies. "Whiteness" came to signify the inner purity and self-control of modern society, whereas "blackness" encompassed the licentiousness and wilfulness that modernity suppressed.

MORGAN examined the social relations of slavery in the colonial period, as they affected class relations among southern whites. The preference of Virginia planters for white indentured servants ended only when the rebellion led by Nathaniel Bacon in 1676 exposed deep and dangerous class divisions between tidewater planters and the white laborers they endeavored to command. African slavery helped to bridge these gaps by insuring that the propertyless laboring class, which otherwise could constitute a mob, were enslaved Africans. All white men, by contrast, were free and equal in their status as independent producers. Racial slavery thereby provided social stability and white equality for the South in the new American nation.

The modern historical debate over slavery has obvious implications for the history of race in America. For many years, that debate centred on PHILLIPS's study of the antebellum plantation system. Phillips acknowledged, abstractly, the injustice of the Atlantic slave trade, but he insisted that slavery in the American South extended the benefits of civilization to a people who otherwise would have languished in the "African jungle." Whatever its economic impact, slavery also "left a permanent and increasingly complex problem of racial adjustments." Fundamental to Phillips's perspective were three propositions: that slavery was "less a business than a life"; that slavery made "fewer fortunes than it made men"; and, that as a "picturesque" way of life for whites and blacks, neither its "basis" nor its "operation" were "wholly evil."

STAMPP wrote in direct rebuttal to Phillips, contradicting at every turn characterizations of plantation slavery as largely benevolent and benign. As described by Stampp, slavery had no saving graces. "When freedom came," he concluded, "the Negro, in literal truth, lost nothing but his chains." Moreover, Stampp dismissed the notion that race fitted the African American to servitude. Whereas Phillips had treated unruliness among slaves in a chapter entitled "Slave Crime," Stampp described a wide array of slave resistance and rebellion. The slave felt the cruelty of his situation keenly, Stampp insisted, and resisted his oppressors at every opportunity."I have assumed," wrote Stampp in a famous introductory line, "that innately Negroes "are, after all, only white men with black skins." Stampp intended thereby to set aside white racial prejudice against blacks, although it seemed to some critics that he overlooked the significance of race in the process.

GENOVESE placed the psychology of racism within a structure of racial paternalism and examined slavery as a dialectical bond between whites and blacks, a bond that made the expression of the "simplest human feelings" of the one a "reference to the other." The "picturesque" society described by Phillips became in Genovese's analysis a unique pre-capitalist society. Slavery, argued Genovese, was a system of "class rule" involving two races; the social relations of slavery were essentially relations of class.

The destruction of slavery in the Civil War marked the beginning of an era of radical transformation in race relations in the South. The capacity of slavery to maintain an equality and unity among whites of all classes ceased to exist and the social status and economic independence of white yeoman farmers declined dramatically. WOODWARD, the leading historian of the post-emancipation South, emphasized the promise of the southern populist movement in the late 19th century and the devastating consequences of its defeat. In the early populist movement pauperized white farmers formed political alliances with freedmen in a common pursuit of economic justice. However, the manipulation of racial divisions and antipathies by economic elites broke apart the populist alliances and opened the way to a new era of racial segregation. Segregation imposed by whites reconstructed a racial border and in the process defined an arena of white privilege independent of slavery. Woodward has modified but not abandoned his interpretation of Jim Crow in the light of criticism from various directions.

Although less severe, racism and racial segregation permeated the North as well. FREDRICKSON (1971) examined the intellectual history of white racial thought from the early national period into the Darwinian age of evolution. He found two principal themes: "hierarchical biracialism," which

required a system of enforcing and maintaining white supremacy; and, "racial homogeneity," which envisioned the disappearance of the African American from the United States. Slavery and segregation provided mechanisms for maintaining white supremacy (and preventing "miscegenation" or race mixing) in a biracial society; colonization schemes and Darwinian visions of biological extinction illustrated the white dream of a racially homogeneous nation. White racial thought interacted with both themes over time and managed to accommodate antislavery as well as proslavery interests. Slaveholding paternalism fit comfortably within hierarchical biracialism whereas the "romantic racialism" of abolitionism (derived from racial Anglo-Saxonism) could express its fond, if condescending, view of African Americans as a simple, warmhearted, joyous people in biracial or homogeneous terms. Fredrickson has continued to write extensively on racial themes, often in the context of comparison with South Africa. A collection of his essays which shed light on a variety of topics – from slavery to Jim Crow and on to the comparative dimension – are conveniently brought together in FREDRICKSON (1988).

TAKAKI defined white racial thought in 19th-century America as the legitimating ideology of empire. He linked the racial subordination of African Americans (who produced the export commodities of the American continental empire) with the near extermination of the Indian (who stood in the path of westward expansion) and with the exploitation of Chinese labor in the West (as American imperial ambitions reached across the Pacific). Takaki also linked race and gender (ideals of womanhood and masculinity), a topic of widening interest to historians of the late 20th century.

The capacity of white racial thought to distort African American history and to misdirect public policy animated GUTMAN's study of the black family. Specifically, Gutman responded to Daniel Patrick Moynihan's controversial 1965 report to President Lyndon Johnson which linked the perceived breakdown of the black family to the heritage of slavery. Moynihan initially called for government intervention, but soon changed his mind. In a memo to President Richard Nixon in 1970, Moynihan argued that slavery had so deeply damaged the African American family that federal "Great Society" programs of uplift were inappropriate and ineffective. Moynihan concluded that the time had come "when the issue of race could benefit from a period of 'benign neglect.'" Gutman insisted that the so-called breakdown of the black family in urban America resulted not from slavery but from the mid-20th century uprooting of southern sharecroppers by mechanized cotton pickers and from the oppressive effects of the welfare policies that Moynihan alternately wished to expand and contract. Gutman argued that African Americans responded with healthy human ingenuity to the oppressive conditions of slavery. For example, although bondage made legally binding marriages among slaves impossible, Gutman uncovered long-lasting de facto marriages, and argued that the slave family helped to spread a "common slave culture" over the antebellum South. That culture moved into the North, drawn to its industrial centers during World War I, where the family structure changed but showed no signs of the general breakdown widely noted by the mid-20th century. As a public discussion of race and family values began in earnest, Gutman's work argued forcefully that diverse family structures reflected human responses to specific, and changing, circumstances.

The "Great Migration" of southern black sharecroppers to the industrial North insured that the "Negro problem," so long associated with the South, became a national problem. In 1937, the Carnegie Corporation commissioned the Swedish sociologist Gunnar Myrdal to produce a detailed report on "The Negro Problem" in the United States. MYRDAL wrote at a time of national and international crisis. His study extolled an underlying "American creed" of liberty and equality. Within this creed, racial injustice persisted as an anomaly that Myrdal predicted would end as the United States developed a sense of its own mission in the world. The 1954 Supreme Court decision ending racial segregation in public schools seemed to Myrdal a confirmation of his predictions. Myrdal concluded that black Americans, denied identification with the national group, held on to a variety of contradictory opinions. MEIER explored both radical and conservative ideologies in the era of segregation and into the first wave of southern black migration northward. The dominant racial ideology among Negroes in the "Age of Booker T. Washington" was one of self-help and racial solidarity. It gave rise to Negro accommodation to segregation. However, the Harlem Renaissance of the 1910s and 1920s and the rise of the "New Negro" (confident, northern, urban, and middle class) generated a contradictory ideology of individualism, upward mobility, and integration into white culture.

The New Negro raised the issue of African American ethnic identity and it was in this context that DU BOIS developed his influential concept of "double-consciousness." The "veil" of race obscured "true self-consciousness" because it demanded that the Negro see himself through the alienating perspective of white society. Efforts to see beyond the racial veil required an African American ethnic identity, but it was precisely here, argued HUGGINS, that the Harlem Renaissance was most problematic. African Americans, unlike other immigrant groups in the late 19th and early 20th centuries, remained unavoidably native Americans and enmeshed in ethnic representations often created and enacted by whites. The participation of black performers in blackface minstrelsy seemed to Huggins to be an unavoidable but pathological expression of double-consciousness, ensuring that theatrical expressions of African American ethnicity could not rise above the level of travesty.

The growing attention paid by scholars in the late 20th century to ethnicity – that is, to cultural cohesion shaped by consent, in contrast to the biological determinism of racial descent – reflected the fact that race in the 20th century lost the explanatory power that 18th and 19th century science had claimed for it. The social order that race had once defined collapsed; lacking social legitimacy, racial patriarchy lost its capacity for benevolence and its capacity to elicit deference. The language of race became simply a language of anger and resentment. Writing for a popular audience, LEMANN recounted the history of the Great Migration and focused attention on northern responses to it. Liberal outrage over a history of enslavement and a heritage of southern poverty and oppression – the latter made violently clear in southern white resistance to the civil rights movement in the 1950s and 1960s – produced efforts at the national level to sweep aside

segregation and with it the poverty and hostility of racial isolation. Lemann focused on the failure of well-intentioned programs of racial integration, and on mounting white opposition to affirmative action remedies for past patterns of racial discrimination. In Lemann's view, liberal programs for racial justice succeeded only in alienating much of the white working class from the social programs of the Democratic party. Lemann chronicled the collapse of 1960s confidence and idealism, but left untold the story of African American immigrant success in urban America, the effects of which would undoubtedly shape the future of ethnic awareness and assimilation.

LOUIS S. GERTEIS

See also African American History entries; Jim Crow; Slavery entries

Radio and Television

Aitken, Hugh G.J., *The Continuous Wave: Technology and American Radio, 1900–1932*, Princeton: Princeton University Press, 1985

Boddy, William, *Fifties Television: The Industry and Its Critics*, Urbana: University of Illinois Press, 1990

Douglas, Susan J., *Inventing American Broadcasting, 1899–1922*, Baltimore: Johns Hopkins University Press, 1987

Hilmes, Michele, *Hollywood and Broadcasting: From Radio to Cable*, Urbana: University of Illinois Press, 1990

MacDonald, J. Fred, *One Nation under Television: The Rise and Decline of Network Television*, New York: Pantheon, 1990

Smulyan, Susan, *Selling Radio: The Commercialization of American Broadcasting, 1920–1934*, Washington, DC: Smithsonian Institution Press, 1994

Udelson, Joseph H., *The Great Television Race: A History of the American Television Industry, 1925–1941*, University: University of Alabama Press, 1982

AITKEN examines American radio from the perspectives of technological development and corporate history. His approach emphasizes the interaction between science, technology, and the economy in the process of technological development. The first half of the book examines the maturation of "continuous wave" technology, which made possible the transmission of voices. The second part focuses on the creation and expansion of early radio's dominant corporate enterprise, the Radio Corporation of America. This account is less concerned with the impact of radio than with the shift in control of radio technology from individual inventors to large corporate entities such as RCA. Figuring prominently in the account is the role of patent law and government support.

Focusing on the social and cultural trends through 1922, DOUGLAS explains radio's evolution toward entertainment broadcasting. This "social construction" approach delineates how radio moved away from initial perceptions of its usefulness as an alternate form of telegraph or telephone, and came to be incorporated into popular culture. A burgeoning middle-class consumer culture, the increasing control that large corporations exercised over new technologies, and society's increasing tendency to look to the government for regulatory purposes emerge as central forces in the evolution of American radio. Douglas is particularly effective in discussing the role of popular perceptions and representations, and also of gender, in early American radio.

SMULYAN continues Douglas's story of the evolution of American radio through the 1920s and into the 1930s. She examines how advertising came to be incorporated into radio broadcasting, and assesses the impact of that development upon the radio industry, as well as the larger social implications. In general, Smulyan examines how "social and cultural choices affect technology at the same time that technology affects society and culture." The role of the broadcasting industry, advertisers, economic factors, the state, the demands of the audience, and the protestations of those with alternative views of radio's potential all figure in the rise of commercial broadcasting. According to the author, the 1934 Communications Act epitomized and reinforced the prevailing trend in American radio by not questioning the commercial orientation of radio. Smulyan concludes with an examination of today's mass media, the parallels that exist with radio's earlier development toward commercial broadcasting, and the continuing influence of the 1934 Communications Act.

UDELSON maps the technological development of television through 1941. The precedents set by the radio industry, combined with a consumer demand for high quality technology, exercised great influence over the course of television's development. As radio and movies were incorporated into popular culture, improvements in television's technological capabilities were made with an eye toward capturing a share of the mass entertainment market. As with the obstacles that radio faced, low-quality transmission and regulatory problems needed to be overcome before a mass audience would accept the highly anticipated new medium. The necessary technological improvements were in place by 1941, though the medium's successful introduction into society at large was delayed by World War II. Udelson is strong on the political and corporate dynamics of television's development. Less attention is paid to the dynamics of the potential audience within its larger social context.

Following World War II, television situated itself in the American social landscape. By the 1950s, the "Golden Age" of television had dawned. Declaring that so-called "Golden Age" a myth, BODDY examines television's transition from "theater television" supported by a single sponsor, to Hollywood-dominated film programming underwritten by multiple sponsors. In mapping this transition, he examines the precedents set by the closely related radio industry, the economic and promotional strategies of the networks, changes in advertising and marketing strategies, and the interaction between corporate power and the Federal Communications Commission. These developments culminated in greater network control over the content and style of programming. Boddy concludes with the quiz show scandals of 1959 to highlight the growing criticism directed toward commercial television and its programs, criticisms that continue to sound familiar today.

MacDONALD is a comprehensive history of television from its inception up to the present. The corporate giants, the industry's decision makers, the society in which they operated, the political possibilities and resistance which they faced, and the programs they aired form the broad parameters of this study. The television industry evolves against a backdrop of inefficiency and corruption. In this balanced study, MacDonald praises television's ability to entertain and inform the public, though criticism is aimed at the medium's tendency to misrepresent, even "brutalize," reality. The story is taken into the dramatically changing telecommunications environment of the 1980s and the subsequent options and challenges facing network television. A concluding discussion of the need for a radical restructuring of commercial television to compete in the "new video order" anticipates the media mergers of the present.

In an examination of the mass entertainment industry, HILMES focuses on the Hollywood film industry's interactions with radio and television broadcasting. The author demonstrates how the various media influenced each other over the course of their development. A central theme throughout the study is Hollywood's ability to use radio and television to strengthen its own position. Through advertising, program production, and the selling of broadcast rights, Hollywood has maintained an influential presence in entertainment programming broadcast into the home. Over the course of the 20th century, Hollywood has consistently demonstrated its ability to adapt to technological and structural changes which affect the mass entertainment industry, most recently evidenced by the mutually beneficial association established with "pay-cable." Not unlike Douglas and Smulyan, Hilmes is concerned with the process by which the institutions and content of this country's mass entertainment industry took shape. In similar fashion to MacDonald, Hilmes concludes her study with a look at the dramatic changes occurring by the late 1980s in America's telecommunications market. Most of these studies suggest that the future form which America's mass entertainment industry assumes will reflect the continuing interactions between science, technology, the economy, and society.

MICHAEL A. KRYSKO

See also Communications and Media

Railroads: General

Adler, Dorothy R., *British Investment in American Railways, 1834–1898*, Charlottesville: University Press of Virginia, 1970

Chandler, Alfred D., Jr., *The Railroads: The Nation's First Big Business: Sources and Readings*, New York: Harcourt Brace, 1965

Cochran, Thomas C., *Railroad Leaders, 1845–1890: The Business Mind in Action*, Cambridge, MA: Harvard University Press, 1953

Fishlow, Albert, *American Railroads and the Transformation of the Antebellum Economy*, Cambridge, MA: Harvard University Press, 1965

Fogel, Robert William, *Railroads and American Economic Growth: Essays in Econometric History*, Baltimore: Johns Hopkins Press, 1964

Grodinsky, Julius, *Transcontinental Railway Strategy, 1869–1893: A Study of Businessmen*, Philadelphia: University of Pennsylvania Press, 1962

Kirkland, Edward C., *Men, Cities, and Transportation: A Study in New England History, 1820–1900*, 2 vols., Cambridge, MA: Harvard University Press, 1948

Kolko, Gabriel, *Railroads and Regulation, 1877–1916*, Princeton: Princeton University Press, 1965

Licht, Walter, *Working for the Railroad: The Organization of Work in the Nineteenth Century*, Princeton: Princeton University Press, 1983

Martin, Albro, *Railroads Triumphant: The Growth, Rejection and Rebirth of a Vital American Force*, New York: Oxford University Press, 1992

Olson, Sherry H., *The Depletion Myth: A History of Railroad Use of Timber*, Cambridge, MA: Harvard University Press, 1971

Scott, Roy V., *Railroad Development Programs in the Twentieth Century*, Ames: Iowa State University Press, 1985

Stover, John, *American Railroads*, Chicago: University of Chicago Press, 1961

Taylor, George Rogers, *The Transportation Revolution, 1815–1860*, New York: Rinehart, 1951

Taylor, George Rogers and Irene D. Neu, *The American Railroad Network, 1861–1890*, Cambridge, MA: Harvard University Press, 1956

Wilkins, Mira, *The History of Foreign Investment in the United States to 1914*, Cambridge, MA: Harvard University Press, 1989

American railroad histories range from the celebratory and the descriptive to the highly political and economically analytical. The subject touches land policy, business enterprise, the raising of capital on an unprecedented scale, the development of corporate organization, labour in all its aspects – and, of course, the significance of railroads for American economic development.

STOVER provides a straightforward narrative account of American railroad history, including two chapters on railroad problems after 1920. A similar descriptive account is to be found in TAYLOR and NEU, though its chronological span is more limited. They examine the vast technological changes, particularly in the 1880s, which transformed the fragmented lines of 1860 into an integrated network of 160,000 miles of standard gauge, with most of the physical obstacles to the free flow of traffic overcome. KIRKLAND's two volumes incorporate much of the 19th-century history of New England within the framework of his study of all forms of transport – but with railroads taking pride of place. The books are vigorous in style, and encyclopedic in content.

The construction of the railroads placed heavy requirements on raw material supplies, not least on timber. In the first phase of building, wood was used wherever possible. The greatest need was for ties and, when the lines were being laid across the treeless prairies, timber had to be transported over vast distances. The "myth" about which OLSON writes is that railroad demand was one reason for the international concern in the 1890s of a timber famine. Olson concludes that the fears were unfounded because of research in timber technology which extended the range of usable timbers, and the experimental plantations started by the railroads themselves.

A different kind of "myth", that the farm community was the exploited victim of railroad monopolists, is examined by GRODINSKY. He, too, sees the 1880s as crucial, when the massive building, especially in 1886–89, led to the most widespread rate reductions in American railroad history. This occurred in the context of inadequate supplies of capital, requiring business leaders to be primarily capital-raisers; the initial aim was to avoid loss rather than make profit, and the main method was to secure satisfactory rates. Territorial monopolies were generally vulnerable and short-lived, a continuing story of positions established and demolished, or agreements reached and abandoned. What eventually brought rate stability was the rapid growth of traffic from 1890 onwards, resulting mainly from heavy movements of farm produce.

Railroad business leaders are examined by COCHRAN in a pioneering study in entrepreneurship. The theme of capital-raising and the associated development of the railroad corporation has attracted considerable attention. CHANDLER sees the railroad as the prototype of the subsequently widespread business corporation. Both ADLER and WILKINS examine the importance of foreign, especially British, capital in the process. LICHT examines every conceivable aspect of labour on the railroads, including recruitment, work practices, injuries, social life and unionization. The subject is viewed solely from the point of view of railroad employees, but the treatment is extremely comprehensive.

TAYLOR is a general textbook in the multi-volume Rinehart series, on The Economic History of the United States. Now widely acknowledged as a classic, it examines the role of transport in general, and the railroad in particular, in industrialization and general economic development during the period 1815–60. It was this question of the railroads' contribution to growth that brought "new" economic historians into the discussion. FISHLOW's methodology was new, using advanced statistical and mathematical techniques applied to a remarkable range of source materials. His conclusions supported the traditional view that railroads were of crucial significance. While rejecting the more extravagant claims of Jenks or Rostow, he reached precise and judicious conclusions: at least up to the Civil War, railroads did reduce costs of freight and passenger travel, generated resource development through construction and operation (what he termed "backward linkages"), created responses in other sectors through "forward linkages" as new transport facilities were made available and, not least, helped to disseminate industrial skills through the need for widely dispersed repair and maintenance facilities.

In contrast, FOGEL, using even more complex methodology, challenged all previous assumptions. He asserted that the effect of railroads could only be assessed by first constructing a counterfactual model of what conditions would have been in 1890 in their absence. Accordingly he calculated the likely consequences for the American economy had no railroads been built, the most important assumption being that far more canals would have been constructed. Concentrating almost solely on the grain trade, he concluded that the difference made to the gross national product in 1890 was not of great significance. His controversial methodology and conclusion provoked a very considerable subsequent literature.

KOLKO was similarly controversial on the politics of railroad regulation, suggesting that the mechanisms which developed placed power in the hands of the railroad barons themselves, a thesis vigorously contested by MARTIN and other writers. SCOTT is one of several writers examining aspects of railroad history in the 20th century. He claims that no other institution has been engaged in development work for so long or in such diverse forms as railroads, and asserts that no other private enterprise has invested as much in the promotion of economic development.

JIM POTTER

See also Transport

Railroads: Legislation and Court Cases, 1880s–1920s

Benson, Lee, *Merchants, Farmers, and Politics: Railroad Regulation and New York Politics, 1850–1887*, Cambridge, MA: Harvard University Press, 1955

Hoogenboom, Ari and Olive Hoogenboom, *A History of the ICC: From Panacea to Palliative*, New York: Norton, 1976

Kerr, K. Austin, *American Railroad Politics, 1914–1920*, Pittsburgh: University of Pittsburgh Press, 1968

Kolko, Gabriel, *Railroads and Regulation, 1877–1916*, Princeton: Princeton University Press, 1965

Martin, Albro, *Enterprise Denied: The Origins of the Decline of the American Railroads, 1897–1917*, New York: Columbia University Press, 1971

Miller, George H., *Railroads and the Granger Laws*, Madison: University of Wisconsin Press, 1971

Skowronek, Stephen, *Building a New American State: The Expansion of National Administrative Capacities, 1877–1920*, Cambridge and New York: Cambridge University Press, 1982

Railroad regulation was one of the central issues in political debate during both the Gilded Age and the Progressive Era. Not surprisingly, it is also a topic that has aroused fierce disagreement among historians. Of all the surveys of federal railroad policy, undoubtedly the most controversial has been KOLKO, which argues that the primary purpose of government policy was to aid the big railroads. The carriers welcomed the creation of the Interstate Commerce Commission (ICC) in 1887, hoping that it would provide them with some protection from the ravages of competition. Moreover, in practice regulation vindicated these hopes. The members of the ICC were sympathetic towards the railroads, using their powers to protect the latter's profits. Most importantly, America's political leaders consistently supported the interests of the major carriers. Kolko is particularly emphatic that "Progressives", such as Roosevelt and Wilson, were as determined to protect the interests of railroads as their "conservative" counterparts.

However, the author fails to substantiate this argument fully. He does prove that America's political leaders were keen that the railroads should be financially strong, but he provides less evidence that they were prepared to subordinate the interests of all other groups to those of the railroads.

While MARTIN is equally dismissive of railroad regulation, the basis of his critique is radically different from Kolko's. He accuses the federal government of conducting a vindictive and repressive policy towards the railroads, a policy that contributed materially to the decline in railroad services that has taken place in the 20th century. He argues that the ICC's repeated refusal to allow rate increases deprived railroads of vital revenue, preventing them from carrying out necessary investment. He also condemns the government's refusal to allow the railroads to engage in pooling. Martin makes no secret of his total disdain for many of the policymakers, and parts of his account are positively splenetic. But he is a skilled business historian and is able to produces a mass of convincing evidence in support of his major conclusions.

SKOWRONEK approaches railroad regulation from a very different perspective from either Kolko or Martin. He examines the history of the ICC as part of a wider attempt to chart how the American government adapted to the increasingly complex tasks facing it in the four decades after Reconstruction. He highlights the hesitancy and ineffectiveness of the government's attempts at regulation during the Gilded Age. The desire of Congress to appeal to diverse economic interest groups prevented it from formulating a clear, effective policy, while judicial hostility obstructed the ICC's attempts to impose order on the railroads. The author shows that during the Progressive Era, by contrast, the ICC was allowed to expand its authority dramatically, ensuring that it was able to establish itself as a powerful regulatory agency. Although Skowronek's discussion of railroad policy is relatively brief, the clarity and rigour of his analysis ensure that his accounts adds greatly to our understanding of the dynamics of regulation.

In their survey of the ICC's history HOOGENBOOM and HOOGENBOOM provide a short, straightforward account of the Commission's policies during the Gilded Age and Progressive Era. In general, their assessment of the Commission's performance is critical. They admit that judicial hostility weakened the ICC during the 1890s, but they insist that it was the mediocre quality of the Commissioners and their staff that was responsible for the ICC's ineffectiveness during the Progressive era. Instead of trying to impose a clear policy, Commissioners were prepared to react in an ad hoc manner to individual crises. The Hoogenbooms' study is based primarily upon secondary sources, rather than upon extensive primary research, and it lacks the analytical vigour that characterises the works of Kolko, Martin and Skowronek. But it does, nevertheless, provide a very clear and balanced introduction to the complex history of regulation.

As well as these general surveys, there are several more specialised studies which shed light on the history of railroad policy during this period. Several writers focus on the development of regulation during the Gilded Age. MILLER looks at the efforts of states in the upper Mississippi Valley to impose controls on the railroads during the 1870s. He argues that the principal promoters of these measures were merchants who hoped to prevent the carriers from charging discriminatory rates. Miller plays down the farmers' role in campaigning for railroad reform, and shows that agrarian leaders tried to restrain merchants from passing more stringent measures. All in all, his account of the development of railroad regulation in these states is deft and convincing. As well as looking at the development of state regulation, BENSON provides a detailed account of the origins of federal control. He emphasizes that many groups felt threatened by the uncontrolled power of the railroads, thus ensuring that there was widespread support for state and federal regulation. He argues, in particular, that the leading role in promoting the Interstate Commerce Act of 1887 was played by New York merchants who believed that regulation would prevent carriers from discriminating in favour of traders in other cities.

Other historians focus on the dramatic impact of World War I upon the railroads. In the fullest account of the evolution of federal policy during the war and its aftermath, KERR questions whether the war should be seen as a watershed in railroad policy, marking a shift between the Progressive policies of the pre-war era and the conservative, pro-business policies of the 1920s. Like Kolko, he denies that federal regulation ever acted to protect the public interest against the interests of business; rather, he insists, it simply enabled diverse economic groups to reconcile their clashing interests. Parts of Kerr's analysis seem questionable: in particular, he deploys relatively little evidence to support his bold claims about the character of regulation in the Progressive Era. But his analysis of the way in which the struggles between rival carriers, shippers and labour shaped policy between 1917 and 1920 is superb.

PHILIP J. CULLIS

See also Antitrust Legislation and Court Cases

Reagan, Ronald 1911–
40th President of the United States

Anderson, Martin, *Revolution*, San Diego: Harcourt Brace, 1988; revised as *Revolution: The Reagan Legacy*, Stanford, CA: Hoover Institution Press, 1990

Cannon, Lou, *Reagan*, New York: Putnam, 1982

Dallek, Robert, *Ronald Reagan: The Politics of Symbolism*, Cambridge, MA: Harvard University Press, 1984

Hogan, Joseph (editor), *The Reagan Years: The Record in Presidential Leadership*, Manchester: Manchester University Press, 1990

Jones, Charles O. (editor), *The Reagan Legacy: Promise and Performance*, Chatham, NJ: Chatham House, 1988

Kymlicka, B.B. and Jean V. Matthews (editors), *The Reagan Revolution?*, Chicago: Dorsey Press, 1988

Mervin, David, *Ronald Reagan and the American Presidency*, London: Longman, 1990

Rogin, Michael Paul, *Ronald Reagan, the Movie, and Other Episodes in Political Demonology*, Berkeley: University of California Press, 1987

Schaller, Michael, *Reckoning with Reagan: America and Its President in the 1980s*, New York: Oxford University Press, 1992

Vaughn, Stephen, *Ronald Reagan in Hollywood: Movies and Politics*, Cambridge and New York: Cambridge University Press, 1994

White, John Kenneth, *The New Politics of Old Values*, Hanover, NH: University Press of New England, 1988

Wills, Garry, *Reagan's America*, New York: Penguin, 1988

Ronald Reagan's multi-faceted career as radio, movie and television actor, California governor, spokesman for a resurgent Republican right, and finally United States president has made him one of the most written-about personalities of the 20th century. Much of this literature is broadly interpretive, synthetic and sometimes polemical, rather than based on the primary sources conventionally used by historians but not yet available for research on Reagan.

To date, CANNON is the best study of Reagan's pre-presidential life in its entirety and has been much drawn upon by students of his presidency. It is particularly good on Reagan's governorship, which the author covered as a Los Angeles *Times* journalist, and highlights the distinction between the conservatism of his rhetoric and the pragmatism of his actual policy.

Through his films Reagan left behind a more visible record before entering elective office than any other major politician, and his Hollywood career has therefore attracted much scholarly attention. VAUGHN promises to be the definitive study. Based on vast primary research and focusing on the period from 1937 to 1952, it shows Reagan's political transformation from shallow liberal to avowed conservative within the mid-20th century Hollywood environment. Vaughn's analysis of the cultural themes of Reagan's films draws parallels between their use of history and their message regarding communism, liberalism, welfare, patriotism, national defense, individualism, and family values and his later rhetoric as president on many of the same issues. Reagan's central role in the Hollywood Red Scare and his emergence as a skilled propagandist for the movie industry receive detailed coverage. ROGIN deals more impressionistically but still convincingly with the same themes, and portrays Reagan and the politics he represented as the product of the films that were so much a part of American mass culture. Drawing on the paranoid fear of conspiracy which some historians see as central to American political history, this study suggests that Reagan's anti-Soviet "evil empire" rhetoric reflected the nation's collective psychological focus on "demons", and that movies, beginning with D.W. Griffith's racist masterpiece *Birth of a Nation* (1915), have done much to weaken the barriers between popular paranoia and social reality.

Many studies suggest that Reagan's personal appeal and political success as president were based on the values which he represented. For WILLS, his greatest strength was that he made Americans feel good about themselves as a nation. His ability to do this was dependent not simply on communication skills, but also on an unquestioning belief in the values and cosy vision of the American past, derived from his midwestern small-town upbringing and career in the Hollywood "dream factory". The book focuses predominantly on Reagan's pre-presidential career, and readers need to be well informed about the broad outlines of administration policies if they are to derive full benefit from Wills's interpretive and relatively brief coverage of them, and from his argument that, as president, Reagan not only represented the past, but resurrected it as the promise of the future. In a more accessible interpretation, DALLEK suggests that Reaganite Republicanism was a complex phenomenon: tax cuts, less government and strong defence were more important as symbols of traditional values rather than as material goals designed to appeal to voters' rational self-interest. WHITE offers a sophisticated and highly readable analysis of Reaganite rhetoric and poll data to reach a similar conclusion. In his view, Reagan's political genius was to convey a sense of shared values with the American people that provided an antidote to the problems and uncertainties that had beset the nation since the late 1960s. His appeal was philosophical rather than political. Polls showed that many voters had doubts about his policies, but still supported him because he had shown a world that Americans had wanted to see, even if they could no longer live there.

It is too early for a definitive assessment of Reagan's presidency. ANDERSON offers a highly partisan account, but he merits attention as a *bona fide* scholar who was Reagan's domestic policy adviser. In contrast to those emphasizing the primary significance of values in understanding Reagan's political appeal, he argues that it was the worldwide intellectual renaissance of conservatism in the 1970s that make Reaganism possible. Anderson also claims that the policy achievements of the Reagan presidency on free-market economics, tax reform, welfare reform, and foreign policy added up to a revolution. However, this view gains little support from more objective analysts.

There are two very useful brief interpretive studies of the Reagan presidency. MERVIN, a British political scientist, argues that Reagan was the most successful president since Franklin D. Roosevelt, because he restored presidential prestige and leadership in the wake of Watergate, Vietnam and the weak presidencies of Gerald Ford and Jimmy Carter. This judgement reflects the book's emphasis on policy process rather than policy substance, and Mervin concludes that Reagan had far more success in transforming the terms of political debate than in achieving his policy objectives. SCHALLER is much more critical. Though praising Reagan for restoring national pride and confidence, he suggests that his legacy was complicated and contradictory on issues like taxation (social security tax increases outweighed personal income tax cuts in the lower half of the income distribution), new federalism (which transferred costs but not power to state government), and balancing the budget. Schaller even attributes Cold War victory more to internal Soviet developments than to Reagan's "peace through strength" approach.

Three of the numerous essay collections published at the end of Reagan's presidency offer good instant analysis of his legacy. All are agreed that the political changes of the 1980s did not constitute a revolution and that their true significance will depend on whether the course of public policy in the 1990s and beyond sees the expansion or rejection of conservatism. HOGAN offers a mainly British perspective on a wide range of institutional and political issues, such as Reagan's revitalization of the presidency, his judicial appointments and his role as party leader. It has especially good essays by Hogan (on the budget deficit) and Nigel Ashford (on the new conservatism). JONES proffers the views of a group of eminent American political scientists on the same range of issues, and contains a famous essay by Aaron Wildavsky on Reagan as a political strategist. More polemical and therefore more lively than either of these two is KYMLICKA and MATTHEWS. This set of essays adopts a broad perspective and includes contributions by historians, sociologists, economists and political scientists. It contains a lively essay by Richard Polenberg comparing the impact of FDR and Reagan, and a savage diatribe against Reaganomics by the Keynesian *doyen*, James Tobin.

IWAN W. MORGAN

Recent American History (since 1945): General

Barone, Michael, *Our Country: The Shaping of America from Roosevelt to Reagan*, New York: Free Press, and London: Collier Macmillan, 1990

Boyer, Paul S., *Promises to Keep: The United States since World War II*, Lexington, MA: Heath, 1995

Chafe, William H., *The Unfinished Journey: America since World War II*, New York: Oxford University Press, 1986, 3rd edition, 1995

Dubofsky, Melvyn and Athan Theoharis, *Imperial Democracy: The United States since 1945*, Englewood Cliffs, NJ: Prentice Hall, 1983, 2nd edition, 1988

Leuchtenburg, William E., *A Troubled Feast: American Society since 1945*, Boston: Little Brown, 1973, revised 1979 and 1983

Rosenberg, Norman and Emily S. Rosenberg, *In Our Times: America since World War II*, 3rd edition, Englewood Cliffs, NJ: Prentice Hall, 1987; 5th edition, 1995

Schaller, Michael, Virginia Scharff, and Robert D. Schulzinger, *Present Tense: The United States since 1945*, Boston: Houghton Mifflin, 1992

Unger, Irwin and Debi Unger, *Postwar America: The United States since 1945*, New York: St. Martin's Press, 1990

The first histories of America since 1945, written in the 1950s and 1960s, contrasted the affluence and international involvement of postwar America with the depression and isolation of pre-war America. As the period since 1945 has lengthened, recent histories of America since 1945 have tended to pay less attention to the contrasts with the pre-war period, but instead have contrasted the relative homogeneity and self-confidence of the first two decades after 1945 with the greater degree of turmoil, uncertainty and division in America since the late 1960s. All histories of postwar America have emphasized the pervasive influence of the Cold War.

SCHALLER, SCHARFF and SCHULZINGER provide quite comprehensive coverage, in a moderate degree of depth and detail, of the major issues in the political, social, economic and cultural history of America since World War II. Events are dealt with for the most part in chronological order, though some chapters deal separately with developments in foreign affairs. The early chapters develop the themes of the legacy of the New Deal, the rise of a large, activist federal government and the domestic and international impact of the Cold War. Later chapters develop such aspects as the protest movements of women and African Americans and the impact of the mass media, especially television, in shaping American ideas and values. The book places special emphasis on the role of the courts as engines of social change, on the ways in which migration to the Sunbelt affected economics and politics, and on the pivotal role of immigration, especially of Hispanics and Asians, in shaping American society in recent decades.

CHAFE is a longer account, written from a liberal viewpoint. Chafe argues that federal government activism since World War II has brought great progress to America in such fields as civil rights, reduction of poverty levels and protection of the environment, but that America's journey to the fulfilment of liberal goals is unfinished. He portrays the liberal reforms of political figures of the postwar years very favourably, especially Harry Truman and Lyndon Johnson, while more conservative figures, particularly Richard Nixon and Ronald Reagan, are more severely criticized. Issues related to civil rights and feminism are given particularly detailed attention.

A more conservative standpoint informs BARONE's survey. The book begins in 1930 and its account of the Depression years and of America in World War II provides useful background to the postwar period. The author suggests that American history since 1945 is not simply a story of progress from the New Deal onwards, away from isolationism and laissez-faire to internationalism and the welfare state. He gives more sympathetic treatment to conservative figures such as Ronald Reagan. On foreign policy, Barone demonstrates that the period began with an unusual degree of national unity as a result of World War II, but suggests that in peacetime there were greater differences over social, cultural and political issues, which were intensified by differences over foreign policy issues in the Vietnam War years.

BOYER devotes less attention to politics, and places more emphasis on social and cultural developments. However, he begins with discussion of the atomic bomb and stresses that America throughout the postwar period has lived in the nuclear age. Although the book is relatively brief, certain issues are given particular attention, such as the relative decline of religion as a force in American life from the 1950s to the 1980s, and the changing ethnic composition of America as a result of the Immigration Act of 1965. Boyer also discusses economic changes, including the decline of manufacturing industry and the impact of new technology such as computers and videos.

Although it is a slightly older work, LEUCHTENBURG is distinguished by its very high quality of analysis, along with the wit and verve of its presentation. The first half discusses social and economic trends in the late 1940s and 1950s, with emphasis on the pressures towards conformity which built up in the 1950s. The second half analyzes the pressures towards liberalization in the 1960s. Leuchtenburg shows how political liberalism in the early 1960s showed great promise, especially in the fields of civil rights and anti-poverty in the administrations of John F. Kennedy and Lyndon Johnson. In contrast, later chapters analyze the destruction of the liberal promise of the early 1960s, the bitter disunity of American society by the late 1960s, the recourse to a more conservative path in the 1970s and to the politics of illusion in the 1980s.

Two briefer surveys are provided by the Rosenbergs and the Ungers. ROSENBERG and ROSENBERG treats in chronological order such topics as the origins of the Cold War, the affluence of the 1950s, Vietnam, cultural liberalism in the 1960s, conservative backlash in the 1970s, Reagan's presidency, and social problems such as crime and drugs. Social, economic and cultural issues are interrelated with issues of politics and foreign affairs. Although its relative brevity does not permit detailed discussion of particular issues, the book provides a useful, reasonably comprehensive introduction to the period. UNGER and UNGER helps to place the postwar years in context in an opening chapter on the period 1900–1945. Each chapter includes a short primary source document, such as the Supreme Court Ruling on Public School Desegregation or the National Organization for Women's Statement of Purpose. Otherwise, the book provides brief coverage in chronological order of the main developments in American political, social, economic and cultural history from Truman's inauguration in 1945 to the end of the 1980s.

DUBOFSKY and THEOHARIS cover all of the major issues in American history since 1945, but emphasis is placed on national security issues and their impact on domestic affairs. Moreover, there is more emphasis on economic issues than in most other surveys of the period. The major theme of the book is the clash between objectives at home and ambitions abroad. It is suggested that the United States has pursued essentially imperialist policies abroad and that this has led to a great increase in the power of national security and intelligence agencies, thereby undermining the liberties of the American people. There is a useful discussion of the changing American economy since the 1970s, with emphasis on the decline of manufacturing industry, and the stagnation in living standards of the majority of the American people.

PETER G. BOYLE

Reconstruction: General

Beale, Howard K., *The Critical Year: A Study of Andrew Johnson and Reconstruction*, New York: Harcourt Brace, 1930

Belz, Herman, *Reconstructing the Union: Theory and Policy During the Civil War*, Ithaca, NY: Cornell University Press, 1969

Benedict, Michael Les, *A Compromise of Principle: Congressional Republicans and Reconstruction, 1863–1869*, New York: Norton, 1974

Benedict, Michael Les, *The Fruits of Victory: Alternatives in Restoring the Union, 1865–1877*, Philadelphia: Lippincott, 1975; revised, Lanham, MD: University Press of America, 1986

Bowers, Claude G., *The Tragic Era: The Revolution after Lincoln*, Boston: Houghton Mifflin, 1929

Du Bois, W.E.B., *Black Reconstruction: An Essay Toward a History of the Part Which Black Folk Played in the Attempt to Reconstruct Democracy in America, 1860–1880*, New York: Harcourt Brace, 1935; as *Black Reconstruction in America*, Cleveland: World, 1964, London: Cass, 1966; reprinted New York: Atheneum, 1992

Dunning, William Archibald, *Reconstruction: Political and Economic, 1865–1877*, New York: Harper, 1907

Foner, Eric, *Reconstruction: America's Unfinished Revolution, 1863–1877*, New York: Harper, 1988, abridged as *A Short History of Reconstruction*, 1990

Franklin, John Hope, *Reconstruction: After the Civil War*, Chicago: University of Chicago Press, 1961, 2nd edition, 1994

Gillette, William, *Retreat from Reconstruction, 1869–1879*, Baton Rouge: Louisiana State University Press, 1979

McKitrick, Eric, *Andrew Johnson and Reconstruction*, Chicago: University of Chicago Press, 1960

Milton, George Fort, *The Age of Hate: Andrew Johnson and the Radicals*, New York: Coward McCann, 1930

Perman, Michael, *The Road to Redemption: Southern Politics, 1869–1879*, Chapel Hill: University of North Carolina Press, 1984

Perman, Michael, *Emancipation and Reconstruction, 1862–1879*, Arlington Heights, IL: Harlan Davidson, 1987

Stampp, Kenneth M., *The Era of Reconstruction, 1865–1877*, New York: Knopf, 1965

Summers, Mark W., *Railroads, Reconstruction, and the Gospel of Prosperity: Aid under the Radical Republicans, 1865–1877*, Princeton: Princeton University Press, 1984

The Republican effort to reconstruct southern state governments and the American Union after the Civil War on terms of racial equality in civil and political rights has been among the most controversial subjects of American history. DUNNING provides a very useful general history that reflects the view common at the turn of the 20th century that the entire effort had been misguided. Motivated by a combination of misplaced idealism and hostility to former Confederates, Republicans overcame the opposition of President Andrew Johnson and imposed a regime of civil and political equality on the South. They were aided in this by the failure of Johnson and former Confederates to recognize the political realities and deal flexibly with them. Dunning accepted the view of white southerners that the former slaves were inherently incapable of participating in democratic government, and that the Republican program had therefore led to the imposition of corrupt and incompetent governments in the South, run by northern "Carpetbaggers" and native white "Scalawags," backed by ignorant black voters. Like most white southerners, Dunning sees the collapse of the Republican governments as a "redemption" of the South.

Arguing that Radical Republicans repudiated Abraham Lincoln's moderation on Reconstruction, BOWERS and MILTON are fiery indictments of the Radical program, suffused with early 20th century racism. The former work was particularly aimed at a popular audience and is a well-written, highly partisan (anti-Republican) account. According to both Bowers and Milton, northerners' war-induced hatred of the South allowed Radical Republicans to use Reconstruction to crush out the Jeffersonian and Jacksonian ideals of states rights and political and economic equality (for white people). These ideals were heroically but vainly defended by President Andrew Johnson. Both treat Johnson as a great champion of the common man, while the Republicans represented the anti-democratic, commercial elite of the nation. Milton is primarily

an account of Johnson's effort to resist the Radical Republican policy. Bowers goes on to describe the consequences of the Radical victory: horribly corrupt governments that pillaged the South as well as an orgy of corruption in the North. Bowers describes the Republican era as one of "Negro rule" and justifies the violent southern resistance through which the South was "redeemed" from mis-government.

BEALE revised earlier histories by stressing the economic influences that affected Reconstruction and downplaying the importance of race. He argues that northeastern business interests used the Reconstruction issue to take control of the government and harness it to the use of capitalism. According to Beale and other "revisionists," before the war an alliance of western and southern agrarians had frustrated these efforts. During Reconstruction, northeastern capitalists, working through the Republican party, appealed to Civil War passions to turn westerners against their natural southern allies. President Johnson failed to make the real issue clear, enabling the northeasterners to succeed in their efforts.

In a seminal work, largely ignored when published, DU BOIS reaches almost opposite conclusions from the same starting point. Writing from a Marxist perspective, Du Bois argues that during Reconstruction the capitalists of the North forged an alliance with the freedpeople and poor whites of the South, who attempted to create democratic societies within their states. In the 1870s northern business interests abandoned this unnatural alliance in favor of a more comfortable one with the white southern elite, who agreed to accept northern business domination of the nation in exchange for local control of their region. In the course of his work, Du Bois attends closely not only to political and social reform in the South during Reconstruction, but to northern economic interests in the South.

New overviews that appeared in the 1960s, sometimes called "neo-revisionist," rejected such concentration upon the economic influences at work during Reconstruction. In brief, readable accounts, both FRANKLIN and STAMPP reinterpreted Radical Reconstruction as an earlier version of the contemporary civil rights movement's effort to establish racial, civil and political equality. Both minimize the amount and importance of corruption among southern Republicans and point out how progressive their policies were.

Belz, McKitrick, and Benedict (1974) look closely at the private correspondence of the leading actors, at newspapers and journals of opinion, and at the congressional debates, to provide detailed accounts of how Republicans arrived at their Reconstruction policy. All three pay close attention to constitutional issues. They point out significant disagreements among the so-called Radical Republicans, distinguishing among conservatives, moderates, and radicals. BELZ describes how Republican visions of a restored Union grew more radical in the early years of the Civil War, moving from an immediate restoration of the Union as it was to one that required abolition of slavery and potentially the long-term territorialization of the South. As the war came to an end, Republicans moved back to a more conservative position. McKitrick and Benedict both argue that Republicans were united primarily by concern that Johnson was placing the South back in the hands of disloyal, proslavery leaders. McKITRICK argues that the concern was largely psychological, with northerners demanding clear signs of southern acceptance of defeat. BENEDICT (1974) argues that Republicans were sincerely concerned with securing the basic rights of African Americans, with conservatives and radicals disagreeing on how far they could go to do so. Both stress Johnson's racism rather than his commitment to Jacksonian ideals, and chronicle how Johnson's intransigence forced the Republican factions to cooperate to produce a compromise Reconstruction program that fell short of what the most radical Republicans wanted. Benedict challenges the traditional view that Republican Reconstruction policy worked a radical change in American government, arguing that it was basically conservative from a constitutional point of view, with most Republicans committed to maintaining a federal system balanced between state and national power.

GILLETTE describes the collapse of Republican Reconstruction policy during the Grant administration (1869–77). Paying close attention to the administration's reaction to political events in each southern state, he attributes the failure of Reconstruction to Grant's lack of commitment and to endemic northern racism. PERMAN (1984) offers a careful account of political developments in the reconstructed South. He argues that Republicans and Democrats competed for the support of a crucial mass of floating leaders and voters, many of them former Whigs, who liked neither party. He attends closely to divisions among centrists and extremists, regulars and reformers, in both the Republican and Democratic/Conservative camps, and he goes on to describe the battle between agrarians and more modern commercial interests in the Democratic party after they "redeemed" the South from Republican rule. SUMMERS explains how Republicans hoped to secure the support of such people through a program of economic development, and details developmental efforts throughout the South. Although this program failed primarily because of the economic depression of 1873, corruption was endemic and serious, he insists, helping to alienate the groups Republicans had hoped to attract.

FONER is the most important general study of Reconstruction. Drawing upon research in the original sources and upon the outpouring of work on Reconstruction from 1960 to 1985, Foner covers the development and consequences of Reconstruction policy in detail, from its beginning during the Civil War to its denouement in the 1870s. He attends not only to the origins and conflict over the political program and constitutional issues, but to social and economic change, paying special attention to the role of African Americans and women in seeking to secure their own autonomy and interests. His highly nuanced interpretive framework parallels Du Bois. However, Foner does not describe the Republican party as the representative of business interests. The party was an independent political entity, seeking to maintain its hold on power. It appealed to a northern "free labor" ideology that retained powerfully democratic elements. Farmers, workers, and businesspeople all adhered to different versions of it. Foner chronicles how the Republicans sought to expand their free labor ideology into the South, how the freedpeople molded that ideology into a more radically egalitarian one, how women and workers in the North utilized it to demand greater equality and control of their lives, and how northern business interests reacted by abandoning many of the ideology's democratic elements and compromising with southern conservatives. Thus

Foner stresses class and economic issues more than race in explaining the erosion of northern support for Reconstruction, while he argues that both class and race motivated white southern resistance. Republicans responded to the new configuration of political forces, leading to the end of Reconstruction in 1877. Foner also stresses the essential radicalism of Reconstruction, arguing that the United States was the only formerly slave society that attempted to give real political power to freedpeople after emancipation.

Although Foner's is the standard synthetic history of Reconstruction, the most useful shorter surveys, based on the recent Reconstruction historiography, and aimed at students and those who want a sophisticated introductory summary, are BENEDICT (revised 1986) and PERMAN (1987), which also include helpful bibliographic essays.

M. LES BENEDICT

Reconstruction: Policy and Politics

1) 1861–1869

Belz, Herman, *Reconstructing the Union: Theory and Policy During the Civil War*, Ithaca, NY: Cornell University Press, 1969

Benedict, Michael Les, *A Compromise of Principle: Congressional Republicans and Reconstruction, 1863–1869*, New York: Norton, 1974

Carter, Dan T., *When the War Was Over: The Failure of Self-Reconstruction in the South, 1865–1867*, Baton Rouge: Louisiana State University Press, 1985

Dunning, William Archibald, *Reconstruction: Political and Economic, 1865–1877*, New York: Harper, 1907

Foner, Eric, *Reconstruction: America's Unfinished Revolution, 1863–1877*, New York: Harper, 1988, abridged as *A Short History of Reconstruction*, 1990

McKitrick, Eric, *Andrew Johnson and Reconstruction*, Chicago: University of Chicago Press, 1960

Rose, Willie Lee, *Rehearsal for Reconstruction: The Port Royal Experiment*, Indianapolis: Bobbs Merrill, 1964

Stampp, Kenneth M., *The Era of Reconstruction, 1865–1877*, New York: Knopf, 1965

Trefousse, Hans L., *The Radical Republicans: Lincoln's Vanguard for Racial Justice*, New York: Knopf, 1968

Virtually from the secession of South Carolina on 20 December 1860 debate began on how the nation would be reunited, or reconstructed. Historians have sustained this debate, generally focusing on the years of the Civil War to the inauguration of Ulysses S. Grant as president, 1861–69, or the years of Grant's administration to the controversial inauguration of Rutherford B. Hayes as president, 1869–1877, after which the federal government ceased direct intervention in southern state political affairs.

The debate over Reconstruction was dominated for several decades by DUNNING and his followers. He presented the South as "subjugated by an alien power" and condemned Reconstruction measures passed by an extremist Radical

Republican congressional majority over President Andrew Johnson's objections. These laws gave freedmen the vote, the ability to hold public office, direct support from the federal government through the Freedmen's Bureau, and full civil rights while denying former Confederates political privileges. Such vengeful actions inflamed social and racial antagonisms by imposing on capable and proud whites incompetent and corrupt rule by three groups: uneducated blacks; scalawags, detested white southerners loyal to the Union; and carpetbaggers, greedy opportunists from the North. Misguided congressional policies engendered white enmity leading to political violence, economic turmoil, and bloodletting on a large scale.

The reaction against the Dunning school, long in the making, found powerful expression in McKitrick and Stampp in the 1960s. Clearly influenced by the civil rights movement, STAMPP offered a view of Reconstruction which is a mirror image of Dunning. He is sympathetic to the motives and objectives of the Republican Reconstruction program, and regrets that it was not radical enough in its implementation.

Johnson's obstructions of the Radical Republican program instigated his impeachment and consigned him to contemporary infamy. McKITRICK looks to strike a balance between such castigation and 20th-century efforts to rehabilitate Johnson's historical character. Neither devil nor angel, Johnson did, however, forfeit his authority as president and party leader, manage unwittingly to block reconciliation of North and South, and disrupt the political life of the nation. Johnson was a pivotal actor in the tragedy of Reconstruction, and his role as champion of amnesty for Confederates, speedy restoration of southern states to representation in Congress, and social conservatism receives scrutiny.

In a pathbreaking book, ROSE gives a reminder that, before Johnson and Radical Republicans dominated the scene, a practical experiment on the Sea Islands surrounding Beaufort and Port Royal, South Carolina, had explored answers to the most vexing Reconstruction question: How could former slaves live within southern society? Abandoned by Confederate planters to their slaves and the United States military in November 1861, the rich plantations of the Sea Islands became a field of missionary activity for sectarian antislavery educators. Their principal mission was to teach freedom and free enterprise, but they, in turn, learned about the ways and culture of their students. Sea Island blacks went to war on the Union side, entered schools, gained title to land, engaged in political activities, and experienced the mixed blessings of being wage laborers. Their story in the end contained more sadness than joy, but what politicians, military officers, and philanthropists observed at Port Royal influenced subsequent federal Reconstruction policies.

The politicians who were most engaged with the racial aspects of Reconstruction are the subjects of TREFOUSSE. Rather than authors of vindictive misrule, Radical Republicans in and out of Congress like Thaddeus Stevens, Charles Sumner, Salmon P. Chase, and Edwin M. Stanton were innovators, friends of freed slaves, believers in democracy as well as enlarged national power, and principled political reformers. While part of the book recounts Radical Republican interest in military operations, most of it centers on their struggle for emancipation, their efforts to achieve Reconstruction on their terms, and their bitter conflict with Johnson. Their precipitous

decline as a governing bloc after Grant's inauguration completes the study.

BELZ is oriented more toward constitutional and legislative theory than practical politics. Questions concerning the fundamental nature of the Union and the civil status of emancipated slaves highlighted complex problems confronting lawmakers during the Civil War. Congress receives credit for prompting consideration of Reconstruction issues, and their initiatives – ranging from plans to reconfigure Confederate states as territories to requirements that reorganized state governments should write new constitutions prohibiting slavery – compelled a series of responses from President Abraham Lincoln. Friction between Congress and Lincoln over the best approach to Reconstruction in changing political and military circumstances enlivens the narrative.

BENEDICT subjects congressional wrangling over Reconstruction policy to quantitative as well as historical analysis. He concentrates on the tensions and divisions within the Republican ranks, and finds in this group, easily perceived as monolithic, a mixture of conservatives, moderates, and radicals. The level of commitment to racially egalitarian principles fundamentally delineated each lawmaker. Recognition of these divisions within the Republican camp helps to explain the development of Reconstruction legislation and leads to the conclusion "that radicals never controlled the processes of Reconstruction" because "moderates and conservatives dominated the institutional mechanisms of Congress." Alongside the use of quantitative methods, one great feature of this book is the parade of personalities seen from new and provocative vantage points.

The focus of Reconstruction shifts from Congress to the southern states in CARTER. Trying to assess fairly the efforts of southern white leaders such as Lewis Parsons of Alabama and William L. Sharkey of Mississippi to restore their states to the Union under Johnson's provisional state governments, he finds that they failed to exercise meaningful political, economic, or social leadership largely because they were unable to accept the revolutionary consequences of emancipation and unwilling to tolerate any federal involvement in local affairs. He refrains from skewering these white leaders for their failure on account of the catastrophic conditions plaguing the region in the immediate postbellum period. While strained at times, this book argues convincingly that not all southerners resisted all change following the Civil War.

Magisterial in scope, FONER keeps blacks in the forefront of the Reconstruction story while synthesizing a generation of scholarship. His sweeping investigation of the political, economic, social, and ideological dimensions of Reconstruction contains specific commentary on southern and border states without slighting an increasingly activist national government. A conviction that "blacks were active agents in the making of Reconstruction," responsible for forcing their own emancipation, pressing claims for equal civil rights, and altering traditional class relationships among white planters, merchants, and yeomen, provides narrative coherence. Unlike most Reconstruction studies, changes during these years in northern society – where capitalists and manufacturers triumphed over farmers and artisans – also receive attention.

WILLIAM M. FERRARO

2) 1869–1877

Abbott, Richard H., *The Republican Party and the South, 1855–1877*, Chapel Hill: University of North Carolina Press, 1986

Bensel, Richard Franklin, *Yankee Leviathan: The Origins of Central State Authority in America, 1859–1877*, Cambridge and New York: Cambridge University Press, 1990

Dawson, Joseph G. III, *Army Generals and Reconstruction: Louisiana, 1862–1877*, Baton Rouge: Louisiana State University Press, 1982

Gillette, William, *Retreat from Reconstruction, 1869–1879*, Baton Rouge: Louisiana State University Press, 1979

Keller, Morton, *Affairs of State: Public Life in Late Nineteenth Century America*, Cambridge, MA: Belknap Press of Harvard University Press, 1977

McFeely, William S., *Grant: A Biography*, New York: Norton, 1981

Perman, Michael, *The Road to Redemption: Southern Politics, 1869–1879*, Chapel Hill: University of North Carolina Press, 1984

Sefton, James E., *The United States Army and Reconstruction, 1865–1877*, Baton Rouge: Louisiana State University Press, 1967

Seip, Terry J., *The South Returns to Congress: Men, Economic Measures, and Intersectional Relationships, 1868–1879*, Baton Rouge: Louisiana State University Press, 1983

Summers, Mark W., *Railroads, Reconstruction, and the Gospel of Prosperity: Aid under the Radical Republicans, 1865–1877*, Princeton: Princeton University Press, 1984

From 1869 to 1876, the federal government tried to sustain the new political order in the South, with each state under Republican control, that had been established by 1868 under the Reconstruction Acts.

Although most of Reconstruction occurred during the presidency of Ulysses S. Grant, 1869–77, historians have focused overwhelmingly on the Andrew Johnson years, 1865–68. To remedy this oversight, GILLETTE provides a thorough description and analysis of the policy on Reconstruction of both the executive and legislative branches after 1868. Despite claiming that the federal government still had power and options in dealing with the reorganized and readmitted South, Gillette's study actually catalogues a steady erosion of interest and involvement, with withdrawal a virtual *fait accompli* as early as 1874. In his view, Grant's policy was "a study in incongruities", while the Republicans in Congress were uncertain in their commitment to preserving the newly-installed governments in the South, especially if that meant losing support and control in the politically more crucial North.

The creation of a viable Republican party in the South would seem a primary concern of northern Republicans and a good reason for active involvement in southern Reconstruction. Yet ABBOTT finds that, remarkably, this was not the case. While Republicans wanted to ensure that the defeated South did not return to the control of the former Confederates, now Democrats, and that the former slaves were not returned to slavery or left unprotected, they had no agenda for a Republicanized South. Surprisingly, the investment of money, organization and energy needed to create a permanent Republican presence was not forthcoming. Without a long-term or specific southern strategy, Republicans soon lost interest when whites did not flock to the party in the South, and when the attempt to maintain Republicanism in the South threatened their northern base.

Further evidence for the northern Republicans' unwillingness to sustain their southern counterparts is offered by SEIP's study of how the southern delegation was treated once it returned to Congress in 1869. The South's new Republican congressmen desperately needed to be able to show their supporters as well as their Democratic opponents that they could "bring home the bacon." The region needed a more flexible and available currency and also appropriations for internal improvements. Yet its Republican congressmen were constantly rebuffed because the northern states had different financial interests and were actually competing with the South for federal largesse. Even on measures for sustaining the Reconstruction governments in the South, they met with little support.

Grant's views and positions on Reconstruction are discussed, though not systematically analyzed, in McFEELY's biography. In general, he concurs with Gillette's view of Grant's inconsistency and lack of perseverance. But he does emphasize some of the general's more decisive and positive actions. Grant broke with Johnson and his approach to Reconstruction in 1867; he tried to sustain the Republican governments in the South during his first term; he lobbied vigorously and effectively for legislation against Klan violence in 1871; and he was always moved, and often angry, when told about southern outrages and violence. But still he offered no firm or clear policy.

Even though the southern states were self-governing after 1868, United States troops were still stationed there, though in decreasing numbers. SEFTON's study covers the entire period after 1865 but, disappointingly, he has only one chapter on the post-1868 phase. He sums up the role of the military as one of executing, rather than shaping, a policy that was aimed at maintaining the Reconstruction governments and not at occupying or controlling the South. Anomalous and unique in the history of the United States military, the Reconstruction episode was, nevertheless, in Sefton's view, a creditable performance by the army.

In contrast, DAWSON focuses on one state only and pays a lot of attention to the post-1868 years. Yet his book is most useful, because the army's role in Louisiana was continuous and important – far more so than in any other southern state. As elsewhere, the army's role after 1868 was to maintain peace and order, but the turbulence of Louisiana's politics compelled the army to intervene in elections, to resolve contests between rival legislatures, and to put down the White League's paramilitary coups in New Orleans and in outlying parishes. Despite the continuity in its leadership – with the same commander from 1871 to 1875 – the army's performance was reactive rather than consistent and, like the federal policy it was administering, also limited and defensive.

The political system that emerged in the South as a result of federal Reconstruction policy is analyzed by PERMAN. Besides explaining the nature and composition of the two parties and their interaction, Perman suggests that post-1868

Reconstruction politics in the South passed through two phases. In the first, there was the possibility of a competitive, two-party system, as both parties attempted to control the political center. But, after 1873, this broke down when the Democrats played the "race card", used political violence and emphasized the distinctiveness and exclusiveness of the two parties, a policy aimed at destroying the Republicans, not just defeating them. Also emphasized in this study is the persistence of the planter/agrarian element in the resurgent Democratic party.

Another region-wide analysis is SUMMERS's very detailed study of the role of economic development, particularly railroad-building, in the Reconstruction South. Republicans saw the creation of railroads as a key element in consolidating their party and shifting the political focus from racial and sectional issues to economic progress. Although they placed major emphasis on railroads, their initiative ran into such difficulties that the Democrats were handed a ready-made bill of particulars with which to charge their opponents with extravagance, incompetence and corruption – an indictment that Summers acknowledges was not entirely unfounded.

More general studies of American government and politics in this period perform a useful service in placing the specific problems of Reconstruction in a wider and deeper context. BENSEL examines the role of the national state in mid-19th century America. At the heart of his book is the question of the impact of the sectional crisis and the massive war it generated on the growth of the central, or national, state in America. If the federal government had been able to extend its authority into the South through political reorganization and economic development, then the considerable wartime expansion of the nation-state would have continued. But the failure of the reconstruction of the South stalled American state-building, giving rise to anti-statist forces in the South and compelling the government to devote its energy to countering southern separatism, rather than building a more consolidated state apparatus, as European nations were doing at the time.

KELLER offers a wide-ranging discussion of public life and policy after the Civil War that shows how the centralization of power during wartime gave way to decentralization and laissez-faire policies as well as to an organizational form of politics in which issues and principles declined in importance. The South shared in this experience, and so its reconstruction and redemption, Keller argues, were just regional variations on a nationwide theme, rather than an aberration or major disjunction.

MICHAEL PERMAN

Reconstruction: in the Southern States

Ash, Stephen V., *Middle Tennessee Society Transformed, 1860–1870: War and Peace in the Upper South*, Baton Rouge: Louisiana State University Press, 1987

Fitzgerald, Michael W., *The Union League Movement in the Deep South: Politics and Agricultural Change During Reconstruction*, Baton Rouge: Louisiana State University Press, 1989

Holt, Thomas, *Black over White: Negro Political Leadership in South Carolina During Reconstruction*, Urbana: University of Illinois Press, 1977

Jaynes, Gerald David, *Branches Without Roots: Genesis of the Black Working Class in the American South, 1862–1882*, New York: Oxford University Press, 1986

Morris, Robert C., *Reading, 'Riting, and Reconstruction: The Education of Freedmen in the South, 1861–1870*, Chicago: University of Chicago Press, 1981

Powell, Lawrence N., *New Masters: Northern Planters During the Civil War and Reconstruction*, New Haven: Yale University Press, 1980

Richardson, Joe M., *Christian Reconstruction: The American Missionary Association and Southern Blacks, 1861–1890*, Athens: University of Georgia Press, 1986

Roark, James L., *Masters Without Slaves: Southern Planters in the Civil War and Reconstruction*, New York: Norton, 1977

Trelease, Allen W., *White Terror: The Ku Klux Klan Conspiracy and Southern Reconstruction*, New York: Harper, 1971; London: Secker and Warburg, 1972

Tunnell, Ted, *Crucible of Reconstruction: War, Radicalism and Race in Louisiana, 1862–1877*, Baton Rouge: Louisiana State University Press, 1984

Wayne, Michael, *The Reshaping of Plantation Society: The Natchez District, 1860–1880*, Baton Rouge: Louisiana State University Press, 1983

Wiener, Jonathan M., *Social Origins of the New South: Alabama 1860–1885*, Baton Rouge: Louisiana State University Press, 1978

Nowhere is David Potter's distinction between "lumpers" and "splitters" more evident than in writing about Reconstruction in the southern states, because the people of the ex-Confederate states, white and black, native and immigrant, found a wide variety of ways of defining the economic and social meanings of free labor, and of managing the political demands and the consequences of their return to the Union – common processes that often began before and continued after the postwar decade of "Reconstruction".

For ROARK, who considers the socioeconomic dimension from the perspective of native southern planters, the dominant theme was the continuing search for a substitute for slavery. Although planters were accepting patterns of black behaviour in the mid-1870s that they had found insupportable earlier, the price of this acceptance was the decay of paternalism, and a desire for distance from freedpeople as strong as that felt by blacks for whites. Planters, though, could be immigrant northerners, numbering in POWELL's estimate between twenty and fifty thousand in the early years after the war. Expecting work on the northern pattern from their labourers and finding it difficult to come to terms with black traditions, many were pushed out by successive crop failures and the onset of Radical Reconstruction.

Some northern planters established schools, and MORRIS shows that the idealism of the northern educational effort was tempered by pragmatism and an emphasis on order and gradualism. Educational objectives often addressed the civic needs of the ex-slaves, and educators themselves took prominent political roles. The real investment for the future, stressed by

RICHARDSON, was the teacher training programme of the American Missionary Association, which, in spite of paternalism and some racial prejudice, came closer to a recognition of black rights and needs than most organizations.

If freedpeople wanted education, they wanted land more; and JAYNES rigorously analyzes the economic evolution of "decentralized tenant farming" (his generic term for the sharecropping and renting that appeared in the late 1860s). Using Freedmen's Bureau records he ingeniously presents the southern transition from centralized plantation factories to decentralized domestic production units as a mirror image of British industrial development. Most important for the labourer was time, its allocation and control; while for the landowner the availability of credit with its implications for payment by share or wage, was crucial.

The timing of this economic transition in 1867–68, and some of its most immediate political consequences are illuminated by FITZGERALD, who argues that, while the Union League's emphasis on the politics of dignity, access to land and resistance to gang labour focused resistance to planters' economic coercion, its secrecy and politicization also heightened the white sense of crisis. As a result, it helped to precipitate the terrorism of the Ku Klux Klan in the spring of 1868 – to which, ironically, blacks' success in renting family plots of land made them more vulnerable.

TRELEASE provides the standard narrative account of the Klan. While systematically documenting the atrocities that have often been ignored in the pursuit of social and economic transformations, he is cautious about the political effectiveness of the Klan's violence. Although he strips away the mantle of "southern chivalry" – it is a historiographic point of some interest that this was still thought necessary in the early 1970s – he gives more credence to the Klan's rationalization of defensive action in the face of Union League provocation than most historians would today.

Though the Klan had first been organized in Tennessee, in the variegated landscape and economy of its heartland portrayed by ASH fewer than half the farmers had held any slaves at all. One of the most contested theatres of war, the state subsequently went through the shortest period of political reconstruction. Its small planter elite retained its social position, but buttressed from a rather different direction, as important occupational shifts moved freedpeople from farms to towns and villages, while white workers became farm labourers or tenants.

WIENER uses his local study of Alabama to argue that Reconstruction was the culmination of a bourgeois revolution and that the Black Belt and the city of Birmingham were the sites of a developmental conflict between the democratic capitalist and the "Prussian Road" to the modern world – as discussed in Barrington Moore, *The Social Origins of Dictatorship and Democracy* (1966). The first historian to quantify the extent of planter persistence in postwar society, Wiener sees them assuming many functions of a merchant class, but remaining opposed to any industrial development that threatened to remove black labour from the plantation.

The greatest concentration of the richest planters, however, was probably in the Natchez region (the adjacent river counties of Mississippi and Louisiana). Here WAYNE finds that although the pre-war elites remained in control, their authority had to come to terms with the priorities of their former slaves, their families, churches, schools and voluntary organizations. Most importantly, the dissolution of plantation law meant that for the first time the state began to shape the patterns of daily life.

Politics therefore became fundamental to the working out of Reconstruction, and it was in South Carolina that black political power was exercised most impressively. Paving the way for much subsequent work, HOLT demonstrated just how much material on black leaders and politicians could be exhumed. Nevertheless their power was circumscribed particularly by the governor's patronage, and by colour, caste and economic cleavages among themselves. Holt also argues that the causes of Radical Republican decline and defeat in the state were the product of local circumstances rather than of national political patterns.

In Louisiana, the state where Reconstruction was most protracted and most tortuous, state politics extensively reflected national patterns. TUNNELL's interpretive essays are concerned to integrate the military, political and socio-economic dimensions into a narrative of cultural identity. Just as important as national influence was the decentralization of the American political system which made control of state politics rest on local bases in the hinterland – both points resonating far beyond the southern states during Reconstruction.

S.G.F. SPACKMAN

Reconstruction: Economic Aspects

Foner, Eric, *Nothing but Freedom: Emancipation and Its Legacy*, Baton Rouge: Louisiana State University Press, 1983

Glymph, Thavolia and J.J. Kushma (editors), *Essays on the Post-Bellum Southern Economy*, College Station: Texas A & M University Press, 1985

Hahn, Steven, *The Roots of Southern Populism: Yeoman Farmers and the Transformation of the Georgia Upcountry, 1850–1890*, New York: Oxford University Press, 1983

Higgs, Robert, *Competition and Coercion: Blacks in the American Economy, 1865–1914*, Cambridge and New York: Cambridge University Press, 1977

Mandle, Jay R., *Not Slave nor Free: The African-American Experience since the Civil War*, Durham, NC: Duke University Press, 1982

Ransom, Roger L. and Richard Sutch, *One Kind of Freedom: The Economic Consequences of Emancipation*, Cambridge and New York: Cambridge University Press, 1977

Wayne, Michael, *The Reshaping of Plantation Society: The Natchez District, 1860–1880*, Baton Rouge: Louisiana State University Press, 1983

Wiener, Jonathan M., *Social Origins of the New South: Alabama 1860–1885*, Baton Rouge: Louisiana State University Press, 1978

Wright, Gavin, *Old South, New South: Revolutions in the Southern Economy since the Civil War*, New York: Basic Books, 1986

The central problems that have preoccupied economic historians in their analysis of the postbellum South have been, first of all, the character of the new institutions (sharecropping and the crop lien system) that replaced slavery; and, second, the reasons for the poverty and economic backwardness from which the section suffered for generations after Appomattox. HIGGS is representative of a group of economic historians, using quantitative methods grounded in neo-classical economic theory, who explain these developments in terms of the operation of market forces, only slightly constrained by racism and legal discrimination, although it is difficult to see how a methodology which assumes the operation of a free market can effectively test for its absence. This is a succinct, thought-provoking and relatively readable example of the New Economic History.

RANSOM and SUTCH is widely regarded as the most persuasive analysis of the changes in southern agriculture. The authors also employ quantitative methods, as well as a variety of documentary sources, but they are much less restrictive in their assumptions. They examine the ways in which the economic opportunities available to freedmen and women were restricted by racism. Central to their thesis is a detailed examination of the operation of the crop lien system. By allowing merchants and landlords who held local monopolies of credit to appropriate the economic surplus, the crop lien system, they believe, trapped African American farmers in a condition akin to peonage. By stifling initiative, discouraging investment, and promoting cotton monoculture, it also trapped the whole "Cotton South" in a state of arrested development.

WAYNE is one of several more detailed case-studies of plantation communities, in this case the district around Natchez. It traces the development of new economic and social relationships in the years following emancipation. While planters maintained their dominant position in the cotton economy, their former slaves' freedom to move in search of employment and bargain for better terms forced them to develop new techniques of labour management based on control of credit and, in due course, access to state power. Thus Wayne finds both continuity and discontinuity in the organisation of southern agriculture.

On the other hand, MANDLE, operating from Marxist premises, believes that the social changes traced by Wayne and others did not shake the hold of the plantation as a "mode of production." In the sense of a system based on the production of staple crops for the market and employing labourers who were forced to work for less than a free market wage, the plantation, in Mandle's view, retained its dominant position in southern agriculture. WIENER also finds evidence for the persistence of the planter class in postbellum Alabama. A high proportion (though not, in comparative terms, an unusually high proportion) of the planter elite in 1860 retained their land, if not their slaves, in 1870 and 1880, and he believes that they maintained a political and economic, as well as ideological, hegemony which, among other things, enabled them to hold back the development of industry. This is a clearly articulated, though perhaps overstated, challenge to C. Vann Woodward's "New South" thesis.

FONER is a collection of three essays on the social and economic effects of emancipation. Drawing on a comparison with the experience of emancipation in other plantation societies, Foner points out that the United States was unique in conferring political power on the freedmen. The period of Reconstruction, therefore, saw a continuing struggle between planters and freedmen to utilise the power of the state to enforce their rights in the economic arena. The essays, ranging from a high-level comparative study to a detailed analysis of a rice-workers' strike in the South Carolina Low Country, are each highly suggestive and thought-provoking.

Whereas most of the works listed deal with the plantation South, HAHN is a study of the Georgia upcountry from the antebellum decade to the eve of the Populist revolt. This region, formerly occupied by self-sufficient yeoman farmers, was after 1865 thrust into the vortex of commercial agriculture by the coming of the railroads, new laws regulating grazing and the use of common land, and the spread of indebtedness. Hahn examines the manner in which a community's whole way of life was transformed by these processes.

GLYMPH and KUSHMA is a valuable collection of essays on the postbellum southern economy. Armistead L. Robinson examines the experience of wage labour during the war years; Thavolia Glymph traces the origins of sharecropping between 1865 and 1868; Harold Woodman offers a broader analysis of the development of the plantation system; and Barbara Jeanne Fields relates the evolution of capitalist agriculture in the postbellum South to the spread of bourgeois social relations on a world scale.

WRIGHT is by far by the most impressive and influential study of the southern economy since 1865. Although he generalizes over a wide chronological sweep, his insights shed light on immediate postwar developments. He considers the implications that followed from the conversion of slaveholders, or "labor lords," into landlords, and he analyzes the causes and consequences of what he believes to be the most striking characteristic of the postbellum southern economy, namely the extraordinary wage differentials between the South and the rest of the nation. The South constituted an isolated labour market and, in many respects, an isolated economy. His imaginative analysis of this phenomenon lies at the heart of a comprehensive and revealing interpretation of the whole postbellum Southern economic experience.

ROBERT HARRISON

Red Scare, 1919–1920

Brody, David, *Labor in Crisis: The Steel Strike of 1919*, Philadelphia: Lippincott, 1965

Coben, Stanley, *A. Mitchell Palmer: Politician*, New York: Columbia University Press, 1963

Coben, Stanley, "A Study of Nativism: The American Red Scare of 1919–1920", *Political Science Quarterly*, 79(1), 1964

Higham, John, *Strangers in the Land: Patterns of American Nativism, 1860–1925*, New Brunswick, NJ: Rutgers University Press, 1955, corrected reprint, 1963; 2nd edition, 1988

Jaffe, Julian F., *Crusade Against Radicalism: New York During the Red Scare, 1914–1924*, Port Washington, NY: Kennikat Press, 1972

Murray, Robert K., *Red Scare: A Study in National Hysteria, 1919–1920*, Minneapolis: University of Minnesota Press, 1955

Noggle, Burl, *Into the Twenties: The United States from Armistice to Normalcy*, Urbana: University of Illinois Press, 1974

Preston, William, *Aliens and Dissenters: Federal Suppression of Radicals, 1903–1933*, Cambridge, MA: Harvard University Press, 1962; 2nd edition, Urbana: University of Illinois Press, 1994

Tuttle, William M., Jr., *Race Riot: Chicago in the Red Summer of 1919*, New York: Atheneum, 1970

The aftermath of World War I was marked by an outbreak of widespread social disturbance including race rioting, labour conflict, and clashes between returning servicemen and other groups. The uncertainty of the period contributed to the anti-radical campaign of 1919–20, known as the Red Scare. Few detailed studies have been made of this subject. MURRAY provides a short, but still the only full-length, survey based on a range of primary and secondary material. He locates the anti-radical hysteria firmly within the chaos of post-war demobilization and labour strife, but concentrates on description more than explanation. His use of hyperbole is problematic when, for example, he claims "In 1919 America's soul was in danger."

COBEN (1964) is a seminal article which draws upon psychological studies to argue that while the Red Scare was brought on by severe social and economic dislocations after the war, America possesses a latent tendency to such action due to inherent fear of social change. However, not a great deal of solid evidence is presented to support these claims, and in fact the author points to factors, such as the rising cost of living and postwar depression, that helped to create an environment in which the anti-radical mood could thrive. He also argues that politicians were prepared to take advantage of the mood for their own ends. This particular feature is a major concern of COBEN (1963), a study of A. Mitchell Palmer, the attorney general who gave his approval, and name, to the raids on suspect radical groups, and the subsequent deportations in 1919 and 1920. In this full-length biography of the Quaker progressive reformer turned Red crusader, Coben suggests that, although Palmer hoped to ride the fear of Bolshevism into the presidency, he nonetheless shared the feelings of many Americans rather than merely exploiting them. After initial criticism of his inactivity against the "red threat", the bombing of his own home and the influence of advisers such as J. Edgar Hoover are seen as significant factors in leading Palmer to initiate the rounding up of supposed radicals in November 1919.

PRESTON is much less neutral in tone, but like Coben he suggests that the Red Scare was not an aberration, but born of the twin fears of radicalism and aliens. This is a detailed narrative of the development of federal security policies ("the national security state") based on official records. The author locates the beginnings of the anti-radical campaign in the attacks on the Industrial Workers of the World and attempted deportations which pre-dated 1919. The microscopic study of debates, and conflicts, within the Justice Department and the Immigration Bureau is revealing, but there is little reference to the events of 1919 and the strikes and bombings which, as other authors point out, provided the context.

JAFFE's local study, which sees the Red Scare as "largely the result of wartime developments", provides a useful insight into both the nature of some of the radical organizations in New York State, and the activities of the Lusk committee which was established to investigate the extent of revolutionary radicalism. Jaffe demonstrates not only the way in which local politicians both contributed to and exploited the postwar mood, but also the limits to such actions. For a short time the Committee threatened to undermine the democratic processes by unseating five duly elected Socialist representatives. However, this move itself contributed to the decline of the Red Scare, and following the election of Al Smith the various repressive Lusk acts were repealed.

A broad narrative synthesis based largely on secondary sources is offered by NOGGLE in his account of the transition from war to peace. He claims to offer an alternative to Coben's theoretical approach, but in truth the rational explanation of events based on a fear of revolution, encouraged by strikes and bombings, is only slightly different in emphasis. He does include other factors which helped to create a general sense of social disorder, such as the changes affecting black Americans and women.

A longer and broader perspective, necessarily less detailed, is provided by HIGHAM. His brief coverage of 1919–20 is placed within the history of the anti-immigrant movement of the late-19th and early 20th centuries and the "crusade for Americanization." He stresses the continuity between wartime and postwar hysteria and the quest for 100 per cent Americanism, and outlines the various shifts in mood from the attempt to expel aliens, through redemption, to exclusion, culminating in the immigration acts of the 1920s.

Two other works are indirectly relevant to this subject. BRODY's study of the steel strike shows clearly the impact of the Red Scare on labour relations. The strike, a major test of union strength after the war, was characterized as revolutionary, and posing a choice between the American system and Bolshevism. The postwar strikes – and particularly the involvement of immigrant workers – appeared to underline the failure of wartime Americanization programmes and to increase the mood of hysteria. In that environment, without public or government support and with a leader identified by previous statements as pro-Bolshevik, the strike was doomed to failure.

TUTTLE examines postwar race relations amid the climate of "unrest, anxieties, and dislocations that plagued the United States," and argues that it was no coincidence that racial violence occurred at this time. He sees the attack on blacks as a continuation of wartime xenophobia, and also shows the role of African Americans in labour disputes to be a major factor in the outbreak of violence which disrupted Chicago in the summer of 1919. Black militancy was characterized as radical, and for some Americans race violence was the work of Bolsheviks. Tuttle's brief account of the Red Scare provides an appropriate introduction to his main concern.

NEIL A. WYNN

See also Anticommunism

Reform Movements, 1820s–1850s

Abzug, Robert H., *Cosmos Crumbling: American Reform and the Religious Imagination*, New York: Oxford University Press, 1994

Cole, Charles C., Jr., *Lion of the Forest: James B. Finley, Frontier Reformer*, Lexington: University Press of Kentucky, 1994

Davis, David Brion (editor), *Ante-Bellum Reform*, New York: Harper, 1967

Griffin, C.S., *The Ferment of Reform, 1830–1860*, New York: Crowell, 1967; London: Routledge, 1969

Nissenbaum, Stephen, *Sex, Diet, and Debility in Jacksonian America: Sylvester Graham and Health Reform*, Westport, CT: Greenwood Press, 1980

Roth, Randolph A., *The Democratic Dilemma: Religion, Reform and the Social Order in the Connecticut River Valley of Vermont, 1791–1850*, New York: Cambridge University Press, 1987

Walker, Robert H., *Reform in America: The Continuing Frontier*, Lexington: University Press of Kentucky, 1985

Walters, Ronald G., *American Reformers, 1815–1860*, New York: Hill and Wang, 1978

Yacovone, Donald, *Samuel Joseph May and the Dilemmas of the Liberal Persuasion, 1797–1871*, Philadelphia: Temple University Press, 1991

Abolitionism, women's rights and feminism, temperance, utopianism, unionism, dietary and health reform, communitarianism, prison and asylum reform, millennialism, antimasonry, nativism, and sabbatarianism among others were movements during the 1820s through the 1850s and beyond that were driven by what is often identified, rather nebulously, as the "reform impulse." Scholars routinely argue over the origins, goals, ideologies, nature, meanings, modes, diversity, continuity, and consequences of reform as well as the personalities, motivations, and methods of reformers. The numerous movements and reformers provide a fertile field for varying interpretations of social change in America.

GRIFFIN is a good starting point for those interested in reform in the United States during the antebellum period. In a clear, concise historiographical essay of less than 100 pages, he examines several of the different interpretations among historians on the nature and meaning of reform. Quoting liberally from Ralph Waldo Emerson, who was both reformer and critic of reform, Griffin analyzes how Americans, at their best and worst, attempted to bring concrete meaning to the ideals of democracy and freedom. He notes the large degree of diversity among reformers and reform movements and offers conclusions that may be either challenged or endorsed.

In a similar vein, a series of essays on reform edited by DAVIS provide a variety of perspectives. In the introductory essay, Davis gives a brief but useful historiography that highlights the complexities and ambiguities of terms associated with reform such as conservatism, liberalism, and radicalism. He poses a series of questions designed to provoke and guide further study of reform. The other essays examine the personalities, motives, and changing attitudes of reformers; the effect of evangelical revivalism and Jacksonian democracy on reform; and the diverse themes present within specific movements.

Especially interesting is the influential essay on "Romantic Reform in America, 1815–65" in which John L. Thomas examines the transition from conservative revivalism to radical reform.

The diversity of motives, commitments, and needs among various reformers underscores WALTERS's synthesis, which briefly examines the rhetoric, tactics, patterns and changes of most of the major reform personalities and organizations. Asserting that reformers, confident in progress and human will, were representative of an American society that sought to maintain old values amidst the forces of modernization, Walters contends that reform helped people adapt to a changing world by serving a variety of needs. Limited within the period yet broad in the various types of reform covered, Walters maintains that lack of continuity and failure to build lasting institutions and tradition were among the major characteristics of the reform impulse of the era. He also includes an extremely useful bibliographical essay.

WALKER challenges the thesis of discontinuity in American reform and emphasizes the uninterrupted cumulative impact of reform ideas and social movements. Walker examines the common features among reformers – such as creative imagination, consistent rationales, and optimistic assumptions – and places reform in the period from the 1820s to the 1850s within the larger scope and context of reform in American society. Mixing analysis and narrative, Walker introduces new approaches, and a taxonomy of terms for the study of reform.

For those interested in the quantitative method, ROTH examines church, municipal, and voting records for a statistical analysis of nine communities within Vermont's "burned-over" district. He asserts that although unable always to reconcile democratic ideals with communitarian traditions, the citizenry of this region, dedicated to reform, was more successful in attempts to create a Christian, reformed, republican society than anywhere else in the Western world. Rather than examine the republican-liberal tension as the context of reform during this era, Roth explores the tensions among the diverse aspirations and promises which were the legacy of the American Revolution.

The role of religion in reform takes center stage as ABZUG analyzes how many of the originators of reform movements applied cosmological thinking and religious imagination to the political, economic, and social problems of a secular world in an unsuccessful attempt to sacralize human affairs. He maintains that reformers helped to reformulate the sacred understanding of society by combining the language of religion, republicanism, and the natural sciences. A useful companion to Abzug would be YACOVONE's biography of the New England minister and reformer Samuel May. Yacovone asserts that reformers such as May acted on religious principles, but centered their concept of reform around the liberal persuasion which emphasized individual rights, while at the same time condemning the social evils such as slavery and war that arose from unrestricted economic freedom. Together both works provide a useful examination of reform as it evolves from a New England phenomenon to a national one.

Biography offers an attractive way to study the various movements and organizations, and much has been written about the leading abolitionists, feminists, and reformers. Examining the life of Sylvester Graham and the new anxieties

Americans began to harbor about the human body, NISSENBAUM places dietary and health reform within the larger context of American reform, especially the relationship with temperance and evangelism. COLE examines education, prison, antislavery, and temperance reform on the Ohio frontier through the life of James Finley, a Methodist circuit rider. He also analyzes the devastating effect of reform on the traditions and culture of Native Americans. Together these works offer insights into little explored areas of the reform impulse.

These varied approaches furnish the reader with a multifaceted look at an impulse that continues to drive American society. The reform movements during the period from the 1820s to the 1850s provide fertile ground for further study.

LAWRENCE S. LITTLE

Religion: General

Ahlstrom, Sydney E., *A Religious History of the American People*, New Haven: Yale University Press, 1972

Bonomi, Patricia U., *Under the Cope of Heaven: Religion, Society, and Politics in Colonial America*, New York: Oxford University Press, 1986

Butler, Jon, *Awash in a Sea of Faith: Christianizing the American People*, Cambridge, MA: Harvard University Press, 1990

Gaustad, Edwin Scott, *A Religious History of America*, New York: Harper and Row, 1966, revised 1990

Hatch, Nathan O., *The Democratization of American Christianity*, New Haven: Yale University Press, 1989

Hopkins, Charles Howard, *The Rise of the Social Gospel in American Protestantism, 1865–1915*, New Haven: Yale University Press, and London: Oxford University Press, 1940

Hudson, Winthrop S., *American Protestantism*, Chicago: University of Chicago Press, 1961

Marsden, George M., *Fundamentalism and American Culture: The Shaping of Twentieth-Century Evangelicalism, 1870–1925*, New York and Oxford: Oxford University Press, 1980

Miller, Perry, *The New England Mind: The Seventeenth Century*, New York: Macmillan, 1939

Miller, Perry, *The New England Mind: From Colony to Province*, Cambridge, MA: Harvard University Press, 1953

Montgomery, William E., *Under Their Own Vine and Fig Tree: The African-American Church in the South, 1865–1900*, Baton Rouge: Louisiana State University Press, 1993

Moore, R. Laurence, *Religious Outsiders and the Making of Americans*, New York: Oxford University Press, 1986

Noll, Mark A., *A History of Christianity in the United States and Canada*, Grand Rapids, MI: Eerdmans, 1992

Raboteau, Albert J., *Slave Religion: The "Invisible Institution" in the Antebellum South*, New York: Oxford University Press, 1978

Turner, James, *Without God, Without Creed: The Origins of Unbelief in America*, Baltimore: Johns Hopkins University Press, 1985

The history of religion in the United States has been, first and foremost, the history of Protestant Christianity. Whether Calvinist, evangelical, fundamentalist or even occult, American religious diversity has often meant diversity within a Protestant tradition. To be sure, other religious groups have been influential at different times in America's history, but to understand religion in the United States one must start by studying the development of Protestant Christianity.

HUDSON provides such a starting point. In a short and compelling interpretation of American Protestantism, Hudson argues that Protestantism's desire to maintain its dominant place in American culture has ironically allowed the American environment to shape Protestant traditions in the United States. He identifies the ability to adapt to the rich diversity in America as the distinguishing and unifying characteristic of American Protestantism.

While readers interested in a concise interpretation of religion in America should first turn to Hudson, Noll and Gaustad also provide two other important introductions to religion in the United States. GAUSTAD's expressed goal is "to portray the role of religion in all stages of this country's development – from the moment that America was only a gleam in the eye of an Italian sailor to the full-blown and often bewildering present." While he concentrates on Protestant Christianity, Gaustad devotes attention to a host of other religious movements, such as Spanish and French Catholicism, Judaism, and Mormonism. Comparing the United States and Canada, NOLL's central focus is the rise and decline of Protestant dominance in America. Noll, a proponent of the new social history, concentrates on "'ordinary' people who did not leave extensive written records." Both Noll and Gaustad rank among the most up-to-date of the general works on religion in America.

A massive survey of religion in the United States, AHLSTROM attempts to move beyond mere "church history" by placing American religion in world history and by including a number of "secular" movements in his discussion. Although Ahlstrom is at his best in describing ideas and theology, he also notes the remarkable religious diversity and the changing social conditions of American life. While some argue that the growth of social history in recent years renders Ahlstrom's balance of theology and societal context somewhat outdated, it still stands as the most comprehensive and authoritative general account of American religious history.

Perry Miller has sparked research and debate in American religious history for more than fifty years. MILLER (1939) "discovered" that the Puritans were anything but the unenlightened, single-minded religious simpletons hailed in the common stereotype. While their main source of inspiration naturally came from their Calvinist theology, Miller argued that they also drew heavily on the changing intellectual milieu of the 17th century. From within the new tradition of humanism, the Puritans drew upon classical culture and, especially, natural philosophy in the creation of their intellectual world. Despite this breadth and sophistication, however, Miller argued that covenant theology, the centerpiece of the Puritans' creative effort, was foredoomed to failure. Unable to hold the thin line between the omnipotence of almighty God and the growing spirit of rationalism in the early modern world, covenant theory, in Miller's view, subtly encouraged confidence in human action and thereby led the Puritans into an age that undermined arbitrary authority in favor of "explicit rationalism and constitutionalism." MILLER (1953) traces the decline (or declension) of covenant theology in New England. He is able to show that the ideas of the Puritans, despite their declining impact on American religion, had a great impact on the social and political culture of America. The greatest legacy of the covenant theology was to bestow upon America the myth of a national covenant, the belief that America holds a special and divine mission in the world. Miller remains the starting place for all scholarly investigation of early American religious and intellectual life.

Revising Miller's argument that American religion entered a period of declension in the late 17th century, BONOMI's important study argued for the continuing growth of American religion during the 18th century. The 17th century was a period of disorder, transformation, and creation. The 18th century was an era of growth and stabilization. Whereas Miller focused on the ideas and doctrine of the Puritans, Bonomi understands religion primarily as an institutional, not a spiritual, structure. She argues that the Great Awakening gave Americans a forum in which to experiment with notions of individualism, democratization, and resistance to authority. When the political crisis of the American Revolution developed, Bonomi concludes, the Great Awakening provided the experience necessary for the development of colonial resistance to England.

Where Bonomi ends, HATCH begins. He argues that, between 1780 and 1840, a rebellious people, frustrated with the reigning religious order, led a charge that democratized American Christianity. Examining five egalitarian movements of the early republic, the Christian Connection, Mormons, African Americans, Methodists, and Universalists, Hatch argues that the "sovereign audience" demanded that religious leaders abandon their Calvinist moorings, profess confidence in private judgment and millennialism, and call for the restitution of the primitive church order of the New Testament. The Second Great Awakening, far from being the conservative reaction described in some accounts, was the rise of the populist masses against the religious culture of early America. Although Hatch recognizes that the movements he describes relied upon their own authoritative and coercive church hierarchy, he believes that they could not prevent the triumph of the egalitarian idea in American religion once it was unleashed.

More comprehensive than either Bonomi or Hatch, BUTLER offers a major reinterpretation of the first three hundred years of American religious history. Agreeing with Bonomi, Butler challenges all claims of Puritan hegemony in the 17th century by claiming that "the story of religion in America after 1700 is one of Christian ascension rather than declension." Most notably, Butler argues, occult practices successfully vied with the churches for patronage in the first century of settlement. In the 18th century, however, Butler challenges Bonomi's interpretation of the Great Awakening. In his view, the revivals of the early 18th century were so utterly distinct from one another that any attempt to lump them together is an "interpretive fiction." Furthermore, Butler finds the impetus behind growing Christianization, not in Bonomi's and Hatch's notions of increased individualism and democratization, but in a desire for authority and stability. One group, however, remained outside of this increasing Christianization: the African slaves. Stripped of their pre-Christian beliefs in an "African spiritual

holocaust," black Americans came slowly to Christianity. By the time they finally joined Christian America in the early 19th century, Butler believes that antebellum America had become a "spiritual hothouse." Although he does not delve deeply into the era after 1865, Butler assures us that religious growth continued because "Americans increasingly turned to Christian congregations and church membership as a means of formulating and rationalizing their own religious convictions amid the vagaries of modern life." The historical verdict is still out on Butler's revisionism, but his interpretation is likely to inspire a new generation of scholars.

While both Hatch and Butler give considerable attention to America's numerous under-studied religious minorities, MOORE offers a full-length treatment of these religious "outsiders." Examining Mormons, Catholics, Jews, Christian Scientists, Pentecostals, Fundamentalists and a number of other lesser-known groups, Moore argues that religious minorities have been marginalized by historians who have seen them too often as mere aberrations rupturing a progressive, Protestant tradition. From the American Revolution to the present, Moore argues that defining oneself as outside of the mainstream has been a vital part of the American experience.

In the story of the religious growth of the American people, few stories are as compelling and absorbing as the development of African American Christianity. RABOTEAU chronicles the development of Christianity among the slaves in the antebellum South. Reinforcing the notion that religion played a crucial role in the development of African American culture, Raboteau's comprehensive account covers the West African background, contrasts religion among the various slave societies of the New World, and recounts the origins and growth of slave religion in the United States. Raboteau argues that African culture did survive in slave religion, but he claims that the cultural meaning of those survivals had been transformed. Although he would not agree with Butler's stark depiction of an "African spiritual holocaust," Raboteau admits that, for American blacks, "the gods of Africa died." MONTGOMERY takes up the story of the growth of black church after the Civil War. The "cornerstone" of black life after emancipation, the church served the needs of a complex and diverse African American community. "The church," argued Montgomery, "helped to perpetuate the sense of group identity" that had been nurtured by the common experiences of life in the slave South.

While African American churches proliferated in the late 19th century, TURNER argues that unbelief became, for the first time in the history of America, a viable intellectual and cultural alternative to theism. He suggests that theologians themselves paved the way for unbelief by adapting doctrines to keep pace with the rise of science and rationalism. Encouraged by the rising secularism and rationalism of society, religious leaders attempted to incorporate some of the new ideas of modernity into their doctrines. In particular, Turner claims that theologians adopted new attitudes toward morality and de-emphasized the mysterious nature of religious knowledge. In the late 19th century, these adaptations opened the door to a system of unbelief. Changes in morality and sources of knowledge led agnostics to revere secular ideals instead of God and to construct a moral code independent of God.

Although Turner outlines an important change in American religion, fundamentalists, among others, did not fall victim to the tide of modernization. In his analysis of the fundamentalists of the late 19th and early 20th centuries, MARSDEN dispels the myth of the fundamentalists as small-town or rural anti-intellectuals. Noting the importance of pre-Civil War evangelical Protestantism, Marsden emphasizes both Scottish Common Sense realism and Baconian philosophy in fundamentalist thought. Marsden notes that "militant opposition to modernism was what most clearly set off fundamentalism from a number of closely related movements." The crucial moment in the origins of fundamentalism, says Marsden, came at the close of World War I. The war produced a cultural crisis that propelled the fundamentalists into a self-conscious campaign to halt the onset of modernism.

HOPKINS chronicles another religious movement that arose out of the cultural crisis of modern America, the Social Gospel. As liberal Protestants who had embraced the developments of capitalism in the late 19th century, most leaders of the Social Gospel movement did not hope to reverse the course of America's forward march. Instead, they hoped that religion, through a more active participation in the political and social world, could help curb the abuses and the problems that had arisen between capital and labor in industrial America. The Social Gospel, concludes Hopkins, played an enormously important role in making the social reforms of the Progressive period respectable and successful.

While Protestantism, indeed Christianity, no longer holds the central place in American culture that it held in the 19th century, religion has continued to remain an important part of the United States' social, moral and intellectual fabric. In the 20th century, the number of denominations and churches has continued to increase, and the varieties of religious experience, both Christian and non-Christian, have mushroomed. In spite of a powerful and growing secular culture, historians will continue to have much work to do in chronicling this most important American institution.

WILLIAM CARRIGAN

See also African American History: Religion; Catholic Church; Fundamentalism; Judaism; Protestantism entries; Puritanism; Revivalism; Social Gospel

Republican Party

Benedict, Michael Les, *A Compromise of Principle: Congressional Republicans and Reconstruction, 1863–1869*, New York: Norton, 1974

Edsall, Thomas Byrne and Mary D. Edsall, *Chain Reaction: The Impact of Race, Rights, and Taxes on American Politics*, New York: Norton, 1991

Foner, Eric, *Free Soil, Free Labor, Free Men: The Ideology of the Republican Party Before the Civil War*, New York: Oxford University Press, 1970

Gienapp, William E., *The Origins of the Republican Party, 1852–1856*, New York: Oxford University Press, 1987

Mayer, George H., *The Republican Party, 1854–1966*, 2nd edition, New York: Oxford University Press, 1967

Montgomery, David, *Beyond Equality: Labor and the Radical Republicans, 1862–1872*, New York: Knopf, 1967

Moos, Malcolm Charles, *The Republicans: A History of Their Party*, New York: Random House, 1956

Rae, Nicol C., *The Decline and Fall of the Liberal Republicans: From 1952 to the Present*, New York: Oxford University Press, 1989

Sherman, Richard B., *The Republican Party and Black America from McKinley to Hoover, 1896–1933*. Charlottesville: University Press of Virginia, 1973

Summers, Mark W., *Railroads, Reconstruction, and the Gospel of Prosperity: Aid under the Radical Republicans, 1865–1877*, Princeton: Princeton University Press, 1984

Weed, Clyde P., *The Nemesis of Reform: The Republican Party during the New Deal*, New York: Columbia University Press, 1994

The Republican party has long been a popular subject for historians and political scientists alike. MOOS is an early general account of the history of the party, which analytically documents the major developments of the party in its first 100 years, including: the formation of the party in the 1850s, the party and Lincoln, the changes in the party's constituencies in the late 19th century, the party split in 1912, and the defeats of the post-Depression years. Moos, himself a lifelong Republican and political science professor, gives a generally sympathetic account of the intellectual and ideological past of the party.

MAYER is also a chronological history of the party, but offers a more comprehensive coverage, with details of the party's conventions, campaigns, elections, and policies from the party's beginnings to 1964. Essentially a narrative survey, Mayer does not explore in any depth more fundamental issues relating to party ideology, fluctuating electoral fortunes, and relations between the national and the state and local levels of the party.

Since its first publication, FONER has been regarded as a classic study of the political ideology of the Republican party before the Civil War. Based on substantial research in primary sources, Foner provides an insightful analysis of the political outlooks of the main components of the Republican party – former Democrats, Whigs, Abolitionists, Free Soilers, Know-Nothings – and what brought these disparate forces together to form the new party. Foner argues that free labor was the essential idea that united the party and dictated the new party's ideological vision on several other crucial issues including the expansion of slavery, race relations, and preservation of the Union. While Foner has corrected the traditional view that the Republican party was merely a coalition of sectional forces without a coherent ideological commitment of its own, he in turn has been criticized for paying insufficient attention to practical questions of party organization and electoral priorities.

Examining the complex process by which the Republican party came into being and became the main challengers to the Democrats between 1854 and 1856, GIENAPP presents a powerful study which has woven together traditionally often contradictory approaches – ideological, ethnocultural, political, and social-intellectual. Focusing on the formation of the

Republican organization at the grassroots level in several northern states, Gienapp argues that the political realignment of the 1850s resulted from the inadequate responses of the second party system to many northern popular concerns, such as temperance, nativism, and anti-Catholicism, as well as anti-slavery. In particular, he highlights the importance of the nativist Know-Nothing Party in this crucial and complex process of political realignment. Gienapp regards the realignment of the 1850s as a mass-based revolt from the beginning, which was transformed into an organized political force by the work of party leaders who established a party organization, and reached out to various groups of potential supporters.

Among numerous studies of the Republican party during the Civil War and Reconstruction, BENEDICT stands out. With his very comprehensive, meticulous, detailed account and analysis of hundreds of roll-call votes in the 38th through 40th Congress, Benedict is able to provide a precise and persuasive breakdown of factional alignments within both the Republican and Democratic parties. Such treatment allows him to document the crucial movements in Reconstruction legislation backed with a precise calculation of the Republican strengths, thus reinforcing the argument advanced by such revisionist historians as Eric McKitrick and W.R. Brock, that the "radical" Reconstruction program was in fact shaped by moderate Republicans.

SUMMERS offers a critical assessment of the workings of the Republicans in the former Confederate states (except Virginia and Tennessee), and examines the Republican-led attempt at economic revitalization in the South (with the railroad-aid policy as the centerpiece). Summers credits Republicans for their genuine and ambitious effort to promote railway construction in the South, but concludes that the program was a failure, owing to the poor economic and financial infrastructure of the South, the impact of the national depression of 1873, and the Republicans' own factionalism and corruption.

MONTGOMERY examines the connections between the labor movement and the political realignment during Reconstruction. In Montgomery's view, workers had earlier identified themselves with the Republican ideological commitment to equality and the Union, but when workers asked for something "beyond equality" – for example, the demand for the eight-hour day – the Radicals regarded the labor movement as a threat to property rights and social stability. Such labor challenges shattered the Radicals' confidence in unlimited democracy and caused them to abandon their egalitarianism in 1868. Radicals consequently gave way to the leadership of the Stalwarts in a new political alignment dedicated to stabilization of the status quo. Not all critics are convinced that the relationship between the labor movement and the Republican party was anything like as close as Montgomery suggests.

Of the studies of the Republican party at the turn of the century, SHERMAN occupies a special place, as it is devoted to examining the party's attitudes and policies toward racial matters. Covering six presidents – from McKinley to Hoover – and a span of almost forty years, Sherman's research carefully explains how the party of Lincoln alienated African American voters by its wavering between wooing southern white votes and maintaining black suffrage, its indifference toward race matters, its toleration and acceptance of racial

segregation, and its opportunistic use of black votes. Sherman's study helps to explain why black voters overwhelmingly left the Republican party in 1936.

WEED is a study of the behavior and policies of the Republican party as a minority party during the New Deal years. He discusses the way in which the party elites worked to reunite the party's key interest groups, which refused to compromise with New Deal principles and policies. He examines in detail the congressional Republican response to the major New Deal innovations.

As one of the limited number of studies concerning the Republican party in the post-1945 era, RAE provides a good account of the party's history from 1952 to the end of the 1980s, with a particular emphasis on its liberal elements. He argues that the liberals lacked both a cohesive philosophy and the organizational skills to capture the national party machinery. In the mean time, rank-and-file Republicans increasingly embraced the prevailing conservative philosophy.

EDSALL is a compelling and highly readable account, written in a lively journalistic style, of how the Republican party re-emerged, and was able to win five of the six presidential elections from 1968 to 1988. Focusing on the development of the party's ideological rhetoric and organizing strategy, Edsall concludes that the Republican victories of the period resulted largely from the party's skilful exploitation of two pivotal yet explosive issues – race and taxes – in order to construct a new populist coalition of Republican conservatism. The Republicans sought to realign the electorate by adding to their traditional constituencies many formerly Democratic supporters, who were disappointed by their leaders' inability to offer viable solutions to new problems.

XI WANG

Republicanism

Adams, Willi Paul, *The First American Constitutions: Republican Ideology and the Making of the State Constitutions in the Revolutionary Era*, translated by Rita Kimber and Robert Kimber, Chapel Hill: University of North Carolina Press, 1980

Appleby, Joyce, *Liberalism and Republicanism in the Historical Imagination*, Cambridge, MA: Harvard University Press, 1992

Bailyn, Bernard, *The Ideological Origins of the American Revolution*, Cambridge, MA: Belknap Press of Harvard University Press, 1967, revised 1992

Banning, Lance, *The Jeffersonian Persuasion: Evolution of a Party Ideology*, Ithaca, NY: Cornell University Press, 1978

Kramnick, Isaac, *Republicanism and Bourgeois Radicalism: Political Ideology in Late Eighteenth-Century England and America*, Ithaca, NY: Cornell University Press, 1990

McCoy, Drew R., *The Elusive Republic: Political Economy in Jeffersonian America*, Chapel Hill: University of North Carolina Press, 1980

Pocock, J.G.A., *The Machiavellian Moment: Florentine Political Thought and the Atlantic Republican Tradition*, Princeton: Princeton University Press, 1975

Rahe, Paul A., *Republics Ancient and Modern: Classical Republicanism and the American Revolution*, Chapel Hill: University of North Carolina Press, 1992

Wood, Gordon S., *The Creation of the American Republic, 1776–1787*, Chapel Hill: University of North Carolina Press, 1969

Wood, Gordon S., *The Radicalism of the American Revolution*, New York: Knopf, 1992

Until the 1960s, intellectual historians described the political history of the American Revolution by referring primarily to the ideas expressed by John Locke in the second of his *Two Treatises of Government*. BAILYN transformed the study of the Revolutionary era by focusing instead on the thoughts of the radical writers and opposition politicians of 18th-century England. According to Bailyn, these theorists, more than Locke, were responsible for shaping the attitudes and assumptions of the Revolutionary generation. The central characteristic of the independence movement, then, was not a reasoned defense of natural rights, the consent of the governed, and the contractual basis of government, but an impassioned fear of corruption, official conspiracies, and enslavement.

WOOD (1969) demonstrates that the so-called radical Whig conceptualization of the dangers of power and corruption affected not only the movement for independence but the entire history of the Confederation. The Revolutionaries' perception of the benefits of mixed government and bicameralism, puzzlement over the rise of democratic despotism, and appreciation of the advantages of constitutional federalism were shaped by the promise of moral regeneration which they assumed to be inherent in their commitment to republican self-rule. The distinctively American contribution to the science of politics resulted from the realization among Americans that they had no special claim to virtue, but that a judicious arrangement of the institutions of government could manage an unvirtuous citizenry and perpetuate the life of the republic.

Independence and the collapse of the monarchical order in America did not end in the triumph of republican principles. WOOD (1992) argues that the popularization of postwar politics and culture dismayed many of the leaders of the Revolution. The Founding Fathers had hoped to construct a republic based on virtue, selflessness, and deference to natural aristocrats. However, the liberating rhetoric of the Revolution, coupled with the reality of popular participation in an expanding circle of political and economic activities, led inevitably to the celebration of democracy in the early 19th century.

In his discussion of the role of republican ideology in state constitution-making, ADAMS offers an oblique criticism of Bailyn and Wood. Adams argues that those who describe American republicanism as though it were the product of a single mind have understated the dynamic nature of the doctrine. American republicanism must be understood as a spectrum of attitudes and beliefs that can be separately identified by the positions disputants took during the drafting and ratification of the several state constitutions.

Bailyn, Wood, and Adams focus on the elements of republicanism and their significance for the Revolutionary generation. It was left to POCOCK to describe the historical context of the hopes and fears expressed by Americans. In his extended analysis of political thought from the 16th to the late 18th centuries, Pocock traces the revival of classical republican ideals by the civic humanists of the Florentine republic, their Anglicization by the commonwealthmen of the English Civil War, and their adoption by the Founding Fathers during the American Revolution. At the center of the civic humanist ideal was the virtuous citizen – active, independent, and selfless. The crucial problem confronting all republican theorists, then, was the problem of forestalling the decline of the republic by delaying the onset of habits detrimental to civic virtue.

In Pocock's formulation, the involvement of citizens in commerce, which invariably entails the extension of credit, creation of dependent relationships, and selfish pursuit of personal gain, was antithetical to republicanism. BANNING, Pocock's student, interprets the history of the 1790s along these lines. He attributes the success of the Jeffersonians in 1800 in large part to their ability to indict the Hamiltonian financial program and Federalist foreign policy as anti-republican.

McCOY argues persuasively, however, that American republicans embraced the idea of free trade. Although they believed that virtue was the lifeblood of the republic, they rejected the classical definition of the concept. Not Spartan forbearance and primitive simplicity, but industriousness was the essence of virtue for the Revolutionaries. And in a naturally bountiful land, where a comfortable sufficiency was easily achieved, forsaking foreign trade would have the unwelcome effect of encouraging idleness. Commerce, by providing the necessary incentives for farmers to remain diligent in their labor, was indispensable in the American republic.

Historians who question the pervasiveness of republican ideas in Revolutionary America have gone beyond McCoy's redefinition of the concept of virtue. They insist that Lockean liberalism was never displaced by classical republicanism. Otherwise, how is one to account for the triumph shortly after independence of individualism, materialism, and interest-group politics? APPLEBY has been a persistent critic of the republican synthesis, and essays that she has written over the past two decades have been conveniently re-published in her latest book. Appleby argues that republicanism and liberalism were competing ideologies in the early modern Anglo-American world and that, given the economic growth of the colonies in the half century before the Revolution, it is not surprising that the latter prevailed in America.

KRAMNICK agrees with Appleby that liberalism constituted a viable alternative to republicanism in the late 18th century. Although theorists who emphasized civic virtue, self-abnegation, and public good over private interest found ready audiences on both sides of the Atlantic, emerging economic imperatives gave moral sanction to expressions of competitive individualism, acquisitiveness, and personal ambition. In America, Kramnick argues, the Antifederalists were the champions of classical republicanism and the Federalists, ultimately victorious, were the proponents of liberalism.

Unlike Appleby and Kramnick, who posit the existence of two opposing camps of ideologues, RAHE argues that republican and liberal ideas existed in tandem in the mind of the Founding Fathers. Revolutionary Americans acknowledged the nobility of public spiritedness but redefined the concept of virtue to accommodate the emergence of a capitalist economy. In a sprawling 1,200-page tome, Rahe contends that this redefinition of virtue, and the institutionalization of self-interest that accompanied it, mark a decisive break between ancient and modern republicanism.

MELVIN YAZAWA

See also American Revolution: Character, Scope, and Significance

Reuther, Walter 1907–1970
Labor leader

Barnard, John, *Walter Reuther and the Rise of the Auto Workers*, Boston: Little Brown, 1983

Carew, Anthony, *Walter Reuther*, Manchester: Manchester University Press, and New York: St. Martin's Press, 1993

Cormier, Frank and William J. Eaton, *Reuther*, Englewood Cliffs, NJ: Prentice Hall, 1970

Halpern, Martin, *UAW Politics in the Cold War Era*, Albany: State University of New York Press, 1988

Howe, Irving and B.J. Widick, *The UAW and Walter Reuther*, New York: Random House, 1949

Lichtenstein, Nelson, "Walter Reuther and the Rise of Labor-Liberalism," in *Labor Leaders in America*, edited by Melvyn Dubofsky and Warren Van Tine, Urbana: University of Illinois Press, 1987

Reuther, Victor G., *The Brothers Reuther and the Story of the UAW: A Memoir*, Boston: Houghton Mifflin, 1976

Zieger, Robert H., *The CIO, 1935–1955*, Chapel Hill: University of North Carolina Press, 1995

Walter Reuther was clearly the most important American labor leader of the post-World War II era, and a large amount of scholarship has been devoted to various aspects of his career. The central theme of much of it has been the debate over whether Reuther was a social or a business unionist. Many accounts, especially biographies, have been fascinated with their subject and praised Reuther's social reformism, integrity, and positive achievements. This view has been challenged by work stressing Reuther's role in the bureaucratization and de-radicalization of the labor movement.

The first major biography of Reuther was by HOWE and WIDICK. Written in 1949, this account concentrates on Reuther's early career and rise to the presidency of the United Automobile Workers, but does not deal with his important achievements in the postwar period, especially his heyday in the 1950s. While dated and lacking access to detailed primary sources, this is nonetheless a good source of information on Reuther's early politics and ideas.

CORMIER and EATON is a sympathetic account that provides a sound overview of Reuther's whole career. One of its main assets is its extensive use of interviews with Reuther, members of his family, and close associates, as well as with a number of his opponents. These interviews help to make the book lively and readable, and also provide a close insight into Reuther's character. This account, however, is also restricted by its scant use of UAW archives, some of which were not available at the time of writing. Cormier and Eaton is a useful but not definitive work.

REUTHER is a lengthy memoir written by Walter Reuther's brother Victor, and tells of how the three Reuther brothers – Victor, Walter, and Roy – played a prominent role in the UAW and the wider American labor movement. It is a forceful defense of the Reuther legacy that tends to view Walter in a favorable light, especially portraying his rise to the union presidency as virtually pre-ordained. This said, it contains a great deal of valuable and detailed information, especially on Walter Reuther's family background and ideas, his bargaining achievements, and his relationships with George Meany, the CIA, and leading politicians. This account stresses Walter Reuther's social reformism, and also explores his contribution to international affairs, an area that other works largely ignore. The book is generally well-written and makes for entertaining reading.

BARNARD is a concise, scholarly account that provides an able introduction to Reuther's career. It concentrates mainly on his earlier years and his rise to power. Barnard provides a very sympathetic account of Reuther that portrays him as a social reformer whose aims outdistanced those of the labor movement. As a contribution to a series aimed at providing short and accessible biographies, it lacks the richness and depth of detail that a larger treatment could provide, and fails to explore many of the paradoxes of Reuther's legacy.

LICHTENSTEIN offers a far more critical assessment of Reuther in a thoroughly researched and important essay that precedes the argument of a forthcoming book. He claims that Reuther's presidency of the UAW helped rob the labor movement of its radical potential, by cementing a "social compact" between capital and labor that brought contract gains to postwar workers but limited union power. A related argument is put forward by HALPERN, who details Reuther's role in isolating the leftwing of the UAW, and argues that Reuther exploited the anticommunist threat to cement his leadership of the union. Halpern claims that the loss of the Communists limited the vitality of the union, although he also recognizes the considerable benefits that Reuther won for UAW members at the bargaining table. Halpern's work deals purely with the ouster of the left from the union in the immediate postwar years, especially the victory of the Reuther faction at the 1947 UAW convention.

CAREW is a concise and accessible account of Reuther's career that successfully utilizes Reuther's papers and recent scholarship. Carew provides a positive assessment of the labor leader, repeatedly refuting the arguments of Lichtenstein and Halpern. He argues that the Cold War gave Reuther little freedom of choice as UAW president, making it impossible for him to resist the isolation of the left since "genuine radical politics" were no longer an option. Carew also stresses that the loss of the Communists was positive because it meant an end to the damaging factionalism that had plagued the UAW. He also argues that Reuther was a "victim" rather than an initiator of the bureaucratization of the CIO. Carew portrays Reuther as a figure with both practicality and vision, who built the UAW into the most powerful labor union in America.

Given this debate about the significance of Reuther, ZIEGER is a helpful account because it provides a balanced and perceptive overview of the labor leader. It is more helpful than other studies in placing Reuther in a wider context, and considers his contribution not just to the UAW but to the industrial union movement as a whole. This work is especially valuable for information on Reuther's presidency of the CIO, and his role in the expulsion of Communists in the late 1940s. It contains many valuable insights into the strengths and limitations of Reuther's thinking, especially in showing his commitment to capitalism, his fierce anticommunism, and the failure of his presidency to revitalize the CIO.

TIM MINCHIN

See also Congress of Industrial Organizations; Labor Unions

Revivalism

Boles, John B., *The Great Revival, 1787–1805: The Origins of the Southern Evangelical Mind*, Lexington: University Press of Kentucky, 1972

Carwardine, Richard J., *Transatlantic Revivalism: Popular Evangelicalism in Britain and America, 1790–1865*, Westport, CT: Greenwood Press, 1978

Harrell, David Edwin, *All Things Are Possible: The Healing and Charismatic Revivals in Modern America*, Bloomington: Indiana University Press, 1975

Johnson, Paul E., *A Shopkeeper's Millennium: Society and Revivals in Rochester, New York, 1815–1837*, New York: Hill and Wang, 1978

McLoughlin, William G., *Modern Revivalism: Charles Grandison Finney to Billy Graham*, New York: Ronald Press, 1959

McLoughlin, William G., *Revivals, Awakenings, and Reform: An Essay on Religion and Social Change in America, 1607–1977*, Chicago: University of Chicago Press, 1978

Ryan, Mary P., *Cradle of the Middle Class: The Family in Oneida County, New York, 1790–1865*, Cambridge and New York: Cambridge University Press, 1981

Smith, Timothy L., *Revivalism and Social Reform in Mid-Nineteenth-Century America*, New York: Abingdon Press, 1957

Revivals of religion, in which the unregenerate are called to convert and the backsliders to renew their lives, are features of many religious movements, but have been especially characteristic of American evangelical Protestantism since the 18th century. Usually confined to a single church, community, or region, revivals may become national or even international in scope. For these larger movements some historians prefer the term "awakening" but have disagreed over their timing and whether particular awakenings even occurred.

There is no adequate general history of revivals from the colonial period to the present. The best place to begin is McLOUGHLIN (1959), which locates the emergence of modern revivalism in the 1820s when Charles Grandison Finney began to popularize those "new measures" which acknowledged human ability to work up a revival and accept God's freely offered grace, in contrast to the traditional Calvinist and 18th-century view of revival and conversion as entirely the work of God. The book is particularly good in showing how the great evangelists, such as Finney, Dwight L. Moody, Billy Sunday, and Billy Graham, adapted the techniques of revivalism to new circumstances. McLoughlin is critical of revivalism, particularly in the 20th century, suggesting that it fostered materialism, anti-intellectualism, and self-interested individualism.

Most historians have placed revivalism in the Calvinist and post-Calvinist traditions of New England and have developed a cyclical model of awakenings beginning with the mid-18th century First Great Awakening. By way of contrast SMITH traces the sources of revivalism to the Wesleyan (Methodist) movement and examines such neglected figures as Phoebe Palmer. Focusing on the revivals of 1857–58, previously not included by historians in any of the awakenings, the book stresses the growing strength of perfectionist evangelicalism during previous years, especially in urban areas. It thus abandons both the lingering impression of revivals as rural phenomena nurtured on the frontier and by implication the dominant model of cyclical awakenings. Moreover, Smith argues that the quest for personal holiness provided the energy for reform movements concerned with poverty, drunkenness, and slavery, and, more problematically, laid the groundwork for the later social gospel.

In contrast to his 1959 book, which concentrated on revivalists and their methods, McLOUGHLIN (1978) is an extended essay that identifies five American awakenings, the last projected to end about 1990. Moving beyond the generally negative appraisal of the former study, the 1978 book interprets these awakenings as "revitalization movements" (anthropologist Anthony Wallace's concept) that respond to cultural anxiety and can alter the world view of an entire people. The Second Great Awakening (1800–1830), for example, led to the rise of participatory democracy during the Jacksonian era. Although the connection between religious revivals and broader societal developments is not always convincingly made, the book provides an insightful comparative and interdisciplinary analysis.

Also appearing in 1978, CARWARDINE demonstrates the importance of the exchange of ideas, techniques, and personnel between Britain and the United States. Like Smith, the book focuses on cities and gives particular attention to the Methodists, concluding that McLoughlin and others have exaggerated the Presbyterian Finney's role in the development of the new measures. Unlike Smith, Carwardine concludes that the 1857–58 revival was not a genuine awakening, but was mainly a response to the anxieties of businessmen during the financial panic of those years. Time series data on Methodist church membership present a more complex picture of revivalism than the Presbyterian-Congregationalist (neo-Calvinist) derived model of awakenings.

The southern phase of the second awakening, from the late 1790s into the first decade of the new century, was largely neglected until the appearance of BOLES. This very carefully documented study emphasizes the ecumenical nature of the revivals, in which Methodists, Presbyterians, and Baptists were active. Although the revivals began in the West and absorbed much of the colour of the frontier, they were based on eastern precedents and quickly spread throughout the South. The book takes seriously the belief system of the participants, which emphasized God's sovereignty and His ordering of all earthly events. Whatever might have been the case in the North, Boles insists that the southern revivals helped shape a regional orthodoxy, centering on individual conversion and personal morality, that came to terms with slavery and left little room for social reform.

Implicitly accepting a neo-Calvinist framework, Johnson and Ryan examine the sites of two of Finney's greatest successes, respectively Rochester and Oneida County, both in upstate New York. Although their interpretations differ, they offer the most sophisticated accounts of the relationship of revivalism to social change, an enterprise first begun for this so-called "burned-over district" by Whitney R. Cross more than four decades ago. Recognizing the contribution of Finneyite revivalism to such reform movements as abolitionism and temperance, JOHNSON seeks to explain how the great revival of 1830–31, with its assertion of moral free agency and its millennialist expectations, helped both to consolidate a middle class of entrepreneurs and professionals, who regarded social disorder as essentially a religious problem, and to impose discipline on a growing class of industrial workers. The book is especially useful for its careful delineation of a society in flux and its quantitative analysis of church membership, tax, and occupational data.

Critical of Johnson's emphasis on class and social control, RYAN insists that questions of gender and family were also central to revivalism. Broadly concerned with shifting understandings of power, responsibility, and moral authority in middle class households, the book argues that the revivals helped loosen the traditional constraints of patriarchal authority and expand women's sphere both with respect to moral influence within the home and charitable work in the community. Since women and youth constituted most of the converts, the revivals created a new web of associations between mothers and children. Contrary to Johnson, Ryan finds few workingmen converts to evangelical Protestantism, a result that may hinge on her primary reliance on Presbyterian data.

Revivals in the 20th century have become associated with more conservative evangelical movements, epitomized since the 1950s by the Billy Graham crusades, and with perhaps the most dynamic branch of Christianity, Pentecostalism. Claiming such gifts as healing and speaking in tongues, well-known Pentecostals such as Oral Roberts and Jimmy Swaggart have achieved public attention largely through their effective use of the mass media. Although they have been much discussed by sociologists and journalists, the best historical introduction to these movements, especially for the period after World War II, is HARRELL. The book distinguishes two phases: the healing revival, which peaked in the early 1950s and appealed to more marginal members of society, and the later charismatic revival which emphasized all the gifts of the spirit and attracted more diverse groups, including Episcopalians and Roman Catholics. By the 1970s old-fashioned tent revivalists were confined mainly to small towns and rural areas. New tendencies, such as the gospel of prosperity, flourished, while personal and financial scandals gained media attention.

FREDERICK A. BODE

See also Great Awakening; Second Great Awakening

Revolutionary War *see* War of Independence

Riots

Avrich, Paul, *The Haymarket Tragedy*, Princeton: Princeton University Press, 1984

Bernstein, Iver, *The New York City Draft Riots: Their Significance for American Society and Politics in the Age of the Civil War*, New York: Oxford University Press, 1990

Capeci, Dominic J., Jr., and Martha Wilkerson, *Layered Violence: The Detroit Rioters of 1943*, Jackson: University of Mississippi Press, 1991

Cortner, Richard C., *A Mob Intent on Death: The NAACP and the Arkansas Riot Cases*, Middletown, CT: Wesleyan University Press, 1988

Feldberg, Michael, *The Turbulent Era: Riot and Disorder in Jacksonian America*, New York: Oxford University Press, 1980

Fine, Sidney, *Violence in the Model City: The Cavanagh Administration, Race Relations, and the Detroit Riot of 1967*, Ann Arbor: University of Michigan Press, 1989

Gilje, Paul A., *The Road to Mobocracy: Popular Disorder in New York City, 1763–1834*, Chapel Hill: University of North Carolina Press, 1987

Gilje, Paul A., *Rioting in America*, Bloomington: Indiana University Press, 1996

Gordon, Michael A., *The Orange Riots: Irish Political Violence in New York City, 1870 and 1871*, Ithaca, NY: Cornell University Press, 1993

Hair, William Ivy, *Carnival of Fury: Robert Charles and the New Orleans Race Riot of 1900*, Baton Rouge: Louisiana State University Press, 1976

Senechal, Roberta, *The Sociogenesis of a Race Riot: Springfield, Illinois, in 1908*, Urbana: University of Illinois Press, 1990

Slaughter, Thomas P., *Bloody Dawn: The Christiana Riot and Racial Violence in the Antebellum North*, New York: Oxford University Press, 1991

Tuttle, William M., Jr., *Race Riot: Chicago in the Red Summer of 1919*, New York: Atheneum, 1970

The study of riots in U.S. history provides scholars with an opportunity to explore the manner in which Americans relate to one another and their institutions, as well as the social, economic, and political conditions that produce discontent and protest. The use of collective violence to alleviate perceived or actual wrongs has had a long tradition in American society, as shown by GILJE's (1987) social history of riots in New York City during the Revolutionary and post-Revolutionary eras. Analyzing numerous riots through extensive research, Gilje maintains that during the Revolutionary era, the ideal of a corporate community legitimized and sanctioned riots against deviants or outsiders. Rioters respected lives and property and often used symbols and effigies as targets of their outrage or grievances. After the American Revolution, according to Gilje, community interests were challenged by diverse goals and religious, ethnic, racial, and class differences, often leading to unsanctioned violent conflict and attacks on persons and property.

Complementing Gilje, FELDBERG briefly surveys riots mainly but not exclusively in Philadelphia during the Jacksonian era – a period of increased urban collective violence. Feldberg contends that riots usually consisted of two groups of citizens battling one another, but they could also be triggered by groups attacking isolated individuals or confronting official forces. The success of riots, he maintains, led to the formation of professional police departments. Classifying riots as those that furthered a political cause and those that fulfilled emotional or recreational needs, Feldberg asserts that riots stemmed from a number of sources, and attempts, with some success, to apply theories of collective violence in the 1960s to the Jacksonian era.

Although most racial riots during the 19th century consisted of white citizens attacking black communities in an urban setting, SLAUGHTER examines the Christiana riot in 1851 that consisted of organized black Americans, fugitive and free, defending themselves from slave catchers in rural Lancaster County, Pennsylvania. He analyzes the various conditions, attitudes, and perceptions that contributed to a pattern of violence which increased with the Fugitive Slave Law of 1850, and he scrutinizes the treason trial that blurred lines between the law and politics in the aftermath of the riot. To place the riot in a broader context of a culture of violence in antebellum America, Slaughter examines court records of collective and individual cases of violence among ethnic groups, races, classes and across gender lines.

The New York city draft riots in July 1863 cost over 100 lives, and still remain the bloodiest outbreak of urban violence in American history. BERNSTEIN not only traces the process by which a protest against the draft escalated into something much more complex and more violent, but he also places the riots into their broader historical context. He uses the riots to illuminate the tensions in mid-19th century New York between rich and poor, native born and immigrants, and blacks and whites, and also between city and nation. The riots brought to the surface explosive issues of class, race, government and politics. Even if some of his conclusions are controversial, Bernstein provides a model of how to use a study of one episode in one city to achieve greater insight into some of the major themes of 19th-century American history.

Ethnic, class, and religious differences take center stage as GORDON examines the political and economic circumstances that precipitated the Orange riots in New York in 1871 and 1873. He maintains that contending visions of the nation's past, present, and future, and differing perceptions of republicanism, pitted Irish Catholic immigrants against nativist Protestant elites. Taking into account the effects of industrialization and political corruption, Gordon offers many insights into life among the Irish working class as well as the forces that attempted to control them.

Viewed by AVRICH as the culmination of years of labor disputes, strikes, and agitation, the events surrounding the Haymarket riot of 1886 reveal a pattern of labor unrest quelled by government muscle that lasted well into the 20th century. Using collective biography, Avrich focuses on the hopes, dreams, passions, and opinions of the leading personalities in the Chicago anarchist movement. Characterizing the events surrounding the riot and the subsequent trial as the first "red scare," Avrich asserts that the tragedy exposed the inequities of American capitalism and the limitations of the American justice system.

Much of the recent historiography on riots in the 20th century attempts to understand the differing attitudes and perceptions of white and black Americans, as well as the nature and meaning of collective violence. HAIR traces the life of Robert Charles – an all but obscure African American whose actions sparked rioting in New Orleans in 1900 – as a means of exploring racial repression, intimidation, and violence in the deep South. Hair cites economic factors, especially job competition, as a major contributor to racial tensions and hardening white attitudes that created the conditions for a riot. In a sense, Hair's study actually covers two riots – one by white citizens and a one-man riot by Charles who, Hair maintains, was a "harbinger" of rising assertiveness among African Americans.

CORTNER analyzes the role of the NAACP in strengthening the criminal procedure requirements of due process, by helping to litigate the release of 79 African Americans sentenced to prison or death in the wake of racial violence in 1919, in Phillips County, Arkansas (where blacks constituted a majority of the population). Cortner describes local conditions of peonage and sharecropping against a background of growing postwar disillusionment and discontent across the nation. Clearly illustrating how black demands for economic justice provoked racial attacks by white citizens, Cortner maintains that a legal riot also occurred in a wave of hysteria that convicted innocent men and women without due process.

On conditions and attitudes in the urban North, TUTTLE's social history of the Chicago riot in 1919 analyzes the effects of migration and urbanization, that increased black assertiveness and white apprehension in areas such as job and housing. Maintaining that riots occur more often in times of economic and social stress, Tuttle places the Chicago riot within the context of the "Red Summer of 1919," and the postwar recession, which led to growing anti-radicalism and xenophobia throughout the nation. He also gives a good account of efforts by African Americans to create a viable community in Chicago.

Examining the Springfield, Illinois riot in 1908, SENECHAL takes a different approach that focuses on the social characteristics of the participants, victims, and non-participants rather than the background conditions. She emphasizes the importance of perceived black violation of place, and concludes that those whites who had little contact with African Americans and who had jobs that excluded African Americans were more likely to riot. The victims were not random, but were African Americans who had gained a degree of success. Senechal maintains that white racism was not monolithic but covered a variety of attitudes and responses.

Since the 1940s, riots have usually been characterized as the work of African Americans destroying white businesses and property in black communities with a few roving white mobs on the periphery. Analyzing police arrest records, court files, and probation records from the Detroit riot in 1943, CAPECI and WILKERSON argue persuasively that, rather than the "black hoodlums" and "white hillbillies" identified in official reports, rioters were ordinary men and women from diverse backgrounds who rioted for various reasons. Capeci and Wilkerson examine factors such racial pride, political awareness, and long-time residency that led to a new aggressiveness in the black community.

Asserting that the Detroit riot in 1967 was a form of protest intended to highlight the conditions under which African Americans lived, FINE provides an excellent and exhaustive analysis of many aspects of urban collective violence during the turbulent 1960s. He explores race relations, public policies and programs, police and community relations, and the response from the criminal justice system of what many considered a model city that had resolved its racial problems. Fine profiles the rioters, counter-rioters, and the non-involved, suggesting that no single model of collective behavior can explain why some rioted but most did not. Fine, Capeci and Wilkerson, and Senechal all give useful reviews of the historiography and theories of collective violence.

The need for a historical overview of rioting in America has been met, at least in part, by GILJE (1996), which ranges from the colonial period to Los Angeles in 1992. Aiming at comprehensive coverage, from ritual public protests in the colonies, through labor and ethnic violence to 20th-century race riots, Gilje may strive too hard to include every kind of social disturbance in his relatively brief survey. However, he performs a valuable service in linking together numerous episodes of rioting in American history and seeking to place them in a broader context.

LAWRENCE S. LITTLE

Rivers and Canals

Allen, Michael, *Western Rivermen, 1763–1861: Ohio and Mississippi Boatmen and the Myth of the Alligator Horse*, Baton Rouge: Louisiana State University Press, 1990

Goodrich, Carter, *Canals and American Economic Development*, New York: Columbia University Press, 1961

Haites, Erik F., James Mak, and Gary M. Walton, *Western River Transportation: The Era of Early Internal Development, 1810–1860*, Baltimore: Johns Hopkins University Press, 1975

Hunter, Louis C., *Steamboats on the Western Rivers: An Economic and Technological History*, Cambridge, MA: Harvard University Press, 1949

Mahoney, Timothy R., *River Towns in the Great West: The Structures of Provincial Urbanization in the American Midwest, 1820–1870*, New York: Cambridge University Press, 1990

Scheiber, Harry N., *The Ohio Canal Era: A Case Study of Government and the Economy, 1820–1861*, Athens: University of Ohio Press, 1969; with new preface, 1987

Shaw, Ronald E., *Canals for a Nation: The Canal Era in the United States, 1790–1860*, Lexington: University Press of Kentucky, 1990

Way, Peter, *Common Labour: Workers and the Digging of North American Canals, 1780–1860*, Cambridge and New York: Cambridge University Press, 1993

The history of rivers and canals has long been a popular subject among American historians. In particular, the steamboats on the western rivers and the opening of the Erie Canal were seen as symbols of the technological and practical achievements of an American empire on the march. While many historians explored the economic and political consequences of such growth, few examined the social or environmental forces at work.

HUNTER wrote his history of the steamboat in response to such celebratory histories of American waterways. His wide-ranging study discusses the economic, social, and technological developments in the mid-to-late 18th century which prepared the way for the steamboat. Hunter gave considerable attention to the specifics of steamboat construction, and provides much information on the development of organized services, and on the crews, passengers and cargoes of the steamboats. He describes moves to regulate the operation of steamboats, and depicts the railroads as the nemesis of the river trade.

GOODRICH built a career around the study of early American transportation. In his view, canals were the primary factors in the development of the trans-Appalachian West. He portrayed a decentralized government which actively promoted internal improvements, but which had to depend largely on voluntary civic organization and the leadership of private entrepreneurs. Most importantly, Goodrich's interpretation challenged the popular historiography of his day – the idea that, during the first half of the 19th century, the federal government operated according to a strictly laissez-faire philosophy. SCHEIBER's study of Ohio during the canal era bears out the importance in such developments of public enterprise – in this case promoted by an individual state – at least until financial difficulties, competition between various localities, and then the coming of the railroad, brought the heyday of the canals to an end.

While Goodrich emphasized the effects of canals on opening the trans-Appalachian West, HAITES, MAK and WALTON returned to the rivers of the West to investigate whether canals really proved so crucial to western development. This econometric study of Mississippi and Ohio River trade offered little new information and reiterated much of Goodrich's findings. Yet, the book did provide additional evidence on the private sources of funding, the direct and indirect methods of government support, and the interdependency of the flatboat and steamboat trade. The latter topic alone makes the book worthwhile.

SHAW's comprehensive study of canal-building up to the Civil War is probably the best synthesis of the subject. Urbanization along canal routes, construction procedures, private and public funding, and the role of engineers are among the topics covered. But he examines wider issues too. He carefully evaluates the relationship between canals and railroads, and analyzes the influence of canals in fostering national unity and a sense of national identity.

In his study of river boatmen, ALLEN challenges some of the mythology of the flatboat and keelboat trade of the Mississippi and Ohio Rivers. He examines the social and economic aspects of their lives, including the impact of the steamboat and urban growth on their livelihoods. One of the first social histories of rivers, Allen's study also discusses the roles of river towns and economic growth in the development of a laboring subculture. MAHONEY places the river towns, rather than the rivers themselves, at the center of his story. He shows the influence of geography and of market dynamics in the development of the river towns, and their role in the wider development of the Midwest. Mahoney traces the symbiotic relationship between urban growth and river trade. The regional identity was initially shaped by natural transportation routes, but, when the railroad came to dominate the Midwest in the 1850s, a new midwestern identity and economy formed around Chicago.

WAY's award-winning study is concerned not so much with the canals as with the men whose labor built them. He paints a remarkable picture of the varied make-up of the work force, the appalling conditions in which they often lived and worked, the violence and insecurity which constantly plagued them, their various forms of protest, and their basic helplessness in face of the power of the employers, backed when necessary by the civil and military authorities. Because of their rough, tough and peripatetic way of life, few canal workers participated in the formal political system, and they found little scope for the commitment to republicanism and the craft pride, which other labor historians have discerned in urban workers in the same period. The underside of canal history has never been revealed in this way before.

CRAIG THOMPSON FRIEND

See also Internal Improvements; Transport

Roads and Road Transport, to 1900

Coleman, J. Winston, *Stage-Coach Days in the Bluegrass, Being an Account of Stage-Coach Travel and Tavern Days in Lexington and Central Kentucky, 1800–1900*, Louisville, KY: Standard Press, 1935

Davis, William, *A Way Through the Wilderness: The Natchez Trace and the Civilization of the Southern Frontier*, New York: HarperCollins, 1995

Durrenberger, Joseph Austin, *Turnpikes: A Study of the Toll Road Movement in the Middle Atlantic States and Maryland*, Valdosta, GA: Southern Stationery and Printing Company, 1931

Rouse, Parke, Jr., *The Great Wagon Road from Philadelphia to the South*, New York: McGraw Hill, 1973

Rutman, Darrett B. and Anita H. Rutman, *A Place in Time: Middlesex County, Virginia, 1650–1750*, 2 vols., New York: Norton, 1984

Southerland, Henry DeLeon, Jr., and Jerry Elijah Brown, *The Federal Road Through Georgia, the Creek Nation, and Alabama, 1806–1836*, Tuscaloosa: University of Alabama Press, 1989

Roads in American history have been taken for granted. While historians are aware of the importance of the Great Wagon Road, the Wilderness Road, and the National Road to the development of the American nation, few have paid serious scholarly attention to these highways. Antiquarian studies abound, but offer little of real historical value. Surprisingly, in those instances when historians have ventured down a specific road, they have often attempted to portray it less as a transportation route than as a venue for the transmission of cultural or social change.

In his early study of turnpikes – toll roads regulated through legislative acts – DURRENBERGER explored the social and economic conditions which led to the creation of turnpike companies. State governments necessarily became involved in road improvements because they were regarded as so crucial to community life. They connected population centers and they tied the developing West to the more established East. Therefore, the boom in turnpike construction in the early 19th century reflected the expansion of the nation itself.

The focus of COLEMAN's study of 19th-century Kentucky is not so much on the roads, as on the means of transport on them – the stagecoach. Coleman discovered an extensive system of transport-related economic activities which made roads more than transportation routes. Taverns, inns, stores, coach-lines, and tollgates contributed to road-oriented micro-economies which in turn contributed to the larger economic structure of the region. Coleman's colorful descriptions are a feature of the book.

Since Durrenberger and Coleman, historians have looked beyond road construction and transport to explore the wider economic and social impact of roads. The Great Wagon Road was most important in the peopling of the back country in the colonial and revolutionary era. ROUSE explored the road as an instrument of military, economic, religious and cultural developments. He examined the migration of the Quakers of Pennsylvania into Virginia and North Carolina; the use of the road to mobilize American troops during the southern campaigns of the War of Independence; early attempts at establishing stage routes; and the evolution of the log cabin as an architectural form.

RUTMAN and RUTMAN use a road as the organizing principle of a study of a colonial Virginia county. The road tied together segments of a complex rural community. Three Anglican churches lined the road, thereby ecclesiastically connecting the county's population, despite the distances separating neighbors and families. Another road in the county, referred to by residents as "the negro road," served even less as a transportation route. Instead, the Rutmans explored it as a metaphor for the move towards slavery in the region in the late 17th century. The Rutmans skilfully use the road to explore the nuances of colonial Virginia life.

While Rouse and the Rutmans explored their roads in cultural, economic and even metaphorical senses, SOUTHERLAND and BROWN studied the Federal Road through the Old Southwest as an extension of the federal government into a previously ungoverned land. The road proved controversial on both national and local levels. Originally a mail route, the road quickly became part of a federal military road system. As it crossed through Creek Indian territory, the road enabled the federal government, the military, and a series of unscrupulous white Americans, to undermine Creek society and contribute to the eventual removal of these peoples in the 1830s.

The Old Southwest also elicited attention from the most recent contributor to the history of American roads. DAVIS traveled one of the oldest American roads, the Natchez Trace which connected Nashville, Tennessee to Natchez, Mississippi.

The trace, claimed Davis, was the means by which education, religion, and enlightenment spread into the uncivilized southwest. In his analysis, however, Davis concludes that, central though the road may have been to the settlement and development of a region, its importance was short-lived. The Natchez Trace remained important only until it was replaced by the steamboat and railroad as the major means of transport, by which time the Indians had been removed, and white American society and culture predominated.

CRAIG THOMPSON FRIEND

See also Transport

Roads and Road Transport, 20th century: Automobiles, Buses, and Trucks

Belasco, Warren James, *Americans on the Road: From Autocamp to Motel, 1910–1945*, Cambridge: Massachusetts Institute of Technology Press, 1979

Berger, Michael, *The Devil Wagon in God's Country: The Automobile and Social Change in Rural America, 1893–1929*, Hamden, CT: Archon, 1979

Finch, Christopher, *Highways to Heaven: The Auto Biography of America*, New York: HarperCollins, 1992

Flink, James J., *The Automobile Age*, Cambridge: Massachusetts Institute of Technology Press, 1988

Jackson, Carlton, *Hounds of the Road: A History of the Greyhound Bus Company*, Bowling Green, OH: Bowling Green University Popular Press, 1984

Lewis, David L. and Laurence Goldstein (editors), *The Automobile and American Culture*, Ann Arbor: University of Michigan Press, 1983

McShane, Clay, *Down the Asphalt Path: The Automobile and the American City*, New York: Columbia University Press, 1994

Rae, John B., *The American Automobile: A Brief History*, Chicago: University of Chicago Press, 1965

Rae, John B., *The Road and the Car in American Life*, Cambridge: Massachusetts Institute of Technology Press, 1971

Wren, James A. and Genevieve J. Wren, *Motor Trucks of America*, Ann Arbor: University of Michigan Press, 1979

In his groundbreaking work, RAE (1965) describes the automobile as a social force that affects every American. Not only is it the instrument for rapid and modern transportation, but it also serves as a means of moving up the social ladder. It was the agent of social as well as physical mobility. Furthermore, the method of low-cost, high volume assembly line production invented to produce automobiles meant "drastic transformations in the economy and society of the United States." The main thrust of Rae's book is the way in which a mechanical invention shaped a whole way of life. In RAE (1971) this argument is expanded to include highway transportation, like trucks and buses, and also the roads and highways which they use. In the face of contemporary criticism of highway transportation, Rae rejects the idea that the personal motor vehicle and bulk transportation carriers will be replaced in the foreseeable future. Despite the adverse conditions created by increasing traffic, he argues that the economic efficiency of motor vehicles, and the freedom of mobility that they provide for individuals, are factors that will prevent them from disappearing.

In a considerably revised version of his earlier book *The Car Culture*, FLINK brings his study of the car culture in America up to date by including a survey of the events of the late 1970s and 1980s, when the American automobile industry was under assault by Japanese and other foreign car manufacturers. Convinced of the staying power of "mass personal automobility," Flink defends the American auto industry and refutes critics who predict that passenger cars are becoming obsolete. Unlike Rae, who examines the American auto industry without taking European or foreign experience into account, he studies the influence of the automobile as an international phenomenon. He contends that, in order to understand the automobile revolution on a global scale, an examination of the United States, the world's "foremost automobile culture," is essential.

In 1979, recognizing that the automobile has exerted a "potent influence" on American culture and concerned that up to the late 1960s there had been a paucity of studies of the subject, the *Michigan Quarterly Review* devoted two combined issues to the topic of the influence of automobiles on American culture. The overwhelming response to the special journal edition led to the publication of the book edited by LEWIS and GOLDSTEIN. The essays cover a wide array of topics, including the influence of the motor car on fashion, the city, the farmer, love and sex, women, film, art, the novel and poetry, and popular music. This is a valuable overview of the cultural impact of the automobile and adopts a broad approach to the study of cultural change.

The most recent study of the tremendous influence of the car on American society and culture is FINCH. His wideranging study includes not only the automobile itself but also roads, trucks, shopping malls, suburbs, motels, cruising, smog, tailgate parties, and fast food franchises. One major theme centers around the sexual allure and eroticism of the automobile. Finch attempts to contrast European and American auto history, but does not maintain this comparative approach. Instead, he concentrates on Los Angeles, a town he considers to be the nation's "automoville." Similar to other works that try to cover all aspects of the automobile in American culture, Finch only touches on important facets, such as the emergence of chain franchises in the 1950s, or the major innovations in body design and styling.

While most studies of the automobile in the United States, particularly Rae and Flink, argue that the automobile "progressed logically and inevitably," some recent historians have refuted the belief that technological determinism alone served as the engine for progress. McSHANE argues that the success of the automobile in the United States was the result, not of technological improvements in the combustion engine, but of changes in American urban culture. McShane argues that people living in the city began to view streets not as open public spaces but as traffic ways. They also began to perceive the automobile as both a status symbol and a symbol of liberation.

Most studies of the emergence of the automobile culture in the United States concentrate on the effect which cars had on the American consumer. BELASCO demonstrates that what Americans did with their cars was just as important in the process of changing American culture into a state of dependence on the automobile. In the early years of the car, touring, or auto-camping, became a national recreation. At first it was seen as a way to escape the drudgery of work routines and the bureaucratic institutions of urban civilization but, as the number of cars increased and touring became more popular, the Gypsy nature of touring gave way to a controlled "conservative commercial" system. Belasco traces this metamorphosis from the early days of touring by examining the beginnings of the motel industry, a more bourgeois, sanitized, and safe form of touring. Belasco provides an interesting perspective on the causes and effects of the growth of the car culture in the United States.

One area particularly affected by the introduction of the automobile was rural America. Building on the work of Rae and Flink, BERGER sees the car as the "greatest revolutionizing force" in rural society. The impact of the auto caused a loosening of rural family ties, and broke down the "insularity" of the rural community. Berger examines the effect of the auto on rural leisure activities, churches and religion, education, and improved health care, and its wide-ranging impact on the rural environment.

Automotive history generally concentrates on cars, and gives only passing attention to the history of bus manufacturing or the emergence of intercity bus lines. JACKSON describes the founding of Greyhound in 1913 as a result of a transportation need in the northern Minnesota mining region and the entrepreneurial effort of a first-generation American. From these small beginnings, it grew into a national corporation. Attention is paid to the bureaucratization and systematization of the company as it grew in the 1920s, development of a network of national terminals in the 1930s, 1940s, and 1950s, the role of the bus and of company policy towards discrimination during the civil rights movement, and the importance of bus lines in African American migration patterns out of the South from the 1950s to 1970s. Jackson also mirrors automobile historians writing in the 1970s who express concern for the effects of the oil embargo on transportation.

In the history of combustion engine transportation, the truck too has played an important part. WREN and WREN do not provide a narrative historical account but they do offer a starting point, and a useful guide to information on the history of trucks. The work is divided into four sections: "Milestones" from 1895 to 1979 lists chronologically facts relating to such topics as patents, engineering developments, production and sales, innovations, federal legislation, standardization, and new models; "Pioneers" provides brief biographies of individuals, such as Clessie L. Cummins and August C. Fruehauf, who are closely associated with the trucking industry; "Roll Call" lists names of motor trucks produced and their production years; and "Highlights" offers motor vehicle statistics like unit sales, and bus and truck registration.

CRAIG S. PASCOE

See also Transport

Rockefeller, John D. 1839–1937
Industrialist and philanthropist

Collier, Peter and David Horowitz, *The Rockefellers: An American Dynasty*, New York: Holt, Rinehart, 1976
Harr, John E. and Peter J. Johnson, *The Rockefeller Century*, New York: Scribner, 1988
Hawke, David Freeman, *John D.: The Founding Father of the Rockefellers*, New York: Harper, 1980
Hidy, Ralph W. and Muriel E. Hidy, *History of the Standard Oil Company (New Jersey)*, volume 1: *Pioneering in Big Business, 1882–1911*, New York: Harper, 1955
Nevins, Allan, *John D. Rockefeller: The Heroic Age of American Enterprise*, 2 vols., New York: Scribner, 1940
Nevins, Allan, *Study in Power: John D. Rockefeller, Industrialist and Philanthropist*, 2 vols., New York: Scribner, 1953; abridged by William Greenleaf, as *John D. Rockefeller*, New York: Scribner, 1959
Tarbell, Ida M., *History of the Standard Oil Company*, New York: McClure Phillips, 1904
Winkler, John K., *John D.: A Portrait in Oils*, New York: Vanguard Press, 1929

John Davison Rockefeller, captain of industry and philanthropist, epitomizes the self-made millionaire of the Gilded Age. He started work following high school as a bookkeeper-clerk in a commission house in Cleveland and built a billion-dollar fortune by creating and developing the Standard Oil Company of New Jersey in 1870. As early as 1880 Rockefeller controlled 90 per cent of the American oil industry. Such an accumulation of power and wealth fostered worldwide fascination.

For some writers this interest turned into severe criticism of Rockefeller. TARBELL, the "muckraking" journalist, launched an attack, uncovering his ruthless, "non-Christian" practices that built the Standard Oil monopoly: his espionage and harassment of competitors, manipulation of state legislatures, and use of transportation rebates. In her history of Standard Oil of New Jersey, Tarbell denounces Rockefeller's oil trust and his ruthless practices in railroads, shipping, gas, copper, iron, steel, and banks. Such diversity gave Rockefeller unprecedented power in state and federal government. Tarbell's attack was presented in an antitrust progressive rhetoric that masks her serious journalistic research.

The end of the Progressive era dampened the passionate hatred of Rockefeller and gave WINKLER the opportunity to produce a less hostile portrait of the millionaire. Winkler was interested in bringing Rockefeller to life through journalistic inquiries into the industrialist's private affairs. Rockefeller's success, in Winkler's view, grew out of frugality, Baptist piety, remorseless elimination of competition, and the complete devotion of his time and intelligence to business. The author notes that it was the press campaign by Rockefeller's publicity adviser, Ivy Lee, together with the millionaire's philanthropy that changed the industrialist's negative public image. Winkler concludes that Rockefeller's lust for money, shrewd judgment of men, and piety were passed on to future generations.

Serious academic work on Rockefeller begins with the two-volume biography by NEVINS (1940), which gives a detailed account of Rockefeller's early life and apprenticeship, and traces the rise of the petroleum industry as he built and consolidated his trust. Nevins attempts to justify the magnate's unethical behavior. With the discovery of a great mass of Rockefeller correspondence previously thought to have been lost, NEVINS (1953) published a second biography. He is more critical of his subject in this more concise and better balanced academic study, argues that monopoly of the type achieved by Standard Oil at the height of its power, though odious, was yet in some way desirable and certainly inevitable. The company and its creator were models for the age of industrialization. Rockefeller was, in a sense, the chief of the robber barons, aloof and alone. Nevins also offers an insightful account of the development of the Rockefeller philanthropy ranging from his gift to the University of Chicago to the establishment of the Rockefeller Institute and Foundation. The 1959 abridged version gives a clear and informative synopsis of Rockefeller's life.

HAWKE is a refreshing and thoughtful biography based on exhaustive research, which portrays a more complex Rockefeller than is depicted in Tarbell's harsh tones or Nevins's sometimes apologetic and admiring ones. Hawke understands Rockefeller's contractual relationship to God, his ability indirectly to control every decision of the trust, his firm belief in monopoly as a simple matter of enlightened business and godly virtues, and his admiration for Napoleon's genius for organization and the emperor's thorough understanding of men.

For those interested in the history of Standard Oil, the definitive work of HIDY and HIDY is a thorough academic study, retracing in detail the history of the company from its development in the United States to its worldwide expansion. This sound narrative account is a good tool for understanding the economic dynamics behind the expansion of Rockefeller's business empire and its influence in national and international spheres.

The most recent studies focus less on Rockefeller than on his legacy: his family and philanthropy. COLLIER and HOROWITZ concentrated their work on the Rockefeller "dynasty" from John D. Senior through the fourth generation, the cousins. Theirs is a social history of the nature of Rockefeller philanthropy and power, the rise and decline of the family as an institution, and the relentless effects of the family legend on its members. Their study is impressive, even though it too often accepts its sources uncritically. Except for a few documents released to the writers by the cousins, the authors did not use any new material.

John Harr worked for over a decade as a close associate of John D. III, and Peter Johnson, a historian, had just joined the Rockefeller office when they decided to collaborate on a study of John D. Senior, Junior and the Third. HARR and JOHNSON were privy to previously unrevealed private material from the family's office, but their study was greatly influenced by their close relationship with John D. Rockefeller III. The writers also made extensive use of the Rockefeller archives. They focus on the family's charitable contributions and the interaction of family members, rather than business endeavors and tactics. The authors describe each succeeding

generation's evolving philanthropy, the organizations they created to distribute funds, and the parts they played in inculcating a social conscience in their successors.

ANNE-MARIE GRIMAUD

See also Business History: Individual Corporations; Oil and Natural Gas

Rocky Mountains

Bakken, Gordon Morris, *The Development of Law on the Rocky Mountain Frontier: Civil Law and Society, 1850–1912*, Westport, CT: Greenwood Press, 1983

Gould, Lewis L., *Wyoming: A Political History, 1868–1896*, New Haven: Yale University Press, 1968

Lamar, Howard Roberts, *The Far Southwest, 1846–1912: A Territorial History*, New Haven: Yale University Press, 1966

Larson, Robert W., *Populism in the Mountain West*, Albuquerque: University of New Mexico Press, 1986

Larson, Taft Alfred, *History of Wyoming*, Lincoln: University of Nebraska Press, 1965, 2nd edition, 1978

Lyman, Edward Leo, *Political Deliverance: The Mormon Quest for Utah Statehood*, Urbana: University of Illinois Press, 1986

Paul, Rodman W., *The Far West and the Great Plains in Transition, 1859–1900*, New York: Harper, 1988

Smith, Duane A., *Rocky Mountain West: Colorado, Wyoming, and Montana, 1859–1915*, Albuquerque: University of New Mexico Press, 1992

Spence, Clark C., *Territorial Politics and Government in Montana, 1864–89*, Urbana: University of Illinois Press, 1975

The history of the Rocky Mountain West involves the settlement of a vast arid territory, the rise of extractive enterprises such as mining, the exploitation of the earth and water, the formation of politics and public policy in territories struggling to become states, the struggle against economic and political colonialism, and the economic and social transitions leading to urbanism and tourism. PAUL emphasizes the role of mining and irrigation in the economic development of the region, and notes the significance of transportation in the creation of cities and towns. Salt Lake City and Denver became significant urban centers for processing, handling and manufacturing. These two cities were major regional distribution centers for goods coming from the East. Local merchants supplied the army, settlers, and entrepreneurs. Politics in Colorado were disruptive, confused, intensely combative and highly personal in the 1860s. The economic maturation of Denver and the drive for statehood brought some degree of political maturity to the territory. In Salt Lake, Mormons dominated in government, and politics was dominated by a vicious argument between the Mormons and the gentile territorial officials. That struggle would lead to federal military intervention and territorial status until 1896.

SMITH covers some of the same ground, but notes how mining rushes as well as materialism, urbanism, transportation, exploitation, industrial capitalism, and social change overwhelmed the frontier in areas of intense economic activity leaving vast territory lingering in underdevelopment. Conservation, preservation, and the national park system enabled the region to attract tourists in large numbers and slowly move away from the environmentally damaging industries of the 19th century. The major themes of federalism, corporate dominance, conservation and environmentalism, the exploitation of the land, urban versus rural controversies, and colonialism were well established in the 19th century. In the 20th century these issues were even more intensely contested. The advent of environmental controls called unrestrained development to a halt at the cost of jobs, but the rise of tourism refocused economic and social hopes.

LAMAR traces the political development of New Mexico, Colorado, Utah, and Arizona from territorial status to statehood. Each territory developed singular political traditions, but all followed American political habits, customs, and institutions. For each, the local struggle was for money and power and the territorial struggle was for statehood and freedom from vassalage administered by a feudal lord in Washington, DC, or so the local politicians argued.

Robert LARSON argues that regional Populism was diverse and complex, focusing on more than free silver. In Montana, Colorado, and Utah, Populism focused on antimonopolism and improved working conditions for labor. Colorado Populists were interested in agrarian issues while Arizona Populists were more interested in local issues. One issue that did unify Rocky Mountain Populists, except in New Mexico, was advocacy of woman suffrage.

In his examination of Montana territorial politics, SPENCE describes a no-party system dominated by coalitions of territorial governors and powerful economic interests. Political conflicts were over local and national issues as well as personalities, patronage, and spending policy. LYMAN demonstrates that Utah's political struggle for statehood was complicated by the dominant position of the Church of Jesus Christ of Latter Day Saints. The Mormon position favoring polygamy further complicated politics, causing federal intervention with troops and an army of federal prosecutors. The public change of position on polygamy and politics in 1890 resulted in statehood in 1896. In addition to positioning the territory for statehood, Mormon politicians forged numerous links with highly placed members of both national parties. These friendships proved to be the best insurance available against anti-Mormon politics in the White House and in Congress.

GOULD demonstrates that Wyoming's territorial politics were factional, but adjusted to national economic and political trends like many other states in the nation.

T.A. LARSON chronicles a political struggle against corporate and federal governmental influence in territorial life, statehood, the economic depressions and prosperity of the 20th century, and an emergent Wyoming with a positive self-image. In 1970 Wyoming was rated as one of the six best states in quality of life.

BAKKEN argues that law evolved from a recognition that the region was environmentally challenged by aridity, and socially enabled by distance and culture to make rapid change. Innovations in water law, labor law, and female suffrage resulted. Legislators and judges changed the English common law of waters from riparian rights to prior appropriation in recognition of the changed circumstances caused by aridity.

Legislators passed protective labor law for miners and started to protect women and children in the mines, a change approved by the United States Supreme Court. Women received the vote in Wyoming, but this singular act was part of a larger legislative and judicial movement to protect women's property rights and civil rights. Law was the glue which held social and economic change together in the West.

GORDON MORRIS BAKKEN

Roosevelt, Eleanor 1884–1962
Campaigner for reform causes, and First Lady

Black, Ruby, *Eleanor Roosevelt: A Biography*, New York: Duell Sloan and Pearce, 1940

Chafe, William H., "Anna Eleanor Roosevelt", in *Notable American Women, The Modern Period: A Biographical Dictionary*, edited by Barbara Sicherman and Carol Hurd Green, Cambridge, MA: Belknap Press of Harvard University Press, 1980

Cook, Blanche Wiesen, *Eleanor Roosevelt*, volume 1: *1884–1933*, New York: Viking, and Harmondsworth: Penguin, 1993

Hareven, Tamara, *Eleanor Roosevelt: An American Conscience*, Chicago: Quadrangle, 1968

Hickok, Lorena A., *Eleanor Roosevelt: Reluctant First Lady*, New York: Dodd Mead, 1980

Hoff-Wilson, Joan and Marjorie Lightman (editors), *Without Precedent: The Life and Career of Eleanor Roosevelt*, Bloomington: Indiana University Press, 1984

Kearney, James, *Anna Eleanor Roosevelt: The Evolution of a Reformer*, Boston: Houghton Mifflin, 1968

Lash, Joseph P., *Eleanor and Franklin: The Story of Their Relationship*, New York: Norton, 1971; London: Deutsch, 1972

Lash, Joseph P., *Eleanor: The Years Alone*, New York: Norton, 1972

Scharf, Lois, *Eleanor Roosevelt: First Lady of American Liberalism*, Boston: Twayne, 1987

Snowman, Daniel, *Eleanor Roosevelt*, London: Heron, 1970

Steinberg, Alfred, *Mrs. R.: The Life of Eleanor Roosevelt*, New York: Putnam, 1958

Biographers have swarmed upon the life of Eleanor Roosevelt. Sustained by plentiful records, including her own extensive journalism and memoirs, they have feasted on the complexities of America's most influential First Lady. Born into privilege in the 19th century, growing up with the prejudices of her class and initially focused on homemaking, by degrees Mrs. Roosevelt transformed her 40-year marriage to Franklin Delano Roosevelt into an extraordinary political partnership, and successfully continued in public life after the president's death in 1945. She was reviled as a radical and loved as a humanitarian, but her lofty idealism and imposing presence were balanced by an endearing sense of fun. As one enthusiast noted in 1946, she "swims like a lifeguard, can catch a baseball hot off the bat, is a first-class horsewoman, loves the movies and dances hot rumbas with the same zest as Strauss waltzes."

BLACK, a pioneering study published when Eleanor Roosevelt was 56, was written with her co-operation but without authorized status or scholarly apparatus. As one of the women journalists whom Mrs. Roosevelt pointedly encouraged when she was in the White House, Black was not a detached witness and she predictably highlighted the First Lady's political role. But she did shrewdly foresee that Mrs. Roosevelt would continue to develop her interests, acknowledging the contradictions in her life and stressing the "Spartan strain" that helped her to work and play. In the spirit of the times, the Roosevelts' personal relationship was not probed.

Some eighteen years later, and still before Eleanor Roosevelt's death, STEINBERG produced a similarly full and unannotated biography, which drew on her personal papers and correspondence. The president's affair with his wife's social secretary was hurried over, and Mrs. Roosevelt was not presented as a woman whose life was transformed by a critically timed personal trauma, but rather as a lonely person who took refuge in crowds, as an ugly duckling who turned into a swan. While finding Eleanor Roosevelt in "many ways as good a politician" as her husband, Steinberg concluded that FDR had the edge because of his practicality and ability to take the long view.

By the late 1960s and early 1970s, as the position of American women changed, feminism made an impact on the academy, and the achievements of liberal reform were reassessed, the time was ripe for new evaluations of Mrs. Roosevelt. Her death in 1962 also gave such reappraisals an increasing degree of perspective. All commentators continued to be influenced by Eleanor Roosevelt's writings, with their careful modesty, calculated revelations, preoccupation with duty, and interest in "every manifestation of life, good or bad." But it was now possible to place Mrs. Roosevelt more securely in her turbulent times.

For SNOWMAN, in his short, lively and unfootnoted volume, Eleanor Roosevelt is more important because of what she was than what she did. He plays down Mrs. Roosevelt's political role, rather unfairly, but persuasively shows the limitations inherent in acting as a lightning and divining rod for FDR. Snowman's irritation with her persistent self-deprecation is understandable to the modern reader; his cursory treatment of sexual issues is less so.

HAREVEN, KEARNEY and SCHARF have all written professional biographies which locate Eleanor Roosevelt in the evolving American reform tradition, manifested at home and abroad. So too does the collection of articles edited by HOFF-WILSON and LIGHTMAN. These writers, like CHAFE, pay tribute to Mrs. Roosevelt's wide-ranging activism, networking skills and status as the most successful woman in American politics. Yet it is the work of Lash and Cook which stands out among the modern studies of Eleanor Roosevelt, with the former enjoying the warm support of the Roosevelt family, and the latter able to consult the largest array of public and personal papers and to utilize the insights of years of feminist scholarship.

In a comprehensive, minutely researched two-volume biography (supplemented by a short memoir and two books on Mrs. Roosevelt and her friends), LASH deploys knowledge which has accumulated since he was one of the youth leaders she turned to in the 1930s, terrified of seeing the younger generation sink into jobless alienation. His work gives us a full account of Eleanor Roosevelt's personal and public development, treating her difficult childhood, relations with FDR, their children and her own circle of friends with affectionate candour, and her intellectual growth on issues like the position of women, the treatment of minorities and internationalism with the critical seriousness they deserve. In the process, we learn more about Mrs. Roosevelt's difficult husband: a man who loved the limelight, thought politics was a masculine business, liked to relax with pretty, supportive women, but who nonetheless could appreciate his wife's "really brilliant mind and spirit". And we follow the transformation of a woman who once declared that she had "no talents, no experience, no training for anything" into a skilful lobbyist, a successful journalist and lecturer, and a respected ambassador for the United States throughout the world.

It is left to COOK, however, to show how effectively Eleanor Roosevelt's motherly and self-controlled demeanour concealed her passionate and unconventional side from the inquisitive public gaze. As a result, it is only recently that we have been able to do full justice to Mrs. Roosevelt's work as a social feminist and teacher, as well as to her love of politics, personal ambitions, relish for power, delight in adventure, and loving friendships with individuals as diverse as her bodyguard, Earl Miller, and the influential reporter, Lorena HICKOK, author of another very personal account of a remarkable First Lady, who remains a fascinating public figure in her own right.

CHRISTINE BOLT

See also First Ladies

Roosevelt, Franklin D.   1882–1945
32nd President of the United States

Burns, James MacGregor, *Roosevelt: The Lion and the Fox*, New York: Harcourt Brace, and London: Secker and Warburg, 1956

Burns, James MacGregor, *Roosevelt: The Soldier of Freedom, 1940–1945*, New York: Harcourt Brace, and London: Weidenfeld and Nicolson, 1970

Davis, Kenneth S., *F.D.R.*, 4 vols. to date, New York: Putnam, 1971 (vol. 1), and Random House, 1985–93 (vols. 2–4)

Freidel, Frank, *Franklin D. Roosevelt*, 4 vols., Boston: Little Brown, 1952–73

Freidel, Frank, *Franklin D. Roosevelt: A Rendezvous with Destiny*, Boston: Little Brown, 1990

Graham, Otis L. and Meghan Robinson Wander (editors), *Franklin D. Roosevelt, His Life and Times: An Encyclopedic View*, Boston: Hall, 1985

Hofstadter, Richard, *The American Political Tradition and the Men Who Made It*, New York: Knopf, 1948; London: Cape, 1962

Lash, Joseph P., *Eleanor and Franklin: The Story of Their Relationship*, New York: Norton, 1971; London: Deutsch, 1972

Leuchtenburg, William E., *In the Shadow of F.D.R: From Harry Truman to Ronald Reagan*, Ithaca, NY: Cornell University Press, 1983, revised as *In the Shadow of F.D.R.: From Harry Truman to Bill Clinton*, 1993

Maney, Patrick J., *The Roosevelt Presence: A Biography of Franklin Delano Roosevelt*, New York: Twayne, 1992

Morgan, Ted, *F.D.R: A Biography*, New York: Simon and Schuster, 1985

Perkins, Frances, *The Roosevelt I Knew*, New York: Viking, 1946

Rosenman, Samuel Irving, *Working with Roosevelt*, New York: Harper, and London: Hart Davis, 1952

Sherwood, Robert E., *Roosevelt and Hopkins: An Intimate History*, New York: Harper, 1948, revised 1950; as *The White House Papers of Harry L. Hopkins*, 2 vols., London: Eyre and Spottiswoode, 1948–49

Tugwell, Rexford G., *The Democratic Roosevelt: A Biography of Franklin D. Roosevelt*, New York: Doubleday, 1957

Ward, Geoffrey C., *Before the Trumpet: Young Franklin Roosevelt, 1882–1905*, New York: Harper, 1985

Ward, Geoffrey C., *A First-Class Temperament: The Emergence of Franklin Roosevelt*, New York: Harper, 1989

The greatest president of the 20th century, matched only by Washington and Lincoln overall, uniquely elected four times for a momentous twelve-year tenure of the White House, it is not to be wondered that Franklin Roosevelt has attracted the attention of innumerable biographers. Although most of any lasting value have been broadly sympathetic, the contentiousness of the issues and events of his presidency have inevitably occasioned considerable debate, which seems likely to continue. A great creative president has also stimulated much historical controversy.

One may begin, if not always in strict chronological order, with the "Court" historians, those who knew Roosevelt from working with him and carried on the cause after his relatively early death. PERKINS first met Roosevelt in 1910, watched him as a young politician and later served him when he was governor of New York, and then throughout his presidency as Secretary of Labor. Her book is aptly titled, by no means uncritical in places, but overall generous in detailing his growth in stature. It is not strictly a formal biography, but essentially thematic, particularly good on social issues but relatively thin on the war years. It is written with considerable perception and provides a valuable, easily read introduction to his character and personality.

ROSENMAN, another of Roosevelt's associates from his days in the governorship, edited his Public Papers and Addresses, to which some of this book was originally intended as an introduction, but it outgrew its conception. His account of their relationship is also appropriately named for it provides a useful description of the actual mechanics of Roosevelt's presidency, the day to day procedures required, and is especially good in its portrayal of his human side. It is a careful blending of recollection and information, avowedly written from a supportive standpoint.

TUGWELL was a member of the Brain Trust and always one of the New Dealers that right-wing critics loved to hate.

His book is a substantial study of Roosevelt, a sort of personalized history based in part on his own experience, but replete with analysis rather than descriptive narrative. It is naturally partisan but not uncritically so. Perhaps reflecting the focus of Tugwell's interests, it is least effective on the war years. This last is the concern of SHERWOOD, a professional author and Roosevelt speechwriter, who utilized the forty filing cabinets of papers that Harry Hopkins left at his death to provide a unique portrait of life inside the White House, where Hopkins actually lived for three years, serving as Roosevelt's alter ego and general political handyman. Passing briefly over the pre-World War II years, the book provides as close an insight into the formulation of Roosevelt's policies from 1940 as one could have expected, had he left his own memoirs. Immensely readable, concentrating on the big issues and themes of World War II, Sherwood paints a portrait of Roosevelt as the indispensable man for the times, speaking for humanity at its darkest hour. Although reinforced by interviews and recollections of innumerable participants in these momentous events, it lacks the critical, detached eye of subsequent scholars.

HOFSTADTER provides an engaging down-to-earth corrective, in the chapter on FDR in a highly influential book cast in the form of a series of biographical essays. His Roosevelt is a man of flexibility and charm, of breadth rather than depth, self-confident in his belief in the efficacy of improvisation. Admiring but critical, Hofstadter draws in a mere 35 pages a deft and stimulating portrait that captures the essential humane pragmatism of the man, unshackled by theory, who symbolized for his era liberalism at home and internationalism abroad.

FREIDEL (1952–73) began the task of utilizing the immense resources of the Franklin D. Roosevelt Library at Hyde Park for a detailed and authoritative record. There are an estimated forty tons of papers and Roosevelt himself boasted, "I have destroyed practically nothing". The immensity of Freidel's task may be illustrated by the fact that it took him until the third volume (1956) to reach Roosevelt's first election to the presidency in 1932, and that the whole project of a multi-volume life petered out after the fourth in the series, more than twenty years after the publication of the first. The fourth volume (1973) deals with the period from Roosevelt's election in 1932 through the 100 Days to the London Economic Conference in the summer of 1933; it is the longest and the most useful of the four, partly reflecting the outpouring of New Deal scholarship since Freidel began writing. FREIDEL (1990) is a one-volume work that partially fulfilled his original ambition, and which was completed shortly before his death. Freidel was a good scholar who has put all subsequent historians of Roosevelt in his debt, but the earlier volumes at least are somewhat two-dimensional, more concerned with facts than ideas. It is, for example, rather frustrating that, while Roosevelt's affliction with infantile paralysis is exhaustively itemized, the effects of the illness and the suffering are dismissed in one brief paragraph and a quoted Roosevelt brush-off to a journalist. Clearly Freidel lets the facts speak for themselves, though rather gently when they tend to Roosevelt's disadvantage. Thus Roosevelt's affair with Lucy Mercer is dismissed in the first volume, referred to in passing in the fourth, and briefly discussed in the 1990 one-volume account. Yet if one wants to know what happened and when, Freidel is usually indispensable and, ironically, some of his best writing in Freidel

(1990) is on World War II which he had not tackled earlier. This is a substantial work, but still, like its predecessors, one whose real strength lies in detailed narrative.

Burns is both an absorbing biography and a probing study in political leadership. The writing is compelling, and is perhaps aided by the fact that Burns has a thesis to advance. In BURNS (1956), dealing with the period to 1940, it is the problem posed by the Machiavellian dichotomy of being "a fox to recognize traps, and a lion to frighten wolves". How far is the democratic politician justified in compromise? In this context Burns unusually sees the frustrations of Roosevelt's second term as "by far the most significant phase of his career". In BURNS (1970), he further pursues the ambiguity that Roosevelt "as war leader was a deeply divided man" – for whom short-term goals were too often preferred to long-term needs. Nevertheless Burns provides a magnificent panorama of Roosevelt's presidency, sweeping up all its issues into an over-arching thesis supported by several subordinate ones. One may question whether Roosevelt enjoyed the freedom of action that Burns would ideally postulate, and whether there must not always be a gap between what a president should be and what, of necessity, he has to be. There can, however, be no question that this is historical writing at its finest.

One of the most interesting and novel accounts is provided by LASH, a uniquely detailed record of a presidential marriage that became a political partnership. Although the order of the names in the title is significant, for it is written from Eleanor Roosevelt's papers by one of her young protégés who later became a journalist, it is a sensitive, sympathetic study that illuminates much of the private life of a president who more than most had a public wife and family. It is all the more revealing, for Roosevelt is generally regarded as ultimately unknowable as a man in the inmost core of his personality; Lash at least sets the context, even if he cannot penetrate the hidden interior.

DAVIS is now one volume short of completing his massive political biography. Although written largely from published sources and thus dependent on their predecessors, the four volumes' collective strength lies in their vigorous writing which, although sometimes overdone, succeeds in portraying with life and colour many of the personalities of the period. Written with the general reader in mind though without detracting from its scholarly reliability, it is well disposed towards Roosevelt but still quite critical. Davis has a view of what Roosevelt might have done, and finds his pragmatism indicative of an unwillingness to act always as the times demanded; equally he recognizes FDR's ability to adapt to circumstance. Although less useful than other works, Davis is often more stimulating.

Ward is the best treatment of Roosevelt's early life up to his election as governor of New York state. WARD (1985) recreates the upper-middle-class family background from which Roosevelt sprang. The security which it gave him was crucial in endowing him with the self-assurance of his later years as president. WARD (1989) deals with the years from his marriage to his re-entry into politics after his battle with polio. Roosevelt remains at the centre, but Ward also recreates the world in which he moved. The work is largely based on primary sources, and no other biographer is quoted unless he knew Roosevelt personally. The two volumes stand complete in themselves, and Ward has manifested no wish to take the story further. If the detail is immense, so too is the readability.

MORGAN can make a claim to be the first comprehensive one-volume biography that gives evenly balanced treatment to all aspects of its subject's life and career. It is the work of a professional writer, clearly dependent in part on previous historians, sourced but not footnoted, and written for the general reader. Perhaps this latter intent helps explain the speculative, circumstantial "conjecture" about an early girlfriend who, having allegedly been made pregnant by Roosevelt, thereupon sailed to Europe for an abortion – or the full discussion of the Newport naval scandal involving the entrapment of homosexuals on which Roosevelt was grilled by a Senate committee. Indeed Morgan's portrait generally contains a fair number of warts. Still, if it could be said to be quite critical in places, Morgan does not fail to see the "capacity for growth" that "became the core of his character". His chapter on the effects of Roosevelt's illness, in particular, is a finely wrought tribute to his subject.

GRAHAM and WANDER is a most useful compendium for anyone wishing to read up piecemeal on Roosevelt and his times. Some 125 contributors have written on well over 300 topics ranging from relatives, colleagues and enemies to legislation, elections, wartime conferences and New Deal agencies. Odd by-ways are also illuminated. Thus all Roosevelt's honorary degrees are listed (31) and even the Roosevelt Dime gets an entry. Each signed article has a brief supporting bibliography.

MANEY is a synthesis of just over 200 pages, aimed at the student market. It is quite a feat to incorporate so much in so short a space. Based almost entirely on secondary sources, the book does not aim to offer any particular new information and is not over-enthusiastic about Roosevelt's undoubted greatness. Perhaps it reflects the sixty years that elapsed between Roosevelt's first election as president and its publication. Roosevelt has finally passed into history; and perhaps the assessment of him is coloured by a more astringent view of the presidency, inspired by the record of more recent incumbents. Still it might act as a stimulant for further exploration.

So stupendous was Roosevelt's tenure of the White House that even in death he loomed over his successors. LEUCHTENBURG examines this phenomenon in a brilliant exploration of how ten Presidents from Truman to Clinton have adjusted to this experience. The book is scintillatingly written, based on an enormous range of sources, full of pointed anecdotes, above all enjoyable. It is perhaps a tribute to Roosevelt's many-faceted personality that among those of his successors on whom he cast his spell, as Leuchtenburg effectively demonstrates, none was a greater admirer than Ronald Reagan who, having voted for him four times, subsequently endeavoured to wrap himself in his mantle. It would have appealed to Roosevelt's considerable sense of humour.

JOHN KENTLETON

See also New Deal entries; World War II entries

Roosevelt, Theodore 1858–1919
26th President of the United States

Beale, Howard K., *Theodore Roosevelt and the Rise of America to World Power*, Baltimore: Johns Hopkins Press, 1956

Blum, John Morton, *The Republican Roosevelt*, Cambridge, MA: Harvard University Press, 1954, 2nd edition, 1977

Cooper, John Milton, Jr., *The Warrior and the Priest: Woodrow Wilson and Theodore Roosevelt*, Cambridge, MA: Belknap Press of Harvard University Press, 1983

Gould, Lewis L., *The Presidency of Theodore Roosevelt*, Lawrence: University Press of Kansas, 1991

Harbaugh, William H., *Power and Responsibility: The Life and Times of Theodore Roosevelt*, New York: Farrar Straus, 1961; revised, New York and Oxford: Oxford University Press, 1975

McCullough, David, *Mornings on Horseback*, New York: Simon and Schuster, 1982

Morris, Edmund, *The Rise of Theodore Roosevelt*, New York: Coward McCann, and London: Collins, 1979

Mowry, George E., *Theodore Roosevelt and the Progressive Movement*, Madison: University of Wisconsin Press, 1947

Mowry, George E., *The Era of Theodore Roosevelt, 1900–1912*, New York: Harper, and London: Hamish Hamilton, 1958

Pringle, Henry F., *Theodore Roosevelt: A Biography*, New York: Harcourt Brace, 1931, London: Cape, 1932; revised, Harcourt Brace, 1956

Though there were some biographies that appeared in the years immediately following his death in 1919, Theodore Roosevelt did not attract a serious student of his life until PRINGLE published his prize-winning one-volume account in 1931. Pringle portrayed Roosevelt as a perpetual adolescent, and many parts of his narrative have come under serious attack from later Roosevelt scholars. The book does capture well an aspect of Roosevelt's character, and its sceptical interpretation of Roosevelt's importance influenced work on the president for a quarter of a century.

MOWRY (1947) began his research on Roosevelt before World War II. His book had a very positive effect upon the way that the reform phase of Roosevelt's career was appraised for another two decades. The book is now very dated, and its melodramatic style has not worn well. Like so many books on Roosevelt, it told the story from his point of view and did not delve carefully into the attitudes of his adversaries. MOWRY (1958) is more of a synthesis about the great period of Roosevelt's career than his earlier volume had been. It is impressively researched and has many useful insights, a number of errors limit the book's utility for the general reader. Mowry was an important Roosevelt scholar and this book shows why his impact on the field was so significant.

BLUM grew out of the author's work on the publication between 1951 and 1954 of Roosevelt's collected letters. With a dazzling series of chapters on Roosevelt as president, politician, and diplomat, Blum's book rehabilitated him as a historical figure, and launched a serious assessment of his place in United States history. The book is brilliantly written and crammed with perceptive insights. In many ways, it remains the most accessible means of learning about Roosevelt's public life. Everyone who has written on Roosevelt since has worked in Blum's shadow.

BEALE embarked on a monumental biographical project about Roosevelt during the late 1940s, but the work was left unfinished at his death. As part of the biography, Beale delivered the Albert Shaw lectures on diplomatic history at Johns Hopkins University, and his 1956 book grew out of the lectures. The voluminous notes attest to the wide range of Beale's research. The text itself is crammed with information and is aimed at the specialist. Beale makes a good case for Roosevelt's realism in foreign policy, but the author is less than sympathetic towards his subject's accomplishments in that field. As a result, the evidence and conclusions of Beale go in opposite directions.

HARBAUGH first published his book in 1961, but that volume is now unobtainable. The later revised edition, which is still in print, is the best one-volume treatment of Roosevelt's whole life. Harbaugh is judicious and balanced on every aspect of what Roosevelt did, and his work reflects the best scholarship that was available to him. His interpretation has gained general acceptance among serious students of Roosevelt and his age.

MORRIS won the Pulitzer Prize for biography for his 1979 study of Roosevelt's early life, and he has been working on the remaining two volumes since that time. The book depicts Roosevelt as he wished history to see him, colorful, larger-than-life, and on the right side of every controversy. Morris's command of the details of Gilded Age politics was not secure, and he did not incorporate much of the available literature on the Spanish-American War into his analysis of Roosevelt's role in the McKinley administration and the fighting in Cuba. Morris's biography achieved a wide popularity, but it has had little effect on scholarly judgments about Roosevelt and his times.

McCULLOUGH focused on the formative years of Roosevelt's early life, and his narrative ends in the mid-1880s. The most notable contribution of the book is its emphasis on the nature and extent of Roosevelt's childhood asthma. Using the diaries of Roosevelt and his family, McCullough advances a psychosomatic interpretation of the illness and connects it to Roosevelt's relationship with his imposing father. Although other Roosevelt students have challenged this interpretation, McCullough's biographical study has many perceptive insights about the young Roosevelt.

Woodrow Wilson and Theodore Roosevelt are a natural pairing for a joint biography, but no one had done it before COOPER. The thrust of the narrative is more sympathetic to Wilson than to Roosevelt, but the juxtaposition of the two careers often yields important judgments about their respective effect on domestic and foreign policy. Cooper makes a good case for the value of a medical and psychological treatment of Roosevelt's life. This book is an excellent way to get into the issues of the period when Roosevelt and Wilson dominated American politics.

GOULD contributed an examination of Roosevelt's record as president to the Kansas series on the American presidents. He argued that Roosevelt personalized the presidency even as he was modernizing it for the 20th century. Stressing the continuities between Roosevelt and William McKinley during the first Roosevelt term, Gould showed how Roosevelt became a legislative and foreign policy prototype for the modern presidency during his second term. The book endeavored to incorporate as much as possible of the scholarly writing about Roosevelt into the analysis, and the bibliography will offer the general reader guidance about what else to read on Roosevelt through early 1991.

Popular biographies of Roosevelt still appear, and there are several new scholarly treatments under way. There remains a need for a new analysis of his entire life based on the rich body of available manuscripts. While few presidents have been more examined than Theodore Roosevelt, the fascinations of his life and the importance of his political achievements will attract writers and interested readers for years to come.

LEWIS L. GOULD

See also Gilded Age and Progressive Era; Imperialism and Anti-Imperialism; New Nationalism and New Freedom; Progressivism

Rush, Benjamin 1745–1813
Medical scientist, publicist and social commentator

Binger, Carl, *Revolutionary Doctor: Benjamin Rush, 1746–1813*, New York: Norton, 1966

D'Elia, Donald J., *Benjamin Rush: Philosopher of the American Revolution*, Philadelphia: American Philosophical Society, 1974

Good, Harry G., *Benjamin Rush and His Services to American Education*, Berne, IN: Witness Press, 1918

Goodman, Nathan G., *Benjamin Rush: Physician and Citizen, 1746–1813*, Philadelphia: University of Pennsylvania Press, 1934

Hawke, David Freeman, *Benjamin Rush: Revolutionary Gadfly*, Indianapolis: Bobbs Merrill, 1971

Benjamin Rush, often called the father of American psychiatry, was not just the most famous American physician of his day, he was also a zealous Revolutionary who promoted the Patriot cause as a radical pamphleteer, member of the Second Continental Congress, signer of the Declaration of Independence, and surgeon general of the Continental Army. In addition, he was an outspoken leader of the temperance and antislavery movements, and a vigorous advocate of educational and medical reforms. It is surprising that a man of such diverse interests and accomplishments should have attracted so little scholarly interest. Perhaps it is because Rush's dogmatic medical theory, which posited a simple, unitary explanation of disease and an equally simplistic remedy of heavy bloodletting and purging, came into universal disfavor among later generations of medical professionals. Rush's strong association with the repudiated theory, together with his alleged involvement in the Conway Cabal to overthrow George Washington as head of the Continental Army, assured his historical obloquy.

Though very dated, GOOD deserves mention because it is the first serious and objective scholarly study of Rush. The author makes good use of the documentary sources available at the time and offers a judicious evaluation of his subject's life and work. He absolves Rush of any complicity in the Conway Cabal, and insists upon judging Rush's medical theories and practices by the standards of his own day, not those of the 20th century.

Although it too is somewhat dated after more than sixty years, GOODMAN is the standard biography of Rush. It is the first full-length study to provide a comprehensive and balanced treatment of the man as a Revolutionary leader, physician, educator, and reformer. Goodman paints a sympathetic portrait of an intense Patriot who cared as deeply about American independence as did George Washington. He challenged Washington only when the military chief pursued policies that he, as surgeon general, considered detrimental to the welfare of the wounded and sick soldiers for whom he was responsible. Goodman argues that Rush was in no way involved in the Conway Cabal. Echoing Good's earlier arguments, he maintains that Rush's seemingly preposterous reliance on phlebotomy in treating his patients must be judged in the medical context of the 18th century, when purging and bleeding were widely accepted medical practices in Europe no less than in America.

HAWKE, the most recent biography, is the best study available of Rush's life and career up to 1789. Based on careful research in Rush's papers and writings, the volume illuminates not just the many facets of the controversial doctor's life and career but also the tumultuous times in which he lived. The volume is well written and offers fresh insight and useful new data on the subject. Its portrayal of Philadelphia during and after the Revolution is especially rich in detail. As biography, its principal limitation is its scope, which is limited to the first half of Rush's life. Hawke does not treat that very important period of his subject's life when Rush established his strongest claim to fame as a physician and reformer. It was after 1789, for example, that Rush undertook his most important work with the mentally ill patients at the Pennsylvania Hospital and published his *Medical Inquiries and Observations upon the Diseases of the Mind*, America's first treatise on psychiatry. Rush's most noteworthy and enduring contributions in the field of psychiatry are thus not explored by Hawke.

BINGER covers what Hawke omits – Rush's role and contributions as a medical reformer, especially his groundbreaking work with the mentally insane. He writes skillfully about Rush's heroic work during the yellow fever epidemic of 1793, and offers a new perspective for understanding Rush's pioneering work in diagnosing and treating mental illness. Rush challenged the prevailing view of his day that lunatics were devil-possessed, and argued that mental disorders often issued from physical causes and were as subject to the healing arts as were physical ones. Binger, a prominent psychiatrist himself, writes with perception and insight about medical aspects of Rush's life. But in some ways the volume is more a series of commentaries by a modern psychiatrist about the life and work of a pioneering psychiatrist than it is a serious biography. Binger's research in Rush materials is superficial, and he does not try to understand Rush in the context of his world. Rather he imposes on his subject the language and terms of modern psychiatry. The book is written with the general reader in mind. Its weakness is that it is fitfully organized, impressionistic, and lacks originality of interpretation.

D'ELIA is a historian's brief for the historical importance of Rush. The author laments the fact that the historical record, by and large, depicts Rush as a figure of secondary importance in Revolutionary America, memorable only because of a few significant isolated political activities in which he participated, some limited success as a social reformer, and considerable notoriety for his zealous advocacy of phlebotomy. He deserves better, says D'Elia. A systematic examination of Rush's thought and writing, the author continues, discloses that "far from being a secondary historical character, [he] was a leading – perhaps the chief – philosophical exponent of the American Revolution." The claim, he admits, is large, but he attempts to back it up with arguments that Rush's philosophy of the American Revolution was more original, comprehensive, and visionary than that of any other Patriot thinker. It is an interesting but not always convincing argument.

D'Elia fills a void in Rush literature but does not satisfy the need for an up-to-date comprehensive biography of an important figure who has indeed been slighted by the historical record.

CHARLES D. LOWERY

S

San Francisco

Broussard, Albert S., *Black San Francisco: The Struggle for Racial Equality in the West, 1900–1954*, Lawrence: University Press of Kansas, 1993

Burchell, R.A., *The San Francisco Irish, 1848–1880*, Manchester: Manchester University Press, and Berkeley: University of California Press, 1980

Chinn, Thomas W., *Bridging the Pacific: San Francisco Chinatown and Its People*, San Francisco: Chinese Historical Society of America, 1989

DeLeon, Richard Edward, *Left Coast City: Progressive Politics in San Francisco, 1975–1991*, Lawrence: University Press of Kansas, 1992

Ethington, Philip J., *The Public City: The Political Construction of Urban Life in San Francisco, 1850–1900*, Cambridge and New York: Cambridge University Press, 1994

Godfrey, Brian J., *Neighborhoods in Transition: The Making of San Francisco's Ethnic and Nonconformist Communities*, Berkeley: University of California Press, 1988

Issel, William and Robert W. Cherny, *San Francisco, 1865–1932: Politics, Power, and Urban Development*, Berkeley: University of California Press, 1986

Kazin, Michael, *Barons of Labor: The San Francisco Building Trades and Union Power in the Progressive Era*, Urbana: University of Illinois Press, 1987

Lotchin, Roger W., *San Francisco, 1846–1856: From Hamlet to City*, New York: Oxford University Press, 1974

McDonald, Terrence J., *The Parameters of Urban Fiscal Policy: Socioeconomic Change and Political Culture in San Francisco, 1860–1906*, Berkeley: University of California Press, 1986

San Francisco's role as the pre-eminent city on the Pacific Coast during the 19th century and its modern reputation as an exemplar of cosmopolitanism have stimulated a variety of accounts. LOTCHIN initiated recent scholarship with his comprehensive history of the urbanization process in the decade following the transfer of the San Francisco Bay Area to the United States from Mexico. Detailing both the rapid growth and the diverse population that made the city so remarkable to contemporaries in the Gold Rush era, Lotchin also shows how the city's economic, cultural, and political affairs were shaped by events and issues common to American cities in general.

The urbanization process is examined by ISSEL and CHERNY, with particular attention to the conflicts between business organizations, labor unions, and the municipal government, which shaped the political and economic decisions that determined the city's growth and development in the period between the middle 1850s and the beginning of the Great Depression. In a postscript, the authors describe the social, economic, and political developments from the New Deal years to the middle of the 1980s and describe a shift from polarized politics between business and labor to a "politics of hyperpluralism."

KAZIN chronicles one part of organized labor during the period from the 1890s to the beginning of the 1920s in his study of how the skilled craftsmen in the building trades sought, exercised, and then lost control of their workplace, and also lost their influence in the city government. His meticulous examination of the best organized of the city's wage-earners demonstrates both their heterogeneity and their departure from the principle that placed political party activity off-limits to members of American Federation of Labor unions during the period. He shows both how San Francisco became the home of the nation's strongest union movement and how a determined business community gradually reduced labor to a political nonentity by the early 1920s.

Two studies shed considerable light on the ways in which political traditions and governmental institutions shaped the city's public life in the 19th century. In a successful challenge to a stereotype that suggests that urban political bosses and their "machines" pursued spendthrift policies, McDONALD shows that in San Francisco such leaders were constrained by an ideology of fiscal restraint that originated in the Vigilance Committee actions of 1856. McDonald also demonstrates the importance of city charters and election rules, as well as the influence of non-elected public officials. ETHINGTON analyzes political discourse and public communication, and he argues that the actions and institutions of "the public sphere" played a more important role in shaping the city's history than did the tensions, conflicts and accommodations between business, labor, and government. Ethington also extends the influence of the ideology of republicanism into the middle of the 19th century and finds that it played a key role during the "Republican Terror" of the Vigilante actions of 1856. He sees the "republican liberalism" of that period being replaced during the 1890s with a "pluralist liberalism," created by leaders of political parties with a new vision of politics shaped not by notions of civic virtue but by theories of social group needs.

Given San Francisco's historic racial and ethnic diversity and its post-1960s reputation as a haven for gay and lesbian migrants, there is a growing literature on particular groups. GODFREY provides a survey of "ethnic and nonconformist communities" from the perspective of a cultural geographer. Although it is stronger on the period since World War II than on the pre-war years, the book provides a wealth of information on all of the European, Asian, and Latin American ethnic communities, as well as on the black residents and the various nonconformists, including beats, hippies, and gays.

The Irish have left their social, cultural and political imprint on the city to a greater extent than any other ethnic group. BURCHELL describes their experience in the forty years after the Gold Rush, and does so in a way that shatters what is left of the older notions about how the immigrant experience was uniformly one of disappointment and immiseration. Using manuscript census records of individuals and families, as well as more literary evidence, Burchell is able to examine closely the private and public lives of the immigrants and their children. While United States-born Protestants maintained their dominant status in San Francisco as elsewhere, the Irish suffered neither the public opprobrium nor the limits on private success that were an integral feature of their experience in most American cities during the period.

For most of its history, the Chinese constituted the largest Asian population in San Francisco, and for over one hundred years the city was the most important destination for Chinese immigrants to the United States. CHINN provides an insider's account of the evolution of the Chinese community from the earliest days during the Gold Rush to the 1980s. Based on both Chinese- and English-language sources and illustrated with dozens of photographs, the book also includes extensive maps and capsule biographies of community leaders.

BROUSSARD analyzes the social, cultural, economic, and political history of the African American residents with a particular interest in the process of community building and civil rights reform politics. He concludes that, although San Francisco went further than any other western American city in the creation of biracial efforts to end racial discrimination, the typical black resident in the middle of the 1950s still found significant obstacles blocking access to equality in jobs, housing, education, and political participation.

The contentious politics of the fifteen years following the well-publicized murders of George Moscone and Harvey Milk, the city's liberal mayor and its first gay supervisor (city councilman) in 1975 are examined by DeLEON. He finds conservative business leaders and homeowners confronted with a tripartite reformist population divided into what he calls populists, liberals, and environmentalists. DeLeon's detailed analysis provides an illuminating explanation of the unstable and volatile – and colorful – political culture of contemporary San Francisco.

WILLIAM ISSEL

Sanger, Margaret 1879–1966
Birth control advocate

Chesler, Ellen, *Woman of Valor: Margaret Sanger and the Birth Control Movement in America*, New York: Simon and Schuster, 1992

Douglas, Emily Taft, *Margaret Sanger: Pioneer of the Future*, New York: Holt Rinehart, 1970

Gordon, Linda, *Woman's Body, Woman's Right: A Social History of Birth Control in America*, New York: Grossman, 1976, Harmondsworth: Penguin, 1977; revised, New York: Penguin, 1990

Gray, Madeline, *Margaret Sanger: A Biography of the Champion of Birth Control*, New York: Marek, 1979

Kennedy, David M., *Birth Control in America: The Career of Margaret Sanger*, New Haven: Yale University Press, 1970

Lader, Lawrence, *The Margaret Sanger Story and the Fight for Birth Control*, New York: Doubleday, 1955

Reed, James, *From Private Vice to Public Virtue: The Birth Control Movement and American Society since 1830*, New York: Basic Books, 1978

As with so many public figures who have spent their lives courting controversy, biographical treatments of birth-control activist Margaret Sanger range from the hagiographical to the sensationalist. LADER exemplifies the first approach. Clearly enamoured of the aging Sanger, Lader ceded complete editorial control to his subject, and this is reflected in the markedly uncritical tone of the completed biography. Unindexed and inadequately documented, it perpetuates many of the myths and distortions which punctuate Sanger's two ghost-written autobiographies, *My Fight for Birth Control* (1931) and *An Autobiography* (1938), while skirting around the details of her complex personal life. Even though it rests upon a more solid documentary foundation (Sanger's personal papers in the Library of Congress and the Sophia Smith Collection at Smith College), the DOUGLAS biography is written in the same celebratory mode. The first posthumous study of Sanger, it presents her as a latter-day Joan of Arc, downplaying her early radicalism and sanitizing her numerous extramarital affairs by referring to them throughout as "friendships." GRAY takes entirely the opposite tack. Although sympathetic to her subject, she is less concerned with analyzing Sanger's lifelong crusade for birth control than with exploring those aspects of her life which previous biographers had chosen to ignore. Adopting a style more suited to popular romance than serious biography, she attempts to document the details of Sanger's intimate relationships (even going so far as to assert at one point that her commitment to the cause of birth control sprang from a desire to satisfy her own voracious sexual appetite), her interest in spiritualism and the occult, and the addiction to alcohol and prescription drugs which allegedly marred her old age. Although it is based on extensive interviews with family members, friends, and professional associates, Gray's work is lacking in analytical depth and fraught with factual inaccuracies. Consequently, it is of little use either to the researcher or to the serious general reader.

Standing as she does, however, at an historiographical intersection where a number of histories converge – the history of gender, the history of sexuality, the history of radicalism, the history of American medicine, and the history of the social sciences as well as the history of birth control – Margaret Sanger has also attracted considerable scholarly attention. KENNEDY was the first social historian to undertake an in-depth assessment of her life and work. Rather than attempting to write an exhaustive biography, he opted to focus on Sanger's public career between 1912 and World War II – the period when she was the leading voice in the American birth-control movement. He pays scant attention to her propagandizing work on the world stage, and ignores entirely her role in winning funding for the research which led to the development of the oral contraceptive during the 1950s. In contrast with Lader and Douglas, he is not inclined to place Sanger on a pedestal. While acknowledging the magnitude of her achievement, he does not hesitate to point out what he perceives as her flaws. He argues that she exaggerated the lack of public knowledge regarding contraception prior to her campaign, in order to bolster her own position within the movement. He criticizes her for her decision to seek middle-class acceptance for her ideas, rather than engaging in an education campaign to reach the lower classes who were her original concern. He claims that her willingness during the 1920s to pander to social scientists, particularly eugenicists, hindered medical research into contraception. He also asserts that, by encouraging women to define themselves primarily as sexual beings, she offered them a false sense of liberation and planted the seeds of an ideology which Betty Friedan would later term the "feminine mystique."

GORDON endeavours to place Sanger's work in its broader socio-historical context. Written at the height of the "second wave" of American feminism, it traces the history of birth control in the United States from the 1870s and the campaign for "voluntary motherhood" to the 1970s and the struggle for legalized abortion. Taking as her starting point the idea that birth control has always been an issue of politics as opposed to technology, Gordon documents the struggle of American women for sexual and reproductive self-determination, but consciously downplays the contribution of prominent individuals. Thus, she pays tribute to Sanger's effectiveness as an organizer, but is careful to emphasize that "in all respects, she was part of a movement, not its inventor". She goes on to condemn Sanger for her retreat from radicalism in the years after 1917 and for cooperating with professional elites who would ultimately neutralize the feminist potentialities of birth control.

Subsequent studies have presented Sanger in a more favourable light. Rejecting Gordon's rather negative assessment of her career, REED argues that it was Sanger who first gave expression to the feminist impulse which underpinned the successes of the American birth-control movement in the 1920s and 1930s. He compares her contribution to the movement with those of Robert Latou Dickinson, a prominent gynecologist and sometime Sanger ally who championed birth control as a means of strengthening the American family, and Clarence Gamble, heir to the Proctor and Gamble fortune, who saw it primarily as a means of reducing fertility rates among the lower classes. By no means uncritical of Sanger, Reed is a useful introduction to the public dimension of her life.

As the first scholar to profit in full from the invaluable work of the Margaret Sanger Papers Project at New York University and Smith College, CHESLER has written what is without

question the definitive biography of Sanger. Although she recapitulates some familiar material, her narrative is thoroughly grounded in the relevant secondary literature, particularly the important work that has been done over the last twenty years in the field of women's history. Moreover, unlike earlier biographers, she pays careful attention to the links between Sanger's public life and her private life, concluding that she saw her revolt against conventional morality and sexual behaviour as a serious political act. Always balanced and objective, Chesler is able to maintain a critical distance from her subject without ever belittling her accomplishments.

SEAN P. HOLMES

See also Birth Control

Scandinavian Americans

Blegen, Theodore C., *Norwegian Migration to America*, 2 vols., Northfield, MN: Norwegian-American Historical Association, 1931–40
Gjerde, Jon, *From Peasants to Farmers: The Migration from Balestrand, Norway, to the Upper Middle West*, Cambridge and New York: Cambridge University Press, 1985
Hansen, Marcus Lee, *The Immigrant in American History*, edited by Arthur M. Schlesinger, Jr., Cambridge, MA: Harvard University Press, 1940
Haugen, Einar, *The Norwegian Language in America: A Study in Bilingual Behavior*, 2 vols., Philadelphia: University of Pennsylvania Press, 1953
Hvidt, Kristian, *Flight to America: The Social Background of 300,000 Danish Immigrants*, New York: Academic Press, 1975
Ostergren, Robert C., *A Community Transplanted: The Experience of a Swedish Immigrant Settlement in the Upper Middle West, 1835–1915*, Madison: University of Wisconsin Press, 1988
Runblom, Harald and Hans Norman, *From Sweden to America: A History of the Migration*, Minneapolis and Uppsala, Sweden: University of Minnesota Press/Acta Universitatis Upsaliensis, 1976
Semmingsen, Ingrid, *Veien mot vest: Utvandringen fra norge til amerika*, 2 vols., Oslo: Aschehoug, 1942–50

The literature of Scandinavian America has consistently been colored by the over-arching questions of ethnic relations in the United States. Its very existence is located in a heavy immigration to America wherein the Scandinavian nations contributed significant numbers to the citizenry of the United States. In a century of migration beginning in 1830, roughly 2.5 million people from the nations of Sweden, Norway, Finland, Denmark, and Iceland emigrated to the United States. Prior to 1890, Ireland was the only nation to exceed the transoceanic emigration rates of Norway, Iceland, and Sweden. Since Scandinavian Americans were among the most likely among immigrant nationalities to live in rural locales, moreover, they have been examined as exemplars of a great settler migration to the agricultural frontiers of the Americas.

A central thread running through the historiography of Scandinavian Americans, like many other ethnic groups in the United States, is the issue of acculturation to American life and integration into the American nation. The earliest histories of Scandinavians in America tended to be filiopietistic tracts written by immigrants or their children that affirmed the loyalty and value of Scandinavian Americans to the United States. By the 1930s, however, a group of Scandinavians and Scandinavian Americans, trained in professional graduate schools, contributed significantly to the developing field of immigration study in the United States that was principally assimilationist in content.

HANSEN, steeped in the tradition of Frederick Jackson Turner which had underscored the significance of the frontier in shaping American development, folded the European immigrant experience into the larger frontier narrative. Hewing to the Turnerian argument that the frontier was an environment that Americanized immigrants, Hansen nonetheless was sensitive to the different cultural and social patterns exhibited by Yankee and immigrant settlers on the edge of American settlement. By arguing that immigrants followed the American pioneer westward, purchasing and "filling in" land broken by the American-born, he illustrated how immigrants differed from American-born settlers but also how they played a central role in frontier narrative.

In his magisterial two-volume study of Norwegians in America, BLEGEN also invoked the Turnerian tradition to focus primarily on the 19th-century rural immigrant narrative. Like Hansen, he stressed the process of transition from immigrant to American. Practitioners of other disciplines, such as linguist HAUGEN illustrated how immigrant traditions – such as language – were a combination of the maintenance of old cultural forms and the diffusion of new impulses. The outcome of these interactions was the creation of new cultural forms, such as a Norwegian American linguistic tradition that Haugen identified in the densely settled immigrant communities of the Middle West.

As Americans at mid-century wrote about immigration to the United States, scholars in Scandinavia "discovered" the emigration. At one time an embarrassment that so many would forsake the fatherland, emigration was eventually perceived to be a central element in the modernization of Scandinavia and a critical ingredient of the story of the Scandinavian people. In a richly detailed study of Norwegian emigration, SEMMINGSEN focused on the social and economic crises that racked Norway and contributed both to a transformation of the Norwegian peasantry and the backdrop of emigration to the Americas.

Recent scholarship on Scandinavian America has been informed by two forces. First, the "new social history" reaffirmed the centrality of the inarticulate in the study of the American past, and encouraged historians to seek methods that gave voice to those such as immigrants who tended to leave only a very limited documentary record for historians to use. Using recently developed computer technologies, HVIDT analyzed the behavior of Danish immigrants. He illustrated changing patterns of rural and urban origins, the shifts from family to individual migration, the occupational structure of the immigrant group, and their adaptation to and reception in the United States.

Evidence of increasing interest is best illustrated in the work of "Sweden and America after 1860: Emigration, Re-migration, Social and Political Debate", a project in Uppsala that produced a group of dissertations. Summarized in RUNBLOM and NORMAN, the project attempted to understand the underlying psychology and patterns of migration, and concentrated on issues, such as the urban Swedish experience and re-migration of immigrants to Sweden, that had received short shrift from scholars in the past. In this project, historians connected urbanization and industrialization in the homelands to international migration. In painstaking detail, they quantified the patterns and process of migration.

A second trend has seen historians stress the centrality of understanding immigration as a process that linked people across space. As such, historians have attempted to cut through what has been called the "salt water curtain" and analyze both the origins and the destinations of the migrants. GJERDE examines the social and economic development of a region in Norway from which a large migration would emanate. He then explores who chose to emigrate, and the world that the immigrants created in the United States. As the title suggests, economic mobility is central to the story as immigrants entered a world of greater wealth and altered social customs.

OSTERGREN, a historical geographer, provides a similar portrait of emigration from a region of Sweden. Rich in spatial detail, Ostergren focuses on how families used emigration as a tactic to maintain or extend their economic condition, but also on how it set in motion routes of cultural change that were not initially envisioned by the immigrants. In the tradition of Hansen, these works focus on the rural world of the immigrant. Because they examine communities transplanted, they stress the continuities – rather than the uprootedness – of the immigration. But because they must focus on clustered settlements of immigrants of common European roots, they are unable to concentrate on the outliers, those who did not move in migrating chains.

JON GJERDE

Schools: from the Revolution to 1900

Anderson, James D., *The Education of Blacks in the South, 1860–1935*, Chapel Hill: University of North Carolina Press, 1988

Boylan, Anne M., *Sunday School: The Formation of an American Institution, 1790–1880*, New Haven: Yale University Press, 1988

Coleman, Michael C., *American Indian Children at School, 1850–1930*, Jackson: University Press of Mississippi, 1993

Cremin, Lawrence A., *American Education: The National Experience, 1783–1876*, New York: Harper, 1980

Kaestle, Carl F., *Pillars of the Republic: Common Schools and American Society, 1780–1860*, New York: Hill and Wang, 1983

Katz, Michael B., *Reconstructing American Education*, Cambridge, MA: Harvard University Press, 1987

Perko, F. Michael (editor), *Enlightening the Next Generation: Catholics and Their Schools, 1830–1980*, New York: Garland, 1988

Solomon, Barbara Miller, *In the Company of Educated Women: A History of Women and Higher Education in America*, New Haven and London: Yale University Press, 1985

Woody, Thomas, *A History of Women's Education in the United States*, 2 vols., New York: Science Press, 1929; reprinted, New York: Octagon, 1980

Education has always been considered a mainstay of the American democratic system. As a field of scholarly inquiry its history has experienced a significant rebirth. Among the most important works on the 19th century is CREMIN, the second volume in a sweeping trilogy of American education. It explores not only the educative influences of schools but also of less formal agents of learning such as newspapers, the family, the church, voluntary associations, libraries, fairs and museums. While Cremin acknowledges the ideological baggage of many modes of instruction, and the grave injustices wrought against blacks and Native Americans, he holds an overall laudatory opinion on the course of education. In his view, the 19th century witnessed an unprecedented popularization of education through the rapid expansion and increasing accessibility of a wide range of educational institutions. The result was a "liberating literacy" that advanced personal choice and thus equality for the majority of Americans.

KATZ presents a challenge to Cremin's optimistic account of American schooling. This eminent and controversial educational historian argues that 19th-century school reforms were chiefly guided by a desire to discipline a fast increasing and diversifying workforce. The common school bureaucracies that were created for the purpose perpetuated American inequality, as they paid little attention to the education of the socially disadvantaged among students.

KAESTLE is a superb analysis of the evolution of public schools and their ideology up to the eve of the Civil War. In nine rich yet concise chapters that reflect current thinking on the subject, he compares rural with urban schooling in the early Republic, charts the regional differences in the development of common schools, and treats in some depth the ideological justification and reform efforts that accompanied the expansion of public education. As "pillars of the Republic" common schools were to provide equality of opportunity, educate for democratic citizenship, and contain the 19th-century explosion of ethnic and cultural diversity through the teaching of a universal gospel of republican Protestant values. Kaestle places emphasis on the social context in which school systems evolved. Thus he reminds us that, while reform programs were similar throughout the United States, the systematization of common schooling did not occur in the South because of the opposition of the region's entrenched planter elite.

Specialist studies on particular themes and groups significantly enlarge the perspective of the general literature. WOODY is a classic on female education, its reissue in 1980 testifying to a lasting importance. Pioneering in its time, this sprawling survey remains an impressive storehouse of information, not least due to its abundant use of primary documents and quotations. The organization is topical, including discussions of the various modes of female higher education, the economic and social conditions of women, women in teaching and the professions, vocational and physical education, coeducation, and the woman's club movement. As might be expected, Woody omits many themes pertinent to the new social history such as the roles of class, race, ethnicity and religion in the shaping of formal education. An excellent revisionist supplement to Woody is SOLOMON, which focuses on the experiences of women in higher education – their fight for access to academies, seminaries, and colleges, their experiences at school, and the impact of their academic training on their lives after graduation.

ANDERSON's thorough study examines how black education in the post-Civil War South was shaped by the determination of the region's upper class to subordinate blacks both politically and economically. Sections on the 19th century outline the initial efforts of freed slaves to seize control of their education, and the mounting white campaign for black industrial training schools. Anderson rejects the traditional interpretation of the role of northern philanthropists in the establishment of southern black schools, suggesting that they were not disinterested agents who secured the best possible compromise for African-Americans in the face of racism. Instead they were willing accomplices in the southern wish to create an efficient labour force which would lend stability to a class- and effectively race-based economic system.

Despite the importance of Catholic schools to 19th-century American education, few good book-length explorations of the subject exist. PERKO is a collection of previously published essays which brings together much recent scholarship on Catholic education. Over half of the volume addresses the 19th century and includes, in addition to general treatments of the development of elementary and higher education, discussions about the Americanization of parish schools, foreign language instruction, the nature of Catholic textbooks, and the attitudes of prominent Catholics towards their educational institutions. Together the articles illustrate the reasons why Catholics founded separate schools, and they throw light on the tensions that existed between Catholic opponents and proponents of parochial schools.

A growing body of literature has emerged on the schooling of Native Americans. COLEMAN is novel in that it approaches the subject from the pupils' viewpoint. Based on first-hand accounts by members of thirty tribal groups, it highlights the varied and often ambivalent responses of Indian students to the culturally alien government and mission schools, and the conflict of values encountered by many on the return home from boarding school. It also contains an interesting summary of traditional Indian modes of education.

Throughout the 19th century Sunday schools complemented public schools in major ways and occupied a firm place within the web of 19th-century education. BOYLAN demonstrates this in what is the best general exploration of the role of Sunday Schools during the first one hundred years of their existence. Originally founded, like their British counterparts, to teach basic literacy to the poor, Sunday schools switched with the spread of common schooling to a purely religious curriculum which filled the gap left by the toned down "moral education" Protestantism of the public schools. They also continued to provide elementary instruction in the absence of other opportunities. Most importantly, their concern for raising a virtuous republican citizenry supported directly a chief educational aim of American public schools.

NIKOLA BAUMGARTEN

See also Education

Schools: 20th century

Cremin, Lawrence A., *American Education: The Metropolitan Experience, 1876–1980*, New York: Harper, 1988

Fass, Paula S., *Outside In: Minorities and the Transformation of American Education*, New York: Oxford University Press, 1989

Kliebard, Herbert, *The Struggle for the American Curriculum, 1893–1958*, New York and London: Routledge, 1987, 2nd edition, 1995

Krug, Edward A., *The Shaping of the American High School*, volume 1: *1880–1920*, New York: Harper, 1964, reprinted Madison: University of Wisconsin Press, 1969; volume 2: *1920–1941*, University of Wisconsin Press, 1972

Ravitch, Diane, *The Troubled Crusade: American Education, 1945–1980*, New York: Basic Books, 1983

Spring, Joel, *The Sorting Machine Revisited: National Educational Policy since 1945*, New York and London: Longman, 1989

Tyack, David B., *The One Best System: A History of American Urban Education*, Cambridge, MA: Harvard University Press, 1974

CREMIN provides a broad account and interpretation of education, in which schools are only part of the vast array of institutions in American society seeking to educate its citizens. In the third volume of his comprehensive history of American education, Cremin argues that education, in all its forms, is a central element in the quest for cultural self-definition. Formal schooling in the 20th century is examined in great detail and placed within the context of urbanization, industrialization and modernization. Three themes appear throughout the book as characteristics of American education: popularization, multitudinousness of curricula and social services, and the politicization of education. These three themes are central to Cremin's sometimes idealistic view. In contrast, notable by its absence from Cremin's description of schooling is any detailed analysis of continuing inequality and the reasons for it. However, Cremin's work is essential to understanding schooling in 20th-century America; its breadth and highly detailed bibliographic essays are unmatched.

KLIEBARD examines the struggle to define the guiding principles for organizing the school curriculum. Rather than viewing curricular reform as a monolith, Kliebard argues that it is highly contested terrain. Humanists sought to develop mental discipline in students largely through the study of traditional academic subjects. Developmentalists, under the growing influence of child psychology theories, aimed to tie curriculum development and subject matter to the natural mental development of the child. A third group, social efficiency educators, attempted to use the ideas of Frederick Taylor to rationalize the curriculum, by ridding it of wasteful items while concurrently providing the most efficient way of fitting an increasingly heterogeneous student population for their future roles. Finally, social meliorists, challenging Social Darwinists, pushed for a curriculum that would turn schools into active agents of positive social change. In the course of the 20th century these four groups of curriculum advocates vied for control of the curriculum. As no one school of thought triumphed over the other three, the result was a "loose, largely unarticulated, and not very tidy compromise."

TYACK examines schools in the 20th century from an organizational perspective. The urban model of school organization, for the most part, became the standard for the country. A growing cadre of professional educators in the early 20th century borrowed organizational concepts from the business world to create institutions that would better fit their students into the rapidly transforming economy. Reform from the top down was the order of the day as education professionals, armed with new social and scientific theories, attempted to wrestle control of schools from local political authorities, and create a new type of schooling that would provide the needed link between family and economic position in the larger world. Creating the "one best system," however, has had damaging effects; despite the rhetoric, children of the poor remained ill-served by schools, equal opportunity did not extend to all students, and the effort to escape politics in school decisions has often had the unintended effect of preserving the status quo.

Concentrating on the institution of the high school, KRUG (1964, 1972) is able to chart the ebb and flow of educational reform during the first half of the 20th century. The tremendous physical and curricular growth of secondary schooling after 1900 was the result of a combination of demographic and, more importantly, social and cultural factors that placed increasing responsibility on high schools to mold efficient, skilled, and moral citizens. The marked contradictions in progressive educational thought between attention to the individual and social efficiency are highlighted by Krug as he traces a wide variety of national and local debates over the shaping of the high school.

RAVITCH explores what happened to American public schools and institutions of higher education after World War II. She argues that the convergence of various social, economic, and political forces after the war led to the end of federal non-involvement in local and state controlled school systems. Through richly detailed narratives of how the Cold War, the civil rights movement, and the social uprisings of the 1960s affected education, Ravitch takes a probing look not only at American schools but at larger social forces acting upon the schools. The effort to further the crusade for equal educational opportunity was transformed by pressure from special interest groups representing minorities, women, the handicapped, and non-English speaking ethnic groups, into a crusade for special privilege and federal intervention and protection. Reforms became sweeping, federally controlled, and based on questionable social science research instead of being incremental and locally or state controlled. Ravitch's critique became the prominent philosophy of the Reagan administration that sought to scale back the federal role in educational matters. The goal of educational excellence was not to be achieved by federal initiative and power, but through local action and choice.

In the expanded version of his 1976 book, SPRING examines the same postwar period as Ravitch, but with different emphases and conclusions. Like Ravitch, Spring analyzes the increasing power of the federal government over education. Rather than finding the explanation in special interests and social fragmentation, Spring points to the natural inclination of the state to use schools to further its own economic and foreign policy goals. The growth of federal policymaking in relation to schools was the natural result of the state attempting to win the Cold War and retain global economic dominance. Schools, for Spring, are "sorting machines" used by economic and political elites to channel students of varied abilities into the most desirable social functions by the most efficient means possible. Whereas Ravitch called for the return of local control to strengthen schooling in a democratic society, Spring sees the answer in complete government non-interference in school issues. The only way equal access to knowledge will be provided, for Spring, is through this libertarian solution.

Unlike the revisionists who view schooling as a means of social domination imposed from above, FASS explores the role of minority groups in shaping the structure and goals of schools in the 20th century. Specifically, Fass looks at immigrants in the early 20th century, blacks in the 1930s and 1940s, women in the 1950s, and Catholic efforts to establish autonomous educational institutions. All these groups played a vital role in shaping schools that accepted diversity and pluralism. The organization and curricula of schools in the 20th century is not an imposition from above. Rather, it is the result of interaction between minorities and educators. Fass's book is groundbreaking in the imaginative use of non-traditional source material such as student yearbooks and newspapers. It is also representative of the ongoing historiographical process of placing schools in a wider social context that yields a richer understanding not only of American education but of American society.

ALEXANDER URBIEL

See also Education

Schurz, Carl   1829–1906
Political leader, reformer, soldier and author

Beisner, Robert L., "Carl Schurz: The Law and the Prophet," in his *Twelve Against Empire: The Anti-Imperialists, 1898–1900*, New York: McGraw Hill, 1968

Easum, Chester V., *The Americanization of Carl Schurz*, Chicago: University of Chicago Press, 1929

Fuess, Claude M., *Carl Schurz, Reformer*, New York: Dodd Mead, 1932

McFarland, Gerald W., *Mugwumps, Morals, and Politics, 1884–1920*, Amherst: University of Massachusetts Press, 1975

Simpson, Brooks D., LeRoy P. Graf, and John Muldowny (editors), *Advice after Appomattox: Letters to Andrew Johnson, 1865–1866*, Knoxville: University of Tennessee Press, 1987

Sproat, John G., *"The Best Men": Liberal Reformers in the Gilded Age*, New York: Oxford University Press, 1968

Trefousse, Hans L., *Carl Schurz: A Biography*, Knoxville: University of Tennessee Press, 1982

The career of German-born Carl Schurz has fascinated historians, even if it has attracted few biographers. From Republican politician to mugwump and anti-imperialist, his experiences as a diplomat, Civil War general, senator, and cabinet member made him an important and visible – although not central – figure of American political life in the second half of the 19th century. Among initial efforts to chronicle his life, two studies stand out: EASUM's examination of Schurz's "Americanization" as the German revolutionary adjusted to new circumstances, and FUESS's biography. However, these studies hold far more interest as evidence of how historians' treatment of Schurz has changed rather than on their own merits.

The only significant scholarly biography of Schurz of recent vintage, by TREFOUSSE, takes as its major theme its subject's identity as a German American leader. Exploiting Schurz's correspondence in both German and English, Trefousse recounts Schurz's escape from Germany, followed by a mercurial career of highs and lows. Recalling Schurz's support of Radical Republican principles on slavery and race during the Civil War, Trefousse has some difficulty in explaining why Schurz came to turn against continued federal protection for blacks in the 1870s. Nor does Schurz's identity as a German American leader provide a compelling explanation of his career, for German Americans tended to divide along religious lines when it came to casting their votes. It is probably closer to the truth to say that Schurz manipulated his image as a German American leader to gain political influence: he exercised far more leverage upon his fellow political independents. Nevertheless, readers seeking to know more about Schurz should turn first to Trefousse's study.

It was as a political independent that Schurz made his most significant impact. Two studies offer contrasting impressions of his political associates, often labelled mugwumps. According to SPROAT, the liberal reformers of the 1870s were out of touch with their world, unable to grapple with the problems of an industrial society, and nostalgic for government of, by, and for the elite. Quick to pounce upon the inconsistencies of Schurz and his allies, Sproat constructs a rather severe indictment of them. McFARLAND presents a somewhat more sympathetic perspective, detailing the accomplishments as well as the shortcomings of the mugwumps, from their official "christening" during the election campaign of 1884 through the Progressive era. These independents could help to shape the outcome of closely-contested elections during the Gilded Age. Their influence declined after the realignment of the 1890s which created solid Republican majorities throughout the North, where most mugwumps resided.

Schurz sought to advise American presidents on matters of politics and policy. Some presidents, such as Lincoln, tolerated him; one, Hayes, actually appointed him to the cabinet as secretary of the interior. Other chief executives found him irritating. Nowhere was this more evident than in his willingness in 1865 to offer Andrew Johnson advice on how best to pursue Reconstruction. Eventually the president directed him to visit the South and report on what he saw. SIMPSON, GRAF and MULDOWNY provide the most complete description of Schurz's tour (along with annotated texts of his letters to President Johnson) and set it in the context of other fact-finding missions undertaken at Johnson's behest. They conclude that from the beginning Schurz presumed too much in undertaking to advise the president, and, while acknowledging that Schurz did not exaggerate or fabricate his findings – indeed, he secured supporting testimony when he could to buttress his observations – from the beginning he intended to act as an adviser rather than an observer, hoping that his reports would cause Johnson to have second thoughts about the wisdom of his policy.

Another one of Schurz's causes was opposition to American imperialism. BEISNER demonstrates the continuity between Schurz's opposition to the annexation of the Dominican Republic during the Grant administration and his later anti-imperialism at the end of the century. However, he also highlights Schurz's egotism and self-righteousness, and suggests that these characteristics as well as his political independence marginalized his influence upon American policymakers. Nor did Schurz oppose American territorial expansion out of concern for the people who would come under United States authority; rather, he was concerned about the impact of so-called "inferior" races upon American society, and doubted that such people were fit for democratic institutions.

BROOKS D. SIMPSON

See also German Americans

Scientific Management

Aitken, Hugh G.J., *Taylorism at Watertown Arsenal: Scientific Management in Action, 1908–1915*, Cambridge, MA: Harvard University Press, 1960

Brandeis, Louis D., *Scientific Management and Railroads, Being Part of a Brief Submitted to the Interstate Commerce Commission*, New York: Engineering Magazine, 1911

Copley, Frank Barkley, *Frederick W. Taylor: Father of Scientific Management*, 2 vols., New York: Harper, 1923

Kakar, Sudhir, *Frederick Taylor: A Study in Personality and Innovation*, Cambridge: Massachusetts Institute of Technology Press, 1970

Nadworny, Milton J., *Scientific Management and the Unions, 1900–1932: A Historical Analysis*, Cambridge, MA: Harvard University Press, 1955

Nelson, Daniel, *Frederick W. Taylor and the Rise of Scientific Management*, Madison: University of Wisconsin Press, 1980

Taylor, Frederick W., *The Principles of Scientific Management*, New York: Harper, 1911

Thompson, C. Bertrand, *Theory and Practice of Scientific Management*, Boston: Houghton Mifflin, 1917

Wrege, Charles D. and Ronald G. Greenwood, *Frederick W. Taylor, the Father of Scientific Management: Myth and Reality*, Homewood, IL: Business One Irwin, 1991

Scientific Management, or Taylorism, refers to the method and process of systematic management developed by Frederick Winslow Taylor (1856–1915). As advanced and outlined by TAYLOR, the principles of scientific management deal with such issues as the organization and use of knowledge and planning, defining and performing work tasks, the interaction between labor and management, and the monitoring and assessment of work performed. Significantly, decisions regarding the operations and the arrangement of work were thus removed from the shop-floor and transferred to central management while workers were selectively assigned to prescribed tasks. Taylor used time studies to measure and evaluate the amount of time or effort needed to complete each component operation in a production process. Since these studies relied upon techniques of observation and statistical measurements they were labeled *scientific*. In fact, despite that label, these studies, which were intended to assess and ultimately improve productivity and reduce unit costs, were not necessarily objective. The precise significance and extent of Scientific Management, as a theory or in practice, remains controversial. THOMPSON, which includes an extended bibliography of the early literature, claims that during Taylor's lifetime Scientific Management was adopted in some two hundred institutions, although not always successfully.

BRANDEIS, who popularized the phrase scientific management over Taylor's preferred phrase of task management, argued in the *Eastern Rate Case* in 1910 that, since eastern railroads relied upon outdated managerial methods, they were as a result operated inefficiently. Accordingly, instead of a freight rate increase, all these railroad companies needed to do was install a modern, systematic management system to improve their rates of profitability. Brandeis, who was at the time a celebrated lawyer and would later serve as an associate justice of the U.S. Supreme Court (1916–39), brought ample notoriety to Taylor and helped make Taylorism more conspicuous throughout the United States.

Taylor and Taylorism have been the subject of numerous biographies, monographs, and journal articles. Indeed, at the peak of their notoriety, literally hundreds of articles and numerous books were published in the popular and academic presses in the years between 1910 and 1914. Shortly after Taylor's death COPLEY was authorized to prepare the official biography. Despite being a substantial work in two volumes, it suffers somewhat because of the restraints and demands placed on Copley by Taylor's family, influential associates, disciples and followers. Copley's biography is overly sympathetic and somehow contrives to be too lengthy and yet not detailed enough on aspects of Taylor's life and work. In a recent study, WREGE and GREENWOOD do an admirable job in separating myth from reality, and discuss in more detail the ideological leanings and biases of Taylorism and Scientific Management. They outline not only Taylor's contributions but also some of his shortcomings. Given the advantage of hindsight and the extensive use of personal correspondence, manuscripts, and contemporary records, Wrege and Greenwood are both discerning and balanced.

KAKAR adopts a kind of applied psychoanalytical and psycho-historical approach to re-interpret Taylor's personality and techniques of systematic factory management. His study investigates the life, work, and character of Taylor by placing them in the context of his culture and his innovations. Kakar concludes that in resolving his own internal struggles, Taylor helped to resolve and define a broader agenda of social and economic issues.

NELSON places Taylor and Taylorism within the context of the emerging factory system in the United States, and depicts both the origins and consequences of systematic or Scientific Management. Nelson concludes that Taylor's career and thus his legacy remain paradoxical; in some areas Taylor was a reformer and in others he was a reactionary. Nelson's study is a scholarly and thoughtful investigation of the repercussions of combining an influential innovator and unlikely revolutionary within the context of an evolving industrial structure. It uses original sources effectively and incorporates a useful and extensive review of the literature.

NADWORNY concludes that while Scientific Management effectively challenged existing methods of industrial management, its most striking and lasting consequence was in the area of industrial relations. The relationship between unionism and Taylorism was problematic, and unions often viewed Scientific Management with anxiety and resentment. However, Nadworny suggests that the open hostility between management and labor that existed prior to 1920 eventually gave way to a more cooperative environment during the 1920s.

The consequences of attempts to adopt or introduce the methods of Scientific Management have been the subject of several case studies. Among the more notable of these is AITKEN who examines not only the stated objectives of Taylorism but also some of its unanticipated consequences. He analyzes the installation of the Taylor system at the Watertown (Massachusetts) Arsenal and the resulting labor dispute. The strained relationship between Taylorism and labor unions can therefore be examined in a specific location rather than simply generalized. This case study is particularly interesting since, after the introduction of time studies at the Watertown Arsenal and a strike by its machinists, the House of Representatives initiated hearings on Scientific Management in 1911–12.

TIMOTHY E. SULLIVAN

Scott, Winfield 1786–1866
Military commander and presidential candidate

Cunliffe, Marcus, *Soldiers and Civilians: The Martial Spirit in America, 1775–1865*, Boston: Little Brown, 1968; London: Eyre and Spottiswoode, 1969

Elliott, Charles Winslow, *Winfield Scott: The Soldier and the Man*, New York: Macmillan, 1937

Gienapp, William E., *The Origins of the Republican Party, 1852–1856*, New York: Oxford University Press, 1987

Mansfield, Edward D., *The Life and Military Services of Lieut.-General Winfield Scott*, New York: N.C. Miller, 1862

Smith, Arthur D.H., *Old Fuss and Feathers: The Life and Exploits of Lt.-General Winfield Scott*, New York: Greystone Press, 1937

Weigley, Russell F., *Quartermaster-General of the Union Army: A Biography of M.C. Meigs*, New York: Columbia University Press, 1959

Weigley, Russell F., *History of the United States Army*, New York: Macmillan, 1967; revised, Bloomington: Indiana University Press, 1984

Weigley, Russell F., *The American Way of War: A History of United States Military Strategy and Policy*, New York: Macmillan, 1973

The neglect of General Winfield Scott by historians is one of the most perplexing features of 19th-century American historiography. Scott lacks a modern, scholarly biography. In one sense, this is not surprising for Scott was insufferably vain and pompous. He was also humourless, haughty and not one to admire the hoi polloi, though he was loyal to friends and those he admired. He was not, in short, a typical figure of the age of the "common man". His most striking attributes are hardly likely to place him very high up on a list of figures admired by today's academic historians. Yet Scott was an important figure and he does not deserve this neglect.

ELLIOTT is the only substantial biography worthy of its subject, and it is appropriately massive. Written firmly in the Uptonian tradition of American military history, it carries a foreword by Brigadier-General George E. Leach who, though a volunteer himself, complains that American military policy is "atrocious". Elliott's biography now has a rather quaint air, with old-fashioned chapter headings. A typical example heads Chapter 14: "General Scott Garners Additional Laurels on the Battlefield, but an Unknown British Marksman Does Him a Serious and Painful Disservice". Elliott skirts tactfully around Scott's somewhat tense marriage, though he is not blind to Scott's numerous and glaring faults. Nonetheless, he is suitably indulgent, and believes that a seam of "solid worth . . . lay like bedrock beneath the top soil of harmless foibles and egotism". There are full accounts of Scott's many feuds, especially with Generals Pillow and Worth. Elliott criticizes Scott for "unnecessarily immoderate use of language" in stigmatizing their offences. If this book has a weakness it is prolixity, and a somewhat simplistic, one-dimensional approach to the American military tradition.

The other two biographies are of little value. MANSFIELD is a piece of hasty journalism devoted to applauding Scott's military achievements in the Mexican War. Although not without some useful information, it is uncritical and is of more use as a gauge of how some of his contemporaries (and Scott himself) viewed his potential as a presidential candidate than as an accurate portrait of the general. The book was enlarged in 1861 when Scott once again came into public prominence on the outbreak of the Civil War; regrettably, he had departed as general-in-chief in November 1861 by the time the book appeared. SMITH is rather shallow and never replaced Elliott as the standard biography. It is a competent popular treatment, lacking any real scholarly flair or insight into its subject's life.

Altogether more sophisticated in delineating the political context in which Scott operated is CUNLIFFE. Winfield Scott was the dominating single personality in the period Cunliffe covers. He discusses Scott's attitudes towards politics and patronage, his vexed relationship with President James K. Polk, and the effect of political rivalries and jealousies on the conduct of the Mexican War, culminating in Scott's relief, and the appointment of a court of inquiry, October 1847–July 1848. "To the Mexicans", Cunliffe observes drily, "the inquiry was baffling in the extreme". Cunliffe also details Scott's feuds – notably with General Edmund P. Gaines and with Franklin Pierce's Secretary of War, Jefferson Davis. All of Cunliffe's points require further attention. GIENAPP is the best treatment of Scott as the Whig presidential candidate in the 1852 contest with Pierce. This was an ill-fated foray, not just for Scott personally, but for the party he represented. Gienapp demonstrates that Scott's wooing of the immigrant vote, especially the Irish, exacerbated nativist tensions within the Whig party. Discontented Whigs began to desert their party and support the anti-immigration American party, or Know Nothings.

Scott's military achievements are discussed most ably in the three books by Weigley. In his two general surveys, WEIGLEY (1967, 1973) considers Scott against the background of the development of American military institutions and doctrine. Scott is justly credited with having a major impact on the consolidation of those infant institutions, professional ethos and the officer corps. Weigley perhaps over-emphasizes the influence of theoreticians on Scott's generalship – though this is a common weakness of American historians in writing about 19th-century military operations. Weigley discusses convincingly the revival of the position of general-in-chief, but emphasizes that its weakness and ambiguity remained. If the Secretary of War chose, the general-in-chief was rendered powerless. In Scott's case, relations were worsened because, in the 1850s, he represented the defeated political party – a unique circumstance. Perhaps the most revealing of the three books is WEIGLEY (1959), his biography of Montgomery Meigs. Here, the ailing, gloomy general-in-chief is seen through the eyes of an ambitious, forceful subordinate. Scott was mentally alert, facile with the pen, and strategically subtle, but crippled with physical infirmities. Weigley's is an excellent account of the Sumter Crisis.

BRIAN HOLDEN REID

See also Civil War: Campaigns 1; Mexican War entries

Second Bank of the United States

Catterall, Ralph C.H., *The Second Bank of the United States*, Chicago: University of Chicago Press, 1902, reprinted 1968

Govan, Thomas Payne, *Nicholas Biddle: Nationalist and Public Banker, 1786–1844*, Chicago: University of Chicago Press, 1959

Hammond, Bray, *Banks and Politics in America, from the Revolution to the Civil War*, Princeton: Princeton University Press, 1957

McFaul, John M., *The Politics of Jacksonian Finance*, Ithaca, NY: Cornell University Press, 1972

Remini, Robert V., *Andrew Jackson and the Bank War: A Study in the Growth of Presidential Power*, New York: Norton, 1967

Schlesinger, Arthur M., Jr., *The Age of Jackson*, Boston: Little Brown, 1945; London: Eyre and Spottiswoode, 1946

Schweikart, Larry, *Banking in the American South from the Age of Jackson to Reconstruction*, Baton Rouge: Louisiana State University Press, 1987

Shade, William G., *Banks or No Banks: The Money Issue in Western Politics, 1832–1865*, Detroit: Wayne State University Press, 1972

Sharp, James Roger, *The Jacksonians Versus the Banks: Politics in the States after the Panic of 1837*, New York: Columbia University Press, 1970

Temin, Peter, *The Jacksonian Economy*, New York: Norton, 1969

Wilburn, Jean Alexander, *Biddle's Bank: The Crucial Years*, New York: Columbia University Press, 1967

Most of the 19th-century discussions of the Second Bank of the United States tended to repeat contemporary arguments, often resulting in criticism of Andrew Jackson's actions by the Whiggish historians who dominated the field and generally emphasized the question of the Bank's constitutionality. CATTERALL produced the first modern history of the Bank. He examined in detail the administration of the Bank under William Jones, Langdon Cheves, and Nicholas Biddle and included several chapters on the "Last Days of the Bank" in the years following Jackson's veto of the bill to recharter. Catterall's general assessment of the Bank's behavior as a quasi-public agency was quite favorable, while he criticized the economic reasoning in Jackson's veto of the recharter bill as "beneath contempt."

In general the Progressive historians in the first half of the 20th century were far more pro-Jackson and their views were synthesized and amplified by SCHLESINGER who portrayed the Bank as a private monopoly and Jackson's veto as a democratic blow against the bastion of economic privilege in the interest of "the other sectors of society" – namely, the farmers and the workingmen who distrusted banks and paper money. It represented the positive use of the federal government by a strong president to restrain the excessive power of the business community and constituted one of the defining moments of the history of American liberalism.

Almost immediately this interpretation came under criticism from historians in the 1940s and 1950s who emphasized Jackson's reactionary economic views and the positive economic role of the Bank before the veto. HAMMOND portrayed the Bank as a central bank fulfilling some of the functions of the Federal Reserve. As such the Bank under Biddle had performed well and promoted the national interest. State bankers and their representatives influenced Jackson to destroy the Bank in order to free themselves from its restraints. For Hammond and the other advocates of this interpretation, the veto represented an episode in the history of "entrepreneurial radicalism" and ushered in the age of laissez-faire that democratized American business.

While Hammond had praised Biddle's behavior as president of the Bank, he took a more critical stance toward his activities during the Bank War and as president of the Bank of the United States of Pennsylvania. In contrast, GOVAN defends Biddle every step of the way and is highly critical of Jackson. He describes the Bank in 1832 as a successful and generally popular public institution that deserved recharter and argues that Biddle, who had voted for Jackson in 1828, attempted to meet Jackson's criticisms and to cooperate with the administration. The veto resulted from Jackson's personal animosity towards banks and paper money, and once he acted his supporters then fell into line. The Bank War initiated a policy that led not only to the Panic of 1837 and the subsequent depression, but also the disorderly state of the currency and financial system through the remainder of the 19th century.

WILBURN closely examines public opinion and congressional behavior in 1832 and emphasizes the importance of the political situation. She argues that, at the time of the passage of the recharter, the Bank was generally popular (particularly with state bankers) and the vote of Congress in favor of recharter reflected that popularity. However once it was made a political issue Democrats who had favored the Bank turned against it. Of particular importance was the rejection of Martin Van Buren as minister to Britain, and the subsequent shift of attitude of the New York Democrats on the issue.

REMINI's study, which was later incorporated into his three-volume biography of Jackson, tells the story from the president's point of view. He suggests that "the destruction of the Bank occurred because it got caught in the clash between two wilful, proud, and stubborn men." Jackson distrusted the political influence of the Bank and when Biddle's attempt to gain a new charter for the institution coincided with the nomination of Henry Clay to oppose Jackson in the election of 1832, the president set himself against recharter. For Remini the importance of the veto – which he acknowledges was flawed economics, but masterful propaganda – was the heightened role claimed for the president in the legislative process.

In marked contrast, TEMIN praises Biddle's Bank, but argues that it "gets higher ratings on its aspirations to be a central bank than on its accomplishments." Jackson did not understand the Bank's functions and his destruction of the Bank had relatively little impact on the American economy. Rather it was outside forces – China's need for silver, the policies of the Bank of England, and the fluctuation of the world cotton market – which produced the boom of the 1830s, the Panic of 1837, and the subsequent deflation. Neither Jackson nor Biddle was to blame for the economic crisis. The Bank probably could have done nothing about the situation even if Jackson had followed an enlightened policy. The "political importance of Jackson's destruction of the Second Bank of the United States far outweighed the economic."

McFAUL returns the focus of the controversy to the political realm. He challenges the idea that bankers influenced Jackson's actions and analyzes the evolution of economic policy within the Democratic party that led eventually to the "divorce of bank and state" through the implementation of the Independent Treasury scheme. While he sees this as an attempt to control the banking and currency system, McFaul admits that the independent treasury cannot be seen as a substitute for a central bank, because of the Jacksonians' basic commitment to a hard money, anti-bank policy, and to decentralization.

The fight over the currency and credit system after the destruction of the Bank took place primarily within the states. SHARP extends McFaul's analysis by using case studies from the major regions to show the way in which the Jacksonians moved increasingly against banks and paper money during these years. He portrays a Democratic party increasingly dominated by its radical anti-bank majority, seeking to remove the abuses of the banking system by eliminating banking corporations and restricting the circulation of bank notes. The "hards" within the party were never entirely successful, because they faced opposition not only from the Whigs but also from the pro-bank "softs" within their own ranks. SHADE emphasizes the emergence of the Whig policy of "free" banking which was implemented (with the aid of "soft" Democrats) in most of the states and became the model for the National Banking System established during the Civil War.

SCHWEIKART offers a detailed analysis of banking in the South following the Panic of 1837 and takes issue with those who associate the Jacksonians with laissez-faire. He argues that from the time of Jackson's veto, his followers were unwitting advocates of a strong central government and government control over banking that prevented American banks from ever being freely governed by market forces.

WILLIAM G. SHADE

See also Financial History, 1780s–1930s; Jackson, Andrew; Jacksonian Era

Second Great Awakening

Bilhartz, Terry D., *Urban Religion and the Second Great Awakening: Church and Society in Early National Baltimore*, Rutherford, NJ: Fairleigh Dickinson University Press, 1986

Butler, Jon, *Awash in a Sea of Faith: Christianizing the American People*, Cambridge, MA: Harvard University Press, 1990

Carwardine, Richard J., *Transatlantic Revivalism: Popular Evangelicalism in Britain and America, 1790–1865*, Westport, CT: Greenwood Press, 1978

Cross, Whitney R., *The Burned-Over District: The Social and Intellectual History of Enthusiastic Religion in Western New York, 1800–1850*, Ithaca, NY: Cornell University Press, 1950

Finke, Roger and Rodney Stark, *The Churching of America, 1776–1990: Winners and Losers in Our Religious Economy*, New Brunswick, NJ: Rutgers University Press, 1992

Foster, Charles I., *An Errand of Mercy: The Evangelical United Front, 1790–1837*, Chapel Hill: University of North Carolina Press, 1960

Griffin, C.S., *Their Brothers' Keepers: Moral Stewardship in the United States, 1800–1865*, New Brunswick, NJ: Rutgers University Press, 1960

Hatch, Nathan O., *The Democratization of American Christianity*, New Haven: Yale University Press, 1989

Johnson, Curtis D., *Islands of Holiness: Rural Religion in Upstate New York, 1790–1860*, Ithaca, NY: Cornell University Press, 1989

Johnson, Paul E., *A Shopkeeper's Millennium: Society and Revivals in Rochester, New York, 1815–1837*, New York: Hill and Wang, 1978

McLoughlin, William G., *Revivals, Awakenings, and Reform: An Essay on Religion and Social Change in America, 1607–1977*, Chicago: University of Chicago Press, 1978

Mathews, Donald G., *Religion in the Old South*, Chicago: University of Chicago Press, 1977

Ryan, Mary P., *Cradle of the Middle Class: The Family in Oneida County, New York, 1790–1865*, Cambridge and New York: Cambridge University Press, 1981

Sellers, Charles, *The Market Revolution: Jacksonian America, 1815–1846*, New York: Oxford University Press, 1991

Historians are broadly agreed that the sequence of religious revivals from the 1790s to the 1840s constituted the most profound religious upheaval in American history. It is also acknowledged that the flowering of abolitionism and other reform movements cannot be understood in isolation from the Awakening. But there is no consensus about the roots, function and significance of this New World Reformation; nor, despite much fine scholarship and the proliferation of sophisticated local studies, is there an overarching work which comprehends the movement as a whole.

Two principal and closely inter-related fault-lines mark the historiography. The first separates those historians who celebrate the Awakening's liberating, counter-cultural energies from those who interpret the movement as a product of conservative social thought and an instrument of control. FOSTER and GRIFFIN both see the revivals, and the benevolent reform societies associated with them, as the weapons of traditional ecclesiastical elites bent on preserving authority in the face of church disestablishment, demographic change and the forces of secularization.

This particular version of the social control thesis – open to the charge that it depends too heavily on Presbyterian and Congregationalist experience, and understates the postmillennialist optimism of the moral reformers – has lost influence in recent years. But the repressive aspects of evangelical religion in the early republic have continued to receive attention, especially from "new social historians" concerned with the experience of ordinary people during an era of market transformation, nascent industrialization and class formation. In the most vigorous and influential of these studies, Paul JOHNSON places Charles Finney's stunning Rochester revival of 1831 in the wider context of the class tensions accompanying the young city's commercial and industrial development. Johnson explains the revival, and the temperance reform it spawned, as the means by which Rochester's entrepreneurs imposed bourgeois discipline and values on a fast-increasing and potentially fractious workforce. Johnson's critics have questioned the representativeness of Rochester in both socioeconomic and religious terms; moreover, by underestimating the strength of lower-class religion in Rochester's early years he arguably obscures the autonomous involvement of the proletariat in the revival.

MATHEWS's study of the Old South, by contrast, points to the liberating aspects of evangelicalism, at least in the Awakening's early phases. Taking as his starting-point the personal esteem and egalitarianism that evangelical religion nourished, he stresses the rebellion of poor and rising lower-middle-class people, including many women and blacks, against the traditional elite. Mathews is not blind to the darker, more authoritarian potentiality of evangelicalism; but even when the antebellum generation of socially entrenched southern white evangelicals generally endorsed slavery, the earlier ethos lived on in a black Christianity fashioned by a sense of hope, victory and "liberty".

The liberating possibilities for women in the proliferation of evangelical churches and voluntary bodies has been a frequent theme, especially of feminist historians. One of the best of these is RYAN's elegant case study of changing social structure and emergent middle-class family life in Utica during the Canal Era. Evangelical women in Oneida County, active in revivals, maternal associations and moral reform, created a community in which they fashioned a new ideology of domesticity, one which supplanted traditional patriarchal authority.

The Awakening's counter-cultural significance has been most fully elaborated by HATCH, in what has been justly acclaimed as the single most influential work on religion in the early republic. Hatch shows how American Christianity, in the face of a popular passion for equality, was democratised and fragmented; how new, populistic movements, especially Methodism and New Light forces in older churches, sustained revivalists of youth, vigour and sometimes genius, men and women who encouraged common sense in interpreting Scripture and celebrated the sovereignty of the audience. The argument is powerfully and imaginatively worked out.

A debate over the importance of economic change to the religious awakening constitutes the second fault line in the historiography. In his classic pioneering study of upstate New York's "Burned-Over District", a model for many later works, CROSS attributed the region's unique religious and social "ultraisms" to a particular combination of demographic and economic changes after 1815: specifically, he contended that enthusiasm was a feature of areas of Yankee settlement which were moving from a frontier to a mature commercial economy. In a path-breaking attempt to integrate religion into the political history of Jacksonian America, SELLERS similarly finds an economic explanation for the proliferation of revivalist movements: Methodist, Baptist and other "New Light" churches expressed the anxieties of the subsistence world over the advance of the capitalist market; Finneyite "Moderate Lights", by contrast, helped men and women make the transition to the commercial order. The book is wonderfully provocative, but is at the very least open to the charge that it seriously overstates New Light opposition to the market.

Curtis JOHNSON represents the other side of the divide. In a measured, thoughtful study of rural religion in upstate New York, he shows that, demographically and economically, little separated evangelicals from non-evangelicals. What explained the promotion of revivals were changes in religious ideas and outlook: the advance of a profound, Arminianized belief in both the importance and attainability of salvation, particularly as women sought to control male behaviour and secure the conversion of children before they left home.

McLOUGHLIN blends economic and ideological elements in a fertile mix. Borrowing from anthropology, he interprets the Awakening principally as a period of "cultural revitalization." At the core of his analysis he places the ideological shift from Calvinism to Arminianism, from a theory of election and inability to one of universal atonement and ability, a transition which brought society's prevailing religious message into line with people's daily perceptions of the reality of human autonomy in political and economic spheres. McLoughlin identifies five such awakenings in American history, each of which resolved tensions between day-to-day behaviour and traditional norms.

Whereas for McLoughlin the revivals were the product of external demands, BILHARTZ's study of religion in early national Baltimore explains religious enthusiasm principally in terms of the internal, institutional needs, character and ambitions of the churches. The most successful denomination (the Methodists) was the most single-mindedly revivalist. There is value in this approach, though it does not explain the experience of the "failed" revival, or why revivalist churches were only variably successful.

While most studies of the Second Great Awakening adopt a local or regional focus, CARWARDINE places the rolling waves of revival from the late 1790s to the 1850s in a wider, transatlantic context, and demonstrates a number of parallel developments in theology and religious practice in Britain and America. His perspective confirms the primary importance of Methodism as an engine of revival and theological change.

Two recent works, neither exclusively concerned with the Awakening, nor necessarily convinced of the value of the term itself, provide challenging perspectives on religious change in this era. BUTLER draws attention to the coercive power of denominational and inter-denominational agencies; attributes the success of some evangelical groups partly to their syncretising of popular magic and Christianity; and points to a renewal of African American religion. FINKE and STARK examine the factors that made the Baptists and Methodists ("the upstart sects") such effective competitors in the "free market religious economy" of the early republic, and contend that the Awakening "was no more (or less) than a series of local revival meetings, organized and led by professional evangelists."

RICHARD J. CARWARDINE

See also Great Awakening; Protestantism entries; Religion; Revivalism

Sectionalism/Regionalism

Banner, James M., Jr., *To the Hartford Convention: The Federalists and the Origins of Party Politics in Massachusetts, 1789–1815*, New York: Knopf, 1970
Bensel, Richard Franklin, *Sectionalism and American Political Development, 1880–1980*, Madison: University of Wisconsin Press, 1984
Bradshaw, Michael, *Regions and Regionalism in the United States*, Jackson: University Press of Mississippi, and London: Macmillan, 1988
Davis, Joseph L., *Sectionalism in American Politics, 1774–1787*, Madison: University of Wisconsin Press, 1977
Degler, Carl N., *Place over Time: The Continuity of Southern Distinctiveness*, Baton Rouge: Louisiana State University Press, 1977
Fischer, David Hackett, *Albion's Seed: Four British Folkways in America*, New York: Oxford University Press, 1989
Freehling, William W., *The Road to Disunion: Secessionists at Bay, 1776–1854*, New York and Oxford: Oxford University Press, 1990
Jensen, Merrill (editor), *Regionalism in America*, Madison: University of Wisconsin Press, 1952
O'Brien, Michael, *The Idea of the American South, 1920–1941*, Baltimore: Johns Hopkins University Press, 1979
Potter, David M., *The South and the Sectional Conflict*, Baton Rouge: Louisiana State University Press, 1968
Steiner, Michael and Clarence Mondale (editors), *Region and Regionalism in the United States: A Source Book for the Humanities and Social Sciences*, New York: Garland, 1988
Turner, Frederick Jackson, *The Significance of Sections in American History*, New York: Holt, 1932

The terms "sectionalism" and "regionalism" pose problems of definition, and, in the context of American history, a distinction has generally been made between them. Sectionalism, according to David Potter, "involves the interplay of more or less opposing human groups, geographically set apart but operating within a common political organization. The understanding of sectionalism, therefore, involves an understanding of the forces involved in this adverse relationship." As far as the United States is concerned, the two dominant "sections" involved in this "adverse relationship" have traditionally been perceived as North and South. However, as Frederick Jackson Turner, one of the earliest writers on sectionalism, noted, "the Civil War was only the most drastic and most tragic of sectional manifestations" in America's history. Regionalism is generally considered to be a less disruptive phenomenon. Although not always or necessarily non-confrontational, regional differences have not, historically speaking, been regarded as posing any fundamental threat to the Union.

Discriminating guidance on the debate over definition may be found in section 1 of POTTER. Not only does he discuss sectionalism – in his famous essay "The Historian's Use of Nationalism and Vice Versa" – but he also examines "The Enigma of the South," and traces the development of the sectional theme in southern history. TURNER, most often associated with his "frontier thesis," was also one of the first to develop the idea of sections in American history. His thinking can be traced either in his original work, or in various later anthologies or commentaries – for example, *Frontier and Section: Selected Essays*, introduced by Ray Allen Billington (1961), or Billington's biography, *Frederick Jackson Turner: Historian, Scholar, Teacher* (1973).

Both regionalism and sectionalism are perceived to have been "present at the creation" of America – Washington's Farewell Address is a frequently cited warning of the dangers of such divisions – but some authorities seek their origins much further back in time. FISCHER traces the roots of American regional distinctiveness back to Britain in his ambitious, although controversial, study. He examines four main immigrant groups: the Puritans from eastern counties of England who arrived in Massachusetts between 1629 and 1640; the Royalist elites and the indentured servants from the south of England who settled the Chesapeake between 1642 and 1675; the migrants to the Delaware Valley between 1675 and 1725, most of whom came from the North Midlands and from Wales; and the North British and Irish migrants who settled in the Appalachian backcountry between 1718 and 1775. These groups, Fischer argues, "carried across the Atlantic four different sets of British folkways which became the basis of regional cultures in the New World," cultures which "were fully established" by the time of the Revolution. Many historians take issue with Fischer's thesis, and question whether any of these groups was anything like as homogeneous as his argument requires them to be. A valuable collection of diverse reactions to Fischer's thesis is conveniently gathered in the *Forum* discussion in the *William and Mary Quarterly*, July 1991.

In a study of the Revolutionary period, DAVIS examines the "role that sectional identity, sectional differences, and sectional interests, rivalries, and jealousies played in the political life of the new nation," and more particularly the impact that sectionalism had on "the forces of federalism and nationalism" at this time. Ultimately, he concludes, sectionalism was only very briefly put aside during the Revolution, and constituted the main threat to the Union until the Civil War. This is not an especially new idea, but in his argument that sectionalism "complicated the struggle between the proponents and opponents of stronger central government," effectively preventing the latter "from defending their ideology and the Articles of Confederation against attack," Davis is on more original, and extremely persuasive, ground.

Although the South is perceived as that part of the Union where sectionalism was strongest, the Northeast, too, enjoyed a brief flirtation with this destructive concept at the time of the War of 1812. The causes and consequences of New England sectionalism – or separatism – are examined by BANNER, who argues that the Massachusetts Federalist Party was, among other things, "an expression of political and regional culture." Ultimately the move for separation was defeated because it would have "ruptured the intimate and indisputable economic links between New England and the rest of the nation."

For the century after 1815, the dominant sectional forces that historians have examined in any depth relate to the North-South divide. This is not to say that the East-West divide is wholly ignored, but here the debate often focuses on the West as contested ground between North and South, rather than on sectional sentiment in the West itself. Much of the literature on the coming of the Civil War is inevitably concerned with the politics of sectionalism, and the South's sense of its distinct sectional identity. In his sweeping account of the history of the South during the first half of the 19th century, FREEHLING stresses diversity and internal contradictions within the South. Would-be secessionists faced a formidable task in seeking to convince different groups of Southerners of the paramount importance of commitment to one united South, based on a proslavery ideology. Freehling's interpretation is stimulating but controversial, and it is debatable whether internal diversity is necessarily incompatible with a sense of a shared sectional identity and common sectional interests.

DEGLER surveys southern history over a longer period, and argues for the persistence of a southern sense of sectional distinctiveness, which stemmed from its experience of slavery. In a study of the period between the two world wars of this century, O'BRIEN develops the theme of the South as "common property," and examines the idea of the South as interpreted by, among others, southern agrarians such as John Crowe Ransom, Allen Tate, Frank Owsley and Donald Davidson.

BENSEL defies the widespread assumption that, in the 20th century, such factors as class, race and ideology have supplanted sections as formative influences on American politics. He insists that sectional competition has remained a (or even *the*) dominant influence on the political system. The most significant sectional divide, he argues, reflected the division of labour between the advanced northern core and the underdeveloped southern and western periphery. He pursues his controversial line of argument through a series of political events from tariffs and imperialism at the turn of the century, through world wars, the New Deal, civil rights and on to the economic issues of the 1970s. With the help of numerous maps and tables, he focuses his study on intense and persistent sectional conflict in the House of Representatives, where, he claims, sectional competition and alignments have changed little during the last hundred years. This is a challenging study, if not altogether a persuasive one.

On the subject of regionalism, the most comprehensive discussion is still contained in the JENSEN collection of essays by the foremost early writers on the topic, including Fulmer Mood, Merle Curti and Howard W. Odum. As an interdisciplinary study of "the regional-sectional concept" this collection of essays may be somewhat dated now, but it has not been surpassed. Mood's essay, in particular, shows that the sectional-regional concept, although potentially destructive, was also an administrative necessity for a country as large as the United States. For most of the time – at least up to 1860 – it had the effect of holding the Union together at the same time as it threatened to pull it apart.

The continuing administrative benefits, as well as the limitations, of regionalism in the 20th century are viewed through the eyes of a geographer in BRADSHAW. From an examination of regional stereotypes, which he perceives as not entirely helpful media creations, Bradshaw moves on to consider such examples of the regional idea as the rise of the Sunbelt, a concept that has prompted the emergence of "oppositional" constructs, such as the Frostbelt, the Snowbelt, and the Rustbelt. The East/West divide is also examined in some depth, as are two examples of regional programmes: the Tennessee Valley Authority (TVA) and the Appalachian Regional Commission (ARC). These, Bradshaw concludes, were successful but limited in their influence since there remains "a conflict between national and regional (or local) needs – at least as perceived by the people."

A valuable guide to further reading on a wide range of topics relating to regions and regionalism is to be found in STEINER and MONDALE, a comprehensive annotated bibliography of books and articles. It includes a lengthy section devoted to historical studies of regionalism.

S-M. GRANT

Segregation *see* Jim Crow

Settlement House Movement

Carson, Mina, *Settlement Folk: Social Thought and the American Settlement Movement, 1885–1930*, Chicago: University of Chicago Press, 1990

Chambers, Clarke A., *Seedtime of Reform: American Social Service and Social Action, 1918–1933*, Minneapolis: University of Minnesota Press, 1963

Crocker, Ruth Hutchinson, *Social Work and Social Order: The Settlement Movement in Two Industrial Cities, 1889–1930*, Urbana: University of Illinois Press, 1992

Davis, Allen F., *Spearheads for Reform: The Social Settlements and the Progressive Movement, 1890–1914*, New York: Oxford University Press, 1967

Lasch-Quinn, Elisabeth, *Black Neighbors: Race and the Limits of Reform in the American Settlement House Movement, 1890–1945*, Chapel Hill: University of North Carolina Press, 1993

Lissak, Rivka Shpak, *Pluralism and Progressives: Hull House and the New Immigrants, 1890–1919*, Chicago: University of Chicago Press, 1989

Muncy, Robyn, *Creating a Female Dominion in American Reform, 1890–1935*, New York: Oxford University Press, 1991

Trattner, Walter I., *From Poor Law to Welfare State: A History of Social Welfare in America*, New York: Free Press, 1974

Trolander, Judith Ann, *Professionalism and Social Change: From the Settlement House Movement to Neighborhood Centers, 1886 to the Present*, New York: Columbia University Press, 1987

Until relatively recently, the settlement house movement has received little attention from historians except as part of wider studies of the Progressive movement. There were early works written by the pioneer settlement house workers themselves, but these need to be treated with caution. Though the best of them certainly offer an insight into the motivations and the work of these reformers, they are largely uncritical.

In a study which began to fill the gap, CHAMBERS argues that the reform impulse of the Progressive Era did not die during World War I, but that it continued through the conservative climate of the 1920s into the New Deal. The settlement houses were essential in maintaining this continuity, although much of their enthusiasm for reform was lost in the face of demands for conformity and the loss of funding from those who had sponsored their efforts before the war. Chambers gives a fair assessment of the holding action conducted by the settlements during the 1920s, but this is a traditional work on social reform which, while not actually eulogizing them, accepts the settlements very much at face value.

DAVIS concentrates much more on the early years of the settlement houses when they were at their most innovative, and, he would argue, their most influential. He sees the settlements as "spearheads for reform" and as a force behind many

of the social welfare and urban reforms of the Progressive Era. This too is a rather traditional work on social reform, giving a very positive assessment of the settlement workers and little critical analysis of their motives. Nonetheless, it remains the standard work on the settlements, and, while it concentrates mostly on the most famous houses, it still offers a clear and insightful study of one element of Progressive Era reform. Two more recent studies both try to put the settlement houses of the Progressive Era into a wider context. TRATTNER is possibly the more successful of the two, placing the settlements in the context of the history of social welfare reform, but he does not really offer any new perspectives on the movement. TROLANDER concentrates on the post-World War II period when the settlements declined in influence and lost much of their sense of purpose. A well-researched study which once again places the settlements in the wider context of social reform, it does not offer any clear or striking re-evaluation of the movement.

Among the more recent books, there have been several more specialized studies which look at specific aspects of the settlements' work. Influenced by the "new social history", they have considered the settlement movement with reference to the analytical frameworks provided by race, ethnicity, class and gender. Thus, LISSAK sees Hull House, and by implication many of the other settlements, as an agency concerned primarily with the Americanization of the immigrant. Hull House sought to play a leading role in preparing immigrants for successful assimilation into American society. Although Hull House leaders recognized that the immigrants needed to create their own segregated ethnic environment, they saw this as only a temporary expedient in the process of the immigrants' adaptation to American ways. In this sense Hull House was not advocating cultural pluralism. The quest by Hull House to become the community centre of the neighbourhood was ultimately unsuccessful and it remained only a marginal institution despite its location in the middle of an ethnic neighbourhood. This is, at times, a heavily theoretical study, but despite occasional overdoses of jargon, it is generally well-written and persuasive.

CARSON is also concerned with the relationship of the settlements with their immigrant neighbours. She argues that the settlements were a product of Victorian ideas of service and a "religion of humanity." Though many of the settlements' activities constituted an attempt at social control, settlement leaders made very real efforts towards cultural pluralism and the recognition of the positive contribution which could be made by immigrant groups towards solving the problems of urban America. Although limited by its concentration only on the most famous settlements, this study does successfully illuminate the tensions between the middle-class settlement workers and their working-class neighbours.

MUNCY is more concerned with the fact that a substantial number of settlement residents and leaders were women – a fact that had been noted in earlier works, but which had not been developed. Placing the settlements within the framework of women's history, Muncy argues that the settlements provided an ideal setting for educated women to pursue new careers in social reform in a situation where they received the help of other women and were not dominated by men. She suggests that the settlement ethos was carried into the Federal

Children's Bureau, an agency which was itself the product of lobbying by settlement workers and their allies. Muncy tends to underplay the role of male reformers in the settlement movement in order to elevate that of the women, who are generally treated highly sympathetically. This is, however, an innovative study which offers new insights into both the settlement movement and the role of women in social welfare reform.

In a somewhat old-fashioned case study of two Indiana settlements, in Indianapolis and Gary, CROCKER argues that settlements such as Hull House were far from typical, and that the less well-known settlements were not centres of feminist reform networks, nor were they primarily secular institutions. Rather, religion played a much more important role in the settlement movement than has previously been recognized, and, though women were involved, they were not the dominant influence. Crocker suggests that settlement workers entered the slums both to help the poor and to control poor people, and that the reform activity of settlements was fairly limited. The problem with Crocker's study is that neither of the settlements she looks at were members of the National Federation of Settlements and therefore cannot really be described as representative of the movement. Though well-researched, the book does not contribute a great deal to the broader study of the settlement house movement.

LASCH-QUINN's study examines one of the conspicuous failures of the settlement houses – their inability to formulate a policy to deal with the influx of blacks into settlement environs in the early 20th century. While some settlements provided segregated facilities for their black neighbours, others moved out of the neighbourhood when blacks entered in large numbers. Lasch-Quinn argues that by blurring traditional definitions of settlement work, and by looking at institutions of black social reform as settlements, a new perspective can be developed. Thus, "settlement work" was often carried out by African American women's clubs, churches and other institutions. This study offers a critique of the settlement house movement from a different viewpoint. By placing race at the centre of its analysis, it illustrates a major "blindspot" of the movement.

ELIZABETH J. CLAPP

See also Addams; Social Work/Social Reform

Seven Years' War, 1754–1763

Anderson, Fred, *A People's Army: Massachusetts Soldiers and Society in the Seven Years' War*, Chapel Hill: University of North Carolina Press, 1984

Frégault, Guy, *Canada: The War of the Conquest*, translated by Margaret M. Cameron, Toronto: Oxford University Press, 1969

Gipson, Lawrence Henry, *The British Empire Before the American Revolution*, vols. 6–7: *The Years of Defeat, 1754–1757* and *The Victorious Years, 1758–1760*, New York: Knopf, 1946–49, revised 1958–70

Jennings, Francis, *Empire of Fortune: Crowns, Colonies, and Tribes in the Seven Years' War in America*, New York: Norton, 1988

Leach, Douglas E., *Roots of Conflict: British Armed Forces and Colonial Americans, 1677–1763*, Chapel Hill: University of North Carolina Press, 1986

Nash, Gary B., *The Urban Crucible: Social Change, Political Consciousness, and the Origins of the American Revolution*, Cambridge, MA: Harvard University Press, 1979

Parkman, Francis, *Montcalm and Wolfe* (France and England in North America, part 7), Boston: Little Brown, 1884; numerous subsequent editions, including *Montcalm and Wolfe: The French and Indian War*, New York: Da Capo Press, 1995

Rogers, Alan, *Empire and Liberty: American Resistance to British Authority, 1753–1763*, Berkeley: University of California Press, 1974

The changing nomenclature of this conflict reveals much about its historiography. For many years it was called the French and Indian War – itself a 19th-century term – and many historians have focused on the role of the war as a cause of the Revolution. Recent studies have tended to employ the term for the European phase of the war – the Seven Years' War – and have placed the conflict in its broader context, utilising changes in both ethno-history and new military history.

PARKMAN is a classic study of the war. Writing in a grand literary style, Parkman was one of the first historians to examine the war in detail and to explore its relationship to the American Revolution. However, the work is important not because of its content, but because of the influence it has had upon later historians. It must be read with great care as it is almost as much story as history. Parkman is extremely selective in his use of sources, and all but caricatures Frenchmen as evil and scheming adversaries, and Native Americans as brutal savages.

JENNINGS is an example of a work heavily influenced by Parkman, and written partly as a corrective to his work. Examining the course of Indian-European relations from the late 1740s to the Treaty of Paris in 1763, Jennings stresses the importance of pressure from both local and imperial sources on the native inhabitants of North America. Jennings concludes that the origins of the war lay almost exclusively in the greed of colonial and British officials. The work is a good study of the involvement of the Indian peoples in the conflict and provides an expert analysis of diplomacy between Europeans and Indians and among the Indian peoples themselves. Unfortunately the book is weaker in its analysis of the acts of imperial officials, and tends to reduce them to a series of conspiracies and plots.

FRÉGAULT provides a French Canadian perspective on the war, paying particular attention to military affairs. He sees the origins of the conflict in the underlying tensions between the British and French Empires, claiming that the British were determined to destroy French Canada. He thus portrays the war as a struggle for the survival of French Canada, and depicts French Canadians as desperately struggling to retain control of their future against the overwhelming might of the British colonies. However, Canada was conquered not because of the might of the British – Frégault stresses the inability of British and Anglo-American forces to win a decisive victory – but rather because of the unwillingness of France to provide adequate support for its North American colony.

GIPSON provides an extremely detailed view of the military and naval aspects of the war in its global and imperial perspective, a perspective reflected in his name for the conflict the Great War for the Empire. He argues that the war was a crucial turning point in the history of North America, for it removed the possibility that the French would block western expansion and gained the security which Americans required as a precondition of a bid for independence. He pays particular attention to the many logistical and tactical problems faced by the British, and stresses the extent of the military failures before 1757. The work emphasizes the degree of colonial dependence upon Great Britain for military and financial support, and refutes the notion that the colonists were capable of defending themselves. Victory in North America was won by British blood, according to Gipson, blood spilt because of concern for the North American colonies rather than for the British Empire as a whole.

LEACH analyses the many problems faced by the British in waging war in North America. Although this work examines warfare throughout the colonial period, over half of it is devoted to the Seven Years' War. Leach argues that the colonists' innate dislike of a standing army created tensions with the British army, heightened by a basic rivalry between colonists and Englishmen. Conflicts multiplied as the need for colonial participation in warfare increased in the mid-18th century. The colonists increasingly viewed the British as tyrannical despots, while the British viewed colonists as cowardly profiteers. Such tensions naturally served to undermine the ties of the empire, and contributed to the Revolutionary movement.

ROGERS also examines how the war generated tensions between colonists and British army officers and how it laid the foundations for the Revolution. He provides a less sympathetic view of the British, arguing that the oppressive methods used by British officers to recruit men and obtain supplies and transport provided many colonists with a view of arbitrary government. He argues that this created a fertile ground for the development of Whig ideology. Colonial assemblies quickly found themselves cast in the role of defenders of traditional liberties against the tyranny of the British military machine. Once the assemblies had taken this stance they continued to make these claims after the war, with disastrous consequences for the British Empire.

ANDERSON provides another perspective on how the war generated social tension and change. Making use especially of the muster rolls and orderly books of the Massachusetts forces, he provides an important case study of the experience of army life for colonial New Englanders. In particular Anderson shows how the close contact between colonial forces and troops of the regular British army led to tensions between the two. The work goes further to examine the nature and composition of the Massachusetts forces, and to study the methods used by the provincial governments to raise forces. Anderson stresses that the success of New England recruiters lay in the temporary service of the men, and the contractual limitations placed on their service – and also in the wartime economic conditions of New England.

Like others, NASH sees many of the origins of the Revolution lying in the Seven Years' War. In a study of popular unrest that contributed to the Revolutionary movement, he examines the impact of the war on the populations of Boston, New York and Philadelphia. The work stresses the social dislocation caused by the deaths of so many adult men, and the swing from wartime boom to postwar depression. After the war the seaports were left in economic depression, and poverty spread throughout the "lower classes" creating a pool of popular discontent.

MATTHEW C. WARD

See also British-French Rivalry in North America; Native Americans: Indian Wars

Seward, William H. 1801–1872
Political leader and Secretary of State

Bancroft, Frederic, *The Life of William H. Seward*, 2 vols., New York: Harper, 1900; reprinted, Gloucester, MA: P. Smith, 1967

Brock, William R., *Parties and Political Conscience: American Dilemmas, 1840–1850*, Millwood, NY: KTO Press, 1979

Crofts, Daniel W., *Reluctant Confederates: Upper South Unionists in the Secession Crisis*, Chapel Hill: University of North Carolina Press, 1989

Ferris, Norman B., *Desperate Diplomacy: William H. Seward's Foreign Policy, 1861*, Knoxville: University of Tennessee Press, 1976

Lothrop, Thornton Kirkland, *William Henry Seward*, Boston: Houghton Mifflin, 1896; reprinted, New York: AMS Press, 1972

Paolino, Ernest N., *The Foundations of the American Empire: William Henry Seward and US Foreign Policy*, Ithaca, NY: Cornell University Press, 1973

Potter, David M., *Lincoln and His Party in the Secession Crisis*, New Haven: Yale University Press, and London: Oxford University Press, 1942

Taylor, John M., *William Henry Seward: Lincoln's Right Hand*, New York: HarperCollins, 1991

Van Deusen, Glyndon G., *William Henry Seward*, New York: Oxford University Press, 1967

William H. Seward is a major 19th-century figure who has attracted less attention from modern historians and biographers than he deserves. The first "biography" of him was compiled by his son, Frederick, based on his autobiography and personal papers, all of which were quoted at length. BANCROFT is significant because for nearly seventy years it was the sole biography. It is less partisan than the family biography, less detailed and a more digestible piece of writing, which includes useful information. LOTHROP contains material on Seward's diplomacy, though it is filtered through a prism of assumptions about American dominance in the Western Hemisphere that would no longer be advanced by historians, at any rate quite so crudely.

BROCK is the best study of the dilemmas that beset the Whig party, and led to its failure to achieve a durable settlement of the slavery question in the 1840s, culminating in the Compromise of 1850. It traces Seward's career in relation to

Antimasonry and the Free Soil movement. Brock does not think highly of President Zachary Taylor and the "elderly" Whig leadership of 1848–50, but he judges Seward as "one of the wisest and most farsighted statesmen of the age". This is arguably the best book of an original and influential historian.

Seward's controversial policy during the secession crisis is discussed in detail in two books which focus on these critical months. POTTER is convinced that the war was avoidable, and that Lincoln failed to make sufficient effort to keep the Unionists of the Upper South sympathetically aligned with the new Republican administration. Seward gains high praise for his single-handed effort to negotiate with them, and with Confederate emissaries. Potter is too intolerant of the difficulties posed by the cumbersome electoral system – there were four months between Lincoln's election and his inauguration – and his southern bias is pervasive. Scholarship has moved on since 1942. CROFTS essentially updates this interpretation in a stimulating and challenging book. He defends Seward against charges that he was naive in relying on southern Unionism as a moderating influence during the secession crisis. He was knowledgeable about the Upper South, so Crofts claims, and understood that a new Union party could gain in influence if it was given time. He therefore argues that the Upper South would "become more unconditionally pro-Union" the longer the secession crisis was strung out. This is a respectable hypothesis, although it is not very novel, and Crofts cannot equal Potter's book for verve and eloquence. Yet the longer the crisis continued the more likely were secessionist sceptics to side with the seceded states. The case is far from proven; we cannot assume that Seward's policy would have brought enduring peace.

VAN DEUSEN remains the most important biography of Seward. He devotes considerable space to Seward's consistent opposition to Know Nothingism. His book was completed before the "ethno-cultural" interpretation of American politics became influential. Van Deusen sees Know Nothingism and Republicanism as in competition, and this aspect of his interpretation requires modification. But Van Deusen still provides a sympathetic and authoritative account of Seward's period as secretary of state. He concedes that Lincoln kept a careful eye on the conduct of foreign affairs, but believes that he delegated to Seward responsibility for executing American policy. Van Deusen provides careful and favourable assessments of Seward's wartime diplomacy, especially towards the French intervention in Mexico, the *Alabama* claims, and Pacific expansion. This is a solid and trustworthy rather than inspired biography. It is rather solemn in tone, and the mischievous, raffish side of Seward's personality is underplayed. There is no doubt that Seward was a gifted administrator, a versatile diplomat, and a statesman who was sensitive to, but not intimidated by, public opinion. The international standing of the United States did not decline during the Civil War. Yet he was also a bon viveur, a man who enjoyed life, and this sparkling side of his personality is crushed by the weight of Van Deusen's earnest scholarship.

FERRIS makes a brave and creditable attempt to explain Seward's aggressive and abrasive – sometimes apparently erratic and irrational – conduct of American policy during the early weeks and months of the Lincoln administration. However, the best overall study of Seward's diplomacy is

PAOLINO. His is an admirable monograph, cogent, economical and shrewd. He is especially good on Seward's expansionist impulse, and how its force varied depending on the audience that he was addressing. Paolino discusses Seward's frustration in 1869 at not completing his programme of expansion – not least, his failure to acquire San Domingo or build a canal across the Panama isthmus. Seward, he argues, lacked the naval power to consummate these ambitious plans.

The most recent biography is TAYLOR. This is nicely shaped, shrewd, and attractively written, but less heavyweight than Van Deusen. But because he writes with a lighter touch, Taylor is more successful in capturing Seward's elusive personality. The best part of the book covers Seward's complicated marriage, his relations with his sons (Frederick was assistant secretary during his tenure of the State Department), and his taste for "society" (he was an engaging host). Although Taylor is critical of Van Deusen's account of Seward's diplomacy, his chapters do not constitute an advance on it. He does devote proportionately more space to Seward's role in the suspension of civil liberties, and the arrest of suspected, disloyal "Copperheads". Yet the overall effect is disappointing. Taylor has sampled the Seward Papers, but his book rests on the standard secondary authorities, including Van Deusen. Also, his book lacks a bibliography, and all newcomers to the subject should consult Van Deusen first.

BRIAN HOLDEN REID

See also Civil War, Approach to entries; Civil War: International Aspects; Expansionism

Sherman, William Tecumseh 1820–1891
Union general in Civil War

Athearn, Robert G., *William Tecumseh Sherman and the Settlement of the West*, Norman: University of Oklahoma Press, 1956

Castel, Albert, *Decision in the West: The Atlanta Campaign of 1864*, Lawrence: University Press of Kansas, 1992

Glatthaar, Joseph T., *The March to the Sea and Beyond: Sherman's Troops in the Savannah and Carolina Campaigns*, New York: New York University Press, 1985

Lewis, Lloyd, *Sherman, Fighting Prophet*, New York: Harcourt Brace, 1932

Liddell Hart, B.H., *Sherman: Soldier, Realist, American*, New York: Dodd Mead, 1929; London: Eyre and Spottiswoode, 1933

Lucas, Marion Brunson, *Sherman and the Burning of Columbia*, College Station: Texas A & M University Press, 1976

Marszalek, John F., *Sherman's Other War: The General and the Civil War Press*, Memphis: Memphis State University Press, 1981

Marszalek, John F., *Sherman: A Soldier's Passion for Order*, New York: Free Press, 1993

Merrill, James M., *William Tecumseh Sherman*, Chicago: Rand McNally, 1971

Reston, James, Jr., *Sherman's March and Vietnam*, New York: Macmillan, 1984

Royster, Charles, *The Destructive War: William Tecumseh Sherman, Stonewall Jackson, and the Americans*, New York: Knopf, 1991

William T. Sherman was one of the leading generals in the American Civil War, and an early proponent of the total warfare that would become the staple of 20th century conflict. The first biographical accounts of Sherman appeared while the Civil War was still being fought. Newspapers and popular magazines fed the public appetite for information on this successful general who had sprung so recently into the public imagination. Northern sources were complimentary, southern ones very critical.

In 1875 Sherman himself interpreted his role in the war when he published two volumes of memoirs. Here, in a matter-of-fact way which emphasized his own key role and downplayed the roles of some others, he enraged his former opponents and even some of his former colleagues. A battle of reviews ensued, with Sherman alternately lambasted and praised. In 1886 he responded with an expanded version of his memoirs which added material on his non-Civil War years and included an appendix which contained letters he had received from critics of the first edition.

Sherman's death in 1891 resulted in a flurry of books meant to profit from the publicity surrounding his demise, and from the increasingly sentimental view of the war as it receded further into the past. An adequate biography did not result, however, and, instead, Sherman's reputation as a brute grew, as Americans increasingly accepted a Lost Cause view of the Civil War.

In 1929, LIDDELL HART, the leading British military theorist, used Sherman's life to trumpet to a post-World War I generation the indirect approach to warfare that the author believed Sherman so brilliantly exemplified, an approach which he thought the military should have copied in the recent conflict. Three years later, LEWIS published what was to remain the standard biography until the 1990s. He provided important insight into Sherman's personality, sharing the anti-black attitude of his subject and the anti-Reconstruction dislike of his generation.

Because Liddell Hart and Lewis only touched on Sherman's life after the Civil War, ATHEARN partially filled the gap with a factual book on Sherman's major role in the Indian Wars, the construction of the transcontinental railroad, and the settling of the West. MERRILL, the first biographer to utilize family papers not available to earlier scholars, published the first full biography of Sherman to cover his whole life, but did not seriously challenge Lewis's place as the general's pre-eminent biographer.

A series of books published during the last twenty years has produced insights into key aspects of Sherman's wartime career. LUCAS studied the 1865 burning of Columbia, South Carolina, arguing persuasively that Sherman did not bear primary responsibility for the conflagration. He blamed the Confederate torching of cotton bales, a high wind, and Union soldiers' consumption of widely available alcohol. MARSZALEK (1981) studied Sherman's important relationship with newspaper reporters, showing how the animosity between the two reflected the recurring problem of military-press debate over national security. He concluded that personality more than First Amendment issues drove the battle between Sherman and the reporters.

Three books analyzed Sherman's concept of total war. RESTON studied it within the framework of the Vietnam War. His inadequate research and his present-mindedness limited the effectiveness of his argument. GLATTHAAR presented a sympathetic view of Sherman in his study of Union troops during the March to the Sea and through the Carolinas. He showed that the general and his soldiers agreed on the need for the war of destruction which they fought in the later years of the war. Going even further, ROYSTER studied "destructive war" not only through the eyes and actions of Sherman and his men but also through the attitudes of Stonewall Jackson and the American people in general. He argued that this kind of warfare developed not out of the brutality of one Union general but out of the American character as a whole.

The best study of Sherman's ability in conventional warfare is CASTEL, who concluded that Sherman let too many military opportunities slip through his fingers during the Atlanta Campaign to receive universal praise for his efforts. Still, he recognized the importance of Sherman's generalship to the major Union victory.

MARSZALEK (1993) is the most complete biography of Sherman. Based on in-depth research in primary sources, it argues that Sherman was not a one-dimensional brute but a humane individual whose need for personal and public order drove him throughout his life. His war of destruction was his way of ending the conflict as quickly as possible with the fewest casualties to his own soldiers and to his southern friends.

Despite these many past studies, Sherman's historical reputation remains captive to the image of brutality portrayed in the folklore of the Lost Cause, best exemplified in the classic motion picture, *Gone with the Wind*. The future holds promise, however, that a more objective view of the general will emerge in the public mind once the important scholarship of recent years becomes more widely disseminated.

JOHN F. MARSZALEK

See also Civil War: Campaigns 2

Shipping

Albion, Robert Greenhalgh, *Square Riggers on Schedule: The New York Sailing Packets to England, France and the Cotton Ports*, Princeton: Princeton University Press, 1938

Albion, Robert Greenhalgh, with Jennie Barnes Pope, *The Rise of New York Port, 1815–1860*, New York: Scribner, 1939

Albion, Robert Greenhalgh, *Naval and Maritime History: An Annotated Bibliography*, privately printed, 1951; 4th edition, Mystic, CT: Munson Institute of American Maritime Studies, 1972, and supplement, 1971–1986, by Benjamin W. Labaree, 1988

Albion, Robert Greenhalgh, William A. Baker, and Benjamin W. Labaree, *New England and the Sea*, Middletown, CT: Wesleyan University Press, 1972

Bauer, K. Jack, *A Maritime History of the United States: The Role of America's Seas and Waterways*, Columbia: University of South Carolina Press, 1988

Baughman, James P., *The Mallorys of Mystic: Six Generations of American Maritime Enterprise*, Middletown, CT: Wesleyan University Press, 1972

Bonsor, N.R.P., *North Atlantic Seaway: An Illustrated History of the Passenger Services Linking the Old World with the New*, Prescot, Lancashire: T. Stephenson, 1955; revised (5 vols.), Newton Abbot, Devon: David and Charles, 1975–80

De La Pedraja, René, *The Rise and Decline of US Merchant Shipping in the Twentieth Century*, New York: Twayne, 1992

Fischer, Lewis R. and Gerald E. Panting (editors), *Change and Adaptation in Maritime History: The North Atlantic Fleets in the Nineteenth Century*, St. Johns, Newfoundland: Maritime History Group, Memorial University of Newfoundland, 1985

Haites, Erik F., James Mak, and Gary M. Walton, *Western River Transportation: The Era of Early Internal Development, 1810–1860*, Baltimore: Johns Hopkins University Press, 1975

Hyde, Francis E., *Cunard and the North Atlantic, 1840–1973: A History of Shipping and Financial Management*, London: Macmillan, and Atlantic Highlands, NJ: Humanities Press, 1975

Maddocks, Melvin, *The Great Liners*, Alexandria, VA: Time-Life Books, 1978

There are various accounts of the rise and decline of the American merchant marine. BAUER is a well-written general survey, which covers the whole span from the age of exploration and the colonial period to the 20th century, and which deals with rivers and canals as well as the high seas. For the more recent period, it can be supplemented by DE LA PEDRAJA which focuses on the oceanic merchant fleet, and attributes its decline to excessive devotion to free market competition.

The golden age of American shipping was between 1783 and 1860, when American vessels were second to none, and the United States fleet in the mid-1850s was temporarily larger than the British. The driving force was the rise of the American cotton and grain trades, the transatlantic migration and the Gold Rush demand for passage to California. American merchant shipping suffered badly in the Civil War and never recovered in the late 19th century. During the 20th century, the United States government has mounted huge shipbuilding campaigns during the world wars, but in peacetime, apart from in the protected coastal trades, American shipping has declined.

ALBION (1938) is the classic study of the elite New York-Liverpool packet ships at the height of American maritime power. These ships carried high-value passengers and freight as well as much general cargo. They shipped American staples – especially cotton and grain – to Europe, and British manufactured goods to the United States. Albion provides short descriptions of the leading ships, merchants and packet owners. There are no detailed studies of individual early 19th-century packet lines such as the Black Ball, or of many important commodities like cotton or wheat. ALBION (1939) is still the

best historical study of a large American port. The rise of shipping on the western rivers, also driven by the cotton and grain trades, is surveyed in HAITES, MAK and WALTON. The map, on p. 2–3 shows the huge area covered. The authors analyze how improvements in steamboat design and the commercial organisation of the trade allowed freight rates to fall dramatically between 1815 and 1860.

The United States made the technical transition to steam and to iron and steel ships far more slowly than Britain and Germany. Hence an increasing proportion of American exports were carried by foreign ships. FISCHER and PANTING include an analysis by Safford of American decline, and good surveys of the other national fleets. The huge rise of American cotton and grain exports, in the years 1865–80, preserved many old American sailing ships long after their natural span. However, by 1870 most American capitalists had found higher returns in domestic industry and western railroads, and maritime issues were no longer high on the national agenda. The American government attempted to help by restricting imports of cheap foreign ships and reserving the coastal trade for American shipping, but, while this limited the decline, it created a high cost industry that could not possibly compete overseas.

ALBION, BAKER and LABAREE survey the long maritime history of New England from colonial times to the present, with chapters on the "Heroic and Golden Ages, 1775–1860", the "Dark Age, 1865–1914", and the present. New England had been the leading shipbuilding area in North America – but was ill-equipped to compete with the heavy industry of Glasgow and Hamburg. BAUGHMAN traces the progress of one versatile New England firm, Mallorys of Mystic, Connecticut, which survived many changes, from early 19th-century sail-making and whaling, through wooden shipbuilding, to operating steamship companies on the protected coastal routes. The firm finally closed in 1941. Mystic itself has now become an attractive maritime museum.

British, Canadian and European shipping dominated the Atlantic in the late 19th century. HYDE is a detailed business history of the leading British line, Cunard. In the 1850s Cunard's main rivals were the New York-based Collins Line which had built several powerful steam-driven wooden side-wheelers. The ocean sailing packets, lovingly chronicled by Albion, had often raced each other across the Atlantic, but Collins and Cunard provided the first steam contest. However, Hyde reveals that Cunard was in secret collusion with Collins. At first, both companies received large mail subsidies, but the Collins Line collapsed in 1858 when the United States withdrew its subsidy. Britain, too, withdrew subsidies after 1865, but Hyde shows how Cunard survived by finding the right balance between the key luxury passenger, migrant and freight trades.

In the early 20th century, European shipping lines such as Cunard continued to build the biggest and most impressive ships, and to take large shares of the Atlantic emigrant and passenger trades. Between the wars the freight and migrant markets collapsed, leaving the liner trade unbalanced. Hyde shows how the British government subsidized Cunard, but the American government was less generous. The last great ships on the Atlantic run were therefore the luxury passenger vessels. MADDOCKS provides a good pictorial survey of these "Great Liners". The book opens with several pages of large contemporary advertisements of the French Line's *Normandie*, the Cunard Line's *Queen Mary*, and the United States Line's *Leviathan* – which was originally the Hamburg-America *Vaterland*. There are excellent colour illustrations of the interiors. The essential history is neatly summarized between the photographs. In the long run the airlines have taken the passenger trade and foreigners the freight.

There are many general surveys of Atlantic shipping. BONSOR is a bulky five-volume, 2100 page directory of transatlantic passenger shipping, ship by ship, line by line, from 1816 to 1970. He provides basic details of construction, costs, ownership, trades, commercial success and demise. There is a huge literature on maritime history. Fortunately, ALBION (1951, 1972, 1988) has left a well-organized series of annotated bibliographies. These are exhaustive listings of all types of literature covering the many diverse aspects of international maritime history.

JOHN R. KILLICK

See also Foreign Trade; Transport

Slater, Samuel 1768–1835

Industrial innovator and manufacturer

Bagnall, William R., *Samuel Slater and the Early Development of the Cotton Manufacture in the United States*, Middletown, CT: J.S. Stewart, 1890

Batchelder, Samuel, *Introduction and Early Progress of the Cotton Manufacture in the United States*, Boston: Little Brown, 1863; reprinted, Clifton, NJ: A.M. Kelley, 1972

Cameron, E.H., *Samuel Slater: Father of American Manufactures*, Freeport, ME: Bond Wheelright, 1960

Conrad, James L., Jr., "The Making of a Hero: Samuel Slater and the Arkwright Frames," *Rhode Island History*, 45, February 1986

Conrad, James L., Jr., "'Drive That Branch': Samuel Slater, the Power Loom, and the Writing of America's Textile History," *Technology and Culture*, 36, January 1995

Jeremy, David J., *Transatlantic Industrial Revolution: The Diffusion of Textile Technologies Between Britain and America, 1790–1830s*, Cambridge: Massachusetts Institute of Technology Press, 1981

Prude, Jonathan, *The Coming of Industrial Order: Town and Factory Life in Rural Massachusetts, 1810–1860*, Cambridge and New York: Cambridge University Press, 1983

Tucker, Barbara M., *Samuel Slater and the Origins of the American Textile Industry, 1790–1860*, Ithaca, NY: Cornell University Press, 1984

White, George S., *Memoir of Samuel Slater, Father of American Manufactures, Connected with a History of the Rise and Progress of the Cotton Manufacture in England and America*, Philadelphia, 1836; reprinted, New York: A.M. Kelley, 1967

Samuel Slater, a former apprentice in Jedediah Strutt's cotton textile mills in Belper, England, is always included in any discussion of the early American cotton textile industry. Quite surprisingly, however, he has not been the subject of a major full-length biography. Consequently Slater biographical details must be pieced together from a number of differently focused sources.

A Slater contemporary who was also born in England, WHITE provides the first important view of Samuel Slater in 1836. His powerful presentation continues to set the tone and provide the focal points that frame discussions of Slater, in spite of its exaggerated and eulogistic approach, incomplete coverage, and occasional inaccuracies. White utilizes recollections of his meetings with Slater, discussions with Slater's associates and contemporaries, and newspaper accounts of the textile industry's earliest days to develop a laudatory assessment of his friend's achievements. Not intending a full examination of Slater's life, White's stated purpose is to establish Slater as "The Father of American Manufactures." Slater is credited with single-handedly and from memory constructing the water-powered spinning machinery of Richard Arkwright at Pawtucket, Rhode Island in 1790. He then establishes a system of mill management and operation, including child labor, similar to that which existed in England. For White, who had been assisted in his efforts by members of the Slater family, the mill environment introduced by Slater brings a strong and positive moral force to American society.

While concentrating on a broader view of the textile industry and especially of the Lowell mills during the mid-19th century, BATCHELDER refers to mills established by Slater and those which he influenced as the Rhode Island system. Disagreeing with White, Batchelder strongly criticizes Slater's mill management approach because of its reliance on the family system of labor and limited use of power-weaving technology.

Writing on the 100th anniversary of the American cotton textile industry in 1890, BAGNALL emphasizes Slater's background, and the first days at Pawtucket, and praises his feat of memory. Slater is described as honorable, courageous, and patient, and is credited with the initial development of his industry and the growth of industrial New England. More informative than White, especially about Slater's later years, Bagnall adds significantly to an emerging picture of Slater by explaining that his skill as a "spinner" and his intent on remaining in this branch limited his contributions to the textile industry after 1816. This refers to Slater's apparent rejection of the power loom. Together with White, Bagnall completes the 19th-century view of Slater as heroic, hardworking, and somewhat conservative.

CAMERON provides a later but similarly sympathetic view by focusing on Slater's personal life, his relationship with his family, and his mill properties outside of Pawtucket. Slater is portrayed as confident, forward-looking at all times, a pioneering industrialist, and an affectionate parent and husband. Although Cameron utilizes specific manuscript collections, he does not provide any specific citations. Like White, Cameron acknowledges support received from the Slater family.

Since 1980, standard views of Slater have been both broadened and questioned. JEREMY's study of the transfer of early textile technologies in the transatlantic community includes Slater as an important example of this process. Jeremy refines some details regarding Slater's early American period while accepting limitations suggested by Bagnall. By placing Slater in the broadest possible context, Jeremy provides the basis for a better understanding of his contributions.

More specifically, the heroic view of Slater and his mill system has recently been challenged. PRUDE examines social patterns inherent in the industrialization of south central Massachusetts where Slater began to build mills in 1812 and eventually lived after 1832. Although Prude is more concerned with the impact of mills in a rural environment, he presents Slater as charismatic, shrewd, pragmatic, devoted to business, and a key figure in the class struggle that Prude sees as intrinsic to industrialization.

Writing like Prude and Jeremy in the late 1970s and 1980s, TUCKER is most interested in Slater's interaction with American culture and values, as they influenced his approach to industry building. Her assessment of Slater's early years in Pawtucket is more revealing than others although she does not deal directly with his introduction of Arkwright technology. Slater is described as taking advantage of American values and traditions, thus countering whatever potential existed for class struggle. Tucker's Slater is a complex figure – ambitious, determined, but bound too much by traditional values and past practices, and unable to delegate authority to others. His direction was as much towards the past as it was towards the future. Slater monopolized power at first and became even less adaptable in his later years when confronted by a changing economy. Because Tucker's focus shifts away from Pawtucket by 1806 and follows Slater's mill system into Smithfield, Rhode Island and then into south central Massachusetts, she cannot consider Slater's later life in Pawtucket where he lived until 1832.

In separate articles, Conrad challenges two traditional views of Slater. CONRAD (1986) rejects the belief that Slater worked alone in 1790 as he built Arkwright machinery and then set it in motion. Slater is pictured using some machinery already in place when he arrived, and receiving help from skilful Rhode Island artisans as well as his partners, William Almy and Moses and Smith Brown. This conclusion is supported by others. CONRAD (1995) determines that Slater did not reject power-weaving technology as suggested by Bagnall, Jeremy, Prude, and Tucker. Basing his conclusions on numerous Slater manuscript collections, Conrad finds Slater supporting the early use of the power loom and steam power in his own mills. For Conrad, Slater is less heroic, but more consistent in his aggressive use of machine technology.

JAMES L. CONRAD, JR.

See also Manufacturing Industry entries; Technology and Invention

Slavery: General

Berlin, Ira, *Slaves Without Masters: The Free Negro in the Antebellum South*, New York: Pantheon, 1974; Oxford: Oxford University Press, 1981

Berlin, Ira and Ronald Hoffman (editors), *Slavery and Freedom in the Age of the American Revolution*, Charlottesville: University Press of Virginia, 1983

Blassingame, John W., *The Slave Community: Plantation Life in the Antebellum South*, New York: Oxford University Press, 1972, revised 1979

Clinton, Catherine, *The Plantation Mistress: Woman's World in the Old South*, New York: Pantheon, 1982

Curtin, Philip D., *The Rise and Fall of the Plantation Complex: Essays in Atlantic History*, Cambridge and New York: Cambridge University Press, 1990

Davis, David Brion, *The Problem of Slavery in the Age of Revolution, 1770–1823*, Ithaca, NY: Cornell University Press, 1975

Elkins, Stanley M., *Slavery: A Problem in American Institutional and Intellectual Life*, Chicago: University of Chicago Press, 1959, 3rd edition, 1976

Fogel, Robert William, *Without Consent or Contract: The Rise and Fall of American Slavery*, New York: Norton, 1989

Fox-Genovese, Elizabeth, *Within the Plantation Household: Black and White Women of the Old South*, Chapel Hill: University of North Carolina Press, 1988

Frey, Sylvia R., *Water from the Rock: Black Resistance in a Revolutionary Age*, Princeton: Princeton University Press, 1991

Genovese, Eugene D., *Roll, Jordan, Roll: The World the Slaves Made*, New York: Pantheon, 1974; London: Deutsch, 1975

Goodheart, Lawrence B., Richard D. Brown, and Stephen G. Rabe (editors), *Slavery in American Society*, 3rd edition, Lexington, MA: Heath, 1993

Gutman, Herbert G., *The Black Family in Slavery and Freedom, 1750–1925*, New York: Pantheon, and Oxford: Blackwell, 1976

Harris, J. William, *Society and Culture in the Slave South*, London and New York: Routledge, 1992

Jordan, Winthrop D., *White over Black: American Attitudes Toward the Negro, 1550–1812*, Chapel Hill: University of North Carolina Press, 1968; abridged as *The White Man's Burden: Historical Origins of Racism in the United States*, New York: Oxford University Press, 1974

Kolchin, Peter, *American Slavery, 1619–1877*, New York: Hill and Wang, 1993; London: Penguin, 1995

Morgan, Edmund S., *American Slavery, American Freedom: The Ordeal of Colonial Virginia*, New York: Norton, 1975

Oakes, James, *The Ruling Race: A History of American Slaveholders*, New York: Knopf, 1982

Parish, Peter J., *Slavery: History and Historians*, New York: Harper, 1989

Phillips, Ulrich Bonnell, *American Negro Slavery: A Survey of the Supply, Employment, and Control of Negro Labor as Determined by the Plantation Regime*, New York: Appleton, 1918; reprinted Baton Rouge: Louisiana State University Press, 1966

Rose, Willie Lee, *Slavery and Freedom*, New York and Oxford: Oxford University Press, 1982

Stampp, Kenneth M., *The Peculiar Institution: Slavery in the Ante-Bellum South*, New York: Knopf, 1956; London: Eyre and Spottiswoode, 1964

White, Deborah Gray, *Ar'n't I a Woman? Female Slaves in the Plantation South*, New York: Norton, 1985

In the past thirty years our understanding of slavery in North America has been revolutionized by an outpouring of outstanding scholarship. PARISH is a convenient starting point for students new to this scholarship, as he combines an overview of the subject with an excellent discussion of its historiography. Though judicious and fair in his treatment of conflicting points of view, the author is quite willing to make firm judgments on the value of individual works.

The recent scholarship is daunting enough in scope, variety, and quantity to have discouraged attempts at a comprehensive synthesis. The only recent one, KOLCHIN, is fortunately a good one. As the book is relatively short, it inevitably neglects some of the regional and temporal variety of slavery's history, but it does cover the entire time period and the major topics. Kolchin usually adopts a middle point of view on the historiographical debates. His interpretation is informed by comparative studies, including his own earlier comparison of American slavery with Russian serfdom.

A different kind of survey is FOGEL, the first half of which covers slavery, the second half abolition. In part one Fogel focuses primarily on the economics of slavery, an area to which Fogel himself has been a distinguished, and at times controversial, contributor. This work is in many ways a response to the massive criticism of Fogel's earlier *Time on the Cross*, co-authored with Stanley Engerman. The newer volume retreats from some of the most debatable points of the earlier one, without however abandoning its basic argument: that agriculture based on slavery, while morally repugnant, was a thoroughly rational capitalist enterprise. Because of its lucid explications of the technical work of the economists who now dominate most areas of economic history in the United States, the book is a good starting point for a consideration of their work.

Three collections of essays also offer good starting points for new students. GOODHEART, BROWN and RABE bring together an excellent selection of articles and book excerpts. Many of the authors discussed here are represented; aside from those, essays by Lawrence Levine on slave spirituals, Albert Raboteau on folk religion, and Drew Faust on slave management can be highly recommended. There is a smaller selection of readings from recent work on slavery in HARRIS, carefully chosen to provide an introduction to various aspects of southern slave society. Another book of essays – this time all the work of one author – is ROSE, which includes beautifully written analyses of particular periods or aspects of slavery in the United States. Especially important is her "The Domestication of Domestic Slavery," focusing on the early national period and offering more insights than many large books on the subject.

Two older comprehensive works deserve continued attention. PHILLIPS was the first truly scholarly synthesis. This pioneering volume dominated the scholarship on slavery for a generation. Phillips's interpretation was severely skewed by his racism and southern background. He argued that most masters were benevolent paternalists and that slavery was the "best school yet invented" for the training of an "inert and backward people"; he was unable to regard African American culture as a subject deserving serious study. The modern edition cited here is to be preferred because of the introduction by Eugene Genovese, who makes the best case he can for Phillips's continuing relevance. STAMPP summed up the liberal reaction to Phillips's interpretation, and remains an outstanding treatment of slavery as an institution. While Stampp uncompromisingly condemned slavery for its injustice and cruelty, he, too, paid little attention to African American culture, arguing that it had largely been destroyed by slavery.

Partially inspired by Stampp's work, ELKINS carried to an extreme the argument that slavery in the United States was a uniquely destructive institution. The book is a loosely connected series of interpretive essays, based on relatively little primary research. In the most provocative section Elkins compared slave plantations to Nazi concentration camps and argued that many slaves had been reduced in fact, as well myth, to emasculated "Sambos". Some of the best work on slavery originated as a response to Elkins's arguments, and most of it has discredited the Sambo thesis. The most recent edition of the book is useful for the appendix in which Elkins reflects on this more recent scholarship.

Slavery in the United States was part of an economic system that embraced much of the Atlantic world – and part of Elkins's book is devoted to comparisons, or contrasts, between the United States and Latin America. CURTIN is a brief synthesis, by one of the most influential historians of that system, of much of the work on the "plantation complex" that embraced Africa, Europe, South America and the Caribbean, as well as North America. While Curtin largely ignores the United States itself, his book provides the indispensable broader context for the study of slavery there.

JORDAN is a study of attitudes and ideas about race, rather than slavery itself, but for the period covered the two are inextricably linked. He offers what is still the most comprehensive discussion of white views on race and slavery in the colonial and early national periods. He argues that ideas about African inferiority, while vague and not always coherent, were a crucial prerequisite for the rise of slavery. His long and deeply researched book traces the ways in which these vague ideas ultimately hardened into a racialism that provided slavery's most important intellectual bulwark after the American Revolution. MORGAN, which covers much of the same chronological ground, emphasizes the class issues at work in slavery's rise. This gracefully written study of the most important of the North American colonies that came to depend on slave labor argues that African slavery became attractive precisely when white indentured servitude became both expensive and socially threatening to elite planters. Morgan's suggestion that American ideas about liberty flourished in part because racially-based slavery allowed white men permanently to exclude a large working class from the political sphere has influenced much subsequent work.

The era of the American Revolution has produced less scholarship than it deserves as a key turning point in the history of slavery. The essays in BERLIN and HOFFMAN include some of the best available scholarship on the period. They cover all major geographical regions, and emphasize demographic as well as ideological developments. One common theme is the rise of a new African American culture in the newly independent United States. FREY is a comprehensive treatment of slavery in the southern colonies in the revolutionary era. The book is notable for the way in which slaves themselves play a central role in Frey's analysis of what she terms a "triagonal" war involving British, slave, and white American protagonists. An important theme is the transformation of African American culture by the combined forces of revolutionary ideology and the rise of evangelical Christianity. The fusion of these two, she argues, created the foundations of black culture and black resistance to slavery in the future.

Most of the more comprehensive treatments of American slavery focus on the period from about 1830 to the outbreak of the Civil War. BLASSINGAME was one of the first to treat the culture of slaves as an important topic in its own right. Based especially on an analysis of the writings of escaped slaves, this book is organized as a refutation of Elkins's arguments (see above) that slaves were reduced to dependent "Sambos". Blassingame's emphases on the strengths of slave families and communities and the consistency of slave resistance have been followed in most subsequent work.

Still more comprehensive and influential is GENOVESE. While to some degree echoing Blassingame's arguments on family and resistance, Genovese places even greater stress on the importance of religion. It is in this book that Genovese works out most fully his neo-Marxist analysis, drawing especially on the work of Antonio Gramsci, of the slave South. Genovese sees slaves as powerfully influenced by the paternalist ideology of their masters; they were, he argues, enmeshed in a reciprocal system of obligation even while they resisted that system. The range and depth of Genovese's research, his lively style, and his theoretical approach have made this book the single most important study of slavery in the United States, and given it an influence far beyond specialists in the subject.

Much of the best work on slavery has focused on special topics or particular social strata in slave society. GUTMAN analyzes the slave family in depth and at length. This book, like Blassingame's, was conceived in part as a refutation of the Elkins thesis that slavery had, among other things, destroyed slave family life. Gutman also takes issue with Genovese, arguing that the evidence shows that slave culture was more autonomous and independent of master class influence than Genovese allows. This large and sprawling book does not always hang together well, but Gutman's passionate defense of African American cultural values and his often ingenious use of sources have made it a cornerstone of many subsequent interpretations.

WHITE focuses more narrowly on slave women. Her argument goes even further than Gutman in the direction of claims that slave culture and values were largely autonomous from masters; indeed her slave women often seem autonomous from slave men as well. Her relatively brief treatment has opened up what is certain to be a major line of research in the future. Both CLINTON and FOX-GENOVESE focus mainly on the women of the master class. Both these books tend to read all the evidence in one direction, though they choose different directions. Much of Clinton's argument springs from a modern feminist's conviction that white slave mistresses, despite their privileged positions, suffered under many disabilities in a patriarchal society, and that many of them became, in effect, anti-slavery. Fox-Genovese takes the opposite point of view, that mistresses were largely satisfied with their roles as a subordinate part of the ruling class. Fox-Genovese gives more attention than Clinton to slave women and to the relationships between mistresses and their slaves; like Genovese, Fox-Genovese stresses the influence of planter hegemony on slave life.

In his study of slave masters (not mistresses) OAKES emphasizes that most masters were not planters at all, but operators of smaller farms with few slaves – a distinguishing characteristic of slavery in the United States when seen in comparative perspective. For Oakes, slave masters were thoroughly American types – capitalists on the make, political liberals, evangelical Protestants, often guilt-ridden about the contradictions inherent in their situation. This sometimes polemical work overstates its case, but provides a valuable corrective to the tendency of most works to limit their attention to larger plantations.

Two books that deal with the larger social and intellectual context of slavery in the United States deserve inclusion here, because of the importance of their subjects and the influence of their work. BERLIN is a history of free, rather than slave, African Americans in the South. As his title indicates, he sees free blacks in the South as an integral part of slave society; he suggests that "the status and treatment whites afforded the free Negro are an especially revealing gauge of Southern society." By exploring the lives of people at slavery's social and legal boundaries, Berlin sheds fresh light on slavery itself. DAVIS is a history of slavery's abolition rather than slavery itself. Like Jordan (see above), Davis is primarily concerned with white thought and action. He shows how ideas about slavery were intimately related to ideas about much else – politics, economics, the nature of "free" society. The second volume of what is planned as a three-volume history of abolition, this book is remarkable for the depth of its research and the subtlety of its analysis. It forms part of one of the unquestionably great works of scholarship by an American historian.

J. WILLIAM HARRIS

See also Colonial History: Slavery and Indentured Servitude

Slavery: Economics of

Bateman, Fred and Thomas Weiss, *A Deplorable Scarcity: The Failure of Industrialization in the Slave Economy*, Chapel Hill: University of North Carolina Press, 1981

Conrad, Alfred H. and John R. Meyer, "The Economics of Slavery in the Ante Bellum South," in their *The Economics of Slavery and Other Studies in Econometric History*, Chicago: Aldine, 1964, as *Studies in Econometric History*, London: Chapman and Hall, 1965

David, Paul A. and others, *Reckoning with Slavery: A Critical Study in the Quantitative History of American Negro Slavery*, New York: Oxford University Press, 1976

Fogel, Robert William, *Without Consent or Contract: The Rise and Fall of American Slavery*, New York: Norton, 1989

Fogel, Robert William and Stanley L. Engerman, *Time on the Cross: The Economics of American Negro Slavery*, Boston: Little Brown, 1974

Genovese, Eugene D., *The Political Economy of Slavery: Studies in the Economy and Society of the Slave South*, New York: Pantheon, 1965; London: MacGibbon and Kee, 1968

Genovese, Eugene D., *The Slaveholders' Dilemma: Freedom and Progress in Southern Conservative Thought, 1820–1860*, Columbia: University of South Carolina Press, 1992

Kilbourne, Richard H., *Debt, Investment, Slaves: Credit Relations in East Feliciana Parish, Louisiana, 1825–1885*, Tuscaloosa: University of Alabama Press, 1995

Phillips, Ulrich Bonnell, *American Negro Slavery: A Survey of the Supply, Employment, and Control of Negro Labor as Determined by the Plantation Regime*, New York: Appleton, 1918; reprinted Baton Rouge: Louisiana State University Press, 1966

Wright, Gavin, *The Political Economy of the Cotton South: Households, Markets, and Wealth in the Nineteenth Century*, New York: Norton, 1978

The economics of slavery have been the subject of one of the great historiographical debates of modern times. Argument has centred on questions of efficiency and profitability, and the place of profit in the overall motivation of slaveholders.

PHILLIPS's classic study of American slavery was founded upon the argument that masters were motivated, not by an urge to maximize profit, but by an attachment to paternalistic values. His thesis was built on the racist premise that blacks were inherently lazy and could not be overworked. Supposedly, then, slackness and crude labour were the norm. The real benefits of slavery, Phillips argued, were social – an accommodation between black and white, and the comfortable preservation of white supremacy. Slavery, he wrote, "was less a business than a life; it made fewer fortunes than it made men." Beyond his racist premises, Phillips built up a series of closely-linked arguments – and these arguments have run throughout the long debate on the slave economy. Slave owning, he argued, tied up capital, and shortage of capital blocked the development of southern industry. This in turn discouraged urban growth; and, since slavery undermined the price and status of labour, the South attracted few white immigrants. The region failed to diversify and relied heavily on northern manufactures and credit. With slaves bought for status reasons, slave prices were dangerously inflated. There were, supposedly, more irrationalities. Cotton monoculture exhausted land, and led to a wild career of constant westward expansion into virgin soil; and concentration on cotton led to unhealthy overproduction.

By the 1950s, several studies had been made of the profitability of individual slave plantations, but such work was limited by the incompleteness of data and by questions over the typicality of the slave holdings selected. Using econometrics (economic theory, with quantitative methods), CONRAD and MEYER brought a methodological breakthrough. Instead of looking at individual plantations, estimates were made for average input costs (above all, slaves, and land) and for average outputs (notably staple crops, and natural increase among slaves). Rates of return in all parts of the South were found to be healthy, and to be comparable with those on northern investments. In the slave-exporting states an important part of profits was seen as deriving from slave breeding and from the sale of slaves. Slave prices, these writers found, were realistic, and were not inflated by conspicuous consumption.

FOGEL and ENGERMAN dramatically launched a new phase in the debate. Scholarship was combined with entrepreneurial flair to promote a major econometric reinterpretation of slavery. Fogel and Engerman's main claims include the following. The slave system was highly profitable (10 per cent annual profit typically, from 1820 to 1860), and did not rely on slave breeding. Profit came from efficient use of resources, and southern agriculture was 35 per cent more efficient than northern free farms. The long-run economic prospects of slavery were good. There was no conflict between slavery and urbanization; per capita incomes were very high in world terms; and long-run viability was shown by the continued expansion of cotton acreages well after slavery had ended. Slavery's economic strength, Fogel and Engerman continued, came partly from the routine of the gang labour system, partly from the high participation rate in the work force (including women and children), but also from the skills and (especially controversially) from the high morale of the slaves. Individual slaves were rewarded for hard work, and could aspire to skilled jobs or "managerial" positions. The slave family, supposedly, was encouraged, and forcible family separations were rare. Diet and accommodation compared well with those of northern free workers.

FOGEL restated most of these claims, but gave more emphasis to the advantages of assembly-line techniques in gang labour (and seemed to place somewhat less emphasis than before on the zeal of individual slaves). He claimed that slaves' hours of work were no longer than those of northern free workers, but that the gang system of slavery produced more efficiency. New material was presented on the height of slaves, and slaves were found to be taller (and therefore better fed) than European workers. Little attention was paid to the possibility that the "efficiency" of the gang system might actually have constituted brutality. The samples used on slave heights raise questions about typicality. This data is especially puzzling because it suggests extremely low birth weights, undersized children, and yet an unlikely transformation into tall adults. Overall, Fogel and Engerman's work saw slavery as flexible capitalism, brought down, not by economic forces, but by political and military weight.

The techniques used by Fogel and Engerman have brought important new dimensions, challenges, and insights to the study of slavery. Their work has been controversial, however, and several volumes of criticism, including DAVID et al., appeared in response to *Time on the Cross*. David and his colleagues challenged Fogel and Engerman's claims to scientific rigour, disputed their data, and questioned inferences made. They challenged the notion that slaves had identified with masters in a common economic endeavour, and they radically reinterpreted evidence on punishment, incentives, diet, material conditions, slave sales, and sexual exploitation. They challenged the appropriateness of a "geometric index of total factor productivity" which compared northern free farms with the slave South – but which took little account of factors like the impact of industry on land and labour prices in the North.

WRIGHT trailed his ideas on slave economics in his critical essay in David et al., but developed them more fully in his book. Rather than sharing Fogel and Engerman's emphasis on the efficiency of slavery, Wright attributed the profitability of antebellum slavery to the soaring world demand for cotton and to the South's virtual monopoly in its supply. Even without the Civil War, the stagnation in demand for cotton in the late 19th century would, he argued, have brought slavery into crisis. Slave units had advantages over free farms in that they could collectivize food preparation and child care, and could devote a high percentage of their labour to cash crops rather than to safety-first subsistence production. But, according to Wright, the slave economy was flawed, and the plantation South lacked the creative tension to stimulate industry, urbanization, and economic diversification.

For GENOVESE's Marxist analysis, technical debates about levels of profit were largely irrelevant when searching for the essential nature of slavery. Slaveholders, he argued, were pre-capitalist or anti-capitalist, and their priorities were family, status, and honour, not profit maximization. For Genovese, capitalism meant a system where labour was a commodity commanding its hire in the market, and that commodity was detached from notions of duties and reciprocal rights. In slavery, though, slaveholders owned their labour, and mutual paternalistic ties supposedly developed between master and slave. The system, Genovese argued, was enmeshed in the capitalist world – providing essential staples, and drawing on northern banking, manufacturing, and commercial services. But slavery, he claimed, had produced its own class structure and ideology, and was thoroughly hostile to bourgeois values. Like Phillips, he argued that slavery tended to exhaust the soil, tied up capital, and inhibited industry, urbanization, and the domestic market. In a series of studies (including Genovese 1965 and 1992), he developed the idea that slaveholders dreaded industrialization, feared the growth of a proletariat and of an industrialist class, and saw slavery as the one way to prevent chaos, and to protect liberty and orderly progress.

BATEMAN and WEISS have provided the most rigorous investigation into the failure of the South to develop an extensive industrial base. They found that the profits of southern industries were high, and suggested that such profits should have drawn in more investors. They reached a mixed conclusion, giving some comfort to Genovese and some to his critics. Fear that factory development might threaten slavery was, they suggested, not enough to deter individual investors, but a more personal threat – that of being ostracised by planter society – might have deterred some investors. But the South, they emphasized, did have a comparative advantage in cotton production. Cotton generally produced good profits, and substantial economic risks were involved in switching to industrial investment. Social factors, Bateman and Weiss concluded, discouraged industry to some extent, but economic rationality was also at work.

KILBOURNE's Louisiana case study argued that the slave South was not crippled by debt, and that it did not heavily depend on the North for credit. Slaves were the overwhelmingly important form of collateral, and were used to produce an economically healthy and flexible credit system. With the abolition of slavery, however, the basis for southern credit was shattered, greatly exacerbating economic dislocation.

MICHAEL TADMAN

Slavery: Legal Aspects

Campbell, Stanley W., *The Slave Catchers: Enforcement of the Fugitive Slave Law, 1850–1860*, Chapel Hill: University of North Carolina Press, 1970

Cover, Robert M., *Justice Accused: Antislavery and the Judicial Process*, New Haven: Yale University Press, 1975

Fede, Andrew, *People Without Rights: An Interpretation of the Fundamentals of the Law of Slavery in the U.S. South*, New York: Garland, 1992

Fehrenbacher, Don E., *The Dred Scott Case: Its Significance in American Law and Politics*, New York: Oxford University Press, 1978; abridged as *Slavery, Law, and Politics*, 1981

Finkelman, Paul, *An Imperfect Union: Slavery, Federalism and Comity*, Chapel Hill: University of North Carolina Press, 1981

Finkelman, Paul (editor), *Fugitive Slaves*, New York: Garland, 1989 (Articles on American Slavery, vol.6)

Finkelman, Paul (editor), *Law, the Constitution, and Slavery*, New York: Garland, 1989 (Articles on American Slavery, vol.11)

Finkelman, Paul, *Slavery and the Founders: Race and Liberty in the Age of Jefferson*, Armonk, NY: Sharpe, 1996

Hall, Kermit L. (editor), *The Law of American Slavery: Major Historical Interpretations*, New York: Garland, 1987 (United States Constitutional and Legal History, vol. 9)

Higginbotham, A. Leon, Jr., *In the Matter of Color: The Colonial Period*, New York: Oxford University Press, 1978 (Race and the American Legal Process, vol. 1)

Hyman, Harold M. and William M. Wiecek, *Equal Justice under Law: Constitutional Development, 1835–1875*, New York: Harper, 1982

Morris, Thomas D., *Free Men All: The Personal Liberty Laws of the North, 1780–1861*, Baltimore: Johns Hopkins University Press, 1974

Morris, Thomas D., *Southern Slavery and the Law, 1619–1860*, Chapel Hill: University of North Carolina Press, 1996

Schafer, Judith Kelleher, *Slavery, the Civil Law, and the Supreme Court of Louisiana*, Baton Rouge: Louisiana State University Press, 1994

Schwarz, Philip J., *Twice Condemned: Slaves and the Criminal Laws of Virginia, 1705–1865*, Baton Rouge: Louisiana State University Press, 1988

Tushnet, Mark V., *The American Law of Slavery, 1810–1860: Considerations of Humanity and Interest*, Princeton: Princeton University Press, 1981

Watson, Alan, *Slave Law in the Americas*, Athens: University of Georgia Press, 1989

Wiecek, William M., *The Sources of Antislavery Constitutionalism in America, 1760–1848*, Ithaca, NY: Cornell University Press, 1977

The literature on American slavery and the law may be divided into two general parts: private and state law, and constitutional law. There is, of course, a great deal of overlap between the two, and a number of books listed above – for example, Cover, Finkelman (1981), and Wiecek – discuss both aspects of slavery and the law. Some studies, such as Schafer and Schwarz, focus on a particular state, while others, like Tushnet, are more national in scope. For the sake of coherence, this essay deals first with non-constitutional law, then looks at constitutional law, and finally at other legal topics.

HIGGINBOTHAM is a mammoth study of the development of the law of race relations in the colonial period, and, naturally, most of it is concerned with the law of slavery. The book begins with a very poignant discussion of the author's own experiences when he was placed in segregated housing as a college student. Higginbotham was not trained as a historian, and he wrote the book at a time when he was a sitting federal judge. There are some shortcomings to this book, especially in its failure to place laws regulating blacks adequately in the context of other legal and social developments. Nevertheless, this is the best available study of the evolution of race and law in the colonial period, and it may be supplemented by important articles by Higginbotham in various law reviews in the late 1980s and early 1990s.

WATSON is a study of the evolution of slave law in all of the colonies in the Americas. For its comparative analysis alone, this is a scholarly tour de force. Watson worked from original sources in Dutch, Spanish, Portuguese, Danish, and French, as well as English. He argues that most of colonial slave law was borrowed from continental European, especially Roman, law. This is a provocative thesis that not all scholars fully accept, at least for the English colonies.

SCHWARZ considers criminal prosecutions of slaves in Virginia from the colonial period to the end of the Civil War. Relying almost entirely on manuscript court records, he examined thousands of cases and offers unusual information and insight into the way slave law was actually implemented. He argues that all slave crime was "political" in the sense that it was directed at an oppressive system, and also that all slave criminals were "twice condemned." Some scholars have criticized parts of this thesis, but all recognize the formidable research that has gone into the book, and the valuable contribution that it makes.

Like Schwarz, SCHAFER concentrates on a single jurisdiction – in her case, Louisiana. On the basis of meticulous research into previously unknown archival records of some 1200 cases appealed to the Louisiana Supreme Court between the territorial period and the Civil War, she is able to show how that court dealt with slavery, and how, when confronted with the contradiction between slaves as persons and slaves as property, it generally gave priority to the latter. Louisiana developed what is a unique jurisprudence which combined the civil law traditions inherited from France and Spain with the common law jurisprudence borrowed from other American states, and Shafer demonstrates how the latter gradually became predominant, as Louisiana law became "Americanized."

Tushnet and Fede offer broad interpretations of the American law of slavery. TUSHNET sees American judges as struggling between seeing slaves as property and seeing them as people. While his approach is sophisticated, Tushnet is at times more intent on using slave law to explore Marxist theory than he is on explaining what really happened. In a book marred by innumerable typographical errors, FEDE offers a no-holds-barred assault on almost all scholars of slavery for failing to be critical enough of southern judges.

Much of the literature on the law of slavery has been published in law reviews, rather than in book form. However, many of the key articles are reprinted in HALL, a valuable collection of important historical interpretations, and in two volumes edited by FINKELMAN, both published in 1989 in the series Articles on American Slavery. Finkelman has also edited a steady stream of other books on the law of slavery, some bringing together articles and essays, and others being collections of source material, including pamphlets, statutes and records of important cases.

A thorough and well-informed historical overview of the law of slavery has long been needed, and MORRIS (1996) has filled this gap admirably. He absorbs into the broader historical picture the unavoidable mass of detail which study of the law entails. He places much emphasis on local variations in slave law, and he suggests that serious tensions emerged within the law of slavery during the 19th century, under the pressure of rapid social and economic change. Some of Morris's conclusions may be contested, but the encyclopedic coverage and the overall authority of the work make it invaluable. It also includes a superb bibliography.

Beyond the criminal and private law of slavery, there is a literature on the place of slavery in constitutional law, international law, and legal ethics. Some of the works in this area also deal with the private and criminal law of slavery. COVER, a Yale Law professor, raises questions about the morality of judges who heard cases involving slavery. For example, he discusses attempts by one Virginia judge to use the state constitution to end slavery, and the responses of other Virginia judges to masters who tried to free slaves through their wills. Cover also discusses how southern judges dealt with issues arising from the African slave trade, and how northern judges responded to the fugitive slave laws of 1793 and 1850. His theme is "justice" and morality, and he is less interested in the history *per se*, than in how it can be used to inform jurisprudence.

CAMPBELL is the only modern book-length study of the fugitive slave law of 1850. Arguing that the law was successfully enforced, Campbell shows that it led to the return of scores of slaves to their owners. On the other hand, he does not adequately consider either the vast number of slaves not returned or the impact of resistance to that law. MORRIS (1974) is a valuable study of the northern legislative response to fugitive slaves. This book examines the laws – known as personal liberty laws – that the northern states passed to protect their own free black citizens from being kidnapped. Such laws also served to delay or prevent the return of fugitive slaves.

Tied to the return of fugitive slaves was the problem of slaves taken into the free states by their masters. FINKELMAN (1981) is a careful study of all the northern states and how they responded to the presence of slaves-in-transit. By 1860 in all but two northern states, slaves-in-transit became free the moment they entered a free state. The most famous slave to live in a free jurisdiction was Dred Scott, who in fact lived in two – the free state of Illinois and then Wisconsin territory (where slavery was forbidden under the terms of the Missouri Compromise). FEHRENBACHER is a Pulitzer Prize winning study of this important case, in which the Supreme Court ruled that Congress had no power to prohibit slavery in the territories, and Chief Justice Roger B. Taney ruled that, as a black American, Dred Scott could not be a citizen. In his elegantly written and closely argued study, Fehrenbacher places the case in the larger context of American constitutional development and antebellum politics. In effect, he uses the Dred Scott case as the focal point of a masterly interpretive history of slavery and the further extension of slavery as constitutional and judicial issues, from the origins of the republic to the outbreak of the Civil War.

HYMAN and WIECEK is an authoritative synthesis of the modern historiography of American constitutional development in the middle decades of the 19th century. They are able to place the Dred Scott case and the whole complex of problems surrounding slavery, the law and the Constitution in this larger context. WIECEK is a sensitive and careful examination of how and why antislavery groups used Constitutional doctrine and arguments in their struggle against slavery. He traces the process by which they broke down the consensus that slavery was subject to state, rather than federal control.

In a book with a different emphasis, based on previously published essays, FINKELMAN (1996) presents an indictment of the Constitution as a proslavery document. He extends his attack to the first fugitive slave law of 1793, and to the provisions and the implementation of the Northwest Ordinance of 1787, and is particularly critical of Jefferson's record on slavery. Taken together, a number of these studies build up a strong case that much of the Constitution was written with slavery in mind, and that the Supreme Court further shaped the Constitution into a proslavery compact, especially in the period from 1836 to 1861.

PAUL FINKELMAN

Slavery: Slave Trade, External

Coughtry, Jay, *The Notorious Triangle: Rhode Island and the African Slave Trade, 1700–1807*, Philadelphia: Temple University Press, 1981

Curtin, Philip D., *The Atlantic Slave Trade: A Census*, Madison: University of Wisconsin Press, 1969

Inikori, Joseph E. and Stanley L. Engerman (editors), *The Atlantic Slave Trade: Effects on Economies, Societies, and Peoples in Africa, the Americas, and Europe*, Durham, NC: Duke University Press, 1992

Klein, Herbert S., *The Middle Passage: Comparative Studies in the Atlantic Slave Trade*, Princeton: Princeton University Press, 1978

Mannix, Daniel P. with Malcolm Cowley, *Black Cargoes: A History of the Atlantic Slave Trade, 1518–1865*, New York: Viking, 1962; London: Longman, 1963

Rawley, James A., *The Transatlantic Slave Trade: A History*, New York: Norton, 1981

Solow, Barbara L. (editor), *Slavery and the Rise of the Atlantic System*, Cambridge, MA: Du Bois Institute for Afro-American Research, Harvard University, 1991

For those seeking an introduction to the history of the Atlantic slave trade, and its impact in North America, from the colonial period onwards, MANNIX and COWLEY provide a useful starting point. An older study, more narrative than analytical in its approach, and more concerned with the big picture than the minutiae, it is clearly written with the general reader

in mind – and it has attracted some criticism from specialists in the field. It does not, unfortunately, include an especially full bibliography – and in any event that is rather dated by now – but the bibliographical information that is provided offers a useful introduction to some of the sources and secondary material. Organised chronologically, the work covers the 17th through 19th centuries, from the beginnings of the Atlantic slave trade up to the Civil War and the destruction of slavery in the United States. In the process, it examines the growing reliance upon a slave-labour force in colonial America, the experience of the Middle Passage and the personalities involved in the trade, including active participants – willing and unwilling – and those who consistently and vigorously opposed it.

CURTIN's work is of a quite different order, and is now widely recognized as a classic. In the author's own words, this study "seeks to explore old knowledge, not to present new information." In brief, Curtin's aim is to offer some hard and fast facts and figures relating to the Atlantic slave trade, including the numbers of people transported, when they were brought across, where they originated and where they ended up. His conclusions are backed by a wealth of quantitative evidence. Inevitably, in a work published in 1969, some of the evidence presented has been challenged, and knowledge of the subject has been expanded by other historians. The debate about the actual scale of the Atlantic slave trade has continued during the years since Curtin wrote. However, the continuing value of Curtin's work lies in its synthesis of so much of the early material, the attempt to establish a firm base from which to pursue the subject, and the long- and short-term trends which he identifies.

Another wide-ranging, comparative examination of the Atlantic slave trade and the various nations involved in it is provided by KLEIN. His aim is to examine both the trade's demographic features and the experience of the Middle Passage. Klein begins with an assessment of the demand for slaves in America, before moving on to examine the trade to Brazil and the internal trade of that country, paying particular attention to details such as the numbers involved, the mortality rates and the size of the ships used. The second part of the work covers the importation of slaves into Virginia, as well as the English, French and Cuban slave trades. What Klein shows is that all these trades had a surprising amount in common, from the size of ships employed to the treatment which the slaves received – although the United States directly imported only some 5 per cent of the total number of slaves taken to the New World. The book includes a substantial amount of historiographical information, both in the text and in the accompanying notes.

The early 1980s saw the publication of several works on the external slave trade. RAWLEY is another general history, but a very different one from Mannix and Cowley. Rawley's is a much larger, far weightier study and is clearly aimed at a more specialist market. Indeed, the introduction makes it clear that this is intended as the first comprehensive one-volume study of the Atlantic slave trade "by a professional historian," as opposed to the "journalists and popularizers" whose work has served to misrepresent the trade. To a great extent Rawley fulfils the expectations that he raises with this statement. This is an extremely well-constructed study, which presents an impressive amount of material and a wide range of arguments in an objective, coherent and fluent manner. Regrettably, it does not include any bibliography or guide to further reading. The focus of the work is the trade between West Africa and the New World from the 15th century onwards, with particular emphasis given to the 18th century, "stressing the roles of England and the United States" in that period. As Rawley shows, despite the fact that the United States – or what was to become the United States – imported such a relatively small percentage of the total number of slaves brought across the Atlantic, the trade "was fundamental to the country's colonial and national development." Ultimately, Rawley reminds us, the trade influenced not just the American economy "but also its Constitution, its social makeup, its reformist outlook, and its political allegiances."

COUGHTRY's study of the Rhode Island slave trade shows clearly the deep involvement of colonial merchants in "the notorious triangle" which traded rum, slaves and molasses. Based on a careful study of some 934 slaving voyages from Rhode Island between 1709 and 1807, Coughtry's is no dry, statistical work. Supporting the impressive quantitative material which he has uncovered, he has used a wide range of additional source material, including contemporary newspapers, merchants' correspondence and eyewitness testimony. As a result, he is able to present a far more rounded picture of the Rhode Island slave traders, although he does not lose sight of the fact that these were men who put profits firmly before any other consideration. Although the Rhode Island legislature abolished the slave trade in 1787, many of the merchants continued to trade illegally. Indeed, some 30 per cent of the voyages which Coughtry has examined occurred after the slave trade was officially abolished. The earlier trade had been principally with Barbados and Jamaica, whereas after the Revolution the Rhode Island merchants established closer links with Cuba, and with the southern states, notably Georgia and South Carolina. A detailed Appendix, which sets out Coughtry's quantitative evidence, accompanies the volume.

There are two important recent collections of essays on the Atlantic slave trade. SOLOW has edited papers which were originally presented at a Harvard conference in 1988. They explore and develop many points made by Rawley and others concerning the importance of the Atlantic trade to the economic and social development of the United States and Western Europe, from the 16th through 19th centuries. This is a varied collection, ranging from Solow's own opening essay on "Slavery and Colonization," through essays on the Portuguese and Dutch slave trades (by Franklin W. Knight and P.C. Emmer, respectively), to David Richardson's examination of "Slavery, Trade, and Economic Growth in Eighteenth-Century New England" and David Galenson's study of the growth of slavery in the 17th-century Chesapeake. INIKORI and ENGERMAN edited another collection of conference papers, this time from a 1988 gathering at the University of Rochester, and includes papers from Martin Klein, Patrick Manning and Seymour Drescher. This collection is primarily concerned with the international dimensions and impact of the Atlantic trade, and has less to say about the North American experience – there is no essay devoted to the southern United States here, for example, although Ronald Bailey's contribution focuses on the effects of slavery on the New England elites, and Thomas Wilson and Clarence Grim examine the legacy of

the Middle Passage for 20th-century African Americans. There is more emphasis on the impact that the trade had on Africa. In their different ways, both collections are extremely valuable as indications of recent work on the Atlantic slave trade, and its economic, social and political impact on the United States.

S-M. GRANT

Slavery: Slave Trade, Internal

Bancroft, Frederic, *Slave Trading in the Old South*, Baltimore: Furst, 1931
Collins, Winfield H., *The Domestic Slave Trade of the Southern States*, New York, Broadway Publishing, 1904
Drago, Edmund L. (editor), *Broke by the War: Letters of a Slave Trader* [i.e., A.J. McElveen], Columbia: University of South Carolina Press, 1991
Fogel, Robert William and Stanley L. Engerman, *Time on the Cross: The Economics of American Negro Slavery*, Boston: Little Brown, 1974
Phillips, Ulrich Bonnell, *American Negro Slavery: A Survey of the Supply, Employment, and Control of Negro Labor as Determined by the Plantation Regime*, New York: Appleton, 1918; reprinted Baton Rouge: Louisiana State University Press, 1966
Stephenson, Wendell H., *Isaac Franklin: Slave Trader and Planter of the Old South*, Baton Rouge: Louisiana State University Press, 1938
Tadman, Michael, *Speculators and Slaves: Masters, Traders, and Slaves in the Old South*, Madison: University of Wisconsin Press, 1989, revised 1996

In 1904, COLLINS produced the first book-length study of the internal slave trade of the antebellum South. By comparing the growth rates of slave populations in different states, he established that there was a massive inter-regional movement of slaves. He suggested however, though with little evidence, that the vast bulk of this westward movement of slaves came, not by slave trading, but by planter migrations. He rejected the abolitionist claim that slavery in the older-established southern states relied for its economic survival on the breeding of slaves for sale.

In his studies of slavery, PHILLIPS – like Collins, a white supremacist – sought to make the white South confident about itself and its past, and skilfully reworked proslavery arguments through the extensive use of manuscript records from slaveholders. Reflecting the proslavery tradition, he presented slavery as a benign institution in which there was little place for the internal slave trade or for the break up of slave families by that traffic. Although he identified a few slave traders "of solid worth," he argued that generally traders were shunned. Like Collins, he argued that the trade was small, and comprised mainly unruly slaves, and a few others who were released by impoverished masters.

In 1931 BANCROFT published a richly detailed study of the trade, and designed his work as a major challenge to Phillips's thesis of benign slavery. Bancroft's work, reflecting the abolitionist tradition, emphasized slave breeding, the pervasive nature of slave trading and of family separations, and the cruelty of slavery. The great foundation of his work was the compiling of vast numbers of slave traders' advertisements from the files of southern newspapers. To this he added the results of interviews he had conducted (about 1902) with black and white southerners who remembered the slave trade. His book provides still unrivalled profiles of slave traders in towns and cities across the South; and he found that many of those traders were men of the highest social standing.

A few years after Bancroft's book was published, STEPHENSON, a follower of Phillips, produced a study of the trader Isaac Franklin. Using the evidence of one or two antebellum witnesses, he assumed that Franklin avoided family separations and that he had a reputation for unusually honest dealing. Franklin was portrayed as an interesting anomaly, rather than as part of a massive and cruel traffic in slaves.

FOGEL and ENGERMAN argued that slave families were protected and encouraged, and that slaves – with high morale, and enjoying positive incentives – co-operated in a highly profitable economic system. Fogel and Engerman's evidence on profitability cut much of the ground from the thesis that the older states had relied on slave breeding for their economic survival. Their analysis of the slave trade and separations was based on the coastal traffic between the Chesapeake ports and New Orleans. They found that males constituted about 60 per cent of that trade, but made up only about 51 per cent of the total movement of slaves between the states. They therefore concluded that, since slave trading had little effect on the sex ratio of total slave movements, it could only have made up, at most, 16 per cent of the long-distance movement of slaves. In order to estimate the scale of family separations – and using the New Orleans trade – they counted numbers of children sold without parents and numbers of slaves sold in mother-and-offspring units (without husband). It seemed from this sort of evidence that only about 2 per cent of the marriages of slaves involved in the westward trek were destroyed by that movement. TADMAN's work makes clear, however, that the New Orleans trade was unique. Sales to the sugar plantations of southern Louisiana skewed the New Orleans trade towards sturdy, adult males. Tadman's work shows that sex ratios are no guide to the scale of the trade, since the internal slave trade to all areas except southern Louisiana carried equal numbers of males and females. Furthermore, the composition of the New Orleans trade (with exceptionally low percentages of young women and children) gives no useful guide to the general pattern of separations in the trade.

In sharp contrast to Fogel and Engerman, Tadman argued that fully 60 to 70 per cent of inter-regional slave movements were the result of slave trading. He estimated that the trade broke one in five marriages of slaves born in the exporting states, and separated one in three of that region's children from one or both of their parents. Calculations of the scale of the trade were based partly on an analysis of the highly age-selective nature of the total inter-regional slave movement – a pattern which fitted very closely with the age-selective slave trade, but which did not fit with the basically non-selective character of planter migrations. Further evidence on the scale of the trade came from a detailed count of slave traders operating in South Carolina in the 1850s. Tadman found traders to be intensely active, not just in major urban areas, as documented by Bancroft, but throughout every county of the rural South. He found the trade to be overwhelmingly an overland affair, with the Chesapeake-New Orleans coastal trade being highly exceptional. Even more than Bancroft, he found that traders were generally men of high status. Further, those who sold to the trader usually did so simply in order to make a profit, rather than to stave off economic distress. Tadman argued that the slave trade showed that a profound gulf existed between the slaveholders' benevolent self-image and their behaviour towards slaves and their families. A resilient slave community, he argued, rejected the values of their masters, especially since those values paid so little respect to slave families.

DRAGO is an edited collection of letters from a slave-buying agent of the prominent Charleston slave trader, Ziba Oakes. The letters give revealing insights into an important aspect of the sordid business of slave trading.

MICHAEL TADMAN

Slavery: Slave Culture and Community

Blassingame, John W., *The Slave Community: Plantation Life in the Antebellum South*, New York: Oxford University Press, 1972, revised 1979

Boles, John B., *Black Southerners, 1619–1869*, Lexington: University Press of Kentucky, 1983

Frey, Sylvia R., *Water from the Rock: Black Resistance in a Revolutionary Age*, Princeton: Princeton University Press, 1991

Genovese, Eugene D., *Roll, Jordan, Roll: The World the Slaves Made*, New York: Pantheon, 1974; London: Deutsch, 1975

Gutman, Herbert G., *The Black Family in Slavery and Freedom, 1750–1925*, New York: Pantheon, and Oxford: Blackwell, 1976

Joyner, Charles, *Down by the Riverside: A South Carolina Slave Community*, Urbana: University of Illinois Press, 1984

Kolchin, Peter, *American Slavery, 1619–1877*, New York: Hill and Wang, 1993; London: Penguin, 1995

Levine, Lawrence W., *Black Culture and Black Consciousness: Afro-American Folk Thought from Slavery to Freedom*, New York: Oxford University Press, 1977

Miller, Randall M. and John David Smith (editors), *Dictionary of Afro-American Slavery*, Westport, CT: Greenwood Press, 1988, revised 1997

Mullin, Michael, *Africa in America: Slave Acculturation and Resistance in the American South and the British Caribbean, 1736–1831*, Urbana: University of Illinois Press, 1992

Raboteau, Albert J., *Slave Religion: The "Invisible Institution" in the Antebellum South*, New York: Oxford University Press, 1978

Stuckey, Sterling, *Slave Culture: Nationalist Theory and the Foundations of Black America*, New York and Oxford: Oxford University Press, 1987

Wood, Peter H., *Black Majority: Negroes in Colonial South Carolina from 1670 Through the Stono Rebellion*, New York: Knopf, 1974

For the past quarter century or more students of American slavery have moved away from an emphasis on slave treatment, where slaves were often seen as objects largely controlled by masters, to an emphasis on slave culture and community, where slaves are recognized as active agents shaping their own world. As Eugene Genovese put it, the question was no longer what was done to the slaves but what they did for themselves. BLASSINGAME led the way with a pioneering book using slave autobiographies and objects that slaves made to reconstruct a vigorous slave culture, based on an African grammar in voice and crafts, that freed the slaves from the master's ascriptions of status and personality. For Blassingame, different slaves responded in different ways to bondage, and arrived at their balance between assertiveness and submissiveness.

The use of slave-created documents drove the scholarship. GENOVESE relied heavily on WPA ex-slave narratives and planters' accounts to fit slave culture into a model of hegemony, drawn from Marxist Antonio Gramsci, that emphasized an ongoing dialectic between master and slave. But even as slaves claimed social and cultural space from supposedly paternalistic masters, they vitiated their revolutionary power by accepting the terms of engagement defined by the master. Genovese places religion at the center of the dialectic, with masters feeding their own Christian beliefs into the slaves' religion, while the slaves gained a sense of moral superiority over masters who did not follow their own precepts.

Most scholars rejected Genovese's Marxism, but many accepted the dialectic. LEVINE, for example, argues that as a pre-literate people slaves expressed their values through music, stories, material culture, and religion, and crafted a sense of self as a separate and worthy people. Like Genovese, he characterizes slaves as "pre-political," resisting bondage more by forging their own internal culture than by any organized, overt action. Slave culture turned slaves inward, but in the context of responses to bondage.

GUTMAN dissented from those who argued that slave culture was principally a survival mechanism and a response to whites. Rather, by examining the "last generation of slaves," he insisted that slave culture, as embodied in conceptions of "family" and "community," had grown from African roots and American experience, and that most slaves maintained kin associations over time and space. The two-parent slave family, however endangered by bondage, provided the foundation for blacks' identities in freedom.

The argument for a self-generating slave culture reached its apotheosis in STUCKEY's inquiry into the question of how a single African American culture was formed out of many African sources. He claims a greater universality of slave culture in America, in northern and southern settings, because he casts African culture in almost pan-African terms. He also warns that too much contact with whites undermined black leadership coming from the churches. In his view, only those who kept their ties to slave culture offered a truly nationalistic vision.

The character of slave religion stood at the center of any assessment of culture and community. RABOTEAU locates slave religion in self-created, independent, African-rooted beliefs and practices and sees the religion of the quarters as the springboard for black leadership. As something which the slaves made by and for themselves, even in adapting Christianity to their own folk beliefs, slave religion became the nucleus of community and the means whereby slaves judged one another.

In a skilful synthesis of the scholarship, BOLES assumes a longitudinal perspective to mark the environmental, social, and cultural factors shaping Africans' and African Americans' adaptations. He finds much creativity and diversity within the slave community, but, as in his collection, *Masters and Slaves in the House of the Lord* (1988), he also emphasizes the shared religious experience between black and white. For Boles, the critical moment for African American community development occurred in the mid-18th century, when slave population density and sexual parity made communication easier and family life possible, and when slaves became self-conscious about ritual.

Tracking the story of African American culture back to its colonial taproot became an important focus of scholarship. WOOD makes the case that, in the early years of settlement, the "black majority" defined many of the ways in which black and white carved out a new society in frontier South Carolina. The Africans' comparative advantages in technical skills allowed them to acculturate more readily to a semi-tropical environment than their masters, but such skills also made them at the same time more valuable and more dangerous to their masters. Wood anticipated very recent interest in African American-Indian cultural interaction, but his main focus was on the uneasy and often contradictory relationship between black and white.

Comparison of the acculturating experiences in different settings promised to show how place affected culture. MULLIN examines the formation of family life, religious expressions, and local economies in Virginia, South Carolina, and the West Indies, and concludes that acculturation varied according to crop grown, climate, population density, attitudes of planters, the household economy of the slaves, and more. He rejects Genovese's and others' insistence on a growing paternalism among North American planters, stressing instead how any patriarchy faded as planters put business above all else by the 19th century.

The insistence on place resounded among folklorists, anthropologists, and archaeologists who were increasingly entering the discussion. Using folklore, especially from the WPA slave narratives, ethnography, architecture, and more, JOYNER excavates the lives of slaves in All Saints Parish, South Carolina, in a model study emphasizing the importance and peculiarity of place and time and cautioning against large generalizations about slave culture.

Critical moments, the time of interactions, also occasioned scholarly interest. The era of the American Revolution increasingly came to be seen as the defining moment for the creating of an African American slave culture and community. FREY shows that an emerging African American culture in the pre-revolutionary South, due to dramatic demographic growth and the formation of black families, increased the cultural distance between black and white, yet in the Revolutionary age blacks became both more American with their embrace of evangelical Protestantism and Revolutionary ideology and more African American with their creation of large free black communities and churches.

A major effort to bring together the variegated and expansive scholarship was made by MILLER and SMITH in their dictionary, which distils much of the enormous literature on slavery from the 1960s through the 1980s in more than 200 entries on virtually every aspect of slavery, from Africanisms to whipping. Collectively, the essays suggest the variety of slave responses to bondage culturally and socially based on place and time, and also the dynamic, syncretic nature of slave culture in North America.

With so much scholarship at hand, a new synthesis was required. KOLCHIN identifies the growth of slave families, the occupational diversity and socioeconomic differentiation among slaves, and the Christianization of slaves as the critical processes that transformed Africans into African Americans and informed slave communities. By paying much attention to colonial America and by taking a comparative historical perspective, he, like Boles, sees culture as an evolutionary process and, like Mullin, asks how different political, economic, and social systems shaped slavery and slave culture. Therein lie the concerns that continue to invite inquiry into the measure and meaning of slave culture and community.

RANDALL M. MILLER

See also Colonial History: Slavery and Indentured Servitude

Slavery: Slave Resistance and Rebellion

Aptheker, Herbert, *American Negro Slave Revolts*, New York: Columbia University Press, and London: King and Staples, 1943

Bauer, Raymond and Alice H. Bauer, "Day to Day Resistance to Slavery," *Journal of American Negro History*, 27(2), 1942

Blassingame, John W., *The Slave Community: Plantation Life in the Antebellum South*, New York: Oxford University Press, 1972, revised 1979

Elkins, Stanley M., *Slavery: A Problem in American Institutional and Intellectual Life*, Chicago: University of Chicago Press, 1959; 3rd edition, 1976

Fogel, Robert William and Stanley L. Engerman, *Time on the Cross: The Economics of American Negro Slavery*, Boston: Little Brown, 1974

Genovese, Eugene D., *Roll, Jordan, Roll: The World the Slaves Made*, New York: Pantheon, 1974; London: Deutsch, 1975

Genovese, Eugene D., *From Rebellion to Revolution: Afro-American Slave Revolts in the Making of the Modern World*, Baton Rouge: Louisiana State University Press, 1979

Phillips, Ulrich Bonnell, *American Negro Slavery: A Survey of the Supply, Employment, and Control of Negro Labor as Determined by the Plantation Regime*, New York: Appleton, 1918; reprinted Baton Rouge: Louisiana State University Press, 1966

Stampp, Kenneth M., *The Peculiar Institution: Slavery in the Ante-Bellum South*, New York: Knopf, 1956; London: Eyre and Spottiswoode, 1964

Tadman, Michael, *Speculators and Slaves: Masters, Traders, and Slaves in the Old South*, Madison: University of Wisconsin Press, 1989, revised 1996

In interpreting the scale and character of slave resistance and rebellion in North America, three basic frameworks have been important – slave submission to their masters and to the system of slavery, rejection of the system by slaves, and accommodation within the system. Because there seem to have been few major revolts in North America, but at the same time there is much evidence of day-to-day resistance, most historians have worked with some sort of accommodation theory. Such theories, however, have ranged from models of close accommodation (with substantial sharing of values between slaves and masters) to models of strictly limited accommodation (with slave values being largely independent of those of masters).

From the 1920s to the 1950s, PHILLIPS's conservative, racist version of accommodation was highly influential. Blacks were seen by Phillips as being innately lazy, and this supposed laziness was presented as a fundamental restraint on the master and on the nature of slavery. Supposedly, masters had to accept slow and inefficient work, and came to do so happily – so that slavery became, it was claimed, a "school" for the gradual education of "primitive" blacks. In such an analysis, slave resistance had little place, and a tradition of revolt was unthinkable. Slaves were seen as being naturally docile and contented, and were said to be intimately linked with their owners by ties of strong mutual affection. Such a theory served to turn the legacy of slave exploitation into a comfortable foundation for white southern history.

The Marxist historian APTHEKER sought, by cataloguing slave revolts across the history of North American slavery, to establish – contrary to Phillips – that slaves were far from being docile, and that they resisted their masters and rejected their masters' values. Aptheker found evidence to suggest some 250 slave revolts in North America. Much of this material (drawn from contemporary newspapers) seems to have concerned rumours of revolts and panics about possible risings – with very few cases indeed of insurrections which succeeded in destroying white lives and property. This evidence does not establish that North American slaves had a tradition of revolt, but it does cast doubt on the claim that masters saw their slaves as being uniformly docile.

In the 1940s a pioneering article by BAUER and BAUER proposed a theory of very limited accommodation, and argued for a very vigorous tradition of "day-to-day" resistance, short of revolt. Such resistance included slowing down of work, destroying slave-owners' property, feigning illness, and even self-mutilation. Docility was seen as a myth fostered by pro-slavery propaganda, and inadvertently bolstered by the anti-slavery tactic of presenting slaves as good workers who were unfairly exploited. The thesis of day-to-day resistance is of great importance, but it is difficult to establish how widespread such forms of resistance were, and whether such activity represented a communal pattern of solidarity against slavery.

In 1956 STAMPP launched a major counter-attack against the Phillips thesis, in which day-to-day resistance was of great importance. Slaveowners, however, were seen as having powerfully destructive effects on slave families and communities. Slave culture and community were seen as being deeply compromised, and slaves according to Stampp lived in confusion "between two cultures" (African and white), unable to gain stability from either.

ELKINS put forward a highly controversial "submission" argument – that slaves in North America became infantilized, and subordinated their wills to those of their masters. According to Elkins, Latin American slavery saw major restraints on the power of masters, because of the influence of the Catholic Church, of legal traditions, and of the Iberian colonial authorities. In contrast, we are told, North American masters had absolute power. An analogy was drawn with Nazi concentration camps, where Elkins argued that, because of their extreme powerlessness, inmates identified with their oppressors. Elkins rejected Phillips's notion of innate black docility, but maintained that extreme powerlessness turned North American slaves into docile "Sambos." This argument, however, was not supported by empirical evidence, was founded on a highly dubious comparison with Latin America, and – as numerous historians have now shown – ignored much evidence of slave resilience and community.

BLASSINGAME, a black historian, issued an all-out challenge to Elkins, and used evidence from slaves and ex-slaves to see slavery from the perspective of the slave quarters. Although he accepted that open revolts were extremely rare, he argued for a vigorous slave community in which various forms of resistance were widely practised.

In their controveresial 1974 study, FOGEL and ENGERMAN launched a major accommodation thesis, seeing slavery as an efficient capitalist system, and seeing slaves as working diligently in response to positive incentives. Masters, we are told, encouraged and protected families and provided good material treatment for their slaves, and offered the attraction of a hierarchy of skilled jobs at which to aim. According to this thesis, an important sharing of values greatly limited the scale of resistance and rebelliousness.

GENOVESE (1974) elaborated a profoundly important thesis of close accommodation. This Marxist thesis saw southern slave owners as anti-bourgeois paternalists. Masters owned their labour force (the slaves), and this special relationship with labour was seen as leading to more personal labour relations than in free-market capitalism. Violence was seen as the vital guarantee of slave-owner power, but the routine of slavery was seen as being based on a paternal "hegemony." Masters and slaves were locked in a class struggle, and slaves saw slavery as wrong. But masters gave slaves certain "privileges," such as extensive protection of marriages, and moderation of work regimes. Masters developed a confident, paternal self-image, and slaves worked within slavery to maintain what they saw as "rights" – and what masters saw as privileges. Slaves and masters were, therefore, seen as sharing important values. Day-to-day resistance was seen as being mainly individualistic, and as non-threatening to the slave owners' hegemony. GENOVESE (1979) compared patterns of revolt across the Americas, and explored the higher incidence of revolt in Latin America and the West Indies, compared with North America. Critically important explanatory factors included the larger size of plantation units, higher ratios of

black to white, and higher percentages of African-born slaves in the West Indies and in Latin America. Genovese also argued, rather speculatively, that, across the Americas, revolts before the French Revolution generally aimed at escape, while from the French Revolution onwards they aimed fundamentally to challenge the system of slavery.

In his 1989 book, and more explicitly in the 1996 edition, TADMAN questioned theories of close accommodation, and suggested a thesis of strictly limited accommodation, with slaves rejecting the values of masters. He argued that the internal slave trade and family separations were pervasive in antebellum slavery. The scale of separations led him to suggest that there was a gulf between the slaveholders' benevolent self-image and their actual behaviour. Limited privileges to "key slaves" (defined as drivers and their wives, and certain senior domestic slaves) allowed masters to see themselves as being benevolent, while in fact they acted with racist indifference, especially towards the great bulk of non-key slaves.

MICHAEL TADMAN

Slavery: Proslavery Thought

Faust, Drew Gilpin, *A Sacred Circle: The Dilemma of the Intellectual in the Old South, 1840–1860*, Baltimore: Johns Hopkins University Press, 1977

Fredrickson, George M., *The Black Image in the White Mind: The Debate on Afro-American Character and Destiny, 1817–1914*, New York: Harper, 1971

Genovese, Eugene D., *The World the Slaveholders Made: Two Essays in Interpretation*, New York: Pantheon, 1969

Genovese, Eugene D., *The Slaveholders' Dilemma: Freedom and Progress in Southern Conservative Thought, 1820–1860*, Columbia: University of South Carolina Press, 1992

Greenberg, Kenneth S., *Masters and Statesmen: The Political Culture of American Slavery*, Baltimore: Johns Hopkins University Press, 1985

Jenkins, William S., *Pro-Slavery Thought in the Old South*, Chapel Hill: University of North Carolina Press, 1935

Oakes, James, *The Ruling Race: A History of American Slaveholders*, New York: Knopf, 1982

Shore, Laurence, *Southern Capitalists: The Ideological Leadership of an Elite, 1832–1885*, Chapel Hill: University of North Carolina Press, 1986

Tise, Larry E., *Proslavery: A History of the Defense of Slavery in America, 1701–1840*, Athens: University of Georgia Press, 1987

Dismissed as an abhorrent ideology, and neglected as an area of study, proslavery thought was until quite recently the subject of only one serious book-length study. The standard, but now dated, account is JENKINS which offers a lengthy but useful catalogue of the various strands of the proslavery argument – religious, legal, ethical, scientific, moral and political. He demonstrates how the movement developed and became more systematically defensive in the South after the 1830s, in the face of a radical northern abolitionist assault. Jenkins is partly responsible for furthering the early stereotypes of proslavery thought as little more than a regional oddity, and as a superficial and deceptive vehicle for propaganda.

More recently, historians have recognised the importance of proslavery thought as a genuinely felt and coherent ideology, and therefore a critical window into the southern mind. TISE is only the second full-length book devoted specifically to proslavery thought, and his sometimes convoluted account is notable for tracing the historical origins and evolution of the defence of slavery back to the colonial period. Moreover, Tise detects a consistent and significant strand of northern proslavery thought, and he also gives the proslavery argument a comparative, transatlantic perspective.

For further elucidation of this crucial element of antebellum American thought, it is necessary to turn to chapters or sections of wider studies of southern politics and society. In their different ways, many such studies examine the political and moral dilemmas faced by slaveholders in articulating an elaborate justification of human bondage in southern society, which would serve the dual purpose of maintaining a white consensus (and the loyalty of nonslaveholding whites through opportunities for upward mobility), and securing the power of the planter elite. According to SHORE, in a work which deals with the broader framework of a capitalist "transvaluation" in the ideology of the ruling elite, the primary argument for the virtues of slavery was that, rescued from the drudgery of labor in subtropical conditions for which they were ill-suited, slaveholders were assured the leisure and freedom to concentrate on the cultivation of mind and manners. Thus, in rejecting northern critiques of southern "backwardness," planters presented slavery in a positive, progressive light, as the bulwark of southern civilization, and the basis of a successful agricultural economy.

Exploration of the moral dilemma behind the proslavery argument is further enhanced by FAUST in a brilliant and highly readable study of southern intellectual leadership. Faust skilfully describes how the "Sacred Circle," a network of five alienated, elite southern thinkers, adapted a national evangelical reform creed to define a "sacred vocation" of moral stewardship and Christian duty, which in the process led to an idiosyncratic defence of slavery. Scornful of the Old South's disregard for the role of transcendent "men of mind" in practical life, these self-absorbed and ambitious intellectual "exiles" used the defence of slavery as a vehicle to prescribe a powerful social role for themselves, as well as a moral leadership, guiding and educating their region, through the civilizing of slaves and the "elevating" of masters.

In a landmark assessment of southern political culture and the tensions within the master-slave relationship, GREENBERG demonstrates how slaveholders attempted to reconcile their genuine belief in liberty with the realities of human bondage. To their way of thinking, the defence of slavery helped to ensure liberty for all whites. To counter the critical stereotype of abusive slaveholders, and also to offer a favorable contrast to the precarious existence of northern wage laborers, planters proclaimed their responsibility to protect and care for their chattels – and not just as a matter of economic self-interest. By removing the threat of antagonism within the framework of slavery and emphasizing a paternalistic ideal, slaveholders could present an organic, harmonious and interdependent community, as well as define the parameters of their own power.

Few historians have projected the world-view of slaveholders more convincingly than Eugene D. Genovese – which on the surface seems ironic given the political perspective that he presents. In GENOVESE (1969), he links together George Fitzhugh's blistering critique of northern capitalism and the suffering of "wage slaves" and his own Marxist interpretation of a pre-bourgeois, seigneurial southern slave society. Genovese is keen to stress the importance of proslavery thought as a political ideology perpetuating the hegemony of a master class. This is a stimulating and provocative work marred in places by an intrusive ideological framework, and the over-application of class analysis at the expense of questions of race. In a much more recent brief study, based on a series of lectures, GENOVESE (1992) considers a problem addressed by Shore and others: the ambiguous response of southern conservative intellectuals and slaveholders to progress. Genovese explores their dilemma of how to welcome the positive benefits of progress – in the shape of material wealth and greater freedom – without losing the traditional social order upon which their authority and wealth rested. In a challenging and compelling study, Genovese demonstrates how southern thinkers backed themselves into a dark ideological corner from which there was no escape.

Proslavery thought has often been interpreted by historians as being created to allay the South's own deeply-held anxieties about the moral contradictions inherent in slavery. OAKES is concerned with the troubled consciences of slaveholders who attempted to shake off their guilt and remorse over slavery, as well as their fear of divine retribution. Torn between their religious convictions and the lure of the accumulation of wealth, they devised a progressive, secular ideology, fusing a "gospel of prosperity," which stressed the divine sanctioning of slavery, upward mobility for all whites, westward expansion and material success, with a firm endorsement of white supremacy.

It is this latter idea which concerns FREDRICKSON, who detects, from the 1840s onwards, a more explicit and virulently racist strain of proslavery sentiment. Unresponsive to the traditionally hierarchical and paternalistic arguments of the aristocratic Old South, more abrasive, egalitarian slaveholders of a newer generation, located in the newer frontier regions of the Southwest, utilized new scientific and ethnological theories of black inferiority to develop the idea of what Fredrickson calls a "herrenvolk" democracy for the master race, based on white supremacy. Not all observers see such a clear distinction between one school of proslavery thought and another, but Fredrickson presents his case forcefully, and suggests the broad appeal of this kind of herrenvolk democracy to the mass of the southern white population.

WAYNE J. JOHNSON

See also Race; South: Colonial Period to Civil War

Small Towns

Atherton, Lewis E., *Main Street on the Middle Border*, Bloomington: Indiana University Press, 1954

Bailey, Barbara Ruth, *Main Street, Northeastern Oregon: The Founding and Development of Small Towns*, Portland: Oregon Historical Society, 1982

Carlton, David L., *Mill and Town in South Carolina, 1880–1920*, Baton Rouge: Louisiana State University Press, 1982

Crockett, Norman L., *The Black Towns*, Lawrence: Regents Press of Kansas, 1979

Daniels, Bruce C., *The Connecticut Town: Growth and Development, 1635–1790*, Middletown, CT: Wesleyan University Press, 1979

Doyle, Don Harrison, *The Social Order of a Frontier Community: Jacksonville, Illinois, 1825–70*, Urbana: University of Illinois Press, 1978

Faragher, John Mack, *Sugar Creek: Life on the Illinois Prairie*, New Haven: Yale University Press, 1986

Hickey, Joseph V., *Ghost Settlement on the Prairie: A Biography of Thurman, Kansas*, Lawrence: University Press of Kansas, 1995

Lingeman, Richard, *Small Town America: A Narrative History, 1620–the Present*, New York: Putnam, 1980

Lockridge, Kenneth A., *A New England Town, the First Hundred Years: Dedham Massachusetts, 1636–1736*, New York: Norton, 1970, revised 1985

Underwood, Kathleen, *Town Building on the Colorado Frontier*, Albuquerque: University of New Mexico Press, 1987

In United States history, a great deal of attention has been paid to the growth of America's urban areas, and how they have contributed to the economic, political, and cultural growth of the country. The small town, however, has also played a pivotal role in American history. Traditionally, historical examination of American small towns has been limited to a study of their commercial and political life, and how the social structure of those towns reflected the so-called "American character". In the last thirty years, however, more comprehensive studies have emerged, studies that examine a wide range of social and cultural, as well as economic and political factors that not only situate the small town within a broader social and cultural context, but question some of the traditional notions of what small-town America was like.

LOCKRIDGE is widely known as one of the best early studies of a small American community. In his history of Dedham, Massachusetts from 1636 to 1736, Lockridge discusses the utopian and communal goals of the town's founders and traces the transformation of these goals over the years. The township of Dedham was originally conceived as the hoped-for embodiment of many of the Puritan ideals of egalitarianism and order, and for many years land availability, geographic isolation, and a relatively homogeneous population served to make Dedham a small, stable, and economically self-sufficient community. As Dedham grew from a small village of several hundred people to a provincial town of nearly 2000 inhabitants in the mid-18th century, and land and resources became scarce, class differences became more pronounced and threatened the stability of the community. Lockridge also explores how the rise of individualistic ideals began to undermine the original communal orientation of the town's leaders and inhabitants.

DANIELS discusses the development of the Connecticut town in the colonial period. He explores the process of town settlement and formation, the political and economic life of small communities in New England, and the transformation of the relationships between church and government at this time. Although primarily a demographic study, Daniels does discuss the communal framework of these communities. Arguing that historians cannot generalize about the history of the small New England towns, he shows that even towns within the same region were often very different in their structure and their political, economic, and religious life.

The transformation of communal ideals in the late 18th and early 19th century was due in large part to changing economic circumstances in the United States. However, these conceptions of community were not restricted to Puritan New England; such goals and ideals could also be seen in other towns across the country, as studies such as Doyle and Faragher show. DOYLE focuses on the question of community-building in a period of headlong westward expansion, and with a highly mobile population. He suggests that a core population who settled and stayed in the town, promoted and protected a sense of community, amid all the comings and goings of other groups. Doyle also includes fascinating discussions of the role of boosterism in promoting small towns, ethnic and racial tensions in Jacksonville, and the relationship between local and national issues, particularly at the time of the Civil War. FARAGHER examines a community of small towns in the Sugar Creek valley of Illinois in the 19th century, and traces the transformation of life in rural America. A comprehensive and highly readable social history, Faragher uses a wide variety of sources such as newspapers, account books, and personal accounts. He examines the economic base of these communities, exploring the often adversarial economic relationships between small farmers and "progressive agriculturalists", those individuals interested in transforming agriculture into a capitalist enterprise. Faragher also devotes considerable attention to family and social life, particularly the social status of women, in rural communities. He includes an extensive discussion of marriage and kinship, childbirth, social perceptions of death, and relationships between men and women.

HICKEY also explores the dynamics of rural small town life in his "biography" of Thurman, Kansas. Located in the heart of the Kansas Flint Hills, Thurman was, in 1900, a thriving farming and ranching community. By 1944, Thurman was virtually extinct, as the impact of agricultural changes and the economic hardship of the Great Depression resulted in the closing of its schools, churches, and stores, and eventually in the town's desertion. Hickey focuses on the social, political, and economic ramifications of the rise of commercial agriculture in the late-19th and early 20th centuries, as well as the changes confronting the western cattle industry at this time. Hickey also places Thurman within a broader context, exploring how the life (and death) of a community like Thurman reflected changes occurring in communities across the country.

In histories of small-town America, issues of race and the role of the many ethnic groups who participated in small town formation are often neglected. Although town settlement by European immigrants is often explored, many studies often fail to acknowledge that a great many of America's small towns were settled and run by native non-whites. CROCKETT is one of the few histories to examine the founding and growth of African American towns. After the Civil War and

Emancipation, many former slaves, as well as free men and women from the northern states, weary of persistent racial persecution and violence, sought safe haven in communities of their own. Many African American leaders at this time felt that the only solution was to form stable, economically viable, isolated communities in which black families could live and prosper without the constant threat of racial discrimination. Crockett examines the black town "experiment" that took place in the late 19th century, focusing on the formation, growth, and eventual demise of five black towns in Kansas, Mississippi, and Oklahoma. He explores the impact of isolation on these towns, as well as the impact of the regional and national social and economic transformations that eventually resulted in their demise.

CARLTON examines the economic and social developments of towns in South Carolina in the late 19th and early 20th centuries. This study focuses primarily on the response to the rise of the textile industry, and the resulting political and social changes, within small South Carolina towns. As men and women moved into towns from rural areas to work in the textile mills, communities which had formerly been divided solely along racial lines were rapidly becoming divided also along class lines. Carlton does not devote much attention to the social or cultural implications of this new divisiveness, preferring to focus more extensively on the economic impacts of industrialism.

UNDERWOOD explores the process of town building in the West in her study of community formation on the Colorado frontier. As men and women moved west in the 19th century, the process of community formation that had been accomplished so long ago in the East had to begin anew. Underwood examines the economic, political, and demographic factors affecting town settlement and formation in the West through the turn of the century, including a discussion of the communal goals and ideals brought to town formation by settlers. This is one of the few studies to focus extensively on the role of the family and social interaction in these small towns, as well as the settlers' interactions and relationships with the Native American tribes in the region.

BAILEY looks even further west to town development and small town life in northeastern Oregon. This study is sometimes overly simplistic in its narrative focus and does not explore larger social and cultural issues. However, Bailey is nonetheless a straightforward demographic study of the founding and growth of towns in this region, and is useful especially for its exploration of the economic history of the far western communities during the age of western expansion and settlement.

Finally, LINGEMAN provides a useful resource for examination of small towns throughout America, from the 17th century to the present. This study is a compilation of the author's essays on small town life in New England, the southern states, and the frontier towns in the 19th century. There is no visible link between the essays included in this volume, and Lingeman provides few hints of any overarching theme. Nonetheless, this study is especially useful for its extensive list of bibliographic references, and provides much insight into the economic, political, and social life of small towns in the United States. Another general history of small town life is ATHERTON, a mainly descriptive – and sometimes nostalgic

and sentimental – account of the economy, society and culture of midwestern small towns from the mid-19th to the mid-20th century.

ROBIN L.E. HEMENWAY

Smith, Alfred E. 1873–1944
Political leader, reformer and presidential candidate

Eldot, Paula, *Governor Alfred E. Smith: The Politician as Reformer*, New York: Garland, 1983

Handlin, Oscar, *Al Smith and His America*, Boston: Little Brown, 1958

Hapgood, Norman and Henry Moskowitz, *Up from the City Streets: Alfred E. Smith, A Biographical Study in Contemporary Politics*, New York: Harcourt Brace, 1927

Josephson, Matthew and Hannah Josephson, *Al Smith, Hero of the Cities: A Political Portrait Drawing on the Papers of Frances Perkins*, Boston: Houghton Mifflin, 1969

O'Connor, Richard, *The First Hurrah: A Biography of Alfred E. Smith*, New York: Putnam, 1970

Perry, Elisabeth Israels, *Belle Moskowitz: Feminine Politics and the Exercise of Power in the Age of Alfred E. Smith*, New York: Oxford University Press, 1987

Pringle, Henry F., *Alfred E. Smith: A Critical Study*, New York: Macy-Masius, 1927; reprinted, New York: AMS, 1970

Alfred E. Smith is remembered primarily as the man who lost the 1928 presidential election to Herbert Hoover, and as the first Roman Catholic to receive the nomination of a major political party. He has also been characterized as the first product of an urban political machine to rise through the ranks from precinct runner to presidential candidate, as a distinguished Progressive Era legislator, as the four-term progressive governor of the country's most important state during the generally reactionary era of the 1920s, and as the architect of the "Al Smith revolution" which brought millions of immigrant-stock voters into presidential politics for the first time.

The most widely known account of Smith's career is HANDLIN, essentially an extended interpretive essay, in which Smith stands as the archetype of the immigrant version of the "American Dream" of nearly unlimited social mobility. Writing prior to the election of John F. Kennedy, Handlin presents Smith's failure to attain the presidency in 1928 as a personal and national tragedy that demonstrated the sad fact that "no Catholic or Jew could aspire to be President, whatever other avenues of advance might be open" (p.189). Handlin's writing style and point of view are so highly personalized that it frequently seems as if he is writing Smith's autobiography. While highly sympathetic to Smith up through the 1932 presidential election, Handlin nevertheless concludes that "from 1933 onward ... the man lost his grip." For all the book's familiar tone and paucity of detail, it provides a perceptive analysis of Smith's strengths and weaknesses, and of his accomplishments and failures.

Much richer in detail, though less acute in interpretive insights, is JOSEPHSON. The Josephsons were requested by the daughter of Frances Perkins, FDR's famed Secretary of Labor, to complete a manuscript begun by her mother, a pioneer social worker and intimate collaborator of Al Smith as legislator and governor. The Josephsons supplemented Perkins's three draft chapters, extensive notes, and tape-recorded recollections with their own researches into Smith's papers, official records, newspaper files and personal interviews with surviving associates of both notables. Of particular significance is their exposition of Smith's ethnic origins, which reveals that "this country's most famous Irish-American, was not after all a 'pure Irishman' at all, but a fine mixture of Italian, German, English, and Irish strains, a true product of the melting pot of New York." The Josephsons also explore the post-1926 struggle for Smith's soul fought between his "kitchen cabinet" of party leaders, intellectuals, and social workers, and his "golfing cabinet", composed of wealthy and successful Catholics and Jews seeking political recognition and clout. While the former, of whom Perkins was a charter member, receive a great deal of the credit for Smith's advanced progressivism, the latter reap much of the blame for his seemingly inexorable turn to the right after 1928, and for his increasingly strident alienation from Roosevelt and the New Deal. The Josephsons conclude with Perkins that he was "the man responsible for the first drift in the United States toward the conception that political responsibility involved a duty to improve the life of the people."

Even more influential than Frances Perkins in Smith's "kitchen cabinet" was Belle Moskowitz, another prominent social worker. Smith himself acknowledged that she "had the greatest brain of anyone I ever knew." The story of their highly effective collaboration is recounted by PERRY, who is Moskowitz's granddaughter and a distinguished historian in her own right. The author delineates the evolution of the "partnership" between Moskowitz and Smith, beginning with his first campaign for governor of New York in 1918 and ending with her death in 1932. Perry subscribes to the sentiment, attributed to Democratic official Molly Dewson, that Moskowitz was "Al Smith's tent pole," the real author of many of the social programs for which Smith was celebrated. Perry offers an inside look, both at the evolution of the social policy initiatives that made New York the nation's banner progressive state, and a model for the New Deal, and at "the selling of Al Smith" in 1928, a campaign in which Moskowitz served as the New Yorker's publicity director. She is also revealing on the subject of Smith's unsuccessful efforts to wrest the 1932 Democratic nomination from Franklin D. Roosevelt.

Far less complicated is HAPGOOD and MOSKOWITZ, the product of a collaboration between a literary critic and the husband of Belle Moskowitz. Written before Smith's nomination for the presidency, the book has all the enthusiasm and subjectivity of a campaign tract. It contains neither footnotes nor bibliography, and is valuable primarily for understanding the excitement and loyalty which Smith was able to generate in his followers. The authors present Smith as "the son of the city", the product of "the loves and hopes of fathers and mothers measured in millions; not of its surface changes, but of its continuing needs."

Filled with interesting anecdotes, but deficient in critical analysis, is O'CONNOR who stresses the role of Smith's Catholicism in his 1928 defeat, as well as his ongoing feud with publisher William Randolph Hearst. He also compares and contrasts Smith's life and career with those of two contemporaries: flamboyant New York Mayor James J. Walker and President Franklin D. Roosevelt. O'Connor argues that no American political leader conducted himself more honorably, and that his eventual defeat and isolation from the political mainstream were both a personal and a national tragedy.

PRINGLE provides perhaps the most balanced assessment of Smith by one of his contemporaries. Written in 1927, Pringle's matter-of-fact assessment of Smith's motivation, accomplishments and impact serve as a healthy antidote to the largely uncritical accounts of the Josephsons, Moskowitz and Hapgood, and O'Connor. Pringle sees Smith's performance as governor as a phenomenon, in that a man who owed his position and his power to control of a personal machine actually used that power chiefly in the interests of good government. Particularly interesting is Pringle's contemporary analysis of Smith's "presidential yearnings", his chances of election, and the type of president that he might become.

Welcome evidence that modern-day historians are discovering and reinterpreting Alfred E. Smith is provided in ELDOT, who concentrates intensively on the gubernatorial years, from 1919 to 1929, and on assessing Smith's reputation as a "reformer". She focuses tightly on the areas of political and governmental restructuring, taxing and spending, state parks, housing regulation, labor and welfare measures, water power, civil liberties and prohibition enforcement. Eldot concludes that Smith was a "selective" reformer, "accepting those elements of progressivism that appealed to him on rational, humanitarian, or expedient (they won votes) grounds and rejecting those that appeared detrimental to the party to which he owed an intense loyalty." More importantly, she presents Smith as an indispensable conduit between the Progressive Era and the "urban liberalism" of the New Deal. She concludes that Smith's "place in American history is secured by the deeds of the governor – not the works of the ex-governor," and agrees with FDR that Smith's New York was a model for the New Deal, and that the "Happy Warrior" would have done what Roosevelt did, if he had been elected president.

JOHN D. BUENKER

Smith, John 1580-1631
Colonial pioneer and promoter

Barbour, Philip L., *The Three Worlds of Captain John Smith*, Boston: Houghton Mifflin, and London: Macmillan, 1964

Barbour, Philip L. (editor), *The Complete Works of Captain John Smith, 1580–1631*, 3 vols., Chapel Hill: University of North Carolina Press, 1986

Brown, Alexander, *The Genesis of the United States: A Narrative of the Movement in England, 1605–1616*, 2 vols., Boston: Houghton Mifflin, 1890; reprinted, New York: Russell and Russell, 1964

Emerson, Everett H., *Captain John Smith*, New York: Twayne, 1971

Morgan, Edmund S., *American Slavery, American Freedom: The Ordeal of Colonial Virginia*, New York: Norton, 1975

Rountree, Helen C., *The Powhatan Indians of Virginia: Their Traditional Culture*, Norman: University of Oklahoma Press, 1989

Smith, Bradford, *Captain John Smith: His Life and Legend*, Philadelphia: Lippincott, 1953

Vaughan, Alden T., *American Genesis: Captain John Smith and the Founding of Virginia*, Boston: Little Brown, 1975

John Smith remains one of the most intriguing and controversial figures in the period of early American settlement. No less than thirty biographies have depicted his life, but few were based on sound scholarship. A popular folk hero, John Smith has been variously identified as a soldier of fortune, a self-made man, the saviour of Jamestown, the first American writer and the ideal American hero, but even his staunchest advocates admit that at times he was a bully and braggart, prone to exaggeration and deeply frustrated by his failure to return to America after 1614. During his lifetime, he published eight works in which he gradually developed a new model of colonization based on stronger, more stable settlements rather than the small commercial outposts hitherto prescribed, and recounted a life so colourful and packed with incident that it raised questions about his veracity. Though many lacunae in his life remain, especially in the period between 1617 and 1631, modern scholars have tended to be more sympathetic to Smith than his earlier critics.

Among the "Brief Biographies" included in BROWN's pioneering two-volume compilation of original documents, is an influential and hostile portrait of Smith which contributed further to Smith's already declining reputation at the hands of Charles Deane, Lewis Kropf and Henry Adams in the late 19th century. Writing in 1890, Brown dismissed Smith as a mere adventurer, who, aggrandizing his own role at the expense of the true founders of the colony, denied Virginia the glorious beginning and genteel origins worthy of its name. Far from being a hero – his rescue by women at critical junctures in his life precluded that – Smith compounded Jamestown's many problems. What appears to have most offended Brown was Smith's total lack of deference and complete disregard for authority. It was precisely these qualities in Smith that appealed to his two most successful and substantial biographers, Bradford Smith and Philip Barbour.

The modern re-evaluation of John Smith began with the work of Bradford SMITH. Intent on restoring John Smith's reputation, he sought to substantiate as much as possible of his hero's account of his Hungarian and Transylvanian exploits which would in turn allay suspicions about other parts of his narrative. With the assistance of Laura Polyani Striker, who contributed an appendix based on research conducted in Hungarian archives, Bradford Smith fashioned the first coherent account of these inchoate years. Smith's role in Virginia was less problematic. It was John Smith who injected a steely and much needed realism into the Jamestown venture, and his success was evident from the debacle which followed his departure, while his tough-minded policy towards the indigenous population was distinguishable from the atrocities

which followed. As for the Pocahontas story, which ensured Smith his place in American folklore and which he omitted from his earliest writings, there was no evidence to disprove it and many compelling reasons to accept it. For Bradford Smith, John Smith was the ideal American hero and the way Smith told it was probably the way it was in Europe as well as America.

The authoritative life of John Smith is BARBOUR (1964) which is lengthy, detailed and prodigiously researched, and even more partisan than Bradford Smith's. Though half of Barbour's biography is devoted to Smith's two and a half years as a colonist in Virginia, his earlier career as an adventurer in Europe, Asia and Africa, and his subsequent role as a promoter and publicist of English expansion, are fully covered. Barbour endorses Smith's version of his early career on the grounds that it fits well into what is known about the events of these years. As a member of the first Virginia Council and as President of the colony from September 1608 to August 1609, Smith's was the major role in the initial settlement, exploration and survival of Jamestown. Barbour defended Smith's policies towards the local population, noting that they involved much posturing but little violence, and was the first to suggest that central to the Pocahontas story was an adoption ritual which Smith himself failed to understand, a view widely accepted by other historians. Smith's achievements were not limited to Virginia, for in 1614 he explored and mapped the New England coast, naming the region and making plans for its settlement. Thwarted by his inability to return to America, he found a meaningful role for himself in later life as a propagandist and writer.

An admirable introduction to what Smith published is the slim volume by EMERSON, another fervent admirer, which set out to establish the context necessary for understanding Smith's works before examining and analysing the works themselves. An adventurer and writer in the Elizabethan tradition, Smith was also, and more importantly, America's first writer, a man whose vision of the promise of life in the new world, regardless of status, was characteristically American. Among Smith's writings, of which only one was a full-length book, Emerson identified his *Description of Virginia* which formed the first part of the *Map of Virginia*, as his most enduring work. Egotistical as they might appear to some, Smith's writings reflected not only his successes, but his frustrations. Smith wrote, according to Emerson, because he had once had adventures and could no longer have any more.

VAUGHAN draws heavily on the earlier work of Bradford Smith and Barbour in a short and well balanced account of the founding years of Virginia, though there is, additionally, some reference to Smith's activities along the New England coast. This is not a conventional biography, but a broader study in which Smith is deployed as a symbol of Elizabethan and Jacobean England, and of the country's imperial impulse. Not surprisingly, Vaughan also ascribes a critical role to Smith in the survival of Jamestown. For a year, Smith ruled the English colony almost single-handedly, putting men to work, reducing the level of sickness, securing supplies and holding off attack by the local population whose numbers were vastly superior. On the story of Pochahontas and Smith Vaughan remained neutral; whatever the truth, it was buried with the participants.

The reorientation of early American history which began in the late 1960s made it unlikely that, as a subject, John Smith would appeal to a new generation of students trained in the methodologies of the new social history, which was already transforming perceptions of New England society, and would subsequently do the same for the Chesapeake. Nevertheless, MORGAN, whose study of the relationship between freedom and slavery in colonial Virginia anticipated much of the new work on the Chesapeake, subjected the Jamestown fiasco (his term) to a trenchant analysis from which Smith emerges with credit.

There was one area, however, in which Smith continued to be a player – his dealings with and observations on Native Americans. ROUNTREE acknowledges Smith as one of the principal sources of her study of the Powhatan Indians, but notes that, in common with other European observers, only certain things interested him, most obviously questions of military strength and food supply. Like Brown a hundred years earlier, Rountree is less impressed by Smith's talents and energy than by his egotism and abrasiveness. She is also sceptical about the trustworthiness of his writings, especially the later ones, a scepticism which extends to his account of his rescue by Pocahontas for which, as she rightly points out, there is no confirmatory evidence.

The publication of a modern edition in three volumes of Smith's complete writings in BARBOUR (1986), along with a revival of interest in the contact period among scholars in the 1990s, and the continuing efforts of anthropologists and ethnohistorians to interpret the culture of Native Americans in the pre- and post-conquest periods, undoubtedly presage a revival of interest in the life and works of John Smith.

GWENDA MORGAN

See also Colonial History: Colonies 1

Smith, Joseph *see* Young, Brigham and Joseph Smith

Social Darwinism

Bannister, Robert C., *Social Darwinism: Science and Myth in Anglo-American Social Thought*, Philadelphia: Temple University Press, 1979

Degler, Carl N., *In Search of Human Nature: The Decline and Revival of Darwinism in American Social Thought*, New York: Oxford University Press, 1991

Fredrickson, George M., *The Black Image in the White Mind: The Debate on Afro-American Character and Destiny, 1817–1914*, New York: Harper, 1971

Goldman, Eric, *Rendezvous with Destiny: A History of Modern American Reform*, New York: Knopf, 1952

Hofstadter, Richard, *Social Darwinism in American Thought, 1860–1915*, Philadelphia: University of Pennsylvania Press, 1944; London: Oxford University Press, 1945; revised, Boston: Beacon Press, 1955

Wyllie, Irvin G., *The Self-Made Man in America: The Myth of Rags to Riches*, New Brunswick, NJ: Rutgers University Press, 1954

Though he did not invent the term, which originated in continental Europe in the latter part of the 19th century, it was HOFSTADTER's work which introduced Social Darwinism into common historical discourse as a brief means of referring to a complex of ideas in late 19th century social thought. The ideas themselves were the consequence of an attempt to apply Charles Darwin's theories on the evolution of species to human society. Humans in their social and economic environment, according to the Social Darwinists, were involved in a "struggle for existence" in the same way as every other biological organism. They evolved, also in the same way, by "natural selection" and "the survival of the fittest" – the latter phrase first used by the English philosopher Herbert Spencer but acceptable to Darwin himself.

Hofstadter's account began with an analysis of the arrival of first Darwinism and subsequently Social Darwinism in America. Only two Social Darwinist thinkers, however, were analyzed in any detail: Spencer himself and William Graham Sumner of Yale University. Moreover, while asserting that Social Darwinist thinkers were telling the business elite in postbellum America what they wanted to hear in order to justify the "tooth-and-claw" economic competition of the time, he provided little or no proof of his claim.

The Social Darwinism of Spencer and Sumner undermined the case for reform. Society was evolving, with near-glacial slowness, towards inevitable perfection by means of the "survival of the fittest." Efforts to interfere with this process were impossible or at least would have unfortunate consequences – helping the "unfittest" to survive artificially by means of legislation would retard the development of society as a whole. In their work, therefore, Spencer and Sumner re-emphasized the message of laissez-faire economics that government should not become involved in economic or social affairs.

Many thinkers, however, were soon challenging this attempt to apply Darwin's biological theories by analogy to human societies. Hofstadter actually discussed the views of these critics at far greater length than he did those of Spencer and Sumner. Sociologist Lester F. Ward pointed out that while animals were transformed by their environment, man had the capacity to transform his own environment. Human evolution, therefore, as opposed to animal, had the potential to be mental and purposeful. Ward and other critics maintained that, far from promoting the survival of the fittest, competition was wasteful and retarded progress. By the end of the 19th century, a new trend in social thought – John Fiske in America, Henry Drummond, T.H. Huxley, and Prince Peter Kropotkin in Europe – had turned its back on selfish individualism and embraced the view that the natural outcome of human evolution was greater cooperation and social solidarity. This found echoes in the Social Gospel movement in American Protestantism, together with the work of economists such as Richard T. Ely, sociologists including Edward A. Ross, and pragmatic philosophers, most significantly John Dewey. As Social Darwinism in the sense of competitive individualism declined, Hofstadter saw the survival of the fittest argument mobilized to justify the eugenics movement and also in defense of racism, militarism, and imperialism.

GOLDMAN coined the term "Reform Darwinism" to describe the point of view of those who attacked "Conservative Darwinism" of the Spencerian variety. The most crucial element in Reform Darwinism, he maintained, was the way in which it analyzed Social Darwinism as merely a rationalization of economic interests. This theme was obvious, for example, in Henry George's work and Charles A. Beard's later investigation of the Constitution. A second element was the way in which Reform Darwinists applied a more thorough-going evolutionism across a wide range of fields: Walter Rauschenbusch in theology, Edward A. Ross in ethics, Richard T. Ely in economics, Roscoe Pound and Louis D. Brandeis in the law, Franz Boas in anthropology, and David Graham Phillips in novels about women.

While Goldman extended Hofstadter's analysis of those who criticized Social Darwinism, FREDRICKSON further developed the linkage he had made between Darwinian evolutionary theory and race. Fredrickson suggested that the racist arguments developed in support of slavery were re-formulated on Darwinian lines in the closing years of the 19th century. Instead of a paternalistic vision on the part of middle-class advocates of the New South, who saw African Americans progressing in a world of mutual accommodation, the new Darwinian dogma emphasized the manner in which blacks were losing out in the struggle for survival against whites. In depicting them as a degraded race condemned to ultimate extinction, it prepared the ground for the policy of segregation which became formalized across the South during the early 20th century.

While, for the most part, the authors discussed so far took Hofstadter's view of Social Darwinism, other writers have dissented from it. In his examination of how Gilded Age businessmen explained and defended themselves, WYLLIE maintained that they used arguments based on the Bible far more than those drawn from Darwin and Spencer. Since America appeared to offer many opportunities, men became successful less by struggling with competitors than with their own baser natures. Wyllie argued that Darwinism was accepted only very slowly in the United States, and that most businessmen remained ignorant of Social Darwinist ideas in anything but the very vaguest sense.

Wyllie's criticism of Hofstadter's interpretation of Social Darwinism was developed much further by BANNISTER. Despite the insistence of reformers during the last years of the 19th century that Social Darwinism dominated the thought of the conservative opposition, Bannister found very few American business leaders or intellectuals who were "Social Darwinists" in any meaningful sense. While many Americans were committed to notions of competition and individual success, this had little to do with Darwinism. Hofstadter in any case failed, in Bannister's opinion, to distinguish sufficiently between Darwinism and Spencerianism – the former actually undercut the latter in several respects. The work of Spencer himself was not widely known or understood – even by Andrew Carnegie and others who were supposedly his disciples. Sumner was not really a Spencerian, disliked plutocracy as much as socialism, opposed imperialism, and in the end became a kind of progressive. While Hofstadter had conceded that imperialism, militarism, and racism had roots in other

things besides Social Darwinism, Bannister went much further – arguing, for example, that there was little evidence of Darwinian rhetoric in the 1890s debates over imperialism. He also emphasized that the "anti-image" of Social Darwinism – the notion of a society organized on the basis of brutal competition – was a powerful antidote to economic selfishness as well as imperialist and militarist thought.

The writers so far discussed had one thing in common: they all assumed that Social Darwinism, as a doctrine, belonged to the past. DEGLER, who analyzed the return of biological explanations to social science in recent decades, insisted that Social Darwinism itself had been killed off. However, this is to ignore the re-emergence in the United States during the 1980s of a right-wing rhetoric of economic individualism, racism, and militarism that was in many ways analogous to the Social Darwinism of the later 19th century – a development awaiting its own historian.

MELVYN STOKES

See also Imperialism and Anti-Imperialism; Race

Social Gospel

Carter, Paul Allen, *The Decline and Revival of the Social Gospel: Social and Political Liberalism in American Protestant Churches, 1920–1940*, Ithaca, NY: Cornell University Press, 1954

Curtis, Susan, *A Consuming Faith: The Social Gospel and Modern American Culture*, Baltimore: Johns Hopkins University Press, 1991

Dorn, Jacob Henry, *Washington Gladden: Prophet of the Social Gospel*, Columbus: Ohio State University Press, 1966

Gorrell, Donald K., *The Age of Social Responsibility: The Social Gospel in the Progressive Era, 1900–1920*, Macon, GA: Mercer University Press, 1988

Hopkins, Charles Howard, *The Rise of the Social Gospel in American Protestantism, 1865–1915*, New Haven: Yale University Press, and London: Oxford University Press, 1940

Luker, Ralph E., *The Social Gospel in Black and White: American Racial Reform, 1885–1912*, Chapel Hill: University of North Carolina Press, 1991

McDowell, John Patrick, *The Social Gospel in the South: The Woman's Home Mission Movement in the Methodist Episcopal Church, South, 1886–1939*, Baton Rouge: Louisiana State University Press, 1982

May, Henry Farnham, *Protestant Churches and Industrial America*, New York: Harper, 1949

Minus, Paul M., *Walter Rauschenbusch: American Reformer*, New York: Macmillan, and London: Collier Macmillan, 1988

Sharpe, Dores Robinson, *Walter Rauschenbusch*, New York: Macmillan, 1942

White, Ronald C., Jr., *Liberty and Justice for All: Racial Reform and the Social Gospel, 1877–1925*, San Francisco: Harper, 1990

In the first major book on the social gospel, HOPKINS traced the term itself to a communal experiment in Georgia in the mid-1890s. For more than three years, the members of the community produced a religious monthly with this title. Scattered use of the term had occurred before, but it now increasingly caught on as the description of a particular social and theological point of view. To Hopkins, the social gospel itself had its roots in movements to liberalize theology, a number of British influences (including Christian socialism), the consequences of industrialization, the emotional traditions of evangelicalism, and the cooler effects of Unitarianism. More pragmatically, it had its origins in the attempts made by a number of Protestant ministers, confronted in the late 19th century by increased conflict between capital and labor, to work out solutions of their own. These turned, for the most part, on a new emphasis on the importance of Christian ethics in regulating human behavior, and the quest to secure a terrestial Kingdom of Heaven in which social harmony would be the dominant characteristic.

MAY also used the impact of the labor conflicts of the last years of the 19th century to explain the emergence of social criticism in the main Protestant denominations which, until 1876, had formed an almost unbroken front in defense of the conservative status quo. Subsequent years, he maintained, saw the growth of a "social Christianity" movement split into three principal sections: conservative, radical (often socialist), and progressive. It was the last of these which May thought to have had the most influence, and which he described in terms of the social gospel.

Both Hopkins and May saw the social gospel as emerging in the final decades of the 19th century and attaining its peak in the years before World War I. GORRELL traced how social gospel ministers reached leadership positions in a range of Protestant institutions during the early years of the 20th century and, in association with progressive politicians, including Theodore Roosevelt, persuaded Americans that they were faced with a major social crisis. He divided his analysis of social gospel ideas into five periods, the last coinciding with the World War I shift from domestic reform to a preoccupation with reconstruction on the international scene.

CURTIS explained the appearance and rise of the social gospel – with its emphasis on social rather than individual salvation, its view of an immanent, more indulgent God, and its preoccupation with this life rather than an afterlife – as having more to do with a late Victorian cultural crisis than with the response to the social realities of urbanization and industrialization. In its emphasis on religion as a guarantor of psychological well-being, as a commodity to be acquired or rejected, and as a form of entertainment, it embraced and excused many of the ideals of an emerging consumer society. By 1920, the social gospel was no longer critical of capitalist exploitation, and supported the idea of corporate abundance.

CARTER explored what happened in the following two decades. During the 1920s, the churches' preoccupation with prohibition, the popularity of business, increased secularism, and the growth of fundamentalism, worked together to marginalize the critique of existing society that had underpinned much of the social gospel. In the following decade, however, under the impact of economic depression and international instability, it began both to revive and to change. Under the influence of Reinhold Niebuhr and other advocates, it became noticeably more realistic in its perception of human nature and – on the whole – less optimistic.

Most of the early books on the Social Gospel pay tribute to the influence of Washington Gladden in articulating many of its early ideas and Walter Rauschenbusch in advancing its more systematic theology. In his biography of Gladden, DORN maintained that – while not an original or very profound thinker – he played a major part in popularizing liberal theology and the social application of Christian thought. A Congregationalist minister in Columbus, Ohio, from 1882, Gladden advocated – in innumerable speeches, sermons, writings, and books – the Christianization of all aspects of life. Although Gladden was optimistic and idealistic by nature, Dorn pointed out, he was well aware that existing social, economic, and political reality came nowhere near his vision of things as they should be. SHARPE, who had been a student of Rauschenbusch's and later became his secretary, published the first major biography of him. It dealt, in some detail, with the main outlines of his career as a Baptist minister and his subsequent work as an academic theologian, but it was primarily conceived as an affectionate homage and lacked critical distance. In a briefer study, MINUS demonstrated how Rauschenbusch's liberal theology – grounded, among other sources, in the thought of Horace Bushnell – came before, and influenced the form of, his faith in social salvation. To attain his dream of social harmony, defined in terms of the Kingdom of Heaven on earth, Rauschenbusch endorsed a two-pronged strategy of structural change and personal change. The former was to be achieved through scientific administration, the latter as a result of religious inspiration. While advocating social equality, he did not attack men who had achieved great wealth. Gladden had criticized John D. Rockefeller's philanthropy as "tainted money"; Rauschenbusch, Minus showed, had had Rockefeller himself, a fellow-Baptist, as a benefactor for much of his career.

Partly as a response to the slowness of industrialization there, together with the lack of large-scale immigration, the South appeared originally to have been largely unaffected by the social gospel. Yet, in his analysis of the leaders of the women's home missionary movement in the Methodist Episcopal Church, South, McDOWELL suggests that many of the women concerned were influenced by – and had connections with – the northern leaders of the social gospel. They engaged in campaigns for temperance, child labor laws, international peace, and improved race relations. Yet how important they deemed each of these to be – particularly the concern for race relations – is not entirely clear from McDowell's work. In contrast, WHITE, examining the thought and actions of major prophets of the social gospel, finds that racial justice was far more important as an issue among social gospellers – both north and south of the Mason-Dixon line – than has hitherto been acknowledged. Concentrating mostly on the quarter-century before 1912, LUKER traces the way black and white reformers, many of them believing in the social gospel, explored a variety of solutions to the problems of racial conflict and growing urbanization. While some advocates of the social gospel espoused racial separatism, others – black as well as

white – were encouraged by the impact of theological person-
alism to attack the assumptions at the core of racism.

MELVYN STOKES

See also Progressivism

Social Mobility

Edel, Matthew, Elliott D. Sclar, and Daniel Luria, *Shaky
    Palaces: Homeownership and Social Mobility in Boston's
    Suburbanization*, New York: Columbia University Press,
    1984
Griffen, Clyde and Sally Griffen, *Natives and Newcomers:
    The Ordering of Opportunity in Mid-Nineteenth-Century
    Poughkeepsie*, Cambridge, MA: Harvard University Press,
    1978
Kaelble, Hartmut, *Social Mobility in the 19th and 20th
    Centuries: Europe and America in Comparative
    Perspective*, Leamington Spa, Warwickshire: Berg, 1985;
    New York: St. Martin's Press, 1986
Kessner, Thomas, *The Golden Door: Italian and Jewish
    Immigrant Mobility in New York City, 1880–1915*, New
    York: Oxford University Press, 1977
Nash, Gary B., *The Urban Crucible: Social Change, Political
    Consciousness, and the Origins of the American
    Revolution*, Cambridge, MA: Harvard University Press,
    1979
Pessen, Edward (editor), *Three Centuries of Social Mobility
    in America*, Lexington, MA: Heath, 1974
Thernstrom, Stephan, *The Other Bostonians: Poverty and
    Progress in the American Metropolis, 1880–1970*,
    Cambridge, MA: Harvard University Press, 1973
Ueda, Reed, *Avenues to Adulthood: The Origins of the
    High School and Social Mobility in an American Suburb*,
    Cambridge and New York: Cambridge University Press,
    1987

Social mobility studies generally seek to discover whether
America was truly the land of opportunity, characterized by
social fluidity rather than class stratification. A good overview
of the history of social mobility in the United States can be
found in PESSEN. The articles which it contains represent the
work of the most significant scholars in the field and they
clearly set forth many of the key debates and alternative interpretations. These essays not only cover the entire span of
American history, from colonial times to the 20th century, but
also demonstrate some of the different methodologies used in
studies of this subject, including the exploration of the social
origins of elites and occupational and residential mobility.

Another key study of the subject is THERNSTROM's examination of late 19th century Boston. Relying heavily upon quantitative information derived from census schedules and city
directories, he looks at social mobility in the context of both
spatial and occupational mobility. In terms of the former,
Thernstrom finds a considerable degree of movement in and
out of Boston in the decades since the 1880s. More significant
are his conclusions about occupational mobility and what they
reveal about the traditional image of the United States as a
socially fluid society. He contends that movement up the occupational ladder from unskilled blue-collar work to white-collar
employment was limited, but nonetheless real, and sufficient
to give a degree of substance to the American dream. His
pioneering use of sophisticated quantitative techniques and his
conclusions inspired a flood of literature which both emulated
and challenged his work.

GRIFFEN and GRIFFEN expand upon Thernstrom's study
of occupational mobility, while taking care to replicate his
methods in order to ensure comparability of their conclusions.
Their examination of Poughkeepsie, New York in the late 19th
century also attempts to address some of the criticisms which
were leveled at Thernstrom's work, particularly concerning
his rigid definition of "upward mobility" as movement from
blue-collar to white-collar occupations, without adequate
consideration of how different ethnic, racial and gender
groups themselves defined social success. They argue that while
there was considerable upward mobility for all groups, there
was also a distinct gap between the opportunities available to
the native-born inhabitants on the one hand, and those available to either foreign-born immigrants or African Americans,
on the other.

KESSNER's comparative study of Italian and Jewish
communities in New York at the turn of the century moves
away from a pure reliance on statistical analysis of occupational change. Instead, he uses literary sources to place his
study carefully in the cultural context of these disparate immigrant groups and what they brought to the New World in
terms of skills and expectations. This approach makes his work
highly readable and more easily digested by the general reader.
Although he finds a relatively high degree of mobility, sufficient to justify the characterization of America as a land of
opportunity, he also observes that Italians and Jews did move
upward on the occupational ladder at different rates, owing
to differences in the cultural baggage which they brought from
the Old World. Many Italians, for instance, had limited expectations of social change either because they anticipated a return
to Italy, or because their largely agricultural background did
not provide them with the skills necessary to climb into white-
collar positions.

Much of the work on social mobility has concentrated on
immigrant urban communities in the late 19th and early 20th
centuries, but there are also important studies of earlier
periods. NASH's exhaustive study of Boston, Philadelphia
and New York in the 18th century is an excellent example.
Historians of the earlier period have generally examined
changes in wealth distribution among different classes rather
than attempting to trace occupational mobility. Nash uses
quantitative evidence on changes in wealth distribution as part
of a larger and more ambitious effort to analyze the role of
class formation in the political radicalism of the American
Revolution. He concludes that, instead of becoming more
socially fluid, American urban society in this period was rapidly
becoming stratified, with wealth progressively concentrated at
the top. The end result, he argues, was a society in which class
and consciousness of class increasingly became significant in
shaping critical political events, including the Revolution itself.

More recent studies have built upon the pioneering work
of the 1970s. KAELBLE's slender volume, for example, provides an excellent synthesis of much earlier work, and his

comparison with European data directly addresses the issue of whether America really was the golden land of opportunity at the turn of the century. He asserts that the chances for upward mobility in the United States were somewhat greater than in other industrial societies, particularly for unskilled workers – a difference which he attributes largely to a more accessible educational system. He further argues that occupational mobility in both the United States and Europe increased only modestly during the industrial age, though in later periods of "organized capitalism" and the "post-industrial society" these mobility rates became more significant. Drawing upon extensive secondary sources, Kaelble may be rather difficult reading for those not already familiar with the literature of social mobility.

Two other books expand upon two particularly popular strategies for social advancement: education and home ownership. While somewhat cluttered with statistics, UEDA's brief examination of the high school system in suburban Somerville, Massachusetts, from the 1850s to the 1920s, does provide a clear, chronological account of its development. He contends that for much of the 19th century the public high school primarily served to preserve the social and economic status of native-born elites. After the turn of the century, however, a significant minority of the immigrant working-class were able to use these schools as an avenue to upward occupational mobility.

EDEL, SCLAR and LURIA paint a less rosy picture in their examination of blue-collar home ownership in 19th- and 20th-century Boston. Although a challenging book because of its heavy use of Marxist theory and its chronological jumps, it provides a striking critique of conventional social mobility studies. The authors argue that working-class homeownership represented a compromise with industrial elites which muted social and economic conflict in the United States. They further assert that this blue-collar investment in real estate more often than not provided only a false promise of social advancement. The American urban system, characterized by the repeated abandonment of older settlement areas and the continuous development of new suburbs, has progressively devalued working-class neighborhoods. Trapped by their initial investment, the authors suggest, blue-collar workers have been unable to move to take advantage of new economic opportunities, and have instead seen their economic position eroded, particularly in recent decades.

DANIEL J. JOHNSON

See also Class

Social Welfare/Social Security

Abramovitz, Mimi, *Regulating the Lives of Women: Social Welfare from Colonial Times to the Present*, Boston: South End Press, 1988

Achenbaum, W. Andrew, *Social Security: Visions and Revisions*, Cambridge and New York: Cambridge University Press, 1986

Gordon, Linda, *Pitied but Not Entitled: Single Mothers and the History of Welfare, 1890–1935*, New York: Free Press, 1994

Lubove, Roy, *The Struggle for Social Security, 1900–1935*, Cambridge, MA: Harvard University Press, 1968; 2nd edition, Pittsburgh: University of Pittsburgh Press, 1986

Patterson, James T., *America's Struggle Against Poverty, 1900–1980*, Cambridge, MA: Harvard University Press, 1981, revised as *America's Struggle Against Poverty, 1900–1994*, 1994

Piven, Frances Fox and Richard Cloward, *Regulating the Poor: The Functions of Public Welfare*, New York: Pantheon, 1971

Quadagno, Jill, *The Transformation of Old Age Security: Class and Politics in the American Welfare State*, Chicago: University of Chicago Press, 1988

Skocpol, Theda, *Protecting Soldiers and Mothers: The Political Origins of Social Policy in the United States*, Cambridge, MA: Belknap Press of Harvard University Press, 1992

Trattner, Walter I., *From Poor Law to Welfare State: A History of Social Welfare in America*, New York: Free Press, 1974

As TRATTNER observed in his study of social welfare in the United States, broad theoretical generalizations are difficult to come by. His history of social welfare sticks to what he describes as "the facts." It gives a chronological overview of social provision for the less affluent from the colonial period to the 1970s. It includes accounts of both state and private provision, providing ample bibliographic references and analyses of the work of other scholars in the field. There is some sensitivity to matters of gender and race and provision for the young and old.

Subsequent scholars have greatly increased the attention paid to women and minorities. ABRAMOVITZ explicitly examines social welfare policy in terms of what it did to women and people of color. Thus she explicitly writes gender into social history in contrast to earlier commentators who either treated it inadequately or ignored it altogether. She follows the analytical path pioneered by PIVEN and CLOWARD who regard social welfare provision as a tool for social control of the poor and as a means of providing a cheap labor supply. While there are some references in their work to social welfare provision in colonial and early America, the bulk of their study examines the welfare activities of the federal government. Reflecting the time in which it was written, the analysis focuses on the racial and racist dynamics of the American welfare state rather more than it concentrates upon matters of gender.

GORDON's history of welfare provision for single mothers takes a social structuralist approach to explore the topic with particular attention to matters of race, class, and gender. She considers the extent to which women were both actors and acted upon in welfare legislation, federal bureaus, and welfare organizations. Covering the period from 1900 through 1940, she also explores the social dynamics of welfare, the dominance of maternalist thought in the Progressive Era, and the power struggles which influenced the Social Security Act of 1935. Organized women had a substantial role in the Children's Bureau and the creation of welfare policy at state and federal levels in the 1910s and 1920s, but little in the 1930s, as the role of the federal government expanded. This study provides a detailed examination of the political infighting and economic and social values which shaped the Social Security Act and accounted for the particularities of its coverage.

SKOCPOL focuses upon the political origins of social welfare legislation. She traces the role of the federal government in supplying pensions provision for injured and aged Civil War veterans, the widows and orphans of those fatally wounded in combat, and survivors' benefits. She also explores the role of women as lobbyists for widows' pensions, especially the work of the National Congress of Mothers and the General Federation of Women's Clubs. The primary interest here is in the expansion of the role of government, the battles for political control over pensions, and the distinctive nature (or not) of the American welfare state. Too little is made here of the racial dynamics of welfare provision, and too much reliance placed upon the passage of legislation rather than its enforcement, but this remains an essential work for understanding the structure of public provision.

The Social Security Act of 1935 is the single most important piece of social welfare legislation in American history. It provided for old age assistance, retirement insurance, aid to the blind and disabled, and Aid to Dependent Children (ADC). Forged in the crucible of the Great Depression, but drawing upon attitudes towards assistance dating from the Progressive Era, it established the role of the federal government in providing for the jobless, dependent young, and old. It had two tiers: the first based upon contributions from workers in covered occupations (primarily white men in the early years), including retirement and unemployment compensation, and the second based upon relief (ADC, old age assistance, aid to the blind and disabled).

LUBOVE details the major pieces of legislation and the welfare movements which led up to the Social Security Act, tracing the antecedents for each part of this omnibus measure. He focuses upon voluntarism in welfare provision, the reluctance of labor unions to rely upon a state which seemed hostile to them, and the opposition to publicly supported medical care from both the medical and insurance establishments. The account of mothers' pensions concentrates upon the competition between private and public sectors to aid needy widows and children and the revulsion against institutional care. Similarly, the analysis of old age pensions explores the question of the adequacy of private provision, and the revulsion against placing the elderly in almshouses.

Paying attention to regional variations in the passage and implementation of welfare legislation, QUADAGNO examines the role of the South in defining federal welfare efforts. She provides a general history of old age security in industrial America, believing the relatively late unionization of mass production workers and the malign influence of southern racism combined both to shift the burden of pension provision on to the federal government and to restrict retirement coverage to workers in certain occupations.

ACHENBAUM examines the early years of Social Security in order to determine who gained and how the political exigencies of the 1930s and thereafter have influenced the distribution of pensions and the other benefits. Carrying his analysis through the Great Society, he provides a detailed account of the changes which the Social Security programs have undergone, especially the additions of Medicaid and Medicare. He pays particular attention to the status of women in society, the economy, and social welfare. As Achenbaum concludes, the way in which the Social Security Act treats people mirrors "the essential quality of the American experiment." One might add that the treatment of social security and social welfare by historians encapsulates views of what constitutes history, matters of race, gender, and class, and long-term social trends.

In his wide-ranging and authoritative survey of the problem of poverty, and attempts to combat it, in 20th century America, PATTERSON pays particular attention to the New Deal years, and to the War on Poverty in the 1960s. He discusses not only the development of the welfare state but also the mounting problems of welfare dependency during recent decades, and the widespread reaction against the welfare system.

S.J. KLEINBERG

Social Work/Social Reform

Ehrenreich, John H., *The Altruistic Imagination: A History of Social Work and Social Policy in the United States*, Ithaca, NY: Cornell University Press, 1985

Higginbotham, Evelyn Brooks, *Righteous Discontent: The Women's Movement in the Black Baptist Church, 1880–1920*, Cambridge, MA: Harvard University Press, 1993

Kunzel, Regina G., *Fallen Women, Problem Girls: Unmarried Mothers and the Professionalization of Social Work, 1890–1945*, New Haven: Yale University Press, 1993

Lasch-Quinn, Elisabeth, *Black Neighbors: Race and the Limits of Reform in the American Settlement House Movement, 1890–1945*, Chapel Hill: University of North Carolina Press, 1993

Lubove, Roy, *The Professional Altruist: The Emergence of Social Work as a Career, 1880–1930*, Cambridge, MA: Harvard University Press, 1965

Rothman, David J., *The Discovery of the Asylum: Social Order and Disorder in the New Republic*, Boston: Little Brown, 1971, revised 1990

Trolander, Judith Ann, *Professionalism and Social Change: From the Settlement House Movement to Neighborhood Centers, 1886 to the Present*, New York: Columbia University Press, 1987

In the late 19th century, "social work" was an imprecise term that could refer to a wide range of activities, some of which were driven by a belief in reform. At that early date, social work and social reform might be said to have been in their closest, least antagonistic relationship. The story of social work and social reform is very much the story of the growing distance, and growing conflict, between the two. The literature has generally been concerned with four major issues: the professionalization of social work and its effect on reform; the question of "social control" versus "social welfare"; the tensions frequently present between the goals of social work and those of social reform; and, most recently, the role of gender and of race in shaping social work and social reform.

LUBOVE examined the relationship between the charity organization movement and the professionalization of social work, and found much to criticize. Charity organizers invented "casework," and thus contributed to the professionalization of social work. Yet they also injected elements of Social Darwinism and a fundamental distrust of the poor into their relief efforts. Charity organizers focused on the flawed "character" of the poor, rather than the destructive environments in which they lived. Lubove recognized the class tensions between charity organizers and their "clients," and suggested that social work often served the interests of business, while charity organization work often did more for the philanthropists who gave donations, and the middle-class social workers, than it did for those actually in need.

ROTHMAN focused on the sudden devotion to institutionalization as the cure for poverty that emerged in Jacksonian America. Nineteenth-century reformers believed that poverty need not exist in America, and moved to eliminate it. A "cult of asylum" swept the country, as reformers concluded that institutionalization was a positive good, Institutions for the poor would rehabilitate them by teaching them the critical skills needed for the modern age – especially discipline and work. Institutions would socialize the poor out of dependence. However, reform sentiment was confronted by a changing social context, as immigration and urban growth affected the nature of poverty and the characteristics of the poor. The native-born middle class grew distant from, and suspicious of, the increasingly foreign-born poor. Existing institutions were in danger of becoming places where the poor could be locked away, with little effort at real reform, rehabilitation, or socialization. Indeed, institutions could be made so unappealing that the poor would avoid them, and taxpayers would benefit from the reduced costs.

Both Lubove and Rothman, and other scholars at the time, were interested in the reforms, the reformers, and the institutions which they created. The analyses concentrated on understanding the ideology behind social work, the intellectual currents supporting social reform, and the legislative history of the various reforms. This approach – what Raymond Mohl has called "mainstream social welfare history" – began to be supplemented, or even supplanted, during the 1980s by new attention to the world of the poor, their responses to reform, and their role in bringing about change.

EHRENREICH explored more fully the question of the tension between social work and social reform. He suggested that the commitment to social reform could only be successful during periods when social movements provided the massive support necessary to institute them and make them work. In the absence of such support, reforms often ended up serving the interests of the wealthy and the powerful, and social workers then acted as the instrument of the political and economic elites. In the Progressive Era, for example, social work served as an instrument of social control over the poor by the middle class.

Focusing even more directly on the poor and the working class, TROLANDER stressed the ways in which the poor used institutions to suit their own needs. "Acculturation" or "Americanization" activities of the early settlement workers may have been instruments of social control, but the poor embraced them for their own reasons. Although still giving coverage to the issue of professionalization of social work, Trolander suggested that a continuing shortage of trained social workers postponed full professionalization of the field until after World War II. Like some other scholars, she tended to consider professionalization as part of the context, not the central concern. In another emerging trend of the literature of the 1980s, Trolander also paid careful attention to the ways in which gender and ethnicity shaped the relationship between settlement house workers and their neighbors. Gender affected the settlements' approach to reform; dominated by women, settlements practised a passive approach to neighborhood organizing, a consensus style of reform work, and an emphasis on programs for women and children. Ethnicity played its part, too; Italians were under-represented in the clubs and activities at Hull House, in part because the Catholic Church resented the settlement's role in establishing a public school at a time when the church was attempting to establish a parochial one.

In another notable example of the sophisticated use of gender as an analytic tool, KUNZEL examined the complex relationships between three different groups of women: evangelical reformers, professional social workers, and unmarried (usually working-class) mothers. Pitted against one another in the contested territory of the maternity home, these three groups had very different understandings of gender – understandings which were further complicated by class distinctions. Professional social workers adopted the supposedly gender-neutral rhetoric of science to gain the upper hand over the competing evangelical reformers, but in the process inadvertently established psychiatrists as the experts in understanding "illegitimacy." Since psychiatry remained a male professional monopoly, female social workers ultimately lost control over the field of unmarried motherhood.

Like several others in the early 1990s, LASCH-QUINN re-examined the thorny question of race and social reform. She offered a more complex interpretation of the racial views of the progressive reformers. While settlements were committed to cultural pluralism, they were unable to redirect their energies towards urban blacks who were needy and desirous of their services. Race and racism proved an insurmountable problem for most settlement workers, who found their efforts at inter-racial activities stymied by forces both within and without the movement. Lasch-Quinn also suggests that the reliance of historians on Jane Addams as the "typical" settlement worker has contributed to a misinterpretation of the racial views of such workers. While Addams was extremely liberal, others were not so open-minded.

HIGGINBOTHAM's examination of African American women in the progressive era reform movements suggests that, for black women, social reform could not be separated from the struggle for social equality. Mostly middle-class, black women reformers practised and preached racial uplift; they established schools and kindergartens, day care centers and settlement houses for the benefit of poor and working-class blacks. But, for the women who led these efforts, reform work had several meanings. It helped to establish these middle-class women as leaders of the African American community, giving them authority and political power; it helped the cause of racial equality, by providing education and other services not available from white sources; and it helped the cause of women's rights as well, as this "social work" gave women an organizational base from which to challenge male authority for leadership in the black church and the black community.

By the mid-1990s then, the literature on social work and social reform had shifted on its axis. While certainly not abandoning class relations and class tensions as a defining concept, the most recent literature has added gender, race and ethnicity to the matrix. Moreover, the current generation of scholarship remains interested in uncovering the views, the opinions, and the experiences of the poor and the working class. Resistance to efforts at social control, rather than social control itself, is at the heart of the new literature.

ELNA C. GREEN

See also Settlement Houses

Socialism and Communism

Buhle, Mari Jo, Paul Buhle, and Dan Georgakas,
 Encyclopedia of the American Left, New York: Garland,
 and London: St. James Press, 1990
Buhle, Paul, *Marxism in the United States: Remapping the
 History of the American Left*, London: Verso, 1987,
 revised 1991
Diggins, John Patrick, *The American Left in the Twentieth
 Century*, New York: Harcourt Brace, 1973; revised as
 The Rise and Fall of the American Left, New York:
 Norton, 1992
Draper, Theodore, *The Roots of American Communism*,
 New York: Viking, 1957
Draper, Theodore, *American Communism and Soviet Russia:
 The Formative Period*, New York: Viking, 1960
Isserman, Maurice, *Which Side Were You On? The
 American Communist Party During the Second World
 War*, Middletown, CT: Wesleyan University Press, 1982
Klehr, Harvey, *The Heyday of American Communism: The
 Depression Decade*, New York: Basic Books, 1984
Klehr, Harvey and John Earl Haynes, *The American
 Communist Movement: Storming Heaven Itself*, New
 York: Twayne, 1992
Weinstein, James, *The Decline of Socialism in America,
 1912–1925*, New York: Monthly Review Press, 1967

The most accessible introduction to the history of the American Left is DIGGINS. In a narrative interspersed with vivid portraits of leading radicals and illuminating discussions of the ideas which influenced them, Diggins relates the rise and fall of four leftist movements: the "Lyrical Left," the Greenwich Village rebellion of the 1910s; the "Old Left," the Communist movement born of the Great Depression; the "New Left," the youth uprising of the 1960s; and the "Academic Left," the institutionally-based radicalism of the 1970s and 1980s. By employing this generational approach, Diggins highlights what he believes is one of the most important characteristics of the history of the American Left – its discontinuity. He also tends to accentuate the domestic as opposed to the European origins of the leftist impulse. Of the four movements he describes, he is unmistakably more sympathetic with the Lyrical and New

Lefts than with the Old and Academic Lefts. Indeed, he is highly critical of the last. The main weakness of this very well written and generally reliable account is that, by concentrating so heavily on the intellectual articulations of the American Left, it tends to marginalize the activities of ordinary rank-and-file members.

More demanding but no less rewarding is BUHLE's history of Marxism in the United States. In contrast with Diggins, Buhle foregrounds the European contribution to the American Left, portraying Marxism in the United States principally as a means by which "new" immigrants expressed their dissatisfaction with aspects of their adopted country. The best passages are those in which the author draws on his vast knowledge of the German and Yiddish-language radical press to recreate the intellectual world of early immigrant socialism. However Buhle is also at pains to show how Marxism's popularity in America has always depended on the ability of its adherents to identify themselves with indigenous radical traditions. The Debsian Socialists of the pre-World War I period were highly successful in this respect, for example harnessing the strength of the American women's movement by sponsoring female suffrage, whereas the Communists of the 1920s, who disregarded women's rights, failed conspicuously.

A number of studies deal with specific aspects of American Socialism and Communism. Still the most authoritative treatment of the former in its period of greatest influence, the 1910s, is WEINSTEIN. Based on extremely extensive research into primary sources, this study reveals how during World War I the Socialist party garnered major support among both industrial workers and small farmers, native stock and immigrant. It then traces the process by which, in the years 1919–25, the Socialist movement, while still retaining some popular appeal, began to fragment, until after 1925 Communism replaced Socialism as the central force in American radicalism.

Early scholarly debate on American Communism was dominated by the work of DRAPER (1957, 1960). Like other contributors to the Fund for the Republic "Communism in American Life" series, Draper viewed Communism as an alien and undesirable presence in the United States, and accordingly emphasized the subordination of the American Communist Party (CPUSA) to the authority of the Soviet Union. Any appearance of authentic popular enthusiasm for Communism, such as during the "Popular Front" phase of the mid-1930s, was, Draper argued, deceptive, the result of automatic obedience by the movement's Stalinist leadership to a new directive from Moscow. Another distinctive feature of Draper's two books was that they dealt almost exclusively with Party elites, and had little to say about the mass of the movement's ordinary members.

More recent, "revisionist" studies of Communism in the United States have typically employed a social history approach to the topic, as opposed to the political or institutional perspective favored by Draper, and have stressed the domestic origins of the American Communist movement, rather than external influences. One of the best examples of this more sympathetic tendency is ISSERMAN. Among the virtues of this book is the evidence it provides of popular involvement in Party activities, and its sensitivity to the ways in which American Communists interpreted Soviet directives according to their own particular needs and interests. However the narrative of Party history during World War II which occupies the main part of the text, documenting as it does a series of policy reversals by the CPUSA in the wake of the Nazi-Soviet Pact, the German invasion of the Soviet Union, and the beginning of the Cold War, has the unintended effect of confirming Draper's claim that American Communists were inordinately obedient to the "Moscow line."

American Communism during the 1930s, supposedly years of "Americanization" and significant popular support, is the topic of KLEHR. However, this volume is "Draperian" rather than revisionist in its approach, in that it privileges leadership over membership, and relations with Moscow over indigenous factors. Beginning with a brief recapitulation of events in Party history during the 1920s, and ending with a look forward to World War II, the rest of the book is devoted to the various stages of CPUSA policy in the 1930s. Although extremely well researched, and more acute in its observations than much recent scholarship, Klehr could nonetheless be criticised for failing to utilize some of the more advantageous aspects of revisionism, such as the methods of social and, particularly, oral history.

Similar criticism could be levelled at KLEHR and HAYNES, which echoes Klehr's earlier study in its emphasis on Soviet control and on party leaders. For example, it fails to give satisfactory explanations of the experiential basis of ordinary Party members' allegiance to Communism, and the interaction between Comintern policies and local American conditions. These flaws notwithstanding, this short volume constitutes the most up-to-date, dependable account currently available of the history of the American Communist movement.

Finally, despite some omissions and its occasionally celebratory tone, BUHLE, BUHLE and GEORGAKAS is an immensely useful research tool for students of all aspects of the American Left, especially when used alongside Bernard K. Johnpoll and Harvey Klehr's *Biographical Dictionary of the American Left* (1986).

HUGH WILFORD

South: General

Boles, John B., *The South Through Time: A History of an American Region*, Englewood Cliffs, NJ: Prentice Hall, 1995

Boles, John B. and Evelyn Thomas Nolen (editors), *Interpreting Southern History: Historiographical Essays in Honor of Sanford W. Higginbotham*, Baton Rouge: Louisiana State University Press, 1987

Cash, W. J., *The Mind of the South*, New York: Knopf, 1941

Cooper, William J. Jr., and Thomas E. Terrill, *The American South: A History*, New York: Knopf, 1990, 2nd edition, 1996

Escott, Paul D. and David R. Goldfield (editors), *Major Problems in the History of the American South: Documents and Essays*, 2 vols., Lexington, MA: Heath, 1990

Franklin, John Hope and Alfred A. Moss, Jr., *From Slavery to Freedom: A History of African Americans*, 7th edition, New York: McGraw Hill, 1994 (originally published, by Franklin only, as *From Slavery to Freedom: A History of American Negroes*, New York: Knopf, 1947)

Hill, Samuel S. (editor), *Encyclopedia of Religion in the South*, Macon, GA: Mercer University Press, 1984

Link, Arthur S. and Rembert W. Patrick, *Writing Southern History: Essays in Historiography in Honor of Fletcher M. Green*, Baton Rouge: Louisiana State University Press, 1965

Miller, Randall M. and John David Smith (editors), *Dictionary of Afro-American Slavery*, Westport, CT: Greenwood Press, 1988, revised 1997

Roller, David C. and Robert W. Twyman (editors), *The Encyclopedia of Southern History*, Baton Rouge: Louisiana State University Press, 1979

Wilson, Charles Reagan and William Ferris (editors), *Encyclopedia of Southern Culture*, Chapel Hill: University of North Carolina Press, 1989

Woodward, C. Vann, *The Burden of Southern History*, Baton Rouge: Louisiana State University Press, 1960, 3rd edition, 1993

The geographical region of the United States known as the South has attracted far more than its share of distinguished scholarship because it has long been the most exotic, most different section of the nation. It was, after all, the area of the United States that most depended on slavery, that separated from the rest of the nation, and on whose soil was fought the American Civil War, the bloodiest conflict in the nation's history. By a whole battery of cultural, demographic, and sociological measures, it has long been the most distinctive portion of the nation. Its very "differentness," when contrasted with the nation as a whole, serves to illuminate signficant aspects of the history both of the South and of the nation. Moreover, to the degree that the South's historical experience is more universal than that of the United States – in the world context, the United States has greater claims to uniqueness than does the South – the study of southern history offers a potential bridge of understanding to the historical experiences of people worldwide.

Two modern works offer the best introductions to the general history of the entire South, from European discovery to the present. BOLES is somewhat shorter, pays more attention to cultural, social, religious, and intellectual history, and is written as a series of five lengthy interpretative essays. COOPER and TERRILL is longer, with more emphasis on political, economic, and labor history, and is more encyclopedic in coverage. Both textbooks have very extensive bibliographical essays that are useful guides to the secondary literature upon which the general histories have been constructed. Both textbooks discuss all the major issues of southern history, including the rise of slavery, the causes and consequences of the Civil War, the nature of race relations, and the evolution of the modern South (the so-called Sun Belt). Neither of these books has a defensive, provincial tone. ESCOTT and GOLDFIELD is primarily intended for classroom use, but its imaginative integration of interpretative introductions by the authors, apt selection of primary documents, excerpts from important interpretative writings, and a series of bibliographies following each section of the book give it a utility far beyond its original purpose. It very appropriately complements the general interpretations of Boles and of Cooper and Terrill by providing a range of voices and viewpoints.

CASH is a classic interpretation of the South, almost an icon of southern studies, written by a journalist on the eve of World War II. Its influence has been immense, as much for its powerful writing style as for its bold and critical interpretation of the region. In recent decades Cash has been seriously criticized and is now generally recognized to be greatly flawed, yet every serious student of the region should read it because it has so shaped other discussions of the South's history. But no one should accept Cash's interpretations as sufficient. An important critic of Cash has been WOODWARD, who in a series of brilliant essays collected here has offered the most influential general interpretation of the South's overall historical experience. Woodward has, more than any other scholar, helped historians to contextualize the South's history in the broader history of the rest of the world. He has written a number of significant books on the South, referenced in several of the bibliographies to books here discussed, but these eloquently written essays indicate why the history of the South has proven so endlessly fascinating.

The best overall guides to the outpouring of scholarship on the South are collections of essays, one in honor of a distinguished teacher of southern history, Fletcher M. Green, and another in honor of a distinguished editor, Sanford W. Higginbotham. LINK and PATRICK contains seventeen bibliographical essays covering the work – books, articles, and dissertations – written on the South up to 1961; the essays are arranged chronologically, though several address particular topics over a broad chronological period. BOLES and NOLEN contains thirteen historiographical essays covering the scholarship written between 1961 and 1983, with the exception of the essay on women, which surveys the historical writing since the early 20th century. Both volumes are intensively indexed and serve as indispensable guides to what has been written on the history of the South.

Four specialized encyclopedias are essential both for the information they provide and for their bibliographical references to a very specialized literature on virtually every topic in southern history. The oldest and in many ways still the most useful is ROLLER and TWYMAN, which contains, in strict alphabetical arrangement, treatments of varying length on practically every significant southern person, event, period, intellectual or cultural artifact, and movement. A strength of the volume is its treatment of basic political and economic history. The entries are signed and are accompanied by a brief guide to sources, and the volume is carefully indexed. WILSON and FERRIS is similar, though its coverage emphasizes topics that have had a cultural (high and low) impact, ranging from William Faulkner to moon pies. The arrangement is alphabetical by topic, though sometimes the trick is to determine the topic. The detailed index is essential. Religion has been especially important to the South's history, and HILL offers the most complete coverage of the topic, again with each entry, arranged alphabetically, concluding with a brief guide to reading. Slavery has also had an enormous role in the history of the region, and the most complete introduction to the topic

is provided in MILLER and SMITH. The best introduction to black history in general, from colonization to the civil rights movement and beyond, is FRANKLIN and MOSS. The most up-to-date coverage of all of southern history, with highly analytical, well-documented articles, book reviews, and an annual guide to periodical literature, is provided by the *Journal of Southern History*, which has been published quarterly since 1935.

JOHN B. BOLES

South: Colonial Period to Civil War

Coclanis, Peter A., *The Shadow of a Dream: Economic Life and Death in the South Carolina Low Country, 1670–1920*, New York and Oxford: Oxford University Press, 1989

Collins, Bruce, *White Society in the Antebellum South*, London and New York: Longman, 1985

Cooper, William J., Jr., *Liberty and Slavery: Southern Politics to 1860*, New York: Knopf, 1983

Eaton, Clement, *The Growth of Southern Civilization, 1790–1860*, New York: Harper, and London: Hamish Hamilton, 1961

Freehling, William W., *The Road to Disunion: Secessionists at Bay, 1776–1854*, New York: Oxford University Press, 1990

Genovese, Eugene D., *The Political Economy of Slavery: Studies in the Economy and Society of the Slave South*, New York: Pantheon, 1965; London: MacGibbon and Kee, 1968

Harris, J. William, *Plain Folk and Gentry in a Slave Society: White Liberty and Black Slavery in Augusta's Hinterlands*, Middletown, CT: Wesleyan University Press, 1985

Klein, Rachel N., *The Unification of a Slave State: The Rise of the Planter Class in the South Carolina Backcountry, 1760–1808*, Chapel Hill: University of North Carolina Press, 1990

Lebsock, Suzanne, *The Free Women of Petersburg: Status and Culture in a Southern Town, 1784–1860*, New York: Norton, 1984

Mathews, Donald G., *Religion in the Old South*, Chicago: University of Chicago Press, 1977

Oakes, James, *Slavery and Freedom: An Interpretation of the Old South*, New York: Knopf, 1990

Wyatt-Brown, Bertram, *Southern Honor: Ethics and Behavior in the Old South*, New York and Oxford: Oxford University Press, 1982

Historians of the antebellum South have understandably concentrated on the two grand topics of slavery and the coming of the Civil War. Indeed, it is not clear that "the South" as a subject of historical inquiry would exist if, say, slavery had been abolished there in the era of the American Revolution. The result, in any case, is truly an embarrassment of riches in the depth and breadth of scholarship. As both slavery and the Civil War receive considerable attention elsewhere in this volume, discussion here focuses on books with broad interpretive themes, that encompass multiple social strata, or that illustrate recent approaches to the subject. Among surveys of the period between the Revolution and the Civil War, the best remains EATON. While much of its content has been superseded, it offers both comprehensiveness and attention to the diversity of southern life.

Two books limited to the study of a single state help to show how the social and economic institutions of the 19th century grew from colonial antecedents. COCLANIS traces the long history of the Atlantic coast rice kingdom from its origins to its disappearance after the Civil War. It emphasizes the importance of market forces in explaining the economic rise and eventual fall of this area marked by huge plantations. Though based on impressive quantitative research, the interpretation is presented in graceful essay form. KLEIN nicely complements Coclanis. She shows how the South Carolina backcountry, originally isolated from markets and populated mainly by nonslaveowning whites, evolved into an important part of a single polity dominated by large planters. Her emphasis on class power and its political consequences provides a counterpoint to Coclanis's stress on market forces.

Two books offer sweeping interpretations of southern politics in the long antebellum period. Within a brief compass, COOPER provides a clear and relatively comprehensive synthesis of the South's political history. He makes a strong case for a fundamental continuity and uniformity in southern politics over the period from the Revolution to the Civil War, based on two overriding concerns: that "liberty" for whites must be preserved, and that black slavery must be protected as an essential element of that liberty. FREEHLING covers the same chronological ground in quite different fashion. After discussing the social roots of southern politics and the consequences for slaveholders of the Revolutionary heritage, Freehling analyzes a series of national political conflicts rooted in slavery, from the Missouri controversy in 1819 to the Kansas-Nebraska Act in 1854. Unlike Cooper, Freehling stresses the diversity of the South and the difficulty of uniting southerners politically around a consistent defense of slavery. His sometimes quirky prose may deter some readers, but Freehling's work adds importantly to what we know about all the major conflicts he discusses.

GENOVESE has become the most influential current historian of the antebellum South. In his first major publication, a volume of loosely interrelated essays, he introduces his basic argument: that the antebellum South was a "slave civilization" created by the special class relationships arising from slavery. In his later work Genovese has filled in and sometimes modified his arguments, but the brevity and clarity of this first attempt at interpretive synthesis make it a good introduction to his argument.

Other interpreters of the south have disputed Genovese's claims in one fashion or another. WYATT-BROWN, like Genovese, argues that the South was fundamentally distinct from the rest of the United States, but he attributes this to a culture of "honor," rooted in a particular constellation of family values, that united whites regardless of class throughout the south. COLLINS makes an argument along somewhat similar lines, but sees a more wide-ranging set of ligaments, including religion and social mobility, tying together white southerners. In addition to offering this particular interpretation, Collins provides a useful synthesis of a good deal of the secondary literature, particularly on nonslaveholding whites. A third recent interpretive work is OAKES. Here the author argues that slavery created not a distinct "civilization" in the South, as Genovese would have it, but a distorted variation of the liberal capitalism which the South shared with other regions. Like Collins, this volume provides in brief compass a helpful synthesis of a great deal of secondary literature.

HARRIS takes up some of these same themes through a local study of an area encompassing cotton plantations in Georgia and South Carolina. Its central subject is the set of inter-relationships – social, economic, and political – among slaves, slave owners, and white nonslaveholders; it concludes that republican ideology was one of the crucial ligaments uniting, somewhat tenuously, different white classes. It can be taken as one example of the local studies that have informed much of the new scholarship.

The study of women's history, though it took hold more slowly for the study of the South than for the Northeast, has become central to investigations of the antebellum era. An early and excellent example is LEBSOCK, another local study. With often ingenious use of sources such as wills and deeds, Lebsock argues that the evidence tends to show the existence of a distinct "women's culture" in Petersburg, Virginia. Among its virtues, this book deals lucidly with questions about the nature of southern distinctiveness without starting from the usual point, slavery.

Protestant evangelical religion was central to antebellum southern life and culture for blacks and whites, rich and poor. MATHEWS provides an outstanding interpretive synthesis of this important subject. This book is a study of the many ways in which southern culture and society were affected by evangelical values rather than by churches, denominations, or theology, and thus it illuminates many areas outside the normal purview of the religious historian. It can also be recommended for its attention to change over time and its inclusion of slave as well as white religion.

J. WILLIAM HARRIS

South: since 1865

Ayers, Edward L., *The Promise of the New South: Life after Reconstruction*, New York: Oxford University Press, 1992

Boles, John B. and Evelyn Thomas Nolen (editors), *Interpreting Southern History: Historiographical Essays in Honor of Sanford W. Higginbotham*, Baton Rouge: Louisiana State University Press, 1987

Branch, Taylor, *Parting the Waters: America in the King Years, 1954–63*, New York: Simon and Schuster, and London: Macmillan, 1988

Cash, W.J., *The Mind of the South*, New York: Knopf, 1941

Flynt, J. Wayne, *Dixie's Forgotten People: The South's Poor Whites*, Bloomington: Indiana University Press, 1979

Reed, John Shelton, *The Enduring South: Subcultural Persistence in Mass Society*, Lexington, MA: Lexington Books, 1972

Scott, Anne Firor, *The Southern Lady: From Pedestal to Politics, 1830–1930*, Chicago: University of Chicago Press, 1970

Tindall, George Brown, *The Emergence of the New South, 1913–1945*, Baton Rouge: Louisiana State University Press, 1967

Wilson, Charles Reagan and William Ferris (editors), *Encyclopedia of Southern Culture*, Chapel Hill: University of North Carolina Press, 1989

Woodward, C. Vann, *Origins of the New South, 1877–1913*, Baton Rouge: Louisiana University Press, 1951, updated by Charles B. Dew, 1971

Woodward, C. Vann, *The Strange Career of Jim Crow*, New York: Oxford University Press, 1955, 3rd revised edition, 1974

Woodward, C. Vann, *The Burden of Southern History*, Baton Rouge: Louisiana State University Press, 1960, 3rd edition, 1993

The American South, like Wales and Ireland, represents a peripheral region often out-of-step with its politically/economically/culturally dominant neighbor. Aspects of this relationship included quasi-imperialism, negative stereotyping and patronizing self-righteousness which in turn inspired cultural resentment, political defensiveness, and economic frustration. Few historians doubt that the South is different from the rest of America, though they vigorously debate the extent of that difference and whether it is increasing or decreasing during the late 20th century. More troubling to historians has been the issue of continuity or discontinuity between the antebellum and postbellum "Souths." Was the southern factory merely a plantation within walls, continuing and even deepening class and racial divisions through policies of paternalism, racism, and sexism? Or was it a dramatic departure from agrarianism?

At the heart of historical debate has been the work of Woodward. Generally considered one of the ten most influential historians of 20th century America, he challenged the predominant notion that little changed in the South after the Civil War. Whether in race relations or political and economic leadership, he sees dramatic change: hardening racial lines, a new generation of industrialists who dominate, the rise of one-party politics challenged by radical agrarian movements. As the South pursued its separate course, its history evolved in distinctly un-American fashion: a region of poverty within a nation of plenty; a section constructing a system of racial apartheid within a nation that affirmed equality; a people rooted in place, community, and tradition within a nation increasingly renowned for historical rootlessness and modernity; a religion famous for its Calvinism, sense of guilt, and evangelicalism in contrast to America's sense of innocence, tolerance, and optimism. Although racism had long been a theme of southern history, rigid segregation was as much a northern import in the late 19th century as indigenous to the South. And the drive for racial integration of the 1950s became a drive for racial separatism by the 1970s.

Many of these themes were developed in WOODWARD (1951), a superb, wide-ranging general study (volume 9 in the *History of the South*), which virtually re-wrote southern history for the period from 1877 to 1913. Similar themes are explored more briefly in WOODWARD (1960, 1993), a collection of essays of remarkable elegance, clarity and insight, some of which, for example on "The Search for Southern Identity" and "The Irony of Southern History," have become recognized as classics. WOODWARD (1955, 1974) focuses on the history of legally enforced segregation, and the challenge to it in the 1950s and 1960s. The book has shaped modern historical debate on the subject, and its many challengers attest to its enduring influence.

CASH presents quite a different view of the region. Journalist by profession and very much a product of the Great Depression, he portrayed the South in static terms. The man at the center of southern history was a "hell-of-a-fellow" yeoman farmer. The region was characterized by a sense of honor transmuted by poverty into the "savage ideal" of lynching, aversion to new ideas, religious emotionalism, sentimentality, lack of realism, and excessive individualism. The New South no less than the Old manifested such negative characteristics. AYERS does not entirely disagree with Woodward or Cash, portraying a region where change occurred within the broader context of continuity. In the struggle between old and new, Ayers tends to emphasize modernizing forces such as railroads, mass produced goods, and a more fluid economy. But he also writes perceptively about continuing folkways, particularly music and religion.

If the years between 1865 and 1920 reveal a region struggling with its identity, the following quarter century was one of devastating confrontation with American patterns. The assault on southern life by religious and cultural modernism, liberal Democratic politics and changing racial policies, the Great Depression, and the integrating economic forces unleashed by the New Deal and World War II, is the subject of TINDALL's work. At the same time that poverty and intolerance thrived, William Faulkner, Eudora Welty, Flannery O'Connor and a host of other writers began a half-century dominance of American literature. Tindall's encyclopedic history of the era is the companion piece to Woodward's history of the immediately preceding period.

Most scholars assumed that the integration of the South into the racial, political, and economic mainstream after 1945 would gradually eradicate Southern distinctiveness. Sociologist REED built his productive writing career around a counter theme: though history no longer formed the core of Southern exceptionalism, middle-class preferences, values, and patterns demonstrated remarkable regional resilience. And to the degree that America and the South converged, it was as likely a result of the "southernization" of America (in matters of sports, religion, violence, and politics) as in the "Americanization" of the South. Reed focuses on the persistence of localism, violence, and conservative religion.

Works on particular aspects of southern history contribute to the broader picture. SCOTT provides a useful corrective to accounts that tend to be largely devoted to white males. She explores the unfolding women's movement in the South from church to women's clubs to suffrage activists. Although southern culture attempted to confine women to a pedestal of ladyhood, many women were forced by economic necessity, or freely chose, a life of community activity.

FLYNT broadens the portrait of southern history by adding yet another dimension often omitted, in his study of poor whites. Centered in Appalachia but found throughout the region, they generated and sustained a rich folk culture with strong ties to the United Kingdom at the same time that they experienced economic indigence and political powerlessness. The book explores their lives through chapters on their primary occupations – tenant farming, coal mining, textile work – and their politics, religion, and folkways. This work also explores the out-migration of poor whites who moved north in search of better economic opportunities, taking their folkways with them.

BRANCH explores the civil rights movement in America during the 1950s and 1960s. Although the movement was primarily southern, and particularly was nourished by black evangelical religion, racism was by no means a regional problem. The study focuses on Martin Luther King, Jr. and the major civil rights groups he formed. But it also explores conflicts between these groups and the federal government as well as with each other.

BOLES and NOLEN provide the best guide to what historians have written about the South. Their volume is an invaluable guide to interpretations of southern history and contains additional historical discussions of thirteen topics as diverse as race relations, women, and Sun Belt prosperity. WILSON and FERRIS provide a companion volume that is as richly illuminating as it is eccentric. Twenty-four senior editors introduce each section of the encyclopedia with overview essays. These are followed by insightful brief discussions of topics as diverse as football, air-conditioning, Elvis Presley, Tallulah Bankhead, Blues, Eudora Welty, gumbo, possums, and grits.

WAYNE FLYNT

Southwest

Acuña, Rodolfo, *Occupied America: The Chicano's Struggle Toward Liberation*, San Francisco: Canfield Press, 1972; 3rd edition, as *Occupied America: A History of Chicanos*, New York: Harper, 1988

Faulk, Odie B., *Land of Many Frontiers: A History of the American Southwest*, New York: Oxford University Press, 1968

Gómez-Quiñones, Juan, *Roots of Chicano Politics, 1600–1940*, Albuquerque: University of New Mexico Press, 1994

Hollon, Eugene W., *The Southwest: Old and New*, New York: Knopf, 1961

Luckingham, Bradford, *The Urban Southwest: A Profile History of Albuquerque, El Paso, Phoenix, Tucson*, El Paso: Texas Western Press, 1982

Meinig, D.W., *Southwest: Three Peoples in Geographical Change, 1500–1970*, New York: Oxford University Press, 1971

Spicer, Edward H., *Cycles of Conquest: The Impact of Spain, Mexico, and the United States on the Indians of the Southwest, 1533–1960*, Tucson: University of Arizona Press, 1962

Spicer, Edward H. and Raymond H. Thompson (editors), *Plural Society in the Southwest*, Albuquerque: University of New Mexico Press, 1972

Scholars have often disagreed over how to define the Southwest as a region, except in the simplest geographical terms. One of the classic narrative accounts of the Southwest as a geographically defined region can be found in HOLLON's history of Colorado, Texas and Arizona. Although limited in that it does not cover the entire Southwest, its theme of progressive development under American rule represents the traditional interpretation of the southwestern experience. While less well known, FAULK also provides a straightforward descriptive account of economic and political change, particularly in the period since the American conquest. His work is particularly useful because it covers a broader area, including California and New Mexico.

LUCKINGHAM is a study of four major southwestern cities which uses urbanization as the central theme of its overview of the region's progressive growth. While tracing in brief the history of these urban centers from the 17th century to recent times, he discusses the impact of changes in the regional economy and the introduction of new transportation technologies, as well as the impact of national policies and the boosterism of local elites. Like the authors previously cited, he provides a mainly chronological narrative rather than a deep analysis of the region's development.

A more analytical attempt to understand the region's history may be found in MEINIG's brief examination of its economic, political and cultural geography. One of the most important studies of the Southwest published in the past few decades, his work focuses on the spatial development of the area, examining the changing flow of immigration, transportation and trade patterns and the geographic and social relationships of the region's three "peoples": Anglo, Native American and Mexican. This discussion of the interaction between various peoples and the landscape which they inhabited is well illustrated with maps depicting the changing spatial dynamics of demographic and economic forces. It also offers a useful step towards an alternative definition of the American Southwest which concentrates on its status as a unique cultural landscape where diverse peoples and traditions have come into juxtaposition.

The contributors to SPICER and THOMPSON provide various viewpoints on the creation of this landscape. Based on a series of papers presented at an Arizona conference, these essays address the question of how the non-dominant ethnic groups of the Southwest, particularly Native Americans and Mexican Americans, interacted with the dominant Anglo society and accepted, or resisted, cultural transformation. Although the introductory essays provide a measure of overall cohesion, the fragmented nature of the individual pieces, which deal with different time periods and employ different methodological approaches, make this a somewhat difficult book for those who are not already familiar with southwestern history.

SPICER's own work is critical to the study of cultural pluralism in this region. Despite its length, his seminal study of the interaction between Native Americans and successive waves of conquerors is very readable, mainly because he avoids cumbersome technical language. Spicer documents both the attempts of conquering societies to "civilize" the native people and transform their culture, and the reaction of Native Americans to these assaults upon their traditional folkways. Comparing the policies of Spain, Mexico and the United States, he argues that Spanish missionaries were the most successful in transmitting their cultural values. Overall, however, he concludes that, despite repeated conquests and the undoubted transformation of Native American society, the original inhabitants of the region have stubbornly retained a distinctive religious, linguistic, and communal identity as a people. This argument contradicts the assertions of Hollon and Faulk that the Southwest can be characterized simply by the progressive absorption of minorities into the dominant Anglo society.

This theme of cultural resistance, as it relates to the region's Mexican American population, has become one of the principal topics of southwestern studies. Now in its third edition, ACUÑA provides a useful survey text for an alternative cultural definition of the region. In the course of a careful narrative account of the history of each of the states in the greater Southwest, he reverses the image presented by Anglo scholars; rather than a story of inevitable progress, this is a story of conquest, oppression and resistance. As in Spicer's study of Native Americans, Acuña emphasizes the extent to which the Chicano peoples of the Southwest have retained a separate cultural and social identity – an identity created out of the struggle to survive in a hostile society. He offers an even more radical conclusion. Using Marxist-Leninist theories of international colonial domination, he argues that, far from being a "pluralist" society, the Anglo- dominated society in the Southwest has exploited the subordinate Chicano community as an internal "colonial" dependency.

A more recent attempt to deal with this subject can be found in GÓMEZ-QUIÑONES's sweeping and ambitious study. As the title suggests, this lengthy work focuses on the political development of the Hispanic Southwest, covering both the periods of Spanish and Mexican rule, and the subsequent American conquest. In the later period, Gómez-Quiñones meticulously documents the creation and maintenance of autonomous Chicano movements and communities within the dominant Anglo political order. Building on much of the recent scholarship on the Southwest, he discusses the entire span of strategies used by Mexican Americans to cope with their political, social, and economic marginalization. He also includes a sensitive examination of the creation of ethnic identity and the significance of gender and class relationships both within the Mexican American community and in their interaction with the dominant society. For the reader interested in the southwestern history, as defined by the Chicano experience, this is an extraordinarily useful book, although it can be a difficult text for the newcomer to the subject.

DANIEL J. JOHNSON

See also California; Mexican Americans; Native Americans: Cultures 4

Space Policy and Program

Chaikin, Andrew, *A Man on the Moon: The Voyages of the Apollo Astronauts*, New York: Viking, and London: Joseph, 1994

Collins, Martin, J. and Silvia D. Fries (editors), *A Spacefaring Nation: Perspectives on American Space History and Policy*, Washington, DC: Smithsonian Institution Press, 1991

Divine, Robert A., *The Sputnik Challenge: Eisenhower's Response to the Soviet Satellite*, New York and Oxford: Oxford University Press, 1993

Lambright, W. Henry, *Powering Apollo: James E. Webb of NASA*, Baltimore: Johns Hopkins University Press, 1995

Logsdon, John M., *The Decision to Go to the Moon: Project Apollo and the National Interest*, Cambridge: Massachusetts Institute of Technology Press, 1970

McDougall, Walter A., *The Heavens and the Earth: A Political History of the Space Age*, New York: Basic Books, 1985

Murray, Charles and Catherine Bly Cox, *Apollo: The Race to the Moon*, New York: Simon and Schuster, and London: Secker and Warburg, 1989

Ordway, Frederick I. and Randy Liebermann (editors), *Blueprint for Space: Science Fiction to Science Fact*, Washington, DC: Smithsonian Institution Press, 1992

Smith, Robert W., *The Space Telescope: A Study of NASA, Science, Technology, and Politics*, Cambridge and New York: Cambridge University Press, 1989

The American civilian space programme has been one of the defining aspects of the 20th century, and is potentially of interest to almost all students of recent American history. What began as a manifestation of Cold War competition became sustained by bargaining among domestic policymakers in a process that can serve as a useful microcosm of American politics in general. But surprisingly, perhaps, given the wealth of documentation and oral history interviews available, specific works on the history of the space programme remain relatively rare. A lack of quantity, however, does not mean a loss of quality.

For many, space exploration is synonymous with the Apollo moon landing programme, which was initiated by President Kennedy in 1961 and put Neil Armstrong on the lunar surface in 1969. CHAIKIN, and MURRAY and COX, both offer reliable and readable accounts of Apollo, the former from the point of view of the astronauts and the latter from that of their ground controllers and engineers. Both are also good at setting out the technical, political, and organisational challenges that faced the National Aeronautics and Space Administration (NASA) during the period, making them useful introductions to the issues involved in space exploration.

For a more detailed study of the political impetus behind Apollo, LOGSDON remains the standard work, despite its pioneering, and now venerable, status: its argument, that Apollo grew out of a unique set of political circumstances that prevailed in early 1961, remains sound. The other aspect of Apollo, the practice rather than the purpose, is well covered in LAMBRIGHT which highlights the role of James Webb, NASA's administrator during the 1960s. For Lambright,

Webb is worth studying not only as the personal dynamo whose managerial skill brought together the many different components of Apollo into a coherent whole, but also as a central figure in the evolving relationship between government, industry and the scientific community.

The best treatment of the pre-Apollo period is DIVINE, which makes good use of recently available material on military as well as civilian space projects. It covers the impact of Sputnik on the American public, the establishment of NASA and the development of the space race from the perspective of the White House. He argues, persuasively, that Eisenhower was prepared to pay the heavy domestic price for appearing lackadaisical about Soviet space successes in order to preserve the secrecy surrounding the development of the reconnaissance satellite.

While coverage of the 1970s and 1980s remains understandably sparse, SMITH offers a detailed study of the evolution of one particular project, the space telescope. A historian who is happy to borrow some analytical tools from political science, he charts the means by which the small group of astronomers who initially conceived the telescope were able to build a coalition of support, first among other scientists, then among NASA officials and finally among politicians, that would sustain the huge cost of the venture. A less detailed version of Smith's study appears in COLLINS and FRIES, a collection of essays covering several aspects of space exploration from a historical perspective. Particularly worth noting, together with Fries's introduction, are those by Howard McCurdy on NASA's strategy to sell its space station project to the White House, and Pamela Mack on the use of space for environmental monitoring. (As with Smith, these are useful distillations of book-length studies.)

ORDWAY and LIEBERMANN, a wide-ranging and well-illustrated survey of the idea of spaceflight and its advocates from antiquity onwards, is a desirable if eclectic companion to any study of the history of space exploration. Especially useful for the development of the American space programme are chapters on the media's enthusiasm for space in the 1950s, the public relations skills of the German rocket designer Wernher Von Braun which helped to spark interest in space among public and politicians alike, and a discussion of why Apollo failed to lead to the permanent moon bases and missions to Mars that once seemed inevitable.

McDOUGALL is perhaps the best single-volume history of the space programme. Although over a decade old, the breath of its research is unrivalled and splendidly enhanced by judiciously chosen anecdotes and felicitous writing, and it thoroughly deserved its Pulitzer Prize. However, readers seeking an introductory volume should note that its dazzling account of the American and Russian space programmes is quickly subsumed within McDougall's larger theme – that in striving to outdo the communist system in the exploration of space, the United States, lamentably, began to adopt its rival's state direction of technological development. The ideas which flow from this framework are elegant and powerful, creating a book which any serious student of America in the Cold War period can read with profit, but it is best appreciated with some prior knowledge of the highlights of space history.

GILES ALSTON

Spanish-American War, 1898

Foner, Philip S., *The Spanish-Cuban-American War and the Birth of American Imperialism, 1895–1902*, 2 vols., New York: Monthly Review Press, 1972

Karnow, Stanley, *In Our Image: America's Empire in the Philippines*, New York: Random House, 1989

LaFeber, Walter, *The New Empire: An Interpretation of American Expansion, 1860–1898*, Ithaca, NY: Cornell University Press, 1963

May, Ernest R., *Imperial Democracy: The Emergence of America as a Great Power*, New York: Harcourt Brace, 1961

Millis, Walter, *The Martial Spirit: A Study of Our War with Spain*, Boston: Houghton Mifflin, 1931

Offner, John L., *An Unwanted War: The Diplomacy of the United States and Spain over Cuba, 1895–1898*, Chapel Hill: University of North Carolina Press, 1992

O'Toole, George J.A., *The Spanish War: An American Epic, 1898*, New York: Norton, 1984

Pérez, Louis A., Jr., *Cuba Between Empires, 1878–1902*, Pittsburgh: Pittsburgh University Press, 1983

Smith, Joseph, *The Spanish-American War: Conflict in the Caribbean and the Pacific, 1895–1902*, London and New York: Longman, 1994

Trask, David F., *The War with Spain in 1898*, New York: Macmillan, and London: Collier Macmillan, 1981

There are several very readable overviews of the war between the United States and Spain. For many years the best-known was MILLIS. The work of a celebrated journalist, and a popular bestseller during the 1930s, it depicts the conflict as a brief and exciting episode in which Americans fought unselfishly to liberate the people of Cuba from Spanish oppression. Influenced by World War I, Millis does not neglect to mention the horrors that occurred during the 1898 war, and he is also generally scathing about the quality of leadership on both sides. However, he believes that the call to arms brought out the best in the character of the American people and resulted in a brilliant victory. There have been numerous attempts at producing similar stirring and rousing accounts for a general audience. One of the most successful is O'TOOLE, which adopts an effective narrative style that includes copious quotations from contemporary sources and at times even gives a day-by-day account of events. The advantage – and also the limitation – of this approach is that the story of the war unfolds chronologically almost in the form of a diary and is presented from the point of view of the participants.

The most authoritative modern study of the actual fighting is TRASK. A substantial volume of more than 600 pages, based upon impressive historical research, it is especially insightful on American military strategy, and highlights the woeful lack of preparedness for war and the damaging effects of interservice rivalries between the army and the navy. The military campaigns against Puerto Rico and the Philippines are also examined in meticulous detail. SMITH is a more concise and more accessible work which teachers and students will find useful. It also stresses the military aspects of the war, but gives more discussion of the revolt in Cuba that began in 1895 and preceded American intervention.

Professional historians in the United States have shown much less interest in studying the details of the military campaigns than in poring over the question why America went to war in 1898, and thereby assumed the status of a world power. This is exemplified in an influential study by LaFEBER which argues that the decision to intervene in 1898 represented the culmination of more than three decades of national preparation in which the search for overseas markets and raw materials had pushed the American business frontier beyond the boundaries of the continental United States. Consequently, the war against Spain and the resulting extension of American influence throughout the Caribbean and Pacific are seen as part of a deliberate and logical process. Although LaFeber underlines the significance of economic influences, his analysis takes account of political and diplomatic factors. FONER, however, gives an orthodox Marxist interpretation of events. He singles out American capitalism as the determining influence on the decision to intervene in Cuba in 1898, and dogmatically asserts that the ensuing conflict was an imperialistic war fought for imperialistic reasons.

A number of historians have rejected the economic interpretation as too simplistic and have preferred to concentrate instead on the diplomatic background as the key to understanding why war occurred. These studies usually focus on the role of President McKinley and consider the controversial question whether he was a strong or a weak leader. The complex diplomatic activity of the period is competently described in MAY. The author was the first American historian investigating this subject to conduct extensive research in several European archives, and was therefore able to provide an extremely well-informed and balanced analysis of the international efforts to achieve a diplomatic settlement of the pre-war crisis in Cuba. May gives particular weight to domestic political factors in both Spain and the United States and concludes that they created a diplomatic impasse in which war became inevitable. But McKinley does not escape criticism, and is portrayed by May as a president who ultimately lacked courage and was pushed into war. This particular interpretation is effectively challenged in OFFNER. Despite being only 300 pages long, Offner's monograph is the result of a massive amount of archival research and provides the definitive account of diplomatic relations between the United States and Spain from the outbreak of rebellion in Cuba in 1895 to the signing of the Peace Protocol in August 1898. Offner agrees with May that McKinley did not want war, but he argues that the President was consistent and positive in his attempts to bring peace to Cuba.

Although Cuba was the dominant issue in the 1898 war, American military expeditions were also despatched to fight in the other Spanish colonies of Puerto Rico and the Philippines. These particular campaigns are competently described in Millis, O'Toole, Trask and Smith. The adoption of a broader geographical perspective to events has resulted in some writers suggesting that the conflict be renamed the "Spanish-American-Cuban-Filipino War". For example, Foner has emphasised the military contribution of the Cuban rebels to winning the war. Notably, he presents the challenging thesis that they were on the point of defeating the Spaniards in 1898, and did not need American military assistance. The relations between Americans and Cubans are expertly analyzed by PÉREZ, who describes in impressive detail the growing divergence between the two sides, and explains why the United States insisted that the new Cuban republic accept the notorious Platt Amendment. A readable introduction to similar difficulties encountered by the American occupation forces in the Philippines is KARNOW. The author is sympathetic to the pressures placed upon the McKinley and Roosevelt administrations, but he is highly critical of American policy for inflicting a cruel war of conquest upon the Filipinos.

JOSEPH SMITH

See also Cuba and the United States; Imperialism and Anti-Imperialism; McKinley

Spoils System see Patronage/Spoils System

Sport: General

Adelman, Melvin L., *A Sporting Time: New York City and the Rise of Modern Athletics, 1820–70*, Urbana: University of Illinois Press, 1986

Cahn, Susan K., *Coming on Strong: Gender and Sexuality in Twentieth-Century Women's Sport*, New York: Free Press, 1994

Gorn, Elliott J., *The Manly Art: Bare-Knuckle Prize Fighting in America*, Ithaca, NY: Cornell University Press, 1986

Guttmann, Allen, *From Ritual to Record: The Nature of Modern Sports*, New York: Columbia University Press, 1978

Hardy, Stephen, *How Boston Played: Sport, Recreation, and Community 1865–1915*, Boston: Northeastern University Press, 1982

Rader, Benjamin G., *American Sports: From the Age of Folk Games to the Age of Spectators*, Englewood Cliffs, NJ: Prentice Hall, 1983, 3rd edition, as *American Sports: From the Age of Folk Games to the Age of Televised Sports*, 1995

Riess, Steven A., *City Games: The Evolution of American Urban Society and the Rise of Sports*, Urbana: University of Illinois Press, 1989

Tygiel, Jules, *Baseball's Great Experiment: Jackie Robinson and His Legacy*, New York: Oxford University Press, 1983

Prior to the 1970s, academics generally ignored American sports history. This situation changed sharply in the following two decades when scholars began writing numerous monographs and articles on the subject. In his 1978 study of the nature of modern sports and their relationship with society, GUTTMANN produced a major pioneering work in the field. Critical of Marxist interpretations of sport history, he uses theory from sociologist Max Weber to analyze seven distinguishing characteristics of modern sports. They are: secularism, equality, specialization, rationalization, bureaucracy, quantification and a concern for records. Guttmann then examines the American fascination with baseball and football in these terms, and suggests that they both contain a mix of primitive and modern characteristics specifically appealing to Americans. While many of Guttmann's arguments are speculative, his book employs sophisticated sociological theory and marks a turning point in the scholarly study of sport history.

RADER is the best general history of American sports. Pioneering in the identification of a 19th-century sporting fraternity and the role of television in modern sports, his work reflects much of the recent academic progress in the field. Beginning with the English sporting traditions of the colonists, he traces the evolution of sport from the age of folk games to the modern sports of today. To accomplish this, Rader examines developments in American social, cultural and economic history, explaining how these were related to the evolution of sport. He also describes the internal changes in the sports themselves as they became more bureaucratic, organized and specialized. Rader treats nearly all levels of this topic from youth sports to professional leagues and includes discussions of class, race and gender in his analysis. Although the book is very inclusive, some leisure activities, such as hunting, fishing and chess, are not covered.

Many of the best works on American sport focus on its relationship with urban developments. One good example is HARDY who examines the topic in Boston during the half-century after the Civil War. He finds that Bostonians in the late 19th century used sport and recreation to provide community order in their ever-changing city. This book contains useful material on the politics surrounding the development of playgrounds and parks as well as the establishment of athletic clubs in the schools. Hardy's case study was the first complete work to provide detailed evidence of how in the late 19th century city residents, from nearly all social classes, used sport and recreation to advance their various agendas of achieving community stability. ADELMAN's discussion of developments in New York City from 1820 to 1870 also examines how urbanization and sport were related. Influenced by Guttmann, he uses modernization theory as an analytical framework for his study. Departing from previous assessments of the antebellum years which found limited sports activity, Adelman shows that organized sports did exist in New York City in that period, and that many of them achieved a modern character by the 1860s. His work explores the changing nature of the city along with the internal development of sport, and recognizes both as dynamic processes. Although dogged at times by rigid adherence to its analytical framework, Adelman's study provides the most detailed history of sport in the antebellum era.

RIESS also argues that urbanization played an active role in the emergence of American sports. Tracing the development of sport in the evolving American city between 1820 and 1980, he incorporates the findings of many urban and social historians into his analysis. Covering several major American cities, Riess presents an interesting discussion of government, business, and underworld activity in such sports as baseball, boxing and horse racing. While this work's treatment of the antebellum and post-World War II years is less comprehensive, Riess still provides the best overall account of the city's connection to the changing nature of American sports.

The study of sport has also been useful in examining the history of social class in America. GORN's study of bare-knuckle prize fighting in the 19th century gives important insights into the working-class culture of that time. He not only describes the boxing heroes and their major bouts in detail, but he also explains the larger social significance of the sport. Gorn shows how the values associated with prize fighting helped to define the ethos of the laboring classes, as the sport became a manifestation of the workingman's opposition to the dominant Victorian values of the day. Furthermore, by describing how the middle class eventually accepted boxing and its values of masculinity and courage, this study reveals how American attitudes about manliness had changed by the final decades of the 19th century.

CAHN's examination of women's sport in the 20th century also explores the country's conception of gender norms. Her book shows how Americans have generally associated sport with manliness, a phenomenon which has limited the opportunities of female athletes. She also argues that prevailing gender stereotypes were manifested when successful female athletes were unfairly classified as "abnormal" or "mannish" by the sporting community. Cahn thoroughly documents the battles waged over both the control and suppression of women's sport in this century. Like most good scholarly works on sport history, this book transcends mere description of athletic competition as it shows how American attitudes about gender and sexuality have persisted in the 20th century.

Developments in sport have also reflected prevailing American racial attitudes. The best study of this topic is TYGIEL, which examines the integration of professional baseball. His discussion of Branch Rickey and Jackie Robinson is balanced and insightful. In addition, Tygiel documents the stories of other black baseball pioneers, including their early careers in the Negro Leagues. In the process, this book paints a vivid picture of the Jim Crow South where African American athletes had to endure bigoted taunts and threats throughout the years following integration. This well researched study provides a broad coverage of baseball's desegregation along with a revealing commentary on American society in the 20th century.

KENT M. KRAUSE

Stanton, Elizabeth Cady 1815–1902

Campaigner for women's rights

Banner, Lois W., *Elizabeth Cady Stanton: A Radical for Woman's Rights*, Boston: Little Brown, 1980

Griffith, Elisabeth, *In Her Own Right: The Life of Elizabeth Cady Stanton*, New York: Oxford University Press, 1984

Hersh, Blanche Glassman, *The Slavery of Sex: Feminist-Abolitionists in America*, Urbana: University of Illinois Press, 1978

Lutz, Alma, *Created Equal: A Biography of Elizabeth Cady Stanton, 1815–1902*, New York: John Day, 1940

Lutz, Alma, "Elizabeth Cady Stanton", in *Notable American Women, 1607–1950: A Biographical Dictionary*, volume 3, edited by Edward T. James and others, Cambridge, MA: Belknap Press of Harvard University Press, 1971

Pellauer, Mary D., *Toward a Tradition of Feminist Theology in the Religious Social Thought of Elizabeth Cady Stanton, Susan B. Anthony and Anna Howard Shaw*, New York: Carlson, 1991

Riegel, Robert E., *American Feminists*, Lawrence: University Press of Kansas, 1963

Stanton, Theodore and Harriot Stanton Blatch (editors), *Elizabeth Stanton as Revealed in Her Letters, Diary and Reminiscences*, 2 vols., New York: Harper, 1922

Elizabeth Cady Stanton is the most contentious and impressive of the 19th-century American feminists. Arousing controversy in her own time because of her radicalism and independence, she has since been a challenge to biographers because she has not left an easily managed body of records or a definite summary of her ideology. What is more, two of her children, STANTON and BLATCH, carefully edited her papers and presented the image they favoured to the world. But if Stanton was often irked by fellow feminists towards the end of her career, she would have relished the attention that she has belatedly received.

LUTZ (1940), the first modern biography, is a full and well-researched account of Stanton's life. It stresses her wide interests, independence of thought, courage, aversion to compromise and devotion to the ideal of freedom; and there is a nice contrast between Stanton's long experience of criticism and the eventual tributes to her as the mother of women's suffrage and the greatest woman the world had ever produced. The famous friendship with fellow reformer and feminist, Susan B. Anthony, is given appropriate attention, and an even-handed approach is evident in Lutz's judgements on the two women and the two wings of the suffrage movement. Stanton's drawbacks as a thinker or leader are not highlighted here, any more than they are in LUTZ (1971), which nonetheless usefully points up Stanton's international activities and reform apprenticeship, as well as her move away from Presbyterianism, growing commitment to writing, and neglect after her death, because she left behind no loyal organisation to cherish and publicise her achievements.

Three studies which allow one to compare Stanton with her contemporaries are those by Riegel, Hersh and Pellauer. Since RIEGEL seeks to revise the "usual glorified picture of early feminists", Mrs. Stanton comes out rather well from his account. She is acknowledged to have enjoyed success in her lifetime, and to have been the "dynamo of feminism, the centrifugal force that held the movement together, and the most effective propagandist in the drive to expand the opportunities of women." In assessing Stanton's character, Riegel, like other scholars, is influenced by the children's presentation of their mother as blessed with physical and mental vitality, "unconquerable optimism", organising ability, humour, a love of play, personal charisma and dignity. Given the importance of the marriage question to Stanton, he is right to give prominence to her own experience of it. Of the formative relationships in her life, there is only space to do justice to her father. Riegel's judgment that Stanton was not a philosopher might have been moderated if he had been able to treat her ideas, especially on religion, at greater length. This PELLAUER does, of course, and it is very helpful to see religious influences discussed as an integral part of feminism, rather than simply as a factor leading women to reform, or against which they did or did not react in reaching maturity as social activists. For HERSH, as for Riegel, Stanton is a celebrator of women's moral and spiritual gifts, whose charm and brilliance set her apart from her contemporaries. Hersh is well aware of what Stanton shared with other feminists, notably her elevation of women's role in the family, her sympathy with the claim that women were morally superior to men, and her elitism. However, we do not lose sight of the fierce determination to achieve both equality in the home and access to the wider world that have generally made unorthodoxy seem to be Stanton's most striking characteristic.

BANNER is a biography which builds on these earlier works and is, though quite short, securely grounded in primary sources. The key individuals and environments that shaped Stanton's development are interestingly presented, and status discontent is rightly discounted as a motivation. Stanton is rather explained in terms of her upbringing, experience, intelligence, reading, maternal instincts and sensitivity to others. We also learn how she responded positively to successive crises in her desire to prove that "all is well, grand, glorious, triumphant"; how she discovered early the difficulty of allying with conservative groups; and how she survived by adopting moderate strategies for change or even abandoning causes that proved too unpopular or personally trying: dress reform being a case in point. More than any other biographer before her, Banner is able to establish Mrs. Stanton as a thinker, sometimes original, frequently borrowing from such intellectual currents as eugenics, utopianism, Fabian socialism and the social gospel. Like her predecessors, she does not dwell on Stanton's prejudices and inconsistencies.

The most recent life of Stanton is GRIFFITH, which is based on a systematic search through surviving records, and an intelligent use of social learning theory, which emphasizes the importance of role models. Seeking to integrate Stanton's public and private lives, Griffith presents her as a famous woman, dedicated to achieving independence and aware of her place in history. Her behaviour patterns are seen as being based on successive role models, among whom her powerful but domestic mother and the nationally revered feminist-abolitionist Lucretia Mott are accorded welcome prominence. In an era when we are fully aware of the way in which sexual images are socially constructed, Griffith shows us how Stanton deliberately constructed her dual image as matriarch and revolutionary. Sensibly, the author also admits that all the facts of Stanton's life will not fit into a single theory. Moreover, she is willing to reveal that her eventually autonomous heroine was capable of self-indulgence and ingratitude, besides being affected by the class and race prejudices of her time.

CHRISTINE BOLT

See also Feminism; Women's History: Suffrage

State Constitutions and State Politics, 1776–1789

Adams, Willi Paul, *The First American Constitutions: Republican Ideology and the Making of the State Constitutions in the Revolutionary Era*, translated by Rita Kimber and Robert Kimber, Chapel Hill: University of North Carolina Press, 1980

Becker, Robert A., *Revolution, Reform, and the Politics of American Taxation, 1763–1783*, Baton Rouge: Louisiana State University Press, 1980

Daniell, Jere R., *Experiment in Republicanism: New Hampshire Politics and the American Revolution, 1741–1794*, Cambridge, MA: Harvard University Press, 1970

Hall, Van Beck, *Politics Without Parties: Massachusetts, 1780–1791*, Pittsburgh: University of Pittsburgh Press, 1972

Hoffman, Ronald, *A Spirit of Dissension: Economics, Politics, and the Revolution in Maryland*, Baltimore: Johns Hopkins University Press, 1973

Hoffman, Ronald and Peter J. Albert, *Sovereign States in an Age of Uncertainty*, Charlottesville: University Press of Virginia, 1981

Main, Jackson Turner, *Political Parties Before the Constitution*, Chapel Hill: University of North Carolina Press, 1973

Main, Jackson Turner, *The Sovereign States, 1775–1783*, New York: New Viewpoints, 1973

Morrill, James R., *The Practice and Politics of Fiat Finance: North Carolina in the Confederation, 1783–1789*, Chapel Hill: University of North Carolina Press, 1969

Nevins, Allan, *The American States During and after the Revolution, 1775–1789*, New York: Macmillan, 1924

Wood, Gordon S., *The Creation of the American Republic, 1776–1787*, Chapel Hill: University of North Carolina Press, 1969

Young, Alfred F., *The Democratic Republicans of New York: The Origins 1763–1797*, Chapel Hill: University of North Carolina Press, 1967

Before the American Revolution created a new nation, it transformed thirteen British provinces into American states with new governments and constitutions, the first fruits of the Revolution. Although somewhat outdated, NEVINS still offers perhaps the most comprehensive survey of that transformation. This large volume provides detailed coverage of constitutional, political, social and fiscal developments. Nevins largely follows the method of progressive historians such as Charles Beard and Merrill Jensen in emphasizing conflict, particularly sectional factionalism. But unlike many progressives, he stresses continuity between colonial and state governments, and he is highly disapproving of the more radically popular state constitutions, which he argues were dangerously unbalanced.

Written half a century later, MAIN's two surveys share some of Nevins's progressivism, if not his elitism. Aimed at the non-specialist, *The Sovereign States* offers a lively, readable summary of the economic, social and political histories of the states. Throughout, Main stresses change over continuity,

arguing that the state governments with their strong legislatures and innovative constitutional conventions marked a break with their pre-revolutionary predecessors. Main's emphasis on factions and competing interests is clearer in *Political Parties Before the Constitution*. In this more technical volume he uses roll call analysis of voting in the state legislatures to show the existence of two primitive parties – localist and cosmopolitan – in every state after 1776.

HALL's study of Massachusetts politics also uses roll call analysis to demonstrate the existence of political divisions in the years immediately after the Revolution. In this highly quantitative example of social science history, Hall discovers essentially two interest-based divisions in Massachusetts politics, one very cosmopolitan and commercially-oriented and the other localist and less commercially-oriented. He sees the federal Constitution as an effort by the out-of-power cosmopolitans to regain power and as the catalyst for true party politics in the 1790s.

The first 105-page section of YOUNG's important book focuses on the formation of two proto-parties or "interests" in New York following the ratification of the state constitution of 1777. These interests, initially the conservative Whigs and the popular Whigs were split essentially along class lines, according to Young. He argues that the bulk of the conservative whigs evolved into federalists while the popular whigs became anti-federalists in the debate over the federal Constitution. Later, Young argues, the anti-federalists merged into the Democratic Republicans, the subject of the rest of the book.

HOFFMAN's study of revolutionary Maryland politics shares with Main, Hall, and Young an emphasis on economic interests and political divisions. Hoffman focuses on the whiggish Popular Party led by Charles Carroll of Carrollton and Samuel Chase which created the notably conservative 1776 constitution. But in order to gain support for their constitution, Carroll and his fellow elite members were forced to pass a radically popular fiscal program. And so, despite a conservative constitution, Maryland's new government also had its radical side, according to Hoffman. His narrative ends with the dissolution of the Popular Party in 1785.

WOOD's masterful and massive volume marks a departure from the old progressive preoccupation with interests and political faction for a new emphasis on republican ideology. At its core, it is a study of the first state constitutions and the political culture that produced them. The constitutions were the embodiment of Whig republican ideology and as such made a clean break from the colonial governments. But they did not long satisfy people, and calls for still more representative government eventually prompted the reactionary, conservative movement for the federal Constitution of 1789, which marks for Wood the end of classical republicanism. Although he has been criticized for overlooking conflict in his portrayal of a unified revolutionary republican ideology, Wood set the agenda for the scholarship of the next two decades.

DANIELL's short narrative study of New Hampshire politics shares Wood's emphasis on ideology. While political and regional interests are not absent, the stress is on the republicanism of the Granite State's founders. Popular dissatisfaction with the constitution of 1784 represented a crisis of confidence in republicanism that was favorably resolved only after the ratification of the federal Constitution, according to Daniell.

ADAMS's book, originally written in German, criticizes the ideological school for creating a false image of political consensus and for failing to understand that the founders were pragmatic men chiefly concerned with the science of government. Yet he follows Wood's method of close analysis of the language of the state constitutions and other documents, largely eschewing discussions of politics or factions. One chapter offers a useful state-by-state summary of constitution making. Adams concludes that the state constitutions were revolutionary, especially in their conception of the idea of "constituent power" as opposed to legislative power. Unlike many of the historians of this period, he argues that the federal Constitution of 1789 was not a conservative reaction but rather the logical extension of the ideas of the state constitutions.

A secondary theme in nearly all these books, the creation of state fiscal policy, takes center stage in BECKER's study of state taxation. In this state-by-state account, he finds that the revolution brought both continuity and change in taxation, with New England the least changed and the middle Atlantic and southern states the most. MORRILL offers a detailed study of North Carolina's fiscal policy from 1783 to 1789. He finds a basic division between fiat (or paper) money men and hard money men, with the fiat men generally triumphing until ratification of the federal Constitution.

The essays collected by HOFFMAN and ALBERT stress the central role of the states in the politics of the Confederation period. Of consistently high quality, they focus chiefly on the politics and fiscal policies of several states from Massachusetts to South Carolina.

LAWRENCE A. PESKIN

See also American Revolution: Character, Scope, and Significance; Articles of Confederation

States Rights

Bartley, Numan V., The Rise of Massive Resistance: Race and Politics in the South During the 1950s, Baton Rouge: Louisiana State University Press, 1969

Bowman, Ann O'M. and Richard C. Kearney, The Resurgence of the States, Englewood Cliffs, NJ: Prentice Hall, 1986

Elazar, Daniel J., American Federalism: A View from the States, New York: Crowell, 1966; 3rd edition, New York: Harper, 1984

Ellis, Richard E., The Union at Risk: Jacksonian Democracy, States' Rights, and the Nullification Crisis, New York: Oxford University Press, 1987

Freehling, William W., Prelude to Civil War: The Nullification Controversy in South Carolina, 1816–1836, New York: Harper, 1966

Lowry, William R., The Dimensions of Federalism: State Governments and Pollution Control Policies, Durham, NC: Duke University Press, 1992

Mason, Alpheus T. (editor), The States Rights Debate: Antifederalism and the Constitution, Englewood Cliffs, NJ: Prentice Hall, 1964; 2nd edition, New York: Oxford University Press, 1972

States rights, as a constitutional theory in American history, began with the antifederalists, "Founding Fathers" who feared a central government having, or potentially acquiring, too much power. The origins and evolution of this debate are ably traced in a slender volume by MASON. The author supplements his commentary with documents, and succeeds in making the states rights debate intelligible. Mason's work, which appeared during the civil rights struggle, was consciously presentist. He hoped to place the contemporary debate into historical perspective by pointing out the uncertainty that characterized the Constitution's formation and early interpretation. The antifederalists themselves, Mason concluded, were guided by personal motives rather than grand legal theories. He also emphasizes their considerable achievements, such as elimination of the proposed Congressional veto over state legislation.

One celebrated case of states rights was the Nullification crisis of 1832–33 in South Carolina, when state leaders invoked the constitutional theory to "nullify" federal laws, in this case the tariffs of 1828 and 1832. The classic work on this episode is FREEHLING, whose interpretation has remained authoritative. He traces the ideological heritage of South Carolina's nullifiers, from Jefferson and Madison to the Hartford Convention, which their intellectual leader John C. Calhoun fashioned into a coherent philosophy, eventually embraced by southern secessionists in 1860. Freehling concludes that the nullifiers actually cared little about the tariff, but rather used it as an excuse to test their states rights theories and challenge majority rule. They believed that the federal government would inevitably strike at slavery; Nullification was simply a "prelude" to that confrontation.

In a more recent study of Nullification, ELLIS builds on Freehling's work and focuses on the interaction between states rights doctrine, as a constitutional argument, and Jacksonian politics. Ellis conceives the crisis as a three-way discussion between nullifiers, "mainstream" states rights advocates, and nationalists. He also focuses, more than Freehling, on President Andrew Jackson's ideology, which, he says, supported both states rights and majority rule. Jackson viewed Nullification as a potentially fatal strike against majority rule, and thus the foundation of America's democratic constitutional government. His "Nullification Proclamation," which declared it to be an "impractical absurdity," alienated many southerners and mainstream states righters. In essence, Ellis argues, Jackson's response aligned the federal government against the "compact theory" of constitutional formation. The crisis in South Carolina linked slavery and states rights together for the rest of the antebellum period. Even though Jackson isolated South Carolina and the nullifiers, who got little support from other slaveholding states, many southerners came to embrace their arguments as a viable basis for defence of their peculiar institution.

BARTLEY shows how states rights became a central tenet of white resistance to civil rights, in particular federally mandated desegregation, in the 1950s. He portrays states rights as essential to the "ideological cover" for "neo-Bourbonism," his term for the reactionary and exceptionally racist upper-class white leadership that opposed the Brown decision. The origins of neo-Bourbonism lay in the 1930s and 1940s, when the southern power elite became increasingly hostile towards

Franklin Roosevelt's centralizing New Deal, and outraged by Supreme Court decisions that undermined white hegemony. The Dixiecrat movement was the political forerunner of neo-Bourbonism, and tested the strength of states rights sentiment in the South. Ultimately, Bartley contends, massive resistance and states rights faded before a resurgent "moderate" faction that opted for economic stability and tokenism rather than for pushing states rights to another showdown with federal authorities – after the disaster in Little Rock.

Any discussion of the nature of American federalism, a recurrent topic for many political scientists, naturally includes states rights. In a widely read and controversial work, ELAZAR examines the federal system from the states' perspective. His basic argument is that constitutionally, administratively and politically, states are discrete "civil societies." They serve certain well-defined functions in the federal system, and each has a unique political heritage. Elazar argues that when a particular state enjoys a high degree of "internal unity," in terms of politics and cultural ideology, it can effectively forestall federal authority, as in the cases of South Carolina in 1832 or Mississippi in the 1960s. Contrary to many other scholars, he maintains that increasing federal authority has not subsumed the states' identity. Rather, they behave, in many ways, as self-governing entities, in a system of operative states rights.

A more recent work that celebrates the renewed vigor of state governments is BOWMAN and KEARNEY. The authors do not argue for the "New Federalism" of Nixon and Reagan, but rather explain why it happened, and how state governments have become more "progressive" and effective. They cite escalating conflicts with federal authority, a willingness to confront mandates from Washington, and interstate cooperation as evidence of the revitalized states. They attribute the resurgence partly to increasing professionalization and reform in the executive branch in many states, as well as reinvigorated state legislatures and judiciaries. Furthermore, many states have made constitutional changes that afford citizens greater access to politics and government, which has helped facilitate harmonious cooperation between state and increasingly moribund local authority, all of which has enhanced the power and prestige of state governments. Finally, public alienation and dissatisfaction with the federal government has prompted many people to place greater faith in their states. Not surprisingly, the authors conclude that most states have exercised their new power with great skill and success, although they admit that smaller, less financially secure, states will have increasing difficulty adapting to new responsibilities.

A number of studies examine federal/state relations in specific policy fields. A representative work is LOWRY, which looks at pollution control. The author tests the hypothesis that states are in fact resurgent, using a four-cell model that assesses "vertical involvement" (the degree of federal oversight) and "horizontal competition" (the amount of cooperation or conflict between different states). He concludes that federal administrators have practiced a flexible management style, exercising a greater presence in some areas than in others.

CHRISTOPHER J. OLSEN

See also Federalism; Nullification Crisis

Stephens, Alexander H. 1812–1883

Political leader; Vice President of Confederate States of America

Cleveland, Henry, *Alexander H. Stephens in Public and Private*, Philadelphia: National Publishing, 1866

Hendrick, Burton J., *Statesmen of the Lost Cause: Jefferson Davis and His Cabinet*, Boston: Little Brown, 1939

Howe, Daniel Walker, *The Political Culture of the American Whigs*, Chicago: University of Chicago Press, 1979

Johnson, Michael P., *Toward a Patriarchal Republic: The Secession of Georgia*, Baton Rouge: Louisiana State University Press, 1977

Johnston, Richard Malcolm, *Life of Alexander H. Stephens*, Philadelphia: Lippincott, 1878; revised, with William Hand Browne, 1883

Rable, George C., *The Confederate Republic: A Revolution Against Politics*, Chapel Hill: University of North Carolina Press, 1994

Schott, Thomas E., *Alexander H. Stephens of Georgia: A Biography*, Baton Rouge: Louisiana State University Press, 1988

Von Abele, Rudolph, *Alexander H. Stephens: A Biography*, New York: Knopf, 1946

Wilson, Edmund, *Patriotic Gore: Studies in the Literature of the American Civil War*, New York: Oxford University Press, and London: Deutsch, 1962

Alexander Stephens was a central figure in southern and national politics throughout the mid-19th century sectional crisis, yet he has had few biographers. During his lifetime, two lives of Stephens appeared. The first was a campaign biography produced by his publisher and friend, CLEVELAND, in 1866 to help restore his reputation after his vice presidency of the defeated Confederacy. The second was put together by one of his closest friends in Georgia, JOHNSTON, and later revised by the editor of the *Southern Messenger*, William H. Browne. The result was a long and highly eulogistic book.

The first serious biography, by VON ABELE, is succinct and sympathetic, although by no means uncritical. In fact, Von Abele concludes that, in view of its length, Stephens's political career had little to show for it, principally because Stephens invariably backed the losing side. Moreover, he feels that Stephens made three serious errors of judgment – endorsing the fateful Kansas-Nebraska bill in 1854, throwing himself into the fight for the Lecompton constitution in 1857–58, and confronting the Davis administration in 1864. Stephens's personal qualities – his generosity and the enormous affection and respect he inspired in Georgia and the South – are treated approvingly.

More recently, a thorough and scholarly one-volume life has appeared that, in its length and detail, is appropriate to Stephens's importance. Heavily weighted toward his pre-war career and giving only slight attention to his record during Reconstruction, SCHOTT captures very well the public and private Stephens. His profound melancholy and his physical afflictions are given due stress, as are his generosity and capacity for deep personal attachments – for example to his half-brother, Linton. Driving his public career, so Schott feels, was a longing for recognition, rather than fame or fortune. Stephens's practical skill as a politician is recounted and acknowledged, while his abstract and uncompromising constitutional theorizing is analyzed and explained. But the larger significance, the contribution, and the representativeness of Stephens are, alas, not really addressed in this carefully recounted life.

More interpretative are two essays that treat Stephens as a representative of particular themes or trends. In his study of the literature of the Civil War, WILSON singles out Stephens as the figure who embodied and articulated the essence of southern separatism. Writing admiringly of his intellect and of his purity of principle that led him to take uncompromising positions that the author describes approvingly as "impossibilist," Wilson saw Stephens as the exponent, in its extreme form, of the South's protest against domination and bureaucracy, a universal cause that he felt always required clear and forceful articulation. The exact opposite of Lincoln, the practical wielder of power, Stephens was always at odds with the majority and always challenging orthodoxy with ideals and principles.

HOWE's essay on "Alexander H. Stephens and the Failure of Southern Whiggery" is paired with "Abraham Lincoln and the Transformation of Northern Whiggery" as concluding chapters of his study of Whig political thought and practice. The Whigs' espousal of economic development and diversity became unviable in the South, as the region came increasingly under the sway of pre-modern values and the cotton-based plantation sector. Accordingly, Howe argues, the southern Whigs, of whom Stephens was a leading and representative figure, were unable to stem the drift toward secession. Nevertheless, the debate between Jefferson Davis and Stephens over the appropriate means to wage a war for independence was really a replay of the earlier Whig-Democrat ideological contest, as Stephens emphasized economic strength and public confidence, while Davis relied totally on military means.

Stephens's Confederate role is also examined in HENDRICK's chapters on the dissident "Georgia Triumvirate" at the core of which was Stephens himself. Unlike some of the others in this powerful challenge to the Davis administration, who acted out of personal distaste or contempt for Davis himself, Stephens was driven by his fear that the president was despotic. Hendrick describes Stephens as a "fanatic" with "the intensity of a William Lloyd Garrison" who was plotting, with Governor Joseph E. Brown of Georgia, against President Davis. Unlike Wilson, Hendrick finds little to admire in Stephens's principles, seeing them as mere egotism, a conviction that he alone was right.

In RABLE's study of the Confederate political system, Stephens is a leading figure representing one of the two political cultures that he finds vying for ascendancy. Although the Confederates eschewed parties as sources of corruption and division, they nevertheless confronted differences between the cultures of national unity and of liberty, and Stephens was clearly identified with the latter. Thus, the feud between Davis and Stephens could be seen as involving nothing less than the contest between the fundamental political cultures of the Confederacy.

Although he became Confederate vice president a few months after his own state seceded, Stephens was actually one of the leaders of the antisecessionists in Georgia. JOHNSON's study of Georgia's secession movement describes Stephens's role. After giving one of the speeches against secession before the legislature, he took no action in the campaign for a convention. He then reappeared at the convention itself, though soon withdrew again. Yet the vote to secede was quite close, 166–130, raising the possibility that, with activism on the part of Stephens and the other leading antisecessionists, perhaps the outcome might have been different. This is yet another of the puzzling features of Stephens's career, but Johnson offers no explanation for Stephens's seemingly fatalistic course.

MICHAEL PERMAN

See also Confederate States of America: Constitution, Government, and Politics; Whig Party

Stevens, Thaddeus 1792–1868
Political leader

Brodie, Fawn M., *Thaddeus Stevens: Scourge of the South*, New York: Norton, 1955
Current, Richard N., *Old Thad Stevens: A Story of Ambition*, Madison: University of Wisconsin Press, 1942
Current, Richard N., "Love, Hate, and Thaddeus Stevens," in his *Arguing with Historians*, Middletown, CT: Wesleyan University Press, 1987
Korngold, Ralph, *Thaddeus Stevens: A Being Darkly Wise and Rudely Great*, New York: Harcourt Brace, 1955
McCall, Samuel W., *Thaddeus Stevens*, Boston: Houghton Mifflin, 1899
Miller, Alphonse B., *Thaddeus Stevens*, New York: Harper, 1939
Woodburn, James Albert, *The Life of Thaddeus Stevens: A Study in American Political History*, Indianapolis: Bobbs Merrill, 1913
Woodley, Thomas Frederick, *Great Leveler: The Life of Thaddeus Stevens*, New York: Stackpole, 1937

In a 1992 address to a conference celebrating the bicentennial of Thaddeus Stevens's birth, Eric Foner remarked that "Thaddeus Stevens remains one of the most controversial and enigmatic individuals in the history of American politics," "whose unusual complexity of motivations and unique blend of idealism with political pragmatism make him almost impossible to categorize." Best remembered as one of the leaders of the Radical Republicans in the House of Representatives during Reconstruction, and most memorably depicted in D.W. Griffith's 1915 film, *Birth of a Nation*, as a vindictive monster with a bad wig and a bad limp, Stevens consistently fought for legislation that would ensure the equality and prosperity of freedmen while punishing white southerners for slavery and the Civil War. To some, he was an avenging champion; to others, a spiteful destroyer. Historians themselves can rarely agree on the man and his role in American history.

The first significant biography to appear was McCALL. A part of the popular American Statesmen series, it focused on the public man and, in particular, his national career, relying on the *Congressional Globe*, newspapers, and government documents. McCall admired Stevens and firmly believed that all his actions were based on strongly-held moral convictions. WOODBURN, published fourteen years later, echoed this sentiment but also anchored his life in the context of a troubled postwar America and the complexities of changing race relations. These two books would be the last positive view taken of Stevens for some time, as William Dunning, Claude Bowers, and other historians revised opinions of Reconstruction and declared it a "tragic era," one for which they held Stevens and his colleagues primarily responsible. They depicted him as a bitter and angry man who took out his personal frustrations on the South.

WOODLEY began by challenging this view, but ironically reinforced it by his belief that Stevens's clubfoot explained his public life. Like Dunning, Bowers, and others he ascribed a personal motive to Stevens's public actions. MILLER, published two years later, steered away from such psychological explanations. Although he relied a great deal on Woodley's factual information, he believed that Stevens had been motivated by a deep-seated belief in the equality of all men. Following up his earlier work, *Two Friends of Man* (1950), on Wendell Phillips and William Lloyd Garrison, KORNGOLD followed in Miller's footsteps, but was excessively laudatory and discounted all but the purest ideological motives for any of Stevens's actions.

The two best biographies of Stevens are very different in their orientation and conclusions. In his elegantly written study, CURRENT (1942) found personal motives for Stevens's actions, but ascribed them to economics rather than emotions. Current examined Stevens's business interests and early career and gave Americans a portrait of an early entrepreneur who sought to consolidate his gains through legislation. Influenced by the work of Charles Beard, Howard Beale, and his adviser, William Hesseltine, Current portrayed Stevens as a capitalist who exploited political power for his enrichment. Although he takes this too far, he did an invaluable service in focusing on Stevens as a pragmatic businessman and politician. CURRENT (1987), an article first published in 1947 in *Pennsylvania History*, seeks to correct this over-emphasis on business motives, and focus more on Stevens's political beliefs. Its insights, combined with those in his book, are a refreshing change from previous studies.

The other important work on the "great leveler" is BRODIE. Now better known for her controversial 1974 book on Thomas Jefferson's private life, Brodie used her interest in the new school of "psychobiography" to analyze Stevens's life, and to come up with new insights into the man. She wrote in detail on his family, his early life and background, and his physical deformity, assigning each a role in his personal and political development. She also speculated on the role of his relationship with his long-time housekeeper, Lydia Smith, who was black. Convinced that Smith and Stevens were lovers, Brodie postulated that it was this relationship that accounted for Stevens's hatred of racial prejudice and the South. But by finding motives for Stevens's behavior in his personal life rather than in ideology, she discredited their purity even while she revealed more of Stevens as a human being. Brodie's work reflects a current obsession with the private lives of public figures, a preoccupation which, when carried too far, can distort the historical record.

There has been no recent biographical work on Stevens to incorporate the large and influential body of Reconstruction historiography that has emerged since the 1960s, much of which has questioned the importance of radical Republicans in the establishment of the postwar order. In the light of these writings, it is important to reassess Stevens and his role in Reconstruction. That task is in the hands of Hans Trefousse, who is currently working on a biography of Stevens.

JEAN V. BERLIN

See also Reconstruction: Policy and Politics 1

Stevenson, Adlai E. 1900–1965
Politician, orator and presidential candidate

Baker, Jean H., *The Stevensons: A Biography of an American Family*, New York: Norton, 1996

Davis, Kenneth S., *A Prophet in His Own Country: The Triumphs and Defeats of Adlai E. Stevenson*, New York: Doubleday, 1957; as *The Politics of Honor: A Biography of Adlai Stevenson*, New York: Putnam, 1967

Johnson, Walter (editor), *The Papers of Adlai Stevenson*, 8 vols., Boston: Little Brown, 1972–79

McKeever, Porter, *Adlai Stevenson: His Life and Legacy*, New York: Morrow, 1989

Martin, John Bartlow, *Adlai Stevenson of Illinois: The Life of Adlai E. Stevenson*, New York: Doubleday, 1976

Martin, John Bartlow, *Adlai Stevenson and the World: The Life of Adlai E. Stevenson*, New York: Doubleday, 1977

Sievers, Rodney M., *The Last Puritan? Adlai Stevenson in American Politics*, Port Washington, NY: Associated Faculty Press, 1983

Adlai Stevenson has generated more biographical literature than his public positions as a one-term Illinois governor from 1949 to 1953, his two unsuccessful campaigns as the Democratic party's presidential candidate in 1952 and 1956, and his four-year ambassadorship at the United Nations might seem to merit. Partly the abundant commentary is the result of the devotion of his literate friends; partly it is the result of his emergence as a symbol of issue politics and political campaigning conducted to inform and educate American voters.

DAVIS is the most distinguished example of the adulatory biographical studies of Stevenson by men who worked with him on campaigns and wanted to promote his ideas of liberalism. It was published shortly after Stevenson's second presidential campaign and after the author's extensive interviews with his subject. A professional historian, Davis does not mask his admiration for a man he believes one of the most important historical figures of his generation – more significant, in fact, than Eisenhower and Nixon. Davis emphasizes Stevenson's commitment to transforming American elections into "reasoned and precise debate" at a time when television sound bites and negative campaigning were becoming election fixtures.

Thirty years later, McKEEVER, another close friend who was national publicity director for the Volunteers for Stevenson in 1952, covered the same territory in a pedestrian biography that does little to extend either an understanding of Stevenson the liberal or Stevenson the man. A practitioner of biography without warts, McKeever made little effort to place Stevenson in his times, though he did provide a devastating portrait of Ellen Borden Stevenson, who divorced Stevenson in 1949.

In the early 1970s, JOHNSON, another Stevenson veteran who had worked on the draft- Stevenson movement in 1952, began publishing Stevenson's papers in what eventually grew to eight volumes and nearly 5000 pages. Johnson's textual notes and commentary provide a portrait of Stevenson as the liberal internationalist who was sometimes at odds with the Kennedy and Johnson administrations which he served as United Nations ambassador. Having known and worked with Stevenson, Johnson also reveals the charm and wit of the man.

At the same time that Johnson was collecting the letters and speeches that in published form have assured Stevenson's place in history, MARTIN, the author of some of Stevenson's best speeches in 1952, was commissioned by the Stevenson family to write an authorized biography. In time Martin's work expanded into a 1500-page, two-volume study. In the first volume Martin covers Stevenson's early family life. What other biographers avoided, he developed into explanatory material critical of Stevenson's neurasthenic mother and invalid father. Concentrating on Stevenson's personal dilemmas, he includes the famous episode when twelve-year-old Stevenson accidentally shot a neighbor. Martin uses this event and others as the context for Stevenson's tortured decisions as to whether to run for governor of Illinois in 1948 and, four years later, president of the United States. From this background, according to Martin, came an uncertain politician who was not at home in national politics. At the end of Martin's first volume, Stevenson, defeated for the presidency, has become a national figure, but one whose contributions to American political life are impermanent.

In many ways Martin's first volume carries the admiring tone of most of the Stevenson literature. So does much of the second volume which covers Stevenson as a Democratic leader from 1952 to the 1956 campaign, and after this second defeat by Eisenhower, as a party leader from 1956 until his appointment as Ambassador to the United Nations in 1961, and his death in 1965. But Martin's version of the middle-aged Stevenson is increasingly that of an overweight, perplexed public servant who wants to retire from the United Nations, but who cannot give up his status as a celebrity. Martin is especially incisive on Stevenson's limited role in the shaping of American foreign policy during the years of the Bay of Pigs, Cuban Missile Crisis and the early years of American involvement in Vietnam.

The work of a talented journalist with an exhaustive capacity for research, Martin's impressive biography is sometimes overwhelmed by details. There is no core to the book, but it remains an example of the vacuum-cleaner, non-conclusive style of writing lives to which Sievers offers an analytic counterpoint.

For SIEVERS, Stevenson is by no means a commanding historical presence. Instead Sievers tries to limn "the relationship between what Stevenson believed and how he behaved, the linkage of thought and action." There is, in Sievers's topical account of what Stevenson believed about foreign and domestic policy, a gap on civil rights and even foreign policy matters where he seemed torn between his internationalism and understanding of Third World countries and his stance as a committed Cold Warrior. Sievers concentrates on Stevenson's moralism and concludes that his subject may be the last American Puritan, as full of jeremiads as a 17th-century Massachusetts preacher. Ultimately Sievers gives Stevenson credit for the spotlight that he shone on concerns such as nuclear disarmament, even while he failed to have any comprehensive understanding of policy and public affairs in post-World War II America.

Taking another approach, BAKER places Stevenson in the context of his family, whose members had been involved in elective and appointive offices for over a half-century before Stevenson was born. While Stevenson is the centerpiece of her family biography, almost half of the book covers preceding and succeeding generations of the family. The book ends with the political career of Stevenson's son, Adlai III. For Baker, Stevenson is not a major historical figure whose public accomplishments need to be reviewed. Rather Stevenson the man and the Stevenson family studied over time are as significant as Stevenson the public figure. Only through a discovery of his private life can readers understand his public worlds. Besides politics, Baker emphasizes the houses, schooling, and even reproductive lives of four generations of Stevensons, in an effort to use one American family as a means of viewing a sweep of American history.

JEAN H. BAKER

Stock Market

Beckman, Robert, *Crashes: Why They Happen – What To Do*, London: Sidgwick and Jackson, 1988

Ferris, Paul, *Gentlemen of Fortune: The World's Merchant Banks and Investment Bankers*, London: Weidenfeld and Nicolson, 1984

Insana, Ron, *Traders' Tales: A Chronicle of Wall Street Myths, Legends, and Outright Lies*, New York: Wiley, 1996

Kindleberger, Charles P., *Manias, Panics, and Crashes: A History of Financial Crises*, 3rd edition, New York: Wiley, and London: Macmillan, 1996

Lewis, Michael, *Liar's Poker: Rising Through the Wreckage on Wall Street*, New York: Norton, 1989; Harmondsworth: Penguin, 1990

Magill, Frank N. (editor), *Chronology of Twentieth-Century History: Business and Commerce*, Chicago and London: Fitzroy Dearborn, 1996

Miller, Merton H., *Financial Innovations and Market Volatility*, Oxford and Cambridge, MA: Basil Blackwell, 1991

Schwager, Jack D., *Market Wizards: Interviews with Top Traders*, New York: New York Institute of Finance, 1989

Stewart, James B., *Den of Thieves*, New York: Simon and Schuster, 1991

Sobel, Robert, *Panic on Wall Street*, New York: Macmillan, 1968; revised, New York: Dutton, 1988

Toporowski, Jan, *The Economics of Financial Markets and the 1987 Crash*, Aldershot: Elgar, 1993

Train, John, *The New Money Masters*, New York: Harper, 1989

The wide variety of books on the US stock market illustrates its importance to the global economy. Interested readers will find many different versions of its history, from high-brow economic analysis to popular "get-rich-quick" schemes, and from highly personal accounts of individual careers to a narrative history of the stock market since traders first met under the buttonwood tree near Wall Street in 1792.

SOBEL, a prolific writer on the North American business world, describes the constantly repeating cycle of boom and bust that has characterized both the US stock market and the American economy. His description of the 18th-century stock speculator William Duer provides a role model for all the fraudulent traders of the following 200 years. Insider dealing, bribes for government officials, personal avarice and corporate greed made a fortune for Duer. Unfortunately, he was also to become the first great victim of over-confidence in his investments when the market turned against him in 1792. Sobel illustrates the great crises that have afflicted Wall Street and provides good summaries of the causes of the Jacksonian crisis (1837), the gold crisis (1873), the Great Crash (1929) and Black Monday (1987).

Other writers who have concentrated on financial crises can be read in conjunction with Sobel's book. BECKMAN presents an anecdotal account of financial disasters over the last 250 years and, despite the unnecessary emphasis he places on his own forecast of Black Monday, the book is a readable account of how the hysteria of the crowd can blind individuals to reality. KINDLEBERGER, an economist, produces a more academic study of the nature of financial crashes than either Sobel or Beckman. The emphasis is again on how economic cycles of boom and bust are endlessly repeated by investors. Kindleberger analyses all the major financial crises from the Dutch Tulipmania boom of 1636 to the bursting of the Nikkei bubble of 1990. His dissection of typical stages in a crisis and his analysis of speculative manias are essential reading. Both MILLER and TOPOROWSKI provide more theoretical examinations of recent crashes; their reliance on economic theory and numerical analysis makes their books challenging reading, but these are sound additions to the Wall Street canon.

Of the many books dealing with traders, two collections of interviews are particularly illuminating. TRAIN describes in detail the investment strategies of consistent stock market outperformers, such as George Soros, Jim Rogers and Peter Lynch. Train shows that hard work, intelligence and good fortune are the essential attributes of the world's top traders. SCHWAGER's interviews are less formal and, consequently, tend to reveal more about the psychology of trading. Different trading strategies for currencies, equities and commodities are all explained by protagonists in the US markets.

FERRIS is a good introduction to the major stockbroking and investment banking firms that have molded the US Stock Exchange. His brief accounts of Wall Street giants such as Morgan Stanley, Salomon Brothers and Goldman Sachs bring out their individual characteristics. As something of a sceptical outsider, Ferris is freed from the public relations considerations and the tendency towards the hagiographic that mar many of the more extensive corporate histories. INSANA fleshes out many of the personalities that have passed into Wall Street lore. Some of the short biographies are colored by nostalgia and several of the tales are too far-fetched to be believable. None the less, as an introduction to the occasionally crazy world of Wall Street, Insana makes a readable companion to more formal Wall Street histories.

The late 1980s were years of great change in Wall Street. The rampant bull market of the early 1980s came to an abrupt end with the Black Monday crash. Allegations of insider dealing, market rigging, and the falsification of records became commonplace. A plethora of books describing the excesses of the Yuppie era appeared. Foremost among them, LEWIS's account of his time at financial powerhouse, Salomon Brothers, is as fascinating as it is worrying. He describes how he managed to get a trainee position as the only non-MBA in his year and ended up as a bond salesman, trading millions of dollars of other peoples' money. Lewis's account of the recruitment process, training and salesmanship hilariously highlights the differences between the American and English ways of doing business. Power dressing, personality clashes, ostentatious spending on status symbols and the replacement of experience with youthful aggression are all well-documented.

STEWART tells the story of Ivan Boesky and Michael Milken, who were convicted on charges of massive insider trading while working at Drexel Burnham Lambert. Boesky, who was conservatively estimated to be worth $130 million at the time of his arrest, helped to convict Milken whose personal wealth was an astonishing $700 million. Stewart, an editor on the *Wall Street Journal*, describes the heady days of junk-bond dealing in the 1980s when new methods of financing takeovers made millions for investment banks. The book documents the extent of insider trading and the inability of the Stock Exchange and merchant banks to police the market. The excessive bonuses and salaries, the inner workings of the trading desk and the personal relationships that shaped deals are all well detailed. The Stock Exchange Commission investigations, and the resulting media coverage, led to the downfall of Drexel Burnham Lambert.

MAGILL presents a series of readable articles on major events on the US stock market from the beginning of the 20th century.

ANDREAS LOIZOU

See also Financial History entries

Story, Joseph 1779–1845
Jurist and Supreme Court justice

Dunne, Gerald T., *Justice Joseph Story and the Rise of the Supreme Court*, New York: Simon and Schuster, 1970

Eisgruber, Christopher, "Justice Story, Slavery and the Natural Law Foundations of the American Constitution," *University of Chicago Law Review*, 55, 1988

Leslie, William R., "The Influence of Joseph Story's Theory of the Conflicts of Laws on Constitutional Nationalism," *Mississippi Valley Historical Review*, 35, September 1948

McClellan, James, *Joseph Story and the American Constitution: A Study in Political and Legal Thought*, Norman: University of Oklahoma Press, 1971

McDowell, Gary L., "Joseph Story's 'Science of Equity'," *Supreme Court Review*, 1979

Newmyer, R. Kent, *Supreme Court Justice Joseph Story: Statesman of the Old Republic*, Chapel Hill: University of North Carolina Press, 1985

Story, William W. (editor), *Life and Letters of Joseph Story*, Boston: Little Brown, and London: J. Chapman, 1851; reprinted, Freeport, NY: Books for Libraries Press, 1971

Story, William W. (editor), *The Miscellaneous Writings of Joseph Story*, Boston: Little Brown, 1852; reprinted, New York: Da Capo Press, 1972

Joseph Story's remarkable career as lawyer, teacher, legal commentator and Justice of the Supreme Court for nearly 34 years (1811–45) has languished in the shadow of his more famous senior colleague, Chief Justice John Marshall. They were opposites in many ways. Marshall was a southerner appointed by a Federalist and uninterested in detailed legal study or writing. Story was a northerner appointed by a Democratic Republican who wrote nine major treatises on law, which alone would have guaranteed him a place in American intellectual history. Their closeness and Story's importance to Marshall is summarized in Marshall's comment: "These seem to be the conclusions to which we are drawn by the reason and the spirit of the law. Brother Story will find the authorities." Story's near-adoration of Marshall should not obscure his vital role during the nearly 25 years they served together. Story, however, had to watch as Jacksonian America dismantled much of the edifice that he and Marshall created; he was, he knew, "the last of the old race of judges".

His son knew this too, and this is the main theme of STORY (1851, 1971; and 1852, 1972). Each of these two-volume works was reprinted in the early 1970s, a period which saw the publication of an astonishing amount of scholarship on Story. The loyal son claimed that his father supplied the intellectual underpinnings of the simple, logical opinions for which Marshall is remembered. These volumes are invaluable for the large amount of conveniently accessible material by Story which they contain. Much of Story's thought is revealed in both his letters and the autobiographical study included in *The Miscellaneous Writings*. Even if the reader is not convinced that Story is as important as his son believed, these volumes ought to be consulted, along with his opinions in the reports of the Supreme Court.

NEWMYER has written what looks to be the standard life. He focuses on Story's public career, and sees him as a defender of the Enlightenment values of the Revolution that appeared to be an anachronism in a country increasingly beset by the divisions caused by slavery and capital in the mid-19th century. The national jurisprudence that he tried to create through his commentaries, opinions, and his oversight of the Harvard Law School reflected that view. Writing for an audience far wider than lawyers, Newmyer provides an account of Story's career which is much more than a loosely connected series of judicial opinions. He describes this multi-faceted life in detail, and concludes that the unity of Story's juridical views could not survive the centrifugal forces of a rapidly changing society. The certitudes of the established order of eastern Massachusetts and the Revolutionary generation were fragile, and Story knew it. When the mid-20th century looked for a new national framework, too much had changed to allow a return to Story's principles.

The other two book-length studies focus on specific issues, while giving more than adequate coverage in other areas. Reflecting his own background in banking, DUNNE is particularly interested in Story's central role in the creation of a national economic order, as part of his attempt to build nationwide institutions in law and politics. He sees connections between Story's work and the embrace of a strong national structure in the 20th century. Newmyer has some sympathy with this view, but warns against too much reliance on such connections when one is trying to understand the changes in the 20th century. McCLELLAN offers a robust defense of Story, in what he admits is a "revisionist" view of his career. The author is eager to bring Story out of Marshall's shadow. He argues forcefully that Story was Marshall's legal braintrust, and that Marshall's natural leadership talents and Story's self-effacement combined to make Marshall seem a towering figure. Without denying Marshall's greatness, McClellan claims the same recognition for Story. After a biographical overview, McClellan divides his book into chapters on natural law, religion, the Constitution, property, and nationalism, and concludes with a discussion of Story's legacy. If the reader bears in mind the author's strongly-held views, this is a thoughtful and stimulating interpretation.

Three important articles focus on aspects of Story's work. LESLIE explores Story's views on conflicts of laws, with particular reference to the case of *Prigg v. Pennsylvania* in 1842, which defended exclusive federal jurisdiction over fugitive slaves. Ironically, this furnished a precedent for Taney's decision in the Dred Scott case fifteen years later. EISGRUBER defends Story's opinion against the criticisms of Newmyer and others, on the ground that Story realised that only federal action would ever make possible the eradication of slavery. Therefore, he had to uphold the federal law against all challenges – even from abolitionists, as in the Prigg case. McDOWELL underlines the importance of Story's commentaries on the law of equity as an attempt to counter the Jacksonian movement for codification of the law, the purpose of which was to assert democratic control of the courts, against the power of a conservative judiciary.

GEORGE CONYNE

See also Marshall, John; Supreme Court

Strikes

Adams, Graham, Jr., *Age of Industrial Violence 1910–15: The Activities and Findings of the United States Commission on Industrial Relations*, New York: Columbia University Press, 1966

Bernstein, Irving, *The Lean Years: A History of the American Worker, 1920–1933*, Boston: Houghton Mifflin, 1966

Bernstein, Irving, *Turbulent Years: A History of the American Worker, 1933–1941*, Boston: Houghton Mifflin, 1970

Brody, David, *Steelworkers in America: The Nonunion Era*, Cambridge, MA: Harvard University Press, 1960

Brody, David, *Labor in Crisis: The Steel Strike of 1919*, Philadelphia: Lippincott, 1965

Clegg, Hugh Armstrong, *Trade Unionism under Collective Bargaining: A Theory Based on Comparison of Six Countries*, Oxford: Blackwell, 1976

Dubofsky, Melvyn and Warren Van Tine, *John L. Lewis: A Biography*, New York: Quadrangle/New York Times, 1977

Edwards, P.K., *Strikes in the United States, 1881–1974*, Oxford: Blackwell, and New York: St. Martin's Press, 1981

Fine, Sidney, *Sit-Down: The General Motors Strike of 1936–37*, Ann Arbor: University of Michigan Press, 1969

Morgan, David, "Terminal Flight: The Air Traffic Controllers' Strike of 1981," *Journal of American Studies*, 18(2), 1984

Petersen, Florence, *Strikes in the United States, 1880–1936*, Washington, DC: Government Printing Office (Bureau of Labor Statistics), 1938

Renshaw, Patrick, *American Labour and Consensus Capitalism, 1935–1990*, London: Macmillan, and Jackson: University Press of Mississippi, 1991

Seidman, Joel, *American Labor from Defense to Reconversion*, Chicago: University of Chicago Press, 1953

Seidman, Joel (editor), *Trade Union Government and Collective Bargaining: Some Critical Issues*, New York: Praeger, 1970

Wolff, Leon, *Lockout: The Story of the Homestead Strike of 1892: A Study of Violence, Unionism, and the Carnegie Steel Empire*, New York: Harper, and London: Longman, 1965

Strikes have deep roots in American history. A bakers' dispute in 1741 is sometimes taken as the first true strike, though others argue that the first withdrawal of labour by wage earners did not occur until 1786. In any case, the place to start the study of this phenomenon is EDWARDS, recommended to anyone who can read only one book on strikes. In a comparatively brief book of impeccable scholarship, backed by appendices, graphs, and tables, he summarizes the whole state of play on the subject, and makes a fundamental point: strikes in the United States have always been long and, as a result, their overall volume has been greater than elsewhere. Measurement of strikes by duration, number, days lost, numbers involved or other yardsticks can yield quite different results. The two large volumes of *Historical Statistics of the United States*, published by the US Department of Commerce, Bureau of the Census, list all these measurements, and many more, in scores of tables, summarized conveniently in PETERSEN. Despite all these figures, the first serious attempt to count strikes was not made until 1880, as part of the population census taken in that year.

This coincided with the birth of the American Federation of Labor (AFL) between 1881 and 1886, and two decades of great industrial unrest which followed, as working people struggled to establish unions to bargain collectively through representatives of their own choosing. Employers violently resisted these attempts to organize, raise wages and reduce hours. In consequence, many bloody battles occurred. The most important, at Homestead, Pennsylvania in 1892, is vividly described in WOLFF. His title raises an important point: workers were often *locked out* by employers for refusing to accept new contracts imposing lower wages, longer hours or worse conditions. At a time of rapid technical innovation and cost-cutting in the steel industry, the Carnegie company reduced the sliding-scale of pay agreed earlier with the amalgamated union of skilled craftsmen. After months of conflict, in which dozens of strikers were killed, Carnegie imposed his pay cuts and smashed the union. As so often in such conflicts, this proved a lasting victory. In 1901 the United States Steel Corporation was established, and it ruthlessly smashed all further attempts at unionization and kept America's largest basic manufacturing industry an open shop until 1937.

Though employers still held the whip hand, strikes continued and indeed became such a serious and persistent problem that the federal government was forced to step in and seek to regulate the situation. ADAMS discusses this era of industrial unrest, when National Guardsmen attacked a striking coalminers' camp in Colorado and killed 17 women and children. This outrage led to greater use of federal commissions and mediation during strikes, while after 1914 the insatiable demands of the war economy forced both government and employers to try to reduce causes of unrest. Yet strikes continued, and after 1918 employers embarked on a powerful counter-offensive.

BRODY (1960) is a classic study of steelworkers in the non-union era down to 1920. Following Homestead, only two strikes occurred involving more than 10,000 workers: one in 1901 and the other, the "great strike" of 1919, which lasted more than 3 months and involved 365,000 workers. BRODY (1965) explains how the steel bosses crushed the 1919 strike and maintained the open shop. This defeat had decisive consequences for both the steel industry and the whole labour movement. Union membership declined steeply during the 1920s, while the open shop became known as the "American plan". Seduced by prosperity, workers saw no reason to join unions, while employers forced them to sign "yellow dog" contracts which forbade them to do so, and used court injunctions to stop strikes. Yet strikes occurred, especially in coal mining and southern textiles, where Gastonia, North Carolina, became a by-word for industrial violence. BERNSTEIN (1966) provides a superb narrative of this period.

Mass unemployment during the Great Depression drove the strike rate down to a record low level. Only 180,000 workers went on strike in 1933, compared with 4.6 million in 1919 and 4.75 million in 1946. Yet when economic recovery began in the mid-1930s rank-and-file militancy was used to secure radical political ends. The 1935 Wagner Act legalized collective bargaining; sit-down strikes in the car and other mass-production industries tripled union membership; while New Deal reforms, vigorously backed by resurgent labour, laid the basis for a welfare state. All this, and the creation of the

Congress of Industrial Organizations (CIO), is best studied in BERNSTEIN (1970), and in FINE's meticulous analysis of the 1936–37 sit-down strike. This most momentous industrial dispute in American history forced General Motors to recognize the United Automobile Workers (UAW) and helped end the open shop in steel, chemicals, rubber, textiles and most mass-production industries. RENSHAW argues that these strikes, and subsequent war experience, consolidated labour's economic position in the Keynesian-style managed capitalism which lasted until the 1970s. DUBOFSKY and VAN TINE is a magnificent analysis of coal strikes which John L. Lewis led during the New Deal and the war years.

SEIDMAN (1953) paints the broader picture of wartime strikes and highlights the decisive importance of the postwar strike wave, especially the 1946 General Motors strike, when GM withstood a 113-day stoppage to resist UAW demands that it open its books to the union. That employers did not use violence to try to crush these strikes, as they had in 1919 and 1936–37, shows how much stronger unions had become. Between 1933 and 1950 union membership grew five-fold. Despite the anti-union Taft-Hartley Act of 1947, American labour was infinitely stronger than it had ever been.

Unions now enjoyed the support of law and government, the cooperation of management, long-term contracts and elaborate disputes procedures. Yet none of this reduced the strike rate. As Philip Taft's contribution to SEIDMAN (1970) shows, the American strike-rate remained remarkably constant over time, despite such peaks as occurred in 1919, 1936–37, or 1945–46, and troughs in the 1920s and the early 1930s. The American labour movement is strangely paradoxical: politically conservative, and fully accepting capitalism, it is nevertheless unusually militant and strike-prone. CLEGG's penetrating and sophisticated analysis explains why this remained so, even during the years of union maturity between 1950 and 1980. In the absence of a labour or socialist party, some historians describe strikes as bids to act on the political front. Clegg doubts this, arguing instead that the elaborate bargaining systems evolved in America since the 1930s themselves stimulate strikes when renewal time comes round, especially since such systems are strongly decentralized and local. Moreover, unofficial strikes are as frequent as official ones. MORGAN's vigorous account of such a landmark unofficial strike, the disastrous 1981 air traffic controllers' dispute, also reveals American labour's failure to gain that very support among high-tech, white-collar workers that it most needs to survive into the next century.

PATRICK RENSHAW

See also Labor History entries

Suburbs

Binford, Henry C., *The First Suburbs: Residential Communities on the Boston Periphery, 1815–1860*, Chicago: University of Chicago Press, 1985

Ebner, Michael, *Creating Chicago's North Shore: A Suburban History*, Chicago: University of Chicago Press, 1988

Fishman, Robert, *Bourgeois Utopias: The Rise and Fall of Suburbia*, New York: Basic Books, 1987

Jackson, Kenneth T., *Crabgrass Frontier: The Suburbanization of the United States*, New York and Oxford: Oxford University Press, 1985

Marsh, Margaret S., *Suburban Lives*, New Brunswick, NJ: Rutgers University Press, 1990

Stilgoe, John R., *Borderland: Origins of the American Suburb, 1820–1939*, New Haven: Yale University Press, 1988

Warner, Sam Bass, *Streetcar Suburbs: The Process of Growth in Boston, 1870–1900*, Cambridge, MA: Harvard University Press, 1962

Surprisingly the suburb, that quintessential American residential form, has only recently become an object of interest to American historians. In the post-World War II suburban boom, novelists and sociologists examined this unprecedented phenomenon, but there was no useful history of American suburbanization until the publication of JACKSON's work in 1985. His account deployed a mixture of technological explanations (for example, transportation innovations, and balloon frame housing), economic explanations (such as long-term mortgages), and political explanations (for example the Federal Housing Agency under the New Deal) for the dramatic growth and unique form of the American suburb. He identified evolving transportation technology from the ferry to the automobile as the dominant force creating the possibilities within which uniquely American economic and political practices created a culturally specific suburban form.

Except for a brief look at the early 19th century ideologies of domestic rural architecture, Jackson focuses on the suburbs as a rejection of the city. He attributes the popularity of suburbs largely to middle-class flight from urban blight and from those poorer than or different from themselves. Thus Jackson judges the suburbs negatively, for leading to the destruction of community by a "drive-in," privatized, suburban culture which separated people by class and race. He provides a very convincing historical companion to the sociological and literary critique of the 1950s, one that is the standard work in the field.

Jackson's emphasis on technology built on WARNER's pioneering study of Boston's evolution from a "walking city" of 200,000 inhabitants within a radius of two or three miles, into a sprawling metropolis of over one million extending to a radius of 10 miles. The later decades of the 19th century witnessed a middle-class consensus on the desirability of dividing work and residence, and created the possibility for growing numbers to achieve that ideal. In the process the rural ideal and city life blended into a new image – the suburb, the home of the middle class, transported to and from the city by street car. The detached, front-facing, wooden house with colonial adornment was standard by 1900. Upward social mobility and movement outward from the old "walking city" were synonymous, as more and more people were able to afford the suburbs. Boston's "street car suburbs" increased class separation while breaking down ethno-religious divisions. Warner's critique of the class separation and unplanned sprawl of Boston's suburbs foreshadowed Jackson's criticisms.

Following in the footsteps of Warner and Jackson, EBNER studied the history of the eight prestigious Chicago suburbs conventionally dubbed the North Shore. Although writing for a wider audience, he draws upon professional historiography and his work was published by a university press. Ebner focuses on the railroads as the main force shaping the North Shore, and his focus on transportation and public health innovations supplements Jackson. One major contribution of Ebner is in detailing each suburb's uniqueness (for example, Evanston's temperance or Winnetka's education), implicitly disputing the impression that suburbs were homogeneous. These suburbanites had overlapping identities with their individual suburb, the North Shore, and Chicago. The multilayered approach is suggestive, but it is not clear how the different loyalties were integrated.

Published in the same year as Jackson, BINFORD disputes his interpretation of the origins of suburbs. Using Somerville and Cambridge, Massachusetts as case studies, he places the origins of suburbs before the principal developments in transportation. He finds the origins of the suburbs not in the city, but in developments on the fringe of the metropolis. Most of these suburbanites were not commuters, rather they sought to take advantage of their proximity to the city without being part of it. Instead of a transition from village to suburb, Binford found politically self-conscious, residential suburban entities outside the walking city. He effectively suggests that, in looking backwards for the origins of the later suburb, Jackson and Warner overlook earlier structures and attitudes that can be called "suburban."

All of these studies examined the mechanisms of suburbanization rather than the experience of suburban living. The major thrust of the spate of works that followed Jackson and Binford is to address the nature of that experience, and with that change of emphasis comes a more positive evaluation of the place of the suburbs in American history. FISHMAN is the most important of these later studies. In a work that spends considerable time on British antecedents, he agrees with Binford that suburbs preceded mass commuting, but finds the origins in England, especially London, rather than in Jacksonian America. He portrays the suburban ideal as a utopian attempt of the Anglo-American bourgeois to create a livable environment within reach of the city.

STILGOE's term "borderland" offers an escape from using the term "suburb" to cover historically different forms, and moves the focus to visual and cultural concerns. He found that, from the Jacksonian era to World War II, the core of suburban attraction lay in the abiding desire of families to shape private space. MARSH also examines the suburbanites' experience on their own terms. She found that men initially promoted suburban ideals while female domesticity was still urban-centred. But by the 20th century these merged into doctrines of togetherness and companionate marriage which were assumed to be best achieved in suburbs. In contrast to Jackson's view, Fishman, Stilgoe and Marsh portray suburbanites' assertion of a laudable ideal as more significant than their rejection of the city.

Historical inquiry into the suburbs effectively ends with the 1960s. Several authors refer to fundamental changes in suburbs after 1970, but historians have yet to tackle that more recent phenomenon. Paradoxically, Jackson predicted the end of suburbs as we know them, and the suburbanization of America. Fishman intriguingly poses suburbanization as an interlude between two de-centralized periods: the rural and the "technoburb." But the fate of suburbs since 1970 awaits its historians. Using history to understand the post-World War II suburb remains the primary point of interest and debate. The most interesting historiographical development has been the evolution from histories decrying suburbs which reflect the sociological and literary critiques of the 1950s, to histories that focus on the suburban experience and give suburbs a more honoured place in the American past and present.

W. BRUCE LESLIE

Suffrage

Chute, Marchette, *The First Liberty: A History of the Right to Vote in America, 1619–1850*, New York: Dutton, 1969; London: Dent, 1970

DuBois, Ellen Carol, *Feminism and Suffrage: The Emergence of an Independent Women's Movement in America, 1848–1869*, Ithaca, NY: Cornell University Press, 1978

Field, Phyllis F., *The Politics of Race in New York: The Struggle for Black Suffrage in the Civil War Era*, Ithaca, NY: Cornell University Press, 1982

Flexner, Eleanor, *Century of Struggle: The Woman's Rights Movement in the United States*, Cambridge, MA: Belknap Press of Harvard University Press, 1959, revised 1975

Gillette, William, *The Right to Vote: Politics and the Passage of the Fifteenth Amendment*, Baltimore: Johns Hopkins Press, 1965

Kousser, J. Morgan, *The Shaping of Southern Politics: Suffrage Restriction and the Establishment of the One-Party South, 1880–1910*, New Haven: Yale University Press, 1974

Lawson, Steven F., *Black Ballots: Voting Rights in the South, 1944–1969*, New York: Columbia University Press, 1976

McKinley, Albert Edward, *The Suffrage Franchise in the Thirteen English Colonies in America*, Philadelphia: University of Pennsylvania, 1905

Porter, Kirk H., *A History of Suffrage in the United States*, Chicago: University of Chicago Press, 1918

Rogers, Donald W. with Christine Scriabine (editors), *Voting and the Spirit of American Democracy: Essays on the History of Voting and Voting Rights in America*, Urbana: University of Illinois Press, 1992

Williamson, Chilton, *American Suffrage: From Property to Democracy, 1760–1860*, Princeton: Princeton University Press, 1960

There has not been a one-author, single-volume, comprehensive account of the history of suffrage in the United States, but ROGERS might be used as a concise substitute. This collection of eight revised public lectures examines crucial phases of the historical development of voting and voting rights from the founding of the British American colonies down to the present day, including: suffrage reform from 1787 to 1860

(Sean Wilentz), immigration and suffrage in antebellum America (Paul Kleppner), blacks and the right to vote during the Reconstruction era (Eric Foner), and participation in American elections (Everett C. Ladd). The suggested reading list attached after each lecture is helpful.

Well after its first appearance in 1918, PORTER remains the only comprehensive and informative, but not error-free, account of the development of American suffrage from colonial times to 1918. Following a succinct review of the suffrage in the colonies, Porter discusses a series of important subjects, including the removal of property qualification between the 1820s and the 1840s, aliens and suffrage, black suffrage and the Civil War, black disfranchisement at the turn of the century, and the women's suffrage movement. In a work largely based on the secondary sources of his time, Porter uncritically accepts many of the contemporary interpretations regarding suffrage history, particularly the Dunning school interpretation of black suffrage during the Reconstruction period.

McKINLEY offers a comprehensive and detailed picture of the evolution of voting rights and practice in each of the original thirteen British colonies in North America. Relying exclusively on published records and laws, McKinley gives a meticulous account of how each colony developed its own voting qualifications and regulations, but offers little critical commentary on the subject.

WILLIAMSON coherently delineates the development of the suffrage from the eve of the American Revolution, when suffrage was largely property-based, to the beginning of the Civil War, by which time most states had removed property qualifications for voting. Based on considerable primary research, Williamson challenges the Turnerian argument that the westward movement was responsible for the coming of universal white manhood suffrage. He attributes the liberalization of suffrage regulation before the Civil War largely to the results of the American Revolution, which generated and enhanced the spirit of democracy. Williamson regards the disappearance of property qualifications in voting as a demonstration of democracy, even though blacks and women were largely excluded from voting during the period he covers.

Written primarily for a general audience, CHUTE makes a good survey of the growth of representative institutions from the first meeting of the General Assembly at Jamestown to the aftermath of the 1840 Dorr Rebellion in Rhode Island. In comparison with Williamson, Chute gives more attention to the pre-Revolutionary period, and broadly agrees with Williamson that the American Revolution lent force to the movement toward greater voting participation.

FIELD is a well-researched and well-focused case study of the politics surrounding black suffrage in New York from 1821 to 1870. Specifically, it documents the details of the complex relations between race, party politics, and ideology at grass-roots level before and during the Civil War. Through skilful analysis of the data collected from three state referenda (1846, 1860, 1869) on black suffrage, Field examines public attitudes toward black voting rights and argues that parties manipulated the social fears of their constituent elements and used these fears as a kind of cement to bind the party together at local level. Given the function of the Republican party as a mediator trying to accommodate diverse interests, Field acknowledges a certain degree of opportunism on the part of the party in the interest of maintaining unity, by omitting black suffrage from its commitments in 1860 and upholding it in 1869.

GILLETTE is still the major study of the making of the Fifteenth Amendment. Drawing from his careful examination of the congressional debate in 1869, Gillette concludes that the driving force behind the amendment was the political calculation of northern Republicans that enfranchisement of northern blacks would help to secure Republican control of national and state governments. In a way, Gillette is a corrective to the traditional view that the amendment was introduced to consolidate Republican strength in the South, but he does not share the revisionist view that black suffrage was motivated more by Republican idealism. In Gillette's view, it was considerations of political expediency that impelled moderate Republicans in the North to take an active part in the process of making and ratifying the amendment.

Like Field, a superb combination of historical analysis and quantitative sophistication, KOUSSER examines the political and legal origins of the black disfranchisement movement in the eleven former Confederate states from 1880 to 1910. Based on his exhaustive research in state records regarding voting, and the painstaking computation of election returns at the state and national levels, Kousser disputes the traditional view that black disfranchisement resulted from the voluntary surrender by black voters of their voting rights and, instead, argues that the systematic implementation of electoral devices and procedures in the South – white primary, poll tax, educational qualifications, registration and multiple-box laws, and the Australian ballot – effectively excluded most blacks from voting until the coming of the New Deal, and created one-party politics in the South. In Kousser's view, the successors to the antebellum patrician class, rather than the poor whites, were the main disfranchisers, because of their determination to eliminate or reduce any opposition regardless of race or color.

LAWSON is a comprehensive and detailed account of how black suffrage as a political and constitutional issue revived at local and national level between 1944 and 1969. Starting where Kousser ends, Lawson examines such important developments as the fall of the white primary and the poll tax, the NAACP-led crusade for black re-enfranchisement, the efforts of the federal government (from Roosevelt to Johnson) to reform suffrage, and the congressional actions on black voting rights in the 1950s and 1960s. In Lawson's view, the success of the "second Reconstruction" lay in a combination of many factors: the joint black-white struggle for the vote (in which blacks played a greater leadership role than in the first Reconstruction), the black migration from 1940 to 1970 which helped to build the political muscle needed to break the congressional stalemate – as blacks selectively congregated in strategic locations in the middle Atlantic and east north central states, and in California – the impact of various protest activities, and the responses from federal administrations under pressure.

DuBOIS is an excellently written and highly readable study of the evolution of the women's suffrage movement from 1848 to 1869. DuBois identifies the women suffrage movement as essentially a movement driving for the creation of a truly democratic society. Suffragists, in her view, were more radical in their demands than traditionally thought, and their aspiration for enfranchisement represented a much more advanced program for improving women's social position, but the vitality of the movement during the pre-Civil War period was restrained by the organizational connection of its leaders with the antislavery movement, which kept them from concentrating on the struggle for their own rights. She believes that Civil War-generated radical ambitions for social change and the Republican party's refusal to include women's suffrage in its political agenda were directly responsible for the birth of an independent feminist movement.

FLEXNER traces important developments in women's suffrage from the Seneca Falls Convention of 1848 to the adoption of the Nineteenth Amendment in 1920. Compared to DuBois, Flexner pays more attention to the work of both grassroots and national organizations, and gives considerable attention to the role of black women (such as Sojourner Truth and Ida B. Wells-Barnett) in the movement.

XI WANG

See also Jim Crow; Women's History: Suffrage

Sumner, Charles 1811–1874
Senator and antislavery and civil rights campaigner

Blue, Frederick J., *Charles Sumner and the Conscience of the North*, Arlington Heights, IL: Harlan Davidson, 1994

Donald, David, *Charles Sumner and the Coming of the Civil War*, New York: Knopf, 1960

Donald, David, *Charles Sumner and the Rights of Man*, New York: Knopf, 1970

Du Bois, W.E.B., *Black Reconstruction: An Essay Toward a History of the Part Which Black Folk Played in the Attempt to Reconstruct Democracy in America, 1860–1880*, New York: Harcourt Brace, 1935

Dunning, William Archibald, *Reconstruction: Political and Economic, 1865–1877*, New York: Harper, 1907

Haynes, George H., *Charles Sumner*, Philadelphia: G.W. Jacobs, 1909

Nason, Elias, *The Life and Times of Charles Sumner: His Boyhood, Education, and Public Career*, Boston: B.B. Russell, 1874

Pierce, Edward Lillie, *Memoir and Letters of Charles Sumner*, 4 vols., Boston: Roberts, 1877–93

Schurz, Carl, *Charles Sumner: An Essay*, edited by Arthur Reed Hogue, Urbana: University of Illinois Press, 1951

Storey, Moorfield, *Charles Sumner*, Boston: Houghton Mifflin, 1900

Charles Sumner's death in 1874 met with an outpouring of adulation that rivaled the mourning of Abraham Lincoln a decade earlier. In public memory, both men represented the moral strength and noble purpose of the victorious North in the Civil War. The decline of Sumner's reputation, and its rehabilitation, reflected changing American attitudes regarding the once rebellious South, the emancipated slaves, and federally protected civil rights.

NASON completed his biography within a few days of Sumner's death and presented in it the man that New England and much of the North then revered. PIERCE, still adulatory in tone, provided the first scholarly treatment of Sumner. He had entered Sumner's reformist circle in the late 1840s as a young Harvard-educated lawyer with a keen interest in antislavery politics. He remained close to Sumner throughout his friend's life and was named literary executor of Sumner's estate. Pierce constructed his biography from raw materials extracted from Sumner's vast collection of private correspondence. The biography provided readers with lengthy extracts from letters sent and received by Sumner and with a chronological narrative of Sumner's public life. Pierce's biography provided subsequent historians with ready access to a significant portion of Sumner's private papers. SCHURZ wrote his biographical essay in 1894 drawing extensively from the Pierce biography. The essay was never completed. Schurz, weakened by age, devoted his waning energies to his own *Memoirs* (which he completed shortly before his death). The Schurz biography remained unpublished for more than fifty years, but it revealed to readers of a subsequent generation Schurz's interest in resurrecting Sumner's memory as a corrective to the dominating historical presence of Lincoln in the conservative Republican political hegemony of the late 19th century.

Biographies by Storey and Haynes marked a major turning point in Sumner's historical reputation. STOREY, a reform-minded "mugwump" Republican, viewed Sumner from much the same perspective as Schurz. Writing for the "American Statesmen" series which celebrated New England's moral leadership in the Civil War era, Storey explored in Sumner's public career the interlocking characteristics of antislavery and Liberal Republican reform. But Storey's biography marked the end of an historiographical era. Racism dominated historical scholarship in the early 20th century and Sumner the champion of equal rights quickly became Sumner the deluded and dangerous fanatic. Reflecting this change of attitude, HAYNES presented a picture of Sumner very different from Storey's. According to Haynes, Sumner outlived his best days. His greatest accomplishments (in the struggle against slavery) preceded the Civil War; his greatest "mistakes" were his post-emancipation efforts to secure equal rights for blacks. Particularly burdensome to future generations, observed Haynes, was Sumner's role in the passage of the Fifteenth Amendment to the United States Constitution which granted equal voting rights to the emancipated slaves.

Haynes's biography was very much in tune with a revisionist assault on abolitionism and Radical Republicans. DUNNING, the leading historian of Reconstruction in the early 20th century, dominated a generation of historical research and writing that denounced the kind of antislavery radicalism which Sumner personified as dangerous "fanaticism." Although DU BOIS, in his impassioned critique of the Dunning school, wrote approvingly of Sumner's struggle for emancipation and civil rights, black historians found few allies in their efforts to stem the revisionist tide.

It was not until DONALD's two-volume biography that Sumner fully regained the principled high ground that had been denied to him for a half century. When Donald's first volume appeared, however, it was not entirely clear that this would be the result. This first volume, treating Sumner's antebellum career, won the Pulitzer Prize, but it also drew criticism from historians who were themselves civil rights activists, because it depicted Sumner's sudden enthusiasm for moral reform as an antidote to a deep personal malaise. Radical historians in the early 1960s traced the historical roots of their own struggle against southern segregation and racial discrimination to the determined and courageous 19th-century fight against slavery. By linking Sumner's reform zeal with a personality disorder, Donald recalled to these critics Dunning's racist vitriol. But Donald's second volume, treating Sumner's role during the Civil War and Reconstruction, amply recovered whatever balance had been lost in the earlier discussion of motivation. Self-righteous and yet courageous, secure in the affections of his reformist circle and yet humbled by a brief, humiliating marriage, Sumner re-emerged in Donald's masterful biography as the man whom Pierce had known and as the statesman that a nation had alternately admired and reviled.

In a work of admirable brevity BLUE confirms Donald's judgments, and the judgments of a subsequent generation of historical scholarship treating antislavery reform, emancipation, and the struggle for civil rights during the Civil War era. In the second half of the 20th century Sumner's reputation had been restored to its pre-revisionist eminence. "Despite his egotism and self-righteousness," concludes Blue, "Sumner is best remembered as the moral conscience of the North."

LOUIS S. GERTEIS

Supreme Court

Currie, David P., *The Constitution in the Supreme Court*, 2 vols., Chicago: University of Chicago Press, 1985–90

Friedman, Leon and Fred L. Israel (editors), *The Justices of the United States Supreme Court, 1789–1969: Their Lives and Major Opinions*, 5 vols., New York: Chelsea House/Bowker, 1969–78

Friedman, Leon (editor), *The Justices of the United States Supreme Court, 1969–1978: Their Lives and Major Opinions: The Burger Court*, New York: Chelsea House, 1978

Haines, Charles Grove, *The Role of the Supreme Court in American Government and Politics, 1789–1835*, Berkeley: University of California Press, 1944

Haines, Charles Grove and Foster H. Sherwood, *The Role of the Supreme Court in American Government and Politics, 1835–1864*, Berkeley: University of California Press, 1957

Hall, Kermit L. and others (editors), *The Oxford Companion to the Supreme Court of the United States*, New York and Oxford: Oxford University Press, 1992

Holmes Devise: Paul Freund and Stanley N. Katz (general editors), *History of the Supreme Court of the United States*, New York: Macmillan, 1971–; volumes published to date, in order of subject:
  1. Goebel, Julius, *Antecedents and Beginnings to 1801*, 1971
  2. Haskins, George Lee and Herbert A. Johnson, *Foundations of Power: John Marshall, 1801–15*, 1981
  3. White, G. Edward, *The Marshall Court and Cultural Change, 1815–35*, 1988; abridged New York: Oxford University Press, 1991
  4. Swisher, Carl Brent, *The Taney Period, 1836–64*, 1974
  5–7. Fairman, Charles, *Reconstruction and Reunion, 1864–88*, 2 vols., 1971–87; supplemented with *Five Justices and the Electoral Commission of 1877*, 1988
  8. Fiss, Owen M., *Troubled Beginnings of the Modern State, 1888–1910*, 1993
  9. Bickel, Alexander M. and Benno C. Schmidt, Jr., *The Judiciary and Responsible Government, 1910–21*, 1984

Kelly, Alfred H. and Winfred A. Harbison, *The American Constitution: Its Origins and Development*, New York: Norton, 1948; 7th edition, with Herman Belz, 2 vols., 1991

McCloskey, Robert G., *The American Supreme Court*, Chicago: University of Chicago Press, 1960, revised by Sanford Levinson, 1994

Mason, Alpheus T., *The Supreme Court from Taft to Warren*, Baton Rouge: Louisiana State University Press, 1958, 3rd edition, as *The Supreme Court from Taft to Burger*, 1979

New American Nation series, New York: Harper, 1971–; volumes to date, in order of subject:
  Hyman, Harold M. and William M. Wiecek, *Equal Justice under Law: Constitutional Development, 1835–1875*, 1982
  Beth, Loren P., *The Development of the American Constitution, 1877–1917*, 1971
  Murphy, Paul L., *The Constitution in Crisis Times, 1918–1969*, 1972

Pfeffer, Leo, *This Honorable Court: A History of the United States Supreme Court*, Boston: Beacon Press, 1965

Schwartz, Bernard, *A History of the Supreme Court*, New York: Oxford University Press, 1993

Swindler, William F., *Court and Constitution in the Twentieth Century*, 3 vols., Indianapolis: Bobbs Merrill, 1969–74

Warren, Charles, *The Supreme Court in United States History*, 3 vols., Boston: Little Brown, 1922, revised, 2 vols., 1926

White, G. Edward, *The American Judicial Tradition: Profiles of Leading American Judges*, New York: Oxford University Press, 1976, revised 1988

Wiecek, William M., *Liberty under Law: The Supreme Court in American Life*, Baltimore: Johns Hopkins University Press, 1988

Surprisingly few histories of the United States Supreme Court exist, and none written before the 20th century. This would be odd, given the importance of the Supreme Court in American national life, were it not for the fact that there is a similar dearth of institutional studies of Congress and the presidency. A more striking peculiarity of the corpus of Supreme Court histories is that almost none were written by historians. In a narrow view, only three of the authors noted here would be identified primarily as historians, the others being political scientists and lawyers. Finally, only two of the works noted here were published before 1950. The Court's historiography is predominantly the product of recent scholarship.

The great classic and model for Supreme Court histories is WARREN's two-volume study. Warren combined scholarship of the gentleman amateur's sort, but of the highest quality, with an active professional life. He served as an assistant attorney general of the United States and was a leader of the American bar – and the author of one of its earliest histories. Thus his historical writing is informed by the outlook of one deeply engaged as a lawyer with the issues of his day. Warren was politically and ideologically conservative; he despised abolitionists, reflected the racism of his era, regarded Jacksonian critics of the Supreme Court with contempt, was an ardent nationalist, and was determined to rehabilitate the reputation of Chief Justice Roger B. Taney from the slurs of antislavery advocates. Warren exploited contemporary newspaper commentary and archival manuscript sources, especially correspondence, establishing a high standard for historical research and writing. He integrated doctrinal and political history well and brought the story up to the threshold of his own time, 1918.

HAINES, a political scientist at UCLA, brought to his study of the antebellum Court the perspective of one who had already had a major scholarly impact with *The American Doctrine of Judicial Supremacy* (2nd edition 1932) and *The Revival of Natural Law Concepts* (1930). Themes from these earlier works influenced his treatment of the Marshall and Taney Courts: a neo-Progressive scepticism about the primacy of judicial review and the power of the courts, a political scientist's assumption that the Court is merely one institution of government among others, and an emphasis on political theory, especially the separation of powers. Haines and his student/colleague SHERWOOD, who completed most of the second volume after the senior author's death in 1948, enjoyed the benefit of a well-developed body of secondary literature. Their work, much more than Warren's (who wrote in lofty, lawyerly isolation), reflected engagement in a mature scholarly dialogue among students of the Court.

The *Holmes Devise* is a unique collective scholarly project, now in its fifth decade. Subsidized by a bequest from Justice Oliver Wendell Holmes's estate, conceived largely by Justice Felix Frankfurter, the project has had only two general editors, law professor Paul Freund and historian Stanley N. Katz. The first five volumes reflected Freund's legal-academic orientation, all but one of their authors being primarily law professors: GOEBEL, HASKINS and JOHNSON (a historian as well), SWISHER (a political scientist), FAIRMAN, and BICKEL and SCHMIDT. Thus these volumes reflect the doctrinal orientation of lawyers, sometimes producing a peculiar historical astigmatism, which ignores or neglects cases which had very important broader historical implications. The reader should bear this lawyer's perspective in mind when using these volumes and compensate accordingly. The two volumes published under Katz's editorship – WHITE and FISS, with three more in preparation – reflect a much surer historical sensibility, including an attention to social context missing in some of the earlier volumes.

The three constitutional volumes (of a projected four) published to date within the multi-volume *New American Nation* series devote so much attention to the Supreme Court that they may fairly be taken to constitute a coherent institutional history. Embedded in a series of forty-plus volumes covering all aspects of the American experience, the contributions of HYMAN and WIECEK, BETH, and MURPHY take care to relate the Supreme Court's functioning to the larger society, stressing political and ideological implications of judicial doctrine. The three volumes have a distinctly liberal outlook, warmly sympathetic to the causes of civil liberties and civil rights. Murphy is, indeed, a leading exemplar of the liberal approach that dominated American constitutional historical scholarship for the half-century after the New Deal.

The reader seeking to follow up Haines's two volumes will find that the three-volume set by SWINDLER integrates nicely. (The major gap, unfortunately, is Reconstruction.) Swindler was a journalist before he became a lawyer and law teacher. His writing thus has a lively quality that reaches the reader more directly and successfully than much of what is written within the conventions of academic prose. Yet Swindler makes no scholarly sacrifices for the sake of popular appeal; his *Sources and Documents of United States Constitutions* (1973–79) is a 14-volume collection of federal and state constitutional texts that has become the standard resource for state constitutions. Swindler went to great lengths to present judicial doctrine against a full, richly-detailed backdrop of social and economic history, and integrates the Court more effectively into its times than other works discussed above.

MASON's work is also a survey of the modern Court. Successor at Princeton to the towering constitutional authority Edward S. Corwin, Mason also wrote standard biographies of Justices Taft, Brandeis, and Stone, as well as interpretive texts in the public-law genre of political science. Unabashedly partisan in his admiration, approaching adulation, for Brandeis, Mason nevertheless transcended both ideology and scholarly discipline to provide a coherent, reliable history of the 20th-century Court.

CURRIE's volumes betray their law-school origins. In striking contrast with, say, Swindler, Currie writes with total indifference to the social, economic, and political context in which the Court does its work. He proceeds case-by-case, providing analysis and critiques of the Court's decisions, arranged topically within an overall chronological order. The result is what would be found in an American law school classroom: doctrinal autopsies of leading and less-significant cases. Currie's sole concern is to analyze how the Court evolved doctrine. He indulges himself in repeated critiques of judicial reasoning, evoking memories of Holmes's characterization of Christopher C. Langdell as a legal theologian. The reader seeking a lawyer's abstract doctrinal analysis will be well served here.

McCLOSKEY has had an incalculable influence on the way that Americans think about the Supreme Court, because his slender volume – 260 pages in its original edition – served for a generation as a standard text in undergraduate political science and history courses on American constitutional development. He economized in his discussion of topics, pursuing a strategy of *multum in parvo* to consider only a score or so of major cases, concluding with *Brown* v. *Board of Education*. He did not shrink from judgment, and his evaluations were all the more impressive to the undergraduate mind for being so relatively few, packaged in a volume of quite finite length that lent itself well to classroom use. The undergraduates of the 1960s weaned on his book are today's judges, lawyers, law professors, and political scientists who shape American law and educate those who will succeed them. Though McCloskey's judgments hold up well, it was inevitable that his book should age, as events overtook its assumptions. One of his last graduate students, Sanford Levinson, today a law professor, rescued the book from encroaching obsolescence, bringing out a revised edition that preserved the original intact, but that added two updating chapters and a thoughtful bibliography. McCloskey's book was thus launched into a second life, and its influence goes on.

WIECEK has produced another short interpretive history of the Supreme Court. In no sense a replacement of McCloskey, Wiecek's book was offered as a more finely-textured, detailed survey of the Court's history that reflected a generation of scholarship that had completely revised the study of the Court since McCloskey wrote.

SCHWARTZ, a remarkably prolific legal scholar, has done much to promote an understanding of the Court among the general lay public. One of his most valuable contributions is his history of the Court. Dissatisfied with excessively detailed and lengthy studies like those in the Holmes Devise series and with what he considered brief, superficial works like McCloskey's, Schwartz wrote a 400-page survey for the "general reader", organizing it, as lawyers are wont to do, by the periods of chief justiceships, plus four case studies. The greatest utility of Schwartz's study lies in its survey of the entire topic. It contains not so much major interpretations as the author's judgments about the cases he discusses.

PFEFFER is a more dated, yet more interpretive, study of the same length as Schwartz's. The author, a practising lawyer who has prepared numerous amicus briefs representing a strict-separationist position on church-state cases before the Supreme Court, presents an explicitly liberal interpretation of the Court's history. The reader who seeks an authoritative survey, reflecting the climate of the mid-1960s, and examining the issues before the Court from a civil libertarian perspective, will find it here.

Four specialized works warrant mention. While none of them is a history of the Court as such, each contributes significantly in its own way to our understanding of the Court's past. The first, KELLY, HARBISON and BELZ, is an undergraduate text. Now in its 7th edition and expanded to two volumes, this classic reflects two distinctive interests that the current author, Belz, brings to what had been a standard liberal-nationalist interpretation of the Court: neo-conservatism and an extended use of political theory. A plus for the user of this work is an exceptionally good bibliography of books on the Court.

FRIEDMAN and ISRAEL is a collection of biographical sketches, together with excerpts from major opinions, of each of the justices, prepared by different authors. It might be said that the history of the Court is the sum of the works of its members. To the extent that is true, this collection of mini-biographies presents the life of the court, one justice at a time.

A shorter version of this approach, without excerpted opinions, but with greater analytical insight and judgment, is presented in WHITE, an excellent series of vignettes, almost all of which are of justices of the Supreme Court. White brings the training of an intellectual historian to the enterprise, and though he is also a lawyer who teaches at a law school, he has continually reaffirmed his origins as an historian of thought throughout his career. This book represents one of his ablest achievements, and is the one most useful to the non-specialist.

Finally, the *Oxford Companion*, edited by HALL *et al.* is an invaluable ancillary reference. Though it is organized as a one-volume encyclopedia and not a historical work, it contains among its one thousand entries brief, accurate sketches of the justices and their major opinions. The volume's most lengthy entry, a four-part history of the Court, provides the single most accessible brief survey of the subject.

WILLIAM M. WIECEK

T

Taft, William Howard 1857–1930

27th President of the United States, and Chief Justice of the Supreme Court

Anderson, Donald F., *William Howard Taft: A Conservative's Conception of the Presidency*, Ithaca, NY: Cornell University Press, 1973

Anderson, Judith Icke, *William Howard Taft: An Intimate History*, New York: Norton, 1981

Coletta, Paolo E., *The Presidency of William Howard Taft*, Lawrence: University Press of Kansas, 1973

Duffy, Herbert S., *William Howard Taft*, New York: Minton Balch, 1930

Manners, William, *TR and Will: A Friendship That Split the Republican Party*, New York: Harcourt Brace, 1969

Mason, Alpheus T., *William Howard Taft: Chief Justice*, New York: Simon and Schuster, and London: Oldbourne, 1965

Minger, Ralph Eldon, *William Howard Taft and United States Foreign Policy: The Apprenticeship Years, 1900–1908*, Urbana: University of Illinois Press, 1975

Pringle, Henry F., *The Life and Times of William Howard Taft*, 2 vols., New York: Farrar and Rinehart, 1939

Ross, Ishbel, *An American Family: The Tafts, 1678 to 1964*, Cleveland: World, 1964

Scholes, Walter and Marie V. Scholes, *The Foreign Policies of the Taft Administration*, Columbia: University of Missouri Press, 1970

Vivian, James F. (editor), *William Howard Taft: Collected Editorials, 1917–1921*, New York: Praeger, 1990

Wedged between the strong presidencies of Theodore Roosevelt and Woodrow Wilson, William Howard Taft has usually been depicted as a failure in office because of his inability to emulate the success of Roosevelt as a champion of reform and to achieve re-election in 1912. The scope of his presidential papers has also inhibited serious scholarship about his years in office. The best biography is almost sixty years old, and there is no thorough study of his years in the White House.

DUFFY was a biography that came out in the year of Taft's death. It was not a serious work of historical inquiry, and was superseded within a decade by PRINGLE. A distinguished biographer of Theodore Roosevelt, Pringle received full access to the Taft Papers. He produced a very sympathetic biography that made a strong case for Taft's competence as president, defended his role in the feud with Roosevelt, and rehabilitated Taft in such episodes as the Ballinger-Pinchot controversy over conservation policy. Pringle was quickly recognized as the standard life of President Taft, though his interpretive insights did not change the existing historical interpretation of Taft as a mediocre president.

ROSS wrote a lively and well-documented family history of the Tafts that contained much interesting information from the Taft Papers about the president and his relations with his wife and children. Because of the popular audience at which it was aimed, Ross's book had almost no impact on how historians evaluated Taft in office.

MANNERS wrote a popular treatment of the split between Taft and Theodore Roosevelt that had such significant consequences for the Republican party during the presidential election of 1912. The book made no systematic use of the papers of either president, and the interpretation accepted the accuracy of Roosevelt's criticisms of his successor's performance in the White House. The book is of relatively little analytic value, but has not been superseded either.

During 1973, two studies of Taft as president appeared. COLETTA came at Taft from the perspective of a multi-volume biographer of William Jennings Bryan. The result is a book that treats Taft as a presidential failure, and endeavors to understand why he did not achieve the same success as Theodore Roosevelt. The book makes only occasional use of the Taft Papers, and covers many aspects of the administration, such as the struggle over the Payne-Aldrich Tariff of 1909, in a superficial way. The volume is one of Coletta's lesser efforts, and a new study of Taft as president is very much needed.

Donald ANDERSON approached Taft's presidency as a political scientist interested in how chief executives function in office. He drew on the president's own letters and speeches for the primary source material of the narrative. Anderson accepted as a working principle that Taft had been a failure, and the text then endeavored to account for his lapses. Ironically, when Anderson's book appeared, the effects of Vietnam and the Watergate scandal were raising questions about strong presidents and their excesses. From that perspective, Taft's emphasis on the constitutional limits of the presidency would acquire greater appeal to historians.

Judith Icke ANDERSON wrote a biography of Taft from the perspective of political psychology. Rather than re-examining what Taft did in office, she too adopted the position that the difficulties of Taft's presidency needed to be explained. To do so, she constructed an interpretation of the Tafts' marriage that made the president more ardent than his wife in the relationship. When denied all the love he needed, Taft compensated by overeating and procrastination. The book's thesis did not command wide respect when it appeared, the sources used for the study were relatively limited, and the impact of Anderson's work on Taft's historical reputation was marginal.

MINGER used a number of episodes in Taft's pre-presidential career to consider his record in foreign policy during the McKinley and Roosevelt administrations. Each individual chapter is well-researched and clearly written, but the book is less than the sum of its parts. Like other authors writing about Taft, Minger does not escape seeing him as a foil for Roosevelt and a potential failure in the White House. SCHOLES and SCHOLES used the Taft Papers and other primary sources to write a detailed and thorough treatment of Taft's foreign policy as president. The book shows how much Taft involved himself in diplomatic issues, and is valuable for its comprehensive survey of the problems that the president encountered in world affairs. Written for a specialist audience, the book is important but dated.

VIVIAN is a documentary collection of the editorials Taft wrote for the *Philadelphia Ledger* during World War I and afterward. The extensive and well-researched annotation makes the volume a useful guide to the recent writings about Taft, and sheds new light on a neglected period in his public career.

MASON explored an aspect of Taft's career that had not received much attention, his service as Chief Justice of the Supreme Court during the 1920s. In addition to setting out Taft's views on constitutional issues, Mason treated in detail the Chief Justice's work for the Supreme Court as an institution, most notably the construction of the new building for the Justices.

William Howard Taft is worthy of a modern biographical study that does justice to his conservative and limited theory of the presidency, his important role as a leader of the Republican party, and his constitutional impact as Chief Justice during the 1920s.

LEWIS L. GOULD

Taney, Roger B. 1777–1864
Chief Justice of the Supreme Court

Fehrenbacher, Don E., *The Dred Scott Case: Its Significance in American Law and Politics*, New York: Oxford University Press, 1978; abridged as *Slavery, Law, and Politics: The Dred Scott Case in Historical Perspective*, 1981

Finkelman, Paul, "Hooted Down the Page of History: Reconsidering the Greatness of Chief Justice Taney," *Journal of Supreme Court History 1994*, 1995

Frankfurter, Felix, *The Commerce Clause under Marshall, Taney, and Waite*, Chapel Hill: University of North Carolina Press, 1937

Lewis, Walker, *Without Fear or Favor: A Biography of Chief Justice Roger Brooke Taney*, Boston: Houghton Mifflin, 1965

Schumacher, Alvin J., *Thunder on Capitol Hill: The Life of Chief Justice Roger B. Taney*, Milwaukee: Bruce, 1964

Smith, Charles W., Jr., *Roger B. Taney: Jacksonian Jurist*, Chapel Hill: University of North Carolina Press, 1936

Swisher, Carl Brent, *Roger B. Taney*, New York: Macmillan, 1935

Swisher, Carl Brent, *The Taney Period, 1836–64*, New York: Macmillan, 1974

Tyler, Samuel, *Memoir of Roger B. Taney, LL.D.: Chief Justice of the Supreme Court*, Baltimore: J. Murphy, 1872

Wiecek, William M., "Slavery and Abolition Before the United States Supreme Court, 1820–1860," *Journal of American History*, 65(1), June 1978

Roger B. Taney is best known as the Justice who wrote the decision in *Dred Scott* v. *Sandford* (1857), declaring that blacks could never be citizens of the United States and that they had no rights which whites were bound to respect. He is also remembered for his many decisions on economic rights, which tended to decentralize power, and allowed states to regulate their economies. His most important role before joining the Court centered on his involvement in the destruction of the Second Bank of the United States. While serving as Andrew Jackson's attorney general, Taney drafted Jackson's message that accompanied his veto of the recharter of the Bank. Later, as an interim secretary of the treasury, Taney began the process of withdrawing federal funds from the bank. Since his death in 1864 his reputation as a judge has waxed and waned, as historians, lawyers, and society as a whole have considered the role of the Supreme Court in issues of race, economics, and national versus state power.

At his death most northerners despised Taney. Charles Sumner opposed an appropriation for a bust of the late Chief Justice, declaring that "the name of Taney" would "be hooted down the page of history." This popular dislike for Taney stemmed almost entirely from the *Dred Scott* decision, which Republicans campaigned against in 1858 and 1860. Most historians writing about Taney in the late 19th century described him as a supporter of slavery and secession. Despite this hostility to Taney because of the *Dred Scott* decision and his wholesale attacks on the Lincoln administration, most biographers and many constitutional scholars, at least until the 1970s, have been favorable, even laudatory. TYLER is a typical late 19th century "memoir" of a great man, written by a friend and published in Taney's home town. It contains sketches of an autobiography that Taney drafted, as well as letters and other primary material. It lacks any analysis, but is useful as a primary source and gives some insights into Taney's personality.

Swisher, Frankfurter and Smith all contributed to the successful rehabilitation of Taney's reputation as a Justice. SWISHER (1935) remains the standard biography, despite its age and many of its interpretations, which are now outdated. It is the starting place for reading about Taney's career and life. SMITH is a much briefer life of Taney, overshadowed by Swisher, while FRANKFURTER is a much more specialized study of one particular issue. All three volumes portray Taney as a "democrat" who fought for the "rights of the people" against "special interests." These three authors make Taney into something of a New Deal Democrat, battling the Bank of the United States and other powerful economic interests. Frankfurter was obsessed with Supreme Court decisions striking down economic regulations from the late 1890s to 1937. Because Taney allowed the states to experiment with economic regulation and development, Frankfurter finds him a great judge. All three authors downplay or ignore the importance of race, and show little or no sympathy for the rights of blacks, slave and free, in the age of Taney. They see *Dred Scott* as a small "mistake," which should not be allowed to overshadow his otherwise admirable career. As Swisher concludes, "Had he [Taney] died at some time before March 6, 1857" – the day *Dred Scott* was announced – "he would have gone to his grave to the accompaniment of unanimously laudatory obituaries."

LEWIS's unabashedly favorable account, and the unscholarly SCHUMACHER, follow in the tradition of Swisher, and add little to his biography. SWISHER (1974) places Taney in the larger context of the history of the Supreme Court. This book is a central source for studying the Supreme Court during this period; but its value is limited by Swisher's generally uncritical approach to Taney, and his hostility towards those who opposed slavery.

Fehrenbacher, Wiecek and Finkelman challenge the sympathetic views of Taney. FEHRENBACHER's elegantly written Pulitzer Prize winning book is much more than just a study of *Dred Scott*. It places the case itself in the context of a masterly study of the significance in both law and politics of the issues of slavery and its further extension, from the Revolution to the Civil War. Fehrenbacher portrays Taney as a seething proslavery southern nationalist, who saw *Dred Scott* as an opportunity to undermine the Republicans and anyone else who threatened slavery. WIECEK shows how the Supreme Court had supported slavery throughout the four decades leading up to the Civil War. FINKELMAN argues that Taney's actions during the Civil War went beyond the traditional role of the Justice and that he was openly helpful and sympathetic to the self-proclaimed enemies of the United States. Both Fehrenbacher and Finkelman show that *Dred Scott* was not an aberration, but was consistent with Taney's career beginning with his tenure as Andrew Jackson's attorney general. These three authors also demonstrate that Taney's economic decisions, praised so much by Frankfurter and Swisher, were in fact tied to his career-long defense of slavery and opposition to rights for blacks. Thus, he defended states rights in order to lay the groundwork for protecting slavery; and, when he opposed states rights in a few rare cases, like *Prigg* v. *Pennsylvania* (1842) and *Ableman* v. *Booth* (1859), it was only because, in those instances, that position protected slavery.

PAUL FINKELMAN

See also Supreme Court

Technology and Invention

Colton, Joel and Stuart Bruchey (editors), *Technology, the Economy, and Society: The American Experience*, New York: Columbia University Press, 1987

Corn, Joseph J. (editor), *Imagining Tomorrow: History, Technology, and the American Future*, Cambridge: Massachusetts Institute of Technology Press, 1986

Gramsci, Antonio, "Americanism and Fordism," in *Selections from the Prison Notebooks of Antonio Gramsci*, edited and translated by Quintin Hoare and Geoffrey Nowell Smith, London: Lawrence and Wishart, 1971; New York: International, 1972

Hounshell, David A., *From the American System to Mass Production, 1800–1932: The Development of Manufacturing Technology in the United States*, Baltimore: Johns Hopkins University Press, 1984

Marcus, Alan I. and Howard P. Segal, *Technology in America: A Brief History*, San Diego: Harcourt Brace, 1989

Marx, Leo, *The Machine in the Garden: Technology and the Pastoral Ideal in America*, New York and London: Oxford University Press, 1964

Mayr, Otto and Robert C. Post (editors), *Yankee Enterprise: The Rise of the American System of Manufactures*, Washington, DC: Smithsonian Institution Press, 1981

Mottram, Eric, *Blood on the Nash Ambassador: Investigations in American Culture*, London: Hutchinson, 1989

Mowery, David C. and Nathan Rosenberg, *Technology and the Pursuit of Economic Growth*, Cambridge and New York: Cambridge University Press, 1989

Reynolds, Terry S. (editor), *The Engineer in America: A Historical Anthology from Technology and Culture*, Chicago: University of Chicago Press, 1991

Rosenberg, Nathan, *Technology and American Economic Growth*, New York: Harper, 1972

Smith, Merritt Roe, *Harpers Ferry Armory and the New Technology: The Challenge of Change*, Ithaca, NY: Cornell University Press, 1977

The history of the United States, perhaps more than any other country, could be read as a history of technology. Yet it is only comparatively recently that the subject has begun to approach a position at the heart of academic debate. This is not to say that technology had been previously ignored. Critics such as Lewis Mumford and Marshall McLuhan, and novelists from Herman Melville to Kurt Vonnegut, have stressed its centrality to any analysis of society. In his pathbreaking work of literary and cultural history, MARX examines the powerful appeal of the pastoral ideal in America, and the impact of technology and industrialisation upon it. He set the terms of much of the debate on the relationship between technology and American society and culture for the next thirty years.

As for the history of technology itself, there have been various works on particular inventions, such as the railroad, telegraph, automobile and radio. But in the broader fields of historical study, there have been few thematic works on the subject, and technology has often remained on the margins. Perhaps because of increasing concerns about the computer, the microchip and information transmission, this has begun to change significantly over the last fifteen years. A good example – and a useful and by no means superficial introduction to a range of issues – can be found in the collection of thematic essays edited by COLTON and BRUCHEY, which place major developments in American history within the context of changes in technology. The impressive list of contributors includes such historians as Alfred Chandler and Kenneth Jackson. Some essays deal with largely uncharted areas, notably in Harry Scheiber's discussion of the historical tensions between technology and the law.

Most studies tend to concentrate on either the role of technology in economic development or on the relationship between technology and American society and culture. On the former subject, ROSENBERG provides a concise and authoritative introduction for non-specialists, written by one of the leading authorities in the field. It is now 25 years old, and inevitably a little dated, but it sets out the issues clearly. It links technological change to such important features of the American condition as the land-labour ratio, abundant natural resources, and widespread popular education. Rosenberg examines the United States as both a borrower and an initiator of technological advances, and in his conclusion he discusses such topics as the growth of the knowledge industry and the importance of environmental issues, which are more than ever relevant today.

The essays in MAYR and POST discuss the development of the "American system" of manufactures, based on the use of interchangeable parts, and its contribution to American industrial development in the 19th century. Technological development is related to such matters as business management and labour relations. The impressive list of contributors includes Nathan Rosenberg, David Hounshell, Merritt Roe Smith, Alfred Chandler and Neil Harris. HOUNSHELL's own book is an outstanding work of synthesis, covering a wide range of subject matter. Very well-written, and backed by excellent illustrations and diagrams, it traces the 19th-century production techniques of key inventions – guns, sewing machines and bicycles – up to the 20th-century factory organisation of Henry Ford and Frederick Taylor. These two men were key figures in understanding the implementation of technological innovations, and Hounshell is particularly perceptive in identifying the major differences between the two. This is a well-researched and comprehensive study, which is also very readable.

In the 20th century, the pursuit of profit through technological superiority found expression in the form of Research and Development (R+D) departments in big corporations. The progression from the small-scale inventors of the 19th century into the highly sophisticated organisation of the modern corporation provides the subject matter of MOWERY and ROSENBERG. However, the authors stress that, both within firms and in society in general, it is not the impetus to innovation that matters, but rather how such innovations are utilized. This is a highly detailed and often technical analysis, and those who are not well-versed in such matters may find the text tough going at times.

The engineer has long been a central character in both the economy and the culture of the United States. REYNOLDS addresses the growth in importance of this figure, especially his or her (but usually his) rise to the status of professional. A series of essays shows how a distinctly American style of engineering emerged out of the different approaches inherited from France and Britain, and how, by the 20th century, this new style became subordinate to the needs of large corporations and industry. These essays are generally readable but they do not tie together as well as those in Colton and Bruchey – and there is a disappointing paucity of illustrations.

Broader questions of the role of technology in American society and culture have attracted particular attention from non-American observers. Though now more than fifty years old, and at times confusing and apparently contradictory, GRAMSCI still offers one of the most succinct and original assessments of the collision of technology and culture in the United States. According to this influential Italian Marxist commentator, the United States succeeded in creating a new rationalised populace who put their faith in the promise of technological consumerism, and who were willing to sacrifice personal and sexual freedom in return for the high wages of the production line, and the fruits that such income might bring. (Gramsci also attributes much importance to Frederick Taylor and Henry Ford.) MOTTRAM is a very personal collection of eclectic and provocative essays. Focusing on American obsessions with speed, power and efficiency, he examines how these desires became enmeshed within technologies, particularly those relating to guns and automobiles. There is much discussion of the exploration of these themes in literature and film.

CORN contains a fascinating collection of essays that attempt to reassess contemporaneous popular attitudes to technology and invention. Implicit are the utopian notions attached to such devices as the X-ray machine and plastics. Such faith may now seem laughable, but, at the time, as Corn argues in an excellent epilogue, they provided the United States with a new technological frontier that helped to compensate for the loss of its geographical counterpart. This is a very well written and sophisticated inquiry into why, as some claim, "the future ain't what it used to be."

The question of whether technology was enthusiastically welcomed in the United States is expertly investigated by SMITH in an acclaimed case study of one community. He uses Harpers Ferry and the presence of the armory there as a microcosm of the bitter-sweet American relationship with the machine. In this small community in a rural area of Virginia, he finds a hesitant and equivocal response to new technology – a mixture of wonder and fascination on the one hand and anxiety and derision on the other. In the minds of many people, there was a reluctance to adapt to new disciplines and a desire to preserve existing lifestyles. Smith's fascinating study has wider significance in the national context, not least because he contrasts the situation in Harpers Ferry with the readier acceptance of technological change in Springfield, Massachusetts, home of a more famous armory.

The writing of a textbook survey of technology and society in American history is a daunting task. MARCUS and SEGAL have made one such brave attempt, and have chosen to focus more on the impact of American society and culture on technology, rather than vice versa. The handling of the subject would have benefited from more sustained critical analysis, and at times the book is in danger of falling between two stools, and failing to satisfy either the technically-minded or the student in the social sciences and the humanities. However, in 350 pages of text, it offers a compact and wide-ranging survey, and it has the merit of bringing the story right up to date in its discussion of matters of current concern, including nuclear power, space, robotics and biotechnology.

DREW WHITELEGG

See also Economic Growth; Industrialization

Telegraph and Telephone

Blondheim, Menahem, *News over the Wires: The Telegraph and the Flow of Public Information in America, 1844–1897*, Cambridge, MA: Harvard University Press, 1994

Brooks, John, *Telephone: The First Hundred Years*, New York: Harper, 1975

Coe, Lewis, *The Telegraph: A History of Morse's Invention and Its Predecessors*, Jefferson, NC: McFarland, 1993

Fischer, Claude S., *America Calling: A Social History of the Telephone to 1940*, Berkeley: University of California Press, 1992

Garnet, Robert W., *The Telephone Enterprise: The Evolution of the Bell System's Horizontal Structure, 1876–1909*, Baltimore: Johns Hopkins University Press, 1985

Marvin, Carolyn, *When Old Technologies Were New: Thinking about Electric Communication in the Late Nineteenth Century*, New York: Oxford University Press, 1988

Pool, Ithiel de Sola (editor), *The Social Impact of the Telephone*, Cambridge: Massachusetts Institute of Technology Press, 1977

Thompson, Robert Luther, *Wiring a Continent: The History of the Telegraph Industry in the United States, 1832–1866*, Princeton: Princeton University Press, 1947

Although the development of the telegraph, and later the telephone, was to effect some considerable change in the lives of virtually everyone in America, as elsewhere, there is surprisingly little written about either. BROOKS is a straightforward, narrative account of the rise to power of the American Telegraph and Telephone Company (AT&T), rather than a history of the telephone *per se*. The study was supported by AT&T, who gave Brooks access to its archives and who encouraged its shareholders to purchase the paperback edition. In these circumstances, it is hardly surprising that the result is not an entirely objective account. There is little on other, independent telephone companies, and although the author is critical of the regulated monopoly – still in force when the work was written – he does not develop the point. There is also little on the actual impact of the telephone, beyond the author's recognition that it introduced "a new habit of mind" to Americans, "a habit of tenseness and alertness, of demanding and expecting immediate results" in all areas of life and work. For all its limitations, the book is as good a place as any to start. Brooks does cover a large period in a reasonably succinct 350 pages, and, if it is not quite a business history, it is nevertheless a valuable and well-written introduction to an important, if neglected, subject.

Another useful, if very different, introduction to the subject is the volume of essays edited by POOL. This is, in many ways, an extremely eclectic collection, and only a couple of the essays relate to the American experience. The essays cover such subjects as: the sociology of early telephone usage; the role of the telephone as the "Creator of Mobility and Social Change"; "Women and the Switchboard"; the telephone and the city; and "The Use of the Telephone in Counseling and Crisis Intervention." Taken as a whole, this is a fascinating, if slightly disjointed, analysis of the telephone in the modern world.

During the 1980s, two further useful books on the telephone were published. GARNET is another study that has delved into the AT&T archives for its material, since the author was asked by AT&T "to examine the impact of regulation on the configuration of Bell operating company boundaries," a project which developed into the author's dissertation for Johns Hopkins. In the process it expanded well beyond its original remit, and became a more general history of the Bell System. It is very much an economic or business history, wider in scope than Brooks's study but along similar lines. Garnet focuses on the individuals who helped steer the Bell System through the changing landscape of state and federal legislation, and who promoted organisational changes that would sustain its technological and financial momentum into the 20th century. AT&T, Garnet shows, was far more heavily influenced by the political environment than some other businesses in the late 19th and early 20th centuries, a fact that strongly influenced the pattern of its development. It should be stressed that this is not a work for the general reader – although the short bibliography will be useful for those wishing to pursue the subject – nor is it a history of the telephone and its impact on society. It is, rather, a well-researched study of one company's response to the changing business environment of modern America.

MARVIN is a study of technological change from the late 19th century onwards, which deals not only with the telephone, but is more concerned with the impact of electricity on communication, and is really a study of the background to the mass-media of the late 20th century. In what is, in many ways, a fascinating study, Marvin examines issues of representation, access and authority, and the impact of mass communication on these issues. She pays particular attention to electric light and to the telephone, and to "how electrical experts and their publics projected their respective social worlds on to technology in the late 19th century." In brief, Marvin's is an impressive study of the telephone's impact on society, how it has been used and abused, how it altered the nature of social intercourse, and how it changed forever the expectations that people originally had of it.

There are two more recent studies, one devoted to the telegraph and the other to the telephone. FISCHER examines the impact that the telephone had on American society, although – contrary to Marvin's argument – he contends that society had a greater impact on the telephone than vice versa. Unlike those studies which enjoyed the financial support of AT&T, Fischer's is on the whole a more critical work, with much of the criticism aimed at the telephone companies themselves. However, Fischer does not devote much attention to the business side of the equation; his book might well be used in conjunction with one of the earlier studies by Brooks or Garnet, to provide an overview of the communications revolution. For his part, Fischer has isolated the automobile as a point of comparison with the telephone, since both were relatively new methods of communication in the period which he covers. He gives special attention to three case studies of relatively small towns in California: Palo Alto, San Rafael and Antioch. Although this emphasis on small-town America rather calls into question some of his conclusions, the work is nevertheless a well-crafted study, with a substantial, and up-to-date, bibliography.

BLONDHEIM is the most recent study of the precursor of the telephone, the telegraph. As he shows, America was actually quite slow to grasp the benefits of this new form of communication, which in its early days was often beaten to the post by the humble carrier pigeon. Information management was slower to develop than the information transfer process itself, a problem that became acute during the American Civil War. Blondheim devotes much of his analysis to this period, and to the changes that the telegraph brought to politics both during and after the war, and particularly in the disputed election of 1876, when the telegraph did so much to help Rutherford B. Hayes secure the presidency. Like Fischer, Blondheim sees the new technology as bolstering, rather than altering, existing social and political arrangements. A somewhat older history of the early years of the telegraph in America is THOMPSON which is still useful as a standard account of the industry from its first beginnings to the end of the Civil War. A much more recent, brief and informative survey is provided by COE, which ranges from the pioneer work of Samuel F.B. Morse and others, and the early development of the telegraph, to consideration of its longer-term influence and significance.

S-M. GRANT

Television *see* Radio and Television

Temperance

Blocker, Jack S., Jr., *"Give to the Winds Thy Fears"*: The Women's Temperance Crusade, 1873–1874, Westport, CT: Greenwood Press, 1985

Blocker, Jack S., Jr., *American Temperance Movements: Cycles of Reform*, Boston: Twayne, 1989

Bordin, Ruth, *Woman and Temperance: The Quest for Power and Liberty, 1873–1900*, Philadelphia: Temple University Press, 1981

Clark, Norman H., *Deliver Us from Evil: An Interpretation of American Prohibition*, New York: Norton, 1976

Epstein, Barbara Leslie, *The Politics of Domesticity: Women, Evangelism, and Temperance in Nineteenth-Century America*, Middletown, CT: Wesleyan University Press, 1981

Giele, Janet Zollinger, *Two Paths to Women's Equality: Temperance, Suffrage, and the Origins of Modern Feminism*, New York: Twayne, 1995

Gusfield, Joseph, *Symbolic Crusade: Status Politics and the American Temperance Movement*, Urbana: University of Illinois Press, 1963

Krout, John Allen, *The Origins of Prohibition*, New York: Knopf, 1925

Rorabaugh, W.J., *The Alcoholic Republic: An American Tradition*, New York: Oxford University Press, 1979

Tyler, Alice Felt, *Freedom's Ferment: Phases of American Social History from the Colonial Period to the Outbreak of the Civil War*, Minneapolis: University of Minnesota Press, 1944

Tyrrell, Ian, *Sobering Up: From Temperance to Prohibition in Antebellum America, 1800–1860*, Westport, CT: Greenwood Press, 1979

Tyrrell, Ian, *Woman's World/Woman's Empire: The Woman's Christian Temperance Union in International Perspective, 1880–1930*, Chapel Hill: University of North Carolina Press, 1991

Early scholarship on temperance tended to ask whether it represented the fulfilment of a tradition of intolerance or an aberration from reform impulses in American history. Recent historians, especially those concentrating on issues of gender, have reacted against a general public impression that temperance advocates were grim, puritanical, and unrealistic, and have argued that they addressed real and potentially destructive problems.

KROUT initiated scholarly study of the topic with a narrative concentrating on the varieties of antebellum temperance reformers. The practice of drinking alcohol was firmly established and rarely challenged in the colonial period. In the antebellum progression from New England elites to religious enthusiasts to businessmen to educated women, and on to urban workers, 19th-century reforms adhered to American legacies of perfectionism, interest in securing democratic government, and a sense of self-conscious mission. TYLER is the earliest academic work that treats temperance positively. Countless religious, utopian, and reform movements were part of the antebellum effort to purify and perfect America. Temperance emerged from the goals of keeping people sober enough to vote wisely, become economically successful, and look after the morality of their neighbours.

In an essential book, GUSFIELD emphasizes the importance of status saving in the temperance movement, but does not view the movements as empty substitutes for more meaningful reform. A work of sociology, it is most interested in the functions which temperance performed in the lives of different groups, and thus does not study economic or other power issues. Early temperance advocates were old elites worried about their declining status, and mid-century Washingtonians who were struggling workers attempting to improve their status. Arguing aggressively against Gusfield, CLARK places temperance in the "American reform tradition" in its attempt to solve problems of loneliness, poverty, violence, "disorder and near chaos" in antebellum America. An earlier America could solve problems in community settings, but economic individualism and the increasing mobility of antebellum society caused problems which communities could no longer handle. Religion, optimism about America's future, and fears of individual failure, all played roles in the rise of temperance. Clark argues that liquor was part of a rough male world of fast, angry drunkenness and urban prostitution – a world in need of reform.

TYRRELL (1979), shows that there were several temperance movements in antebellum America. While the first temperance leaders in the early 19th century were New England Federalists, the most powerful groups in the 1820s and 1830s were economic entrepreneurs, evangelical preachers, and technologically innovative farmers, and, by the 1840s, self-reforming workers in the Washingtonian movement. Depicting most temperance leaders as "improvers" hoping to better themselves and their country, he argues against Gusfield's notion that they were traditional groups defending themselves against the forces of change. RORABAUGH does the most effective job in linking temperance and changes in drinking habits. In the first third of the 19th century, consumption of spirits increased dramatically, as the anxieties of frontier settlement and new economic opportunities and fears led to cycles of sobriety and binge drinking. Rorabaugh speculates that temperance commitments, in the 1830s and later, emerged from a new generation of self-controlled and ambitious Americans who mixed temperance and religion with the goal of upward mobility.

BORDIN is the leading interpretation of temperance as the effort of middle-class women to extend virtues that they associated with home and motherhood into the public sphere. Problems of male drunkenness, poverty, and violence demanded solutions, and middle-class women responded with the ideology of the affectionate family. While seeing temperance as a safe reform that did not challenge the basis of 19th-century class or gender relations, Bordin argues that the "Do Everything" programme of the Women's Christian Temperance Union led women into new areas of public life, as they addressed issues of kindergarten and vocational education, recreation, poverty, and peace. In an interpretative work, EPSTEIN also places women's temperance activities in the context of northeastern middle-class gender relations. Studying the personal papers and periodical writing of women from the colonial period through the mid-19th century, the author concludes that the growing notion of separate spheres stimulated new antagonisms and resentments between men and women. Temperance thus emerged at the height of the Second Great Awakening as a proto-feminist movement in response to those resentments, but Epstein also stresses the limits on the autonomy of women in Victorian America.

BLOCKER (1985) is a quantitative study of the women's temperance movement at the time of the origins of the WCTU in 1873 and 1874. On the basis of a study of 911 crusades on the national level and local crusades in Ohio, he concludes that the temperance crusade tried to include groups like Catholics, immigrants, and African Americans, and that opposition to male drinking in saloons was a far more important motivation than status or economics. TYRRELL (1991) relates gender issues to efforts to spread temperance throughout the world by means of a campaign for a worldwide petition against alcohol, international conventions of female temperance workers, and the efforts of an impressive number of women who became temperance missionaries. With his emphasis on internationalism as an expression of millennialism, he seeks to refute old notions that opponents of alcohol were defenders of a pristine older America. In contrast to Epstein, he argues that, while the temperance workers showed commitments to homosocial sisterhood, they were also committed to the ideal of the perfect affectionate male-female relationship. GIELE agrees with Bordin and Tyrrell that women's involvement in temperance, despite the apparent limitations of its upper-class and religious roots, constituted a feminist movement. In demanding that men change their behaviour, temperance efforts expanded the activities of women beyond the home and ultimately led them to demand the right to vote.

BLOCKER (1989) is the outstanding synthesis of modern scholarship, and emphasizes change and diversity within various forms of opposition to alcohol, in part as responses to changes in drinking habits. It identifies five "cycles of reform": a call for temperate drinking habits among working people and their employers in the early 1800s, a more harsh middle-class turn to the law in the 1840s and 1850s, the rise of the WCTU in the middle and later decades of the 1800s in response to new male behaviour, followed by the prohibition movement and modern emphases on medicine and treatment.

TED OWNBY

See also Feminism; Prohibition; Reform Movements

Tennessee Valley Authority

Creese, Walter L., *TVA's Public Planning: The Vision, the Reality*, Knoxville: University of Tennessee Press, 1990

Droze, Wilmon Henry, *High Dams and Slack Waters: TVA Rebuilds a River*, Baton Rouge: Louisiana State University Press, 1965

Grant, Nancy L., *TVA and Black Americans: Planning for the Status Quo*, Philadelphia: Temple University Press, 1990

Hargrove, Erwin C., *Prisoners of Myth: The Leadership of the Tennessee Valley Authority, 1933–1990*, Princeton: Princeton University Press, 1994

Hargrove, Erwin C. and Paul Keith Conkin (editors), *TVA: Fifty Years of Grass-Roots Bureaucracy*, Urbana: University of Illinois Press, 1983

Hubbard, Preston J., *Origins of the TVA: The Muscle Shoals Controversy, 1920–1932*, Nashville: Vanderbilt University Press, 1961

McCraw, Thomas K., *TVA and the Power Fight, 1933–1939*, Philadelphia: Lippincott, 1971

McDonald, Michael J. and John Muldowny, *TVA and the Dispossessed: The Resettlement of Population in the Norris Dam Area*, Knoxville: University of Tennessee Press, 1982

Pritchett, C. Herman, *The Tennessee Valley Authority: A Study in Public Administration*, Chapel Hill: University of North Carolina Press, 1943

Selznick, Philip, *TVA and the Grass Roots: A Study in the Sociology of Formal Organization*, Berkeley: University of California Press, 1949

Talbert, Roy, Jr., *F.D.R.'s Utopian: Arthur Morgan of the TVA*, Jackson: University Press of Mississippi, 1987

Wheeler, William Bruce and Michael J. McDonald, *TVA and the Tellico Dam, 1936–1979: A Bureaucratic Crisis in Post-Industrial America*, Knoxville: University of Tennessee Press, 1986

Wildavsky, Aaron B., *Dixon-Yates: A Study in Power Politics*, New Haven: Yale University Press, 1962

A federal agency established by Congress in 1933 to develop the Tennessee River and its tributaries, the Tennessee Valley Authority (TVA) was one of the most striking and successful of all New Deal projects. Its multipurpose approach to regional planning attracted widespread attention and stimulated extensive reportage and analysis by journalists, social scientists, and historians. The best general history of the enterprise is a comprehensive collection of essays edited by HARGROVE and CONKIN. Though somewhat uneven, the essays provide an authoritative synthesis of earlier scholarship and a balanced interpretation of the undertaking.

HUBBARD is the definitive study of the long congressional struggle in the 1920s over the development of the Tennessee River, a fight eventually won by progressives led by Senator George W. Norris. Hubbard concentrates on the public side of this famous legislative controversy rather than behind-the-scenes efforts. An older but still useful work by PRITCHETT reviews the agency's integrated development of the river during its first decade and offers a favorable appraisal of its administrative organization.

TALBERT perceptively examines the role of Arthur E. Morgan, the first chairman of the TVA board, emphasizing his moral reformism and responsibility for most of TVA's social experiments. Talbert describes the bitter feud between Morgan and David E. Lilienthal over hydro-electric power policy, the chairman's departure in 1938, and Lilienthal's emergence as the dominant figure in the Authority. McCRAW tells the story of the "power fight" between TVA and the private utility companies in the 1930s. His treatment of the battles in the federal courts, in propaganda campaigns, and in the scramble for markets is illuminating but too brief to be altogether satisfactory. After 1939 public power reigned supreme in the valley, and by the end of World War II TVA had become the nation's largest producer of electricity. In the 1950s the Eisenhower administration attempted unsuccessfully to limit the Authority's power program by authorizing a consortium of private utilities to relieve the demands for more TVA power. WILDAVSKY analyzes the so-called Dixon-Yates affair, which precipitated a dramatic political struggle over the agency's financing and the issue of public versus private power. The result is an instructive case study of the controversy, marred only by a weak and redundant concluding chapter.

Navigation, flood control, and maximum production of electric power, centering in the great dams on the Tennessee, were the TVA's principal mandates. DROZE's careful study shows how the agency proceeded to make the river navigable by creating a 650-mile waterway, which became an important stimulus to the valley's economy. Droze places navigation improvement in the larger context of the Authority's multipurpose management.

Early studies of the Tennessee Valley Authority tended to be uncritical and approving. This changed in 1949, however, when SELZNICK published a notable revisionist work. Focusing on TVA's agricultural program, he pointed out that slogans like decentralized administration and "grass roots democracy," which were celebrated in David E. Lilienthal's TVA: Democracy on the March (1944), served as a "protective ideology" for the Authority. In order to meet its needs, the organization allowed the existing agricultural leadership – the land grant colleges, extension service, and American Farm Bureau – to co-opt its farm programs and give them a conservative and undemocratic cast.

McDONALD and MULDOWNY are also critical of TVA in their evaluation of the agency's population relocation policies in the construction of Norris Dam. The authors demonstrate TVA's inadequacies as a planning and resettlement agency, although they may neglect some long-term benefits to residents of the region. In a study of the treatment of African Americans as employees and clients of the Authority, GRANT concludes that racial discrimination was an integral part of TVA operations, even though the agency announced a policy of fair treatment of blacks and introduced a racial quota to ensure proportional representation of blacks in the work force. In the 1960s TVA decided to build the Tellico Dam as a means of reviving the stagnant economy on the Little Tennessee River. It would be "the showcase" of a new economic development mission. WHEELER and McDONALD ably reconstruct the protracted struggle to complete the task. The project provoked strong opposition from environmentalists, sportsmen, and others, and before the dam was finished in 1979 the organization had lost much of its luster.

Two recent works provide still other perspectives on the TVA experience. HARGROVE analyzes the leadership of the nine TVA chairmen between 1933 and 1990. No other writer has made such a penetrating and convincing interpretation of the agency's leadership, and no previous student has so clearly marked out the distinctive periods of its history. TVA leaders, Hargrove suggests, became prisoners of myths about the organization – like that of "grass roots democracy" – and a changed environment prevented them from duplicating the technological and political successes of their early predecessors. CREESE is interested in TVA's architecture and public planning. He uses photographs and maps as well as more conventional sources in analyzing the transformation of the environment in the Tennessee Valley and the changing designs for dams and power plants, communities, and recreational facilities. Creese's rendering of TVA history raises some questions, and his definition of the agency's public planning seems unduly narrow. But he is persuasive in arguing that, after the success of its first phase, the Authority's alternative vision of what American life might be like was gradually overwhelmed by the reality of producing cheap electrical power.

DEWEY W. GRANTHAM

Texas, Annexation of

Adams, Ephraim Douglass, *British Interests and Activities in Texas, 1838–1846*, Baltimore: Johns Hopkins Press, 1910

Billington, Ray Allen, *The Far Western Frontier, 1830–1860*, New York: Harper, 1956

Freehling, William W., *The Road to Disunion: Secessionists at Bay, 1776–1854*, New York: Oxford University Press, 1990

Garrison, George Pierce, *Westward Extension, 1841–1850*, New York: Harper, 1906

Merk, Frederick, *Slavery and the Annexation of Texas*, New York: Knopf, 1972

Pletcher, David M., *The Diplomacy of Annexation: Texas, Oregon, and the Mexican War*, Columbia: University of Missouri Press, 1973

Sellers, Charles, *James K. Polk: Continentalist, 1843–1846*, Princeton: Princeton University Press, 1966

Smith, Justin H., *The Annexation of Texas*, New York: Baker and Taylor, 1911

Tutorow, Norman E., *Texas Annexation and the Mexican War: A Political Study of the Old Northwest*, Palo Alto, CA: Chadwick House, 1978

The Anglo Americans living in the northeast corner of Mexico rebelled and established an independent republic of Texas in 1836. Although it was quickly recognized by the United States, Texas was not annexed for another decade. Secret negotiations by the Tyler administration produced a treaty that was defeated in the Senate, but after the election of 1844, Congress passed a joint resolution of annexation that was subsequently accepted by the Texans. The entire process faced bitter opposition from those who believed that annexation was a plot by an "aggressive slavocracy" and, as a consequence, the various interpretations of historians have been closely connected to their understanding of the coming of the Civil War.

Three older accounts helped to set the scene in their different ways. GARRISON denied the importance of slavery and portrayed annexation as part of the "forward movement" of an "adventurous and aggressive people" extending democracy into new areas. He discussed the background of the rebellion and his chapter on the boundary question supports the position of the Polk administration. In response to British meddling, the Tyler administration reopened negotiations and, after the people had spoken in the election of 1844, Congress extended the offer and the Texans gained the annexation which they had long wished.

ADAMS clarified the British role in Texas, showing the mixed policy that hoped to sustain an independent Texas that would act as a barrier to American expansion, and also serve British economic interests. At the same time, the reformist element wanted an independent Texas rid of slavery and hoped to exchange recognition for emancipation. In other words the British had both strategic and humanitarian goals that would be furthered by an independent Texas. SMITH argued that this British interest in Texas ultimately determined the Tyler administration's movement toward annexation in defense of American interests and American destiny. Based on extensive and meticulous research, his account forms a brief for the defense of the actions of the Tyler and Polk administrations, portraying annexation as principled, popular, and patriotic. Smith argued at length that there was no conspiracy and that the ill-merited prestige of annexation's opponents prejudiced previous historians.

In the mid-1950s, BILLINGTON extended Smith's interpretation within a Turnerian mold, emphasizing expansion as a natural process sustained by public opinion that "awakened to" America's Manifest Destiny. Southerners fearful of English encroachment, northern and western commercial interests, land speculators and pioneers, acting through the Democratic party, sustained the bold policies that reached fruition under Polk, who was looked upon at the time as one of the nation's "near-great" presidents.

The second volume of SELLERS's superb biography of Polk deftly summarizes the activities of the Tyler administration, emphasizing the fear of British meddling and the desire to protect slavery and unite the South, but he focuses primarily on the intrigue within the Democratic party that led to the nomination and election of Polk. He presents a measured evaluation of the election and the relative importance of the Texas issue, and a particularly good discussion of Polk's dealings with, and deception of, the Van Burenite Democrats. He sketches the "continental vision" that underlay Polk's decision to assert "extravagant boundary claims" over Texas, in his desire to acquire California.

MERK revives the Whig and abolitionist charges that annexation was the product of a small group of southerners around Tyler, who were involved in land speculation in Texas, but were primarily concerned with the protection of slavery and the westward expansion of the Cotton Kingdom. He highlights the role of Abel P. Upshur, Tyler's secretary of state, and the northern-born Mississippi Senator, Robert John Walker, whose propaganda efforts attempted to elicit both southern and northern support for annexation. When the treaty, which was primarily Upshur's work, was defeated by the Whigs and Van Burenite northern Democrats, Tyler changed strategy and with the aid of Walker pushed the Joint Resolution through Congress. The newly elected Polk both before and after his inauguration pressed for annexation and influenced the final decisions of both the Senate and the Texans.

PLETCHER places annexation in a larger diplomatic context within which he emphasizes the actions of the Mexicans, the British, and the French, as well as American diplomats and policymakers. His emphasis is less on motivation than on assessing the "gains and losses" associated with alternative policies. Thus while he offers a great deal of information on French and British responses to American actions, he is ambivalent on the main matters of dispute between historians. Aside from being somewhat unimaginative, Pletcher's main weakness is an inadequate understanding of American party politics at the time.

TUTOROW focuses on the popular response to expansion in the states of Ohio, Indiana, Illinois and Michigan which, in the view of most historians, strongly supported the idea of Manifest Destiny and which, he believes, represented a microcosm of the nation as a whole. In the 1830s the urge for expansion was bipartisan, but the issue caused divisions within the parties. In 1844 the region responded like the rest of the country, with the Democrats favoring annexation and Whigs opposed. At the same time, the Texas issue pitted the North against the South as the antislavery elements in both parties turned against the annexation of Texas because they believed it would extend slavery. The episode offered a foretaste of the realignment of parties in the region around the slavery issue, which led to the Civil War.

FREEHLING's remarkable analysis of the events leading to the Civil War presents the most detailed and intelligent examination of the decision-making process leading to the annexation of Texas. At each step of the way he focuses on those individuals or groups that acted to produce the result, and then probes their motivation. Annexation resulted from the actions of a "President and his main diplomatic lieutenants [who] were coherent ideologues who used established patterns of slavery politics to secure the latest dubiously democratic consolidation of the Slavepower." He then shows how the push for Texas progressively moved out of the cabinet to the southern

Democrats and then the Democratic party and eventually to the Democratic voters who supported Polk. Polk revived Jacksonian fortunes in the South and did far better than Van Buren in the Old Northwest, where arguments emphasizing Manifest Destiny nationalized the appeal of annexation.

WILLIAM G. SHADE

See also Expansionism; Manifest Destiny; Polk; Tyler

Textbooks on United States History

Bailey, Thomas A. and David M. Kennedy, *The American Pageant: A History of the Republic,* 10th edition, Lexington, MA: Heath, 1994

Bailyn, Bernard, Robert Dallek, David Brion Davis, David Herbert Donald, John L. Thomas, and Gordon S. Wood, *The Great Republic: A History of the American People,* 4th edition, Lexington, MA: Heath, 1992

Berkin, Carol, Christopher L. Miller, Robert W. Cherny, and James L. Gromly, *Making America: A History of the United States,* Boston: Houghton Mifflin, 1995

Bernhard, Virginia, David Burner, Elizabeth Fox-Genovese, Eugene D. Genovese, and John Clymer, *Firsthand America: A History of the United States,* 3rd edition, St. James, NY: Brandywine, 1994

Blum, John Morton, William S. McFeely, Edmund S. Morgan, Arthur M. Schlesinger, Jr., Kenneth M. Stampp, and C. Vann Woodward, *The National Experience: A History of the United States,* 8th edition, New York: Harcourt Brace, 1993

Brinkley, Alan, *American History: A Survey,* 9th edition, New York: McGraw Hill, 1995; abridged as *The Unfinished Nation: A Concise History of the American People,* New York: Knopf, 1993

Brogan, Hugh, *The Longman History of the United States of America,* London: Longman, and New York: Morrow, 1985; as *The Penguin History of the United States of America,* Harmondsworth: Penguin, 1990

Davidson, James West, William E. Gienapp, Christine Leigh Heyrman, Mark H. Lytle, and Michael B. Stoff, *Nation of Nations: A Narrative History of the American Republic,* 2nd edition, 2 vols., New York: McGraw Hill, 1994

Divine, Robert A., T.H. Breen, George M. Fredrickson, and R. Hal Williams, *America: Past and Present,* 4th edition, New York: HarperCollins, 1995; brief 3rd edition (with Randy Roberts), 1994

Faragher, John Mack, Mari Jo Buhle, Daniel J. Czitrom, and Susan Armitage, *Out of Many: A History of the American People,* Englewood Cliffs, NJ: Prentice Hall, 1994; brief edition, 1995

Henretta, James A., W. Elliot Brownlee, David Brody, and Susan Ware, *America's History,* 2nd edition, New York: Worth: 1993

Jones, Maldwyn A., *The Limits of Liberty: American History, 1607–1980,* New York and Oxford: Oxford University Press, 1983, 2nd edition, 1995

Kennedy, David M., Thomas A. Bailey, and Mel Piehl, *The Brief American Pageant: A History of the Republic,* 3rd edition, Lexington, MA: Heath, 1993

Norton, Mary Beth, David M. Katzman, Paul D. Escott, Howard P. Chudacoff, Thomas G. Paterson, and William M. Tuttle, Jr., *A People and a Nation: A History of the United States,* 4th edition, Boston: Houghton Mifflin, 1994; brief 3rd edition (with William J. Brophy), 1991

Tindall, George Brown and David E. Shi, *America: A Narrative History,* 3rd edition, 2 vols., New York: Norton, 1992; brief 3rd edition, 1993

United States history textbook publishing is a commercial enterprise driven by the competition to sell books to more than one million undergraduates enrolled in over 3000 American colleges and universities. Most are written by academic historians, but may actually be the product of a close collaboration among authors, editors, and marketing specialists. Typically 1000 pages of text, they are lavishly illustrated with color maps, photographs, illustrations, and other visually engaging graphics, and are attractively packaged in an 8 by 10-inch format. Virtually all are narrative chronologies firmly grounded in standard political, economic, and diplomatic events, however much attention they may also devote to social and cultural issues. The most elaborate ones have pages liberally divided by headings and subheadings, often in color or distinctive typeface, and may include sidebars that survey historiography, provide capsule biographies of interesting persons, or present excerpts from source documents. Texts generally include lists of suggested readings that make useful bibliographies of the monographic literature. The full wording of the Declaration of Independence, the Constitution, and other basic documents are placed in appendices, along with tables of presidential election results, cabinets, basic data on population, and the admission of states into the union.

Most United States history texts are published simultaneously in a single hardcase volume, which covers 1607 to the near present, and a two-volume paperback version, divided at the Civil War or Reconstruction. Texts are differentiated primarily by reading level, emphasis on social or political history, historiographic orientation, use of color and illustrations, and to a lesser extent by the quality and sophistication of the writing. As a consequence of the heady competition, more than a dozen full-size, attractive, color textbooks are published in the United States and another dozen available with black-and-white illustrations. Several leading publishers also offer condensed versions of their standard works that dispense with color and reduce the number of illustrations. These concise editions generally follow closely the organization of the parent text, but are about 60 per cent the length of the originals, somewhat smaller in physical size, and less costly.

Typical of the mass-market textbook is BRINKLEY (1995). First published in 1959 and now in its 9th edition, Brinkley offers a traditional narrative of American history built around a core of political and economic events. This attractive color text contains a good selection of illustrations, maps, charts, and other graphics, as well as other features designed to make it stand out among the competition. In response to criticism that United States history texts had neglected social and cultural history, especially dealing with minorities and the non-elites, this latest edition has integrated additional material on immigrants, Native Americans, African Americans, and women into the political narrative. The end-of-chapter suggested readings provide a basic selection of recent monographs. The concise edition of Brinkley follows closely the organization of the full-length version, but as with many such abridgments, it sacrifices supporting details for the sake of brevity. DIVINE *et al.* shares many of the characteristics of Brinkley and similar texts trying to position themselves in the center of the mass market, including a parallel brief edition. There are attempts to augment sometimes outdated or one-sided interpretations with separate historiographic essays, but these are not included in every chapter. BLUM *et al.* is an older and more traditional text with a distinguished cast of authors, but unfortunately it has not kept abreast of recent publishing or historiographic trends. Its only concession to color is a distracting reddish tint used in headings, sidebars, and some graphics, while the illustrations themselves are old-fashioned. The authors stoutly defend their emphasis on questions of public policy as the best means of understanding American society and thus have made little attempt to broaden their coverage of social and cultural history. Their interpretive touchstone, which assesses how well government has fulfilled the promises of individual liberty and opportunity over the years, is a limited principle that leads the authors to espouse the middle ground of liberal politics without seriously considering historic criticisms from both wings.

Several publishers have made particular efforts to make their offerings more approachable to beginning students, primarily by using a basic vocabulary, simple concepts, and features specifically designed to aid learning. The venerable text by BAILEY and KENNEDY, first published in 1956 and now in its 10th edition, falls into this category because of its easy syntax, unsophisticated interpretations, and limited coverage of controversial issues. The slightly larger-than-average typeface, generous page layout, and ample color illustrations further mark this as an elementary text. This basic political narrative rarely strays from great men and significant events, despite the inclusion of more material designed to broaden themes of pluralism and American diversity. It is at heart a patriotic work that celebrates American progress and the free enterprise system, while largely ignoring dissenting political viewpoints outside the mainstream. Sidebars present broader historiographic interpretations, but the context seems clearly intended to convey the notion that these other views are mistaken in some way, without indicating why or suggesting that an honest debate is involved. KENNEDY, BAILEY, and PIEHL offer the same features in a cramped black-and-white-plus-one-color brief edition. Even greater efforts to appeal to unsophisticated students can be found in DAVIDSON *et al.* This college-level text features a simplified writing style characterized by clear, short, didactic sentences, fundamental vocabulary, and uncomplicated ideas. Strong colorful illustrations, marginal notes, and well-designed pages support the authors' goal to make "pedagogical points easier to grasp." Social history is well integrated into the basic political narrative, but the interpretations are somewhat dated – the Cold War is explained largely as American response to Soviet aggression, for example. The authors convey little sense of

historiography and provide few opportunities for students to reflect on historic questions, much less to discuss or argue with the text's point of view. Pedagogical concerns are taken a step further by BERKIN *et al.* In addition to use of vivid color throughout, including textual subheadings, the writing is crafted to avoid unusual vocabulary, complex ideas, or other stumbling blocks to comprehension. Nearly every page uses bold-face type to highlight important or unfamiliar terms, which are then defined in set-off boxes at the foot of the page. Chapters begin with a series of "critical thinking questions," which unfortunately are more likely to elicit factual responses than to provoke real thought. The historical narrative is organized around a four-part progression that presents a menu of expectations, constraints, choices, and outcomes for each important historical era or event. This schema neatly structures complex issues, but it also constrains history into a preconceived formula that is often ill-suited to the questions involved. The outcome is a distorted and oversimplified approach to American history, yet one that might be useful as a stepping stone for students unprepared for more traditional texts.

Other authors have sought to carve out a niche by paying greater attention to social and cultural history, often neglected in traditional narratives. NORTON *et al.* is an attractive, engaging, and balanced work that pays more than usual attention to women, minorities, and to social history generally, while retaining a strong political narrative core. Significantly less space is devoted to accounts of wars and battles. Chapters include brief chronologies, excerpts from source documents, set-off historiographic discussions, and excellent selections of recent monographs in the suggestions for further readings. The brief edition follows the original nearly chapter for chapter, but the condensation sacrifices details and examples, making a more choppy and disconnected text in comparison. HENRETTA *et al.* have successfully integrated social history into a basic political chronology, sometimes even to the extent of sacrificing space devoted to discussion of political events. The coverage of the frontier West, women, working class life, and minorities is excellent. Their assumptions about the preeminence of economic conditions in explaining history leads to some distortions. The authors conveniently overlook abuses during late 19th century industrial consolidation, for example, because they argue that every other sort of progress depended on the general prosperity brought by industrialization. Similarly, they defend aggressive American foreign policy by suggesting that the United States, as the rightful leader of the capitalist world, had a right to follow its own economic interests. This economic imperative undermines the authors' otherwise sympathetic treatment of the working class, minorities, immigrants, and neglected Americans. FARAGHER *et al.* have incorporated the idea of community as an organizing principle in their text by offering the notion that shared feelings about values and history have established a basis for common American identity. Thus their history is largely an account of how the nation was contrived out of many different and often seemingly diverse communities – a sort of neo-melting pot thesis. Despite the excellent treatment of social issues generally and the West particularly, the core of the text relies primarily on a narration of the standard political, diplomatic, and economic issues. A brief edition is also available.

Several texts have explored new territory without resorting to expensive color features. BERNHARD et al. have written a first-rate history that is noteworthy for its excellent coverage of Native Americans, the working class, everyday life, amusements, consumer society, and minority politics. It contains the fullest and most lucid account of socialism, Watergate, Reaganomics, and other controversial issues. It is regrettably weak in the pre-revolutionary period, which is allocated fewer than 100 of the total 965 pages. Clymer's essay "Succeeding in History Courses," included in the appendix, is a clear and forthright explanation of the nature of historical explanations and the value of history. Clymer's invitation for students to enter into the discussion of history is carried through in the text, not only through the well chosen questions posed at the end of each chapter, but also by the candor in dealing with conflicting interpretations. The relatively sparse black-and-white illustrations are generally poor quality, perhaps as a consequence of the inexpensive printing method used. BAILYN et al. is an important text by a formidable team of authors, that provides excellent historical analysis and interpretation. The first edition, published in 1977, created a stir because of its sophisticated and elegant writing, lucid arguments, and strong historiographic framework. Bailyn and his colleagues depended on informed readers to follow their subtle arguments involving the interactions of politics, ideology, and society. The current 4th edition has preserved these distinctive characteristics, but the vocabulary has been simplified, sentences shortened, and other changes have brought it closer to the mainstream without destroying its strongest points. The sections on the colonial and revolutionary periods remain outstanding. The annotated suggested readings provide an excellent guide to the recent monographic literature. The reputation of TINDALL and SHI lies in quite the opposite direction. Published in a handbook format, this engaging and balanced narrative of American history is rich in detail and unencumbered by historiographic debate or harsh judgments. Traditional political, economic, and diplomatic events form the backbone of this text, while social and cultural issues are relegated to separate chapters. Tindall and Shi include a judicious selection of black-and-white illustrations, maps, and photographs, but clearly the strength of this work rests on the writing itself. The careful detail and full coverage of political events makes this an excellent single-volume reference work. The brief edition is 30 per cent shorter, but preserves the format and all of the strong points of the original.

Two United States history texts by British authors provide a distinct contrast to the more lavish American products. BROGAN emphasizes the traditional fare of political and diplomatic history in a single-volume text devoid of illustrations, save for line maps. He provides a strong interpretive framework that focuses on the actions of great men and economic concerns from a generally consensus point of view. The text is weak on factual details and the chronology sometimes falters into abstraction. The cursory treatment of the century and a half prior to independence provides a shaky foundation for understanding what followed. Brogan makes up for this omission by his unabashed admiration for the rise and progress of American nationhood and the unfolding of American values. His generally optimistic approach to the nation's history nevertheless failed him as he struggled to understand the problems facing the country at its Bicentennial. Brogan thus ends his account rather awkwardly and abruptly in 1976, as if betrayed by the values he had so enthusiastically endorsed. JONES also provides a traditional narrative that is narrowly focused on the political mainstream of American history. Like Brogan, the text has none of the illustrations or special features common to American productions, save for a selection of appendix maps and tables. It also devotes less than 10 per cent of its 600 pages to the period prior to 1783. The interpretations are traditional, save that Jones criticizes the Progressive Era, New Deal, and other reform movements for not going far enough to solve all of the problems facing the country – as if this were an actual possibility. While this criticism may true enough, it may not sufficiently recognize the realities of American politics.

EMIL POCOCK

Third Parties

Black, Gordon S. and Benjamin D. Black, *The Politics of American Discontent: How a New Party Can Make Democracy Work Again*, New York: Wiley, 1994

Ceaser, James and Andrew Busch, *Upside Down, Inside Out: The 1992 Elections and American Politics*, Lanham, MD: Rowman and Littlefield, 1993

Gillespie, J. David, *Politics at the Periphery: Third Parties in Two-Party America*, Columbia: University of South Carolina Press, 1993

Herbst, Susan, *Politics at the Margin: Historical Studies of Public Expression Outside the Mainstream*, Cambridge and New York: Cambridge University Press, 1994

Hesseltine, William B., *Third-Party Movements in the United States*, Princeton: Princeton University Press, 1962

Hofstadter, Richard, *The Age of Reform: From Bryan to FDR*, New York: Knopf, 1955; London: Cape, 1962

Klehr, Harvey, John Earl Haynes, and Fridrikh Igorevich Firsov, *The Secret World of American Communism*, New Haven: Yale University Press, 1995

Kruschke, Earl R., *Encyclopedia of Third Parties in the United States*, Santa Barbara, CA: ABC-CLIO, 1991

Mazmanian, Daniel A., *Third Parties in Presidential Elections*, Washington, DC: Brookings Institution, 1974

Rosenstone, Steven J., Roy L. Behr, and Edward H. Lazarus, *Third Parties in America: Citizen Response to Major Party Failure*, Princeton: Princeton University Press, 1984

Schlesinger, Arthur M., Jr. (editor), *History of US Political Parties*, 4 vols., New York: Chelsea House, 1973

Cultural dualism, structural constraints, and other features of the Anglo American experience set patterns of two-party dominance. American third parties have rarely achieved or sustained a tertiary share of elite power comparable even to that of third parties in the British House of Commons. The American third-party tradition dates from the 1820s. Its significance seems now beyond serious dispute. In addition to their role performance in (mainly non-elite) tasks traditionally assigned to political parties, U.S. third parties have been steam-venters for dissidents and for dissenting perspectives. In presenting their visions, third parties have contributed mightily to the nation's democratization. When they have proved popular, third-party ideas have often been appropriated (or stolen) by major parties, and thereafter implemented either as public policy or as constitutional reform.

Significant treatments of third parties as a general phenomenon appear infrequently, at a rate of perhaps one per decade. ROSENSTONE, BEHR and LAZARUS stands out as among the most important. Just two of their eight chapters feature descriptive accounts of important 19th- and 20th-century third-party eruptions. The principal value of this work lies in its contribution to the construction of a theoretical explanation of the third-party phenomenon. It is argued that voters calculate the costs and the benefits of voting for a major party as well as of defecting to a third-party nominee. The Rosenstone model presents major-party failure, low levels of public affection for the major parties, and well-known, attractive third-party candidates as the principal determinants of the strength of third-party movements.

An earlier work by the political scientist MAZMANIAN makes its own contribution to the understanding of third parties. He contends that opportunities for third parties arise as the major parties chase, and seek to co-opt, the transient spatial domain of majority opinion. Thus, for example, George Wallace's right-wing populist 1968 American Independent Party movement was a reaction against the Democratic and Republican shared embrace of civil rights. Opposing many of the onerous structural burdens upon third-party electoral participation, Mazmanian recommends uniform and achievable legal requirements for ballot access. He holds up as a model the "modified two-party system" in New York State, where a candidate may run (and his/her ballot totals may be accumulated) as the nominee both of a major and of one or more third parties.

In his last major work, the prolific historian HESSELTINE highlighted important national third parties from the Antimasons of the 1820s through the 1948 Dixiecrats and Progressives. He emphasizes the impact of third parties upon major-party programs and upon public policy. All of these works focus upon nationally-organized transient or shortlived parties. These are the parties, arising as independent protest movements or as seceding splinters from a major party, that rise but also die out quickly. Often they leave behind a substantial legacy in mainstream politics.

These transient parties are but one of three third-party types. Some scholars prefer the term minor party to designate long-lived doctrinal third parties. These doctrinal parties – Prohibition, Communist, and others – manage to sustain themselves for decades, often at distances far removed from the mainstream. Third parties also arise in non-national politics. Occasionally one of these non-national parties transforms itself into a major force, or even a governing party, in a local community or an entire state.

GILLESPIE provides a comprehensive and accessible recent overview of past and present third parties of all these three types. Two of the book's eight chapters add a theoretical perspective. There are also two chapters on the transient parties (including the nominally "independent" campaign of H. Ross Perot in 1992), one each on long-lived doctrinal parties and

on non-national parties, and a chapter on women, African Americans, and the third-party option. For those seeking information on a wide range of topics, KRUSCHKE offers a brief encyclopedic guide to 81 historic and contemporary American third parties.

SCHLESINGER is a multi-volume, multi-author work, containing information and analysis of considerable benefit to those with an interest in third parties. It provides a valuable combination of extensive documentary materials with lengthy interpretive essays by leading authorities on fourteen third parties from the Antimasons through the American Independents. There are also valuable case studies of particular parties. HOFSTADTER, a prime example of the case study genre, treats both the Populists and Progressives. It has aroused much controversy, but still offers many insights into the history of reform movements in the late 19th and early 20th centuries. HERBST's study of political marginality features the Libertarian party in its fifth chapter. The author's interviews with twenty Illinois Libertarian activists are of note. A controversial 1995 book charges that, in the 1930s and 1940s, the Communist Party of the U.S.A. recruited a spy network on behalf of Soviet espionage – a network that penetrated the Manhattan Project, the State Department, and the Office of Strategic Services. KLEHR, HAYNES and FIRSOV – a combination of two American historians and a Russian colleague – drew upon evidence from the newly-opened Comintern files in Russia, in their efforts to back up their remarkable claims.

BLACK and BLACK, written in the aftermath of the 1992 Perot campaign, was intended as a manifesto for the creation of a new party to smash the Democratic-Republican duopoly. On that campaign itself, the retrospective monograph by CEASER and BUSCH brings clarity and interpretive insight. For third parties, the 1990s did indeed afford a window of opportunity seemingly more open than any that had come since the Great Depression. Evidence of this centered on the 1992 campaign of Perot, whose 19 per cent vote share was the third highest ever for a presidential candidate not the standard-bearer of a major party. It was the highest share in history for any such candidate not running as an ex-president.

There were other signs too. In the 1980s, ex-Mayor of Burlington, Bernie Sanders, an avowed socialist, ran as an independent and won Vermont's only seat in the United States House of Representatives. Independent or third-party candidates won gubernatorial contests in Connecticut, Alaska, and Maine. Progressives, Libertarians, and independents grew in number in state legislative bodies. During the presidential campaign of 1996, opinion polls showed many Americans welcoming the prospect of a new third major party with the political muscle to battle the Democrats and Republicans.

J. DAVID GILLESPIE

Tocqueville, Alexis de, 1805–1859
French political thinker and commentator on the United States

Brogan, Hugh, *Tocqueville*, London: Fontana, 1973
Commager, Henry Steele, *Commager on Tocqueville*, Columbia: University of Missouri Press, 1993

Drescher, Seymour, *Dilemmas of Democracy: Tocqueville and Modernization*, Pittsburgh: University of Pittsburgh Press, 1968

Eisenstadt, Abraham S. (editor), *Reconsidering Tocqueville's Democracy in America*, New Brunswick, NJ: Rutgers University Press, 1988

Jardin, André, *Tocqueville: A Biography*, translated by Lydia Davis and Robert Hemenway, New York: Farrar Straus, and London: Halban, 1988

Mancini, Matthew, *Alexis de Tocqueville*, New York: Twayne, 1994

Pierson, George Wilson, *Tocqueville and Beaumont in America*, New York: Oxford University Press, 1938

Reeves, Richard, *American Journey: Traveling with Tocqueville in Search of Democracy in America*, New York: Simon and Schuster, 1982

Schleifer, James T., *The Making of Tocqueville's Democracy in America*, Chapel Hill: University of North Carolina Press, 1980

Siedentop, Larry, *Tocqueville*, New York and Oxford: Oxford University Press, 1994

Following in Hector Crèvecoeur's footsteps as a French interpreter of the American experience, Alexis de Tocqueville is best known among historians of America for his study of American society during the Age of Jackson, *Democracy in America* (1835–40). This was far from being all that he wrote, but any student of Tocqueville's political thought and writings could do worse than begin with some of the studies that concentrate on his experiences in, and conclusions about, 19th-century America.

The Tocqueville "revival" of the 20th century really began with PIERSON's 1938 study, which traces the background to, and progress of, Tocqueville's travels, as well as offering a substantial and detailed assessment of *Democracy* itself. Pierson is not blind to the failings of the work, and argues for example that Tocqueville did not adequately define "democracy" and yet viewed the process as inevitable, and that he failed to recognise the impact that industrialization and the two-party system were having on America, and consequently overestimated the tendency for democracy to degenerate into the "Tyranny of the Majority." The first sustained study of what had been a somewhat obscure subject, this work is rightly considered a classic, although late 20th century readers will find Pierson's suggestion that "perhaps a suppression of individual or minority rights *is* possible, and even in times of peace," more than slightly ironic given the work's publication date, and may well conclude that Tocqueville knew better than his commentator the nature of the process he was describing.

Tocqueville's understanding of democracy and the historical process is examined more fully by DRESCHER, a leading Tocqueville scholar who has written widely on the subject. He offers not only a succinct analysis of the thoughts of Tocqueville and his travelling companion, Gustave de Beaumont, on a wide variety of American topics, but also an excellent starting-point for anyone seeking a guide through the maze of Tocqueville scholarship prior to 1968. Drescher does not focus solely on *Democracy*, but also examines Tocqueville and Beaumont's writings on prison reform, Beaumont's novel *Marie*, and their voluminous correspondence. Inevitably, the study is somewhat dated now, but anyone seeking to understand the impact of the American experience on Tocqueville's ideas cannot afford to ignore Drescher's work.

The 1980s saw a new surge of interest in Tocqueville and his writings. One of its products was a major study of *Democracy in America* by SCHLEIFER, who argues that, as an interpreter of the American experience, Tocqueville was largely replaced by James Bryce's *The American Commonwealth* (1888). However, this does not prevent Schleifer from providing a valuable study of *Democracy*, which examines the influence of American thinkers and writers – notably James Madison and Jared Sparks – on Tocqueville's work. Schleifer skilfully traces the sources of Tocqueville's information, and the uses which he made of it. His examination of the development of Tocqueville's ideas on democracy, and specifically of the precise meaning which he attached to it, is also very illuminating. Towards the end of the 1980s, a collection of essays on Tocqueville and *Democracy* appeared, under the editorship of EISENSTADT. The proceedings of a conference held in 1985 to mark the 150th anniversary of the publication of *Democracy in America*, they vary widely in quality and outlook. Some of the contributors praise Tocqueville as a prophet of American democracy, while others concentrate rather more on *Democracy*'s shortcomings. However, the very range of treatment makes this an extremely valuable contribution to Tocqueville scholarship.

The 1980s also saw the publication of JARDIN's biography of Tocqueville, the most comprehensive to date. As the general editor of the thirty-volume *Complete Works* of Tocqueville, Jardin is uniquely well-qualified to write on his subject, as is evident in this substantial work, which is solid and well-researched, although anyone seeking startling new revelations on Tocqueville will be disappointed. Instead, Jardin concentrates on Tocqueville's life and career, offering an extremely perceptive analysis of his political views and ambitions which does not focus entirely on *Democracy*, but includes a valuable assessment of *L'Ancien Régime et la Révolution*, although in neither case does Jardin attempt to comment on the contemporary relevance of Tocqueville's work.

Several studies of Tocqueville do, however, have as their main aim a consideration of the 20th century relevance of his thought. One such is REEVES, an account of the author's experiences as he retraces Tocqueville's journey around the United States, "asking the questions that Tocqueville had asked." The result is a stimulating, if not wholly successful, study, which concludes that there is, after all, some hope for democracy in America. COMMAGER is a more recent work by an eminent American historian, which, in the author's own words, is less "concerned with what Tocqueville had to say about America and democracy in the 1830s [than] with what he has to say about democracy and America in the 1990s and after." Extracts from *Democracy* are brought in periodically, but only to serve as points of departure for comments on slavery, the proslavery argument, racism in general, the Cold War and what America was really doing in Vietnam.

BROGAN, one of the very best short studies of Tocqueville, is extremely critical of the tendency to "use" Tocqueville to comment on the concerns of our own day. Although too brief to be in any sense comprehensive, this work should nevertheless be the starting-point for anyone interested in *Democracy in America* and its impact, particularly during the Cold War when Tocqueville's "prophecy" about Russia and America seemed most prescient. Brogan stresses the importance of placing Tocqueville firmly in his own time, and this work is particularly insightful when it comes to an assessment of Tocqueville's impact on 19th-century thought, on the process whereby Tocqueville's ideas of democracy were fed into the European mind, and on the development of "Tocqueville's most famous contribution to political thought," the concept of the "Tyranny of the Majority." Brogan concludes that Tocqueville hoped, ultimately, for the best of both worlds: democracy with aristocratic virtues.

So far the 1990s have seen the appearance of two general studies which, following in Brogan's footsteps, attempt to offer a comprehensive yet concise assessment of Tocqueville's life and work. Both trace the background to, and development of, Tocqueville's political ideas, before moving on to a consideration of *Democracy* and other writings. SIEDENTOP is a succinct study which sticks close to its subject, whereas MANCINI is more wide-ranging in his assessment of Tocqueville's political and ideological development, the people and ideas which influenced him, and those whom he in turn influenced. As a volume in the "Past Masters" series, Siedentop looks set to be the more accessible of the two, but Mancini is rather better in terms of its arrangement, argument and approach. It also includes the most up-to-date annotated guide to Tocqueville scholarship, which will be invaluable to anyone new to the subject.

S-M. GRANT

Transcendentalism

Boller, Paul F., Jr., *American Transcendentalism, 1830–1860: An Intellectual Inquiry*, New York: Putnam, 1974

Buell, Lawrence, *Literary Transcendentalism: Style and Vision in the American Renaissance*, Ithaca, NY: Cornell University Press, 1973

Carafiol, Peter, *The American Ideal: Literary History as a Worldly Activity*, New York: Oxford University Press, 1991

Howe, Irving, *The American Newness: Culture and Politics in the Age of Emerson*, Cambridge, MA: Harvard University Press, 1986

Matthiessen, F.O., *American Renaissance: Art and Expression in the Age of Emerson and Whitman*, New York and London: Oxford University Press, 1941

Rose, Anne C., *Transcendentalism as a Social Movement, 1830–1850*, New Haven: Yale University Press, 1981

Critical works on Transcendentalism tend to examine the term in three interconnected ways: first, as a theological, reformist and literary movement based in New England during the 1830s and 1840s; second, as a constellation of philosophical and aesthetic ideas which derive from European Romanticism but which are distinctively American in character; and third, as a conceptual marker representative of an idealistic current running throughout American culture.

BUELL directs his study to the literary theme of his subtitle through a "combination of intellectual history, critical explication, and genre study." He traces the complex term Transcendentalism through from its early derogatory connotations (suggesting "outlandishness" and "vagueness") to the moment of Ralph Waldo Emerson's resignation as a Boston pastor in 1832 and the founding of the Transcendentalist club in 1836, which represented a radical break with Unitarianism and the Lockean psychology on which it was based. Buell examines its various "rhetorical structures" and forms which correlate to post-Kantian thought, but which also mark Transcendentalist writing as a distinct "outgrowth" of New England culture. The book focuses on how the central themes of revelation, spiritual truth and Nature are expressed in the writings of Emerson, Henry David Thoreau and Margaret Fuller, through to a concluding section on Walt Whitman, who, while he is not associated directly with Transcendentalism, pursues parallel Romantic themes.

The central concern of BOLLER is the Transcendentalists' break with the Unitarian Church and the roots of their discontent, which he claims to derive from "a quest ... to find meaning, pattern, and purpose in a universe no longer managed by a genteel and amiable Unitarian God." The study begins with an appraisal of Emerson's Divinity School Address of 1838, in which he praised the "moral sentiment" of intuition against reason as the foundation of religious faith. Boller goes on to examine various aspects of Transcendentalist thought, paying particular attention to "transcendental idealism", moral philosophy and the social reformist writings of Thoreau and Emerson. The book concludes with a consideration of the "excesses" of Transcendentalism with reference to Nathaniel Hawthorne's short story, "The Celestial Railroad" (1843).

Some of these themes are further pursued in HOWE's critique of Emersonian thought, and particularly what he characterizes as Emerson's "devotion to inwardness." This short and provocative book begins by praising the scepticism of Hawthorne as a more critically engaged response to the "newness" of the age than that of Emerson's idealistic individualism. For Howe, this "newness" represents America in its infancy, before the toll of slavery, civil war and industrialization had tempered such idealistic yearnings. Thus, other figures such as Hawthorne, and later Melville and Orestes Brownson, are each set up as "a 'control' of realism, shadowing hopes with doubts, enthusiasms with quizzical silence." However, the author also detects self-doubt in Emerson's more mature work, for example the essays "Experience" (1844) and "Fate" (1852), in which Howe claims Emerson addresses the "circumstance, loss, [and] depletion" of the age more authentically than in his work of the 1830s. Howe concludes his study by calling for a re-examination of Emerson's influence on contemporary American intellectual thought.

In a finely written "social and intellectual history" ROSE views the reformist ethos of Transcendentalism as a crucial "part of the social life of antebellum America." She maps the influence of Boston Unitarianism from the end of the 18th century to the dissent of the Transcendentalists in the 1830s. From the early skirmishes with Unitarian doctrine, she views the late 1830s as a period of transition for the major radical intellectuals, marking a shift from an engagement with religion to issues of wider social reform. These impulses are illustrated by Rose's consideration of the two experimental communities associated with Transcendentalism – Bronson Alcott's anarchic Fruitlands and George Ripley's Fourierist Brook Farm – in contrast to Thoreau's and Emerson's individualist departures from such social ideals. The period under consideration closes with the coming of age of American Victorianism in the 1850s, at which time Rose states "the Transcendentalist movement ended in deflated hopes and cheerful acquiescence."

MATTHIESSEN is a classic study of mid-19th century literature, which, within a cultural and intellectual framework, examines a selection of American texts written between 1850 and 1855. Influenced by the school of New Criticism, Matthiessen is primarily interested in the aesthetic and "imaginative value" of these works, and he attempts to trace in them recurrent themes germane to an understanding of the epoch, and what he discerns as a "re-birth" of American literature. Although his studies of Emerson and Thoreau are interesting, and the tenor of Transcendentalism is central to the work, it is his reading of the other writers, Hawthorne, Whitman and Melville, which constitute the most important sections of the book.

CARAFIOL traces to its Transcendentalist roots a belief in American exceptionalism and an idealized national identity, which he claims to have dominated American literary scholarship since the last quarter of the 19th century. In many of the critical works on Transcendentalism he detects the persistence of an "American ideal", a myth which "continues to legislate the kind of questions Americanists ask." He claims that this has resulted in a widespread scholarly project to tell a "coherent story" of American cultural history, to the exclusion of "disorderly" readings of texts. He asserts that we need to wrestle with dissenting voices, even those which have been formerly included in the American canon, through a revisionist and historicist reading of Transcendentalist writing and criticism. Carafiol attempts this through what he calls a "structured conversation about selected texts", including readings of Matthiessen and Buell and re-readings of Emerson's "The Transcendentalist" (1842) and Thoreau's *A Week on the Concord and Merrimack Rivers* (1849), in an attempt to rescue the latter two from the label of Transcendentalism, which he understands to be an "obsolete fiction."

MARTIN HALLIWELL

Transport: General

Bauer, K. Jack, *A Maritime History of the United States: The Role of America's Seas and Waterways*, Columbia: University of South Carolina Press, 1988

Cudahy, Brian J., *Cash, Tokens, and Transfers: A History of Urban Mass Transit in North America*, New York: Fordham University Press, 1990

De La Pedraja, René, *The Rise and Decline of US Merchant Shipping in the Twentieth Century*, New York: Twayne, 1992

Finch, Christopher, *Highways to Heaven: The Auto Biography of America*, New York: HarperCollins, 1992

Hunter, Louis C., *Steamboats on the Western Rivers: An Economic and Technological History*, Cambridge, MA: Harvard University Press, 1949

Martin, Albro, *Railroads Triumphant: The Growth, Rejection, and Rebirth of a Vital American Force*, New York: Oxford University Press, 1992

Petzinger, Thomas, Jr., *Hard Landing: The Epic Contest for Power and Profits That Plunged the Airlines into Chaos*, New York: Times Business, 1996

Rae, John B., *The Road and the Car in American Life*, Cambridge: Massachusetts Institute of Technology Press, 1971

Shaw, Ronald E., *Erie Water West: A History of the Erie Canal, 1792–1854*, Lexington: University Press of Kentucky, 1966

Smith, Henry Ladd, *Airways: The History of Commercial Aviation in the United States*, New York: Knopf, 1942

Taylor, George Rogers, *The Transportation Revolution, 1815–1860*, New York: Rinehart, 1951

Walker, Henry Pickering, *The Wagonmasters: High Plains Freighting from the Earliest Days of the Santa Fe Trail to 1880*, Norman: University of Oklahoma Press, 1966

Despite the geographical expanse of the United States and the concomitant historical importance of transportation in the development of the nation, transportation history is, today, a fragmented field, composed of a small number of specialized academic historians and a larger number of generalist-popularizers. Many of the standard works are old, out of print, and often difficult to acquire. In addition, there is no single scholarly work on general United States transportation history.

The classic survey of antebellum transportation is TAYLOR, which surveys roads, bridges, canals, steamboats, railroads, the merchant marine, and domestic and foreign trade, and examines the interrelationship of the "transportation revolution" and government, workers, manufacturing, finance, and the national economy generally. In addition, Taylor provides an extensive bibliographic essay. Unfortunately, there is no comparable volume for the postbellum period or the 20th century.

It is particularly difficult to find a completely satisfactory survey of American maritime history. Most of the attempts have produced mixed results, but BAUER, the most recent, is the best of the genre. Arranged topically and chronologically, it covers the age of exploration and the colonial era, the maritime (mainly deep water) growth of the new republic, early American shipbuilding, the antebellum coastal trade, antebellum canals, western rivers, inland seas, fishing, maritime decline after the Civil War, 20th-century programs for revival, and the post-World War II merchant marine. The writing is lively and the analysis sharp. An excellent supplement to Bauer is DE LA PEDRAJA, which focuses on the 20th-century oceanic merchant fleet. The work examines liners, tramp shipping, proprietary companies, and flags of convenience. Throughout, the author sees the decline of the merchant marine as a by-product of an obsession with free market competition and a fear of government ownership or operation of a fleet.

There is no single work on American river transportation, but the best introduction to the topic, and at the same time the classic study of the impact of steamboats on the development of the antebellum West, remains HUNTER, which is old

but still unequaled. Hunter's focus is economic and technological. He provides a carefully-documented economic analysis
that is buttressed by an equally careful portrait of the human
aspects of western steamboats. He first examines technological
developments, turning then to the business side of steamboat
operations, including organization, finance, and labor, and
passenger conditions aboard steamboats.

To understand canal development in the antebellum United
States, the reader need look no further than the Erie Canal in
New York. A well-written scholarly account is SHAW, which
examines political issues, construction, operation, travel and
commerce, and the canal's social and cultural significance.
Shaw takes his monograph to the end of the Canal Age and
beginning of the Railroad Age in the mid-1850s.

Transcontinental transportation, before and even during the
heyday of the railroads, depended upon overland wagon trains.
WALKER conveys the drama and sweep of the wagon
trains, telling a good story supported by solid scholarship.

The best general survey of the role of railroads in American
development is MARTIN, a briskly written and passionately
argued work. The bulk of the book focuses on the 20th
century. Martin traces the rise and decline of passenger transportation, a decline that he attributes to excessive government
regulation. In addition, the book examines the impact of railroads on coal mining, transportation of produce to market,
and the development of the steel and automobile industries. It
also discusses railroad management and the role of railroads
in politics. The work is particularly strong in providing a broad
context for the development of the railroad industry.

The history of transportation in the United States during
the 20th century is above all the history of the nation's love
affair with the automobile. FINCH tells that story with all its
technological, social, political, and economic components. The
book examines individual companies, the advertising that made
their products famous, and the impact of "car culture" on
cities, families, and gender roles. An excellent supplement is
RAE, which studies the social and economic effects of highway
transportation, sketching first the historical significance of
highways and highway vehicles, and then their economic and
social impact, the movement of goods, the "enrichment of rural
life," the growth of suburbs, and the location of industry.

For a survey of air transport, an old but still valuable and
comprehensive study is SMITH, which begins with the Wright
Brothers at Kitty Hawk and takes the story to the early 1940s.
Smith covers the development of mail lines, the evolution of
federal aviation regulations, the planes, the lines, and the major
designers and entrepreneurs. A necessary epilogue to Smith is
PETZINGER, a survey of the industry's troubles during the
latter decades of the 20th century. In particular, Petzinger
emphasizes the costs of destructive labor-management relations
and suggests that the roots of the industry's problems are to
be found in four decades of fare and route regulation.

As the United States has urbanized, transport within and
between cities has grown in importance. A readable introduction to the history of urban mass transportation is CUDAHY.
This brief survey includes numerous photographs and is clearly
aimed at a broad audience. Nevertheless, the author, who
comes to the subject with experience in the mass transportation industry, demonstrates solid scholarship. The book covers
motor buses, street cars, subways, and elevated lines, explains

the basic innovations – especially electrification – describes key
features of labor-management relations, and sketches the
debate over private vs. public ownership. In all, this is a brief
and enjoyable survey of an important subject.

KENNETH J. BLUME

Truman, Harry S. 1884–1972
33rd President of the United States

Donovan, Robert J., *Conflict and Crisis: The Presidency of Harry S. Truman, 1945–48*, New York: Norton, 1977
Donovan, Robert J., *Tumultuous Years: The Presidency of Harry S. Truman, 1949–1953*, New York: Norton, 1982
Ferrell, Robert H., *Harry S. Truman and the Modern American Presidency*, Boston: Little Brown, 1983
Gosnell, Harold F., *Truman's Crises: A Political Biography of Harry S. Truman*, Westport, CT: Greenwood Press, 1980
Jenkins, Roy, *Truman*, London: Collins, and New York: Harper, 1986
Kolko, Joyce and Gabriel Kolko, *The Limits of Power: The World and United States Foreign Policy, 1945–1954*, New York: Harper, 1972
Leffler, Melvyn P., *A Preponderance of Power: National Security, the Truman Administration, and the Cold War*, Stanford, CA: Stanford University Press, 1992
McCoy, Donald R., *The Presidency of Harry S. Truman*, Lawrence: University Press of Kansas, 1984
McCullough, David, *Truman*, New York: Simon and Schuster, 1992
Pemberton, William E., *Harry S. Truman: Fair Dealer and Cold Warrior*, Boston: Twayne, 1989

Studies of Harry Truman and his presidency tend to emphasize a number of common themes. They all highlight the fact
that Truman owed his political fortunes to his activity as a
"machine" politician who valued loyalty and cooperation
within the system. Most studies also acknowledge his fighting
spirit. They generally agree that his domestic Fair Deal and
his fertile foreign policy owed their success to Truman's pugna-
cious style and his tendency to hold out for the things he
believed were right. While assessments of his presidency as a
whole are still few in number, they may be supplemented by
the rich variety of studies on aspects of his presidency, particularly in foreign policy.

In his two-volume history of the Truman presidency,
DONOVAN offers a detailed account of the most important
episodes of the period. Donovan is sympathetic to Truman and
tends to write uncritically, but he provides an excellent work
of reference and a most comprehensive guide to the Truman
presidency. McCOY also views Truman through sympathetic
eyes. A conventional history, based on research in the archives,
it does not address the major historiographical issues that have
been raised by other writers in the field. Because it is very
compact, each aspect of the Truman presidency gets only
limited treatment. Truman's handling of the economy after the
war is judged to have been "impressive." Although, in McCoy's

view, Truman lacked charisma and used the wrong body language, he had good political instincts and had the knack of choosing a good team, particularly in the area of foreign policy.

In contrast, PEMBERTON is much more critical. In this very readable short political biography, he argues that Truman's reputation for decisiveness is exaggerated, and that he could be too often manipulated by subordinates. He remained faithful to the New Deal's commitment to social reform not out of ideology but out of loyalty to the coalition that supported the Democrats. Pemberton criticizes Truman for an inability to see the world in complex terms. The Cold War, he believes, might have taken a different course if Truman had resorted to fewer slogans and aphorisms. Certainly Joseph McCarthy would not have found such fertile ground for his anticommunist inquisition.

Perhaps the best introduction to Truman is JENKINS. Although the research base is rather narrow, the British politician compensates by providing thoughtful insights which are fuelled by eloquent prose. He holds the president in very high regard and embarked on the biography in the first place as a result of his own deep and personal commitment to NATO and the western alliance. He believes that Truman was "in some ways the superior of Roosevelt": he was more decisive and had more "sustained energy." Truman had the ability to distinguish the big issues from the little ones and "was generally right" on those big issues. Unlike Pemberton, Jenkins believes that Truman was decisive and possessed that rare quality: foresight.

GOSNELL, on the other hand, chooses to be more equivocal. He treats each issue on its own and reserves judgment either way. He draws on published sources and, like Donovan, tries to cover most of the major problems confronted by Truman. He argues that the Hiroshima bomb was dropped for military reasons only and that generally Truman's foreign policy was shaped by circumstances that were largely beyond his control. He is critical of the Truman Doctrine with its resonance of indiscriminate commitments overseas, but is effusive about the Marshall Plan.

The short biography by FERRELL in the Library of American Biography series argues that Truman tried to cooperate with the Soviets at first. But his hands were tied, and Ferrell contends that it was unlikely that things would have turned out differently if Truman had altered his style. Ferrell argues that containment was a piecemeal policy, often improvised. Truman was less certain about himself in private than he was in public. But Ferrell admires his basic decency, and believes that his championship of civil rights was an "emotional matter for him", rather than a sophisticated political strategy. He concludes that "No political figure . . . not even Franklin Roosevelt . . . proved as willing as Truman to stand up for what he believed."

The most recent work is the bestselling biography by McCULLOUGH. This massive biography, running to over 1000 pages, traces Truman's life from his childhood in a racially segregated Independence, Missouri, to his retirement there. McCullough likes his subject. When Truman erred, as he did by showing interest in the Ku Klux Klan in the 1920s, McCullough sees it as "out of character." He concurs in the widely held opinion that Truman was decisive and determined,

and abhorred hesitancy and weakness. He thought J. Robert Oppenheimer was a "cry-baby" because of his stricken conscience over the atomic bomb. Truman was capable of great anger, but usually confined it to letters that were not intended to be seen, and did not allow himself to be driven by it.

Some of the most challenging studies of the period are in the field of foreign policy. KOLKO and KOLKO is perhaps the most comprehensive "revisionist" history of the period. The Kolkos argue that the Truman years saw a huge attempt by the United States to extend its sphere of interest in Europe and the Far East. The administration was impelled not by personal ambition but by the demands of America's capitalist economy. It was as impervious to emerging nationalism as it was to the sheer extent of the destruction that had been wreaked upon the Soviet Union by World War II.

LEFFLER is an exhaustive account of national security policy in the Truman years. This highly acclaimed book casts its research net wide. Leffler shows that the foreign policy of the postwar years has to be understood as an exercise in geopolitics. Key policymakers wanted to thwart the Kremlin in any design it might have over forward bases, critical industries and raw materials. The United States had emerged from the war as the "preponderant power" and it had no intention of relinquishing that power. It wanted to create an international environment that was hospitable to America's interests. Truman and his advisers were shrewd men who understood the source of Soviet weakness and its strength. They saw that their main brief was to fill the vacuums of power left in the wake of the war and to promote economic reconstruction. As the task became more difficult, a number of serious choices had to be made, but Truman and his advisers were always in full command of their decisions.

ROBERT GARSON

See also Cold War; World War II, United States and 5

Truth, Sojourner c.1797–1883
Evangelist and abolitionist

Johnson, Paul E. and Sean Wilentz, *The Kingdom of Matthias*, New York: Oxford University Press, 1994

Mabee, Carleton with Susan Mabee Newhouse, *Sojourner Truth: Slave, Prophet, Legend*, New York: New York University Press, 1993

Painter, Nell Irvin, "Truth, Sojourner," in *Black Women in America: An Historical Encyclopedia*, edited by Darlene Clark Hine and others, 2 vols., New York: Carlson, 1993

Painter, Nell Irvin, "Representing Truth: Sojourner Truth's Knowing and Becoming Known," *Journal of American History*, 81(2), September 1994

Stewart, Jeffrey C. (editor), *Narrative of Sojourner Truth, a Bondswoman of Olden Time: with a History of Her Labors and Correspondence Drawn from Her "Book of Life"* (1878 edition), New York: Oxford University Press, 1991

Washington, Margaret (editor), *Narrative of Sojourner Truth* (1850 edition), New York: Vintage, 1993

Born a slave in Ulster County, New York, between 1797 and 1799, known as Isabella and then Isabella van Wagenen until she changed her name in the 1840s, Sojourner Truth was one of the first African American women to speak out publicly for the abolition of slavery and for women's rights. She was known in abolitionist and reform circles during her lifetime, but the residual curiosity about her that remained after her death in 1883 has recently been fanned into new life by interest in civil rights and feminism, and she has become a symbol of blacks' and women's struggles for freedom. More is being written about her today than at any previous time. Sojourner Truth's story is not only intrinsically interesting; it has been reshaped from time to time to serve different purposes, and Truth herself took an important role in influencing the ways she has been represented to a wider public.

After years of servitude Isabella took her freedom as New York was finally abolishing slavery in 1827, and in about 1829 moved to New York City. There she combined domestic work with a deepening commitment to evangelical Christianity; this led to three years' attachment to the prophet Robert Matthews, who called himself Matthias and headed a communitarian sect known as The Kingdom. JOHNSON and WILENTZ throw light on this previously obscure stage of Isabella van Wagenen's life and on the religious world of New York in the 1830s with which she was involved. Though she is not the main focus of their book, and they melodramatically conceal her identity until its final page, they provide valuable background for understanding her later emergence as a speaker and campaigner.

A poor, black woman, she had by 1835 several times demonstrated the courage and tenacity that shaped her life: seizing her own freedom when her owner refused to release her; suing successfully for the return of her son who had been illegally sold to a slaveholder in Alabama; and suing, again successfully, for libel over allegations of involvement in a murder scandal that led to the break-up of Matthias's Kingdom. In 1843 she left New York to spread the Word as an itinerant preacher, and adopted the name Sojourner Truth to mark the break with her past. Although she was a notable camp-meeting speaker, this would not be the only avenue for the wise sayings and sharp wit that became her hallmark. Joining, from 1843 to 1846, a community founded by radical abolitionists in Northampton, Massachusetts, she emerged as an antislavery speaker and from 1850 onwards as an advocate of women's rights too.

With the help of the abolitionist Olive Gilbert, she published that year an account of her life, the *Narrative of Sojourner Truth*, successive editions of which contributed to her support and spread her fame in reform circles. Until very recently, writing about her was largely based on this and other documents published in her lifetime. Readers should note that a number of modern dramatized biographies, books for children and young people, and short historical studies of Sojourner Truth derive from these sources or perpetuate traditions initiated by them, and can be misleading; they are not cited here. STEWART's introduction to the reprinted 1878 edition of the *Narrative* was among the first to provide a critical evaluation of Truth's career. WASHINGTON's introduction to the 1850 edition adds new research findings and a thoughtful commentary, particularly on the *Narrative*'s context and influence. But these two editions also reflect the interpretive problems facing those interested in Sojourner Truth: each reproduces a different 19th-century account of what is now her most famous speech, at the Akron women's rights convention of 1851. Comparison of the two suggests how conjectural the conventionally-accepted version of that speech is, and how cautiously such sources need to be used.

Harriet Beecher Stowe's romanticization of Sojourner Truth as a mysterious "Libyan Sibyl" in an 1863 article for *Atlantic Monthly* spread her fame, but also belied the forthrightness and practicality of a career that was just then taking another new turn. From 1864 Truth worked among refugees in Washington with the National Freedman's Relief Association, and later ran an agency to find employment in the North for former slaves. She campaigned for women's suffrage, arguing that the Fifteenth Amendment should extend rights to women as well as to black men. She was active during the 1870s in efforts to obtain land for the resettlement of freed slaves in the West, and – at the age of at least eighty – travelled to Kansas in 1879 as a volunteer relief-worker with "Exodusters" arriving from the South, whose migration she viewed as a providential sign of redemption for black Americans.

New research on Sojourner Truth, now being published, is at last untangling the webs of tradition and mythology that have grown up around her. MABEE provides a factual discussion of the various aspects of Truth's life, not least of her relief work and campaigning of the 1860s and 1870s that had received short shrift in earlier accounts. The book's emphasis on the correction of the historical record concerning Sojourner Truth is both a strength and a weakness: on one hand it is a useful reference tool, on the other it falls short of being a powerful overall interpretive biography.

For that we shall have to await the work of others, notably Nell Irvin Painter, whose book-length study, *Sojourner Truth: A Life, a Symbol* (New York: Norton, 1996) has been published too recently to be considered here. The two articles by PAINTER cited here nevertheless present different facets of her attempt to recover a deeper understanding of Truth's life by tracing both the factual record and the shaping of her story by Truth herself and her contemporaries. Painter throws valuable light on the emergence of a figure who had trenchant things to say about gender, race and class in American society and so has become a role-model to modern generations. She also shows how modern accounts can selectively downplay issues that the 19th century would have emphasized, especially the evangelical, messianic roots of Sojourner Truth's faith, work and expression.

CHRISTOPHER CLARK

Tubman, Harriet c.1820–1913
Abolitionist and helper of fugitive slaves

Boyer, Richard O., *The Legend of John Brown: A Biography and History*, New York: Knopf, 1973

Bradford, Sarah H., *Scenes in the Life of Harriet Tubman*, Auburn, NY: Moses, 1869; 2nd edition, as *Harriet, the Moses of Her People*, New York: Lockwood, 1886; reprinted as *Harriet Tubman: The Moses of Her People*, Secaucus, NJ: Citadel Press, 1974

Buckmaster, Henrietta, *Let My People Go: The Story of the Underground Railroad and the Growth of the Abolition Movement*, New York: Harper, 1941

Conrad, Earl, *Harriet Tubman*, Washington, DC: Associated Publishers, 1943

Hine, Darlene Clark (editor), *Black Women in American History: From Colonial Times Through the Nineteenth Century*, 4 vols., New York: Carlson, 1990

Oates, Stephen B., *To Purge This Land with Blood: A Biography of John Brown*, New York: Harper, 1970

Petry, Ann, *Harriet Tubman: Conductor on the Underground Railroad*, New York: Crowell, 1955; as *The Girl Called Moses*, London: Methuen, 1960

Siebert, Wilbur H., *The Underground Railroad from Slavery to Freedom*, New York: Macmillan, 1898; reprinted, New York: Russell and Russell, 1967

Sterling, Dorothy, *Freedom Train: The Story of Harriet Tubman*, New York: Doubleday, 1954

Villard, Oswald Garrison, *John Brown, 1880–1859: A Biography Fifty Years After*, Boston: Houghton Mifflin, 1910; revised, New York: Knopf, 1943

Yee, Shirley J., *Black Women Abolitionists: A Study in Activism, 1828–1860*, Knoxville: University of Tennessee Press, 1992

Harriet Tubman is without doubt one of the most important icons in African American history. Her life and her legend have been immortalized by songwriters and storytellers, poets and playwrights. And yet serious scholarly works about her are still in short supply. Of the books listed above, both STERLING and PETRY were written for young people. Sterling is also one of those strange hybrids that combines fact with fiction. That she should have resorted to such an approach raises a crucial issue. By far the biggest problem confronting any would-be biographer of Tubman is the lack of available sources. Despite the fact that she lived most of her life in freedom, Tubman never learned to read and write. Unable to put her opinions and experiences to paper, she was equally reluctant to reveal her story to others. It seems that we shall never be able to delve deep enough into Tubman's mind to understand what exactly drove this remarkable woman.

Originally published in 1869 under the title *Scenes in the Life of Harriet Tubman*, BRADFORD transformed her subject into a living legend. This is anything but dispassionate biography. Profits from sales of the book were used by Tubman to pay off a mortgage. Bradford can at best be described as impressionistic. Far from drowning readers in a wealth of detail, she instead forces them to wade through wave after wave of empty rhetoric. The fault is not entirely hers. Since secrecy was essential to the success of the Underground Railroad, information on its operations is extremely scarce. The second edition of the book, reprinted in 1974, sought to address this issue. Contained in its appendix is a series of character references written on behalf of Tubman by such eminent antislavery activists as Gerrit Smith and Frederick Douglass. Although this does nothing to invalidate earlier criticisms of the book, it does offer a clear estimation of the esteem in which Tubman was held.

The last freightload of fugitive slaves to be transported along the Underground Railroad had long since arrived at its destination by the time SIEBERT was published. Since its operations no longer needed to be safeguarded, Siebert was able to lift the veil of secrecy that surrounded the Railroad. The surest means of avoiding detection was to venture across the sparsely populated Appalachians, a route regularly taken by Tubman. She would stop often at a series of stations in Delaware before escorting slaves on to Philadelphia. Although he acquired this information from Tubman, Siebert makes little use of his interview with her. Instead, he disappointingly draws many of his observations from the pages of Bradford.

BUCKMASTER borrows heavily from both Bradford and Siebert, retracing the steps of the two authors more successfully than she does those of Tubman herself. However, neither Buckmaster nor Siebert set out to write a biography of Tubman, and neither book can really be criticized for its failure to offer detailed accounts of all nineteen expeditions which Tubman is alleged to have made to the South. Nor does CONRAD fare much better. Despite his diligent efforts to track down every available source on his subject, Tubman eludes the author as successfully as she would a slave catcher. Nonetheless, Conrad is a far better biography than Bradford. He does offer a reasonably detailed account of her escape to freedom. As he also clearly illustrates, Tubman's activism did not end with the abolition of slavery. On the contrary, she campaigned tirelessly on such issues as temperance, welfare and women's suffrage.

Women's suffrage is an issue more commonly associated with another black female activist of the 19th century. YEE offers some intriguing if undeveloped comparisons between Tubman and her contemporary, Sojourner Truth. Both were individualists who refused to play the role that society had prescribed for them. Despite the social circles in which they moved, neither conformed to conventional ideas about ladylike behaviour. As poor women, Truth and Tubman also challenged the essentially male and middle-class leadership of the African American community.

Tubman had a closer association with the notorious white abolitionist John Brown. As BOYER, OATES and VILLARD all elaborate, the two were more than just mutual admirers. Tubman agreed to recruit supporters for Brown's raid on Harpers Ferry from among the slaves that she had helped to escape to Canada. She herself was to act as the "shepherd" who would lead the bondsmen liberated by Brown's army to freedom. Only illness prevented her eventual participation. Entirely academic as the question may be, it is irresistible to ask what the effect on her reputation would have been, had she gone.

More useful still are some of the essays on Tubman, previously published elsewhere, which appear in HINE. The piece by Benjamin Quarles is perhaps the best brief overview of Tubman's life available, although infuriatingly there are no footnotes. Priscilla Thompson offers an engaging account of the working relationship between Tubman and the Quaker abolitionist Thomas Garrett. His home in Wilmington, Delaware was one of the main stations at which Tubman stopped for sanctuary and supplies when working along the Underground Railroad.

CLIVE WEBB

See also Abolitionism

Turner, Nat 1800–1831
Leader of slave uprising

Aptheker, Herbert, *Nat Turner's Slave Rebellion*, New York: Humanities Press, 1966

Clarke, John Henrik (editor), *William Styron's Nat Turner: Ten Black Writers Respond*, Boston: Beacon Press, 1968

Drewry, William Sidney, *The Southampton Insurrection*, Washington, DC: Neale, 1900; reprinted, Murfreesboro, NC: Johnson, 1968

Duff, John B. and Peter M. Mitchell (editors), *The Nat Turner Rebellion: The Historical Event and the Modern Controversy*, New York: Harper, 1971

Foner, Eric, *Nat Turner*, Englewood Cliffs, NJ: Prentice Hall, 1971

Johnson, F. Roy, *The Nat Turner Slave Insurrection*, Murfreesboro, NC: Johnson, 1966

Johnson, F. Roy, *The Nat Turner Story: History of the South's Most Important Slave Revolt*, Murfreesboro, NC: Johnson, 1970

Oates, Stephen B., *The Fires of Jubilee: Nat Turner's Fierce Rebellion*, New York: Harper, 1975

Stone, Albert E., *The Return of Nat Turner: History, Literature, and Cultural Politics in Sixties America*, Athens: University of Georgia Press, 1992

Styron, William, *The Confessions of Nat Turner*, New York: Random House, 1967; London: Cape, 1968

Tragle, Henry Irving, *The Southampton Slave Revolt of 1831: A Compilation of Source Material*, Amherst: University of Massachusetts Press, 1971

Two distinct themes have emerged from the works written on Nat Turner and the slave revolt which he led in Southampton County, Virginia in 1831. Some authors have sought to understand the man, and to assess the origins, events and outcomes of the rebellion. Others have explored more fully the meaning of Turner in the context of later African American history and of contemporary culture and politics.

In the first full-length account of the insurrection, DREWRY skilfully and dramatically reconstructs the events of August 1831, using both written sources and the personal reminiscences of black and white witnesses. Less impressive are his efforts actually to explain why the insurrection occurred. Drewry was himself a white native of Southampton County, his attitudes on race a reflection of his birthright. Slavery, he believed, was a benign institution, as much a benefit to bondsmen as it was to their masters. Compelled by such logic to discount revenge as a motive, Drewry was at a loss to understand what drove Turner to revolt. His only suggestion is that Nat was so spoilt by his masters as to suffer delusions of grandeur. From such a perspective, the insurrection could be seen as nothing other than an unprovoked act of barbarism.

Despite its limitations, Drewry was for decades regarded as the last word on Nat Turner. Not until the civil rights movement was in full swing did historians start to question his thesis. APTHEKER shatters the assumption that slaves were contented with the system. The Turner rebellion, he argues, was anything but an isolated incident. On the contrary, it was just one expression of the increasing slave unrest which was sweeping not only through Southampton County, but across the entire Western hemisphere. What little evidence Aptheker is able to offer is nowhere near sufficient to substantiate his argument. Nonetheless, the book is not without merit. Although he refers readers to Drewry for a blow by blow account of the rebellion, Aptheker is better in assessing its repercussions.

JOHNSON (1966) is another study where the shortcomings outweigh the successes. The reproduction of some forty folktales about the rebellion is useful as a basis for speculation about its symbolic meaning. As for a specific account of the insurrection, JOHNSON (1970) seeks to provide it, but he does not succeed. He interviewed a number of informants whose ancestors had survived the rebellion, but their testimony cannot be taken as totally reliable. Worse still is the fact that Johnson too often lapses into speculation rather than staying close to the sources. More useful are the photographs of old Southampton County buildings, which help towards an imaginative re-creation of the world in which Turner and the other actors in the story lived.

All of these earlier authors would have benefited from reading two important anthologies published in the early 1970s. Between them, FONER and TRAGLE unearthed an abundance of hitherto unused sources, including oral testimonies and contemporary newspaper accounts. It was OATES, however, who actually incorporated these materials into a new narrative of the Nat Turner rebellion. He himself uncovered other significant sources, including census records, which enables him to describe the key protagonists – including Nat Turner himself – in much richer detail. Oates also makes impressive use of existing research on slavery as a means of placing the rebellion in its proper context. The studies of other historians into social control and alternative forms of slave resistance, for instance, enable him to explain why Turner failed to recruit a larger band of followers.

Turner's failings are also unflinchingly described by STYRON in his Pulitzer Prize winning novel. Although his tone is sympathetic, he portrays Turner as a tormented soul, plagued by confusion and guilt. Published as it was during the height of the Black Power movement, the book provoked a storm of controversy. CLARKE contains a series of savage critiques penned by such militant black writers as Mike Thelwell and Vincent Harding. All ten of the authors decry the notion that Styron had performed a heroic rescue mission in retrieving Turner from obscurity. On the contrary, they argue that the spirit of Nat Turner had continued to live on in the collective folk memory of African Americans, long after his martyrdom. This was a completely exaggerated claim. More important was what Turner meant to the militants themselves. His courageous rebellion served as an inspiration in their own revolutionary struggle against the forces of white racism. In depicting Turner as deluded and indecisive, Styron denied African Americans their rightful heritage. Clarke was an important signpost pointing towards the later argument that blacks alone should write their own history.

STONE places the controversy surrounding Styron's novel into historical perspective. He is especially insightful in exposing the severe limitations of Styron's research for the book. Equally interesting are the defences of the novel made by such eminent white historians as C. Vann Woodward and Eugene Genovese. These are reprinted in DUFF and MITCHELL, yet another useful anthology.

CLIVE WEBB

See also Slavery: Slave Resistance and Rebellion

Tyler, John   1790–1862
10th President of the United States

Chitwood, Oliver Perry, *John Tyler: Champion of the Old South*, New York: Appleton Century, 1939

Cooper, William J., Jr., *The South and the Politics of Slavery, 1828–1856*, Baton Rouge: Louisiana State University Press, 1978

Lambert, Oscar Doane, *Presidential Politics in the United States, 1841–1844*, Durham: Duke University Press, 1936

Merk, Frederick with Lois Bannister Merk, *Fruits of Propaganda in the Tyler Administration*, Cambridge, MA: Harvard University Press, 1971

Merk, Frederick, *Slavery and the Annexation of Texas*, New York: Knopf, 1972

Morgan, Robert J., *A Whig Embattled: The Presidency under John Tyler*, Lincoln: University of Nebraska Press, 1954

Peterson, Norma Lois, *The Presidencies of William Henry Harrison and John Tyler*, Lawrence: University Press of Kansas, 1989

Seager, Robert II, *And Tyler Too: A Biography of John and Julia Gardiner Tyler*, New York: McGraw Hill, 1963

Tyler, Lyon G., *The Letters and Times of the Tylers*, 3 vols., Richmond: Whittet and Shepperson, 1884–85

Burned in effigy by his adversaries, John Tyler stands in the pages of American history as an enigma in the presidential office. A Virginian by birth, a Jeffersonian by principle, a Whig by adoption, and a President by accident, Tyler, his opponents claimed, deceived his party and even disgraced his office. Tyler's historical reputation remains, to the present day, mediocre at best.

It was the President's son, Lyon G. TYLER, who wrote the first full-scale biography of his father. Published in three volumes, *The Letters and Times of the Tylers* is a storehouse of facts and a good guide to the Tyler family correspondence. A predictable family bias, however, diminishes its historical value, for Lyon Tyler surely wrote to defend his father's name and vindicate his record. Tyler emerges as an impeccable Jeffersonian, a loyal southerner, and a steadfast guardian of constitutional values throughout his long political career.

CHITWOOD similarly argues that Jeffersonian strict construction and states rights served as the two pillars of Tyler's ideology. This is a distinctly political biography, analyzing Tyler's persistent battle against federalism, but critical of his poor record in domestic politics. While emphasizing the presidential years, Chitwood remains the only modern biographer to describe Tyler's entire career in considerable detail.

Though published many years later, SEAGER is a full-scale life-and-times biography of the traditional kind. Commanding a mass of information, Seager details the social life and history of John and Julia Gardiner Tyler. Replete with dozens of vignettes of society life in Washington, New York, and Virginia, this is a veritable treasure trove of information on the Tyler family. Building on the scholarship of Chitwood and others, Seager portrays Tyler as a moderate states-rights Jeffersonian, but his analysis of the Texas issue, and Tyler's foreign policy in general, is superior to earlier treatments of the subject.

A number of studies concentrate upon the Tyler presidency. LAMBERT asserts that Tyler was an ambitious, though weak and vacillating, executive who fell prey to the political maneuverings of the Democratic party. Devoting approximately one-half of his book to Tyler's controversies with the Congressional Whigs and the other half to Tyler's ambitions for re-election in 1844, Lambert concludes that poor leadership ultimately accounts for Tyler's ineffectual administration. MORGAN is a concise, yet perceptive, analysis of Tyler's theory and practice of presidential rule. Adopting a topical rather than a chronological approach, he examines the question of presidential succession, the use of the veto, relations with the cabinet, the extent of executive power, foreign relations, and party politics. Like Chitwood, he concludes that the administration was a partial failure in domestic policy though a success in foreign affairs. Morgan astutely portrays Tyler as a Jacksonian who vigorously redefined executive power by use of the veto, yet whose presidency was marred by an absence of leadership and initiative in proposing legislation.

In her much more recent study, PETERSON also highlights the foreign policy achievements of Tyler's "flawed presidency." In a lucid and well-written examination of presidential politics, she discusses comprehensively the struggle for supremacy between the legislative and executive branches of government. Like Morgan, she personifies this conflict in the figures of Tyler and his chief nemesis, Henry Clay. Petulant, ambitious, bitter, and determined to "bring down Tyler," Clay hoped to destroy the administration and elevate himself to the presidency in 1844. Failing in the latter, Clay, Peterson suggests, was more than successful in the former. Despite the paralysis of domestic legislation, Webster and Tyler fashioned a successful foreign policy that sought open trade relations with China and the German states, an expansion of the Monroe Doctrine to include the Hawaiian kingdom, and peace with Britain.

The annexation of Texas and its subsequent admission as a state in 1845 dominated the latter stages of the administration. Hotly debated by contemporaries, Texas remains a contentious point among historians. Seager's pioneering work contends that Tyler's third-party movement in 1844 forced the Democrats into adopting a pro-annexation platform. Fearful that a "Tyler and Texas" ticket might cost them victory, Democratic leaders looked to Polk and a pro-annexation stand. Tyler's third-party strategy, Seager concludes, was a political coup guaranteeing annexation and demolishing Clay's presidential candidacy.

Through a study of propaganda, Merk concludes that Tyler employed deception, intrigue, and secrecy in the acquisition of Texas. Impressed by the validity of northern charges against the president, MERK (1972) contends that Tyler, Upshur, and

Calhoun were extremists who sought only to aggrandize southern power through the acquisition of Texas. With the use of supporting documents, MERK (1971) illustrates how the president built upon his propaganda successes in Maine in utilizing a national propaganda campaign on the Texas issue.

Rather than characterizing Tyler as a southern extremist, COOPER's novel portrait is of an ambitious yet committed southern politician who sought to unify the South behind his presidential campaign for 1844. By appearing to protect slavery and the South through the acquisition of Texas, Tyler found a provocative and emotional issue that would unite the South behind him. The politics of slavery, Cooper maintains, were absolutely central to the Texas issue and to the man at the vanguard of it, John Tyler. Texas, Cooper continues, crushed the Whigs and assured the supremacy of the politics of slavery.

In contrast with Cooper's portrayal of Tyler as the architect of Texan annexation, Peterson takes the unorthodox view that an ineffectual Tyler exerted little influence over a cabal of southern extremists bent on annexation. From the secretary of state's office, Upshur and Calhoun "played 'fast and loose' with Tyler, who naively was unaware of what was happening." Eager and ambitious southern radicals, Peterson contends, seized the Texas issue as their own.

Despite his ineffectiveness in domestic politics, Tyler's biographers generally conclude that he was a more accomplished and successful statesman in foreign affairs, and that the annexation of Texas was his greatest achievement as president.

RICHARD J. FOLLETT

See also Texas, Annexation of

U

United Nations, United States and

Coate, Roger A., *Unilateralism, Ideology, and US Foreign Policy: The United States in and out of UNESCO*, Boulder, CO: Rienner, 1988

Fasulo, Linda M., *Representing America: Experiences of US Diplomats at the UN*, New York: Facts on File, 1984

Finger, Seymour Maxwell and Joseph R. Harbert (editors), *US Policy in International Institutions: Defining Reasonable Options in an Unreasonable World*, Boulder, CO: Westview Press, 1978, revised 1982

Franck, Thomas M., *Nation Against Nation: What Happened to the UN Dream and What the US Can Do about It*, New York: Oxford University Press, 1985

Gati, Toby Trister (editor), *The US, the UN, and the Management of Global Change*, New York: New York University Press, 1983

Gregg, Robert, *About Face? The United States and the United Nations*, Boulder, CO: Rienner, 1993

Imber, Mark F., *The USA, ILO, UNESCO, and IAEA: Politicization and Withdrawal in the Specialised Agencies*, London: Macmillan, and New York: St. Martin's Press, 1989

Karns, Margaret P. and Karen A. Mingst (editors), *The United States and Multilateral Institutions: Patterns of Changing Instrumentality and Influence*, London and Boston: Unwin Hyman, 1990

Kay, David A. (editor), *The Changing United Nations: Options for the United States*, New York: Academy of Political Science, 1977

The task of analyzing and characterizing the United States' long and varied relationship with an organization as multifaceted and changing as the United Nations presents great problems for researchers and authors. GREGG offers one of the most accessible and comprehensible approaches. His study isolates American expectations of the United Nations, and the extent to which the UN meets these expectations, as being a primary determinant of United States policy towards the UN. American expectations are measured in terms of a range of factors from perceptions of United States leadership and influence to aspects of the American character. Gregg demonstrates that the United Nations' increasing development away from these expectations coincided with a steady alienation of the United States from the organisation. Two case studies are employed – the antagonistic Reagan years and the later Gulf

War cooperation – in order to demonstrate the importance of American conceptions and expectations in determining its policy towards the United Nations.

FRANCK's investigation into the souring of United States-United Nations relations is more polemical and less analytical, but very readable. It also begins by characterising early high expectations of the United Nations as a result of the "over-selling" of the organization to the postwar American public. Adopting a chronological approach, Franck demonstrates that early positive developments were soon overshadowed by worrying trends in the willingness of states to resort to force, and the impotence of the United Nations to keep the peace. Through an examination of the crises in Guatemala, Hungary, and Czechoslovakia, the growing dominance of the organization by a radical Third World majority, the financial crisis, and the withdrawal of the UNEF (United Nations Emergency Force) peacekeeping force, Franck shows clearly that the United Nations "dream" of preserving global peace became a casualty of the traditional pursuit of self-interest by its member-states.

FASULO provides a valuable primary source for research into United States policy towards the United Nations by compiling a comprehensive collection of short accounts by former United States representatives to the UN of their experiences, recollections and perceptions of the organization. These are divided into sections according to the administrations the representatives served under: Truman-Eisenhower, Kennedy-Johnson, Nixon-Ford, Carter, and Reagan. Fasulo provides a comprehensive context for these recollections through an introductory overview of the United Nations system, and the United States mission structure and its position within the United States foreign policy establishment, and then a brief overview of developments in United States-United Nations relations during each administration. The accounts of representatives including Averell Harriman, Arthur Goldberg, George Ball, George Bush, Daniel Patrick Moynihan, Andrew Young, and Jeanne Kirkpatrick, provide intriguing reading and important background material for understanding the personalities, dynamics and motivations behind United States actions within the United Nations.

Another common approach used to examine United States-United Nations relations is through edited collections of studies of discrete aspects of the relationship. The collection edited by GATI divides into five sections. It begins with a comprehensive overview of the nature of the United Nations system and the general outlines of the American approach to it, and is followed by evaluations of the UN's security competence, the confrontation of the United States and the West by an increasingly radical Third World majority, prospects for reforming the UN, and comments on the Reagan administration's more abrasive approach to the United Nations.

FINGER and HARBERT similarly rely on a number of discrete studies to deliver a more intensive examination of important aspects of the United States-United Nations relationship. The approach of this volume is to examine the pursuit of American foreign policy interests, in the areas of security, economic and Third World relations, and human rights, through the UN system. The various essays evaluate the problems and opportunities of United States action through the UN, and conclude that the United Nations remains a useful, if fragile, instrument for American policymakers.

Similarly, KARNS and MINGST impose a framework of utility and influence indicators on their edited collection to explore the motives and causes behind a variety of United States relationships with aspects of the United Nations system. Security and human rights are explored in general terms, while other essays focus on United States relations with particular institutions, including the IAEA (International Atomic Energy Agency), UNESCO (United Nations Educational, Scientific, and Cultural Organization), and the IMF (International Monetary Fund). The editors conclude that both the character of the international institution and domestic determinants within the United States have a crucial impact in determining American policy towards the institution.

KAY assembles a large team of authoritative contributors, whose essays cover a very broad range of aspects of United States-United Nations relations, from human rights to the impact of the United Nations on nuclear diplomacy. While few areas of importance escape attention, the essays tend to be too brief to afford the depth of insight and attention to detail of other edited volumes of this kind.

There are also studies of American interaction with particular United Nations bodies or forums. Because of the dramatic nature of the American withdrawals or boycotts of a number of specialized agencies, these tend to attract the more intensive case study analyses. IMBER investigates the circumstances of the United States' withdrawal from, or boycott of, the ILO (International Labour Organisation), UNESCO, and the IAEA, and in each case evaluates its charges of politicization against the agency, as well as the particular reasons for the rupture. COATE concentrates on the United States' withdrawal from UNESCO to investigate the more general ideological influence of the anti-United Nations school in the American foreign policy establishment. Both authors conclude that the ruptures of relations were motivated by a mixture of ideological commitment and frustration due to the long poisoning of United States-United Nations relations.

MICHAEL WESLEY

Universities and Colleges: 1783–1900

Allmendinger, David F., Jr., *Paupers and Scholars: The Transformation of Student Life in Nineteenth-Century New England*, New York: St. Martin's Press, 1975

Burke, Colin F., *American Collegiate Populations: A Test of the Traditional View*, New York: New York University Press, 1982

Gordon, Lynn D., *Gender and Higher Education in the Progressive Era*, New Haven: Yale University Press, 1990

Hoeveler, J. David, Jr., *James McCosh and the Scottish Intellectual Tradition: From Glasgow to Princeton*, Princeton: Princeton University Press, 1981

Leslie, W. Bruce, *Gentlemen and Scholars: College and Community in the "Age of the University," 1865–1917*, University Park: Pennsylvania State University Press, 1992

Noll, Mark A., *Princeton and the Republic, 1768–1822: The Search for a Christian Enlightenment in the Era of Samuel Stanhope Smith*, Princeton: Princeton University Press, 1989

Palmieri, Patricia Ann, *In Adamless Eden: The Community of Women Faculty at Wellesley*, New Haven and London: Yale University Press, 1995

Potts, David P., *Wesleyan University, 1831–1910: Collegiate Enterprise in New England*, New Haven: Yale University Press, 1992

Stameshkin, David M., *The Town's College: Middlebury College, 1800–1915*, Middlebury, VT: Middlebury College Press, 1985

Stevenson, Louise L., *Scholarly Means to Evangelical Ends: The New Haven Scholars and the Transformation of Higher Learning in America, 1830–1890*, Baltimore: Johns Hopkins University Press, 1986

Veysey, Laurence R., *The Emergence of the American University*, Chicago: University of Chicago Press, 1965

Williams, Roger L., *The Origins of Federal Support for Higher Education: George W. Atherton and the Land-Grant College Movement*, University Park: Pennsylvania State University Press, 1991

The history of American higher education briefly flourished in the late 1960s and early 1970s as an academic analogue to the attention received by campuses in that politically charged time. But the academic interest disappeared almost as suddenly as the student movement. Classes that drew large enrollments in the late 1960s and early 1970s were soon superseded by more traditional history courses. Higher education was again relegated to scattered pages in texts and specialized courses rarely survived except in graduate educational administration programs.

Scholarship was similarly sidetracked. But in the 1980s the field began a modest recovery. The founding of *History of Higher Education Annual* in 1980 provided a home, and a number of books, most conceived during the student movement, finally came into print. Many addressed either the antebellum years or the period between the Civil War and World War I.

Since Richard Hofstadter published *Academic Freedom in the Age of the College* in 1955, much research has been structured around his depiction of a "great retrogression" in colleges, as they went through a period of stagnation influenced by either elitism or religious fundamentalism. ALLMENDINGER refuted the former charge which was based largely on Harvard and Yale. He found that even at eight other prestigious New England colleges there was a very different social class mix. Ironically many students fit the modern definition of "non-traditional": older, part-time, non-residential, and working. Elitism more accurately labels the residential, better equipped, more expensive colleges of the late 19th century. Supporting Allmendinger's slim volume, BURKE demonstrated in exhaustive detail that the remarkable spread of colleges facilitated accessibility and proved that colleges had become a popular institutional expression of identity for locales, denominations, voluntary associations, and states. Rather than isolated elitist institutions on the brink of extinction, Burke persuasively portrayed vibrant multipurpose institutions that overlapped high schools and professional schools.

The secularity of modern academia has guaranteed a secularized history of colleges whose existence was inspired by religious motivations. George M. Marsden's *The Soul of the American University* (1994) offers a thoughtful overview by a committed Christian that extends beyond the chronology of this essay. NOLL's study of Princeton provides a case study of denominational higher education from a similar perspective. He sensitively examines the ultimately unsuccessful attempt of Samuel Stanhope Smith to harmonize the Enlightenment, Calvinism, and republicanism. Noll reinforces Allmendinger's and Burke's dismissal of Hofstadter's retrogression thesis.

VEYSEY has dominated the postbellum history of higher education for three decades. His depiction of colleges dominated by discipline and piety being succeeded by universities divided by commitments to utility, research, and liberal culture has structured our understanding of the emergence of research universities. His depiction of "the price of structure" brilliantly placed the well-known story of growth, "captains of erudition", and professionalization into a context of continuing contradictions and dilemmas in higher education. Veysey remains the touchstone for interpreting university growth to 1900. However, research universities constituted only a small minority of institutions of American higher education. Veysey too easily accepted the traditional view of colleges as the dinosaurs of postbellum higher education. A series of books have corrected that image. Although he concentrated on antebellum developments, Burke offered provocative hints for the rest of the century.

The institutional "house history," long a despised form, offered one test. Leading examples of a new variety of institutional history are Stameshkin and Potts. STAMESHKIN placed a small Vermont college's struggle in the context of small town boosterism, denominational identity, and near extinction before Middlebury College became a prestigious and highly selective institution. He sensitively describes a uniquely American story of the unlikely institutions that often became elite defenders of liberal education in the 20th century. POTTS details a similar story for a Methodist institution in Connecticut whose support, shifting from town to denomination to metropolitan backers, enabled it to become Wesleyan University. LESLIE develops similar themes in a comparative study of four Middle Atlantic colleges (Princeton, Franklin and Marshall, Bucknell, and Swarthmore) which also struggled on small budgets underwritten by local support, denominationalism, and serendipitous bequests, until they attracted the sons of the emerging industrial upper middle and upper classes. He placed this search for prosperity within a cultural context; the four colleges were, first, valued expressions of specific ethno-religious and local identities and then of the generalized Protestantism of affluent *fin-de-siècle* metropolitan culture.

While these works identified colleges as important social and cultural expressions, two others demonstrated their intellectual vitality. STEVENSON described the "New Haven Scholars" of Yale creatively combining scholarship and piety. It was a vibrant academic community that may not have created a lasting solution, but was intellectually engaged; this was not anachronistic stagnation. HOEVELER resurrected James McCosh, one of the villains in previous portrayals of the rise of the university. In a sensitive intellectual and social history, he demonstrated that McCosh wrestled creatively with fundamental problems to create a viable amalgam which dealt seriously with issues often ignored by heroes of earlier historiography like Charles Eliot of Harvard. While most scholarship continues to focus on Eastern private colleges and a few major public research universities, WILLIAMS brought land grant colleges into the historiographic mainstream. He demonstrated that, like denominational colleges, these institutions creatively struggled with the issues of the day.

Gender has produced much of the liveliest scholarship in recent years. GORDON took the debate beyond the previous focus on pioneers and access to write a social analysis of the second generation of women at five colleges, the University of California, University of Chicago, Vassar College, Sophie Newcomb College, and Agnes Scott College. She found that they rejected the first generation's separatism, and used college to launch a life that combined marriage and a socially useful public life. PALMIERI offers a model case study of a faculty community. Examining the first academic generation, she found a close self-sustaining community of women who eschewed marriage and made Wellesley their family. Like the faculty in many of the male colleges, their ideas would be largely rejected by the next generation, but Palmieri argues convincingly that they left a valuable legacy.

The history of American higher education has been transformed since 1970 by a small group of specialists. But no synthesis of the new work comparable in influence to Veysey, or, earlier, Frederick Rudolph's *The American College and University* (1962), has yet been written. Consequently most outsiders draw their knowledge from books now discounted or strongly revised by specialists. The scholarly generation spawned by the student movement has failed to bring the history of higher education into the center of serious historical debate.

W. Bruce Leslie

See also Education

Universities and Colleges: 20th century

Freeland, Richard M., *Academia's Golden Age: Universities in Massachusetts, 1945–1970*, New York: Oxford University Press, 1992

Geiger, Roger L., *To Advance Knowledge: The Growth of American Research Universities, 1900–1940*, New York: Oxford University Press, 1986

Geiger, Roger L., *Research and Relevant Knowledge: American Research Universities Since World War II*, New York: Oxford University Press, 1993

Hawkins, Hugh, *Banding Together: The Rise of National Associations in American Higher Education, 1887–1950*, Baltimore: Johns Hopkins University Press, 1992

Heineman, Kenneth J., *Campus Wars: The Peace Movement at American State Universities in the Vietnam Era*, New York: New York University Press, 1993

Herbst, Jurgen, *And Sadly Teach: Teacher Education and Professionalization in American Culture*, Madison: University of Wisconsin Press, 1989

Kett, Joseph F., *The Pursuit of Knowledge under Difficulties: From Self-Improvement to Adult Education in America, 1750–1990*, Stanford, CA: Stanford University Press, 1994

Leslie, Stuart W., *The Cold War and American Science: The Military-Industrial-Academic Complex at MIT and Stanford*, New York: Columbia University Press, 1993

Levine, David O., *The American College and the Culture of Aspiration, 1915–1940*, Ithaca, NY: Cornell University Press, 1986

Noble, David F., *America by Design: Science, Technology, and the Rise of Corporate Capitalism*, New York: Knopf, 1977

Schrecker, Ellen W., *No Ivory Tower: McCarthyism and the Universities*, New York: Oxford University Press, 1986

Veysey, Laurence R., *The Emergence of the American University*, Chicago: University of Chicago Press, 1965

American institutions of higher education grew nearly two orders of magnitude from 1900 to the 1990s – from roughly 170,000 students to 14,000,000. In this process they assumed multiple institutional forms, embraced burgeoning realms of knowledge, multiplied the services which they provided, and became central institutions in American society. Recent historiography has scarcely comprehended the magnitude of all these changes. It is important to highlight the few studies that encompass major themes or episodes in this transformation, at the expense of passing over the large literature devoted to single institutions and prominent individuals.

American universities were the engines of historical change in higher education at the dawn of the 20th century. The classic interpretation of VEYSEY divided their emergence into two stages – debate and experiments concerning the relative roles of utility, research, and liberal culture prior to 1890 and the ascendancy of institutional forces that produced the standard American university by 1910. However, Geiger's studies of 20th century research universities depict a continuous, complex evolution. GEIGER (1986) shows how professionalization and discipline formation initially provided powerful stimuli toward academic standardization, but sources of financial support nevertheless differentiated institutions. After World War I in particular, public universities continued to grow and serve a broad clientele, while private universities controlled the size and (to varying extents) the social composition of their students through selective admissions. Lavish voluntary support in the 1920s, largely from alumni, permitted the leading private universities to establish elite undergraduate colleges, but they also sought excellence in faculty scholarship and graduate education. These latter developments were notably encouraged and shaped by foundation philanthropy, which greatly expanded faculty research at the leading universities.

Another novel development was the emergence of technological universities like Massachusetts Institute of Technology (MIT) and California Institute of Technology (Caltech). NOBLE has interpreted the eagerness of universities, especially MIT, to work for industry as indicative of an enduring corporate domination of university research. However, Geiger (1986) considered the Caltech pattern more characteristic, where foundation emphasis on academic science prevailed over direct services to industry. At the end of the 1920s, MIT too deliberately fashioned a more academic orientation.

Voluntary associations of colleges and universities, HAWKINS has shown, proved to be an important source of coordination and standardization. Formed around 1900, these entities performed as a kind of private, consensual government – a deliberate alternative to government controls. After World War II, though, the associations largely assumed the responsibility of mediating between the federal government and their constituents.

Enrollment growth has been a ubiquitous feature of the American experience, and its consequences during the interwar years are the central concern of LEVINE. Three distinctive types of institution – junior colleges, municipal universities, and teachers colleges (upgraded from normal schools, whose history is explored in HERBST) – explicitly catered to this influx. Levine, however, remains ambivalent about this development. Although such institutions brought the opportunity for advanced education to a multitude of new students from diverse social strata, the growing elitism of the leading colleges, which he also covers, tended to keep the most highly valued opportunities still out of reach. By making the late 20th-century ideal of "equality of educational opportunity" his standard, Levine finds little solace in the considerable educational advancements of this era.

The ramifications of the vast postwar educational expansion have received no comparable treatment. FREELAND nevertheless elucidates the dynamics of variegated student demand on the "institutional complex" of higher education. Examining the postwar development of eight institutions in eastern Massachusetts – Harvard, MIT, Tufts, Brandeis, Boston College, Boston University, Northeastern, and the University of Massachusetts – this unique study depicts how each institution occupied a particular niche in the market for higher education. Such market differentiation is a widespread but rarely analyzed phenomenon in the American system. Freeland also describes institutional reactions to common developments affecting students, finances, faculty, and the zeitgeist for higher education.

Many of these latter topics are also analyzed from the perspective of research universities in GEIGER (1993). This study traces the growth and fluctuations of the federal role in university research, as well as such key topics as the boom and bust of graduate education in the 1960s and the role of foundations in shaping academic social science. Institutional development is studied through critical junctures at eight institutions – MIT, University of California at Berkeley, Yale, Stanford, University of California at Los Angeles, Pittsburgh, Georgia Tech, and Arizona. The historical significance of the 1980s is also described, for example in the impact of biotechnology and industrial linkages with academic research. Some recent studies have been more critical than Geiger of the role of American universities in the Cold War. On the important issue of Defense Department sponsorship of university research, LESLIE depicts the emergence of key laboratories at MIT and Stanford. The benefits to both parties of these relationships are persuasively demonstrated, although it is less clear, as the author alleges, that the military-university nexus might have been detrimental to other areas of academic science. University complicity in McCarthyism is minutely portrayed by SCHRECKER. Such blanket condemnation of the academy, however, tends to obscure a basic ambivalence: the pathology of McCarthyism was soon condemned, but the Cold War mentality from which McCarthyism had sprung was nevertheless internalized.

These Cold War proclivities were essentially shattered by the student rebellion of the late 1960s. Geiger (1993) appraises its effects at the principal research universities, where it ultimately fostered, rather hypocritically, a posture of moral superiority and ivory-tower aloofness. HEINEMAN focuses on the peace movement at four state universities – Kent State, Michigan State, Penn State, and State University of New York at Buffalo. Having sympathy for neither the Pentagon nor university administrators, Heineman finds a sincere Christian pacifism among working-class students subverted by the deluded radicalism of would-be revolutionaries from affluent families.

Finally, in a category by itself, KETT provides a rich and penetrating analysis of the many forms of instruction lying between self-improvement and adult education. At least half of this substantial study deals with the 20th century, covering such topics as training for law and business and the evolution of junior/community colleges. Kett takes adult and community college educators to task for assuming that vocational subjects were appropriate for their students, even though many of the students themselves sought further education largely for cultural and economic advancement.

In higher education as elsewhere, the history of the 20th century challenges the historian with overabundance of both primary sources and subsequent commentary. Virtually any aspect of higher education can be illuminated through recourse to institutional histories and biographies (of widely varying value), and (occasionally excellent) historical studies of science, various academic disciplines, and the professions. Still, vital topics remain problematic, less for want of monographic writings than for need of synthesis and interpretation.

ROGER L. GEIGER

See also Education

Urban History: General

Callow, Alexander B., Jr. (editor), *American Urban History: An Interpretive Reader with Commentaries*, 3rd edition, New York and Oxford: Oxford University Press, 3rd edition, 1982

Chudacoff, Howard P., *The Evolution of American Urban Society*, Englewood Cliffs, NJ: Prentice Hall, 1975, revised, with Judith E. Smith, 1994

Chudacoff, Howard P. (editor), *Major Problems in American Urban History: Documents and Essays*, Lexington, MA: Heath, 1994

Glaab, Charles N. and Theodore A. Brown, *A History of Urban America*, New York: Macmillan, and London: Collier Macmillan, 1967, 3rd edition, 1983

Goldfield, David R. and Blaine A. Brownell, *Urban America: From Downtown to No Town*, Boston: Houghton Mifflin, 1979; 2nd edition as *Urban America: A History*, 1990

Miller, Zane L., *The Urbanization of Modern America: A Brief History*, New York: Harcourt Brace, 1973

Monkkonen, Eric H., *America Becomes Urban: The Development of US Cities and Towns, 1790–1980*, Berkeley: University of California Press, 1988

Schlesinger, Arthur Meier, *The Rise of the City, 1878–1898*, New York: Macmillan, 1933

Teaford, Jon C., *The Twentieth-Century American City: Problem, Promise, and Reality*, Baltimore: Johns Hopkins University Press, 1986, 2nd edition, 1993

Thernstrom, Stephan and Richard Sennett (editors), *Nineteenth-Century Cities: Essays in the New Urban History*, New Haven: Yale University Press, 1969

Warner, Sam Bass, *Urban Wilderness: A History of the American City*, New York: Harper, 1972

A subject of peripheral interest to most historians a half-century ago, the study of – and teaching about – American urban development has burgeoned in popularity to such an extent that the subject is now a staple topic of mainstream history. Its growth and maturation as a historical sub-discipline, however, was a particularly difficult one, and indeed today the field is still characterized by an absence of consensus on the terms "urban" and "city", and consequently on what the subject of "urban history" is, or should be, about – a divergence of view which is reflected in the eclecticism which marks the range of works published under the subject's banner.

SCHLESINGER Sr. was one of the first to argue that cities should be given more attention by historians. The importance of his inquiry, however, lies more in its historical significance – as a landmark in the emergence of urban history and the inspiration it gave to others – than in its description of how social, economic and technological changes affected the late 19th century city.

Interest in the subject developed along with both the realization that many of the nation's postwar problems stemmed from urbanization, and the growing interest on the part of historians in history "from the bottom up." The need for a basic text on the subject was met by GLAAB and BROWN who produced the first – and arguably still the best – textbook on the subject. A well-written chronological narrative organised around the theme of urban growth, it offers a systematic and comprehensive "synthesis" of America's urban past.

A number of other studies were produced over the sixteen years between the original publication and the third revised edition of their work; few, however, go beyond this pioneer text. Of these, CHUDACOFF (1975), MILLER, and GOLDFIELD and BROWNELL offer lucid, readable and authoritative accounts on selected themes in American urban history – the evolution of urban social and spatial systems and the process of urbanization – by some of the best practitioners in the field.

CALLOW does much the same, though by way of anthology rather than textbook narration. Arranged both chronologically (for example "The City in the Antebellum Period") and topically (for example "The City in Social Conflict") into nine sections – each with their own interpretive commentary – his interdisciplinary collection of 33 essays provides the reader with a stimulating introduction to the "organizing ideas" and concepts that have fashioned American urban history.

This period also witnessed the emergence of a (self-proclaimed) new departure in the subject: the so-called trend towards the "new urban history," which is best exemplified in the work of THERNSTROM and SENNETT. The focus of their study, however – a quantitative exploration of geographical and social mobility – is far more narrow than the title of their work implies. Nor are these issues, as the editors subsequently admitted, ones which are necessarily exclusive to the urban environment. In applying computer technology to a mass of hitherto neglected primary sources – manuscript census schedules, city directories, tax lists and the like – the twelve contributors to this well-presented volume do, none the less, yield considerable insight into the experience of ordinary people in the 19th-century city.

In similar vein, though from a different (ecological) perspective, WARNER, the other leading contemporary figure in the field, examines the relationship between behaviour and the urban environment at three different historical stages, as a means of shedding light on the latter-day "urban crisis". Given Warner's conviction that "privatism" (by which he means capitalism and the culture it spawns) was responsible for the "ills" that bedevil modern urban America, his skilfully crafted and extensively illustrated study is consequently more a discussion of the need to transform the American city, than it is a history of the American city. Like Sennett and Thernstrom's study of mobility, it also views the city as a passive backdrop (or dependent variable) to the subject of central concern; that is to say, they both approach their work from an "Urban as Site" perspective.

MONKKONEN, like Warner, is motivated by a contemporary sense of purpose – though in his case it is to redress, as he sees it, urban America's lack of self-understanding. In almost every other aspect, however, his study is the antithesis of Warner's. He approaches the subject: from an "Urban as Process" perspective, or one that places the city centre stage (as an independent variable) in the inquiry. He concludes that the American city was (and is) consciously shaped by human action and human organizations, and not, therefore, merely the "inevitable" outcome of a process driven by impersonal economic and technological forces. Clearly written, and persuasively argued, Monkkonen posits an innovative and powerful new synthesis of America's urban past.

In contrast, both TEAFORD and CHUDACOFF (1994) return to the more conventional approach and familiar themes that characterized earlier work on the subject. The former, a selective and slender study, is aimed at demonstrating the author's thesis that the modern metropolis is irredeemably fragmented, economically and socially. The latter is a wide-ranging and detailed interpretive reader in the Callow mould; in accordance with the series of which it is a part, its treatment of urban development is structured as a discussion of "major problems".

PETER McCAFFERY

Urban History: Government and Politics

Green, Paul M. and Melvin G. Holli (editors), *The Mayors: The Chicago Political Tradition*, Carbondale: Southern Illinois University Press, 1987

Hammack, David C., *Power and Society: Greater New York at the Turn of the Century*, New York: Russell Sage Foundation, 1982

McDonald, Terrence J., *The Parameters of Urban Fiscal Policy: Socioeconomic Change and Political Culture in San Francisco, 1860–1906*, Berkeley: University of California Press, 1986

Rice, Bradley Robert, *Progressive Cities: The Commission Government Movement in America, 1901–1920*, Austin: University of Texas Press, 1977

Schiesl, Martin J., *The Politics of Efficiency: Municipal Administration and Reform in America, 1880–1920*, Berkeley: University of California Press, 1977

Teaford, Jon C., *The Unheralded Triumph: City Government in America, 1870–1900*, Baltimore: Johns Hopkins University Press, 1984

Teaford, Jon C., *The Rough Road to Renaissance: Urban Revitalization in America, 1940–1985*, Baltimore: Johns Hopkins University Press, 1990

In the context of the rapidly growing interest in all aspects of urban history, much recent work on city government and politics has focused on the crucial period of the later 19th century and the early 20th century. A number of works published in the 1980s reinterpreted American municipal government and politics, and attempted to shed new light on a subject too long dominated by the boss-reformer dichotomy. For example, HAMMACK seeks to discover who governed the nation's largest city during the late 19th century. In a richly detailed study, he dissects the city's political structure and specifically considers who wielded the most influence in the determination of four questions. First, he considers who governed the choice of mayoral nominees, before proceeding to the struggle to create Greater New York through the consolidation of New York City, Brooklyn, Queens, and Staten Island. Then he identifies the decision-makers in the conflict over the construction of the New York subway and in the battle over the centralization of school government. He discovers a number of distinct social, economic, and political elites which shared power – bargaining and compromising with one another in an effort to determine the course of city rule. Though his study deals only with late-19th-century New York, it offers a model which scholars could apply in other cities as well.

McDONALD provides a detailed examination of municipal fiscal policy, a topic too often ignored by historians who feel more comfortable dealing with rhetoric than with hard financial data. Using quantitative analysis, McDonald attempts to identify the factors that influenced the spending pattern of San Francisco's city government between 1860 and 1906. He finds that neither industrial and commercial growth nor the ethnic or occupational background of officeholders was decisive in determining spending levels. Instead, certain institutional and ideological constraints limited the options of city rulers and dictated the fiscal future of San Francisco. He also discovers that machine politicians who dominated the politics of the 1880s were actually less willing to expand the public sector to serve constituents than reformers of the late 1890s. Though a case study, McDonald's work surveys urban historiography and offers challenging suggestions for the future investigation of politics and government in cities throughout the United States. Reading the work, however, can prove a daunting task to those not enamored of the quantitative approach.

TEAFORD (1984) presents a more comprehensive account, examining municipal government throughout the country rather than in a single city. He discusses the changing structure of municipal government in the late 19th century. Plebeian ward representatives dominated the boards of aldermen or city councils and focused their attention on satisfying neighborhood demands. Meanwhile, upper-middle-class members of independent commissions and executive officers gained greater control over city-wide questions. Moreover, an emerging corps of professional civil servants entrenched in city hall played a growing role in the development of municipal parks, libraries, and public works. The city's delegation to the state legislature also wielded power over urban public policy, usually dictating the fate of any state legislation affecting solely the city. The second half of Teaford's study deals with municipal services. He argues that upper-middle-class Americans could have boasted of some of their urban services, but they chose to emphasize the negative aspects because the accommodation and compromise vital to American urban rule offended their sense of honorable and respectable government.

SCHIESL focuses on the efficiency crusade of the early 20th century, discussing how devotees of efficient administration transformed city government throughout the nation. The goal was "businesslike" government dominated by non-partisan policymakers and an expert professional bureaucracy. Though his chronicle of municipal accounting and civil service reform may not make the most compelling reading for the novice in American history, anyone concerned with Progressive-era developments can benefit from Schiesl's work. "Honesty and efficiency" was the battle cry of myriads of municipal reformers across the nation, and Schiesl accurately summarizes their proposals and achievements.

RICE offers a straightforward account of one of the most notable reforms in American municipal government, the commission plan. He ably traces the commission plan from its origins in Galveston, Texas, through its heyday during the second decade of the 20th century. He then discusses its relative decline as the city manager plan largely superseded commission government on the reform agenda. A relatively short work, this study packs a great deal of information into a compact format and is one of the best studies on municipal reform in America. Anyone who wishes to understand the development of 20th-century city government in the United States should read it.

GREEN and HOLLI is a collection of essays on thirteen of Chicago's most significant mayors. Beginning with Joseph Medill, the mayor who took charge following the Great Fire of 1871, this collection examines such significant and controversial figures as Carter Harrison II, Edward Dunne, Big Bill Thompson, Anton Cermak, Edward Kelly, Richard J. Daley, Jane Byrne, and Harold Washington. Together the essays offer the reader a valuable survey of Chicago government and politics. Though this volume deals with only a single city, it presents insights and information useful to an understanding of American municipal government as a whole. Urban scholars would benefit from similar compilations surveying the municipal leaders of other cities.

TEAFORD (1990) examines efforts to revitalize older American cities after World War II. It looks at this issue from the vantage point of city hall, focusing on the response of municipal governments to the specter of decline facing central cities in the northeastern quadrant of the United States. Thus it describes how city government coped with the changing times, embracing public works schemes which would supposedly boost urban fortunes and revamping the structure of municipal finance to stave off bankruptcy and fiscal disgrace. It also examines the changing style of municipal leadership. Mayors of the 1950s sold themselves as builders who would create a new physical environment for the city. By the 1960s "glamor-boy" mayors of the ilk of New York's John Lindsay had taken charge, capitalizing on an upbeat, attractive media image to pump fresh life into the cities and dampen the seething hostilities which threatened to erupt in riots and disorders. By the late 1970s and the 1980s, a new breed of hard-headed budget-cutters were winning elections, promising to restore the financial position of the cities and to nurture private-public partnerships which might result in the long-sought revitalization of the older centers.

JON C. TEAFORD

See also Municipal Government: Corruption and Reform

Urban History: Economic and Social Aspects

Abbott, Carl, *The New Urban America: Growth and Politics in Sunbelt Cities*, Chapel Hill: University of North Carolina Press, 1981, revised 1987

Berman, Marshall, "In the Forest of Symbols: Some Notes on Modernism in New York", in his *All That is Solid Melts into Air: The Experience of Modernity*, New York: Simon and Schuster, 1982; London: Verso, 1983

Boyer, Paul S., *Urban Masses and Moral Order in America, 1820–1920*, Cambridge, MA: Harvard University Press, 1978

Chudacoff, Howard P., *The Evolution of American Urban Society*, Englewood Cliffs, NJ: Prentice Hall, 1975, revised, with Judith E. Smith, 1994

Davis, Mike, *City of Quartz: Excavating the Future in Los Angeles*, London: Verso, 1990

Ford, Larry R., *Cities and Buildings: Skyscrapers, Skid Rows, and Suburbs*, Baltimore: Johns Hopkins University Press, 1994

Frieden, Bernard J. and Lynne B. Sagalyn, *Downtown Inc.: How America Rebuilds Cities*, Cambridge: Massachusetts Institute of Technology Press, 1991

Goldfield, David R. and Blaine A. Brownell, *Urban America: From Downtown to No Town*, Boston: Houghton Mifflin, 1979; 2nd edition as *Urban America: A History*, 1990

Warner, Sam Bass, *The Urban Wilderness: A History of the American City*, New York: Harper, 1972

There is a vast body of literature on urban areas in the United States. Indeed most major cities, along with their inhabitants, have been the subject of individual studies. However the study of cities is not a confined discipline, and those interested in thematic approaches should be aware of important current developments, especially within the field of cultural geography, and associated with the work of people like David Harvey, Ed Soja and Doreen Massey.

It is fortunate that possibly the best general introductory history, CHUDACOFF and SMITH, has recently been updated, and now spans the period from the early colonies right up to the Los Angeles uprising of 1992. The emphasis of the book is very much on people, and on the city as a product of the human desire to interact both socially and economically. Work patterns, housing, sanitation, recreation and the problems created by urban growth are analysed succinctly. A recurring backdrop to the text is the theme of the city possessing both centripetal and centrifugal characteristics, often as a product of technology. Special mention should be given to the excellent bibliographies accompanying each chapter.

The centripetal-centrifugal theme is developed more extensively by GOLDFIELD and BROWNELL. Four distinct phases in urban growth are identified. First there is the city as an "act of faith" in the colonial period. This was replaced by the city as market centre in the early days of the nation. The increasing importance of transportation led to the city as a radial centre. Finally, more recent developments have led to the ultimate displacement of the city, for many Americans, by the urban fringe. This is a neatly compartmentalised work that conveys a sense of process in urban development.

If urban centres were becoming increasingly irrelevant in the post-World War II period, there were some groups trying to spark their renaissance. FRIEDEN and SAGALYN assess the economics of recent downtown redevelopment schemes, specifically those in Boston, Seattle, San Diego and Pasadena. They assess the social forces behind the malling of the country and the success with which downtown projects such as Boston's Quincy Market revitalized central city areas. They deal at length with the growth from the 1970s of an alliance between private developers and city halls. There is, however, a tendency to overstate the image of the city as a profit-maximizing enterprise; little empathy seems to be extended to the less well-off central city areas. The thoroughness of detail in the discussion of wheeler dealing by developers is commendable, but some may find it unduly technical.

FORD focuses on the ways in which people have experienced North American cities through the buildings constructed in them. Changes in the spatiality of urban form are contextualized with changes in architecture. This includes the rise of downtowns and central business districts, and more recently shopping centres and the commercial strip. Ford deliberately avoids "esoteric jargon" as he puts it, but, while this makes the work accessible, it also renders it slightly superficial. When Ford does attempt to inject some theory his chosen models are confusing.

Though somewhat older, WARNER retains much of its merit and its influence. Writing at the start of the 1970s, a time of much soul-searching with regards to the future of cities, Warner makes an attempt to understand the future by understanding the past. An elegy to how far North American cities have consistently fallen short of their goals of community, innovation and open competition, Warner's lyrical prose is matched by a superb selection of photographs.

BOYER is a thoughtful evaluation of the responses of middle-class and elite groups to the perceived threat of moral collapse and social disintegration in the rapidly growing cities. He traces a change from early 19th century attempts to re-create the village or small town environment in the city, through attempts to come to terms with the new urban environment, to the moral crusades, attempts to restore moral and social control, and schemes of environmental improvement in the Progressive era.

Since World War II, the most spectacular growth in the United States has been in the so-called Sunbelt. ABBOTT emphasizes that this growth was almost exclusively urban, and analyzes its impact in the boom cities of Atlanta, Portland, Denver, Norfolk and San Antonio. He concludes that the most successful cities were those that were able to diversify economically, while functioning as business centres for private and public administration. Backed by strong quantitative analysis he argues that cohesive business elites in the 1960s were able to fly the flag of civic boosterism to buy off potential resistance to urban renewal projects in sunbelt cities at exactly the time that such programmes were being increasingly criticized in the North.

BERMAN paints a tragic yet beautiful picture of such projects in New York City under the planning control of Robert Moses. In his desire to perform "necessary surgery" on the city Moses ploughed the Cross Bronx Expressway through an integrated but poor community (and also through Berman's home). Berman contextualizes his essay within a wider debate about modernism and modernity that may appear, at first glance, to step beyond the realms of economic and social history. But his central thesis, that one condition of modern life is to live in a world where, as Marx said, "all that is solid melts into air", is of direct applicability to the history of the built environment of the last hundred years or more in the United States.

Finally, there has been no better work on one city than DAVIS's study of Los Angeles. Though some may dismiss him as polemical, he has constructed a cogent and brilliantly written analysis of the economic power structure of the city from the mid-1800s. Financed first by real estate, then by oil and lastly by aerospace, the elite, as he sees it, has maintained its control by various devices. Davis is particularly knowledgeable on the role of the Los Angeles Police Department, on the growth of gangs and on the social implications of recent architectural developments within the city. Like Berman, Davis adopts a multidisciplinary cultural approach, with history being placed squarely within contemporary concerns about urban public space.

DREW WHITELEGG

Utopian and Communitarian Movements

Berry, Brian J.L., *America's Utopian Experiments: Communal Havens from Long-Wave Crises*, Hanover, NH: University Press of New England, 1992

Clark, Christopher, *The Communitarian Moment: The Radical Challenge of the Northampton Association*, Ithaca, NY: Cornell University Press, 1995

Fogarty, Robert S., *All Things New: American Communes and Utopian Movements, 1860–1914*, Chicago: University of Chicago Press, 1990

Fogarty, Robert S., *Dictionary of American Communal and Utopian History*, Westport, CT: Greenwood Press, 1980

Foster, Lawrence, *Women, Family, and Utopia: Communal Experiments of the Shakers, the Oneida Community and the Mormons*, Syracuse, NY: Syracuse University Press, 1991

Guarneri, Carl J., *The Utopian Alternative: Fourierism in Nineteenth Century America*, Ithaca, NY: Cornell University Press, 1991

Hayden, Dolores, *Seven American Utopias: The Architecture of Communitarian Socialism, 1790–1975*, Cambridge: Massachusetts Institute of Technology Press, 1976

Klaw, Spencer, *Without Sin: The Life and Death of the Oneida Community*, New York: Allen Lane, 1993; London: Penguin, 1994

Spann, Edward K., *Brotherly Tomorrows: Movements for a Cooperative Society in America, 1820–1920*, New York: Columbia University Press, 1989

Stein, Stephen J., *The Shaker Experience in America: A History of the United States Society of Believers*, New Haven: Yale University Press, 1992

The forming of communes or "intentional communities" to further religious, social or political objects outside the main strands of society has been a recurring theme in American history. Though by no means unique to the United States, it is a tendency that has had peculiar resonance in a culture that so often defined itself as a part of a "New World" venture in social organization, and utopian communities have long exercised a fascination for scholars and general readers. The colonial period witnessed the creation of a number of religious communities, but there was a sharp increase during the antebellum years, particularly in the 1820s and 1840s, in communitarian ventures designed to pioneer wider social change; another upsurge in community-founding accompanied the social unrest of the 1890s. Altogether between 1800 and 1914 at least 260 communities were founded in the United States. The 20th century has seen no decline in the movement. Above all, the "counter-culture" of the 1960s produced many thousands of urban and rural communes. In the fading afterglow of these efforts there has been unprecedented scholarly attention to the history of such movements; the 19th century, in particular, is increasingly well covered by good recent scholarship.

FOGARTY (1980) is an indispensable reference tool emphasizing the period 1787–1919. Its brief biographical and institutional sketches provide a lucid introduction to the scope and variety of communal movements, their aims and their contrasting patterns of failure and success. General historical surveys of utopian communities in this period have also started to appear. SPANN focuses largely on secular movements, including Owenism and Fourierism, and discusses the relationships between communal efforts and the wider socialist movement in the late 19th and early 20th centuries. It draws largely on printed and secondary sources, but is the best of these general works to cover most of the period. FOGARTY (1990) deals with the often-neglected postbellum period, noting that fresh research has emphasized the continuing presence of a significant number and increasing variety of communal groups. This variety, even in a supposedly "secular" age, included a significant number of religious movements, and Fogarty provides an invaluable introduction to them. Indeed, except during the "peak" periods of communal founding, such as the 1840s, the 1890s and the 1960s, communes as institutions have been particularly favoured by those seeking spiritual renewal or religious revival.

Surveys of diverse movements face the insoluble challenge of balancing completeness against cohesiveness. Several historians have instead taken thematic approaches that throw light on the purposes and character of utopian communities from particular perspectives. BERRY offers a general material explanation for American utopias by tracing a correlation between economic depression, millennial expectations and community-founding from the late 18th century to the New Age movements of the 1990s; his is a lively, thought-provoking argument, but open to the objection that it attributes insufficient weight to the wider contexts in which communal groups are founded. HAYDEN's lucid and imaginative book examines the landscape, buildings and design of selected groups, arguing that the means by which communities created the built environment in which they lived not only reflected the organizational ideals they espoused but influenced their ability to succeed as viable institutions. FOSTER joins a growing literature on gender, family relations and sexuality that traces not only on the internal relationships in communities but the similarities and contrasts between communal experience and that of the wider society.

The most traditional approach to utopias is the monographic study of a particular individual, group or movement. KLAW's study of the Oneida Community, though heavily focused on its leader John Humphrey Noyes, is an excellent, lively account in this genre that succeeds in conveying some of the flavour of communal life. Many new works, however, are moving beyond a focus on institutions and individual leaders to explore the wider social and cultural roots of communal movements. STEIN provides a sophisticated but accessible account of one of the longest-lasting and best-known of American communal groups; he includes discussions of Shaker theology and of the movement's recent history that other studies have tended to omit. Similarly impressive is GUARNERI's book on American Fourierism, that not only traces the rise and decline of the most influential secular communal movement of the period, but explores its connections with a wide variety of contemporary reform efforts, including abolitionism and the labour movement. CLARK explores the history of a little-known Massachusetts community through a study of the lives of the men and women who founded it. He locates a particular period of communitarian effort within the context of broader social changes, particularly in rural America, and of reform movements, particularly radical abolitionism. He also identifies the decline of 1840s utopian communities with a wider "retreat from radicalism" that embraced both a shift to more conventional political activity and the beginnings of managerial capitalism.

Utopian communities will continue to exercise fascination, even though their numbers, size and longevity usually seem to justify their consignment to the margins of American history. The combination of rich stories of human eccentricity with often heroic efforts to establish new kinds of social organization has an intrinsic appeal. But just as communes themselves might be divided into those that sought to withdraw from the world and those that sought to change it, so their histories fall into two main categories: those that look inward to the movements themselves, and those that look outward to their connections with the wider society. The future of utopian scholarship lies with the latter.

CHRISTOPHER CLARK

V

Van Buren, Martin 1782–1862
8th President of the United States

Cole, Donald B., *Martin Van Buren and the American Political System*, Princeton: Princeton University Press, 1984

Curtis, James C., *The Fox at Bay: Martin Van Buren and the Presidency, 1837–1841*, Lexington: University Press of Kentucky, 1970

Hofstadter, Richard, *The Idea of a Party System: The Rise of Legitimate Opposition in the United States, 1780–1840*, Berkeley: University of California Press, 1969

Latner, Richard B., *The Presidency of Andrew Jackson: White House Politics, 1829–1837*, Athens: University of Georgia Press, 1979

Meyers, Marvin, "Old Hero and Sly Fox: Variations on a Theme," in his *The Jacksonian Persuasion: Politics and Belief*, Stanford, CA: Stanford University Press, 1957

Niven, John, *Martin Van Buren: The Romantic Age of American Politics*, New York: Oxford University Press, 1983

Remini, Robert V., *Martin Van Buren and the Making of the Democratic Party*, New York: Columbia University Press, 1959

Remini, Robert V., *Andrew Jackson and the Course of American Freedom, 1822–1832*, New York: Harper, 1981

Remini, Robert V., *Andrew Jackson and the Course of American Democracy, 1833–1845*, New York: Harper, 1984

Schlesinger, Arthur M., Jr., *The Age of Jackson*, Boston: Little Brown, 1945; London: Eyre and Spottiswoode, 1946

Shepard, Edward M., *Martin Van Buren*, Boston: Houghton Mifflin, 1888, revised 1899

Wilson, Major L., *The Presidency of Martin Van Buren*, Lawrence: University Press of Kansas, 1984

For almost a hundred years after his death Martin Van Buren remained one of the most neglected figures in American political history. The only scholarly biography during those years was a volume in the American Statesmen series by SHEPARD, who describes him favorably as a believer in laissez-faire. Even after the acquisition of Van Buren's papers by the Library of Congress and the publication of his autobiography in the early 20th century the neglect continued. The 19th-century Whig image of Van Buren as an unscrupulous party spoilsman – the Sly Fox or Little Magician – persisted down to World War II.

SCHLESINGER was the first to reassess the image by attributing the success of the Jackson movement as much to the political strategy of Van Buren as to the popularity of Andrew Jackson. In his provocative reinterpretation of Jacksonian Democracy, Schlesinger devotes more space to Van Buren's one term as president than he does to Jackson's two, and describes the passage of Van Buren's Independent Treasury bill as the climax of Jacksonism. He portrays Van Buren as a radical Locofoco Democrat who separated the banks from the government and reduced the hours of labor on federal public works.

REMINI (1959) continued the reassessment in his study of Van Buren's political career in the 1820s. According to Remini, Van Buren was responsible for creating the Democratic party and for bringing about a new party system. The party, he argues, did not evolve gradually from economic and social changes, but was planned and organized by Van Buren and a few other Jackson supporters during the election campaign of 1828. Remini also believes that Van Buren established a new rationale for parties by saying they were indispensable for preserving democracy. Although Remini intended to follow this study with a full-length biography of Van Buren, he instead shifted his attention to Jackson.

HOFSTADTER expands on Remini's interpretation in his study of the rise of the theory and practice of political parties in the United States. Hofstadter had planned to restrict his work to the first generation of American political leaders, but he soon realized that he would have to include Van Buren and his state political organization, the Albany Regency. In his final chapter he credits Van Buren and his colleagues with formulating a remarkably well-rounded defense of political parties that was based more on experience than theory.

MEYERS too recognizes Van Buren's pre-eminence as a party politician, but believes that his reputation hurt rather than helped his presidential career. Won over by the agrarian ideals of Jacksonianism, the American people wanted plain republicans – not politicians – as their candidates. They were intrigued by party politicians, but did not honor them. Van Buren managed to win the election of 1836, but his reputation as the "Sly Fox" doomed him to defeat in 1840.

In his two volumes dealing with Jackson as president REMINI (1981, 1984) places a great deal of emphasis on the role of Van Buren. Jackson, he says, was impressed by Van Buren's political wisdom, his caution, and his loyalty, and listened to him throughout his two terms. LATNER on the other hand believes that the westerners Amos Kendall and Francis Preston Blair had more influence than Van Buren. Both historians, however, agree that Jackson made his own final decisions and was controlled by no one.

In his study of the Van Buren presidency, CURTIS praises the Magician for his moderation and consistency in dealing with Mexico, and in maintaining neutrality during the Canadian Rebellion. He is more critical, however, of Van Buren's successful three-year fight to win passage of the Independent Treasury bill. Although Democrats called the bill a new Declaration of Independence, Curtis considers its passage a "hollow victory," which split the Democratic party and contributed to Van Buren's defeat in the fall.

In another account of the Van Buren presidency, WILSON treats the Independent Treasury as an economic rather than a political issue. He concludes that Van Buren won a real victory in getting the bill passed, and he rejects the idea that the Democrats were badly divided. Most Democrats, he writes, agreed that the Treasury should be separated from the state banks, even though they disagreed over the question of paper money. In addition, he praises Van Buren for his republicanism in framing a system for controlling the banks that would perform many of the functions previously handled by the Bank of the United States.

The two full-length biographies of Van Buren by Niven and Cole are in some respects similar. Both authors write traditional political history, with little of the statistical analysis used by the new political historians. They both give Van Buren credit for building the national Democratic party and for following Jeffersonian Republican principles. In so doing they defend him against Whig charges that he was nothing but an unprincipled political manager.

NIVEN, whose book is longer, tells the story of Van Buren's life in a dramatic narrative style and is more interested in the man than in historical interpretation. He spends comparatively little time on Van Buren's presidency, but devotes almost a quarter of his text to the years that followed. Believing Van Buren sincerely opposed to slavery, he considers him more committed to the Free Soil platform in 1848 than many believed. COLE believes that Van Buren played a vital role in American political history. More representative of his era than Jackson, he set the standard for the new style of party politician. He had a moderating effect on the Jackson presidency, and did not follow Jackson's policies slavishly during his own. His greatest contribution lay in reconciling old republican traditions with the demands of the new society.

DONALD B. COLE

See also Democratic Party; Jacksonian Era

Veblen, Thorstein 1857–1929
Social and economic thinker

Diggins, John Patrick, *The Bard of Savagery: Thorstein Veblen and Modern Social Theory*, New York: Seabury Press, and Hassocks, Sussex: Harvester Press, 1978
Dorfman, Joseph, *Thorstein Veblen and His America*, New York: Viking, 1934; London: Gollancz, 1935
Dos Passos, John, *The Bitter Drink: A Biography of Thorstein Veblen*, San Francisco: Sherwood and Katharine Grover, 1939
Qualey, Carlton C. (editor), *Thorstein Veblen: The Carleton College Veblen Seminar Essays*, New York: Columbia University Press, 1968
Riesman, David, *Thorstein Veblen: A Critical Interpretation*, New York: Scribner, 1953
Teggart, Richard Victor, *Thorstein Veblen: A Chapter in American Economic Thought*, Berkeley: University of California Press, 1932
Tilman, Rick, *Thorstein Veblen and His Critics, 1891–1963: Conservative, Liberal, and Radical Perspectives*, Princeton: Princeton University Press, 1992

Thorstein Bunde Veblen remains a "reticent and evasive" intellectual figure despite the plethora of studies covering his philosophy and life. A critic of orthodox economic theory, Veblen, who many believe held a "peculiar animus" against capitalism and industrialization, gained that reputation because of his scathing criticism of the society of his time, and his belief that "whatever is, is wrong." Although most often considered a social critic and economist, Veblen defied being cast in any one role. Veblen's theories and work are interdisciplinary, covering fields such as history, sociology, government, psychology, anthropology, and philosophy. His concepts of the machine process, pecuniary culture, absentee ownership, conspicuous consumption, and the nature of private property still evoke heated debate.

DORFMAN provides an excellent introduction to Veblen which places the development of his views within the context of his experiences and the historical period in which he lived. Dorfman argues that Veblen, having grown up in isolated rural northern Minnesota surrounded by the Norwegian small farmer culture of his father and neighbors, possessed a permanent detachment from modern society which gave him the ability to criticize capitalism and society more objectively.

In a more critical interpretation of Veblen, TEGGART provides an "unsympathetic" approach to the study of Veblen's philosophy and published works. In order to gain a better understanding of Veblen's ideas, Teggart places him alongside other lines of economic thought in the late 19th century. This short work is divided into four sections: the cultural and intellectual influences affecting both Veblen's life and work; a summary of his career in which Teggart contends that Veblen's ideological outlook was influenced by his agrarian, premodernist upbringing and by the ideological influence of, among others, Kant, Hegel, Marx and Darwin; a discussion of his unique and critical approach to economic science; and a section on the positive contributions of Veblen's ideas in creating a "technique for social criticism."

In contrast to the earlier critical approach of Teggart, DOS PASSOS typifies the passionate support from liberal social critics who believed Veblen championed their struggle against capitalism and the industrial process. This very brief study is a defense of Veblen's refusal to conform to the process of reconciling Christian ethics with the accumulation of property and excessive profits, and a celebration of his "dissecting out the century with a scalpel so keen, so comical, so exact," in an effort to expose the dangers of the machine process.

Again, as in Dorfman and Teggart, the importance of Veblen's agrarian background plays an important role in the development of his ideas.

Even critics of Veblen are unable to deny the influence which he exerted over their intellectual development. RIESMAN admits that he is not a "devotee" of Veblen, but concedes that Veblen's mysterious personality, intentional vagueness, immense range of social science interests, concern for society, and topical and contemporary social criticism merit serious consideration and re-interpretation. Riesman examines Veblen's major works and major theories, and his analysis challenges many of Veblen's ideas. Written in 1953, during a period when American capitalism was seemingly healthy and progressing at a rapid pace, this study reinterprets Veblen's work in order to understand better the "flavor of his hatreds and affections" towards a system that Riesman believed to be working quite well.

One question concerning Veblen is the validity of his work as it applies to social and economic life in later 20th century America. This is the theme of a book of essays, edited by QUALEY, that focuses on Veblen as a major social critic and assesses the relevance of his work to understanding America in the 1960s. The essays were the result of an American studies seminar in the fall of 1966 at Carleton College, where Veblen had been an undergraduate student. Charles Friday writes of Veblen's ability to foresee the future of capitalism; Thomas Cochran examines the business environment during Veblen's life; Joseph Dorfman describes the ideas that served as the "background of Veblen's thought;" David Noble argues that Veblen's social criticism was driven by his belief in a "mythical prehistoric Eden" that was destroyed by the growth of business institutions; Isador Lubin, a former student of Veblen, denies that he had a "skeptical animus" toward capitalism and argues that he remained a detached social observer; and Carlton Qualey offers a summary of the seminar's evaluation of Veblen's thought.

DIGGINS shares Lubin's view that Veblen was a "detached social scientist and an engaged social critic." The problem with Veblen, Diggins believes, is that he is misunderstood by both critics and supporters. Diggins attempts to clarify Veblen's "ambiguous nature" by comparing his ideas with those of other social thinkers of the period. Using Veblen as the ideological center, Diggins presents the ideas of Marx and Weber and to a lesser degree Tocqueville, Durkheim, Summel, Sombart, Mead, and others for purposes of comparison or contrast. Diggins considers Veblen to be one of the most "original" and "inner-directed" of American social critics and he seeks to clear up any confusion caused by Veblen's eccentricities and ideological ambiguities. This work provides a useful contrast to the earlier work by Riesman.

In the first of an intended three-part series, TILMAN takes a different approach to understanding Veblen and his ideology. By analyzing and assessing both the positive and negative weight of radical, conservative, and liberal criticism of Veblen's writing between 1891 and 1963, Tilman hopes to convey how the perceptions of various critics of Veblen's ideas "have played an important part in the distortion" of both Veblen and American intellectual history. Some of the critics included by Tilman in this study are Paul Sweezy, Richard Ely, John R. Commons, David Riesman, Daniel Bell, Talcott Parsons, and

Richard V. Teggart. In chronological order, Tilman presents each critic's reaction to Veblen's ideas on political economy and social thought, such as status emulation, conspicuous consumption, and pecuniary versus industrial employment.

CRAIG S. PASCOE

Versailles, Treaty of, and League of Nations

Ambrosius, Lloyd E., *Woodrow Wilson and the American Diplomatic Tradition: The Treaty Fight in Perspective*, Cambridge and New York: Cambridge University Press, 1987

Bailey, Thomas A., *Woodrow Wilson and the Lost Peace*, New York: Macmillan, 1944

Bailey, Thomas A., *Woodrow Wilson and the Great Betrayal*, New York: Macmillan, 1945

Floto, Inga, *Colonel House in Paris: A Study of American Policy at the Paris Peace Conference, 1919*, Aarhus, Denmark: Universitetsforlaget i Aarhus, 1973; Princeton: Princeton University Press, 1980

Knock, Thomas J., *To End All Wars: Woodrow Wilson and the Quest for a New World Order*, New York and Oxford: Oxford University Press, 1992

Levin, N. Gordon, Jr., *Woodrow Wilson and World Politics: America's Response to War and Revolution*, New York: Oxford University Press, 1968

Link, Arthur S., *Woodrow Wilson: Revolution, War, and Peace*, Arlington Heights, IL: Harlan Davidson, 1979

Mayer, Arno J., *Politics and Diplomacy of Peacemaking: Containment and Counterrevolution at Versailles, 1918–1919*, New York: Knopf, 1967; London: Weidenfeld and Nicolson, 1968

Walworth, Arthur, *Wilson and His Peacemakers: American Diplomacy at the Paris Peace Conference, 1919*, New York: Norton, 1986

Widenor, William C., *Henry Cabot Lodge and the Search for an American Foreign Policy*, Berkeley: University of California Press, 1980

President Wilson's articulation of a peace programme, of which the most striking features were the principle of national self-determination and a league of nations, his attempt to implement this through his unprecedented personal participation in the Paris peace conference of 1919, and the failure of the Senate to ratify the consequent Treaty of Versailles including the League of Nations, constitute a dramatic episode in the history of America's foreign relations, and one that has seemed to most of those who have studied it to have enduring significance and relevance.

BAILEY's twin works, which appeared as World War II was ending, were explicitly directed to finding out what "went wrong" so that "we may not make the same mistakes twice". In both books, but especially *The Great Betrayal*, he focuses on the extent to which Wilson's own actions contributed to his failure to achieve a lasting peace and secure America's adherence to the League of Nations. Although dated in their outlook and based only on the printed sources available at the time, Bailey's books contain many acute observations and still provide a lucid and highly readable introduction to the subject.

Postwar developments provided new perspectives. The Senate's rejection of the League of Nations seemed of less long-term significance as the United States came to adopt a world role. By contrast, the course followed by the Wilson administration in 1917–19 was seen by LEVIN as having "laid the foundations" of American foreign policy later in the century. Surveying Wilson's wartime diplomacy, conduct of the negotiations in Paris and response to the Bolshevik revolution, he argues that it represented "an effort to construct a stable world order of liberal-capitalist internationalism, at the center of the global ideological spectrum, safe from both the threat of imperialism on the Right and the danger of revolution on the Left". While stressing the ideological consistency of Wilson's policy, Levin's rigorous analysis also brings out aspects of it, such as the belief in 1919 that Germany should be punished, that are often overlooked. MAYER, too, interprets the events of 1918–19 in terms of a trans-national ideological conflict between the right, the revolutionary left and Wilsonian liberalism. His massive study is distinguished by the way it relates the peacemaking process to political developments in the various countries of Europe. Throughout, he emphasizes the concern of all those at the peace conference with the threat of Bolshevism and its impact on their decisions.

That this emphasis is somewhat exaggerated and anachronistic is the view of the Danish scholar, FLOTO, whose book is concerned with broader issues than its title indicates. Although it focuses on the role of Wilson's key adviser, Colonel House, and the question of when and why his relationship with Wilson broke down, it provides a comprehensive and thoughtful analysis of the American conduct of the peace negotiations. Arguing that Wilson's actions can best be understood in the context of American domestic politics, Floto concludes that it was the combined opposition of Republicans at home and the Allied leaders in Paris that compelled the President to compromise his liberal principles. A more favourable picture of House is presented by WALWORTH, who is also more sympathetic to the statesmen of the Allied countries. However, Walworth's large book is primarily a very detailed narrative of the proceedings in Paris, based on extensive research in private papers in American, British and French archives as well as the great array of published material and scholarship on the subject.

Recent scholarship on the League of Nations issue has placed it in a broader chronological framework. AMBROSIUS traces the story from Wilson's adoption of the ideal while the United States was still neutral through the Paris negotiations and the proceedings in the Senate to the election of 1920 which, he convincingly argues, represented the emphatic repudiation of Wilson and his League. This thoroughly researched account brings out the real political interests that shaped attitudes to the subject, such as the British and French desire for an American guarantee of the peace, and the American concern that the United States should control the League rather than vice versa. Criticizing Wilson's view of the League as an inconsistent combination of "universalism" and "unilateralism", Ambrosius sees it as epitomizing a much longer "American diplomatic tradition".

By contrast with this cool appraisal, KNOCK is sympathetic to Wilson's ideals. Whereas Ambrosius highlights what he sees as common elements in Americans' attitudes to foreign policy, Knock stresses the differences not only between isolationists and internationalists but also between the conservative and progressive varieties of internationalism. Just as, in Knock's view, Wilson's domestic progressivism was the product of an "age of socialistic inquiry", so his approach to international relations was shaped by the ideas current in liberal, socialist and pacifist circles in America and Britain. Having triumphed in the 1916 election, Knock argues, this progressive coalition was weakened by divisions over American belligerency and the administration's own repression of dissent. Wilson was thus deprived of the political support which he needed to achieve his goals in 1918–19; ideological as well as partisan differences meant that conservative internationalists, such as William Howard Taft, would never be reliable allies for the president.

That there were profound differences between Americans who favoured international involvement is confirmed by WIDENOR's penetrating study of Wilson's principal foe in the fight over Senate ratification. Widenor analyzes the development of Lodge's thinking about foreign policy, showing both its intellectual consistency and the way it grew out of concerns about the character of American society. Although he endorsed a league to enforce peace in 1915, Lodge envisaged it as a means by which the United States could stand with the Allies, whose cause he passionately supported; when Wilson associated the idea with "peace without victory", Lodge became an opponent. Since he regarded a universal commitment to collective security as mischievous and unrealistic, Lodge's reservations in 1919 were designed to destroy what Wilson saw as the League's animating principle. In this interpretation, there was no real possibility of compromise.

The last two chapters of LINK's short book give a brief, lucid and authoritative account from a point of view sympathetic to Wilson.

JOHN A. THOMPSON

See also Wilson

Vietnam War: Military and Diplomatic History

Berman, Larry, *Planning a Tragedy: The Americanization of the War in Vietnam*, New York: Norton, 1982

Berman, Larry, *Lyndon Johnson's War: The Road to Stalemate in Vietnam*, New York: Norton, 1989

Fitzgerald, Frances, *Fire in the Lake: The Vietnamese and the Americans in Vietnam*, New York: Vintage, and London: Macmillan, 1972

Gelb, Leslie H. and Richard K. Betts, *The Irony of Vietnam: The System Worked*, Washington DC: Brookings Institution, 1979

Goodman, Allan E., *The Lost Peace: America's Search for a Negotiated Settlement of the Vietnam War*, Stanford, CA: Hoover Institution Press, 1978; 2nd edition, as *The Search for a Negotiated Settlement of the Vietnam War*, Berkeley: Institute of East Asian Studies, University of California, 1986

Halberstam, David, *The Best and the Brightest*, New York: Random House, and London: Barrie and Jenkins, 1972

Herring, George C., *America's Longest War: The United States and Vietnam, 1950–1975*, New York: Wiley, 1979; 2nd edition, Philadelphia: Temple University Press, 1986; 3rd edition, New York: McGraw Hill, 1996

Karnow, Stanley, *Vietnam: A History*, New York: Viking, and London: Century, 1983; revised, New York: Viking, 1991, Harmondsworth: Penguin, 1992; updated, London: Pimlico, 1994

Kolko, Gabriel, *Anatomy of a War: Vietnam, the United States, and the Modern Historical Experience*, New York: Pantheon, 1985; as *Vietnam: Anatomy of a War, 1940–1975*, London: Unwin, 1987

Lewy, Guenter, *America in Vietnam*, New York: Oxford University Press, 1978

Palmer, Bruce, *The 25-Year War: America's Military Role in Vietnam*, Lexington: University Press of Kentucky, 1984

Podhoretz, Norman, *Why We Were in Vietnam*, New York: Simon and Schuster, 1982

Summers, Harry G., Jr., *On Strategy: A Critical Analysis of the Vietnam War*, Novato, CA: Presidio Press, 1982

Werner, Jayne S. and Luu Doan Huynh (editors), *The Vietnam War: Vietnamese and American Perspectives*, Armonk, NY: Sharpe, 1993

Young, Marilyn Blatt, *The Vietnam Wars, 1945–1990*, New York: Harper, 1991

The ever-growing body of literature on Vietnam testifies both to the lack of consensus on any of the major questions surrounding American involvement, and to the wealth of evidence that is available. However, only relatively recently have professional historians begun to write significantly on this issue. Some of the earliest attempts to understand Vietnam came from journalists and were highly personal and highly condemnatory of American involvement in Southeast Asia. Of these FITZGERALD is the most outstanding. This Pulitzer Prize winner is a passionate yet sensitive examination of how Americans failed to understand Vietnamese culture, and how this impacted on America's relationship with its ally in the South and its conduct of a counter-insurgency war. While undoubtedly groundbreaking in its time, Fitzgerald is now viewed as being somewhat simplistic and too sympathetic to the North Vietnamese communists. Nevertheless, it is a landmark work and one which still has the ability to move the reader. HALBERSTAM is another journalistic account which achieved classic status. Although over-long and discursive, it skilfully portrays the men that were brought to power by President Kennedy, many of whom remained during the Johnson years. The arrogance of the "can-do" generation of policymakers and advisers – born of innate intelligence and a belief in the supremacy of the United States – is fully explored and ultimately blamed for mistakes that contributed to the tragedy of Vietnam.

The belief that America had in some way blundered or slipped into the Vietnam crisis – the "quagmire" thesis – faced a major challenge from GELB and BETTS, who advanced the "stalemate" theory in their analysis of how the United States was led into ever-deeper participation in Vietnam. Successive presidents sought to balance the dangers of fighting a land war in Asia against the fear of being blamed for "losing" Vietnam, as the Democrats were blamed for the loss of China to communism.

Many revisionist accounts that appeared in the late 1970s and early 1980s sought to justify America's involvement in Southeast Asia and defend military conduct in Vietnam. New works questioned the view that Vietnam was an immoral war and argued that the war could have been won. PODHORETZ is a forcefully argued defence of America's reasons for participation in the Vietnam war. Vehemently challenging the writings and logic of the antiwar movement – attacking Frances Fitzgerald, Susan Sontag and Mary McCarthy in particular – he concludes that America was in Vietnam trying to save the southern half from the evils of communism and that this action was as morally defensible an act as fighting against Nazism.

PALMER is one of the best analyses of the military dimension of the war. As Vice Chief of Staff of the U.S. Army from 1968 to 1973 he provides an insider's view of the military conduct of the war, and the possible lessons to be learned from it. He contends that the military leadership failed to convey its reservations about the possibility of success to the civilian leadership. SUMMERS, an army strategist and infantry squad leader in the Korean War, takes a theoretical approach, comparing military strategy during the Vietnam War with Clausewitzian principles of war. He shows that logistically and tactically the United States succeeded in Vietnam but nevertheless lost the war due to a failure in strategy. Summers contends that a conventional war along the lines of World War II and Korea would have greatly increased the chances of victory, and that Johnson made a fundamental mistake by not declaring war and mobilizing the American people for the fight against the communists.

On the basis of a detailed analysis of classified records, LEWY examines the sense of national guilt over Vietnam and concludes that it was misplaced. Unlike Palmer and Summers, Lewy contends that the United States should have applied more effort to fighting a counter-insurgency war, rather than applying traditional military concepts to what was essentially a guerrilla war. Lewy seeks to refute antiwar claims of an American policy of genocide; indeed he finds that the overall death toll in Vietnam was much lower than in World War II and Korea. This is an impressive, well-argued volume, perhaps too clinical in tone for some tastes. WERNER and HUYNH include several excellent essays on the military battle in Vietnam which investigate the war from both an American and a Vietnamese perspective. Their analysis suggests that the war was neither a conventional conflict nor strictly an unconventional, guerrilla war, and challenges many of the assertions made by Summers and Palmer.

A concise, if somewhat one-sided, discussion of how Washington and Hanoi viewed peace negotiations can be found in GOODMAN. Drawing on off-the-record interviews with U.S. diplomats – but denied equivalent North Vietnamese interviews – Goodman simplifies and analyzes the many attempts to initiate peace talks during the 1960s and the January 1973 peace agreement. He concludes that both sides in the conflict believed in force rather than diplomacy, and that such attempts at peace were, as a result, half-hearted at best. However, "negotiating while fighting" proved a better strategy for the communist side.

Post-revisionist works have tended to be more dispassionate accounts. BERMAN (1982) is a brief study of the July 1965 decision to "Americanize" the Vietnam war, based largely on declassified documents from the Lyndon Baines Johnson Presidential Library, and including long extracts from key memoranda and recorded conversations. It underlines the stalemate thesis by arguing that Johnson went to war not necessarily believing he would win a military victory there, but in order to deny a communist victory, largely because he feared that a partisan debate over the loss of Vietnam would sabotage his Great Society programs. Thus domestic politics had a large impact on the American decision to commit to major combat in Vietnam. Moreover, this was Johnson's decision and thus the war was very much Johnson's war – a theme further developed in BERMAN (1989), which traces the president's increasing preoccupation with the conflict.

KOLKO, a New Left critic of the war, offers a radical and challenging critique. From an in-depth study of the three main protagonists in the Vietnam war – the Communist Party of Vietnam, the Republic of Vietnam and the United States – he concludes that the war revealed the limitations of United States power, and the failure of the containment policy in the face of a determined and able revolutionary force.The length, style and organization of the book do not make it an easy read, but its provocative interpretation of American imperialism has sparked fierce debate.

The best introductory texts, aimed at undergraduates and the general reader, are Young, Herring and Karnow. Of these, KARNOW is probably the best-known and most widely-read. Based largely on interviews carried out for a PBS documentary series on Vietnam, it is rich in anecdotes and vivid characterizations of the key protagonists (often based on Karnow's contemporary contact with them), but lacks any coherent overall thesis. Its comprehensive coverage includes the French colonial legacy in Vietnam, and the long history of Chinese domination, as well as the years of direct United States involvement. The book is generally well-balanced, for example in dealing with atrocities on both sides. A major disappointment to historians is the lack of footnotes.

HERRING is a more traditional historical text and benefits from material released from the presidential libraries as well as the Pentagon papers. He argues persuasively that American involvement in Vietnam was the logical culmination of the containment policy formulated during the Truman administration, and he maintains that successive administrations never questioned the assumption that the American national interest required the denial of South Vietnam to communism. Herring pays closer attention to the Washington policymakers and military strategy than to the Vietnamese and to Americans on the ground.

YOUNG is a succinct, clearly structured and brisk historical synthesis. Drawing on a wealth of primary and secondary material, her readable narrative begins with the French attempts to regain their colonies in Indochina and concludes

with a useful chapter on the years after America left Vietnam (something missing from many works). This work blends political, diplomatic and cultural history, and includes cartoons, photographs, comprehensive notes and a bibliography that are useful for the general reader.

SYLVIA ELLIS

Vietnam War: Political and Social Consequences

DeBenedetti, Charles with Charles Chatfield, *An American Ordeal: The Antiwar Movement of the Vietnam Era*, Syracuse, NY: Syracuse University Press, 1990

Gitlin, Todd, *The Sixties: Years of Hope, Days of Rage*, New York: Bantam, 1987, revised 1993

Hellman, John, *American Myth and the Legacy of Vietnam*, New York: Columbia University Press, 1986

Lake, Anthony (editor), *The Vietnam Legacy: The War, American Society, and the Future of American Foreign Policy*, New York: New York University Press, 1976

MacPherson, Myra, *Long Time Passing: Vietnam and the Haunted Generation*, New York: Doubleday, 1984; Sevenoaks, Kent: Sceptre, 1988

Morgan, Edward P., *The 60s Experience: Hard Lessons about Modern America*, Philadelphia: Temple University Press, 1991

Rowe, John Carlos and Rick Berg (editors), *The Vietnam War and American Culture*, New York: Columbia University Press, 1991

Shafer, D. Michael (editor), *The Legacy: The Vietnam War in the American Imagination*, Boston: Beacon Press, 1990

Small, Melvin and William D. Hoover (editors), *Give Peace a Chance: Exploring the Vietnam Antiwar Movement*, Syracuse, NY: Syracuse University Press, 1992

Wells, Tom, *The War Within: America's Battle over Vietnam*, Berkeley: University of California Press, 1994

Zaroulis, Nancy and Gerald Sullivan, *Who Spoke Up? American Protest Against the War in Vietnam, 1963–1975*, New York : Doubleday, 1984

The literature on the domestic social and political impact of the Vietnam War is most voluminous in two areas : first, the history of the antiwar movement and, second, the war's cultural reception. Almost all discussions of the subject, even those published a decade or more after the war's conclusion, are to some degree polemical, and all are deeply evocative of the period's social and political divisions. Essay collections and participant memoirs constitute two of the most valuable staples in the literature. One of the earliest essay collections concerned with the war's legacy, LAKE is perhaps most interesting as a period piece. Edited by a former White House assistant on Southeast Asia policy (later to be President Clinton's National Security Adviser), these essays attempt to analyse the "lessons" of the war, relating them both to U.S. foreign policy options and to domestic social change.

The antiwar movement has attracted some outstanding historical writing, generally by movement veterans or (as in the case of Wells) by younger scholars sympathetic to the movement's ideals. ZAROULIS and SULLIVAN provide a detailed narrative of antiwar protest and its impact in institutions as various as American churches, the United States Congress and the military. They emphasize the movement's status as a home-grown, patriotic and authentic expression of the American left. Their narrative is stronger on illuminating detail than it is on analysis. DeBENEDETTI lays stress on the pre-1965 (pre-hippie) phase of the movement, tracing the emergence of antiwar arguments and organisation from the anti-nuclear middle-class activism of the late 1950s and early 1960s. The author's sympathies (and those of Charles Chatfield, who completed the manuscript after DeBenedetti's death) are clearly with radical and religious pacifism, rather than with the students' anti-draft and New Left activism. The essays in SMALL and HOOVER, assembled in memory of Charles DeBenedetti and introduced by 1972 antiwar presidential candidate George McGovern, concentrate far more on the later 1960s and early 1970s. The book is divided into four sections: antiwar strategies and tactics (including analysis of the movement's student, religious, pacifist, countercultural and civil disobedience wings); the military (the antiwar GI movement and veterans against the war); the neglected area of women's opposition to the war; and the antiwar movement in schools and colleges.

WELLS provides the most balanced, readable and judicious treatment of the antiwar movement. Based on extensive interviewing and on an impressive range of primary sources, Wells exposes and clarifies the movement's internal divisions over tactics and wider aims (essentially Democratic party reformism vs. leftist revolutionism). He also emphasizes the movement's resilience, self-doubts and substantial impact on the war managers. As with most other studies, Wells finds it especially difficult to assess the effect of antiwar activity on wider public opinion. He does, however, provide a convincing analysis of the relationship between movement protest and the elite dissidence of various political and business leaders. Two fascinating sub-themes are: the extent to which the movement was illegally penetrated and harassed by agents of the Johnson and Nixon administrations; and the role played by antiwar sympathisers in the families of many top war managers.

Most general accounts of the American left in the 1960s and early 1970s have important sections on the war's domestic impact. A leading figure in Students for a Democratic Society (SDS), GITLIN examines the history and ideas of the New Left in the context of the Vietnam War, civil rights and youth culture. Though weak in some areas (such as African American contributions to antiwar protest), Gitlin vividly chronicles the energetic fertility of the student movement. He also provides a persuasive analysis of the 1969 disintegration of SDS amid self-advertising extremism and the destructive pulls of anarchism and Leninism. MORGAN offers a more balanced (less SDS-oriented) synthetic history of 1960s leftist activism, setting antiwar protest against the backcloth of campus revolt, the civil rights awakening, the counterculture and the early women's movement. He interprets the 1960s political experience in terms of tension between values of community and personal authenticity.

The most cogent and influential account of the war's impact on American culture is provided by HELLMAN. Alongside detailed studies of Vietnam-related novels and films, he evokes and interprets that radical questioning occasioned by the war of America's redemptive national myth. He examines how the notion of Southeast Asia as a new frontier developed in American culture, even before the election of John Kennedy. Post-1968 novels and films are presented as attempts to re-mythologize America's "city on a hill" mission in the light of the defeat and domestic divisions. Various essays in the collections edited by Rowe and Berg, and by Shafer, expand and amplify Hellman's approach. Contributions to ROWE and BERG range from film to historiographical and popular music criticism. Strongly opposed to the Reaganite attempt to rehabilitate the war as an honourable cause, most of the essays seek to establish and illustrate the complex, often evasionary, nature of the war's cultural reception. SHAFER's collection includes important essays on the myth of the heroic veteran, on the postwar experience of Vietnamese immigrants and refugees, and on journalistic treatments of the war. MacPHERSON, though a little self-indulgent in style, traces the impact of the war on the generation who fought and protested against it. Among the many interviews and personal narratives, MacPherson develops the case that the war's social and political impact at home was complex and unpredictable. Her discussion is strongest on American working-class experiences of the war.

JOHN DUMBRELL

Violence

Brown, Richard Maxwell, *Strain of Violence: Historical Studies of American Violence and Vigilantism*, New York: Oxford University Press, 1975

Brown, Richard Maxwell, *No Duty to Retreat: Violence and Values in American History and Society*, New York and Oxford: Oxford University Press, 1991

Brundage, W. Fitzhugh, *Lynching in the New South: Georgia and Virginia, 1880–1930*, Urbana: University of Illinois Press, 1993

Graham, Hugh Davis and Ted Robert Gurr, *Violence in America: Historical and Comparative Perspectives*, 2 vols., Washington, DC: Government Printing Office, 1969; revised, Beverly Hills, CA: Sage, 1979

Lane, Roger, *Roots of Violence in Black Philadelphia, 1860–1900*, Cambridge, MA: Harvard University Press, 1986

McGrath, Roger D., *Gunfighters, Highwaymen, and Vigilantes: Violence on the Frontier*, Berkeley: University of California Press, 1984

Nerone, John, *Violence Against the Press: Policing the Public Sphere in US History*, New York: Oxford University Press, 1994

Nieman, Donald G. (editor), *Black Freedom/White Violence 1865–1900*, New York: Garland, 1994

Pleck, Elizabeth H., *Domestic Tyranny: The Making of Social Policy Against Family Violence from Colonial Times to the Present*, New York: Oxford University Press, 1987

Shapiro, Herbert, *White Violence and Black Response: From Reconstruction to Montgomery*, Amherst: University of Massachusetts Press, 1988

Utley, Robert M., *High Noon in Lincoln: Violence on the Western Frontier*, Albuquerque: University of New Mexico Press, 1987

Wyatt-Brown, Bertram, *Honor and Violence in the Old South*, New York: Oxford University Press, 1986

Violence is a diffuse and difficult subject to define, yet it has played a fundamental part in the American experience. BROWN (1975) explores America's historical tradition of violence and vigilantism from the colonial period to the late 20th century. In this influential work, he views the doctrine of popular sovereignty, developed by the revolutionary generation, as the powerful philosophical rationale for subsequent extralegal violence. He dates American vigilantism to the South Carolina back country of 1767, and views it as a constant factor in American life until the 1900s, as illustrated by the extensive list of vigilante movements in Appendix 3. In Brown's view, the typical frontier vigilante movement was socially conservative, and committed to defending community order. Two of Brown's chapters appear in the revised edition of GRAHAM and GURR's classic collection of essays covering a broad range of issues, including American Indian resistance, labor violence, 1960s political protest, and interracial clashes, all of which underscore violence as an integral part of the American value system.

For many, images of the 19th-century American West and violence are synonymous, but there is considerable scholarly debate over "frontier violence" and its historical legacy. UTLEY's superb reconstruction of the Lincoln County War, in New Mexico, in 1878–79 is a significant case study in frontier violence perpetuated by cattle-merchant rings seeking money and power, which provided the springboard for Billy the Kid's immortal fame. Utley regards the "Code of the West," a tradition of violent self-redress and self-defense with its roots in Texas, as well as inadequate law enforcement, as two important underlying factors responsible for the predominance of violence in 1870s Lincoln County life.

In a rather disappointing work, BROWN (1991) describes the Americanization of the common law doctrine of "duty to retreat" into "no duty to retreat," or the "Texas rule" (Texas being the central state in the gunfighter culture of the West), which prevailed in the frontier states west of the Appalachian Mountains. He sees it as a significant development in American culture because it sanctioned killing in self-defense. For Brown, the legal doctrine of "no duty to retreat" is the basis of the violent character of the contemporary United States and even permeates American foreign policy.

An alternative school of thought on "frontier violence" is illustrated by McGRATH who asserts that the frontier was unmistakably violent but less so than the 1980s urban United States. Using the towns of Aurora and Bodie on the trans-Sierra mining frontier in the second half of the 19th century as case studies, McGrath argues that the frontier was characterized by low rates of burglary, robbery, and theft, but experienced high numbers of fist-fights and gunfights, in which the victims were usually roughs or badmen. McGrath attempts a much fuller picture of frontier violence than previous scholars, with attention to the role of women and minorities. The appendix contains a valuable summary of the two schools of thought on the historical legacy of "frontier violence."

The South also has a historical reputation for violence. In an abridged but equally intriguing version of his *Southern Honor* (1982), WYATT-BROWN examines the southern "Code of Honor," its role in maintaining white supremacy in slave-based society, and its relationship to individual and collective violence including duelling, lynching, charivari, and vigilantism. BRUNDAGE's seminal multi-disciplinary examination of the rise and decline of lynching in Georgia and Virginia over a fifty-year period, complete with statistical tables and extensive lists of the victims of mob violence in these states, addresses many important questions regarding geographical variations in mob violence, the character of the victims and mob members, and the reasons for the decline of extralegal mob activity by the mid-20th century.

In volume 7 of a 12-volume series on African American life, NIEMAN brings together a useful collection of 22 essays on interracial violence, most of which focus on the role of violence in the South during the Reconstruction period. In contrast, LANE's ambitious and highly readable analysis of black criminal violence in a northern city in the same period explores the relationship between urban-industrial growth, black marginalization, and the long-term effects of a flourishing black criminal subculture, in order to explain the continued increase in violent behavior within the American black community in contrast to the experience of native-born whites and immigrants.

In a sobering and compelling work, SHAPIRO provides a methodically researched broad narrative analysis of interracial violence between Reconstruction and the 1950s. Through an examination of direct physical acts of violence generated by white racism, and sanctioned by the inaction of federal government and the complicity of newspaper editors and law enforcement agencies, Shapiro explores issues of race and class in the perpetuation of white supremacy. African Americans, however, did not passively accept white violence: they employed a variety of strategies of resistance, including electoral support for the Republican party during Reconstruction, consistent demands for federal anti-lynching legislation, calls for separatism, and organization of black self-defense groups. Shapiro evaluates the origins and leadership of each strategy.

PLECK's challenging analysis of family violence focuses on the efforts to relieve abused children and battered wives in three periods of statutory and institutional reform. She explores the passage of the first statutes against wife-beating and child abuse by the Puritans; the emergence of private societies for the protection of abused women and children in the late 19th century together with the movement to punish wife-beaters at the whipping post; and the feminist push for legislative remedies for wife-beating and marital rape in the 1970s. Pleck argues that the persistent belief in the "family ideal" over three centuries effectively blocked cogent responses to family violence, except when changing social and political conditions propelled these issues into the public arena.

NERONE examines the relationship between the press and the bourgeois public sphere; the role of violence in the "culture of public expression" from the mid-18th century to the late 20th century; and the changing nature of violence against the press, paralleling changes in newspaper production, from editorial duelling to attacks on abolitionist and African American newspapers and labor periodicals, and since World War II, attacks on "the media" as a seemingly monolithic institution.

VIVIEN M.L. MILLER

See also Riots

Voting *see* Suffrage

W

Wallace, George C. 1919–

Politician and agitator; presidential candidate

Bass, Jack, *Taming the Storm: The Life and Times of Judge Frank M. Johnson and the South's Fight over Civil Rights*, New York: Doubleday, 1993

Carter, Dan T., *The Politics of Rage: George Wallace, the Origins of the New Conservatism, and the Transformation of American Politics*, New York: Simon and Schuster, 1995

Clark, E. Culpepper, *The Schoolhouse Door: Segregation's Last Stand at the University of Alabama*, New York and Oxford: Oxford University Press, 1993

Crass, Philip, *The Wallace Factor*, New York: Mason Charter, 1976

Frady, Marshall, *Wallace*, New York: World, 1968

Lesher, Stephan, *George Wallace: American Populist*, Reading, MA: Addison Wesley, 1994

George Corley Wallace may well be the most important "loser" in 20th-century American politics. The stormy petrel of Barbour County, Alabama, fashioned a populistic record in the 1940s and 1950s Alabama legislature, then transformed himself into the chief defender of racial segregation in America during the 1960s and 1970s. During his four terms as Alabama governor (and an additional half term served by his wife, Lurleen), Wallace fashioned the most powerful state political machine since the legendary Huey Long, the "Kingfish" of Louisiana. During his three presidential races (1964, 1968, 1972), he redefined American politics. By his incessant attacks on the encroachments of federal power, and on overseas commitments from Vietnam to foreign aid, he drove both national parties to the right, seeded the fertile soil of American politics for Ronald Reagan to harvest, and drained millions of blue-collar workers out of the Democratic party. This migration into a third party was their way station into the Republican party of the 1980s. Wallace tapped a subterranean vein of alienation (the "Archie Bunker" vote, the "angry white male") that still thrives in American politics. Both the major parties and the Perot movement in the 1990s contained major elements of the American Independent movement that Wallace led so successfully.

LESHER's biography, the first serious attempt to record Wallace's life, is unfortunately marred by too close association with its subject. Lesher, a journalist who covered Wallace's national campaigns, relied too heavily on interviews with Wallace and his associates, and with blacks who forgave Wallace after an assassin's bullets left him paralyzed, near death, and contrite over his career of racism. After Wallace asked forgiveness for his strident defense of racial injustice, Lesher de-emphasized race and substituted populism as the dominant theme in his career. He drew little of his information from Wallace's Alabama opponents, notably former governor Albert Brewer, whom Wallace defeated in 1970 in a campaign of demagoguery without precedent in recent Alabama politics.

By far the best study of the Wallace phenomenon is CARTER. Portraying Wallace as a shrewd opportunist who hitched his fortunes to whatever rising star appeared on America's political horizon, Carter provides masterful historical context for his biography. Weaving Wallace into the tapestry of the civil rights movement, Carter portrays him as the counterpoint to Martin Luther King, Jr. Each man sought to mobilize a previously impotent and ignored constituency: in the one case, blacks who could not vote; in the other, the white southern working class, and northern ethnic voters taken for granted by the Democratic party. The sources of alienation were diverse: affirmative action programs; busing of school children to obtain racial balance; a no-win war in Vietnam; the antiwar protest movement; increasing inflation; rising job insecurity; and a counterculture youth movement that challenged traditional family values. Gradually these forces eroded Democratic party strength and led masses of ordinary Americans to back Wallace in an outraged protest against the course of American life and public policy. Though Wallace was the vehicle of this protest, he was by no means its chief beneficiary. That honor went to Richard Nixon, who shrewdly used code words ("law and order") to soften the hard edges of Wallace's racism without obscuring its meaning to alienated blue-collar Democrats.

If Carter is the best work specifically about Wallace, CLARK is the best contextual piece. Taking a single incident, the 1963 integration of the University of Alabama, Clark weaves a fascinating portrait of the shrewd George Wallace. Always stopping just short of outright legal defiance and violent confrontation, Wallace thought of himself as preventing the sort of violence which had occurred at the University of Mississippi in 1962. In truth his fiery rhetoric and flamboyant demagoguery fueled the politics of resistance and created a fertile environment for angry whites teetering on the brink of psychopathic violence. Clark also reveals how Wallace's "stand in the schoolhouse door" first brought Wallace to national attention and galvanized a vast national audience of angry whites into an army that would later lead his presidential campaigns in a variety of non-southern states. Although Wallace stands squarely in the foreground of this volume, two courageous black college students, Vivian Malone and James Hood, precipitated the confrontation with their admission to the college and became the victims of Wallace's crusade on behalf of segregation and states rights.

BASS is, like Clark, rich in context. Federal Judge Frank M. Johnson, Jr. was a college friend of Wallace's at the University. But as a Republican judge from the predominantly white hill country of north Alabama, Johnson followed a different course from Wallace on the federal bench. Many of the most important legal cases affecting race during the 1960s and 1970s arose in his court. Despite a constant stream of invective from Wallace and physical threats from white supremacists, Johnson held steady to a course of implementing desegregation in all aspects of southern life. This judicial activism made him anathema to his neighbors but a beacon of justice to blacks. That Alabama could produce two such contradictory national figures as Frank M. Johnson and George C. Wallace is a remarkable tribute to the complexity of the state's public life and political debates.

FRADY was the first attempt at serious biography. The book provides a colorful portrayal of the governor at the peak of his national influence. Although it contains many useful anecdotes and some thoughtful analysis, the biography was too close to the events to offer much depth. CRASS is a thoughtful work that focuses on Wallace's influence on national politics. He examined the Wallace constituency and his influence on both national parties. His summary is particularly useful concerning Wallace's influence on the Nixon administration.

WAYNE FLYNT

War Debts and Reparations, 1920s–1930s

Clarke, Stephen V.O., *Central Bank Cooperation, 1924–31*, New York: Federal Reserve Bank of New York, 1967

Costigliola, Frank, *Awkward Dominion: American Political, Economic, and Cultural Relations with Europe, 1919–1933*, Ithaca, NY: Cornell University Press, 1984

Eichengreen, Barry, *Golden Fetters: The Gold Standard and the Great Depression, 1919–1939*, New York: Oxford University Press, 1992

Kindleberger, Charles P., *The World in Depression, 1929–1939*, Berkeley: University of California Press and London: Allen Lane, 1973

Leffler, Melvyn P., *The Elusive Quest: America's Pursuit of European Stability and French Security, 1919–1933*, Chapel Hill: University of North Carolina Press, and London: Allen Lane, 1979

McNeil, William C., *American Money and the Weimar Republic: Economics and Politics on the Eve of the Great Depression*, New York: Columbia University Press, 1986

Schuker, Stephen A., *American "Reparations" to Germany, 1919–33: Implications for the Third-World Debt Crisis*, Princeton: Princeton University Press, 1988

The relationship between the pattern of international indebtedness which emerged after 1918 and the alarming instability which engulfed the world economy during the inter-war period has been the subject of intense investigation by both historians and economists. Before World War I the United States was the world's leading debtor nation, a position totally transformed by the close of hostilities, by which time it had become the leading creditor nation. An obvious question posed by scholars was whether an all-powerful America, by pursuing narrow self-interests, lost the opportunity to restore the war-ravaged economies to a sound footing and, instead, helped create the flimsy structure which collapsed, with such devastating effect, in 1929.

During the 1950s and 1960s it was common for historians to portray the United States as a selfish power seeking to dominate the world economy during the decade after 1918. Since then scholars have adopted a different stance and LEFFLER is an excellent example of the new breed of historians who emphasize the desire of America to stabilize rather than to exploit this new world. American officials tried to resolve war debt and reparation controversies, alleviate French anxieties and create the environment in which private American capital could be freely exported. Unfortunately, these aims were constrained by domestic issues, for example, by the insistence of Congress on the collection of all war debts, which heavily influenced foreign policy options. In any conflict between domestic priorities and the implementation of measures designed to revitalize or to stabilize the international economy, the former was always the victor.

In a work which integrates cultural, political and economic history, COSTIGLIOLA shows that American policy, although often creative, was ultimately flawed because it was dependent upon continuing prosperity. The United States saw the need for a strong and stable Germany as both a market for its exports and as a counter to French influence. Pressure was put upon the principal players in the European economic drama to accept the Dawes Plan, but for its success and indeed for that of the gold standard, U.S. capital exports were essential. Once American investors shunned Europe, there was no alternative policy other than the short run response of the Hoover Moratorium.

McNEIL points out that American private bankers lent nearly $3 billion to German borrowers between 1925 and 1930, a sum which was about double that flowing from the Marshall Plan after World War II. As a result, reparations could be paid without putting pressure on Germany to balance its budget. By the late 1920s, there was a growing American concern about United States lending to Germany and about the domestic policies being pursued by the Weimar Republic. The United States government could not influence German economic policy, and American banks, which in any case were not equipped to impose conditions, were happy to lend money with no strings attached. The American Reparations Agent, S. Parker Gilbert, tried to curb Weimar public borrowing, which he feared was potentially harmful, but without success. The attempts of American bankers and their representatives to resolve difficulties by removing them from the political arena was doomed to failure, since all the most pressing problems were intractably political.

SCHUKER is an excellent example of the new international history of the 1920s. In this short work, which contains an excellent bibliography, the massive transfer of wealth from the United States to Weimar is emphasized. Foreigners who bought marks during the great inflation, who bought German bonds or who loaned money got little or nothing in return. Germany, on the other hand, after defaulting on her international obligations, received far more from foreigners than was paid out in reparations. American money was a massive subsidy to Germany which enabled the population to enjoy a much higher standard of living than could be justified by economic growth. Schuker adds that many New Dealers were indifferent to the substantial losses suffered by American lenders because of an antipathy to Wall Street and high finance.

The interactions between domestic politics and the international economy are at the core of EICHENGREEN's study. He believes that the gold standard should be analyzed as a political as well as an economic system. A government confronted with severe domestic political pressure with which it is unable to cope could face a progressive loss of credibility. Under such circumstances, when investors become anxious, international cooperation becomes very important. Reparations, however, were one of the imbalances caused by World War I which made international cooperation much more difficult. After 1928, the collapse in U.S. lending imposed a terrible strain on those countries trying to obey the rules of the gold standard. One solution would have been greater international cooperation, but political factors made this increasingly difficult. Eventually Britain and the United States decided that the costs of remaining on gold were too great and abandonment was the only realistic option. In a volume which discusses economic problems in a way intelligible to the lay person, KINDLEBERGER believes that reparations and war debts were not directly responsible for the Great Depression. However, they served to complicate and distort the international economy throughout the 1920s and during the worst years of the economic collapse in the early 1930s. In a pioneering study of central bank relationships, CLARKE finds that up to the summer of 1928 cooperation seems to have been working well. From that date the failure, possibly due to the inability of bankers to control their domestic economic problems, had serious consequences for the whole world.

All these studies stress the inter-relationships between economics and politics. Indeed there would be widespread agreement with Clarke's observation that the main obstacle to stability during the inter-war years was the failure of the western democracies to deal with the major political and economic problems.

PETER FEARON

See also Foreign Policy: Financial and Economic Aspects; Foreign Policy, 1919–1941

War of 1812: Causes

Adams, Henry, *History of the United States of America During the Administrations of Jefferson and Madison*, 9 vols., New York: Scribner, 1889–91; edited by Earl N. Harbert, 2 vols., New York: Library of America, 1986

Brown, Roger H., *The Republic in Peril: 1812*, New York: Columbia University Press, 1964
Burt, A.L., *The United States, Great Britain, and British North America: From the Revolution to the Establishment of Peace after the War of 1812*, New Haven: Yale University Press, and London: Oxford University Press, 1940
Egan, Clifford L., *Neither Peace nor War: Franco-American Relations, 1803–1812*, Baton Rouge: Louisiana State University Press, 1983
Hatzenbueler, Ronald L. and Robert L. Ivie, *Congress Declares War: Rhetoric, Leadership, and Partisanship in the Early Republic*, Kent, OH: Kent State University Press, 1983
Horsman, Reginald, *The Causes of the War of 1812*, Philadelphia: University of Pennsylvania Press, 1962
Perkins, Bradford, *The First Rapprochement: England and the United States, 1795–1805*, Philadelphia: University of Pennsylvania Press, 1955
Perkins, Bradford, *Prologue to War: England and the United States, 1805–1812*, Berkeley: University of California Press, 1961
Pratt, Julius W., *The Expansionists of 1812*, New York: Macmillan, 1925
Spivak, Burton, *Jefferson's English Crisis: Commerce, Embargo, and the Republican Revolution*, Charlottesville: University Press of Virginia, 1979
Stagg, J.C.A., *Mr. Madison's War: Politics, Diplomacy, and Warfare in the Early American Republic, 1783–1830*, Princeton: Princeton University Press, 1983
Watts, Steven, *The Republic Reborn: War and the Making of Liberal America, 1790–1820*, Baltimore: Johns Hopkins University Press, 1987

The second war between Britain and the United States has never ceased to arouse controversy. Contemporary battles between Federalists and Republicans over the merits of the war have been succeeded in this century by differing interpretations of its causes. Every account of the conduct of the war, every biography of those involved, contains its own explanation, and valuable anthologies of articles – notably *The War of 1812: Past Justifications and Present Interpretations* edited by George Rogers Taylor (1963) – have demonstrated the range of views.

The traditional 19th-century interpretation blamed the conflict on British outrages against American commerce during the Napoleonic wars. ADAMS's classic study emphasized the weakness and incompetence of Republican leaders in the United States, but otherwise its deep research in diplomatic sources on both sides of the Atlantic modified the traditional emphasis on British intransigence only slightly, though Adams also detected an imperialist desire to conquer Canada among some American proponents of war.

The early 20th century eagerly took up the suggestion that materialist motives lay behind the cries of injured national honour. Territorial ambition, land hunger, and the need of American farmers to recover markets closed by British measures, all found their advocates. The most influential statement of this approach came in PRATT, who detected a sectional intrigue to secure Canada for the North and Florida for the South, though evidence of the bargain was flimsy. More pertinently, he suggested that westerners were stirred by growing Indian hostility which they blamed on the Canadian authorities.

BURT's volume in the Carnegie Endowment's "Relations of Canada and the United States" series decisively rejected the expansionist thesis. Setting American-Canadian relations in the context of Anglo-American diplomacy, Burt's judicious if relatively brief account insisted that Canada was not the cause of the war, only the obvious target for the United States once war had been declared, essentially because of maritime grievances.

A more careful grounding in the primary sources was provided by Bradford Perkins's trilogy on Anglo-American relations between 1795 and 1815. PERKINS (1955) destroyed the image of persistent Anglo-American ill will stemming from the Revolution. He argued that, in the decade following the Jay treaty of 1794, the two countries found mutual benefit in good relations, in the face of a common French threat. PERKINS (1961) then explained why this "first rapprochement" collapsed in the new situation created as Napoleon seized control of continental Europe and Britain exploited her control of the seas. This most comprehensive and scholarly account since Adams agreed with him that Madison made serious miscalculations and was responsible for taking a divided nation into the war.

More argumentative than Perkins, HORSMAN insisted that the 1812 conflict was the direct consequence of the war in Europe and of British policy decisions. Critically, after 1807 the British government was controlled by a faction determined not only to defeat Napoleon at any cost but also to maintain British commercial supremacy. The resulting friction with the United States made many Americans, including westerners, eager for war as early as 1807, long before Tecumseh's Indian confederation became a source of anxiety.

This debunking of "western" or imperialist explanations of the war was underlined by BROWN. His particular interest lay in understanding the psychology and motivation of those who felt driven to demand war in 1812. The failure to force the belligerents to relax their commercial regulations challenged American confidence that they had established a republican experiment capable of providing the basis for a viable, truly independent nation. War became the only alternative to submitting to externally-imposed rules, and popular unrest raised the danger that the Federalists might come to power and pervert republicanism if the ruling Republican party did not do something decisive.

Thus by 1964 the old argument had played itself out. Though the growing interest in Indian studies has subsequently emphasized the significance of growing Indian hostility to America's westward movement, there is little evidence that it influenced sentiment in favour of war with Britain. After 1979 a new string of interpretations broadened understanding of the Napoleonic crisis. The problem was now seen as one of explaining not why war came in 1812 but why it had not come five years earlier. SPIVAK explained the commitment to peaceful commercial measures during Jefferson's presidency. Initially the Embargo was purely defensive in purpose, protecting American shipping, but increasingly it became used as a means of coercing the belligerents, however futile this proved to be.

EGAN's detailed account of America's relations with France during the pre-war decade further explained the situation which the American government faced. French policy attempted to embroil the United States in war with Britain, but the objective was thwarted again and again by Napoleon's erratic and short-sighted actions. American leaders, on their side, looked to a settlement with France as a means of putting pressure on Britain and securing advantage in any armed conflict.

Recent advances in Madison's reputation have meant that American policy in 1809–12 has been viewed more sympathetically. Brown, for example, argued that Madison, far from vacillating, made up his mind that war was inevitable more than a year before it happened. STAGG gave a controversial twist to the old argument by suggesting that Madison saw that commercial coercion could not work, because Canada, after 1808, began to provide Britain with supplies that the United States was trying to interdict. Hence the conquest of Canada was necessary if commercial coercion were ever to work. HATZENBUELER and IVIE tried to explain how a majority in favor of war was built up in the 1811–12 session of Congress. Largely ignoring external events and constituency pressure, their interdisciplinary approach suggested that the combination of a leadership program of preparedness measures, loyalty to the Republican party, and belligerent rhetoric persuaded waverers to vote in favor of war.

Finally, Brown's emphasis on the cultural expectations and frustrations that made national assertion necessary was connected by WATTS with America's transition from agrarian republic to liberal capitalist economy. Thus the war became the defining moment that served to reconcile the internal contradictions and tensions generated by economic expansion and avaricious individualism, and provided an opportunity to energize and validate such liberalizing tendencies. By implication, the war was brought about in order to achieve this transformation. Such a view operates at a level of motivation, and requires a reading of evidence, unknown to traditional diplomatic historians.

DONALD J. RATCLIFFE

War of 1812: Course and Consequences

Adams, Henry, *History of the United States of America During the Administrations of Jefferson and Madison*, 9 vols., New York: Scribner, 1889–91; edited by Earl N. Harbert, 2 vols., New York: Library of America, 1986

Brown, Wilburt S., *The Amphibious Campaign for West Florida and Louisiana, 1814–1815: A Critical Review of Strategy and Tactics at New Orleans*, University: University of Alabama Press, 1969

Dowd, Gregory Evans, *A Spirited Resistance: The North American Indian Struggle for Unity, 1745–1815*, Baltimore: Johns Hopkins University Press, 1992

Graves, Donald E., *The Battle of Lundy's Lane: On the Niagara in 1814*, Baltimore: Nautical and Aviation Publishing, 1993

Hickey, Donald R., *The War of 1812: A Forgotten Conflict*, Urbana: University of Illinois Press, 1989

McKee, Christopher, *A Gentlemanly and Honorable Profession: The Creation of the US Naval Officer Corps, 1794–1815*, Annapolis, MD: Naval Institute Press, 1991

Mahan, Alfred Thayer, *Sea Power in its Relations to the War of 1812*, Boston: Little Brown, and London: Sampson Low Marston, 1905; reprinted, New York: Greenwood Press, 1968

Owsley, Frank Lawrence, *Struggle for the Gulf Borderlands: The Creek War and the Battle of New Orleans, 1812–1815*, Gainesville: University Presses of Florida, 1981

Skelton, William B., *An American Profession of Arms: The Army Officer Corps, 1784–1816*, Lawrence: University Press of Kansas, 1992

Stagg, J.C.A., *Mr. Madison's War: Politics, Diplomacy, and Warfare in the Early American Republic, 1783–1830*, Princeton: Princeton University Press, 1983

Stanley, George F.G., *The War of 1812: Land Operations*, Toronto: Macmillan/National Museums of Canada, 1983

A century after its first publication, ADAMS's pro-Federalist history dominates the war of 1812 historiography. Most subsequent histories of the war reflect or contradict Adams's contentions of Madison's ineptitude as president and commander-in-chief. For depth of insight, personality sketches, and personal bias, these volumes remain the place to begin one's study of the war at the level of Washington politics.

Both Stagg and Hickey reflect the Vietnam War's impact upon scholarly analysis. Each is concerned with political intrigue from a different point of view. STAGG is a superb study of the interworkings of Washington politics and the impact of Republican infighting upon the prosecution of the war. For grand strategy, it is without peer and serves as a useful antidote to Adams. HICKEY takes an opposite tack, concentrating on the war's critics and overemphasizing the importance of the Federalists in the war's outcome. But his book constitutes a fine, brief overview of the conflict with an antiwar bias, and his conclusions are particularly effective. Neither of these two works is particularly useful for tactical analysis.

Too often professional historians reduce wars to causes, statistics, strategies, and consequences. A few continue to emphasize the human side of conflict and to analyze the motivations, feeling, tragedies, and triumphs of combat. Writing from a Canadian viewpoint, STANLEY provides the best overall analysis of the military effort along the international border. He does not discuss the British blockade and the Chesapeake and Gulf campaigns and those operations must be followed elsewhere. We await Canadian scholar Frederick Drake's study of naval operations for a modern study of a subject not significantly revised since Admiral Mahan's study of nine decades ago. MAHAN's line-of-battle fleet prejudices still dominate the interpretation of the naval actions, but greater appreciation of the role of privateering has emerged in recent years. GRAVES's study of Lundy's Lane brings home to the reader the reality of linear formation combat in a well-researched and well-written analysis of the bloodiest encounter of the war. A veteran of several amphibious operations, US

Marine Corps General BROWN shows considerable expertise in his acute analysis of the Gulf campaign. It should be used in conjunction with OWSLEY's study of the Creek War to obtain a full understanding of the war in the Southeast. Owsley effectively highlights the role which Native Americans played in the conflict and its outcome. In a different vein, DOWD develops a most successful integrated analysis of the last major attempt to combined Indian resistance to American encroachment on the trans-Appalachian frontier, especially in the Old Northwest. He demonstrates authoritatively how the advocates of nativism and accommodation struggled to control the political, cultural, and military agendas of their peoples. In the end, both camps failed.

While Stagg and Hickey adeptly summarize its economic, social, and political consequences, both McKee and Skelton are necessary to comprehend the impact of this war upon the professional military in the United States. McKEE's superbly researched and written analysis of the United States Navy's officer corps provides an excellent introduction to the question of why the American naval team could hold its own with the Royal Navy. SKELTON does much the same for the United States Army, and he conclusively demonstrates how the war brought a degree of professionalism and non-partisanship into the army's officer corps that would characterize it for the rest of its history. These two superb examples of the "new" military history must be consulted by anyone seeking a detailed study of the war's military and naval consequences.

DAVID CURTIS SKAGGS

War of Independence, 1775–1783: Military History

Black, Jeremy, *War for America: The Fight for Independence, 1775–1783*, New York: St. Martin's Press, and Stroud, Gloucestershire: Sutton, 1991

Black, Jeremy, *European Warfare, 1660–1815*, New Haven: Yale University Press, and London: UCL Press, 1994

Conway, Stephen, *The War of American Independence, 1775–1783*, London: Arnold, 1995

Higginbotham, Don, *The War of American Independence: Military Attitudes, Policies, and Practice, 1763–1789*, New York: Macmillan, and London: Collier Macmillan, 1971

Huston, James A., *Logistics of Liberty: American Services of Supply in the Revolutionary War and After*, Newark: University of Delaware Press, 1991

Mackesy, Piers, *The War for America, 1775–1783*, London: Longman, and Cambridge, MA: Harvard University Press, 1964

Rodger, N.A.M., *The Insatiable Earl: A Life of John Montagu, 4th Earl of Sandwich*, London: HarperCollins, and New York: Norton, 1993

Royster, Charles, *A Revolutionary People at War: The Continental Army and American Character, 1775–1783*, Chapel Hill: University of North Carolina Press, 1979

Syrett, David, *The Royal Navy in American Waters, 1775–1783*, Aldershot, Hampshire: Scolar Press, 1989

Wood, W.J., *Battles of the Revolutionary War, 1775–1781*, Chapel Hill: University of North Carolina Press, 1990

Amid the wealth of studies on the American Revolution, it is all too easy to treat the military dimension as marginal and to forget that the result of the war was not inevitable, for both political and military reasons. The number of general studies of the conflict have been relatively limited. For some time the standard British account was MACKESY, a work that was stronger on strategic issues than on the details of conflict and that was largely written from the British perspective. In contrast, HIGGINBOTHAM, the most comprehensive American treatment, was stronger on the Revolutionaries and weaker on the British, especially on the naval and global aspects of the conflict.

Among more recent studies, BLACK (1991) draws on both American and British archival sources and emphasizes the fallacy of assuming that for contemporaries the outcome of the war was inevitable. Along with the problems that the British faced, first in fighting the colonists and then in also fending off the challenge of their European enemies, he stresses the need to note the stresses and strains which the war imposed on the American rebels. Many of the actual battles can be followed in detail in WOOD.

CONWAY places considerable emphasis on the global context and on strategic questions. He also sees the conflict as prefiguring the French Revolutionary and Napoleonic Wars in the degree of popular commitment and involvement: "the first appearance, on a significant scale, of a people's war". There is considerable weight in this analysis, but it is also necessary to note the degree of commitment that earlier 18th-century conflicts could elicit or reflect.

The question of novelty is also addressed in BLACK (1994), a work that emphasizes the vitality of *ancien régime* military methods and also includes a discussion of whether the British could have won. Black argues that although the British could use their maritime power to blockade and occupy strategic points, the issue was not going to be settled until an army was landed that could destroy the American Continental Army. Thus, a greater emphasis can be placed on American skill and determination in avoiding such a defeat. The British were unable to exploit battlefield advantages because of deficiencies on their part, but also thanks to American fighting quality.

An important aspect of that quality was a degree of determination that reflected ideological commitment. ROYSTER is a study of the ideals that Americans defined for themselves in creating, recruiting and fighting in the Continental Army and of the relationship of these ideals to their experience with their army. In what was both a revolutionary and a civil war, it is necessary to explain what led people to kill and risk death. Royster demonstrates the intensity of the Revolutionaries' reaction to the struggle for independence, and argues that they constantly invoked their ideals to redefine their experience in a heroic fashion, and thus helped to sustain their commitment.

A different form of sustenance is discussed by HUSTON who provides both an analytical study and a narrative account of the logistics of the war. He concludes that, in light of the inexperience of the Revolutionary leaders in logistical questions, the lack of an adequate central executive authority or centralized governmental machinery, the rivalries between the colonies and the active defence of local interests, logistical support for the army was as could be expected: at times, when vigorously managed, adequate, but at other times, as a consequence of incompetence and selfishness, inadequate. French aid was indispensable, but so also was the capacity of the Americans to go on bearing the strain of providing supplies.

Huston draws attention to the logistical consequences of British control of the sea. The naval dimension is addressed at length by SYRETT, who shows how the fighting on land cannot otherwise be understood. His account of the British navy is a critical one, blaming poor political and military planning and indifferent commanders. This argument can be taken too far. Mistakes clearly were made, but Syrett tends to adopt the perspective too frequently shown when British generalship in the conflict is considered: that generals or admirals were either very good or failures. Instead, it is necessary to place more weight on the problems of fighting a trans-oceanic war that was simultaneously civil and international.

The most important recent naval contribution is to be found in RODGER's study of the First Lord of the Admiralty. In his positive re-evaluation of Sandwich, he argues that Lord George Germain, the Colonial Secretary, in his quest to establish himself as the dominant war minister, sought to undermine Sandwich and was temperamentally unsuited to creating the necessary co-operation between army and navy. In addition, Rodger suggests that after the entry of France into the war, America became a strategic backwater, but that Germain was unwilling to accept the political and strategic consequences, as it threatened his position. The navy had already efficiently carried out its share in the ministerial strategy for 1776 and 1777, but the Cabinet thwarted Sandwich's wish for full mobilization against the French threat. Late mobilization meant that for most of the war the British navy was fighting on the defensive against heavy odds and the only real possibilities of taking the initiative were before Spain entered the war in 1779, and in 1782, by which time Britain was winning the naval race. Rodger's observation that historians must be prepared to discuss what might have been, if they are to assess realistically the judgement of ministers whose decisions had to be based on such considerations, is very pertinent.

JEREMY BLACK

War of Independence, 1775–1783: Diplomacy

Bemis, Samuel Flagg, *The Hussey-Cumberland Mission and American Independence: An Essay in the Diplomacy of the American Revolution*, Princeton: Princeton University Press, 1931

Bemis, Samuel Flagg, *The Diplomacy of the American Revolution*, New York: Appleton Century, 1935; revised, Bloomington: Indiana University Press, 1957

Dull, Jonathan R., *The French Navy and American Independence: A Study of Arms and Diplomacy, 1774–1787*, Princeton: Princeton University Press, 1975

Dull, Jonathan R., *A Diplomatic History of the American Revolution*, New Haven: Yale University Press, 1985

Harlow, Vincent T., *The Founding of the Second British Empire, 1762–1793*, volume 1: *Discovery and Revolution*, London: Longman, 1952

Hutson, James H., *John Adams and the Diplomacy of the American Revolution* Lexington: University Press of Kentucky, 1980

Morris, Richard B., *The Peacemakers: The Great Powers and American Independence*, New York: Harper, 1965

Scott, H.M., *British Foreign Policy in the Age of the American Revolution*, Oxford: Clarendon Press, and New York: Oxford University Press, 1990

Stinchcombe, William C., *The American Revolution and the French Alliance*, Syracuse, NY: Syracuse University Press, 1969

Stourzh, Gerald, *Benjamin Franklin and American Foreign Policy*, Chicago: University of Chicago Press, 1954, 2nd edition, 1969

Like its military dimension, the diplomatic history of the War of Independence has received insufficient attention. Yet any emphasis on the military and political value of French, Spanish and Dutch intervention on the side of the Revolutionaries necessarily directs attention to the reasons for the breakdown in their relations with Britain, the process by which links with the Revolutionaries were established and subsequently developed, and their influence on the conduct of the war and on the negotiations for peace. For long the classic and most popular diplomatic history of the Revolution was BEMIS (1957). This was a slightly revised version of an edition first published in 1935. Although succinct and wide-ranging, it has for long been dated, not least because of its failure to appreciate the priorities of French diplomacy. However, it is still of value, not least because of its thorough coverage of the issues of neutral shipping and international law. BEMIS (1931) is a more specialized work, but neglects important British documents and exaggerates the importance of the Anglo-Spanish negotiations of 1780, especially for the British.

Bemis has been supplanted as a synthesis by DULL (1985). He integrates the war into its European context and shows how French diplomacy was motivated by the desire to weaken Britain so as to be able to deal better with Russia's growing power in eastern Europe. Dull explains why Britain was unable to find any allies and how France, Spain and the Netherlands came to fight on the Revolutionaries' side. The book is weakest on British policy and strongest on that of France. On the latter subject, it builds upon the extensive archival research undertaken for DULL (1975), which studied the interrelationship between the naval and diplomatic history of the American Revolution, and provided a sound account of the causes, chronology and limitations of French intervention.

Drawing essentially on French material and perspectives, this work supplemented STINCHCOMBE, the standard history of the Franco-American alliance from the American standpoint. Further light on the alliance is provided by STOURZH, an acute analysis of Franklin's beliefs and attitudes about foreign policy. Franklin faced rivalry within the American diplomatic mission in Paris and, more generally, in the American diplomatic corps. HUTSON's study of John Adams is a valuable account of another crucial American diplomat, which extends to cover the entire course of American revolutionary diplomacy.

The position of the other side must never be forgotten. The best narrative is provided by SCOTT, which will doubtless serve as the standard work on the subject for many years. His emphasis, however, is diplomatic and he fails to probe the public debate over foreign policy and, more generally, offers a less than complete account of the domestic dimension. Although, in line with other recent work on the period, the role of the Crown is emphasized, mercantile, parliamentary and popular pressures receive less attention, and are, in general, minimized or dismissed. Scott emphasizes the extent to which the absence of allies created problems for Britain. This is correct, but it was not necessarily fatal. Britain had been handicapped by its continental commitments earlier in the century, for example during the War of the Austrian Succession (1740–48), and again when Hanover was overrun by France in 1757. There is need for fresh thinking on the military and diplomatic consequences of isolation during the War of American Independence.

The peace negotiations can be approached from the British perspective by using HARLOW. He supports the views of the British minister, the Earl of Shelburne, and is perceptive on the wider colonial dimension, but does not fully understand French policy. He tends to fit his analysis into his general theme of a reorientation of British imperial ambitions towards the Indian Ocean. Shelburne's statesmanship and magnanimity towards America are emphasized.

In contrast, MORRIS adopts an American perspective. Based on very extensive archival research, this is an account of diplomatic history between 1780 and the end of the war. However, the value of the work is limited because of its hostility to France and Spain. Morris doubted the value of the French alliance, and has been criticized for showing only limited knowledge of the nature of diplomacy in this period.

JEREMY BLACK

Warren, Earl 1891–1974
Chief Justice of the Supreme Court

Katcher, Leo, *Earl Warren: A Political Biography*, New York: McGraw Hill, 1967

Kluger, Richard, *Simple Justice: The History of Brown v. Board of Education and Black America's Struggle for Equality*, New York: Knopf, 1975; London: Deutsch, 1977

Levy, Leonard W., *The Supreme Court under Earl Warren*, New York: Quadrangle, 1972

Lewis, Anthony, *Gideon's Trumpet*, New York: Random House, 1964; London: Bodley Head, 1966

Pollack, Jack Harrison, *Earl Warren: The Judge Who Changed America*, Englewood Cliffs, NJ: Prentice Hall, 1979

Schwartz, Bernard, *Super Chief: Earl Warren and His Supreme Court, A Judicial Biography*, New York: New York University Press, 1983

Severn, Bill, *Mr. Chief Justice Earl Warren*, New York: McKay, 1968

Tushnet, Mark V. (editor), *The Warren Court in Historical and Political Perspective*, Charlottesville: University Press of Virginia, 1993

Weaver, John D., *Warren: The Man, The Court, The Era*, Boston: Little Brown, 1967; London: Gollancz, 1968

White, G. Edward, *Earl Warren: A Public Life*, New York: Oxford University Press, 1982

Earl Warren is best known as the Chief Justice of the United States Supreme Court (1953–69) who wrote the decision in *Brown* v. *Board of Education of Topeka, Kansas* (1954) which made segregated schools unconstitutional. Warren was also a vice presidential candidate of the Republican party (1948), and governor of California (1944–53). Warren is also remembered for presiding over a Supreme Court that strengthened civil liberties, especially in the areas of freedom of speech, freedom of the press, religious freedom, separation of church and state, and the right to protest against the government, expanded individual liberties, developed the right to personal and marital privacy, struck down legally sanctioned racial discrimination, and expanded due process protections for criminal defendants.

Warren also chaired the commission – popularly known as the Warren Commission – which investigated the murder of President John F. Kennedy. In addition to his court career, Warren was the first three-term governor of California, and a progressive, reforming district attorney and a state attorney general, noted for his successful prosecution of corrupt officials and his modernization of law enforcement in California. He is also remembered for his strong advocacy of the World War II internment of Japanese Americans (most of whom were American citizens) and his sometimes overzealous prosecutions of accused criminals, especially if they were tied to the Communist party.

President Eisenhower, a middle-of-the-road Republican, appointed Warren, an equally moderate Republican, to the Court in 1953. By the end of his Court years Warren was one of the most liberal justices in Court history. He was also, next to John Marshall (1801–35), the most important Chief Justice in American history. One of the central questions of Warren historiography is to explain how this rather conventional, mundane, conservative, and intellectually unimpressive politician metamorphosed into a great liberal leader of the Court.

The literature on Warren is almost universally laudatory, as SCHWARTZ's title, *Super Chief*, illustrates. This huge volume provides important details on the evolution of all the important, and many of the minor, cases that came before the Court during Warren's chief justiceship. The book is mostly a summary of Warren's decisions and a somewhat gossipy account of internal Court politics based on undocumented interviews with former Supreme Court clerks. Schwartz devotes only 15 pages to Warren's important pre-court career, and has only a 6-page discussion of the Warren Commission. This book tells us little about Warren as an individual, or what might have motivated him as a judge, and does not even attempt to evaluate the subject or place him in any historical context.

WHITE, the best overall biography, combines a fine account of his early life and pre-court career with an expert, law professor's analysis of Warren's court years. White provides a balanced assessment of Warren, pointing out his inconsistencies, his early racism, and his ability to overcome his rather provincial, small-town California upbringing. White argues that Warren's pre-court career is consistent with his court years, but this position seems somewhat strained. There is a particularly fine account of Warren's relationship with Justice Felix Frankfurter, who came to hate the Chief Justice. White's conclusion, that Warren was "not an ideologue," but was motivated by "instincts for what was fair, honorable, politically feasible and sensible" is itself fair, reasonable, and sensible. White finds Warren to be a "great man" for "what he embodied" and "for what he accomplished." While focusing on Warren's judicial career, White downplays (and almost ignores) the persistent right-wing campaign against the Chief Justice coming from extremist groups, Republican politicians, and the American Bar Association. White offers an extremely useful appendix which organizes Warren's opinions by topic. He cites a wide variety of primary sources, scholarly articles, and dissertations, but unfortunately he uses the frustrating law review footnoting style which may baffle many readers.

POLLACK, the least critical and least scholarly of the major posthumous biographies, lacks footnotes, a comprehensive bibliography, a list of cases decided by Warren, or even a useful index. Pollack has a journalist's eye for details, but many of his anecdotes and facts are not entirely on the mark. Pollack downplays and ignores Warren's racism and red baiting during his California years, and is constantly searching for hints in Warren's earlier life of what Pollack calls "the Warren-to-be." He devotes only a few paragraphs to Warren's role in the Japanese internment, trying to explain it away as an almost legitimate response to Pearl Harbor. Similarly, he explains away Warren's use of warrantless wiretaps and coerced confessions in a murder case involving labor radicals by saying that Warren honestly believed the men were guilty. By contrast, White's sophisticated analysis of these issues illustrates both Warren's limitations and his ability to grow as Chief Justice.

Lively and well-written, WEAVER is the best biography by a contemporary, and surpasses White as a source for Warren's pre-court career. Like most of the other biographies, Weaver uses the theme of equality and justice to interpret Warren's life, but at least confronts the more problematic aspects of Warren's pre-court career, including the internment. Weaver provides a fine, well-documented account of Warren's California career as well as the best discussion available of the right-wing attacks on Warren after he joined the Court.

Like Weaver, KATCHER focuses mostly on Warren's pre-court years. Although it is not footnoted, Katcher is useful for some of the details of Warren's life and career in California (some of these details are corrected in White). He downplays Warren's role in the Japanese internment and his sometimes overly aggressive actions as a prosecutor. Katcher begins his book with the controversy over Warren's chief justiceship that led the right-wing John Birch Society to call for his impeachment, and he provides the flavor of the contemporary political attacks on the Chief Justice. Like Katcher, SEVERN is journalistic in tone, and lacks any scholarly pretenses, but offers a good deal of information about Warren's early life and political career, while ignoring many controversial aspects. Severn praises Warren for his character, comparing him to Chief Justice John Marshall, and concluding that "By any reasonable standard, allowing for small faults that make a man big, Chief Justice Earl Warren also is a giant of his time."

While not biographies, Lewis and Kluger offer excellent insights into Warren's role in shaping the Court. LEWIS's classic study of *Gideon* v. *Wainwright* (1963), which led to the guarantee of legal counsel for all criminal defendants, describes how Warren devoted special energy to ensuring that petitions from prisoners and poor defendants – *in forma pauperis* applications – gained a full hearing before the Court. KLUGER is the best study of the *Brown* case; it places Warren's appointment in the context of the internal court debate over desegregation, and describes his role in creating a unanimous decision.

Both TUSHNET and LEVY provide useful perspectives on the Court and its personnel under Warren. Both are collections of essays by prominent scholars and journalists. Tushnet argues that the "Warren Court" did not actually emerge until 1962, when the liberal and progressive-thinking Arthur Goldberg replaced Frankfurter on the bench. The various biographies and other studies may be usefully compared with Warren's own memoirs, published posthumously in 1977, which reveal much about the pressures under which he worked.

PAUL FINKELMAN

See also Civil Rights Movement; Kennedy, John F., Assassination of; Supreme Court

Washington, Booker T. 1856–1915
African American leader and educator

Bontemps, Arna, *Young Booker: Booker T. Washington's Early Days*, New York: Dodd Mead, 1972

Harlan, Louis R., *Booker T. Washington*, 2 vols., New York and Oxford: Oxford University Press, 1972–83

Harlan, Louis R., *Booker T. Washington in Perspective: Essays of Louis R. Harlan*, edited by Raymond W. Smock, Jackson: University Press of Mississippi, 1988

Mathews, Basil, *Booker T. Washington: Educator and Interracial Interpreter*, Cambridge, MA: Harvard University Press, 1948; London: SCM Press, 1949

Meier, August, *Negro Thought in America, 1880–1915: Racial Ideologies in the Age of Booker T. Washington*, Ann Arbor: University of Michigan Press 1963

Spencer, Samuel R., Jr., *Booker T. Washington and the Negro's Place in American Life*, Boston: Little Brown, 1955

The most famous and controversial African American leader and educator of his day, Booker T. Washington gained national attention by his "Atlanta Compromise" address of 1895 which offered a pragmatic solution to the race problem in the South. The autobiographical *Up from Slavery* (1901) presented him as the black exemplar of self-help, good sense and rationality. Subsequent commentators have reached differing estimates of Washington's life and times, but the man and his motives

remain matters of conjecture. MATHEWS's now dated and decidedly sympathetic account is also rich in detail. It includes interviews with surviving members of the Washington family, and Tuskegee staff and former students. It applauds Washington's heroic "attempt to lift a whole people" from the debilitating legacy of slavery, and endorses his advocacy of agricultural and vocational training for the mass of southern blacks – as well as rural and industrial workers on both sides of the Atlantic. But, Mathews maintains, his speeches and correspondence also reveal that Washington envisioned eventual economic, political and social equality for African Americans. Aware of the animosity which Washington aroused during his lifetime, Mathews concludes that "Men shall remain divided as to whether reform should be attempted in the main by denunciation and political pressures or by the flank approach of education, persuasion and compromise" – leaving little doubt as to his own preferences and those of his subject.

Washington is similarly depicted as a racial realist/diplomat by SPENCER (in an undocumented study), but he also offers a more critical appraisal of the principal of Tuskegee Institute as a "benevolent despot" who exercised rigid control over his faculty, students, the Negro press and the distribution of federal patronage in the South. An optimistic exponent of the unabashedly materialistic Gospel of Wealth, Washington was a practitioner of Christian humility and a democratic educationalist, who "did what was possible, given the time and place in which he lived." In a caustic review of Spencer's book. W.E.B. Du Bois, Washington's leading African American critic, dismissed its portrayal of "a martyr appreciated mainly by Southern whites and not by his fellow Negroes" as a "fairy tale" certain to please "the present rulers of Mississippi and Georgia."

The political, intellectual and racial climate in which Washington functioned is examined in MEIER's penetrating, scholarly and semi-sociological analysis. Unlike earlier commentators, he demonstrates that the principle of industrial education for African Americans was well-established before Washington's ascendancy, while his attacks on opponents – and notably W.E.B. Du Bois – involved issues of power and prestige as much as profound ideological differences. Alert to the paradoxes which Washington presented, Meier also stresses his influence and public friendships with white politicians and philanthropists, and the clandestine actions he took against discrimination and segregation, while overtly expressing a philosophy of accommodation to racial prejudice.

The inspirational example of Washington's life, as retailed in *Up from Slavery*, informs (and distorts) BONTEMPS's imaginative reconstruction – intended for younger readers – of the progress from slave cabin to national and international fame of a black boy who embodied the precepts of the Protestant ethic. It offers no real insights into those forces which shaped the complexities and ambiguities of the adult Washington.

With the rise of the civil rights and Black Power movements of the 1950s and 1960s, Washington's popular reputation was as a passive and "Uncle Tom" leader. Scholarly and informed reappraisal of his life and times, incorporating new materials, was initiated by Harlan (an editor of the 13 volumes of Washington's Papers), who emerged as his most distinguished biographer – the winner of two Bancroft Prizes and the Pulitzer Prize for Biography in 1984. HARLAN (1972) offered an account and interpretation of Washington's life from his earliest years in Virginia to his dinner at the White House with Theodore Roosevelt in 1901. Washington's association with a succession of influential white mentors (or surrogate fathers), and his shrewd grasp of the path to personal advancement, received detailed attention. His "incorrigible humility," Harlan suggests, made him acceptable to whites, but the role-playing and deception which this entailed also brought "a loss of innocence." Moreover, his rise to fame "coincided with a setback of his race." Sectional reconciliation after the traumas of the Civil War and Reconstruction was achieved not only at the expense of the Negro but also with Washington's public blessing. But Harlan recognizes and wrestles with the enigmas of Washington's many-sided personality, all of which were bent to the service of an insatiable quest for power: "Ideas he cared little for. Power was his game and he used ideas simply as instruments to gain power."

The second volume, HARLAN (1983), reaches similar conclusions. At the height of his fame "The Wizard of Tuskegee" possessed a set of "multiple personalities to fit his various roles" – educationalist, interracial diplomat, political boss, presidential adviser, New South ideologue, and companion of millionaires. At the end of his life he was also a more outspoken (but always circumspect) opponent of white racism. Yet whatever guise he adopted, Washington was unable simultaneously to challenge and accommodate to white supremacy. Possessed of a remarkable ability to make virtues out of necessities, Washington "always lacked the capacity for the highest registers of indignation." His real and tangible achievements – particularly the benefits bestowed on its students and the local community by Tuskegee's innovations and the securing of philanthropic funds for southern schools and colleges – are dutifully recorded, but Harlan appears to hold Washington personally responsible for the worsening American racial situation in the first two decades of the 20th century. Readers of either or both volumes of this meticulously researched biography of "the last black leader born in slavery" may arrive at conclusions different from those of the author.

Harlan's 25 years of research and writing on Washington are distilled in Smock's collection of his essays in HARLAN (1988). Particularly valuable are the pieces "Booker T. Washington in Biographical Perspective", "The Secret Life of Booker T. Washington" and "Booker T. Washington's Discovery of the Jews." They are fitting tributes to the acumen and industry of their author and the monumental stature of their subject.

JOHN WHITE

Washington, George 1732–1799
Leader of the Revolution and 1st President of the United States

Alden, John R., *George Washington: A Biography*, Baton Rouge: Louisiana State University Press, 1984

Cunliffe, Marcus, *George Washington: Man and Monument*, Boston: Little Brown, 1958, revised 1982

Ferling, John E., *The First of Men: A Life of George Washington*, Knoxville: University of Tennessee Press, 1988

Fleming, Thomas, *First in Their Hearts: A Biography of George Washington*, New York: Norton, 1968

Flexner, James Thomas, *George Washington*, 4 vols., Boston: Little Brown, 1965–72; vols. 1–2, London: Leo Cooper, 1972–73

Flexner, James Thomas, *Washington: The Indispensable Man*, Boston: Little Brown, 1974; London: Collins, 1976

Freeman, Douglas Southall, *George Washington*, 7 vols., New York: Scribner, and London: Eyre and Spottiswoode, 1948–57 (vol. 7 by John Alexander Carroll and Mary Wells Ashworth); abridged by Richard Harwell as *Washington: An Abridgment in One Volume*, Scribner, and Eyre and Spottiswoode, 1968

Higginbotham, Don, *George Washington and the American Military Tradition*, Athens: University of Georgia Press, 1985

Jones, Robert F., *George Washington*, Boston: Twayne, 1979; revised, New York: Fordham University Press, 1989

Ketchum, Richard M., *The World of George Washington*, New York: American Heritage, 1974

Knollenberg, Bernhard, *Washington and the Revolution, A Reappraisal: Gates, Conway, and the Continental Congress*, New York: Macmillan, 1941

Longmore, Paul K., *The Invention of George Washington*, Berkeley: University of California Press, 1988

McDonald, Forrest, *The Presidency of George Washington*, Lawrence: University Press of Kansas, 1974

Marling, Karal Ann, *George Washington Slept Here: Colonial Revivals and American Culture, 1876–1986*, Cambridge, MA: Harvard University Press, 1988

Morgan, Edmund S., *The Genius of George Washington*, New York: Norton, 1980

Phelps, Glenn A., *George Washington and American Constitutionalism*, Lawrence: University Press of Kansas, 1993

Schwartz, Barry, *George Washington: The Making of an American Symbol*, New York: Free Press, and London: Collier Macmillan, 1987

Smith, Richard Norton, *Patriarch: George Washington and the New American Nation*, Boston: Houghton Mifflin, 1993

Wills, Garry, *Cincinnatus: George Washington and the Enlightenment*, New York: Doubleday, 1984; London: Hale, 1985

Biographies of George Washington began to appear almost immediately after his death. These early works were full of praise for the great man, a few based more on imagination than actual fact. Parson Weems's 1807 book, written to instruct children on the proper values for living, is the most extreme example. He created the cherry tree legend and other tall tales. Jared Sparks censored his hero's life in 1839, as well as his writings in an extensively edited edition of his letters, to ensure a blameless reputation. More sound but still outdated are biographies by John Marshall (5 vols., 1804–07), Washington Irving (5 vols., 1855–59), Woodrow Wilson (1903), and Henry Cabot Lodge (2 vols., 1889), among others.

These were followed by debunking works that discussed Washington's battle losses, hot temper, use of strong language, love of Sally Fairfax, his wealthy neighbor's wife, greedy acquisition of land, and supposedly padded expense accounts. The result of both laudatory and debunking traditions was to make Washington a public figure who was particularly difficult to understand – either perfect or fundamentally flawed. More recent books have tried to deal with him as a real person and a politician. What has emerged from these efforts is the portrait of an interesting but complex man who played a central role in early American history, and who has become an integral part of American culture.

There are currently two notable multi-volume biographies of Washington, by Douglas Southall Freeman and James Thomas Flexner. The more detailed is FREEMAN (1948–57), a massive work, in seven lengthy volumes. The last volume was written after Freeman's death by Mary W. Ashworth and John A. Carroll. The entire set was then condensed by Richard Harwell from 3,582 to 754 pages in a single volume without footnotes, FREEMAN (1968). The original work reflects Freeman's great scholarship, painstaking organization, and concern for accuracy; it is a model of the genre. Although a few specific interpretations have been supplanted, this remains the most comprehensive study of Washington and the best place to check for specific activities, military movements, and decisions. Washington is followed in minute detail through the battles of the French and Indian War as well as the American Revolution, as he fusses over his crops at Mount Vernon, and during his two terms as president. The volumes range from a discussion of the settlement of Virginia's Northern Neck and of Washington's own ancestors, to a description of his death bed scene and burial arrangements.

In contrast, in his four-volume biography FLEXNER (1965–72) is less concerned with Washington's actions and more with his "emotions." FLEXNER (1974) is a re-written and condensed single-volume biography, without footnotes. This author concentrates on Washington's life as a warrior and planter, on what interested and concerned him whether in uniform or while at home, even including efforts to raise mules at Mount Vernon. He was the first to present a discussion of Washington and slavery, based on previously unused material, showing how the president quietly arranged for his slaves to be freed after Martha's death.

While trying to treat Washington in an even-handed manner, both Freeman and Flexner clearly admire him, and only occasionally offer any criticism. Flexner's briefer biography is even subtitled *The Indispensable Man*, and he refers to Washington as "a great and good man." Freeman contends that the "great" man had only two flaws, excessive ambition and the "lack of strong affection for his mother." Flexner ascribes questionable actions during the later years of his presidency to mental decline and "periods of senility."

Those readers wanting to go beyond the detailed rendering of Washington's life by Freeman and Flexner can turn to several editions of his papers. The most complete is the extensive multi-volume set currently being produced by the University Press of Virginia in three series: Colonial, Revolutionary War, and Presidential (1983–). Washington's diaries have also been published and are a useful source when trying to find out what he did on a particular day, or whether he actually visited a certain place, slept or ate in the region. Barring the need for this kind of information, the multi-volume sets should satisfy most serious readers.

There are a number of one-volume biographies of Washington aimed at the general reader, including works by Richard Ketchum, Marcus Cunliffe, Thomas Fleming, and Robert Jones. KETCHUM alternates well written biographical chapters with sections that contain wonderful illustrations of items from Washington's lifetime or earlier (such as maps of Virginia, family artifacts, portraits of a variety of figures, pages from books and documents, and paintings of battles). All of this reflects what the publisher, American Heritage, does well, producing quality works for a popular audience. In his book appropriately subtitled *Man and Monument*, CUNLIFFE briefly evaluates the "real" man behind the legends. He concludes that Washington was a "good man, not a saint; a competent soldier, not a great one; an honest administrator, not a statesman of genius." Yet in summing up Cunliffe holds that he was "an exceptional figure."

FLEMING's Washington is more, a man of great courage in battle and politics, who had a "first class mind." He describes young George trying to break a colt, provides a series of "amazing" stories of questionable validity, and includes a chapter called "Strength Versus Guile" on tricks and spies used by the General to fool the British during the Revolutionary War. This book is appropriate only for the very young, harking back in some ways to Parson Weems. A much better choice would be JONES who synthesizes modern research in a short book which is balanced both in terms of interpretation and format, managing briefly to cover Washington's entire life. He sees Washington as a "great military leader," skilled administrator and diplomat, but overly sensitive to criticism and too concerned with his reputation. To Jones he was an ordinary man with "extraordinary self-discipline and devotion to duty."

There are two single-volume biographies which are more scholarly efforts at synthesis. ALDEN tries to make Washington human by discussing his sense of humor and his loves, until at times his tone becomes almost gossipy. But, appropriately for an expert on the American Revolution, he also concentrates on Washington's military experiences, and discusses them in some detail. The major part of this book deals with Washington, the military leader. FERLING also emphasizes Washington the military man. It is the longest and most comprehensive recent single-volume biography, and is both judicious in its judgments and well balanced in its coverage of his whole life. His Washington is both a soldier and planter, but not a politician. On the whole Ferling fruitfully mines recent scholarly work, as well as Washington's diaries and letters, to present a first president who is a truly complex figure. He discusses the private and public man, starting with a youth who was "callow, pompous ... obsequious ... humorless," proceeding to a soldier who was distant and singularly friendless, a president who was no one's (not even Hamilton's) dupe, and concluding that he truly accomplished much. This was done at a price, for the presidency took its toll, and aged him seriously. Ferling pictures Washington as uninterested in politics before the Revolution, not playing an active political role even during his first administration, and taking a partisan stand only at the very end of his life. This is a portrait contradicted by several recent studies, including those of Glenn Phelps and Paul Longmore.

There are several books which are evaluations of Washington's role in the Revolution, rather than biographies. The narrowest in scope is KNOLLENBERG's reappraisal of the 1777–78 "Conway Cabal," in which he rejects the idea that this was a conspiracy to replace Washington, and pictures him negatively – as being, at this point, paranoid. This needs to be read in conjunction with more recent works by Richard H. Kohn (Eagle and Sword, 1975) and others on the American military. In works that started as lectures, both Higginbotham and Morgan take a broader perspective and offer much more complimentary assessments. HIGGINBOTHAM examines Washington's colonial and Revolutionary war experiences, compares him to World War II General George Marshall, and concludes that his "foremost contribution to the American military tradition" was respect for civilian control. MORGAN also sees this deference to Congress as Washington's "genius," the consequence of his republicanism and understanding of power. This short essay distils the essence of Washington. It is followed by a selection of his letters designed to prove Morgan's points.

Other books, while including biographical information, focus on Washington as president. In a volume which is part of a series on the American presidency, McDONALD actually emphasizes the role played by Alexander Hamilton and reduces Washington's significance to such an extent that he disappears from much of the book, to the point of becoming irrelevant to many of the policies and accomplishments of his two terms. The bank, the debt issue, and foreign policy are treated, in conceptualization and implementation, as the work of the secretary of the treasury. Many of these matters, McDonald states, were "clearly beyond Washington's ken and outside his area of interest."

In contrast, SMITH makes Washington a stronger figure, absolutely central to the events of the 1790s. Although strictly chronological in its treatment, this book seems at times disjointed, as it sandwiches personal and social information between political issues, or accounts of the president on his travels through the new nation. More clearly focused is the work of the political scientist PHELPS. He insists that Washington made substantive constitutional contributions, based on his experiences as a Virginia planter, and as commander-in-chief during the Revolution. Washington emerges as a republican and an ultra-nationalist, who had a vision of the form that the new nation's government should take. As president he took a leadership role on foreign policy and war issues, but deferred to Congress on legislative matters.

The value of studies by Schwartz, Longmore and Wills lies in their combination of biography and intellectual history, and their overlapping discussions of Washington's life and image. SCHWARTZ examines how and why Washington became a hero, a symbol of the republican virtues of modesty, industry, and wisdom. He argues that Washington was actually a man of "modest accomplishments," revered because such reverence served the needs of the new nation. LONGMORE utilizes biographical details more specifically to show that Washington deliberately cultivated his role as a republican symbol. He was an ambitious man, a politician and an actor, always concerned with furthering his reputation. Longmore sees these characteristics in evidence even in the period before 1758 when, he argues, Washington fully participated in the political life of Virginia. He was never content to be only a planter, and never

the reluctant politician that others (including Freeman) have portrayed. The book contains a fascinating appendix on what Washington read, which is designed to show that he had a self-taught, deliberately acquired, understanding of the republican ideal hero of his time.

WILLS is also concerned with Washington as a symbol, and with how he perceived himself, but the primary emphasis is on the way contemporary "artists and propagandists" used his image. This book is based on a series of lectures that dealt with three acts in Washington's life – his resignation as commander-in-chief, his role in presiding over the Constitutional Convention, and his farewell as president – and how they have been illustrated in paintings, sculptures, poems, and written accounts. The lectures were accompanied by slides, a number of them reproduced here as illustrations. Wills shows that hero worship, and the desire for fame, were important to the Revolutionary generation. Washington shared these ideas and was the master of appropriate gestures made at significant times, but he was also used by others to create a "Washington cult."

MARLING goes one step further than Wills in looking at Washington in the context of American culture. Like Wills, she is interested in the uses made of Washington's image, but unlike him she is not really interested in Washington himself. The man is gone, only the symbol remains. The message, actually shared by all the works discussed here, is that Washington is difficult to understand precisely because he is so much a part of American culture.

A reader interested in the details of Washington's life should consult Freeman, one looking for a quick understanding should examine either Cunliffe or Ketchum, which are both very readable. The best and most up-to-date single-volume biography is Ferling, while Phelps ably sums up Washington's political ideas. There is also, of course, important material on Washington in numerous other books, including general works on the Revolution and the early Republic, and specialized studies of particular topics or events, but a comprehensive list would be enormous.

MAXINE N. LURIE

Washington, DC

Goode, James M., *Capital Losses: A Cultural History of Washington's Destroyed Buildings*, Washington, DC: Smithsonian Institution Press, 1979

Green, Constance McLaughlin, *Washington*, 2 vols., Princeton: Princeton University Press, 1962–63

Green, Constance McLaughlin, *The Secret City: A History of Race Relations in the Nation's Capital*, Princeton: Princeton University Press, 1967

Jacob, Kathryn Allamong, *Capital Elites: High Society in Washington, D.C., after the Civil War*, Washington, DC: Smithsonian Institution Press, 1995

Leech, Margaret, *Reveille in Washington, 1860–1865*, New York: Harper, 1941

Lessoff, Alan, *The Nation and Its City: Politics, "Corruption," and Progress in Washington, D.C., 1861–1902*, Baltimore: Johns Hopkins University Press, 1994

Whyte, James H., *The Uncivil War: Washington During the Reconstruction, 1865–1878*, New York: Twayne, 1958

Young, James Sterling, *The Washington Community, 1800–1828*, New York: Columbia University Press, 1966

From its founding as part of a political and sectional bargain, Washington, DC – the capital of the United States – has held a peculiar fascination. Over its two centuries of existence, the city has evolved from a swampy backwater of dubious architectural and social distinction to a sprawling urban center with government and public buildings on a heroic scale and a population representing a sweep of values and conditions.

No book adequately covers the full history of Washington down to the present. The best synthesis is GREEN (1962–63). In two dense but readable volumes, the first winning a Pulitzer Prize, she chronicles the city's origin, planning, and development, paying close attention to the erratic relationship between the national government and residents, local humanitarian and cultural attitudes, tensions related to a location on the border between North and South, expansion during periods of war and national crisis, and the challenge to build an infrastructure and to provide social services without compromising aesthetic appeal or moral sensibilities. Personalities assume a lesser role as the city becomes a megalopolis, and the prevailing style of writing mutates from narrative to analytical. On balance, though, Green supplies a wonderful feel for Washington as a place and a community, albeit one cleft along lines of class and race, as well as conveying a strong sense of change over time.

Inspired by her longer work, GREEN (1967) is a more specialized study of the history of race relations in Washington. A black community, initially both free and slave, existed in the area from 1791. While far too often the object of white "discrimination and intolerance," this local black community maintained a vibrancy and identity through the efforts of its own educated and prosperous leaders. Divisions within the black community, however, complicated frictions between black and white. Green's account ends, unfortunately, on the eve of the profound civil rights protests of the mid-1960s, which heralded stark new realities for race relations.

The changing architectural and physical landscape of Washington receives plaintive treatment in GOODE. Life in the city from the 18th century to the 1970s passes in view thanks to hundreds of photographs and accompanying text explaining who designed and constructed a building, how it was used, and why it was razed. Contents include residences, fancy and plain, from every era, and nonresidential structures – government buildings, churches, clubs, stores, offices, theaters, schools, hospitals, transportation centers, and fire stations. There is no better way to take a walking tour of Washington through the decades.

The best histories of Washington have focused on particular periods and people, especially the years before 1900 when colorful characters strode upon a stage that had not yet grown beyond human dimensions. YOUNG looks at the political community of the early 19th century. He endeavors to understand the behavior of "the governing group" – legislators, executives, judges – during the Jeffersonian era by exploring in detail its "inner life and values." By making judicious use of political science approaches and mining published histories, memoirs and correspondence, and travel accounts, Young recreates the early working and leisure world of Washington with the many personal, social, and official rivalries, often based on regional or state identities, within and among legislative, executive, and judicial personnel. His analysis of life in local boardinghouses is particularly illuminating.

The Civil War severely disrupted established social and political patterns in Washington. LEECH provides a grand narrative portrait of these wartime years. President Abraham Lincoln is the dominant character, but his supporting cast of politicians, generals, bureaucrats, and locals is immense. In the finest tradition of narrative history, Leech conveys sights, sounds, and emotions with force and verve, but seldom probes very deeply.

With much less flair, WHYTE takes up the story of Washington after the Civil War. The existence of a territorial government in Washington from 1871 to 1874 – complete with a governor, legislature, and special boards – was a feature of this period. Alexander Shepherd, responsible for using territorial authority to upgrade the city's infrastructure, perhaps to excess, emerges as both hero and villain. Whyte also considers the question of voting for district residents, and the fluid place of blacks in a community coming to grips with constitutional amendments which emancipated slaves, guaranteed due process and equal protection, and secured suffrage for black males.

LESSOFF is an ambitious study that brings the eye of a modern scholar to the same ground covered in Leech and Whyte, while adding excellent chapters on the District Commission, a local governing board established in 1878, that extends the account into the early 20th century. Drawing inspiration from other urban histories, Lessoff focuses on the seemingly mundane construction of streets, curbs, sidewalks, sewers, bridges, and parks to depict relationships among leaders, residents, and taxpayers. Either through interest or lack of interest, the federal government influenced almost everything. Sensitive to indiscretion and scandal, Lessoff finds enough evidence of rascality to warrant a remark about rediscovering "a parcel of long-dead rogues." A lively prose style, sprinkled with irreverence, makes engaging even the inherently dull.

Nothing is dull about JACOB. She portrays a high society in Washington during the second half of the 19th century that flourished despite a diversity of geographical origin and a high rate of population turnover, usually fatal to an aristocratic class. The Civil War displaced the southern elite from the city and opened the way for rich northern and western newcomers, eager to vie for social leadership through ostentatious displays of opulence. The new matrix of social relationships, composed of these newcomers, government officialdom, and old residents, had important political consequences, but Jacob steers clear of politics to delve into the different social factions and groupings among elite whites. This is a revealing, gossipy and sometimes titillating look at the high and mighty in dress and undress.

WILLIAM M. FERRARO

Washington Treaties, 1921–1922

Buckley, Thomas H., *The United States and the Washington Conference, 1921–1922*, Knoxville: University of Tennessee Press, 1970

Dingman, Roger, *Power in the Pacific: The Origins of Naval Arms Limitation, 1914–1922*, Chicago: University of Chicago Press, 1976

Iriye, Akira, *After Imperialism: The Search for a New Order in the Far East, 1921–1931*, Cambridge, MA: Harvard University Press, 1965

Nish, Ian H., *Alliance in Decline: A Study in Anglo-Japanese Relations, 1908–23*, London: Athlone Press, 1972

Vinson, John Chalmers, *The Parchment Peace: The United States Senate and the Washington Conference, 1921–1922*, Athens: University of Georgia Press, 1955

The Washington Conference of 1921–22 has tended to be neglected by recent scholarship. This is unfortunate since the Conference had considerable significance for the inter-war world. As Thomas Buckley argues, Washington was probably the most successful disarmament conference in history, being responsible for the effective long-term limitation of one of the most important contemporary weapons systems. The Conference ranged far beyond naval disarmament, for the Washington treaties codified the conduct of international relations in China, crafted a cosmetic means to end the embarrassing alliance between Britain and Japan and cleared up a number of outstanding issues in the Pacific and east Asia which had been left over from World War I. It was also one of those rare occasions before World War II in which the United States voluntarily played the leading role in world politics. The Washington treaties not only modulated military and political relations between several of the great powers for nearly two decades but the naval treaty shaped the early progress of the Pacific War, after Pearl Harbor.

The only modern general study of the origins and, especially, the course of the Conference is BUCKLEY, which focuses on the role of the United States. Buckley concentrates his attention on naval disarmament, but there is good coverage of the ending of the Anglo-Japanese alliance, and Chinese and other east Asian concerns. It may be supplemented by the rather older work of VINSON who provides an exhaustive account of the Senate's debates, particularly on the Four Power Treaty, a meaningless consultative treaty between the United States, Britain, Japan and France which was the diplomatic device used to camouflage the killing of the Anglo-Japanese alliance.

First and foremost, Washington was a disarmament conference, a point given symbolic force by the decision to postpone its opening for a day to allow for the interment of the American Unknown Soldier at Arlington National Cemetery. The most dangerous phenomenon which the Conference sought to alleviate was the naval rivalry and consequent tensions between the United States and Japan in the Pacific. The best guide to the Pacific naval dimension of the Washington Conference is DINGMAN who, working from British and Japanese as well as American sources, provides a comprehensive and clear picture of the intricacies of Japanese-American naval rivalry in the Pacific and east Asia.

The most dramatic part of the Conference came on the first day when in his opening speech, Charles Evans Hughes, the American secretary of state, put forward a plan to the astonished delegates which would set the relative capital ship strengths of the United States, British and Japanese navies at a ratio of 5:5:3; this proposal entailed scrapping of large numbers of existing warships (or ships under construction) by the three major naval powers. As Buckley and Dingman show, Hughes and the American negotiators pushed their naval disarmament plans to a successful conclusion as much for domestic as for international reasons, hoping to boost the electoral appeal of Warren Harding and the Republican party, by associating them with successful disarmament. At the Conference, Hughes and his colleagues maintained their initial momentum, pushing through the Washington Naval Treaty which set the desired ratios in capital ships for the five major naval powers (which included France and Italy) and, significantly, put a moratorium on the development of naval bases in large parts of the western Pacific. This non-fortification clause of the naval treaty meant that the United States and Britain were unable to build bases within striking distance of Japan.

The immediate origins of the Washington Conference lay in the fate of the Anglo-Japanese alliance which the United States government and public opinion had come to see as a shield behind which Japan extended its position at the expense of China. NISH is the acknowledged authority on that alliance, and his work on its demise provides powerful insights into the American role in ending the Anglo-Japanese alliance. Nish points up the decisive role of the United States in bringing the British government to the decision that the alliance had outlived its usefulness. Nish also details the way in which Washington hijacked the British suggestion for an international conference and made it essentially an American project.

No very recent work focuses specifically upon the Chinese and east Asian dimensions of the Washington Conference, but the treatment of China at Washington and the fate of the so-called Washington system is ably surveyed in IRIYE's study of international relations in east Asia in the 1920s. Iriye describes the creation of the nine power treaty on China at Washington, and chronicles the operation of the treaty provisions, which were essentially a codification of the "open door" policy, during the turbulent 1920s when its principles came under fierce attack from Chinese nationalists, from the Soviet Union and Chinese communists, and finally by the Japanese themselves. Although invoked frequently by the United States in the 1930s, both the Nine Power Treaty and the rest of the Washington framework were killed by Japanese expansionism and Japanese-American alienation after 1931.

DENNIS B. SMITH

See also Hughes; Open Door Policy

Watergate

Ben-Veniste, Richard and George Frampton, Jr., *Stonewall: The Real Story of the Watergate Prosecution*, New York: Simon and Schuster, 1977

Bernstein, Carl and Bob Woodward, *All the President's Men*, New York: Simon and Schuster, and London: Secker and Warburg, 1974

Colodny, Len and Robert Gettlin, *Silent Coup: The Removal of a President*, New York: St. Martin's Press, and London: Gollancz, 1991

Emery, Fred, *Watergate: The Corruption and Fall of Richard Nixon*, London: Cape, 1994

Hougan, Jim, *Secret Agenda: Watergate, Deep Throat and the CIA*, New York: Random House, 1984

Kutler, Stanley I., *The Wars of Watergate: The Last Crisis of Richard Nixon*, New York: Knopf, 1990

Lang, Gladys Engel and Kurt Lang, *The Battle for Public Opinion: The President, the Press and the Polls During Watergate*, New York: Columbia University Press, 1983

Lukas, J. Anthony, *Nightmare: The Underside of the Nixon Years*, New York: Viking, 1976

Schudson, Michael, *Watergate in American Memory: How We Remember, Forget, and Reconstruct the Past*, New York: Basic Books, 1992

Woodward, Bob and Carl Bernstein, *The Final Days*, New York: Simon and Schuster, and London: Secker and Warburg, 1976

Watergate was the most serious constitutional crisis faced by the United States since the Civil War. What began as the obstruction of justice in a trivial burglary case ended up as a direct conflict over fundamental constitutional principles between the executive and the judicial powers, and the resignation of the president in the face of impeachment.

Contemporary reporting still shapes much public perception of the issues and the personalities involved. BERNSTEIN and WOODWARD made folk-heroes out of its authors, not so much for its account of their own assiduous reporting, but as the basis for the film which starred Robert Redford and Dustin Hoffman. The authors had also created a mystery of their own – the identity of their White House source, Deep Throat. Two years later, they were Pulitzer-prize winning celebrities in their own right, and their dramatic reconstruction of the closing months of the administration in WOODWARD and BERNSTEIN still remains valuable, even though it privileges the role of Alexander Haig, and has been challenged in particulars.

The account of LUKAS began life as two full issues of the *New York Times Magazine* (July 1973 and January 1974) on the unfolding crisis. This narrative of what Gerald Ford called "our long national nightmare" was the first to put the burglary and its consequences into the context of an abuse of presidential power that began almost immediately after Nixon took office in January 1969. Building on the reporting of Seymour Hersh, it also raised serious questions about the role of the CIA and its domestic surveillance.

This has proved fertile ground for conspiracy theorists. The most responsible investigation has been that of HOUGAN, who gained access to FBI material that was not available to the Ervin Committee. His identification of Haig as Deep Throat (denied by Haig himself) and his argument that the break-in was a bungled CIA operation to spy on the clients of prostitutes operating out of a neighbouring apartment building have both been taken further by COLODNY and GETTLIN. They

substantiate the personal connections between Woodward and Haig, and they shed more light on the anxieties of the Joint Chiefs of Staff about the Nixon-Kissinger foreign policy and their resultant spying on the National Security Council (the Moorer-Radford affair). However, it was John Dean, they allege, who organized the break-in and cover-up, in order to protect his wife's connection with the call-girl ring.

This all makes for compelling reading, but it ignores the ample evidence in both tapes and memoirs of the political inspiration for the break-in, and Nixon's personal responsibility for the cover-up from its earliest stages. Nor does it explain why Nixon had to face impeachment or resign. Ultimately, the President's fall was determined by the gradual unfolding of the legal process and the concomitant loss of public trust in anything that he had to say on Watergate. BEN-VENISTE and FRAMPTON provide the fullest account of the one constitutional innovation produced by the crisis, the Special Prosecution Force, and they illuminate the technicalities of building a case that would stand up in court, and the legal dilemmas involved in granting immunity in return for evidence.

Right to the end, Nixon treated Watergate as a public relations exercise as much as a political problem or a legal process. LANG and LANG caution against reading too much into the press reporting, or the televisual impact of the Ervin Committee hearings, both of which involved self-selected public participation. Nixon's standing was also affected by foreign affairs (Vietnam, the Middle East and the summit conferences) and the domestic economy. Nonetheless, the spontaneous "firestorm" of protest at the firing of Archibald Cox, the expressions of public disgust at the language of the tapes and the extraordinary viewing figures for the House Judiciary Committee impeachment debate show public opinion acting as an extraconstitutional but legitimating check and balance within the political system, in the manner of James Madison's "second sense of the community".

This is a typically perceptive point made by KUTLER, in what is by far the most comprehensive and balanced treatment of Watergate yet to appear. He sets the crisis in the contexts both of Vietnam and of Nixon's own political career and personal character; and although the Washington *Post* is strikingly absent from this account, Kutler's legal and constitutional emphasis is able to show where the determining opinions were formed, and the crucial decisions were taken, and how the political system responded to a series of wholly unprecedented tests. He makes Nixon's own memoirs very revealing, and demonstrates convincingly that whatever historical revisionism has accompanied the ex-president's campaign for rehabilitation, Watergate remains "the spot that will not out".

Kutler was also the historical consultant for the Brian Lapping Associates' five-part television documentary on Watergate prepared to mark the twentieth anniversary of Nixon's resignation (and, as it turned out, his death). Written by the then London *Times* Washington bureau chief, EMERY is the book of the series. While its claims to the production of new evidence are sometimes exaggerated, it does provide a solid narrative account of the action, and systematically compares the conflicting memoir accounts.

SCHUDSON addresses the ways in which Watergate has been used in American public and political life in the last two decades. It is not very helpful in sorting out the more obvious questions of its impact on political behaviour such as voter participation and attitudes towards government, but it does clarify the processes (such as the institutionalization of the Special Prosecutor, the careers made out of the crisis, and the "lessons" learned from it) which have ensured its continuing presence in American culture. With three thousand hours of tapes still to be made public, the historiography of Watergate has hardly begun.

S.G.F. SPACKMAN

See also Nixon

Wealth

Amory, Cleveland, *Who Killed Society?*, New York: Harper, 1960

Baltzell, E. Digby, *The Protestant Establishment: Aristocracy and Caste in America*, New York: Random House, 1964; London: Secker and Warburg, 1965

Chester, Ronald, *Inheritance, Wealth, and Society*, Bloomington: Indiana University Press, 1982

Jones, Alice Hanson, *Wealth of a Nation to Be: The American Colonies on the Eve of Revolution*, New York: Columbia University Press, 1980

Lapham, Lewis H., *Money and Class in America: Notes and Observations on Our Civil Religion*, New York: Weidenfeld and Nicolson, 1988

Pessen, Edward, *Riches, Class, and Power Before the Civil War*, Lexington, MA: Heath, 1973; as *Riches, Class, and Power: America Before the Civil War*, New Brunswick, NJ: Transaction, 1990

Soltow, Lee, *Men and Wealth in the United States, 1850–1870*, New Haven: Yale University Press, 1975

Williamson, Jeffrey G. and Peter H. Lindert, *American Inequality: A Macroeconomic History*, New York: Academic Press, 1980

Writing on wealth often takes the form of writing on closely allied subjects such as inequality, class, caste, elites and aristocracy. WILLIAMSON and LINDERT provide a good overview of the historical distribution of wealth through their investigation of rates of inequality in wealth-holding since the colonial period. They are very aware of the difficulties in establishing just who owned what, and in what amounts at any period, including the most recent, but conclude that rates of inequality among free Americans before the Revolution were not too different from those of today; that there was increasing inequality between 1820 and 1860; that the Civil War reduced inequality within regions but increased it between North and South; that rates of inequality stabilized between the war and 1900, but increased up to America's entrance into World War I. The war helped redistribute wealth downward, but this trend was reversed in the 1920s. There was notable equalization between 1929 and 1950 and stability thereafter to the point at which they wrote. Latest figures, however, would show that rates of inequality have turned upward again since 1980. The authors discuss the principal variables which, they argue,

correlate with inequality, including technology, demography and capital accumulation. They discuss two associated factors which they argue are often overlooked, immigration and fertility. This is a highly statistical survey but not inaccessible to the non-specialist. There are eleven appendices and a substantial bibliography. The authors deal with the importance of inheritance in a footnote in order to discount it.

CHESTER can be read as an antidote to this view. This is a work of intellectual history, surveying the expressed attitudes of literate elites. It is also mildly polemical, since it has an expressed purpose to help ensure equal starting places for American children. It surveys attitudes toward the inheritance of wealth in western European thought before turning to the United States, where it is very useful in exploring the courts' acceptance of the state's right to tax inheritance, when opponents of this taxation claimed it was an attack on property itself. The chapter on the perpetuation of dynastic trusts is particularly important in showing how both discretionary and support trusts escape taxation. (Discretionary trusts are those where the trustee has absolute discretion on whether to pay anything at all to the beneficiary; support trusts those where the trustee is bound only to provide means to the extent of supporting the beneficiary directly, as opposed to his or her assignees or creditors.) The author argues that the levels of inequality and poverty resulting from the present levels of property distribution are socially expensive, not least in promoting crime. Overall the work is informed by the beliefs of John Stuart Mill who felt that individuals should not inherit unreasonable amounts of wealth.

JONES studies the distribution of wealth in the colonies on the eve of the Revolution, principally in 1774. She applies statistical sampling techniques to probate records and, in an important advance on previous analyses, considers the credits and liabilities of decedents' estates. She concedes that the subject is shrouded in some statistical obscurity, and that the New York material is particularly sparse and difficult to use, but is confident that her estimations may be relied upon. An important chapter analyzes net worth and financial assets and liabilities and shows how the two latter were far more important than cash, in estates. She investigates debtor and creditor classes and overturns the conventional wisdom by showing that the rich owed more than the poor. In all she suggests that during the colonial period wealth inequality grew in the South, as a result of the development of slavery, to such a degree as to outstrip the steady increase in inequality in the Middle and New England colonies.

PESSEN investigates Alexis de Tocqueville's assertion that in the United States of the 1830s most rich men had originally been poor, and finds little cause to agree with it. His basic source is the tax assessment roll, and he studies New York City, Boston, Brooklyn and Philadelphia in the period from 1810 to the Civil War. Since Philadelphia tax records have disappeared, he studies that city differently, using largely qualitative sources like city histories and memoirs. He believes that the incompleteness of wills and probate inventories makes them less useful than tax records. His findings are clear, that there was a high and growing inequality in the "Era of the Common Man," and that few rose or fell great distances. There is no close investigation of who was being taxed at what point in the life cycle, and two crucial assumptions are made about total wealth. The first is that since under-assessment of taxes was rife it is proper to multiply assessment by six; the second is that, since tax assessments hide corporate wealth, which is likely to consist of the investments of the wealthy, 50 per cent of corporate wealth should be assigned to the elite, a figure some may find low. Further refinement of his methods would not, however, seem likely to have produced significantly different conclusions.

SOLTOW uses the manuscript schedules of the 1850, 1860 and 1870 censuses to establish the distribution of wealth in the mid-19th century. The 1850 census surveyed real estate, the latter two real and personal estate. Comparisons by decade are therefore hampered by the lack of figures for personal estate in 1850 and by the abolition of slavery in 1865, for slaves had been counted as property in 1860. Figures are presented for the proportions of total wealth held by each one per cent of the richest ten per cent and by decile thereafter. They are based on random samples of around 10,000 cases in 1850 and 1870 and 13,000 in 1860. Since findings are not correlated with age, they are a little misleading, because individuals can be shown to grow wealthy as they age. Soltow argues that individuals could look for "handsome rates of accumulation of wealth" during a lifetime, though handsome is undefined.

BALTZELL takes as his basic assumption the inevitability of inequality and therefore the fact that some will be richer than others. As befits a Philadelphian from a prominent family whose entry in Who's Who openly admits support for the Democratic party, his attitude to inequality is not particularly unusual. He accepts it but argues that it is the obligation of the wealthy both to lead by example and to admit new members to their class as freely as possible. As long as they do this, they may rightly call themselves an aristocracy, but if they do not they must be termed a caste. His work is a survey of familiar social, cultural and political history, seen from the point of view of the struggle between the two ideas of caste and aristocracy for the soul of the nation's wealthy. Something of his loyalties may be seen in the title of one of the chapters: "The Aristocratic Counterattack on Caste: President Eliot and the two Roosevelts." The work closes with the early 1960s, having been finished at the time of John F. Kennedy's assassination. At the very least it is an interesting defence of wealth in a meritocratic democracy.

LAPHAM is the work of a journalist, twice editor of Harper's magazine. Like Baltzell, the author is a self-confessed member of the United States upper class but he studies what he terms the equestrian class, which might be read as the plutocracy. There are no footnotes in the classic style and the work often reads like a cross between Thorstein Veblen and Gore Vidal, but as this should suggest, when the wit is good it is very good indeed. Both Lapham and Baltzell may be read simultaneously as secondary and primary sources, illuminating the usually obscured world of American wealth.

AMORY falls into the same category. Though completed in 1960 and badly in need of updating, it is an almost encyclopedic introduction to the world of the American rich in the 19th and early 20th centuries. There are no footnotes and the style is highly anecdotal, but the work is the product of a sure-footed analyst of American social conventions when based on wealth and family. It also includes a list of the "Four Hundred" and those American families entitled to a coat of arms. Some

may find this a little too like gossip masquerading as history, but no one wanting to know how the wealthy have behaved can overlook this work.

R.A. BURCHELL

See also Class; Equality; Poverty

Webster, Daniel   1782–1852
Political leader, lawyer, orator and senator

Bartlett, Irving H., *Daniel Webster*, New York: Norton, 1978

Baxter, Maurice G., *Daniel Webster and the Supreme Court*, Amherst: University of Massachusetts Press, 1966

Baxter, Maurice G., *One and Inseparable: Daniel Webster and the Union*, Cambridge, MA: Harvard University Press, 1984

Brown, Norman D., *Daniel Webster and the Politics of Availability*, Athens: University of Georgia Press, 1969

Current, Richard N., *Daniel Webster and the Rise of National Conservatism*, Boston: Little Brown, 1955

Curtis, George Ticknor, *Life of Daniel Webster*, 2 vols., New York: Appleton, 1870

Dalzell, Robert F., Jr., *Daniel Webster and the Trial of American Nationalism, 1843–1852*, Boston: Houghton Mifflin, 1972

Erickson, Paul D., *The Poetry of Events: Daniel Webster's Rhetoric of the Constitution and Union*, New York: New York University Press, 1986

Fuess, Claude M., *Daniel Webster*, 2 vols., Boston: Little Brown, 1930

Jones, Howard, *To the Webster-Ashburton Treaty: A Study in Anglo-American Relations, 1783–1843*, Chapel Hill: University of North Carolina Press, 1977

Nathans, Sydney G., *Daniel Webster and Jacksonian Democracy*, Baltimore: Johns Hopkins University Press, 1973

Peterson, Merrill D., *The Great Triumvirate: Webster, Clay, and Calhoun*, New York: Oxford University Press, 1987

Shewmaker, Kenneth E. (editor), *Daniel Webster, "The Completest Man"*, Hanover, NH: Dartmouth College/University Press of New England, 1990

Daniel Webster's long career in politics, law, and diplomacy, and the contrast between his olympian reputation as champion of the Union and the flaws in his character and personal life, have inspired a wide range of biographical and other studies. Earlier biographies were generally very sympathetic, and often eulogistic. CURTIS was a close friend of Webster, and his literary executor, and his two volumes are a conventional 19th-century "authorized" biography, but much better than many of the kind. Later biographers have drawn heavily upon it. More than half a century later, FUESS, a distinguished New England schoolmaster, produced another very traditional biography on the grand scale. It is a well-written narrative, and includes much valuable detail, but it is almost entirely uncritical of its subject. It looks very dated in the light of modern studies of the political history of the Jacksonian period.

The gap before the publication of major modern biographies was partly filled by CURRENT. His brief study mixes concise narrative with analysis of Webster's conservatism and his nationalism. Through all the phases of Webster's career, Current detects an underlying consistency in political thinking, based on the relationship between property and power, a harmony of interests among various groups and sections in society, active promotion of economic development by the federal government, profound reverence for the Constitution, and staunch defence of the Union.

There are two notable modern biographies of Webster. BARTLETT is the more lively and readable, and looks closely at the relationship between the private and the public man. Bartlett is fascinated by the contrasting images of "Black Dan" and "the God-like Daniel," and he is sometimes tempted into highly speculative psychological explanations of the contradictions in Webster's personality and character. The book is not full enough to give adequate coverage to all aspects of Webster's career, but contains shrewd judgments on many issues, and a thoughtful evaluation of Webster's nationalism.

BAXTER (1984) is a more substantial and comprehensive biography, and the first to profit, in full measure, from the superb Dartmouth College edition of the Webster Papers, under the general editorship of Charles M. Wiltse. This is a sound, thoughtful, if somewhat unexciting, biography, in which Baxter strives, with considerable success, to weave together the various strands of Webster's life – personal, political, diplomatic, legal, and oratorical. This is the most dependable modern study, but cautious rather than searching in its judgments.

Webster also figures, along with Henry Clay and John C. Calhoun, in PETERSON's grand-scale collective biography. This is a detailed and balanced account of the political history of the four decades from 1810 to 1850 when these three near-contemporaries often dominated the scene. Although published as recently as 1987, it is somewhat old-fashioned in both content and approach, and adds little to the understanding of the subject.

Much of the best work on Webster in the last thirty years has been in specialized studies of particular phases or aspects of his career. BROWN examines Webster's vain pursuit of the presidency during the early and mid-1830s, and traces the process through his flirtation with Jackson during the Nullification Crisis (1832–33), his switch to the Clay-Calhoun anti-Jackson alliance, and his futile bid for the presidency in 1836. Brown sees Webster as the victim of the change from the natural progression of "the best men" into the presidency to the selection by party strategists of the "available man." NATHANS develops a similar thesis over a longer period, in a more sustained and penetrating analysis, and in a more critical spirit. He sees not only Webster but a whole generation of political leaders as victims of change in the political climate. He is particularly interesting on the subject of Webster's "anti-partyism." Even while engaged in relentless pursuit of the presidency on a party ticket, he hankered after a return to a situation where harmony of interests, orchestrated by an elite leadership, would remove the need for parties.

This is also one of the themes of DALZELL's illuminating study of the difficult and often disappointing final decade of Webster's life. He argues that Webster's nationalist ideology, articulated in his major speeches, cannot be separated from his everyday political activities and his presidential ambition. More than half of Dalzell's book is devoted to the final two years of Webster's life, and, in particular, to his role in the Compromise of 1850 – above all, his notorious 7 March speech, which brought him such violent condemnation from antislavery New Englanders. Dalzell provides by far the best account and analysis of the closing chapter of Webster's life, when his lifelong commitment to that balance of interests, which he regarded as essential to national unity, was shattered by the destructive force of the slavery issue.

Three other monographs cover diverse aspects of Webster's public life. BAXTER (1966) is a meticulous study of Webster as a great advocate, pleading cases before the Supreme Court. He lists 168 such cases, between 1814 and 1852, and claims that Webster had a decisive influence in the development of the legal rules and constitutional doctrines laid down by the Court in this formative period. JONES is the authoritative study of Webster's major achievement as secretary of state, in negotiating the treaty with Britain which settled the Maine boundary and other outstanding issues. There is no definitive modern study covering both of Webster's two periods as secretary of state.

Webster's reputation has taken some heavy blows in the later 20th century. Even his set-piece oratory, which long survived as one enduring claim to fame, may strike the modern ear as over-elaborate and often ponderous. ERICKSON offers a clear and careful examination of Webster's major speeches, highly laudatory in tone. His grasp of the historical context is often uncertain, and there is no sustained analysis of Webster's impact on his audiences.

SHEWMAKER is the editor of a collection of lively essays based on the papers delivered at a conference to mark the completion of the Webster Papers project. Contributions from Bartlett, Baxter, Current, and Jones provide neat summaries of contemporary scholarly appraisals of Webster. In the spirit of such an occasion, their assessments err on the side of generosity, but are far from uncritical.

PETER J. PARISH

Webster, Noah   1758–1843
Educator, lexicographer and journalist

Andresen, Julie Tetel, *Linguistics in America, 1769–1924: A Critical History*, London and New York: Routledge, 1990

Landau, Sidney I., *Dictionaries: The Art and Craft of Lexicography*, New York: Scribner, 1984; Cambridge: Cambridge University Press, 1989

Monaghan, E. Jennifer, *A Common Heritage: Noah Webster's Blue-Back Speller*, Hamden, CT: Archon, 1983

Rollins, Richard M., *The Long Journey of Noah Webster*, Philadelphia: University of Pennsylvania Press, 1980

Rollins, Richard M. (editor), *The Autobiographies of Noah Webster, from the Letters and Essays, Memoir and Diary*, Columbia: University of South Carolina Press, 1989

Shoemaker, Ervin C., *Noah Webster, Pioneer of Learning*, New York: Columbia University Press, 1936

Warfel, Harry R., *Noah Webster, Schoolmaster to America*, New York: Macmillan, 1936

Wood, Gordon S., *The Creation of the American Republic, 1776–1787*, Chapel Hill: University of North Carolina Press, 1969

Noah Webster had a very long and varied career that encompassed politics, journalism, education, and lexicography. A young man during the American Revolution, he lived until the mid-19th century and was both a witness to, and a participant in, a vast expanse of early American history. Traditionally under-appreciated by most cultural and political historians who, like so many others, consider only the dictionary that bears his name, Webster's achievements and activities were numerous. His spelling book was one of the best-selling books ever, and his ability to make a living on its proceeds made him one of the few authors of that time to subsist on writing alone. His activities in local politics and his early but quickly fading influence in early national politics are important aspects that should not be neglected.

The dictionary which Webster laboured on for many years was largely "corrected" by his son-in-law after his death. While his definitions are outstanding and today are widely respected as such, both his etymology and the theory of linguistics which backed them up largely disappeared after his death. In fact, the huge success of his dictionary had more to do with clever marketing by his publishers for its "American-ness" than with its quality or uniqueness. In general, it is difficult to find a book that can successfully encompass the breadth and complexity of Webster's life without becoming fixated on Webster the person. Accounts vary from rapturous praise to bitter iconoclasm, and this makes a balanced assessment difficult.

The most popular starting point for study of Webster has often been WARFEL. His enthusiastic and unreferenced book lies within the genre of historiography that seeks to describe "Great Men and their Deeds," and it would not make a very good academic introduction to Webster's life. Its very readable style does provide an entertaining account of Webster's achievements that has provoked and informed many subsequent accounts. The uncritical nature of most of the book hinders its wider utility. Despite these problems, Warfel remains useful because he draws on some 19th-century sources which are now hard to track down, and he remains a pleasure to read.

SHOEMAKER is contemporary with Warfel and shares many of the same methodological weaknesses of historical biography at that time. This book, while presenting Webster in the most favourable light possible, does manage at times to separate itself from the subject in a somewhat more critical manner. Particularly useful is the attempt to connect Webster's pedagogic theories to the wider 18th-century milieu. Scholarly and somewhat dry, the book is of most interest to those with an interest in 18th-century linguistic and educational theories. It is also very useful for its extensive use of examples from primary sources.

One modern revisionist scholar has focused intensively on Webster's life. ROLLINS (1980) is a stark, psychological portrait of Webster which seeks to show that Webster ended his life bitter and disillusioned, having abandoned all that motivated him in his earlier years. It is valuable for its description of the major events of Webster's life, and his relation to the society around him. The psychoanalytical approach adopted by Rollins is much less useful than the material it presents. ROLLINS (1989) continues this revisionist approach, using valuable and extensive excerpts from Webster's letters, diaries and autobiography. Again Rollins seems intent on showing Webster as a bitter old man who failed in his life goals. The book is particularly weak in its presentation of Webster's business and family activities.

A most welcome corrective to Rollins's 1980 account is MONAGHAN. Her book is particularly valuable, as the title suggests, on Webster's speller, which as she points out, was actually a primary reader. The influence of the "speller," and Webster's intermittent acumen as an entrepreneur are extensively covered in a readable and well-referenced study. However, Monaghan is much less convincing on Webster's lexicographical and political endeavours, and ignores completely the difficulties he was to have with one of his editors, Joseph Worcester. She is excellent on Webster's orthography and the wider intellectual basis on which it rested. Her descriptions of its broader implications are especially well done. Particularly welcome is her account of Webster's relationship with his immediate family, although a wider coverage of his son-in-law Chauncey Goodrich might have helped. All in all, this book is the most illuminating study of Webster as an individual.

The context of Webster's lexicographical efforts is explored in LANDAU. In particular his coverage of the "War of the Dictionaries" is concise and instructive, particularly for his references to further sources. Drawing on his extensive lexicographical experience, he also presents very clearly the social and political questions that lexicographers must encounter.

Webster's contributions to American linguistics are well covered in ANDRESEN. Her attempt to see Webster as part of an American linguistic tradition is particularly welcome. She provides a good account of Webster's intellectual and political dispute with Thomas Jefferson, although she is rather too fixated on Webster's character flaws. Her thoughtful coverage of Webster's linguistic efforts demonstrates, among other things, his dependence on English scholars such as Horne Tooke.

A good but brief introduction to Webster's political beliefs may be found in WOOD. His mammoth and authoritative study sets Webster's political contributions in a wider American context. Of course, Wood is dealing with a very much broader subject, but he is very helpful in drawing attention to Webster's political importance, which is often overlooked.

DAVID J. MIKOSZ

Weld, Theodore Dwight 1813–1895

Abolitionist

Abzug, Robert H., *Passionate Liberator: Theodore Dwight Weld and the Dilemma of Reform*, New York: Oxford University Press, 1980

Barnes, Gilbert Hobbs, *The Antislavery Impulse, 1830–1844*, New York: Appleton Century, 1933

Lesick, Lawrence Thomas, *The Lane Rebels: Evangelicalism and Antislavery in Antebellum America*, Metuchen, NJ: Scarecrow Press, 1980

Lumpkin, Katharine Du Pré, *The Emancipation of Angelina Grimké*, Chapel Hill: University of North Carolina Press, 1974

Merrill, Walter McIntosh, *Against Wind and Tide: A Biography of William Lloyd Garrison*, Cambridge, MA: Harvard University Press, 1963

Thomas, Benjamin P., *Theodore Weld: Crusader for Freedom*, New Brunswick, NJ: Rutgers University Press, 1950

For many years, Theodore Weld was the forgotten man of the abolitionist movement. Much of this was his own doing. Throughout his career, Weld endeavoured to avoid the limelight. His published writings were sporadic and unsigned. Although Weld's reputation has long since been resuscitated, those who seek to study him are in no danger of being deluged by the volume of available material. Those works which do exist concentrate equally on aspects of his political and personal life.

BARNES attempted to lift Weld from his self-imposed obscurity, and restore him to his rightful place in history. Contrary to what was then conventional wisdom, he questions the influence which William Lloyd Garrison and his associates in New England exerted over the abolitionist movement as a whole. Garrison is portrayed as an insensitive individual, lacking real leadership qualities, who did less to attract new supporters than he did to alienate existing ones. Long eclipsed by Garrison, Weld's star begins, by contrast, to shine brilliantly through the pages of the book. His involvement in abolitionism is attributed to his conversion by revivalist preacher Charles Grandison Finney, who argued that man achieved his own salvation through acts of "disinterested benevolence" towards others. Despite the uncertainties of his own mentor, Weld saw in this doctrine the need to champion the cause of enslaved African Americans. Attention is focused on his work as a field agent for the American Anti-Slavery Society in Ohio, Vermont, western Pennsylvania and New York. Barnes asserts that Weld's talents were inspirational rather than organizational. His genius lay in the ability "to make missionaries of his converts", encouraging in them the impulse to spread the word through the establishment of their own abolitionist societies and newspapers. Groundbreaking as Barnes was, it is too cruel in its characterization of Garrison, and too kind in its championing of Weld.

Nonetheless, Barnes left an important legacy. Although future historians might refute the idea that Weld had a greater influence on abolitionism than Garrison, they would have been foolish to ignore him altogether. MERRILL is a clear example. His biography of Garrison includes an entire chapter on Weld. Merrill depicts the differences between the two men by emphasizing the contrast in both their appearances and their personalities. Where Garrison was dapper, Weld was dishevelled; where one was self-righteous, the other was self-effacing. Their personalities reflected their politics, as their politics reflected their personalities. Merrill neatly distinguishes the differing philosophies of the two abolitionists. Both men believed that abolition should begin immediately: for Garrison, on a universal scale; for Weld, on a gradual basis.

Although it was Barnes who first outlined the influence of Charles Finney over abolitionists such as Weld, it is LESICK who offers the fullest appraisal. The slavery debates organized by Weld while he was a student at Lane Seminary are one example. As Lesick intriguingly reveals, the debates took the form of one of Finney's revivalist meetings. It is insights such as this which make Lesick an indispensable source for the Weld scholar.

There are only two biographical studies which focus entirely on Weld. It was seventeen years after the publication of Barnes that the first biography of the abolitionist appeared. THOMAS adopts a similar vein in placing revivalist-based abolitionism at the vanguard of the movement. The insights which it offers into Weld the man add richer shades to the rather sketchy portrait painted by Barnes. Nonetheless, it is not a complete picture. The formative experiences which helped to shape Weld receive only cursory analysis. His growing from infancy to mid-adolescence is disposed of within the first three pages.

ABZUG attempts to restore the balance. Psychoanalytical in approach, it suggests that Weld's career was shaped in response to his troubled experiences as a child. Growing up in a competitive household, Weld struggled to gain the attentions of his Calvinist father. Weld's entire adult life was a quest for emotional security, an attempt to resolve his ambivalent feelings about paternal authority. Intriguing as this emphasis on personal experience is, it does not always convince. The only source available on Weld's childhood is his own recollection of it, made as an old man. This lack of empirical evidence occasionally leads Abzug to somewhat speculative conclusions. It is also too insular an argument. In stressing the uniqueness of Weld's individual experience, Abzug overlooks the larger social and political forces which simultaneously led so many like-minded Americans to organize an antislavery movement in the 1830s. Nonetheless, the book is still by far the richest work available on Weld.

LUMPKIN offers an altogether uglier image of Weld than the one projected by Abzug. In a revealing analysis of his marriage to fellow abolitionist Angelina Grimké, she suggests that Weld was not so much tormented, as tormentor. Weld believed that self-abnegation was the only sure way to godly perfection. His rejection of public office and refusal to have his writings published were a reflection of this position. When Weld suspected others of courting public attention, he was unsparing in his criticism. Despite his supposed support for sexual equality, Weld attacked Grimké when she spoke on women's rights, rather than concentrating exclusively on slavery. Not until she had learned, like him, to suppress self-seeking ambition, should she return to public speaking. In crushing the confidence of his wife, Lumpkin persuasively argues, Weld robbed the abolitionists of one of their most articulate and effective speakers.

CLIVE WEBB

See also Abolitionism; Grimké

Wells-Barnett, Ida B. 1862–1931

Campaigner for racial justice and women's rights

Duster, Alfreda M. (editor), *Crusade for Justice: The Autobiography of Ida B. Wells*, Chicago: University of Chicago Press, 1970

Grossman, James R., *Land of Hope: Chicago, Black Southerners, and the Great Migration*, Chicago: University of Chicago Press, 1989

Hendricks, Wanda, "Wells-Barnett, Ida Bell," in *Black Women in America: An Historical Encyclopedia*, edited by Darlene Clark Hine and others, 2 vols., New York: Carlson, 1993

Holt, Thomas, "The Lonely Warrior: Ida B. Wells-Barnett and the Struggle for Black Leadership," in *Black Leaders of the Twentieth Century*, edited by John Hope Franklin and August Meier, Urbana: University of Illinois Press, 1992

Kellogg, Charles Flint, *NAACP: A History of the National Association for the Advancement of Colored People*, volume 1: *1909–1920*, Baltimore: Johns Hopkins Press, 1967

Spear, Allan H., *Black Chicago: The Making of a Negro Ghetto, 1890–1920*, Chicago: University of Chicago Press, 1967

Thompson, Mildred I., *Ida B. Wells-Barnett: An Exploratory Study of an American Black Woman, 1893–1930*, New York: Carlson, 1990

Thornbrough, Emma Lou, *T. Thomas Fortune, Militant Journalist*, Chicago: University of Chicago Press, 1972

Zangrando, Robert L., *The NAACP Crusade Against Lynching, 1909–1950*, Philadelphia: Temple University Press, 1980

A pioneering black feminist, educator, social worker and outspoken critic of lynching, Ida B. Wells (born a slave in Holly Springs, Mississippi), also campaigned against racial segregation and the disfranchisement of African-Americans. At the Chicago World's Columbian Exposition in 1893, she protested against the exclusion of blacks (apart from Haitians) from its displays, and circulated 10,000 copies of an acerbic pamphlet, *The Reason Why the Colored American Is Not in the Colombian Exposition* – in her own words, "a clear, plain statement of the facts concerning the oppression put upon the colored people in this land of the free and home of the brave." In 1895, she married Ferdinand L. Barnett, owner of the *Chicago Conservator* and a strong advocate of racial equality. An accomplished journalist and debater, she was a fierce critic of Booker T. Washington's accommodationism, a supporter of Marcus Garvey, a founder of the National Association of Colored Women in 1896, and one of the two black women who signed the call which resulted in the formation of the National Association for the Advancement of Colored People (NAACP) in 1909.

Wells-Barnett has yet to be accorded a major biography, but THOMPSON provides a well-documented and engaging account – originally presented as a Ph.D. dissertation in 1979 – which traces Wells-Barnett's public career and stresses "the relationship between her declining influence and the increasing significance of organizational powers in the black community," together with a judicious selection of her essays.

Wells-Barnett's uncompleted memoirs were edited nearly forty years after her death, by her daughter, DUSTER, who also assisted Thompson with her research. An invaluable source on the life and times of a remarkable critic of racial and economic injustice, this posthumously published autobiography reveals the public and private faces of its protagonist. There are graphic accounts of Wells's early life in rural Mississippi, her association with Timothy Thomas Fortune, editor of the New York *Age*, lecture tours across the United States and in Europe, and associations with such luminaries as Frederick Douglass, Booker T. Washington, W.E.B. Du Bois, and the African American bishops Henry McNeal Turner and Alexander Walters. Several chapters describe her two visits to Britain, in 1892 and 1894, where she helped to organize the British Anti-Lynching Society and, on the second occasion, criticized British supporters of the African American cause for addressing racially segregated audiences, and for their ambivalent pronouncements on lynching. Wells-Barnett's assertiveness, inability to tolerate criticism and seemingly boundless egotism also emerge from the pages of this carefully-edited memoir. For example, she reflects that had Marcus Garvey listened to her advice concerning the problems involved in launching a shipping company – the ill-fated Black Star Line – "he need not have undergone the humiliations which afterward became his." In Duster's view, her mother would "be remembered most for her fight against the lynching of Negroes, and for her passionate demand for justice and fair play for them." Most remarkable, however, was the fact that she opposed lynching and other outrages inflicted on African Americans "with the single-mindedness of a crusader, long before men or women of any race entered the arena."

In her judicious biography of journalist T. Thomas Fortune, THORNBROUGH records that he assisted Wells when she was forced to leave Memphis, after denouncing a multiple lynching, and his enormous admiration for a woman "who showed courage and ability." Wells-Barnett's conflicts with members of the NAACP – her resentment "of the patronizing assumptions of the academic few who wanted to keep the organization in their own hands" – are recounted by KELLOGG in his history of the early years of this interracial protest movement.

Wells-Barnett's activities in Chicago as the "leading militant" in the Afro-American Council, involvement in local politics, and relations with the white reformer Jane Addams in social settlement work, are duly noted by SPEAR, who typifies Wells-Barnett as a racial "militant long before militancy found a national spokesman in W.E.B. Du Bois," and a "natural leader" of those opposed to Booker T. Washington's perceived conservatism. More recently, in his excellent analysis of African American migration to Chicago, GROSSMAN mentions Wells-Barnett's assistance to black migrants through the Negro Fellowship League (before its efforts were eclipsed by those of the better-funded Chicago chapter of the National Urban League, and the black YMCA), and notes "her feminism and refusal to take a back seat to male leadership, and her apparently abrasive personality."

Wells-Barnett's impassioned denunciations of and campaigns against lynching – or what she called "color line murder" – receive passing notice in ZANGRANDO's important book. HOLT's incisive essay offers a succinct account of the life of a "Lonely Warrior" and suggests that the "turning point in her career" came in 1892, after the lynching of three of her friends who had operated a "People's Grocery" on the outskirts of Memphis. When she later exposed the myth that most lynchings of African American men occurred because of their (alleged) rape of white women – and suggested obliquely that white women might well be attracted to black men – Wells-Barnett could no longer live safely in the South. Holt argues plausibly that, although she is usually seen as an implacable opponent of Booker T. Washington, Wells-Barnett actually shared his emphasis on self-help and economic accumulation, but saw economic power "not as a reward achieved by accommodating to the status quo, but [as] a weapon to use against it." Concerning the often bitter and disillusioned reflections in her memoirs, Holt suggests that these could be dismissed "as the carpings of a disappointed sexagenarian, except that the rejections she described were real enough, even though her interpretations of them were not necessarily valid." Her repeated public exposure of lynching was, Holt observes, the tactic eventually adopted by the organization about which she became so disillusioned – the NAACP.

HENDRICKS adopts a slightly less critical approach in an informative profile which provides some detail on her subject's childhood experiences, precocious reading habits, early forays into journalism (under the pen name "Lola") and subsequent crusade against lynching. Hendricks also notes Wells-Barnett's engagement in the women's suffrage movement and, notably, her refusal to march with African American delegates in the National American Woman Suffrage Association's parade in Washington DC in 1913. Instead, she joined her white colleagues in the Illinois delegation – an action which "successfully integrated the suffrage movement" in America. Wells-Barnett, Hendricks concludes, was not only a major reformer, but also "one of the first Black leaders to link the oppression and exploitation of African Americans to white economic opportunity." Both Hendricks and Holt include useful bibliographies of references to and selected works by Ida B. Wells-Barnett – who, as John Hope Franklin has remarked – was "for more than forty years one of the most fearless and one of the most respected women in the United States."

JOHN WHITE

See also African American History: 1870s–1954 entries

Westward Expansion

Billington, Ray Allen, *Westward Expansion: A History of the American Frontier*, New York: Macmillan, 1949, 5th edition, with Martin Ridge, 1982
Cronon, William, *Changes in the Land: Indians, Colonists, and the Ecology of New England*, New York: Hill and Wang, 1983
Jeffrey, Julie Roy, *Frontier Women: The Trans-Mississippi West, 1840–1880*, New York: Hill and Wang, 1979
Limerick, Patricia Nelson, *The Legacy of Conquest: The Unbroken Past of the American West*, New York: Norton, 1987
Rohrbough, Malcolm J., *The Trans-Appalachian Frontier: People, Societies, and Institutions, 1775–1850*, New York: Oxford University Press, 1978
Unruh, John D., Jr., *The Plains Across: The Overland Emigrants and the Trans-Mississippi West, 1840–1860*, Urbana: University of Illinois Press, 1979
Weber, David J., *The Mexican Frontier, 1821–1846: The American Southwest under Mexico*, Albuquerque: University of New Mexico Press, 1982
White, Richard, *"It's Your Misfortune and None of My Own": A New History of the American West*, Norman: University of Oklahoma Press, 1991

For generations the basis of American history rested with the idea that westward expansion into successive frontier regions had determined the settlement of the North American continent, and shaped the character of American society. Historian Frederick Jackson Turner became the primary exponent of this belief, and among his later disciples, BILLINGTON remained a persistent advocate of the formative influence of the frontier process. Land and opportunity attracted pioneers into each new frontier – colonial, trans-Appalachian, and trans-Mississippi – and these settings determined the boundaries of development. Consequently, these frontiers also define the categories of Billington's history as he discusses elements of settlement activity in each region. This book orginally appeared in 1949, and Billington studiously revised and updated each subsequent edition, including the extensive and impressive bibliography. The fifth edition, with RIDGE as coauthor, is again updated but still reveals Turner's influence in determining the book's conception of westward expansion.

ROHRBOUGH's work reflects Turner's lingering presence, especially in his use of terms, but demonstrates the changing views of historians who study migration and settlement. Interested in how societies and institutions developed in the region between the Appalachian Mountains and the Mississippi River, Rohrbough shows that "frontier people were generally less concerned with democracy (whether political or economic) than they were with the acquisition and protection of property." Arriving in a place, pioneers sought security first, then stability. To establish their permanent institutions, he argues, people relied on "shared values and priorities" as well as models from older societies. The population also shared an interest in generating commerce, and Rohrbough believes that, in this period, only Florida, Michigan, and Arkansas remained isolated and outside the range of "economic prosperity" longer than other areas.

Relying on Turnerian definitions, historians equated westward expansion with the advance of civilization, and this notion of progress justified exploiting natural resources and displacing Native Americans. Proponents of a "new" western history, however, view the experience differently. To consider the impact of human influence on the landscape, CRONON examines the "process of ecological change that followed the Europeans' arrival" in New England. This is not to assume, he notes, that Native Americans existed in a virgin wilderness. They had already altered the land to their way of living, and

Europeans modified the ecosystem to suit themselves. From the European perspective, New England represented abundance, particularly in resources that had become scarce in Europe. Unfortunately, argues Cronon, colonists "assumed the limitless availability of more land to exploit," and using resources as marketable commodities, they became "ecologically self-destructive." Native Americans soon entered the European economic nexus and, as a consequence, was disrupted every aspect of their lives. The result of their participation, says Cronon, left them victims "to disease, a demographic collapse, economic dependency, and the loss of a world of ecological relationships they could never find again."

This emphasis on the consequences of settling North America represents one of LIMERICK's concerns in her influential and provocative study. The frontier as defined by Turner, she asserts, negates the West as a place and fixes it in time so that its history becomes only a nostalgic past in the popular mind. The western experience, counters Limerick, produced a "legacy of conquest" that still exists. A positive image of brave pioneers subduing savages or winning California to fulfill their Manifest Destiny, for example, ignores the poverty facing many Native Americans and Hispanics in parts of the West today. An engaging writer, Limerick presents new ways to think about the West and its history.

Agreeing with Limerick, WHITE views the American West "as a product of conquest and of the mixing of diverse groups of people." His study represents a synthesis of the changing ideas about western history and offers an alternative to Billington's traditional approach. Like Cronon, White considers the ecological and social impact of Europeans in North America. The advent of horses and weapons, for example, disrupted tribal balances and altered alliances among Native Americans. He also refutes the popular, though often rhetorical, belief that westerners were "beholden to no one" in developing their region. Instead, writes White, the federal government "guided and molded" western settlement by sponsoring scientific exploration, building transportation networks, subjugating and controlling native tribes, and distributing land. The effort necessitated that government become more centralized and powerful, while it created federal bureaucracies that continue to be fixtures in the modern-day West. White's concern with 20th-century issues in the West, such as debates about controlling water or energy, demonstrates changing impressions about the region's history.

Most historical perceptions about westward expansion have stemmed from an Anglo-American perspective, but WEBER reminds his readers that the borderlands region of the American West had once been another country. Examining events from the Mexican viewpoint, he discusses the development of the Santa Fe trade, the impact of an Anglo-American presence in California and Texas, and the Texas Revolution. The frontier of northern Mexico, notes Weber, suffered from Indian threats, a weak government, economic difficulties, quarrels between church and state, and intrigues by military leaders. Even worse, the Mexican government ignored the region until sensing that settlers from the United States posed a threat.

One of many fine histories about women in the West, JEFFREY's book considers the experience of "young married women who made up the bulk of adult female emigrants." Westward migration, she says, threatened standards of domesticity. Pioneer life allowed women to take part in making decisions and regain "economic importance" within the subsistence economy of the frontier. Women also brought institutions (schools and churches) to developing communities and understood their role in doing so. In Wyoming, Jeffrey points out, the legislature granted women's suffrage in order to attract "responsible" settlers and counter lawless elements.

In the popular mind, western expansion has been symbolized by a train of covered wagons moving along the Oregon-California trail. Writing the definitive statement on the history of overland migration, UNRUH discusses motives for migrating, public attitudes about wagon travel, interaction among emigrants, and relations with Native Americans. Among his conclusions, Unruh shows that because emigrants treated Indians along the trail "with suspicion and distrust," travelers provoked depredations and killed more Indians than vice versa. This fear of hostile tribes invoked demands for military protection which initiated and increased the federal presence in the West.

J. THOMAS MURPHY

Whig Party

Bartlett, Irving H., *Daniel Webster*, New York: Norton, 1978

Benson, Lee, *The Concept of Jacksonian Democracy: New York as a Test Case*, Princeton: Princeton University Press, 1961

Carwardine, Richard J., *Evangelicals and Politics in Antebellum America*, New Haven: Yale University Press, 1993

Cooper, William J., Jr., *The South and the Politics of Slavery, 1828–1856*, Baton Rouge: Louisiana State University Press, 1978

Gienapp, William E., *The Origins of the Republican Party, 1852–1856*, New York: Oxford University Press, 1987

Holt, Michael F., *The Political Crisis of the 1850s*, New York: Wiley, 1978

Howe, Daniel Walker, *The Political Culture of the American Whigs*, Chicago: University of Chicago Press, 1979

Remini, Robert V., *Henry Clay: Statesman for the Union*, New York: Norton, 1991

Sellers, Charles, *The Market Revolution: Jacksonian America, 1815–1846*, New York: Oxford University Press, 1991

Wallace, Anthony F.C., *Rockdale: The Growth of an American Village in the Early Industrial Revolution*, New York: Knopf, 1978

Watson, Harry L., *Jacksonian Politics and Community Conflict: The Emergence of the Second American Party System in Cumberland County, North Carolina*, Baton Rouge: Louisiana State University Press, 1981

The antebellum Whig party has provided fertile ground for historians seeking explanations not only for the coming of the American Civil War but also for the triumph of commercial and industrial capitalism in the middle decades of the 19th century. Although we still lack a convincing general survey of the party, topics such as Whig ideology, leadership, and policies have provided the focus of several important books. These include HOWE, a thoughtful biographical exploration of Whig political culture which rejects the traditional view that the party was largely devoid of principles. Whiggery, argues Howe, was essentially a vehicle for bourgeois interests (broadly defined). Its objectives were ordered social and economic development and the attainment of a disciplined and morally upright republic. Howe's sympathetic interpretation of Whiggery is rejected by SELLERS, a controversial and polemical book which depicts the Whigs as purveyors of an intolerant Protestant morality and the corrosive values of modern industrial capitalism. Sellers's allegedly countercultural distaste for Whiggery and fondness for Jacksonian Democracy frequently blind him to the latter's faults and the former's virtues.

CARWARDINE is an elegant account of the impact of evangelical Protestantism on antebellum politics. It highlights the extent to which Whiggery was grounded in the dominant subculture of the day, and furnishes plentiful evidence on the way in which Whig politicians appealed to evangelical voters during the presidential campaigns of the 1840s. Its nuanced and sophisticated depiction of Whig political culture is a refreshing contrast to the rather crude, reductionist approach – to Whiggery and religion – contained in Sellers.

A number of excellent state and local studies furnish further insights into Whiggery. These include BENSON, a pioneering and hugely influential "ethnocultural" interpretation of New York politics, which depicts Whigs as advocates of a "positive liberal state," in which government was perceived as an essential tool of moral and material progress. Although the book lacks a convincing analysis of grassroots confessional allegiances, it suggests that ethnic and religious conflicts lay close to the heart of party politics in antebellum America.

More sophisticated is WATSON, a pathbreaking account of Jacksonian-era politics in Cumberland County, North Carolina, which has contributed significantly to the developing Market Revolution synthesis. Watson asserts that the bulk of support for the Whig party was located in Fayetteville where local merchants led the fight for banks and internal improvements. The finding that urban Whigs spearheaded capitalist progress in North Carolina, however, needs to be balanced by an awareness that Whigs also drew significant support from the undeveloped and rural western counties of the state. WALLACE attempts to demonstrate how a group of Whig textile entrepreneurs transformed the economy and society of Rockdale, a small village in southeast Pennsylvania. A splendidly detailed and evocative community study which draws heavily on the techniques of social and historical anthropology, it links support for Whiggery with the evangelical Protestant drive for "a Christian, capitalist nation" dedicated to manufacturing and progress, and inhabited by free men equipped with the tools to compete successfully in the race of life. Unfortunately the book is deeply flawed by an alarming lack of persuasive evidence to support the central thesis that antebellum Rockdale was the scene of a fateful struggle between Whiggish industrialists and secular supporters of the rational Enlightenment.

Southern Whiggery is best approached through COOPER. Controversial in some quarters for its insistence on the pre-eminence of the slavery question, it contends that southern Whigs were able to compete effectively with the Democrats only by depicting themselves as the staunchest defenders of southern rights within the Union. Although this lucid study lacks a convincing discussion of the socioeconomic basis of Whiggery below the Mason-Dixon line, its contention that growing sectional tensions played a key role in destroying the party as a viable national force is incontestable.

REMINI is the fullest modern biography of Henry Clay, the foremost Whig statesman of the age. Encylopedic in length and focusing entirely on high politics, it depicts the famous slaveholding nationalist as a flawed genius. Clay's great strengths, it is convincingly argued, were his rhetorical skills, his mastery of parliamentary tactics and his devotion to the Union. His weaknesses were his political ambition, his lack of the popular touch, his reputation as a conniving and immoral politician, and his inability to win the confidence of northern antislavery Whigs. BARTLETT is the most accessible life of Daniel Webster, the Massachusetts politician who vied with Clay for leadership of the Whig party during the late 1830s and 1840s. Less scholarly in tone than Remini, it nonetheless highlights the complexities of Webster's character and provides a convincing analysis of his celebrated Unionism.

Holt and Gienapp are essential reading for anyone attempting to understand why the Whig party disappeared so quickly in the 1850s after proving so competitive in the previous decade. Rejecting Cooper's emphasis on the slavery issue, HOLT's characteristically bravura contention is that the Whig party collapsed primarily because it failed to convince American voters of its relevance – specifically, that it could protect the republic from cultural and political degradation at the hands of foreign-born Roman Catholic immigrants. GIENAPP shares Holt's view that nativism was the chief cause of the Whigs' collapse and provides in-depth quantitative and qualitative analysis of the party's demise in the North. This book also contains the most reliable account of the 1852 presidential election – the last contest in which the Whigs fought as a trans-sectional political organization.

ROBERT COOK

White, William Allen 1868–1944
Newspaper editor and political commentator

Crunden, Robert M., *Ministers of Reform: The Progressives' Achievement in American Civilization, 1889–1920*, New York: Basic Books, 1982

Griffith, Sally Foreman, *Home Town News: William Allen White and the Emporia Gazette*, New York: Oxford University Press, 1989

Jernigan, E. Jay, *William Allen White*, Boston: Twayne, 1983

Johnson, Walter, *William Allen White's America*, New York: Holt, 1947

McKee, John DeWitt, *William Allen White: Maverick on Main Street*, Westport, CT: Greenwood Press, 1975

Quandt, Jean B., *From the Small Town to the Great Community: The Social Thought of Progressive Intellectuals*, New Brunswick, NJ: Rutgers University Press, 1970

Rich, Everett, *William Allen White: The Man from Emporia*, New York: Farrar and Rinehart, 1941

White, William Allen, *The Autobiography of William Allen White*, New York: Macmillan, 1946; edited by Sally Foreman Griffith, Lawrence: University Press of Kansas, 1990

Chameleon-like, William Allen White's reputation has varied over the years, revealing as much about the changing attitudes of his biographers as about the multi-faceted man himself. RICH is the earliest scholarly biography, by a teacher at a local college in Emporia, Kansas – the home town that White made famous as a symbol for small-town America. Written when White was well-known throughout the United States and Europe as the chairman of the Committee to Defend America by Aiding the Allies, which helped swing public opinion behind the Lend-Lease Act, it presents his life as the embodiment of American virtues of optimism, decency and pragmatism. Setting a pattern followed by all later biographers, Rich treats White as both an exemplary individual and a representative American. His narrative of White's life depicts the sweep of American history between the Civil War and World War II – his childhood in frontier Kansas, his youth in the heady days of Gilded Age speculation, his early manhood as participant in Progressive reform movements and supporter of American entry into World War I, to his later years as world traveller and bemused but mellowed observer of the passing scene in the 1920s and 1930s. As a professor of literature, Rich is often insightful in his treatment of White's novels and short stories.

JOHNSON is the most substantial biography, offering greatest detail on White's more than fifty years as a Republican political insider. A diplomatic historian, Johnson is most interested in identifying the circumstances that produced a midwestern Republican who was willing to challenge effectively his region's and party's isolationism in the late 1930s. Like many New Deal liberals, Johnson is critical of White's emphasis upon moral rather than environmental reform, and his refusal to abandon the Republican party in the 1930s. He concludes that White was "a strange mixture of broad, kindly tolerance and small, narrow provincialism – a composite American."

Subsequent historians have shown greater interest in White's contributions as a writer of fiction and non-fiction, particularly his brilliance as a political commentator, and his leading role in the Progressive movement. Both Crunden and Quandt have included White among a distinguished cast of Progressive intellectuals. QUANDT analyzes White's ideas about community, a significant preoccupation of the period. An intellectual historian, she sometimes overlooks important distinctions between White's more ephemeral, journalistic purposes and those of philosophers like John Dewey. CRUNDEN argues that progressivism was "a climate of creativity" that united several generations of writers and artists who shared similar Protestant backgrounds and a commitment to a democratic civil religion.

JERNIGAN presents an overview of White's life, then provides a synopsis and brief analysis of White's major publications. McKEE is a readable, shorter biography that focuses on White's adroit use of all means to "make his private opinion public opinion." It adds little new information or interpretation. Like Johnson, he tends to become embroiled in fruitless debates over whether White should be classified as a liberal or conservative.

GRIFFITH, on the other hand, argues that White's ideas can best be understood as rooted in a 19th-century American tradition of community-building boosterism that predates 20th-century definitions of liberalism. Her account does not attempt to cover every aspect of White's life, but focuses upon his life-long role as editor and publisher of a small-town newspaper, the Emporia *Gazette*. By placing White's career in journalism within the context of a social history of Emporia, Griffith paints a detailed portrait of small-town life in turn-of-the-century America. She uses White's life to illustrate the sweeping social and cultural transformations of the period, as major economic and technological changes, especially in communications and the media, substantially altered both politics and community life.

None of these studies of White, nor many other historical accounts of the period, could have been written without extensive quotations from White's own writings. Most significantly, WHITE bears inclusion here because it is a classic work of American autobiography and still one of the best descriptions available of the many-sided Progressive era. Reflecting upon his experiences from the Olympian perspective of the early years of World War II, he offers a largely accurate and highly evocative account of his first fifty years, including dramatic narratives of significant political events such as the formation of the Progressive Party in 1912 and vivid first-hand portraits of many of the leading political and literary figures of his time. Considered in terms of literary merit, White's self-portrait surpasses that of any of his biographers.

SALLY FOREMAN GRIFFITH

See also Newspapers and Magazines; Progressivism

Whitney, Eli 1765–1825
Inventor and manufacturer

Britton, Karen Gerhardt, *Bale o' Cotton: The Mechanical Art of Cotton Ginning*, College Station: Texas A & M University Press, 1992

Chaplin, Joyce E., *An Anxious Pursuit: Agricultural Innovation and Modernity in the Lower South, 1730–1815*, Chapel Hill: University of North Carolina Press, 1993

Green, Constance McLaughlin, *Eli Whitney and the Birth of American Technology*, Boston: Little Brown, 1956

Hounshell, David A., *From the American System to Mass Production, 1800–1932: The Development of Manufacturing Technology in the United States*, Baltimore: Johns Hopkins University Press, 1984

Mirsky, Jeanette and Allan Nevins, *The World of Eli Whitney*, New York: Macmillan, 1952

Smith, Merritt Roe, "Eli Whitney and the American System of Manufacturing," in *Technology in America: A History of Individuals and Ideas*, edited by Carroll W. Pursell, Cambridge: Massachusetts Institute of Technology Press, 1981

Woodbury, Robert S., "The Legend of Eli Whitney and Interchangeable Parts," *Technology and Culture*, 1, Summer 1960

In the pantheon of early American inventors, no one matches Eli Whitney's stature. For three generations and more he has been on the tips of our schoolchildren's tongues. The dimensions of his history are epic. In inventing the cotton gin Whitney changed the course of the Old South. Upland cotton could now profitably be grown in mass and the expansion of the cotton kingdom reinvigorated slavery and assured that moral qualms would be swept aside in the pursuit of profit. As the inventor of interchangeable parts, Whitney established at his Mill Rock armory the basis for the American system of mass production, and put his country on the road to industrial greatness. And Whitney's legend has always aided Americans in the reaffirmation of their self-belief; in inventing a way around the labor shortage that plagued the early republic he proved the native charm, keen wit, and wily adaptiveness of this "new man," this new American.

Until relatively recently historians have carried this portrait of Eli Whitney triumphantly forward. Two separate biographies published in the 1950s provided the scholarly underpinnings for this epic version of the inventor. MIRSKY and NEVINS admirably detailed the national and international economic context for Whitney's labors, though Whitney himself remained a somewhat obscure figure. GREEN took a more popular approach to biography, and while not inattentive to the importance of historical context, her sympathy for the inventor borders on the hagiographic.

By 1960 historians of technology were interested in the impersonal forces and processes of economy and market; the study of the individual contributions of "great men" had fallen into disrepute. Though much of the latest scholarship in this area does not focus on Whitney directly, several works do an excellent job of providing the larger context for Whitney's developments. BRITTON presents the history of cotton ginning from the 1770s to modern times. Whitney's contributions are sketched out in a single chapter, but with glossy pictures and easy prose the book succeeds in placing cotton at the center of the story, where it belongs. A more academic treatment of the southern context for Whitney's invention is provided by CHAPLIN. While the South's plantation elite is sometimes seen as standing against the modernity that would bring factory production and industrial might to the United States, Chaplin proves that, from 1730 to 1815 at least, successful southern planters were deeply involved in the modernization and mechanization of agriculture. Chaplin's planting class is not a seignorial elite, content with a life of ease and luxury, but a group of agricultural innovators with a dynamic and enlightened view of technological progress. For Chaplin, Whitney is just one of a score of adapters and innovators participating in the headlong rush to find profitability in upland cotton. HOUNSHELL provides an excellent framework for interpreting Whitney's other pursuit, the mass manufacture of

firearms. While Whitney materials are scant in this volume, nowhere else would one find an explanation of how French 18th-century military rationalism played a large role in convincing American armorers, including Whitney, of the revolutionary possibilities of interchangeable parts. From cotton gins to sewing machines, McCormick reapers to Model Ts, Hounshell's book is both rigorous and sprightly, and ably places Whitney and his contemporaries into the wider context of American technological advancement.

This is not to suggest that nothing since 1960 has been written on Whitney as inventor. The focus, however, has not been on building up his legend but on tearing it down. The first to dismantle the Whitney myths was WOODBURY in his quietly excoriating article, "The Legend of Eli Whitney and Interchangeable Parts." In a close examination of the evidence, Woodbury proved that Whitney was at his most inventive when scheming to make money. Using a specially prepared set of muskets, Whitney duped the American government into believing that he had mastered a system of interchangeability and used the money from the federal contract to pursue his many lawsuits against those who had infringed on his ginning patent. Far from pioneering interchangeable parts, the self-promoting inventor actually lagged significantly behind a host of others in developing these technologies. Does this mean that Whitney should be cast from the pantheon? SMITH addressed this exact question in, "Eli Whitney and the American System of Manufacturing." Granting and in some ways underscoring Woodbury's conclusion that Whitney was a sham inventor, Smith went beyond demythologizing and addressed Whitney's important contributions to the promotion of a fundamentally American technological agenda. In Smith's analysis Whitney was a consummate businessman and promoter. However bogus his actual achievements in the interchangeability of musket parts, he had the government's ear and helped them to develop and popularize the notion that through mechanization, standardization, and steady work habits, the fledgling republic might one day be an economic powerhouse. In a nation desperate for affirmation, Whitney's was a self-fulfilling prophecy, and one for which he should be honorably remembered.

STEPHEN W. BERRY

See also Agriculture, to 1860; Technology and Invention

Willard, Frances 1839–1898
Campaigner for temperance and women's rights

Blocker, Jack S., Jr., *Retreat from Reform: The Prohibition Movement in the United States, 1890–1913*, Westport, CT: Greenwood Press, 1976

Bordin, Ruth, *Frances Willard: A Biography*, Chapel Hill: University of North Carolina Press, 1986

Earhart, Mary, *Frances Willard: From Prayers to Politics*, Chicago: University of Chicago Press, 1944

Epstein, Barbara Leslie, *The Politics of Domesticity: Women, Evangelism, and Temperance in Nineteenth-Century America*, Middletown, CT: Wesleyan University Press, 1981

Gordon, Anna A., *The Beautiful Life of Frances E. Willard: A Memorial Volume*, Chicago: Woman's Temperance Publishing Association, 1898; revised and abridged edition, as *The Life of Frances E. Willard*, Evanston, IL: National Woman's Christian Temperance Union, 1912

Leeman, Richard W., *"Do Everything" Reform: The Oratory of Frances E. Willard*, New York: Greenwood Press, 1992

Strachey, Ray, *Frances Willard: Her Life and Work*, London: Unwin, 1912; New York: Revell, 1913

Tyrrell, Ian, *Woman's World/Woman's Empire: The Woman's Christian Temperance Union in International Perspective, 1880–1930*, Chapel Hill: University of North Carolina Press, 1991

Although no longer widely remembered, Frances E. Willard was one of the most highly respected and influential women in late 19th century America. For nineteen years she served as president of the Woman's Christian Temperance Union (WCTU), the largest women's organization of that era. During most of that time, Willard also worked for the Prohibition party, campaigned for the vote and other rights for women, and aided a host of other reform causes.

Because of her immense popularity and distinguished career, several biographies – some for adults and others for young readers – appeared during her lifetime or shortly after her death. Two of these are still frequently cited and merit mention. GORDON should be a major source because its author, Anna Gordon, was Willard's private secretary for 21 years and an extremely close confidante for most of that time. Yet her biography proves disappointing. Part I provides a surprisingly superficial overview of Willard's life and career that leaves out much that Willard did. Gordon quotes at length from Willard's journals and speeches, but adds little from her own observations or understanding of Willard. Part II offers memorial tributes from many of Willard's friends and associates. STRACHEY proves a more useful, though still limited, biography. Rachel Strachey, a British journalist, did not know Willard but did have access to Willard's journals and the aid of several of her colleagues, including another of Willard's close companions, Lady Henry Somerset, whose views appear to have shaped Strachey's own. In any case, Strachey provides an admiring portrait, which has only brief accounts of Willard's various causes, but a full and compelling portrait of her personality that helps to explain her popularity. Strachey provides a useful discussion of Willard's religious views, temperament (stressing Willard's slowness to take offense), and her organizational skills. She presents Willard as driven by an intriguing blend of self-sacrifice and ambition, and concludes that Willard's greatness lay in her character rather than her work.

Two later biographies provide fuller descriptions of Willard's public role and greater acknowledgment of the importance of her reform activities. EARHART did not have access to Willard's journals, which had been lost. Believing that Willard's colleagues in the WCTU had created a legend that exaggerated Willard's support for temperance, Earhart minimizes the importance of Willard's role in the fight for prohibition and instead stresses her battle for women's rights and her support for labor and socialism. Earhart portrays Willard as a successful, in many ways radical, leader who pushed a conservative group of women to support suffrage and labor reform. In 1891–92, Earhart argues, Willard almost succeeded in bringing together a reform coalition, made up primarily of Populists and Prohibitionists, that could have taken power. While emphasizing Willard's public life, Earhart does not ignore the personal; her biography has an excellent chapter on Willard's sexuality.

BORDIN's much more recent biography also discusses Willard's private life while focusing primarily on her public role. Bordin's account has three advantages over Earhart's. Having rediscovered the lost journals as well as using additional Willard papers, she was able to provide a more fully-documented and definitive account. She also had access to a far more extensive and sophisticated scholarship on the history of women in America that enabled her to put Willard into a fuller historical context. And, perhaps most important, Bordin, who had earlier written a history of the WCTU, rightly restores the temperance crusade to the center of Willard's career. At the same time, she realizes the importance of Willard's role in the battle for women's rights as well as her efforts in the Prohibition party and for broader reforms. In all these causes, Bordin concludes, Willard remained a true Victorian, but one who used traditional conceptions of womanhood, especially female responsibilities in home and church, to make her radical ideas more acceptable. Bordin also contends that Willard herself was a model of womanhood even as she used that ideal to expand women's role. She thereby synthesized women's rights feminism with the ideal of a separate women's culture. Thus Bordin makes Willard's character central to her work, rather than greater than her work as Strachey does.

Bordin is the best single authority on Willard's life, although Earhart and even Strachey remain useful. So too do four other books, three of which do not focus specifically on Willard but rather analyze causes in which she participated. The most important of these, TYRRELL, analyzes the work of the International WCTU, which Willard founded. He not only provides the fullest account of Willard's efforts outside of the United States, a topic which all the biographies discuss, but he also offers shrewd insights on Willard herself. Tyrrell proves especially astute in his comments on Willard's Christianity, her attitude toward her mother, and the importance she placed on changing the behavior of men as well as of women. BLOCKER provides helpful context and additional detail for understanding Willard's role in the Prohibition party and the attempt to unite it with the Populists. In one chapter EPSTEIN uses Willard and the WCTU to explore the role of domestic ideals in creating what she considers a "protofeminism." LEEMAN brings together several of Willard's speeches, and introduces them with an extended analysis of her role as a public speaker – an extremely important aspect of her career, which the biographies do not examine so systematically.

GAINES M. FOSTER

See also Prohibition; Temperance

Williams, Roger 1603?–1683
New England religious leader and dissenter

Camp, L. Raymond, *Roger Williams, God's Apostle of Advocacy: Biography and Rhetoric*, Lewiston, NY: Mellen Press, 1989

Gaustad, Edwin Scott, *Liberty of Conscience: Roger Williams in America*, Grand Rapids, MI: Eerdmans, 1991

Gilpin, W. Clark, *The Millenarian Piety of Roger Williams*, Chicago: University of Chicago Press, 1979

Gura, Philip F., *A Glimpse of Sion's Glory: Puritan Radicalism in New England, 1620–1660*, Middletown, CT: Wesleyan University Press, 1984

Miller, Perry, *Roger Williams: His Contribution to the American Tradition*, Indianapolis: Bobbs Merrill, 1953

Miller, William Lee, *The First Liberty: Religion and the American Republic*, New York: Knopf, 1986

Morgan, Edmund S., *Roger Williams: The Church and the State*, New York: Harcourt Brace, 1967

Skaggs, Donald, *Roger Williams' Dream for America*, New York: Lang, 1993

Spurgin, Hugh, *Roger Williams and Puritan Radicalism in the English Separatist Tradition*, Lewiston, NY, and Lampeter, Dyfed: Mellen Press, 1989

The historiography of Roger Williams is divided into two eras – that which preceded Perry Miller and that which came after his book. Most scholars agree that Perry MILLER rescued Williams from 19th-century secular liberalism and restored him to the world of 17th-century Calvinism. In Miller's hands, Williams gained the image that no scholar would dispute today, as the "most passionately religious of men" and "an explorer into the dark places" of justice and conscience. Although some of his assertions have been modified or disputed – Williams's use of typology comes to mind – Miller continues to set the questions, and a serious student of Williams must begin here.

Still cited by recent scholars, MORGAN's highly readable contribution to the Williams historiography provides a succinct analysis of the 17th-century radical ideas that produced such a troublesome man. Far from being an eccentric intellectual wanderer, Williams, according to Morgan, drew on his English Puritan, separatist heritage for his ideas about church and state. His was an odyssey in search of perfection, but it was perfection based on established dissenter ideas – not sharply different from conventional New England theology. Some of Williams's insights blended nicely with Enlightenment thought. As Morgan points out, however, that did not make him a proto-liberal.

GILPIN continues the work begun by Miller and Morgan by focusing on Williams's conception of the millennium. For him, Gilpin points out, millennialism constituted the framework of God's plan for humankind. All else was supported by that framework – past, present, future. Williams's extreme separatism fed his millennial vision, and Gilpin shows how this brand of religious radicalism undergirded his concept of political and social order. Williams saw his times as a transitional period between the corruption of the old church and its salvation through the second coming of Christ, and he therefore emphasized discontinuities rather than the gradual progression of more conventional millennialism. This vision justified his separatism and placed it in proper relation to other aspects of Williams's thought.

Calling his study an intellectual biography "pure and simple," GURA focuses on several radical religious leaders, including Williams, and relates them to Puritan culture in America and England. He argues for a dialectical development between radicals and reformists which "continuously revitalized" New England's religious culture. Unlike some other scholars, Gura believes that it would be a mistake to think of Williams as an isolated case. He presents strong evidence that New England town, church, and colony records reveal frequent disciplinary actions against those who expressed deviant opinions on religious issues. What authorities feared most was the spread of radical ideas, and Williams made it his business to do just that.

William MILLER, like Gura, places Williams in a broader context, the development of religious liberty. He devotes one chapter to Rhode Island's founder. Pointing out that freedom of religion was not just a question of expediency in the United States, Miller sees it as part of a radical tradition within the Protestant reformation and notes that Williams has come to embody that tradition in popular and church (especially Baptist) history. Miller concedes that he belongs there, despite erroneous popular ideas of who Williams was and how he became an advocate of "soul liberty." With engaging style and forceful arguments, Miller shows how Williams's intense exclusivity turned in on itself to become inclusive. He also includes an excellent discussion of Vernon Louis Parrington's 1920s portrait of Williams as a secular liberal and his subsequent revitalization by Perry Miller and Morgan.

Like most historians today, SPURGIN sees Williams as a visionary, a "conscientious troubler" who irritated and upset religious leaders in New England and Old. Though previous scholars credited separatism as an important influence on Williams, none had analyzed this aspect in depth. Spurgin asserts that Williams instigated a major reinterpretation of separatism simply by following through the principles of that tradition to their logical conclusion, and by applying those principles to political and social thought.

SKAGGS also builds on the work of others in making explicit the acceptance and dissemination of Williams's ideas on separation of church and state and freedom of conscience. He shows how Rhode Islanders and Baptists put Williams forward as the champion of these ideas in the 18th century as did liberal historians and others in the 19th and early 20th centuries. Although his analysis is at times somewhat eccentric, Skaggs also provides a valuable review of the Williams historiography. No Williams scholars today would take issue with Skaggs's contention that millennialism holds the key to Williams's thought.

Because of the lack of sources, little has been written on Williams's early life. CAMP provides the best account of those years, paying close attention to the milieu at Charterhouse School and Pembroke College, Cambridge, where Williams received his education. He also offers a useful picture of Sir Edward Coke's influence on Williams, and Williams's short stint as a private chaplain. Camp's primary goal, however, is to study Williams as a rhetorician in order to gain a better understanding of his ideas and impact on American culture.

Less satisfactory concerning Williams's career in New England and the relationship between his ideas and rhetorical strategy, the book nevertheless achieves other more modest goals established by the author.

Witty and readable, GAUSTAD is the best recent account of Williams's life. The author combines able analysis with a synthesis of much of the excellent work on Williams done in the last forty years. Styling Williams an exile, Gaustad points out that his exile, to a great extent, was self-imposed. He provides useful commentary on Williams's major publications, noting, for example, that despite his poor writing style, his ideas come through with force and clarity. Regardless of his status as an outcast, Williams did not entirely isolate himself from the ecclesiastical establishment or from experiments in religion undertaken in New England or elsewhere. Instead, Gaustad shows that he engaged orthodoxy on both sides of the Atlantic in a lifelong debate over principles he felt were absolute and undeniable, and it was this engagement, not his isolation, that secured Williams's place in history.

ELIZABETH E. DUNN

See also Colonial History: Religion

Wilson, Woodrow   1856–1924

28th President of the United States

Baker, Ray Stannard, *Woodrow Wilson: Life and Letters*, 8 vols., New York: Doubleday, 1927–39

Bragdon, Henry Wilkinson, *Woodrow Wilson: The Academic Years*, Cambridge, MA: Belknap Press of Harvard University Press, 1967

Calhoun, Frederick S., *Power and Principle: Armed Intervention in Wilsonian Foreign Policy*, Kent, OH: Kent State University Press, 1986

Clements, Kendrick A., *Woodrow Wilson: World Statesman*, Boston: Twayne, 1987

Clements, Kendrick A., *The Presidency of Woodrow Wilson*, Lawrence: University Press of Kansas, 1992

Cooper, John Milton, Jr., *The Warrior and the Priest: Woodrow Wilson and Theodore Roosevelt*, Cambridge, MA: Belknap Press of Harvard University Press, 1983

Heckscher, August, *Woodrow Wilson*, New York: Scribner, 1991

Link, Arthur S., *Wilson*, 5 vols., Princeton: Princeton University Press, 1947–65

Link, Arthur S., *Woodrow Wilson: Revolution, War, and Peace*, Arlington Heights, IL: Harlan Davidson, 1979

Mulder, John, *Woodrow Wilson: The Years of Preparation*, Princeton: Princeton University Press, 1978

Schulte Nordholt, Jan Willem, *Woodrow Wilson: A Life for World Peace*, translated by Herbert H. Rowen, Berkeley: University of California Press, 1991

Thorsen, Niels Aaga, *The Political Thought of Woodrow Wilson, 1875–1910*, Princeton: Princeton University Press, 1988

Weinstein, Edwin A., *Woodrow Wilson: A Medical and Psychological Biography*, Princeton: Princeton University Press, 1981

Modern scholarship on the 28th President has been dominated by the work of Arthur S. Link, whose magnificent 69-volume edition of *The Papers of Woodrow Wilson* (Princeton, 1966–94) falls outside the rubric of this *Guide*. An unfortunate consequence of his involvement with this project over three and a half decades is that his own major study, LINK (1947–65) remains incomplete. The first volumes that exist constitute both less and much more than a biography. They are less not only because they stop in 1917 but also because the first 45 years of Wilson's life are dealt with in a brief, introductory chapter of *The Road to the White House*. They are much more because they treat fully the various issues and events with which Wilson was concerned from his election as president of Princeton University in June 1902 to America's entry into World War I. As the series progresses, Link's attitude towards his subject changes. The first volume contains some harsh criticism of Wilson's thought and action but the latter three present matters from the president's own standpoint, with implicit sympathy. Based upon broad and deep research, Link's work contains extensive quotations from primary documents. It provides an authoritative and detailed account of Wilson's first term in the White House, including the development of the domestic legislative programme of "the New Freedom" and the complex stories of the administration's response to the Mexican revolution and its conduct of American neutrality during World War I. Link has supplemented his *magnum opus* with several shorter works, perhaps the most important of which is LINK (1979), a compact and lucid review of Wilson's evolving policy towards World War I and its aftermath that represents Link's most considered interpretation – and assessment – of its character.

For the years which it covers in detail, Link's major study clearly supersedes the earlier multi-volume biography by BAKER, the journalist (and former "muckraker") who served as Wilson's press secretary during the Paris peace conference of 1919. But Baker's first two volumes deal much more fully than Link with Wilson's early life and include material, derived from personal acquaintance and correspondence, that is not available elsewhere. Wilson himself gave Baker, who was a devoted admirer, first access to his papers. Baker seems to have become swamped by the quantity of these; his last two volumes, on the period of American belligerency in World War I, consist almost entirely of documents, arranged in chronological order.

Like Baker, BRAGDON makes use of interviews and personal correspondence with those who knew Wilson, in his narrative of Wilson's life up to the point in 1910 when he left Princeton to become governor of New Jersey. This lengthy but very readable book contains extensive summaries and assessments of Wilson's writings as well as the details of his academic career at Bryn Mawr, Wesleyan and Princeton. It is based on a wide range of sources and presents a vivid picture of college life in the late 19th century, and of the way in which Princeton developed. Like many others, Bragdon sees Wilson's record as president of Princeton as presaging his performance in the nation's highest office – impressive feats of leadership based on co-operative endeavour, being followed by high-handed attempts to achieve over-ambitious goals, ending in defeat and failure. Bragdon concludes that the bitter controversies which marked the later years of Wilson's tenure had a hardening effect on his personality.

More recent works have benefited from the appearance of the successive volumes of the *Papers*, and, indeed, those by Mulder, Weinstein and Thorsen have been published as "Supplementary Volumes" to the series. MULDER's book, which covers the same years as Bragdon's, is briefer, more interpretative and more sharply focused on the evolution of Wilson's thought. A student of church history, Mulder emphasizes Wilson's religious faith and the influence upon him of the "covenant theology" that he imbibed from his father, a minister and prominent figure in the southern Presbyterian Church. While recognizing that Wilson showed little direct interest in theology, Mulder argues that his heritage shaped his "way of understanding the world – a predisposition to see things in synthetic, holistic terms and a tendency to make all issues reducible to well-defined moral categories". In Mulder's view, the rebuffs which Wilson experienced at Princeton over his "quad plan" and the location of the Graduate College inspired in him a new hostility to wealth and privilege that turned him into a political progressive.

An explanation for the apparent change in Wilson's style of leadership at Princeton is offered by WEINSTEIN, in the most well-informed of the several psychological biographies to which Wilson has been subjected. According to Weinstein, a neurologist, Wilson's judgement had been affected by the medical problem that he suffered in May 1906, and his psychological response to it. Weinstein believes this incident, in which Wilson temporarily lost the sight of one eye, to have been a "major stroke" – the consequence of progressive arteriosclerosis that, in Weinstein's view, manifested itself in several other small strokes before the disabling one that struck Wilson down in October 1919. Though accepted by Link and others, this version of Wilson's medical history has been disputed. Weinstein also suggests that Wilson suffered from dyslexia in his youth, which would explain why he was very late in learning to read and always read slowly. In addition to furnishing these medical diagnoses, Weinstein seeks to illuminate Wilson's psychological history through interpretations of the language he used at different times.

The tendency to concentrate upon Wilson's weaknesses and failures was stemmed by COOPER, one of the leading historians of the Progressive era, in his dual biography of Wilson and his great contemporary and rival, Theodore Roosevelt. Expressing a higher opinion than most previous biographers of Wilson's scholarly writings, especially *Congressional Government* (1885), Cooper calls him "the finest American political scientist of the period of his academic career". In contrast to Mulder, Cooper discounts the influence of Wilson's religious faith upon his political attitudes, arguing that it was the processes of politics that interested him and that he took a detached view of substantive issues until he entered the arena himself – which he did by associating himself with anti-Bryan Democrats in the 1900s. Wilson's later espousal of progressive reform is seen as just one example of the political pragmatism that Wilson, an admirer of Burke, adhered to in theory as well as practice. Although a bold and confident leader, Wilson set his course, Cooper argues, by seeking consensus and responding to circumstances. Cooper devotes comparatively little attention to Wilson's fight for the League of Nations, which has done the most to create a very different image of him, and stresses the deterioration of his health in

1919. However, contextual reinterpretations of many of Wilson's other important actions, including his decision to ask for war against Germany in 1917, contribute to this sympathetic but unconventional portrait.

That Wilson was a strong, shrewd and effective president is also the impression conveyed by CALHOUN's study of the manner in which he employed armed force abroad. In particular, Calhoun emphasizes the firmness with which Wilson maintained civilian control and, while avoiding interference in the details of operations, prevented military attitudes from producing "mission creep". Reviewing the interventions in Mexico, Haiti, Santo Domingo, World War I and Russia, Calhoun praises Wilson for recognizing the limits of military power and always using it in conjunction with other means of achieving his objectives. In suggesting that a few broad purposes, such as promoting democracy, upholding international law or nurturing collective security, lay behind Wilson's resorts to force, Calhoun tends to disregard the great differences between the various interventions (not least in their scale) as well as to simplify the reasons for embarking on them. However, his detailed analysis of individual episodes, particularly those in Latin America and Russia, is penetrating and valuable.

Wilson's prominence on the international stage made him a world figure, and the continuing interest he has aroused among Europeans, in particular, has led to some notable contributions to the literature on him. Using material made available for the first time in the *Papers*, a Danish scholar, THORSEN, has produced a thorough analysis of Wilson's unpublished as well as published writings on political matters in the years before he entered politics himself. Arguing that Wilson's scholarly works have too often been interpreted within the inappropriate categories of Beardian historiography or modern political science, Thorsen maintains that they reflect a continuing and evolving engagement with the problems of the American polity and the means by which these might be addressed. In Thorsen's view, Wilson, an early admirer of Hamilton and the Federalists, was never an adherent of laissez-faire liberalism; rather, he was a believer in effective national government, who was preoccupied by the role of leadership in a diverse, organically developing, modern democracy. Whether or not Wilson's writings can always bear the weight of interpretation Thorsen places upon them, this careful and sophisticated study clearly supersedes previous ones.

Wilson's nationalism is also emphasized by SCHULTE NORDHOLT, a Dutch historian, but he highlights its sentimental character. This accords with the rather different picture which he presents of Wilson as not so much a systematic thinker as a great orator who was "temperamentally a poet". Although in the form of a biography, Schulte Nordholt's lengthy study concentrates upon Wilson's role during and after World War I, with the rest of his life being examined for the light it can throw upon this critical period. Based primarily upon the *Papers* (by this time almost complete) and other printed sources, it contains insights and judgements that reflect the author's unabashedly European perspective. Baffled by the "strange phenomenon" of a Calvinist who came "to expect so much of mankind", Schulte Nordholt concludes that Wilson's religion was a simple faith that centred on hymn-singing. He focuses on the recurring motifs of Wilson's rhetoric and comments that "the longer we listen to this unworldly voice, this unhistorical lyricism, the stranger it sounds". A certain ambivalence seems to lie at the heart of this engagingly personal book; while portraying Wilson as the embodiment of American naivete, Schulte Nordholt responds positively to what he sees as the president's noble vision of "world peace".

Less idiosyncratic and more respectful of Wilson is the full-scale biography by HECKSCHER. This, too, is based largely on *The Papers of Woodrow Wilson*, with which project Heckscher was associated as a member of the editorial committee, and it includes much material not previously known. Focused on Wilson himself, it presents a sophisticated and persuasive analysis of his character that is sympathetic without being uncritical. Heckscher emphasizes the influence of Wilson's health upon his behaviour, especially in 1919. Here, as on most questions, his interpretation accords with that of Link, for whose uncompleted biography this comprehensive narrative may be seen as a kind of substitute – although it engages much less thoroughly and knowledgeably with the historical context of Wilson's career. Nevertheless, this gracefully written and nicely illustrated volume provides the most authoritative complete account of Wilson's life now available.

CLEMENTS (1987) is a much briefer biography which devotes a somewhat greater proportion of its attention to the issues and events with which Wilson was concerned. Its brisk narrative style conveys much sound information lucidly and concisely; the author's judgements, while sympathetic to Wilson, are balanced. CLEMENTS (1992) is more detailed and concentrates upon Wilson's presidency, stressing its domestic achievements. It includes path-breaking chapters on the Departments of Agriculture and Commerce that throw an unusual light upon the administration. Clements's interpretations of Wilson's foreign policy are more developed (and slightly different) than those in this earlier book, and he also incorporates the findings of the later volumes of the *Papers*, particularly on the effects of Wilson's major stroke in October 1919. A full and up-to-date bibliographical essay adds to the value of this first-rate survey.

JOHN A. THOMPSON

See also New Nationalism and New Freedom; Progressivism; Versailles, Treaty of, and League of Nations; World War I entries

Winthrop, John 1588–1649

Puritan leader and governor of Massachusetts Bay colony

Dunn, Richard S., *Puritans and Yankees: The Winthrop Dynasty of New England, 1630–1717*, Princeton: Princeton University Press, 1962

Morgan, Edmund S., *The Puritan Dilemma: The Story of John Winthrop*, Boston: Little Brown, 1958

Moseley, James G., *John Winthrop's World: History as a Story; the Story as History*, Madison: University of Wisconsin Press, 1992

Power, M. Susan, *Before the Convention: Religion and the Founders*, Lanham, MD: University Press of America, 1984

Rutman, Darrett B., *Winthrop's Boston: Portrait of a Puritan Town, 1630–1649*, Chapel Hill: University of North Carolina Press, 1965

Rutman, Darrett B., *John Winthrop's Decision for America: 1629*, Philadelphia: Lippincott, 1975

Schweninger, Lee, *John Winthrop*, Boston: Twayne, 1990

One of a number of books written in the 1950s which were designed to rescue the Puritans from their reputation as "killjoys in tall-crowned hats," MORGAN's biography of Winthrop remains a classic and the best starting point for anyone curious about him. Exploring fundamental issues of Puritan society in particular and human society in general, Morgan has made the founder of Massachusetts accessible to several generations of college students. The governor's dilemma, according to Morgan, was actually twofold. First, what does an individual owe society – that is what sorts of compromises of one's principles must be made for the sake of civil society. Second, and this is the distinctly "Puritan dilemma" of the title, how does one live in the world and not be captured by it. Overall, Morgan succeeds in his effort to humanize the Puritans while paying sufficient attention to their particular religious mission. Winthrop emerges as a man devoted to God while not forgetting the context of the world around him.

DUNN's multi-generational study of the Winthrops portrays John the elder as the "first keeper of the New England conscience." Sketching a portrait of someone capable of a wide range of emotions and moods, Dunn also depicts a Winthrop who tried to control and manipulate others and who demanded discipline and moral uprightness from his fellow colonists. Seeing a parallel between his struggles against external attacks on Massachusetts and those against internal critics, Dunn finds that both encouraged Winthrop to seek power and autonomy for his provincial government. Of the three generations considered, John receives the least attention as the focus of only two of fourteen chapters, but Dunn ably shows his crucial role as governor of Massachusetts and its foremost guardian of orthodoxy.

Contending that Winthrop's talent as a writer has often been neglected, SCHWENINGER sets out to explore his most important works, and analyzes them in straightforward informative prose. After a brief survey of Winthrop's life in England and America, Schweninger looks at several of his writings in detail, including his early journal and later conversion narrative, pieces he wrote in preparation to migrate, his version of the antinomian controversy in Massachusetts, and finally his historical and political writings. Schweninger contends that the "Modell of Christian Charity," transformed the Puritan migration into a mission to perfect church-state relations. In addition, within Winthrop's framework of mutual bonds, he unknowingly provided the initial justification for participatory democracy in the colonies. Many historians have compared Winthrop's writings unfavorably with those of Plymouth governor William Bradford, but Schweninger views them as representative of different approaches and ideals. His compact book offers a sympathetic look at the Massachusetts Bay leader's ideas and literary skills.

The best study of Winthrop's journals is MOSELEY's slim but complex volume. Describing him as an individual who could be moralistic, self-denying, and humorless but also temperate, firm, and even witty, Moseley first relates Winthrop's odyssey as a writer and then analyzes what happened to those writings at the hands of historians. He shows how Winthrop's character developed over time and through the writing of his journals. In his youth and early adulthood, Winthrop gradually resigned himself to his Puritan faith. The deaths of his first two wives taught Winthrop to even out his moods – something Winthrop recognized as a problem after reviewing his journal. In Massachusetts, Winthrop grew as a man of action, and he further developed his philosophy of moderation. At the same time, he became more conscious of his journal as a history of New England rather than just a personal chronicle. Moseley also relates a long history of misreadings of Winthrop's journals but sees this story as our one remaining link to their author.

POWER gives Winthrop a prominent place in her study of the interrelationship of politics and religion in early America, and devotes about one third of her book to his writings. Overall, she finds Winthrop to be a moderate who opposed rigidity and literal-mindedness in either religion or the law. She also contrasts Winthrop's ideal of a homogeneous covenanted community to Elisha Williams's notion of a Christian commonwealth with limited pluralism and more emphasis on the individual. Though she falls short of her larger goal of redefining political labels, Power offers some creative analysis of the interaction between Winthrop's religious principles and political attitudes.

Rutman's two books approach Winthrop from two different perspectives. One encompasses Winthrop's role in the development of Boston, and the other concentrates on that narrow slice of time when Winthrop made his decision to migrate to America. In his somewhat dated but still provocative work on Boston, RUTMAN (1965) uses Winthrop's ideals as a starting point for the growth of the city and traces its divergence away from that lofty beginning. Although Winthrop outlined an organic community of mutual obligations with individuals working toward a common goal, Rutman contends that divisions set in at the very beginning. By locating Boston on a small, narrow-necked peninsula, Winthrop guaranteed the spread of villages and land seeking that violated the goals he had so carefully described in the "Modell of Christian Charity." Commerce and trade brought economic divisions to add to the political and religious differences that beset the city as soon as it was founded. For his part, Winthrop never saw Boston as a failure; he never complained that it had not developed as he planned. Instead, according to Rutman, he accepted human failings and weakness as God's will.

The intention of RUTMAN (1975) is to introduce students and general readers to Winthrop through an interpretive essay (about half of the book) and a selection of documents related to the problem at hand. The essay focuses on the choices available to Winthrop as he made his decision for America. His early years had been ones of gradually expanding geographic, economic, educational, and religious horizons. Rutman sees Winthrop's choice to relocate as the culmination of his increasing dissatisfaction with life in England, coupled with an increasing awareness of the potential for a new life in the colonies. Eventually these factors worked together to overcome his doubts and propel Winthrop to America.

ELIZABETH E. DUNN

See also Boston; Colonial History: Colonies 2; Puritanism

Women's History: General

Amott, Teresa L. and Julie A. Matthaei, *Race, Gender, and Work: A Multicultural Economic History of Women in the United States*, Boston: South End Press, 1991

Armitage, Susan and Elizabeth Jameson (editors), *The Women's West*, Norman: University of Oklahoma Press, 1987

Degler, Carl N., *At Odds: Women and the Family in America from the Revolution to the Present*, New York and Oxford: Oxford University Press, 1980

DuBois, Ellen Carol and Vicki L. Ruiz (editors), *Unequal Sisters: A Multicultural Reader in US Women's History*, New York: Routledge, 1990, 2nd edition, 1994

Evans, Sara M., *Born for Liberty: A History of Women in America*, New York: Free Press, 1989

Guy-Sheftall, Beverly, *Daughters of Sorrow: Attitudes Toward Black Women, 1880–1920*, New York: Carlson, 1990

Kerber, Linda K., *Women of the Republic: Intellect and Ideology in Revolutionary America*, Chapel Hill: University of North Carolina Press, 1980

Riley, Glenda, *Inventing the American Woman: A Perspective on Women's History*, Arlington Heights, IL: Harlan Davidson, 1987, 2nd edition, 1995

Scott, Anne Firor, *The Southern Lady: From Pedestal to Politics, 1830–1930*, Chicago: University of Chicago Press, 1970

Sklar, Kathryn Kish, *Catharine Beecher: A Study in American Domesticity*, New Haven: Yale University Press, 1973

Solomon, Barbara Miller, *In the Company of Educated Women: A History of Women and Higher Education in America*, New Haven and London: Yale University Press, 1985

White, Deborah Gray, *Ar'n't I a Woman? Female Slaves in the Plantation South*, New York: Norton, 1985

It is an impossible task to encapsulate the history of women in the United States within a list of a dozen or so volumes. This general entry should be used in conjunction with entries on more specific topics (such as feminism, women's work, and women's liberation). Women's history emerged as part of the new social history of the 1960s and 1970s and shares with it a concern for the diversity of experiences, the typical and ordinary, and the impact of grand events upon every day folk as well as elites. The books discussed here capture the richness and diversity of women's experience, emphasizing how those experiences varied by race, region, and ethnicity while still exploring the common threads of education, employment, and political participation.

Among the many texts providing a general overview of women's lives in the United States, RILEY stands out for her breadth of coverage and inclusiveness, as well as her useful suggestions for further reading. This is a textbook which takes a gender-specific approach to American history, concentrating upon the events the author deems to be particularly germane to women's changing lives. The focus is upon women's work, socialization, roles and activities, and the cultural values which shaped women's behavior. Stronger on early history than on the last two decades, the book encompasses the sweeping changes occurring in American women's lives, even if it touches on some topics more lightly than others. It successfully incorporates the histories of women of color and white working-class women into its analysis.

EVANS gives a detailed account of women's political activities, emphasizing the evolving boundaries between private and public lives from pre-conquest North America until the present day, and noting that these boundaries not only changed over time but also varied for different activities in which women participated. In this she challenges the public-private dichotomy which has dominated women's history as being too simplistic a framework for understanding women's lives. She begins with an account of women's role in Native American cosmology, agriculture, and governance, then moves on to the impact of colonization on Indian and white women. She explores the way that the American Revolution politicized women and the domestic arena. The book is structured both thematically and chronologically, but the emphasis on politics, organizing, and organizations limits the amount of attention devoted to economics and demography.

Other works explore these aspects in greater detail. DEGLER provides a comprehensive demographic history of women's lives, concentrating upon women's roles within the family and the potential conflict between traditional family structures, rising levels of female employment, and other activities outside the home. As with a number of other historians sensitive to the separate but intertwined histories of women and the family, he writes women back into the history of the family itself and sees them as agents of change within the family circle as well as outside it. The issue that Degler reflects upon, and which he regards as crucial in the combined histories of women and the family, is whether women should be seen as individuals with their own separate agendas or as people who serve their families, defined by and deriving their identities from their family status. By combining an analysis of fertility, family structure, employment, and political and social activism, Degler helps to integrate women's experience with changes in the economic, social, and demographic structures of American life.

AMOTT and MATTHAEI shift the emphasis more toward employment inside and outside the home, and women's free and enforced labor, but retain the emphasis on diversity of experiences. They explore the racial, ethnic, and class variations of women's working lives, including paid and unpaid labor in the home. This economic history provides a theoretical framework for considering the class/race/ethnicity/gender dynamics of labor, then goes on to analyze women's work in the major ethnocultural groups. Each group is evaluated in terms of the constraints placed on women, the relation (if any) between economic activity and political and social power, and the group's place in the economic/political hierarchy of the United States. While the histories of each group cover the relevant time frames (pre-European conquest to the present in the case of Native American women), most of the tabular data comes from the 20th century, so that readers would do well to consult other works for a detailed analysis of women's employment in earlier periods.

Other studies of the history of women also select narrow time frames in which to illuminate specific aspects of women's lives. KERBER's account of the Enlightenment, the American Revolution, and the early years of the Republic recasts this period in gendered terms. The American Revolution depended upon women's ability to farm, nurse, and raise funds as well as men's ability to shoot and to write fine, albeit exclusionary, documents. The role of women in the early Republic as republican mothers, educated in order to educate their children in letters and civic virtue, underpinned the development of women's education and expansion into political and social activism which occurred in the mid-19th century.

SKLAR's study of Catharine Beecher follows on from Kerber, in the same way that the Cults of True Womanhood and Domesticity derived from aspects of Republican Motherhood. Sklar examines the life of this pioneer of female education, women's employment as teachers, and domesticity as a female vocation. First published in 1841, Beecher's *Treatise on Domestic Economy* established the parameters of middle-class housekeeping in the highly mobile, urbanizing nation. It glorified women's role as the center of the home and made domesticity into an ideology and the plank from which women could influence the world, even over matters as contentious as slavery. While this is essentially a biography of Catharine Beecher, it also looks at the writing of her sister Harriet Beecher Stowe and the role of women in 19th century reform movements. By exploring the life of one of the leading apostles of female domesticity, Sklar illuminates the dilemmas faced by antebellum women, the dominant ideologies of the period, and the rebellion of some women against the gender constraints of the era.

The crucial role of education in the advancement of women's status forms the subject of SOLOMON's study. She begins with a consideration of the difficulties encountered by women who wished to progress beyond the educational basics, looking at the colonial and early Republican attitudes towards female education. She examines the founding of seminaries for young ladies, including Catharine Beecher's work in Hartford and in the West to advance female education and the efforts to establish schools for black girls in the North. Solomon details the struggle for higher education by women of diverse backgrounds, and the particular difficulties encountered by African American women who wanted an advanced education. She also examines the ambivalent attitude of many educators towards their female pupils, both at the elementary and advanced levels.

WHITE explores the world of female slaves in the plantation South, where very few learned to read or write. She investigates their work routines, family lives, and relations with whites, using slave narratives, the testimony of ex-slaves collected during the Great Depression, and the writings of other historians. She differentiates between matrifocal and matriarchal worlds, finding that the exigencies of plantation slavery led to an emphasis on female interdependence, and also the creation of some leadership roles for women within the slave community. White considers how whites constructed their images of African American women slaves in order to justify their treatment of them. She also explores the interactions of black and white women under slavery and the gendered dynamics of plantation life. Her analysis of why relatively few slave women tried to escape to freedom illuminates a neglected aspect of slavery. White sees slave women as showing great resourcefulness in a dauntingly difficult world.

In examining the lives of African American women after slavery (most of whom lived in the rural South and were involved in sharecropping), GUY-SHEFTALL contrasts their world with that of urban, white middle and working classes. She details black women's attempts to defend themselves and to improve the standing of their race. She also explores constructs of motherhood, whether as mammy to white families or as mother to her own children. The efforts of African American women on behalf of their race and their sex are discussed at length. The author reflects upon the public-private dichotomy as applied to African American women, the role of black women in the suffrage struggle, and the struggle for public education for black women and girls. The focus is upon the intellectual thought of African American women, their self-conception, and the ambivalent attitudes towards all women during the Gilded Age and Progressive Era.

SCOTT focuses on the world made possible by slavery and later the cheap labor of African American women, namely the world of the southern white lady. She examines how these women moved from a world bounded by the Cult of True Womanhood, to one in which they participated in the affairs of home, church, and community on an increasingly sure footing. Noting the discontent felt by many white women over slavery, sexual double standards, and limited educational opportunities, she then discusses southern white women's participation in the Civil War, their responses to the postbellum world, and their political and club activities. She explores the economic role of white women from all class backgrounds both before and after the Civil War, the growing interest in female education in the postbellum period, and the development of higher education for white women in the South. Despite the conservative attitude of most southern churches on women's roles at home and in church, southern women organized missionary societies, settlement houses, and branches of the Women's Christian Temperance Union. Scott illuminates the suffrage struggle in the South, and its implications for wider gender roles as she discusses pro- and anti-suffrage sentiment among southern whites. She also deals with women's role in race relations and the role of race in such gender issues as suffrage.

The essays in ARMITAGE and JAMESON also have a regional focus, challenging the stereotypes and general neglect of women in the study of the West. Traditional histories of the West document white men's conquest, ignoring women of all races or relegating them to a few general (and frequently ahistorical) remarks. The essays presented here challenge that neglect, exploring women's lives in a multicultural history of the West which examines the westering process, depictions of white and Native American women, economic roles, child-rearing, and sexual practices. They also explore the ways in which the myths of the West have recreated women's experience in an ahistorical fashion. Cowboy Art, realistic and representational, presents women as passive and genteel, while men are active and rough. Native American women were rarely depicted in paintings or postcards and were caricatured and stereotyped when they were. Several essays question the applicability of the Cult of True Womanhood to western women, finding that roles were permeable even if frequently separate, and that women took an active part in community affairs and farm politics. The value of the regional approach to women's history is that it takes concepts and constructs developed largely to describe the experience of northern and eastern women and tests them in different socioeconomic and political climates.

Similarly, the essays in the volume edited by DuBOIS and RUIZ cover a wide range of economic, social, and political topics in women's history. Several provide useful theoretical and historiographical frameworks, analyzing the various theoretical perspectives used in women's history, such as separate spheres, the family wage ideology, and the public-private role dichotomy. Many explicitly focus on the employment, educational, and sexual experiences of women of color. The uses of history as a means of validating contemporary perceptions are explored by several authors. This volume raises the questions of what history is and how the incorporation of women into the historical record may alter it. By incorporating diverse experiences and perceptions, writing the history of all women, not just those of the elite, the politically active, or the participants in the grand events of any period, women's history expands the historical canvas and helps it to reflect more fully the events and forces of the past.

S.J. KLEINBERG

Women's History: Education

Burstall, Sara A., *The Education of Girls in the United States*, London: Swan Sonnenschein, and New York: Macmillan, 1894; reprinted, New York: Arno Press, 1971

Hine, Darlene Clark and others (editors), *Black Women in America: An Historical Encyclopedia*, 2 vols., New York: Carlson, 1993

Horowitz, Helen, *Alma Mater: Design and Experience in the Women's Colleges from Their Nineteenth Century Beginnings to the 1930's*, New York: Knopf, 1984; 2nd edition, Amherst: University of Massachusetts Press, 1993

Kerber, Linda K., *Women of the Republic: Intellect and Ideology in Revolutionary America*, Chapel Hill: University of North Carolina Press, 1980

Palmieri, Patricia Ann, *In Adamless Eden: The Community of Women Faculty at Wellesley*, New Haven and London: Yale University Press, 1995

Scott, Anne Firor, "The Ever Widening Circle: The Diffusion of Feminist Values from the Troy Female Seminary, 1822–1872," *History of Education Quarterly*, 19, 1979

Sklar, Kathryn Kish, *Catharine Beecher: A Study in American Domesticity*, New Haven: Yale University Press, 1973

Solomon, Barbara Miller, *In the Company of Educated Women: A History of Women and Higher Education in America*, New Haven and London: Yale University Press, 1985

Woody, Thomas, *A History of Women's Education in the United States*, 2 vols., New York: Science Press, 1929; reprinted, New York: Octagon, 1980

The study of women's education in the United States, like investigations of other aspects of schooling, has taken a new direction in the last thirty years. Previous work focused on curriculum (with special attention given to the physical education considered so problematic for women), setting, numbers, and comparisons between private and public schools. The English scholar BURSTALL's monograph on the education of girls is typical of this genre, although Burstall's international perspective encourages comparative insights such as her claims that American schools do not develop the individual talents of female students and that the excessive demands on students' time in United States women's colleges discourage intellectual inquiry.

The most substantial of these earlier institutional studies that focus on the externals of women's education is WOODY, a two-volume study published in 1929. Woody's comprehensive coverage of female education is organized chronologically and regionally, as the author covers topics from 19th-century academies to professional education for women. Woody offers the standard view that the motives for schooling a population whose future required domesticity were rooted in Europe, that the 19th century was the watershed for more academic training for American girls, and that changes in economics and politics accounted for the increase in female teachers and college students at the end of the 19th century. In this descriptive work education is a dependent variable. But Woody remains an indispensable, if encyclopedic, introduction to the field.

In the 1960s American historians expanded their understanding of education to include socialization – both in and out of the classroom. Simultaneously, under the general rubric of social history, investigations of women's history proliferated. Girls' schooling was often evaluated, as in an article by SCOTT on the Troy seminary in New York, as advancing feminism and the 19th-century women's movement. Investigations of women's education were no longer centered in male attitudes, but rather in female perceptions, the kinds of discrimination against women in schools and colleges and the dilemmas of educated women in a society that privileged motherhood and child-raising.

In KERBER's account of women during the American Revolution, political changes in society at large led to expanded and improved facilities for women, especially in the North. Alert to the exclusionary motives of male seminaries based on single-sex bonding, Kerber notes the different reasons for educating women who were no longer schooled solely to be interesting companions for their spouses. In the new Republic, more emphasis was placed on self-reliance for women, as an educated mother was expected to place her learning in service to her family's – and particularly her sons' – civic education, thereby making her contribution to the new nation. Unlike earlier studies, Kerber also extends the schooling of women – who were frequent autodidacts throughout the 19th century – to include reading.

Several biographies of women worthies have made important contributions to this field. Among these are Helen Horowitz's study of M. Carey Thomas, of Bryn Mawr College (1994), Elizabeth Green's *Mary Lyon and Mount Holyoke: Opening the Gates* (1979), and SKLAR's outstanding biography of a truly exceptional woman, Catharine Beecher. Her life, writings and especially her advocacy of women as moral educators both shaped and reflected 19th-century attitudes. Beecher's career as a teacher along with her insistence that women not be educated to be mere ornaments were important contributions to a field often incorrectly perceived as a progress from exclusion to equality.

Several excellent studies focus on one of the more abiding artifacts of women's separate sphere – the women's college. Mabel Newcomer's 1959 *A Century of Higher Education for American Women* takes an institutional approach to the subject. In a study of female professors at Wellesley, one of the most influential women's colleges in the United States, PALMIERI revises the standard wisdom that these colleges reinforced conventional notions of domesticity. Palmieri highlights Wellesley's separatist community which encouraged educated women to avoid marriage and instead enter careers of public service.

While also covering higher education, SOLOMON concentrates on the connections between education and the extent of choice in women's lives. Unlike Newcomer, Solomon also investigates women's struggles for access to institutions of higher learning, the nature of the college experience, and the links between feminism and women's higher education. She completed her book at a moment in the history of women's education when most women preferred coeducation, and the single-sex colleges of the past were abandoning their original mission. The historical meaning of single-sex college education for generations of Americans remains a neglected area of study in the field.

HOROWITZ, conscious of the hidden dimensions of education, imaginatively probes the limits of higher education for women as reflected in the architectural settings of the campuses of the Seven Sisters, together with three notable spin-offs – Sarah Lawrence, Bennington, and Scripps. Clearly women's education is for her more than intellectual development. As Horowitz makes clear, while the male founders of women's colleges offered demanding courses of liberal arts study, college life was more secluded and limited than that on male campuses, even as female students broke with conventions of femininity.

Just as women's education in the United States has significantly differed from that of men, so does black women's schooling differ from that of white women. HINE examines the segregated history of African American women, stressing the contributions of black women to education even before Reconstruction. Hine also includes biographical accounts of important African American educators.

JEAN H. BAKER

See also Education; Universities and Colleges entries

Women's History: Suffrage

Bolt, Christine, *The Women's Movements in the United States and Britain from the 1790s to the 1920s*, London: Harvester Wheatsheaf, and Amherst: University of Massachusetts Press, 1993

Buhle, Mari Jo and Paul Buhle (editors), *The Concise History of Woman Suffrage: Selections from the Classic Work of Stanton, Anthony, Gage, and Harper*, Urbana: University of Illinois Press, 1978

DuBois, Ellen Carol, *Feminism and Suffrage: The Emergence of an Independent Women's Movement in America, 1848–1869*, Ithaca, NY: Cornell University Press, 1978

Flexner, Eleanor, *Century of Struggle: The Woman's Rights Movement in the United States*, Cambridge, MA.: Belknap Press of Harvard University Press, 1959, revised 1975

Kraditor, Aileen S., *The Ideas of the Woman Suffrage Movement, 1890–1920*, New York: Columbia University Press, 1965; 2nd edition, New York: Norton, 1981

Melder, Keith, *Beginnings of Sisterhood: The American Woman's Rights Movement, 1800–1850*, New York: Schocken, 1977

O'Neill, William L., *Everyone Was Brave: The Rise and Fall of Feminism in America*, Chicago: Quadrangle, 1969; with new afterword as *Everyone was Brave: A History of Feminism in America*, 1971

Scott, Anne Firor and Andrew M. Scott, *One Half the People: The Fight for Woman Suffrage*, Philadelphia: Lippincott, 1975, 2nd edition, Urbana: University of Illinois Press, 1982

Sinclair, Andrew, *The Better Half: The Emancipation of the American Woman*, New York: Harper, 1965; London: Cape, 1966

Wheeler, Marjorie Spruill, *New Women of the New South: The Leaders of the Woman Suffrage Movement in the Southern States*, New York and Oxford: Oxford University Press, 1993

The woman's suffrage movement was the focus of historical analysis long before women's history became an accepted area for academic inquiry. It has been the subject of a considerable range of books, some more carefully researched than others. The first history of the movement was compiled by its early leaders, published in six volumes between 1881 and 1921. It is more readily accessible to modern readers in BUHLE and BUHLE's one-volume selection from the work. This includes a useful introductory essay, which describes the main trends and themes of the movement, explaining its origins and eventual success as a result of World War I. In editing the text of the original history, the Buhles have skilfully distilled the essence of the original work into a more manageable form. The selection reflects the spirit of the original volumes, both in its concentration only on the main suffrage organisations and its largely uncritical assessment of the suffrage movement.

FLEXNER, written before the second wave of American feminism and therefore not informed by it, was recognised at the time as a landmark in the history of the women's rights movement and remains one of the best works on the subject. It is impressive in its range, and places the suffrage movement in the wider context of social and economic change. It also recognises the depth of the achievement of the suffrage leaders, and the difficulty of the struggle – a fact which tends to be obscured by later works which seek to explain why the vote achieved so little for women.

Both SINCLAIR and O'NEILL reflect changing perceptions of women's place in American society as the second wave of American feminism began to develop. Both see the fight for the suffrage as part of the wider movement for women's rights and are critical of the suffrage movement's concentration on the single issue of the vote. O'Neill, in particular, is very judgmental, blaming the suffrage movement for its failure to achieve any real improvements in women's status with the vote. Though his work has much to commend it, it tends to judge the earlier movement too much from the perspective of the feminist movement of the 1960s. In what is essentially a collection of documents, SCOTT and SCOTT provide a useful introductory essay which places the documents in their context, and offers some insights into the movement. The focus is upon the suffrage campaign and the tactics of the main suffrage organisations, with little indication of the extent of the opposition to or support for the movement. It is suggested that the splits in the suffrage movement might actually have contributed to its eventual success. The Scotts also suggest that the vote helped women to advance their cause materially and provided a foundation upon which other efforts were able to build.

KRADITOR is a more specialized study of the ideas of the suffrage movement as they developed in the Progressive Era. She suggests that the ideas of the suffragists reflected their aspirations but were also their weapons, often developed in response to their opponents. Kraditor argues that the Progressive Era was crucial to the movement, as the suffragists repositioned themselves. Thus, they shifted their argument from an insistence upon natural justice to one based on expediency and women's special qualities. This is a well-researched book, and offers some provocative, if occasionally doubtful, conclusions.

MELDER locates the origins of the suffrage movement in the reform movements of the antebellum period. He argues that since much of women's reform activity in these years focused upon the particular problems of women, the 1830s were vital in the development of the issues which would eventually lead to the creation of an organised women's movement. As reformers of various kinds, women came into direct confrontation with male traditions and behaviour patterns. Antislavery was, however, the key reform movement in the creation of an independent women's rights movement. Melder's work is useful in placing the women's rights movement in the context of antebellum reform, but he needs to explain more fully why so few women actually embraced the cause before the Civil War.

In contrast, DuBOIS sees the post-Civil War years as the crucial period. She suggests that failure to achieve the suffrage in the 1870s was far less the result of hostilities within the suffrage movement, than an aspect of the defeat of Reconstruction radicalism. Conflict within the movement during the late 1860s significantly advanced the movement and liberated it from its subservience to abolitionism. Such a positive interpretation of events does not, however, fully explain why it took the suffrage movement so long to secure the vote.

Interestingly there have been few books written during the last few years specifically on the national woman's suffrage movement. There have, though, been an increasing number of local and regional studies, as well as a few comparative studies. One excellent example of the former is WHEELER's study of the southern woman suffrage movement. Meticulous in its research and compelling in its analysis, it convincingly connects the rise of the suffrage movement in the South with the issues of race, rights and reform. Wheeler draws upon the current scholarship in women's history to produce an impressive study of the ideas and actions of eleven southern leaders of the movement. BOLT is a useful synthesis of more recent work on the women's movements in Britain and the United States, with much of its focus on the suffrage movements. The comparative perspective offers a fresh look at the issues and a useful overview.

ELIZABETH J. CLAPP

See also Suffrage

Women's History: Women at Work

Andolsen, Barbara Hilker, *Good Work at the Video Display Terminal: A Feminist Ethical Analysis of Changes in Clerical Work*, Knoxville: University of Tennessee Press, 1989

Benson, Susan Porter, *Counter Cultures: Saleswomen, Managers, and Customers in American Department Stores, 1890–1940*, Urbana: University of Illinois Press, 1986

Boydston, Jeanne, *Home and Work: Housework, Wages and the Ideology of Labor in the Early Republic*, New York: Oxford University Press, 1990

Cantor, Milton and Bruce Laurie, *Class, Sex, and the Woman Worker*, Westport, CT: Greenwood Press, 1977

Dublin, Thomas, *Transforming Women's Work: New England Lives in the Industrial Revolution*, Ithaca, NY: Cornell University Press, 1994

Goldin, Claudia, *Understanding the Gender Gap: An Economic History of American Women*, New York and Oxford: Oxford University Press, 1990

Hart, Vivien, *Bound by Our Constitution: Women, Workers, and the Minimum Wage*, Princeton: Princeton University Press, 1994

Jensen, Joan M., *Loosening the Bonds: Mid-Atlantic Farm Women, 1750–1850*, New Haven and London: Yale University Press, 1986

Jones, Jacqueline, *Labor of Love, Labor of Sorrow: Black Women, Work, and the Family from Slavery to the Present*, New York: Basic Books, 1985

Kessler-Harris, Alice, *Out to Work: A History of Wage-Earning Women in the United States*, New York and Oxford: Oxford University Press, 1982

Kleinberg, S.J., *The Shadow of the Mills: Working-Class Families in Pittsburgh, 1870–1907*, Pittsburgh: University of Pittsburgh Press, 1989

Oppenheimer, Valerie Kincade, *The Female Labor Force in the United States: Demographic and Economic Factors Governing Its Growth and Changing Composition*, Berkeley: University of California Press, 1970

The historical interest in women's work surged from the 1970s onwards, pursuing several related themes, with new ones emerging as the interests of the research community expanded. In one of the first monographs to explore the structural changes in the female labor force, OPPENHEIMER analyzes supply and demand factors, the discrete nature of the male and female labor markets, and the demographic factors which led to the expansion of employment for older and married women. The work tends toward the schematic, structural and quantitative. Based upon United States Census data, it details basic quantitative data about which women were in the labor market between 1900 and 1960.

Most of the initial histories of working women defined work as paid employment whether it occurred inside or outside the home. KESSLER-HARRIS provides a comprehensive overview of female labor force participation from the colonial era through the 1970s. She integrates the study of laboring women with major economic, social, political, and cultural events to provide a comprehensive overall text on the topic of female employment. If one had to chose only one text on women's work, this would be it.

GOLDIN's study of the economic history of American women also covers a long time span, stretching from the colonial era to the present day. It makes use of econometric data and numerous case studies in order to track the developments in female employment patterns. Goldin explores the reasons for the gender gap in earnings and analyzes the racial and ethnic patterns in women's work. She correlates employment with specific stages of women's life cycles, the changing economic role of married women, and the political economy of gender. Some readers may find the econometric techniques difficult to follow, but the textual explanations are clear.

The essays included in CANTOR and LAURIE concentrate on trade union organizing, the labor market experience of women in different ethnic groups, cross class organizing, and some of the methodologies used in the study of working women. The emphasis is on northern and western industrial workers, particularly those from Irish, Italian, and Jewish backgrounds, but there is little on southern women or African Americans.

One specialized source which remedies this omission is JONES, who concentrates on the labor and family situations of African American women during slavery and freedom. She sets work in its widest context, probing the gendered and racial meanings of the term and the range of women's experiences. This study traces that experience from toil as plantation hands under slavery to work as free laborers, and domestic servants, and on through employment and geographical transitions within the bounds of a racially biased society.

Women worked in a variety of settings and at a variety of tasks. JENSEN explores women's role in the development of agriculture in the Mid-Atlantic region between 1750 and 1850. She devotes particular attention to women's production of butter for market in the context of the rural domestic economy. She also considers the ways in which this market orientation contributed to women's engagement in affairs outside the home, especially in the Quaker churches and early reformist activities in the antebellum era.

BOYDSTON explores the changing nature of work as a concept in the colonial and antebellum eras. Commercial agricultural production and industrialization altered how both sexes regarded domestic labor. When the production of goods and services moved outside the household, the activities carried on by women within the home were no longer regarded as work. That term described paid wage labor, while what housewives did for their families became a labor of love. By considering how societies regard work inside and outside the home, Boydston indicates that it is a fluid construct susceptible to a wide variety of economic, social, and political factors. This book provides insight into the origin of the separate spheres for women and men which underpinned much of female reform activity outside the home.

The structure of the local economy strongly influenced whether women would hold jobs outside the home, and also the domestic work which they performed. As KLEINBERG shows, in late 19th and early 20th century Pittsburgh, heavy industry – iron, steel, mining and railroading – employed no women. An economy dependent upon those industries marginalized women's non-domestic employment, and reinforced a narrow set of roles. In the Steel City, married women took in boarders to supplement uncertain male incomes, while unmarried women worked in shops, offices, food processing, and other women's kitchens. Kleinberg examines women's economic activity in the context of family life and the structure of the local economy, exploring the interaction between men's and women's economic contributions to working-class families. She also analyzes the impact of urbanization on working-class women and children, and the way different social classes experienced urban life.

Work and working are cultural and economic constructs rather than terms with definitions valid for all times and places. HART's examination of the campaign for minimum wages for women working in the sweated trades explores the fundamental issue of gender-based legislation, and social assumptions about women's work. Set primarily in the Progressive Era and Great Depression, her comparative analysis of the family wage economy incorporates new theoretical perspectives in women's history. Examining the different means employed to regulate women's work in Britain and the United States, Hart compares the two political and legal systems, and their significance in formulating social policy.

There are many analyses of women's employment in specific industries, including textiles, shoes, department stores, offices, and domestic service, references to which can be obtained through the general historical texts already cited. DUBLIN considers women's role in the industrial revolution, noting that many of the first modern labor histories gave the impression that men formed the bulk of the early industrial labor force, when, in fact, women comprised the majority of textile workers and were well represented in the shoe industry. He traces the processes by which women became an industrial labor force, the social significance of their work, and the diversity of female employment in New England in the 19th century.

In the 20th century, white-collar work, particularly secretarial and clerical jobs, have become the dominant mode of employment for women. BENSON details one area of expanding female employment, the shops and stores which accompanied the commercial revolution in the United States in the early 20th century. The new emporia of consumption witnessed a three-way battle for primacy between the sales clerks, the management, and the customers. This contest reflected the gendered, racial, and class hierarchies of American society and is explored here in the context of labor and management relations, and the social acceptability of certain forms of employment and certain potential employees.

In an examination of the other prevalent form of white collar work for women, ANDOLSEN investigates the changes in clerical work and the meaning of office automation. She notes the continued gendering of the work place so that work done by women receives lower pay regardless of the skills involved. She places clerical work in an international context, since the computer communications revolution means that data entry does not need to occur in the same site as data production. This exerts a downward pressure on wages and working conditions.

S.J. KLEINBERG

Women's History: Women in Ethnic Minority Groups

Amott, Teresa L. and Julie A. Matthaei, *Race, Gender, and Work: A Multicultural Economic History of Women in the United States*, Boston: South End Press, 1991

DuBois, Ellen Carol and Vicki L. Ruiz (editors), *Unequal Sisters: A Multicultural Reader in US Women's History*, New York: Routledge, 1990, 2nd edition, 1994

Giddings, Paula, *When and Where I Enter: The Impact of Black Women on Race and Sex in America*, New York: Morrow, 1984

Hine, Darlene Clark (editor) *Black Women in United States History*, 16 vols., New York: Carlson, 1990

Jones, Jacqueline, *Labor of Love, Labor of Sorrow: Black Women, Work, and the Family from Slavery to the Present*, New York: Basic Books, 1985

Mirandé, Alfredo and Evangelina Enríquez, *La Chicana: The Mexican-American Woman*, Chicago: University of Chicago Press, 1979

Nakano, Mei, *Japanese American Women: Three Generations, 1890–1990*, Berkeley, CA: Mina Press, 1990

Niethammer, Carolyn, *Daughters of the Earth: The Lives and Legends of American Indian Women*, New York: Collier, 1977

Seller, Maxine Schwartz (editor), *Immigrant Women*, Philadelphia: Temple University Press, 1981; 2nd edition, Albany: State University of New York Press, 1994

Weinberg, Sydney Stahl, *World of Our Mothers: Lives of Jewish Immigrant Women*, Chapel Hill: University of North Carolina Press, 1988

Historical literature concerning women in America has exploded during the last three decades, and an increasingly large part of that explosion includes works that discuss the experiences of women in different ethnic groups. Some of the best of this work can be sampled in two general readers, one edited by DuBois and Ruiz, the other by Amott and Matthaei. The anthology edited by DuBOIS and RUIZ provides a wonderful overall introduction to the field. Among important contributions by leading authorities, the second edition includes essays on the experiences of African American, Asian American, Native American and Mexican American women. There is also an outstanding introduction which discusses the issues and difficulties involved in multicultural women's history, and there are four excellent bibliographies. AMOTT and MATTHAEI adopt a somewhat different approach in their predominantly economic history. Not only do they choose to focus on the relationship between women and work, but they do so from a "theoretical framework of radical political economics." Their volume gives a general overview of the role of wage work in women's lives and includes chapters on Native American, Chicana, African American, European American, Asian American, and Puerto Rican women.

The area which has received the most scholarly attention to date is African American women's history. GIDDINGS represents one of the first attempts to chronicle the lives of African American women and remains one of the most comprehensive works. Its main drawback is that it does not include any discussion of how slavery affected the lives of African American women, but JONES remedies this oversight. In addition, whereas Giddings tends to focus on the role and contributions of individuals, Jones is more concerned with the experiences and lives of the general population of African American women. Her volume explores the interconnection between the personal and public lives of African American women, and the effect of that interconnection on their families. With its emphasis on wage labor, there is a strong emphasis on economic history in this volume. The most monumental study is HINE's 16-volume anthology, which consists largely of collections of scholarly essays previously published elsewhere. These include work by some of the most important figures in the field and span the period from slavery to the present.

The experiences of immigrant women in the United States have received less scholarly attention. In an attempt to fill this gap, SELLER offers a good introduction. This is another anthology of scholarly essays, but it is organized thematically, and includes sections devoted to the reasons for immigration, employment, family and community life, education, political activism, and generation conflict. An excellent bibliographical essay covering both general works and more specialized studies dealing with the experiences of European, Middle Eastern, Asian, Caribbean, Latina and Pacific Asian immigrants, adds to the usefulness of this volume.

There are various studies of particular ethnic groups. WEINBERG describes the experiences of Jewish immigrant women, told from their own perspectives. Utilizing oral history interviews with 47 women, this study focuses on the issues that these women found important – family, work, and education – and explores how women's attitudes differed from those of their male counterparts. The lives of Mexican American women, or Latinas/Chicanas, have also attracted scholarly

interest during the last two decades. Much of the work in this field is highly theoretical, but MIRANDÉ and ENRÍQUEZ provide an accessible introduction. Divided into seven parts, their study explores the impact of Mexican culture as well as family life, employment and education among Latinas. They conclude with sections exploring the images of Latinas in literature and discussing Chicana feminism. The bibliography is very full, but without any categorization of the books, it can be rather overwhelming.

Finally, two groups of women who are just now beginning to be studied are Japanese and Native American women. NAKANO is an exploration of three generations of Japanese American women, and the ways in which cultural assimilation varies between generations. It is another volume which utilizes oral history interviews, and the result is a highly readable volume in which the lives of individual women are the main focus. NIETHAMMER is another non-traditional history, in that it is organized around women's life cycle events – menarche, marriage, childbirth, menopause, death – instead of a traditional chronological approach. The result is a readable and fascinating study which explores all facets of Native American women's lives.

VANESSA L. DAVIS

See also Immigration and Ethnicity

Women's History: Women's Liberation Movement

Collins, Patricia Hill, *Black Feminist Thought: Knowledge, Consciousness, and the Politics of Empowerment*, Boston: Unwin Hyman, and London: Routledge, 1990

Davis, Flora, *Moving the Mountain: The Women's Movement in America since 1960*, New York: Simon and Schuster, 1991

Evans, Sara M., *Personal Politics: The Roots of Women's Liberation in the Civil Rights Movement and the New Left*, New York: Knopf, 1979

Faludi, Susan, *Backlash: The Undeclared War Against American Women*, New York: Crown, 1991; London: Chatto and Windus, 1992

Friedan, Betty, *The Feminine Mystique*, New York: Norton, and London: Gollancz, 1963

Harrison, Cynthia, *On Account of Sex: The Politics of Women's Issues, 1945–1968*, Berkeley: University of California Press, 1988

Mansbridge, Jane J., *Why We Lost the ERA*, Chicago: University of Chicago Press, 1986

Mathews, Donald G. and Jane Sherron DeHart, *Sex, Gender, and the Politics of ERA: A State and the Nation*, New York and Oxford: Oxford University Press, 1990

The books discussed here provide a chronological account of the events leading up to the Women's Liberation Movement of the 1960s and 1970s. They encompass the economic, social, and political conditions which gave rise to the movement and discuss its consequences for gender relations and women's status. HARRISON places women's issues in the context of economic and political developments after World War II in her exploration of the demobilization backlash against women, the subsequent widening of their employment opportunities, and women's involvement in social protest movements such as the peace and civil rights movements. She notes that governmental policies about women altered despite the absence of a mass social movement. She provides a detailed analysis of the President's Commission on the Status of Women set up by President John F. Kennedy and the inclusion of a ban on discrimination against women in the Civil Rights Act of 1964.

A number of works shed light on the disparate perspectives and issues behind the Women's Liberation Movement. FRIEDAN, first published in 1963, documented the "problem that had no name," the dissatisfaction that many middle-class women experienced with their suburban domestic existence in the late 1950s and early 1960s. Based upon questionnaires distributed to Smith College alumnae, media portrayals of women, and the pervasive employment discrimination encountered even by educated women, the book became a rallying cry for one group of feminists, mostly white, middle-aged, and middle-class. It attacks Sigmund Freud's attitudes towards women, biases in education, and advertisers' attempts to sell housewifery as a female vocation. Friedan documented what many women felt about their lives, namely that "having it all" did not provide happiness. Her remedy for the dissatisfied housewife was for her to find a job which would put her education and talents to real use, rather than the make-work that many women undertook. Friedan went on to found the National Organization for Women, which battles for equal rights on a wide variety of issues.

Many women in the African American community had jobs, but found that the discrimination in employment still endemic in American society in the postwar era prevented work from being a panacea. Employment as experienced by many black and poor white women was not necessarily liberating. In a social and intellectual history, COLLINS examines another group of feminists, African American women, many of whom came to feminism through frustration with the civil rights movement, in which they did much of the work but were excluded from most leadership and policymaking positions. She locates the experience of black women at the center of her analysis, exploring the origins of black feminist thought, the sometimes uneasy relationships between white and black feminists, and the sexual politics of relationships within the African American community.

The interconnectedness of social movements underpins EVANS's analysis of the origins of the Women's Liberation Movement. She examines the activism of black and white women in the civil rights and antiwar movements, and the ways in which white feminists drew upon civil rights metaphors in order to situate the oppression of women in the context of the exploitation of African American men and women. Written from both an academic and personal standpoint, this work also reflects upon the conflict within the New Left and antiwar movements in which women were treated as second-class citizens and radicalized on that account. Evans concentrates on women's liberation as it existed upon the university campuses

of the 1960s and 1970s, but has relatively little to say about the more middle-of-the-road organizations which outlasted the radical alternatives.

DAVIS provides an overview of the Women's Liberation Movement from 1960 onwards which both details the origins of the movement in other social movements and examines its expansion from a largely campus-based protest movement to a much broader challenge to economic, social, political, and sexual norms. This study also explores the opposition to feminism, some of it from women and much of it from the political and religious right of the American political spectrum. Davis demonstrates the broad scope and far-reaching impact of the Women's Liberation Movement on all aspects of American life. She documents the pervasive discrimination which women encountered in many areas, reminding us that as late as the early 1960s airline stewardesses (as they were then called) were routinely fired if they got married, turned 32, or gained a few pounds. Largely because of women's activism, it has been made illegal to discriminate on account of sex, marital status, or age and, as a result, the rules of employment and welfare, among other areas, have been fundamentally altered.

Where the movement failed was in its attempts to incorporate an anti-discrimination amendment into the American Constitution. Both Mathews and DeHart, and Mansbridge, examine the reasons why a sufficient number of states refused to ratify the Equal Rights Amendment (ERA). MANSBRIDGE analyzes the weakening base of support for the ERA from 1982. She documents the confusion over equal rights and proscribed gender roles which anti-feminists and conservatives exploited and against which feminists fought unsuccessfully. She also explores the tensions within the Women's Liberation Movement which reduced its effectiveness as a national lobbying effort. MATHEWS and DeHART's account of the failure to pass the ERA begins with the women's suffrage movement and then focuses primarily on the supporters and opponents of the ERA in North Carolina. They allow both groups to speak for themselves, and give their reasons for their stance. In their analysis, sex and how people understood it, rather than political or economic rights, was the underlying issue in people's position on the ERA. The conservative and religious right was particularly successful in depicting the ERA as a threat to conventional family forms and gender relations. The battle over the constitutional amendment was thus fought over roles and values rather than legal issues.

The failure to pass the Equal Rights Amendment was but one aspect of what has come to be termed the backlash against women and feminism, exploited by newspapers, magazines, cinema, and television as a means of selling products and satisfying the men in charge. FALUDI documents the pervasive anti-women sentiment of the media as well as the emergence of a right-wing political and social agenda which uses anti-feminist rhetoric as a means of mobilizing public opinion and support. She also examines the legal decisions which have undercut the equal treatment of women and men in the marketplace.

S.J. KLEINBERG

Woodhull, Victoria   1838–1927

Campaigner for women's rights

Brough, James, *The Vixens: A Biography of Victoria and Tennessee Claflin*, New York: Simon and Schuster, 1980

Johnston, Johanna, *Mrs. Satan: The Incredible Saga of Victoria C. Woodhull*, New York: Putnam, 1967

Marberry, M.M., *Vicky: A Biography of Victoria C. Woodhull*, New York: Funk and Wagnalls, 1967

Meade, Marion, *Free Woman: The Life and Times of Victoria Woodhull*, New York: Knopf, 1976

Sachs, Emanie, *The Terrible Siren: Victoria Woodhull*, New York: Harper, 1928

Underhill, Lois Beachy, *The Woman Who Ran for President: The Many Lives of Victoria Woodhull*, Bridgehamton, NY: Bridge Works, 1995

Victoria Claflin Woodhull, spiritualist, writer and publisher of *Woodhull & Claflin's Weekly*, friend and confidante of millionaire Cornelius Vanderbilt, and women's rights activist, was one of the most flamboyant and radical women of the late 19th century. An advocate of free love, she married, divorced, and co-habited with men in an era dominated by a belief in marital monogamy and female purity. Woodhull's beliefs and actions prevented her from operating within the most powerful circles of the suffrage movement, yet she actively cultivated friendships with suffrage leaders such as Elizabeth Cady Stanton, and spent much of her own money on suffrage causes.

In 1872 she exposed Elizabeth Tilton's affair with Henry Ward Beecher, setting off a scandal that rocked the intellectual and religious community of the East Coast. She also announced her candidacy for President of the United States, which caused great debate both inside and outside the suffrage movement. Defeated in her bid for the presidency, plagued by obscenity lawsuits stemming from her exposure of Beecher's infidelities, and discouraged that the American public did not appreciate her use of "truth," Woodhull left the United States for England in 1877. There she met the banker John Biddulph Martin, married him in 1883 after a stormy courtship, and spent the rest of her life in England trying to live as a respectable gentlewoman.

Woodhull's colorful life has proved a challenge to biographers, who have thus far focused on a chronological rather than analytical approach. In both cases utilizing an impressive array of contemporary sources, SACHS and JOHNSTON provide the two most comprehensive accounts of Woodhull's beliefs and actions, but neither provides an interpretation within a historical context. Sachs, Woodhull's first biographer, is generally unsympathetic towards her subject.

MEADE provides a mildly critical but softer view of Woodhull, arguing that her radical activities, while well-intentioned, set back the cause of women's rights. The book is basically a chronological narrative, but includes little on the last twenty years of Woodhull's life. BROUGH is similar in style and approach, although he includes Tennessee Claflin, Woodhull's sister and business partner, as a major character. Resembling a novel rather than a scholarly biography, the book incorporates dialogue which is taken from contemporary but uncited sources.

MARBERRY organizes his chapters around the most dramatic events in Woodhull's life, highlighting the Tilton-Beecher scandal, and allegations of attempted blackmail of prominent New Yorkers. He portrays her not only as a radical but also as a prima donna, referring to her as "The Woodhull" – as did some of her contemporaries. Marberry is clearly amused by his subject.

In much the most recent study, UNDERHILL comes closest to providing a historical analysis of Woodhull's actions and beliefs, and acknowledges the larger forces that may have influenced her. In a well-organized chronological narrative, presented in short, readable chapters, Underhill shows Woodhull's calculated manoeuvres for power both in the New York business world and in the suffrage movement. This book is intended to be a feminist biography, and includes an introduction by the feminist writer Gloria Steinem.

THERESA KAMINSKI

Working Classes

Dublin, Thomas, *Women at Work: The Transformation of Work and Community in Lowell, Massachusetts, 1826–1860*, New York: Columbia University Press, 1975

Gutman, Herbert G., *Work, Culture, and Society in Industrializing America: Essays in American Working-Class and Social History*, New York: Knopf, 1976; Oxford: Blackwell, 1977

Gutman, Herbert G., *Power and Culture: Essays on the American Working Class*, edited by Ira Berlin, New York: Pantheon, 1987

Peiss, Kathy, *Cheap Amusements: Working Women and Leisure in Turn-of-the-Century New York City*, Philadelphia: Temple University Press, 1986

Rosenzweig, Roy, *Eight Hours for What We Will: Workers and Leisure in an Industrial City, 1870–1920*, Cambridge and New York: Cambridge University Press, 1983

Rubin, Lillian B., *Worlds of Pain: Life in the Working-Class Family*, New York: Basic Books, 1976

Slayton, Robert A., *Back of the Yards: The Making of a Local Democracy*, Chicago: University of Chicago Press, 1986

Stansell, Christine, *City of Women: Sex and Class in New York, 1789–1860*, New York: Knopf, 1986

Wilentz, Sean, *Chants Democratic: New York City and the Rise of the American Working Class, 1788–1850*, New York: Oxford University Press, 1984

Zonderman, David A., *Aspirations and Anxieties: New England Workers and the Mechanized Factory System, 1815–1850*, New York: Oxford University Press, 1992

While numerous works have been written which examine the subjects of industry and labor in American history, it is surprising to find that fewer works – until recently, at least – concern themselves primarily with the development of a working-class identity. However, there are a number of important studies which examine in a general manner the working lives of industrial workers in the United States. Foremost among the historians to have explored this topic in a comprehensive manner is Herbert Gutman, America's principal historian of the working class. GUTMAN (1976 and 1987) are two excellent and profoundly influential collections of essays on working-class and social history, which range over many aspects of the working-class experience. Among the topics considered are the demographic composition of the American working class in the 19th century, the working and family lives of African Americans, both enslaved and free, and the clash between industrial work regimens and workers from traditional, pre-industrial societies. These works are probably the best place to start for a reader new to the topic who wishes to acquire an overview of the major themes and topics in working-class history.

Although not in the same league as Gutman, ZONDERMAN provides an excellent generalized study of the working lives of early New England mill and factory hands, and analyzes the complex relationship which existed between New England industrial workers, their employers, and their work sites and work regimens. Zonderman examines in great detail workers' relationships with their employers and supervisors, their attempts to hold on to pre-industrial work routines and environments, and the impact of differences in age, gender, ethnicity, class, and country of birth on workers' relationships with one another, and on their interaction with the many complex parts of the industrial system. Zonderman's work provides a wealth of detail on all aspects of the early 19th century work experience, and serves as an excellent introduction to the topic of workers' lives during the early stages of industrialization.

While Zonderman's work provides a good discussion of the lives of female textile operatives, STANSELL's study of the lives of working-class women in New York City in the early to mid-19th century is by far the best examination of the historical interaction of class and gender. Stansell explores all facets of the lives of working-class women, including their work within the home, their relationships with their husbands and children, the formation of female networks and friendships with other women, their leisure-time activities, their work regimens in factories, shops, and sweatshops, and their encounters with the representatives of middle-class charitable organizations. Stansell examines in depth the double burden which working-class women encountered in their roles as working wives and mothers.

Among the few American historians to have tackled the subject of class consciousness, WILENTZ describes the formation of a working-class identity among American artisans in the period following the American Revolution. He examines in exhaustive detail working-class politics, the clash between wage labor and early capitalist entrepreneurs, and the development of working-class political culture. Wilentz analyzes the use of revolutionary language and republican rhetoric by workers angered by their loss of status as a result of the growth of industrial capitalism. Of particular interest is the Introduction in which Wilentz reviews past historical scholarship on the interaction between class and politics in American history. This is perhaps the best study of the early development of class-consciousness in America. Although Wilentz does consider the role of women in class formation,

DUBLIN is a much more thorough and insightful study of the growth of working-class consciousness, and its relationship to issues of nativity and ethnicity, among female workers in New England textile mills.

While many historians have presented workers as victims of industrial capitalism, others have concentrated on portraying members of the working class as active, innovative historical agents. In his study of Slavic immigrant workers in Chicago's stockyards district (the same community portrayed in Upton Sinclair's The Jungle), SLAYTON concludes that the abuses of industrialization did not prevent these workers from forming a true community, or from developing alternative systems of support which helped them to survive economic crises and preserve their Slavic heritage. Slayton examines in depth the role played by family, immigrant benevolent societies, schools, political organizations, the foreign-language press, and the Catholic church in providing networks of support and buffers against the brutalities of industrial employment. While there is much of value in Slayton's study, it becomes bogged down at times in lengthy discussions of Chicago politics which will test the patience of many readers.

One area of working-class culture that has received particular attention is the role and use of leisure in working-class communities. PEISS examines the effect which the entry of large numbers of young, working-class women into the work force had on working-class leisure. She examines the substantial role played by these young women in transforming working-class leisure culture from being homosocial to heterosocial in nature. Peiss describes the ways in which leisure activities provided young, working-class women with an opportunity to rebel against parental authority, and to assert their own sense of female autonomy and style. This independence and style appealed to middle-class youth as well, and influenced the adoption of working-class leisure patterns by the middle class. Peiss's work makes an interesting contribution both to working-class history and to women's history.

In a similar vein, ROSENZWEIG examines the clash between the working and middle classes over the definition of suitable leisure activities. Rosenzweig examines efforts by the native-born, Protestant middle class to control or eliminate such sources of working-class leisure as saloons and raucous Fourth of July celebrations. It is suggested that, while workers achieved some success in resisting middle-class attempts to control their leisure-time behavior, new forms of recreation (specifically motion pictures) arose in the early 20th century, which ultimately erased differences between classes and within them. Rosenzweig concludes that, by replacing ethnically homogeneous saloons as centers of recreation, and imparting "American," middle-class values to diverse social groups, mass amusements worked to eliminate ethnic differences between workers, and thus helped to create a consolidated, non-ethnic working class and working-class culture.

There has been less historical study of working-class life or consciousness in the 20th century. However, a few excellent sociological works do exist. For example, RUBIN explores the effect which limited education and little opportunity for economic advancement have on working-class marriages. She concludes that the tensions created by increased material expectations in an age of declining job security and decreasing financial rewards for blue-collar workers are directly responsible for the conflict, disappointment, apathy, and loneliness that characterize the marital relationships of many working-class Americans.

ANN KORDAS

See also Class

World War I: American Neutrality, 1914–1917

Cohen, Warren I., *The American Revisionists: The Lessons of Intervention in World War I*, Chicago: University of Chicago Press, 1967

Coogan, John W., *The End of Neutrality: The United States, Britain, and Maritime Rights, 1899–1915*, Ithaca, NY: Cornell University Press, 1981

Devlin, Patrick, *Too Proud to Fight: Woodrow Wilson's Neutrality*, New York: Oxford University Press, 1974

Link, Arthur S., *Wilson: The Struggle for Neutrality, 1914–1915*, Princeton: Princeton University Press, 1960

Link, Arthur S., *Wilson: Confusions and Crises, 1915–1916*, Princeton: Princeton University Press, 1964

Link, Arthur S., *Wilson: Campaigns for Progressivism and Peace, 1916–1917*, Princeton: Princeton University Press, 1965

Link, Arthur S., *Woodrow Wilson: Revolution, War, and Peace*, Arlington Heights, IL: Harlan Davidson, 1979

May, Ernest R., *The World War and American Isolation, 1914–1917*, Cambridge, MA: Harvard University Press, 1959

Osgood, Robert E., *Ideals and Self-Interest in America's Foreign Relations: The Great Transformation of the Twentieth Century*, Chicago: University of Chicago Press, 1953

Smith, Daniel M., *The Great Departure: The United States and World War I, 1914–1920*, New York: Wiley, 1965

Discussions of American diplomacy, 1914–17, are inevitably shaped by the question of why the United States entered World War I. This question has been of more than academic interest since it has generally been taken to have a direct bearing on the wider issues of whether American involvement in world politics has been either wise or necessary. In the interwar years, the historiographical running was made by those who thought it was neither, and who traced American belligerency to the unneutral character of United States policy, variously attributed to the pro-Ally bias of President Woodrow Wilson and his advisers, Allied propaganda, the influence of arms manufacturers and bankers directly involved in supplying Britain and France with munitions and loans, or the extent to which the whole nation's prosperity had become dependent on its greatly expanded trade with the Allied powers. Such "revisionist" literature, in its significantly different forms, is probably best approached through COHEN's lucid and judicious account and assessment.

The ascendancy of such interpretations was manifested in the Neutrality Laws of 1935–37, and, just as the events of 1939–41 led to the gradual dismantling of this legislation, so they gave rise to different interpretations of the earlier experience. Publicists who favoured throwing America's weight against the Axis powers now argued that United States intervention in World War I had been inspired by a realistic concern with the nation's security – which they saw as once again at stake. This perspective influenced much of the writing of the 1940s and 1950s but, in the most thorough investigation of the thesis, OSGOOD, while maintaining that a concern with national security *ought* to have guided American policy, concludes that in fact it did not play any significant part in forming the attitudes of Wilson, his advisers, other leading political figures, Congress, or the great majority of contemporary commentators.

Whereas Osgood focuses on the domestic debate over the course which the nation should follow, MAY analyzes the interaction of policymaking in Washington, London and Berlin on the basis of documentation from all three countries. In his view, Wilson's decision for war was determined neither by economic nor by security considerations, but by the need to preserve America's prestige so that the country could use its influence to secure a lasting peace. May sees American diplomacy as reflecting the contradictory pressures of nationalism and neutralism – a determination to uphold American rights and honour co-existing with a strong desire to avoid involvement in the conflict. While recognizing that Wilson was clearly in command of policy, May stresses the president's concern for national unity, and thus the influence upon him of public opinion.

As the biographer of Wilson, LINK (1960–65) naturally concentrates more on the thought-processes of the president himself. However, the three large volumes which cover the period of neutrality are much more wide-ranging than might be expected and provide the most detailed and authoritative account of the whole complex story. These volumes are based not only on Wilson's own voluminous papers but also on a vast array of other unpublished as well as published sources. Among the aspects which Link's narrative illuminates are the elements of flexibility in United States policy towards submarine warfare and the extent to which the Allies had by 1916 become dependent on American financing. The chief points in Link's interpretations are clearly set out in LINK (1979), an extensively revised version of lectures originally published under the title *Wilson the Diplomatist* (1957). Link argues that Wilson's objective from the start of the war was to maintain the neutrality of the United States in accordance with international law. Increasingly, however, his policy was governed by the desire to bring the war to an end and establish a lasting peace – and this was "the impelling reason" for his "acceptance of belligerency" in 1917.

Subsequent works have been written in the shadow of Link's scholarship. The debt is generously acknowledged by DEVLIN, whose substantial book is based almost entirely on printed sources. It is nonetheless a thoroughly scholarly as well as elegantly written piece of history, the product of over two decades' private study by an eminent British judge. As a committed Christian, Devlin seems to have been attracted to the subject by the idea that "Wilson in the 20th century represents idealism in action", and his analysis of American policy in these years focuses on the role of the president and the light which this throws on his character. Consequently, Devlin probes more insistently than other writers the reasons for Wilson's changes of course, and for the occasional discrepancy between the president's public position and that adopted in his secret diplomacy. Although Devlin's conclusion that Wilson entered the war to enhance his influence over the peace accords with those of May and Link, he presents the case for it more fully and clearly than they do.

By contrast, COOGAN is more critical of Wilson and explicitly takes issue with Link's claim that the president was guided by international law in his handling of the issues of neutrality. By reviewing the official positions of both the British and American governments on maritime rights before the war, Coogan shows how far the "blockade" of Germany imposed by Britain in 1914–15 departed from these. He attributes the effective acquiescence of the United States in such clearly illegal actions to Wilson's pro-British bias. However, Coogan's neo-revisionist suggestion that this paved the way for American belligerency is necessarily undeveloped as he does not carry the story beyond March 1915 or discuss the dispute with Germany over submarine warfare.

There are several brief introductions to the subject, of which the best is probably still SMITH's lucid and thoughtful account – though in highlighting the issue of national security, it reflects the era in which it was written.

JOHN A. THOMPSON

World War I: the United States at War, 1917–1918

Braim, Paul F., *The Test of Battle: The American Expeditionary Forces in the Meuse-Argonne Campaign*, Newark: University of Delaware Press, 1987

Breen, William J., *Uncle Sam at Home: Civilian Mobilization, Wartime Federalism, and the Council of National Defense, 1917–1919*, Westport, CT: Greenwood Press, 1984

Clark, John Maurice, *The Costs of the World War to the American People*, New Haven: Yale University Press, and London: Oxford University Press, 1931

Coffman, Edward M., *The War to End All Wars: The American Military Experience in World War I*, New York: Oxford University Press, 1968

Conner, Valerie Jean, *The National War Labor Board: Stability, Social Justice, and the Voluntary State in World War I*, Chapel Hill: University of North Carolina Press, 1983

Cooper, John Milton, Jr. (editor), *Causes and Consequences of World War I*, New York: Quadrangle, 1972

Cuff, Robert D., *The War Industries Board: Business-Government Relations During World War I*, Baltimore: Johns Hopkins University Press, 1973

Greenwald, Maurine Weiner, *Women, War, and Work: The Impact of World War I on Women Workers in the United States*, Westport, CT: Greenwood Press, 1980

Kennedy, David M., *Over Here: The First World War and American Society*, New York: Oxford University Press, 1980

Schaffer, Ronald, *America in the Great War: The Rise of the War Welfare State*, New York: Oxford University Press, 1991

Thompson, John A., *Reformers and War: American Progressive Publicists and the First World War*, Cambridge and New York: Cambridge University Press, 1987

Trask, David F., *The AEF and Coalition Warmaking, 1917–1918*, Lawrence: University Press of Kansas, 1993

Vaughn, Stephen, *Holding Fast the Inner Lines: Democracy, Nationalism, and the Committee on Public Information*, Chapel Hill: University of North Carolina Press, 1980

Wynn, Neil A., *From Progressivism to Prosperity: World War I and American Society*, New York: Holmes and Meier, 1986

For many years the main focus in the history of the United States and World War I was on either foreign policy and the events leading up to 1917, or the negative impact of the conflict on domestic affairs, with the stifling of dissent and the apparent end of progressivism. Something of this tone is captured in the title of CLARK's contribution to the Carnegie Endowment "Economic and Social History of the World War". The author's aim is to examine the view that the United States made a profit from the war; he concludes "Perhaps all we can be sure of is that nothing has remained untouched by the war." The old-fashioned tone and emphasis on economics, ultimately linking the war with the Depression, limit this work, but it does touch on a broad range of concerns including labour and race which later writers developed more fully.

COOPER has compiled an extremely useful collection of essays selected chiefly from historical journals. Only three of the fourteen articles deal with causes, and the aim to show the impact of the war on American society and provide an alternative to the view that the conflict "replaced political reform with reaction, social tolerance with prejudice, intellectual optimism with disillusionment", is largely accomplished. Several of the contributions point the way for later study on issues such as war and reform, war and the intellectuals, and war and women. The editor provides a brief overview of the subject and an extensive bibliography.

The impact of the war on government has been an area of some considerable interest. CUFF's rather narrow but readable organizational history details the faltering development of the major war mobilization agency, the War Industries Board. Drawing attention to the limitations of centralized authority, he reveals the complex interplay between corporate capitalism, government, and progressive thinking, which determined the nature of wartime business-government relations. BREEN looks at the organization at the local level and points to the decentralized system of voluntary organization which lay behind much of America's war effort. Although this is a rather uneven book, it does reveal the variety of wartime responses and mixed achievements at state level. The implicit lesson is that the reality of power had shifted to Washington, DC.

The combination of centralized federal control with voluntary cooperation is the concern of CONNER's examination of the war's impact on labour policy. While she clearly demonstrates the implementation of progressive thinking in the formation of the National War Labor Board, and its major significance in establishing precedents for the 1930s, she also reaches down to the shop-floor level and considers the board's effects on labour relations in practice. Her detailed research concludes with the second industrial conference established to address postwar labour problems in 1920.

GREENWALD covers similar ground in her valuable study of the war's effects on female employment. After examining the development of government labour policy as it effected women, she concentrates on key sectors, such as railroads and communications. Her argument, that the war provided new opportunities for women, increasing government recognition, and "shifts within the female labor force" which raised expectations of further change, appears well-grounded; her claim that disappointed women workers were at the forefront of postwar strike action is perhaps more questionable.

The traditional negative view of wartime government propaganda activities, and particularly of the Committee on Public Information, is modified by VAUGHN who demonstrates that the emphasis on communicating "a national ideology" had its origins in progressivism. He argues convincingly that reform-minded journalists and intellectuals participated in the propaganda effort in the hope of further reforming American society, and he gives at least some idea of what the propagandists actually did. The relationship between reformers and the war is more fully examined in THOMPSON's substantial account of the intellectual response, particularly of those associated with *New Republic*, such as Walter Lippmann. He demonstrates that liberal disillusionment lay in the high hopes and expectations with which they entered the conflict and which were ultimately shattered by the peace settlement.

The themes of war and reform are taken up in different ways in three general studies of American society and World War I. KENNEDY's wide-ranging, thoroughly researched, and stimulating book has an impressive breadth. It includes the political economy of wartime mobilization, wartime politics, a summary of the impact on social groups, and a thoughtful consideration of the cultural significance of the American military experience. In the end his conclusion echoes the traditional view of the war as "a sad story, a tale of death, broken hopes, frustrated dreams . . ." In a very readable book largely based on secondary sources (and lacking footnotes), SCHAFFER covers similar ground to Kennedy, but has a slightly different emphasis and conclusion. In focusing on the links between war and welfare, he suggests that the war brought about a high point of social reform, and sees the long-term significance of the war as an indicator "of what America would become during most of what remained of the twentieth century." He also uses military experiences, including the treatment of shell-shock victims, to illustrate the style of management adopted by the federal government.

Using a variety of primary sources, WYNN concentrates on the home front and allows more space to social groups, with individual chapters on labour, women, and African Americans. However, his concern is much like the other authors in that he demonstrates how progressive thinking on a range of issues was affected and re-shaped by war. Rather than seeing the war as a "turning point" or just marking the end of one period, he stresses continuity and suggests that the war accelerated modernization, and helped to bring about the transition from progressivism to the 1920s.

There is a separate literature on the actual military participation of the American armed forces in the final stages of the war. COFFMAN is a wide-ranging survey which covers military preparations and organisation, and the war at sea and in the air, as well as the role of the United States army on the western front. Although he is critical of Pershing's misjudgments and his frequently uncooperative behaviour as an ally, he generally shares the prevailing assumption at the time when he wrote that it was the presence of American forces which tipped the balance, and decided the war on the western front. TRASK is a brief history of the operations of the American Expeditionary Forces in France in 1918, viewed primarily from the highest level of field command. He stresses the importance of the inter-allied perspective, and insists that the AEF cannot be studied in isolation. He is very critical of earlier accounts which accepted Pershing's own view that the AEF decided the war. In Trask's view, the impending arrival of large numbers of American troops was very important, but such was the unpreparedness of the American forces that it would have taken them at least two years to achieve full operational efficiency. One good example of studies of American troops in action on the western front is provided by BRAIM who focuses on their performance under battle conditions in one particular area.

NEIL A. WYNN

See also Pershing

World War II, Approach to

1) European War and American Neutrality

Beard, Charles A., *President Roosevelt and the Coming of War, 1941: A Study in Appearances and Realities*, New Haven: Yale University Press, 1948

Cull, Nicholas John, *Selling War: The British Propaganda Campaign Against American "Neutrality" in World War II*, New York: Oxford University Press, 1995

Dallek, Robert, *Franklin D. Roosevelt and American Foreign Policy, 1932–1945*, New York: Oxford University Press, 1979; with new afterword, 1995

Divine, Robert A., *Roosevelt and World War II*, Baltimore: Johns Hopkins Press, 1969

Heinrichs, Waldo H., *Threshold of War: Franklin D. Roosevelt and American Entry into World War II*, New York: Oxford University Press, 1988

Kimball, Warren F., *The Most Unsordid Act: Lend-Lease, 1939–1941*, Baltimore: Johns Hopkins Press, 1969

Langer, William L. and S. Everett Gleason, *The Challenge to Isolation, 1937–1940*, New York: Harper, 1952

Langer, William L. and S. Everett Gleason, *The Undeclared War, 1940–1941*, New York: Harper, 1953

Reynolds, David, *The Creation of the Anglo-American Alliance, 1937–1941: A Study in Competitive Co-operation*, London: Europa, 1981; Chapel Hill: University of North Carolina Press, 1982

Wilson, Theodore A., *The First Summit: Roosevelt and Churchill at Placentia Bay, 1941*, Boston: Houghton Mifflin, 1969; revised, Lawrence: University Press of Kansas, 1991

When the European war began in September 1939, the United States was formally neutral. After France fell in June 1940 President Franklin D. Roosevelt's policy became overtly pro-Allied, and during 1941 increasing material aid was offered to Britain, especially via the Lend-Lease Act of March 1941 and naval patrolling in the Atlantic. But public attitudes, though pro-Allied, remained antiwar. It was not until after Pearl Harbor in December 1941 that America joined the European war, and then only following a declaration of war by Nazi Germany.

Central to understanding the evolution of American policy is the figure of Roosevelt himself who conducted his own foreign policy, often bypassing the State Department entirely. Early postwar critics, such as BEARD, made use of documentation unearthed by the congressional inquiries into Pearl Harbor to accuse an already imperious presidency of manoeuvring the country towards war in Europe and Asia while professing a policy of peace and self-defense. Concerned at the criticism, the Council on Foreign Relations in New York – non-partisan but establishment – secured Rockefeller Foundation money and State Department approval to commission from LANGER and GLEASON a two-volume semi-official history based on unique and extensive access to government and personal papers. The combination of archival sources and 1,800 pages of text gave the work immense authority and it can still be read with profit, especially concerning bureaucratic policymaking. The authors explained the gulf between Roosevelt's words and actions by reference to the president's temporizing nature and his tendency to exaggerate the strength and cohesion of the opposition.

In DIVINE's incisive little book, the emphasis is on personality not politics. Divine interprets Roosevelt as a genuine isolationist in the 1930s, whose equivocations even in 1941 reflect his continued aversion to war as much as political calculation. In his full-length, archivally-based study of foreign policy throughout the Roosevelt era, DALLEK judged that the president had accepted the necessity of war by the spring of 1941 but always remained conscious that "effective action abroad required a reliable consensus at home," which in turn depended on time and events. Whereas Beard had denounced the power of the modern presidency, Dallek stressed its limitations.

During this period relations with Britain were the main axis of American policy towards Europe. KIMBALL's detailed study of the evolution of the Lend-Lease Act was based on American sources, before those in Britain were opened, but it still stands up well. Kimball finds Roosevelt a sloppy administrator but a shrewd politician, though his "lack of candor" remained disturbing. Another 1969 monograph by WILSON also set a specific episode (the Atlantic Meeting of August 1941 between Roosevelt and Churchill) within a broader analysis of Anglo-American relations. Unlike Kimball's work, however, Wilson's

has been revised to take account of British archives and subsequent historiography.

The fullest account of Anglo-American interaction in the period is by REYNOLDS, who explores the ambivalence of the relationship by reference to continued economic rivalries as well as growing military cooperation. He, like Divine, draws attention to Roosevelt's own equivocations about America's role in the war. Although CULL's book is primarily about British propaganda policy, it is based on extensive work in American archives and it highlights the effect of changing media images of Britain in shaping American debate on the war in 1940–41.

American policy towards the European war has to be understood in the broader context of relations with Japan, and of American isolationism in the 1930s. Most of the books discussed here insist on the interaction of events in Europe and Asia and of American responses to them. The Navy is a case in point, because the United States did not yet have a two-ocean capability and choices therefore had to be made between force postures in the Atlantic and the Pacific. The most detailed analysis of this global jigsaw, for the period March to December 1941, is by HEINRICHS who also integrates intelligence data into the picture. He underlines the importance of Hitler's attack on the Soviet Union in June 1941 and the successful Russian resistance in making Europe less critical and the Pacific more urgent.

Even in such an intricately bureaucratic account as that of Heinrichs, however, "all the threads of policy ultimately led to the White House." Like him or not, Roosevelt remains at the center of the historiographical debate and, despite the long scholarly paper-chase, his intentions are still tantalizingly elusive.

DAVID REYNOLDS

2) Japan and the United States, 1931–1941

Borg, Dorothy and Shumpei Okamoto (editors), *Pearl Harbor as History: Japanese-American Relations, 1931–1941*, New York: Columbia University Press, 1973

Butow, Robert J.C., *The John Doe Associates: Backdoor Diplomacy for Peace, 1941*, Stanford, CA: Stanford University Press, 1974

Conroy, Hilary and Harry Wray (editors), *Pearl Harbor Reexamined: Prologue to the Pacific War*, Honolulu: University of Hawaii Press, 1990

Feis, Herbert, *The Road to Pearl Harbor: The Coming of the War Between the United States and Japan*, Princeton: Princeton University Press, 1950

Heinrichs, Waldo H., *American Ambassador: Joseph C. Grew and the Development of the United States Diplomatic Tradition*, Boston: Little Brown, 1966

Ike, Nobutake (editor), *Japan's Decision for War: Records of the 1941 Policy Conferences*, Stanford, CA: Stanford University Press, 1967

Neu, Charles E., *The Troubled Encounter: The United States and Japan*, New York: Wiley, 1975

Utley, Jonathan G., *Going to War with Japan, 1937–1941*, Knoxville: University of Tennessee Press, 1985

In September 1931 the Japanese army in northeast China began the takeover of Manchuria. This marked the beginning of a new phase of expansion on the Asian mainland which brought Japan into conflict not only with China and various European powers but also increasingly with the United States. In July 1937 Japan and China stumbled into full-scale war with each other and the clash between Japanese expansionism and United States interests and ideals caused a steep deterioration in American-Japanese relations. In 1940–41 the creation of the Axis of Japan, Germany and Italy, and gathering American alarm at the danger of that Axis, produced a freeze in United States-Japanese relations which led to war in December 1941. Of course, Japanese-American relations had been on the slide at least since the end of the Russo-Japanese War in 1905, and NEU gives the decade before Pearl Harbor its vital historical perspective, providing a succinct and reliable account of the issues which blighted American-Japanese relations before, during and after World War I.

Taken together, the volumes edited by Borg and Okamoto, and by Conroy and Wray, provide extensive coverage of the issues and forces which brought the United States and Japan into conflict. Both have the advantage of combining contributions from American and Japanese scholars, so that the two sides of the story are adequately covered. BORG and OKAMOTO is a formidable piece of scholarship which has paired chapters on the institutions and individuals concerned with Japanese-American relations in the decade before Pearl Harbor. Thus there are accounts of the role of the Japanese and United States army and navy, their foreign policy bureaucracies and other state institutions, the Japanese and American legislatures and non-governmental institutions, such as political groups, business interests and the press. CONROY and WRAY is a less closely structured collection, consisting of a number of loosely linked chapters by Japanese and American scholars, on various aspects of the two countries' relationship. Highly skilled editing links the individual contributions, highlighting and explaining points of difference between the scholars involved. In sum, these two collections provide a comprehensive account of Japanese-American relations between 1931 and 1941, linking foreign policy in both the United States and Japan to their essential domestic backgrounds. Perhaps the most serious drawback is that the two volumes combined total nearly one thousand pages of text.

One thread which ran through Japanese-American relations from the Manchurian crisis of 1931–33 to Pearl Harbor was provided by Joseph Grew, who was the American ambassador in Tokyo from 1932 to 1942. HEINRICHS offers a sensitive portrayal of Grew which provides a human dimension to the deterioration of American-Japanese relations. The biography gives a clear insight into the problems experienced by a member of the American decision-making elite, committed to trying to avert a war between Japan and the United States, when confronted with the complex, often obscure, developments within Japan and in Japanese foreign policy during this crucial decade.

The classic work on the descent into war is FEIS, whose pioneering narrative of Japanese-American relations from the mid-1930s continues to influence scholarship, and remains a reliable factual account. Feis is sympathetic to American perceptions and policies between 1937 and 1941, and therefore represents a useful corrective to some of the more recent revisionist interpretations of American conduct, which allege that Roosevelt provoked Japan into war.

UTLEY is a well-written and precise study of American decision-making in the four years up to Pearl Harbor. His account is firmly rooted in Washington and skilfully traces the influence of politicians, civil servants, the army and navy and other groups upon the shaping of United States policy towards Japan. It is particularly enlightening in its description of the process by which the non-confrontational policies of Cordell Hull, Roosevelt's cautious secretary of state, were steadily eroded by his administration colleagues and by shifting bureaucratic balances, often at quite low levels, which reoriented American policy towards a resolute stand against Japan in the second half of 1941.

The final months of peace were obviously the crucial time in Japanese-American relations. This period may be followed in detail in two books which cover 1941 from the Japanese and American sides. The best way to follow the slide to war from the Japanese perspective is to use the translated documents, and in particular the outstanding commentary, provided by IKE. The records of the key meetings that decided on a line of policy which led to confrontation and war highlight the increasing Japanese sense of being hemmed in. They also show that, after the freezing of Japanese assets in July 1941 which cut off Japan's vital oil supplies, decision-makers in Tokyo believed they had little option but to seize the vital strategic materials, even if this meant war with the United States. In fascinating detail, BUTOW tells the other side of the story by following the ultimately futile efforts of an unlikely collection of clerics, diplomats, officials and members of the administration who tried to pull Japan and the United States out of the abyss of their engulfing conflict.

DENNIS B. SMITH

See also Pearl Harbor

World War II, United States and

1) Campaigns in Europe

Ambrose, Stephen E., *D Day, June 6, 1944: The Climactic Battle of World War II*, New York: Simon and Schuster, 1994

Ambrose, Stephen E., *Eisenhower: The Soldier*, New York: Simon and Schuster, 1983; London: Allen and Unwin, 1984

Bradley, Omar N. with Clay Blair, *A General's Life: An Autobiography*, New York: Simon and Schuster, and London: Sidgwick and Jackson, 1983

D'Este, Carlo, *Bitter Victory: The Battle for Sicily, 1943*, New York: Dutton, and London: Collins, 1988

D'Este, Carlo, *Decision in Normandy*, New York: Dutton, and London: Collins, 1991

Gelb, Norman, *Ike and Monty: Generals at War*, New York: Morrow, and London: Constable, 1994

Keegan, John, *Six Armies in Normandy: From D-Day to the Liberation of Paris*, London: Cape, and New York: Viking, 1982

Macdonald, Charles B., *The Mighty Endeavor: American Armed Forces in the European Theater in World War II*, New York: Oxford University Press, 1969

Macdonald, Charles B., *The Battle of the Bulge*, London: Weidenfeld and Nicolson, 1984

Parker, Danny, *Battle of the Bulge: Hitler's Ardennes Offensive, 1944–1945*, Philadelphia: Combined Books, and London: Greenhill, 1991

Weigley, Russell F., *Eisenhower's Lieutenants: The Campaign of France and Germany, 1944–1945*, Bloomington: Indiana University Press, and London: Sidgwick and Jackson, 1981

The American contribution to victory over Germany can be assessed in terms of military leadership, the conduct of ground operations, and the air offensive against the Third Reich. As a component of an alliance two difficulties arise: first, the need to differentiate the peculiarly American aspects of the conflict, and second, the national bias which is difficult to eliminate from studies of the Allied war effort. The works of both American and British authors suggest various approaches to these problems.

The one overall view of the American contribution in a single volume is provided by MacDONALD (1969) who was one of the team of United States Army official historians. Condensation tends to eliminate analysis of strategic controversies and leads to the avoidance of critical comment. As an account of ground operations, and of the achievements of the American soldier, MacDonald provides a useful narrative. He gives little attention to allies, or to naval and air operations, in order to produce a work of manageable proportions.

The American high command is analyzed closely by WEIGLEY, who presents a sympathetic account of the tasks carried out between Normandy and Germany by the various corps and division commanders. He is less happy with the performance of Eisenhower and his principal subordinates, such as Bradley and Patton, whom he criticises for their predilection for mass firepower rather than manoeuvre as a means of solving battlefield problems. He recognises the major difficulty in making an assessment of Eisenhower: that he was too remote from the battlefield for the normal indices of successful generalship to apply. He exhibits national bias in his comments on Eisenhower's most difficult subordinate, Montgomery. GELB's more recent work on the Eisenhower-Montgomery relationship encounters the same problems and exhibits the same bias against the prickly British general. Such works should be balanced by recent British accounts by Hamilton and by Lamb. More detailed studies of two leading American generals are AMBROSE (1983) on Eisenhower and BLAIR on BRADLEY. These studies are sufficiently lengthy to provide the detailed information required to arrive at a balanced assessment of their subjects' performance as military commanders. Blair makes a commendable effort to draw attention to the qualities of a general who is often overshadowed by Eisenhower, Montgomery, and Patton in popular imagination.

One American historian who overcomes national bias to write authoritative accounts of aspects of war in Europe is D'Este. As an American army officer, he reveals commendable balance in discussion of the military politics of the alliance and in his assessment of the performance of the respective armies. In his study of Sicily D'ESTE (1988) points to the scattered nature of the various headquarters which hindered planning and impeded Eisenhower's control of the headstrong Montgomery and Patton. This suggests a lack of firmness as the Supreme Allied Commander learned his trade. D'ESTE (1991) is a superb analysis of the Normandy campaign which not only brings measured judgment to the Eisenhower-Montgomery relationship but highlights the manpower restraints which inhibited the allied conduct of the battle for Normandy. This work is rivalled by KEEGAN in style and maturity of judgment. Keegan extends the analysis to the often forgotten role of the Canadians and Poles – and especially of the Germans – in this crucial campaign. AMBROSE (1994) is one of a number of anniversary studies of D-Day. It is not quite up to this distinguished author's usual standard, and, understandably perhaps, his choice of material is excessively weighted towards the Americans.

In the latter stages of the war, the Battle of the Bulge presented Eisenhower and his forces with a major challenge. Once again, MacDONALD (1984) attempts to reduce the material from the official history to manageable levels. In the process, he presents a solid narrative of the difficulties encountered by the American forces. His work needs to be supplemented by PARKER which is liberally illustrated by photographs, and more especially, by a good selection of maps. Without such maps the reader may find the fighting in the difficult terrain of the Ardennes as confusing as the GIs did in 1944–45.

GRAHAM E. WATSON

2) War Against Japan

Barbey, Daniel E., *MacArthur's Amphibious Navy: Seventh Amphibious Force Operations 1943–1945*, Annapolis, MD: Naval Institute Press, 1969

Blair, Clay, *Silent Victory: The US Submarine War Against Japan*, Philadelphia: Lippincott, 1975; abridged as *Combat Patrol*, Toronto and London: Bantam, 1978

Chwialkowski, Paul, *In Caesar's Shadow: The Life of General Robert Eichelberger*, Westport, CT: Greenwood Press, 1993

Connaughten, Richard, John Pimlott, and Duncan Anderson, *The Battle for Manila*, Novato, CA: Presidio, and London: Bloomsbury, 1994

Costello, John, *The Pacific War*, New York: Rawson Wade, and London: Collins, 1981; revised, London: Pan, 1985

James, D. Clayton, *The Years of MacArthur*, volume 2, Boston: Houghton Mifflin, and London: Leo Cooper, 1975

Leary, William M. (editor), *We Shall Return! MacArthur's Commanders and the Defeat of Japan, 1942–1945*, Lexington: University Press of Kentucky, 1988

McNalty, Bernard, *War in the Pacific: Pearl Harbor to Tokyo Bay*, New York: Mayflower, and London: Sidgwick and Jackson, 1978

Morison, Samuel Eliot, *The Two-Ocean War: A Short History of the United States Navy in the Second World War*, Boston: Little Brown, 1963

Reynolds, Clark G., *The Fast Carriers: The Forging of an Air Navy*, New York: McGraw Hill, 1968

Rogers, Paul P., *The Good Years: MacArthur and Sutherland*, New York: Praeger, 1990

Rogers, Paul P., *The Bitter Years: MacArthur and Sutherland*, New York: Praeger, 1991

Schaller, Michael, *Douglas MacArthur: The Far Eastern General*, New York and Oxford: Oxford University Press, 1989

Spector, Ronald H., *Eagle Against the Sun: The American War with Japan*, New York: Free Press, and London: Viking, 1985

Van der Vat, Dan, *The Pacific Campaign, World War II: The US-Japanese Naval War, 1941–1945*, New York: Simon and Schuster, 1991; London: Hodder and Stoughton, 1992

The essential starting point is a good general survey which brings together the geographically dispersed naval, ground and air operations into a coherent digestible whole. COSTELLO provides a sound overall perspective with the inclusion of sufficient detail in his narrative to whet the appetite for more detailed consideration of individual campaigns. McNALTY is a more recent comprehensive account which combines incisively written chapters by various historians with a wealth of photographs, maps and diagrams to provide an authoritative reader-friendly introduction to the war against Japan. He does not neglect the contributions of British Commonwealth forces, nor of China. The text of each chapter represents a successful condensation of the official histories, and this lends weight to the comments and judgments offered by the authors. MORISON condenses his 15-volume official history of naval operations into a single volume in which activities in the Pacific are presented in some detail, alongside naval operations against the European Axis. This volume reminds readers of the restraints placed on operations against Japan, especially in terms of resources, by the higher priority accorded to the war against Germany. VAN DER VAT provides a more recent readable narrative of naval operations in the Pacific. Neither he nor Morison gives equal weight to ground and land-based air operations. SPECTOR stands out as an overall single-volume history of the war in the Pacific, which places particular battles and campaigns in the broader context of grand strategy, logistics and productive capacity. He describes and discusses the different approaches favoured by General MacArthur and Admiral King, the decision to combine elements of both, and the escalating scale of naval and amphibious operations against Japan.

The naval conflict in the Pacific broke new ground in three areas: naval air power, submarine warfare, and amphibious warfare. REYNOLDS examines the development of the fast carrier forces which gave the Allies the confidence to range widely across the ocean, destroy the Japanese fleet, and isolate the island garrisons in the drive towards Japan. He fully supports the Navy's wartime emphasis on the Central Pacific and deplores the diversion of resources to MacArthur in the South West Pacific. The manner in which the Japanese economy was crippled, together with the increased obstructions to Japanese strategic mobility, is outlined in BLAIR's very detailed account of United States submarine operations. He demonstrates how, after initial technical difficulties with torpedoes were overcome, the Americans became more effective than the German submarine campaign in the Atlantic. As an amphibious force commander under MacArthur, BARBEY provides a personal recollection of how the Navy and Marines built up a wealth of operational experience in amphibious warfare. He provides a lucid but uncritical account of MacArthur's campaign in the South West Pacific.

The dominant and most controversial American in the Pacific War was Douglas MacArthur, around whom debate has swirled. In his two-volume study, JAMES offers a sympathetic but not uncritical assessment of MacArthur. He makes allowances for the character deficiencies in his attempt to evaluate MacArthur's military skills, of which the most important was his grasp of tri-service amphibious warfare. SCHALLER places MacArthur in the context of American policy in the Far East and sees his subject as being as much politically motivated as driven by military considerations. He highlights MacArthur's craving for publicity and the manner in which such publicity was used to obscure military incompetence. He reveals MacArthur's paranoia about the publicity accorded to Roosevelt, Marshall and Eisenhower, his former subordinate. ROGERS (1990, 1991) looks as MacArthur's relations with Sutherland, his chief of staff, in a two-volume study of high command. He is very knowledgeable on the details of personal relations, and concludes that the creation of his own personal image was the main determinant of the general's military strategy. As part of the process the "American Caesar" discouraged individual publicity for his subordinates as well as for his fighting troops.

CHWIALKOWSKI is one of a small number of recent works which focus on Robert Eichelberger, commander of 8th Army. It is suggested that the subservient behaviour of otherwise capable generals was explained by personal animosities among them which were exploited by MacArthur. The process of bringing generals out from under MacArthur's shadow is facilitated by LEARY's collection of essays which deals with seven individual naval, air, and army commanders. The technical and tactical contributions of all seven need to be examined in relation to MacArthur's claims to military greatness.

MacArthur's obsessions form an important theme of the recent account of the destruction of Manila which has been attributed to Japanese barbarity. CONNAUGHTEN, PIMLOTT and ANDERSON place most blame on the Japanese and raise questions about the American methods of firepower during the battle for Manila. They indicate how the pressure to succeed which MacArthur placed on his subordinates increased the use of aircraft and heavy artillery within the city, with consequent heavy loss of civilian lives. They highlight MacArthur's desire to regain possession of the city by his personal leadership of the assault, in order to regain his own pre-war apartment, and his possessions, which had been left intact by the Japanese – the most extreme example of the manner in which his personal obsession affected the conduct of military operations.

GRAHAM E. WATSON

3) Naval War

Abbazia, Patrick, *Mr. Roosevelt's Navy: The Private War of the US Atlantic Fleet, 1939–1942*, Annapolis, MD: Naval Institute Press, 1975

Baer, George W., *One Hundred Years of Sea Power: The US Navy, 1890–1990*, Stanford, CA: Stanford University Press, 1994

Dull, Paul S., *A Battle History of the Imperial Japanese Navy, 1941–1945*, Annapolis, MD: Naval Institute Press, 1978

Morison, Samuel Eliot, *The Two-Ocean War: A Short History of the United States Navy in the Second World War*, Boston: Little Brown, 1963

Roskill, S.W., *The War at Sea, 1939–1945*, 3 vols., London: Her Majesty's Stationery Office [HMSO], 1954–61

Runyan, Timothy J. and Jan M. Copes (editors), *To Die Gallantly: The Battle of the Atlantic*, Boulder, CO: Westview Press, 1994

Spector, Ronald H., *Eagle Against the Sun: The American War with Japan*, New York: Free Press, and London: Viking, 1985

Willmott, H.P., *The Barrier and the Javelin: Japanese and Allied Pacific Strategies, February to June 1942*, Annapolis, MD: Naval Institute Press, 1983

For the U.S. Navy, World War II was the major turning point in its development. From that time on, the United States was to possess a navy that was truly second to none, and which was to become a dominating instrument of its security policy. In his survey of the Navy's history during the century from 1890 to 1990, BAER places this process in its broader context. He focuses on the linkages between naval development and the national policy of the United States, arguing that the Americans' geographic isolation from Europe, their disinclination to spend resources on armaments and the workings of their domestic politics all conspired to produce a navy that was in 1941, despite desperate last-minute efforts to recapture lost ground, seriously unprepared for war. The United States Navy did not have the resources for a global war fought simultaneously in the Atlantic and in the Pacific.

This theme is further developed by ABBAZIA who shows that President Roosevelt's navy reflected the preoccupations and uncertainties of a great democracy in an era of uneasy peace. He describes its strengths and weaknesses, and shows the extent to which a fleet engagement with the navy of Imperial Japan, and the consequent necessity for a strategic advance across to the western Pacific, dominated the deliberations of the navy's planners. Despite the strategic decision to give the Atlantic top priority, the United States was forced to fight an active war in the Pacific with the few resources immediately available.

MORISON was the U.S. Navy's semi-official historian of World War II. The work cited here is a distillation of his monumental but readable 15-volume series, *History of United States Naval Operations in World War II* (1947–62). Significantly, twelve of the fifteen volumes concern the Pacific. He is clear, comprehensive, rather uncritical of his subject and committed to a navy that conducted itself on the whole gloriously in "the greatest of all wars in which it has ever been engaged." The navy learned quickly from its earlier mistakes and recovered from its initial unreadiness. It was soon to develop concepts of anti-submarine and amphibious warfare and became adept at the conduct of fleet engagements not just with battleships but with carriers often playing the dominating role.

Since there is as yet no single volume which focuses on the role and experience of the United States Navy in the Atlantic war, perhaps because this was so much more of a true coalition war with the British, Canadians and other allies, ROSKILL still provides an indispensable background review. As the Royal Navy's Official Historian, he had access to all the official papers and also – although he made no specific reference to it – to the tactical and strategic effects of the information provided by ULTRA intelligence. For this reason, and despite the fact that his three-volume history was written more than thirty years ago, it has stood up well to modern scholarship and still provides an excellent context against which the American contribution to the Atlantic war should be judged. He discusses frankly various Anglo-American differences, for example over strategic priority and the conduct of the war against the U-boat, and his conclusions remain authoritative.

Perhaps the critical campaign of the Atlantic war was the battle against the U-boat and surface raiders that sought to prevent the passage of soldiers, military supplies, food and fuel across to Britain. As RUNYAN and COPES show rather graphically, this was a multi-faceted, many-layered campaign in which victory was the product not only of the endurance, fighting skills and weaponry of the allied sailors (merchant as well as naval) on the spot, but also upon operational intelligence, on logistical and organizational expertise and on the industrial productivity, especially, of the United States.

While in the early days of the war, the nation's top strategists were preoccupied with the strategic situation in Europe, the Atlantic and the Mediterranean, the U.S. Navy from the start was convinced of the need to launch offensive actions against the still expanding Japanese as soon as possible. In his still unsurpassed single-volume survey of the Pacific War, SPECTOR describes the way in which the United States was torn between General MacArthur's option of approaching Japan from the southwest, or Admiral King's alternative of a drive across the central Pacific. Scarcely having the resources for either, the United States compromised by attempting them both simultaneously. Spector shows that what led to Japan's ultimate defeat was America's awesome industrial power. This compensated for the weaknesses in America's strategic decision-making processes. It also allowed the U.S. Navy to move smoothly from the initial phase of the war which, despite Admiral Halsey's hit-and-run tactics, was largely defensive, to an ever-increasing offensive in which large-scale fleet engagements cleared the way for the greatest sweep of amphibious operations the world has ever seen.

In one volume of a projected four-part series, WILLMOTT examines the critical year of 1942 in some detail. His approach is exhaustive, correcting many of the factual errors that characterize previous accounts, especially on the Japanese side. He shows that the United States was sucked into campaigns earlier than planned because of the unexpected initial scale of the Japanese success and because of the catastrophic weaknesses of America's allies. But Willmott also shows how deeply flawed was the Japanese approach to maritime war, and finds in such flaws some of the seeds of their later downfall.

One of the major reasons for previous mistakes in discussing the Japanese side of the campaign was the relative inaccessibility of Japanese sources. In a pioneering work, DULL did much to rectify matters – although a comparison with Willmott may still make some of his conclusions look debatable. He shows that the American victories at Coral Sea and Midway were far from being the end of the dangers represented by the Japanese Navy. There were many significant naval battles afterwards, especially around Guadalcanal, and the Japanese won their share of them.

GEOFFREY TILL

4) Air Power

Coffey, Thomas M., *Hap: The Story of the US Air Force and the Man Who Built It, General Henry H. "Hap" Arnold*, New York: Viking, 1982

Copp, DeWitt S., *A Few Great Captains: The Men and Events That Shaped the Development of US Air Power*, New York: Doubleday, 1980

Craven, Wesley Frank and James Lea Cate (editors), *The Army Air Forces in World War II*, 7 vols., Chicago: University of Chicago Press, 1948–58

Freeman, Roger, *The Mighty Eighth: Units, Men and Machines: A History of the US 8th Army Air Force*, London: Macdonald, and New York: Doubleday, 1970; revised as *The Mighty Eighth: A History of the Units, Men and Machines of the US 8th Air Force*, London: Jane's, 1986

McFarland, S.L. and W.L. Newton, *To Command the Sky: The Battle for Air Superiority over the Germans, 1942–1944*, Washington, DC: Smithsonian Institution Press, 1991

MacIsaac, David, *Strategic Bombing in World War II: The Story of the United States Strategic Bombing Survey*, New York: Garland, 1976

Sherry, Michael S., *The Rise of American Air Power: The Creation of Armageddon*, New Haven and London: Yale University Press, 1987

The rise of American air power is one of the major legacies of World War II. By 1945, the United States Army Air Corps possessed a fleet of strategic bombers capable of destroying targets irrespective of their size or distance from America's shores. By 1947, this new force had proven worthy of its own military service branch, the United States Air Force. Because the story of American air power during World War II must be understood in the context of the larger history of American aviation, most books on the subject begin with the development of American military air power since World War I.

This is the starting point of the classic seven-volume official history written by CRAVEN and CATE in the decade following World War II. After describing the evolution of air power doctrine from World War I to the late 1930s, these volumes offer a detailed account of how the American Army Air Forces went about building a bomber force capable of fighting a major war. In their first five volumes, Craven and Cate meticulously describe how the Army Air Forces played a significant role in almost every American campaign from 1941 to 1945, from providing air cover for the invading forces in North Africa to landing paratroops on the beaches of Normandy on 6 June 1944. This vivid detailed narrative is accompanied by Volumes VI and VII, entitled *Men and Planes* and *Services Around the World*, respectively. In *Men and Planes*, the authors discuss the organizational structure of the Army Air Force, and in *Services Around the World*, they explore the individual overseas bases maintained by the American Army during World War II. Those readers who are daunted by the sheer scale of the official history may turn to a history of one major bomber force. FREEMAN is a detailed factual account of the operations of the Eighth Air Force in Europe, full of detailed information on men, machines and individual raids.

SHERRY begins what is to date the most comprehensive study of this subject by giving an account of the evolution of the manned bomber from 1917 to 1945. He adopts this approach because he contends that one cannot understand how American air power came to be what it was by 1945 without understanding what the creators of the United States Army Air Corps thought about air power. Chief among these men was Henry H. "Hap" Arnold, whom COFFEY credits as "the father of the modern American Air Force," and who was appointed Chief of the Army Air Corps by President Franklin D. Roosevelt in 1940, on the eve of America's entrance into World War II. In August 1941, just months before the Japanese attack on Pearl Harbor, Arnold initiated a massive build-up of the American air forces which wreaked much destruction on the Germans and Japanese from 1941 to 1945.

Arnold is also a major subject of COPP's book. But unlike Coffey, Copp examines the small group of air officers who directed American air power during World War II. He argues persuasively that a handful of daring men risked their reputation, and their lives, to make American air power a significant factor in the Allied victory in World War II. Copp explains that men like Claire Chennault placed the major focus of America's air forces, both in Europe and Asia, on long-term strategic bombing. These operations proved very important in weakening both Germany and Japan.

Many of the decisions of the leaders discussed in Copp's study were a result of the conclusions drawn by the Strategic Bombing Survey, the focus of MacISAAC's fine book. MacIsaac credits the Strategic Bombing Survey, the organization which evaluated the effects of America's long-range bombing in order to plan the future of the aerial campaign during the war, with setting the foundation for the strategy and tactics of the modern American air force. During the war itself, the major concern within the Strategic Bombing Survey was the question of future targets for America's bombers. This question is taken up in all these books. Arguably the most important of these was whether to fire-bomb German and Japanese cities in 1944 and 1945. Because this decision was made by Henry Arnold, it is discussed by Coffey and Copp, but they do not delve deeply into the matter.

A far deeper analysis appears in Sherry. By analyzing the issue in the context of the development of the modern American air force, he uncovers what he believes to be the larger meaning behind Arnold's fateful decision, a decision which has stirred much ethical debate. Sherry argues that Arnold thought that fire-bombing cities would have a great psychological impact, thus making strategic bombing a winning weapon of war. Because Sherry engages in such searching analysis, his is by far the most useful history of American air power during World War II.

Focus on strategic bombing has tended to obscure discussion of the tactical application of air power. McFARLAND and NEWTON supply an important corrective in their thoroughly documented account of the struggle between the Luftwaffe and the Allied air forces for mastery of the skies over western Europe, the outcome of which was crucial not only for strategic bombing but for the effective operation of the Allied armies below.

PETER K. PARIDES

5) Atomic Bomb

Alperovitz, Gar, *Atomic Diplomacy: Hiroshima and Potsdam: The Use of the Atomic Bomb and the American Confrontation with Soviet Power*, New York: Simon and Schuster, 1965, London: Secker and Warburg, 1966; revised, New York and Harmondsworth: Penguin, 1985; 2nd revision, London: Pluto, 1994

Alperovitz, Gar with Senho Tree and others, *The Decision to Use the Atomic Bomb, and the Architecture of an American Myth*, New York: Knopf, 1995

Bernstein, Barton, "The Atomic Bombings Reconsidered," *Foreign Affairs*, 74(1), 1995

Butow, Robert J.C., *Japan's Decision to Surrender*, Stanford, CA: Stanford University Press, 1954

Feis, Herbert, *Japan Subdued: The Atomic Bomb and the End of the War in the Pacific*, Princeton: Princeton University Press, and London: Oxford University Press, 1961; revised as *The Atomic Bomb and the End of World War II*, 1966

Giovannitti, Len and Fred Freed, *The Decision to Drop the Bomb*, New York: Coward McCann, 1965; London: Methuen, 1967

Herken, Gregg, *The Winning Weapon: The Atomic Bomb in the Cold War, 1945–1950*, New York: Knopf, 1980

Rhodes, Richard, *The Making of the Atomic Bomb*, New York: Simon and Schuster, 1986; Harmondsworth: Penguin, 1988

Sherry, Michael S., *Preparing for the Next War: American Plans for Postwar Defense, 1941–45*, New Haven and London: Yale University Press, 1977

Sherwin, Martin J., *A World Destroyed: The Atomic Bomb and the Grand Alliance*, New York: Knopf, 1975

The American use of the atomic bomb against Japan during the last stage of World War II has been the subject of heated debates among historians. In his classic account of this subject, FEIS argues that it may not have been essential for the United States to drop two atomic bombs on Japan. He agrees with the conclusion reached by the United States Strategic Bombing Survey in 1946 that Japan would have surrendered sooner rather than later, without the atomic bomb, or Soviet participation, or an American invasion of the Japanese mainland. On the other hand, Feis believes that, despite these qualifications, the decision to drop the atomic bomb was inevitable and justifiable, given that Washington was preoccupied with the idea of ending the war quickly and at minimum cost. BUTOW's work is more concerned with events inside Japan and he concludes that the atomic bomb, even if not decisive, was the catalyst which quickened Japan's decision to surrender in August.

ALPEROVITZ (1965, revised 1985 and 1994) presented a quite different interpretation of this subject. He dismisses the need to deploy atomic bombs to defeat Japan, and claims that the bomb was in fact used to blackmail the Soviet Union into accepting concessions in Central and Eastern Europe and in the Far East. In the revised editions of his work in 1985 and in 1994, Alperovitz attempts to reinforce this thesis by including more material. As additional evidence in support of his theory, the 1994 edition contains an intelligence report by the War Department, which was submitted to the Chief of the Strategic Policy Section of the Operations Division on 30 April 1946. The report was written after the war and it contains a rather inaccurate description of events in Japan. Alperovitz does not make much effort to examine whether the Japanese leaders were really capable of accepting surrender without the shock of atomic bombs and/or Soviet entry. However, he still insists that the atomic bomb was the first shot of the Cold War rather than the final shot of World War II. ALPEROVITZ (1995) returns to the same themes in a huge, sprawling book, packed with quotations from sources which lend support to his viewpoint. He condemns as vehemently as ever the decision to drop the bomb, and adds a detailed discussion of the public relations campaign, carefully designed, as he sees it, to promote public acceptance of this highly questionable decision.

GIOVANNITTI and FREED is a narrative of the Truman administration from April 1945 down to the decision to drop the atomic bombs in August 1945. The book stems from a project sponsored by the National Broadcasting Company, and benefits from a wealth of material from United States archives. The conclusion is that, while the principal motive for using the bomb was to end the war, the Truman administration also hoped that the availability of the atomic bomb after July would enhance American diplomatic leverage on the Soviet Union. HERKEN also suggests that the decision to drop the bomb was influenced by both military and political considerations.

RHODES's prize-winning book is a history of the development of the atomic bomb from its origins at the beginning of the 20th century to its first use in August 1945. This exhaustive study is primarily concerned with the theoretical and technical aspects of the production of the bomb, and has much of value to say on the American scientific community and on the Manhattan project. SHERRY is concerned with the thinking of the American military on the atomic bomb in the summer of 1945. He points out that the military leaders did not believe that the new American weapon would deter a Soviet advance in the Far East. Indeed, the use of the atomic bomb on Japan's mainland could hardly affect the situation in Japanese-occupied Manchuria and Korea, where the Russians advanced rapidly after they declared war against Japan on 8 August. Sherry also argues that the American military leadership was unclear in the summer of 1945 which countries were most likely to pose a threat to the United States after the end of World War II. A resurgent Germany or Japan was still regarded as the most likely threat to the United States in the future.

Sherry thus directly challenges Alperovitz by placing the military considerations far above the political considerations in the decision to use the atomic bomb against Japan.

SHERWIN, on the other hand, carefully analyzes both the diplomatic and strategic factors which influenced the Truman administration after April 1945. He supports part of Alperovitz's thesis that the bomb changed Truman's thinking by persuading him that it made the Soviet Union's entry into the war against Japan unnecessary. He argues that the atomic bomb increased Truman's confidence in dealing with Japan and the Soviet Union and probably his optimism about the postwar world. Sherwin stresses that Truman and his close advisers did not question that the atomic bomb must be used against Japan once it had been successfully tested. There was not sufficient interest in pursuing alternative approaches or in discussing moral questions. Sherwin thus gives further support to the view that military considerations were uppermost in Truman's mind.

BERNSTEIN has written numerous authoritative articles on this subject. In the most recent of them, he summarizes the main points succinctly, arguing that the decision to drop the atomic bomb was conceived merely as an extension of existing Allied air bombing strategy. The atomic bomb was clearly intended to be used during the war. He points out that Germany and Japan had already killed innocent civilians by massacre and bombing and that by early 1945, the war had become "virtually total war." He contends that, under these circumstances, there could be no question of imposing moral restraints on the use of the bomb. Bernstein also stresses the negative domestic consequences for the Truman administration if it were to waste nearly $2 billion on developing atomic bombs, and were then to opt, instead, to invade Japan, thus prolonging the war and costing many thousands of American lives. Bernstein explains convincingly why there were no politically feasible and militarily acceptable alternatives to the dropping of the atomic bomb. The Truman administration did discuss whether a demonstration or a warning should be given to the Japanese prior to the use of the bomb, but, given the record of Japanese fanaticism, the possibility that the bomb might not explode, and the increasing pressure to end the war quickly, such preliminaries were thought to involve too much risk. Overall, Bernstein supports the consensus among most scholars that the bomb was used in the belief that this might hasten the end of the war, while at the same time offering the "powerful bonus" of making the Soviets "more manageable."

SAKI DOCKRILL

6) Relations with Allies

Dallek, Robert, *Franklin D. Roosevelt and American Foreign Policy, 1932–1945*, New York: Oxford University Press, 1979; with new afterword, 1995

Feis, Herbert, *Churchill, Roosevelt, and Stalin: The War They Waged and the Peace They Sought*, Princeton: Princeton University Press, 1957

Kolko, Gabriel, *The Politics of War: The World and United States Foreign Policy, 1943–1945*, New York: Random House, 1968; London: Weidenfeld and Nicolson, 1969

Louis, William Roger, *Imperialism at Bay: The United States and the Decolonization of the British Empire, 1941–1945*, Oxford: Clarendon Press, 1977; New York: Oxford University Press, 1978

McNeill, William Hardy, *America, Britain and Russia: Their Cooperation and Conflict, 1941–1946*, London: Oxford University Press, 1953

Reynolds, David, Warren F. Kimball, and A.O. Chubarian (editors), *Allies at War: The Soviet, American and British Experience, 1939–1945*, New York: St. Martin's Press, and London: Macmillan, 1994

Smith, Gaddis, *American Diplomacy During the Second World War, 1941–1945*, New York: Wiley, 1965; 2nd edition, New York: Knopf, 1985

Snell, John L., *Illusion and Necessity: The Diplomacy of Global War, 1939–1945*, Boston: Houghton Mifflin, 1963

Thorne, Christopher, *Allies of a Kind: The United States, Britain, and the War Against Japan, 1941–1945*, New York: Oxford University Press, and London: Hamish Hamilton, 1978

Relations between the United States and its major allies during World War II have long been a highly controversial topic in American historical literature. Most of the controversy has focused on relations with the Soviet Union. Over the last two decades, however, numerous scholars have substantially revised the traditional, Churchillian approach to Anglo-American relations, as well as the questions and issues being addressed.

Written during the first decade of the Cold War, early studies of United States relations with its World War II allies sharply criticized Roosevelt and his advisers for supposedly appeasing Stalin, most notoriously but far from exclusively at the 1945 Yalta Conference, and thereby allowing a massive and unnecessary extension of Soviet power at war's end. Proponents of this interpretation included Roosevelt's political opponents, former advisers who had disagreed with his approach, and journalists who saw in Churchill's rejected policies the ones that the United States should have followed. Although, in his memoirs, Churchill downplayed Anglo-American wartime differences so as not to damage postwar relations, the memoirs nevertheless provided substantial ammunition for some of these attacks on American policy, and exercised an extraordinary influence over subsequent volumes because of their exceptional quality and early publication before the release of many documents.

Roosevelt's defenders countered that his Soviet policies had been motivated by military necessity and the need to maintain the Grand Alliance to defeat the Axis. The growth in Soviet power had resulted not from those policies, but rather from the Axis defeat itself and the military realities created by the advancing Red Army. Simultaneously, however, most of these defenses, written during and influenced by the height of the Cold War, agreed that Roosevelt had been naive to think that postwar cooperation with Stalin had ever been possible. This duality was clearly visible in both McNeill and Feis, two of the earliest histories of the Grand Alliance. Written before the release of much archival information, McNEILL was nevertheless an exceptionally detailed, comprehensive and insightful volume that viewed the alliance as extraordinarily successful in compromising national differences so that the Axis could be defeated and its breakup be a logical if not inevitable consequence of victory. Yet it assailed Roosevelt for his naive belief that he could work with Stalin to create an idealistic new postwar order, and for separating military from political issues during the war. Similar criticisms emerged in the work of FEIS, a former State Department official granted special access to government files and private papers. However, he placed less emphasis on the inevitability of postwar conflict and more on Stalin's responsibility and on the naive and mistaken assumptions that had governed American policy.

The release of extensive documentation, and the changing political climate in the 1960s and 1970s, led to two major challenges to this interpretation. The first, as originally presented by SNELL and then most comprehensively by DALLEK, argued that given the wartime situation Roosevelt's policies actually constituted a highly realistic and pragmatic attempt to mesh military means with political ends and to maximize the national interests of the United States, while reconciling Allied differences in order to keep the coalition together. The second, originating in the so-called "New Left" school of historiography and deeply affected by the Vietnam War, attacked United States rather than Soviet policy for aggressiveness and for shattering the alliance. This case was most comprehensively presented by KOLKO, who argued that the United States had sought to create a postwar world conducive to its own capitalist expansion, and that this effort had led it to define as adversaries both of its major allies as well as the indigenous left throughout the world.

During the 1970s and 1980s historians began to make use of both the enormous archival record of the war years being declassified in Britain as well as the United States and the perspectives being offered by the new social/cultural history to expand and redefine the study of American wartime diplomacy. Particularly noteworthy was a new focus on Anglo-American relations that directly attacked Churchill's approach, by emphasizing the extensive conflicts that had existed between the two nations during the war. LOUIS examined some of the most notable and bitter of these conflicts, and those within each government, as they related to decolonization of the British Empire. THORNE's pioneering work examined numerous aspects of Anglo-American relations in the war against Japan with special focus not only on their conflicts, but also on racial and cultural factors and relations with other Pacific/Asian nations.

The impact of this enormous expansion of scholarly research and redefinition of U.S. wartime diplomacy was most visible in the second, 1985 edition of SMITH. The first, 1965 edition had followed McNeill, Feis and others in their intense criticism of Roosevelt's postwar policies, particularly in regard to the Soviet Union. The second edition severely modified these criticisms while placing much greater emphasis on Anglo-American conflicts and United States policies toward the Third World.

The thaw in, and then demise of, the Cold War between 1986 and 1991 resulted in the partial opening of the Soviet archives, without which all histories of Allied relations had been woefully incomplete, and the beginnings of a fundamental reassessment of Soviet policy. It also led to new scholarly contacts between Russian World War II scholars and

their Anglo-American colleagues, and efforts to produce comprehensive and comparative histories of the alliance. The collection of essays edited by REYNOLDS, KIMBALL and CHUBARIAN is a recent result of such contacts and attempted collaboration. Based upon contemporary archival research, it includes contributions by scholars in all three countries that cover the diplomatic, military, economic and social experiences of the allies, both individually and in relation to each other.

MARK A. STOLER

7) Economic Impact

Bureau of the Budget, *The United States at War: Development and Administration of the War Program by the Federal Government*, Washington, DC: Government Printing Office, 1946

Craf, John R., *A Survey of the American Economy, 1940–1946*, New York: North River Press, 1947

Janeway, Eliot, *The Struggle for Survival: A Chronicle of Economic Mobilization in World War II*, New Haven: Yale University Press, 1951

Milward, Alan S., *War, Economy and Society, 1939–1945*, London: Allen Lane, and Berkeley: University of California Press, 1977

Nash, Gerald D., *The Great Depression and World War II: Organizing America, 1933–1945*, New York: St. Martin's Press, 1979; 2nd edition, as *The Crucial Era*, 1992

Nash, Gerald D., *World War II and the West: Reshaping the Economy*, Lincoln: University of Nebraska Press, 1990

Nelson, Donald M., *Arsenal of Democracy: The Story of American War Production*, New York: Harcourt Brace, 1946

Vatter, Harold G., *The US Economy in World War II*, New York: Columbia University Press, 1985

Wilcox, Walter W., *The Farmer in the Second World War*, Ames: Iowa State College Press, 1947

Studies of the American economy in World War II have necessarily concerned themselves, to some degree, with the federal government's efforts to organize the economy for purposes of waging war. Two of the earliest accounts, by the BUREAU OF THE BUDGET and by NELSON, stem from within the war administration itself. These have proved indispensable sources for subsequent interpretations, yet are generally apologetic and celebratory in tone. The Bureau of the Budget is the more reliable of the two, as Nelson, the Sears-Roebuck executive who headed the War Production Board from 1942 to 1944, is notably self-serving and disingenuous in his memoir.

The stated purpose of CRAF is to promote a broad understanding of the subject among the reading public, and he endeavours to present it in a concise and readable form. Accordingly, his survey, though offering little in the way of interpretation or critical assessment, is a handy source of reference for numerous aspects of the economy during the war years. It provides a useful synopsis of the various wartime agencies, and clarifies such complicated topics as processes of industrial conversion, the significance of machine tools, rationing, and the war's impact on the federal budget. American attempts to meet overseas food shortages, and the domestic debate over retention of price controls, serve to conclude the survey in 1946.

Writing in the early years of the Cold War, JANEWAY wants his chronicle to serve as a morality tale of the superiority of democracy over dictatorship, and sings the praises of Franklin Roosevelt for having the wisdom to trust in the self-mobilizing energy of the masses, rather than in compulsion from above. Yet he laments failures within the war administration which rendered this momentum from outside Washington so necessary, and which, he warns, would have to be avoided in the event of a direct confrontation with the Soviet Union. The litany of wartime production bottlenecks, shortages, hoarding, and under-utilized capacity which he recounts are viewed as avoidable results of a persistent failure to coordinate the productive capacity of the various sectors of the American economy with United States and Allied military and civilian requirements. He ascribes this failure as much to the vices as to the folly of wartime administrators, and spices his narrative with anecdotes of perpetual power-jockeying in the corridors of Washington.

More recent work has attempted to place the subject within the broader perspective of previous and subsequent American history. For NASH (1979), the war economy was pivotal in bringing giant public and private institutions, which had been developing since the turn of the century, into a dominant position in American society. He argues that the American public came to credit big business, big government, and their special wartime relationship with the return of prosperity. The experience of the war economy thus serves to explain many basic characteristics of the postwar era – Keynesian economic policies, the "military-industrial complex", big labour, and large-scale agriculture – by way of the broader public support which they now enjoyed. Yet Nash also points to the too-rapid urbanization of the war years as an underlying cause of many of the problems of urban blight in the postwar decades.

VATTER offers a wealth of statistical information in support of his analysis of wartime and postwar trends. Not until the years during and immediately following the war does he see changes in the role of the federal government, initiated under the New Deal, crystallize into features of American political economy sufficiently durable to survive even the stagflation of the 1970s. The founding of the Bretton Woods agencies between 1944 and 1947 serves as his point of departure for a lengthy concluding discussion of the continuing integration of the international economy, and the related linkage between domestic and foreign economic policymaking.

In his remarkably thorough worldwide survey, MILWARD, an authority on the national economies of Europe during the war, uses a comparative perspective to account for the great success of the American wartime economy, as well as for postwar American economic hegemony. The key American advantages, he argues, were a comparatively substantial domestic supply of most important raw materials, as well as a level of gross output which, even prior to the wartime recovery from depression, exceeded the combined output of the Axis powers. Milward maintains, furthermore, that as early as 1940–41, the Roosevelt administration made a strategic decision to take advantage of this American productive

superiority by fighting the war as a war of production. Accordingly, he devotes much attention to the resulting United States-British efforts, without parallel on the Axis side, at cooperation in such matters as munitions, raw materials, food, and shipping space. He considers the enormous share of world output attained by the United States, as a result of its wartime productive effort, to be perhaps the war's most important legacy for the postwar world. His international approach makes clear to American readers the wartime roots of the postwar crisis in European agriculture, which would provide much of the impetus behind the Marshall Plan by 1947.

The historiography also includes more specialized studies, for example on specific sectors and regions. WILCOX, an agricultural economist who briefly served in the War Food Administration, tries to tie together the various wartime developments in agriculture in order to promote a better understanding of the problems of postwar farm policy. Already the object of much federal attention and money before the war, American agriculture enjoyed the same notable expansion of output and incomes felt throughout the economy, buttressed by rising consumer purchasing power and by federal policies of price supports and controls. At the same time, this sector differed from others in that it experienced virtually none of the difficulties of conversion and reconversion. Wilcox stresses, however, that although the family farm had retained its predominant position in American agriculture at war's end, it found itself more dependent than ever on the market and on government programmes. Meanwhile, even as the wartime diffusion of improved technology helped compensate for losses in the agricultural workforce, wartime urban growth siphoned off professional skills from rural areas, which consequently suffered a deterioration in schools and medical facilities.

For NASH (1990), the war's prime significance for American economic history consists in its promotion of a better regional balance in levels of economic development. Previously sustained by what he describes as a colonial economy, providing raw materials and food to the more industrialized Northeast and Midwest, the West underwent an extraordinary process of diversification during World War II, which enabled it to narrow the gap in standard of living with the rest of the country. According to Nash, federal money was the major driving force behind this process, financing the establishment of numerous military installations, the expansion of existing operations in mining, shipbuilding, and aircraft, and the development of entirely new western industries, such as steel and aluminum. Most significant for the future economy of the region, however, was the creation of several centres for scientific research and technological development. Big business also provided much of the necessary capital for such ventures, and Nash notes that the West was typical of the whole country in the war's acceleration of concentration in business. Yet he also considers the region's tradition of hostility to monopoly, partly a legacy of dependence on the East, and devotes much attention to western champions of small business during the war.

RONALD MACKINNON

8) Home Front

Anderson, Karen, *Wartime Women: Sex Roles, Family Relations, and the Status of Women During World War II*, Westport, CT: Greenwood Press, 1981

Bernstein, Alison R., *American Indians and World War II: Toward a New Era in Indian Affairs*, Norman: University of Oklahoma Press, 1991

Berube, Allan, *Coming Out under Fire: The History of Gay Men and Women in World War Two*, New York: Free Press, 1990

Blum, John Morton, *V Was for Victory: Politics and American Culture During World War II*, New York: Harcourt Brace, 1976

Campbell, D'Ann, *Women at War with America: Private Lives in a Patriotic Era*, Cambridge, MA: Harvard University Press, 1984

Clive, Alan, *State of War: Michigan in World War II*, Ann Arbor: University of Michigan Press, 1979

Daniels, Roger, *Prisoners Without Trial: Japanese Americans in World War II*, New York: Hill and Wang, 1993

Nash, Gerald D., *The American West Transformed: The Impact of the Second World War*, Bloomington: Indiana University Press, 1985

O'Neill, William L., *A Democracy at War: America's Fight at Home and Abroad in World War II*, New York: Free Press, 1993

Polenberg, Richard, *War and Society: The United States, 1941–1945*, Philadelphia: Lippincott, 1972

Terkel, Studs, *"The Good War": An Oral History of World War Two*, New York: Pantheon, 1984; London: Hamish Hamilton, 1985

Tuttle, William M., Jr., *"Daddy's Gone to War": The Second World War in the Lives of America's Children*, New York and Oxford: Oxford University Press, 1993

Wynn, Neil A., *The Afro-American and the Second World War*, New York: Holmes and Meier, 1975, London: Elek, 1976; revised, Holmes and Meier, 1993

Few events have so electrified the United States as the Japanese attack on Pearl Harbor on 7 December 1941. Americans who lived during World War II knew that that their world, and their lives, would never be the same again – and they never were. How their lives did change has been the subject of a rich body of historical writing. In recent years historians studying change on the home front have shifted their scholarly focus; instead of looking at the ostensibly united home front, they have disaggregated the population and examined how the war affected different groups in society. From this perspective, "The Good War" is a much more complex phenomenon.

"The Good War" is the ironic title which TERKEL has given to his popular oral history which demythologizes World War II. These interviews show that, while patriotism was deeply held and goals were widely shared, national unity papered over deep ethnic, religious, and racial divisions, including the race riots that swept the country in 1943. Rapid and immense social change on the home front was evident on every hand from 1941 to 1945; there were millions of fathers going to war, millions of mothers going to work in war factories, and millions of families migrating from one part of the country to another. World War II resulted in victory for the United States and its allies, but as recent histories of the home front have demonstrated, the social costs were high.

In addition to Terkel, among the most perceptive and widely read histories of the home front are POLENBERG, BLUM, and O'NEILL. These books all deal with people of color, and with race relations, as important indicators of social strain during the war, but they should be supplemented by other works. Helpful studies of wartime civil rights activism, race riots, and the black press have been published; the most comprehensive general history of African Americans during the war is WYNN. There is also a rich body of literature, both scholarly and autobiographical, on the Japanese American internment. The most recent history by the leading scholar on the topic is DANIELS. BERNSTEIN is the first book-length history of American Indians during the war.

Scholars with an interest in social history have focused on how the war affected women and children. Histories disagree whether the war was "a turning point" in American women's history. Some contend that it was because of the unprecedented job opportunities that arose in defense industries. ANDERSON sees continuity in the persistence of salary discrimination against women and of job segregation by sex as well as race and class, but she also sees great change. For her, the decision of large numbers of married women, and mothers, to take war jobs, was "a profoundly important event in American social history." CAMPBELL disagrees, contending that the war "did not mark a drastic break with traditional working patterns or sex roles." In presenting the children's home front history, TUTTLE examines father absence and father return along with other aspects of girls' and boys' wartime lives, emphasizing gender differences in their war games, schooling, popular culture, and other experiences. The war left an indelible imprint on the dreams and nightmares of an American generation not only in childhood, but in adulthood as well.

World War II was a time of fundamental change on the home front; some scholars have called it a watershed period in United States history. Although the war usually did not initiate new changes, it rapidly accelerated those already under way. Appropriations for the war lifted the country out of the Great Depression and stimulated the building not only of defense plants, but also of war-boom communities for newly-arrived migrants. CLIVE focuses on "the worker's war" in Michigan, including the migration to Detroit of both African Americans and whites from the South. Not only cities and towns, but entire regions of the country were changed by the war. NASH shows how the war transformed the American West socially and culturally. It was also a time of massive personal change. BERUBE is an illuminating history of gay men and lesbians who served their country in the war, and came out in the process. In this way and in countless others, Americans discovered not only new talents and new horizons on the home front, but also new identities.

WILLIAM M. TUTTLE, JR.

Wright, Frances 1795–1852
Reformer, orator and campaigner for women's rights

Bartlett, Elizabeth Ann, *Liberty, Equality, Sorority: The Origins and Interpretation of American Feminist Thought: Frances Wright, Sarah Grimké, and Margaret Fuller*, New York: Carlson, 1994

Eckhardt, Celia Morris, *Fanny Wright: Rebel in America*, Cambridge, MA: Harvard University Press, 1984

Heineman, Helen, *Restless Angels: The Friendship of Six Victorian Women: Frances Wright, Camilla Wright, Harriet Garnett, Frances Garnett, Julia Garnett Pertz, Frances Trollope*, Athens: Ohio University Press, 1983

Kissel, Susan S., *In Common Cause: The "Conservative" Frances Trollope and the "Radical" Frances Wright*, Bowling Green, OH: Bowling Green State University Popular Press, 1993

Mullen, Richard, *Birds of Passage: Five Englishwomen in Search of America*, New York: St. Martin's Press, and London: Duckworth, 1994

Perkins, A.J.G. and Theresa Wolfson, *Frances Wright, Free Enquirer: The Study of a Temperament*, New York: Harper, 1939

Stiller, Richard, *Commune on the Frontier: The Story of Frances Wright*, New York: Crowell, 1972

Waterman, William Randall, *Frances Wright*, New York: Columbia University Press, 1924

Utopian reformer and free thinker Frances Wright is widely known for her curious relationship with the Revolutionary War hero Lafayette, for setting up the experimental bi-racial community of Nashoba, and for her belief in free love. Her devotion to antislavery, free thinking, educational reform and women's rights, coupled with her public presence as a speaker in support of these reforms, resulted in the widespread adoption as near-synonymous terms of "Fanny Wrightism" and "radicalism." Yet like other woman's rights activists, Wright had considerable difficulty in reconciling her private life with her intellectual beliefs.

Two older biographies take somewhat differing views of the character, activities and influence of Wright. PERKINS and WOLFSON view her as a heroic figure. While they are mildly critical of her for her "failure" as a wife and mother, they present a cogent defence of her contributions to social reform in the first half of the 19th century. WATERMAN equivocates on Wright's influence, pointing out that, while she was a pioneer for some causes, she also participated in others that were already well established. He does, however, credit her with furthering the causes of free thought, revised marriage laws, and changes in property rights for married women. Published just at the dawn of the development of women's history and incorporating some previously unpublished letters, STILLER is nonetheless a mostly uncritical narrative, adding little to the previous biographies.

These earlier biographies have been largely superseded by ECKHARDT's more recent study. Clearly influenced by the field of women's history yet mindful of overall historical context, Eckhardt portrays Wright as passionately devoted to important social causes, but because she was so far ahead of her time she was unable to accomplish much of what she set out to do. This is an ambitious and generally sympathetic biography, which makes large claims for the enduring importance of its subject, and which skilfully interweaves Wright's troubled private life and her controversial public career.

Emphasizing the trans-Atlantic connection, MULLEN focuses on Wright as a travel writer but also provides a readable narrative of her life. While he admires her high ideals, he criticizes her lack of common sense. HEINEMAN, a literary scholar, positions Wright within a composite biography of six influential, though not all well-known, 19th-century women. She dedicates a chapter to Wright's work at Nashoba, but, with her emphasis on friendship and women's agency, she neglects the cultural and historical importance of Wright's contributions.

Utilizing feminist theory, BARTLETT examines the ways in which Wright's feminist ideology was connected to the Enlightenment. She highlights how various modes of thought (moral sense philosophy, Epicurean utilitarianism, and utopian socialism) influenced Wright's beliefs about the role of women. KISSEL also examines Wright's feminism, clearly showing her radical tendencies but pointing out how terms such as "radical," "conservative," and "liberal" shift not only in time but also with subject matter.

THERESA KAMINSKI

Wright, Orville 1871–1948 and Wilbur Wright 1867–1912
Aviation pioneers

Bilstein, Roger E., *Flight in America, 1900–1983: From the Wrights to the Astronauts*, Baltimore: Johns Hopkins University Press, 1984; revised (without dates in title) 1994

Corn, Joseph J., *The Winged Gospel: America's Romance with Aviation, 1900–1950*, New York: Oxford University Press, 1983

Crouch, Tom D., *A Dream of Wings: Americans and the Airplane, 1875–1905*, New York: Norton, 1981

Crouch, Tom D., *The Bishop's Boys: A Life of Wilbur and Orville Wright*, New York: Norton, 1989

Hallion, Richard P. (editor), *The Wright Brothers: Heirs of Prometheus*, Washington, DC: Smithsonian Institution Press, 1978

Howard, Fred, *Wilbur and Orville: A Biography of the Wright Brothers*, New York: Knopf, 1987; London: Hale, 1988

Jakab, Peter L., *Visions of a Flying Machine: The Wright Brothers and the Process of Invention*, Washington, DC: Smithsonian Institution Press, 1990

The story of Wilbur and Orville Wright, two bicycle mechanics from Dayton, Ohio, who beat the world to the secret of flight, has been an inspiration to Americans since Wilbur made the first controlled, powered flight on the dune of Kitty Hawk, on the North Carolina coast, in December 1903. Not only did the Wrights usher in a new era, but they did so while embodying such admirable American virtues as diligence, daring, modest pioneering, and the successful combination of science with commerce.

CROUCH (1989) is indisputably the best biography we have, and is likely to remain so for the foreseeable future. It successfully weaves together the central strands of the Wrights' story – family support, technological innovation, and the impact of aviation on society – to explain why the brothers proved capable of making their breakthrough. As the title suggests, Crouch offers a new and persuasive portrait of their father, a minister of religion who instilled in them the deep self-assurance which enabled them to pursue their own route to success, as well as a disinclination to leave the family home that kept them together. They lived with their father and were cared for by their sister until Wilbur's death in 1912. HOWARD takes a more conversational tone, and chooses to concentrate on the post-1903 period rather more than does Crouch. While neither as detailed nor considered as Crouch, it is a satisfactory introduction for those seeking a straightforward and readable account of the brothers' life and work.

An appreciation of the extensive research under way into aeronautics in the last quarter of the 19th century helps to put the Wrights' workings into context while in no way diminishing their achievement. CROUCH (1981) gives a thorough account of the active American pursuit of heavier than air flight, with due weight given to pioneers like Samuel Pierpont Langley and Octave Chanute. JAKAB is a short but clearly written monograph which sets out the extremely methodical way in which the Wrights approached the problems associated with flight, including building their own wind tunnel. It is particularly good at showing why a background in bicycles equipped them to tackle crucial questions of propulsion and balance, and covers their work in 1904 and 1905 when they perfected the original Wright Flyer to produce a fully controllable aeroplane.

Two useful books that cover the impact of the Wrights' work on the development of aviation and on American society are Bilstein (1994) and Corn. CORN's theme is that aviation chimed with both a uniquely American faith in social progress through technological innovation and an appreciation of the brave individual pioneer, an identification which sustained a great wave of enthusiasm for all things aeronautical during the 1920s and 1930s. If at times the argument is rather over-emphasized, the book captures well the awed early reaction to the sight and potential of the airplane. BILSTEIN (1984, 1994) starts with a useful summary of the Wrights' work, before moving on to a comprehensive survey of all aspects of aeronautics in the United States.

A worthy collection of essays by Wright scholars, the chief value of HALLION (1978) now lies in Hallion's photographic essay on the Wrights and their machines. A few minutes with these photographs and illustrations can add greatly to the reader's understanding of what it was, in technical terms, that the Wrights actually achieved.

GILES ALSTON

See also Aviation and Aerospace

Y

Young, Brigham 1801–1877 and
Joseph Smith 1805–1844
Mormon leaders

Arrington, Leonard J., *Brigham Young: American Moses*, New York: Knopf, 1985

Bringhurst, Newell G., *Brigham Young and the Expanding American Frontier*, Boston: Little Brown, 1986

Brodie, Fawn M., *No Man Knows My History: The Life of Joseph Smith the Mormon Prophet*, New York: Knopf, 1945, London: Eyre and Spottiswoode, 1963; revised, New York: Knopf, 1971

Bushman, Richard L., *Joseph Smith and the Beginnings of Mormonism*, Urbana: University of Illinois Press, 1984

Foster, Lawrence, *Religion and Sexuality: Three American Communal Experiments of the Nineteenth Century*, New York and Oxford: Oxford University Press, 1981

Hansen, Klaus J., *Mormonism and the American Experience*, Chicago: University of Chicago Press, 1981

Hill, Donna, *Joseph Smith: The First Mormon*, New York: Doubleday, 1977

Newell, Linda King and Valeen Tippetts Avery, *Mormon Enigma: Emma Hale Smith, Prophet's Wife, "Elect Lady," Polygamy's Foe, 1804–1879*, New York: Doubleday, 1984; 2nd edition, Urbana: University of Illinois Press, 1994

O'Dea, Thomas F., *The Mormons*, Chicago: University of Chicago Press, 1957

Van Wagoner, Richard S., *Mormon Polygamy: A History*, Salt Lake City: Signature, 1986

In view of all that has been written about Joseph Smith and Brigham Young, the charismatic early leaders of the Church of Jesus Christ of Latter-Day Saints (the Mormon Church), the paucity of good biographies is surprising. This may be due, in part, to the unique place that these men hold in American religious history. Both proclaimed themselves to be prophets charged with establishing God's kingdom on earth – a kingdom that contained such radical changes to the Protestant tradition as revelation and new scripture, polygamy, and a return to the mixing of church and state. Few of the early biographers of Smith and Young had the training or inclination to step beyond facile defenses or condemnations of these men. Even recent scholarly works are still shaped by the authors' scepticism or belief concerning religious experiences; believers tend to accept religious experience at face value, and generally portray the prophets sympathetically, while non-believers find naturalistic explanations for Mormon origins, but often slight the impact of religious experiences on the development of these men and their followers.

BRODIE is an in-depth study, which quickly became one of the most popular of all the biographies of Joseph Smith. Although raised in a prominent Mormon family, Brodie came to reject Mormonism and all supernatural explanations of Smith's revelations. She believed that, through his charisma and skill in drawing on the culture of the time, Smith gradually evolved from a "bucolic scryer" given to using folk magic into the "preacher-prophet" of his later years. Elegantly written, the book presents a view of Smith informed by psychoanalysis that non-Mormons can understand and accept. But Brodie's extensive reliance on published sources, even to the exclusion of important manuscript collections, biased her story towards Smith's detractors. Historians will also be uncomfortable with Brodie's use of the biographer's license to add assumed dialogue and thoughts of key characters.

In his sociological study of Mormonism, O'DEA eschewed psychological explanations, and argued that Joseph Smith was simply a product of the religious excitement of his era. This "common-sense explanation" is inadequate, however, when O'Dea attempts to explain Smith's innovations such as polygamy, plurality of gods, and temple rituals for the dead. O'Dea is at his best when charting the church's continued separation from American society under Brigham Young, and the stresses and conflicts felt by the church as it has attempted to return to mainstream America in the 20th century.

HANSEN's brief treatment of Smith in his larger study of Mormonism is one of the latest in a line of psychological studies. Like Brodie, Hansen has a background in the Mormon church but chooses to find the source of the Book of Mormon and Smith's visions in the church leader's psyche. Hansen, however, rejects psychoanalysis and similar theories because of their tendency to categorize Smith's genius as mental illness. Unfortunately, Hansen's alternative framework, Julian Jaynes's controversial hypothesis of the "breakdown of the bicameral mind," is even less accepted by experts, and leaves too many questions unanswered. However, there is a valuable discussion of Smith's part in the development of Mormon doctrine, politics, racial views and polygamy.

HILL is perhaps the best biography of Smith written by a sympathetic Mormon. She takes advantage of the large manuscript collections owned by the church to produce an in-depth and readable narrative of Smith's life. Arguing that it is impossible to prove or disprove spiritual experience, Hill accepts Smith's basic contention of divine inspiration and instead focuses on the results of those experiences. Unfortunately, this framework limits Hill's analysis of Smith's place in the religious culture of the time. BUSHMAN also acknowledges the validity of Smith's claim to religious experiences but is more successful in placing him in the larger context of American religious history. A Mormon and well-known historian of colonial New England, Bushman agrees that Smith was influenced by early 19th century religious culture, but suggests that Smith can best be understood as someone who outgrew that culture. He contends that Mormonism lacks the strong evidences of 19th-century republicanism, congregationalism, the Enlightenment or evangelical revivalism which would be needed to support a cultural explanation. Unfortunately, the book, originally conceived as part of a series on Mormonism, ends with Smith's move to Ohio, thirteen years before his death.

In an exhaustively researched study of Joseph Smith's first wife, Emma Hale Smith, NEWELL and AVERY fill key gaps in our understanding of Smith. They examine closely Joseph's domestic life, his institution of the practice of polygamy, and Emma's break with Brigham Young after Joseph was killed. The practice of Mormon polygamy is examined by both Van Wagoner and Foster. Using a narrative approach, VAN WAGONER focuses on administrative history, carrying the story from Joseph Smith's introduction of the practice in the 1830s through to present-day polygamous Mormon splinter groups. Many, however, will find FOSTER's multi-disciplinary approach and firm grounding in American communal and religious history more valuable. He rejects the notions that Smith and Young were driven by either lust or divine influence, arguing instead that Mormon polygamy must be seen as part of an earnest attempt to bring order to 19th-century America by restructuring the family and the larger society.

The best biography of Brigham Young is ARRINGTON. Making good use of the vast primary source material generated by Young during his presidency, Arrington paints a picture of a strong, natural leader, a consummate businessman and a kingdom builder who, unlike Joseph Smith, had little interest in doctrinal innovation. Arrington is a devout Mormon and former Church Historian who views Young sympathetically. Although surprisingly objective on most issues, he tends to gloss over Young's occasional heavy-handed use of power. This lengthy book also contains too much on the history of the church, and not enough about Young's private thoughts on such issues as his polygamous marriages, violence perpetrated by Mormons on non-members in Utah, and Mormon conflict with the United States government.

In his much shorter study, BRINGHURST is more willing to broach such topics and keeps the spotlight more on Brigham Young himself. However, his portrayal of Young lacks the depth of Arrington's, and it does not fulfil the promise of its title by illuminating Young's place in the history of the expanding American frontier.

SHAWN JOHANSEN

See also Mormons

INDEXES

BOOKLIST INDEX

Books and articles discussed in the entries are listed here by author/editor name. The page numbers refer to the lists themselves, where full publication information is given. Journal articles and essays from collections are indicated by the word "article" in parentheses.

GENERAL INDEX

Page numbers in **bold** indicate subjects with their own entries.

Twain, Mark, 296
Tweed Ring, New York City, 473, 512
Tweed, William Marcy, 473, 512
two-party system, 696
Tydings, Joseph, 418
Tyler, John, 136, 691, 704–05
Tyler, Julia Gardiner, 704

U-boats, in World War II, 776
U-2 flights, 101, 102
U.S. v. Carolene Products, 175
UAW, *see* United Automobile Workers
Ulster, 143, 350
underclass, 428, 553
underground railroad, 119, 702
UNEF, *see* United Nations Emergency Force
unemployment insurance, 503
UNESCO, *see* United Nations Educational, Scientific, and Cultural Organization
UNIA, *see* Universal Negro Improvement Association
Union League, 585
Union Pacific Railroad, 8
unions: 382, **392–93**, 594, 675; craft unions, 193, 302, 382, 389, 392; emergence of, 300; German American involvement in, 295; industrial unions, 193; during New Deal, 503, 504, 506, 507; during 1920s, 517; in railroad industry, 575, 577; and Taylorism, 619; trade unions, 382
Unitarian church, 43, 82, 230, 308, 566, 651, 697
United Artists, 251
United Automobile Workers (UAW), 166, 250, 594, 676
United Electrical Workers, 167
United Fruit Company, 274
United Fund, 543
United Mine Workers of America, 166, 401
United Nations, 671, 672, 707–08
United Nations Educational, Scientific, and Cultural Organization (UNESCO), 708
United Nations Emergency Force (UNEF), 707
United States Information Agency, 270
United States Military Academy (West Point), 306
United States Naval Academy (Annapolis), 370
United States Steel Corporation, 92, 433, 464, 675
United States v. *Peters*, 440
United Steel Workers, 167
United Way, 543
UNIVAC computer, 160, 550
Universal Military Training and Service, 204
Universal Negro Improvement Association (UNIA), 14, 289, 290
Universalist church, 566, 590
universities: 200, 218, 258, 345, 559, **708–11**, 755; McCarthyism in, 40, 230, 711
University of Alabama, 727
University of Arizona, 710
University of California, Berkeley, 709, 710

University of California, Los Angeles, 710
University of Chicago, 258, 602, 709
University of Massachusetts, 710
University of Mississippi, 727
University of Notre Dame, 258
University of Pittsburgh, 710
Upham, Charles Wentworth, 281
Upshur, Abel P., 691, 704, 705
Upton, Emory, 46, 457, 619
urban historiography, 326, 472, 473
urban history: 472, 473, 474, 653, **711–14**; African American, 13, 17, 21
Urban League, 18, 747
urban minorities, 229
urban planning, 472, 473
urbanization: 296, 297, 344, 376, 424, 434, 436, 463, 472, 473, 488, 509, 513, 550, 551, 561, 597, 598, 599, 600, 602, 603, 611, 614, 616, 635, 651, 661, 665, 711, 781; and Native Americans, 496
Utah, 449, 494, 495, 528, 551, 603, 786
Ute Indians, 494
Utica (NY), 241, 436, 453, 622
utilities, public, 474
Uto-Aztecan peoples, 494
utopian movements, 58, 312, 588, 645, 666, 688, **715–16**, 783
Utrecht, Treaty of (1713), 74

vagrancy, 186
Van Buren, Martin, 90, 354, 363, 407, 459, 557, 691, 692, **717–18**
Vance, Zebulon, 162
Vanderbilt, Cornelius, 767
Vanzetti, Bartolomeo, 278
Vassar College, 709, 761
Vatican II, 98, 169
Vaughan, Alden, 483
Vaux, Calvert, 525
Veblen, Thorstein, 218, 400, 437, **718–19**
Venezuela, 462
Venezuelan Boundary Dispute (1895–96), 395
Vera Cruz (Mexico), 448, 450
Vermont, 42, 355, 509, 588, 695, 709, 746
Verrazano, Giovanni da, 212
Versailles, Treaty of (1919), 207, 264, **719–20**
veterans: 542; pensions, 242, 305, 654; Veterans Bureau, 319
vice, commercialization of, 563
Vicksburg campaign, 126, 306
Vidal, Gore, 80, 175
videos, 579
Vienna summit (1961), 377
Viereck, George Sylvester, 295
Vietnam: 102; immigration from, 723
Vietnam War: 3, 14, 47, 101, 106, 137, 205, 239, 260, 265, 266, 267, 272, 273, 304, 316, 366, 368, 369, 376, 377, 386, 404, 518, 519, 528, 529, 557, 579, 629, 672, **720–23**, 727; protests against, 181, 182, 579; Vietnam veterans, 529, 723
Vigilance Committee, in San Francisco, 611

vigilantism, 724
Viking settlements in North America, 211
Vinson, Fred, 331
violence: 186, 643, 660, 688, 689, **723–25**, 786; against blacks, 365; collective or mob, 376, 476, 596, 597
Virgin Islands, 457
Virginia, 17, 48, 72, 123, 134, 135, 141, 147, 149, 152, 156, 186, 199, 212, 307, 350, 366, 396, 397, 412, 413, 457, 460, 461, 483, 521, 571, 599, 637, 638, 641, 648, 649, 704, 724, 736, 737, 738
Virginia Company, 141
Virginia Council, 648
Virginia Resolutions, **27–28**, 426
Voltaire, 277
voluntary motherhood, 613
volunteer armies, 456
Von Braun, Wernher, 663
von Neumann, John, 160
voodoo, 511
Voting Rights Act (1965), 111, 113, 476
Voyager space probe, 52

Wade, Benjamin F., 367
Wadsworth, Jeremiah, 467
Wagenen, Isabella van (Sojourner Truth), 701
wages, 391, 431
Wagner, Robert, 111
Wagner Act, *see* National Labor Relations Act
wagon trains, 699, 749
waitresses unions, 29, 393
Walker, David, 65
Walker, James J., 647
Walker, Robert John, 691
Wall Street Crash, 253, 308, 673
Wallace, George, 198, 420, 695, **727–28**
Wallace, Lurleen, 727
Wallis, George, 432
Walpole, Sir Robert, 70
Walters, Alexander, 747
Waltz, Kenneth, 266
Wanamaker's store, 436
war debts, 181, 350, **728–29**
War Eagle (Cornelius C. Cusick), 491
War Food Administration, 781
War Industries Board, 770
War of 1812: 7, 46, 51, 213, 248, 260, 277, 278, 287, 363, 426, 484, 492, **729–31**; and citizenship, 109
War of Independence: 14, 30, 46, 260, 276, 370, 415, 599, **731–33**, 737, 738; and citizenship, 109
War of the Austrian Succession, 733
War on Poverty, 311, 553, 654
War Production Board, 780
Ward, Lester F., 649
Warner, Charles Dudley, 296
Warren Commission, 377, 378, 734
Warren, Earl, 20, 111, 170, 177, 178, 377, **733–35**
Warren, Mercy Otis, 4
Washington state, 495, 527

NOTES ON ADVISERS
AND CONTRIBUTORS

Adams, David. Professor Emeritus of American Studies; Chair, David Bruce Centre for American Studies, Keele University, Staffordshire. Author of *America in the Twentieth Century* (1967) and *An Atlas of North American Affairs* (1969, 1979). Editor of *British Documents on Foreign Affairs: Reports and Papers from the Foreign Office Confidential Print* (25 vols., 1986–95). Series editor, *European Papers in American History* (1994–). **Essays:** Isolationism; Perkins.

Alston, Giles. Formerly Lecturer in Government, University of Essex, Colchester. Contributor to *The Bush Presidency: First Appraisals* edited by Colin Campbell and Bert A. Rockman (1991) and *Re-examining the Eisenhower Presidency* edited by Shirley Anne Warshaw (1993). **Essays:** Space Policy and Program; Orville Wright and Wilbur Wright.

Aspinwall, Bernard. Senior Lecturer in Modern History, University of Glasgow, until 1995. Author of *Portable Utopia: Glasgow and the United States, 1820–1920* (1984), *USA* (1985), and *Reinido Unido y América: Influencia Religiosa* (1992). Contributor to *Contemporary Irish Studies* (1983), *The Scots Abroad* (1985), *Mormons in Early Victorian Britain* (1989), *Irish Immigrants and Scottish Society* (1991), *Dictionary of Scottish Church History* (1993), and *The Church Faces the Modern World: Rerum Novarum and Its Impact* (1994). **Essays:** Catholic Church; Catt; Nation; Pacifism.

Badger, Anthony J. Paul Mellon Professor of American History, University of Cambridge. Author of *Prosperity Road: The New Deal, North Carolina, and Tobacco* (1980), *North Carolina and the New Deal* (1981), and *The New Deal: The Depression Years, 1933–40* (1989). Editor of *The Making of Martin Luther King and the Civil Rights Movement* (with Brian Ward, 1996) and *Southern Landscapes* (with Walter Edgar and Jan Gretlund, 1997).

Bailey, Fred Arthur. Professor of History, Abilene Christian University, Texas. Author of *Class and Tennessee's Confederate Generation* (1987), *William Edward Dodd: The South's Yeoman Historian*, and *Southern Censorship and the Search for a Suitable Past* (forthcoming). Contributor to numerous journals including *Southwestern Historical Quarterly, Georgia Historical Quarterly, Tennessee Historical Quarterly, Florida Historical Quarterly, Journal of Southern Studies*, and *Journal of Southern History*. **Essays:** Class; McGuffey.

Baker, Jean H. Professor of History, Goucher College, Baltimore. Author of *The Politics of Continuity* (1973), *Ambivalent Americans: The Know Nothing Party in Maryland* (1977), *Affairs of Party: The Political Culture of Northern Democrats in the Mid-Nineteenth Century* (1983), *Mary Todd Lincoln: A Biography* (1987), and *The Stevensons: A Biography of an American Family* (1996). **Essays:** Civil War: the North 1; Stevenson; Women's History: Education.

Bakken, Gordon Morris. Professor of History, California State University, Fullerton. Author of *The Development of Law on the Rocky Mountain Frontier: Civil Law and Society, 1850–1912* (1983), *The Development of Law in Frontier California* (1985), *Rocky Mountain Constitution Making, 1850–1912* (1987), *California Legal Manuscripts in the Huntington Library* (1989), and *Practicing Law in Frontier California* (1991). **Essays:** Pacific Northwest; Rocky Mountains.

Barney, William L. Professor of History, University of North Carolina at Chapel Hill. Author of *The Road to Secession* (1972), *The Secessionist Impulse* (1974), *Flawed Victory* (1975), *The Passage of the Republic* (1987), and *Battleground for the Union* (1990). Editor of *Learning History in America* (with Lloyd Kramer and Donald Reid, 1994). **Essays:** Civil War: Approach to 4; Civil War: Debate on Causes.

Barrow, John C. III. PhD candidate, Vanderbilt University, Nashville. Author of *The Moral Equivalent of War: Jimmy Carter and the Quest for a National Energy Policy* (dissertation). **Essay:** Carter.

Baumgarten, Nikola. Former Research Fellow, Hughes Hall, University of Cambridge. Contributor to *Historical Dictionary of Women's Education* edited by Linda Eisenmann (forthcoming) and to the journal *History of Education Quarterly*. **Essay:** Schools: from the Revolution to 1900.

Benedict, M. Les. Professor of History, Ohio State University, Columbus. Author of *The Impeachment and Trial of Andrew Johnson* (1973), *A Compromise of Principle* (1974), and *The Blessings of Liberty* (1995). **Essays:** Legal History: Special Aspects; Reconstruction: General.

Berlin, Jean V. Author of *A Confederate Nurse: The Diary of Ada W. Bacot* (1994), and assistant editor of *The Correspondence of William T. Sherman* (in progress).

Contributor to *Proceedings of the South Carolina Historical Association*, and to the journals *Documentary Editing*, *Hayes Historical Journal*, and *Pennsylvania History*. **Essays:** Beecher Family; Crandall; Fulton; Stevens.

Berry, Stephen W. PhD candidate, University of North Carolina at Chapel Hill. **Essays:** Kit Carson; Whitney.

Biles, Roger. Professor of History, East Carolina University, Greenville, North Carolina. Author of *Big City Boss in Depression and War: Mayor Edward J. Kelly of Chicago* (1984), *A New Deal for the American People* (1991), *The South and the New Deal* (1994), and *Richard J. Daley: Politics, Race, and the Governing of Chicago* (1995). **Essay:** Chicago.

Black, Jeremy. Professor of History, University of Exeter, England. Author of numerous books including *War for America: The Fight for Independence* (1991) and *Pitt the Elder* (1992). **Essays:** War of Independence: Military History; War of Independence: Diplomacy.

Blume, Kenneth J. Associate Professor of History, Albany College of Pharmacy, Albany, New York. Contributor to *Historical Dictionary of Oceania* edited by Robert D. Craig and Frank P. King (1981), *Biographical Dictionary of Internationalists* edited by Warren F. Kuehl (1983), and *American National Biography*, and to the journals *Civil War History* and *American Neptune*. **Essays:** Foreign Policy, 1865–1918; Transport: General.

Bode, Frederick A. Professor of History, Concordia University, Montreal. Author of *Protestantism and the New South* (1975) and *Farm Tenancy and the Census in Antebellum Georgia* (with Donald E. Grinter, 1986). Contributor to *Journal of Southern History*, *Journal of Interdisciplinary History*, *Historical Methods*, and *Research in Economic History*. **Essays:** Finney; Protestantism: General; Revivalism.

Boles, John B. William P. Hobby Professor of History, Rice University, Houston. Author of *The Great Revival, 1787–1805: Origins of the Southern Evangelical Mind* (1972), *Black Southerners, 1619–1869* (1983), *The Irony of Southern Religion* (1995), and *The South Through Time: A History of an American Region* (1995). Editor of *Interpreting Southern History* (with Evelyn Thomas Nolen, 1987) and *Masters and Slaves in the House of the Lord: Race and Religion in the American South, 1740–1870* (1988). Editor of *Journal of Southern History*. **Essay:** South: General.

Bolt, Christine. Professor of American History, University of Kent at Canterbury. Author of *The Anti-Slavery Movement and Reconstruction* (1969), *Victorian Attitudes to Race* (1971), *A History of the USA* (1974), *Power and Protest in American Life* (with A. T. Barbrook, 1980), *American Indian Policy and American Reform* (1987), *The Women's Movements in the United States and Britain* (1993), and *Feminist Ferment* (1995). Editor of *Anti-Slavery, Religion and Reform* (with Seymour Drescher, 1980). Pro Vice Chancellor of the University of Kent, 1988–91. **Essays:** Mott; Eleanor Roosevelt; Stanton.

Bonwick, Colin. Professor of American History, Keele University, Staffordshire. Author of *English Radicals and the American Revolution* (1977) and *The American Revolution* (1991), and various articles on British and American aspects of the American Revolution. **Essays:** American Revolution: Causes; Declaration of Independence; Federal Government: Establishment of; Jefferson.

Bowers, Jerome D. II. PhD candidate and Associate Instructor, Department of History, Indiana University, Bloomington. Contributor to *American National Biography*. **Essays:** British Americans; Middle Atlantic States.

Boyle, Peter G. Senior Lecturer, Department of American and Canadian Studies, University of Nottingham. Author of *American-Soviet Relations: From the Russian Revolution to the Fall of Communism* (1993). Editor of *The Churchill-Eisenhower Correspondence, 1953–55* (1990). **Essays:** Dulles; Eisenhower; Foreign Policy: General; Foreign Policy, Special Aspects 5; Recent American History.

Bradford, James C. Professor, Air War College, Maxwell Air Force Base, Alabama. Author of *The Reincarnation of John Paul Jones: The Navy Discovers Its Professional Roots* (1984), *Admirals of the New Steel Navy: Makers of the American Naval Tradition, 1880-1930* (1990), and of several articles on Jones. Editor of *Command under Sail: Makers of the American Naval Tradition, 1775-1850* (1985), *The Papers of John Paul Jones* (1986), *Captains of the Old Steam Navy: Makers of the American Naval Tradition, 1840-1880* (1986), *Crucible of Empire: The Spanish-American War and Its Aftermath* (1993), and the Library of Naval Biography series, Naval Institute Press. Vice President of the North American Society for Oceanic History. **Essay:** Jones.

Brands, H. W. Professor of History, Texas A&M University, College Station. Author of numerous books, including *Cold Warriors: Eisenhower's Generation and American Foreign Policy* (1988), *India and the United States: The Cold Peace* (1990), *The Devil We Knew: Americans and the Cold War* (1993), and *The Wages of Globalism* (1995). **Essays:** Foreign Policy: Special Aspects 4; Kissinger; Mahan.

Brereton, T. R. Lecturer, Texas A&M University, College Station. Author of *1001 Things Everyone Should Know about the Civil War* (with Frank E. Vandiver, forthcoming), and *Dictionary of the Civil War* (forthcoming). **Essays:** Armed Services; Military History: General; Pershing.

Brewer, Teri F. Senior Lecturer in Anthropology, University of Glamorgan, Pontypridd, Wales. Contributor to *Seven Rock Art Sites in Baja California* edited by Clement W. Meighan and V. L. Pontoni (1978), and to the journals *Lore & Learning*, *Journal of Cherokee Studies*, *Folklore*, and *Folk Music Journal*. Editor of *A Women's Studies Reader* (with Stevi Jackson and others, 1993); managing editor of *Folklore*. **Essays:** Native Americans: General; Native Americans: Cultures 4; Native Americans: Cultures 5.

Buenker, John D. Professor of History, University of Wisconsin–Parkside, Kenosha. Author of *Urban Liberalism and Progressive Reform* (1978), *The Income Tax and the Progressive Era* (1985); co-author of guides to Progressivism, immigration and ethnicity, urban history, and multi-culturalism. Contributor to collections on midwestern history, to biographical reference books, and to many journals, including *Mid-America, Journal of American History, American Historical Review, American Quarterly,* and *New England Quarterly.* Contributing editor of *Journal of American History.* **Essays:** Gilded Age and Progressive Era; La Follette; Alfred E. Smith.

Bullock, Steven C. Professor of American History, Worcester Polytechnic Institute. Author of *Revolutionary Brotherhood: Freemasonry and the Transformation of the American Social Order, 1730–1840* (1996). **Essays:** Antimasonry; Early National Period; Franklin; Cotton Mather and Increase Mather.

Burchell, R. A. Director, Eccles Centre for American Studies, British Library, London; former Professor of American Studies, University of Manchester. Author of *Westward Expansion* (1974), *The San Francisco Irish, 1848–1880* (1979), and *Harriet Martineau and America* (1995). Editor of *The End of Anglo-America* (1991) and *American Studies in Europe.* **Essays:** California; Gold Rushes; Hispanic Americans; Native Americans: Indian Wars; Public Land Policy; Wealth.

Burton, Orville Vernon. Professor of History, University of Illinois at Urbana. Author of *In My Father's House Are Many Mansions: Family and Community in Edgefield, South Carolina* (1985) and *A Gentleman and an Officer: A Military and Social History of James B. Griffin's Civil War* (with Judith N. McArthur, 1996). Co-editor of two collections on southern communities and of works on social science computing. Contributor to *Encyclopedia of American Social History* and *Encyclopedia of the Confederacy,* and to *Journal of Social History, Journal of Southern History,* and *Journal of Southern Studies.* **Essays:** Confederate States of America: Home Front.

Carrigan, William. PhD candidate, Emory University, Atlanta. **Essays:** Mexican War, 1846–1848: Politics and Diplomacy; Religion: General.

Carroll, Francis M. Professor of History, St. John's College, University of Manitoba, Winnipeg. Author of *American Opinion and the Irish Question* (1978), *Crossroads in Time: A History of Carlton County, Minnesota* (1987), *The WPA Guide to the Minnesota Arrowhead Country* (introduction, 1988), and *The Fires of Autumn* (with Franklin R. Raiter, 1990). Editor of *American Commission on Irish Independence, 1919* (1985). **Essays:** *Alabama* Claims and Treaty of Washington; Canada and the United States; Civil War: International Aspects; Irish Americans.

Carson, James Taylor. Member of the Department of History, Queen's University, Kingston, Ontario. Contributor to *Ethnohistory* and *Journal of Mississippi History.* **Essays:** Colonial History: Non-English Settlements in North America; Early Exploration of North America; Great Plains; Native

Americans: White Encounter with; Native Americans: Federal Policy towards; Native Americans: Cultures 2; Native Americans: Cultures 3.

Carwardine, Richard J. Professor of History, University of Sheffield. Author of *Transatlantic Revivalism: Popular Evangelicalism in Britain and America, 1790–1865* (1978) and *Evangelicals and Politics in Antebellum America* (1993). Contributor to *Journal of American History, Journal of Ecclesiastical History,* and *Journal of American Studies.* **Essay:** Second Great Awakening.

Castle, Kathryn. Principal Lecturer in History, University of North London. Author of *Britannia's Children: Reading Colonialism Through Children's Books and Magazines* (1996), and an essay on India in British history in *The Imperial Curriculum* edited by J.A. Mangan (1993). **Essay:** Federal Bureau of Investigation.

Channon, Geoffrey. Professor of History, University of the West of England, Bristol. Editor of *Studies in Transport History: Railways* (1996), and contributor to the journals *Economic History Review, Business History Review,* and *Journal of Transport History.* **Essay:** Du Pont Family.

Clapp, Elizabeth J. Lecturer in American History, University of Leicester. Contributor to the journals *Mid-America* and *Journal of American Studies.* **Essays:** Addams; Children and Youth; Kelley; Prostitution; Settlement House Movement; Women's History: Suffrage.

Clark, Christopher. Professor of History, University of York, England. Author of *The Roots of Rural Capitalism: Western Massachusetts, 1780–1860* (1990) and *The Communitarian Moment: The Radical Challenge of the Northampton Association* (1995). **Essays:** Bellamy; Market Revolution; Truth; Utopian and Communitarian Movements.

Clarke, Sally H. Associate Professor of History, University of Texas at Austin. Author of *Regulation and the Revolution in United States Farm Productivity* (1994). **Essay:** Agriculture, since 1860.

Clinton, Catherine. Fellow, W.E.B. Du Bois Institute, Harvard University, Cambridge, Massachusetts. Author of a number of books on women's history, including *The Plantation Mistress* (1982), *The Other Civil War: American Women in the Nineteenth Century* (1984), and *Tara Revisited: Women, War, and the Plantation Legend* (1996). Editor of *Portraits of American Women* (with G.J. Barker-Benfield, 1991) and *Divided Houses: Gender and the Civil War* (with Nina Silber, 1992).

Coates, Peter A. Lecturer, Department of Historical Studies, University of Bristol. Author of *The Trans-Alaska Pipeline Controversy: Technology, Conservation and the Frontier* (1991), *In Nature's Defence: Americans and Conservation* (1993), and *Environment and History: The Taming of Nature in the USA and South Africa* (with William Beinart, 1995). Contributor of a chapter on oil and environmentalism in

Alaska in *Politics in the Postwar American West* edited by Richard Lowitt (1995). **Essays:** Rachel Carson; Cattle Kingdom; Conservation; Muir; National Parks.

Cole, Donald B. Professor Emeritus, Phillips Exeter Academy, Exeter, New Hampshire. Author of *Immigrant City: Lawrence, Massachusetts, 1845–1921* (1963), *Jacksonian Democracy in New Hampshire, 1800–1851* (1970), and *Martin Van Buren and the American Political System* (1984). Editor (with John J. McDonough) of *Witness to the Young Republic: A Yankee's Journal* (1989) and *The Presidency of Andrew Jackson* (1993). **Essays:** Andrew Jackson; Nullification Crisis; Polk; Van Buren.

Collins, Bruce W. Dean and Deputy Principal, University College, Scarborough, Yorkshire. Author of *The Origins of America's Civil War* (1981) and *White Society in the Antebellum South* (1985). **Essays:** Civil War, 1861–1865: General; Financial History, since 1940s.

Conrad James L., Jr. Professor of History, Nichols College, Dudley, Massachusetts. Contributor to *Rhode Island History*, *Business and Economic History*, and *Technology and Culture*. **Essay:** Slater.

Conyne, George. Lecturer in History and American Studies, University of Kent at Canterbury. Author of *Woodrow Wilson: British Perspectives, 1912–1921* (1992). **Essays:** Constitution: the Document; Constitutional History: General; Constitutional History, 1789–1877; Constitutional History, since 1877; Hughes; Story.

Cook, Emily Walker. Member of the History departments, University of Massachusetts, Boston, and Babson College, Babson Park, Massachusetts. Contributor to *College Language Association Journal*. **Essays:** Anthony; Eddy; Friedan; Goldman.

Cook, Robert. Lecturer in American History, University of Sheffield. Author of *Baptism of Fire: The Republican Party in Iowa, 1838–1878* (1994) and a forthcoming book on the civil rights movement. **Essays:** African American History: since 1954; Know Nothings; Whig Party.

Coopey, Richard. Research Fellow, London School of Economics. Author of *The Wilson Governments, 1964–70* (with S. Fielding and N. Tiratsoo, 1993), *3i: 50 Years of Investing in Industry* (with D. Clarke, 1995), and *Britain in the 1970s: The Troubled Economy* (with N. Woodward, 1996). **Essay:** Ford.

Crawford, Martin. Reader in American History, Keele University, Staffordshire. Author of *The Anglo-American Crisis of the Mid-Nineteenth Century: The Times and America, 1850–1862* (1987), and *William Howard Russell's Civil War: Private Diary and Letters, 1861–1862* (1992). Contributor to numerous journals including *Civil War History*, *Journal of Southern History*, *Slavery and Abolition*, and *North Carolina Historical Review*. General Editor of the British Association for American Studies Pamphlets series, 1989–93. **Essay:** Appalachia.

Cressey-Hackett, Maureen. PhD student in American History, University of Cambridge. **Essay:** Hamer.

Cullis, Philip. Lecturer in American History, University of Edinburgh. Author of *Antitrust in America: The Scholarly Debate, 1910–1943* (dissertation, 1993). **Essays:** Antitrust Legislation and Court Cases; Economic Thought; Industrialization; New Deal: Legislation and Agencies 2; Populism; Railroads: Legislation and Court Cases.

Curtin, Neil. Lecturer in History and American Studies, King Alfred's College of Higher Education, Winchester. **Essays:** Benton; Federalist Party; Jeffersonian Republican Party.

Daniels, Roger. Charles Phelps Taft Professor of History, University of Cincinnati. Author of *The Politics of Prejudice* (1962), *The Bonus March* (1971), *Concentration Camps, North America* (1981), *Coming to America* (1990), and *Prisoners Without Trial* (1993). Editor of the Asian American Experience series and chair of the board of editors, Statue of Liberty/Ellis Island Centennial series, University of Illinois Press. **Essays:** Asian Americans; Immigration and Ethnicity: General; Immigration: Federal Policy towards.

Davies, Gareth. Lecturer in American Studies, University of Lancaster. Author of *From Opportunity to Entitlement: The Transformation and Decline of Great Society Liberalism* (1996), and contributor to the *Journal of American Studies*. **Essay:** Great Society.

Davis, Michael G. PhD candidate, Vanderbilt University, Nashville. **Essay:** Foreign Policy since 1945: General.

Davis, Vanessa L. PhD candidate and Teaching Fellow, Vanderbilt University, Nashville. **Essays:** Bethune; Gay and Lesbian Movements, since 1960s; Women's History: Women in Ethnic Minority Groups.

Dawson, Joseph G. III. Associate Professor of History, Texas A&M University, College Station. Author of *Army Generals and Reconstruction* (1982). Editor of *Commanders in Chief* (1993) and *The Texas Military Experience* (1995). Director of the Military Studies Institute at Texas A&M University. **Essay:** Mexican War: Campaigns.

de Zoysa, Richard. Senior Lecturer in Politics, South Bank University, London. Author of numerous magazine and journal articles. **Essay:** New York City.

Dietle, Robert L. Assistant Professor of History, Western Kentucky University, Bowling Green. **Essay:** France and America, 1763–1815.

Dirck, Brian. Member of the Department of History, University of Kansas, Lawrence. Contributor to *Missouri Historical Review*, *Houston Review*, and *East Texas Historical Journal*. **Essays:** Confederate States of America: General; Legal History: General.

Dockrill, Saki. Lecturer in War Studies, King's College, London. Author of *Britain's Policy for West German Rearmament, 1950–1955* (1991) and *The Challenge of Power: Eisenhower's New Look National Security Policy, 1953–1961* (1996). Editor of *From Pearl Harbor to Hiroshima: The Second World War in Asia and the Pacific, 1941–1945* (1994). Contributor to the journal *Diplomacy and Statecraft*. **Essays:** Acheson; Marshall Plan; World War II: United States and 5.

Dumbrell, John. Senior Lecturer in American Studies, Keele University, Staffordshire. Author of *The Making of US Foreign Policy* (1990), *Vietnam: American Involvement at Home and Abroad* (1992), and *The Carter Presidency: A Revaluation* (1993). Editor of *Vietnam and the Antiwar Movement: An International Perspective* (1989). **Essays:** Central Intelligence Agency; Vietnam War: Political and Social Consequences.

Dunn, Elizabeth E. Assistant Professor of History, Baylor University, Waco, Texas. Contributor to *Benjamin Franklin, Jonathan Edwards, and the Representation of American Culture* edited by Barbara B. Oberg and Harry S. Stout (1993) and to the journals *Pennsylvania History* and *Pennsylvania Magazine of History and Biography*. **Essays:** Abigail Adams; Williams; Winthrop.

Eden, Douglas. Head of American Studies, and Director of the Centre for Study of International Affairs, Middlesex University, London. Author of *Political Change in Europe* (1981) and contributor to the journal *American Interests*. Editor of *The Future of the Atlantic Community* (1997). **Essay:** Democracy.

Ellis, Richard E. Professor of History, State University of New York at Buffalo. Author of *The Jeffersonian Crisis: Courts and Politics in the Young Republic* (1971) and *The Union at Risk: Jacksonian Democracy, States' Rights, and the Nullification Crisis* (1987). **Essays:** Articles of Confederation; Bill of Rights; Constitution: Ratification; Era of Good Feelings; Madison; John Marshall; Morris.

Ellis, Sylvia. Temporary lecturer, Sunderland University and PhD candidate, University of Newcastle upon Tyne. **Essays:** Foreign Policy: Special Aspects 3; Vietnam War: Military and Diplomatic History.

Emsley, Clive. Professor of History, Open University, Milton Keynes. Author of *Policing and Its Context, 1750–1870* (1983) and *Crime and Society in England, 1750–1900* (1996). Editor of *Crime History and Histories of Crime* (with Louis A. Knafla, 1996). **Essay:** Police and Law Enforcement.

Fairclough, Adam. Professor of American History, University of East Anglia, Norwich. Author of *To Redeem the Soul of America: The Southern Christian Leadership Conference and Martin Luther King, Jr.* (1987), *Martin Luther King, Jr.* (1990, 1995), and *Race and Democracy: The Civil Rights Struggle in Louisiana, 1915–1972* (1995). **Essays:** Civil Rights Movement; King; Thurgood Marshall.

Fearon, Peter. Senior Lecturer and Head of the Department of Economic History, University of Leicester. Author of *War,*

Prosperity and Depression: The US Economy, 1917–1945 (1987) and contributor to *Capitalism in Crisis: International Responses to the Great Depression* edited by W. R. Garside (1993). **Essays:** Economic Growth; Great Crash and Great Depression; New Deal: Economic Impact; War Debts and Reparations.

Feller, Daniel. Associate Professor of History, University of New Mexico, Albuquerque. Author of *The Public Lands in Jacksonian Politics* (1984) and *The Jacksonian Promise* (1995). Contributor to *Journal of the Early Republic*, *Reviews in American History*, and *Documentary Editing*. Assistant editor of *The Papers of Andrew Jackson, 1983–86*. **Essays:** Calhoun; Jacksonian Era: General.

Ferraro, William M. Assistant Editor, Ulysses S. Grant Association, Southern Illinois University, Carbondale. Editor of *The Papers of Ulysses S. Grant*, vols. 19–20 (1995), and *The Salmon P. Chase Papers*, vols. 1–2 (1995). Contributor to *South Atlantic Quarterly*, *Rhode Island History*, and *New Jersey History*. **Essays:** Grant; "Money Question"; Patronage/Spoils System; Reconstruction: Policy and Politics 1; Washington, DC.

Finkelman, Paul. Joseph C. Hostetler–Baker & Hostetler Visiting Professor, Cleveland-Marshall College of Law, Cleveland. Author of many books, most recently *"His Soul Goes Marching On": Responses to John Brown and the Harpers Ferry Raid* (1995), *Slavery and the Founders: Race and Liberty in the Age of Jefferson* (1996), *Slavery and the Law* (1996), and *Dred Scott v. Sandford: A Brief History with Documents* (1997). Editor of *American Legal History: Cases and Materials* (with Kermit L. Hall and William M. Wiecek, 1991) and *Toward a Usable Past: Liberty under State Constitutions* (with Stephen E. Gottlieb, 1991). Contributor to numerous journals and collections including *Supreme Court Review*, *Stanford Law Review*, *American Political Trials*, *Albany Law Review*, and *Brooklyn Journal of International Law*. **Essays:** Slavery: Legal Aspects; Taney; Warren.

Flynt, Wayne. Distinguished University Professor, Department of History, Auburn University, Alabama. Author of *Duncan Upshaw Fletcher: Dixie's Reluctant Progressive* (1971), *Cracker Messiah: Governor Sidney J. Catts of Florida* (1977), *Dixie's Forgotten People: The South's Poor Whites* (1979), *Montgomery: An Illustrated History* (1980), *Southern Poor Whites: A Selected Annotated Bibliography* (1981), *Mine, Mill, and Microchip: A Chronicle of Alabama Enterprise* (1987), and *Poor but Proud: Alabama's Poor Whites* (1989). Editor of *Alabama: The History of a Deep South State* (with William Warren Rogers and others, 1994). **Essays:** Poverty; South: since 1865; Wallace.

Follett, Richard J. Junior Lecturer in American History, University College, Galway, Ireland. Fulbright scholar at Louisiana State University, Baton Rouge, 1991–93. **Essays:** Historical Geography; Tyler.

Forbes, Robert P. Independent scholar, New Haven, Connecticut. Author of *Slavery and the Meaning of America:*

The Missouri Crisis and Its Aftermath (forthcoming). Contributor to *The Reader's Encyclopedia of the American West* edited by Howard R. Lamar (1977) and *New Essays on Slavery, Religion, and Sectionalism* (forthcoming). **Essays:** Missouri Compromise; Monroe.

Foster, Gaines M. Associate Professor of History, Louisiana State University, Baton Rouge. Author of *Ghosts of the Confederacy: Defeat, the Lost Cause, and the Emergence of the New South, 1865–1913* (1987) and contributor to *Bonds of Affection: Americans Define Their Patriotism* edited by John Bodnar (1996). **Essays:** Lost Cause / Southern Memories of the Civil War; Willard.

Fried, Richard M. Professor of History, University of Illinois at Chicago. Author of *Men Against McCarthy* (1976) and *Nightmare in Red: The McCarthy Era in Perspective* (1990). **Essay:** McCarthyism.

Friend, Craig Thompson. Assistant Professor of History, Georgetown College, Kentucky. **Essays:** Internal Improvements; Rivers and Canals; Roads and Road Transport: to 1900.

Frost, Dan R. Assistant Professor of History, Dillard University, New Orleans. Co-author of *The LSU College of Engineering: Origins and Establishment, 1860–1908* (1995), and contributor to *Southern Historian* and *Maryland Historian*. **Essays:** Civil War: the North 2; Education.

Garson, Robert. Reader in American Studies, Keele University, Staffordshire. Author of *The Democratic Party and the Politics of Sectionalism, 1941–48* (1974), *The Uncertain Power: A Political History of the US since 1929* (with C. J. Bailey, 1990), and *The United States and China since 1949: A Troubled Affair* (1994). **Essays:** Foreign Policy: Special Aspects 2; Truman.

Geiger, Roger L. Professor of Education, Pennsylvania State University, University Park. Author of numerous books, including *To Advance Knowledge: The Growth of American Research Universities, 1900–1940* (1986) and *Research and Relevant Knowledge: American Research Universities since World War II* (1993). Contributor to *Science in the 20th Century* edited by J. Krige and D. Pestre (1997) and the journals *Minerva, Review of Higher Education, History of Higher Education Annual, Higher Education Policy,* and *History of Education Quarterly.* **Essay:** Universities and Colleges: 20th century.

Geiter, Mary K. Lecturer in American Studies, College of Ripon and York St. John, York. Editor of *The Memoirs of Sir John Reresby* (with W. A. Speck, 1991) and contributor to the journal *Northern History.* **Essays:** Anne Hutchinson; Penn.

Gerteis, Louis S. Professor of History, University of Missouri, St. Louis. Author of *From Contraband to Freedman: Federal Policy Toward Southern Blacks, 1861–1865* (1973) and *Morality and Utility in American Antislavery Reform* (1987); contributor to *Civil War History, Union and Emancipation,* and *Journal of American History.* **Essays:** Chase; Race; Sumner.

Gillespie, J. David. Charles A. Dana Professor of Political Science, Presbyterian College, Clinton, South Carolina. Author of *Politics at the Periphery: Third Parties in Two-Party America* (1993); contributor to numerous journals, including *American Political Science Review, Policy Studies Journal, Australian Journal of Politics and History, Arab Studies Quarterly, Journal of Palestine Studies, Social Science, Operant Subjectivity,* and *Phylon.* **Essay:** Third Parties.

Gjerde, Jon. Professor of History, University of California, Berkeley. Author of *From Peasants to Farmers: The Migration from Balestrand, Norway to the Upper Middle West* (1985) and *The Minds of the West: Patterns of Ethnocultural Evolution in the Rural Middle West, 1830–1917* (1997). **Essays:** Midwest; Scandinavian Americans.

Goff, Philip K. Assistant Professor of History, California State University, Los Angeles. Contributor to the journals *Religious Studies Review* and *Excursus.* **Essay:** Adams Family.

Gordon, John Steele. Staff member, *Audacity* magazine, New York. Author of *Overlanding: How to Explore the World on Four Wheels* (1975), *The Scarlet Woman of Wall Street* (1988), and *Hamilton's Blessing: The Extraordinary Life and Times of Our National Debt* (1997); currently editing the letters and non-dramatic works of Oscar Hammerstein II. **Essays:** Astor; Morgan.

Gould, Lewis L. Eugene C. Barker Centennial Professor in American History, University of Texas at Austin. Author of *The Presidency of William McKinley* (1980), *Lady Bird Johnson and the Environment* (1988), *The Presidency of Theodore Roosevelt* (1991), and *1968: The Election that Changed America* (1993). Editor of *American First Ladies: Their Lives and Their Legacy* (1996). **Essays:** First Ladies; McKinley; New Nationalism and New Freedom; Theodore Roosevelt; Taft.

Graham, Hugh Davis. Holland N. McTyeire Professor of American History, Vanderbilt University, Nashville. Author of *The Uncertain Triumph* (1984), *The Civil Rights Era* (1990), and *Civil Rights and the Presidency* (1992). Editor of *Civil Rights in the US* (1994). Member of the editorial board, *Journal of Policy History.* **Essays:** Civil Rights Acts; Long.

Grant, S-M. Lecturer in United States History, University of Newcastle upon Tyne. Contributor to *Nations and Nationalism* and *Journal of American Studies.* Editor of *The British-American, 1989–93.* **Essays:** African American History: Civil War, Emancipation, and Reconstruction; Bell; Civil War: Approach to 1; Civil War, Approach to 2; Draft/Conscription; Equality; Mann; Nationalism; New England; Olmsted; Sectionalism/Regionalism; Slavery: Slave Trade, External; Telegraph and Telephone; Tocqueville.

Grantham, Dewey W. Holland N. McTyeire Professor of History Emeritus, Vanderbilt University, Nashville. Author of *Southern Progressivism: The Reconciliation of Progress and Tradition* (1983), *Recent America: The United States since 1945* (1987), and *The South in Modern America: A Region at*

Odds (1994). General editor of the Twentieth-Century America series, University Press of Mississippi. **Essay:** Tennessee Valley Authority.

Green, Elna C. Assistant Professor, Sweet Briar College, Virginia. Author of *Southern Strategies: Southern Women and the Woman Suffrage Question* (1997), and contributor to *North Carolina History Review* and *Louisiana History*. **Essays:** Family; Social Work/Social Reform.

Greene, Daniel P. Instructor, McLennan Community College, Waco, Texas. Contributor to *Statesmen Who Changed the World* edited by Frank W. Thackeray and John E. Findling (1993) and contributor to *Diplomatic History*. **Essay:** Foreign Policy since 1945: Special Aspects 1.

Griffith, Sally Foreman. Associate Professor of History, Villanova University, Pennsylvania. Author of *Home Town News: William Allen White and the Emporia Gazette* (1989), and contributor to the *Pennsylvania Magazine of History and Biography*. Editor of *Autobiography of William Allen White* (1990). **Essay:** White.

Grimaud, Anne-Marie. PhD candidate, State University of New York at Stony Brook. Contributor to *Protest, Power, and Change: An Encyclopedia of Nonviolent Action* edited by Roger S. Powers and William B. Vogele (1997). **Essay:** Rockefeller.

Halliwell, Martin. PhD candidate, Department of English Studies, University of Nottingham; part-time lecturer, De Montfort University, Leicester. Contributor to *Reader's Guide to Literature in English* edited by Mark Hawkins-Dady (1996) and to the journals *Over Here* and *Journal of American Studies*. **Essays:** Pragmatism; Transcendentalism.

Harris, J. William. Associate Professor of History, University of New Hampshire, Durham; Fulbright Professor, University of Genoa, 1997. Author of *Plain Folk and Gentry in a Slave Society* (1985). Editor of *Society and Culture in the Slave South* (1992). **Essays:** African American History: 1870s-1954, the South; Slavery: General; South: Colonial Period to Civil War.

Harrison, Lowell H. Professor Emeritus of History, Western Kentucky University, Bowling Green. Author of *John Breckinridge, Jeffersonian Republican* (1969), *The Civil War in Kentucky* (1975), *George Rogers Clark and the War in the West* (1976), *Antislavery Movement in Kentucky* (1978), *Western Kentucky University* (1987), and *Kentucky's Road to Statehood* (1992). Editor of *A Kentucky Sampler* (1977) and *Kentucky's Governors* (1985). **Essays:** Boone; George Rogers Clark

Harrison, Robert. Lecturer in History, University of Wales, Aberystwyth. Contributor to *Journal of Urban History*, *Pennsylvania Magazine of History and Biography*, *Pennsylvania History*, and *Wisconsin Magazine of History*. **Essays:** Elections: General; Government and the Economy; Labor History: Legal and Political Framework; Reconstruction: Economic Aspects.

Hawkins, Richard A. Senior Lecturer in History, University of Wolverhampton. Contributor to *International Directory of Company Histories* and to the journals *Economic History Review*, *Business History*, and *Australian Studies*. **Essays:** Advertising; Japan: Matthew Perry and the Reopening of.

Hawley, Ellis W. Professor Emeritus, Department of History, University of Iowa, Iowa City. Author of *The New Deal and the Problem of Monopoly* (1966) and *The Great War and the Search for a Modern Order* (1979, 1992). Editor of *Herbert Hoover as Secretary of Commerce* (1981). Contributor to the journals *Business History Review*, *Journal of Economic History*, and *Journal of Policy History*. **Essay:** Mellon.

Heinig, R. J. PhD candidate, Department of History, University of Notre Dame, Indiana. **Essay:** Niebuhr.

Hemenway, Robin L. E. Faculty member, Program in American Studies, University of Minnesota, Twin Cities campus, Minneapolis. Managing editor of *American Studies Journal*. **Essays:** Barton; Cowboys; Native Americans: Recent History; Native Americans: Chiefs; Small Towns.

Hepworth, Candida N. Teaches American literature in American Studies programme, University of Wales, Swansea. Contributor to *Over Here* and *Studies in History and Contemporary Culture*. **Essay:** Mexican Americans.

Holden Reid, Brian. Senior Lecturer in War Studies, King's College, London, and Resident Historian, The Staff College, Camberley, Surrey. Author of numerous books including *J. F. C. Fuller: Military Thinker* (1987, 1990), *Debates with Fuller and Liddell Hart* (1995), and *The Origins of the American Civil War* (1996), and of many essays on American history. Editor of *American Studies: Essays in Honour of Marcus Cunliffe* (with John White, 1991), *Military Strategy in a Changing Europe* (with Michael Dewar, 1991), and *The Science of War* (1993). Teaching Fellow, Institute of United States Studies, University of London. **Essays:** Buchanan; Thomas J. ("Stonewall") Jackson; Lee; McClellan; Scott; Seward.

Holland, Max. Freelance writer based in Washington, DC. Author of numerous books, including *The Militarization of the Middle East* (1982), *When the Machine Stopped: A Cautionary Tale from Industrial America* (1989), *The CEO Goes to Washington: Negotiating the Halls of Power* (1994), and *The Commission* (forthcoming). Contributor to *Reviews in American History*, *The Nation*, *Los Angeles Times Magazine*, *Common Cause*, *Washington Post*, *New York Times*, and other newspapers and journals. **Essay:** John F. Kennedy: Assassination of.

Holmes, Sean P. Lecturer in American Studies, Brunel University, Twickenham, Middlesex. Author of *Weavers of Dreams, Unite! Constructing an Organizational Identity in the Actors' Equity Association, 1913–1934* (dissertation). Former researcher on the Margaret Sanger Papers project. **Essay:** Sanger.

Holt, Michael F. Professor of American History, University of Virginia, Charlottesville. Author of *Forging a Majority: The Formation of the Republican Party in Pittsburgh, 1848–1860* (1969), *The Political Crisis of the 1850s* (1978, 1983), *Political Parties and American Political Development* (1992), and a forthcoming history of the Whig Party.

Hopkins, Michael F. Senior Lecturer in History, Liverpool Institute of Higher Education. Author of *Sir Oliver Franks and the Washington Embassy* (forthcoming). Editor of *Intelligence, Defence and Diplomacy* (1994). **Essays:** Britain and the United States: General; Korean War: Military and Diplomatic History; MacArthur.

Ickringill, S. J. S. Lecturer in History, University of Ulster, Coleraine. Contributor to *Sport, Culture and Politics* edited by J. C. Binfield and John Stevenson (1993) and *The Insular Dream* (1995). Editor of three volumes in the European contributions to American Studies series (1988–92). Member of the editorial board for *The Sports Historian*; former Chair, Irish Association for American Studies, and Vice President, European Association for American Studies. **Essay:** Baseball.

Issel, William. Professor of History, San Francisco State University. Author of *Social Change in the United States, 1945–1983* (1985), *San Francisco, 1865–1932: Politics, Power, and Urban Development* (1986), and contributor to *Western History Quarterly*. Co-editor of the Contemporary USA series, and member of the editorial board, *Pacific Historical Review*. **Essays:** Liberalism; San Francisco.

Jeffrey, Jonathan. Special Collections Librarian, Western Kentucky University, Bowling Green. Contributor to *Filson Club History Quarterly*, *Register of the Kentucky Historical Society*, *Shaker Messenger* and *Encyclopedia USA*. **Essay:** Dix.

Johansen, Shawn. Member of the Department of History, Frostburg State University, Maryland. Contributor to *Gender and History* edited by Linda J. Nicholson (1986) and *Fatherhood in Industrializing America* (forthcoming). **Essays:** Birth Control; Marriage and Divorce; Mormons; Brigham Young and Joseph Smith.

Johnson, Daniel J. PhD candidate, University of California at Los Angeles. **Essays:** Social Mobility; Southwest.

Johnson, Wayne J. Lecturer in American Studies, University College of Ripon and York St. John, York. Contributor to *The Blackwell Dictionary of Evangelical Biography* edited by Donald M. Lewis (1995), and to *Studies in Church History* and *Staffordshire Studies*. **Essay:** Slavery: Proslavery Thought.

Jones, Peter d'A. Professor of History, University of Illinois at Chicago. Author of *An Economic History of the USA since 1783* (1956), *The Consumer Society* (1965), *The Christian Socialist Revival, 1877–1914* (1968), *Since Columbus: Poverty and Pluralism in the History of the Americas* (1975), and

Henry George and British Socialism (1991). Editor of *Ethnic Chicago* (with Melvin G. Holli, 1977, 1995). **Essays:** Foreign Trade; George; Lyndon Baines Johnson; Pinchot.

Kaminski, Theresa. Assistant Professor of History, University of Wisconsin, Stevens Point. **Essays:** Gilman; Woodhull; Frances Wright.

Kentleton, John. Lecturer in History, University of Liverpool. Contributor to *Vietnam: The History and the Tactics* edited by John Pimlott (1982), *Dwight D. Eisenhower: Soldier, President, Statesman* edited by Joann P. Krieg (1987), and *Annual Bulletin of Historical Literature*, *Journal of American Studies*, and *History*. **Essays:** Elections 3; George C. Marshall; New Deal: Political and Constitutional Issues; Franklin D. Roosevelt.

Kersten, Andrew E. PhD candidate, University of Cincinnati. Contributor to *The Filson Club History Quarterly*, *Southern Historian*, and *Queen City Heritage*. **Essay:** New Deal: Social Impact.

Kidd, Stuart. Director of American Studies, University of Reading, England. Author of essays and articles on the cultural history of the United States, and especially on the South during the interwar years. **Essays:** Anti-Evolution Crusade; Bryan.

Killick, John R. Lecturer in Economic History, University of Leeds. Contributor to *Business History of General Trading Companies* edited by Shin'ichi Yonekawa and Hideki Yoshihara (1987), *The USA and Canada* (1993), and to the journals *Business History Review* and *Journal of Southern History*. **Essays:** Foreign Policy: Financial and Economic Aspects; Foreign Trade; Investment: Foreign Investment in the United States; Investment: United States Investment Abroad; Shipping.

Kirk, John A. Lecturer in American History, University of Wales, Lampeter, Dyfed. Contributor to *The Making of Martin Luther King and the Civil Rights Movement* edited by Brian Ward and Anthony J. Badger (1996). **Essay:** National Association for the Advancement of Colored People.

Kleinberg, S. J. Reader in American Studies, Brunel University, Twickenham, Middlesex. Author of *The Shadow of the Mills: Working Class Families in Pittsburgh, 1870–1907* (1989), *Women in American Society* (1990), and *Women of the United States* (forthcoming). Editor of *Retrieving Women's History* (1988, 1992). Associate editor, *Journal of American Studies*. **Essays:** Feminism; Philanthropy; Social Welfare/Social Security; Women's History: General; Women's History: Women at Work; Women's History: Women's Liberation Movement.

Kordas, Ann. PhD candidate, Temple University, Philadelphia. **Essays:** Gender; Homosexuality; Working Classes.

Krause, Kent M. Member of the Department of History, University of Nebraska, Lincoln. **Essays:** Basketball; Football; Sport.

Krysko, Michael A. PhD candidate, Department of History, State University of New York at Stony Brook. **Essays:** Communications and Media; Open Door Policy; Radio and Television.

Lambert, Andrew D. Lecturer, Department of War Studies, King's College, London. Author of *Battleships in Transition: The Creation of the Steam Battlefleet, 1815–1860* (1984), *Warrior: The First Ironclad* (1987), *The Crimean War: British Grand Strategy, 1853–1856* (1990), *The Last Sailing Battlefleet: Maintaining Naval Mastery, 1815–1850* (1991), *Steam, Steel and Shellfire: The Steam Warship, 1815–1905* (1992), and *The Crimean War* (with Stephen Badsey, 1994). Contributor to numerous journals, including *War and Society* and *Journal of Strategic Studies*. **Essay:** Civil War: Naval War.

Laver, Harry S. PhD candidate, University of Kentucky, Lexington. Contributor to *The American Revolution, 1775–1783: An Encyclopedia* edited by Richard L. Blanco (1993). **Essays:** Continental Congress; Federalist Papers.

Lay, Shawn. Assistant Professor of American History, Coker College, Hartsville, South Carolina. Author of *War, Revolution, and the Ku Klux Klan: A Study of Intolerance in a Border City* (1985), *The Invisible Empire in the West: Toward a New Historical Appraisal of the Ku Klux Klan of the 1920s* (1992), and *Hooded Knights on the Niagara: The Ku Klux Klan in Buffalo, New York* (1995). **Essay:** Ku Klux Klan.

Leonard, Thomas C. Professor, Associate Dean, and Director of Mass Communications Program, Graduate School of Journalism, University of California, Berkeley. Author of *Above the Battle: War-Making in America from Appomattox to Versailles* (1978), *The Power of the Press: The Birth of American Political Reporting* (1986), and *News for All: America's Coming-of-Age with the Press* (1995). Associate editor, *American National Biography*. **Essays:** Hearst; Pulitzer.

Leslie, W. Bruce. Associate Professor of History, State University of New York at Brockport. Author of *Gentlemen and Scholars: College and Community in the "Age of the University", 1865–1917* (1992). Contributor to *History of Education Quarterly*. Member of the editorial board, *History of Higher Education Annual*. **Essays:** Eliot; Food; German Americans; Middle Classes; Professions; Suburbs; Universities and Colleges: 1783–1900.

Levy, David W. David Ross Boyd Professor of American History, University of Oklahoma, Norman. Author of *Herbert Croly and the New Republic: The Life and Thought of an American Progressive* (1985) and *The Debate over Vietnam* (1995). Editor of *The Letters of Louis D. Brandeis* (with Melvin I. Urofsky, 5 vols., 1971–78), *Half Brother, Half Son: Letters of Louis D. Brandeis to Felix Frankfurter* (with Melvin I. Urofsky, 1991) and *FDR's Fireside Chats* (with Russell D. Buhite, 1992). Contributor to *Oklahoma Law Review*, *Michigan Law Review*, *Yale Review*, *Journal of Thought*, *Teaching History*, *Phylon*, and *Intellectual Digest*. **Essays:** Brandeis; Holmes.

Little, Lawrence S. Assistant Professor of History, Villanova University, Pennsylvania. **Essays:** African American History: Religion; Phillips; Reform Movements; Riots.

Loizou, Andreas. Stock market analyst and freelance financial journalist based in London. Editor (with Michael Sheimo) of *International Encyclopedia of the Stock Market* (forthcoming). Articles published in *Financial Times*, *Sunday Times*, *The Times* and *The Evening Standard*. **Essay:** Stock Market.

Lowery, Charles D. Professor of History and Head of Department, Mississippi State University. Author of *James Barbour: Jeffersonian Republican* (1984). Editor of *Encyclopedia of African American Civil Rights* (with John F. Marszalek, 1992). **Essays:** John Adams; Erie Canal; Meriwether Lewis and William Clark; Louisiana Purchase; Northwest Ordinances; Rush.

Lurie, Maxine N. Assistant Professor of History, Seton Hall University, Orange, New Jersey. Editor of *A New Jersey Anthology* (1994), *Minutes of the East Jersey Proprietors, 1764–1794* (1985), and contributor to *AHA Newsletter*, *Docet*, *New Jersey History*, *Pennsylvania Magazine of History and Biography*, *Maryland History*, *Rutgers University Library Journal*, and *New Jersey Lawyer*. **Essays:** Pilgrim Fathers; George Washington.

McAllister, Ted V. Lecturer, Vanderbilt University, Nashville. Author of *Revolt Against Modernity: Leo Strauss, Eric Voegelin, and the Search for a Post-Liberal Order* (1996). **Essays:** Conservatism; Lippmann.

McCaffery, Peter. Teaching Resources Manager, School of Creative, Cultural and Social Studies, Thames Valley University, London. Author of *When Bosses Ruled Philadelphia: The Emergence of the Republican Machine, 1867–1933* (1993), and contributor to *Urban History* and *Journal of Interdisciplinary History*. **Essays:** Philadelphia; Urban History: General.

McConnell, Stuart. Associate Professor of History, Pitzer College, Claremont, California. Author of *Glorious Contentment: The Grand Army of the Republic, 1865–1900* (1992) and contributor to *Bonds of Affection: Americans Define Their Patriotism* edited by John Bodnar (1996) and *Encyclopedia of the United States in the Twentieth Century* edited by Stanley Kutler (1996). Editor of *Magazine of History*, special issue on the Civil War, 1993. **Essay:** Grand Army of the Republic.

MacKinnon, Ronald. Teaching assistant, State University of New York at Stony Brook. Contributor to *Historical Dictionary of World War II France* edited by Bertram M. Gordon (forthcoming). **Essay:** World War II: United States and 7.

McKivigan, John R. Associate Professor of History, West Virginia University, Morgantown. Author of *The War Against Proslavery Religion* (1984) and *The Moment of Decision* (with Randall M. Miller, 1994). Co-editor of *The Speeches of*

Frederick Douglass, vols. 4–5 (1992), and editor of *The Correspondence of Frederick Douglass*. **Essays:** Brown; Douglass.

Major, John. Reader in History, University of Hull. Author of *The New Deal* (1968), *The Contemporary World: A Historical Introduction* (1970), *The Oppenheimer Hearings* (1971), and *Prize Possession: The United States and the Panama Canal, 1903–1979* (1993). Contributor to *The Cambridge History of Latin America* (vol. 7, 1990) and *Pearl Harbor: A Fifty-Year Perspective* edited by Robert Love (1993), and to *Review of International Studies, Historical Journal, Diplomatic History,* and *Journal of Strategic Studies*. **Essay:** Panama Canal.

Mann, Anthony. PhD candidate, Keele University, Staffordshire. **Essay:** Boston.

Marszalek, John F. W. L. Giles Distinguished Professor, Department of History, Mississippi State University. Author of *Court-Martial: A Black Man in America* (1972, also published as *Assault at West Point*, 1994) and *Sherman: A Soldier's Passion for Order* (1993). Editor of *The Diary of Miss Emma Holmes, 1861–1866* (1979) and *Encyclopedia of African American Civil Rights* (with Charles D. Lowery, 1992). **Essay:** Sherman.

Mason, Fran. Lecturer in Cultural Studies, King Alfred's College of Higher Education, Winchester. Contributor to *Journal of Popular Culture*. **Essay:** Los Angeles.

Mason, Keith. Lecturer in History, University of Liverpool. Author of *The American Revolution* (in progress) and *Slavery and Emancipation in North America, the British West Indies, and St. Dominque/Haiti* (in progress). Contributor to *Journal of Southern History, Virginia Magazine of History and Biography,* and *Bulletin of the John Rylands Library*. **Essays:** American Revolution: Development of a Crisis, 1763–1770; American Revolution: Development of a Crisis, 1770–1775; Colonial History: Economic Development; Constitution: Philadelphia Convention; Loyalists; Paine.

Matray, James I. Professor of History, New Mexico State University, Las Cruces. Author of *The Reluctant Crusade: American Foreign Policy in Korea, 1941–1950* (1985), *Historical Dictionary of the Korean War* (1991), *Korea and the Cold War: Division, Destruction, and Disarmament* (1993), and contributor to the journals *Korean Studies, Journal of American History, Prologue,* and *Diplomatic History*. **Essay:** Korean War: Political and Economic Impact.

Middleton, Richard. Reader in American History, Queen's University of Belfast. Author of *The Bells of Victory: The Pitt-Newcastle Ministry and the Conduct of the Seven Years' War 1757–1762* (1985) and *Colonial America: A History, 1585–1776* (2nd edition, 1996). **Essay:** Colonial History: Government and Politics.

Mikosz, David J. Research student in Social and Political Sciences, Churchill College, University of Cambridge. **Essays:** Mencken; Noah Webster.

Miller, Andrew Thompson. Assistant Professor of History and Director of Africana Studies, Union College, Schenectady, New York. Contributor to *The Underclass Debate: View from History* edited by Michael B. Katz (1993) and *After Ellis Island: Newcomers and Natives in the 1910 Census* edited by Susan Cotts Watkins (1994). **Essay:** Black Power.

Miller, Randall M. Professor of History, Saint Joseph's University, Philadelphia. Editor of *"Dear Master": Letters of a Slave Family* (1978, 1990), *Dictionary of Afro-American Slavery* (with John David Smith, 1988, 1997), and *Catholics in the Old South* (with Jon L. Wakelyn, 1983). Editor of the *Pennsylvania Magazine of History and Biography*, 1987–91. **Essays:** Civil War: the Common Soldiers; Slavery: Slave Culture and Community.

Miller, Vivien M. L. Lecturer in American Studies, Middlesex University, London. **Essays:** Crime and Punishment; Prisons and Asylums; Violence.

Minchin, Tim. Mellon Research Fellow, University of Cambridge. Author of *What do We Need a Union For? The TWUA in the South, 1945–1955* (1997). **Essays:** John L. Lewis; Reuther.

Moore, Deborah Dash. Professor of Religion, Vassar College, Poughkeepsie, New York. Author of *B'nai B'rith and the Challenge of Ethnic Leadership* (1981), *At Home in America: Second Generation New York Jews* (1981), and *To the Golden Cities: Pursuing the American Jewish Dream in Miami and Los Angeles* (1994). Editor of the *YIVO Annual*, and former Research Director, YIVO Institute for Jewish Research. Co-editor of *Jewish Women in America: An Historical Encyclopedia* (forthcoming). **Essays:** Jewish Americans; Judaism.

Morgan, Gwenda. Reader in Historical Studies, University of Sunderland. Author of *The Hegemony of the Law: Richmond County, Virginia* (1989). Contributor to *The End of Anglo-America* edited by R. A. Burchell (1991), and to *Virginia Magazine of History and Biography*. **Essays:** Colonial History: Colonies, settlement and growth 4; John Smith.

Morgan, Iwan W. Professor of American History and Head of Department of Politics and Modern History, London Guildhall University. Author of *Eisenhower Versus "The Spenders": The Eisenhower Administration, the Democrats and the Budget, 1953–60* (1990), *Beyond the Liberal Consensus: A Political History of the United States since 1965* (1994), and *Deficit Government: Taxing and Spending in Modern America* (1995). Editor of *America's Century: Perspectives on United States History since 1900* (with Neil A. Wynn, 1993). **Essay:** Reagan.

Morrison, Malcolm F. Lecturer in History, University of Reading, England. **Essays:** British-French Rivalry in North America; Colonial History: Religion; Great Awakening; Thomas Hutchinson.

Murphy, J. Thomas. Independent historian based in Texas. Contributor to *William Tecumseh Sherman and the Settlement* *of the West* by Robert G. Athearn (reissue, 1995); assistant editor of *The Papers of Ulysses S. Grant*, vols. 17–20 (1991–95). Contributor to *Annals of Iowa* and *Journal of the West*. **Essays:** Cowboys; Custer; Westward Expansion.

Neather, Andrew. Former staff writer, United Auto Workers' *Solidarity* magazine, Detroit; now freelance writer based in London. Contributor to *Bonds of Affection: Americans Define Their Patriotism* edited by John Bodnar (1996). **Essays:** Agrarian Discontent; American Federation of Labor; Anticommunism; Labor History: General; Labor Unions.

Newman, Mark. Lecturer in American Studies, University of Derby, England. Contributor to *Southern Landscapes* edited by Anthony J. Badger and others (1997), and to the journals *Virginia Magazine of History and Biography*, *Journal of Mississippi History*, *Arkansas Historical Quarterly*, and *North Carolina Historical Review*. **Essay:** Protestantism: Denominational Histories.

Oatham, Julia L. Teaching Assistant in Politics and research student, University of Wales, Swansea. Author of an article on the American image of Cuba. **Essays:** Cuba and the United States; Imperialism and Anti-Imperialism.

Olsen, Christopher J. Member of the Department of History, Virginia Wesleyan College, Norfolk. Contributor to *Southern Historian* and *Florida Historical Quarterly*. Associate editor of *Southern Historian*. **Essays:** Conventions, Political; Davis; States Rights.

Olson, Bruce A. Associate Professor, Del Mar College, Corpus Christi, Texas. Contributor to *Labor's Heritage*, *Houston Review*, *Forward Observer*, *Military Review*, and *Texas Handbook*, and author of occasional papers for the Institute for International Business Analysis, University of Houston. **Essay:** Militia/National Guard.

Osborn, Shari L. PhD candidate, State University of New York at Stony Brook. Contributor to *Firsthand America: A History of the United States* edited by Virginia Bernhard and others (3rd edition, 1994) and *The Encyclopedia of the United States Congress* edited by Don Bacon and others (1995). Editor of a collection of Nixon presidential documents (with Stanley Kutler, forthcoming). **Essay:** Nixon.

Ostrander, Richard. Instructor, University of Notre Dame, Indiana. Contributor to *Church History* and *Fides et Historia*. **Essay:** Fundamentalism.

Ownby, Ted. Member of the faculty, University of Mississippi, Oxford. Author of *Subduing Satan: Recreation, Religion and Manhood in the Rural South, 1865–1920* (1990), editor of *Black and White: Cultural Interaction in the Old South* (1993), and contributor to *Faulkner and Ideology* edited by Ann Abadie and Donald Kartiganer (1995) and *Haunted Bodies: Gender and Southern Texts* edited by Anne Goodwyn Jones and Susan Donaldson (1997). **Essays:** Graham; Prohibition; Temperance.

Palmer, Niall Andrew. Lecturer in American Studies, Brunel University, Twickenham, Middlesex. **Essay:** Harding.

Parides, Peter K. PhD candidate, and Adjunct Lecturer, Department of History, State University of New York at Stony Brook. Contributor to *Protest, Power, and Change: An Encyclopedia of Nonviolent Action* edited by Roger S. Powers and William B. Vogele (1997). **Essays:** Expansionism; World War II: United States and 4.

Parish, Peter J. Director of the Institute of United States Studies, University of London, 1983–92; now Mellon Senior Research Fellow in American History, University of Cambridge. Author of *The American Civil War* (1975) and *Slavery: History and Historians* (1989). Editor of *Abraham Lincoln: Speeches and Letters* (Everyman edition, 1993). **Essays:** Emancipation Proclamations; Lincoln; Daniel Webster.

Pascoe, Craig S. PhD candidate, University of Tennessee, Knoxville. Contributor to *American Cities and Suburbs: An Encyclopedia*, and the journals *Essays in Economic and Business History* and *Southern Historian*. **Essays:** New Orleans; Roads and Road Transport, 20th century; Veblen.

Patterson, James T. Professor of History, Brown University, Providence, Rhode Island. Author of *Congressional Conservatism and the New Deal* (1967), *The New Deal and the States: Federalism in Transition* (1969), *Mr. Republican: A Biography of Robert A. Taft* (1972), *The Dread Disease: Cancer and Modern American Culture* (1987), *America since 1941: A History* (1994), *America's Struggle Against Poverty* (revised, 1994), and *Grand Expectations: The United States, 1945–1974* (1996).

Perman, Michael. Professor of History and Research Professor in the Humanities, University of Illinois at Chicago. Author of *Reunion Without Compromise: The South and Reconstruction, 1865–1868* (1973), *The Road to Redemption: Southern Politics, 1869–1879* (1984), and *Emancipation and Reconstruction, 1862–1879* (1987). Editor of *Perspectives on the American Past: Readings and Commentary* (1989), *Major Problems in the Civil War and Reconstruction* (1991), and *The Coming of the American Civil War* (2nd edition 1992). Associate editor, *American National Biography*. **Essays:** Reconstruction: Policy and Politics 2; Stephens.

Peskin, Lawrence A. PhD candidate, University of Maryland, College Park. **Essays:** Gallatin; State Constitutions and State Politics.

Phelan, Craig. Lecturer in American Studies, University of Wales, Swansea. Author of *William Green: Biography of a Labor Leader* (1989) and *Divided Loyalties: The Public and Private Life of Labor Leader John Mitchell* (1994). **Essays:** Debs; Gompers; Knights of Labor.

Pinsker, Matthew. Adjunct Instructor, Haverford College, Pennsylvania. Contributor to *Jewish American History and Culture: An Encyclopedia* (1992), and to *Journal of the*

Abraham Lincoln Association. **Essays:** Civil War, Approach to 3; Douglas.

Pocock, Emil. Associate Professor of History, Eastern Connecticut State University, Willimantic. Contributor to *The Pursuit of Public Power: Political Culture in Ohio, 1787–1861* edited by Jeffrey P. Brown and Andrew R. L. Cayton (1994), and to *Indiana Magazine of History, Journal of the Early Republic,* and *American Historical Review.* **Essays:** Bushnell; Historiography; Textbooks.

Porter, Joy. Lecturer in American History, Anglia Polytechnic University, Cambridge, England. Author of *American Indian Identity in the Life of Arthur Caswell Parker, 1881–1955* (forthcoming), and contributor to *Over Here* and *Journal of American Studies.* **Essay:** Native Americans: Cultures 1.

Potter, Jim. Reader Emeritus in Economic History, University of London. Author of *The American Economy Between the World Wars* (1974), and contributor to *Lessons from America* edited by Richard Rose (1974), *Other Voices, Other Views: An International Collection of Essays from the Bicentennial* edited by R. W. Winks (1978), *La Revolution Americaine et l'Europe* edited by C. Fohlen (1979), *American Immigration: Its Variety and Lasting Imprint* edited by R. Kroes (1979), and *Colonial British America* edited by Jack P. Greene and J. R. Pole (1984). **Essays:** Business Cycle; Economic History: General; Energy; Financial History, 1780s–1930s; Marketing and Distribution; Population; Railroads: General.

Przybyszewski, Linda C. A. Assistant Professor, Heyman Center for the Humanities, Columbia University, New York. Contributor to *Abortion, Medicine, and the Law* edited by J. Douglas Butler and David Walbert (1992), *Great Justices of the US Supreme Court: Ratings and Case Studies* edited by William D. Pederson and Norman W. Provizer (1993), *Biographical Dictionary of United States Supreme Court Justices* edited by Melvin I. Urofsky (1994), and *Chinese Immigrants and American Law* edited by Charles McClain (1994). **Essay:** Harlan.

Rabe, Stephen G. Professor of History, University of Texas at Dallas. Author of *The Road to OPEC: United States Relations with Venezuela, 1919–1976* (1982), *Eisenhower and Latin America* (1988), and *Imperial Surge: The United States Abroad, the 1890s to Early 1990s* (with Thomas G. Paterson, 1992). **Essay:** Foreign Policy: Special Aspects 6.

Rabinowitz, Howard N. Professor of History, University of New Mexico, Albuquerque. Author of *Race Relations in the Urban South, 1865–1890* (1978), *The First New South, 1865–1920* (1992), *Race, Ethnicity, and Urbanization: Selected Essays* (1994). Editor of *Southern Black Leaders of the Reconstruction Era* (1982). Associate editor, *American National Biography.* **Essay:** Jim Crow.

Rable, George C. Professor of History, Anderson University, Indiana. Author of *But There Was No Peace: The Role of*

Violence in the Politics of Reconstruction (1984), *Civil Wars: Women and the Crisis of Southern Nationalism* (1989), and *The Confederate Republic: A Revolution Against Politics* (1994). **Essay:** Confederate States of America: Constitution, Government, and Politics.

Ralph, James. Assistant Professor, Middlebury College, Vermont. Author of *Northern Protest: Martin Luther King, Jr., Chicago, and the Civil Rights Movement* (1993). **Essay:** Jesse Jackson.

Ratcliffe, Donald J. Senior Lecturer in American History, University of Durham, England. Contributor to *The Pursuit of Public Power* edited by Jeffrey P. Brown and Andrew R. L. Cayton (1994) and *The Market Revolution in America* edited by Melvyn Stokes and Stephen Conway (1996), and to the journals *Ohio History, Journal of American History, Journal of the Early Republic,* and *Timeline.* **Essays:** John Quincy Adams; Burr; John C. Frémont and Jessie Benton Frémont; War of 1812: Causes.

Renshaw, Patrick. Senior Lecturer in American History, University of Sheffield. Author of *The Wobblies* (1967), *American Labour and Consensus Capitalism, 1935–1990* (1991), and *The Longman Companion to America in the Era of the Two World Wars, 1910–1945* (1996). **Essays:** Industrial Workers of the World; Strikes.

Reynolds, David. Fellow, Christ's College, University of Cambridge. Author of *The Creation of the Anglo-American Alliance, 1937–1941: A Study in Competitive Cooperation* (1982), *An Ocean Apart: The Relationship Between Britain and America in the Twentieth Century* (with David Dimbleby, 1988), *Britannia Overruled: British Policy and World Power in the Twentieth Century* (1991), and *Rich Relations: The American Occupation of Britain, 1942–1945* (1995). Editor of *Allies at War: The Soviet, American, and British Experience, 1939–1945* (with Warren F. Kimball and A. O. Chubarian, 1994), and *The Origins of the Cold War in Europe: International Perspectives* (1994). **Essay:** World War II: Approach to 1.

Saillant, John. Editor of IEAHCNET, based at Brown University, Providence, Rhode Island. Contributor to the journals *New England Quarterly, Journal of the History of Sexuality, Journal of the Early Republic, Early American Literature, Vermont History,* and *Religion and American Culture.* **Essay:** Edwards.

Sarson, Steven J. Lecturer, Department of History, University of Wales, Swansea, and PhD candidate, Johns Hopkins University, Baltimore. Contributor to *The Blackwell Encyclopedia of the American Revolution* edited by Jack P. Greene and J. R. Pole (1991), and to the journals *New Comparison, Journal of American Studies, History,* and *Southern Historian.* **Essays:** African American History: Colonial Beginnings to 1860; American Revolution: Character, Scope, and Significance; Colonial History: Colonies, settlement and growth 1; Colonial History: Society; Colonial History: Slavery and Indentured Servitude.

Scribner, Christopher MacGregor. Teaching Fellow, Vanderbilt University, Nashville. Contributor to *Alabama Review* and *Tennessee Historical Quarterly*. Essays: Democratic Party; Federalism; Judiciary; Mumford; Newspapers and Magazines.

SenGupta, Gunja. Assistant Professor of History, East Texas State University, Commerce. Author of *For God and Mammon: Evangelicals and Entrepreneurs, Masters and Slaves in Territorial Kansas, 1854–1860* (1996), and contributor to *Civil War History* and *Kansas History*. Essays: Angelina Grimké and Sarah Grimké; Paul.

Shade, William G. Professor of History, Lehigh University, Bethlehem, Pennsylvania. Author of *Banks or No Banks* (1972) and *The Evolution of Electoral Systems* (with Paul Kleppner, 1981). Contributor to *Social Science Quarterly, Journal of American History, Journal of Interdisciplinary History, Social Science History*, and *Journal of Southern History*. Essays: Alien and Sedition Acts; Manifest Destiny; Second Bank of the United States; Texas: Annexation of.

Sicilia, David B. Assistant Professor of History, University of Maryland at College Park. Author of *The Entrepreneurs* (with Robert Sobel, 1986) and *Labors of a Modern Hercules: The Evolution of a Chemical Company* (with Davis Dyer, 1990). Essays: Business History: General; Edison; Manufacturing Industry: General; Manufacturing Industry: Individual Industries.

Silbey, Joel H. President White Professor of History, Cornell University, Ithaca, New York. Author of *The Shrine of Party, 1841–1852* (1967), *A Respectable Minority* (1977), *The Partisan Imperative* (1985), and *The American Political Nation, 1838–1893* (1991). Essays: Congress; Elections 1; Parties and Political Movements.

Simpson, Brooks D. Associate Professor of History and Humanities, Arizona State University, Tempe. Author of *Let Us Have Peace: Ulysses S. Grant and the Politics of War and Reconstruction, 1861–1868* (1991), *The Political Education of Henry Adams* (1995), and *America's Civil War* (1996). Essays: Henry Adams; Civil War: Campaigns 1; Civil War: Campaigns 2; Compromise of 1877; Andrew Johnson; Schurz.

Skaggs, David Curtis. Professor of History, Bowling Green State University, Ohio. Author of *Roots of Maryland Democracy, 1753–1776* (1973) and *A Signal Victory: The Lake Erie Campaign, 1812–1813* (with Gerard T. Altoff, 1997). Editor of *In Defense of the Republic: Readings in American Military History* (1991) and *Treatise on Partisan Warfare* by Johann von Ewald (1991). Essay: War of 1812: Course and Consequences.

Smith, Dennis B. Senior Lecturer in History, University of Ulster, Coleraine. Author of *Japan since 1945: The Rise of an Economic Superpower* (1995) and contributor to *Britain and Japan, 1859–1991* edited by Hugh Cortazzi and Gordon Daniels (1992). Essays: China and the United States; Pearl Harbor; Washington Treaties; World War II, Approach to 2.

Smith, Joseph. Senior Lecturer, University of Exeter, Devon. Author of *Illusions of Conflict* (1979), *The Cold War* (1989), *Unequal Giants* (1991), and *The Spanish-American War* (1994). Editor of *Annual Bulletin of Historical Literature*. Essays: Latin America and the United States; Mexico and the United States; Monroe Doctrine; Spanish-American War.

Smith, Mark M. Assistant Professor of History, University of South Carolina, Columbia. Author of *Mastered by the Clock: Time, Slavery, and Freedom in the American South* (forthcoming) and contributor to the journals *Time and Society, South Carolina Historical Magazine*, and *Immigrants and Minorities*. Essay: Agriculture, to 1860.

Spackman, S.G.F. Lecturer in Modern History, University of St. Andrews, Fife. Author of *Wallingford Riegger* (1982) and articles on 19th- and 20th-century American politics and music history. Essays: Reconstruction: in the Southern States; Watergate.

Spark, Alasdair. Head of American Studies, King Alfred's College of Higher Education, Winchester. Author of several articles on the cultural impact of the Vietnam War, including "Flight Controls: The Social History of the Helicopter as a Symbol of the Vietnam War" in *Vietnam Images* edited by Jeff Walsh and Jim Aulich (1988); has also written on Anglo-Americanism and on science fiction. Essay: Counterculture.

Speck, W. A. Professor Emeritus of Modern History, University of Leeds. Author of *Reluctant Revolutionaries: Englishmen and the Revolution of 1688* (1988) and *The Birth of Britain: A New Nation, 1700–1710* (1994). Editor of *History: The Journal of the Historical Association*, 1986–92. Essays: Britain and the American Colonies, 1651–1763; Colonial History: Colonies, settlement and growth 3.

Stokes, Melvyn. Lecturer in American History, University College, London. Editor of *Race and Class in the American South since 1890* (with Rick Halpern, 1994) and *The Market Revolution in America: Social, Political, and Religious Expressions, 1800–1880* (with Stephen Conway, 1996). Essays: Darrow; Dewey; Film; Muckrakers; Progressivism; Social Darwinism; Social Gospel.

Stoler, Mark A. Professor of History, University of Vermont, Burlington. Author of *The Politics of the Second Front: American Military Planning and Diplomacy in Coalition Warfare, 1941–1943* (1977), *Explorations in American History: A Skills Approach* (1986), and *George C. Marshall: Soldier-Statesman of the American Century* (1989). Essay: World War II: United States and 6.

Stowell, Daniel W. Member of the Department of History, University of Florida, Gainesville. Author of *Rebuilding Zion: The Religious Reconstruction of the South, 1863–1877* (forthcoming); contributor to *Georgia in Black and White* edited by John C. Inscoe (1994), and to *Georgia Historical Quarterly*. Essays: Church and State; Moody.

Sullivan, Timothy E. Assistant Professor of Economics, Towson State University, Baltimore. Contributor to the *Handbook of*

American Business History edited by David O. Whitten (1990) and to the journals *Business and Economic History, Canadian Papers in Business History*. **Essays:** Elections 2; McCormick; Scientific Management.

Sylla, Richard. Henry Kaufman Professor of the History of Financial Institutions and Markets, and Professor of Economics, New York University. Author of *The American Capital Market, 1846–1914* (1975), *A History of Interest Rates* (with Sidney Homer, 1991), and *The Evolution of the American Economy* (with Sidney Ratner and James H. Soltow, 1993). Contributor to *Patterns of European Industrialization* edited by W. G. Toniolo (1991). Editor, *Journal of Economic History*, 1978–84. **Essays:** Hamilton; Alexander Hamilton: Financial and Economic Program.

Tadman, Michael. Lecturer, Department of Economic and Social History, University of Liverpool. Author of *Speculators and Slaves: Masters, Traders, and Slaves in the Old South* (1989, 1996), and of a new introduction to *Slave Trading in the Old South* by Frederic Bancroft (1996). **Essays:** Slavery: Economics of; Slavery: Slave Trade, Internal; Slavery: Slave Resistance and Rebellion.

Teaford, Jon C. Professor of History, Purdue University, West Lafayette, Indiana. Author of several books, including *The Rough Road to Renaissance: Urban Revitalization in America, 1940–1985* (1990) and *Cities of the Heartland: The Rise and Fall of the Industrial Midwest* (1993). Member of the editorial boards of *Urban Affairs Quarterly* and *Journal of Urban History*. **Essays:** Municipal Government: Corruption and Reform; Urban History: Government and Politics.

Thompson, John A. Lecturer in History, St. Catharine's College, University of Cambridge. Author of *Progressivism* (1979) and *Reformers and War* (1987). **Essays:** Versailles, Treaty of; Wilson; World War I: American Neutrality.

Till, Geoffrey. Professor of History and International Affairs, Royal Naval College, Greenwich, and Visiting Professor in Maritime Studies, Department of War Studies, King's College, London. Author of numerous books, including *Air Power and the Royal Navy* (1979), *Maritime Strategy and the Nuclear Age* (1984), *Modern Sea Power* (1987), and *The Sea in Soviet Strategy* (with Bryan Ranft, 1989). Editor of *East-West Relations in the 1990s: The Naval Dimension* (with D. J. Pay, 1990), *The Centennial Volume* of the Navy Records Society (1993), *Coastal Forces* (1994), and *Sea-Power: Theory and Practice* (1994). **Essays:** Nimitz; World War II: United States and 3.

Tulloch, Hugh. Senior Lecturer in History, University of Bristol. Author of *James Bryce's American Commonwealth: The Anglo-American Background* (1988) and *Acton* (1988). **Essay:** Bryce.

Turley, David. Senior Lecturer in History, University of Kent, Canterbury. Author of *The Culture of English Antislavery* (1991); contributor *Slavery and Abolition* (1993) and *Race and Class in the South since 1890* edited by Melvyn Stokes

and Rick Halpern (1994). **Essays:** Abolitionism/Antislavery Movement; Du Bois; Garrison.

Tuttle, William M., Jr. Professor of History and American Studies, University of Kansas, Lawrence. Author of *Race Riot: Chicago in the Red Summer of 1919* (1970), *W. E. B. Du Bois* (1973), *Plain Folk* (with David H. Katzman, 1982), *"Daddy's Gone to War": The Second World War in the Lives of America's Children* (1993), and *A People and a Nation* (with Mary Beth Norton and others, 4th edition, 1994). **Essay:** World War II: United States and 8.

Tweedale, Geoffrey. Senior Research Fellow, International Business Unit, Manchester Metropolitan University. Author of *Southern Steel and America* (1987) and *Steel City* (1995). **Essays:** Carnegie; Computers and Data Processing.

Urbiel, Alexander. PhD candidate, Indiana University, Bloomington. Contributor to *Encyclopedia of Indianapolis* edited by David J. Bodenhamer and Robert G. Barrows (1994) and *Hoosier Schools Past and Present* (forthcoming). Editorial assistant, *History of Education Quarterly*. **Essays:** Nativism; Schools: 20th century.

Vecoli, Rudolph J. Professor of History, and Director of the Immigration History Research Center, University of Minnesota, St. Paul. Author of *A Century of European Migrations, 1830–1930* (1991), and contributor to *The Statue of Liberty Revisited* edited by Wilton S. Dillon and Neil G. Kotler (1994) and *Journal of the Canadian Historical Association*. General editor, *Research Collections in American Immigration* (microfilm editions), and contributing editor, *Encyclopedia of Multicultural America* (1995). **Essay:** Italian Americans.

Venn, Fiona. Senior Lecturer in History, University of Essex, Colchester. Author of *Oil Diplomacy in the Twentieth Century* (1986) and *Franklin D. Roosevelt* (1990). **Essays:** Business History: Big Business; Business History: Individual Corporations; Foreign Policy, 1919–1941; Oil and Natural Gas.

Vorenberg, Michael. Assistant Professor of History, State University of New York at Buffalo. Contributor to *Journal of the Abraham Lincoln Association*. **Essays:** Bennett; Child; Greeley; Morse.

Waddell, Steve R. Assistant Professor of History, United States Military Academy, West Point, New York. Author of *US Army Logistics: The Normandy Campaign, 1944* (1994), and of articles on the Soviet military; contributor to *Reference Guide to United States Military History* edited by Charles Reginald Shrader, vols. 1–5. **Essay:** Patton.

Wang, Xi. Associate Professor of History, Indiana University of Pennsylvania. Author of *The Trial of Democracy: Black Suffrage and Northern Republicans, 1860–1910* (1997). **Essays:** Citizenship; Lodge; Republican Party; Suffrage.

Ward, Matthew C. Lecturer in American History, University of Dundee, Scotland. Contributor to *Virginia Magazine of*

History and Biography and *Pennsylvania Magazine of History and Biography*. **Essays:** Colonial History: Colonies, settlement and growth 2; Colonial History: Relations with Native Americans; Colonial History: Westward Expansion; Seven Years' War.

Watson, Graham. Former Lecturer in American History, University College, Cardiff. Specialist in military history, and author of histories of units in the British Army. **Essays:** World War II: United States and 1; World War II: United States and 2.

Watson, Harry L. Professor of History, University of North Carolina, Chapel Hill. Author of *Jacksonian Politics and Community Conflict: The Emergence of the Second American Party System in Cumberland County, North Carolina* (1981) and *Liberty and Power: The Politics of Jacksonian America* (1990). Joint editor of *Southern Cultures Quarterly*. **Essay:** Clay.

Watts, Trent A. Member of the Department of History, Hillsdale College, Hillsdale, Michigan. Author of the foreword to *Men Working* by John Faulkner (new edition, 1996); contributor to *Encyclopedia of American Decades: 1910–1919* edited by Victor Bondi (1996), *American National Biography*, and the journals *North Carolina Historical Review*, *Presidential Studies Quarterly*, *Florida Historical Quarterly*, *Southwestern Historical Quarterly*, and *Atlanta History*. **Essay:** Coolidge.

Webb, Clive. Lecturer in American History, University of Reading, England. **Essays:** Tubman; Turner; Weld.

Wesley, Michael. Research Fellow, Asia-Australia Institute, University of New South Wales, Sydney. Author of articles on Cambodia in *Terrorism and Political Violence* (forthcoming). **Essay:** United Nations.

White, John. Reader in American History, University of Hull. Author of *Reconstruction after the American Civil War* (1977), *Black Leadership in America* (1985, 1990), and *Billie Holiday: Her Life and Times* (1987). Editor of *Martin Luther King, Jr., and the Civil Rights Movement in America* (1991) and *American Studies: Essays in Honour of Marcus Cunliffe* (with Brian Holden Reid, 1991). **Essays:** African American History: General; African American History: 1870s-1954, the North; Garvey; Malcolm X; Booker T. Washington; Wells-Barnett.

White, Mark J. Assistant Professor of History, Eastern Illinois University, Charleston. Author of *The Cuban Missile Crisis* (1996), and of articles in *Journal of Strategic Studies*, *Mid-America*, *Illinois Historical Journal*, *Maryland Historian*, and other journals. **Essays:** Cold War; Cuban Missile Crisis; John F. Kennedy; Kennedy Family.

Whitelegg, Drew. PhD candidate, King's College, London. **Essays:** Aviation and Aerospace; Technology and Invention; Urban History: Economic and Social Aspects.

Wiebe, Robert. Professor of American History, Northwestern University, Evanston, Illinois. His books include *The Search*

for Order, 1877–1920 (1967), *The Opening of American Society* (1984), and *Self-Rule: A Cultural History of American Democracy* (1995).

Wiecek, William M. Professor of Law and Professor of History, Syracuse University, New York. Author of *The Guarantee Clause of the Constitution* (1972), *The Sources of Antislavery Constitutionalism in America, 1760–1848* (1977), *Equal Justice under Law* (with Harold M. Hyman, 1982), *Constitutional Development in a Modernizing Society* (1985), and *Liberty under Law* (1988). **Essays:** Frankfurter; Legal Thought/Jurisprudence; Supreme Court.

Wilford, Hugh. Lecturer in American Studies, Middlesex University, London. Author of *The New York Intellectuals: From Vanguard to Institution* (1995) and contributor to *Journal of American Studies*. **Essays:** Immigration: Acculturation and Americanization; Intellectual History; McCarthy; Socialism and Communism.

Williams, Robert. Principal, St. Aidan's College, and Senior Lecturer in Politics, Durham University, England. Editor of *Explaining American Politics: Issues and Interpretations* (1990). Contributor to *Roosevelt to Reagan: The Development of the Modern Presidency* edited by Malcolm Shaw (1987), and to the journals *Political Studies*, *Public Administration*, and *Journal of American Studies*. Member of the editorial board, *Corruption and Reform*. **Essays:** Civil Service; Presidency.

Wynn, Neil A. Head of History and Reader in History, University of Glamorgan, Pontypridd, Wales. Author of *The Afro-American and the Second World War* (1976, 1993) and *From Progressivism to Prosperity* (1986); contributor to *Afro-American History*, *Journal of Contemporary History*, and *Peace and Change*. Editor of *America's Century: Perspectives on United States History since 1900* (with Iwan W. Morgan, 1993). **Essays:** Nineteen-Twenties; Red Scare; World War I: the United States at War.

Yazawa, Melvin. Associate Professor of History, University of New Mexico, Albuquerque. Author of *Representative Government and the Revolution: The Maryland Constitutional Crisis of 1787* (1975) and *From Colonies to Commonwealth: Familial Ideology and the Beginnings of the American Republic* (1985). **Essays:** American Revolution: General; Colonial History: General; Colonial History: Education; Puritanism; Republicanism.

Young, Nancy Beck. Member of the Department of History, Southwest Missouri State University, Springfield. Author of articles on economic and business history. **Essays:** Hoover; New Deal: General; New Deal: Legislation and Agencies 1.

Zelko, Frank. PhD candidate, University of Kansas, Lawrence. Author of *Generation, Culture, and Prejudice: The Japanese American Decision to Cooperate with Evacuation and Internment During World War II* (1992). **Essays:** Environment; Nature; Powell.

Zieger, Robert H. Professor of History, University of Florida, Gainesville. Author of *American Workers, American Unions, 1920–1985* (1986), *John L. Lewis* (1988), and *The CIO, 1935–1955* (1995). **Essay:** Congress of Industrial Organizations.